Oxford Dictionary of National Biography

Volume 9

Oxford Dictionary of National Biography

IN ASSOCIATION WITH

The British Academy

From the earliest times to the year 2000

Edited by

H. C. G. Matthew

and

Brian Harrison

Volume 9

Burt–Capon

OXFORD
UNIVERSITY PRESS

Great Clarendon Street, Oxford OX2 6DP

Oxford University Press is a department of the University of Oxford.
It furthers the University's objective of excellence in research, scholarship,
and education by publishing worldwide in

Oxford New York

Auckland Bangkok Buenos Aires Cape Town
Chennai Dar es Salaam Delhi Hong Kong Istanbul Karachi
Kolkata Kuala Lumpur Madrid Melbourne Mexico City Mumbai Nairobi
São Paulo Shanghai Taipei Tokyo Toronto

Oxford is a registered trade mark of Oxford University Press
in the UK and in certain other countries

Published in the United States
by Oxford University Press Inc., New York

First published 2004

British Library Cataloguing in Publication Data
Data available

Library of Congress Cataloging in Publication Data
Data available: for details see volume 1, p. iv

ISBN 0-19-861359-8 (this volume)
ISBN 0-19-861411-X (set of sixty volumes)

Text captured by Alliance Phototypesetters, Pondicherry
Illustrations reproduced and archived by
Alliance Graphics Ltd, UK
Typeset in OUP Swift by Interactive Sciences Limited, Gloucester
Printed in Great Britain on acid-free paper by
Butler and Tanner Ltd,
Frome, Somerset

LIST OF ABBREVIATIONS

1 *General abbreviations*

AB	bachelor of arts
ABC	Australian Broadcasting Corporation
ABC TV	ABC Television
act.	active
A$	Australian dollar
AD	*anno domini*
AFC	Air Force Cross
AIDS	acquired immune deficiency syndrome
AK	Alaska
AL	Alabama
A level	advanced level [examination]
ALS	associate of the Linnean Society
AM	master of arts
AMICE	associate member of the Institution of Civil Engineers
ANZAC	Australian and New Zealand Army Corps
appx *pl.* appxs	appendix(es)
AR	Arkansas
ARA	associate of the Royal Academy
ARCA	associate of the Royal College of Art
ARCM	associate of the Royal College of Music
ARCO	associate of the Royal College of Organists
ARIBA	associate of the Royal Institute of British Architects
ARP	air-raid precautions
ARRC	associate of the Royal Red Cross
	against tuberculosis]
BCh	bachelor of surgery
BChir	bachelor of surgery
BCL	bachelor of civil law

BCnL	bachelor of canon law
BCom	bachelor of commerce
BD	bachelor of divinity
BEd	bachelor of education
BEng	bachelor of engineering
bk *pl.* bks	book(s)
BL	bachelor of law / letters / literature
BLitt	bachelor of letters
BM	bachelor of medicine
BMus	bachelor of music
BP	before present
BP	British Petroleum
Bros.	Brothers
BS	(1) bachelor of science; (2) bachelor of surgery; (3) British standard
BSc	bachelor of science
BSc (Econ.)	bachelor of science (economics)
BSc (Eng.)	bachelor of science (engineering)
bt	baronet
BTh	bachelor of theology
bur.	buried
C.	command [identifier for published parliamentary papers]
c.	*circa*
c.	*capitulum pl. capitula*: chapter(s)
CA	California
	Cantabrigiensis
	capitulum pl. capitula: chapter(s)
	companion of the Bath
	commander of the Order of the British Empire
	Columbia Broadcasting System
	cubic centimetres
	Canadian dollar
	compact disc
	command [identifier for published parliamentary papers]
	Common (*or* Christian) Era
	century
	compare
	Companion of Honour
	chapter
	bachelor of surgery
	Imperial Order of the Crown of India
	Central Intelligence Agency
	Criminal Investigation Department
	companion of the Order of the Indian Empire
	Compagnie
CLit	companion of literature
CM	master of surgery
cm	centimetre(s)

Cmd	command [identifier for published parliamentary papers]
CMG	companion of the Order of St Michael and St George
Cmnd	command [identifier for published parliamentary papers]
CO	Colorado
Co.	company
co.	county
col. *pl.* cols.	column(s)
Corp.	corporation
CSE	certificate of secondary education
CSI	companion of the Order of the Star of India
CT	Connecticut
CVO	commander of the Royal Victorian Order
cwt	hundredweight
$	(American) dollar
d.	(1) penny (pence); (2) died
DBE	dame commander of the Order of the British Empire
DCH	diploma in child health
DCh	doctor of surgery
DCL	doctor of civil law
DCnL	doctor of canon law
DCVO	dame commander of the Royal Victorian Order
DD	doctor of divinity
DE	Delaware
Dec	December
dem.	demolished
DEng	doctor of engineering
des.	destroyed
DFC	Distinguished Flying Cross
DipEd	diploma in education
DipPsych	diploma in psychiatry
diss.	dissertation
DL	deputy lieutenant
DLitt	doctor of letters
DLittCelt	doctor of Celtic letters
DM	(1) Deutschmark; (2) doctor of medicine; (3) doctor of musical arts
DMus	doctor of music
DNA	dioxyribonucleic acid
doc.	document
DOL	doctor of oriental learning
DPH	diploma in public health
DPhil	doctor of philosophy
DPM	diploma in psychological medicine
DSC	Distinguished Service Cross
DSc	doctor of science
DSc (Econ.)	doctor of science (economics)
DSc (Eng.)	doctor of science (engineering)
DSM	Distinguished Service Medal
DSO	companion of the Distinguished Service Order
DSocSc	doctor of social science
DTech	doctor of technology
DTh	doctor of theology
DTM	diploma in tropical medicine
DTMH	diploma in tropical medicine and hygiene
DU	doctor of the university
DUniv	doctor of the university
dwt	pennyweight
EC	European Community
ed. *pl.* eds.	edited / edited by / editor(s)
Edin.	Edinburgh
edn	edition
EEC	European Economic Community
EFTA	European Free Trade Association
EICS	East India Company Service
EMI	Electrical and Musical Industries (Ltd)
Eng.	English
enl.	enlarged
ENSA	Entertainments National Service Association
ep. *pl.* epp.	*epistola(e)*
ESP	extra-sensory perception
esp.	especially
esq.	esquire
est.	estimate / estimated
EU	European Union
ex	sold by (*lit.* out of)
excl.	excludes / excluding
exh.	exhibited
exh. cat.	exhibition catalogue
f. *pl.* ff.	following [pages]
FA	Football Association
FACP	fellow of the American College of Physicians
facs.	facsimile
FANY	First Aid Nursing Yeomanry
FBA	fellow of the British Academy
FBI	Federation of British Industries
FCS	fellow of the Chemical Society
Feb	February
FEng	fellow of the Fellowship of Engineering
FFCM	fellow of the Faculty of Community Medicine
FGS	fellow of the Geological Society
fig.	figure
FIMechE	fellow of the Institution of Mechanical Engineers
FL	Florida
fl.	*floruit*
FLS	fellow of the Linnean Society
FM	frequency modulation
fol. *pl.* fols.	folio(s)
Fr	French francs
Fr.	French
FRAeS	fellow of the Royal Aeronautical Society
FRAI	fellow of the Royal Anthropological Institute
FRAM	fellow of the Royal Academy of Music
FRAS	(1) fellow of the Royal Asiatic Society; (2) fellow of the Royal Astronomical Society
FRCM	fellow of the Royal College of Music
FRCO	fellow of the Royal College of Organists
FRCOG	fellow of the Royal College of Obstetricians and Gynaecologists
FRCP(C)	fellow of the Royal College of Physicians of Canada
FRCP (Edin.)	fellow of the Royal College of Physicians of Edinburgh
FRCP (Lond.)	fellow of the Royal College of Physicians of London
FRCPath	fellow of the Royal College of Pathologists
FRCPsych	fellow of the Royal College of Psychiatrists
FRCS	fellow of the Royal College of Surgeons
FRGS	fellow of the Royal Geographical Society
FRIBA	fellow of the Royal Institute of British Architects
FRICS	fellow of the Royal Institute of Chartered Surveyors
FRS	fellow of the Royal Society
FRSA	fellow of the Royal Society of Arts

FRSCM	fellow of the Royal School of Church Music
FRSE	fellow of the Royal Society of Edinburgh
FRSL	fellow of the Royal Society of Literature
FSA	fellow of the Society of Antiquaries
ft	foot *pl.* feet
FTCL	fellow of Trinity College of Music, London
ft-lb per min.	foot-pounds per minute [unit of horsepower]
FZS	fellow of the Zoological Society
GA	Georgia
GBE	knight or dame grand cross of the Order of the British Empire
GCB	knight grand cross of the Order of the Bath
GCE	general certificate of education
GCH	knight grand cross of the Royal Guelphic Order
GCHQ	government communications headquarters
GCIE	knight grand commander of the Order of the Indian Empire
GCMG	knight or dame grand cross of the Order of St Michael and St George
GCSE	general certificate of secondary education
GCSI	knight grand commander of the Order of the Star of India
GCStJ	bailiff or dame grand cross of the order of St John of Jerusalem
GCVO	knight or dame grand cross of the Royal Victorian Order
GEC	General Electric Company
Ger.	German
GI	government (*or* general) issue
GMT	Greenwich mean time
GP	general practitioner
GPU	[Soviet special police unit]
GSO	general staff officer
Heb.	Hebrew
HEICS	Honourable East India Company Service
HI	Hawaii
HIV	human immunodeficiency virus
HK$	Hong Kong dollar
HM	his / her majesty('s)
HMAS	his / her majesty's Australian ship
HMNZS	his / her majesty's New Zealand ship
HMS	his / her majesty's ship
HMSO	His / Her Majesty's Stationery Office
HMV	His Master's Voice
Hon.	Honourable
hp	horsepower
hr	hour(s)
HRH	his / her royal highness
HTV	Harlech Television
IA	Iowa
ibid.	*ibidem*: in the same place
ICI	Imperial Chemical Industries (Ltd)
ID	Idaho
IL	Illinois
illus.	illustration
illustr.	illustrated
IN	Indiana
in.	inch(es)
Inc.	Incorporated
incl.	includes / including
IOU	I owe you
IQ	intelligence quotient
Ir£	Irish pound
IRA	Irish Republican Army
ISO	companion of the Imperial Service Order
It.	Italian
ITA	Independent Television Authority
ITV	Independent Television
Jan	January
JP	justice of the peace
jun.	junior
KB	knight of the Order of the Bath
KBE	knight commander of the Order of the British Empire
KC	king's counsel
kcal	kilocalorie
KCB	knight commander of the Order of the Bath
KCH	knight commander of the Royal Guelphic Order
KCIE	knight commander of the Order of the Indian Empire
KCMG	knight commander of the Order of St Michael and St George
KCSI	knight commander of the Order of the Star of India
KCVO	knight commander of the Royal Victorian Order
keV	kilo-electron-volt
KG	knight of the Order of the Garter
KGB	[Soviet committee of state security]
KH	knight of the Royal Guelphic Order
KLM	Koninklijke Luchtvaart Maatschappij (Royal Dutch Air Lines)
km	kilometre(s)
KP	knight of the Order of St Patrick
KS	Kansas
KT	knight of the Order of the Thistle
kt	knight
KY	Kentucky
£	pound(s) sterling
£E	Egyptian pound
L	lira *pl.* lire
l. *pl.* ll.	line(s)
LA	Lousiana
LAA	light anti-aircraft
LAH	licentiate of the Apothecaries' Hall, Dublin
Lat.	Latin
lb	pound(s), unit of weight
LDS	licence in dental surgery
lit.	literally
LittB	bachelor of letters
LittD	doctor of letters
LKQCPI	licentiate of the King and Queen's College of Physicians, Ireland
LLA	lady literate in arts
LLB	bachelor of laws
LLD	doctor of laws
LLM	master of laws
LM	licentiate in midwifery
LP	long-playing record
LRAM	licentiate of the Royal Academy of Music
LRCP	licentiate of the Royal College of Physicians
LRCPS (Glasgow)	licentiate of the Royal College of Physicians and Surgeons of Glasgow
LRCS	licentiate of the Royal College of Surgeons
LSA	licentiate of the Society of Apothecaries
LSD	lysergic acid diethylamide
LVO	lieutenant of the Royal Victorian Order
M. *pl.* MM.	Monsieur *pl.* Messieurs
m	metre(s)

m. *pl.* mm.	membrane(s)
MA	(1) Massachusetts; (2) master of arts
MAI	master of engineering
MB	bachelor of medicine
MBA	master of business administration
MBE	member of the Order of the British Empire
MC	Military Cross
MCC	Marylebone Cricket Club
MCh	master of surgery
MChir	master of surgery
MCom	master of commerce
MD	(1) doctor of medicine; (2) Maryland
MDMA	methylenedioxymethamphetamine
ME	Maine
MEd	master of education
MEng	master of engineering
MEP	member of the European parliament
MG	Morris Garages
MGM	Metro-Goldwyn-Mayer
Mgr	Monsignor
MI	(1) Michigan; (2) military intelligence
MI1c	[secret intelligence department]
MI5	[military intelligence department]
MI6	[secret intelligence department]
MI9	[secret escape service]
MICE	member of the Institution of Civil Engineers
MIEE	member of the Institution of Electrical Engineers
min.	minute(s)
Mk	mark
ML	(1) licentiate of medicine; (2) master of laws
MLitt	master of letters
Mlle	Mademoiselle
mm	millimetre(s)
Mme	Madame
MN	Minnesota
MO	Missouri
MOH	medical officer of health
MP	member of parliament
m.p.h.	miles per hour
MPhil	master of philosophy
MRCP	member of the Royal College of Physicians
MRCS	member of the Royal College of Surgeons
MRCVS	member of the Royal College of Veterinary Surgeons
MRIA	member of the Royal Irish Academy
MS	(1) master of science; (2) Mississippi
MS *pl.* MSS	manuscript(s)
MSc	master of science
MSc (Econ.)	master of science (economics)
MT	Montana
MusB	bachelor of music
MusBac	bachelor of music
MusD	doctor of music
MV	motor vessel
MVO	member of the Royal Victorian Order
n. *pl.* nn.	note(s)
NAAFI	Navy, Army, and Air Force Institutes
NASA	National Aeronautics and Space Administration
NATO	North Atlantic Treaty Organization
NBC	National Broadcasting Corporation
NC	North Carolina
NCO	non-commissioned officer

ND	North Dakota
n.d.	no date
NE	Nebraska
nem. con.	*nemine contradicente*: unanimously
new ser.	new series
NH	New Hampshire
NHS	National Health Service
NJ	New Jersey
NKVD	[Soviet people's commissariat for internal affairs]
NM	New Mexico
nm	nanometre(s)
no. *pl.* nos.	number(s)
Nov	November
n.p.	no place [of publication]
NS	new style
NV	Nevada
NY	New York
NZBS	New Zealand Broadcasting Service
OBE	officer of the Order of the British Empire
obit.	obituary
Oct	October
OCTU	officer cadets training unit
OECD	Organization for Economic Co-operation and Development
OEEC	Organization for European Economic Co-operation
OFM	order of Friars Minor [Franciscans]
OFMCap	Ordine Frati Minori Cappucini: member of the Capuchin order
OH	Ohio
OK	Oklahoma
O level	ordinary level [examination]
OM	Order of Merit
OP	order of Preachers [Dominicans]
op. *pl.* opp.	opus *pl.* opera
OPEC	Organization of Petroleum Exporting Countries
OR	Oregon
orig.	original
OS	old style
OSB	Order of St Benedict
OTC	Officers' Training Corps
OWS	Old Watercolour Society
Oxon.	Oxoniensis
p. *pl.* pp.	page(s)
PA	Pennsylvania
p.a.	per annum
para.	paragraph
PAYE	pay as you earn
pbk *pl.* pbks	paperback(s)
per.	[during the] period
PhD	doctor of philosophy
pl.	(1) plate(s); (2) plural
priv. coll.	private collection
pt *pl.* pts	part(s)
pubd	published
PVC	polyvinyl chloride
q. *pl.* qq.	(1) question(s); (2) quire(s)
QC	queen's counsel
R	rand
R.	Rex / Regina
r	recto
r.	reigned / ruled
RA	Royal Academy / Royal Academician

RAC	Royal Automobile Club
RAF	Royal Air Force
RAFVR	Royal Air Force Volunteer Reserve
RAM	[member of the] Royal Academy of Music
RAMC	Royal Army Medical Corps
RCA	Royal College of Art
RCNC	Royal Corps of Naval Constructors
RCOG	Royal College of Obstetricians and Gynaecologists
RDI	royal designer for industry
RE	Royal Engineers
repr. *pl.* reprs.	reprint(s) / reprinted
repro.	reproduced
rev.	revised / revised by / reviser / revision
Revd	Reverend
RHA	Royal Hibernian Academy
RI	(1) Rhode Island; (2) Royal Institute of Painters in Water-Colours
RIBA	Royal Institute of British Architects
RIN	Royal Indian Navy
RM	Reichsmark
RMS	Royal Mail steamer
RN	Royal Navy
RNA	ribonucleic acid
RNAS	Royal Naval Air Service
RNR	Royal Naval Reserve
RNVR	Royal Naval Volunteer Reserve
RO	Record Office
r.p.m.	revolutions per minute
RRS	royal research ship
Rs	rupees
RSA	(1) Royal Scottish Academician; (2) Royal Society of Arts
RSPCA	Royal Society for the Prevention of Cruelty to Animals
Rt Hon.	Right Honourable
Rt Revd	Right Reverend
RUC	Royal Ulster Constabulary
Russ.	Russian
RWS	Royal Watercolour Society
S4C	Sianel Pedwar Cymru
s.	shilling(s)
s.a.	*sub anno*: under the year
SABC	South African Broadcasting Corporation
SAS	Special Air Service
SC	South Carolina
ScD	doctor of science
S$	Singapore dollar
SD	South Dakota
sec.	second(s)
sel.	selected
sen.	senior
Sept	September
ser.	series
SHAPE	supreme headquarters allied powers, Europe
SIDRO	Société Internationale d'Énergie Hydro-Électrique
sig. *pl.* sigs.	signature(s)
sing.	singular
SIS	Secret Intelligence Service
SJ	Society of Jesus
Skr	Swedish krona
Span.	Spanish
SPCK	Society for Promoting Christian Knowledge
SS	(1) Santissimi; (2) Schutzstaffel; (3) steam ship
STB	bachelor of theology
STD	doctor of theology
STM	master of theology
STP	doctor of theology
supp.	supposedly
suppl. *pl.* suppls.	supplement(s)
s.v.	*sub verbo* / *sub voce*: under the word / heading
SY	steam yacht
TA	Territorial Army
TASS	[Soviet news agency]
TB	tuberculosis (*lit.* tubercle bacillus)
TD	(1) *teachtaí dála* (member of the Dáil); (2) territorial decoration
TN	Tennessee
TNT	trinitrotoluene
trans.	translated / translated by / translation / translator
TT	tourist trophy
TUC	Trades Union Congress
TX	Texas
U-boat	*Unterseeboot*: submarine
Ufa	Universum-Film AG
UMIST	University of Manchester Institute of Science and Technology
UN	United Nations
UNESCO	United Nations Educational, Scientific, and Cultural Organization
UNICEF	United Nations International Children's Emergency Fund
unpubd	unpublished
USS	United States ship
UT	Utah
v	verso
v.	versus
VA	Virginia
VAD	Voluntary Aid Detachment
VC	Victoria Cross
VE-day	victory in Europe day
Ven.	Venerable
VJ-day	victory over Japan day
vol. *pl.* vols.	volume(s)
VT	Vermont
WA	Washington [state]
WAAC	Women's Auxiliary Army Corps
WAAF	Women's Auxiliary Air Force
WEA	Workers' Educational Association
WHO	World Health Organization
WI	Wisconsin
WRAF	Women's Royal Air Force
WRNS	Women's Royal Naval Service
WV	West Virginia
WVS	Women's Voluntary Service
WY	Wyoming
¥	yen
YMCA	Young Men's Christian Association
YWCA	Young Women's Christian Association

2 *Institution abbreviations*

All Souls Oxf.	All Souls College, Oxford
AM Oxf.	Ashmolean Museum, Oxford
Balliol Oxf.	Balliol College, Oxford
BBC WAC	BBC Written Archives Centre, Reading
Beds. & Luton ARS	Bedfordshire and Luton Archives and Record Service, Bedford
Berks. RO	Berkshire Record Office, Reading
BFI	British Film Institute, London
BFI NFTVA	British Film Institute, London, National Film and Television Archive
BGS	British Geological Survey, Keyworth, Nottingham
Birm. CA	Birmingham Central Library, Birmingham City Archives
Birm. CL	Birmingham Central Library
BL	British Library, London
BL NSA	British Library, London, National Sound Archive
BL OIOC	British Library, London, Oriental and India Office Collections
BLPES	London School of Economics and Political Science, British Library of Political and Economic Science
BM	British Museum, London
Bodl. Oxf.	Bodleian Library, Oxford
Bodl. RH	Bodleian Library of Commonwealth and African Studies at Rhodes House, Oxford
Borth. Inst.	Borthwick Institute of Historical Research, University of York
Boston PL	Boston Public Library, Massachusetts
Bristol RO	Bristol Record Office
Bucks. RLSS	Buckinghamshire Records and Local Studies Service, Aylesbury
CAC Cam.	Churchill College, Cambridge, Churchill Archives Centre
Cambs. AS	Cambridgeshire Archive Service
CCC Cam.	Corpus Christi College, Cambridge
CCC Oxf.	Corpus Christi College, Oxford
Ches. & Chester ALSS	Cheshire and Chester Archives and Local Studies Service
Christ Church Oxf.	Christ Church, Oxford
Christies	Christies, London
City Westm. AC	City of Westminster Archives Centre, London
CKS	Centre for Kentish Studies, Maidstone
CLRO	Corporation of London Records Office
Coll. Arms	College of Arms, London
Col. U.	Columbia University, New York
Cornwall RO	Cornwall Record Office, Truro
Courtauld Inst.	Courtauld Institute of Art, London
CUL	Cambridge University Library
Cumbria AS	Cumbria Archive Service
Derbys. RO	Derbyshire Record Office, Matlock
Devon RO	Devon Record Office, Exeter
Dorset RO	Dorset Record Office, Dorchester
Duke U.	Duke University, Durham, North Carolina
Duke U., Perkins L.	Duke University, Durham, North Carolina, William R. Perkins Library
Durham Cath. CL	Durham Cathedral, chapter library
Durham RO	Durham Record Office
DWL	Dr Williams's Library, London
Essex RO	Essex Record Office
E. Sussex RO	East Sussex Record Office, Lewes
Eton	Eton College, Berkshire
FM Cam.	Fitzwilliam Museum, Cambridge
Folger	Folger Shakespeare Library, Washington, DC
Garr. Club	Garrick Club, London
Girton Cam.	Girton College, Cambridge
GL	Guildhall Library, London
Glos. RO	Gloucestershire Record Office, Gloucester
Gon. & Caius Cam.	Gonville and Caius College, Cambridge
Gov. Art Coll.	Government Art Collection
GS Lond.	Geological Society of London
Hants. RO	Hampshire Record Office, Winchester
Harris Man. Oxf.	Harris Manchester College, Oxford
Harvard TC	Harvard Theatre Collection, Harvard University, Cambridge, Massachusetts, Nathan Marsh Pusey Library
Harvard U.	Harvard University, Cambridge, Massachusetts
Harvard U., Houghton L.	Harvard University, Cambridge, Massachusetts, Houghton Library
Herefs. RO	Herefordshire Record Office, Hereford
Herts. ALS	Hertfordshire Archives and Local Studies, Hertford
Hist. Soc. Penn.	Historical Society of Pennsylvania, Philadelphia
HLRO	House of Lords Record Office, London
Hult. Arch.	Hulton Archive, London and New York
Hunt. L.	Huntington Library, San Marino, California
ICL	Imperial College, London
Inst. CE	Institution of Civil Engineers, London
Inst. EE	Institution of Electrical Engineers, London
IWM	Imperial War Museum, London
IWM FVA	Imperial War Museum, London, Film and Video Archive
IWM SA	Imperial War Museum, London, Sound Archive
JRL	John Rylands University Library of Manchester
King's AC Cam.	King's College Archives Centre, Cambridge
King's Cam.	King's College, Cambridge
King's Lond.	King's College, London
King's Lond., Liddell Hart C.	King's College, London, Liddell Hart Centre for Military Archives
Lancs. RO	Lancashire Record Office, Preston
L. Cong.	Library of Congress, Washington, DC
Leics. RO	Leicestershire, Leicester, and Rutland Record Office, Leicester
Lincs. Arch.	Lincolnshire Archives, Lincoln
Linn. Soc.	Linnean Society of London
LMA	London Metropolitan Archives
LPL	Lambeth Palace, London
Lpool RO	Liverpool Record Office and Local Studies Service
LUL	London University Library
Magd. Cam.	Magdalene College, Cambridge
Magd. Oxf.	Magdalen College, Oxford
Man. City Gall.	Manchester City Galleries
Man. CL	Manchester Central Library
Mass. Hist. Soc.	Massachusetts Historical Society, Boston
Merton Oxf.	Merton College, Oxford
MHS Oxf.	Museum of the History of Science, Oxford
Mitchell L., Glas.	Mitchell Library, Glasgow
Mitchell L., NSW	State Library of New South Wales, Sydney, Mitchell Library
Morgan L.	Pierpont Morgan Library, New York
NA Canada	National Archives of Canada, Ottawa
NA Ire.	National Archives of Ireland, Dublin
NAM	National Army Museum, London
NA Scot.	National Archives of Scotland, Edinburgh
News Int. RO	News International Record Office, London
NG Ire.	National Gallery of Ireland, Dublin

NG Scot.	National Gallery of Scotland, Edinburgh
NHM	Natural History Museum, London
NL Aus.	National Library of Australia, Canberra
NL Ire.	National Library of Ireland, Dublin
NL NZ	National Library of New Zealand, Wellington
NL NZ, Turnbull L.	National Library of New Zealand, Wellington, Alexander Turnbull Library
NL Scot.	National Library of Scotland, Edinburgh
NL Wales	National Library of Wales, Aberystwyth
NMG Wales	National Museum and Gallery of Wales, Cardiff
NMM	National Maritime Museum, London
Norfolk RO	Norfolk Record Office, Norwich
Northants. RO	Northamptonshire Record Office, Northampton
Northumbd RO	Northumberland Record Office
Notts. Arch.	Nottinghamshire Archives, Nottingham
NPG	National Portrait Gallery, London
NRA	National Archives, London, Historical Manuscripts Commission, National Register of Archives
Nuffield Oxf.	Nuffield College, Oxford
N. Yorks. CRO	North Yorkshire County Record Office, Northallerton
NYPL	New York Public Library
Oxf. UA	Oxford University Archives
Oxf. U. Mus. NH	Oxford University Museum of Natural History
Oxon. RO	Oxfordshire Record Office, Oxford
Pembroke Cam.	Pembroke College, Cambridge
PRO	National Archives, London, Public Record Office
PRO NIre.	Public Record Office for Northern Ireland, Belfast
Pusey Oxf.	Pusey House, Oxford
RA	Royal Academy of Arts, London
Ransom HRC	Harry Ransom Humanities Research Center, University of Texas, Austin
RAS	Royal Astronomical Society, London
RBG Kew	Royal Botanic Gardens, Kew, London
RCP Lond.	Royal College of Physicians of London
RCS Eng.	Royal College of Surgeons of England, London
RGS	Royal Geographical Society, London
RIBA	Royal Institute of British Architects, London
RIBA BAL	Royal Institute of British Architects, London, British Architectural Library
Royal Arch.	Royal Archives, Windsor Castle, Berkshire [by gracious permission of her majesty the queen]
Royal Irish Acad.	Royal Irish Academy, Dublin
Royal Scot. Acad.	Royal Scottish Academy, Edinburgh
RS	Royal Society, London
RSA	Royal Society of Arts, London
RS Friends, Lond.	Religious Society of Friends, London
St Ant. Oxf.	St Antony's College, Oxford
St John Cam.	St John's College, Cambridge
S. Antiquaries, Lond.	Society of Antiquaries of London
Sci. Mus.	Science Museum, London
Scot. NPG	Scottish National Portrait Gallery, Edinburgh
Scott Polar RI	University of Cambridge, Scott Polar Research Institute
Sheff. Arch.	Sheffield Archives
Shrops. RRC	Shropshire Records and Research Centre, Shrewsbury
SOAS	School of Oriental and African Studies, London
Som. ARS	Somerset Archive and Record Service, Taunton
Staffs. RO	Staffordshire Record Office, Stafford
Suffolk RO	Suffolk Record Office
Surrey HC	Surrey History Centre, Woking
TCD	Trinity College, Dublin
Trinity Cam.	Trinity College, Cambridge
U. Aberdeen	University of Aberdeen
U. Birm.	University of Birmingham
U. Birm. L.	University of Birmingham Library
U. Cal.	University of California
U. Cam.	University of Cambridge
UCL	University College, London
U. Durham	University of Durham
U. Durham L.	University of Durham Library
U. Edin.	University of Edinburgh
U. Edin., New Coll.	University of Edinburgh, New College
U. Edin., New Coll. L.	University of Edinburgh, New College Library
U. Edin. L.	University of Edinburgh Library
U. Glas.	University of Glasgow
U. Glas. L.	University of Glasgow Library
U. Hull	University of Hull
U. Hull, Brynmor Jones L.	University of Hull, Brynmor Jones Library
U. Leeds	University of Leeds
U. Leeds, Brotherton L.	University of Leeds, Brotherton Library
U. Lond.	University of London
U. Lpool	University of Liverpool
U. Lpool L.	University of Liverpool Library
U. Mich.	University of Michigan, Ann Arbor
U. Mich., Clements L.	University of Michigan, Ann Arbor, William L. Clements Library
U. Newcastle	University of Newcastle upon Tyne
U. Newcastle, Robinson L.	University of Newcastle upon Tyne, Robinson Library
U. Nott.	University of Nottingham
U. Nott. L.	University of Nottingham Library
U. Oxf.	University of Oxford
U. Reading	University of Reading
U. Reading L.	University of Reading Library
U. St Andr.	University of St Andrews
U. St Andr. L.	University of St Andrews Library
U. Southampton	University of Southampton
U. Southampton L.	University of Southampton Library
U. Sussex	University of Sussex, Brighton
U. Texas	University of Texas, Austin
U. Wales	University of Wales
U. Warwick Mod. RC	University of Warwick, Coventry, Modern Records Centre
V&A	Victoria and Albert Museum, London
V&A NAL	Victoria and Albert Museum, London, National Art Library
Warks. CRO	Warwickshire County Record Office, Warwick
Wellcome L.	Wellcome Library for the History and Understanding of Medicine, London
Westm. DA	Westminster Diocesan Archives, London
Wilts. & Swindon RO	Wiltshire and Swindon Record Office, Trowbridge
Worcs. RO	Worcestershire Record Office, Worcester
W. Sussex RO	West Sussex Record Office, Chichester
W. Yorks. AS	West Yorkshire Archive Service
Yale U.	Yale University, New Haven, Connecticut
Yale U., Beinecke L.	Yale University, New Haven, Connecticut, Beinecke Rare Book and Manuscript Library
Yale U. CBA	Yale University, New Haven, Connecticut, Yale Center for British Art

3 *Bibliographic abbreviations*

Adams, *Drama*	W. D. Adams, *A dictionary of the drama*, 1: *A–G* (1904); 2: *H–Z* (1956) [vol. 2 microfilm only]
AFM	J O'Donovan, ed. and trans., *Annala rioghachta Eireann / Annals of the kingdom of Ireland by the four masters*, 7 vols. (1848–51); 2nd edn (1856); 3rd edn (1990)
Allibone, *Dict.*	S. A. Allibone, *A critical dictionary of English literature and British and American authors*, 3 vols. (1859–71); suppl. by J. F. Kirk, 2 vols. (1891)
ANB	J. A. Garraty and M. C. Carnes, eds., *American national biography*, 24 vols. (1999)
Anderson, *Scot. nat.*	W. Anderson, *The Scottish nation, or, The surnames, families, literature, honours, and biographical history of the people of Scotland*, 3 vols. (1859–63)
Ann. mon.	H. R. Luard, ed., *Annales monastici*, 5 vols., Rolls Series, 36 (1864–9)
Ann. Ulster	S. Mac Airt and G. Mac Niocaill, eds., *Annals of Ulster (to AD 1131)* (1983)
APC	*Acts of the privy council of England*, new ser., 46 vols. (1890–1964)
APS	*The acts of the parliaments of Scotland*, 12 vols. in 13 (1814–75)
Arber, *Regs. Stationers*	F. Arber, ed., *A transcript of the registers of the Company of Stationers of London, 1554–1640 AD*, 5 vols. (1875–94)
ArchR	*Architectural Review*
ASC	D. Whitelock, D. C. Douglas, and S. I. Tucker, ed. and trans., *The Anglo-Saxon Chronicle: a revised translation* (1961)
AS chart.	P. H. Sawyer, *Anglo-Saxon charters: an annotated list and bibliography*, Royal Historical Society Guides and Handbooks (1968)
AusDB	D. Pike and others, eds., *Australian dictionary of biography*, 16 vols. (1966–2002)
Baker, *Serjeants*	J. H. Baker, *The order of serjeants at law*, SeldS, suppl. ser., 5 (1984)
Bale, *Cat.*	J. Bale, *Scriptorum illustrium Maioris Brytannie, quam nunc Angliam et Scotiam vocant: catalogus*, 2 vols. in 1 (Basel, 1557–9); facs. edn (1971)
Bale, *Index*	J. Bale, *Index Britanniae scriptorum*, ed. R. L. Poole and M. Bateson (1902); facs. edn (1990)
BBCS	*Bulletin of the Board of Celtic Studies*
BDMBR	J. O. Baylen and N. J. Gossman, eds., *Biographical dictionary of modern British radicals*, 3 vols. in 4 (1979–88)
Bede, *Hist. eccl.*	*Bede's Ecclesiastical history of the English people*, ed. and trans. B. Colgrave and R. A. B. Mynors, OMT (1969); repr. (1991)
Bénézit, *Dict.*	E. Bénézit, *Dictionnaire critique et documentaire des peintres, sculpteurs, dessinateurs et graveurs*, 3 vols. (Paris, 1911–23); new edn, 8 vols. (1948–66), repr. (1966); 3rd edn, rev. and enl., 10 vols. (1976); 4th edn, 14 vols. (1999)
BIHR	*Bulletin of the Institute of Historical Research*
Birch, *Seals*	W. de Birch, *Catalogue of seals in the department of manuscripts in the British Museum*, 6 vols. (1887–1900)
Bishop Burnet's History	*Bishop Burnet's History of his own time*, ed. M. J. Routh, 2nd edn, 6 vols. (1833)
Blackwood	*Blackwood's [Edinburgh] Magazine*, 328 vols. (1817–1980)
Blain, Clements & Grundy, *Feminist comp.*	V. Blain, P. Clements, and I. Grundy, eds., *The feminist companion to literature in English* (1990)
BL cat.	*The British Library general catalogue of printed books* [in 360 vols. with suppls., also CD-ROM and online]
BMJ	*British Medical Journal*
Boase & Courtney, *Bibl. Corn.*	G. C. Boase and W. P. Courtney, *Bibliotheca Cornubiensis: a catalogue of the writings … of Cornishmen*, 3 vols. (1874–82)
Boase, *Mod. Eng. biog.*	F. Boase, *Modern English biography: containing many thousand concise memoirs of persons who have died since the year 1850*, 6 vols. (privately printed, Truro, 1892–1921); repr. (1965)
Boswell, *Life*	*Boswell's Life of Johnson: together with Journal of a tour to the Hebrides and Johnson's Diary of a journey into north Wales*, ed. G. B. Hill, enl. edn, rev. L. F. Powell, 6 vols. (1934–50); 2nd edn (1964); repr. (1971)
Brown & Stratton, *Brit. mus.*	J. D. Brown and S. S. Stratton, *British musical biography* (1897)
Bryan, *Painters*	M. Bryan, *A biographical and critical dictionary of painters and engravers*, 2 vols. (1816); new edn, ed. G. Stanley (1849); new edn, ed. R. E. Graves and W. Armstrong, 2 vols. (1886–9); [4th edn], ed. G. C. Williamson, 5 vols. (1903–5) [various reprs.]
Burke, *Gen. GB*	J. Burke, *A genealogical and heraldic history of the commoners of Great Britain and Ireland*, 4 vols. (1833–8); new edn as *A genealogical and heraldic dictionary of the landed gentry of Great Britain and Ireland*, 3 vols. [1843–9] [many later edns]
Burke, *Gen. Ire.*	J. B. Burke, *A genealogical and heraldic history of the landed gentry of Ireland* (1899); 2nd edn (1904); 3rd edn (1912); 4th edn (1958); 5th edn as *Burke's Irish family records* (1976)
Burke, *Peerage*	J. Burke, *A general* [later edns *A genealogical*] *and heraldic dictionary of the peerage and baronetage of the United Kingdom* [later edns *the British empire*] (1829–)
Burney, *Hist. mus.*	C. Burney, *A general history of music, from the earliest ages to the present period*, 4 vols. (1776–89)
Burtchaell & Sadleir, *Alum. Dubl.*	G. D. Burtchaell and T. U. Sadleir, *Alumni Dublinenses: a register of the students, graduates, and provosts of Trinity College* (1924); [2nd edn], with suppl., in 2 pts (1935)
Calamy rev.	A. G. Matthews, *Calamy revised* (1934); repr. (1988)
CCI	*Calendar of confirmations and inventories granted and given up in the several commissariots of Scotland* (1876–)
CClR	*Calendar of the close rolls preserved in the Public Record Office*, 47 vols. (1892–1963)
CDS	J. Bain, ed., *Calendar of documents relating to Scotland*, 4 vols., PRO (1881–8); suppl. vol. 5, ed. G. G. Simpson and J. D. Galbraith [1986]
CEPR letters	W. H. Bliss, C. Johnson, and J. Twemlow, eds., *Calendar of entries in the papal registers relating to Great Britain and Ireland: papal letters* (1893–)
CGPLA	*Calendars of the grants of probate and letters of administration* [in 4 ser.: *England & Wales, Northern Ireland, Ireland*, and *Éire*]
Chambers, *Scots.*	R. Chambers, ed., *A biographical dictionary of eminent Scotsmen*, 4 vols. (1832–5)
Chancery records	chancery records pubd by the PRO
Chancery records (RC)	chancery records pubd by the Record Commissions

CIPM	*Calendar of inquisitions post mortem*, [20 vols.], PRO (1904–); also *Henry VII*, 3 vols. (1898–1955)
Clarendon, *Hist. rebellion*	E. Hyde, earl of Clarendon, *The history of the rebellion and civil wars in England*, 6 vols. (1888); repr. (1958) and (1992)
Cobbett, *Parl. hist.*	W. Cobbett and J. Wright, eds., *Cobbett's Parliamentary history of England*, 36 vols. (1806–1820)
Colvin, *Archs.*	H. Colvin, *A biographical dictionary of British architects, 1600–1840*, 3rd edn (1995)
Cooper, *Ath. Cantab.*	C. H. Cooper and T. Cooper, *Athenae Cantabrigienses*, 3 vols. (1858–1913); repr. (1967)
CPR	*Calendar of the patent rolls preserved in the Public Record Office* (1891–)
Crockford	*Crockford's Clerical Directory*
CS	Camden Society
CSP	*Calendar of state papers* [in 11 ser.: *domestic*, *Scotland*, *Scottish series*, *Ireland*, *colonial*, *Commonwealth*, *foreign*, *Spain* [at Simancas], *Rome*, *Milan*, and *Venice*]
CYS	Canterbury and York Society
DAB	*Dictionary of American biography*, 21 vols. (1928–36), repr. in 11 vols. (1964); 10 suppls. (1944–96)
DBB	D. J. Jeremy, ed., *Dictionary of business biography*, 5 vols. (1984–6)
DCB	G. W. Brown and others, *Dictionary of Canadian biography*, [14 vols.] (1966–)
Debrett's Peerage	*Debrett's Peerage* (1803–) [sometimes *Debrett's Illustrated peerage*]
Desmond, *Botanists*	R. Desmond, *Dictionary of British and Irish botanists and horticulturists* (1977); rev. edn (1994)
Dir. Brit. archs.	A. Felstead, J. Franklin, and L. Pinfield, eds., *Directory of British architects, 1834–1900* (1993); 2nd edn, ed. A. Brodie and others, 2 vols. (2001)
DLB	J. M. Bellamy and J. Saville, eds., *Dictionary of labour biography*, [10 vols.] (1972–)
DLitB	Dictionary of Literary Biography
DNB	*Dictionary of national biography*, 63 vols. (1885–1900), suppl., 3 vols. (1901); repr. in 22 vols. (1908–9); 10 further suppls. (1912–96); *Missing persons* (1993)
DNZB	W. H. Oliver and C. Orange, eds., *The dictionary of New Zealand biography*, 5 vols. (1990–2000)
DSAB	W. J. de Kock and others, eds., *Dictionary of South African biography*, 5 vols. (1968–87)
DSB	C. C. Gillispie and F. L. Holmes, eds., *Dictionary of scientific biography*, 16 vols. (1970–80); repr. in 8 vols. (1981); 2 vol. suppl. (1990)
DSBB	A. Slaven and S. Checkland, eds., *Dictionary of Scottish business biography, 1860–1960*, 2 vols. (1986–90)
DSCHT	N. M. de S. Cameron and others, eds., *Dictionary of Scottish church history and theology* (1993)
Dugdale, *Monasticon*	W. Dugdale, *Monasticon Anglicanum*, 3 vols. (1655–72); 2nd edn, 3 vols. (1661–82); new edn, ed. J. Caley, J. Ellis, and B. Bandinel, 6 vols. in 8 pts (1817–30); repr. (1846) and (1970)
DWB	J. E. Lloyd and others, eds., *Dictionary of Welsh biography down to 1940* (1959) [Eng. trans. of *Y bywgraffiadur Cymreig hyd 1940*, 2nd edn (1954)]
EdinR	*Edinburgh Review, or, Critical Journal*
EETS	Early English Text Society
Emden, *Cam.*	A. B. Emden, *A biographical register of the University of Cambridge to 1500* (1963)
Emden, *Oxf.*	A. B. Emden, *A biographical register of the University of Oxford to AD 1500*, 3 vols. (1957–9); also *A biographical register of the University of Oxford, AD 1501 to 1540* (1974)
EngHR	*English Historical Review*
Engraved Brit. ports.	F. M. O'Donoghue and H. M. Hake, *Catalogue of engraved British portraits preserved in the department of prints and drawings in the British Museum*, 6 vols. (1908–25)
ER	The English Reports, 178 vols. (1900–32)
ESTC	*English short title catalogue, 1475–1800* [CD-ROM and online]
Evelyn, *Diary*	*The diary of John Evelyn*, ed. E. S. De Beer, 6 vols. (1955); repr. (2000)
Farington, *Diary*	*The diary of Joseph Farington*, ed. K. Garlick and others, 17 vols. (1978–98)
Fasti Angl. (Hardy)	J. Le Neve, *Fasti ecclesiae Anglicanae*, ed. T. D. Hardy, 3 vols. (1854)
Fasti Angl., 1066–1300	[J. Le Neve], *Fasti ecclesiae Anglicanae, 1066–1300*, ed. D. E. Greenway and J. S. Barrow, [8 vols.] (1968–)
Fasti Angl., 1300–1541	[J. Le Neve], *Fasti ecclesiae Anglicanae, 1300–1541*, 12 vols. (1962–7)
Fasti Angl., 1541–1857	[J. Le Neve], *Fasti ecclesiae Anglicanae, 1541–1857*, ed. J. M. Horn, D. M. Smith, and D. S. Bailey, [9 vols.] (1969–)
Fasti Scot.	H. Scott, *Fasti ecclesiae Scoticanae*, 3 vols. in 6 (1871); new edn, [11 vols.] (1915–)
FO List	*Foreign Office List*
Fortescue, *Brit. army*	J. W. Fortescue, *A history of the British army*, 13 vols. (1899–1930)
Foss, *Judges*	E. Foss, *The judges of England*, 9 vols. (1848–64); repr. (1966)
Foster, *Alum. Oxon.*	J. Foster, ed., *Alumni Oxonienses: the members of the University of Oxford, 1715–1886*, 4 vols. (1887–8); later edn (1891); also *Alumni Oxonienses … 1500–1714*, 4 vols. (1891–2); 8 vol. repr. (1968) and (2000)
Fuller, *Worthies*	T. Fuller, *The history of the worthies of England*, 4 pts (1662); new edn, 2 vols., ed. J. Nichols (1811); new edn, 3 vols., ed. P. A. Nuttall (1840); repr. (1965)
GEC, *Baronetage*	G. E. Cokayne, *Complete baronetage*, 6 vols. (1900–09); repr. (1983) [microprint]
GEC, *Peerage*	G. E. C. [G. E. Cokayne], *The complete peerage of England, Scotland, Ireland, Great Britain, and the United Kingdom*, 8 vols. (1887–98); new edn, ed. V. Gibbs and others, 14 vols. in 15 (1910–98); microprint repr. (1982) and (1987)
Genest, *Eng. stage*	J. Genest, *Some account of the English stage from the Restoration in 1660 to 1830*, 10 vols. (1832); repr. [New York, 1965]
Gillow, *Lit. biog. hist.*	J. Gillow, *A literary and biographical history or bibliographical dictionary of the English Catholics, from the breach with Rome, in 1534, to the present time*, 5 vols. [1885–1902]; repr. (1961); repr. with preface by C. Gillow (1999)
Gir. Camb. opera	*Giraldi Cambrensis opera*, ed. J. S. Brewer, J. F. Dimock, and G. F. Warner, 8 vols., Rolls Series, 21 (1861–91)
GJ	*Geographical Journal*

Gladstone, *Diaries*	*The Gladstone diaries: with cabinet minutes and prime-ministerial correspondence*, ed. M. R. D. Foot and H. C. G. Matthew, 14 vols. (1968–94)
GM	*Gentleman's Magazine*
Graves, *Artists*	A. Graves, ed., *A dictionary of artists who have exhibited works in the principal London exhibitions of oil paintings from 1760 to 1880* (1884); new edn (1895); 3rd edn (1901); facs. edn (1969); repr. [1970], (1973), and (1984)
Graves, *Brit. Inst.*	A. Graves, *The British Institution, 1806–1867: a complete dictionary of contributors and their work from the foundation of the institution* (1875); facs. edn (1908); repr. (1969)
Graves, *RA exhibitors*	A. Graves, *The Royal Academy of Arts: a complete dictionary of contributors and their work from its foundation in 1769 to 1904*, 8 vols. (1905–6); repr. in 4 vols. (1970) and (1972)
Graves, *Soc. Artists*	A. Graves, *The Society of Artists of Great Britain, 1760–1791, the Free Society of Artists, 1761–1783: a complete dictionary* (1907); facs. edn (1969)
Greaves & Zaller, *BDBR*	R. L. Greaves and R. Zaller, eds., *Biographical dictionary of British radicals in the seventeenth century*, 3 vols. (1982–4)
Grove, *Dict. mus.*	G. Grove, ed., *A dictionary of music and musicians*, 5 vols. (1878–90); 2nd edn, ed. J. A. Fuller Maitland (1904–10); 3rd edn, ed. H. C. Colles (1927); 4th edn with suppl. (1940); 5th edn, ed. E. Blom, 9 vols. (1954); suppl. (1961) [see also *New Grove*]
Hall, *Dramatic ports.*	L. A. Hall, *Catalogue of dramatic portraits in the theatre collection of the Harvard College library*, 4 vols. (1930–34)
Hansard	*Hansard's parliamentary debates*, ser. 1–5 (1803–)
Highfill, Burnim & Langhans, *BDA*	P. H. Highfill, K. A. Burnim, and E. A. Langhans, *A biographical dictionary of actors, actresses, musicians, dancers, managers, and other stage personnel in London, 1660–1800*, 16 vols. (1973–93)
Hist. U. Oxf.	T. H. Aston, ed., *The history of the University of Oxford*, 8 vols. (1984–2000) [1: *The early Oxford schools*, ed. J. I. Catto (1984); 2: *Late medieval Oxford*, ed. J. I. Catto and R. Evans (1992); 3: *The collegiate university*, ed. J. McConica (1986); 4: *Seventeenth-century Oxford*, ed. N. Tyacke (1997); 5: *The eighteenth century*, ed. L. S. Sutherland and L. G. Mitchell (1986); 6–7: *Nineteenth-century Oxford*, ed. M. G. Brock and M. C. Curthoys (1997–2000); 8: *The twentieth century*, ed. B. Harrison (2000)]
HJ	*Historical Journal*
HMC	Historical Manuscripts Commission
Holdsworth, *Eng. law*	W. S. Holdsworth, *A history of English law*, ed. A. L. Goodhart and H. L. Hanbury, 17 vols. (1903–72)
HoP, *Commons*	*The history of parliament: the House of Commons* [*1386–1421*, ed. J. S. Roskell, L. Clark, and C. Rawcliffe, 4 vols. (1992); *1509–1558*, ed. S. T. Bindoff, 3 vols. (1982); *1558–1603*, ed. P. W. Hasler, 3 vols. (1981); *1660–1690*, ed. B. D. Henning, 3 vols. (1983); *1690–1715*, ed. D. W. Hayton, E. Cruickshanks, and S. Handley, 5 vols. (2002); *1715–1754*, ed. R. Sedgwick, 2 vols. (1970); *1754–1790*, ed. L. Namier and J. Brooke, 3 vols. (1964), repr. (1985); *1790–1820*, ed. R. G. Thorne, 5 vols. (1986); in draft (used with permission): *1422–1504*, *1604–1629*, *1640–1660*, and *1820–1832*]
IGI	*International Genealogical Index*, Church of Jesus Christ of the Latterday Saints
ILN	*Illustrated London News*
IMC	Irish Manuscripts Commission
Irving, *Scots.*	J. Irving, ed., *The book of Scotsmen eminent for achievements in arms and arts, church and state, law, legislation and literature, commerce, science, travel and philanthropy* (1881)
JCS	*Journal of the Chemical Society*
JHC	*Journals of the House of Commons*
JHL	*Journals of the House of Lords*
John of Worcester, *Chron.*	*The chronicle of John of Worcester*, ed. R. R. Darlington and P. McGurk, trans. J. Bray and P. McGurk, 3 vols., OMT (1995–) [vol. 1 forthcoming]
Keeler, *Long Parliament*	M. F. Keeler, *The Long Parliament, 1640–1641: a biographical study of its members* (1954)
Kelly, *Handbk*	*The upper ten thousand: an alphabetical list of all members of noble families*, 3 vols. (1875–7); continued as *Kelly's handbook of the upper ten thousand for 1878* [1879], 2 vols. (1878–9); continued as *Kelly's handbook to the titled, landed and official classes*, 94 vols. (1880–1973)
LondG	*London Gazette*
LP Henry VIII	J. S. Brewer, J. Gairdner, and R. H. Brodie, eds., *Letters and papers, foreign and domestic, of the reign of Henry VIII*, 23 vols. in 38 (1862–1932); repr. (1965)
Mallalieu, *Watercolour artists*	H. L. Mallalieu, *The dictionary of British watercolour artists up to 1820*, 3 vols. (1976–90); vol. 1, 2nd edn (1986)
Memoirs FRS	*Biographical Memoirs of Fellows of the Royal Society*
MGH	Monumenta Germaniae Historica
MT	*Musical Times*
Munk, *Roll*	W. Munk, *The roll of the Royal College of Physicians of London*, 2 vols. (1861); 2nd edn, 3 vols. (1878)
N&Q	*Notes and Queries*
New Grove	S. Sadie, ed., *The new Grove dictionary of music and musicians*, 20 vols. (1980); 2nd edn, 29 vols. (2001) [also online edn; see also Grove, *Dict. mus.*]
Nichols, *Illustrations*	J. Nichols and J. B. Nichols, *Illustrations of the literary history of the eighteenth century*, 8 vols. (1817–58)
Nichols, *Lit. anecdotes*	J. Nichols, *Literary anecdotes of the eighteenth century*, 9 vols. (1812–16); facs. edn (1966)
Obits. FRS	*Obituary Notices of Fellows of the Royal Society*
O'Byrne, *Naval biog. dict.*	W. R. O'Byrne, *A naval biographical dictionary* (1849); repr. (1990); [2nd edn], 2 vols. (1861)
OHS	Oxford Historical Society
Old Westminsters	*The record of Old Westminsters*, 1–2, ed. G. F. R. Barker and A. H. Stenning (1928); suppl. 1, ed. J. B. Whitmore and G. R. Y. Radcliffe [1938]; 3, ed. J. B. Whitmore, G. R. Y. Radcliffe, and D. C. Simpson (1963); suppl. 2, ed. F. E. Pagan (1978); 4, ed. F. E. Pagan and H. E. Pagan (1992)
OMT	Oxford Medieval Texts
Ordericus Vitalis, *Eccl. hist.*	*The ecclesiastical history of Orderic Vitalis*, ed. and trans. M. Chibnall, 6 vols., OMT (1969–80); repr. (1990)
Paris, *Chron.*	*Matthaei Parisiensis, monachi sancti Albani, chronica majora*, ed. H. R. Luard, Rolls Series, 7 vols. (1872–83)
Parl. papers	*Parliamentary papers* (1801–)
PBA	*Proceedings of the British Academy*

Pepys, *Diary*	*The diary of Samuel Pepys*, ed. R. Latham and W. Matthews, 11 vols. (1970–83); repr. (1995) and (2000)
Pevsner	N. Pevsner and others, Buildings of England series
PICE	*Proceedings of the Institution of Civil Engineers*
Pipe rolls	*The great roll of the pipe for …*, PRSoc. (1884–)
PRO	Public Record Office
PRS	*Proceedings of the Royal Society of London*
PRSoc.	Pipe Roll Society
PTRS	*Philosophical Transactions of the Royal Society*
QR	*Quarterly Review*
RC	Record Commissions
Redgrave, *Artists*	S. Redgrave, *A dictionary of artists of the English school* (1874); rev. edn (1878); repr. (1970)
Reg. Oxf.	C. W. Boase and A. Clark, eds., *Register of the University of Oxford*, 5 vols., OHS, 1, 10–12, 14 (1885–9)
Reg. PCS	J. H. Burton and others, eds., *The register of the privy council of Scotland*, 1st ser., 14 vols. (1877–98); 2nd ser., 8 vols. (1899–1908); 3rd ser., [16 vols.] (1908–70)
Reg. RAN	H. W. C. Davis and others, eds., *Regesta regum Anglo-Normannorum, 1066–1154*, 4 vols. (1913–69)
RIBA Journal	*Journal of the Royal Institute of British Architects* [later *RIBA Journal*]
RotP	J. Strachey, ed., *Rotuli parliamentorum ut et petitiones, et placita in parliamento*, 6 vols. (1767–77)
RotS	D. Macpherson, J. Caley, and W. Illingworth, eds., *Rotuli Scotiae in Turri Londinensi et in domo capitulari Westmonasteriensi asservati*, 2 vols., RC, 14 (1814–19)
RS	Record(s) Society
Rymer, *Foedera*	T. Rymer and R. Sanderson, eds., *Foedera, conventiones, literae et cuiuscunque generis acta publica inter reges Angliae et alios quosvis imperatores, reges, pontifices, principes, vel communitates*, 20 vols. (1704–35); 2nd edn, 20 vols. (1726–35); 3rd edn, 10 vols. (1739–45), facs. edn (1967); new edn, ed. A. Clarke, J. Caley, and F. Holbrooke, 4 vols., RC, 50 (1816–30)
Sainty, *Judges*	J. Sainty, ed., *The judges of England, 1272–1990*, SeldS, suppl. ser., 10 (1993)
Sainty, *King's counsel*	J. Sainty, ed., *A list of English law officers and king's counsel*, SeldS, suppl. ser., 7 (1987)
SCH	Studies in Church History
Scots peerage	J. B. Paul, ed. *The Scots peerage, founded on Wood's edition of Sir Robert Douglas's Peerage of Scotland, containing an historical and genealogical account of the nobility of that kingdom*, 9 vols. (1904–14)
SeldS	Selden Society
SHR	*Scottish Historical Review*
State trials	T. B. Howell and T. J. Howell, eds., *Cobbett's Complete collection of state trials*, 34 vols. (1809–28)
STC, 1475–1640	A. W. Pollard, G. R. Redgrave, and others, eds., *A short-title catalogue of … English books … 1475–1640* (1926); 2nd edn, ed. W. A. Jackson, F. S. Ferguson, and K. F. Pantzer, 3 vols. (1976–91) [see also Wing, *STC*]
STS	Scottish Text Society
SurtS	Surtees Society
Symeon of Durham, *Opera*	*Symeonis monachi opera omnia*, ed. T. Arnold, 2 vols., Rolls Series, 75 (1882–5); repr. (1965)
Tanner, *Bibl. Brit.-Hib.*	T. Tanner, *Bibliotheca Britannico-Hibernica*, ed. D. Wilkins (1748); repr. (1963)
Thieme & Becker, *Allgemeines Lexikon*	U. Thieme, F. Becker, and H. Vollmer, eds., *Allgemeines Lexikon der bildenden Künstler von der Antike bis zur Gegenwart*, 37 vols. (Leipzig, 1907–50); repr. (1961–5), (1983), and (1992)
Thurloe, *State papers*	*A collection of the state papers of John Thurloe*, ed. T. Birch, 7 vols. (1742)
TLS	*Times Literary Supplement*
Tout, *Admin. hist.*	T. F. Tout, *Chapters in the administrative history of mediaeval England: the wardrobe, the chamber, and the small seals*, 6 vols. (1920–33); repr. (1967)
TRHS	*Transactions of the Royal Historical Society*
VCH	H. A. Doubleday and others, eds., *The Victoria history of the counties of England*, [88 vols.] (1900–)
Venn, *Alum. Cant.*	J. Venn and J. A. Venn, *Alumni Cantabrigienses: a biographical list of all known students, graduates, and holders of office at the University of Cambridge, from the earliest times to 1900*, 10 vols. (1922–54); repr. in 2 vols. (1974–8)
Vertue, *Note books*	[G. Vertue], *Note books*, ed. K. Esdaile, earl of Ilchester, and H. M. Hake, 6 vols., Walpole Society, 18, 20, 22, 24, 26, 30 (1930–55)
VF	*Vanity Fair*
Walford, *County families*	E. Walford, *The county families of the United Kingdom, or, Royal manual of the titled and untitled aristocracy of Great Britain and Ireland* (1860)
Walker rev.	A. G. Matthews, *Walker revised: being a revision of John Walker's Sufferings of the clergy during the grand rebellion, 1642–60* (1948); repr. (1988)
Walpole, *Corr.*	*The Yale edition of Horace Walpole's correspondence*, ed. W. S. Lewis, 48 vols. (1937–83)
Ward, *Men of the reign*	T. H. Ward, ed., *Men of the reign: a biographical dictionary of eminent persons of British and colonial birth who have died during the reign of Queen Victoria* (1885); repr. (Graz, 1968)
Waterhouse, *18c painters*	E. Waterhouse, *The dictionary of 18th century painters in oils and crayons* (1981); repr. as *British 18th century painters in oils and crayons* (1991), vol. 2 of *Dictionary of British art*
Watt, *Bibl. Brit.*	R. Watt, *Bibliotheca Britannica, or, A general index to British and foreign literature*, 4 vols. (1824) [many reprs.]
Wellesley index	W. E. Houghton, ed., *The Wellesley index to Victorian periodicals, 1824–1900*, 5 vols. (1966–89); new edn (1999) [CD-ROM]
Wing, *STC*	D. Wing, ed., *Short-title catalogue of … English books … 1641–1700*, 3 vols. (1945–51); 2nd edn (1972–88); rev. and enl. edn, ed. J. J. Morrison, C. W. Nelson, and M. Seccombe, 4 vols. (1994–8) [see also *STC, 1475–1640*]
Wisden	*John Wisden's Cricketer's Almanack*
Wood, *Ath. Oxon.*	A. Wood, *Athenae Oxonienses … to which are added the Fasti*, 2 vols. (1691–2); 2nd edn (1721); new edn, 4 vols., ed. P. Bliss (1813–20); repr. (1967) and (1969)
Wood, *Vic. painters*	C. Wood, *Dictionary of Victorian painters* (1971); 2nd edn (1978); 3rd edn as *Victorian painters*, 2 vols. (1995), vol. 4 of *Dictionary of British art*
WW	*Who's who* (1849–)
WWBMP	M. Stenton and S. Lees, eds., *Who's who of British members of parliament*, 4 vols. (1976–81)
WWW	*Who was who* (1929–)

Burt family (*per. c.*1830–1964), building contractors and civil engineers, achieved prominence with **John Mowlem** (1788–1868), contractor. He was born at Carrants Court Cottages, Swanage, Dorset, on 12 October 1788, the third child and eldest son of John Mowlem (1751–1837), quarryman, of a family long established there, and his wife, Hannah Froom (1764–1836). 'His father and his three brothers and himself were the last gang of quarrymen who worked at Tilly Whim', an ancient Purbeck stoneworking (Hardy, 121).

Though he himself told of quitting home for London almost penniless, travelling free on a stone-brig, it appears that when employed as a mason at Norris Castle, Isle of Wight, Mowlem was recommended by the architect to the master mason Henry Westmacott with a wharf in King's Row, Pimlico, near where Mowlem lodged on his arrival in London about 1807. 'He was a big, strong young fellow'—aged only twelve, but tall for his age, he had been obliged to hide from a press gang—'with a splendid eye and hand for work' (Hardy, 122). Despite working for 'beggarly wages' he married Susannah (1788–1849), daughter of George Manwell of Swanage, at St George's, Hanover Square, on 29 February 1812. They lived at various addresses in King's Row, Pimlico, for several years; his wife soon became indisposed, suffering poor health the rest of her life. Mowlem, 'honest, industrious and sober', was 'taken from the number of journeymen to complete a job in Whittlebury Forest at the house of General Fitzroy', as foreman about 1815. 'This being completed', he recalled, 'I was made foreman over all the works then going on in London' (Baines, 1.7–8).

Responding to the emerging demand for macadamizing London's streets, Mowlem set up as a paving contractor and stone merchant about 1823, though it took several years to establish himself. He moved from Pimlico in 1825 to share a house in Upper Quebec Street, Marylebone, with his wife's brother, Henry, parish rate collector. In 1831–6 the Mowlems lived in Chester Place, Regent's Park (partly sublet), by which time he enjoyed a substantial interest in several metropolitan paving contracts, including the West End parishes. But the competition was intense; failure to maintain an adequate supply of stone sometimes lost a contract, though his rivals suffered similarly, and there is evidence of collusion. It was by close attention to detail that Mowlem made his profits in a trade of large turnover but narrow margins—in 1838 his turnover was probably rather more than £12,000. Perennially short of cash, he operated on bills of exchange.

In 1839–40 Mowlem undertook his first work of national importance, paving Blackfriars Bridge with the granite sets known as 'narrow cubes', of which he was the first manufacturer. He realized that this could establish him in the first rank of paving contractors. 'This contract', he wrote, 'is one of the best I have ever had and will place me above harm and in that situation in the Metropolis where I shall be much envied' (that is, by rival contractors; Baines, 1.72–3). Leaving his ordinary business to be managed by his wife's nephew George Burt and Burt's brother-in-law, Joseph Freeman, he moved to Guernsey (where he had long been a major purchaser) for eight months in November 1839 to ensure the vital supplies of granite. 'Although this is the devil's own battle to fight, I will stick here; for if the job is completed well, all will be well afterwards … I *will* have a large share of the Metropolis' (ibid.).

Contending with hostile merchants, Mowlem leased and bought quarries; faced with incessant rain, he introduced tarpaulins into the quarries, and himself often took a double turn at the pump; 'I am so fatigued in the evening I can scarcely get home' (Baines, 1.72–3). Lacking sufficient stone-dressers, he raised piece-rates, brought quarrymen from the mainland, reduced his charge for dressing stones from 4*d.* to 3*d.*, and sent some stones for dressing in London. His gamble succeeded: he prised the St Clement Danes' paving contract from the firm that had held it for twenty years, succeeded George Manwell as office of works contracting mason for the London district, responsible for maintaining government property, and in 1842 recovered the St Martin's paviour's and mason's contract. When in January 1845 he took George Burt and Joseph Freeman into partnership, the firm's stock was valued at £4668, including stone, barges, horse-trucks, horses, a crane, and a travelling scaffold; by 1850 the valuation had more than doubled.

Despite retiring in 1845 to Swanage, where he bought property (most extensively from 1857), became a public benefactor, and found time for an all-over wash in cold water every morning—'I have been too busy through the whole of my life to indulge in this sort of cleanliness' (Baines, 1.224)—Mowlem kept a close eye on the metropolitan paving contracts. He attended committees himself when necessary, and travelled to inspect quarries—in 1847 alone he needed 50,000 tons of Guernsey stone. Coal provided freight for his brigs when they were not carrying stone. 1848 saw a notable expansion in the firm's activities, and Mowlem secured a dominant position in the supply of granite. In May 1851 the firm was 'very successful' (*John Mowlem's Swanage Diary*, 120) in bidding for the London vestries' contracts—some for only hundreds of pounds—that provided nearly all the firm's work into the 1870s, earning it the sobriquet of London John. Work for ten major local authorities in the 1860s grossed an average of over £50,000 per annum.

Mowlem's manuscript diary shows that, although he had little formal education, he wrote a clear round hand, and expressed himself clearly and pithily ('as demure as an old whore at a christening'; *John Mowlem's Swanage Diary*, 73). Physically tough—at fifty-two he described himself as 'waterproof. I stand my ground, blow high, blow low, and am as hearty as a buck, never destined for a drawing-room' (Baines, 1.79–80)—, 'too fond of money to gamble' (*John Mowlem's Swanage Diary*, 83), he yet found time to go to the Derby. He enjoyed wine and music, particularly Handel and German chorales. Travelling in France and Germany in 1846 for the benefit of his wife's health, he noted the high quality of German masonry and acquired a liking for warm baths which led him to install a bathroom on his return home. 'Very respectful to upper ranks' (Baines, 1.217) and lacking sympathy for the Chartists he none the less contemned aristocratic superciliousness and sympathized with the Anti-Corn Law League. In 1849 he was elected an assistant of the Glass-Sellers' Company. Though brought up a Methodist, he became a churchgoer and was a connoisseur of sermons. He was a freemason. As a Dorset magistrate he found his colleagues 'a set of old ladies', half a millennium behind the times (*John Mowlem's Swanage Diary*, 123). He died, childless, at Purbeck House, Swanage, on 8 March 1868 and was buried at Swanage cemetery.

Mowlem's principal partner, **George Burt** (1816–1894), contractor, was born at Swanage on 2 October 1816, the eldest son of Robert Burt (*d.* 1847), stone merchant, and his wife, Laetitia Manwell (*c.*1787–1861), sister of Mowlem's wife. After starting work as a stonemason in the Swanage quarries, at the age of nineteen George Burt was summoned to join his uncle in London, becoming his partner in 1844. Burt presided over a change in the character of the firm's work: the financial crisis of 1866–7 that brought down many great speculative contractors left Mowlems unimpeded, so that they were able to enter the list of major public-works contractors, landing one of the biggest contracts then offered, for building Queen Victoria Street in the City (1869). Their new status was secured by rebuilding Billingsgate Market (1874–7); thereafter they played a leading role in London (notably the City of London School in 1880, Smithfield fruit market in 1882, and the Imperial Institute in 1887, as well as major sewerage and railway works).

George Burt married Elizabeth (*b.* 1812), daughter of John Hudson of Stow, Norfolk, on 19 May 1840; they had two sons and three daughters. In 1850 he leased a five-bedroomed house in Cambridge Place, Paddington, where his family lived with a governess and two female servants. Tall, with broad forehead, deepset eyes, and long, curved nose, in later life he wore a full beard and moustache. According to Thomas Hardy, who met him in 1892, Burt 'had a good profile, but was rougher in speech than I should have expected after his years in London' (Lewer and Smale, 138). He continued his uncle's transformation of Swanage into a seaside resort, buying property and planning to develop Durston Park as a villa estate; he established gas and waterworks as well as a pier from which his paddle-steamer plied to Bournemouth, and he built a pretentious mansion, Purbeck House, in the main street, and was satirized in Elizabeth Godfrey's novel, *The Cradle of a Poet* (1910), as a vulgarian flaunting his wealth. He left a reputation as 'the amazing Burt, in whose nature eccentricity and business capacity, and the instincts of the pedagogue, the philanthropist and the money-maker seem to have been strangely mixed' (Lewer and Smale, 139).

Collecting relics of old London, often from his firm's own demolitions, Burt re-erected many in Swanage, notably the porch for the post-fire Mercers' Hall, now adorning the town hall. He was a JP in the metropolis and Dorset, a prominent freemason, an active member of the Metropolitan Asylums Board, three times master of the Glass-Sellers' Company, and in 1878–9 sheriff of London. Although he paid for the building of St Aldhelm's Anglican church in Swanage (1892), Burt also subscribed to rebuilding the Methodist church (1886), where his face was carved over the entrance. He died suddenly, of heart disease, at Purbeck House on 18 April 1894, but was buried at Kensal Green cemetery in London. He established a Purbeck Estate Trust to perpetuate the house for his family's residence, its contents devolving as heirlooms with the estate. His other extensive property in Swanage he bequeathed to his children to be developed for building.

George Burt's elder son, **Sir John Mowlem Burt** (1845–1918), contractor, born in Paddington on 2 February 1845, godson of John Mowlem, took up his dominant role. Physically, John Mowlem Burt strongly resembled his father. Educated privately and at Marischal College, Aberdeen, he began as a mason in the company's Aberdeen yards (acquired in 1858), before returning to London; instructed in all the departments, he proved 'a quick learner and an active man in carrying forward work', as well as a 'kind-hearted lad' (*Aberdeen Free Press*). He became a partner in 1875, overseeing such major works as the Admiralty extensions and arch (1896–1901, 1906–14); New Scotland Yard (1908); Institution of Civil Engineers (1911); and refronting Buckingham Palace (1913). As contractor for the coronation annexe at Westminster Abbey he was knighted in 1902. The firm was incorporated in 1903 but reverted to a private company in 1908.

John Mowlem Burt married Marion (1847–1903), daughter of Robert Ker Aitchison, merchant, on 9 February 1869; they had one son and two daughters. The year after her death he married Grace Emma, daughter of Joseph Blackstone, a doctor. Like his father, Burt was a freemason. In 1881 he was living with his wife and children, three servants, and a nurse, at 18 Grosvenor Road, adjoining Mowlem's extensive leasehold premises. On his second marriage he bought Durlston, Elsworthy Road, Hampstead. In 1916 he moved to his house at Swanage, where he had long been active in local government. He died on 20 February 1918 at his Swanage house, Carthion. He divided the bulk of his estate equally among his three children, his son having the option of taking his holding in J. Mowlem & Co.

His nephew, **Sir George Mowlem Burt** (1884–1964), contractor and civil engineer, made still greater advances. Born in Grosvenor Road, Westminster, on 10 January 1884, he was the elder son of George Burt (1851–1919)—younger son of George Burt (1816–1894) and a governing director of the firm—and his wife and cousin, Emily, daughter of James Arbon and his wife, Susannah Manwell, John Mowlem's favourite. George Mowlem Burt was educated at Clifton College and followed his father's and uncle's path into the family firm in 1902, becoming an apprentice in the joiners' shop. His progress was rapid. Promoted assistant foreman on the Admiralty Arch in 1906 and an outside superintendent in 1911, he was appointed to the board in 1913 at a salary of £600. On his father's death he became supervising director. In 1911 he married Olave Charlotte Sortain, daughter of Frederich E. Hulbert of Rotherfield, Sussex; they had one son.

A rich crop of contracts immediately after the First World War included the Port of London Authority (PLA) offices at Tower Hill, the Star and Garter Home at Richmond, and Bush House, Aldwych (1929 and 1934), followed by a great deal of dock reconstruction for the Port of London Authority; dock, jetty, and factory for Fords at Dagenham; and the King George V graving dock, Southampton. Other major London contracts included the Peter Robinson department store, the new Lloyds building, titanic office-blocks on Millbank for Imperial Chemical Industries (1927–8), power stations (Fulham and Battersea), and hospitals (St Mary's, Paddington, and the Royal Masonic).

Such a scale of operations called for a wider capital base: George Mowlem Burt took the company public in 1925 with a capital of £500,000 (£350,000 issued), paying a 7.5 per cent dividend. The annual turnover rose from an average of £1,530,000 in the 1920s to £3,470,000 in the 1930s. Rearmament and war brought yet greater increases: construction of the Royal Ordnance Factory, Swynnerton (1939–42), alone cost £4 million. From 1940 to 1945 Mowlems won over £29 million worth of contracts, including airfield runways and concrete units for Mulberry harbours. Similarly, Mowlems played an important role in post-war reconstruction, notably power stations and refineries. When Burt retired as chairman in 1961 (becoming president), his company ranked eleventh in the British construction industry.

Knighted in 1942, and appointed KBE in 1955, Sir George Mowlem Burt actively promoted the interests of the construction industry. A notable committee man, he was a founding member of the Federation of Civil Engineering Contractors, serving as chairman in 1932–3 and president in 1946–8 and 1951–6. He also served as president of the London Master Builders Association (1921), and of the International Federation of Building and Public Works (1930). On the board of the Building Research Station from about 1936 to 1956, he was chairman for ten years. In addition he served on several important committees under the ministries of Health and Works, accompanied Lord Portal to the USA in 1942 to study building methods, and chaired the interdepartmental committee on alternative forms of house construction. He was an Olympic fencer (1920 and 1924) and British épée champion in 1922. Enthusiastic for traditional country gentry sports, from 1931 to 1937 he was master of the Old Surrey and Burstow hunt. He died at his home, Comforts Place, Tandridge Lane, Lingfield, Surrey, on 1 September 1964.

For several generations the Burt family exemplified the characteristics of the founder of their firm. Self-educated, John Mowlem had slowly built up a considerable and profitable contracting business with a high degree of vertical integration, largely confined to a particular sector, on the basis of small unit profits on a steadily increasing turnover. The Burts further expanded the firm, and seized an opportunity afforded by their conservative financial policy to break into major public building contracting. They, like Mowlem, made an enduring impact on their native Swanage, but although they established estates they remained primarily public-works contractors. After the First World War the enormous cost of public works demanded a widening of their capital base to be obtained only by a public flotation, but the family's predominance in the company was maintained for nearly half a century longer. M. H. Port

Sources F. Baines, history of John Mowlem & Co., 2 vols., [n.d.], LMA, Ac. 2809/58 [includes excerpts from John Mowlem's diary] · LMA, John Mowlem & Co. archives, Ac. 2809 · D. Lewer and D. Smale, *Swanage past* (1994) · *John Mowlem's Swanage diary, 1845–1851*, ed. D. Lewer (1990) · *PICE*, new ser., 34 (1965), 301 [Sir George Mowlem Burt] · *ILN* (9 Nov 1878), 442 [George Burt] · census returns, 1851, 1881, 1891 · wills of John Mowlem, George Burt and Sir John Mowlem Burt · W. M. Hardy, *Old Swanage, or, Purbeck past & present*, 2nd edn (1910) · *Mowlem 150th year, 1822–1972* [company brochure] · *Aberdeen Free Press* (13 Feb 1868) · m. cert. [John Mowlem Burt and Emma Grace Blackstone] · m. cert. [John Mowlem Burt and Marion Aitchison] · d. cert. [George Mowlem Burt] · *CGPLA Eng. & Wales* (1918) [John Mowlem Burt] · *The Times* (3 Sept 1964) [George Mowlem Burt] · parish register, Swanage, 9 Nov 1788 [baptism, John Mowlem] · parish register, Swanage, 2 Oct 1816 [George Burt]

Archives LMA, John Mowlem & Co. archives, Ac. 2809

Likenesses G. R. Black, lithograph?, 1879 (George Burt), London Metropolitan Archives · photograph, *c.*1880 (George Burt), repro. in '150 years of construction Mowlem' (1972) [leaflet] · C. H. Mabey, bust, 1889 (George Burt), Swanage Town Council · R. R. Reinagle, oils (John Mowlem), John Mowlem & Co.

Wealth at death £40,000—John Mowlem: probate, 1868, *CGPLA Eng. & Wales* · £125,697 8*s.* 1*d.*—George Burt: resworn probate, 1894, *CGPLA Eng. & Wales* · £206,453 14*s.* 11*d.*—John Mowlem Burt: probate, 1918, *CGPLA Eng. & Wales* · £294,247—George Mowlem Burt: probate, 1964, *CGPLA Eng. & Wales*

Burt, Albin Roberts (1783–1842), portrait and miniature painter, was born, probably in London, on 1 December 1783, the son of Harry Burt (1725–1785), a grocer, and his Welsh wife, Mary, *née* Roberts (1739–1825). He trained as an engraver under Robert Thew and Benjamin Smith, but later turned to portrait painting. On 31 December 1810 he married Sarah Jones (1785–1854). They settled in Chester, whence Burt travelled about the country, working in Bath and Worcester (1812), Birmingham and Warwick (1814), Oxford (1817), and, at intervals, London, painting people of all classes 'from a lord down to a "boots"', apparently 'equally at home with all' (Uwins, 16). From 1830 he lived at Reading, though he moved briefly to Southampton in 1834.

A versatile artist with an eye for detail, Burt executed shell and stone cameos, cabinet portraits in oil, silhouettes, and miniatures on card, ivory, and copper in oil or watercolour; he also taught miniature painting, and cleaned and repaired old paintings. One of his advertisements stated that he had 'a new-invented machine by which the most accurate likenesses can be taken' (Foskett, *Miniatures*, 189). His charge for coloured profiles was a half to 1 guinea for quick half-hour sittings, 3 guineas upwards for miniatures on ivory, and 5 to 10 guineas for small full-length portraits. He signed his works 'Burt' followed by a date, or 'A. R. Burt' followed by a date and place. He exhibited at the Royal Academy in 1807 and 1830. Distinguished sitters included Mary Mitford and the poet and hymn writer Edward Caswell. An engraving after John Jackson of Lord Nelson, with whom he was acquainted through Sir

William Hamilton, is held in the National Maritime Museum, London. (According to family legend, Burt's brother, Henry Frederick Burt, was Nelson's secretary.) *Britannia Unveiling the Bust of Nelson*, a stipple engraving after the celebrated porcelain painter Thomas Baxter (who was married to Burt's cousin Anne Roberts), representing Lady Hamilton, whom his mother knew when a girl in Wales, secured him many new subscribers. Some verses by Richard Llwyd, 'Lines Written on Seeing Mr Burt's Likenesses', begin:

Is there a Youth who his Adora loves?
Whose every step his partial eye approves?
Till Time shall place her on the Bridal Throne,
Let BURT portray the charmer—Lover's own.
(R. Llwyd, *At Drigolion Caredig Cymru*, n.d.)

A large income enabled Burt to maintain a family of eight children 'in good style' (Uwins, 16), and to leave money to his widow on his death. One son, Henry Wellington Burt, also a portrait painter, opened a drawing school at Reading in 1830 when he was sixteen. A daughter, Emma Hamilton Burt, married John White, a well-known Reading artist; their child Sydney Victor White was a noted photographer. Burt died on 16 March 1842 of consumption at his home, 3 Conduit Crescent, Reading. Collections of his work are held at the Chester Record Office, the Museum of Reading, and the National Museum and Gallery of Wales, Cardiff. JOANNA SELBORNE

Sources D. Foskett, *A dictionary of British miniature painters*, 1 (1972) · D. Foskett, *Miniatures: dictionary and guide* (1987) · Redgrave, *Artists* · B. Stewart and M. Cutten, *The dictionary of portrait painters in Britain up to 1920* (1997) · S. McKechnie, *British silhouette artists and their work, 1760–1860* (1978) · D. O'Brian, *Miniatures in the 18th and 19th centuries* (1951) · S. Uwins, *A memoir of Thomas Uwins*, 2 vols. (1858) · Graves, *RA exhibitors* · Graves, *Artists* · *Engraved Brit. ports.* · J. Johnson, ed., *Works exhibited at the Royal Society of British Artists, 1824–1893, and the New English Art Club, 1888–1917*, 2 vols. (1975) · J. O. Wilstead and B. Morris, *Thomas Baxter: the Swansea years, 1816–1819* (1997) · B. S. Long, *British miniaturists* (1929) · Mallalieu, *Watercolour artists* · private information (2004) · S. Houfe, *The dictionary of 19th century British book illustrators and caricaturists*, rev. edn (1996)
Archives Ches. & Chester ALSS · NMG Wales · NMM · priv. coll., family MSS · Reading Museum Service
Likenesses A. Burt, self-portrait (copy), priv. coll.

Burt, Sir Cyril Lodowic (1883–1971), psychometric psychologist and eugenicist, was born in London on 3 March 1883, first child of Cyril Cecil Barrow Burt (*b.* 1857), a medical practitioner, and Martha Evans of Monmouth. His younger sister, Marion Burt (1891–1978), became a doctor like her father. From 1893 to 1923 the family lived at Snitterfield, Warwickshire, a country village where Burt's father had his practice.

Education and early researches Burt's education was in the classics, although he tried more than once to change to science. He attended King's School, Warwick, and later Christ's Hospital, which was then in London. In 1902 he went up to Jesus College, Oxford, to read Greats, graduating with second-class honours in 1906, which he followed by a teaching diploma and a summer visit to the University of Würzburg in 1908. There he met the psychologist Oswald Külpe, who was developing an experimental psychology that attempted to deal with the higher functions of the mind such as intelligence. At Oxford he had gone to lectures by the psychologist William McDougall, who opened an important door for him in 1907 by getting him involved in the anthropometric survey of the British people proposed by Francis Galton, in which he was to work on the standardization of psychological tests. This project brought him into contact with the world of eugenics, Charles L. Spearman, and Karl Pearson.

In 1909 Burt made use of Spearman's model of general intelligence to analyse his data on the performance of schoolchildren in a battery of tests. He arranged the results in a rank order matrix, and tested Spearman's hypothesis of a unitary general factor, *g*, which he found to work fairly well. This first research project was to define Burt's life's work in quantitative intelligence testing, eugenics, and the inheritance of intelligence, and to link him with the Galton–Pearson school of thought. One of the conclusions in his 1909 paper was that upper-class children in private preparatory schools did better in the tests than those in the ordinary elementary schools, and that the difference was innate. The discussion of intelligence and its relation to class was a product of the establishment of universal education in Britain. Intelligence added a new indicator to the eugenicists' discussion of the significance of fertility differentials between classes. If the lower class, along with all its other supposed faults, was less intelligent as well as more fertile, and if intelligence, as the eugenicists claimed, was genetically determined, then the excess fertility of this class would soon pull down the intelligence of the entire population. It was in this context that Cyril Burt's work took place.

Burt's first post was as a lecturer in psychology at the University of Liverpool, where he was attached to Charles Sherrington's department of physiology. In 1913, with the help of the Eugenics Society, the Mental Deficiency Act was passed. This act stipulated that defective children were to be removed from elementary schools and transferred to special schools for the feeble-minded. Burt was appointed psychologist to the London county council (LCC) with the responsibility of picking out the feeble-minded children. At first he tested only those who were known to be behind their classmates, but later he organized a more general programme, designing and standardizing the tests used and investigating the distribution of learning difficulties in children. In one of his early papers, written for the *Eugenics Review* in 1912, Burt stated that the evidence was conclusive that intelligence was mainly inherited. This was a position that he was to defend to the end of his long life.

Educational philosophy Burt's quantitative psychology of individual differences was meant as a way of grading children, selecting those that would be suitable for scholarships as well as those that were to be sent to the special schools, allocating children of appropriate ability to appropriate vocations, and fitting education to the child's future status as a worker belonging to a specific class. The LCC post gave him access to very large numbers of children, and he took full advantage of it to found what was essentially a new science of quantitative educational psychology. He was allowed to work in Spearman's laboratory, and the National Institute of Industrial Psychology helped him with research assistants. In 1917 he published *The Distribution and Relations of Educational Abilities*, in 1921, *Mental and Scholastic Tests* (which gave details of the type of tests he used), and in 1925, *The Young Delinquent*, in which he proposed a complete child guidance clinic staffed by psychologists and social workers. Following up on this suggestion a child guidance council was set up with Burt in the chair, and by 1928 the London Child Guidance Training Centre opened in Islington, providing training for psychiatrists, psychologists, and social workers. As a part-time professor of educational psychology at the London Day Training College, Burt also trained child guidance specialists at postgraduate level. In the new field of child guidance Burt's influence was paramount. He also made contributions to vocational psychology through a scheme that correlated occupation with intelligence.

Burt believed that social inequality had a biological basis, but since he found that the correlation between the IQs of fathers and sons was only 0.50, there had to be considerable social mobility for IQ distribution by class to persist: as it was, nearly half the population was in a class too high or too low. Like other psychometrists, Burt believed in a meritocracy of intelligence, with an educational ladder that would lead the misplaced child up or down to his true place in society. However, through the twenties and early thirties he acted as chair for the Eugenics Society's long-running Pauper Pedigree Project, which was designed to show that the pauper class was a closed, inbreeding group of interrelated families, and that pauperism could be traced to a heritable biological defect of temperament, showing itself in moral imbecility, feeble-mindedness, nervousness, and criminality. The results of the study were published in 1933.

As an educational psychologist, Burt contributed to a series of policy-making reports on secondary education by the Board of Education consultative committee through the twenties and thirties, beginning with the Hilton Young report of 1919, which introduced the 11+ examination, up to the Spens Report of 1938, which prepared for the introduction of tripartite secondary education in 1944. It should be said that Burt did not originate these educational policies, although they coincided with his point of view. It is not completely clear how much psychometry was actually used in the assessment of the aptitude of children for the different types of education available. By 1939 about one third of the local education authorities still did not have an IQ test as part of the selection process, and many of those that did used very non-standard procedures. By 1952 almost all included some kind of IQ test in their exams. By the mid-1960s, however, a wave of discontent with selection had begun which was to culminate in the introduction of more egalitarian comprehensive schools to replace the several types of elite and not-so-elite secondary school then in existence.

On 9 April 1932 at the age of forty-nine, Burt married Joyce Muriel Woods (*b.* 1908/9), a former student of his, then aged twenty-three. The marriage was not a success and the couple lived separately for most of it, although they never divorced. There were no children.

University College years In 1932 Burt succeeded Spearman as professor of psychology at University College, London, continuing the Galton–Pearson line that was the heart of the college's statistical tradition. He cut back on his large-scale collection of data and turned instead to theoretical problems concerned with the technique of factor analysis and its mathematical basis, regarding it as one of a number of possible ways of dealing statistically with variance broken down into separate factors, and comparing it to R. A. Fisher's analysis of variance—Fisher had succeeded Pearson himself at University College as Galton professor of eugenics in 1933. He also applied it in new areas, to temperament, physique, and the marks of examiners. His major work *Factors of the Mind* appeared in 1940. It was about this time that Burt began to suffer from severe Ménière's disease. From about 1947 onwards, Burt became concerned to link his work historically with that of Karl Pearson, emphasizing the early contribution of Pearson's mathematics to factor analysis.

In 1946 Burt was knighted. He retired in 1950 at the height of his fame. Soon afterwards, opinion in education began to swing against him. Ideas which had been progressive in his early years came under attack. Educational psychometry came to be seen as no more than an attempt to justify a class society, at one with the outdated assumptions of the eugenics movement. The inheritance of IQ was now associated with psychologists who argued for genetically determined differences in IQ between races. It is possible that his two new twin studies of 1955 and 1966, and the one that appeared in 1958 under the name of an assistant, J. Conway, were rejoinders to attacks on Burt's position by environmentalist critics. The twin studies argued strongly for a very high degree of heritability for IQ: his data for separated monozygotic twins reared together and apart showed correlations of 0.944 and 0.771.

Death and reputation Within a year of his death from cancer on 10 October 1971, Burt's reputation suffered a further blow. The problem concerned the twin studies. Leon Kamin of Princeton pointed out that the number of pairs of twins cited in Burt's papers grew over the years from twenty-one to fifty-three, but the correlations remained constant, an impossible degree of reproducibility. Kamin argued that psychometry was scientifically worthless, and politically pernicious. Other psychologists questioned the perfect regression to the mean found by Burt in the relationships between the IQ of parents and children, and pointed out that his papers were full of errors and inaccuracies. Finally, Oliver Gillie, writing in the *Sunday Times* in 1976, accused him of outright fraud, including the invention of two assistants and several pairs of twins, as well as much of his published data, an accusation that created storms of support and protest for and against Burt. Leslie Hearnshaw, one of Burt's erstwhile supporters, added further damaging details in his intimate official biography of

1979, suggesting that Burt had suffered from personality changes that had resulted in his fabricating data and inventing assistants.

However, later writers began a process of rehabilitation. Robert Joynson, a psychologist (1989), and Ronald Fletcher, a sociologist (1991), reviewed the evidence once again. Joynson in fact devoted a whole book to countering Hearnshaw's book page by page. Like Fletcher, he argues in high adversarial style as Burt's council for the defence. Joynson glosses over the errors and omissions in Burt's figures and in his explanations of the sources of his data by pointing out that, of course, this was not modern data gathering. The IQ results themselves were often no more than roughly estimated, with the tests carried out by very imperfectly trained helpers. The thirty-two new sets of separated monozygotic twins that turned up after Burt's data gathering presumably ceased may have been found in Burt's own attic after much searching, rather than being lost in the blitz (when University College was evacuated to Aberystwyth), and subsequently reinvented, as Hearnshaw suggested. Of the three 'missing' co-workers, M. G. O'Connor, M. Howard, and J. Conway, who worked with Burt on his twin studies, none could have worked with Burt after the war, and O'Connor was never traced. But they might have collected data at an earlier period that were still in Burt's possession. Joynson argues that the unvarying coefficients that first caught Kamin's attention referred mainly to physical and educational measures, in which Burt was no longer very interested, and probably had not bothered to do for the most recent pairs of twins.

N. J. Mackintosh in dealing with the same problem in 1995 is more critical, though he avoids the accusation of outright fraud. He suggests that Burt's muddle of changed and unchanged correlations was due to multiple careless mistakes, the result of copying figures at different times from different sources; that was clearly the case in his inaccurate quotations from earlier twin studies by other authors. The tables are full of misprints and other errors. Burt's 1966 figures as they stand are completely unreliable; in Mackintosh's view, there can be no innocent explanation of this that leaves Burt's reputation as a careful scientist unscathed. The question of his assistants, however, seems to have been fairly well resolved. It is unlikely that Burt was actually collecting more twin data after his retirement, but it is possible that he was able to find some of his old material bit by bit in the various places where it had been stored. Unfortunately, several boxes of Burt's papers were destroyed after his death.

The role of politics It is difficult to separate the problem of Burt's science from the political stance of his attackers and defenders. Burt himself was formed in an era when hereditarianism and eugenics were the norm. His interest in eugenics was shared by an entire intellectual class up to the thirties, and especially by bearers of the Galton–Pearson tradition. But in the post-war climate of egalitarianism selectivity in education began to seem both antiquated and unjust. The movement towards comprehensive schools mirrored the movement to end the segregation of handicapped people. The attack on hereditarianism became an attack on its most prominent exponent, and was led largely by psychologists who were passionate environmentalists. Similarly, attempts to rehabilitate Burt's reputation, though not completely successful, came at a time when egalitarianism and the comprehensive school were under attack, and interest in measurement of ability increasing. Indeed, confidence in IQ testing generally coincides with peaks in popularity of the political right. Adrian Wooldridge in reviewing the controversy in 1994 very convincingly linked this reassessment to a swing against egalitarianism that was powered by Margaret Thatcher's education policies, which depended upon many of the same ideas that Burt had espoused in the 1930s and 1940s.

PAULINE M. H. MAZUMDAR

Sources R. Fletcher, *Science, ideology and the media: the Cyril Burt scandal* (1991) • S. J. Gould, *The mismeasure of man* (1981) • L. S. Hearnshaw, *Cyril Burt, psychologist* (1979) • R. B. Joynson, *The Burt affair* (1989) • L. Kamin, *The science and politics of IQ* (1977) • N. J. Mackintosh, *Cyril Burt: fraud or framed?* (1995) • P. Mazumdar, *Eugenics, human genetics and human failings: the Eugenics Society, its sources and its critics in Britain* (1992) • G. Sutherland and S. Sharp, *Ability, merit and measurement: mental testing and English education, 1880–1940* (1984) • A. Wooldridge, *Measuring the mind: education and psychology in England, c.1860–c.1990* (1994) • *WWW* • *CGPLA Eng. & Wales* (1972)

Archives U. Lpool, corresp. and papers | Bodl. Oxf., corresp. with C. D. Darlington • Bodl. Oxf., corresp. with the Society for the Protection of Science and Learning • ICL, corresp. with Herbert Dingle • UCL, corresp.

Likenesses W. Stoneman, photograph, 1947, NPG

Wealth at death £24,657: probate, 6 Jan 1972, *CGPLA Eng. & Wales*

Burt, Edmund (*d.* 1755), author and rent collector, is known to have been born in England and in 1725 to have referred to his wife's being in London. On 31 May of the same year he was appointed receiver-general and collector of rents on the unsold forfeited estates in Scotland, from 24 June, with £400 per annum to cover salary and expenses. Virtually all the Scottish estates forfeited after the Jacobite rising of 1715 had been sold except for those of Glenmoriston and Seaforth, and Burt was concerned with collecting rents on them until they too were sold, in 1730 and 1741 respectively. His work involved close co-operation with General George Wade, the commander-in-chief in Scotland, but (in spite of later reports to the contrary) he had no part in the building of the 'Wade roads' in the highlands. A letter by a magistrate of Inverness dated 1 January 1726 reveals that Burt was then a justice of the peace, part of the 'haughty, keen and unsupportable government of these military and stranger judges set over us' (Salmond, 104). By 1733 he had also become manager of the lead mines at Strontian in Argyll, and he continued to be employed in the highlands for some years after 1741.

Between about 1727 and 1728 Burt wrote a series of letters, later published as *Letters from a Gentleman in the North of Scotland to his Friend in London* (including a further letter written in around 1737), in which he summarized Wade's road-building achievements. Burt realized that the earlier correspondence describing conditions in the areas of

Scotland in which he was working would be regarded as highly offensive by Scots, and he swore his unknown correspondent in London to secrecy: publicity would create difficulties in his work, earn him enemies, and 'It would do me no great honour to be known to have made a collection of Incidents, mostly low, and sometimes disagreeable' (Burt, 1.3). When the letters were published anonymously in London in 1754, the editor stated that he had bought them from the author, though he respected Burt's desire for anonymity by claiming not to know the writer's identity, only that he had 'died some time ago, and through Losses, unsuccessful Law-Suits, and other Disappointments, left his Family in none of the best of Circumstances' (ibid., 1.vii). Although the report of his death was somewhat premature, Burt may well have decided to publish the letters as a result of financial problems, and he may have entrusted the work to a relative, the publisher being Samuel Birt. All attempts at maintaining anonymity failed, and after his death in London on 4 January 1755 his obituarists in the *Gentleman's Magazine* and the *Scots Magazine* had no hesitation in ascribing authorship to him.

The emphasis in the *Letters* on dirt, poverty, barbarity, and superstition caused indignation among patriotic Scots. David Dalrymple, Lord Hailes, denigrated Burt as 'an ignorant creature who drew together materials for a book in order to procure a bit of bread' (Doig, 131–2). This and other information led Richard Gough to call Burt a sutler or contractor, 'a poor illiterate, hireling scribbler, who was reported to have hanged himself at his lodgings at Charing Cross' (Gough, 2.573). However, the *Letters* is a major source of information about conditions and customs in Scotland, especially in Inverness-shire and the Great Glen area. Burt had a talent for precise observation, and at times showed considerable understanding of those whose lifestyles he described, but his strong sense of the ludicrous inclined him to anecdotes and comments that in entertaining some readers were bound to arouse the fury of others. David Stevenson

Sources [E. Burt], *Letters from a gentleman in the north of Scotland to his friend in London*, 2 vols. (1754) • K. S. MacKenzie, 'General Wade and his roads', *Transactions of the Inverness Scientific Society and Field Club*, 5 (1895–9), 145–77 • D. Stevenson, 'Who was Edmund Burt?', *Essays for Professor R. E. H. Mellors*, ed. W. Ritchie, J. C. Stone, and A. S. Mather (1986), 250–59 • register of the privy seal of Scotland, 1711–31, NRA Scotland, PS3/7 • J. B. Salmond, *Wade in Scotland* (1904) • R. P. Doig, 'A bibliographical study of Gough's *British topography*', *Edinburgh Bibliographical Society Transactions*, 4 (1960–74), 103–36 • R. G. [R. Gough], *British topography*, [new edn], 2 vols. (1780) • *GM*, 1st ser., 25 (1755), 92 • *Scots Magazine*, 17 (1755), 52

Archives NRA Scotland, forfeited estate MSS, rentals and other papers relating to work in the highlands, E633, E655

Burt, George (1816–1894). *See under* Burt family (*per.* c.1830–1964).

Burt, Sir George Mowlem (1884–1964). *See under* Burt family (*per.* c.1830–1964).

Burt, Sir John Mowlem (1845–1918). *See under* Burt family (*per.* c.1830–1964).

Burt, Thomas (1837–1922), trade union leader and politician, was born on 12 November 1837 at Murton Row near North Shields, the elder of two sons of Peter Burt, coalminer, and his wife, Rebecca, daughter of Thomas Weatherburn, colliery engineman. He had twin sisters who died in infancy and a brother who predeceased him at the age of thirty-three. Burt's father moved to the Durham coalfield with his family in 1844 after being victimized for taking part in trade union activities. Burt received little formal education, but became an avid reader during his late teenage years, and attributed much of the learning that he did acquire to the interest shown in him by his maternal grandfather.

Burt began work underground at the age of ten, first as a trapper and then as a pony driver, and worked in a number of local collieries before returning with his family to Northumberland, where he was a hewer at various collieries around Cramlingon and Choppington. He became involved in trade unionism from the age of about sixteen, was victimized, and joined the Northumberland and Durham Mutual Confidence Association when it was founded in 1863. He became delegate for Choppington, moved the resolution that led to the secession of Northumberland from the association in 1865, and was elected full-time secretary and agent of the new Northumberland Miners' Mutual Confident Association, remaining secretary until 1905 and agent until 1913.

These were the years that saw the formation and growth of county mining unions, the foundation of the Miners' Federation of Great Britain, and the adoption (and abandonment) of the system of tying wages to selling-price sliding scales, but Burt remained firmly wedded to the principles of industrial co-operation and class harmony which he had advocated since the beginning of his career. It was his adherence to these principles that explains Burt's refusal to join the Labour Party, and helps to explain the strained relations that developed between the Northumberland Miners' Mutual Confident Association and the Miners' Federation of Great Britain: Burt and his colleagues, unlike the leaders of the federation, continued to believe that the sliding scale, or some form of arbitration or conciliation, provided the best way of dealing with the north-east coalfield's particular sensitivity to changing market conditions.

In 1873 Burt was adopted as the Liberal candidate for Morpeth, and in the following year he was returned as MP, retaining the seat for forty-four years until his retirement in 1918, by which time he had become the 'father of the House'. Like other radicals, Burt supported issues such as Irish home rule, household suffrage, the reform of trade union law, and the disestablishment of the Church of England. He was a member of several parliamentary committees and commissions (including the royal commission on accidents in mines, 1879–86, the royal commission on mining royalties, 1890–91, and the royal commission on labour, 1891–4); he was parliamentary secretary to the Board of Trade between 1892 and 1895; and he was made a privy councillor in 1906. His career 'illustrates better than [that of] almost any other labour leader the phenomenon of the Liberal–Labour alliance in the closing decades of the nineteenth century' (Bing and Saville, 61).

Unlike many other miners' leaders, Burt was physically frail, and he was described, by supporters and opponents alike, as meek, gentle, and pacific. He turned down several opportunities to augment his income, but received an annuity under the will of his friend Andrew Carnegie, who died in 1919. He married his cousin, Mary Weatherburn, in 1860 and they had four sons and four daughters. He described his wife, who predeceased him, as a 'daughter of the people', who was 'in complete sympathy with my public work, and throughout what was destined to be a long, happy married life … proved in every sense a brave and loving helpmate' (Burt, 139). Burt died at his home, 20 Burdon Terrace, Newcastle upon Tyne, on 12 April 1922, having been bedridden for three years, and was buried in Jesmond cemetery, Newcastle, on 19 April.

JOHN BENSON

Sources R. P. Arnot, *The miners: a history of the Miners' Federation of Great Britain*, 1: … *1889–1910* (1949) • J. Benson, *British coalminers in the nineteenth century: a social history* (1980) • T. Burt, *Pitman and privy councillor: an autobiography with supplementary chapters by Aaron Watson* (1924) • H. F. Bing and J. Saville, 'Burt, Thomas', *DLB*, vol. 1

Archives BL, letters to W. E. Gladstone and others • CAC Cam., letters to W. T. Stead • University of Sheffield, letters to A. J. Mundella

Likenesses B. Stone, photograph, 1901, NPG • wood-engraving (after photograph by W. & D. Downey), NPG; repro. in *ILN* (7 March 1874)

Wealth at death £5128 17*s*. 5*d*.: probate, 27 July 1922, *CGPLA Eng. & Wales*

Burt, William (1778–1826), writer, son of Joseph Burt of Plymouth, was born in Plymouth on 23 August 1778, educated at Exeter grammar school, and afterwards articled to a banker and solicitor at Bridgwater. Subsequently he practised at Plymouth as a solicitor for the rest of his life, while at the same time editing the *Plymouth and Dock Telegraph* for several years. At one period he also held a commission in the 38th foot.

Eventually Burt became well known on account of his publications, the best of them being perhaps *Christianity: a Poem*, published posthumously in 1835. He wrote two books on literary subjects, *Preface to Notes on N. T. Carrington's Poem 'Dartmoor'* (1826) and *Observations on the Curiosities of Nature*, once again published posthumously in 1836, both of which were edited by his nephew, Major Thomas Seymour Burt. Most of his other works were of a general or technical nature, as for instance, *Desultory reflections on banks in general, and the system of keeping up a false capital by accommodation* (1810), *The Consequences of the French Revolution to England Considered* (1811), and *A review of the mercantile, trading and manufacturing state, interests and capabilities of the port of Plymouth* (1816). This knowledgeable and versatile writer died at Plymouth on 1 September 1826.

THOMPSON COOPER, *rev.* NILANJANA BANERJI

Sources Allibone, *Dict.* • T. Seymour Burt, 'Memoir', in W. Burt, *Christianity: a poem in three books* (1835) • J. Davidson, *Bibliotheca Devoniensis* (1852) • [J. Watkins and F. Shoberl], *A biographical dictionary of the living authors of Great Britain and Ireland* (1816)

Burthogge, Richard (*bap.* **1638**, *d.* **1705**), philosopher, was baptized on 30 January 1638 at Plympton St Maurice, Devon, son, presumably not the eldest, of Richard and Honour Burthogg. His father, a 'gunner', was commissioned captain of foot in the parliamentarian garrison of Plymouth in 1643, at £300 per annum, with a family member, Thomas, as his lieutenant. Under the Commonwealth he bought, with Henry Hatsell, sequestrated crown land at Portloe in Cornwall. Burthogge went to Exeter grammar school, and was admitted as a servitor at All Souls College, Oxford, in 1654; he graduated BA from Lincoln College in 1658. He studied medicine at Leiden (admitted, 1661; MD, 1662). It is said that a sister Mary was married to Edward Giles of Bowden, then a sizable Tudor residence, in the parish of St Mary, Totnes. Some time after 1662 Burthogge himself went to live at Bowden, where he set up a medical practice (an early patient was James Harrington, republican author of *Oceana*). The Gileses were a leading Totnes family, merchants and financiers before they were also landowners. John Giles had been the richest merchant in Devon in 1523, and a second cousin, Sir Edward Giles, was high sheriff under James I. Edward died in 1666, Bowden going to his brother, John, but Burthogge remained for at least some years. He may have moved, at least temporarily, into Totnes (he paid for 'posts' in front of the present 18 High Street in 1675). He seems to have lived at Bowden in the 1690s, although his will of 1705, written from Bowden, describes him as 'late of the town of Totnes'. Two of Burthogge's early works are addressed to Andrew Trevill of Tongesland, Plymouth, and by 1677 he had married Trevill's daughter, Mary. This may not have been his first marriage, or hers. According to Anthony Wood he had buried a first wife and married a widow by 1691, and a wife Mary died in 1695.

Burthogge's published works place him squarely within the anti-dogmatic, broad-church, tolerationist tradition of such Anglican writers as William Chillingworth, Henry More, John Locke, and Joseph Glanvill (another native of Plymouth and close contemporary), opposed both to intolerance and to 'enthusiasm', and seeing the institutional arrangements of the church as a practical, rather than doctrinal matter. Burthogge's background, training, and interests were close to those of Locke, with whom he had west country friends in common. Like Locke's, his outstanding intellectual achievement was a general theory of knowledge and enquiry consonant with his politico-religious and scientific proclivities. In Burthogge's case this was an unequivocal and comprehensive idealism, perhaps the first to be propounded in modern Europe.

A difference from Locke was that the exigencies of local politics in Totnes and the west country put Burthogge firmly and openly on the side of nonconformity, as created by the Act of Uniformity of 1662. A minister ejected from St Mary's gave a weekly lecture at Bowden, one extruded from a Cornish parish was housed there with his family for two years, and Bowden was registered for nonconformist worship in 1672. In 1675 Burthogge was presented for non-attendance at Totnes church, as was his wife, together with Mary Giles, in 1684. His remark 'A persecuting furious Spirit is none of Christ's; [but] Antichrist's' (*Organum vetus et novum*, 1678), probably alludes less to Philip II or Louis XIV than to local tories who used the law to harass their political opponents.

Burthogge's earliest works, on divine goodness (1672 and 1675), are directed as much against Calvinism as against atheism, their purported target. Seemingly harsh doctrine is defended, but interpreted 'reasonably' (if sometimes sophistically) in accordance with the axiom that God cannot justly demand of us what is beyond our power to give. Such philosophy as appears is vaguely Platonist. *Organum*, however, focuses on what it is to be 'reasonable'. Burthogge argues that all the immediate objects of thought are 'entia cogitationis' or 'appearances', shaped by the faculties of sense and reason or judgement. His arguments probably drew on the error theory of Arnold Geulincx, whose lectures he could have attended at Leiden. Geulincx had elaborated the common charge against scholastic philosophy that it took merely notional or logical distinctions and entities for real ones—that is, ignored how far the content and structure of everyday beliefs are due to the ways in which we perceive and think of reality, rather than to reality itself. Burthogge, however, argued that the very nature of a cognitive faculty entails that we are locked into the notional. The categories we employ, 'the meanings and notions under which the understanding apprehends its objects', are 'no more without it or in the things themselves than colours are without the eye'. Anyone who, 'not contented with the knowledge of things according to appearances, is always attempting to know them in their realities' will be led into contradictions, as one who tries to look behind the 'common notion' of quantity 'is confounded with the composition of the continuum'. The everyday distinction between what is, and what is not 'real' is properly understood as a distinction between notions, since we cannot get behind our notions to compare them with reality. Predication itself involves comparison and analogy, and the only available criterion of truth ('logical truth', since 'metaphysical truth' is beyond us) is the place of a proposition in a harmonious and coherent system. As with a broken plate, when all the pieces fit together perfectly, they strike us as correctly placed. When some parts of an otherwise coherent scheme are missing, there is probability. Science aims to match the coherence and unity of reality, so that 'the more large, general and comprehensive our knowledge is, the more assured and evident it is'. In 'science as it is in arch-work, the parts uphold one another'. Yet any system is in principle vulnerable to replacement by a more comprehensive and coherent system, which is why 'the best way of confuting error, is … by shewing the truth'. We should subject the credentials and interpretation of revelation to the same principles of reasonableness, bearing in mind that divine truth, like all truth, is analogical, and that the point of divine analogies is spiritual and moral.

Burthogge's later works all appeal to this 'method wholly new'. Politically the most timely was a passionate, cutting advocacy of toleration, published with government approval in 1687. When James II replaced many county officials opposed to the repeal of the penal and test acts, Burthogge became a JP for Devon and member of Totnes corporation, one of many whigs who decided that toleration was worth tactical support of James. He also served on a commission investigating the Anglican exactions. Paradoxically, the revolution of 1688 that brought many other whigs, including Locke, into central government had the reverse effect at local level. Although Burthogge remained JP, he and his friends, tainted by their association with James and 'the papists', were largely ousted by tories. But he continued to engage in politico-religious controversy on bishops, infant baptism, and the elect, dealing blows left and right. He also dedicated two philosophical works to Locke, evidently seen as a prestigious ally. *An Essay upon Reason, and the Nature of Spirits* begins with an effective restatement of his idealism, emphasizing the role of categorial concepts and making some use of Lockean argument. There are interesting suggestions as to the nature of consciousness, leading into a somewhat Spinozistic, 'harmoniously' speculative panpsychism, which was further defended in 1699. In the last years of both their lives Burthogge corresponded with Locke, whose commentary on St Paul adopts the interpretation of Romans 8: 28–30 (a major source of the doctrine of the elect) argued for in Burthogge's last work, published in 1702.

Burthogge's (presumably) third wife, Honour, was thought to be expecting a child in 1705 when, after a 'great sickness at Bowden', Burthogge died. He was buried at St Mary's Church, Totnes, on 24 July. As Wood judged, he had 'attained a pretty full estate', including farms and other properties in Plymouth, Modbury, and Ashprington (where the Giles owned property) but none in Totnes. These he left in the first instance to the expected child, if a son, in effect to his daughter Sarah, wife of Edward Stephens of Lygrove in Gloucestershire. Eventually the land, or some of it, passed to Burthogge Mayo (or Mayow), son of another daughter, Mary, and Philip Mayo of Bray. A third daughter, Ann, had died, leaving a young son to whom Burthogge left provision for an apprenticeship, and to be set up in a trade; he was Richard Babbage, ancestor of Charles Babbage, inventor of the calculating machine. Honour Burthogge died in 1723.

Burthogge has received some recognition by historians of philosophy, both in the past, as by Sir William Hamilton and Ernst Cassirer, and in recent work. But it has been summary and in passing, generally with emphasis on his 'anticipation' of Kant or, less commonly, of Locke. His thought deserves fuller consideration, however, both as an illustration of what modern idealism owed to error theory and toleration theory, and for his revealing, strangely compelling arguments themselves—in their simplicity, at least, in sharp contrast to Kant's.

MICHAEL AYERS

Sources *DNB* • Wood, *Ath. Oxon.: Fasti* (1815), 214 • Wood, *Ath. Oxon.*, new edn, 4.581–2 • *Transactions of the Devonshire Association*, 28, 326–9 [transcription of will] • parish register, Plympton St Maurice, 30 Jan 1638 [baptism] • parish register, Totnes, 24 July 1705 [burial] • private information (2004) [Devon RO, Totnes Museum] • *Transactions of the Devonshire Association*, 28, 737; 32, 2–3; 19, 538–42; 79, 123 • 'Eveleigh's rentals', Totnes Museum [copy] •

'Devon pedigrees', Totnes Museum [copy] • M. Goldie, 'John Locke's circle and James II', *HJ*, 35 (1992), 557–86 • PRO, SP 28/128 pt 1 • PRO, E 121/1/6/10 • G. Nuchelmans, *Judgement and proposition: from Descartes to Kant* (1983), chap. 6 • *The correspondence of John Locke*, ed. E. S. de Beer (1979–82), vols. 5–7
Archives Exeter Cathedral, dean and chapter library, collection
Wealth at death 'a pretty full estate'; properties in and near Plymouth and Modbury, and in parish of Ashprington; also farm rent from Manor of Ashprington: will, repr. in *Transactions*

Burton. For this title name *see* individual entries under Burton; *see also* Bass, Michael Arthur, first Baron Burton (1837–1909).

Burton [*née* Charnock], **Beryl** (**1937–1996**), cyclist, was born on 12 May 1937 at 3 Howard Avenue, Halton, Leeds, the second daughter in the family of three children of John Henry Charnock, motor engineer, and his wife, Jessie May, *née* Williamson. As a child she suffered from chronic ill health. Chorea and rheumatic fever kept her in hospital and then in a convalescent home for fifteen months. She had resultant speech difficulties and for a while was paralysed down one side of her body. Her education suffered and she left Stainbeck secondary school, Leeds, at fifteen. She was working as a clerk in a clothing factory when she met Charles Robert (Charlie) Burton, eight years her senior. He was also a clerk, and the son of Abraham Burton, labourer. They married on 2 April 1955. Charlie introduced her to club cycling and then competitive racing, a sport that she dominated for over quarter of a century by winning fifteen world championship medals and 120 British national titles.

Burton's first season of serious competition was 1957, when she finished second in the national 100 mile time trial. Two years later, at Liège, BB—as she was affectionately known within the cycling fraternity—became world 3000 metres track pursuit champion. She successfully defended that title in 1960 in Leipzig and won it three more times, and also gained three second and four third places. Domestically she was national pursuit champion thirteen times. Yet distance-cycling on the road, either in bunched racing or time trials, rather than the shorter track events was her real love. She was world road-racing champion twice and national champion twelve times. In unpaced time trials her record was formidable. Although there were no world or European titles in this genre of the sport, she was British 25 mile champion twenty-five times, 50 mile champion twenty-three times, 100 mile champion eighteen times, and best all-rounder—where all three events are taken into consideration—for twenty-five successive years. She was the first woman to beat one hour for 25 miles, two hours for 50 miles, and four hours for 100 miles. In 1967 she became the only woman ever to beat a men's record when in twelve hours she rode 277.25 miles.

Although she was appointed MBE in 1964 and was advanced to OBE four years later, Burton never felt that her accomplishments were adequately recognized by the media. In Europe she was acclaimed, but in Britain the poor coverage given to women's cycling meant that few heard of her outstanding performances. Charlie Burton worked as an accounts clerk but devoted much of his time to managing his wife's cycling career and acting as her mechanic. Beryl herself earned some income and helped her physical fitness by labouring in local market gardens and rhubarb farms. The Burton family were not well off, especially when they had to finance many of her early trips abroad themselves, but she refused to turn professional despite the entreaties of Raleigh, the British cycle manufacturers. She also stayed loyal to her first club, Morley cycling club, even though it never became one sponsored by the cycle industry.

Burton's daughter, Denise, was born in January 1956 and was almost literally brought up in the saddle, on a rear seat of her mother's bicycle. As a family the Burton trio cycled the country for pleasure and established a Christmas routine of cycling and staying in youth hostels. Almost inevitably Denise became a competitive cyclist, and mother and daughter twice lined up together to represent Britain in world road-race championships. However, relations became strained as they emerged as racing rivals in the 1970s, a situation aggravated by domestic circumstances, as Denise still lived at home. After Denise outsprinted her mother to win the national road-race title in 1975, the fiercely competitive Beryl Burton refused to shake hands with her on the podium. Nevertheless an emotional public reconciliation followed, and eight days before Burton's death the pair won the team prize in a local time trial.

In 1978 Burton broke her right leg and shoulder blade and had fifty-six stitches in her face when a motorist knocked her off her bike, but this did not deter her and she continued to ride competitively, always seeking to beat targets that she had set herself. She won her last national title in 1988. Later, although she had no chance of titles, she continued to ride in national championships because she loved the sport. Indeed she was scheduled to ride in the national 10 mile time trial the day before her fifty-ninth birthday. However, on 5 May 1996 she failed to return from a training run and was found lying beside her bike in Skipton Road, Harrogate. She was pronounced dead on arrival at Harrogate District Hospital. An inquest found that she died of natural causes, of heart problems perhaps associated with her childhood illness. She was survived by her husband, Charlie, and daughter, Denise.

WRAY VAMPLEW

Sources B. Burton, *Personal best: the autobiography of Beryl Burton* (1986) • *The Times* (6 May 1996) • *The Times* (8 May 1996) • *The Independent* (7 May 1996) • *The Guardian* (7 May 1996) • *Daily Telegraph* (7 May 1996) • b. cert. • m. cert. • d. cert.
Likenesses photograph, 1961, repro. in *Daily Telegraph* • J. Pratt, photograph, *c.*1962, repro. in J. Huntington-Whiteley, ed., *The book of British sporting heroes* (1998), 57 [exhibition catalogue, NPG, 16 Oct 1998 – 24 Jan 1999] • group portrait, photograph, repro. in *The Times* (8 May 1996) • photographs, Hult. Arch.
Wealth at death under £180,000: administration, 5 Aug 1996, *CGPLA Eng. & Wales*

Burton, Cassibelan (**1609–1682**), translator, was born on 19 November 1609 at Weddington, Warwickshire, the only son of William *Burton (1575–1645), barrister and historian of Leicestershire, and his wife, Jane (1589–1632), daughter of Humfrey Adderley of Weddington, and nephew of Robert Burton, author of *The Anatomy of Melancholy.* William Burton had inherited Dadlington Manor in the village of Dadlington, Leicestershire, from his father, Ralph, who had himself purchased it from John Grey in 1585; from William it passed to his son Cassibelan on the former's death in 1645. Wood (3.154), however, accuses Burton of extravagance, claiming he 'consumed the most, or better part of the estate which his father had left him', and, indeed, Dadlington Manor had passed into the ownership of a certain William Cox by 1659. Nichols (4.932) preserves a memorandum of his payments over a few days in April 1649, which records outlays, often large, to various individuals, including one of £6 15*s.* 'to my wife, for odd disbursements' and another of £20 'to sir Charles Egerton, for a mare'. Burton was in the commission of the peace for Leicestershire on 19 April 1647 and in 1650 possessed the lordship of Lindley in that county, which had descended to him from his father (Nichols, 4.647). He also inherited his father's collections, which he passed to Walter Chetwynd to be used by him in writing *The Antiquities of Staffordshire*.

Burton rendered Martial into English, but his translation remained in manuscript, prompting his 'boon companion' (Wood, 3.154) Sir Aston Cokayne to remark in his *Small Poems of Several Sorts &c.* (1658):

> When will you do yourself so great a right,
> To let your English Martial view the light?

Burton married on 8 August 1639 Helen (*d.* 1680), daughter and coheir of Sir Nicholas Trott of Quicksword, Hertfordshire. His unusual name, due perhaps to his father's interest in history, might be derived from Cassivellaunus, the English warlord who opposed Julius Caesar. The appeal of Roman history was evidently felt also by the son: Burton's own eldest (*b.* 9 December 1642) was called Constantine. Burton died on 28 February 1682.

ROSS KENNEDY

Sources Wood, *Ath. Oxon.*, new edn, 3.154–6 • J. Nichols, *The history and antiquities of the county of Leicester*, 4/2 (1811), 635, 647, 714, 932 • A. Cokain [A. Cokayne], *Small poems of divers sorts* (1658) • *DNB*

Burton, Catharine [*name in religion* Mary Xaviera of the Angels] (**1668–1714**), Carmelite visionary and prioress of the English Carmel, Hopland, was born on 4 November 1668 at Beyton, near Bury St Edmunds, Suffolk, the daughter of the devout recusant yeoman Thomas Burton and his wife, Mary Suttler. The Burton household was a refuge for Jesuits, and many of Catharine's siblings also entered religion, her brother Christopher (1671–1744) becoming a Jesuit and working on the mission in Lancashire (1709–28), her eldest sister an Augustinian canoness in Bruges, and two other sisters Carmelites, the widowed Anne Woolmer in Antwerp and Agnes (*d.* 1744) in Hoogstraten, where she was elected prioress (1727–33). Suffering debilitating illness between the ages of nineteen and twenty-five, Catharine developed a particular devotion to St Francis Xavier. On regaining her health she left England, and on 8 December 1693 entered the English Carmel at Hopland in Antwerp, where she made her profession, as Mary Xaviera of the Angels, on 9 December 1694. She was elected subprioress in 1697, novice mistress soon afterwards, and prioress in 1700, serving in that capacity almost continuously until her death in the English Carmel, after a final illness, on 9 February 1714 NS. She was buried in the convent. Her spiritual autobiography, recording her visions and angelic visitations, was edited in manuscript by Thomas Hunter SJ.

PAUL ARBLASTER

Sources T. Hunter, *An English Carmelite: the life of Catharine Burton, Mother Mary Xaviera of the angels, of the English Teresian convent at Antwerp*, ed. H. J. Coleridge and others (1876) • J. S. Hansom, ed., 'A list of convicted recusants in the reign of King Charles II. British Museum Additional MS. 20739', *Catholic Record Society Miscellanea V* (1909), 299–301 • G. Holt, *The English Jesuits, 1650–1829: a biographical dictionary*, Catholic RS, 70 (1984), 49 • 'Engelse Karmelitessen', Oud Kerkarchief Antwerpen (Antwerp University) ['English Carmelites', old church archives of Antwerp, Antwerp University Library]

Archives Antwerp University Library, Oud Kerkarchief, record of election; accounts signed as subprioress and prioress

Burton, Charles (**1793–1866**), Church of England clergyman and theologian, was born on 18 January 1793 at Rhodes Hall, Middleton, Lancashire, the youngest of five sons of Daniel Burton, founder of a substantial calico-printing business and a prominent Wesleyan Methodist, and his wife, Esther. In early adulthood Burton was a keen poet, publishing several volumes of poetry and hymns, including *Horae poeticae* (1815), *A Selection of Psalms and Hymns, Including Original Compositions* (1820), and *The Bardiad: a Poem in Two Cantos* (1823). During his adolescence Burton absorbed his father's zealous Methodism, and became an itinerant preacher. He was soon, however, attracted by the apostolicity and parochial system of the Church of England. He was educated at the University of Glasgow, St John's College, Cambridge, and Magdalen College, Oxford (graduating LLB in 1822, and being incorporated BCL and then DCL in October 1829), and was ordained to the Anglican ministry in 1816. He was married at about this time; his wife may have been named Sarah. The couple had at least two children: a son, Charles Henry, who followed his father into the priesthood, and a daughter, Louisa Sarah.

The whole of Burton's ministerial life was spent in Manchester, initially as curate. In 1819–20 he built himself All Saints' Church in what was then the pleasant suburban district of Chorlton upon Medlock, where he remained as incumbent and then rector until his death. The church, which cost £18,000 to build, was largely destroyed by a fire in 1850. Burton was a cleric of traditional cast, with much of the zeal of the convert. His energies were channelled primarily into parochial work. Throughout his ministerial life he was an active visiting minister, and worked hard to maintain a comprehensive and efficient system of parochial district visiting. This was made increasingly difficult as the rapidly expanding working-class population of the city spread in the 1830s and 1840s into what had been a middle-class district. Burton, however, unlike many of his fellow clerics, did not retreat to the new suburbs, but toiled to meet the challenge through an efficient system of parochial schools and ancillary organizations.

Although firmly evangelical, Burton had little sympathy for the aggressive low-church campaigns of those such as the Revd Hugh Stowell; the 'political parson' was anathema to him. He was deeply suspicious of popular controversy, and throughout his Manchester life rarely strayed into the public limelight. The few exceptions to this derived from his popularity as a preacher. From the 1830s to the 1850s he gave several series of popular Sunday evening lectures: the series of 1836, 'The world before the flood', delivered at All Saints', attracted congregations of over 2000. In many cases these lectures formed the basis of Burton's more substantial theological works. The most important of these, *Lectures on the Millennium* (1841), *Lectures on the World before the Flood* (1844), and *Lectures on the Deluge and the World after the Flood* (1845), reflected his interest in science, which led eventually to his election as a fellow of the Linnean Society, as a result of a botanical discovery on Anglesey. Nevertheless, as he was at pains to point out, his writings largely represented book learning rather than any kind of practical scientific knowledge.

The thrust of Burton's works was to oppose the incipient rationalism of Charles Lyell and the geologists; 'the scriptures cannot be broken', and the reiteration of Paleyite evidences of divine design, were his constant themes. In line with perhaps the majority of educated churchmen, Burton did not attempt to uphold the literalist view that the world had been created in 4004 BC. Instead he advanced a variant of the 'gap' theory of Thomas Chalmers and J. B. Sumner, that creation involved first the creation of chaos, within which the older geological strata and their fossils might have been laid down, but then, at some much later date, the six-day intervention during which God made man. Although these volumes, appearing by chance just as Chalmers's *Vestiges* challenged the various bases of natural theology, were welcomed as a vigorous defence of the Bible, and continued to be sold into the 1850s, they made no original contribution to the debates over geology or palaeontology.

Although Burton remained a popular lecturer after 1850, he produced no further substantial work. He died on 6 September 1866 at Western Lodge, Durham, having caught typhus fever while on a visit there. On 11 September he was buried at his church, All Saints', Manchester.

M. HEWITT

Sources biographical cuttings, Man. CL • *Manchester Guardian* (1816–66) [passim] • visitation returns Archdeacon Rushton, Man. CL • All Saints' Church, Chorlton upon Medlock file, National Society records • *Church of England Magazine*, 18 (1843), 1–30, 257–87 • *Manchester Courier* (8 Sept 1866) • *Manchester Courier* (12 Sept 1866) • *DNB* • Venn, *Alum. Cant.* • *CGPLA Eng. & Wales* (1867) • *IGI*

Archives Church of England Record Society, National Society records, All Saints' Church, Chorlton upon Medlock file

Likenesses photograph, 1863, Man. CL

Wealth at death under £100: probate, 16 Jan 1867, *CGPLA Eng. & Wales*

Burton, Charles Edward (1846–1882), astronomer, was born on 16 September 1846 at Barnton, Cheshire, the son of the Revd Edward W. Burton, incumbent of Barnton. The family moved to Ireland while he was young. He showed from childhood a marked taste for astronomy, and in February 1868 entered Lord Rosse's observatory at Parsonstown as assistant, where he specialized in the grinding of specula. Some months later he took a BA degree at the University of Dublin. Compelled by poor health to resign the post in March 1869, he joined the Sicilian expedition to observe the total solar eclipse of 22 December 1870, and on 13 February 1871 read a paper on its results before the Royal Irish Academy. The observations and drawings made by him at Agosta were included in the volume published by the Royal Astronomical Society devoted to total eclipses (*Memoirs of the Royal Astronomical Society*, 41, 1879). In 1874 he was attached as photographer to the transit of Venus expedition, and profited by his stay at Rodriguez to observe southern nebulae (30 Doradûs and that surrounding η Argûs) with a 12 inch silvered glass reflector of his own construction. On his return he spent nearly twelve months at Greenwich measuring photographs of the transit, then worked from 1876 at the observatory of Dunsink, near Dublin. He retired in August 1878, once more through ill health, to his father's parsonage at Loughlinstown, co. Dublin, where he made diligent use of his own admirable specula. His observations on Mars, during the opposition of 1879, were of especial value as confirming the existence, and adding to the numbers, of the 'canals' discovered by Schiaparelli two years previously.

Burton was a skilled instrumentalist as well as a good observer. Together with Howard Grubb he devised a 'ghost micrometer', so called because it used 'the images of fixed and moveable lines, instead of the material lines' employed in conventional micrometers (*Monthly Notices of the Royal Astronomical Society*, 41, 1880–81, 59). His experiments on lunar photography were interrupted by preparations to travel to South Africa to observe again the transit of Venus. But within a few weeks of starting for his assigned post at Aberdeen Road, Cape Colony, he died suddenly, of heart disease, in Castle Knock church, on Sunday 9 July 1882. A. M. CLERKE, *rev.* JOSEPH GROSS

Sources *Copernicus: an International Journal of Astronomy*, 2 (1882), 158 • *Astronomical Register*, 20 (1882), 173–4

Burton, Decimus (1800–1881), architect, was born on 30 September 1800 in the parish of St Pancras, London, and baptized in the parish church there on 18 July 1802, the son of James *Burton (1761–1837), speculative developer, and his wife, Elizabeth, *née* Westley (1761–1837). His brothers included the Egyptologist James *Haliburton. Burton benefited greatly from his father's success and wealth, which cushioned his own professional life. He began his career with his foot firmly on the social ladder, and after attending Tonbridge School, Kent, enjoyed several years in the Royal Academy Schools, which he entered in November 1817 with a design for a national museum. However, the fact that he was not articled to an architect, possibly because of his father's rise in status, nor went on the grand tour early in life are anomalies in the training of an architect, such as it was at this time. As a consequence of this, Burton stands slightly outside the

Decimus Burton (1800–1881), by Maxim Gauci (after Eden Upton Eddis)

growing circle of professionally educated practitioners in early nineteenth-century Britain. This is confirmed by James Burton's retrospective diary, held in Hastings Museum, Sussex, which sums up his most famous son's formative years thus: 'born 30 Sept. 1800 left School Sept 1816—& became my assistant in the Office—Commenced his Career as an Architect in Carlton Chambers April 1823. Then built his and adj [adjacent] house in Spring Garden'. During his time as his father's assistant Decimus received drawing lessons from George Maddox, but more importantly he learned about efficient working practices from his father's productive career and their work together is testament to this. The qualities of efficiency, professionalism, and an educated sensitivity to the wider implications of design for the creation of distinct urban environments rather than any kind of 'genius' are the hallmarks of Decimus Burton's architecture.

Training and early career Burton's training at the Royal Academy comprised lectures delivered by John Soane, professor of architecture, and the use of casts as models from which to draw and learn about the architecture of the ancients, and both remained an important influence on Burton. When he set up his own practice in 1823 in Carlton Chambers, a multi-purpose block built by his father as part of the Regent Street development, Soane recommended a Mr Grant (capacity unstated) for Burton's new offices. Not long afterwards Burton designed and built two houses on Spring Gardens, where from 1827 he lived and had his office. Burton's house had a 'Grecian Room' which contained the substantial collection of casts he purchased *en bloc* through a Mr Brown in Rome and delivered to Spring Gardens in November 1827. These were donated by Burton to the Victoria and South Kensington Museum (now the Victoria and Albert Museum) in 1879, and are now held there in the sculpture archive. Here again Soane and the Royal Academy were likely influences, not least as Soane's own house (Sir John Soane's Museum, Lincoln's Inn, London) and collection of casts were used as a source book for architectural details and part of the training of his pupils.

The other essential tool of the architect in the early nineteenth century was his library. Burton had intended to leave his extensive collection to the Royal Institute of British Architects but it passed instead to his nieces, who sold at least part of it at auction when the sale catalogue listed 347 separate lots, some of which ran into many volumes. The collection indicates a range of interests beyond architectural theory and practice: it contained the *Proceedings of the Camden Society* complete in 135 volumes and transactions of many of the learned societies of which Burton was a member or fellow, including the Royal Society of Arts, the Society of Antiquaries, and the Royal Society, as well as a complete set of the *Histoire naturelle* (70 vols.) of G. L. L. Buffon and B. G. E. Lacépède. The architectural texts comprised mostly standard works on classical architecture, such as the five volumes of Colen Campbell, *Vitruvius Britannicus* by John Woolfe and James Gandon, James Gibbs's *Book of Architecture*, and William Kent's *The Designs of Inigo Jones*. Alongside these, topographical views and surveys of cities and counties pepper the collection. There were also some foreign-language texts, including volumes by C. Percier and J.-B. Rondelet, a complete set of G. Piranesi's works, and several dictionaries. Although Burton travelled to France and Spain, about which journey little is known, the absence of an educative grand tour early in his career meant that his books and casts were his sources for design. This goes some way towards explaining the rather stiff and academic character of his architecture.

A leading Greek revival architect Despite his lack of direct contact with antique architecture, Burton was widely fêted in the contemporary press as a significant exponent of the Greek revival style and his individual works—including the Hyde Park screen (1823–5), which was heralded as the 'new Propylaea', and the Athenaeum (1827–30)—were much praised. Both of these buildings were decorated with a copy of the Panathenaic procession from the Parthenon frieze executed by the sculptor John Henning. Burton also used this motif in the interior of The Grove (1822–4), a spectacular and well-positioned villa in Regent's Park which he designed for his friend the geologist George Bellas Greenough MP, a founder member of the Athenaeum and the Geological Society through whom Burton met many of his clients. The Acropolis at Athens provided further inspiration for this villa as its exterior form is a reworking of the Erechtheion. Despite his renown as a Greek revivalist, Burton's architectural sources were more diverse and included ancient Rome. Alongside the arch (1825) at Constitution Hill, based on the arch of Titus, he designed the Colosseum (1823–7) in

Regent's Park for Thomas Horner. This was based on the Pantheon, with a Greek doric portico (a replica of the Pantheon at Oxford Circus). As the taste for the Gothic revival gathered pace in the late 1830s praise for Burton's Greek revival designs turned to scorn. His disappointing church designs show that he never mastered the Gothic style, although his work in the 'old English' style and the *cottage orné* was well received.

Burton's public standing Evidence given by Burton to two parliamentary select committees shows the diversity of his experience and, by virtue of his being asked, the esteem in which his opinion was held by contemporaries. The report of the select committee on the office of works (1828) included an inquiry into payment to tradesmen by measure and value or payment in gross. Here Burton's rather traditional views on the organization of work are revealed as he favoured payment by measure, a reflection of his reputation for working professionally and to estimate, skills he developed in his father's office.

Burton's evidence to the select committee of the House of Commons (1840), which discussed plans to develop Trafalgar Square (of which the proceedings were reported in the *Civil Engineer and Architect's Journal*, 7, September 1840), gave a more public platform to his views on urban planning. This is one of the first examples of public discussion about an urban space with acknowledged national and political significance. Moreover, Burton's involvement gave him an equal voice to the other expert witnesses called to give evidence, including Edward Blore, Francis Chantrey, T. L. Donaldson, Joseph Gwilt, Philip Hardwick, Sidney Smirke, R. Westmacott, C. R. Cockerell, and John Deering. Indeed, Burton's relationship to his peers and interest in the broader issues of architectural practice were already evident as he was a founder member (in 1834) and later vice-president of the Institute of British Architects, an organization founded to establish and raise the status of the profession. Right at the beginning of his career, Burton's involvement in 1823 with a competition for designs for the completion of King's College, Cambridge, and subsequent exhibition of some of the entries in the Great Room of the Western Exchange, had shown that he agreed with the way in which many architects were thinking about the nature and status of architectural drawing at this time. The exhibition catalogue stated that 'the object of architecture as we all know, is the building and not the drawing which represents it, the latter is quite the secondary object'. Visitors to the show were asked to imagine the designs as built as 'without this act of mind, architectural drawings can communicate comparatively little pleasure'. Fellow exhibitors included other architects at the forefront of the profession: Lewis Vulliamy, T. L. Donaldson, J. L. Wolfe, Charles Barry, Ambrose Poynter, Thomas Rickman, and Henry Hutchinson.

The relationship between Burton and John Nash One of the most problematic areas of Burton's early career is his relationship with John Nash, favoured architect of George IV. It has been assumed that Burton worked in Nash's office, but there is no evidence to support this. Rather, his working relationship with Nash began through his father's work on the Regent Street and Regent's Park projects for which Nash was the architectural 'overseer'. In this, James Burton enabled the building work and Decimus provided the architectural styling. This relationship reveals Burton's developing independence as he emerges as the dominant force in the construction of these distinctive urban spaces.

The Athenaeum is perhaps Burton's best-known and most fully documented building and played a key role in the development of 'clubland' and the evolution of a new building type. His good friend John Wilson Croker was secretary of the club and Burton was one of its earliest members. The building history forms part of the continuing relationship between Burton and Nash as its design was intended to follow Nash's scheme for the United Services Club, to which it was a kind of pendant piece, situated opposite it at the foot of Regent Street on the former site of Carlton House.

Burton's work in Regent's Park As an independent practitioner Burton was responsible for much of the architecture and landscaping of Regent's Park, where he worked not only with his father but also with other developers and organizations. In addition to the Colosseum he was responsible for the design and layout of the Zoological Society gardens (1826–41) and those of the Botanical Society (1840–59). Many of the villas which contribute to the architectural character of the park were designed or redesigned by Burton. These include: The Holme (1818), built for his father; South Villa (1819); the marquess of Hertford's villa (designs exh. RA, 1822, 1825; MS book of drawings of the villa now in the Architectural Association Library, London); and Grove House, where Greenough lived until his death in 1856. Hanover Lodge was designed by Burton for the Napoleonic veteran Sir Robert Arbuthnot, who took up residence in 1827; St John's Lodge, owned by John Mabberley MP, was let in 1829 to Marquess Wellesley, who employed Burton to enlarge it. The last villa to be built in the park was a large house (1832–3) for Sir James Holford for which Burton drew on his earlier design for Holwood House in Kent.

Burton's work at Hyde Park Corner Burton's most important work in London was carried out for the office of woods. This began at the conjunction of Hyde Park, St James's Park, and Green Park at the area known as Hyde Park Corner, and shows him to be one of the main executants of the vision of George IV and his ministers of London as a royal city rivalling its European counterparts. In collaboration with the king and his chief officials Burton planned to create an urban space dedicated to the celebration of the Hanoverian dynasty, national pride, and the nation's heroes. The project, which evolved in the 1820s, comprised creating two aligned entrances, the arch at Constitution Hill into Green Park, and the Hyde Park screen at Hyde Park Corner. These two entrances would form part of a processional route for the monarch from

Buckingham Palace to Hyde Park, an increasingly significant public space. The work required the removal of the toll-gate which had defined Hyde Park Corner as the entrance to London from the west, and the levelling of the approach road to make the site more amenable to development. This set piece of urban planning was, however, never completed. The arch at Constitution Hill was left devoid of decorative sculpture as a result of the moratorium in 1828 on public building work, and was used instead, much to Burton's chagrin, as a plinth for an oversized and much ridiculed equestrian statue of the duke of Wellington by Matthew Cotes Wyatt, which was later removed to Aldershot. In 1883 the arch at Constitution Hill was turned and resited to make way for increased traffic, and Burton's two aligned entrances were thus knocked off their axis.

In 1825 Burton began work on the three royal parks that met at Hyde Park Corner. The spread of the city westwards highlighted the social and political importance of these open landscapes. Positive reactions to Regent's Park as a public open space to which Burton had made a substantial contribution encouraged him to make a similar statement about urban planning in his designs for Hyde Park and Green Park; these, though in a poor state, bordered and halted the development of fashionable west London. Repair and much remedial work and replanting were necessary alongside Burton's new designs for the Stanhope, Grosvenor, and Cumberland gates. More ambitious plans for the parks that were not realized include the dramatic circular Bayswater Gate and Lodge and an entrance to Green Park from Piccadilly based on a Greek temple design. In their relationship to the new royal residence, Buckingham Palace, Hyde Park, Green Park, and St James's Park constituted collectively the kind of landscape that surrounded country houses. Owned by the crown, these parks were redesigned by Burton both as a way of enhancing the status of the monarch and the nation, and as a way of ensuring effective communication between important public buildings. In 1850–51 Burton returned to work on Buckingham Palace, where he was responsible for the removal of Nash's Marble Arch facing the building to its present site and the subsequent enclosure of the palace forecourt.

Phoenix Park, Dublin Burton's last major public commission took him to Dublin, where he was employed by the reformed Irish board of works to redesign Phoenix Park, which lies to the north-west of the centre of Dublin. The scale and significance of the work, carried out between 1832 and 1849, is comparable to that carried out in the royal parks in London and included new lodges, entrances, and landscaping. Burton played a central role in the work; other figures involved in its implementation and execution, many of whom were key figures in contemporary politics, had worked on the royal parks in London.

Private commissions Alongside his public career Burton carried out many private commissions in addition to the villas in Regent's Park, namely small country houses such as Holwood House, Kent (designs exh. RA, 1824), for John Ward MP, and Grimstone, Yorkshire (1840–50), for the second Lord Howden. He also furnished designs for important urban schemes including: St Leonards near Hastings, Sussex, built by his father in the late 1820s; the Calverley estate in Tunbridge Wells, Kent (from 1828), for John Ward MP; Fleetwood, Lancashire (1836–43), for Sir Peter Hesketh Fleetwood; and Cobh, co. Cork, Ireland (1843–50), for the fifth Viscount Midleton. Later in his career Burton became involved with innovative glasshouse design including the Palm House (1845–8) and the Temperate House (1859–62) at Kew Gardens, where he also designed the Museum of Economic Botany. His earlier work on the 'Great Stove' or conservatory at Chatsworth for the sixth duke of Devonshire caused much controversy as a public row blew up between Burton and his collaborator Joseph Paxton about who had been responsible for the design. Although opinion favoured Paxton, Burton expressed his frustration and anger at the appropriation of his work in letters to his close friend John Wilson Croker. Burton retired from professional life in 1869 (his nephew Henry Marley Burton took over his practice) and lived quietly at his houses in St Leonards, Sussex, and 1 Gloucester Houses, Kensington, where he died twelve years later, on 14 December 1881. He was buried in Kensal Green cemetery.

Decimus Burton never married and on his death his estate passed mainly to his two spinster nieces, Helen (*d.* 1892) and Emily Jane Wood (*d.* 1903), whose estates were split up on their deaths. Partly as a result of this there is more circumstantial than documentary evidence about Burton, and his remaining papers are in a fragmentary state. Most primary source material exists in the form of letters copied into government and committee minute and correspondence books. The imbalance between the scale and significance of his work and lack of related documentary evidence has tended to relegate Burton to the margins of architectural histories. Largely through his endeavours, however, Burton's principal employer, the office of woods, made a significant contribution to the shaping of London in the early nineteenth century.

DANA ARNOLD

Sources D. Arnold, 'The architect and the metropolis: the work of James and Decimus Burton in London and Dublin, 1800–1840', PhD diss., U. Lond., 1997 • D. Arnold, *Re-presenting the metropolis: architecture, urban experience and social life in London, 1800–1840* (2000) • D. Arnold, *The re-imaging of London, 1880–1840* [forthcoming] • D. Arnold, 'A family affair: Decimus Burton's designs for Regent's Park villas', *The Georgian villa*, ed. D. Arnold (1996) [repr. 1998] • D. Arnold, 'Decimus Burton's work in the Phoenix Park, 1832–49', *Bulletin of the Irish Georgian Society*, 37 (1995), 57–75 • D. Arnold, 'The arch at Constitution Hill: a new axis for London', *Apollo*, 138 (1993), 129–33 • D. Arnold, 'Decimus Burton and the urban picturesque', *The picturesque in late Georgian England*, ed. D. Arnold (1995), 51–6 • J. Bohan, 'James and Decimus Burton: architectural trends in England exemplified by their work 1760–1860', PhD diss., Yale U., 1961 • J. Mordaunt Crook, 'The villas in Regent's Park', *Country Life*, 144 (1968), 22–5, 84–7 • J. McCullen and B. Arnold, *Decimus Burton, 1800–1881* (Dublin, 1988) [exhibition catalogue, Royal Hospital, Kilmainham, Dublin, 1 July – 1 August

1988] · G. Meynell, 'The Royal Botanic Society's garden, Regent's Park', *London Journal*, 6 (1980), 135–46 · P. Miller, *Decimus Burton, 1800–1881* (1981) [exhibition catalogue, Building Centre Trust, London, 1981] · P. Chalmers Mitchell, *Centenary history of the Zoological Society of London* (1929) · B. Pool, ed., *The Croker papers, 1808–1857*, new edn (1967) · A. Saunders, *Regent's Park: a study of the development of the area from 1086 to the present day*, 2nd edn (1981) · A. Saunders, *The Regent's Park villas* (1981) · H. Scherren, *The Zoological Society of London* (1905) · H. C. Smith, 'Vicissitudes of Marble Arch', *Country Life*, 112 (1952), 38–9 · D. Stroud, 'Hyde Park Corner', *ArchR*, 106 (1949), 397–9 · J. Summerson, *Georgian London*, rev. edn (1962) · d. cert. · *CGPLA Eng. & Wales* (1882) · *IGI*

Archives CKS, corresp., plans and accounts relating to The Grove, Penshurst · V&A, letterbook relating to British embassy, Paris | BL, corresp. with Charles Babbage, Add. MSS 37185–37188 · CUL, letters to the Royal Society of Literature · NA Ire., corresp. relating to Phoenix Park, Dublin · PRO, CRES papers, letter-books, and some designs relating to royal parks · RIBA BAL, letters to John Wilson Croker

Likenesses M. Gauci, lithograph (after E. U. Eddis), BM, NPG [*see illus.*]

Wealth at death £62,887 9*s*. 6*d*.: resworn probate, April 1883, *CGPLA Eng. & Wales* (1882)

Burton, Edward (1794–1836), Church of England clergyman and theologian, the son of Major Edward Burton, was born at Shrewsbury on 13 February 1794. He was educated at Westminster School, matriculated as a commoner of Christ Church, Oxford, on 15 May 1812, gaining a studentship the next year, and in 1815 obtained a first class in both classics and mathematics. Having taken his BA degree on 29 October 1815, he was ordained to the curacy of Tettenhall, Staffordshire. On 28 May 1818 he proceeded MA, and paid a long visit to the continent, chiefly occupying himself in work at the public libraries of France and Italy. In 1824 he was select preacher in Oxford. On 12 May 1825 he married Helen, daughter of Archdeacon Corbett, of Longnor Hall, Shropshire. After his marriage he lived at Oxford. In 1827 he was made examining chaplain to the bishop, and in 1828 preached the Bampton lectures. On the death of Charles Lloyd, bishop of Oxford and regius professor of divinity, Burton was appointed to succeed him in the professorship in 1829, and took the degree of DD the same year. As professor he was also canon of Christ Church and rector of Ewelme, where, ahead of his contemporaries, he introduced open seats into the church in the place of pews. In other respects, his was a conservative appointment in every sense, and in 1834 he led the opposition to the admission of dissenters to the university. He died at Ewelme on 19 January 1836, in his forty-second year.

Burton published widely on Greek and Latin literature, his first work being the superintended publication of some of Charles Lloyd's works. As professor, he attacked unitarianism in *Testimonies of the Ante-Nicene Fathers* (1826) and extreme evangelicalism in a pamphlet dispute with Henry Bulteel. He published on the Greek New Testament (1830), *An Introduction to the Metre of the Greek Tragedians* (1814), *The Three Primers … of Henry VIII* (1834), *Lectures on Ecclesiastical History* (1831), and *Thoughts on the Separation of Church and State* (1834). Among the works on which he was engaged at the time of his death was an edition of Eusebius, published in 1838. Burton was an energetic but not an innovative scholar.

William Hunt, *rev.* H. C. G. Matthew

Sources *GM*, 2nd ser., 5 (1836), 310 · W. R. Ward, *Victorian Oxford* (1965) · Allibone, *Dict.*

Archives Shrewsbury School | BL, correspondence with Samuel Butler and others

Likenesses P. Corbet, oils, 1838, Christ Church Oxf. · marble medallion, Christ Church Oxf.

Burton, (Frances) Elaine, Baroness Burton of Coventry (1904–1991), politician, was born on 2 March 1904 at 17 Royal Avenue, Scarborough, Yorkshire, the only child of Lesley Aubrey Burton and his wife, Frances Butler. She remembered her father as an upper-class wastrel who squandered his inheritance, yet he was also a hurdler in the 1908 Olympics and gave her a lifelong enthusiasm for sports. He paid local boys a penny each to race her, and at sixteen she became the girls' world champion sprinter. After attending Leeds Girls' Modern School she trained as a teacher at Leeds City Training College and taught in primary schools and evening classes in Leeds from 1924 to 1935, coached city sports teams, and played county hockey and cricket. However, she realized that she was a political animal, if not necessarily a good party person, and amid the economic insecurity of the 1930s she abandoned her career to study unemployment first hand. She spent two years (1935–7) as a social worker in south Wales before becoming an organizer of keep fit classes for the National Fitness Council.

Upon the outbreak of the Second World War, Burton was laid off and spent over six months seeking work. Reluctant to teach again, she presented an article about women's unemployment to a newspaper editor and her initiative resulted in a weekly column in *The Star* on women's wartime difficulties; these articles were published in 1941 as *What of the Women?*. This was followed in 1942 with *And your Verdict?*, which accused the government of denying women their full role in the war effort. She also worked for the John Lewis Partnership. Her interest in politics blossomed and in June 1943 she stood as a Common Wealth candidate in the Hartlepool parliamentary by-election, where she was soundly defeated by the Labour candidate. After Labour rejected an alliance with the young left-wing movement in 1944 many Common Wealth members, including Elaine Burton, switched parties to ensure a united front against the Conservatives. While the Labour landslide and the magnanimous endorsement of Common Wealth's leading light, J. B. Priestley, did not help her win Henden South in 1945, she defeated the former Conservative minister Leslie Hore-Belisha five years later in Coventry South.

As a late convert to Labour, Burton aroused some suspicion among her new colleagues, though one sceptic—Jean Mann—was soon impressed by her doughty advocacy of women's issues in the face of an indifferent party leadership. An ardent but not aggressive feminist, Burton urged equal pay and had a talent for rapidly asking ministers follow-up questions before the speaker could move on.

Though she personally hated housework and cooking she became the housewives' voice in parliament, making her an authority on consumer protection. In 1955 she delivered a political broadcast on value for money. She also successfully sponsored a Disposal of Uncollected Goods Bill, enabling shopkeepers to sell abandoned goods left for cleaning or repair. For example, she told MPs, there were 450,000 uncollected pairs of shoes at cobblers' shops in the country and this bill would help such tradesmen to recoup some of the resulting costs.

Burton championed Coventry's needs, particularly its employment problems. None the less her local party threatened to deselect her in 1955 after she defied their instructions and voted to deny Aneurin Bevan the party whip over his perceived challenge to Clement Attlee's leadership. The controversy soon subsided, and at that year's general election Coventry's anti-Labour swing was smallest in her constituency, perhaps because voters respected her independent stand, but in 1959 she was defeated and felt 'gutted' at losing her platform in parliament. For two years she worked as an adviser at John Waddington Ltd, which had produced a card game invented by her, based on the coronation. She returned to parliament on her creation as Baroness Burton of Coventry in April 1962. For years her trademark had been her large and colourful veiled hats, known as the 'bride's mother's hat'—she had even worn them on the dole queue—but in the upper house she ran into a seventeenth-century rule forbidding headwear. In 1965 she persuaded the house to abolish the rule and enlivened the chamber with her millinery as she had done in the Commons.

Burton made many more substantial contributions to the Lords' work, including the continuation of a crusade she had begun as an MP. Remembering her own experience of buying clothes horses in order to practise hurdling, abandoning her dream of swimming the channel, and seeing athletically talented students unable to fulfil their potential owing to lack of resources, she argued vigorously for improved funding of amateur athletics (though she was staunchly opposed to tobacco sponsorship). She warned that a ministry of sport would be meddlesome, but as early as 1956, in one of her numerous letters to *The Times*, she urged the creation of an independent grant supported body like the Arts Council. After she had raised questions and initiated debates on the issue the government agreed to subsidize amateur athletes who wished to compete internationally. In 1965 she was appointed to the newly formed Sports Council, which served only to advise the government but in 1971, the year she retired, it was given independence and responsibility for allocating funds.

Baroness Burton also spoke on such favourite topics as women's opportunities in business and public life, initiating a debate on the matter at the age of eighty (she had been a founding member of the Federation of Business and Professional Women). She championed the rights of air travellers, campaigned to protect children from flammable nightwear, and took an interest in broadcasting, having served on the Independent Television Authority between 1964 and 1969. Throughout the 1970s she worried about the Labour Party's direction and urged fellow moderates to actively resist the encroachment of the far left. Feeling that her pleas were in vain she and eight other peers left the party in January 1981, declaring her inability to accept such policies as unilateral nuclear disarmament, withdrawal from the EEC, and the party's proposed new method of choosing its leader. She became the Social Democratic Party's spokesman in the Lords on civil aviation and consumer affairs, and remained active until she died, unmarried, on 6 October 1991 at her home, 18 Vincent Court, Seymour Place, Westminster.

DUNCAN SUTHERLAND

Sources *The Times* (3 March 1981) · *The Times* (9 Oct 1991) · Burke, *Peerage* · M. Phillips, *The divided house: women at Westminster* (1980) · J. Mann, *Woman in parliament* (1962) · newspaper clipping collection, Labour Party Archive, 103 Princess Street, Manchester · *Hansard 5C* (1950–59) · *Hansard 5L* (1962–91) · 'Spinster on the war path', *Evening Standard* (9 Dec 1950) · A. Sampson, *Richard Crossman* (1990) · W. D. Rubinstein, ed., *The biographical dictionary of life peers* (New York, 1991) · *CGPLA Eng. & Wales* (1992) · *WWW* · b. cert. · d. cert.

Archives U. Warwick Mod. RC, political corresp. | U. Warwick Mod. RC, Coventry borough labour party papers · UCL, Gaitskell papers, letters and a brochure

Wealth at death £346,847: probate, 15 April 1992, *CGPLA Eng. & Wales*

Burton, Sir Frederic William (1816–1900), watercolour painter and art administrator, was born on 8 April 1816 at Clifden House, Corofin, near Inchiquin Lake, co. Clare, Ireland. He was the third son of Samuel Frederic Burton (*b.* 1786), a country gentleman, and his wife, Hannah Mallet, the daughter of a Dublin civil engineer. The Burtons owned a large estate at Mungret, co. Limerick, and had been living at Corofin since the 1780s. The family were descendants of Sir Edward Burton of York, who, for his loyalty and military services in the Wars of the Roses, was knighted by Edward IV in 1460.

Samuel Burton was an amateur landscape painter who exhibited work in Dublin from 1809 to 1814, and he encouraged his son to paint. In 1826 the Burtons went to live in Dublin to further their sons' education; they sent the ten-year-old Frederic to the Dublin Society's drawing schools, where he studied under Henry Brocas the elder and Robert Lucius West. At sixteen he exhibited his first work, *Abraham on his Journey to Sacrifice Isaac*, at the Royal Hibernian Academy. The artist and writer Samuel Lover taught him to paint miniature portraits on ivory and gave him lessons in the technique of watercolour painting. Burton spent the first part of his career as a miniaturist and portrait painter.

In 1837, at the age of twenty-one, Burton was elected an associate of the Royal Hibernian Academy; he became a full member in 1839. The other important influence in his life was the antiquarian and artist George Petrie, who encouraged him to look to the Irish landscape and antiquities for inspiration and to study the history of art. Through Lover and Petrie he met the leaders of Irish literary, musical, and artistic life. As a prolific portrait painter, he produced a visual record of intellectual life: he was commissioned to paint portraits of Sir Samuel Ferguson (National Gallery of Ireland, Dublin), Helen Faucit in the role of Antigone (National Gallery of Ireland, Dublin), and Thomas Davis (National Gallery of Ireland, Dublin). His chalk portrait of George Eliot is now in the National Portrait Gallery in London.

At this time the study of Irish antiquities, landscape, and culture was undergoing a revival. Burton was a serious and highly regarded scholar in this field: his knowledge of antiquities and archaeology was recognized with his membership of the council of the Royal Irish Academy, and he was invited to become a founder member of the Irish Archaeological Society in 1840. He went on tours of Howth in co. Dublin, Connemara, Achill Island, and co. Kerry where he sketched the landscape and studied rural life. In 1839 Burton visited the Aran Islands with Petrie, making sketches in pencil and watercolours of everyday life, ruins, and landscape. These were later used as sources for his larger compositions and subject pictures such as *Blind Girl at the Holy Well* (1839), *Aran Fisherman's Drowned Child* (1841; National Gallery of Ireland, Dublin), and *Connaught Toilette: Connemara Girls on their Way to Market* (1841). These pictures were exhibited and engraved, which further increased their popularity.

Burton was a close friend of Thomas Davis, the leader of the Young Ireland movement, and he designed a frontispiece for the magazine the *Spirit of the Nation*. He also illustrated his brother the Revd Robert Burton's *History of the Royal Hospital Kilmainham* (1843). Objects designed by Burton include the ceremonial mace for the King and Queen's College of Physicians in Ireland (1850–53), for which there are fourteen designs in the National Gallery of Ireland, a seal for St Columba's College (1843), and a fibula brooch of Irish gold based on an antique Celtic model (National Museum of Ireland, Dublin).

In 1842 Burton went on an extended tour of Germany, sketching Bavarian peasants and medieval architecture. He returned in 1844, but from 1851 to 1856 was employed by King Maximilian II of Bavaria as curator of the royal collection in Munich. There he came under the influence of the German Nazarene painters and his genre and historical subject pictures became more Romantic in spirit. A literary theme provided a source for his most famous work, *The Meeting on the Turret Stairs* (1864) (National Gallery of Ireland, Dublin), which depicts the lovers Hellelil and Hildebrand. It was inspired by a Danish ballad which had been translated by his friend Whitley Stokes. The Romantic medieval treatment of the subject matter and strong colours make this Burton's most Pre-Raphaelite work. In 1855 Burton was elected an associate of the Watercolour Society; he became a full member in 1856. From 1858 he lived in London, where he was part of Rossetti's circle. In 1863 he was elected a fellow of the Society of Antiquaries.

Burton gave up painting in 1874 when he was appointed director of the National Gallery, London, in succession to his friend Sir William Boxall. Burton was the third director of the gallery and the last to have total power over the trustees in the purchasing of artworks. As a result, his career may be judged by the acquisitions which he authorized during his twenty years' tenure. These included some of the most significant works in the gallery: Duccio's *Annunciation* from the *Maestà*, Leonardo da Vinci's *Virgin of the Rocks*, Botticelli's *Venus and Mars*, Piero della Francesca's *Nativity*, Raphael's *Ansidei Madonna*, Hans Holbein the younger's *Ambassadors*, Vermeer's *Young Woman Standing at a Virginal*, and Velázquez's *Philip IV*. Also during his directorship, a series of extensions was added to the gallery building in 1876 and 1887, and the National Gallery Loan Act of 1883 was secured, authorizing the loan of pictures to museums outside London. Burton was knighted in 1884 and in 1886 received the honorary degree of LLD from the University of Dublin. He retired from the gallery in 1894 and lived at 43 Argyle Road, Kensington, where he died on 16 March 1900. He never married. He was buried on 22 March in Mount Jerome cemetery, Dublin. An exhibition of his work was held at the National Gallery of Ireland later that year. PAUL CAFFREY

Sources W. G. Strickland, *A dictionary of Irish artists*, 1 (1913), 130–42 · *DNB* · NG Ire., Burton Archive · M. Stokes, draft biography of Burton, NG Ire. · J. McFarlane, 'Sir Frederic William Burton RHA (1816–1900): his life and work', BA diss., TCD, 1976 · H. Potterton, 'A director with discrimination', *Country Life*, 155 (1974), 1140–41 · Lady Gregory [I. A. Gregory], 'Frederick William Burton', *The Leader* (8 Dec 1900) · M. Bourke, 'Frederic William Burton, 1816–1900, painter and antiquarian', *Éire–Ireland*, 28/3 (1993), 45–60 · P. Caffrey, 'Samuel Lover: his life and work', BA diss., TCD, 1985 · *The Times* (27 March 1900) · A. Crookshank and the Knight of Glin [D. Fitzgerald], *The watercolours of Ireland: works on paper in pencil, pastel and paint, c.1600–1914* (1994) · P. Caffrey, 'Samuel Lover's achievement as a painter', *Irish Arts Review*, 3/1 (1986), 51–4 · P. Caffrey, 'Irish portrait miniatures, c.1700–1830', PhD diss., Southampton Institute, 1995 · A. Le Harivel, ed., *National Gallery of Ireland: illustrated summary catalogue of drawings, watercolours and miniatures* (1983) · M. Bourke, 'The Aran fisherman's drowned child', *GPA Irish Arts Review Yearbook*, 5 (1988), 190–96

Archives NG Ire., archive · U. Texas, MSS | BL, letters to Sir Austin Layard, Add. MSS 39037–39040 · Bodl. Oxf., letters to F. G. Stephens · National Gallery, London, letter-books and minutes of trustees, NG7 · National Gallery, London, corresp. with Ralph Nicholson Wornum · Ransom HRC, letters to Charles Fairfax Murray

Likenesses attrib. G. F. Mulvany, oils, *c.*1840, NG Ire. · Allen & Co., photograph, *c.*1845, NG Ire. · J. Cundall, photograph, *c.*1845, NG Ire. · Cundall, Downes & Co., carte-de-visite, 1860–69, NPG · T. Farrell, portrait, 1860–69, NG Ire. · H. T. Wells, oils, 1863, NPG · Lombardi, photograph, 1880, NG Ire. · H. J. Brooks, group portrait, oils (*Private view of the Old Masters Exhibition, Royal Academy, 1888*), NPG · F. W. Burton, self-portrait, chalk drawing, NG Ire. · J. Hughes, marble bust (after plaster life mask, *c.*1850), NG Ire.

Wealth at death £10,451 16*s.*: probate, 23 April 1900, *CGPLA Eng. & Wales*

Burton, George (*bap.* **1717**, *d.* **1791**), Church of England clergyman and biblical scholar, was baptized on 14 March 1717 at Owston, Lincolnshire, the second son of George and Elizabeth Burton of Burton Lazars, Leicestershire. His niece Felicia Burton, daughter of his elder brother, Philip, married George Horne, bishop of Norwich. In 1733 George matriculated from St Catharine's College, Cambridge, whence he graduated BA in 1737; four years later he proceeded MA from King's College, Cambridge. He was ordained priest at Norwich in August 1740, and was presented to the rectory of Eldon the same year. In 1751 he became rector of Herringswell, also in Suffolk. He retained both livings until his death. Burton also taught, and generally had three or four pupils boarding in his house. He married, on 9 July 1743, Anne Reeve of Melton Mowbray, who was the sister of William Reeve.

In 1766 Burton published his ambitious *Essay towards reconciling the numbers of Daniel and St. John, determining the birth of Our Saviour, and fixing a precise time for the continuance of the present desolation of the Jews, with some conjectures and calculations pointing out the year 1764 to have been one of the most remarkable epochas in history*, to which he added a supplement in 1768. His tables fixing the paschal feast and linking the chronologies of all ages and nations were published together in 1787. In addition to his chronological work, Burton compiled materials for a history of Eldon, and possibly left a manuscript of such a study at his death. Burton's chronological principles seem to have been rather obscure, though he was an assiduous scholar. The antiquary George Ashby claimed Burton's chronological writings were comprehensible and persuasive only to Burton himself. Another antiquary, William Stukeley, was Burton's friend and correspondent, and reputedly gave him Charles Bertram's ingenious forgery, *Richard of Cirencester*.

Burton died at Bath on 3 November 1791, aged seventy-four, and was buried in Walcot church.

THOMPSON COOPER, *rev.* EMMA MAJOR

Sources Venn, *Alum. Cant.* • *ESTC* • J. Nichols, *The history and antiquities of the county of Leicester*, 2 (1795–8), 228, 268 • *IGI* • Watt, *Bibl. Brit.* • Nichols, *Illustrations*, 6.880–87 • W. Stukeley, *Medallic history of Marcus Aurelius Valerius Carausius*, 2 vols. (1757–9), 116

Archives Bodl. Oxf., antiquarian notes and collections • Suffolk RO, Ipswich, collections for a history of Elveden | Bodl. Oxf., letters to William Stukeley

Burton, Henry (*bap.* 1578, *d.* 1647/8), Independent minister and religious controversialist, was born at Birdsall in the East Riding of Yorkshire, and baptized on 9 October 1578, the son of William Burton and Mary (*née* Holme). He matriculated as sizar of St John's College, Cambridge, in 1595, probably graduated BA early in 1600, and proceeded MA in 1603.

Early career and writings After his graduation Burton tutored the sons of Sir Robert Carey, who recommended him to Prince Henry as his clerk of the closet. He took up this position in 1605 and, after Henry's death in 1612, continued in this office for Prince Charles. That year he was also incorporated at Oxford. On 14 November 1618 he was ordered to show his licence for lecturing at St Matthew's, Friday Street, London, and on 3 October 1621 he was appointed rector of that parish. It must have been during this period that he married his first wife, Anne; their daughter Anne was baptized on 21 September 1621 and son Henry on 13 May 1624.

Shortly after the death of King James, Burton presented a letter to Charles accusing the bishop of Durham, Richard Neile, and Bishop William Laud of being 'popishly affected', and as a result of this was dismissed from his

M: Henry Burton, for preaching againſt Po
piſh innovations and printing his 2 Sermons
For God & the King, was much vexed in the high
Commiſsion Court, afterward cenſured in the
Starr-Chamber to be deprived of his Miniſtrie,
degraded in the Vniverty, loſt both his Eares on
the pillorie, was fined 5000,# baniſhed into the Ile
of Gernſey, there Comitted to perpetuall cloſs im
priſonment, where no freinds, no not ſo much
as his wife or Children, might once ſee or come
into the Iſland where hee was on pain of im
priſonment to them, Which Corporall puniſh
ment was Executed on him, and his two other bleſsed
Brethren or fellow-Sufferers. June 30th 1637.

Henry Burton (*bap.* 1578, *d.* 1647/8), by Wenceslaus Hollar

post. Later he claimed that because of their 'popish practices' he became a nonconformist. The majority of Burton's sermons and printed writings from 1621 to 1636 were directed against the perceived threat of Arminian tendencies within the English church. In 1626 he joined the assaults on Richard Mountague's books *New Gagg* and *Appello Caesarem*. Mountague attempted, among other things, to stress the obscurity of the Calvinist doctrine of predestination and argued that it was possible for believers to fall away from grace in such a way as to lose faith and be damned. Such assertions challenged Burton's own conviction of election that Christ died only for the elect and that once elected it was not possible to fall from grace. As he said in *A Plea to Appeale* (1626), Mountague's 'Heresy overthroweth the whole tenure and truth of the Gospell; it turneth upside downe the very foundation of our salvation, grounded upon God's eternall love in electing and predestinating us in Christ to Grace and Glory'. During this year, for his continuing attacks on the ecclesiastical establishment, Burton was cited before high commission but no proceedings were taken against him.

Burton's deep hostility to Roman Catholicism was given full expression in *The Baiting of the Popes Bull* (1627). It was a response to a papal bull, probably sent to England in 1626, which he saw as an effort to incite Catholics to subversive activity and which thus consolidated his fear of possible covert activities by the Jesuits. In *Israels Fast* (1628) he called for the execution of all Jesuits and seminary priests and 'because they seduce the people from God they shall be put to death' (fol. B1). His assaults on the Catholic church were clearly linked to his apocalyptic vision in *The Seven Vials* (1628), dedicated to Charles I. A commentary on the sixteenth and seventeenth chapters of the book of Revelation which, according to Burton's interpretation, describe the destruction of the beast and the fall of the whole papal hierarchy, it also serves as a 'Propheticall Chronologie' to the end of the world and 'was purposely penned for these last times, as to forewarne, so to forearm God's people against the last and extremist perills'. Burton perceived himself to be living in a time when God's elect would inevitably defeat the 'popish' princes of the world and the pouring of the seventh vial would bring about the ultimate destruction of Babylon. This would usher in the end of the world and the second coming of Christ to final judgment. *The Seven Vials* also took him into the rather confused controversy over the precise nature of the Church of Rome and led him to condemn Bishop Joseph Hall's book *The Old Religion*. Burton took offence over Hall's assertion that salvation could be achieved within the Roman Catholic church and accused him of encouraging protestants to convert to Catholicism. In the same year Burton also attacked John Cosin's book *A Collection of Private Devotions of the Hours of Prayer*. Burton objected to a number of issues raised by Cosin, including the mention of angels acting as intermediaries before God and prayers for the dead. This provoked him to ask for a petition to be presented to the king and parliament calling for a prohibition against all 'popish' and Arminian books and against any Arminians holding senior positions within the English church.

Trial and imprisonment Following the publication of his *Babel No Bethel* (1629), Burton was brought before the high commission. The charge was that in dedicating it to the House of Commons, he was attempting to divide Commons from the king. In his *A Narration of the Life of Mr. Henry Burton* (1643) however, Burton thought that the real reasons were that he had attacked the 'Church of Rome as no true Church of Christ, and because such kind of Bookes were printed without licence when none could be obtained'. On 15 June he came before Bishop William Laud of London on charges which included preaching against the canonical duty of bowing at the name of Jesus. Laud temporarily suspended him from preaching and he was subsequently imprisoned in the Fleet for twelve days. Burton appealed his case to Archbishop George Abbott who reinstated him on 10 July. In 1634 Burton preached at Thomas Cotton's conventicle in Colchester and in 1636 he collaborated with William Prynne on the tract *A Divine Tragedy*, a collection of 'authentic' tales of the punishment given to sabbath breakers and a vehement attack on the newly reissued Book of sports.

During this time there were widespread rumours that the Laudian bishops 'were denying the orders of non-episcopal churches and unchurching them for their failure to uphold episcopacy' (Milton, 487). Burton subsequently published a tract criticizing this policy, saying that those who 'make no bones even in open court, to vilify the prime pillars of those Churches themselves, as having no lawful ministers, because no prelates to put them in order' (*The Lord's Day*, 1636, 46). In the same year, in his *An Apology of an Appeal* (1636), Burton commented on the idea of a just balance between the king's prerogative and the liberty of his subjects, implying that the king's prerogative was limited and defined by the law. As he declared, 'the King's prerogative, his just laws, and the People's liberties, are so combined together, that they must be altogether preserved entire' (p. 28). Burton's views on this subject were severely criticized by Peter Heylin in a tract published in 1637. It was also between 1633 and 1637 that Burton began to consolidate his collaboration with William Prynne in their attacks on the Laudian church. A witness states that during Prynne's imprisonment in the Tower of London during this time Burton visited him regularly and they both began to publish their works with the same printer in Amsterdam.

On 5 November 1636 at St Matthew's, Friday Street, Burton preached two sermons to commemorate Guy Fawkes's day where he identified all bishops with the Roman Catholic church and attacked the claim that episcopacy was *jure divino*. He argued that it was a usurpation of the king's authority for the bishops to derive their authority from an unbroken chain of apostolic succession. As he told his parishioners, 'the bishops are the most dangerous enemies of the King who under a pretense of honour and love do machinate the overthrow of his Kingdom and State, as by altering his State of religion'. For these two sermons Burton was charged with sedition and on 3 December 1636 was summoned to the Chiswick house of Dr Arthur Duck, one of the members of the high commission, who administered an *ex officio* oath, which Burton refused to take. He then took his leave and appealed to the king. After this a special session of the high commission was called in London which Burton, after being invited twice to appear, refused to attend. In his absence he was suspended from his ministerial function and ordered to be apprehended. Burton subsequently barricaded himself into his house. As he narrates, 'I shut myself up in my house, as in my prison, and there did compile my two said sermons, with my Appeale, in one Book, to the end it might be published in print, as it was'. The sermons were eventually published as *For God and the King* shortly before 1 February 1637, when the sheriff of London, William Abell, arrived at Burton's house with pickaxes and swords, broke down his door, ransacked his study, and threw him once again in the Fleet.

Burton was joined in prison by John Bastwick and William Prynne and all three appeared before the Star Chamber on 14 June to answer charges of libel and sedition. During the trial Burton posed as an upright minister of the word and at one point said to the court that 'I pray God that this honorable court in the judgment of this cause do nothing this day whereby they may sin against God'. The lord keeper informed him that they were not sitting there to hear him preach, but Burton replied that:

> I am brought into a great strait, that of necessity I must desert my cause and my conscience, or undergoe the censure of this Honorable Court: and therefore I do without any further deliberation choose rather to abide the censure … than to desert my cause and conscience. (Burton, 12)

At these words Burton tells us that 'the audience gave a great humme' (ibid.). At the conclusion of the trial Lord Cottington censured the three to lose their ears in the palace yard at Westminster, to be fined £5000 each, and to suffer perpetual imprisonment. They were also denied access to their family, friends, pen, ink, and paper. It is reported that when the sentence was executed on 30 June 1637, Burton's ears were cut so close that his temporal artery was opened and blood gushed out upon the scaffold. On 28 July, after his ears had healed, Burton was transported to Lancaster Castle and was imprisoned there on 7 August. He was eventually transferred to Castle Cornet on Guernsey on 1 November. It is said that his parishioners, in protest against his punishment, refused to pay their tithes and also molested their new rector, Robert Chestlin.

Burton's later years On 7 November 1640 a petition from Burton's second wife, Sara, seeking his release was read in the House of Commons, and on 21 November he was released together with Prynne. According to one report they made their triumphal entry into London carrying sprigs of rosemary in their hands closely followed by an estimated ten thousand people. In March 1641 all previous penalties against Burton were reversed, and he was awarded a BD and voted £6000 by the House of Commons (although he never received this). On 8 June the Commons voted that he should be restored to 'his former liberty of preaching', but because the rectory was blocked by the presence of a legal incumbent, Robert Chestlin, he was not readmitted until 4 June 1643.

After his release Burton continued his assaults on bishops and episcopacy, but this time he attacked not only the abuses of the prelates but the very system itself. In his *A Replie to a Relation of the Conference between William Laude and Mr Fisher the Jesuit* (1640) he had told Laud that the 'erection of Prelacie or Hierarchy was that Mystery of Iniquity which Satan began to brood and hatch even in the Apostles days' (p. 53). On 20 June 1641 Burton preached a fast sermon before the House of Commons where he declared the need for a complete reform of the English church and a need to purge the universities and schools so that 'the church of God may be furnished with able ministers, able to pray and able to preach' (*England's Bondage*, 1641, 29). Also in this sermon Burton reiterated his claims that Christ's return to judgment was imminent, followed by the beginning of a heavenly New Jerusalem. When parliament drew up the protestation to be taken by the members of both houses and all office-holders in church and state, Burton published an anonymous pamphlet *The Protestation Protested* (1641), in which he accused the Church of England of being anti-Christian. He argued for the forming of Independent congregations 'who are fitted and who desire to draw unto Christ in a holy-communion with him'. The tract was severely criticized by a number of clergymen, among them John Geree and Thomas Edwards, who both feared that the growth of Independent churches would breed disunity within church and state. Following Robert Chestlin's departure from St Matthew's, Friday Street, Burton began to reorganize the congregation as a gathered church. According to Edwards, Burton's church was full of internal disruption and disputes, with Burton supposedly quarrelling with a butcher, suspending the singing of psalms, and agreeing to forbear baptism of some of his parishioners' children. Burton's former ally William Prynne launched a full-scale attack on Independency, which initiated a bitter pamphlet controversy between them.

On 17 April 1645 the separatists John Duppa, David Brown, and Samuel Chidley, who were offended by Burton's brand of Independency, met in Burton's house to 'better know the differences of our professions and practices, and so endeavor (if possible) to be one of mind concerning the truth' (Brown, sig. A3*v*). During their discussions Burton defended his form of separation from the church and informed them that he had renounced his ordination in the Church of England because there was no holiness in the parish churches, but the meeting was concluded by Brown and his colleagues completely dissociating themselves from Burton. The latter's willingness to operate within the parish structure and to use church buildings represented to them unacceptable compromise. Meanwhile Burton's parishioners had petitioned the committee for plundered ministers that he had refused to officiate in accordance with the *Directory for the Publique Worship of God*. As a result he was summoned to attend their next meeting on 26 April, when he was questioned as to whether he would officiate according to the directory. Apparently his reply was: 'It is a large question.' In that year he appeared three more times before the committee to be examined about his attitude to the directory and at a meeting on 19 August some of the petitioners attended and declared 'that the said differences are composed and settled by agreement between them', and the case was dismissed. Despite this outcome eleven days later the committee appointed Daniel Dyke to St Matthew's, Friday Street, as Burton 'hath quit the said place'. In the same year a committee of underwriters appointed Burton to deliver a regular catechetical lecture every two weeks at St Mary Aldermanbury and he used this opportunity to preach Independency. Because of this the rector, Edmund Calamy, whose sympathies were presbyterian, prevented Burton from preaching by instructing the churchwardens to debar his entry into the church. This led to a minor pamphlet war between Calamy and Burton and it seems the issue was not resolved as Calamy denied all knowledge of him being locked out, stating that he had no power over the keys.

When Burton made his will on 4 December 1647 he was already sick. Bequests to relatives and friends totalling

£140 were to be paid from the principal of a loan made to parliament on 28 November 1646. His congregation received £5 for a supper and £10 to be distributed to its poor by the deacons. His son Henry received a £700 addition to his previous portion, while Burton's second wife, Sara, was to enjoy the residue of the estate, including land in Sunbury and in Shepperton, Middlesex. Burton was buried at St Mary Aldermanbury on 7 January 1648.

KENNETH GIBSON

Sources R. T. Hughes, 'Henry Burton: a study in religion and politics, 1604–1640', PhD diss., Iowa, 1972 • R. T. Hughes, 'Henry Burton: the making of a puritan revolutionary', *Journal of Church and State*, 16 (1974), 421–34 • M. Tolmie, *The triumph of the saints: the separate churches of London, 1616–1649* (1977) • A. Milton, *Catholic and Reformed: the Roman and protestant churches in English protestant thought, 1600–1640* (1995) • H. Trevor-Roper, *Archbishop Laud, 1573–1645* (1940) • H. Burton, *A narration of the life of Mr. Henry Burton* (1643) • Venn, *Alum. Cant.* • T. Edwards, *Gangraena, or, A catalogue and discovery of many of the errours, heresies, blasphemies and pernicious practices of the sectaries of this time*, 3 vols. in 1 (1646) • D. Brown, *Two conferences between some of those that are called separatists and independents* (1650) • will, PRO, PROB 11/203, sig. 9

Archives BL, Sloane MS 1983 • BL, Add. MS 5/540 • BL, Add. MS 11/308 • BL, Add. MS 28/011

Likenesses G. Glover, line engraving, BM, NPG; repro. in Burton, *Narration* • W. Hollar, etching, NPG [*see illus.*] • woodcut, BM; repro. in H. Burton, *A divine tragedie lately acted* (1641)

Burton, Hezekiah (*bap.* 1632, *d.* 1681), Church of England clergyman, was baptized in the village of Sutton-cum-Lound, Nottinghamshire, on 23 April 1632, the son of Hezekiah Burton, a clergyman, and his wife, Anne. He attended school in Sutton-cum-Lound before being admitted to Magdalene College, Cambridge, as a sizar in 1647, aged fifteen. Here he came under the care of the presbyterian divine Francis Tallents. Burton graduated BA in 1651 and in the same year was appointed Wray fellow on parliamentary authority, replacing the ejected John Dacres. He proceeded MA in 1654, incorporating his degree at Oxford University in the same year. During the interregnum he established a considerable reputation as a tutor. His circle of friends at Magdalene included the philosopher Richard Cumberland and Samuel Pepys. He also corresponded with the Platonist Henry More.

After the Restoration, Burton retained his fellowship at Magdalene and earned further ecclesiastical preferments. In February 1661 he was ordained deacon and in 1663 he became vicar of Lilford in Northamptonshire. A prebend's stall at Norwich followed in 1667. In the autumn of the same year Magdalene granted Burton leave of absence for one year to become chaplain to the new lord keeper of the seal, Orlando Bridgeman. He never returned to Magdalene. In January 1668, together with John Wilkins, Burton represented Bridgeman in abortive negotiations with dissenters over their possible accommodation within the established church. Wood records that Wilkins's 'Club for a Comprehension' met in Essex House, in the chamber of 'that great Trimmer and Latitudinarian, Dr Hezekiah Burton' (Wood, *Ath. Oxon.*, 4.512–13). Burton was subsequently rector of the urban parish of St George's, Southwark, from 1668 to 1680, where he was noted for his charity to imprisoned debtors. He was also allowed a dispensation to

Hezekiah Burton (*bap.* 1632, *d.* 1681), by Mary Beale, *c.*1674

hold the rectory of Taplow in Buckinghamshire in plurality. Through the influence of John Tillotson, he became rector of Barnes in Surrey in 1680. After he moved to Barnes he was stricken with a fever which proved fatal to him and other members of his family (he was certainly married, but we have no details of his wife or children). He died at his rectory in August or September 1681.

Burton published nothing during his lifetime except for an *alloquium ad lectorem* ('address to the reader') to the work of his friend Richard Cumberland, *De legibus naturae* (1672), for whom he acted as editor. Two volumes of his *Discourses*, edited and prefaced by Tillotson, were published posthumously from his notes in 1684 and 1685. The *Discourses* reflect Burton's latitudinarian desire to emphasize the moral theology of a natural religion against what he saw as counterfeit and superficial modes of formal religious devotion. They also explore latitudinarian preoccupations with creating an ethical language which could reconcile self-interest and moral duty. Burton's emphasis upon natural sociability and benevolence recall the thesis of his friend Cumberland as well as the arguments of Tillotson and John Wilkins. The *Discourse Concerning the Authority of Men in the Kingdom of Christ* was reprinted by itself in 1718.

JON PARKIN

Sources Venn, *Alum. Cant.*, 1/1 • P. Cunich and others, *A history of Magdalene College, Cambridge, 1428–1988* (1994) • J. Tillotson, 'preface', in H. Burton, *Several discourses*, 1 (1684) • Wood, *Ath. Oxon.*, new edn, 4.512–13 • T. Birch, *The life of the Most Reverend Dr John Tillotson, lord archbishop of Canterbury* (1752), 42, 76, 77, 93, 124–6 • Pepys, *Diary*, 1.67–8; 3.21; 10.50 • *Letters and the second diary of Samuel Pepys*, ed. R. G. Howarth (1932) • J. Lightfoot, *Some genuine remains of the late pious and learned John Lightfoot DD* (1700), li • *The Conway letters: the correspondence of Anne, Viscountess Conway, Henry More, and their friends, 1642–1684*, ed. M. H. Nicolson, rev. edn, ed. S. Hutton (1992),

478–9 · *The diary and correspondence of Dr John Worthington*, ed. J. Crossley and R. C. Christie, 2 vols. in 3, Chetham Society, 13, 36, 114 (1847–86), vol. 2, pt 1, p. 246; vol. 2, pt 2, pp. 352, 360 · W. Kennett, *A register and chronicle ecclesiastical and civil* (1728), 375

Archives Bodl. Oxf., letters to Dr Astley, Tanner MS 134, fols. 206, 233 · LPL, admission to Barnes, MS VG1/3 · LPL, dispensation to hold Taplow in plurality, MS VB1/3, fol. 3

Likenesses M. Beale, oils, *c*.1674, Magd. Cam. [*see illus.*] · R. White, line engraving, 1684 (after M. Beale), BM, NPG; repro. in Burton, *Several discourses* · attrib. M. Beale, red chalk drawing, BM

Burton [*née* Arundell], **Isabel**, **Lady Burton** (**1831–1896**), author and traveller, was born at 14 Great Cumberland Place, London, on 20 March 1831. Descended from an old Roman Catholic family, her father was Henry Raymond Arundell, a lineal descendant of the sixth Baron Arundell of Wardour; her mother, Eliza, was a sister of the first Baron Gerard. While living at Trieste she claimed and used the title *Gräfin* by virtue of her descent from the first Baron Arundell of Wardour, hereditary count of the Holy Roman empire. She was educated at New Hall School, run by the Convent of the Canonesses of the Holy Sepulchre, near Chelmsford, and afterwards at Boulogne, where she first met Sir Richard Francis *Burton (1821–1890) in 1851. She immediately formed a romantic attachment for him. They met again in 1856, but her parents opposed their match; not until 1861 did she consent to marry him without their approval. After obtaining a dispensation for a mixed marriage from Cardinal Wiseman, they were married in a Roman Catholic ceremony at the Royal Bavarian Chapel, Warwick Street, London, on 22 January 1861, in the necessary presence of the civil registrar. Their marriage, surely one of the most studied of Victorian marriages, appears to have been genuinely companionate, as she and Burton rode, swam, and fenced together. She shared much of his life of literature and travel, seeing many of his books through press, and being instructed on several occasions to 'pay, pack, and follow' before they settled in Trieste, where they lived from 1872 to 1890.

Although she lived in Burton's literary shadow, referring to herself as 'the mere bellows player to the organist', Isabel Burton was a good writer. Her *Inner Life of Syria, Palestine, and the Holy Land* (2 vols., 1875) compares favourably with her husband's book about Syria, to which she also contributed, and her *AEI, Arabia, Egypt, India* (1879) is a notable travel account. She appears as editor of Burton's translation of the Portuguese poet Luis Vaz de Camõens's *Lusiads* (2 vols., 1880) and as author of 'The reviewer reviewed', a postscript to his commentary on Camõens's life and work (2 vols., 1881). When she saw his *The Highlands of the Brazil* (2 vols., 1869) through publication, she added a preface without his knowledge that warned against his references to polygamy and sexual practices. The reader should, she said, 'steer through these anthropological sand-banks and hidden rocks as best he or she may' (R. F. Burton, *Highlands*, 1.viii). She vigorously supported issuing his famous translation of *The Arabian Nights* by subscription and deserves credit for its financial success. Her own expurgated 'household' edition of that work failed, a fact that Burton himself noted with some satisfaction, although he assisted her in the preparation of it.

Isabel Burton, Lady Burton (1831–1896), by unknown photographer, 1869

Isabel Burton was noted for her concern for animals, of which she usually kept many. Her menagerie at Damascus was so varied that only with difficulty did she keep its members from devouring each other. At Trieste one of her chief interests was a local society for the prevention of cruelty to animals. Any coachman who flicked his horses with a whip was likely to receive a jab from her umbrella.

Isabel Burton worked constantly to further her husband's career. He requited her devotion with an absolute confidence that no male friend obtained from him. During the last years of his life she nursed him devotedly. Her actions after his death, however, outraged many of their friends as well as subsequent scholars, for she burnt most of his enormous collection of private papers, including his manuscript translation of 'The scented garden', which he considered 'the crown of my life' (Wright, 2.217). She later claimed that his apparition repeatedly appeared to her and ordered its destruction.

In 1891 Lady Burton received a civil-list pension of £150. She published her *Life of Captain Sir Rich*[d]*. F. Burton, K.C.M.G., F.R.G.S.* (2 vols.) in 1893. Drawing on material available only to her, it is an indispensable source for Burton, but it is also selective and possibly distorted. Devoting herself to his memory, she published certain of his book manuscripts that she had spared, and envisaged a memorial edition of all of his published works, of which seven volumes appeared before her death. Portions of her unfinished autobiography were incorporated into *The Romance of Isabel Lady Burton* (2 vols., 1897) by W. H. Wilkins, who also edited and published her *Passion-Play at Ober-Ammergau* (1900). Lady Burton died on 22 March 1896 at the house at 67 Baker Street, London, which she shared with her widowed sister. She was buried beside her husband in the mausoleum, shaped like an Arab tent, that she had designed for him in the cemetery of St Mary Magdalene at Mortlake, remembering his wish, 'I should like us both to lie in a tent, side by side.'

J. S. COTTON, *rev.* JASON THOMPSON

Sources M. S. Lovell, *A rage to live: a biography of Richard and Isabel Burton* (1998) • W. H. Wilkins, *The romance of Isabel, Lady Burton*, 2 vols. (1897) • J. Burton, *Sir Richard Burton's wife* (1941) • L. Blanch, *The wilder shores of love* (1954), 9–130 • G. M. Stisted, *The true life of Capt. Sir Richard F. Burton* (1896) • F. M. Brodie, *The devil drives: a life of Sir Richard Burton* (1967) • T. Wright, *The life of Sir Richard Burton*, 2 vols. (1906)

Archives Hunt. L., letters • Syracuse University, New York, corresp. with publishers, etc. | Bodl. Oxf., letters to J. J. Fahie • Hunt. L., letters to Leonard Smithers • Royal Asiatic Society, London, letters to Bernard Quaritch

Likenesses L. Desanges, watercolour, 1861, Orleans House Gallery, Twickenham; repro. in Brodie, *The devil drives*, following p. 222 • photograph, 1869, repro. in I. Burton, *Inner life of Syria*, 1 (1875), frontispiece • photograph, 1869, repro. in Wilkins, *The romance of Isabel, Lady Burton [see illus.]* • photograph, 1887, repro. in Wilkins, *The romance of Isabel, Lady Burton*, vol. 2, p. 686 • photograph, 1890–93, repro. in R. Burton, *Personal narrative of a pilgrimage*, memorial edition (1893), frontispiece • portrait (aged seventeen), repro. in Wilkins, *The romance of Isabel, Lady Burton*, vol. 1

Wealth at death £12,473 9*s*. 2*d*.: probate, 8 June 1896, *CGPLA Eng. & Wales*

Burton [Haliburton], **James** (1761–1837), builder and developer, was born on 29 July 1761, probably in London, the son of William Haliburton, a Southwark-based builder of Scottish descent. He was articled to a surveyor named James Dalton in 1776, and subsequently became his partner. Burton (he preferred this version of his surname from an early age) began his career as a speculative builder in 1785, with the construction of four houses in Southwark. He went on to become the most successful developer in late Georgian London, responsible for some of its most characteristic architecture.

Burton received some architectural training, but few buildings are known to have been designed by him. One was the Southwark Institution (formerly the Leverian Museum), in Blackfriars Road, built in 1786 but later demolished; another was the earliest part of the Royal Veterinary College in Camden, of 1792–3. Burton's energies went into building, and as early as 1790 he was approaching the Foundling Hospital estate with a request to undertake single-handedly the development of their Bloomsbury lands. This was refused, but it did not take long for the dynamic Burton to become the most important builder on the hospital's estate: 586 houses were built under his supervision between 1792 and 1802, and over £400,000 was expended during a period otherwise difficult for speculative building. Owners of the adjacent estates, including the duke of Bedford and the Skinners' Company, engaged him to continue the development of Bloomsbury. His only work exhibited at the Royal Academy was a drawing of the south side of Russell Square, shown in 1800.

Burton's construction methods were subsequently criticized, and he was unfairly regarded as the epitome of the Georgian jerry-builder. His early developments are characterized by a uniformity and austerity of elevation, allied to spacious formal layouts consisting of terraces, squares, and crescents. There is certainly no doubt about his energy and financial acumen. Between 1785 and 1823 he was responsible for the erection of 2366 houses in London, with an estimated value of some £1,848,900. Numerous other developments were constructed under his supervision.

Burton was master of the Tylers' and Brickmakers' Company in 1801–2, and in 1804 he raised a company of volunteers, the Loyal British Artificers, at his own expense, and recruited from the large body of artificers that were in his employ; Burton was colonel of the unit. He bought Mabledon Park, outside Tonbridge, in the same year, and in 1810 served as sheriff of Kent. His other activities in that county included some development at Tunbridge Wells in 1805–7, and his considerable investment in the Ramhurst (later Tonbridge) powder mills from 1811 onwards; Sir Humphry Davy was also involved in this gunpowder-manufacturing enterprise, which subsequently passed wholly into the ownership of the Burton family.

James Burton played a vital part in the major London building projects of John *Nash. In 1815 Burton began to build part of Waterloo Place, and in 1816 he allied himself firmly with Nash by taking many of the leases for the proposed terraces around Regent's Park, and for a number of the villas within it; one, The Holme, was designed by his youngest son, Decimus *Burton, for Burton's own occupation in 1818. The alliance was further cemented in 1817, when he took on the leases of five of the largest blocks on Regent Street. The crown estate was reluctant to advance moneys to speculative developers but Burton's considerable financial involvement effectively guaranteed the success of the project. His alliance with Nash was continued in the construction of the grand terraces built around Regent's Park in 1823–6. The last of these, Chester Terrace, was completed in 1825. Nash was highly critical of Burton's interpretation of his designs, and in vain sought the complete rebuilding of the terrace.

Burton's final major development was the creation of the coastal resort of St Leonards. He purchased an estate in 1828, and proceeded to lay out a town on the twin principles of classical formality and picturesque irregularity. Much of the building was complete by 1830. Described in 1833 as 'a conceited Italian town' (Clarke, 42), St Leonards was a development of considerable ambition, conceived and designed by the elderly James Burton to be a rival to Brighton.

Burton was married in 1783 to Elizabeth Westley (1761–1837). Ten children survived infancy: Eliza, James *Haliburton, Henry, Jane, William Ford, Alfred, Septimus, Octavia, Jessy, and Decimus. He was a direct, shrewd, and energetic man. Following his death on 31 March 1837 he was buried in the churchyard of St Leonards under a pyramidal memorial. A monument to his memory was also erected in the town. ROGER BOWDLER

Sources P. A. Clarke, 'James and Decimus Burton', RIBA thesis, 1949 • P. Miller, *Decimus Burton, 1800–1881* (1981) [exhibition catalogue, Building Centre Trust, London, 1981] • Colvin, *Archs.* • D. J. Olsen, *Town planning in London: the eighteenth and nineteenth centuries*, 2nd edn (1982) • A. Saunders, *Regent's Park: a study of the development of the area from 1086 to the present day* (1969) • E. Melling, ed., *Kentish Sources III* (1961) • *Sussex*, Pevsner (1965)
Archives Hastings Museum, Sussex
Likenesses J. Cochran, engraving, *c.*1820 (after drawing by A. Wivelk) • watercolour, *c.*1830, repro. in *RIBA Journal* (6 March 1939), 454 • bronze monument, *c.*1837, Marina and Grand Parade, St Leonards, East Sussex • E. U. Eddis, portrait, Hastings Museum, East Sussex • pen-and-ink drawing, NPG
Wealth at death £60,000: PRO, death duty registers, IR 26/1440

Burton, James Daniel (1784–1817), Wesleyan Methodist minister, was born on 25 July 1784, in Manchester, the son of Daniel Burton, of Rhodes, near Manchester. The Burton family were affluent calico printers and enthusiastic Methodists: three of Daniel Burton's sons and his son-in-law became Methodist preachers (two itinerant and two local), and, according to his memoir, James Burton was baptized by John Wesley. Burton received a good education, although not one particularly directed towards the ministry. While making allowances for the impact of stereotypes in conversion narratives, it would seem that in his early adulthood Burton turned away to some degree from the religious influences of his background. In February 1801 he was brought to reassess his course in life by 'an awful Providence' (*Methodist Magazine*, Sept 1817, 708): on leaving the theatre in Manchester he encountered the bearers of a corpse, recently and suddenly deceased. This set in train a new religious seriousness, manifested in sick-visiting close to his father's country house.

Burton began preaching, and became a Wesleyan itinerant in 1805, working at first under the supervision of the venerable John Pawson at Wakefield. Pawson described Burton as 'a pious, modest, humble young man' (Bowmer and Vickers, 3.126). Burton grew in ability as a preacher as he grew in experience, concentrating in his sermons on practical Christianity rather than controversy or dogma. Despite his affluent upbringing, he remained open to the poor. At a period of tension within the movement, his memorialist lauded him as a firm upholder of Methodist discipline (Grindrod, 884). In 1814 he published *A guide for youth, recommending to their serious consideration vital piety, as the only rational way to present happiness and future glory.*

Burton's health declined in 1814. Following three years of illness, he died on 24 March 1817, leaving a widow, Margaret, and several children. MARTIN WELLINGS

Sources E. Grindrod, 'Memoir of Mr. James Burton', *Methodist Magazine*, 40 (1817), 881–91 • *Methodist Magazine*, 40 (1817), 708–9 • *The letters of John Pawson*, ed. J. C. Bowmer and J. A. Vickers, 3 vols. (1994–5), vol. 3, p. 126 • *Early Victorian Methodism: the correspondence of Jabez Bunting, 1830–1858*, ed. W. R. Ward (1976), 300 • *DNB*

Burton, John (1696–1771), Church of England clergyman and tutor, was born at Wembworthy, Devon, the son of Samuel Burton (*d.* 1707), rector of that parish. He was educated at schools in Okehampton and Tiverton, and—following his father's death—in Ely, where he was placed under the guardianship of the Revd Samuel Bentham, his mother's first cousin. His mother remarried—her next husband was Dr John Bear (1673/4–1762), rector of Shermanbury, Sussex—and died on 23 April 1755, aged eighty.

Burton matriculated from Corpus Christi College, Oxford, on 21 October 1713, graduated BA in 1717, and proceeded MA in 1721. Having been a college tutor since 1717 he was elected probationary fellow of his college in 1721, full fellow in 1723, and proceeded BD (1729) and DD (1752). He was an able and diligent tutor whose approach to teaching Greek is set out in a letter to his nephew Edward Bentham published as *De litterarum graecarum institutionibus dissertatio critica* (1758). His desire to see his pupils acquire a correct usage and scholarly understanding of Greek prose led him to produce sample compositions for them to emulate, and to encourage them to study Greek authors without recourse to editions with Latin cribs. To this end he published *Pentalogia* (1758), a collection of five Greek tragedies by Sophocles, Euripedes, and Aeschylus, which became a standard edition in the university. In the logic and metaphysics schools Burton has been credited with introducing Locke into the curriculum.

In 1733 Burton was nominated by Eton College to succeed to the living of Mapledurham, Oxfordshire, on the death of Dr Edward Littleton (*bap.* 1698, *d.* 1733), and was elected a fellow of Eton. He took up residence in Mapledurham vicarage in March 1734, yet allowed his predecessor's widow, Frances, *née* Goode (*d.* 1748), and her three young daughters to continue living there. He and Frances married the following year; they had no children. Always free with his money, Burton spent large sums on improving the vicarage house, gardens, and glebe lands. In 1766 he left Mapledurham to be rector of Worplesdon, Surrey, where he promoted the building of a causeway over the River Wey to enable his parishioners easier access to Guildford.

Throughout his life Burton published a vast number of tracts and sermons. Most of his sermons were reprinted in *Occasional Sermons Preached before the University of Oxford* (2 vols., 1764–6); they are long and formal in style, in keeping with Burton's preference, stated in the preface, for 'the old fashioned methodical elaborate sermon, with all its formalities to the modern plausible loose essay' (*Biographia Britannica*, 49). Towards the end of his life he undertook to gather together his Latin theological dissertations as *Opuscula miscellanea theologica* and *Opuscula miscellanea metrico-prosaica*. Among his most important pieces was 'Commentariolus Thomae Secker, archiep Cantuar memoirae facer', which attracted much attention and was severely criticized by Archdeacon Francis Blackburne on behalf of the latitudinarians, and by Dr Philip Furneaux on behalf of the nonconformists.

Though a tory Burton was not so extreme as Dr William King, principal of St Mary Hall, and under the pseudonym Phileleutherus Londinensis he criticized King's celebrated speech at the dedication of the Radcliffe Library, in

Oxford, on 13 April 1749. King responded with a fierce *Elogium famae inserviens Jacci Etonensis, or, The praises of Jack of Eton, commonly called Jack the Giant* (1750), in which he satirized 'the Burtonic style'. In *The Genuineness of Lord Clarendon's 'History of the Rebellion' Vindicated* (1750) Burton rebuffed the criticisms levelled by John Oldmixon against the editors of Clarendon's history. His encaenia oration of 1763 attacked John Wilkes and prompted stinging criticism from Charles Churchill, who dismissed his verse as 'pantomime thoughts and style full of tricks' (C. Churchill, *The Candidate*, 1764, verse 716 ff.).

At the time of his death Burton was living at Eton College, having suffered increasingly from erysipelas in his latter years. He recovered sufficiently to teach a few pupils, whom in the evening before his death 'he harangued with more than usual elegance and perspicuity, on some important subjects in Divinity' (Bentham, 308). He died at the college on 11 February 1771 and was buried at the entrance to its inner chapel.

W. P. Courtney, *rev.* M. J. Mercer

Sources *Biographia Britannica, or, The lives of the most eminent persons who have flourished in Great Britain and Ireland*, 3 (1750), 46–9 • E. Bentham, 'Memoirs of the late Rev. and learned John Burton', *GM*, 1st ser., 41 (1771), 305–8 • Foster, *Alum. Oxon.* • P. Quarrie, 'The Christ Church collection of books', *Hist. U. Oxf.* 5: *18th-cent. Oxf.*, 495–8 • M. L. Clarke, 'Classical studies', *Hist. U. Oxf.* 5: *18th-cent. Oxf.*, 513–34, esp. 518–21 • J. Aitkin, *General biography*, 10 vols. (1799–1815) • *IGI*
Archives BL, letters to William Wogan, Add. MS 21428
Likenesses stipple (after Cosins), BM, NPG

Burton, John (1710–1771), antiquary and physician, was born on 9 June 1710 at Colchester, the elder son of four children of John Burton (1669/70–1743), a merchant from London, and Margaret (1690/91–1713), daughter of the Revd John Leake, of Kirkthorpe or Warmfield, near Wakefield. He was educated at Merchant Taylors' School, London (1725–6), and at St John's College, Cambridge, where he was admitted in 1727 and graduated MB in 1733. In 1734 he was practising medicine at Heath, on the outskirts of Wakefield. Already displaying the strong support for the tory party that he maintained throughout his life, he was vigorous on his party's behalf at the bitterly contested county election of 1734. His activities lessened the success of the Revd Dr Jaques Sterne in the whig interest at York and thus sowed the seeds of the animosity between the two men that was to bedevil him.

On 2 January 1735, in York Minster, Burton married Mary (*c.*1715–1771), only child of Samuel Henson (*d.* 1716) and his wife, Mary (*d.* 1743); their only son, John, became an army officer. It was probably his wife's income that enabled Burton to continue his medical studies, under Herman Boerhaave at Leiden University, where he became acquainted with Heinrich van Deventer's teachings on midwifery; he was awarded MD from Reims. His first medical articles were published by the Edinburgh Philosophical Society in 1734 and 1736, and his *Treatise of the Non-Naturals* was printed at York in 1738. By then he had established his practice as physician and man-midwife in York, and he was a prime mover in establishing in 1740 the York County Hospital, where he was honorary physician until 1746. Burton actively campaigned for the tory interest in the elections of 1741, further incurring the hostility of Sterne, now precentor of York Minster, and his nephew and political assistant, Laurence Sterne.

Burton's position was financially improved in 1743, when he inherited substantial estates on the deaths of his father and mother-in-law. Two years later he suffered a setback from which his reputation and his pocket never fully recovered. The occasion was the rising of 1745. Burton travelled late in November to Lancashire, where Charles Edward Stuart's forces were marching south after their capture of Carlisle. His motives were unclear but his absence from York at this critical time strengthened the suspicion, fuelled by his whig enemies, that he was going over to the Young Pretender. Burton was arrested on his return to York, and committed to York Castle on 30 November on a charge of treason. After three months' imprisonment he was summoned to London to be examined before the privy council, who finally released him on bail after examination in March 1747. He was tried at York assizes in July, but on account of the Act of Indemnity passed in June his prosecution was abandoned and he was discharged. He had been declared bankrupt and his furniture and books sold, leaving him with his wife's modest fortune.

Burton's political rehabilitation was marked by his appointment as commissioner for the land tax in 1750, 1765, and 1766, and by the offer in 1754 of the freedom of the city of York (which he did not accept). This is in spite of the fact that he was visited by two of his fellow prisoners from London, Flora Macdonald and Captain Malcolm McLeod, in 1747, 1748, and 1749. In 1749 he published two pamphlets to justify his conduct and proclaim his innocence. His medical practice took longer to resurrect. In 1751 he published *An Essay towards a Complete System of Midwifery*, in which the engraved plates are the earliest published work of George Stubbs. Burton's text shows signs of hasty composition which were perhaps partly due to his attempt to recover his damaged professional status but were principally due to his wish to forestall a book being written by the eminent London man-midwife, William Smellie, which was sure to publicize Smellie's improved obstetrical forceps. Smellie's *Treatise on the Theory and Practice of Midwifery* (1751) received warm praise from the *Monthly Review*, whereas Burton's *Essay* had been given a long, but cool review. Burton reacted by publishing *A letter to William Smellie, M.D., containing critical and practical remarks upon his treatise on midwifery* (1753). While a few of his criticisms are valid, most are mere carping. Smellie did not respond but a former pupil of his, Giles Watts, published a successful defence against Burton's criticisms in 1755. Burton's reputation does not seem to have suffered, and his own improved forceps remained in use for many years.

Burton now turned his attention to antiquities. His curiosity about the past was fostered by his friendship with his fellow physician and tory Francis Drake, the historian of York. In the spring of 1745 Burton and Drake explored the country east of York to find the site of the Roman fort of

Delgovitia, which they agreed was at Millington; on 28 May 1747 Burton read a paper on the subject before the Royal Society. He took the opportunity of being detained near the Tower of London to study the historical records there and compiled an account of the archives (Bodl. Oxf., MS Top. Yorks. b.6). In 1754 he and Drake explored the so-called Danes' hills on Skipwith common. In 1755 he began a tour, cut short by an attack of gout, of Yorkshire antiquities, and collected material from archives in Oxford and Cambridge, from cathedral, archiepiscopal, episcopal, and capitular records, and from private collections. He even applied to Rome for drawings or paintings of Yorkshire monasteries 'in their flourishing state'. In 1758–9 he published his magnum opus, *Monasticon Eboracense*, in which he surveyed the history of most of the monastic houses of Yorkshire and in many cases detailed their properties. He dedicated the work to the Society of Antiquaries, to which he was elected a fellow. The enduring importance of Burton's history is that he calendars the charters by which the monasteries held their numerous properties; most importantly he uses over 2000 charters formerly in St Mary's Tower in York but by then in his possession. He hoped to publish the contents of these charters in a second volume but failed to attract enough subscribers to finance it. He none the less continued to amass materials and paid for transcripts from manuscripts in the British Museum. Ten years later, enfeebled by gout, he abandoned his projected second volume and hoped to sell his own collection of manuscripts, preferably to the British Museum. Failing to find a buyer he threatened to burn his manuscripts, 'for I cannot bear the thoughts of any other person having the profits of my labour for near forty years, and at several hundred pounds expense'. Finally, about 1770, he succeeded in selling his collection to William Constable, of Burton Constable, in the East Riding of Yorkshire, for a lump sum said to have been £2000 and an annuity of £55 for Burton and his wife. Constable did not have much, if anything, to pay in the way of annuity.

Burton died in the parish of Holy Trinity, Micklegate, York, on 19 January 1771, and Mary Burton died on 28 October following. At his death he was living in or near Micklegate in York; he was buried at Holy Trinity Church, Micklegate, on 21 January. Burton is commonly supposed to have resembled Laurence Sterne's satirical description of him as Dr Slop—'a little, squat, uncourtly figure … of about four feet and a half perpendicular height, with a breadth of back, and a sesquipedality of belly'—but a sworn testimony of 1746 describes him as 'a tall Well sett Gentleman' (A. H. Cash, *Laurence Sterne: the Early and Middle Years*, 1975, 180, 290). C. BERNARD L. BARR

Sources [G. J. Armytage and F. Barber], 'Inscriptions on mural monuments in the parish church of S. Peter at Warmfield, otherwise Kirkthorp', *Yorkshire Archaeological Journal*, 1 (1870), 58–60 · C. B. L. Barr and B. A. English, 'The records formerly in St Mary's Tower, York', *Yorkshire Archaeological Journal*, 42 (1970), 198–235, 359–86, 465–518 · W. H. F. Bateman, ed., *The parish registers of Holy Trinity, Micklegate, in the city of York*, 2 vols. (1894–5) · A. H. Cash, 'The birth of Tristram Shandy: Sterne and Dr Burton', *Studies in the eighteenth century*, ed. R. F. Brissenden (Canberra, 1968), 133–54 · C. Collyer, 'John Burton, a York rebel: notes on a lecture', *Report for the year 1956–57*, York Georgian Society (1957), 15–22 · R. Davies, 'Memoir of John Burton', *Yorkshire Archaeological Journal*, 2 (1873), 403–40 · R. Davies, *A memoir of the York press* (1868); repr. (1988) [with new introduction by B. Barr] · A. Doran, 'Burton ("Dr. Slop"): his forceps and his foes', *Journal of Obstetrics and Gynaecology of the British Empire*, 23 (1913), 3–24, 65–86 · J. B. Morrell, *York monuments* (1944) · E. B. Newsome and W. R. Newsome, *An index of marriage bonds and allegations in the peculiar jurisdiction of the dean and chapter of York, 1613–1839* (1985) · C. J. Robinson, ed., *A register of the scholars admitted into Merchant Taylors' School, from AD 1562 to 1874*, 2 vols. (1882–3) · R. F. Scott, ed., *Admissions to the College of St John the Evangelist in the University of Cambridge*, 3: *July 1715 – November 1767* (1903) · A. R. Simpson, 'The invention and evolution of the midwifery forceps', *Scottish Medical and Surgical Journal*, 7 (1900), 465–95 · R. H. Skaife, ed., 'The register of marriages in York Minster', *Yorkshire Archaeological Journal*, 2 (1873), 97–128 · B. Whitehead, 'York and the Jacobite rebels', *York Historian*, 6 (1985), 59–71 · *York Courant* (11 Jan 1743) · *York Courant* (19 April 1743) · *York Courant* (17 Nov 1745) · *York Cournat* (3 Dec 1745) · *York Courant* (8 April 1746) · *York Courant* (9 Dec 1746) · *York Courant* (2 April 1751) · *York Courant* (31 Dec 1751) · *York Courant* (30 March 1756) · *York Courant* (22 Jan 1771) · *York Courant* (29 Oct 1771) · R. Forbes, *The lyon in mourning, or, A collection of speeches, letters, journals … relative to … Prince Charles Edward Stuart*, ed. H. Paton, 3 vols., Scottish History Society, 20–22 (1895–6) · R. G. [R. Gough], *British topography*, [new edn], 2 vols. (1780) · Mrs E. P. Hart, ed., *Merchant Taylors' School register, 1561–1934*, 2 vols. (1936) · *Memorials of John Murray of Broughton*, ed. R. F. Bell, Scottish History Society, 27 (1898) · Nichols, *Illustrations* · Nichols, *Lit. anecdotes* · I. P. Pressly, *A York miscellany* (1938) · *An inventory of the historical monuments in the city of York*, Royal Commission on Historical Monuments (England), 5 vols. (1962–81) · *An account of what passed between Mr George Thompson of York, and Dr John Burton, of that city, physician and man-midwife, at Mr Sheriff Jubb's entertainment, and the consequences thereon* (1756) · W. Upcott, *A bibliographical account of the principal works relating to English topography*, 3 vols. (1818); repr. (1978) · Venn, *Alum. Cant.*

Archives BL, medical reports and essays, Sloane MSS 3984, 3835 · BL, travel notes, Add. MS 11571 · Bodl. Oxf., collections relating to York's history · Bodl. Oxf., index to pedigrees of nobility and gentry in the Harley MSS · NA Scot., historical notes relating to Billingborough · W. Yorks. AS, letters concerning his behaviour during '45 | Lincs. Arch., corresp. relating to his behaviour during the '45 · W. Yorks. AS, Leeds, Yorkshire Archaeological Society, Yorkshire pedigrees made by John Hopkinson with annotations by Burton

Burton, John Hill (1809–1881), historian and political economist, was born in the Gallowgate, Aberdeen, on 22 August 1809, the second of six children of William Kinninmont Burton (*d.* 1819), a lieutenant in the army, and of Elizabeth (*d.* 1848), daughter of John Paton of Grandholm, Aberdeenshire. The father was an only son with no close kin, and nothing is known of his further connections. The mother came of a family of lairds. Mary *Burton, the educational and social reformer, was his sister.

Burton's parents were poor, but in Scotland that presented no bar to a good education. He attended Aberdeen grammar school from about 1819, then went with a bursary to Marischal College, Aberdeen, in 1823. After graduating MA in 1826, he applied himself to the law, first in articles to a writer in his native city, then in reading for the bar in Edinburgh. He qualified, but scarcely ever practised. Instead he turned to letters, which provided him with an inevitably precarious income until 1854, when he was appointed secretary to the Scottish prison board. In early life, much of his output was mere hackwork, often appearing under a pseudonym, such as elementary histories, articles in almanacs, and incidental editorial matter for the work of others. At a somewhat more elevated level he wrote a series of manuals of Scottish law, a general one published in 1839, afterwards divided into separate treatises on civil and criminal jurisprudence. He also produced much journalism, for the *Westminster Review*, *Edinburgh Review*, *Blackwood's Edinburgh Magazine*, and *The Scotsman*. He later brought out collections of his best pieces, notably in *The Book-Hunter* (1862). These literary reminiscences contained a vivid portrait of Thomas De Quincey, and were supplemented in the second edition by his widow's memoir of himself. He had married in 1844 Isabella, daughter of Captain Lauder of Flatfield, Perthshire. They had three daughters before she died in 1849. His second wife, married on 3 August 1855, was Katharine, daughter of Cosmo *Innes, professor of constitutional law at the University of Edinburgh, who bore him two sons and two daughters, and survived him.

Journalism formed a respectable part of intellectual life in Edinburgh, and Burton had been drawn into the circle round Sir William Hamilton, last of the line of Scottish common-sense philosophers. Burton and his friends, especially James Ferrier and John Cairns, were often called Young Scotland. Conscious of philosophical developments elsewhere in Europe, they yet failed to develop a new synthesis with the native tradition which might have preserved its former prestige and influence.

The problems of any such synthesis can be illustrated by the disparate nature of Burton's own activity. His prime claim to a place in the circle lay in his *Life of Hume* (1846), followed by his edition of *Letters to Hume* (1849). The common-sense school was concerned with criticism of Hume's positions, and Burton helped to extend its scope by not only surveying the published works but also drawing for the first time on the unpublished manuscripts. If Burton failed to amplify the criticism himself, he at least brought out Hume's contributions to political economy, unsystematic yet anticipating Adam Smith.

Burton approached political economy from a utilitarian point of view. He collaborated with Sir John Bowring in editing *The Works of Jeremy Bentham* (1838–43), then compiled *Benthamiana* (1843), a selection of his writings. Later he wrote a survey of *Political and Social Economy* (1849). His enthusiasm did not meet with entire approval from his friends in Young Scotland, who tended to think that this new philosophy lost in intellectual catholicity what it gained in logical rigour compared with the classical tradition of the Scottish Enlightenment. John Stuart Mill's merciless *Examination of Hamilton* (1865) brought out their latent discord. Unable to resolve it, their circle broke up, not without acrimony.

That was perhaps why Burton's philosophical interests steadily yielded to his historical ones. His work here also started early, with an edition of the *Jacobite Correspondence of the Atholl Family* (1840). He went on with *Lives of Lovat and Forbes of Culloden* (1847), and editions of *Darien Papers* (1849) and of the *Autobiography of Alexander Carlyle* (1860). His survey of *The Scot Abroad* (1864) remains in some respects unsurpassed. The appearance of his *History of Scotland*, following Hume's practice of publication by instalments, began in 1867 and ended posthumously in 1890. Here again, however, a satisfactory synthesis was wanting. Burton, an Episcopalian, seemed to sectarian compatriots to have taken up at many points in this work the unacceptable positions of his defeated religious minority. His greatest undisputed achievement was editorial, the *Register of the Privy Council of Scotland*, of which he brought out the first volume in 1877 and a second before his death; the series was not completed by David Masson until 1907. Burton's *History of the Reign of Queen Anne* (1880) showed failing powers. He had been appointed historiographer-royal of Scotland in 1867.

Patriotic as Burton's labours were, they also signalled a fragmentation of Scottish intellectual tradition, especially of philosophical history. His philosophy, felt to be rather alien by his countrymen, was simply not related to his history, which took on a drily critical, not to say antiquarian, character. Even his widow called him unimaginative, and his painfully shy, irascible nature precluded much convivial meeting of minds with contemporaries. On 10 August 1881 he died of bronchitis at his home, Morton House, in the Pentland Hills, and was buried on 13 August at Dalmeny, Midlothian.

MICHAEL FRY

Sources K. Burton, 'Memoir', in J. H. Burton, *The book-hunter*, new edn (1882) · G. E. Davie, *The democratic intellect: Scotland and her universities in the nineteenth century* (1961) · *Fasti academiae Mariscallanae Aberdonensis: selections from the records of the Marischal College and University, MDXCIII–MDCCCLX*, 2, ed. P. J. Anderson, New Spalding Club, 18 (1898)

Archives NL Scot., corresp. and papers | NL Scot., corresp. with Blackwoods · UCL, SDUK MSS, letters to the SDUK · UCL, corresp. with Sir Edwin Chadwick

Likenesses W. B. Hole, portrait, 1882, Messrs Blackwood & Sons Ltd, Edinburgh · A. Rhind, marble bust, 1885? (after W. Brodie), Scot. NPG · W. Brodie, stone bust, Dean cemetery, Edinburgh

Wealth at death £3248 10s. 7d.: confirmation, 16 Nov 1881, *CCI*

Burton, Margaret (*d.* 1488). *See under* Women in trade and industry in York (*act. c.*1300–*c.*1500).

Burton, Mary (*bap.* 1819, *d.* 1909), educational and social reformer, was baptized on 7 February 1819 in Aberdeen, the youngest of four children of William Kinninmont Burton (*d.* 1819), lieutenant in the Rutlandshire fencible cavalry, and Elizabeth Paton (*d.* 1848), daughter of John Paton, laird of Grandholme, Aberdeen. The details of her early life are unknown. In 1832 she moved to Edinburgh with her widowed mother and brother, John Hill *Burton, historian and advocate. Mary Burton never married. After her mother's death she considered becoming a nurse on the staff of Florence Nightingale, but found her true vocation at home: here she combined a lifetime's work on behalf of women with her responsibilities to raise orphaned nephews and nieces 'and to see that they were trained alike on the intellectual and practical side of life' (*The Scotsman*, 22 March 1909). This commitment to practical as well as academic attainment was the hallmark of her contribution to education in Edinburgh.

In 1869 she persuaded the directors of the Watt Institution and School of Arts of Edinburgh, a pioneering technical college and forerunner of Heriot-Watt University, to open its classes to female students for the first time. Her niece, Ella, daughter of John Hill Burton, was one of the pioneering intake. Mary Burton followed up this achievement by becoming the first woman director of the Watt Institution in 1874. When the Watt Institution merged with George Heriot's trust to form Heriot-Watt College in 1885, she became a life governor of the college. She was an active supporter and honorary president of the Watt Literary Society. As befitted the governor of an institution that described itself as a 'people's college', she maintained that universities should open in the evening to admit working people.

Mary Burton was among the first women to be elected to public bodies responsible for money raised from local rates. From 1884 she served for many years on the St Cuthbert's parochial board, later Edinburgh parish council. The board managed poorhouses, asylums, and the allocation of clothing grants, school fees, apprenticeships, widows' pensions, and other provisions to poor and destitute people. In 1889 she unsuccessfully urged the board to petition parliament to enable county and town councils to provide schooling free of charge. This was typical of the then radical proposals she championed as a member, from 1885 to 1897, of the Edinburgh school board, which provided compulsory education for the city's children. On the election hustings she made a robust case for providing practical training for domestic responsibilities. Girls, she argued, should learn to use a sewing machine and boys the use of a saw and plane, adding that 'she herself could work with these tools and she had mended a floor before now' (*Edinburgh Evening News*, 24 March 1885). Once elected, she promoted classes in cookery and laundry, and the teaching of knitting and sewing to boys. She helped increase provision of school evening classes and argued that they should be open to all. Despite persistent opposition from some of her colleagues, she ensured that the board met in the evenings, so that 'working men' members could attend.

An energetic landlord of tenement properties in Edinburgh's old town, Burton encouraged her tenants to embrace thrift and cleanliness and abstain from alcohol. In summer she held parties for them at her home, Liberton Bank, south of the city. A kindly, spare figure with 'fresh bright face and Quaker like garb', often seen driving her pony cart to meetings, Mary Burton was well known and fondly regarded by her contemporaries (*Edinburgh Evening News*, 22 March 1909). She died at Elmhill House Royal Asylum, Aberdeen, on 19 March 1909, and was buried in Dean cemetery, Edinburgh, three days later. Her lifelong commitments were reflected in her will. This included legacies of £100 to provide prizes for students attending evening classes at Heriot-Watt College, and to the Edinburgh Women's Suffrage Society to campaign 'for the admission of women to sit as members of parliament, either at Westminster or in a Scottish Parliament' (ibid., 23 March 1909). ANN JONES

Sources *The Scotsman* (19 March 1909) • *The Scotsman* (22 March 1909) • *Edinburgh Evening News* (22 March 1909) • *Edinburgh Evening News* (23 March 1909) • minutes of the directors of the Watt Institution and School of Arts, 1869–85, Heriot-Watt University Archive, SA1/2/2 • *Edinburgh Evening News* (20 March 1885) • *Edinburgh Evening News* (21 March 1885) • *Edinburgh Evening News* (24 March 1885) • *Edinburgh Evening News* (31 March 1891) • *Edinburgh Evening News* (1 April 1891) • minutes of meetings of the governors of George Heriot's Trust, Heriot-Watt College Committee, 1887–1909, Heriot-Watt University Archive, HWC 1/1–2 [esp. 2 April 1909] • Heriot-Watt College Literary Society, *A history of Heriot-Watt College Literary Society, 1868–1928*, 1929, Heriot-Watt University Archive, HWC 4/1/23, 10–11, 44, 55 • minutes of Edinburgh school board, 1885–97, City of Edinburgh Central Library, Edinburgh Room, YL 353 [esp. 19 Oct 1885, 16 April 1887, 17 March 1890, 13 Oct 1890] • minutes of St Cuthbert's parochial board, 1884–97, City of Edinburgh Archive, SL/10 [esp. meeting 17 July 1889] • S. A. Tooley, 'Notable Victorians, some recollections of Edinburgh's foremost women; third article: Miss Louisa Stevenson, Miss Flora Stevenson, Miss Hill Burton', *Weekly Scotsman* (20 Feb 1932) [YDA 1818 City of Edinburgh Central Library, Edinburgh Room] • S. A. Tooley, 'A slum landlady: an interview with Miss Hill Burton', *Young Woman*, 4 (Oct 1895–Sept 1896) • memorial inscription, Dean cemetery, Edinburgh, plot H15 • b. cert. • m. cert. [William Burton] • d. cert.

Likenesses G. Tunny, photographs, repro. in Tooley, 'A slum landlady'

Wealth at death £1289 3*s*. 8*d*.: confirmation, 30 April 1909, *CCI*

Burton, Sir Montague Maurice [*formerly* Meshe David Osinsky] (**1885–1952**), clothing manufacturer and retailer, was born on 15 August 1885 in the town of Kurkel, Kovno province, Russia (now Lithuania), the only son of Chaim Judah Osinsky (*b*. 1825), bookseller, and his wife, Rachel Elky Osinsky. Of Jewish parentage, he was raised as Meshe David Osinsky by an uncle. He entered a Kovno *yeshiva* in his early teens, with the apparent intention of becoming a rabbi, but in 1900 emigrated to England thus escaping the escalating Russian pogroms.

The earliest details of Burton's life in England reveal him trading from a small ready-made clothing shop at Chesterfield, Derbyshire, in 1904, using the adopted name of Morris (occasionally Maurice) Burton. A second shop was opened in 1908 at Mansfield by which time Burton, who had settled on the forenames Montague Maurice, had also acquired a small clothing factory in Leeds. In March of 1909 he married Sophia Amelia (*d*. 1957), daughter of Maurice Marks, a Worksop furniture dealer. They set up home in Sheffield and had one daughter and three sons.

In the following years Burton oversaw the rapid development of his business despite prolonged periods of ill health. Concentrating on the provision of affordable bespoke clothing for the working man, he added shops in industrial towns such as Sheffield, Manchester, and Leeds, opening a total of fourteen branches by 1914. The firm also acquired additional factory capacity in Leeds, which became the new base for the head office, and by 1917 when it adopted limited liability status the business was employing about 400 workers. Burton was exempted from military service, as a result both of his continuing

Sir Montague Maurice Burton (1885–1952), by unknown photographer

poor health and of his work as a wartime contractor supplying military uniforms. Indeed, the extraordinary pressures placed on the firm by the demand for uniforms and subsequently for demobilization clothing provided a considerable stimulus to business and revealed Burton's particular ability to co-ordinate the manufacturing and retailing functions of his company.

On the retail side, the number of shops increased rapidly during the inter-war years from 40 in 1919 to more than 250 in 1927, reaching a pre-war peak of 595 in 1939. With the exception of Éire (and an abortive attempt to establish the chain in Denmark), the United Kingdom remained the sole focus for retail development. The chain of shops had spread to north-east England by 1914, the first London branch was opened in 1916, and similar developments soon followed in Belfast and Dublin (*c*.1918) and Edinburgh (1922). Growth on this scale needed considerable capital and required Burton to convert his business into a public company in March 1929. The company went public as 'Montague Burton, The Tailor of Taste, Ltd' with an authorized capital of £4 million. By 1931 the level of representation in large towns throughout the United Kingdom was such that attention was turned instead to the construction of branches in smaller centres.

The success of the rapid and extensive shop development of the inter-war period confirmed Burton's views on the emergence of an increasingly homogeneous market for multiple bespoke clothing. More particularly, such developments also reflected his belief in the value of retail property as a business asset and his acumen in the property market. As a consequence Montague Burton Ltd entered the post-war years with a considerable and extremely valuable property portfolio which included the offices, restaurants, billiard halls, and the like which were developed above the shop space. Peacetime witnessed a slow increase in the number of Burton branches and the acquisition in 1946 of the department store retailers Peter Robinson Ltd and Stagg and Russell Ltd. The purchase of these stores in the West End of London and the subsequent development of similar outlets in Bristol, Gloucester, and Cheltenham signalled a limited expansion into women's fashion retailing but remained insignificant in comparison to the firm's traditional trade at the time of Burton's death in 1952.

Burton sought to maintain the symbiotic relationship between production and distribution during the inter-war years by greatly expanding productive capacity. Most significant was the acquisition and massive redevelopment of a clothing factory at Hudson Road, Leeds, which began in 1922. By 1925, nine years before completion of the final stage of development, the company could rightly claim that Hudson Road was the largest clothing factory in Europe. Employing 10,500 people at its peak, Hudson Road enabled Burton to realize his principles on industrial co-operation and employee welfare in an industry frequently vilified for the inhumane treatment of its workers. Emphasis was placed on staff welfare from the outset with the construction of a large, modern staff canteen and employee rest-room. By 1934 these had been augmented with the provision of a doctor's surgery and medical clinic, dental and ophthalmic surgeries, and a sun-ray clinic. In addition, the firm provided facilities for various sporting activities, sponsored operatic and drama societies, and encouraged the establishment of sick benefit and holiday saving clubs.

Similar facilities and initiatives were provided in three other new smaller clothing factories opened during the later 1930s as the company continued to expand its productive capacity in order to meet the demand emanating from the still rapidly growing chain of shops. Wartime saw the acquisition of a button factory in Kent, but most activity was concentrated on the production of as much as one-quarter of the armed services' requirement for uniforms. Further expansion of manufacturing capacity occurred during the final years of the 1940s when the relaxation of development controls permitted the construction of two new factories in Yorkshire and Lancashire. This period also witnessed backward integration into cloth production.

Throughout his career Montague Burton remained a committed and vocal advocate of collective bargaining and arbitration in industry, and willingly dealt with his employees' chosen representatives. He thought that low wages were a false economy, and maintained from 1921 that his employees received the highest wages in the tailoring trade in Europe. Burton also insisted on working conditions of the highest possible standard. In consequence, the company suffered only two strikes during his lifetime, the first in 1927, the second while he was abroad in 1936, and it was generally recognized for its enlightened attitude toward employee welfare. By way of contrast, however, Burton remained highly autocratic in his dealings with senior management and, like many entrepreneurial founders of large businesses, was highly reluctant to delegate responsibility. He was directly responsible for most of the major policy decisions throughout his long career as founder and subsequently chairman of the company. This control was exercised most resolutely in relation to the firm's real estate department which he ran in an almost secretive fashion from the library at his home in Kent Road, Harrogate. Burton personally co-ordinated many property transactions and dealt directly with his firm's property agents in London. He conducted his business with a 'steely' personality and with great self-assurance.

The tenacity of Burton's management style stood in sharp contrast to his otherwise retiring and self-effacing personality. Noted for his private generosity, Burton was something of a loner, shunning personal publicity and limiting his own contact with people. A keen advocate of temperance, he displayed simple tastes and disliked ostentation. He claimed to live his life at 60 miles an hour, and maintained a gruelling work schedule, holding office as non-executive director of four other companies, as well as serving as vice-president of the Multiple Shops Federation.

Playing golf provided Burton with a regular form of relaxation, combining his passions for fresh air and exercise, and he enjoyed playing bridge with members of his family. Interested in scholarship, Burton was also a voracious reader of the classics, an occasional literary critic, a sponsor of several prizes in the arts and literature, and a member of the PEN club. He considered himself a modernist by temperament. He also wrote in some detail on topics related to his long-held interests in travel, industrial co-operation, and the international order.

Burton acted as chairman of the Industrial Welfare Society's delegation to the United States and Canada in 1930 and made frequent fact-finding visits to retail and manufacturing firms in North America between the wars and after. He visited Russian factory plants in 1935 and was chosen as Leeds chamber of commerce's delegate to attend the Federation of Commonwealth and British Empire Chambers of Commerce meeting at Wellington, New Zealand, in 1936. He went round the world four times in total, recording his travels between 1933 and 1936 in two volumes of published diaries entitled *Globe Girdling* (1935, 1937).

These diaries reveal Burton's immense pride in his Jewish ancestry and his optimism for Palestine despite the worsening international situation. A generous supporter of educational and charitable institutions there, he was particularly gratified with the success of the new Hebrew University which he endowed with fifty scholarships. An acquaintance of Chaim Weizmann and close friend of Selig Brodetsky, president of the Zionist Federation of Great Britain and Ireland from 1948, Burton also provided financial and practical support to numerous Jewish educational and charitable institutions in Britain. He was honorary life president of the Jewish congregation in Harrogate, vice-president of the Jewish Peace Society, and a popular representative of the Leeds Zionist Central Council.

Burton's wider concerns for international and industrial harmony were summarized in his book *The Middle Path* (1943). Reflecting many of his liberal inclinations, this book advocates arbitration in both industrial and international affairs. It builds on his long-held opinions of the need for a world federation with the power and authority to decide and implement international political decisions, and reflects on the importance of free and fair trade and industry. Burton also provided practical and financial support to initiatives designed to bolster international understanding. This included the establishment of branches of the League of Nations at his factories and the endowment of chairs of international relations at universities in Jerusalem, Oxford, Edinburgh, and London, and of lectureships at Nottingham and Leeds. Similarly, his interest in industrial relations was reflected in the establishment of chairs at the universities of Leeds, Cardiff, and Cambridge. Burton was knighted in 1931 in acknowledgement of his efforts to further industrial relations and international peace and received an honorary doctorate from the University of Leeds in 1944.

Although a justice of the peace in Leeds from 1924, Burton largely eschewed calls for his greater involvement in public life, declining an invitation to be lord mayor of Leeds in 1930. He preferred instead to concentrate his time and energy on his business and private interests and also expressed a wish to spend more time with his daughter and three sons, believing that the pressures of his early career had deprived him of some of the pleasures of fatherhood. None the less, Montague Burton continued to play a pivotal role in the development of the company he founded, devoting the greater part of his time to its management until his death on 21 September 1952 at the Great Northern Hotel, Leeds. A funeral was held at Harrogate synagogue, probably on 25 September.

ANDREW ALEXANDER

Sources E. M. Sigsworth, *Montague Burton the tailor of taste* (1990) • R. Redmayne, ed., *Ideals in industry* (1951) • M. Burton, *Globe girdling*, 1 and 2 (1935–7) • *The Times* (23 Sept 1952) • S. Brodetsky, tribute, *The Times* (30 Sept 1952) • W. Yorks. AS, Leeds, Burton papers • private information (1971) • *WWW* • *DNB* • certificate of naturalization, W. Yorks. AS, Leeds, Burton papers • d. cert.

Archives W. Yorks. AS, Leeds | Bodl. Oxf.

Likenesses R. G. Lewis, oils, Burton Group Ltd, Leeds • photograph, repro. in Sigsworth, *Montague Burton* [*see illus.*] • photographs, Burton Group Ltd, Leeds

Wealth at death £687,495 16*s*. 10*d*.: probate, 28 May 1953, *CGPLA Eng. & Wales*

Burton, Richard [*formerly* Richard Walter Jenkins] (**1925–1984**), actor, was born on 10 November 1925 at Pont-rhyd-y-fen, a village in the Afan valley, 4 miles from Port Talbot,

Richard Burton (1925–1984), by Bob Penn, 1959

the sixth son and twelfth of the thirteen children of Richard Jenkins, a miner, and his wife, Edith Maud Thomas, who had been a barmaid. His mother died in October 1927, and he was brought up by his eldest sister, Cecilia, and her husband, Elfed James. He was often unhappy and ill at ease, and at fourteen he wrote in his diary 'I am sure that wherever I go, I will not be wanted' (Bragg, 57). The family spoke both Welsh and English, and Richard remained fluent in Welsh throughout his life. He was educated at the eastern primary school, Port Talbot, and at Port Talbot secondary school. At fifteen he left school and went to work in the men's outfitting department of the local co-operative store. Bored, he joined a youth club and experienced the exhilaration of amateur dramatics. He was already a gifted and enthusiastic rugby player, with a reputation as a fearless, if dirty, player whose vindictiveness on the field could be boundless. He was a brawler, and it was to the injuries he sustained in one particularly bruising street fight that he traced the spinal problems that in later life were to cause him great pain. In appearance, the young Richard Jenkins was of medium height, with fine, wide eyes. Sturdily built, he had the body of a rugby half-back, long and solid in the trunk with short legs. He was troubled by boils and his skin was pitted by acne. Nevertheless, he was considered extremely attractive. Convinced that in education lay escape from his job, he focused all his charm on Philip Burton, a teacher at Port Talbot secondary school and an instructor in the local Air Training Corps which Richard had joined, and in September 1941 he went back to school. Burton became Richie Jenkins's legal guardian, and in 1943 Jenkins legally renounced his own surname to become Richard Burton.

Recognizing his ward's abilities, Philip Burton pointed Richard towards a career as an actor, and arranged an audition for him in Cardiff with the actor and dramatist Emlyn Williams. Richard Burton made his début as Glan in Williams's comedy *The Druid's Rest* at the Royal Court Theatre, Liverpool, in November 1943, making his first London appearance in the same part at the St Martin's Theatre on 26 January 1944. When the play closed, he was called up by the RAF, and spent six months on a special, six-month wartime course at Exeter College, Oxford, where he read English in addition to undergoing RAF training. His tutor, Neville Coghill, a gifted amateur director, was captivated by him. Casting Burton as Angelo in his Oxford University Dramatic Society production of *Measure for Measure*, Coghill proclaimed him 'a genius'. Demobilized in 1947, Burton returned to the theatre, under contract to H. M. Tennent Ltd, and appeared as Mr Hicks in *Castle Anna* at the Lyric, Hammersmith, in February 1948. Later that year, while filming Emlyn Williams's *The Last Days of Dolwyn*, he met actress Sybil Williams, the daughter of an under-manager in a coal mine at Ferndale, another Welsh mining village. They were married in 1949, and had two daughters, Kate (*b.* 1957) and Jessica (*b.* 1959).

In 1949, in Christopher Fry's *The Lady's not for Burning*, the stillness and simplicity that were to be Burton's trade mark attracted favourable attention, not least from his director, John Gielgud. He made his New York début in the same part when the production transferred there in 1950. After his Prince Hal in the Stratford upon Avon history cycle in 1951, his future was assured. Kenneth Tynan wrote of him 'Burton is a still, brimming pool, running disturbingly deep; at twenty-five he commands repose and can make silence garrulous' (Gielgud, 302). He joined the Old Vic in 1953 to play Hamlet for the first time, and remained with the company until 1956. His beautifully modulated voice and controlled physical presence created an impression of sensitivity combined with a startling virility. In 1955 his Henry V won him the *Evening Standard* best actor award. When he alternated the roles of Iago and Othello with John Neville in 1956, his reputation as the most exciting classical actor of his generation looked unassailable. Burton was notorious for his romantic exploits off the stage. He also had a reputation as both a compelling storyteller in the Welsh tradition, and as a fierce drinker. Asked where his ambition lay next—Macbeth perhaps, or Lear?—no one took his reply seriously: 'I want to be a millionaire'. However, when the Old Vic season finished, he settled in Switzerland; he would never appear on the London stage again.

Burton's first Hollywood film had been *My Cousin Rachel* (1953), a version of the Daphne du Maurier story, in which he played opposite Olivia de Havilland. It brought him the first of his seven Academy award nominations (he never won an Oscar), and brought him the coveted main role in the biblical drama *The Robe* (1953). His films in this period included *The Desert Rats* (1953) and a version of John Osborne's play *Look Back in Anger* (1959). In 1960 he played

King Arthur in the Lerner and Loewe musical *Camelot* in New York, for which he received the New York drama critics' award in 1961 for the best performance in a musical. In 1961 he flew to Rome to play Mark Anthony in the film *Cleopatra*, which also starred Elizabeth Taylor (*b.* 1932), the English-born daughter of Francis Taylor, art dealer, who had moved to America on the outbreak of the Second World War. Within a few months, Burton had separated from his wife. The film, one of the most expensive ever made, met with critical disdain.

During the next thirteen years, Burton made over twenty films, including *The Comedians* (1967), *Where Eagles Dare* (1969), and *Bluebeard* (1972), few of which pleased him or the critics, but in the John Le Carré thriller *The Spy who Came in from the Cold* (1965) he was superb, and his performance opposite Elizabeth Taylor in Edward Albee's *Who's Afraid of Virginia Woolf?* (1966) was justifiably acclaimed; both Burton and Taylor were nominated for Academy awards, Taylor winning the Oscar. They had been married in Canada in 1964 after Burton's divorce was finalized. The romance had been conducted under intense press scrutiny; their 1963 film, *The VIPs*, exploited public interest in their real-life affair. Burton was Taylor's fifth husband. She had two sons and a daughter from previous marriages; together they adopted another daughter.

In April 1964 Burton opened as Hamlet at the Lunt-Fontanne Theatre in New York, directed by John Gielgud. The controversial production ran for seventeen weeks, to mixed critical acclaim and immense box-office success. A film of the live performance was made, and although Burton ordered all the prints to be destroyed, one was discovered after his death. In 1966 he returned to Oxford to raise money for the university dramatic society, appearing in the title role in Marlowe's *Dr Faustus* with Elizabeth Taylor as Helen of Troy. They gave their services freely, but the critics savaged him. The Burton–Taylor Theatre in Oxford was established as a direct result of this production. When Burton said he yearned to be an academic, an honorary fellowship was arranged at St Peter's College, Oxford.

Burton was appointed CBE in 1970. His drinking was now addictive, and in 1974 his marriage to Elizabeth Taylor was dissolved; they remarried a year later in Botswana, and divorced again in 1976. Burton married Susan Hunt, the daughter of Frederick Miller and former wife of racing driver James Hunt in 1976, while he was playing in Peter Shaffer's *Equus* on Broadway. *Equus* impressed the critics, and was filmed. He continued to make films, most of them routine, such as *Exorcist II: the Heretic* (1977) and *The Wild Geese* (1978). In 1980 he recreated his role of King Arthur on tour in *Camelot*. The back problems which had long troubled him intensified: his right arm hung useless at his side, and he was unable to raise the left above his shoulder. Only his closest intimates knew that the stillness on stage that had always been his trade mark was now the stillness of disability. Not until he collapsed in Los Angeles could he be persuaded to undergo surgery on his spine. Fighting a losing battle with alcoholism, he returned to Switzerland to convalesce. His marriage was dissolved in 1982 while he was filming *Wagner*, and in 1983 he married Sally Hay, a continuity girl he had met on the film set. She was the daughter of Jack Hay, motoring correspondent for the *Birmingham Post*. In the television mini-series *Ellis Island* (1984) Burton played the father of his real daughter, the actress Kate Burton. It would be his last work. He died of a cerebral haemorrhage on 5 August 1984 in hospital in Geneva, and was buried at Celigny, Switzerland, where he lived.

Richard Burton had made his first appearance in London when the theatre was dominated by actors of flamboyant lyricism, such as Michael Redgrave, John Gielgud, and Laurence Olivier. His robust sexuality had confounded and excited critical opinion, and his explosion onto the scene was unsettling. Here, for the first time in the twentieth century, was a great classical actor whose plebeian roots were unashamedly apparent. Ever since Irving, leading actors had been assiduously disguising their humble origins and insinuating themselves into the upper echelons of society: knighthoods were commonplace, soon there would be peerages. Burton was a throwback to a much older tradition, the actor as rapscallion. The tabloid press loved him, celebrating his boozy extravaganzas and his torrid personal life, and ignoring the sensitivity and erudition that lay beneath his 'roaring boy' exterior. The new generation of British actors welcomed him too, many of them imagining that his example licensed their own attempts to express Hamlet's neuroses in the raw accents of their native dialects. They did not appreciate that, although Burton was the son of a Welsh miner (and used his native accent to great advantage in the celebrated recording, and somewhat less celebrated film, of Dylan Thomas's *Under Milk Wood*), the glorious cadences of his mature voice were the result of subordinating himself to rigorous training and discipline. Burton's obituarists deplored his failure to fulfil their expectations, but their ambitions were not necessarily his. He had done what he wanted with his life: he had achieved fame and riches, and had experienced passion. His fortune allowed him to be generous, and his largesse was boundless. He retained a certain natural simplicity, and never forgot his family and roots in the small mining community in south Wales. KEITH BAXTER

Sources P. Ferris, *Richard Burton* (1981) · M. Bragg, *Rich: the life of Richard Burton* (1988) · D. Jenkins and S. Rogers, *Richard Burton: a brother remembered* (1993) · P. Junor, *Burton* (1985) · J. Cottrell and F. Cashin, *Richard Burton* (1971) · J. Gielgud, J. Miller, and J. Powell, *An actor and his time* (1979) · personal knowledge (2004)

Archives NL Wales, Emyr Humphreys MSS · NL Wales, Emlyn Williams MSS | FILM BFI NFTVA, 'In from the cold? A portrait of Richard Burton', 20 Sept 1988 · BFI NFTVA, *Parkinson: the interviews*, BBC 1, 2 Aug 1995 · BFI NFTVA, *Great romances of the 20th century*, BBC 2, 22 Nov 1997 · BFI NFTVA, *Reputations*, BBC 2, 10 July 2001 · BFI NFTVA, news footage · BFI NFTVA, performance recordings | SOUND BL NSA, performance recordings · BL NSA, oral history interviews

Likenesses I. Penn, gelatine silver print, 1950, NPG · D. Farson, bromide print, 1954, NPG · B. Penn, photograph, 1959, NPG [*see illus.*]

Wealth at death £692,456 in England and Wales: probate, 13 May 1985, *CGPLA Eng. & Wales* · total estate approx. £3,500,000

Burton, Sir Richard Francis (1821–1890), explorer and author, was the son of Colonel Joseph Netterville Burton and Martha Beckwith, daughter and coheir of Richard Baker of Barham House, Hertfordshire. The eldest of three children, he was born on 19 March 1821 at Torquay. His sister was Catherine Eliza Burton, later Lady Stisted; his brother, Edward Joseph Netterville Burton, served in the Indian army. After Colonel Burton was placed on half pay for refusing to testify against Queen Caroline in 1820, he moved his family to the continent, where Burton spent his youthful years in France and Italy, with a brief interlude in 1829 in an English preparatory school. Determined that Burton should become a clergyman, a career choice that seems preposterous in retrospect, Colonel Burton insisted that he go to Oxford, where he matriculated from Trinity College in 1840. Although his intellectual accomplishments exceeded those of most undergraduates of the day, Burton's behaviour, ranging from unconventional Latin and Greek pronunciation to increasingly rebellious activities, denied him academic recognition. An unauthorized steeplechase outing finally caused his rustication in 1842.

Early experiences in India Colonel Burton then acquiesced to his son's requests and purchased a commission for him in the Bombay army. Burton arrived in India on 28 October 1842 and was posted to the 18th regiment of Bombay infantry. In 1844 his regiment was sent to the newly annexed Sind, where Burton spent much of his Indian service. Besides infantry duties, Burton served as a staff interpreter, surveyor, and intelligence officer during his Indian years. His phenomenal gift for mastering languages, apparent from childhood, flowered in India as he periodically exhibited proficiency in the East India Company's language examinations. Within a year of his arrival, he had scored first in both the Hindustani and Gujarati examinations, administered under the strict supervision of the accomplished orientalist Major-General Vans Kennedy. Altogether Burton passed seven language examinations in India; over the course of his lifetime, he mastered more than forty languages and dialects.

Besides languages, Burton also mastered cultures with such proficiency as to enable him to pass among native peoples in disguise. His favourite persona was that of Mirza Abdullah of Bushehr, half Arab and half Iranian, practitioner of various trades and professions, whichever best suited the needs of the moment. 'What scenes he saw!' Burton wrote of himself. 'What adventures he went through! But who would believe, even if he ventured to detail them?' (*Falconry in the Valley of the Indus*, 1852, 103). This ability was of great service to General Sir Charles Napier, who greatly influenced Burton, as Napier imposed order on the Sind. Besides providing political intelligence, Burton informed Napier's attempts to stamp out such abuses as wife murdering, infanticide, and pederasty while establishing a British-style legal system. Concerned about stories of male brothels, Napier again turned to Burton, who observed them in disguise and provided a report that enabled Napier to suppress them. This report, which was supposed to remain secret, was circulated by officers hostile to Burton after Napier's departure. Attempts to have Burton dismissed from the service failed, but his prospects in India were permanently blighted, a fact that became apparent when he applied to be official interpreter only to see the post awarded to an incomparably less qualified officer. Still unwell from an earlier bout of cholera, Burton was granted sick leave and returned to England in 1849.

Sir Richard Francis Burton (1821–1890), by Frederic Leighton, Baron Leighton, *c.*1872–5

As he recovered Burton turned to literary pursuits. His first book, *Goa and the Blue Mountains* (1851), was quickly followed by three more: *Scinde, or, The Unhappy Valley* (2 vols., 1851), *Sindh, and the Races that Inhabit the Valley of the Indus* (1851), and *Falconry in the Valley of the Indus* (1852), the last containing a remarkable autobiographical postscript. Although Burton is most often thought of as a traveller, explorer, or linguist, he is probably best understood as a writer. During four decades of literary production, he published dozens of books, many of them multi-volumed, and over 100 articles or their equivalent, besides writing several book-length manuscripts that were never published. He accumulated voluminous notes and sketches while keeping two series of diaries, one of research and observations, the other of his innermost thoughts. Burton was a brilliant conversationalist and a riveting lecturer: it was said that his conversation was better than his books and his diaries better than his conversation. Few ever saw the diaries, however, for they were destroyed along with most of his other papers, some in a warehouse fire in 1861, others after his death. Despite the scale of his literary output, Burton's expectations of deriving a substantial income from it were usually disappointed.

In forbidden cities In 1852 Burton proposed to the Royal Geographical Society that he make the *hajj*, or pilgrimage, to the Islamic holy cities of Mecca and Medina. Forbidden to non-Muslims, less than half a dozen Europeans were known to have visited them and lived, and of those only the Swiss explorer J. L. Burckhardt had left a detailed account. Burton intended to make the pilgrimage in complete disguise as a Muslim native of the Middle East. While his experiences in India provided good preparation, this was an exploit of linguistic and cultural virtuosity which carried considerable risk for its perpetrator. With support from the Royal Geographical Society and a leave from the East India Company, Burton sailed from England in April 1853.

Burton first travelled to Egypt, where he spent a month in Alexandria and some further weeks in Cairo renewing his familiarity with Islamic mannerisms. He modified his former persona to become Sheikh Abdullah, a wandering Sufi dervish and practitioner of medicine. So successful was he in the latter role that he soon developed a thriving practice. He also perfected his Arabic, which he had learned in India, at venerable al-Azhar University. After the fasting month of Ramadan he proceeded by camel to Suez, whence a tumultuous voyage on a pilgrim boat took him to the Arabian port of Yanbuᶜ al-Bahr. He then travelled by caravan to Medina, arriving on 25 July 1853. There he remained for some weeks as he explored the city, visiting the Prophet's tomb and venturing to nearby sites such as the battlefield at Uhud. On 31 August he departed Medina with the Damascus caravan and reached Mecca early on 11 September 1853. Later that morning he proceeded to the Great Mosque and stood before the Kaaba.

> There at last it lay, the bourn of my long and weary pilgrimage, realising the plans and hopes of many and many a year … I may truly say that, of all the worshippers who clung weeping to the curtain, or who pressed their beating hearts to the stone, none felt for the moment a deeper emotion than did the Haji from the far north …. But, to confess humbling truth, theirs was the high feeling of religious enthusiasm, mine was the ecstasy of gratified pride. (*A Personal Narrative of a Pilgrimage*, 3, 1855–6, 199–200)

During the several days that Burton spent in Mecca, he performed the associated rites of the pilgrimage such as circumambulating the Kaaba, drinking the Zemzem water, and stoning the devil at Mount Arafat. All the while, as at Medina, he secretly made the detailed notes that enabled his resulting book to surpass all preceding Western accounts of the holy cities. Burton had originally hoped to continue east into the unexplored regions of central Arabia, but unrest among the Bedouin tribes prevented him, so he returned to Egypt in the early autumn of 1853. *A Personal Narrative of a Pilgrimage to Al-Madinah & Meccah* (3 vols., 1855–6) made Burton famous and became a classic of travel literature.

Instead of going on to Britain, where he would have received a hero's welcome at the Royal Geographical Society and the applause of the general public, Burton lingered in Cairo until November 1853, when his leave expired. Even as he completed the manuscript of his *Personal Narrative* after returning to Bombay, he was planning the penetration of another forbidden city. This time his objective was Harar, an important religious centre and notorious base for the slave trade in Somalia. No European had ever entered Harar, and its inhabitants believed that should any Christian do so, the city would fall. Burton now proposed an expedition into Somalia, until then only tentatively explored, intending to travel inland to Harar, survey the coast around Berbera, and then strike south-east across the Somali peninsula, ending in Zanzibar. The Bombay council, with the enthusiastic support of its senior member James Grant Lumsden, approved the expedition. Besides Burton, who would be leader, it was to include Lieutenant William Stroyan of the Indian navy, Lieutenant G. E. Herne of the Bombay infantry, and assistant surgeon J. E. Stocks, but Stocks died just before leaving India and was replaced by infantry Lieutenant John Hanning *Speke. However, when the party assembled at their staging point at Aden on 1 October 1854, the political resident, Colonel James Outram, dismissed their plan as excessively dangerous and liable to stir up hostility. He insisted that the expedition be limited to coastal areas. Burton accordingly revised the plan, sending Speke to explore the possibly gold-bearing Wadi Nogal, and Herne and Stroyan to investigate Berbera and its environs. He reserved the trip inland to Harar for himself.

Burton sailed from Aden on 29 October 1854, disguised as a Turkish merchant. After some pleasant preparatory weeks in the town of Zayla on the Somali coast, he started for Harar. As he approached the city, however, he fell under suspicion of being a foreign spy. Reasoning that his Turkish identity would afford little protection from the amir of Harar, who was notorious for capriciously executing people or leaving them to languish in his dungeons, he decided to present himself as a British agent on a diplomatic mission, forging a letter to that effect, in hopes that the amir would be unwilling to offend the British government. On 3 January 1855 he entered Harar. The amir received him courteously, although Burton spent an uneasy ten days in the city before being allowed to depart. After a difficult trip back to the coast, where he met Herne and Stroyan at Berbera, he returned to Aden on 9 February 1855. Speke, having failed to reach his objective, had arrived a short time earlier. As was becoming customary with Burton, his experience translated directly into a book, *First Footsteps in East Africa, or, An Exploration of Harar* (1856). The experience also whetted Burton's appetite for further African exploration.

The Nile Soon after Burton reached Aden, he applied for another leave, this time to look for the source of the Nile, the greatest geographical mystery of the time. Of Burton's many adventures, this is probably the one best remembered by the general public. The origin of the eastern branch of the river, the Blue Nile, in the Ethiopian highlands, was fairly well understood, but that of the great western branch, the White Nile, lay somewhere in one of those blank spots on the map that irresistibly beckoned to nineteenth-century explorers. Burton now proposed to march inland via Harar and on to the Nile. He returned to Berbera on 7 April 1855 where he joined Speke, Stroyan, and Herne. Encamped a short distance from the town, they were attacked and overwhelmed by a large party of Africans early on 19 April. Herne, though badly beaten, escaped relatively unscathed, but Speke was severely wounded, and Stroyan was killed. Burton, hit in the face with a javelin, acquired his distinctive scar. A friendly African vessel rescued the three survivors and brought them back to Aden on 22 April 1855. There the attending physician recommended Burton's immediate return to England.

Return to Britain, and the Crimean War Burton was probably disappointed at his reception in London. He read his Harar paper before the Royal Geographical Society on 11 June 1855 and he was later awarded the society's gold medal, but the pilgrimage to Mecca was old news, and the significance of his adventures in little-known Somalia was not understood. Public attention was focused to the Crimean War, where British forces appeared to be faring poorly. Burton obtained permission to volunteer for service and travelled to Constantinople, where he became chief of staff to General W. F. Beatson's contingent of bashi bazouks, although he remained a captain, the highest military rank he ever held. The bashi bazouks, irregular horsemen from the Turkish provinces, were a promising if unruly body of cavalry, but they were never sent into action. A well-developed plan by Burton to use them to relieve the beleaguered city of Kars in Armenia was dismissed out of hand, while he rightly rejected an ill-prepared proposal that he undertake a solitary mission into the Caucasus. After General Beatson was replaced, Burton sailed for England on 18 October 1855, having seen little of the front during his four months in the Crimea. His short, critical memoir of his experiences was not published until many years later.

Exploring east Africa, and the quarrel with Speke In London, Burton revived his plan for exploring the sources of the Nile. His objective was the great lakes of central Africa, from which he correctly believed the Nile flowed, but their location, or even their existence, was uncertain. The Royal Geographical Society and the Foreign Office supported the expedition, as did the East India Company, which gave Burton two years' leave at full pay. Burton, as leader of the expedition, invited John Speke and another friend, the physician and linguist John Steinhäuser, to join him, although delays prevented the latter's participation. Steinhäuser would be doubly missed, both as a physician and a stabilizing influence. Burton and Speke arrived at Zanzibar, the staging area for the expedition, on 20 December 1856. There they spent several months of preparation and made preliminary probes along the coast, looking for the best point to strike inland. Burton also compiled an enormous quantity of notes about Zanzibar, including a book manuscript, which he entrusted to an official of the East India Company for dispatch to the Royal Geographical Society.

Burton and Speke sailed from Zanzibar to Kaole on 17 June 1857. They headed east with a caravan of more than 100 bearers heavily laden with supplies and instruments for an expedition that was expected to last as long as two years. The journey was arduous, as both Burton and Speke became too ill to manage their men who stole, deserted, and mishandled materials. Arriving at the Arab slaving post of Tabora on 7 November, they paused for a month to refit and gather additional information before resuming their march east. When they did so, Burton became so ill that he could no longer walk and had to be carried about for nearly a year. On 13 February 1858 they discovered Lake Tanganyika. This alone would have been remembered as a momentous event in African exploration, had it not been overshadowed by what ensued.

On leaving Lake Tanganyika on 26 May, they returned to Tabora, where Burton devoted himself to linguistic and anthropological studies as preparatory steps for further explorations. Speke, who had no interest in these subjects, proposed to travel north and verify stories of an enormous lake there. Burton, still ill, chose not to go. That turned out to be a serious mistake, for Speke discovered Lake Victoria, which he decided was the source of the Nile. It is indeed the major source of the river, although Speke had no way of verifying that fact after only a brief visit to the lake's southern shore. The exhaustion of their supplies prevented further explorations. On the arduous return trip Speke became desperately ill and was nursed back to health by Burton. Not until 4 March 1859 did they reach Zanzibar, where Burton learned that most of his papers, including the Zanzibar book manuscript, had not been forwarded to London and were apparently lost. On 22 March he and Speke sailed for Aden.

Although Burton later wrote that Speke's attitude towards him altered immediately after the latter's return from Lake Victoria, their outward relations still seemed amicable. When Speke sailed on to London, Burton remained in Aden for further recuperation—another mistake as it turned out, although Speke promised to make no announcement of the expedition's results until Burton joined him. When Burton arrived in London on 21 May 1859, he was dismayed to find that Speke had lectured before the Royal Geographical Society, had proposed another expedition to Africa, and was claiming by far the greater share of credit for his and Burton's accomplishments. Speke became the hero of the moment and continued to extol his own achievements in speech and print; Burton, though usually an avid controversialist, made no public attack against Speke for several months. Not until early 1860 did he set forth his position with the publication of *The Lake Regions of Central Africa* (2 vols., 1860). By then Speke had returned to Africa, but a rift had opened between them that would never be closed.

The dispute between Burton and Speke became one of the most celebrated scholarly controversies of the nineteenth century. Although Speke can be faulted for his conduct, the episode ultimately did little credit to either man. As each sought to strengthen his own claims and diminish the other's, the scientific purpose of their labours, elucidation of the sources of the Nile, was obscured. Meanwhile they were incited by malicious individuals who found cruel sport in watching two famous explorers destroy each other's reputation. The initial course of the argument went in favour of Speke, who received lavish funding for a return expedition to Africa in company with Captain James Augustus Grant to establish the connection between Lake Victoria and the Nile. Burton was left in the background. He had the further misfortune of finding that his brother, Edward, had lapsed into mental illness from which he never recovered.

In North America Burton sailed for North America in April 1860 and travelled in Canada and through the United States. The first portion of the trip is poorly documented, but the obscurity lifts with the material contained in *The City of the Saints and across the Rocky Mountains to California* (1861), which begins with a stagecoach journey across the American West to Salt Lake City. There Burton remained for nearly a month, noting Mormon institutions and enjoying a lengthy interview with the Mormon prophet, Brigham Young. Burton's *City of the Saints* is by far the best account of Mormonism of its day, exceeding in judgement and detail those of Remy, Twain, and Emerson. From Salt Lake City, Burton proceeded to San Francisco and returned to England via the Isthmus of Panama, arriving late in 1860.

Marriage, minor consular posts, and further dispute with Speke On 22 January 1861 Burton married Isabel Arundell (1831–1896), the descendant of an old Roman Catholic family [*see* Burton, Isabel]. She had been in love with Burton since their first meeting ten years earlier, but the match had been impeded by her parents, who disapproved of Burton's character and financial prospects. She, to the chagrin of Burton's family and many of his friends, remained a staunch Roman Catholic, while Burton, though initiated into many religions during his life, persisted in agnosticism. Each probably hoped to convert the other; if so, neither succeeded. Nevertheless, Isabel Burton adored her husband, even as she disapproved of some of his work; he in turn was devoted to her and, during his final years, heavily dependent on her. Shortly after his marriage Burton suffered a serious misfortune when a warehouse fire destroyed most of his papers and memorabilia from India, the Middle East, and east Africa. The disaster prefigured the similar fate that befell his papers after his death.

Newly married and needing employment, Burton approached the Foreign Office for a consular position, hoping for the post at Damascus. Instead, he was offered the consulship at Fernando Po, a small, unhealthy island in the Bight of Biafra on the west African coast. When he accepted the position on 27 March 1861 he requested to retain his commission in the Bombay army, but he was struck from the list, thereby losing not only his half pay but also any prospect of a pension or sale of his commission, an action about which he always complained bitterly.

Burton did not permit Isabel to accompany him to Fernando Po, which he described as 'the very abomination of desolation'. He slipped away from the post at every opportunity for excursions on the African mainland or to meet Isabel in the Canaries or England. Although he loathed Fernando Po, he worked continuously at his writing with *Wanderings in West Africa* (2 vols.) and *Abeokuta and the Cameroons Mountains* (2 vols.), both appearing in 1863. *Two Trips to Gorilla Land and the Cataracts of the Congo* (2 vols.), though written in 1862, was not published until 1876. He also compiled a collection of aphorisms, *Wit and Wisdom of West Africa* (1865). The most remarkable of his exploits during this time was a mission to Dahomey, where he was instructed to take diplomatic measures to suppress the slave trade. He was there during, though he did not actually witness, the human sacrifices that he described in *A Mission to Gelele, King of Dahome* (2 vols., 1864). In August 1864 he returned to England on home leave.

When Burton arrived in London, the Nile controversy was raging again. Speke and Grant, so long overdue that they were feared lost, had reappeared. When Speke addressed the Royal Geographical Society on 23 June 1863, he announced his discovery of a major outlet on the north of Lake Victoria, which, he claimed, established that lake as the source of the Nile. Again he attacked Burton. After the initial excitement, however, public opinion, previously so favourable to Speke, slowly swung to Burton as questions were raised about the accuracy of Speke's findings. Most damaging, although Lake Victoria does flow into the Nile, Speke could not demonstrate that fact incontrovertibly, for he had not followed the river continuously from the lake. In neglecting to do so, he had not explored Lake Albert to ascertain its contribution to the Nilotic system. That left the further possibility that Lake Tanganyika, which Burton incorrectly held to be the source of the Nile, was somehow involved. Speke's conduct also alienated many. It was proposed that Burton and Speke debate their differences at a scholarly meeting soon to convene in Bath. Goaded by a manipulative third party, Burton agreed. The debate was scheduled for 16 September 1864, but on the day before the meeting Speke was killed in an apparent shooting accident that may well have been suicide. Burton certainly believed it was so. *The Nile Basin* (1864) is a statement of Burton's position at that stage of the controversy.

Burton did not return to Fernando Po, for in September 1864 he was transferred to the consulate in Santos, Brazil. Considering Santos unhealthy, Burton established a pleasant retreat at São Paulo, 45 miles distant. At Rio de Janeiro he and Isabel enjoyed the favour of emperor Dom Pedro II, a student of Arabic and other Eastern languages. A leave in Minas Gerais resulted in *The Highlands of the Brazil* (2 vols., 1869). Another literary production of Burton's Brazilian years was *Vikram and the Vampire* (1870), a translation of Hindu folk tales. In April 1868 Burton fell dangerously ill. When he was granted sick leave he sent Isabel to London to lobby for a better post while he set off on a tour of South America. Two visits to the theatre of war between Paraguay and its neighbours provided material for *Letters from the Battle-Fields of Paraguay* (1870). He was wandering through Peru in February 1869 when he learned that he had been appointed consul at Damascus. On arriving in England on 1 June 1869, Burton obtained some additional months of sick leave, some of which he spent on the continent with his friend Algernon Charles Swinburne.

At Damascus The consulship at Damascus was the realization of Burton's diplomatic dreams. In contrast to his previous postings, Burton closely involved himself in his duties. Once again he resumed his old practice of disguise, mixing with the people at night to gather information. When tensions between Christians and Muslims threatened a repetition of the massacre of 1860, Burton took effective action. Meanwhile, he and Isabel enjoyed some of the happiest moments of their lives. For the first time, Burton displayed an active interest in archaeology, correctly identifying some inscriptions as Hittite in origin. But he also encountered serious opposition. Burton's immediate superior, the consul-general at Beirut, was an enemy, and the ambassador at Constantinople, who apparently feared that Burton might take his job, undermined Burton's authority. The Turkish pasha of Syria, Muhammad Rashid, was invariably hostile. Burton believed the pasha attempted to have him murdered on one occasion; on another, the pasha certainly forged a document damaging to Burton. Although Burton was generally popular at Damascus, he made a number of local enemies among various ethnic and religious groups who were vocal in their complaints. Especially damaging were those of the Jewish moneylenders whom Burton refused to assist in debt collection. In London, Sir Moses Montefiore and Sir Francis Goldsmid accused Burton of antisemitism. There seems to have been little foundation to any of these reports, but by spring 1871 the Foreign Office was considering transferring him to another post. At that moment, Burton's name became associated with an exceedingly ill-advised attempt to facilitate the conversion and resettlement under British protection of several hundred Shazlis, members of a Muslim mystical sect. When the Turkish authorities heard of this, they successfully demanded Burton's immediate recall. Instructing Isabel to 'pay, pack and follow', he left Damascus on 18 August 1871 (Burton, 1.569).

For a year Burton was without employment while the Foreign Office awaited a suitable vacancy. As always, he continued to write, quickly publishing *Unexplored Syria* (2 vols., 1872). Resentful over his recall, he vented his anger in another manuscript that contained many antisemitic sentiments, something previously absent from his writing. Isabel dissuaded him from publishing it, but she preserved the manuscript, and it appeared posthumously as *The Jew, the Gypsy, and El Islam* (1898) when the Dreyfus affair was at its height. In need of income, he accepted a lucrative offer to explore for sulphur in Iceland, where he spent the summer of 1872. As usual, his experiences turned into a book, *Ultima Thule, or, A Summer in Iceland* (2 vols., 1875), but the sulphur venture failed.

The scholar and poet While in Iceland, Burton was offered the consulship at Trieste, for which he sailed on 24 October 1872. He frequently complained about the post and long hoped for a loftier position in a place more suited to his talents, but it was a virtual sinecure that gave him plenty of leisure to write. Sometimes he worked on as many as eleven literary projects simultaneously. He translated Francisco Lacerda's *Lands of the Cazembe* (1873) and annotated and wrote a long preface to Albert Tootal's *The Captivity of Hans Stade of Hesse* (1874). *Etruscan Bologna* appeared in 1876 as did *A New System of Sword Exercise for Infantry*. An interest in the Portuguese poet Luis Vaz de Camões, dating from his Indian days, resulted in a two-volume translation of Camões's *Lusiads* in 1880, followed by a commentary on Camões and his work, also in two volumes, in 1881.

Besides being a translator of poetry, Burton was also a poet himself. His *Kasidah of Haji Abdu el-Yezdi, a Lay of the Higher Law* (1880) is by far his most notable poetic effort. Unlike most of Burton's compositions, which were hastily written and carelessly (if at all) edited, this is a polished work that contains many fascinating autobiographical insights. Unfortunately, it was perceived as an echo of Edward Fitzgerald's *Rubaiyat of Omar Khayyam* and only half of its print run of 200 copies was sold, although after Burton's death it became quite popular, going through many editions and long remaining in print. Nor was this Burton's only poetic effort, for poetry is often interspersed in his works. He had also published another volume of poetry entitled *Stone Talk* in 1865, but Isabel, who disapproved of its satiric nature, bought up the copies and destroyed them.

Isabel Burton approved even less of Burton's presentation of sexual material in his writing, for he was determined to challenge public mores. This had motivated him to participate in the establishment of the Anthropological Society of London, the Anthropological Institute, and the short-lived London Anthropological Society. These, however, were too timid to suit him. With his friend Foster Fitzgerald Arbuthnot, he developed a plan for translating and publishing classic Eastern erotic works. Because of the danger of prosecution, in 1882 they formed the Kama Shastra Society, ostensibly an organization based in Benares but in reality consisting entirely of Burton and Arbuthnot. Aided by Indian pandits, the society's first publication, the *Kama sutra*, appeared in 1883. Of all of Burton's works, this is probably the most widely read, but since almost all of its uncounted editions were pirated, Burton did not profit. The *Ananga ranga* (1885) was mostly translated by Arbuthnot, with Burton helping to polish the manuscript. The Kama Shastra Society's third publication, *The Perfumed Garden of the Cheikh Nefzaoui* (1886), was translated by Burton from a French translation of the Arabic original. In collaboration with Leonard Smithers, Burton also produced his translations of erotic classical literature, the *Priapeia* (1890), and the posthumous *Carmina of Gaius Valerius Catullus* (1894).

Burton received frequent leave during his Trieste years. In December 1875 he and Isabel sailed for India, a journey that he recorded in *Sind Revisited* (2 vols., 1877). He also absented himself from the consulate on several occasions to go hunting for gold, much to the annoyance of his superiors. With the support of Khedive Ismaʿil, he twice went into the Midian during 1877–8 to look for its ancient goldmines. When this failed, the khedive reneged on his promise to pay the expenses, leaving Burton with a substantial loss. Burton returned to Egypt in the autumn of 1879 in a futile effort to press his claims for reimbursement. While there he explored the Faiyûm and the Natron lakes with William Robertson Smith, compiler of the *Dictionary of the Bible*. The sight of a slave caravan in the desert so moved him that he forwarded a plan to London for the suppression of the slave trade in the Red Sea, but the government was not interested. Despite Foreign Office warnings, he made yet another gold-hunting expedition to the Gold Coast in 1881–2. This one actually looked promising, but when the Foreign Office heard of it he was ordered to desist, causing yet more loss. Even so, the trips inevitably resulted in books, *The Gold Mines of Midian and the Ruined Midianite Cites* (1878), *The Land of Midian (Revisited)* (2 vols., 1879), and *To the Gold Coast for Gold* (2 vols., 1883). Official business again brought him to the Middle East in 1882, when he was sent to search for his friend Edward Henry Palmer, who had been murdered in the desert. Burton's long account of this journey found no publisher.

Although the volume of Burton's literary production remained large, its quality seemed to be diminishing. The two best books published during his first years at Trieste had mostly been composed earlier: *Zanzibar* (2 vols., 1872), after the long-lost manuscript was found, and *Two Trips to Gorilla Land* (2 vols., 1876). Publishers became increasingly reluctant to accept his work. Shortly after the appearance of *The Book of the Sword* (Burton was a master fencer) in 1884, Burton had his first heart attack. With deteriorating health and apparently declining literary power, he was in fact about to publish his greatest work.

The *Arabian Nights* had been an important part of Burton's life for decades. In 1882 he began translating it in earnest. Although there were other translations of the *Nights* in English, Burton's was distinguished by his retention of the sexual content of the original Arabic versions, while his extensive footnotes drew on a lifetime of travel and research. Unable to get an acceptable offer from a publisher, he decided to print it himself, a venture that must have seemed more speculative than any of his searches for gold. He and Isabel announced a limited subscription of 1000 copies, hoping for 500 responses; to their surprise, they received 2000, but kept their word and accepted only 1000. At last Burton's literary efforts were rewarded with financial success, as he got 16,000 guineas from an outlay of 6000 . According to Isabel, he reflected,

> I have struggled for forty-seven years, distinguishing myself honourably in every way that I possibly could. I never had a compliment, nor a 'thank you', nor a single farthing. I translate a doubtful book in my old age, and I immediately make sixteen thousand guineas. Now that I know the tastes of England, we need never be without money. (Burton, 2.442)

Despite its deliberately archaic style, *The book of the thousand nights and a night: A plain and literal translation of the Arabian nights entertainments* (16 vols., 1885–8) has become the pre-eminent English translation of the Middle Eastern classic. It is the keystone of Burton's literary reputation.

In 1886 Burton was made KCMG, but later that year his application to be ambassador to Morocco was rejected. He then requested early retirement; this too was refused, although his already light workload was reduced. In 1888 he completed the six volumes of the *Supplemental Nights*, including the famous 'Terminal essay'. The last months of Burton's life were devoted to a new translation of *The Perfumed Garden*, this one to be made directly from the original Arabic text. He called it 'The scented garden' to distinguish it from its predecessor. 'I have put my whole life and all my life blood into that *Scented Garden*', he said, 'and it is my great hope that I shall live by it. It is the crown of my life' (Wright, 2.217). Burton was one day from completing it when he died at the consulate in Trieste on 20 October 1890. On 15 June 1891 he was buried in the cemetery of St Mary Magdalene, Mortlake, Surrey, in a mausoleum shaped like an Arab tent, designed by Lady Burton. After his death, she burned most of his vast accumulation of personal papers, including the more than 1000 pages of 'The scented garden' manuscript.

A fascinating person to the many who knew him, Sir Richard Burton has also captured the interest of succeeding generations. There have been more than a dozen Burton biographies and at least three of Lady Burton. Virtually all of these have been published by trade presses and marketed to broad audiences. Burton has also been the subject of documentary films and fiction, perhaps most notably in William Harrison's novel *Burton and Speke* (1982), from which the film *Mountains of the Moon* (1990) was made. Many of Burton's books have been reprinted since his death, attaining a level of success far greater than during his lifetime. His wide range of accomplishments and enigmatic character, yet to be fully defined, make him continually attractive to researchers, writers, and readers. JASON THOMPSON

Sources M. S. Lovell, *A rage to live: a biography of Richard and Isabel Burton* (1998) · F. M. Brodie, *The devil drives: a life of Sir Richard Burton* (1967) · B. Farwell, *Burton: a biography of Sir Richard Francis Burton* (1963) · N. M. Penzer, *An annotated bibliography of Sir Richard Francis Burton K.C.M.G.* (1923) · I. Burton, *The life of Captain Sir Richard F. Burton*, 2 vols. (1893) · G. M. Stisted, *The true life of Capt. Sir Richard F. Burton* (1896) · J. A. Casada, *Sir Richard F. Burton: a bibliographical study* (1990) · B. J. Kirkpatrick, ed., *A catalogue of the library of Sir Richard Burton, KCMG, held by the Royal Anthropological Institute* (1978) · E. Rice, *Captain Sir Richard Francis Burton* (1990) · M. Hastings, *Sir Richard Burton: a biography* (1978) · G. S. Burne, *Richard F. Burton* (1985) · J. Hayman, ed., *Sir Richard Burton's travels in Arabia and Africa: four lectures from a Huntington Library manuscript* (1993) · A. H. Jutzi, ed., *In search of Sir Richard Burton: papers from a Huntington Library symposium* (1993) · F. McLynn, *Burton: snow upon the desert* (1990) · F. McLynn, *From the sierras to the pampas: Richard Burton's travels in the Americas, 1860–69* (1991) · T. Wright, *The life of Sir Richard Burton*, 2 vols. (1906)

Archives BL, books and pamphlets from library; MSS, RP 3236; papers of and relating to Burton, Add. MS 49380, fols. 54–72 · Harvard U., Houghton L., notes for translation of Camoens, etc. · Hunt. L., annotated books; corresp. and papers; letters; literary

MSS; MSS of lectures • Orleans House Gallery, London, annotated books; corresp.; papers • RGS, letters to the RGS; other papers intended for publication by the RGS; travel notebooks • Richmond Local Studies Library, corresp. • Syracuse University, New York, corresp. and literary MSS | BL, letters to Henry Spencer Ashbee, Add. MS 38808C • Bodl. Oxf., letters to J. J. Fahie • Mitchell L., Glas., Glasgow City Archives, letters to Sir William Stirling-Maxwell • Royal Asiatic Society, London, letters to Bernard Quaitch • Trinity Cam., letters to Lord Houghton • UCL, letters to Sir Francis Galton • Wilts. & Swindon RO, papers, mainly photograph albums and newspaper cuttings

Likenesses portrait, 1848, repro. in W. H. Wilkins, *The romance of Isabel Lady Burton*, 2 vols. (1897) • photograph, *c.*1850–1859, repro. in Burton, *Life* • Jacquand, oils, 1851 (with sister), repro. in Brodie, *The devil drives* • R. F. Burton, self-portrait, *c.*1855, repro. in R. F. Burton, *Personal narrative of a pilgrimage to El Medinah and Meunh* (1855–6) • L. Desanges, watercolour, 1861, Orleans House Gallery, Twickenham; repro. in Brodie, *The devil drives* • E. Edwards, photograph, 1865, NPG • F. Leighton, oils, *c.*1872–1875, NPG [*see illus.*] • Lock & Whitfield, woodburytype photograph, 1876, NPG • M. Collier, pencil drawing, 1878, NPG • G. de Benvenuti, oils?, 1879, repro. in Burton, *Life* • M. de Gutmansthal, portrait, 1879, SOAS • Ape [C. Pellegrini], watercolour, before 1885, NPG • A. Letchford, portraits, 1889, Orleans House Gallery, Twickenham • F. G. Baker, photograph, 1890 (with Lady Burton), repro. in Brodie, *The devil drives* • Ape [C. Pellegrini], chromolithograph, NPG; repro. in *VF* (24 Oct 1885) • A. Letchford, ink drawing (on his deathbed), Orleans House Gallery, Twickenham • photograph (with al-Haji Adullah signature), priv. coll.

Wealth at death £188 15*s.* 1*d.*: probate, 23 March 1891, *CGPLA Eng. & Wales*

Burton, Robert (1577–1640), writer, was born on 8 February 1577 in Leicestershire, the fourth child and second son of Ralph Burton (1547–1619) and his wife, Dorothy, *née* Faunt (1560–1629).

Family and education Burton's parents had settled on their marriage at Lindley Hall, a property which had come into the family through Ralph's grandmother; the original family home was at Falde in Staffordshire. Lindley Hall, of which nothing now remains above ground, was a moated manor house lying close to Watling Street and not far from Nuneaton. The Burton family was of some antiquity, if no great distinction: Ralph appears to have lived the quiet life of a country gentleman until his death in 1619, but he fathered two sons distinguished for their learning in Robert and his elder brother, William *Burton, the antiquary. Robert appears to have attended both the local grammar schools, Bishop Vesey's at Sutton Coldfield and King Edward VI's at Nuneaton; he gives no reason why he changed from one to the other, although there is a suggestion in *The Anatomy of Melancholy* that he was not happy as a schoolboy.

In 1593 Burton matriculated as a member of Brasenose College, Oxford, of which his brother was already a member, but there is no surviving evidence that he actually came into residence at that time. Sixteen would seem an unusually young age to come up today, but many became undergraduates before that age in the sixteenth century. He did not in fact take his first degree until 1602, by which time he had been a member of Christ Church for three years. Migration from one college to another was not unusual, but the period from 1593 to 1599 remains an unfilled gap in Burton's life. He was not out of the country;

Robert Burton (1577–1640), by Gilbert Jackson, 1635

interested as he undoubtedly was in geography, he notes that he has never travelled 'but in a Mappe or Card' (Burton, 1.4, l. 9). Perhaps he was ill: a record has in fact been found of one 'Robert Burton', age twenty, who consulted the astrologer–doctor Robert Forman in London in the summer of 1597 and was diagnosed as suffering from melancholy. When he was admitted a student of Christ Church, Burton was treated as a freshman although he was twenty-two, and according to Anthony Wood was placed under the tuition of John Bancroft 'for form sake, tho' he wanted not a tutor' (Wood, *Ath. Oxon.*, 3rd edn, 2.652); at the time Bancroft, who afterwards became bishop of Oxford, was only three years older than his pupil. Burton proceeded to his BA on 30 June 1602 and to the MA on 9 June 1605. He took his BD in May 1614, as may have been required by the college statutes; he did not proceed further to the DD.

Pursuit of patronage Burton remained a student of Christ Church until his death. He blames his lack of advancement on his failure to find patrons; he sought their aid in vain, describing himself as 'left behind, as a Dolphin on shore, confined to my Colledge, as *Diogenes* to his tubbe' (R. Burton, *The Anatomy of Melancholy*, 1621, 4). As time went on he seems to have become reconciled to his lack of worldly success. He did obtain some appointments. In 1616 he was nominated by the dean and chapter of Christ Church to the college living of St Thomas's in what was then a western suburb of Oxford and held this vicarage until he died; his family arms (three talbots' heads), placed in 1621 on the south porch of the church, still remain, although all other records have been lost. Apparently he discharged the duties of parish priest himself. In 1624 he was presented by Frances, the dowager countess of Exeter, to the benefice of Walesby in Lincolnshire; he may have tutored Robert Smith, her son by her first marriage. He never resided at Walesby, which was entrusted to a curate. In 1631 he resigned this living, which was apparently required for someone else, but in the following year he was presented by Lord Berkeley to a richer benefice, the rectory of Seagrave in the county of Leicester (he had been given the advowson of this living in 1624, but had had to wait for the death of the previous incumbent). The barons Berkeley were local magnates in Leicester, and the Burton family held part of the manor of Lindley from them; it was reasonable that Burton should look for patronage to this quarter. George, the eighth Baron Berkeley, matriculated as a 'canon-commoner' of Christ Church in 1619 at the age of eighteen and was very possibly a pupil of Burton's; in 1621 Burton dedicated the first edition of *The Anatomy of Melancholy* to him with a dedication which is respectful but not, by the standards of the day, unduly flattering. Once again Burton's pastoral duties would have been discharged by a curate, but Seagrave was only 20 miles from Lindley, and it is likely that he visited it more often than Walesby.

Walesby and Seagrave represent the sum total of what may be termed Burton's external appointments, but he did hold positions in Oxford in addition to his studentship at Christ Church. In 1615, 1617, and 1618 he was one of the clerks of the market—nowadays a virtual sinecure, but in his time an important office responsible for guarding the interests of members of the university in their dealings with the traders of Oxford. More to his taste, it may be supposed, was his appointment on 27 August 1624 as librarian of Christ Church, an office which he held until his death. To describe Burton as 'bookish' can only be called ridiculous understatement. Most of his personal library survives; in all, some 1700 titles are known—a reasonable collection, though not vast, as compared, for example, to the library credited to John Dee. It is interesting that in his will he directed that, after some personal bequests to friends, the first choice of his books should go to Bodley's librarian, and only those not selected for the Bodleian should revert to his own college library (where they are still preserved). When writing the *Anatomy* he had depended for material in the first instance on the university library and from his will the Bodleian acquired some rare books.

All in all, although Burton complains of the lack of patronage, as scholars and writers in the Renaissance were wont to do, it is doubtful whether he would have wished to leave Oxford and the Bodleian. He might perhaps have really wanted the headship of a college. But he cannot really have regretted having, as he put it in the third edition of the *Anatomy*, 'been brought up a Student in the most flourishing Colledge of *Europe, Augustissimo collegio*' (Burton, 1.3, ll. 16–17). In 'Democritus to the reader', the introductory section of the *Anatomy*, he states that part of his motive for writing it was that he was 'loth … to be an unprofitable or unworthy Member of so learned and noble a Society' (ibid., 1.3, ll. 21–2), but did not feel himself suited to studies in divinity, which he felt led to unnecessary argument and controversy, and 'saw no such great neede' (ibid., 1.20, ll. 31–2) for a contribution from himself. He contributed several short poems to different collections of verse, mainly commemorative, published in Oxford; he wrote part of one play, *Alba*, now lost, which was acted before King James in Oxford in 1605; and in the following year he began another, *Philosophaster*, which was not completed until 1615 and not acted until 1618. This last, which survives in two holographs, may be classified as a cross between an academic drama and a comedy of humours and is not without genuine merit, particularly in the satirical portraits of pretenders to learning, including alchemists. These passages are reminiscent of Ben Jonson's *The Alchemist*: this was staged in 1610 and in his introduction Burton points out that his play was written first. But such of his time as was not taken up by his college and pastoral duties must have been fully occupied by compiling his one great work.

The Anatomy of Melancholy Large encyclopaedic works were common in the Renaissance, often treating exhaustively of a single subject. In publishing the *Anatomy* Burton was competing for recognition as a serious scholar, and no doubt judged himself prepared for his task by the wide-ranging, though not well-organized, course of reading which he states he had followed (Burton, 1.3, l. 23ff.). But why should he have chosen melancholy as his subject? There is no doubt that what in general terms might be called morbid psychology was a topic of great interest in his time and much had been written on it. Whether in fact there was actually a greater incidence of mental illness in the Europe of the sixteenth and seventeenth centuries it is difficult to say, although modern scholars have adduced some reasons why that might have been the case. Interestingly, Burton does not seem to have been troubled by some causes that have been suggested; he appears, for example, to be unaffected by the gloom some are supposed to have felt at the deposition of the earth by recent astronomical discoveries (in which he was keenly interested) from a supposedly favoured position at the centre of the universe. It may be that the interest in melancholy is a particular example of the new curiosity in the Renaissance about the workings of the human mind: to be fascinated by one's own mental processes, as Montaigne was, is to become aware of the oddity and irrationality of mental experiences. This was exacerbated by new religious sensibilities, and specifically it became of vital interest for both Catholics and protestants to be able to distinguish in themselves between proper seriousness of mind and the potentially disastrous deadly sin of despair, and this is a subject to which Burton devotes especial attention.

Beyond this, to be a melancholic was something of a fashionable condition, having been so at least since Ficino noted in his *De vita* (1482) that melancholia was prone to attack students and artists. Some have suggested, indeed, that the *Anatomy* is in fact a disguised encomium in praise of the condition, but although Burton notes briefly that melancholia was associated with intellectual distinction he never suggests that anyone should cultivate it, and never speaks of it but as a cruel disease, one 'which crucifies the Soule in this life and everlastingly torments in the world to come' (Burton, 3.49, ll. 15–16). He never describes his own symptoms, unless the poem 'The Authors Abstract of Melancholy', added in 1628, is meant to be taken as autobiographical; if so, it might be suspected that he had suffered from manic depression. He describes some of the more grotesque behaviour of the mentally sick, but he makes plain that he does so 'not to upbraid any miserable man, or by way of derision (I rather pity them) but the better to discerne; to apply remedies unto them' (ibid., 1.408, ll. 12–14). An attempt to ameliorate, if not to cure, illness was a pastoral duty perfectly consonant with his vocation as a priest. His clearest statement about his motive for writing is unequivocal: 'I write of Melancholy by being busie to avoid Melancholy' (ibid., 1.6, ll. 29–30); being himself 'not a little offended with this maladie' (ibid., 1.7, ll. 20–21), and followed the advice given at the very end of the *Anatomy* to those threatened by the illness: '*be not idle*'.

Having settled on his subject, Burton as a scholar would naturally have aspired to treat it in a properly academic manner, but he seems to have determined to achieve as exhaustive a study as he could manage, given the material available to him—printed material, that is, for he never records any attempt at clinical research or practical healing. His pursuit of new information was relentless. The first edition of *The Anatomy of Melancholy, What it Is; with All the Kindes, Causes, Symptomes, Prognostickes and Several Cures of it* (1621) contained some 353,369 words and more material was added with each subsequent edition until the sixth, posthumous edition in 1651, which contains corrections and additions made before his death and totals some 516,384 words. It is indeed a long and detailed work, but its scheme is logical: the first partition, following on the general introduction, is concerned with defining the different kinds of melancholy, their causes and symptoms; the second partition deals with cures; and the third with the two special cases of love and religious melancholy. It has been alleged that Burton never defines his subject, yet he quotes the common definition: 'a kinde of dotage without a fever, having for his ordinary companions, feare and sadnesse, without any apparent occasion' (Burton, 1.162, ll. 25–6; it is the definition of 'dotage' which justifies his inclusion of love and religious mania) . He certainly does not confine himself strictly to the limits suggested, and there are digressions on subjects other than melancholy, but the progress of the work is regular. The reader, however, is likely to be overwhelmed by the sheer mass of material, and to have difficulty, which would not have been experienced by the better educated of its original readership, from the amount of quotation in the learned tongues. To Burton, of course, Latin was his second language and his handling of it was fluent, though it must be said that his footnotes in particular can be very difficult to follow (some of the obscurities may be the fault of the printer). He had less Greek, in common with many of his contemporaries, who habitually read Greek authors in Latin translations; he does not seem to have mastered any other languages: modern authors such as Montaigne or Ariosto are quoted in English (or Latin) translations.

Burton proclaims that his style is unpremeditated and that he writes as he spoke, 'in an extemporean stile … out of a confused company of notes' (Burton, 1.17, ll. 15–16). If he had a stylistic ideal it must have been what was known to his period as 'copiousness'—fullness and richness of detail—and in his determination not to leave out any relevant information from as many branches of knowledge as were relevant he paid scant regard to consistency. This causes especial difficulty in his additions, where he was liable in each new edition to patch in a new quotation or reference which does not agree at all with what was already there. Although he boasts of having acknowledged all his sources (which is largely, though not absolutely, true) he does not, except infrequently, give precise references. But he was able to rival the great encyclopaedist scholars of Europe, and there were not many Englishmen of his time who could do that.

Death and reputation Notwithstanding its difficulties and length, the *Anatomy* was a popular work; altogether there were eight editions in the seventeenth century. It was apparently favoured by some as a quarry for learned quotations to add an appearance of erudition to their own works, but no doubt it attracted many other readers by its rich collection of anecdotes and curious facts. States of what Burton would have recognized as melancholy, even if not more than instances of mild depression, are common enough, and there is always a market for books which explain us to ourselves. The *Anatomy* fell out of favour in the eighteenth century, although it retained one very distinguished reader in the shape of Dr Johnson (himself melancholic), and interest in it was revived by the publication of John Ferriar's *Illustrations of Sterne* (1798) which revealed the borrowings from Burton in *Tristram Shandy*. From that time until the end of the eighteenth century several editions were published, and the book became greatly admired by the Romantics, especially Lamb and Coleridge. Lamb may in fact have done Burton a disservice by paying tribute to him in his essay 'Detached thoughts on books and reading' as 'that fantastic great old man'; from that time onwards there has been a tendency to portray Burton as an ineffectual and eccentric scholar, remote from real life, and at worst a scatter-brained pedant with a streak of frivolity, and to regard the *Anatomy* as simply 'a curiosity of literature', possibly even a joke.

There is no evidence that Burton was a recluse, and testimony that he had some real practical interests. He was known as a mathematician and as both an astrologer and an astronomer, and even had some reputation as a surveyor. Nor in real life did he always appear a melancholic; Anthony Wood says of him:

> As he was by many accounted a severe student, a devourer of authors, a melancholy and humorous [i.e., moody] person; so by others, who knew him well, a person of great honesty, plain dealing and charity. I have heard some of the antients of Ch[rist] Ch[urch] often say that his company was very merry, facete and juvenile [i.e., humorous and lively]. (Wood, *Ath. Oxon.*, 3rd edn, 2.653)

But it is fitting that his epitaph in Christ Church Cathedral states (in the Latin composed by himself) that 'he devoted his life and death to Melancholy'. He died on 25 January 1640. There was a rumour that he hanged himself in order to conform with his own astrological calculations about his date of death, but this was a story told about other astrologers, and had it been true he would not have been buried in the cathedral at all. J. B. BAMBOROUGH

Sources R. Burton, *The anatomy of melancholy*, ed. T. C. Faulkner and others, 6 vols. (1989–2000) · J. R. Simon, *Robert Burton (1577–1640) et L'anatomie de la mélancolie* (Paris, 1964) · N. K. Kiessling, *The library of Robert Burton*, Oxford Bibliographical Society, new ser., 22 (1988) · N. K. Kiessling, 'Robert Burton's will: holograph copy', *Review of English Studies*, new ser., 41 (1990), 94–101 · R. L. Nochimson, 'Studies in the life of Robert Burton', *Yearbook of English Studies*, 4 (1974), 85–111 · B. H. Traister, 'New evidence about Burton's *Melancholy?*', *Renaissance Quarterly*, 29 (1976), 66–70 · C. McQuillen, ed. and trans., *Philosophaster: a critical edition with English translation* (Binghampton, N.Y., 1993) · C. McQuillen, 'Burton's *Philosophaster*: holograph status of the manuscripts', *Manuscripta*, 29 (1985) · J. Nichols, *The history and antiquities of the county of Leicester*, 3/1 (1800), 415–19; 4/2 (1811), 635, 668 · Wood, *Ath. Oxon.*, new edn · K. J. Höltgen, 'Robert Burton and the rectory of Seagrave', *Review of English Studies*, new ser., 27 (1976), 129–36 · J. Ferriar, *Illustrations of Sterne* (1798) · C. Lamb, 'Detached thoughts on books and reading', *The last essays of Elia* (1833) · W. G. Hiscock, *A Christ Church miscellany* (1946)

Likenesses G. Jackson, oils, 1635, Brasenose College, Oxford [*see illus.*] · C. Le Blon, engraving, repro. in R. Burton, *The anatomy of melancholy*, 3rd edn (1628) · marble bust, Christ Church Oxf.

Wealth at death calculated at £1200: Nochimson, 'Studies in the life of Robert Burton'

Burton, Robert. *See* Crouch, Nathaniel (*c.*1640–1725?).

Burton, Simon (*bap.* **1613**, *d.* **1663**), publisher, was baptized on 18 July 1613 in the parish of St Augustine, Watling Street, London, the eldest child of Francis Burton (*c.*1578–1617) and Joane (*fl.* 1597–1617). His father was the son of William Burton of Onibury, Shropshire, and a freeman of the Stationers' Company. Formerly an apprentice of Thomas Adams, Francis Burton sold books from several addresses in St Paul's Churchyard and was linked to a group of stationers. In June 1616, shortly before his death, he was admitted to the livery of the Stationers' Company. Henry Featherstone acted as overseer of his will.

Simon Burton was bound apprentice on 26 March 1628 to William Aspley, and made free of the Stationers' Company on 2 May 1636. His first publication was Jacob Reuff's *The Expert Midwife* (1637). This work was printed by Edward Griffin and sold by Thomas Alchorn at the Green Dragon in St Paul's Churchyard. With the death in 1640 of his grandmother, Joanne Bright, Burton appears to have acquired the lease of the Green Dragon. One of the shop's tenants was Octavian Pulleyn, at this time a business partner of the London stationer George Thomason. Thomason, formerly an apprentice of Henry Featherstone, was appointed an overseer of Joanne Bright's will. The other appointed overseer of the will was a goldsmith called Thomas Totney. A freeman of the Fishmongers' Company, Totney had married Alice Burton (1615–1648), Burton's younger sister, by licence, most likely on 25 March 1636; Burton's other sister, Joan (1614–1663), married Richard Taylor (*fl.* 1606–1663), graduate of Trinity College, Cambridge, and afterwards clerk of St James's, Duke's Place, London, and vicar of Ramsay, Essex. In the later 1630s Totney had been living in the parish of St Katharine Cree, and by 1640 Burton was keeping a publisher's shop in the parish. The shop was next to the Mitre tavern near Aldgate, and it was from this address that Burton issued *Visions, or, Hels Kingdome Strangely Displaied* (1640), Robert Chamberlaine's translation of a work by Francesco Quevedo, reissued as *Hell Reformed* (1641). Perhaps Burton enjoyed modest success as a publisher for in 1642 he invested £50 in Irish land; his lot of 111 acres was to fall in the south-west quarter of the barony of Decies, co. Waterford (Munster province).

Little is known of Burton's publishing activities in the civil wars. Some time between December 1645 and September 1646 he married Judith, widow of James Alford, citizen and grocer of London. In May 1649, together with his brother-in-law Totney, Burton stood bound by recognizance for £80 for the orphaned children of his wife's former husband. Burton evidently maintained contact with Totney, for in February 1651 he published a book by Totney, now, after a prophetic revelation, calling himself Theaurau John Tany. This was known as *His Aurora in Tranlagorum in Salem gloria*. On 13 August 1651 Tany was convicted on the charge of blasphemy at the London sessions of the peace held at the Old Bailey; Burton, the publisher of the *Aurora*, appears to have escaped unpunished.

Though Burton's whereabouts in 1651 are unknown, it is clear that by March 1652 he was living in the parish of St Katharine Cree; his wife was buried in the church on 3 February 1653. Notwithstanding his failure to pay tithes, Burton served as a parish constable in 1654, questman in 1655, ancient in 1660, and was twice nominated as a collector for the poor. On 21 March 1661 he took out a lease for twenty-one years at 40s. per annum for a shop at the sign of the Green Dragon in St Paul's Churchyard. When making his will in May 1663, Burton described himself as living in Whitechapel, London. His death some weeks afterwards was recorded in the obituary of Richard Smith, which described him as 'an oyleman wthout Algate' (H. Ellis, ed., *The Obituary of Richard Smyth*, CS, 1849, 58). In accordance with his dying wish, he was buried on 23 July 1663 in the parish of St Katharine Cree. He was survived by three daughters and a son. These were Alice, Frances (*d.* 1678), who married Augustine Steward, Elizabeth (*d.* in or after 1677), who married Thomas Crosse, and Simon (*d.* 1677), who was made free of the Stationers' Company by patrimony on 1 April 1672. ARIEL HESSAYON

Sources A. Hessayon, *'Gold tried in the fire': the prophet Theaurau John Tany and the puritan revolution* [forthcoming] · will of Simon Burton, PRO, PROB 11/312, fols. 12*v*–14*r* · court of judicature, proceedings, BL, Add. MS 5081, fols. 79*r*–84*r* · will, probate, 9 Dec 1640, GL, MS 9171/29, fols. 175*v*–176*v* [Joanne Bright] · Aldgate ward, first precinct, 1623–1851, GL, MS 1162/1A, fols. 24*r*, 24*v*, 25*r*, 27*r* · St Katharine Cree, vestry minute book, 1639–1718, GL, MS 1196/1, fols. 75*r*, 80*r* · D. F. McKenzie, ed., *Stationers' Company apprentices*, [1]: *1605–1640* (1961), 36 · letter-book, 1648–51, CLRO, 55, fol. 72*r* · orphans' finding book, CLRO, vol. 1, fol. 103*r*; vol. 2, fol. 127*r* and fol. 255*r*

Burton, Simon (1690?–1744), physician, was born in Caresly, Warwickshire, the eldest son of Humphrey Burton, of Caresly, near Coventry, and Judith, daughter of the Revd Abraham Bohun. He was educated at Rugby School, and at New College, Oxford, where he proceeded BA 1710; MA 1714; MB 1716; and MD 1720. After practising for some years at Warwick, he moved to London, where he established himself in Savile Row and acquired a large practice. He was admitted on 12 April 1731 as a candidate of the College of Physicians, of which he became a fellow on 3 April 1732 and was censor in 1738; he delivered the Harveian oration in 1740. Burton was appointed physician to St George's Hospital in 1733, and subsequently royal physician-in-ordinary. He was one of the physicians who attended Alexander Pope in the diagnosis and treatment of his last illness, which led to a dispute between Burton and Thomas Thompson; reference is made to the dispute in a satire entitled *Discord, or, One thousand seven hundred and forty-four, a poem, by a great poet lately deceased* (1744). The story circulated that Burton and Thompson quarrelled in Pope's sickroom, Pope quietening them with an instruction that a postscript should be added to 'The Dunciad':

> Dunces, rejoice! forgive all censures past,
> The greatest dunce has kill'd your foe at last
> (Mack, 807)

The epigram has also been attributed to Burton. Pope was survived somewhat less than a fortnight by Burton, who died after a few days' illness on 11 June 1744, at his house in Savile Row, London.

ARTHUR H. GRANT, *rev.* MICHAEL BEVAN

Sources Munk, *Roll* · *General Advertiser* (13 June 1744) · *Penny London Morning Advertiser* (13–15 June 1744) · *GM*, 1st ser., 14 (1744) · S. C. Lawrence, *Charitable knowledge: hospital pupils and practitioners in eighteenth-century London* (1996) · *A catalogue of all graduates … in the University of Oxford, between … 1659 and … 1850* (1851) · M. Mack, *Alexander Pope: a life* (1985)

Burton, Thomas (*d.* 1437), chronicler and abbot of Meaux, was the author of the most authoritative Cistercian chronicle to be written in late medieval England. The place of his birth, and the details of his early life are unknown. Although the continuator of his chronicle described him as 'well educated', there is no evidence that he studied at a university. Late in the fourteenth century he became a monk at Meaux, Yorkshire, where his name first appears in two lists of members of the abbey in 1394 and 1396. In the first list he is described as 'bursar and sergeant of the abbey'. In the second list no office appears after his name, but in 1396 Burton was elected abbot in a disputed election which was referred to the papal curia. As abbot of Meaux he attended the general chapter of the Cistercian order in Vienna in 1397. None the less, despite a papal judgment in his favour Burton resigned his position as abbot in 1399. According to the evidence of an incised slab now in Wawne church, Yorkshire, he died on 4 October 1437 at what must have been an advanced age, having lost his sight during the final years of his life. He was buried in Meaux Abbey.

Burton's chronicle survives in two manuscripts which contain an early and a revised version of his text respectively. He appears to have begun his work *c.*1388, and to have completed the first version of his chronicle by 1396. He then revised his text, probably between 1397 and 1402. The Meaux chronicle, which is built around the history of Meaux, is divided into sections dealing with the tenure of each abbot. It possesses the unique feature that each section is further divided into local and general history, and each of these subsections further subdivided to deal with particular aspects of their subject matter. Burton also included in his chronicle a list of abbots of Meaux, of chapter-headings, and a table denoting the properties of each abbot. A continuation to his chronicle which was written during the time of Abbot John Horton (1445) is found in the revised version only. This continuation omits the sections on general history.

Although certain of his sources appear to be lost, Burton took his account of general history mainly from a number of well-known chronicles. Many of these were of northern origin, and would have been readily available in the Meaux Library, whose catalogue survives as part of Burton's collectanea. The sections on general history contain useful information, but the most valuable parts of his work are undoubtedly those that deal with the history of Meaux. In these parts of his chronicle Burton provided an exceptionally detailed account of a Cistercian community, describing such matters as the numbers of monks, the state of religious observance, dissensions in the monastery, particularly during the time of Abbot William Scarborough (1372–96), and, most importantly, an account of the abbey's properties and finances. As a former bursar Burton possessed an expert knowledge of the finances of the house, and it was this knowledge that gives his work its unique value.

Because he could draw on his own practical experience, Burton's description of the community at Meaux constitutes the best extant account of the domestic history of a Cistercian monastery during the later middle ages. His work is also of some interest because of his skilled use of charter evidence, and his antiquarian outlook. Burton based his account upon a thorough examination of the records of the house, and his critical examination of these documents marks him out as a historical writer of unusual ability. Not surprisingly, he included a register of documentary material relevant to Meaux in the revised version of his chronicle. He was also interested in the topographical changes in the area around Meaux, and in the history of the abbey's buildings. Altogether his work, which stands at the end of a long tradition of Cistercian writing in the north, shows how effectively the history of a corporate body could be written by an individual with an enduring interest in its past.

JOHN TAYLOR

Sources *Chronica monasterii de Melsa, a fundatione usque ad annum 1396, auctore Thoma de Burton*, ed. E. A. Bond, 3 vols., Rolls Series, 43 (1866–8) · A. Gransden, *Historical writing in England*, 2 (1982), 355–71 · A. Gransden, 'Antiquarian studies in fifteenth-century England', *Antiquaries Journal*, 60 (1980), 75–97 · *Yorkshire: York and the East Riding*, Pevsner (1995), 613, 738 · *Yorkshire: York and the East Riding*, Pevsner (1972), 312

Archives BL, MS Egerton 1141 · JRL, MS Lat 219

Likenesses effigy on monument, Wawne church, East Yorkshire

Burton, Thomas. *See* Bell, Thomas (*b. c.*1551, *d.* in or after 1610).

Burton, Thomas (*fl.* **1656–1661**), diarist, of Brampton Hall, Westmorland, was the 'heir at law' of Richard Burton, his grandfather. On 20 August 1656 Thomas Burton was returned as MP for Westmorland, in the second protectorate parliament (1656–8). On 16 October he successfully rebutted a charge of disaffection to the then government. He was, indeed, among the Westmorland 'ejectors' and a commissioner for the 1656 monthly assessment. In 1657 he acquired a portion of the manor of Brough, sequestered from the papist Blenkinson family (a 'business' mentioned *en passant* in the diary). Burton sat, again for the county, in Richard Cromwell's parliament (27 January to 22 April 1659). He stood, having pressed a poll, unsuccessfully for the county for the Convention Parliament of 1660. He supported the king and was probably the Thomas Burton who petitioned for office and was given the post of under-searcher in the Port of London, and 'though an Oliverian', was later knighted.

Burton's anonymous manuscript diary, comprising six volumes, came into the British Museum early in the nineteenth century (Add. MSS 15859–15864), most likely from among the papers of Henry Hyde, second earl of Clarendon, via the London Institution. Covering the periods from 3 December 1656 to 27 June 1657, 20 January to 4 February 1658, and 27 January to 22 April 1659, it was transcribed and annotated by John Torrill Rutt (1760–1841), an experienced editor and a member of the Society for Constitutional Information, who enhanced the edition with extracts from Guibon Goddard's diary for the 1654–5 parliament. Rutt ascribed the diary to Burton on internal evidence. In 1845 this was peremptorily challenged by Thomas Carlyle in his *Letters and Speeches of Oliver Cromwell*, who made a guess, no more than that, that the 'very dull man' who had compiled it was 'one of the Suffolk Bacons, most probably Nathaniel Bacon, Master of the Court of Requests'. In 1861 it was 'identified' on the basis of handwriting as the work of the first earl of Clarendon, a pleasant notion ruled out by Hyde's exile throughout the 1650s. Burton's authorship was clinched by Mrs C. S. Lomas's meticulous pursuit of both internal and external evidence, notably the diarist's interest in northern affairs, (*The Athenaeum*, 3808, 513–14, reprinted as appx 2, vol. 4, of the 1974 edn of the diary).

Burton's *Diary* is a prime source for what was said and done in two protectorate parliaments. It puts flesh on the bones of the *Commons Journals*. It is a reminder, too, that many later Stuart politicians served a political apprenticeship in those years. But its value was not immediately appreciated when it came into print. Carlyle assailed 'the thing called Burton's diary' as 'wearisome ephemera and cast-clashes of facts gone all to dust and ashes … a Book filled …, with mere inanity and moaning wind', which might, though, if reduced to 'one readable sheet of sixteen pages', be useful (Carlyle, 3.17, 73). Ironically Carlyle cites Burton often in his *Cromwell*. The article on Burton in the *Dictionary of National Biography* dismisses the diarist as 'a mere reporter'. But that is precisely his value. A more involved Burton might have attempted his own evaluation of what he heard, crying up his own and his friends' speeches, omitting what seemed at the time irrelevant or did not chime with his own estimate of things, tidying up the actual record of the debates, cutting out seeming trivialities which, in fact, give colour, showing how MPs respected traditional procedures, going about their multifarious business in a corporate sense of the Commons' institutional significance, while not without an eye to posterity. Whatever Burton's purpose may have been in writing his diary, the record of the debates on 'the case of James Nayler' the Quaker (*Diary of Thomas Burton*, vol. 1, *passim*) alone commands respect for his assiduity.

Ivan Roots

Sources *Diary of Thomas Burton*, ed. J. T. Rutt, 4 vols. (1828); repr. (1974) • C. S. Lomas, 'The authorship of Burton's diary', *The Athenaeum* (Oct 1900), 513–14 • *The letters and speeches of Oliver Cromwell*, ed. T. Carlyle and S. C. Lomas, 3 vols. (1904) • HoP, *Commons, 1660–90* • C. H. Firth, *The last years of the protectorate, 1656–1658*, 2 vols. (1909) • *CSP dom.* • M. A. E. Green, ed., *Calendar of the proceedings of the committee for compounding … 1643–1660*, 5 vols., PRO (1889–92) • J. Nicolson and R. Burn, *The history and antiquities of the counties of Westmorland and Cumberland*, 2 vols. (1777) • I. Roots, 'Lawmaking in the 2nd protectorate parliament', *British government and administration: studies presented to S. B. Chrimes*, ed. H. Hearder and H. R. Loyn (1974) • *N&Q*, 2nd ser., 11 (1861), 12

Archives BL, Add. MSS 15859–15864

Burton, William (*c.*1545–1616), Church of England clergyman, was born within the soke of Winchester, and in 1556, aged eleven, he entered Winchester College as a scholar. He proceeded to New College, Oxford, where he was admitted perpetual fellow on 5 April 1563 and graduated BA on 14 April 1565. He has been identified as the William Bereton, vicar of Hanney, Berkshire (from 1570, resigned by 26 January 1581), and as William Burton MA, admitted vicar of Coleshill, Berkshire, on 23 August 1580. The first ministry to which Burton the writer himself alludes was a period of five years at Norwich, which must have occupied the later 1580s. One of this name was vicar of Aylesham, Norfolk, and a preacher at the puritan exercise at Wiverton in October 1585. The Burton who ministered at Norwich was certainly of this party, and he wrote warmly of the godly regime which operated in the city from 1575 under the direction of John More, and with the enthusiastic support of the civic leadership. For Burton this was a time of 'heavenly harmony and sweete amitie' when all important decisions in local government were preceded by consultation with the preachers. The city fathers in their turn gave daily attendance at the sermons, and the commons obliged with 'due reverence, & obedience' to their municipal and spiritual leaders (Erasmus, sigs. A2, A2*v*).

Burton's encomium of puritan Norwich recalled a cherished era of the recent past, in which he can have been only a junior figure. His signature appears fifty-sixth of the sixty-two ministers of Norfolk who in 1584 declined to subscribe to the three articles whereby Archbishop Whitgift endeavoured to enforce conformity; but he was not among the larger number of Norwich men who in the previous year had petitioned the queen in more general terms against the existing government of the church. Burton's five-year spell in the city must have extended to 1589, for in January that year he witnessed (with approval) the burning of the alleged Arian heretic Francis Kett, and on 21 December he preached in the cathedral. It was presumably at this point that Burton himself was in trouble ('about matters of my Ministrie' as he puts it). He was, he claimed, publicly defended by the city authorities, especially the then mayor; and 'when all meanes fayled', the city stepped in to maintain him (Erasmus, sig. A3).

By 1591, when he published *Certaine Questions and Answeres … by Way of Catechising* (STC 4167), Burton had shifted to Bristol at the instigation of Bishop Fletcher, to whom the work is dedicated. When he preached in St Thomas's Church there, he defended the destruction of stained glass, of which the church retained a notable example, on the seemingly Islamic principle that no human image could adequately represent the divine form. In general, however, Burton's sermons and catechetical works had gentler themes, expressed in a lucid and homely style which won him a considerable readership, not least among persons of quality. Yet he was a firm critic of social religion, scorning those who went to hear, or be seen to hear, a fashionable preacher, and then laughed at him 'at … belly's full' (Burton, *A Sermon Preached in the Cathedral Church of Norwich, 1589*, after 1591; STC 4178; quoted in Knappen, 410). In his own sermons there were echoes of the mid-century 'commonwealth' preachers Lever and Latimer, arguing for a radical redistribution of wealth. He was, however, equally critical of those reformers whose patience with the established church was exhausted; he himself remained within the structure.

On 25 November 1591 Burton was instituted to the vicarage of St Giles, Reading. Here, as at Bristol, his congregations urged him to publish his works, and from his time at Reading come *A Caveat for Sureties* (1593; STC 4166: two sermons he had given in Bristol); *Conclusions of Peace, between God and Men* (1594; STC 4169); *An Exposition of the Lord's Prayer* (1595; STC 4174); *David's Evidence* (1596; STC 4170); *David's Thanksgiving … Two Sermons* (1598; repr. with two further sermons 1602; STC 4172–3); *The Rowsing of the Sluggard* (1595; 2nd edn 1595, 1598, 1634; STC 4175–7); and *God Wooing his Church* (1599; STC 4174.5). The *Exposition* is dedicated to the second earl of Essex, and *David's Evidence* to the third Baron Wentworth and his wife, in whose household Burton had lived at a time when he was 'as a drie roote removed and unlikely to finde a place to grow in' and was there protected from unspecified 'stormes and tempestes' by which he was threatened (sig. A2v). On departure he was given books from Wentworth's library and other assistance, presumably financial. Another prominent patron was Sir William Periam, lord chief baron of the exchequer and son-in-law of Lord Keeper Bacon. A lost work, *The Anatomy of Belial* (1602), was dedicated to Ralph Warcupp of English, Oxfordshire. A collection of Burton's writings was published in 1602 (STC 4165a), demonstrating his popular appeal. He also produced a translation of seven dialogues of Erasmus, dedicated to the corporation of Norwich (1606; issued the same year as *Utile dulce*, and reprinted in 1624; STC 10457–8); he hoped he might show that Catholics had no exclusive claim to Erasmus as their man. Finally, in 1608 Burton published *The Christians Heavenly Treasure* (STC 4168), which he dedicated to Sir Dru Drury, gentleman usher of the privy chamber and one of the most forceful of the Norfolk puritan gentry. Burton evidently spent his last years in London, and died in 1616, intestate, in the parish of St Sepulchre, Holborn, where he was perhaps buried. Administration of his goods was granted first, on 17 May, to his son Daniel, but later (2 December 1618), following appeal against the previous grant, to his widow Dorothy Jones, alias Burton.

C. S. KNIGHTON

Sources T. F. Kirby, *Winchester scholars: a list of the wardens, fellows, and scholars of … Winchester College* (1888), 133 • Wood, *Ath. Oxon.*, new edn, 2.1–2 • Foster, *Alum. Oxon.*, *1500–1714*, 1.219 • A. Peel, ed., *The seconde parte of a register*, 2 vols. (1915), vol. 1, p. 244; vol. 2, p. 145 [vol. 1, pp. 157–60 for negative information only] • *The papers of Nathaniel Bacon of Stiffkey*, ed. A. H. Smith and G. M. Baker, 2: 1578–1585, Norfolk RS, 49 (1983), 316 • M. M. Knappen, *Tudor puritanism* (1939), 409–10, 419, 435 • P. Collinson, *The Elizabethan puritan movement* (1967), 141, 176, 188 • [D. Erasmus], *Utile-dulce, or, Trueths libertie: seven wittie-wise dialogues, full of delight … seasonable for all ages, till roomes idolatrie, and womens delicacie be reformed*, trans. W. Burton (1606); repr. (New York, 1973) • registers Gheast and Piers (unclass.), Wilts. & Swindon RO, 3rd foliation, fols. 6v, 7v • administration, PRO, PROB 6/9, fols. 68, 202 • wills, PRO, PROB 11/132, fols. 440v–441

Burton, William (1575–1645), antiquary, was born on 24 August 1575, the eldest son of Ralph Burton (1547–1619) of Lindley, Leicestershire, and Dorothy (*b.* 1550), daughter of William Faunt of Foston, Leicestershire. He was educated, along with his younger brother Robert *Burton (1577–1640), author of *The Anatomy of Melancholy*, at Nuneaton grammar school and then at Brasenose College, Oxford, where he graduated BA on 22 June 1594. He was admitted to the Inner Temple on 20 May 1593 and was called to the bar in 1603, although soon after, because of ill health, he retired to his estate at Fauld in Staffordshire. On 12 May 1607 he married Jane (1589–1632), daughter of Humphrey Adderley of Weddington, Warwickshire, with whom he raised one son, Cassibelan *Burton, and on his father's death in March 1619 he inherited his main estate at Lindley.

Burton was the pivotal figure in a circle of antiquaries operating in the midlands from the 1590s to the 1650s. Initially his main interest was in classical scholarship. He wrote an unpublished Latin comedy, 'De amoribus Perinthii et Tyanthes', in 1596 and the following year, with Thomas Creede, published a translation from the Greek of *The History of Cleitophon and Leucippe*. By this date, however, he had also begun research on the history of his family and its estates. This was to lead to the antiquarian studies that were to be the dominant concern of the remainder of his life. To start with he worked closely with the Staffordshire historian Sampson Erdeswicke, and his assistant William Wyrley, in 1604 writing the preface to a collection

William Burton (**1575–1645**), by Francis Delaram, 1622

of church notes for Leicestershire, intended to be published in Wyrley's name. Over the following years he built a reputation locally as an authority on all things antiquarian and also developed a wide network of correspondents with whom he exchanged and copied manuscripts. These included Sir Robert Cotton, John Selden, and the herald Augustine Vincent. His most prized possession was the text of John Leland's *Itinerary*, which he did much to popularize among his contemporaries and which he eventually donated to the Bodleian Library.

The publication of *The Description of Leicestershire* in 1622 further enhanced Burton's reputation and established him as a father figure to the next generation of local historians. William Dugdale later declared that this work had done much to spark his own interest in local history and during the late 1620s and early 1630s Burton was the driving force in a co-operative project to produce comparable histories of other midland shires. He himself began work on Warwickshire and got halfway through an account of Staffordshire; but by 1636 he was looking to Sir Simon Archer, Thomas Habington, and Sir Christopher Hatton to take on Warwickshire, Worcestershire, and Northamptonshire respectively. *The Antiquities of Warwickshire* was finally completed by Dugdale in 1656, using some of the notes made by Burton forty years earlier. Over the same period Burton was also preparing a second edition of his *Leicestershire*, which had been criticized for genealogical inaccuracies when it first appeared. This was ready in 1638 and, because of illness, he entrusted oversight of its publication to his friend Sir John Lambe, the Laudian dean of the arches. For reasons which are unclear, it never appeared in print. The only surviving manuscript, updated to 1642, was presented by his son to the Staffordshire antiquarian Walter Chetwynd, among whose papers it remained.

Publication of *The Description of Leicestershire* marked an important advance in the writing of county history. It was similar to earlier works, such as Erdeswicke's *Survey of Staffordshire*, in that it combined observation of local topography and curiosities with an account of the descents and achievements of the leading county families; but it set much higher standards of historical scholarship. Burton adopted the sceptical and questioning approach to his source materials befitting a trained lawyer, and provided a rudimentary system of referencing. He also ranged more widely than before, drawing extensively on the public records in the Tower of London, as well as deeds and cartularies in the collections of local gentry. The second edition of *Leicestershire* offered a much expanded account, with more historical and archaeological material and extensively revised genealogies. It incorporated new evidence from the public records and local repositories, material communicated by his friends—such as Sir Thomas Shirley's work on the history of his family—and a new section on the ecclesiastical and secular government of the shire. The end result still fell some way short of Dugdale's *Warwickshire* in terms of the thoroughness of its research and the completeness of its manorial and family histories; however, it was the most comprehensive county history available hitherto.

Like those of many of his fellow antiquaries, Burton's religious sympathies were essentially conservative. He can best be described as a Laudian protestant, in that he had a deep loathing of puritans and strongly approved of efforts to promote 'the beauty of holiness'. In 1623 he restored his own chapel at Lindley and he praised similar schemes elsewhere, notably Laud's refurbishment of St Paul's Cathedral. Several members of his mother's family were Catholics, including his uncle and godfather, Arthur Faunt, a leading Jesuit intellectual whom he greatly admired. This may have influenced his religious attitudes; but they were probably also shaped by his nostalgia for a settled past. He looked back with longing across the divide of the Reformation and associated Calvinism with the destruction of the rich intellectual and artistic heritage of the pre-Reformation church.

Burton was wealthy and prominent enough to have served in local office, but showed no inclination to do so. Nor did he display any interest in politics more generally. His *Leicestershire* was dedicated to the royal favourite, the duke of Buckingham; but this was probably because Buckingham was the county's most famous son rather than out of any ambition for court preferment. During the civil war he sided with the royalists and according to Anthony Wood 'suffered much' (Wood, *Ath. Oxon.*, 3.154). Burton died at Fauld on 6 April 1645 and was buried in the parish church at Hanbury, Staffordshire. RICHARD CUST

Sources J. Nichols, *The history and antiquities of the county of Leicester*, 4 vols. (1795–1815) · W. Burton, 'Leicestershire', Staffs. RO, Chetwynd papers, D649/3/2 [second version in manuscript] · P. Styles, *Studies in seventeenth century west midlands history* (1978) · R. P. Cust, 'Catholicism, antiquarianism and gentry honour: the writings of Sir Thomas Shirley', *Midland History*, 23 (1998) · W. Dugdale, *The antiquities of Warwickshire illustrated*, rev.

W. Thomas, 2nd edn, 2 vols. (1730) • J. R. Broadway, 'Antiquarianism in the midlands and the development of county history, 1586–1656', PhD diss., U. Birm., 1997 • J. R. Broadway, *William Dugdale and the significance of county history in early Stuart England*, Dugdale Society, 39 (1999) • S. A. E. Mendyk, *Speculum Britanniae: regional study, antiquarianism and science in Britain to 1700* (1989) • *The itinerary of John Leland in or about the years 1535–1543*, ed. L. Toulmin Smith, 5 vols. (1906–10); repr. with introduction by T. Kendrick (1964) • D. Williams, 'William Burton's 1642 revised edition of the *Description of Leicestershire*', *Leicestershire Archaeological and Historical Society Transactions*, 50 (1974–5) • T. E. Cogswell, *Home divisions: aristocracy, the state and provincial conflict* (1998) • Wood, *Ath. Oxon.*, new edn • *DNB*

Archives BL, church notes, Warwickshire and Leicestershire collections, Egerton MS 3510 • BL, commonplace book, Add. MS 6046 • BL, notes on Falde, Add. MS 31917 • Staffs. RO, genealogical and historical notes; notes and papers incl. authorial copy of *History of Leicestershire* with annotations and MS notes for second edition; pedigrees | Bodl. Oxf., corresp. with Sir Simon Archer • Coll. Arms, Vincent collection, church notes, pedigrees

Likenesses oils, 1604, S. Antiquaries, Lond. • F. Delaram, line engraving (aged forty-seven), BM, NPG, V&A; repro. in W. Burton, *The description of Leicestershire* (1622), frontispiece [*see illus.*]

Burton, William (*c.*1608–1673), merchant and naval administrator, came from an obscure and probably humble Norfolk family. Nothing is known of his parents. He was apprenticed to a Yarmouth merchant and became a freeman of the town in 1630, a common councillor by 1641, and an alderman in 1649. Burton married in 1644; his wife, Martha, died in 1684 and several of their children also survived him. Yarmouth had a strong puritan element in its population, and Burton was a member of William Bridge's congregationalist church. His part in the civil war is not recorded, but he was clearly a parliamentarian supporter. In 1650 he was commissioned as a major of foot in the Norfolk militia, and he served as bailiff of Yarmouth (equivalent to mayor elsewhere) in 1652–3.

Burton's entry on the national scene came with his choice as a member of the nominated assembly (the Barebone's Parliament) in July 1653, when he was also appointed an admiralty and navy commissioner. The commission had been set up at the end of 1652, after the Commonwealth's initial reverses in the First Dutch War, combining the authority of previously separate admiralty and navy commissions and committees, and was important in turning the war in England's favour during 1653. Although he was dropped from the commission in 1654, Burton's activity as a naval contractor and organizer in charge on the east coast continued unabated.

Burton was classified as a radical in the Barebone's Parliament, but he was not a Fifth Monarchy extremist, and he served as agent for the then admiralty commissioners during the Spanish war in 1656–60. He sat in the protectorate parliaments of 1656–8 and 1659 and his speeches suggest that he was a republican but not an anti-Cromwellian; after the protector's death he was noted to be remembered for funeral mourning. Along with other leading radicals he withdrew from the government of Yarmouth corporation in the spring of 1660. He was temporarily arrested after the Restoration, and was included by the Convention Parliament among the twenty non-regicides who were disqualified for life from ever holding any office again.

Burton's service on the high court of justice, to try royalist rebels and conspirators in East Anglia (December 1650–January 1651), may well have made him enemies among subsequently influential cavaliers. He spent much of the 1660s as a political and religious exile in the Netherlands. His son-in-law was accused of having tried to obtain a pardon by bribery in 1666, and Burton may have been offered one in 1668–9; however, he did not take this up and return home until 1672. His will shows clear evidence of his continuing puritan commitment. In spite of having had to surrender confiscated property acquired during the interregnum and the serious interruption to his business as a merchant and shipowner, his assets were still considerable; his will included an ingenious provision whereby the legacies for his grandchildren by one daughter were to be paid, as far as possible, out of the debt owing to him by the son-in-law who was married to his other daughter—and vice versa. His eldest surviving son, John, later married the daughter of Oliver Cromwell's brother-in-law, Major-General John Desborough, and was to be active in nonconformist whig politics from the 1680s to the early 1700s. At his death in Yarmouth on 8 April 1673 Burton was described locally as 'the late great rebel'. His career exemplifies both the strength of East Anglian puritanism and the role of notables from the middling sort in sustaining the power of the short-lived English republic. He was buried on 10 April. G. E. Aylmer

Sources *CSP dom.*, *1649–72* • C. H. Firth and R. S. Rait, eds., *Acts and ordinances of the interregnum, 1642–1660*, 3 vols. (1911) • A. Woolrych, *Commonwealth to protectorate* (1982) • B. Capp, *Cromwell's navy: the fleet and the English revolution, 1648–1660* (1989) • P. Gauci, *Politics and society in Great Yarmouth, 1660–1722* (1996) • Burton's parliamentary diary • S. R. Gardiner and C. T. Atkinson, eds., *Letters and papers relating to the First Dutch War, 1652–1654*, 6 vols., Navy RS, 13, 17, 30, 37, 41, 66 (1898–1930) • P. Millican, ed., *A miscellany comprising … Baptisms and deaths recorded in the church book of the Great Yarmouth Independent church, 1643–1705*, Norfolk RS, 22 (1951) • *JHC*, 7–8 (1651–67)

Archives Bodl. Oxf., letter-book of the admiralty and navy commissioners, Rawl. MS A461 • Norfolk RO, Yarmouth Assembly MSS

Wealth at death considerable wealth by seventeenth-century provincial standards; £100 to each of ten grandchildren; £200 and £50 plus Yarmouth property to his wife; residue to his son; £50 to another relative: will, PRO, PROB 11/342, sig. 18

Burton, William (1609–1657), antiquary and philologist, was born in Austin Friars, London, the son of William Burton of Atcham in Shropshire. Educated at St Paul's School, he went to Queen's College, Oxford, at Easter 1625. His proficiency in Greek attracted the notice of Thomas Allen of Gloucester Hall, who invited him to take up a lectureship in Greek there. This was not only well earned but also fortunate, for it enabled Burton to continue his studies which he might otherwise have abandoned because of his financial circumstances. He was a Pauline exhibitioner from 1624 to 1632. Although he received the degree of bachelor of civil law in 1630 his financial difficulties necessitated his becoming an assistant to Thomas Farnaby, a famous schoolmaster of Kent.

This experience with Farnaby stood Burton in good stead when he himself became master of the free school at Kingston, Surrey. While working as a teacher he heard of the death of his previous benefactor, Thomas Allen, and this occasioned his first work, his funeral sermon *Laudatio funebris in obitum viri excellentiss. D. Thomae Alleni*, published in London in 1632 and in Oxford in 1633. He may also have been the author of a dedication to another possible patron, Charles Howard, *Nobilissimi herois Dn. Caroli Howardi comitis Nottinghamiae … apotheōsis ad illustrissimum V. Dn. C. Howardum, comitem Nottinghamiae … fratrem superstitem* (1643) which exists only as a single sheet folio. He remained as master of the free school until 1655, when, on being stricken with a palsy, he decided to retire to London, where he lived for a further two years and managed to see the majority of his last book printed: *A commentary on Antoninus his itinerary, or, Journeys of the Roman empire, so far as it concerneth Britain* (1658), which includes an engraving of the author by Wenceslas Hollar.

Burton was above all a noted philologist, and, Wood tells us, 'was an excellent critic and antiquary, and therefore beloved of all learned men of his time, especially of the famous Usher, archbishop of Armagh' (Wood, *Ath. Oxon.*, vol. 3, col. 439). His links with other correspondents of Ussher are reflected in his works: his treatise *Annotations on the First Epistle of Clement the Apostle to the Corinthians* (1647) took Patrick Young's Latin edition of 1633 and translated it; his *Veteris linguae Persicae historia* of 1657, printed with his *Graecae linguae historia* (1657), was thought by some to be by his friend Gerald Langbaine but included an epistle by the same addressed to Burton. Burton's concentration in these works on searching for possible methods to avoid dissension within the church would likewise have commended him to this friendship circle. His decision to translate the utopian work of Johan Heinrich Alsted, *The beloved city, or, The saint's reign on earth a thousand years, asserted and illustrated from 65 places of holy scripture* (1643), points to more eschatological preoccupations.

Burton died on 28 December 1657 and was buried the same day in a vault under the church of St Clement Danes, in the Strand. Wood mentions receiving information about his education from a daughter named Apollonia, who later married a Mr Calverly of Pewter Street in Westminster (Wood, *Ath. Oxon.*, vol. 3, col. 439); it seems likely that she was the child baptized at Kingston on 31 March 1643. Burton's manuscripts and coin collection later came into the hands of Thomas Thynne, who had been his pupil at Kingston. Burton has sometimes been confused with another contemporary antiquarian, the topographer William Burton of Leicestershire, who is best known for his *Description of Leicestershire*. Certainly one of his later biographers, Andrew Kippis, conflated the two authors, but, as Anthony Wood related, the name was a common one during the period, for he himself could list as authors not only our William Burton, but also 'William Burton of Leicestershire, William Burton a divine, and William Burton a pretender to astronomy' (Wood, *Ath. Oxon.*, vol. 3, col. 440). ELIZABETHANNE BORAN

Sources Wood, *Ath. Oxon.*, new edn, 3.438–40 • Foster, *Alum. Oxon., 1500–1714*, 1.219 • R. G. [R. Gough], *British topography*, [new edn], 2 vols. (1780), vol. 1, p. 5 • W. T. Lowndes, *The bibliographer's manual of English literature*, 1 (1834), 309 • S. Knight, *The life of Dr. John Colet, dean of St. Paul's in the reigns of K. Henry VII and Henry VIII, and founder of St Paul's School: with an appendix containing some account of the masters and more eminent scholars of that foundation, and several original papers relating to the said life* (1724), 403–4 • J. Granger, *A biographical history of England from Egbert the Great to the revolution*, 5th edn, 6 vols. (1824), vol. 4, p. 56 • *British Museum general catalogue of printed books … to 1955*, BM, 263 vols. (1959–66), vol. 4, p. 759 • A. Kippis and others, eds., *Biographia Britannica, or, The lives of the most eminent persons who have flourished in Great Britain and Ireland*, 2nd edn, 3 (1784), 41–3 • parish registers, St Clement Danes, City Westm. AC, 28 Dec 1657 [burial]

Archives Hunt. L., papers relating to Roman Britain

Likenesses W. Hollar, etching, BM, NPG; repro. in W. Burton, *A commentary on Antoninus his itinerary, or, Journies of the Romane Empire, so far as it concerneth Britain* (1658)

Burton, William Evans (1804–1860), actor and theatre manager, was born in London on 24 September 1804, the son of William Burton, sometimes called William George Burton (1774–1825), a printer and bookseller and the author of *Researches into the Religion of the Eastern Nations as Illustrative of the Scriptures* (2 vols., 1805). He received a classical education at St Paul's School, and is said to have matriculated at Christ's College, Cambridge, with the intention of entering the church; but at the age of eighteen he was obliged to take charge of his father's printing business. On 10 April 1823 he married Elizabeth, the daughter of John Loft, with whom he had a son, William Shakespeare Burton, an artist. His success in some amateur performances led him to adopt acting as a profession, and in 1825 he joined the Norwich circuit, where he remained for some years. In February 1831 he made his first appearance in London at the Pavilion Theatre, as Wormwood in Samuel Beazley's *The Lottery Ticket*; the following year he played Marrall to the Overreach of Edmund Kean at the Haymarket.

In 1834 Burton went to America, and appeared at the Arch Street Theatre, Philadelphia, on 3 September 1834 as Doctor Ollapod in Colman's *The Poor Gentleman*. His first engagement in New York was at the National Theatre on 31 October 1837, as Guy Goodluck in *John Jones*. On 13 April 1841 he took over the management of the National in New York, but a few weeks later, on 29 May, the building was destroyed by arson; Burton lost his private wardrobe, which had arrived from Philadelphia two days before. For a period he managed theatres in Philadelphia and Baltimore, and in July 1848 he leased Palmo's Opera House, New York, which he renamed Burton's Theatre. Here he produced, with extraordinary success, John Brougham's version of *Dombey and Son*, in which he played Captain Cuttle. In April 1853 he was married to Jane Livingston Hill, an actress, who died, aged thirty-nine, in New York on 22 April 1863, after a period of mental illness. The Metropolitan Theatre, Broadway, New York, came under Burton's management on 8 September 1856, with the title of Burton's New Theatre. Not satisfied with his success in this new house, and unable to compete successfully with Wallack's Lyceum, he gave up its direction in 1858, and commenced starring engagements, his name at this point being familiar throughout the country.

In literature Burton was almost as industrious as in acting. He wrote several plays, the best known being *Ellen Wareham, a Domestic Drama*, produced in May 1833, which was performed at five London theatres at the same time. He was editor of the *Cambridge Quarterly Review*, editor of and entire prose contributor to the *Philadelphia Literary Souvenir* (1838–40), founder and proprietor of the *Philadelphia Gentleman's Magazine*, which he sold after disagreements with his editor, Edgar Allan Poe, and a contributor to many periodicals. His prose sketches were collected in *Waggeries and Vagaries* (1848).

In December 1859 Burton made his last stage appearance, in Hamilton, Ontario. His health was failing for many months before his death, which occurred at 174 Hudson Street, New York, on 9 February 1860. As an actor, he was generally associated with comic characters; his humour was broad and deep, and sometimes approached coarseness, but at the same time was genial and unforced. His power of altering his facial expression was apparently greater than any other actor of his day.

Burton's library, reputedly the largest and best in New York, and especially rich in Shakespearian and other dramatic literature, was sold in the autumn after his death in more than six thousand lots, ten to twenty volumes often forming a lot; a manuscript list of the plays contained in it is held at Harvard University Library. His two residences housed a large collection of paintings, including some rare Italian and Flemish works. His large fortune was ultimately divided among his three daughters, Cecilia, Virginia, and Rosine. G. C. BOASE, *rev.* JOHN WELLS

Sources J. N. Ireland, *Records of the New York stage, from 1750 to 1860*, 2 vols. (1866–7) · Adams, *Drama* · T. A. Brown, *A history of the New York stage from the first performance in 1732 to 1901*, 3 vols. (1903) · G. Ripley and C. A. Dana, eds., *The American cyclopaedia*, 16 vols. (1873–6), vol. 3, p. 479 · F. S. Drake, *Dictionary of American biography, including men of the time* (1872), 147 · *The Era* (4 March 1860), 14 · *Willis's Current Notes* (1852), 38 · W. E. Burton, ed., *The cyclopaedia of wit and humour*, 2 vols. (New York, 1858–64)

Likenesses Homer, engraving?, 1858 (after photograph), repro. in *Ballou's*, 15 (1858), 353 · portrait, *c*.1889, repro. in *Cent.*, 17 (1889), 198 · portrait, *c*.1901, repro. in *The Bookman*, 14 (1901), 55 · portrait, *c*.1901, repro. in *Scribner's Magazine*, 29 (1901), 179 · Inman, portrait (as Dr Ollapod), repro. in *Cent.*, 17 (1889), 197 · T. B. Welch, engraving (after Valentine), Harvard TC · engraving?, repro. in W. E. Burton, *Cyclopædia of wit and humour of America, Ireland, Scotland, and England* (1857)

Wealth at death large fortune: *DNB*

Burton, William Paton (1828–1883), watercolour painter, was born at Madras, the son of William Kinnmont Burton, an officer in the Indian army, and his wife, Maria, *née* Sutter. He was educated in Edinburgh and after a short time studying as a draughtsman in the office of David Bryce, the architect, he turned to painting. He travelled widely in France, the Netherlands, Italy, and Egypt, and produced many drawings of landscapes and old buildings there. In the early 1860s he moved from Edinburgh to London, and about 1867 from London to Witley, in Surrey, where he made studies of the surrounding landscape.

Burton's paintings, of which most are in watercolour but some in oil, have been described as 'confident although generally uninspired' (McEwan). Burton exhibited numerous works at the Royal Scottish Academy, including *View of the Coliseum, Rome* (1855), *Glasgow Cathedral* (1859), *A November Day in Surrey* (1863), and *Antwerp from the River* (1876). He first exhibited at the Royal Academy in 1862, with *Autumn Evening*, and was afterwards a frequent exhibitor there, his works including *Gloaming* (1870), *Semenood, on the Nile* (1875), and *Farm at Cults, Near Aberdeen* (1883). In 1882 he was elected to the Royal Scottish Society of Painters in Watercolour, and in 1883 to the Society of British Artists. He exhibited nine works at Suffolk Street, including *Sunrise and Sunset* (1867) and *Near Amberley, Sussex* (1883–4). He also exhibited at the Glasgow (later Royal Glasgow) Institute of the Fine Arts, where his works included *Haymaking on Meadow Land* (1882).

Burton married Elizabeth Sheild, who predeceased him. He died suddenly on 31 December 1883 at Dumbreck Cottage, Cults, Banchory-Devenick, Kincardineshire.

L. A. FAGAN, *rev.* MARK POTTLE

Sources *The Athenaeum* (Jan 1884) · Bryan, *Painters* (1903–5) · C. B. de Laperriere, ed., *The Royal Scottish Academy exhibitors, 1826–1990*, 4 vols. (1991), vol. 1 · R. Billcliffe, ed., *The Royal Glasgow Institute of the Fine Arts, 1861–1989*, 1 (1990) · J. Johnson, ed., *Works exhibited at the Royal Society of British Artists, 1824–1893, and the New English Art Club, 1888–1917*, 2 vols. (1975) · Graves, *RA exhibitors*, vol. 1 · Mallalieu, *Watercolour artists*, vol. 1 · J. Halsby, *Scottish watercolours, 1740–1940* (1986) · P. J. M. McEwan, *Dictionary of Scottish art and architecture* (1994) · Wood, *Vic. painters*, 2nd edn · d. cert.

Burton, Sir William Westbrooke (1794–1888), colonial judge, was born on 31 January 1794 at Daventry, Northamptonshire, fifth son of Edmond Burton, solicitor, and his wife, Eliza, daughter of the Revd John Mather. When thirteen he left Daventry grammar school to be a midshipman. He was wounded in action in HMS *Conqueror* off Toulon in July 1810, and sought a civil career when peace curtailed naval promotions. He entered the Inner Temple in November 1819, and was called to the bar in November 1824. Chiefly a special pleader, he showed judicial promise as recorder of Daventry between 1826 and 1827.

In 1827 Burton was appointed senior puisne judge at the Cape, where Roman-Dutch law prevailed; he visited Holland to master the language. The Colonial Office, meanwhile, commissioned over his head a Scot, William Menzies, familiar with Roman law. Burton, chafing at his subordinate position (occupied from 1 January 1828), soon had to mediate in disagreements between his two seniors. The Cape's acting governor (later governor of New South Wales), General Richard Bourke, liked Burton and relied on his informal advice.

In 1832 Burton was sent to New South Wales, again as junior of three judges, lamenting his enforced transfer to a judgeship 'not worth holding' in an expensive colony. Bourke, as incumbent governor, renewed their friendship. Sworn in on 22 December 1832, Burton was a competent sole judge, though 'overspeaking' in full court often in dissent. He influenced local legal practice to accord more with English practice.

In 1834 Chief Justice Forbes sought sick leave. Burton so insistently claimed to act in his stead that Forbes deferred departing. Burton's grounds revealed a special pleader's skill, but the Colonial Office dismissed them. When Forbes retired in 1837, Burton pressed to succeed him, supported by Bourke and the Macarthur family with whose 'tory' policies Burton sympathized. He hampered his cause by injudicious court statements seemingly critical of Bourke's administration. James Dowling, who, as senior judge, invoked Lord Brougham's patronage to secure his own promotion, found in Burton an 'unfriend … sadly cut by his disappointment'.

Burton took leave in 1839. In London he published his *State of Religion and Education in New South Wales* (1840) and was presented to the queen. He returned in 1841 to judicial duties, revised the colony's bankruptcy statutes, and published a text on insolvency law. His transfer to Melbourne in 1843 was countermanded by Dowling who wanted a politically neutral appointee.

In 1844 Burton left Australia to join the Madras court, and to receive a coveted knighthood. Soon disliking India, he became preoccupied with domestic concerns. His ailing wife, Margaret, daughter of Leny Smith of Homerton, London, whom he had married on 15 April 1827, went to England and died in September 1846. Likening his future to a 'London November fog', Burton became morose until marrying, on 11 June 1849, Maria Alphonsine, daughter of John Beatty West, MP for Dublin.

Pensionable in 1855, Burton contemplated returning to Sydney but feared the expense. Friends encouraged him. He resigned from the Madras bench he had served well, went to Sydney, and, on 11 August 1857, was appointed to the legislative council, becoming its president in 1858. He added patrician qualities to his reputation as 'a Conservative of the Conservatives'. In 1861 he resigned when a 'swamping' of the legislature was attempted.

An influential Church of England layman, Burton failed to secure establishment of the church in Australia, and attracted controversy because of his perceived religious bias as judge. He returned in frail health to England in 1861, and led a secluded retirement overtaken by blindness. He died, childless, in London on 6 August 1888.

J. M. BENNETT

Sources [E. Digby], ed., *Australian men of mark*, 2 vols. [1889] • K. G. Allars, 'Sir William Westbrooke Burton', *J. Royal Aust. Soc.*, 37 (1951), 257 • H. King, *Richard Bourke* (1971) • C. H. Currey, *Sir Francis Forbes* (1978) • J. M. Bennett, *A history of the supreme court of New South Wales* (1974) • [F. Watson], ed., *Historical records of Australia*, 1st ser., 17–19 (1923) • *Gipps–La Trobe correspondence, 1839–1846*, ed. A. G. L. Shaw (1989) • J. N. Molony, *An architect of freedom* (1973) • *The Times* (13 Aug 1888) • *AusDB*

Archives Mitchell L., NSW, Bourke, James Mitchell, E. Deas Thomson, and Dowling MSS • NL Aus., Dowling MSS

Likenesses lithograph (in old age), repro. in Digby, *Australian men of mark*, facing p. 58 • portrait (in judicial robes), New South Wales, Former Government Printer's collection

Burtt, Joseph (1818–1876), archivist and archaeologist, was born in the parish of St Pancras, London, on 7 November 1818. He was educated by his father, a private tutor, who was a Greek scholar and the author of a Latin grammar. He entered the public service in 1832 under Sir Francis Palgrave, by whom he was employed on work for the record commission at the chapter house of Westminster Abbey. He continued there for more than twenty years, arranging and making inventories of the exchequer and other records then housed in that building. He was taken on to the staff of the Public Record Office in 1840, and in August 1851 was promoted to assistant keeper of the records of the second class. In June 1859 he became a first-class assistant keeper, a position that he held to his death. Over those years Burtt superintended the removal from the chapter house to the new repository in Fetter Lane of the vast mass of documents, many of them unsorted and uncatalogued, which had been kept at Westminster since the Middle Ages. In addition to his ordinary official duties Burtt listed and calendared the chancery records of the palatinate of Durham. He was also employed in his private capacity by Dean Stanley and the chapter of Westminster in sorting and arranging the muniments of the abbey, and began the work of examining and arranging the muniments of the dean and chapter of Lincoln.

In his later years Burtt felt slighted by the appointment of a junior colleague as secretary of the Public Record Office, and was at odds with his seniors. By that time, however, he had begun a second, and by no means subsidiary, career in the emergent discipline of archaeology. In 1862 he became secretary of the Royal Archaeological Institute, and subsequently he took on in addition the editorship of the *Archaeological Journal*. He was for many years a prime mover in the institute and was especially active in organizing its annual congresses. Burtt died, after a protracted illness, at his home, Crofton Lodge, Upper Tulse Hill, London, on 17 December 1876, and was buried in Nunhead cemetery. His wife, Sarah, survived him.

Besides his wide-ranging archival work Burtt contributed archaeological and historical papers to the *Archaeological Journal*, the *Gentleman's Magazine*, *The Athenaeum*, *Archaeologia Cantiana*, and other periodicals. He also edited the 'Household expenses of John of Brabant and of Thomas and Henry of Leicester' for volume 2 of the *Miscellany* (1853) of the Camden Society.

EDMUND VENABLES, *rev.* G. H. MARTIN

Sources E. Venables, *Journal of the Archaeological Institute*, 34 (1877), 90–92 • J. D. Cantwell, *The Public Record Office, 1838–1958* (1991) • private information (1886) • *CGPLA Eng. & Wales* (1877)

Archives Bodl. Oxf., Phillipps MSS

Wealth at death under £600: probate, 5 Jan 1877, *CGPLA Eng. & Wales*

Burwell family (*per. c.*1500–1684), gentry, are of particular interest in demonstrating the ability of merchants and yeomen of enterprise to rise socially in coastal Suffolk, a region largely free from the close attention of resident gentry, by exploiting the opportunities arising from trade and local office. Descending in two lines, based in Sutton and Woodbridge, the family first came to local prominence through the marriage of **Edmund Burwell** (*c.*1500–1561) and Alice (*d. c.*1550), daughter of Thomas Alvard (*d.* 1504) of Woodbridge and Ipswich. Alvard had made a career for himself in Ipswich, being twice elected bailiff and twice MP, the last time in the year of his death. Although he had spent most of his life developing his interests on a wider stage, it was to the Augustinian priory of Woodbridge that his mind returned when he came to make provision for his soul's welfare in masses to be said for himself and his forebears. By his will his three daughters shared the family property in Sutton, consisting of the manors of Fen Hall and Pistries (or Pettistree) with Osmonds. The marriage of Alice Alvard and Edmund Burwell took place about 1515. According to the subsidy list of 1524, an Edmund Burwell was living in Butley, a parish close to Woodbridge, but by the time of his death in 1561 he was established in Woodbridge as yeoman and grocer, with a shared interest in the shipping which sailed from the Deben estuary with the Iceland fishing fleet. He also partnered more substantial Woodbridge and Ipswich merchants in provisioning the English garrison at Calais in its last days. Details are scanty, but he was able to use the profits of his wife's dowry and connections to establish himself as a man of moderate substance. He divided his possessions in such a way that his eldest son, William, and his descendants regarded themselves as landowners rather than merely landholders in Sutton. Nicholas, the second son, inherited the Woodbridge grocery business; the other two sons were given cash payments of £20, two riding horses each, and household equipment and furnishings for the houses in which they were already living, Richard in Sutton and John in Wickham Market, where he also was carrying on a grocer's business.

William Burwell (1515/16–1596) of Sutton developed the potential of the land he had inherited from his father. In 1561 Pistries, in which he had a third share through his mother's dowry, consisted of 52 acres of land, 8 of pasture, 7 of meadow, and 80 of heath and produced cattle and corn. In 1574 and 1579 he purchased the shares of the other Alvard daughters and the adjoining manor of Osmonds. He exploited the poor clay soil on the bank of the estuary by building a kiln to make bricks and tiles, and improved the heathland by foldcourse farming of sheep. The manor house in which he lived was extended and a new parlour and its upper chamber added, equipped with substantial furnishings which he planned should remain in the house as heirlooms. His table silver was engraved with his initials and he habitually wore a gold ring. By 1587 he felt sufficiently socially secure to apply for and receive a grant of arms consisting of a newly designed coat of argent, a saltire gules between four oak leaves, quartered with Alvard. Perhaps his most farsighted action was to establish what became a family custom of sending sons to Cambridge and Gray's Inn. But William's mind was not wholly directed to material prosperity. His wife, Love (*d.* 1609), whom he married in 1560, was the daughter of Thomas Willson, vicar of Sutton. The religious character of the parish was moderately puritan and the children of William's marriage were brought up in this tradition. He died aged eighty on 24 March 1596 and was buried the following day; his memorial brass tablet in Sutton parish church described him as 'gentleman'.

In his will William Burwell remembered the poor, not only of Sutton but also of the neighbouring parishes, with a bequest of 20*s.*, and he gave a further 20*s.* for the repair and maintenance of the church. His wife received for her lifetime the rents of all his purchased lands, once various generous annuities had been allowed for. The main estate was inherited by his eldest son, Francis, while his second son, Thomas, who later became president of the College of Physicians and at the time of his father's death was well launched on his career, received £100 and an annuity of £5. William, the third son, was given his father's gold ring and the spoons marked WB in addition to furniture for his house and the reversion of some land with its foldcourse after his mother's death; he also received an annuity of £5. The testator's surviving brother, John, whose business seems not to have prospered, was given an annuity of 40*s.* Grandchildren, nieces, nephews, and godchildren were all remembered with cash gifts. Francis's legacy, in addition to the family manors, provided the means to sustain the family's prestige: a flock of 200 wethers, the profits of the brick kiln. His wife, Jane Mawe, had her dowry secured to her with an annuity of £20 during her mother-in-law's lifetime. Thus by the end of the sixteenth century the Sutton branch of the Burwell family was established in the ranks of the minor gentry with sons rising in their chosen professions, while maintaining a firm base in the inherited and augmented estate. William Burwell's grandsons were all Cambridge educated: William (*b.* 1593) proceeded to Gray's Inn and was called to the bar in 1640; Thomas *Burwell (1603/4–1673) became a fellow of Trinity Hall and later chancellor of the diocese of Durham; Francis, who inherited the Sutton estates in 1626, was also at Gray's Inn and was subsequently called to the bar.

The grocer's business in Woodbridge inherited by Edmund Burwell's second son, **Nicholas Burwell** (*c.*1517–1583), was also prospering. By his father's will Nicholas had confirmed to him the freehold tenements and premises in Woodbridge:

> according to the tenor and effecte of my granncers will and testament … a fetherbedd with all that thereto longethe which [he] hath in his possession and custody at this present day and a dyaper tabell clothe with a dyaper towell and all these particular parcells as followeth, that is to say my fetherbedd stonding in the parlor with all that thereto is belonging: a silver goblett too silver spoons too brass potts too chislylls too latten candelsticks too buffett stools a counter table too large chistes 12 pieces of pewter too great cobirons and four curtaines of saye colored red and green all which said legacies and giftes to my said sonne Nicholas before beqeathed I will he shall have immeaditly after my decease. (Norfolk RO, Cowlles 39)

There was clearly no disparagement of the second son in entering into a town property that had been held in the same family for four generations. Nicholas married at least twice; his first recorded marriage, to a woman named Agnes (*d.* 1570), took place *c.*1560, the eldest child being born in 1561. He and his second wife, Alice Curtis (*b.* 1549), had four children, all of whom profited from the generous will of their grandmother Margery, widow of William Curtis, a wealthy Woodbridge draper. Ignoring her daughter's step-children, Margery Curtis made handsome bequests to her grandsons John, Anthony, and Edmund and made Margery, her only granddaughter, her residual legatee. **Edmund Burwell** (*bap.* 1574, *d.* 1652) was fortunate in the various legacies he received, not only from his grandmother and father, but also from other members of the extended Burwell family. He was considered to be a suitable husband for Mary Pitman, eldest daughter and eventually coheir of **Jeffrey Pitman** (*bap.* 1561, *d.* 1627) of Woodbridge, draper and haberdasher.

The Pitman family was well established in Woodbridge, although Jeffrey's father, William Pitman, was a citizen of London and member of the Mercers' Company with a house in Fetter Lane and city interests which he passed on to his son. Both had shares in shipping out of Woodbridge and Harwich and were prominent in Woodbridge affairs. The town had a strong corporate sense, and gifts and endowments for the common good were made by the wealthy. Jeffrey Pitman made over tenements whose rents were to be added to the charitable funds of the town. Either he or one of his forebears had presented two silver cups engraved with the Pitman arms to the parish church. But life had dealt hardly with Jeffrey and Alice Pitman. Of their seven children, three died in infancy and their two sons, both students at Gray's Inn, died there in 1613 and 1626. It can hardly have been a consolation to Jeffrey to be made high sheriff of Suffolk in 1625. Alice Pitman died in 1613 and Jeffrey married again; his second wife was Anne Bencher, a widow who was the daughter of Henry Strong of London. They had no children, and when Jeffrey died in 1627 the Pitman inheritance passed to his daughters, Avice, who married William Allston, later the Independent minister of Woodbridge, and Mary, who in 1605 married Edmund Burwell. Although the Pitman family name was lost to Woodbridge with the death of Jeffrey Pitman in 1627, his grandson **Sir Jeffrey Burwell** (1606–1684) not only perpetuated his forename, but also continued to take an active part in the affairs of the town. Educated at the grammar school in Bury St Edmunds, he followed the family tradition through Cambridge and Gray's Inn to become a successful lawyer. In 1629 he acted for the Woodbridge charity trustees over a disputed legacy to the town's Seckford bequest and, having received a fee of £42 for his expenses from the churchwardens, paid for the installing of a west gallery bearing his coat of arms in the parish church.

The profits of Jeffrey Burwell's legal practice must have been considerable, as in 1645 he and his younger brother Nicholas were parties to the sale to Jeffrey of Rougham Hall, near Bury St Edmunds. This then became the family home, where Jeffrey's father, Edmund, died in 1652. The purchase may have been made in anticipation of his marriage to Elizabeth Derehaugh (*d.* 1678), only daughter and heir of Thomas Derehaugh of Colston Hall, Badingham, which took place in 1648. He was knighted in 1663; the grocer's son had broken into the circle of county gentry, and it was by no means an unequal match when Mary Burwell (1654/5–1711), his only daughter and heir, married Robert Walpole of Houghton, Norfolk, MP for Castle Rising and later for King's Lynn. When her father died in 1684 Mary Burwell sold the Rougham estate, but his memory was perpetuated in charitable bequests to the poor of Rougham as well as by a handsome memorial in the parish church.

Robert and Mary Walpole had a family of thirteen children. Their second son was given the forename Burwell; he was killed in 1690 at the battle of Beachy Head. Edward Walpole, their fourth son, started his education in 1674 at Woodbridge School, founded in 1662 with the assistance of a substantial donation from Francis Burwell of Sutton. But the most lasting memorial to the Burwell family of Woodbridge and Sutton was erected on the stable block of the great house at Houghton, built in 1721 by the third son of Mary Burwell and Robert Walpole, Robert Walpole, first earl of Orford. There the arms of Alvard and Burwell of Woodbridge and Sutton were displayed alongside those of Norfolk's gentry and notabilities. JOY ROWE

Sources J. C. Wedgwood and A. D. Holt, *History of parliament*, 1: *Biographies of the members of the Commons house, 1439–1509* (1936), 10 • parish register, Sutton [baptisms, marriages, and burials of Burwells of Sutton] • parish register, Woodbridge, 18 Nov 1574 [baptism, Edmund Burwell] • parish register, Woodbridge, 13 May 1605 [marriage, Edmund Burwell and Mary Pitman] • parish register, Rougham, 1652 [burial, Edmund Burwell] • parish register, Woodbridge, 16 March 1561 [baptism, Jeffrey Pitman] • parish register, Woodbridge, 20 July 1606 [baptism, Jeffrey Burwell] • W. C. Metcalfe, ed., *The visitations of Suffolk made 1561, 1577 and 1612* (1892), 119 • W. H. Rylands, ed., *The visitation of the county of Suffolk, begun … 1664, and finished … 1668*, Harleian Society, 61 (1910) • W. A. Copinger, *The manors of Suffolk*, 7 vols. (1905–11), vol. 4, pp. 11–12, 322; vol. 6, pp. 322–4; vol. 7, pp. 270–76 • F. W. Steer, *The Dandy pedigree*, Proceedings of the Suffolk Institute of Archaeology and History, 27 (1943), 143 • D. MacCulloch and J. Blatchly, *The Wimbill chancel and Rush-Alvard chapel*, Proceedings of the Suffolk Institute of Archaeology and History, 36, pt 2 (1986) • V. B. Redstone, *Bygone Woodbridge* (1893) • Venn, *Alum. Cant.*, 1/1.269 • A. Hervey, ed., *Suffolk in 1524, being the return for a subsidy granted in 1523*, Suffolk Green Books, 10 (1910) • A. Hervey, ed., *Suffolk in 1569, being the return for a subsidy granted in 1566*, Suffolk Green Books, 12 (1909) • A. Hervey, ed., *Suffolk in 1674, being the hearth tax returns*, Suffolk Green Books, 11 (1905) • S. H. A. H. [S. H. A. Hervey], *Biographical list of boys educated at King Edward VI Free Grammar School, Bury St Edmunds, from 1550 to 1900* (1908) • M. A. Weaver and J. N. Stevens, *St Mary's Church, Woodbridge guide* (1981) • A. Simpson, *East Anglian studies: the wealth of the gentry* (1961) • D. MacCulloch, *Suffolk and the Tudors: politics and religion in an English county, 1500–1600* (1986) • J. Corder, *Dictionary of Suffolk arms*, Suffolk RS, 7 (1965) • J. Corder, *Dictionary of Suffolk crests*, Suffolk RS, 40 (1998) • Suffolk RO, Ipswich, Calais account 1556–7, HA 411/1/1/1/1 • will, Norfolk RO, wills register, Cowlles 39 [Edmund Burwell] • will, Suffolk RO, Ipswich, 1C/AA1/27/142 [will of Nicholas Burwell] • will, Suffolk RO, Ipswich, 1C/AA1/34/44 [will of William Burwell] • will of John Burwell, Suffolk RO, Ipswich, 1C/AA1/58/61 • will of Jeffrey Pitman, PRO, PROB 11/152, fols. 67–70 • will of Francis Burwell, PRO, PROB 11/152, fols. 271*v*–273*r* • memorial, Sutton parish church [William Burwell] • memorial, Woodbridge parish church [Jeffrey Pitman] • memorial, Rougham parish church [Jeffrey Burwell]

Likenesses attrib. G. Janssen, group portrait, marble effigies, *c.*1627 (Jeffrey Pitman and family), Woodbridge parish church • J. Hoskins, miniature (Nicholas Burwell) • double portrait, crayon drawing (Sir Jeffrey Burwell with his wife)

Burwell, Edmund (*c.*1500–1561). *See under* Burwell family (*per.* *c.*1500–1684).

Burwell, Edmund (*bap.* 1574, *d.* 1652). *See under* Burwell family (*per.* *c.*1500–1684).

Burwell, Sir Jeffrey (1606–1684). *See under* Burwell family (*per.* c.1500–1684).

Burwell, Nicholas (c.1517–1583). *See under* Burwell family (*per.* c.1500–1684).

Burwell, Thomas (1603/4–1673), civil lawyer, was the fifth son of Francis Burwell of Sutton, Suffolk, and his wife, Jane, daughter of Simon Mawe of Rendlesham, Suffolk. He was admitted to Peterhouse, Cambridge, aged sixteen, in 1620, graduating BA in 1624 and proceeding MA from Trinity Hall in 1627. He was a fellow of Trinity Hall, the nursery of civilian (ecclesiastical) lawyers from 1626 to 1632. As such he gained experience of civil law and practice by sitting a good deal between 1629 and 1631 as surrogate to the chancellor of the Ely consistory court. In 1632 Burwell was appointed chancellor of the diocese of Durham, and on 19 February 1633 he married Anne, daughter of Seth Chapman of Bury St Edmunds, with whom he had three daughters and three sons. At Durham Burwell aligned himself with the Laudian faction led by John Cosin, then a canon of the cathedral—so much so that in 1642 he was impeached for sending a puritan canon to London in a cart. In the interregnum he was sheltered by his brother in Suffolk.

At the Restoration Burwell was created LLD at Cambridge. He resumed his duties at Durham and was also appointed chancellor of York. This was a strange choice, as there was a long-standing rivalry between York and Durham arising from conflicting jurisdictions between the two dioceses. Durham claimed that the archbishop had no right of visitation in Durham as he had in Chester and Carlisle. More serious was the dispute over the jurisdiction of the spiritualities of Durham during a vacancy, which affected the consistory court and the fees for the administration of the diocese going to York or remaining in Durham. The dispute went back to 1286 and was exacerbated by the Reformation. Third, there were difficulties which arose from two peculiars in the York diocese where Durham had ecclesiastical jurisdiction. In 1638 Burwell had been summoned to the high commission in York for not recognizing York testamentary jurisdiction and had declared that he would 'answer and try it with Dr Leggatt', the judge of the York court (Borth. Inst., HC, CP. ND/12 and Rvii, PL 138). However, on his appointment to York he did not resign his post at Durham. At York he was the archbishop's chief lay officer, presiding (in the prelate's invariable absence) over the archbishop's three courts. He could also be involved in purely administrative matters: for example, in 1661 he was appointed to the commission to oversee the restoration of the see's temporalities or possessions. To add to all this Burwell was in 1661 elected as MP for Ripon through the good offices of the archbishop. He remained an MP until his death in 1673. He was described as a 'very active committee man', serving on no fewer than 126 committees (Bolton, 1.753). At Durham he was again closely associated with the Laudian Cosin, now bishop. In parliament he was involved with the passing of the Clarendon code and voted against toleration for dissenters, pronouncing 'a puritan was ever a rebel'. He was naturally concerned mainly with church matters: the maintenance of the urban clergy; the Act of Uniformity; and the revised prayer book. In 1668 he defended the ecclesiastical courts when they came under fire and he strongly resisted the enfranchisement of Durham as being against the prince bishop's interests.

Parliament normally sat from the end of September until Easter. This left only the summer (Trinity) term (plus occasional and irregular visits at other times) for Burwell to attend his two northern dioceses. In fact Durham had the lion's share, because his main home was there; indeed his wife was the stepdaughter of the dean, John Sudbury. In York the work was left mainly to the two resident advocates, an unsatisfactory arrangement, against which there were some appeals, as one of them might be sitting in a case where he also represented one of the litigants. So matters continued until the death of Bishop Cosin on 15 January 1672. It was the first Durham vacancy since the Restoration and the match was laid to the tinder. On 20 January the Durham dean and chapter were inhibited by Richard Sterne, the archbishop of York, from assuming the administration of the diocese during the vacancy. Burwell ignored this and acted for the dean and chapter, only to be cited to York for contempt in ignoring the inhibition. The case was not heard until 18 April, when Sterne sat himself at Bishopthorpe, and Burwell and Dean Sudbury were represented by proctors. On 17 May Sterne excommunicated his own chancellor. The archbishop's case was prohibited at the court of king's bench on the grounds of a 1587 judgment in favour of Durham. From this time, and until March 1673, Burwell reversed the pattern of twelve years and sat regularly in his York courts, hoping, no doubt, to re-establish his authority there. He was helped in this by the fact that parliament was prorogued from 24 March 1672 to 25 March 1673. Despite the unusual length of the Durham vacancy the case was not concluded at that time, nor at any time since. An informal arrangement between the two dioceses has in more recent vacancies avoided bad blood, but in fact the *Guinness Book of Records* lists the dispute as 'the most protracted (unresolved) litigation' in English history (*Guinness Book of Records*, 1993, 184).

Burwell returned to London for the reopening of parliament in March 1673 but died immediately, his funeral being held in St Margaret's, Westminster, on 25 March. His career exemplifies many of the weaknesses of the church courts after the failure to reform them at the Restoration: the overlapping and competing jurisdictions; the danger of prohibitions from the secular courts; the plurality of offices held by a single person; the frequent absences of the principal officers which led to inefficiency, delays, and consequently increased fees, and even serious abuses. These problems were not addressed at the next opportunity for reform in 1688. BARRY TILL

Sources B. D. Till, 'The ecclesiastical courts of York' (typescript), Borth. Inst. • B. D. Till, *York against Durham: the guardianship of the spiritualities in the diocese of Durham 'sede vacante'*, Borthwick paper, no. 84 (1993) • P. A. Bolton, 'Burwell, Thomas', HoP, *Commons, 1660–90*, 1.752–3 • I. M. Green, *The re-establishment of the Church of England*,

1660–1663 (1978) • A. Whiteman, 'The restoration of the Church of England', *From uniformity to unity, 1662–1962*, ed. G. Nuttall and O. Chadwick (1962), 19–88 • J. Spurr, *The Restoration Church of England, 1646–1689* (1991) • W. J. Sheils, 'The restoration of the temporalities: Archbishop Frewen's commissioners, 1661–1662', *Borthwick Institute Bulletin*, 1 (1975), 17–30 • D. Marcombe, 'The dean and chapter of Durham, 1558–1603', PhD diss., U. Durham, 1973 • archbishop's register, 33, Borth. Inst. • LPL, MS 3403 • U. Durham L., archives and special collections, Misc C, dean and chapter loose papers • Durham Cath. CL, Hunter MSS • dean and chapter act book, York Minster Library, H4 • York high commission papers, Borth. Inst., HC.CP.ND/12 • articles, Borth. Inst., Rvii, PL 138 • CUL, EDR D2/43 and 44 • W. A. Copinger, *The manors of Suffolk*, 7 vols. (1905–11), vol. 7, pp. 270, 272 • J. Keble, *Reports in the court of king's bench … from the 12th to the 30th year of the reign of … Charles II*, 3 vols. (1685), vol. 3 • *The reports of Sir Peyton Ventris, kt.*, 2 vols. (1726), vol. 2 • Venn, *Alum. Cant.* • *Calendar of the manuscripts of Major-General Lord Sackville*, 2 vols., HMC, 80 (1940–66), vol. 1, p. 322

Burwell, William (1515/16–1596). *See under* Burwell family (*per.* c.1500–1684).

Bury. For this title name *see* Keppel, William Coutts, seventh earl of Albemarle and Viscount Bury (1832–1894).

Bury, Arthur (1623/4–1713), college head and writer on theology, was probably born at Sidbury, Devon, the son of John *Bury (1580–1667), the vicar there, and his wife, Agnes (*d.* 1644). He matriculated at Exeter College, Oxford, on 5 April 1639, aged fifteen, graduated BA on 29 November 1642, and became fellow the following year. Deprived of his fellowship by the parliamentary visitors in 1648, he went to live with his father in Devon, probably in Exeter. While in the county he married his first wife, whose name is unknown. They had two sons, John, the elder, born in 1654, and Arthur.

At the Restoration Bury regained his fellowship at Exeter College, along with a prebend of Exeter and a royal chaplaincy. At the prompting of Charles II he was elected rector of his college on 27 May 1666. His first wife having died, on 5 May 1669 he was licensed to marry Mary Southcote, widow of George Southcote of Exeter. His son John, who had matriculated at Exeter College in 1668, became a fellow in 1672, but died in 1685. Bury proved a considerable benefactor to his college, spending £700 to improve its buildings, but although Humphrey Prideaux, dean of Norwich, considered him one of the more able heads of houses, the rector often clashed with his fellows and the university authorities. He became embroiled in serious difficulties in October 1689 when he expelled James Colmer, a fellow, for fornication. Colmer responded by charging Bury with 'heresy, taking of bribes, and grievous incontinency' (*Hist. U. Oxf.* 5: *18th-cent. Oxf.*, 396). When the visitor, Sir Jonathan Trelawney, bishop of Exeter, arrived to investigate in July 1690, the rector and his supporters refused him entry.

Bury's position had already become untenable following his publication in spring 1690 of *The Naked Gospel*. Intended as a persuasive to prayer book reform and doctrinal comprehension, this treatise sought to revive primitive Christianity, freed of later corruptions. The doctrine of the Trinity, Bury argued, was one such accretion. Not only was it irrelevant but actually counter-productive, in that the disputes it engendered frustrated protestant union and distracted sincere Christians from cultivating practical holiness.

The *Naked Gospel* provoked a flurry of responses, including pamphlets by William Nichols and Thomas Long. The ensuing Trinitarian controversy shook Oxford for the rest of the decade, particularly after two champions of orthodoxy, Robert South and William Sherlock, accused one another of heresy. Though applauded by liberals like John Locke and the unitarian philanthropist Thomas Firmin, who had reportedly subsidized its publication, the work was condemned by the university's convocation and publicly burnt on 19 August 1690 for its alleged Socinianism. Bury was deposed and excommunicated, but still refused to leave his college. His defenders also included the notorious Oxford whig James Parkinson, who hailed the rector as a victim of tory persecution in his *Fire's Continued at Oxford* (1690). Bury justified his conduct and attempted to clarify his ideas in *The Account Examined* (1690). In *The Danger of Delaying Repentance* (1692), a sermon preached in the university church, he not only denied the charge of Socinianism but issued a scathing indictment of Calvinism and the gloomy introspection he claimed it fostered. Indeed, his dissatisfaction with contemporary Calvinism, rather than an attachment to any particular notions of the Trinity, lay at the heart of Bury's theological radicalism, which was evident well before *The Naked Gospel*, especially in his sermon before the Sons of the Clergy, *Not Fear, but Love* (1683). Not surprisingly it was he who cast one of only two votes in favour of the Arminian George Bull for Lady Margaret professor in 1691.

Bury was finally forced to leave Exeter College when, in January 1695, the House of Lords upheld his deprivation. He then settled in Westminster, though he still held a portion of the vicarage of Bampton, Oxfordshire, until his resignation in 1707. He died at Compton Durville, in the parish of South Petherton, Somerset, on 3 May 1713 and was buried three days later. His widow was probably the Maria Bury buried there on 8 June 1714. Both were survived by Bury's younger son Arthur, a fellow of King's College, Cambridge, and then a physician at Exeter, who died in 1725.

Jim Benedict

Sources C. W. Boase, ed., *Registrum Collegii Exoniensis*, new edn, OHS, 27 (1894), cxxviii–cxxxiii, 77, 107–8, 118–19, 271, 371 • W. Cotton and J. Dallas, eds., *Notes and gleanings: a monthly magazine devoted chiefly to subjects connected with the counties of Devon and Cornwall*, 4 (1888–92), 65–71 • [A. Bury], *The account examined, or, A vindication of Dr. Arthur Bury* (1690) • [J. Parkinson], *The fire's continued at Oxford* (1690) • Wood, *Ath. Oxon.*, new edn, 4.482–3 • *The life and times of Anthony Wood*, ed. A. Clark, 2, OHS, 21 (1892), 78, 319 • *The life and times of Anthony Wood*, ed. A. Clark, 3, OHS, 26 (1894), 53, 68, 325, 329–30, 330, 334, 337–41, 345, 364, 425, 440, 452, 474, 479 • N. Tyacke, 'Religious controversy', *Hist. U. Oxf.* 4: *17th-cent. Oxf.*, 569–620, esp. 616–17 • *Letters of Humphrey Prideaux … to John Ellis*, ed. E. M. Thompson, CS, new ser., 15 (1875), 111–12 • *Remarks and collections of Thomas Hearne*, ed. C. E. Doble and others, 1, OHS, 2 (1885), 231, 241–2, 301 • *Remarks and collections of Thomas Hearne*, ed. C. E. Doble and others, 2, OHS, 7 (1886), 72 • *Remarks and collections of Thomas Hearne*, ed. C. E. Doble and others, 8, OHS, 50 (1907), 144–5 • F. W. Weaver and C. H. Mayo, *Notes and Queries for Somerset and Dorset*, 3 (1893), 98 • *N&Q*, 7 (1853), 473–4 • *N&Q*, 3rd ser., 1 (1862), 264 • Greaves & Zaller, *BDBR*, 282–4 [T. Firmin] • *Fifth report*, HMC, 4 (1876), esp. 376 [J. R.

Pine-Coffin] • *Hist. U. Oxf.* 5: *18th-cent. Oxf.*, 394–6 • *The correspondence of John Locke*, ed. E. S. De Beer, 4 (1979), 12, 22, 150–51 • *CSP dom.*, *1665–6*, 375 • J. Spurr, *The Restoration Church of England, 1646–1689* (1991), 276, 385 • J. Walker, *An attempt towards recovering an account of the numbers and sufferings of the clergy of the Church of England*, pt 2 (1714), 115–6 • J. A. I. Champion, *The pillars of priestcraft shaken: the Church of England and its enemies, 1660–1730* (1992), 107–8, 116, 120 • Foster, *Alum. Oxon.*

Archives BL, account of *The naked gospel* | BL, testimonial for M. Cartier, Add. MS 4275, fol. 42 • Bodl. Oxf., examination of one Arthur Berry, May 1655, as a royalist

Likenesses portrait; formerly in the Corporation of the Poor, New Buildings, Exeter, in 1893

Bury, Charles Kenneth Howard- (1883–1963), mountaineer and army officer, was born at Charleville Castle, King's county, Ireland, on 15 August 1883, the only son of Captain Kenneth Howard-Bury (1846–1885), army officer, and his wife, Lady Emily Alfreda Julia (1856–1931), youngest daughter of Charles William Bury, third earl of Charleville. He had one sister, Marjorie (1885–1907). His mother had become heir to the estates at Charleville Forest, King's county, after the last of her brothers and uncles died in 1875, and the peerage became extinct. His father, a grandson of the sixteenth earl of Suffolk and Berkshire, assumed the additional surname of Bury after their marriage in 1881; on his death in 1885, Lord Lansdowne, viceroy of India and a relative, was appointed to be Howard-Bury's guardian. He was educated privately at Charleville, at Eton College, and at the Royal Military College in Sandhurst (1902–4).

Howard-Bury joined the 60th rifles in 1904 and was posted to India, where he went travelling and big game-hunting. In 1905 he secretly entered Tibet without permission and was rebuked by Lord Curzon. His early travel diaries date from 1906 and show his keen powers of observation, encyclopaedic knowledge of natural history, and linguistic ability. In 1912 he inherited Belvedere House, Mullingar, co. Westmeath, from a cousin, Charles Brinsley Marlay. In that year he spent six months in the Tien Shan (Tianshan) Mountains. Although he prepared a draft book from his diaries, it was not published until 1990, as *The Mountains of Heaven*. He resumed army duties in 1915 and commanded the 7th and 9th battalions of the King's Royal Rifles (dispatches seven times; DSO in 1918). He served at Arras, the Somme, Passchendaele, and Ypres, where he was captured; he remained a prisoner of war at Fürstenberg until 1919.

After the war the Royal Geographical Society was eager to attempt the ascent of Mount Everest, but political opposition from Tibet and from the British government remained an obstacle. In 1920 Howard-Bury travelled to India at his own expense to lobby the government of India. He met the viceroy and other British officials, including Charles Bell, the political officer in Sikkim, who shortly afterwards received permission from Tibet for an Everest expedition in 1921. Though not an experienced climber, Howard-Bury was offered the leadership of the first Everest expedition partly in recognition of his role in persuading British officials to obtain permission from Tibet. Howard-Bury led a diverse expedition of surveyors, climbers, and military officers, which achieved the goals of surveying Everest and finding a route to the summit for later climbers. He wrote *Mount Everest: the Reconnaissance, 1921* (1922), which later appeared in French and Dutch and a shorter version in 1991. A variety of white primula discovered during the expedition was named after him, *Primula buryana*. He was awarded the founders' medal of the Royal Geographical Society and gold medals from the French Geographical Society and Club Alpin Français (French Alpine Club).

The Everest expedition made Howard-Bury a public figure and in 1922 he was elected to parliament for Bilston (South Wolverhampton) as a Unionist. He served as parliamentary private secretary to the under-secretary of state for war from 1922 to 1924, when he lost his seat. He was elected as MP for Chelmsford in 1926, but retired in October 1931, after he inherited his ancestral castle at Charleville on the death of his mother. He served as deputy lieutenant and JP in co. Westmeath and also honorary colonel to the 85th East Anglian field brigade of the Territorial Army from 1927 to 1932. During the Second World War he was appointed an assistant commissioner of the British Red Cross.

About 1940 Howard-Bury met Rex Beaumont (1914–1988), an actor with the Royal Shakespeare Company then in the Royal Air Force, who became his close friend and heir. In the post-war period Howard-Bury and Beaumont restored Belvedere House and gardens and built a villa at Dar al-Oued in Hammamet, Tunis. Dar al-Oued became a meeting-place for creative personalities and authors such as André Gide, Sacheverell Sitwell, and Dame Freya Stark. Howard-Bury and Beaumont continued to entertain many writers, explorers, politicians, and clerics at Dar al-Oued and at Belvedere, and became close friends with Colonel H. al Bourguiba, first president of Tunisia. The only known portrait of Howard-Bury was painted at Dar al-Oued by Paul Hannaux. He was 6 feet 2 inches tall, had the appearance of a distinguished gentleman, and was widely known as 'Monsieur Le Colonel'. Howard-Bury died of old age at Belvedere House on 20 September 1963 and was buried in his family's vault in St Katherine's Church, Tullamore. He bequeathed Charleville to a cousin and Belvedere to Rex Beaumont. He never married.

MARIAN KEANEY

Sources Westmeath county library, Mullingar, Howard-Bury MSS • private MSS, priv. coll., Mullingar, Westmeath • private information (2004) • A. Reynolds, 'The man who walked off the map', MA diss., Maynooth University, 1991 • *The Times* (21 Sept 1963) • R. Illingworth, 'The political career of Charles Howard-Bury' [unpublished typescript] • sale catalogue (1980) [Belvedere House sale; Christies, Westmeath, 1980] • W. Unsworth, *Everest*, another edn (1991) • Burke, *Gen. Ire.* (1976) • C. K. Howard-Bury, *Mountains of heaven: travels in the Tian Shan Mountains, 1913*, ed. M. Keaney (1990) • C. Howard-Bury and G. L. Mallory, *Everest reconnaissance: the first expedition, 1921*, ed. M. Keaney (1991)

Archives NL Scot., notebooks relating to the Everest expedition • priv. coll. • RBG Kew, *Primula buryana* • RGS • TCD, papers, incl. prisoner-of-war diaries • Westmeath county library, Mullingar, family papers | U. Nott., Marlay MSS, ed. R. Warwick Bond | FILM National Film Archive, Dublin, film of Howard-Bury's villa and gardens at Dar al-Oued, Hammamet, Tunis

Likenesses P. Hannaux, oils, 1950 • photographs, Westmeath county library, Mullingar, Ireland • photographs, priv. coll.
Wealth at death £58,964: probate, 13 April 1964, *CGPLA Éire*.

Bury, Charles Rugeley (1890–1968), chemist, was born in Northfield End, Henley-on-Thames, on 29 June 1890, the first child of Charles Rugeley Bury (1849–1916), a non-practising solicitor, and his wife, Aimee Gwynneth Pryse (1867–1963). His mother was a direct descendant of Sir Richard Pryse of Plas Gogerddan Manor near Aberystwyth, who was created a baronet by Charles I. Her second name is a typical Welsh forename and she was very proud of her pedigree. Bury was nicknamed Dick by his nanny and this name persisted within the family. In 1895 they moved to Ellfield in Wotton under Edge in the Cotswolds. He was educated at a Leamington preparatory school and Malvern College, thence gaining an entrance scholarship to Trinity College, Oxford (1908), where he graduated in 1912 with first-class honours in chemistry. He then spent a year demonstrating in the joint Trinity–Balliol chemical laboratory and during 1912/13 spent some months at Göttingen University before being appointed assistant lecturer in chemistry in the University of Wales at Aberystwyth.

Immediately the First World War started Bury volunteered for the 5th Gloucestershire regiment, was soon commissioned, and experienced a variety of active service in the western front trenches, the Middle East, and eventually as captain of an independent command which traversed Persia to the southern Caspian to secure the Baku oilfields. He suffered a skull wound at Kut in 1917 but recovered completely.

After being demobilized in 1919 Bury returned to Aberystwyth to teach physical chemistry in an understaffed department heavily overcrowded with ex-service students and inadequately equipped for such numbers. In these difficult circumstances he composed his first and by far his most important publication, entitled 'Langmuir's theory of the arrangement of electrons in atoms and molecules', published in the *J. Amer. Chem. Soc.*, (43, 1921, 1602–8). This momentous advance in understanding electronic atomic and molecular structure was written independently with no opportunity for consultation with any chemist of like interest. In this very concise paper Bury corrected Langmuir's conclusions and gave an alternative unifying summary of the chemical properties of all the elements up to uranium in terms of his new electronic structures. This version, often attributed to Niels Bohr, appeared in many subsequent chemistry texts.

Bury predicted that an, as yet unknown, element of atomic number 72 should exist, and that it would not be a rare earth but would resemble zirconium. The discovery of element no. 72 (hafnium) was announced by Hevesy and Coster in *Nature* in 1923. There can be no doubt that their successful search was prompted by Bury's paper but there is no mention of the latter's prediction in their report. Another Bury prediction was that there would be a further series of elements heavier than uranium; twenty-five years later the transuranic elements were discovered.

Bury's second major contribution to chemical theory, entitled 'Auxochromes and resonance', appeared later in *J. Amer. Chem. Soc.* (57, 1935, 2115–17). By applying the concept of 'resonance' (later termed electron delocalization) he proposed a rational electronic correlation of the effects of structural variations on the colours of diverse classes of organic dyes. The London Chemical Society rejected this paper on the ground that it 'had no new experimental data' (Davies, 87). However, immediately after its American publication, Bury's ideas provoked the initiation of intense research activity in dye chemistry in Britain, Switzerland, and especially at the Eastman Kodak Laboratories in the USA.

The laboratories at Aberystwyth possessed little sophisticated equipment. Nevertheless, Bury showed exceptional ingenuity in devising elegant research schemes requiring little beyond precise temperature control, accurate chemical analysis, and competent use of the sensitive Beckmann thermometer. These involved accurate measurements of physico-chemical properties such as freezing points, densities, specific heats, and viscosities, as well as phase rule studies; they were the basis of his third, less spectacular, but very substantial contribution to physical chemistry, recorded in some thirty publications over two decades. By using butyric acid solutions as a model system he unravelled fundamental aspects of soap and soap–acid chemistry. The intensely rancid odour of butyric acid pervading his research laboratories and lingering on clothing caused his research students occasional embarrassment in college social events and may well have terminated some budding romances.

Soon after returning to Aberystwyth, Bury met Emily Frances Margaret Adams, known as Peggy, a striking golden-redhead who lectured in the agricultural botany department. They married on 11 July 1922. Their son, John (1925–2000), was keenly interested in theatre design and eventually became head of design in the National Theatre. Their daughter, Anne (*b.* 1927), worked at Barclays Bank.

Bury was a tall, handsome man of upright military bearing but of few words, with a rather retiring, modest personality; he never quoted his own publications to his student classes. He did not seem to enjoy lecturing but was at his best in small tutorial groups which he conducted for final-year students. These were enjoyable occasions when he relaxed completely, and his criticisms of student essays were always constructive and encouraging, occasionally spiced with his logical, dry humour. He was a very individual, markedly unconventional character, especially in dress, hairstyle, and general appearance, and his ancient cars were often the subject of humorous student pranks.

An acknowledged expert on the phase rule, Bury left Aberystwyth in 1943 to become leader of the phase rule section at ICI in Billingham. On retirement from ICI in 1952 he and his wife moved to a pretty old cottage in East Dean on the South Downs. Here he enjoyed his hobby as an amateur painter of considerable merit; he donated one of his canvases to the art department at Aberystwyth.

Although Bury's major papers commanded worldwide interest there was little public recognition for his work apart from his election to the council of the prestigious Faraday Society. This may partly be due to his own retiring disposition and to the fact that these papers were published in America and fourteen years apart. However, there is no record of his having expressed any disappointment or bitterness. Bury died of a stroke at his home, Walnut Tree Cottage, East Dean, Sussex, on 24 December 1968 and was buried at East Dean church. J. B. Bowen

Sources M. Davies, 'Charles Rugeley Bury and his contribution to physical chemistry', *Archive for History of Exact Sciences*, 36 (1986), 75–90 • annual reports of the University College of Wales, Aberystwyth to its court of governors, 1921–41, U. Wales, Aberystwyth, archive • personal knowledge (2004) • private information (2004) • *Nature*, 222 (1969), 805

Wealth at death £94,351: probate, 6 March 1969, *CGPLA Eng. & Wales*

Bury [*née* Campbell], **Lady Charlotte Susan Maria** (**1775–1861**), novelist and diarist, was born on 28 January 1775 at Argyll House, Oxford Street, London, the youngest child of John Campbell, fifth duke of Argyll (1723–1806), army officer and politician, and Elizabeth (1734–1790), second daughter of John Gunning of Castle Coot in co. Roscommon, widow of James Hamilton, sixth duke of Hamilton, and at one time lady of the bedchamber to Queen Charlotte. As a young woman, Lady Charlotte was noted for her beauty: in 1791 Horace Walpole wrote that 'everyone admires' her 'person and understanding' (Walpole, 188). Her contemporaries also praised her 'charming manners, all ease and simplicity' (*Memoir*, ed. Grant, 137). Maria Edgeworth, who met her in 1830, thought her 'agreeable—unaffected—free from authorship pretension or pretension of any sort' (*Letters from England*, 448).

Until 1809 Lady Charlotte was frequently in Edinburgh, where she entertained many of the literary celebrities of the day. It was at one of her parties that Sir Walter Scott met Matthew Lewis, and she was also a long-standing friend of the novelist Susan Ferrier. Her first publication, *Poems on Several Occasions*, appeared anonymously in 1797, when she was twenty-two. The poems are mainly sentimental and melancholic, written on such fashionable topics of the day as the simple virtues of highland peasants and the transitory nature of fame and happiness. In 'An Ode to Evening' Lady Charlotte describes her work as 'artless lines' which

> impart
> The soften'd feelings of the heart.
> (*Poems*, 5)

On 14 June 1796 Lady Charlotte married her distant cousin Colonel John Campbell (eldest son of Walter Campbell of Shawfield and his first wife, Eleanora Kerr), who, at the time of his death in Edinburgh on 15 March 1809, was member of parliament for the Ayr burghs. The couple had nine children, of whom only two—Lady A. Lennox and Mrs William Russell—survived Lady Charlotte.

In 1810 Lady Charlotte was appointed lady-in-waiting in the household of the princess of Wales, afterwards Queen Caroline, and began keeping a diary, in which she recorded the foibles and failings of the princess and other members of the court. Lady Charlotte also began her career as a novelist at this time, publishing *Self-Indulgence* anonymously in 1812. She left her position at court in May 1815, and on 17 March 1818, in spite of the reservations of friends such as Sir Walter Scott, she married the Revd (Edward) John Bury, the only son of Edward Bury of Taunton. Educated at University College, Oxford (BA 1811, MA 1817), John Bury became rector of Lichfield, Hampshire, in 1814. Lady Charlotte Bury had two daughters from this marriage, but throughout it she was short of money, and it was probably her financial difficulties which led her to begin writing fiction again in the 1820s. She published *Conduct is Fate* in 1822, following it by more than a dozen other novels, the last of which, *The Two Baronets*, was published posthumously in 1864.

Some of Lady Charlotte's novels were once very popular, including *Flirtation* (1827), which went into a third edition in 1828; *The Divorced* (1837), which was also published in both France and America; and *The History of a Flirt* (1840), which was reissued in the Parlour Novels series in the 1850s. According to one commentator, she earned as much as £200 for a novel at the height of her career (Steuart, ix), but the books were less successful with critics. They were not extensively reviewed, and Lady Holland wrote dismissively of *Alla giornata* (1826) that 'it is said to be better than her former publications. It had need be so to be worth anything' (Adburgham, 121). Most of these works originally appeared without her name, but even at the time there does not seem to have been any secret as to the identity of the writer. The novels have attracted some scholarly attention in studies of the 'silver fork' literature of the 1820s and 1830s, but none of them has been reissued in the twentieth century. In addition to her fiction, Lady Charlotte also wrote *Suspira santorum, or, Holy Breathings* (2 vols., 1826), a collection of prayers, and a year after her husband's death at Ardenample Castle, Dunbartonshire, in May 1832, she published *The Three Great Sanctuaries of Tuscany* (1833), a poem illustrated by him. She also edited two novels, Caroline Lucy Scott's *Marriage in High Life* (1828), and Catherine Gore's *Memoirs of a Peeress, or, The Days of Fox* (1837).

Lady Charlotte Bury was best-known, however, for her *Diary Illustrative of the Times of George IV* (2 vols.); when it appeared anonymously in 1838, it was thought to bear evidence of a familiarity with the scenes depicted which could only be attributed to Lady Charlotte. It was reviewed with much severity, and attributed to her by both the *Edinburgh* and the *Quarterly* reviews. Thackeray also mocked the *Diary* in his 'Skimmings from the Dairy of George IV', even though he used gossip from it when writing *The Four Georges*. Probably helped by the controversy, the volumes sold rapidly, and the book was soon republished in an expanded edition. The charge of the authorship was not at the time denied, and the *Diary* was published under her name in 1908. It was largely sympathetic to Queen Caroline, and Lady Charlotte was called as a defence witness at her trial. Lady Charlotte Bury died at 91 Sloane Street, Chelsea, London, on 31 March 1861.

G. C. Boase, *rev.* Pam Perkins

Sources A. F. Steuart, introduction, in *The diary of a lady-in-waiting, by Lady Charlotte Bury*, ed. A. F. Steuart, 1 (1908) • A. Adburgham, *Silver fork society* (1983) • *Maria Edgeworth: letters from England, 1813–1844*, ed. C. Colvin (1971) • *Memoir and correspondence of Mrs Grant of Laggan*, ed. J. P. Grant, 2nd edn, 3 (1845) • Walpole, *Corr.*, vol. 11 • *The Times* (2 April 1861) • *The letters of Sir Walter Scott*, ed. H. J. C. Grierson and others, centenary edn, 12 vols. (1932–79), vol. 6 • *GM* • Burke, *Peerage*

Archives BL, diary, M/497 [microfilm] • UCL, letters | Bodl. Oxf., letters to Mary Anne Disraeli • NL Scot., letters to Gordon-Cumming family

Likenesses J. Opie, oils, *c.*1784, Inveraray Castle, Strathclyde • lithograph, 1795, NPG, BM • T. Wright, stipple, 1830 (after T. Lawrence), BM, NPG; repro. in *La Belle Assemblé* (1830) • A. Blakley, chalk drawing, 1841, Scot. NPG • J. Hoppner, oils (as Aurora), Inveraray Castle, Strathclyde • J. Posselwhite, stipple (after G. Hayter), BM, NPG; repro. in C. Bury, *The three great sanctuaries of Tuscany, Valombrosa, Camalodi, Laverna: a poem* • J. W. Tischbein, oils, Scot. NPG • engraving, repro. in *New Monthly Magazine* (Jan 1837)

Bury, Edward (1615/16–1700), clergyman and ejected minister, was born in Worcestershire, if John Walker is to be credited, though in 1665 all his extended family were living in north-west Shropshire; the names of his parents are not known. 'At five years old he was adopted by an uncle to a fair estate: but such was the profaneness of the family that when God had touched his heart, he desired to be removed' and as a result was disowned by both father and uncle (Calamy, *Abridgement*, 2.557). He attended grammar school in Coventry, though there is no evidence to support either Edmund Calamy's claim that he was a student of Oxford University or Walker's contemptuous charge that he was a tailor.

Bury was curate of Bewdley, Worcestershire, in 1649–50 but by 1654 he had been instituted to the rectory of Great Bolas in Shropshire. This probably followed the ejection of Isaac Martin, who had signed the testimony of Shropshire presbyterian ministers in 1648 but who in 1651 was charged with stirring up the parish in favour of the invading troops of Charles II. He had also married by 1654, when the first of the five children he was to have with his first wife, Margaret, between then and 1663 was born. For a time Bury lived peacefully at Great Bolas, 'till once being suspected of desiring the king's return, his house was searched, his goods plundered, and his life threatened and much endangered' (Calamy, *Abridgement*, 2.558). The alleged royalist, however, survived in his living only as long as the other ministers ejected in August 1662. He continued to live in the parish for some years until forced to move by the Oxford Act. Calamy records that about 1665 Bury's mother, father, and ten brothers and brothers-in-law were all resident close by. By 1672 he had moved to the adjacent parish of Stoke upon Tern, where his own house was licensed as a meeting-house, while he himself was licensed to preach as a presbyterian at the house of William Smallwood at Ranton, Staffordshire. The books he published between 1674 and 1681 and the will he made the month before he died all give him as living in Eaton, a township of Stoke upon Tern.

Despite his religious nonconformity Bury was a political and social conservative. His distaste for lower-class indiscipline is particularly evident in *England's Bane, or, The Deadly Danger of Drunkenness* (1677), which warns that 'the taverns and alehouses are the devil's schools, where his language of hell is taught, and his shop, where men are trained up in his work' (p. 13). Bury was able to make influential connections in Shropshire and surrounding counties. *A Help to Holy Walking* (1675) included a preface signed on 2 November 1674 which was to Lady Wilbraham, the wife of Sir Thomas Wilbraham JP of Woodhay, Cheshire, to whom he dedicated in the same year *Death Improved and Immoderate Sorrow for Deceased Friends and Relations Reproved*. Bury also dedicated books to Lady Penelope Paget and Lady Frances Paget, daughters of William, fifth Lord Paget. He dedicated *The Husbandman's Companion* (1677) to Lady Frances Paget's husband, 'the right worshipful his much honoured friend, Rowland Hunt of Boare Eaton [Boreatton] in the County of Salop', while *A Soveraign Antidote Against the Fear of Death* (1681) was dedicated to Philip Foley of Prestwood, esquire, and his wife, Lady Penelope Paget.

The years of tory reaction, however, seem to have brought considerable hardship to Bury. During the drought of June 1681 he presided at a fast service at Hodnet, Shropshire. Though the law prohibited only preaching, the justices 'fined Mr Bury £20, though he only prayed, and did not speak one word', and since he did not have more than £7, took the rest in goods (*Calamy rev.*, 92). Philip Henry heard that they had taken sheets, dishes, books, and two beds from Bury in distraint. In the winter of 1683–4 the earl of Bedford sent £50 to Richard Baxter for distribution among distressed ministers, and Bury was one of the beneficiaries. Evidently, for a time, his titled friends were unwilling or unable to protect him. Perhaps the tory enemies of William, sixth Lord Paget, a defender of Algernon Sidney, were eager to damage his clients and relations in Shropshire.

The events of 1688–9 improved the situation for nonconformist preachers. In 1690–92 Bury received £5 a year from the common fund set up by the united body of presbyterians and congregationalists, but he was by now over seventy years old, and was losing or had lost his sight. When *Death Improved* was reissued in 1693 it revealed that Lady Wilbraham's recent loss of a daughter had coincided with the death of one of Bury's sons, but four of his children, including Samuel *Bury, vicar of Bury St Edmunds, survived him, as did his second wife, Mary (*d.* 1704). Edmund Bury died on 5 May 1700, probably at Eaton upon Tern, at the age of eighty-four, and was buried at Great Bolas two days later. STEPHEN WRIGHT

Sources E. Calamy, ed., *An abridgement of Mr. Baxter's history of his life and times, with an account of the ministers, &c., who were ejected after the Restauration of King Charles II*, 2nd edn, 2 vols. (1713) • *Calamy rev.* • *Walker rev.* • J. Walker, *An attempt towards recovering an account of the numbers and sufferings of the clergy of the Church of England*, 2 pts in 1 (1714) • A. Gordon, ed., *Freedom after ejection: a review (1690–1692) of presbyterian and congregational nonconformity in England and Wales* (1917) • E. Calamy, *A continuation of the account of the ministers … who were ejected and silenced after the Restoration in 1660*, 2 vols. (1727) • J. B. Williams, *Life of Philip Henry* (1974) • *Calendar of the correspondence of Richard Baxter*, ed. N. H. Keeble and G. F. Nuttall, 2 vols. (1991) • E. Bury, *Death improved and immoderate sorrow for deceased friends and*

relations reproved (1674) [and 1693] • E. Bury, *England's bane, or, The deadly danger of drunkenness* (1677) • E. Bury, *A help to holy walking* (1675) • E. Bury, *The husbandman's companion* (1677) • E. Bury, *A soveraign antidote against the fear of death* (1681) • *DNB*
Wealth at death £81 17*s.*: *Calamy rev.*

Bury, Edward (**1794–1858**), engineer, was born at Salford, near Manchester, on 22 October 1794. His early education was received at a school in the city of Chester. From an early age he was interested in machinery and showed ingenuity in constructing models. After school and an apprenticeship in engineering he eventually established himself at Liverpool as a manufacturer of engines.

On 4 March 1830, at St Mary's, Walton on the Hill, Bury married the botanical artist Priscilla Susan *Bury, *née* Falkner (1799–1872). In the same year the Liverpool and Manchester Railway was opened, and for several years after this Bury devoted his attention to the construction of engines for railways. He supplied many of the first engines used on the Liverpool and Manchester and on the London and Birmingham railways, and his important paper 'On the locomotive engines of the London and Birmingham Railway' appeared in the *Transactions of the Institution of Civil Engineers* (17 March 1840). In this he provided detailed drawings of the engines, and elaborate tables of data on the operation of the railway, showing, for example, the quantity of coke consumed by each of the engines. He also discussed the relative advantages of four and six wheels. This paper was of importance in the history of locomotive traction, and of considerable interest in the theory of steam-drawing engines. About this time he introduced a series of improved engines for the steamboats employed on the Rhône, which attracted much attention on the continent and led to his being consulted by the directors of many railways then being constructed in Europe.

For some years after the opening of the London and Birmingham Railway in September 1838, Bury had the entire charge of the locomotive department of that line. He subsequently undertook the management of the whole of the rolling stock for the Great Northern Railway. By his engineering capabilities, his mechanical knowledge, his good judgement, and his tact, he won the complete confidence of the directors and of those who were employed under him.

On 1 February 1844 Bury was elected a fellow of the Royal Society, his claim being founded on the great improvements which he had introduced, especially in adjusting the dimensions of the cylinder and driving wheels, and the effective pressure of the steam. He resigned from the Institution of Civil Engineers in 1857, having retired from his professional work. During his later years he lived at Crofton Lodge, Windermere. He died at East Villa, Scarborough, on 25 November 1858 and was survived by his wife.

Robert Hunt, *rev.* Desmond King-Hele

Sources *PRS*, 10 (1859–60), 12 • J. C. Poggendorff and others, eds., *Biographisch-literarisches Handwörterbuch zur Geschichte der exacten Wissenschaften*, 1 (Leipzig, 1863), 220 • *PICE*, 16 (1856–7), 98 • *CGPLA Eng. & Wales* (1858) • *IGI* • private information (2004) • d. cert. [Priscilla Susan Bury, wife]
Wealth at death under £45,000: probate, 23 Dec 1858, *CGPLA Eng. & Wales*

Bury [*née* Lawrence], **Elizabeth** (**1644?–1720**), diarist, was probably born on 2 March 1644, and was baptized on 12 March 1644 at Clare, Suffolk, one of four children of Captain Adams Lawrence of Linton, Cambridgeshire, and Elizabeth Cutts of Clare. Her father died in 1648, and in 1651 her mother married Nathaniel Bradshaw, minister of a church in the neighbourhood. In 1662, her stepfather being one of the ejected ministers, the family moved to Willingham, Cambridgeshire. A committed dissenter, Elizabeth rejected several advantageous offers of marriage from members of the established church (*Account*, 38). On 1 February 1667 she married Griffith Lloyd of Hemingford Grey, Huntingdonshire, who died on 13 April 1682. She remained a widow for fifteen years, residing part of the time in Norwich. In Bury on 29 May 1697 she married Samuel *Bury (*bap.* 1663, *d.* 1730), Presbyterian minister. This union provided the couple 'many comforts of our lives, our mutual Endearments, and unbroken affection to each other' (*Account*, 26).

About 1654 the young Elizabeth described herself as 'coverted' and began the practice of introspective meditation which would shape her later diary entries. She appears to have been largely self-educated with the encouragement of her stepfather and a Dr Fulwood (*Account*, 8). In spite of her delicate health, she routinely rose at four in the morning to pursue her studies, which included Hebrew, divinity ('her Darling Study'), philosophy, philology, history, anatomy, medicine, and mathematics, as well as French, music, and heraldry (*Account*, 6). She later kept a stock of bibles and practical books to be distributed as she saw fit. Although she herself read several languages, her husband notes that she regretted that:

> so many Learned Men should be so very uncharitable to her Sex, as to speak so little in their Mother-Tongue … especially (as she often argued) since they would all so readily own, *That Souls were not Distinguished by Sexes*. (*Account*, 7)

In 1664, Elizabeth began writing her diary, initially in shorthand (which her husband states he could not decipher), and continued it until her death.

About 1712 Bury's health declined, and in 1719 she travelled with her husband for the cure to Bath and then Bristol, where she died on 8 May 1720. She was buried in Bristol on 22 May. Bury published his account of her life the same year, with William Tong's funeral sermon and Isaac Watts's elegy. The text reached a third edition in 1721. In his elegy Watts called Bury 'a pattern for the Sex in ages yet unborn' for her exemplary piety and management of her life.

In his account Samuel Bury described Elizabeth as quick-witted and eloquent in conversation and correspondence, noting that her 'great Aptness and Felicity of Expression' made her a valued correspondent 'by some of the Brightest Minds, even in very distant Countries' (*Account*, 5). Included with her life were portions from her large collection of papers composed after 1690 which had been written in longhand. Samuel Bury organized them under headings such as 'her self-examinations', 'remarks on the sacraments', and 'answers to prayers and deliverances in dangers', the last of which records numerous providential escapes from house fires, highwaymen, and sickness by herself and her family. He also included several of her letters offering advice on instructing children, getting married, and negotiating religious disputes, which show a practical application of her intensely spiritual vision to the events of everyday life.

MARGARET J. M. EZELL

Sources *An account of the life and death of Mrs Elizabeth Bury*, ed. S. Bury (1720) · G. Ballard, *Memoirs of several ladies of Great Britain* (1752) · *DNB*

Likenesses G. Burder, line print, pubd 1777, BM, NPG

Bury, John (*c.*1400–*c.*1480), prior of the Augustinian convent, London, and theologian, was born at Bury St Edmunds. He became an Augustinian friar, probably entering the order in his late teens, and first joining the London convent, where he was ordained subdeacon on 18 December 1417. He must have shown early promise as a scholar, because less than two years later, on 30 August 1420, he was granted leave by the prior-general to study at the Oxford convent for three years. In the event he remained in Oxford for much longer, becoming a doctor in theology in the 1430s or 1440s, and acquiring a considerable reputation as a theologian and preacher in London as well as in Oxford.

In 1458–9 Bury composed the *Gladius Salamonis*, a reply to Reginald Pecock's *Repressor of Overmuch Blaming of the Clergy*. Pecock, bishop of Chichester, had been under increasing attack since 1450 for propounding schemes for church reform whose radical nature exposed him to suspicions of heresy. The opposition to his writings had been led by the London clergy, and it was under their influence that Bury began work on his treatise. It was once thought that the *Gladius* was commissioned by Thomas Bourchier, archbishop of Canterbury, as part of his proceedings against Pecock in 1457. There is however no evidence for this. In his examination of the bishop, Bourchier showed little interest in the detail of Pecock's arguments. He was eager to bring a swift end to the controversy, and to have Pecock restored to his see. Nevertheless, Bury did dedicate his treatise to Bourchier, and in the text he did present a methodical and comprehensive examination of Pecock's conclusions. He had planned the *Gladius* in two books, but he published the first before the second was completed. Only a single copy, of book 1, survives (Bodl. Oxf., MS Bodley 108) and it may be that the second book was never finished.

John Bury attracted the attention of Henry VI, who granted him an annual pension on 15 April 1458, describing him as 'oon of the preests of our chapelle' (PRO, PSO 1/20/1057). Further advancement quickly followed. He was elected prior provincial of the order in England on 5 August 1459, the election being confirmed by the prior-general in February 1460. At this point, or shortly before, he had joined the community at Clare, Suffolk, the order's premier convent, renowned for its scholarship. He was certainly at Clare in 1460, but by 1471 he had become prior of the London convent. He continued to produce theological works and sermons, including a commentary on St Luke's gospel and a collection of scholastic *quaestiones*, though none survives. His books, which he bequeathed to the Carthusians at Sheen, included a copy of Chaucer's translation of Boethius. He died at the London convent, probably *c.*1480.

JAMES G. CLARK

Sources Emden, *Oxf.*, 1.323 · Bale, *Cat.*, 1.595 · R. Pecock, *The repressor of over much blaming of the clergy*, ed. C. Babington, 2, Rolls Series, 19 (1860), 567–613 · Tanner, *Bibl. Brit.-Hib.*, 431 · J. Catto, 'The king's government & the fall of Pecock, 1457–1458', *Rulers and ruled in late medieval England: essays presented to Gerald Harriss*, ed. S. Walker and R. E. Archer (1995), 201–22 · C. W. Brockwell, *Bishop Reginald Pecock and the Lancastrian church* (1985), 162 · V. H. H. Green, *Bishop Reginald Pecock* (1945)

Archives Bodl. Oxf., MS Bodley 108 [copy]

Bury, John (1535–1571), translator, was the son of William Bury (*d.* 1563), draper of London and merchant of the staple, and Christian (*d.* in or before 1559?), daughter of William Wilkinson. He is said to have been educated at Cambridge, although his name does not appear in the university records. It may have been at Cambridge that he produced his only surviving work, an English translation of Isocrates' speech *Ad demonicum*. This translation, *The Godly Advertisement or Good Counsell of the Famous Orator Isocrates*, was made from the original Greek, and it is the first printed English rendering of this speech. It was published by William Copland in January 1559, with Benedict Burgh's English verse translation of Cato's *Distichs*, although Bury confesses in his preface that he did not know the name of the author of this earlier translation. He dedicated this small volume to his uncle Sir William Chester. In August 1558 another uncle, James Bury, bequeathed his law books to John, who entered the Inner Temple in November 1559.

Bury's mother probably died before 14 November 1559 for at this time William Bury arranged a second marriage, to Christian, widow of Edward Wilmot. John inherited his father's estate at Water Eaton in Oxfordshire on his father's death on 12 July 1563. Sir William Chester was the chief mourner at the funeral. Six weeks later, on 30 August, Bury married Elizabeth Stafford. He was to have inherited the estate at Culham, Oxfordshire, on the death of his father's second wife, but she outlived him. In August 1570 he fell from his horse and broke his leg, and he died from the consequences of this injury on 22 February 1571. He was survived by Elizabeth, and by his four-year-old son, Thomas.

P. BOTLEY

Sources R. E. C. Waters, *Genealogical memoirs of the extinct family of Chester of Chicheley*, 2 vols. (1878), 64–6 · Venn, *Alum. Cant.* · Cooper, *Ath. Cantab.*, 3.75 · W. H. Cooke, ed., *Students admitted to the Inner Temple, 1547–1660* [1878], 32 · Arber, *Regs. Stationers*, 1.79 · H. B. Lathrop, *Translations from the classics into English from Caxton to Chapman, 1477–1620* (1933); repr. (1967), 44–6

Bury, John (1580–1667), Church of England clergyman, was born at Tiverton, Devon, and baptized there on 25 July 1580; his father was probably a weaver in the town. On 9 February 1597 he was elected scholar of Corpus Christi

College, Oxford, and in 1602, shortly after having graduated BA on 13 February, was appointed first Blundell fellow of Balliol College by Lord Chief Justice Sir John Popham. He proceeded MA on 16 May 1605 and was incorporated at Cambridge in 1608.

From 1609 Bury was vicar of Sidbury, Devon. Probably before 1615 he married Agnes (*d.* 1644), with whom he had two sons, Arthur *Bury (1623/4–1713) and John, subsequently a parliamentarian colonel, and four daughters, Gertrude, Ann, Margaret, and Elizabeth (*d.* 1676), who married Humphrey Saunders in December 1632. In 1615 Bury published a sermon delivered at the Exeter assizes, *The Schole of Godly Feare*.

On 12 May 1626 Bury was admitted to the vicarage of Heavitree, Devon. In July 1630 he resigned Sidbury to his son-in-law Richard Babington. His sermon preached at the bishop's visitation in Exeter in 1630, published as *The Moderate Christian* (1631), was dedicated to Bishop Joseph Hall, whose evangelizing priorities he seems to have shared. Like Hall, Bury insisted that the business of saving souls take precedence over attempts to enforce outward conformity. Puritans, however, ought not to scruple at indifferent ceremonies, but bear with their weaker brethren for the sake of church unity. In March 1632 Bury received a canonry in Exeter Cathedral.

On 29 May 1643, while Bury was 'absent in the king's service' (Wood, *Ath. Oxon.*, 3.777) the Oxford convocation voted to create him DD. Threatened with sequestration in 1646, he resigned Heavitree in favour of his daughter Margaret's husband, William Banks (*d.* 1697). Bury remained in Devon, where he was joined by his son Arthur, who left his Oxford fellowship at the parliamentary visitation. Eventually, in 1659, he was admitted by the committee of triers to the rectory of Widworthy in the county. In 1661 he published a catechism, *God's Method for Man's Salvation*, for the use of his parishioners there.

In 1662, while his son-in-law Humphrey Saunders was ejected from Holsworthy, Devon, Bury himself succeeded to the rectory of St Mary Major, Exeter, following the deprivation on 23 September of John Bartlet for nonconformity. Bury died on 5 July 1667 and was interred in Exeter Cathedral on 9 July. He made bequests to the public workhouse at St Sidwell's, Exeter, endowed a school in the same parish, and left funds for the maintenance of thirteen poor persons in St Catherine's Almshouse in Exeter, and for the poor in Tiverton. JIM BENEDICT

Sources W. Jones, 'John Bury, canon-residentiary of Exeter Cathedral, and his sons-in-law and descendants', *Notes and Gleanings: a Monthly Magazine Devoted Chiefly to Subjects Connected with the Counties of Devon and Cornwall* [ed J. Dallas and W. Cotton] (1888–92), 4.65–71 • J. Prince, *Danmonii orientales illustres, or, The worthies of Devon*, 2nd edn (1810), 152–4 • Wood, *Ath. Oxon.*, new edn, 3.777 • J. Walker, *An attempt towards recovering an account of the numbers and sufferings of the clergy of the Church of England*, pt 2 (1714), 28 • *Walker rev.*, 108, 110 • G. Oliver, *Ecclesiastical antiquities in Devon*, 1 (1840), 49 • K. Fincham and P. Lake, 'Popularity, prelacy and puritanism in the 1630s: Joseph Hall explains himself', *EngHR*, 111 (1996), 856–81, esp. 873 • *Fasti Angl.* (Hardy), 1.423–4 • Foster, *Alum. Oxon.* • *Calamy rev.*, 426 • *The registers of baptisms, marriages, and burials of the city of Exeter*, 1, ed. W. U. Reynell-Upham and H. Tapley-Soper, Devon and Cornwall RS (1910), 68, 149 [17 Nov 1644, 9 July 1667] • J. Jones, *Balliol College: a history*, 2nd edn (1997), 84–5, 326 • I. Gowers, 'The clergy in Devon, 1641–62', *Tudor and Stuart Devon … essays presented to Joyce Youings*, ed. T. Gray, M. Rowe, and A. Erskine (1992), 200–26

Likenesses J. Gandy?, portrait (formerly in the Corporation of the Poor, New Buildings, Exeter, 1891)

Bury, John (1925–2000), theatre designer, was born on 27 January 1925 at a nursing home in Aberystwyth, Cardiganshire, the only son of Charles Rugeley *Bury (1890–1968), an industrial and academic chemist, and his wife, Emily Frances Margaret Adams, a botanist. He had a happy childhood, and was encouraged by his parents to take an interest in many subjects. He was educated at Hereford Cathedral school and briefly at University College, London, before his call-up into the Fleet Air Arm in 1942. On 19 September 1947 he married Margaret Leila Greenwood (*b.* 1925), a schoolteacher, daughter of Arthur Alexander Greenwood, a tailor. They had a son. The marriage was dissolved in 1964.

Somewhat unsure of his direction after his demobilization in 1946, Bury drifted into short-term jobs in London until he came across the Theatre Workshop company, run by Joan Littlewood and beginning its tenancy of the rundown Theatre Royal at Stratford in the East End. It was hardly London's most glamorous theatrical address, yet the company's work helped to transform the costive postwar English theatre.

Bury's bear-like, burly frame and buoyant personality were ideally suited to Littlewood's company-based, improvisational style; he was happy to act (badly, by his own admission), drive the van, or hang the lights (he developed into an expert lighting designer too). Although without Littlewood's knowledge of Brecht and Stanislavski, he was as committed as she to breaking away from the romantic, painterly style which then dominated British theatrical design.

Bury's first credited design work was a simple wooden flexible structure for Ibsen's *An Enemy of the People* (Stratford East, 1954), and this was followed by a series of innovatory productions as Theatre Workshop entered a genuinely golden age. Brendan Behan's *The Quare Fellow* (1956) was contained within Bury's bleak, arid prison walls, he devised a cunningly fluid composite set for Shelagh Delany's *A Taste of Honey* (1958), and he captured a colourfully exuberant East End canvas for Lionel Bart's joyous musical *Fings ain't wot they used t'be* (1959). The vigorous E15 style was a sharp antidote to the prevailing genteel Shaftesbury Avenue theatre; Bury's designs, using minimal scenery and props to suggest the world of each production, were refreshing and influential. Perhaps the finest summation of his work with Littlewood was *Oh, what a lovely war* (1963). This treatment of the First World War, using period songs in the style of a Pierrot show, was a diamond-hard reappraisal of history, with Bury's design—including the unforgettably potent device of a newsreel sign constantly updating the war-dead statistics—a vital element of a historic evening.

In 1964 Bury joined the fledgeling Royal Shakespeare Company (RSC), initially working with various directors including Peter Brook—for whose production of Dürrenmatt's *The Physicists* (Aldwych, 1964) he designed a startling, laboratory-clinical room—before forming the second major partnership of his career, with Peter Hall. This work coincided with another golden age as Hall led the RSC into a legendary period. The Hall–Bury partnership's major feat was the revisionist epic of the Wars of the Roses Shakespeare history-play cycle (Stratford, 1964), for which Bury used then unconventional materials of steel and wire-mesh to help conjure up a clamorous, smoky world of ferocious tribal energy. He became chief designer for the company in 1965.

With Hall, as with Littlewood, Bury's work was remarkable for its variety. It included classics and premières: his vast, tubular factory for Henry Livings's *Eh?* (Aldwych, 1964), the David Warner *Hamlet* (Stratford, 1965), set in menacingly glittering blackness, his ashy-grey, cavernous room for the feral household of Pinter's *The Homecoming* (Aldwych, 1965), a crowded, Daumieresque world for *The Government Inspector* (Aldwych, 1966), and his dark landscape of chrome and leather for Pinter's *Old Times* (Aldwych, 1971). He also worked with Hall on opera productions, including the monumental demands of Covent Garden's *Moses and Aaron* and some of Glyndebourne's most haunting Mozartian designs. The team also memorably re-examined the baroque repertoire, using elements drawn from the Jacobean masque, in Cavalli's *Calisto* and Monteverdi's *Il ritorno d'Ulisse* for Glyndebourne. Bury married on 20 January 1966 Elizabeth Duffield (*b.* 1941), designer, daughter of Thomas Henry Duffield, a businessman; they had two sons and a daughter.

Bury loved travelling and working overseas, although the brashly commercial world of 1970s Broadway held little joy for him on two musicals: *The Rothschilds* (New York, 1970), an overblown saga, bedevilled by endless rewrites and sackings on the road, and a hilariously pretentious rock-musical flop directed by Hall, *Via galactica* (New York, 1972), involving malfunctioning trampolines.

After joining Hall to move with the National Theatre from the Old Vic to the South Bank (as head of design, 1973–85), Bury's early work there coincided with a period of unexciting stateliness in Hall's work. Their *The Tempest* (1974), featuring John Gielgud's last Prospero, used ideas from Inigo Jones more effective in the earlier Glyndebourne Monteverdis, while a *Hamlet* (1975) with Albert Finney was an uncharacteristically drab bore. A new Pinter galvanized the partnership to another triumph (1975) with Gielgud and Ralph Richardson in *No Man's Land*, for which Bury carved out the essential Pinter space with carpet and beautifully textured silk upholstery, following a favourite dictum: 'The poetry is in the geometry.' Their finest commercial hour came with Peter Shaffer's *Amadeus* (1975; New York, 1980), a demanding play for the designer, its many scenes ranging from imperial receptions to intimate episodes of Mozart's dreams. Bury's solution—using silvers and blues—was typically flexible and sensitive to the play's shifting moods.

Poor health—asthma and heart trouble—in his later years cut down Bury's workload, although he still took on major projects. He continued to work abroad—a *Hamlet* (1993) for Tokyo's Shiki Theatre was a personal highlight—and in the world's opera houses. He took on one of the first productions at L'Opéra de Paris Bastille with a monumental, stark *Elektra* (1992) and he worked again with Hall on a *Salome* (Royal Opera House, 1992) of luscious decadence.

At the time of his death Bury was working—helped, as so often, by his second wife, Elizabeth—on a re-scrutiny for the new Glyndebourne of one of the Hall–Bury team's finest productions, Benjamin Britten's *A Midsummer Night's Dream*, first seen in the old house in 1981. The design had a triumphant posthumous reception during the 2001 season, enchanting audiences anew with its magical black and white crepuscular forest. It looked even better in the new house, the success of which owed so much to Bury's advice and enthusiasm. He was passionate about theatre spaces; he was crucially involved also with the progress of the Barbican Theatre and the National Theatre's most flexible auditorium, the Cottesloe. In that area, as well as in his own constantly innovative design work, he was one of the most influential of twentieth-century designers.

Bury served twice (1960–68 and 1975–85) on the Arts Council drama panel and was chairman of the Society of British Theatre Designers (1975–85). He was appointed OBE in 1979. He died on 12 November 2000 in the Winfield Medical Centre, Tewkesbury Road, Gloucester, as a result of congestive cardiac failure. He was buried four days later in Brimscome cemetery, Stroud. ALAN STRACHAN

Sources J. Goodwin, ed., *British theatre design* (1989) · *Daily Telegraph* (15 Nov 2000) · *The Times* (15 Nov 2000) · *The Guardian* (15 Nov 2000) · *The Independent* (17 Nov 2000) · b. cert. · m. certs. · d. cert. · private information (2004)

Archives Theatre Museum, London, model for Hamlet · V&A, model for Tristan and Isolde | Glyndebourne, East Sussex, photographic archives · National Theatre, London, photographic archives · priv. coll. · Royal Shakespeare Company, Stratford upon Avon, photographic archives

Bury, John Bagnell (1861–1927), classical scholar and historian, was born in co. Monaghan, Ireland, on 16 October 1861. His father, the Revd Edward John Bury, curate of Monaghan, subsequently rector of Clontibert and canon of Clogher, had married Anna Rogers of Monaghan, 'a very clever woman and a great reader' (*DNB*). Edward Bury was a sound classicist, and introduced his son to Greek and Latin at a precocious age: John began Latin at four, and as a youth his command of Greek was such that Professor Robert Yelverton Tyrrell was unable to disconcert him during an examination in Greek grammar.

After attending Monaghan diocesan school and Foyle College, Londonderry, Bury entered Trinity College, Dublin, in 1878 and in 1879 came first in examinations for classical scholarships. In 1880 he spent six months in Germany at Göttingen, studying Sanskrit, Syriac, and Hebrew; in the same year he visited Italy for the first time, and won the Bishop Berkeley medal for Greek, a distinction of

John Bagnell Bury (1861–1927), by Walter Stoneman, 1919

which he remained proud. In 1881, while still an undergraduate, he collaborated with Professor John Pentland Mahaffy in editing Euripides' *Hippolytus*; in his introduction Mahaffy gave Bury the main credit for 'sifting the materials and composing the notes', whereas 'the critical suggestions, the illustrations and the opinions propounded' were a joint effort. In 1882 he graduated with a double first, taking first place in classics and fourth in mental and moral philosophy; his especially distinguished answers in classics earned him a large gold medal and a studentship of £700. He now embarked on a campaign, which lasted three years, to secure a fellowship at Trinity: in the 1883 examinations he obtained third prize; he spent the autumn of 1883 in Leipzig, working for the 1884 examinations when he was awarded the Madden prize for classics; his labours were rewarded in the 1885 diet when he became a fellow. As he confessed to a friend, Nathaniel Wedd of King's College, Cambridge, he had worked 'to the extreme limit of his powers' (Baynes, 3). The publication in *Hermathena* of emendations on Pindar, Euripides, Sophocles, Diogenes Laertius, Hesychius, Sappho, Catullus, Cicero's letters to Atticus, and Plautus reflects the breadth of his reading. In September 1885 Bury married his second cousin, Jane, daughter of John Carleton Bury, physician of Mitchelstown, co. Cork; they spent their honeymoon in north Italy, where they visited Ravenna, but an epidemic prevented a planned visit to Greece. The marriage produced one son, Edward Basil, born in 1891.

Early intellectual interests Bury's intellectual interests were always wide. Philosophy was part of his undergraduate studies, and he remained under the influence of his preferred master, Hegel. Music inspired him with its ability to transcend the constraints of time and space, but poetry was an even greater interest and pleasure. Swinburne was one favourite, even if he came to feel that the poet's romanticism was an obstacle to recovering the cheerful spirit (*euphrosynē*) of the ancient Greeks. In 1882 he delivered a paper on Browning's philosophy to the Browning Society in London, which attracted the poet's attention; Bury presented Browning as a writer who helped his readers make the transition from the world of experience to the realm of eternal truths, and who recognized the universality of the individual. He addressed the society again in 1886. One result of this devotion to poetry, in combination with his linguistic skills and lively sense of humour, is the sequence of translations into Greek and Latin verse, published in the magazine *Kottabos* between 1888 and 1895 (Bury himself was editor from 1888 to 1891). He regarded verse composition as a training in the virtue of words, whose disappearance from British scholarship would be a sad day. A similar approval for the educational virtues of useless learning informed his reaction to the retention of compulsory Greek at Cambridge in 1891: universities should not be converted into utility institutions for technical, commercial, or other training—transferable skills and graduate employability did not concern him.

Bury's commitment to interpreting classical texts produced numerous publications, of which the most substantial are editions of Pindar's *Nemean Odes* (1890) and *Isthmian Odes* (1892). In spite of his philological skills, these editions did not have a major impact since much of Bury's commentary was devoted to the ingenious tracing of verbal responsions within the poems as an attempt to recover the texture of Pindar's poetry. Critical reaction to the *Nemean Odes* forced him to adopt a much more defensive position in the *Isthmian Odes*; thereafter, even though he asserted that he would confront the objectors, he abandoned his projected edition of the rest of Pindar. The editions, however, remain interesting since they reveal Bury's conception of the essential spirit of ancient Greece: he was attracted by Pindar as a poet whose celebration of the victories of great men of old would not tempt readers to modernizing interpretations; Pindar reflected the authentic quality of the Hellenic spirit through his depiction of the bright place in which his heroes lived. Bury's evocation of the life of the Aeginetan élite is more readable than his intricate literary theory.

Bury's enduring claim to fame is as a historian of the late Roman and Byzantine empires, though the epithet Byzantine would have been anathema, and his involvement with these topics is manifest in publications in 1888: he reviewed de Boor's edition of Theophylact and Sotiriadis' study of John of Antioch, and wrote his first article devoted to a Byzantine topic, on Theophylact Simocatta's chronology; he also demonstrated his familiarity with Gibbonian rhetoric by composing a stylistic parody devoted to the theme of home rule. These preliminaries scarcely suggested the magnitude of his achievement in the following year, when he published a long article on the emperors of the eleventh century, based on the narrative of Michael Psellus, as well as his first major work, *A history of the later Roman empire from Arcadius to Irene* (*A.D. 395 to A.D. 800*), an account in two volumes, over 1100 pages. For Bury, eastern Roman history was a phase of Hellenic history, and so the *History* stresses continuities from the classical world: 'No "Byzantine Empire" ever began to exist; the Roman Empire did not come to an end until 1453' (*A History of the Later Roman Empire*, v). But his lack of sympathy with Christianity entailed that one of the major forces shaping the development of the eastern Roman empire received inadequate attention, and his preference for the deeds of the great, evinced in his editions of Pindar, ensured that there would be little attention to social history: Bury missed the value of hagiography for illuminating the lives of lesser individuals, and thereby for achieving a fuller understanding of the development of those societies to whose constitutional and institutional continuities he was devoted. However, the 1889 *History* at once established his international reputation: Henry Tozer, writing to congratulate him, stated, 'I have good hopes that your graphic manner of presenting your subject, and your agreeable style, will do much towards awakening a general interest in the history of the Eastern Empire' (Baynes, 6). The expectations may have been too sanguine, but the assessment of Bury's literary qualities is accurate.

Chairs at Dublin and Cambridge In 1893 Bury was elected professor of modern history at Trinity, a post which he was allowed to retain even after appointment as regius professor of Greek in 1898. In 1902 he received an honorary Doctor of Letters from Oxford and was appointed regius professor of modern history at Cambridge, the position which he occupied until his death. He was elected to a fellowship at King's, where he was pleased to find colleagues who shared his anti-clerical views. His inaugural lecture was devoted to the independence of history as a scientific discipline; history was not to be the servant of literature, a source of background information about a sequence of 'great works'; nor was it the educator of public figures, even though this view had been proclaimed by his two favourite Greek historians, Thucydides and Polybius. Rather, history deserved to be studied because of its value to human life, since the present can only be understood through reference to the past. The lecture's message was the triumph of rational investigation, a belief propounded in his earliest publications when he had attacked the superstitions and orthodoxy of 'maw-filled, crop-full Christians' (*Browning Society Papers*, 1, 1882, 261). Study of history offered mankind a chance to advance through the progress of knowledge, but, for history to supplant the institutionalized power of centuries of religious restraint, it would need to be conducted with exceptional rigour, hence the need for scientific history. By emancipating itself from the literary approach to historical evidence advocated by Jowett in the nineteenth century, history could proclaim its independence and, though remaining a humanist discipline, attain to the precision and objective truth with which the sciences were currently credited.

Bury's inaugural attracted such attention that numerous latecomers could not find space in the hall, but he did not have a great impact on undergraduates. He disliked the constraints of the Cambridge historical tripos, which focused on set books: instead he proposed a system of open-book examinations. If in this respect Bury anticipated academic developments by almost a century, other aspects of his professorial service are now less favoured: he had a healthy contempt for university bureaucracies, and declined to sacrifice the time and thought demanded by administrative duties. On the other hand, he did encourage those interested in research, being generous with time and advice: the young Norman Baynes and Stephen Runciman both benefited from the intimidating stimulation of such contacts. Professor Fay of Toronto commented that 'a talk with Bury was almost like being present at the making of history' (Baynes, 51).

Histories of the classical world and Byzantium During the 1890s Bury continued to publish on classical topics. In 1893 there appeared his *History of the Roman empire from its foundation to the death of Marcus Aurelius* (27 *B.C.–A.D. 180*), a work commissioned by the publisher John Murray. Bury had a low opinion of Romans: 'Their intelligence was solid and commonplace, moving rigidly on old lines; they were incapable of striking a new vein or of conceiving a new idea' (Baynes, 15). He was a Hellenist, and this preference is evident in the preparations which attended his other major contribution to the history of the classical world, the *History of Greece to the Death of Alexander the Great* (1900). Bury travelled extensively in Greece in 1895: Mr Bosanquet, who accompanied his tour of the classical sites of central Greece, commented that Bury was:

> a delightful companion with his mind full of everything in history and literature that bore upon the places we visited. He knew just what he wanted to see or verify on each site and carried the classical authorities in his head and quoted them with wonderful precision. He had a thought-out programme and adhered to it with placid obstinacy. (Baynes, 20–1)

Bury's good humour rendered tolerable a tour undertaken in bad weather through a region where facilities were often rudimentary and banditry an alleged threat. After this trip he published a series of articles which demonstrated his ability to fuse his critical mastery of textual evidence and familiarity with Greek geography. The *History of Greece* has stood the test of time far better than its Roman counterpart, and, as revised by Russell Meiggs, is still widely used as a text book for first-year undergraduates: if it fails to impart a notion of the diverse development of Greek societies and cultures, its clear exposition of a series of historical problems still makes a useful introduction to the principles of studying ancient history.

At the same time, however, Bury was even more active

in later periods of Hellenic history, namely the later Roman empire and Byzantium. Between 1896 and 1900 he brought out a seven-volume edition of Gibbon's *Decline and Fall*, providing the great work of another rationalist anti-clerical writer with a scholarly apparatus of notes and appendices which discussed the views adopted in the text and presented contemporary scholarship. He also wrote a series of articles on historical problems, especially from the sixth century: his study of the Nika riot (*Journal of Hellenic Studies*, 1897) remains the fullest analysis of the complex sources for this incident, and displays his sympathetic knowledge of the chronicle of John Malalas on whose text he had worked in the Bodleian Library at Oxford. In 1905 he published *The Life of St. Patrick and his Place in History*, whose scholarly basis had been established in numerous detailed studies published in the preceding four years. For Bury, Patrick was part of his study of the late Roman world, where the influence of Christianity served to spread Roman practices beyond the empire's frontiers; this classical approach to Patrick, coupled with his distaste for Christianity, meant that Bury, despite his precise scholarship, ignored the Irish dimension to the construction of Patrick and so failed to comprehend his inspirational power.

Patrick could be seen as a distraction from Byzantium, to which he had only devoted brief notes or reviews during these years, but Bury returned to his main theme in 1906 with an article, 'The treatise De administrando imperio', in the *Byzantinische Zeitschrift*. His interest in the writings of Constantine VII Porphyrogenitus is already evident in his 1889 *History* and in appendices to Gibbon, while in 1898 he had promised a new edition of these in the series Byzantine Texts which he was co-ordinating. He did not embark on this labour, and parts of Constantine's writings still require a modern edition, but this interest produced his most enduring scholarship: in 1907 Bury published 'The ceremonial book of Constantine Porphyrogennetos' (*EngHR*); this article was followed in 1910 by *The Constitution of the Later Roman Empire* (publication of the 1909 Creighton lecture) and in 1911 by *The imperial administrative system in the ninth century, with a revised text of the Kleterologion of Philotheos*. This last was identified by Norman Baynes as 'probably the greatest single piece of pure scholarship that he ever produced: it would be difficult to praise this masterpiece too highly' (Baynes, 34), a judgement which remains true. It exploited Bury's talents as masterly philologist, sensitive elucidator of administrative structures, and devotee of the history of eastern Rome; it is essential reading for those interested in the structures of the middle Byzantine world, but also repays consultation by those concerned with other periods of eastern Roman history, since Bury was alert to the changes in institutional hierarchies over the centuries.

Bury's other major Byzantine work of this period, *A history of the eastern Roman empire from the fall of Irene to the accession of Basil I (A.D. 802–867)* (1912), continued the story of the Hellenic Roman world from his 1889 volumes; this could be praised as 'a revelation of the method of the scientific historian', though this rigorous approach has resulted in 'a collection of monographs rather than a history' (Baynes, 35), a work which lacks an artistic unity. Even during this period of late Roman preoccupation, Bury continued to publish notes on classical texts and in 1908 delivered a course of lectures at Harvard entitled 'The ancient Greek historians'; in reality a series of historiographical essays, these were published in the following year. His historical range was revealed by a contribution on Russia 1462–1682 to the *Cambridge Modern History*, as well as a projected biography of Catherine II.

A scientific historian In 1910 Bury began to experience health problems, whose seriousness was disguised from all but a small circle of friends by his own determination and the support of his wife; he never fully recovered from eye trouble which afflicted him in the winter of 1910–11, and thereafter there were periods when he was unable to read. Ill health perhaps spurred him to produce a historiographical testament, the *History of the Freedom of Thought*, which expounded most explicitly the rationalist beliefs that had always spurred his approach to historical study. It charted the progress of mankind from the freedom of the Greeks, through the servility of the middle ages, to the emancipation of the modern period. In this work, composed 'with fire and force', Bury was concerned with the grand theme, and hostile reviewers, especially those alienated by his animosity to the church as an agent of repression, found plenty of scope for criticism on details. His rationalist views on the nature of history were further expounded in the *History of the Idea of Progress* (1920), which developed some of the themes of his inaugural lecture. But it is appropriate that Bury's last major composition was devoted to east Rome, the *History of the later Roman empire from the death of Theodosius I to the death of Justinian (A.D. 395 to A.D. 565)* (1923), 1000 pages in two volumes; the period covered is less than half that of his 1889 *History*, and the treatment is necessarily much denser. Equally appropriate for the philhellene is his commitment in his last years to the *Cambridge Ancient History*, of which he was editor-in-chief and to whose earlier volumes he contributed numerous chapters on classical Greek history and literature. From 1918 Bury spent every winter in Rome for his health, and it was there, at the Hotel Ludovisi, that he died on 1 June 1927.

Bury's assessment of Thucydides in his *Ancient Greek Historians* (1909) is applicable to his own achievements as a historian: he was not concerned to entertain but to establish a record whose truth would ensure its permanent utility; accuracy was of prime importance. As a scientific historian Bury rigorously excluded his own personality and opinions from his writings; events should be followed rather than moulded to fit an artistic plan; chance played a key role in determining the course of history so that it was misleading to search for general causes for grand sequences of events, especially in the remote past. One example of the avoidance of personal judgements is his refusal to portray any major character from later Roman history, although he admitted the relevance of personal qualities and motivations in the historical process: even for Justinian, who dominates the second volume of the

1923 *History*, Bury contented himself with providing readers with materials to form their own character assessment while not committing himself. To the last he was a classical philologist who had converted to History. As a result many of his works fragment into collections of articles: particular issues are dispassionately dealt with in meticulous detail, but the place of each discussion in the wider work is overlooked. However, the fact that the best of these monographs are still required reading for specialists is testimony to the importance of Bury's historical scholarship. If his objectivity and precision suggest a dry personality, this was belied by his lively wit and happy conviviality, which endured even through his long battle against illness. His boyish good looks remained famous, and Bury seems to have delighted in exploiting them to surprise the unwary: Norman Baynes, on first encountering the distinguished professor, mistook him for a fellow undergraduate. MICHAEL WHITBY

Sources N. H. Baynes, ed., *A bibliography of the works of J. B. Bury, with a memoir by Norman H. Baynes* (1929) • H. Temperley, 'The historical ideas of J. B. Bury', in *Selected essays of J. B. Bury*, ed. H. Temperley (1930) • *DNB* • *CGPLA Eng. & Wales* (1927)
Archives BL, corresp. with Macmillans, Add. MS 55120 • Bodl. Oxf., letters to Gilbert Murray • King's AC Cam., letter to Oscar Browning
Likenesses Lafayette Ltd, photograph, 1913–14, repro. in Temperley, 'Historical ideas' • W. Stoneman, two photographs, 1919, NPG [*see illus.*]
Wealth at death £7286 14*s*.: administration with will, 7 Sept 1927, *CGPLA Eng. & Wales*

Bury, Katherine (*fl.* 1346–1348?). *See under* Women traders and artisans in London (*act. c.*1200–*c.*1500).

Bury [*née* Falkner], **Priscilla Susan** (1799–1872), botanical artist, was born on 12 January 1799 in Rainhill, Lancashire, the daughter of Edward Dean Falkner (1750–1825), a wealthy Liverpool trader, who had been high sheriff of Lancashire in 1788, and his wife, Bridgett Tarleton (*d.* 1819), only daughter of John Tarleton, merchant and shipowner; Priscilla Falkner was named after her maternal grandmother, Susan Precilla Bertie.

Priscilla Falkner drew plants raised in the greenhouses of her family home, Fairfield (demolished 1913), 2 miles east of Liverpool and, by 1829, had enough studies of lilies and allied plants for publication, a venture promoted by her friend, William Swainson. She modelled her proposed book, then tentatively named 'Drawings of lilies', on William Roscoe's *Monandrian Plants* (1824–8), with the plates to be accompanied by brief letterpresses based on her notes. Indeed, she even used Roscoe's book prospectus as a model for her own. In it, she advertised her 'Drawings of Liliaceous Plants arranged by Botanists in the genera Crinum, Amaryllis, Pancratium …', to appear in ten numbers, each of five plates to be lithographed by Hullmandel, subscribers paying a guinea a number, others 27*s*.

On 4 March 1830, at Walton on the Hill, Priscilla Falkner married Edward *Bury (1794–1858), a railway engineer; the couple had at least three sons, born between 1831 and 1835. In 1831 Priscilla Bury's drawings began to be published as *A Selection of Hexandrian Plants*, the large (64 cm x 48 cm) plates being engraved by Robert Havell; the work had only seventy-nine subscribers. Fifty-one plates appeared in ten fascicles, the last in 1834, but whether or not the text is Bury's is unclear. The plates are fine-grained aquatints, partly printed in colour and retouched by hand: the original drawings later went to Dumbarton Oaks, Washington. The published work has been praised as 'certainly one of the most effective colour-plate folios of its period' (Blunt and Stearn, 248).

After 1836 Priscilla Bury contributed eight plates to (originals now in NHM) Maund and Henslow's *The Botanist* and, in 1860–1, brought out *Figures of Remarkable Forms of polycystins, or Allied Organisms, in the Barbados Chalk deposit*, with twelve plates of photographic prints of drawings made from microscopic preparations mounted by Christopher Johnson (1782–1866) of Lancaster, from specimens collected by John Davy (1790–1868). About 1865 there was a second edition with twenty-four plates with a photograph of diatoms by Bury and she seems to have issued further separate plates. M. C. Cooke (1825–1914) brought out another edition in 1869 and that included another plate of diatoms, signed P. S. Bury 1869.

In 1860 Priscilla Bury issued a memoir of her husband, *Recollections of Edward Bury*, privately published by John Garnett of Windermere, and by 1866 she was living at Fairfield, Thornton Heath, Croydon. She died at Fairfield, of bronchitis and cerebral congestion, on 8 March 1872.

D. J. MABBERLEY

Sources N. F. McMillan, 'Mrs Edward Bury (*née* Priscilla Susan Falkner), botanical artist', *Journal of the Society of the Bibliography of Natural History*, 5 (1968–71), 71–5 • W. Blunt and W. T. Stearn, *The art of botanical illustration*, new edn (1994) • Desmond, *Botanists*, rev. edn • *IGI* • d. cert.
Archives Liverpool Central Library, Roscoe collection, letters
Wealth at death under £8000: probate, 17 April 1872, *CGPLA Eng. & Wales*

Bury [Aungerville], **Richard** (1287–1345), administrator and bishop of Durham, was the son of Sir Richard d'Aungerville of Willoughby, Leicestershire. He was born on 24 January 1287 near Bury St Edmunds, Suffolk (whence his name). After the death of his father he was raised and educated by his uncle, John Willoughby. Bury studied in the arts faculty at Oxford from *c.*1302 to *c.*1312, and although he apparently did not incept as a master, he acquired a lifelong interest in books and learning. He entered royal service in 1312 as a clerk under Walter Langton, royal treasurer and bishop of Coventry and Lichfield, and by the end of that year held two rectories, the identifiable one being Melton in Suffolk. In October 1316 he joined the administrative staff of Prince Edward of Windsor (the future Edward III), then a child of three, as a clerk in the exchequer of his earldom of Chester, becoming a clerk to the justices of Chester in 1319, and chamberlain of Chester from 1320 to 1323 or 1324. Bury may also have served as tutor to the young Edward from *c.*1323 to *c.*1326. In March 1325, when Queen Isabella and her son went to France to arrange a treaty with Charles IV, Bury probably travelled with them as a counsellor to the prince, under

Richard Bury (1287–1345), seal

whom he served as constable of Bordeaux from 19 February to 16 April 1326.

When Edward was crowned king in place of his father in January 1327, Bury was appointed cofferer of the wardrobe. He rose in royal service to the office of keeper and treasurer of the wardrobe (21 August 1328–23 September 1329) and keeper of the privy seal (24 September 1329–7 April 1333). He also acquired numerous benefices, among them the rectory of Croydon (1327–9), prebends of Crediton College in Devon (1327–30), Chichester (1328–34), York (1329–34), Exeter (1330–34), Salisbury (1330–34), Lincoln (1330–33), the archdeaconry of Northampton (January–March 1331), prebends of London (1331–3), Lichfield (January–June 1331) and St Patrick's, Dublin (1332–3), and the deanship of Wells (March–December 1333). With the exception of the last, none of the preferments Bury held in or before 1333 required residency. Whether as a means of keeping himself canonically free for royal service or as a sincere attempt to return to a university for further study, the king sought and received in August 1333 on Bury's behalf a three-year papal dispensation, allowing him to use his income as dean of Wells for university study. These plans, if such they were, were almost immediately bypassed. In response to a royal supplication Bury was made bishop of Durham (one of the very richest sees in England) by papal provision on 24 October 1333, quashing the election by the monks of Durham of their fellow monk and Oxford theologian, Robert Graystanes. Bury was consecrated into that office at Chertsey Abbey, Surrey, on 19 December 1333, and was installed at Durham in June 1334.

Bury's diplomatic skills had been useful in gaining papal support for Edward at the beginning of his reign. Bury was sent as envoy to the papal court at Avignon in 1330 and helped negotiate papal support for the *coup d'état* in October 1330 that ended the regency and gave Edward III freedom to rule. Bury was made a papal chaplain in 1331, and again served as royal envoy to Avignon from February to November 1333. After Bury became bishop of Durham he served as treasurer of the exchequer from 3 February to 1 August 1334 and ultimately as chancellor of the realm from 28 September 1334 to 6 June 1335. He was frequently employed in diplomatic service as royal envoy to Philippe VI (July to September 1336); adviser to the royal council at York on the Scottish war (March 1337); companion to the king in Flanders and the Rhineland to negotiate with Ludwig IV (1338); envoy to France (November 1338, July 1339, April 1341); and truce-maker with the Scots (April 1340, July 1341, April 1342, August 1343). Bury died at Auckland on 14 April 1345 and was buried shortly afterwards at the east end of Durham Cathedral.

One of the results of Bury's years in royal and episcopal administration was a formulary-book of letters, compiled about 1324 and containing approximately 1500 letters in all. This *Liber epistolaris quondam Ricardi de Bury* survives in a manuscript which in the mid-twentieth century was in the collection of Lord Harlech. It was edited by Noel Denholm-Young for the Roxburghe Club in 1950.

Throughout the period of his episcopate, when not actually travelling with or on behalf of the king, Bury divided his time between occasional visits to Durham and residence at the London inn of the bishops of Durham. By 1331 Bury had assembled a large household of clerks and chaplains who travelled or resided with him. During his episcopate this *familia* came to include the Mertonian scholars and theologians Thomas Bradwardine and Walter Burley, two other Mertonians, Walter Seagrave and John Maudith, the Oxford masters and doctors of law Richard Bentworth and John Atton, the Oxford theologians Richard Fitzralph and Richard Kilvington, and the Dominican theologian and proto-humanist Robert Holcot. The circle may also have included, for a time, the Franciscan theologian Walter Chatton. Not all of these figures resided with Bury at the same time, yet even so they represent the single most notable circle or sequence of scholars under the patronage of one person in fourteenth-century England. These clerics and learned table companions provided a high level of intellectual exchange in Bury's household, and he in turn supported their careers in royal and ecclesiastical service, which in the case of Thomas Bradwardine led to his appointment as chancellor of St Paul's in London. Indeed, four years after the death of his patron Bradwardine was made archbishop of Canterbury.

Bury assembled a large private library during his lifetime, some of it commissioned through scribes, much of it acquired by purchase or gift from monastic communities and the second-hand book market. He is known to have borrowed books from St Albans Abbey and from Bermondsey Priory. Bury's attitudes towards books and his plan to establish a library for a college he would endow at Oxford are revealed in his *Philobiblon* (chs. 18–19), which may have been written with the help of Robert Holcot. In that work his preferences for literary and theological works are prominent, along with his belief in the importance of language study in Greek and Hebrew. The liberal arts remained central to his understanding of learning and far more rewarding and important than the study of law.

Bury's *Philobiblon* contains more than expressions of his love of books, his methods of acquiring his library, and his plans for endowing a college at Oxford that would house his collection. It contains abundant criticisms of contemporary scholarly and religious practices. The *Philobiblon* was cast as an episcopal letter to the Christian faithful, admonishing various groups for their neglect or misuse of learning. Cast in the form of a complaint (*planctus*) voiced by books themselves, it accuses secular clerks, particularly those who have left the schools for a church career, of forgetting what little training they have received, or allowing their books to fall into disreputable hands by being pawned to non-believers. Two contemporary practices attract particular scorn. One is a practice, becoming common by the middle of the fourteenth century, of putting forward as one's own lectures and books the works created by an earlier author. The second is the translation of Greek or Latin works into the vernacular by clerks of insufficient learning. Bury is similarly critical of monks and mendicant friars, whom he sees as more concerned with food, wine, and comfortable accommodation than with the content of books. In the context of a chapter on the ancients and moderns (that is, his contemporaries), Bury makes one of his most famous ironic observations:

> The zeal of that noble university [Paris], whose rays once shed light into every corner of the world, has grown lukewarm, nay, is all but frozen. There the pen of every scribe is now at rest, generations of books no longer succeed each other, and there is none who begins to take [his] place as a new author. They wrap up their doctrines in unskilled discourse, and are losing all propriety of logic, except that our English subtleties [referring to Oxford logic], which they denounce in public, are the subject of their furtive vigils. (Bury, *Philobiblon*, trans. Thomas, 70–71)

The *Philobiblon* was printed several times in the fifteenth and sixteenth centuries (Cologne, 1473; Speyer, 1483; Paris, 1500; Leipzig, 1574; and Oxford, 1599).

Petrarch, who had met Bury in Avignon, describes him with kind but carefully chosen words as 'an ardent amateur'—'a man of eager mind and not unlearned, from his youth unusually inquisitive concerning abstruse matters' (Emden, *Oxf.*, 1.325), and one of his own clerks, Walter Burley, expresses a similar view, calling him 'a most fervent enthusiast for the increase of knowledge' (ibid.); however, William Chambre, a monk at Durham, describes him only as 'adequately learned' (ibid.). It was thus Bury's enthusiastic support of learning more than his own learning that impressed his contemporaries. His plans for a college that would house his library, consisting of hundreds of manuscripts, was never fulfilled because of the debts he left at the time of his death. While his episcopal income was substantial, his consecration as bishop in 1333 required him to give up his benefices and canonical prebends, and his lifestyle as prelate, royal envoy, and patron of learning exceeded his familial and episcopal revenues. His books, filling more than five large carts, were sold by the executors of his estate.

W. J. Courtenay

Sources *Chancery records* [researches in foreign archives, Italy] · *CEPR letters*, 2.392 · *The liber epistolaris of Richard de Bury*, ed. N. Denholm-Young, Roxburghe Club (1950) · R. Bury, *Philobiblon*, ed. and trans. E. C. Thomas (1888); repr. as *The love of books: the Philobiblon of Richard de Bury* (New York, 1966) · R. Bury, *Philobiblon*, ed. A. Altamura (Naples, 1954) · Emden, *Oxf.* · N. Denholm-Young, 'Richard de Bury', *TRHS*, 4th ser., 20 (1937), 135–68; repr. in *Collected papers on mediaeval subjects* (1946), 1–25 · J. de Ghellinck, 'Un évêque bibliophile au XIVe siècle: Richard d'Aungerville', *Revue d'Histoire Ecclésiastique*, 18 (1922), 271–312, 482–508 · B. Smalley, *English friars and antiquity in the early fourteenth century* (1960), 66–74 · Tout, *Admin. hist.*, 3.25n., 26n. · W. J. Courtenay, *Schools and scholars in fourteenth-century England* (1987), 133–7

Likenesses seal, U. Durham L., Durham Cathedral muniments, 3.6.Pont.4 [*see illus.*]

Bury, Samuel (*bap.* 1663, *d.* 1730), Presbyterian minister, fifth and last child of Edward *Bury (1615/16–1700), an ejected minister, and his first wife, Margaret, was born at Great Bolas, Shropshire, where he was baptized on 21 April 1663. He was educated at Thomas Doolittle's academy, which was then at Islington. Here he was contemporary with Matthew Henry, who entered in 1680 and remained long enough to contract a strong friendship with Bury. Edmund Calamy (1671–1732), who entered in 1682, remembered Bury as a student of philosophy, not divinity. On 29 May 1697 Bury married Elizabeth [*see* Bury, Elizabeth (1644?–1720)], diarist, second daughter of Captain Adams Lawrence and Elizabeth Cutts, of Linton, Cambridgeshire, and the widow of Griffith Lloyd of Hemingford Grey, Huntingdonshire. No children were born to the marriage but Elizabeth's diary shows it to have been a long and happy union. After her death Bury published an account of her life based on the diary, which she kept from 1679 until her death.

Bury's first ministry was at Bury St Edmunds, where he took up his duties probably before the passing of the Toleration Act of 1689. In 1690 the first Presbyterian Trust, of which Bury was a trustee, took a lease on, and then purchased, a house in Churchgate Street to use as a chapel. By 1710 the congregation had outgrown this building and the trustees, with Bury as treasurer, built a new chapel, which was opened on 30 December 1711. On this occasion Bury preached two sermons which were subsequently published. The chapel survives as a grade one listed building and was fully restored in 1991. Between 1699 and 1714 Bury published a number of funeral and ordination sermons and a catechism for a charity school in Bury St Edmunds.

By 1696 Bury was engaged in collecting a list of the nonconforming ministers; Oliver Heywood supplied him on 14 August with the names in Yorkshire and Lancashire, through Samuel Angier. Bury was involved in promoting the protestant interest in Suffolk, and was the recognized leader of protestant dissent in the county. In the Lady Hewley suit of 1830–42, great pains were taken by the Unitarian defendants to collect indications of concessions to heterodox opinion on the part of Bury, as a representative Presbyterian of his time. However, the evidence that they used, which was taken from a farewell letter from Bury to his Bristol congregation, demonstrates that Bury was closer to Richard Baxter's 'middle-way' than to a unitarian faith, for he wrote, 'I never was prostituted to any party, but have endeavoured to serve God as a catholic Christian', and spoke of requirements which have no good scripture warrant as making 'apocryphal sins and duties' (Bury, 'Dying pastor's last legacy'). This address was essentially practical, avoiding controversy, and the strain is fervently evangelical.

In 1718 Bury was joined at Bury St Edmunds by his nephew Samuel Savage as his assistant. By this date both Bury and his wife were in poor health, and in 1719 he left Bury St Edmunds to take a cure at Bath. Before leaving the town he gave the chapel four silver chalices, four silver plates, and two large communion flagons, and in his will left it a set of Matthew Henry's *Expositions* upon the scriptures to be kept in the vestry. The flagons were sold, but the rest of the plate was placed with the borough council for safe keeping.

While Bury was in Bath he was approached by Henry Chandler, a contemporary from Doolittle's academy, to take over the pastorship of Lewin's Mead Chapel in Bristol. This was the larger of the two Presbyterian congregations in Bristol, and it had been vacant since the death of Michael Pope in 1718. It counted 1600 adherents. Some of its members had been sheriffs of the city; others were 'persons of condition; divers very rich, many more very substantial, few poor. The whole congregation computed worth near 400,000*l*' (Murch, 107). Bury agreed to go to Bristol for six months, and arrived there on 8 April 1720. A month later he lost his wife, who died on 8 May. His stay at Bristol was permanent; he got as assistant, probably in 1721, John Diaper, who succeeded him as pastor and resigned in 1751. Under Bury's ministry the congregation increased both in numbers and in wealth.

Bury died on 10 March 1730 at Lewin's Mead, and was buried on 15 March in St James's churchyard, where formerly there stood an altar tomb with Latin epitaphs to Bury and his wife. ALEXANDER GORDON, *rev.* E. LORD

Sources S. Bury, 'The dying pastor's last legacy to his flock, 1729/30', *Protestant Dissenter's Magazine*, 1 (1794), 235–7 • *An account of the life and death of Mrs Elizabeth Bury*, ed. S. Bury (1720) • *An account of the life and death of the late Reverend Mr. Matthew Henry*, ed. W. Tong (1716) • E. Calamy, *An historical account of my own life, with some reflections on the times I have lived in, 1671–1731*, ed. J. T. Rutt, 2 vols. (1829) • J. Hunter, *The rise of the old dissent, exemplified by the life of Oliver Heywood* (1842) • J. Toulmin, *An historical view of the state of the protestant dissenters in England* (1814) • J. Duncan, 'Samuel Bury, 1663–1729/30', 1957, DWL • J. Murch, *A history of the Presbyterian and General Baptist churches in the west of England* (1835) • *Calamy rev.* • J. Browne, *A history of Congregationalism and memorials of the churches in Norfolk and Suffolk* (1877) • J. Hunter, *A historical defence of the trustees of Lady Hewley's Foundation* (1834) • J. Corry and J. Evans, *The history of Bristol, civil and ecclesiastical*, 2 vols. (1816) • parish register (baptism), 21 April 1663, Great Bolas, Shropshire • parish register (burial), 15 March 1730, Bristol, St James • Churchgate Chapel book, Bury St Edmunds, Suffolk RO, Bury St Edmunds, E5/5/2.1

Archives Suffolk RO, Bury St Edmunds, Churchgate Chapel book

Likenesses oils; formerly at Simpson & Son Auctioneers, Bury St Edmunds

Bury, Sir Thomas (*bap.* **1652**, *d.* **1722**), judge, was baptized on 29 February 1652 in Grantham, the youngest son of Sir William Bury (1605–1669) of Linwood, Lincolnshire, and his second wife, Jane, daughter and coheir of George Ellis of Wyham, Lincolnshire. He entered Lincoln College, Oxford, on 13 May 1664, the same day as his elder brother, Gilbert. He gained a BA on 1 February 1668 and on 24 April following was admitted to Gray's Inn. He was called to the bar on 12 June 1676. In August 1681 Bury was made counsel for the city of Lincoln; he was made a freeman of the city on 25 February 1699 and was elected recorder on 7 September 1700. In November 1700 he was made a serjeant-at-law—two of his patrons being his distant relative Sir William Ellys, second baronet, a prominent Lincolnshire whig, and the whig grandee the duke of Newcastle. Bury resigned his recordership on 1 March 1701 following his appointment on the 26 January as a baron of the exchequer. He had been knighted on 16 February 1701.

Bury's epitaph says that he 'by his Great Application to the Study of the Law, raised himself to one of the highest Degrees in that Profession' (epitaph, parish church, Grantham), but Mr Speaker Arthur Onslow, in his notes to Bishop Burnet's *History*, affirms that it appeared from Bury's book of accounts (a most unlikely place for such a revelation) that he gave the lord keeper, Sir Nathan Wright, a bribe of £1000 for elevating him to the bench. Bury was reappointed following the accession of Queen Anne, and for fifteen years he continued to discharge the duties of a puisne judge. In judicial matters he was inclined towards the whigs, giving his opinion in support of Lord Chief Justice Holt, and on the same side as Baron Somers, in the celebrated *Ashby* v. *White* case which had been brought before the Lords on a writ of error following a case in queen's bench in which several whig voters sued the returning officers of the borough for disfranchising them. On 20 and 22 April 1710 he—with Lord Chief Justice Parker and Mr Justice Tracy, at the Old Bailey—tried Daniel Dammarree and others for riot and being the ringleader of a mob during the Sacheverell riots of 1–2 March.

No doubt Bury's political sympathies led to his reappointment on the accession of George I. Indeed, on the death of Sir Samuel Dodd, Bury was raised to be chief baron of the exchequer on 10 June 1716. On 1 December 1718 he was elected a member of the Royal Society. Bury died of the palsy at his house in Serjeants' Inn on 4 May 1722, having carried on working until within a few hours of his death. He was buried on 18 May in the parish church of Grantham, where a handsome tomb was erected to his memory. His will of 1715 left £10,000 to be laid out in land for the benefit of his brother Gilbert and his son William. The ultimate beneficiary of this and of his estates at Irby, near Wainfleet, was his grand-nephew William Bury of Linwood Grange. STUART HANDLEY

Sources A. R. Maddison, ed., *Lincolnshire pedigrees*, 1, Harleian Society, 50 (1902), 213–5 • Sainty, *Judges* • Baker, *Serjeants* • Foss, *Judges*, 7.17–18 • A. Boyer, *The political state of Great Britain*, 23 (1722), 552 • N. Luttrell, *A brief historical relation of state affairs from September 1678 to April 1714*, 6 (1857), 572–3 • *Bishop Burnet's History*, 5.224 • will, PRO, PROB 11/585, sig. 89 • HoP, *Commons*, 1690–1715 [draft] • Foster, *Alum. Oxon.* • *The record of the Royal Society of London*, 4th edn (1940), 394 • J. Foster, *The register of admissions to Gray's Inn, 1521–1889*,

together with the register of marriages in Gray's Inn chapel, 1695–1754 (privately printed, London, 1889), 304
Likenesses J. Richardson, oils, 1719, Gray's Inn, London • J. Smith, mezzotint, 1720 (after J. Richardson), BM, NPG
Wealth at death wealthy; £10,000 to be laid out in land after death: will, PRO, PROB 11/585, sig. 89, 1722

Bury, Thomas Talbot (*bap.* **1809**, *d.* **1877**), architect and engraver, was baptized on 26 November 1809 in the parish of St Botolph, Aldgate, London, the son of Richard Samuel Bury (*b. c.*1777) and his wife, Caroline (*née* Talbot). In 1824 he was articled to Augustus Charles Pugin, and in 1830 he commenced practice at 7 Gerrard Street, Soho. He was in partnership with Charles Lee (1803/4–1880) from 1845 for about four years. He was also assistant to Louis Vulliamy. In addition to his architectural practice, Bury was often engaged in engraving and lithographing his own and other architects' drawings, notably those of Augustus Welby Pugin and Owen Jones. With the former he worked on designing the details of the houses of parliament under Sir Charles Barry. He was particularly skilful in colouring architectural studies, and his aid in this respect was often sought by the most eminent architects of the day when they were engaged in preparing designs for competition. He was described by H. R. Mallalieu as 'an architect and topographer who produced Parisian views somewhat in the manner of W. [William] Callow' (Mallalieu, *Watercolour artists*, 1.49). He frequently exhibited his works at the Royal Academy between 1846 and 1872; and sent to the international exhibition of 1862 a large picture representing, at one view, all the churches, schools, public and other buildings erected by him (now in the RIBA collection). Among his principal works were thirty-five churches and chapels, fifteen parsonages, twelve schools, and twenty other large public buildings and private residences in various parts of England and Wales. These are listed in Bury's obituary (*The Builder*, 205). Bury was elected an associate of the Institute of British Architects in 1839, and a fellow in 1843. In 1876 he was elected a vice-president. He was in 1863 made a fellow of the Society of Antiquaries, and was also a member of the council of the Royal Archaeological Institute of Great Britain and Ireland, a member of the Cambrian Archaeological Association, and an associate of the Society of Civil Engineers.

A handsome facsimile of the first edition of his *Coloured Views of the Liverpool and Manchester Railway*, published by Rudolph Ackermann in 1831, was published in Oldham in 1976. These are considered to be the finest of the various series of prints published to commemorate the opening of the Liverpool and Manchester Railway, on 15 September 1830, and include thirteen hand-coloured aquatint plates engraved by H. Pyall (or Ryall) and S. G. Hughes 'from drawings made on the spot' (*Coloured Views of the Liverpool and Manchester Railway*, vii.) by Bury. His collections of architectural and antiquarian books, his pictures, drawings, cabinets, and armour, were sold at Christies on 29 June 1877. In 1847 Bury published *Remains of Ecclesiastical Woodwork*, illustrated by his own engravings, which are signed with his characteristic monogram which consisted of three superimposed initials followed by the rest of his surname, the whole in capital letters. This was followed in 1849 by his *History and description of the styles of architecture of various countries, from the earliest to the present period*. On 23 February 1877 he died at home at 50 Welbeck Street, Cavendish Square, London, a widower and childless. He was buried at Norwood cemetery.

W. H. TREGELLAS, *rev.* ANNETTE PEACH

Sources *Dir. Brit. archs.* • *The Builder*, 35 (1877), 205 • Mallalieu, *Watercolour artists* • *RIBA drawings collection* • *IGI* • Graves, *RA exhibitors* • *CGPLA Eng. & Wales* (1877)
Archives RIBA BAL, drawings collection • RIBA BAL, biography file, RIBA nomination papers, Av1 p. 102; Fv2 p. 0; Fv2 p. 5
Wealth at death under £6000: probate, 4 March 1877, *CGPLA Eng. & Wales*

Bury St Edmunds, Hugo of (*fl. c.*1130–*c.*1150), artist, was active at the abbey of Bury St Edmunds under abbots Anselm (1121–48) and Ording (1148–56). Documents written at the abbey record that he worked in several media. He cast a bell for the newly rebuilt abbey church. He 'painted incomparably' a large Bible, for which he obtained vellum from Ireland. He 'carved incomparably' a cross and figures of the Virgin and St John. For the west front of the church he made a pair of decorated bronze doors, of which it was judged that 'as he surpassed all others in other works, in this work he wonderfully surpassed himself' (Arnold, 2.289–90). Some other works may be his. A lead seal of *c.*1150, which portrays an unnamed abbot of Bury, shows the hallmarks of his style. A wall painting of *c.*1160 in the chapel of St Anselm at Canterbury Cathedral, which shows St Paul bitten by a viper on the island of Malta, has been attributed to Hugo, although it may be the work of a follower.

Hugo's career at Bury probably lasted from the late 1120s until the 1150s. Talbot, the prior, and Hervey, the sacrist, who commissioned Hugo to illuminate the large Bible, held office between *c.*1125 and *c.*1136. Elias, sacrist during most of Ording's abbacy, commissioned the cross, the latest of Hugo's recorded works. The title of 'master', repeatedly applied to Hugo in the Bury *Gesta sacristarum*, implies that he was probably not a monk, but a secular artist hired by the abbey.

Hugo's cross may be identifiable as the walrus-ivory cross at the Cloisters in New York. The first part of the Bible which Hugo illuminated is preserved as MS 2, Corpus Christi College, Cambridge. This despoiled manuscript, containing the Old Testament up to the book of Job, still preserves six large-scale pictures of biblical scenes, a decorative page of script, and forty-one decorated initials. A fragment of one leaf is all that is known to survive of the second part of the Bible.

Hugo's figure style in the Bible derives from the art of the Alexis Master, who may have worked at Bury during his career. Hugo's use of double frames and panelled backgrounds also recalls that master's pictures, but Hugo's palette is richer, and his figures have greater weight and grace. His 'damp fold' technique for rendering draperies derives from Byzantine art, while the curvilinear patterns of his folds show an unprecedented degree of stylization. The style which he created strongly influenced English art for the remainder of the twelfth century, and found echoes on the continent.

Whether or not Hugo was a wall painter, the records of his activities as carver and manuscript painter attest his versatility. His surviving work in the Bury Bible shows that he was worthy of the admiration which the written sources accord him. TIMOTHY GRAHAM, *rev.*

Sources C. M. Kauffmann, 'The Bury Bible', *Journal of the Warburg and Courtauld Institutes*, 29 (1966), 60–81 · R. M. Thomson, 'Early Romanesque book-illustration in England: the dates of the Pierpont Morgan *Vitae sancti Edmundi* and the Bury Bible', *Viator*, 2 (1971), 211–25 · R. M. Thomson, 'The date of the Bury Bible reexamined', *Viator*, 6 (1975), 51–8 · C. R. Dodwell, *The pictorial arts of the West, 800–1200* (1993), 341–7 · E. C. Parker and C. T. Little, *The Cloisters cross: its art and meaning* (1994) · T. A. Heslop, 'The production and artistry of the Bury Bible', *Bury St Edmunds: medieval art, architecture, archaeology, and economy*, ed. A. Gransden (1998), 172–85 · 'Gesta sacristarum', *Memorials of St Edmund's Abbey*, ed. T. Arnold, 2, Rolls Series, 96 (1892), 289–96
Archives CCC Cam., MS 2

Bury St Edmunds, Mabel of (*fl.* 1239–1256), embroiderer, is known to have been an embroiderer of ecclesiastical vestments directly commissioned by Henry III in the years 1239–44. Evidence for these commissions is to be found in the close and liberate rolls in a succession of payments for work in progress, for materials, or for work completed.

Mabel's first commission from the king was in 1239, for a chasuble and offertory veil. Work on the chasuble took two years and when complete Henry ordered that it be appraised 'by the better workers of the city of London' so that a valuation, fair to both parties, could be arrived at (*CClR*, *1237–42*, 372). The chasuble was probably of samite, a twill-weave silk; it was embroidered in gold thread and enriched with pearls. A great orphrey, an edging orphrey, and fringe were supplied for the chasuble by Adam of Basing (*d.* 1262x6), who also arranged for it to be lined with canvas and fine silk. The chasuble was offered at the shrine of St Edward at Westminster Abbey, by the king and queen. While working on this chasuble Mabel seems also to have completed a set of 'ornaments for the King's [private] chapel', that is, the offertory cloth, apparels, stole, fanon, amice, collar, and cuffs, paid for in 1241 (*Calendar of the Liberate Rolls*, 1240–1245, 49). In 1243–4 Mabel embroidered a banner, again commissioned by Henry III, to hang in Westminster Abbey. This was made of red samite and embroidered in gold with the figures of the Virgin and St John.

Where Mabel lived and worked is not known. Some believe that she spent her working years in London, others that she always resided in Bury St Edmunds. Nothing is heard of her between 1245 and 1256 when the king, visiting Bury St Edmunds, commanded that she be given six ells of a suitable cloth and a lining of rabbit skin in recognition of her past services to himself and his queen. That Mabel was a very skilled embroiderer is certain. It is possible that she may have been particularly skilled in the gold thread embroidery technique known as underside couching; by drawing the thread into the body of the silk a solid, yet flexible, ground was achieved. This is one of the notable techniques of English medieval embroidery (*opus anglicanum*). Henry III commissioned embroideries from several other women, but his association with Mabel was unique. It is not possible to identify her chasuble and banner in the 1388 inventory of vestments at Westminster Abbey though both must have been very fine pieces.

KAY STANILAND

Sources *CClR*, *1237–56* · *Calendar of the liberate rolls*, 1–2, PRO (1916–30) · R. C. Stacey, ed., *Receipt and issue rolls for the … reign of King Henry III, 1241–42*, PRSoc., new ser., 87 (1992) · R. K. Lancaster, 'Artists, suppliers and clerks: the human factors in the art patronage of King Henry III', *Journal of the Warburg and Courtauld Institutes*, 35 (1972), 81–107 · J. W. Legg, 'On an inventory of the vestry in Westminster Abbey, taken in 1388', *Archaeologia*, 52 (1890), 195–286

Busby, Charles Augustin (1786–1834), architect, was born on 27 June 1786 in Poland Street, London, one month before the wedding of his parents, Dr Thomas *Busby (1754–1838), musician and author, and Priscilla Angier (*bap.* 1760, *d.* before 1838), daughter of Charles Angier of Earls Court; Augustus has invariably yet erroneously been given as his middle name. Educated at home with six younger brothers and sisters, he exhibited at the Royal Academy from 1801, entered the Royal Academy Schools in 1803, and won the gold medal four years later. Two volumes of designs by Busby followed in 1808: *A Series of Designs for Villas and Country Houses* and *A Collection of Designs for Modern Embellishments*. Bingham called the latter 'one of the prettiest pattern books produced during the Regency' (Bingham, 32), and they brought the young unknown several commissions, but open competition found him his first significant contract: the Commercial Coffee Rooms, Corn Street, Bristol (1809; exh. RA, 1810). On 3 July 1811, as the building neared completion, he married Louisa Mary Williams, with whom he had two children.

Attracted by the intellectual rigour of the Greek revival, Busby also possessed a lifelong fascination for everything mechanical; he patented a hydraulic system to save water in canals (1813) and worked up designs for cast-iron roofs, and always described himself as an 'architect and engineer'. Following his apprenticeship to Daniel Alexander, Busby received a commission to create a Gothic castle at Gwrych, Denbighshire (exh. RA, 1814), which he hoped would launch a successful country house practice. In 1816–17, however, the castle was taken from him and one of his iron roofs may have collapsed; the allegation comes from a later hostile source, and cannot be substantiated. Within months he was in America, where, based in New York, he experimented with the propulsion of steamboats and studied prison design. Yet he apparently received only one commission in America: the Bolingbroke Theatre, Petersburg, Virginia (1817–18), and was obliged to return to Britain to a lowly clerkship under Francis Goodwin (1784–1835), whose office was then flush with projects for the commissioners for new churches. Part-way through a shabby scheme to secure additional contracts by circumventing commission regulations the venal pair fell out. Without delay, Busby secured his own commissioners' jobs in Leeds and Oldham (1821; exh. RA, 1822), only to see the plans rejected on the advice of Nash and Smirke, because the iron roofs were seen to be weak and insecure.

Again Busby quit London, this time at the invitation of Thomas Read Kemp.

Kemp provided Busby with high-profile work in Brighton and brokered a partnership with a talented local architect, **Amon Henry Wilds** (*bap.* 1790, *d.* 1857), not, as was long thought, with his father, Amon Wilds (1762–1833), carpenter and then builder. He was baptized at All Saints', Lewes, Sussex, on 4 November 1790, the son of Amon Wilds and his wife, Sarah Dunn (1764–1822); the date of 1784 universally given for Wilds's birth is presumably incorrect. In Brighton the Wildses had built for Kemp a chapel (Holy Trinity, Ship Street, 1817) and possibly a residence, The Temple (1819), while for the Unitarians they created a majestic Doric temple in New Road (1820). In 1823 Kemp commissioned the younger Wilds and Busby to create a homonymous speculative development. From Kemp Town they continued sometimes together, often individually, to establish such an ascendancy that Regency Brighton, judged in the 1830s 'alone to be equalled at St Petersburg' (Dale, 10), was essentially their creation. While lack of surviving documentary evidence has made it difficult to distinguish the works of Busby in Brighton from those of Wilds (almost invariably, their drawings are signed 'Wilds & Busby'), the inclusion of Egyptian details, ammonite Ionic capitals, and bold scallop shells recessed over windows, and later, Italianate designs, characterize the work of Wilds. Individual works by Busby include the chapels of St Margaret (1824; dem. 1959) and St George (1824–5), and Portland Place (1824–8; plans exh. RA, 1830). After only twenty-five months the partnership between Busby and Wilds was dissolved amid considerable acrimony in June 1825, with Busby claiming many buildings as his own. By contrast, Wilds was in partnership with his father from *c.*1806 to 1823.

Kemp Town (plans exh. RA, 1825) is an exceptional piece of urban planning: a self-sufficient community of 250 socially graded houses with amenities arranged (had all been built) in three squares, a crescent, and fourteen terraces. The enterprise was grandiose and comparable with Nash's Regent's Park. The span of Lewes Crescent is 200 feet wider than the Royal Crescent, Bath. Architecturally, as well as financially, however, Kemp Town was not a success. The architects were allowed no part in the building, while lengthy delays compromised their design. Mediocre façades failed to discipline the provocative width of Lewes Crescent and unify the whole. Kemp Town underwhelms. On a similar scale, Busby repeated this vision in Brunswick Town, Hove (plans exh. RA, 1825). Designed in 1824, it is said to have been Busby's own brainchild and, in contrast to the lack of organization in Kemp Town, Brunswick surged ahead under Busby as architect, builder, and manager. Until at least the devising of the ground-plan, however, Wilds was still a full partner; he withdrew the very day the building agreement was signed in November 1824. Whereas Brunswick Terrace and the upper half of Brunswick Square surely bear the incisive flourish of Busby's talent, the mannered façades lower down the square and the intemperate group numbered 1–6 Brunswick Terrace are too vulgar to be his.

Busby was active in local politics, and served on the Hove vestry and the Brunswick commission. In 1831 he became high commissioner of Hove and helped prepare the local petition in favour of the Reform Bill; his Brighton votes in 1832 show him a radical whig. He was also a keen astronomer, and was often seen off the beach in the small paddle-steamer he designed and built. Inventive to the end, he intended the Brunswick houses to have running hot and cold water, and gained Faraday's approval for a steam-driven central heating system (patented 1832). During the later 1820s Busby overstretched himself. Arrested for debt in 1829 and sued in 1832, his nemesis came in February 1833, when he was declared bankrupt, owing £12,644. Through the generosity of friends the debts were soon paid, but Busby was a broken man. He died intestate in his house at 1 Stanhope Place, Hove, on 18 September 1834 and was buried seven days later in St Andrew's churchyard, Hove.

Meanwhile, Amon Henry Wilds continued in practice in Brighton, with substantial activity in Gravesend, Kent, in the 1830s. The Brighton houses he built for himself reveal flamboyant à la mode tastes: the Gothic House, Western Terrace (*c.*1822–5), was followed by a foray into the oriental style with the Western Pavilion (*c.*1828). The unexecuted design of a pyramid for his extension to St Nicholas's churchyard (1840–41) and the cast-iron Victoria fountain (1845) demonstrate his delight in the picturesque. At the same time, his use of coade stone, his patented method of cleaning chimneys without climbing boys (1843), and his scheme for a floating Brighton breakwater (*c.*1843) point to a progressive, utilitarian mind. Wilds's most important works were his sequences of linked villas: Hanover Crescent (1822–7), Montpelier Crescent (1843–7), and Park Crescent (1849–55) in Brighton, and Park Crescent, Worthing (1825–9; exh. RA, 1830). His recreation was archery, and briefly he involved himself in local government, serving in 1845–8 as a Brighton commissioner. He died on 13 July 1857 at his home, Old Shoreham Cottage, Old Shoreham, Sussex.

Rapidly forgotten, much of the Brighton work of Wilds and Busby was under threat of demolition from the 1930s. The researches of Anthony Dale, and the pioneering conservation work of the Regency Society he co-founded, helped to restore their reputations locally, and an exhibition at the RIBA in 1991 reintroduced Busby to a wider public, though perhaps at the expense of allowing him to overshadow Amon Henry Wilds.

MARTIN D. W. JONES

Sources N. Bingham, *C. A. Busby: the Regency architect of Brighton and Hove* (1991) · A. Dale, *Fashionable Brighton, 1820–1860*, 2nd edn (1967) · S. Colman, 'The linked villas of Amon Henry Wilds', DipArch diss., Brighton Polytechnic, 1989 · Colvin, *Archs.* · M. H. Port, *Six hundred new churches: a study of the church building commission, 1818–1856, and its church building activities* (1961) · Brighton poll book (1832) · M. Ray, 'Who were the Brunswick Town commissioners?', *Sussex Archaeological Collections*, 127 (1989), 211–28 · *GM*, 1st ser., 81/2 (1811), 84 · *GM*, 1st ser., 84/1 (1814), 248 · *Brighton Gazette* (24 Feb 1831), 1 · PRO, B3/738 [bankruptcy proceedings, February 1833] · parish register, Lewes, All Saints', 4 Nov 1790, E. Sussex RO [baptism] · *Brighton Herald* (25 July 1857) · directories, Brighton, 1822–

34 · directories, Sussex, 1819–57 [Amon Henry Wilds] · gravestone, churchyard, St Nicholas's, Brighton [parent of Amon Henry Wilds]
Archives NRA, priv. coll.
Likenesses J. Fruman, miniature, 1807, V&A
Wealth at death under £200: administration, E. Sussex RO, W/B22.199

Busby, Sir Matthew [Matt] **(1909–1994)**, football manager, was born on 26 May 1909 at 28 Old Arbiston, one of thirty-two two-room cottages near Bellshill, Lanarkshire. He was the eldest child of Alexander Busby, a coalminer, and his wife, Helen Greer. It was a hard life made harder when his father was killed at the battle of Arras in 1916. His mother took a job at the pit top and later at a nearby steelworks in order to keep her young family. Matthew went to the local elementary school, St Bride's, Bothwell, where he showed such promise that he was transferred to the Motherwell higher grade school, which offered some secondary education to those children unable to afford grammar school. However, by the time he was sixteen he was working down in the pit.

The player Football was a popular recreation for many young pitmen in the 1920s. Busby played for Orbiston Cannibals and then Alpine Villa, which won the Scottish junior cup for players under eighteen. Scouts from the professional clubs were always on the look-out for talent and Busby had trials first for Denny Hibernian and then Manchester City. The Denny club secretary was friendly with one of City's Scottish professionals and Busby played for the reserve team against Burnley reserves in February 1928. He was impressive enough to be signed on at wages of £5 per week during the season and £4 in summer. But he was not a success either as an inside forward or on the wing. Moreover he was homesick. Manchester City were then the top dogs of local football, while their nearby rivals Manchester United were struggling both on and off the field. United might have signed Busby in 1930 but they could not afford the £150 transfer fee. It was soon after this that he had a moment of good fortune that changed his life: he was moved from inside forward to wing-half when the normal incumbent failed to turn up for a third team match. Busby played well enough to win a place in the reserve team and when Matt Barrass, the first team right-half, got injured Busby took his place. Poor Barrass was never able to regain it. On 12 January 1931 Busby married Jeanie Philips Menzies (1908/9–1988), daughter of Jeanie Macvie, a typist.

Busby became a probing, skilful, and attacking wing-half who had good ball control, a shrewd and often well-disguised pass, and a box of dribbling and feinting tricks which earned him a cap for Scotland against Wales in 1934. He was not so good defensively, being slightly slow, but he and Eric Brook inspired Manchester City's FA cup final victory in 1934 when the *Manchester Guardian* identified him as a certain choice for that select eleven of 'Footballers Who Obviously Love Football'. Busby moved to Liverpool in 1936 for a fee of £8000, and helped the club both to avoid relegation and to play a more thoughtful and effective game in the two seasons before war broke out.

Sir Matthew Busby (1909–1994), by Sefton Samuels, 1969

Like many other leading professional footballers, Busby was an army physical training instructor during the war. He also played a lot of football, and in October 1945 was given command of a star-studded army side which went to Italy to help entertain the troops. There had been talk of his taking a coaching job at Liverpool but on his demobilization in 1946 he accepted an offer to manage Manchester United.

Into management Although the job was hardly a poisoned chalice, it was a definite challenge. The club had an overdraft of £15,000, and their Old Trafford ground was unusable after being bombed in 1941. United were forced to play their home matches at Manchester City's Maine Road ground until August 1949. Nevertheless, the team was not a bad one and Busby made two or three signings which improved it. Busby was thirty-six, and his long years in professional football had shown him many of the things that were wrong with the game. First team players looked down on the rest, and even they saw the manager only once a week and the only team talk they were likely to get was just before Saturday's match. Directors were prone to interfere too much in football matters, on which few had any useful knowledge. Clubs also tended to treat their players in a rather disdainful manner. Busby wanted to adopt a more humane approach. He believed in taking training (and is often thought of as the first tracksuit manager), favoured regular team talks, and, like Herbert Chapman, sought the players' views. He also made it clear to the directors that it would be he, not they, who picked the team. And although Busby recognized that football was a physical game he felt that the development of skills had been neglected. This he sought to remedy.

Busby made a good start to his managerial career. United were fourth in the temporary Northern League in 1945–6 and when the first division was restarted in 1946–7 the club were runners-up for three seasons in a row, though they did win the FA cup in 1948. Spurs offered Busby their manager's job at a salary of £2750 but he turned them down. Finally, after seven years in which they were never out of the first division's top four, United won the championship in 1951–2 for the first time in forty years. But it was done with an ageing team and the scheme to find replacements was already in the making.

In 1947 Manchester United reserves had won the central league, but it was felt that none of the players was good enough for the first team. Busby and his assistant, Jimmy Murphy, decided that something had to be done. Their aim was to develop young players in a more sophisticated and systematic way than any club had done before. If boys were recruited at fifteen, they could not only be taught how to play but also have instilled in them a loyalty to the club and its methods which would build the team spirit and solidarity necessary for success. The objective was to identify the best young players in the country and to sift them through four or five teams, each representing a rung on a ladder to the first eleven. The club had no large staff to achieve this. In addition to Murphy and Busby there was Bert Whalley, a recently retired centre-half, who was employed as coach to the young; a former Post Office engineer, Joe Armstrong, who had an eye for discovering footballing talent; and eight part-time scouts. Over time, contacts and networks were established. By the late 1950s three-quarters of the tips about young players came from supportive schoolteachers and by the late 1960s the club was receiving hundreds of letters a week suggesting the names of boys to be looked at. This structure was supported by a network of landladies carefully chosen to provide the stability and comforts that the boys had left at home.

The Busby Babes The scheme was a great success and bore fruit in the so-called *Busby Babes. But how was it done? Manchester United was not a household name in the late 1940s and early 1950s. Why should Mark Jones and David Pegg, both south Yorkshire boys with connections to Sheffield Wednesday, join Manchester United? Why should Duncan Edwards from Dudley, just down the road from Wolverhampton Wanderers, one of the most successful clubs of the 1950s, sign for United? And why did Bobby Charlton, a star of the east Northumberland schoolboys team, with eighteen clubs anxious for his signature, opt for Manchester rather than Newcastle United? The hard work of that team at Old Trafford—Busby, Murphy, Whalley, and Armstrong—is obviously one answer. But some who have seen the club accounts say that they show that inducements were offered to parents to encourage them to let their sons sign for the club. Payments were made, though it is not clear by whom, and it is hard to believe that Busby would not have known about it. No other English club was as good at recruiting and bringing forward the young talent as Manchester United, who won the FA youth cup five times in a row between 1953 and 1957.

The first real test for the system was at hand. By the end of 1952 United were at the bottom of the first division. In came the youngsters Jackie Blanchflower, Eddie Colman, Duncan Edwards, David Pegg, and Jeff Whitefoot, and by the end of the season the club had risen to eighth. During the next two seasons they were fourth and fifth, with an average age of twenty-three. Some of them—Colman and Tommy Taylor, for example—looked particularly young, and the newspaper men's addiction to alliteration produced the nickname the Busby Babes, though more serious thinkers could see that such a sobriquet was inappropriate. The experience and training that United had given them bestowed, perhaps like Busby himself, a maturity beyond their years. These were the first products of a system that owed comparatively little to the buying and selling of players. Moreover the next generation was already at the club. The league championship was won in 1955–6 and 1956–7. The double of FA cup and league, not achieved since 1897, almost certainly would have been completed in 1957, had United not lost their goalkeeper in the cup final to a reckless challenge. A third successive championship seemed, if not certain, very likely. Moreover Busby had pioneered English entry to the European cup in 1956–7 against the wishes of the Football League management committee, and reached the semi-final before being defeated by the formidable Real Madrid.

In the following season victories in the European cup against Shamrock Rovers and Dukla Prague were followed by a third-round tie with Red Star of Belgrade (won 5–4 on aggregate). It was on 6 February 1958, while returning from the second leg of that match, that their Elizabethan aircraft crashed attempting a third take-off from Munich airport, where it had made a refuelling stop. Twenty-three passengers died, including eight players: Geoff Bent, Roger Byrne, Eddie Colman, Duncan Edwards, Mark Jones, David Pegg, Tommy Taylor, and Billy Whelan. The club secretary Walter Crickmer, the trainer, Tom Curry, and the coach, Bert Whalley, also died. Nine players survived, although two never played again. Busby also escaped, although he had severe injuries, including a collapsed lung and a crushed foot. Twice he received the last rites from a Roman Catholic priest.

It was here that Busby's wife, Jean, played an important part, not only in nursing him back to health, but helping in her husband's struggle to find the will to continue the work. Misfortune was not a stranger to the Busby household. Four of their sons had died soon after birth. Busby admitted later that he had prayed for death, but eventually saw that what he must do for the sake of those who had died was to try to succeed again.

Post-Munich success The patched-up team reached the 1958 FA cup final with most of the nation behind them. Busby had not long been out of hospital but he saw the match, lost to Bolton Wanderers, and received the CBE in the following month. Rebuilding the team had to be done quickly and players were bought to provide solidity and experience. But virtuosity was purchased too in the dynamic skills of Pat Crerand and Denis Law. The FA cup was won in 1963, by which time the next generation of the youth policy, together with the remains of the pre-Munich side, were ready. United won the championship in 1964–5 and 1966–7 and were runners-up in 1967–8. But in 1968, on home soil at Wembley Stadium, the team finally won the European cup, defeating Benfica 4–1. Of that team only four had been bought: Stepney, Dunne, Crerand, and Law. The remainder were home grown Brennan, Foulkes, Sadler, Stiles, Best, Charlton, Kidd, and Aston. It was a remarkable testimony both to the system and to the men who made it. It was an emotional moment at which many tears were shed. The trophy that had become something of a holy grail for the club had been won. Public recognition descended on manager and players. Busby had been given the freedom of Manchester in 1967; in 1968 he was knighted and was voted manager of the year.

The European cup-winning team was an ageing one and Busby was having to spend more of his time dealing with some of his more temperamental stars. He had already had problems with both George Best and Denis Law, and had been criticized for not curbing the on-field indiscipline of some of his players. Busby announced his retirement in January 1969. For the next two years he stayed on at the club as general manager, perhaps not the most helpful thing for his successor. The club opted for continuity with the internal appointment of Wilf McGuinness, a former player whose career had been cut short by injury. McGuinness lacked Busby's authority and was unable to control some of the bigger egos in the dressing-room. From appearing to be football's easiest job, managing Manchester United became the toughest. A succession of incumbents tried and failed. Busby became a director in 1971, relinquishing the title of general manager. He retired from the board in 1982, and became president of the club from 1980 to 1993.

Busby managed Manchester United for just over twenty-three years. In that time he earned them an aggregate profit of over half a million pounds. But much more than that, by his example and success he made them into England's, indeed Britain's, first modern glamour club. No English football team had come near to the average attendances which United could boast in the 1960s: 54,854 in 1966–7 and a record 57,352 in 1967–8. Between the mid-1960s and the mid-1980s they were the best-supported side in the country and remarkably suffered only a 1 per cent fall in attendances when crowds in the first division as a whole fell by nearly a third. Even relegation to the second division for one season in the 1970s made no difference to the strength of their support. Fans came not only from Manchester, but from all over the north-west—indeed from all corners of the country—in order to be associated with the Red Devils. Munich obviously had something to do with the affection felt for the club but other post-Munich factors were probably more important.

First, there was the huge publicity generated by their European cup campaigns, particularly after the spectacular victory over Benfica in Lisbon in March 1966. United won 5–1 after scoring three goals in the first fifteen minutes, two of them by George Best, whom the *Daily Mirror* dubbed El Beatle. Best was a huge media star and he played for United. Second, the mid-1960s were good times for English football. England's world cup victory of 1966 generated fresh interest in new places and was both part of and contributory to the rapid growth of football on television. And 1966–7 was also one of United's championship seasons. Moreover, it was an outstanding team, symbolized by the attacking and creative trinity of Best, Charlton, and Law. At a time when football was becoming more defensive, United scored eighty-four league goals in 1966–7, almost twenty more than anyone else. Their football was full of the excitement and flair for which Busby always aimed. They were easily the biggest attraction in English football. If there was one period when Manchester United became everyone's second team, this was it. Indeed some commentators have convincingly argued that it was only after this time that the Munich disaster became an important part of the brand mystique.

Qualities and characteristics How did Busby achieve such success as a manager? In some ways he was forward-looking, in his attitudes towards European football, for example, and in the welcome he gave to the spread of the sport worldwide. He knew, from his own experience, that players could and should be treated better. He therefore took a close interest in their welfare, something which had not been common in his own playing days. Busby did not invent the idea of a youth policy but he probably believed in it more than any other manager, and largely built his reputation on it. However, he was not a coach in the modern sense of that term. He regularly took training until the 1960s but he offered no tactical innovations. He was a believer in creative football and had a somewhat romantic attachment to the game. When his players were on the field he gave them a very long, and very loose, rein, anxious that 'too much mind' might rob their football of its spectacular attractions. On the other hand he was gradually made aware that his teams might have to play defensively sometimes, although this was never a notable trait in his sides. Busby was keen to remind players how important were tackling, positioning, and communication on the field. And, like all good managers, he was an excellent judge of a player. He also had his fair share of luck.

What was Busby like as a man? At Liverpool, where he was team captain in the 1930s, it was said that he looked more like a bank manager than a professional footballer, as he walked to the ground in an overcoat and trilby hat, smoking a pipe. He was intelligent and authoritative, and, it was often said, imperturbable. During the Second World War he achieved the rank of company sergeant major. A practising Catholic and a good family man, he was perhaps also a father figure to his players: protective, understanding, and compassionate, qualities which were perhaps easier to exhibit when he was forty rather than sixty. He drove a solid Rover in 1968 but replaced it later with a Jensen sports car. It was Busby's style, warmth, and charisma that people noticed when they met him. Yet warm as he was, he also possessed a certain detachment which proved an invaluable managerial tool. He was certainly not easy-going, and he could be ruthless when defending the interests of the club. According to one biographer,

> Busby's toughness was well known in the dressing-room. Those who didn't fall under his charismatic spell eventually saw a glint of steel. In this too he was subtle. An exasperated sigh was a bad sign. His eyes, never warmly engaged with yours, would focus coldly as it became clear that ground was not being conceded on the other side of the desk. (Dunphy, 263)

Denis Law recalled being summoned to Busby's office after requesting a pay rise.

> He was stern. You've caused a lot of problems for this club, he told me, a lot of heartache. Nobody's going to hold Manchester United to ransom. Then he reached into his drawer and pulled out a typed apology which he told me I'd have to read at a press conference he'd called for later that morning. We'd always got on well. But he was a hard man … and crafty. He said he was protecting the wage structure at the club. But we did a deal which nobody knew about. He told me that if I apologized in public for the trouble I'd caused he'd give me half the rise I'd asked for. So I went out and ate humble pie. (ibid., 302–3)

These were the foundations on which Busby's managerial career were built.

Busby died in the Alexandra Hospital, Cheadle, on 20 January 1994. He was survived by one son and one daughter. The Sir Matt Busby Suite at Old Trafford and Sir Matt Busby Way leading to the stadium bear his name. A statue also stands in front of the ground, a monument to arguably the greatest British football manager of all time.

TONY MASON

Sources D. Miller, *Father of football: the story of Sir Matt Busby* (1994) • A. Hopcraft, *The football man: people and passions in soccer* (1968) • E. Dunphy, *A strange kind of glory: Sir Matt Busby & Manchester United* (1991) • M. Busby, *Soccer at the top: my life in football* (1974) • *The Times* (21 Jan 1994) • *The Independent* (21 Jan 1994) • *The Guardian* (21 Jan 1994) • b. cert. • m. cert. • d. cert.

Likenesses S. Samuels, photograph, 1969 [*see illus.*]

Wealth at death £224,982: probate, 8 Sept 1994, *CGPLA Eng. & Wales*

Busby, Richard (1606–1695), schoolmaster, was born at Lutton, Lincolnshire, on 22 September 1606, the second son of Richard Busby, churchwarden there, and Dorothy, sister of Henry Robinson of Westminster. It is likely that Busby belonged to a family which had long been tenants of Westminster Abbey in Rutland. At Westminster School he became captain of the king's scholars. Elected from Westminster in 1624 to a studentship at Christ Church, Oxford, he matriculated on 10 February 1626, graduated BA on 21 October 1628, and proceeded MA on 18 June 1631. These graduations were supported by gifts from the vestry of St Margaret's, Westminster. Busby remained at Christ Church as a tutor, establishing a reputation as an 'exact Latinist and Grecian' (Wood, *Ath. Oxon.*, 4.418). In August 1636 he acted before the king and queen in Cartwright's *Royal Slave*, and had some notion of making the stage his career, but in 1638 he returned to Westminster as head master.

At first Busby's appointment was provisional, following the deprivation of Lambert Osbaldeston for libelling Archbishop Laud. On 1 July 1639 Busby was collated to the prebend of Cudworth in Wells Cathedral, having the previous day received the diaconate from the bishop of Bath and Wells. On 23 December 1640 the dean and chapter of Westminster granted Busby the patent of his office. This was probably occasioned by the return to the abbey of the dean, Bishop John Williams; Busby, who rarely volunteered such opinions, acknowledged Williams as a 'stout defendant of his order' (*Correspondence of Isaac Basire*, 39).

For the next twenty years Busby steered Westminster through a succession of awkwardnesses with tact and firmness. Parliament took several measures to ensure that the school did not suffer from sequestration of the dean and chapter's revenues and the eventual dissolution of the collegiate body of which the school was part. It appears that Busby evaded subscription to the solemn league and covenant which was enjoined on all officers of Westminster College, in 1644; he may also have avoided signing the engagement in 1649. In place of the dean and chapter there were appointed governors to regulate Westminster School, with whom Busby achieved a working relationship, though he demonstrated his adherence to the proscribed Anglican rite. Busby quietly assisted impoverished royalists, but remained scrupulously observant of the *status quo*. Much has been made of prayers being said for Charles I in the school 'an hour, or two (at most)' before his execution (South, 5.58), but there is no record of prayers there for Charles II during the next eleven years. (Busby was to walk in Cromwell's funeral procession, leaving it to one of his pupils to spoil the occasion by snatching a banner from the hearse.) Busby's chief difficulty was with his second master, Edward Bagshaw, who in 1657 complained of being relegated to teach the lowest forms, and contrived to have the head master ridiculed before the school. Busby (not without using force against Bagshaw's person and premises) eventually drove his opponent to resign. It was not the last of Busby's troubles, but he was beginning to coast on his own legend. Even by 1659 the speaker of the Commons could be called 'a Busby amongst so many school-boys' (*Diary of Thomas Burton*, 4.243).

At the Restoration Busby recovered his Wells prebend and, on 3 July 1660, was appointed to a stall at Westminster. Two days later he was ordained priest in Henry VII's chapel. On 19 October Oxford allowed him to proceed directly to the degree of DD. He bore the ampulla at Charles II's coronation, as he would the orb at that of James II. A more substantial perquisite of his Westminster canonry was a house in the precincts, which he rebuilt and filled with boarders. There was some talk of his profiteering, and he had, as an officer of the chapter, a business acumen unkindly interpreted as 'devilish covetousness' (Pepys, 8.199). At Wells his only prolonged visit was in 1670 when his emoluments were at risk. He explained to the chapter there on 6 July that he was too ill to reside, and in any case was fully employed at Westminster. He was allowed to retain his income as if resident, nobody daring to question how a man incapable of the modest work of a cathedral canon in one place could run a school in another. Busby did serve Wells as proctor in convocation, and gave fifty-six volumes and more than £300 to the cathedral library. His intended benefactions to Oxford were less successful. In 1667 he proposed lectureships in mathematics and oriental languages at Christ Church; the latter was seemingly held for a time by his pupil Humphrey Prideaux. In 1682 the university rejected Busby's repeated offers to found a catechetical lecture.

There were occasional rumours that Busby would retire or was about to die, but he showed little inclination to do either. He continued in office at Westminster until he was eighty-five, when he died, unmarried, on 5 April 1695. He was buried in Westminster Abbey beneath the marble pavement (itself his gift) of the choir. He bequeathed an estate at Willen, Buckinghamshire, and other property worth altogether over £5500 to various causes at Willen itself, Oxford, Wells, and Westminster, and to the sustenance of poor clergy. Trustees still administer his charities.

Many of the stories told of Busby cannot be authenticated. That he boasted of having educated sixteen of the bench of bishops is demonstrably impossible (and in any case the teacher of Dryden, Locke, and Wren needed to count no other heads). It hardly matters if he actually told Charles II that he kept his hat on in the royal presence lest his boys see him acknowledge a higher authority than his own: George V so liked the story that he allowed the incumbent head master the same privilege. Busby's spirit permeates Westminster still in countless ways: in the name of a house, and of the library he established, and in the school's determination to stay rooted to its cramped but lively site.

Busby's reputation derives from more than simple longevity. It is based on solid classical learning, to which he added the magnetism of a great teacher, well attested by many of his pupils. With the assistance of his ushers he published grammars, which he was ever revising. He introduced mathematics and modern and oriental languages, hiring specialist assistants. He established the Latin pronunciation still current at Westminster. As a disciplinarian he was feared by his charges (and their mothers), though in this respect he was to be outclassed by Keate of Eton. It is not quite accurate to say he founded the public-school system. What he above all did was to make Westminster a school to which the political nation sent its sons for a century. The trust reposed in Busby by those of all political colours was the key to this. His discreet conduct in the 1640s and 1650s earned him the name of 'complier' from some of his own side, but it was the basis of his own and his school's triumph.

C. S. KNIGHTON

Sources Westminster Abbey, London, muniments, 5543, 43062–77, 66903–6 et al. • G. F. R. Barker, *Memoir of Richard Busby, D.D.* (1895) • J. Sargeaunt, *Annals of Westminster School* (1898), 79–134 • Wood, *Ath. Oxon.*, new edn, 4.417–20 • A. Wood, *The history and antiquities of the colleges and halls in the University of Oxford*, ed. J. Gutch (1786), 436–7 • *Diary of Thomas Burton*, ed. J. T. Rutt, 4 vols. (1828), vol. 2, p. 522; vol. 4, p. 243 • *Letters of Humphrey Prideaux … to John Ellis*, ed. E. M. Thompson, CS, new ser., 15 (1875), 12, 59, 132 • E. M. Thompson, ed., *Correspondence of the family of Hatton*, 2, CS, new ser., 23 (1878), 216 • *The correspondence of Isaac Basire*, ed. W. N. Darnell (1831), 36, 37–9, 41–2, 60–62 • E. Bagshaw, *A true and perfect narrative of the differences between Mr Busby and Mr Bagshawe* (1659) • R. South, *Twelve sermons and discourses on several subjects and occasions*, 5 and 6 [these only so titled] (1717), 5.48 • *Report on the manuscripts of Allan George Finch*, 5 vols., HMC, 71 (1913–2003), vol. 1, pp. 229–30 • *Calendar of the manuscripts of the dean and chapter of Wells*, 2, HMC, 12 (1914), 421–2, 446, 452, 455, 460–61, 465–7 • *Calendar of the manuscripts of the marquis of Bath preserved at Longleat, Wiltshire*, 5 vols., HMC, 58 (1904–80), vol. 3, pp. 22–4, 423 • D. S. Bailey, ed., *Wells Cathedral Chapter Act Book, 1666–83*, Somerset RS, 72 (1973) • D. S. Bailey, ed., *The canonical houses of Wells* (1982), 32–3; 162–3 • E. G. W. Bill, *Education at Christ Church, Oxford, 1660–1800* (1988), 198, 205–6, 248–9, 271–2, 303 • L. E. Tanner, *Westminster School: its buildings and their associations* (1923) • L. E. Tanner, *Westminster School* (1934), 12–22 • J. D. Carleton, *Westminster School* (1965), 9–23 • J. C. D. Field, *The king's nurseries: the story of Westminster School* (1987), 32–44 • *Hist. U. Oxf.* 4: *17th-cent. Oxf.*, 457, 460n. 32, 484 • *Old Westminsters*, vols. 1–2 • E. Wetenhall, *Of gifts and offices in the publick worship of God* (1679), 205–6 • Pepys, *Diary*

Archives Westminster Abbey, London, muniments • Westminster School, London

Likenesses F. Bird, marble effigy on monument, 1695 (after death mask), Westminster Abbey, London • attrib. J. Riley, oils, Christ Church Oxf. • attrib. J. M. Rysbrack, marble bust, Christ Church Oxf. • J. Watson, mezzotint (after oils attrib. J. Riley ?, 1775) • R. White, line engraving (after H. Tilson), BM • oils (after R. White), NPG; versions, Christ Church Oxf. and Westminster School, London • portrait, Willen vicarage, Buckinghamshire • portraits, Christ Church Oxf. • three portraits, Westminster School, London

Wealth at death £5565 5*s.* 6½*d.*: will, Barker, *Memoir of Richard Busby*, 131–47

Busby, Thomas (1754–1838), composer and author, was born on 26 December 1754 in Westminster, the son of Thomas Busby, a coach painter, and his wife, Ann. As a boy he had a fine treble voice and attempted at the age of twelve or thirteen to join the choir of Westminster Abbey, but was turned down because he was considered too old. He then had some singing lessons from Samuel Champness and Jonathan Battishill, and learned harpsichord from Charles Knyvett. In the summer of 1769 he sang as a boy treble at Vauxhall Gardens at a salary of 10 guineas per week. Shortly afterwards his voice broke, and he was articled for five years as a resident pupil to Battishill; he found him negligent as a teacher, but took the opportunity when not pursuing music to study in his exceptionally well-stocked library.

On the expiry of his articles Busby returned home and began to make his living from music and from journalism and literature. About 1778 he wrote the music to *The Man the Master*, by William Kenrick. He also started an oratorio on Alexander Pope's *Messiah*; this was eventually performed in 1799 as *The Prophecy*. Between about 1783 and 1785 he brought out his *Universal Dictionary of Music*, a serial work written in conjunction with Samuel Arnold, which appeared as an insert in the *New Musical Magazine*; it remained uncompleted but none the less ran to 197 numbers. In March 1784 he was appointed organist of St Mary, Newington Butts, and he moved to a similar position at St Mary Woolnoth in March 1798. He took part as a tenor in the 1784 Handel commemoration festival. In June 1786 he married Priscilla Angier (*bap.* 1760), daughter of Charles

Thomas Busby (1754–1838), by R. White

Angier of Earls Court; they had seven children, including the architect Charles Augustin *Busby.

Busby was for a time parliamentary reporter for the *London Courant* and assisted in editing the *Morning Post*. In 1786 he published *The Age of Genius!*, a satirical poem of over 800 lines in the style of Charles Churchill, one of his favourite authors. His next major musical work was *The divine harmonist, or, Sunday associate, containing elegant extracts, and original compositions, of sacred music* (1788), consisting of twelve numbers of sacred music by various composers, including Busby himself. This was again successful, but *Melodia Britannica, or, The Beauties of English Song*, his attempt at an equivalent secular collection, was a failure.

Busby was a member of the Wittinagemot Club that met at the Chapter Coffee House. Through this connection he encountered in 1795–6 Sir Richard Phillips, and came to write for many of Phillips's publications, including the *Monthly Magazine* and *Public Characters*, an annual collection of biographical articles on prominent men of the day. From about this time he also contributed to the *European Magazine*, the *Analytical Review*, the *Attic Miscellany*, and the *Whitehall Evening Post*. In 1799 his early oratorio *The Prophecy* was finally performed at Covent Garden. After *The Prophecy* he attempted a number of other choral works. The music of these is lost and it is doubtful if any of them, apart from *Britannia*, a patriotic oratorio to words by John Gretton, were ever performed. In 1801 he received a doctorate in music from the University of Cambridge; his doctoral exercise was a thanksgiving ode on the British naval victories, thus continuing the theme of *Britannia*.

In 1803 a lengthy biographical article on Busby appeared in *Public Characters*. There is little doubt that Busby wrote it himself: it is certainly difficult to imagine anyone else writing about him at such length, and in such unremittingly laudatory terms. In it he describes himself as having 'always been a friend to charitable institutions of every description' (Busby, 5.398) and goes on to list his involvement in, and musical compositions for, the Surrey Dispensary, the Philanthropic Society, the Royal Humane Society, and the Literary Fund, of which he became a fellow in 1800. Much of this charitable work was doubtless also shrewdly calculated to raise his public profile and to advance his career. The composition of *Britannia* is a case in point. In early 1800 Busby proposed to the committee of the charitable fund for the erection of a 'Grand Naval Pillar' to commemorate recent naval victories that he should compose a new 'secular oratorio', which should then be performed, 'upon a scale adequate to the great occasion' (Busby, 5.406), at a charity concert at the King's Theatre. The concert was arranged, but in the end the committee decided not to perform *Britannia* in its entirety, preferring to combine extracts from it with selections from Handel and hoping thereby to increase the chances of attracting the attendance of George III. The delayed première of the complete work was at Covent Garden the following month, for the benefit of the Royal Humane Society.

Busby's literary activities continued with his *Complete Dictionary of Music*, published about 1801. His *Monthly Musical Journal*, intended to supply the public with 'the best new foreign music, Italian, German, and French, interspersed with original compositions by himself, Dr Arnold, Dr Callcott, and other eminent composers' (Busby, 5.408), rapidly became a casualty of wartime conditions and was discontinued after only four numbers. Busby also wrote theatre music for several plays, of no great originality or merit. The only score which survives is that for Matthew Lewis's *Rugantino, or, The Brave of Venice* (*c*.1802), now in the British Library.

The Nature of Things, Busby's translation of Lucretius's *De rerum natura*, on which he had been working for many years, was published in 1813. It gained him some notoriety and was much discussed, reviewed, and parodied. Thereafter, apart from a lengthy work published in 1816 in which he argued that the letters of Junius were written by John Lewis de Lolme, he restricted himself to writing about music. Among his subsequent publications were a *Grammar of Music* (1818), *A General History of Music* (2 vols., 1819), the entertaining and informative *Concert Room and Orchestra Anecdotes* (3 vols., 1825), and *A Musical Manual* (1828). The *General History of Music* was the subject of a forthright article in the *Edinburgh Review*, which pointed out that it was drawn almost entirely from the histories of Burney and Hawkins. Although the charge of plagiarism was well founded, and Busby had undoubtedly been less than candid about the relationship of his own text to those of Burney and Hawkins, the criticism missed the essential point about the *History*: its value was as a popularizing work which brought the writings of Burney and Hawkins in simplified form within the reach of many without access to the originals.

Busby published nothing after 1828. In his latter years he lived with a married daughter at Queen's Row, Pentonville, London, where he died on 28 May 1838.

PHILIP OLLESON

Sources [T. Busby], 'Thomas Busby, Mus.D. LLD. &c.', *Public characters of 1802–1803*, 5 (1803), 388–411 · K. G. F. Spence, 'The learned Doctor Busby', *Music and Letters*, 37 (1956), 141–53 · D. Dawe, *Organists of the City of London, 1666–1850* (1983), 85 · J. C. Kassler, *The science of music in Britain, 1714–1830: a catalogue of writings, lectures, and inventions*, 1 (1979), 141–7 · review of *A general history of music*, *EdinR*, 33 (1820), 351–5 · *Musical World* (17 May 1838), 45–6 · *The Times* (29 May 1838) · W. Van Lennep and others, eds., *The London stage, 1660–1800*, 5 pts in 11 vols. (1960–68) · Highfill, Burnim & Langhans, *BDA* · *IGI*

Likenesses J. Lonsdale, oils, Magd. Cam. • R. White, engraving, BL • R. White, soft-ground etching, BM [*see illus.*]

Busby Babes (*act.* **1953–1958**), footballers, were a group of talented young players assembled by Sir Matt *Busby at Manchester United during the 1950s. They formed one of the best club teams in the history of English football, and twice won the Football League championship, but the side was effectively destroyed when eight players were killed in an air crash at Munich on 6 February 1958.

The Busby Babes first won the Football League championship in 1955–6 with a record eleven-point margin over the runners-up, Blackpool. In the following season, 1956–7, they won the league again and came close to the elusive double, but lost the FA cup final 2–1 to Aston Villa after the United goalkeeper was injured early in the game. They were also the first English team to compete in the new European cup, and astonished Europe by beating the Belgian champions, Anderlecht, 10–0 in only their second game in the competition. They were knocked out in the semi-finals by the formidable Real Madrid side which won the European cup every year between 1956 and 1960.

It is believed that the term Busby Babes was first used by the *Manchester Evening Chronicle* Saturday night edition, the *Football Pink*, after Matt Busby had fielded several promising youngsters in a league game at Huddersfield Town on 31 October 1953. 'Busby's Bouncing Babes Keep All Town Awake', the paper proclaimed after a goalless draw. Busby himself disliked the term, as it gave the impression of callow youths whereas he felt that he had made them into mature players at a far earlier age than most of their contemporaries at other clubs. Nor does Busby deserve all the credit. The origins of United's youth policy can be traced back to the 1930s, and particularly to the formation of the Manchester United Junior Athletics Club in 1938, well before Busby's arrival at Old Trafford at the end of the war. Busby was also greatly assisted in finding and developing his teenagers by his assistant Jimmy Murphy, chief scout Joe Armstrong, and the United coach Bert Whalley.

The Busby Babes epitomized English football at the end of the era before money and television came to dominate the game. English players were still limited to a maximum wage of £17 a week during the season and £14 in summer (a restriction which was eventually abolished in 1961). In 1957, for example, the most successful year so far in Manchester United history, the captain Roger Byrne [*see below*] earned only £1189, including bonuses. Even allowing for inflation, most of the team earned less money in their entire careers than some of their Manchester United successors would be paid in a single week. Few of them could afford cars, and so they regularly used public transport. It was quite common for United supporters travelling to matches by bus to find themselves sitting next to one of the players they were about to watch.

Matt Busby's reliance on grooming his own players proved highly effective: between 1951 and 1957 the club bought only three recruits from outside. Apart from being extremely talented, they also benefited from their great team spirit; they socialized together and were all good friends. Typical young men of the 1950s, the players spent much of their time listening to the latest rock and roll records in each others' homes, which in most cases were lodgings, or 'digs' arranged by Manchester United. One legendary club landlady, 'Ma' Watson, looked after several of the Babes in her large house near to the Manchester United ground.

The Babes would frequent Manchester cinemas, snooker halls, the dog track at Belle Vue, and on Friday and Saturday nights the Locarno Ballroom in Sale or the Plaza dance-hall in Manchester, where managers happily gave their celebrity guests free admission. After going to the pictures in the evening they would often return to Ma Watson's and devour cornflakes and milk sitting round

Busby Babes (*act.* **1953–1958**), by unknown photographer, 1958 [back row (left to right) Duncan Edwards, Bill Foulkes, Mark Jones, Ray Wood, Eddie Colman, and David Pegg; front row (left to right) John Berry, Billy Whelan, Roger Byrne, Tommy Taylor, and Dennis Viollet]

her kitchen table. Mrs Watson's United contract was ended, however, one December when she found her husband in bed with a maid, and reacted by serving the whole household Spam for Christmas dinner instead of turkey.

Many of the Babes learned outside trades—Duncan Edwards [*see below*] as a joiner, for example. And like all young men of that era, they were also obliged to complete two years' national service in the armed forces. Professional footballers, however, were excused many of the military duties of other national servicemen and spent much of their time on physical training and football practice. The authorities would usually release them to play for their clubs, on the understanding that they were also available for the British army team, which therefore reached a very high standard. In Duncan Edwards's case, with his commitments to the United first team, combined with army games, England matches, and other representative fixtures, he played more than 180 serious games in his two years as a soldier.

One of the Babes' finest performances was when they beat the London club Arsenal 5–4 on Saturday 1 February 1958. In the following week they travelled to Yugoslavia for a European cup quarter-final with Red Star Belgrade and drew another exciting game 3–3 after being 3–0 ahead at one point. On their way home the following afternoon, Thursday 6 February 1958, United's charter flight stopped to refuel at Riem airport in Munich in freezing weather. Twice the pilot aborted take-off half-way down the runway. On the third attempt the plane barely got off the ground, crashed through the fence at the end of the airfield, and crossed a minor road before hitting a house and a tree. Seven players (Byrne, Bent, Colman, Jones, Pegg, Taylor, and Whelan) died immediately and an eighth (Edwards) later that month.

Roger William Byrne (1929–1958), the captain, was born at 15 Mitchell Street, Gorton, Manchester, on 8 September 1929, the son of William Henry Byrne (*d.* 1974), clerk to a furniture dealers, and his wife, Jessie, *née* Barlow. After attending Burnage grammar school, Byrne played for Ryder Brow youth club before signing as a professional for Manchester United in 1949. He made his first team début in November 1951 at left back, his normal position though he often played at outside left, and won his first league championship medal in the following April. He became United captain in 1954, played 280 competitive games for the club, and scored twenty goals, of which thirteen were penalty kicks. After winning his first cap for England against Scotland in April 1954, he played in every subsequent England match up to the time of his death in 1958, and won thirty-three caps in total. Byrne was known for his speed, his quick reading of the game, and his overlapping runs. He was not a great tackler, but according to his colleague Bill Foulkes, he just had to show opponents 'that he was twice as fast as they were and they would be panicked into making a hasty pass' (Roberts, 40–41). He married Joy Weatherall Cooper (*b.* 1932/3), a physiotherapist, the daughter of Arthur Cooper, a cinema manager, at Droylsden parish church on 15 June 1957.

The reserve full back **Geoffrey** [Geoff] **Bent** (1932–1958) went to Belgrade only because of last-minute doubts about Roger Byrne's fitness. He was born at 2 Stott Lane, Salford, on 27 September 1932. One of the four Munich victims who came from coalmining families, he was the son of Clifford Bent, a colliery surfaceman, and his wife, Clara, *née* Dunning (*d.* 1972). He attended St John's junior school, Swinton, and Tootal Road Grammar School, Swinton. On 27 June 1953 he married at Pendlebury parish church Marion (*b.* 1930/31), a typist, the daughter of Harold Mallandaine, an engine driver. Bent played just twelve times for United, but would have enjoyed a regular first team place at most other clubs.

Edward [Eddie] **Colman** (1936–1958) was born at 9 Archie Street, Salford, on 1 November 1936, the son of Richard Colman, a general labourer, and his wife, Elizabeth, *née* Purcell (*d.* 1971). A small, cheeky lad, who often wore a flat cap and duffle-coat, Colman was brought up in Archie Street, which was later used as the model for the famous ITV soap opera *Coronation Street*, and attended Ordsall council school. The England captain Billy Wright described Colman as the 'creative genius of the team' (Arthur, 34). Supporters called him Snakehips or Swivelhips because of his distinctive dribbles, ball control, and body swerves. He was buried at Weaste cemetery, Salford.

Mark Jones (1933–1958) was born at 21 Elliott's Terrace, Wombwell, Barnsley, on 15 June 1933, the son of Amos Jones, a coalminer, and his wife, Lucy, *née* Fox (*d.* 1957), and attended Darfield Foulstone Modern School. The United centre half, he was regarded as the team's rock in defence: with blond hair and broad shoulders, he stood 6 feet 1½ inches tall and weighed 14½ stone. He would almost certainly have played for England one day. Jones, who had a wife, June, was known for his slight eccentricities: he had smoked a pipe since he was eighteen, wore a trilby hat, owned more than fifty budgerigars, and loved shooting rabbits in the countryside.

Left-winger **David Pegg** (1935–1958) was born at 11 Market Street, Highfields, Adwick-le-Street, Doncaster, on 20 September 1935, the son of Thomas William Pegg, a colliery surface worker, and his wife, Jessie, *née* Day. He was educated at Highfields modern school and Doncaster technical school. Famous for his accurate crosses and strong left-foot shot, Pegg gained a solitary cap for England, though at the time of Munich he had lost his place in the United side through a dip in form. Cocky, cheerful, and good-looking, he was famous for mixing with girls.

The centre forward **Thomas** [Tommy] **Taylor** (1932–1958), like Jones and Pegg, came from a south Yorkshire mining background. He was born at 4 Quarry Street in the village of Smithies, near Barnsley, Yorkshire, on 29 January 1932, the son of Charles Joseph Taylor, a coalminer, and his wife, Violet, *née* Hodgkins. After attending Raley secondary modern school, he played for Barnsley between 1949 and March 1953, when he signed for Manchester United for a new British record fee of £29,999—a pound was knocked off to avoid the pressure of being the first £30,000 player. Of strong physique, and an accurate header of the ball, he was 6 feet tall, had black, wavy hair, and always seemed to be smiling. At the time of his death he had a fiancée, Carol. Taylor scored 131 goals in 191 games for United, the second highest ratio for any player in the club's history, and sixteen times in nineteen appearances for England.

The Irish international forward **William Augustine** [Billy, Liam] **Whelan** (1935–1958) was born at 28 St Attracta Road, Cabra, Dublin, on 1 April 1935, the son of John William Whelan (*d.* 1943), a labourer, and his wife, Elizabeth, *née* McGuirk, and attended St Peter's School, Phibsboro, Dublin. Signed from the Dublin club Home Farm, Whelan was known for his dribbling, accurate finishing, and his trick of pushing the ball through opponents' legs. 'He had everything', said Bobby Charlton, 'except an extra bit of pace' (Roberts, 124). At the time of his death he was engaged to Ruby McCullough.

By common consent the finest footballer in this team, and one of the greatest players of all time, was **Duncan Edwards** (1936–1958). The only child of Gladstone Edwards, a metal polisher, and his wife, Sarah Ann, *née* Harrison, he was born at 23 Malvern Crescent, Woodside, Dudley, Worcestershire on 1 October 1936. On leaving Wolverhampton Street secondary school, Dudley, he joined Manchester United in June 1952 despite determined approaches from his local team, Wolverhampton Wanderers, and several other first division clubs. Edwards made his first team début against Cardiff City in April 1953, aged only sixteen and a half, and won a regular place the following autumn. He also captained the Manchester United teams which won the FA youth cup in 1953 and 1954. Edwards first played for England in April 1955 at the age of only eighteen years and 183 days, and remained the youngest England international of the twentieth century until Michael Owen broke the record in 1998. Edwards usually played at wing-half, what would later be called midfield, but was famous for filling any position; he often appeared at centre forward, and once scored four goals for the England under-23 team against Scotland. Weighing 13 stone, he was powerful in appearance and described as 'a tank'; he was surprisingly gentle in temperament, introverted and shy, and yet did not seem to suffer any nervousness before a game. Busby described Edwards as the 'most complete footballer in Britain—if not the world' (Taylor, 131), while his team-mate Bobby Charlton once said that 'compared to Duncan, the rest of us are just like pygmies. He had the lot' (ibid., 10). Edwards's footballing talents included speed, tackling, ball control, heading, passing, shooting, and leadership qualities. In 1957 he came third in the poll for European footballer of the year. Edwards played 177 games for Manchester United, and scored twenty-one goals; he also won eighteen caps and scored five times for England. The multiple injuries which he suffered in the crash would probably have killed most men much sooner. Doctors at the Rechts der Isar Hospital in Munich were astonished at Edwards's stamina and will to live, but he died after fifteen days on 21 February 1958 and was buried at Queen's Cross cemetery, Dudley.

Two other players, half-back Jackie (John) Blanchflower (1933–1998) and winger Johnny (John) Berry (1926–1994), were so badly hurt that they never played professional football again. Fifteen other passengers and crew also died in the crash, including the former England and Manchester City goalkeeper Frank Swift (1913–1958), who had travelled to Belgrade as a journalist for the *News of the World*. The dead also included three Manchester United officials: club secretary Walter Crickmer, trainer Tom Curry, and coach Bert Whalley.

Matt Busby spent more than two months in hospital recovering from serious injuries. He returned to England to see the hastily reconstructed Manchester United lose 2–0 to Bolton Wanderers in the 1958 FA cup final, but it took Busby five years to restore his side to their past glory. Manchester United then won the FA cup in 1963, the league championship in 1965 and 1967, and in 1968 became the first English club to win the European cup.

Among the young players who survived the crash were Sir Bobby Charlton (*b.* 1937), who was a member of England's 1966 world cup-winning team, won a then record 106 international caps, and scored a record forty-nine goals for England. Other survivors included the Northern Ireland goalkeeper Harry Gregg (*b.* 1932) and the defender Bill Foulkes (*b.* 1932).

The skill, entertainment, and innocent enthusiasm of the Busby Babes captured the imagination of the general public in the 1950s. Manchester United's improvised, swashbuckling football often produced high scores; the team earned huge affection well beyond traditional Manchester United followers and drew huge crowds wherever they played. The great tragedy was that they had yet to reach their full potential, and might easily have succeeded Real Madrid as the dominant side in Europe. Byrne, Edwards, and Taylor would all have been leading members of the England team for many years, joined possibly by Eddie Colman, Mark Jones, and David Pegg. Without the missing United players the previously promising England side failed even to reach the quarter-finals of the world cup played in Sweden in the summer of 1958.

The Babes are also remembered as symbols of Matt Busby's two pioneering policies: putting extra emphasis on grooming his own young players, and taking English clubs into Europe. Both would be adopted with equal enthusiasm and success by Busby's most prominent successor as Manchester United manager, Sir Alex Ferguson (*b.* 1941).

The main memorial to the Busby Babes is a plaque on the wall of the east stand at the Manchester United stadium at Old Trafford. Seven of the players are commemorated in street names on a small housing estate in Newton Heath, east Manchester, not far from the site where Manchester United was originally founded (as Newton Heath) about 1878; and two blocks of flats in Salford are named after Duncan Edwards and Eddie Colman. There is also a small shrine in the Kirchtrudering district of Munich next to the now disused airfield where seven of the Busby Babes died. MICHAEL CRICK

Sources J. Roberts, *The team that wouldn't die: the story of the Busby Babes* (1975) · F. Taylor, *The day a team died* (1983) · M. Arthur, *The*

Manchester United aircrash (1983) • E. Dunphy, *A strange kind of glory: Sir Matt Busby and Manchester United* (1991) • M. Busby, *Soccer at the top* (1973) • G. Dykes, *The Manchester United alphabet* (1994) • I. McCartney, *Roger Byrne: captain of the Busby Babes* (2000) • I. McCartney and R. Cavanagh, *Duncan Edwards* (1988) • I. McCartney, *Duncan Edwards: the full report* (2001) • B. Hughes, *The Tommy Taylor story* (1996) • R. Cavanagh and B. Hughes, *Viollet: the life of a legendary goalscorer* (2001) • J. Kennedy, *Tommy Taylor of Manchester United and Barnsley* (1994) • W. Foulkes, *Back at the top* (1965) • H. Gregg, *Wild about football* (1961) • b. certs. • m. certs. [Geoffrey Bent; Roger William Byrne] • *CGPLA Eng. & Wales* (1958)

Archives Manchester United, Old Trafford, Manchester, archive and museum | Dudley Leisure Centre, Duncan Edwards memorabilia • PRO, official papers on the cause of the Munich crash | FILM BFI NFTVA

Likenesses photograph, 1958, Popperfoto, Northampton [*see illus.*] • bronze statue (Matt Busby), Manchester United football ground, Old Trafford, Manchester • photograph (David Pegg), Hult. Arch. • photograph (Thomas Taylor), Hult. Arch. • photographs (Roger Byre), Hult. Arch. • photographs (Duncan Edwards), Hult. Arch. • photographs (Mark Jones), Hult. Arch. • stained-glass windows (Duncan Edwards), St Francis Church, Dudley, Worcestershire • statue (Duncan Edwards), town centre, Dudley

Wealth at death £1493 11*s.* 1*d.*—Geoffrey Bent: administration, 15 April 1958, *CGPLA Eng. & Wales* • £9073 1*s.* 1*d.*—Roger William Byrne: administration, 16 July 1958, *CGPLA Eng. & Wales* • £2294 17*s.* 6*d.*—Edward Colman: administration, 15 April 1958, *CGPLA Eng. & Wales* • £4368 9*s.* 6*d.*—Duncan Edwards: administration, 7 Aug 1958, *CGPLA Eng. & Wales* • £800 3*s.* 7*d.*—Mark Jones: administration, 23 April 1958, *CGPLA Eng. & Wales* • £2250 4*s.* 0*d.*—David Pegg: administration, 21 April 1958, *CGPLA Eng. & Wales* • £3549 13*s.* 5*d.*—Thomas Taylor: administration, 20 May 1958, *CGPLA Eng. & Wales* • £1210 3*s.* 10*d.*—William Augustine Whelan: administration, 7 June 1958, *CGPLA Eng. & Wales*

Busfeild, William. *See* Ferrand, William (1809–1889).

Bush, Alan Dudley (**1900–1995**), composer, was born in Dulwich, London, on 22 December 1900, the son of Alfred Walter Bush (1869–1935), director of W. J. Bush & Co., manufacturing chemists, and his wife, Alice Maud Brinsley (1870–1951). He was educated privately, then at Highgate grammar school (1911–17). He studied composition under Frederick Corder and piano with Tobias Matthay at the Royal Academy of Music (1918–22), gaining a Thalberg scholarship, the Phillimore piano prize (both 1920), and a Carnegie award for his first string quartet (1923). After leaving the Royal Academy of Music, his piano studies continued with Benno Moiseiwitsch, Mabel Lander, and Artur Schnabel. As a pianist he had a heavy touch, although his technique was strong and reliable. He studied composition (1927–32) with John Ireland, a formative influence on his music. Meanwhile he returned to the Royal Academy of Music as professor in 1925, remaining there until 1978. Of his numerous students, most who have made a mark came from his last teaching years, including the composers Edward Gregson and Roger Steptoe, and the pianist Graham Johnson. He studied philosophy and musicology at Berlin University under Johannes Wolf and Friedrich Blume (1929–31); close contact with Bertolt Brecht and Hanns Eisler influenced his political views. On 31 March 1931 he married Nancy Rachel Head (*c.*1905–1991), daughter of Frederick Dewas Head,

Alan Dudley Bush (1900–1995), by Elliott & Fry, 1946

lawyer and journalist, and sister of the song composer Michael Head. She was a writer and librettist, who collaborated with Bush on all of his operas and operettas, and on many vocal works. They had three daughters, one of whom, Alice, died in a road accident at the age of seven.

Bush joined the Communist Party in 1935, having dallied briefly with the Independent Labour Party and the Labour Party. Surprisingly, the conservative Royal Academy of Music proved a haven for the staunch Marxist: a few liberally minded admired him, and he was observed by many as something of a novelty. He rarely attended formal occasions such as prize day, or any function where royalty might be present, but uncharacteristically, at a special dinner in London, he was once seen carrying a flaming Christmas pudding from the kitchens, followed by a long stream of tailcoated serving staff. Believing too much patriotism a bad thing, he once said, 'It's high time we had a revolution in this country', unconcerned about the inevitable loss of life, despite having been a private in the Royal Army Medical Corps (1941–5). In a less tolerant country he would certainly have been imprisoned, or worse. But he was merely ignored, both politically, and, which is a pity, as a composer. He nevertheless played an active role: as adviser and conductor of the London Labour Choral Union (1929–40); founder (1936) and president (1941–76) of the Workers' Music Association; founder of the William Morris Musical Society (1941); chairman of the Composers' Guild (1947–8), later vice-president; and examiner for the Associated Board (Ceylon, India, and

Australia, 1932–3). On concert tours to eastern and western Europe and the USSR he conducted British music, including his own.

Bush was tall, handsome, straight-backed, and, when avoiding politics, which was rare, had great charm. Towards both sexes his manners were impeccable. He had a touch of charisma as conductor and speaker, though shyness sometimes made him clumsy. There was no noticeable sense of humour, but when challenged (which he seemed to like) he grinned wryly. The dogmatic Bush never said 'You may be right', but rather 'That's all very well, but …', and there was a plethora of 'buts'. He was dictatorial, convinced that he was right: when examining he believed his own pupils to be best, nominating them for special mention. His four operas were all overtly political; the first, *Wat Tyler*, won an Arts Council award (1951). A notable early work was the energetic *Dialectic* for string quartet (1929), but the late 1940s were his best period, with the moving *Lidice* for unaccompanied chorus (1947), the violin concerto (1948), and the remarkable *Nottingham Symphony* (1949). Other landmarks were *Voices of the Prophets* (1953), commissioned by Peter Pears, and a choral work, *Mandela Speaking* (1985).

Bush's sight failed towards the end of his life. Nancy, his devoted wife, died in 1991; he ceased composing in 1992. He died on 31 October 1995 in Watford General Hospital; he was survived by two daughters, Catherine and Rachel. He was cremated at Golders Green on 7 November after a well-attended service. During his last years he was not informed about changes in the USSR, his family and friends not wishing to upset him. RICHARD STOKER

Sources B. Morton, 'Alan Bush', *Contemporary composers* (1990) · *Alan Bush*, Workers' Music Association, bulletin special supplement (1996) · C. Mason and H. Cole, 'Bush, Alan (Dudley)', *New Grove* · S. Sadie, ed., *The new Grove dictionary of opera*, 4 vols. (1992) · *The Times* (4 Nov 1995) · *The Independent* (3 Nov 1995) · *Composer News* (winter 1995) · B. Stevens, 'Alan Bush's *Wat Tyler*', *Composer*, 51 (1974), 5 [see also letter, *Composer*, 56 (1975–6), 31–2] · M. V. Searle, *John Ireland: the man and his music* (1979) · R. Stoker, *Open window—open door* (1985) · *WWW*, 1991–5 · L. Ronald, ed., *Who's who in music* (1935) · *Who's who in music*, 3rd edn (1950) · Grove, *Dict. mus.* · J. O. Ward, ed., *The concise Oxford dictionary of music*, 2nd edn (1964) · H. Rosenthal and J. Warrack, *The concise Oxford dictionary of opera*, 2nd edn (1979) · *Cambridge biographical dictionary* (1998) · personal knowledge (2004) · private information (2004)

Archives BL, corresp. and music MSS · British Music Information Centre, London | Birm. CA, letters to Katherine Thompson · BL, letters to Bernard Stevens, Add. MS 69025 · Goldsmiths' College, London, music scores from eastern Europe | FILM BBC TV Archives, 'Alan Bush—a life', Anna Ambrose, London Co-operative Society, 1983 [film of Bush conducting] | SOUND British Music Information Centre, London, recordings of Bush's music on vinyl and CD

Likenesses PBJ, oils, 1940, Alan Bush Trust, Sutton Coldfield · Elliott & Fry, photograph, 1946, NPG [*see illus.*] · D. Chittock, pencil drawing, Alan Bush Trust, Sutton Coldfield · I. Walters, bust, priv. coll. · L. Winters, bust, Alan Bush Trust, Sutton Coldfield · photograph, repro. in *The Independent* · photograph, repro. in *The Times* · photograph, repro. in R. Rapaport, *Thomas Armstrong: a celebration by his friends* (1998) · photographs, Alan Bush Trust, Sutton Coldfield · photographs, Marx Memorial Library, London · photographs, Camera Press, London

Wealth at death £86,239: probate, 28 March 1996, *CGPLA Eng. & Wales*

Bush, Eric Wheler (1899–1985), naval officer, was born on 12 August 1899 at Simla, the younger son and younger child of the Revd Herbert Wheler Bush, chaplain to the forces, and his wife, Edith Cornelia, daughter of Dr George Cardew, inspector-general of the Indian Medical Service. Mrs Bush returned to England in 1908 with her two sons, leaving her husband as the principal of the Lawrence Memorial School, Murree, until he too returned, to become vicar of Bathford, in 1912. Eric Bush was educated in England at Stoke House, Stoke Poges, and on 10 May 1912 entered the Royal Naval College, Osborne, as a naval cadet.

After two years' general education, 'Blake term', of which he was a member, proceeded to the Royal Naval College, Dartmouth, but the course was interrupted at the end of the first term by the mobilization of the fleet, on 1 August 1914. Bush was appointed to the armoured cruiser *Bacchante*, the flagship of the 7th cruiser squadron, and on 28 August 1914 was present at the battle of the Heligoland Bight. After service in the North Sea and English Channel, the cruiser joined the Mediterranean Fleet and was part of the Dardanelles expeditionary force. On 25 April 1915 Midshipman Bush (promoted in the previous October), commanded a picket-boat which towed boats of the first assault wave to land on Anzac beach and for his services on this day and during the month which followed he was awarded the DSC, besides receiving the first of four mentions in dispatches. In August Bush was similarly engaged during the Suvla landings.

In March 1916 he joined the new battleship *Revenge*, in which he remained until the end of the war, seeing action only at the battle of Jutland. A sub-lieutenant since July 1917, he was one of the 370 naval officers—Kipling's 'gentlemen tired of the sea'—whose education had been interrupted and who were sent to Cambridge University in January 1919 for two terms. By his own account, his main achievement appears to have been the hoisting of a large white ensign on the lantern above his college, Trinity.

Bush's inter-war career was typical for the period, with service aboard a destroyer in the Baltic and Home Fleet being followed by commissions in the East Indies, where he qualified as an interpreter in Hindustani in 1924, and on the China station, where, in 1932, he joined his first command, the Yangtze (Yangzi) gunboat *Ladybird*. Between sea jobs he served as a training officer, his infectious enthusiasm for the service producing an exceptional term (two of whose members were to win VCs), attended the Royal Navy staff course, and, from 1934 to 1936, occupied the naval intelligence division's Japanese desk.

At the end of 1936 Commander Bush was appointed as executive officer of the Mediterranean Fleet cruiser *Devonshire*. Observation of the fighting during the Spanish Civil War and evacuation of refugees gave the Royal Navy much useful experience, but Bush also found time to get married, on 20 May 1938, during a visit to Cannes, to Mollie Noël, daughter of Colonel Brian Watts DSO, of the Royal Army Medical Corps. They had two sons.

Promoted in June 1939, Bush became captain, auxiliary patrols, on the outbreak of war commanding the variegated collection of minor warships and conscripted fishing vessels which closed the Strait of Dover to German submarines and dealt with the early magnetic mines. His tireless efforts during the Dunkirk evacuation, at which he was responsible for the La Panne beaches, earned him the first of three DSOs. In June 1941 he returned to sea, in command of the anti-aircraft cruiser *Euryalus*, in which he remained until September 1943, taking part in all the more notable eastern Mediterranean actions during the period and the invasions of Sicily and Salerno.

Acquaintance with amphibious operations was renewed by Bush's appointment in command of the Force Sword assault group, which he trained and led for the Normandy invasion, where he was responsible for landing 8th infantry brigade at Ouistreham, on the exposed eastern flank of the assault area. After brief command of the battleship *Malaya* in the autumn of 1944, he returned to combined operations as the chief staff officer of Force W, the amphibious component of the south-east Asia command. He commanded the assaults on Akyab and the Arakan coast operations and was largely responsible for the planning and execution of the invasions of Ramree Island and Rangoon and for the unopposed reoccupation of Malaya and Singapore.

From late 1945 until June 1948, Bush commanded HMS *Ganges*, the boy seamen's training establishment at Shotley, near Harwich. This was to be his last naval appointment, for he was not selected for promotion to flag rank and was retired from the service, shortly before his forty-ninth birthday.

An enthusiast for all matters maritime and dedicated to the encouragement of youth, Bush became the secretary of the sea cadet council (1948–59). Towards the end of this time he wrote and had published (in 1958) his autobiography, *Bless our Ship*. His character and personality show through this modest account of a substantial naval career: patriotic without a trace of jingoism or bigotry, his determination and dedication to duty were tempered by kindliness, a keen sense of humour, and love for his wife and two sons, both of whom followed him into the Royal Navy.

Leaving the sea cadet council, Bush next became the general manager of the Red Ensign Club, in Stepney, which he ran until 1964. Even in retirement he continued his association with the sea, being engaged for several years by the British-India Steam Navigation Company as a liaison officer and lecturer accompanying educational cruises. So well received were his lectures on the Gallipoli expedition, he was persuaded to write an excellent account of the campaign (*Gallipoli*, 1957) based on meticulous research as well as his own experience. Prior to this, he had compiled two anthologies of poetry and prose, one nautical (*The Flowers of the Sea*, 1962) and the other military (*Salute the Soldier*, 1966). Bush finally retired from the sea to Tunbridge Wells, Kent, where he died on 17 June 1985.

DAVID BROWN, *rev.*

Sources *The Times* (20 June 1985) · *Navy List* (1912–48) · E. Bush, *Bless our ship* (1958) · *CGPLA Eng. & Wales* (1985) · *WWW* · private information (1990)

Archives King's Lond., Liddell Hart C., papers relating to his career | SOUND IWM SA, recorded lecture

Wealth at death £8928: probate, 22 Nov 1985, *CGPLA Eng. & Wales*

Bush, Geoffrey (1920–1998), composer, was born on 23 March 1920 at 84 Strode Road, Kilburn, London, the son of Charles Christmas Bush, schoolmaster and author, and his wife, Winifred, *née* Chart. His parents separated soon after his birth, and he never saw his father again. Brought up by his mother, he was a chorister in Salisbury Cathedral (1928–33), where under Walter Alcock he learned to admire the centuries-long tradition of English church music, and where the foundations of his enduring Christian faith were laid. At Lancing College (1933–8) his early efforts at composition came under the critical discipline of Jasper Rooper. However, his real musical mentor was John Ireland, who helped to strengthen his sense of an English identity even when his interests broadened to include, especially, French and Russian music. In 1938 he went up on a scholarship to Balliol College, Oxford, where he gained a second class in classical moderations and took his BMus in 1940; he was awarded the MA and DMus in 1946. While at Oxford he became a close friend of the composer Bruce Montgomery, already making a name for himself as a detective story writer under the name Edmund Crispin. Bush even lent a hand with a genre he always enjoyed, and earned a fleeting appearance in one of Montgomery's stories as a hard-pressed film composer. A pacifist, he spent the Second World War as assistant warden of a Welsh children's hostel before returning to Oxford.

Bush had continued to compose, and the first of his six operas, *The Spanish Rivals*, was produced at Brighton in 1948 and for the Festival of Britain in 1951. He meanwhile married, on 15 April 1950, Julie Kathleen McKenna (*b.* 1924/5), physiotherapist, daughter of Curtin McKenna, chartered secretary; they had two sons, Andrew and Paul. Bush's distinguished career as a teacher began with extramural lecturing in Oxford in 1947. In 1952 he moved to the extra-mural department of London University, where he remained in various capacities until 1987. He was also visiting professor at King's College, London, for twenty years from 1969. There he was a much admired lecturer, adept at conveying the importance of strict disciplines and serious ideas with the urbanity and wit that were also to make him a popular broadcaster.

Bush's first symphony had its première at the 1954 Cheltenham festival, where a number of his works were played and where he was a familiar and popular figure. It includes a blues-influenced slow movement in memory of Constant Lambert, some of whose tastes Bush shared; he enjoyed jazz as well as American musicals. The same festival saw the première of what was to be his most popular work, the overture *Yorick*, which had already won the 1949 Royal Philharmonic Society prize. A second symphony followed in 1957, but its neglect until a recording in 1994 contributed to his abandoning the form. In any case, some of his most characteristic music, in a long and wide-ranging list of works, was in smaller forms, and reflected the breadth but discrimination of his literary tastes. These included settings of Chaucer, Herrick, Shakespeare, Jonson, Shelley, Wilde, Kathleen Raine, and Stevie Smith, as well as medieval lyrics and modern limericks. His operas ranged from pacifist subjects, including *The Equation* (1967), a bleak work for the Sacred Music Drama Society, to *Lord Arthur Savile's Crime* (1972), a piece for students with a wealth of witty and sly musical allusions that well suit Wilde's story. He admitted to being happiest writing songs and operas, when he could find the right words.

Bush's championship of English music also took him to scholarly work: he edited several volumes of the series Musica Britannica, works by John Ireland and other English composers, among them Elgar, and an anthology of English song. He also served on the Composers' Guild of Great Britain, the Arts Council, and the Performing Right Society. He was made an honorary fellow of the University College of Wales, Aberystwyth, in 1986.

Though his music ranged wide and encompassed many forms, Bush's most characteristic works were shorter ones in which the lyrical qualities and directness of utterance he sought were most naturally realized. His books included a lively collection of essays, partly autobiographical, *An Unsentimental Education*. The appreciation and affection he enjoyed in the musical world were demonstrated at a seventieth birthday concert presented at the Wigmore Hall, London, by the Songmakers' Almanac, 'A celebration of English song, 1850–1990', its title referring to a tradition to which he had made a valuable contribution. In person, he was a genial, bespectacled man, usually bow-tied, quick and intelligent in conversation, witty and far from uncritical about contemporary developments he deplored, but essentially kind and generous. He died at his home, 43 Corringham Road, Golders Green, London, on 24 February 1998, of prostate cancer. He was survived by his wife, Julie, and their two sons. JOHN WARRACK

Sources G. Bush, *An unsentimental education and other musical recollections* [n.d., c.1990] · *Contemporary composers* [inc. full list of works] · *The Times* (27 Feb 1998) · *The Independent* (2 March 1998) · *The Guardian* (3 March 1998) · *Daily Telegraph* (5 March 1998) · *New Grove* · *Balliol College register* · personal knowledge (2004) · b. cert. · m. cert. · d. cert.

Likenesses photograph, 1962, repro. in *Daily Telegraph* · photograph, repro. in *The Times* · photograph, repro. in *The Independent*

Wealth at death £81,378: probate, 6 April 1998, *CGPLA Eng. & Wales*

Bush, Paul (1489/90–1558), bishop of Bristol, was born at Dilton, near Westbury, Wiltshire, the second son of William Bush, who leased a farm and fulling mill from the Bonshommes (a community of priests living according to the Augustinian rule) at nearby Edington. It is probable that Paul Bush received his early education at Edington. He went on to St Mary's, the Augustinian college in Oxford, where he graduated BA in 1518. Later he received the degrees of BTh and DTh, and was ordained priest, remaining at Oxford, where he established a reputation in the study of theology and medicine, and for his Latin poetry.

In 1525 Bush returned to Wiltshire, and became a member of the community of Bonshommes at Edington. Soon afterwards he became corrector, or deputy, to John Ryve, the rector, or head, of the community. Bush was also appointed a royal chaplain, and by June 1539 had become a canon of Salisbury Cathedral, holding the prebend of Bishopstone. During these years he produced numerous theological and devotional works written in both English and Latin. Products typical of their period in conveying an entirely orthodox late medieval spirituality, they include *A Lyttel Treatise in Englyshe Called the Exposycyon of Miserere mei Deus* (1525); *Notes on the Psalms* (1525); *Dialogus inter Christum et Mariam* (1525); *A Lyttel Treatise in Englyshe called the Extirpacion of Ignorancy*, a poetical work dedicated to the Princess Mary by the author, 'prest and bonhomme of Edynden' (1526); *Certayne gostly medycynes necessary to be used among wel disposed peple, to eschew and avoid the comen plage of pestilence* (1531).

When John Ryve died in May 1538 the influential Wiltshire landowner Walter, Lord Hungerford of Farleigh Castle wrote to Thomas Cromwell strongly recommending that Bush should be nominated as rector. Bush was duly appointed, and shortly afterwards Lord Hungerford became steward of most of the priory lands, while Paul Bush's elder brother, John Bush of Dilton, became steward of the house's lands in west Wiltshire.

Edington Priory was dissolved on 31 March 1538, and Bush received an annual pension of £100, together with property at Coleshill, Berkshire. When the diocese of Bristol was established by Henry VIII on 4 June 1542 Bush was chosen to become the first bishop, with the former church of the Augustinian canons as the cathedral. He was consecrated on 25 June 1542. His writings, and his answers to questions proposed by Cranmer in 1548, make it clear that Bush was conservative in his religious views. None the less, he accepted the successive changes of Edward VI's reign. He supported the introduction of an English Bible, and he did not oppose the introduction of English prayer books in 1549 and 1552. In the House of Lords he voted unsuccessfully against clerical marriage in February 1549, but when the clergy were permitted to marry he was quick to take advantage of the new freedom. His wife was Edith Ashley, daughter of Henry Ashley, gentleman, of Monkton Up Wimborne, Dorset. Paul Bush's sister, Margaret, was married to one of Edith Ashley's relatives in Dorset.

Bush appears to have fought to uphold the rights of his poorly endowed bishopric (its revenues in 1559 amounted to little more than £300 per annum), and in 1551 he certainly made a determined effort to prevent the crown from seizing the manor of Leigh or Abbots Leigh near Bristol. In February 1551 he was summoned before the privy council at Greenwich to answer for his refusal to surrender the property, 'yet would he in no wise yield thereunto but departed refusing to commune of the matter' (*APC*, 1550–52, 210). Eventually he was overruled and was obliged to grant the manor to the crown in May 1551.

With the accession of Queen Mary in 1553 Bush found himself in an impossible situation as a married bishop. He appears to have had no difficulty in reconciling himself to the restoration of Catholicism, and may indeed have welcomed it, but the queen would tolerate neither a married bishop nor an ex-religious who had broken his vow of celibacy. The situation was not altered by the death of his wife, Edith, in October 1553. Bush was summoned before a commission appointed by the queen and was forced to resign his bishopric. He retired to Winterbourne in south Gloucestershire, where he became rector. While there he wrote an *Exhortation* addressed to Margaret, wife of John Burgess, a clothier from nearby Kingswood. Published in London in 1554 this was a spirited defence of the mass and the doctrine of the real presence against, in the words of its title, 'the rasshe fantastycall myndes of the blynd and ignorante'. His will, drawn up on 25 September 1558, is couched in traditional Catholic form, and gives detailed instructions about his funeral. His bequests included lands and property at Winterbourne and the manor house of 'Eastlinges Court' (now Gastlings Court) in the neighbouring parish of Frampton Cottrell; he also left gold rings, plate, cattle, corn, and good quality possessions which indicate that he lived in considerable style. The bulk of his property was bequeathed to his relatives.

Bush died at Winterbourne on 11 October 1558. His wife had been buried at the east end of the north choir aisle in Bristol Cathedral, and his own tomb was now erected nearby. The effigy of the bishop appears on the tomb as a scantily clad, tonsured, emaciated figure, lying on a rush mat, with his head resting on a mitre which retains some traces of colour. By his side is his pastoral staff. The inscription reads

> Hic jacet Dominus Paulus Bushe, primus huius ecclesiae episcopus qui obiit XI die Octobris Anno Domini MDLVIII, aetatis suae LXVIII. Cuius Animae Propitietur Deus Christus, Amen. ('Here lies Paul Bushe, first bishop of this church, who died 11 October Anno Domini 1558, aged 68. May the Lord Christ have mercy on his soul, Amen'.)

J. H. Bettey

Sources J. H. Bettey, 'Paul Bush, the first bishop of Bristol', *Transactions of the Bristol and Gloucestershire Archaeological Society*, 106 (1988), 169–172 • *Wiltshire Notes and Queries*, 4 (1902–4), 97–107, 145–56 • Emden, *Oxf.*, 4.89 • G. Burnet, *The history of the Reformation of the Church of England*, rev. N. Pocock, new edn, 7 vols. (1865), vol. 2, pp.127, 168, 440; vol. 5, pp.198–213, 386 • will, PRO, PROB 11/42A, sig. 3 • *VCH Wiltshire*, 3.323; 8.153 • *STC, 1475–1640*, nos. 4184–6 • *LP Henry VIII*, vols. 13, 15–16 • *APC*, 1550–52, 210 • F. Heal, *Of prelates and princes: a study of the economic and social position of the Tudor episcopate* (1980)

Likenesses effigy, Bristol Cathedral • portraits (Paul Bush?), bishop of Bristol; repro. in *Wiltshire Notes and Queries*, 97, 100–01

Wealth at death see will, PRO, PROB 11/42A, sig. 3

Bush, Percy Frank (1879–1955), rugby player, was born at 37 Rawdon Place, Cardiff, on 23 June 1879, the third son of James Bush (1844–1923), headmaster of the Cardiff School of Science and Art, and his wife, Fanny Rogers (1847–1923). He had an elder sister, Ethel M. Bush (1874–1947), who became a well-known pacifist. He was already playing for Pen-y-graig, one of the leading Rhondda clubs, when a student at University College, Cardiff, between 1896 and 1899, in preparation for his career as a schoolmaster. Although he made his début for Cardiff Rugby Football Club in October 1899, he did not establish himself in the side until 1903, when he struck up an effective partnership at half-back with R. J. (Dicky) David. He was one of the eight Welsh players selected for the 1904 British rugby union tour of Australia and New Zealand during which his speed, skill, and audacity were much admired: he appeared in all four test matches and emerged as the top scorer with 104 points. Small but compact at 5 feet 6 inches and 10½ stone, his running, dodging, and swerving, allied to a remarkable ability to stop dead in his tracks as his would-be tacklers shot past, marked him out as the most dangerous opponent the New Zealand All Blacks were likely to face on their 1905 tour of the British Isles.

It was indicative of the strength of Welsh rugby at that time, when Wales won the triple crown and championship six times between 1900 and 1911, that Bush had yet to make an international appearance when he went on tour in 1904, and was still overlooked by the Welsh selectors for the 1904–5 season on his return. When he did make his first international appearance it was in the most historic circumstances, as Wales beat New Zealand 3–0 at the Cardiff Arms Park on 16 December 1905, the only defeat suffered by the powerful All Blacks in the course of their thirty-five match tour. It was the New Zealanders' constant fear of Bush that led to the only score of the game when from a scrum 30 yards out he moved on a decoy run to the right while the ball was moved sharply to the left for Dr Teddy Morgan to score the winning try in the corner. Ten days later (26 December 1905) Bush was responsible for his club's narrow defeat by the tourists when, with characteristic but on this occasion fatal nonchalance, he delayed a clearance kick from his in-goal area and a grateful New Zealander pounced on the ball to score. Bush's failure to kick the ball as hard as he kicked himself afterwards resulted in a 10–8 defeat which haunted him for the rest of his career. He made amends on new year's day 1907, when he captained Cardiff to a historic 17–0 victory over the visiting South Africans, whose only other defeat on tour was by Scotland (6–0).

As Cardiff club captain between 1905 and 1907, and again from 1908 to 1909, Bush, served by the dependable Dicky David at scrum-half, was able to direct and orchestrate the entire back division from his position at outside-half. This was why he did not enjoy a longer international career, for the scrum-half position for Wales was occupied by the brilliant R. M. Owen of Swansea, who was used to controlling events himself. The conflicting individualism of Bush and Owen disabled them from developing a successful international partnership. Significantly, it was with his club partner Dicky David at scrum-half that Bush had his finest game for Wales, on 7 March 1907, against Ireland, when he had a hand in all of the six Welsh tries and dropped a goal in the 29–0 victory, capping an extraordinary all-round performance with a try so audacious it made one of his team-mates, R. T. Gabe, laugh out loud. Gabe, a fellow schoolteacher who played with Bush for Cardiff and Wales, and called him 'Trix', reckoned that while many could side-step one way or the other, Bush did it both ways 'all the time' (Smith and Williams, 149). He was equally impudent in the game with England played at Bristol on 18 January 1908 in a dense mist. Asked beforehand which way Wales would be playing, Bush replied 'We will play with the fog' (ibid., 193), and at one point in the game itself he transferred the ball quickly to Gabe then dashed off shouting, pursued by Englishmen, while Gabe ran in the opposite direction to touch down unopposed. In all he won ten caps for Wales.

Bush married, on 23 June 1909, Adeline Jane (1883/4–1941), daughter of Henry Wood, with whom he had a son and a daughter. His international career came to an end in 1910, when he resigned his teaching post at Cardiff's Wood Street School to take up a commercial appointment in Nantes, a major bunkering port for Welsh coal, where he continued playing and became captain of the Stade Nantais club, once scoring fifty-four points against Le Havre. After serving the French government during the war, on 19 October 1918 he was appointed British proconsul at Nantes; he became vice-consul in December 1924, and was effectively acting consul until he resigned on grounds of ill health in 1937 and later returned to Cardiff. In 1952 at a banquet at Cardiff city hall he was presented by the French consul with the medaille d'argent de la reconnaissance française in recognition of his contribution to Welsh–French relations and commercial links.

Bush, one of the most gifted and outrageous individuals to grace the international rugby field, also played minor counties cricket for Glamorgan between 1900 and 1903. He died at his home, Bryn Asaph, Romilly Road, Cardiff, on 19 May 1955 and was cremated at Thornhill two days later. GARETH WILLIAMS

Sources D. Smith and G. Williams, *Fields of praise: the official history of the Welsh Rugby Union, 1881–1981* • W. Thomas, *A century of Welsh rugby players, 1880–1980* (1980) • D. E. Davies, *Cardiff rugby club: history and statistics, 1876–1975* (1975) • J. Billot, *History of Welsh international rugby* (1970) • C. Thomas, *The history of the British Lions*, pbk edn (1996) • *South Wales Echo* (19 May 1955) • *Western Mail* [Cardiff] (20 May 1955) • private information (2004) • m. cert.

Likenesses photograph, repro. in Davies, *Cardiff rugby club* • photograph, repro. in A. Hignell, *A who's who of Glamorgan county cricket club (1881–1991)* (1992), 48

Bush, Rice (*c.*1610–1649), pamphleteer on poor relief, came to prominence in the public debates about new institutions for social welfare which took place in London at the end of the civil war. Little is known about his early life. The son of John Bush, yeoman, of Regil or Ridgehill, a hamlet in Winford parish, Somerset, he was bound apprentice to Baptiste Trott, a London draper, in 1628, and he became a freeman of the Drapers' Company in 1638. On 4 February 1640 he married Elizabeth Berriford in St John's, Hackney, probably her home parish, since from at least 1641 he was trading in silk in or near Cheapside, eventually with apprentices of his own.

In 1647 Bush became a member of the select vestry of St Mary Magdalen, Milk Street, a parish notable for its Presbyterianism; and the title Captain sometimes given to him there suggests that he may have seen service in the London trained bands. He was also involved in City politics, though on its fringes, as an activist in a pressure group, not as a member of the political élite. In 1645 he joined Samuel Hartlib and others in Hartlib's circle in petitioning the lord mayor for a new corporation to centralize and reinvigorate parochial poor relief throughout the metropolis. The result was a Corporation of the Poor employing and relieving the poor across the city, established by parliamentary ordinance in 1647 and revised by an act of parliament in 1649. Bush was active in lobbying MPs on both occasions, and he was named as one of the corporation's governing assistants in the 1649 statute.

In March 1649, during the second campaign, Bush published *The poor man's friend, or, A narrative of what progress many worthy citizens of London have made in that godly work of providing for the poor.* Like other tracts at this time by members of the Hartlib group, including William Petty and Peter Chamberlen, it articulated the wider vision behind local municipal activity. Bush advocated what amounted to a welfare state: registers of the poor, employment for them, and public provision of cheap loans, medical assistance, and education 'in religion, arts and mysteries'. Only the first two of these, registers and employment schemes, were realized by the corporation (which itself collapsed at the Restoration). But the tract was an influential contribution to contemporary and later debate on reform of the poor law. Bush showed an educated knowledge of earlier projects, both in London and the provinces, and an ambition that 'improvement' for 'the public good' in the capital would set an example for the rest of the country, including his 'native county'. He also expressed a novel sensibility, more widely shared later, towards 'the miseries of the poor': 'the cries of poor creatures for bread' (1649 was a year of high prices), and 'the secret mournings of poor families, to the heart-breaking of the truly pitiful and compassionate Christians'.

Bush's role in the parliamentary lobbying of the later 1640s was acknowledged by Edward Odling, solicitor to the Corporation of the Poor, in a broadsheet of about 1652 (*The Humble Remonstrance*), which describes him as 'now at rest in the Lord'. Bush had been buried on 9 August 1649 on the south side of the church of St Mary Magdalen, Milk Street, alongside three of his young children, interred in February and March of the same year. The causes of death are unknown. He left a widow, who remarried in 1654, a son, also christened Rice (in 1642), who died in 1661, and perhaps two other children. Private tragedy accompanied, and cut short, the public achievements which the political circumstances of the later 1640s made possible for this public-spirited and compassionate London citizen.

PAUL SLACK

Sources [R. Bush], *The poor man's friend* (1649) • V. Pearl, 'Puritans and poor relief: the London workhouse, 1649–1660', *Puritans and revolutionaries: essays in seventeenth-century history presented to Christopher Hill*, ed. D. Pennington and K. Thomas (1978), 206–32 • P. Slack, *From Reformation to improvement: public welfare in early modern England* (1999), ch. 4 • Drapers' Hall, London, Drapers' Company Records, Apprenticeship Binding Book, F.B.2 • P. Boyd, ed., *Roll of the Drapers' Company of London* (1934), 32 • A. H. Johnson, *The history of the Worshipful Company of the Drapers of London*, 5 vols. (1914–22), vol. 4, p. 158 • A. W. Hughes Clarke, ed., *The registers of St Mary Magdalen, Milk Street, 1558–1666, and St Michael Bassishaw, London, 1538–1625*, Harleian Society, register section, 72 (1942) • vestry minutes, St Mary

Magdalen, Milk St, 1619–68, GL, MS 259 · The humble remonstrance of Edward Odling citizen, broadsheet, *c.*1652, BL, 190.g.12(185) · parish register, St John, Hackney, 4/2/1640 [marriage] · *IGI*

Bushe, Charles Kendal (1767–1843), judge, born on 13 January 1767 at Kilmurry, co. Kilkenny, Ireland, was the only son of the Revd Thomas Bushe (1727–1795), of Kilmurry, rector of Mitchelstown, co. Cork, and Catherine, daughter of Charles Doyle, of Bramblestown, co. Kilkenny. Bushe went to school at Mrs Shackleton's academy, Ballintore, and at the French Huguenot school, Portarlington, before matriculating at Trinity College, Dublin, in July 1782. At university he excelled both in classics and in mathematics, and he was a scholar of the university and a gold medallist. Bushe won early renown for oratory at the College Historical Society, a debating society founded by Henry Grattan. Among other orators of the time were William Plunket, John Curran, and Richard Lalor Sheil.

Bushe was called to the Irish bar in 1790, and he soon acquired a good practice. However, he was saddled with the debts of his father. He also married relatively soon, becoming the husband of Nancy Crampton (1768–1857) in 1793. This meant that for most of his early career he had little money to spare, as he and Nancy had a large family of four boys and six girls; the eldest, John, later followed his father into the law.

In 1796 Bushe entered the Irish parliament as member for Callan. He held his seat until 1799, when he was returned for Donegal. Bushe was a fervent opponent of the Act of Union and spoke against it in the union debate in 1800, despite the offer of money, an earldom, and the position of master of the rolls if he would support the government and vote in its favour. Such integrity prompted Grattan to dub the young Bushe 'the incorruptible'. Bushe wrote as well as spoke against the union, and his satirical pamphlet, *Cease your Funning*, is well known. Bushe was an emancipist and decided to continue to serve despite the passing of the Act of Union in 1801. For his efforts in defence of legislative independence, he received the freedom of the city of Dublin.

Bushe's prominence as an opponent of the union did not affect his appointment as a law officer, and he was made third serjeant in July 1805. On the promotion of solicitor-general Plunket to the attorney-generalship in October 1805, Bushe, though opposed to the government on the question of Catholic emancipation—a measure which he steadily advocated—accepted the office of solicitor-general for Ireland, and held it until 1822, when, on the retirement of Lord Downes, he was appointed lord chief justice of the king's bench. Bushe resigned in 1841, having struggled in ill health to place the chief justiceship at Peel's disposal when he should enter office. Despite the well-established custom, no peerage was granted him on his retirement.

Bushe died in early July 1843 at his son's residence, Furry Park, Howth Road, Dublin, and was buried on 10 July in Mount Jerome cemetery, where a monument was erected to him. G. V. Benson, *rev.* Sinéad Agnew

Charles Kendal Bushe (1767–1843), by Martin Cregan, 1828

Sources E. OE. Somerville and M. Ross [V. F. Martin], *An incorruptible Irishman: being an account of Chief Justice Charles Kendal Bushe, and of his wife Nancy Crampton, and their times, 1767–1843* (1932) · F. E. Ball, *The judges in Ireland, 1221–1921*, 2 vols. (1926) · 'Chief Justice Bushe', *A new biographical dictionary of 3000 cotemporary [sic] public characters, British and foreign, of all ranks and professions*, 2nd edn (1825) · W. B. S. Taylor, *History of the University of Dublin* (1845) · J. F. Waller, ed., *The imperial dictionary of universal biography*, 3 vols. (1857–63) · 'Art III — Charles Kendal Bushe', *Irish Quarterly Review*, 3 (1853), 51–120 · H. Brougham, 'Lord Chief Justice Bushe', *Historical sketches of statesmen who flourished in the time of George III*, 3rd ser. (1843), 223–36 · *The Nation* (22 July 1843) · *Legal Reporter* (6 Nov 1841) · J. S. Crone, *A concise dictionary of Irish biography* (1928) · H. Boylan, *A dictionary of Irish biography* (1978)

Archives TCD | BL, correspondence with Sir Robert Peel, Add. MSS 40226–40487 · priv. coll., seal of the court of king's bench, presented to Bushe 1822

Likenesses T., plaster bust, 1816, NG Ire. · P. Turnereth, plaster bust, 1816, NG Ire. · M. Cregan, oils, 1828, NG Ire. [*see illus.*] · M. Cregan, oils, 1830, NG Ire. · J. Kirkwood, etching, pubd 1841 (after C. Grey), NG Ire. · D. Lucas, mezzotint, pubd 1842 (after W. Stevenson), NG Ire. · Edouard, silhouette, repro. in Somerville and Ross, *Incorruptible Irishman* · J. Heath, stipple (after J. Comerford), BM, NPG; repro. in J. Barrington, *Historic memoirs* (1809)

Bushe, Sir (Henry) Grattan (1886–1961), lawyer and colonial governor, was born in Trinidad on 1 January 1886, the son of John Scott Bushe, colonial secretary of Trinidad and acting governor at the time. An ancestor was Charles Kendal Bushe (1767–1843), solicitor-general for Ireland (1805) and chief justice of the king's bench and queen's bench in Ireland (1822–43). Henry Grattan Bushe was educated at Aysgarth School and Denstone College.

Called to the bar in 1909, Bushe was a member of the south-eastern and western circuits in 1910–16 and of the

Hertfordshire and Essex sessions in 1916, and a member of Marshall Hall's chambers. He then began a public service career as secretary to the royal commission investigating the contracts between the War Office and Sir John Jackson Ltd (1916–17). On 14 April 1914 he married Mary Kenrick Gibbons Chambers. They had one son (killed in action in 1944). In 1917 he joined the Dominions and Colonial Office as acting legal assistant; he subsequently became assistant legal adviser (1919–31) and legal adviser (1931–41).

A junior colleague, William Dale (who eventually became legal adviser to what became the Foreign and Commonwealth Office), later described Bushe in his memoirs. He was:

> a small spare man with flat grey hair, glinting brown eyes, and an impish look … Brooding over the legal scene sat Bushe, in his large room overlooking Downing Street. He was of Irish extraction, a penetrating lawyer, outspoken; he hit hard at humbug, and could be sarcastic, not to say cynical. (Dale, 57)

Bushe was deeply committed to the rule of law and sound administration in the colonies. He introduced the professional magistracy to take over the magistrates' courts from the district officers in east and west Africa. In the 1930s he was much involved in the problem of Palestine, where Britain had assumed the mandate from the League of Nations after the First World War. Bushe had little sympathy for the concept of a national home for the Jews as outlined in the Balfour declaration, and little or no patience with the very serious tensions between Arabs and Jews. In the abdication crisis in 1936 he was principally concerned to ascertain the views of the colonies, to advise, and to preserve the constitutional monarchy.

In 1941 Bushe was appointed governor and commander-in-chief of Barbados. This transfer to a governorship was a promotion without precedent in the colonial service, for governors had rarely been chosen from the ranks of practising lawyers and never before from the legal staff of the colonial office. It was neither an easy post nor an easy period. Bushe was sent to administer a community which, while itself highly critical, took unkindly to criticism from others and was very conscious of the fact that its House of Assembly was, next to the House of Commons and the Bermuda House of Assembly, the oldest legislature in the British empire. But it could hardly be expected that a constitution devised for an infant white settlement in the reign of Charles I would be flexible enough to meet conditions in the twentieth century with a large ethnic population—of rapidly growing political consciousness—living side by side with the descendants of the original white settlers. Indeed, the rigidity of the constitution and other defects had long given rise to friction between governors and elected members.

As a trained constitutional lawyer, Bushe was quick to see where the constitution could be improved, and was able before the end of his term of office to prepare the way for improvements. He had also to contend with all the security measures necessitated by the war and with the difficult questions of conserving and distributing food stocks seriously restricted by the enemy submarine blockade. The ethnic element, sharing the general West Indian political desires, wanted a wider franchise; labour demanded wider recognition; and the planters were unsure of the future for their sugar. All these insistent problems Bushe handled shrewdly, skilfully, and with success; and his administration proved to have been a significant stage in the history of the colony. He retired in 1946, returning to Britain.

Bushe was appointed CMG in 1927 and CB in 1932, and was advanced to KCMG in 1936. He was also a knight of grace of the order of St John. His club was the Union Club. Lady Bushe, a trained musician and keenly interested, as a dame of the order of St John of Jerusalem, in the work of the St John Ambulance Brigade and of the Girl Guides, actively supported her husband in everything that made for the encouragement in the colony of music, drama, and cultural activities. Sir Grattan Bushe died at Guy's Hospital, London Bridge, London, on 23 August 1961. His wife survived him. ALEC SAMUELS

Sources W. Dale, *Time past, time present* (1994) • affairs in Barbados: dispatch from the governor, G. Bushe, March–June 1942, PRO, CO 28/326/13 • affairs in Barbados: dispatches from the governor, G. Bushe, June 1942, PRO, CO 28/327/14 • broadcasts by the governor, G. Bushe, April–Aug 1943, PRO, CO 28/330/7 • affairs in Barbados: dispatches from the governor, G. Bushe, Dec 1943–Jan 1945, PRO, CO 28/332/4 • affairs in Barbados: dispatches from the governor, G. Bushe, Dec 1944–March 1946, PRO, CO 28/332/5 • visit of H. G. Bushe to west Africa: report, 1932, PRO, CO 554/90/13 • inquiry into administration of justice: Bushe report: printing of report, 1938, PRO, CO 822/86/7 • proposed appointment of Sir Grattan Bushe, legal adviser at the colonial office, as governor in succession to Sir John Waddington, PRO, CO 967/129 • *The Times* (26 Aug 1961) • m. cert. • d. cert.

Archives PRO, CO 850/187/20 • PRO, CO 850/200/14 | Bodl. RH, corresp. with Judge Thacker

Likenesses photograph, repro. in *The Times*

Wealth at death £18,598 16*s*.: probate, 1 Nov 1961, *CGPLA Eng. & Wales*

Bushell, Browne (*bap.* **1609**, *d.* **1651**), royalist naval officer, was baptized on 17 May 1609, the eldest son of Nicholas Bushell (*c.*1551–1632) of Bagdale Old Hall, Whitby, and his wife, Dorothy (*bap.* 1587), daughter of Sir Henry Cholmley (1553–1616), of Abbey House, Whitby. Browne was the maiden name of his paternal grandmother. With his share from the sale of Bagdale Old Hall to his brother-in-law, Isaac Newton, he bought the *John* and in 1632 he was carrying Newcastle coals to Dunkirk. It was probably in the Spanish Netherlands that in 1633 he married his sixteen-year-old wife, but their son Nicholas was buried at Whitby in 1639. According to his final testament, delivered from the scaffold on Tower Hill, Bushell served the king of Spain for ten years, yet as late as 1634 he was described as a merchant of Newcastle and captain of the *Mary Anne* of that port. When he returned to England from Dunkirk in August 1642 his experience of continental warfare explains why parliament immediately gave him a commission on the *Martin*, then engaged in the siege of Portsmouth. Bushell soon justified parliament's trust. On the night of 9–10 August 1642 he led a group of longboats into the strongly-defended harbour and seized the *Henrietta Maria*, a royalist pinnace, without a shot being fired. Soon after he made a dawn attack on Southsea Castle—a formidable fortress commanding the sea channel into Portsmouth—and again achieved a brilliant coup: the royalist garrison surrendered without resistance. Within days Portsmouth fell to parliament, thereby depriving the king of an essential port of entry from the continent. Soon after Sir Hugh Cholmley became parliament's governor of Scarborough, he was joined there by his cousin, Bushell. Under the captain's professional directions Scarborough Castle—a semi-derelict anachronism—was converted into a modern fortification. The artillery platform outside the barbican is still called Bushell's battery. He was at Hull when Cholmley secretly changed sides in March 1643, but he promised Hotham that he would retake Scarborough for parliament. Again Bushell won a bloodless victory: during Cholmley's absence at York, castle and town were restored to parliament. However, when his cousin met him at the town gates on 29 March Bushell was persuaded also to change sides. As Sir Hugh later explained, Bushell's nature was 'rash but flexable and good' (Cholmley, 'Memorials tuching Scarbrough', fol. 10*r*), and he was reminded of all the favours he owed to his mother's family. From then on Bushell's loyalty was fixed. Out of Scarborough in the *Cavendish*, a 12-gun warship, he led a squadron of royalist privateers which gained notoriety for daring raids on parliament's ships in the North Sea. When Scarborough harbour was lost, he operated out of Ostend and Dunkirk. In July 1645, while attempting to supply Goring at Exeter, the *Cavendish* was intercepted and boarded, but Bushell escaped by swimming ashore. He was at Boulogne in 1647 and from there took refuge in Jersey when Mazarin expelled all privateers from French ports; but it was off Tynemouth that he was finally taken in April 1648, probably by his former shipmate, Captain John Lawson of Scarborough. Bushell was imprisoned in Windsor Castle and allowed 5*s*. a week for his maintenance. The attorney-general decided to try him not for his acts of piracy but for his surrender of Scarborough to Cholmley. His trial took place at Westminster on Lady day 1651. The evidence against him was conclusive and he was sentenced to die on 29 March 1651, the eighth anniversary of his treason. Browne Bushell died as bravely as he had lived: he regretted only that he had not fought for the king from the beginning of the wars, he declared himself a faithful son of the Church of England, and he was pleased to be told that the same block and axe had been used to execute Charles I. Seconds later he became a royalist martyr.

JACK BINNS

Sources J. Binns, 'Captain Browne Bushell: North Sea adventurer and pirate', *Northern History*, 27 (1991), 90–105 • J. Hotham, *A true and exact relation of … Sir Hugh Cholmleys revolt, deserting the parliament, and going to the queen* (1643/4) [Thomason tract E 95(9)] • *The speech and confession of Capt. Brown-Bushel* (1651) [Thomason tract E 626(14)] • J. R. Powell, *The navy in the English civil war* (1962) • J. R. Powell and E. K. Timings, eds., *Documents relating to the civil war, 1642–1648*, Navy RS, 105 (1963) • Pannett Park Museum, Whitby, Yorkshire, Whitby Literary and Philosophical Society Library, Shaw Jeffrey MSS, Box A; Percy Burnett MSS • M. Y. Ashcroft, ed., *Scarborough records, 1600–1640: a calendar* (1991) • M. Y. Ashcroft, ed., *Scarborough records, 1641–1660: a calendar* (1991) • J. Charlesworth, ed., *The parish register of Whitby* (privately printed, Leeds, 1928) • H. Cholmley, 'Memorials tuching Scarbrough', Bodl. Oxf., MS Clarendon 1669 [pubd in *EngHR*, 32 (1917)] • D. E. Kennedy, 'Parliament and the navy, 1642–1648: a political history of the navy during the civil war', PhD diss., U. Cam., 1959 • T. Hinderwell, *The history of Scarborough*, 3rd edn (1832) • J. Rushworth, *Historical collections*, 3–4 (1692–1701) • H. Cholmley, 'Memoirs', 1656, York Minster Library, Add. MS 343 [privately printed, 1787 and 1870] • K. R. Andrews, *Ships, money, and politics: seafaring and naval enterprise in the reign of Charles I* (1991) • J. Webb, *The siege of Portsmouth in the civil war* (1977) • J. Foster, ed., *The visitation of Yorkshire made in the years 1584/5 … to which is added the subsequent visitation made in 1612* (privately printed, London, 1875) • W. Dugdale, *The visitation of the county of Yorke*, ed. R. Davies and G. J. Armytage, SurtS, 36 (1859) • *Diary of Lady Margaret Hoby*, ed. D. M. Meads (1930)

Archives PRO, account book of the *John*, HCA 30/638, no. 2

Likenesses oils, 1633, Pannett Park Museum, Whitby • medallion, repro. in W. Winstanley, *The Loyall martyrology* (1665), frontispiece

Wealth at death gave his executioner 20*s*. and wished it had been more; 'inheritance', the Bushell estate, in Bagdale and Ruswarp, sold to brother-in-law by 1632

Bushell, Seth (**1620/21–1684**), Church of England clergyman, was born the only son of Adam Bushell (*d. c.*1627) and Alice Bushell, *née* Loggan, of Cuerden, near Preston in Lancashire. He entered St Mary Hall, Oxford, as a commoner in 1639. When Oxford was occupied by the king's forces in the civil war he returned to Lancashire. Bushell was a parliamentarian puritan who in 1650 was minister in Euxton, Lancashire, where parliamentary inspectors appraised him as 'a godly, preachinge minister, and conformable to the present government' (Fishwick, *Lancashire and Cheshire Church Surveys*, 102). At some point he married Mary Farington, daughter of Roger Farington of Leyland, a place near his family home. In 1654, the year in which he published a preface to Robert Towne's *A Re-Assertion of Grace*, Bushell went back to Oxford where he graduated BA, proceeding MA in February 1655. By that time he was curate or incumbent of Whitby, Yorkshire, where a branch of his family was established. On 23 July 1657 he was married again, this time to Mary Stansfield, daughter of William Stansfield of Euxton. In 1658 he published a sermon which produced a riposte from the Quaker founder George Fox. Throughout these years he seems to have continued to occupy the living of Euxton, up to and beyond the point, probably in 1664, when he took up the vicarage of Preston. By that juncture he had conformed to the Church of England, as required by the 1662 Act of Uniformity. However, he retained some of the flavour of his earlier puritan views. Preston parish church was in the gift of the decidedly protestant Hoghton family, whose custom it was to appoint men of puritan orientation, which in Bushell's case embraced a strong advocacy of religious tolerance.

During his eighteen-year tenure as vicar of Preston, Bushell was probably married once more (to a woman named Elizabeth who died in 1697), took his Oxford DD in

June 1672, and in the following year published, as *A Warning-Piece for the Unruly*, two sermons that he delivered on the occasion of the archbishop of York's metropolitical visitation. Another sermon, given at the funeral of his patron Sir Richard Hoghton, was published as *The Believer's Groan for Heaven* in 1678. Upon his resignation from Preston in October 1682 he became vicar of Lancaster, providing a brief interval of tolerant churchmanship between the occupancy of two vicars described by the local Quaker William Stout as 'seveire' (*Autobiography of William Stout*, 78). Indeed, 'a person of a moderate disposition … [who] much discuraged persecution for religion … and [was] very corteous to Dissenters of all denominations', Bushell acted as an antidote to the ferocity of the Anglican-tory reaction in Lancashire in the 1680s (ibid., 78). In 1682 he published his major work, *Cosmos-meros, the worldly-portion, or, The best portion of the wicked and their misery in the enjoyment of it opened and applied: together with some directions and helps in order to a heavenly and a better portion, enforced with many useful and divine considerations*.

Bushell died in Lancaster on 6 November 1684. His memorial in Lancaster Priory church reinterpreted his career as that of a man 'most devoted to the reformed Church of England' and also to the crown, though in fact the legacy of his earlier radicalism lived on in his espousal in difficult times of principles of religious understanding and freedom. MICHAEL MULLETT

Sources H. Fishwick, *The history of the parochial chapelry of Goosnargh in the county of Lancaster* (1871), 120–4 · M. Mullett, '"To dwell together in unity": the search for agreement in Preston politics, 1660–1690', *Transactions of the Historic Society of Lancashire and Cheshire*, 125 (1974), 61–81, esp. 71 · M. A. Mullett, 'Conflict, politics and elections in Lancaster, 1660–1688', *Northern History*, 19 (1983), 61–86, esp. 62 · *The autobiography of William Stout of Lancaster, 1665–1752*, ed. J. D. Marshall, Chetham Society, 3rd ser., 14 (1967), 78–9, 250 · Wood, *Ath. Oxon.*, new edn, 4.162 · H. Fishwick, ed., *Lancashire and Cheshire church surveys, 1649–1655*, Lancashire and Cheshire RS, 1 (1879), 102 · Foster, *Alum. Oxon.*

Bushell, Stephen Wootton (1844–1908), physician and art historian, born on 28 July 1844 at Woodnesborough, near Sandwich, Kent, was the third son of William Bushell, a farmer, and his wife, Sarah Frances Wootton. After education at Tunbridge Wells School and at Grange Court, Chigwell, he studied medicine at Guy's Hospital, and in 1866 graduated MB of the University of London, where he won several scholarships and gold medals. He was appointed house surgeon at Guy's Hospital in 1866 and in the following year became resident medical officer to Bethlem Royal Hospital. In 1868 he went to Peking (Beijing), as physician to the British legation there. Bushell married on 26 November 1874 Florence Jane (*b.* 1851/2), daughter of Robert Mathews, a surgeon; they had one son.

Bushell became a considerable connoisseur of Chinese art, architecture, books, and coins. He studied the Chinese language and Chinese literature, and in the early 1870s travelled through the country with the photographer John Thomson, collaborating with him to produce a collection of photographs of Peking architecture and artefacts which is now in the Oriental Museum at the University of Durham. He also bought Chinese ceramics for A. W. Franks, the director of the British Museum, who presented his collection to the British Museum in 1876. In 1882–3 Bushell bought for the South Kensington Museum (later the Victoria and Albert Museum). His purchases for Franks and for South Kensington became the nuclei of both museums' Chinese collections. Bushell retired from his post, owing to ill health, in 1900. The services which he rendered to the Zongli yamen and other Chinese government departments had received formal acknowledgement in 1894, and in 1897 he had been made a CMG.

After returning to England, Bushell devoted himself to writing on Chinese art and archaeology, and quickly won recognition as the leading authority of his day on Chinese ceramics. Bringing to the subject both his scientific training and his experience as a connoisseur, as well as an adequate grasp of the Chinese language, he was able to study, and in many cases publish in translation, classic Chinese works on arts and handicrafts. These publications included *Porcelain of Different Dynasties* (1908), a reproduction with translation of a sixteenth-century Chinese collector's album with coloured illustrations (the original by Xiang Yuanpian was destroyed by fire in 1887, and the illustrations, taken from a copy, are therefore of questionable value); Bushell had in 1886 published a translation of the text of this album in the *Journal of the Peking Oriental Society*. His *Chinese Pottery and Porcelain* (published posthumously in 1910) was a translation of the classic *Tao shuo* ('Speaking of pottery'), and ranked in significance with Stanilaus Julien's translation of *Jingdezhen tao lu* (1856). *Jade in China* (1906), an illustrated catalogue of the Heber Reginald Bishop collection (now in the Metropolitan Museum, New York) also included translations of *Yu shuo* ('Discussion of jade') by Tang Rongzuo, and *Yuzuo tu* ('Illustrations of the manufacture of jade') by Li Shichuan. Other works by Bushell include *Oriental Ceramic Art*, a description of the W. T. Waters collection in Baltimore, published in ten richly illustrated volumes in 1897, followed by a separate edition in 1899, and a catalogue of the J. Pierpont Morgan collection of Chinese porcelain in the Metropolitan Museum of New York, which he prepared with W. M. Laffan in 1907. He also wrote *Chinese Art* (1904), a general introduction to the field, and edited Cosmo Monkhouse's book *Chinese Porcelain* (1901).

Bushell died on 19 September 1908 at his house, Ravensholt, Mount Park, Northolt. He was survived by his wife and son. As a contemporary observer of late nineteenth-century Chinese art, he was outstanding; his accounts of the kilns at Jingdezhen of that period are invaluable, and his catalogues are still important reference works on the later Qing porcelains. His translations may not be unquestioned, but they offered models for the scholarly handling of his subject. Bushell's own collection of Chinese artefacts was probably inherited by his family: in 1975 a granddaughter, Dorothy Bushell, presented a gift of twenty-five pieces to the Victoria and Albert Museum; the remainder of her collection was donated to the National Trust and is held at Beningbrough Hall, Yorkshire.

R. L. HOBSON, *rev.* M. TREGEAR

Sources *Journal of the Royal Asiatic Society of Great Britain and Ireland* (1909), 239–40 • *WW* (1908) • private information (1912) • N. Pearce, 'Photographs of Beijing in the Oriental Museum, Durham', *Apollo*, 147 (March 1998), 33–9 • R. Kerr, 'The Bushell gift', *Oriental Art*, 44/2 (summer 1998), 36–8 • J. Ayers, 'Enlightened decisions: the founding of the V&A's far eastern department', *Orientations*, 26 (Nov 1995), 64–8 • b. cert. • m. cert. • d. cert. • *CGPLA Eng. & Wales* (1908)
Archives V&A, MSS | Bodl. Oxf., letters to Sir Aurel Stein • U. Durham, Oriental Museum, John Thomson photographic collection
Wealth at death £12,141 17*s*. 9*d*.: resworn administration with will, 22 Oct 1908, *CGPLA Eng. & Wales*

Bushell, Thomas (*b*. before **1600**, *d*. **1674**), mining entrepreneur and mint-master, was born into a minor gentry family of Cleeve Prior, near Evesham, in Worcestershire. In Aubrey's words he had a good wit and a working and contemplative head; but his education was neglected—he admits an ignorance of Latin in the first of his many pamphlets, *Youths Errors* (1628), and for that reason Anthony Wood's notion that he had had some education at Oxford cannot be true. He also fell into bad ways, reminding his brother Edward in the same volume of a childhood theft which may have driven him from home. At fifteen he entered the service of Sir Francis Bacon. There a showy lifestyle, very different from that of Cleeve Prior, encouraged debts far beyond his own means, and which were paid by Bacon. Bacon, however, at the height of his powers as a philosophical writer, found in Bushell an apt and admiring pupil. With him he shared his enthusiasm for mining, probably stimulated by his share in a lease of eight granges of Strata Florida Abbey, together with their mineral rights, in 1617. He expounded the techniques of driving dewatering adits at the lowest possible level, and of conveying a forced draught of air in ducting. These techniques he appears to have allowed Bushell to assume were of his own devising, and in later years Bushell was to make the most of this; but the fact is they are described and illustrated as early as 1556 in Agricola's *De re metallica*.

Bacon's fall as chancellor in 1621 involved allegations of corruption among his staff, and Bushell fled to the Isle of Wight, returning after a while to serve Bacon until his death in 1626. These years of reflection culminated in an eremitical sojourn—he says, three years—in a cabin on the Calf of Man. *Youths Errors* was the *mea culpa* for misspent years, and is equipped with a woodcut portrait of 'the Superlative Prodigall' as he called himself, hands folded in prayer, a cross tucked in. All through his life Bushell seems to have required the dramatic, the flamboyant gesture, even when the occasion was personal and private.

Thus purged, Bushell reappeared in London and obtained the farm of the duties on silk dyeing, and a fifteenth share in the notorious soap monopoly. He had married an heiress—we know only her name, Isabell—found by Bacon, and lavished money on a small estate at Enstone, near Chipping Norton, in Oxfordshire. Here the register records the baptism and burial on 8 June 1626 of a son, Francis, named after Bacon; another son, Arthur, was married in 1640. Bushell was a widower by 1642, for in that year he mortgaged the lease of Belsize Manor, which had come to him with a second wife, Anne, widow of Sir William Wade, lieutenant of the Tower until displaced during the Overbury affair.

The 'Rock of Enstone' was a conceit typical of the age, designed after the hydraulic works of Isaac de Caus at Wilton, and of others elsewhere. During the clearing of ground at the foot of a hillock a spring of fine water appeared, which, augmented from other sources, enabled Bushell to create a fantastic grotto (illustrated by Plot in his *Oxfordshire*, and with a valuable description of 1635 by Lieutenant Hammond). A pleasure house in a rustic gothic style was erected above, with rooms to either side, one hung with black, the 'hermit's' study; the other Bushell's bedroom. The whole was set amid orchards and gardens, and Hammond records his astonishment that a man should spend so much money in this way without possessing the freehold: 'a mad gim-cracke sure' (Thacker, 32), yet something central to Bushell's personality.

A royal visit in 1636 was taken by Bushell as an opportunity to explore the possibility of a lease of the Cardiganshire mines royal, in the hands of Sir Hugh Myddleton until his death in 1631, and thus in his widow's. Bushell had begun to interest himself in the idea of successful working by the principles he recalled from his days with Bacon, and certainly Myddleton had done very well. Mine royal was a term applying to mines which produced lead–silver ore in such a proportion that the silver left after burning off the lead exceeded the value of the loss and the costs of production. Lessees under the aegis of the Mines Royal Company, established in 1568, had a right to enter upon any land and work such mines, to the obvious disarray and often violent objections on the landowners' part. In Cardiganshire the main productive mines had been known for many years. They lay in the hilly country to the east of Aberystwyth, where the region has a rainfall of sixty to eighty inches a year, rendering Bushell's scheme to drive adits to drain the workings practicable and attractive. But what was never considered, by any of the early modern entrepreneurs, was the total cost. Expenditure on dead work and labour was never deducted—at least not in the specious and brief accounts and claims put in front of the public. Myddleton in a private letter said his costs were £200 a week—£10,400 a year; and that may be set against the £28,000, almost all in Welsh silver, struck at the Tower mint between 1627 and 1631. Whether lead sales balanced his books no one can say.

Only one of Bushell's adits at the 'five mountains' succeeded—dramatically—in 1641, at Tal-y-bont. The cost of these workings was immense, and his personal fortune, with whatever he could raise by borrowing from individuals, would have been poured into them. When fired by enthusiasm, 'his tongue was a chaine and drew in so many to be bound for him and to be ingaged in his designes that he ruined a number' (*Brief Lives*, 43). In 1637 a further application to the crown brought about letters patent establishing a branch mint, with himself as warden and master worker, in the royal castle at Aberystwyth, to coin the silver produced locally instead of sending to the Tower. The technical staff were seconded from the Tower, as were the dies: Bushell's coinage carried, in addition, the feathers badge of the prince of Wales on both sides, and his personal mark, an open book. The rough book of the mint survives and records that between January 1639 (when the mint started work) and September 1642 £10,500 worth of sterling silver coin was produced.

In that September Charles I ordered the mint to be moved to Shrewsbury, his first civil war base. Here not only fine Welsh bullion but all manner of plate contributed by supporters or acquired in other ways could be reduced to coin. Bushell eked out Aberystwyth dies with newly cut ones of his own, rough indeed, but stamping coin as good as any. A dearth of gold forced him to strike huge medals of 20*s*. and 10*s*. in silver, as well as 5*s*., 2*s*. 6*d*., and some shillings. These were ready for him to distribute in person to the army on the eve of Edge Hill (October 23)—a typically flamboyant gesture. In January 1643, when Charles had settled himself at Oxford, Bushell moved the mint to that city, where he became joint warden with Sir William Parkhurst, the royalist warden of the Tower mint up to that time. And when Rupert captured Bristol in July 1643, Bushell was sent to erect a mint in the castle there. Some time before 11 September 1645, when Fairfax recaptured the city, he slipped away and next appears as the commandant of Lundy island in the mouth of the Bristol Channel. In July 1646 he was obliged to surrender, one of the last royalist holds. Bushell lavished expenditure on the king's cause, but like many another was ill-requited after the Restoration. A consolidated claim for £36,000 for lead and clothing, attested by Parkhurst and others, was never paid. He received only half of the £2000 tardily authorized in 1663. As early as 1641 he mortgaged the finest lead mine—not mine royal—at Cwmystwyth, and this marks the beginning of the deluge of debts for which he was pursued until the end of his life.

Bushell never went back to Wales. As soon as Lundy had been surrendered he began fresh overtures for mining in the west country, pretending to be able to drain the rich but drowned mine of Combe Martin. Capitalizing ever more on his relationship with Bacon, he had a medal struck showing the sage on one side; on the other his own name and the motto *Deus est qui clausa recludit* ('God it is who throws open the hidden things') surround the figure of a miner. Purchasers were supposed to bind themselves to pay Bushell a set sum if he succeeded in maintaining a steady £500 of production per annum after eighteen months. It was a 'gimcrack' scheme; a few specimens of the medal survive. Most of his later schemes centred on Hingston Down, near the Cornwall–Devon border, and on Mendip. Only in the latter leadfield are there signs that anything was done. Aubrey met Bushell about this time in the latter's house at Lambeth, and describes him as 'a handsome proper gentleman … he was about 70 … he had a perfect, healthy constitution, fresh, ruddy face, hawke-nosed, and was temperate' (*Brief Lives*, 44).

Bushell's last years were sad and lonely. 'Lady Wade' had died in 1645. He was for most of the time on the run from creditors, at one time being imprisoned by them in Newgate; at other times he lay low at Lambeth and elsewhere, occasionally worrying authority about confirmation of his civil war grant of the customs on lead. But in 1663 he was sworn as a 'gentleman of the privy chamber extraordinary', and this, at least, put an end to the fear of arrest. His last lodging was in Scotland Yard, and there he died on 21 April 1674; he was buried on the 24th in Westminster Abbey cloisters, but no sign remains.

GEORGE C. BOON

Sources G. C. Boon, *Cardiganshire silver and the Aberystwyth mint in peace and war* (1981) • J. W. Gough, *The superlative prodigall: a life of Thomas Bushell* (1932) • T. Bushell, *The first part of youths errors* (1628) • T. Bushell, *A just and true remonstrance of His Majesties mines-royall …* (1642) • T. Bushell, *The case of Thomas Bushell* (1649) • C. Thacker, 'An extraordinary solitude', in S. Raphael and others, *Of Oxfordshire gardens* (1982), 27–48 • *Aubrey's Brief lives*, ed. O. L. Dick (1949), 43–4 • C. E. Challis, '1603 to 1660: court and Commonwealth', *A new history of the royal mint*, ed. C. E. Challis (1992), 267–335 • E. Besly, *Coins and medals of the English Civil War* (1990)

Archives BL, Add. MSS 18760–18761 • NMG Wales, Aberystwyth mint and civil war coins • PRO, Aberystwyth mint MSS | BL, Harley MS 6833 • BL, Harley charters 111.B.61, 111.E.10

Likenesses woodcut, *c*.1628, repro. in Gough, *Superlative prodigall*, frontispiece • medals, BM

Busher, Leonard (*bap.* **1573**, *d.* in or after **1651**), advocate of toleration, was baptized at Wotton under Edge, Gloucestershire on 24 April 1573, the son of William Busher (*d.* 1607), tradesman, and his wife Janet. After an apprenticeship in the Grocers' Company in London, he was made free in 1604. It was probably soon after becoming a London citizen that he married, for his daughter Elizabeth was baptized at St Dunstan in the East on 29 July 1606. Shortly thereafter he emigrated to the Netherlands. There he embraced Baptist tenets, and on 8 July 1611 was described by Matthew Saunders and Cuthbert Hutten as belonging to a different group of Anabaptists than those of John Smyth and Thomas Helwys respectively. Busher's party accepted the Hoffmanite (monophysite) doctrine of Christ's incarnation. There is no evidence to support the tradition that Busher returned to London with Helwys in 1612. The following year he was working on the manuscript of his classic *Religions Peace, or, A Reconciliation, between Princes & Peoples, & Nations*, published in Amsterdam in 1614. Before composing this work he had written two other pieces, the first an attack intended to expel Antichrist and the professional clergy from the church, and the second a declaration against inaccurate translations in the New Testament. He lacked the funds to publish these works, but it was probably one of these that he sent to John Robinson a year before completing *Religions Peace*; Robinson refused to reply, prompting Busher to chide him for cloaking his errors in silence.

Addressed to James I and parliament, *Religions Peace* is a powerfully argued case for religious toleration, resting on the principle that no sovereign or bishop can compel conscience or command faith. Laws that repress freedom of religion are antichristian and contrary to both the gospel and natural reason. Ministers of Christ, Busher averred, rely solely on the word and spirit, not fire and sword, to win and sustain converts. He pointedly contrasted the toleration allowed to Christians by the Turks with the repression of believers in England by *de facto* tyrants. But religious freedom did not mean the withdrawal of magistrates from the religious sphere, for he urged crown and parliament to unite in repressing persecuting prelates and clerics. Although toleration should not exclude Catholics, Busher rejected any claim that Rome was a true church and attacked the separatist Francis Johnson for maintaining such a position. By his call for Jews to enjoy liberty to worship and the right to defend publicly their views, and for the gathering of Jews and Gentiles into congregations of the faithful, Busher effectively made a case for the Jews' legal readmission to England. *Religions Peace* is not a narrow polemical work, for it contains only a passing reference to believers' baptism by immersion. The tract manifests not only Busher's working knowledge of Greek but his extensive reliance on the New Testament, the source of approximately 200 of his 240 biblical citations.

Busher reappears on 8 December 1642, when he wrote a letter, in Dutch, from Delft to a Mennonite friend in Amsterdam, Abram Derikson, describing himself as weak, elderly (aged seventy-one), lonely, and in need of assistance; he signed the letter a 'desolate broeder in cristo, Mark Leonard Busher' (Burrage, 2.259). On 1 January 1644 Robert Baillie referred to a work by Busher, whom he depicted as an old English Anabaptist in Amsterdam. This was *An exhortation unto the learned divines assembled at Westminster* (Amsterdam, 1643), in which he again appealed for toleration. The following year Busher's *Wholesome Severity Reconciled with Christian Liberty* was published in London, apparently in a very small run since only one copy (now in the Bodleian) has been found. Busher's classic was reproduced in 1646 (again published in London) under the title *Religions Peace, or, A Plea for Liberty of Conscience*, with a preface to 'the Presbyterian reader' by H. B., probably the Independent minister Henry Burton. Apparently H. B. made no attempt to contact Busher, who was still living. About this time Busher was reading John Archer's *The Personall Raigne of Christ upon Earth* (1641) as well as reflections by the Baptist minister James Toppe seeking 'to prove Christes Monarchicall reigne over all the Kingedomes of this world' (Burgess, 3.203). Repudiating both men, Busher argued in 1647 that Christ governed his heavenly realm but would not personally rule the earth's kingdoms. Apparently no copy of Busher's book has survived. Toppe responded in an unpublished manuscript, 'Christs monarchicall, and personall reigne uppon Earth' (1648?). Busher was still alive in 1651, when his name appeared in the archives of the Waterlander Mennonites. He was one of the earliest English proponents of religious toleration, though it was not without restrictions, for he insisted that appeals to authority in religious debate must be confined to scripture. RICHARD L. GREAVES

Sources C. Burrage, *The early English dissenters in the light of recent research (1550–1641)*, 2 vols. (1912) • E. B. Underhill, ed., *Tracts on liberty of conscience and persecution, 1614–1661*, Hanserd Knollys Society (1846) • S. Wright, 'Leonard Busher: life and ideas', *Baptist Quarterly*, 39 (2001), 175–92 • K. L. Sprunger, *Trumpets from the tower: English puritan printing in the Netherlands, 1600–1640* (1994) • W. T. Whitley, 'Leonard Busher, Dutchman', *Transactions of the Baptist Historical Society*, 1 (1908–9), 107–13 • *The letters and journals of Robert Baillie*, ed. D. Laing, 3 vols., Bannatyne Club, 73 (1841–2), vol. 2, p. 121 • W. H. Burgess, 'James Toppe and the Tiverton Anabaptists', *Transactions of the Baptist Historical Society*, 3 (1912–13), 193–211 • W. K. Jordan, *The development of religious toleration in England*, 4 vols. (1932–40), vol. 2 • W. M. Lamont, *Godly rule: politics and religion, 1603–60* (1969) • L. Busher, *Religions peace*, 2nd edn (1614)

Archives BL, letters, Sloane MS 63, fols. 36–57 • Mennonite Archives, Amsterdam, MS B1378

Wealth at death very poor: Burrage, *The early English dissenters*, 1.71, 278–9

Bushnan, John Stevenson (1807–1884), physician, was born at Guildhall, London, on 28 February 1807, the eldest of the five children of Joseph Bushnan (1773–1831), controller of the chamber, City of London, and his wife, Mary Newton, *née* Osborn. He studied medicine at Edinburgh where he became MRCS and MRCP in 1830. Bushnan settled in Dumfries, Scotland, where, on 2 February 1832, he married Mary Farquhar Connell. They had three children. While there he took on work for the middle-class radical organization the Society for the Diffusion of Useful Knowledge, although he was disappointed in their ability or willingness to fund his research. He also found it difficult to reconcile the need to popularize his work with his desire to produce an academic publication. Like others before him, Bushnan attempted to use his connection with the secretary, Thomas Coates, to secure a post at University College, London, or the attached hospital. In 1836 he graduated MD at Heidelberg University after a period of residence and an examination, and returned to England to settle at Castle Cary, Somerset, where he practised medicine from 1837 to 1841. From 1841 to 1848 he travelled abroad, returning to practise in London. The following year he was appointed editor of the *Medical Times and Gazette*, a post he held until 1852. In this post he became a strong advocate of private asylums and the network of service industries which supported the private madhouse system. He also promoted the appointment of medical men, rather than lay superintendents, to manage asylums. Under his editorship the *Medical Times and Gazette* was very critical of the lunacy commission and the inquisitorial nature of its inspection system, reflecting his earlier progressive politics.

In 1852 Bushnan was appointed senior physician of the Metropolitan Free Hospital in Devonshire Square in the City, but he held the post for only one year. In the same year he was also appointed medical superintendent of the private asylum Wyke House, in Middlesex, but by 1857 this had passed to Robert Gardiner Hill, the famous proponent of non-restraint, and in 1858 Bushnan purchased an interest in Laverstock House Asylum in Salisbury, Wiltshire, where he became the sole licensee and resident physician in 1860. He remained the proprietor there until 1867. In 1868 he had returned to London and was living at the Medical Club in Pall Mall, but in 1871 he moved to Southampton where he took up general medical practice working until his retirement in 1882.

Besides his editorials in the *Medical Times and Gazette*, Bushnan published sporadically throughout his career. Between 1833 and 1860 he produced some sixteen publications on a variety of medical, philosophical, natural history, and social topics, many for the general reader. Bushnan had an early interest in phrenology and phrenological societies but by the 1830s was disenchanted as they had patently failed to refine cerebral physiology. In 1833 he published *A History of a Case of Animals in the Blood of a Boy*, and in the same year, from Dieffenbach's German original, *Surgical Observations on the Restoration of the Nose*. Bushnan was a firm Christian and in 1851 engaged in a controversy with Harriet Martineau over remarks in her book *Letters on the Laws of Man's Social Nature*, which was so agnostic that it gave widespread offence.

Bushnan was the son and grandson of City freemen from the Paviors' and later, more prestigious, Merchant Taylors' guilds. As comptroller, his father received an income of £1600 to £1800 a year, and it seems likely that Bushnan's career was kept afloat by his father's support. Like many doctors in the first half of the nineteenth century Bushnan appears to have struggled to establish a career in medicine. In later life his financial affairs collapsed, his sight failed, and returning from Southampton in 1884 he ended his days as a poor brother of the Charterhouse, in the City of London, where he died on 17 February 1884.

Nick Hervey

Sources *Medical Times and Gazette* (8 March 1884), 339 • Boase, *Mod. Eng. biog.*, 1.497 • *Medical Circular*, 2 (1853), 149–50 • *London and Provincial Medical Directory* (1851–84) • burial registers, Dumfries, 1819–54, frame 2127, M118219 [old parish registers, CD-ROM] • St Lawrence Jewry, baptisms, 1813–1914, GL, MS 10442A • d. cert.
Archives UCL, SDUK MSS, corresp. with Thomas Coates • UCL, letters to Society for the Diffusion of Useful Knowledge

Bushnell, John (*bap.* **1636**, *d.* **1701**), sculptor, was baptized in St Andrew's, Holborn, London, on 22 April 1636, the son of Richard Bushnell, a plumber, and his wife, Mary. Bushnell was apprenticed to the mason Thomas Burman about 1650, but completed only six years of his training. According to George Vertue, Burman made a servant girl pregnant and tried to coerce Bushnell into marrying her; Bushnell absconded with £15 of Burman's money and fled abroad. He later stated that between 1657 and 1668 he worked in 'Rome, Venice & other greate & ffamous cities in Italy, Spain, France and Kingdomes & parts beyond the seas' (PRO, C10/129/26). His subsequent work shows that, while abroad, he became acquainted with the latest innovations in Roman and Venetian sculpture. He spent some years in Venice, where he worked on the vast monument to Alvise Mocenigo in the church of San Lazzaro dei Mendicanti. The sculpture was designed by Giuseppe Sardi and was the work of a number of artists, including Bushnell, who contributed two large reliefs representing the siege of Martinengo and the battle of Paros, for which he was paid 2500 ducats.

Having settled in Hatton Garden in London, in 1669 Bushnell received a private order for three garden statues for Sir Robert Gayer of Stoke Poges Manor, Buckinghamshire; he was to be paid £125 in total. Long before completing them, however, he was given the public commissions for the four royal figures on new Temple Bar (for which he was paid at least £110 each) and asked to model the plaster face-mask of George Monck, duke of Albemarle, for his state funeral in 1670. He was next commissioned to carve the statues of Sir Thomas Gresham, the martyred Charles I, and the imperious Charles II for the Royal Exchange, which are now housed in the Old Bailey. He expected such 'particular honours' as his due (Vertue, *Note books*, 1.86), but these royal figures were not necessarily received with approbation. The Stuart kings wore their hair long and were dressed in Roman tunics with their garters under bare knees, anachronisms that were not tolerated for long. Bushnell began work on six of the replacement line of kings for the courtyard at the exchange, but they were rejected, much to his chagrin, because they too were in classical dress.

Gayer's garden statues had been forgotten, and it was only after Gayer brought a suit for £1000 damages that Bushnell finally produced them in 1675. He continued to accept many private commissions throughout his career. To commemorate Elizabeth Pepys (*d.* 1669), the diarist's wife, Bushnell carved the speaking marble bust in St Olave, Hart Street, London. He made the monuments to Abraham Cowley and Sir Palmes Fairborne in Westminster Abbey (though the latter has been altered). His monument *Sir William Ashburnham and his Wife* in Ashburnham church, Sussex (1675), which was damaged in transit by sea before its installation, is a dramatic memorial which was influenced by the Venetian work of the Fleming Giusto de Corte. The same year Bushnell carved his masterpiece, *John, Viscount Mordaunt*, a monument in All Saints, Fulham, which earned him £250. Like the Ashburnham monument, it comprises a number of separate parts in contrasting marbles. His later monument *Elizabeth, Lady Myddleton*, and two other Myddleton busts, are in Chirk church, Denbighshire. *Elizabeth* was carved posthumously from a painted portrait, and Bushnell portrayed her suckling an infant. *Lady Mary May*, who ordered her own tomb for Mid Lavant church, Sussex, while she was still alive, was given the marks of smallpox from which she died in 1681. Bushnell's work became increasingly quaint: the figures on the monument to Henry, earl of Thomond in Great Billing, Northamptonshire, are caricatures, possibly completed by the sculptor's sons after his death.

From various legal arguments it is known that Bushnell moved twice between 1669 and 1675 to increasingly bigger workshops, first to Whitehall and then to Wandsworth. Because he led a peripatetic career it has been impossible to establish when he married Mary (*d.* 1704), his wife, or to pinpoint the births of all of their children. His eldest son was called John and another son, Richard, was baptized on 14 December 1679 in All Saints, Wandsworth High Street. Vertue mentions in his *Note Books* that Bushnell had one or two daughters. In 1685 he bought a large plot (96 by 420 feet) in Tyburne Lane, near Hyde Park

Corner. The poor rates show that he paid taxes there between 1686 and 1694, but nothing thereafter.

Bushnell suffered from dementia; his many financial catastrophes contributed to his ill health. According to Vertue the sculptor speculated in coal, but three of his ships foundered. He also built a cavernous house on his plot at Hyde Park Corner, where he constructed a giant Trojan horse which was to serve as a tavern, the head big enough to seat twelve men inside. He expected to earn £500 but the horse blew down in a storm and he refused to start again. In 1690 he inherited a property near Reading which caused him endless legal trouble, and he bought another in Kent, although he allowed it to run down so badly that the tenant took him to court. He entered into complex financial arrangements involving his properties which backfired; consequently he became a vexatious litigant. He was also vain and capricious in character. He died impoverished and mad, and was buried in Paddington on 15 May 1701. Vertue attributed his death to 'gout which got in his stomach' (Vertue, *Note books*, 1.87); presumably drink contributed to his downfall. After his death his sons continued to live in the Hyde Park Corner house, 'like Hermitts or Brutes' (ibid.), and there in 1725 Vertue saw the six rejected statues from the exchange, a model of an equestrian *Charles II* never cast, the remains of the Trojan Horse, an *Alexander the Great* which Bushnell had modelled to prove he could cope with nude anatomy, and a bust of the architect William Talman.

Bushnell's skills were variable, and his quirky style often difficult to accept, but his monuments have a narrative quality hitherto unknown in English tomb sculpture. Along with Caius Cibber, he introduced to post-Restoration England a dramatic visual language already common in continental sculpture.

KATHARINE GIBSON

Sources Vertue, *Note books*, 1.86–7, 128–9, 142; 2.8–9 • K. Esdaile, 'John Bushnell, sculptor', *Walpole Society*, 15 (1926–7), 21–41 • K. Esdaile, 'Additional notes to John Bushnell', *Walpole Society*, 21 (1932–3), 105 • R. Gunnis, *Dictionary of British sculptors, 1660–1851*, new edn (1968), 72–4 • M. Whinney, *Sculpture in Britain, 1530 to 1830*, rev. J. Physick, 2nd edn (1988), 95–102 • L. Borean, 'John Bushnell in Venice', *Church monuments*, 14 (1999), 88–103 • K. Gibson, '"The kingdom's marble chronicle": the embellishment of the first and second buildings, 1600 to 1690', *The Royal Exchange*, ed. A. Saunders (1997), 138–73 • court of chancery: *Bushnell* v. *Gayer*, Middlesex, 1676, PRO, C10/129/26 • chamberlain of London's accounts, GL, MS 6667/2; MS 1888; MS 1894; MS 184/4, 1667–1676, fol.30 • court of chancery, PRO, C3/342/33; C5/211/16; C9/115/22; C9/117/16; C9/145/16; C9/150/24; C9/204/10; C9/245/7; C9/432/67; C22/964/31; C22/965/27 • CLRO, Misc. MSS 135.27 • City Westm. AC, Westminster City Archives, F3584–3691, F417–418, F423 • LMA, X102/110 • PRO, PROB 6/78, fol. 93; PROB 6/87, fol. 45, 1711; PROB 6/107, fol. 52v, 1730

Wealth at death very poor except for property: administration, PRO, PROB 6/78, fol. 93; PROB 6/87, fol. 45; PROB 6/107, fol. 52*v*

Bushnell, Walter (*bap.* **1609**, *d.* **1667**), Church of England clergyman, was baptized at Corsham, Wiltshire, on 15 January 1609, the son of William Bushnell; he had at least one brother and two sisters. Having matriculated on 12 December 1628 aged nineteen from Magdalen Hall, Oxford, he graduated BA on 20 October 1631, proceeded MA on 11 June 1634, and was ordained. In 1644 he became vicar of Box, also in Wiltshire. He was apparently undisturbed during the civil war, but was removed from his living in 1656. At this date, or earlier in his career, he went to live in Bath. After the Restoration in 1660 Bushnell regained his living and he achieved brief fame in July that year when he published a 256 page account of his treatment at the hands of the local commissioners for the ejection of scandalous ministers in 1656.

After accusations had been made against him the commissioners had summoned Bushnell on 21 January 1656. According to John Walker he insisted on a public hearing. Between 14 February and 14 July he appeared before them on six separate occasions—at Marlborough, Market Lavington, and Calne. He faced six charges: profaning the sabbath; drinking to excess in alehouses; using the Book of Common Prayer and baptizing infants with the sign of the cross; playing dice and cards; attempting to seduce a serving woman; and being disaffected to the government and associating with former royalists. Accusations were batted back and forth until the commissioners resolved to deprive him. A further hearing 'touching his sufficiency' took place at Salisbury on 23 July. With difficulty, he managed to secure £12 per annum as the one fifth allowed to unmarried deprived ministers by ordinance, although the living was worth far more than £60. Stern, his replacement, was installed in December. Bushnell claimed that in all he lost some £400 through his deprivation and the proceedings leading up to it.

The validity of the allegations is difficult to assess, not least because some crimes of 1656 were badges of pride in 1660. The evidence was flimsy and contradictory, and the prosecutors, whether through malice or principle, paid little attention to legal proprieties. The bad character of some of the accusers further undermines their credibility. All that was established was that Bushnell sometimes held parish meetings in alehouses, that he did play cards and dice, though not for money, and that he probably used the sign of the cross in baptism. Much of the rest Bushnell effectively disproved.

It is striking that his narrative barely even names any commissioners. His main enemies were nearby ministers: Dr Humphrey Chambers, rector of Pewsey and first assistant minister to the commissioners; William Blisset of Salisbury; Mr Byfield, whose living is not recorded; Thomas Baylie, rector of Mildenhall; and William Hughes, vicar of St Mary's, Marlborough. Bushnell believed that these men and the parishioners who testified against him were motivated by greed. At the final hearing, he claimed, he was surrounded by relatives of commissioners, all angling for rich livings. He also claimed that Stern had been curate to Chambers's brother-in-law, though this was denied. Byfield, who attended every minute of the hearings, appears especially vindictive and cavalier in his attitude towards the law.

The tone of Bushnell's writing is unsurprisingly bitter and he does not come across as a particularly sympathetic character, but there are flashes of humour in his debunking of the more absurd allegations and his description of

Byfield's constant interjections 'when the pipe was out of his Mouth' (*Narrative*, 16). Chambers and Blisset printed a riposte to Bushnell's work in September 1660, contending that they had made no gains through the proceedings and that his 'spiteful, jeering, groundless and most uncharitable' work made unjustified assumptions about their motives (*Answer of Humphrey Chambers*, 24). Blisset's son, the clerk who had recorded the proceedings, proved Bushnell's allegation that Stern had given his father £20 for securing Box for him to be false; in fact, he said, Stern paid him, the son, for interceding with the original patron of the living, who had been angry at Stern for petitioning Cromwell directly for it. Byfield was already dead by 1660, but Bushnell saw Chambers, Baylie, and Hughes ejected from their livings in turn.

When Bushnell drew up his will on 19 February 1667 he was already ill. He died, unmarried, some time that spring, and his will was proved on 7 May by his executors, his brother William Bushnell and his friend Thomas Hulbert. ANDREW WARMINGTON

Sources *A narrative of the proceedings of the commissioners … in the case of Walter Bushnell, clerk* (1660) • *An answer of Humphrey Chambers … to the charge of Walter Bushnell* (1660) • J. Walker, *An attempt towards recovering an account of the numbers and sufferings of the clergy of the Church of England*, 2 pts in 1 (1714) • *Walker rev.*, 371 • Foster, *Alum. Oxon.* • PRO, PROB 11/323, fols. 460r–460v • parish register, Corsham, Wiltshire, Wilts. & Swindon RO, 15 Jan 1609 [baptism]

Wealth at death £274 cash; moveables and chattels: will, PRO, PROB 11/323, sig. 58

Busia, Kofi Abrefa (1913–1978), sociologist and politician, was born on 14 April or 11 July 1913 (he stated 11 July) at Wenchi, in the Asante region of the Gold Coast. He was the son of Yaw Bosea, a prominent member of the royal Safoase Yefre matrilineage of Wenchi, and Yaa Pokuaa. During his primary and secondary education he was taught by Methodists; in 1927, after a period at Wesley College, Kumasi, he studied at the prestigious Methodist school Mfantsipim, in Cape Coast. A spell of teacher-training was followed by his appointment to the staff of Wesley College in February 1933. Having left under a cloud he then studied at Achimota School. There he met his first wife, Helena Poku (Amma Appiaa), from Bekwai, who tragically died shortly after the marriage.

In 1939 Busia was awarded a scholarship to read philosophy, politics, and economics at University College, Oxford, and gained a BA in 1941. In July 1942 he was appointed one of the first two African assistant district commissioners (the other was A. L. Adu) in the Gold Coast. For contested reasons he left his post after a short period. He returned to Oxford, where with Carnegie and Nuffield scholarships and the supervision of Meyer Fortes (1906–1983), he completed his DPhil thesis, 'The position of the chief in the modern political system of Ashanti', published with the same title four years later, in 1951. Appointed a Gold Coast government sociologist, he supervised the social survey of Sekondi-Takoradi, which was published in 1950. In that year he married Victoria Naa Morkor King Bruce (Naa Morkor), a nurse, with whom he had two daughters. Having been appointed to the staff of the new University College of the Gold Coast in 1949, he established its department of sociology in 1954, and became the country's first African professor.

As the rush to independence gathered pace Busia's radical conservatism—he remained close to Moral Rearmament and was always a strong advocate of the abiding value of Ghana's traditional order as opposed to socialism—made him a natural opponent of Kwame Nkrumah (1909?–1972), whose left-leaning Convention People's Party dominated politics in the 1950s. Busia led the ill-organized, self-destructive Ghana Congress Party, and only just managed to be elected for his home constituency of Wenchi in the general election of 1954—his party's sole electoral success. By the end of 1954 a more powerful opposition alliance, the National Liberation Movement (NLM), emerged in central Ghana, and in 1956 Busia was its leader. Despite driving the country close to civil war in the immediate run-up to independence the NLM ultimately failed to halt Nkrumah and his CPP, who led the Gold Coast into independence, as Ghana, in 1957. The CPP government's increasing authoritarianism, which included imprisonment without trial, forced many NLM activists into exile. After leading a shrinking and increasingly cowed opposition in the national assembly Busia was disqualified as a member of the assembly in April 1959 by new legislation removing those who had been absent for more than twenty consecutive sittings, a measure almost certainly aimed at him personally. Harsh as this was it revealed a consistent tension in his political life between the demands of an academic career that required him to lecture and attend seminars overseas and the political imperative of being physically close to his putative constituency. Fearful, with reason, of returning to immediate detention, Busia remained in the Netherlands, where he taught at the Institute of Social Studies in The Hague and the African Studies Centre in Leiden. He was also professor of sociology at St Antony's College, Oxford (1964–6).

Nkrumah was overthrown by a military coup in February 1966 and Busia returned in triumph to Ghana. He chaired the military government's political committee, which was charged, among other things, with drafting a new constitution and establishing the many commissions of enquiry that exposed the excesses of Nkrumah's period in office. With the CPP outlawed and Busia and his new Progress Party favoured by the military, few were surprised when they triumphed in the elections that returned Ghana to civilian rule in 1969. Though his *Africa in Search of Democracy*, a book written in exile and published in 1967, had promised a radical return to parliamentary decency and social justice Busia's period as prime minister was brief and undistinguished. The increasingly rapid decline of an already weakened economy created harsh social tensions. As intolerant of opposition as Nkrumah's governments had been, that of Busia clashed with labour unions, with hard-pressed rural producers, and—when they disagreed with him—with the judiciary. In April 1972 the army took power again. Busia once more went into exile, and lived at Standlake, in

Oxfordshire. He died on 28 August 1978, having been a diabetic for most of his adult life. His body was returned to Ghana for a state funeral and burial.

RICHARD RATHBONE

Sources C. E. Donkoh, *Nkrumah and Busia of Ghana* (Accra, 1972) • D.-B. Kwaku, *The political biography of Dr Kofi Abrefa Busia* (Accra, 1996) • R. Rathbone, ed., *Ghana*, 2 vols. (1992), ser. B/1 of *British documents on the end of empire* • H. K. Akyeampong, ed., *K. A. Busia: Ghana's struggle for democracy and freedom speeches, 1957–69* (Accra, 1979) • R. Rathbone, *Nkrumah and the chiefs: the politics of chieftaincy in Ghana, 1951–1960* (2000) • *WWW*, 1971–80 • D. Owusu-Ansah and D. M. McFarland, *Historical dictionary of Ghana* (1995)
Archives Bodl. Oxf., letters to Sir Alfred Zimmern • CUL, corresp. with Meyer Fortes
Likenesses photographs, after 1952, Ghanaian press

Busino, Horatio [Orazio] (*fl.* **1617–1621**), Roman Catholic priest and visitor to England, was the rector of Piazzola, a small town north-west of Padua, the location of a grand palace belonging to the Contarini family. In 1617 Pietro Contarini was appointed Venetian ambassador to the court of St James, and among the twelve people who accompanied him from Piazzola to London was Busino, to serve as his chaplain and his private secretary for public affairs.

Reaching the Low Countries on 11 September, Busino was told that as he was entering among heretics he must doff his gown to avoid being insulted; he therefore put on a leather jerkin, which, as he remarks, gave him the air of a soldier and probably preserved him from abuse in London where, he noted, 'most sensible people dress in the English fashion' (PRO, 31/14/141, p. 108). The party landed at Gravesend in early October, and in London occupied a house in Bishopsgate belonging to Sir Paul Pindar, a merchant with long-standing contacts with Venice. Busino celebrated mass at an altar set up in the long gallery of the house which served as a chapel. Busino, who held the degree of doctor of law, was assigned 186 ducats for salary and board for a year (1 ducat being equivalent to 5s.), which compared favourably with the 100 ducats paid to Giovanni Baptisto Leonello, Contarini's public secretary for private matters and state interests. Leonello had been in London with the previous ambassador and spoke English.

While Contarini reported back to the doge on matters of state Busino, who found himself 'residing well-nigh idle here' (PRO, 31/14/142, p. 61), wrote long informal letters to Contarini's three brothers, supplementing these with his 'Anglopotrida', a pun on the culinary term denoting a dish of odds and ends not fit for reheating. He did however suggest that the Contarinis might wish to pass his dish around and perhaps even keep it. The letters remained in the Contarini archive until 1843, when they were bequeathed to the Library of St Mark, Venice.

With the unexpected death of Contarini's young butler shortly after their arrival Busino was minded 'to think of myself who am the senior and perhaps the most feeble in this household' (PRO, 31/14/142, p. 49). Leonello took him to the Fortune Theatre to cheer him up, but as Busino could not understand the speech he could only gaze on the antics and listen to the songs. He was surprised at the freedom allowed to single ladies, one of whom sat next to him and tried in English and French to converse, showing him her jewellery. Fortunately Busino was ignorant of her profession, and took the laughter of his master and secretary seated behind him in good part. On twelfth night they went to the Banqueting Hall to watch Ben Jonson's masque *Virtue* performed at the royal court, and later that year saw *The Duchess of Malfi*, which Busino, a secular priest, did not care for, complaining that friars were always portrayed unfavourably on the stage.

The major event following the embassy's arrival was the lord mayor's inauguration in early November. They watched the spectacular procession from a house in Cheapside, proceeding to Whitehall to see the fleet of decorated barges passing along the Thames—a subject which Busino described at length, comparing the splendour with similar events at Venice and Piazzola. There were other entertainments: across the Thames in Southwark they went to see cock-fighting and bull-baiting, while the noise of military parades, archery practice, and the firing of guns in nearby Finsbury fields were audible in their house. A short walk beyond the city brought them to the ducking ponds at Islington.

While disapproving of the protestant religion Busino was equally critical of the Spaniards he saw in London, conspicuous in their own costume and generally hated by the populace, as they were in Italy. Busino was impressed by London's militia, describing the City as a sort of republic of wholesale merchants. Alongside this he noted the cramped housing, filthy streets, and lack of clean water. He praised the night-watch in the City, but found the penal code very sanguinary. Viewing a public execution at Tyburn and ignorant of English psalmody he took the hymns as catches or glees and thus misinterpreted the attitude of the onlookers.

During the summer Busino suffered a period of illness, either before or after the six days in June during which he accompanied Contarini to Oxford, where he admired the university library, and Cambridge, where they were harangued by a drunken student who invaded their lodging. 'All youth flocks there who desire advancement through literature', he wrote, adding 'These universities produce good doctors but bad ministers of heresies' (*CSP Venice*, 1617–19, 247). They called at Audley End and Theobalds on the way back; on other occasions Busino visited Wanstead House and Burleigh. They were summoned to the royal palaces of Oatlands and Greenwich, and at Deptford were shown the skeletal remains of Drake's *Golden Hind*.

Antonio Donato, the next ambassador, arrived in London at the beginning of November 1618. Contarini's party left at the end of the month, being delayed by light winds at Dover but finally sailing in early December. Busino remained with Contarini while he was ambassador in Madrid, finally reaching Piazzola in February 1621.

ANITA MCCONNELL

Sources R. L. Brown, transcripts and translations of Venetian document in St Mark's Library, Venice, PRO, PRO 31/14/10, 11, 141–2, 144–6 • 'Diaries and despatches of the Venetian embassy at the court of King James I in the years 1617, 1618', *QR*, 102 (1857), 398–

438 · 'Relazioni d'Inghilterra di Pietro Contarini ambasciatore straordinaria a Giacomo I', *Relazioni degli stati Europei lette al senato dagli ambasciatori Veneziani nel secolo decimosettimo*, 3: *Inghilterra* (1859), 189–210 · *CSP Venice*, 1617–19

Busk, George (1807–1886), naval surgeon and naturalist, was born on 12 August 1807 at St Petersburg, the second son of Robert Busk (1768–1835), merchant of St Petersburg, and his wife, Jane, daughter of John Westly, a customs house clerk at St Petersburg. Sir Wadsworth Busk (1730–1811), attorney-general of the Isle of Man, was his grandfather, and Hans Busk the elder (1772–1862), Radnorshire squire and poet, was his uncle.

Busk was educated at Dr Hartley's school, Bingley, Yorkshire. He then served six years as an articled student of the College of Surgeons under George Beaman before completing his medical education as a student at St Thomas's Hospital, London, and, for one session, at St Bartholomew's Hospital. He became a member of the Royal College of Surgeons, in 1830 acted as apothecary on board the *Grampus*, the seamen's hospital ship at Greenwich, and in 1831 was appointed to the Seamen's Hospital Society. By 1832 he was transferred from the *Grampus* to the *Dreadnought*, where he was engaged as assistant surgeon. In time he became resident surgeon (by 1837), first surgeon (1841), visiting surgeon (1854), and then consulting surgeon (from 1866). During his service he successfully employed the microscope in the investigation of pathological subjects such as cholera, and also made some important observations on scurvy. On these subjects, and on cases of smallpox and typhus fever, he contributed a number of reports to the Seamen's Hospital Society.

On 12 August 1843 Busk married his cousin Ellen, youngest daughter of Jacob Hans Busk of Theobalds, Hertfordshire; the couple had two daughters. In the winter of 1843, during a post-mortem examination conducted on board the *Dreadnought*, he discovered in the intestine of an East Indian seaman a new type of fluke. The parasite was later named *Distoma buskii* by the zoologist Edwin Ray Lankester (1847–1929). Also in the surgeon's honour the name *Buskia* was given to a genus of Bryozoa by Joshua Alder in 1856 and by Julian Tenison-Woods in 1877.

In 1855, having spent twenty-five years at Greenwich, Busk retired from active service, and settled in central London, living first at 15 and later at 32 Harley Street. He discontinued private practice in order to devote himself to natural history. About 1861 he became interested in palaeontology; in April that year, his translation of a paper by D. Schaaffhausen appeared in *Natural History Review* as 'On the crania of the most ancient races of man'. This dealt with an unusual cranium recently discovered in the Neander valley, raising the question whether it was a deformed *Homo sapiens* or some new species of hominid. Busk was convinced of its similarity to a cranium found some years previously in Gibraltar and now sent with associated material for his study. His visit to the Gibraltar caves in 1864 in the company of Hugh Falconer (1808–1865) convinced him that the crania were not the result of some deformity, but bore characteristics of modern man. At the 1863 conference held in Paris to discuss the circumstances surrounding a mandible found at Moulin Quignon on the Somme in association with various prehistoric stone tools, Busk was among those who suspected that it was a modern bone, fraudulently planted in order to gain a reward, and this indeed proved to be the case. He subsequently devoted much time and attention to the study of cave fauna. He recognized the Forbes Quarry skull as another example of what had become known as Neanderthal man, and his work on the Windmill Hill cave at Brixham established the contemporaneity of humankind and extinct animals. A monograph, *Crania typica*, was projected and the plates drawn, but the text was never completed.

Busk's first natural history studies centred on the microscopic investigation of the lower forms of life: he was the first to formulate a scientific arrangement of Bryozoa (Polyzoa), for an article in the *English Cyclopaedia* (1856). His major works included: the *Catalogue of Marine Polyzoa in the Collection of the British Museum* (3 vols., 1852–75); descriptions of Bryozoa contributed to John MacGillivray's *Narrative of the Voyage of H.M.S. Rattlesnake* (1852), and of Mazatlán shells to Philip Pearsall Carpenter's *Catalogue of the Collection of Mazatlán Shells, in the British Museum* (1857); *A Monograph of the Fossil Polyzoa of the Crag* (Palaeontological Society Monograph), published in 1859; and *Catalogue of the Cyclostomatous polyzoa in the Collection of the British Museum* (1875). His most important work was considered to be his *Report on the Polyzoa Collected by H.M.S. Challenger during the Years 1873–1876* (2 vols., 1884–6), which was completed with the assistance of his elder daughter, Jane, during his last illness. In addition, he wrote some seventy to eighty papers on botany, zoology, and medicine, and published translations of various important reports and papers.

Busk was editor of the *Microscopical Journal* (1842), the *Quarterly Journal of Microscopical Science* (1853–68), *Natural History Review* (1861–5), and the *Journal of the Ethnological Society* (1869–70). He was also involved with a number of medical and scientific societies. He was elected FRCS on 11 December 1843, Hunterian professor from 1856 to 1859, a member of council from 1836 to 1880, examiner from 1868 to 1872, president in 1871, and vice-president (1872–73, 1879–80).

Busk was a founder of the Microscopical Society in 1839, and was the society's president (1848–9) and an honorary fellow from 1869. In 1846 he was elected FLS; he acted as the society's zoological secretary from 1857 to 1868 and was vice-president between 1869 and 1882. On 6 June 1850 he was elected FRS; he served on the society's council four times and in 1871 received the royal medal. He was for some years treasurer of the Royal Institution, and was the first Home Office inspector of laboratories under the Cruelty to Animals Act. He was a member of the Geological Society from 1859, and was the recipient of the Lyell medal in 1878 and the Wollaston medal in 1885. He was also a member of the Anthropological Institute from 1871 and its president in 1873–4. He was a member of the X Club formed in 1864 to bring together like-minded science enthusiasts.

Busk died at his home, 32 Harley Street, on 10 August

1886. A bed at the Dreadnought Hospital was endowed in his memory by his daughters, and his collection of Bryozoa was presented to the British Museum (Natural History), South Kensington, London.

B. B. WOODWARD, *rev.* YOLANDA FOOTE

Sources *Medico-Chirurgical Transactions*, 70 (1887), 23–7 · J. W. Judd, *Quarterly Journal of the Geological Society*, 43 (1887), 40–41 · *Proceedings of the Linnean Society of London* (1886–7), 36–8 · *The Times* (11 Aug 1886) · private information (1901) · catalogue, NHM · *Catalogue of scientific papers*, Royal Society, 1 (1867), 741–2 · Boase, *Mod. Eng. biog.* · C. Knight, ed., *The English cyclopaedia: biography*, 6 vols. (1856–8) · G. C. Cook, 'George Busk FRS, 1807–1886, nineteenth-century polymath: surgeon, parasitologist, zoologist, and palaeontologist', *Journal of Medical Biography*, 5 (1997), 88–101 · *CGPLA Eng. & Wales* (1886) · E. Trinkhaus and P. Shipman, *The Neanderthals: changing the image of mankind* (1993)

Archives NHM, drawings, notebooks, and papers · NHM, notes relating to Royal Society's expedition to Kerguelen's land · RCS Eng., diary, notes, and papers | NHM, Bryozoan collection · Sheff. Arch., letters to Margaret Gatty

Likenesses T. H. Maguire, lithograph, 1849, RS · E. M. Busk, oils, Burlington House, London · E. M. Busk, oils, Linn. Soc.; copy, RCS Eng. · lithograph, RS · portrait, Seamen's Hospital Society, London

Wealth at death £46,933 7*s.* 2*d.*: resworn probate, Dec 1886, *CGPLA Eng. & Wales*

Busk, Hans, the elder (1772–1862), scholar and poet, was born on 28 May 1772, the youngest son of Sir Wadsworth Busk (1730–1811), attorney-general of the Isle of Man and treasurer of the Middle Temple, and Alice (*d.* 1776), daughter and coheir of Edward Parish of Ipswich and Walthamstow. In his youth he spent some time in Russia, where he was a member of Catherine the Great's chevalier guard. He owned an estate at Glanalder, Radnorshire, and took an active interest in county business; he was a justice of the peace, and high sheriff in 1837. On 28 April 1814 he married Maria, daughter and heir of Joseph Green; they had two sons and five daughters. Their elder son was Hans *Busk, pioneer of the volunteer movement; their daughters Rachel Harriette *Busk and Julia Clara *Byrne were both authors on European subjects. Busk's leisure was devoted to classical studies and general literature, and he published several volumes of light verse. He died at Great Cumberland Place, Hyde Park, on 8 February 1862.

T. F. HENDERSON, *rev.* K. D. REYNOLDS

Sources Boase, *Mod. Eng. biog.* · Burke, *Gen. GB* (1972) · M. Dolley, 'Procurator extraordinary - Sir Wadsworth Busk (1730–1811)', *Proceedings, Isle of Man Natural History and Antiquarian Society* (1980), 8. 207–45

Wealth at death under £8000: probate, 5 March 1862, *CGPLA Eng. & Wales*

Busk, Hans, the younger (1815–1882), army reformer, the son of Hans *Busk (1772–1862) and his wife, Maria, daughter of Joseph Green, was born in London on 11 May 1815. Rachel Harriette *Busk and Julia Clara *Byrne were his sisters. He was educated at King's College, London, and matriculated from Trinity College, Cambridge, in 1835 (BA 1839, MA 1844, LLD 1873). He was called to the bar at the Middle Temple in 1841.

While still an undergraduate Busk proposed to the government the advantage of forming rifle clubs for defence against invasion, and on receiving a discouraging reply from Lord Melbourne in 1837 started a model rifle club in the university, and published a popular pamphlet, *The Rifle and how to Use it*. In 1858 he joined and revived the Victoria Rifles, then the only volunteer corps in existence, and his lectures throughout the country were instrumental in extending the movement, as contemporaries acknowledged. He published several treatises and pamphlets of great practical value to the movement, which were frequently reprinted. They include *The Rifleman's Manual*, *Tabular Arrangement of Company Drill*, and *Rifle Volunteers: how to Organise and Drill them*.

Busk was also interested in the navy. He had intended a naval career, and, being forced to abandon it, devoted much time to yachting. He mastered the principles of naval construction, and designed several successful yachts. He was the first to advocate lifeboat stations, and fitted out a model lifeboat at his own expense, which he presented to Brixham. In 1859 he published *The Navies of the World, their Present State and Future Capabilities*, which described the principal European navies and proposed improvements in the British navy. In 1869 a large public subscription was raised in recognition of his services; he used it to buy a lifeboat and lifeboat station at Ryde, Kent.

Highly regarded by his friends as a gastronome, Busk assisted in the establishment of a school of cookery at South Kensington. He also published several minor pamphlets. He was high sheriff of Radnorshire in 1847 and deputy lieutenant of Middlesex in 1859. He succeeded his father at Glanalder, Radnorshire, and Culverden Grove, Kent, in 1862. Honorary degrees were awarded to him by Oxford and Cambridge, and he was a fellow of the Royal Geographical Society. He founded in 1874 and edited the *New Quarterly Review*. Reportedly he married a Miss Dunbar, and they had one daughter, Annie Mary; his wife died not long after their marriage. Busk died at his home, 21 Ashley Place, Westminster, on 11 March 1882.

T. F. HENDERSON, *rev.* JAMES LUNT

Sources *Annual Register* (1882), 119–20 · *Men of the time* (1875) · Burke, *Gen. GB* · Venn, *Alum. Cant.* · I. F. W. Beckett, *Riflemen form!* (1982) · Beresford family tree, Coll. Arms · private information (2004)

Likenesses G. W., portrait, 1833 (as a young man), priv. coll. · H. J. Fleuss, portrait, 1860 (in Victoria rifles uniform), priv. coll. · H. J. Fleuss, engraving (after portrait, 1860) · wood-engraving, NPG; repro. in *ILN* (25 March 1882)

Wealth at death £25,306 8*s.* 6*d.*: resworn probate, Jan 1883, *CGPLA Eng. & Wales* (1882)

Busk [*née* Blair], **Mary Margaret** (1779–1863), writer and translator, was born at Portland Place, London, in 1779, the daughter of Alexander Blair (1737–1815/16), a wealthy nonconformist soap manufacturer and timber trade merchant from Birmingham, and his wife, Mary Johnson (1749–1827). Her father, a proprietor of the Royal Institution, numbered among his friends the distinguished members of the Birmingham Lunar Society, and possessed homes in Staffordshire near his businesses and in Portland Place, where his wife was a society hostess. Mary Margaret married William Busk (1769–1849), a barrister of the Temple (and later a member of parliament), at Beaconsfield on 2 August 1796. They lived in London, though they travelled frequently and at length on the continent, where Mrs Busk became very proficient in German, French, Spanish, and Italian. Their one child, a daughter, died in infancy in 1801.

By 1819 William Busk's financial position became difficult, due to election expenses and loans to family members, and his wife began to write for publication. Mary Busk's younger brother, Alexander Blair (one of twins), was an intimate college friend of the Scottish writer John Wilson, and it was through this connection that in the mid-1820s she became one of the very few women contributors to the early volumes of *Blackwood's Edinburgh Magazine*, beginning with an essay on Schiller in 1825, and running to thirty-two articles by 1838. At her best, as in 'Modern German school of irony' (September 1835), she unfolds for the British public the genealogy of German idealist thought. During these years her reviews of continental works also regularly appeared in the *Foreign Quarterly Review* and the weekly *Athenaeum*. While most women reviewers assumed either a genderless or male stance, Busk's reviews create 'complex personae' in which the voices are 'so ironically self-conscious that we sense underlying mockery and deliberate confusion of gender' (Curran, 10)

Busk's first books, however, were two didactic works of fiction: *Zeal and Experience: a Tale* (1819) and the better-known *Tales of Fault and Feeling* (1825). A more congenial venue for her work appeared in the late 1820s, with the founding of the Society for the Diffusion of Useful Knowledge. Busk's insatiable reading in history and knowledge of languages allowed her to diffuse *A history of Spain and Portugal from B.C. 1000 to A.D. 1814* (1833), and translations of such works as Philip Siebold's *Manners and Customs of the Japanese* (1841). Her work as a historian culminated in the four extraordinarily detailed volumes of *Mediaeval popes, emperors, kings, and crusaders, or, Germany, Italy, and Palestine, from A.D. 1125 to A.D. 1268* (1854–6).

In 1836 William Busk's business affairs became embarrassed, perhaps due to his gambling, and the couple may have legally separated to protect her income. Mrs Busk cancelled plans to publish a collection of poems and plays with Blackwood and instead successfully brought out the work by subscription. The two volumes of *Plays and Poems* (1837) have been remembered for 'Sordello', a narrative in tetrameter couplets that caused the young Robert Browning to rewrite his own long poem on the troubadour and delay publication of his *Sordello* until 1840. Afterwards William lived chiefly on the continent, and Mary Margaret took London lodgings for part of the year when she was not with him. When he died in Hamburg in 1849, she returned to a house in Queen Anne Street, London, though after seeing *Mediaeval Popes* through the press she published little. A lifelong asthmatic, she died at home on 11 January 1863. Along with London contemporaries such as Sarah Austin, Mary Margaret Busk served as an intermediary between intellectuals on the continent and in Britain, through both review essays and translations, and helped broaden the cultural climate after the end of the Napoleonic wars. D. E. LATANÉ, JR.

Sources E. Curran, 'Holding on by a pen: the story of a lady / reviewer Mary Margaret Busk (1779–1863)', *Victorian Periodicals Review*, 31 (1998), 9–30 · G. T. Prigmore, 'The letters of Mrs Mary Margaret Blair Busk to Blackwood's Magazine', MA diss., Texas Tech, 1952 · M. Oliphant, *William Blackwood and his sons*, 3 vols. (1897) · *The Times* (2 April 1801) · *The Times* (4 Aug 1796) · *GM*, 2nd ser., 31 (1849) · *GM*, 1st ser., 66 (1796) · *GM*, 3rd ser., 14 (1863) · E. Swann, *Christopher North (John Wilson)* (1934) · M. Howard, 'Pioneering intercultural interpretation: Mary Margaret Busk and German literature', *Connections: essays in honour of Eda Sagarra*, ed. P. Skrine and others (Stuttgart, 1993) · private information (2004) [Eileen Curran]

Archives NL Scot., letters to Blackwoods · UCL, SDUK MSS, corresp.

Wealth at death negligible, if any

Busk, Rachel Harriette (1831–1907), folklorist, was born at 22 Cumberland Street, London, the youngest of the five daughters of Hans *Busk the elder (1772–1862), scholar and poet, and his wife, Maria (1788–1840), daughter of Joseph Green. An elder sister of Rachel's was Mrs Julia Clara *Byrne (1819–1894), wife of the editor of *The Times* and the *Morning Post*, and Hans *Busk the younger (1815–1882) was the elder of her two brothers. Rachel Busk was educated by her father, and from an early age she spent much time in foreign travel, becoming an excellent linguist. Brought up as a protestant, she joined the Roman Catholic church in 1858, an enthusiastic convert of H. E. Manning (later second archbishop of Westminster), and her example was later followed by her four sisters.

Rachel Busk lived much at Rome from 1862 onwards, and gained an intimate knowledge of the city and of society there in the days of papal independence. Among her wide circle of friends was Cardinal Giacchino Pecci, afterwards Pope Leo XIII. She contributed a series of letters on Roman politics and society to the *Westminster Gazette* (a weekly Roman Catholic paper that ran from February 1859 until April 1879); some of these were reprinted in 1870 in a volume entitled *Contemporary annals of Rome: notes political, archaeological and social, with a preface by Monsignor Capel*. Her reports covered Garibaldi's invasion of Rome, and the calling of the general council (known as the First Vatican Council, 1869–70), including an account of Manning's attendance.

Travelling in outlying parts of Italy, Spain, and Austria, Rachel Busk became an authority on folklore, collecting thousands of folk tales and songs by word of mouth. She published anonymously *Patrañas, or, Spanish Stories* (1870); *Household Stories from the Land of Hofer, or, Popular Myths of Tirol* (1871); and *Sagas from the Far East: Kalmouk and Mongol Tales* (1873). Under her own name she published *The Folk-Lore of Rome* (1874); *The Valleys of Tirol* (1874); and *The Folk-Songs of Italy* (1887), a well-edited selection, giving a specimen from each province with a line-for-line translation and notes.

The London home shared by Rachel Busk with her sister Julia Pitt Byrne was known for its hospitality, and in 1898 she edited and published material for further volumes of Julia Pitt Byrne's *Gossip of the Century*, giving these the title *Social Hours with Celebrities*, fittingly called by her 'a chronicle of slight incidents'. They contained many reminiscences, autobiographical and biographical. Portraits included one of Nicholas Wiseman (first archbishop of Westminster), who, Rachel Busk claimed, had based the published version of his London lectures on the notes she had taken at his request. Among others of interest were such notable Catholic figures as Charles Waterton, Mrs Fitzherbert, Charles Lavigerie, and Theobald Mathew. Hilaire Belloc dedicated his *The Path to Rome* to her in 1902.

Rachel Busk maintained a worldwide correspondence with fellow folklorists, horticulturists, and archaeologists. She died at her residence in Members' Mansions, Victoria Street, Westminster, on 1 March 1907, and was buried in the family vault at Frant, near Tunbridge Wells.

ELIZABETH LEE, *rev.* G. A. ELWES

Sources [R. H. Busk], *Contemporary annals of Rome … by the Roman correspondent of the 'Westminster Gazette'* (1870) • J. C. Byrne, *Social hours with celebrities*, ed. R. H. Busk, 2 vols. (1898) • J. C. Byrne, *Gossip of the century*, 2 vols. (1892) • *The Times* (8 March 1907) • Burke, *Gen. GB* (1972)

Wealth at death £28,175 10*s*. 9*d*.: administration, 17 April 1907, *CGPLA Eng. & Wales*

Buss, Frances Mary (1827–1894), headmistress, was born in London on 16 August 1827, the eldest child of Robert William *Buss (1804–1875), a painter and etcher, and his wife, Frances Fleetwood (*d. c.*1860). Frances and her four brothers were the only survivors to adulthood among their ten children. She later described how her education began: her grandparents, whom she was visiting in Aldersgate, sent her to a private school housed in the most rudimentary accommodation 'to get me out of the way' (Ridley, 3). She was next sent to a similar school in Kentish Town kept by a Miss Cook, which she remembered as simply consisting of children learning Murray's *Grammar*. At the age of ten she proceeded to a more advanced school in Hampstead presided over by a Miss Wyand. By the age of fourteen she herself was teaching there and by sixteen was sometimes left in sole charge of the school. Her father was not a particularly successful artist nor, it appears, a good manager of money. To help the family finances her mother, who was the strongest influence on her early life, set up a private school in Clarence Road, Kentish Town, in 1845.

Frances Buss assisted with the teaching in her mother's school, which was based on the ideas of Pestalozzi, while attending during 1848–9 evening lectures at the newly opened Queen's College in Harley Street, London. She was taught by F. D. Maurice, Charles Kingsley, and R. C. Trench, and gained certificates in French, German, and geography. To Dorothea Beale, a contemporary at Queen's, she described the education gained there as opening 'a new life to me, I mean intellectually' (Buss to Beale, 13 Jan 1889, North London Collegiate School archives). She was strongly influenced by the ideas and concerns of Revd David Laing (1800–1860), one of the founders of the college and secretary from 1843 of the Governesses' Benevolent Institution. The poverty of many governesses made him aware of the plight of middle-class women forced onto the labour market, and he aimed to provide education and certification to enable such women to qualify as

Frances Mary Buss (1827–1894), by James Russell & Sons, *c.*1875

teachers. Frances Buss's own experience of having to earn a living as a teacher continuously from her teens to help support her family (two of her younger brothers, Alfred Joseph Buss and Septimus Buss, were enabled to attend King's College, London, and enter the church) lent a particular immediacy to Laing's objectives.

North London Collegiate School The Busses' school, renamed the North London Collegiate School for Ladies, moved to 46 Camden Street, with Frances Buss as its head, on 4 April 1850. She was to be head of the school, which started with thirty-five pupils, for over forty years. It was started under the auspices of the clergy of St Pancras. Laing, as vicar of Holy Trinity, Haverstock Hill, taught divinity there and was a close adviser until his death. Buss's first speech to parents paid tribute to Queen's College, which was 'in all respects equivalent to a university course for gentlemen' (North London Collegiate School archives), and indicated her intention to prepare her students for further study there. She presented the school as being principally concerned with the education of girls intending to become governesses. Her purpose was not so much inspired by an egalitarian ideology (indeed, she still saw the chief role of women as that of homemaker) but a pragmatic one, and fits with much of the language of the women's movement at this time. Her aim was to provide 'a useful education' based on 'an authorised system', justifying her new school in terms of economic necessity, 'so as to fit them for the important position in society they will be called upon to follow' (ibid.). The first prospectus stressed that the school was for 'daughters of limited means, clerks and private offices and persons engaged in trade and other pursuits'. She insisted that a sound education was as essential for the daughters from such families as it was for the sons. Unlike Miss Beale, the contemporary headmistress with whom she was often associated, she did not exclude tradesmen's daughters. At governors' meetings she regularly delighted in demonstrating the wide range of social backgrounds from which her students were drawn. Her denominational policy was similarly inclusive: non-Anglicans were admitted, and a 'conscience clause' allowed parents to withdraw their children from the religious instruction.

By 1865 the school had 200 day girls (there were a few boarders), but was still run as a private, family concern, R. W. Buss and Septimus Buss teaching art and scripture respectively. A feature of North London Collegiate was the organization of lectures outside the ordinary curriculum, notably a series on political economy by Professor W. B. Hodgson, a close associate. In July 1870 Frances Buss handed over the school to trustees, and in the following year a second school, the Camden School, was established in Kentish Town with lower fees to cater especially for girls from lower-middle-class families. Making the case for an additional school, she argued that the 'increasing number of girls who, as they grow up, must become breadwinners as certainly as boys, makes their claim to education more pressing than ever' (D. Burchell, *Miss Buss' Second School*, 1971, 20).

Miss Buss's efforts to establish publicly accountable girls' schools were hampered by lack of funds. She raised only £47 by an appeal, at a time when boys' schools received lavish support. Her campaign to secure an endowment for the two schools was assisted by the endowed schools commissioners, who sympathized with her object, and they were able to obtain funds from the Platt charity belonging to the Brewers' Company. In 1875 a scheme to administer the schools under the Endowed Schools Act was laid down by the charity commissioners, and in the following year a successful inspection was carried out by London University. As the first public day school for girls, the North London Collegiate School was a model for the schools founded by the Girls' Public Day School Company, established in 1872, and new headmistresses at the company's schools were sent to observe its methods.

The teaching profession Miss Buss quickly gained a reputation as one of the leading authorities on girls' education. On 30 November 1865, on the same day as Emily Davies, she gave evidence to the schools inquiry commission (the Taunton commission) both about her own school and the two wider educational missions for which she is best remembered: the importance of the training and professional standing of teachers, and the value of competitive, external examinations for girls. From the outset she was concerned about the training of her staff, sending them to the Home and Colonial Institute, where her mother had attended a training course, for further instruction. She bemoaned the lack of properly trained teachers, calling for every teacher to be taught the art of teaching and the 'power of imparting knowledge'. In 1869 she became the first woman fellow of the College of Preceptors, helping to establish the college's professorship of the science and art of education in 1872. Her election to a fellowship of the college in 1873 was the only public recognition she ever received. She was also a member of the council of the Teachers' Training and Registration Society. Rather than establish a training department attached to her school, as Miss Beale had done at Cheltenham, Miss Buss promoted separate training institutions, including the Maria Grey Training College and the Cambridge Training College. At her own school she made a policy of appointing only staff trained in the theory and practice of education, using staff meetings as opportunities for further training. The minutes for 6 June 1887 record that 'a lesson on teaching decimals was given' (North London Collegiate School archives).

Miss Buss regarded teaching as 'one of the noblest professions, not second even to medicine' (*Educational Review*, February 1895). She gave much time and energy to promoting professional associations among her fellow teachers. At the first meeting of the Teachers' Guild, intended to unite all branches of the profession, held at the North London Collegiate in 1883, she urged that teaching should 'cease to be a trade—where in return for so much coin so many hours were grudgingly given—and that instead it should be a learned profession' (ibid.), though one measure of her own success was a high salary, which reached £1454 a year by 1893. In 1866 she was one of the founder members of the London Association of Schoolmistresses. With Dorothea Beale she established the Association of Head Mistresses, which first met at her house in 1874, with the purpose of holding conferences 'in order to know what we ought to assert and what surrender' (*DNB*). She had a sometimes fiery relationship with the governors of her own schools, especially the first chairman, Dr John Storrar. Given the economic reasons she advanced for female education, it was appropriate that she should also have been influential in establishing the Teachers' Provident Association and the Teachers' Loan Society to assist teachers in financial need.

Girls' education Frances Buss saw competitive external examinations as the best preparation of her students for professional life, and was adamant that girls should compete to the same standard as boys. In December 1863, when the Cambridge local examinations were opened to girls on an experimental basis, twenty-five of the eighty-three candidates who took part were pupils of Miss Buss. She helped Emily Davies to organize the memorial sent to Cambridge in 1864 calling for this arrangement to be made permanent, which was granted in 1865. Her annual speeches to parents explained her emphasis on these external examinations: in 1868 she spoke of their importance in setting a standard; in 1870 she pointed to their impartiality as a relative measure of schools; and in 1871 she insisted on their good effects upon girls' education. She saw no harm in competition and had no objection to prizes, also encouraging games such as hockey and gymnastics. 'I would like girls trained to match their brothers', she reiterated in an interview (*Women's Penny Paper*, 8 June 1889). She made a point of ensuring that mathematics, a subject some thought unsuited to girls, was well taught, appointing Sophie Bryant (whom she groomed to be her successor as headmistress) to teach the subject. Many of her former pupils went on to study at the women's colleges founded at Cambridge; twelve were at Girton in 1879. Clara Collet became the first former North London Collegiate pupil to obtain a degree when she took a London BA in 1880.

The women's movement Frances Buss was a supporter of reform movements, taking an interest in anti-slavery, Italian unity, the National Indian Association, and later Irish home rule. She assisted in the temperance work of her brother Septimus, an east London vicar. She believed in the importance of women taking part in public life, organizing leaflets to women ratepayers in support of Elizabeth Garrett's candidature for the London school board in 1870 and encouraging the candidature of one of her staff, Jane Chessar, to the same body in 1873. Her association with Emily Davies dated from a shared interest in the Society for Promoting the Employment of Women. As a headmistress she had a keen eye for the development of employment opportunities for women, and would change curricula accordingly, introducing lessons on the working of municipal government after the 1888 Local Government Act. Active in the campaign to admit women to the medical profession, she was a governor of the London School of Medicine for Women. In 1874 she hosted a meeting of the Friends of the Women's Peace Movement, where a paper on 'the best way for women to use their influence to prevent war' was read. Although she sympathized with Josephine Butler's purity campaigns, her position prevented her from taking a public stand. She belonged to the Central National Society for Women's Suffrage, and saw a link between the difficulties encountered in securing satisfactory educational opportunities for women and their exclusion from the parliamentary franchise: 'If we had only had the vote some of the difficulties I have described would never have existed' (*Women's Penny Paper*, 8 June 1889). She was convinced that the full effects of these movements would be felt over the long term: 'I should like to revisit the earth at the end of the twentieth century to see the result of the great revolution of the nineteenth—the women's rights movement' (*Woman's Signal*, January 1896).

Character and reputation Pupils remembered Miss Buss with a mixture of respect and fear; she was a strict disciplinarian, boasting to Dr Thring of Uppingham School that she had no need for corporal punishment since she could reduce a girl to tears in minutes. Although she was extremely nervous on public occasions, and was by her own admission not a good speaker, she grew to value public occasions, especially the annual prize-givings. She had a keen eye for publicity and cultivated the press. Her regular addresses to her pupils on moral and philosophical questions were published after her death as *Leaves from the Note-Books of Frances M. Buss*, edited by G. Toplis (1896). She was well travelled, often taking younger members of staff with her on trips to Italy, her favourite destination, and Sweden, where she made a study of the school system in 1871. Described as 'short of stature and heavy of figure', she was said to possess 'the artist's gift of knowing how to dress', favouring garments of lace (Burstall, 39). Her unremitting work as a teacher prematurely aged her—she was white-haired in her forties—and she became worn down by a debilitating kidney ailment. Frances Buss died at her home, 87 King Henry's Road, Hampstead, London, on 24 December 1894, and was buried in the churchyard at Theydon Bois, Essex, near the country cottage where she spent her vacations. Memorial windows were placed in the school hall of North London Collegiate School for Girls (as it was named in 1870) and in Theydon Bois church.

Frances Buss's ideas laid the foundations for girls' day education in England. They were absorbed by a whole generation of headmistresses and schoolmistresses, many of whom were taught by her. One of them, Sara Burstall, who was both a pupil and an assistant mistress under her, spoke of Miss Buss's decisive influence, 'which was destined to shape my whole life, as it has of many others' (S. A. Burstall, *Retrospect and Prospect*, 1933, 43).

ELIZABETH COUTTS

Sources A. E. Ridley, *Frances Mary Buss and her work for education* (1895) • S. A. Burstall, *Frances Mary Buss* (1938) • J. Kamm, *How different from us: a biography of Miss Buss and Miss Beale* [1958] • *DNB* • Boase, *Mod. Eng. biog.* • F. Hays, *Women of the day: a biographical dictionary of notable contemporaries* (1885) • *Englishwoman's Review*, 26 (1895), 47–50 • reports at prize-giving, staff meeting minutes, correspondence, North London Collegiate School archives • R. M. Scrimgeour, ed., *The North London Collegiate School, 1850–1950* (1950) • M. Forster, *Significant sisters* (1984) • S. Fletcher, *Feminists and bureaucrats* (1980) • J. Roach, *A history of secondary education in England, 1800–1870* (1986) • J. Roach, *Secondary education in England, 1870–1902* (1991) • P. Hollis, *Ladies elect: women in English local government, 1865–1914* (1987) • P. Levine, *Victorian feminism* (1987)

Archives North London Collegiate School, corresp. and papers

Likenesses photographs, 1860–72, repro. in Ridley, *Frances Mary Buss*, facing pp. 87 and 273, frontispiece • J. Russell & Sons, photograph, *c.*1875, NPG [*see illus.*] • portrait, repro. in *ILN* (5 Jan 1895), 11 • portrait, repro. in *Education* (Nov 1890) • portrait, repro. in *Educational Review* (Jan 1895)

Wealth at death £19,794 17*s.* 9*d.*: probate, 21 Jan 1895, *CGPLA Eng. & Wales*

Buss, Robert William (1804–1875), painter and etcher, the eldest son of William Church Buss (*d.* 1832) and his wife, Mary, was born at 60 Jewin Street, Cripplegate, London, on 4 August 1804. He was named after his grandfather, an excise officer who turned schoolmaster in Tonbridge. Buss served an apprenticeship with his father, a master engraver and enameller, and then studied painting under George Clint, a miniaturist, watercolour and portrait painter, and mezzotint engraver. In 1826 Buss married Frances Fleetwood (*d.* *c.*1860), a handsome, dignified woman whose practical resourcefulness and strong character complemented Buss's gentle, humorous temperament, love of colour and form, and exacting attention to painting realistic details. The couple settled in Mornington Crescent, Hampstead Road, London, where of their ten children five survived infancy. The only girl, Frances

Mary *Buss (1827–1894), became a distinguished educationist; she was assisted for many years by her father and her clergyman brothers Alfred and Septimus.

At the start of his career Buss, like Clint, specialized in painting theatrical portraits. Many of the leading actors of the day sat to him, including William Charles Macready, John Pritt Harley, and J. B. Buckstone. Fifteen of these portraits, prepared for *Cumberland's British Theatre*, were exhibited at the Colosseum in Regent's Park, London. Later Buss essayed historical and humorous subjects. He exhibited a total of 112 pictures between 1826 and 1859: twenty-five at the Royal Academy, twenty at the British Institution, forty-five at the Suffolk Street gallery of the Society of British Artists, seven at the New Watercolour Society, and fifteen in other locales. Of these, twenty-five were engraved, evidence of considerable popularity. Among them were *Soliciting a Vote*, engraved by T. Lupton in 1834; *The Bitter Morning*, lithographed by T. Fairland, also in 1834; and *The Stingy Traveller*, engraved by J. Brown in 1845. Buss also entered a cartoon, *Prince Henry and Judge Gascoigne*, into the Westminster Hall competition and for the music salon of Charles Philip Yorke, fourth earl of Hardwicke at Wimpole Hall, Cambridgeshire, he executed vast representations (9 ft x 20 ft) of the origin and triumph of music.

Buss began his career as an illustrator on an inauspicious note. Based on having carved into the block Buss's design illustrating Dickens's 'A Little Talk about Spring, and the Sweeps' for the *Library of Fiction* (published June 1836), the wood-engraver John Jackson recommended Buss in late April 1836 to the publishers Edward Chapman and William Hall. They needed someone to replace Robert Seymour, who had committed suicide, as illustrator to Charles Dickens's serial fiction *Pickwick Papers*. Buss set aside his painting and worked up a dozen or so preliminary sketches (five are in the Pierpont Morgan Library, New York) for the fledgeling novel, then in its second of twenty instalments. His drawings were adequate, but the process of biting in a steel plate was unfamiliar to him so he hired an expert etcher. Buss saw that the 'free touch of an original work was entirely wanting,' and that the printed images seemed lifeless and uninspired. But, he concluded, 'Time was up' and the unsatisfactory illustrations for part 3 had to be issued (R. W. Buss, 124). The publishers summarily dismissed him—something that vexed Buss throughout the rest of his life, as he revealed in a statement written on 2 March 1872. But he never held his dismissal against Dickens; indeed, for his own pleasure Buss subsequently painted three oils and two small watercolours and made several other drawings from subjects in Dickens's fiction.

Shortly after the *Pickwick* fiasco Saunders and Otley hired Buss to illustrate a new edition of Frederick Marryat's *Peter Simple* (1837) and Henry Colburn hired him to illustrate Frances Trollope's *The Widow Married* (1840). These the artist managed to etch satisfactorily, and thereafter he obtained several commissions for illustrating fiction. For some years Buss worked for Charles Knight, designing wood-engravings for Knight's editions of *London* (1841–4), *William Shakespeare* (1842–3), and *Old England* (1845–6).

In 1845, burdened by 'money anxieties' (Kamm, 20), Buss's wife started a school for young boys and girls, and his daughter established on the same premises, 14 Clarence Road, Kentish Town, a morning school offering young ladies a liberal education. When four years later the two schools moved into larger quarters near by in Holmes Terrace, Buss assisted—first teaching drawing and later expanding his repertory to include science, literature, and elocution. In 1850 Buss's wife retired, and on 4 April in that year his daughter launched a more ambitious venture, in the family house at 46 Camden Street, Camden Town: the North London Collegiate School for Ladies. A former pupil recalled that Buss's 'Chemistry series was marvellous, especially for smells and explosions, while his Elocution lessons and the little plays he arranged for us with costumes made us his devoted pupils' (Kamm, 43). He also researched earlier British printmakers, lecturing on the subject in his daughter's schools and, from 1853, he delivered a series of four talks, accompanied by 300 examples reproduced on sixty scrolling cartoons, at literary and scientific institutions in London and the provinces. These he published privately in 1874 as *English Graphic Satire*, a book for which he supplied in various mediums examples of his predecessors' work. Buss also gave lectures on fresco painting and on the picturesque and the beautiful, though these were never published, and from 1850 to 1852 he edited *The Fine Art Almanack*.

After his wife's death Buss did little further teaching. When Dickens died in June 1870, the ageing artist was moved to attempt a large watercolour, *Dickens's Dream* (Dickens House Museum, London), depicting the dozing author seated in his Gad's Hill study and enveloped by his creations. It was Buss's last bid to illustrate Dickens's characters, and with typical modesty he replicated the images of the artists who succeeded him. But before he could finish the painting, he died peacefully at his home, 14 Camden Street, on 26 February 1875 and was buried at Highgate cemetery, Middlesex. ROBERT L. PATTEN

Sources J. Kamm, *How different from us* (1958) · F. G. Kitton, *Dickens and his illustrators* (1899) · R. W. Buss, 'My connexion with *The Pickwick papers*' (2 March 1872), in W. Dexter and J. W. T. Ley, *The origin of 'Pickwick'* (1936) · J. R. Cohen, *Charles Dickens and his original illustrators* (1980) · S. Houfe, *The dictionary of British book illustrators and caricaturists, 1800–1914* (1978) · C. Knight, *Passages of a working life during half a century*, 3 vols. (1864–5) · J. D. Champlin and C. C. Perkins, eds., *Cyclopedia of painters and paintings*, 4 vols. (1887) · Graves, *Artists*, new edn · G. Everitt, *English caricaturists and graphic humourists of the nineteenth century* (1893) · Boase, *Mod. Eng. biog.* · A. G. Buss, 'R. W. Buss', *N&Q*, 5th ser., 3 (1875), 330–31, 451 · *The Athenaeum* (13 March 1875), 366 · J. Grego, *Pictorial Pickwickiana*, 2 vols. (1899) · J. W. T. Ley, 'Robert William Buss: a tribute to an unlucky artist', *The Dickensian*, 6 (1910), 71–5 · J. W. T. Ley, 'Fair play for Buss', *The Dickensian*, 28 (1932), 258–64 · J. W. T. Ley, 'Buss's *Pickwick* pictures: an important letter', *The Dickensian*, 32 (1936), 101–4 · F. F. Buss, 'Dickens's dream: the last picture of R. W. Buss', *The Dickensian*, 28 (1932), 265–6 · G. S. Layard, 'Our graphic humourists: Robert William Buss', *Magazine of Art*, 26 (1901–2), 361–4 · *IGI*

Likenesses R. W. Buss, self-portrait, bust, 1837, Boston Athenaeum; repro. in Cohen, *Charles Dickens*, 51
Wealth at death under £4000: probate, 20 March 1875, *CGPLA Eng. & Wales*

Busse, Dorothy Adelaide. *See* Braddell, Dorothy Adelaide (1889–1981).

Bussell, John Garrett (1909–1985). *See under* Hogarth, Ann (1910–1993).

Bussy [*née* Strachey], **Dorothea** [Dorothy; *pseud.* Olivia] (**1865–1960**), translator and author, was born on 24 July 1865 at Willenhall, near Barnet, London, the third of the ten children (three others died in infancy) of Lieutenant-General Sir Richard *Strachey (1817–1908), scientist and administrator in India, and his wife, Jane Maria *Strachey (1840–1928), writer [*see under* Strachey, Sir Richard]. Twenty-seven years separated the eldest from the youngest child, Dorothy being fourteen years older than her adored brother Lytton *Strachey; Ralph *Strachey, Oliver *Strachey, and James *Strachey were also her brothers. Her younger sister, the future French scholar (Joan) Pernel *Strachey, was eleven years her junior; her other sister was Philippa *Strachey. Ray *Strachey (*née* Costelloe) was the wife of Oliver. Owing to paternal journeyings to India the family had no settled residence until 1872, when they bought Stowey House on Clapham Common, moving, in 1884, to 69 Lancaster Gate, London, memorably described by Lytton in his essay of that title. Dorothy was in India with her mother from 1867 to 1870 and from 1878 to 1879, living in Simla. Otherwise, her early childhood was spent between London, Fife, Edinburgh, and Rothiemurchus, the home of her maternal grandfather. She was educated by her energetic mother on a diet of English and French literature, unpurged of roughage. *Tom Jones*, unabridged, was read to her when she was fifteen. French nursery maids helped with day-to-day French. Despite the family's militant agnosticism, which Dorothy espoused for life, at about thirteen she was sent to Laleham Lea, Hannah Pipe's Wesleyan boarding-school, on King's Avenue, Clapham, London, where she read Shelley in secret. At sixteen she was enrolled for three terms at Les Ruches School at Avon, Fontainebleau, France, headed by Marie Souvestre, a brilliant and admired family friend. Les Ruches kindled her lifelong devotion to the spirit of France and inspired her short novel *Olivia*. When Marie Souvestre re-established her school as Allenswood in Wimbledon Park, Dorothy took a part-time post there in 1885, teaching mainly Shakespeare.

Dorothy Strachey's emotional life was complex. 'Love', wrote Olivia, 'has always been the chief business of my life' (Olivia, 10). As an adolescent she fell in love with Marie Souvestre. From her late twenties to her mid-thirties she conducted an intense platonic affair with Sydney Foster, a married cousin. Having spurned a sequence of appropriate suitors, Dorothy, pretty, petite, and sharp-witted (later befringed and bespectacled), but something too of a rebel, stunned her family by her engagement to (Albert) Simon Aimé Bussy (1870–1954), a talented but penniless French painter to whom the Stracheys had been patrons. Their contented marriage, celebrated at Paddington register office on 18 April 1903, was to last until Simon's death, despite Dorothy's later desperate love for André Gide. An only daughter, Jane Simone, was born on 6 March 1906.

From 1903, apart from the period from 1937 to 1951, when the Bussys moved to 40 rue Verdi, Nice, La Souco, a delightful house overlooking Monte Carlo Bay at Roquebrune-Cap-Martin (sketch in R. Fry, *Letters*, 2, 1972, 622), became their home and a warm Riviera haven for family and visiting writers, Lytton and Julia Strachey, Gide, Martin du Gard, Valéry, Malraux, among others. When not travelling elsewhere in Europe or north Africa, the Bussys habitually spent summers in Britain, the upper floor of 51 Gordon Square (to which the Stracheys had moved) becoming theirs after the death of Lytton in 1932. They were part of Bloomsbury and regular summer visitors at Charleston.

Dorothy Bussy's first writings were translations, in 1904 of Auguste Bréal's *Velasquez*, in 1906 of Camille Mauclair's *Antoine Watteau, 1684–1721*. Her own essay *Eugène Delacroix* appeared in 1907. A three-act drama, *Miss Stock's School*, written probably towards 1910, was never produced or published. A playlet for puppets, *The Marionettes' Tragedy* (*Bulletin des Amis d'André Gide*, 47, July 1980) was home-produced in 1922. Occasional short pieces appeared in *Horizon*, *Time and Tide*, and the *Nouvelle Revue Française*. A feminist, she was a regular reviewer in *The Englishwoman*.

Befriending André Gide in 1918 in Cambridge altered the direction of Bussy's life and re-ignited her energies as translator. The often violent but unreciprocated passion she felt for him lasted until her death and fuelled the more than a thousand letters which they exchanged between 1918 and 1951.

Only two short works by Gide had been put into English—one badly—by the time *Strait is the Gate*, Bussy's felicitous version of *La porte étroite*, appeared in 1924. This was followed in 1925 by *The Vatican Swindle*. By 1951, having become his trusted translator and friend, she had published English versions of all his major fiction and travel literature, including *The Coiners* and his autobiography, *If it Die*. Her acute literary sensitivity, deep culture, near perfect command of French, immersed as she was in French and English artistic life (she became the main link between Bloomsbury and the *Nouvelle Revue Française* group), infused her accurate and stylish renderings which are alive not only to meaning but to the formal subtleties and musicality (though she herself was unmusical) of Gide's French. Her close friendship with the man allowed for full mutual collaboration. The art of her novella, *Olivia*, subsequently revealed that, while literally labours of love, her translations, which remain standard, could safely have freed themselves further from their revered originals. She also translated works by Jean Schlumberger, Paul Valéry, André Malraux, and Louis Guilloux.

Bussy's one novel, begun in late 1931, completed by December 1933, then neglectfully entombed by Gide, appeared pseudonymously as *Olivia* by Olivia, in 1949 at the Hogarth Press, the author collaborating with her friend the novelist Roger Martin du Gard on the French translation (1949). Jacqueline Audry directed a successful film version in 1951. Not only feminist criticism has convincingly constructed for *Olivia* an increasing reputation as a telling early example of the female voice deftly analysing transgressive female love in an exclusively female environment. In 1950 Dorothy published *Fifty Nursery Rhymes, with a Commentary on English Usage for French Students*, a curiously original language-teaching book.

Six years after Simon's death and a bare fortnight after the accidental death of her daughter, Janie, Dorothy Bussy, 'little bowed old marmoset' (Strachey and Partridge, 245), died of old age on 1 May 1960 at 28 Kenilworth Road, Ealing, London. She had bequeathed all to her daughter, who left no will. The inheritance was divided among indirect family descendants. In October and December 1963 her books were sold at Sothebys and in May 1964 her letters and manuscripts. Correspondence with Gide was purchased by the Bibliothèque Nationale which also acquired by donation her letters from Martin du Gard. D. A. STEEL

Sources *Correspondance André Gide–Dorothy Bussy*, ed. J. Lambert, 3 vols. (Paris, 1979–82), vols. 9–11 of *Cahiers André Gide* · J. Lambert, ed., *Selected letters of A. Gide and D. Bussy* (1983) · *Bulletin des Amis d'André Gide*, 84 (Oct 1989) [*Les Bussy: le pinceau et la plume*] · Olivia [D. Bussy], *Olivia* (1949) · M. Holroyd, *Lytton Strachey: a biography*, rev. edn (1971) · Z. Walter, *Pour Sylvie* (1975) · *The Times* (13 May 1960) · *Figaro Littéraire* (18 June 1960) · P. Loisel, *Simon Bussy, l'esprit du trait: du zoo à la gentry* (Paris, 1996) [exhibition catalogue, Musée Départemental de l'Oise, Beauvais, 3 April – 16 June 1996, Musée des Beaux-Arts, Dole, 25 June – 8 Sept 1996, Musée d'Art et d'Industrie, Roubaix, 20 Sept – 10 Nov 1996] · B. Askwith, *Two Victorian families* (1971) · O. Garnett, 'Simon Bussy: an Anglo-French painter', *Charleston Magazine*, 6 (1992–3), 15–21 · J. Strachey and F. Partridge, *Julia: a portrait of Julia Strachey* (1983) · C. R. Sanders, *The Strachey family, 1588–1932* (1953) · m. cert. · d. cert.

Archives Bibliothèque Littéraire Jacques Doucet, Paris · Bibliothèque Nationale, Paris · BL OIOC, corresp. | BL OIOC, Strachey MSS · Tate collection, letters to Philippa Strachey · Women's Library, London, letters to Philippa Strachey

Likenesses S. Bussy, pastel, *c*.1901–1902, AM Oxf. · S. Bussy, pastel, *c*.1920–1925, Musée de L'Oise, Beauvais, France · R. Strachey, oils, NPG

Wealth at death £1380 7*s*. 6*d*. in England: administration with will, 11 Oct 1962, *CGPLA Eng. & Wales*

Bussy, Sir John (*d*. **1399**), speaker of the House of Commons and courtier, was the son and heir of Sir William Bussy of Hougham, Lincolnshire, and Thistleton, Rutland, and Isabel, daughter of John Paynell of Boothby. Bussy first appears in the records in 1378, when he served overseas under the command of John of Gaunt. Early in 1382 (shortly before he was knighted) Bussy was retained by Gaunt with a fee of £40 per annum, and it was as a servant of the house of Lancaster that he rose to prominence. His principal interests were in Lincolnshire, where he was sheriff in 1383–4, 1385–6, and 1390–91. He was also MP for Lincolnshire ten times between 1383 and 1397; he sat for Rutland in 1391. Having helped Maud Neville to obtain a pardon for joining her lover in the murder of her first husband, in 1382 Bussy became her third husband, and thus secured lands in Yorkshire as well. On Maud's death, he married Mary, widow of Sir Ralph Daubeney, another Lincolnshire landowner. Mary died in 1398 shortly after the couple had received a papal licence allowing them use of a portable altar.

Bussy became chief steward of the duchy of Lancaster north of the Trent in 1394 and held the post until 1398; he actively served Gaunt as late as February 1397. He was also associated with Michael de la Pole, earl of Suffolk, but he helped to secure the earl's estates after their confiscation by the Merciless Parliament in 1388. It was probably as a result of his Lancastrian ties that Bussy was chosen speaker of the Commons in 1394. He enjoyed royal patronage from 1390 when he secured a reversion on the keepership of Somerton. He may have been speaker of the Commons again in 1395, when he was one of six, including Sir William Bagot, selected to convey the Commons' proposals to Richard II, who was in Ireland. In 1397 he received a grant of £100 per annum for as long as he remained a member of the king's council. He was joined by Bagot and Sir Henry Green in the secret council meetings to determine what 'loans' should be exacted by Richard II from those who had opposed him in 1388. He was certainly speaker for the January 1397 parliament, when he forced the Commons to abandon their attack on the king's household expenditures represented by Thomas Haxey's petition. Bussy was again speaker when the earls of Arundel and Warwick were appealed of treason in September 1397, and he may have been behind the device of appealing the former appellants. Arundel berated him as one who 'was always false'. Bussy was clearly instrumental in moving the Commons to petition for the repeal of pardons previously granted to the appellants, and in the insistence of the Commons that the clergy should appoint a proctor who could render a verdict of blood. Bussy was also active in securing the impeachment of Arundel's brother, Thomas, archbishop of Canterbury.

Naturally Bussy shared in the spoils of Arundel's and Warwick's fall as well as the spoils of Sir Thomas Mortimer, an appellant partisan condemned in the next parliamentary session. When parliament reassembled at Shrewsbury on 27 January 1398 Speaker Bussy led the Commons in making an unprecedented grant to Richard II of the wool custom for life, as well as in the annulment of the proceedings of the Merciless Parliament. Although he did not sit in the Merciless Parliament, in 1398 Bussy felt it prudent to secure a royal pardon for his activities in support of Henry Bolingbroke and the appellants. At the dissolution of this parliament he was a member of the parliamentary commission of eighteen empowered to deal with unanswered petitions and to settle the quarrel that had broken out between the remaining appellants, Henry Bolingbroke and the duke of Norfolk. It was Bussy in September 1398 who declared to them the sentence of banishment which superseded the announced duel at Coventry. He was again rewarded, from Norfolk's estates. When the parliamentary committee moved beyond its original powers by authorizing confiscation of the Lancastrian inheritance, Bussy was yet again involved.

Bussy was active in negotiations with the Scots in 1398 and 1399, and when Richard II left for Ireland in the latter year, Bussy and Green remained at home. By this time Bussy was a deeply unpopular figure, and a favourite target for Richard II's opponents. As such he was the subject of a thinly veiled attack in the poem 'On King Richard's Ministers':

> Ther is a busch that is forgrowe;
> Crop hit welle, and hold hit lowe,
> Or elles hit wolle be wilde.
> (T. Wright, ed., *Political Poems and Songs Relating to English History*, 1, 1859, 363)

When Henry Bolingbroke landed Bussy attempted to raise support for Richard at St Albans, but eventually he and Green fled with the earl of Wiltshire to Bristol Castle, where the keeper handed them over to Henry Bolingbroke. On 29 July 1399 Sir John Bussy was beheaded. Henry IV was still issuing commissions in 1402 for the confiscation of Bussy's goods. His son, John, did recover much of the family land in Lincolnshire, but he remained a local figure. JAMES L. GILLESPIE

Sources C. Rawcliffe, 'Bussy, Sir John', HoP, *Commons* • J. S. Roskell, 'Two medieval Lincolnshire speakers: Sir John Bussy of Hougham and Sir Henry de Retford', *Lincolnshire Architectural and Archaeological Reports and Papers*, 7/1 (1957–8), 117–25 • J. S. Roskell, *The Commons and their speakers in English parliaments, 1376–1523* (1965) • S. Walker, *The Lancastrian affinity, 1361–1399* (1990) • A. Goodman, *John of Gaunt: the exercise of princely power in fourteenth-century Europe* (1992) • *Chancery records* • *RotP*, vol. 3 • C. M. Barron, 'The tyranny of Richard II', *BIHR*, 41 (1968), 1–18 • G. B. Stow, ed., *Historia vitae et regni Ricardi Secundi* (1977) • J. L. Gillespie, 'Thomas Mortimer and Thomas Molineux: Radcot Bridge and the appeal of 1397', *Albion*, 7 (1975), 161–73 • *CIPM*, vols. 14, 16

Bustamante [*formerly* Clarke]**, Sir (William) Alexander (1884–1977)**, prime minister of Jamaica, was born William Alexander Clarke on 24 February 1884 at Blenheim, Hanover, Jamaica, the elder son and second of the five children of Robert Constantine Clarke, an Irish planter, of Hanover, and his second wife, Mary Wilson, a Jamaican. In later life he shrouded his upbringing in legend. He attended elementary school. In 1904 he was a store clerk, and went to Belmont, St Catherine, to train as an overseer. In 1905 he left for Cuba, where a tramway company employed him. They transferred him as inspector to Panama, where he courted Mildred Edith Blanck, the widow of an English engineer, who had two sons. In 1910 they married at Kingston, Jamaica. He thus had two stepsons, but no children of his own. He worked for the tramway company in Panama certainly until 1919, and reportedly joined the Cuban special police in 1919 or 1920. In 1932 he went to New York as Alejandro Bustamanti, a Spanish gentleman, apparently becoming a hospital attendant. He claimed he made his fortune on the New York stock exchange, but once said he left New York to avoid having to establish his legal status to the American immigration authorities.

In 1934, as Alexander Bustamante, he opened a money-lending office in Kingston, Jamaica. His secretary was Gladys Maud Longbridge JP, daughter of Frank Longbridge; he married her in 1962. He wrote anti-government letters to the press, sympathizing with the underprivileged. In 1937 he became treasurer of the Jamaica Workers' and Tradesmen's Union.

By May 1938 Bustamante was undisputed labour leader. He was arrested on 24 May on a sedition charge, which was later withdrawn. He was a key figure in the development between 1938 and 1943 of two rival trade union blocs and two political parties supported by trade union wings. He registered the Bustamante Industrial Trade Union in 1939, installing himself as life president-general. After a waterfront address he was interned on 8 September 1940, but released on 8 February 1942. The hierarchy of the People's National Party of Norman Manley looked after the Bustamante Industrial Trade Union, but on release Bustamante repudiated them. He left the People's National Party to form the Jamaica Labour Party (JLP) in 1943. To avoid disqualification from nomination as a candidate under a name not legally his own, he became William Alexander Bustamante by deed poll. His party won the 1944 elections, and he became leader of government business and minister of communications from 1945 to 1953.

In 1947 Bustamante was elected mayor of Kingston. The JLP won the 1949 elections with a reduced majority. In 1951 its constitution stated the goals as self-government, British Caribbean federation, and dominion status within the Commonwealth. Bustamante, however, never supported federation strongly. He became chief minister and minister of local government in 1953, but after his party's defeat in 1955, led the opposition. He was president of the West Indies Democratic Labour Party from 1958 to 1960, but resigned to campaign for Jamaica's withdrawal from the federation. His opposition led to the 1961 referendum which decided on secession. The JLP won the 1962 elections. With independence in 1962 he became the first prime minister, keeping responsibility for external affairs and defence. He was sworn of the privy council in 1964. He retired in 1967, at the age of eighty-three.

Bustamante was a Roman Catholic with deep respect for the church's guidance. He was tall, striking, flamboyant, vigorous, and courageous. His recreations were farming, swimming, motoring, and, in youth, horse-breaking. He was a spellbinding, clowning demagogue with great authority over the masses. He was economically and politically conservative, and led a conservative labour-based party. He opposed socialism and upheld the traditional values of Jamaican society. In 1962 he told the house: 'I am for the West. I am against communism'.

Bustamante had deep compassion for the working classes and strove to improve their economic lot. He said: 'I belong to no class. I belong to all classes. But I plead for the poor of the poor, for I come from the gutter of poverty and I once knew what hunger was and what nakedness was.' He shared working-class affection for the British monarchy.

Bustamante was knighted in 1955, appointed GBE in 1967, and became a National Hero (Jamaica) in 1969. He was made an honorary doctor of laws of Fairfield University, A, in 1963 and of the University of the West Indies in 1966. He held the national order of cedars, Lebanon; the distinguished order of the brilliant star with special grand cordon, Republic of China; the grand gold cross, Order Gran Heraldica de Cristobal Colon, Dominican Republic; and the gran cordon, order of Liberatador, Venezuela. Bustamante died at his residence in Irish Town, Jamaica, on 6 August 1977. I. M. CUMPSTON, *rev.*

Sources G. E. Eaton, *Alexander Bustamante and modern Jamaica* (1975) • R. M. Nettleford, ed., *Norman Washington Manley and the new Jamaica* (1971) • *Personalities Caribbean*, 6th edn (1977–8) • *WWW* • *The Times* (8 Aug 1977)

Butchell, Martin van (*b.* 1735, *d.* in or after 1812), empiric, was born in Eagle Street, near Red Lion Square, London, in February 1735, the son of Martin van Butchell, tapestry maker to George II. Having shown an aptitude for the study of medicine and anatomy he became a pupil of John Hunter, and after successfully practising as a dentist for many years he became eminent as a maker of trusses. He acquired celebrity by his skill in treating cases of fistula; he was still more noted for the eccentricity of his manners. His long beard and extraordinary costume attracted much attention, as did his custom of riding in and about Hyde Park on a white pony, which he sometimes painted purple and sometimes with purple or black spots. To defend himself against assault he carried a large white bone, which was said to have been used as a weapon of war in Tahiti. For many years he lived in Mount Street, Berkeley Square, and attracted numerous patients by his quaintly worded newspaper advertisements.

On the death in 1775 of his first wife (details of whom are unknown) Butchell applied to the anatomists William Hunter and William Cumberland Cruikshank to exercise their skill to preventing the decay of the corpse. The mode of embalmment used involved injecting the vascular system with oil of turpentine and camphorated spirit of wine, which had been coloured so that, when filled, the vessels of the cheeks and lips exhibited their original hue. The body's cavities were filled with powdered nitre and camphor and glass eyes inserted. The corpse was then deposited in a bed of thin plaster of Paris in a box with a removable glass lid. For many years Butchell kept his first wife's embalmed body in his parlour and frequently exhibited the corpse to his friends and visitors. On his second marriage, of which again no details are known, the body was removed to the museum of the Royal College of Surgeons in Lincoln's Inn Fields.

Butchell's precise date of death is unknown although he appears to have been alive in 1812. His first wife's corpse, 'a repulsive-looking object' (*DNB*), remained at the Royal College until its destruction during air raids on the night of 10–11 May 1941.

THOMPSON COOPER, *rev.* PHILIP CARTER

Sources *GM*, 1st ser., 63 (1793), 5–6, 165 • *GM*, 1st ser., 76 (1806), 681 • *GM*, 1st ser., 82/1 (1812), 326 • H. Lemoine and J. Caulfield, *The eccentric magazine, or, Lives and portraits of remarkable persons*, 1 (1812), 109 • *Kirby's wonderful … museum*, 6 vols. (1803–20) • R. Malcolm, ed., *Curiosities of biography, or, Memoirs of wonderful and extraordinary characters* (1855) • J. Timbs, *Doctors and patients, or, Anecdotes of the medical world and curiosities of medicine*, 2 vols. (1873); new edn (1876) • *IGI*

Likenesses stipple, pubd 1803, NPG • J. Mills, line engraving (after A. Mills), NPG; repro. in Kirby, *Wonderful and scientific museum*, vol. 1, p. 191

Butcher, Edmund (1757–1822), Unitarian minister and author, was born on 28 April 1757 at Colchester, the only son of John Butcher, an unsuccessful builder and carpenter who had early to struggle for a living. His family came originally from Feering, Essex, and was descended from John Butcher, vicar there about 1667. His primary education was conducted by Dr Thomas Stanton, Presbyterian minister at Colchester. At fourteen years of age he gave sign of precocious talent in an unpublished heroic poem, the 'Brutaeis', which was written on the subject of the mythical Trojan occupation of Britain and illustrated with pen-and-ink drawings. He was soon apprenticed to a London linen draper. His leisure time was spent cultivating his taste for literature and writing for periodicals, the profits from which were sent home to his parents and sister. Subsequently the family inherited the small estate of their ancestors at Feering and their fortunes improved.

Butcher attended the ministry of Hugh Worthington, the eloquent Arian of Salters' Hall, who, together with Richard Wright, Presbyterian minister at Atherstone, prepared him for the ministry. He entered Daventry Academy, under Thomas Belsham, in 1783. As a child he had been instructed in orthodox Calvinism but he later claimed he never gave credence to the Trinitarian doctrine, and his studies at Daventry confirmed him in Arian views. On leaving Daventry Academy in 1788 he settled at Sowerby, near Halifax, but remained there for only six months before moving to London, where Worthington got him temporary engagements at Monkwell Street and Carter Lane. He was ordained on 19 March 1789 as successor to Michael Pope at Leather Lane, Holborn. The ordination service was conducted by such Unitarian and Arian luminaries as Andrew Kippis, Thomas Belsham, Hugh Worthington, Theophilus Lindsey, and Robert Jacomb. While at Leather Lane, Butcher took part with others in the Wednesday evening lecture established by Worthington after 1792 at Salters' Hall. Although he revived his congregation, his feebleness of voice, which was the result of a lung affliction, precluded him from popularity. His condition deteriorated and in 1797 he was obliged to leave London for the cleaner air of Sidbury Vale, near Sidmouth, where his health improved, and in 1798 he was able to accept the invitation to become minister at the Presbyterian chapel in Upper High Street, Sidmouth. By now Butcher was married to Elizabeth Lowe (*d.* 1831), the widow of Samuel Lowe, and the daughter of John Lawrence, a wealthy Shropshire landowner. They had married on 6 July 1790 and had two children: Edmund, who became a Church of England clergyman and alderman of Bristol, and Emma.

Butcher remained at Sidmouth until 1820, and built a house there on a piece of land presented to him by a member of a wealthy Jewish family who attended his services. Relinquishing all belief in a propitiatory atonement, his views gradually passed from the Arian to the form of unitarianism associated with Lindsey, that affirmed Christ's humanity and denied his divinity. According to Murch the congregation at Sidmouth, which during Butcher's time became decidedly unitarian, 'did not become numerous under his care [for] he was not what is called a popular preacher' (Murch, 347).

Butcher was a prolific writer and author of numerous published works including many sermons, of which the most admired was his *Sermons for the Use of Families* (3 vols., 1819). He wrote over 100 hymns 'but few have attained to any position in modern hymnals' (Julian, 198). His most popular hymns are 'From north and south, from east to west' and 'From Christ my lord shall I depart'. He also contributed articles and poetical pieces to the *Protestant Dissenter's Magazine*, of which he was sometime editor. His writings were not confined exclusively to religious and moral themes. He published two topographical works, *A Picture of Sidmouth*, which ran to a fourth edition (1830), and *An Excursion from Sidmouth to Chester in the Summer of 1803* (2 vols., 1805). His style was described as 'simple and familiar; the sentences short and sometimes striking' (*Monthly Repository*, 309).

Within the last few years of his life Butcher was afflicted with a form of paralytic stroke which produced great debility and eventually in 1820 forced him to retire. Early in 1821 he went to reside with his son at Bristol, and from there moved to Bath in November. A fall, which dislocated his hip, confined him to bed. He died in Bath on Sunday 14 April 1822 and was buried at Lyncombe Vale, near Bath, in the cemetery belonging to the Bath Unitarian Chapel. A tablet to his memory was placed in the Old Meeting-House, Sidmouth, and reads: 'His congregation erect this tablet as a lasting tribute of respect and admiration for the piety, zeal and unremitting fidelity with which he fulfilled his pastoral duties in this place during 23 years'. He was survived by his wife, who died in Bath on 25 November 1831. ALEXANDER GORDON, *rev.* M. J. MERCER

Sources J. Murch, *A history of the Presbyterian and General Baptist churches in the west of England* (1835) • C. Surman, index, DWL • J. Julian, ed., *A dictionary of hymnology*, rev. edn (1907) • Watt, *Bibl. Brit.* • J. Evans, *Monthly Repository*, 17 (1822), 247, 309–12 • R. Spears, *Record of Unitarian worthies* (1877) • Allibone, *Dict.*

Archives Bristol RO, corresp. and family papers • DWL, New College archives, essays written while a student at Daventry Academy, L12/3 [written in shorthand]

Butcher, Richard (1586/7–1664), antiquary and lawyer, came from an unknown family. In 1646, as town clerk of Stamford, he published *The survey and antiquitie of the towne of Stamford, in the county of Lincolne; with its ancient foundation, grants, priviledges, etc.*, probably the result of work done to support the town council's claims presented to parliament in the 1640s. Butcher's account of Stamford extended its history back to pre-Christian Britain. The conclusion claimed that he had written the work 'through times of trouble, Prisonment and all Distractions, which can wretched man befall' (p. 46) trusting that the town would soon return from its current predicaments to its medieval fortunes. The book was reprinted in 1717 and in 1727. Butcher's two-volume manuscript 'Antiquity revived', concerned with the genealogies and homes of the British aristocracy, also survives (St John's College, Cambridge). With his wife, Dorothy, Butcher had several children including a son, Robert, who matriculated from St John's College, Cambridge, in 1653 aged seventeen, and was ordained at Peterborough in 1663. A portrait of Butcher aged sixty-one in 1648 was engraved by Clamp. He died in 1664 and was buried in September at All Saints, Stamford. THOMPSON COOPER, *rev.* PETER SHERLOCK

Sources J. Granger, *A biographical history of England from Egbert the Great to the revolution*, 5th edn, 3 (1824), 152–3 • R. G. [R. Gough], *British topography*, [new edn], 2 (1780), 29, 523 • C. Holmes, *Seventeenth-century Lincolnshire*, History of Lincolnshire, 7 (1980), 33, 36 • Venn, *Alum. Cant.* • parish register (burial), Stamford, All Saints, Sept 1664

Archives St John Cam., 'Antiquity revived'

Likenesses R. Clamp, stipple (after portrait, St John Cam.), BM, NPG; repro. in Harding, *Biographical mirrour* (1795)

Butcher, Samuel (1811–1876), Church of Ireland bishop of Meath, was the eldest son of Vice-Admiral Samuel Butcher and his wife, Elizabeth, the daughter of Richard Townsend Herbert, of Cahirnane, co. Kerry. He was born at his parents' residence at Danesfort, near Killarney, co. Kerry, on 9 October 1811. He was educated at home until about 1827, when his father moved to Cork and he was sent to the school of Drs Hamblin and Porter. In 1829 he entered Trinity College, Dublin, where he was awarded a foundation scholarship for classics in 1832. He graduated BA in 1834, became a fellow in 1837, and was then appointed tutor and lecturer. He was made MA in 1839 and DD 1849 and was appointed Donnellan lecturer for 1848 and 1849. Butcher was ordained into the priesthood in 1840. In 1847 he married Mary, the second daughter of John Leahy of South Hill, Killarney. They had two sons (one of whom, Samuel Henry *Butcher became a professor of Greek at Edinburgh University and then MP for Cambridge University) and four daughters.

In 1850 Butcher was made professor of ecclesiastical history at Trinity College, and two years later resigned his fellowship and became regius professor of divinity. In 1854 he accepted the college living of Ballymoney, co. Cork, which he continued to hold along with his professorship until August 1866, when, on the recommendation of Lord Derby, he was appointed to the vacant see of Meath, the premier bishopric of Ireland. Butcher ably defended the Irish church against the attacks which were made on it from all quarters. He could be termed a moderate whose avoidance of extreme partisanship helped to avert some of the dangers which threatened the church after disestablishment. He worked hard to reorganize the affairs of the church throughout Ireland and especially in his own diocese and also took an active lead in promoting the movement to secure an endowment for the divinity school in Trinity College. On the important question of the revision of the prayer book he sided with the revision party, to which position, according to a contemporary, 'his character, position, and learning contributed very considerable weight' (*Freeman's Journal*, 31 July 1876). He also became involved in the debate surrounding Tyndall's

Belfast address to the British Association of 1874, publishing his response in a *Charge* in October 1874. Other publications included various addresses, sermons, and charges to his clergy, and a treatise, *Theory and Construction of the Ecclesiastical Calendar* (1877).

Amid these various activities and while still in very good health Butcher became suddenly ill with congestion of the lungs and bronchitis. Perhaps in a delirious state, he inflicted a fatal injury upon himself. He died on 29 July 1876, at his episcopal residence, Ardbraccan House, Navan, and was buried in the churchyard there. His public life was marked by commitment and ability whether in university or in church affairs. He was highly esteemed in both the general synod and at Trinity College.

G. V. BENSON, *rev.* DAVID HUDDLESTON

Sources H. Cotton, *Fasti ecclesiae Hibernicae*, 6 (1878), 94–5 · W. M. Brady, *Clerical and parochial records of Cork, Cloyne, and Ross*, 1 (1863), 42 · Burtchaell & Sadleir, *Alum. Dubl.*, 2nd edn · [J. H. Todd], ed., *A catalogue of graduates who have proceeded to degrees in the University of Dublin, from the earliest recorded commencements to … December 16, 1868* (1869) · J. Healy, *History of the diocese of Meath* (1908) · R. B. McDowell and D. A. Webb, *Trinity College, Dublin, 1592–1952: an academic history* (1982) · H. E. Patton, *Fifty years of disestablishment* (1922) · Boase, *Mod. Eng. biog.*

Wealth at death under £30,000 (in Ireland): probate, 29 Aug 1876, *CGPLA Ire.*

Butcher, Samuel Henry (1850–1910), classical scholar, was born in Dublin on 16 April 1850. His father, Samuel *Butcher (1811–1876), was then professor of ecclesiastical history at Trinity College. His mother was Mary, *née* Leahy, from a Kerry family. His early years were spent in Dublin, or at Ballymoney, co. Cork, where his father held a college living, and after 1866, when his father became bishop of Meath, at Ardbraccan, near Navan. His only brother, John George (1851–1935), became a KC, Conservative MP for the city of York, and Baron Danesfort. The eldest of his four sisters, Elizabeth (1849–1908), became Lady Monteagle. Butcher was educated at home until the age of fourteen, then at Marlborough College. His progress was rapid: in 1865 he won a senior scholarship. He also won many prizes for Latin and Greek composition, and ultimately became senior prefect. Later he acknowledged his debt to the teaching of George Granville Bradley, then headmaster. He was a fair cricketer, and football captain. In 1869 he won a classics open scholarship at Trinity College, Cambridge, and began residence that autumn. His undergraduate career was an unbroken success. In 1870 he won the Bell scholarship, in 1871 the Waddington scholarship, in 1871 and 1872 the Powis medal. In 1873 he graduated senior classic, and was awarded a chancellor's medal. As an undergraduate he was the centre of a brilliant group of friends, and a member of the exclusive society, the Apostles. In 1874 he was elected fellow of Trinity.

After graduating Butcher was an assistant master at Eton (1873–4). He then returned to Cambridge, as lecturer in classics at Trinity. There he might have remained, but for his engagement in 1875. Under the statutes, a fellowship was forfeited by marriage. Dr Bradley, master of University College, Oxford, offered him a tutorship there with a 'married' fellowship attached. He therefore moved to Oxford, and in 1876 married Rose Julia (*d.* 1902), youngest daughter of Richard Chenevix *Trench, archbishop of Dublin; the couple had no children. At Oxford his teaching rapidly made its mark. His scholarship, brilliant and solid, his enthusiasm, his interest in the matter as well as the language of his authors, made his lectures attractive and profitable. Among his pupils were J. W. Mackail, Cecil Spring-Rice, and others who later won distinction, and to whom he was friend as well as teacher. A university commission was appointed in 1877, and Butcher gained acquaintance with academic problems which was later useful to him. He actively supported female education, and was honorary secretary to the council of the Association for the Higher Education of Women at Oxford (1879–82). He also began to distinguish himself as an author. In 1879 he published, with Andrew Lang, a translation of the *Odyssey* which was considered the most successful prose reproduction yet. In the same year Butcher published a small book on Demosthenes, giving the political context and the rhetorical methods of the orator.

These works, and his growing reputation as a scholar and teacher, gained Butcher, in 1882, the chair of Greek at Edinburgh University. He met at first some opposition as a non-Scot; but his charm and teaching ability soon overcame all obstacles. Popular among his students, with whom he was closer than was usual in Scottish universities, he soon gained a leading position in the senatus. In 1889 the Scottish Universities Bill became law; and a royal commission was nominated to draw up new statutes and reform the Scottish university system. Its chairman was Lord Kinnear, and Butcher was chosen to represent the professors. The work of the commission, an executive not advisory body, was difficult and onerous. The commissioners had to draw up for all the four Scottish universities not only statutes but ordinances or regulations, and the constitutions of the universities had to be harmonized and, so far as possible, made identical. This laborious task lasted nearly eleven years, during which the commission held 251 meetings. Its general report was not issued until April 1900. It was generally recognized by the commissioners and by the academic body that Butcher's experience, industry, and tact were of great value in achieving a beneficent, far-reaching reform.

Meanwhile Butcher took an active part in Edinburgh society; and his house, with his wife's conversational powers, became a brilliant social centre. Among his closest friends were Professor and Mrs W. Sellar. In 1891 Butcher published a volume of essays and addresses, *Some Aspects of the Greek Genius*, on the nature of the Greek mind. The most notable essay was that on Aristotle's conception of fine art and poetry, the germ from which grew Butcher's most important work, *Aristotle's Theory of Poetry and Fine Art* (1895).

At Edinburgh, Butcher was first drawn into politics. Of liberal views but strong conservative instincts, during the Irish home-rule controversy, he took a leading role in organizing the Unionist Party in Edinburgh. When, with Gladstone's return to power in 1892, the home-rule threat reappeared, he actively promoted the election of his friend Lord Wolmer (later second earl of Selborne) for West Edinburgh.

In 1902 Rose Butcher died after a brief illness. This loosened his ties to Edinburgh; and, having held his professorship long enough for a pension, Butcher resigned in 1903. A. J. Balfour presided at his farewell dinner in January 1904. He moved to London, residing the rest of his life at 6 Tavistock Square. In 1904 he lectured at Harvard and elsewhere in the United States, and published *Harvard Lectures on Greek Subjects* (1904), a sort of sequel to *Some Aspects of the Greek Genius*. He worked on a critical edition of Demosthenes' speeches, two volumes of which were published (1903, 1907), and in improving successive editions of the *Poetics*.

Before leaving Edinburgh, Butcher had been appointed to the royal commission on university education in Ireland (1901), of which Lord Robertson was chairman. In its discussions Butcher took a prominent part. Believing in the justice of the Roman Catholic demands, he aimed at satisfying the Catholic authorities without infringing the independence of Trinity College. He therefore aided the chairman in excluding it from the discussion, while doing his utmost to elicit the exact views of Catholic witnesses as to the extent of ecclesiastical control which they considered advisable. He also tried to secure the attendance of the Maynooth students in the new university. When in 1903 the report appeared, it was accompanied by eight 'reservations'; and the chairman himself dissented. The report produced no result.

Another royal commission was appointed on the same subject in June 1906. Sir Edward Fry was chairman. Butcher was the only person who served on both royal commissions. This time, Trinity College was expressly included, and its financial and other conditions were carefully examined; but in their report (January 1907) the commissioners declared that, in their opinion, it was impossible to make that foundation available for the higher education of Catholics. They therefore recommended the establishment in Dublin of a separate college. When Augustine Birrell's bill for the creation of a new university was introduced in parliament (31 March 1908), Butcher opposed the granting of indefinite powers of affiliation to the senate, but in vain. Although the scheme differed in many ways from what he wanted, he accepted membership of the senate of the new university, and took an active part in its proceedings.

In 1906, on the death of his old friend Sir Richard Jebb, Butcher became Conservative MP for Cambridge University. His first speech was on the Irish University Bill; an impassioned appeal to substitute for the existing royal university a real teaching university where the Catholic Irish layman could obtain the education he desired. Butcher seldom spoke in the Commons, and mostly on educational and Irish questions. In addition to his classical works, he published speeches on Ireland.

In 1903 Butcher had been a principal founder of the English Classical Association. He was chairman of its council from then on, and president in 1907. He was instrumental in bringing about, through the association, a reform Latin pronunciation. He was also the first president of the Irish Classical Association. He was a prominent member of the Hellenic Society and the committee for the British School at Athens. He opposed the abolition of compulsory Greek at the older universities, but was willing to make concessions for students specializing in other subjects. When the British Academy was founded in 1902, he was one of its original fellows, and became president in 1909. In July 1908 he was appointed a British Museum trustee, and six months later a member of its standing committee. He was continually consulted on educational questions and appointments. He received honorary degrees from Oxford, Dublin, St Andrews, Edinburgh, Glasgow, Manchester, and Harvard. He was a corresponding member of the American Academy. In 1910 he received the Greek order of the Redeemer. He was an honorary fellow of University College, Oxford, and Trinity College, Cambridge.

Of middle height, well but rather slightly built, Butcher was considered handsome. His eyes were large, of a deep brown, and very brilliant. His hair was black and abundant, later slightly grizzled. His conversation was fluent, vivacious, and energetic, but playful as well as vigorous, argumentative on occasion, but never overbearing. Generous to others, he was capable of fiery indignation against public or private wrongs. He had a strong sense of humour, delighting especially in the wit of his countrymen.

Butcher's varied labours eventually harmed his health. Although naturally somewhat delicate, he generally appeared healthy. He spent the summer vacation of 1910 at Danesfort, near Killarney, on a little property inherited from his father, where he loved to spend his holidays. In October he had an attack of internal haemorrhage, which led to suffusion of blood on the brain. He died in a nursing home, 7 Mandeville Place, Marylebone, London, on 29 December 1910, and was buried in the Dean cemetery, Edinburgh, beside his wife.

G. W. PROTHERO, *rev.* ROGER T. STEARN

Sources *Classical Review*, 25 (1911) · *Gryphon* (Feb 1911) · A. W. Verrall, 'S. H. Butcher, 1850–1910', *PBA*, [4] (1909–10), 393–9 · private information (1912) · Venn, *Alum. Cant.* · *WWW*, *1897–1915* · *WWBMP* · *CGPLA Ire.* (1911) · *CGPLA Eng. & Wales* (1911)

Archives U. Edin. L., 1882–1900 lecture notes and papers, Special collections Gen 802–03, 807–08, 1891–93, 1992, 2051–56, 2073 · NRA782 Gore, corresp. | King's AC Cam., 1876–1909 letters (15) to Oscar Browning · NA Scot., corresp. with members of the Balfour family · UCL, Galton MSS, 1905–06 letters to Sir Francis Galton

Likenesses W. Hole, double portrait, etching, 1884 (with J. S. Blackie), NPG; repro. in W. Hole, *Quasi cursores* (1884)

Wealth at death £29,945 12*s.* 8*d.*: resworn probate, 13 Feb 1911, *CGPLA Eng. & Wales* · £1783 5*s.* 10*d.*: resealed probate, 14 June 1911, *CGPLA Ire.*

Butchill, Elizabeth (*c.*1758–1780), child murderer, was raised in Saffron Walden, Essex. Nothing is known of her parents. Roughly three years before her offence Butchill, 'a decent plain young woman' (Laurie, 958), moved to Cambridge to live with her aunt Esther, a college bed maker, and wife of William Hall, the brewer to Trinity College. On the night of 6 January 1780 Butchill was heard making terrible groans and was attended to by her aunt.

The next morning the body of a new-born female was found in the river near Trinity College bogs. The coroner's inquest determined that the child had suffered a fractured skull before it was drowned. Butchill's uncle William suspected the child to be hers and she was brought before the mayor and coroner for examination. Butchill confessed that she had been delivered of a female child and that she had thrown the child down the necessary into the river and buried the placenta and other evidence of the birth in a nearby dunghill. Butchill's trial is unusual in so far as the coroner's jury charged her with murder, but not as the birth mother. Unwed mothers suspected of infanticide were usually charged under a 1624 act to prevent the murdering of bastard children, which made the mere act of concealing the birth of the child a capital offence (21 Jas. I, c. 27). Women who could not produce one witness to confirm that the child had been born dead, and who concealed the birth, were presumed to have killed it, though a conviction for concealment seldom led eighteenth-century judges to pass the death sentence. Butchill, though indeed the unwed mother, was not charged as such, nor with concealing the birth under the 1624 act, and instead faced the common law charge of murder. Tried and convicted before Judge Buller, she was executed at Cambridge on 17 March 1780. GREG T. SMITH

Sources B. Laurie, *The Newgate calendar, or, Malefactors' bloody register* (1932), 956–8

Bute. For this title name *see* Stuart, John, third earl of Bute (1713–1792); Stuart, John, first marquess of Bute (1744–1814); Stuart, John Crichton-, second marquess of Bute (1793–1848); Stuart, John Patrick Crichton-, third marquess of Bute (1847–1900); Stuart, John Crichton-, fourth marquess of Bute (1881–1947); Stuart, John Crichton-, sixth marquess of Bute (1933–1993).

Butler [*née* Ramsay], **Agnata Frances** (1867–1931), classical scholar, was born on 28 January 1867 at 13 Upper Seymour Street, Marylebone, London, the third and youngest daughter of Sir James Henry *Ramsay, tenth baronet (1832–1925), of Bamff, historian, and his first wife, Elizabeth Mary Charlotte (*d.* 1868), daughter of William Scott-Kerr of Sunlaws. She was brought up in Perthshire in a distinguished family of Scottish academics, her uncle George Ramsay holding the chair of humanities at Glasgow in succession to his uncle, William Ramsay. Educated at St Leonards School, St Andrews, in which her father took a particular interest, she went to Girton College, Cambridge, in 1884.

Agnata Ramsay was remembered for her remarkable tripos result in 1887. Women students were officially allowed to enter the university examinations only in 1881, following the success of another Girtonian, Charlotte Angas Scott (1858–1931), who had been ranked as equal to the eighth wrangler in the mathematical tripos in 1880 (her scripts having been informally marked 'by courtesy'). Agnata Ramsay was therefore among the first generation of women students at Cambridge to take the classical tripos, and her achievement in being placed in division one of the first class in 1887 was unequalled by any man in that

Agnata Frances Butler (1867–1931), by Eveleen Myers

year. But for her gender, she would have received the accolade of senior classic. *Punch* marked her supremacy with a famous cartoon in which Mr Punch ushered a gowned female into a first-class railway compartment labelled Ladies Only with the text 'Honour to Agnata Frances Ramsay' (2 July 1887). She, and those who followed her, such as Phillipa Fawcett of Newnham College, who was placed above the senior wrangler in 1890, and Margaret Alford (*b.* 1868) of Girton, who, also in 1890, was bracketed with the senior classic, demonstrated that women could benefit from Cambridge and were entitled to be admitted to the same courses and examinations as men.

Agnata Ramsay subsequently disproved the then commonly held contention that women who undertook rigorous academic study would be unattractive to potential husbands. Remaining in Cambridge to work on an edition of Herodotus, she 'captured' the master of Trinity College, Henry Montagu *Butler (1833–1918), a widower of fifty-seven whom she had met in November 1887 at a production of Sophocles' *Oedipus Rex*. They married on 9 August 1888. He claimed 'It is her goodness, not her Greek and Latin, which have stolen my heart', but on their honeymoon they 'read a great deal of Greek together' (Butler, 30, 32). Marrying the master of Trinity at the age of twenty-one, she stepped at once into the demanding role of the leading hostess in Cambridge. For thirty years, in spite of her retiring disposition, she fulfilled the heavy duties expected of her with poise and dignity. She bore three sons, James Ramsay Montagu *Butler (later regius professor of modern history at Cambridge) in 1889, Gordon in

1891, and Nevile in 1893. The publication of her edition of the seventh book of Herodotus' *History* in the same year as the birth of her first son provoked a further *Punch* cartoon, punning on 'a crib for Herodotus' (7 Dec 1889). After her husband's death in 1918 she remained in Cambridge, where she played an active part in the life of the local Christian Science church, which she had helped to found. Agnata Butler died at Sunny Lodge, Mount Park, Harrow, Middlesex, on 27 May 1931. SARA DELAMONT

Sources K. T. Butler and H. I. McMorran, eds., *Girton College register, 1869–1946* (1948) • J. R. M. Butler, *Henry Montagu Butler: master of Trinity College, Cambridge, 1886–1918* (1925) • J. Grant and others, *St Leonards School, 1877–1927* (1927) • B. Stephen, *Emily Davies and Girton College* (1927) • R. Strachey, *The cause: a short history of the women's movement in Great Britain* (1928) • I. Bradley, 'Cambridge without a Butler: like a master without a servant', *The Times* (24 July 1978) • M. Bradbrook, *That infidel place* (1969) • b. cert. • d. cert.
Likenesses E. Myers, photograph, NPG [*see illus.*]
Wealth at death £2957 18*s*. 6*d*.: resworn probate, 21 July 1931, *CGPLA Eng. & Wales*

Butler, Alban (1709–1773), Roman Catholic priest and hagiographer, was born on 13 October 1709, the second son of Simeon Butler of Appletree, Aston-le-Walls, Northamptonshire, and his wife, Ann, daughter of Henry Birch of Goscote, Walsall, Staffordshire. His nephew and biographer was Charles *Butler (1750–1832), lawyer and secretary of the Catholic Committee.

Alban Butler was educated at Dame Alice Harrison's school at Fernyhalgh, Lancashire, which he entered in 1722, and then from 14 June 1724 at the English college, Douai, Flanders. While a student he copied manuscripts for the use of Richard Challoner in compiling his *Memoirs of Missionary Priests* (1741). He was ordained priest at Cambrai in April 1734. Appointed professor of philosophy at the English College, Douai, he taught Newton's system of natural philosophy rather than Leibniz's, which was the more fashionable on the continent but which Butler regarded as irreconcilable with Catholicism. He went on to become professor of divinity and vice-president of the college. His care for British soldiers wounded in the battle of Fontenoy in 1745 won him the protection of their commander, the duke of Cumberland. In the same year he accompanied the earl of Shrewsbury and his sons the Hon. James Talbot and Thomas Talbot on their grand tour of France and Italy.

In 1749 Butler was sent on the English mission, becoming chaplain to Lord Langdale at Painsley, Draycott in the Moors, Staffordshire. He then became chaplain to Francis Gage at Warkworth, Northamptonshire in 1751, and then in 1754 chaplain to Edward Howard, ninth duke of Norfolk, and tutor to his nephew and heir presumptive, Edward Howard, at the Duke's Palace, Norwich. A trunk sent to Butler at Norwich was mistakenly delivered to the Anglican bishop's palace, and its contents, including not only Catholic books but also the instruments of his asceticism, a hairshirt and a scourge, would have incriminated him but for the intervention of the duke of Cumberland. A voracious reader and prolific writer, he was able to visit London to consult its libraries. According to Charles Butler,

Alban Butler (1709–1773), by unknown engraver, pubd 1781

> All his day was spent in reading. When he was alone, he read; when he was in company, he read; at his meals, he read; in his walks, he read; when he was in a carriage, he read; when he was on horseback, he read; whatever he did, he read. (Butler, 8)

He subsequently accompanied Edward Howard to the continent.

Butler's *Lives of the Saints* was completed in Paris in 1759. Its full title was *Lives of the fathers, martyrs and other saints, compiled from the original monuments and other authentic records; illustrated with the remarks of judicious modern critics and historians* (4 vols); it was his *magnum opus*. At the suggestion of Richard Challoner the first edition was published without the author's notes, but this omission was remedied in subsequent editions. Gibbon described it as 'a work of merit: the sense and learning belong to the author—his prejudices are those of his profession' (Gibbon, 5.36n.) Arranged to follow the calendar so as to give the lives of the saints on their feasts, the biographies were accompanied by homilies which inculcated Catholic spirituality, derived from devotional writers such as St Francis of Sales. Addressed to farmers and shopkeepers, it proved a popular work, which went through several editions and remained in print for two centuries, as well as being translated into French and Italian.

The bulk of Butler's published works related to the biographical, hagiographical, liturgical, and devotional themes of his *Lives of the Saints*. They included an exercise in biographical controversy, *Remarks on the two first volumes of the late 'Lives of the popes' by Mr Archibald Bower in 'Letters to a gentleman'* (1754), the hagiographical *A short account of the life and virtues of the venerable and religious mother, Mary of the Holy Cross, abbess of the English Poor Clares at Rouen* (1767), and the biographical *The Life of Sir Tobie Mathews* (1795). *The Moveable Feasts and Fasts, and other Annual Observances of the Catholic Church* (1774) dealt with aspects of the liturgical calendar. *Mediations and Discourses on the Sublime Truths and Important Duties of Christianity* (3 vols., 1791–3) elaborated similar themes. His sole work not on a devotional theme, *Travels through France and Italy, and part of the Austrian, French, and Dutch Netherlands, during the years 1745 and 1746* (1803), was an account of the grand tour he had undertaken.

Some of Butler's works, edited by Charles Butler, were published posthumously. Others, also on hagiographical and theological subjects, remain unpublished, including 'Collections for the lives of Bishop Fisher and Sir Thomas More', 'Memoirs of missionary priests', and *A Treatise of Revealed Religion*. In 1765 Butler returned to Douai. Following the expulsion of the Jesuits from France the English Jesuit College, a boarding-school for boys, at St Omer was handed over to the English secular clergy, and in 1766 Butler was appointed president. He also acted as vicar-general for the dioceses of Arras, Boulogne, St Omer, and Ypres, presumably with responsibility for English Catholic visitors and residents.

Butler died on 15 May 1773 at the English College, St Omer, where he was buried. The bulk of his papers, including those concerning the English Catholic martyrs, became part of the archives of the archdiocese of Birmingham. He left his books to the English colleges at Douai and St Omer, to his friends and family, and especially to his nephew Charles Butler. J. A. Hilton

Sources G. Anstruther, *The seminary priests*, 4 vols. (1969–77) · Gillow, *Lit. biog. hist.* · B. C. Foley, *Some other people of penal times* (1991) · F. O. Blundell, *Old Catholic Lancashire*, 3 vols. (1915–39) · will, Ushaw College, Durham, UCM II/122 · C. Butler, *An account of the life and writings of the Rev. Alban Butler* (1799) · *Butler's Lives of the saints*, rev. H. Thurston and D. Attwater, 2nd edn, 4 vols. (1956) · E. Gibbon, *The history of the decline and fall of the Roman empire*, ed. J. B. Bury, 7 vols. (1909–14) · J. A. Hilton, 'The science of the saints: the spirituality of Butler's *Lives of the saints*', *Recusant History*, 15 (1979–81), 189–93 · J. Kirk, *Biographies of English Catholics in the eighteenth century*, ed. J. H. Pollen and E. Burton (1909) · M. Sharratt, 'Alban Butler: Newtonian in part', *Downside Review*, 96 (1978), 103–11 · B. Ward, *The dawn of the Catholic revival in England, 1781–1803*, 2 vols. (1909)

Archives Roman Catholic Archdiocese of Birmingham · Ushaw College, Durham · Westm. DA

Likenesses stipple, pubd 1781 (after engraving), NPG [*see illus.*] · Finden, engraving, repro. in A. Butler, *Lives of the saints* · portrait, St Edmund's College, Ware, Hertfordshire

Wealth at death over £650; bequests of books, church plate, clothes, furniture; value cannot be established: will, 1771, Ushaw College, Durham, UCM II/122

Butler, Arthur Gray (1831–1909), headmaster, born at Gayton rectory, Northamptonshire, on 19 August 1831, was the third son of George *Butler, dean of Peterborough, and his wife, Sarah Maria, eldest daughter of John Gray of Wembley Park, Middlesex. After attending Eagle House at Hammersmith, he entered Rugby School under A. C. Tait in August 1844. In a novel *The Three Friends* (1900), Butler later described school life there, recording friendships between Matthew Arnold, A. H. Clough, and Theodore Walrond, and the effect produced on his Rugby contemporaries by the early poems of Tennyson. At school and college he was distinguished in both work and games, and Butler's Leap at Rugby commemorates a youthful athletic feat.

In March 1850 Butler was admitted as a scholar of University College, Oxford. At Oxford he was an original member of the Essay Club founded in 1852 by his friend G. J. Goschen, and was president of the union in 1853. In the same year he won the Ireland scholarship, and graduated BA with a first class in the final classical school. He was elected a fellow of Oriel in 1856, proceeding MA in the following year. Like his brothers, George *Butler and Henry Montagu *Butler, he became a schoolmaster, returning to Rugby in 1858 as assistant master under Frederick Temple. He was ordained deacon in 1861 and priest in 1862.

On the reconstitution of Haileybury College in 1862 Butler was appointed the first headmaster. In September the school took over the buildings of the East India Company's college near Hertford, which had been founded in 1805 for the training of its civil servants. Haileybury had no endowment, and from the outset Butler was hampered by inconvenient buildings and lack of modern appliances. Nevertheless he set himself to infuse into the school something of the strenuous vitality of the Rugby system, appointing Rugby men as masters and introducing the Rugby football game, which was made compulsory. He himself served as chaplain. He provided racquet and fives courts. He encouraged the growth of corporate spirit in the dormitories, with which he replaced the existing study bedrooms, and maintained the continuity of associations by naming the various houses after prominent Anglo-Indian civilians. Pupil numbers rose rapidly in a few years from 54 to 360. Butler's attractive personality, his enthusiasm, his eloquence, and thoroughness exercised a considerable influence over boys and masters. He was a stimulating classical teacher, and had the faculty of throwing new light on familiar passages. A nervous breakdown caused by overwork compelled his resignation in December 1867. He had by then raised Haileybury to a recognized place among the leading English public schools.

On resuming work in 1874 Butler served as chaplain of the Royal Indian Civil Engineering College at Coopers Hill near Egham. Returning to Oxford in 1875, he settled down to the more congenial duties of dean and tutor of Oriel, where his pupils included Cecil Rhodes. On 4 April 1877 he married Harriet Jessie, who was twenty years his junior, daughter of Michael Pakenham Edgeworth and niece of Maria Edgeworth. Re-election to his fellowship in October 1877 confirmed his place among the first generation of married dons at Oxford. He was disappointed to be passed over for the provostship in 1882; an anti-clerical sentiment among the governing body favoured D. B. Monro, a layman. After resigning his official position at Oriel in 1895 he maintained close relations with his college and was elected to an honorary fellowship in 1907. It was partly owing to his suggestions that both Oriel and Oxford benefited by the will of Cecil Rhodes.

Although not a productive scholar in the narrow academic sense, Butler cherished strong literary instincts, which found expression mainly in verse. He published two dramas, *Charles I* (1874; 2nd edn, 1907) and *Harold* (1892; 2nd edn, 1906), and two volumes of poetry entitled *The Choice of Achilles* (1900) and *Hodge and the Land* (1907). The latter reflected a long-standing interest in land reform. A broad-churchman in religion, and a lifelong friend of A. P. Stanley, Butler was a liberal in politics, though, like his friends from the Essay Club, Goschen and G. C. Brodrick, his opposition to Irish home rule led him into Liberal Unionism. In Oxford he was a supporter of women's education, and of social causes such as the housing of the poor. He and his wife were active in the Oxford Cottage Improvement Society.

Butler died at GlenFinnan, Belgrave Road, Torquay on 16 January 1909, and was buried in Holywell cemetery, Oxford. He left one son, Harold Edgeworth Butler (1878–1951), professor of Latin at London University, and three daughters, Olive Harriet Edgeworth Butler (1879–1951), warden of Lady Margaret Hall Settlement in Lambeth; Ruth Florence Butler (1881–1982), tutor in history and vice-principal of the Society of Oxford Home Students; and (Christina) Violet *Butler (1884–1982), tutor in economics to the Society of Oxford Home Students.

G. S. Woods, *rev.* M. C. Curthoys

Sources *The Times* (17 Jan 1909) · *The Haileyburian*, 17/389 (16 Feb 1909), 169–71 · L. S. Milford, *Haileybury College, past and present* (1909) · *Oxford Magazine* (21 Jan 1909) · I. Thomas, *Haileybury, 1806–1987* (1987) · C. Colvin, 'A don's wife a century ago', *Oxoniensia*, 50 (1985), 267–78 · K. Tillotson, 'Rugby, 1850: Arnold, Clough, Walrond, and *In memoriam*', *Review of English Studies*, new ser., 4 (1953), 122–40 · private information (1912) · J. Foster, *Oxford men and their colleges* (1893) · *CGPLA Eng. & Wales* (1910)

Archives Bodl. Oxf. · Royal Entomological Society, London, corresp. and papers | CUL, letters to Darwin

Likenesses G. Richmond, oils, 1867, Haileybury College, Hertfordshire

Wealth at death £30,328 15*s.* 7*d.* in UK: resworn probate, Sept 1910, *CGPLA Eng. & Wales* (1909)

Butler, Arthur John (1844–1910), Italian scholar and mountaineer, born at Putney, Surrey, on 21 June 1844, was the eldest of the six children of William John *Butler (1818–1894), at that time curate of Puttenham, near Guildford, Surrey, but best-known as the dean of Lincoln, and Emma Barnett (*d.* 1894), daughter of George Henry Barnett, banker, of Glympton Park, Woodstock, Oxfordshire. Through both parents he was connected with Stratford Canning, first cousin of George Canning—Stratford being his mother's maternal grandfather, and his father's great-great-uncle (by marriage).

After a childhood at Wantage, Berkshire, affectionately dominated by parents of strong if differing characters, both devoted pioneers of the Tractarian movement, Arthur took a scholarship to St Andrew's College, Bradfield, in 1853. At Easter 1857 he proceeded to Eton College, and subsequently to Trinity College, Cambridge, where he

Arthur John Butler (1844–1910), by Frederick Hollyer

obtained a scholarship. He won the Bell university scholarship in 1864, and graduated eighth classic in the tripos of 1867, and as a junior optime in mathematics. He was elected a fellow of Trinity in 1869. In the following year he reluctantly left Cambridge on accepting a post as examiner under the Board of Education. On 6 April 1875 he married Mary Caroline Humphrey, daughter of William Gibson Humphrey, vicar of St Martin-in-the-Fields. Butler worked in the education office, Whitehall, until 1887, when an invitation to become salaried partner in the publishing firm of Rivington tempted him from a routine which had never been congenial. After the amalgamation of Messrs Rivington with the firm of Longman he transferred his services to Messrs Cassell & Co. as their chief editor. In 1894 he relinquished business, and was appointed an assistant commissioner on secondary education. Subsequently from 1899 until his death he was engaged at the Public Record Office in editing calendars of foreign state papers from 1577 onwards: he published four volumes between 1901 and 1909. In 1898 he became professor of Italian language and literature at University College, London, and likewise filled that office until his death.

Butler was an accomplished scholar. His most important work was his contribution to the study of Dante. He was the first Englishman to replace the old dilettante enjoyment of the *Divine Comedy* by exact and disciplined study, and to treat it as scholars treated a Greek or Latin classic. His *Purgatory of Dante*, a prose translation with notes, appeared in 1880; his *Paradise* in 1885; his *Hell* in

1892. In 1890 he edited the Italian text. In 1893 he published a *Companion to Dante*, a translation of Scartazzini's work, and in 1895 a small book, *Dante: his Times and his Work. The Forerunners of Dante* (1910), an annotated selection from the Italian poets before 1300, was finished a few days before his death.

Butler also devoted much leisure to translating French and German works. Among others, he published the *Memoirs of Baron de Marbot* (1892); *Select Essays of Sainte-Beuve* (1895); *Memoirs of Baron Thiébault* (1896); and *The History of Mankind*, from Professor Friedrich Ratzel's work (1896). He also edited the English version of *Bismarck: the Man and the Statesman* (1898). At the same time, for thirty-five years Butler wrote for *The Athenaeum*, and was an occasional contributor to magazines on his favourite topics: Dante, mountaineering, Eton, and the Napoleonic campaigns. However, much of his most characteristic writing was spent in fugitive contributions to the press, which were always trenchant, original, and humorous, and exhibited an unusual blend of inborn churchmanship with an outspoken and militant liberalism.

From his school days Butler was also a mountaineer, delighting in alpine expeditions off the beaten track. In 1886, when he became a member of the Alpine Club, he brought to it an intimate knowledge—beyond challenge by any mountaineer in Europe—of the Ötzthal alps, which he first attacked in 1874, and revisited many times, up to 1890, with an ardour that was almost a passion. Butler became the editor of the *Alpine Journal* in 1890, and supervised it until the end of 1893 (vols. 15 and 16). He delighted in the dinners of the Alpine Dining Club. He was a member of the band of 'Sunday Tramps' which Leslie Stephen organized in 1882, ranking number ten on the original list. Butler died at his home, Wood End, Weybridge, on 26 February 1910, survived by his wife, one son, and six daughters, and was buried at Wantage.

A. T. Quiller-Couch, *rev.* Nilanjana Banerji

Sources *The Times* (28 Feb 1910) • *The Times* (8 March 1910) • *The Athenaeum* (5 March 1910), 275–6 • *Eton College Chronicle* (10 March 1910), 660 • F. Pollock, 'Arthur John Butler', *Cambridge Review* (3 March 1910), 315–16 • *Life and letters of William John Butler*, ed. A. J. Butler (1897) • F. W. Maitland, *The life and letters of Leslie Stephen* (1906) • Venn, *Alum. Cant.* • *CGPLA Eng. & Wales* (1910)

Likenesses F. Hollyer, photograph, NPG [*see illus.*] • Lady Holroyd, oils, priv. coll.

Wealth at death £12,937 11*s*.: resworn probate, 7 April 1910, *CGPLA Eng. & Wales*

Butler, Basil Edward [*name in religion* Christopher Butler] (**1902–1986**), Roman Catholic bishop and theologian, was born in Reading on 7 May 1902, the second of four sons and third of six children of William Edward Butler, wine merchant, and his wife, Bertha Alice Bowman, a schoolteacher originally from Suffolk. His intellectual gifts revealed themselves early, and he proceeded from Reading School to St John's College, Oxford, on a scholarship. At Oxford he received the Craven scholarship and Gaisford Greek prose prize and was *proxime accessit* for the Hertford scholarship, as well as taking first classes in classical honour moderations (1922), *literae humaniores* (1924), and theology (1925).

In 1925 Butler began his life as a clerical don with a tutorship at Keble College, and the following year was ordained an Anglican deacon. His high-church upbringing came to maturity at university, but he was becoming increasingly convinced by Catholicism. He taught classics at Brighton College in 1927–8 and (after his reception into the Roman communion in 1928) at Downside School, Somerset, in 1928–9. Downside was to be his home until 1966. He entered the Benedictine community there in 1929, assuming the religious name Christopher, and was ordained priest in 1933. He was headmaster of Downside from January 1940 until his election as seventh abbot of Downside on 12 September 1946. He was re-elected in 1954 and 1962, remaining abbot until 1966, and he presided over the extensive building programme which followed the great fire at Downside in 1955. In August 1961 he was elected president of the English Benedictine congregation, a post he held until 1966. It was in this capacity that he attended all four sessions of the Second Vatican Council from 1962 to 1965, during which he emerged as perhaps the leading English-speaking participant. His fluency in Latin, and his wide theological learning, neither of which was shared by many of the anglophones at the council, gave him great authority. He was also assisted by his independence from local episcopal concerns. He was present as a major religious superior, not as a bishop. He was a member of the commission for doctrine and contributed to the chapter on the Virgin Mary, which was included (principally, it is said, at his instigation) in the decree on the church, *Lumen gentium*, rather than appearing as a separate document. He also interested himself in the discussions on war and peace, with particular reference to nuclear deterrence. If Cardinal J. H. Newman was the 'invisible father' of the Second Vatican Council, then no one was better suited to be his spokesman than Butler. His Sarum lectures at Oxford in 1966 (published in 1967) presented his thoughts on *The Theology of Vatican II* and he was made an honorary fellow of St John's, the first Catholic priest to be so honoured by an Oxford college since Newman.

The Vatican Council made Butler a public figure and in 1966 he left Downside to go to Westminster as auxiliary bishop to Cardinal J. C. Heenan. He was consecrated with the title of bishop of Nova Barbara in Westminster Cathedral on 21 December 1966. As auxiliary he became the first area bishop of Hertfordshire, last resident president of St Edmund's College, Ware, and vicar capitular of the archdiocese in the interregnum between Cardinal Heenan and Cardinal Basil Hume. He became an elder statesman among the English hierarchy and an official Roman Catholic representative on many ecumenical bodies, including the Anglican–Roman Catholic International Commission. He was co-chairman of 'English ARC' (English Anglican–Roman Catholic Committee) from 1970 to 1981, and was twice honoured with the cross of St Augustine by the archbishop of Canterbury. In February 1980 he was appointed an assistant to the pontifical throne by Pope John Paul II.

The breadth of Butler's activities and his popularity as a

radio personality, especially on the *Any Questions?* programme in the 1960s, conceal from view the fact that his was chiefly an intellectual genius. In his books—which ranged in subject from scripture (he consistently supported the priority of St Matthew's gospel, as he demonstrated in *The Originality of St Matthew*, 1951) to spirituality via theology, ecumenism, and autobiography—and in the many hundreds of reviews and articles which he wrote, he revealed a wide sympathy. He owed most to the scriptures and the fathers, but he had a great attachment to the spiritual teaching of the French Jesuit master of contemplative prayer, Jean-Pierre de Caussade (1675–1751), and also, in later years, to the Canadian Jesuit Bernard Lonergan (1904–1985). Like the abbot in the rule of St Benedict, he made full use of things *nova et vetera* and always retained much of that balance of the middle way, which distinguishes classical Anglicanism and to some extent English Catholicism. From 1972 he was a member of the editorial board of the *New English Bible*.

Butler was a man of deep spirituality, who put prayer at the centre of a timetable which always remained fixed and unvaried throughout his adult life. He loved, as a Benedictine, the stability of the regular life, and all he wrote and said reflected his deep life of prayer. As a junior monk he had been a disciple of Dom David Knowles and had sought a deeper asceticism. He was of slightly more than average height, and as a young man he had an ascetic appearance. Advancing years made him more corpulent. His hair was always close-cropped, which gave great prominence to his head, very suitable given his intellectual gifts. He lived a simple life, although he enjoyed smoking a pipe, and was an expert chess player as well as a devotee of detective novels. He was a reserved man but became easier and more relaxed as a bishop. He remained a true Benedictine, one whose central vocation is seeking God. He died on 20 September 1986, at the Hospital of St John and St Elizabeth, St John's Wood, London, and was buried at Downside Abbey, Stratton on the Fosse.

DOMINIC AIDAN BELLENGER, *rev.*

Sources B. C. Butler, *A time to speak* (1972) • A. T. Flood, *B. C. Butler's developing understanding of the church: an intellectual biography* (1981) • Ceredig [D. Rees], *Bishop Christopher Butler, seventh abbot of Downside and bishop of Nova Barbara* (1986) • V. Rice, *Dom Christopher Butler, the abbot of Downside* (1965) • *The Tablet* (27 Sept 1986) • *The Times* (22 Sept 1986) • personal knowledge (1996) • *CGPLA Eng. & Wales* (1986)

Archives Downside Abbey Archives • Westm. DA

Likenesses Van Zeller, caricature, Downside • J. Ward, oils (as abbot), Downside • oils (as headmaster), Downside

Wealth at death under £40,000: probate, 18 Nov 1986, *CGPLA Eng. & Wales*

Butler, Charles (1560–1647), philologist and apiarist, was born at High Wycombe in Buckinghamshire. He entered Magdalen Hall, Oxford, in 1579, and afterwards became a bible-clerk at Magdalen College, where he took his BA in 1584, and MA in 1587. After leaving the university he became master of the Holy Ghost School in Basingstoke, Hampshire (1593), and held the living at Nateley Scures. In 1600 he moved to Wootton St Lawrence (3 miles from Basingstoke), where he served until his death. He was married, though his wife's name is not known.

Butler was the author of *The Feminine Monarchie, or, A Treatise Concerning Bees* (1609). A second edition appeared in 1623. The third edition (1634) is printed in Butler's phonetic spelling, under the title of *The feminin Monarchi', or, The Histori of Bee's*. Two Latin translations (1673 and 1682) were published, followed by a retranslation into English (1704). *The Feminine Monarchie* is an outstanding contribution to the literature of apiculture, particularly on the keeping of bees in traditional domed skep hives where the combs created by the bees adhere to the wall. Butler provides a commentary both on then current apicultural methods and on improved techniques based upon his own careful observations. In the 1609 edition he tried to indicate the piping noise of unmated queen bees by a system of musical notation. In the 1623 edition he expanded this into a four-part madrigal. The text still merits study by the serious beekeeper, although many of his technical terms fell out of use in the nineteenth century.

Butler also wrote a Latin treatise on rhetoric, *Rhetoricae libri duo: quorum prior de tropis & figuris, posterior de voce & gestu praecipit* which is not known to have been published before 1629, although the dedication is dated from Basingstoke '5 Idus Martii 1600'. In 1625 he published a treatise displaying considerable learning on the topic of affinity as a bar to marriage. The title of the work is *Syngeneia. de propinquitate matrimonium impediente regula, quæ una omnes quæstionis hujus difficultates facile expediat*. In 1633 appeared *The English grammar, or, The institution of letters, syllables, and words in the English tongue, whereunto is annexed an index of words like and unlike* (2nd edn, 1634). There he dwells upon the capriciousness of English orthography ('neither our new writers agreeing with the old, nor either new nor old among themselves'), and proposes the adoption of a system whereby men should 'write altogether according to the sound now generally received.' His last work was *The principles of musik in singing and setting. With the two-fold vse thereof, ecclesiasticall and civil* (1636).

Butler died on 29 March 1647 and was buried in an unmarked grave in the chancel of his church at Wootton St Lawrence. He is commemorated in two pictorial memorial windows dedicated on 14 November 1954 to mark the coronation of Elizabeth II. His wife had died in 1628, but he was survived by three sons and a daughter, Elizabeth, who in 1633 married the Revd Richard White; their great-grandson was the Revd Gilbert White of Selborne.

A. H. BULLEN, *rev.* KARL SHOWLER

Sources J. P. Harding and others, *British bee books: a bibliography, 1500–1976* (1979) • H. M. Fraser, *History of beekeeping in Britain* (1958) • F. R. Money, *Charles Butler, vicar of Wootton, 1600–1647* (*c.*1953) [pamphlet] • Wood, *Ath. Oxon.*

Butler, Charles (1750–1832), Roman Catholic layman and lawyer, was born in London on 14 August 1750, the son of James Butler, a successful linen draper who had a shop on Pall Mall. His mother, whose maiden name was Blandecque and whose family came from St Omer, had enjoyed a wide education including study of Greek and Latin. His uncle was the priest and hagiographer Alban *Butler.

Butler began his education at Mr Plunkett's school at

Charles Butler (1750–1832), by Robert William Sievier, pubd 1817 (after John Barry)

Hammersmith about 1756, and after three years was moved to a school established on the country estate of the English College of Douai at Esquerchin. About 1763 he entered the English College itself as a lay pensioner. He returned to England in 1766, and after consultation with his family rejected a religious career in favour of secular advancement in the law.

In 1769 he was apprenticed to study law under Mr Maire, presumably a member of the leading co. Durham Catholic family. Maire was a conveyancer, the only field in which Catholics could practise. Upon Maire's death in 1773 Butler moved to work under the Catholic layman, eminent conveyancer, and art patron Matthew Duane. The story, apparently originated by the *Dictionary of National Biography*, that Butler established a close friendship with another pupil of Duane's, John Scott, later lord chancellor and first earl of Eldon, is almost certainly erroneous. Scott joined Duane only about the time that Butler left, and Scott was a longstanding opponent of Catholic emancipation, although Butler later wrote of him with respect.

In 1775 Butler set up his own conveyancing practice and entered Lincoln's Inn, although as a Catholic he could not take the oath of supremacy and could not proceed to the bar. He developed a reputation as a political writer, publishing a (now lost) pamphlet opposing the workhouse reform projects of the Norfolk clergyman Robert Potter and, in 1777, another supporting naval impressment, which brought him to the attention of the first lord of the Admiralty, John Montagu, fourth earl of Sandwich. His growing prosperity was marked by his marriage to Mary (*b.* 1754/5), daughter of John Eyston of East Hendred in Berkshire, a member of a distinguished Catholic family. In accordance with the Marriage Act (1753), which required all marriages to take place before a Church of England clergyman, they were married on 10 February 1777 at St Martin-in-the-Fields, almost certainly following a Catholic ceremony; they had two daughters and a son. In 1779 he appeared as Sandwich's counsel at a parliamentary inquiry into the management of Greenwich Hospital. When asked whether he had taken the oaths prescribed by the Test Act, he replied that it was 'a question which this House will have the humanity not to ask of me, because it leads to an explanation rather inconvenient to myself' (Abercrombie, 'Early life', 287).

Butler seems to have withdrawn from general political activity after 1779 and devoted himself to his practice and to writing. Butler habitually left his home at four in the morning, went to his office, and wrote on one of his literary projects until breakfast, after which he would proceed to the business of the day. He maintained his political friendships, and in June 1782 became secretary to the Catholic Committee, formed in the hope that the Rockingham ministry would prove sympathetic to extensions of the toleration granted to Catholics by the Catholic Relief Act (1778). The committee's primary focus was the establishment of a regular hierarchy by the appointment of bishops-in-ordinary instead of vicars apostolic; the vicars apostolic were thought to be more offensive to the British state than bishops as their authority was directly derived from the papacy. Although from 1787 the committee included three clerical members, including one of the vicars apostolic, tension remained between the vicars apostolic and the committee.

Following a favourable response to the idea from William Pitt the younger, Butler was appointed in 1788 by the committee to prepare a new relief bill. Included with this bill was a declaration of Catholic principles, the protestation, which Butler composed from suggestions made by Pitt's brother-in-law Charles, third Earl Stanhope, who had proposed that further Catholic relief be part of a general scheme to include protestant dissenters. The bill included a new oath and defined Catholics as 'Protesting Catholic Dissenters'. Although the bill was ready by May 1789 it was not discussed for two years for lack of parliamentary time; in the meantime the vicars apostolic formally condemned the oath and controversy raged between the vicars apostolic and the committee, in which Butler played a prominent part. His 'Appeal' was addressed to the Catholics of England, defending the protestation and the oath, and was signed by two clerical and five lay members of the committee, which together with the responses and other writings of the committee, provided the contents of the 'blue books', so called from the colour of their bindings. Butler and his colleagues failed to persuade clergy and laity to support the committee's interpretation of English Catholicism. John Milner emerged as Butler's chief antagonist, beginning a lengthy feud. Under pressure from the clergy, parliament discarded the proposed oath and the 'Protesting Catholic Dissenters' were once more 'Roman Catholics'. The Irish oath of 1778 was substituted, and the bill passed on 24 June 1791.

The act of 1791 included a clause removing the requirement that a barrister take the oath of supremacy or make a declaration against transubstantiation. In that year Butler was able to become the first Catholic to be called to the bar since the revolution of 1688. Butler only argued one case at the bar, that of *Cholmondeley* v. *Clinton* in the House of Lords in 1819, which set a decisive precedent for later judgments on questions of land removal. By the time that he was called to the bar Butler had already built up a substantial reputation as a legal writer. In 1785 he took over the editing of Edward Coke's *The Institute of the Laws of England* (usually known as 'Coke upon Littleton') from Francis Hargrave. Hargrave had completed the commentary upon 190 folios, having begun work in 1774; Butler edited the remaining 203 for publication in 1787, and there were seven further editions in his lifetime, the last in 1831.

Following the passage of the 1791 act, Butler was a founder of the Cisalpine Club, established in 1792 'to resist any ecclesiastical interference which may militate against the freedom of English Catholics'. Butler's search for a close relationship between the state and English Catholics, to the exclusion of the hierarchy, did not prevent him taking part in the resettlement in England of religious communities displaced from their continental homes by the French revolutionary government. His literary projects during this period included *Horae biblicae*, a commentary on the old and new testaments and the sacred texts of non-Christian religions, first published in 1797, and *Horae juridicae subsecivae* (1799), comparing the evolution of the Grecian, Roman, feudal, and canon law.

Efforts to repair relations between the vicars apostolic and the Cisalpine Club eventually resulted in the period known as the 'mediation' and the establishment of a new committee, the Catholic Board, in 1807. Butler did not serve as secretary but remained active: *An Address to the Protestants of Great Britain and Ireland* (1813) sought to assure non-Catholics that they should not see the campaign for Catholic emancipation as a movement directed against them. Butler was responsible for the draft of another Catholic relief bill that year but this failed, partly through disagreement among the bill's parliamentary supporters and also through opposition among the vicars apostolic led by John Milner, who argued that the bill's provision for a veto by the British state on the appointment of Catholic bishops would effectively create a new schismatic church. Butler's support in 1816 for Catholic involvement in non-denominational education, and in 1819 for an amendment to the oath of supremacy so that Catholics might take it, only served to show the distance between him and the ecclesiastical leadership. On 8 May 1822 Milner censured Butler as 'a rebel to ecclesiastical authority and a public sinner' (B. Ward, *The Eve of Catholic Emancipation*, 1911–12, 3.102) who wanted to transfer the pope's spiritual sovereignty to the British monarch. Butler was at the time engaged in correspondence with Rome to explain that he supported the independence of the state only in temporal matters, where he believed it had no bearing upon the pope's spiritual authority; although a formal resolution was never achieved Rome did accept that Milner's attacks were unjustified.

At this late stage in his career, Butler's literary output was reaching its peak. Among his many other works, including legal texts, history, and pamphlets on the Catholic issue, came the four-volume *Historical memoirs respecting the English, Irish and Scottish Catholics from the Reformation to the present time*, which appeared between 1819 and 1821. Perhaps inevitably, Butler's interpretation of Catholic history was met with a rejoinder from Milner in *Supplementary Memoirs of English Catholics* (1820). Butler followed with the publication of his autobiographical *Reminiscences* (1822) and his *Continuation of the Rev. Alban Butler's Lives of the Saints to the Present Time* (1823). He continued to defend the Catholic position: *The Book of the Catholic Church* appeared in 1825, a reply to Robert Southey's *Book of the Church* (1824), an ecclesiastical history hostile to Catholicism. It was followed by a further exchange of pamphlets between Butler and critics of Catholicism, who included Henry Phillpotts, later bishop of Exeter, and the philologist Richard Garnett.

Butler's failing eyesight led to his withdrawal from business from 1825 onwards, and he did not play a leading role in the winning of Catholic emancipation in 1828. His contribution was rewarded when he was presented to George IV, and he revised the *Historical Memoirs* to include an account of the emancipation struggle. In 1831 he was appointed king's counsel on the recommendation of the attorney-general, Sir Thomas Denman: the letter from William IV said the king was 'happy to confer an honour on so learned and worthy a person' (Ward, *The Eve of Catholic Emancipation*, 3.278). He died on 2 June 1832 at his house in Great Ormond Street, London. He was survived by his widow and their two daughters, Mary, who married Charles Stonor, an army officer, and Theresia, who married Andrew Lynch of Lynch Castle, co. Galway, barrister in England. DOROTHY M. MOORE

Sources *Annual Register* (1832), 206–8 • N. J. Abercrombie, 'The early life of Charles Butler', *Recusant History*, 14 (1977–8), 281–92 • N. Abercrombie, 'Charles Butler and the English Jesuits, 1770–1823', *Recusant History*, 15 (1979–81), 283–301 • Gillow, *Lit. biog. hist.* • A. Polson, *Law and lawyers, or, Sketches and illustrations of legal history and biography*, 2 vols. (1840) • B. Ward, *The dawn of the Catholic revival in England, 1781–1803*, 2 vols. (1909) • B. Ward, 'Butler, Charles', *The Catholic encyclopedia*, ed. C. G. Herbermann and others, 3 (1908) [internet edn, www.newadvent.org/cathen/ (2000)] • R. A. Melikan, *John Scott, Lord Eldon, 1751–1838: the duty of loyalty* (1999) • *DNB* • *GM*, 1st ser., 102/2 (1832), 269–71 • *IGI*

Archives BL, letter-books on legal, literary, and Roman Catholic matters, Add. MSS 25127–25129 • BL, minutes and papers as secretary of the Catholic committee, Add. MSS 5416, 7961–7962 • BM • U. Birm. L., lectures on Littleton • Westm. DA, family and other corresp. and papers • Westm. DA, papers relating to Stonyhurst College; literary papers | Bodl. Oxf., letters to E. H. Barker • Bodl. Oxf., letters to Isaac Disraeli • Hunt. L., letters to Charles O'Conor • NL Ire., letters to Denis Scully • Warks. CRO, corresp. with Sir John Throckmorton • Westm. DA, corresp. with J. Kirk • Westm. DA, corresp. with Bishop Poynter

Likenesses R. W. Sievier, line and stipple, pubd 1817 (after J. Barry), BM, NPG [*see illus.*] • Mrs D. Turner, lithograph, 1829, NPG • bust, 1832, Lincoln's Inn, London • miniature, engraving, repro. in

C. Butler, *Historical memoirs respecting the English, Irish and Scottish Catholics from the Reformation to the present time*, 4 vols. (1819–21) · miniature, oils (as a child at Douay), priv. coll.; repro. in Ward, *Dawn of the Catholic revival in England*, vol. 1

Butler, Charlotte (*fl.* 1674–1693), actress and singer, was said to have been 'the Daughter of a decay'd Knight' and recommended to the stage by Charles II, by whom she was named (Cibber, 97). The theatre prompter John Downes remembered that she joined the Duke's Company at about the time when the operatic version of *The Tempest* was staged (spring 1674). No theatre roles are known for her at this time, but she sang Plenty and an African woman in the court masque *Calisto* in February 1675.

From early in 1680, when she acted the *ingénue* Serina in the première of Thomas Otway's *The Orphan* and spoke its sexually teasing epilogue, Mrs Butler became an increasingly popular actress. Aphra Behn wrote the role of the heroine Charlot in *The City Heiress* (1682) for her, with opportunities to display her singing and dancing. The first breeches role she created was in Otway's comedy *The Atheist* (1683), where she played Lucretia, disguised as 'a very pretty Fellow' in the last act. She appears to have spent five years off the stage, returning in 1689 to create over a dozen roles in three years by authors including Thomas Shadwell (Philadelphia in *Bury Fair*, Levia in *The Amorous Bigotte*), John Crowne (Airy in *The English Frier*), and Thomas Southerne (Floriante in *Sir Anthony Love*). Thomas D'Urfey wrote Betty Jiltall for her in *Love for Money* (January 1691), 'a cunning, singing, weeping, wheedling, toying, chattering, mercenary Town Jilt', and gave her yet another sexually provocative epilogue. She was viciously attacked by the satirists. The 'Satyr on both Whigs and Tories' (1683) accused her of giving the clap to her lover, the 'Satyr on the Players' (*c*.1684) mocked her pretensions as a singer—'mony is the Syren's chiefest Aym' (BL, Harleian MS 7319)—and 'The Wedding' (*c*.1689) accused the 'Strumpet Termagant' of disgracing even her own profession (Harvard, MS Eng. 633).

Many of Mrs Butler's roles featured her singing and William Mountfort's *The Successful Strangers* included '*Mrs.* Butlers *Dance*' even though she had no part in the play. Cibber comments that she was 'allow'd, in those Days, to sing and dance to great Perfection' and was 'a capital, and admired Performer' in Henry Purcell's dramatic operas *Dioclesian* and *King Arthur* (Cibber, 97). Her singing partner was the bass John Bowman and they sang dialogues by Purcell in *Sir Anthony Love* and in John Dryden's *Amphitryon* (1690). In *King Arthur* (1691) Mrs Butler acted and sang the airy spirit Philidel to Bowman's earthy spirit Grimbald. She also sang Cupid in this opera and years later Roger North remembered Cupid's invocation of the Cold Genius, when, with her back turned to the audience, she 'performed it admirably, even beyond any thing I ever heard upon the English stage' (Wilson, 217).

Mrs Butler was an attractive brunette (Jiltall is called 'my sweet pretty charming Black Eyes') with the figure and panache for breeches roles. Cibber admired her as an actress in tragedy but particularly praised her in comedy, where 'she had a manner of blending her assuasive Softness, even with the Gay, the Lively, and the Alluring' (Cibber, 97). In January 1692 she created the affected La Pupsey, carrying and kissing her lapdog throughout, in D'Urfey's comedy *The Marriage Hater Matched*; soon after this the satirical pamphlet *Poeta infamis, or, A Poet not Worth Hanging* (1692), attacking D'Urfey, his play, and Butler herself, claimed that she was expecting 'to lie in within this Month'. In May 1692 she sang in Purcell's *The Fairy Queen*, appearing as Spring in the 'Masque of the Seasons' and performing the song 'When I have often heard young maids complaining', but she left the London stage at the end of the season because the managers would not increase her salary from 40*s*. to 50*s*. a week. She joined Joseph Ashbury's company at the Smock Alley Theatre, Dublin, and all that is known of her after this is that in late spring 1693 she spoke an epilogue at the lord lieutenant's final visit to the theatre before his return to England.

Olive Baldwin and Thelma Wilson

Sources W. Van Lennep and others, eds., *The London stage, 1660–1800*, pt 1: *1660–1700* (1965) · C. Cibber, *An apology for the life of Mr. Colley Cibber* (1740) · J. Wilson, ed., *Roger North on music* (1959) · J. Downes, *Roscius Anglicanus*, ed. J. Milhous and R. D. Hume, new edn (1987) · *Poeta infamis, or, A poet not worth hanging* (1692) · O. Baldwin and T. Wilson, 'Purcell's stage singers: a documentary list', *Performing the music of Henry Purcell* [Oxford 1993], ed. M. Burden (1996), 276–7 · E. Boswell, *The Restoration court stage (1660–1702): with a particular account of the production of 'Calisto'* (1932) · P. Danchin, ed., *The prologues and epilogues of the Restoration, 1660–1700*, 7 vols. (1981–8), vols. 2–3 · 'Satyr on both whigs and tories', 1683, BL, Harleian MS 7319 · 'Satyr on the players', *c*.1684, BL, Harleian MS 7319 · 'The wedding', *c*.1689, Harvard U., Houghton L., MS Eng. 633

Butler, Christopher. *See* Butler, Basil Edward (1902–1986).

Butler, Sir Clifford Charles (1922–1999), physicist, was born on 20 May 1922 at Dellwood, Liebenrood Road, Reading, Berkshire, the son of Charles Hannington James Butler, a wholesale grocer's clerk, and his wife, Olive, *née* Pembroke. His father was later a buyer for the wholesale grocer William Kingham of Reading. Butler was educated at Reading School and Reading University, where he gained his BSc and PhD. From 1942 to 1945 he was a demonstrator in physics at Reading University. In the latter year he joined the University of Manchester as assistant lecturer in physics, and in 1947 he became lecturer.

At Manchester, Patrick Blackett had established a leading research school for cosmic ray physics. Butler worked with G. D. Rochester, studying cosmic rays using a counter-controlled cloud-chamber. Among the photographs obtained, they found two unexpected events, one in October 1946 and one in May 1947, showing previously unknown particles. These 'V-particles', as they came to be called, were a thousand times heavier than the electron, but, strangely, they were enormously long-lived on nuclear timescales. No further examples were found up to the summer of 1949, so to obtain a higher flux of cosmic rays the equipment was moved to the Pic-du-Midi observatory in the Pyrenees. Carl Anderson and colleagues from the California Institute of Technology confirmed the existence of the V-particles, but it was the Butler group that systematically studied them and found that there were two types, hyperons and mesons. Their long life, explained in 1952 by Abraham Pais, arose because they were created by fast nuclear reactions in pairs—once separated from their partner they no longer interacted rapidly. Murray Gell-Mann and K. Nishijima clarified this picture by identifying a quantity, called 'strangeness', in recognition of their apparently strange behaviour. The particles were created in pairs in order to balance positive and negative values of strangeness in fast interactions; subsequent decay could violate strangeness, but only slowly. Butler's and Rochester's discovery may be seen as the first step towards understanding of the quark structure of matter. Considering the importance of the discovery, it is hard to understand why they were never recognized by the Nobel committee.

Butler married, on 5 July 1947, Kathleen Betty Collins (*d.* 1999), the daughter of Sydney Charles Collins, a clerk. They had two daughters. In 1953 Blackett left Manchester to head the physics department at Imperial College, and Butler went with him to lead a high-energy nuclear physics group. He was appointed assistant director of the physics department in 1955, promoted to professor in 1957, and elected a fellow of the Royal Society in 1961. When Blackett withdrew as departmental head in 1963, Butler succeeded him. While head, he reorganized the departmental structure, forming several departmental committees, with the heads of research groups meeting under his chairmanship to determine policy. These arrangements remained in place. Between 1966 and 1969 Butler also served as dean of the Royal College of Science.

Throughout his time at Imperial College Butler remained as head of the high-energy nuclear physics group. As the era of cloud-chambers came to an end he recognized the importance of the hydrogen bubble chamber, and the first to operate in western Europe was at Imperial College. However, he saw that building large chambers needed resources beyond those of any one British university. He therefore organized a consortium of universities funded by the Department of Scientific and Industrial Research to construct the British Hydrogen Bubble Chamber, with himself as 'spokesman'. Meanwhile, a smaller French chamber had been moved to the Conseil Européen de Recherches Nucléaires (CERN), and Butler's group used it in an international collaboration which probably set the tone now regarded the norm for CERN experiments. (Previously it had been assumed that experiments would be done by national teams.) The British chamber went to CERN in 1963 and was the main source of photographs until a larger CERN chamber became operational. It then returned to the Rutherford laboratory to be used at the Nimrod accelerator. There a flexible track-sensitive target, filled with liquid hydrogen inside a neon-hydrogen mixture, was used in experiments for the first time.

Meanwhile, Butler had become interested in education policy. He joined the academic planning board of the University of Kent in 1963, the Schools Council in 1965 (serving for nineteen years), and the University Grants Committee in 1966. He took a leading part in a reappraisal of sixth-form examinations by the Schools Council and the standing conference on university entrance, and was co-author of the Butler and Briault report. He also chaired the Royal Society's standing education committee from 1969 to 1979 and served on the physics consultative committee of the Nuffield Foundation, which had started a major programme aimed at producing new teaching material. The foundation soon became influential in education circles, and Butler left Imperial College to become its director in 1970. He was there during a period of considerable funding uncertainty but, despite that, set up three ambitious projects: the group for research and innovation in higher education, the programme for law and society, and the centre for agricultural strategy at the University of Reading.

Butler's role in the establishment of the Open University was also important, since the foundation gave a significant grant to create a course on genetics as a test bed for other courses. Butler was appointed to the council of the Open University in 1971, the year it admitted its first students, and stayed as a member until 1995; he served as vice-chairman from 1986 to 1995. He represented the council on a critical Department of Education and Science (DES) review at a time when it was argued that, with many courses now established, staff numbers could be reduced. The case for maintaining the level of support was won, and funding issues were resolved.

In 1975 Butler was appointed vice-chancellor of Loughborough University, where he stayed until his retirement at the end of 1985. The major development in the earlier years was the merger with the neighbouring college of education. The DES decided upon the merger in 1974, and it took place in 1977. The college had been a pure teaching institution, and Butler needed to recruit a team of professors to establish research activities. Fortunately there was little overlap of subject departments in the two institutions, and the merger went very smoothly. Student numbers and research income increased, and new facilities were implemented, with a new students' union and library. As financial pressures on the universities grew, Loughborough was fortunate in having a vice-chancellor well known and trusted by the DES. Indeed, Butler had become a national figure, knighted in 1983 for his services to education. He chaired the council for the education and training of health visitors (1977–83), the advisory committee on the supply and education of teachers (1980–85), and the steering committee of the DES educational counselling and credit transfer information service project (1983–9).

Although he was no longer directly involved in particle physics research after 1970, Butler never lost his interest in physics, and he played a vital role in the International Union of Pure and Applied Physics, being its secretary-general (1963–72), vice-president (1972–5), and president (1975–8) during years when the union was of great importance in maintaining relations between physicists on both sides of the Iron Curtain. After his retirement he chaired an ABRC/Natural Environment Research Council study to assess the role, structure, and programme of the British

Geological Survey and a working party on research selectivity for the department of education for Northern Ireland, Queen's University, Belfast, and the University of Ulster. However, with the worsening health of his wife, Kathleen, he became less involved in public matters. Kathleen had been admitted into hospital when Butler was himself suddenly taken ill. He died at the Glenfield Hospital, Groby Road, Leicester, on 30 June 1999, of renal failure, and Kathleen died shortly after him. They were survived by their two daughters. IAN BUTTERWORTH

Sources I. Butterworth, *Memoirs FRS*, 47 (2001), 39–54 • *The Independent* (28 July 1999) • *The Times* (26 Aug 1999) • *Daily Telegraph* (12 July 1999) • *WWW* • personal knowledge (2004) • private information (2004) • b. cert. • m. cert. • d. cert.
Archives RS, corresp. with Lord Blackett
Wealth at death £647,803: probate, 21 Dec 1999, *CGPLA Eng. & Wales*

Butler, Dorothy. *See* Middleton, Dorothy (1909–1999).

Butler, Edmund, earl of Carrick (*d.* **1321**), justiciar of Ireland, was a younger son of Theobald Butler (*d.* 1285), butler of Ireland, and Joan, daughter of John Fitzgeoffrey. He may have visited England as early as 1289, and was certainly of age at the death of his childless elder brother, Theobald (V), in 1299. The death of his mother in 1303 brought him a share of the Fitzjohn lands in England and Ireland, and he also acquired some of the English and Irish estates of the Pippards. In 1302 he married Joan, a daughter of John fitz Thomas Fitzgerald (*d.* 1316), later first earl of Kildare.

In 1303 Butler was ready to join an Irish expeditionary force to Scotland, but was asked to remain in Ireland for its security. He acted as deputy justiciar from November 1304 to May 1305, when John Wogan was out of the country. During a visit to England in 1309–10 he was knighted by Edward II. He was deputy again from August 1312 to June 1314. In the winter of 1312–13 he organized a major campaign in Leinster which brought the Uí Bhroin of Wicklow to the peace. At a Michaelmas feast in Dublin in 1313 he is said to have dubbed thirty knights. He served once more as justiciar from February 1315 to April 1318, for the last year under Roger Mortimer, who had been appointed king's lieutenant. His period of office coincided both with the invasion of Ireland by the Scots under Edward Bruce and with the great famine of 1316–17. He brought the magnates of Ireland to Dundalk to confront Bruce in July 1315. When the Scots retreated north, he did not follow, assuming (reasonably but wrongly) that the earl of Ulster was capable of defeating them. When Bruce came south early in 1316, he was present at an inconclusive battle at Skerries in Kildare, after which he and other magnates gave hostages and assurances of loyalty to John Hotham, the king's emissary. A year later, when Robert Bruce had joined his brother in Ireland, Butler left Dublin to its own devices and concentrated upon mustering Munster against the Scots. The army he raised confronted them near Limerick in April 1317, leaving King Robert's forces no choice but to retreat, starving. Shortly before Butler died, Edward II issued a declaration 'to clear the fair fame of Edmund le Botiller who has been accused of having assisted the Scots in Ireland, that he has borne himself well and faithfully towards the king' (*CPR, 1317–21*, 535). Any suspicions seem groundless. It fell to Butler to organize a highly regionalized country in the most difficult circumstances; if his performance was not glorious, it compared favourably with that of Edward II himself and of those who defended the north of England at the same period.

On 1 September 1315 Edward II had granted Butler the manors of Carrick-on-Suir and Roscrea in Tipperary, with the title of earl of Carrick. He was also given return of writs in three Tipperary cantreds, a grant that foreshadowed the later liberty of Tipperary. He was occasionally referred to as earl by the king (and in April 1317 by Pope John XXII); but, perhaps because of its limited endowment, his comital status failed to gain acceptance, and he did not normally use the title. In 1320 the pope released him from a vow to undertake a pilgrimage to Santiago de Compostela because of the state of Ireland. He spent his last months in England, in March 1321 arranging a marriage (which was outrun by events) between his daughter, Joan, and Roger, the second son of Roger Mortimer, involving the settlement of the Mortimer lands in Ireland on the couple. He died in London on or shortly before 13 September 1321, and was buried the following November at Gowran (Kilkenny), where the bishop of Ossory and the prior of the hospitallers had earlier agreed to supply four priests to pray for his soul and those of members of his family. He was succeeded by his son, James *Butler, who in 1328 became first earl of Ormond. ROBIN FRAME

Sources *Chancery records* • E. Curtis, ed., *Calendar of Ormond deeds*, IMC, 1: *1172–1350* (1932) • J. T. Gilbert, ed., *Chartularies of St Mary's Abbey, Dublin: with the register of its house at Dunbrody and annals of Ireland*, 2, Rolls Series, 80 (1884) • A. J. Otway-Ruthven, *A history of medieval Ireland* (1968) • R. Frame, 'The Bruces in Ireland, 1315–18', *Irish Historical Studies*, 19 (1974–5), 3–37 • R. Frame, 'The campaign against the Scots in Munster, 1317', *Irish Historical Studies*, 24 (1984–5), 361–72 • R. Frame, *English lordship in Ireland, 1318–1361* (1982) • J. R. S. Phillips, 'The mission of John de Hotham to Ireland, 1315–1316', *England and Ireland in the later middle ages*, ed. J. Lydon (1981), 62–85 • *The annals of Ireland by Friar John Clyn and Thady Dowling: together with the annals of Ross*, ed. R. Butler, Irish Archaeological Society (1849) • *CEPR letters*, 2.196, 415, 439 • PRO • GEC, *Peerage*
Archives NL Ire., deeds

Butler, Edmund (*d.* **1551**), archbishop of Cashel, was the illegitimate son of Piers *Butler, eighth earl of Ormond. According to Wood he was 'bred a canon regular of the order of S. Austin, and for some time studied, as is supposed, among those of his order in Oxon' (Wood, *Ath. Oxon.*, 3rd edn, 2.757). By 1516 he was archdeacon of Ossory. Butler was nominated by the pope to Cashel in 1524 but his consecration did not take place until 1527, owing to a quarrel with his father; Edmund opposed Piers's levying of taxes in his archdiocese, which he saw as contrary to his own rights to tax. Edmund's own taxations and the fervour with which his retainer Desmond Duff pursued claims resulted in complaints to Dublin. This extended to accusations of robbing a boat laden with merchandise and holding the owners to ransom, made all the more scandalous by happening within 4 miles of the city of Waterford. In 1526 owing to the poverty of his see he was made prior *in commendam* of Athassel, co. Tipperary. This drew him into a dispute with the town of Clonmel over the property rights of the priory in the town. Dissension within the church was provoked by Butler's 1529 provincial council at Limerick which gave the mayor of Limerick the power to imprison clerical debtors.

Butler was regularly resident in Dublin and may have been there more frequently than in Cashel. He was a privy councillor, and while combative about property and other rights was more circumspect in his relations with the civil authorities. Neither opposing Henry VIII's ecclesiastical policy nor actively promoting it, he did not take the oath of supremacy until 1539 (at Clonmel, together with the archbishop of Tuam and eight other bishops). Butler's powerful position was probably strengthened by the newly extended influence of the house of Ormond, a product of the eclipse of the Geraldines after the Kildare revolt and Edmund's father being the first non-absentee earl in a century. Edmund's associations with the house of Desmond, partly a product of his preconsecration dispute with his father, further compounded his influence. He attended the parliament of 1541 at which the act making Henry VIII king of Ireland was passed. Ordinances for the reformation of the inhabitants of the south of Ireland, which he was to assist Ormond and Desmond in implementing, were also passed in this parliament but actually contain little of a specifically 'reforming' mould. Recognition of his co-operation with royal policy may be seen in the fact that Athassel was one of only two religious houses not to be dissolved in 1541 (ultimately it passed into the hands of the earl of Ormond in 1558). Butler held a further council at Limerick the following year.

It is not clear how far Butler's involvement with implementing royal policy extended to promoting reform within his diocese. The late 1520s suggest that he was not interested in pastoral matters: Kildare complained that services were not said in Cashel diocese and the state of morals at Athassel was condemned. That the law officers of the crown, the attorney-general and the solicitor-general, sought in 1549 to get him to accompany them on an expedition to 'abolish Idolatry, papistry, the mass sacrament, & the like' (Edwards, 32) suggests he was similarly less than active during the latter parts of his episcopate. According to John Lynch's *De praesulibus Hiberniae II* (allegedly drawing on a volume by Patrick Fleming, a contemporary parish priest in Butler's Cashel), his allegiance to the reformed church was temporary and his religious practice did not change. However, it may have been less a case of conviction and more of the pragmatic acceptance of a change of authority. Lynch certainly goes too far in crediting a story which has Butler carrying the sacrament in procession, an act hardly credible of a man who cautiously dropped the conventional greeting *sedis apostolicae gratia* from his letters.

Butler died on 5 March 1551. After his death no appointment was made to his see until the reign of Mary. Fragments of his tomb can still be seen on the east side of the north transept of Cashel Cathedral.

MIHAIL DAFYDD EVANS

Sources J. B. Leslie, Church of Ireland succession lists, general index, Representative Church Body Library, Dublin • A. O'Donnell, 'Edmund Butler, archbishop of Cashel (1524–51), and the Reformation', *Irish Ecclesiastical Record*, 5th ser., 100 (1963), 137–49 • J. Hunt, 'The tomb of Archbishop Edmund Butler at Cashel', *Journal of the Royal Society of Antiquaries of Ireland*, 83 (1953), 199 • R. D. Edwards, *Church and state in Tudor Ireland* (Dublin, 1935) • R. Bagwell, *Ireland under the Tudors*, 1 (1885) • C. E. Maxwell, *Irish history from contemporary sources* (1923) • *CSP Ire.*, 1509–73 • Wood, *Ath. Oxon.*, new edn, 2.757 • Emden, *Oxf.*, 4.90

Butler, Edward (1823–1879), barrister and politician in Australia, was born in co. Kilkenny, Ireland, the son of Michael Butler, tenant farmer, and his wife, Mary, *née* Joyce. He was educated at St Kieran's College, Kilkenny, where he was encouraged to prepare for the Catholic priesthood. Thomas Carlyle, for whom he acted as a Galway guide on his 1849 journey to Ireland, suggested that he had been rejected as unsuitable. But it is uncertain whether the career decision was his own or that of church authorities. As an adult he remained secretive about this and other details of his early life.

When Butler met Carlyle he was already a Young Ireland enthusiast and a devoted follower of Charles Gavan Duffy, editor of the nationalist *Galway Vindicator* and active organizer of potential insurrection. In the 1848 crisis he had been arrested and briefly imprisoned. Duffy later brought him to Dublin to be sub-editor of *The Nation*. He was one of the most active campaigners in Duffy's League of North and South, organized to secure election of candidates committed to vote for land reform. But even before Duffy himself had been disillusioned by the parliamentary performance of the Independent Irish Party (1852–5) Butler, lacking the means to prepare himself for a legal career or sustain himself in a political career, had decided to start a new life in New South Wales.

Butler arrived in Sydney in May 1853 and supported himself by working as a journalist while he studied law. Armed with an introduction from Duffy (who later migrated to Victoria), he was offered work on the radical *Empire* by Henry Parkes, an admirer of Duffy's, and joined other liberals in challenging the local 'bunyip aristocracy'.

Carlyle described the young Butler as 'a burly thick-necked sharp-eyed man' (Carlyle, 189). Later colonial descriptions repeated the emphasis on physical bulk but often mentioned 'kindly eyes' and 'a rich brogue and humorous style of address' (*Sydney Morning Herald*, 10 June 1879). Colonial conditions stimulated reassessment of his Young Ireland ideas and experience. He seemed always to believe that his liberalism could be reconciled with his Catholicism. In 1858 he gained fourth position in the election of twelve laymen to govern the Catholic college, St John's, within the newly established University of Sydney.

Though he joined in criticism of clerical maladministration and of church reliance on state support he was not an anti-clerical, and in the 1870s he became a friend of the new archbishop, Roger Vaughan, who made him one of his four executors. He remained a fellow of St John's from 1858 until his death.

Butler's admission to the bar on 16 October 1855 began a distinguished legal career which ended abruptly twenty-four years later when he collapsed and died while presenting a case in the same court. He was appointed a Sydney district crown prosecutor on 21 January 1859 and prosecuted regularly in both district and supreme court jurisdictions until 1870. He appeared in common law and commercial cases, but was especially admired by fellow professionals for his skill in cross-examination in criminal cases. In one famous case, following a defence address by his friend W. B. Dalley, he began his summing up for the jury: 'My learned friend has presented the poetry of the case. I shall now give you the facts' (Dowd, 250). The accused received a sentence of seven years. By the 1870s he was the recognized leader of the colonial bar. In 1871 he was one of three lawyers appointed with three judges to review legal procedures in the colony. He was made a queen's counsel on 19 November 1873.

It was in association with reforming liberals that Butler was first appointed to the legislative council in September 1861. He resigned from the council in 1863 to concentrate on his legal career, and declined a subsequent offer of the attorney-generalship. When he first contested a seat in the legislative assembly (December 1869) it was in the increasingly bitter sectarian atmosphere of colonial politics following the 1868 attempted assassination of the visiting duke of Edinburgh. He was a popular and successful campaigner: a contemporary observed that 'if he had held up an umbrella his people would vote for it' (Martin, 272). He was re-elected for the seat of Argyle in March 1872, May 1872 (ministerial), and December 1874. When he retired from the assembly in October 1877 he was again appointed to the council, of which he remained a member until his death.

Butler deplored sectarian conflict and its destructive impact on united efforts for reform: 'my longing is inexpressible … for the cessation of [these] terrible animosities' (Butler to Parkes, 5 Sept [1871], Parkes MSS). His friend Parkes, deeply distrusted by most Catholics, described Butler in 1870 as 'the most sterling man in parliament, uncompromised' and the best qualified to lead a 'crusade' for liberal reform (Parkes to Cooper, 28 Jan 1871, Parkes MSS). In a peacemaker role, Butler became Parkes's 'greatest electoral asset' in the 1872 campaign which produced a reforming coalition. He was ably assisted by a younger brother, Thomas, who had followed him to Sydney and had, in 1869, become editor of the local Catholic newspaper, the *Freeman's Journal*. Parkes offered Butler the office of attorney-general, in which he successfully carried through reform of property law during the following year but was notably less successful with criminal law and equity.

As attorney-general Butler expected to have the traditional first offer when the position of chief justice became vacant in November 1873. The governor, Sir Hercules Robinson, considered him to be 'well fitted by character and ability' (Robinson to Parkes, 24 Oct 1873, Parkes MSS). But, having promised the job to Butler, Parkes then offered it to his conservative political rival James Martin. Butler immediately resigned from the ministry. The unscrupulous Parkes exploited sectarian prejudices and suggested that Butler was part of a 'church party' that tried to take over the legal system. Butler, who had first shown willingness to reconsider his candidacy, told Parkes that, once his appointment was opposed on religious grounds, his withdrawal 'would compromise in my own person the civil rights of my Roman Catholic fellow citizens' (Butler to Parkes, 10 Nov 1873, Parkes MSS). The affair greatly exacerbated sectarian conflict in the colony and became part of local Catholic political mythology. However, Butler himself emerged with an enhanced reputation as the most principled of politicians: he was described as a public figure of 'transparent honesty of purpose' by Roger Vaughan (*Sydney Morning Herald*, 12 June 1879), and as 'the most attractive of New South Wales nineteenth-century politicians' (Nairn, 312) in a later historian's assessment.

In 1878 Butler was urged to reduce his workload after heart disease was diagnosed. In the following year he was seriously injured in an accident while driving in the country to investigate a pastoral investment. On his first day back in court, 9 June 1879, he suffered a massive heart attack and 'literally died in [legal] harness' (*Sydney Morning Herald*, 10 June 1879). He was buried in Petersham cemetery two days later after a requiem in St Mary's Pro-Cathedral presided over by Archbishop Vaughan, from which Henry Parkes was a noted absentee.

Five years after arrival in the colony Butler had married Ellen May Connolly at Parramatta on 1 May 1858 (with W. B. Dalley as witness). They had three sons and five daughters. When Ellen Butler died in 1871 there were seven surviving children, of whom the eldest was only ten. Butler regretted that his busy political and legal life restricted the time he could spend with 'my poor little ones' (Butler to Parkes, [1871], Parkes MSS). On 22 April 1875, in the chapel of St John's College, he married Marion Daintrey, who had converted to Catholicism. They had one daughter, Winifred, whose upbringing became the subject of a bitterly contested equity case after the death of her mother in 1889, highlighting the deep religious divisions in New South Wales society which Butler himself had tried to bridge. A. E. Cahill

Sources *Sydney Morning Herald* (12 June 1879) · *Freeman's Journal* [Sydney] (28 June 1879) · *Sydney Mail* (14 June 1879) · B. Nairn, 'Butler, E.', *AusDB*, vol. 3 · B. T. Dowd, 'Edward Butler QC', *Royal Australian Historical Society Journal and Proceedings*, 49 (1963–4), 241–57 · M. Rutledge, 'Edward Butler and the chief justiceship, 1873', *Historical Studies: Australia and New Zealand*, 13 (1967–9), 207–22 · A. Martin, *Henry Parkes: a biography* (1980) · J. M. Bennett, *A history of the New South Wales bar* (1969) · C. G. Duffy, *My life in two hemispheres*, 2 vols. (1898) · T. Carlyle, *Reminiscences of my Irish journey in 1849* (1882) · Mitchell L., NSW, H. Parkes MSS

Archives University of Sydney, St John's College | Mitchell L., NSW, H. Parkes MSS • State Library of Victoria, Melbourne, La Trobe manuscript collection, C. G. Duffy MSS
Likenesses photograph, New South Wales Parliamentary Library, Sydney, Australia

Butler, Edward Dundas (1842–1919), linguist and librarian, was born on 15 October 1842 at 6 Cheyne Walk, Chelsea, London, the son of Thomas Butler and his wife, Jane Isabella, *née* North. Having been educated at Blue Coat School, London, he joined the department of printed books of the British Museum as a transcriber on 31 December 1859 at the age of seventeen. When a separate department of maps was set up in 1867 he was transferred to it, and promoted in 1869, becoming second in command to the keeper. In 1880 he was promoted assistant, first class, and transferred with the map collection back to the main library. His duties included examining and arranging accessions to the collection of maps, preparing the map catalogue for printing, and cataloguing general works in the so-called 'difficult languages', which, in his case, included Hungarian, Finnish, and Romanian. He retired probably on his sixtieth birthday in 1902.

It may be assumed that Butler's interest in the lesser literatures of eastern Europe originated in his training in the British Museum, where Thomas Watts laid special emphasis on acquiring material in neglected languages. Butler proved himself an able translator from Hungarian and Finnish in particular. His translations included a collection of poems and fables from the Hungarian (1877), which *The Academy* (23 June 1877) found 'as suggesting a hope that the Museum still continues to Hungarian literature the enlightened patronage which distinguished it in the time of the late Mr Thomas Watts', as well as a longer piece by János Arany (1881). Butler was also responsible for the first history of Finnish literature in English, translated from the Finnish original of B. F. Godenhjelm (1896). His contributions to the *Encyclopaedia Britannica* (9th edn, 1875–89) and miscellaneous pieces in periodicals revealed the range of his interest.

It is not known whether Butler ever visited the countries whose literature he studied; he certainly established good connections with Hungary, where his activity was followed with interest. As a result of his literary activity he was elected corresponding member of the Kisfaludy Társaság (2 February 1879) and external member of the Hungarian Academy of Sciences (19 May 1881). Contemporary British opinion praised the 'conscientious and faithful rendering of both spirit and form of the original' in his translations (*The Athenaeum*, 3 Nov 1877).

Butler died of heart failure on 11 February 1919 at his home, 66 Whitehall Park, Islington, London, leaving at least one son, Frank. LÓRÁNT CZIGÁNY

Sources L. Czigány, *A magyar irodalom fogadtatása a viktoriánus Angliában, 1830–1914* (1976), 185–90 • L. Czigány, 'Magyar irodalom az Encyclopaedia Britannica tükrében', *Új Látóhatár*, 4 (1961), 369–74 • L. Czigány, 'The László Waltherr Collection', *British Museum Quarterly*, 33 (1968–9), 92–102 • *Révai nagy lexikona*, 4 (1912), 146 • b. cert. • d. cert.
Archives BL
Likenesses photograph, repro. in L. Felberman, ed., *A British tribute to Hungary and its kings* (1907)
Wealth at death £574 5*s*. 3*d*.: probate, 2 April 1919, *CGPLA Eng. & Wales*

Butler, Sir Edward Gerard (1770–1825), army officer, entered the army by purchasing a cornetcy in the 15th light dragoons in 1792. He was at once sent to Flanders on the outbreak of the war in 1793, and on 24 April 1794 was one of the officers of the two companies of his regiment which helped to save the life of the Austrian emperor. Landrecy was closely invested by the Austrian and British armies, when a large French corps endeavoured to raise the siege. This force had moved so rapidly that it was close to the allied lines and on the point of taking the emperor himself prisoner as he was riding along the road almost unattended; General Otto, perceiving the danger, ordered the only cavalry he had at hand—160 of the 15th light dragoons and 112 Austrian hussars—to charge the French, the aim being to save the emperor rather than defeat the enemy. The French panicked and fled, leaving three guns behind. The emperor conferred on the eight British officers present the order of Maria Theresa, and King George III, at the emperor's request, knighted them.

Butler was promoted lieutenant in the 11th light dragoons in May 1794, and he was in 1796 gazetted major without purchase in the newly raised 87th regiment. With it he served in the West Indies in 1797 at Trinidad and Puerto Rico, and he remained in garrison there until 1802. In 1804 he was promoted lieutenant-colonel, and in 1806 the 87th was ordered to form part of the expedition to South America. In both the attack on Montevideo and Whitelocke's attempt on Buenos Aires, where the 87th had 17 officers and 400 men killed or wounded, Butler especially distinguished himself.

From 1807 to 1810, while the 2nd battalion, under Colonel Hugh Gough, was serving in the Peninsula, the 1st battalion of the 87th, under Butler, garrisoned the Cape of Good Hope. In 1810 he was second in command of a force ordered from the Cape to assist Major-General Abercromby in the capture of Mauritius, but it was already taken when they arrived. Although he saw no more service, Butler was promoted colonel in 1811 and major-general in 1814, and made a CB in 1815. He died in Normandy in June 1825.

H. M. STEPHENS, *rev.* DAVID GATES

Sources J. Philippart, ed., *The royal military calendar*, 3 vols. (1815–16) • R. Cannon, ed., *Historical record of the eighty-seventh regiment, or royal Irish fusiliers* (1853) • A. B. Rodger, *The war of the second coalition: 1798–1801, a strategic commentary* (1964)

Butler, Edward Joseph Aloysius [*name in religion* Cuthbert] (1858–1934), abbot of Downside and scholar, was born in Dublin on 6 May 1858, the only child of Edward Butler (*d.* 1902), barrister, and his wife, Mary Cruise (*d.* 1897). His father had been professor of mathematics in Newman's recently established Catholic University in Dublin. Educated at Downside near Bath in Somerset from 1869 to 1875, Butler entered the Benedictine noviciate at Belmont Priory, Hereford, in 1876, taking in religion the name of Cuthbert. There he acquired his lifelong attachment to the spiritual teaching of Augustine Baker and the ascetical practice of manual labour.

In 1880 Butler returned to Downside, where the young Aidan Gasquet was prior, and the liturgical scholar Edmund Bishop—like Butler himself, a virtual autodidact—was a frequent visitor. Butler was ordained priest in 1884 and taught in the school, but his principal interest was the contemporary movement to win traditional monastic autonomy for Downside and the other houses of the English Benedictine congregation. The congregation was at that time a highly centralized body, and the monasteries were viewed principally as 'feeders', providing priests for the numerous Benedictine parishes. The movement's objective was in large part achieved in 1900, when the monasteries became abbeys, and their independent liturgical and intellectual life began to flower.

Meanwhile, in 1896, Butler was sent to Cambridge as the first superior of Benet House, where Downside monks could study at the university, under the auspices of Christ's College. There he edited the *Lausiac History of Palladius* (1898, 1904). After returning to Downside as sub-prior in 1904, he was elected abbot in 1906. Re-elected in 1914 he was also abbot president of the congregation from 1914 to 1921. He published a critical edition of the rule of St Benedict in 1912 and in 1919 published his most respected work, *Benedictine Monachism*, which combines judicious scholarship with many reflections on his own experience. He also published the more controverted *Western Mysticism* (1922).

In the same year Butler resigned the abbacy on a matter of monastic principle: it seems that he failed to win the community's support for his proposal that no monk should be liable under obedience to serve in the outlying Benedictine parishes. Thereafter he lived at Ealing Priory, writing *The Life and Times of Bishop Ullathorne* (2 vols., 1926) and *The Vatican Council* (2 vols., 1930), which is drawn almost entirely from Ullathorne's letters, a narrative that is detailed, fair-minded, and free of all party spirit. He died suddenly of heart failure at Clapham on Easter day, 1 April 1934, and was buried at Downside.

By temperament Butler was a scholar rather than an administrator, and impressed everyone he encountered with his intellectual honesty and sincere piety. As abbot, though he held strongly that a monastery should be a family, he was not himself gifted with the necessary fatherly qualities. Some have also criticized him for allowing the development of Downside School to endanger the monastic observance he restored. But as a teacher and practitioner of a sane and balanced monasticism, it would be hard to find his equal, and his written works on this subject have not dated. Butler received the honorary degree of doctor of letters from Trinity College, Dublin, in 1908.

David Daniel Rees

Sources *Downside Review*, 52 (1934) • private information (1949) • Fasti book, Downside Abbey, near Bath

Archives Downside Abbey, near Bath | Bodl. Oxf., letters to Sir James Marchant

Likenesses W. C. Symons, portrait, 1909, Downside Abbey, near Bath

Butler, Sir Edwin John (1874–1943), plant pathologist and mycologist, was born on 13 August 1874 in Kilkee, co. Clare, the youngest of three sons of Thomas Butler, of Suirville, co. Tipperary, resident magistrate, and his wife, Annie Barry. He was educated first in Gainsborough, Lincolnshire, and from 1897, owing to illness, at home where he had the run of a large library. In 1890 he went to the Christian Brothers' School in Cork, after which he studied medicine at Queen's College, Cork. In 1898 he took the degrees of MB, BCh, and BAO of the Royal University of Ireland, but he never practised. His main interest lay in botanical research and especially in aquatic phycomycetes. Awarded an 1851 Exhibition two-year travelling scholarship, from 1899 he worked in Paris, Antibes, Freiburg, and finally the Jodrell Laboratory of the Royal Botanic Gardens, Kew.

At the end of 1900 Butler was appointed to the new post of cryptogamic botanist to the government of India. Before leaving England he married, in February 1901, Nina, daughter of Alfred John Le Mesurier, head of an old Guernsey family. They had one son and two daughters. On arrival in India Butler's first posting was to Calcutta. In 1902 he was transferred to Dehra Dun, and in 1905 he became the first imperial mycologist at the new agricultural research station at Pusa, Bengal. While in India he published some forty scientific papers on diseases of tropical crops, investigations which provided an authoritative background for his textbook, *Fungi and Disease in Plants* (1918), a landmark for tropical plant pathologists. He also published his classic account of the genus *Pythium* (1907). At the same time, he and his Indian staff, in collaboration with European taxonomic mycologists, began the census which culminated in Butler and G. R. Bisby's *The Fungi of India* (1931).

In 1920 Butler left India to become director of the newly founded Imperial Bureau of Mycology at Kew. After assembling a small staff and laying plans for the abstracting journal, the *Review of Applied Mycology*, Butler visited plant pathologists in the United States and Commonwealth countries to obtain support for the bureau, which flourished. In 1927 it became a unit of the Imperial Agricultural Bureaux as the Imperial Mycological Institute and in 1930 moved into purpose-built accommodation on land leased from the Royal Botanic Gardens, Kew.

In 1935 Butler resigned from the institute in order to join the Agricultural Research Council, of which he became the first paid secretary. After leaving the institute, where he retained a small laboratory which he visited at weekends, Butler's administrative duties were so heavy that he had little time for mycological research. He did, however, find time to complete, with S. G. Jones, the general part of the textbook, *Plant Pathology*, published in 1949.

Butler had an easy manner but his searching cross-questioning gave him a reputation as a somewhat intimidating examiner or assessor for appointments. He was also a practised diplomat, often getting his own way by inducing others to propose the course of action he desired. He was appointed CIE in 1921 and CMG in 1932; he was knighted in 1939, and was elected FRS in 1926. He was president of the British Mycological Society in 1927 and the Association of Economic Biologists in 1928–9, and in 1938, the University of Aberdeen awarded him an honorary LLD. Butler died in the Shiel Nursing Home, Elgin Road, Weybridge, following an attack of influenza, on 4 April 1943. G. C. AINSWORTH, *rev.*

Sources E. W. Mason, *Obits. FRS*, 4 (1942–4), 455–74 · personal knowledge (1993) · *CGPLA Eng. & Wales* (1943)
Wealth at death £5433 12*s*. 4*d*.: probate, 7 July 1943, *CGPLA Eng. & Wales*

Butler, Lady (Charlotte) Eleanor (1739–1829), elder of the two Ladies of Llangollen, was born at Cambrai, the youngest daughter of Walter Butler of Garryricken (1703–1783) and his wife, Eleanor (*d*. 1794), daughter of Nicholas Morres of Latargh, co. Tipperary. Her father was the only lineal representative of James Butler, second duke of Ormond, attainted in 1715 for his Jacobite sympathies, and his estates and titles forfeited. The Irish titles were later claimed by Eleanor's brother, John (1740–1795), and were restored in 1791, when he was acknowledged sixteenth earl of Ormond and his sisters granted the rank of earl's daughters.

Like many upper-class Catholics of the time Eleanor Butler was educated abroad. Under the influence of the French Enlightenment, the intellectual climate of the convent of English Benedictines at Cambrai was both liberal and anti-clerical, and gave her not only 'a certain degree of refinement in literature' according to a friend, but 'a distaste for Irish priests and Irish popery' (Mavor, 27). This was to become uncomfortably evident on her return from France to live at the castle of Kilkenny, where her parents were now ensconced in impoverished and priest-ridden grandeur, and where she was to spend upwards of twelve frustrating and unhappy years. Apparently of too 'satirical' and 'masculine' a cast of mind to make the advantageous marriage that might help restore the family fortunes, she seemed doomed to a life of narrow solitude when, in 1769, and aged almost thirty, she met Sarah Ponsonby.

Sarah Ponsonby (1755–1831), second of the Ladies of Llangollen, was the orphaned daughter of Chambre Brabazon Ponsonby, a cousin of the earl of Bessborough, and had newly arrived to attend school in Kilkenny. She met Eleanor Butler soon after, and it was not long before the Butlers had the strange experience of seeing their difficult bluestocking daughter embarking on a friendship with a schoolgirl of thirteen. Over time the relationship became closer, not only on account of their mutual love of the arts and their strong inclination to lead a life of Rousseauesque 'retirement', but because both women were, in their separate ways, unhappy.

On leaving school Sarah Ponsonby, shy, bookish, and with little money of her own, had gone to live with distant relations at Woodstock House, near Kilkenny. Here her

Lady (Charlotte) Eleanor Butler (1739–1829), by unknown artist, *c*.1810–23 [left, with Sarah Ponsonby]

life was soon plagued by the unwanted attentions of her middle-aged guardian. Meanwhile Eleanor Butler's family, despairing of ever finding her a suitable husband, had, in the interests of economy, determined to send her back to Cambrai. These difficulties drove both women to make secret plans to run away to England and find a cottage where they might live together. Accordingly, on the night of 30 March 1778, disguised as men and armed with pistols, they fled their homes and made for Waterford and the boat for England. Their families caught up with them 2 miles from the port, and they were ignominiously brought back as prisoners. Nothing daunted, Eleanor Butler made a second escape shortly afterwards and joined Sarah at Woodstock. Here, after a lengthy psychological war of attrition, their exasperated relatives at last gave them permission to go away together. Accompanied by Mary Carryll, the devoted Woodstock housemaid, they for a time toured north Wales, finally settling at Plas Newydd, a rented cottage on the outskirts of the village of Llangollen. This, either by luck or good judgement, happened to be one of the main staging posts for travellers between England and Ireland.

They now began to live the 'retirement' that would make them famous. It was a life almost conventual in its simplicity, lived according to a strict timetable, regulated by careful, if not always very accurately kept, accounts, concentrating on good works (though in moderation), self-improvement, reading, gardening, and delicious meals. Two years after setting up house together Queen Charlotte, having heard of them from an increasing number of visitors and admirers (though the terms were not always synonymous), was writing for plans of their cottage and garden. The duke of Wellington was to become a treasured friend; Wordsworth, Southey, and Anna Seward, 'Queen Muse of Britain', were to compose poems upon them beneath the cottage roof. Josiah Wedgwood lectured them on rock formations, Erasmus Darwin called on them with Charles, and John Lockhart with Sir Walter Scott. Mrs Thrale (now Piozzi) wrote of them admiringly, as did Madame de Genlis in *Souvenirs de Félicie*, and there were many others.

In time their comparative poverty was relieved by special pensions from George III, while Louis XVI honoured Lady Eleanor, as she had by then become, with the coveted decoration of the Croix St Louis, and Prince Pückler-Muskau would soon dub them 'the most celebrated Virgins in Europe' (*N&Q*, 4th ser., 4, 1869, 220–21). Yet apart from their aristocratic connections the two women were not, as often supposed, either artists or writers, though Lady Eleanor kept a voluminous journal. Nor, judging from sketches of them and a late double portrait, were they particularly handsome (though their devotees thought otherwise), both ladies being inclined to the embonpoint.

For some, it seems, their fascination lay in the myths of their retirement: that they had both been born on the same day of the same year, that both were orphans, that they later never spent one night away from home—all of which were false—and that they dressed always as men, when in fact they only wore the usual Welsh countrywoman's riding habit and beaver hat. Later down the years and even to modern times they were rumoured to be spies, men dressed as women, suffragettes, or nymphomaniacs. For others their charm lay in the rumoured story of their elopement and the tantalizingly ambiguous nature of their relationship. To yet more the picturesque elegancies and, later, the Gothic extravaganzas of their cottage and its garden proved irresistible. All were convinced, or affected to be, that the two women were perfect living examples of devoted friendship and romantic retirement. They had become icons.

In fact the retirement was not always romantic: it had to survive jealousies, unnerving rows with tradesmen, unpleasant newspaper reports about their private life, disastrous bills, and far too many visitors. Yet it had its highlights, the highest perhaps when they finally managed to purchase their cottage, thus ensuring the continuing safety of their quiet life together. It was a life attached to the seasons, so somewhat repetitive, but a repetition they loved and savoured, finding in it always, as Lady Eleanor regularly insisted, 'Pleasures unknown to Vulgar minds' (Mavor, 157). Lady Eleanor died at Plas Newydd on 2 June 1829, and her friend died there on 9 December two years later. They are buried with their maid, Mary Carryll, beneath a substantial neo-Gothic tombstone in Llangollen churchyard. ELIZABETH MAVOR

Sources E. Mavor, *The ladies of Llangollen* (1971)

Archives CUL, letters • NL Wales, Peniarth MSS, Hamwood MSS (2296–2296); corresp. and household accounts; diaries and papers, SY23.3BU | Denbighshire RO, Ruthin, letters to Thomas Yoole • Essex RO, Harvey MSS • Harvard U., Houghton L., letters to Lady Frances Douglas • JRL, letters to Hester Lynch Piozzi

Likenesses silhouette, *c*.1810–1823, NPG [*see illus.*] • Lady Sitwell, double portrait, watercolour, 1819 (with S. Ponsonby), NL Wales • M. Leighton, double portrait, engraving, *c*.1828 (with S. Ponsonby), Plas Newydd, Llangollen • M. Leighton, double portrait, pencil, 1828 (with S. Ponsonby), priv. coll. • R. J. Lane, lithograph (after M. Leighton), BM, NPG • M. Leighton, portrait, Loton Hall, Shrewsbury • J. H. Lynch, double portrait, lithograph (with S. Ponsonby; after M. Leighton), NG Ire., NPG

Butler [*née* Preston]**, Elizabeth, duchess of Ormond and *suo jure* Lady Dingwall (1615–1684)**, noblewoman, was born on 25 July 1615, the only child and heir of Richard Preston, Lord Dingwall (*d*. 1628), one of James I's gentlemen of the bedchamber, and Elizabeth Butler (1582x1600–1628), the only surviving child of Thomas Butler, tenth earl of Ormond. When the tenth earl died in 1614 a dispute over the Ormond estate was settled by James so that it was divided between the eleventh earl and the Dingwalls, and by the influence of George Villiers, subsequently duke of Buckingham, Dingwall was made Baron Dunmore and earl of Desmond in 1619. Through this award Elizabeth Preston became heir to much of the Ormond estate and the title Lady Dingwall on her parents' deaths in 1628. There had earlier been plans for her to marry George Feilding, Buckingham's nephew, but she showed a preference for her cousin, James *Butler, Viscount Thurles (1610–1688), also a grandchild of the tenth earl, and heir to the title. In return for £15,000 the earl of Holland used his influence in 1629, after Buckingham's death, to persuade Charles I to permit this match and the marriage took place at Christmas of that year. In 1630 the couple went to live at Carrick-on-Suir, co. Tipperary, and between 1632 and 1646 Elizabeth, who became countess on her husband's succession in 1633, gave birth to eight sons, including Richard *Butler, five of whom died as children, and two daughters.

The family was living at Carrick when the 1641 rebellion broke out, and although the earl went to Dublin to command the army, Elizabeth and her children moved to Kilkenny Castle, the Ormond seat but also the confederate capital. Nevertheless she was able to assist English settlers fleeing the rebellion and filled the castle with refugees. She was permitted to rejoin her husband in Dublin in 1642, which she did in the company of some of these refugees, and continued her work of looking after those, particularly children, who had lost all as a result of the rebellion. When, in 1646, the city was under siege, she led a team of women carrying earth in baskets to reinforce the fortifications.

When Ormond departed for England, after surrendering Dublin to the English parliament in 1647, he left his wife behind for a month to discharge his debts. She then joined him in England, but on his decision to go into exile she took up residence at Caen, in France, with the family, where he joined her in 1651 after the failure of his campaign against the Commonwealth forces in Ireland. It became evident that there would not be enough money to support the family, and therefore in August 1652 she left for England with her family to plead with Cromwell for some support from her own Irish estates. Through the intervention of friends, and because she had assisted protestants during the rebellion, in 1653 the English parliament issued an order to permit her to live in her house at Dunmore, co. Kilkenny, and receive £2000 per annum from her estate on condition that she sent no funds to, nor had any contact with, her husband. In fact she received much less than the agreed amount and it was not until 1657 that she was able to move her family to Ireland.

After the Restoration, Lady Ormond rejoined her husband in England, after sending useful political advice from Ireland. Subsequently, as duchess of Ormond (from March 1661), she maintained a household that she deemed in keeping with her husband's rank and the office of lord lieutenant, which he held from 1662 to 1669 and from 1677 to 1685. This at times led to lavish expenditure—one dinner for Charles II cost £2000—but her correspondence also shows that she was anxious to reduce her husband's debts and those of her sons and she spent much time trying to restore as well as beautify the family's estates. Her health began to fail in 1681 and although a visit to Bath in 1683 induced an improvement she died on 21 July 1684 at St James Square, London. She was buried in Westminster Abbey on 24 July, deeply mourned by her husband, who was buried beside her four years later.

M. Perceval-Maxwell

Sources Baroness Burghclere [W. Gardner], *The life of James, first duke of Ormonde, 1610–1688*, 2 vols. (1912) • V. Treadwell, *Buckingham and Ireland, 1616–28: a study in Anglo-Irish politics* (1998) • GEC, *Peerage*, new edn, vols. 2, 4, 10 • *Calendar of the manuscripts of the marquess of Ormonde*, new ser., 8 vols., HMC, 36 (1902–20), vols. 1–7 • W. P. Kelly, 'The early career of James Butler, twelfth earl and first duke of Ormond (1610–1688), 1610–1643', PhD diss., U. Cam., 1997

Archives NL Ire., MSS | Bodl. Oxf., Carte MSS

Wealth at death owned substantial estates in her own right

Butler [*née* Thompson], **Elizabeth Southerden**, Lady Butler (**1846–1933**), military painter, was born on 3 November 1846 at Villa Claremont, Lausanne, Switzerland, the elder daughter of Thomas James Thompson (1812–1881) and his second wife, Christiana Weller (1825–1910). Unusually, her education and that of her sister, the poet and essayist Alice *Meynell (1847–1922), was not entrusted to a governess but was undertaken by her father, a man of independent means and artistic leanings. After spending much of her childhood in Italy, she began receiving professional art training in 1862 and entered the Female School of Art, South Kensington, London, in 1866; she supplemented her studies there with attendance at a private 'undraped female' life class which enabled her to draw figures with confidence in her later work as a battle painter. In 1869 the family moved to Florence and converted to Roman Catholicism. Her first notable work, *The Magnificat* (1872; St Wilfrid's Church, Ventnor), was of a religious subject.

On a visit to Paris in 1870 Elizabeth Thompson found her true métier when she encountered the new, more realistic portrayal of battle being pioneered by painters such as Edouard Detaille and Jean Louis Ernest Meissonier. Her first successful Royal Academy submission, *Missing* (exh. 1873)—a scene of the suffering of ordinary soldiers in the

Elizabeth Southerden Butler, Lady Butler (1846–1933), self-portrait, 1869

aftermath of a battle in the Franco-Prussian War—was an exercise in this manner. The next year, the lessons she had learned in France were applied to a British military subject, *Calling the Roll after an Engagement, Crimea* (exh. RA, 1874; Royal Collection). 'The Roll Call', as it quickly became known, proved to be one of the most popular paintings of the nineteenth century: at the academy, a policeman had to be stationed in front of it for its protection. The painting was subsequently taken on a highly successful solo tour of a number of provincial cities, and engravings of the work and carte-de-visite photographs of the artist—looking young and pretty, completely contrary to what the public would expect a successful battle painter to be like—were sold by the thousand.

During the next few years Elizabeth Thompson exhibited a series of scenes from the Crimean and Napoleonic wars, which were similar in character and composition to 'The Roll Call' with individualized but anonymous soldiers arranged across the canvas and the minutiae of dress and equipment recorded with the utmost accuracy. These works, *The 28th Regiment at Quatre Bras* (exh. RA, 1875; National Gallery of Victoria, Melbourne), *Balaclava* (exh. Fine Art Society, London, 1876; Manchester City Galleries), and *The Return from Inkerman* (exh. Fine Art Society, London, 1877; Ferens Art Gallery, Hull) were also immensely popular. Much was made of the unprecedented sympathy for the suffering and heroism of the ordinary British soldier which they seemed to display, a quality which was deemed especially remarkable because she had never witnessed war at first hand, but explicable in view of her sex; she was a 'Florence Nightingale of the brush' as someone commented. Nevertheless, with hindsight one can see that these works also benefited from the interest in the plight of the less fortunate in society, which was a feature of contemporary art in the 1870s.

In 1879 the success of these works brought Thompson within two votes of election as associate of the Royal Academy, the nearest any woman came to receiving such an honour in the nineteenth century. However, this proved to be the summit of her career. She never again stood for election at the academy, perhaps sensing that the reformist climate of the 1870s, which had seen the academy almost countenance a female associate member, had passed. Subsequently, only *Scotland for Ever!* (exh. Egyptian Hall, Piccadilly, London, 1881; Leeds City Art Gallery), today her best-known painting, enjoyed the kind of acclaim her previous work had received. An important reason for this sudden slump in her popularity was undoubtedly her marriage on 11 June 1877 to an up-and-coming army officer, Sir William Francis *Butler (1838–1910). This brought in its train the duties of child-rearing (she had five children) and the requirement to travel to distant parts of the globe. It also encouraged her to continue with her bleak, untriumphalist approach when tackling subjects drawn from contemporary colonial wars at a time when public taste was for scenes of imperial conquest. Because of his Catholic Irish background William Butler became increasingly critical of Britain's 'imperial mission' and appears to have encouraged her to refrain from glorying in the defeat of ill-equipped native troops in works such as *The Defence of Rorke's Drift, January 22nd, 1879* (exh. RA, 1880); Royal Collection) and *'After the Battle': arrival of Lord Wolseley and staff at the bridge of Tel-el-Kebir at the close of action* (exh. RA, 1885; priv. coll.). By contrast, rival battle painters such as Richard Caton Woodville, Charles Fripp, and William Barnes Wollen—all of whom had learned from her successes of the mid-1870s—felt no qualms about catering to popular taste.

Although Lady Butler continued to paint until 1929 her work was largely ignored—except for a period in the 1890s when she enjoyed something of a revival with Napoleonic subjects such as *Dawn of Waterloo: the 'Reveille' in the Bivouac of the Scots Greys on the Morning of Battle* (exh. Royal Academy, 1895; priv. coll.) and *'Steady the Drums and Fifes!': the 57th (Die-Hards) Drawn up under Fire on the Ridge at Albuera* (exh. RA, 1897; the Queen's regiment, Canterbury). It was not that the character of her work had fundamentally changed, for she continued to celebrate the stoicism of the ordinary British soldier in adversity and danger just as she had half a century before. It was more that as a response to the conditions of modern warfare, particularly those of the First World War, her kind of battle painting now seemed old-fashioned and inappropriate. She died at her residence, Gormanston Castle, co. Meath, Ireland, on 2 October 1933.

Lady Butler has a dual claim to fame. She pioneered a new, more realistic depiction of warfare in British painting, one which was to prove immensely influential at the end of the nineteenth century. And she briefly enjoyed critical and popular success of such magnitude that, for a while, it seemed a new era for women artists in Britain was about to dawn. PAUL USHERWOOD

Sources P. Usherwood and J. Spencer-Smith, *Lady Butler: battle artist, 1846–1933* (1987) • E. Butler, *An autobiography* (1922) • E. Butler, *From sketch-book and diary* (1909) • P. Usherwood, 'Elizabeth Thompson Butler: the consequences of marriage', *Woman's Art Journal*, 9/1 (spring–summer 1988), 30–34 • P. Usherwood, 'Tokenism: the case of Elizabeth Thompson Butler', *Woman's Art Journal*, 11/2 (autumn 1990), 14–18 • J. Oldcastle, 'Our living artists: Elizabeth Butler (née Thompson)', *Magazine of Art*, 2 (1878–9), 257–62 • W. Meynell, 'The life and work of Lady Butler', *Art Annual* (1898), 1–31 [Christmas] • J. W. M. Hichberger, *Images of the army: the military in British art, 1815–1914* (1988) • *The Times* (4 Oct 1933) • *CGPLA Eng. & Wales* (1934)

Archives Hove Central Library, Sussex, letters to Viscount Wolseley and Lady Wolseley

Likenesses E. Butler, self-portrait, oils, 1869, NPG [*see illus.*] • Fradelle & Marshall, carte-de-visite, NPG • lithograph, NPG

Wealth at death £325 2*s.* 2*d.*—in England: probate, 5 Jan 1934, *CGPLA Eng. & Wales* • £310 18*s.* 8*d.*: probate, 14 Dec 1933, *CGPLA Éire*

Butler, Eliza Marian [Elsie] (**1885–1959**), German scholar, was born on 29 December 1885 in Bardsea, Lancashire, third daughter and third of the seven children of Theobald Fitzwalter Butler (1845–1914), a coal owner and iron manufacturer at Barrow in Furness, and his wife, Catherine Elizabeth Barraclough (*d.* 1946). Her father wanted his children educated abroad, and Eliza (Elsie) was dispatched to Hanover. This led to a lifelong preoccupation with German literature and a lifelong scepticism about the Germans. She became a German scholar in spite of herself.

After Hanover, a spell in Paris, and a year at Cheltenham, Butler entered Newnham College, Cambridge, in 1908 and obtained first-class honours in the medieval and modern languages tripos in 1910. Some schoolteaching was followed by research on Friedrich Hebbel in Bonn, where she was put off by what she saw as Germanic academic pettiness and was dismayed by nationalist attitudes. The outbreak of the First World War sent her home, and she taught French, then German at Newnham (with more detested schoolteaching in between), and was once almost arrested as a spy. In 1917–18 she served in the Scottish women's hospitals unit in Russia and Macedonia. Then, after she had taught for two years at Avery Hill Training College, Newnham offered her a lectureship in German. She would have preferred French or Russian.

Still seeking a research topic, Butler turned to Professor J. G. Robertson (1867–1933) in London. He suggested Heine (who also disliked the Germans), and the result was *The Saint-Simonian Religion in Germany* (1926), a large book which she claimed nobody ever read. Her second book was again out of the mainstream, a biography of the eccentric aristocrat Hermann von Pückler-Muskau, *The Tempestuous Prince* (1929), whose ghost she claimed to have met, briefly, in Berlin. Still eager to escape from German, her next involvement, juxtaposing literary and psychological analysis, was with another flamboyant writer in *Sheridan: a Ghost Story* (1931).

After a sabbatical year visiting India with the Pali

Eliza Marian Butler (1885–1959), by Elliott & Fry

scholar Isaline Blew Horner (1896–1981), her companion from 1926 onwards, there appeared Butler's finest work, *The Tyranny of Greece over Germany* (1935). The book is broad in its literary coverage; it is scholarly but highly readable; and it is a polemic. Whatever their own views on the matter, Butler argued, the Germans had not been liberated by Greek ideals, but had become obsessed with a distortion of those ideals while assimilating them less than any other nation. How, she asked, could German Hellenism have produced only pain and dionysiac frenzy, and she raised doubts about accepted views of Goethe and German classicism. The book was, predictably, not translated into German. A visit to Germany in 1936, too, was soured by antisemitism and swastikas.

In 1936 Butler took the Henry Simon chair of German at Manchester University. Though increasingly depressed by the contrast between Germany's literature and its political present, she wrote a biography of another literary individualist, *Rainer Maria Rilke* (1941), aiming again not just to present the poetry, but to dispel some of the Rilke myths. She was appointed in 1944 to the Schroeder chair of German in Cambridge, where her elder sister Kathleen Teresa *Butler was mistress of Girton College. Her inaugural lecture, 'The direct method in German poetry' (25 January 1946) again tried to match German literature with a national psyche that produced Nazism. This led to three books on the ambivalent figure of the magus, which had always fascinated her: *The Myth of the Magus* (1948), *Ritual Magic* (1949), and *The Fortunes of Faust* (1952). These interests prompted her to visit Aleister Crowley (1875–1947), the once-notorious diabolist, and her autobiography makes clear her strong sense of the supernatural. Her not infrequent encounters with ghosts are recounted in her autobiography in a deliberately doubting tone that has the effect of making them entirely believable.

Butler was president of the Conference of University Teachers of German in 1948–9, and retired in 1951, living until her death in London, where she wrote two short novels, *Daylight in a Dream* (1951) and *Silver Wings* (1952), summed up in *The Times* obituary as 'not very good' (14 Nov 1959), a judgement that she had herself ruefully accepted. *Heinrich Heine: a Biography* and *Byron and Goethe: Analysis of a Passion*, both in 1956, were followed by a sparkling autobiography, *Paper Boats* (1959); an incomplete study, *Napoleon and the Poets*, remains in manuscript in the Institute of Germanic Studies, London. Elsie Butler was sceptical but always scholarly, a feature overlooked by those who dismissed her work as frivolous. Her position as an outside observer allowed her to address problems that nationalist literary approaches did not even recognize. While able to respond to the essence of cultures (India, Greece, Russia), she was clearly attracted to a particular type of forceful literary individual, and with Heine, Byron, Pückler-Muskau, Rilke, and the others, she recognized beside their 'star quality' the conflicts between the inner self, the writings, and the image. London and Oxford gave her honorary doctorates in 1957 and 1959. She died at her home, 30 Dawson Place, Bayswater, London, on 13 November 1959, and a memorial service was held on 7 December in King's College chapel, Cambridge. BRIAN MURDOCH

Sources E. M. Butler, *Paper boats* (1959) • W. Muschg, 'Germanistik? In memoriam Eliza M. Butler', *Euphorion*, 59 (1965), 18–45 • *The Times* (14 Nov 1959) • E. Purdie, 'Eliza Marian Butler', *German Life and Letters*, new ser., 13 (1959–60), 154 • I. B. Horner, 'Eliza Marian Butler', *Newnham College Roll Letter* (1960), 34–6 • E. Sagarra and P. Skrine, *The department of German at the Victoria University of Manchester: a brief history, 1895–1996*, rev. J. Purver (1996) • *WWW* • private information (2004) [Newnham College, Cambridge; Institute of Germanic Studies, London] • Burke, *Gen. Ire.* (1958) • *CGPLA Eng. & Wales* (1960)

Archives U. Lond., Institute of Germanic Studies, corresp. and papers | King's AC Cam., letters to G. H. W. Rylands

Likenesses A. R. M. Todd, pastel, 1947, Newnham College, Cambridge • Elliott & Fry, photograph, NPG [*see illus.*] • photograph, Beit Library, Sidgwick Avenue, Cambridge

Wealth at death £11,513 17*s.* 6*d.*: probate, 9 March 1960, *CGPLA Eng. & Wales*

Butler, Fanny Jane (1850–1889), physician and medical missionary, was born on 5 October 1850 at 6 Cheyne Walk, Chelsea, London, the eighth of the ten children of Thomas Butler (*b.* 1809), who worked at the British Museum, and his wife, Jane Isabella North. Only the Butler boys received formal schooling; Fanny, like her sisters, was mostly tutored at home. She spent one year in a girls' school in 1856 and was then taught by her elder brothers and sisters until she attended West London College as a day girl in 1865. At the age of fifteen Fanny became a stay-at-home daughter, helping her mother with the younger children and housework. She regularly attended St Simon Zelotes Church in upper Chelsea, became a Sunday school teacher, and began to admire the heroism and sacrifice of missionaries.

In 1872 Butler was sent to Birmingham to nurse her eldest sister, who showed her an article by William Elmslie, a well-known medical missionary to Kashmir, calling for women medical missionaries to serve the women of India. Butler at first rejected the idea because she did not like the medical women's movement, but later, encouraged by her sisters and parents, she applied to and was accepted by the Indian Female Normal School and Instruction Society in 1874. She passed the preliminary arts examination with the second highest grades out of a total of 123 students, only four of whom were women.

In October 1874 Butler entered the newly opened London School of Medicine for Women (LSMW) with the first batch of fourteen students. The LSMW provided a full course of study even though no medical school in the United Kingdom admitted women to the examinations. Three years later, in 1877, the King and Queen's College of Physicians in Ireland opened the examinations to women. Throughout the debate about providing women with these credentials, stories of suffering zenana-confined women in India had helped to legitimize medical training for British women. Life at the LSMW transformed Butler. No longer confined to the home and domestic duties, she had to overcome her fear of travelling alone and of meeting different people. To promote religious contemplation among her colleagues, Butler started the Bible and Prayer Union. She went to Dublin in 1877 for her first exam, won the first Ernest Hart scholarship, and began attending clinical lectures and hospital practice at the London (later Royal Free) Hospital in the first year that women from the LSMW were admitted to its wards. She won the prize for pathology in the summer session, 1879. In 1880, the year she passed her final exam in Dublin and was awarded the licence of the King and Queen's College of Physicians in Ireland and the licence of midwifery, she also won the prize for anatomy. She went on to become the first qualified English woman medical missionary.

Butler left England on 24 October 1880 under the auspices of the Church of England Zenana Missionary Society, a group which seceded from the Indian Female Normal School and Instruction Society over matters of dogma. She arrived in Jubbulpore, Central Provinces, in December of the same year but language training and a fall from a pony delayed her work. In June 1882 Butler left for Calcutta, where she worked in a small dispensary in a Muslim district of the city. She joined the Zenana Mission House in Bhagalpur, capital of Bihar, in March 1883. During her four years at this dispensary Butler estimated that medical staff saw more than 30,000 patients. Butler left Bhagalpur in March 1887 for an eleven-month furlough. Most of her time was spent in England, visiting family and giving public lectures about conditions in India, but she also studied in the Allegemeine Krankenhaus in Vienna for four months. While on furlough Butler learned that the Church of England Zenana Missionary Society had agreed to send her to Kashmir. In March 1888 she left England, arriving in Srinagar in May.

When Butler arrived missionaries were allowed to winter in Kashmir but not to live in Srinagar. A new clinic, opened on 13 August 1888 in the centre of the city, served patients three days a week when Butler travelled 4 miles from the mission quarters by boat or pony. Hundreds of women and children came to see the woman doctor; Butler estimated that she had seen more than 5000 patients before the year was out. Butler did not know Kashmiri and had to use a translator for both her medical and religious work. She began the day with prayers that included her servants and boatman, delivered a religious address to those assembled for morning treatment, and then again in the afternoon to a new group of patients. She spoke in Hindustani while her Muslim porter translated. In her account of how many patients had been seen since the opening of the clinic, Butler claimed that at least 2000 had heard 'the Word'. In December 1888 Miss Newman, a nurse, and Miss Rainsford, a woman with some medical knowledge, joined Butler. This team saw 8832 outpatients, had 75 hospital patients, and performed 500 operations in the first seven and a half months of 1889. Butler commented most frequently on two medical problems in Kashmir: eye diseases and burns resulting from the indigenous practice of carrying containers of hot ashes and coals inside clothing for warmth.

By the summer of 1889 most of the small mission staff were ill. However, by September they were all recovered sufficiently to undertake a tour—setting up tents, seeing thousands of people who needed medical attention, and preaching. When they returned to Srinagar for the laying of the foundation stone for a new building, on 12 October, the first of a complex to include a dispensary, mission house, and hospital, Butler was too ill to attend. Her dysentery became worse during the week and by the 25th she had peritonitis. On 26 October 1889 she collapsed and died that same day at 5.30 p.m. Her boatman, accustomed to taking her to the city to see patients, now rowed her body to the small cemetery in Srinagar where she was buried. Butler's early death in Kashmir made her a martyr to the cause of saving Indian women through a double cure: medical and spiritual. Following her death a scholarship was established at the LSMW and her story inspired others to take up work in India.

As a child Butler had impressed people with her practical approach to duty. Throughout her medical training she was praised for her diligence but seemed to enjoy herself only when caring for infants in the hospital. In India she was well known for her hard work, seeing patients from sunrise to sunset with little time for relaxation. Her only relief from work came with prayer, alone or with her patients. During these years she wrote about her work for mission publications and while on furlough made some presentations but neither articles nor speeches thrilled people. Her directness has been called by one biographer a real hindrance to her success; to some she seemed harsh and cold. At the same time her contemporaries praised her devotion to people in need. Butler's own writing about the people she helped suggests that, while she treated their medical and spiritual bodies with compassion, she deplored their habits and had no respect for their social and religious institutions. GERALDINE FORBES

Sources E. M. Tonge, *Fanny Jane Butler: pioneer medical missionary* (Church of England Missionary Society) · J. L. M., 'Fanny Jane Butler, L.K.Q.C.P.I. and L.M.', *Medical Missions at Home and Abroad*, 3 (1890), 52–9 · F. J. Butler, 'A letter from Kashmir', *Medical Missions at Home and Abroad*, 2 (1889), 279–81 · 'Editorial jottings', *The Indian Female Evangelist*, 10/73 (1890), 205–8 · A. Burton, 'Contesting the zenana: the mission to make "lady doctors for India", 1874–1885', *Journal of British Studies*, 35 (1996), 368–97 · R. Fitzgerald, 'A "peculiar and exceptional measure": the call for woman medical missionaries for India in the later nineteenth century', *Missionary encounters: sources and issues*, ed. R. A. Bickers and R. Seton (1996), 174–97 · R. Fitzgerald, '"Rescue and redemption": the rise of female medical missions in colonial India during the late nineteenth and early twentieth centuries', *Nursing history and the politics of welfare*, ed. A. M. Rafferty, J. Robinson, and R. Elkan (1996), 64–79 · 'The Women's Medical Mission, Kashmir', *Medical Missions at Home and Abroad*, 3 (1889), 5–6 · 'The C.E.Z.M.S. Medical Missions', *Medical Missions at Home and Abroad*, 9/5 (1902), 69–73 [by the editor] · *Medical Missionary Record*, 5/3 (1890), 57–62 · Mrs J. T. Gracey [A. R. Gracey], 'Miss Fanny Jane Butler, MD: first medical woman to Kashmir', *Eminent missionary women* (1898), 132–41 · b. cert.
Likenesses drawing, repro. in Tonge, *Fanny Jane Butler* · drawing (after photograph), repro. in Gracey, 'Miss Fanny Butler, M.D.', 133 · photograph, repro. in J. L. M., 'Fanny Jane Butler', 52–9, 53
Wealth at death £68 1s. 6d.: administration with will, 27 June 1890, *CGPLA Eng. & Wales*

Butler, Frank Hedges (1855–1928), motorist and aviator, was born in London on 17 December 1855, the fifth son of James Butler, wine merchant, of Hollywood, Wimbledon Park, and his wife, Frances Mary, eldest daughter of William Hedges. He was educated at private schools at Brighton and Upper Clapton to 1870 and, after travelling in Europe, Africa, and South America, entered the family business of Hedges and Butler (founded in 1667), Regent Street, London, in which he became a partner in 1882. He married in 1880 Ada (*d.* 1905), daughter of Joseph Bartholomew Tickle, wool broker, of London and Sydney, and with her had one daughter, Vera (later Vera Nicholl), who shared many of his motoring and ballooning adventures.

Hedges Butler was one of the first people in Britain to own a motor car. He acquired a Benz car in 1897, joined the Automobile Club de France, and then was appointed first honorary treasurer of the newly formed Automobile Club of Great Britain, a post which he held until 1902. With the Hon. Charles Stewart Rolls, he helped to organize races from 1898. It was the shortcomings of a motor car, and the consequent abandonment of a motor tour in Scotland in September 1901, which led Hedges Butler to turn his attention to the air. A balloon ascent was suggested instead of the tour, and Butler, his daughter, and Rolls went up in a balloon, the *City of York*, from the Crystal Palace, with Stanley Spencer in control. While in the air over London, he suggested the formation of an aero club as a branch of the Automobile Club. The Aero Club of the United Kingdom was registered at Somerset House in October 1901, and the first balloon ascent organized by the club took place on 15 November.

Frank Hedges Butler (1855–1928), by William Morris, 1923

The club (which in 1910 became the Royal Aero Club) brought together inventors and recreational balloonists, and supplied them with a ground at Shell Beach, Isle of Sheppey, suitable for their experiments. Hedges Butler also took a keen interest in the beginnings of powered flight, and in 1908, when the American inventor Wilbur Wright arrived in France to demonstrate his aeroplane, Butler was one of the first two Englishmen to fly as passenger with him.

By 1907 Hedges Butler had completed one hundred balloon ascents, including a solo flight which established a record for distance in Britain (1902), and what was then the world's longest cross-channel balloon voyage (London to Caen, 1905).

As a result of the successful flights by Wilbur Wright in France in 1908, the Aero Club undertook the training of aeroplane pilots, to whom, from 1910 onwards, it issued its certificates; these were recognized by the government when it was decided to establish the Royal Flying Corps. The Aero Club, inspired by Hedges Butler, in fact played an all-important part in fostering the early development of flying in England. Hedges Butler's concern with the air diminished in no way his interest in travel. In the course of his business he often visited the wine-producing regions of Europe—including Champagne in 1914–18, even when fighting was only a few miles away—but these journeys only stimulated his enthusiasm, and with great enjoyment he moved widely about the world. He had been elected FRGS in 1877.

Hedges Butler had still other interests. He was a violinist of merit, and in 1894 founded the Imperial Institute Orchestral Society, in which he played one of the first violins. He was a man of hospitable nature with a gift for friendship, who enjoyed splendid health, as well as ample means to indulge his many enthusiasms. He died in a nursing home at 29 Wimpole Street, London, on 27 November 1928 and was buried in Norwood cemetery three days later. H. A. JONES, *rev.* JULIAN LOCK

Sources C. G. G., *The Aeroplane* (5 Dec 1928), 912 · *The Times* (28 Nov 1928) · F. Hedges Butler, *Fifty years of travel by land, water, and air*

(1920) • *WWW, 1916–28* • L. T. C. Rolt, *The aeronauts: a history of ballooning, 1783–1903* (1966) • D. D. Jackson, *The aeronauts* (1981) • private information (1937) • *CGPLA Eng. & Wales* (1929)

Likenesses W. Morris, bronze medal, 1923, NPG [*see illus.*] • Spy [L. Ward], caricature, Hentschel-colourtype, NPG; repro. in *VF* (11 Dec 1907) • photograph, Hedges & Butler Ltd, London

Wealth at death £5,261 8*s*. 2*d*.: probate, 30 Jan 1929, *CGPLA Eng. & Wales*

Butler, Sir (George) Geoffrey Gilbert (1887–1929), historian and politician, was born at 55 Harrington Gardens, Kensington, London, on 15 August 1887, the ninth son of Spencer Perceval Butler, conveyancing counsel of Lincoln's Inn, and his wife, Mary Kendall. He belonged to a distinguished academic family: he was a nephew of Henry Montagu Butler, George Butler (1819–1890), and Arthur Gray Butler. Sir Montagu Sherard Dawes *Butler and Sir (Spencer) Harcourt *Butler were his brothers. Educated at Clifton College, where he later became a school governor, Butler matriculated at Trinity College, Cambridge, in 1906, taking first class in both parts of the historical tripos, and was elected to a major college scholarship in his third year. He won the chancellor's medal for English verse, edited the *Cambridge Review*, and was president of the union in his fourth year. In June 1910 he was offered a fellowship at two colleges simultaneously. He chose that at Corpus Christi College where, as college lecturer and director of studies in history, he 'set out to make the teaching of that subject a vital factor in the college as a whole' (Bury, 241). In 1912 he became librarian, taking charge of the college's inestimable collection of manuscripts and incunabula created by Matthew Parker at the dissolution of the monasteries.

In 1913 Butler published an edition of the Edmondes papers and in 1914 a series of lectures, *The Tory Tradition*. He was, however, first and foremost a historian of international relations and of modern diplomatic history. According to his friend Sir William Spens, 'He regarded a European war in the near future as highly probable … [and] he did his best to ensure that the undergraduates of his college should have some idea of what war would mean' (*DNB*). When the First World War broke out he was prevented by disability from military service. In the spring of 1915 he went to the Foreign Office, where he joined the news department, which was at the forefront in presenting the British perspective to the new media of foreign neutrals, especially to the United States. Here he had the advantage of knowing America, for in 1913 and 1914 he had been a visiting lecturer at the University of Pennsylvania. In 1916 he returned to lecture at the same university, and while there he married, on 17 November 1916, Elizabeth Levering Jones (*b*. 1892), eldest daughter of Joseph Levering Jones, a corporate lawyer of Philadelphia. They had no children. In 1917 he returned to America as part of the foreign secretary Arthur Balfour's mission. He remained in New York until 1919 as director of the British bureau of information, a post in which he fostered Anglo-American relations and for which he was made KBE (1919).

Butler returned to Cambridge in 1919, and was soon afterwards appointed praelector in diplomatic history at Corpus. He devoted himself to three things: 'to his duties as librarian of Corpus, and in particular to rearranging and cataloguing the incunabula and making the manuscripts more accessible; to his historical teaching; and to promoting conservative principles, as he understood these, among the undergraduates of the university' (*DNB*). During these post-war years Butler published a number of books: *Studies in Statecraft* (1920); *Guide to an Exhibition of Historical Authorities of British History* (1920), derived from the college manuscript collection; *A Handbook to the League of Nations* (1925); and in 1928 *The Development of International Law*, written in conjunction with one of his former pupils. The first-named expounded to a wider audience his views on international relations and international law, particularly on the developing League of Nations. In it he argued strongly that the league should move cautiously and not to try to do too much before it had established its influence and authority.

A convinced Conservative, Butler saw that the coming of representative democracy at the end of the First World War had transformed the British parliamentary system, and realized that in order to meet these new challenges his party had to embrace a reformist platform. An obituarist described him as a 'Conservative of the new school' (Bury, 242). Within the university Butler tried to ensure the political education of like-minded undergraduates by developing the then new Cambridge University Conservative Association (CUCA) into 'a regular school for young Conservatives of ever growing value to the party' (Bury, 242). At the general election of 1923 he was returned as the Conservative MP (burgess) for the university. His talents were quickly recognized, and in 1925 he joined the Conservative ministry as parliamentary private secretary to Sir Samuel Hoare, the secretary of state for air. Butler introduced Hoare to his college, which quickly became his intellectual base. Butler's skills were also put to use in a number of other ways. He was a member of a Home Office committee on legal aid and a prominent member of the 1927 Donoughmore commission, which investigated the constitution of Ceylon. During these years Butler served on the council of the Royal Historical Society, as a syndic of the Cambridge University Press, and as secretary of the university's newly created board of research studies. His government and university duties came together with the formation of the Cambridge University air squadron, the first ever at a British university and one that trained many of the fighter pilots who later distinguished themselves in the Second World War.

Butler's health failed in the late 1920s, and after a business trip to the United States he died of cancer of the liver and of the stomach at 21 Bentinck Street, Marylebone, London, on 2 May 1929. He was commemorated by Corpus Christi College through several benefactions, and what was then the new students' library was named after him. Family members presented the college with his portrait together with a tankard with his chancellor's medal inset. PETER MARTLAND

Sources *DNB* • P. Bury, *The college of Corpus Christi and of the Blessed Virgin Mary: a history from 1822 to 1952* (1952), 240–42 • Templewood papers, CUL • b. cert. • m. cert. • d. cert.
Archives CCC Cam., papers • Trinity Cam., corresp. and papers | CUL, Templewood papers, corresp. • King's Lond., Liddell Hart C., corresp. with Sir B. H. Liddell Hart
Likenesses photograph, repro. in Bury, *The college of Corpus Christi*, pl. 40 • portrait, CCC Cam.
Wealth at death £11,022 6s. 1d.: probate, 1929, *CGPLA Eng. & Wales*

Butler, George (1774–1853), headmaster and dean of Peterborough, was born in Pimlico, London, on 5 July 1774, being the second son of the Revd Weeden *Butler the elder (1742–1823), and Anne, daughter of Isaac Louis Giberne. He was educated in his father's school, Cheyne Walk School, Chelsea, and then became a foundation scholar of Sidney Sussex College, Cambridge, where he was senior wrangler and senior Smith's prizeman (January 1794), graduated BA in the same year, and took his MA in 1797 and his BD and DD in 1804 and 1805 respectively. He was admitted at Lincoln's Inn in 1794. In the same year his college elected him a fellow. On his subsequent appointment as a mathematical lecturer, and later as classical tutor, he abandoned the law as a career. In these years he travelled extensively, undertaking a tour of Germany on foot in 1795, and acting as tutor to B. P. Blachford (*c*.1784–1816), later an MP, in France, Italy, and Sicily during 1802. He was elected a public examiner at Cambridge in 1804, and in 1805 was nominated one of the eight select preachers before the university. In April 1805 he became headmaster of Harrow School in succession to Dr Joseph Drury after a highly contentious election in which the boys favoured the internal candidate, Mark Drury. The subject of virulent poetical attacks by Byron, Butler experienced disciplinary problems throughout his headmastership, including a rebellion by the boys in 1808. He frequently resorted to flogging, as Anthony Trollope later attested. He introduced competitive examinations and encouraged physical exercise. A succession of scandals and misfortunes led to a serious fall in pupil numbers during the 1820s, and the school governors persuaded him to resign in 1829. The accumulation of fees and income from boarders during his twenty-four years as headmaster left him comfortably off. He retired to the rectory of Gayton, Northamptonshire, to which his college had presented him in 1814. In November 1836 he was named chancellor of the diocese of Peterborough, and he was appointed by Sir Robert Peel to the deanery of Peterborough on 3 November 1842.

Few men could compete with Butler in versatility of mind and in the variety of his accomplishments. Besides his great mathematical attainments he was also a distinguished classical scholar, and spoke German, French, and Italian with correctness and fluency. He was practically versed in chemistry and other branches of physical science. He excelled in all athletic activities, and was awarded, when nearly seventy, the medal of the Royal Humane Society for rescuing a woman from drowning. His affection for Harrow School, in the service of which so many of the most active years of his life had been passed, amounted to a passion, and he published in 1849 a selection of the school lists, 1770–1828.

Butler married, on 18 March 1818, Sarah Maria, eldest daughter of John Gray of Wembley Park, Middlesex. They perpetuated a fruitful dynasty of academics and public servants. Four sons obtained distinguished honours at the universities: George *Butler, Spencer Perceval, Arthur Gray *Butler, and the youngest, Henry Montagu *Butler, who was headmaster of Harrow from 1859 to 1885. Butler's latter years were years of suffering; in 1849 he developed heart trouble, and a gradual failure of sight ensued, ending in almost total blindness. His death was quite sudden; while seated at table with his family he became rapidly insensible, and in the course of ten minutes passed away, almost without a struggle, at the deanery, Peterborough, on 30 April 1853. He was buried at Gayton church. A monument by Richard Westmacott to the memory of Butler was erected in Harrow church in July 1854.

G. C. Boase, *rev.* M. C. Curthoys

Sources *GM*, 2nd ser., 39 (1853), 559, 662–4 • *GM*, 2nd ser., 42 (1854), 153–4 • *ILN* (7 May 1853), 343 • *ILN* (18 June 1853), 483 • *ILN* (16 Sept 1854), 257–8 • Venn, *Alum. Cant.* • N. G. Annan, 'The intellectual aristocracy', *Studies in social history: a tribute to G. M. Trevelyan*, ed. J. H. Plumb (1955), 241–87 • E. Graham, *The life of Henry Montagu Butler DD* (1920) • Boase, *Mod. Eng. biog.* • C. Tyerman, *A history of Harrow School, 1324–1991* (2000)
Archives Bodl. Oxf., corresp. • Harrow School, Middlesex, corresp. and papers as headmaster of Harrow | BL, corresp. with Sir Robert Peel, Add. MSS 40245–40605, *passim* • Devon RO, letters to Sir Thomas Dyke Acland
Likenesses R. J. Lane, lithograph (after F. W. Wilkin), BM, NPG

Butler, George (1819–1890), headmaster and Church of England clergyman, born at Harrow, Middlesex, on 11 June 1819, was the eldest of the ten children of George *Butler (1774–1853), headmaster of Harrow School, and his wife, Sarah Maria, eldest daughter of John Gray of Wembley Park, Middlesex. Butler attended Harrow School from April 1831 and in October 1838 went up to Trinity College, Cambridge. He and his father felt he had made a poor start there (despite being placed in the first class in the first-year examinations) and, after tutoring from Augustus Short, he migrated to Exeter College, Oxford, matriculating in October 1840. In 1841 he won the Hertford scholarship at Oxford, and was elected a scholar of Exeter College. In 1842 he was elected Petrean fellow in that college, and in 1843 he took a first class in classics, graduating BA in 1845 and MA in 1846. Among his friends at Oxford were J. D. Coleridge, J. A. Froude, and George Ferguson Bowen. He visited Ireland with Froude during the famine in 1845 (both catching smallpox). He then tutored Lord Hopetoun in Scotland, and took reading parties to Germany and the Lake District. To his father's disappointment, he declined to be ordained, having 'no internal call, nor inclination for the Church' (Wainwright, 118). In 1848 he was appointed to a tutorship at Durham University; while working there, he met his future wife.

In 1850 Butler returned to Oxford, where he was for several years a public examiner, and in 1852 he vacated his fellowship at Exeter by his marriage, on 8 January 1852, to Josephine Elizabeth (1828–1906) [*see* Butler, Josephine

George Butler (1819–1890), by unknown photographer, in or before 1890

Elizabeth], fourth daughter of John *Grey (1785–1868) and his wife, Hannah Annett. They had three sons and a daughter, Eva, whose early death in 1864 greatly upset both parents. His marriage made George Butler more decisive and he seems also to have gained conviction from his wife's strong, sometimes mystical, faith. Butler's religion can be best described as broad-church in the tradition of Arnold and Stanley. In 1852 he introduced the first geography lectures at Oxford (writing on the subject in *Oxford Essays*), and afterwards gave lectures on art in the Taylor building, publishing his lectures in 1852 as *Principles of Imitative Art*. Butler treated his wife as an equal in scholarly life: they collated editions of Chaucer's poems in the Bodleian and worked on Italian art. They began to take on cases of social injustice. They 'prayed together that a holy revolution might come about and that the Kingdom of God might be established on the earth' (Butler, 102). The Butlers met W. E. Gladstone at Exeter College in 1853, and played some part in the movement to reform the university. In 1854 Butler was ordained deacon as curate of St Giles's, Oxford, and in 1855 priest, publishing *Village Sermons* (1857). In 1855 he was classical examiner to the secretary of state for war, and in 1856 examiner for the East India Company's civil service. Butler continued to be active in Oxford. He was honorary secretary to the new University Museum and from 1856 to 1858 he was principal of Butler's Hall, a private college at Oxford, to which he gave his name; it was one of the few private halls to be founded under the 1854 Oxford University Act.

The damp Oxford climate affected his wife's health, and in 1857 Butler accepted the post of vice-principal of Cheltenham College. As a schoolmaster, Butler was seen as one of the century's most progressive. He was an intellectual muscular Christian, as well known for coaching sports as the classics and geography—for which he compiled *The Public Schools Atlas* of modern geography (1872) and of ancient geography (1877). He was seen as a natural headmaster and when an invitation came in 1865 to be principal of Liverpool College he accepted it, his wife recalled, 'as providential' (Butler, 164); they also welcomed the change from Cheltenham because of its associations with the death of Eva.

The Butlers flourished in Liverpool, whither they moved in January 1866; tory Cheltenham had been politically stifling. In Liverpool Butler reorganized the school, reformed the curriculum, introducing systematic science, and raised educational standards. He failed to persuade his governors to arrange that Liverpool College students might be granted degrees after one year at Durham, but in 1878 he was one of those who founded a University College in Liverpool. Butler's emphasis on winning scholarships to Oxbridge colleges gained Liverpool College much acclaim but was felt by some to unbalance it. The college declined in the late 1870s and numbers fell: 'Butler was tired and exhausted: indiscipline was rife … and he had almost lost control' (Wainwright, 150). Meanwhile, his wife involved herself in social action, frequently away from home. Together they supported the North of England Council for the Higher Education of Women and assisted James Stuart, who organized in Liverpool what became the university extension scheme. In the holidays, the Butlers travelled widely in the UK and Europe.

George Butler was a staunch participant in the campaign for the abolition of the Contagious Diseases Acts, which made his wife famous. He supported her unwaveringly, often discreetly but sometimes openly, as with his paper 'The duty of the Church of England in moral questions', which was partly read to the church congress in Nottingham in 1872, but was howled down. Butler met this onslaught laconically. In 1873 he organized a clerical memorial on the acts, which was presented to Gladstone as prime minister. The Butlers were active in other causes also, and were strongly liberal in politics (though they made little headway with Gladstone personally over contagious diseases). With Josephine quite often absent campaigning, George readily played a leading role in dealing with the destitutes and prostitutes who found the Butlers' home a welcome place of refuge.

By the early 1880s George Butler was exhausted by teaching, and suffered from depression. Moreover, the Butlers' involvement in the contagious diseases campaign was not well regarded by many of his college's governors, who were in addition alarmed at the college's decline. In March 1882, under pressure from them, he resigned. Gladstone, who with his father had been a founder of the college, and had spoken at the prize-giving of 1872 (Butler's best year for Oxbridge awards) was sympathetic to his friend's plight. In the face of blistering opposition on the contagious diseases question from Queen Victoria, he appointed Butler a canon of Winchester in 1882, the installation being on 7 August 1882. The same year Butler was given an honorary DD at Durham. His health revived, though he continued to be periodically depressed. In Naples in 1889 he caught influenza during the great epidemic. He returned to London seriously ill and died at the Grosvenor Hotel, Victoria, on 14 March 1890. He was buried in the cemetery at Winchester. His wife's memoir of her husband (n.d. [1892]) reflects a burning love, but is as much autobiography as biography. For all his many gifts, George Butler was eclipsed by his wife's bright light in the memoir as much as in his life; certainly he did not regret the latter. H. C. G. Matthew

Sources J. E. Butler, *Recollections of George Butler* (1892) • J. E. Butler, *An autobiographical memoir*, ed. G. W. Johnson and L. A. Johnson (1909) • *DNB* • D. Wainwright, *Liverpool gentlemen: a history of Liverpool College* (1960) • P. McHugh, *Prostitution and Victorian social reform* (1980) • J. R. Walkowitz, *Prostitution and Victorian society: women, class and the state* (1980) • Gladstone, *Diaries* • R. Symonds, *Inside the citadel: men and the emancipation of women, 1850–1920* (1999) • *CGPLA Eng. & Wales* (1890)
Archives Northumbd RO, Newcastle upon Tyne, family corresp.; papers; sermons | BL, corresp. with W. E. Gladstone, Add. MSS 44374–44503, *passim*
Likenesses photograph, in or before 1890, NPG [*see illus.*]
Wealth at death £8903 8*s*. 6*d*.: probate, 19 April 1890, *CGPLA Eng. & Wales*

Butler, George Slade (**1821–1882**), antiquary, was born on 4 March 1821 at Rye, Sussex, the son of Richard Weeden Butler, surgeon, and his third wife, Rhoda Jane, only daughter of Daniel Slade. He was educated at a private school in Brighton, was admitted a solicitor in Hilary term 1843, and built up a considerable practice in Rye, where he served as clerk of the peace from 1843 and as town clerk from 1875.

Butler became an early member of the Sussex Archaeological Society in 1846–7. In its *Collections* he published four papers on the history of Rye (1861–70), and, in four parts (1863–6) later reprinted as a single volume, *Topographica Sussexiana*. This was the first published attempt at a bibliography for the county and drew heavily on lists prepared in the British Museum Library by Sir Henry Ellis. He was elected a fellow of the Society of Antiquaries in March 1862. He died in Rye on 11 April 1882.

Gordon Goodwin, *rev.* John H. Farrant

Sources *Hastings and St Leonards News* (21 April 1882) • *Hastings and St Leonards Independent* (13 April 1882) • *Kelly's directory of Sussex* (1862); (1874); (1878) • L. A. Vidler, *A new history of Rye* (1934) • BL, Sir Henry Ellis's lists of Sussex books, Add. MS 37039 • *CGPLA Eng. & Wales* (1882)
Wealth at death £3105 8*s*.: administration, 22 May 1882, *CGPLA Eng. & Wales*

Butler, Sir (**Spencer**) **Harcourt** (**1869–1938**), administrator in India, was born in London on 1 August 1869, the second of the nine sons of Spencer Perceval Butler, barrister, of Lincoln's Inn, conveyancing counsel to the office of works, and his wife, Mary, only child of the Revd Nicholas

Sir (Spencer) Harcourt Butler (1869–1938), by Walter Stoneman, 1930

Kendall of Bodmin. He was the brother of Sir (George) Geoffrey Gilbert *Butler and Sir Montagu Sherard Dawes *Butler. He was educated at Harrow School, then under the headmastership of his uncle Henry Montagu *Butler and, after passing the Indian Civil Service examination in 1888, spent his probation at Balliol College, Oxford. In October 1890 he began his Indian career in the North-Western Provinces (renamed in 1902 the United Provinces of Agra and Oudh). In 1894 he married Florence, daughter of Francis Nelson Wright of the Indian Civil Service. Butler first received particular notice as secretary in 1901 of the famine commission presided over by Sir Antony (afterwards Lord) MacDonnell. The report which he drafted was for many years the standard authority on Indian famine prevention and relief. For this work he was appointed CIE. Later honours were the CSI (1909), KCSI (1911), GCIE (1923), and GCSI (1928).

As deputy commissioner of Lucknow district (1906–8) Butler enhanced the beauty and amenities of the capital of Oudh. At the close of 1907 the viceroy, Lord Minto, took him from this post to be secretary of the foreign department, which then had charge of both external relations and those with the Indian states. Three years later (1910) he was appointed to the viceroy's executive council in charge of the new department of education, which included within its scope public health, local self-government, archaeology, and several minor branches. In 1913 he formulated a memorable government resolution which reshaped policy towards higher education. From now on the principle of expansion through five affiliating institutions was abandoned in favour of the establishment of independent teaching and residential universities. This set the pattern for the expansion of university education in India for the rest of the century.

In 1915 Butler went to Rangoon as lieutenant-governor of Burma. By his development for the use of the allies of the output of wolfram concentrates from the Tavoy fields he broke the virtual monopoly which the Germans had acquired in the manufacture of tungsten, a valuable agent in the production of munitions. Butler also did much to awaken a new spirit in Burma, notably by raising a large sum by public subscription for the foundation of Rangoon University, thereby ending the inconvenient and unsatisfactory affiliation of the colleges of Burma to Calcutta University, across the Bay of Bengal.

Early in 1918, when his term in Burma had run only half its course, Butler went as lieutenant-governor to the United Provinces. He allayed serious agrarian unrest in Oudh by reconciling the landowning *talukdars* to a policy of tenancy reform. The Montagu–Chelmsford reforms, coming into force under the 1919 Government of India Act on 1 January 1921, initiated the system of provincial 'dyarchy', which gave elected Indian ministers considerable authority over fields of government 'transferred' to them; and the heads of provinces became governors. Like Lord Willingdon in Madras, Butler encouraged joint consultations between the two halves of his government—the 'reserved', with executive councillors, and the 'transferred', with ministers responsible to the legislature.

Butler had the unique experience of introducing the dyarchical system into two great provinces. The second of these was Burma, where the reforms took effect two years later than in peninsular India. As governor from the beginning of 1923, he nursed the area's public consciousness, but never concealed from higher authority the dangers of instability and the need for less exiguous defence measures. He took prompt steps to bring to an end slavery and human sacrifice, as practised by the Nagas in the unadministered territory bordering on the Hukawng valley, which he visited in 1925.

Butler left Rangoon at the end of 1927, and accepted the chairmanship of the Indian states committee, which looked into relations between the Indian princes and British power. Reporting in 1929, it reaffirmed the doctrine of 'paramountcy', but laid down guiding principles on its application and on equitable financial relations between British India and the states. In 1931 he accepted the chairmanship of the governing body of the School of Oriental and African Studies, London University. He joined the boards of the Peninsular and Oriental Steamship Company, the National Provincial Bank, and other concerns. His occasional writings include his concise and fascinating *India Insistent* (1931).

Sir Harcourt Butler died from heart disease and gout in the Hospital for Tropical Diseases, St Pancras, London, on 2 March 1938. He was survived by his wife and only son, Victor. His gifted personality was well summed up by Sir John Hewett, one of the most distinguished of his predecessors in the headship of the United Provinces:

> He had a brilliant intellect, boundless energy, and wonderful capacity for getting at the root of a matter, ability to express his conclusions so as to be clear to all, and a very practical head in carrying them out. Butler was a wonderful host. His fondness for music added greatly to the charm of his entertainments.

Indeed, his social skills were an important factor in his successful career.

F. H. BROWN, *rev.* FRANCIS ROBINSON

Sources *The Times* (3 March 1938) · *The Times* (7 March 1938) · *Journal of the Royal Central Asian Society*, 25 (1938) · BL, Harcourt Butler MSS · private information (1949) · personal knowledge (1949) · d. cert.

Archives BL OIOC, corresp. and papers, MS Eur. F 116 | BL, corresp. with Sir John Clague, MS Eur. E 252 · BL, letters to Lord Reading, MS Eur. E 238, F 118 · BL OIOC, letters to Sir Basil Blackett, MS Eur. E 397 · BL OIOC, letters to Y. FitzRoy, MS Eur. E 312 · Bodl. Oxf., corresp. with Sir Aurel Stein · CUL, corresp. with Lord Hardinge · Isle of Wight RO, Newport, letters to Joan Oglander · News Int. RO, letters to Geoffrey Dawson · NL Scot., corresp. with fourth Earl Minto · U. Hull, Brynmor Jones L., letters to Forbes Adam | SOUND IWM SA, oral history interview

Likenesses G. H. Thomas, statue, *c.*1925, Lucknow, India · W. Stoneman, photograph, 1930, NPG [*see illus.*] · G. H. Thomas, statue, *c.*1931, Rangoon, Burma

Wealth at death £22,785 6*s.* 7*d.*: resworn probate, 25 March 1938, *CGPLA Eng. & Wales*

Butler, Sir Harold Beresford (1883–1951), civil servant, was born in Oxford on 6 October 1883, the elder son in the family of two sons and two daughters of Alfred Joshua Butler (1850–1936), fellow and bursar of Brasenose College and a noted Coptic scholar, and his wife, Constance Mary Heywood, a granddaughter of Marcus G. Beresford, archbishop of Armagh. He was a scholar of Eton College and a Brackenbury scholar and Jenkyns exhibitioner of Balliol College, Oxford, where he was captain of the hockey eleven. After obtaining a first class in *literae humaniores* he was elected a fellow of All Souls College in 1905.

Butler's early ambition was to enter the Foreign Office and after a year at All Souls he went to Germany and France, where he obtained a knowledge of the countries and their languages which later proved of great value to him. There were, however, no vacancies in the Foreign Office and he entered the Local Government Board in 1907, transferring to the Home Office in the following year.

In 1910 he married Olive Augusta Newenham, daughter of Samuel Abraham Walker Waters, assistant inspector-general of the Royal Irish Constabulary, of Stillorgan, co. Dublin. They had one daughter and two sons. Their younger son was the historian Rohan D'Olier *Butler.

Butler had his first experience of international work as secretary to the British delegation to the conference on aerial navigation in 1910. Although he was a captain in the Inns of Court Officers' Training Corps, he was refused permission to join the forces on the outbreak of war in 1914. His section of the Home Office, concerned with blockade measures, was ultimately merged with the corresponding section of the Foreign Office as the foreign trade department, of which he became secretary in 1916. A year later he was transferred to the newly created Ministry of Labour at the insistence of the parliamentary secretary and fellow Etonian, W. C. Bridgeman. His role was to inject some administrative expertise, denied to the ministry by the political appointment of two trade unionists as minister and permanent secretary, and to develop a long-term industrial strategy. For two years he exerted a radical influence, about which he was later wistful (Butler, 134, 145). He recruited committed Labour sympathizers to compile weekly reports for the war cabinet, to counter its relative ignorance of industrial matters, and to encourage industrial self-government, particularly through the spread of Whitley councils and trade (wages) boards. His commitment to 'home rule for industry' placed him at odds with the centralizing bias of existing labour administrators such as William Beveridge. 'No system of bureaucratic control', he argued, could succeed in Britain because of people's innate belief in 'their competence to manage their own affairs' and the effective resolution of problems being dependent on the genuine commitment of those involved (Lowe, 67–8). These were the firmly held views which guided him as he moved from the national to the international stage.

In 1918, with Edward Phelan and in a somewhat more tense relationship with Malcolm Delevingne, Butler drafted a programme for the labour section of the Versailles peace conference. It was adopted and he was appointed secretary to the organizing committee and then the secretary-general of the first labour conference, held in Washington in 1919. Here the constitution of the International Labour Organization was agreed, based on Butler's novel principle of equal representation for government, employers, and workers. The conference faced serious difficulties as it had neither independent staff nor funding and the American government, having failed to ratify the peace treaty, was unable to participate. Its eventual success was largely due to Butler's diplomatic and administrative skill. He narrowly failed, however, to be elected the provisional director because there were obvious objections to men of the same nationality holding the senior posts in both the League of Nations (of which Sir Eric Drummond was the first secretary-general) and the International Labour Office. Instead he was appointed deputy director of the office, based in Geneva, under Albert Thomas, with particular responsibility for administration and finance. He was able to build up an efficient international staff and to counteract any tendency to over-centralization.

Butler succeeded Thomas as director in 1932 in the depths of the depression which made international co-operation increasingly difficult. His term of office demonstrated his commitment to international co-operation, although he was realistic about the possibilities for change. He showed himself to be a man of vision, but not a visionary: a Conservative with strong Labour sympathies and a man of deep-rooted principle.

Butler's first practical concern was to induce America to join the organization, which it did in 1934. Believing that the centre of gravity in the world was shifting away from Europe, he sent his staff to give technical advice to overseas governments, established an overseas section of the office, and in 1934 induced the conference to enlarge the governing body so that seven non-European countries were among the sixteen governments represented. He initiated regional conferences in the belief that many problems were of regional rather than universal significance. Throughout his term of office he also insisted that attention be paid to the economic conditions which lay behind the social problems.

In 1938 Butler resigned under pressure from the French government (Alcock, 155) and shortly afterwards accepted the post of first warden of Nuffield College, Oxford. There he had time only to lay plans, as on the outbreak of war he was appointed southern regional commissioner for civil defence and, after returning to the college in January 1942, he went to Washington, DC, in May of that year as head of the British information service. He resigned from the wardenship in June 1943, having helped to initiate the Social Reconstruction Survey, directed by G. D. H. Cole, to inform the planning of the transition from peace to war. He remained in Washington until his retirement in 1946, after which he was prominent in the movement for closer European co-operation. He was appointed CB in 1919 and KCMG in 1946.

During the Second World War Butler wrote the first of his three books, *The Lost Peace* (1941), on the inter-war years. This was followed in 1947 by *Peace or Power* and in 1950 by *Confident Morning*, the first volume of an uncompleted autobiography. He died at the Dunedin Nursing Home, Bath Road, Reading on 26 March 1951.

RODNEY LOWE

Sources *International Labour Review* (April 1951) • H. Butler, *Confident morning* (1950) • *The Times* (28 March 1951) • personal knowledge (1971) [*DNB*] • private information (1971, 2004) • R. Lowe, *Adjusting to democracy: the role of the ministry of labour in British politics, 1916–1939* (1986) • A. Alcock, *History of the International Labour Office* (1971) • H. Scott, *Your obedient servant* (1959), 38 • *The modernisation of conservative politics: the diaries and letters of William Bridgeman, 1904–1935*, ed. P. Williamson (1988) • I. Elliott, ed., *The Balliol College register, 1833–1933*, 2nd edn (privately printed, Oxford, 1934) • N. Chester, *Economics, politics, and social studies in Oxford, 1900–85* (1986) • *CGPLA Eng. & Wales* (1951)

Archives BLPES, corresp. with Lord Beveridge • Bodl. Oxf., corresp. with L. G. Curtis • Bodl. Oxf., letters to Sir Alfred Zimmern • PRO, ministry of labour papers, LAB 2/218/16, LAB 2/212/7, LAB 2/212/13, LAB 2/454/1, LAB 2/1804/1

Likenesses W. Stoneman, photograph, 1948, NPG • F. Eastman, oils, Nuffield Oxf.

Wealth at death £18,876 3*s*. 6*d*.: probate, 4 July 1951, *CGPLA Eng. & Wales*

Butler, Henry [Enrrique Botelero] (*d.* **1652**), composer and viol player, was identified by Spanish court documents as a native of Sussex and a gentleman of quality in England before taking service as a musician in the royal court of Spain from 7 September 1623; his life prior to this is otherwise unknown. His employment began while the prince of Wales was in Madrid seeking to marry the Infanta Maria, but no connection has been established between the prince's arrival at the court and Butler's position there. In 1625 James Wadsworth the younger described Butler among English fugitives in the Spanish court, stating: 'Moreover there is one M. *Henry Butler*, which teacheth his Catholike Maiesty to play on the Violl, a man very fantasticall, but one who hath his pension truely payd him for his fingers sake' (Wadsworth, 63).

Philip IV elevated Butler to the position of *gentilhombre de casa* on 28 February 1637. This honour entitled him to a more generous clothing allowance than that of many other musicians or of the painter Diego Velázquez. Trips to England were approved in 1632 and 1636. On one occasion the king sent Butler to Portugal to escort some Irishmen, and in 1644 Butler travelled to Rome, possibly on diplomatic business (Subirá, 223).

Confirmation of Butler's musical accomplishments came from the seventeenth-century writers Christopher Simpson and Jean Rousseau. His twenty known works include two preludes and thirteen sets of divisions on grounds for bass viol (viola da gamba) and basso continuo, and an aria and three sonatas for violin, bass viol, and basso continuo. (A set of divisions and one sonata are also ascribed to other composers.) The remaining work, an untitled sonata-like composition for bass viol and basso continuo, may be the earliest 'sonata' for solo instrument and basso continuo written by an English composer. Other distinguishing aspects of Butler's music are its demand for a virtuoso bass viol technique and its use of features of both English and Italian musical styles. Details surrounding Butler's death at the end of March 1652 remain unknown. He left an heir and executor, Don Juan Isidro de Butler. ELIZABETH V. PHILLIPS

Sources Archivio General de Palacio, Madrid, Spain, Sección Administrativa, MSS Capilla, legajos 1115, 1135, 1137; MS Casa. Mercedes, raciones, gages, legajo 866; MS Casa. Vestuarios, legajo 973; MSS Expedientes personales, cajas 137/20, 150/4; MS Oficios de la Real Casa, Guardajoyas, legajo 902 • J. Wadsworth, *The English Spanish pilgrime* (1629); 2nd edn (1630); 2nd edn corrected (1630) • C. Simpson, *Chelys, minuritionum artificio exornata: the division-violist, or, The art of playing ex-tempore upon a ground*, 3rd edn (1712) • J. Rousseau, *Traité de la viole* (Paris, 1687); facs. edn (1965) • E. V. Phillips, 'The divisions and sonatas of Henry Butler', PhD diss., Washington University in St Louis, 1982 • *Henry Butler: collected works*, ed. E. V. Phillips (1991) • J. Subirá, 'Dos músicos del Rey Felipe IV: B. Jovenardi y E. Butler', *Anuario Musical*, 19 (1964), 201–23

Archives Bibliothèque du Conservatoire Royal de Musique, Brussels, MS Litt. XY, no 24.910 • Bodl. Oxf., Mus. Sch. MSS C.71, D.249 • Durham Cath. CL, Mus. MSS D.2, D.5, D.10 • GL, Gresham Music Library, Mus. MS 369 • priv. coll. • Royal College of Music, London, II.F.10 (2) | NYPL, Drexel 3551

Butler, Henry Montagu (1833–1918), college head, was born at Gayton, Northamptonshire, on 2 July 1833. Ninth child of Dr George *Butler (1774–1853), headmaster of Harrow School and dean of Peterborough, and his wife, Sarah Maria, daughter of John Gray of Wembley Park, Middlesex, he was the grandson of Revd Weeden *Butler the elder. His brother George *Butler (1819–1890), canon of Winchester, married the social reformer Josephine Butler (1828–1906). Educated at Olney School, Olney, Eagle House School, Hammersmith, and Harrow School (1846–51) under Dr C. J. Vaughan, Butler was a high achiever,

Henry Montagu Butler (1833–1918), by Sir William Rothenstein, *c*.1916

becoming head of school and Gregory scholar. He entered Trinity College, Cambridge, in 1851, where he excelled, winning the Battie prize (1853) and Porson prize (1854). President of the Union Society, scholar of the college, Bell university scholar, senior classic, BA and fellow in 1855, and DD in 1865, Butler was assistant tutor at Trinity in 1855–6 and 1858–9, spending the year between touring the Far East. Between 1856 and 1858 he was private secretary to William Francis Cowper at the Board of Health; secretary to the 1857 royal commission on the National Gallery; curate at Great St Mary's, Cambridge; and ordained a deacon in 1859.

Aged twenty-six, following the unexpected resignation of Dr Vaughan, Butler was appointed headmaster of Harrow School, and remained there for twenty-six years. Over thirty published testimonials praised his suitability to be the first Old Harrovian headmaster. A traditionalist, sensitive to the entrenched views of able, long-established staff, yet aware of the need to modernize, he adopted a patient, pragmatic approach. Butler made some important curricula reforms: in science, influenced by his brother-in-law, Francis Galton, and in music, by appointing John Farmer, who inaugurated the famous Harrow songs. Butler selected other distinguished staff, including Reginald Bosworth Smith and Frederick William Farrar. Noted for the variety, morality, and thoroughness of his teaching, Butler established good relationships with boys and staff, taking a personal interest in their welfare. He initiated new building at Harrow, notably the Vaughan Library, established in 1861, which later included a stained-glass memorial window to his first wife. Butler appealed to Old Harrovians for funds to build a sanatorium, and extended the headmaster's house and the cricket fields. He gave lengthy evidence to the 1864 Clarendon commission into public schools, which recognized improvements at Harrow under himself and Vaughan. He piloted the school through a difficult period after the commissioners' controversial recommendation that governors should have more say in the curriculum. The demands of school management led to serious illness in 1881. His wife, Georgina, died in 1883, and when offered the deanery of Gloucester in 1885 he accepted. However, he never settled, remaining only fifteen months, but he did manage to introduce popular music into cathedral services to appeal to the general public. When the opportunity arose to become master of Trinity in 1886 he was delighted.

As master, Butler presided rather than ruled over deans, tutors, and fellows in an increasingly lay society. Noted for his conciliatory skills and stature as the public face of Trinity, his pre-eminence was such that he became vice-chancellor of the university in 1889/90. Butler was an Apostle, a member of the select Cambridge debating society dominated by Harrow and Trinity intelligentsia, of which he was president in 1865.

As at Harrow, Butler's meticulous memory and attention to detail ensured impeccable organization of college functions. His sense of history was strong; he added considerably to Trinity memorabilia but was disappointed when his plan to extend the Wren Library was rejected and a simpler annexe built instead. Although Butler always strove for moderation and unity, beneath a mild exterior he could be firm and resolute, adopting an independent approach to outside interference. At Harrow he frequently preferred his colleagues' views to those of the governors; in 1861 he married without consulting the governing body. Not afraid openly to criticize colleagues, he castigated Bertrand Russell's condemnation of the First World War as a dereliction of duty, Russell being relieved of his lecturership in 1916. Butler himself sometimes took personal criticism badly, becoming depressed when he was unable to convince others of his opinions. On his eightieth birthday, however, his Trinity colleagues praised his charm, dignity, style, and good humour. A warm, sympathetic, and loyal friend and employer, Butler could be disarmingly self-deprecating. At Harrow he confessed to deficiencies in mathematics and natural sciences; at Trinity he agreed he was not as academically pre-eminent as his predecessors.

Butler was Christian rather than sectarian, and at Cambridge became a practical link between different denominations. A Liberal, he advocated national schooling to tackle the problem of deprivation. Influenced in his youth by F. D. Maurice, he was committed to the cause of working-class education and helped establish a working men's college in Cambridge; he supported the university extension scheme and, as *ex officio* manager of Roxeth national school, promoted scholarships for elementary school boys. He founded the Harrow Mission in 1882, bringing aid to a poor area of west London, and advised the 1895 Bryce commission on secondary education that poor students should receive financial help. With the aid of his second wife, Agnata, who was placed by examiners above the senior classic at Cambridge in 1887, Butler supported degrees for women and was a member of Girton College council. Criticized as a shallow popularist who favoured his friends, his unswerving self-confidence was seen by some as vanity. A caricature in *The Granta* (1889) depicted Butler as very aware of his own goodness—and the failings of others. Although he campaigned to foster modern languages at both school and university, Butler was criticized for allowing classical composition to predominate. He was essentially a teacher, not an educationist.

On 19 December 1861 Butler married Georgina Isabella (*d*. 1883), daughter of Edward Francis Elliot of Madras and granddaughter of Hugh Elliot (1752–1830), minister at the court of Frederick the Great. Georgina died in December 1883. On 9 August 1888, a few months after he had met her at a performance of a Greek play, Butler married Agnata Frances [*see* Butler, Agnata Frances (1867–1931)], daughter of the historian Sir James Henry *Ramsay, bt (1832–1925) of Bamff, the classical scholar, and his first wife, Elizabeth Mary Charlotte. There were two sons and three daughters from the first marriage, three sons from the second. Butler had a wide social circle, with Alfred Tennyson, Matthew Arnold, Charles Kingsley, John Ruskin, A. E. Housman, and G. O. Trevelyan among his friends. With a phenomenal memory and wit, he was a popular after-dinner speaker. Tall and slender as a young man, he was talented at cricket, football, and boxing, but restricted from playing through poor health. He loved Italy, enjoyed mountaineering, and belonged to an alpine club; in later life he enjoyed walking in the Cambridge countryside. Strongly opposed to smoking, regarding it as unseemly, later portraits show him as a benign elder statesman. Although feeble in his final years, his mind remained active.

Butler excelled at classics, writing and translating Latin and Greek poetry and memorial epitaphs. He was a passionate composer of sermons, which were highly praised as eloquent and uplifting. An excellent letter writer, his correspondence with people of various persuasions revealed many interests, but his publications were meagre. His chief works included volumes of school and university sermons, *Chatham as an Orator* (1912), *Some Leisure Hours of a Long Life* (1914), and *Ten Great and Good Men* (1909), which he acknowledged was light reading. Butler was honorary chaplain to the queen (1875–7); examining chaplain to archbishops Tait and Benson (1879–83); select preacher at Oxford (1877, 1878, 1882, 1899); select preacher at Cambridge (1879, 1885, 1887, 1889, 1890, 1895–8, 1903, 1906, 1913); prebendary of Holborn in St Paul's Cathedral (1882–5); honorary canon of Ely (1897); and governor of Harrow (1901).

Following a short bronchial attack, Butler died at Trinity lodge, Cambridge, on 14 January 1918. The archbishop of Canterbury officiated at his funeral at Trinity, and A. E. Housman composed a Latin inscription for the commemorative brass in the ante-chapel. Among the condolences was one from George V. He was buried at Harrow School on 17 January, survived by his wife. The first son from his second marriage, Sir James Ramsay Montagu *Butler (1889–1975), historian, lived his life in Trinity and was his father's biographer. Sir Nevile Montagu Butler (1893–1973), diplomatist, was another of his sons from this marriage. H. M. Butler was thus a central figure of Noel Annan's 'intellectual aristocracy'. JANET SHEPHERD

Sources *DNB* · *The funeral of the Reverend Henry Montagu Butler, DD*, Harrow School, Middlesex, archives · *Harrow School register*, Harrow School, Middlesex, archives · H. M. Butler, *Some leisure hours of a long life* (1914) · 'Oh the pity of it', *The Granta* (1889), 8–9 · *Testimonials in favour of the Rev. H. Montagu Butler: fellow and assis. tutor of Trinity College, Cambridge … candidate … headmastership … Harrow School* · CUL, Acton MSS, Add. MS 8119 · CUL, Stewart MSS · E. Graham, *The Harrow life of Henry Montagu Butler, D.D.* (1920) · J. R. M. Butler, *Henry Montagu Butler: master of Trinity College, Cambridge, 1886–1918* (1925) · *The Times* (15 Jan 1918) · W. C. Lubenow, *The Cambridge Apostles, 1820–1914* (1998) · N. G. Annan, 'The intellectual aristocracy', *Studies in social history: a tribute to G. M. Trevelyan*, ed. J. H. Plumb (1955), 241–87 · J. R. de S. Honey, *Tom Brown's universe: the development of the Victorian public school* (1977) · J. Roach, *Secondary education in England, 1870–1914* (1987)

Archives Harrow School, Middlesex, corresp., headmaster's book, and sermons · Trinity Cam., corresp., diaries, and papers | BL, letters to W. E. Gladstone, Add. MSS 44413–44526 · BL, corresp. with Macmillan & Co., Add. MS 55111 · Bodl. Oxf., letters to Sir William Harcourt · Bodl. Oxf., letters to Hastings Rashdall · Bodl. Oxf., corresp. with J. G. Wilkinson [incl. some copies] · CUL, letters to Lord Acton · CUL, corresp. with Lord Hardinge · CUL, Kelvin MSS · CUL, letters to H. F. Stewart · CUL, letters to Sir George Stokes · Durham Cath. CL, letters to J. B. Lightfoot · King's Cam., letters to Oscar Browning · Leics. RO, letters to R. F. Martin · LPL, corresp. with Edward Benson · LPL, letters to A. C. Tait and papers · NL Scot., letters to Sir Charles Dalrymple · Trinity Cam., George Butler MSS · Trinity Cam., Fitzgerald MSS · Trinity Cam., Frazer MSS · Trinity Cam., Houghton MSS · Trinity Cam., W. Lamb MSS · Trinity Cam., Pethick Lawrence MSS · Trinity Cam., Myers MSS · Trinity Cam., letters to Sir Henry Babington Smith · Trinity Cam., R. C. Trevelyan MSS

Likenesses G. F. Browning, drawing, 1851, Trinity Cam. · photograph, 1855, Trinity Cam. · H. von Herkomer, oils, 1885, Harrow School, Middlesex · caricature, lithograph, 1889, repro. in *The Granta* [Cambridge] · lithograph, 1903, repro. in *VF* · W. Orpen, oils, 1911, Trinity Cam. · W. Orpen, oils, 1911, FM Cam. · E. O. Hoppé, photograph, 1913, Trinity Cam. · W. Rothenstein, chalk drawing, 1916, Trinity Cam. · W. Rothenstein, pencil drawing, *c*.1916 (version of chalk drawing, 1916), NPG [*see illus.*] · Elliott & Fry, photographs, Trinity Cam. · E. Glazebrook, four photographs, Trinity Cam. · Hay, caricature, watercolour study, NPG; repro. in *VF* (18 May 1889) · Hills & Saunders, carte-de-visite, Trinity Cam. · W. Orpen, oil study, RA · F. Sternberg, engraving, Trinity Cam. · F. Sternberg, mezzotint (after H. von Herkomer, 1887), BM, NPG · F. Sternberg, photograph (after W. Orpen), Trinity Cam. · E. Walker, oils (after W. Orpen), Trinity Cam. · W. B. Wollen, oils (after H. von Herkomer), Trinity Cam. · cartoons, Trinity Cam., Wren Library · pencil sketches, Trinity Cam., Wren Library · photograph (as young man), Trinity Cam. · photographs, Trinity Cam., Wren Library

Wealth at death £12,656 12*s*. 1*d*.: probate, 1 March 1918, *CGPLA Eng. & Wales*

Butler, James, first earl of Ormond (*c*.1305–1338), magnate, was the eldest surviving son of Edmund *Butler (*d*. 1321) and his wife, Joan, daughter of John fitz Thomas *Fitzgerald (*d*. 1316), who was created earl of Kildare in 1316. He married in 1328 Eleanor de Bohun (*d*. 1363), daughter of Humphrey (VII) de Bohun, earl of Hereford (*d*. 1322), and granddaughter of Edward I, an alliance that augmented the Butlers' English properties. James's name may reflect his father's devotion to Santiago de Compostela, for in 1320 Edmund, his wife, and son were released from a vow to visit the shrine of St James. James, who was in Ireland when Edmund died at London, was summoned to England and by February 1323 was a yeoman (*valettus*) in Edward II's household. In 1325 the king granted him his lands and marriage before he was of full age and the court speeded his return to Ireland where his lordships in Munster and Leinster were threatened by Irish raids. The first steps of his career were thus taken during the ascendancy of the Despensers, who established links with several leading Anglo-Irish families. Their fall in 1326 left Ireland unstable and the new rulers of England uncertain of the allegiance of the magnates. James Butler was drawn into regional feuds and was among those who received reprimands from England between December 1326 and June 1328. At that point, however, his father's close relations with Roger Mortimer (Edmund had been justiciar of Ireland during Mortimer's lieutenancy in 1317–18 and they had negotiated a marriage alliance in 1321), and the search for stability in Ireland on the part of the Mortimer regime, worked to his advantage. At the Salisbury parliament in October 1328, where Mortimer became earl of March, James Butler was created earl of Ormond and given a life-grant of the liberty of Tipperary, which in the event his descendants were to hold until 1716. At the same time his marriage to Edward III's cousin drew him towards the apex of aristocratic society.

The new earl's career was often dominated by campaigns against the native Irish who threatened his lands in Tipperary and south Leinster. In 1329, for instance, he burnt the territory of the Ó Nualláin family in Carlow in revenge for the capture of his brother; and in 1336 he made a compact with the Ó Ceinnéidigh family of north Tipperary, in which they agreed to provide rent and military service, while Ormond accepted arrangements for mutual compensation between the Irish and the English settlers. His role in Irish marcher society was compatible with a career on a wider stage and could indeed be used to advertise his indispensability. The fall of Mortimer in 1330, and the resumption of grants made under his influence, rendered Ormond's gains of 1328 vulnerable. Faced by the strong methods of the justiciar, Anthony Lucy, the earl crossed to England and spent part of 1332 at his town of Aylesbury, subjecting Edward III to petitions in which he stressed his military services in Ireland, his relationship to the royal house, and the antiquity of his family and its possession of the butlerage of Ireland since the time of King John. As well as protecting his threatened endowments, he obtained financial rewards. His relations with

Edward were further advanced when he led a retinue of 318 men from Ireland to the Scottish campaign of 1335.

Ormond died on 16 or 18 February 1338 at Gowran, Kilkenny, before his intention to endow a Franciscan house at Carrick-on-Suir in Tipperary was carried through. The Kilkenny chronicler, Friar John Clyn, an admirer of the Butler family, lamented his death: he was 'a generous and amiable man, elegant and courteous; in the bloom of youth the flower withered' (*Annals of Ireland*, ed. Butler, 28). Ormond was buried with his father at Gowran. Inquisitions taken at his death show that, besides his Irish lordships, he had property in ten English counties, all held jointly with his wife, who by 1344 had married Sir Thomas Dagworth. The earl was succeeded by his surviving son, James *Butler, who was granted his lands in 1347 while still under age. ROBIN FRAME

Sources *Chancery records* • PRO • E. Curtis, ed., *Calendar of Ormond deeds*, IMC, 1: *1172–1350* (1932) • C. A. Empey, 'The Butler lordship', *Journal of the Butler Society*, 1 (1970–71), 174–87 • R. Frame, *English lordship in Ireland, 1318–1361* (1982) • *The annals of Ireland by Friar John Clyn and Thady Dowling: together with the annals of Ross*, ed. R. Butler, Irish Archaeological Society (1849) • J. T. Gilbert, ed., *Chartularies of St Mary's Abbey, Dublin: with the register of its house at Dunbrody and annals of Ireland*, 2, Rolls Series, 80 (1884) • *CEPR letters*, 2.196; 3.263–4 • G. O. Sayles, ed., *Documents on the affairs of Ireland before the king's council*, IMC (1979) • *RotP* • *CIPM*, 8, no. 184
Archives NL Ire., deeds

Butler, James, second earl of Ormond (1331–1382), magnate and justiciar of Ireland, was the only surviving son of James *Butler, the first earl of Ormond (*c.*1305–1338), and his wife, Eleanor de Bohun (*d.* 1363), a granddaughter of Edward I. His kinship to Edward III, his extensive lordships in southern Ireland, and the fact that he was the only Irish magnate with significant estates in England, made him a crucial link between the two countries at a time when the colony was badly affected by plague and by a Gaelic military and cultural recovery. According to the annals of John Clyn, he was born at Kilkenny in 1331. After his father's death in 1338 he remained with his mother until 1344. A tussle then ensued for his custody between the dowager countess and her husband, Sir Thomas Dagworth, and Maurice fitz Thomas Fitzgerald, first earl of Desmond (*d.* 1356); as a by-product of this Desmond ravaged the Butler lands in Tipperary. Early in 1346 Edward III gave the custody to John Darcy, the former justiciar of Ireland, and in the same year James married Elizabeth, daughter of Darcy and his wife, Joan de Burgh, widow of the second earl of Kildare. In February 1347 the king admitted him to his inheritance, saying he wished for his service overseas, and he crossed to France.

Ormond was back in Ireland by 1350, when he had a life grant of the constableship of Dublin Castle. His career made progress in 1355–6, when he attended the Michaelmas parliament at Westminster and served on the Scottish expedition. It suffered no long-term harm in 1357, when he arrested John Bolton, the deputy justiciar, and held him captive at Waterford. This action may have been provoked by a dispute over military policy, since Ormond had been appointed chief keeper of the peace throughout Kilkenny and Tipperary. The king reprimanded him and summoned him to England. But in 1358 he had the keeping of the peace throughout all Munster; and in March 1359 he was appointed justiciar in succession to Almaric de St Amand. By this time he was an experienced warrior and marcher diplomat who had created a web of alliances in the southern midlands. He made contracts with English and Irish leaders, including members of the Howell, de Burgh, Purcell, Power, Ó Ceinnéidigh, Ó Mechair, Ó Cearbhaill, and Mac Con Mara lineages. Most involved military service. Those with the Irish often included agreements about the occupation of land and arrangements for the settlement of disputes according to the custom of the marches. One was sealed in his mother's presence at his manor of Shere Vachery in Surrey during his visit to England in 1358, when he brought Edmund Ó Ceinnéidigh with him.

Ormond's service as justiciar from March 1359 to September 1360 was the most significant phase of his career. He quickly summoned great councils at Waterford and Dublin to obtain taxation for the war in Leinster, and established garrisons on the routes around Carlow and Gowran which were threatened by Art Mac Murchadha and his allies. In the summer of 1359 he commanded a force which confronted Mac Murchadha and the Ó Mórdha near Athy in Laois. It was probably this episode that was recalled some sixty years later, when James Yonge of Dublin, writing a work of instruction for the fourth earl, bade him emulate:

> the deeds of the noble, victorious earl, Sir James, your grandsire, which in all his time lechery hated. And therefore God in all his time granted him marvellous victory upon his enemies with few people, namely upon the O'Mores, of which he slew huge people in the red moor of Athy, a little afore the sun going down, standing the sun marvellously still till the slaughter was done. (Steele, 129)

In July 1360 Ormond summoned a great council to Kilkenny where a petition was drawn up, itemizing the problems Ireland faced and begging Edward III to send a powerful leader, backed with English troops and money. Ormond crossed to England in the autumn and attended the Westminster parliament early in 1361. There the expedition of the king's son, Lionel, was announced, in terms that echoed the Kilkenny petition. Ormond was closely associated with Lionel's rule, acting as justiciar during his absence between April 1364 and January 1365.

The earl held the justiciarship again between 1376 and 1379, supported by 120 men-at-arms and 200 archers whose wages were charged on the English exchequer. The Dublin government was virtually bankrupt at this period, but his own affairs were in better shape. In 1372 he had received a grant of the liberty of Tipperary, which he had held for life, for himself and his heirs. At the same period he was expanding his influence on the south coast by acquiring the trading town of Youghal and the manor of Inchiquin from its absentee lords. The impression he made on some may be seen in an action of Richard Wye, bishop of Cloyne. Preaching in Dublin Castle before the king's lieutenant, the earl of March, in December 1380, the bishop created a scandal by interpolating into the mass the words 'eternal God, there are two in Munster who destroy us and our goods, the earl of Ormond and the earl of Desmond with their followers, whom in the end the Lord will destroy' (Curtis, 2.173). When March died suddenly a year later, Ormond refused the justiciarship, ostensibly because of the need to defend his own lands, but more probably because of the expense the office entailed.

Ormond, who in 1379 had made his will at Shere, where he wished to be buried if he died in England, died at his castle of Knocktopher in Kilkenny on 18 October or 6 November in 1382, and was buried at Gowran. The Dublin annals describe him as 'a strong and eminent knight at arms, whom no enemy ever conquered' (Gilbert, 2.285). In 1364 he had granted protection and privileges to the Cistercian abbey of Holycross, close to Cashel, which flourished under his successors. He left his gold and silver vessels to his wife, who lived until 1390, and to his son, James *Butler, who succeeded him. ROBIN FRAME

Sources *Chancery records* • E. Curtis, ed., *Calendar of Ormond deeds*, 6 vols., IMC (1932–43), vols. 1–2 • PRO • H. G. Richardson and G. O. Sayles, eds., *Parliaments and councils of mediaeval Ireland*, IMC, 1 (1947) • A. J. Otway-Ruthven, *A history of medieval Ireland* (1968) • R. Frame, *English lordship in Ireland, 1318–1361* (1982) • C. A. Empey, 'The Butler lordship', *Journal of the Butler Society*, 1 (1970–71), 174–87 • GEC, *Peerage* • R. Steele, ed., *Three prose versions of the 'Secreta secretorum'*, EETS, extra ser., 74 (1898) • *A descriptive catalogue of ancient deeds in the Public Record Office*, 3 (1900), 440 • R. Stalley, *The Cistercian monasteries of Ireland* (1987) • *CIPM*, 15, nos. 696–709 • J. T. Gilbert, ed., *Chartularies of St Mary's Abbey, Dublin: with the register of its house at Dunbrody and annals of Ireland*, 2 vols., Rolls Series, 80 (1884–6) • *The annals of Ireland by Friar John Clyn and Thady Dowling: together with the annals of Ross*, ed. R. Butler, Irish Archaeological Society (1849)

Archives NL Ire., deeds

Butler, James, third earl of Ormond (*c.*1360–1405), magnate and justiciar of Ireland, was the son of James *Butler, second earl of Ormond (1331–1382), and Elizabeth (*d.* 1390), daughter of Sir John Darcy. He was about twenty-three when he was granted custody of his lands on 2 March 1383. As head of a great lordship centred on Tipperary and Kilkenny, Ormond played a key role in Anglo-Irish affairs. He was justiciar in 1384–5, 1394–5, and in 1404. Richard II clearly regarded him as the premier Irish earl when he appointed him as justiciar during his first expedition to Ireland. The Irish annalists readily acknowledged him as 'head of the chivalry of Ireland' at his death.

This leadership did not go unchallenged. Like his father, Ormond became embroiled in a lifelong struggle against his neighbours and tenants, the earls of Desmond, notwithstanding the fact that Gerald fitz Maurice Fitzgerald, third earl of Desmond (*d.* 1398), was married to his sister Eleanor and was father of Katherine of Desmond, who bore Ormond four sons out of wedlock. In October 1384 the king's lieutenant established a high-ranking commission to treat for peace between Desmond and Ormond. One of the members of the commission, the earl of Kildare, was ordered to intervene again in March 1387. In 1396 Ormond's brother Thomas was killed by John Fitzgerald, son of the earl of Desmond, in a dispute in Waterford. Peace was eventually restored when Desmond agreed to forfeit 800 marks to the earl of Ormond for the death of Thomas. War broke out again in 1399 when, shortly after the arrival of King Richard's second expedition, some English magnates (apparently at Ormond's instigation) captured the Desmond castle of Dungarvan, devastating the surrounding region. In response John Fitzgerald, now earl of Desmond, ravaged the barony of Cahir. Peace was re-established when the earls with their opposing armies met near the monastery of Inishlounaght (Tipperary). Desmond was drowned some days later (11 October) crossing the River Suir.

Ormond restored the fortunes of the family lordship, diminished by territorial losses suffered at the hands of the renascent Irish. He secured his borders through marriage alliances with Tadhg Ó Cearbhaill, lord of Ely (Éile), and with the Burkes of Clanricarde (1401). An indenture between the earl and the Ó Braonáin family of Odogh (1401) provided for the adjudication of frontier disputes in time of peace. Doubtless similar political and military indentures with Irish and Gaelicized Anglo-Norman lords, since lost, extended the earl's influence well beyond his borders. No less significant was the purchase of the Despenser purparty in Kilkenny in 1391, making the Butlers undisputed lords of the strategic Barrow–Nore–Suir basin.

Richard's choice of Ormond as justiciar in Ireland on 24 July 1394, before his own arrival there in October, must be seen in this context. Besides being a fluent Irish speaker, Ormond's network of alliances with Irish and Gaelicized Anglo-Norman lords was a decisive factor in inducing them to submit to the king.

Ormond married Anne (*fl.* 1386–1397), daughter of John Welles, before 17 June 1386; to her James *Butler, fourth earl of Ormond (the White Earl), was born. A younger son, Richard, was ancestor of Piers Butler, eighth earl of Ormond. Another son, Thomas Butler, prior of Kilmainham, may have been illegitimate. Ormond had in addition four sons—James, ancestor of the Butlers of Cahir, Edmund, Gerald, and Theobald—with Katherine of Desmond. Later tradition, emanating from sources sympathetic to Piers Butler, eighth earl of Ormond, suspected Katherine of incestuous relations with her own brother and of attempting to poison the countess of Ormond together with her children. In December 1399 Katherine offered to surrender £200 granted to her by Ormond if he were successful in securing in Rome a dispensation for their marriage. A curious agreement (18 January 1399) between the earl and the bishop of Cloyne, who undertook among other things to act as the earl's agent in the Roman curia, may represent the opening moves in a legal campaign to clear the way for a marriage that, in the event, never took place. Ormond died on 6 September 1405 and was buried at St Mary's Church, Gowran, Kilkenny. C. A. EMPEY

Sources E. Curtis, ed., *Calendar of Ormond deeds*, IMC, 2: 1350–1413 (1934), vols. 2–3 • E. Tresham, ed., *Rotulorum patentium et clausorum*

cancellariae Hiberniae calendarium, Irish Record Commission (1828) · K. W. Nicholls, 'Late medieval Irish annals: two fragments', *Peritia*, 2 (1983), 87–102 · E. Curtis, ed., *Richard II in Ireland, 1394–1395, and submissions of the Irish chiefs* (1927) · GEC, *Peerage* · *CPR*, 1381–5; 1396–9 · J. Graves, *A roll of the proceedings of the King's Council in Ireland, for a portion of the sixteenth year of the reign of Richard the second, AD 1392–93, with an appendix*, Rolls Series, 69 (1857); repr. (Wiesbaden, 1965) · C. A. Empey, 'The Butler lordship', *Journal of the Butler Society*, 1 (1970–71), 174–87

Butler, James, fourth earl of Ormond [*called* the White Earl] (**1390–1452**), magnate and administrator, later known as the White Earl, was the elder son of James *Butler, third earl of Ormond (*c*.1360–1405), and his wife, Anne Welles (*fl*. 1386–1397), daughter of the Lincolnshire peer John, Lord Welles (*d*. 1361).

Background and early career James Butler was born in Ireland, probably in the summer of 1390, into a family also connected with such Gaelic and Gaelicized lineages as the Ó Cearbhaills and Clanwilliam Burkes and subsequently the Mac Murchadhas, Ó Raghallaighs, and Ó Néills. His mother tongue was English, but his possession of an early fifteenth-century Irish manuscript, 'The book of the White Earl', and later patronage of the Gaelic bard, Tadhg Óg Ó hUiginn, who wrote him a notable praise poem *c*.1448–9, suggests that he also learned Irish. On his father's death in 1405, his wardship, marriage, and the custody of his inheritance were granted by Henry IV to the then lieutenant of Ireland, Thomas of Lancaster, later duke of Clarence.

Ormond's service as chief governor in Ireland, ultimately more extensive than that of any previous Irish earl, began only two years later. At seventeen, after serving under Lancaster's deputy, Stephen Scrope, on an expedition against the Leinster Irish, he became Scrope's deputy on 18 December 1407 when the latter returned to England. He summoned his first parliament to Dublin in the spring of 1408 and remained in office until Lancaster's arrival on 2 August. He sailed for England, either with Lancaster in March 1409, or soon after—the first of some nine visits there during his adult career—and was absent when livery of his Irish lands was granted, on proof of his majority, in August 1411. He gained livery of his English lands the following May and took part in Clarence's French expedition of 1412–13, before being dispatched back to Ireland with forty men-at-arms and 160 archers in September 1413 to support the short-lived lieutenancy of John Stanley. Service under Stanley's successor, John Talbot (later earl of Shrewsbury), on campaign and, from May 1415, as keeper of the peace for Kilkenny, Tipperary, and Waterford, ended in 1416 in the first hostilities of the long-running Talbot–Ormond feud. Ormond crossed from England to France with Clarence in 1418 and served at the siege of Rouen, then at Pontoise in 1419. His memories of the English victories in France in this period and related events in England (either set down in his lifetime or retold by his youngest son) provided source material a century later for the first English biography of Henry V. In 1430 Ormond returned to France again with Henry VI's coronation expedition before arranging a pilgrimage to Rome in 1431. He may have joined the Calais expedition under Humphrey, duke of Gloucester, in 1436. But his main concerns remained in Ireland.

Lieutenant and justiciar, 1420–1427 On 10 February 1420 Ormond was appointed to a two-year Irish lieutenancy in his own right on terms which represented a new royal initiative to reduce English financial support for the Dublin government and encourage more effective exploitation of local resources. The prospect of redress for the confiscation of his Irish lands in his absence in July 1417 by John Talbot for the non-payment of mid-fourteenth-century Butler debts to the Irish exchequer gave the earl a pressing incentive to co-operate. Celebrating his appointment by commissioning *The Governance of Prynces*, a new English version by James Yonge of Dublin of the treatise for rulers, *Secreta secretorum*, Ormond held office in Ireland from 22 April 1420 to 10 April 1422. He increased both the efficiency and the receipts of the Irish exchequer. By promising to avoid coign (forced purveyance) and to use his personal resources to meet any debts outstanding at the end of his lieutenancy, he secured more generous defence subsidies from general and local assemblies. With only £1270 received from England, he mounted energetic campaigns not only in Leinster, but also in Ulster, Munster, and Connacht. His success caused broadly similar funding arrangements to be adopted for all appointments to the lieutenancy between 1425 and 1442. The resumption of regular English auditing of Irish treasurers' accounts continued until 1446. But the lieutenancy also embittered Talbot–Ormond antagonism. Ormond purged the administration of supporters of Talbot and his brother, Richard Talbot, archbishop of Dublin. A petition to the king from parliament in Dublin in 1421 criticized Talbot's lieutenancy. In England in 1422–3, Ormond was accused by Talbot of treasonable activities in Ireland in 1414–16, including collusion with Ó Conchobhair Failghe, one of several occasions when it was alleged that, both in and out of office, he used his influence with Gaelic leaders against his political opponents. Committed to the custody of the earl marshal (John (V) Mowbray, earl of Norfolk), Ormond claimed that Talbot's lieutenancy had subjected him to systematic persecution.

After the quarrel was temporarily quashed in parliament at Westminster in November 1423, Ormond served in Ireland from May to September 1424 as deputy lieutenant for Edmund (V) Mortimer, earl of March. After March's death on 19 January 1425, Ormond was appointed lieutenant on 1 March for a year, serving from 28 April. On 15 April 1426 he was elected in Ireland as justiciar, serving, during the ensuing delay in England in appointing a new lieutenant, until 31 July 1427. These years further demonstrated his ability to govern Ireland with minimal English financial support, his readiness to do so contrasting with the reluctance shown by late fourteenth-century Irish magnates. Receiving less than the £1000 offered from England for the lieutenancy, he negotiated submissions in 1425 from the Mac Mathghamhnas, from Eóghan Ó Néill, and from the Ó Tuathail and Ó Broin families, combining strong-arm tactics with sensitivity to Gaelic concerns. The frequently threatened route from Dublin to the south was sufficiently secure to hold parliament at Kilkenny in February 1426, the last time it was to meet there before the 1530s. The justiciarship, entirely dependent on local resources, saw no slackening of military effort and a further rise in revenue at the Irish exchequer.

Later career Despite efforts to regain office, Ormond did not serve as chief governor again for nearly fourteen years. His exclusion from power was largely due to the resurgence of the Talbot–Ormond feud, reported by 1428 to have divided the gentry and common people of Ireland into two opposing factions. A petition praising Ormond from the Dublin parliament which was held in November 1428 by his close ally, the lieutenant, John (VI) Sutton, was followed to England by anonymous articles hostile to them both. In 1429 it was reported in England that Ormond and Sutton were burning church property in Ireland. Ormond retaliated with complaints of numerous attacks on himself and his servants by Archbishop Talbot and his supporters in Dublin, Meath, and Kildare, estimating his losses at over £3500. He was the subject of another attack in Dublin in 1434. In 1438 a proposed deputy lieutenancy for his cousin, Lionel, Lord Welles, was vetoed by the king because the feud with the Talbots remained unsettled. Not until 15 March 1441, when an agreement was negotiated in Dublin between Welles, Archbishop Talbot, and the earl, designed to prevent the last from using the chief governorship for factional advantage, did Ormond return to office. As deputy he then presided in June 1441 over the great council at Naas, which successfully petitioned against the classification of the English of Ireland as aliens for the purposes of the alien tax imposed in England in 1440.

Ormond's appointment as lieutenant on 27 February 1442 nevertheless provoked such controversy that the seven-year term agreed was never completed. He rebutted the charges of misgovernment and incompetence which Archbishop Talbot immediately pressed at Westminster. Some of the accusations were supported by the Irish chancellor, Richard Wogan, who described him as 'a grete growen man of flesh' whose 'indignacion', 'hevy lordshipe', and power in office quelled opposition; all were denied by a great council at Dublin which maintained that none but Ormond was 'so mighty and so hable to kepe [Ireland] to the kinges availle' (PRO, E101/248/16; Graves, 287). Although plans for an investigation in England came to nothing in 1443, Ormond had to abandon office to a deputy, Richard Nugent, Lord Delvin, in August 1444 to obey a summons there to answer new charges. Thomas Fitzgerald, prior of Kilmainham, had accused him of treason and, apparently, necromancy; Giles Thorndon, the Irish treasurer, of misappropriation of exchequer funds. After considerable delay, during which Ormond participated in the reception of the French embassy at court in July 1445 and received royal licence for pilgrimage to Canterbury, while abortive preparations were twice made to settle the Fitzgerald case by judicial duel, he was eventually acquitted of the charges against him in September 1447. It was probably no accident that this kept him in England until after the settlement of the Talbot–Ormond feud in Ireland in 1446–7.

In 1449–50 Ormond gave his support in Ireland to Delvin's deputyship for Richard, duke of York, and to York's personal rule as lieutenant. He stood godfather to the latter's son, George (the future duke of Clarence), in Dublin in October 1449, then sealed indentures as York's annuitant on 28 July 1450. The terms of this agreement, binding him to service in war and peace in England and Ireland for 100 marks a year, were superseded a month later. On 23 August he accepted £1000 a year and the profits of York's earldom of Ulster for a deputy lieutenancy which he held until his death.

Lordship in Ireland Ormond's personal rule of the Butler lordship is best known for his seigneurial ordinances (1428–35, 1447–9), unparalleled in Ireland, for the government, defence, and regulation of coign and livery in Tipperary and Kilkenny, all with local consent. In his absences he delegated protection of the lordship to leading relatives including his illegitimate half-brother, Thomas Butler, prior of Kilmainham (*d.* 1419), and his nephew, Edmund mac Richard Butler (*d.* 1464). His own acquisition of Castlewarden and Oughterard in Kildare, granted to him and his heirs in 1412 for his support for Lancaster's lieutenancy, increased the Butler landholding nearer Dublin. A much later claim that he gave lands in England to the royal heralds seems doubtful. His first marriage (before 28 August 1413) to Joan (*d.* 1430), daughter of William Beauchamp, Lord Bergavenny, significantly extended his English connections, but at the cost of weakening Butler power in Ireland in the next generation. Besides James *Butler (1420–1461), the fifth earl, John *Butler (*d.* 1476/7), the sixth, and the seventh earl, the marriage produced two daughters. Anne (who apparently died young) was betrothed in May 1429 to Thomas, son and heir of James Fitzgerald, sixth earl of Desmond (*d.* 1462/3), strengthening an alliance of considerable importance to Ormond from the early 1420s to 1444, when its rupture (until 1449) added to the problems of his third lieutenancy and subjected the Butler lordship to attack from the west. Her sister Elizabeth's marriage (*c.*1444–5) to Shrewsbury's heir, John Talbot, was a crucial step towards the ending of the Talbot–Ormond feud. Through his own second marriage, in 1432, to Elizabeth (1398?–1452), widow of John, Lord Grey of Codnor, and only legitimate child of Gerald fitz Maurice Fitzgerald, fifth earl of Kildare (*d.* 1432), Ormond acquired the bulk of the Kildare lands for life and also the animosity of the collateral heirs.

Edmund Curtis, in a history of medieval Ireland first published in 1923, hailed Ormond as the first of a succession of great leaders of a fifteenth-century, aristocratic, home-rule movement against English unionism. Ormond was unquestionably the dominant Irish magnate of his day, but, notwithstanding his appetite for office and a readiness to circumvent unwelcome royal orders, his separatist credentials now seem less clear-cut. Constitutional principle was not conspicuously at issue in his power struggle with the Talbots. Twice an advocate of a major

English military effort to complete the conquest of Ireland under the crown (1421 and *c*.1436–8), he apparently sent Henry V a carefully researched justification of the legitimacy of royal lordship over both English and Gaelic Ireland. In 1451–2, when moves were being made against York's adherents in England, he prudently professed his loyalty to Henry VI.

Ormond died at Ardee, Louth, on 23 August 1452, possibly of plague, after an arduous, six-week campaign beginning in Tipperary. A devotee of St Thomas Becket, from whose family his claimed descent, he had close links with Canterbury Cathedral priory and the London hospital of St Thomas of Acre, burial-place of Countess Joan, but his body remained in Ireland. Although also a patron of St Canice's Cathedral, Kilkenny, and the abbeys of Jerpoint, near Thomastown, and Holy Cross, Tipperary, he was buried at St Mary's Abbey, Dublin, of which he had claimed (*c*.1423) to be 'on of the chef founders nexte the kyng' (Griffith, 395). ELIZABETH MATTHEW

Sources E. A. E. Matthew, 'The governing of the Lancastrian lordship of Ireland in the time of James Butler, fourth earl of Ormond, *c*.1420–1452', PhD diss., U. Durham, 1994 • E. Curtis, ed., *Calendar of Ormond deeds*, 6 vols., IMC (1932–43), vols. 2–5 • *Chancery records* • E. Tresham, ed., *Rotulorum patentium et clausorum cancellariae Hiberniae calendarium*, Irish Record Commission (1828) • J. Graves, ed., *A roll of the proceedings of the King's Council in Ireland … AD 1392–93*, Rolls Series, 69 (1877) • M. C. Griffith, 'The Talbot–Ormond struggle for control of the Anglo-Irish government, 1414–47', *Irish Historical Studies*, 2 (1940–41), 376–97 • C. A. Empey and K. Simms, 'The ordinances of the White Earl and the problem of coign in the later middle ages', *Proceedings of the Royal Irish Academy*, 75C (1975), 161–87, esp. 167–87 • 'Henry Marleburrough's chronicle of Ireland', *Two histories of Ireland*, ed. [J. Ware] (1633), 207–223; facs. edn (1971) • N. B. White, ed., *Irish monastic and episcopal deeds, 1200–1600* (1936) • U. Nott. L., MiL 1c/17 • E. Curtis, *A history of medieval Ireland from 1086 to 1513*, 2nd edn (1938) • T. Carte, *An history of the life of James, duke of Ormonde*, 3 vols. (1735–6); new edn, pubd as *The life of James, duke of Ormond*, 6 vols. (1851), vol. 1 • K. Simms, 'Bards and barons: the Anglo-Irish aristocracy and the native culture', *Medieval frontier societies*, ed. R. Bartlett and A. MacKay (1989), 177–97 • BL, Add. MSS 4789, 4797 • Ormond deeds, NL Ire. • NL Ire., Harris collectanea, MS 4 • T. W. Moody and others, eds., *A new history of Ireland*, 2: *Medieval Ireland, 1169–1534* (1987); repr. with corrections (1993) • Coll. Arms • PRO, E101/248/16

Archives Coll. Arms • NL Ire., deeds | Birm. CL, Hampton MSS • Bodl. Oxf., MS Laund misc. 610 • NL Ire., Harris collectanea, MS 4 [incl. details of documents relating to Ormond's chief governorships]

Wealth at death see PRO, C 139/148/11; E 149/193/5

Butler, James, first earl of Wiltshire and fifth earl of Ormond (1420–1461), magnate, was the eldest son of James *Butler, fourth earl of Ormond (1390–1452), and Joan *Beauchamp (*d.* 1435), daughter of William *Beauchamp, first Baron Bergavenny. He was born on 24 November 1420, probably in Ireland, and was among the large number of knights dubbed by Henry VI at the parliament of 1426. Some time before 1435 he was sent to France, where he is listed as a member of the duke of Bedford's retinue, though since he was still a child at this time it is most likely that he was simply receiving an education in the duke's household. In the next few years two key events provided the young knight with the means for a political career independent of his father. The first was the death of his grandmother, also Joan, in 1435, which placed at his disposal a substantial collection of manors in Cambridgeshire, Leicestershire, southern Staffordshire, and elsewhere, and gave him an entrée to the networks of gentry in these counties. The second was the marriage to Avice Stafford (1423–1457), a major heiress in the west country, which he contracted some time before July 1438.

Although some of Avice's lands were placed in the couple's hands soon after the marriage, her twenty-one manors in Devon, Dorset, and Somerset were not apparently among them, and Butler was not active in this area until the 1440s, when he had come of age. Instead, his first sphere of activity seems to have been Cambridgeshire, where he settled at his late grandmother's manor of Fulbourn in the late 1430s and began to establish a presence in the county. Here he became embroiled in a dispute between lords Bardolf and Tiptoft, over control of the local estates of the honour of Richmond. Accused of overawing the parliamentary elections in 1439, Butler was dealt with sharply by the government, but he seems to have gained the support of many local gentry, and his links with Bardolf, the king's chamberlain, probably helped in his efforts to restore himself to grace. Although he spent part of 1441 serving in France for his family's traditional lord, the duke of York (with a retinue drawn mainly from Cambridgeshire and the Ormond lands in Ireland), he was also developing associations at court. By 1442, when he acquired the life shrievalty of Cardiganshire and Carmarthenshire, he was a king's knight, and it was more as a courtier than as a soldier that he was to distinguish himself in the ensuing decade. It is a sign of his position in the household that he was included in Suffolk's expedition to France to collect the new queen in the autumn of 1444.

By the early 1440s Butler was becoming a prominent figure in the politics of Warwickshire, joining forces with the courtier-magnate Henry Beauchamp, earl of Warwick, and his allies lords Sudeley and Beauchamp of Powick—men to whom he could be useful both as a member of the royal household and as the political heir of Lady Bergavenny. In the middle of the decade, however, Butler seems to have focused his attention on the Somerset–Dorset region, where he acquired a grant of his wife's lands in fee (in 1445) and was placed on the local benches (in 1443). As far as his territorial interests were concerned, this was an obvious area for Butler to seek dominance, and it may be that the government concurred, since some time in the mid-1440s he was granted the reversion of the stewardship of the southern forests (many of which were clustered in the south and the near south-west), while on 8 July 1449 he was created earl of Wiltshire. Butler's earldom may have been meant to signify his succession to the waning power of the Hungerford family and to the late Humphrey, duke of Gloucester, but he was to find it hard to establish himself locally. He had virtually no land in Wiltshire itself until after the attainders of 1459, and he faced competition for authority in the region as a whole: from his own lord, the duke of York, who snatched away the reversion of the forests in September 1446; and from the earl of Devon, another major landowner in Dorset and Somerset, who turned on Wiltshire following the latter's alliance with Lord Bonville in 1451. As Devon marched towards his manor house at Lackham, near Bath, Wiltshire fled to the king, leaving his lands undefended. It was a humiliating episode; and the more so as Wiltshire's craven show of obedience did not save him from a brief spell of imprisonment for his own part in the conflict.

By the early 1450s Wiltshire had had a busy, if rather ineffectual, career, but now his circumstances were to change. On 23 August 1452 his father died, so endowing him with the earldom of Ormond and its extensive holdings in southern Ireland. At the same time, English politics were becoming more heated and, as Richard of York turned against the duke of Somerset and Henry VI's household, so these men cast around for allies. Wiltshire, well connected in the court and active in the council from 1449, a landowner of substance in England, and now a possible counterweight to the duke of York in Ireland, was an obvious candidate. The earl faced a difficult choice. His father had died in office as York's deputy, and there was every reason for him to hope for the same patronage from the duke: he had been York's steward and fee'd man in Dorset since 1446, and was closely involved with the duke's men both there and in the east midlands. In the autumn of 1450, while York was riding high, Wiltshire seems to have hesitated: he joined in the duke's parade through London on 3 December 1450, and was on sufficiently good terms with York to continue to receive his annuity (until 1453).

As the duke's prospects declined, however, Wiltshire made up his mind. In February 1452 he joined the royal army that resisted York at Dartford, and received a pardon for the events of 1451 in return. Later in the year he became a regular witness to royal charters, attended council meetings, and took an active part in the judicial commission that toured York's estates in the summer and autumn. In May 1453 he was rewarded with a ten-year grant of the lieutenancy of Ireland, and received the votes of all the peers at that month's chapter of the Order of the Garter (though Sir Edward Hull was actually elected, Wiltshire joining only in 1458–9). By the time of the king's madness in 1453–4, Wiltshire's identification with Somerset and the queen was complete, and the breach with York an open one: in January 1454 he was raising troops in alliance with York's enemies, and in the following March, as Yorkist power grew, he lost the lieutenancy of Ireland. During York's protectorate, he was excluded from the council and may well have gone to Ireland. He did not actively defy the regime—and, interestingly, received the custody of some lands in Somerset and a commission as keeper of the sea—but (as one of the mainpernors) he was clearly involved in the restoration of Edmund Beaufort which followed the king's recovery at the end of 1454.

Now a central figure in the anti-Yorkist party, Wiltshire was appointed treasurer on 15 March 1455, and on 22 May bore the king's standard at the battle of St Albans. He now set about earning his principal claim to fame, as a coward. According to one chronicler, he 'fought manly with the helys' (*Historical Collections of a Citizen of London*, 198), and fled from every one of the battles at which he was present. On this occasion he quitted the battlefield dressed as a monk, but cheekily petitioned the victorious Yorkists afterwards for permission either to resume his place around the king or to reside on his estates in Ireland. What response this elicited is unknown, but the earl seems to have stayed away from the centre until York's power began to crumble in the early months of 1456. Even then Wiltshire seems to have remained fearful of the Yorkists, whose soldiers had apparently sought to kill him at St Albans. In March 1456 he sought permission to go on pilgrimage, and in the following month his fears were vindicated, when Sir William Herbert and Sir Walter Devereux attacked his lands in Herefordshire.

For Wiltshire there was no going back. As the 1450s wore on, he became more closely associated with the queen and the Lancastrian party she was building, joining the prince of Wales's council in January 1457, and marrying Eleanor Beaufort (*d.* 1501), daughter of the dead duke of Somerset, after Avice died later in that year (the marriage may have taken place in April 1458). Wiltshire's evident partisanship may be the reason why a council of lords, meeting at Coventry in March–April 1457, reappointed York to the lieutenancy of Ireland in preference to him. As any last chances of consensus evaporated, however, his commitment to Lancaster made him more and more important, culminating in his appointment as treasurer on 30 October 1458 and chief steward of the duchy of Lancaster on 12 February 1459. As treasurer, Wiltshire seems to have been exceedingly unpopular, doubtless because of the unorthodox means he was forced to adopt in order to fund the faltering government. He benefited directly from the attainders of the Yorkists in 1459, acquiring a mixture of annuities, custodies, and estate offices in Wiltshire and the adjoining counties, and once again replacing York (on paper, at least) as lieutenant of Ireland. Within a few weeks he was harrying York's former tenants at Newbury, receiving small sums of money and large amounts of condemnation—the latter from pro-Yorkist chroniclers and from the Yorkist lords themselves, who identified the earl as one of their three 'mortalle and extreme enemyes' (*English Chronicle*, 88).

About the time of the Yorkist invasion of June 1460 Wiltshire set out to sea with a number of Genoese ships, allegedly stuffed with soldiers and his own treasure. His aims are uncertain: possibly to try to head off the Yorkists; possibly to raise support in France; possibly simply to escape. In any event, he is recorded as having been in sanctuary at Utrecht in October 1460, though by early 1461 he was in Wales with the earl of Pembroke and a detachment of foreign troops. There, on 2 or 3 February, he encountered the earl of March at Mortimer's Cross. On this occasion Wiltshire quite surpassed himself, fleeing—once again in disguise—at the very beginning of the battle. He managed to reach the Lancastrian army in the north, but seems to have avoided direct participation in its defeat at Towton on 29 March. Soon after, however, he was captured by the Yorkists and taken to Newcastle upon Tyne, where he was executed on 1 May. Fate had finally caught up with the flying earl. His head was displayed on London Bridge, and he was posthumously attainted in the parliaments of 1461 (England) and 1462 (Ireland).

JOHN WATTS

Sources GEC, *Peerage*, new edn, 10.126–9; 12/2.734 • J. L. Watts, *Henry VI and the politics of kingship* (1996) • *Chancery records* • *The Paston letters*, AD *1422–1509*, ed. J. Gairdner, new edn, 6 vols. (1904) • C. Carpenter, *Locality and polity: a study of Warwickshire landed society, 1401–1499* (1992) • R. Virgoe, 'The Cambridgeshire election of 1439', *BIHR*, 46 (1973), 95–101 • R. L. Storey, *The end of the house of Lancaster* (1966) • J. S. Davies, ed., *An English chronicle of the reigns of Richard II, Henry IV, Henry V, and Henry VI*, CS, 64 (1856) • P. A. Johnson, *Duke Richard of York, 1411–1460* (1988) • C. L. Scofield, *The life and reign of Edward the Fourth*, 2 vols. (1923) • J. Gairdner, ed., *The historical collections of a citizen of London in the fifteenth century*, CS, new ser., 17 (1876) • *Itineraries [of] William Worcestre*, ed. J. H. Harvey, OMT (1969) • C. A. J. Armstrong, 'Politics and the battle of St Albans, 1455', *BIHR*, 33 (1960), 1–72 • R. Somerville, *History of the duchy of Lancaster, 1265–1603* (1953) • PRO

Wealth at death lands in Ireland and England

Butler [Bocach], **James, ninth earl of Ormond and second earl of Ossory** (*b*. in or after **1496**, *d*. **1546**), nobleman, was the eldest son of Piers *Butler, eighth earl of Ormond and first earl of Ossory (*b*. in or after 1467, *d*. 1539), and Margaret [*see* Butler, Margaret (*d*. 1542)], daughter of Gerald *Fitzgerald, eighth earl of Kildare. Some historians have estimated that he must have been born *c*.1485, others reckon 1504, but surviving evidence indicates that he was born about 1496 when his mother was recorded soon after marrying his father as 'greate with childe'. He spent his early years in and around the Ormond country in counties Kilkenny and Tipperary, not engaging in public affairs until 1513, when as a teenager he went overseas to participate in Henry VIII's invasion of northern France. While serving at the siege of Thérouanne he received a serious leg wound which caused him to limp for the rest of his life—hence his epithet *bocach* ('the lame').

Butler's first official involvement in Ormond family affairs came in March 1518 when the feudal baron of Loughmoe in Tipperary granted possession of the important manor of Templemore to Piers, earl of Ormond, and 'James le Butler, his son and heir'; this transaction almost certainly marked James's entry into adulthood, as he would have turned twenty-one shortly beforehand (Curtis, no. 43). Over the next two years he remained in the shadows, following his father around the country, learning above all to take command of the large Ormond army, as conditions around the Ormond territories dictated he be groomed as a warlord as well as a landlord. His military capacity was soon widely recognized, and it was noted that, despite his youth, the Butler soldiers would take their orders only from him or his father.

The appointment of Thomas Howard, earl of Surrey, as the new lord lieutenant of Ireland in 1520 brought James Butler back into direct contact with the monarchy of Henry VIII. For reasons of his own, Surrey was well disposed towards the Butler family, and agreed to support a suggestion that James be sent to the royal court to marry Anne Boleyn. Had this arrangement been realized it would have helped to solve the greatest problem then facing the Butlers, namely the possibility of a successful Boleyn bid for the earldom of Ormond. In the event, nothing came of the marriage proposal—how different might English history have been had a wedding gone ahead!—but even so, James was forced to prolong his residence at court. He probably entered the household of Thomas Wolsey, perhaps for as much as a year's duration, becoming one of the cardinal's entourage of young noblemen; extant sources refer to his being with Wolsey in autumn 1520 and again in summer 1521. Some historians suspect that Wolsey saw an opportunity to influence events in Ireland by keeping James close, virtually as a hostage, in order to direct the actions of his father and put the Butler army to use in the king's service. As Wolsey himself put it, Piers Butler could be manipulated: 'Not doubting but his said sonne being [in England] … he woll doo ferre the better the rather to get him home' (*State Papers, Henry VIII*, 1.91–2). After accompanying Wolsey on his embassy to Calais in August 1521, James's hopes of a return to Ireland were repeatedly delayed. By the following October he had been recruited into the royal household itself, becoming an esquire-at-arms to the king. He remained at Whitehall a further six years, making a favourable impression on King Henry, who in September 1527 referred to him as 'our faithful servant, James le Butler', and rewarded him with a rent-free grant of crown land in Meath.

Butler eventually returned home after February 1528, taking up residence at Keappahedin Castle in co. Kilkenny, and in 1530 he married Joan (*d*. 1565), sole daughter and heir of James Fitzgerald, the late earl of Desmond (*d*. 1529). Increasingly involved with his father and younger brothers in confronting the Fitzgeralds of Kildare in Leinster, in May 1528 he was temporarily held prisoner by Brian O'Connor Faly, an ally of Kildare, but was soon set free. He subsequently added to his reputation as a warlord, in 1532–3 raiding the estates of Fitzgerald supporters in co. Wexford and imposing the illegal military exaction known as coign and livery on the inhabitants of Fethard-on-Sea, where allegedly he 'did menace the commonalty' (Hore and Graves, 45–6). Instead of being reprimanded he was rewarded by the crown, and in 1532 he was made lord treasurer of Ireland with a seat on the Irish council. He and his family succeeded eventually in goading the Fitzgeralds into violent retaliation. He narrowly escaped being killed in September 1532 when attacked by pro-Fitzgerald MacGillapatrick forces in Upper Ossory; his youngest brother, Thomas, was not so fortunate and was killed. Hunting the culprits 'to their stalls' he discovered a Geraldine encampment nearby, and saw the murderers welcomed by the earl of Kildare's brother and other senior Fitzgerald commanders (Curtis, no. 191). His testimony about the killing contributed to the king's decision to summon Kildare to England for what proved to be the final time.

With the outbreak of the Kildare revolt in 1534 Butler greatly increased his standing with the crown, for his forces played a major part in securing southern Ireland against the rebels. His defence of Kilkenny town in August 1534 has been identified as an early turning point in the war; likewise his seizure of Dungarvan Castle, co. Waterford, in October 1535, effectively ended Geraldine hopes in the south. Reward soon followed. In May 1535 he was appointed lord admiral of Ireland and warden of the ports, a new government position that apparently required him to act as the Irish representative of the recently expanded English admiralty, and the following autumn he was raised to the peerage as Viscount Thurles.

The destruction of the Kildare dynasty in 1534–5 ushered in a new era in Ireland in which the Butlers of Ormond were manifestly the most powerful lineage in the country. Their pre-eminence presented new problems for a crown anxious that no Irish family should ever emulate the threat that had been posed to England's security by the Fitzgeralds. James's connections with the royal court helped to allay royal suspicion of his family. So too did his evident approval of the early stages of the Henrician reform of the church: in 1538 he wrote to Henry VIII expressing his disdain of 'the longe fraudulent tradicions and detestable abusyons of the papisticall secte' and praising the king 'as a lanterne to all other good Christian Princes' for setting 'furthe the Worde of God to the people' (*State Papers, Henry VIII*, 2.563). Historians have disputed how far he embraced a truly protestant position, but his friendly relations with Bishop Hugh Latimer about 1538 and his later political links to the Dudley–Seymour faction at court suggest that at the very least he was not opposed to the first exponents of protestantism in England. In political terms, of course, whether he had genuinely protestant leanings did not greatly matter. Rather, his ready compliance with the break from Rome was enough to guarantee him the king's favour. For the most part, criticism of the military racketeering practised by the Butlers in southern Ireland was easily deflected.

Shortly before succeeding his father as ninth earl of Ormond in August 1539 Butler stared down a serious challenge to his family's position by Lord Deputy Leonard Grey. In a letter to Cromwell in 1538 he contended that far from governing Ireland in the best interests of the crown 'my lord deputie is the Erle of Kildare newly born again' (*State Papers, Henry VIII*, 3.32), and he entered into a conspiracy to have Grey kicked out of office. The most interesting aspect of what was essentially a crude power struggle was how far James gained the backing of leading members of the Irish council, some of whom had previously been among his sternest critics. A magnate with a large private army, he convinced them of his willingness to co-operate in the long-term reform, or demilitarization, of the Irish polity; Grey was dismissed in 1540 and executed a year later.

The appointment of Sir Anthony St Leger as Grey's replacement should have augured well for the Ormond interest in Ireland. St Leger and Ormond had established a mutual understanding before 1540, and may even have conspired to effect Grey's disgrace. Initially relations between them were positive, with Ormond adding his weight to St Leger's policy of extending crown authority in Ireland through assimilating the Irish local lords and chieftains. It has been argued, for instance, that in 1540 he persuaded James fitz John Fitzgerald, earl of Desmond, to make peace with St Leger and embrace the re-emergence of royal power in Munster, an agreement that greatly boosted St Leger's status. Likewise in June 1541 it was Ormond who acted as St Leger's spokesman in the Irish House of Lords when the revolutionary Act for the Kingdom of Ireland was introduced, explaining the act to a select group of native Irish chieftains who were present at parliament as guests of honour, addressing them in Gaelic. Ever mindful of his court lobby, in return for his support Ormond gained access to St Leger's allies among the conservative faction that dominated King Henry's court after the fall of Thomas Cromwell.

Gradually, however, the coalition with St Leger came asunder as the new lord deputy realized Ormond wanted to gain control of his political programme. The two were at loggerheads by June 1542 when St Leger, attempting to establish a following of his own, granted a royal protection to one of Ormond's enemies, a former rebel. Ormond was further enraged shortly afterwards when St Leger furthered Desmond's interests in Munster at his expense. Having first neutralized St Leger's main patron at court, the duke of Norfolk, and befriended another leading conservative, Thomas Wriothesley, Ormond retaliated, forming a formidable alliance with other malcontents on the Irish council who resented St Leger. Henry VIII's decision to go to war with France worked strongly in the earl's favour, enabling him to nullify St Leger's attempts to discredit him as an overmighty subject in command of an unruly private army by demonstrating that, unlike other Irish lords, his soldiers were ready to serve the king. In 1544 at his own expense he fitted out 300 men from Kilkenny and Tipperary to serve in France, 200 more than originally required. In November 1545 he assumed joint command with Matthew Stewart, earl of Lennox, of an Irish army raised by King Henry for the invasion of western Scotland. Comprising a force of 2000 kerne, it was reckoned to be the largest Irish levy to serve the English monarchy outside Ireland for 200 years. Although the invasion was aborted near Dumbarton in response to political developments in Scotland, Ormond had attained a position of great importance as one of the king's most trusted and most experienced military commanders.

St Leger was understandably alarmed by Ormond's growing eminence, and following the earl's return to Ireland early in 1546 the rivalry between the two men spilled over into bitter mutual denunciation. With the Irish council divided by the feud, King Henry was compelled to intervene, ordering them both to Whitehall where their allegations and counter-allegations might be subjected to an official inquiry. According to the Irish annals, before his departure for court St Leger was heard to declare that only one of them would survive the investigation—prophetic words, as events transpired. The following October, when the inquiry was over and St Leger had been exonerated, Ormond and seventeen of his followers died of poison after attending a banquet given in the earl's honour at Limehouse in London. Unsurprisingly, the manner of his death, which occurred at Holborn, has caused historians to suspect that Ormond and his servants had been murdered at the instigation of the lord deputy, but a close examination of the evidence surrounding the fatal banquet does not support this suspicion, revealing that St Leger had neither the motive nor the opportunity to plot such an outcome. On his deathbed the earl himself did not suspect St Leger of foul play, even naming his former adversary as a supervisor of his will, all differences between them having been settled to their mutual satisfaction. Rather, the best explanation for the earl's mysterious death is probably that given by the near contemporary chronicler, Richard Stanihurst, who in 1577 recorded that some foolish rogue or 'caytife' had accidentally poisoned the meat. If true, then Ormond and his party were the victims of probably the worst case of accidental food poisoning in sixteenth-century London.

Ormond died on 28 October 1546, and was survived by his wife and their seven sons: Thomas *Butler, the eldest, his successor as tenth earl; Edmund, later of Cloghgrenan, co. Carlow; John, of Kilcash, co. Tipperary; Walter, of Nodstown, co. Tipperary; James, of Duiske, co. Kilkenny; Edward of Ballinahinch, co. Tipperary; and Piers, of Grantstown, co. Tipperary and Leix Abbey in Offaly. He also had an illegitimate daughter by an unknown partner, Síle Butler. He was buried in a Butler family tomb (long since destroyed) in the chapel of St Thomas the Martyr in Holborn. A second tomb to his memory still exists in Kilkenny, in the choir of St Canice's Cathedral; according to Stanihurst, this contained his heart, which was removed from his body and conveyed to Ireland after his death. A drawing of the earl, made about 1537 and attributed to Holbein, has been identified in the Royal Collection at Windsor; in 1951 a portrait, possibly a copy, was listed among the contents of the marquess of Ormond's English home. DAVID EDWARDS

Sources GEC, *Peerage*, new edn, 10.142–4 • NL Ire., Ormond collection • *State papers published under … Henry VIII*, 11 vols. (1830–52) • D. Edwards, 'The Ormond lordship in county Kilkenny, 1515–1642', PhD diss., TCD, 1998 • D. Edwards, 'Malice aforethought? The death of the ninth earl of Ormond, 1546', *Butler Society Journal*, 3/1 (1987), 30–41 • D. Edwards, 'Further comments on the strange death of the ninth earl of Ormond', *Butler Society Journal*, 4/1 (1997), 58–64 • D. Starkey, 'Holbein's Irish sitter?', *Burlington Magazine*, 123 (1981), 300–03 • W. F. Butler, 'The descendants of James, ninth earl of Ormond', *R.S.A.I.*, 59 (1929), 29–44 • D. G. White, 'Henry VIII's Irish kerne in Scotland and France, 1544–1545', *Irish Sword*, 3 (1957–8), 213–25 • E. Curtis, ed., *Calendar of Ormond deeds*, IMC, 4: *1509–1547* (1937) • H. Hore and J. Graves, eds., *The social state of the southern and eastern counties of Ireland in the sixteenth century* (1870) • R. Dudley Edwards, *Church and state in Tudor Ireland* (1935) • G. V. Jourdan, 'The breach with Rome', *History of the Church of Ireland*, ed. W. A. Phillips, 2 (1934), 169–227 • J. Kirwan, 'A portrait of James Butler, ninth earl of Ormond', *Butler Society Journal*, 3/4 (1994), 512–13 • P. Wilson, *The beginnings of modern Ireland*, another edn (1914) • B. Bradshaw, *The Irish constitutional revolution of the sixteenth century* (1979) • T. B. Butler, 'King Henry VIII's Irish army list', *Irish Genealogist*, 1 (1937), 1–13, 36–8 • *Holinshed's Irish chronicle*, ed. L. Miller and E. Power, new edn (1979)

Likenesses H. Holbein, drawing, *c*.1537, Royal Collection

Butler, James (*fl.* **1631–1634**), army officer, was one of the very numerous Butlers of Ireland who in the seventeenth century gained reputation as soldiers; his parents' names are unknown. At least six officers of that name served in the imperial army during the Thirty Years' War. James Butler is said to have been descended from Richard Butler, first Viscount Mountgarret (*d.* 1571). He is first met with in Poland, where he levied at his own expense an unusually large regiment of at least fifteen companies. Gustavus Adolphus is said to have hated him, so it may be that he was the Butler who in 1627 helped to defeat the Poles near Danzig but then changed sides, fighting with the Polish army in its victory over the Swedes at Osterode.

It was certainly James Butler who commanded a regiment, largely officered by Irishmen, and including his kinsman Walter *Butler, that marched early in 1631 to Frankfurt an der Oder, in Silesia, where the imperial army, under Tiefenbach, awaited the approach of Gustavus Adolphus with a larger force. Before the arrival of the Swedes, James Butler rode to the camp of Tilly, who was marching upon Magdeburg, in the hope of securing reinforcements for Frankfurt. Butler was too late to prevent the fall of the city but appears to have taken part in the siege and sack of Magdeburg, in which a terrible revenge was exacted. After its capture, and before the battle of Breitenfeld, he appears to have rejoined Tiefenbach in Lusatia and then in Bohemia, at Nimburg on the River Elbe in November 1631. A Saxon army under Hans Arnim having taken position on the other side of the river, Butler and his Irish regiment sent across a wooden bridge to fortify and hold the *tête de pont* on the enemy's side; his defence, ending with the burning down of the bridge, was so vigorous that finally Arnim returned to Prague.

Not long afterwards, however, Butler, a colonel who had many adversaries or rivals, left the imperial service and returned to Poland, where he fought against the Muscovites in the war of 1632–4. After this nothing certain is known of him, though he was possibly either the James Butler said to have fallen at Ross in March 1643, fighting on the side of the Irish catholics under General Preston against the royal troops under the command of James Butler, twelfth earl of Ormond, or the Colonel James Butler who commanded ninety-nine men at Wexford in the confederate army at the end of 1646. STEPHEN WRIGHT

Sources *DNB* • A. von Wrede, *Geschichte der k. und k. Wehrmacht*, 5 vols. (Vienna, 1898–1905), vol. 2, pp. 40, 109; vol. 3 pt 2 p. 614 • *CSP Ire.*, *1633–47*, 573

Butler, James, first duke of Ormond (**1610–1688**), lord lieutenant of Ireland, was born at Clerkenwell, Middlesex, on 19 October 1610.

Lineage and upbringing Butler was the eldest son of Thomas Butler, Viscount Thurles (*b.* in or before 1596, *d.* 1619), son and heir of Walter Butler, eleventh earl of Ormond, and Elizabeth Poyntz (*c*.1588–1673) from Iron Acton, Gloucestershire. At the time of his birth the affairs of the Butlers, one of the principal families of Anglo-Norman settlers to survive in Ireland from the middle ages, were disordered. In the early sixteenth century Butlers had been entrusted with the government of Ireland as lord deputy of the English monarch. The fortunes of the house had also been helped by kinship with Anne Boleyn,

James Butler, first duke of Ormond (1610–1688), by Sir Peter Lely, 1678

and so with Elizabeth I, with whom the tenth earl stood high. However, the continuing Catholicism of the Butlers made them suspect, as loyalty came to be associated with confession. In addition, their large estates, concentrated in but not confined to counties Kilkenny and Tipperary, were envied. Furthermore, by the seventeenth century their palatine jurisdiction over Tipperary was looking more anachronistic, and raised fears that the Butlers might exercise regalian rights against rather than on behalf of the English crown.

A pretext for the monarchy to interest itself directly in the affairs of the Ormonds was offered when the tenth earl died in 1614, leaving as his heir a single daughter, Elizabeth. James VI and I pressed Lady Elizabeth Butler into a marriage with a royal favourite, Sir Richard Preston, subsequently Baron Dingwall and earl of Desmond. On the tenth earl's death the king had adjudicated on how the great Butler patrimony should be apportioned. The bulk was awarded to Lady Dingwall. When Walter Butler, the eleventh earl, protested he was imprisoned for eight years at the Fleet prison in London. These privations destroyed his health and truncated Earl Walter's estates. Fresh interference by the crown was provoked by the drowning in a shipwreck of the earl's heir, Viscount Thurles, on 15 December 1619. In 1621 the palatine jurisdiction over Tipperary was suppressed. The young James Butler was claimed as a royal ward, and was removed from the Catholic school in Finchley to which his devout mother had sent him and from the Fleet prison where he was lodging with his grandfather. On the initiative of the privy council, the youth was placed in the household of the severely Calvinist archbishop of Canterbury, George Abbot.

Subsequently it did not suit memorialists of Butler to acknowledge how Abbot had moulded the future duke. He was said to have neglected the boy's general education. A scheme to send him to Eton College seems not to have been adopted. But in spiritual matters the impact of the dour prelate was greater. Butler was detached from the Catholicism of his forebears and immediate kindred. Henceforward he—and his descendants—adhered steadfastly to the reformed religion. Indeed he manifested a personal piety, evident in the prayers which he composed for his own use. It was proof against the efforts of his Catholic relations and disappointed those who hoped that he would revert to the faith of his fathers. Much else in this formative decade remains shadowy. The king continued to strip the Ormond patrimony and to favour the Prestons. In 1628 the death of the duke of Buckingham, who had intended that the Preston heir marry his own nephew, George Fielding, allowed the Ormonds to recover. By a single, simple act James Butler overcame the worst difficulties. The heir to the much enlarged Preston holdings was another fatherless child, whose wardship was granted in 1628 by an avaricious monarch to the courtier Lord Holland. At Christmas in the following year the ward, Elizabeth Preston (1615–1684) [*see* Butler, Elizabeth], was permitted to marry her cousin James Butler, and the wedding took place on Christmas day. Holland apparently extorted £15,000 from the Butlers for this arrangement. The price, hardly cheap, allowed the reunion of the divided Ormond inheritance, and improved the prospect that the couple could resume a position at the apex of the Irish aristocracy. Two measures vital to the survival and revival of Ormond power—conversion to protestantism and the reuniting of the estates—had been taken. They betokened a willingness to adapt to the current situation which marked James Butler's long career.

The newly married pair speedily returned to Ireland, where, from their residences at Carrick-on-Suir, co. Tipperary, and Kilkenny, they began the repair of their neglected apanage. This work was redoubled when, on the death of his grandfather, the eleventh earl, on 24 February 1633, full control of the inheritance came to the new earl. His estate policies resembled those of others, such as Antrim in north-east Ulster or Cork in south Munster, anxious to increase rentals. In Ormond's case an even sharper spur was his debts. Most were bequeathed by the troubles which had bedevilled and reduced the estate since 1614. However, others were incurred through his own incurable extravagance. By 1641 the lands notionally yielded £8000, making the earl one of the richest proprietors in the kingdom. Ormond found himself separated from the traditional followers of the family by his new religion. In Kilkenny and Tipperary he favoured the more recently arrived who shared his protestantism. These actions strained and may have ruptured older ties of affinity. The Catholic bishop of Ossory, David Rothe, led attacks in the locality on the heretic earl. But that very attribute, protestantism, which complicated dealings with his traditional followers, recommended him to the government.

Peace and war in Ireland, 1633–1647 The arrival of Wentworth as lord deputy coincided with Ormond's succession to the earldom. Ormond quickly attracted the viceroy's favourable interest. State service was a necessary supplement for many Irish landowners, whose rents seldom matched their ambitions. The administration in Dublin was one source of profitable employments, the court in England a better one. Already in 1631 Ormond had secured the command of a troop of horse: a post agreeable to any young aristocrat. Wentworth expected Ormond to put his local influence at the disposal of the regime: a reasonable expectation on the part of any Irish governor, but one not always fulfilled by waywardly independent Irish grandees. Ormond behaved circumspectly. In January 1635 he was sworn of the Irish council. In August 1637 he welcomed the viceroy to his city of Kilkenny, where he was lavishly entertained. Greater opportunities beckoned once Ireland became involved in the war which had broken out in Scotland. Wentworth encouraged Charles I to regard Ireland as a supplier of loyal troops to suppress the uprising. As the Irish army was expanded and prepared for fighting in 1638, Ormond was commissioned as lieutenant-general of horse. He was never required to campaign against the covenanters. However, he was reappointed to the same post when, in 1640, a new descent on Scotland was planned. The trust reposed in Ormond by Wentworth was indicated when the latter, during his absence in 1639, named the earl as his deputy as commander-in-chief of the Irish army.

Too great a dependence on a single patron, no matter how mighty, could prove dangerous, especially when that patron, as in Wentworth's case, routinely aroused controversy. Ormond had collaborated enthusiastically in the assault mounted by the lord deputy on the proprietors of Idough and Lower and Upper Ormond, some of whom were themselves Butlers. Ormond received at least £2000 as reward for his assistance in this shabby process. Any monetary gain was offset by the future damage through too intimate an association with the Wentworth regime. In 1640, once it was clear that Wentworth's power, first in Ireland but then in England, was waning, Ormond sought, not altogether successfully, to distance himself. Unless he did so, he might be involved in the viceroy's fall, especially if episodes such as the expropriation of Idough were to be included in his indictment. Certainly, kinsmen of Ormond, particularly when Catholic, notably Viscount Mountgarret, were prepared to exploit his present discomfiture. Despite these problems, outwardly Ormond remained a devoted adherent of the king's administration in Ireland. For example, he had put his electoral influence at its disposal in preparation for the 1640 parliament. But as yet the earl lacked the political arts to prevent instability increasing in Wentworth's absence. He was unable to dissuade an aggrieved Irish parliament from pursuing the fallen Wentworth and his minions in Ireland, and Ormond was reckoned to be one of the latter. Suggestions that Ormond might succeed as lord deputy in December 1640 were blocked by Wentworth's enemies at the English court, who were threatening also to become Ormond's. Instead two lords justices, Sir John Borlase and Sir William Parsons, were appointed. Subsequently they emerged as opponents of Ormond and the king whom he served.

Ormond's activities in the summer of 1641 later excited controversy. The plan with which earlier Wentworth had been associated and which featured in his trial—to ship part of the Irish army to assist the king—was now resurrected. The force would allow Charles to rout his critics in the Westminster parliament. Such a scheme was mooted, and a driving force behind it was Randal MacDonnell, second earl of Antrim. Subsequently Antrim contended that Ormond was also heavily involved. The latter denied involvement. This was not the only occasion when there was debate on how far Ormond was privy to the innermost counsels of the king. In this affair as in others, Ormond resented any aspersion cast on his honesty and fealty. A mutual antagonism crackled between the two peers. On Antrim's side it may have led him to try to besmirch Ormond. Certainly Ormond thought it had. This early effort to blacken Ormond's character warns that many never subscribed to the legend of his unblemished nobility which was artfully constructed in his later years and which flourished after his death. Other signs of the animosity which he could excite appeared when rebellion reached his own strongholds of Kilkenny and Tipperary. Ormond escaped to Dublin, but much of his estate was seized and wasted, in some cases by his Catholic kinsfolk. Only after tricky negotiations were his wife and family allowed to leave Kilkenny. This town, the centre of his power, was soon transformed into the headquarters of the insurgents, who became known as the confederated Catholics of Kilkenny. Those aggrieved by his policies in the 1630s now vilified the absent earl.

In November 1641 Ormond had hastened from the country back to Dublin. Differences over how best to respond to the insurrection split the government, and prevented any decisive action. This indecisiveness allowed the rebellion to engulf much of the island. Soon the moment for compromises had passed, and instead Ormond was required to lead forces into the hinterlands of Dublin. At Kilrush in co. Kildare on 15 March 1642 he defeated the insurgents, who included his kinsman Mountgarret. He also raised the siege of the important port of Drogheda. Most of his campaigning took place in the pale adjacent to Dublin, but he did venture into the western province of Connaught in pursuit of the rebels. Calculations by the king's supporters in Ireland had always been complicated by the swiftly changing events in Scotland and England. If Irish critics of recent policies sought to exploit the king's disarray and reverse what Wentworth and his predecessors had done, the widening rebellion faced the Dublin government with the dilemma of where best to turn for aid. Few supposed that the scanty resources of the small and scattered protestant communities would suffice to defeat the rebels. But as England also descended into civil war in August 1642, the likelihood of either the king or the parliament sparing troops or much money to relieve Ireland receded. Even so, Ormond, unlike the lords justices, looked still to Charles to quell the Irish troubles.

In recognition of this loyalty the king advanced Ormond to a marquessate on 30 August 1642. Yet, over the succeeding years Ormond's fidelity to the Stuarts was sorely tested. Charles was never in a condition materially to assist the besieged Irish protestants. Indeed he looked to Ireland to provide the resources which would deliver him from his enemies in England and Scotland. The troops under the command of Ormond and other loyalists, if freed for English service, would be welcomed. To this end, Ormond and other royal emissaries were empowered to conclude truces with the Irish insurgents. The resulting pacifications—in 1643, 1646, and 1649—disappointed the more extravagant hopes of English cavaliers. It became clear to the king's English advisers that the confederates might supply him with more. Thus, as Charles's plight in England, Wales, and Scotland worsened, so the attractions of an understanding with the Irish Catholics increased. Ormond, uncertain as to the king's true wishes, was perplexed about how best to reconcile obedience to his distant master with defence of English and protestant Ireland. Throughout the summer of 1643 he negotiated the cessation which was finally concluded on 15 September.

Ormond was rewarded by being named by the king as lord lieutenant, and was sworn on 21 January 1644. But this public demonstration of royal confidence did not still criticism or bring supplies. In regional theatres of war, such as Munster and Ulster, local generals refused to be bound by the peace. In contrast, Charles, uninterested in the fate of his Irish subjects, wished only to have the cessation made permanent. As intended, the peace of 1643 enabled some forces from Ormond's army to be dispatched to England. Their record proved a sorry one: those who were not quickly killed or captured mostly deserted to the enemy. Desperate for further help, the king authorized his lord lieutenant to reopen discussions for a more durable treaty with the confederates at Kilkenny. These talks were hampered by uncertainty as to just what Charles was willing to barter and by the divisions on both sides over tactics and conditions. Ormond himself may have been reluctant to see Catholics regain control of church buildings. He hesitated about provoking a fresh rift with England by allowing an unequivocal assertion of Ireland's legislative sovereignty. Moreover, he was encouraged not to give way too readily by his awareness of the serious divisions among the confederates themselves. Many within the supreme council at Kilkenny had been well known to him before 1641; some, indeed, were kinsmen. Ormond maintained unofficial contact with those, such as Lord Muskerry, most eager for a negotiated peace.

On 27 February 1645 the king ordered Ormond to make peace at all costs. However, Charles I's behaviour, often mystifying to his devoted servants, reached a new level of opacity when he sent the Catholic earl of Glamorgan as a special ambassador to the Kilkenny confederates. Glamorgan arrived in June 1645. The king continued to profess greater trust in Ormond than in Glamorgan. What he had not revealed to his viceroy was the latitude allowed to Glamorgan to concede much in order to make the peace. By December 1645 Glamorgan had secured a secret deal which would have restored Catholics to land, government, and office, and Catholicism as the state religion. In return, 10,000 confederate troops would be shipped to England. When, later in the month, the terms of the treaty were leaked, Ormond arrested and imprisoned Glamorgan in Dublin. All too soon Ormond realized that he had been bypassed and hoodwinked by his sovereign. Quickly he released his embarrassing prisoner. The king, sensitive to the hostility directed on the Glamorgan treaty, disavowed what had been done in his name (and at his behest). Sole responsibility for renewing overtures to the confederates was returned to Ormond. The latter's exertions produced a fresh peace, proclaimed on 30 July 1646. It failed in its aims. Immediately Rinuccini, the powerful papal nuncio to the confederation, condemned it and excommunicated its supporters. Confederate armies obedient to Rinuccini and the Ulster commander, Owen Roe O'Neill, launched an offensive which seemed on the verge of securing the objective which had hitherto eluded them: the capture of Dublin.

Ormond, chastened by these rebuffs and reverses, struggled to know how best to satisfy the seemingly irreconcilable. Charles I, defeated in England, was a prisoner of the Scots, but still dreamed of deliverance by force of arms. Protestant Ireland, in the defence of which Ormond had spent heavily and mortgaged his future prospects, seemed in greater peril than ever. Ormond himself, having suffered severe financial losses with his estates in enemy hands since the end of 1641, feared also loss of reputation. He was obliged to face the unpalatable conclusion that now, with the English parliament victorious, it, rather than the king, offered the better chance of rescuing something from the wreck of English and protestant Ireland. Accordingly he was forced into the strategy which earlier he had condemned others in the Dublin government for proposing. He explored what the English parliament might offer. Ormond was assisted by well-placed contacts, particularly among the presbyterian party at Westminster. But his close affinity with a particular grouping naturally carried risks as the advantage shifted unpredictably from the presbyterians to their opponents. By October 1646 the dire straits of Dublin made Ormond put out fresh feelers. He was prepared to contemplate the surrender of the capital so long as the safety of deserving protestants was guaranteed. He also expected recompense for the £13,877 from his own funds which he had allegedly spent since 1643. By 1646 it was suggested that his rents had dwindled to a mere £600, less than 10 per cent of their notional value in 1641, and inadequate for his expenses as lord lieutenant and commander. Parliament sent commissioners to Dublin to talk with Ormond in November 1646, but hobbled them with instructions to grant much less than Ormond demanded. One sticking point arose from the lord lieutenant's continuing allegiance to the king whose commission he held. Ormond would surrender the office only with Charles's approval. In February 1647 Ormond again approached parliament. Now he was prepared, so long as other details satisfied, to resign the viceroyalty without having the king's prior consent. The political pendulum at Westminster had swung back to Ormond's presbyterian friends. Meanwhile, at Kilkenny, the executive council of the confederation now included Antrim, Ormond's inveterate enemy. Although Ormond continued to discuss the possibility of a treaty with the confederates, the better prospect lay decidedly with parliament. Commissioners from the Westminster parliament landed in Dublin on 7 June 1647, accompanied by 2000 soldiers to reinforce the garrison. Articles were signed on 18 June by which Dublin was ceded to the English parliament, while Ormond was permitted to retire to England and was compensated.

Exile, 1647–1660 By July 1647 Ormond, together with his wife and children, had arrived in England. They divided their time between his maternal home of Iron Acton in Gloucestershire and London. Ormond was able to see and advise the king, in custody at Hampton Court. The Ormonds also refreshed themselves with city pleasures. The marquess had his portrait painted by both the young Lely and John Hoskins. But soon he moved to France—first to Caen and then by March 1648 to Paris—where he worked with others to construct a coalition on behalf of Charles. Suspicions of both Ormond and his monarch abounded and impeded this design. However, Charles's position improved briefly when his Scottish supporters, the engagers, invaded England. Also, sporadic uprisings disturbed England. But the decisive defeat of these royalists at Preston on 17 August 1648 rendered Stuart prospects dismal. Nevertheless, Ormond persisted with the scheme of creating an Irish royalist coalition which might yet save Charles. On 30 September 1648 Ormond returned to Ireland. It seems that he had again been commissioned as lord lieutenant by Charles. There he renewed offers to the confederates. A treaty, generous towards the Catholics, was agreed on 17 January 1649. By then, however, Charles I's trial impended. Before the month ended he had been executed. Despite the regicide, Ormond remained in Ireland trying belatedly to rally more to the Stuart cause. His commission as viceroy had lapsed on the king's death, but Charles II is reputed to have renewed it on 17 February 1649. His signal services to the Stuarts were further recognized by his appointment to the select company of the knights of the Garter. It was said that earlier Wentworth, as he faced execution in 1641, had wanted Ormond to succeed to the stall which he would soon vacate, but the younger man demurred.

Military successes, with the fall of such strategic towns as Dundalk, Newry, Trim, and Drogheda, by the summer of 1649 had reopened the tantalizing prospect that Dublin might succumb to the royalists. In the event, Ormond was routed on 2 August 1649 at Rathmines, close to Dublin. This dashed any likelihood that he would beat the forces of the new English Commonwealth and prepared the ground for the subjugation of the island by Oliver Cromwell, who landed a few days later with an army of 12,000. In many quarters, this defeat discredited Ormond. His martial prowess was contrasted unfavourably with Cromwell's and O'Neill's. As a campaign of vilification against him gathered momentum, certain themes soon prevailed. His abilities as a general were questioned; he owed his high command to heredity alone. Pusillanimity and dishonourable conduct were woundingly imputed to him. Interwoven in these attacks was anger at his earlier apostasy, which had turned him into an enemy of Catholic Ireland. Despite these increasingly shrill denunciations from the Catholics with whom he wanted to ally, Ormond persevered. He resisted the reconquest of the kingdom by those who had so lately killed his king. But all too soon loyalty to the successor, Charles II, was strained when the latter took the solemn league and covenant and repudiated the peace made by Ormond in January 1649. After this volte-face the fragile coalition of Irish royalists disintegrated. Recognizing that he was losing the little support he retained among the Irish Catholics, on 6 December 1650 Ormond named the marquess of Clanricarde (a Catholic) as his deputy. Five days later he sailed back into continental exile.

Years of privation followed. Caen was again chosen as an economical location. Soon Ormond moved to the exiled court in Paris, where by virtue of his experience and rank he enjoyed an almost automatic eminence. His finances were in disarray. He had been unable to pay off the accumulated debts on his inheritance before the uprising. The wars then denied him much of his landed revenues. To raise cash in order to pay the king's soldiers and his own urgent expenses, lands had been leased on easy terms to tenants, mortgaged, and even sold. The emoluments of office, pay as an army officer, and the compensation awarded him by parliament in 1647 were not adequate recompense. In a bid to improve affairs, his wife, herself the heir to much of the property, returned to Ireland. There, resourceful and energetic, in 1653 she persuaded the authorities to allow her £2000 per annum from the lands which had been commandeered by the state. How much of this found its way to her husband is uncertain. Finance necessarily came to dominate the thinking of the couple, sometimes jarring with their notions of what constituted true nobility.

At court Ormond joined those, notably Edward Hyde, the future earl of Clarendon, and Edward Nicholas, who believed that in time the Cromwellian order would collapse and the king would come into his own. They wished to keep free of damaging commitments to presbyterians, Catholics, or foreign powers which had so complicated Ormond's tasks as lord lieutenant in Ireland. Ormond had also to counter the refugees from Catholic Ireland whose charm and pathos induced the king to promise them much. In 1655 Ormond's staunch protestantism led to his being sent by the king to prise his younger brother, Prince Henry, away from their mother, who was determined to have the prince reared as a Catholic. In common with others in the king's entourage, especially as exile lengthened, Ormond craved action. Rumours that the usurpers might be toppled regularly cheered the dispirited refugees. In response to one of these stories, in January 1658 Ormond dyed his hair and met royalist conspirators in London. Nothing came of the enterprise, and Ormond returned to the continent on 8 February 1658. The government was well aware of the plans. Earlier, in 1655, it had taken the precaution of putting Ormond's eldest son, Thomas *Butler, earl of Ossory, in the Tower of London. After his release he went to France and then joined his father in the Southern Netherlands.

New configurations on the part of the Cromwellians obliged the exiles to find fresh billets. In 1655, when the protectorate allied with France, Charles's friends were obliged to move. After a spell in Cologne most, including Ormond, headed for the Southern Netherlands. Charles II's alliance with Spain encouraged the active to seek service with the Spaniards, now the declared enemy of the Cromwellian state. Ormond took this course. In 1656 he was in Flanders as colonel of a regiment of foot under Charles's younger brother, the duke of York. How far it relieved his frustration and his financial difficulties can only be guessed. The enforced foreign stay throughout the 1650s enlarged his horizons. Later he expressed dislike of foreign (especially French) habits, and was alarmed by the ambitions and activities of Louis XIV. At the same time, he admitted that the Spanish and French offered the best models of virtue and nobility. True to this belief, he insisted that offspring complete their education on the continent. Moreover, his tastes, always inclined to the grandiose, converged with those of an increasingly internationalized aristocracy, often to the disadvantage of his finances. Western Europe was valued as a source not just of paintings, books, and stylish artefacts, but also of artificers who could improve Irish manufactures. After 1660 he introduced them onto his estates in an effort to revive the textile industries.

Throughout the 1650s Ormond had difficulty in keeping closely in touch with developments in Ireland and England. Correspondence with his wife and servants was monitored by the authorities. As the protectorate and then the revived Commonwealth hastened towards dissolution in 1659 the hopes of exiles soared. By the spring of 1660 Charles II's court was thronged with informants and aspirants. Acquaintances told Ormond what was happening in Dublin, where a convention representing all protestant Ireland had assembled in February 1660. Once the king had returned to England in May 1660, his boon companions, such as Ormond, were much courted. Ormond received handsome recompense for his steadfastness. He was appointed to one of the great offices of state, the lord stewardship, which gave him control over the king's household below stairs, a necessary intimacy with the king, and ample opportunities for patronage. He was advanced in the peerage, receiving on 20 July 1660 an English earldom of Brecknock, so that he could sit in the English House of Lords in the coming parliamentary session, as well as the subsidiary title of Baron Butler of Llanthony. More spectacular was his elevation to an Irish dukedom, of Ormond, on 30 March 1661. A unique distinction, it confirmed his standing as Charles's foremost subject in that kingdom. Other honours, such as the lord lieutenancy of Somerset and the stewardships of Westminster and Bristol, were also conferred.

Office in England and Ireland, 1660–1688 At this juncture, although Ormond was much consulted about the outlines and detail of policy, especially towards Ireland, it seemed as if the king designed others for its government. But the proposed nominees were never invested with the viceroyalty, suggesting that it was fiercely battled over by the partisans of opposed factions. In the interim, authority rested with lords justices in Dublin, of whom Orrery, a past and future antagonist of Ormond, was the chief. On 21 February 1662 uncertainty ended when Ormond was named as the new lord lieutenant. But he delayed his departure for Ireland until July 1662. His continuing presence at the court and council offered chances to mould the coming settlement of Ireland. Subsequently Ormond, in conjunction with his ally Clarendon, was blamed by the disgruntled. Former Catholic landowners in particular felt that he was responsible for their meagre compensation. Such strictures, however, attributed more power to Ormond than he then possessed. Chronic lack of money may have slowed his progress to Dublin. In order to leave London and enter the Irish capital with the appropriate splendour he had to borrow not just cash, but also horses and clothes. After his arrival on 27 July the Irish parliament, prodded by the deferential and astute, gave timely relief in the form of a gift of £30,000. This hardly offset what the duke had lost in the preceding decades. Nor could it underwrite the expansive and expensive style which the viceregal couple felt they should adopt. More solid supports were provided in the land settlement. Later it was reckoned that the new lands bestowed on Ormond raised his rentals from an estimated £8000 in 1641 to £25,000. Not all agreed that Ormond deserved such generosity. Protestants whose acquisitions in the 1650s were now reduced, together with Catholics who were reinstated in little or nothing of what they had owned in 1641, compared the largesse towards the duke with their own shabby treatment. At first, in the euphoria of the king's return to London and Ormond's to Dublin, these complaints were muted, but soon they were aired publicly. Also, Ormond was to be faced with more co-ordinated opposition—including, in 1663, a bungled plot to seize Dublin Castle and overthrow his government.

Some of the joy with which the wanderer was welcomed may have been fabricated, but his viceroyalty promised both favour for those traduced during the 1650s and a governor familiar with the personalities and problems of the kingdom. In the last regard, of course, some remembered how unpopular and contentious Ormond had been. In the early 1640s he had been obstructed by members of his own council. Some of those opponents, or their heirs, survived in the Irish council of the 1660s. Thought by the unfriendly a disciple of Wentworth, Ormond was watched apprehensively for signs that he wished to erect the absolutism of which his mentor had dreamed. After 1662 old animosities were rediscovered and new ones created. Yet the choice of Ormond to govern Ireland marked a regression to a practice not seen since the 1530s: that of entrusting government to a member of the indigenous landed élite. The habit had been abandoned owing to the high risk of such a viceroy playing the overmighty subject. In 1662 Charles II was happy to gamble that Ormond's strong sense both of personal fealty to him as king and of his Englishness would curb any unruliness. There remained dangers that the duke would advance his own servants and friends and so aggravate the problems of factionalism within Ireland: these fears came to be realized in some measure over the next thirty years.

The political and administrative problems which confronted the Dublin government after Charles II's restoration were intractable. The preceding decades bequeathed protestant nonconformity, much of it among the Scottish presbyterians of Ulster, but also serious in Dublin and other towns. Ormond shared with other returned royalists a conviction that the obstinacy and beliefs of the presbyterians had caused the troubles of the 1640s and the king's execution. Some protestants, more understanding of the dissenters, accused Ormond and his government of subjecting these nonconformists to greater severity than the Catholics. Ormond, having throughout the 1640s exploited the divisions among the confederate Catholics, knew that they were no more a monolith than the protestants. He also accepted that some, often of the same Old English lineage as the Butlers, put devotion to the English sovereign before obedience to the pope and his agents. In 1649 he had tried to create an alliance based on this shared allegiance which would cut across ethnic and confessional differences. The modest results cautioned him against supposing that it could ever be achieved easily. Yet he appreciated that Ireland would never be stable so long as Catholics, the bulk of its inhabitants—between 75 and 80 per cent of its people—were excluded from full citizenship on the basis simply of their religion. He therefore encouraged fresh moves to see whether an undertaking, a 'loyal formulary', could be devised by which, in return for Catholic assurances of fidelity, the well-affected might be readmitted to a share of power. In the end the search, led by Peter Walsh, generated a public outcry. Protestants were outraged that the authorities were contemplating any concessions to Catholics, and the latter divided as to how best to respond, with the majority opposing what they denounced as a dangerous Gallicanism through which greater weight was accorded to the civil than to the religious power. So far as protestants were concerned, Ormond's encouragement of Walsh's activities, coupled with his easy social relations and kinship with Catholic grandees, reawakened doubts about his commitment to protestantism. Ormond never indulged in the rabid anti-Catholicism which some of his political rivals, notably Orrery, made their credo. He may, indeed, have been unduly indulgent of what the well-born Catholics did in private. But he accepted the need to enforce the laws, especially at moments of domestic and international danger.

More positively Ormond assisted the re-established Church of Ireland. One companion in exile had been John Bramhall, bishop of Derry and Wentworth's chief adjutant in ecclesiastical affairs. After the Restoration, Bramhall was translated to the archbishopric of Armagh, and so to the formal primacy. Others who had suffered for their attachment to the liturgy and government of the Church of England were rewarded with dignities in the Irish church. These sufferers, many of them aged and ill-informed about Irish conditions, did little to tackle either the material or spiritual deficiencies of the Church of Ireland. Ormond's enthusiasm—although it was not his alone—for promoting such clerics burdened the Irish church at a moment when it needed to respond vigorously to the new challenge from the dissenters. The duke also looked after his clerical dependants. Of his twenty-two identified chaplains, eleven were later consecrated as Irish bishops. In some (if not all) cases, the personal tie rather than outstanding spiritual or organizational gifts recommended them for advancement. Not until the 1680s did there emerge a younger generation of Church of Ireland clergymen, such as William King, Nathanael Foy, and Samuel Foley, able to identify pressing problems and devise workable remedies. In contrast to the bishops of English birth wished on Ireland in the 1660s, many of their successors had been born and educated in Ireland.

Indirectly Ormond might claim some credit for these Dublin graduates who went on to revitalize the Church of Ireland. One of his first appointments after returning in 1660 was that as chancellor of Dublin University. Most of the labour of reviving and remodelling this academy fell to its vice-chancellor, provost, and fellows. Nevertheless, the chancellor took his duties seriously. Keen to ensure that it became, and remained, a seminary for loyalists in state and church, he urged the prosperous of protestant Ireland to enter sons in the college. From 1669 Ormond held the same position at the University of Oxford. There, too, he backed his auxiliaries among the resident dons eager to align the institution unshakeably behind the monarchy and doctrines of non-resistance. Grandees from Ireland were encouraged to send their sons to Oxford. More expensive—perhaps four times more so—than the Dublin establishment, Oxford catered to a different Irish constituency. Ormond himself set an example by putting his unruly grandson, James Butler, already his heir and eventually his successor as duke, into Christ Church. The vigilance of John Fell, the dean, was expected to accomplish the reformation which France had not.

On occasion Ormond depicted himself as the simple soldier and man of action. Yet, as his appreciation of books, prayer, and education all hinted, he was more reflective than he pretended. Admirers extolled Ormond's apparent insouciance, as—for example—at moments of Catholic intrigue. Critics, deceived by the casualness, lamented it. Ormond disarmingly denied any expertise in the more recondite spheres of government. In particular, he shrugged off the complexities of finance as beyond his comprehension. Especially in the 1670s, when much of the running and collection of the revenues was contracted to a syndicate of farmers, in which Lord Ranelagh was prominent, Ormond's professions were entirely credible. Even so, he knew that trickery was afoot and bestirred himself to limit and eventually to end Ranelagh's interference. Yet Ormond's tardy and ineffectual response to the scandals of the revenue farm exemplified two problems of his rule after 1660, one personal, the second structural. In some tricky matters he affected indifference, but in others the indifference was all too real.

The numerous calls on Ormond's time meant that issues were neglected. His aristocratic addictions—hunting, gambling, and playgoing—distracted from irksome tasks. Over the years, and especially while soldiering throughout the 1640s and 1650s, Ormond built up a personal band of junior and aspirant officers. These comrades, such as William Flower, John Stephens, and Thomas Worsopp, expected further gratification. Once Ormond was again lord lieutenant, regimental commands were his to dispose. As he bestowed military preferment, the honouring of reciprocal obligations shaded into easy cronyism and perhaps downright venality. Defensive preparedness inevitably suffered. Orrery had warned of this in 1666. In 1669 Ormond's successor in the Irish government, the grizzly Lord Robartes, censured the corruption which marked the duke's superintendence of the Irish army. Robartes contended that in Ireland the king had 'but a painted army', owing to Ormond's tricks (Lord Robartes to O. Bridgman, 23 Oct 1669, Staffs. RO, D. 1287/18/3). Army patronage cemented Ormond's following in Ireland. However, by the early 1680s the most important military dispositions for Ireland were decided in England. Ormond, although still lord lieutenant, found his patronage alarmingly curtailed.

This diminished power paralleled developments in the administration of Irish finances. Again early in the 1680s, the lords of the Treasury in London were exercising closer oversight. In part this was a response to the disappointments over the much vaunted claims that Ireland could help England out of its financial difficulties. It also told of the dissatisfaction—shared ironically by Ormond—with the revenue farms, particularly Ranelagh's. Such moves accentuated but hardly originated the political subordination of Ireland to England. Increasingly Irish administration was integrated into a system run from London. The freedom of the king's deputy in Dublin, or of the council and other advisers, to initiate policies had long been small. After 1660 what happened in Ireland, particularly how forfeited lands and remunerative offices were allocated, interested several of those highly placed at the English court. Because the direction and many details of policy for Ireland were decided in London, both protestants and Catholics congregated there. Many had hastened thither from Dublin in May 1660. Thereafter they lobbied assiduously. They could weaken the incumbent viceroy. Ormond, intermittently absent in Ireland between 1662 and 1669, worried about confuting his detractors at Charles's court. Further, he belonged—and had done since the early 1650s—to a grouping at court centred on Clarendon and composed of traditionalists keen to uphold the rights of the established church. Clarendon's dismissal and exile in 1667 left Ormond exposed and vulnerable to attack. The king contemplated new courses in domestic, religious, and foreign policy, some of which, it was supposed, Ormond would not approve. These changes brought about his enforced resignation in 1669.

It was inevitable that Ormond should supply material for his attackers by his behaviour in the Irish government. Serious problems had arisen over the enactment and implementation of the land settlement. Ormond, capable in the right company of bonhomie, could also manifest a haughtiness worthy of his ducal rank. A contemporary remarked that 'he wanted the small arts of familiarity and caressing which men of many designs could not be without' (Dublin Public Libraries, Gilbert MS 207, p. 37). He was willing to entertain the important in the viceregal apartments in Dublin Castle. Keen to impress and even overawe, he—in collaboration with his wife—brought them to a new pitch of magnificence. The favoured might also be charmed or intimidated at his own Kilkenny Castle. This too was modernized and enlarged to accord better with the Ormonds' idea of how the king's surrogate should be housed. Admirers naturally approved; doubters had their reservations about Ormond's intentions and abilities confirmed.

The tiresome business of managing a restless parliament was readily delegated by Ormond to others, such as Orrery. The strength of opposition in the supposedly loyalist assembly took Ormond aback, as did the 1663 conspiracy to surprise Dublin Castle. Once the essentials of the restoration settlement in Ireland—land, church, and money—had been agreed, in no small degree thanks to Orrery's wiles, Ormond was happy to rule without the distraction of a Dublin parliament. Nevertheless, fresh problems quickly arose: the threat of foreign invasion and an army mutiny at Carrickfergus in 1666. In each case Ormond's responses were censured: in the first instance as too unruffled, in the second as unduly harsh. Fumbling in handling public issues encouraged scrutiny of personal failings. His and his followers' profiteering from recent measures was remarked upon. Ormond's characteristic nepotism in the distribution of civil and military offices was aptly symbolized by the choice of his eldest son, Ossory, to act as his deputy during his absences in 1664–5 and 1668–9. It looked as though he were treating the government of Ireland as if it were the exclusive preserve of himself, his family, and followers. In similar fashion, because the Ormonds lacked any grand residence in Dublin, they treated Dublin Castle as theirs.

Removal from the viceroyalty in 1669 left Ormond with the prestigious lord stewardship. If it reduced his scope for patronage, it also lessened the costly obligations to live in state which threatened to cripple him financially. The feeling that the Ormonds must live in a fashion equal to that of the other notables at Charles II's court had led them early in the 1660s to purchase the Hertfordshire seat of Moor Park. In 1670 this was sold, at a profit, and expenses were cut by hiring a house. Other economies included the sale of the duke's post as a gentleman of the bedchamber. But with an accumulation of debts—in 1660 they had been set at £130,000—and the mounting costs of servicing them, it was impossible to bring expenditure into line with revenues. Frequent absence from Ireland, the rarity of any lengthy stay at Kilkenny, the cumulative impact of leasing policies adopted in the 1640s, and the duke's temperamental distaste for the minutiae of estate business all meant that the Irish holdings were haphazardly overseen. Much authority on the spot was delegated to Ormond's half-brother Captain George Matthews. Ormond's widowed mother, Lady Thurles, in 1626 had married George Matthews of Thurles in co. Tipperary. She did not die until May 1673: an imperious matriarch within the family, she also consumed its attenuated revenues.

Out of favour and out of sympathy with much of the ethos of the royal court in the 1670s, Ormond retained his high office and was careful not to parade his resentments. This dignity in adversity won plaudits. It also helped him towards reappointment as lord lieutenant in 1677. Ranelagh, fearful that Ormond's return might augur the end of his revenue fraud, intrigued to prevent it. The scheme, supported also by the lord treasurer, Danby, which might have installed Monmouth as viceroy failed. The duke of York, jealous of Monmouth's popularity and fearful lest it be increased by a tour of duty in Ireland, promoted Ormond's claims. In Ireland, Ormond's immediate task was to prepare for a new parliament which, it was hoped, would close the land settlement. This programme was rapidly overtaken by the unfolding of the Popish Plot in 1678. Potentially, this threatened to envelop and unsettle Ireland. Protestant opportunists saw the allegations of continuing Catholic treachery as a pretext to complete the expropriation and emasculation of their Catholic neighbours. The latter, it was feared, even if not part of an international conspiracy, might protect themselves by pre-emptive actions. Ormond's refusal to panic ensured that the episode disturbed Ireland far less than had been predicted. In the aftermath of the crisis, from 1681, he presided over something akin to the tory reaction which engulfed England. But, notwithstanding his strongly tory outlook, he remodelled the army and civil administration less thoroughly than some ultras had urged. His caution told of his understanding that the Irish protestant community was scarcely large enough to serve as the sole foundation for the regime. Wilfully to divide it, and to exclude many from office on the basis of origins or past behaviour in the interregnum, would be to add gratuitously to the already considerable impediments to governing the kingdom. Forbearance of this sort, deemed politic in the 1660s when clearly the regime in Ireland needed all the backers it could muster, by 1684 irritated the intolerant. Ardent royalists wanted privilege to be confined to the unequivocal supporters of a divine-right Stuart monarchy. Increasingly, Ormond came to be viewed as an obstacle to the realization of this vision in Ireland. As one contemporary observed, 'divers reformations to be made in Ireland, which His Majesty thinks will be too hard a thing to put on my Lord of Ormond' (P. Maddocks to Sir R. Southwell, 14 Nov 1684, Bodl. Oxf., MS Eng. Lett. C.53, fol. 131). The duke struggled to avoid a humiliating removal. By 1684 he too sensed what many others suspected: that dismissal was inevitable. Yet he postponed it until February 1685 when Charles's death terminated his commission.

In the later stages of this final tour of duty Ormond had seen much of the lord lieutenant's authority over the army and finances transferred to functionaries in Whitehall. Nevertheless, he put his imprint on the city where for so long he had presided. At Kilmainham, on the outskirts of Dublin, he established a military hospital modelled closely on Les Invalides and the Chelsea Hospital. In default of any complete rebuilding of the viceregal accommodation, this project gave Dublin its largest and most conspicuous public monument in the modern classical idiom. Although termed the Royal Hospital, in its conception and iconography it was as much a celebration of Ormond's long reign over Ireland as of the Stuarts. Otherwise, the reefs of the Popish Plot and exclusion negotiated, he had contentedly handed government to his son, now the eldest surviving, Richard, earl of Arran, who served as his lord deputy between 1682 and 1684. The deaths in 1680 of his popular and able heir Ossory and on 21 July 1684 of his redoubtable wife deepened the duke's wish to concentrate more on the education and settlement of his close family. His wife had at least lived long enough to enjoy the final accolade bestowed on him. On 9 November 1682 Ormond had been created an English duke. Thereby he was distinguished from, and elevated higher than, all others in Ireland. But even this honour brought worrying obligations. In 1682 the Ormonds purchased from Lord St Albans the largest mansion in the recently completed West End development of St James's Square. It cost £9000, and had then to be furnished with fitting splendour. By the standards of their social equals, the peers in the higher degrees of the nobility and the knights of the Garter especially esteemed by the king, these were not thought extravagances. But such expenditure worsened the fiscal problems of the duke. By the time he died his debts were calculated variously at £100,000 and £150,000.

Once free of office and a widower, the ageing duke preferred the country to the city, but it was too late to retrench dramatically. With characteristic self-knowledge Ormond prepared himself for gradual physical decline and death. Allowed the use successively of Cornbury, Oxfordshire, and Badminton, Gloucestershire, he settled more permanently in the Bankes's Dorset house of Kingston Lacy. There he died on 21 July 1688, and was interred on 4 August alongside his wife in Westminster Abbey.

Character and reputation During his life Ormond was criticized by individuals who felt aggrieved by their treatment and—more concertedly—by groups such as Cromwellian collaborators, protestant dissenters, and Irish Catholics who blamed him for their disappointments after 1660. Despite this undercurrent of dissatisfaction, Ormond's posthumous reputation remained high while the Stuarts ruled and while his grandson, the second duke, retained favour. However, the latter's exile in continental Europe after 1715 and his involvement with the Jacobites retrospectively tarnished the first duke as well. The Butlers were damaged by their close association with the Stuarts and—by extension—with their absolutist ambitions. Late in the 1720s the process of rehabilitation began. A deprived English clergyman, Thomas Carte, also a Jacobite sympathizer, planned a biography of the first duke. It was intended to exculpate both Charles I and Ormond from collusion in the Irish uprising of 1641. Carte's *Life of James, Duke of Ormonde* was published in three volumes in 1735 and 1736. From his exile in France, the second duke thanked Carte. Ormond, brought to the notice of a new generation, was extolled. Mary Delany, having read the *Life*, in 1751 adjudged the duke 'the completest fine gentleman and the loyalist subject I ever read of' (*The Autobiography and Correspondence of Mary Granville, Mrs Delany*, ed. Lady Wanover, 6 vols., 1861–2, 1st ser. 3.6). Such a response attested to Carte's success, especially among those who still esteemed the Stuarts.

In compiling the account, Carte had collected numerous original documents, many of which were included in his unwieldy text. The quest for materials had taken him to Ireland, where he was assisted by antiquaries, bibliophiles, and descendants of Ormond's contemporaries. Most valuably, he was allowed not only access to the Ormond archive in Kilkenny Castle, now abandoned by the family, but also to carry away materials. The principles on which Carte selected what to take were haphazard. What he removed from Ireland found its way into the Bodleian Library between 1753 and 1757, and was catalogued in the mid- and later nineteenth century. The remainder of the family papers, supposedly the elements relating to local, personal, and estate affairs, were left at Kilkenny. There, from 1870, they were calendared by J. T. (later Sir John) Gilbert. Ten volumes, dedicated to the collection and continued by others after Gilbert died, appeared between 1895 and 1920. The originals of the documents were transferred from Kilkenny to the National Library of Ireland in Dublin when the Butlers finally left the castle in 1935. Even then, some estate materials, apparently of continuing use in the locality, stayed behind.

The division of the papers, together with the bulk of Carte's biography, for long discouraged any sustained assessment of Ormond's career. In addition, records important to an understanding of his finances and political stance have disappeared, through either planned or accidental destruction. Modern writers have with difficulty escaped the hagiographical tone of Carte, and, in reaction, have sometimes accepted uncritically the hostile estimates of Ormond's adversaries.

Longevity gave Ormond's reputation a lustre which his discharge of office alone could not always justify. As early as the 1630s local victims of his ruthlessly exploitative estate policies rounded on him. His identification first with Wentworth between 1633 and 1640 and then with Charles I's cause in the 1640s attracted opprobrium from both protestants and Catholics with divergent loyalties. His surrender of Dublin in 1647 and sorry showing at Rathmines in 1649 were impugned. The connection with Wentworth rose up and haunted him during his later viceroyalties because some hailed—or derided—him as the heir of the would-be absolutist. If anything, Ormond shared with Wentworth a lofty conception of the viceregal office which should be embodied in the physical arrangements of the state apartments in Dublin Castle. Ormond's involvement in the factious politics of Charles II's court revived old and created fresh enmities. Particularly as the Catholics seemed likely to be handled more gently, from the 1670s onwards pamphleteers rehearsed what had or had not happened in the Ireland of the 1640s. Because of Ormond's continuing importance and his supposed friendliness towards Catholic ambitions, his past behaviour was minutely scrutinized. Attacked by, among others, the earl of Anglesey, who as Arthur Annesley had been one of the parliamentary commissioners to whom Dublin was ceded in 1647, Ormond vindicated himself. His protégé and confidant Sir Robert Southwell was set to answer more elaborately with a life and times of the duke. This, never published while Ormond lived, proved reticent. Nor were all convinced by the defences which did appear in the 1680s. Roger Morrice, a London whig, remembered the duke as 'a ready and obsequious tool'. Having outlived his usefulness to the crown, he was unceremoniously laid aside.

Undoubtedly Ormond enjoyed popularity in Ireland. This stemmed from the fact that he could be accounted Irish (despite his repeated protestations of his Englishness), and so conversant with and sympathetic to the troubles of the island. Especially as he was edged into the antechambers of Charles II's and James II's palaces, his refusal to pander to the newly important or to compromise his Anglican principles was applauded. However, the adjustments which he had been obliged to make over his longer career may have strained him. One annalist, not blind to the duke's weaknesses, declared that 'he loved splendour when it could be come at. Yet when crosses rushed upon him and [he] could not prevent it, he bore them with a talent to be admired' (Dublin Public Libraries, Gilbert MS 207, p. 2). Such stoicism in adversity enabled him to endure the reverses of the 1650s, the 1670s, and after 1685. He admitted also that he had an eye to posterity, determined to lie well in the chronicle. On occasion, certainly, he was prepared to enlist propagandists to state his case. They seldom did so with great aplomb. It was left to Ormond, through his own carriage, to comport himself according to his ideals of noble conduct. These were not necessarily consistent, perhaps inevitably in a long career pursued in such variegated settings. He regretted how adversity beset and disabled so many in Ireland. He regarded lineage and loyalty as the touchstones by which the claims to office and influence should be decided. However, this outlook was increasingly at odds with the attitude of the English rulers of Ireland. Ruefully he accepted that those, including many of his name, who could not abandon Catholicism disqualified themselves from state service. He was saddened that they could not make the leap which he had, in the otherwise uncongenial household of Archbishop Abbot. Reluctant to pry into people's souls, he nevertheless subscribed to the conventional wisdom of the day that public separation from the state cult weakened that state. As a result, although he remained tolerant of the promptings of private conscience, he resolutely applied the laws which required conformity with the established church and penalized those who did not conform. This attitude incurred the wrath of both devout Catholics and precisians.

Some thought Ormond too unbending as he upheld his notion of chivalric and noble conduct. Others despised him for the accommodations into which he entered, profitable alike to himself and his progeny. The interest of his life comes partly from the many years which it spanned, and also from the abundant but still patchy documentation of him as the type of the Anglo-Irish aristocrat. In the end it is impossible to decide whether Ormond harked back to an anomalous idea of nobility, in which allegiance to the sovereign overrode religious faith and ethnic classification, or, alternatively, advocated precociously the politics of inclusion. If he adhered to the second proposition, he evinced the same pragmatism as Charles II, in which present and future manoeuvrability mattered more than the ballast of confession and ancestry.

Issues on which Ormond openly dissented from his monarch were few. During the 1640s his reluctance to concede much to the ultramontane Catholics at Kilkenny may have hampered negotiations and led to his supersession by Glamorgan. Throughout the 1660s and 1670s he resisted, but in the end unsuccessfully, the bid to reopen the Irish land question. In the English House of Lords during 1666 he joined other Irish landowners by proxy in protesting against the planned inhibitions on Irish trade. However eloquent, he could not prevent a statutory ban on the export from Ireland of live cattle. After 1685 he watched apprehensively and amazed as James II and his deputies in Ireland dismantled some of the incipient protestant ascendancy. These changes endangered the commanding position in which Ormond had so laboriously re-established himself and his family. Yet, whatever his fears, they were usually concealed behind his habitual courtliness and deference. This restraint hastened his elevation among staunch tories and Anglicans into 'the good old duke'. As lord high steward he carried the crown at James's coronation, as he had at that of Charles in 1661. Otherwise, age as much as disinclination excused him from regular involvement in the ceremonial of the new king's court. Moreover, as for others from Ireland in his position, such as Lord Cork and Burlington, the impact of James's pro-Catholic policies was likely to be more immediate and disruptive on their Irish than on their English interests. This he knew and dreaded, but before the irrevocable choices of allegiance had to be made, he died. It was left to his grandson and heir, the second duke, to assess how the interests of the family and its fortune would best be served. TOBY BARNARD

Sources Bodl. Oxf., MSS Carte • NL Ire., Ormonde MSS • V&A NAL, Forster Library, Ormonde papers • *The manuscripts of the marquis of Ormonde*, [old ser.], 3 vols., HMC, 36 (1895–1909) • *Calendar of the manuscripts of the marquess of Ormonde*, new ser., 8 vols., HMC, 36 (1902–20) • R. Southwell, 'Life of Ormond', in Lord Mountmorres, *The history of the principal transactions of the Irish parliament from 1634 to 1666*, 2 vols. (1792), 1 • T. Carte, *An history of the life of James, duke of Ormonde*, 3 vols. (1735–6) • J. T. Gilbert, ed., *A contemporary history of affairs in Ireland from 1641 to 1652*, 7 vols. (1880) • J. C. Beckett, *The cavalier duke* (1990) • account of Restoration politics in Ireland, Dublin Public Libraries, Gilbert MSS 207, 227 • T. C. Barnard and J. Fenlon, eds., *The dukes of Ormonde, 1610–1745* (2000) • R. Armstrong, 'Protestant Ireland and the English parliament, 1641–1647', PhD diss., TCD, 1995 • S. Egan, 'Finance and the government of Ireland, 1660–85', PhD diss., TCD, 1983 • D. Edwards, 'The Ormond lordship in county Kilkenny, 1515–1642', PhD diss., TCD, 1998 • W. P. Kelly, 'The early career of James Butler, twelfth earl and first duke of Ormond (1610–1688), 1610–1643', PhD diss., U. Cam., 1997 • P. A. Morris, 'Ormond's army: the Irish standing army, 1640–69', PhD diss., Vanderbilt University, 1980 • J. E. Ayledotte, 'The duke of Ormonde and English government in Ireland, 1677–85', PhD diss., Iowa University, 1975 • T. C. Barnard, '"Parlour entertainment for an evening": histories of the 1640s', *Kingdoms in crisis: Ireland in the 1640s, essays in honour of Dónal Cregan*, ed. M. Ó Siochrú (2001), 20–43 • T. C. Barnard, 'Sir John Gilbert and Irish historiography', *Sir John T. Gilbert, 1829–1898*, ed. M. Clark, Y. Desmond, and N. P. Hardiman (1999), 92–110 • C. W. Russell and J. P. Prendergast, *The Carte manuscripts in the Bodleian Library, Oxford: a report* (1871) • GEC, *Peerage*

Archives Bodl. Oxf., corresp. and papers • Bodl. Oxf., corresp. [copies] • Dorset RO, accounts • Hunt. L., letters and corresp. • Magd. Cam., corresp. • NL Ire., corresp. and papers • TCD, corresp. [letter-book as chancellor of Oxford University and steward of the king's household] • V&A NAL, letters and papers relating to his career in Ireland | BL, letters to Lord Essex, Stowe MSS 200–212, *passim* • BL, letters to Sir Edward Nicholas, Egerton MSS 2533–2537, 2539 • BL, corresp. with Lord Orrery, Add. MSS 37206–37208, *passim* • BL, corresp. with Sir Philip Perceval, etc., Add. MSS 46920–46956 • BL, letters to Sir Robert Southwell, Add. MS 21484 • Bodl. Oxf., Clarendon MSS • Bodl. Oxf., letters to Sir Cyril Wyche • PRO, state papers, domestic • PRO, state papers, Ireland • Worcester College, Oxford, corresp. • Yale U., Beinecke L., letters to William Legge

Likenesses J. van Egmont, oils, 1648, Claydon House, Buckinghamshire • oils, *c*.1655 (after P. Lely), NPG; version, Buccleuch estates, Selkirk, Scotland • J. M. Wright, oils, *c*.1670, Hardwick Hall, Derbyshire • P. Lely, portrait, 1678, Kedleston Hall, Derbyshire [*see illus.*] • P. Lely, oils, *c*.1680, Euston Hall, Suffolk; version, Chatsworth House, Derbyshire • R. Dunkarton, mezzotint, pubd 1815 (after D. Loggan), BM, NPG • E. Scriven, stipple, pubd 1824 (after G. Kneller), NG Ire. • E. Ashfield, pastel drawing, NG Ire. • attrib. P. Lely, oils, NG Ire. • P. Lely, oils, NG Ire. • R. Williams, mezzotint (after W. Wissing), NG Ire. • portrait, repro. in J. Fenlon, *The Ormonde picture collection* (2001) • portraits, repro. in Barnard and Fenlon, eds., *The dukes of Ormonde* • portraits, repro. in R. Ormond and M. Rogers, eds., *Dictionary of British portraiture*, 1 (1979), ii, 102

Butler, James, second duke of Ormond (1665–1745), army officer, politician, and Jacobite conspirator, was born in Dublin Castle on 29 April 1665, the second and eldest surviving son of Thomas *Butler, sixth earl of Ossory (1634–1680), soldier and politician, and his wife, Aemilia

James Butler, second duke of Ormond (1665–1745), by Sir Godfrey Kneller, *c.*1695

van Nassau (*d.* 1688), the daughter of Lodewijk van Nassau, lord of Beverweerd, a Dutch army officer and administrator. His paternal grandfather was James *Butler, first duke of Ormond (1610–1688).

Early years Lord James Butler, as he was known until 1680, was educated privately, including a period spent in Orange in 1677/8. Just before France annexed the principality in 1680 he matriculated at Christ Church, Oxford, on 4 March 1679. However, he was not suited to an academic life—Peter Drelincourt, his Swiss companion and tutor, reported in August 1679 that his young charge:

> being born of such illustrious a family, and to such a great estate as he is, and being not intended for a doctor, he needeth neither much learning neither a governor, being both old and wise enough to govern himself, and to do what he pleaseth. (*Hist. U. Oxf.* 4: *17th-cent. Oxf.*, 233)

He also spent lavishly, a characteristic trait throughout his career, getting through £1100 in his first year at Oxford and prompting his grandfather to thoughts of providing him with a military career. On 30 July 1680 he had succeeded his father as Baron Butler of Moore Park in the English peerage, but he was known by his superior Irish title of earl of Ossory. He proceeded MA from Oxford on 6 September 1680, the year in which he received an MA from Dublin University.

On 20 July 1682 Ossory married Anne (*bap.* 1667, *d.* 1685), daughter of Laurence *Hyde, then Viscount Hyde of Kenilworth, and from November 1682 earl of Rochester. They had one daughter who died in 1688. In February 1683 both Ossory and his grandfather were admitted to the Middle Temple and in May Ossory received a DCL from Oxford. In August 1683 he was appointed colonel of an Irish regiment of horse, and he gleaned important military experience as part of the French forces besieging Luxembourg in May 1684.

In July 1684 Ossory inherited the Scottish title Lord Dingwall from his grandmother Elizabeth *Butler, *née* Preston, duchess of Ormond, although he did not claim the title until 1711. His wife died in Dublin Castle on 25 January 1685 following a miscarriage. On 14 March 1685 he was summoned by writ to the English parliament and on 19 May he took the oaths as Baron Butler of Moore Park. On 16 May he was appointed a gentleman of the bedchamber to James II. He was present at the battle of Sedgemoor on 6 July. On 3 August at Badminton, Gloucestershire, Ossory married Lady Mary Somerset (1664/5–1733), daughter of Henry *Somerset, first duke of Beaufort. A son, Thomas, died in infancy, but two daughters reached adulthood, Elizabeth (1688/9–1750), who died unmarried, and Mary (1689/90–1713), who married John, third Baron Ashburnham. Ossory also fathered at least one illegitimate son, William Butler, who served as a captain in Brigadier Echlin's dragoons. Ossory was made colonel of a regiment of Irish foot guards in January 1686, although by then he was living in London in a separate establishment in St James's Square.

On 21 July 1688 Ossory succeeded his grandfather as duke of Ormond in the Irish and English peerages. Almost immediately opponents of James II's religious policies moved on 23 July to elect Ormond to the chancellorship of Oxford University in order to forestall a royal nominee. The earl of Rochester then proceeded to court to persuade James II to accept the decision, which was accomplished when Ormond took up the post with royal approval in August. He also succeeded his grandfather as chancellor of Dublin University, and as high steward of both Westminster and Bristol. In September 1688 he was nominated to the Garter, but he was clearly ill at ease with James II's policies, and on 17 November signed a petition to the king asking him to call a free parliament. He then joined William of Orange on 25 November and subsequently attended meetings of peers in London in December designed to facilitate the calling of a free parliament and secure public order.

Reign of William III Ormond voted on 31 January 1689 against the motion to declare William and Mary king and queen, and on 4 and 6 February against the motion to declare that James had abdicated the throne. These stances aligned him with high toryism and Jacobitism; however, his Dutch connections (his mother was William's second cousin) and his friendship with William saw him reconciled to the new regime. He was appointed a gentleman of the bedchamber (1 March), had his Garter confirmed (installed on 5 April), and was named lord high constable of England for the coronation on 11 April. On 20 April he was named colonel of the second troop of Life Guards. James II's successful invasion of Ireland saw him attainted by the Irish parliament in May 1689, but Ormond spent the summer campaigning in Holland, Henry Prescott recording that he had 'conducted himself splendidly' (*Diary of Henry Prescott*, 1.737) in a battle near Till. In the following year he joined William's Irish campaign and was present at the battle of the Boyne on 12 July. He was then sent to take possession of Dublin, and on 19 July was able to welcome the king to his main Irish residence, Kilkenny Castle. In December 1690 he was sworn of the Irish privy council and in February 1691 he was named lord lieutenant of Somerset.

Ormond spent the next few summers on campaign with William III in the Low Countries. He was named a major-general for the campaign of 1692 and he was present at the battle of Steenkerke in July 1692. In March 1693, possibly piqued at the failure to secure promotion, he offered to resign his commission 'in regard the campaign would be a great charge, and his affairs required his presence in Ireland' (Luttrell, 3.66–7). This was a plausible reason because Ormond had inherited debts of approximately £98,500 (some estimates put the figure as high as £150,000) from his grandfather which took £6000 per annum in interest payments out of an estimated income of £17,000 a year in 1690/91. This debt burden was constantly rising and his lavish expenditure on campaign (over £2000 per annum) only accentuated his difficulties. Not surprisingly, William decided that he could not be spared and Ormond took part in the campaign, seeing action in July 1693 at Landen, where he was wounded and taken prisoner by the French, before being exchanged for James FitzJames, duke of Berwick, James II's illegitimate son. He was raised to the rank of lieutenant-general in 1694. Following two failed attempts by commissioners (in 1691 and 1694) to bring his debts under control, the Irish parliament in 1695 passed the first of many private acts (both English and Irish) aimed at restoring the Butler family finances. It provided for lands to be vested in trustees to be sold or leased to pay debts. Ormond returned to the campaign in 1695 and was present at the siege of Namur. On 9 April 1696 he was sworn of the English privy council before again serving in Flanders in the summer. Ormond remained a tory in domestic politics and he voted against the attainder of the Jacobite plotter Sir John Fenwick in the Lords in November 1696. Early in October 1697 Ormond joined his duchess in Ireland, and on 10 November 1697 he took his seat in the Irish House of Lords. This may have been an economy measure coupled with the need to sort out his finances, for in 1697 the English parliament passed a private act to permit the sale of woods and the granting of leases for lives renewable for ever. He rented Clancarty House in Dublin, and there were reports that the mansion in St James's Square was being rented out to the French ambassador. Ormond stayed in Ireland until November 1698.

In February 1699 Ormond resigned his place in the bedchamber, which William then gave to his brother Charles, earl of Arran. Ormond always had a finely developed sense of his own honour, and when the Dutch favourite Arnold Joost van Keppel, earl of Albemarle, was promoted colonel of the 1st troop of Horse Guards, ahead of Ormond, he resigned his colonelcy of the second troop. This played well among tories in parliament keen to show their disapproval of the king's preference for all things Dutch, but in the event Ormond withdrew his resignation. In 1701 the English parliament passed yet another private act to protect Ormond's estate, managed through the House of Lords by Rochester.

Reign of Queen Anne Following the accession of Queen Anne, Ormond was employed in April 1702 to command the land forces for the attack on Cadiz. After initial success the main objective of the attack was not achieved amid much looting by Ormond's troops. On 26 September the troops re-embarked and only the fortuitous sighting of the Spanish treasure fleet at Vigo enabled some military advantage to be gained with much of the French escort destroyed and a large haul of treasure captured. Ormond himself had led the detachment which had landed to seize the batteries commanding the bay at Randa Fort. However, Ormond and Admiral Sir George Rooke had disagreed throughout the campaign and, despite favourable votes from both houses praising both men, Ormond complained of Rooke's conduct. As the duke of Marlborough wrote in November 1702, an inquiry into Cadiz 'ought not to be desired by anybody that was there, so that I hope the Duke of Ormond will be discreter than to complain of Sir George Rooke' (*Marlborough–Godolphin Correspondence*, 1.146). Having been the origin of proceedings against Rooke, Ormond declined to give evidence in the matter and the admiral was exonerated.

In February 1703 Ormond was appointed lord lieutenant of Ireland. This was a popular appointment given the aura surrounding his grandfather and the fact that Ormond was the first Irish viceroy since the revolution. Not everyone was confident that he had the requisite qualities for the post. John Isham summed up the feelings of many when he wrote 'he is generally very well beloved here, but unless he has some better heads about him than he usually converses with, I much question whether he will govern this kingdom long to the satisfaction of England' (Barnard, 17). The new fields of patronage open to Ormond at least helped to stave off the encroaching financial crisis which he faced, although even this advantage was offset by his belief in the ostentatious display appropriate to his governmental position. He arrived in Dublin in June 1703, and after a difficult first session (including the passage of an estate act on his behalf) left Ireland in March 1704. By this date he had been allowed to breach the principle that serving lieutenants should not command Irish regiments by obtaining permission to raise a horse regiment. Ormond returned to Ireland in November 1704, and left again in June 1705.

In September 1705 Ormond invited the lord treasurer, Sidney Godolphin, first earl of Godolphin, and other leaders of the English ministry to a lavish treat at the villa in Richmond Park, Surrey, that he had leased the previous year. This may have been good politics because the Marlborough–Godolphin duumvirate found Ormond a difficult man to deal with, particularly as they felt that he was unduly influenced by tories such as his former father-in-law, Rochester. Thus in June 1706 Marlborough wrote, 'he is so poor a man, that the hands he is in will never let him serve the Queen as he ought to do' (*Marlborough–Godolphin Correspondence*, 2.590). The political difficulty for Godolphin was to find a replacement acceptable to the ministry's whig allies who wanted the viceroyalty for Thomas, Baron Wharton. In the event Ormond was replaced as lord lieutenant of Ireland by Thomas Herbert, eighth earl of Pembroke, in April 1707, not that this change of administration prevented another private bill to protect his finances from being passed by the Irish parliament. Ormond remained valuable to the ministry—so much so that upon hearing rumours of his wish to sell his regiments in December 1708 Marlborough hoped to persuade the queen not to permit it, 'since it must turn to her disservice' (ibid., 2.1185). On party issues Ormond still supported the tories, voting in March 1710 against the impeachment of Dr Henry Sacheverell. Ormond's finances were if anything getting worse, as he was deprived of the emoluments of high office and in 1710 the Irish parliament passed an act vesting all his estates in the hands of trustees.

The return of the tories to power in the autumn of 1710 presaged Ormond's return to high office. At first there was some talk that he preferred a household post, the mastership of horse, to a return to the Irish lieutenancy, as it 'would have been as much to his liking', and 'he having the character of a generous good natured fine gentleman, and not one that would set up for a politician, those that are in possession of the Queen's ear could have suffered him near there without any jealousy' (*Wentworth Papers*, 149). However, he was evidently of more use in Ireland and he was duly appointed lord lieutenant on 26 October 1710. It was Ormond's prompt action on 8 March 1711 which prevented the marquis de Guiscard from being killed on the spot following his attempt to assassinate Robert Harley. Ormond duly arrived in Dublin in July 1711 and left in November, following the prorogation of the Irish parliament. The dismissal of the duke of Marlborough from his military employments on 1 January 1712 saw Ormond appointed colonel of the first troop of foot guards, commander-in-chief of the armed forces in England and Holland, and, most prestigious of all, captain-general. Meanwhile, in 1712 the British parliament passed an act granting Ormond permission to surrender to the crown his palatine jurisdiction in Tipperary in return for financial compensation. Ormond travelled to Flanders to take command of the British troops, but on 25 April he received instructions from the secretary of state, Henry St John, Viscount Bolingbroke, advising him to take great caution in taking military action. These anticipated the more specific 'restraining orders' that Ormond received in May, which debarred him from active campaigning against the French without further approval. These instructions were to be kept secret from the allies, but the ministry informed the French. Ormond agreed to operations covering Prince Eugene of Savoy's siege of Quesnoy, but with the fall of the town imminent Ormond had to inform Prince Eugene that he had to suspend operations for two months. In July 1712 Ormond marched the British contingent away from the allied army only to find most towns in the Low Countries closed against him. Rather grudgingly, Louis XIV permitted their entry into Dunkirk, having previously refused admittance on the ground that the German troops paid by the British remained in the field.

By 1713 sales had reduced the gross rental on Ormond's estates to approximately £11,000 per annum. However, Ormond continued to accumulate offices, adding the lord lieutenancy of Norfolk in April 1713, and in June was made lord warden of the Cinque Ports. He continued to support the tory ministry in the Lords, voting in June 1713 for the commercial treaty with France. He was replaced as lord lieutenant of Ireland on 22 September 1713. In October 1713 Ormond began regular contact with the exiled Jacobite court. By early 1714 he was being seen as the key to a Jacobite restoration on the death of Queen Anne, partly no doubt because his military position made it possible for him to play a role comparable to that of George Monck at the restoration of Charles II in 1660. On the accession of George I Ormond lost all his offices and became part of the tory effort to reverse the sudden decline in their fortunes. He attended meetings hosted by Francis Atterbury, bishop of Rochester, aimed at uniting the tories before the general election of 1715. The whig triumph at court, followed by a crushing victory at the polls, set the scene for the pursuit of those responsible for the policies of the 1710–14 tory ministry, including Ormond, who was vulnerable for having carried out the restraining orders.

Exile Ormond was impeached for 'high treason and other high crimes and misdemeanours' by the House of Commons on 21 June 1715. There is a suggestion that whig ministers used the Spanish ambassador to persuade Ormond to leave the country, but Ormond may have thought it prudent to do so anyway. He left at the end of July and arrived in Paris on 8 August. Ormond's removal disrupted plans for a Jacobite rising in the west of England, which was subsequently abandoned by the arrest of its putative leaders, such as George Granville, Baron Lansdowne. Ormond's flight served only to assist his enemies in parliament and he was given until 10 September 1715 to surrender or face attainder by act of parliament and forfeiture of his estates to the crown. His debts were now estimated at £110,500, with a notional rental income of £16,000 per annum which was in reality less than half of that. His English and Irish estates were now administered by the forfeited estates commissioners until a private act of 1721 allowed Ormond's brother, Arran, to buy them back. The duchess of Ormond remained in England and was to benefit from efforts on her behalf to protect her jointure from confiscation. A clause on her behalf was in 1716 added to the bill appointing commissioners for forfeited estates, and the following year another clause was added to the bill enabling the king to grant relief to the wives of forfeited persons. After 1720 she settled in Paradise Row, Chelsea.

Once in France Ormond requested assistance from Louis XIV and attempted to reactivate the western rising, which was to coincide with the Scottish expedition under John Erskine, earl of Mar. He was duly appointed captain-general by the Pretender in October 1715. However, this plan proved abortive following the betrayal of the plans to the ministry in England. With the Pretender no longer welcome in France, in April 1716 Ormond accompanied the exiled court to the papal enclave at Avignon, where he was made a knight of the Thistle in April. In July 1716 he was derogated from the Order of the Garter. However, when the exiled court moved to Rome early in February 1717 Ormond soon left for Paris and then became embroiled in attempts to obtain support from Sweden against George I. Ormond was dispatched on an embassy to Russia in the autumn of 1717 in an attempt to gain succour for the Jacobite cause. However, plans for a Russian bride for the Pretender and attempts to compose Russo-Swedish differences fell through and by June 1718 Ormond was back in Paris.

The defeat of the Spanish fleet at Cape Passaro in 1718 led Philip V's chief minister, Cardinal Alberoni, to seek an alliance with the Jacobites. Ormond was summoned to Madrid in November 1718 and made a general in the Spanish army. Plans were concocted for an invasion of the west country headed by Ormond, with a secondary expedition to the highlands of Scotland. However, the fleet intended for the invasion was damaged by storms in the Bay of Biscay at the end of March 1719. On 10 March the House of Commons was informed of the preparations and a royal proclamation issued offering a reward of £5000 for Ormond's capture. He continued in Spanish service until 1723, although this did not prevent him from becoming heavily involved in the Jacobite efforts at a restoration, loosely described as the Atterbury plot. Ormond was to lead an invasion spearheaded by Irish officers in Spanish service which was timed to coincide with the British general election due in 1722. However, parallel plans in England failed to materialize so that although the small flotilla of ships was ready to sail in April 1722, by the time it reached Bilbao in June the expedition had been cancelled.

In 1729 *The Life and Character of James Butler* was published in order to advance any possibility of Ormond acquiring a pardon following the death of George I. Ormond remained resident in Spain until 1732, when he settled in Avignon. There his presence was tolerated by the papal authorities despite the occasional complication caused by his devout Anglicanism. His duchess died on 19 November 1733. Ormond paid a visit to Spain in 1740 and thereafter remained in Avignon, where he spent his declining years in very pleasant surroundings. Lady Mary Wortley Montagu described his existence there in 1743: 'he keeps an assembly where all the best company go twice a week, lives here in great magnificence, is quite inoffensive, and seems to have forgotten every part of his past life and to be of no party' (Dickson, lviii). Appearances could be deceptive, however, for in 1744 Ormond was prepared to travel to Dunkirk to assist Prince Charles Edward's invasion fleet.

Ormond died in Avignon on 16 November 1745 NS, although some contemporary reports placed his death in Madrid. His body was taken back to England for burial on 22 May 1746 in Westminster Abbey. He was succeeded in his Irish peerages by his brother, the earl of Arran, who did not assume them.

Significance Ormond's appearance was slightly unprepossessing: according to St Simon 'he was rather short, stout and short-necked'. However, these physical attributes were overshadowed because he 'bore himself very gracefully, with the air of a *grand seigneur* and great politeness and nobility of manner' (Cruickshanks, 'The second duke', 248). Ormond was a landed aristocrat to whom good manners and courtly accomplishments came easily, but he lacked the qualities to be a major political figure; above all, he lacked political judgement. As John Macky wrote, Ormond was

> one of the most generous, princely, brave men that ever was, but good-natured to a fault; loves glory, and consequently is crowded with flatterers; … hath all the qualities of a great man, except that one of a statesman, hating business. (GEC, *Peerage*)

Jonathan Swift concurred with the view that Ormond allowed himself to be imposed upon by lesser, self-seeking men, noting that he was 'governed by fools and has usually much more sense than his advisers, but never proceeds by it' (Simms, 4). Field Marshal James Keith, although critical of Ormond's timidity in military matters, saw him as 'a man of a very easy temper, and of an ordinary understanding, so diffident of himself that he often followed the advice of those who had a smaller share of sense than himself' (Dickson, xx). However, James Barry, fourth earl of Barrymore, summed up his prestige in Jacobite circles when he noted on his death that 'the Duke's age and rank set him above all jealousies and envy, an advantage no other subject can pretend to' (Cruickshanks, *Political Untouchables*, 96).

STUART HANDLEY

Sources GEC, *Peerage* • *The Jacobite attempt of 1719: letters of James Butler, second duke of Ormonde, relating to Cardinal Alberoni's project for the invasion of Great Britain on behalf of the Stuarts, and to the landing of a Spanish expedition in Scotland*, ed. W. K. Dickson, Scottish History Society, 19 (1895) • D. Szechi, *Jacobitism and tory politics, 1710–1714* (1984) • C. I. McGrath, *The making of the eighteenth-century Irish constitution: government, parliament and the revenue, 1692–1714* (2000) • D. Szechi, *The Jacobites: Britain and Europe, 1688–1788* (1994) • C. Dalton, ed., *English army lists and commission registers, 1661–1714*, 6 vols. (1892–1904) • N. Luttrell, *A brief historical relation of state affairs from September 1678 to April 1714*, 6 vols. (1857) • *The Marlborough–Godolphin correspondence*, ed. H. L. Snyder, 3 vols. (1975) • G. V. Bennett, *The tory crisis in church and state, 1688–1730: the career of Francis Atterbury bishop of Rochester* (1975) • R. Beddard, ed., *A kingdom without a king: the journal of the provisional government in the revolution of 1688* (1988) • M. de Ruvigny, *The Jacobite peerage* (1904) • A. D. Francis, *The*

First Peninsular War, 1702–1713 (1975) · *Hist. U. Oxf.* 4: *17th-cent. Oxf.* · T. C. Barnard, 'Introduction: the dukes of Ormonde', *The dukes of Ormonde, 1610–1745*, ed. T. C. Barnard and J. Fenelon (2000), 1–53 · J. Fenelon, 'Episodes of magnificence: the material worlds of the dukes of Ormonde', *The dukes of Ormonde, 1610–1745*, ed. T. C. Barnard and J. Fenelon (2000), 137–59 · D. W. Hayton, 'Dependence, clientage and affinity: the political following of the second duke of Ormonde', *The dukes of Ormonde, 1610–1745*, ed. T. C. Barnard and J. Fenelon (2000), 211–41 · E. Cruickshanks, 'The second duke of Ormonde and the Atterbury plot', *The dukes of Ormonde, 1610–1745*, ed. T. C. Barnard and J. Fenelon (2000), 243–53 · R. Moulins, 'James Butler, second duke of Ormonde in Avignon', *The dukes of Ormonde, 1610–1745*, ed. T. C. Barnard and J. Fenelon (2000), 255–62 · L. B. Smith, 'Spain and the Jacobites, 1715–16', *Ideology and conspiracy: aspects of Jacobitism, 1689–1759*, ed. E. Cruickshanks (1982), 159–77 · E. Cruickshanks, *Political untouchables: the tories and the '45* (1979) · *The Wentworth papers, 1705–1739*, ed. J. J. Cartwright (1883) · *The diary of Henry Prescott, LLB, deputy registrar of Chester diocese*, ed. J. Addy and others, 3 vols., Lancashire and Cheshire RS, 127, 132–3 (1987–97) · J. G. Simms, 'The establishment of protestant ascendancy, 1691–1714', *A new history of Ireland*, ed. T. W. Moody and others, 4: *Eighteenth-century Ireland, 1691–1800* (1986), 1–30

Archives BL, letter-book, Add. MS 33950 · Bodl. Oxf., corresp. · Bodl. Oxf., letter-books · NL Ire., corresp. and papers · NL Ire., letter-books · NL Ire., letters · Northants. RO, corresp. · Royal Arch., corresp. and related material · Yale U., Farmington, Lewis Walpole Library, corresp. relating to Jacobite intrigues | BL, corresp. with John Ellis, W. Chapman, Lord Longford, and others, Add. MSS 28875–28927, *passim* · Bodl. Oxf., letter-book of corresp. with Cardinal Jules Alberoni · CAC Cam., corresp. with Thomas Erle · V&A NAL, corresp. and papers

Likenesses G. Kneller, oils, *c.*1695, Examination Schools, Oxford [*see illus.*] · mezzotint, 1700–40 (after M. Dahl, 1714), NG Ire. · J. Smith, mezzotint, pubd 1701 (after G. Kneller), BM; NG Ire., NPG · J. Smith, mezzotint, pubd 1702 (after G. Kneller), NG Ire., NPG · G. Kneller, oils, 1713, NG Ire. · attrib. M. Dahl, oils, 1714, NPG; version, Deene Hall, Northamptonshire · J. Brooks, group portrait, mezzotint, pubd *c.*1747 (*The battle of the Boyne, 1st July 1690*; after J. Wyck), NG Ire. · J. H. Robinson, stipple and line engraving, pubd 1834 (after G. Kneller), NG Ire. · attrib. M. Dahl, oils, Badminton Park, south Gloucestershire · J. Faber senior, mezzotint, BM, NPG · P. Pelham, mezzotint (after M. Dahl, 1714), NG Ire. · P. Pelham, mezzotint (after G. Kneller), BM, NPG · P. Schenck, mezzotint (after unknown portrait, 17th cent.), NG Ire. · P. Schenck, mezzotint (after G. Kneller), NPG · J. Simon, mezzotint (after M. Dahl, 1714), BM, NG Ire., NPG

Butler, James (1830–1913). *See under* Heaton, Clement (1824–1882).

Butler, James Armar (1827–1854), army officer, was the fourth son of Lieutenant-General the Hon. Henry Edward Butler (1780–1856), who served in the 27th regiment in Egypt and afterwards as a colonel in the Portuguese army at Busaco, where he was wounded, and of his wife, Jane (*d.* 1834), daughter of Clotworthy Gowan. Somerset Richard Butler, third earl of Carrick, was his uncle. Educated on the continent and at Sandhurst, Butler was commissioned ensign in the 90th regiment in 1843. He served in the Cape Frontier War of 1846–7, was promoted lieutenant in 1847, and purchased his captaincy in the Ceylon rifle regiment in May 1853.

Butler and his friend Lieutenant Charles Nasmyth of the Bombay artillery went to the Crimean War in 1854, initially not under military command. They visited the siege at Silistria, and soon found themselves actively assisting the Turkish command, which was under strong pressure from the besieging Russian troops. Butler's energy and courage helped maintain the morale of the garrison. On 13 June he was wounded in the forehead and died on 22 June, just before the Russian troops retired. On 14 July, before the news of his death arrived, he had been promoted a major in the army, and lieutenant and captain in the Coldstream Guards.

H. M. Stephens, *rev.* James Lunt

Sources A. W. Kinglake, *The invasion of the Crimea*, 8 vols. (1863–87) · J. H. Lehmann, *Remember you are an Englishman: a biography of Sir Harry Smith* (1977) · *The autobiography of Lieutenant-General Sir Harry Smith*, ed. G. C. Moore Smith, 2 vols. (1901); repr. (1902) · A. J. Smithers, *The Kaffir wars* (1973) · C. Nasmyth, letters, *The Times* (1854) · E. H. Nolan, *The illustrated history of the war against Russia*, 1 (1855) · Boase, *Mod. Eng. biog.* · Burke, *Peerage* · *GM*, 2nd ser., 42 (1854), 304

Butler, James Edward (*d.* 1709). *See under* Butler, Pierce, styled third Viscount Galmoye, and Jacobite earl of Newcastle (1652–1740).

Butler, Sir James Ramsay Montagu (1889–1975), historian, was born in the master's lodge, Trinity College, Cambridge, on 20 July 1889. Both his grandfather and his father, Henry Montagu *Butler (1833–1918), had been headmaster of Harrow School, and in 1886 the latter was appointed master of Trinity College. His first wife had died three years earlier, and in 1888 he married second a 21-year-old former Girton student who had recently graduated in top place in classics, Agnata Ramsay, daughter of Sir James Henry *Ramsay, tenth baronet, of Bamff, Perthshire [*see* Butler, Agnata Frances (1867–1931)]. Jim Butler, as he was always known to his friends and in his family, was the eldest of the three sons born of the second marriage. Of the first marriage there were two sons and three daughters.

At the age of thirteen Butler moved from St Faith's preparatory school, Cambridge, to Harrow School with an entrance scholarship and quickly showed great ability and brilliant promise. Four years later he became head of the school. In 1905 Butler took the Trinity College examination and was awarded a scholarship; but he did not matriculate until October 1907. As an undergraduate his great ability was further confirmed by the award of a long succession of university scholarships and prizes for Latin and Greek verse and prose, culminating in the chancellor's classical medal (1911). In 1910 he was elected president of the union, and he crowned his successes by gaining first class honours in part one of the classical tripos (1909) and in part two of the history tripos (1910). In 1913 his college elected him to a prize fellowship, and the thesis which he submitted for the competition was published as *The Passing of the Great Reform Bill* (1914, reprinted 1964).

On the outbreak of war in 1914 Butler joined the Scottish Horse, a yeomanry regiment with which he served in the Gallipoli campaign of 1915 and in Egypt. In 1916 he joined the directorate of military operations in the War Office, and then served on the general staff in France. He was twice mentioned in dispatches and in 1919 was appointed OBE (military division) 'for services in connection with operations in France'.

Sir James Ramsay Montagu Butler (1889–1975), by Walter Bird, 1962

On demobilization Butler returned to Trinity College. He was one of the tutors to Prince Albert (later George VI) and Prince Henry (later duke of Gloucester) when they went to Cambridge for a year, for which he was appointed MVO (4th class) in 1920.

In 1922 Butler was nominated for one of the two parliamentary seats then allocated to the ancient universities and was elected as an independent. He played a prominent part in the debates leading to the passing of the Oxford and Cambridge Universities Act in July 1922, whereby commissions were set up with powers, for a limited period, to amend the universities' and colleges' statutes and ordinances. This ultimately led to the admission of women to full membership of Cambridge University. In the general election of December 1923, fought on the issue of tariff reform, Butler stood again as an independent Liberal; but he was narrowly defeated by his cousin, Sir G. G. G. *Butler, on the second ballot under the transferable vote system then in force.

Soon after his father's death in 1918 Butler moved from the lodge of Trinity College to the set of rooms at the top of the spiral staircase at the north-west corner of the Great Court, with lovely views over the Backs. There almost for the rest of his life he delighted to entertain his friends, especially to small lunch and dinner parties. Though a teetotaller himself, he was always a generous and delightful host. In 1925 he published a memoir of his father's thirty-one years as master of Trinity College, which remained a valuable social history of the politics and mores of Cambridge in that period. He was appointed a tutor by his college in 1928, and in the following year a university lecturer in history. In 1931 Trinity appointed him senior tutor, a responsible post which he held with success for seven years.

In the Second World War Butler served in the army intelligence corps, and from 1942 at the civil affairs and military government central organization. His work for France was recognized by his appointment as chevalier of the Légion d'honneur. In 1947 he was appointed regius professor of modern history in succession to G. N. Clark, and he held that chair until 1954. In his inaugural lecture, delivered on 26 January 1949, he argued that 'History has a strong claim to rank as one staple of a liberal education' and outlined the plans for the military histories of the war (*The Present Need for History*, 1949). Meanwhile in 1946 C. R. Attlee as prime minister had announced the government's intentions on the latter subject, and that Butler had been appointed chief military historian and editor of the whole series. It finally comprised forty-one volumes on grand strategy, the principal campaigns, and civil affairs and military government after the end of hostilities. Butler himself wrote the two grand strategy volumes covering September 1939 to August 1942 (vol. 2, 1957, and vol. 3, part 2, 1964). For his work on this project he was knighted in 1958.

In February 1955 Butler was elected vice-master of his college, an arduous and responsible post which he held with distinction for five years. When he resigned the regius chair in 1954, the university promptly elected him an emeritus professor of modern history. Having thus shed some of his responsibilities, he accepted a request that he should write the authorized biography of Philip Kerr, eleventh marquess of Lothian, a wartime ambassador in Washington (*Lord Lothian*, 1960).

In his very full life Butler's chief recreations were rock climbing and long walks in wild country—on the continent as well as in the British Isles. He never married, and his college and university always stood first in his interests and affections. He made a generous benefaction to Trinity College in his lifetime and another under his will. As a young man he left the Anglican church of his father and adopted the doctrines of Christian Science, to which he adhered strictly to the end of his life. When in 1975 he apparently suffered an accident and was obviously in great pain, it was only with difficulty that he was persuaded to enter a nursing home in Cambridge—for a rest and not for treatment. He died there on 1 March, and on 10 May 1975 a large congregation in the college chapel was bidden to recall 'the rare beauty of his character' and 'the gentle humorous charm of his manner'. No one who knew him would challenge that encomium.

STEPHEN W. ROSKILL, *rev.*

Sources *WWW* · Trinity Cam., Butler MSS · personal knowledge (1986) · private information (1986)

Archives Trinity Cam. | CAC Cam., A. V. Hill MSS · CAC Cam., Roskill MSS · CUL, Butterfield MSS · HL, Beaverbrook MSS

Likenesses W. Stoneman, photograph, 1948, NPG · H. Lamb, pencil drawing, 1949, Trinity Cam. · W. Bird, photograph, 1962, NPG [*see illus.*]

Wealth at death £95,217: probate, 9 April 1975, *CGPLA Eng. & Wales*

Butler, John, sixth earl of Ormond (*d.* **1476/7**), magnate, was the second son of James *Butler, the fourth earl (1390–1452). He served in Normandy under his elder brother in 1440, and was squire for the king's body when taken prisoner by the French in August 1449. He supported the Lancastrians in the civil war, serving under Henry Beaufort, duke of Somerset, at Guînes and Dieppe, and was attainted by Edward IV's first English parliament. He styled himself earl after the execution of his brother,

James *Butler, the fifth earl (1420–1461), and invaded Ireland in 1462, where he seized the family estates and captured Waterford. This Lancastrian revival in Ireland ended with the Butler defeat by the earl of Desmond at the battle of Piltown, after which the sixth earl fled to Portugal and was attainted by the Irish parliament. He returned to England in February 1471 during Henry VI's readeption, when his English attainder was annulled and he was recognized as earl of Ormond. He visited Portugal again in 1472, but was pardoned by Edward IV before 23 November 1474, recognized as earl, and accompanied the king to France in July 1475. His attainder was annulled by the Irish parliament the same month. Allegedly, Edward IV used to say of him that he was 'the goodliest knight he ever beheld and the finest gentleman in Christendom' (*DNB*). According to family tradition, Ormond died unmarried in the Holy Land, on pilgrimage, before 15 June 1477, possibly on 14 December 1476; but his illegitimate son with Raynalda O'Brien, Sir James *Ormond (*d.* 1497), later became joint governor of Ireland. Ormond was succeeded as seventh earl by his brother, Thomas Butler. STEVEN G. ELLIS

Sources E. Curtis, ed., *Calendar of Ormond deeds*, 6 vols., IMC (1932–43) • GEC, *Peerage*, new edn • H. F. Berry and J. F. Morrissey, eds., *Statute rolls of the parliament of Ireland*, 4 vols. (1907–39) • A. Cosgrove, 'The execution of the earl of Desmond, 1468', *Journal of the Kerry Archaeological and Historical Society*, 8 (1975), 11–27 • J. Warkworth, *A chronicle of the first thirteen years of the reign of King Edward the Fourth*, ed. J. O. Halliwell, CS, old ser., 10 (1839) • E. B. Fryde and others, eds., *Handbook of British chronology*, 3rd edn, Royal Historical Society Guides and Handbooks, 2 (1986) • *DNB*

Archives NL Ire., deeds

Butler, John (1717–1802), bishop of Hereford and pamphleteer, was born in Hamburg, the son of John Butler. He matriculated at University College, Oxford, as a plebeian, on 10 May 1733, aged fifteen, and graduated BCL in 1746 and DCL in 1752. Butler then took holy orders and was appointed rector of Ashley, Hampshire, in 1750 (held to 1777). In 1751, while acting as chaplain to Bishop Thomas Hayter of Norwich, he obtained additionally the major parish of Great Yarmouth, and showed himself a conscientious incumbent during the ten years for which he held the post. Butler's relentless ambition and Hayter's post as preceptor to Prince George led him into Leicester House circles during the 1750s. He held office as chaplain to the princess dowager of Wales, and he struck up a close association with Henry Bilson-Legge, chancellor of the exchequer in the Pitt–Newcastle coalition of 1757–61. His connection with Leicester House presaged a career of importance, which was confirmed when he was chosen to preach before the House of Commons on the occasion of the general fast in 1758.

At this stage of his life Butler was a staunch whig churchman, sceptical about making the established church more comprehensive, and he was further rewarded by installation as canon of the tenth prebend of Winchester Cathedral on 18 December 1760 (held to 1788). This preferment revealed that Butler was attracting notice from the duke of Newcastle and the 'old corps' whigs via his main patrons, the Onslow family, for his preaching and journalism. He had little sympathy with the new order represented by Lord Bute. In 1762 he issued an anonymous pamphlet, entitled *An Address to the Cocoa Tree from a Whig*. It attacked Bute for relying on tory support and not possessing the public's confidence which, Butler argued, was retained by the old corps. The pamphlet quickly ran to three editions.

The Onslow connection (notably George, fourth baron and first earl) helped to ensure Butler's survival, and he followed them in gradually transferring his loyalties from the Rockingham faction to the court. So did his nomination as one of George III's chaplains, in the late 1760s, after the Walpole family had recommended his promotion to Lord Hertford, the lord chamberlain. His courtier-like behaviour thereafter damned him forever with Horace Walpole. 'Is there a yard of lawn in England more dirty than Butler's?', Walpole later demanded of William Mason (Walpole, *Corr.*, 29.134). Butler hardly concealed his careerism. On 24 November 1769 he was installed as archdeacon of Surrey yet discharged the office diligently. His ascent was also helped by a successful second marriage. His first wife, whose name is unknown, had kept a school at Westminster, whereas his second, Ann, whom he married about 1763, was the daughter and coheir of Sir Charles Vernon of Farnham, Surrey. Butler thus further consolidated his position in the Winchester diocese.

By the 1770s Butler was careful not to upset the court and he made a point of opposing the dissenters' claims for relief in 1772. He had not abandoned the writing of polemical literature but, under the name of Vindex, spoke out for Lord North's policies towards the rebellious American colonists. Ambition was leading him to articulate sentiments on the imperial crisis that barely differed from clergy colleagues with tory pedigrees. In his private correspondence with Lord Onslow he was no less stern when rejoicing in the sending of Hessian troops to New York and in the slaughter of citizens that followed the fall of that city: 'Mankind cannot suffer by the extirpation of them', he observed (5 Nov 1776, Onslow MSS, Surrey HC, G173/2/1, p. 128). As archdeacon of Surrey he took the lead in drawing up the address of loyalty to the crown from the Winchester diocesan clergy in November 1775, and was an obvious choice to preach the fast day sermon before the House of Commons at St Margaret's, Westminster, on 13 December 1776. Butler took a firm but moderate line on the rebellious Americans, declaring that they had 'brought the mischiefs of War upon themselves and us, by taking up arms against a legal Authority, legally exercised' (Butler, *Sermon*, 7). While commentators including Horace Walpole still thought that his tone was too understanding to commend it to the court the sermon turned out not to have damaged his hopes of a mitre.

Butler was consecrated bishop of Oxford on 25 May 1777. His time in the see was relatively uneventful, apart from his rebuilding the episcopal house at Cuddesdon and his helping Charles Woide to transcribe the Alexandrine manuscript of the Bible. Butler had hoped for a deanery to supplement the low episcopal income of Oxford and, though he finally resigned as archdeacon of Surrey on 1 April 1782, he was not rewarded for his sacrifice until translation to the see of Hereford in 1788 (elected 13 February). This last episcopate was his finest hour, in pastoral terms, and he threw himself into overhauling the workings of the diocese, 'being determined', as he told Lord Onslow, 'to crowd as much useful work as possible into the remaining part of my life' (1 May 1788, Onslow MSS, G173/2/2, p. 46). His three published visitation charges show that he combined pastoral concern with administrative competence and that he was strict in enforcing clerical residence and in recommending catechetical instruction. Most of his sermons appeared in *Select Sermons* (1801). Butler died on 10 December 1802, leaving no children but much property. NIGEL ASTON

Sources *GM*, 1st ser., 68 (1798), 804 · *GM*, 1st ser., 72 (1802), 233–5, 1170 · A. Chalmers, ed., *The general biographical dictionary*, new edn, 7 (1813), 455 · Foster, *Alum. Oxon.* · Nichols, *Lit. anecdotes*, 9.10 · W. R. Ward, ed., *Parson and parish in eighteenth-century Hampshire*, Hampshire RS, 13 (1995), 162 · C. J. Palmer, *The perlustration of Great Yarmouth*, 1 (1872), 167 · C. J. Palmer, *The history of Great Yarmouth* (1856), 183 · *Fasti Angl.* (Hardy), 1.473 · *Fasti Angl.*, 1541–1857, [Canterbury], 89, 103 · O. Manning and W. Bray, *The history and antiquities of the county of Surrey*, 3 (1814), 160 · *Fasti Angl.*, 1541–1857, [Bristol], 78 · [J. Butler], *Account of the character of the Rt. Hon. H. B. Legge* (1762?) · [J. Butler], *An address to the cocoa tree from a whig*, 3rd edn (1762) · J. Butler, *A sermon preached before the honourable House of Commons at the church of St. Margaret's, Westminster, on Friday, December 13, 1776*, 2nd edn (1777) · *Critical Review*, 43 (1777), 73–4 · *Monthly Review*, 56 (1777), 78 · *The last journals of Horace Walpole*, ed. Dr Doran, rev. A. F. Steuart, 2 vols. (1910), vol. 1, pp. 103, 594; vol. 2, p. 136 · Walpole, *Corr.*, 29.134, 188, 192 · P. Langford, 'The English clergy and the American revolution', *Political culture*, ed. Helmuth (1990), 275–307
Archives Hereford Cathedral Library, letters to his wife, MS 3391 | NL Scot., letters to Lord Hailes · Oxon. RO, Oxfordshire archives, diocese book, diocesan MSS, MS Oxf. dioc. papers c.327, c.654 · Surrey HC, letters to first earl of Onslow, G173/2/1–2 · Yale U., Beinecke L., New Haven, Connecticut, letters to Thomas Balguy
Likenesses line engraving, pubd 1783, NPG · W. Pether, pastel drawing, *c.*1800, bishop's palace, Hereford · P. J. Simon, stipple (after T. H. Hall), BM, NPG · engraving (after W. Pether, *c.*1800), repro. in J. Butler, *Select sermons* (1801), frontispiece

Butler, John (1728–1796), army officer in America, was born in Connecticut. Little is certain of his early life except that he married Catherine Bratt, with whom he had at least one son, Walter *Butler (1752–1781). By the eve of the American War of Independence, he had long established himself as a prominent landholder, merchant, and liaison with Native Americans in the Mohawk valley, New York. In the climate of rising tensions between Britain and its North American colonies, he also established himself as a leading loyalist in a divided region.

When war erupted in 1775, most of Butler's family was held in Albany, while he and his son, Walter, managed to flee to Montreal. A region that was crucial to both sides in the war was the area between Albany and Canada; the Mohawk valley was a significant part of this, because it offered the American patriots the most feasible route into Canada and the British a passage through which to strike at the centre of the rebellious colonies. Any success in the region could be won, however, only with the assistance of the power of the Iroquois confederacy and its tributaries. Britain's department of Indian affairs, however, had been thrown into disarray the previous year with the death of its northern superintendent, Sir William Johnson, who for two decades dominated the scene and placed the affection of the Iroquois above all else. Matters were worsened with the departure of Johnson's heirs and closest allies for England, where they would secure his former position and wealth as a benefit to be passed down to the next Johnson generation. In their absence the Iroquois confederacy, along with the vast majority of Native Americans in the region, declared their neutrality. Butler was given the unhappy position of acting superintendent of Indian affairs by Quebec's military governor, General Guy Carleton, and assigned the difficult task of persuading the Iroquois to fight with the British until Johnson's replacement arrived in July 1776.

Butler's competence, either as a diplomatist or as a military commander, is unclear. He certainly had the confidence of Carleton, but Johnson's heirs, which included Sir William's official replacement and probable nephew, Guy Johnson, and Joseph Brant, Sir William's brother-in-law and a prominent leader of the Mohawk (a component of the Iroquois confederacy), clearly had a low opinion of him. Operating primarily out of Niagara, Butler certainly abused his position, allowing merchants such as Edward Pollard to exercise lucrative monopolies over the distribution of supplies to Native Americans, but such activities were par for the course. His tactics of recruiting the wary Iroquois were equally unsavoury. His primary device was said to have been rum, which he distributed freely before signing up young braves, and in diplomatic encounters he mixed lies about American patriot intentions to annihilate the natives with threats of British military might. On one such occasion, in May 1776, he concluded:

> You had better recall your resolutions and determine to keep the Kings peace, and the King will then be glad to hear from you. What a wretched situation must you be in when the King attacks all the seaports in America and comes in earnest to sweep off the Americans, if he finds you supporting the Americans. (Graymont, 96)

It should be noted, however, that such tactics were not unique to either the British or the whites.

After the return of Sir William's heirs, who were far more familiar and trusted by the Iroquois leaders (and in fact included a number of them), recruiting drives met with much greater success. The jealous Butler continued his efforts to rally the Iroquois to the British cause, but his intoxicated and ill-equipped recruits were more of an annoyance to Brant and the Johnsons than a help. Nevertheless, in the following year Butler was assigned the charge of raising a new corps of loyalists, aptly called Butler's rangers, who were to be used as special forces units on the New York frontier. They were expected to be highly mobile guerrilla fighters who spoke Native American languages and used native methods of wilderness warfare. Such skills were essential, as these men were expected to fight side by side with Native Americans. They took the scalps of the enemy dead and wounded, tortured captives, and even used the chilling war whoop of native warriors as their battle cry. As leader of this force Butler rose to the rank of lieutenant-colonel.

Butler's rangers were used in the brutal engagements that were the hallmark of the New York frontier campaigns fought by divided communities and families that were intent on dealing out the most brutal punishments for perceived disloyalty. Nor was this a white affair, as the Iroquois confederacy itself was drawn indecisively into the conflict and consequently torn apart, and its warriors found themselves defending their homes against former relatives and allies. The rangers were at virtually all of the major engagements in the region, among them the infamous attack on Cherry valley, commanded by Walter Butler, in November 1777, in which thirty-two civilians, mostly women and children, were massacred. Butler himself commanded the assault on Wyoming valley, Pennsylvania, in the following summer; there his rangers and native allies, primarily Seneca and Mohawk warriors of the now broken Iroquois confederacy, boasted taking 227 scalps. Despite capitulation terms to the contrary, Butler's victorious forces plundered the area's settlements, which included upwards of a thousand abodes, a greater number of cattle, and all of the mills. Recounting the events after withdrawing to Niagara, as was the case each autumn after a spring and summer of raids, Butler proudly remarked to Carleton:

> But what gives me the sincerest satisfaction is that I can with great truth assure you that in the destruction of this settlement not a single person has been hurt of the Inhabitants, but such as were in arms, to those indeed the Indians gave no Quarter. (Graymont, 172)

At the conclusion of the war Butler and his rangers were justly wary of returning home to the frontier communities they had pillaged, and so most of them accepted royal land grants in the Niagara peninsula once the corps was disbanded in June 1784. Butler retained his leadership role, serving as the district judge and deputy superintendent of Indian affairs. He died there in 1796.

TROY O. BICKHAM

Sources E. Cruikshank, *The story of Butler's rangers and the settlement of Niagara* (1893); repr. (1975) · B. Graymont, *The Iroquois in the American Revolution* (1972) · C. G. Calloway, *The American Revolution in Indian country: crisis and diversity in Native American communities* (1995) · R. S. Allen, *His majesty's Indian allies: British Indian policy in defence of Canada, 1774–1815* (1992) · D. Ritcher, 'Butler, Walter', *ANB* · J. Potter, *The liberty we seek: loyalist ideology in colonial New York and Massachusetts* (1983)

Archives BL, Haldimand papers, Add. MSS 21661–21892 · Hist. Soc. Penn., Yeates papers, corresp. · PRO, Carleton papers, 28, vols. 1–10 · PRO, Carleton papers, 30, vol. 55

Wealth at death substantial lands in Canada

Butler, John, styled twelfth Baron Dunboyne (1731–1800), Roman Catholic bishop of Cork, was the third son of Edmond Butler, styled eighth Baron Dunboyne (*d.* 1732), of Grange, co. Tipperary, and Anne Nagle, *née* Grace, widow of Richard Nagle, and daughter of Oliver Grace, of Shanganagh, co. Tipperary. The Grange Butlers, a landed family, were part of the network of Butler families and dependants which covered much of south Leinster and Munster. The title of Dunboyne had been forfeited by James, fourth Baron Dunboyne, for his implication in the Irish rising of 1641; he was outlawed, yet the title continued to be used and the estates were retained by the family. Butler's older brothers, Pierce and Edmond, were already soldiering in France when he decided on a career in the church. He travelled to Rome via Cadiz, Genoa, and Leghorn, and took up residence in the Irish College in the via degli Ibernesi. During his student years he attended lectures at the Congregatio de Propaganda Fide, and, in an obscure incident, lost his left eye. He was ordained priest on 20 December 1755 in the Lateran basilica, and appears to have completed his doctoral studies before returning to Ireland in 1758. On his way home he was delivered over to a justice of the peace at Whitehaven in Cumberland, but was not detained. He returned to his native diocese of Cashel and was appointed parish priest of Ardmayle in 1759. He also took up duty as bishop's secretary and was made an archdeacon. During the following four years he re-established himself in the Butler social network.

When the diocese of Cork fell vacant, Butler, supported by local bishops, emerged as a strong candidate. He was nominated bishop by Pope Clement XIII on 16 April 1763, and his consecration in June elicited a praise poem in Gaelic by Eadbhárd de Nógla. He took up residence at Monkstown, outside Cork city, had a city house at Pope's Quay, and was parish priest of St Mary's. The beginning of his episcopal ministry coincided with the gradual emergence of the Catholic community from civil and economic disadvantage. The Catholic church underwent reorganization, following the Tridentine model, as it adapted to more tolerant conditions. Butler was heavily involved in this process and, in the first ten years of his episcopate, three new chapels were built in Cork. He was, however, careful not to alienate the protestant establishment, with whom he had many contacts. When the pioneering local educationist Nano Nagle engaged to introduce the Ursuline Sisters to the city, Butler delayed their arrival until 1771 so as not to offend protestant sensibilities. His episcopate witnessed widespread urban and rural agitation which often turned into violence. He condemned the coopers' riots in Cork in an 'exhortation' published in the *Hibernian Chronicle* (2 July 1766). Rural Whiteboy anger in Munster was sometimes directed against Catholic clergy over stole fees and other dues, and, in his *Statuta synodalia pro dioecesi Corcagiensi* (1768), he declared that association with the Whiteboys was a reserved sin. He subscribed to the Test Act of 1774 and gave strong financial support to the Catholic committee.

In December 1785 Butler inherited the title and estate of Lord Dunboyne, following the death of his nephew Piers Butler, usually called the eleventh Baron Dunboyne. As a Catholic priest he had taken a vow of celibacy but, if he did not produce an heir, the direct line in the lordship of Dunboyne was in danger of extinction. He resigned his see in December 1786, petitioned the pope for a dispensation from celibacy, and married in 1787 Maria Butler (1764/5–1860), of Wilford, co. Tipperary, daughter of Theobald Butler and Elizabeth Lee. His request to the pope was rejected and he took the oaths of allegiance, abjuration, and supremacy in Clonmel on 19 August 1787. His is the sole authenticated instance of the apostasy of a member of the Catholic Irish hierarchy. He moved to the family seat in Dunboyne, co. Meath, shortly afterwards. A daughter was born to the couple but died young. They later moved to Lesson Street in Dublin. Butler's attitude towards the rising of 1798 is unknown, though the village of Dunboyne was burned in the disturbances, including the Catholic chapel, which was later rebuilt on land granted by the Butler family. In 1800, worn down by age and illness, he addressed a letter of repentance to the pope and made his will. He was confessed by the Augustinian preacher William Gahan, and died in Lesson Street, Dublin, on 7 May 1800. He was interred in the Augustinian friary in Fethard, co. Tipperary. Litigation over his will, by which he left his Meath estates to the Catholic college at Maynooth, commenced almost immediately. A compromise between the college and the Butler family was reached in 1808 which permitted the setting up of the Dunboyne establishment at Maynooth College to maintain and endow selected scholars for additional studies. The title of Dunboyne was restored on 26 October 1827 when the attainder was reversed and James Butler (1780–1850) was confirmed as thirteenth Baron Dunboyne.

THOMAS O'CONNOR

Sources C. Costello, *Faith or fatherhood? Bishop Dunboyne's dilemma: the story of John Butler, Catholic bishop of Cork (1763–1787)* (2000) · GEC, *Peerage* · *DNB*

Archives Cashel diocesan archives · Sacra Congregazione di Propaganda Fide, Rome, scritture riferite mei congressi, Irlanda | Dublin diocesan archives, Troy MSS · Blackrock, Cork, annals of Ursuline convent

Wealth at death see will, Costello, *Faith or fatherhood?*, 163–71

Butler, Joseph (1692–1752), moral philosopher and theologian, was born on 18 May 1692 in Wantage, Berkshire. He was the youngest among the eight children of Thomas Butler (*d.* 1731), variously described as a prominent cloth merchant or linen draper in the town and as 'gentleman' in the records of Oriel College, Oxford, on Butler's admission as an undergraduate there in 1715. Six of the children—three boys and three girls—survived infancy, and the family lived in a house now called The Priory, leased from the dean and chapter of Windsor, at the south-west corner of the parish churchyard. The eldest child, Robert, who died in 1749, helped Butler financially during the early part of his career. Robert's son Joseph was ordained by Butler in 1741, and it was this branch of the family that settled at Kirby House, Inkpen, Berkshire, and provided information about Butler's life to Thomas Bartlett, his biographer. Butler's other brother, Jonathan, and his eldest sister, Deborah, are also named by Bartlett. The Butler family was Presbyterian, part of a thriving community in Wantage with its own chapel.

Early years and education, 1692–1718 Butler stipulated in his will that all his papers should be destroyed after his death, and as he did not marry there is little surviving correspondence or manuscript evidence to provide details of his personal life. He was sent to the grammar school in Wantage, which was situated alongside the parish church, just

Joseph Butler (1692–1752), by Mr Taylor of Durham, 1750–52

a few yards from his home. The schoolmaster, the Revd Philip Barton, clearly had a significant influence on Butler, who was to appoint him to the living of Hutton, Essex, in 1740, although no evidence survives of the curriculum followed at the school.

It is likely that Butler originally intended to be ordained as a Presbyterian minister, and in 1711 or 1712 he was sent to the dissenting academy recently opened by Samuel Jones in Gloucester, which moved to Tewkesbury in 1713. Jones had been a student at Leiden and brought to his teaching a depth and range that soon gave his academy a high reputation. One of his pupils was Thomas Secker, the future archbishop of Canterbury, whom Butler met when he went to Gloucester and who was to become a significant figure in his life. Secker's autobiography attests to the range of Jones's teaching, which included study of the ancient languages, logic, mathematics, geography, and biblical studies. Through Jones's lectures on logic Butler was introduced to John Locke's *Essay Concerning Human Understanding*.

It is clear that Butler was also reading contemporary theological texts, for it is from this time that his correspondence with Samuel Clarke dates. Clarke's Boyle lectures of 1704, *A Demonstration of the Being and Attributes of God*, were first published in 1705 and caused a great deal of interest, generating intense debate about the nature of God's existence, the relationship between God and space, and the immateriality of the soul. Butler was one of many who challenged Clarke on particular aspects of his argument, in a series of anonymous letters in 1713 and 1714, to which Clarke replied. The correspondence concerned matters of divine omnipresence and divine necessity. Clarke was so impressed by the perspicacity and manner of his young critic that the correspondence was published in an appendix in 1716 as *Several letters to the Reverend Dr Clarke from a gentleman in Gloucestershire relating to the 'Discourse concerning the being and attributes of God'*. A French translation of *A Demonstration*, which included the exchange with Butler, appeared in Amsterdam in 1717. The relationship thus established with Clarke, cemented by further correspondence, was to serve Butler well in his future career.

By 1714 Butler had acquired a sound general education, together with a familiarity with contemporary philosophical and theological literature. It was at this point that he took the decision to conform to the Church of England. There is no surviving evidence to cast light on his reasons for conforming, although Secker's autobiography refers to correspondence that he himself, who had not yet conformed, had with Butler over subscription to the Thirty-Nine Articles. An early biographer connected with the Butler family suggests that Butler's father tried to dissuade him from this course of action and then relented. Membership of the Church of England opened up the ancient universities to Butler and he entered Oriel College, Oxford, on 17 March 1715. After the depth and rigour of his education at Jones's academy Oxford was something of a disappointment to him. He wrote to Clarke that he had to 'mis-spend so much time here in attending frivolous lectures and unintelligible disputations' (30 Sept 1717, *Works*, 1.332), and considered the possibility of moving to Cambridge. That he stayed in Oxford may have been due to his friendship with Edward Talbot, a fellow of Oriel since 1712 and second son of William Talbot, bishop of Salisbury and, later, of Durham. Until his early death, in 1720, Talbot did much to advance the prospects of Butler and, later, Secker and their mutual friend Martin Benson. Butler graduated BA from Oriel on 11 October 1718, and on 26 October was ordained deacon by William Talbot. His ordination to the priesthood, again by Talbot, took place on 21 December 1718 in Clarke's church, St James's, Piccadilly.

London and Stanhope, 1718–1738 It was not long before the patronage of the Talbot family bore further fruit. After a brief period assisting Edward Talbot in the parish of East Hendred, near Wantage, at that time in the diocese of Salisbury, Butler was appointed preacher at the Rolls Chapel, in London, in 1719 by Sir Joseph Jekyll, the independently-minded whig MP and master of the rolls, on the recommendation of Bishop Talbot and Samuel Clarke. Jekyll, himself the product of a dissenting academy, was known for his sympathy with unorthodox theological opinions and was a patron of William Whiston and Thomas Chubb. The Rolls Chapel, which no longer survives, was assigned by Edward III in 1377 to the keeper of the rolls of chancery and eventually became a chapel for the legal profession as well as a record repository. The chapel, in Chancery Lane, was rebuilt by Inigo Jones in 1617, and in the early eighteenth century attracted a sophisticated congregation receptive to the careful and reasoned discourses that Butler preached to them. From his six or seven years at the Rolls Chapel only the *Fifteen Sermons*, published in 1726 and dedicated to Jekyll, survive. Secker helped Butler to prepare the sermons for publication and also assisted with the clarification of Butler's argument in the preface to the second edition in 1729.

Butler was now established in London and was beginning to move in prominent ecclesiastical and legal circles. His place in the legal establishment was marked by his proceeding to the BCL degree at Oxford on 10 June 1721, and he was made a prebendary of Salisbury Cathedral in the same year. Yet he soon had additional responsibilities outside London as the patronage of the Talbots expanded. In November 1721 William Talbot was translated from Salisbury to Durham and soon took advantage of his new position to help the friends whom his son Edward had commended to him. In 1722 Bishop Talbot presented Butler to the living of Haughton-le-Skerne, near Darlington, and in 1724 presented Secker, who had now conformed and been ordained by Talbot, to the benefice of Houghton-le-Spring, providing Benson with a prebendal stall at the cathedral in the same year. Thus began Butler's long association with the diocese and county of Durham. From 1722 he began to divide the year between his living and his duties at the Rolls Chapel but was hampered by the dilapidated state of the rectory at Haughton until Secker persuaded Talbot to allow Butler to exchange the living for the richer benefice of Stanhope, in Weardale, where the income was boosted by tithes from lead mining and where the rectory was in good order. The generous income of Stanhope, where he moved in 1725, allowed Butler to resign the Rolls preachership, and he resided entirely at Stanhope until 1733, working as a diligent parish priest and writing his most famous work, the *Analogy of Religion*.

Very little evidence remains of the routine of Butler's life at Stanhope. He was known throughout his adult life for his modest lifestyle, his generosity with money, and his sense of obligation towards the needy, and these characteristics were probably evident in his work as a parish priest. There is evidence that he was visited in Stanhope more than once by the Seckers and the Talbots—Edward Talbot's widow, Mary, and their daughter Catherine, who lived with Secker and his wife, Benson's sister. Catherine Talbot, a future member of the Bluestocking Circle, became a close friend. Butler's father died in 1731, and Butler was joint executor of the will with his brother Robert. Much time must have been spent in the writing of the *Analogy*. Although written as a defence of the Christian religion against the criticisms of deist and freethinking writers such as Matthew Tindal and Anthony Collins, it is also possible to see in the *Analogy* a more personal attempt by Butler to position himself with respect to the influences of his youth, such as Locke and Clarke, and to debates within the Church of England in the 1720s and 1730s about the nature of Christian belief and the place of the church. For Butler, as for Secker, the breadth of his formative education, his journey from dissent to conformity, and his familiarity—through the Talbots—with thinkers and writers on the verge of heterodoxy, such as Whiston and

Thomas Rundle, provided additional motivation for a statement of Christian belief that took careful account of criticisms and that was cast in an empirical mould rather than a rationalistic one.

Secker, who had become a royal chaplain in 1732 and rector of St James's, Piccadilly, in 1733, was concerned that his old friend was becoming isolated in Stanhope and commended him to Queen Caroline, the philosophically literate consort of George II. Caroline, a former pupil of Leibniz, was interested in following contemporary theological debates, summoning churchmen such as George Berkeley, Samuel Clarke, and Benjamin Hoadly to discuss theology with her. The queen expressed some surprise, thinking that Butler was dead, but the archbishop of York, Lancelot Blackburne, is believed to have replied, 'No, Madam; but he is buried' (*Works of the Right Reverend Father in God, Joseph, Late Lord Bishop of Durham*, ed. S. Halifax, 1849, 1.xlviii). An opportunity soon presented itself, in November 1733, when Charles Talbot, the elder brother of Edward, became lord chancellor. He immediately made Butler his chaplain, at Secker's suggestion, which Butler accepted on the understanding that he would continue to reside in Stanhope for half the year. Butler proceeded to the degree of DCL at Oxford on 8 December 1733, which was presumably the occasion of his presenting a silver claret jug to Oriel College.

Now that Butler and his friends were back under Talbot and royal patronage they soon succeeded to prominent positions in the church, at a time of some turbulence in its relationship with the government. A number of government measures, such as the Mortmain Bill and the Quaker's Tithe Bill, were thought to erode the status and privileges of the Church of England in favour of nonconformity and anticlericalism. The nomination of Thomas Rundle, another Talbot protégé, to the see of Gloucester in December 1733 was blocked by Edmund Gibson, bishop of London and Walpole's principal ecclesiastical adviser, on the grounds of Rundle's suspected deistic tendencies. In the event Butler's friend Benson was appointed in Rundle's place and Benson and Secker were consecrated bishop together—Secker to the neighbouring diocese of Bristol—in January 1734.

It is from about this time that there is evidence of a cooling in relations between Secker and Butler. Secker, according to his autobiography, clearly thought Butler did not sufficiently appreciate his efforts to commend him to Lord Chancellor Talbot:

> on his telling me & my Wife & Mrs Talbot, how well he was in the Chancellors Family we told him how much we had suffered on account of our getting him into it; & that we had concealed it from him, to prevent his being uneasy. But we could never get him, in several Conversations which we had with him on the Subject, [to say] either that he was obliged to us, or that he was sorry for us: but he rather appeared to slight us, & take the Part of Dr Rundle & Mr William Talbot against us. (*Autobiography of Thomas Secker*, 15–16)

In the early years of his episcopate Secker was regarded by Walpole and others as an unreliable supporter in the House of Lords and it is possible that this caused some tension between him and Butler.

1736 was an important year for Butler. *The Analogy of Religion* was published in May. Again Secker had helped with the preparation of the text, 'which cost me a great deal of time & pains' (*Autobiography of Thomas Secker*, 16), improving some of the style and language. A second, corrected, edition appeared in the same year. Queen Caroline appointed Butler as her clerk of the closet—the head of her ecclesiastical household—and he administered the sacrament privately to her on 4 July 1736. His duties included daily attendance on the queen between 7 and 9 in the evening to take part in theological discussion, and necessitated the renting of lodgings near the court (both at Kensington Palace and Hampton Court). His income was boosted by his appointment on 16 July 1736, through the influence of Lord Chancellor Talbot, to a prebendal stall at Rochester Cathedral, of which he was elected vice-dean on 25 November 1738. This was the last act of Talbot patronage that Butler received: William Talbot had died in 1730 and Lord Chancellor Talbot died in December 1736.

Queen Caroline died on 20 November 1737, and it was reported by Lord Hervey that on her deathbed she commended Butler to John Potter, the archbishop of Canterbury. It is clear that in his brief tenure of office as her clerk of the closet Butler had been highly regarded by the queen and it was not long before her wishes were fulfilled. On Secker's translation to Oxford, Butler was nominated to the see of Bristol, on 19 October 1738, and consecrated in the chapel of Lambeth Palace on 3 December 1738.

Major works By the time that he became a bishop Butler had written and published the writings that made a major contribution to philosophy and theology in the English language. The *Fifteen Sermons Preached at the Rolls Chapel* and *The Analogy of Religion* were the fruit of the years between 1719 and 1736, although they also drew on the intellectual exploration of Butler's years in Tewkesbury and Oxford, which is evident in the correspondence with Clarke.

The *Fifteen Sermons* were first published in 1726, although Butler added an important preface to the second edition, in 1729, in which he says that the sermons were chosen from among his preaching output at the chapel rather than having been written as a series of discourses to argue a particular case. The book is widely accepted as one of the most significant ethical writings of the eighteenth century; in it Butler uses a searching analysis of human nature as the foundation of an ethical theory that propounds that virtue consists in following nature, while vice is deviation from nature. One of Butler's targets is the psychological egoism of writers such as Thomas Hobbes and, more recently, Bernard de Mandeville. Yet he is not an uncritical follower of the 'moral sense' theory of the third earl of Shaftesbury, who tended to emphasize feeling rather than reason as the basis for morality and posited an innate human capacity to distinguish virtue from vice.

In his analysis Butler puts forward an essentially hierarchical view of human nature in which the various motivational principles in the human personality are ranked and need to be integrated properly if virtuous action is to ensue. Thus conscience, implanted by God, is the most important principle, which 'pronounces determinately some actions to be in themselves just, right, good; others to be in themselves evil, wrong, unjust' (J. Butler, *Fifteen Sermons*, 2.8). Self-love and benevolence are principles that are not entirely consistently handled by Butler, although it is reasonably clear that he regards 'cool self-love' as superior to benevolence, which in its turn holds greater sway than particular appetites and passions such as hunger, thirst, love, and hate. The relationship between conscience and self-love is crucial in Butler's attempt to provide an account of moral behaviour that avoids the extremes of psychological egoism on the one hand and a highly abstract metaphysical system on the other. Butler the preacher is concerned to help his congregation to lead virtuous lives by stripping away the moral and intellectual confusion that may hinder them. His theological presuppositions—the existence of an ordered universe created by God and the existence of a future life—enable him to minimize the possibility of conflict between conscience and self-love, between duty and long term self-interest:

> Conscience and self-love, if we understand our true happiness, always lead us the same way. Duty and interest are perfectly coincident; for the most part in this world, but entirely and in every instance if we take in the future and the whole; this being implied in the notion of a good and perfect administration of things. (ibid., 3.9)

The careful and nuanced approach to complex issues of the *Fifteen Sermons* is also apparent in Butler's principal contribution to contemporary theological debate, *The Analogy of Religion, Natural and Revealed, to the Constitution and Course of Nature*, published in 1736. In the *Analogy* Butler does not attempt to create an imposing intellectual system *de novo*. He is, rather, the calm apologist grappling with contemporary arguments that challenged the Christian faith and dealing methodically with their errors and inconsistencies. In particular he deals with the challenge of deism, of which the principal recent expression was Tindal's *Christianity as Old as the Creation*, published in 1730. Deism cannot be presented as a clearly defined or systematic philosophy but was a term used to describe an outlook in contemporary religious thought that asserted the supremacy of reason over revelation in understanding and explaining the Christian faith. The deists, who as individuals ranged from active Christian ministers to those on the verge of atheism, typically based their estimate of religious truth on what could be known to the enquiring mind through the use of reason alone. For them reason can at best prove the existence of a God who is an impersonal and distant creator necessary for the maintenance of the laws of nature. Such central beliefs of revealed religion as the doctrine of the Trinity, the divinity of Christ, and the authority of the church are rejected by them as irrational and incoherent. Together with this intellectual critique of revealed religion goes an anticlerical attack on the power and institutions of the church and, in some instances at least, a radical political outlook.

There is some evidence that Butler engaged in correspondence, now lost, with Lord Kames during the 1730s on the evidences of natural and revealed religion. This is the subject of the *Analogy*, in which Butler counters the deist critique by arguing both that the investigation of nature can show us more than the deists allow—such as the existence of a future life and that this life is a time of moral probation—and that the difficulties apparent in Christian revelation are analagous to the difficulties apparent in the account of natural religion offered by the deists. Butler criticizes his opponents for setting standards of proof for revelation that are not satisfied either by the deistic beliefs that they proclaim or by a range of commonsense beliefs that they do not question. The evidence of Christianity is

> the kind of evidence upon which most questions of difficulty in common practice are determined: evidence arriving from various coincidences, which support and confirm each other, and in this manner prove, with more or less certainty, the point under consideration. (J. Butler, *Analogy of Religion*, pt 2, chap. 7, para. 30)

Butler constantly directs attention to the way that we ordinarily think and insists that we cannot and should not proceed differently in matters of religion. In religion as in ordinary life what is needed for reasonable belief is not certainty but enough probability to warrant action. The arguments about the need to rely on probabilities—'probability is the very guide of life'—and the necessity of deciding in practice between alternatives that can none of them be proved beyond doubt have a more general application than Butler's particular argument with the deists.

Butler appended two dissertations, 'Of personal identity' and 'Of the nature of virtue', to the *Analogy*, the first of which has become influential, arguing against Locke and others for the existence of a real identity throughout a person's life. The second, originally intended to form part of the main text of the *Analogy*, clarifies Butler's account of the role of conscience by placing it in the realm of God's providence and so restricting its sphere of authority.

Bishop of Bristol, 1738–1750 Butler did not greet his preferment to Bristol with unalloyed enthusiasm. Writing to Robert Walpole on receiving the news that he was to be appointed to Bristol he commented: 'Indeed, the bishoprick of Bristol is not very suitable either to the condition of my fortune, or the circumstances of my preferment; nor, as I should have thought, answerable to the recommendation with which I was honoured' (Bartlett, 73–4). Bristol was the poorest diocese in England, yielding an annual income of between £300 and £450 for much of the eighteenth century, insufficient for Butler's needs. He therefore retained his incumbency at Stanhope, which provided an income almost twice that of Bristol, and his prebendal stall at Rochester. In addition to Bristol and Stanhope, however, he had to maintain a household in London during parliamentary sessions, which he did by hiring lodgings. It was not until 1740 that a convenient solution was found and Butler was appointed to the deanery of St Paul's Cathedral, where he was installed on 24 May 1740, providing him with a realistic income and a house in London. He was then able to resign from his posts at Stanhope and Rochester.

It is unlikely that Butler took up residence in Bristol until after the parliamentary session of 1739, which ended on 14 June. He conformed to contemporary practice and resided in his diocese during the summer months and on other special occasions, moving to London in the autumn for the parliamentary session. After the first two or three years of his episcopate his normal custom was to come to London in mid-October and stay there until the end of June, moving back to his diocese for three months or so in the summer. Incumbents who wished to be instituted to their livings had therefore in many cases to travel to London to go through the formalities with their bishop—until 1740 in St James's, Piccadilly, and latterly in the deanery of St Paul's. On occasion such duties were carried out in Bristol by the bishop's commissary.

The diocese of Bristol consisted of the deanery of Bristol, roughly coterminous with the city, and the county of Dorset. Bristol was the second city and second port in the kingdom. Its port dominated the Irish and West Indian trade and was the principal centre for the slave trade, though there was a marked decline in the volume of trade during the middle years of Butler's episcopate. The city had an active civic and social life with a prosperous merchant community and a growing working population on the margins of the city, who provided a willing congregation for George Whitefield and John Wesley from 1739 onwards. The evidence suggests that Butler was among the more diligent of eighteenth-century bishops in the regularity of his ordinations, visitations, and confirmations. Surviving records suggest a primary visitation of the diocese in 1739 or 1740, and further visitations in 1743, 1746, and 1749, a triennial pattern of visitations that matched the requirements of canon law.

An eighteenth-century bishop was expected to provide hospitality both to his clergy and to the leading citizens of the diocese. As Butler's later practice in Durham was to keep open house three days a week it is probable that he instituted a similar regime in Bristol, particularly when he was able to use his income from the deanery of St Paul's to refurbish his palace. His relations with the mercantile community were good and he received a gift of cedar wood from the merchants of Bristol, some of which he used in the renovation of his chapel and the rest he took to Durham, where it was later used by Bishop Barrington for furniture.

An important intermediary in Butler's relations with the city of Bristol was Josiah Tucker, whom Butler made his domestic chaplain. Tucker was Butler's frequent companion—he later wrote of Butler's habit of taking nocturnal walks in the garden of the bishop's palace—and was, like his bishop, closely involved in the development of the new Bristol Infirmary, for which Butler preached a sermon, now lost, in 1747. It was a sermon by Tucker that triggered a series of meetings between Butler and John Wesley in August 1739, at one of which Butler said to Wesley, 'Sir, the pretending to extraordinary revelations and gifts of the Holy Ghost is a horrid thing, a very horrid thing' (H. Rack, *Reasonable Enthusiast*, 2nd edn, 1992, 209). Butler's attempts to respond to the increasing activity of the Methodists in Bristol took a number of forms. He prompted Tucker to write a pamphlet, *A Brief History of the Principles of Methodism*, one of the most balanced and perceptive of the many attacks on Methodism at the time. The popularity of Wesley and Whitefield in the mining area of Kingswood Chase also convinced Butler that something should be done for the unchurched working people on the margins of Bristol society. He therefore spent time and money, buying the land himself for £400, to secure the necessary financial and parliamentary support for the establishment of the new parish and church of St George, built after he had left Bristol.

As a bishop of the Church of England, Butler had a seat in the House of Lords and sat in fourteen parliamentary sessions, from February 1739 to March 1752. After the first session, when he was frequently in the house, his attendance record was not notably regular or frequent. In every other session, with the exception of 1742–3, he was absent more often than he was present, with attendance tailing off in the second half of his episcopate. The king's ministers sought to appoint to the bench of bishops those who would provide political support for the government. On the whole the bishops were compliant with ministerial pressure of this kind and were usually to be relied upon in the lobby. Butler was among the more compliant and usually voted with the government when he was present, although he joined Secker, Benson, and two other bishops to vote against the Spirituous Liquors Bill on 25 February 1743. However, this was an unusual act of opposition and Secker was later to contrast Butler's support for the government with his own more principled stance:

> As my Favour with the Court & Ministry declined, his [Butler's] friendship did. He said to me, at the End of the first Session, in which he sat in the House of Lords [1739], that the ministers were both wicked Men & wicked Ministers. Yet he not only always voted with them, but expressed Contempt & Dislike of me for doing otherwise: & never, that I could hear, spoke a Word by way of Apology for me to any other Person. (*Autobiography of Thomas Secker*, 22)

That Butler's consistent support for the government was part of a carefully considered political stance is probable; his sermons display a sophisticated and nuanced support for the *status quo* and a characteristic horror of political disorder, the prospect of which was raised by events such as the Jacobite rising of 1745. At the same time many junior bishops in the eighteenth century recognized the spur of ministerial pressure as an incentive to preferment. As clerk of the closet after 1746 Butler was once again a member of the royal household, and in contention for promotion to a wealthier and more significant see.

Another body with which Butler had a connection was the Society for the Propagation of the Gospel in Foreign Parts (SPG). His attendance at the monthly meetings between November 1738 and December 1750 was erratic but he left the society £500 in his will and took a close interest in its affairs. A particular cause in which the SPG was involved in the late 1740s and early 1750s was the proposal to introduce the episcopate in the American colonies, and Butler was one of a number of bishops to present suggestions. His scheme, dating from 1750, was very cautious and would only have given bishops spiritual jurisdiction over their clergy and not civil powers over the large dissenting population. Yet it was not possible to win the support of Newcastle's government for any of the proposals, and the episcopate was not established until after American independence.

An important feature of Butler's public ministry as a bishop was the preaching of sermons before public institutions, many of which had an annual sermon or sermons. His *Six Sermons on Public Occasions*, published in a collected edition in 1749, were preached in London churches between 1738 and 1749, forming a small fraction of his preaching output as bishop. Of the six sermons three are concerned with the responsibility for charitable giving, two—preached before the House of Lords, in 1741 and 1747—raise questions about political society, while the first addresses the mission of the church. They display the same characteristics as his other writing: a cautious approach to the complexity of the issues, an awareness of the other side of the argument, and careful attention to criticisms that have been raised. Butler sees his teaching function as a bishop as being to strengthen the religious cement that holds a civilized society together and provides it with shared assumptions and a common moral discourse. He stresses the need to steer a middle course—of true religion, rather than atheism on the one hand or superstition on the other; and of civil liberty—that 'severe and … restrained thing' (J. Butler, *Six Sermons*, 3.17)—rather than tyranny or licentiousness. And he is acutely aware of the danger of disorder whenever people stray from the middle way, both religiously and socially; the danger of excess is a constant theme of his preaching, as it is of his writing.

Bishop of Durham, 1750–1752 By the late 1740s Butler's name was being mentioned in connection with a number of episcopal appointments and his appointment as clerk of the closet in 1746, which involved more frequent attendance at court, was an indication of the regard in which he was held by George II. When Edward Chandler, who had succeeded Butler's old patron William Talbot as bishop of Durham in 1730, died on 20 July 1750 Butler was rapidly nominated to the vacant see. The appointment was confirmed in October and Butler did homage and was enthroned by proxy at Durham on 9 November. However, he did not take possession of the see until the following June, and died only a year later. Butler's characteristic scrupulousness had threatened to delay the appointment. He objected to Newcastle's wish to detach the bishopric from the lord lieutenancy of the county palatine and said that he would not accept the bishopric on those terms. He also resisted Newcastle's attempt to appoint Thomas Chapman to a prebendal stall at Durham lest Chapman's appointment should be seen as a condition of his own preferment. His apprehension was expressed in a letter to a friend:

> It would be a melancholy thing in the close of life, to have no reflections to entertain oneself with, but that one had spent the revenues of the bishoprick of Durham, in a sumptuous course of living, and enriched one's friends with the promotions of it, instead of having really set one's self to do good, and promote worthy men. (Bartlett, 116)

When his appointment was announced it was thought that Butler was 'a man of unexceptionable character in private life' who would 'be much loved in the County' (Shuler, 116). His arrival in Durham on 28 June 1751 was a happy occasion, with its attendant official dinners and social functions. Butler then immediately began the primary visitation of his new diocese, which covered the counties of Durham and Northumberland—a gruelling schedule of travel with occasional periods of rest. Starting in Newcastle on 17 July he travelled as far north as Berwick before returning to Durham on 27 July. The visitation of the deaneries in co. Durham was completed in August.

The middle of the eighteenth century saw the church in the diocese of Durham under severe pressure. Decaying buildings, especially in Northumberland, and significant population changes demanded a level of flexibility of response that it proved very difficult to provide. Wesley's activity in Durham and Northumberland between 1742 and 1753 increased the pressure on the established church and its leaders, prompting the long-serving archdeacon of Northumberland, Thomas Sharp, to report on the 'visible decay of religion' (Shuler, 204) in his archdeaconry by 1752. It was this sense of decay and of a growth in scepticism about the claims of the Christian religion that had fuelled much of Butler's preaching over the previous decade and was the context for his primary visitation charge of 1751, one of the most significant pastoral documents written by a member of the eighteenth-century episcopate.

The Butler of the 1751 *Charge to the Clergy of the Diocese of Durham* is the Butler of the confrontation with Wesley: wary of religious enthusiasm; reticent in his own articulation of the Christian faith, which is not a matter for common conversation; aware of the part played by external forms of religion in generating a settled and confident faith. It is not that he doubts the truth of what he preaches but that he is acutely aware of the risks involved in communicating a religion, the evidence for which 'is complex and various' (J. Butler, *Charge*, para. 5), to an audience with the alarming capacity to misinterpret the message. This concern lies behind his practical suggestions about handling religious subjects when they arise in conversation and his conviction that sermons are inappropriate vehicles for open theological speculation. Butler's aim is to encourage his clergy to make constructive use of the opportunities available to them to press the claims of the Christian religion on a sceptical, or simply apathetic, society. He is aware of the difficulty of the task, as he states at the beginning of the *Charge*:

> It is impossible for me, my brethren, upon our first meeting of this kind, to forbear lamenting with you the general decay of religion in this nation; which is now observed by every one, and has been for some time the complaint of all serious persons. (ibid., para. 1)

This is not, however, a situation in which to despair. Butler stresses the absurdity of taking 'the supposed doubtfulness of religion for the same thing as proof of its falsehood' (ibid., para. 4). The author of the *Analogy* is well equipped to expose the slipshod thinking of those who demand knock-down proofs of religious truth. It is in conscientious pastoral practice that the clergy should be engaged. This will be difficult. Some parishes are very large, many people will resist the kind of serious conversation in which Butler wishes his clergy to engage them, and many parents will not be interested in their children's welfare. However, the task is sufficiently important to be persevered with.

As in Bristol, Butler was concerned with the social and charitable aspects of Christian witness. His interest in charity schools stood out among eighteenth-century bishops of Durham and he maintained his support for the hospital movement. On 5 September 1751, as its grand visitor, he laid the foundation stone of the new infirmary in Newcastle. The sermon that he had preached before the governors of the London Hospital in 1748 was reprinted in Newcastle, together with a covering letter from Butler to Archdeacon Sharp, as a way of raising interest and money for the infirmary. In the initial list of subscribers his was the most generous gift: £100 a year for five years and then £20 a year for life. He was to leave the infirmary £500 in his will.

Butler continued the tradition of episcopal hospitality and generosity that he had established at Bristol. He kept open house at Auckland Castle or Durham Castle, his two residences, for three days a week. He was always happy to retire to Auckland Castle, where the extensive park gave him some escape from the rigours of his work, 'my Park being a favourite article with me as, before I had one, my garden was' (Shuler, 119). His time there saw the addition of the South Park and the rebuilding of the garden wall; 'Butler's Steps' still survive in the castle. There is a charming tradition, too, that Butler, when tired, sat in the chapel at Auckland Castle, listening to the organ being played by his secretary. He also had work done at Durham Castle, in particular the decoration of the dining room in the Strawberry Hill Gothic style. Butler's generosity to those in need became legendary also, with much of his greatly increased income—Durham was the second wealthiest see in the Church of England—being spent on worthy causes. It was not in his nature to be profligate, however, and generosity with his own income went hand in hand with a firm and shrewd oversight of diocesan property.

Death and influence Only four months after his arrival in Durham Butler returned to London, to Vane House, the house in Hampstead that he bought after leaving the deanery of St Paul's, for the new session of parliament, which began on 14 November 1751. There is no evidence that he ever returned to Durham. He sat in the House of Lords on only eight occasions during the session, which ended on 26 March 1752—an indication of his declining health. He wrote his will on 22 April, added a codicil on 25 April, and by the end of May his health was causing sufficient concern to his doctors for a visit to Bath to be recommended. He arrived there on 3 June, having stayed for two nights at Cuddesdon, with Secker, on the way. Although it was Secker's impression that Butler was not alarmed by his condition he deteriorated rapidly, displaying the symptoms of acute liver disease. Benson reported to Secker on 12 June that Butler's case was hopeless. He died in Bath on 16 June, attended by his chaplain, Nathaniel Forster.

Butler's last days were a harrowing time for his friends. Benson interrupted his diocesan duties to visit Butler at least once, and he and the fretful and exhausted Forster kept Secker in constant touch with Butler's progress, detailing the treatment prescribed, agonizing over the adequacy of the medical attention, coping with those of Butler's relatives who were present, and making tentative arrangements for the funeral. Benson found his leave-taking exceptionally painful and it was left to Forster to announce tersely to Secker: 'This morning about eleven o'clock my best of Friends exchang'd this life for a far better' (LPL, MS 1373, fols. 18–19). Butler's body was taken to Bristol, where it was buried in the chancel of the cathedral (now the lesser lady chapel) on the afternoon of 20 June 1752. The news of his death did not reach Durham until three days after the funeral, although it had been known that he was beyond recovery. At 'about 6 the great bell in the Abbey tolled a short space on account of the bishop's death' (Gyll, 191). At Bristol Butler is commemorated by a memorial with an inscription by Robert Southey, and at Durham by a late-nineteenth-century memorial in the choir with an inscription by W. E. Gladstone.

Butler's defence of the external forms of religion in the Durham *Charge* was attacked by Francis Blackburne in *A Serious Enquiry into the Use and Importance of Religion* (1752). The *Charge*, together with Butler's refurbishment of his chapel at Bristol and the use of stained glass at Vane House, later led to a rumour that he had died a Roman Catholic. This occasioned a flurry of pamphlet and periodical exchanges in 1767 into which Secker, by now archbishop of Canterbury, was drawn in order to issue an authoritative refutation.

Butler left an intellectual legacy that was refracted through many different lenses. Ten editions of the *Analogy* were published in England, and five in Scotland, during the eighteenth century, while there were six English editions of the *Fifteen Sermons*, three of which were combined with the *Six Sermons*. During his lifetime Butler's work had attracted the attention of Kames and of Hume, who sent Butler a copy of his *Treatise on Human Nature* and tried to meet him. It was also reviewed in the learned journals of the time. The Scottish dimension was particularly significant, as Butler took his place in the debate about the relationship between religion and ethics generated by Shaftesbury's followers and their critics. In this context his influence on Francis Hutcheson, Kames, David Fordyce, Thomas Reid, and Adam Smith was pervasive. In England his moral philosophy had a marked influence on the work of David Hartley, who was a friend, and Richard Price, while the *Analogy* continued to attract attention in theological discussion. The German theologian J. J. Spalding translated the *Analogy* in 1756 and used it to defend the Lutheran church against the attacks of secularist critics while also distancing himself from the conservative pietism of many contemporary German clergy.

It was in the nineteenth century that Butler's influence became more institutionalized, as his work appeared on university syllabuses in Oxford and Cambridge from the 1830s, with R. D. Hampden in Oxford and William Whewell in Cambridge as influential proponents. John Henry Newman famously described Butler as 'the greatest name in the Anglican Church' (J. H. Newman, *Apologia pro vita sua*, 1959, 103) and wrote appreciatively of his influence. Yet Butler was also read outside university circles. Samuel Taylor Coleridge introduced William Hazlitt to Butler's work in 1798 and Hazlitt, who gave a public lecture on Butler, was later to write:

> the *Analogy* is a tissue of sophistry, of wire-drawn, theological special-pleading; the *Sermons* (with the Preface to them) are in a fine vein of deep, matured reflection, a candid appeal to our observation of human nature, without pedantry and without bias. (A. C. Grayling, *The Quarrel of the Age*, 2000, 56)

Coleridge's enthusiasm for Butler was influential in Cambridge and was also apparent in the work of F. D. Maurice.

Given that both the *Analogy* and the *Fifteen Sermons* had become set texts it is not surprising that many editions appeared during the nineteenth century and that they were translated into a number of languages. This was also the century of important collected editions of *Butler's Works*—most notably those by W. E. Gladstone (1896) and J. H. Bernard (1900)—and a number of books about Butler, culminating in W. A. Spooner's study (1901). Gladstone's edition was the culmination of a lifetime's enthusiasm for Butler, whose *Analogy* he had read as a set text at Oxford and whose thought provided him with a framework for his understanding of personal and political conduct as well as the relationship of Christianity to the modern world. His *Studies Subsidiary to the Works of Bishop Butler* (1896) was published as a companion volume to the *Works* and contained some material originally written in 1845, offering a somewhat conservative and defensive account of Butler's significance. Gladstone had earlier written to his son about Butler: 'I place him before any other author, the spirit of wisdom is in every line' (D. Lathbury, ed., *Correspondence on Church and Religion of W. E. Gladstone*, 1910, ii, 163).

Despite a period of relative decline in its reputation in the middle of the twentieth century Butler's moral philosophy continues to attract attention in the Anglo-American literature, not least because of his acute psychological insight into the human condition. If many of his theological preoccupations and strategies are now regarded as outdated, theologians and philosophers of religion are taking a greater interest in what might be extracted from his apologetic methodology and applied more generally, particularly in the use of probabilistic arguments. Spooner's judgement that Butler was apart from his own time in his life and modes of thinking, and was therefore misunderstood by his contemporaries, hints at the allure of a figure whose subtlety of thought and seriousness of purpose continue to attract attention.

CHRISTOPHER CUNLIFFE

Sources *The works of Bishop Butler*, ed. J. H. Bernard, 2 vols. (1900) • T. Bartlett, *Memoirs of the life, character and writings of Joseph Butler* (1839) • E. Steere, ed., *The sermons and remains of … Joseph Butler* (1862) • E. C. Mossner, *Bishop Butler and the age of reason* (1936) • T. Penelhum, *Butler* (1985) • C. Cunliffe, ed., *Joseph Butler's moral and religious thought* (1992) • *DNB* • I. Rivers, *Reason, grace, and sentiment: a study of the language of religion and ethics in England, 1660–1780*, 2 (2000) • J. C. Shuler, 'The pastoral and ecclesiastical administration of the diocese of Durham, 1721–1771: with particular reference to the archdeaconry of Northumberland', PhD diss., U. Durham, 1975 • *The autobiography of Thomas Secker, archbishop of Canterbury* (1988) • W. A. Spooner, *Bishop Butler* (1901) • J. B. Schneewind, *The invention of autonomy* (1998) • S. Clarke, *A demonstration of the being and attributes of God and other writings*, ed. E. Vailati (1998) • institution book, 1739–61, Bristol RO, EP/A/5/1/2 • 1746 visitation process, Bristol RO, EP/V/1 • confirmation schedule, Bristol RO, EP/A/21/1 • correspondence of Benson and Forster to Secker, LPL, MS 1373, fols. 5–24 • LPL, SPG papers, vols. 3–5 • will, U. Durham L., department of palaeography and diplomatic, SGD 35/14 [copy] • W. M. Jacob, *The making of the Anglican church worldwide* (1997) • *JHL*, 25–7 (1736–52) • D. E. White, *A Butler bibliography* (privately printed, 1993) • J. G. A. Pocock, 'Josiah Tucker on Burke, Locke, and Price', *Virtue, commerce, and history* (1985) • G. Shelton, *Dean Tucker and eighteenth-century economic and political thought* (1981) • N. Hope, *German and Scandinavian protestantism, 1700–1918* (1995) • T. Gyll, 'Diary', *Six north country diaries*, ed. [J. C. Hodgson], SurtS, 118 (1910) • *VCH Berkshire*, vol. 2 • H. C. G. Moule, *Auckland Castle: a popular history and description* (1918)

Archives BL, letters and other papers, Add. MSS • U. Durham L., department of palaeography and diplomatic, papers • U. Durham L., register | Bristol RO, Bristol diocesan records • LPL, letters; SPG minute books

Likenesses attrib. W. Fayram, oils, *c.*1730, Auckland Castle, Bishop Auckland, co. Durham • J. Vanderbank, oils, 1732, Auckland Castle, Bishop Auckland, co. Durham • T. Hudson, oils, *c.*1740; formerly at Kirby House, Inkpen, Berksire • Mr Taylor of Durham, oils, 1750–52, Newcastle Infirmary; various versions • Mr Taylor of Durham, oils, another version, 1750–52, Auckland Castle, Bishop Auckland, co. Durham [*see illus.*] • British school, oils, 1751–1752?, Auckland Castle, Bishop Auckland, co. Durham; repro. in Cunliffe, ed., *Joseph Butler's … thought* • R. Cooper, stipple engraving, 1816 (after W. Fayram), BM • oils (as young man), Magd. Oxf.

Wealth at death £9000–£10,000: will, U. Durham, department of palaeography and diplomatic, SGD 35/14

Butler [*née* Grey], **Josephine Elizabeth** (1828–1906), social reformer and women's activist, born on 13 April 1828 at Milfield Hill, Glendale, Northumberland, was the fourth daughter and seventh child of John *Grey (1785–1868) and Hannah Eliza, *née* Annett (*d.* 1860). She was unusual among nineteenth-century feminists in having family ties to the whig aristocracy: Lord Grey, the whig prime minister during the passage of the Reform Act of 1832, was her father's cousin. Except for two years at a school in Newcastle, Josephine was educated at home. As a young girl, she participated in county society events: she and her sister Harriet were belles at the hunt and county balls of Northumberland. Despite her gentry connections, Butler always distanced herself from fashionable society, preferring to identify herself as a member of the provincial middle classes. 'Democratic in all her instincts', she preferred the company of honest working men to members of the

Josephine Elizabeth Butler (1828–1906), by George Frederic Watts, 1894

'refined "better" classes': 'my sympathies are wholly with the non-privileged, even when they drop every "h"' (Bell, 105).

Beautiful and histrionic, meticulously dressed and coiffed, Butler was adored by men and women alike. A charismatic leader and gifted speaker, she could inspire intense personal loyalty among her co-workers. When Mary Priestman and her friend Mary Estlin went to hear Butler in Bristol in 1870, they waited 'amidst silence for the speaker'. A few minutes later, the door opened and Butler entered, 'slight and graceful—almost young & very beautiful'.

> As she moved to the table she raised her eyes with such a look of inexpressible sadness, as if the weight of the world's sin & sorrows rested on her innocent head. A woman Christ to save us from our despair was the involuntary thought that came into my head & has never left it. (Butler collection, n.d.)

Men also responded to Butler's magnetic appeal. 'She bore the marks of a sad and terrible consecration', wrote Canon Henry Scott Holland. 'She had a magnetic influence over the spirit, and she laid on us the compulsion of a call to the service of the broken and wounded' (Fawcett, 442). Even men who disagreed with her responded to her personal charisma. After her testimony before the royal commission of 1871, one member of the committee, Peter Rylands, was moved to remark, 'I am not accustomed to religious phraseology, but I cannot give you an idea of the effect produced except by saying that the spirit of God was there' (Walkowitz, *Prostitution*, 114).

Family background Butler credited her family with endowing her with a lifelong commitment to humanitarian reform, republican values, and vital Christianity. Religion was central to the Grey family life. From her mother, a descendant of Huguenot silk weavers, Josephine was imbued with a devout religiosity, free of any allegiance to a particular sect or creed. From her father, an agricultural reformer and anti-slavery advocate, she gained a love of justice and social compassion as well as a horror of slavery and arbitrary power. Along with republicanism, humanitarianism, and an abiding concern for individual liberty, Josephine also inherited her father's sense of national destiny, his evangelical belief that the English 'seem to be a people distinguished in the plan of Providence … to accomplish God's great designs upon the Earth' (J. Butler, *John Grey*, 27–8).

By the time she was eighteen, Josephine Grey had suffered an intense religious crisis, precisely because she could not yet envisage those 'great designs'. 'Haunted' by stories of suffering and poverty, she sought answers to her 'soul's trouble' and a solution to its 'dark questioning' (Caine, 162, 163). Josephine Grey resolved this religious doubt through a conversion that left her with a mystical sense of calling, and a fervent belief in the efficacy of prayer and in her power to communicate directly with God. Her sense of divine mission, formed in her youth and ultimately finding its political cause two decades later, made her, in the words of one commentator, 'constitutionally unable to separate theory from practice' (Uglow, 149). For her, Christian understanding implied action, whether it be at the level of personal philanthropy or national political agitation. Like a number of other Christian feminists, Butler endeavoured to implement a feminist political theology that would erode divisions between a secular public and a privatized spirituality. In her later political campaigns, she presented herself as a spiritual campaigner empowered by God to fight injustice: she 'had often thought of this saying that God and one woman make a majority' (ibid., 151).

Besides her mother, two other female relatives were important influences in Josephine's life. Her aunt, Margaretta Grey, was a strong-minded feminist in the Enlightenment tradition. She also formed strong attachments with all her sisters, but particularly with her sister Harriet, who later married a Swiss banker and settled in Naples. Through her father, sister, and future husband, she subsequently gained an entrée into republican circles throughout western Europe.

Marriage and Oxford In 1852 Josephine Grey married George *Butler (1819–1890), a university teacher and Anglican clergyman. They both shared a broad Christianity, a cultural attachment to Italy, as well as a strong commitment to liberal reforms. George Butler encouraged his wife in her public work, and he would suffer set-backs in his own career on account of his wife's notoriety. Although she became the leader of a campaign widely characterized as the 'revolt of the women', Butler gave special credit to the support of her husband and sons: 'It seems strange that I should have been engaged in taking up the cudgel against men when my father, brothers, and sons have all been so good' (Walkowitz, *Prostitution*, 121).

The Butlers first lived in Oxford, where George Butler was appointed examiner to the university and where their three sons were born. Josephine Butler remembered the Oxford of the 1850s as a narrow and misogynist community of celibate men, 'with little or no leaven of family life', women's colleges, and domestic sociability (Caine, 165). As a young wife, Josephine Butler was deeply offended by the open acceptance of the double standard by the gentlemen of the university. She listened in silent anger to the denunciation of Mrs Gaskell's *Ruth* (a novel in which the heroine is seduced and abandoned) by the masculine company who assembled at her home in the evenings.

> A moral sin in a woman was spoken of as immensely worse than in a man; there was no comparison to be found between them. A pure woman, it was reiterated, should be absolutely ignorant of a certain class of ills in the world, albeit those evils bore with murderous cruelty on other women.

Inwardly furious at the audacity and arrogance of one young man who 'seriously declared that he would not allow his own mother to read such a book', she 'resolved to hold [her] peace', and to speak 'little with men, but much with God' (Walkowitz, *Prostitution*, 87, 88). With the support of her husband, she began to seek out 'ruined' women and welcome them into her home. Her rescue work extended to one young mother, seduced and abandoned by an Oxford don, who was in Newgate for the murder of her baby.

Cheltenham and Liverpool The Butlers' stay in Oxford was cut short by Josephine Butler's respiratory illness; a lesion on her lung had been diagnosed when she was eighteen, and the Butlers were now warned that the climate of Oxford might be fatal to her health. Josephine would suffer physical and nervous breakdowns of this sort throughout her long life. To escape the Oxford damp, George Butler accepted the post of vice-principal at Cheltenham College in 1857. Their daughter Eva was born in Cheltenham. In these new surroundings, they continued to take a lively interest in international liberal causes. Although their support for Garibaldi was well received, their support for the cause of American abolition was not. When the American Civil War broke out in 1861 the Butlers, who supported the Union cause, found themselves socially ostracized. This was Mrs Butler's first experience of political support for an unpopular cause: 'The feeling of isolation … was often painful … but the discipline was useful' (Petrie, 44).

The accidental death of her daughter Eva in 1864 was a 'turning point' in Josephine Butler's life. When the Butlers moved to Liverpool in 1864, she 'became possessed with an irresistible urge to go forth and find some pain keener than my own, to meet with people more unhappy than myself' (Walkowitz, *Prostitution*, 116). 'It was not difficult to find misery in Liverpool', she wrote of her early social work there (ibid.). In 1866 she began to work among the women of the Liverpool workhouse in the 'oakum shed', a women's vagrant ward and bridewell. Here she practised her transformative skills on the 'wretched, draggled, ignorant outcasts of the casual ward, persuading them to fall down on their knees and pray to Jesus' (Walkowitz, *City*, 88).

From the workhouse, gaols, and streets of Liverpool, Mrs Butler brought poor 'ruined' young women, friendless, all physically worn out from their hard lives, to be nursed by her in her home. Her widowed sister helped her in this 'work without a name that came upon us' (Walkowitz, *Prostitution*, 116). She had the help of Mrs Cropper, a Quaker and a pioneer 'in the advocacy and practice of the modern methods of kindness in rescue work', who had recently established a family 'home' in Liverpool (ibid.). A few months later, with financial support from a number of Liverpool merchants, she established a small envelope factory as an industrial home for friendless girls.

Feminism During the late 1860s Butler became increasingly involved in the campaign for women's rights. She was one of the signatories of the petition for women's suffrage presented to parliament by John Stuart Mill in 1866. From 1867 to 1873 she served as president of the North of England Council for Promoting the Higher Education of Women. In 1868 she petitioned Cambridge to provide special examinations for women. She also joined the Married Women's Property Committee in 1868, remaining on the committee until the passage of the Married Women's Property Act of 1882. In 1868 she published her first pamphlet, *The Education and Employment of Women*, the first of ninety books and pamphlets she would publish over the next forty years, in which she pleaded for the higher education of women and the removal of legal and customary restrictions on their employment. 'Economics', she wrote, 'lie at the very root of practical morality' (Caine, 179).

In 1869 Josephine Butler edited a collection of essays entitled *Woman's Work and Woman's Culture*. Her introduction to the volume constituted her most comprehensive, theoretical statement about the woman question. In this essay, she endeavoured to reconcile a series of beliefs and commitments, most notably liberalism and Christianity; sex equality and sexual difference; and an evolutionary theory of historical development and Christian eschatology. Butler's introduction also constituted her first public effort to integrate the discussion of prostitution and the double standard into a general discussion of the condition of women.

Butler's introduction to *Woman's Work and Woman's Culture* (1869) upholds a liberal ideal of companionate marriage and sex equality. It also details the detrimental effects of women's economic dependence on men and their need for public and meaningful work. Beginning on a conciliatory note, Butler explains that the essays in the volume would not exclusively treat 'women's questions', nor was the cause they advocated 'solely of women'—but also 'the cause of men' (*Woman's Work*, viii). She did not intend to 'reiterate any accusation' against men of the present or past generations, or charge 'any living being with a conscious and wilful participation in any existing social wrong' (ibid., ix). Rather the 'evils in society' that oppressed women were 'to a great measure' the result of accident, and of the 'halting and unequal progress of society' (ibid.). Women were victims of a 'transitional' period of industrialization, 'stranded' by the elimination of many of their traditional employments while being prohibited from pursuing new opportunities (ibid., xv).

A critique of male domination none the less seeps through. While writing her pamphlet on women's employment, Butler received a letter from the positivist Frederic Harrison defending restrictions on women's labour on the grounds that women's place was in the home. Butler's introduction to *Woman's Work and Woman's Culture* sets out to detail how wrong-headed, how 'Satanic', that radical position appeared to her. Quoting from the census, Butler documented the increasing number of women, outside of marriage, who had to work for 'starvation wages' (*Woman's Work*, xv). The closing off of occupations to women precipitated poor women 'downwards' into prostitution and resulted in the 'destruction of bodies, of consciences, of souls'—a fate that had no analogue for men. Economic dependence on men also corrupted women of the better classes, forcing them into mercenary marriages and destroying their dignity 'in the scramble for husbands' (ibid., xxiii). This dignity could be restored by education and employment in useful public work.

Without challenging the importance of women's spiritual influence in the home, Butler called for the diffusion of the 'home influence' in the general society. Like other feminists of her time, Butler only partially challenged orthodox Victorian assumptions about women's separate sphere. She defended the right of women to maintain legal, political, and economic identities outside the family, but she also sought to exploit the notion of women's moral pre-eminence. She celebrated the feminine form of philanthropy, 'the independent, individual ministering, the home influence', against the masculine form, 'the large comprehensive measure, the organization, the system planned by men and sanctioned by Parliament' (*Woman's Work*, xxix–xxx). Butler thus tried to mark out a specific area of public activity for women of the better classes. This feminine form of philanthropy was, in her mind, the best method of stemming the decline in moral values among 'our vast population' of the poor (ibid., xxxvi).

Although she joined forces with secular liberals such as John Stuart Mill to defend women's rights, Butler tried to infuse her liberalism with the spiritual authority of 'essential Christianity'. Like other Christian feminists, she looked to Christ's teachings as a model of sex equality, while also claiming a special spiritual relationship between women and their saviour. Not only were women among Christ's earliest followers, but their love for him 'exceeds the love which it is possible for any man to feel for Him' (*Woman's Work*, lx). Butler's effort to meld liberal feminism and Christianity generated significant tensions in her writings. However much the ethics of Christ seemed to validate liberal feminism, Christian eschatology, as Butler presented it, did not fit comfortably with liberal visions of progress. Butler ended her essay on a dark prophetic note that called into question the social efficacy of her applied Christianity. Struggling in the cause of 'suffering humanity' might not succeed in rectifying social evils, but it might hasten the Second Coming—'the advent of the Day which we long for' (ibid., lxiv).

The Contagious Diseases Acts In 1869 Butler was approached by Elizabeth Wolstenholme Elmy to serve as honorary secretary of the Ladies National Association for the Repeal of the Contagious Diseases Acts. The Contagious Diseases Acts of 1864, 1866, and 1869 provided for the medical and police inspection of prostitutes in garrison towns and ports. Although the acts had been in force for a number of years, it was not until the late 1860s that public agitation against them mounted, in response to efforts to extend the acts to the north. One organization, the National Association, had already formed to demand the repeal of the acts, but the fledgeling repeal movement did not gain attention and notoriety until a 'Ladies' protest' was published in the *Daily News*, with 124 signatures of leading female members of the Society of Friends and of prominent feminists, including Elizabeth Wolstenholme Elmy, Florence Nightingale, Harriet Martineau, and Ursula Bright. This was soon followed by the formation of the Ladies National Association. Female participation in the repeal campaign astonished and perplexed the press and the British public, unused as they were to women speaking before mixed audiences on such matters as prostitution, venereal disease, and internal gynaecological examination.

Over the next sixteen years repeal groups proliferated, reflective of the regional, political sectarian, class, and gender distinctions in the movement. Overall, repeal drew its power from its alliance of middle-class nonconformists, radical working men, and middle-class feminists, who had previously engaged in a range of liberal mid-Victorian reforms, such as anti-slavery, temperance, medical reform, and women's suffrage. Butler operated as the charismatic leader of the campaign, leaving everyday details and political lobbying to others, notably to the male leaders of the campaign, such as James Stansfeld, Henry J. Wilson, and James Stuart. Using the Ladies National Association as her platform, Butler pushed liberal feminism in new directions, developing theories and methods of political agitation that would directly affect future campaigns for the emancipation of women. She sponsored new forms of feminist activism, expanding beyond drawing-room meetings to promote a range of out-of-door political activities. She also elaborated the concerns of women's rights to include a defence of female bodily integrity.

Butler repeatedly declared in public that she could never view the question of state regulation as 'fundamentally more a woman's question than it is a man's' (J. Butler, *The Constitution Violated*, 1871, 153). Yet, her 'revolt of the women' was infused with a sense of sexual grievance. In her public writings, she tended to mute expressions of sex antagonism or to displace them onto working-class women. In one of her 'public letters' on the 'Garrison Towns of Kent', for instance, she allowed a Chatham prostitute to deliver a powerful denunciation of men and male power, a denunciation that conveniently incorporated the entirety of Butler's brief against the acts:

> It is *men, only men*, from the first to the last that we have to do with! To please a man I did wrong at first, then I was flung about from man to man. Men police lay hands on us. By men we are examined, handled, doctored. In the hospital it is a man again who makes prayer and reads the Bible for us. We are had up before magistrates who are men, and we never get out of the hands of men till we die! (Walkowitz, *City*, 92)

In private correspondence, Butler complained of the tendency of male leaders to dominate the movement and to shut out female initiatives, particularly when it came to policy matters and public appearances. Political differences led Butler to cultivate an inter-class alliance with working men and to identify a special mission for women in the repeal camp.

During the repeal campaign, Butler resorted to daring acts of personal heroism that showed her solidarity with her fallen sisters. Many of these performances occurred during parliamentary by-elections in the early 1870s, when repealers challenged Liberal Party candidates who supported the acts. In 1870 repealers successfully opposed the candidacy of Henry Storks in Colchester and were elated by his defeat. Butler's activities during the Colchester by-election substantially contributed to this victory. In her *Personal Reminiscences of a Great Crusade* (1896) she recalled how she was chased by a crowd of brothel-keepers and their flunkies in Colchester, forcing a Mrs Hampson and herself to seek refuge in the cellar of a 'Methodist' grocer, who installed them 'amongst his bacon, soap, and candles' (J. Butler, *Personal Reminiscences*, 33). She later encountered the same kind of opposition in Pontefract, when repealers opposed the candidacy of a member of the government, H. C. E. Childers, who had offered himself for re-election. A women's meeting was held in a hayloft; hired bullies 'led by two persons whose *dress* was that of gentlemen' set bundles of straw afire while the Metropolitan Police casually looked on. Fortunately, 'two or three working women placed themselves in front' of Butler and Mrs Charlotte Wilson, so that they could make their escape by jumping down the hatch of a trapdoor.

> It was not so much personal violence that we feared as what would have been to any of us *worse than death*; for the indecencies of the men, their gestures and threats, were what I would not like to describe. (Walkowitz, *City*, 91)

'The people', Butler insisted, were 'more just, more manly, than those who rule them', a position she reiterated in *The Constitution Violated*, a pamphlet published in 1871 and 'Dedicated to the Working Men and Women of Great Britain' (Walkowitz, *Prostitution*, 142; *Constitution Violated*). Butler condemned police power under the Contagious Diseases Acts as a violation of the rule of law and of the English constitution. She characterized supporters of the acts as latter-day embodiments of 'Old Corruption', as adherents of a 'deadly materialism' that merely transferred 'the power of the deprivation of human rights from the hands of a monarch or hereditary aristocracy' into those of 'official experts' (*Constitution Violated*, 206). At the same time, she situated the repeal campaign in a tradition of radical political protest, summoning up a range of earlier 'champions of liberty' from Wat Tyler to John Wilkes, who had served as icons of the Chartist struggle (ibid., 3, 4). Butler also condemned the unequal treatment of men and women under the acts, arguing that it was inhumane to regard fallen women as 'foul sewers' rather than as 'moral agents'. In framing the repeal campaign as a defence of the 'Ancient Constitution' Butler incorporated women, even prostitutes, into the body politic, and she made the health and bodily integrity of women essential to the welfare of the nation at large.

Catherine of Siena Butler offers a different kind of historical justification for her own political activism in *Catherine of Siena*, published in 1878. In her biography of the fourteenth-century saint, Butler celebrated St Catherine as a pioneering example of a female activist and Christian mystic. Butler explained that she wished to link Catherine's 'spiritual life' to her 'public action in connection with contemporary events' (*Catherine of Siena*, 2nd edn, 1879, vii). Not only did she personally identify with Catherine's struggle to carve out a public role for herself, she also represented the 'contemporary events' of Catherine's day as harbingers of the political and social problems that beset Victorian Britain. Medieval Siena, despite its beauty and sunny clime, suffered from many of the maladies that plagued the Victorian body politic. These included epidemic disease, political factions, a falling away of old-fashioned virtues, a tyrannical democracy, and a corrupt church and government.

Having set the historical scene, Butler presents Catherine as a plebeian and medieval variant of herself. She introduces Catherine as a 'daughter of the people', descended from a 'race' of stern, republican artisans, an untutored woman who ultimately became the trusted adviser to political and religious leaders. Called out of her solitude by God to devote herself to 'active ministrations', Catherine encountered many of the same forms of prejudice and slanders about her 'virtue' that, many centuries later, were levelled at Butler (*Catherine of Siena*, 1879, xii). Like Butler, Catherine overcame social resistance to her public activities, and she too went on to assume an ever widening circle of influence. Over time, Catherine extended her 'active ministrations' from personal philanthropy among the poor to mediating between political factions in Siena and advising the pope. Catherine's physical martyrdom—her 'spareness in diet'—served as another point of identification for Butler, as did Catherine's 'constant converse with God' (ibid., 32, 33, 38). According to Butler, Catherine cultivated a 'science of prayer', a practice that was 'experimental' and 'methodical'. There was nothing hysterical about Catherine's ecstasies and communions with God; they required 'sustained self-denial' and 'untiring diligence' (ibid., 38, 39).

Europe, social purity, and empire Besides celebrating a female tradition of Christian activism and prophecy, *Catherine of Siena* also signalled Butler's romance with contemporary Italy and her engagement with European affairs. In 1874, when the repeal campaign was politically stalled in Britain owing to the fall of Gladstone's Liberal government, Butler undertook a mission to the continent to spark abolitionist efforts there. 'God', Butler wrote in 1875, 'has been training us, not for our battles in England alone, but for this battle of principles all over Europe' (Butler, *Autobiographical Memoir*, 109). Butler's example inspired men and women in almost every European country, as well as the United States, to take up the question of state-regulated prostitution. Butler was the moving force behind the formation of the British, Continental and General Federation for the Abolition of Government Regulation of Prostitution, founded in 1875. Not all of her followers shared her libertarian views. Whereas Butler advocated self-restraint and rescue work among prostitutes as an alternative to state regulation or repression, members of the German Moral Associations condemned prostitution as a crime and demanded the prosecution of women involved in the trade.

More repressive modes of reform were also superseding repeal efforts at home. After the regulation system was suspended in England in 1883, Butler and her female allies shifted their attention to the foreign traffic in women and the entrapment of children into prostitution in London. They persuaded the journalist W. T. Stead to publish a sensational exposé of child prostitution, the 'Maiden tribute of modern Babylon', in the *Pall Mall Gazette* in 1885. 'Maiden tribute' had an electrifying effect on public opinion and forced parliament to pass the Criminal Law Amendment Act of 1885, raising the age of consent for girls to sixteen and giving the police greater summary power to repress brothel-keepers and streetwalkers. An additional clause of the bill made indecent acts between consenting male adults illegal. Throughout Britain, grass-roots social purity groups were formed to oversee the local enforcement of this act. Purity groups soon turned their attention to the suppression of obscene books, birth control literature and advertisements for abortifacients, music-hall entertainment, and nude statuary.

Repeal leaders of all persuasions initially filled many of the committee positions of the National Vigilance Association, which oversaw many of these legal prosecutions. However, this collaboration was short-lived for Butler and for some of her libertarian friends. In 1897 she explicitly warned her workers to beware 'of "Purity Societies" which seek affiliation with our Society' on the grounds that they persecuted individuals and that they were

> ready to accept and endorse any amount of coercive and degrading treatment of their fellow creatures, in the fatuous belief that you can oblige human beings to be moral by force, and in so doing that you may in some way promote social purity. (Walkowitz, *Prostitution*, 252)

Her warnings were not heeded by many feminist leaders, including Millicent Fawcett, who remained actively engaged in the purity campaign throughout the first two decades of the twentieth century.

During the late 1880s and 1890s Butler's attention shifted to India. After the repeal of the Contagious Diseases Acts in Great Britain in 1886, Butler led the campaign to end the regulation of prostitution in India through the cantonment regulations. When her husband died at Winchester in 1890, she temporarily ceased public activities. She soon resumed her agitation on behalf of her 'suffering sisters in India' by writing pamphlets about regulation in India, by contributing articles in repeal journals, and by corresponding with missionaries. Although she condemned the 'imperially imposed degradation' of Indian women under cantonment regulations, she did not condemn British imperial rule *per se* (J. Butler, *The New Godiva: a Dialogue*, 1888, 13). On the contrary, she stoutly defended British manifest destiny and enunciated for feminists a special imperial mission of representing female colonial subjects, akin to their special role in representing the interests and sufferings of poor women within the nation.

Although the 'new abolitionists' applauded and supported Butler's efforts on behalf of her 'Indian sisters', they were deeply critical of her support for the British cause during the Second South African War. In *Native Races and the War* (1900) Butler defended the British empire against the criticism of our 'Continental friends' who regard 'British Colonization' as a 'series of acts of aggression, solely inspired by the love of conquest and desire for increased territory' (*Native Races*, 138, 139). Butler acknowledged the greedy ambition of Rhodes and Jameson, as well as the harsh treatment of 'natives' by individual settlers, but she reiterated her conviction, that 'with all her faults, looked at from God's point of view, England is the best, and the *least* guilty of nations' (Burton, *Burdens*, 12). As an old abolitionist and daughter of an abolitionist, she proudly pointed to the fact that British law made slavery illegal, whereas the Boers accepted no such law. Great Britain, she predicted, 'will in future be judged condemned, or justified, according to her treatment of those innumerable, colored races, heathen or partly christianized, over whom her rule extends' (*Native Races*, 152).

After her husband's death Josephine Butler moved into a number of lodgings around the country. In 1903 she took up residence near her eldest son, George Grey Butler, at Wooler, Northumberland, where she died at her home, 2 Victoria Villas on 30 December 1906. She was buried at Kirknewton, Northumberland. Her three sons survived her.

Historical scholarship on Butler A few full-length biographies of Josephine Butler have been written, but most historical studies have tended to concentrate on Butler's role in the repeal campaign. Historians have long acknowledged the campaign against the Contagious Diseases Acts as a critical event in the history of feminism, and they have credited Butler with playing an instrumental role in articulating a feminist position on prostitution and in gaining public support for the repeal cause. Since the 1970s, the work of social historians has offered a deeper and more contextualized account of Butler and the political mobilizations she spearheaded. McHugh and the present author have highlighted the campaign against the Contagious Diseases Acts as part of a network of influential middle-class nonconformist pressure groups in the mid-Victorian era, while the studies of Banks and Levine have successfully located Butler as a member of a generation of feminist friends and political collaborators. Historians influenced by Michel Foucault, such as Mort, Kent, and the present author, have stressed the importance of the Contagious Diseases Acts and their opposition as a massive mobilization over sexuality issues that not only reshaped gender, class, and sexual subjectivities in late Victorian Britain but also informed national political history and state-building.

Whereas the social histories of the 1970s and 1980s concentrated on Butler's participation in the repeal movement, later cultural histories have paid closer attention to her rhetoric and political thought in the overall body of her writings. Hadley and the present author have inquired into Butler's use of melodramatic narrative and performance, while Uglow, Caine, and Yeo have examined Butler's uneasy synthesis of liberalism and Christian feminism. In another direction, Burton has highlighted a set of allegiances left unexplored by earlier historians of repeal, notably Butler's investment in nationalism and British imperialism. This recent historical work not only highlights Butler as a distinguished exemplar of feminist humanitarianism, it also reveals the complex cross-currents of libertarianism and Christianity, ethnocentrism and internationalism, performance and politics at work in that humanitarian tradition.

JUDITH R. WALKOWITZ

Sources J. E. Butler, *Personal reminiscences of a great crusade* (1896) • J. E. Butler, *An autobiographical memoir*, ed. G. W. Johnson and L. A. Johnson (1909) • J. E. Butler, *Memoir of John Grey of Dilston* (1869) • J. E. Butler, *Recollections of George Butler* (1892) • J. R. Walkowitz, *Prostitution and Victorian society: women, class and the state* (1980) • J. R. Walkowitz, *City of dreadful delight: narratives of sexual danger in late-Victorian London* (1992) • J. Uglow, 'Josephine Butler: from sympathy to theory, 1828–1906', *Feminist theorists: three centuries of key women thinkers*, ed. D. Spender (1983), 146–67 • B. Caine, *Victorian feminists* (1992) • A. Burton, *Burdens of history: British feminists, Indian women, and imperial culture, 1865–1915* (1994) • A. Burton, 'States of injury: Josephine Butler on slavery, citizenship, and the Boer War', *Social Politics*, fall (1998), 337–61 • E. M. Bell, *Josephine Butler: flame of fire* (1962) • A. S. G. Butler, *Portrait of Josephine Butler* (1954) • P. McHugh, *Prostitution and Victorian society* (1979) • P. Levine, *Feminist lives in Victorian England* (1990) • E. J. Yeo, 'Protestant feminist and Catholic saints in Victorian Britain', *Radical femininity: women's self-representation in the public sphere*, ed. E. J. Yeo (1998), 127–48 • G. Petrie, *A singular iniquity: the campaigns of Josephine Butler* (1971) • M. Forster, *Significant sisters* (1984) • N. Boyd, *Three Victorian women who changed their world: Josephine Butler, Octavia Hill, Florence Nightingale* (1982) • S. Kent, *Sex and suffrage in Britain, 1860–1914* (1987) • F. Mort, *Dangerous sexualities: medico-moral politics in England since 1830* (1987) • O. Banks, *Becoming a feminist: the social origins of 'first wave' feminism* (1986) • M. Fawcett, *Contemporary Review*, 133 (1928), 442–6 • E. Hadley, *Melodramatic tactics: theatricalized dissent in the English marketplace, 1800–1885* (1995) • Women's Library, London, Butler collection

Archives Balliol Oxf., corresp.; papers relating to Benjamin Jowett • Northumbd RO, Newcastle upon Tyne, corresp. and diaries • U. Leeds, Brotherton L., letters to Hannah Ford and Emily Ford • U. Lpool L., Sydney Jones Library, corresp. and papers • U. St Andr., family corresp. • Women's Library, London, corresp. and papers • Women's Library, London, National Vigilance Association collection | RIBA BAL, letters to Edith Rhoda and Arthur Stanley Butler and others • University of Sheffield, Henry J. Wilson collection • Women's Library, London, Fawcett Collection

Likenesses G. Richmond, pastel, 1851, NPG • G. Richmond, portrait, 1852, Women's Library, London • G. F. Watts, portrait, 1894, NPG [*see illus.*] • Elliott & Fry, photograph, U. Lpool • A. Munro, marble bust, Walker Art Gallery, Liverpool • A. Munro, marble bust, Girton Cam. • 550 photographs, Women's Library, London, Josephine Butler Society collection • bust, Walker Art Gallery, Liverpool • plaster relief, Walker Art Gallery, Liverpool • portraits, U. Lpool, Sydney Jones Library

Wealth at death £1753 5*s*. 7*d*.: resworn probate, 29 June 1907, *CGPLA Eng. & Wales*

Butler, Kathleen Teresa Blake (1883–1950), Italian scholar, was born at Bayview, Bardsea, Urwick, Lancashire, on 26 September 1883, the eldest of the four daughters and three sons of Theobald Fitzwalter Butler (1845–1914), iron merchant, deputy lieutenant for Lancashire, and mayor of Barrow in Furness (1906–11), and his wife, Catherine Elizabeth Barraclough (*d*. 1946). She was proud of her descent from a Norman baron in Ireland in the twelfth century and revelled in stories of her ancestors' wild exploits. Her father took an enthusiastic interest in the languages and cultures of the countries he visited, both for business and on family holidays. Most of his children were educated abroad. Kathleen began with a Norwegian governess. At the age of fourteen she moved on to schools in Hanover, Saxony, and Paris. In 1907 she entered Cambridge Training College for Women and taught at Stamford high school for a year. She then became a student at Newnham College, Cambridge (1909–13), following her younger sister Eliza Marian *Butler. Here her exceptional intellectual qualities were quickly recognized by her dons, but she made her friends among the less intellectual students, who are said to have envied greatly her green silk tartan stockings from Paris.

From Newnham, where she gained a first in the medieval and modern languages tripos (French and German) in 1911 and a second in 1913 (Italian and Romance philology), Butler went straight to a lectureship in French at Royal Holloway College and again made her mark with her red hair, emerald green jacket, and small scholarly handwriting. It was said of her that she had no time for students who would not think but much patience with those who could not. Girton College, Cambridge, claimed her in 1915 as director of studies in modern languages, a post she held for twenty-three years. She soon became known among her new colleagues as Blazing Butler, the redhead whose impatience with bureaucracy and rigid rules was liable to boil over at staff meetings: a tendency which her professionalism and sense of duty tamed over the years, making her an excellent and restrained chairman. Her prodigious capacity for work was boosted by her ability to catnap. She created a fellows' garden at Girton and for many years served with her friend Lady Stephen on the curators' committee of the college, where her flair for flower arranging and interior decorating contributed much to the new fellows' rooms built in 1932.

From 1926, when Cambridge opened its lectureships to women, until 1948 Butler was university lecturer in Italian. In 1919 and 1935 she organized a summer school for Italian studies. She helped to found the journal *Italian Studies* (1937) and chaired the Italian committee of the Modern Languages Association for many years. Her scholarly works included *A History of French Literature* (2 vols., 1923) and, jointly with her Girton colleague Henriette Bibas, *Les premières lettres de Guez de Balzac, 1618–27* (2 vols., 1933–4). She was joint editor with Barbara Reynolds of *Tredici novelle moderne* (1947).

In 1942 Butler was elected mistress of Girton. At the vice-chancellor's request, she postponed her retirement to pilot through the measure by which, in 1948, Cambridge finally conceded to women full membership of the university. KTB, as she was affectionately known, took great and deserved delight in representing the college at this time, particularly when the queen, later the queen mother, the college visitor, came up in October 1948 to receive an honorary doctorate, the first woman to be so honoured by Cambridge. Kathleen Butler died from renal failure in Addenbrooke's Hospital, Cambridge, on 2 May 1950. Between bouts of pain she had worked for months to complete her final work: *'The Gentlest Art' in Renaissance Italy: an Anthology of Italian Letters, 1459–1600* (published posthumously in 1954). She was buried in Girton churchyard, Cambridgeshire, on 8 May.

BARBARA E. MEGSON

Sources K. T. Butler and H. I. McMorran, eds., *Girton College register, 1869–1946* (1948) • H. I. McMorran and I. Wall, *Girton Review*, Michaelmas term (1950) • M. G. L. Thomas, 'A selection of impressions', *Girton Review*, Michaelmas term (1950) • J. I. W., 'Kathleen Teresa Blake Butler (N. C., 1909–1913)', *Newnham College Roll Letter* (1951), 48–50 • *Evening News* (3 May 1950) • *The Times* (4 May 1950) • *Manchester Guardian* (4 May 1950) • *Daily Graphic* (4 May 1950) • K. T. Butler, 'Women at Cambridge: a retrospective, 1869–1947', *Girton Review*, Lent term (1948) • Burke, *Gen. Ire.* (1958) [Blake Butler, formerly of Millbrooke] • b. cert. • d. cert.

Archives Girton Cam., corresp. and papers

Likenesses R. Moynihan, oils, 1949, Girton Cam. • photographs, Girton Cam.

Wealth at death £17,654 14*s*. 5*d*.: administration, 13 July 1950, *CGPLA Eng. & Wales*

Butler [*née* Reid], **Lois** (**1897–1970**), aviator and skier, was born on 3 November 1897 at 275 Drummond Street, Montreal, Canada, the only daughter and second of the five children of Sir William Duff Reid (1866–1924) and his wife, Minnie Cormack (*d*. 1949). Taken to Canada in 1873, when his father undertook railway projects, William Duff Reid later joined him on the Canadian Pacific Railway. On the death of Reid senior in 1908 he became president of the Reid Newfoundland Co. Ltd, based at St John's.

Lois Reid was sent to England to be educated at Abbots Langley School, and returned in 1913 to complete her education at Havergal College, Toronto. She met her future husband, Lieutenant-Colonel Hugh William Knox-Niven (*d*. 1923), when he arrived as aide-de-camp to the governor of Newfoundland. They married in 1918; there was one daughter of this marriage, which ended in 1923 with Knox-Niven's death. In 1925 Lois married Alan Samuel Butler (1898–1987), chairman of the De Havilland Aircraft Company. He ran an air-survey firm in Newfoundland and had been involved in carrying the first airmails there. They had a daughter and a son. Alan Butler owned a succession of De Havilland aircraft in which he toured and raced. In 1928, with Lois as passenger, he set a world speed record for two-seater light aeroplanes, of 119.77 m.p.h. In 1929 Lois gained a private pilot's licence (no. 1963), and in the following year acted as second pilot to her husband, flying a twin-engined Gloster Survey biplane (G–AADO) from London to Cape Town. Designed for aerial survey and photo-mapping by De Havilland for the Aircraft Operating Company, Cape Town, the AS31 was a unique aircraft required for an urgent four months' contract to cover 63,000 square miles in Northern Rhodesia. The Butlers left Heston Aerodrome on 20 March 1930, accompanied by an engineer, the plane laden with spare parts. Lois kept a diary and photographic record of the 8000-mile trip, which involved twenty-three stops for refuelling and repairs and took twenty-seven days. They arrived in Cape Town on 15 April, Lois having undertaken approximately one quarter of the flying each day. On her return she competed in the king's cup air race and the Europa *Rundflug*, a 7000 mile race around Europe.

The years between the wars were truly golden for those with means, leisure, and a sense of adventure; the Butlers possessed all these. Lois Butler joined the Kandahar Ski Club in 1930 and, already a first-class skier, was awarded her gold K in 1931 and an alpha for downhill racing in 1933. The UK was largely responsible for starting downhill and slalom racing, and Lois was a member of the British ladies' team, taking part in European ski championship meetings that later became world cup events. When Canada sent a team to these international ski meetings she naturally transferred her affections and ski prowess to the Canadian team, representing Canada at the 1936 winter Olympics at Garmische Partenkirchen, and many other important international meetings, until all sports came to a full stop with the advent of the Second World War.

By 1939 Lois Butler had accrued over 300 hours as a pilot and was among the first eight women asked to join the Air Transport Auxiliary (ATA), formed in September to ferry aircraft from the manufacturers' airfields to RAF bases. A reluctant Air Ministry had finally agreed that women pilots could be allowed to fly small trainer aircraft, and by the bitter January of 1940 they were ferrying open Tiger Moths from the factories. The weather and visibility was always bad, but spring found them adept at flights from the south of England to the north of Scotland. The group having proved itself, Lois Butler was among the first to be selected later that year for conversion to light operational aircraft at the Central Flying School of the RAF. As the pressures of war increased so did the intake of women to the ATA, and eventually they were flying all types of operational aircraft. By VE-day (3 May 1945), Lois Butler had flown more than 1000 hours, handling 36 types of Royal Navy and RAF aircraft, including the Mosquito, the fastest of them all. This was a range of experience obtained by very few service pilots.

After the war the Butlers sold their home in London and the family moved to Salisbury, Rhodesia. They also acquired tobacco farms near Bulawayo, but Lois did not settle, and they returned to Studham Hall, in Bedfordshire, leaving their son, David, in Rhodesia. Lois Butler returned to skiing at the Kandahar Club, renewing her friendships in Europe. The summers were spent sharing her husband's passion for boats; they would go down the French canals to the Mediterranean each summer and visit the Greek islands. It was during one of these holidays that Lois Butler died, of a heart attack, in Piraeus, Greece, on 17 August 1970. She was buried in St Mary's Church, Studham. ENID DEBOIS

Sources private information (2004) [Carol Horton, daughter; J. Riddell, president of Kandahar Ski Club and the Ski Club of Great Britain] • *Aeroplane* (March–April 2000) • L. Butler, memoir, 1945, priv. coll. [account of her years in ATA] • *The Times* (23 Sept 1970) • will • *CGPLA Eng. & Wales* (1970)

Archives De Havilland Aircraft Heritage Centre, Salisbury Hall, Hertfordshire, pilot's logbook

Likenesses S. Elwes, portrait, before 1939, Studham Hall, Bedfordshire • photographs (in ATA), Salisbury Hall Museum, London

Wealth at death £481,638: probate, 14 Sept 1970, *CGPLA Eng. & Wales*

Butler [*née* Fitzgerald]**, Margaret, countess of Ossory and Ormond** (*d.* **1542**), noblewoman, was the second daughter of Gerald *Fitzgerald, eighth earl of Kildare (1456?–1513), lord deputy of Ireland, and his first wife, Alison (*d.* 1495), daughter and coheir to Roland Eustace, baron of Portlester. Margaret married Piers *Butler, eighth earl of Ormond and first earl of Ossory (*b.* in or after 1467, *d.* 1539), about 1485. In March 1509 she and her husband were admitted to the confraternity of the convent of Osney, near Oxford. She exercised a personal role in aspects of the administration of the Ormond patrimony: in March 1515 and again in November 1516 she presided at hearings held in Christ Church, Dublin, regarding the earldom of Ormond being entailed to male heirs. In March 1517 she appeared in the presence of a notary and the bishop of Ferns at St Saviour's Church in New Ross, co. Wexford, with regard to a case concerning the disputed possession of a house in the town.

Throughout her life, in her capacity as countess, Margaret Butler was party to successive indentures, bonds, and agreements concerning the transfer or ownership or custodianship of land, chiefly in counties Kilkenny, Tipperary, and Carlow. In 1526 letters patent were issued to Piers, earl of Ormond, and to his wife, granting them various castles, honours, and lands in counties Kilkenny and Tipperary to be held in tail male. Her preservation of Geraldine interests is evident in her interception of a letter written in 1525 by her brother Gerald *Fitzgerald, ninth earl of Kildare, to the earl of Desmond. In it, Kildare entreated Desmond to join forces with him, unaware, as he claimed, of the fact that Desmond was engaged in continental intrigue against Henry VIII at this time. In 1537 a grand jury of the commons of co. Kilkenny complained that Ossory, his wife, and their children indiscriminately imposed coign and livery exactions in their lordship.

In his will, dated 28 May 1539, Piers Butler appointed Margaret his executor, along with two of their sons, Richard and James *Butler, later ninth earl of Ormond and second earl of Ossory. In September 1539 she and her second son, Richard, were granted all profits arising from Piers's property since his death in the previous August. In April 1540 she was resident at Kilkenny and in May of that year she signed an indenture to secure one-third of the land which James Butler was to inherit. One gains some insight into the extent of her wealth from the terms of this agreement. She was to receive the castles, towns, and manors of Donmore, Donfert, Bennitsbridge, Ballykive, and Whitsbrownstown in co. Kilkenny, Tullow and Bynecorre in co. Carlow, and Killenaule in co. Tipperary. At that time she also presented James with Ir£100, twenty-four milk cows, and twenty-four stud mares. In July 1540 Margaret was in Waterford, from where she sent Henry VIII a gift of hawks. Up to her death she continued her personal participation in the administration of the Ormond estate.

In the Jacobean era Margaret and her husband were celebrated for having brought civilization to Tipperary and Kilkenny and for having provided a good example to the inhabitants of both counties by bringing artificers from Flanders and other countries to make tapestries, cushions, and carpets. Margaret was patron of a school near the churchyard of St Canice's Cathedral, Kilkenny, and the reconstruction of Gowran Castle, co. Kilkenny, is attributed to her. Contemporaries acknowledge that the countess was the dominant party in the marriage. The ninth earl of Kildare referred to his sister as 'my lady, his [Piers's] wife, by whom he is only ruled' (*State Papers, Henry VIII*, vol. 2, pt 3, 123). Richard Stanihurst's account is of a formidable woman whose husband governed well:

> through the singular wisdom of his Countess, a lady of such port, that all estates in the realm crouched unto her; so politique, that nothing was thought substantial debated without her advice. She was man like, and tall of stature, very liberal and bountiful.

He describes her as a sure friend and a bitter enemy, and praises her for having been 'the only means at those days whereby her husband's country was reclaimed from sluttish and unclean Irish custom to English habits, bedding, house-keeping, and civility' (*Holinshed's Chronicles*, 6.280). Margaret and Piers had three sons, James (Piers's successor), Richard, and Thomas, and six daughters, Margaret, Catherine, Joan, Ellice, Eleanor, and Ellen. In her final years she is said to have lived in a manner 'most Godly, in contemplation and prayer, giving alms bountifully to poor and needy people' (BL, Add. MS 4792). The countess died in early August 1542, and was buried in St Canice's Cathedral, Kilkenny, along with her husband; their tomb is adorned by a mensa monument which portrays both as idealized in features. MARY ANN LYONS

Sources *Holinshed's chronicles of England, Scotland and Ireland*, ed. H. Ellis, 6 (1808), 280 • *LP Henry VIII*, 13/2, no. 181; 15, nos. 551, 558,

857; 16, no. 777; 18, no. 688 • *State papers published under … Henry VIII*, 11 vols. (1830–52), vol. 2, pt 3, 123–4; vol. 3, pt 3, 146, 222, 411 • *CSP Ire., 1509–73*, 5, 32, 54, 64 • E. Curtis, ed., *Calendar of Ormond deeds*, 6 vols., IMC (1932–43), 3.309; 4.23–4, 27, 36–7, 186–91, 194–5, 216 • J. S. Brewer and W. Bullen, eds., *Calendar of the Carew manuscripts*, 5: *1603–1623*, PRO (1871), 176 • N. B. White, ed., *Irish monastic and episcopal deeds* (1936), 239 • D. Bryan, *Gerald Fitzgerald, the great earl of Kildare* (1933), 91 • Burke, *Peerage* (1976) • J. Lodge, *The peerage of Ireland*, rev. M. Archdall, rev. edn, 7 vols. (1789), vol. 1, p. 87; vol. 4, pp. 21–2 • T. W. Moody and others, eds., *A new history of Ireland*, 2: *Medieval Ireland, 1169–1534* (1987); repr. with corrections (1993), 774; 9: *Maps, genealogies, lists: a companion to Irish history, part 2* (1984), 169 • GEC, *Peerage*, new edn • J. Graves and J. G. Prim, *The history, architecture and antiquities of the cathedral church of St Canice, Kilkenny* (1857), 248 • S. G. Ellis, *Tudor frontiers and noble power: the making of the British state* (1995), 136 • C. Lennon, *Sixteenth-century Ireland: the incomplete conquest* (1994), 61, 73 • S. G. Ellis, *Ireland in the age of the Tudors* (1998), 84 • Robert Rothe's account of Margaret Butler's final years, BL, Add. MS 4792

Archives NL Ire., indenture (20/1/1509), D. 1947

Likenesses tomb effigy, St Canice's Cathedral, Kilkenny, Ireland

Butler, Mary Joseph (1641–1723), abbess of Ypres, was born in Callan, co. Kilkenny, the daughter of Theobald (Toby) Butler (*d.* 1649) of Callan and his wife, Anne (*née* Audley), of Attebridge, Norfolk. She was a descendant on her father's side of Edmund, earl of Carrick, through his son John, the younger brother of the first earl of Ormond. After her father's death in 1649 she was sent by her mother to be educated at the Benedictine convent in Ghent, where her aunt Lady Mary Knatchbull was abbess. She proved to be an extremely religious child, and from the age of twelve expressed her intention of becoming a nun. She was subsequently transferred to the order's house at Boulogne, where she was professed on 4 December 1657, taking the name in religion Mary Joseph. In 1658 she moved to Pontoise, where the Boulogne community migrated, and remained there until 1683, when she was sent to boost the falling numbers at the Irish Benedictine convent in Ypres, then run by Abbess Dame Flavia Cary. Following Cary's death in 1686, Butler was elected abbess of Ypres on 29 August 1686, and was blessed by the bishop of Tournai the following year. The convent again faced a crisis for a time, but its future was secured by the arrival of nuns from other houses.

Soon after establishing herself at the head of the Ypres community Butler was requested by Richard Talbot, earl of Tyrconnell and lord lieutenant, to return to Ireland and found a convent in Dublin (1687). His invitation came at the demand of James II, who wished to see a Benedictine community under his patronage established in the city. Her departure for Ireland was initially delayed by serious illness, and it was not until the autumn of 1688 that she left Ypres. Before arriving in Dublin on 31 October she broke her journey in London, and waited on the queen in Whitehall, who promised her royal protection for the new foundation. In Dublin she was met by the members of her community originally from Pontoise who had been based in Dublin since September 1687. While in the city Butler retained her position as abbess of Ypres. The new convent, located in Great Ship Street near Dublin Castle, was not a welcome addition to the existing Dublin Benedictine house in Channel Row. Its abbess, Dame Mary Joseph O'Ryan, had the support of Patrick Russell, Catholic archbishop of Dublin, and the Dunkirk Benedictines. Butler's convent, however, had the obvious backing of the king, who issued it with a royal patent on 5 June 1689. This preference may have stemmed from the fact that Butler's brother Francis served as the king's cup bearer. Known as the Royal Monastery of Gratia Dei, the convent also had an attached school which initially took in thirty girls from gentry and noble families.

The community faced an uncertain future after the defeat of James's army at the battle of the Boyne in July 1690. Victorious Williamite troops subsequently entered Dublin and sacked the convent. Having disbanded the school and hidden the church's ornaments in neighbouring houses, Butler resolved to leave Ireland, despite promises of protection from the duke of Ormond. She did accept passes secured by the duke from King William, which guaranteed her and her sisters a safe journey home. On her return to a depleted community in Ypres, she lived for several years in extreme poverty with four lay sisters. She rejected advice from her family and the church hierarchy to sell the house and move to a more comfortable and established convent, and instead remained on in Ypres despite the hardships. While their situation began to improve with the arrival of four novices in 1695 (two of whom were professed in 1700), their position remained precarious, and in 1696 they were granted permission to beg from the bishop. Their numbers continued to grow gradually, aided by the arrival of four nuns from Pontoise, and in 1699 they received financial help from Pope Innocent XII. Further donations from the French monarchy and Mary of Modena, with whom Butler maintained a correspondence, further improved their circumstances, so that by the time of her death at Ypres on 22 December 1723 the convent was once again successful.

FRANCES CLARKE

Sources J. J. Butler, 'The Irish dames of Ypres and the Butler connection', *Journal of the Butler Society*, 3/2 (1988–9), 152–9 • H. Concannon, *Irish nuns in penal days* (1931) • P. Nolan, *The Irish dames of Ypres* (1918) • Mrs T. Concannon, *Daughters of Banba*, [another edn] (1930) • B. Whelan, *Historic English convents* (1936)

Likenesses portrait, repro. in Nolan, *Irish dames of Ypres*

Butler, Sir Montagu Sherard Dawes (1873–1952), administrator in India and college head, born at Julian Hill, Harrow, on 19 May 1873, was the third son of Spencer Perceval Butler, barrister, of Lincoln's Inn, later conveyancing counsel to the High Court of Justice and the office of works, and his wife, Mary, only child of the Revd Nicholas Kendall of Bodmin. As such he belonged to one of the famous Cambridge academic families, Henry Montagu *Butler (1833–1918) being his uncle. Sir (Spencer) Harcourt *Butler and Sir (George) Geoffrey Gilbert *Butler were his brothers. Montagu Butler was at school at Haileybury College and was admitted to Pembroke College, Cambridge, in 1891. He gained first classes in both parts of the classical tripos (1894–5) with distinction in the second part; he was president of the union, coxswain of the college boat, and one of the founders of the May week ball. Elected into a fellowship in 1895, he decided to enter public service; in

Sir Montagu Sherard Dawes Butler (1873–1952), by Walter Stoneman, 1932

1896 he headed the examination list for the Indian Civil Service, and was awarded the Bhaunagar medal.

Late in 1896 Butler went to the Punjab, where his administrative ability was quickly recognized. In 1901 he married Anne Gertrude (1876–1954), daughter of George Smith, and sister of George Adam Smith. They had two sons and two daughters, the elder son being Richard Austen *Butler, the politician, and one of the daughters Dorothy *Middleton (1909–1999), author of *Victorian Lady Travellers*. Butler was settlement officer of Kotah state in 1904–9, and in 1912–15 was joint secretary of the royal commission on public services in India. During the First World War, when he was deputy commissioner of Attock, he was active in the recruitment drive for the Indian army in the Punjab. In 1921, after the constitutional reforms enacted in 1919 had reconstituted the Indian legislatures, he became president of the legislative council of the province. In the next year he was appointed secretary to the government of India in the department of education, health, and lands, and in 1924 he was made president of the council of state.

Butler was transferred to Nagpur as governor of the Central Provinces in 1925 and had to face the many problems created by the nationalist non-co-operation movement in the legislature. Butler aimed always at government by agreement, and would exercise infinite patience in the reconciliation of opposing views. He drove a wedge into the phalanx of non-co-operation by appointing a *swarajist* leader as home member and succeeded in bringing other non-co-operators into responsible posts. During his second term of office as governor he was confronted by a revival of civil disobedience under the leadership of M. K. Gandhi, and endeavoured, wherever possible, to deal with offenders under the ordinary law, without invoking the aid of the special powers given by the government of India.

Butler's consistent record of work for the welfare of India was recognized by his appointment as CIE (1909), CVO (1911), CB (1916), CBE (1919), and KCSI (1924). In 1933 he resigned to become lieutenant-governor of the Isle of Man. There, his insistence on a balanced budget provoked some preliminary opposition, but it was not long before his measures of reform were accepted, and he remained there for four years. Of his many appointments, none gave him such intense pleasure as his election to the mastership of his old college, Pembroke, in 1937, for which he had always harboured great affection. He had been made an honorary fellow in 1925 and had sent both his sons there. The mastership was no sinecure: Pembroke was only just beginning to recover from a series of disastrous losses in 1935, and Butler set about reorganizing its finances. He willingly accepted invitations to serve on the borough council as well as on the council of the senate and the financial board of the university.

The outbreak of war upset many of Butler's plans for the college, but it served to intensify rather than to diminish his activity. Shortly after his election as mayor of Cambridge in November 1941 he was knocked down by an ambulance and severely injured during a tour of air-raid posts in the blackout; he recovered to serve an additional term as mayor. Similarly, he was delighted when the college extended his tenure of the mastership to the statutory limit. He retired in 1948, but even then retained his seat on the borough council as an alderman. He died suddenly in the Evelyn Nursing Home, Cambridge, on 7 November 1952.

SYDNEY C. ROBERTS, *rev.* FRANCIS ROBINSON

Sources *The Times* (8 Nov 1952) · personal knowledge (1971) · b. cert. · d. cert.

Archives BL OIOC, corresp. and papers, Eur. MS F 225 | BL OIOC, corresp. with John Simon, Eur. MS F 77 · King's AC Cam., letters to Oscar Browning

Likenesses W. Stoneman, photograph, 1932, NPG [*see illus.*] · F. Dodd, drawing, Pembroke Cam.

Wealth at death £33,413 7*s*. 1*d*.: probate, 10 Jan 1953, *CGPLA Eng. & Wales*

Butler [Boteler], **Nathaniel** (*b*. **1577**, *d*. in or after **1643**), colonial governor and maritime author, was the elder son of the second marriage of John Butler (*d*. 1614) of the Toft, in Sharnbrook, Bedfordshire, and Mary, daughter of James Gedge and widow of Christopher Harris. On John Butler's death the family's holdings in Sharnbrook passed to Butler's elder half-brother, Sir Oliver. Butler joined the Virginia Company, where he became a supporter of Robert Rich, second earl of Warwick. On 28 April 1619 he was elected, by 297 votes to three, governor of the Virginia Company's sister organization, the Bermuda Company. His elevation was the result of a bargain struck between

Warwick and another leading Virginia Company member, Sir Edwin Sandys. Warwick helped Sandys to become the company's treasurer, and in return Sandys delivered the votes of his followers to Butler, who shortly afterwards was also appointed to the board of the Virginia Company (9 June 1619). Butler's governorship of Bermuda lasted three years, during which time he began work on his *Historye of the Bermudaes*. At his departure on 25 October 1622 he journeyed to Virginia, evidently on behalf of Warwick, who had now turned against Sandys. There Butler helped to lead an expedition of eighty men against local natives, but his main purpose in travelling to the colony was to gather evidence of its deteriorating condition and misgovernment. When he eventually returned to England, in 1623, Butler presented his findings to the privy council in a 900-word paper entitled 'The unmasked face of our colony as it was in the winter of the year 1622' (PRO, SP 16/526/98). His scathing criticisms, reinforced by additional findings gathered by Warwick, persuaded the king to establish a commission of inquiry into Virginia's government in May 1623.

Like Warwick, Butler was a Hispanophobe, and when in 1624 war with Spain was imminent he proposed that Bermuda should be used as a base from which to attack the Spanish West Indian fleets. His idea was not taken up but when hostilities began in 1625 he was appointed captain of an armed merchantman, in which capacity he participated in the ill-fated expedition to Cadiz. On 27 October the expedition's commander, Sir Edward Cecil, ordered him to organize the fleet's boats in preparation for the evacuation of the troops from Port Puntal. He returned to England by way of Ireland and on 27 June 1626 he was appointed captain of another armed merchantman in the fleet led by Robert Bertie, Lord Willoughby. The expedition sailed in October but was quickly abandoned after encountering severe storms in the Bay of Biscay. Shortly afterwards Butler wrote, but did not publish, a treatise entitled 'A discourse of the miscarriages of our two late expeditions, and the cares propounded for the future'. Again he advocated using Bermuda as a springboard from which to intercept the Spanish West Indian fleets, and this time strongly hinted that he himself possessed the qualities needed to take charge of such a base. He also argued for the capture of Gibraltar, an idea which Cecil had considered and rejected in 1625. However, if Butler's views were brought to the notice of the government they were ignored. In the following year he commanded yet another merchantman, this time on the expedition to the Île de Ré when he lay off the western side of the island. His final naval service, between 10 June and 31 December 1628, was as captain of one of the king's own ships, during which time he participated in the earl of Lindsey's unsuccessful expedition to relieve the Huguenots of La Rochelle.

In 1634 Butler was invited by the head of the admiralty commission, Richard Weston, first earl of Portland, to apply for a captaincy in the forthcoming ship money fleet, but by the time he did so in March 1635 Portland had died and he had missed his opportunity. 1634 also saw Butler complete a series of six 'dialogues', of which two were based on his treatise of 1626/7. These took the form of an extended conversation between a fictional admiral and a captain on a wide range of maritime topics, including the naval expeditions of the 1620s. Butler did not regard this work as finished, however, and continued to revise it into the early 1640s. It is not known whether he continued to seek naval employment after 1635. On 23 April 1638 he was appointed governor of the Providence Island Company, of which his former patron the earl of Warwick was a member. On 6 June 1639 he seized Truxillo, in Honduras, which he surrendered to the Spanish only after payment of a large ransom. He subsequently returned to England to answer charges in connection with the raid. After a hearing on 19–20 June 1640 he was cleared of misconduct. He disappears from the record thereafter, but evidence from one version of his *Dialogues* suggests that he was still living in 1643.

Butler may never have married. His place of settled residence in England has not been established, but his letter to Portland of March 1635 was written from Coventry. His *Dialogues* were not published until 1685, while his *Historye of the Bermudaes* did not appear in print until 1882. Boteler, the more archaic spelling of his surname, was adopted by his 1685 publisher, Moses Pitt; he himself spelt his name Butler. ANDREW THRUSH

Sources *Boteler's dialogues*, ed. W. G. Perrin, Navy RS, 65 (1929) · BL, Add. MS 41616, fols. 25–35 · F. A. Blaydes, ed., *Genealogica Bedfordiensis* (1890), 250 · J. Glanville, *The voyage to Cadiz in 1625*, ed. A. B. Grosart, CS, new ser., 32 (1883), 72, 125 · [N. Butler?], *The historye of the Bermudaes or Summer Islands*, ed. J. H. Lefroy, Hakluyt Society, 1st ser., 65 (1882) · report by Butler, 1627, PRO, SP 16/526/98 · W. F. Craven, *Dissolution of the Virginia Company: the failure of a colonial experiment* (1932) · T. K. Rabb, *Jacobean gentleman: Sir Edwin Sandys, 1561–1629* (1998) · *CSP col.*, vol. 1

Archives BL, diary, history of the Bermudas, corresp., and discourse of marine affairs, Sloane MSS 750, 758, 2449

Butler, Pierce, styled third Viscount Galmoye, and Jacobite earl of Newcastle (1652–1740), army officer, was born on 21 March 1652, the son of Edward Butler, second Viscount Galmoye (*c.*1627–1667), and Eleanor, daughter of Charles White of Leixlip, co. Kildare, and widow of Sir Arthur Aston; he was a descendant of Thomas Butler, tenth earl of Ormond. On 6 August 1677 Butler was created DCL of Oxford. James II appointed him a privy counsellor of Ireland and lord lieutenant of the county of Kilkenny. As colonel of the 2nd regiment of horse in the Irish army he participated at the siege of Londonderry, during which he led an unsuccessful attempt to capture Enniskillen (March 1689). During the siege of Enniskillen he ordered the execution of a prisoner, Captain Woolstan Dixie, after the defenders had sent over a captured Jacobite in supposed exchange, thus causing the protestants to accuse him of barbarity and treachery, that 'infamous wretch whom no titles could honour' (Wauchope, 64). He later fought at the battles of the Boyne and Aughrim, gaining the ranks of brigadier and major-general of horse respectively. Although subsequently outlawed (11 May 1691), he was one of the Irish commissioners at the capitulation of Limerick and was included in the amnesty of 3 October 1691. He could have regained his family's extensive estates in Kilkenny and Wexford had he agreed to remain in Ireland, but instead he chose to join James II in France. His loyalty was rewarded by his being created earl of Newcastle and later first lord of the bedchamber to James at the court of St Germain. Consequently Butler's English estates were forfeited and he was attainted in 1697. Following the death of his first wife, Anne Mathew, daughter of Theobald Mathew of Thomastown, co. Kilkenny, he married, in March 1695, Henrietta Fitzjames (1666/7–1730), widow of Henry Waldegrave, first Baron Waldegrave, and natural daughter of James II and of Arabella Churchill.

Appointed colonel of the 2nd or Queen's regiment of horse in James's exiled Irish army in 1692, Butler served in Normandy and then at the siege of Roses (1693). He was breveted brigadier in the French army on 28 April 1694, and in 1694–7, at the head of his regiment, served with distinction in the armies of Germany, the Moselle, and the Meuse. While his regiment of horse was reduced in 1698, he was compensated by Louis XIV with command of a new regiment of infantry, Galmoye's. He served in Italy (1701–2) and then Germany, being appointed maréchal-de-camp on 3 December 1703. Having been passed over for the rank of lieutenant-general in the French army, he received this rank from Philip V and passed into Spanish service on 1 March 1705. He served in Italy, Germany, Flanders, and Spain, serving with distinction in various engagements in 1705–14, including the battles of Cassano, Calcinato, and Turin, and the sieges of Douai, Quesnoy, Bouchain, and Barcelona. Although the régiment de Galmoye was incorporated into the régiment Dillon in 1715, he returned to French service on 10 May 1722 with the rank of lieutenant-general, dated from 1 March 1705. Henceforth effectively retired, he died in Paris on 18 June 1740 and was buried there, in St Paul's Church. His son by his first marriage, **James Edward Butler** (*d.* 1709), army officer in the French service, had risen to the rank of colonel. He had been killed at the battle of Malplaquet on 11 September 1709, and a nephew, Colonel James Francis Richard Butler, assumed the title of Viscount Galmoye despite the attainder.

T. F. HENDERSON, *rev.* P. J. C. ELLIOT-WRIGHT

Sources GEC, *Peerage*, new edn, vol. 5 • J. C. O'Callaghan, *History of the Irish brigades in the service of France*, [new edn] (1870), 149–50 • Burke, *Gen. Ire.* (1976), 199 • B. Burke, *A genealogical history of the dormant, abeyant, forfeited and extinct peerages of the British empire*, new edn (1883), 97–8 • J. Lodge, *The peerage of Ireland*, 4 (1754), 48–9 • M. H. Massue de Ruvigny, ed., *The Jacobite peerage* (1904), 217, 238 • R. Hayes, *Biographical dictionary of Irishmen in France* (1949), 20 • P. Wauchope, *Patrick Sarsfield and the Williamite war* (1992), 57, 64 • J. G. Simms, *Jacobite Ireland* (1969), 114

Butler, Piers [*called* Red Piers], **first earl of Ossory and eighth earl of Ormond** (*b.* in or after **1467**, *d.* **1539**), magnate and lord deputy of Ireland, was born after May 1467, at Pottlerath, co. Kilkenny (or possibly at Kilkenny), the third son of Sir James Butler (*d.* 1487), landowner, of Callan, co. Kilkenny, and his wife, Sawe (Sabina), daughter of Donnell Reagh MacMurrough Kavanagh. Piers Butler's career was concerned chiefly with acquiring legitimate title to the Irish estates of the earldom of Ormond. The Pottlerath Butlers were cousins to the earls of Ormond, and as head of the most prominent junior branch of the Butler family, Sir James Butler was deputy to the absentee earls.

Early years, c.1485–1516 The prolonged absence from Ireland during the Wars of the Roses of John *Butler, sixth earl of Ormond (*d.* 1476/7), and his brother Thomas Butler, seventh earl of Ormond (*c.*1424–1515), made Sir James Butler regard the lordship as his own. His Geraldine alliance increased his ambitions. About 1485 Piers Butler married Lady Margaret [*see* Butler, Margaret (*d.* 1542)], noblewoman, second daughter of Gerald *Fitzgerald, eighth earl of Kildare (1456?–1513), and his first wife, Alison. The couple had three sons, including James *Butler, ninth earl of Ormond and second earl of Ossory (*b.* in or after 1496, *d.* 1546), magnate, and Richard Butler, first Viscount Mountgarret [*see below*], and six daughters. This marriage had political implications. Kildare, acting as lieutenant to Lambert Simnel, named Piers Butler sheriff of co. Kilkenny on 13 August 1487. Sir James Butler appointed Piers Butler as deputy in the same year without the seventh earl of Ormond's consent. By the time of his death, on 16 April 1487, Sir James Butler had made his family the dominant Butler lineage in Ireland. However, their authority was dependent on continued Kildare support, and when Ormond, furious at Piers Butler's appointment, sent Sir James Butler (*d.* 1497), an illegitimate son of James *Butler, first earl of Wiltshire and fifth earl of Ormond, to Ireland as his official deputy in 1492, the other junior branches of the Butlers, resentful of Pottlerath ambitions, assisted him. Piers Butler was rehabilitated by Henry VII after supporting Simnel, and the king appointed him sheriff of co. Kilkenny on 20 March 1489.

With Kildare under royal order to refrain from interference on Piers Butler's behalf, Sir James Butler quickly gained the upper hand. He arrested Piers and kept him 'in prison by a long season' (Curtis, vol. 4, appendix, no. 31). Following his release Piers refused to accept Sir James's authority and fought on. Enjoying little support within the Ormond lordship and because of Sir James's promise to kill him, he was forced to hide in the woods. By 1495 Kildare was able to discredit Sir James at court and thereafter Piers Butler began to regain a foothold in the lordship. The dispute was only finally ended when Piers chanced upon Sir James near Kilkenny on 17 July 1497 and 'with a couragious charge gored the Basterd through with his speare' (Brewer and Bullen, 5.177). Piers Butler was knighted before 7 September 1497. The protection afforded him by Kildare secured Butler a pardon (28 February 1498) and he wasted little time in benefiting from his rival's death: he immediately re-occupied Kilkenny Castle, whence he informed the seventh earl of Ormond of his resumption of control over the Irish estate. Although Ormond tried to ignore his kinsman, by 1500 Butler had overrun the earl's Kilkenny manors, seizing Callan, Rosbercon, Grannagh, and Dunfert to his own use, as well as imposing coign and livery in Carrick-on-Suir, co.

Tipperary, 'contrary to the old use and custom there' (Curtis, vol. 4, appendix, no. 48). Between 9 and 20 July 1505 the ageing and sonless earl had little option but to lease Butler the lands he already occupied and appoint him his Irish deputy. However, Ormond's refusal to sell him the lands denied Piers any legal foothold on the estate.

A further weakness in Butler's position was the prior claims to the lordship of two older brothers, Edmund and Theobald Butler, who although born before their parents' marriage, had been legitimized by the Irish parliament in 1468. These weaknesses in no way swayed him from the conviction that he could obtain the Irish estate, but he knew he would have to prove the earldom was entailed, that his line was the legitimate one, and that his older brothers were illegitimate. He set out to establish his dominance throughout the earldom before Ormond's death to ensure that no local challengers emerged from the other Butler branches. In this he was greatly advantaged by his marriage connection because he alone of the Butlers could offer protection from Geraldine raids.

Upon Ormond's death on 3 August 1515, Butler, while supreme within the lordship, had not managed to extinguish his relatives' claims to the earldom, much less established that the Irish estates were entailed. Yet he felt confident that he could rely on his brother-in-law Gerald *Fitzgerald, ninth earl of Kildare (1487–1534), to press his suit. Initially Kildare did so—granting Butler livery of the inheritance in April 1516 on the basis that the Irish estates descended by tail male. This ran counter to Henry VIII's December 1515 grant of the Ormond estates in England, Wales, and Ireland to the seventh earl's daughters and heirs general. Henry's subsequent demand that Kildare advance the heiresses' claim transformed the earl's relationship with Butler. Although Kildare persuaded the Irish privy council to adjourn the case, pending further instruction from England, and it was allowed to rest until 1528, Butler, who was forced to continue in uncertain possession in Ireland, felt betrayed.

'I feare nothing thErle of Kildare', 1516–1528 Butler was forced late in 1516 to reconsider his strategy, aware that his Geraldine link had advanced him as far as it could and that he was regarded dubiously at court because of it. He sought a court connection to further his claims. At that juncture a remarkable convergence of interests occurred: Cardinal Thomas Wolsey, anxious to curb Kildare and identifying Butler as the perfect agent for the task, offered him the tantalizing possibility of secure possession of the Irish estates to oppose the earl. Piers, sensing a profound change in royal policy, grasped the opportunity, sending his son James Butler to be raised in Wolsey's household.

Butler also renegotiated his position *vis-à-vis* the Old English gentry and townsmen of the Ormond lordship. This was crucial, for although he enjoyed the support of its Gaelic inhabitants, he was for that very reason distrusted by the lordship's Old English population. His new approach won him the support of the Old English, who hankered after the re-emergence of strong Butler rule. Butler himself was given 'of their awne free wills' the prerogative of the 'erles of Ormounde' both for 'the defence of your Majesties said subjects' from 'the Irishe disobeysaunts adjoyning to the said shire [Kilkenny] as for his assistennce in doing his dutie to your Highnes in ministration of justice and servying of processe … so longe as need shulde require' (Curtis, vol. 4, addenda, no. 267).

Butler had re-invented himself, going from Gaelic chieftain to aspiring noble, and the lordship's Old English reinforced this by thereafter supporting his claim as rightful heir. Aware that the Old English could act as a lobby on his behalf, Butler sought to convince them of his Anglicized disposition: recruiting 'out of Flanders & other countryes diverse Artificers who … made, Diaper, Tapistrey, Turkey-carpetts, Cushions, & other like workes … to give good example to the people of that country'. His wife proved a 'help mete' in the Anglicization process and Richard Stanihurst credited her with reclaiming the lordship 'from sluttishnesse and slovenrie, to cleane bedding and civilitie'. After Butler's death she established a school-house at Kilkenny.

By 1517 Butler felt strong enough to move against Kildare. Recognizing that Kildare's strength lay in his ability to summon reinforcements from his Gaelic allies, Butler began supporting anti-Geraldine factions in the lordships that ringed his own. He intrigued with the O'Mores, O'Carrolls, MacMurrough Kavanaghs, O'Connors, and MacGiollapadraigs. By 1519 Butler's intrigues had forced Kildare to overstep the mark when retaliating. He was summoned to England to answer charges of oppressive behaviour, while Butler was free to pursue a private war without fear of royal censure. This was partly to do with Butler's close friendship with the lord lieutenant, Thomas Howard, earl of Surrey. The failure of Surrey's administration forced Henry to revert to government by aristocratic delegation, and, with Kildare ostracized, Butler was appointed deputy lieutenant after 21 December 1521. This was on the basis of Surrey's resounding endorsement of him as having 'a true English hert … the man of moost experience of the feautes of warre of this countrey', and his status as the only resident magnate of sufficient standing to govern in Kildare's stead (*State Papers, Henry VIII*, 2.49). His deputyship was not a success, however, despite appointment as lord deputy on 6 March 1522, largely because the government's decision to reduce English subventions left him little freedom of action. Moreover, the distance of his lordship from Dublin meant that Butler could not adequately protect the pale, and in May 1523 Kildare was sent to govern his own lordship, which the lord deputy could not control. Butler's continued feud with Kildare crippled his government, and commissioners were sent from England in summer 1524 to settle the dispute between them. They recommended Kildare's restoration as lord deputy and Butler was removed on 4 August 1524.

The rivalry between Butler and Kildare intensified as the struggle for mastery over the midlands escalated. The Butler junior branches, supported by Kildare, grew restive. In desperation Butler sought to discredit the Geraldines at court, claiming Kildare was complicit in the treasonous contact with France of James fitz Maurice Fitzgerald, tenth earl of Desmond. In August 1526 Butler and Kildare were summoned to court to answer the charges each made against the other. Through Wolsey's intercession Butler was exonerated and allowed to return to Ireland in February 1528.

Earl of Ossory, 1528–1534 Butler's sojourn yielded two positive results. First, it persuaded the king, on whom he had made a favourable impression, to grant him vast estates in counties Kilkenny and Tipperary on 5 November 1526. Second, in 1528 a compromise between Butler and the heirs general of the seventh earl of Ormond was brokered, whereby Butler received fourteen of the Ormond manors on a thirty year lease and elevation to the peerage, while Sir Thomas Boleyn, one of the heirs general, was elevated as ninth earl of Ormond on 8 December 1529 and retained the English estates. At Windsor Castle, on 23 February 1528, Butler was created first earl of Ossory. He had yielded—convinced that the path to political survival lay in compromise. Furthermore, he had exchanged uncertainty for secure title and possession of the wealthiest areas of the lordship; and he had used the years of his illegal occupancy of the Ormond estates to greatly expand his demesne possessions within the lordship. In 1487 he had inherited the Pottlerath estate of 4500 acres, and by 1527 he had amassed 16,970 acres, and now could further expand his estate. Significantly, the last act of his London sojourn was a visit to Wolsey, whose intervention on his behalf had proved crucial.

There was another reward: Butler's reluctant acceptance of Henry's ruling revealed him to be pliable and persuaded the government to maintain him as a foil to Kildare. The king and Wolsey disagreed over whether or not Ossory or his heir should be appointed as Kildare's deputy. Ossory was reappointed lord deputy on 4 August 1528. Although he again proved incapable of defending the pale, and was replaced on 4 September 1529, Ossory's star continued to rise. His increased influence continued to undermine the Geraldine hegemony. By 1528 Cahir Ruadh O'Connor, the tánaiste (designated heir) of Brian O'Connor—Kildare's most important Gaelic ally—was supporting Ossory. Soon after, Brian MacGiollapadraig, chief of Upper Ossory, a former Kildare client, married Ossory's daughter Margaret. Confronted by the collapse of his faction, Kildare was forced to throw caution to the wind and confront Ossory directly in the early 1530s.

The excessive violence Kildare employed, culminating in his procurement of the murder of Thomas Butler, Ossory's younger son, in 1532, ultimately cost him dear. Initially, however, he recovered the deputyship from 1532 to 1534, despite Ossory, by utilizing his connections at court, including Surrey (now third duke of Norfolk) and Boleyn (now earl of Wiltshire). In 1533 Kildare was summoned to England to answer charges of maladministration. In May 1534, during Kildare's detention, Ossory and his heir concluded a compact with the government in which 'both in jopardie of their bodies to deathe, spending of the rentes of their landes, and all their goodes' they undertook to aid the lord deputy, Sir William Skeffington, and promised to resist 'the Bisshop of Roomes usurped jurisdiction … and enduce … others … to doo likewise' (*State Papers, Henry VIII*, 2.194–7). In return, Ossory was authorized to order the midlands: this agreement was one of several crucial factors in pushing the Geraldines into rebellion in June 1534.

Securing the Ormond legacy, 1534–1539 During the Kildare rebellion, Ossory supported the crown. Despite Geraldine devastation of his estates he twice rejected overtures from his nephew, Thomas *Fitzgerald (1513–1537), to join him. During 1534–5 he held the south for the crown, before joining the royal army that crushed the rebels. The Irish privy council acclaimed Ossory and his heir, Lord James Butler, as the saviours of the lordship. Thereafter rewards came thick and fast: Lord James Butler was made high admiral of Ireland and warden of the ports and was elevated, as Viscount Thurles, on 2 January 1536. The 1536 parliament secured the Ormond inheritance for Ossory. The Act of Absentees (1536) extinguished the tripartite agreement he had been forced into with the now disgraced Boleyns and the second heirs general, the St Legers. The claims of his older brothers' heirs general were finally extinguished with the repeal of the 1468 Act of Legitimisation. Late in 1537 Ossory's claim to the earldom of Ormond was finally admitted. On 22 January 1538 he was styled earl of Ormond, and down until the mid-seventeenth century he and his heirs were known as earls of Ormond and Ossory.

To reinforce his position Ormond endorsed the royal supremacy. The Butlers were rewarded during the dissolution of the monasteries, and by 1542 the Ormond inheritance had been augmented by the addition of 14,000 acres of former church lands. In 1537 the Ormond estates were valued at Ir£388 17*s*. 7¼*d*. From the late 1530s Ormond, then in his early seventies, was content to allow Thurles to emerge as the leader of the Butler faction. He did not completely retire. It was he who frustrated the efforts of the lord deputy, Leonard Grey, Viscount Graney, to provoke the Butlers into opposing the government, by negotiating the composition of March 1538 with the crown commissioners, appointed at Graney's instigation, to look into alleged Butler extortions within the Ormond lordship. Ormond undertook to plant 'good civilitie', 'extinguisshing of abusions and enormyties' within his lordship (*State Papers, Henry VIII*, 2.563–4). By 1538 Ormond's health was failing and, described as 'now but a consumed man', he was unable to attend upon the lord deputy in Dublin and was thereafter confined to Kilkenny Castle, where he died on 26 August 1539 (*State Papers, Henry VIII*, 3.72). His last act was to entail the earldom to ensure that his successors were secure from the heirs general of the seventh earl of Ormond. He was interred in the chancel of St Canice's Cathedral in Kilkenny in a tomb that fittingly matched his confidence in his dynasty's future.

Ormond's achievement was based on two factors. First, by attaining control of the crucial Butler lordship through martial endeavour and shrewd negotiation, he made himself a powerful political figure; second, and more crucially, to retain what he had won he made subservience to the crown his guiding tenet. In this he was the first of the new breed of Irish nobles. His flexibility ensured his ultimate success, for whenever necessary he re-invented himself—hence his transformation from closest Geraldine ally to bitterest enemy after 1516.

Richard Butler, first Viscount Mountgarret (*d.* 1571), nobleman, was the second son of Piers Butler and his wife, Margaret. He married, first, Eleanor, daughter of Theobald Butler, of Neigham, co. Kilkenny, then Katherine, daughter and heir of Patrick Barnewall, of Stackallan, co. Meath. His third wife, whom he married in 1541, was Anne, daughter of John Plunket, fourth Baron Killeen, and his first wife, Margaret. However, the couple divorced that year and she married William Fleming. Butler was knighted in 1546 or 1547. He was created Viscount Mountgarret on 23 October 1550. He died on 20 December 1571, and was buried in St Canice's Cathedral. He was succeeded by his heir from his first marriage, Edmund Butler, second Viscount Mountgarret (*d.* 1602). DAVID FINNEGAN

Sources E. Curtis, ed., *Calendar of Ormond deeds*, 6 vols., IMC (1932–43) • D. Edwards, 'The Ormond lordship in county Kilkenny, 1515–1642', PhD diss., TCD, 1998 • C. A. Empey, 'From rags to riches: Piers Butler, eighth earl of Ormond, 1515–39', *Butler Society Journal*, 2/3 (1984), 299–314 • J. Graves and J. G. A. Prim, *The history, architecture and antiquities of the cathedral church of St. Canice, Kilkenny* (1857) • C. A. Empey and K. Simms, 'The ordinances of the White Earl and the problem of coign in the later middle ages', *Proceedings of the Royal Irish Academy*, 75C (1975), 161–87 • D. B. Quinn, ed., 'Ormond papers, 1480–1535 in the Public Record Office, London, and the British Museum', appx, *Calendar of Ormond deeds*, ed. E. Curtis, IMC, 4: 1509–1547 (1937) • 'Calendar of fiants, Henry VIII to Elizabeth', *Report of the deputy keeper of the public records in Ireland*, 7–22 (1875–90), appxs; repr. in *The Irish fiants of the Tudor sovereigns*, 4 vols. (1994) • *State papers published under … Henry VIII*, 11 vols. (1830–52), vols. 1–3 • R. Stanihurst, 'Third booke of the Historie of Ireland, comprising the raigne of Henry the Eyght', *The chronicles of England, Scotlande and Irelande*, ed. R. Holinshed and others, 2 (1577), 76–115 • S. Ellis, *Tudor frontiers and noble power: the making of the British state* (1995) • J. S. Brewer and W. Bullen, eds., *Calendar of the Carew manuscripts*, 6 vols., PRO (1867–73) • GEC, *Peerage*

Likenesses tomb effigy, St Canice's Cathedral, Kilkenny, Ireland

Wealth at death approx. 35,000 acres; drew much income from prohibited practice of coign and livery.

Butler, Reginald Cotterell (1913–1981), sculptor, was born on 28 April 1913 at Buntingford, Hertfordshire, the only child of Frederick William Butler and his wife, Edith Barltrop, the master and matron of the Buntingford workhouse. His father was a distant relative of the Irish poet William Butler Yeats, and his grandfather had been a gardener at Chatsworth under Sir Joseph Paxton. His mother was of Anglo-French extraction and a distant relative of the poet George Crabbe. From the age of fourteen he was educated at the Hertford grammar school. He learned a great deal about the crafts and handling of tools in his father's Buntingford community.

Reg Butler (as he preferred to be known) entered architectural practice locally in 1933 and was sufficiently successful to be elected ARIBA in 1937. He was a lecturer in architecture at the Architectural Association School (1937–9), and continued with architectural journalism throughout the war and until 1951. In 1938 he married (Mary) Joan (Jo), daughter of Robert Child, a farmer; they had no children. With his friend Rosemary, a sculptor, daughter of Matthew Young, doctor of medicine, he had two daughters. During the Second World War, as a conscientious objector, he worked as a blacksmith in Sussex. He was interested in sculpture from 1937 onwards, initially being influenced by African primitive art and the work of Henry Moore. His first one-man show was at the Hanover Gallery, London, in 1949. He was awarded the first Gregory fellowship in sculpture at the University of Leeds (1951–3), and in 1951 also became a lecturer at the Slade School of Fine Art, London, eventually becoming head of the department, a post he held until 1980. The Arts Council of Great Britain and the Greater London council commissioned work from him for the Festival of Britain in 1951. In 1952 the British Council invited him to take part in an exhibition at the British pavilion at the Venice Biennale.

Butler was awarded the *grand prix* in an international competition for an intended monument, entitled 'The Unknown Political Prisoner', in 1953, for a sculpture to be placed on the Russian–German frontier in Berlin. The sculpture was never built and the maquette was destroyed by a Hungarian refugee when it was exhibited at the Tate Gallery in London. Butler was able to make a second small model.

Butler's earlier work shows an acute awareness of trends in Britain and Europe after the war and has close affinities to sources as diverse as Henry Moore, Graham Sutherland, and Francis Bacon, as well as to Picasso, Julio González, Germaine Richier, Alberto Giacometti, and at a later stage, Balthus and Hans Bellmer. This suggests a certain eclecticism in his nature, but it is fair to say that he was equal to the sources of his inspiration, and at times excelled them. He enjoyed argument and was a stimulating and respected teacher. He loved fast cars and was excited by modern technology and by science fiction. He was one of a number of sculptors working with forged and welded metals in the 1950s. Critics tended to find the work harsh and threatening, reflecting a mood of post-war anxiety which Sir Herbert Read summed up as 'the Geometry of Fear'.

In the mid-1950s Butler's work turned from spiky biomorphic metaphors towards a more realist concern with the female figure. Increasingly its erotic nature suggested that the sculptor was searching to invent a series of modern Venuses. In his William Townshend lecture at University College, London, in November 1980, Butler talked at length about his admiration of Stone Age fertility figures. His own last series of doll-like figures, owing something to Indian and Japanese inspiration, seemed to relate twentieth-century sexual fantasies to an ancient tradition. The bronze casts were painted with a sugar-almond surface and were not unlike the treatment of female flesh in the paintings of Lucas Cranach. Heads and limbs were made in interchangeable units, the eyes were made of painted resin and covered with a glassy lens, and human hair was implanted in the skulls, but not in the pubic areas. His creations, combining both lust and compassion, achieved the potency of their primitive ancestors.

Butler continued to be a prominent and controversial

figure whose work was admired throughout Europe and in the United States. He is represented in the Tate collection, the Museum of Modern Art in New York, and the Hirshhorn Museum and Sculpture Garden in Washington, DC, as well as in many other museums. In 1965 he was elected to the Royal Academy of Belgium. A posthumous memorial exhibition took place at the Tate Gallery in November 1983. Reg Butler died on 23 October 1981 at Berkhamsted, Hertfordshire, where he had lived since 1953. JOHN READ, *rev.*

Sources BBC film (1958) • R. Calvocoressi, *Reg Butler* (1983) [exhibition catalogue, Tate Gallery, London, 1983] • personal knowledge (1990) • *CGPLA Eng. & Wales* (1982)
Archives Museum of Modern Art, New York, works • Tate collection, letters, broadcast transcript • Tate collection, works • Washington, Hirshhorn collection | FILM BBC, film (1958)
Likenesses C. Hewitt, photograph, 1953, Hult. Arch.
Wealth at death £33,954: probate, 25 Oct 1982, *CGPLA Eng. & Wales*

Butler, Richard, first Viscount Mountgarret (*d.* 1571). *See under* Butler, Piers, first earl of Ossory and eighth earl of Ormond (*b.* in or after 1467, *d.* 1539).

Butler, Richard (*d.* 1612), Church of England clergyman, was of unknown parentage. Having matriculated as a sizar at St John's College, Cambridge, in Michaelmas term 1580, he graduated BA in 1584 and proceeded MA in 1587. He was ordained deacon and priest at Peterborough on 2 February 1588, and in 1591 was appointed vicar of Spratton, Northamptonshire, a living he held until his death. In 1594 he proceeded BD. He obtained the rectory of Ashton-in-the-Wall in 1602. In 1608 he received a DD and was incorporated at Oxford on the day that William Laud became DD.

Very early on in his clerical career Butler was seen as one who could be relied upon by those in authority. He was successively employed as a surrogate in the Peterborough church courts by Bishop Richard Howland (*d.* 1600) and Bishop Thomas Dove, both active against puritans, and as commissary to the latter 'caused a furore by maintaining that infants dying unbaptized were damned' (Tyacke, 16). Associated with that group of clerics identified as 'proto-Arminians'—men such as John Buckeridge, Benjamin Carier, and Richard Neile—Butler worked diligently with them and with civil lawyers such as John Lambe in the run-up to the Hampton Court conference of 1604. He was remembered at the conference for his description of a puritan as a 'Protestant frayed out of his wits' (W. Barlow, *The Summe and Substance of the Conference*, 1638, 38), and was subsequently active in the subscription campaign of 1604–5. With strict views on the observance of ceremonies prescribed in the Book of Common Prayer, he clashed with puritans such as Robert Catelin, rector of All Saints, Northampton, and was in turn accused of popery. Apparently even Archbishop Bancroft later harboured suspicions about Butler's theological views, which came under the spotlight after a sermon on justification and penance given at court (where he had become a chaplain) in 1610.

Butler's association with Neile continued. In 1611 he assisted the bishop in examining the case of Edward Wightman, the last heretic to be burned at the stake in England. That year he was also appointed archdeacon of Northampton in succession to his friend Buckeridge, for whom he had already deputized in the courts. In his will, dated 10 September 1612, Butler left money to Neile's wife, Dorothy, donated his books to Buckeridge, now bishop of Rochester, and left a collection of medieval manuscripts to St John's College, Oxford. He died shortly afterwards, and was buried on 14 September at Spratton.

ANDREW FOSTER

Sources W. J. Sheils, *The puritans in the diocese of Peterborough, 1558–1610*, Northamptonshire RS, 30 (1979) • E. A. Irons, 'A calendar of a court book', *Northants Notes & Queries*, new ser., 3 (1911), 171 • BL, Sloane MS 271, fols. 23r–23v • BL, Add. MS 8978, 94 • K. Fincham, *Prelate as pastor: the episcopate of James I* (1990) • J. Fielding, 'Arminianism in the localities: Peterborough diocese, 1603–1642', *The early Stuart church, 1603–1642*, ed. K. Fincham (1993), 93–113 • PRO, SP 14/12/69, 74, 77, 90, 96 • PRO, SP 14/70/66 [will] • Bodl. Oxf., MS Ashmole 1521 (B) VII • N. Tyacke, *Anti-Calvinists: the rise of English Arminianism, c.1590–1640* (1987)

Butler, Richard, third Viscount Mountgarret (1578–1651), soldier, was the son of Edmund Butler, second Viscount Mountgarret (*d.* 1602), and Grany, or Grizzel, daughter of Barnaby, first lord of Upper Ossory. Shortly before 8 October 1596 he married Margaret O'Neill, daughter of Hugh *O'Neill, earl of Tyrone, with whom he had three sons and six daughters. He joined his father-in-law's rebellion, and is said to have specially distinguished himself by his defence of the castles of Ballyragget and Cullihill, but, like his own father who had also rebelled, he made his peace with Queen Elizabeth and was pardoned in August 1600.

Butler succeeded his father on 24 November 1602, and obtained livery for his patrimony, and pardon for intrusion thereon, on 22 February 1606. In 1607 he was among those falsely accused by Lord Howth in connection with a suppositious rising. In 1611 Mountgarret sued for a share in the plantation of Ulster. In the following year James VI and I authorized a re-grant to him of his castles and lands with power to hold courts at Ballyragget, and a yearly fair and weekly market. But if he showed himself willing to submit to the prerogative authority of the crown in Ireland, he was clearly considerably less circumspect with regard to the policies of the Dublin government. He sat in the Irish parliament of 1613, joining with the other recusant lords in their protest at the packing of that assembly by the protestant administration.

In 1619, amid the fall-out from the partition of the Ormond inheritance and the loss of the palatinate authority of Tipperary by the Butler family, Sir Robert Naunton, secretary to the king, was warned anonymously that the eleventh earl, Walter, as well as his brother, Mountgarret, and others were plotting insurrection with 'all the principal Irish', and that Mountgarret's son and heir, Edmund, had taken to wearing 'Irish trouses … which is still observed to be a forewarning of rebellion when they change their habit' (Canny, 271). In 1624 the lord deputy, Viscount Falkland, urged that Mountgarret, then heir to the earldom of Ormond, ought to be removed to England 'during these doubtful times' (*CSP Ire.*, *1615–25*, 478). Falkland subsequently embellished his suspicions of Mountgarret as 'a man powerful in the parts where he lives, one that all the last rebellion was out, and then a very dangerous man, and one of the last that came in' (*CSP Ire.*, *1625–32*, 235). In August 1626, however, Mountgarret took an oath of loyalty to the king, and in the following May he went to Whitehall to obtain leave to travel.

It is not clear whether Mountgarret was granted permission to go abroad, but in 1627 he was also reportedly appointed one of the commissioners for collecting the subsidy intended for the maintenance of the army with which the Old English enticed the English crown into negotiations on 'matters of grace and bounty' granting certain rights to Catholics in Ireland.

After the death of his first wife, mother of his heir, Edmund, Mountgarret had married twice more. Some time before 1618, he married Thomasine Freeman (*d.* 1625), widow of Sir Francis of Billing, Northamptonshire, and daughter of Sir William Andrews of Newport Pagnell, or else of Lathbury, Buckinghamshire. At her confirmation in 1619 she adopted the name Elizabeth. Then, at some point before 31 July 1631, Mountgarret married Margaret Spencer (*d.* 1655), widow of Sir Thomas of Yarnton, Oxfordshire, and daughter of Richard Branthwaite, serjeant-at-law. These marriages were childless.

Mountgarret was in London in 1632. In 1635 he fell victim to an attempt by the new lord deputy, Sir Thomas Wentworth, to establish a plantation on certain Butler lands in the territory of Idough or Ideagh in co. Kilkenny. Mountgarret angrily complained that an inquisition had upheld the claims of the crown over these lands 'by undue and sinister means', and the patents of June 1619 on which he based his own claim were simply ignored (Clarke, 109). Wentworth intimidated Mountgarret into submitting his claim to the commission for defective titles, which resulted in a fine of £300, and forced him to release his interests in the land to Sir Christopher Wandesford. Despite his efforts to obstruct the process of plantation which then ensued, Mountgarret's opposition was eventually overborne, but he remained implacable, sending his son to London in 1640 to seek redress, the whole episode ultimately finding its way into the articles of impeachment against Wentworth.

When a rising broke out in Ireland in 1641 Mountgarret and James, twelfth earl of Ormond, were jointly commissioned to govern Kilkenny. Towards the end of December, Mountgarret, Ormond's great-uncle, assumed command of the disorganized forces in the area himself because of 'the apprehensions he had of the height to which the meaner sort of people might grow up against the nobility and gentry' (Clarke, 196). Within a week of Mountgarret's defection the rebels had taken most of the strategic points in the counties of Kilkenny, Tipperary, and Waterford. His combined forces now marched into Limerick and joined with lords Brittas and Castleconnell before taking Kilmallock. Mountgarret now headed south and took Mallow before an argument with Lord Roche and the rebels of co. Cork, one of the earliest signs of tension within the confederate camp, sent him back to Kilkenny.

In March, Mountgarret explained to Ormond why he had thrown in his lot with the rebels, referring to the hostility with which the lords justices, Sir William Parsons and Sir John Borlase, had greeted Old English pleas to arm themselves in defence against the rebels. If he was to be suspected as a rebel he might as well act like one, having no doubt, after the experience of James Touchet, the earl of Castlehaven, that he could expect to be treated like one. On 15 April 1642 an exceedingly dishevelled and miscellaneous force, the command of which Mountgarret shared with at least half a dozen kinsmen and others, was decisively beaten by the earl of Ormond at the battle of Kilrush. Two months later the first meeting of the lords and gentry of the confederate Catholics took place at Kilkenny. Mountgarret, as the most influential Catholic lord then in rebellion, was appointed president of the supreme council established to lend direction to the unity of purpose which the confederates professed themselves to feel. His son-in-law, Richard Bellings, was appointed secretary.

Shortly after a further military defeat at Liscarrol in September 1642 Mountgarret waived his prior claim to the command of the Leinster army, which was entrusted instead to Colonel Thomas Preston. Mountgarret was present at the defeat of the confederate army at the battle of Ross on 18 March 1643. In the following May, assisted by the fortuitous arrival of two Spanish 24-pounders and a mortar, Mountgarret and his son captured Borrass Castle and Ballynakilly. Evidently as part of the talks which led to the cessation of arms of September 1643, Mountgarret was nominated for the earldom of Wexford, but any intention that the grant be made was never carried out.

In 1646 Mountgarret resisted the opposition of the papal nuncio, Rinuccini, who excommunicated all those observing the confederates' treaty with Ormond, and was equally supportive of the second treaty in 1649, opposing any rapprochement with his kinsman Owen Roe O'Neill and the other partisans of the Catholic clerical party.

Mountgarret died in 1651 and was buried in the chancel of St Canice's Cathedral, Kilkenny, under a monument with a eulogistic Latin inscription. SEAN KELSEY

Sources *DNB* • GEC, *Peerage* • *CSP Ire.* • A. Clarke, *The Old English in Ireland, 1625–1642* (1966) • T. W. Moody and others, eds., *A new history of Ireland*, 3: *Early modern Ireland, 1534–1691* (1976) • N. Canny, *Making Ireland British, 1580–1650* (2001)

Butler, Richard, first earl of Arran (1639–1686), army officer, was born on 15 June 1639, probably in Ireland, the fifth son of James *Butler, twelfth earl and later first duke of Ormond (1610–1688), and his wife, Elizabeth *Butler (1615–1684), Lady Dingwall in her own right, daughter and heir of Richard Preston, earl of Desmond and Lord Dingwall (*d.* 1628), and his wife, Elizabeth Butler (*d.* 1628), only daughter of Thomas Butler, tenth earl of Ormond. His early childhood was spent in Ireland, but in 1647, with the collapse of the royalist fortunes, he went with his mother and siblings to London and later to Caen. In 1653 they returned to England, where Butler lived for a time at

Acton in Gloucestershire, the home of his father's uncle Sir Robert Poyntz. In 1657 he went with his elder brother Thomas *Butler, earl of Ossory (1634–1680), to the Netherlands. He was reunited with his father, and they returned to England at the Restoration in 1660.

In May 1662 Butler was created Baron Butler of Cloughgrenan, Viscount Tullogh, and earl of Arran, the last title coming from the Aran Islands in Galway Bay, which he had purchased. Later that year he preceded Ormond to Ireland on the latter's appointment as lord lieutenant, and in 1663 he was made an Irish privy councillor. Ireland henceforth was the main centre of his activity, but he was frequently in England on both private and public business and had some involvement in court politics on behalf of Ormond in 1677, and again in 1680–82 following the death of his brother Ossory. He returned to Ireland to become lord deputy, a post he held from 13 April 1682 to 19 August 1684, while Ormond was in England. During this time he courageously directed in person efforts to control a serious accidental fire which destroyed much of Dublin Castle. As a politician he never enjoyed the confidence of his father to the same extent as Ossory, and his own preference was for soldiering. In 1662 he was commissioned colonel of the new 1200-strong regiment of Irish footguards. Subsequently he was made governor of Dublin, where he made a substantial contribution to the repair of St Audoen's Church for the use of his regiment. His competence as a commander was shown in his firm suppression of a serious mutiny at Carrickfergus with four companies of his regiment in 1666. In 1670, at the head of his footguards and the ceremonial battleaxe guard, he 'most nobly' welcomed to Dublin Lord Berkeley, one of his father's successors as viceroy. In 1673 he commanded his regiment with distinction on board ship at the battle of the Texel and in the other naval operations of that year against the Dutch, in recognition of which he was created Baron Butler of Weston in the English peerage. He was awarded the degree of DCL by Oxford University in 1677.

After Ormond's reappointment as lord lieutenant, Arran played a leading role in the reorganization of the Irish army into regiments in 1683–4, and introduced dragoons and grenadiers into the force. On 10 September 1684 he was appointed marshal of the army in Ireland. He was colonel of a cavalry regiment for a time, but in 1685 lost this appointment to Richard Talbot, James II's Irish favourite. Arran had an estate at Sherwood Park in co. Carlow. He obtained the civil appointments of aulnager of Ireland (1666) and *custos rotulorum* of co. Carlow (1675), and received a grant of the Irish lighthouses in 1667. His financial position was strengthened by his two marriages to substantial heiresses. The first, in September 1664, was to Mary, Baroness Clifton of Leighton Bromswold in her own right (*bap.* 1651, *d.* 1668), daughter of James Stuart, third duke of Richmond (1612–1655), and his wife, Mary (1622–1662), daughter of George Villiers, first duke of Buckingham. There were no children. His second marriage, which took place before 7 June 1673, was to Dorothy (*d.* 1716), daughter of John Ferrars of Tamworth Castle and his wife, Anne, daughter of Sir Dudley Carleton. They had five children, but were predeceased by all except Charlotte (1678–1725), who in 1699 married Charles, fourth Baron Cornwallis of Eye (1675–1722). In character Arran was convivial and good-natured but of a somewhat indolent disposition. At court he displayed 'a singular address in all kinds of exercises, played well at tennis and on the guitar, and was pretty successful in gallantry' (Hamilton, 88). After his first wife's early death, by which he was much affected, he drank heavily for a time, but eventually recovered his self-control. In Ireland he took an interest in horse-racing. He died of pleurisy in London on 25 January 1686, and was buried two days later in Westminster Abbey.

HARMAN MURTAGH

Sources GEC, *Peerage*, new edn · J. Lodge, *The peerage of Ireland*, rev. M. Archdall, rev. edn, 4 (1789), 55–6 · R. J. Hayes, ed., *Manuscript sources for the history of Irish civilisation*, 1 (1965), 77 · *The manuscripts of the marquis of Ormonde*, [old ser.], 3 vols., HMC, 36 (1895–1909) · *Calendar of the manuscripts of the marquess of Ormonde*, new ser., 8 vols., HMC, 36 (1902–20) · *CSP Ire., 1660–70* · *CSP dom., 1671–86* · A. Hamilton, *Memoirs of the Count de Grammont* (1906) · C. Dalton, ed., *Irish army lists, 1661–1685* (privately printed, London, 1907) · C. L. Falkiner, *Illustrations of Irish history and topography* (1904), 80–89 · J. C. Beckett, *The cavalier duke: a life of James Butler, first duke of Ormond, 1610–1688* (1990) · T. Carte, *An history of the life of James, duke of Ormonde*, 3 vols. (1735–6); new edn, pubd as *The life of James, duke of Ormond*, 6 vols. (1851), vol. 4, pp. 679–80 · *Sixth report*, HMC, 5 (1877–8), 720–23

Archives Bodl. Oxf., letter-books and papers | Bodl. Oxf., Carte MSS

Likenesses oils, Royal Hospital, Kilmainham, Dublin

Butler, Richard (1743–1791), revolutionary army officer in America, was born on 1 April 1743 in St Bridget's parish, Dublin, the son of Thomas Butler, supposedly the son of a baron, possibly Thomas Butler, sixth Baron Cahir, and Eleanor Parker. He and his family emigrated to America in 1748, settling in Lancaster, Pennsylvania. In 1764, during the rising of the Ottawa under Pontiac, he served as an ensign in Henry Bouquet's expedition against the American Indians. Subsequently he and his brother William became Indian traders. In a border dispute between Pennsylvania and Virginia in 1774 he led militia against Virginians at Pittsburgh. He married Mary (or Maria) Smith; they had three children. In 1775 he was appointed an Indian agent by the revolutionary American government to negotiate the neutrality of tribes in the Ohio country.

On 5 January 1776 Butler was commissioned captain of the 2nd Pennsylvania battalion, and was promoted to major of the 8th Pennsylvania regiment on 20 July. He was advanced to lieutenant-colonel on 12 March 1777. At Bound Brook, Pennsylvania, on 13 April he commanded the 8th Pennsylvania regiment, and was appointed colonel of the 9th Pennsylvania regiment on 7 June. He joined Daniel Morgan's rifle corps later in 1777 as a lieutenant-colonel and second in command, and fought at Saratoga. He was in the battle of Monmouth on 28 June 1778 and a skirmish at King's Bridge on 30 September 1778. He fought gallantly in Anthony Wayne's storming of Stony Point on 16 July 1779 and was praised for his conduct. In January 1781 he helped Wayne quell a mutiny among Pennsylvania troops, then joined the marquis de Lafayette in Virginia. He acquitted himself well when his force surprised the Queen's rangers, commanded by John Simcoe, at Spencer's Ordinary on 26 June. In 1782 he served with Wayne in Georgia and on 30 September 1783 was commissioned a brevet brigadier-general.

In March 1784 congress appointed Butler an Indian commissioner to negotiate cessions of land from the northwestern Indians. Over the next two years he helped finalize three treaties that compelled the natives to cede vast territories to the new republic. For his services congress rewarded him in August 1786 with the superintendency of Indian affairs for the northern district. Two years later he was appointed a lieutenant and judge of the court of common pleas in Allegheny county, Pennsylvania. In 1790 he was elected to the Pennsylvania state senate, and the following year presided over a court of inquiry that acquitted Josiah Harmar of responsibility for his army's defeat by Indians.

In 1791 Butler was appointed second in command, with the rank of major-general, in Arthur St Clair's army sent to avenge Harmar's defeat. As the army advanced northward into Indian country he and St Clair quarrelled over how the campaign should be conducted. On 3 November, about 100 miles north of the Ohio River, Butler learned that an Indian attack might be imminent, but did not inform St Clair. The following day the Indians unleashed their assault. Butler, commanding the army's right wing and fighting bravely, was mortally wounded. Realizing that he was dying, he insisted on being left behind when St Clair retreated. He was killed by a tomahawk blow to the head; he was scalped, and his heart was eaten by warriors. On 25 December 1793 his body was recovered by Anthony Wayne's army, and it was buried the following day on the battlefield. PAUL DAVID NELSON

Sources *American state papers: military affairs*, 1 (1832) · *American state papers: Indian affairs*, 1 (1832) · *Military journal of Major Ebenezer Denney*, ed. W. H. Denney (1860) · *The St Clair papers*, ed. W. H. Smith, 2 (1882) · T. M. Green, *Historic families of Kentucky* (1889) · P. G. Williams, 'Butler, William', *ANB* · S. Gratz, 'Biography of General Butler', *Pennsylvania Magazine of History and Biography*, 7 (1883), 7–10 · C. Stillé, *Major-General Anthony Wayne and the Pennsylvania line in the continental army* (1893) · P. D. Nelson, *Anthony Wayne: soldier of the early republic* (1985) · W. Sword, *President Washington's Indian war: the struggle for the old northwest, 1790–1795* (1985) · E. G. Williams, 'The journal of Richard Butler, 1775: continental congress envoy to the western Indians', introduction and notes, *Western Pennsylvania Historical Magazine*, 46 (1963), 381–95; 47 (1964), 31–46, 141–56 · B. Burke, *A genealogical history of the dormant, abeyant, forfeited and extinct peerages of the British empire*, new edn (1866)
Archives Detroit Public Library, Michigan, MSS
Likenesses engraving, U. Mich., Clements L.

Butler, Richard Austen [Rab], **Baron Butler of Saffron Walden (1902–1982)**, politician, was born at Attock Serai, Punjab, India, on 9 December 1902, the eldest of a family of two sons and two daughters of Sir Montagu Sherard Dawes *Butler (1873–1952) and his wife, Anne Gertrude Smith (1876–1954). His father, who had passed top into the Indian Civil Service, was a member of a remarkable academic dynasty (since 1794) of Cambridge dons, which

Richard Austen [Rab] **Butler, Baron Butler of Saffron Walden** (1902–1982), by Walter Stoneman, 1941

included a master of Trinity, two headmasters of Harrow, and one of Haileybury. He later became governor of the Central Provinces and, finally, of the Isle of Man. His mother, warm, sympathetic, and encouraging, and to whom Butler was always devoted, was one of ten talented children of George Smith CIE, a Scottish teacher, journalist, and editor in India. She was the sister of Sir George Adam *Smith.

Education, marriage, and entry into politics When Butler was six he fell from his pony and broke his right arm in three places, an injury which was aggravated by a hot-water bottle burn. The arm never fully recovered, and successful games playing was thus ruled out, though he became a keen shot. Returning to be educated in England, Butler attended the Wick preparatory school at Hove. Having rebelled against going to Harrow School because of a surfeit of Butlers there and having failed a scholarship for Eton College, Butler (by now known as Rab as his father had intended) went to Marlborough College. After a final year learning modern languages, which were better taught than the classics he had earlier endured, Butler went to France to improve his French with the diplomatic service in mind. He won an exhibition to Pembroke College, Cambridge—the money was needed—which, after a first class in the modern and medieval languages tripos (1923), was converted into a scholarship. He became secretary of the union as a Conservative. An unsuccessful love affair and a mainly nervous collapse did not stop him becoming president of the union (1924). In his fourth year

Butler gained a first in history (1925) and a fellowship at Corpus Christi College.

While an undergraduate Butler had met Sydney Elizabeth Courtauld (*d.* 1954), a capable, strong-minded girl, who became his wife on 20 April 1926. Her father, Samuel *Courtauld, an industrialist, settled £5000 a year on Butler for life tax-free. This financial independence enabled him to decide on a parliamentary career, though his father told him that strong personal executive decisions were not his forte and he should aim for the speakership. While the honeymooners went round the world, the Courtauld family secured for them a fairly safe seat, Saffron Walden in Essex, and on their return Butler was duly selected without the complication of competing candidates. He had a comfortable victory in the general election of 1929 and held the seat until his retirement in 1965. Before the election he had become private secretary to Sir Samuel Hoare, and he soon became known to the party hierarchy. His first notable public act was a sharp exchange in *The Times* with Harold Macmillan, who was advised to seek 'a pastime more suited for his talents' than politics (*The Times*, 28 May 1930; Howard, 41).

A junior minister In the National Government in 1931 Hoare became India secretary and Butler his parliamentary private secretary. At the second round-table conference Butler was deeply impressed by M. K. Gandhi, the current hate figure of many Conservatives and of his father. After a tour of India, Butler became Hoare's under-secretary in September 1932. His support of constitutional reform and knowledge of the Indian scene made him a natural choice, even though he had been in parliament only three and a half years and was easily the youngest member of the government. India was the issue on which Winston Churchill was challenging Stanley Baldwin, and in the Commons Butler compared himself to 'the miserable animal', a bait 'in the form of a bullock calf tied to a tree, awaiting the arrival of the lord of the forest' (*Hansard* 5C, vol. 276, col. 1011, 29 March 1933; Howard, 376). Yet he was never devoured by Churchill and proved himself Hoare's able lieutenant in defending the India Bill throughout the fierce two and a half year war waged against it by the Conservative right wing.

The Butlers had since 1928 lived in the constituency, first at Broxted and then at Stansted Hall, Halstead, where their three sons and a daughter were largely brought up, and where in 1935 Baldwin came for the weekend and Churchill was invited—something which the new prime minister remembered in 1940. They also had a flat in Wood Street, London, until they moved to 3 Smith Square in 1938. They entertained generously in both London and the country.

Foreign Office: appeasement Neville Chamberlain's accession to the premiership in May 1937 brought Butler a welcome release from the India Office but not a department of his own. Nevertheless, his stint as parliamentary secretary at the Ministry of Labour gave him a useful acquaintance with the depressed areas and with mass unemployment. After nine months he went to the Foreign Office as under-secretary of state in February 1938. With the foreign secretary, the first earl of Halifax, in the House of Lords he was once again prominent—in the long run, indeed, too prominent. The policy of appeasement cut across the Conservative Party much more deeply than India or unemployment, and, when Churchill took over, Butler was on the wrong side of the divide. Appeasement was held against him in a way it was not against those more minor supporters of the Munich agreement, Lord Dunglass (Alec Douglas-Home) and Quintin Hogg.

Butler was an enthusiastic Chamberlainite and like Chamberlain regarded Munich not as a means of buying time but as a way of settling differences with Adolf Hitler. Winding up for the government in the House of Commons on the day that Churchill had earlier delivered a powerful polemic against the Munich agreement, Butler maintained that Britain had 'two choices—either to settle our differences with Germany by consultation, or to face the inevitability of a clash between the two systems of democracy and dictatorship', unwisely adding that war settled nothing (*Hansard* 5C, vol. 339, col. 453, 5 Oct 1938). He was disposed, however, to interpret Benito Mussolini's invasion of Albania as a general threat to the Balkans, until Chamberlain told him not to be silly and to go home to bed. Butler remained an appeaser down to the outbreak of war. He did not favour an alliance with Russia, and he opposed the Polish alliance signed on 25 August 1939 because it would have 'a bad psychological effect on Hitler' (Howard, 85). Indeed even after Britain had declared war Butler remained something of an appeaser. After Chamberlain's fall he, together with Alec Dunglass and two friends, drank to the 'King over the Water' and described Churchill as the greatest political adventurer of modern political history (Colville, 122).

Despite his conspicuous identification with the *ancien régime*, Butler survived Churchill's reconstruction of the government in May 1940. 'I wish you to go on', Churchill told him, 'with your delicate manner of answering parliamentary questions without giving anything away'; the prime minister also expressed appreciation of having been asked to 'Butler's private residence'. The Foreign Office was now a backwater, whose calm was only disturbed by Butler's imprudent conversation with Dr Bjorn Prytz, the Swedish minister in London in June 1940. 'Britain's official attitude', Prytz telegraphed Stockholm after his interview, 'will for the present continue to be that the war must go on, but [Butler] assured me that no opportunity for reaching a compromise would be neglected if the possibility were offered on reasonable conditions'. When Prytz's telegram came to the prime minister's notice, he complained to Halifax that Butler's 'odd language' indicated a lukewarm attitude to the war if not defeatism. Even so, Churchill magnanimously accepted Butler's highly unconvincing explanation of the damaging incident (Roberts, 232–4). Butler was lucky to keep his job. Bombed out of both Smith Square and his father-in-law's house, Butler went for a time to stay in Belgrave Square with Henry (Chips) Channon, his parliamentary private secretary since 1938.

Education and post-war reconstruction Butler remained at the Foreign Office against his wishes when Sir Anthony Eden, whom he did not admire, succeeded Halifax in December 1940. But in July 1941 after nine years as an under-secretary he became president of the Board of Education. Even further removed from the war than the Foreign Office, education was nevertheless a political minefield and had seen no major reform since 1902. Ignoring Churchill's warnings not to stir up either party politics or religious controversy, Butler decided on comprehensive reform. Although in the end he had to exclude the public schools, every child was given the right to free secondary education and, to make that right a reality for the poor, provision was made for the expansion of both nursery and further education and for the raising of the school-leaving age. All Butler's formidable diplomatic and political skills were needed to secure the agreement of the churches as well as the acquiescence of Churchill and Conservative back-benchers, whom Butler thought 'a stupid lot'. The 1944 Education Act, which Butler believed would 'have the effect of welding us into one nation—instead of two nations as Disraeli talked about' (Timmins, 92, 95), was Butler's greatest legislative achievement and was deservedly called after him.

Butler became chairman of the Conservative Party's post-war problems central committee in 1941, and in November 1943 he joined the government's reconstruction committee. The only leading Conservative clear-sighted enough to oppose an early election, he became minister of labour in Churchill's 'caretaker' government in May 1945. After the electoral defeat in July—Butler's own majority fell to 1158—Churchill made him chairman of the Conservative Research Department, although his own bizarre preference was for Duncan Sandys. At that time there was little to be chairman of, but with the considerable assistance of David Clarke, and later, Michael Fraser, whom Butler rightly described as 'the best adjutant the party has ever had', the department was up to strength by the end of 1946 (R. A. Butler, 140). Like Churchill, who thought it would tie the hands of the next Conservative government and cripple the party now, Butler was chary of embarking upon detailed policy-making, though for different reasons. He thought the time was not yet ripe for it, wanting to make sure that the party was facing in the right direction before it made firm commitments. In 1946 Butler also became chairman of the industrial policy committee, whose members included three future chancellors of the exchequer as well as Oliver Stanley and three other future cabinet ministers.

From these two positions Butler exerted the major influence in reshaping Conservative policy and producing the civilized Conservatism of the post-war party. In 1947 the industrial policy committee produced the *Industrial Charter*, which, Butler told Lord Woolton in 1949, 'placed the party on the fairway of modern economic and political thought' (Ramsden, *Age of Churchill*, 134). His later more detailed verdict was that 'the *Charter* was … an assurance, that in the interests of efficiency, full employment, and social security, modern Conservatism would maintain strong central guidance over the operation of the economy'. Mass unemployment was to be a thing of the past; as Butler put it, those who advocated 'creating pools of unemployment should be thrown into them and made to swim' (R. A. Butler, 146, 61). The right wing regarded Butler's efforts as 'pink socialism', a recurring charge under various names in his later career. He himself believed that, without the rejection of unemployment and the acceptance of the welfare state, the spectre of the thirties would not be exorcized and the Conservative Party would remain in opposition. Accordingly Butler was happy in 1950 to welcome 'as a healthy piece of constructive work' *One Nation*, the first pamphlet of a group of nine new tory MPs, among whom were Iain Macleod, Angus Maude, Edward Heath, and Enoch Powell. The pamphlet described full employment as 'a first responsibility of government', and called on the Conservative Party 'to act as a balancing force, to ensure that liberty and order reinforce one another'.

Since Marlborough, painting had been Butler's chief hobby; after the war he occasionally painted with Churchill, once being commanded by him to 'take the mountains', while his leader would 'take the sea' (R. A. Butler, 33). Butler thought their paintings were of about the same standard.

Chancellor of the exchequer Contrary to the general expectation and his own, Butler became chancellor of the exchequer in October 1951 and inherited the usual economic crisis. He tackled it by import controls and the resurrection of monetary policy. Butler himself favoured more drastic measures, having accepted a plan cooked up in the Bank of England and the Treasury. Under this plan, known as Robot, the pound was to be allowed to float (or rather sink); it was to be made (partially) convertible into dollars; and most of the sterling balances held in London were to be blocked. While Robot's first two provisions seem reasonable in retrospect, they would not have worked in 1952. As the British economy was then overloaded because of the excessive rearmament programme bequeathed by the Labour government, devaluation was inappropriate. Exports would scarcely have increased and imports would have been made more expensive. Britain's trading position would have been made still worse by the proposed very limited convertibility. Even the Treasury admitted that much of Britain's export trade might be faced with conditions of great difficulty. The third element of Robot was scarcely less damaging. Although Australia and other members of the sterling area were to be allowed to convert 10 per cent of their reserves into dollars, they would hardly take kindly to 90 per cent of their reserves being frozen. Apart from its effect on Britain, the plan broke the rules of the International Monetary Fund from which the government proposed to borrow money, would probably have killed the newly formed European Payments Union from which it had also just borrowed on a large scale, would have broken up much of the sterling area, and would have infuriated the west Europeans, the Commonwealth, and the United States. Nevertheless, had it not been for the opposition of Lord Cherwell and his chief economist, Donald MacDougall, Robot would have been accepted. Fortunately, after Cherwell had put to Churchill a paper, drafted by MacDougall, pointing out that Robot would produce a sharp rise in food prices and unemployment, the plan was defeated in cabinet.

Butler's wholehearted embrace of Robot, even though, as he admitted to his colleagues, his economic advisers were violently opposed to it, was markedly out of character. An innately cautious and prudent politician, he had spent much of the six years in opposition repudiating the kind of economics and the kind of Conservatism that Robot embodied and implied. To adopt his own earlier metaphor, Robot would have put the Conservative Party back 'in the rough'. It would have been disastrous politically and economically, undoing at a stroke all Butler's efforts and achievements of the last six years. Not surprisingly, therefore, despite what he said in his memoirs, Butler later admitted that his opponents had been right all along (Cairncross, 270). The next few months showed that not only had Robot prescribed the wrong remedies for the putative crisis but there had never been a crisis. As was becoming customary, the Treasury's assumptions and estimates all turned out to be mistaken. Not long after a cautious budget in March, when Butler raised the bank rate to 4 per cent and cut food subsidies by 40 per cent, but also cut income tax and increased pensions and welfare benefits to help the worst off, the reserves began to increase not drain away.

By September such was Butler's standing that in the absence of both Churchill and Eden he was left in charge of the government. Later in the autumn he was able to tell the lord mayor's banquet that the country had gained an invaluable breathing space; and he was the star of the tory party conference at Scarborough. By the end of the year the reserves were much higher than anybody in the Treasury had thought possible. By 1953 Butler had more scope to promote expansion and in his second budget was able to cut income tax and purchase tax and to promise the abolition of the excess profits levy. In the summer when, with Eden ill in Boston, Churchill was felled by a stroke, Butler again took charge of the government. The gravity of Churchill's illness, concealed by his entourage, was known to Butler; this was perhaps the first occasion on which he could have become prime minister had he striven for the job. He had no such thoughts and ran the government well.

After Robot's demise Butler 'reverted', as he said, 'to normal Keynesian economics' (Seldon, 559), and initially his policy differed little from Labour's. This led *The Economist* to introduce 'Mr Butskell … a composite of the present Chancellor and the previous one' who spoke up for the course of moderation from both sides of the house. Butler had long been regarded by the Conservative right as being little better than a socialist, while the Labour left tended to regard Gaitskell as rather worse than a Conservative. Certainly both Gaitskell and Butler favoured Keynesian techniques and sought to maintain full employment. Both were moderates and both had good political manners. Both, too, had considerable respect for each other, but Gaitskell had (in Butler's words) 'unquenchably socialist' convictions and a strong belief in equality; Butler had no such convictions or beliefs (R. A. Butler, 160). Moreover, he had in contrast to Gaitskell a belief in monetary policy and much less interest in planning. Butler favoured convertibility; Gaitskell defended exchange controls and the sterling area. They differed, too, on the far greater emphasis that Gaitskell (rightly) gave to the need for Britain to invest more and consume less.

At the Treasury, Butler, who was one of the two best post-war chancellors, had two special difficulties. Sir Walter Monckton had been made minister of labour by Churchill to conciliate the unions, and conciliation entailed conceding excessive wage claims, sometimes in concert with the prime minister and without consulting the chancellor. 'Walter and I', Churchill told Butler one morning in 1954, 'settled the rail strike in the early hours of the morning on their terms. We did not think it necessary to keep you up' (R. A. Butler, 164). In any case, the government had no alternative but to rely on what Butler in his 1954 budget speech called 'voluntary moderation'. That policy had in fact worked well in 1952 and 1953 when rises in wages were small, but then it broke down, leaving what Butler later called 'a gaping hole in our armour' (ibid.). Butler's second special difficulty was the Conservatives' pledge to build 300,000 houses a year, which Macmillan, the minister of housing, never allowed the chancellor or the cabinet to forget. In consequence, too many of the nation's resources went into the housing drive. In 1954 Butler's third budget was, as he said, a 'carry-on affair' with few changes, but later in the year he predicted the doubling of the country's standard of living within twenty-five years.

Important mistakes On 9 December 1954 Butler's wife died after a long and painful illness. His grief and the loss of her influence as well as the effects of three gruelling years affected Butler's political judgement. His troubles were in any event growing: inflation and balance of payments difficulties necessitated a 'stop', and in February 1955 Butler raised the bank rate and brought back hire-purchase restrictions. Contrary to the later right-wing orthodoxy, Butler's fault was not to interfere too much but too little. Until 1955 industrial investment was inadequate, and virtually nothing was done to make particular industries more efficient. All the same, the record of the chancellor and of the government was one to be envied by all their successors. Apart from the mess they inherited from Labour, the Churchill administration avoided the sort of economic crises that plagued its predecessor and future governments. Butler loosened the economy without endangering social peace. The welfare state was protected and improved. By pursuing 'one nation' centrism the government engineered a contented country.

The electorate's response in 1955 was to say it wanted more of the same. Butler produced for Eden an electioneering budget, taking 6*d.* off income tax. That was his first mistake. After the election Eden invited him to give up the Treasury, but Butler refused, which was his second mistake. Butler then had what he called 'a very disagreeable summer', being the target of criticism both from his own side and the opposition (R. A. Butler, 179). Gaitskell accused him of having deliberately deceived the electorate, while his Treasury advisers slowly awoke to the growing danger of inflation which their bad budgetary advice had acutely exacerbated. After Butler had failed to persuade the cabinet of the need to cut the bread subsidies and take other drastic measures, a run on the pound compelled an autumn budget whose unimaginativeness underlined the errors of its predecessor—Butler's third mistake. In December 1955 Eden decided to replace him with Macmillan, who showed by his stipulated terms for his transfer, to which the prime minister weakly submitted, that he was determined also to replace Butler as Eden's heir apparent. Disregarding the advice of Harry Crookshank, Macmillan's oldest friend, that he was committing 'sheer political suicide', Butler consented to become merely lord privy seal and leader of the house—his fourth and biggest mistake (Howard, 221). He needed a change, but ministerial power in British politics rests with the big departments and for Butler to allow himself to be left without a department was a gratuitous act of unilateral disarmament.

Macmillan later admitted that in the light of subsequent events his demands implied that he was 'actuated by some degree of personal rivalry with Butler' (Macmillan, 693). Though Macmillan was to the left of him on economics, there was no issue on which Butler was, in the eyes of the Conservative Party, seen to be right wing. Many Conservatives saw him as a 'Butskellite'. Hence he was always more popular in the country than in his own party. His appearance was not charismatic, with his damaged arm, his sad, irregular features, and his clothes, described by Channon as 'truly tragic'. But behind it there was a Rolls-Royce mind and a sharp sardonic wit which he enjoyed exerting at the expense of his colleagues. He was the master of many types of ambiguity—'there is no one's retirement party Mollie [his second wife] and I would like more to attend'—and occasionally the cause of ambiguity in others. In the autumn Eden's colleagues, his supporters, and the newspapers had become increasingly disenchanted with the prime minister; and his mishandled reshuffle, whose most conspicuous features were the moves of Butler and Macmillan, brought a renewed press bombardment. Butler watched the prime minister's travails with detachment; 'I have been very calm', he said. But, unlike Macmillan, he was indiscreet in public. Questioned at Heathrow airport about articles hostile to Eden in the Sunday papers, Butler expressed his 'determination to support the Prime Minister in all his difficulties'. While Eden could have done without that sort of support, it was another of Butler's declarations which won the headlines: Eden, he said, is 'the best Prime Minister we have' (Howard, 222). No doubt the new lord privy seal was correct in saying that those words were not his but the reporter's; he had merely given his assent to them—and a denial to the reporter would of course have been even worse. Yet they sounded like a typical 'Rabism', and had Butler felt more warmly to Eden he would probably have been more careful. Describing the episode in his autobiography, Butler said that Eden's reshuffle did not receive a favourable press, characteristically adding that 'a series of articles began to appear assessing [Eden's performance] in decidedly unflattering and somewhat unfair terms' (Howard, 222; R. A. Butler, 183).

Suez, and missing no. 10 Butler was ill when President Nasser of Egypt nationalized the Suez Canal Company in 1956 and was in no danger of being infected by the collective hysteria that followed in Britain and France. He missed the first cabinet meeting at which the fatal route to Port Said was mapped and he was not included in the Egypt committee that Eden set up, though he occasionally attended it. His freedom from departmental responsibilities would for once have been an advantage, but cool, detached advice was not what Eden wanted. Over Suez Butler's predicament was acute. Far too intelligent to accept Eden's likening of Nasser to Mussolini, he had nevertheless an 'appeasing' past to live down. Believing that party and public opinion required action of some sort, Butler also believed that Britain should act in accordance with international law.

Hence Butler was in a similar position to John Foster Dulles, the American secretary of state, and was driven to similar deviousness: as the international position altered, different expedients had to be produced to prevent Eden launching an attack on Egypt. But what was permissible in Dulles, trying to divert an ally from folly, looked less so in the cabinet's nominal number two seeking to restrain his leader, sick and unbalanced though Eden was. Butler would probably have done better to state his position unequivocally or to keep quiet or to resign; doubts were not enough. Even so, if he had succeeded, as his phrase went, in keeping Eden 'in a political strait-jacket' he would have done the prime minister and the country a great service. But by October Butler had run out of strait-jackets, and he used the wrong tactics for defeating the Anglo-French-Israeli plan. Instead of joining with Monckton in direct opposition to a grubby conspiracy which was bound to fail, Butler implausibly advocated that Britain, France, and Israel should mount an open attack on Egypt which would have been scarcely less disastrous. After the UN had voted for an emergency force and an Israeli-Egyptian cease-fire seemed imminent, Butler tried to prevent the Anglo-French invasion as it was by then redundant; and when two days later Eden told the cabinet that a cease-fire was essential, Butler like Macmillan strongly supported him.

Butler's deviousness over Suez was honesty itself compared with the duplicity of Eden and some colleagues; and he was more consistent than Macmillan whose fire-eating bellicosity first drove Eden on towards destruction and who then suddenly demanded peace. Yet Butler's lack of enthusiasm for the use of force had offended the party's large pro-Suez element (many of whom disliked him anyway), and his failure to prevent it had disappointed the antis. He ended up pleasing virtually no one. By contrast, Macmillan, whose record on Suez was far worse—he later admitted that it was 'a very bad episode' in his life (Horne, 1.447)—had pleased the gunboat-minded by his initial fire-eating and then disarmed the opponents of force by his sudden switch to favouring a cease-fire. Unlike Butler, Macmillan was thought at least to know his own mind, even if he changed it. Butler had made matters still worse for himself by being, even by his standards, inordinately indiscreet. While in public he robustly defended Suez, he said very different things in private, being almost suicidally imprudent at a dinner of right-wing MPs. Butler's varying indiscretions to different back-bench groups gave the impression that he was not playing the game. Others were playing a deeper one.

Eden's retreat to the West Indies to recuperate left Butler to do the salvage work at the head of a weak and divided government. Inaccessible in Jamaica, Eden to his intense annoyance was largely ignored. 'I know', Butler condescendingly telegraphed to him, 'how difficult it must be for you to form a judgement on all that has gone on since you left' (Lamb, *Eden Government*, 297–8). Eden, who probably thought it would have been easier to do so if he had been kept fully informed, can have been little more comforted to hear from Butler that there were 'many who would like to see you back, including members of the Cabinet' (Ramsden, *Winds of Change*, 320–21). In Whitehall Butler was at his best, running the government as competently as he had done when Churchill was incapacitated. Yet as acting head of the government he was saddled with what he called 'the odious duty of withdrawing the troops' (R. A. Butler, 194). While Selwyn Lloyd thought that in Eden's absence he had been 'splendidly supported' by Butler (Lloyd, 252), Rab gained little credit for limiting the damage he had not caused. Instead, the salvage man was blamed for the wreckage.

Home secretary Butler did not mount a leadership campaign after Suez. Maybe he was too busy; maybe he thought it was unnecessary because he was bound to win; or, more probably, he thought Eden would be able to hold on until Easter or even the summer, so that a campaign would be premature. All the same, when Eden resigned on 9 January, Butler spent the evening pondering what he should say in his first broadcast to the nation as prime minister. In reality his chances had faded in the aftermath of Suez. The cabinet voted overwhelmingly for Macmillan, and back-bench soundings gave a similar result. Churchill preferred Butler personally but gave his backing to Macmillan, as did the chief whip, the chairman of the party, and the chairman of the 1922 committee. Eden gave no advice to the queen: he disliked both men but he preferred Butler. Butler took his defeat well. Macmillan refused him the Foreign Office, and Butler did not insist, accepting the Home Office while remaining leader of the house. At least he now had a department. He also, as under Churchill and Eden, had the government to run from time to time. When Macmillan in 1958 went on his Commonwealth tour after settling his 'little local difficulties' over the resignation of his entire Treasury team in January, Butler was left, as he said, 'to hold the baby'. As usual he held it well, and this time was popular. As home secretary he was a reformer, which was less popular.

After the October 1959 election Butler became chairman of the Conservative Party in addition to being home secretary and leader of the house. Other than demonstrating that there was almost no limit to his capacity for transacting public business at which he was indeed the unrivalled master, there was little point in Butler's new job. It was in any case scarcely compatible with his existing ones. His leadership of the house entailed trying to get on with the opposition in the Commons, while his chairmanship of the party entailed attacking the opposition in the country. Further, as home secretary, Butler was intent on penal reform, while many of his party faithful were intent on the return of flogging. However Butler was always adept at squaring circles, and he squared those three. Much more important to him than the acquisition of offices was his wedding, in the presence of the couple's ten children, on 21 October 1959 to Mollie, a relative by marriage of his late wife, and widow of the polar explorer Augustine Courtauld; she was the daughter of Frank Douglas Montgomerie of Castle Hedingham, Essex. The marriage was strikingly happy and gave Butler renewed strength.

Butler was an outstanding home secretary, making few mistakes in handling a notoriously tricky department and initiating much useful legislation. He was stuck with the government's Homicide Bill, which introduced degrees of murder, since it was already on its way through parliament when he was appointed. The bill, which had been made necessary by the disagreement between Lords and Commons, was difficult to defend, but Butler deftly put it on the statute-book. While he was at the Home Office, he became a convinced abolitionist, though that did not cause him to err on the side of leniency, when considering whether or not to grant a reprieve. Even at the time, many thought his decision to allow the hanging of James Hanratty a serious misjudgement.

Elsewhere the prime minister allowed him 'a completely free hand' with his reforms (R. A. Butler, 197), a liberality probably assisted by Macmillan's awareness that they would make the home secretary a target of right-wing abuse. When home secretary, Winston Churchill had laid down that 'the mood and temper of the public with regard to the punishment of crimes and criminals is one of the unfailing tests of the civilisation of any country' (Howard, 255). Butler took Churchill's dictum as his text and, undeterred by signs that many on the right of his party would fail that test, he embarked on a comprehensive plan of penal reform. Pointing out that after examining all the available evidence the pre-war Cadogan committee had concluded that flogging was not a deterrent, Butler declined to reintroduce corporal punishment. His refusal annoyed the new MP for Finchley, Margaret Thatcher, who voted to bring back the birch or the cane for violent young offenders, the only time in her Commons career that she voted against the party line. It was then, as Butler wrote, that he had his main controversy with elements in the Conservative Party, 'Colonel Blimps of both sexes—and the female of the species was more deadly, politically, than the male' (R. A. Butler, 200). The annual seaside outing of the hangers and floggers at the Conservative Party conference in full cry against the home secretary was not a spectacle for the squeamish, but at Brighton in 1961 Butler routed his opponents with a brilliant speech.

Much of the legislation for which the Home Office was responsible, Butler told a Conservative Party conference meeting in 1959, was still 'laced in Victorian corsetry' (R. A. Butler, 202). After the Wolfenden committee had recommended the effective removal of prostitutes from the streets and the legalization of homosexual acts between consenting adults in private, Butler found that the Colonel Blimps of the parliamentary party would allow him to enact only the first part of the committee's recommendations. Elsewhere, however, he could loosen the Victorian corsets without over-exciting the darker emotions of the Conservative right. The law on charities was reformed, and licensing hours and the law on obscene publications were both liberalized. In addition, by the introduction of betting shops, Butler's Betting and Gaming Act for the first time enabled the poorer classes to place a bet without breaking the law.

Butler's modernizing social legislation was broadly supported by the left wing of the party and by centrist and liberal opinion in the country; it was opposed or grudgingly endured by the Conservative right. On immigration Butler was supported by the right and opposed by those who were usually his allies. Churchill had favoured legislation to curb it, the Eden government had come close to introducing restrictions in 1955, and Macmillan had considered legislation in 1958. Between 1959 and 1961 the annual number of immigrants from the West Indies, Africa, and the Indian subcontinent grew from 21,000 to 136,000; so, although immigration had been scarcely an issue at the 1959 election, legislation had become inescapable by 1961. Even so, both Butler and Macleod, by then leader of the house, who together piloted the Immigration Bill through the Commons, found their task distasteful. The bill was bitterly attacked by the serious press and savaged by Gaitskell, who denounced Butler and Macleod as hypocrites for failing to stop it by threatening resignation. None the less Labour, a little later, abandoned its opposition to restricting immigration, and the Wilson government soon introduced controls which were stricter than Butler's.

In October 1961 Butler lost two of his offices, retaining only the Home Office, but after making what he later called 'a staunch decision to back the Common Market' he was made overseer of the Common Market negotiations which in practice meant little (Howard, 296). In March 1962 Macmillan, tired of the squabbling between the Colonial and Commonwealth offices, formed a new central Africa department and persuaded Butler to take charge of it. This was a real job, if a thankless one; characteristically, Butler merely added it to his other one. But in the cabinet massacre of July 1962 he lost the Home Office and was left with his central African responsibilities, with the honorific title of 'first secretary of state' plus the intimation that he would be serving as deputy prime minister. Macmillan was thus able both to heap burdens onto the good-natured Butler and to strip him of them again almost at will. For nearly all his long parliamentary career Butler had been a minister: this gave him a unique experience of administration but made him too addicted to Whitehall ever to think of withdrawing. He had, too, the character and quality of a great public servant.

Macmillan weakened his government by banishing Butler from the home front. Yet the government gained in Africa. At the Victoria Falls conference in July 1963 Butler achieved the seemingly impossible feat of an orderly dissolution of the Central African Federation without conceding full independence to Southern Rhodesia.

Missing the leadership again Butler made no attempt to take advantage of Macmillan's considerable troubles in the first half of 1963, and the prime minister's revived fortunes had persuaded him to fight the next election, when his prostate operation altered that decision. Butler was yet again asked to deputize. In January 1962 the prime minister had told Butler that if he went before the election 'all falls to you', but those words of reassurance were soon broken. In the summer of 1963 Macmillan told Hailsham that if he resigned before the election he wished Hailsham to be his successor, and when Hailsham asked about Rab, since he was surely the most obvious successor, Macmillan replied that 'Rab simply doesn't have it in him to be Prime Minister' (Howard, 290; Walters, 111). Macmillan was determined to prevent Butler succeeding him and played an unprecedented part in choosing his own successor, at first supporting Hailsham and then switching to Home. At the Conservative Party conference at Blackpool, where the first round of the leadership struggle was fought, Butler ostentatiously and probably misguidedly kept himself aloof from all that was going on. But he successfully put forward his claim to make the leader's speech in place of Macmillan on the Saturday. The Homes and the Butlers lunched together before that final rally. Home told them that he was going to see his doctor for a medical examination the following week because he had been approached about being the party's leader. Both Rab and his wife were 'amazed' by this intelligence, having thought like other cabinet ministers that Home had ruled himself out when he avowed in cabinet that in no circumstances would he be a candidate (M. Butler, 97). At the rally that afternoon, by reading out a long letter from Macmillan and by some remarks of his own, Home upstaged Butler, whose speech flopped. His text was good but, probably unnerved by Home's revelation and conduct, he eschewed all the oratorical arts, and the applause was more dutiful than wholehearted.

The second round of the leadership contest was fought in London but not under Queensberry rules. The prime minister devised a procedure under which he kept control of events. By naïvely or negligently agreeing to his proposals, the cabinet effectively abdicated in favour of Macmillan and his choice—a grave misjudgement by all the leadership contenders, except of course Home. And after fudged consultations with cabinet ministers by the lord chancellor, Lord Dilhorne, and with MPs by the whips, some of whom knew the answer they wanted and went on until they got it, Macmillan adjudged his contender—Home—the winner.

When Dilhorne's figures of the cabinet's voting—ten for Home and only three for Butler—were published many years later, they were seen to be 'impossible', as Macleod had judged them at the time. Dilhorne's claim that both Boyle and Macleod himself supported Home was self-evidently absurd. His phoney figures were presumably caused more by the faulty procedure, wishful thinking, incompetence, and, possibly, deafness than by outright chicanery; otherwise they would have been more plausible. Although in giving Home 87 first-choice votes of MPs to 86 for Butler, the legerdemain of the chief whip, Martin Redmayne, was less blatant than that of the lord chancellor, his accountancy, too, was creative. The news of Home's victory was leaked on 12 October 1963, the day before Macmillan was to see the queen. There was still, nevertheless, an opportunity for a third round, since a decision reached by such dubious means inevitably caused a row. That evening a meeting of cabinet ministers at Enoch Powell's house telephoned Butler urging him to fight. Hailsham did the same, telling him 'you must don your armour, dear Rab'. Butler, who was, he said, 'just dozing off', merely undertook to take note of what Hailsham had said and possibly act on it; but his only response the next morning, after his doze, was to ask the lord chancellor to call a meeting of all the leading candidates (Walters, 132–3; personal knowledge). Home felt like withdrawing, but was dissuaded by Macmillan, who ignored the opposition to his 'compromise' choice and did not change his intended advice to the queen. Shortly afterwards Home was on his way to the palace, where he was asked to see if he could form a government. Even then Butler could have prevailed. Had Butler 'stood firm', as he later agreed with Boyd-Carpenter, he would have been prime minister (Boyd-Carpenter, 178–9). Home could not have formed a government without Butler, and without Hailsham, Maudling, Macleod, Boyle, and Powell, all of whom would have refused to serve if Butler had given a lead. Powell later spoke graphically of having handed Butler 'a loaded revolver and told him that all he had to do was pull the trigger' (R. Shepherd, *Enoch Powell*, 1996, 260). His wife, too, was urging him on, but his heart was not in the fight, and after reserving his position Butler became foreign secretary on 20 October. Perhaps, as his father had long ago told him, he could not take strong personal executive decisions. Perhaps, like his old chief in 1940, Halifax, he did not really want the job. More likely he was inhibited by fears of splitting the party; and Home had been a friend since their Chamberlain days. Yet certainly their 'friendship' did not lead Butler to think that Home was fitted to be prime minister. He told Home on the day of his triumph that he spoilt the image of modernization, and shortly afterwards he described the prime minister as 'an amiable enough creature' who did not understand economics or even education at all (Ramsden, *Winds of Change*, 209; Howard, 332).

In any case Butler's forbearance did not help the Conservatives. The supporters of both Butler and Hailsham thought their man would win the election of 16 October 1964, and both were probably right. Even Home only just lost it. Later Alec Home came to believe it might have been better had Butler got the top job, since anybody else was seen as a somewhat 'unnatural' successor (Thorpe, 310). After painful second thoughts, Macmillan in the eighties came to a similar conclusion (Horne, 2.582).

Life peer and master of Trinity The rest, politically, was anticlimax. The job Butler had wanted in 1957 and 1960 no longer presented much of a challenge. He ran the Foreign Office easily, but had no opportunity or inclination to do anything of note. Had the Conservatives won the 1964 election, he would not have been reappointed. Butler was given no part in the election preparations and only a bit part in the election itself, though he gave one rather unfortunate interview, in which he agreed with a *Daily Express* journalist that the election might slip away from the tories in the last few days. After the election he lost his chairmanship of the Conservative Research Department, which he had held for twenty years. Home offered him an earldom which he refused; in 1965 the new prime minister, Harold Wilson, offered him the mastership of Trinity College, Cambridge, which he accepted. He then accepted a life peerage in 1965 and took his seat on the cross-benches. Butler was the first non-Trinity man to become master for 250 years, and his appointment was at first not wholly welcome in the college. Nevertheless he and his wife were pre-eminently successful there, and in 1972 91 out of 118 fellows present voted for the maximum extension of Butler's term of office. In 1971 he published his autobiography. Lively, wise, and relatively accurate, *The Art of the Possible* was a strong contrast to the multi-volume efforts of Eden and Macmillan and was one of the very few political autobiographies to enhance its author's reputation. This was followed in 1977 by *The Conservatives*, a history of the party, which Butler edited and introduced. In the same year he retired from Trinity.

Butler was sworn of the privy council in 1939, and was appointed CH in 1954 and KG in 1971. He was awarded honorary degrees by thirteen universities (including Oxford and Cambridge, both in 1962), and elected an honorary fellow of Pembroke College, Cambridge, in 1941, Corpus Christi College, Cambridge, in 1952, and St Antony's College, Oxford, in 1957. He was rector of Glasgow University (1956–9), high steward, Cambridge University (1958–66), chancellor of Sheffield University (1960–78), chancellor of Essex University from 1962, and high steward of the city of Cambridge from 1963. He was president of the Modern Language Association and of the National Association of Mental Health from 1946, and of the Royal Society of Literature from 1951. He was given the freedom of Saffron Walden in 1954.

His son, Adam, was a member of the 1979 Conservative government, but Butler like Macmillan had no great liking for the new Conservative regime. In February 1980 he successfully opposed in the Lords the government's proposal to allow local authorities to charge for school transport, which he saw as a breach of the 1944 act's promise to provide free secondary education for all. Butler's portrait was painted by Margaret Foreman for the National Portrait Gallery, where he was last seen in public. He finished *The Art of Memory* (1982), which was little more than a footnote to its predecessor and was published after his death. He died on 8 March 1982 at his home, Spencers, in Great Yeldham, Halstead, Essex.

Achievement A Baldwinian Conservative, opposed to drastic change and dedicated to compromise, Rab Butler, even more than Macmillan, was chiefly responsible for the humane and moderate 'one nation' toryism of the post-war period. Others, of course, played an important part. But Butler did more than anybody else to slough off the Conservatives' dismal legacy of the thirties, to commit the party to full employment and the welfare state, and hence to secure its early return to power. Similarly his failure to win the party leadership in 1963 proved a delayed but fatal blow to 'one nation' toryism—at least in the twentieth century.

In his farewell message to the 1963 party conference, Macmillan hailed the coming into existence of 'the party of our dreams', which accepted a 'pragmatic and sensible compromise between the extremes of collectivism and individualism'; yet at the very same time he was blocking from the leadership the man who had done even more than himself to establish that compromise. The 1964 election was crucial. A Conservative victory would have consolidated such a party and probably produced a Labour realignment. Defeat led to the later polarization of the parties and an abandonment of Macmillan's 'compromise'—as Macmillan and Butler both lived long enough to see. By barring Butler's way in 1963 Macmillan had inadvertently helped to turn the 'party of our dreams' into one more like his nightmare. By the 1980s much of the party's leadership had not only repudiated 'the pragmatic and sensible compromise between the extremes of collectivism and individualism', it had stigmatized the governments of Macmillan himself and of other tory prime ministers as misguided collaborators with the socialist enemy.

A man of great intelligence, Butler was in most respects superbly equipped for politics. He was sometimes accused of deviousness, but he was often more honest (and more indiscreet) than his colleagues. His trouble was not that he was more devious than them, merely that he was worse at it. Indeed he retained a strong vein of innocence, rare in sophisticated politicians. He was also abnormally good-natured, and inspired great affection. Yet at crucial periods he was unable fully to mobilize his support in the parliamentary party and he was inept at advancing his own claims. Hence Eden and Macmillan were able to push him around almost at will and to land him with unsuitable offices; that was made easier for them, too, by Butler being more a public servant than a politician. His achievement as both, however, was immense. IAN GILMOUR

Sources Baron Butler of Saffron Walden [R. A. Butler], *The art of the possible: the memoirs of Lord Butler* (1971) • M. Butler, *August and Rab: a memoir* (1992) • A. Howard, *RAB: the life of R. A. Butler* (1987) • J. Ramsden, *The age of Churchill and Eden, 1940–1957* (1995) • J. Ramsden, *The winds of change: Macmillan to Heath, 1957–1975* (1996) • J. Ramsden, *The making of conservative party policy: the conservative research department since 1929* (1980) • R. Blake, *The conservative party from Peel to Major* (1997) • I. Gilmour and M. Garnett, *Whatever happened to the tories: the conservative party since 1945* (1997) • A. Cairncross, *Years of recovery: British economic policy, 1945–51* (1987) • A. Seldon, *Churchill's Indian summer: the conservative government, 1951–55* (1981) • A. Horne, *Macmillan*, 2 vols. (1988–9) • H. Macmillan, *Tides of fortune, 1945–1955* (1969) [vol. 3 of autobiography] • N. Timmins, *The five giants: a biography of the welfare state* (1996) • D. Walters, *Not always with the pack* (1989) • J. Colville, *The fringes of power: Downing Street diaries, 1939–1955* (1985) • D. R. Thorpe, *Alec Douglas-Home* (1996) • S. Lloyd, *Suez, 1956: a personal account* (1978) • J. Boyd-Carpenter, *Way of life: the memoirs of John Boyd-Carpenter* (1986) • K. Middlemas, *Power, competition and the state*, 3 vols. (1986–91) • *Chips: the diaries of Sir Henry Channon*, ed. R. R. James, new edn (1993); pbk edn (1996) • A. Roberts, *The holy fox: a life of Lord Halifax* (1992) • E. Pearce, *The lost leaders* (1997) • R. Lamb, *The failure of the Eden government* (1987) • R. Lamb, *The Macmillan years, 1957–1965* (1995) • personal knowledge (2004) • private information (2004)

Archives PRO, MSS, FO 1109 • Trinity Cam., corresp. and MSS | BL OIOC, corresp. with Lord Brabourne, MS Eur F.97 • Bodl. Oxf., corresp. with Lord Monckton • Bodl. Oxf., corresp. with third earl of Selborne • Bodl. Oxf., corresp. with Lord Woolton • Bodl. RH, corresp. with Sir R. R. Welensky and some misc. MSS rel. to Rhodesia • CAC Cam., corresp. with P. G. Buchan-Hepburn • NL Scot., letters to Lord Tweedsmuir • Nuffield Oxf., corresp. with Lord Cherwell • PRO, corresp. with Sir Stafford Cripps, CAB 127/57 • PRO, corresp. with Sir Henry Dale, CAB 127/223 • PRO NIre., corresp. with Lord Dufferin • Tate collection, corresp. with Lord Clark • U. Birm., corresp. with Lord Avon • U. Leeds, corresp. with Henry Drummond-Wolff • Women's Library, London, corresp. with Eleanor Rathbone | FILM BFI NFTVA, profile, 1 June 1956 • BFI NFTVA, news footage • BFI NFTVA, party political footage • BFI NFTVA, propaganda film footage | SOUND IWM SA, oral history interview • IWM SA, recorded lecture

Likenesses W. Stoneman, photograph, 1941, NPG [*see illus.*] • photographs, 1948–52, Hult. Arch. • N. Colvin, pen-and-ink drawing, NPG • M. Foreman, oils, NPG • W. Papas, pen-and-ink drawings, NPG • V. Weisz, pen-and-ink drawing, NPG

Wealth at death £748,789: probate, 21 Oct 1982, *CGPLA Eng. & Wales*

Butler, Sir Richard Harte Keatinge (1870–1935), army officer, was born on 28 August 1870, the son of Colonel E. R. Butler, of the Army Medical Service. Having been educated at Harrow School and the Royal Military College, Sandhurst, Butler was commissioned second lieutenant in the Dorsetshire regiment on 29 October 1890; he became lieutenant on 29 October 1892 and captain on 6 April 1897. On 5 June 1894 he married Helen Frances, second daughter of Major William Benjamin Battiscombe, Argyll and Sutherland Highlanders; they had a son and a daughter. Butler had become adjutant of the 2nd Dorsets in March 1896 and continued in that capacity until September 1900, taking part in the battalion's operations for the relief of Ladysmith. He distinguished himself, rescuing a wounded man from the Tugela River during the retreat from Spion Kop, and again when the battalion stormed Alleman's Nek in June 1900. After being transferred to a mounted infantry unit Butler was severely

Sir Richard Harte Keatinge Butler (1870–1935), by Bassano, 1916

wounded at Fort Itala in September 1901. For his services he had received a brevet majority on 29 November 1900.

After passing from the Staff College, Camberley, in 1906 Butler was brigade-major at Aldershot from April 1906 to April 1910, receiving his regimental majority in February 1910; he returned to Aldershot in November 1911 as general staff officer, grade 2. Having received a brevet lieutenant-colonelcy in May 1913, Butler was selected to command the 2nd Lancashire Fusiliers on 24 June 1914 but was retained at Aldershot until the end of the training season. As a result he joined his new command only in September 1914; but he distinguished himself sufficiently during the first battle of Ypres to be given command of the 3rd brigade in 1st division on 13 November 1914, with the temporary rank of brigadier-general. On 21 February 1915, just three days after receiving his brevet colonelcy, he was appointed brigadier-general, general staff, to succeed the mortally wounded John Gough as Douglas Haig's chief of staff in the first army. On 23 June 1915 he was given the rank of temporary major-general.

Haig had commanded at Aldershot immediately before the war and clearly had confidence in the qualities of vigour, resolution, and drive which made Butler successful in fighting commands with battalion and brigade. Consequently when Haig succeeded Sir John French as commander-in-chief in December 1915, he wanted to appoint Butler as his chief of staff. However, Butler was considered too junior for the post and on 22 December 1915 he was appointed deputy chief of staff at general headquarters (GHQ); he received substantive rank as major-general on 3 June 1916. Butler was to remain at GHQ until February 1918 but he was ill-suited to staff work. His energy made him apt to be impatient and he was not always very helpful with or sympathetic towards subordinates. Indeed he was generally considered excessively rude and, as a result, he only added to the general isolation of GHQ from the army. Nor did Butler have any real understanding of the requirements of a more technologically advanced mode of warfare and he was noticeably lukewarm towards the development of tanks. He would have gladly relinquished his post but Haig declined to release him for an active command, and it was only on 27 February 1918 that he was given the 3rd corps with the rank of temporary lieutenant-general.

The 3rd corps formed part of Hubert Gough's Fifth Army, which was targeted by the major German offensive in March 1918. Butler had a different conception to his neighbouring corps commander, Ivor Maxse, of the kind of defences that should be prepared, favouring holding the front line in strength rather than developing a defence in depth. However, 3rd corps was short of manpower and was forced back towards Noyon, Butler commanding the Amiens sector when the German offensive was finally checked in April. Butler's corps then took part in Haig's counter-attack on 8 August but Butler himself suffered a nervous collapse and was removed at the request of Henry Rawlinson, who had superseded Gough. Butler returned to his command in time for the operations against the Hindenburg line in September but Rawlinson had little confidence in him and he was transferred to the Douai region that same month.

Having been created CB in 1917, KCMG in 1918, and KCB in 1919, Butler commanded a division in the army of occupation from March to October 1919, then a division at Aldershot from November 1919 to February 1923. He was promoted lieutenant-general on 3 January 1923 and was general officer commanding, western command, from June 1924 to June 1928, before retiring on 1 January 1929. Butler died at his home, Roden Lodge, Shrewsbury, on 22 April 1935. He was survived by his wife.

Ian F. W. Beckett

Sources T. Travers, *The killing ground* (1987) · T. Travers, *How the war was won: command and technology in the British army on the western front, 1917–1918* (1992) · R. Prior and T. Wilson, *Command on the western front* (1992) · A. Farrar-Hockley, *Goughie* (1975) · *Army List* · *WWW* · Burke, *Peerage* (1934) · m. cert. · *CGPLA Eng. & Wales* (1935) · *DNB*

Archives IWM, papers | NL Scot., Haig MSS | FILM BFI NFTVA, current affairs footage, G1078–1924

Likenesses Bassano, photograph, 1916, NPG [*see illus.*] · photographs, IWM

Wealth at death £454 11*s.* 1*d.*: probate, 12 July 1935, *CGPLA Eng. & Wales*

Butler, Rohan D'Olier (1917–1996), historian and civil servant, was born on 21 January 1917 at 74 Boundary Road, Hampstead, London, the younger son of Sir Harold Beresford *Butler (1883–1951), civil servant, and his wife, Olive Augusta Newenham, daughter of Samuel Abraham Walker Waters, assistant inspector-general of the Royal

Irish Constabulary. He grew up largely in Geneva, acquiring fluent French and German. He was educated at Summer Fields preparatory school, Oxford, as an oppidan at Eton College under Robert Birley, and privately abroad. He then read modern history at Balliol College, Oxford, where his principal tutor was Benedict Humphrey Sumner. He graduated with first-class honours in 1938, and in the same year was elected a prize fellow of All Souls College, which thereafter remained one of the centres of his life; from 1961 to 1963 he was sub-warden, and from 1984 fellow emeritus.

In 1939 Butler published *The Roots of National Socialism, 1783–1933*, arguing that Nazism derived largely from elements deeply embedded in German history and culture. It was influential during and immediately after the war and underpinned Butler's later arguments for the formal suppression of the state of Prussia, which helped to shape the decisions of the allied council of foreign ministers after the occupation of Germany in 1945. At the outbreak of the Second World War in 1939 he volunteered for the navy but was rejected because of poor eyesight. He worked instead at the Ministry of Information, his time there interrupted by a brief spell in the Special Operations Executive in 1941 and nine months as a pay corps private in 1941–2. He also served in the Home Guard (1942–4). In 1944 he was transferred to the Foreign Office, where he had a major role planning the allied occupation of Germany and Austria. *Inter alia*, he suggested the posthorn design for Austrian stamps.

Butler declined a post-war Foreign Office career and offers of tutorial fellowships at Balliol and Christ Church, Oxford. He was an editor (1945–54) under Sir Llewellyn Woodward, then senior editor (1955–65) of the official, multi-volume *Documents on British Foreign Policy, 1919–1939*. The series showed his rigorous and exacting scholarship. He also planned the succeeding post-war series, *Documents on British Policy Overseas*, and edited the first volume, published in 1984. From 1963 to 1982 he was historical adviser to the secretary of state for foreign affairs, a post in abeyance since 1929. His enthusiasm for this resulted from his belief in the beneficial contribution which historians could make towards formulating foreign policy. As adviser he wrote extensively, especially on German and Russian themes; as Sir Julian Bullard wrote, 'there were few important British ministerial speeches in that period in which the argument was not strengthened and the text not embellished by a contribution from Rohan's distinctive pen' (Bullard and Rogister, 4). A scrupulous historian, he deplored the harm done by official 'weeders'. He was made CMG in 1966.

On 6 August 1956 Butler married, in Copenhagen, Lucy Rosemary (*b.* 1912), daughter of Eric Byron, civil engineer, and sister of Robert *Byron (1905–1941), traveller and writer on art. Through his marriage he gained three stepdaughters, and his wife's family home, White Notley Hall, near Witham, Essex, became his home. Their marriage was happy: she helped sharpen his interest in cultural history, and shared many of his intellectual interests.

Butler contributed to several Festschriften and to the *New Cambridge Modern History*. His *magnum opus* was *Choiseul: Father and Son, 1719–1754* (1980). Massively researched, over 1000 pages long, it embodied his aim of 'history from the inside' and placed Choiseul in his French and international context. It covered only Choiseul's early life, and Butler died before he was able to complete the intended three or four subsequent volumes. In 1981 he graduated DLitt from Oxford and in 1982 he was awarded the prix Jean Debrousse of the Académie des Sciences Morales et Politiques, Paris: a unique distinction for a work written in English. Friends and admirers were surprised that he did not receive further British recognition, and it was suggested that he was 'perhaps the victim of some academic malice' (Bullard and Rogister, 14). He was large and physically impressive, with a memorable, loud laugh. Despite a stammer, he was a brilliant conversationalist and raconteur who enjoyed entertaining friends, and he was generous with his time. He died on 30 October 1996 at the Lawns Nursing Home, Lawn Lane, Springfield, Chelmsford, Essex, of stomach cancer, and was survived by his wife and stepdaughters. ROGER T. STEARN

Sources *The Independent* (5 Nov 1996) · *Daily Telegraph* (6 Nov 1996) · *The Times* (14 Nov 1996) · *The Guardian* · *WWW* · J. Bullard and J. Rogister, memorial service, addresses, 1997, All Souls Oxf. · private information (2004) [Lucy Butler] · b. cert. · d. cert.
Likenesses photograph, repro. in *The Independent* · photograph, repro. in *Daily Telegraph* · photograph, repro. in *The Times* · photograph, repro. in *The Guardian*
Wealth at death under £180,000: probate, 11 Dec 1996, *CGPLA Eng. & Wales*

Butler, Samuel (*bap.* 1613, *d.* 1680), poet, was baptized on 14 February 1613 at Strensham, Worcestershire, the fifth of the eight children of Samuel Butler (*d.* 1626) and his wife, Mary (*d.* 1648). The Butlers were a family of yeoman farmers, increasingly prosperous in recent generations. The poet's father leased his Strensham house and farm from Sir John Russell but owned a house and land at Barbourne as well. He worked for Russell, presumably as a clerk, and left his children an appreciable library of books. To Samuel he willed 'all my Lawe and Latine bookes of Logicke, Rhethoricke, Philosophy, Poesy, phisicke, my great Dodaneus Herball, and all other my lattine and greeke bookes whatsoever' (Worcs. RO, 008.7.1627/29).

By 1626 Butler, whose family then lived at Barbourne, was attending King's School, Worcester. His father died that year, leaving him some Barbourne property, which he may briefly have farmed. Before long he was clerk to a local magistrate, 'Mr. *Jefferys* of *Earls-Croom*' ('Life', sig. a4*r*)—either Leonard Jefferey (*d.* 1629) or his son Thomas. He is said to have taken up painting there, and two 'crudely executed' portraits—reputedly by Butler of Leonard Jefferey and his wife—are preserved in the vestry of Earl's Croome church (Wilding, 17).

According to John Aubrey, who knew Butler, 'He came when a young man to be a servant to the countesse of Kent, whom he served severall yeares' (*Brief Lives*, 1.135). The countess, who lived at Wrest Park, Bedfordshire, and died in 1651, was friendly with the learned John Selden, once the late earl's steward. Selden—a likely source of

Samuel Butler (*bap.* **1613**, *d.* **1680**), by Gerard Soest, 1670s

Butler's fascination with the law and with the out-of-the-way books exploited in *Hudibras*—'tooke notice of his partes and would many times make him write or translate for him' (ibid., 1.138). Butler composed his first surviving poem, 'A Ballad', as early as 1644 and his first prose tract, 'The case of King Charles I. Truly stated', as early as 1649 (Thyer, 1.193–201, 326–68). What he did on leaving Wrest is uncertain. The story goes that he 'liv'd some time also with Sir *Samuel Luke*' ('Life', sig. a4*v*) of Cople, Bedfordshire. This rests on the supposition that Hudibras—who likens himself to someone who must be Luke (*Hudibras*, 1.1.895ff.)—is a satirical portrait of the Presbyterian MP and military commander, and the further supposition that the poet was taking revenge on a past employer. But Butler wrote to Sir George Oxenden (19 March 1663) that Hudibras 'was a West Countrey Knight then a Coll: in the Parliament Army & a Committee man, with whome I became Acquainted Lodging in the same house with him in Holbourne' (Wilders, 450–51). The poem, set 'in Western Clime' (*Hudibras*, 1.1.659), seems to bear this out, and its knowledgeable editor Zachary Grey had evidence deriving from a Gray's Inn bencher that Butler's knight was Sir Henry Rosewell of Ford Abbey, Devon (Butler, *Hudibras*, ed. Z. Grey, 2 vols., 1744, 1.iv).

Gray's Inn played some part in Butler's middle life. According to Aubrey, the poet John Cleveland 'and Sam. Butler, &c. of Grayes Inne, had a clubb every night' (*Brief Lives*, 1.175); Oxenden's sister recalls 'our Old acquaintance Mr Buttler whome wee did use to meete in Grasenn walkes' (Wilders, 450). Aubrey states, 'he studied the Common Lawes of England, but did not practise', and in his next sentence suggests why not: 'He married a good jointuresse, the relict of … Morgan, by which meanes he lives comfortably' (*Brief Lives*, 1.136). Aubrey's statement, repeated by Anthony Wood, is contradicted by the—albeit less authoritative—anonymous 'Life': 'he married one Mrs. Herbert, a Gentlewoman of a very good Family, but no Widow' (Wood, *Ath. Oxon.*, 2.452; 'Life', sig. a5*v*). Besides, the poet was habitually confounded with Hudibras, who courts a widow. Butler refers to 'my wife' in an undated letter (*Prose Observations*, 243–4).

Butler wrote tracts, which he did not publish, on the politics of 1659–60: 'Two speeches made in the *Rump-Parliament*' and 'A speech made at the *Rota*' (Thyer, 1.272–325). The first printed work ascribable to him is *A True and Perfect Copy of the Lord Roos his Answer to the Marquesse of Dorchester's Letter* (1660). With the Restoration his prospects brightened both for finding preferment and for publishing *Hudibras*, which internal evidence suggests he began writing about 1658. In 1661 he was steward at Ludlow Castle to Richard Vaughan, earl of Carberry and lord president of Wales, but gave up that post in January 1662. In Wales he presumably wrote his 'Beneficial Reflections on Milford-Haven'—a plan for its fortification (Thyer, 1.411–18).

Hudibras: the First Part (dated 1663) was licensed on 11 November 1662; Pepys bought a copy of this 'new book of Drollery in verse' on 26 December (Pepys, 3.294). Here the Presbyterian knight Hudibras and his Independent squire Ralpho set out on a godly quest, which is disrupted by their wrangling with each other, and by physical mishaps at the hands of the common people. The book was a prodigious success: five authorized and four pirated editions within the year, plus four editions of a spurious second part. It 'was not only taken into his Majesty's hands, and read by him with great delight, but also by all Courtiers, loyal Scholars and Gentlemen, to the great Profit of the Author and Bookseller' (Wood, *Ath. Oxon.*, 2.453). The genuine *Hudibras: the Second Part* describes the knight's hopeful courtship of a cunning widow and his encounter with the astrologer Sidrophel. Dated 1664, it was licensed on 5 November 1663 and on sale on 28 November (Pepys, 4.400). Two editions were printed; then the two parts together (revised by Butler, who also added satirical and explanatory notes) were printed in 1674 and reprinted in 1678. In view of this success, Pepys, who bought the second part and still could not 'see enough where the wit lies', was an uncommon reader (ibid., 4.411).

Clarendon owned Butler's portrait but never rewarded the poet (*Brief Lives*, 1.136), confirming no doubt Butler's general view that the chancellor had 'layd his Dessignes to depress the Royall Party … and to advance the Rebells'—by preference 'the most perfidious' of them (*Prose Observations*, 197). Perhaps Carberry still employed him; for the earl, who reportedly presented him to Charles II, issued him a protection from arrest in September 1667. Between 1667 and 1669 Butler wrote most of his Theophrastan characters, which numbered at least two hundred, none of them published before 1759. His literary satires on Robert Howard, on Denham, and later on Dryden as heroic dramatist remained unpublished too; so did his poems on

English society, its vices, and French fashions. On 19 July 1668 he was one of the 'eminent men in their way' who dined with Pepys (Pepys, 9.265); another was the painter Samuel Cooper, whose 'great friendship' with Butler is mentioned by Aubrey and to whom a miniature of Butler is attributed (*Brief Lives*, 1.135–6).

On 14 October 1668 William Habington's *Queen of Arragon* (1640) was performed before the duke and duchess of York, with a new prologue and epilogue by Butler addressed to the royal couple. That was all he ever completed for the theatre, although he did sketch another prologue and helped his friend Shadwell (the recipient of his jocular poem 'To Thomas —') with the scientific parts of *The Virtuoso*. Rochester, in 'An Allusion to Horace', names Butler among the writers he respects; Butler's negative remarks about Dryden suggest one reason why.

By 1670 Butler was working for the duke of Buckingham, another of the writers Rochester respected. He went to Paris in the duke's entourage for the negotiation of the *traité simulé* and made some generally disapproving notes on France and the French; in June 1673 he was secretary for Buckingham's affairs as chancellor of the University of Cambridge. Butler could hardly have found his employer's debauched way of life appealing, and he ridicules it in his character of 'A duke of Bucks' (Thyer, 2.72–5).

Two minor works of Butler's were printed at this time: an ironic ode *To the Memory of the most Renowned Du-Vall* (1671) and *Two Letters* (1672), a mock-contribution to William Prynne's argument with John Audland in the mid-1650s. He was also writing 'The Elephant in the Moon'. This poem, his most important after *Hudibras*, makes fun of the Royal Society, one version using heroic couplets instead of the 'hudibrastic' octosyllabic ones. In fact, a number of his unpublished poems use heroics, including a long one he never finished on the imperfection and abuse of human learning. The last original poem he completed, 'Upon Critics who Judge of Modern Plays Precisely by the Rules of the Ancients' (ibid., 1.161–7), answers Thomas Rymer's *Tragedies of the Last Age*, published in the late summer of 1677. In November that year Charles II at last recognized Butler's merit with a £100 grant and £100 annual pension; but the money was not paid, it seems, until Charles gave further orders in September 1678. At this time James Yonge, a Plymouth surgeon, saw Butler at the Wits' Coffee House, Covent Garden: 'the famous old Mr. Butler, an old paralytick claret drinker, a morose surly man, except elevated with claret, when he becomes very brisk and incomparable company' (J. Yonge, *Journal*, ed. F. N. L. Poynter, 1963, 157).

Hudibras: the Third and Last Part (dated 1678) was entered in the Stationers' register on 22 August 1677 and was on sale at the year's end. Four editions had been printed by 1680. It is not as lively as the first two parts, and its middle canto neglects the knight's story altogether to describe the political squabbling after the fall of Richard Cromwell in 1659. However, the satire on republican chaos and earlier career of Shaftesbury had obvious relevance in 1677, and still more when the Popish Plot broke the next year. In February 1680 Butler's 'Cydippe her Answer to Acontius', his last work published before his death, appeared in *Ovid's Epistles Translated by Several Hands*. Butler was at this time impoverished and unwell: he was 'much troubled with the gowt' and 'stirred not out of his chamber' from October 1679 to Easter 1680 (*Brief Lives*, 1.136). He was lodging in Rose Street, Covent Garden, earlier described as 'fitt for mechanicks only and persons of meane qualitie' (*Survey of London*, 36, ed. F. W. H. Sheppard, 1970, 183). The king gave him £20 in 1680, but he had a more constant benefactor in William Longueville (1638–1721), a distinguished bencher of the Inner Temple who lived not far away in Bow Street. 'Mr. *Longueville*', writes Roger North, 'was the last Patron and Friend that poor old *Butler*, the Author of *Hudibras*, had, and, in his old Age, he supported him. Otherwise he might have been literally starved' (R. North, *Life of Francis North*, 1742, 289). The two men had common interests in wit and the law, and Longueville was the talkative company Butler must have needed.

Butler died at Covent Garden 'of a consumption' on 25 September 1680 and was buried two days later at Longueville's expense in the churchyard of St Paul's, Covent Garden. About twenty-five of 'his old acquaintance' attended: Shadwell was a pallbearer together with Aubrey, Sir Robert Thomas, Mr Saunders, 'the countesse of Kent's kinsman', Dr Cole (probably from Worcester), and Dr Davenant, presumably Sir William's son Charles (*Brief Lives*, 1.136–7). In 1721 John Barber erected a monument to Butler in Westminster Abbey, and in St Paul's, Covent Garden, the parishioners erected one in 1786. Butler gave his unpublished writings to Longueville, who arranged the papers and partially transcribed them. In 1759 Robert Thyer, Chetham librarian in Manchester, edited two volumes of Butler's *Genuine Remains*; what survives of the rest was printed in the twentieth century. Aubrey writes that Butler 'was of a leonine-coloured haire, sanguino-cholerique, middle-sized, strong' (ibid., 1.138).

Butler's ideas—about nonconformist subversion, popish plotting, institutional corruption, and other social questions—were conventional, but he expressed them in a brilliantly original way, helped by extraordinary similes drawn from extensive and idiosyncratic reading. The ridiculing of the puritan 'saints' appealed to later generations of Anglicans, while Zachary Grey's annotations, reworked by later editors, kept Butler's world of outmoded learning reasonably accessible. The regular republication of *Hudibras* as a literary classic continued to the beginning of the twentieth century; thereafter Wilders's critical edition of 1967 stands alone.

Butler's distinctive verse and expression were widely imitated in Britain, and in America, up to the early nineteenth century. More than eighty works have been attributed to him, of which only a handful could plausibly be his. He became a byword for neglected genius: Dryden, Oldham, Otway, and others charged his misfortunes on the court and nation. Among the unknown facts of his life the most curious is the strange reluctance of the destitute author to release any of his eminently saleable manuscript works. HUGH DE QUEHEN

Sources J. Wilders, introduction, in S. Butler, *Hudibras*, ed. J. Wilders (1967), xiii–lxi · R. Thyer, ed., *Genuine remains … of Mr. Samuel Butler*, 2 vols. (1759) · H. de Quehen, introduction, in S. Butler, *Prose observations*, ed. H. de Quehen (1979), xvii–lx · H. de Quehen, 'An account of works attributed to Samuel Butler', *Review of English Studies*, new ser., 33 (1982), 262–77 · *Brief lives, chiefly of contemporaries, set down by John Aubrey, between the years 1669 and 1696*, ed. A. Clark, 2 vols. (1898) · [J. Anstry?], 'Life', in [S. Butler], *Hudibras: the first part* (1704), sig. a4r–A1r · M. Wilding, 'Samuel Butler at Barbourne', *N&Q*, 211 (1966), 15–19 · Pepys, *Diary* · Wood, *Ath. Oxon.*, 2nd edn · E. A. Richards, *Hudibras in the burlesque tradition* (1937) · *IGI*

Archives BL, literary papers, Add. MSS 32625–32626 · Rosenbach Foundation, Philadelphia, MSS

Likenesses attrib. P. Borsselaer, oils, *c*.1665, NPG · G. Soest, oils, 1670–79, NPG [*see illus.*] · S. Cooper, watercolour miniature, *c*.1670–1680, repro. in Butler, *Hudibras*, ed. Wilders · E. Lutterel, gouache and pastel drawing, *c*.1680, NPG; copy, Bodl. Oxf. · attrib. J. M. Rysbrack, bust on monument, Westminster Abbey · G. Soest, oils, second version, Bodl. Oxf. · mezzotint (after G. Soest), NPG

Butler, Samuel (1774–1839), headmaster and bishop of Coventry and Lichfield, was born at Kenilworth, Warwickshire, on 30 January 1774, the only son of William Butler, a draper, and his wife, Lucy, *née* Brosell. He was educated at Rugby School, and, from 1791, at St John's College, Cambridge. After an undergraduate career of exceptional distinction (including three Browne medals and a Craven scholarship), he became a fellow of St John's in 1797; in 1798, aged only twenty-four, he was appointed headmaster of Shrewsbury School, a position which he held for thirty-eight years. In the same year, on 4 September, he married Harriet Apthorp, fifth daughter of the Revd East Apthorp, rector of St Mary-le-Bow in London. They had two daughters, Mary and Harriet, and a son, Thomas, born in 1806 and the father of Samuel *Butler (1835–1902); the elder daughter married (27 March 1828) Edward Bather.

It is not too much to say that Butler re-founded Shrewsbury School, with the vital assistance of the liberating Shrewsbury School Act of 1798. It was his triumph at Shrewsbury to turn a virtually moribund school (despite the success which it had long enjoyed after its foundation in 1552) into one of such distinction that, in due course, it would be included among the nine schools investigated by the Clarendon commission as being the leading public schools of England. Yet Butler inherited a school with (by tradition) only one pupil, or more probably a dozen or so; by 1827 there were no fewer than 285. By 1820–21 he was already publicly arguing for Shrewsbury's categorization as one of the foremost public schools.

For thirty-seven years, Butler endured a state of permanently impossible relations with the school's second master, John Jeudwine, 'which embittered both their lives to the detriment of the school, the scandal of the town and the embarrassment of Butler's every action' (Oldham, 73). Right seems to have been on Butler's side, but it is for his achievements in securing scholastic successes for his pupils that his claim to be recognized as one of the greatest headmasters of the nineteenth century lies. Most famously, in 1831 Thomas Brancker, still a sixth-form boy at Shrewsbury, won Oxford's Ireland scholarship, beating both Robert Scott (later one of the editors of Liddell and Scott's great *Greek–English Lexicon*) and W. E. Gladstone; at this point, Salopians had won the Ireland in five successive years. Successes at Cambridge were equally spectacular and even more numerous; Benjamin Hall Kennedy won the Porson prize while still a Shrewsbury schoolboy in 1823. However, undoubtedly the most famous boy to come under Butler's headship at Shrewsbury was no classicist at all—Charles Darwin. Butler instituted regular examinations (seemingly a major innovation), and letters to Butler from the headmasters of Eton and Harrow testify to the interest his methods had aroused; the headmaster of Harrow even came to Shrewsbury to listen to Butler teaching his form. There were severe outbreaks of turbulence and indiscipline during his long reign, but these were by no means unique to Shrewsbury.

In 1802, Butler became vicar of Kenilworth; in 1807 he was instituted to a prebend at Lichfield and his DD followed in 1811. In 1821 he was appointed to the archdeaconry of Derby; his published visitation returns show how seriously he took this office, especially in the matter of the education of the poor. Theologically, he seems to have been equally opposed to the evangelicals and to the Oxford Movement—and indeed to all extremes of opinion, though he had wide-ranging ideas for the reform of church administration. On retirement from his headmastership in 1836, he became bishop of Coventry and Lichfield (shortly to become solely Lichfield), but he was already suffering from ill health related to asthma, and died on 4 December 1839 at his episcopal palace, Eccleshall Castle, in Staffordshire. He was buried at St Mary's Church, Shrewsbury, all business in the town being suspended at the time of his funeral.

Of Butler's numerous publications, his school textbook on modern and ancient geography, first published in 1813, was frequently reprinted. The four-volume edition of Aeschylus (1809–26), produced (under the disadvantageous circumstances of having to use an outdated text) for the Cambridge University Press, calls for mention, mainly because of the severe mauling by C. J. Blomfield which the first volume received (*Edinburgh Review*, 15, 1809, 152–63). It rated no more than a trenchant footnote in E. Fraenkel's great edition of the *Agamemnon* (1949); the claim by his friend Baron Merian in 1824 that Butler was acknowledged to be the best classical scholar of England is simply absurd. Butler's library, which included both manuscripts (sold to the British Museum) and a notable collection of Aldine editions, fetched the then remarkable sum of £10,000 on his death. J. H. C. LEACH

Sources S. Butler, *The life and letters of Dr Samuel Butler*, 2 vols. (1896) · G. W. Fisher, *Annals of Shrewsbury School*, rev. J. S. Hill (1899) · J. B. Oldham, *A history of Shrewsbury School* (1952) · J. H. C. Leach, *A school at Shrewsbury* (1990) · D. S. Colman, *Sabrinae Corolla: the classics at Shrewsbury School under Dr Butler and Dr Kennedy* (1950) · M. R. Austin, ed., *The church in Derbyshire in 1823–4: the parochial visitation returns of the Rev. Samuel Butler* (1974)

Archives BL, Add. MSS 11828–12117 · BL, Add. MSS 34583–34598 · Shrewsbury School Library, corresp., diary, literary papers | BL, corresp. with William Hone, Add. MSS 34585–34586 · BL, letters to Lord Spencer · Bodl. Oxf., corresp. with Sir Thomas Phillipps · Shrops. RRC, corresp. with third Baron Berwick

Likenesses T. Kirkby, portrait, 1819, Shrewsbury School · S. Cousins, mezzotint, pubd 1838 (after T. Phillips), BM, NPG · E. H. Baily, statue, 1843; formerly at Moser Building, Shrewsbury; destroyed 1967 · W. Ward, mezzotint (after T. Kirby), BM, NPG · portrait, bishop's palace, Lichfield
Wealth at death under £30,000: *GM*, 2nd ser., 13 (1840), 670

Butler, Samuel (1835–1902), writer and artist, was born on 4 December 1835 at the rectory at Langar, near Bingham, Nottinghamshire, the eldest son in the family of four children (including another son, Thomas, and two daughters, Henrietta and May) of Thomas Butler (1806–1886), rector of Langar from 1834 and canon of Lincoln, and his wife, Fanny (1808–1873), daughter of Philip John Worsley, a sugar refiner, of Arno's Vale, Bristol. He was the grandson of Dr Samuel *Butler (1774–1839), headmaster of Shrewsbury School, and afterwards bishop of Coventry and Lichfield, whose *Antient Geography* Thomas Butler revised in 1851 and 1855. His aunt Mary, elder daughter of the bishop, was second wife of Archdeacon Bather.

Education and early life These family details were of great significance in Butler's life, in that he was called on to continue a family tradition, as in part he did, by going to Shrewsbury, then under the headmastership of Benjamin Hall Kennedy, his grandfather's successor. He distinguished himself at the family college, St John's, Cambridge (1854–8), coming equal twelfth in the classical tripos, and later wrote the life of his grandfather. More importantly he rebelled against his family by refusing to take orders in the church, as unbelief grew in him while serving as lay reader at St James's, Piccadilly. He recorded his pained and satirical dissent from patriarchal Victorian hypocrisy in his major novel *The Way of All Flesh*.

Butler's first independent wish was to become an artist. He had been taught drawing at Shrewsbury by Philip Vandyck Browne, a friend and associate of the noted watercolourist David Cox, and had executed some still preserved landscape watercolours; and he had attended some classes at the Cambridge School of Art. This was anathema to his father who wrote, 'The artist scheme I utterly disapprove. It will throw you into very dangerous company' (Butler, *Family Letters*, 88–9). After much discussion it was agreed he should go to the colonies, and with approximately £4000 from his father try to make his fortune, after which he would be free to follow his own wish. His father clearly banked on 'all that nonsense' being knocked out of the young man on contact with 'the real world'. Butler chose New Zealand, the most distant of colonies, and set sail from Gravesend aboard the *Roman Emperor* on 30 September 1859. He established himself as a sheep farmer in the Rangitata district of Canterbury Island, describing the new country in his letters home with contrasting references to the English and the European landscape that had made such an impression on him as an eight-year-old boy travelling abroad with his family, and recounting the adventure of his land claim with great vividness. His father had his letters published as *A First Year in Canterbury Settlement* (1863), with a preface by himself. Butler is now regarded as one of the early explorers of New Zealand, having crossed the Rangitata River, and narrowly missed the main pass through the mountains, as he described in the vivid opening to his utopian novel *Erewhon, or, Over the Range*. Butler did not confine himself to sheep farming, but played a considerable role in the cultural life of the colony, organizing the first art exhibitions at the Christchurch Club. He published his first pieces (apart from some slight essays in the St John's magazine *The Eagle*) in the local newspaper, the *Christchurch Press*, especially the witty speculation entitled 'Darwin among the machines', in which he imagined some consequences of the recently published *Origin of Species*.

Samuel Butler (1835–1902), self-portrait, 1873?

Over the range and back: London and art In 1864 Butler returned to England, having realized a tidy profit, and settled in rooms at 15 Clifford's Inn, Fleet Street, London. Although he was still not fully financially independent of his father, the bargain held, and he took up his career in art as a student first at F. S. Cary's in Bloomsbury, in the College of Art in South Kensington, and then at Mr Heatherley's well-known art school in Newman Street. His well-known painting *Family Prayers* (1864) may have been a response to his return to his constricted family circle; it is usually associated with *The Way of All Flesh*, which has a chapter describing such a scene. The art school's informal manner offered an escape. Mr Heatherley himself was the subject of Butler's best-known oil painting, *Mr Heatherley's Holiday* (1873), now in the Tate collection, depicting the genial head seated before the plaster casts of heroic antique statuary, mending a grotesque, frail skeleton with which the students performed the *danse macabre* at parties. There he met Eliza Savage, an independent and witty young woman in a day when there were few female art students, whose correspondence with Butler between 1871 and 1885 is one of the gems of the Butler literature. She encouraged him also in the direction of fiction, which he professed to detest. The correspondence ended with her early death in 1886. He also met the young Johnston Forbes-Robertson, then sixteen, afterwards the noted Shakespearian actor. Wearing the Heatherley's suit of armour, Forbes-Robertson is the subject of one of Butler's earliest known photographs, in the atmospheric style of the Pre-Raphaelite vogue in photography, and foreshadowing the future actor's role as Hamlet.

Forbes-Robertson left an affectionate memoir of Butler, showing him as a diligent student, but one with time for 'happy daily hob-nobs' over lunch at the Horseshoe pub. He notes that Butler was keen to be accepted as a student at the Royal Academy; but Butler's submissions did not lead to his acceptance, though he had at least eleven paintings hung in several exhibitions, including *Mr Heatherley's Holiday* in 1874. J. B. (Jack) Yeats, at Heatherley's in the previous decade, wrote respectfully of Butler's 'emancipated intellect', but dismissed his attempts to paint in a 'Bellini-like' style, as proposed by Ruskin, whose *Seven Lamps of Architecture* had impressed Butler as an undergraduate. Butler later adopted a satirical, even bitter view of the Pre-Raphaelite circles, but a number of Ruskinian aims continued to play a role in his thinking. He also met Charles Gogin, later a successful illustrator, who remained a lifelong friend, and painted the portrait of Butler now in the National Portrait Gallery.

Butler's literary reputation always eclipsed his work as an artist. In 1870 he published *Erewhon* anonymously, to considerable acclaim. This searching and novel utopia was based on a map of an imaginary country inserted into the map of the New Zealand district he had explored. An interest in fictional maps is visible again in his later invention of a new version of the periplus of Odysseus, and in his fascination with the mapping of the geography of Jerusalem onto the Alps that characterized the site of the Sacro Monte at Varallo. This preoccupation may owe something to the classical atlas he saw his father revising when he was a schoolboy. His imaginary society undoubtedly arose from his close scrutiny of the ethical implications of Darwinism, one of the earliest such considerations. He locates the central point in a 'Nowhere' whose citizens are criminalized and punished for contracting and concealing disease, whereas traditional 'sins' and moral failings are cheerfully acknowledged and accepted. This highlights the question of whether 'criminals' are responsible for their crimes; are the causes of crime not what would now be called 'genetic'? And if so, is the self-righteousness of pastors and masters justifiable? In the famous chapter 'Book of the machines', with its museum of the technological innovations Erewhon had banned, Butler foresaw that technology would become overmastering, and that it would have to be controlled. As in all his best work, his topsy-turvy world produces shock, biting humour, and a provocation to fundamental rethinking.

Butler's next book, *The Fair Haven* (1873), like his essay entitled 'The evidence for the resurrection of Jesus Christ as given by the four evangelists critically examined' (drafted in New Zealand, published anonymously in 1865), pressed further on the religious assumptions and claims still being clung to by the churches. It is one of his most complex and least understood books; it purported to be a defence of the miraculous element in Christianity, as edited by William Bickersteth Owen, the brother of the deceased 'author' John Pickard Owen, but it was intended to undermine the proposed views. The chapter 'The Christ ideal' was an oblique attack on current aesthetic substitutes for religion. Formally, it was a subtle deployment of the persona of 'the editor' as developed in the higher criticism of the Bible and in recent fiction. It was, however, taken at face value, and Butler was forced to reveal his authorship and his subversive intention. As the gullible critics had been taken in, they took their revenge in negative reviews.

Evolutionary wits: writings on Darwin and Darwinism Butler pursued his reflections on Darwin and Darwinism in *Life and Habit* (1878), *Evolution, Old and New* (1879), *Unconscious Memory* (1880), and *Luck or Cunning?* (1886). He deserves a more considerable place than he has gained in accounts of Darwin's reception: in English histories of evolutionary thought he is often dismissed as merely idiosyncratic. (An unfortunate personal element entered, when he felt, wrongly, that Darwin had slighted him.) But in France, Butler's Lamarckist interests in the role of forms of heritable memory of experience valuable in the 'survival of the fittest' were welcomed, and his French translators and commentators saw him as an important figure in the history of ideas. George Bernard Shaw was also much influenced by Butler's thinking, and the evolutionary explorations in his plays, most explicitly in *Back to Methuselah*, as well as his social thinking, owe much to Butler, a debt Shaw gladly acknowledged. Butler is due for renewed attention, especially in light of recent developments in molecular biology which make a reconsideration of the subtler modes of inheritance and transmission possible.

Butler's altercations with his father were not yet over. Perhaps the worst of them came in 1879 as a result of his father's discovery that over the years Butler had been giving money to Charles Paine Pauli, a charming rogue whom he had met in New Zealand and who had returned to England at the same time. It emerged at Pauli's funeral in 1897 that he had had a number of such supporters; a late note by Butler reveals his shock. His own financial situation had deteriorated, and he was obliged to travel to Canada, where he had invested his New Zealand gains, to try to put matters right. He felt he had misled Pauli in advising him on investments. His father's discovery of his misplaced generosity or what he construed as an egregious instance of financial mismanagement, and his horror at what this relationship might signify in his unmarried son's life, led to further threats that financial aid would be withdrawn. Finally, however, the elder Butler died in 1886, and Butler came into his inheritance. From that time forward he spent half the year in Italy at Faido and then at Varallo, where he felt both free and at home.

Italian journeys: Alps and sanctuaries Butler's productive travels in Europe, especially Italy, had already begun, and in 1881 he published *Alps and Sanctuaries*, the lively account of his travels to the sanctuaries of the Ticino, Piedmont, and Lombardy. His French translator, Valéry Larbaud (also Joyce's translator), praised his appreciations of Italy, which he rated higher than those of his own countrymen. Amusing and readable, illustrated with Butler's own sketches and paintings, they also had a serious purpose:

the rehabilitation of the sites and artists of the Counter-Reformation, the objects of popular Catholic pilgrimage, but ignored by aristocrats on the grand tour, by the new middle-class tourists, and by the connoisseurs and art historical specialists. He takes up cudgels for a form of art distasteful to the sectarian narrowness and class prejudices of his own family and many of his countrymen. Here he pursues Ruskinian themes in a novel context—the work of anonymous or little known craftsmen who contributed to the pilgrimage sites of Varallo, Varese, Oropa, and Crea—and uses the local villagers as models and pilgrims as participants in a sacred visual drama of events from the life of Jesus or Mary. Having despaired of making a conventional career in art, he successfully brought together his literary and his artistic gifts in *Ex voto: an Account of the Sacro Monte or New Jerusalem at Varallo-Sesia* (1888). *Ex voto* focused on Varallo, the founding site, and contained Butler's most original and sustained contribution to art history, his exposition of the chapel art of Varallo, and his pioneering rediscovery of the work of Gaudenzio Ferrari, painter and major sculptor of the life-size figures of the chapels at Varallo, and several more minor figures such as Tabachetti and the D'Enrico brothers, Giovanni and Antonio (better known as Tanzio da Varallo). While he lauded the unsung craftsmen, he also individualized them and drew their *œuvre* into art history. When the Sacro Monte of Varallo celebrated in 1986 the 500th anniversary of its founding, there was a special exhibition of Butler's letters to and from his many friends in Varallo, with whom he corresponded in Italian, together with one of his paintings of the site.

Only a fraction of Butler's explorations of these themes could be published in the books themselves. He revisited them in depth in the series of paintings, sketches, and photographs of the routes he travelled, the towns and their artworks. The photographs are especially revealing. Butler and his assistant Alfred Cathie preserved a selection of his snapshots in albums left to St John's College, also the repository of the original glass negatives; his most prized album, with large photographs relating to the Sacro Monte, was sold to the Chapin Library at Williams College, Williamstown, Massachusetts. The full range and substance of this joint work of literary and visual art came to light only in the late twentieth century with Elinor Shaffer's *Erewhons of the Eye: Samuel Butler as Painter, Photographer and Art Critic* (1988) and a related travelling exhibition of 1989–90. In 2002, the centenary of his death, St John's College, Cambridge, and Tate Britain held further exhibitions of his photography. The academy reject, the maverick applicant for the Slade professorship (1886), became a pioneer of a new art form.

Classical worlds: new topographies Butler's originality and irreverence were expressed again in the other group of works he published in the 1890s, on the classics. No one could go as unerringly to the heart of Victorian prejudices as he. The very title of his book *The Authoress of the Odyssey* (1897) was calculated to offend the entire establishment nurtured on Gladstone's notion that a classical education, a grounding in the political and military tactics of Homer's *Iliad* and the navigational prowess of the *Odyssey*, was the best preparation for young men whose task was to rule the empire. Butler's sly claim that the *Odyssey* was essentially a domestic tale, the locations were limited to Sicily, the sailing instructions obscure, the adventures told only in recital at the dinner table, summed up in the bold surmise that the author was a woman, had, and even today still has, the desired effect. His project as usual was backed by a variety of related enterprises, in particular his fluent colloquial prose translations of the *Iliad* (1898) and the *Odyssey* (1900), which broke down the stilted pseudo-archaic 'high' style of translation then in vogue and deliberately, as he said, aimed at an ideal audience of young girls uneducated in the classics who would be caught up in the story. No other work of his received such extensive or more strongly divided reviews. Nor did he fail to carry his investigations into the field, trekking to Asia Minor to view the site of Schliemann's excavations of Troy, taking in the Greek sites en route, and photographing along the way.

As usual, Butler was not just being mischievous, but was giving vivid expression to the current state of scholarly controversy. There was a long tradition supporting the position that the *Iliad* and the *Odyssey* were not written by the same hand, and that the former was centred on war and male pursuits, the latter on domestic and female pursuits. Moreover, since the work of F. A. Wolf at the end of the eighteenth century there had been an important critical shift towards the view that the Homeric texts were in any case not written by one author, but were the result of several centuries of oral poetry relating to the events at Troy, brought together in the sixth century BC by a group of editors. There was no single Homer, the 'blind bard' of tradition, and this continued to be the dominant view of scholars in the twentieth century. The Victorian defenders of the unity and greatness of Homer, however, tended to indulge, like Gladstone, and Matthew Arnold, in praise of the 'grand style' and the patriarchal interest. Butler took the most direct route to casting doubt on their values and their grandiloquence when he claimed that their canonical author was in fact a woman. Moreover, Butler presented a photographic record of Sicily as the home of the 'authoress'. It was increasingly held that the classical world of the *Odyssey* was no longer the grand Mycenaean civilization of the time before Troy fell, but the shrunken and impoverished world of the centuries after the Trojan war. Butler's Sicilian photographs accordingly give the flavour of the small, domestic scale of Ulysses' holdings through shots of local sailing boats, dusty courtyards, and farm animals, sleeping men, and especially Circean pigs. These literary reinterpretations intersect with a finely observed current Sicilian landscape. His notable contributions to modernism are again discernible—James Joyce made the argument that the *Odyssey* was 'domestic' his own, reducing the Authoress's journey round Sicily to Bloom's day in Dublin. Paradoxically, Butler's ironic work also gave rise to a succession of modern attempts, by Victor Bérard, the noted French classical scholar, and Jean Bérard, Ernle Bradford, and Tim Severin, to sail in replicas of ancient ships along the routes of the *Odyssey* and to photograph the landfalls.

Last things In *Shakespeare's Sonnets Reconsidered* (1899) Butler's argument that the male object of Shakespeare's interest in the sonnets was a lower-class 'Mr WH' was undoubtedly a gesture of solidarity with Oscar Wilde, tried and imprisoned for a similar interest. There were a number of such gestures at the time, more or less explicit. The ironic championing of the obscure love object of the popular dramatists Shakespeare and Wilde was related to Butler's concern for the little regarded popular artists of the Sacro Monte and their models. In *Erewhon Revisited* (1901) the protagonist, who had succeeded in escaping from Erewhon by balloon, returns to find to his astonishment that he has been made the centre of a new religious cult, based on the 'miracle' of his ascension. This enables Butler to analyse the phenomena of religion from their point of genesis, while disclaiming all responsibility for their uncanny parallels to certain known religions. In thus returning to the beginnings of his writing career, he showed that his wit and his scepticism were as fresh as ever.

Butler's longest-standing friendship was with Henry Festing Jones, whom he regularly visited when in London, and with whom he sometimes travelled. They tried their hands at writing music, first Handelian minuets and gavottes, then an oratorio buffo, *Narcissus* (1888). They studied counterpoint with W. S. Rockstro, and designed a *Ulysses* oratorio (published in 1904). It has been said that for twenty years they shared the favours (for a consideration) of the same woman, on different days of the week. Butler was also accompanied to the end of his life by Alfred Emery Cathie, who had been employed in 1882, at the age of twenty-two, as his valet and clerk, and who became his photographic assistant and his companion.

Samuel Butler fell ill (doctors disagreed on the cause of the malfunction of the digestive tract) and died in St John's Wood Road, London, on 18 June 1902. He had remarked that evening, when Jones, unusually, paid a second daily visit, that it was 'a dark morning'. This small, bookish man, who nevertheless had a strong streak of the intrepid explorer of new worlds about him, was by his own choice cremated at Woking, and his ashes were buried in an unmarked grave. His will appointed his cousin Reginald Worsley his executor and R. A. Streatfeild his literary executor, and stipulated that his pictures, sketches, and studies were 'to be destroyed or otherwise disposed of as they may think best', while Jones was to have 'all interest in musical compositions upon which they had been jointly engaged'. Alfred Cathie was to have £2000, his personal effects, and his photographic cameras.

Afterlife: *The Way of All Flesh* It was the posthumous publication of *The Way of All Flesh* (1902), however, that firmly established Butler's reputation. This powerful autobiographical work was written in the early 1880s but put away in 1886, at the time of his father's death, as he felt that its publication would offend the remaining members of his family (his two surviving sisters were in fact unhappy about it). Had it been published at the time of writing, it would undoubtedly have received a less enthusiastic welcome than it did in the wave of anti-Victorian sentiment that characterized the years after his death. But this uneasy position between two periods has meant that literary scholars and critics of modernism have often remarked on its warm reception, but not in detail on its qualities as fiction, because they felt it belonged to the Victorian period, whereas the Victorianists saw it as falling outside their scope because it was published and received only in the modernist period. Thus it had strong affinities with nineteenth-century fictional forms and concerns, as a *Bildungsroman*, or novel of education, like Goethe's or George Eliot's, and as a study of the loss of religious faith, where comparisons would be to Carlyle and Mrs Humphry Ward. Yet those to whom he spoke most powerfully were not his coevals in fiction, Hardy and Meredith, nor those who came to modernism via aestheticism and decadence, but Shaw, Graves, Forster, Lawrence, Strachey, Wyndham Lewis, and Joyce, and critics like William Empson, heir to his provocative, ingenious, and witty criticism, as well as to men of letters abroad, especially in France. Quite possibly a new, comparative approach is required, looking at Butler's four works of fiction in the context of late-nineteenth-century European naturalism as the stepping-stone to modernism. The status of *The Way of All Flesh* is undisputed, however, and like *Erewhon* it has remained in print without intermission.

Festing Jones advised the executors on the disposition of Butler's estate, and became his first biographer, and the first editor of his notebooks, as well as author of some other pieces about him, including *Darwin and Butler: a Step towards Reconciliation* (1911) and an account of their travels in Sicily. Jones proved a judicious and assiduous adviser, who did his best to place Butler's manuscripts, paintings, photographs, and personal objects in the repositories most appropriate to them: the early watercolours to Shrewsbury School, the bulk of the materials to St John's College, paintings and letters to his New Zealand sitters and correspondents. Butler had himself given away large numbers of his paintings during his lifetime. Jones's biography of Butler (*Samuel Butler, Author of Erewhon*, 1919) was bulky but anecdotal. His best memorial to his friend was his selection of Butler's pithy observations, *The Note-Books of Samuel Butler*, which proved another substantial addition to Butler's reputation when the book appeared in 1912. It still stands its ground against the later selections and the one volume (of five projected volumes) of the modern edition of the notebooks, deftly capturing and juxtaposing Butler's variously passionate, shrewd, quirky, and surprising insights. ELINOR SHAFFER

Sources *The note-books of Samuel Butler*, ed. H. F. Jones (1912) • *Further extracts from the note-books of Samuel Butler*, ed. A. C. Bartholomew (1934) • *Samuel Butler's notebooks: selections*, ed. G. Keynes and B. Hill (1951) • *Letters between Samuel Butler and Miss E. M. A. Savage, 1871–1885*, ed. G. Keynes and B. Hill (1935) • *The note-books of Samuel Butler*, ed. H.-P. Breuer, 1: *1874–1883* (1984) • *The family letters of Samuel Butler, 1841–1886*, ed. A. Silver (1962) • *The correspondence of Samuel Butler with his sister May*, ed. D. F. Howard (1962) • *Butleriana*, ed. A. C. Bartholomew (1932) • S. Butler, *A first year in Canterbury settlement*, ed. T. Butler (1863) • P. Raby, *Samuel Butler: a biography* (1991) • H. F. Jones and A. T. Bartholomew, *The Samuel Butler collection at St John's College, Cambridge: a catalogue and a commentary* (1921) • *Samuel Butler* (1945) [catalogue of the collection in the Chapin Library, Williams College, Williamstown, Mass.] • E. Shaffer, *Erewhons of the eye: Samuel Butler as painter, photographer and art critic* (1988) • *The life and career of Samuel Butler* (1967) [handlist of an exhibition held at Chapin Library, Williams College, Williamstown, Mass.] • *Samuel Butler: a 150th birthday celebration* (1985–6) [handlist of an exhibition held at Chapin Library, Williams College, Williamstown, Mass., 1985–6] • *Samuel Butler and his contemporaries* (1972) [catalogue of an exhibition held at the Robert McDougall Art Gallery, Christchurch, New Zealand] • *Samuele Butler e la Valle Sesia* (1986) [handlist of an exhibition held at the Biblioteca Civica Farinone-Centa, Varallo-Sesia] • *Samuel Butler (1835–1902): the way of all flesh: photographs, paintings, watercolours and drawings* (1989–90) [exhibition catalogue, Bolton Museum and Art Gallery; Royal Museum and Art Gallery, Canterbury; D. L. I. Museum and Art Centre, Durham; University Art Gallery, Nottingham] • *The artist's model from Etty to Spencer*, ed. M. Postle and W. Vaughan (1999) [exhibition catalogue, York City Art Gallery; Kenwood, London; Djanogly Art Gallery, U. Nott.] • *Samuel Butler (1835–1902): centenary exhibition* (2002) [exhibition catalogue, St John Cam.; handlist and notes by E. Shaffer] • *Samuel Butler (1835–1902): photographs* (2002) [exhibition catalogue, Tate Britain, London, Nov 2002 – June 2003]

Archives BL, corresp. and papers, incl. literary MSS, Add. MSS 36711–36713, 38176–38177, 39846–39847, 44027–44054 • BL, notebook, Add. MSS 71695 • Canterbury Museum, letter-book and sketchbook • St John Cam., papers incl. sketches, drawings, and paintings; extensive photographic holdings, including original glass negatives and albums • Williams College, Williamstown, Massachusetts, Chapin Library of Rare Books, corresp. and literary papers, paintings and drawings, 'Sacro Monk' photographic album | Bodl. Oxf., corresp. with Robert Bridges • CUL, letters to Charles Darwin and related papers • CUL, letters, mainly to Henry Festing Jones

Likenesses S. Butler, self-portrait, 1873?, NL NZ, Turnbull L. [*see illus.*] • A. Cathie, photograph, 1890, St John Cam. • C. Gogin, oils, 1896, NPG • S. Butler, self-portrait, Shrewsbury School • S. Butler, self-portrait, St John Cam. • photograph, NL NZ, Turnbull L. • photographs, St John Cam. • photogravure (aged fifty-four), BM

Wealth at death £33,076 18*s*. 6*d*.: resworn probate, Jan 1903, *CGPLA Eng. & Wales* (1902)

Butler, Simon (1757–1797), barrister and Irish nationalist, was born in July 1757, the third son of Edmund Butler, tenth Viscount Mountgarret (*d*. 1779), landowner and barrister, and his wife, Charlotte (*d*. 1778), daughter of Sir Simon Bradstreet and his wife, Ellen. He was called to the Irish bar in Michaelmas term 1778 and was made a king's counsel and a bencher of the King's Inns, Dublin, in Trinity term 1784.

Butler was elected president of the Dublin Society of United Irishmen at their inaugural meeting on 9 November 1791. He served in a number of positions in the society during the early 1790s and attempted to forge close links between reformers and the Catholic lobby. His *Digest of the Popery Laws* (1792) illustrated the extent of the legal disabilities suffered by Irish Catholics. For this work and 'for other professional business' (Plowden, 2.394) the Catholic Committee voted him £500 at their disbandment in April 1793. On 1 March 1793 Butler and Oliver Bond, as chairman and secretary respectively of the Dublin Society of United Irishmen, were summoned before the Irish House of Lords on account of a paper which had been issued by the group. The offending piece had criticized the house's secret committee for compelling witnesses to answer questions on oath. Butler and Bond avowed its publication but submitted that it contained nothing unconstitutional. The Lords, however, voted it a 'false, scandalous, and seditious libel; a high breach of the privileges of this house, tending to disturb the public peace, and questioning the authority of this high court of parliament', and thereupon ordered the defendants to be imprisoned in Newgate gaol for six months and to pay a fine of £500 each. Butler felt that he had been insulted by John Fitzgibbon, earl of Clare, during the proceedings and attempted to challenge him to a duel after his release. He was persuaded not to proceed owing to Fitzgibbon's office as lord chancellor.

In late October or early November 1793 Butler went with his friend Archibald Hamilton Rowan, another prominent United Irishman and close political ally, to Scotland, where they negotiated with Scottish radicals. On 15 November 1793 Butler declared to his fellow United Irishmen that 'he was not only ready when necessary to act but to bleed for his country, and he fears that the time was not far distant when such exertions would be expedient' (McDowell, 93). Though he met with the French spies Eleazor Oswald and William Jackson in 1793–4, Butler severed his links with the United Irishmen during late 1794. In common with other moderates he was unwilling to support the more militant and secretive society which was emerging. On 18 January 1795 he married Eliza, the daughter of Edward Lynch of Hampstead, co. Dublin; they had an only son, Edward. Though Butler's name was erased from the list of king's counsel in 1793, he remained a bencher of the King's Inns until his death, which took place at his lodgings in Brompton Row, Dublin, on 19 May 1797.

Liam Chambers

Sources *DNB* • R. R. Madden, *The United Irishmen: their lives and times*, 1st ser., 2 vols. (1842) • R. B. McDowell, ed., *Proceedings of the Dublin Society of United Irishmen*, IMC (1998) • *The autobiography of Archibald Hamilton Rowan*, ed. W. H. Drummond (1840); facs. edn (1972) • L. M. Cullen, 'The internal politics of the United Irishmen', *The United Irishmen: republicanism, radicalism and rebellion*, ed. D. Dickson and others (1993), 176–96 • *GM*, 1st ser., 67 (1797), 529 • *Annual Register* (1797), 97 • A. C. Kavanaugh, *John Fitzgibbon, earl of Clare* (1997) • R. Musgrave, *Memoirs of the different rebellions in Ireland*, 2nd edn (1801), 94 • F. Plowden, *An historical view of the state of Ireland*, 2 vols. (1803) • M. Elliott, *Partners in revolution: the United Irishmen and France* (1982) • E. Keane, P. Beryl Phair, and T. U. Sadleir, eds., *King's Inns admission papers, 1607–1867*, IMC (1982) • GEC, *Peerage* • Burke, *Peerage* (1970)

Archives NA Ire., Rebellion MSS

Likenesses J. Kay, double portrait, caricature, etching, 1793 (with Hamilton Rowan), NPG • Irish school, stipple, NG Ire.

Butler [Walter], **Theobald** (*d*. 1205), administrator and magnate, was the son of Sir Hervey Walter of Weeton, Lancashire, and of Matilda, daughter and coheir, along with her sister Bertha, of Theobald de Valognes, lord of Parham, Suffolk. Theobald and his brother, Hubert *Walter, who was to become archbishop of Canterbury and justiciar of England, were raised in the household of their aunt Bertha and her husband, Ranulf de *Glanville, justiciar of England.

From about 1180 John, son of Henry II, was also attached to Glanville's household and Theobald was to accompany

John on his expedition to assume the lordship of Ireland in 1185, the freight of Theobald's equipment being paid for by the royal exchequer. Theobald's men, along with an Anglo-Norman party from Cork, were responsible for the assassination of Diarmait Mac Carthaig, king of Desmond, during a parley in 1185. Theobald and Ranulf de Glanville were named by John as joint beneficiaries in a charter granting them 5½ cantreds in north Munster for the service of twenty-two knights' fees, the nucleus of the later holdings of the Butler earls of Ormond. An entry in the annals of Loch Cé, recording the killing in 1185 by Domnall Ó Briain, king of Thomond, of a foster brother of Prince John, suggests that a son of Ranulf de Glanville was included among John's entourage in Ireland. Theobald, who subsequently became the sole beneficiary of the Munster land grant, was to divide this extensive area into four manorial units centred on Nenagh, Thurles, Caherconlish, and Dunkerrin. Additionally, John, as lord of Ireland, granted Theobald two separate landholdings in the lordship of Leinster, the castle and vill of Arklow for the service of one knight between 1185 and 1189, and the manor of Tullach Ua Felmeda, in Carlow, some time between 1189 and 1192. These two grants were made in derogation of the rights of William (I) Marshal as lord of Leinster from 1189 in right of his wife, Isabel, daughter of Richard fitz Gilbert de Clare (Strongbow) and heir of Leinster. It was probably also John, as lord of Ireland, who granted to Theobald Tullach Chiaráin in Osraige (centred on Gowran, Kilkenny). According to the near contemporary *Histoire de Guillaume le Maréchal* the Marshal had to invoke the aid of King Richard against John in order to obtain seisin of all his wife's lands in Leinster; following Richard's intervention, John negotiated that Theobald (styled 'boteillier Tiebaut') might retain the lands in Leinster, to be held of the Marshal and not John.

Between 1185 and 1193 Theobald was in continuous attendance on John, witnessing his charters. He is styled *pincerna* ('butler') when witnessing John's charter to Alard fitz William, chamberlain, issued on the eve of John's departure at Wexford in 1185, the original of which is extant (NL Ire., MS D.8). This reference to Theobald as *pincerna* appears to be an isolated occurrence, however, and Theobald is next so described in John's charter in favour of the city of Dublin (11 May 1192), witnessing alongside John's chancellor and seneschal, suggesting that Theobald may have been *pincerna* of John's personal household rather than holder of an office with any specifically Irish connotations. A charter dating from *c.*1194–9 of John Cumin, archbishop of Dublin, in favour of Theobald refers to him as 'pincerna domini comitis Moretoniae in Hibernia' (Curtis, *Ormond Deeds*, no. 11), indicating that by that stage the office was deemed to be attached to John's lordship of Ireland. In 1194 during the rebellion of John against his brother, King Richard, when John was stripped of the honour of Lancaster, Theobald appears to have been instrumental in securing the submission to King Richard of John's Lancastrian supporters. In February 1194 Theobald delivered the castle of Lancaster, of which he was custodian for John, to Archbishop Hubert, his own brother, acting on behalf of King Richard. King Richard appointed Theobald sheriff of Lancaster, probably at the council held at Nottingham on 30 March, an office for which he accounted until 1198–9, and on 22 April 1194 the king granted him the whole of Amounderness (in which his hereditary fee of Weeton was situated). In August 1194 Theobald was also appointed collector of the revenue raised by licences to hold tournaments, and in 1197–8 he acted as a justice itinerant.

In the financial year 1196/7 Robert le Vavasour, Theobald's father-in-law, accounted as deputy sheriff on his behalf and in 1197/8 and 1198/9 (excepting the Easter quarter) Nicholas Pincerna deputized for him. The identity of this Nicholas is uncertain; he may have been a younger son of the Pincerna family of Warrington, but more probably belonged to that of Warton in Amounderness, to which Theobald may have been related. A number of individuals may be traced in the Amounderness area named Pincerna or le Boteler, which was developing into a surname during the late twelfth century, and this complicates the issue of the origins and significance of Theobald's title. In charters relating to Ireland issued between 1201 and 1205 he himself used the style 'pincerna Hiberniae'.

On John's accession in May 1199 Theobald initially continued as sheriff of Lancaster, but by Michaelmas 1199 he had been removed from office and disseised of Amounderness, as was subsequently claimed, 'because of his many transgressions and … other injuries' (*CIPM*, 1, no. 264). A number of Lancashire complainants against Theobald had travelled to King John at Le Mans. The impact of their advent at court is evidenced by the negotiation of more than twenty fines for the recovery of lands and liberties; some were bold enough to incorporate in their petitions a statement of the wrongs that they had suffered under Theobald's shrievalty. On 12 January 1201 Theobald's Munster lands were included in the grant that King John made to William de Briouze of the kingdom of Limerick, but on the same day Theobald reached an accommodation with Briouze whereby he received a regrant of those lands, which were now to be held of Briouze. The agreement was witnessed by a great number of notables, headed by Archbishop Hubert, whom Roger of Howden claims was instrumental in securing the arrangement and for which Theobald proffered 500 marks to Briouze. On 2 January 1202 Amounderness was restored to Theobald by the king. In the financial year 1203/4 Theobald was granted a licence to go to Ireland. On 3 April 1205 Meiler fitz Henry, justiciar in Ireland, was ordered to take into the hands of the king the lands which were Theobald Walter's 'on the day when he left Ireland' (*Rotuli litterarum patentium*, 60b), suggesting that Theobald was in difficulties with the king, possibly over non-payment of debts.

Theobald died some time after 4 August 1205, when the sheriff of Lancaster was directed to distrain him for a debt of 5 marks, and before Michaelmas 1205 when Gilbert fitz Reinfred, sheriff of Lancaster, answered for the receipts of Theobald's lands in Amounderness, which yielded £10 1*s.* 3*d.* for the king's use for the portion of the year that remained before the Michaelmas audit. On 4 April 1206 the king instructed Meiler fitz Henry, notwithstanding previous directions that he had been given, to allow William Marshal's bailiffs to take charge, along with royal bailiffs, of the lands that Theobald had held of the Marshal, and on 25 May 1206 the king confirmed the reversion of those lands to the Marshal, notwithstanding any contrary mandates he had issued. On or before 20 July 1207 Robert le Vavasour offered the king 1200 marks and two palfreys to have the marriage of his daughter, Matilda, widow of Theobald Walter, and her dower in her late husband's English and Irish estates. On 1 October King John gave Matilda le Vavasour in marriage to Fulk (III) Fitzwarine, with seisin of one-third of Theobald's demesne tenements in dower, Theobald's son and heir, Theobald, being a minor. On 4 February 1214 Gilbert fitz Reinfred was ordered to release Theobald, heir of Theobald Walter, into the care of Peter des Roches, bishop of Winchester. On 24 August 1214 the king ordered Henry, archbishop of Dublin, justiciar in Ireland, to cause Reginald de Pontibus to have seisin of the castles of Theobald Walter in Ireland at Thurles, Roscrea, Lusk, Dublin (originally granted by John as lord of Ireland to Hubert Walter), Ardmullen, and Caherconlish; a mandate was directed on 6 September to Geoffrey de Marisco ordering him to deliver up the castles of Thurles and Roscrea which were in his custody. The younger Theobald had come of age by July 1221 when the king ordered the justiciar of Ireland to give him seisin of those lands of his father which were in the justiciar's custody. In January 1226 arrangements were made with Theobald the younger at the Dublin exchequer about payment of his father's outstanding debts amounting to over £190. The elder Theobald had a daughter, Beatrice, from another union, who married first Thomas of Hereford, who received a marriage grant from Theobald of fifteen knights' fees in Éile; she later (*c*.1220) married Hugh Purcell. About 1196 Theobald established Cistercian monks from Furness at Wryesdale, Lancashire, who some time before 1204 transferred first to Arklow, in Wicklow, and then to Owney (Abington or Wotheney) in Limerick, where Theobald was probably buried. Theobald also founded a priory for Crutched friars at Nenagh, Tipperary, and endowed the Premonstratensian abbey of Cockersand, Lancashire. But his most important monuments were undoubtedly the enduring lordships that he established in large parts of Munster and south Leinster.

M. T. Flanagan

Sources *Chancery records* (RC) • *Pipe rolls* • M. T. Flanagan, *Irish society, Anglo-Norman settlers, Angevin kingship: interactions in Ireland in the late twelfth century* (1989) • A. J. Otway-Ruthven, *A history of medieval Ireland* (1968) • E. Curtis, ed., *Calendar of Ormond deeds*, 6 vols., IMC (1932–43), vol. 1, nos. 7, 10, 11, 17, 20, 21, 22, 26, 27, 31, 33, 34; vol. 2, no. 426 • Giraldus Cambrensis, *Expugnatio Hibernica / The conquest of Ireland*, ed. and trans. A. B. Scott and F. X. Martin (1978), 235 • P. Meyer, ed., *L'histoire de Guillaume le Maréchal*, 3 vols. (Paris, 1891–1901), lines 9581–618 • *Chronica magistri Rogeri de Hovedene*, ed. W. Stubbs, 4 vols., Rolls Series, 51 (1868–71), vol. 3, pp. 237, 268; vol. 4, pp. 152–3 • J. T. Gilbert, ed., *Facsimiles of national manuscripts of Ireland*, 4 vols. in 5 (1874–84), vol. 2, nos. lxvii, lxviii • N. B. White, ed., *Episcopal and monastic deeds, 1200–1600*, IMC (1956), 99–102 • E. Curtis, ed., *Red Book of Ormond*, IMC (1932), 9, 83–7 • W. Farrer, ed., *The Lancashire pipe rolls … also early Lancashire charters* (1902), 81–3, 115, 206, 212, 336–7, 340, 434–6, 438–10, and passim • Dugdale, *Monasticon*, new edn, 6/2.1128, 1137, 1145 • W. Farrer, ed., *The chartulary of Cockersand Abbey of the Premonstratensian order*, 1, pt 2, Chetham Society, new ser., 39 (1898), 375–6 • W. M. Hennessy, ed. and trans., *The annals of Loch Cé: a chronicle of Irish affairs from AD 1014 to AD 1590*, 1, Rolls Series, 54 (1871), 171 • *CIPM*, 1, no. 264, 67 • J. T. Gilbert, ed., *Historic and municipal documents of Ireland, AD 1172–1320, from the archives of the city of Dublin*, Rolls Series, 53 (1870), 55 • T. D. Hardy, ed., *Rotuli litterarum patentium*, RC (1835)

Butler, Sir Theobald [Toby] (**1642/3–1721**), lawyer, was the son of a family from Bolytonrath in co. Tipperary which had fought on the confederate side during the wars of the 1640s and 1650s, but the names of his parents are unknown. His grandfather was executed by the Cromwellians. Butler is said to have been sent to Trinity College, Cambridge, and then to have entered the Middle Temple in 1671. But his presence is not noted in the records of either institution. Similarly, he is thought, five years later, to have shown his intention to practise the law in Ireland by entering the King's Inns, Dublin. Thereafter he combined an agency for his father on estates in co. Clare with a legal career in Dublin. He began to practise in the central Dublin courts about 1682. Thanks to his kinsman the first duke of Ormond, in 1685 he was appointed deputy seneschal of the duke's palatine court of Tipperary. Presumably Ormond's influence also helped secure a knighthood for Butler at an unknown date.

The accession of James II offered a pleasing prospect to Butler, a Catholic with Stuart sympathies. He was made recorder of Clonmel, and then appointed the king's solicitor-general in Ireland. He was also elected as member for the Clare borough of Ennis to the parliament summoned to Dublin in 1689. A signatory of the treaty of Limerick (3 October 1691), Butler was a beneficiary of terms that offered Catholics a degree of security and he continued in Ireland after the defeat of the Jacobites. In 1694 he inherited much of his father's property in co. Clare, and acquired more on his own account, including an estate at Knockgraffon for £1825 from the second duke of Ormond. The ability to buy on this scale reflected Butler's success as a lawyer. However, from the 1690s his lucrative practice was threatened by the legal barriers being erected against Catholics either owning property or following the lettered professions. In 1703 it was rumoured that Butler would take the oath of abjuration and so qualify himself to continue in practice. In 1704, with a Test Act in prospect, he acted as counsel to the Irish Catholics when they argued against the proposal. Perhaps foreseeing that these protests would be unavailing, Butler had taken the precaution of conveying his lands to trustees. Thereafter, with the passage of the Test Act, his activities were circumscribed. It was later reported how he, as 'an old popish lawyer', considered himself too old to convert. He was prepared to rebuild a parish church on his estates, confident that the duty would be served by a Catholic priest in the absence of the protestant incumbent.

Butler remained in touch with the exiled Stuarts, being made a gentleman of the privy council to Mary of Modena. In Ireland, however, he was licensed to carry a sword. This showed his continuing Catholicism, but by 1720 there was a suggestion from Dean Swift that Butler had converted to protestantism. Certainly he continued to plead cases in the Dublin courts after the passage of the Test Act. At his death, aged seventy-eight, on 11 March 1721, he was eulogized as a prominent barrister—probably the best known of Catholic origins and sympathies. He was also credited with talking still with an Irish brogue. He exemplified not only the difficulties faced by professionals from the Catholic community after 1690, but also the ingenuity with which some managed to circumvent legal proscriptions.

TOBY BARNARD

Sources T. Butler, 'Sir Toby Butler', *Journal of the Butler Society*, 5 (1973), 361–76; 6 (1975–6), 455–64 • *An elegy on the very much lamented death of Sir Toby Butler, knight, barrister at law,* [11 March 1720/1], *aet.* 78 (1721) • J. Evans to W. Wake, [21 May 1718], Christ Church Oxf., Wake MS 12, fol. 267 • T. Caulfield to K. O'Hara, 15 June 1703, NL Ire., MS 20388 • chancery bill books, 1682–7, NA Ire. • chancery bill books, 1692–6, NA Ire. • chancery bill books, 1710–12, NA Ire. • chancery bill books, 1713–16, NA Ire. • J. G. Simms, *Treaty of Limerick* (1965)

Butler, Thomas, tenth earl of Ormond and third earl of Ossory (1531–1614), nobleman, was born about February 1531, the eldest of seven sons and heir of James *Butler, ninth earl of Ormond and second earl of Ossory (*b.* in or after 1496, *d.* 1546), and his wife, Joan (*d.* 1565), sole daughter and heir of James FitzMaurice Fitzgerald, tenth earl of Desmond, and his wife, Amy. His assumed date of birth is based on his being 'within one year of full age' in October 1551 and receiving livery of his lands on 10 February 1552 (*Calendar of the Patent and Close Rolls of Chancery in Ireland, of the Reigns of Henry VIII, Edward VI, Mary, and Elizabeth*, ed. J. Morrin, 3 vols., 1861–2, 1.259). He was remembered in Ireland as Tomás Dubh, or Black Thomas, because of his dark complexion.

Early years and education, 1531–1558 Little of Butler's early childhood is known. In 1543 Ormond requested Henry VIII's permission to admit his heir to the circle of young noblemen then being assembled at court around Edward, prince of Wales. The king agreed, thinking it politic for Butler to be raised and educated at court. Butler departed for London early in May 1544 and entered a select group of English and Welsh noble youths groomed by the state as future royal counsellors, courtiers, and servitors, and he was easily convinced of the political virtue of unwavering crown service. Had Ormond lived longer his heir's separation from the Butlers might not have resulted in partial estrangement from his family. However, following his father's sudden death in October 1546, Butler, aged fifteen, became a crown ward, and all hope of his making a swift return to Ireland was extinguished.

Butler, now tenth earl of Ormond and third earl of Ossory, and chief butler of Ireland, was made KB at Edward VI's coronation on 20 February 1547. According to Butler family tradition, he served as a volunteer under Edward Seymour, duke of Somerset and lord protector, distinguishing himself at the battle of Pinkie on 10 September. In truth, his appearance on the battlefield was of political rather than military importance, his presence a

Thomas Butler, tenth earl of Ormond and third earl of Ossory (1531–1614), attrib. Steven van der Meulen

symbol of Edward's (and Somerset's) hold over Ireland. At court he received the finest humanist education available, and proceeded MA at the University of Oxford on 6 September 1566 and was admitted to Gray's Inn on 7 March 1567. A member of Somerset's household, living mainly at Somerset House, Westminster, Ormond survived the lord protector's fall in October 1549 and continued to reside near the court. The new regime, headed by John Dudley, earl of Warwick, was understandably anxious to surround the young king with companions after its own image. Ormond was unsuitable, despite his protestantism, and was not appointed a gentleman of the privy chamber. He was rarely at court in 1550–51. However, he served in the embassy of William Parr, marquess of Northampton, to France in summer 1551 and was rehabilitated during the Christmas festivities of 1551–2. Possibly his personal antipathy towards both Sir Henry Sidney and Barnaby Fitzpatrick, baron of Upper Ossory, so evident in later life, dated from his experiences between 1549 and 1553.

When news of Edward's death reached Kilkenny on 25 July 1553, a rumour circulated that Ormond had been murdered at court, resulting in widespread disruption across the Butler territories. None the less Ormond remained in London, determined to secure his position with the new Catholic monarch, Mary I. Early in 1554 he played a prominent part in defending the queen against the protestant rebel Sir Thomas Wyatt. Mary was grateful. Ormond returned to Ireland in autumn 1554 and the Gaelic annals record 'great rejoicing throughout the greater part of Leath-Mhoga' following his arrival (*AFM*, 5.1531). Sir Anthony St Leger, the lord deputy, did not want him appointed to the Irish privy council but his standing rose when his friend Thomas Radcliffe, Viscount Fitzwalter, arrived in April 1556. Ormond concentrated on establishing his authority in southern Ireland, securing among other things confirmation of his powers as lord of the palatinate liberty of Tipperary *vis-à-vis* the Butlers of Dunboyne and Cahir O'Connor. Fitzwalter used the earl's dominant position in co. Kilkenny to assist his scheme to plant the neighbouring territory of Leix (Laois). Ormond was a prominent member of the earl of Sussex's (Fitzwalter) regime in 1556–8, supporting its policy of military subjugation and colonization. Mary acknowledged his special responsibility for the south-east, granting him extensive lands in counties Kilkenny and Tipperary. However, he was prevented from returning to court. His continued presence in Ireland was necessary as a stabilizing influence, and this stopped him petitioning the queen in person over his disagreements with James FitzJohn Fitzgerald, thirteenth earl of Desmond. He did not return to England until Mary's death in November 1558.

Establishment of power and influence, 1558–1565 Elizabeth I was very well disposed towards Ormond. According to Sir William Cecil, principal secretary, her 'good opinion of Ormond [grew] … from the memory of his education with that holly yong Sallomen, King Edward' (PRO, SP 63/16/71). She encouraged his participation at court festivities, making no secret of her favour. In July 1559 Ormond attempted to reap material benefit from the queen's goodwill, seeking grants and privileges that might establish his supremacy in southern Ireland, especially against his principal adversary, Gerald FitzJames Fitzgerald, fourteenth earl of Desmond. Elizabeth acceded to several of his requests, including writing off debts owed to the crown since 1546 and awarding him leases (on very generous terms) of church property in south-east Ireland. He was appointed lord treasurer of Ireland on 26 August, giving him an *ex officio* place on the Irish privy council. The previous incumbent had been the thirteenth earl of Desmond. Ormond married Elizabeth (1534–1582), daughter and heir of Thomas Berkeley, sixth Baron Berkeley, and his second wife, Anne, about 1559. Elizabeth was reputed 'the fairest [noblewoman] that lived in the court' (J. Smyth, *The Berkeley Manuscripts: the Lives of the Berkeleys*, Bristol and Gloucestershire Archaeological Society, 3 vols., 1883–5, 2.255) and was heir presumptive to the Berkeley estate.

Ormond's close identification with the English crown set him apart from the majority of the Irish peers, some of whom wondered at his easy acceptance of royal policies designed to bring about the Anglicization of local power arrangements. Few of them were willing to curtail coign and livery, the free quartering of dependants on their tenants that lay at the heart of wealth and military power. Ormond was less apprehensive. Confident of crown support, he saw an opportunity to increase his regional power across the south by going along with the government's wishes. In particular, he recognized that the adoption of the English system of local government, including a form of lords lieutenant, would enable him to curb the independence of the cadet Butler branches, who in recent years had broken away from his control, waging war and attacking and plundering neighbours without his consent. Therefore he began to abolish coign and livery and attempted to control his dependants as commander-in-chief in counties Kilkenny and Tipperary. His intended reforms made some progress during the early 1560s: assize courts were held at Kilkenny and Clonmel, co. Tipperary; musters were held by royal commission in counties Kilkenny and Tipperary, paving the way for new, centrally controlled, shire levies; and, crucially, the new government military tax known as the cess was successfully introduced and collected by Ormond's servants. However, he found he could not afford to abolish coign and livery permanently. Early in 1560 Desmond challenged him to battle over a property dispute in co. Tipperary and Ormond accepted. Their armies met near Cashel, co. Tipperary, but probably through the intervention of Ormond's mother, who was married to Desmond, fighting was averted. A pragmatist, Ormond recognized that until such time as Desmond's soldiers were made answerable to government control he needed to retain coign and livery because the alternative, though less oppressive to ordinary people, was hopelessly slow and unwieldy by comparison. His volte-face upset English officials in Ireland and many became suspicious of him, regarding him as a major obstacle to the reduction of the island. He faced mounting opposition from the New English to his involvement in government for the remainder of his life.

Ormond's willingness to serve Sussex against Shane O'Neill in Ulster and against the O'Mores in Queen's county justified continued royal favour towards him. Intransigence on the part of Desmond and himself meant that their dispute was not settled by crown arbitration until the early summer of 1564, when they exchanged promises of 'love and amity'. Ormond resumed immediately the military reform of his lordship and announced the abolition of coign and livery, 'this horrible devouring monster' (PRO, SP 63/11/39 (i)). However, no sooner had his officers implemented his orders than Desmond struck (the restraining hand of his wife having been removed by her death) in the autumn, laying waste Ormond's Athassel estate in co. Tipperary, burning the castle, stealing hundreds of his cattle, and killing his tenants. Vowing revenge, Ormond gathered his kinsmen and followers, re-imposed coign and livery, and went to war. With a force of 500 men, he defeated and captured Desmond at the battle of Affane, co. Waterford, in early February 1565.

Royal favour and the Butler revolt, 1565–1575 Victory marked Ormond's emergence as the most substantial figure in the Irish peerage, although this was not immediately apparent. Elizabeth was furious and even his most steadfast allies in government were unable to defend him.

It seemed his status as an Irish privy councillor and favoured courtier was in jeopardy. Desmond and he were sent to England and placed under house arrest. A royal inquiry was established to examine both men's involvement in military depredations and to settle finally the property disputes between them. Both earls promised to refrain from feuding with one another and each entered into a recognizance for £20,000 on 22 November. In order to prevent bankruptcy, Ormond pressed ahead with his efforts at military reform in his lordship and made his dependants more answerable to his rule. However, his private life caused him difficulties. By the early 1560s Lady Ormond's behaviour had become a source of embarrassment to him. According to Nicholas White, who discussed the matter with him in person, Ormond discovered that she was exchanging love letters with three different gentlemen, 'Morgan, Moore and Mansfield'. The couple separated on bad terms in the spring of 1564, 'divorced from bed and board' (PRO, SP 63/11/39 (i)). They had no children and Ormond was keen to procure a divorce and remarry. He obtained a sentence of divorce in Ireland from Adam Walsh, commissary to his kinsman Patrick Walsh, bishop of Waterford and Lismore, in early 1565. The privy council intervened and appointed a commission, headed by Matthew Parker, archbishop of Canterbury, to hear Lady Ormond's appeal, 'notwithstanding [the] statutes, decrees, orders and constitutions of Ireland' (*CPR, 1563–6*, 258). Under the terms of a special settlement reached four years later, Ormond was compelled to set aside his Irish divorce and retain her as his wife, albeit providing her with an allowance of just £90 per annum for life. He felt the cost of the government's intervention in political not financial terms. This left him vulnerable to the activities of his brothers because he had no heir of his body. From the mid-1560s his next eldest brother, Sir Edmund Butler of Cloghgrenan, and his two youngest brothers, Edward and Piers Butler, openly defied his authority, bringing the Ormond territories to the brink of civil war.

Ormond was quite vulnerable during these years largely because of an improvement in his position in England. He became the new royal favourite by early 1566, especially because of Elizabeth's anger with Robert Dudley, earl of Leicester. Ormond acted as her chief male companion at state ceremonials and their relationship became private and intimate, the queen having several pet names for him, including 'Tom Duff' and 'Lucas', and even dubbing him her 'black husband'. Perhaps his even temperament—what the Spanish ambassador, Diego de Guzman de Silva, called his 'good disposition' (*CSP Spain, 1558–67*, 529)—appealed to her. This intense favour lasted several months and Ormond retained Elizabeth's good graces even after Leicester was restored; she refused to send him back to Ireland. Leicester sought a private understanding with Ormond. Although Ormond lacked an official position about the court he was a permanent fixture all the same, and being 'clever and ingenious', it was noted that he exercised a subtle, insinuating influence over the queen (ibid., 627).

Ormond's difficulties in Ireland grew because his brothers hoped he would remain in England, while elements of the royal government, who either already mistrusted him or else were supporters of Leicester, wished to curb his progress in England by embarrassing him over the state of his Irish lordship. In order to prevent his critics humiliating him over the growing lawlessness of his family in southern Ireland he had to remain in London, close to Elizabeth, but this prevented him from intervening personally to curb his more troublesome kinsmen. Sidney, lord deputy and Leicester's brother-in-law, attempted to exploit Ormond's vulnerability. Never one of the earl's admirers, he intended to increase the authority of his office by revealing in unprecedented detail the evils of Butler military power. His efforts precipitated the Butler revolt of 1569.

About October 1568 Sir Edmund, Edward, and Piers Butler learned that in order to protect himself from criticism at court Ormond had agreed terms with Sidney's representatives for the abolition of coign and livery in his lordship. This, combined with Ormond's inability to prevent Sidney's ally Sir Peter Carew from laying claim to lands held by Sir Edmund Butler in Carlow, signalled the final collapse of the brothers' relationship with the earl. Their subsequent rebellion was as much anti-Ormond as it was anti-government. Late in April 1569 they attacked Clonmel, capital of Ormond's palatinate, robbing and killing burgesses loyal to their brother. Subsequently, during May and June, they turned their attention to co. Kilkenny, targeting Ormond's officials, terrorizing his tenants, besieging the town of Kilkenny itself, and attempting to occupy his most important castles. Elizabeth supported Ormond, especially when he reported Philip II's overtures to him concerning landing a Spanish force in southern Ireland. She sanctioned his return to Ireland by 9 July, extolling his virtues in a letter to Sidney as 'a dutifull noble personage … in whom we have ever found trust and fealty towards us and our crown' (T. O'Laidhin, ed., *Sidney State Papers, 1565–1570*, Dublin, 1962, no. 69).

Ormond was unable to end the revolt quickly and his brothers did not submit or seek Elizabeth's pardon until September. Even then, they did not trust their brother's word and were unwilling to surrender themselves into Sidney's custody. Yet, in a sense, their continued intransigence helped to simplify Ormond's position, persuading him to at last take personal charge of eradicating their military independence. He set about the task with single-minded ruthlessness. Between 1569 and 1571 he oversaw the virtual extermination of his brothers' private armies in counties Kilkenny, Tipperary, and Carlow. This brought his kin to order and paid immediate dividends. The gentry and the burgesses, eager to aid him in imposing a new, more orderly, system of local defence, supported Ormond. Crucially, Elizabeth continued to support him too. Besides granting him further rewards, she blocked Sidney's renewed efforts to undermine him. Ormond achieved the remarkable feat of more or less neutralizing an act of attainder that Sidney had had passed against his brothers in the Irish parliament of 1570. He wanted to handle the problem personally within his family. Possibly Elizabeth's decision to recall Sidney in 1571 was partly a response to Ormond's contention that he had 'over pressed' the earl's family and so incited their rebellion 'upon malice', at enormous crown expense (PRO, SP 63/30/67).

The Butler revolt provided Ormond with the opportunity to demonstrate his strategic importance to the maintenance of English power in southern Ireland, but he was forced to abandon his prominent position at court. Despite this, he spent 1572–3 in London in the vain hope of recovering some of the ground he had lost. However, Elizabeth relied on Ormond's ability to cut the costs of security by providing cheap soldiers for her service, raised and furnished at his own expense from his estates and the lands of his followers. The fact that he had also shown himself a canny commander of the royal forces, able to settle disturbances through negotiation as well as by force, meant that she preferred him to return to Ireland. Through his leadership both the Thomond rebellion of 1570 and the O'More revolt of 1572 were ended quickly, at minimum cost to the exchequer, and the submission of James FitzMaurice Fitzgerald early in 1573 owed much to the efficacy of Ormond's military tactics. He received further rewards between 1573 and 1581, including land grants that brought him new estates in eleven counties across three provinces, from Dublin to Cork to Roscommon.

Ormond's role was ill defined and this led to disputes with other senior figures in the Irish government over military policy and other issues. While serving as general of the queen's army in west Munster he operated without a commission of martial law, and executed only those who opposed him in the field. In contrast, elsewhere, especially around the borders of his territories, the use of martial law against local lords and lineages had become commonplace: thousands were executed without trial. Ormond was disturbed by these developments, seeing many of the martial law commissioners—chiefly English captains and minor gentlemen—as low-born adventurers. He was equally disdainful of the growth of a less inclusive English colonial ideology in government circles, one that viewed all sections of the Irish population, whether Old English or Gaelic, as inherently suspect.

Irish magnate, 1575–1592 Ormond dominated Irish politics in a way that no Irish peer had managed to achieve since Henry VIII's reign. Successive English governors suffered at his hands. Sir William Fitzwilliam, lord deputy, was hopelessly compromised in 1574, his authority eroded when Lord Burghley (Cecil), Sussex, and Elizabeth each reprimanded him for his failure to support Ormond against Upper Ossory. Sidney replaced Fitzwilliam and attempted to disgrace Ormond by stirring up further unrest in the Butler lordship between 1575 and 1578. This failed and he was dismissed at the earl's instigation. Other senior figures to feel Ormond's disapproval included Carew and Marmaduke Middleton, bishop of Waterford.

The second Desmond rebellion broke out in late 1579. Since the mid-1570s Ormond had been attempting to entice Desmond into joining him and other Irish peers in a faction dedicated to achieving greater influence over crown policy in Ireland. Consequently, when Desmond and James Eustace, Viscount Baltinglass, rebelled, Ormond's enemies in government quickly seized the opportunity to challenge his position. His personal reticence over religion, and the fact that his territories were fully in the grip of Counter-Reformation Catholicism, provided some of his severest critics with an ideological justification for opposing him. Despite attempts in August and September 1579 to exclude him from military service he convinced a majority of the Irish privy council of his unique ability to crush the rebels quickly and cheaply. However, as lord-general of the queen's army in Munster, he lacked the government's undivided support. By mid-1580 his efforts to end the rebellion were stalling, partly through lack of co-operation from colleagues. His own force, comprising what annalists described as an 'immense host' recruited from his Catholic tenants, was also criticized heavily (*AFM*, 5.171–3). In June 1581 Elizabeth ordered Ormond to resign his command, having been led to believe that during his various expeditions he had managed to kill just three notable rebels, emboldening Desmond by his apparent leniency and wasting a fortune through excessive expenditure. To set the record straight he compiled a long list of those killed or executed by him. It is a shocking document, revealing that far from being lenient Ormond decimated Desmond's party during his time as lord-general, killing 5650 rebels, their servants, and followers between December 1579 and mid-1581. He justified his actions and pointed out that he might have ended the rebellion had he received sufficient support from the Irish privy council. He wanted to confront his defamers, 'such Machavellis', at court (PRO, SP 63/86/63). Elizabeth was already convinced of the merits of his case by the time he arrived in England early in 1582. On 8 November, Ormond received civil and military power in Munster, making him governor as well as general of the province.

On 1 September 1582 Lady Ormond died at Bristol. Ormond was free to remarry and did so with indecent haste. He took out a marriage licence on 9 November. His second wife was Elizabeth (*d.* 1600), daughter of John Sheffield, Baron Sheffield, and his wife, Douglas Sheffield. After a court wedding he returned to Ireland on 22 January 1583. Ormond and his second wife had one son, James Butler, Viscount Thurles (1583–1590), and a daughter, Elizabeth (*c.*1585–1628).

Ormond ended the war in ten months, offering royal protection and pardon to those who deserted the Geraldine cause and killing those who did not. Desmond was killed on 11 November by Gaelic troops hired by Ormond to track him down. Ormond wrote:

> So is this traitor come to the end I have long looked for, appointed by God to die by the sword to end his rebellion, in despite of such malicious fools as have divers times untruly informed of the service and state of Munster. (PRO, SP 63/105/67)

Rumours were prevalent from late 1582 that Ormond

might be appointed governor, with Sir James Croft as his assistant. This galvanized his enemies. Seemingly unconvinced by his protestantism and concerned that he was much too lenient towards recusants, Sir Francis Walsingham, principal secretary, ordered an investigation that led to the execution of more than 200 people in co. Kilkenny during 1583. Ormond's apparently gentle treatment of the new papal archbishop of Cashel, Dermot O'Hurley, in 1583–4 led to accusations that he was a 'secret maintainer of papistry'.

The outbreak of war with Spain in 1585 served to underline Ormond's importance to the Elizabethan state, and made it more difficult for his government enemies to continue to obstruct him, especially because of his military experience. He was rehabilitated between 1585 and 1588. His influence took hold of Irish affairs and, despite the objections of Sir John Perrot, lord deputy, he was appointed lord admiral of Ireland. Perrot's administration was virtually crippled by Ormond's meddling, especially because the earl advised the curtailment of martial law. Ormond was granted a share of the Munster plantation in co. Tipperary. He remained with Elizabeth during the Armada campaign, acting as marshal and helping Leicester to organize the English army camp at Tilbury, Essex. He was the most important member of the committee of 1589 to draw up a war plan for combating future Spanish threats. In recognition of his services he was made KG on 23 May 1588 in a ceremony at Windsor Castle. Ormond was appointed earl marshal of England, one of the highest honours ever bestowed on an Irish peer, late in 1590 or early in 1591. This may explain why on the publication of *The Faerie Queene* in 1590 he was honoured with a dedicatory sonnet by Edmund Spenser, who hated and feared him in equal measure. The duties attached to this office were such that he worried 'he should be tied to continual attendance in England and thereby to be made a stranger to his country, which he could not endure' (TCD, MS 842, fol. 160*v*). His request to surrender the post was granted some time before September 1592, and within a year he left England for the last time. Elizabeth reassured him that, despite his absence, she would not forget about him, whom she held in 'great and extraordinary estimation', and 'looks to find you always Old Lucas' (CUL, MS Kk.i.15, fol. 48*r*).

The impact of the Nine Years' War, 1592–1603 Ormond was instructed by the privy council to mediate between the Irish privy council and Hugh O'Neill, earl of Tyrone, on his return to Ireland. His intervention was futile because the two sides were already implacably opposed. He advised Sir William Russell, the new lord deputy, on how to conduct relations with Tyrone during the summer of 1594. Ormond preferred to serve in the south-east at the outbreak of the rebellion and was named general of the queen's forces in the pale in August. Family problems influenced his desire to remain in the south. The death of his heir in March 1590 left him again vulnerable to the ambitions of Sir Edmund Butler of Cloghgrenan, and his sons, James and Piers fitz Edmund, who were next in line to the earldom. Late in 1595 Ormond was forced to leave his base in co. Kilkenny to secure the northern frontiers of the pale against Tyrone, and his second-in-command, his cousin Edmund Butler, Viscount Mountgarret, broke free and rebelled, followed in spring 1596 by the fitz Edmunds. Ormond was denounced by hostile English officials as being a 'principall causer and upholder' of his kinsmen's rebellion (BL, Add. MS 34313, fol. 5*r*).

Ormond's subsequent actions gave the lie to such claims. He relieved Blackwater Fort, co. Armagh, before turning on the rebels in south Leinster. Between March and June 1597 he decimated the Butler rebel forces, especially the fitz Edmunds. In recognition of his achievements, and aware that he was willing, at his own cost, to raise a second royal force composed of loyal native auxiliaries while the lord deputy took the main army into Ulster, Elizabeth made him lieutenant-general of the army in September 1597. His promotion antagonized military hardliners, who feared his emphasis on restraint and containment. Ormond assumed overall charge of the prosecution of the war from October 1597 and tried to mediate with Tyrone during cease-fire negotiations in December. This alarmed the New English administrators and planters. Ormond's critics blamed him for Tyrone's victory at the battle of the Yellow Ford on 14 August 1598. In fairness, he had received a serious wound weeks earlier during fighting in the midlands and this prevented him from marching north; the commander in the field, Sir Henry Bagenal, had more experience of campaigning in Ulster; and Ormond's advice was ignored when prior to battle the 'grose error' was committed of 'deviding the armye into six bodies, marching so far asunder as one could not help the other' (PRO, SP 63/202/68). Ormond responded calmly to the news of Bagenal's defeat. He reorganized the army and redeployed it to help garrison the pale's northern frontiers. Within two weeks he had regained the initiative, leading a new expedition towards Farney, co. Monaghan. Rather than confront Ormond, Tyrone dithered and his army began to break up. Consequently, a renewed rebellion in Munster fizzled out in October. Ormond laid the foundations for English victory in the Nine Years' War, doing just enough to prevent Tyrone and his confederates from capitalizing fully on the Yellow Ford and other successes.

Early in 1600 Elizabeth offered Ormond the choice of continuing as lieutenant-general or retiring from the service, 'he being a nobleman so well affected to us … as we would have all the world to know we make extraordinary estimation of him' (LPL, MS 632, fol. 208). Elizabeth was concerned by reports of Ormond's declining health and may have wished to give Charles Blount, Baron Mountjoy, unlimited control of the army, but when Ormond intimated his desire to continue as lieutenant-general and to see the war through, she supported him. Ormond was captured by the O'More rebels on the Kilkenny/Leix frontier during a parley on 10 April 1600. He was imprisoned for more than two months until his Kilkenny and Tipperary clients raised a ransom of £3000. He never recovered from the experience. Though he campaigned again later in the year, he was beginning to go blind and had to spend longer and longer periods in Kilkenny Castle, co. Kilkenny.

Final years, 1603–1614 Ormond spent his final years in retirement on his estates but was still relied on by the new regime. Lady Ormond died in November 1600 and was buried in St Canice's Cathedral, Kilkenny. At some time between 2 and 24 June 1601 Ormond married Helen (*d.* 1642), daughter of David Barry, Viscount Buttevant, and his first wife, Ellen, and widow of John Power. They had no children. He was appointed to the unusual position of vice-deputy in 1604, but the post was largely honorific, his increasing frailty being a barrier to meaningful service. In November he suffered 'a fit of apoplexy', collapsed 'senseless', and was reported dead, only to recover within a few days (*CSP Ire., 1603–6*, 215). His heir was his son-in-law and nephew Theobald Butler (*d.* 1613), Viscount Butler, youngest son of Sir Edmund Butler of Cloghgrenan. However, Theobald predeceased him and his widow, Ormond's daughter and heir, Elizabeth, subsequently commenced proceedings against the eleventh earl, Walter *Butler (1559–1633). The earldom's enormous wealth was a great inducement to litigation. Throughout his long life Ormond managed his estates carefully. By the time of his death rents alone brought in approximately £4000 per annum, with farming profits and the Ormond prisage on wines generating at least as much again. This made him probably the wealthiest man in Ireland. He enjoyed his wealth, commissioning, among others, a fine portrait of himself by Steven van der Meulen (about 1559), and another, possibly by Federico Zuccaro from the 1570s. He had a very notable art collection, with forty-four paintings hanging in the long gallery at Carrick Castle, co. Tipperary, by 1614. This was the largest collection of art in Ireland prior to the late seventeenth century and compared well with those of his English contemporaries, including Henry Fitzalan, earl of Arundel. Ormond carried out major building programmes on several of his properties, including the addition of fine decorative plasterwork at Ormond Castle, co. Kilkenny, and intended by a clause in his will to build and endow a hospital in Kilkenny, partly in order to have masses said for his soul.

Ormond died at Carrick Castle on 22 November 1614 and was buried at St Canice's Cathedral six months later, in May 1615. The celebrated English craftsman Nicholas Stone sculpted his tomb, subsequently reputed the finest in Ireland, at a cost of £230. Only a fragment of the tomb now survives, attached to the base of that of his paternal grandparents. Having been a central figure in the politics of English rule in Ireland under Elizabeth, Ormond was both fêted and reviled by many writers and commentators. Predictably this literature, written in English, Latin, and Gaelic, dates mainly from the 1580s and 1590s, when his influence loomed largest in Anglo-Irish affairs. These works include Thomas Churchyard's *A Scourge for Rebels* (1584), a poem by Sir John Davies in his *The Scourge of Folly* (1611), and *Eolach me ar mheirge an iarla*, written shortly after Ormond's death by Flann Mac Eoin Mac Craith. The most significant text about him was the posthumous Latin panegyric *Ormonius* written by the Butler family physician, Dermitius Meara, and printed in Dublin in 1615. Ormond was a very significant figure in late sixteenth-century Irish history, whose main achievement was the successful prosecution of the Nine Years' War. He was representative of the Old English, yet amenable to more positive aspects of Tudor rule. This can be no surprise considering his upbringing. Equally significant was the emergence of the Butlers as the leading Irish family, having finally eclipsed the Geraldines in the 1580s.

David Edwards

Sources *AFM* · R. Bagwell, *Ireland under the Tudors*, 3 vols. (1885–90) · C. Brady, 'Thomas Butler, tenth earl of Ormond (1531–1614) and reform in Tudor Ireland', *Worsted in the game: losers in Irish history*, ed. C. Brady (Dublin, 1989), 49–59 · Bodl. Oxf., MSS Carte 1, 30, 55–58, 60–62, 131 · G. Butler, 'The battle of Affane', *Irish Sword*, 8 (1967–8), 43–51 · E. Curtis, ed., *Calendar of Ormond deeds*, 6 vols., IMC (1932–43), vols. 3–4 · [T. Carte], *The life of James, duke of Ormond*, new edn, 6 vols. (1851) · J. Curtis, 'The Butler revolt of 1569', MA diss., St Patrick's College, Maynooth, 1983 · D. Edwards, 'The Butler revolt of 1569', *Irish Historical Studies*, 28 (1992–3), 228–55 · D. Edwards, 'The Ormond lordship in county Kilkenny, 1515–1642', PhD diss., TCD, 1998 · C. Falls, 'Black Tom of Ormonde', *Irish Sword*, 5 (1961–2), 10–22 · J. Fenlon, 'The decorative plasterwork at Ormond Castle—a unique survival', *Architectural History*, 41 (1998), 67–81 · J. Graves, 'The taking of the earl of Ormond, 1600', *Journal of the Kilkenny and South East Ireland Archaeological Society*, 2nd ser., 3 (1861–2); 5 (1865), 388–432 · J. Kirwan, 'Thomas Butler, 10th earl of Ormond: his early career and rise to prominence', *Butler Society Journal*, 3/4 (1994), 514–30 · J. Kirwan, 'Thomas Butler, 10th earl of Ormond (*c.*1532–1614): his stewardship of the family estates', *Kilkenny: essays in honour of Margaret Phelan*, ed. J. Kirwan (Kilkenny, 1997), 58–78 · LPL, MS 632, fol. 208 · J. McGurk, 'The battle of Yellow Ford, August 1598', *Dúiche Néill*, 12 (1998), 34–55 · D. Meara, *Ormonius* (1615) · H. Morgan, 'The 1597 ceasefire documents', *Dúiche Néill*, 11 (1997), 9–33 · NL Ire., Ormond MSS 2301, 2506–2509, 11044 · NL Ire., Ormond deeds, D 2640, D 3520 · state papers Ireland, Edward VI, PRO, SP 61 · state papers Ireland, Mary I, PRO, SP 62 · state papers Ireland, Elizabeth I, PRO, SP 63 · state papers Ireland, James I, PRO, SP 63 · Rothe's register of the house of Ormond, TCD, MS 842 · Ormond rentals, *c.*1550–*c.*1650, NL Ire., Ormond MSS 2506, 2509

Archives NL Ire., MSS | Bodl. Oxf., Carte MSS · CKS, letters to Sir Henry Sidney · PRO, state papers

Likenesses S. van der Meulen, *c.*1559, NG Ire. · possibly by F. Zuccaro, 1570–79; formerly at the Château du Jehay, Belgium · attrib. S. van der Meulen, oils; Sothebys, 30 Nov 2000, lot 2 [*see illus.*] · panel painting, St Faith's Church, Gaywood, Essex · portrait, priv. coll.

Wealth at death probably £10,000: Ormond rentals, *c.*1550–*c.*1650, NL Ire., Ormond MSS 2506, 2509

Butler, Thomas (*b.* **1532/3**, *d.* in or before **1591**), Roman Catholic priest and translator, was possibly the son of William Butler (*d.* 1557), who was lessee of the manor at Radley, Berkshire. In 1546, at the age of thirteen, he was sent to Winchester College; in 1551 he became a fellow of New College, Oxford. He took the degree of doctor of canon and civil law, probably at Oxford, but by 1562 he had been expelled from the university for refusal to accept the protestant settlement of Elizabeth I. He stayed for a while at Louvain in the Spanish Netherlands, and may have taken a degree there. He then moved to Rome, where he lived with his friend Thomas Goldwell, exiled bishop of St Asaph. In 1570 Butler published a translation from Italian of a work by the talented Jesuit Antonio Possevino, entitled *A Treatise of the Holy Sacrifice of the Altar Called the Mass*. The book was printed at Louvain and dedicated by Butler to Goldwell. From about the same date, through the patronage of Giovanni Morone, cardinal-protector of the English, Butler acquired a number of legal or administrative positions in the Papal States, and by 1587 he had been appointed prefect of the town of Fabriani. On 27 December 1588 his fellow exile Owen Lewis, bishop of Cassano, was granted a licence to ordain Butler priest, while Butler himself was dispensed for having passed sentences of death and mutilation in the course of his judicial employments. He died in or before January 1591, when Lewis was granted permission to dispose of his effects for pious uses. PETER HOLMES

Sources C. Dodd [H. Tootell], *The church history of England, from the year 1500, to the year 1688*, 2 (1739), 159 • G. Anstruther, *The seminary priests*, 1 (1969) • T. F. Kirby, *Winchester scholars: a list of the wardens, fellows, and scholars of … Winchester College* (1888), 126 • A. Wood, *Historia et antiquitates universitatis Oxoniensis*, trans. R. Peers and R. Reeve, 2 vols. (1674), vol. 1, p. 283 • A. F. Allison and D. M. Rogers, eds., *The contemporary printed literature of the English Counter-Reformation between 1558 and 1640*, 2 (1994), 25 • H. Rashdall and R. Rait, *New College* (1901), 114 • *CSP Rome*, *1558–71*, 152 • [J. Gibbons and J. Fenn], *Concertatio ecclesiae catholicae in Anglia adversus Calvinopapistas et puritanos*, 2nd edn (1588), 405 • N. Sander, *De visibili monarchia ecclesiae libri octo* (Louvain, 1571), iv, 700 • *VCH Berkshire*, 4.410, 412 • A. C. Southern, *Elizabethan recusant prose, 1559–1582* (1950), 47, 53, 396–7 • T. M. Veech, *Dr Nicholas Sanders and the English Reformation, 1530–1581* (1935), 23 • Cooper, *Ath. Cantab.*, 1.294 • Venn, *Alum. Cant.*, 1/1.274 • H. Foley, ed., *Records of the English province of the Society of Jesus*, 6 (1880), 719–20, 723 • Gillow, *Lit. biog. hist.*

Butler, Thomas, sixth earl of Ossory (1634–1680), politician and naval officer, was born at Kilkenny Castle on 8 July 1634, the eldest son of James *Butler, twelfth earl of Ormond and fifth earl of Ossory, later first duke of Ormond (1610–1688), and his wife, Elizabeth *Butler (*née* Preston), *suo jure* Lady Dingwall (1615–1684), sole daughter and heir of Richard Preston, earl of Desmond. Richard *Butler, first earl of Arran (1639–1686), was his brother.

Early life Thomas held the courtesy title of Viscount Thurles until his father's elevation to a marquessate in 1642 when he became earl of Ossory. He went to England with Ormond after Dublin's surrender in 1647, and then (in February 1648) to France, remaining there when his father returned to Ireland in September 1648. Ossory was educated for a year by a French tutor at Caen before proceeding in October 1649 to Monsieur de Camp's academy in Paris, where the diarist John Evelyn first met him. Ossory returned to Caen in December 1650, remaining there with his mother until the summer of 1652, when they returned to England. Ossory was in Ireland from the beginning of 1653 until the end of 1654, when he went back to England with his mother. Sir Robert Southwell, who knew him at this time, described him as 'a young man with a very handsome face … he pleaseth me exceedingly, being very good-natured, talking freely, asking many questions, and humouring the answers … He is temperate, courteous, and excellent in all his behaviour' (Carte, 1.631–2).

In March 1655 Ossory was suddenly arrested and placed

Thomas Butler, sixth earl of Ossory (1634–1680), studio of Sir Peter Lely, *c*.1678

in the Tower on Cromwell's orders, on no firmer ground than his association with known royalist enthusiasts. He remained in the Tower until October, when a serious illness brought his release, partly because of the incessant personal pressure his mother applied to Cromwell. He went at first to Acton, Gloucestershire, with his mother, but in 1657 he was allowed to go abroad after giving security that he would not plot against the protectorate. He stayed chiefly in the Netherlands, though he was at Basel in April 1658. On 7 November 1659 he married Aemilia (*d*. 1688), daughter of Lodewyk van Nassau, heer van Beverweerd, governor of Sluis, an illegitimate son of the stadholder Maurits van Nassau. Although Ormond saw the match as a way of gaining Dutch support for the exiled king, it soon became apparent that it was a genuine love match, and it certainly brought the Butlers no great financial gains: van Nassau gave only £10,000 with his daughter, and insisted on Ossory being given an annuity of £1200. The marriage produced eleven children: of the two sons who survived, the elder, James *Butler (1665–1745), became the second duke of Ormond, while of the four surviving daughters two became countesses, of Derby and Grantham.

After the Restoration At the Restoration, Ossory obtained an impressive array of titles and offices. He served as MP for Bristol from 16 May 1661 to 14 September 1666, and was called to the Irish House of Lords on 8 August 1662, taking precedence over all the other earls. A member of the Irish privy council from December 1660, he served as lord deputy from 21 May 1664 to 3 September 1665, and from 10 April 1668 to 3 May 1669, while Ormond was in England. A friend and confidant of both Charles II and the duke of York, Ossory gave away the bride, Anne Hyde, at York's clandestine marriage on 3 September 1660, and bore the king's train at the coronation on 23 April 1661, causing a stir by claiming the place ahead of Lord Percy, the duke of Northumberland's son.

Ossory's main interest from a very early age had lain in military affairs—according to his father's biographer, Carte, Ossory's first pair of riding boots had kept Ormond awake all night as the boy stamped excitedly on his bedroom floor. The earl became a colonel of foot in the Irish army on 8 February 1661, lieutenant-general of the horse in June, and lieutenant-general of the Irish army on 16 August 1665. In June 1666 he was staying at Euston Hall, Suffolk, with the secretary of state Lord Arlington, who had married the countess of Ossory's sister two months earlier (cementing a close political and personal relationship which was to endure until Ossory's death). Hearing the gunfire from the great 'four days' battle', in which the outnumbered English fleet under the duke of Albemarle slowly retreated towards the Thames, Ossory and Sir Thomas Clifford rushed to Harwich and sailed out to Albemarle's flagship. Ossory brought with him the welcome news that Prince Rupert's detached squadron had been recalled from the west, and on 3 June, the third day of the battle, he was given a commission to command the *St George*. Finding the ship unserviceable, Ossory returned instead to the flagship *Royal Charles* as a volunteer, and fought the rest of the battle in her. When news of his impulsiveness reached Ireland, his family was horrified.

Also in 1666 Ossory became a gentleman of the bedchamber to the king, and a member of the English privy council, and on 14 September he was called to the House of Lords with the English title Baron Butler of Moor Park. These offices, and his new kinship with Arlington, increased his political profile, and he quickly became identified as an opponent of Arlington's fellow 'Cabal' ministers, Lord Ashley and the duke of Buckingham. In October 1666 a bill to ban imports of Irish cattle into England brought the conflict to a head. Buckingham's sarcastic denunciation of the Irish, to the effect that anyone opposing the bill had 'an Irish interest or an Irish understanding' (Pepys, 27 Oct 1666), led Ossory to challenge him to a duel, which the duke avoided. Having been summoned before the House of Lords to explain himself on 29 October, Ossory was imprisoned in the Tower, and was released only after five days, following a petition to the house in which he expressed his regret (31 October). On 19 November, Buckingham and Ashley were the prime movers of another anti-Irish measure, attacking the charity which provided Irish beef for the City of London. After listening to Ashley in silence for some time Ossory exploded, protesting at 'his using such reviling language, aspersions, and misrepresentations of things and persons, as could become none but one of Cromwell's counsellors' (Carte, 2.272). Despite his having broken no rules of the house, the rival faction was too powerful, and the earl was forced to withdraw.

Ossory spent much of 1668 and the first months of 1669 as his father's deputy in Ireland, prior to Ormond's dismissal from the lord lieutenancy. He went with Charles II to Dover in May 1670 but took no part in the secret negotiations there. In October he sailed with a flotilla of yachts to escort William of Orange to England; after taking William back to The Hague in February 1671, Ossory went through Flanders to the French court, intending to volunteer for service with the French army in Alsace. Finding that French intentions had changed, he returned to England in April; he crossed to Flanders once more in June in an attempt to attend the siege of Brunswick, only to find that it was over.

The Third Anglo-Dutch War and service abroad Ossory's obvious impatience to see action finally ended in January 1672, when he was appointed captain of the third-rate *Resolution*. He took part in Sir Robert Holmes's attack on the Dutch Smyrna convoy in March, despite believing that the attack was dishonourable. He also held serious misgivings about the Third Anglo-Dutch War, which the attack precipitated; as well as his family ties, he had struck up a close personal friendship with William of Orange, and they corresponded regularly for the rest of Ossory's life. Nevertheless, Ossory moved to the *Victory* on 11 April 1672 and commanded her at the battle of Solebay (28 May). He was also intended to be second in command to the duke of Monmouth in the proposed invasion of Zeeland, a move which infuriated his old enemy Buckingham, who wanted the leading role in the attack.

On 30 September 1672 Ossory was made a knight of the Garter, and was installed at Windsor on 25 October; in November he went to France as envoy-extraordinary to convey the British court's condolences on the death of the duke of Anjou. According to Carte, he turned down Louis XIV's offer of any command he cared to name in the French army, and returned instead to his naval career in England (albeit with the gift of a jewel worth £2000 from the French king). In May 1673 he was appointed rear-admiral of the Blue squadron, his flag flying in the *St Michael*, despite his father's surprise and his own modest opinion of his lack of seamanship. In fact, the appointment was a stopgap due to the unexpected absence of the designated flag officer, John Narbrough; Ossory's appointment prevented the post from becoming a focus for ambitious claimants and faction-fighting. At the battle of Texel (11 August 1673), Ossory's division was part of Sir Edward Spragge's Blue squadron. Despite his efforts to defend Spragge's flagship, the *Royal Prince*, from successive Dutch attacks, Ossory's conduct was publicly criticized by the squadron's vice-admiral, Sir John Kempthorne, though the charges were quickly retracted when Ossory protested. On 14 August, Ossory hoisted his flag as vice-admiral of the Red squadron. The death of Sir John Harman and return ashore of Prince Rupert led to Ossory's briefly becoming commander-in-chief of the fleet from 14 September for six days, and as a result he was awarded an annual pension of £250. At the end of 1673 Ossory proposed a surprise attack on the Dutch fleet at Hellevoetsluis. During his visits to the Netherlands in

1670–71 he had seen the *Royal Charles* (the flagship captured by the Dutch at Chatham in 1667) lying in that anchorage, and he was determined to avenge that humiliation. An expedition was prepared, but on the night Ossory was due to set out, Charles II countermanded the order—primarily, it was said, because the duke of Buckingham did not want the earl to get the glory, and persuaded the king to abort the scheme.

Ossory vigorously defended Arlington against impeachment in 1674, and in November of that year he went with Arlington to the Netherlands to discuss possible ways of ending the ongoing Franco-Dutch War. The evidence surrounding this mission is contradictory. During it Ossory certainly put to William of Orange the suggestion that he might marry York's daughter Mary, but the prince received the idea coolly and, on his return in January 1675, Ossory was attacked by Charles and York for having exceeded his instructions. Even so, it is quite possible that Charles had wanted Ossory to do exactly what he did, and was dissembling only to save his credit with his brother. On 31 May 1675 Ossory became master of Trinity House, having been an elder brother since 1673, and in August 1675 became a member of the Admiralty board. His attendance at the Admiralty was probably as frequent as his regular visits to the continent and to Ireland would permit: he was present at 62 out of a possible 200 meetings during 1675–9. On 18 November 1676 he was appointed lord chamberlain to the queen, Catherine of Braganza.

Ossory went to Flanders in July 1677 and joined William of Orange at the siege of Charleroi, taking command of 6000 men when the French army approached. After a brief return to England, in January 1678 he became general of all British forces in the Dutch service, winning distinction at the battle of Mons on 4 August. Although several shots hit his armour, he was not wounded. Ossory returned to England on 13 September 1678. Carte states that at this time he was offered the command of the Mediterranean Fleet, but declined as he thought the force too small (owing to a parsimonious Treasury), and that Sir John Narbrough was sent instead. Although the story is plausible, its dating must be wrong; Narbrough had been sent out to deal with the Barbary corsairs on two separate occasions, from early 1674 until late 1676, and then from mid-1677 until mid-1679. As it was, after his return in September 1678 Ossory was quickly plunged into the political crisis surrounding the Popish Plot. Throughout, Ossory defended his father's record in Ireland and vigorously defended the queen against Titus Oates's accusations. On 31 March 1679 he presented a memorial on the state of Ireland to the House of Lords, though Ormond criticized his impulsiveness in doing so without consulting him first.

Ossory was removed from the privy council and the Admiralty in the spring of 1679 as part of Charles II's attempt to placate the whigs, but was restored to the former on 16 April 1680. In September 1679 he had been named envoy-extraordinary to Spain, but after incurring a great deal of expense in preparing for the mission, he found it cancelled as an economy measure by the earl of Essex's Treasury commission.

The Tangier expedition and the death of Ossory In July 1680 Ossory was nominated governor of Tangier, then under siege by the Moors, despite his and his friends' serious reservations about the limited force which a parsimonious Treasury intended to allow him: it was said that his appointment was a ploy by James, duke of York, to get rid of a popular rival. According to his old friend Evelyn, Ossory spoke to him privately of his doubts on 26 July:

> He sent to his secretary for the copy of a letter which he had written to Lord Sunderland (Secretary of State), wishing me to read it; it was to take notice how ill he resented it, that he should tell the King before Lord Ossory's face, that Tangier was not to be kept, but would certainly be lost, and yet added that it was fit Lord Ossory should be sent, that they might give some account of it to the world, meaning (as supposed), the next Parliament … This touched my lord deeply, that he should be so little considered as to put him on a business in which he should probably not only lose his reputation, but be charged with all the miscarriages and ill success … It certainly took so deep root in his mind, that he who was the most void of fear in the world … could not bear up against this unkindness. (Evelyn, 26 July 1680)

Still according to Evelyn, it was at a dinner in Fishmongers' Hall on the same evening that Ossory fell ill with the severe fever, probably typhus, that was to kill him.

Although Ossory and Evelyn might well have had the sort of conversation described by the diarist, Evelyn's recollection of the sequence of events was seriously faulty. The earl had been stricken by the fever about 18 July, and on the 26th he was in the second day of a delirium that lasted until his death. Ossory had been ill in the previous September, and had suffered from pain in his eyes throughout June and July 1680. He died at Arlington's London residence, Arlington House, on 30 July 1680, at about a quarter past seven in the evening. During his last night 'he raved much of Tangier, posting his men, attacking, retrenching and defending, then sighing heavily as in despair, more bewailing the loss of his people's lives than his own' (*Ormonde MSS*, 5.361). Ossory was given what was intended to be a temporary burial on 1 August 1680 in Henry VII's chapel, Westminster Abbey; an intention to move him to a permanent resting place at Kilkenny Cathedral seems never to have been carried out.

Ossory's death triggered a remarkable and genuine outpouring of popular grief. His modesty, affability, courtesy, and loyalty were well known, as was his unwillingness simply to follow the herd in a notoriously cynical and faction-ridden court. When the lord treasurer, Danby, had fallen in 1679, Ossory was the only courtier who made a point of engaging him in conversation, despite the fact that they had often disagreed. A year before he had written to Danby that 'I think it is for the public as well as private good that persons in his Majesty's affairs should be united' (BL, Egerton MS 3331, fol. 5), and this seems to have been no empty rhetoric on his part. His religious views were notably moderate by the standards of the age, advocating a co-existence of Catholics and protestants in Ireland. His frequently reckless and impulsive courage was the despair of his close family, but only raised his standing with the general public still higher. His generosity was a byword: after the battle of Solebay he arranged for one of his agents to distribute up to 40*s.* a head to every seaman recuperating at St Thomas's Hospital. In the last weeks of his life one of his main concerns was to ensure that the officers and men who had served him in the Netherlands were properly provided for. Unlike many of his contemporaries at Charles II's court, Ossory faced few charges of sexual misconduct. Carte noted that 'he was deemed not insensible of the charms of a daughter of Sir C. Swan, with whom he was really in love' (Carte, 2.595), but that he had concealed his feelings so as not to hurt his wife (from whom he was eventually divorced in 1680); in December 1677 he fought a duel over the wife of a Mr Buckley.

Ossory's great failing was implicit in his legendary generosity: his financial management was chaotic, partly because he loved gambling, partly because of his largesse to his subordinates and to any visiting foreign dignitary passing through London or Ireland, and partly because his wife's financial sense was, if anything, even worse than his. Even the distinctly hagiographic Thomas Carte had to acknowledge Ossory's disastrous luck at the gaming tables, though he seems to have exaggerated the countess's financial acumen:

> The earl would come home sometimes thoughtful and out of humour after losses at play, to which he was but too much subject; and when, upon inquiry of the reason, he told her that he was vexed at himself for playing the fool and gaming, and that he had lost one thousand pounds, she still desired him not to be troubled, she would find ways to save it at home. (Carte, 2.594)

As early as 1662 Ossory owed over £2000 to four London merchants, by 1666 this had risen to over £3000, and by 1678 his debts stood at £6184 13*s.* 4*d.*, much of it borrowed from Sir Stephen Fox. Several attempts were made to put his finances on an even keel. From July 1669 he was provided with £3000 a year out of Ormond's estate, and in 1675 he was granted £14,000 by the king, allegedly for losses he had sustained in the royal service. His mother despaired: 'I find [Ossory] indebted to many tradesmen here, who complain of him to be a bad paymaster; and I cannot but fear and suspect him so, because that neither he nor his lady does know what their debts are' (*Ormonde MSS*, 3.439). When he went to France in 1671, she grumbled that it was 'to what purpose unless to spend money I know not, and to satisfy a vaulting and unsettled humour which he still retains' (ibid.). Ossory made occasional gestures towards reformation, as in February 1679 when he wrote to his uncle, 'let my parents see how much our welfare, honour and all, is concerned in well managing our fortune, the doing the contrary having been so fatal to us on many occasions'; this contrition was rendered slightly less impressive by the fact that at exactly the same time the earl was planning to fit out all 3000 of his troops in the Netherlands with new uniform coats at his expense (NL Ire., MS 11047, fols. 35–6).

Unsurprisingly, it took Sir Stephen Fox until well over a year after Ossory's death to get to grips with the state of his accounts. Still, at a time when England was markedly lacking in military heroes, and even more deficient in political ones, Ossory's reputation was unchallenged, and the many eulogies were well deserved. In Dryden's view:

> By Sea, by Land, thy Matchless Worth was known;
> Arms thy delight, and War was all thy Own …
> But Israel was unworthy of thy name:
> Short is the date of all Immoderate Fame.
> (Dryden, ll. 840–41, 846–7)

Burnet was more critical, claiming that Ossory had 'no extraordinary parts, and was too much set on some forbidden pleasures, but was in all other respects the bravest man and the generousest friend that was at court' (*Supplement to Burnet's History*, 62). However, the finest tribute was paid by John Evelyn, the earl's friend of thirty years' standing:

> A loving, generous, good-natured, and perfectly obliging friend; one who had done innumerable kindnesses to several before they knew it … no one more brave, more modest; none more humble, sober, and every way virtuous. Unhappy England in this illustrious person's loss! … He deserved all that a sincere friend, a brave soldier, a virtuous courtier, a loyal subject, an honest man, a bountiful master, and good Christian, could deserve of his prince and country. (Evelyn, 26 July 1680)

J. D. Davies

Sources T. Carte, *An history of the life of James, duke of Ormonde*, 3 vols. (1735–6); new edn, pubd as *The life of James, duke of Ormond*, 6 vols. (1851) • Bodl. Oxf., MSS Carte • NL Ire., Ormonde MSS, esp. MSS 2400 and 11407 • *Calendar of the manuscripts of the marquess of Ormonde*, new ser., 8 vols., HMC, 36 (1902–20) • Evelyn, *Diary* • *The life of Edward, earl of Clarendon … written by himself*, 2 vols. (1857) • GEC, *Peerage* • 'Letters of William of Orange to Ossory, 1672–80', BL, Add. MS 21942 • *Some account of the family of the Butlers* (1716) • *CSP dom.*, *1660–80* • J. P. Ferris, 'Butler, Thomas', HoP, *Commons, 1660–90*, 1.756–7 • J. Dryden, *Absalom and Achitophel* (1681), ll. 817–53 • J. R. Powell and E. K. Timings, eds., *The Rupert and Monck letter book, 1666*, Navy RS, 112 (1969) • R. C. Anderson, ed., *Journals and narratives of the Third Dutch War*, Navy RS, 86 (1946) • J. D. Davies, *Gentlemen and tarpaulins: the officers and men of the Restoration navy* (1991) • *CSP Ire.*, *1660–69* • PRO, admiralty MSS • *A supplement to Burnet's History of my own time*, ed. H. C. Foxcroft (1902) • BL, Egerton MS 3331, fol. 5 • *Sixth report*, HMC, 5 (1877–8) • Pepys, *Diary* • J. R. Tanner, ed., *A descriptive catalogue of the naval manuscripts in the Pepysian Library at Magdalene College, Cambridge*, 4, Navy RS, 57 (1923) • *DNB*

Archives Bodl. Oxf., letters and papers • NL Ire., papers | BL, corresp. with William of Orange, Add. MS 21492

Likenesses P. Lely, oils, *c.*1675–1676, Uffizi Gallery, Florence • studio of P. Lely, oils, *c.*1678, NPG [*see illus.*]

Wealth at death £400 in plate; furniture of little value; was owed £1250 of salary as gentleman of the bedchamber and £562 10*s.* of pension as commander-in-chief of the fleet; owed tradesmen £93 17*s.* 11*d.*, incl. £61 to coachmaker, and £40 to those who embalmed him; in all, the countess was owed £5592 and owed £1968: NL Ire., Ormonde MSS, MS 11047, 71–83

Butler, Thomas Hamly (*c.*1755–1823), composer, was born in London. He was probably the son of the John or James Butler who sang in the first performance of Handel's *Saul*. He was a chorister of the Chapel Royal under James Nares, and studied in Italy for three years with Niccolò Piccinni. Between 1778 and 1780 he was harpsichordist at Covent Garden Theatre, and wrote the music for a masque, *Calypso*, and for an opera, *The Widow of Delphi*, both with words by Richard Cumberland. Neither of these was successful, and in 1782 Butler moved to Edinburgh, where he became a piano teacher and a popular composer. His *Favourite Rondo for the Piano forte* on the Scottish tune 'Lewie Gordon' went through nine editions between 1785 and 1800, and he used Scottish themes in other keyboard works. He also published *A Select Collection of Original Scottish Airs* (1800) with 'symphonies and accompaniments for the flute, violin, and piano forte'. Butler died in Edinburgh in 1823.

W. B. SQUIRE, *rev.* ANNE PIMLOTT BAKER

Sources *New Grove* • R. Fiske, *English theatre music in the eighteenth century*, 2nd edn (1986), 425–6 • D. Johnson, *Music and society in lowland Scotland in the eighteenth century* (1972) • [J. S. Sainsbury], ed., *A dictionary of musicians*, 2 vols. (1824) • Genest, *Eng. stage*, 6.146

Butler, (Christina) Violet (1884–1982), social work trainer, was born on 25 January 1884 at 14 Norham Gardens, Oxford, the youngest child in the family of one son and three daughters of Arthur Gray *Butler (1831–1909), first headmaster of Haileybury College and fellow of Oriel College, Oxford, and his wife, Harriet Jessie, daughter of M. Pakenham Edgeworth, botanist and Indian civil servant, and niece of Maria Edgeworth. With Josephine Butler for an aunt, and with so many relatives in literary, philanthropic, and educational circles, Violet was almost predestined to a life of social service. Deeply fond of her parents, she was educated at home until aged fourteen. She then went to Wycombe Abbey, left at seventeen, and took a first in modern history from the Society of Home Students (later St Anne's College) in Oxford in 1905. Equipped with a knowledge of four languages, she was the first woman to gain a distinction in the diploma in economics and political science; she then took a teaching diploma at London University.

Social work came naturally to an intelligent unmarried Edwardian middle-class young woman, especially since her mother had visited the local workhouse once a week for half a century and her elder sister Olive had become warden of the Lady Margaret Hall settlement in Lambeth, London. Besides, Violet admired the sense of civic duty that inspired seven women, all wives of dons, who were then prominent in Oxford for their voluntary social work: an older trio consisting of Charlotte Green (Mrs T. H. Green), Bertha Johnson (Mrs A. H. Johnson), and Charlotte Toynbee (Mrs A. Toynbee); and a quartet who were Violet's near-contemporaries—Mabel Prichard (Mrs H. A. Prichard), Mary Smith (Mrs A. L. Smith), Frances Wells (Mrs J. Wells), and her much-loved former tutor in economics, Mrs H. A. L. Fisher. A lifelong member of the Oxford Cottage Improvement Society, Violet Butler joined the local branch of the Charity Organization Society, and her links with the Christian Social Union encouraged in her the unsectarian broad-church outlook that was taken for granted within a family so deeply influenced by Thomas Arnold, T. H. Green, and Henry Scott Holland. Throughout her life she operated on the fruitful margin that arbitrarily separates the statutory from the voluntary body.

Butler's *Social Conditions in Oxford* (1912) grew out of her three earlier local preoccupations: housing reform, getting adolescents into skilled work, and (through the Women's Industrial Council) extending women's job opportunities. This work was one of several provincial surveys (of Norwich and Cambridge, for example) inspired by the work of Benjamin Seebohm Rowntree, whose *Poverty: a Study of Town Life* appeared in 1901. Family connections gave Butler an inside view of Oxford's local government, and hers is the best account of it in all the surveys. Suffused with a sense of history, precise yet pragmatic in mood, the book's readability gains from its author's gentle sense of irony and exemplifies an Edwardian affinity between literature and 'social science' that has since been lost. The work also displays the combination of intellectual curiosity, affectionate interest in human nature, and down-to-earth practicality that the Charity Organization Society so often encouraged.

Social Conditions in Oxford gave Butler the academic credentials she needed, and from 1914 to 1945 she combined her local social work with acting as tutor in economics at St Anne's and tutor-secretary (1914–19) for women students at Barnett House, Oxford's centre for training in social work. From 1919 to 1948 she was secretary for social training there, and later she published privately a booklet on its history. The union of social thought and social action at Barnett House admirably suited her temperament. After 1914 she concentrated on teaching, but she found time to compile an attitude survey, the Women's Industrial Council report *Domestic Service* (1916), and her pamphlet *Village Survey-Making* (1929), which encouraged country schools to hunt out information about the past and present of their localities.

Selfless, retiring, and personally somewhat disorganized, Butler founded her influence on friendships. Her determination sometimes degenerated into obstinacy, but her gentle wit and bright eyes softened the impact, and she came to seem the embodiment of practical Christianity. Subtly combining progressive and conservative attitudes, she was cautious in her feminism and rather regretted her college's gradual evolution into an ordinary undergraduate college. She remained active and intellectually alert until well into her eighties, a much-loved figure who was often seen cycling about north Oxford on her many errands, still pursuing her Edwardian aim of using friendly personal contact to draw together paid and voluntary welfare workers, town and gown, and rich and poor. She died in Oxford on 19 May 1982.

BRIAN HARRISON, *rev.*

Sources *The Times* (26 May 1982) • B. Harrison, 'Miss Butler's Oxford Survey', *Traditions of social policy: essays in honour of Violet Butler*, ed. A. H. Halsey (1976) • private information (1993, 2004) • personal knowledge (2004)

Wealth at death £126,693: probate, 24 Aug 1982, *CGPLA Eng. & Wales*

Butler, Walter [*called* Ualtéir na bPaidrín, Walter of the Beads and Rosary], **eleventh earl of Ormond and fourth earl of Ossory** (1559–1633), nobleman, was born about Easter 1559, the second son of John Butler of Kilcash (*d.* 1570) and Catherine, daughter of Sir Cormac MacCarthy

Reagh. He emerged as heir to the Kilcash estate in co. Tipperary some time before September 1576, after the death without issue of his elder brother, James (alive May 1570). He was a ward of his uncle Thomas *Butler, tenth earl of Ormond and third earl of Ossory, until he reached the legal age of maturity at Easter 1580, when Kilcash was restored to him. About 1584 he married Ellen (*d.* 1631), daughter of Edmund Butler, second Viscount Mountgarret, with whom he had three sons and nine daughters. His stock grew steadily as Earl Thomas aged, and following the outbreak of the Nine Years' War he came into his own, displaying his loyalty to the crown as several senior claimants to the earldom of Ormond either died or joined Tyrone in revolt. He received a knee wound fighting against rebel Burkes in 1599, and early in 1600 he helped Ormond to force Tyrone out of the south, services that earned him a knighthood.

When the war ended, however, Butler's devotion to Catholicism (for which he earned the name Walter of the Beads and Rosary) brought him into conflict with the royal authorities. His participation in religious agitation in Kilkenny in 1603 was noted, to be recalled ten years later following his involvement in disturbances at the Irish parliament. The government became alarmed in December 1613 when the unexpected death of Viscount Tulleophelim made him heir to the earldom of Ormond; it was deemed desirable to frustrate his promotion. His protestant cousin Elizabeth Butler, only living legitimate child of Earl Thomas, and Tulleophelim's widow, was encouraged to advance a speculative claim to the Ormond estate as heir, although the lands of the earldom were entailed in the male line. Her claim aroused King James's interest. Late in 1614, having given Walter a cool reception at Whitehall earlier in the year, the king arranged her marriage to her second husband, the Scottish courtier Sir Richard Preston, Lord Dingwall and future earl of Desmond. Under Preston's guidance, and following her father's death and Walter's succession to the title (November 1614), Elizabeth's challenge pressed ahead. In subsequent judicial inquiries no legal cause was found by which to disinherit Earl Walter, but at the suggestion of George Villiers, marquess of Buckingham, Preston's patron, the king agreed to decide the case by arbitration. On 3 October 1618 the main bulk of the Ormond lands was awarded to Elizabeth. Ormond protested and refused to abide by the award, for which he was imprisoned without trial in the Fleet in June 1619. He remained under confinement until 1625, during which time his remaining lands were sequestered into crown hands (February to June 1621), his liberty of Tipperary was seized by writ of *quo warranto* (May 1621), his right to the prisage of wines in Ireland was forfeited (June 1621), and by a legal fiction he lost the custody of his grandson and heir, and eventual successor, James Butler, future duke of Ormond (December 1621). Throughout these proceedings he was denied a defence, and some of his trustees and servants were temporarily incarcerated; an impostor from Galway even attempted to lay claim to his earldom. Moreover, because of the sequestration of his estate, he received no income from his lands, and he was forced to depend on the charity of supporters and to borrow from city merchants in order to meet his prison expenses.

On 18 March 1625, nine days before King James died, Ormond finally submitted to the terms of the 1618 arbitration, thus facilitating a settlement with James's successor, Charles I. His eventual release coincided with Charles's abortive attempt to negotiate a reduction of Irish Catholic grievances. In 1629 Earl Walter reunited the Ormond lands by arranging his grandson's marriage to the Preston heir. The same year, having returned home permanently, he set about frustrating the government's plan to proceed with a plantation in the baronies of Upper and Lower Ormond in co. Tipperary by retaining possession of crucial title deeds to the area. He died on 18 February 1633 and was buried in the Ormond family tomb in St Canice's Cathedral, Kilkenny, bequeathing to his successor an estate heavily encumbered with debt.

DAVID EDWARDS

Sources D. Edwards, 'The Ormond lordship in county Kilkenny, 1515–1642', PhD diss., TCD, 1998 • NL Ire., Ormond MSS • Bodl. Oxf., MSS Carte • *Journal of the Association for the Preservation of the Memorials of the Dead, Ireland*, 7 (1907–9) [funeral] • E. Curtis, ed., *Calendar of Ormond deeds*, 6 vols., IMC (1932–43), vols. 5–6 • LPL, MSS 626, 635 [Carew's Irish genealogies, *c.* 1600] • PRO, state papers, Ireland • CKS, Sackville MSS, Cranfield Irish papers • solved chancery pleadings, NA Ire. • W. F. Butler, 'The descendants of James, 9th earl of Ormond', *Journal of the Royal Society of Antiquaries of Ireland*, 6th ser., 19 (1929) • V. Treadwell, *Buckingham and Ireland, 1616–28: a study in Anglo-Irish politics* (1998) • TCD, Ormond MS 10724 • GEC, *Peerage*

Archives NL Ire., collection

Wealth at death left debts of £45,000: Edwards, 'Ormond lordship', 110–22

Butler, Walter, Count Butler in the nobility of the Holy Roman empire (*d.* **1634**), army officer in the imperial service, was probably born in Roscrea, Tipperary, the second son of Peter Butler of Roscrea, and his wife Catherine De Burgo. His father's family were distant relatives of the dukes of Ormond. Nothing is known of his childhood, but by 1620 he was on the continent and he fought, presumably on the side of the victorious imperialist army, at the battle of White Mountain, outside Prague, on 8 November. Henceforth, his life remains mysterious until 1631, when he became a lieutenant-colonel in his relative Colonel James Butler's regiment then serving in Poland. Walter Butler is one of at least six men by the name of Butler who served in Polish or imperial regiments during the Thirty Years' War (1618–48).

In April 1631 Walter Butler accompanied James *en route* from Poland to the besieged town of Frankfurt an der Oder, and there he took command of a body of troops, perhaps for the first time, for the course of a battle in which at least four other Irish lieutenant-colonels were killed. The encounter proved disastrous for the imperialists, and Butler, having been shot in the arm and wounded by a pike to his thigh, was captured by the Swedes. He was brought on a stretcher to the Swedish king, Gustav Adolf, who is thought to have asked if he were the younger or the elder of the two, by-now-famous, Butler relatives. When Walter replied that he was the younger, Gustav Adolf is said to have replied: 'If you had been the older one, my royal right hand would have struck you' (Fitzsimon, 28). Following this, Butler appears to have been held for at least six months and perhaps for as much as eight months in Swedish captivity.

By 1632 Butler was with General Albrecht von Wallenstein's imperialist army on the Silesian–Bohemian border and was given military control of the general's own duchy of Sagan, while as early as January of that year he was awarded for this purpose the much fought-over Silesian district of Jägerndorf as his winter quarters, marrying there a local countess, Anna Maria von Dohna. After receiving a new contract on 11 February he returned to Poland with the aim of recruiting troops, on top of the 1000 dragoons he appears to have already commanded in Bohemia (a regiment which subsequently captured twelve enemy standards for the imperialists from the Saxon Colonel von Starschettel at Eger). He also established regular correspondence with and made visits to the Irish Franciscan community in Prague, through which he was to meet the Revd Patrick Taaffe, who soon became his regimental chaplain.

By early 1633 Butler's lofty reputation in the imperial military ranks was confirmed in his appointment as colonel of the 'Butler regiment', though little more is heard of him until 27 December that year, when he wrote to the soon-to-become imperial field marshal, Ottavio Piccolomini, expressing his loyalty to the imperial cause, while also providing the first evidence of a veiled criticism of Wallenstein's actions. Certainly, by early 1634, he must have been aware of the widespread dissatisfaction with the general, who was reported to be secretly negotiating with the enemy powers, without the emperor's consent, towards mysterious and treasonable ends. In February Butler was based at Kladrau, west Bohemia, the main route to the lands of the upper Palatinate, where he led nine companies of dragoons and infantry and 900 cavalry. He was ordered by the generalissimo to march with his soldiers to Prague, where negotiations were planned. Butler fearfully reported to Taaffe that he expected to meet with a battle and with his death there, since, by 18 February, Emperor Ferdinand II had called for Wallenstein's capture 'dead or alive' in response to the so-called 'Pilsen reverse', in which most of the leading officers had backed down from a recent token pledge of support for him. When the Prague garrison declared its loyalty to the emperor and his general Matthias Gallas, Wallenstein was left with no other choice than to alter his plans and move himself and his few remaining loyal troops through the Bohemian frontier town of Eger to Saxony.

On 22 February, Butler and his regiment, still heading towards Prague, met Wallenstein and his band of allies at Mies, 4 miles from Pilsen in west Bohemia. He was ordered to spend the night there, away from his troops. The next morning Butler's soldiers joined Wallenstein's, while he dispatched Taaffe to Piccolomini. The message was that the Irishman's loyalty still lay with the emperor, despite present appearances which seemed to suggest the contrary. Indeed Butler sat in the general's coach for at least part of the journey to Eger on 24 February, where he was made privy to Wallenstein's grievances and was promised at first hand, as reward for his assumed loyalty, two regiments and a sum of money to recruit troops in the British Isles. Such a pledge was, understandably, tempting for Butler and he gave assurance, perhaps sincerely, of his continuing trustworthiness as an unwavering ally to the general. On arrival at Eger his troops remained outside the town walls while he and Wallenstein were appointed their quarters separately. The sick general immediately retired to his appointed residence in the burgomaster's house while Butler awaited Taaffe, who was carrying with him the news from Vienna that, if he wished to remain in favour with the emperor, he should arrange the immediate delivery of the 'traitor'. However, this message did not arrive in time to influence the course of that evening's actions which had been planned, not by Butler, but by two little-known Scots, who chose to act decisively on imperial orders. They were Lieutenant-Colonel John Gordon, commander of the Trčka regiment which controlled the Eger garrison, and his second in command, Major Walter Leslie.

Butler appears to have been acquainted with Gordon beforehand, but it seems possible that until the three met that day he had no intention of joining a plot to murder the general who had promised him so much. If so, he appears to have been persuaded with remarkable speed. After holding initial discussions, the well-connected Leslie quickly convinced the others that Wallenstein and his four remaining important allies would have to be killed.

On the afternoon of 25 February 1634 a number of Butler's officers—including the Irishmen Deveroux, Burke, and Geraldine and perhaps a hundred or so soldiers—were let into the town. Meanwhile rumours had spread that the Swedish army was approaching, which may have further pushed the three conspirators towards an immediate resolution. A banquet was announced, to be held at Gordon's lodgings in the town castle, an invitation which Wallenstein's last confidants, Trčka, Ilow, Kinský, and Neumann, gratefully accepted. During the course of the festivities some Irish dragoons waiting outside the dining-hall were given the signal to enter, and all four men were killed. Separately, Deveroux was sent to Wallenstein's residence and, finding him in his bedclothes, stabbed him repeatedly. His corpse was dumped with the others at the castle. The next day Butler revealed Wallenstein's supposedly disloyal intentions to the stunned townspeople and successfully demanded that they and his own regiment swear loyalty to the imperial cause.

Dispatches were sent to the surprised emperor in Vienna with the news: Leslie with Gordon's report and the Irishman Denis MacDonnell with that of Butler, while Duke Francis Albert of Saxe-Launburg, who had been sent from Saxony to meet the exile-bound general, was quickly arrested at the Bohemian border. It is possible that Leslie, being the first to arrive at court, was thus considered the instigator of these loyal actions, since Butler had to press for imperial rewards, even threatening to switch to Polish service if prizes did not come his way, as they quickly did in the form of lavish Bohemian estates and noble titles for Gordon, Leslie, and all the others involved. However, Butler's written requests eventually proved fruitful and besides the titles of count of the Holy Roman empire and imperial chamberlain, the award of a golden chain, and his promotion to the position of regimental 'proprietor' or *inhaber*, he was awarded a large property—Wallenstein's estate in north-west Bohemia at Hirschberg, where the general had kept his library. This property, valued at about 225,000 gulden, along with a separate castle and land at Neuperstein, appears to have henceforth remained in the hands of Butler relatives, until 1722, when they sold their Czech property and moved to Bavaria, remaining there as the Butler-Clonebough-Haimhausen family. It seems that previous sources may be mistaken in recording that Butler was given the entirety of Wallenstein's substantial Friedberg estate.

Butler's continuing military career further confirms his loyalty to the imperial cause, particularly his prominent role at the decisive Spanish-imperial victory of the cardinal-infante and future king of Hungary, Ferdinand III, over the Swedes at Nördlingen on 7 September, for which, according to Thomas Carve, he was widely praised. He also fought elsewhere in Germany, and was at the siege of Regensburg that autumn, before being sent, along with eight regiments, to assault the enemy-held strongholds of Aurach and Schorndorf, a task in which they appear to have been successful. It was at the latter place where he died, still childless, on 25 December 1634, receiving the last sacraments in the presence of Taaffe, his chaplain, and another Irish veteran of Eger, Walter Deveroux. In his will Butler left the significant sum of 30,000 florins towards the construction of the Irish Franciscan abbey in Prague and the support of the community's missionary efforts elsewhere. It is not clear whether the family of his widow, Countess Anna Maria, after arranging for Butler's body to be transferred to Bohemia for burial, initially received control of his Bohemian estates, or if they fell directly, through prior arrangement, into the hands of Richard Butler, a soldier in Spanish service and the son of the count's nephew, Thomas Butler-Clonebough. After 1666, though, ownership appears to have been passed on to Richard's brother Edmund Powelston, who was officially to take up residence in Bohemia as the second Count Butler in 1681.

Meanwhile, following Butler's death, regimental command was handed to Walter Deveroux, who had acquired considerable property himself after the events at Eger in February 1634, with a fellow Irish veteran of that time, Robert Geraldine, now appointed his second in command. After Deveroux's death in 1639 the regiment remained in Irish hands, falling into the proprietorship of Butler's earlier representative at Vienna, Denis MacDonnell.

DAVID WORTHINGTON

Sources F. H. Schubert, 'Butler, Walter, Graf von', *Neue deutsche Biographie*, ed. Otto, Graf zu Stolberg-Wernigerode (Berlin, 1953–) • E. Schmidhofer, 'Das irische, schottische und englische Element im kaiserlichen Heer', PhD diss., University of Vienna, 1971 • *Thomae Carve, Tipperariensis … cum historia facta Butleri, Gordon, Lesley et aliorum*, ed. M. Kerney (1859) • R. D. Fitzsimon, 'Irish swordsmen in the imperial service of the Thirty Years War', *Irish Sword*, 9 (1969–70), 22–31 • *DNB* • T. M. Barker, *Army, aristocracy, monarchy* (1982) • H. von Srbik, *Wallenstein's Ende* (1952) • G. Mann, *Wallenstein* (1971), 242–4, 825–44 • B. Jennings, 'The Irish Franciscans in Prague', *Studies: an Irish Quarterly Review*, 28 (1939), 210–22

Archives Österreichisches Staatsarchiv, Vienna, Kriegsarchiv, Feld Akten • Mestní Archiv, Cheb, Czech Republic

Wealth at death 225,000 gulden—Hirschberg estate in April 1634: Mann, *Wallenstein*, 867

Butler, Walter (1752–1781), army officer in America, was born in Butlersbury (now Fonda), New York, the son of John *Butler (1728–1796), an army officer and official in the British department of Indian affairs, and his wife, Catherine Bratt. Little is known of his early life, but having been brought up in his father's well-to-do household he would have enjoyed the maximum comforts allowed by New York frontier life; he would also have been exposed to the Native Americans who populated his native Mohawk valley and dealt with his father. In the early 1770s he was sent to Albany to study law, and in 1775 he was admitted to the New York bar. However, his legal skills proved of little use in the difficult struggle that lay ahead.

The same year that he was admitted to the bar, Butler and his father, prominent declared loyalists, were forced to flee to Montreal. The rest of the family was rounded up and held by force in Albany. Butler, like most of the young loyalists of the New York frontier, sought to avenge his losses through service in the king's army. In autumn 1775 he was with the combined white and Native American force that captured Ethan Allen near Montreal. If British success on the middle colonies' frontier was to be lasting, however, the full co-operation of the region's Native Americans, most notably the powerful Iroquois confederacy, was essential. Unfortunately, Britain's department of Indian affairs had been thrown into disarray in the previous year with the death of its northern superintendent, Sir William Johnson, who for two decades dominated the scene and placed the affection of the Iroquois above all else. A group of his closest allies and heirs soon departed for England to secure Sir William's position and power. In their absence Butler's father, who was something of a rival to the group, was named acting superintendent. Walter, however, accompanied the party to England. The reasons for his journey are unclear, as there was no love lost between the Butlers and Johnson's heirs, particularly Joseph Brant, who was the brother of Sir William's Mohawk wife, Molly. Perhaps Butler was sent to ensure that the group did not ostracize the Butlers from any affection of the king. Nevertheless, Colonel Guy Johnson, Sir William's nephew, returned with the superintendency, and Butler returned as an ensign in the King's 8th regiment of foot.

Britain's strategy on the middle colonies' frontier was to conduct a series of annual raids with Native American support, which were intended to support the movement of the main armies and drain American patriot resources. This frontier saw some of the most brutal fighting of the conflict, as divided colonial and Native American communities turned on former neighbours, friends, and family members. Butler played an integral part in this. By summer 1777 he had risen to the rank of lieutenant and fought under Sir John Johnson, Sir William's son, in the assault on Fort Stanwix, located in Butler's native Mohawk valley. The siege of the fort failed, but not before the British force, dominated by loyalists from the region and Mohawk and Seneca braves (members of the Iroquois confederacy), attacked an American patriot relief column at Oriskany on 6 August. In the intense fighting that followed, the rebels lost several hundred men, many of whom were scalped, and the British lost a number of key Seneca war leaders. In the aftermath of the battle, a contingent of the British-led force broke away and avenged the loss of the Seneca by burning a village of the neutral Oneida (also a component nation of the Iroquois confederacy)—an action which plunged the already fragile confederacy into civil war.

Butler soon returned to the Mohawk valley on a recruiting campaign, but was captured and taken to Albany. Although he was declared a spy and given a death sentence, he escaped eight months later and fled to the British stronghold at Niagara. Meanwhile his father had been assigned the charge of raising a new corps of loyalists, aptly called Butler's rangers, who were to be used as special forces units on the New York frontier. They were expected to be highly mobile guerrilla fighters who spoke Native American languages and used native methods of wilderness warfare. Such skills were essential, as these men were expected to fight side by side with Native Americans. They took the scalps of the enemy dead and wounded; tortured captives; and even used the chilling war whoop of native warriors as their battle cry. As the major commandant of this force, John Butler could choose his officers, and so his recently returned son was made a captain.

Butler's most remembered service in the rangers was as the leader of the expedition in November 1778 against Cherry Valley, New York. In his command were 321 natives (mostly Seneca), 150 rangers, and 50 British regulars from the 8th regiment of foot. Butler ill-advisedly insulted and mistreated Joseph Brant, who, unlike Butler, had long since earned the respect of Native American war chiefs. Moreover, many of the whites in Brant's party refused to serve under the novice commander, which left Butler at the head of a force that generally wanted confidence in his abilities and wholly lacked respect for him. Unfortunately, Cherry Valley was defended by an equally incompetent force, which had ordered inhabitants to withdraw their possessions from the local fort and had billeted its officers in comfortable houses outside the fort's protection. Butler attacked on 11 November, sending a large body composed mostly of Seneca to deal with the officers in the houses and leading his most disciplined troops to assault the fort. In the chaos that followed, the natives and whites who had little respect for Butler's authority proceeded to pillage the settlement and massacre anyone, loyalist or patriot, who resisted. Despite Butler's pleas, when the force departed the next day the settlement had been destroyed, and thirty-two loyalist and patriot civilians, mostly women and children, lay dead. Only through the intervention of Brant and a handful of other respected men was an even worse atrocity prevented.

Butler vehemently rejected accusations that he could have prevented events at Cherry Valley, but his superiors nevertheless never put so large a force under his command again. He continued to participate in the raids along the frontier until 30 October 1781, when, covering the retreat of the British force, he was shot and scalped at West Canada Creek by an Oneida warrior serving with the American patriots. TROY O. BICKHAM

Sources E. Cruikshank, *The story of Butler's rangers and the settlement of Niagara* (1893); repr. (1975) • B. Graymont, *The Iroquois in the American Revolution* (1972) • C. G. Calloway, *The American Revolution in Indian country: crisis and diversity in Native American communities* (1995) • R. S. Allen, *His majesty's Indian allies: British Indian policy in defence of Canada, 1774–1815* (1992) • D. Ritcher, 'Butler, Walter', *ANB* • J. Potter, *The liberty we seek: loyalist ideology in colonial New York and Massachusetts* (1983)

Archives BL, Haldimand papers, Add. MSS 21661–21892 • PRO, Carleton papers, 30, vol. 55 • PRO, War Office papers, 28, vols. 1–10

Butler, Weeden (1742–1823), author and Church of England clergyman, was born at Margate, Kent, on 22 September 1742. He was articled to a solicitor in London, but left the legal profession for the church. He acted as amanuensis to the Magdalen House chaplain, William Dodd, from 1764 until Dodd's execution for fraud in 1777. In 1776 Butler had succeeded Dodd as morning preacher at Charlotte Street Chapel, Pimlico, London, and he officiated in this fashionable place of worship until 1814. In 1778 he was lecturer of St Clement, Eastcheap, and St Martin Orgar, and for more than forty years he was master of Cheyne Walk School in Chelsea. He also served as chaplain to the duke of Kent and the Queen's Volunteers.

In 1781 Butler began his eclectic literary career with *The Cheltenham Guide*, followed in 1797 by a life of George Stanhope, dean of Canterbury, and a life of Mark Hildesley, bishop of Sodor and Man. Butler also prepared editions of John Jostin's *Tracts, Philological, Critical and Miscellaneous* (1790) and Joseph Wilcocks's *Roman Conversations* (1792), in addition to which he left plays and verse in manuscript.

Butler married Anne, daughter of Isaac Louis Giberne; the couple's children included Weeden *Butler and George *Butler, later headmaster of Harrow School. In 1814 Butler retired to Gayton, Northamptonshire, where he acted as curate to his son Weeden until 1820, when ill health forced him to move first to the Isle of Wight, then Bristol, and finally, Greenhill, near Harrow, where he died on 14 July 1823.

THOMPSON COOPER, *rev.* PHILIP CARTER

Sources *GM*, 1st ser., 93/2 (1823), 182–4 • Nichols, *Lit. anecdotes* • Nichols, *Illustrations*

Archives BL, corresp. and papers, Add. MSS 16381, 16384, 16603, 19024–19025, 19682–19687, 27276, 27577–27578

Butler, Weeden (1772–1831), author, was born on 13 September 1772, at Pimlico, London, the eldest son of the

Revd Weeden *Butler (1742–1823), Church of England clergyman, and his wife, Anne, *née* Giberne. He was educated by his father until 1790 when he entered Sidney Sussex College, Cambridge, graduating BA in 1794 and MA in 1797. He published *Bagatelles, or, Miscellaneous Productions, Consisting of Original Poetry and Translations* in 1795, and also translated several works, including *Prospect of the political relations which subsist between the French republic and the Helvetic body* (1794) and *Zimao, the African* (1800 and 1807). On 26 August 1805 he married Annabella Dundas Oswald in Chislehurst, Kent. Exactly one year later, on 26 August 1806, they had a son, also named Weeden Butler. Of their other children, one more son and three daughters survived into adulthood.

In London, Butler became afternoon lecturer of Charlotte Street Chapel, Pimlico, and evening lecturer of Brompton in 1811, and he was presented to the rectory of Great Woolston, Buckinghamshire, in 1816. Having for nineteen years acted as classical assistant in his father's school, he became head of it on his father's retirement in 1814. He died at home in Cheyne Walk, Chelsea, on 28 June 1831.

THOMPSON COOPER, *rev.* M. CLARE LOUGHLIN-CHOW

Sources Nichols, *Illustrations* • *GM*, 1st ser., 101/1 (1831), 186 • [J. Watkins and F. Shoberl], *A biographical dictionary of the living authors of Great Britain and Ireland* (1816) • Venn, *Alum. Cant.* • will, PRO, PROB 11/1787, sig. 376 • *IGI*

Archives BL, corresp. and papers, Add. MSS 16381, 16384, 16603, 19024–19025, 19682–19687, 27276, 27577–27578

Butler, William (*d.* after **1416**), Franciscan friar and theologian, had become a regent master at Oxford by 1401, when he opposed in the schools the translation of the scriptures into English. He seems to have been elected provincial minister of the Franciscans on 3 May 1406 on the deposition of John Zouche, but, because of Zouche's temporary reinstatement, his appointment was reckoned from 1407; he resigned after his statutory six years in the post, was reappointed by Pope John XXIII, but may not have resumed office. Payments were made to him from the exchequer in May 1408 and in March 1411, but for unclear purposes. In 1416 he seems to have attended the Council of Constance. According to John Bale he was buried at Reading Priory.

Bale lists four works by Butler, two of them with incipits; the second of these, on papal indulgences, Bale saw at the Reading convent, but this has not been found. The other, of which Bale saw a copy, now lost, at the Queen's College, Oxford, was on translation into English; a copy of what is probably the same text, though the incipit cannot be checked since the opening is lost, survives in Oxford, Merton College, MS 68, fols. 202*r*a–204*v*b, where it is ascribed to Butler and dated 1401. Butler's determination was a contribution to the debate on the legitimacy of biblical translation that took place in Oxford in 1401; Richard Ullerston's defence of translation, dated and located in the same way, also survives. While Ullerston favoured translation, Butler considered that translation would foster an undue concern with the literal sense, and diminish the authority of the clergy; neither Butler nor Ullerston refers to the other's contribution to the debate, and neither identifies the proponents of translation as Lollards. Butler's work as it survives reflects a conservative view of the question, lacking the insight into the practice of translation shown by Ullerston's determination. His desire to restrict control of biblical text and exegesis to the clergy anticipates the spirit of Archbishop Arundel's *Constitutions* of 1407.

ANNE HUDSON

Sources A. G. Little, *The Grey friars in Oxford*, OHS, 20 (1892), 254–5 • A. G. Little, *Franciscan papers, lists, and documents* (1943), 199 • E. Déprez, *Études de diplomatique anglaise* (Paris, 1908), 29–30 • M. Deanesly, *The Lollard Bible* (1920), 401–18 • A. Hudson, 'The debate on Bible translation, Oxford 1401', *EngHR*, 90 (1975), 1–18 • *CClR*, *1409–13*, 442, 450 • Bale, *Cat.*, 1.536–7 • Bale, *Index*, 119

Archives Merton Oxf., MS 68, fols. 202*r*a–204*v*b

Butler, William (1535–1618), physician, was born in Ipswich, Suffolk; he possibly matriculated from Peterhouse, Cambridge, in 1558, becoming BA in 1561 and MA in 1564, and was probably incorporated in that degree at Oxford in 1563. He was also a fellow of Clare College, Cambridge. In October 1572 the University of Cambridge granted him a licence to practise physic. He was usually styled 'doctor', though he never took the degree of MD.

Butler acquired an outstanding reputation in his profession, although he became known for his eccentric manner and methods of treatment. He combined traditional Galenical with Paracelsian techniques, representing an intermediate stage in English medicine.

Butler came to royal attention about 1612, partly as a result of his cure of a parson whose wife had inadvertently overdosed him with opium. Butler revived him by putting him into the warm belly of a freshly killed cow. In October of that year he was summoned from Cambridge to attend Henry, prince of Wales, in his last illness. Seeing there was no hope, and not wanting to be associated with the prince's death, Butler had himself removed from the case. He is said to have been among those who suspected that the prince had been poisoned. In November 1614 Butler attended James I at Newmarket for a hunting injury, and when the king was at Cambridge in May 1615 he visited Butler and stayed with him nearly an hour.

Butler lived in the house of John *Crane (1570/71–1652), a celebrated apothecary of Cambridge. It seems likely that they had a long-term sexual relationship, as Butler certainly appears to have had homosexual inclinations. His friend John Aubrey (*Brief Lives*, 1, 1669) tells of Butler 'taking a fancy to' a serving man at an inn. Aubrey also relates how Crane's maid Nell would regularly help Butler stumble home from the local tavern at night.

Many anecdotes are recorded of Butler's unusual methods of therapy. Aubrey writes:

> The Dr. lyeing at the Savoy in London, next the water side where was a balcony look't into the Thames, a patient came to him that was grievously tormented with an ague. The Dr. orders a boate to be in readinesse under his windowe, and discoursed with the patient (a gent.) in the balcony, when on a signall given, 2 or 3 lusty fellowes came behind the gent. and threw him a matter of 20 feete into the Thames. This surprize absolutely cured him. (*Brief Lives*, vol. 1)

Butler died at Cambridge on 29 January 1618, and was

William Butler (1535–1618), by Simon de Passe, 1620

buried there in Great St Mary's Church: on the south side of its chancel there is a mural monument with his bust and a Latin inscription in which he is termed the first among medical men of the time. He was also commemorated by a pub sign at Ye Olde Dr Butler's Head near Guildhall in London, and a sort of ale called Dr Butler's.

Butler left his estate to John Crane, and he was also a benefactor to Clare College, to which he bequeathed many of his books and £260 for the purchase of a gold communion cup. Thirty-five years after his death quacks still made use of his reputation, claiming to have learned their recipes from him.

THOMPSON COOPER, *rev.* SARAH BAKEWELL

Sources *Brief lives, chiefly of contemporaries, set down by John Aubrey, between the years 1669 and 1696*, ed. A. Clark, 1 (1898), 138–43 • J. Boss, 'William Butler (1535–1618): further evidence on a physician between two ages', *Medical History*, 21 (1977), 434–45 • V. Nutton, 'Dr Butler revisited', *Medical History*, 22 (1978), 417–30 • B. Hill, '"The Aesculapius of our age", William Butler, MA (1535–1618)', *The Practitioner*, 210 (1973), 297–301 • R. Thurdlow, 'William Butler, physician extraordinary', *Manchester Medical Gazette*, 46 (1967), 26–8 • Venn, *Alum. Cant.* • Foster, *Alum. Oxon.* • Fuller, *Worthies* (1811), 2.340 • J. Aikin, *Biographical memoirs of medicine in Great Britain: from the revival of literature to the time of Harvey* (1780), 186 • W. Wadd, *Nugae chirurgicae, or, A biographical miscellany* (1824), 31 • *Joannis Lelandi antiquarii de rebus Britannicis collectanea*, ed. T. Hearne, [3rd edn], 6 vols. (1774), vol. 5, p. 197 • J. Granger, *A biographical history of England from Egbert the Great to the revolution*, 5th edn, 2 (1824), 119

Archives Clare College, Cambridge, papers | BL, medical collections and receipts, Sloane MSS 1991, 1087, 1664, 3329, 3756

Likenesses S. de Passe, engraving, 1620, Wellcome L. • S. de Passe, line print, 1620, BM, NPG [*see illus.*] • line engraving, 1620 (after S. de Passe), BM, NPG • bust on mural monument, Great St Mary's, Cambridge • engraving, Wellcome L. • pencil drawing, Wellcome L.

Butler, William Archer (1814?–1848), philosopher, was born of an old and respectable family at Annerville, near Clonmel, co. Tipperary. His father was a member of the established church of Ireland, his mother a Roman Catholic. Through her influence the boy was baptized and educated as a member of the church to which she belonged. While Butler was a child his parents removed to Garnavilla, on the River Suir, about 2 miles from the town of Cahir. The beautiful landscape made a deep impression on his feelings and imagination—an impression which lived in his verse. At nine years old he became a schoolboy at the endowed school of Clonmel. He was a modest, retiring boy, a favourite with the master, and popular with his companions. At school he was an eager, discursive reader, already attracted by metaphysical study, but he also devoted much of his leisure time to poetry and to music, in which he acquired considerable skill. He especially distinguished himself by his public speaking for 'oratory' exhibitions. While at Clonmel, about two years before entering college, Butler passed over from the Roman Catholic to the established church. It is said that his confessor's dealings with his conscience led him to examine the grounds of his creed, and that he found his own way by study and meditation from his early to his later faith.

On entering Trinity College, Dublin, Butler was quickly recognized as a youth of bright intellect, generous sympathies, and broad culture. His prize compositions in prose and verse attracted the attention of the heads of the college, and while still an undergraduate he contributed a considerable body of writings—poems and essays, critical, historical, and speculative—to the *Dublin University Review*. In the debates of the college historical society he took a leading part, and in 1835 delivered, as auditor of the society, an address which was printed. The first examination for the newly instituted moderatorship in logic and ethics took place in November 1834 and Butler graduated in first place. Having thus obtained with honours his BA degree, he continued for two years in residence as a scholar. His friends thought he was destined for the bar, but his tastes and habits were those of a student and a man of letters.

By the exertions of the provost, Bartholomew Lloyd, a professorship of moral philosophy was founded in 1837, and Butler was at once appointed to the chair. At the same time, having been ordained a clergyman of the Church of Ireland, he was presented by the board of Trinity College to the prebend of Clondehorka, in the diocese of Raphoe, Donegal, where he resided, except when his professorial duties required his presence at the university. 'Amongst a large and humble flock of nearly two thousand, he was the most indefatigable of pastors' (Woodward, xxiv). In 1842 he was re-elected to the chair of moral philosophy, and promoted to the rectory of Raymoghy, in the same diocese as Clondehorka. His sermon *Primitive Church Principles not Inconsistent with Universal Christian Sympathy* (1842), preached at the visitation of the united dioceses of Derry and Raphoe in 1842, was published at the request of the bishop and clergy.

Butler's continuing interest in poetry was demonstrated by the publication of his memoir of Felicia Hemans, prefixed to her *National Lyrics and Songs for Music* (1839), and in 1844, on a visit to the Lake District, he made the acquaintance of Wordsworth. It was on a walk to Loughrigg Fells, in which Wordsworth was accompanied by Butler, Archdeacon Hare, and Sir William Rowan Hamilton, that the poet observed the daisy shadow on a stone, which he celebrated in the poem beginning 'So fair, so sweet, withal so sensitive'. In 1845 the Roman Catholic controversy occupied Butler, and beginning in December of that year, he contributed to the *Irish Ecclesiastical Gazette* a series of 'Letters on Mr. Newman's theory of development', collected after his death into one volume (*Letters on the Development of Christian Doctrine*, 1850). During the Irish famine of 1846–7 Butler's exertions were untiring: 'literature, philosophy, and divinity were all postponed to the labours of relieving officer to his parish.' During the closing months of 1847 and the first six months of the following year, Butler was engaged in preparation for a work on faith, and collected with this object a vast mass of theological material; but the work was never to be completed. On Trinity Sunday 1848 he preached the ordination sermon in the church of Dunboe; five days later, on his way home, he was stricken with typhoid fever. On 5 July 1848 he died at Raphoe. He was buried in the churchyard of his own parish.

Butler's lectures as professor (published posthumously in 1856) display a thorough knowledge of Plato, an intelligent approach towards Berkeley, familiarity with the ideas of Kant, and some awareness of Hegel. In his lectures on Plato, perhaps the most important thought is that the Platonic idea was no mere mistaken form of abstract notion, but was Plato's mode of expressing the fact that there is an objective element in perception. Despite his eloquent style and impressive delivery, his lectures were of limited impact. The terms of his professorship did not require him to act as an examiner in philosophy, and students therefore lacked an incentive to attend. The chair remained an uninfluential one until the appointment of Thomas Maguire in 1882. Two volumes of Butler's *Sermons Doctrinal and Practical* were published (1849 and 1856) and reveal the same eloquence as that which characterized his lectures, coupled with an adaptability which enabled him to appeal as much to his rural parishioners as he did to a university audience.

EDWARD DOWDEN, *rev.* C. A. CREFFIELD

Sources T. Woodward, 'Memoir', in W. A. Butler, *Sermons doctrinal and practical* (1849) • R. B. MacDowell, *History of Trinity College Dublin* (1983) • J. T. Ball, *Dublin University Review* (May 1842) • *Dublin University Review* (July 1849)

Archives NL Ire., corresp., diary, and MSS

Likenesses J. Kirkwood, etching, pubd 1842 (after C. Grey), NG Ire. • C. Grey, lithograph, NPG

Butler, Sir William Francis (1838–1910), army officer and author, was born on 31 October 1838 at Ballyslateen, Suirville, co. Tipperary, the seventh child of Richard and Ellen Butler, who were Roman Catholics. Although descended from the earls of Ormond, the family were small landowners and suffered particularly through the famine of 1846–7, which made a lasting impression on Butler himself. His childhood memories also included witnessing evictions and being hoisted onto the shoulders of Daniel O'Connell.

Education and early career Butler's education began at a Jesuit school in Tullabeg, King's county, in 1847 but this was interrupted by his mother's death two years later, and it was some time before the family finances improved sufficiently to send him to Dr James Quinn's school in Dublin.

Watching the frequent departures of British regiments from Dublin during the Crimean War and later reading reports of the Indian mutiny appear to have fuelled Butler's desire for a military career, and he was directly commissioned as an ensign in the 69th foot without purchase on 17 September 1858 on the recommendation of a distant relative, Sir Richard Doherty. After two years in garrison depot at Fermoy, Butler joined the regiment in Burma and served with it there and at Madras. One leave took him to Vellore, where he was instrumental in erecting a monument to those of the 69th killed during the 1806 mutiny. Subsequently his interest in the regiment's past was to bear fruit in *A Narrative of the Historical Events Connected with the 69th Regiment*, published in 1870. A visit to St Helena on the voyage back to Britain in 1864 similarly stimulated an interest in Napoleon, and at his death Butler was to leave an unpublished manuscript on Napoleon's captivity.

Regimental service continued at Gosport and Aldershot, promotion to lieutenant having come on 17 November 1863. In 1866 the 69th went to Guernsey, enabling Butler to make the acquaintance of Victor Hugo. There followed a short period at the Curragh before the threat of Fenian raids from the United States saw the regiment embarked for Canada in August 1867. Inspired by the novels of Fenimore Cooper, Butler spent his first leave travelling the American frontier, and in the spring of 1868 replaced Lieutenant Redvers Buller as the inspecting officer of outposts on the Canadian frontier. Butler engaged in some frontier land speculation, as he was considering leaving the army rather than being purchased over in his regiment. He returned home on leave in September 1869 partly to raise the money required for the investment, and returned to Canada after his father's death in March 1870.

The Red River campaign There appeared little prospect of military advancement, but just before leaving Ireland, Butler had learned that Colonel Garnet Wolseley, whom he had briefly met in Montreal, was organizing an expedition to overthrow a provisional government established by *métis* on the Red River. Butler's celebrated telegram to Wolseley, 'Remember Butler, 69th Regiment', resulted in his being charged with an extended reconnaissance mission to the Red River settlements by way of the United States, involving a descent of the river to Lake Winnipeg. At some personal risk, Butler met the *métis* leader, Louis Riel, at Fort Garry in July, and then traversed some 400 miles of wilderness in twelve days to meet Wolseley. Riel had fled when Butler and the expedition returned to Fort Garry, but Butler remained there after the troops withdrew and undertook a new mission in October to assess the situation in Saskatchewan. Returning to Fort Garry in February 1871, he had accomplished a winter journey of over 2700 miles. His report to the lieutenant-governor of Manitoba recommended the establishment of a special force to keep law and order in the Northwest Territories, the North-West Mounted Police emerging two years later. Butler returned to England and, after visiting France in the latter stages of the Franco-Prussian War, eventually secured a captaincy in an unattached (half-pay) company on 13 April 1872. Butler's earlier land speculation had become fortuitously profitable with the discovery of oil, and he returned to the Canadian north-west, this time navigating the Athabasca, Peace, and Fraser rivers. Tall, strong, energetic, and resourceful, Butler was ideally equipped for exploration, and his literary talents also found full scope in describing his exploits—*The Great Lone Land* (1872) and its sequel, *The Wild North Land* (1873), becoming classic travel narratives.

Asante Returning to Ottawa from the north-west in August 1873, Butler discovered that Wolseley was now to lead an expedition to the Asante kingdom. Another telegram was dispatched and, on reaching England, Butler found orders to follow Wolseley to Asante. Wolseley not only had the gift of recognizing ability but also of fitting individuals into roles within the emerging *Wolseley ring appropriate to that ability. Again, Butler acted on his own initiative by going from Accra to the kingdom of Akim, and leading its fighting men on a parallel course to that of Wolseley from Cape Coast Castle towards the Asante capital at Kumasi. Arriving at Accra in October 1873, Butler had persuaded the Akim chieftains to advance within 20 miles of Kumasi, but his force deserted near to the Asante army Butler hoped to intercept. Wracked with near-fatal fever, Butler was invalided home and spent two months recovering at Netley Hospital. For his services he was promoted major on 1 April 1874 and received the CB. His account of the campaign, *Akim-foo: the Story of a Failure*, was published in 1875.

Africa and marriage Continuing his convalescence in Ireland, Butler was summoned in February 1875 to join Wolseley, who was going to Natal as governor and high commissioner to work towards South African confederation. Butler became protector of (Indian) immigrants and a member of the legislative council, and undertook missions to Bloemfontein, Kimberley, and Basutoland. On returning to England in October 1875 he was appointed deputy assistant quartermaster-general at the War Office, where he remained until February 1879, when he was sent back to South Africa as assistant adjutant-general on lines of communication at Durban during the Anglo-Zulu War.

Butler married on 11 June 1877 a fellow Roman Catholic, Elizabeth Southerden Thompson [*see* Butler, Elizabeth Southerden, Lady Butler], the military painter. They had three sons and three daughters, one of whom died in infancy. Elizabeth's choice of subject, often reflecting her husband's views in depicting less celebratory imperial incidents and controversial Irish scenes such as that in *Evicted*, contributed to a decrease in her popularity. Butler was a more authoritarian husband and father than his radical sympathies for the underdog might suggest.

Butler received a brevet lieutenant-colonelcy on 21 April 1880 for his South African services and he was considered as a possible private secretary to the new viceroy, Lord Ripon, but Gladstone apparently considered that a Roman Catholic viceroy was 'sufficiently experimental' (*Autobiography*, 215). Butler instead became assistant adjutant-general in the western district at Devonport. He held the post from 1 July 1880 until August 1884, with the exception of three months from August to October 1882 when he joined Wolseley's staff in Egypt as assistant adjutant and quartermaster-general, being present at Tell al-Kebir. Butler did not believe the campaign to be justified, and he protested against the possible execution of the Egyptian nationalist leader, Arabi Pasha. This did not damage his career, and he was made aide-de-camp to the queen with the rank of colonel on 18 November 1882. He published anonymously in 1882 *The Invasion of England*, in the popular genre of purposive future-war fiction pioneered by G. T. Chesney's *Battle of Dorking*.

Two years later Butler was again summoned by Wolseley for the expedition to relieve Gordon at Khartoum. Butler had met Gordon briefly in 1876 and greatly admired him. Consulted by Wolseley on the possibility of ascending the Nile in boats in the manner of the Red River campaign, Butler was charged in August 1884 with the provision of 400 boats, to be manned in Egypt by Canadian voyageurs. Butler and the boats—later increased to 800—arrived in September, and for the next three months he toiled to get boats, men, and supplies up the cataracts. It was an arduous task and the relationship between Wolseley and Butler deteriorated. It became more difficult with each campaign for Wolseley to find an adequate role for each of his ring as their individual seniority and reputation advanced. Butler had always worked best alone, and not only resented Herbert Stewart's preferment in a field command but also felt himself excluded by Buller, acting as Wolseley's chief of staff. Wolseley professed to find Butler's faults 'more amusing & less objectionable than the virtues of other men' (PRO, WO 147/8), but he was irritated by Butler's habit of predicting events only in hindsight and resolved not to re-employ one who 'does not pull well in a team' (Wolseley to his wife, 22 Oct 1884; Hove Central Library, Wolseley Collections, W/P 13/27). Having accomplished the task of passing his boats upriver, Butler joined

Wolseley at Korti and was attached to William Earle's river column in December 1884. He persuaded Earle to turn a Mahdist position at Kirbekan on 10 February 1885 rather than attacking it frontally, and when the expedition returned down the Nile he commanded rearguards at Meroe and Dongola.

Butler was given the local rank of brigadier-general on 1 July 1885 and by September, having been mentioned in dispatches, he was back at Wadi Halfa to command the force holding the Egyptian frontier. He repulsed a Mahdist attack at Koshe in December 1885 and that same month also commanded a brigade at Giniss, the last battle in which the British army fought in red coats. He continued to hold the frontier until his troops were replaced by Egyptians in May 1886 and he himself was invalided home in June. With no prospect of immediate re-employment, he spent the next two years in Brittany and Ireland. He was created KCB on 25 November 1886, but this was somewhat overshadowed by his being cited as a co-respondent of Lady Colin Campbell, a friend of his wife, in the sensational 1886 divorce action brought by her husband. There was little evidence that Butler was guilty of impropriety, but he appeared so from his refusal to take the witness stand during the hearings in November and December, for which he was criticized by the jury and the press.

While unemployed Butler completed his account of the Gordon expedition, *The Campaign of the Cataracts* and *Charles George Gordon*, both published in 1887. He was recalled to work on an inquiry into the army ordnance department, but the report he drafted was judged so offensive to the War Office civil authorities that it was suppressed, and his only employment in 1889 was to negotiate the purchase of sites for the new defences of London. However, in February 1890 he was given the Alexandria command, being promoted major-general on 7 December 1892 and moved to command a brigade at Aldershot on 11 November 1893. Transfer to south-east district at Dover followed on 24 February 1896.

To reach high military rank as an Irish Catholic nationalist was unusual, but it was the more so given the sympathy Butler showed for the crown's opponents in many of his campaigns: he later wrote of his regret that 'the majority of our recent wars should have had their origins in purely financial interests or sordid Stock Exchange ambitions' (*Autobiography*, 349). Especially critical of the Egyptian expedition in 1882, he once declared the Gordon relief expedition the only justifiable campaign in which he had participated.

Commander in South Africa In October 1898 Butler was offered command of the troops in South Africa, and this proved the most controversial episode of his career. He was hostile to the tough, assertive policy of the high commissioner towards the Transvaal republic. In Alfred Milner's absence on leave, and without any guiding instructions, Butler temporarily assumed the appointment of high commissioner in November 1898, when Uitlander agitation was increased by the shooting of an Uitlander, Tom Edgar, by a Boer policeman. Sensing 'a colossal syndicate for the spread of systematic misrepresentation' (*Autobiography*, 400), Butler refused to forward the Uitlander petition demanding British intervention. After Milner's return in February 1899 Butler prepared a scheme of defence for the Cape and Natal; later he was accused of negligence in not forwarding it to the War Office until June. Butler's relationship with Milner deteriorated further when Butler made it clear that he would regard any war as a calamity, and Milner insisted the cabinet replace either Butler or himself. Aware of the feeling against him, Butler tendered his resignation on 4 July 1899. It was accepted on 9 August and Butler left South Africa on 23 August, switching commands with Frederick Forestier-Walker at western district.

Last years and death Butler remained at western district for six years, with the exception of four months at Aldershot in late 1900, being promoted lieutenant-general on 9 October 1900. His perceived sympathies for the Boers, however, resulted in his being forbidden to attend the queen on her visit to Bristol in December 1899, and in continuing press hostility. It was not until 1903 that the royal commission on the war in South Africa largely vindicated his pre-war warnings and his defensive preparations. Indeed, Lord Esher concluded that Butler would be an ideal quartermaster-general in a reformed War Office structure. Butler's radicalism precluded any such appointment, although he did preside over a committee on the disposal of war stores in South Africa in 1905. After retiring on 31 October 1905, Butler received the GCB in June 1906 and was called to the Irish privy council in 1909. Made a governor of the Royal Hibernian Military School, Butler was also a member of the senate of the National University of Ireland and a commissioner of the board of national education in Ireland.

In retirement Butler devoted himself to writing, and his works included *The Light of the West with some Wayside Thoughts* (1909) and his *Autobiography*, begun in 1909 but finally edited and published by his daughter in 1911. He was also keenly interested in the Gaelic League. He died of a heart condition on 7 June 1910 at Bansha Castle, co. Tipperary, where he had lived since retirement, and was buried at Killardrigh. IAN F. W. BECKETT

Sources *Sir William Butler: an autobiography*, ed. E. Butler (1911) • E. Butler, *An autobiography* (1922) • E. McCourt, *Remember Butler* (1967) • P. Usherwood and J. Spencer-Smith, *Lady Butler: battle artist, 1846–1933* (1987) • *The South African diaries of Sir Garnet Wolseley, 1875*, ed. A. Preston (1971) • *In relief of Gordon: Lord Wolseley's campaign journal of the Khartoum relief expedition, 1884–1885*, ed. A. Preston (1967) • J. H. Lehmann, *All Sir Garnet: a biography of Field-Marshal Lord Wolseley* (1964) • E. M. Spiers, *The late Victorian army, 1868–1902* (1992) • T. Pakenham, *The Boer War* (1979) • 'Report of the commissioners appointed to inquire into the military preparations … connected with the war in South Africa: minutes of evidence', *Parl. papers* (1904), 41.72–92, Cd 1791 [Butler's evidence 11 Feb 1903, and correspondence] • G. H. Fleming, *Victorian 'sex goddess': Lady Colin Campbell* (1989) • G. Wolseley, Sudan journal, PRO, WO 147/8 • Hove Central Library, Sussex, Wolseley MSS

Archives CUL, Royal Commonwealth Society Library, letters during Asante campaign • NA Canada, account of north-west Canada exploration • Royal Arch., army letters, W15/119, 120 | Hove Central Library, Sussex, letters to Viscount and Lady Wolseley • Killie Campbell Library, Natal, Wood MSS, KCM 89/9/22, 24, 44 • King's

Lond., Liddell Hart C., letter to Maurice • NL Ire., letters to Alice Stopford Green • NL Ire., letters to John Redmond
Likenesses E. Butler, portrait, 1899, priv. coll.; repro. in Butler, *Autobiography* • E. Butler, portrait (from fragment of *After the battle: arrival of Lord Wolseley and staff at the bridge of Tel-el-Kebir at the close of action*), priv. coll.; repro. in Usherwood and Spencer-Smith, *Lady Butler*, 87 and pl. 10 • Spy [L. Ward], cartoon, NPG; repro. in *VF* (9 Jan 1907)
Wealth at death £9031 15s. 9d.: probate, 29 July 1910, *CGPLA Ire.*

Butler, William John (1818–1894), dean of Lincoln, eldest son of John Laforey Butler, a member of the firm of H. and I. Johnstone, merchants and bankers, and his wife, Henrietta, daughter of Captain Robert Patrick, was born in Bryanston Street, Marylebone, Middlesex, on 10 February 1818. His mother was of Irish, and his father of Pembrokeshire, descent. After attending a school in Enfield, he became a queen's scholar at Westminster School in 1830, and was elected to Trinity College, Cambridge, in 1836. He won the Trinity essay in 1839, but, although a reasonably good classical scholar, was unable to give sufficient time to the tripos, and took a pass degree in 1840. He took his MA in 1844, and on 1 July 1847 was admitted *ad eundem* at Oxford (where he was made an honorary canon of Christ Church in 1872).

In 1841 Butler was ordained by Bishop Charles Sumner in Farnham Chapel to the curacy of Dogmersfield, under Charles Dyson. Here he first came under the influence of the Oxford Movement, meeting many of its leaders and beginning a regular correspondence with John Keble. In 1843 he moved to the curacy of Puttenham in Surrey, and in 1844 he accepted the perpetual curacy of Wareside, a poor outlying hamlet of Ware. On 29 July 1843 he had married Emma (*d.* 1894), daughter of George Henry Barnett, head of the banking firm of Barnett, Hoare & Co. They had several children, including Arthur John *Butler, Italian scholar and mountaineer.

In June 1846 Butler was appointed by the dean and chapter of Windsor to the vicarage of Wantage, with which place, as a parish priest, and as the founder (in 1850) and warden of the community sisterhood of St Mary the Virgin, his name is inseparably associated. He supervised the extension of its work throughout Britain and the empire.

Butler transformed Wantage into a model Tractarian parish. He restored the chancel in 1847, and by 1857 had removed the old pews and galleries from the nave and introduced a surpliced choir, which by 1864 numbered some forty men and boys singing the daily service. At the same time, through his large confirmation classes and the building of new schools, he increased the number of communicants: at Easter 1848 he had some ninety-one communicants, but by Easter 1860 this had already risen to 339. Wantage also became one of the most important Tractarian 'training parishes' for the clergy. Among the curates Butler trained were A. H. Mackonochie, G. Cosby White, M. H. Noel, V. S. S. Coles, Canon William Newbolt, and Henry Liddon. However, Butler did encounter much local opposition to his schemes, especially at the time of the 'papal aggression'; this came to a head at the rowdy 1852 Easter vestry which was packed by the local dissenters. But, with tact, diplomacy, and patience, Butler gradually achieved most of his objectives, never losing the support of his bishop, Samuel Wilberforce. Although a committed Tractarian, he always adhered to the Book of Common Prayer, and was careful never to push his parishioners further or faster than was prudent: in the 1860s he refused to introduce the new ritualist practices at Wantage, regarding them as inappropriate to an unsophisticated rural congregation.

Butler's role as the founder, and warden until death, of one of the earliest Anglican sisterhoods was of equal significance with his exemplary work in his parish. One, indeed, was the initial impetus for the other: hoping to gain assistants in his parochial work, he encouraged Elizabeth Crawford Lockhart, sister of William Lockhart, to establish a tiny community in spring 1847 in Wantage. Although Butler intended the community to concentrate its efforts on teaching young children, Elizabeth Lockhart felt drawn to penitentiary work among girls and women. But shortly after a home for penitents was opened in February 1850 the Gorham judgment impelled her to follow her brother into the Roman Catholic church; it was the joint efforts and guidance of Butler and Samuel Wilberforce which ensured the survival of the new sisterhood. In this community of educated women (unlike with his parishioners) Butler was able to give greater play to his modest interest in the details of ceremonial: practices such as reverences to the altar and the use of the sign of the cross were gradually introduced. His extensive knowledge of Catholic monasticism, past and present, was reflected in the community's rule, which—although largely Benedictine in character—showed influence of the rule of the Augustinian canonesses and of the spirituality of Francis of Sales. Under Butler's supervision the community expanded well beyond Wantage, eventually opening houses in India and Africa. It involved itself in a wide range of work: schools for girls were opened in Wantage and Abingdon, plainchant books were printed (the community was much interested in the development of liturgy), a centre for ecclesiastical needlework was established, and maternity homes were opened. The community also gained a body of associates, both clerical and female, among whom from 1868 the high-church novelist Charlotte Mary Yonge was numbered; it was Butler who persuaded her against testing her vocation as a sister with the community.

Upon the deposition of Bishop J. W. Colenso in 1864 by the Cape Town metropolitan synod, Butler was elected to replace him at a synod of the diocese of Natal; but the election was not approved by Archbishop Charles Longley, to whose views Butler loyally subordinated his own wishes. In 1874, however, he was elected to convocation as proctor for the clergy of Oxford. In 1880 he was nominated by Gladstone to a residentiary canonry at Worcester, where he did much to improve the internal government of the cathedral, and to further the establishment of a separate school for the choristers and of a girls' high school in the city. In 1885 Gladstone advanced him to the deanery of

Lincoln. Here he introduced an evening service in the nave and increased the celebrations of holy communion, but shortened Sunday services and reordered the sanctuary.

Butler was an early riser and was unsparing of himself, his time, his trouble, and his purse: 'Prayer, grind, and love' was his description of the requisites of a parish priest. Although austere in appearance he was a deeply compassionate man. He was not afraid of speaking painful truths and his outspokenness extended to the pulpit, but he was never unmerciful except to those whom he regarded as self-indulgent.

Butler's published works were few in number: in 1847 his *Sermons for Working Men* was taken from his time at Wareside; in 1848 *School Prayers* and in 1880 *Plain Thoughts on Holy Communion* were both devotional manuals. However, the Wantage parish diaries, an almost daily record of his work in Wantage, have survived in manuscript and represent one of the most detailed and significant sources for church life in mid-Victorian England.

Butler's health broke down suddenly in January 1894. He died at the deanery in Lincoln on 14 January and was buried on the 18th in the cloister garth, Lincoln. His wife died soon after, on 21 January, and was buried beside her husband in the cloister garth. In 1895 the south chapel of Wantage church was restored in thankful memory for Butler's work there, and in 1896 an alabaster effigy was erected to his memory in Lincoln Cathedral.

George Herring

Sources *Life and letters of William John Butler*, ed. A. J. Butler (1897) · 'The Wantage parish diaries, 1846–80', Berks. RO · P. F. Anson, *The call of the cloister: religious communities and kindred bodies in the Anglican communion* (1955), 242–59 · *Butler of Wantage: an offering from his community of St Mary the Virgin* (1946) · *The Times* (15 Jan 1894) · *The Times* (19 Jan 1894) · *The Times* (22 Jan 1894) · *Church Times* (19 Jan 1894) · *Church Times* (26 Jan 1894)

Archives Berks. RO, journals of parish events and related papers · Community of St Mary the Virgin, Wantage · NRA, sermons and papers | Bodl. Oxf., corresp. with Samuel Wilberforce

Likenesses two portraits, 1843–88, repro. in Butler, ed., *Life and letters* · Chavalliaud, alabaster recumbent effigy, 1896, Lincoln Cathedral · photographs, repro. in Butler, ed., *Life and letters*, frontispiece, p. 1

Wealth at death £15,741 15*s*. 1*d*.: probate, 13 Feb 1894, *CGPLA Eng. & Wales*

Butler, Sir William Waters, first baronet (1866–1939), brewer, was born on 14 December 1866 in his father's newly acquired public house, the London Works tavern, in Smethwick, near Birmingham. He was the eldest son of William Butler, a publican and brewer, and his wife, Mary Jane, *née* Ewing. His rise from these comparatively modest beginnings was assisted by his father's success as a full-scale commercial brewer, following a move in 1876 to The Crown, 36/7 Broad Street, Birmingham, and the purchase of several public houses. He was educated at the city's King Edward VI School and at the Birmingham and Midland Institute, where he qualified as a chemist. He then joined the family brewery and was head brewer and partner by the age of twenty-one. In 1893 he married Emily Mary, daughter of John Brown of Smethwick. They had a son, William Owen Butler, captain in the Royal Warwickshire regiment, who died in 1935, and two daughters.

Butler encouraged an expansionist business strategy which culminated in an agreed merger with Henry Mitchell & Co. of Cape Hill, Smethwick, to form Mitchells and Butlers in 1898. Butler immediately joined the board, became deputy chairman in 1907, and was chairman and managing director from 1914 until his death in 1939. Sound and conservative management kept the company free of the excesses of the property mania of the 1890s and 1900s. Mitchells and Butlers had an impressive growth and profit record, its ordinary dividends averaging 13.6 per cent, excluding bonuses, in 1914–39. The labour force increased from under 300 in 1898 to over 1500 by 1930.

Butler's company distinguished itself by its emphasis on 'fewer but better' public houses, a rationalization strategy in which large outlets, run on efficient lines by managers instead of tenants, were designed to replace several smaller premises. In 1897 Butler was prominent in a consortium of Birmingham brewers which was formed to administer a voluntary 'surrender scheme'. The Birmingham Property Company was established to administer a fund to compensate brewers who agreed to surrender licences on run-down pubs affected by slum clearance schemes. This acted as a model for a national statutory compensation scheme, which was introduced in 1904. Butler and his colleagues went further than merely reducing the number of pubs. They established an informal quid pro quo arrangement with the local licensing magistrates, by which licences were given up in return for new licences on a smaller number of larger, newly built pubs. Mitchells and Butlers, which had given up about three hundred licences by 1925, led the way in Birmingham in building fine new pubs, architecturally impressive, with a whole series of amenities, including gardens, meeting rooms, bowling greens, family rooms, and restaurants. The strategy, which was taken up by brewers and licensing magistrates all over England, did much to divert the hostility of temperance lobbying and to present a more respectable and responsible image of brewing.

Butler was also prominent nationally in the brewing industry. In 1901, as a delegate of the Birmingham and Midland Counties Brewers' Association, he attended his first meeting of the Country Brewers' Society (from 1904 the Brewers' Society), the trade association representing English brewers, and was elected president of the Institute of Brewing in 1906. He acted as chairman of the Brewers' Society in 1907–8, at a critical period for the industry, which was under attack from the temperance and teetotaller interests in the Liberal government. Butler led the defence against the hostile and wide-ranging licensing bill of 1908, which was eventually defeated in the Lords. The First World War increased the pressure on the brewers, adding output and trading restrictions to the general climate of hostility fostered by Lloyd George. Butler was prominent in deflecting opposition. He agreed to serve as a member of the central control board (liquor traffic), a body constituted in 1915 to regulate the trade in wartime, and, more specifically, to manage the state-owned assets of those breweries nationalized in munitions areas. He threw himself into the task with characteristic enthusiasm, helping to transform the Carlisle State Brewery and its tied estate, applying the same 'fewer but better' principles which had served him well in Birmingham. Then, he was prominent with Sir George Younger and Colonel John Gretton in presenting the brewers' response to government proposals to nationalize the whole of the drinks trade. Butler's surprising but disarming reaction—he declared himself happy to accept state purchase provided the compensation terms were adequate—did much to expose the inadequacies of Lloyd George's assault on the industry. Butler was perceived to be one of brewing's staunchest and most able champions.

Butler's other business interests included chairmanship of Birmingham Cold Storage Ltd, but he was also known for his contribution to higher education and training in brewing. In Birmingham, he did much to encourage the fledgeling university, which gained its charter in 1900. His generous benefactions helped to establish the university's school of brewing and malting in 1900, an endowed chair (the Adrian Brown professorship of brewing), and the new biology block of 1927 (Butler personally contributing £50,000). In 1938 he established the Brewers' Society brewing scholarships at the Birmingham Brewing School. He became a member of the council of Birmingham University in 1917, and was also a life governor. Hospitals and a miscellany of charities also benefited from his generosity.

Butler was a genial, kindly man; he loved orchids, and not only attended business meetings with one in his buttonhole, but frequently took prize blooms to distribute at public functions. His many friends included the Birmingham family of Joseph Chamberlain. A baronetcy was conferred on him, in recognition of his philanthropic, national, and political services, in 1926. Butler died suddenly on 5 April 1939, at his home, Southfield, Norfolk Road, Edgbaston, Birmingham, aged seventy-two. He left £552,615 gross and was survived by his wife.

TERRY GOURVISH

Sources T. R. Gourvish and R. G. Wilson, *The British brewing industry, 1830–1980* (1994) • Mitchells and Butlers, *Fifty years of brewing, 1879–1929* (1929?) • *Brewing Trade Review* (May 1939), 247 • K. Hawkins, 'Butler, Sir William Waters', *DBB* • *VCH Warwickshire*, vol. 7 • *Annual Report* [Brewers' Society] (1939) • *Brewers' Journal* (15 Aug 1898), 654 • K. H. Hawkins, *A history of Bass Charrington* (1978) • S. O. Nevile, *Seventy rolling years* (1958) • *WWW* • J. Turner, 'State purchase of the liquor trade in the First World War', *HJ*, 23 (1980), 589–615 • *CGPLA Eng. & Wales* (1939)

Likenesses photograph, 1926, Brewers and Licensed Retailers Association, London

Wealth at death £552,615 0s. 6d.: probate, 11 May 1939, *CGPLA Eng. & Wales*

Butlin, Sir Henry Trentham, first baronet (1845–1912), surgeon, the fourth son of the Revd William Wright Butlin (*b. c.*1813, *d.* 1902), vicar of Penponds, Cornwall, and his wife, Julia Crowther Trentham, was born at Camborne, Cornwall, on 24 October 1845. He was educated at home until, at the age of nineteen, he went to St Bartholomew's Hospital, London, to study medicine, having decided, like his paternal grandfather, to enter the medical profession. After qualifying (1867), he became house surgeon to James Paget. On 27 September 1873 he married Annie Tipping, daughter of Henry Balderson, merchant, of Hemel Hempstead.

After holding several junior posts, Butlin was elected an assistant surgeon to the hospital in 1881, full surgeon in 1892, and in 1897 a lecturer in surgery at the hospital school. For twelve years he had charge of the throat department, and played a great part in its development.

Besides service to St Bartholomew's and its school, Butlin was the first dean of the faculty of medicine of the University of London. He was also successively councillor, treasurer, and president (1910) of the British Medical Association, and councillor and president (1909–11) of the Royal College of Surgeons, but was forced by failing health to resign that office shortly before his death. He was Erasmus Wilson professor of pathology, and later professor of pathology and surgery to the Royal College of Surgeons. The University of Durham conferred on him the honorary degree of DCL, and that of Birmingham, an honorary LLD. He was created a baronet in 1911.

Butlin was an energetic and successful man whose qualities were rewarded by the highest appointments in his profession and a large medical practice. He wrote a large number of papers, addresses, and monographs, dealing for the most part with the pathology of carcinoma and sarcoma, particularly of the larynx and tongue; among others, he wrote a well-known book on *Diseases of the Tongue* (1885). He was an excellent lecturer and teacher.

Butlin was a man of cultured taste, had a keen appreciation of art, was a good linguist, and liked to spend his holidays in travel in France, Spain, or Italy. Riding and driving were among his favourite recreations. He died at his home, 82 Harley Street, London, on 24 January 1912, leaving his wife, two daughters, and a son, who succeeded his father as second baronet; he joined the army while an undergraduate at Trinity College, Cambridge, and was killed in action in 1916.

A. E. GARROD, *rev.* HUGH SERIES

Sources C. B. Lockwood, *St Bartholomew's Hospital Reports*, 48 (1912), 1–8 • *The Lancet* (3 Feb 1912), 331–5 • *BMJ* (3 Feb 1912), 276–80 • private information (1927) • personal knowledge (1927) • *WWW* • Burke, *Peerage* • *BMJ* (10 Feb 1912), 342 • *CGPLA Eng. & Wales* (1912) • N. Weir, *Otolaryngology: an illustrated history* (1990)

Likenesses J. Collier, oils, 1903, St Bartholomew's Hospital, London • photograph, repro. in Weir, *Otolaryngology*, 121

Wealth at death £91,024 19s. 1d.: resworn probate, 5 March 1912, *CGPLA Eng. & Wales*

Butlin, Kenneth Rupert (1897–1965), microbiologist, was born on 3 November 1897 in Kettering, Northamptonshire, the son of Walter Isaac Butlin (*d. c.*1933), footwear manufacturer and later insurance agent, and his second wife, Sarah Jane. He was educated at nearby Oundle School and, after serving with the special brigade Royal Engineers in the First World War, he took first-class honours in chemistry (in 1921) from Trinity College, Cambridge. After five years in Argentina working on the fermentation of sugar for manufacturing rum he spent three years studying vinegar fermentation for a Birmingham company. While at Birmingham, Butlin married, on 27 July 1928, Helen Mary, daughter of Benjamin John Fletcher, principal of Birmingham Art College, and his wife, Mary Joan, *née* Reynolds. They later had one son, Martin.

In 1929 Butlin joined a research group at the Royal Navy cordite factory at Holton Heath, where he worked under A. C. Thaysen studying practical microbiological problems. In 1933 the group moved to the Chemical Research Laboratory, Teddington. Butlin's earliest research papers concerned the acetic acid bacteria, agents of vinegar formation; his 1936 review of these organisms remained definitive into the 1960s. During the Second World War, together with the rest of the Teddington group, he turned his attention to ways of producing *Candida utilis*, an edible yeast, thus converting waste molasses into food protein. The project gave him valuable experience of the large-scale production of microbes and involved an early use of continuous culture. When the war ended Thaysen and some of the staff took the food yeast project to the West Indies for development, and the microbiological research effort at Teddington was left to Butlin with two experimental officers, now investigating the corrosion of iron and steel by bacteria. This common and economically costly process is largely due to sulphate-reducing bacteria, and Butlin's small team rapidly established itself as a leading authority in this area.

About 1948 the director of the Chemical Research Laboratory, Patrick Linstead, perceiving the broader potential of chemical microbiology, initiated an expansion of Butlin's microbiology section. Basic research on sulphate-reducing bacteria was strengthened, new topics were introduced into the research programme, and, in 1950, Butlin was authorized to accept responsibility for a few hundred bacterial cultures of industrial importance which the medically orientated National Collection of Type Cultures proposed to discard, so founding the National Collection of Industrial Bacteria.

In the early 1950s Butlin's team became an independent microbiology group within the laboratory, dedicated to the study of bacteria of industrial and economic importance. The group remit was to tackle such strictly practical topics as the control of water pollution in waterlogged clay and gravel pits, leaching of metal ores by bacteria, bacterial spoilage of petroleum, and the feasibility of producing sulphur on an industrial scale with the aid of sulphur bacteria (the latter project, which involved a newsworthy trip to some north African sulphur lakes to seek appropriate bacteria, received immense publicity at its outset because Britain's post-war industrial recovery was being delayed by a world shortage of native sulphur). It also conducted more fundamental research, though still with a practical background, including the mechanisms of microbial oxidation of phenols, the mechanism of the methane fermentation, the continuous culture of anaerobic bacteria, and the basic biochemistry of sulphate-reducing bacteria.

By 1958 Butlin's group had become the major British research unit in economic microbiology, and it led the world in fundamental knowledge of sulphate-reducing bacteria. Yet late that year the Department of Scientific and Industrial Research, the laboratory's funding body, decided to disband Butlin's group. The reasons were multiple, including administrative economy, a sense that the laboratory was an inappropriate home for such research, poor economic prospects for the sulphur production project, and, arguably, elements of professional jealousy. Despite protests from microbiologists and industrial scientists in Britain and abroad, disbandment went ahead in 1959 and Butlin was compulsorily retired from the scientific civil service. He subsequently undertook consultancy work and continued to attend scientific meetings; the Society for General Microbiology paid him the rare compliment of making him an honorary member.

Butlin was a pioneer of what later came to be called biotechnology: his conviction that the diverse chemical proclivities of microbes made them extremely important to society, not only for industrial production but also for society's civic infrastructure, conditioned his research outlook and informed his writings.

Butlin was a friendly, cultured man who enjoyed opera, travel, good food, wine, and companionship. Colleagues and friends often remarked on his infectious capacity to enjoy life: even quite solemn occasions would take on the character of a party or convivial gathering in his company. Because of his pronounced stammer (which disappeared when he sang) others gave oral presentations such as seminars or lectures on his behalf. He deplored poor scientific writing, and the literary standard of his papers and, perforce, those of his research group, was high. Butlin died of kidney failure at his home, 44D Hampton Road, Teddington, Middlesex, on 1 October 1965, and was cremated at Feltham crematorium; his ashes were interred at Sapperton, Gloucestershire. He was survived by his wife.

John R. Postgate

Sources J. R. Postgate, *Journal of General Microbiology*, 45 (1966), 1–8 [incl. bibliography] · *The Times* (2 Oct 1965), 10 · *Nature*, 208 (1965), 31 · personal knowledge (2004) · private information (2004) [M. Butlin] · *CGPLA Eng. & Wales* (1965)

Likenesses photograph, repro. in Postgate, 'Kenneth Rupert Butlin'

Wealth at death £4561: probate, 15 Nov 1965, *CGPLA Eng. & Wales*

Butlin, Sir William Heygate Edmund Colborne [Billy] (**1899–1980**), fairground proprietor and founder of holiday camps, was born in Cape Town, Cape Colony, where his parents had emigrated, on 29 September 1899, the elder child of William Butlin and Bertha Hill (*d.* 1933). His parents came from contrasting social backgrounds: his father, scion of west-country clergymen, was genteel and preferred playing tennis to running the cycle-importing business which was supposed to support them, while his mother, daughter of a baker turned fairground showman, was left holding the reins of the business as well as the babies. She brought Billy (as he was always known) and his brother back to England, and took up the itinerant life of a gingerbread seller at west-country fairs. Butlin lodged

Sir William Heygate Edmund Colborne [Billy] **Butlin** (1899–1980), by Elliott & Fry, 1961

with his aunt until his brother died of infantile paralysis, whereupon he joined his mother with her horse and caravan. His schooling, which had begun only when he was eight, therefore became intermittent. Bertha then married again and emigrated to Canada with her second husband, Charlie Rowbotham, a Bristol gas fitter, fostering out Billy until they sent for him in 1912.

In Toronto, Butlin started work as a messenger boy, but, realizing that he had an aptitude for art, he studied at night school and graduated to drawing advertisements for Eatons department store. The outbreak of war saw him become one of the Canadian army's youngest (and smallest) soldiers serving in France, where he survived the lousy life of the trenches as a stretcher-bearer. After demobilization, he returned to Eatons to draw, but was lured by memories of the outdoor life of a travelling showman. In 1921 he worked his passage back to England and received a warm welcome from his mother's family on their west-country fair circuit.

Butlin's uncles set him up with a hoopla stall and, from such small beginnings, within thirteen years he rose to become 'one of the most successful showmen in Europe' (Butlin and Dacre, 30). He displayed great business acumen, aiming for quick returns and a memorable image to attract custom. His trade mark of an enormous embroidered B on a white jacket dates from this period. His readiness to innovate was demonstrated in 1922 when he took his (distinctively decorated) stall to the Christmas circus established by Bertram Mills at London's Olympia. Here he met prosperous showmen wintering away from the seaside resorts, and over the next few years he realized that they were benefiting from the new motor charabanc trade which was beginning to damage the vitality of the rural fairs at which Butlin made his summer living. From these contacts he learned about a resort in seemingly remote Lincolnshire, and by early 1927 had visited Skegness, assessed its potential, and established an amusement park there—with hoopla stalls, a helter-skelter, a haunted house, and an electric car track. Butlin observed the public's fondness for birds and animals, and quickly followed the amusement park with a zoo, and another park at nearby Mablethorpe. He was no longer a travelling showman, though he continued to live in a caravan (a luxury one) next to his mother, whom he had brought back to Britain in 1925.

In 1928 Butlin introduced the American-made Dodgems to Skegness. More importantly, he secured the sole European agency for their sale. This was 'a major turning point' in his life, for with that success he 'came into the really big money' (Butlin and Dacre, 89). By the mid-1930s he had a chain of fairgrounds around the coast and complementary winter amusement centres in London, though the trade was sometimes rough, and Butlin carried a cut-throat razor in his top pocket. He also ran the Christmas fairs at Kelvin Hall, Glasgow, and Waverley Hall, Edinburgh, as well as at Olympia. Until her death in 1933 Butlin's finances and several of his ventures were managed by his remarkable mother—'always dressed in black alpaca, with a bunch of keys dangling from a gold chain around her waist … [giving] the impression of being a woman not to be trifled with' (Butlin and Dacre, 100).

Thus Bertha helped Butlin to accumulate the necessary savings towards, but did not live to see the inception of, the venture which made him a national figure—his first holiday camp, opened at Skegness, at Easter 1936. The idea had grown from Butlin's observation of families on sodden seaside holidays sheltering from the rain in amusement parks, forbidden by landladies to return between mealtimes to their boarding-houses. He contrasted this with the happy holiday atmosphere he had enjoyed in 1914 at a lakeside camp provided by Eatons for its employees, and dreamed that he could create a similar camp in Britain, but with provision against the variable British climate.

The idea of summer holiday camps was not new in Britain, as Butlin acknowledged. His scheme had been preceded by numerous private, philanthropic, and self-help ventures. However, although Butlins was aiming at lower- and middle-income groups at this time, he was offering a 'Luxury Holiday Camp'—with electric lighting, and 250 bathrooms for 1000 people. His plans included a theatre, a gymnasium, a swimming-pool, and many other indoor and outdoor sports facilities, all set in landscaped grounds. Such facilities necessitated economies of scale, and large numbers made the desirable camaraderie of a camp initially difficult to achieve, but Butlin's inspired innovation of organized jollity supplied by his 'Redcoats' broke down the campers' reserve. Many became regular visitors, encouraged by winter campers' reunions, the first of which was held at Olympia on new year's eve 1936. They were not deterred by criticisms of the 'Wakey-wakey, rise and shine' atmosphere, which to outsiders seemed like regimentation, but which was regarded by campers as a 'matey' necessity in the organization of their holiday. Moreover, Butlins was unique in making special arrangements for children, allowing husband and wife unparalleled freedom together. The camp was expanded to 2000 beds in the second year, and Butlin instituted Sunday night celebrity concerts by variety theatre and radio stars to entertain and attract them. In his third year he made another brilliant stroke, which gave him mayoral endorsements and publicity throughout England—a regionalized beauty contest with a final at the Skegness carnival.

Butlin's success should also be seen in context. England was recovering from the depression, the Holidays with Pay Bill was under discussion, and, at £3 in high season, he was offering a week's holiday at a new standard for the price of a good week's wage. Butlin lobbied actively for the bill which was passed in 1938. Despite enormous difficulties in the building of the Skegness camp (successfully hidden from his creditors), Butlin achieved his dream, and Butlins Ltd was floated in order to finance further expansion. A second camp was opened at Clacton in 1938, the advertising for which (like that of Skegness) was half funded by the London and North-Eastern Railway, on whose lines the camps lay. Butlin's genius for public relations was displayed again, as he successfully invited prominent figures like Amy Johnson, Victor Sylvester, Len Hutton, and Gracie Fields—to the delight of the campers. In 1938 Butlin also staged the Empire Exhibition at Glasgow. The man who had arrived in 1921 with £5 was now worth tens of thousands.

The Second World War interrupted Butlin's progress. His camps were sequestered for military purposes: Skegness, for instance, was renamed HMS *Royal Arthur* by the Royal Navy (and subsequently claimed by Lord Haw-Haw to have been sunk with all hands!). Nevertheless, Butlin was able to finish building his half-completed third camp, at Filey, for the RAF, and tendered successfully to build two more for the navy, at Pwllheli and Ayr—entering into a risky but valuable contract to buy these three back when the war ended, at three-fifths of their building costs.

During the rest of the war Butlin fulfilled a number of roles. For Lord Beaverbrook at the Ministry of Supply he sorted out problems of morale in the hostels occupied by women workers in the munitions industry, particularly by providing relaxation facilities—so that 'hostels' became 'residential clubs'. In 1943 he brought his fairground rides out of retirement to promote 'Holidays at Home' weeks for workers trapped by wartime travel restrictions. In 1944 he was appointed MBE for his hostel work, and embarked on his final wartime task, as honorary adviser to the Twenty-First Army group regarding leave centres in Europe following the allied invasion. Butlin successfully established nine '21 Clubs', where servicemen could relax with carefully vetted young women, in the Low Countries and Germany.

The return of peace meant Butlin could resume his career as holiday camp caterer. He activated the buy-back clause on Filey, Pwllheli, and Ayr, and thus, with Skegness and Clacton, was well placed to cater for the huge pent-up demand for holidays. Butlin opened Filey, his showplace, with typically flamboyant strokes. Tommy Handley and the *ITMA* cast appeared under the slogan 'Stars You Have Heard—But Seldom Seen'. Music lovers were attracted by an extravagant production of *La Bohème* imported from Naples, and Shakespearian aficionados by the Bristol Old Vic Company. Such ventures helped to counter criticisms of standardization and mass-produced entertainment, and there are indications that large numbers of campers in the 1940s were middle-class. Holidays with pay were now well-nigh universal, but taking an entire family on holiday was still a pricey business, and, with tariffs increased to nearly £1 a day, many working-class families did not find it easy. Nevertheless, Butlin claimed 1.6 million people visited his camps in the late 1940s.

By 1947 Butlin was a millionaire. In 1948, however, he overextended himself, and nearly suffered disaster. Together with A. C. Critchley he set up Butlins (Bahamas) Ltd to create a luxurious holiday village to tempt American tourists. Problems with labour and local politicians, sterling crises, and Critchley's failure to raise a promised reserve of City money, all topped off by the effect of the Korean War on American investors, together conspired to drive the company into liquidation. Butlin himself was 'virtually broke' (Butlin and Dacre, 194). Moreover, he had neglected his British operations. The result was an attempt by City investors to oust him from control of Butlins. He was not a man to back down in the face of difficulties, however, and by mobilizing the small shareholders on his side he kept control of the company.

During the 1950s Butlin reasserted himself in the public eye by sponsoring or taking part in various events such as the cross-channel swim, and the John o' Groats to Land's End walk. His promotion of ballroom dance festivals brought considerable business to his camps as well as contributing to the popularity of the pastime. He maintained that his secret was to give people what he liked, which because he was an ordinary person meant that he gave his customers what they liked. He listened to what they said and learned from it. He bought several chains of hotels, and then opened three more camps, at Bognor Regis in 1960, Minehead in 1962, and Barry Island in 1966, thus establishing a camp within 200 miles of every major centre of population. In 1961 the company's stated aim was to cater for 'the middle income group' (Ward and Hardy, 110), though it also chased the growing youth market, and isolated parts of the camps were given over to big parties of teenagers. A seal of respectability was provided by the visit of the queen to Pwllheli in 1963, and in 1964 'Mr Happiness' was knighted.

Butlin told his associates that his aims in life were 'money, power, and women' ('Billy Butlin', *Secret Lives*,

Channel 4, 26 Nov 1997). He was a short, stocky man, of enormous drive, with an engaging grin and an engrossing personality. However, in his dealings with his staff, bonhomie was sometimes overlaid by a cold autocracy. He demanded total commitment to the business although this had harmed his own private life. On 29 March 1927 he had married Dorothy Mabel (Dolly), daughter of John Cheriton, fish-and-chip shop proprietor, of Tiverton. Their marriage (which produced a daughter) deteriorated as Butlin spent all his time building up his business. By 1938 Dolly's 'sister' Norah Faith (in reality her niece) was acting as his housekeeper and hostess, and then as mother to three children, including Bobby, his successor at Butlins (actually Norah's son from an earlier marriage, whom Billy adopted). Dolly refused him a divorce, but her death in 1958 allowed him to marry Norah on 21 September the following year. The marriage was principally for the sake of their children, for Norah's relationship with Butlin had deteriorated as early as the 1940s, for similar reasons to Dolly's. Butlin soon found solace, however, with Sheila, the nineteen-year-old daughter of Walter Devine, a multiple grocer of Liverpool, who appreciated how far business was always Butlin's priority after he quickly installed her as chief receptionist at his London office. He had two children with her, this time being less of an absentee father, and following his divorce from Norah in 1975 married her in September 1976.

By now Butlin had retired to Jersey. Public tastes and competitors' strategies had begun to change by the mid-1960s; package holidays abroad and self-catering holiday camps at home began to diminish the camps' profitability. In 1968 a cash-flow crisis in the face of a tax demand prompted Butlin suddenly to hand over the company to his son Bobby. Butlin chafed at his non-involvement in the business, and resented changes instituted by Bobby; however, father and son came together to fight off a take-over bid from Phonographic Equipment, a firm which supplied gambling machines, which both regarded as unsuitable to Butlins' family image. By 1972 the company was back in profit, and in a friendly take-over (possibly engineered by Butlin himself) it was sold to the Rank Organization for £43 million.

Butlin devoted time to gardening on a grand scale at Blair Adam House, his Jersey home, and to enjoying his aviary of 1200 budgerigars; but he was incapable of fully retiring, and built up new business interests on Jersey, including several hotels and a holiday village, as well as playing the stock market. He also became more deeply involved in charity work, particularly through the Variety Club of Great Britain (on which he had been a formative influence during the 1950s) and the Grand Order of Water Rats; altogether he donated at least £5 million, chiefly to underprivileged children. His choice of charities was typical of the showman, although his friends and family also recalled his shy and unostentatious side. He died of stomach cancer at Blair Adam House, Jersey, on 12 June 1980, and was buried in St John's cemetery, Jersey.

DOUGLAS A. REID

Sources B. Butlin and P. Dacre, *The Billy Butlin story: 'a showman to the end'* (1982) • R. North, *The Butlin story* (1962) • *DNB* • C. Ward and D. Hardy, *Goodnight campers! The history of the British holiday camp* (1986) • D. J. Jeremy, 'Butlin, Sir William Heygate Edmund Colbourne', *DBB* • H. D. Willcock, 'Boarding house or Butlin's', *Geographical Magazine*, 19 (1946–7), 132–40 • J. Walvin, *Beside the seaside: a social history of the popular seaside holiday* (1978) • m. certs. • 'Billy Butlin', *Secret lives*, 26 Nov 1997 [Channel 4]

Likenesses photographs, 1947–68, Hult. Arch. • D. Low, chalk, *c.*1952, NPG • Elliott & Fry, photograph, 1961, NPG [*see illus.*] • D. Low, pencil, NPG • photograph, repro. in North, *Butlin story*, facing p. 102 • photographs, repro. in Butlin and Dacre, *Billy Butlin story*

Butt, Sir Alfred, first baronet (**1878–1962**), music-hall entrepreneur and racehorse owner and breeder, was born on 20 March 1878, the only son of Frederick Butt, a builder. He was educated at Westminster School and, after leaving school, worked in the accounting department at Harrods as a clerk on a salary of 15*s.* per week. He was then employed by the Palace Theatre, Cambridge Circus.

Butt's subsequent career was built around the management of this theatre, which he made into one of the most prestigious, fashionable, and financially successful variety theatres in London. Appointed company secretary of the Palace Theatre Ltd in 1898, at the age of nineteen, he soon after became assistant manager and, on the death of Charles Morton in 1904, manager of the music-hall. In 1906 Butt was promoted to managing director, a position he retained until 1920. Butt's management of the Palace was characterized by the production of novel and lavish entertainments and he became especially associated with the introduction of foreign performers to British music-hall audiences. The most notable of these included famous continental performers such as Anna Pavlova (1909) and Yvette Guilbert (1910), although he also developed very close business links with American vaudeville which ensured a continuous flow of top American stars to Britain.

In 1910 Butt greatly extended his music-hall business by assuming control of the deceased Thomas *Barrasford's circuit of halls and by merging his interests with those of Walter de *Frece to create the Variety Theatres Controlling Company Limited (VTCC). These developments rapidly made Butt one of the most influential figures in the music-hall industry and enabled him and de Frece to challenge the dominance of Moss Empires within the industry. Butt also became involved in the management of the Globe, Queen's, and Empire theatres (1914), and the Gaiety and the Adelphi (1915), and was responsible for the construction of the Victoria Palace and Glasgow Alhambra.

During the First World War, Butt became involved with the Ministry of Food and oversaw the introduction of compulsory rationing in 1917. In acknowledgement of this role, and also for his contributions to war charities, Butt was knighted in 1918. Having been adopted as the Unionist parliamentary candidate for North Paddington in June 1918, Sir Alfred reduced his involvement in the variety theatre, disposing of his interests in the VTCC (1919) and the Gaiety, Adelphi, and Palace theatres (1920). He did, though, take on the chairmanship of the Theatre Royal, Drury Lane, in 1919, and was its managing director from 1925 to 1931. Butt finally obtained a seat in parliament in November 1922 as the representative for Balham and Tooting. He enjoyed a lengthy parliamentary career, the apogee of which was the award of a baronetcy in the 1929 dissolution honours list for his political and public services. His political career ended in disgrace, however, when in 1936 he was forced to resign after a scandal implicating him in obtaining personal financial gain from leaked budget proposals disclosed to him by his friend J. H. Thomas, the colonial secretary.

Butt held a long-standing interest in gambling and in his younger days he played chemin de fer at casinos in Deauville and other resorts. Horse-racing was another passion, and after his enforced retirement from public life he turned his attention towards the racing world, acquiring the Brook stud in Newmarket. He was a successful owner-breeder, winning the 1946 Oaks with Steady Aim. He was also responsible for the breeding of Petition. As a two-year-old, the horse won the New Stakes at Ascot, and also finished first in the Gimcrack and the Champagne Stakes. Although fancied to win the 2000 Guineas, Petition had an accident at the start. Other successful mares that Butt owned were Quick Arrow, Solar Flower, and Spend a Penny.

Butt married Georgina Mary, daughter of Frederick Say of Norwich, in 1902; they had a son, born in 1908. Georgina died in January 1960 and, in August 1960, Butt married Wilhelmine Wahl, who had been his nurse–companion for a number of years (*Daily Telegraph*, 10 Dec 1962). He died at his home, Clarehaven, Bury Road, Newmarket, on 8 December 1962; his funeral was held at Cambridge crematorium on 12 December. His only son, (Alfred) Kenneth Dudley Butt, succeeded to the baronetcy.

ANDREW CROWHURST

Sources *The Times* (10 Dec 1962) · *Daily Telegraph* (10 Dec 1962) · P. Burton, 'How a variety theatre is run: a day at the Palace Theatre with Mr Alfred Butt', *Strand Magazine* (May 1907), 509–19 · R. Blathwayt, 'The control of a great music hall', *World's Work* (Feb 1911), 250–53 · 'A chat with Alfred Butt', *The Era* (30 July 1904) · A. Crowhurst, 'The music hall, 1885–1922: the emergence of a national entertainment industry in Britain', PhD diss., U. Cam., 1992 · *WWW* · m. cert. · d. cert. · *CGPLA Eng. & Wales* (1963) · *The Times* (13 Dec 1962)

Wealth at death £250,536 6*s*. 5*d*.: probate, 3 Jan 1963, *CGPLA Eng. & Wales*

Butt, Sir Charles Parker (1830–1892), judge, the third son of the Revd Phelpes John Butt of Wortham Lodge, Bournemouth, and his wife, Mary, daughter of John Eddy, vicar of Toddington, Gloucestershire, was born on 24 June 1830. He was educated by private tutors before being admitted on 22 January 1849 as a student at Lincoln's Inn, where he was called to the bar on 17 November 1854, and elected bencher on 11 January 1869.

Butt became a correspondent for *The Times* newspaper while in Constantinople, in Turkey, where he practised in the consular courts, gaining experience of commercial and maritime law. On his return to England, this early experience helped him in his work on the northern circuit and in the Admiralty court where he revealed himself as a skilful advocate, if not a great lawyer. When he became queen's counsel (8 December 1868), he inherited some of the work of Sir William Baliol Brett (afterwards Viscount Esher) who had been made a judge. On 23 December 1878 he married Anna Georgina, the daughter of C. Ferdinand Rodewald.

Butt unsuccessfully contested Tamworth as a Liberal candidate in February 1874, but was returned to parliament for Southampton on 6 April 1880. His maiden speech (1 July) was a vindication of Charles Bradlaugh's right, although a prominent atheist and secularist, to take the oath on broad constitutional grounds. On the Irish question he was an unwavering supporter of the government while in parliament.

Butt succeeded Sir Robert Phillimore as justice of the High Court (Probate, Divorce, and Admiralty Division) on 31 March 1883, and was knighted on 20 April 1883. He succeeded Sir James Hannen as president of the division on 29 January 1891. He was a member, but not an active one, of the royal commission appointed on 1 November 1884 to investigate the causes of loss of life at sea.

Butt's health began to deteriorate, and a serious illness was complicated by his catching flu in the winter of 1891, which led to his death from cardiac paralysis at Wiesbaden in Germany on 25 May 1892. His wife survived him.

J. M. RIGG, *rev.* HUGH MOONEY

Sources *The Times* (27 May 1892) · *Annual Register* (1892), pt 2, p. 174 · *Law Times* (4 June 1892), 97, 120 · *Law Journal* (4 June 1892), 373–4 · *Solicitors' Journal*, 36 (1891–2), 515, 528 · *Men and women of the time* (1891) · *VF* (12 Feb 1887) · *Whitehall Review* (28 May 1892) · *Law reports: appeal cases*, 12 (1887), xviii · 'Judges and law officers: memoranda', *Law reports: appeal cases* (1891), vii · J. Foster, *Men-at-the-bar: a biographical hand-list of the members of the various inns of court*, 2nd edn (1885) · W. P. Baildon, ed., *The records of the Honorable Society of Lincoln's Inn* [incl. *Admissions*, 2 vols. (1896), and *Black books*, 6 vols. (1897–2001)] · Burke, *Peerage* · *Hansard* 3 (1880), 253.1302 · 'Royal commission on loss of life at sea: final report', *Parl. papers* (1887), vol. 63, C. 5227 · *CGPLA Eng. & Wales* (1892)

Likenesses Ape [C. Pellegrini], caricature, chromolithograph, NPG; repro. in *VF* (12 Feb 1887), pl. 16 · portrait, repro. in *ILN* (1892), 679

Wealth at death £9404 4*s*. 4*d*.: administration, 21 June 1892, *CGPLA Eng. & Wales*

Butt, Dame Clara Ellen (1872–1936), singer, was born on 1 February 1872 at 4 Adur Terrace, Southwick, Sussex, the eldest daughter and eldest surviving child of Henry Butt, a captain in the mercantile marine, and his wife, Clara Hook, great-granddaughter of Theodore Hook. Both her parents sang and they encouraged Clara to cultivate her voice, which early showed the richness and compass for which she was to become renowned as a contralto. When her parents moved to Bristol in 1880, the headmistress of South Bristol high school, a Miss Cook, heard her pupil's low notes and asked the bass Daniel Rootham, conductor of the Bristol festival chorus, to hear her. He set about training her voice and enrolled her in his chorus. In January 1890, when she was almost eighteen, she won a scholarship to the Royal College of Music, where she studied with John Henry Blower.

Dame Clara Ellen Butt (1872–1936), by Bassano, 1915

Clara Butt's scholarship was extended for a fourth year. The college sent her to study for three months in Paris with V. A. Duvernoy, the cost being met by Queen Victoria, who had heard of the student's talent through the prince of Wales, then patron of the college. Later in her career Clara Butt studied with the baritone Jacques Bruhy in Paris, with the soprano Etelka Gerster in Berlin, and in Italy. She made her professional début in the Royal Albert Hall, London, as Ursula in Sir Arthur Sullivan's *The Golden Legend* on 7 December 1892. Three days later she sang the title role in Gluck's *Orfeo* when it was staged at the Lyceum Theatre by students of the Royal College of Music. Bernard Shaw wrote in *The World* that she 'far surpassed the utmost expectations that could reasonably be entertained' (Shaw, 14 Dec 1892).

Clara Butt's reputation was soon made, and she became what today would be called 'the flavour of the month', no doubt aided by her imposing presence on the platform—she was 6 feet 2 inches in height. Less than a year after the appearance in *Orfeo*, Shaw reviewed a Royal Choral Society performance of Handel's *Israel in Egypt* conducted by Sir Joseph Barnby at which he singled out Clara Butt's singing of 'Their land brought forth frogs' as magnificent, adding, 'the last fourteen bars came with the true musical and dramatic passion which reduces all purely technical criticism to a mere matter of detail' (Shaw, 29 Nov 1893). After this she was in demand at all the principal festivals and by 1898 was living in London in a flat in Hyde Park Mansions. There, in January 1899, the composer Edward Elgar called on her with a song cycle he had sketched for the forthcoming Norwich Festival. She was in her bath at the time and instructed her woman companion to send him away. Elgar complained to her manager (N. Vert), and a few days later he was received with more warmth. The result was *Sea Pictures*, for contralto and orchestra, of which she gave the first performance at Norwich on 5 October 1899 with the composer conducting. Elgar's host at Norwich, James Mottram, described her 'wonderful dress, the material of which, it was whispered, indicated appropriately the scales of a mermaid's sinuous form' (Mottram, 253). Two days later she sang four of the five songs (with piano accompaniment by Elgar) at St James's Hall in London. Elgar was thrilled with her performance, and there is evidence in his correspondence with A. J. Jaeger, of Novellos, to support her claim in later years that he wrote the part of the Angel in *The Dream of Gerontius* with her voice in mind. Nevertheless, for whatever reason, she did not sing in the first performance of that work at the Birmingham Festival on 3 October 1900, although she sang in *Sea Pictures* on the previous evening at the festival. (She recorded some extracts from *Gerontius* in April 1916.)

In 1900 Clara Butt married the baritone singer Robert Kennerley Rumford (1870–1957), with whom thereafter she gave many highly successful and lucrative concerts, mainly of popular ballads, in Britain and the United States and throughout what was then the British empire. But one of the two songs with which she was most closely associated was by Elgar. Sitting next to him on 26 November 1901 at a concert at which the first two *Pomp and Circumstance* marches were played, after listening to the trio melody of no. 1 she asked him to 'write something like it for me'. After a 'little talk and persuasion on my part, you said "You shall have that one, my dear"' (Clara Butt to Edward Elgar, Elgar birthplace archive, Broadheath). Elgar was planning an opulent final movement for the coronation ode he was writing for the coronation of King Edward VII in 1902. A. C. Benson provided the text for this, beginning with the words 'Land of hope and glory'. As soon as Booseys, the publishers, saw the score, they recognized its potential as a solo song and asked Elgar to revise it accordingly. With slightly different words from those in the ode, Clara Butt sang it for the first time at a concert in the Royal Albert Hall on 24 June 1902. The king's appendicitis postponed his coronation until October, so the ode was not performed until the Sheffield Festival on 2 October 1902 and in London three weeks later. Clara Butt sang in neither performance. The other great tune which she made virtually her own was 'Abide with me', closely followed in the Butt popularity stakes by 'O rest in the Lord' from Mendelssohn's *Elijah*.

During the First World War, Clara Butt was indefatigable in her energy and generosity in organizing concerts for charity and singing in them. Outstanding among these occasions was that from 8 to 13 May 1916, when she sang in six successive performances of *The Dream of Gerontius*, raising £2700 for the Red Cross. In publicity before the performances, the first of which was attended by King George V and Queen Mary, it was announced that Clara Butt believed there was a new attitude towards death. Many of those without faith before the war, she argued, were now hungering to believe that there was life beyond the grave. For her wartime work she was appointed DBE in 1920. This was the year in which she made only her second appearance on the opera stage, when she again sang Gluck's *Orfeo*—this time at Covent Garden with Sir Thomas Beecham conducting.

Clara Butt made many gramophone records, too many of them of the potboilers with which she and her husband filled their recitals. The warm-heartedness of her singing later came to be thought excessive, but undoubtedly it met the taste of the time. Her audiences were thrilled by the booming, trombone-like strength of the tone and by the unashamed emotional portamentos which she imported into her singing. Her voluminous performance of 'Land of hope and glory' has become almost a caricature of an era, but this should not render listeners deaf to its sincerity and noble solemnity. A recording made in September 1920 of 'Where corals lie' from *Sea Pictures* is an example of the lightness of touch she could command, and explains why the composer valued her artistry so highly in his works, when managements could afford her high fees.

Clara Butt knew tragedy in her private life. She and Rumford had two sons and a daughter; both sons predeceased her. From 1901 to 1929 the Rumfords lived at 7 Harley Road, Hampstead, after which they moved to Brooke Lodge, North Stoke, Oxfordshire. In 1931 she had an accident which led, after a painful illness, to her death at North Lodge, North Stoke, on 23 January 1936, three days after King George V. MICHAEL KENNEDY

Sources W. Ponder, *Clara Butt: her life-story* (1928) • J. B. Steane, *The grand tradition* (1974) [2nd edn (1978)] • J. N. Moore, *Edward Elgar: a creative life* (1984) • *New Grove*, 2nd edn (2000) • G. B. Shaw, *The World* (14 Dec 1892) • G. B. Shaw, *The World* (29 Nov 1893) • R. H. Mottram, *Portrait of an unknown Victorian* (1935) • Elgar birthplace archive, Broadheath • *CGPLA Eng. & Wales* (1936)

Archives FILM BFI NFTVA, news footage | SOUND BL NSA, documentary recording; performance recordings; *Talking about music*, 127, BBC, 1LP0153351 S1 BD2/BD3

Likenesses Dinham, double portrait, photograph, *c*.1900 (with her husband, Kennerley Rumford), NPG • Dover Street Studios, photograph, 1911, NPG • Bassano, photograph, 1915, NPG [*see illus.*] • O. Edis, photograph, 1920–29, NPG • waxwork, Madame Tussauds, Warwick Castle

Wealth at death £39,517 6*s*. 11*d*.: probate, 1 May 1936, *CGPLA Eng. & Wales*

Butt, George (1741–1795), Church of England clergyman and poet, was born on 26 December 1741 and baptized on the 30th at St Mary's Church, Lichfield, the son of Dr Carey Butt (*bap*. 1708, *d*. 1781), surgeon and apothecary, and Elizabeth, *née* Marten (*bap*. 1708, *d*. 1789), of Lichfield. Butt was descended from the same family as Henry VIII's physician Sir William Butts. Butt attended Stafford grammar school until he was fifteen. Thanks to the influence of his father's friend and fellow Lichfieldian, Thomas Newton, bishop of Bristol from 1761 to 1782, he was admitted on the foundation at Westminster School in 1756, where he excelled at verse making and public speaking. He ended his schooldays as captain of the school in 1760 and was head of the procession of boys at the funeral of George II. He matriculated at Oxford University on 21 May 1761 as a member of Christ Church, becoming a student (Christ Church's equivalent of fellow) on 24 December 1761, and held several exhibitions. He graduated BA in 1765, MA in 1768, and took the degrees of BD and DD on 29 October 1793.

Butt made a career in the Church of England. He was ordained a deacon in 1765, and was appointed by Sir Walter Bagot to the curacy of Leigh, Staffordshire, which he shortly afterwards resigned for the post of private tutor to Edward, the eldest son of Sir Edward Winnington, first baronet (1728–1791), of Stanford Court, Worcestershire. In October 1767 he returned to Christ Church (acting principally as Edward Winnington's tutor), and mingled easily among the undergraduates without forfeiting their respect. In 1771 he was presented by Sir Edward Winnington to the rectory of Stanford and the vicarage of Clifton-on-Tame, resigned his studentship of Christ Church on 8 October 1772 on the expiry of his year of grace, and on 26 April 1773 at St Mary Magdalene, Richmond, Surrey, married Martha (*d*. 1817), the daughter of Henry Sherwood (*d*. 1790), a London silk merchant with Coventry links. The marriage relieved Butt's financial problems somewhat. He had run up appreciable expenses while in residence in Oxford and his father's ill-fated venture into farming and his own construction of a new parsonage at Stanford made matters worse. The new Mrs Butt came to his rescue by insisting on a methodical approach to future expenditure and on her husband's supplementing his stipend by taking in private pupils, which he did from about 1774 to 1784. These pupils had good family backgrounds and their tutor proved as popular with them as he had earlier been in Oxford, though his 'method of instruction was rather desultory than systematic', as his evangelical daughter rather sternly put it (Sherwood, xiv).

Butt's finances improved further in 1778 when Bishop Thomas Newton appointed him to the vicarage of Newchurch on the Isle of Wight. He remained in residence at Stanford, and exchanged Newchurch in 1783 for the crown living of Notgrove, Gloucestershire. The same year he was appointed chaplain-in-ordinary to George III; he was also chaplain to James Ogilvy, seventh earl of Findlater and fourth earl of Seafield, whom he may have met while acting as Winnington's tutor at Christ Church. In 1787, after endorsement from Archbishop Markham of York (his former headmaster at Westminster) and the marchioness of Stafford (to whose family his brother was chaplain), he was presented to the wealthy vicarage of Kidderminster by the second Lord Foley, Sir Edward Winnington's brother-in-law. Butt held Kidderminster with all his other cures apart from Notgrove (which he resigned), and resided there from 1788 to 1794. His ministry was successful and was marked by excellent relations between him and many of the numerous dissenters in the town who could be seen, in church, on festival days. As his daughter touchingly recalled: 'His countenance was all love, and whether at Stanford or Kidderminster, he loved to speak to his people after service, as a fond father loves the greeting of his children' (*Life of Mrs. Cameron*, 7–8). Butt was well read and published on some scale in most genres. He was conscious of excessive diversification and apologized in his *Poems* for producing effusions rather than solid works such as his proposed book on the defence and display of Christianity. In 1777 Butt submitted a play entitled *Timoleon* to Garrick, who professed himself unable to find fault with it, and considered it would not need adaptation if it was to reach the stage. However, Butt proceeded no further. In the late 1770s Butt was part of the coterie of Anne, Lady Miller (*d.* 1781), at Batheaston near Bath, and dropped verses into her celebrated vase. He made his name with *Isaiah Versified* (1784), a work quite highly estimated by contemporaries; several sermons appeared on special occasions, and a collected two-volume *Sermons* dates from 1791. Butt's *Poems* in two volumes was published in 1793. Though the preface expresses his desire for posthumous fame, Butt's verse is not particularly remarkable, aside from some descriptive and sentimental pieces. At the time of his death he was correcting the text of a religious novel provisionally called 'Felicia'. This was edited and published by his daughter Mary Martha *Sherwood as *The Spanish Daughter*.

Butt's later years were happy ones in private as well as public life. His mother's death in 1789 eased his financial position and, by the time of his death, his finances were at last in credit. Butt moved back to Stanford in 1794 but on 30 June 1795 he suffered a stroke and died on 30 September following at his rectory. He was buried in Stanford churchyard. He left a son, John Martin Butt, and two daughters, including Lucy Lyttelton *Cameron, all three of them minor authors, the most prominent of whom was the aforementioned Mary Martha Sherwood. The girls were educated quite strictly at home by their mother—who never liked the use of the word 'fun'—and their father's less inhibited disposition was appreciated by both in later life as a valuable antidote. He also provided for his younger brother and brought up his nephew like a son. Martha Butt long survived him and died in Worcester on 20 March 1817.

Butt was small in stature, with attractive hands. According to Henry Fuseli (whom he met in London while on chaplaincy duties at St James's), he had a face 'compounded of the features of Sterne and Lavater' (Valpy, 241). He was benevolent, good-natured, and courteous, and had few enemies. Butt's supreme delight (his family apart) was company rather than 'deep solitary study' (ibid., 229), and he took an interest in all the arts, not least painting—he collected pictures and prints—and the theatre. And that love of the theatre he translated into an animated pulpit style. Not the least attractive among Butt's traits was his loyalty to his friends, which he combined with generous but impeccably orthodox religious sympathies. He wrote about 1784 *The Practice of Liberal Piety Vindicated* in defence of a sermon by his friend Richard Valpy of Reading against Calvinist detractors. Butt's artlessness, while charming his friends, may have hindered his rise in the church: he made no secret of his dislike of time-servers. NIGEL ASTON

Sources *GM*, 1st ser., 65 (1795), 969 • *N&Q*, 12th ser., 9 (1921), 351 • *Old Westminsters*, 1.151 • A. L. Reade, *Johnsonian gleanings*, 3 (privately printed, London, 1922), 132 • Foster, *Alum. Oxon.* • archives, Christ Church Oxf. • Nichols, *Lit. anecdotes*, 9.758 • GEC, *Baronetage*, 5.101 • T. Nash, *Collections for the history of Worcestershire*, 1 (1781), 250; 2 (1799), 371 • R. Simms, ed., *Bibliotheca Staffordiensis* (1894) • Glos. RO, D1/201/9 • J. R. Burton, *A history of Kidderminster* (1890), 88, 121–2 • M. M. Sherwood, *Biographical preface to the Spanish daughter*, 2 vols. (1824) • F. J. H. Darton, ed., *The life and times of Mrs. Sherwood (1775–1851)* (1910) • *The life of Mrs. L. L. Cameron, edited by her eldest son* (1862) • R. Valpy, ed., *Poems, odes, prologues, and epilogues* (1804), 225–64 • R. A. Hesselgrave, *Lady Miller and the Batheaston literary circle* (1927)

Likenesses T. Nugent, stipple (after M. Kean), BM, NPG; repro. in G. Butt, *Poems*, 2 vols. (privately printed, Kidderminster, 1793)

Butt, Hamad Masood (1962–1994), multimedia artist, was born in Lahore, Pakistan, on 9 January 1962, one of five children of Masood Aktar Butt (*b.* 1932), civil servant, and his wife, Jamila Masood (*b.* 1942). His parents moved to Britain when he was a child and he was educated in London, where he took A levels in biology, chemistry, mathematics, and art. Between 1980 and 1987 he attended a number of art schools, including Central St Martin's College of Art and Design, where he made paintings, sculptures, prints, and installations. Between 1987 and 1990 he was an undergraduate at Goldsmiths' College, University of London, where he was rewarded with the highest grades ever achieved by a fine art student. His work for his degree show, 'Transmissions' (1990), was exhibited at Goldsmiths' School of Art building in Great Russell Street. Glass books were placed in a circle and rested on an ultraviolet light on the floor. Each book was opened at a different page and had an engraved plant motif. The plant form was borrowed from the cover of *The Day of the Triffids*, by John Wyndham (first published in 1951), and Butt's use of the ultraviolet light imitated the blinding flashes in the sky that proclaimed the arrival of the triffids. 'Transmissions' also touched on scientific experiments: this is evident in the glass books and ultraviolet light, with light rays beyond the limit of visibility at the violet end of the spectrum making contact with crystalized glass. References to scientific light experiments were included on the glass pages.

Butt claimed that the use of popular imagery and scientific experiments challenged conventional views of scientific knowledge. His empirical approach to science became more prominent in a subsequent work, *Familiars*, commissioned in 1992 by Stephen Foster, director of the John Hansard Gallery. This work in three parts is concerned with the properties of matter and spiritual beliefs. Butt worked on preliminary experiments with Dr Garry Rumble of University College, London, to discover at what point iodine vaporized, and continued these experiments with bromine and chlorine in *Familiars* to emphasize their natural instability. His invitation to the private view had an old print of an alembic used for purification by alchemists, showing the connection between alchemy and modern science. Chlorine gas was suspended from the ceiling in glass bubbles that resembled Sir Isaac Newton's cradle. Iodine crystals were heated within a glass ladder until they were transformed into gas. The bromine was housed in a structure reminiscent of 1950s' science fiction. This work was also shown in the Milch Gallery, London, in 1992, and in the 'Rites of Passage' exhibition at the Tate Gallery in 1995.

In his will Butt asked for his unpublished collection of essays entitled *Familiars* to be published: it appeared in 1996, with further essays by Stephen Foster and Sarat Maharaj. Under subheadings such as 'Familiars', 'Fluid and strategic withdrawal', and 'Stress', Butt's essays provided information about his work and revealed how it might have developed. During his last year he became interested in working in sound and film, but his illness prevented him from doing so. He died, unmarried, of AIDS-related bronchopneumonia at St Mary's Hospital, Praed Street, Paddington, London, on 25 September 1994.

PAULINE DE SOUZA

Sources C. Page, 'Hamad Butt: the art of metachemics', *Third Text*, 32 (autumn 1995), 33–42 · S. Morgan and F. Morris, *Rites of passage* (1995) · H. Butt, S. Foster, and S. Maharaj, *Familiars* (1996) · private information (2004) [Jamal Butt] · d. cert.
Archives priv. coll.
Wealth at death under £125,000: probate, 23 May 1995, *CGPLA Eng. & Wales*

Butt, Isaac (1813–1879), politician and lawyer, was the only son of the Revd Robert Butt (*d.* 1829), rector of Stanorlar, co. Donegal, and his wife, Berkeley, a daughter of the Revd R. Cox of Dovish, co. Donegal, through whom he also claimed descent from Bishop Berkeley and the O'Donnells of Ulster. He was born at Glenfin, co. Donegal, on 6 September 1813, and was educated first at Midleton College, Cork, and then at the Royal School, Raphoe. He matriculated at Trinity College, Dublin, in 1828, aged only fifteen, and became a scholar there in 1832. He graduated BA in 1835, was awarded an LLB in 1836, and then received an MA and LLD in 1840. As an undergraduate, Butt amassed a formidable reputation. In 1833 he published an edition of *Fasti*, afterwards seen as evidence of the lengths to which poor scholars of the nineteenth century went to earn a small sum of money. He was an active member of the college historical society, and was successively its secretary, president, and auditor; he also earned recognition as the ablest speaker in several debates and was awarded the gold medal. The society, which had been founded by Edmund Burke and had as one of its auditors Theobald Wolfe Tone, was a stepping stone to influence in Irish political life, and Butt continued to make appearances at its debates after graduation. He also helped to found the *Dublin University Magazine* in January 1833, writing many contributions and serving as editor, except for a few months in early 1836, from August 1834 until he was called to the Irish bar in November 1838.

Early legal and political career Butt's initial foray to London came in 1835, when he went to give evidence before a parliamentary committee. He began to spend part of each year in the capital in order to keep terms at the inns of court, then a prerequisite for a call to the Irish bar. During this time he frequented the gallery of the House of Commons, developing parliamentary ambitions. In February

Isaac Butt (1813–1879), by John Butler Yeats, 1870s

1837 he married Elizabeth Swanzy (*d.* 1897), the daughter of a Monaghan solicitor; they had eight children. In 1836 he had been appointed to the Whately professorship of political economy at Trinity, a post then normally associated with the legal profession, and which he held until 1841 for the fee of £100 per annum. During the 1830s and 1840s he wrote for a number of periodicals, including the *Evening Mail* and a bevy of British newspapers. He was also a founder of the *Protestant Guardian*, and remained associated with it after the journal's amalgamation with *The Warder*.

In 1840, while still a junior barrister, Butt was selected to plead the case of the Dublin corporation before the House of Lords in London. There he skilfully argued against the Municipal Reform Bill, which was intended to reform the corporation and to open its offices to Catholics. Although ultimately unsuccessful, he won respect from Conservatives for his efforts. He was quickly immersed in the affairs of the metropolitan Conservative Association, and acted as its secretary in 1840. In early 1843, at a time when agitation for repeal of the union was exciting interest, he became an alderman in the new corporation. In the great debate on repeal which began on 25 February 1843 and lasted for three days, he was one of the chief speakers against the proposal, and challenged O'Connell to be precise about the authority an Irish parliament would exercise and the future division of powers between Great Britain and Ireland. His reputation as legal counsel grew accordingly, and his stature was recognized when he was called to the inner bar on 2 November 1844, making him one of the youngest barristers to take silk.

The Irish patriot During these early years of his career, Butt's political associations had been typical of a rising protestant politician—Trinity, the bar, the corporation, and involvement in Conservative organizations. His general political ideas, too, appeared to steer him along the predicted course. He spoke against *laissez-faire* principles, supported protection, and presented himself as an upholder of protestantism. However, this picture concealed another and ultimately more influential side of his thinking. Like many others in the circle of contributors to the *Dublin University Magazine*, Butt was an Irish 'patriot' in the mould of leaders of the eighteenth-century Irish parliament. He was concerned about the effects of British policy on Ireland, and about the laggard economic development of his country, and he wished to see Catholics and protestants reconciled. Sympathetic to the plight of the peasantry, he was also acutely aware of the weakness of the Irish economy. In all of these respects, he exemplified a new, admittedly minority, creed of progressive protestant toryism that sought to adapt ascendancy privilege in ways that would make Ireland safe for its own kind. Moreover, he saw Ireland's situation in a wider British context, believing that if the union was to thrive there must be an imperial partnership between his country and the larger neighbour.

Butt's writings were critical of the application of the poor law to Ireland, and of the impact of the land system, and he saw protection as vital to the development of Irish industries. In 1846 he delivered an important lecture on the development of Irish industry; in the following year he considered the impact of the famine—both analyses exhibiting his concern for Ireland's well-being. His outlook was being shaped in the cauldron of political ferment swirling through Ireland in the 1840s. From 1846 onwards, the widespread famine made an immense impression on him; the Young Ireland movement, composed of intellectuals, many of whom were protestant, made its ideas felt. Several men associated with this movement were prosecuted for sedition and treason, especially after the farcical revolution of 1848. Butt was briefed for the defence for a number of cases, including those of William Smith O'Brien and Thomas Francis Meagher. Though sharing none of their politics, Butt's able and eloquent advocacy raised his standing in the eyes of the nationalists.

Political career Butt's political aspirations continued to grow. He stood for parliament as a Conservative in the County Mayo by-election on 29 July 1850 but was defeated, in part because the Catholic clergy worked against him. He was then returned unopposed as a Conservative at the Harwich by-election on 8 May 1852. While declaring himself in favour of protection and maintenance of the church establishment in both England and Ireland, his election address upheld the principle of religious tolerance. However, he had barely taken his seat when parliament was dissolved. He then chose to contest the borough of Youghal in the Conservative interest, winning the seat by two votes on 15 July 1852. Party allegiance in the 1850s and 1860s was fluid; the more so in Butt's case because of his failure to secure appointment as legal adviser to Dublin Castle. He was returned unopposed as a Liberal at Youghal in the general election of 1857, and triumphed again wearing the same livery in 1859. Despite declaring himself in favour of tenant-right and denominational education, he was easily defeated by another Liberal, the wealthy Catholic Joseph N. McKenna, at the general election of 1865 and found himself without a parliamentary seat.

Butt's political record during his long stretch in the House of Commons was nondescript. He supported the demand for tenant-right in Ireland, urged state sponsorship of Irish railway construction, defended Catholic interests against rampant no-popery elements—a substantial element in the heated religious atmosphere of the 1850s and 1860s—and spoke on imperial affairs, being notably concerned about Russian intentions. In future years he retained his interest in foreign policy. During this time he also published a pamphlet on the land problem. Chronically in debt since his student days, his financial and other difficulties mounted in the 1850s. He had an established liaison in London, resulting in at least one illegitimate son—in addition to his eight legitimate children two more were born out of wedlock—and some questionable financial dealings were exposed publicly on more than one occasion. During this troubled time his work at the Irish bar ceased for many years; he was called to the English bar at the Inner Temple on 17 November 1859, before reappearing at the four courts in Dublin in 1864. After losing his parliamentary seat he found himself imprisoned for debt.

Land and home rule, 1865–1874 Butt lost his parliamentary seat just as a sea change was taking place in Irish politics, so that the maturation of his political thinking coincided with fresh opportunities in the second half of the 1860s. Alarmed at the Fenian conspiracy, the British government began in 1865 to arrest and try the conspirators, many of whom Butt defended over the next four years, often at the expense of his lucrative legal practice. Though largely unable to save Fenians from prison, he earned their respect and gratitude, and in the process was transmuted into a nationalist icon. He also spoke at many demonstrations across Ireland and wrote with telling effect on tenant-right, social and economic conditions, denominational education, and, above all else, in favour of an amnesty for Fenian convicts. William Gladstone secured a Liberal victory in the general election of 1868 on the specific platform of remedying Irish disaffection. In 1869 he pushed through legislation disestablishing the Church of Ireland. Rather than staying grievances, it raised Irish expectations. Moreover, though the government released a number of Fenian prisoners in late 1868, this merely heightened demands to free the remainder.

In September 1869 Butt, already head of the Amnesty Association, assumed the leadership of the new Irish Tenant League. There were many divisions within the patriotic community, with the issues of amnesty, tenant-right, and education vying for priority. During autumn 1869 tenant farmer meetings were broken up by Fenians who resented any diversion from the amnesty campaign. The national question held a number of attractions, including the possibility of submerging these differences under a common banner. The self-government ideal might be fashioned into a tool capable of bridging divisions. As Butt told one audience:

> it is a mere question of time when we … ought to strain every nerve to achieve for Ireland national independence. And when I say national independence I don't mean separation. I mean a self-government which gives us the entire right to manage our own affairs. (*The Nation*, 20 Nov 1869)

When Gladstone introduced the Irish Land Bill in February 1870, tenant farming interests were disappointed, thereby encouraging those who saw Ireland's best hope in the formation of a new patriotic organization forged on the anvil of a revived self-government agitation.

On 19 May 1870 forty-nine gentlemen, the majority of whom were protestant, met in Dublin to discuss the future governing arrangements of their country. Those present agreed to promote Butt's plan of federal home rule, and the gathering became the nucleus of the Home Government Association for Ireland. Butt was the guiding light though he never intended it to become a popular body modelled on the Repeal Association. Towards the end of the year, in his *Irish Federalism: its Meaning, its Objects and its Hopes*, he outlined what the concept entailed, distinguishing it from repeal. In his view 'federalism' would offer Ireland an opportunity for 'independence without breaking up the unity of the empire, interfering with the monarchy, or endangering the rights or liberties of any class of Irishmen'. Under it 'Ireland could enjoy all of [the] self-government and distinct national rights which would be necessary for full development of her national life.' He also envisaged self-government as the means of reconciling creeds:

> It is from the joint deliberations of all classes of Irishmen that we may most confidently hope to present a plan of a national legislature, in which the just influence of property and education, and rank may be harmoniously combined with popular privileges and power, so as to make the legislature the real representative of the nation.

This vision set him apart from the bulk of Catholics who took up home rule in the 1870s.

Appreciating the need to secure parliamentary representation to advance home rule, Butt moved into the electoral arena once more. In early 1871 the movement gained some successes though his own candidacy at the by-election for County Monaghan on 22 July ended in defeat. Nevertheless, this proved a temporary setback; he was returned unopposed for the vacancy at Limerick City on 20 September. Support for home rule continued to grow during the next two years, especially after Gladstone's abortive university bill of 1873 evoked the wrath of the Catholic ecclesiastical hierarchy. In its aftermath many priests deserted to the home rule cause. Although initially reluctant, Butt was persuaded to convert the Home Government Association into a popular organization. To effect the transition a national conference was held in Dublin between 18 and 21 November to found the Home Rule League, at which he was the leading figure, making a spirited case for sponsoring federalism rather than repeal and also stressing the benefits of self-government for reconciling classes and creeds. He insisted that the current system of Irish involvement at Westminster was corrupting both his country's representatives and the proper functions of parliament as an institution. In January 1874 Gladstone called a general election. While Butt's own fortunes ebbed, those of the cause of home rule flourished: sixty candidates standing under its banner were returned. On 3 March most of this contingent formed itself into a new independent parliamentary party. Butt accepted the party chairmanship, a position which he retained until his death.

Obstruction and the rise of Parnell Home-rulers began the new parliament in high spirits but their hopes were quickly dashed. Too many home-rulers only adopted the label to save their seats: the movement had very limited financial resources; its roots in the country were tenuous; the means of putting pressure on delinquent members were largely absent. This was not a disciplined party but only one where MPs agreed to consult together; Butt himself, though a gifted speaker and writer, had little appetite for the routine of mundane organizational matters, while his private life and persistent indebtedness diverted his energies away from politics at crucial moments. The new Conservative ministry was not beholden to and, as events proved, was unresponsive to Irish demands. Home rule's fortunes rode heavily on Butt's shoulders. Between 1869 and 1876 he expended immense effort, attending meetings and speaking across the country. Any diminution of his efforts would have had an enervating effect on the cause, but with his energy and finances dissipating, Butt's frame proved too frail. On the positive side, he was popular—indeed he was the foremost politician in the country—and he secured an understanding from Fenians to give parliamentarianism a three-year trial. Butt and the bulk of those who followed him believed that the process of educating public opinion in Britain required a lengthy gestation period. In the meantime he held that the best course was to state within the accepted norms of discourse and behaviour Ireland's case for self-government, express other grievances, and seek ameliorative legislation. His strategy looked in opposite directions: he sought to persuade the Irish people that their interests could be promoted effectively in the House of Commons while demonstrating to observers in Britain that Ireland's claims were reasonable and would be advanced in a dignified fashion.

Butt's formula required a good deal of patience and a substantial degree of political sophistication among supporters, who would have been boosted by a harvest of useful measures. None was forthcoming. Moreover, continuing financial problems constantly dogged Butt's political work: as one member of his party commented in November 1875, 'I would trust him with my cause but not my money. You might as well put water in a colander as money in Butt's pocket' (Joseph Ronayne to John O'Leary, NL Ire., Butt MSS). During 1875 Joseph Biggar resorted to 'obstruction' of parliamentary business. This did not win Butt's approval, though it proved popular in some Irish circles and was applauded by the annual convention of the Fenian-dominated Home Rule Confederation of Great Britain.

This issue which was to mar Butt's final years did not loom large until the spring of 1877. In the meantime, however, he was faced with declining morale and the hostility of some Fenians when the three-year trial period for parliamentarianism expired. To counter this, he enlisted the support of the clergy. In January 1877 the party became the chosen vessel to advocate the Catholic church's education demands in the House of Commons. Collections for a testimonial to ease Butt's financial plight were now aided by the clergy, though the sum achieved proved insufficient for the purpose. During 1877 'obstruction' became the foremost issue in Irish politics, despite its being supported by merely a small section of the parliamentary party. Charles Stewart Parnell was soon the best-known practitioner, quickly gaining a public popularity second only to Butt's own. According to Parnell, he was engaged in an 'active' approach to parliamentary business, not 'obstruction', and he pointed to his efforts to improve bills. Butt was unmoved. By autumn the two men routinely locked horns over parliamentary policy. Butt refused to bend, using his influence in the party, with the Home Rule League, and with the Catholic bishops as well as his deep reserves of support in the country to outmanoeuvre Parnell. In January 1878 a national conference met to iron out differences; it ended with Parnell pledging support to Butt and the party leader promising a more vigorous parliamentary approach.

Relations between the men did not improve, however. Parnell's popularity rose; Butt's declined. However, Butt proved resourceful in marshalling his forces against Parnell and also pinned his hopes on securing legislation from the government. His tactic helped to secure the Intermediate Education Act that year, but his position and health declined and he damaged himself further by speaking in favour of the ministry's stance on the eastern question. He never reappeared in the House of Commons after 1878.

The 'obstruction' episode blighted not only Butt's last years, but also his posthumous reputation. Yet he and Parnell were not very far apart in their respective outlooks. Both men shared a vision of self-government as a reconciling force; both focused Irish attention on the House of Commons, seeing it as a forum for educating opinion; both saw the work of their country's MPs there as crucial. They differed on emphasis. Butt and Parnell concurred on the importance of the expressive and informative aspects of representation though they came to differ on the precise weight and on timing of each. By 1877 Parnell judged that public opinion in Ireland would only continue to support parliamentarianism if MPs acted vigorously. Butt ignored the advice of friends who urged him to direct a more activist campaign in order to thwart the 'obstructionists', partly, no doubt, because he resented Parnell, but also because he preferred 'to teach the country what it does not know', to cite Walter Bagehot's phrase from *The English Constitution*. There was an underlying consistency in his long political life in spite of the veering from toryism to Liberalism and then to nationalism. From his earliest days he was prepared to take unpopular stands, and his intransigence over obstruction and his support in the face of Irish feeling for the ministry's eastern policy in 1878 were late manifestations of this political courage.

Butt's health had been declining for some time and the death of a son in India at the beginning of 1879 weighed on his mind. Following a stroke, he died on 5 May 1879 at Roebuck Cottage, near Dundrum, co. Dublin, and was buried at Stranorlar on 10 May. The obituarist in *The Times* deftly caught the tenor of Butt's life, observing that 'when the choice was between the pleasure of the moment and the fulfilment of a duty, we will not say to others, but to the higher gifts of his own nature, pleasure was sure to gain the day' (*The Times*, 12 May 1879). ALAN O'DAY

Sources T. De Vere White, *The road of excess* (1946) • D. Thornley, *Isaac Butt and home rule* (1964) • L. J. McCaffrey, *Irish federalism in the 1870s* (1962) • E. Larkin, *The Roman Catholic church and the home rule movement in Ireland, 1870–1874* (1990) • E. Larkin, *The Roman Catholic church and the emergence of the modern Irish political system, 1874–1878* (1996) • M. MacDonagh, *The home rule movement* (1920) • *WWBMP* • *The Times* (6 May 1879) • *The Times* (12 May 1879) • *The Nation* (10 May 1879) • *Irish Times* (6 May 1879) • *Irish Times* (12 May 1879) • *Freeman's Journal* [Dublin] (6 May 1879) • R. B. McDowell and D. A. Webb, *Trinity College, Dublin, 1592–1952: an academic history* (1982) • T. S. C. Dagg, *College Historical Society: a history, 1770–1920* (privately printed, [Cork], 1969) • *University Magazine: a Literary and Philosophic Review*, 3 (1879), 710–5 • A. O'Day, 'Defining Ireland's place in parliamentary institutions: Isaac Butt and Parnell in the 1870s', *Government and institutions in the post-1832 United Kingdom*, ed. A. O'Day (1995), 155–90 • R. V. Comerford, *The Fenians in context: Irish politics and society, 1848–82* (1985) • R. V. Comerford, 'Isaac Butt and the home rule party, 1870–77', *A new history of Ireland*, ed. T. W. Moody and others, 6: *Ireland under the Union, 1870–1921* (1996), 1–25 • NL Ire., Butt MSS

Archives BL, letters as sponsor to the Royal Literary Fund, loan no. 96 • NL Ire., corresp. and papers • PRO NIre., corresp. • TCD, Latin orations | BL, corresp. with W. E. Gladstone, Add. MSS 44354–44455 • Bodl. Oxf., letters to Benjamin Disraeli • Glos. RO, letters to Sir Michael Hicks Beach • NL Ire., Daunt MSS • NL Ire., letters to George Delaney • NL Ire., Webb MSS

Likenesses J. B. Yeats, charcoal drawing, 1870–79, NG Ire. [*see illus.*] • Spy [L. Ward], pencil and wash, 1879, NPG; repro. in *VF* (3 May 1873) • Faustin, chromolithograph, NPG • J. Kirkwood, lithograph, NPG • J. B. Yeats, chalk, NPG • cartoons, repro. in White, *Road of excess* • cartoons, repro. in Thornley, *Isaac Butt*

Butt, Mary Martha. *See* Sherwood, Mary Martha (1775–1851).

Butter, John (1791–1877), ophthalmic surgeon, was born at Woodbury, near Exeter, Devon, on 22 January 1791. He was educated at Exeter grammar school, before studying at the Devon and Exeter Hospital. He obtained the MD degree at Edinburgh in 1820, and was elected a fellow of the Royal Society in 1822, with John Abernethy among his proposers. He was a member of the Linnean Society.

Butter was appointed surgeon of the South Devon militia, and ultimately settled at Plymouth, where he specialized in diseases of the eye, becoming surgeon (1814–20) and physician (1820–56) there. Along with Edward Moore, he founded the Plymouth Eye Dispensary. His publications include *Ophthalmic Diseases* (1821) and *Dockyard Diseases, or, Irritative Fever* (1825). In recognition of his services to the dispensary he was, in 1854, presented with his portrait, which was hung in the boardroom. He was a magistrate for the county of Devon.

Butter lost one eye through ophthalmic rheumatism, contracted by exposure while examining recruits for the Crimea, and in 1856 became totally blind. He died at 7 Windsor Villas, Plymouth, on 13 January 1877; his will was proved at nearly £70,000. [ANON.], *rev.* HUGH SERIES

Sources *Western Daily Mercury* (15 Jan 1877) • *Men of the time* (1875) • Boase, *Mod. Eng. biog.* • *CGPLA Eng. & Wales* (1877) • election certificate, RS • N. Weis, *Otolaryngology: an illustrated history* (1990)
Archives RS
Likenesses portrait, 1854, Plymouth Eye Dispensary
Wealth at death under £70,000: probate, 19 Feb 1877, *CGPLA Eng. & Wales*

Butter, Nathaniel (*bap.* 1583, *d.* 1664), bookseller, was baptized on 18 February 1583 at St Augustine, Watling Street, London, the son of Thomas Butter (*c.*1558–1590), also a bookseller, originally of Ludlow, Shropshire, and his wife, Joan. She carried on the business as his widow, as she did after the death of her second husband, the bookseller John Newbery, in 1603. Her daughter Joan Butter married a bookseller named Nathaniel Newbery.

Butter was freed of the Stationers' Company by patrimony on 20 February 1604 and from 1605 was doing business out of his father's shop, the Pied Bull, near St Austin's Gate into St Paul's Churchyard. For the next two years he was treasurer of the lucrative printing and publishing monopoly in vernacular religious and educational texts controlled by the company, known as the English stock. His first independent publication was entered into the Stationers' register on 4 December 1604. From the outset he specialized in small, cheap, ephemeral publications such as news relations, travelogues, and plays, although he did publish a number of theological works, especially the works of Bishop Joseph Hall. Notable early publications include the first edition of Shakespeare's *King Lear* (1607), Thomas Dekker's *The Bellman of London* (1608), and George Chapman's translations of *The Iliad* (1611) and *The Odyssey* (1614).

Despite numerous clashes with the Stationers' Company (one of which ended with a spell in the public pillory), Butter was elected to the company's livery in June 1616 on the same day as his future business partner, the bookseller Nicholas *Bourne. It was Butter's role as a pioneering publisher of news in the 1620s that brought him greatest success and fame. He had published accounts of notable events abroad, sensational stories of murders and monsters at home, and travel narratives from the beginning of his career. When the Thirty Years' War erupted on the continent, Butter was one of several stationers who reprinted the Dutch and Italian *corantos* and *gazettes* imported into England. Their popularity quickly led to the translation and printing of the news in English. He first published news with a group of stationers, but eventually forged a partnership with Bourne that dominated news publishing for the next two decades. Butter seems to have been the public face of the business, while Bourne apparently arranged for financing. They retained Captain Thomas Gainsford, a university-educated professional soldier who was also an author published by Butter, to translate, compile, and edit the newsbooks. Between 1621 and 1632 newsbooks appeared for the most part weekly in sequentially numbered series, printed in quartos of four to forty pages, and generally sold for 2*d.* each. These features caused news to become a sensation in England and led to Butter's appearance in several contemporary literary works (such as Ben Jonson's *The Staple of News*, John Fletcher's *The Fair Maid of the Inn*, and James Shirley's *Love Tricks*).

Butter's news publishing led to further conflicts not only with the company, but also with state and church officials. Between 1620 and 1623 he was arrested more than once for publishing material deemed potentially dangerous, and in 1622 he petitioned to be released because his wife was pregnant and had three other small children, leaving no one to look after his business but a small boy. In March 1627, as England's foreign relations deteriorated, the crown cracked down even harder on news publications, ordering the secretary of state and the Stationers' Company to inform its membership, especially Butter, of new regulations governing the publication of news. None the less, Butter was once again imprisoned in August 1627. From 1628 the news business was clearly slowing down, and it received an even more damaging blow in October 1632, when *corantos* were suppressed by the privy council. Butter and Bourne were called in and warned to cease publication of the weekly serialized newsbooks on account of complaints from ambassadors of Catholic countries. Butter petitioned the secretaries of state for years to revive the *corantos*, promising not to print anything derogatory about countries allied with England, but he was ignored.

On 2 October 1633 Butter and Bourne were elected to the governing body of the Stationers' Company. In place of the weekly newsbooks they began to publish European history, which was actually thinly disguised news of the ongoing Thirty Years' War, in the *Swedish Intelligencer* and the *German Intelligencer*. Butter served as warden of the company for two successive terms in 1636 and 1637. In 1638 he and Bourne were finally granted a patent to revive the *corantos*, but by May 1639 Butter was mortgaging many of his copyrights to secure loans totalling £600. By the end of that year the revived *corantos* had failed for good, although Butter alone published a few in 1640.

Butter was imprisoned by parliament in 1643 and was tried at Windsor by the council of war for committing sedition as an intelligencer. By 1649 he had given up the once prime location of the Pied Bull for less salubrious premises in Cursitors' Alley. In 1651 the company paid out of its poor fund to free him from the Compter prison. He became a serial nuisance over the next decade, constantly haunting the company's meetings with exasperating demands for money, although he did still issue occasional publications. In 1662 he claimed to be on the waiting list for Sutton's Hospital, an institution that cared for the destitute aged, but it seems that he was never admitted. He sold some copyrights in October 1663, but on 22 February 1664 the death was reported of 'Nath. Butter, an old stationer, died very poore' (*Obituary of Richard Smyth*, 60).

S. A. BARON

Sources L. Rostenberg, 'The debut of English journalism: Nathaniel Butter & Nicholas Bourne, first "masters of the Staple"', *Literary, political, scientific, religious & legal publishing, printing & bookselling in England, 1551–1700: twelve studies*, 1 (1965), 75–96 • L. Rostenberg, 'Nathaniel Butter, Nicholas Bourne', *The British literary book trade, 1475–1700*, ed. J. K. Bracken and J. Silver, DLitB, 170 (1996), 31–6 • P. W. M. Blayney, *The texts of King Lear and their origins*, 1 (1982) • *The obituary of Richard Smyth … being a catalogue of all such persons as he knew in their life*, ed. H. Ellis, CS, 44 (1849) • W. C. Ferguson, 'The Stationers' Company poor books, 1608–1700', *The Library*, 5th ser., 31 (1976), 37–51 • W. C. Ferguson, *The loan book of the Stationers' Company with a list of transactions, 1592–1692* (1989) • D. F. McKenzie, ed., *Stationers' Company apprentices*, [2]: *1641–1700* (1974) • H. R. Plomer and others, *Dictionaries of the printers and booksellers who were at work in England, Scotland and Ireland, 1577–1775* (1910–32); repr. (1977) • W. A. Jackson, ed., *Records of the court of the Stationers' Company, 1602 to 1640* (1957) • Stationers' Company records, Stationers' Hall, London, court bks C and D • PRO, state papers domestic, James I, SP14 • PRO, state papers domestic, Charles I, SP16 • W. W. Greg, ed., *A companion to Arber* (1967) • *STC, 1475–1640* • parish register, St Augustine, Watling Street, London

Wealth at death destitute: Stationers' Company court books C and D for the 1640s, 1650s, 1660s; *The obituary*, ed. Ellis

Butter, William (*bap.* **1726**, *d.* **1805**), physician, the son of William Butter and Margaret Mordoch, was baptized on 21 February 1726 at Kirkwall and St Ola, Orkney. He studied medicine at Edinburgh, where he graduated MD in 1761. He became known through his treatises, *On the Kink-Cough* (whooping cough) (1773) and *On Puerperal Fevers* (1775). He also published works on fever and on angina pectoris, and he is said to have attempted to open the carotid artery of a patient at the Edinburgh Infirmary. The attempt was abandoned only when the patient fainted after the first incision.

Butter was described by a contemporary as 'too much under the influence of very favourite hypotheses'. After practising for some years in Derby, Butter moved to London, where he died on 23 March 1805.

G. T. BETTANY, *rev.* CLAIRE L. NUTT

Sources R. Faulder, *New catalogue of living authors* (1799) • *GM*, 1st ser., 75 (1805), 294, 580 • Munk, *Roll* • *IGI* • *Nomina eorum, qui gradum medicinae doctoris in academia Jacobi sexti Scotorum regis, quae Edinburgi est, adepti sunt, ab anno 1705 ad annum 1845*, University of Edinburgh (1846)

Butterfield, Sir Herbert (**1900–1979**), historian, was born at Oxenhope, Yorkshire, on 7 October 1900, the eldest of three children of Albert Butterfield, chief clerk at a Keighley woollen mill, and his wife, Ada Mary Buckland. He was educated at Keighley trade and grammar school, and went up to Peterhouse, Cambridge, as a history scholar in 1919 and graduated first class in both parts of the historical tripos (1921 and 1923). In 1923 he was elected to a fellowship at that college, which he retained continuously, except during his tenure of the mastership, until his death. He married Edith Joyce (Pamela), daughter of the Revd James

Sir Herbert Butterfield (1900–1979), by Ruskin Spear, 1960

E. Crawshaw, a Methodist minister, in 1929; they had three children.

As a young man Butterfield was a voracious reader of plays, novels, and poetry. His first book, *The Historical Novel* (1924), based on a prize-winning undergraduate essay, was a defence of the historical imagination. This literary tendency was still visible in the often rather florid prose of his second and much more substantial book, *The Peace Tactics of Napoleon* (1929). This attempted to restore the sense of contingency and the unexpected to the making of the treaty of Tilsit (1807), the terms of which Butterfield attributed more to incompetent Prussian intrigues than to limitless Napoleonic imperialism. But the breakthrough to national and international recognition came with his iconoclastic *The Whig Interpretation of History* (1931), which purported to show how the traditional teleology of British constitutional development was in fact an invention of sixteenth- and seventeenth-century lawyers. It was a plea not to privilege certain parts of history simply because these appeared to point to the present day, and to understand ideas in their historical rather than their contemporary contexts.

The book established Butterfield in the public mind as the 'hammer of the whigs', not altogether justly. In fact, he entertained a sympathetic preoccupation with the development of liberty, particularly 'English' liberty. This was evident from his engagement with Acton, sometimes described as a Catholic whig. It was disconcertingly apparent in his next sensation, *The Englishman and his History* (1944). Here he argued that: '"wrong" history was one of our assets. The whig interpretation came at exactly the crucial moment, and, whatever it may have done to our history, it had a wonderful effect on English politics' (pp.

6–7). This was much more than a 'piece of wartime spirits-raising' (Elton, 733). It was certainly in no sense a retraction; Butterfield was merely asserting that while the identification of English history with the development of liberty might have been accidental and even misleading, it was also fortuitous. His subsequent attack on the Namierite preoccupation with 'structures' of faction and familial interest, *George III, Lord North, and the People* (1949), was also profoundly whiggish in conception: the people, as represented by the Yorkshire Association, are brought into the political process, thus enabling the avoidance of a French-style revolutionary upheaval in the long run. Eight years later, he returned to the fray with an unusually bitter attack on the Namier school in *George III and the Historians* (1957).

In the meantime Butterfield's interests had expanded dramatically. He had been asked to give a series of lectures on the history of science, which was published as *The Origins of Modern Science, 1300–1800* (1949). It was another sensation, especially when Butterfield argued that the scientific revolution of the sixteenth and seventeenth centuries outshone 'everything since the rise of Christianity and reduces the Renaissance and Reformation to the rank of mere episodes, mere internal displacements, within the system of medieval Christendom' (p. vii). The charge that Butterfield had ignored the experimental side of science was not entirely fair. But it is certainly true that the book, despite his own best intentions, was essentially a whig outline of the growth of scientific progress.

That same year a series of lectures which the Cambridge faculty of divinity had asked him to give was published as *Christianity and History*; much to Butterfield's own surprise this was perhaps his most successful book. With the exception of a brief chapter at the end of *The Englishman and his History*, his work before 1949 had contained very few references to religion. Now Butterfield became something of a sage among many Christian intellectuals, a prophet even. The book was translated into French, German, Spanish, Italian, Chinese, and four Scandinavian languages. The Christianity Butterfield espoused was not so much theological as philosophical, almost anthropological; it was biblical but not exegetical. He eschewed the study of doctrine and of the institutional church(es). His emphasis on human cupidity and sinfulness, but also his underlying humanity and tolerance, struck a deep chord among those who, in the aftermath of the Second World War, were seeking new (or old) faiths after so many other gods had failed.

A year later Butterfield extended his interests yet further into the theory of international history. His earlier studies on Napoleonic diplomacy had already stressed the importance of contingency over inevitability. In 'The tragic element in modern international conflict' (1950) Butterfield began to develop a pessimistically 'Christian' view of international politics. He was particularly critical of national self-righteousness and utopianism in foreign policy: conflict could only be managed, not abolished; and there was no such thing as total security, which could only be bought at the cost of the total insecurity of others. Butterfield could see no pattern in international history, no working towards a preordained goal, only the mysterious workings of 'Providence': all the statesman could do was 'work with Providence'. Once again, Butterfield's work was widely acclaimed not just in Britain—where he soon co-founded and chaired the British Committee on the Theory of International Politics (1958)—but in the United States, where it resonated among 'realist' historically minded political scientists, Christian and unchristian, such as Hans Morgenthau, Kenneth Thompson, and Louis J. Halle. They were taken aback, however, by his temporary advocacy of unilateral western nuclear disarmament.

By 1950, therefore, Butterfield's five main intellectual preoccupations—historiography, the history of science, eighteenth-century constitutional history, Christianity and history, and the theory of international politics—were established. He continued to elaborate them over the next twenty-five years in invited lectures and in essays, such as those published in *History and Human Relations*, *Christianity in European History*, *The Reconstruction of an Historical Episode: the History of the Enquiry into the Origins of the Seven Years War* (all 1951), *Christianity, Diplomacy and War* (1953), *Man on his Past: the Study of the History of Historical Scholarship* (1955), *International Conflict in the Twentieth Century* (1960), *Charles James Fox and Napoleon: the Peace Negotiations of 1806* (1962), and 'Sir Edward Grey in July 1914' (1965), in which he pointedly refused to join the stampede to acclaim Fritz Fischer's one-sided indictment of imperial Germany's responsibility for the outbreak of the First World War.

Underlying these and other diverse projects was a series of interlocking themes. The first was Butterfield's essentially whiggish preoccupation with harmony and balance. Thus he saw the travails of George III 'not as a conflict but as a tide—one which throughout the century is bringing wider classes of Englishmen to intellectual awareness and a realization of the part they might play in politics' (*George III, Lord North, and the People*, 9). He believed that the same virtues might be extended to the sphere of international relations: 'It is the function of foreign policy to create situations in which virtue does not depend on a great power's good intentions, but is ensured on the whole by the general disposition of forces' (*History and Human Relations*, 220). This quest for harmony extended into the historiographical sphere, particularly in his early attempts to reconcile Bury's scientific history with the literary approach of Trevelyan.

At the same time Butterfield was an invincible sceptic. Despite his professional eminence he remained very much the outsider, critical of official collections of documents, which he believed to be designed to mislead as much as to enlighten. Indeed Butterfield was sceptical about the value of all documents, thanks perhaps to his 'distrust of the witnesses by his awareness of original sin' (O. Chadwick, *Acton and his History*, 1998, 213); unlike his teacher Harold Temperley, he produced only one collection of edited documents, volume 3 of *Select Documents of European History*, which covered the years 1715–1920 (1931).

Even more radically, in his first book he had criticized the Rankean documentary method and spoken of the 'impossibility of history' (*Writings*, ed. McIntire, xlvii). Later he doubted whether 'the mere study of antecedents … can ever provide a complete accounting for any decision made by a human being' (introduction to H. Temperley, *Frederic the Great and Kaiser Joseph*, 2nd edn, 1968, xix). To this extent 'all histories' were 'only interim reports'.

Butterfield's scepticism was also reflected in his rejection of all grand designs, both historiographical and contemporary. 'Liberty', he argued, 'comes to the world from English traditions, not from French theories' (*Napoleon*, 18), while the 'real history of freedom is the profounder story of the slow growth of reasonableness among men' (ibid., 44). In particular, he denied that history 'provides us with patterns which we can immediately transpose into the context of contemporary politics' (*History and Human Relations*, 173). Instead, the study of history should promote wisdom, not mechanically but osmotically: Butterfield wanted:

> knowledge not to lie heavily on the mind, not to be used in a narrow or literal spirit, but to sink into the walls of [the historian's] brain so that it was turned into wisdom and experience—then such a person would be able to acquire the right feeling for the texture of events, and would undoubtedly avoid becoming a mere slave of the past. (ibid., 181)

Only by showing the requisite mental 'elasticity of mind' could the historian achieve this.

Butterfield was an unorthodox and original historian, but his intellectual debts were manifold. He took from Acton his distrust of power, from Ranke his celebration of the cultural diversity of the European state system, from Harold Temperley his love of humour and paradox, from Hegel, perhaps, his feel for unintended consequences, and from Max Weber, conceivably, his recognition of the ethics of limitation over the ethics of aspiration.

Butterfield's interests expanded additively rather than substitutively. He was also in constant demand as a speaker and essayist. This meant that he did not escape the accusation of superficiality, nor did his later preference for meditation over production go unremarked upon. He wrote only two longer historical monographs, both of them criticized for their documentary range. The first, *The Peace Tactics of Napoleon*, remains little known, impenetrable and—although it certainly informed his subsequent views on international relations—did not lead to a larger-scale study of Napoleon. It needed a new preface thirty years later (1967) to remind the reader of its central themes. Similarly, his second major work, *George III, Lord North, and the People*, was not followed by the planned biography of Charles James Fox; and with the exception of the work of J. C. D. Clark his writings on the eighteenth century have left no lasting legacy. In the last thirty years of his life Butterfield never wrote another monograph. Many enterprises were left unfinished, especially his projected history of diplomacy, the longer study on Acton, and the biography of Temperley. He was also criticized for ignoring social and economic factors.

In many ways Butterfield's career progressed through co-operation with 'Providence'. He might well have read English literature had the Peterhouse scholarship competition not been for history. He suppressed his early desire to enter the Methodist ministry, when an academic career beckoned. Later he achieved lasting recognition primarily in fields in which he had not shown, and did not profess, any previous expertise. Both *Christianity and History* and *The Origins of Modern Science* were responses to providential invitations. He accepted the mantle of prophet thus thrust upon him neither eagerly nor opportunistically, but with outward humility.

For most of his life Butterfield combined his writing with the supervision and lecturing of undergraduates and research students at Peterhouse and Cambridge University. He was not a dominating supervisor in the conventional sense, but his corrosive questioning of historical presuppositions in discussion sometimes disorientated his pupils as much as stimulated them. From 1938 to 1952 he was editor of the *Cambridge Historical Journal*. He made no attempt to found a school, though his influence on the works of a later generation of Conservative historians, such as Maurice Cowling's *Religion and Public Doctrine in Modern England* (1980), was palpable and acknowledged. Perhaps his most lasting institutional influence was in the Republic of Ireland, where he acted as external examiner to the National University of Ireland, and served on O Dalaigh's commission on higher education. His critique of national historical teleologies was enthusiastically embraced by the new 'revisionist' school of Irish historians, and was singled out for mention by the Revd Dr Brendan Bradshaw in his famous anti-revisionist polemic in *Irish Historical Studies* in 1989.

Although he showed some early ambiguity about charismatic authoritarian leaders, such as Napoleon, Butterfield's personal politics were firmly Liberal: he referred to himself as a 'new whig', of the non-utopian variety. Unlike Harold Temperley, he neither sought nor achieved contemporary political influence.

Butterfield was elected to the chair of modern history in 1944, and appointed to the regius professorship in 1963 and, somewhat belatedly, to a fellowship of the British Academy in 1965. From 1955 to 1968 he was by later standards an unusually uncontroversial master of Peterhouse; and from 1959 to 1961 he was, rather less happily, vice-chancellor of the university, during which period he was a jealous guardian of the independence of the university against the state, and the individual colleges against the university. A knighthood followed in 1968. He received thirteen honorary degrees including an honorary DLitt from Cambridge in 1974.

To those who knew him Butterfield was an engaging, though in many ways an enigmatic, figure. His personal irreverence belied the studied remoteness of much of his later prose and the homespun wisdom of his popular works. He was a teetotaller and a therapeutic pianist. The Christianity which permeates so much of his mature work had been a constant feature of his personal life from a very early age. He was a Methodist lay preacher in Cambridge and the surrounding villages until 1936, and continued to attend Wesley Methodist Chapel on Christ's Pieces every Sunday morning. He was an unconfirmed Anglican communicant in college chapel as master and remained so after his retirement to Sawston in 1968. He died at his home, 26 High Street, Sawston, on 20 July 1979. He was cremated and his ashes were buried beneath a tile in the aisle of Peterhouse Chapel. He was survived by his wife. BRENDAN SIMMS

Sources *DNB* • G. R. Elton, 'Herbert Butterfield and the study of history', *HJ*, 27 (1984), 729–43 • M. Cowling, *Religion and public doctrine in modern England*, 1 (1980) • H. T. Parker, 'Herbert Butterfield', *Essays in modern European historiography*, ed. S. W. Halperin (1970) • *Herbert Butterfield: writings on Christianity and history*, ed. C. T. McIntire (1979) • CUL, Butterfield MSS • A. R. Coll, *The wisdom of statecraft: Sir Herbert Butterfield and the philosophy of international politics* (1985) • K. W. Thompson, *Herbert Butterfield: the ethics of history and politics* (1980)

Archives CUL, papers as vice-chancellor of University of Cambridge; corresp. and papers • priv. coll., diaries | CAC Cam., corresp. with C. B. A. Behrens • CUL, letters to V. N. Datta • King's Lond., Liddell Hart C., corresp. with Sir B. H. Liddell Hart • U. Glas., corresp. with William Collins & Co. | SOUND BL NSA, performance recordings

Likenesses R. Spear, oils, 1960, Peterhouse, Cambridge [*see illus.*]

Wealth at death £33,250: probate, 20 Dec 1979, *CGPLA Eng. & Wales*

Butterfield, (William) John Hughes, Baron Butterfield (1920–2000), medical researcher and university administrator, was born on 28 March 1920 at 22 Yew Tree House, Station Road, Stechford, Birmingham, the son of William Hughes (Billy) Butterfield, engineer and businessman, and his wife, Doris, *née* Pritchard. His father was a director and founder of Levis, a company which made lightweight racing motorcycles, reputed in their time (and still remembered) as the best two-stroke engines ever made. From an early age Butterfield was taken to watch his father's team compete and win in the TT races on the Isle of Man—where, indeed, he may have learned that success depends on individuals working together as a dedicated team, a principle he supported all his life.

By the age of nine Butterfield knew he wanted to be a doctor and in due course he went to Solihull grammar school, where he became head boy and captain of the cricket, hockey, and rugby teams. In 1938 he won a scholarship to Exeter College, Oxford, where he completed his preclinical studies and captained the university cricket and hockey teams. He also played rugby fullback for Oxford and would have been a triple blue but for the outbreak of the Second World War, when blues were temporarily suspended.

Normally, Butterfield would have gone to a London teaching hospital to undertake his clinical studies, but in 1942 London was subjected to almost daily air raids, hospitals were evacuated, and teaching was seriously disrupted. He therefore applied for and won a Rockefeller scholarship to complete his studies in the United States. On his way to Johns Hopkins medical school in Baltimore, the *Loch Catrine*, the merchant ship in which he was sailing, was torpedoed at 11 o'clock at night. The lights went out and Butterfield, keeping his head, went down to his cabin to collect his passport and a bottle of brandy. On deck attempts were being made to lower a lifeboat. Before it was launched the raft attached to it fell off and began to drift away. 'You're young,' said a seaman, 'jump in and catch her.' Butterfield duly jumped in and secured the raft to the now successfully launched lifeboat. The survivors then waited until dawn before being rescued by the Canadian navy, and without the brandy to warm them, the precious bottle having slipped down Butterfield's trouser leg when he plunged into the water. Shortly after his arrival in Baltimore without money or possessions, a bookshop offered Butterfield a modest fee for a talk on his experiences and life in wartime Britain. The invitation was to plague him for many years. Unknown to him the bookshop was under surveillance for communist activities, and every time Butterfield applied for a visitor's visa to America he was regularly subjected to unexplained delays and questioning at the American embassy.

After two years in Baltimore, Butterfield returned to Britain where on 26 January 1946 he married Ann Sanders Berkeley, a 22-year-old American widow working in the economic warfare division of the American embassy and the daughter of Robert Sanders, oil distributor. Shortly after his marriage Butterfield was sent to Germany to complete national service, but he was suddenly recalled and seconded to the Medical Research Council to lead a unit of the Royal Army Medical Corps studying flash burns. Characteristically, Butterfield's experimental model was his own forearm and those of his colleagues. He continued to study flash burns until 1952, when he was invited to join Sir William Penny's team in the Monte Bello islands to observe the biological effects of the first British atomic bomb. For this work he was appointed OBE in 1953. Tragically, his wife Ann had died in childbirth a few years previously, after giving birth to their son, Jonathan. On 16 March 1950 he had married, second, Isabel-Ann Kennedy, a close friend of his first wife and godmother to his son. She was the daughter of Foster Kennedy, physician and neurologist. This second marriage produced two sons, Jeremy and Toby, and a daughter, Sarah.

On his return from Australia, Butterfield moved to Guy's Hospital in London to conduct research with R. T. (Ronald Thompson) Grant. At this time London University and the governors of Guy's Hospital were becoming concerned that the hospital's reputation for medical research (a reputation established in the nineteenth century by Richard Bright, Thomas Addison, and Thomas Hodgkin) was in decline. The governors therefore agreed to introduce a full-time professorship in clinical medicine though the post was initially limited to five years only, because of opposition from within the hospital and university. Butterfield was urged to put his name forward and in 1958 was selected as London University's professor of experimental medicine. Somewhat wryly he rephrased his title the 'experimental professor' of medicine. Five years later he was given tenure.

During work on the drug British Anti-Lewisite (BAL),

used to combat poison gas, Butterfield had become interested in the unexpected effects of the drug on blood-sugar levels—observations which aroused his interest in diabetes. At Guy's he began his investigation of the effects of diabetes and its treatment on muscle and fat metabolism. Once again he used the forearm as a model. For this he employed methods ancient (plethysmography—updated electronically) and modern (arterial catheters and continuous automatic glucose measurements). A singular benefit of these studies lay in the forging of an informal team which worked well together. Butterfield was an exceptionally good communicator, able to clarify a problem with a few simple sketches on a piece of paper or blackboard so that every member of the team—patient, relatives, and research assistants—could easily understand. In 1962 this gift enabled him to persuade the medical officer of Bedford to carry out a survey of diabetes, a disease widely prevalent in Britain and increasing. The ensuing investigations made an important contribution to the global definition of diabetes in terms of blood-sugar levels and became known as the Bedford study. It more than hinted at a relationship between blood-sugar levels and coronary heart disease and proved a gold mine for epidemiologists. The study was also a fine example of Butterfield's ability to run a happy ship, even when the work involved persuading 20,000 citizens of Bedford to leave specimens of urine on their doorsteps, for collection by boy scouts on a Sunday morning, and then testing the resulting 20,000 samples for sugar.

In 1970 Butterfield was invited to be vice-chancellor of Nottingham University. He accepted with enthusiasm because the university had decided to develop its preclinical medical sciences department into a full medical school and teaching hospital, and he took up the post the following year. He set about chairing committees, recruiting teaching staff, recommending names for consultancy posts, and advising on the curriculum. The Queen's Medical Centre which resulted was the first new medical school in England for more than a hundred years. Soon after Butterfield had taken up his duties as vice-chancellor his flair for solving a tricky situation was put to the test when an angry group of undergraduates occupied his office demanding to know what files he kept on their personal sleeping arrangements. Butterfield assured them that if that had been his intent his office would be so full of filing cabinets that he would not be able to get into the room. Satisfied with the logic of this observation, the students departed in a much friendlier frame of mind. The official residence in which the vice-chancellor and his family lived soon became known as Bedside Manor.

Among the recommendations of the royal commission on medical education in 1968 was the establishment of a pre-graduate clinical school in Cambridge based on the new Addenbrooke's Hospital. As an external member of the committee set up to put this into effect, Butterfield was involved at the outset in the planning of the school and its innovative two-year course, which opened in 1976. His appointment that year as regius professor of physic proved him yet again to be the right man in the right place at the right time. There were those in Cambridge who feared the further development of academic clinical medicine. Had it not been for his experience, academic standing, and natural diplomacy, their opposition would not have been assuaged, and the threatened closure of the new school would not have been finally laid to rest. Butterfield considered the foundation of the clinical school in Cambridge to be one of his principal achievements.

In 1978 Butterfield was made master of Downing College—in a leap, which caused some amusement at the time, from junior fellow to master in the space of eighteen months. Under his mastership the college made notable strides in establishing both academic and sporting excellence. He served also as a very effective vice-chancellor of Cambridge University from 1983 to 1985.

Butterfield's expertise, quick wit, and personal warmth served to increase his contacts all over the world and during the last twenty-five years of his life he became deeply involved in the founding of two medical schools in Hong Kong, first at the Chinese University and then at the University of Hong Kong. This led very naturally to a place on the boards of the universities and to the chairmanship of two foundations for Hong Kong student scholarships, the Jardine Educational Trust and the Croucher Foundation. The Jardine connection took him to Japan as well, where in the last year of his life he was given the order of the Sacred Treasure, Japan's highest honour. For the Croucher Foundation, in addition to acting as chairman, Butterfield played an active role in establishing the trust as a primary funding agency for Hong Kong-born citizens wishing to go to universities in Hong Kong, the UK, or elsewhere in the commonwealth. He also, with considerable tact, engineered the handover to the Chinese of the total running and chairmanship of the trust, prior to the handover of Hong Kong in 1997.

Butterfield was much in demand as an adviser on medical and educational subjects abroad, and he received honorary degrees from universities in Hong Kong, Japan, and the USA, as well as the UK. In 1988 his contributions to medicine and education were recognized by his being made a life peer, as Baron Butterfield of Stechford. He was an active member of the House of Lords' committees dealing with environmental and social work, and with science and technology. He also quickly established himself as an expert in medical and educational problems and had a broad input in environmental and social affairs. In particular he won the respect of the house for his explanations of science and ethics in modern medicine, which he delivered not only with clarity but with humour. He was a popular member of visiting parties for the House of Lords, when his expertise and relaxed view of life made him both a knowledgeable and pleasant companion. In addition to his interests in social, environmental, and medical issues, he played a primary role in pressing the needs of schoolteachers and educational matters in general.

Butterfield's door was open to anyone seeking his guidance, and he always gave advice that was in the enquirer's best interest. Despite his public honours he was always known to his students and colleagues as Prof or John. He was noted for his lovable eccentricities: the elegant trilby, the embroidered Chinese baseball cap, and the jaunty panama, worn according to weather or place, and, for his voluminous papers, the wicker flower-basket in summer and nylon string bag in winter. In retirement he so relished his self-imposed advisory and educational tasks that he barely reduced his involvement even when he required major heart surgery and later developed cancer, from which he died at his home in Cambridge on 22 July 2000. The end came slowly and painfully and he bore it with immense courage. He was survived by his wife, Isabel-Ann, and his four children. Lady Butterfield planted a tree in his memory in the fellows' garden at Downing College. The John Butterfield–Harvard University scholarship fund available to undergraduates at Downing College was founded to mark his affection for the United States and his belief in the special relationship between the two countries. ROBERT MAHLER

Sources *Daily Telegraph* (26 July 2000) • *The Guardian* (26 July 2000) • *The Times* (27 July 2000) • *The Independent* (1 Aug 2000) • *The Independent* (5 Sept 2000) • Munk, *Roll* • *WWW* • private information (2004) [Lady Butterfield, Lord Lewis] • personal knowledge (2004) • b. cert. • m. certs. • d. cert.

Archives CUL, corresp. with J. S. Mitchell • Wellcome L., corresp. with Sir Ernst Chain | SOUND Oxford Brookes University, Medical Sciences Video Archive, recorded interviews with Max Blythe (1991 and 1992)

Likenesses W. Evans, portrait, *c*.1975, U. Nott., Trent Building • photograph, 1980, repro. in *The Independent* (1 Aug 2000) • M. V. Foreman, portrait, 1983, Downing College, Cambridge • R. Rubbra, portrait, 1986, Addenbrooke's Hospital, Cambridge, Medical Library, Clinical School • M. Noakes, drawing, Addenbrooke's Hospital, Cambridge, Medical Library, Clinical School • photograph, repro. in *The Guardian* • photograph, repro. in *Daily Telegraph* • photograph, repro. in *The Times*

Butterfield, Michael (1634/5–1724), mathematical instrument maker, was born, according to Martin Lister, in England. Nothing is known of his early life except that he was in France from perhaps 1663. In 1677, when a new form of level made by him was reported in the *Journal des Sçavans*, he was established in the faubourg St Germain, Paris. In the following years other notices of his work concerning levels and hodometers appeared, and his inventiveness and skill brought him into close contact with the Académie des Sciences and its members. By November 1678 he knew Huygens, and in 1680 it was he who constructed Cassini's silver celestial planisphere that was presented to the king. In 1683 he supplied Cassini with instruments for the operations that extended the arc of the meridian measurements to Bourges. It was Butterfield also who oversaw the dividing of the meridian arcs for Coronelli's great globes (4.75 metres in diameter) presented to Louis XIV in 1683 by the Cardinal d'Estrées.

At an unknown date Butterfield became free of the Founders' Corporation of Paris in which he served as *juré* (1702–4). He supplied instruments to the king's observatory, invented a new form of simple microscope (described in *PTRS*, 12, 1678, and in *L'usage du nouveau microscope fait avec une seule et très-petite boulle de verre*, 1679), and a form of sundial that is still known by his name (described in *Description et usage du cadran à boussole portatif universel depuis environ le 54e degré d'elevation du pole jusqu'à environ le 41e degré de l'elevation, c'est à dire le nord d'Angleterre jusqu'au sud d'Italie, & pour tous les pays renfermez entre ces deux terres ou elevations*, Paris, *c*.1701/2). He was particularly noted among contemporaries for his skill in mounting lodestones and for his private collection of the different types thereof. With these he carried out carefully observed experiments, and Nicolas Hartsoeker acknowledged in his *Principes de physique* (1696) that most of the magnetic experiments he described were derived from Butterfield. In 1698 Butterfield received a grant of arms, and in 1717 his was one of four instrument-making workshops visited by Peter the Great.

As Butterfield's investigations into magnetism show, he had a wider interest in natural philosophy than just the production of instruments to be used in its service. In October 1678, he had written to Robert Hooke 'expressing his desire to correspond with [the Royal Society] concerning philosophical, mathematical, and mechanical matters; and offering to communicate such things, as he should meet with [in Paris] of that kind'. The society made an immediate response by ordering a copy of Halley's planisphere of the stars to be sent to Butterfield when this was presented to it on 7 November. Martin Lister's visit to Butterfield in the summer of 1698 offered another chance of creating such contact and a correspondence ensued. The ten letters between 1698 and 1700 that have survived mingle personal and professional matters: settling Lister's affairs in Paris, finding some peach trees for him, distributing copies of his book among Paris acquaintances, news of Butterfield's magnetical activities, and a request to put him in touch with John Sellar. Extracts from one of these letters concerning magnetic sand from Sampierdarena (Genoa) were published in the Royal Society's *Philosophical Transactions* (20, 1698). Butterfield's wife was Pernette Bernier, daughter of the 'Maître Artificier du Roi' Michel Bernier, and with her he had six children: Jean-Dominique (1678–1687), Dorothée (*b.* 1 Feb 1681), Georges-Michel (*b.* 30 Sept 1682), Jean-Baptiste (*b.* 23 Sept 1683), Georges-Michel (*b.* 5 Sept 1687), Jacques-Michel (*b.* 10 Nov 1688). Butterfield died, probably at the Quay de l'Horloge in Paris, where he certainly lived for an extended period, on 28 May 1724. He was probably buried at the church of St Barthélémy. A. J. TURNER

Sources *Journal des Sçavans* (1677) • *Journal des Sçavans* (1678) • *Journal des Sçavans* (1681) • *Journal des Sçavans* (1683) • M. Lister, *A journey to Paris in the year 1698* (1699) • J. Guiffrey, *Comptes des bâtiments du roi sous le règne de Louis XIV*, 5 vols. (1881–1901), vols. 1–2, 4 • M. Butterfield and M. Lister, correspondence, Bodl. Oxf., MS Lister 37 • T. Birch, *The history of the Royal Society of London*, 4 vols. (1756–7), vol. 3, pp. 432–3 • M. Daumas, *Scientific instruments of the seventeenth and eighteenth centuries and their makers*, ed. and trans. M. Holbrook (1972) [Fr. orig., *Les instruments scientifiques aux xvii et xviii siècles* (1953)] • L. Moréri, *Le grand dictionnaire historique*, new edn, ed. [É. F.] Drouet, 10 vols. (1759), vol. 2, p. 392 • Fichiers Léon Laborde 23, nos. 9153–9159, Bibliothèque Nationale de France, MS Na. Fr. 12060

Archives Institut Géographique, Paris • MHS Oxf., instruments • Musée des Arts et Métiers, Paris • Sci. Mus., instruments

Butterfield, Robert (*fl.* 1623–1629), religious controversialist, whose origins are unknown, graduated BA from Trinity College, Cambridge, in 1623, proceeded MA in 1626, and was ordained. Butterfield was one of the conformist divines who defended the moderate Calvinist Bishop Joseph Hall when the puritan divine Henry Burton attacked him after the publication of *The Old Religion* (1628), in which Hall treated Rome as essentially a true church. Butterfield's pamphlet, *Maschil, or, A Treatise to Give Instruction Touching the State of the Church of Rome … for the Vindication of … the Bishop of Exeter from the Cavills of H.B., in his Book Intituled 'The Seven Vialls'*, was published in 1629. Burton replied by publishing *Babel no Bethel … in Answer to Hugh Cholmley's Challenge and Rob Butterfield's 'Maschil', Two Masculine Champions for the Synagogue of Rome* the same year, in which he ridiculed Butterfield as inexperienced and out of his depth. Burton was imprisoned in the Fleet for the pamphlet. Thomas Spencer also replied to Butterfield, abusively, with *Maschil Unmasked* (1629). The debate was closed, not by his defenders, but by Hall himself, with another edition of his treatise including a new appendix called *The Reconciler*. Burton claimed that Butterfield went to Douai and became a Jesuit, but there is no record of this. Nothing is known of his later life.

Gordon Goodwin, *rev.* S. L. Sadler

Sources Venn, *Alum. Cant.* • A. Milton, *Catholic and Reformed: the Roman and protestant churches in English protestant thought, 1600–1640* (1995), 131, 142, 144, 149, 182, 241, 265n. • H. Burton, *Babel no Bethel* (1629) • *STC, 1475–1640*

Butterfield, Swithune (*d.* 1611), author, was born in Uxbridge, Middlesex, and in his will, dated 1608, described himself as a 'gentleman' living in the parish of St Botolph, Cambridge. In 1590 he published in London *The Principles of the True Christian Religion, Breifelie Selected, out of Manie Good Bookes*, a work composed 'for mine owne instruction' but published for others' benefit (Butterfield, sig. A2*r*). An earlier edition of this may have been published in 1582 as *A Summarie of the Principles of Christian Religion*: no copy survives.

Thereafter, his will reveals, Butterfield dedicated 'about twelve years' painful travail' to reading law books, chronicles, histories, political theory, religious polemic, medical, and other books, and making extensive notes under various headings. He appears to have revised these notes and rewritten them in sections in 1604–8. He then had them bound in six volumes and bequeathed them to Pembroke College, Cambridge, of which he is presumed to have been a member. In the order they appear in his will, the six were: his 'Great abridgement of the common lawes of the realm' (vol. 1, undated, but much the largest at '480 leaves' of large folio); his 'Collection out of the civil and canon lawes' of all the laws still valid in England (vol. 2, dated 1608); his 'Policies in peace and war' (vol. 3, 1604), described on the cover as 'Policies in government'; his book of 'Physick and surgerie' (vol. 4, 1607); his 'Principal controversies collected out of Bellarmine' (vol. 5, 1606), described on the cover as 'The differences of the cheif materiall controversies between papists and protestants'; and a book of 'Commonplaces in religion' (vol. 6, 1606), described on folio 2*r* as 'The true Christian religion now professed in England proved by the text of the holy scriptures to bee the true antient Christian religion'. He hoped that volumes 5 and 6 would both be published by a member of Pembroke, and with this in mind was still revising the latter in 1611.

'I know not how these books will be esteemed after my death', Butterfield wrote in 1608. Two volumes have disappeared (1 and 4), but volumes 2, 3, and 5 survive as Pembroke College manuscripts 218, 220, and 219 (held in Cambridge University Library), and volume 6 is still in Pembroke College (MS LC.II.6). All would repay study into how a well-read and enthusiastic layman produced his own idiosyncratic syntheses of what he read. His theology, for example, centred around a justifying faith that was an almost equal mixture of sincere belief and good behaviour. Butterfield also gave Pembroke £10 to buy books for the library, five dozen of his own legal and historical texts, his collection of geometrical instruments (with his own manuscript explanation of how to use them, and a chest to keep them in), and his 'watch with a laram'. In a codicil to his will dated 1611 he bequeathed 'all my wrytten chronicles' to the doctor with whom he then lodged. In another codicil he asked to be buried alongside his father in the north aisle of St Michael's Church, Cambridge. His will was proved on 21 December 1611.

Ian Green

Sources will, CUL, department of manuscripts and university archives, vice-chancellor's court, 1611, bundle 6 • M. Wren, list of benefactors to Pembroke College library, Pembroke Cam., fols. 27*v*–29*v* • S. Butterfield, *The principles of the true Christian religion* (1590) • Cooper, *Ath. Cantab.*, 3.53 • J. Ames, *Typographical antiquities, or, An historical account of the origin and progress of printing in Great Britain and Ireland*, ed. W. Herbert, 3 vols. (1785–90), 1108, 1344, 1378 • *ESTC* • *DNB*

Butterfield, William (1814–1900), architect and designer, was born on 7 September 1814 in London, the second child and eldest son of William Butterfield (1783–1866), chemist and wharfinger, and his wife, Ann (1793–1867), the daughter of Robert Steven, a leather factor of the City of London, and his wife, Jane Dawson. The details of Butterfield's early life are obscure but its circumstances were modest. He was one of nine children in a nonconformist family. At the time of his birth his father kept a chemist's shop at 173 Strand.

At sixteen Butterfield was apprenticed to Thomas Arber, a builder in Pimlico. Two years later, possibly as a result of his father's increased prosperity, he embarked on an architectural training and was articled to E. L. Blackburne, an antiquarian architect. Butterfield later spent a brief time in the office of the Greek revival architects William and Henry Inwood before finding employment in 1838 in a practice in Worcester, probably that of Harvey Eginton. During these years he made a serious, if limited, study of medieval architecture, 'laboriously visiting old buildings' as he later recalled, 'especially churches' (Thompson, 59).

In 1840 Butterfield returned to London, setting up in practice at Lincoln's Inn Fields. Two years later he moved to 4 Adam Street, Adelphi, which was to remain his office for the rest of his life.

William Butterfield (1814–1900), by Jane Fortescue Coleridge, 1874

Butterfield's first significant commission was for his uncle, W. D. Wills, the Bristol tobacco manufacturer, for whom he built the Highbury Congregational chapel. Completed in 1843, its use of rubble stone and irregular quoins shows how quickly he assimilated the ideas expounded by Pugin in his *True Principles of Gothic Architecture* (1841).

Ecclesiology and the high-church party The determining factor in Butterfield's life and work was his involvement from the early 1840s with the ecclesiological movement. It is not clear at what point he became an Anglican, but he had letters published in *The Ecclesiologist* in 1843 and was elected to the Cambridge Camden Society the following year. From this time he was at the heart of the mid-Victorian religious revival and essential to that aspect of it that sought intellectual and aesthetic expression in architecture. He was to become, as George Gilbert Scott wrote, the architect of the 'High Church party'. Yet Butterfield's profound, austere religious faith retained elements of his native nonconformism. He believed in the central importance of the Bible and his distaste for any doctrinal unorthodoxy eventually kept him from worshipping at his own most famous church, All Saints, Margaret Street.

Butterfield began by working in the fourteenth-century English Gothic style, as advocated by Pugin and the Cambridge Camden Society. St Saviour's, Coalpit Heath, Gloucestershire (1844–5), is in this vein. In the vicarage, however, for which precedents were less obvious, Butterfield's own style began to emerge. At the same time he began work on St Augustine's College, Canterbury, built for A. J. Beresford Hope. This was a quintessentially ecclesiological venture, an attempt to revive, on an ancient site, not only the fabric of the middle ages but the spirit as well. According to R. J. E. Boggis, Butterfield intended 'some sort of restoration of the old monastery … and not a mere college' (Boggis, *A History of St Augustine's College Canterbury*, 1907, 55). The resulting buildings show how his strict historicism was becoming modified by a growing interest in solid mass, apparent in the continuous roofline and abrupt punctuation of the wall surfaces by window tracery in the same plane.

Four years later at Great Cumbrae Island in the Firth of Clyde, Butterfield built the College of the Holy Spirit for George Frederick Boyle, later sixth earl of Glasgow, who was committed to reviving the Scottish Episcopal church in the Tractarian spirit. Butterfield's own Gothic language had by now developed, though still in a Puginian idiom. The church at Cumbrae, with its associated buildings, shows his genius for picturesque grouping: the asymmetrical elements drawn tightly round the soaring spire, the whole composition, in pale local stone, set deftly into the side of the island.

With Cumbrae and other substantial commissions that now came to him, Butterfield's career was under way by the late 1840s. He was known, too, through the *Instrumenta ecclesiastica*, published from 1847 by the Ecclesiological Society. Butterfield was its *de facto* editor and hence in a position to publish his own designs for metalwork and furnishings. These became widely known to and favoured by high-church clergy, patrons, and architects.

It was All Saints, Margaret Street, in London, however, that established Butterfield as a national figure. This was the model church of the Ecclesiological Society. It has been since its inception one of the most discussed of nineteenth-century buildings. It marked a turning-point in Butterfield's career and in the Gothic revival, introducing to both the elements of structural polychromy and continental Gothic that were to be defining characteristics of the high Victorian manner.

Once again it was Beresford Hope who engaged Butterfield. One set of designs was already prepared when Ruskin's *Seven Lamps of Architecture* was published, in May 1849. Three months later Hope told his backer Henry Tritton that the plans had been altered to reflect the 'aesthetic possibilities of different materials' that were now becoming clearer to Hope, Webb, and other ecclesiologists (letter from A. J. B. Hope to Henry Tritton, 6 Aug 1850, Tritton collection; Thompson, 349). The result, built in banded brick with a densely elaborated interior, was like nothing before it and liberated Gothic architecture, Charles Eastlake wrote in his *History of the Gothic Revival* (1872), from 'the trammels of … precedent' (p. 253). The church, clergy house, and school are fitted ingeniously into a small site, the church set back but emphasized by its great Germanic spire. Rather than miniaturize details, Butterfield made dramatic play with them, allowing the porch to be cut off where it appears to collide with the house. Each of these elements was striking to contemporaries and divided critical opinion then and since.

Internally the style was still essentially English Gothic, though overlaid with Italianate surface polychromy. The interior is dominated by profuse and in places discordant decoration, the overall effect having suffered from disagreements between Hope and Butterfield, who by the time the building was finished had quarrelled badly. All Saints was completed in 1859, but Butterfield continued to work on it for the rest of his life attempting to correct its faults.

Middle years and major works The 1850s and 1860s were the years of Butterfield's greatest work, much of it ecclesiastical, and all of it developing the polychromatic style of All Saints. St Matthias, Stoke Newington (1849–53), was built as part of the high-church campaign to reconvert the urban poor. The great buttress at the east end, a massively splayed version of the one at Dorchester Abbey, which he had restored, was described by E. A. Freeman, in a letter to *The Ecclesiologist*, as 'depraved' (11, 1850, 208–10; Thompson, 260). This was an early instance of the view of Butterfield's work as wilfully distorted, ugly to the point of sadism, that has subsequently dogged and at times overwhelmed his reputation.

Butterfield's only country house, the austere Milton Ernest Hall, Bedfordshire, was built in 1853–4 for his brother-in-law Benjamin Starey. On its completion he went with Starey on a foreign tour, commenting afterwards to his friend John Duke Coleridge that 'you will think me odd of course but I am more than ever persuaded that an Architect gets but little by travel. I am only glad that I had made up my own mind about a hundred things in art before seeing Italy' (Butterfield, MS letter, 30 Sept 1854, priv. coll.). In his use of precedents—English or continental—Butterfield always made up his own mind. Historicism like functionalism was the servant not the master of his imagination.

At Baldersby in Yorkshire from 1855 to 1857 Butterfield built an estate village for Lord Downe. Here he showed his range along the full scale of architectural propriety, from the dignity of the country church to cottages of distinguished simplicity. In these and in his parsonages—at Coalpit Heath, and Hensall and Pollinton in Yorkshire—he created the simplified vernacular forms from which the domestic Gothic of the next generation, Philip Webb, W. E. Nesfield, and Norman Shaw, would take their cue.

In 1855 Butterfield began work on a new chapel for Balliol College, Oxford (1855–7). St Alban the Martyr, Holborn, London, followed in 1859–62, and St Augustine's, Penarth, Glamorgan, from 1864 to 1866. From the mid-1850s the emphasis in his work began to shift from mass to linearity. The development of his style has been characterized by his biographer Paul Thompson as first a resolution of the Gothic into its geometric elements of circle, square, and triangle and then, in this later phase, a process of abstraction from volume to line. The polychromatic patterns became increasingly complex, often on the diagonal, acting as a counterpoint to the structure.

In 1858 Butterfield began work at Rugby College, Warwickshire, where he built the New Quad in 1867 and the chapel in 1872. Here the tower, an octagon with pyramidal roof, shows, as Thompson, puts it, 'the massive High Victorian forms … veiled, withdrawn, abstracted yet defiant' (Thompson, 287). Though they have sometimes struck critics as chaotic, Butterfield's effects are in fact finely controlled, almost metrical. They play on the rhythms of a familiar architectural language as the 'sprung rhythm' of Gerard Manley Hopkins, who knew and admired Butterfield's work, plays on the spoken word. Hopkins's 'stress' and 'instress' may seem closer to the effect of Butterfield's work than his own notion of 'gaiety', but the view of him as a conscious apostle of ugliness—a contemporary view enlarged upon by historians—was dispelled conclusively by Thompson.

Butterfield's practice was prosperous but not extensive. He disliked competitions or even publication of his work which, in monochrome, tended to give a misleading impression. He maintained close control over every aspect of his buildings. Despite his interest in Ruskin, he firmly discouraged individual expression in his craftsmen. Designing in many media, he had a particular affinity for metalwork, in which he had some practical skill, and stained glass, in which he had none. Here, however, by the sheer force of personality he brought to bear on designers he created a distinct 'Butterfield' style. Characterized by 'clarity, vigour and severity', as Michael Kerney has described it, Butterfield's glass was conceived as integral to his polychromatic interiors, creating mosaic effects with complex leading and jewel-like colour (Kerney, 11). His style was influenced by the growing taste for the Pre-Raphaelite artists Giotto and Fra Angelico. Butterfield worked with several designers, including Pugin, but his most fruitful collaboration was with Alexander Gibbs from about 1861.

The most important church of Butterfield's later career—All Saints, Babbacombe, Devon—was begun in 1867. Here the use of tile, brick, stone, and vivid marbles in the interior reached a height of 'inspired strangeness', as Goodhart-Rendel thought (B. Cherry and N. Pevsner, *The Buildings of England, Devon*, 2nd edn, repr. with corrections 1991, 848). Butterfield's marble font and pulpit enhance a sense of hard, organic integrity. The following year he received the commission for Keble College, Oxford. Completed in 1886, this was the architectural apotheosis of the Oxford Movement in which Nikolaus Pevsner saw 'a summing up of [Butterfield's] ideals as well as his motifs' (J. Sherwood and N. Pevsner, *The Buildings of England, Oxfordshire*, 1974, 225). This is especially true of the chapel, a single, vast space, crowned with some of Gibbs's most successful windows. The classicizing horizontal elements that ground all Butterfield's work are here combined with mannerist details. The columns, half recessed into the walls, have been seen to echo Michelangelo's staircase in the vestibule of the Biblioteca Laurenziana, Florence.

Later life and lesser works Butterfield's personal life had settled early into the spartan routine that was to characterize it. He never married, and spent his life between

Adam Street and the Athenaeum, to which he was elected in 1858. 'A perplexing and challenging' character, as John Coleridge's son Stephen recalled; a shy man 'who carried firmness to the point of obstinacy' (S. Coleridge, *Memories*, 1913, 82–3). The stories of his ruthless perfectionism include his habit, when visiting stained glass workshops, of putting his umbrella through work he disliked.

Yet to his family and few intimates Butterfield was a lovable man who returned the affection he received. To John Coleridge he wrote: 'I am not tempted to wish for general popularity … Steady sympathy like yours through good report & evil report, is alone worth having' (Butterfield to Coleridge, 28 Dec 1874, priv. coll.). General popularity was never his. Not until 1884, after two previous proposals, did he receive the RIBA gold medal.

In his later work there is a lessening of elaboration, then at the end what Thompson characterizes as a 'coarsening' and a failure of invention. Butterfield's influence was considerable, especially on Philip Webb, whom he knew well, but indirect. Of his pupils the only notable architect was Henry Woodyer. Butterfield offered no obvious solution to the late nineteenth century's search for a style. To Norman Shaw it seemed that 'we are all in much the same boat, except Butterfield, who is in a boat of his own all by himself' (A. Saint, *Richard Norman Shaw*, 1976, 219).

Butterfield built St Andrew's, Rugby, in 1875 and provided designs for the cathedral at Melbourne, Australia, in 1877. His most distinguished late work was the Chanter's House, Ottery St Mary, Devon, a remodelling and extension of the family home of the Coleridges. In style it is a work of the 1860s, showing the 'masculine severity' that the patron had long admired in his friend's work. For Coleridge, his son Gilbert said, 'Gladstone must always be right … Butterfield the greatest architect' (Hall, 52).

As well as reflecting the effects of age and an inflexible character, Butterfield's later career also perhaps suffered from that loss of confidence that characterized his generation. The implications of evolutionary theory, to some extent subsumed into a Christian view of creation by the use of minerals and marbles in structural polychrome, were by the end of the century unanswerable. 'The faith & the tradition which made strong men of our fathers are going', Butterfield wrote to Coleridge (letter, 10 June 1883, priv. coll.). 'There will shortly … be nothing left for us to believe in but ourselves, and *that* faith … is comfortless' (ibid.).

Butterfield was the quintessential high Victorian, epitomizing the qualities the age admired: 'reality' and 'go'. His work speaks of both the confidence and the anxieties of the mid-Victorians. Yet he was also an original, with some of the freakishness of genius. Few architects can have been subject to such widely different interpretations.

If some of his contemporaries thought him too individual, too careless of precedent, Butterfield seemed to later critics all too typical. For the generations that found Victorian mores repressive and repulsive, Butterfield's buildings seemed to possess these qualities. John Summerson thought his love of 'ugliness' amounted to 'purposeful sadism' (J. Summerson, 'William Butterfield, or, The glory of ugliness', *Heavenly Mansions and other Essays on Architecture*, 1949, *passim* and 175). Kenneth Clark dared not devote a chapter to him in *The Gothic Revival* published in 1928, at a time when Keble College was a joke and generally believed to have been designed by Ruskin (K. Clark, *The Gothic Revival*, rev. edn, 1950, 3–5). Pevsner saw him as a proto-brutalist (N. Pevsner, *The Buildings of England, Oxfordshire*, 1974, 227). Butterfield's work has come gradually to be better understood but is still arguably undervalued in relation to his contemporaries.

In 1891 Anne Starey, Butterfield's sister, to whom he was deeply attached, died. Butterfield gave up most of his practice the following year. His last known work was in 1895 at All Saints, Margaret Street, London. He had moved, in 1886, to 42 Bedford Square and it was there that he died on 23 February 1900. He was buried in Tottenham cemetery. ROSEMARY HILL

Sources P. Thompson, *William Butterfield* (1971) · W. Butterfield, MS letters to John Duke Coleridge, priv. coll. · M. Kerney, 'The stained glass commissioned by William Butterfield', *Journal of Stained Glass*, 20/1 (1996), 1–30 · P. Thompson, 'All Saints' Church Margaret Street, reconsidered', *Architectural History*, 8 (1965), 73–94 · M. Hall, 'The Chanter's House, Devon', *Country Life* (10 Jan 1991), 50–55 · H. Ricardo, 'William Butterfield', *ArchR*, 7 (1900), 259–63; 8 (1900), 15–23 · *CGPLA Eng. & Wales* (1900)

Archives Arundel Castle, corresp. and plans relating to Arundel church · Balliol Oxf., corresp. relating to Balliol College chapel · Bodl. Oxf., corresp. relating to Keble College chapel [copies] · Devon RO, corresp. relating to Tattershall church and schools · E. Sussex RO, specifications for restoration of St Clements Church, Hastings · Essex RO, Chelmsford, plans, etc., relating to new works at Ardleigh church · priv. coll., Coleridge MSS · priv. coll., Starey MSS · RIBA, Caroë MSS · Winchester College, corresp. relating to Winchester College

Likenesses J. F. Coleridge, charcoal drawing, 1874, Keble College, Oxford [*see illus.*] · J. F. Coleridge, drawing, Chanter's House, Ottery St Mary

Wealth at death £16,369 14*s*.: probate, 17 March 1900, *CGPLA Eng. & Wales*

Butters, Mary [*called* the Carnmoney Witch] (*fl.* **1807–1839**), accused murderer, achieved fame and notoriety on an August night in 1807 when she attempted to work a charm to return the butter to the milk of a cow belonging to a tailor by the name of Montgomery, who lived in the town of Carnmoney, co. Antrim. The events of the night left three people dead: Montgomery's wife, his son, and an old woman by the name of Margaret Lee. Mary Butters, it appears, was known to have the power to cure cattle so afflicted. She duly arrived when sent for, from her home in Carrickfergus, co. Antrim, and set about working her charm. According to the *Belfast News-Letter* account of the event, published on 21 August 1807, just four days after the fatal night in Montgomery's house, Mary Butter's charm consisted of boiling a pot of needles, pins, and crooked nails mixed with some milk over the open fire in Montgomery's house. The subsequent inquest reported that all the occupants, excluding Mary Butters herself, died of suffocation. Butters was imprisoned in Carrickfergus gaol but later discharged by proclamation at the assizes—a verdict implying that the event was seen as an unfortunate accident.

The story of the butter stealing witch has been recorded extensively in Ireland. The witch, often with the aid of supernatural power to transform herself into a hare, steals the milk from her neighbours' cows while they graze in the field and, subsequently, steals the butter from the milk in the churn. The preponderance of this story in Irish tradition is not surprising considering the predominantly agricultural nature of Irish society and the important position of cattle in that society from early times. Fortunately, allied to the story of the butter stealing witch is a body of traditional advice on how the butter might be returned. The two events—the butter stealing and its retrieval—are woven into the international migratory legend 'The Butter Stealing Witch and the Ploughshare' (Christiansen, legend 3058). In the Irish versions of this legend the helper—that is, the person who has the power to return the butter to the milk—is a local wise man. Having blocked all openings and every means of entry to the house, he puts the share or the coulter of the plough into the fire and, when it becomes red hot, a knock is heard on the door. The woman who is knocking repeatedly demands to be allowed to enter. Her request is refused as she is the butter stealer and, once recognized, she is never allowed to return to the farm again.

A fuller and very detailed account of the event of that August night in 1807 was written by William Orr McGraw, who was born in Carnmoney in 1798. He testifies to the veracity of this account by claiming to have seen the pot in which the fatal concoction was brewed. He details information on the important point which led to the deaths by suffocation, namely that Mary Butters ordered that all the openings 'which would admit air' were to be sealed. Orr's account indicates clearly that the migratory legend 'The Butter Stealing Witch and the Ploughshare' was known in the locality, and he firmly places Mary Butters as the witch in the legend. The important difference between Orr's account and the recorded Irish versions of the legend is that Mary Butters is a female witch and not a wise man. There is plenty of evidence elsewhere in Irish tradition, however, that women as well as men had the power to return the milk or the butter. The best-known of these female personages is Biddy Early of co. Clare, while others, whose names have been recorded in folklore, include Moll Anthony from co. Kildare, Brídín or Máirín Cúileann from co. Galway, and Maire Cáitlín Conway from co. Wicklow.

Mary Butters (also known as Mary Buttles or Butlers) has not been found in the Carrickfergus and Carnmoney parish records. Her name does not occur in the tombstone inscriptions for Carrickfergus or in the birth, marriage, and death announcements printed in the *Belfast News-Letter* from 1800 to 1860. Curiously she is not mentioned in the Ordnance Survey memoir for Carrickfergus, while the memoir for the nearby parish of Carnmoney, in which the tragedy took place, records that Mary Butters still resided in Carrickfergus on 28 April 1839, some thirty-two years after the fateful night.

While the event of the August night as reported in the *Belfast News-Letter* did take place, the woman known as Mary Butters and later dubbed the Carnmoney Witch is unidentified. She otherwise acquired her name because of the power she was reputed to have. If William Orr McGraw is correct, Mary Butters died in the town of Carrickfergus 'at an advanced age'. ANNE O'DOWD

Sources *Belfast News-Letter* (21 Aug 1807) · St J. D. Seymour, *Irish witchcraft and demonology* (1913); facs. edn (1989) · S. McSkimmin, *The history and antiquities of the county of the town of Carrickfergus* (1909) · *Parishes of county Antrim, 1838–1839*, 2 vols. (1990), vol. 1/2 of *Ordnance survey memoirs of Ireland* · W. O. McGaw, 'Tragic occurrence, which took place in the parish of Carnmoney and county of Antrim in the year 1807 through belief in witchcraft', *Ulster Journal of Archaeology*, 18 (1955), 113–16 · R. T. Christiansen, *Migratory legends* (1958) · R. M. Young, ed., *Historical notices of old Belfast and its vicinity* (1896) · E. Fitzgerald, 'Moll Anthony of the Red Hills', *Journal of the County Kildare Archaeological Society*, 8 (1915–17), 76–9 · G. W. Saunderson, 'Butterwitches and cow doctors', *Ulster Folklife*, 7 (1961), 72–5 · J. C. Foster, *Ulster folklore* (1951) · private information [C. Doyle]

Butterworth, Edwin (1812–1848), topographer and journalist, was the tenth child of James *Butterworth (1771–1837) and his wife, Hannah Boyton (or Royton; 1774–1836). He was born at Pitses, near Oldham, on 1 October 1812. From childhood Edwin assisted his father, a well-known local historian and publisher, in the preparation of his works, but from the age of sixteen he was writing and publishing on his own account. He produced town histories, cartographical surveys, reports of charities and local societies, and a miscellany of topographical and historical material. By the late 1830s he was becoming particularly interested in the collection and presentation of statistical information on the economic and social trends of Lancashire.

Butterworth wrote six local history books together with some minor works. His *History of Oldham* (1832) and *Historical Sketches of Oldham* (1847) have remained well used and highly regarded, as has his pioneering *A Statistical Sketch of the County Palatine of Lancaster* (1841). None of these books produced much remuneration, however, and the main source of Butterworth's income was therefore writing news items and longer reports about events and current affairs in Oldham and district, which he regularly supplied under contract to several Manchester newspapers and, more sporadically, to the press in other towns. These reports are an important source of information about the fast-growing cotton town during a period of considerable social, economic, and political turbulence.

Butterworth is now perhaps best known for his crucial contribution to Edward Baines's history of Lancashire. Almost all the primary research for the work was undertaken by Butterworth, who travelled on foot to most towns and villages in the county, making meticulous and copious notes on local history and topography. This element of the work was acknowledged by Baines, but it has been apparent to later researchers that Butterworth not only provided the material for the history but also—without any acknowledgement—wrote most of the text. In 1904 Giles Shaw, his first biographer, suggested that 'the work ought properly to be called Butterworth's *History of Lancashire* edited by Baines', noting 'how small a share Baines himself had in the labour of compiling the standard history of the county' (Shaw, 68). Butterworth's own project for the publication of a fifty-part history of Lancashire was abortive.

Butterworth's last years were clouded by ill health and anxiety. He died, unmarried, in Oldham on 19 April 1848, of typhus fever, and was buried on 23 April at Greenacres cemetery in Oldham, where a monument to his memory was erected by public subscription in 1859. He had previously inherited his father's large collection of manuscript local history material and this, with his own voluminous notebooks, diaries, and transcripts, constituted an irreplaceable resource. On his death parts of this collection and of his library were dispersed. Fortunately several friends, among them the Platt brothers, who owned Oldham's largest textile engineering firm, bought the greater part and presented it to the town. The collection now forms one of the most important holdings of the Oldham Local Studies Centre. ALAN G. CROSBY

Sources *DNB* • G. Shaw, 'Edwin Butterworth: his life and labours', *Transactions of the Lancashire and Cheshire Antiquarian Society*, 22 (1904), 61–72 • M. Winstanley, 'News from Oldham: Edwin Butterworth and the Manchester press, 1829–1848', *Manchester Region History Review*, 4/1 (1990), 3–10 • parish register (baptism), Oldham, St Mary, 22 Oct 1812

Archives Oldham Local Studies Centre | Manchester Central L., Shaw MSS

Butterworth, George Sainton Kaye (1885–1916), composer and folk dancer, was born on 12 July 1885 at 16 Westbourne Square, Paddington, London, the only child of Sir Alexander Kaye Butterworth (1854–1946), a solicitor and later general manager of the North Eastern Railway Company, and his wife, Julia Marguerite (1849–1911), the daughter of George Wigan MD of Portishead, Somerset, and a professional soprano before her marriage. His first school was Aysgarth, Yorkshire, from which he entered Eton College as a king's scholar in 1899. He distinguished himself in the athletic and social dimensions of school life as well as in intellectual pursuits; early promise in music was nurtured through study with Charles Lloyd and Thomas Dunhill at Eton, as well as with Christian Padel in York. From 1904 to 1908 he was in residence at Trinity College, Oxford; he took a third class in the honour school of *literae humaniores* and was active in musical circles, holding the presidency of the university musical club from October 1906 to March 1907.

By the time he left Oxford, Butterworth had abandoned plans for a career in the law, and the subsequent years were restless for him. He worked for a short while as a music critic for *The Times*, and as a writer also contributed articles on the composers York Bowen, Henry Balfour Gardiner, and his teacher Dunhill to the second edition of *Grove's Dictionary of Music and Musicians* (1904–10). In 1909 he accepted a teaching post at Radley College but the following year returned to London, and from October 1910 to November 1911 he was enrolled at the Royal College of Music, where he studied the organ with Sir Walter Parratt, the piano with Herbert Sharpe, and theory and composition with Charles Wood.

The most powerful stimulus to Butterworth's artistic development came not from academic study, however, but from two quite different sources: his involvement with the 'rescue' and revival of English folk-music and folk-dance gathering pace at the time, and his intimate friendship with a leading figure of this movement, Ralph Vaughan Williams, both of which had begun in his Oxford days. Butterworth became a major worker in the field, collecting more than 450 items, including songs, dance tunes, and dances; in 1906 he joined the Folk Song Society, and he was a prominent figure in the English Folk-Dance Society, of which he was one of the founders in 1911, as well as a member of its original morris-dance side or team. An accomplished and passionate devotee of folk-dance, he once declared, 'I'm not a musician, I'm a professional dancer' (Barlow, 91). Folk-dancing appears to have been the one activity in which he felt completely assured and fulfilled, and which to some extent knit together the disparate threads of his life up to this point (film of Butterworth dancing survives). He collected and arranged an album of Sussex folk-songs and, in collaboration with Cecil Sharp, published several books of country and morris dances. The friendship with Vaughan Williams encompassed many shared ideals; they admired each other's music, and Butterworth provided both moral and practical support in the composition, performance, and reception of the older man's *London Symphony* (first performed 1914), which was dedicated to Butterworth's memory on its publication in 1920. At his death Butterworth left the majority of his manuscripts to Vaughan Williams.

Butterworth's surviving oeuvre of original compositions dates mostly from the period 1910–14. It is small but distinctive and finely honed, and its core has established a firm hold in the repertory, at least in Britain. (His actual output was larger: a number of works, including songs, piano pieces, and some early chamber music, appear to have been destroyed by the composer in 1915.) It comprises eighteen songs (the majority to words from A. E. Housman's *A Shropshire Lad*, the remainder settings of W. E. Henley, R. L. Stevenson, P. B. Shelley, and Oscar Wilde), three short choral pieces, a suite for string quartet (unpublished), and four orchestral pieces, three of which are idylls partially based on folk-song material, and the fourth a rhapsody thematically connected with two of the *Shropshire Lad* songs. The assimilation of folk-song (in this Vaughan Williams's influence was crucial) is the key to a style that is simple and restrained, yet which distils deep passions that may on occasion emerge with force; folk-song suggested how basic melodic and harmonic vocabulary could be freed from a nineteenth-century tonal syntax (and attendant expressive ethos) that seemed exhausted and blandly cosmopolitan to many composers of the era. The *Rhapsody: a Shropshire Lad* (first performed under Arthur Nikisch at the Leeds festival of 1913) demonstrates impressively that Butterworth was developing both the capability of working on a larger scale without stylistic strain or contrivance and an individual handling of orchestral resources (even if the imprints of Elgar and Sibelius, in addition to Vaughan Williams, can be felt at times).

An unidentified colleague at Radley summed up Butterworth's character in terms echoed closely by other contemporaries:

> He had strength of character, opinions and the courage of them, a rugged directness of manner coupled with a gift of keen criticism and an absence of heroics. Few men can have been worse at making an acquaintance or better at keeping a friend. (Butterworth, 11)

Whether any of Butterworth's friendships were more than platonic is uncertain; although he seems generally to have preferred the company of men, his sexual orientation remains unclear. His modesty, kindness, and natural gifts of leadership were commented on as early as his prep school days. He was a good-looking man, of medium height and build, dark-haired and with the full moustache fashionable in his day, and the most notable feature of his face in photographs is the sensitive and humorous cast of the eyes.

In many respects Butterworth emerges as an almost perfect example of a certain kind of Englishman of his generation—he loved cricket, for instance, as well as country life in general—and the reception of his music has also been dominated by its identification with a ruralist and often elegiac vision of 'Englishness'. Such associations were sealed by the composer's distinguished conduct and sudden death in the First World War; as an example of youthful promise cut short he is the most important musical counterpart of a war poet such as Rupert Brooke (although he did not compose during the conflict). He enlisted on the outbreak of war in August 1914 and was subsequently commissioned in the 13th Durham light infantry. In France in 1916 he took charge of his company after the commanding officer was wounded; during that summer he was three times recommended for, and was twice awarded, the Military Cross. The second decoration honoured conduct on the morning of his death, 5 August 1916; he was killed by a bullet through the head at Pozières during the first battle of the Somme. He was buried on the front line; no grave marking survives, but his name appears on the Thiepval memorial close by, and a trench was named after him. ALAIN FROGLEY

Sources M. Barlow, *Whom the gods love: the life and music of George Butterworth* (1998) · A. Butterworth, ed., *George Butterworth, 1885–1916 (memorial volume)* (privately printed, York and London, 1918) · J. Rippin, 'George Butterworth, 1885–1918', *MT*, 107 (1966), 680–82, 769–71 · M. Dawney, 'George Butterworth's folk music manuscripts', *Folk Music Journal*, 3 (1975–9), 99–113 · S. Banfield, *Sensibility and English song*, 2 vols. (1985) · *DNB* · *CGPLA Eng. & Wales* (1917)

Archives Bodl. Oxf., letters · Eton · Vaughan Williams Memorial Library, London, collected papers | BL, Add. MS 54369 · Bodl. Oxf., MSS Mus. b. 15, c. 297–306 · Vaughan Williams Memorial Library, London, Lucy Broadwood MS collections | FILM Vaughan Williams Memorial Library, London, performance footage | SOUND BL NSA, *Talking about music*, 207, 1LP0202106 S1 BD1 BBC TRANSC · BL NSA, 'To the memory of George Butterworth', M5838BW C1

Likenesses photograph, *c*.1911, Eton; repro. in Barlow, *Whom the gods love*, 97 · photograph, 1913, Vaughan Williams Memorial Library, London, English Folk Dance and Song Society Photograph Collection · Rossmont, photograph, Royal College of Music, London · engraving, Royal College of Music, London

Wealth at death £4701 4*s*. 1*d*.: administration, 1917, *CGPLA Eng. & Wales*

Butterworth, Henry (1786–1860), law publisher, was born on 28 February 1786 in Coventry, Warwickshire, the son of Henry Butterworth, a wealthy timber merchant, and his wife. His grandfather was John *Butterworth (1727–1803), a Particular Baptist minister. Henry was educated at the grammar school at Coventry, but he grew restless. His uncle Joseph *Butterworth (1770–1826), publisher and politician, persuaded him to live with his friends the Stocks, in Bristol. There he briefly attended the school of a Dr Johnson before being employed in the counting house of Mr Stock's sugar refinery. He was soon restless again, however, and at fifteen he entered the bookselling establishment of his uncle Joseph Butterworth, in Fleet Street, London. Living in his uncle's house he became acquainted with William Wilberforce, Nicholas Vansittart, and other leaders of the evangelical movement. He also served in a light volunteer regiment recruited to resist Napoleon. In 1813 Butterworth married Elizabeth Henry Whitehead (*d*. 1853), daughter of Captain Henry Whitehead of the dragoon guards. She published a book of poetry in 1848. They had three sons and four daughters.

In 1818 Butterworth went into business on his own account, perhaps disappointed in his expectation of a partnership. With financial assistance from his father, Henry Butterworth opened premises at 7 Fleet Street, London, and competed with his uncle for business. Butterworth sold his own publications as well as books and reports from other publishing houses. Henry John Stephen's *Commentaries on the Laws of England* (1841), under the Butterworth imprint, became the standard work, superseding the commentaries of Sir William Blackstone, and established Butterworth as the chief London law publisher. Butterworth was active in the Stationers' Company: he was made a liveryman in February 1818 and became a member of its governing body, the court of assistants, in November 1857. In 1823 he was elected a representative of the ward of Farringdon Street Without, London, but declined nomination as an alderman. He later became commissioner of income and property tax and land and assessed taxes for London, and also commissioner of roads. He was made a captain in the London militia in 1841 and was later promoted to colonel.

Following the death of their eldest daughter, Elizabeth (aged sixteen), in 1836, the Butterworths moved to Upper Tooting. Henry continued to visit the business but his son Joshua [*see below*] assumed more and more responsibility. Henry's public offices began to take up most of his time. He was on the building committee for a new church of St Dunstan's and supported church extension generously, particularly in the plans to build a new church at Upper

Tooting. He was made a fellow of the Society of Antiquaries in 1849 and in 1852 was appointed law publisher to the queen. He died at Upper Tooting, London, on 2 November 1860, and was buried at Kensal Green, London. Butterworth's friends proposed a memorial glass window in the choir of St Paul's Cathedral, but instead the cathedral was presented with an alms dish. A stained-glass window was placed in his former parish church of St Dunstan's.

Joshua Whitehead Butterworth (*bap.* 1818, *d.* 1895), second son of Henry Butterworth and Elizabeth Henry Whitehead, baptized on 21 January 1818 at St Pancras's Church, London, inherited his father's business at his death. Joshua had been unofficially running Butterworths for a number of years and made few substantial alterations to the business once he was in charge. He claimed to have found evidence that connected 7 Fleet Street with Shakespeare and Caxton, but he never published on the subject. Like his father he was a fellow of the Society of Antiquaries and he was active in the affairs of the Stationers' Company; he presented the Shakespeare window to the Stationers' Hall. In 1889 he was nominated to the court of the company, and in 1894 became master and presented the Caxton window to the hall. Towards the end of his life he gradually withdrew from the management of the business; he died of pneumonia on 8 January 1895 at his home, 45 Russell Road, Kensington, London.

With no one to succeed Joshua Butterworth the business passed out of the Butterworth family. It was sold to Charles Bond and Richard Shaw Bond but remained at 7 Fleet Street for another four years. Under the Bonds, particularly Charles's second son, Stanley Shaw Bond (1877–1943), Butterworths expanded internationally. As Butterworths Tolley it is still trading as one of the leading legal publishers. It also developed online as Butterworths Lexis Direct. W. B. LOWTHER, *rev.* LESLIE HOWSAM

Sources H. K. Jones, *Butterworths: history of a publishing house* (1980) • H. Curwen, *A history of booksellers, the old and the new* (1873) • *Annual Register* (1860)

Archives GL, Butterworth & Co., Publishers MSS

Likenesses photograph, repro. in Jones, *Butterworths*, 8; formerly at Butterworth & Co. • photograph (Joshua Butterworth), repro. in Jones, *Butterworths*

Wealth at death under £25,000: probate, 18 Dec 1860, *CGPLA Eng. & Wales* • £120,456 4s. 3d.—Joshua Butterworth: resworn probate, March 1896, *CGPLA Eng. & Wales*

Butterworth, James [*pseud.* Paul Bobbin] (1771–1837), poet and local historian, was born on 28 August 1771 at Pitses in the hamlet of Alt, Ashton under Lyne, the youngest of eleven children of James Butterworth and his wife, Jane, *née* Ogden, both hand-loom weavers. Butterworth was sent to school under John Taylor of Alt, who eventually allowed him to share in the teaching of the younger classes. Butterworth attained some skill in ornamental penmanship, and in 1861 wrote a manuscript entitled 'Notes and observations experimental in painting. Made … in my practice'. On 24 June 1792 he married Hannah Boyton (or Royton; 1774–1836), with whom he had ten children; only two sons survived to adulthood, of whom the younger, Edwin *Butterworth (1812–1848), was to become a distinguished topographer.

At first a weaver, by 1799 Butterworth was running a Sunday school at Mumps. At this time he published *A Dish of Hodge Podge, or, A Collection of Poems by Paul Bobbin, Esq.* (1800), and *Rocher Vale* (1804), a poem printed at Oxford. He was postmaster of Oldham from 1812 to 1818, and an Oldham directory of 1814–15 describes him as 'postmaster, bookseller and stationer', while one of 1816–17 gives his profession as 'agent to the Atlas fire office'. In 1818 he reverted to schoolteaching. He continued to write poetry, some of it in dialect, publishing such volumes as *The Rustic Muse* (1818) and *A Sequel to the Lancashire Dialect, by Paul Bobbin* (1819), professedly written in the local dialects of the parishes of Ashton and Rochdale. He also published a *Manufacturer's Companion* (n.d.), and series of books and pamphlets on the history of Oldham and the surrounding area, which record much that would have been forgotten but for his personal observation. Chief among these works of local history were: *An Historical and Descriptive Account of the Town and Parochial Chapelry of Oldham* (1817; 2nd edn, 1826), *The Antiquities of the Town and a Complete History of the Trade of Manchester* (1822; 2nd edn, 1823), *History and Description of the Town and Parish of Ashton-under-Lyne and the Village of Dukinfield* (1823), *A Historical and Topographical Account of the Town and Parish of Rochdale* (1828), and *Tabula Mancuniensis, Chronological Table of the History of Manchester* (1829). This latter work formed the foundation of C. H. Timperley's *Annals of Manchester* (1839) as well as the later *Manchester Historical Recorder* (1874).

Many of Butterworth's books became scarce after his death; indeed, he expressed frustration with the conditions of authorship during his lifetime. In a letter addressed in 1802 to a Manchester bookseller he complained of lack of encouragement: 'How would I exert myself could I find one single friend of genius amongst all the host of Paternoster Row factors!', and, mentioning a work which he might submit, introduced the caveat that 'if like the generality of your tribe, you are not willing to encourage a poor author, I'll commit the work to the flames, and forever renounce the business'.

Butterworth died, one year after his wife, on 23 November 1837, 'sunk into a state of premature dotage and extreme feebleness', and was buried in Oldham parish church (Butterworth MS D-BUT/F/52). In his memoir of Butterworth his son Edwin was somewhat guarded when it came to his father's work as a historian and topographer, stating:

> in his early years he published several poetical pieces … later he produced a number of publications … which he entitled Histories … [which] … bore witness in some degree that the author was calculated to be more successful as a pastoral poet than as a provincial historian. (ibid.)

W. E. A. AXON, *rev.* JOHN LANGTON

Sources Oldham Archives Service, Butterworth MSS, D-BUT • catalogue of Butterworth MSS, Oldham Archives Service • G. Shaw, 'James Butterworth of Oldham', *Transactions of the Lancashire and Cheshire Antiquarian Society*, 26 (1908), 124–32 • G. Shaw, *Annals of Oldham and district*, 2 (1905), 200–04 • G. Shaw, *Local notes and gleanings*, 1 (1887), 204–10, 229–30 • 'Oldham's littérateur: the life struggle of James Butterworth', *Manchester Evening Chronicle* (22

Nov 1884) • 'The James Butterworth centenary: died November 23, 1837', *Oldham Chronicle* (23 Nov 1937)
Archives Oldham Archives Service, corresp. and papers
Wealth at death said to have died in poverty; details of funeral expenses and some possessions at death show this to be untrue: Shaw, *Annals of Oldham*, 203

Butterworth, John (1727–1803), Particular Baptist minister, was born on 13 December 1727, the eldest of five sons of Henry Butterworth, blacksmith, of Goodshaw, Rossendale, in Lancashire. Four of the five sons entered the Baptist ministry. Butterworth received his early education from David Crosley, a Calvinistic minister who had known John Bunyan. After hearing John Wesley preach about 1745, he attended the meetings of the Methodists, but study led him to accept the doctrine of election and to change his sentiments from Arminianism to Calvinism. He then began to preach, and in 1751 was invited to preach at Coventry. As a consequence he received an invitation from the Jordan Well Baptist Church in Coventry to be their minister. He arrived in Coventry in October 1752 and was admitted to membership of the church in the same year. Under him the church's membership increased from 90 to 141, outgrowing the old building. In 1793 a new chapel was built in Butterworth's garden in Cow Lane. He published a *New Concordance and Dictionary to the Holy Scriptures* (1767; reprinted in 1785, 1792, and 1809), which was described by John Rippon as 'the most full and concise of any before published' (*Baptist Annual Register*, 1790, 119). Under the pseudonym Christophilus he also published *A Serious Address to the Revd Dr Priestley* (1790).

Butterworth was married twice, secondly to Ann Heap (1727/8–1808). He died at Coventry on 24 April 1803, aged seventy-five, and was buried on 6 May in the graveyard of Cow Lane Chapel in Coventry. His son Joseph *Butterworth (1770–1826) MP and grandson Henry *Butterworth (1786–1860) ran a successful booksellers' business in London. C. W. Sutton, *rev.* Raymond Brown

Sources J. C. G. Binfield, *Pastors and people: the biography of a Baptist church, Queen's Road, Coventry* (1984), 24–6 • A. J. Parry, *History of the Cloughfold Baptist Church* [1876], 226–32 • T. Newbigging, *History of the forest of Rosendale*, 2nd edn (1893), 237–8 • J. Hargreaves, *Life and memoir of … John Hirst* (1816), 365–6 • A. S. Langley, 'Baptist ministers in England about 1750', *Transactions of the Baptist Historical Society*, 6 (1918–19), 152–3 • [W. T. Whitley], 'An index to notable Baptists', *Transactions of the Baptist Historical Society*, 7 (1920–21), 191 • [W. T. Whitley], 'Three hundred years of Baptist life in Coventry', *Baptist Quarterly*, 3 (1926–7), 137–43, esp. 141 • A. S. Langley, 'Some notable names in midland Baptist history', *Baptist Quarterly*, 3 (1926–7), 280–86, esp. 283 • *Baptist Annual Register* (1790), 119 • I. Morris, *Three hundred years of Baptist life in Coventry: the story of Queen's Road Chapel* (1926) • R. Brown, 'Butterworth, John', *The Blackwell dictionary of evangelical biography, 1730–1860*, ed. D. M. Lewis (1995) • R. G. Thorne, 'Butterworth, Joseph', HoP, *Commons, 1790–1820* • 'Memoir of the late Rev. John Butterworth', *Evangelical Magazine*, 12 (1804), 241–9
Likenesses W. Ridley, stipple (aged seventy-five), BM, NPG; repro. in Binfield, *Pastors and people*, 29

Butterworth, Joseph (1770–1826), publisher and politician, was born on 12 August 1770 in Coventry, the third son of John *Butterworth (1727–1803), Baptist minister, and his second wife, Ann, *née* Heap (1727/8–1808). He was educated by his father, and then attended Coventry Free School. He was apprenticed to a harness plater at Birmingham, and went with his master to London in 1790, where he set up his own business. On 13 October 1791 Butterworth married Anne, the daughter of John Cooke, a clothier of Trowbridge, Wiltshire, and they had one son.

Butterworth then became a law bookseller and publisher at 43 Fleet Street, initially in partnership with Thomas Whieldon, inheriting the business on Whieldon's death. In 1801 he published the first of many editions of *A General Catalogue of Law Books* and his business expanded into a substantial venture.

Meanwhile Butterworth established a reputation as what William Cobbett called 'a sort of Metropolitan of the Methodists' (Cobbett, 201), hosting meetings in his shop and serving as officer of several evangelical organizations including the Bible and Anti-Slavery societies. As the only Methodist MP (for Coventry, 1812–18, and Dover, 1820–26) of his time, he was also notable primarily for opposing Catholic emancipation. Butterworth's professional and religious interests converged in 1803 when he proposed, and later joined, a committee of privileges to defend Methodist rights at law. He was general treasurer of the Wesleyan Methodist Missionary Society from 1819 until his death, although he opposed the Methodist claim to independent church status. In December 1819 Butterworth headed the booksellers' opposition to the Newspaper Stamp Duties Bill. He died of brain fever at his Bedford Square home in London on 30 June 1826. His son had predeceased him, and the publishing tradition was carried on by a nephew, Henry, who had set up business on his own after initially working in Butterworth's office.

Butterworth had been highly thought of during his lifetime: Wilberforce often referred to him as 'honest Butterworth', and his memorial in Wesley Chapel, Church Road, London, states that he was a friend to any organization 'which had for its object the amelioration of man' (Thorne, 349). Leslie Howsam

Sources R. G. Thorne, 'Butterworth, Joseph', HoP, *Commons, 1790–1820*, 3.348–9 • *GM*, 1st ser., 96/2 (1826), 378 • D. Hempton, *Methodism and politics in British society, 1750–1850* (1984) • H. K. Jones, *Butterworth's: history of a publishing house* (1980) • W. Cobbett, *Rural rides* (1967) [first publ. 1830] • W. Ward, 'Joseph Butterworth', *The Blackwell dictionary of evangelical biography, 1730–1860*, ed. D. M. Lewis (1995)
Archives JRL, Methodist Archives and Research Centre, corresp. | Bodl. Oxf., corresp. with William Wilberforce

Butterworth, Joshua Whitehead (*bap.* 1818, *d.* 1895). *See under* Butterworth, Henry (1786–1860).

Butterworth, William. *See* Schroeder, Henry (1774–1853).

Buttevant. For this title name *see* Barry, David fitz James, *de facto* third Viscount Buttevant (1550–1617).

Buttle, Gladwin Albert Hurst (1899–1983), physician and pharmacologist, was born on 11 April 1899 at Park View, Godstone, Surrey, the son of William Buttle, a solicitor, and his wife, Mary Wilby, daughter of William Henry Ward, a builder. He attended Miss Brown's school in Warlingham and went on to the Whitgift Grammar School in Croydon. In 1917 he enlisted in the regular army, trained at the Royal Military Academy, Woolwich, and was commissioned second lieutenant in the Royal Engineers in 1918. A year later he left the army to study medicine at St John's College, Cambridge. His teachers included the physiologists John Newport Langley and Joseph Barcroft, the neurophysiologist Edgar Douglas Adrien, and the biochemist Frederick Gowland Hopkins. In later life he admitted missing lectures in his subjects in order to attend lectures on physics by Ernest Rutherford and on English literature by Arthur Quiller Couch. After graduating BA he entered University College Hospital, London, in 1922, and qualified MB, MRCS, LRCP in 1924. He was awarded the MA in 1927, MD (Louvain) in 1945, and BCh in 1967, and was elected FRCP in 1970.

In 1925, at the suggestion of John Henry Gaddum, a fellow student at Cambridge, Buttle joined the staff of the Wellcome Physiological Laboratories. He was appointed assistant pharmacologist to John William Trevan, with whom he studied the effects of bacterial toxins, the pharmacology of digitalis, and the action of local anaesthetics. He developed a test for scarlet fever anti-serum, then coming into production, and this work led him to the study of the control of streptococcal infection using anti-sera and drugs. In 1935 his attention was drawn to a paper by Gerhard Domagk of the research laboratories of IG Farbenindustrie which showed that the diazo dye known as Prontosil protected mice against virulent strains of streptococci. Buttle experimented with a sample of Prontosil supplied by Domagk but was unable to confirm the observations using the strain of streptococci available to him. After being informed by Dr Leonard Colebrook of Queen Charlotte's Hospital of difficulties in treating puerperal fever in women with streptococcal infection and of the very high mortality rate of the disease he obtained a sample of the virulent strain from the hospital and with this succeeded in reproducing Domagk's results. After December 1935, when workers at the Institut Pasteur in Paris showed that sulphanilamide was the active moiety of the Prontosil molecule, Buttle and his co-workers began research on the chemotherapy of sulphanilamide and its derivatives. They showed that sulphanilamide protected mice against meningococci and gonococci, and revealed the potential of some derivatives in the treatment of pneumococcal and staphylococcal infections.

In 1939 Buttle went to New York to lecture on the research into sulphonamide drugs but had to return to Britain on the outbreak of war as a member of the regular army reserve. He was transferred from the Royal Engineers to the Royal Army Medical Corps, and was appointed to the blood transfusion service, becoming an adviser on blood transfusion to the army. He left the service with the rank of lieutenant-colonel. Early in the war, when serving with the base transfusion unit in Cairo, he recognized that whole blood was essential if battle casualties with excessive blood loss were to benefit from early surgery under anaesthesia. Blood plasma was being sent out from Britain, but not the equipment necessary to collect and store whole blood, and it was necessary to manufacture the apparatus from materials available locally. It was largely due to Buttle's engineering skills that the unit was able to overcome the practical difficulties arising from necessary improvisation. His team of transfusion officers transformed the surgery of the battlefield from El Alamein onwards. He was appointed OBE (military division) in 1942 for his contribution to war medicine.

In 1943 Buttle was sent as an expert in the therapeutic use of sulphonamide drugs to Carthage to assist Lord Moran in treating Winston Churchill for a bronchial infection. On this occasion the prime minister questioned Buttle closely on the new antibiotic penicillin and its potential use in forthcoming military operations.

After the war Buttle and his family settled in London. On 8 November 1936 he had married Eva Karolina Korella (*b.* 1904/5), a talented painter, the daughter of Friedrich Wilhelm Saloman Korella, a retired professor of botany at Danzig University. They had one son, Richard. In 1946 Buttle became the first Wellcome professor of pharmacology at the school of pharmacy, University of London, and held the post to 1966. He was professor of pharmacology at St Bartholomew's Hospital, London, from 1948 to 1966. During this time he researched the chemotherapy of bacterial diseases and cancer. He served on the Medical Research Council's drugs safety committee, the Colonial Office leprosy committee, and the Ministry of Agriculture food additives committee. He was a medical consultant to the Ministry of Defence and president of the therapeutics and experimental medicine section of the Royal Society of Medicine. After his retirement in 1966 he held research posts in Mexico City, 1967–9, Addis Ababa, 1972–4, and Riyadh, 1974–8. On his return to the United Kingdom he became a consultant to the Wellcome laboratories.

Buttle was a short, sturdy, robust man with an original mind that did not run on conventional lines. This latter characteristic was shared by his brother Frank, an Anglican clergyman who combined personal poverty with an interest in the stock market. With the money he made the two brothers set up the Buttle Trust devoted to the education and welfare of deprived children, with Gladwin Buttle acting as chairman of the trust from 1953 to 1974. He died on 3 May 1983 at Charing Cross Hospital (Fulham), London, and a memorial service was held at the church of Christ the King, London. He was survived by his wife.

M. P. Earles

Sources *WWW* · Munk, *Roll* · G. Buttle, 'A full circle', *Trends in Pharmacological Sciences*, 1 (1980), 443–5 · *BMJ* (28 May 1983), 1758 · G. A. H. Buttle, 'Developments in therapeutics during the war', *Pharmaceutical Journal*, 102 (1946), 123–4 · A. M. Barrett, 'Development of British pharmacology', *Pharmaceutical Journal*, 230 (1983), 354–5 · T. E. Wallis, *History of the school of pharmacy, University of London* (1964) · b. cert. · m. cert. · d. cert.

Likenesses photograph, 1939–45, repro. in *BMJ* · photograph (in later life), repro. in Munk, *Roll*, vol. 7

Wealth at death £108,641: probate, 31 Aug 1983, *CGPLA Eng. & Wales*

Button, Ralph (1611/12–1680), nonconformist tutor, was born in Bishopstone, near Salisbury, Wiltshire, the son of Robert Button. He was educated at a local grammar school and then at Exeter College, Oxford, where he matriculated in December 1631, aged nineteen. Button was a favourite pupil of the rector of Exeter and canon of Christ Church, Dr John Prideaux, and after graduating BA in 1633 was recommended to Sir Nathaniel Brent, the warden of Merton College, for a fellowship. He was duly elected a fellow of Merton in 1633 and proved himself a notable tutor. His pupils included Anthony Wood, the antiquary; Wood's brother, Edward, for whom Button gave the funeral address in 1655; and Zachary Bogan, later a fellow of Corpus Christi College, an expert in ancient languages and a zealous puritan. Button proceeded MA in February 1640.

When war broke out in 1642 Button, a puritan, left Oxford for London and was elected the following year to the professorship of geometry at Gresham College to succeed John Greaves. Once Oxford had fallen to parliament in 1646, he returned to Merton College. On 18 February 1648 he was appointed junior proctor by the parliamentary visitors amid some controversy. Wood stated that, in the normal cycle of proctorial appointments, it was the turn of All Souls and New College to select the next holders. Parliament, however, anxious to avoid a repeat of events the previous year when the two proctors refused to assist the visitors, preferred to choose its own men. His new role in Oxford forced Button in June 1648 to resign his Gresham professorship, a position in which he appears to have achieved little of note. On 4 August he was made public orator of the university, and he gave the oration when Fairfax and Cromwell received their DCL degrees in 1649.

Although he was apparently never in orders, Button was made a canon of Christ Church, also on 4 August 1648, in place of Edward Corbet, who had himself briefly replaced the ejected Henry Hammond. The following year Button was appointed sub-delegate to the commission set up to reform the university statutes. He was granted a licence to supplicate for a DD in January 1649 but he chose not to apply. He and his wife, Hester, whom he appears to have married about 1648 or 1649, lived in the canonry in the cathedral cloister. The cartularies of the three main monastic houses dissolved to provide Christ Church's endowment, St Frideswide's Priory, and Eynsham and Osney abbeys, were moved into Button's lodgings so that his former pupil, Wood, could study them at his leisure. From 1652 Button was subdean. In 1660, on the restoration of Charles II, a poem by Button in both Hebrew and Latin was published in *Britannia rediviva*, a collection of works by many Oxford men, a large proportion of whom were from Christ Church and several of whom were, like Button, presbyterians, celebrating the return of Charles II. Button was ejected from his canonry by the visiting commissioners on 27 July 1660. John Fell took his place as canon, and Robert South as orator. According to Wood, as Button was moving his possessions out of his lodgings in Christ Church cloister, 'he would usually say, when he heard the two little bells ring to canonical prayers, There now go the mass-bells, and let those that affected that way go to the church, for be sure I shall not' (Wood, *Ath. Oxon.: Fasti*, 2.159).

Button and his family left Oxford for Brentford, Middlesex, where he took to private tutoring. His presbyterian views resulted in his imprisonment for six months for teaching two knights' sons after refusing to take the Oxford oath which required all ejected ministers and unlicensed teachers to swear that they would not attempt to alter the constitution of church or state. He was also wrongly accused of being the executioner of Charles I, a libel refuted by Thomas Gilbert in a letter to the earl of Anglesey in 1675. Gilbert, himself an ejected minister living in Oxford, cited in defence of Button two leading figures in the university's Anglican establishment, Thomas Barlow and John Fell, now dean of Christ Church. From 1672 Button lived in Islington where he continued to teach young gentlemen privately at home. His pupils were said to include Joseph Jekyll, later master of the rolls, and a Mr Williams, apparently Cromwell's grandson.

Button had three children: Joseph and Hester, whose dates of birth are unknown, and Jonathan, who was baptized at All Hallows Staining in London on 22 February 1655. His wife probably predeceased him as his will of 25 September 1680 makes no mention of her. After Button wrote his first will in June 1679, Joseph, who was heir and executor, fell seriously ill and was close to death. A new will, written on 25 September 1680, made Hester both executor and heir but allowed Joseph, if he survived his father, use of the estate until his death. In the event of Hester's dying before her marriage, the estate was to pass to Button's cousin, William Calovert, of Fordingbridge. In fact, father and son died on the same day, Joseph at five o'clock in the morning of Friday 1 October 1680, and Ralph at 7 a.m. Ralph was buried in Islington parish church. Hester Button married a Dr Boteler, a London physician, and died before 1740. J. H. CURTHOYS

Sources J. Ward, *The lives of the professors of Gresham College* (1740) • G. C. Brodrick, *Memorials of Merton College*, OHS, 4 (1885) • *The life and times of Anthony Wood*, ed. A. Clark, 5 vols., OHS, 19, 21, 26, 30, 40 (1891–1900) • B. Worden, 'Cromwellian Oxford', *Hist. U. Oxf.* 4: *17th-cent. Oxf.*, 733–72 • R. A. Beddard, 'Tory Oxford', *Hist. U. Oxf.* 4: *17th-cent. Oxf.*, 863–906 • Wood, *Ath. Oxon.: Fasti* (1815), 508 • Wood, *Ath. Oxon.: Fasti* (1820), 107, 158–9 • Christ Church Oxf., MSS D&C i.b.3, p. 57; xii.b.103 • will, PRO, PROB 11/364, sig. 125 • *Calamy rev.* • Foster, *Alum. Oxon.*

Wealth at death see will, PRO, PROB 11/364, sig. 125

Button, Sir Thomas (*c.*1575–1634), naval officer, was the fourth son of Miles Button of Worlton, Glamorgan, and Margaret, daughter of Edward Lewis of Y Fan, Glamorgan. During the early 1590s he became a common soldier, and in February 1592 he and two of his brothers were granted a minor office in Glamorgan's shrieval court. His fortunes were transformed soon after, when he married Elizabeth, daughter of Sir Walter Rice of Newton, Carmarthenshire, whereby he became the nephew-in-law of Sir Robert Mansell, from whose patronage he thereafter benefited. In 1599 Button carried dispatches for Mansell, then admiral on the Irish coast, and in 1601 captained a royal pinnace convoying munitions and victuals from Dublin to the forces besieging Kinsale. After a fruitless bombardment of Rincorran Castle, Button blockaded the harbour, a service he performed with distinction. He remained on the Irish station until the spring of 1602, when he was transferred to a larger warship in the channel. In mid-August he sailed for the West Indies in a privateer part owned by Mansell. His quest for plunder proved successful, for on his return in March 1603 it was reported, with some exaggeration, that the expedition had brought back 'three millions of gold' (*CSP dom.*, *1601–3*, 299).

Following the peace with Spain, Button reverted to his former naval employment. Although granted a pension in addition to his salary, he exploited successive commands to line his own pockets, keeping his crew under strength to benefit from surplus wages and victuals. This was a common fraud among captains, but Button acquired a reputation for being especially greedy. In December 1605 he also harboured aboard his ship a notorious pirate, whom he permitted to escape and from whom he received two chests of sugar, which he smuggled ashore and sold for £42. When such naval abuses were investigated in 1608 Button was a principal object of inquiry. Despite a wealth of damning evidence, he and the other leading malefactors escaped punishment.

Shortly thereafter Prince Henry proposed an expedition to discover a north-west passage and in April 1612 Button was given command of two ships, the *Resolution* and the *Discovery*, with which he reached Hudson Bay in August. After discovering the Nelson River (which Button named after his ship's master), and losing the *Resolution*, the expedition wintered, surviving on white partridges. Several men perished and Button himself fell seriously ill, but in the spring the survivors explored the bay into which the river opens, and which Button named after himself. Soon afterwards he abandoned the search, arriving back at Chatham in September 1613. Although his quest had ended in failure, his reputation was now enhanced and in 1614 he was appointed admiral on the Irish station, with instructions to clear the seas of pirates. In January 1615 he escorted a hoy full of artillery to Dunaverty, on Scotland's west coast, after its castle had fallen to local insurgents. While the guns were being disembarked, Button in his longboat rowed back and forth before the castle, while under fire, to inspire the besiegers. Shortly thereafter he returned to his station, and on 30 August 1616 he was knighted by Ireland's lord deputy.

Button fell under renewed suspicion following the establishment of a second commission of inquiry into the navy in 1618. Investigation of his Irish pension revealed that since 1608 he had actually been in receipt of two pensions, prompting navy commissioner John Coke to demand the repayment of £730. However, the charges were dropped after Ireland's lord chief justice explained the peculiar circumstances behind the second grant. Allegations of misconduct laid against Button were thwarted by Bristol's merchants, who extolled his efforts to protect their shipping. By 1620 Button's position was strengthened when Sir Robert Mansell was given the task of destroying the pirate base at Algiers. Mansell bestowed the office of rear-admiral of his small fleet on Button, and would have appointed him vice-admiral had he not initially suspected that Button would be reluctant to quit his Irish command. During the ensuing siege of Algiers, Button, though irritated that he had been passed over for the more senior position, demonstrated his customary bravery under fire, for which he was warmly commended by Mansell. On his return to England he resumed his Irish command, consisting of a single pinnace. In 1622 he complained of the 'bitter and sharp persecutions' to which he had been subjected since the accession of James I (Centre for Kentish Studies, U269/1/ON7124), but his efforts to persuade the navy commissioners to reverse a cut in the size of his crew, and to grant him the right to furnish his ship with stores so as to avoid the usual delays while these were transported from the Kent dockyards to Bristol, went unheeded.

As the prospect of a fresh war with Spain increased Button was appointed on 14 April 1624 to the newly established council of war, taking lodgings in Fulham and entrusting his naval command to a deputy. In May 1625 he carried a banner bearing the crest of Ireland at the king's funeral. By this time his finances were on the verge of collapse. Over the course of the previous thirty-three years he had received only a fraction of the sums he was owed for royal service, and although in January 1625 he had obtained a warrant for £3615 13*s.* 4*d.*, the exchequer was so hard pressed that he remained unpaid. In October, Button complained that for several years he had also funded the victualling of the ship on the Irish station out of his own pocket, but nothing was done to alleviate his condition. Despite illness, he twice attended the House of Commons in March 1626, having been summoned as a member of the council of war, but, like his fellow councillors, he refused to reveal the advice he had given to the lord admiral, the duke of Buckingham. In September he was instructed to escort 2000 troops to the Île de Ré, where Buckingham had laid siege to the citadel. However, severe weather and a leaky ship delayed him, and by the time he reached Plymouth the duke had abandoned the campaign. He subsequently resumed his command on the Irish station.

In August 1627 Button's financial difficulties forced him to mortgage his lands in south Wales, worth £400 per annum. In order to redeem his estate he needed to raise £1243, but by 29 September 1628, when the first repayment on his mortgage was due, he had received only £100 in back pay. His hopes of preventing the seizure of his lands were raised in August 1629, when he intercepted a Dunkirker laden with salt worth around £1400, but despite asking to be allowed her full value he was granted nothing. He illicitly helped himself to some of the cargo and the discovery of this theft in March 1631 cast doubt on his continued employment. In June the admiralty commissioners stripped him of the right to victual the ships under his command, a privilege he had enjoyed since 1614. Furthermore, when he arrived in London in November 1631 to solicit for his arrears, the commissioners denied him an audience. After a wearisome wait lasting twenty-four weeks Button, weakened by illness, returned to his native Glamorgan. His sickness persisted, allowing the admiralty commissioners to entrust the Irish station to another. In February 1634 formal charges were laid against him. For a second time in his career he was accused of having harboured a pirate (in 1630). He was also charged with having relinquished his command to his lieutenant without authorization and with negligence in failing to prevent a devastating raid by pirates on the Irish town of Baltimore in 1631. Button mounted a vigorous defence but his death meant that the matter never came to final judgment. He was buried on 8 April 1634 in St Margaret's, Westminster, and was survived by his wife and five of their seven children. He died intestate and his lands, which were never seized, passed to his eldest son, Miles, who remortgaged them to pay off his debts. Button's widow, Lady Elizabeth, obtained £650 from the exchequer in the three years after her husband's death.

ANDREW THRUSH

Sources *CSP dom., 1591–1634; 1660–61* • *CSP Ire., 1615–32* • *The naval tracts of Sir William Monson*, ed. M. Oppenheim, 2, Navy RS, 23 (1902) • J. S. Brewer and W. Bullen, eds., *Calendar of the Carew manuscripts*, 4: *1601–1603*, PRO (1870), 180, 183 • J. S. Corbett, *England in the Mediterranean: a study of the rise and influence of British power within the straits, 1603–1713*, 1 (1904), 113–14 • J. S. Corbett, *The successors of Drake* (1900), 338–9 • W. J. Smith, ed., *Calendar of Salusbury correspondence, 1553–circa 1700* (1954), 141 • BL, Coke MSS [formerly Derbyshire RO, Coke MSS C173/10; C146/24; C202/16] • *Calendar of the manuscripts of the most hon. the marquess of Salisbury*, 18, HMC, 9 (1940), 149 • A. P. McGowan, ed., *The Jacobean commissions of enquiry, 1608 and 1618*, Navy RS, 116 (1971) • PRO, C66/1952/10 • W. L. Clowes, *The Royal Navy: a history from the earliest times to the present*, 7 vols. (1897–1903), vol. 2, p. 86 • *The autobiography of Phineas Pett*, ed. W. G. Perrin, Navy RS, 51 (1918), 95, 112 • G. T. C. and R. O. J., 'Some account of the parishes of St Nicholas and St Lythan [pt 2]', *Archaeologia Cambrensis*, 3rd ser., 8 (1862), 177–201, esp. 178 • *Report on the manuscripts of the marquis of Downshire*, 6 vols. in 7, HMC, 75 (1924–95), vol. 4, p. 214 • Leeds Public Library, Temple Newsam MS TN/PO 7/2 • *Cabala, sive, Scrinia sacra: mysteries of state and government in letters of illustrious persons*, 3rd edn (1691), 299 • Bodl. Oxf., MS Rawl. A. 455, fols. 122v–123v • *The manuscripts of the Earl Cowper*, 3 vols., HMC, 23 (1888–9), vol. 1 • W. B. Bidwell and M. Jansson, eds., *Proceedings in parliament, 1626*, 2: *House of Commons* (1992) • Carmarthenshire RO, Lort MSS 12/571 and 571a • *APC, 1627–8*, 49, 58, 82 • A. M. Burke, ed., *Memorials of St Margaret's Church, Westminster* (1914), 566 • W. A. Shaw, *The knights of England*, 2 (1906), 159

Likenesses oils, *c.*1610, Coedarhydyglyn, Cardiff; repro. in J. Steegman, *A survey of portraits in Welsh houses: houses in south Wales* (1962), 87

Button [Bitton], **William** (*d.* **1264**), bishop of Bath and Wells, was probably born in the Gloucestershire village of Bitton from which he was named, and in which his nephew Thomas Button, bishop of Exeter (*d.* 1307), built a chapel in 1299. His family was a notable source of competent west-country church officials, and many relatives were promoted under his patronage. His career was launched under Bishop Jocelin of Bath whose official he was by 1231. He also acted as a judge, and displayed a prudence which was characteristic of his pre-episcopal career. By 1235 he had become the cathedral subdean, but it was with his promotion (by 1237) to be archdeacon of Wells that Button emerged as a central figure in the development of the church of Wells. Two lines of activity were crucial: the disciplining of the vicars-choral upon whose conduct the liturgical standards of the church depended, and his work to re-establish Wells's share in the election of bishops of the diocese. Achieving the former underlined the church's particular fitness to become the diocese's liturgical centre; the latter achievement made its centrality a fact. The election of Bishop Roger of Salisbury in 1244 was hotly disputed, because the monks of Bath had elected him by themselves in defiance of a previous agreement on joint election with the canons of Wells. In these fraught circumstances Button acted as a vigorous advocate for his church, travelling to Rome to make its case, but ultimately serving as a mediator, whose acceptance of compromise helped to secure the permanent position of the Wells chapter in future elections. Such service loomed large in his own episcopal election in 1247.

Button's career as bishop was not as happy or successful. He had little long-term national importance, although he was certainly close to those who opposed the king's intervention in ecclesiastical affairs. He was a participant in and signatory to the solemn excommunication of 1251 of all who opposed the strictures of Magna Carta with respect to ecclesiastical privilege. Furthermore, the bishops' remonstrance of 1257 against the king makes particular reference to Button's dispute with the abbot of Glastonbury, in which the king played a key anti-episcopal role. His services to Henry III, which included voyages to Spain to bring the king's prospective daughter-in-law to England (1253), do not indicate a particularly durable or substantial influence. Indeed his main concerns were diocesan and personal. He supervised the codification of diocesan statutes: these clearly articulate the concern of the church, following the Fourth Lateran Council of 1215, to control the laity and clergy by developing clear rules concerning the sacraments and the disciplining of the clergy. He participated with Bishop Bridport of Salisbury in the consecration of Bishop Chause of Carlisle in 1258, after which Wells statutes became the model for Carlisle as well.

In jurisdictional matters Button was less successful, losing a long struggle already fought by several earlier bishops of Wells, including Savaric and Jocelin, to try to assume a visitational and supervisory authority over the great local abbey of Glastonbury. It was in this respect that the king and pope both failed Button, ultimately siding with the abbey and allowing it virtually full exemption from episcopal oversight. Notwithstanding his vigorous offensive, which included forced visitations, the deposition of the abbot, recourse to the courts, and even the use of interdict against communities supporting Abbot Roger Forde, Button was defeated. He was similarly unable to recover control of Congresbury church from the dean and chapter of Wells, the losing battle being his sole and sore point of memory in Wells Cathedral's local history after a seventeen-year career as bishop and distinguished work as cathedral subdean and archdeacon. He died on 3 April 1264 and was buried in the cathedral's lady chapel. His tomb and effigy had been removed by the eighteenth century. His nephew Bishop William *Button, permanently endowed a daily mass and an anniversary service in his uncle's name.

DAVID GARY SHAW

Sources *Calendar of the manuscripts of the dean and chapter of Wells*, 2 vols., HMC, 12 (1907–14) · Paris, *Chron.*, vols. 5–6 · *Chancery records* · John of Glastonbury, *Cronica sive antiquitates Glastoniensis ecclesiae*, ed. J. P. Curley (1985) · F. M. Powicke and C. R. Cheney, eds., *Councils and synods with other documents relating to the English church, 1205–1313*, 1 (1964) · *Ann. mon.*, vols. 1, 3 · Adam of Domerham, *Historia de rebus gestis Glastoniensibus*, ed. T. Hearne (1727), 2 · *The itinerary of John Leland in or about the years 1535–1543*, ed. L. Toulmin Smith, 11 pts in 5 vols. (1906–10) · J. A. Robinson, ed., 'Historia major', *Collectanea I*, ed. T. F. Palmer, Somerset RS, 39 (1924), 57–71
Archives Wells Cathedral, Wells Cathedral MSS, charters

Button [Bitton], **William** (*d.* **1274**), bishop of Bath and Wells, is an elusive yet intriguing figure. Nephew to his namesake William *Button (*d.* 1264), also bishop of the diocese, he received early advancement through his uncle's generosity, becoming vicar of the disputed church of Congresbury. Promoted by 1264 to the key cathedral dignity of archdeacon of Wells during his uncle's episcopate, he succeeded Walter Giffard as bishop in February 1267. He played little part in politics, although in 1269 he attended an ecclesiastical council which objected to royal taxation. Button united with his fellow suffragans of Canterbury in resisting attempts by Canterbury Cathedral priory to exercise metropolitan jurisdiction when the primatial see was vacant in 1271, but made his mark primarily in his diocese and by his pious example. Thus he stands as a bishop renowned for his attention to diocesan concerns, rather than for his activity or ambition in national affairs. He had unusually good relations with his cathedral chapter and it may be that his well-known piety was celebrated by the church through the centuries in part because of the assistance he had given to the cathedral chapter. He helped the canons in the redrafting of their statutes, and particularly required that the singing abilities of the vicars and choristers be kept to a high standard. He also helped to enrich the church, transferring property to the chapter, and overseeing a considerable expansion of the liturgical life of the community by the endowment of several permanent memorial services, including one devoted principally to the memory of his uncle and predecessor, whom the canons remembered less fondly. Naturally these donations brought further property and prestige to the chapter. He also further enriched and expanded the cathedral by giving the church of Dinder to be its last canonical prebend. He died on 4 December 1274 and was buried in the south aisle of the cathedral, covered with an incised slab.

Archbishop Robert Kilwardby lavishly praised Button's piety, and he was the first and perhaps most truly saintly of several late medieval Wells bishops to be celebrated for their piety and sanctity (William of March, Ralph of Shrewsbury, and Thomas Beckington followed). The obituary established for him provided a focus for this cult, and his pyx-box was throughout the fifteenth century the richest source of offerings in the church after those to the Virgin. William Worcester was shown documentary evidence of Button's miracles while travelling through Wells in 1478; Button was believed to be particularly efficacious in remedying toothache. Though his popularity waned somewhat by the end of the fifteenth century, Leland, writing in the 1530s and 1540s, noted that 'the people still venerate' him (*Itinerary*, 293), but Button never received official canonization. DAVID GARY SHAW

Sources *Calendar of the manuscripts of the dean and chapter of Wells*, 2 vols., HMC, 12 (1907–14) · *CClR* · *CPR* · J. A. Robinson, ed., 'Historia major', *Collectanea I*, ed. T. F. Palmer, Somerset RS, 39 (1924), 57–71 · H. R. Luard, ed., *Flores historiarum*, 3 vols., Rolls Series, 95 (1890), vol. 3 · [W. Rishanger], *The chronicle of William de Rishanger, of the barons' wars*, ed. J. O. Halliwell, CS, 15 (1840) · F. M. Powicke and C. R. Cheney, eds., *Councils and synods with other documents relating to the English church, 1205–1313*, 2 (1964) · *Itineraries [of] William Worcestre*, ed. J. H. Harvey, OMT (1969) · *The itinerary of John Leland in or about the years 1535–1543*, ed. L. Toulmin Smith, 11 pts in 5 vols. (1906–10) · *Ann. mon.*, vol. 4
Archives Wells Cathedral, Wells Cathedral MSS, charters
Likenesses sculpture on burial slab, Wells Cathedral
Wealth at death provision of 10 marks for memorial services: *Calendar*, vol. 1, p. 379

Button, Sir William, first baronet (**1585–1655**), politician, was born on 14 July 1585, the second son of William Button (*d.* 1599) of Alton Priors, Wiltshire, and Jane (*d.* in or after 1600), daughter of John Lamb. Taking their name from Bitton Manor, Gloucestershire, which they anciently owned, his family had lived at Alton Priors since the twelfth century; his predecessors included two medieval bishops, of Exeter and Bath and Wells. Button was settled with the greater part of the family's estate in 1591 and four years later further property was purchased from his indebted elder brother. Succeeding his father in 1599, Button matriculated at Queen's College, Oxford, in 1601, and in 1605, when aged nineteen, he was knighted and made colonel of a regiment of foot. Two years later he was granted a licence to travel to France, but this was revoked when the privy council learned that he intended to engage in a duel there. The forestalled duel may have been an indication of his character, for he was later accused in chancery of cruelty towards his tenants and servants. In 1611 he married Ruth, a daughter of Walter Dunch of Avebury, Wiltshire, and in 1621 purchased a baronetcy.

Made a freeman of Marlborough in 1614, Button was elected knight of the shire for Wiltshire in 1628. His decision to embark upon a parliamentary career so late in life had been caused by his need to avoid creditors, for he had recently been arrested for debt in Westminster Hall. During the civil war he sided with the royalists, and in August 1642 was appointed to declare the propositions for raising troops for the king's defence. He later contributed £500 to the royalist cause, but is not known to have taken up arms. His house at Tockenham Court was raided by parliamentary troops in 1643 and again in 1644, when he lost nearly £1300 in chattels and livestock. After the war this property was granted to a parliamentarian. Button witnessed Oxford's surrender in June 1646, and a week later was arrested for disobeying orders to attend the committee for sequestrations in London. He was fined as a delinquent, but recovered most of his estates by 1649. Thereafter he settled at Shaw House, having granted most of his remaining property to his several sons. He died on 28 January

1655 and was buried in a vault he had built for himself in North Wraxall church. His son William succeeded to the title. HENRY LANCASTER

Sources G. D. Squibb, ed., *Wiltshire visitation pedigrees, 1623*, Harleian Society, 105–6 (1954), 33 · Som. ARS, L, DD/WH6/1473, 236, 3128, 3130, 3133, 3147–3150 · Alton [T. C. Button], *Collections relating to the families of D'Annville of Bitton, Gloucestershire, and the Le Grand alias Button, of Wiltshire and Glamorganshire* (1888), 15, 27 · J. Hutchins, *The history and antiquities of the county of Dorset*, 2nd edn, ed. R. Gough and J. B. Nichols, 1 (1796), 363; 2 (1803), 325; 4 (1815), 143 · PRO, WARD 9/348, fol. 131 · J. Rushworth, *Historical collections*, new edn, 3 (1721), 915 · J. Burke and J. B. Burke, *A genealogical and heraldic history of the extinct and dormant baronetcies of England, Ireland, and Scotland* (1838), 94 · will, PRO, PROB 11/249, fol. 109 · PRO, STAC 8/194/25; 8/255/2; 8/50/8 · W. A. Shaw, *The knights of England*, 2 (1906), 138 · GEC, *Baronetage* · PRO, C142/239/123 · Foster, *Alum. Oxon.* · PRO, E 179/199/422 · M. A. E. Green, ed., *Calendar of the proceedings of the committee for compounding … 1643–1660*, 5 vols., PRO (1889–92), 1559

Archives Som. ARS, family MSS, DD/WH6 · Som. ARS, warrants, letters, orders

Wealth at death had already settled most of considerable Wiltshire estate upon children; left only small financial legacies to servants: will, PRO, PROB 11/249, fol. 109

Butts, John (*c.*1728–1765), painter, was born and bred in Cork where he studied with an otherwise unknown painter, Rogers. He developed extraordinary powers in landscape. His compositions, in which figures were often introduced, mainly portray the landscape around Cork, and were executed in a soft, Claudian manner. In 1757 he went to Dublin where, to supply the needs of a large family, he also turned his hand to scene-painting and producing coach panels and signboards. At this period he shared a garret with Chapman, a picture dealer who helped to hasten his early death through drink, in 1765, in Dublin. James Barry RA was a warm admirer of the genius of Butts, and declared, 'his example and works were my first guide and was what enamoured me with the art itself' (*Barry*, 1.20–21). There is one drawing by Butts in the National Gallery of Ireland, Dublin, signed and dated 'Feb 24'. SARAH HERRING

Sources A. Pasquin [J. Williams], *An authentic history of the professors of painting, sculpture, and architecture who have practiced in Ireland … to which are added, Memoirs of the royal academicians* [1796]; facs. edn as *An authentic history of painting in Ireland* with introduction by R. W. Lightbown (1970), 51 · A. Crookshank and the Knight of Glin [D. Fitzgerald], *The painters of Ireland, c.1660–1920* (1978), 111, 115, 116, 235 · A. Crookshank and the Knight of Glin [D. Fitzgerald], *The watercolours of Ireland: works on paper in pencil, pastel and paint, c.1600–1914* (1994), 61–2, 78, 79, 99 · W. G. Strickland, *A dictionary of Irish artists*, 1 (1913), 143 · Redgrave, *Artists*, 2nd edn, 66 · *The works of James Barry*, ed. E. Fryer, 1 (1809), 20–1 · W. L. Pressley, *The life and art of James Barry* (1981), 2, 205, n.8 · M. H. Grant, *A chronological history of the old English landscape painters*, 1 (1926), 39 · A. Le Harivel, ed., *National Gallery of Ireland: illustrated summary catalogue of drawings, watercolours and miniatures* (1983), 44 [with introduction by H. Potterton]

Butts [*married names* Rodker, Aitken], **Mary Franeis** (**1890–1937**), writer, was born on 13 December 1890 at The Salterns, Parkstone, south Dorset, the elder of the two children of Frederick John Butts (1833–1905), captain and gentleman, and his second wife, Mary Jane (1863–1944), daughter of the Revd James Briggs of Parkstone, Dorset, and his wife, Sarah.

Mary Butts spent her first fifteen years at Salterns. She described her childhood in her autobiography, *The Crystal Cabinet* (1937), as a 'perfectness'. Her great-grandfather Thomas Butts had been William Blake's patron, and she grew up among the treasures of Salterns which included a number of Blake's paintings and possessions. The paintings were later sold and are now in the Tate collection but Mary Butts wrote that she inherited 'the kind of seeing that there was in William Blake' (*The Crystal Cabinet*, 34). The countryside around Salterns together with the classical stories and myths her beloved father recounted and acted out with her haunted her imagination and informed her writing, which has a visionary quality akin to Blake's. 'I can write, I want to, should never want to *do* anything else', she wrote in a later diary entry in 1927, but she had discovered her vocation as a child.

Mary Butts was educated locally at The Haven and Sandecotes schools until her father's death. Her mother married Frederick Colville-Hyde and Mary Butts chose to become a boarder at St Leonard's School for Girls in St Andrews. She took the entrance exams for Cambridge but was unsuccessful and registered as a 'general student' at Westfield College, London (1909–12), but left before completing her degree. The following autumn she entered the London School of Economics and graduated in 1914 with a social science certificate, the equivalent of the present-day diploma in social work. She then worked on the Children's Care Committee in the East End of London, before becoming actively involved in the pacifist movement during the First World War, working on the first National Council for Civil Liberties. By this time she had become an atheist and socialist. In her late teens to mid-twenties Mary Butts seems to have had mainly lesbian relationships. This changed, however, when she met the poet and publisher John Rodker (1894–1955). They were married at the Hampstead register office on 10 May 1918 and worked together on Rodker's first publishing house, the Ovid Press (1920). Their only child, Camilla Elizabeth, was born in November 1920, by which time the marriage had broken down, and in early 1921 Mary Butts left for the continent with her lover, the author Cecil Maitland. She divorced Rodker in 1926.

During the first half of the 1920s Mary Butts was based in London at 43 Belsize Park Gardens and her work began to be published in many of the little magazines of the period. *Speed the Plough and other Stories* (1923) was followed by her first novel, *Ashe of Rings* (1925), set in and written during the war. By 1925 her relationship with Maitland had ended and she left for Paris and the French riviera where she stayed until the end of the decade. During the 1920s she knew many of her now more famous modernist contemporaries and is remembered in numerous memoirs for her exuberant personality, her passion for her work (in which she developed an original prose style), and her striking red hair. Jean Cocteau illustrated her epistolary prose sequence, *Imaginary Letters* (1928), which was published a few months after her second novel, *Armed with Madness*, a modernist treatment of the grail myth.

In 1930 Mary Butts collapsed from poverty, alcoholism, and drug addiction and returned permanently to England. On 29 October 1930 in London she married the artist Gabriel William Aitken, otherwise Atkin (1897–1937). In 1932 they moved to Sennen Cove, west Cornwall, to a small cliffside bungalow, which she renamed Tebel Vos (House of Magic). The marriage lasted four years. Aitken moved away in late 1934 in which year Mary Butts converted to Anglo-Catholicism.

The 1930s saw a prodigious output. In addition to becoming a regular reviewer, Mary Butts published her third novel, *Death of Felicity Taverner* (1932); two historical narratives (*The Macedonian*, 1933, and *Scenes from the Life of Cleopatra*, 1935) for which she was highly respected among historians; two further volumes of short stories (*Several Occasions*, 1932, and *Last Stories*, 1938); her autobiography; and numerous poems and articles. The last category includes an appreciation of Aldous Huxley (1931), one of the first critical essays on the supernatural writer M. R. James (1934), a history of supernatural fiction (1933), and two pamphlets which address the psychological and ecological consequences of industrialization, urbanization, and loss of religious faith (*Warning to Hikers*, 1932, and *Traps for Unbelievers*, 1932).

Mary Butts remained in Sennen Cove until her sudden death from general peritonitis at Penzance General Hospital on 5 March 1937. She was buried in Sennen church cemetery. Out of print for several decades, Butts's work has slowly been republished since the late 1980s. Always highly regarded by writers, it is only since the latter part of the twentieth century that her contribution to modern literature has begun to be properly recognized.

NATHALIE BLONDEL

Sources *The journals of Mary Butts*, ed. N. Blondel (2003) • N. Blondel, *Mary Butts: scenes from the life* (1998) [incl. bibliography] • Yale U., Beinecke L., Butts papers • M. Butts, *The crystal cabinet: my childhood at Salterns*, 2nd edn (1988) • private information (2004) • C. Wagstaff, ed., *A sacred quest: the life and writings of Mary Butts* (1995) • b. cert. • m. certs. • d. cert.

Archives Ransom HRC, MSS • Yale U., Beinecke L., corresp., journals, and literary MSS

Likenesses J. Cocteau, two line drawings, 1920–29, repro. in Wagstaff, ed., *Sacred quest*; priv. coll. • Man Ray, photograph, 1920–29, repro. in Wagstaff, ed., *Sacred quest*; priv. coll. • C. Morris, oils, 1924, repro. in R. Morphet, *Cedric Morris* (1984), 43

Wealth at death £213 13s. 3d.: probate, 28 July 1937, *CGPLA Eng. & Wales*

Butts, Robert (1684–1748), bishop of Ely, was the eighth child of William Butts, rector of Hartest, Suffolk, and his wife, Martha Wale. He was educated at Bury St Edmunds grammar school, and matriculated as a sizar at Trinity College, Cambridge, in 1703. He graduated BA in 1707, and proceeded MA in 1711 and DD in 1728. He was ordained deacon by the bishop of London in 1709 and priest by the bishop of Norwich in 1710, to serve as curate of Thurlow in Suffolk. In 1712 the corporation of Bury St Edmunds elected him minister of St Mary's, Bury St Edmunds, which he held until 1725. From 1715 he was also rector of Euston in Suffolk, until 1720. The earl of Bristol, whose chaplain he was, presented him to Ickworth with Wordwell in 1717, which he held until 1733. From 1723 to 1743 he was also preacher of St James's, Bury St Edmunds. In 1728 he became a chaplain to George II. Butts's preferment came through the interest of John, Lord Hervey, son of the first earl of Bristol, a prominent courtier, who was vice-chamberlain and a close associate of Queen Caroline and Sir Robert Walpole. He was reputed to have been a zealous party manager in the Hervey interest in Bury.

In 1731 Butts was appointed dean of Norwich. As dean he seems to have resided regularly at Norwich. Soon after his arrival the dean and chapter agreed to set aside £100 each year from their profits 'to answer any extraordinary calamities that may happen to this Church' (dean and chapter minute book, Norfolk RO, DCN 24/4). Through Hervey's influence with Queen Caroline, Butts was nominated bishop of Norwich in 1733, despite the strenuous opposition of Edmund Gibson, bishop of London, Walpole's chief ecclesiastical adviser. There continued to be strong antipathy between Butts and Hervey, and Gibson. According to Cole, Butts's appointment was a matter of surprise, as he was almost unknown in the ecclesiastical world (*DNB*). Butts himself claimed not to have solicited his own advancement. He was enthroned in person in Norwich Cathedral, a detailed description of which survives (Norfolk RO, DCN 25/3). His welcome outside the city by the dean and prebends, and 'many gentlemen (there being about 10 Coaches and 70 Horse' (ibid.), suggests that he had been well liked as dean.

As bishop, Butts conscientiously spent the summer months of each year, when travel was easier, in his diocese. In his primary visitation charge he spoke strongly against anti-clericalism and defended his clergy against accusations of subverting the government and being 'Disturbers of the People'. He exhorted them to show 'Integrity and Faithfulness in discharge of their duty' and to 'preach not themselves, but Christ Jesus the Lord', and to lead 'an Exemplary and Good Life', encouraging them to 'pray and act for the peace and Prosperity of the Government, upon which, under God, our own security undoubtedly depends' (*The Charge of the Right Reverend Father*, 1736, 22). He trenchantly denounced the apparent growing influence of Roman Catholicism. His visitation records suggest that he carefully monitored non-residence among his clergy, and required non-resident incumbents to provide resident curates. Cole alleges that he was 'universally hated, not to say detested', and that he had a 'haughty manner' (quoted in *DNB*).

Butts disapproved of the bishops' opposition to the mortmain and Quakers tithe bills. He informed his patron, Lord Hervey, that, in spite of Gibson's warm thanks to Sir Robert Walpole for his defence of the church during the House of Commons debate on the repeal of the Test and Corporation Acts, Gibson had immediately begun to work with the other bishops to orchestrate clerical opposition to the bills, although Walpole had informed him that he could not oppose the bills. This contributed to the rift between Gibson and Walpole, and to Gibson's eclipse as Walpole's ecclesiastical adviser.

In 1738 Butts was translated to the richer and smaller diocese of Ely. No evidence survives of his episcopal work at Ely (Owen, viii, 5). In his primary visitation charge Butts reiterated his defence of his clergy against anti-clericalism. He also gave the clergy practical advice about preaching and recommended regular local meetings of clergy, to 'confer together, concerning the Religious State of your Respective parishes, and the best manner of carrying jointly on the common End of your Profession' (*The Charge*, 1740, 22). The spiteful Cole alleged Butts spent very little time in the diocese, and that he had 'sufficient of every necessary language for his episcopal office, but good language', being often heard 'swearing a good round hand'. He is also alleged to have alienated the clergy of Ely diocese by his insolence towards them. A party squib, published after Sir Robert Walpole's death, in 1745, purporting to be Walpole's *Political Will and Testament* bequeathed 'My eloquence … to that Good Shepherd the Bishop of Ely, to persuade the Sheep of his Flock to leave off the Prophaneness, to turn from the evil of their Ways, and to follow the pious example of their leader' (*DNB*).

Butts married, first, Elizabeth Pitches (1686–1734) at Stanton All Saints', Suffolk, on 10 July 1712. They had eleven children, seven of whom died in infancy. Two sons (Eyton and Robert) were ordained, and two daughters married clergymen beneficed in the diocese of Ely. Elizabeth died on 22 August 1734, and was buried in the chapel of the bishop's palace at Norwich. In 1735 Butts married Anne Reynolds, aged twenty-three, daughter of the Revd James Reynolds of Bury. They had six daughters, only one of whom survived infancy. Anne died on 4 December 1795.

During his later years Butts was crippled with gout. He died at Ely House, High Holborn, on 26 January 1748, and was buried in the south choir aisle of Ely Cathedral.

W. M. Jacob

Sources Venn, *Alum. Cant.* • John, Lord Hervey, *Some materials towards memoirs of the reign of King George II*, ed. R. Sedgwick, 2 (1931) • *The charge of the right reverend father in God Robert, lord bishop of Norwich* (1736) • *The charge of the reverend father in God Robert, lord bishop of Ely* (1740) • Butts pedigree, Norfolk RO, X134/1 • 'An account of the enthronement of Bishop Butts', Norfolk RO, DCN 25/3 • Norwich dean and chapter minute book, 1684–1732, Norfolk RO, DCN 24/4 • ordination register, Norfolk RO, NDR 2 • D. M. Owen, *Ely records: a handlist of the records of the bishops and archdeacons of Ely* (1971) • *DNB*

Likenesses H. Cheere, marble bust on monument, 1748, Ely Cathedral • oils, Ely Cathedral, bishop's house

Butts, Sir William (*c.*1485–1545), physician, was born in Norwich, the son of John Butts, auditor of crown revenues, and his wife, Elizabeth. He was educated at Gonville Hall, Cambridge, becoming BA in 1507, MA in 1509, and MD in 1518. In the following year he applied for incorporation into the University of Oxford, but Wood could find no record of his incorporation. Butts married Margaret Bacon, daughter and coheir of John Bacon, of Cambridge, about 1516. She soon became a lady-in-waiting to Princess Mary and later had her portrait painted by Holbein. The marriage produced a daughter and three sons: William, of Thornage, Norfolk; Thomas, of Great Riburgh, Norfolk; and Edmund, of Barrow, Suffolk; William was not killed at the battle of Musselburgh, as Blomefield says, but lived until 1583. All three married daughters of Henry Bury of Suffolk. Edmund's daughter, Anne, married Sir Nicholas Bacon, eldest son of Sir Nicholas Bacon, keeper of the great seal.

Sir William Butts (*c.*1485–1545), by Hans Holbein the younger, *c.*1540–43

In 1524 Butts took a lease of St Mary's Hostel, Cambridge, and was therefore probably principal of the house. At the same time he practised medicine among the nobility, and from 1528 to his death he was constantly employed as physician at the court of Henry VIII. The king, his queens Anne Boleyn and Jane Seymour, the Princess Mary, afterwards Queen Mary, the king's natural son, Henry Fitzroy, duke of Richmond, Cardinal Wolsey, the duke of Norfolk, Sir Thomas Lovell, George Boleyn, and Lord Rochford are all known to have been his patients. His salary as physician to the king was £100 a year, afterwards increased by 40 marks, and an additional £20 for attending the young duke of Richmond. Butts was knighted in 1544. As physician to the Princess Mary he received a livery of blue and green damask for himself and two servants, and cloth for an apothecary. It may fairly be said that the princess owed her life to Butts. Not only did he exert his professional skill in her behalf, but, suspecting that there were plots to poison her, he frightened her governess, Lady Shelton, by telling her that it was commonly reported in London that she was guilty of this crime, and so made her doubly careful of her charge for her own sake.

Butts is sometimes erroneously described as a founder of the College of Physicians: the college was founded in 1518, and he did not join until 1529, when he took up residence in London. He does not seem to have held any collegiate office, but was held in such esteem that he is entered in the college's books as 'vir gravis, eximia literarum cognitione, singulari judicio, summa experientia et prudenti consilio doctor'.

This praise refers more particularly to Butts's medical life; but he was a patron of other branches of learning, and had some influence with the king. When Wolsey was in disgrace Butts tried to reconcile the king to him, and his intervention in favour of Archbishop Cranmer is represented in Shakespeare's *Henry VIII*, v.ii. In religious matters his sympathies were with the Reformation. Butts used his influence to secure advancement for Hugh Latimer, Thomas Thirlby, and Sir John Cheke. He also attempted to convert some of the monks of Syon who refused to acknowledge the king's supremacy. He died on 22 November 1545 at Fulham Manor, Middlesex, after suffering from a 'dooble febre quartanz', and was buried at Fulham church. His tomb was against the south wall, close to the altar, and formerly possessed a brass representing him in armour, with a shield bearing his arms, and a scroll inscribed with the words 'Myn advantage'. Beneath it was a Latin epitaph in elegiacs by his friend Cheke. The tomb and brass are now destroyed, but a slab with Cheke's verses, and an inscription stating that it was restored by Leonard Butts of Norfolk in 1627, was inserted in the wall of the tower. The epitaph wrongly gives the date of death as 17 November.

Butts's will at Somerset House and the inquisitions taken after his death show that he possessed houses at Fulham, and on the site of the White Friars, London; the manors of Thornage, Thornham, Edgefield, and Melton Constable, in Norfolk; and Panyngton, in Suffolk. Other lands with which the king rewarded him had been disposed of before his death. Many of his prescriptions, some devised in consultation with Dr Chambre, Dr Cromer, and Dr Augustine, were preserved in the British Museum (Sloane MS 1047). There are three epigrams on him (nos. 48, 49, 100) in Parkhurst's collection.

C. T. Martin, *rev.* Rachel E. Davies

Sources *LP Henry VIII* • R. J. Popkin, 'Doctor afield: Sir William Butts', *New England Journal of Medicine*, 265 (1961), 32–3 • T. N. Toomey, 'Sir William Butts of Norfolk', *Annals of Medical History*, 6 (1924), 185–94 • F. Blomefield and C. Parkin, *An essay towards a topographical history of the county of Norfolk*, 5 vols. (1739–75), vol. 1 • Munk, *Roll* • Wood, *Ath. Oxon.* • F. Madden, *Privy purse expenses of the Princess Mary, daughter of King Henry the Eighth* (1831), 101, 114 • J. Granger, *A biographical history of England, from Egbert the Great to the revolution*, 2nd edn, 1 (1775), 76, 109 • Cooper, *Ath. Cantab.*, 1.87, 535 • C. Goodall, *The Royal College of Physicians of London founded and established by law* (1684)

Archives BL, Sloane MS 1047 (1886)

Likenesses H. Holbein, group portrait, oils, *c*.1540–1543 (*Henry VIII and the barber surgeons*), Barber's Company, London • H. Holbein the younger, oils, *c*.1540–1543, Isabella Stewart Gardner Museum, Boston, Massachusetts [*see illus.*] • W. N. Gardiner, stipple, 1790 (after S. Harding after H. Holbein), Wellcome L. • C. W. Beck, photogravure, 1917 (after H. Holbein), Wellcome L. • oils (after H. Holbein), NPG

Wealth at death left houses in Fulham and White Friars, London, plus the manors of Thornage, Thornham, Edgefield, and Melton Constable, Norfolk

Buxhull, Sir Alan (1323?–1381), soldier, was the only son of Sir Alan Buxhull, lord of Buxhull in Sussex and tenant-in-chief of Bryanston in Dorset, and of Maud. In 1355 he served on Edward III's mission to Navarre, and went on campaign in France shortly before March 1366. He was named as one of John of Gaunt's lieutenants at the battle of Tournehem in 1369, and was at Calais and Le Mans in 1370, where the English force was defeated by Otto Grandson. It was at this time that Sir Alan was appointed captain of the castle at St Sauveur-le-Vicomte. From 1371 this position was farmed to Thomas Catterton, a squire of William, Lord Latimer, accused of treachery in the Good Parliament. Buxhull was only technically in command when the castle fell in 1375.

A knight of the king's chamber from at least 1358, in 1366 Buxhull was appointed constable of the Tower of London, an office which he held until his death. He had conducted the king of Cyprus, Peter de Lusignan, to London in 1363, and in 1364 he was one of the knights who welcomed the captured king, Jean of France, to England. He witnessed the ultimately unfulfilled contract of marriage between Edmund of Langley and Margaret of Flanders in October 1364. He was already keeper of the Forest of Clarendon in February 1368, and was later appointed keeper of Groveley, Melchet, and Buckholt. In 1372 he was elected fifty-third knight of the Garter upon the death of the earl of Stafford.

In 1374, according to Froissart, Buxhull used his influence at court in favour of John de Montfort, when an expedition was directed to Brittany. He was one of a group of royal courtiers close to Edward III which included William, Lord Latimer, Lord John Neville, Richard Stury, Alice Perrers, and Richard Lyons, but when in December 1377 he was called as a witness at the trial of Perrers, he testified against her. He corroborated the story of Nicholas Carew, who claimed that Alice had influenced the senile Edward III in his decision to pardon Richard Lyons, convicted in the Good Parliament of financial malpractice. His dissociation of himself from the king's mistress may have helped him retain his position in the household after Edward's death.

Buxhull was involved in two scandals later in his life. The first involved a Spanish prisoner, the count of Denia, captured at the battle of Nájera in 1367. The count had granted John Shakell and Robert Hauley, two esquires, his heir as security for a ransom payment. Refusing to give Gaunt custody of this prisoner, they were committed to the Tower. They escaped and sought sanctuary in Westminster Abbey. Buxhull, with Sir Ralph Ferrers and fifty men, killed both the fugitives—Shakell in the main body of the church, and Hauley in the chancel at mass—but avoided discipline for this serious crime. In the second incident Buxhull was ordered, in February 1380 and again in July, to return seisin of the bailiwick of the Forest of Groveley to John Blaunchard and to cease threatening him. Yet Buxhull still appeared to be keeper of Groveley in October 1381 when he was granted wood within the forest for fencing.

Buxhull died on 2 November 1381, and was buried in St Paul's Cathedral by St Erkenwald's shrine with the other Garter knights. The inquisition *post mortem*, taken at Shaftesbury on 14 November and Robertsbridge on 25 November, found that Elizabeth, the wife of Robert Lynde, and Amicia, the widow of John Beverly, were his daughters and heirs, one aged thirty and the other twenty-eight. The mother of these daughters is unknown. Buxhull was survived by his second wife, Maud [*see* Montagu, Maud, countess of Salisbury (*d.* 1424)], daughter of Adam *Fraunceys (*c.*1310–1375), a wealthy mercer and mayor of London, and his wife, Agnes (*d.* after 1392). Maud was pregnant when Buxhull died, and early in 1382 gave birth to a son, Alan, who became his heir. COLIN PAINE

Sources *Chancery records* · *Chroniques de J. Froissart*, ed. S. Luce and others, 15 vols. (Paris, 1869–1975) · G. F. Beltz, *Memorials of the most noble order of the Garter* (1841) · J. Hutchins, *The history and antiquities of the county of Dorset*, 3rd edn, ed. W. Shipp and J. W. Hodson, 4 vols. (1861–74) · M. A. Lower, *The worthies of Sussex* (1865) · C. Given-Wilson, *The royal household and the king's affinity: service, politics and finance in England, 1360–1413* (1986) · G. Holmes, *The Good Parliament* (1975) · *CIPM*, 6, no. 439; 8, no. 393; 15, nos. 191, 304, 306, 378 · J. Weever, *Ancient funerall monuments* (1631)

Wealth at death manor and advowson of Bryanston in Dorset; 1165 acres of land, two messuages, and a watermill in Sussex: PRO, C 6/439; 8/393; 15/191; 15/304; 15/306; 15/378

Buxton [*née* Leupold], **Bertha Henry** (1844–1881), novelist and children's author, was born on 26 July 1844 of German parents. Her father, William Leupold (sometimes spelt Leopold), was a London merchant, and her mother, Therese, was well known in musical circles. From eleven years of age Bertha amused herself and her school friends at Queen's College, Tufnell Park, London, by writing stories. During her early teens she travelled with her parents in America, Germany, and Holland. On 22 December 1860 aged sixteen, she married Henry Buxton, club manager and author, and son of Edward Buxton, merchant. She continued her literary pursuits, translating a German operetta into English, and writing a novel, called *Percy's Wife*, which was published at her husband's expense, under the name B. H. Bee. Afterwards she published short stories in *London Society* and the *Family Herald*.

In 1875 Bertha Buxton's husband deserted her, leaving her poverty-stricken. She turned to writing to support herself and her young son. In order to research her first book, *Jennie of the Prince's*, which appeared in 1876, she studied theatrical life at first hand by taking a walk-on part at the theatre in Exeter. The book was a success. In the following year she wrote a serial for *The World* and brought out during the same period *Won!* The author for these works was given as B. H. B., but a story for children entitled *Rosabella* was published under the name of Auntie Bee. From this period she wrote under her own name, and the following Christmas brought out another children's book, *More Dolls*, which she dedicated to the princess of Wales.

In the autumn of 1877, just as she had achieved a comfortable degree of success, Bertha Buxton was injured in a riding accident which incapacitated her. She forced herself to produce *Fetterless though Bound Together* (1879) and *Great Grenfell Gardens* (1879) before she was fully recovered. She then returned to the stage for subject matter with more success. *Nell—on and off the Stage* (1880) and *From the Wings* (1880) were both serialized in *Tinsley's Magazine*. Bertha Buxton was an industrious and productive writer. Four further novels and a children's story appeared between 1880 and 1881 before her sudden death from heart disease, at her home, Claremont Villa, 12 St Mary's Terrace, Kensington, London, on 31 March 1881.

G. C. BOASE, *rev.* VICTORIA MILLAR

Sources *Carisbrooke Magazine*, 14 (1881) · *Biograph and Review*, 4 (1880), 159–62 · *Tinsley's Magazine*, 28 (1881), 499–500 · *Saturday Review*, 13 (1877), 302 · R. L. Wolff, *Nineteenth-century fiction: a bibliographical catalogue based on the collection formed by Robert Lee Wolff*, 5 vols. (1981–6) · Boase, *Mod. Eng. biog.* · Allibone, *Dict.*

Likenesses photograph, repro. in *Carisbrooke Magazine*, frontispiece

Buxton, Charles (1822–1871), politician, was the third son of Sir Thomas Fowell *Buxton, first baronet (1786–1845), politician and philanthropist, and his wife, Hannah (1783–1872), fifth daughter of John Gurney of Earlham Hall. His sister was Priscilla *Buxton. Born at Cromer on 18 November 1822, he was educated at home until the age of seventeen, and then placed under the charge, successively, of the Revd T. Fisher at Luccombe and the Revd H. Alford (afterwards dean of Canterbury) at Wymeswold. In 1841 he went to Trinity College, Cambridge, where he graduated BA in 1845 and MA in 1850. On leaving the university he became a partner in the well-known brewery of Truman, Hanbury, Buxton & Co. On his father's death in 1845, Buxton wrote his biography (1848), which swiftly passed through thirteen editions, and was translated into French and German. In 1850 he married Emily Mary (*d.* 1871), the eldest daughter of Sir Henry *Holland (1788–1873), of Holland House. They had two sons and four daughters, including Sydney Charles *Buxton.

In 1852 Buxton visited Ireland. He purchased an estate in co. Kerry, and made it a model of cultivation in the course of a few years. In 1853 he published a pamphlet on national education in Ireland, in which he recommended for Ireland 'the system which had answered so admirably in England—that of encouraging each denomination to educate its own children in the best way possible'. In 1854 Buxton delivered a series of lectures on the theory of the construction of birds. In 1855 he published in the *North British Review* an article on the sale and use of strong drink, which attracted much attention as coming from a partner of a great brewing house.

Buxton was elected as Liberal MP for Newport in 1857, for Maidstone in 1859, and for East Surrey in 1865, for which constituency he sat until his death. He made an eloquent appeal in favour of referring the *Trent* question to arbitration; he frequently advocated the principle of the protection of private property during war, and the general amendment of international law in the interests of peace.

Charles Buxton (1822–1871), by London Stereoscopic Co., 1860s

In 1860 he published a work entitled *Slavery and Freedom in the British West Indies*, in which he endeavoured to prove that England had secured the spread of civilization in west Africa, as well as the permanent prosperity of the West Indies.

Buxton advocated the unpopular policy of clemency after the suppression of the Indian mutiny, and in the case of Governor Eyre and the Jamaica massacres. He opposed the Jamaica committee's resolution to prosecute Governor Eyre on a charge of murder, and on 31 July 1866 brought forward in the Commons four resolutions, the first of which declared that the punishments inflicted had been excessive. The government accepted the first resolution, and the others were withdrawn on the understanding that enquiries should be made with the object, if possible, of carrying out the resolutions. Buxton, however, felt it incumbent upon him subsequently to call for an effectual censure and repudiation of the conduct of Eyre and his subordinates.

Buxton was an advocate of church reform, of disestablishment, and of security of tenure in Ireland. In general politics an independent Liberal, he strongly advocated the system of cumulative voting; he took a deep interest in the volunteer movement, but condemned all wars except those of defence.

Buxton inherited his father's intense affection for animals and also his passion for hunting. To these he added a love for architecture; he designed his own seat of Fox Warren, in Surrey, and gained a prize of £100 in the competitive designs for the government offices in 1856. An admirer of the Gothic style of architecture, he also designed the fountain near Westminster Abbey, built by him in 1863, as a memorial of his father's anti-slavery labours. In 1866 Buxton published *The Ideas of the Day on Policy*, and a pamphlet in 1869 on self-government for London.

On 9 April 1867 Buxton was thrown from his horse while hunting, and suffered concussion. During his illness he studied the subject of anaesthetics, and offered a prize of £2000 for the discovery of an anaesthetic agent which would satisfy certain conditions. Early in 1870 Buxton's secretary, Arthur White, attempted to shoot him, and later that year his health suffered a rapid decline. He died away from home, at a hotel in Lochearnhead, Perthshire, on 10 August 1871. His wife died on the same day.

G. B. Smith, *rev.* H. C. G. Matthew

Sources Boase, *Mod. Eng. biog.* • *Notes of thought by C. Buxton [with] … biographical sketch by J. L. Davies* (1883) • Venn, *Alum. Cant.*
Archives Bodl. RH, family corresp.
Likenesses London Stereoscopic Co., photograph, 1860–69, NPG [*see illus.*] • engraving (after photograph by Elliott & Fry), repro. in *The Graphic*, 4 (2 Sept 1871), 237
Wealth at death under £250,000: probate, 18 Dec 1871, *CGPLA Eng. & Wales*

Buxton, Charles Roden (1875–1942), politician and philanthropist, was born at 14 Grosvenor Crescent, London, on 27 November 1875, the seventh child in a family of ten and the third son of Sir Thomas Fowell *Buxton (1837–1915), third baronet and director of a brewery, and his wife, Lady Victoria Noel (1839–1916) [*see* Buxton, Lady Victoria]. He grew up on the family estate at Warlies in Essex. He was educated at Harrow School and at Trinity College, Cambridge, where he took a first in classics in 1897 and was also president of the Cambridge Union. After taking his degree he went to assist his father, who was then governor of South Australia, and travelled extensively in the Far East and India. His health had been poor since childhood, and he spent further periods abroad on medical advice, on the Riviera, in the Cévennes, and even on a cattle ranch in Texas.

Buxton abandoned hopes of an academic career after failing to gain a fellowship at Trinity—one of the great disappointments of his life. Instead he took up law, and was called to the bar in 1902 from the Inner Temple, practising on the south-eastern circuit. From 1901 he also gave lectures in English literature at Morley College for working men and women in south London; he was principal of the college from 1902 to 1910. He wrote and published on a wide range of subjects, and edited the *Albany Review* (formerly the *Independent Review*) from 1906 to 1908.

On 11 August 1904 Buxton married Dorothy Frances Jebb (1881–1963) [*see* Buxton, Dorothy Frances], whom he had met on a Cambridge reading party in the Lake District. The couple adopted a simple, frugal lifestyle. On weekend walking tours in the south of England they were sometimes mistaken for tramps in their old clothes. They had two children, Eglantyne and David. They elected to live in a working-class district of London, at Kennington Terrace, later moving to Golders Green while the children were growing up.

Buxton gave up the law because of ill health, but also in the hope that he might serve the community better as a politician. He stood unsuccessfully as the Liberal candidate in Hertford in 1906, and in Ashburton in Devon in 1908. He was returned to parliament for Ashburton in January 1910, but was voted out again in the second election of that year, and in 1912 was selected as the Liberal candidate for Central Hackney. From 1912 to 1914 he was secretary to the Liberal land inquiry.

Buxton's extensive experience of travelling fostered a strong interest in foreign affairs, particularly in matters concerning the Balkans. In 1914 he went to Bulgaria with his brother Noel [*see* Buxton, Noel Edward Noel-, first Baron Noel-Buxton], on a mission to persuade the country to support the allies, in the course of which both brothers were wounded in an attack by a Turkish would-be assassin; Charles was shot through the lung. Throughout the First World War he argued the (unpopular) case for a reasonable peace by negotiation, and he was a founder member of the Union of Democratic Control. In 1917 he left the Liberals and joined the Independent Labour Party. He attended the conferences of the Socialist International in 1919 and 1920 as an interpreter for the British delegation, and acted as secretary to the Labour Party's delegation to the Soviet Union in 1920. He published an account of his experiences, *In a Russian Village* (1922). He was enthusiastic about the initial achievements of the Russian Revolution, which he described as the most significant event in history since the beginning of Christianity. He was a delegate to the League of Nations assembly in 1924 and 1930, and promoted the international language Esperanto, serving as president of the British Esperantists.

Buxton was defeated when he contested Accrington for the Labour Party in 1918, but won the seat in 1922, only to lose it in the following year. He returned to the Commons as the MP for Elland in 1929, but was unsuccessful in the general elections of 1931 and 1935. He was not a natural election campaigner, being described by friends as more likely to hide from his electors in the company of a good book than go out to solicit for their votes. His work for the Labour Party was mainly in policy discussion, on the advisory committees on foreign affairs and imperial questions, which he chaired from 1926 to 1937. He was also treasurer for the Independent Labour Party from 1924 to 1927. Much of his energy focused on colonial policy. He championed the rights of native peoples in Africa, and travelled to various parts of the continent, including Uganda, Kenya, and Liberia.

Buxton and his wife, Dorothy, who had publicized the sufferings of children in central Europe after the First World War, were frequent visitors to Germany and were highly critical of the Versailles settlement. As late as August 1939 Buxton was in Germany, continuing to argue that efforts should be made to answer German grievances, and that colonial opportunities should be opened up for Germany in west central Africa, always ensuring that the rights of native peoples were protected.

Christian principles informed Buxton's politics and all aspects of his life. His faith embraced a strong sense of social mission, and he moved away from the Church of England over what he saw as its identification with the privileged classes and its attitude towards war. He joined the Society of Friends and became a member of the meeting at Golders Green. It was said that because he had spent so much of his life working for peace, the outbreak of the Second World War broke his heart. He retired from political work in 1939 in poor health, and spent the last two years of his life at his daughter's house, Whingate, Peaslake, Surrey, where he died on 16 December 1942. He was buried in Peaslake cemetery. He left most of his estate to charity. C. V. J. GRIFFITHS

Sources V. A. B. De Bunsen, *Charles Roden Buxton: a memoir* (1948) • J. Bellamy and M. 'Espinasse, 'Buxton, Charles Roden', *DLB*, vol. 5 • *Labour party conference report* (1943) • *The Times* (17 Dec 1942) • C. R. Buxton, *A politician plays truant: essays on English literature* (1929) • C. R. Buxton, *In a Russian village* (1922)

Archives BLPES, corresp., notes, and papers relating to social and economic conditions in post-war Europe • Bodl. RH, corresp. relating to African affairs • Bodl. RH, corresp. and papers • McGill University, Montreal, McLennan Library, family papers | BLPES, corresp. with the Independent Labour Party • Bodl. RH, corresp. with Arthur Creech Jones • Bodl. RH, corresp. with Lord Lugard • Bodl. RH, corresp. with C. W. G. Walker relating to East Africa • Hull Central Library, corresp. with Winifred Holtby

Likenesses photograph, repro. in De Bunsen, *Charles Roden Buxton*

Wealth at death £19,601 18*s*. 0*d*.: resworn probate, 5 March 1943, *CGPLA Eng. & Wales*

Buxton [*née* Jebb], **Dorothy Frances** (1881–1963), humanitarian and social activist, was born on 3 March 1881 at The Lyth, Ellesmere, Shropshire, the youngest daughter of Arthur Trevor Jebb (1839–1894), barrister and philanthropic squire, and his wife, Eglantyne Louisa Jebb (1845–1925), community worker and poet, the sister of Sir Richard Claverhouse Jebb MP, regius professor of Greek at Cambridge. Louisa [*see* Wilkins, Louisa] and Eglantyne *Jebb were her elder sisters. She was educated at Newnham College, Cambridge (1900–04). On 11 August 1904 she married Charles Roden *Buxton (1875–1942), the third son of Sir Thomas Fowell *Buxton, third baronet. The young couple deliberately set up house in the poor London district of Kennington to share those hardships they dedicated themselves as radicals to relieve, if not abolish. Charles Buxton was an educationist with political ambitions to reform the country via parliament; Dorothy was a high-minded social activist, a latter-day Dorothea Brooke, one, in Keats's words:

> to whom the miseries of the world
> Are misery and will not let them rest.

In 1916 she joined both the Independent Labour Party and the Society of Friends.

When the First World War broke out with its concomitant propaganda war Dorothy Buxton could not bear the dehumanization of the German people in the British press which she knew would only worsen and prolong the war and make an eventual genuine peace settlement impossible. She determined to bring before English readers evidence of the fellow humanity of 'the enemy' and, in particular, evidence of the opposition to German chauvinism and militaristic imperialism within Germany. Therefore she set herself to translate and publish in leaflet form extracts from the foreign press, including twenty-five enemy papers which the Board of Trade allowed her to import from Scandinavia—the board was perhaps not unwilling to have such 'intelligence' work done for it voluntarily. She was then invited by C. K. Ogden to publish her unpopular but influential 'Notes from the foreign press' in his weekly *Cambridge Magazine*, which she did from October 1915 to early 1920. She published the news of German socialist anti-war demonstrations and the evidence that the British hardline position on the destruction of Germany only increased support for that country's intransigent military leadership. To translate from French, German, Italian, Russian, Hungarian, Romanian, and Finnish—100 newspapers in all—required a team of scores of expert linguists and translators and shorthand typists, not to mention specialists in foreign affairs; all of the work was supervised and edited by Dorothy Buxton in her own home, which was turned into the daily headquarters. Although she then had two young children, her 'austerity impelled her to make a sacrifice of home-life itself' (Bunsen, 49).

From 1917 Dorothy Buxton received and disseminated the news of appalling privation in Germany. So intolerable did she consider the starving of Germans and Austrians by the allied blockade, even after they had surrendered, that she and her sister Eglantyne, together with Lord Parmoor, Kate Courtney, and Marian Ellis, co-founded the Fight the Famine Committee in 1919 to change that retributive economic policy. Out of the committee came the founding of the international Save the Children Fund.

Dorothy Buxton continued to be a humanitarian activist all her life. During the 1930s she collected and circulated reports on Nazi concentration camps that she had received from the refugees she was aiding, only to have them pigeon-holed by the Foreign Office until after the Second World War had broken out and they were inefficacious. Her husband's peace witness made him an appeaser of Germany's claims to right the wrongs of the treaty of Versailles. But Dorothy insisted on publicizing Nazi atrocities; she even made a quixotic attempt to see Goering in 1935 to confront him with the abominations being perpetrated and so shame him out of his Nazism. He of course only started shouting at her in fury. Both before and during the Second World War she made contact with the Bekennende Kirche—the underground protestant anti-Nazi Christians in Germany, including Bonhoeffer—once again publicizing the existence of humane Germans for British readers. She died, twenty years after her husband, at her home, Whingate, Peaslake, near Guildford, Surrey, on 8 April 1963. SYBIL OLDFIELD

Sources V. A. B. De Bunsen, *Charles Roden Buxton: a memoir* (1948) • F. M. Wilson, *Rebel daughter of a country house: life of Eglantyne Jebb* (1967) • *The Times* (15 April 1963) • D. Buxton, *The white flame: the story of the Save the Children Fund* (1931) • b. cert. • d. cert. • Burke, *Peerage* (1914) • *CGPLA Eng. & Wales* (1963)

Likenesses photograph, c.1904, repro. in Wilson, *Rebel daughter* • photograph, 1922, repro. in general election leaflet [Accrington parliamentary borough]

Wealth at death £44,015 15*s*. 3*d*.: probate, 6 Aug 1963, *CGPLA Eng. & Wales*

Buxton, Edward North (1840–1924), conservationist and brewer, was born on 1 September 1840 at Upton Lane, Stratfield, Essex, the third of six sons born to Sir Edward North Buxton, second baronet (1812–1858), and his wife, Catherine, second daughter of Samuel Gurney of Upton, Essex. He matriculated at Trinity College, Cambridge, in 1859, but seems not to have taken a degree. He was a member of the London school board and its chairman from 1881 to 1885. He unsuccessfully stood for election to parliament in 1880 (Essex South) and 1886 (North-West Suffolk), but was MP for Walthamstow in 1885–6. He was a Liberal and supported free schools, legislation against the enclosure of the commons, the enfranchisement of long leaseholds, and disestablishment in Scotland and Wales. Buxton was partner in the brewing firm Truman, Hanbury, Buxton & Co. and from 1889 chairman of the board of directors. This brought him substantial wealth which, with his strongly religious background, led him to philanthropy. He lived in Essex all his life—at Knighton, Buckhurst Hill, Woodford, from 1862 until his death—and held various offices including those of alderman of the county council and chairman of the local education committee.

Buxton is best remembered for his part in preserving London forests for public recreation. A free-trader (his *ABC of Free Trade*, issued in 1882 by the Cobden Club, went to three editions), he argued that open markets reduced the need to put every acre in Britain to productive use; instead the need for open land, particularly near cities, was pressing. He joined the Commons Preservation Society in 1866, the year after its formation, and with them and his brother Sir (Thomas) Fowell *Buxton fought to save Epping Forest in the 1860s and 1870s when both the crown (the holder of forest rights) and the lords of the manor (holders of manorial rights) were encouraging its enclosure and conversion to arable, or its use for housing or railway developments. Buxton persuaded the society to fight to save all the remaining forest, not a token area of 600 acres. He took direct action, removing fences which had been illegally erected on rights of way, as well as supporting legal battles. The forest was secured for public use in 1878 and, to Buxton's approval, was to 'remain a forest and not be civilised into a park'. He was immediately elected verderer of Epping Forest and remained one until his death. His *Epping Forest* (1884; 9th edn, 1923) shows his affection for the forest and his desire to share it with others. Buxton married, on 23 January 1862, Emily, youngest daughter of the Hon. and Revd Kenelm Henry Digby, rector of Titteshall, Norfolk; they had four sons and five daughters. To celebrate their golden weddings he and his brother Fowell (who had married in the same year) made a joint gift to the Commons Preservation Society and presented Oak Hill at Theydon Bois and Yardley Hill at

Sewardstone (both in the forest) to the public. Their actions aroused the animosity of their landed neighbours who stood to gain from enclosure. After his success in Epping, Buxton turned his attention to Hainault Forest, which in 1851 had been enclosed by act of parliament by the crown acting as lord of the manor. He collected money to buy back enclosed areas and replanted trees to replace the ancient timber that had been felled. And only three weeks before his death he learned that he had secured for the public Hatfield Forest, on which ancient trees still stood.

Buxton had a wide interest in nature and conservation. He was elected fellow of the Royal Geographical Society in 1895 and was a member of the Alpine Club. His *Two African Trips* (1902) included suggestions on the preservation of big game. Appalled at the indiscriminate slaughter of animals, he was one of the earliest and most influential people to suggest shooting big game with the camera rather than the gun. The preservation of forests around London was a milestone in the movement to save open spaces for public recreation, rather than individual commercial profit. Buxton's call, that 'the people of London for all time [may] continue to … profit by the companionship and teaching of Nature' (*Epping Forest*, 21), epitomizes the spirit of the movement. Buxton died at his home on 9 January 1924. Characteristically he scorned suggestions that memorials be raised to him in the forests or that they be renamed after him. ELIZABETH BAIGENT

Sources Venn, *Alum. Cant.* • G. Buxton, 'The Late Mr E. N. Buxton and three Essex forests', *Essex Naturalist*, 21 (1926), 12–14 • Burke, *Peerage* • *WWBMP*, vol. 2 • A. Brimble, *London's Epping forest* (1950) • G. W. E. Russell, *Lady Victoria Buxton* (1919) • W. R. Fisher, *The forest of Essex* (1887) • P. Thompson, 'The Willingales of Loughton', *Essex Naturalist*, 21 (1926), 157–69 • J. Marsh, *Back to the land* (1982) • J. Ryan, 'Photography, geography and empire', PhD diss., U. Lond., 1994 • G. Shaw Lefevre, *English commons and forests: the story of the battle during the last thirty years for public rights over the commons and forests of England and Wales* (1894)

Archives Bishopsgate Institute, London, letters to George Howell

Likenesses photograph, repro. in Buxton, 'Late Mr E. N. Buxton', facing p. 12

Wealth at death £141,318 18s. 3d.: probate, 5 April 1924, *CGPLA Eng. & Wales*

Buxton, Sir (Thomas) Fowell, third baronet (1837–1915), philanthropist, brewer, and colonial governor, was born on 26 January 1837 at West Ham, Essex, the eldest of six sons of Sir Edward North Buxton, second baronet (1812–1858), and his wife, Catherine, second daughter of Samuel *Gurney (1786–1856), of the Quaker family of Upton, Essex. Buxton's paternal grandfather was Sir Thomas Fowell *Buxton, the anti-slavery campaigner. Buxton entered Harrow School in 1850 and matriculated at Trinity College, Cambridge, in 1855, proceeding MA in 1859. On 11 June 1858 he succeeded his father as third baronet and took over landed property and a partnership in the brewing firm Truman, Hanbury, Buxton & Co. of Spitalfields, where he worked until 1889. On 12 June 1862 he married Lady Victoria Noel (1839–1916) [*see* Buxton, Lady Victoria], youngest daughter of Charles Noel Noel, the first earl of Gainsborough. Of their thirteen children, five sons and five daughters survived infancy. His wife was left physically disabled by a spinal illness in 1869. From 1865 to 1868 he was Liberal MP for King's Lynn, but failed to be elected in 1874 (Westminster), 1876, 1879 (North Norfolk), and 1880 (West Essex). In parliament he promoted the Imperial Federation League and he represented Britain at several European conferences on slavery and central African affairs.

Buxton's evangelical faith and his wealth made him an influential figure in the British and Foreign Anti-Slavery Society (of which he was elected president in 1899), the volunteer movement, movements for the welfare of Africans and the improvement of elementary schools, the Church Missionary Society, and Missions to Seamen. He was elected fellow of the Royal Geographical Society in 1858. He was also a member of the Commons Preservation Society and, with his brother Edward North *Buxton, was much involved in its campaign begun in 1866 to save Epping Forest. In particular he contributed to the fund to enable the woodcutter Thomas Willingale to assert his customary rights in a chancery suit.

In 1895 Buxton was appointed governor of South Australia. He was a choice which provoked amazement in England and irritation in South Australia, where the radical premier, Charles Cameron Kingston, made clear his displeasure by cutting the governor's salary and abolishing his expenses—actions which could have only symbolic meaning for the wealthy Buxton. There were also some differences of policy between Buxton and Kingston, but Buxton's quiet good-heartedness and the pleasant manner of his wife and numerous children won over his critics, until Kingston declared 'Governor Buxton and his flock to be the most sociable and commonsense family who have ever inhabited the Adelaide vice-regal mansion' (Howell, 515). Buxton regularly visited prisoners, the insane, the sick, and the destitute; and his wife, also a devout Christian, actively promoted education (particularly for girls), and the welfare of mothers. They clearly enjoyed meeting colonists of all sorts, and regarded the recipients of their very extensive charity as individual people, with their own concerns and needs. Buxton was also remarkable for his interest in Aborigines; he took pains to understand their land-tenure system and to explain it to settlers, whom he exhorted to make amends for past injustices.

While on leave in England in 1898, the health of Buxton's wife and eldest son gave cause for concern and Buxton resigned without returning to Australia, though he continued to be interested in South Australian affairs. In 1899 he was created GCMG for his services. He died at Cromer on 28 October 1915 in a cottage, having characteristically given Colne House, the family home at Cromer, for use as a war hospital. He was succeeded by his eldest son, Thomas Fowell Victor Buxton (1865–1919); his younger sons included Noel Edward Noel-*Buxton, first Baron Noel-Buxton (1869–1948), and Charles Roden *Buxton (1875–1942). His wife's memoirs show Buxton as a man of high principle, prepared to run the risk of

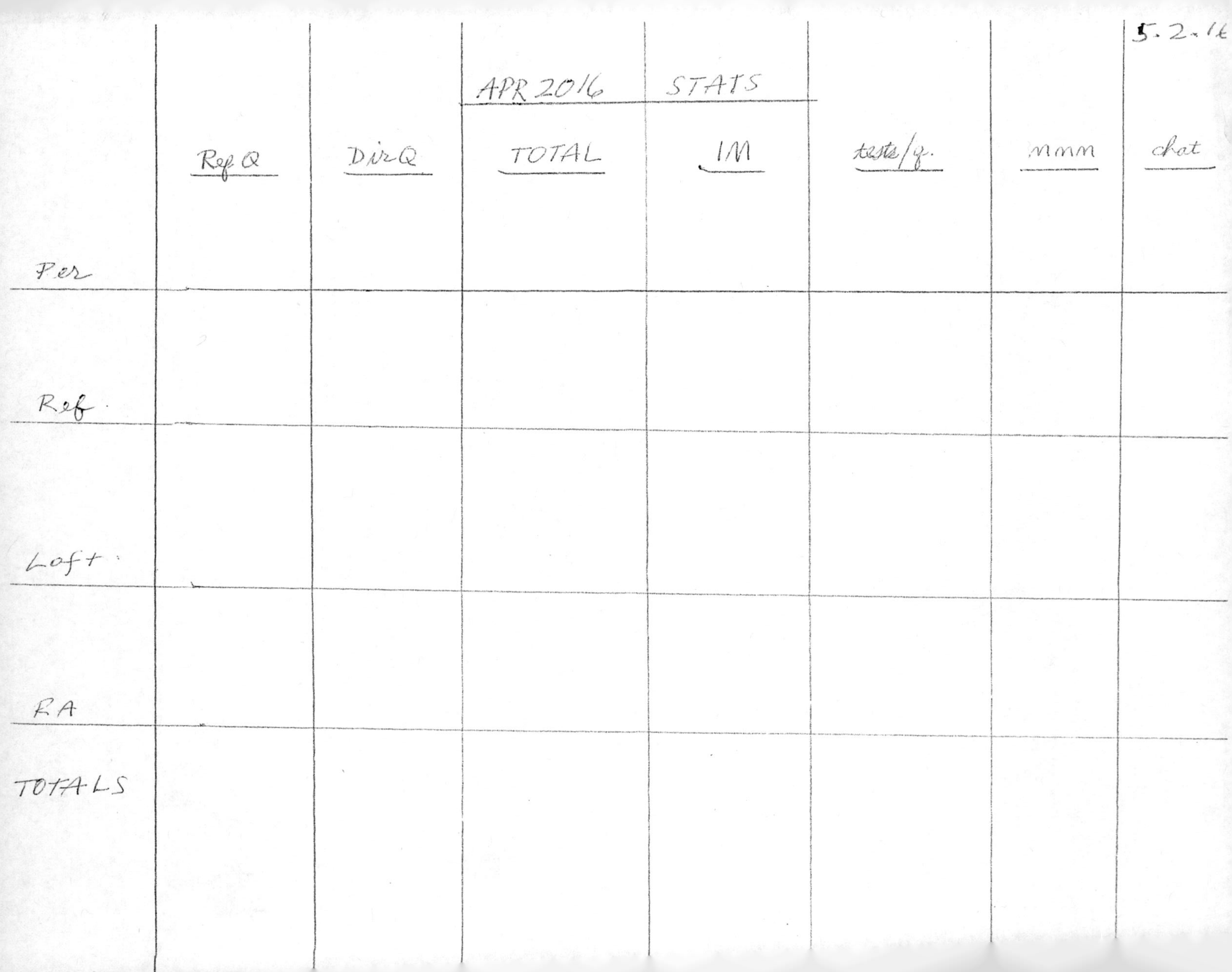

5.2.16

			APR 2016 STATS				
	Ref Q	Dir Q	TOTAL	IM	tests/q.	mmm	chat
Per							
Ref.							
Loft.							
RA							
TOTALS							

unpopularity (as when he opposed his landlord neighbours' wish to enclose Epping Forest), and who put family concerns above office (as when he resigned his governor-generalship). His wealth (he left over £420,000) gave him that freedom of action, but his modesty and generosity made him unusually widely admired and well liked.

ELIZABETH BAIGENT

Sources G. W. E. Russell, *Lady Victoria Buxton* (1919) · P. A. Howell, 'Buxton, Sir Thomas Fowell', *AusDB*, vol. 7 · *The Times* (4 Nov 1915) · *WWBMP*, vol. 1 · *CGPLA Eng. & Wales* (1916) · Venn, *Alum. Cant.* · J. H. Stogdon, ed., *The Harrow School register, 1845–1925*, 4th edn, 2 vols. (1925) · *DNB* · P. A. Howell, 'Varieties of vice-regal life', *Journal of the Historical Society of South Australia*, 3 (1977) · W. R. Fisher, *The forest of Essex* (1887) · Burke, *Peerage*
Archives Bodl. RH, corresp. and papers relating to Anti-Slavery Society · Essex RO, Chelmsford, accounts; diaries; papers · priv. coll., papers
Likenesses W. Holl, stipple, pubd 1835 (after H. P. Briggs), NPG · J. Collier, portrait, Art Gallery of South Australia, Adelaide · Elliott & Fry, photograph, repro. in Russell, *Lady Victoria Buxton*, 112
Wealth at death £420,976 3s. 6d.: probate, 4 March 1916, *CGPLA Eng. & Wales*

Buxton, Jedidiah (1707–1772), mental arithmetician, was born on 20 March 1707 at Elmton, Derbyshire, the eldest of four surviving children of William Buxton (1672–1739), originally from Chelmorton, but then a farmer and schoolmaster of Elmton, and his wife, Sarah (1677–1760), daughter of John Short of Elmton. His paternal grandmother, Ann, was married to John Davenport, vicar of Elmton. Buxton married Alice Eastwood (*d.* 1753) on 4 February 1733 at Kirton, Nottinghamshire; they had at least two children.

Despite his father's profession Buxton never learned to write and throughout his life was employed as a farm labourer. His inability to acquire the rudiments of education seems to have been caused by his absorbing passion for mental calculations, which occupied his mind to the exclusion of all else, and in which he attained a degree of skill that made him the wonder of the neighbourhood. He was first brought into more general notice by a letter in the *Gentleman's Magazine* for February 1751, by George Saxe, a gardener employed by the duke of Kingston, which was shortly followed by further communications in August 1751 and November 1753 from a Mr Holliday, of Haughton Park, Nottinghamshire. Among the many examples of Buxton's arithmetical feats which are given in these letters may be mentioned his calculation of the product of a farthing doubled 139 times. The result, expressed in pounds, extends to thirty-nine figures, and can be verified by the use of a computer. Buxton afterwards multiplied this enormous number by itself. It appears that he had invented an original nomenclature for large numbers, a 'tribe' being the cube of a million, and a 'cramp' a thousand 'tribes of tribes'. In April 1754 he walked to London, where he was entertained by Edward Cave, editor of the *Gentleman's Magazine*, at St John's Gate. He was introduced to the Royal Society, before whom he gave some illustrations of his calculating powers. He was also taken to see Garrick in *Richard III*, but paid no attention to the performance except to count the words spoken by the actors. A memoir of Buxton, with an uncredited portrait in *Gentleman's Magazine*, June 1754, gives his age as forty-nine, which does not agree with the date of his birth in Elmton parish register at the time of his baptism.

After spending some weeks in London, Buxton returned contentedly to his native village. His final years passed in relative obscurity. Local legend tells how he calculated the exact date that he would die, and that after farewells to his employer, family, and friends, he returned home, ate his supper, and died in his chair. He was buried on 5 March 1772 in an unmarked grave in St Peter's churchyard, Elmton.

HENRY BRADLEY, *rev.* GARY WOODHOUSE

Sources *GM*, 1st ser., 21 (1751), 16, 347 · *GM*, 1st ser., 23 (1753), 557 · *GM*, 1st ser., 24 (1754), 251 · parish registers, Elmton, St Peter's, Derbys. RO, D1462, A/PI [birth, baptism], 20 March 1707, 14 April 1707 · *Literary and Biographical Magazine*, 4 (1791), 400 · 'Miner and Sexton: Barlboro' veterans' long and eventful life', *Derbyshire Times* (20 Nov 1909) · parish register, Kirton, 4 Feb 1733, Notts. Arch. [marriage] · parish registers, Chelmorton, Derbys. RO · parish register, Elmton, St Peter's, 5 March 1772, Derbys. RO [burial]
Likenesses oils on wooden panel, 18th cent., Elmton church, Derbyshire · J. Spilsbury, mezzotint, pubd 1773 (after B. Killingbeck), BM, NPG · J. Corner, line print, NPG · M. Hartley, etching (aged fifty-seven), BM · R. Holme, etching (aged sixty), BM · B. Killingbeck, mezzotint (after J. Spilsbury), BM, NPG · Topham, etching (aged sixty-three), BM, NPG · engraving, repro. in *GM*, 1st ser., 25 (1755), 253 · engraving, repro. in *Literary and Biographical Magazine*, 400 · pencil sketch, Derby library

Buxton, Lucy Edith Noel- [*née* Lucy Edith Burn], **Lady Noel-Buxton** (**1888–1960**), politician, was born on 14 December 1888 in Winchester, the eldest daughter of Major Henry Pelham Burn and his wife, Janet Edith (*née* Orr-Ewing). She went to school at St James's, West Malvern, and studied at Westfield College, University of London. Her early politics were Conservative, and she met her future husband, Noel Edward *Buxton (1869–1948), in 1910, while campaigning against him and his liberal politics under the slogan 'No Noel for North Norfolk'; Buxton, twenty years her senior, was returned to Westminster despite her efforts. They married in April 1914 and went to live at Paycockes, in Coggeshall, Essex, an old timbered house which Buxton had restored. They had six children, three boys and three girls, whose childhood was spent mostly at Upshire Bury, near Warlies in Essex, where the Buxtons moved after presenting Paycockes to the National Trust in 1920.

During the First World War, Lucy Buxton's husband became disillusioned with the Liberal leadership and in 1919 he joined the Labour Party. Having lost his seat in 1918, he regained North Norfolk as a Labour MP in 1922. Lucy Buxton became part of the 'Half Circle Club' of Labour women organized by Beatrice Webb. In 1930 she was plummeted into a political career in her own right, when her husband, who had been suffering ill health, retired as constituency MP and took a seat in the House of Lords. Against the wishes of the National Union of Agricultural Workers, the most powerful trade union in the area, Lady Noel-Buxton (as she was now known) was selected as the Labour Party candidate for North Norfolk to fight the resulting by-election in July 1930, which she won by only 179 votes. She made her maiden speech in support of widening the unemployment insurance scheme to include agricultural labourers, at a time when the minister of labour, Margaret Bondfield, had come in for much criticism for failing to address the issue. Her initial experience of Westminster was short-lived, as she lost her seat in the general election in October 1931. She stood again in 1935 but was conclusively defeated, and withdrew in 1936 as Labour's candidate for the seat.

At the 1945 general election Lucy Noel-Buxton was returned as a Labour MP for Norwich. She was regarded as one of the quieter and more reserved female MPs, and spoke in the Commons largely on colonial affairs. She did not stand for re-election in 1950. Her son Christopher had died during the Second World War, and she was widowed in 1948.

Lucy Noel-Buxton had married into a family committed to public and social work, and she shared many of the activities and interests of her husband, Noel, and brother-in-law Charles Roden Buxton. She was one of the foundation trustees of the Noel Buxton Trust, established in 1919, which oversaw the spending of part of the family income on charitable purposes, notably on the causes of child welfare, international peace, and the future development of Britain's African colonies. She also sat on the committee of the Mothercraft Training Society. One of her particular interests was in gardening, and she was active in the London Gardens Guild, which her husband had set up while living in Spitalfields, as a way of improving the quality of life for people living in the city. She was also a fellow of the Royal Horticultural Society. In 1918 she published a book of poems entitled *Hay Harvest and other Poems*. She died in Frinton in Essex on 9 December 1960, and was buried four days later in the churchyard of St Thomas's, Upshire, in Essex, where her husband was also buried.

C. V. J. GRIFFITHS

Sources A. Holt, 'Noel-Buxton, Lucy Edith Pelham, Lady', *DLB*, vol. 5 • M. Anderson, *Noel Buxton: a life* (1952) • P. Brookes, *Women at Westminster: an account of women in the British parliament, 1918–1966* (1967) • *Labour party conference report* (1961) • U. Reading, Rural History Centre, papers of the National Union of Agricultural Workers • PRO, papers of J. Ramsay MacDonald • M. Beard, *The Noel Buxton Trust, 1919–1989: a brief account* (1989) • *The Times* (12 Dec 1960) • *The Times* (14 Dec 1960) • L. Manning, *A life for education: an autobiography* (1970) • *CGPLA Eng. & Wales* (1961)

Archives Duke U., family papers • McGill University, Montreal, Canada, family papers • priv. coll., personal papers | PRO, papers of J. Ramsay MacDonald • U. Reading, Rural History Centre, papers of the National Union of Agricultural Workers, material relating to her candidature in North Norfolk

Likenesses photograph, repro. in *The Times* (12 Dec 1960)

Wealth at death £63,623 0s. 11d.: probate, 20 April 1961, *CGPLA Eng. & Wales*

Buxton, Noel Edward Noel-, first Baron Noel-Buxton (1869–1948), politician, was born in London on 9 January 1869, the second son of Sir (Thomas) Fowell *Buxton (1837–1915), third baronet and director of a brewery company, and his wife, Lady Victoria *Buxton (1839–1916), daughter of the earl of Gainsborough. He grew up in the family house of Warlies in Essex, in a family of ten children. He was educated at Harrow School and Trinity College, Cambridge (1886–9), where he gained a third in the historical tripos. In 1889 he went to work at the family brewery in Spitalfields, and became involved in social work in the area through the missions and the settlement movement. With his brother Charles Roden *Buxton and his cousin Conrad Noel, he used to dress in old clothes and spend nights in 'common lodging-houses' to get closer to the poor (Anderson, 27). In 1901 he contributed to the volume of essays on the problems of city life, *The Heart of the Empire*, edited by C. F. G. Masterman. His social conscience and commitment to charitable work remained constant features in his life, and from 1919 onwards he directed part of his income to the achievement of 'social and economic progress' through a special trust administered by the family. Buxton's social work also developed into ambitions for public service. He became a member of the Whitechapel board of guardians in 1897, and stood unsuccessfully for the London county council. He was unsuccessful in his first parliamentary contest as a Liberal candidate in Ipswich in 1900, but was elected to parliament for Whitby at a by-election in 1905, only to be voted out again the following year in the general election.

Buxton took a year's leave from his work at the brewery in 1892 to travel to Japan, and his encounters with Buddhism in the Far East inspired him to give up blood sports. Travel became an important influence on his life, and he published several books describing his experiences abroad. In 1896 he went to Australia to assist his father, who was then governor of South Australia. A visit to the Balkans in 1899 began a long-lasting fascination with that part of the world and a passion for the cause of oppressed minorities in the region. He helped to found the Balkan Committee in 1902, along with his brother Charles, Noel Brailsford, and James Bryce; he became its first chairman, and later (1907) its president. When the Turks suppressed a revolt in Macedonia in 1903, Buxton travelled with his sister Victoria to see conditions there for himself and to administer aid.

In 1904 Buxton resigned his position as a director at the brewery and began to focus his attention on the eastern counties, taking an interest in the new wave of agricultural trade unionism and encouraging the development of small-holding on his family's Norfolk estate. He was elected Liberal MP for North Norfolk in January 1910, and while campaigning in the constituency he met his future wife, Lucy Edith Burn [*see* Buxton, Lucy Edith Noel- (1888–1960)]; at the time she was canvassing on behalf of his political opponent. He lived first in the family properties of Runton Old Hall and then Colne Cottage, before purchasing Paycockes, a house at Coggeshall in Essex, which had been a home for the Buxton family in the sixteenth and seventeenth centuries. He restored the property to its original timbered appearance and presented the house to the National Trust in 1920.

From 1911 onwards Buxton became increasingly vocal on foreign affairs, launching initiatives to defuse Anglo-German hostility, engaging in relief work in Bulgaria with his brother the Revd Harold Buxton during the hostilities of 1912, and taking up the cause of Armenia in 1913. On the outbreak of war in 1914 he and his brother Charles travelled to Bulgaria on a mission to secure the country's support for the allies or, failing that, its neutrality. Their diplomatic efforts were unsuccessful, but the brothers became local heroes in Bulgaria after they were wounded during a Turkish assassination attempt; a street in Sofia was named Brothers Buxton Street in tribute.

Buxton married Lucy Burn on 30 April 1914 and they had six children: three girls and three boys. During the First World War he worked for the Admiralty, and promoted the Armenian cause on a visit to the United States in 1916. The entry of the US into the conflict seemed to spell an end to any hope of the negotiated peace which he had been promoting, and alongside this disillusionment he was also increasingly disenchanted with the Liberal Party and its leadership. He lost his North Norfolk seat at the 1918 general election, and in 1919 he joined the Labour Party, arguing that it represented what the Liberal Party should be doing but no longer did. He became a close friend and travelling companion of the Labour leader, Ramsay MacDonald. He was active in the party's committee on international questions, calling for the revision of the Versailles settlement and for economic reconstruction, and became treasurer of the Fight the Famine Council.

In 1922 Buxton returned to the House of Commons, winning back his old seat of North Norfolk, this time under Labour colours. Although foreign affairs remained his main political interest, he agreed to take on the agricultural portfolio, which was of particular relevance to his rural constituency. He became minister of agriculture in the first Labour government in 1924. One of the few positive legislative achievements of that short-lived administration was the Agricultural Wages Act which he piloted through parliament, securing the reinstitution of minimum wage legislation in agriculture. He returned as minister of agriculture in the Labour administration of 1929, but retired from the Commons on medical advice in June 1930. Despite his opposition to the principle of hereditary political power, he agreed to take the title Baron Noel-Buxton of Aylsham, Norfolk, on 17 June 1930, changing his surname to Noel-Buxton by deed poll. After he had taken his seat in the Lords, his wife briefly represented his old constituency of North Norfolk in the Commons.

During the 1930s Noel-Buxton's energies were directed largely towards charitable work and campaigns on the international stage. He was president of the Save the Children Fund from 1930 to 1948, and chaired the Miners' Welfare Committee from 1931 to 1934. He agitated for the worldwide abolition of slavery, a cause to which he felt a special obligation as a continuation of the work of his ancestor Sir Thomas Fowell Buxton, the 'Great Liberator'. He visited Abyssinia in 1932, on the invitation of its emperor, to advise on a programme for ending slavery in the country. He remained a critic of the Versailles settlement and was a committed advocate of the appeasement of Germany, arguing that Germany must be given a colonial role in Africa. Even during the Second World War he continued to promote the idea of a negotiated peace. In 1945 he stood down as president of the Balkan Committee, hoping that a younger and more energetic figure would take his place, but the position remained unfilled, and the organization itself collapsed soon afterwards.

Among his papers Noel-Buxton left a list headed 'My lost causes', which included Armenia, Macedonia, and Germany. At the end of his life many of the ideals for which he had campaigned seemed to have been defeated. Although he sat as a Labour MP and later as a Labour peer, he remained a liberal in his social radicalism and his approach towards foreign policy. His manner was restrained and dignified, and colleagues recalled that they had never heard him raise his voice. He wore a beard to cover the scar on his face which was a lasting reminder of the assassination attempt in Bulgaria. He died in London on 12 September 1948, and was buried in the family graveyard at Upshire in Essex. C. V. J. Griffiths

Sources M. Anderson, *Noel Buxton: a life* (1952) • M. 'Espinasse and B. Sadler, 'Buxton, Noel Edward', *DLB*, vol. 5 • *Report of the 48th Annual Conference of the Labour Party* (1949) [report of death] • *The Times* (14 Sept 1948) • *The Labour who's who* (1924) • *The Labour who's who* (1927) • McGill University, Montreal, McLennan Library, Noel-Buxton papers • N. Buxton, *Travels and reflections* (1929) • PRO, MacDonald papers • M. Beard, *The Noel Buxton Trust, 1919–1989* (1989) • R. MacDonald, *At home and abroad* (1936) • *CGPLA Eng. & Wales* (1948)

Archives Duke U., Perkins L., corresp. and papers • McGill University, Montreal, McLennan Library, corresp., memoranda, and notes • NRA, papers | BL, corresp. with Lord Cecil, Add. MS 51140 • Bodl. RH, corresp. with R. Hinden • Bodl. RH, corresp. with Lord Lugard • HLRO, letters to David Lloyd George • King's Lond., Liddell Hart C., corresp. with Sir B. H. Liddell Hart • PRO, corresp. with Ramsay MacDonald, 30/69/1/189 • PRO NIre., corresp. with Edward Carson

Likenesses G. C. Beresford, photograph, 1906, NPG • W. Stoneman, photograph, 1924, NPG • photograph, repro. in Anderson, *Noel Buxton*

Wealth at death £232,848 1s. 3d.: probate, 23 Dec 1948, *CGPLA Eng. & Wales*

Buxton, Patrick Alfred (1892–1955), medical entomologist, was born on 24 March 1892 at 5 Hyde Park Street, Paddington, London, the eldest of the three children of Alfred Fowell Buxton, banker and chairman (1916–17) of the London county council, and his wife, Violet, daughter of the Very Revd Thomas William Jex-*Blake, headmaster of Cheltenham and Rugby schools and dean of Wells, and brother of Sophia Jex-Blake (1840–1912), physician and campaigner for women's rights. Buxton's mother was of Norfolk descent, and his Quaker predecessors were prominent in business, philanthropy, and social reform, and included his great-grandfather, Sir Thomas Fowell Buxton, first baronet (1786–1845), and Sydney Charles, first Earl Buxton (1853–1954). When he was eight, Buxton's family moved to Chigwell, Essex. He was educated at home until he was ten, then spent three years at a preparatory school before attending Rugby School (1905–11).

Buxton entered Trinity College, Cambridge, in 1911, and that year published his first paper (with his brother, Denis) in the *Entomologist's Record and Journal of Variation*. The following year he was elected a fellow of the Royal Entomological Society of London. He graduated from

Cambridge with first-class honours in both parts of the natural sciences tripos (1914/15), and in 1916 was elected to a Trinity College fellowship on a piece of undergraduate research completed in difficult wartime conditions. Having embarked on the study of medicine in November 1913, and served in the field ambulance in the autumn of 1914, Buxton qualified in medicine (MRCS, LRCP) from St George's Hospital in 1917. Taking up a commission in the Royal Army Medical Corps, he was posted to Mesopotamia and north-west Persia, where he devoted as much time as possible to natural history. This was the beginning of a nine-year, semi-peripatetic existence for Buxton and his consanguineous wife, Muryell Gladys, fourth daughter of William Talbot Rice, vicar of Swansea, whom he had married on 16 January 1917.

After returning to England, Buxton spent 1920–21 working under G. H. F. Nuttall at Cambridge and taking a course in tropical medicine in London. In March 1921 he accepted the position of entomologist to the medical department in Palestine, and undertook research on malaria, and on desert and semi-desert faunas. His experiences in north-west Persia and Palestine during and after the First World War led to the publication of what he called that 'vigorous young man's book', *Animal Life in Deserts* (1923). This attractive work became a classic; it was continuously in demand for the next half-century and was reprinted in 1955. Under the auspices of the London School of Tropical Medicine, Buxton led a two-year expedition, from late 1923, to Samoa, the New Hebrides, and Ellice and Tokelau islands to study filariasis. He and his colleague G. H. E. Hopkins made exhaustive collections of the insects of the island, which formed the basis of the *Insect Fauna of Samoa* (9 pts, 1927–35). Their two-volume *Researches in Polynesia and Melanesia* (1927–8), however, represented the official record of the expedition. Encompassing geography, meteorology, and ethnology, Buxton's broad interest in natural history also extended to languages. He mastered Arabic, and endeavoured to learn the 'pidgin' of the south seas while in Samoa.

On his return to London in January 1926 Buxton was appointed head of the department of entomology in the new London School of Hygiene and Tropical Medicine, and in 1933 he became professor in the University of London, where he remained until his death. One of the most widely travelled biologists of his time, he briefly returned to Palestine in 1931, and made a seven-month expedition to northern Nigeria in 1933. At the London School of Hygiene and Tropical Medicine he gave a new direction to his subject by insisting on the necessity for basing applied entomology on a scientific understanding of the physiology of insects. To this end, he published a letter in *Nature* in 1926 that declared that 'real progress will not be made in applied entomology … until we devote time and labour to the study of the fundamentals of insect physiology' (*Nature*, 117, 1926, 624). His appointment of V. B. Wigglesworth (1899–1994) as his assistant in the same year, and subsequent appointments, helped to consolidate this approach. Through his own research he made an impact on the study of mosquitoes and filariasis in the south Pacific, of plague fleas in Palestine, of the tsetse fly in Nigeria, and of the human louse in many parts of the world. More specifically, from 1926 to 1939, Buxton focused on the relations of insects to climate. He identified the importance of the immediate habitat, or 'microclimate', for the understanding and control of insects. By his own researches in this field, and by his examples and the appointments and opportunities which he secured for others, he did much to spread his physiology-based programme for applied entomology.

On the outbreak of war in 1939 Buxton concentrated all his energies on the improvement of insect control in the armed forces and in civilian life under wartime conditions. He established close relations with the medical departments of the War Office, Admiralty, and Air Ministry, and organized series of lectures to nurses and shelter marshals. He convinced Sir Edward Mellanby, secretary of the Medical Research Council, to create an entomological subcommittee of its military personnel research committee, with himself as chairman. Throughout the war, he travelled to the USA, Egypt, and west Africa to investigate and to promote insect eradication measures. Anticipating a repetition of large-scale trench warfare, he turned his attention to the concomitant problem of the louse. His immediate goal was to find a 'lasting' insecticide with which to impregnate clothing. This research resulted in the publication of *The Louse* (1939; 2nd edn, 1947), and prepared the way for the early exploitation of the new insecticide, DDT.

Buxton's career reached its zenith during the war years and the next decade. He was elected to the Athenaeum in 1942 and elected FRS the following year; he was twice president of the Royal Entomological Society of London (1942–3 and 1953–5); and he was awarded the Mary Kingsley medal of the Liverpool School of Tropical Medicine in 1949, and the gold medal of the Linnean Society in 1953. He was appointed CMG in 1947. He also served on the councils of the Royal Society, the Royal Society of Tropical Medicine and Hygiene, the Royal Entomological Society, and the Zoological Society. In conjunction with his work with the colonial medical research committee, Buxton made two exhaustive tours in east Africa in 1945–6, furthering his study of the tsetse fly and trypanosomiasis, and contributing to his *magnum opus*, *The Natural History of Tsetse Flies* (1955). From 1946 to 1949 he served as a member of the Medical Research Council.

Affectionately known as Buggy, Buxton had a strong and distinctive personality. Remembered as 'upright but humane', and prone to a 'slightly explosive temper' (Busvine, *Warmed Both Hands*, 93), he elicited respect and fear from contemporaries: 'Completely honest, considerate, and helpful to others, and with a quick wit and a lively sense of humour, he yet had an ironic and somewhat sarcastic manner which could strongly antagonize those who did not see beyond it' (Wigglesworth). He was intensely interested in all sides of natural history, and he was an enthusiastic and exotic gardener: his buttonhole was often adorned with a rare leaf or flower. All this was combined with a dislike of music, of poetry, and of philosophy, and a curious lack of interest in scientific generalizations. He had a fine command of English and wrote in a lucid unaffected style, and he was equally effective as a speaker, with a vivid descriptive power and a way of presenting even familiar matters in a new light.

After the death of Andrew, one of his two sons and four daughters, in 1952, Buxton seemed weakened. Three years later, he succumbed to bronchopneumonia and cancer of the prostate, and died on 13 December 1955, at his home, Grit Howe, South Park, Gerrards Cross, Buckinghamshire. His funeral was held three days later at St James's, Gerrards Cross. His wife survived him.

V. B. Wigglesworth, *rev.* J. F. M. Clark

Sources personal knowledge (1971) • private information (1971) • V. B. Wigglesworth, *Memoirs FRS*, 2 (1956), 69–84 • *Parasitology*, 47 (1956), 1–15 • *The Times* (15 Dec 1955), 14 • P. Manson-Bahr, *The Times* (24 Dec 1955), 9 • *The Times* (17 Dec 1955), 8 • *WWW, 1951–60* • S. A. Neave, *The centenary history of the Entomological Society of London, 1833–1933* (1933) • J. R. Busvine, *I warmed both hands* (1986) • U. Glas., Archives and Business Records Centre, Edward Hindle collection • P. A. Buxton, 'Applied entomology', *Nature*, 117 (1926), 623–4 • J. R. Busvine, *Disease transmission by insects: its discovery and 90 years of effort to prevent it* (1993) • b. cert. • m. cert. • d. cert. • *CGPLA Eng. & Wales* (1956) • *The Times* (17 Dec 1955), 8

Archives NHM, papers | Bodl. Oxf., corresp. with G. E. Blackman • Royal Entomological Society of London, letters to C. J. Wainwright • U. Glas. L., corresp. with Edward Hindle

Likenesses W. Stoneman, photograph, 1955 • J. R. Busvine, pen-and-ink sketch (after photograph), repro. in Busvine, *I warmed both hands*, 94 • photograph, repro. in Wigglesworth, *Memoirs FRS*, facing p. 69

Wealth at death £23,505 9s. 10d.: probate, 27 Feb 1956, *CGPLA Eng. & Wales*

Buxton [*married name* Johnston], **Priscilla** (1808–1852), slavery abolitionist, was born on 25 February 1808 at Earlham Hall, near Norwich, the eldest of the eight children of Sir Thomas Fowell *Buxton, first baronet (1786–1845), brewer, MP, and leading anti-slavery campaigner, and Hannah (1783–1872), the daughter of John Gurney of Earlham Hall and his wife, Catherine Bell (*d.* 1792). She had seven younger siblings—including the politician Charles *Buxton (1822–1871)—of whom four died in infancy or childhood. Her father was from an Anglican background, while her mother was from a very prominent Quaker family, whose members included anti-slavery campaigner John Joseph Gurney (1788–1847) and prison reformer Elizabeth Fry (1780–1845). Priscilla Buxton lived with her family at their successive homes in London (1808–15), in Hampstead (1815–20), at Cromer Hall, near Cromer, Norfolk (1820–28), and then at Northrepps Hall, near Cromer (1828–34).

Priscilla Buxton's historical importance lies in her activities as an anti-slavery campaigner. Until her marriage in 1834, she acted as her father's main confidante and assistant during the period when he was leader of the parliamentary campaign for the abolition of British colonial slavery. She recommenced her help soon after her marriage, acting as her father's assistant during his leadership of the African Civilisation Society (1839–43), through which he sought to combat the continuation of the Atlantic slave trade by promoting 'legitimate' commerce with west Africa. She compiled information and helped him draft speeches and pamphlets, persuading him to follow her suggestions for substantial revisions to the draft of *The Remedy* (1840), his book promoting the activities of the society. She also co-operated with her father in supporting educational work by missionaries in South Africa, the West Indies, and Mauritius. Fellow anti-slavery campaigner Sir George Stephen later recalled that she was:

> like a guardian angel to him. She acted as his secretary, his librarian, his comforter, and often as his adviser and guide; of her I witnessed, with surprise and admiration, the promptitude of perception with which she comprehended a perplexity, and suggested a solution. (Stephen, 197)

Priscilla Buxton was also an important activist in her own right, promoting national female anti-slavery initiatives. In 1832 she became co-secretary of the London Female Anti-Slavery Society and in 1833 she was involved in organizing the national ladies' anti-slavery petition to parliament: her name, together with that of Amelia Opie (1769–1853), headed the list of 187,000 signatories. The petition was presented to both houses: she described how it needed two men to carry each of the rolls of signatures, which 'were like two great feather beds' and which were presented 'among loud laughing and cheers' (P. Buxton to S. M. Buxton, 16 May 1833, Oxford, Rhodes House, Buxton MSS). It was the largest anti-slavery petition ever presented to parliament and its presentation was carefully timed to coincide with the debate which was to mark the successful culmination of the parliamentary anti-slavery campaign.

Priscilla Buxton married Andrew Johnston (1798–1862) on 1 August 1834, the date when the act emancipating slaves in the British colonies came into force. Johnston, MP for St Andrews, was a close parliamentary ally of Thomas Fowell Buxton, supporting his anti-slavery campaigns until both were defeated in the 1837 general election. Thereafter the Johnstons spent some time at Renny Hill in Fife, before moving south to Halesworth in Suffolk, when Andrew Johnston became a banker in the Gurney family bank in the county. The couple had at least two children. She died on 18 June 1852.

Clare Midgley

Sources P. M. Pugh, introduction, *Calendar of the papers of Sir Thomas Fowell Buxton, 1786–1845* (1980) • G. Stephen, *Anti-slavery recollections: in a series of letters, addressed to Mrs Beecher Stowe* (1854), 197 • C. Buxton, *Memoirs of Sir Thomas Fowell Buxton, baronet, with selections from his correspondence* (1848) • R. H. Mottram, *Buxton the liberator* (1946) • *The letters of William Lloyd Garrison*, ed. W. M. Merrill and L. Ruchames, 1 (1971), 233 • Burke, *Peerage* (1889)

Archives Bodl. RH, Sir Thomas Fowell Buxton MSS

Buxton, Richard (1786–1865), botanist and shoemaker, was born on 15 January 1786 at Sedgley Hall Farm, Prestwich, Lancashire, the second son of the seven children of John Buxton and his wife, Ann (*née* Houghton). His parents, originally from Derbyshire, hit hard times before he turned two, forcing his father to become a labourer in Ancoats, Manchester. After three months at a dame-school and two years of irregular attendance at Sunday school, poverty and sickliness brought the young Buxton's education to a standstill. Barely literate, he wandered the fields near his home, attracted by wild flowers, before being apprenticed to a children's shoemaker in 1798. At sixteen, struck by his ignorance, he taught himself to read. As a journeyman his interest in botany was stimulated by his master, with whom he collected herbs for 'diet drinks'. Buxton, puzzled by unfamiliar plants, consulted Culpeper's *Herbal* then, in 1808, William Meyrick's *New Family Herbal* (1789) from which he learned the Linnaean classification. He later purchased books by William Withering and James Edward Smith and continued to study plants during solitary walks.

From 1821 full-time employment forced Buxton to suspend his botanical pursuits until the depression of 1826. In this year, while botanizing on Kersal Moor, he met John Horsefield, who drew him into the social network of working-men botanists, although Buxton did not attend their pub meetings until 1833.

In 1839 Buxton was invited to join the Manchester Mechanics' Institution natural history class, where, under the editorship of John Bland Wood, together with Leo Hartley Grindon, George Crozier, and James Crowther, he largely compiled the *Flora Mancuniensis* (1840). In 1849, helped by Edward William Binney, he published *A botanical guide to the flowering plants, ferns, mosses, and algae, found indigenous within sixteen miles of Manchester.*

As Buxton's trade declined he had attempted to eke out a meagre existence from delivering newspapers and acting as botanical collector, but from the 1840s his subsistence depended upon charitable donations and sales of his *Guide*. However, his desperate poverty was alleviated by only £10 from the second edition of his *Guide* (1859), rather than the £50 Binney anticipated, because of direct competition from Grindon's *Manchester Flora* (1859). This rivalry placed Buxton at the centre of a violent confrontation between Grindon and Binney. Continuing animosity resulted in Binney's *A Few Remarks Respecting Mr. R. Buxton … and the Subscription Made for him* (1863), a pamphlet defending payments to Buxton from a fund administered by Binney since 1844 for 'the relief and encouragement of scientific men in humble life'. In *Country Rambles* (1882, 173) Grindon even claimed, falsely, that Buxton's *Guide* was largely the work of the shoemaker Thomas Townley.

Buxton was an acknowledged expert on mosses, making collections first with George Crozier and then with John Nowell. With the latter he produced sets of specimens of 'British Mosses, published by Richard Buxton and John Nowell, Lancashire Botanists'. Although widely admired for his botanical skills (William Jackson Hooker was eager to acquire him as a herbarium assistant at Kew), Buxton became better known for his autobiography included in the *Guide*, in which he acknowledged many working-men botanists as well as outlining his own botanical development.

Buxton never married and for much of his life lodged with an older married sister in Ancoats. He died on 2 January 1865 at Limekiln Lane, Ardwick, and was buried at St Mary's, Prestwich, on 5 January. His gaunt appearance was captured on a daguerreotype in 1851 by J. B. Dancer. Invariably described as gentle, mild, and retiring, he combined his interest in botany with a love of poetry and knew John Critchley Prince and Samuel Bamford. He claimed in the *Guide* (Buxton, p. xi) that he was induced to write his autobiography to show 'that the poor can enjoy the pleasures of studying science as well as the rich'.

ANNE SECORD

Sources R. Buxton, *A botanical guide to the flowering plants, ferns, mosses, and algae, found indigenous within sixteen miles of Manchester*, 2nd edn (1859) • E. W. Binney, *A few remarks respecting Mr. R. Buxton, the author of 'The Manchester Botanical Guide'* (1863) • W. Wilson to W. J. Hooker, 23 May 1849, RBG Kew, directors' correspondence, vol. 28, letter 368 • T. Rogers to W. E. A. Axon, 24 May 1882, Man. CL, Axon MS fol. 920.04272 A1 • 'Death of Mr Richard Buxton, the botanist', *Manchester Guardian* (5 Jan 1865) • H. Garnett, 'Richard Buxton: an old-time Manchester botanist', *North Western Naturalist*, 6 (1931), 18–21 • J. B. Wood and others, *Flora Mancuniensis* (1840) • J. Cash, *Where there's a will there's a way! or, Science in the cottage* (1873), 94–107 • J. S. Rowse, 'With nature lovers', *Heywood Advertiser* (26 April 1918) • 'Autobiography of a Lancashire botanist, in humble life', *Manchester Guardian* (7 April 1849) • 'Have working men time to improve? Richard Buxton', *The Economist*, 7 (14 May 1849), 404–5 • L. H. Grindon, *Country rambles, and Manchester walks and wild flowers* (1882), 173

Archives Man. CL, botanical specimens • Manchester Museum, herbarium, botanical specimens • U. Oxf., herbarium, botanical specimens

Likenesses J. B. Dancer, daguerreotype, 1851, repro. in Garnett, 'Richard Buxton', pl. 4 • J. B. Dancer, daguerreotype, 1851, repro. in J. Percy, 'Scientists in humble life: the artisan naturalists of South Lancashire', *Manchester Region History Review*, 5 (1991), 3

Wealth at death destitute

Buxton, Sydney Charles, Earl Buxton (1853–1934), politician, was born in London on 25 October 1853, the younger son (the three subsequent children of the marriage were daughters) of the liberal politician Charles *Buxton (1822–1871) and his wife, Emily Mary (*d.* 1871), eldest daughter of the physician Sir Henry *Holland. He was grandson of Sir Thomas Fowell *Buxton, 'liberator of the slaves'. The family background was one of well-to-do Quaker stock in East Anglia, brewers and bankers. Buxton attended Clifton College (1868–70) and went on to Trinity College, Cambridge (1872), but very soon had to abandon his studies there on account of osteomyelitis of a leg. He then travelled for his health in South America (1873) and Egypt (1875). By 1876 he was strong enough to seek and secure election to the London school board, on which he served until 1882. He also worked from 1882 to 1884 very energetically as an honorary secretary to the fund set up by J. H. Tuke to assist emigration from western Ireland. He was already a fluent writer and publicist, mainly on political and fiscal matters, publishing in 1880 a *Handbook to Political Questions of the Day.* Written as an exercise in self-education, this influential manual eventually passed through eleven editions. In 1888 it was followed by *Finance and Politics: an Historical Study, 1783–1885* (2 vols.), still a work of great value.

Buxton stood unsuccessfully for parliament as a Liberal at Boston (1880), but was elected for Peterborough in 1883. Losing that seat in 1885, he was eventually elected in 1886 for Poplar, which remained his constituency until 1914.

Sydney Charles Buxton, Earl Buxton (1853–1934), by William Strang, 1914

Poplar brought him successful involvement in the great dockers' strike of 1889 as an arbitrator sympathetic to the dockers' case, and he won lasting popularity with his (mainly working-class) constituents in the Isle of Dogs. He maintained a very strong interest in industrial conditions, arising from his involvement in east London, and the question of London's government remained another major preoccupation, together with education. He was a very active member of the royal commission on elementary education, 1886–8. In the Commons he was a member of an informal group of progressive radicals which included Asquith, Grey, and Haldane. When the Liberals came to power in 1892 he was appointed under-secretary at the Colonial Office, a post he held until 1895. The secretary of state, Lord Ripon, being in the Lords, Buxton had to answer on colonial matters in the Commons, besides holding special responsibility for southern Africa, a crucial area in view of the situation in the Transvaal and the problems of relations with Rhodes's South Africa Company. In 1894 he played a role as adviser to Sir William Harcourt in the framing of the innovative Death Duties Bill. Out of office from 1895 to 1905, he remained a frequent speaker in the Commons, was a member of the commission of inquiry into the Jameson raid, followed a moderately 'imperialist' line concerning the Second South African War, and took account of East End opinion in defying Liberal orthodoxy by supporting—contrary to most of his party—the anti-immigration Aliens Bill of 1905.

In December 1905 Buxton became postmaster-general, with a seat in the cabinet. His principal achievements in this office included the purchase for £15,000 of coastal wireless stations from Lloyd's and the Marconi Company (1909), penny postage to the USA, and reduced charges for the postage of literature for blind people. He also won notable success in securing better terms of employment in the Post Office and better relations with the staff (he was responsible for official recognition of the Postal Servants' Union). In February 1910 he was appointed to succeed Winston Churchill as president of the Board of Trade. Here he was responsible for much legislation, notably the important unemployment section (introducing compulsory contributory insurance against unemployment in certain trades) of the National Insurance Act 1911, the Copyright Act (1911), the Miners' Minimum Wage Act (1911–12), the Act Extending Trades Boards to Additional Trades (1913) and the Bankruptcy Act (1913). After the loss of the *Titanic* in 1912 he became much involved in regulations concerned with safety at sea.

Early in 1914 he was named governor-general of the Union of South Africa; he resigned his office and left the cabinet and the Commons. He was appointed GCMG and in May raised to the peerage as Viscount Buxton of Newtimber, in Sussex. He reached South Africa on 8 September and opened parliament the next day. The country was deeply divided, the wounds of the Second South African War of 1899–1902 being by no means healed, and for the first three months of his governor-generalship a party of Boers was in revolt against the government which had declared war on Germany. Buxton's responsibilities were wide, since he was also high commissioner over the protectorates of Basutoland, Bechuanaland, and Swaziland and had a certain (if not clearly delineated) authority in Rhodesia. The South African prime minister was Louis Botha whom he had met in England (1907 and 1911) and the two men greatly liked and esteemed each other. This close friendship was an important factor in the success of Buxton's governor-generalship. He spent much time on the move (frequently by train), getting to know the country and its peoples, making a point of visiting the 'nationalist' Boer strongholds, and winning general popularity, as did Lady Buxton. In 1919 he toured Basutoland and Bechuanaland. His sensitivity to African aspirations made him doubtful about South African plans to have Swaziland transferred to the Union, and Smuts's Native Affairs Bill (1920) tried to meet these doubts by providing for a native affairs commission. Botha died in office in 1919. Buxton's period of office was then prolonged; he finally laid it down in September 1920. On his return to England he was raised to an earldom and he became chancellor of the Order of St Michael and St George. Thereafter he did not play a very prominent role in politics, but in 1923–4 he was an active supporter of Lord Grey of Fallodon's leadership of the Liberals in the House of Lords.

Buxton was twice married: first, in 1882 to Constance Mary (*d.* 1892), the second daughter of John Lubbock, first Lord Avebury, with whom he had two sons and one daughter; both boys predeceased their father, the younger in childhood. In 1896 he married Mildred Anne (*d.* 1955), elder daughter of Hugh Colin Smith, governor of the Bank of England, with whom he had one son, who was killed in action in 1917, and two daughters, the elder of whom predeceased her father. The osteomyelitis from which Buxton had suffered since his schooldays gave him trouble throughout his life and in 1930 he had to suffer the amputation of a leg. He died at his home, Newtimber Place, near Hassocks, Sussex, on 15 October 1934, and was buried at Newtimber.

Buxton was an energetic humanitarian whose temperament accorded well with his family's motto 'Do it with thy might.' His voluminous writings also testify to his industriousness. He did not excel as a public speaker, but people were won over by his modesty and charm. Smuts wrote of his 'simplicity of character and approachableness'. Fishing and shooting were his favoured recreations and he wrote on them also (notably *Fishing and Shooting*, 1902). He shared with his close friend Grey a taste for observing birds. These open-air pursuits gave him refreshment and solace amid the tragedies of his family life.

DANIEL WALEY

Sources Newtimber Place, near Hassocks, Sussex, Sydney Buxton MSS • D. Waley, *A liberal life. Sydney, Earl Buxton, 1853–1934: statesman, governor-general of South Africa* (1999) • M. Cropper and W. Barnes, *Mildred Buxton: a memoir based upon her letters* [1966] • Earl Buxton [S. Buxton], *General Botha* (1924) • H. S. Furniss, *Charles Sydney Buxton: a memoir* (1914) • private information (2004) • *The Times* (16–18 Oct 1934) • H. C. G. Matthew, *The liberal imperialists: the ideas and politics of a post-Gladstonian élite* (1973)

Archives BL

Likenesses W. Strang, etching, 1914, NPG [*see illus.*] • F. H. S., portrait, board of trade office, Newtimber, South Africa • E. Roworth, portrait, House of Assembly, Cape Town, South Africa • Spy [L. Ward], cartoon, repro. in *VF* (2 Jan 1907) • A. Van Wouw, statuette, Newtimber, South Africa

Wealth at death £158,893 10s. 3d.: resworn probate, 17 Jan 1935, *CGPLA Eng. & Wales*

Buxton, Sir Thomas Fowell, first baronet (1786–1845), politician and philanthropist, born on 1 April 1786, was the eldest son of Thomas Fowell Buxton, of Earl's Colne, Essex, and his wife, Anna, daughter of Osgood Hanbury, of Holfield Grange, in the same county. His mother, who was a member of the Society of Friends, was a woman of intelligence and energy. His father, an East Anglian squire, died when he was six years old. At an early age Buxton was sent to a school at Kingston upon Thames, where he was ill treated. His health suffered, and he was moved to the school at Greenwich run by Dr Charles Burney. After leaving school at the age of fifteen, he spent considerable time with the Gurneys, an influential Quaker family, at Earlham Hall, Norwich. He was expected to inherit Irish property (which did not materialize) and entered Trinity College, Dublin, in October 1803 after several months of private tuition in Ireland. He was awarded distinctions in all but one of his examinations at Dublin and received the university gold medal.

Before he had turned twenty-one Buxton was invited to stand as a parliamentary candidate for Trinity College, but declined on account of his intention to enter a business career and his impending marriage to Hannah (*d.* 1872),

Sir Thomas Fowell Buxton, first baronet (1786–1845), by Benjamin Robert Haydon, 1840

fifth daughter of John Gurney of Earlham Hall. Their marriage took place on 13 May 1807, after his return to England. Hannah and her Quaker family (to which Buxton was distantly related) had an important influence on his spiritual life and political career. Elizabeth Fry, the prison reformer, was his sister-in-law, and Joseph John Gurney, the anti-slavery advocate, his brother-in-law. Anna Gurney, Hannah's cousin, was later to help Buxton with his researches into slavery.

In 1808 Buxton joined the brewers Truman, Hanbury & Co. of Spitalfields, London, where his maternal uncle was a partner. His mother had stressed the importance of philanthropy and, encouraged by William Allen, he became involved in various charitable activities in Spitalfields, especially those connected with education, the Bible Society, and the relief of distressed weavers. He defended the Bible Society in 1812 against the attacks of Herbert Marsh, bishop of Peterborough. In 1816, when hunger was widespread in Spitalfields, Buxton delivered a forcible speech, based on his own investigations of conditions, at a meeting at the Mansion House which raised £43,369. An extensive and well-organized system of relief was subsequently set up. Influenced by Elizabeth Fry and his brother-in-law Samuel Hoare, he made several visits to Newgate Prison, and published his findings as *An inquiry whether crime and misery are produced or prevented by our present system of prison discipline* (1818). The book went through five editions in a year, was praised by Sir James Mackintosh in the House of

Commons, and was translated into French and widely circulated in Europe. Its reception in India indirectly led to an inquiry into the scandalous management of Madras gaols. In England its publication led to the formation of the Society for the Reformation of Prison Discipline, of which Buxton was a committee member.

At the general election of 1818 Buxton was elected MP for Weymouth, and he subsequently represented the borough until 1837. During his first session in parliament he took a particular interest in the operation of the criminal law, and seconded Sir James Mackintosh's motion (2 March 1819) for a select committee. He was a member both of this committee and of another on prisons that resulted in legislation to amend the prison laws. In 1820 he supported Mackintosh's motion to abolish the death penalty for forgery. In that year, following the deaths of his eldest son and three daughters, he moved with his wife and four remaining children from Hampstead to Cromer Hall, Norfolk.

Buxton continued his interest in legal and prison reform, and added suttee (the Indian practice of burning widows) to his humanitarian concerns. But it was in the campaign against slavery that he contributed most in his political career. He was an active member of the African Institution, founded in 1807. In May 1821 William Wilberforce, who had long led the anti-slavery group in the House of Commons, formally asked Buxton to become his partner, and then successor, in the crusade against slavery. After some thought Buxton agreed. In 1823 the Anti-Slavery Society was established by abolitionists including Wilberforce, Zachary Macaulay, Thomas Clarkson, Stephen Lushington, Buxton, and others. Buxton was appointed a vice-president of the society, whose publication was the *Anti-Slavery Reporter*. In May 1823 Buxton began the parliamentary campaign against colonial slavery by introducing a motion in the House of Commons for the gradual abolition of slavery. It was carried with the addition of some words proposed by Canning to protect planters' interests. The government issued a circular to colonial authorities, recommending ameliorative reforms, but the proposals needed the support of colonial legislatures, which was not forthcoming. An able researcher, Buxton set about collecting information about slavery and compiling demographic statistics. Public meetings were held throughout the country in denunciation of slavery and petitions were sent to parliament. On 15 April 1831, after the government had declined to take up the issue, Buxton introduced his resolution for the abolition of slavery, fortified with statistics showing a decline in the number of slaves in the West Indies from 800,000 to 700,000 between 1807 and 1830. His initiative was unsuccessful but Buxton continued to push for abolition, especially after the Jamaican slave rebellion of 1831. After the reform of parliament in 1832 the whig government carried a measure to end slavery in the colonies, though it included an apprenticeship period for freed slaves and compensation to the planters. The act received the royal assent on 23 August 1833. In spite of some forebodings, the colonial legislatures carried the act into effect, and emancipation day, 1 August 1834, passed peacefully.

Buxton subsequently concerned himself with the treatment of the aboriginal peoples in South Africa, the foreign slave trade, and the apprenticeship of ex-slaves in the West Indies under the terms of the 1833 act. On 22 March 1836 he successfully moved for a committee of the House of Commons to inquire into the apprenticeship system; his own investigations, gathering a mass of statistical data, showed that the ex-slaves had behaved well under trying circumstances. Apprenticeship was terminated on 1 August 1838, earlier than originally intended. In 1837 he founded the Aborigines' Protection Society, having chaired a select committee on Aborigines in 1835.

Buxton lost his seat at Weymouth in the general election of 1837, but declined numerous offers to stand for parliament again. He turned his attention to the suppression of the slave trade, a cause in which his daughter Priscilla *Buxton assisted him, and published *The African Slave Trade* (1839) and *The Remedy* (1840), later published as one volume. His recommendations included a more efficient naval force off the coast of Africa, treaties with native chiefs, an expedition up the River Niger, and the introduction of commercial agriculture to the Niger region. The idea was to eradicate the African slave trade by substituting Christianity, civilization, and commerce. In 1839 he established the Society for the Extinction of the Slave Trade and the Civilisation of Africa. He persuaded the government to send a costly expedition to explore the Niger and if possible to establish commercial relations with the peoples on its banks.

Later in 1839 Buxton's health gave way and with his wife he toured Italy, where he took time to investigate prison and crime, exposed the deeds of a notorious band headed by Gasparoni, and undertook an investigation of gaols in Rome. On his return to England in 1840, Buxton took part in the planning of the Niger expedition, a venture which had the support of Prince Albert. Three iron steamers, crewmen, scientific specialists, and missionaries of the Church Missionary Society left England in 1841. In Africa the expedition encountered difficulties, and 39 of the 145 Europeans died of fever. Mortified by the failure of his plans, Buxton suffered a relapse of health. In January 1843 the Society for the Extinction of the Slave Trade and the Civilisation of Africa was dissolved, and at its closing meeting Buxton defended himself against charges of imprudence. In the long run the ill-fated Niger expedition might have popularized the idea of substituting legitimate commerce for the slave trade, and opened the way for British commerce in west Africa. But quinine and rapid-fire weapons proved to be more important.

Buxton's evangelical and humanitarian activities in England included his work as treasurer of the London city mission, founded in 1835, and his chairmanship of the Royal Society for the Prevention of Cruelty to Animals, of which he was a benefactor. In his last years Buxton concentrated on the cultivation of his estates, and established model farms at Runton and Trimingham, near Cromer. An essay on his estate management gained the gold medal of the Royal Agricultural Society in 1845. Buxton died at his country seat, Northrepps Hall, Norfolk, on 19 February 1845, and was buried in the ruined chancel of Overstrand church. A deeply religious man, he was a member of the Church of England, though influenced by the Quaker religion of his wife and her family. He was created a baronet on 30 July 1840. Prince Albert headed a movement for a public tribute to his memory, and donations came from the West Indies and from Africa. A statue by Frederick Thrupp was commissioned and placed near the monument to Wilberforce, in the north transept of Westminster Abbey. Buxton's eldest son, Edward North Buxton, succeeded as second baronet. His third son was the politician Charles *Buxton (1822–1871).

Olwyn Mary Blouet

Sources C. Buxton, *Memoirs of Sir Thomas Fowell Buxton, baronet, with selections from his correspondence* (1848) • P. M. Pugh, *Calendar of the papers of Sir Thomas Fowell Buxton, 1786–1845* (1980) • J. Gallagher, 'Fowell Buxton and the new African policy, 1838–1842', *Cambridge Historical Journal*, 10 (1950–52), 36–58 • H. Temperley, *White dreams, black Africa: the antislavery expedition to the River Niger, 1841–1842* (1991) • A. J. C. Hare, *The Gurneys of Earlham*, 2 vols. (1895) • R. H. Mottram, *Buxton the liberator* (1946) • *The Times* (22 Feb 1845), 6 • *GM*, 2nd ser., 23 (1845), 543–6 • HoP, *Commons, 1790–1820*, 3.352–3 • B. Harrison, *Peaceable kingdom* (1982) • I. Bradley, *The call to seriousness* (1976)

Archives Bodl. RH, MSS Brit. Emp. 5.444 | Bodl. RH, letters from T. Clarkson to T. F. Buxton, 1825–8, MSS Brit. Emp. 5.495 • Bodl. RH, Wilberforce MSS • Norfolk RO, copy letters from Colonial Registry Office to Buxton re slavery, 1831–46, MS 11358 • U. Durham, Grey MSS • UCL, Brougham MSS • W. Sussex RO, Gordon Lennox MSS

Likenesses J. Thomson, stipple, 1821 (after drawing by A. Wivell), BM, NPG • G. Hayter, group portrait, oils, 1833–43 (*The House of Commons, 1833*), NPG • H. P. Briggs, stipple, pubd 1835 (after W. Holl), BM, NPG • W. Holl, stipple and line print, pubd 1835 (after H. P. Briggs), NPG • B. R. Haydon, pencil study, 1840, NPG [*see illus.*] • B. R. Haydon, group portrait, oils, 1841 (*The Anti-slavery Society Convention, 1840*), NPG • F. Thrupp, statue, 1846, Westminster Abbey, London • J. Bell, bust, 1848, Freetown Cathedral, Sierra Leone • H. J. Robinson, stipple, 1848 (after painting by G. Richmond), NPG • J. Brain, line print (after G. Hayter), BM, NPG; repro. in J. Saunders, *Political reformers* (1840)

Wealth at death under £250,000: *GM*, 546

Buxton [*née* Noel], **Lady Victoria** (**1839–1916**), philanthropist, was born in her parents' London home in Harley Street on 1 July 1839, the younger child and only daughter of Sir Charles Noel Noel (1781–1866) (later, in 1841, the first earl of Gainsborough) and his fourth wife, Lady Frances Jocelyn (1814–1885), daughter of Robert, earl of Roden. She was named for Queen Victoria, who also acted as one of her godmothers, Lady Frances serving as a lady-in-waiting to the queen. (Subsequently, Lady Victoria served as a bridesmaid when Victoria, the princess royal, married Prince Friedrich Wilhelm of Prussia, the future German emperor Friedrich III, on 25 January 1858.) Her youth was spent at the Noel ancestral home of Exton Park, near Oakham, and at Barham Court, near Maidstone, until it was sold in 1845. She also travelled yearly with her parents on lengthy journeys around the continent.

Lady Victoria's formal education was provided by a governess, but the strongest influence was that of her mother. Her parents' fervent evangelical faith, with its emphasis on good works, became a major influence in her life. As a young woman Lady Victoria visited the sick, ministered to the poor, and taught at Sunday school.

On 12 June 1862 Lady Victoria married Sir (Thomas) Fowell *Buxton, third baronet (1837–1915), a fellow evangelical, whose family name was associated with the British anti-slavery movement. The Buxtons had two country residences, Warlies, near Waltham Abbey, and Colne House, Cromer, as well as a residence in London. The couple had thirteen children, of whom five sons and five daughters survived, including Noel Edward Noel-*Buxton, first Baron Noel-Buxton (1869–1948), and Charles Roden *Buxton (1875–1942).

In 1865 Buxton became the Liberal MP for King's Lynn, but he was defeated when he again contested the seat in 1868. Thereafter he never held a seat in the Commons again, even though he stood for parliament unsuccessfully in 1874, 1876, 1879, and 1880. In the early contests, before she became unable to move among the voters, Lady Victoria helped canvass the electorate. In addition to his political service Buxton's greatest efforts, like those of his wife, were devoted to social services and to the support of various environmental causes and church missions. The Buxtons worked together for the Church Missionary Society and for the YWCA and YMCA.

From 1869 Lady Victoria suffered from 'spinal troubles' and 'osteo-arthritis' (Russell, 68), which often confined her to a waterbed or sofa. When walking she used crutches, and when travelling in a carriage she was obliged to lie down or kneel. Her infirmities, however, did not prevent her from entertaining at large dinner parties and from accompanying her husband to important social functions; despite her serious health problems she was noted for her youthful outlook and her cheerfulness.

An unusually devout woman, Lady Victoria devoted most of her efforts and attention, aside from her home and family responsibilities, to good works. She conducted mothers' meetings at Warlies and established a missionary working party and a branch of the Church of England Mothers' Union; she also served as diocesan president of the Mothers' Union for London. In addition she was president of the Time and Talents Association of young factory girls in Bermondsey. Keenly interested in foreign missions, she conducted mission study circles in her home. She also founded the Waltham Abbey branch of the YWCA.

In 1895 Sir Fowell was appointed governor-general of South Australia, and Lady Victoria accompanied him to the Antipodes. Once in Adelaide she enthusiastically entered the social life expected of the governor, which included a large number of garden parties, dinners, and balls. Within six months of their arrival the radical premier C. C. Kingston declared that the Buxtons were 'the most genial, sociable and common sense family who have ever inhabited the Adelaide vice-regal mansion' (Howell, 'Vice-regal life', 21). As in England, Lady Victoria's chief work in South Australia was philanthropic. She sponsored reading circles in Government House, was keenly interested in facilitating missionary work in Melanesia, New

Guinea, and among the Aborigines in Australia, and pioneered the creation of an association of working girls with the Lady Victoria Buxton Girls' Club. However, she was most closely associated with the Mothers' Union for South Australia, and served as its founding president. During her three years' tenure as president, thirty-nine branches of the Mothers' Union were established in South Australia. Finally, as the niece of Lady Kinnaird, one of the founders of the parent YWCA in Britain, Lady Victoria vigorously supported the work of the YWCA in Adelaide, and for a time served as vice-president of the organization. In Adelaide the Buxtons hosted the first convention in which the constitution of a united Australia was debated and developed. To facilitate the effort the Buxtons held a number of private dinner parties 'where various protagonists could sort out their differences' (ibid., 24).

While on leave in England in 1898 the Buxtons' eldest son developed a life-threatening illness and Lady Victoria's health deteriorated. Sir Fowell resigned his post and the Buxtons never returned to South Australia. But the relinquishment of government life did not mean retirement from an active life for Lady Victoria. In England the Buxtons built St Thomas's Church in Upshire in 1902, and Lady Victoria published the collected edition of the poems written by her brother, Roden Berkeley Noel. In the summer of 1912 the Buxtons celebrated their fiftieth wedding anniversary. Her eyesight nearly gone, Lady Victoria died at North Lodge, Cromer, on 9 August 1916, just ten months after the death of her husband; she was buried on 11 August by his side at Cromer. JOAN B. HUFFMAN

Sources G. W. E. Russell, *Lady Victoria Buxton* (1919) • P. A. Howell, 'Buxton, Sir Thomas Fowell', *AusDB*, vol. 7 • B. Dickey, *Not just tea and biscuits: the Mothers' Union in the diocese of Adelaide, 1895–1995* (1995) • M. Dunn, *The dauntless bunch: the story of the YWCA in Australia* (1991) • P. A. Howell, 'Varieties of vice-regal life', *Journal of the Historical Society of South Australia*, 3 (1977) • *The Times* (10 Aug 1916) • *The Times* (15 Aug 1916) • m. cert. • d. cert. • *CGPLA Eng. & Wales* (1916)

Archives Mary Sumner House, London, Mothers' Union MSS • priv. coll., family MSS • Stafford House, Adelaide, Australia, Mothers' Union (diocese of Adelaide) MSS • University of Melbourne, YWCA of Australia MSS

Likenesses F. W. Carter, drawing, repro. in Russell, *Lady Victoria Buxton*, frontispiece • F. X. Winterhalter, oils (as young woman), repro. in Russell, *Lady Victoria Buxton*

Wealth at death £16,118 14*s*. 5*d*.: probate, 19 Dec 1916, *CGPLA Eng. & Wales*

Buzzard, Sir (Edward) Farquhar, first baronet (1871–1945), physician, was born in Grosvenor Street, London, on 20 December 1871, the eldest of four sons (there were two daughters) of Thomas Buzzard (1831–1919), an eminent neurologist, and his wife, Isabel (*d*. 1901), daughter of Joseph Wass of Lea, Derbyshire. He was educated at Charterhouse School from 1885 and won a scholarship to Magdalen College, Oxford. He excelled in lawn tennis and football. He played for the university (1893–4) and for the Old Carthusian eleven, winners of the amateur cup (1894, 1897), the London senior cup (1895–7), and the London charity cup (1896). After obtaining a fourth class in natural science (physiology) in 1894, he completed his medical training at St Thomas's Hospital, London, where he won the Mead medal in 1898. In 1899 he married May (*d*. 1951), a musician, the daughter of Edward Bliss of Edgbaston, Birmingham. They had two sons and three daughters; the younger son and eldest daughter also became doctors.

Following in his father's footsteps Buzzard went to the National Hospital for Nervous Diseases at Queen Square, London, acting first as house physician to his father's close colleague, J. Hughlings Jackson; later he became assistant physician, a post he held from 1905 to 1922. In 1903 he became assistant physician to the Royal Free Hospital, London, and he was later full physician and lecturer in medical pathology. By 1910 he had made his reputation, having secured his fellowship of the Royal College of Physicians in 1906 and having delivered the Goulstonian lectures of 1907, 'Toxic and infectious diseases of the nervous system'; he had also succeeded to appointments at other London hospitals, including the Queen Alexandra Military Hospital, the Royal Hospital for Incurables, the Throat Hospital, Golden Square, and the Belgrave Hospital for Children. In 1910 he returned to St Thomas's Hospital as a visiting physician, and he remained there until 1928, when he became consulting physician. During the First World War he was consultant to the London command, rising to the rank of colonel, during which time he helped to enlarge the understanding of 'shell shock'.

Although he made no important discoveries, Buzzard surpassed his father in extending knowledge of neurology. He produced many publications but these were mostly in the form of contributions to textbooks, the chief being *Pathology of the Nervous System*, written in 1921 with J. G. Greenfield. Because of the many calls upon his time, original work was abandoned, and he devoted fewer hours to hospital work than his colleagues desired; nevertheless, his clinical opinion was greatly valued, and he excelled by his knowledge and judgement. He was less successful as a teacher: 'Buzzard was usually silent, and his ward teaching was reduced to the essentials of diagnosis' (Munk, *Roll*). This 'contrasted with the polished fluency of his prepared public disquisitions' (ibid.). Students found him awe-inspiring and ponderous. At the Royal College of Physicians he was made councillor (1922–3), censor (1923–4, 1927), and representative on the General Medical Council (1927–9). He was the Lettsomian (1926), Maudsley (1932), and Earl Grey memorial (1939) lecturer. His appointment as physician-extraordinary to King George V in 1923 was followed by his becoming KCVO in 1927, and he was created a baronet in 1929. The pinnacle of his career came when he was appointed regius professor of medicine at the University of Oxford, in 1928.

The Oxford appointment was a turning point in Buzzard's career. Despite his conventional background and manner Buzzard turned out to be 'a consistent ally of innovation and reform' (Webster, 322). As a member of Huntercombe Golf Club Buzzard was one of the group of medical men who had access to Sir William Morris, later Lord Nuffield. With the generous support of Nuffield, to whom he acted as doctor, friend, and adviser, Buzzard did much to further the cause of British medicine. His main aim was to develop a medical school devoted to clinical as well as to laboratory research. This was realized with the creation of the Nuffield Institute for Medical Research in 1936, and the enlargement of the Oxford medical school thereafter.

Buzzard also played a part in the process that led to the creation of the National Health Service in 1948. In his presidential address to the British Medical Association in 1936 he called for reform, indicating the lack of time available to doctors as being the main defect in a disorganized service. Teamwork was needed and this could only come through a co-ordinated hospital system. Starting in Oxford in 1937 and later as the first chairman of the Nuffield Provincial Hospitals Trust, Buzzard helped to develop a regional link between voluntary and municipal hospitals, with the unified staffing of both and the payment of all doctors. The day of honorary service was over, he declared, and he foresaw the end of the voluntary hospital, resulting later in its absorption in a nationalized framework. As for general practitioners, he placed them in the community, furthering the cause of preventive and social medicine to which he attached great importance. This view was set forth forcefully in his Harveian oration for 1941 of the Royal College of Physicians. 'As a skilled politician and effective communicator he was ideally placed to render reform palatable to the conservative establishment, and to mediate with the vested interests threatened by the dramatic changes taking place' (Webster, 322).

As a result of Buzzard's influence an institute of social medicine was created at Oxford, with J. A. Ryle being appointed to the first chair in 1943. Buzzard's views on GPs anticipated the role fashioned for them in 1948 when the profession was sharply divided and consultants were given staffs of their own in the hospital world. Buzzard also had views on the health of the population as a whole. Although he criticized a British Medical Association report on physical education in 1936 because it valued gymnastic exercises over field games, he attached more importance to heredity and hygiene. Every individual, he believed, should develop a 'health conscience' (Cooke, 20). In 1938, influenced by eugenic views current at the time, he opposed marriage of the unfit, envisaging the day when it would be subject to state control.

If Buzzard was effective in committee work, he was less successful in politics, failing in 1937 to secure the university seat as a Conservative. That made no difference to the way he was valued by the university, and his term of office was extended for five years beyond the normal retirement age; he did not become an emeritus professor until 1943. In 1940 he was awarded the Osler memorial medal; many other honours came his way over the years, but he is most remembered for his work in Oxford—no one did more for the medical school. He died at his home, 85 Banbury Road, Oxford, on 17 December 1945, and was succeeded in the baronetcy by his elder son, Anthony Wass (1902–1972).

Frank Honigsbaum

Sources A. M. Cooke, *Sir E. Farquhar Buzzard, Bt, K.C.V.O., D.M., F.R.C.P.: an appreciation* (1975) • *BMJ* (29 Dec 1945), 943–4 • *The Lancet* (29 Dec 1945), 864–5 • *The Times* (19 Dec 1945), 8 • *St Thomas's Hospital Gazette*, 44 (1946), 11–14 • F. Honigsbaum, *The division in British medicine* (1979), 187 • F. Honigsbaum, *Health, happiness and security: the creation of the national health service* (1989), 175 • C. Webster, 'Medicine', *Hist. U. Oxf.* 8: *20th cent.*, 317–43, esp. 322 • Munk, *Roll* • Burke, *Peerage* (1959) • *DNB*

Archives Bodl. Oxf. | Bodl. Oxf., Society for Protection of Science and Learning MSS

Likenesses J. Gunn, portrait, Christ Church Oxf. • photograph, repro. in Cooke, *Sir E. Farquhar Buzzard* • photograph, repro. in *St Thomas's Hospital Gazette*, 11 • photograph, repro. in *The Times*

Wealth at death £47,679 18*s*. 11*d*.: probate, 17 April 1946, *CGPLA Eng. & Wales*

By, John (1779–1836), army officer and engineer, was born in 1779, probably on 7 August, in Lambeth, second son of George By and his wife, Mary, *née* Bryan. After passing through the Royal Military Academy, Woolwich, he was commissioned second lieutenant in the Royal Artillery on 1 August 1799, but was transferred to the Royal Engineers on 20 December. His further commissions were: lieutenant, 18 April 1801; second captain, 2 March 1805; first captain, 24 June 1809; brevet major, 23 June 1814; lieutenant-colonel, 2 December 1824. After serving at Woolwich and Plymouth he went in August 1802 to Canada, where he remained nearly nine years. His duties included work on the Quebec defences, and the construction of a new canal at the Cascades (near Île des Cascades), Lower Canada. In January 1811 he went to Portugal and served in the Peninsular War, taking part in the first and second sieges of Badajoz (May and June 1811).

By was recalled from the Peninsula to take charge of the works at the royal gunpowder mills at Faversham, Purfleet, and Waltham Abbey, a post he occupied with credit from January 1812 until August 1821, when, owing to reductions made in the establishments of the army, he was placed on half pay. While employed in the powder mills he designed a bridge on the truss principle for a span of 1000 feet (described in the *Morning Chronicle*, 14 February 1816). He married first, on 12 November 1801, Elizabeth Baines, and secondly, on 14 March 1818, Esther (*d*. 18 Feb 1838), heir of John March of Harley Street, London, and granddaughter of John Raymond Barker of Fairford Park, Gloucestershire; they had two daughters.

In April 1826 By returned to Canada, having been selected by General Gother Mann (inspector-general of fortifications at the Board of Ordnance) to design and construct a canal system, safe from attack by the United States, between the tidal waters of the St Lawrence and the Great Lakes of Canada. In unexplored territory, where travel was by frail Indian canoe, with a department to be organized, workmen to be instructed, and many difficulties to be overcome, he constructed a remarkable work—the Rideau Canal.

On his arrival in Canada By surveyed the inland route up the Ottawa River to the Rideau affluent, and from there by the Rideau Lake and Catariqui River to Kingston on Lake Ontario. He chose for his headquarters a position near the mouth of the proposed canal, a little below the beautiful Chaudière Falls of the Ottawa River, from where the canal was to ascend 82 feet by a succession of eight locks through a chasm. Here he built himself a house in the bush, there being at that time only two or three log huts at Nepean Point. A town soon sprang up, and was named after him Bytown.

In May 1827, the survey plans and estimates having been approved by the home government, by whom the cost was to be defrayed, By was directed to push forward the work as rapidly as possible, without waiting for the usual annual appropriations of money. Two companies of sappers and miners were placed at his disposal, a regular staff for the works was organized, barracks and a hospital were built in stone, and the foundation-stone of the canal works was laid by Sir John Franklin. The canal was opened in the spring of 1832, when the steamer *Pumper* passed through from Bytown to Kingston. The length of the navigation was 126¼ miles, with forty-seven locks and a total lockage of 446¼ feet. The work proved to be much more expensive than had been anticipated. In 1828 the attention of the British parliament was called to the expenditure, By having recommended that additional money should be granted to increase the size of the locks and build them in stone instead of wood. Colonels Edward Fanshawe and Griffith George Lewis, Royal Engineers, were sent as commissioners from England to report on the subject, and adopted By's views.

Bytown sprang quickly into an important place, and became the centre of a vast lumber trade; after the union of Upper and Lower Canada, its name was changed to Ottawa. The cost of the Rideau Canal—about £800,000—was much above the original estimate. It was criticized by the Treasury, then attempting to increase its power over other departments, including the Ordnance. A Commons select committee, chaired by J. N. Fazakerley, was appointed to investigate. By was recalled, leaving Canada to general regret and widespread tributes. He arrived in England in November 1832. He was examined by the committee, which, while admitting that the works had been carried out with care and economy, concluded its report with a strong expression of regret at the excess of the expenditure over the estimate and the parliamentary votes. By, who had expected commendation on the completion of this magnificent work in so short a time, under so many difficulties, and at a cost by no means extravagant, felt himself much ill-used, and never recovered from the disappointment. His health failing, he was placed on the unemployed list, and died at his residence, Shernfold Park, Frant, Sussex, near Tunbridge Wells, on 1 February 1836, having been most shabbily treated by his political masters. R. H. Vetch, *rev.* James Lunt

Sources *DCB*, vol. 7 • R. Leggett, *John By, lieutenant colonel, royal engineers, 1779–1836: builder of the Rideau canal, founder of Ottawa* (1982) • PRO, War Office records • Royal Engineers Institution, Chatham, royal engineers records • R. H. Bonnycastle, *The Canadas in 1841*, 2 vols. (1842) • W. Porter, *History of the corps of royal engineers*, 2 vols. (1889) • *Parl. papers* (1831–2) [committee reports] • T. W. J. Connolly, *History of the royal sappers and miners*, 2nd edn, 2 vols. (1857) • *Pall Mall Magazine* (June 1898) [article on Ottawa]
Archives NA Scot., Ramsay MSS

Byam, Edward (1583/4–1639). *See under* Byam, Henry (1580–1669).

Byam, Henry (1580–1669), Church of England clergyman, was born on 31 August 1580 at Luccombe, Somerset, one of seven children, and the eldest of four sons of Lawrence Byam (*d.* 1614), rector of Luccombe, and his wife, Anne or Agnes, daughter of Henry Yewings or Ewens, of Capton, Somerset. He matriculated at Exeter College, Oxford, on 10 June 1597 and was elected student of Christ Church on 21 December 1599. He graduated BA on 30 June 1602 and proceeded MA on 9 June 1605 and BD on 9 July 1612. When his father died, Henry succeeded him as rector of Luccombe, and about 1615 he married Susan (*d.* 1642), a daughter of William Fleet, rector of nearby Selworthy. He succeeded his father-in-law at Selworthy in 1618.

Byam's distaste for puritans was evident in a Lenten sermon he preached in Minehead in 1627 on the occasion of the readmission to the Church of England of a Somerset man who had converted to Islam while enslaved by Turkish pirates. Published as *A Returne from Argier* (1628), it complained that 'we have fed our Auditory so long with *Solafides* that Charity is frozen amidst the fire of our Zeale' and that 'new reformers' defamed a truly compassionate reliever of 'his brothers misery' as a follower of the '*old* Religion' (p. 52). William Laud, then bishop of Bath and Wells, refused to accept the accompanying dedication, possibly because of its handling of 'deep points' before a general audience. None the less, Byam subsequently found favour. He was made canon of Exeter on 17 March 1632 and elected clerk for his diocese in the 1640 convocation.

During the civil war four of his five sons became royalist captains and Byam raised troops for Charles I. Robert Blake, then a captain of parliamentarian cavalry, arrested him but Byam escaped to Oxford, where on 31 January 1643, by royal command, he was created DD. His wife and a daughter, fleeing to Wales, had drowned in a shipwreck in 1642. In spring 1645 Byam went as a chaplain to the prince of Wales to the Channel Islands, where his sermons bewailed the times in which 'men gape for new Doctrines, as the Oysters do for new tides' and denounced presbyterians (who 'brought the first Fewel to that prodigious Fire') and Independents (for 'their professed Factions, Fractions, and Independencies') (H. Byam, *XIII Sermons*, 1675, 93, 9). Ousted from his livings in 1647, he remained at Elizabeth Castle in Jersey until its surrender on 12 December 1651, after which he fled to France with two of his sons. Back in England by 1655, he lived with his daughters, having compounded for his estates by paying a fine of £49 4*s.* 8*d.* in 1652. At the Restoration he was made a prebendary of Wells as part of Charles II's plan for filling the cathedral chapters with loyal clerics in preparation for the re-establishment of episcopacy, and may have been considered for a bishopric. Byam died on 16 June 1669 and was buried on 29 June in the chancel of his church at Luccombe. By his will, dated 30 April that year, he bequeathed to his sons William and Francis land in Somerset and to his eldest daughter, Mary, 'a great Bible brought out of France, Archbishop Laud ag[ain]st Fisher, & the French Chronicle' (F. Wood, 21–2).

His brother **John Byam** (1582/3–1653), Church of England clergyman, was the second son of Lawrence Byam. He matriculated at Exeter College, Oxford, on 12 October 1599, aged sixteen, graduated BA on 30 June 1603, and proceeded MA on 25 May 1606. He married Sarah (*d.* 1627), a daughter of William Mascall, rector of Clatworthy, Somerset, whom he succeeded in 1616 when his father-in-law died. In May 1625 he also gained the vicarage of Dulverton, Somerset. He was imprisoned in 1646 when the parliamentarian forces found a letter he wrote to his close friend, Colonel Edmund Wyndham, the royalist governor of Dunster Castle, urging him never to surrender it. In an apparent attempt to avoid sequestration of his parsonage at Clatworthy, Byam claimed to have leased it to a son-in-law in 1639. On 18 March 1648 the county committee ordered his removal from the parsonage. He disputed his sequestration at Dulverton with its parishioners in 1651 and 1652 and died in 1653.

Edward Byam (1583/4–1639), Church of England clergyman, was the third son of Lawrence Byam. On 31 October 1600, aged sixteen, he too matriculated from Exeter College. He was a demy at Magdalen College, Oxford, from 1601 to 1610, graduated BA on 12 December 1604, proceeded MA on 8 July 1607, and was presented to the vicarage of Dulverton on 4 August 1612. He married on 22 July 1613 Elizabeth Eaglesfield, daughter of Anthony Eaglesfield, rector of Walton-cum-Street and prebendary of Wells. He resigned Dulverton to his brother John and moved to Ireland, where he became precentor of Cloyne (30 April 1627), vicar of Castle Lyons, and prebendary of Clashmore (Lismore diocese, 17 April 1639). He died on 6 June 1639 and was buried in the chancel of the church at Castle Lyons. His widow was among the despoiled protestants of 1642. They had six sons and five daughters, and their second son, William, became the governor of Surinam whom Aphra Behn made the villain of her novel *Oroonoko*.

J. Sears McGee

Sources *Walker rev.* • J. Savage, *History of the hundred of Carhampton* (1830) • Wood, *Ath. Oxon.*, new edn, 3.836 • *VCH Somerset*, vol. 5 • E. S. Byam, *Chronological memoir of the reverends Henry, John, and Edward Byam* (1862) • Foster, *Alum. Oxon.* • R. S. Bosher, *The making of the Restoration settlement: the influence of the Laudians, 1649–1662* (1951) • J. R. Bloxam, *A register of the presidents, fellows … of Saint Mary Magdalen College*, 8 vols. (1853–85) • *DNB* • *Fasti Angl.* (Hardy), vol. 1 • *Fasti Angl., 1541–1857*, [Bath and Wells] • F. Wood, *Abstracts of Somersetshire wills* (1890), 21–2

Byam, John (1582/3–1653). *See under* Byam, Henry (1580–1669).

Byard [Bayard], **Nicholas de** (*fl. c.*1300), theologian, was a French Dominican friar active in the second half of the thirteenth century. His writings, especially his *Distinctiones*, appear to have circulated widely, and were known in England—Bishop Ralph Baldock of London owned *Distinctiones Biardi et alii tractatus* when he died in 1313. Their presence in English collections may have persuaded Henry Kirkestede in the fourteenth century, and John Bale, who cites Kirkestede as his authority, in the sixteenth, that Byard was an Englishman. Bale, closely followed by Pits, states that Byard, to whom he gives the name Bayarde, flourished in 1410, and was a Dominican who studied theology at Oxford, and was particularly knowledgeable in matters Aristotelian.

Henry Summerson

Sources T. Kaeppeli, *Scriptores ordinis praedicatorum medii aevi*, 3 (Rome, 1980), 148–53 • R. Sharpe, *A handlist of the Latin writers of Great Britain and Ireland before 1540* (1997), 383 • Bale, *Cat.*, 1.544 • J. Pits, *Relationum historicarum de rebus Anglicis*, ed. [W. Bishop] (Paris, 1619), 588 • Emden, *Oxf.*, 1.134; 3.2148

Byatt, Sir Horace Archer (1875–1933), colonial governor, was born on 22 March 1875 in Avenue Road, Tottenham, Middlesex, the eldest son of Horace Byatt, schoolmaster, of Midhurst, Sussex, and his wife, Laura Archer. He graduated with a BA degree in classical honours at Lincoln College, Oxford, in 1898. There followed a long career in the colonial service, starting in Nyasaland in 1898 and then in Somaliland from 1905, where he rose to commissioner and commander-in-chief in 1911–14. He was colonial secretary, Gibraltar, in 1914; lieutenant-governor and chief secretary, Malta, in 1914–16; and then came the major part of his career, as administrator of former German East Africa in 1916–20 and governor and commander-in-chief of the League of Nations Mandated Territory of Tanganyika in 1920–24. He was finally governor and commander-in-chief of Trinidad and Tobago in 1924–9, after which he retired. He was knighted in 1918. In 1924 he married Olga Margaret Campbell, of Argyll; they had three sons.

In a career notable chiefly for its cautious approach, Byatt's main impact was in the peaceful transfer of power from the Germans to the British in Tanganyika. The country was in a parlous state after the fiercely fought east African campaign; most of the German settlers had fled, and trade and revenue stood at less than half of the pre-war level. Byatt had a very small administrative staff (108 officers) and as a consequence he left much of the German system in place, continuing to employ *akidas*, or German government-appointed chiefs. Auctions of the former German estates were held and these went mainly to the British, Indians, and Greeks, though some land was given back to Africans. Byatt said in 1922 that 'the future of the country lay in developing native cultivation only' (Taylor, 58), and this was in line with the terms of the mandate and the Colonial Office's thinking. He established departments of agriculture, forestry, education, and lands and survey, though the scarcity of the staff meant that progress was slow. Unfortunately he continued the German education policy of having a separate government education system, which ignored and competed with the missionary one, and this was in contradiction to Colonial Office policy, which stressed partnership.

In administration Byatt was criticized for having little interest in the districts, where officers were left to their own devices, using *akidas* or chiefs as agents. However, he replaced the tribute which chiefs collected by government salaries, with Colonial Office approval, as this was a step in the direction of Nigerian-style 'indirect rule'. A well thought out scheme of indirect rule, however, had to wait for his successor, Sir Donald Cameron. Byatt at least had some achievements to his credit: he had finally abolished slavery in 1922, reorganized the police force, introduced the Indian penal code, and managed to curb influenza, sleeping sickness, and yaws. The economy recovered well; by 1925 revenues had begun to equal expenditure and Tanganyika was exporting twice as much as before the war. Some of Byatt's difficulties lay in implementing the mandate, the terms of which were not published until 1922, and he faced delays in receiving answers to amplify details. Cameron was distinctly critical of his work. A later historian commented that Byatt was 'a narrowly competent man, unimaginative, unpopular, and unwell, but he shared the good intentions of the colonial office' (Iliffe, 262).

Byatt spent a shorter period as governor of the crown colony of Trinidad and Tobago, from 1924 to 1929. This was a difficult period to take over the governorship, as the colony faced political unrest with an upsurge of radical labour activity, led by Captain Arthur Cipriani, a white Creole who founded the Trinidad Working Men's Association. In a multi-ethnic population of black people and east Indians, working-class solidarity was beginning to appear above the ethnic divide. Unrest increased with a slump in cocoa prices in the mid-1920s, and the Trinidad Working Men's Association pressed for better wages and working conditions, as well as constitutional reform. In 1925 the first elections in the colony were held, for a new legislative council, though the white planters still exerted political domination. Byatt was involved in a crisis over his power to nominate six of the members. He nominated five but left the sixth place vacant until after the election, claiming he wanted to retain flexibility. In fact he nominated another white member to the three already nominated, and this caused protests in the Indian community who hoped it would be an Indian. The Colonial Office also disapproved of his decision but eventually dropped the matter. Byatt did at least persuade the Colonial Office to raise the limit on individual loans by the agricultural loan bank, so as to assist poorer farmers. He retired to Britain in 1929 and died four years later, at 2 Beaumont Street, St Marylebone, London, on 8 April 1933. His wife survived him. OLIVER FURLEY

Sources V. Harlow, E. M. Chilver, and A. Smith, eds., *History of East Africa*, 2 (1965) • K. Ingham, *A history of East Africa*, 3rd edn (1965) • J. Iliffe, *A modern history of Tanganyika* (1979) • J. C. Taylor, *The political development of Tanganyika* (1963) • J. Cameron and W. D. Dodd, *Society, schools and progress in Tanganyika* (1970) • A. Coulson, *Tanzania: a political economy* (1982) • B. Brereton, *A history of modern Trinidad and Tobago, 1783–1962* (1981) • K. Singh, *Race and class: struggles in a colonial state, Trinidad, 1917–45* (1994) • E. E. Williams, *History of the people of Trinidad and Tobago* (1962) • J. Listowell, *The making of Tanganyika* (1965) • D. Cameron, *My Tanganyika service* (1939) • *WWW* • b. cert. • d. cert. • *CGPLA Eng. & Wales* (1933)

Archives Bodl. RH, diaries

Wealth at death £27,284 0s. 6d.: probate, 28 April 1933, *CGPLA Eng. & Wales*

Byck, Muriel Tamara (1918–1944). *See under* Women agents on active service in France (*act.* 1942–1945).

Byer, Nicholas (*d.* 1681), painter, was a native of Trondheim in Norway. He practised portrait and historical painting, and on coming to England, where he was made a denizen on 2 November 1662, found a steady patron in Sir William Temple, at whose seat at Sheen, in Surrey, he lived for three or four years. His reputation as a face painter must have been considerable; several persons of distinction, including some members of the royal family, sat to him. He died at Sheen in 1681; he is said to have been the first person buried at St Clement Danes, London, after the rebuilding of the church.

GORDON GOODWIN, *rev.* ANNETTE PEACH

Sources E. K. Waterhouse, *The dictionary of British 16th and 17th century painters* (1988) • H. Walpole, *Anecdotes of painting in England: with some account of the principal artists*, ed. R. N. Wornum, new edn, 2 (1849), 479

Byerley, Maria (1787–1843), schoolmistress, was the second daughter and fifth child of Thomas Byerley (1748–1810), nephew, agent, and partner in the pottery works of Josiah Wedgwood, and his wife, Frances, *née* Bruckfield (1761–1838). Katherine *Thomson, the writer, was her younger sister. For the first twenty years of Maria's life the family home was in London, first in Greek Street and then in Sloane Street. Tom and Frances Byerley, who had thirteen children altogether, were not good managers. While Tom's uncle Josiah was alive, he kept a tight grip on the finances of both the family and the firm; after his death in 1795 the fortunes of the Byerleys and of Wedgwood began to go downhill. In 1809 it was agreed that Maria and her elder sister, Frances [*see below*], should try to support themselves by opening a school. A house was rented in Warwick High Street and the school opened its doors to five boarders and two day girls at the end of January 1810.

Despite leasing a second house the Warwick site was cramped and thought to be unhealthy. In 1817 the school moved to Barford House, 3 miles outside Warwick. In 1824 there was a final move to a house called Avonbank, 3 miles outside Stratford. There the school remained until the retirement of Maria and her sister Jane in 1841. It was taken on by the Misses Ainsworth and was still going strong in 1850.

Throughout all this, and the departure through marriage of four of her sisters, Maria was the anchorwoman, the constant presence. She was absent only for two spells of severe illness in 1813 and 1814. She managed the finances not only of the school but also of the family. Initial capital for the school had been raised against the security of legacies to the sisters under the wills of Josiah and Thomas Wedgwood. But pupils did not pay in advance, and until the move from Warwick there was a ceiling on expansion. Josiah Wedgwood the younger helped with loans and an allowance to Mrs Byerley. Maria wrote to him with quiet pride on 12 February 1823, 'I find after making a calculation of our profits this half-year that we are able to send the amount of our debt, I am sorry to say of so long standing, to you. I shall therefore feel very much obliged to you if you will permit your book-keeper to send me an account of all that is owing including interest, so that we may at length feel quite free' (Hicks, 70). She and her brother Samuel also took over the payment of an allowance to their mother.

On paper the school's curriculum was a conventional female one: 'Instruction in English Reading, Spelling, Grammar and Composition, in Geography … and in Ancient and Modern History' (Hicks, 14), with French, Italian, music, dancing, drawing, writing, and arithmetic as extras. However, it appears to have been taught to a standard sufficient to attract those enthusiasts for female education, the Unitarians. Although the Misses Byerley were Anglican, their pupils included Harriet Martineau's niece, Joseph Priestley's granddaughters Marianne and Sarah, sent over from America, Julia Leigh Smith, and from 1821 to 1826 Elizabeth Stevenson, the future novelist Mrs Gaskell.

Maria Byerley died of pneumonia at her sister Katherine's house, 30 Welbeck Street, London, on 2 April 1843. She bequeathed her property to her sisters 'for their separate use & benefit independently & exclusively of any present or future husband & without being in any wise subject to his debts, control or management' (Hicks, 116). The character Maria Bouverie, the vicar's spinster sister in Katherine Thomson's novel *Constance* (1833), set in Warwick, is thought to be a portrait of her sister Maria.

Frances Parkes [*née* Byerley; *known as* Mrs William Parkes] (1786–1842), writer, was the first daughter and fourth child of Thomas and Frances Byerley. She opened the school in Warwick with Maria in 1810. On 21 June 1811 she married the Unitarian textile manufacturer William Parkes (1788–1840). However his uncle's bankruptcy in 1817 brought William down too. They moved from Warwick first to Bloxham and then to Solihull. In 1825 Fanny published *Domestic duties, or, Instructions to young married ladies on the regulation of their conduct in the various relations and duties of married life*, which has generally been taken as reflecting the ethos of the Byerleys' school. It was a considerable success, going into five editions in fifteen years. In the later 1820s they moved to London, where William built up a solicitor's practice. Fanny died at Kilburn Priory, London, of heart disease on 13 September 1842. Two of her six children worked with Florence Nightingale in the Crimea, Maria as a nurse and Edmund Alexander *Parkes as a doctor.

GILLIAN SUTHERLAND

Sources P. D. Hicks, *A quest of ladies: the story of a Warwickshire school* (1949) • J. S. Uglow, *Elizabeth Gaskell: a habit of stories* (1993) • C. de Bellaigue, 'The rise and fall of the domestic model of girls' schools, 1780–1820', BA diss., U. Cam., 1996 • d. cert. • *GM*, 2nd ser., 18 (1842), 441

Archives Wedgwood Museum, Etruria, Wedgwood MSS

Byerley, Thomas [*pseud.* Reuben Percy] (**1789–1826**), journalist, the brother of Sir John Byerley, was descended from an old Yorkshire family. Not much is known about his early career, except that he wrote for the *Monthly Magazine* on subjects of historical and antiquarian interests, and at one point was even engaged in preparing a genealogical chart of the reigning royal family for the duke of Kent. He devoted himself to literary pursuits and finally became editor of the *Literary Chronicle*, an office which he held until his death, and for a time also the assistant editor of the *Star* newspaper. About the year 1818 Byerley married a Miss Mitchell, and in 1823 took on another editorship, that of *The Mirror of Literature, Amusement, and Instruction*, also remaining in this post until the end of his life. Under the pseudonym of Stephen Collet he published *Relics of Literature* (1823), a collection of miscellanies, including a long article, reprinted in 1875, on the art of judging the character of individuals from their handwriting.

Byerley's chief claim to fame was the publication of *The Percy Anecdotes* (20 vols., 1821–3). These volumes, which came out in forty-four monthly parts, were professedly written by 'Sholto and Reuben Percy, brothers of the Benedictine monastery of Mount Benger'. In reality Reuben Percy was Thomas Byerley and Sholto Percy was Joseph Clinton Robertson, editor of the *Mechanics' Magazine*, who died in 1852. Their aim was the compilation of true or probable incidents of daily activities or domestic interests which would strive towards a faithful portrayal of contemporary society and make for instructive and pleasurable family reading, reinforcing moral principles while remaining humorous and enjoyable. The name of the collection was derived from the Percy Coffee House in Rathbone Place, London, where Byerley and Robertson were accustomed to meet. The work was very popular when it was first published; indeed Byron is said to have declared that 'no man that has any pretensions to figure in good society can fail to make himself familiar with the *Percy Anecdotes*'. In later years, however, it was felt to be of no real value.

It was Byerley's last effort at publication. Subsequently his health deteriorated rapidly and he died prematurely at the age of thirty-seven, in London, on 28 July 1826. He was survived by two of his three children. His burial took place at St Bride's, London, on 3 August.

THOMPSON COOPER, *rev.* NILANJANA BANERJI

Sources *The Literary Chronicle and Weekly Review* (5 Aug 1826) • J. Timbs, preface, *The Percy anecdotes*, ed. S. Percy [J. C. Robertson] and R. Percy [T. Byerley], 1 [1868], iii–vi • *N&Q*, 7 (1853), 214 • *N&Q*, 3rd ser., 9 (1866), 168 • *GM*, 2nd ser., 38 (1852), 548 • *British Museum catalogue of printed books*

Byers, (Charles) Frank, Baron Byers (1915–1984), politician, was born in Liverpool on 24 July 1915, the only son (there were two younger daughters) of Charles Cecil Byers (1888–1957), a Lloyds underwriter, vice-chairman of United Molasses Ltd, and one-time Liberal parliamentary candidate, and his wife, Florence May, daughter of James Fairclough of Northenden, Cheshire.

Educated at the Hall School, Hampstead, and at Westminster School, Byers was captain of football and athletics and princeps oppidanorum at the latter. He went up to Christ Church, Oxford, in October 1934, and emerged four years later with a third-class honours degree in politics, philosophy, and economics. He was awarded his blue and international colours as a 220 yard hurdler and held the British universities' record for over twelve years. At Oxford his interest in politics developed. He was a Liberal by temperament, instinct, and upbringing; he became chairman of the Union of Liberal Students and the University Liberal Club (1937), and often recalled with a wry chuckle that his treasurer was one Harold Wilson.

Having left Oxford in 1938 Byers joined Gray's Inn. On 15 July 1939 he married another Liberal stalwart, Joan Elizabeth, daughter of William Oliver, company director of Spicers Ltd of Alfriston, Wayside, Golders Green; they had one son and three daughters. Byers's legal studies ended when on 2 September 1939, the day after the outbreak of the Second World War, and only a few weeks after his marriage, he enlisted in the Royal Artillery. In due course he became a lieutenant-colonel on the staff of the Eighth Army. His courage and determination, which were natural attributes, were recognized when he was appointed OBE in 1944, mentioned three times in dispatches, awarded the Croix de Guerre with palms, and was created a chevalier of the Légion d'honneur.

Byers had been adopted as prospective Liberal parliamentary candidate for the North Dorset constituency at the age of twenty-two and returned to England in July 1945 for the general election. He won a remarkable and unexpected victory, and became one of only twelve Liberals in the Commons. He was at once conspicuous for his political flair, judgement, and administrative ability, and became chief whip in 1946 after only a few months in the house. However, largely because of boundary changes, he narrowly lost his seat in 1950, and failed to regain it in 1951. Already a part-time director of the Rio Tinto Company (later RTZ), he now became full-time, organizing the company's world-wide exploration programme. By 1959 he was in a position to resume his political work, and he became for many years the dominant figure in the Liberal Party as director of its election campaigns, chairman (1950–52 and 1965–7), president, general fund-raiser, and peripatetic speaker. He was responsible almost single-handedly for the survival of the party in a difficult period. He contested, without success, a by-election in Bolton in 1960.

When in 1964 the Liberal Party was offered its first two life peerages, Byers was an obvious choice. In 1967 he became leader of the Liberal peers, a position which he held unchallenged until his death. He was sworn of the privy council in 1972, and became chairman of the Company Pension Information Centre in 1973 and part-time consultant at Marks and Spencer in 1977. He was chairman of the Anglo-Israel Association, a member of the committee on privacy (1970–72) led by Kenneth Younger, chaired a far-reaching report on the organization of British athletics (1968), and was enthusiastically involved in a host of voluntary activities where he was able to demonstrate his passionate concern for people as individuals, particularly the young, the sick, and the deprived.

For twenty years Byers was an outstanding and widely admired party leader in the House of Lords. He was lean, wiry, red-haired, and pugnacious; his carefully prepared speeches were appreciated for their logic, forceful delivery, and conciseness of argument. His Liberalism was both caring and practical, as is shown by his moving contributions to the debates on the Immigration Act in 1971. He had an impish and irreverent sense of humour. His occasional impatience was no more than a reflection of his quickness of mind, as was the brusque bark of 'Byers' with which he answered the telephone. He had a profound and sympathetic knowledge of parliamentary customs and procedures, and made a distinctive contribution to the all-party talks in 1968 on the reform of the upper house.

Byers suffered heart attacks in 1973 and again in 1978 but remained fully active. On 6 February 1984 he had his third and fatal attack when he was working in his room at the House of Lords. It is said that members do not die in the house, because coroners have no jurisdiction in a royal palace, but 'on the way to hospital'. It was the only time that Byers broke a parliamentary convention.

WIGODER, *rev.*

Sources personal knowledge (1990) · private information (1990) · *The Times* (7 Feb 1984) · Burke, *Peerage* (1967) · *CGPLA Eng. & Wales* (1984)

Archives FILM BFI NFTVA, news footage · BFI NFTVA, party political footage | SOUND BL NSA, current affairs recording

Wealth at death £282,299: probate, 15 March 1984, *CGPLA Eng. & Wales*

Byers, James. *See* Byres, James, of Tonley (1734–1817).

Byers [*née* Morrow], **Margaret** (1832–1912), educationist and temperance activist, was born in April 1832 at Windsor Hill, Rathfriland, co. Down, the fourth child and only daughter of Andrew Morrow, a noted temperance activist, and his wife, Margaret Herron. The family engaged in farming and also operated a flax mill. On the death of her father in 1840 Margaret Morrow was sent to live with two paternal uncles in Stoke-on-Trent, England. She was later educated at Mrs Treffry's school in Nottingham, where she taught for a year before her marriage. She returned to Ulster to marry the Revd John Byers, a Presbyterian minister, on 24 February 1852. Immediately after the marriage the couple set sail for Shanghai, where John Byers was to act as a missionary. Her brief visit to America *en route* for China left her deeply impressed by the American high school system of education. Its broad curriculum and the idea that the education of boys and girls should be similar remained central to her educational thinking. After arrival in China in 1853 John Byers became fatally ill and while returning to Ireland, via New York, died at sea.

Margaret Byers, whose only child, a son, had been born in China, returned to Ulster and took up a teaching post in Cookstown, co. Tyrone, in 1854. On moving to Belfast in 1859 she opened an 'establishment for the boarding and education of young ladies'. This was the Ladies' Collegiate School, founded to educate girls over the age of thirteen years. Byers was influenced by the English girls' high school movement of the 1870s, which placed great stress on public examinations and the study of Latin and mathematics, and attempted to downgrade the importance of 'accomplishments' in girls' education. She built a new school in 1873 and this took the name of Victoria College and School from the jubilee year of 1887. In 1878 she took part in a delegation organized by her close friend Isabella M. S. Tod to extend the benefits of the newly introduced Intermediate Education (Ireland) Bill to girls. According to her son it was Byers who persuaded Lord Chancellor Cairns to allow the inclusion of girls in this bill. The introduction of the Intermediate Education Act (1878) proved to be an important step on the way toward making university education available to women. The act also provided money for prizes, scholarships, and exhibitions for girls on the same terms as boys. She took immediate advantage of the intermediate act and the new public examination system it introduced. In the 1880s and 1890s Victoria College and School became one of the top prizewinners. The curriculum of the school was varied and not all the pupils took examinations. Along with the more academic subjects were taught domestic science, art, and music. Nursery, elementary, secondary, and university education, along with teacher training, were all part of the school's work. In 1884, when the Royal University of Ireland admitted women to matriculation for the first time, Byers opened a separate university department in her school.

Byers was a member of the Central Association of Irish Schoolmistresses, founded in January 1882 to ensure that concessions won for girls through the intermediate act would not be diluted or taken away. Its campaign, which ran to 1890, was successful. In 1899 Byers was invited to give evidence before a parliamentary commission to report on the intermediate board. She remained a strong supporter of the intermediate system, arguing that it had revolutionized girls' secondary education in Ireland. Byers was also a member of the first senate of Queen's University, Belfast.

Byers was a strong temperance activist. In 1873 she helped to organize the Belfast Women's Temperance Association (WTA) and Christian Workers' Union, which later affiliated with the British WTA. Part of the work of the Belfast WTA was the founding, in 1876, of the Prison Gate Mission for Women. Byers later became the first president of the Irish Women's Temperance Union, which was founded in 1894. She was opposed to home rule for Ireland and was an active supporter of the Women's Liberal Unionist Association. Byers was also an advocate of the franchise for women and was a committee member of the Ulster branch of the National Society for Women's Suffrage. In 1905 the University of Dublin (Trinity College) conferred an honorary degree of doctor of laws on her; she was the first Ulster woman to be so honoured, in recognition of her outstanding work in education.

Margaret Byers died at her home, 3 Lower Crescent, Belfast, on 21 February 1912 and was buried in Belfast city cemetery. Her son Sir John William Byers (1853–1920), professor of midwifery at the Queen's University of Belfast, survived her. MARIA LUDDY

Sources A. Jordan, *Margaret Byers* [1987] • *The Lady of the House* (15 March 1912) • 'British women at home, Mrs Byers', *Wings*, 11/122 (Feb 1893), 157–8 • *The Times* (22 Feb 1912) • 'Presentation to Mrs Byers', *Englishwoman's Review*, 11 (1880), 312–15

Archives Victoria College, Belfast

Likenesses Hooke, portrait, 1880, Victoria College, Belfast • photographs, Victoria College, Belfast

Wealth at death £12,129 18*s*. 11*d*.: probate, 4 April 1912, *CGPLA Ire*.

Byfield family (*per. c.*1814–1886), wood-engravers, came to prominence with the siblings John, Ebenezer, and Mary, three of the six children of James Byfield (*d.* 1813), carver and gilder in Soho, and his wife, Susanna, *née* Elliott (*c.*1759–1818), whom he had married on 10 September 1775 at St Marylebone, Middlesex. While **John Byfield** (1788–1841) was baptized in St Marylebone Church on 13 April 1788, **Ebenezer Byfield** (1790–1817) and **Mary Byfield** (1795–1871) were baptized on 23 August 1790 and 11 November 1795 respectively in the Providence Chapel, Great Titchfield Street, where the eccentric and charismatic dissenter William Huntington preached. Having been taught, probably by his father, to engrave on wood, John Byfield collaborated with his sister Mary to provide illustrations for several books, including some for the celebrated bibliophile Thomas Frognall Dibdin: *Bibliotheca Spenciana*, 4 vols. (1814); *Bibliographical Decameron* (1817; also with Ebenezer); and *Reminiscences of a Literary Life* (1836). This pair also produced many woodcuts for celebrated publications of William Pickering, printed by Charles Whittingham the younger at the Chiswick Press, including *Icones veteris testamenti* (1830) and Francis Douce's edition of *The Dance of Death* (1833). John alone contributed cuts to John Martin's *Bibliographical Catalogue* (1834) and an edition of Gray's *Elegy Written in a Country Churchyard* (1835). Additionally, he created several bookplates between 1830 and 1840, including a monogram and armorial design for John Gage Rookwood, after designs by Thomas Willement. John lived all his working life in London and several of his addresses are known: Paradise Row (1817) and Cornwall Place, Holloway (1822–7); 4 Brooksby Street (1832–4); and 30 Upper Park Street, Liverpool Road, Islington (1836). He signed his engravings 'J. Byfield'. He married Elizabeth Maylam Tucker of Lydd, Kent, and they had six children. John Byfield died in 1841.

Mary Byfield also conducted work independently of her brother John. She produced engravings for Dibdin's *Typographical Antiquities* (1819) and *Bibliomania Spenciana* (1842), for Joseph Hunter's *South Yorkshire* (1828–31), Orlando Jewitt's *Memorials of Cambridge* (1841), and for Edward Jesse's *A Summer's Day at Windsor, or A Visit to Eton* (1841). In 1841 she also designed a version of the university arms which formed part of the imprint of Oxford University Press. She was given most of her work by the printers Charles Whittingham, nephew and uncle, who employed her almost full time until her death in 1871, aged seventy-six. Consequently, the vast majority of Chiswick Press ornaments were engraved by her. Often she engraved alphabets, witness her work for Oliver Byrne's *First Books of 'Elements' of Euclid* (1847), where each proposition is headed by an initial engraved by her and continues in Caslon italic font, printed in red, yellow, or blue ink. Alternatively, she engraved head and tail-pieces, borders, and vignettes, and this sort of work is best seen in the *Queen Elizabeth's Prayer Book of* 1569 (1853), for which she cut over one hundred blocks, some based on designs by Holbein and Dürer, all of which harmonize perfectly with Whittingham's printing. A number of these engravings were reused in later books printed at the Chiswick Press. Mary taught not only several of her nephews and nieces to engrave on wood, but also Charlotte and Elizabeth Whittingham, the daughters of Charles Whittingham the younger, who often provided the designs for woodcuts. Various of her places of abode are recorded, either in Holloway: Cornwall Place (1822–7), or Islington: 4 Brooksby Street (1832–4), Canonbury Place (by 1842), and 30 Upper Park Street, Liverpool Road (1844). She signed her engravings 'Mary Byfield Sc' or 'BYFIELD SC'; the latter signature is confusing for much of her early work done with John was signed 'BYFIELD, Sc'.

The middle sibling, Ebenezer Byfield, apparently produced less work than his brother or sister. His main contribution was to Dibdin's *Bibliographical Decameron* (1817), although he died in 1817 before its publication that year. One address is known for an 'E. Byfield': Eden Grove, Holloway.

Several of the offspring of this generation followed in their forebears' footsteps. John Byfield had six children of whom Ann, Edward, and Mary were taught to engrave on wood by their aunt Mary. **Edward Byfield** (1838–1860) also engraved borders for Chiswick Press books, the extant proofs of which are marked 'engraved by Mary and her nephew Edward Byfield'. He died, tragically young, on 24 November 1860, at 30 Upper Park Street, Islington. **Ann Byfield** (*b.* 1830) and **Mary Byfield** (*b.* 1840) were active too, producing, for instance, new illustrations for the eighth edition of John William Bradley and J. G. Goodwin's *Manual of Illumination*, published for Winsor and Newton (1861). The sisters advertised themselves as 'artist engravers on wood' at 47 Florence Street, Islington.

Ebenezer Byfield died early, leaving only one son. The boy, **Louis Byfield** (1816–1886), was not only taught to engrave on wood by his aunt Mary, but also brought up by her, and his uncle John. For many years he helped his aunt in her work, producing, for instance, plates of Canonbury House and St Mary's Church for the *Islington Magazine* (July and August 1838) and for Samuel Lewis's *History and Topography of the Parish of St. Mary's, Islington* (1842). His work was signed 'LOUIS BYFIELD SC'. He lived in Islington for some time, at 30 Upper Park Street and 435 Liverpool Road, but died at 230B Queen's Road, Dalston, London, on 18 January 1886. In 1838 he changed profession, thereafter advertising himself as an undertaker and engraver. He was married twice, first to a Mary Ann (*d.* 6 Jan 1879) and then to a Louisa, but left no children.

SUSANNA AVERY-QUASH

Sources J. Butler, 'Ingenious and worthy family: the Byfields', *Private Library*, 3/4 (1980), 148–59 • A. Warren, *The Charles Whittinghams: printers* (1896), 194–6 • G. L. Keynes, *William Pickering, publisher: a memoir and a check-list of his publications*, rev. edn (1969), 30, 32, 36, 72, 86 • W. Chatto, J. Jackson, and H. G. Bohn, *A treatise on wood-engraving*, 2nd edn (1861), 535–8, 544–5, 634 • W. J. Linton, *The masters of wood-engraving* (1889), 99, 175 • H. W. Fincham, *Artists and engravers of British and American book plates* (1897), 15 • *DNB* • R. K. Engen, *Dictionary of Victorian engravers, print publishers and their works* (1979) • S. Houfe, *The dictionary of 19th century British book illustrators and caricaturists*, rev. edn (1996), 84 • R. McLean, *Victorian book design and colour printing*, rev. edn (1972), 7, 11–13, 15–18, 39, 67, 70 • Redgrave, *Artists* • Bryan, *Painters* (1903–5) • *IGI* • *OUP Recorder*, 3/4 (Aug 1998), 1

Archives BM, proofs [John Byfield] • priv. coll., proofs [John Byfield; Mary Byfield, sen.; Edward Byfield] | Bodl. Oxf., John Jackson collection, proofs [John Byfield; Mary Byfield, sen.; Edward Byfield]

Likenesses photograph (Mary Byfield, *c*.1850), repro. in Butler, 'Ingenious and worthy family: the Byfields'

Wealth at death under £100—Edward Byfield: administration, 28 Feb 1861, *CGPLA Eng. & Wales* • £793 6*s*.—Louis Byfield: probate, 23 Feb 1886, *CGPLA Eng. & Wales*

Byfield, Adoniram (*d.* 1658x60), Church of England clergyman, was the third child of Nicholas *Byfield (1578/9–1622), preacher in Chester, and his wife, Elizabeth (*d.* 1623). He matriculated at Emmanuel College, Cambridge, in 1620, graduated in 1624, and was ordained deacon and priest at Peterborough within a year. In 1626 he published an edited version of his father's Calvinistic *The Rule of Faith, or, An Exposition of the Apostles Creed*. On 17 October of the same year he married Anne Smith (*d.* 1656) at St Michael Bassishaw, London, and in 1629 he secured curacies in the London parishes of All Hallows, Staining, Mark Lane, and St Lawrence Jewry. He also preached with Philip Nye at Hackney, where four of his children were baptized. During the 1637 visitation by Archbishop Laud, Byfield's preaching was noted for its irregularities. That year he published a treatise on the 'principles of religion', *The Summe of the Principles*.

In 1642 Byfield became chaplain to Sir Henry Cholmondeley's regiment in the earl of Essex's army, and was possibly the author of *A Letter Sent from a Worthy Divine* (1642), describing the war. On 6 July 1643 he and Henry Roborough were appointed scribes to the Westminster assembly. They were granted the copyright of the *Directory for the Publique Worship of God* (which they later sold for £400) in recognition of their involvement in its compilation, though this was probably limited to recording, in shorthand and cipher, the minutes of proceedings rather than suggesting policies for implementation; Byfield's manuscript notes of the assembly's proceedings were published in 1874. However, another work, *A Brief View of Mr. Coleman his New-Modell of Church Government* (1645), has also been ascribed to him, and if he was its author Byfield also ventured his own opinions on the religious settlement.

In 1646 Byfield was one of the divines appointed to collect proofs from scripture for the confession of faith drawn up by the western association, and two years later was chosen to print *The Reasons Presented by the Dissenting Brethren* against a presbyterian order. At about this time he was presented as vicar and then rector of Fulham by the lord of the manor, Colonel Edmund Harvey, with a stipend of £100 a year paid from the bishop of London's estates. Considered an 'able honest and constant preacher of the gospel' (Feret, 3.287), he probably resigned both posts in 1652, when he was succeeded by Isaac Knight. He moved to Collingbourne Ducis, Wiltshire, a living worth £400 a year; here he openly sympathized with the discipline and organizational tenets of Independent congregations, signing in 1653 the propagation of the gospel petition to the Commons, inspired largely by Independent ministers, which proposed that committees of ministers

Adoniram Byfield (*d.* 1658x60), by unknown engraver

be set up in each county to approve unordained but godly laymen, allowing them to preach and receive maintenance from their congregations without their having to receive the sacraments. In 1654 he was a joint author, with Humphrey Chambers and John Strickland, of *An Apology for the Ministers of the County of Wilts.*, a tract justifying their opposition to the election to parliament of Sir Edward Ludlow. Under the ordinance of 29 June 1654 Byfield was appointed one of the assistant commissioners in Wiltshire for ejecting scandalous and insufficient ministers, and gained notoriety for his conscientiousness. John Walker, in his *Sufferings of the Clergy*, details Byfield's hard usage of Walter Bushnell, who had been ejected from Box, Wiltshire, in 1656. Byfield drew up his will on 29 October 1657. He left his plate and books to his eldest son, also Adoniram. The date of his death is unknown, but must have been between April 1658 and 1 August 1660, when his will was proved. His wife predeceased him; she was buried on 7 November 1656. HENRY LANCASTER

Sources C. J. Feret, *Fulham old and new*, 2 (1900), 18–20; 3 (1900), 287 · A. Laurence, *Parliamentary army chaplains, 1642–1651*, Royal Historical Society Studies in History, 59 (1990), 107 · B. Brook, *The lives of the puritans*, 3 vols. (1813) · P. S. Seaver, *The puritan lectureships: the politics of religious dissent, 1560–1662* (1970) · W. A. Shaw, *A history of the English church during the civil wars and under the Commonwealth, 1640–1660*, 2 vols. (1900) · T. Leishman, *The Westminster directory* (1901) · T. Faulkner, *An historical and topographical account of Fulham* (1813) · Venn, *Alum. Cant.* · Wood, *Ath. Oxon.*, new edn, 3.670 · R. W. Dale, *History of English congregationalism*, ed. A. W. W. Dale (1907) · D. Lysons, *The environs of London*, 4 vols. (1792–6) · H. F. Waters, *Genealogical gleanings in England*, 2 vols (1901) · PRO, PROB 11/300, fol. 31v · A. Mitchell and J. Struthers, *Minutes of the Westminster Assembly* (1874) · parish register (marriages), St Michael Bassishaw, London, 17 Oct 1626 · parish register, Collingbourne Ducis, Wiltshire

Likenesses R. Cooper, stipple (after engraving), NPG · line engraving, NPG [*see illus.*]

Wealth at death over £300: will, PRO, PROB 11/300, fol. 31v

Byfield, Ann (*b.* **1830**). *See under* Byfield family (*per. c.*1814–1886).

Byfield, Ebenezer (**1790–1817**). *See under* Byfield family (*per. c.*1814–1886).

Byfield, Edward (**1838–1860**). *See under* Byfield family (*per. c.*1814–1886).

Byfield, John (**1788–1841**). *See under* Byfield family (*per. c.*1814–1886).

Byfield, Louis (**1816–1886**). *See under* Byfield family (*per. c.*1814–1886).

Byfield, Mary (**1795–1871**). *See under* Byfield family (*per. c.*1814–1886).

Byfield, Mary (*b.* **1840**). *See under* Byfield family (*per. c.*1814–1886).

Byfield, Nicholas (**1578/9–1622**), Church of England clergyman and religious writer, was born in Warwickshire, the son of Richard Byfield, who later became vicar of Stratford upon Avon, and his first wife; Richard *Byfield (*bap.* 1598, *d.* 1664) was his half-brother. In the Lent term of 1596, aged seventeen, he entered Exeter College, Oxford, where he studied for four years without taking a degree. Byfield's religious nature and Calvinist convictions projected him readily towards a life of ministry. It was his intention upon leaving Oxford to secure a living in Ireland but having stopped *en route* and preached at St Peter's in Chester he accepted as providential an invitation to minister there; he remained at St Peter's as lecturer, and from 1608 as curate, where he was 'much followed' despite opposition from the bishop of Chester. During this period he married Elizabeth Tomkyns (*d.* 1623), who bore him ten children, one of whom died in infancy and the last of whom was yet unborn at the time of her father's death. In March 1615, in succession to Thomas Hawkes, Byfield was presented by Sir Horace Vere to the vicarage of Isleworth in Middlesex, a benefice he held and discharged with industry and great effect for the remainder of his life.

In common with the majority of the puritan brotherhood Byfield understood the importance of the pulpit, and both at Chester and at Isleworth he was noted for his preaching. At Isleworth he is said to have preached twice on Sundays, and in the summer, when the city gentry and their families left London for the country, on Wednesdays and Fridays as well. He subsequently consolidated his pulpit ministry with a succession of notable publications. His *Exposition upon the Epistle to the Colossians* (1615) and *The Marrow of the Oracles of God* (1620), as well as his commentary on the first epistle of Peter, published in parts from 1617 onwards and in whole in 1637, continued to strengthen the puritan cause long after his death in 1622. The *Exposition upon … Colossians* among other things emphasized the importance of the pulpit in the experience of the godly,

Nicholas Byfield (1578/9–1622), by unknown artist, 1620

listing ten 'singular benefits' mediated to the faithful through diligent preaching. *The Beginning of the Doctrine of Christ, or, A Catalogue of Sins* (1619) propounded the puritan conviction that a knowledge of oneself was prerequisite to a knowledge of Christ. *The Paterne of Wholesome Words* (1618), in the classic tradition of puritan devotional writing, was still in print in 1671. In all, seventeen works are known to have survived, a remarkable output for a life considerably foreshortened by illness.

Although a puritan leader of some influence, particularly during the Isleworth years, Byfield remained moderate on most contentious issues. While he held a low opinion of church structure and liturgical ceremony and was often outspoken against the ecclesiastical hierarchy, comparing its members to those who had persecuted Christ, he nevertheless conformed for the most part, taking a conservative position in the conformity debates of the early 1620s. He was, perhaps, a nonconformist at heart who conformed for the sake of the gospel and for the sake of the church, disapproving of the 'contentious zeale' of those who 'make needlesse rents in the church' (*Exposition upon … Colossians*, 1628 edn, 194), and advising his parishioners to conform as long as the required ceremonies and customs were not in opposition to the word of God.

Byfield was held in high esteem among the laity, including some of the puritan gentry. At Isleworth Sir Thomas Hoby and his wife were among Byfield's 'most appreciative listeners' (Cliffe, 38), and at Chester he had received a bequest from Thomas Benson, a local businessman, because through Byfield's preaching he 'many times' had 'received comfort' (Richardson, 132). The Veres adopted one of Byfield's children, and it was to them that his widow dedicated his volume of sermons on 1 Peter 3, published posthumously in 1626. On the other hand, it is likely that he would not have been entirely comfortable with having his name associated with the more radical puritans such as Archibald Johnston, Lord Wariston, the Scottish remonstrant who was executed following the Restoration, although Byfield's devotional works greatly influenced Johnston during his formative years.

A significant indication of Byfield's theological leaning was his respect for the sabbath, already evident during his ministry at Chester. In 1611 it brought him into conflict with Edward Brerewood the astronomer and mathematician. Brerewood had accepted responsibility for his nephew following the death of the latter's father and grandfather, and had obtained for him an apprenticeship in London. While on a visit to Chester the boy had come under the influence of Byfield's preaching, and when ordered by his master to perform certain household tasks on Sunday which troubled his conscience had sought Byfield's advice. It was, predictably, to the effect that the fourth commandment enjoined a strict observance of the sabbath and that the tasks in question contravened the law of God. Brerewood, observing that his nephew was deeply troubled and discovering its cause, gave him contrary advice, arguing that the constraints of the fourth commandment applied only to masters.

Brerewood also wrote to Byfield about the matter, refuting Byfield's sabbatarian theology at several points and reminding him that the Lord's day was not the sabbath but an institution of the church by which complete cessation from work on that day was not required. Brerewood feared that Byfield's sabbatarianism contained within it the seeds of social unrest and would lead to 'nothing but disturbance and sedition both in church and commonwealth' (Brerewood, 53). Byfield replied rather curtly, declining to become involved in controversy and claiming that his time would be better spent in the performance of his clerical duties. Brerewood, annoyed at Byfield's attitude, responded with some heat, challenging Byfield to prove his assertion that the sabbath had been transferred from Saturday to Sunday 'by the same authority originally that first commanded it' (ibid., 69). Although this exchange took place in 1611 it was not published until after both Brerewood and Byfield had passed from the scene. Brerewood's *Learned Treatise of the Sabaoth*, which included Byfield's answer and a response from Brerewood, first appeared in 1630, although Byfield's answer to Brerewood had already appeared in its own right in 1626, thus becoming one of the earliest of the many puritan apologies for the Sunday sabbath. The publication of Brerewood's *Learned Treatise* elicited a response from Byfield's half-brother, Richard, by this time vicar of Long Ditton, Surrey, who in 1631 entered the arena with *The Doctrine of the Sabbath Vindicated* in defence of Nicholas's sabbatarian theology.

Byfield died at Isleworth on 8 September 1622 as the result of an enormous 'torturing stone' (Wood, *Ath. Oxon.*,

2.326) in the bladder from which he had suffered continuously for the previous fifteen years. A post-mortem was conducted the following day revealing the presence of a stone, in appearance 'like flint', which measured 15½ inches 'about the edges' and approximately 13 inches long and 13 inches wide (Brook, 2.297; Fuller, *Worthies*, 3.127); it weighed 33 ounces. William Gouge, a fellow puritan of note, was present at the autopsy and initially provided the details in his introductory epistle to Byfield's *Commentary or Sermons upon the Second Chapter of the First Epistle of Saint Peter*, published the following year. That in later life Byfield was 'exceedingly afflicted' (Brook, 2.297) by this unwanted calculus is probably an understatement. His last will, drawn up only two days before his death, reveals him to have been a man of only moderate means with limited financial and property assets. After various small pecuniary and property bequests to his children, including the division of his books equally between his sons Adoniram *Byfield (*d.* 1658x60) and Jonathan, he left the residue of his estate to his wife, Elizabeth, to pass after her decease to his son Benjamin. A small portrait of Byfield at Dr Williams's Library, London, depicts a young and perceptive face, and shows on the lower part of the panel a rather unconvincing representation of the remarkable accretion which brought about his untimely demise.

BRYAN W. BALL

Sources B. Brook, *The lives of the puritans*, 2 (1813) • Wood, *Ath. Oxon.*, 1st edn, vols. 1–2 • T. Webster, *Godly clergy in early Stuart England: the Caroline puritan movement, c.1620–1643* (1997) • Fuller, *Worthies* (1840), vol. 3 • R. Cox, *The literature of the sabbath question*, 1 (1865) • *Diary of Sir Archibald Johnston of Wariston*, 1, ed. G. M. Paul, Scottish History Society, 61 (1911) • J. T. Cliffe, *The puritan gentry: the great puritan families of early Stuart England* (1984) • R. C. Richardson, *Puritanism in north-west England* (1972) • E. Brerewood, *A learned treatise of the sabaoth* (1630) • C. Hill, *Society and puritanism in pre-revolutionary England* (1964) • D. Neal, *The history of the puritans* (1822), vol. 2 • will, LMA, DL/C/361/Nicholas Byfield/1622/Sept. • will, PRO, PROB 11/142, sig. 126 [will of Elizabeth Byfield, wife] • *DNB* • Ches. & Chester ALSS, Calendar of Cheshire quarter sessions, QSE/11/6–7 • parish registers, St Peter's, Chester, Ches. & Chester ALSS

Likenesses oils, 1620, DWL [*see illus.*]

Wealth at death approx. £200, plus property in Isleworth: will, LMA DL/C/361/Nicholas Byfield/1622/Sept.; will, PRO, PROB 11/142, sig. 126 [Elizabeth Byfield]

Byfield, Richard (*bap.* **1598**, *d.* **1664**), clergyman and ejected minister, was baptized on 24 September 1598 at Stratford upon Avon, the son of Richard Byfield, vicar of the parish, and his second wife, Margaret Coats; Nicholas *Byfield (1578/9–1622) was his half-brother. He entered Queen's College, Oxford, in 1615, graduated BA on 19 October 1619, and proceeded MA on 29 October 1622. A brief first marriage to Mary, whose other name is unknown, ended with her death in 1625; she was buried at Kingston, Surrey. Byfield was instituted rector of Long Ditton in Surrey on 17 August 1627, in which year he was licensed to marry Mary Lancasheire of St Laurence Milk Street, London. Byfield's first publication, *The Light of Faith and Way of Holines*, appeared in 1630, and was followed the next year by *The Doctrine of the Sabbath Vindicated*, which was written in answer to Edward Brerewood's *Learned Treatise of the Sabaoth*, a posthumous publication of a letter attacking Nicholas Byfield's views on the sabbath. In 1634 Byfield was suspended for his refusal to read the Book of Sports, the suspension lasting, by his own calculation, four years and four weeks. 'For my part', he later wrote:

> I sate down under their unjust, illegall sentence, with this saying to some of my own acquaintance … There is no coming in for me again, but with the breaking of the whole State, an alteration that must change the Kingdom and the laws thereof. (R. Byfield, *Temple Defilers Defiled*, 1645, foreword)

On the outbreak of civil war Byfield contributed generously to the parliamentarian cause, and in June 1642 was one of the first Surrey inhabitants to lend on the propositions scheme.

Byfield was appointed lecturer at New Brentford, Middlesex, on 13 June 1643. He was active in the meetings of Surrey ministers which took place regularly at Kingston in 1644 and 1645, and he preached at the Thursday lecture at Kingston. On 30 April 1645 the House of Commons nominated him to a seat on the assembly of divines to replace Daniel Featley, who had died earlier that month, and he took his place on 12 May. He preached before the Commons on 25 June, in a sermon extolling the virtues of unity against prelacy, popery, heresy, schism, and profanity. In his Kingston sermons he complained of the failure to establish 'the wholesome food of sound Doctrine' in the church, and denounced those who spread false and dangerous doctrines and advocated toleration; the 'diseasednesse of the Congregation of Kingston' was of particular concern to him (*Temple Defilers Defiled*). In March 1647 Byfield officiated at the wedding at St Giles-in-the-Fields of the London Independent Thomas *Juxon (1614–1672), brother of his third wife, Sarah. The following February he was named a member of the Kingston classis in the unsuccessful attempt by parliament and its Surrey county committee to establish a classical presbyterian system in Surrey.

In 1654 Byfield was appointed an assistant of the Surrey commission for ejecting scandalous ministers. Throughout the 1650s he was obliged to hold services in the parish church of Thames Ditton, the church at Long Ditton having collapsed in 1649. Byfield was to accuse Sir Thomas Evelyn, patron of the living, of having pocketed funds for reparations and of having allowed the church to decay beyond repair. Relations between Byfield and Evelyn were restored briefly in 1654 through the intervention of Oliver Cromwell, who is said to have promised to pay £100 of the £200 needed for rebuilding the church. The new church would, Byfield hoped, be built as 'one entire roome', and not in the 'old superstitious forme of Chancel, Church & church porch'. In April 1657 Byfield renewed his complaints against Evelyn, accusing him of employing a 'prelaticall' household chaplain, and warning the protector and council of the frequent meetings at Evelyn's house of those 'who are potent and against the power of Godlines' (PRO, SP 18/155/44). His opposition to episcopal government and its supporters was to be restated forcefully in *The Gospel's Glory*, which he dedicated in 1659 to Richard Cromwell.

After his ejection in 1662 Byfield retired to East Sheen in the parish of Mortlake, Surrey, where he held property. In a lengthy preamble to his will, which was dated 15 August 1662, he set out as a 'record to all ages' his subscription to orthodox opinions and his 'utter detestation of all Popery as noe other then Antechristianisme, and of all Arminianisme, Socinianisme, Anabaptisme, with all the dreames and furyes of Enthusiasts, Quaqers and ffamalists' (PRO, PROB 11/317, fol. 9). The will mentioned property in Ifield, Sussex, as well as in East Sheen, and also £138 10*s.* still owing to him for loans made to parliament during the civil war. Six daughters and four sons from his third marriage were among the children named in the will, including Nathaniel (*d.* 1733), who was to become a judge of the court of vice-admiralty in Massachusetts and a member of the council of the province. Byfield's eldest sons, Samuel and Richard, children from his second marriage, would later follow him into the church. Byfield died at Mortlake on 26 December 1664 and was buried in the church there. A brass plate on the east wall described him as having 'painfully and constantly taught and kept the Word of God and the Testimony of Jesus Christ' in the thirty-five years he served as rector of Long Ditton (Aubrey, 1.85). Sarah, his widow, died in 1678. JOHN GURNEY

Sources *Calamy rev.*, 96–7 • *The journal of Thomas Juxon*, ed. K. Lindley and D. Scott, CS, 5th ser., 13 (1999) • H. F. Waters, *Genealogical gleanings in England*, 2 vols. (1901) • J. Gurney, 'The county of Surrey and the English revolution', DPhil diss., U. Sussex, 1991 • *DNB* • will, PRO, PROB 11/317, fols. 9–11v • PRO, SP 18/155/44 • *The nonconformist's memorial … originally written by … Edmund Calamy*, ed. S. Palmer, [3rd edn], 3 vols. (1802–3) • J. Aubrey, *The natural history and antiquities of the county of Surrey*, 5 vols. (1718–19) • J. L. Chester and J. Foster, eds., *London marriage licences, 1521–1869* (1887) • A. F. Mitchell and J. Struthers, eds., *Minutes of the sessions of the Westminster assembly of divines* (1874) • Foster, *Alum. Oxon.* • parish registers, Kingston, Surrey HC [transcripts] • *IGI* [citing R. Savage, ed., *The registers of Stratford-on-Avon*, 1897–1905]
Archives PRO, petition, SP 18/155/44
Wealth at death see will, PRO, PROB 11/317, fols. 9-11*v*

Byles, Sir John Barnard (1801–1884), judge and author, was born in Stowmarket, Suffolk, on 11 January 1801. He was the eldest son of Jeremiah Byles, a timber merchant; his mother was the only daughter of William Barnard of Holt, Essex. Little is known about his early education, but before he became a member of the Inner Temple it appears that he was in business. After reading as a pupil in the chambers of Chitty, the great pleader, and practising as a special pleader at 1 Garden Court, Temple, Byles was called to the bar in November 1831, joining the Norfolk circuit. In 1840 he was appointed recorder of Buckingham, and three years later was raised to the degree of serjeant-at-law. When in 1846 the court of common pleas was opened to all members of the bar, Byles received a patent of precedence in all courts. He rapidly acquired a leading practice both on his own circuit, which he led for many years, and also in London.

In 1857, in the last appointments to this office, with Serjeants Shee and Wrangham, Byles was appointed a queen's serjeant. He had strong political and religious beliefs and once stood as a parliamentary candidate as a protectionist Conservative for Aylesbury (December 1850). As a strict practising Unitarian, however, he was unacceptable to the church party and withdrew from the contest before the poll. Despite Byles's beliefs, Lord Cranworth, a whig, selected him, in January 1858, for promotion to the bench. On the resignation of Sir Cresswell Cresswell, Byles took his seat in the common pleas, receiving the customary knighthood. He proved to be a learned and courteous judge, whose 'humour often enlivened the tedium of a trial'. A correspondent in *The Times* recalled an occasion when counsel cited 'Byles on Bills'. 'Does the learned author give any authority for that statement?', asked Byles. 'No, my Lord, I cannot find that he does.' 'Ah then,' replied Byles, 'do not trust him. I know him well.' Known for his special expertise in mercantile matters, he was one of the judges who won for the court of common pleas its high repute among commercial litigants. But he was not the equal of his remarkable contemporary, Willes, in whose judgments are to be found principles of universal validity.

Before he was called, Byles delivered in Lyon's Inn a series of lectures on commercial law. The first, delivered on 3 November 1829, was published unaltered, at the request and risk of friends, as *A Discourse on the Present State of the Law of England*. In the same year appeared *A Practical Compendium of the Law of Bills of Exchange*, his best-known legal work, which was the first systematic analysis of that body of law. This pioneering treatise, which also went into many American editions, was one of the foundation stones of the Bills of Exchange Act of 1882; 'without it the late codification of the law of bills of exchange would have been impossible'. His son Maurice edited the tenth (1870) and later editions, although 'each sheet had passed under the eye of the author'. On Byles's death the work was in its thirteenth edition (1879); it reached its twenty-sixth in 1988.

To a wider world, Byles was known for his pamphlet, *Observations on the Usury Laws, with Suggestions for Amendment and a Draft Bill* (1845), and particularly for his book, *Sophisms of Free Trade* (1849), discreetly entitled *Examined by a Barrister. Sophisms* was a highly successful publication, running through eight editions in two years. Both these works reflected Byles's distrust of the discipline of political economy, still 'in its very infancy', and his suspicion of the 'abstract reasoning' of its exponents, including Ricardo and Malthus; in his opinion, their theories were still to be judged against human experience. *Sophisms* was an unfashionably sceptical questioning of the doctrines of *laissez-faire* political economists and their devotion to the principle of unbridled freedom of contract. Byles considered that the law's refusal to enforce penal bonds and the many statutory provisions protecting the public were a striking refutation of the argument that society should not interfere with man's right to bargain freely. But these views are not reflected in his judgments. In *Hole* v. *Barlow* (1858), for instance, he directed the jury that no action lies for the reasonable use of a lawful trade 'in a convenient and proper place', even though someone may suffer annoyance from its being carried on.

Sophisms may have been ahead of its time. In comparison, Byles's *Foundations of Religion in the Mind and Heart of Man* (1875), written after his retirement and characterized by a lifetime of wide reading, was uncontroversial. He recorded in its preface that it was written at different times over an interval of years.

In January 1873 Byles resigned his judgeship, having served the fifteen years which qualified him for a pension. Moreover he viewed with distaste the forthcoming 'reforms' embodied in the Judicature Acts of 1873–5. In March 1873 he was sworn a member of the privy council, occasionally attending its judicial sittings.

> A very popular figure was lost to Westminster Hall when Sir John Byles ceased to ride down daily to the judges' entrance on his cob, affectionately nick-named 'Bills' by the wits of the junior bar, who thus fitted a new meaning to 'Byles on Bills'.

Byles was twice married, first in 1828 to Hannah, a daughter of James Foster of Biggleswade, who died shortly thereafter, in 1829. His second wife, Emma, daughter of James Weld of Royston, whom he married in 1836, also predeceased him, in 1872; they had several children. Byles lived in Prince's Gardens, South Kensington, and at Harefield House near Uxbridge, where he died on 3 February 1884 in his eighty-fourth year.

GARETH H. JONES and VIVIENNE JONES

Sources *The Times* (5 Feb 1884) • [W. D. I. Foulkes], *A generation of judges* (1886) • P. Atiyah, *The rise and fall of freedom of contract* (1979) • E. Foss, *Biographia juridica: a biographical dictionary of the judges of England … 1066–1870* (1870) • *Solicitors' Journal*, 28 (1883–4), 278 • *Men of the time* (1879) • A. W. B. Simpson, *Leading cases in the common law* (1995) • *'Hole v. Barlow', Comyn's digest: action on case for nuisance* (1858), 4 CBNS 334 • *Bucks Chronicle* (1850) • Boase, *Mod. Eng. biog.*

Wealth at death £201,446 5*s*. 8*d*.: probate, 25 March 1884, *CGPLA Eng. & Wales*

Bylot, Robert (*fl.* 1610–1616), navigator, is first mentioned as a mariner on the *Discovery* (55 tons) in the expedition in search of the north-west passage under Henry Hudson, paid for by Sir Dudley Digges, Sir Thomas Smith, and John Wolstenholme, avid promoters of overseas trade. The expedition sailed from London on 17 April 1610. The boat was swept into Hudson Strait and sailed west towards Hudson Bay. Bylot and others landed near Digges Island at the western end of the strait. Shortly after this Bylot was raised to the rank of mate, the erstwhile mate having been degraded for inciting the crew to disobedience. Bylot's loyalty to Hudson, and the knowledge that they were the only two navigators capable of getting the ship home, kept the restive crew in check, but in the spring of 1611 Hudson degraded Bylot to the rank of seaman and made another man mate, losing Bylot's loyalty and thus removing the last check on the mutineers among the crew. In June 1611 mutineers cast away the captain and some of his followers. They made Bylot mate once again and he piloted the boat to Digges Island and thence to Ireland and finally London.

Bylot's skill and courage first as mate and, after the death of the chief mutineer, Henry Greene, leader of the crew, brought the eight survivors home. On his return he claimed that he had played no part in the mutiny, a claim which perhaps sits ill with the mutineers' having made him mate: but he had undoubtedly saved the ship and the survivors and this made it difficult to charge him with mutiny. This in turn gave protection to the other mutineers, as did the enthusiastic reception for the geographical results of their trip with its hope of finding a north-west passage through Hudson Bay.

Bylot sailed again for Hudson Bay on 14 April 1612 with Sir Thomas Button in the *Resolution* and the *Discovery*, fitted out by the same three men as was the 1610 expedition. They wintered at Port Nelson on the east side of Hudson Bay, having vainly sought a navigable eastern outlet to the bay, and returned in August 1613 to a somewhat muted reception. On 26 July 1612 Bylot, along with Digges, Smith, and Wolstenholme, had become a charter member of the Company of the Merchant Discoverers of the North-West Passage, known as the North-West Passage Company.

Bylot, accompanied by Button's cousin and companion William Gibbons, sailed again in the *Discovery* in March 1614 for the north-west passage. Very little is known of this voyage. They appear to have run into very bad ice off the Labrador coast and spent ten weeks icebound at 'Gibbons his Hole' (about lat. 58° N) before returning home, having achieved nothing.

Despite the lack of results from this voyage Bylot was by this time the most experienced Arctic navigator in the country. On 18 April 1615 he set off again in command of the *Discovery* with William Baffin as his mate in a voyage again paid for by Digges, Smith, and Wolstenholme. By exploring the coasts of Southampton Island, they did much to show that Hudson Bay had no navigable western outlet. They returned home in the autumn of 1615. On 26 March 1616 Bylot, again with Baffin as his pilot, and again with funds from the same three men plus Sir Francis Jones, sailed in the *Discovery* for the north-west passage. They reached 77°45′, which remained the furthest north explored for 236 years. Sailing north around Baffin Bay they found Lancaster Sound, which, however, they did not recognize as the entrance to the north-west passage and the significance of which was also lost on subsequent explorers. Baffin is normally given credit for the scientific and geographical parts of the voyages, but Bylot contributed to their success by his skilful navigation and captaincy. Baffin himself described him as 'a man well experienced that way' (Markham, 111). Nothing more is known of him.

The voyages on which Bylot sailed brought back no knowledge of immediate commercial value, although Hudson Bay was later a focus of trade, but they were of considerable geographical interest. The search for a north-west passage as a route to the Indies was abandoned fairly soon after Bylot's time, but it remained a scientific and strategic goal well into the twentieth century.

ELIZABETH BAIGENT

Sources C. R. Markham, ed., *The voyages of William Baffin, 1612–1622*, Hakluyt Society, 63 (1881) • G. M. Asher, ed., *Henry Hudson, the navigator*, Hakluyt Society, 1st ser., 27 (1860) • L. H. Neatby, 'Hudson, Henry', *DCB*, vol. 1 • L. H. Neatby, 'Bylot, Robert', *DCB*, vol. 1 • A. Eames, 'Button, Sir Thomas', *DCB*, vol. 1 • E. S. Dodge, 'Baffin,

William', *DCB*, vol. 1 • L. H. Neatby, *In quest of the north-west passage* (1958) • E. S. Dodge, *Northwest by sea* (1961) • *DNB*

Byng, Andrew (1574–1652), Church of England clergyman and Hebraist, was born at Cambridge, the second son of Thomas *Byng (*d.* 1599), regius professor of law and master of Clare College, Cambridge, and his wife, Catherine Randolph or Rendell (1553–1627). He matriculated from Clare in 1587, graduated BA from Peterhouse in 1591, was made a fellow of that college in 1592, and proceeded MA in 1594. His godfather Archbishop John Whitgift made him his chaplain, but decided that Byng was too young to succeed his father as master of Clare following the latter's death in 1599. However, Byng rapidly gained preferment. Vicar of Everton, Huntingdonshire, briefly from 1599, in 1600 he secured the rectory of Broughton, Buckinghamshire, and a prebend at York. Two years later he proceeded BD. In 1605 he became a prebendary of Southwell and in 1606 he proceeded DD and became subdean at York. Meanwhile he was chosen by the king as one of the translators for the Authorized Version of the Bible.

In 1618, despite a personal recommendation from the king, Byng again failed to gain a college headship when the fellows of Corpus Christi, Cambridge, elected instead a former fellow, Samuel Walsall. However, on 30 March that year he became archdeacon of Norwich, and about that time secured the rectory of Winterton, Norfolk. In 1627 he added to his other livings the sinecure rectory of East Dereham in the same county. By the summer of 1631 he was implementing at least some aspects of the Laudian liturgical programme: the churchwardens in his archdeaconry were ordered to place their communion tables at the east end of the chancel. His visitation articles of 1638, his only publication, revealed the same priorities as his then bishop, Matthew Wren. Yet in 1640 he was among those archdeacons who objected to the continuation of convocation beyond the parliamentary sitting, and on 28 May he lodged a formal protest against this and against the formulation of the canons. He subsequently lost most, if not all, of his appointments. He died in March 1652 at Winterton, where Nicholas Howlet was then rector, and was buried there on 22 March. He was probably unmarried. NICHOLAS KEENE

Sources Wood, *Ath. Oxon.*, 1st edn, 1.788, 815 • F. Blomefield and C. Parkin, *An essay towards a topographical history of the county of Norfolk*, [2nd edn], 11 vols. (1805–10), vol. 3, p. 641; vol. 11, p. 198 • W. Hargrove, *History and description of the ancient city of York*, 2 vols. (1818), appx, lxxvii • *N&Q*, 3rd ser., 4 (1862), 228 • CUL, Baker MS, xxiv, 349 • T. A. Walker, *A biographical register of Peterhouse men*, 2 (1930), 129 • Venn, *Alum. Cant.* • J. Davies, *The Caroline captivity of the church: Charles I and the remoulding of Anglicanism, 1625–1641* (1992), 219, 255 • K. Fincham, ed., *Visitation articles and injunctions of the early Stuart church*, 2 (1998), xxiii, 270–71 • *Walker rev.* • *DNB*

Byng, George, first Viscount Torrington (1663–1733), naval officer, was born on 27 January 1663, the eldest son of John Byng (*d.* 1683) of a family settled for many centuries at Wrotham, Kent, and Philadelphia Johnson (*d.* 1688) of Loans, Surrey. Having got into financial difficulties, his father was required to part with the Wrotham estate in 1666, and moved to Ireland, where he appears to have

George Byng, first Viscount Torrington (1663–1733), attrib. Jeremiah Davison, *c.*1725

engaged in further unsuccessful speculations as a result of which he lost his remaining money. In 1672 he returned to England, apparently to escape his creditors. During the next few years George was raised and educated by the countess of Middleton, a friend of the family.

Early career, 1678–1687 When George was fifteen his father applied to Lord Peterborough, who presented him to the duke of York. Shortly thereafter, on 31 May 1678, he received the king's letter to be a volunteer on the *Swallow* (Captain Joseph Haddock), carrying troops to Flanders. On 28 November he was transferred to the *Reserve* (Captain David Lloyd) and in June 1679 to the *Mary Rose* (Captain Charles Talbot), which sailed to Newfoundland, then on to the Mediterranean, and finally convoyed merchantmen from Tangier to England.

The *Mary Rose* was paid off on 8 June 1680, and in the following April Byng was entered as a volunteer on the *Phoenix*, commanded by Captain William Blagg. The *Phoenix* was immediately sent back to Tangier, where Byng's maternal uncle, Colonel Johnson, was on friendly terms with Colonel Percy Kirke, the garrison's commander-in-chief. On learning that Byng was dissatisfied with his captain's 'ill-temper' Kirke offered him a cadetship in his 2nd Tangier regiment. This he gladly accepted, and he was discharged from the *Phoenix* on 10 May 1681. Four months later he was appointed ensign (10 September), and early in 1683 Kirke promoted him lieutenant in Colonel Charles Churchill's company. Byng's rapid promotion caused some consternation among his former superiors, and in response Kirke appointed him lieutenant of the galley *Half*, which attended on the garrison, and shortly afterwards to the acting command of the ketch *Deptford*. At Kirke's request, and by order of Lord Dartmouth, he was given a commission as 'lieutenant in the sea-service' later that year, and appointed to the *Oxford* (Captain John Tyrell) on 23 February 1684. On the arrival of the fleet in England the officers and men of the *Oxford* were turned over to the *Phoenix*, fitting for a voyage to Newfoundland. On news that Bombay was in rebellion, her orders were changed to the East Indies, for which she finally sailed from Plymouth on 28 November 1684; she arrived at St Jago, Cape Verde Islands, on 5 January 1685 and at Bombay on 10 June.

The work at Bombay consisted chiefly in suppressing European 'interlopers' and aggressive Indian pirates, by whom Byng was seriously wounded in one confrontation. Tyrell's ill health resulted in Byng's being put in command and provided him with an opportunity to cultivate the goodwill of Sir Josiah Child, the president of Surat and governor of Bombay. On their return to Plymouth (24 July 1687) Child offered him the command of an East India Company ship, which Byng declined, and when the *Phoenix* was paid off he rejoined his regiment, then quartered at Bristol.

The patronage of Admiral Russell, 1688–1701 In May 1688 Byng, still a lieutenant, was appointed to the *Mordaunt* (Captain John Ashby) and in September he followed him to the *Defiance*. In early October, or possibly before, Byng and Captain Matthew Aylmer were involved with a group of conspirators from the army, headed by the duke of Ormond and Colonel Kirke, to secure promises from several influential naval captains not to oppose William III. On Kirke's suggestion and recommendation Byng was particularly involved with the approaches to his own captain and close friend, Captain Woolfran Cornwall. After William's landing at Torbay in November, Byng was deputed by these captains to convey their appeal for recognition and their assurances of goodwill and obedience to the prince. On 28 November Byng found William and Admiral Edward Russell at Sherborne, where the prince 'promised that he would take particular care to remember him' (Laughton, 32), and entrusted him with a reply to the officers of the fleet, and a more confidential letter to Lord Dartmouth, which Byng gave to Aylmer to deliver, asking Dartmouth to join his fleet to Rear-Admiral Edward Herbert's, assuring Dartmouth that he would retain his seniority. This was the turning point of Byng's fortune. Apparently further encouraged by Russell's leadership and the fact that the officers of his own army regiment had also defected to William, Byng had judiciously chosen the winning side. On 22 December 1688 he was appointed captain of the *Constant Warwick*, from which in April 1689 he was removed to the *Reserve*; and on 15 May he moved to the *Dover*, in which he served during the summer in the main fleet under Herbert (now earl of Torrington) and during the autumn and winter in independent cruising, taking several prizes. On 6 May 1690 he was appointed to the *Hope* (70 guns), which was one of the Red squadron under Vice-Admiral Sir John Ashby in the unfortunate action off Beachy Head. In September he was moved into the *Duchess*, which was paid off six weeks later. In November, his naval career now well-established, he resigned his commission in the army to his brother John, and in January 1691 he was appointed to the *Royal Oak* (70 guns), in which he continued until 17 September 1692, but played no part in the victories at Barfleur and La Hogue. On 5 March 1690 he had married Margaret (1670–1756), daughter of James Master of East Langden, Kent, at St Paul's, Covent Garden, London; the couple had a large family of eleven sons, including John *Byng (*bap.* 1704, *d.* 1737), naval officer, and four daughters, including Sarah *Osborn, letter writer. In September 1692 Sir John Ashby hoisted his flag on board the *Albemarle*, to which Byng was appointed second captain, and which he paid off in November 1693. In the spring of 1693 he was offered the post of first captain to the joint admirals, but refused it in a gesture of solidarity to his friend Admiral Russell, then in disgrace. However, he did accept a similar offer made in December 1693 by Russell, who was then commander-in-chief in the Mediterranean. Byng continued in the flagship *Britannia* until May 1696 when he was appointed one of the commissioners for the newly established registry of seamen, an attempted alternative scheme for manning the navy; he held this office until its abolition in 1699.

Mediterranean and North Sea service, 1701–1717 In 1701 Byng was nominated secretary to the earl of Pembroke, the newly appointed lord high admiral. This would have effectively made Byng commander-in-chief, for Pembroke was neither a sailor nor a soldier, and had no experience of commanding men. However, William III's death and the subsequent rise of the Churchill family, critics of Russell, undermined his chances of securing the office. Byng suffered further setbacks under the new regime. His request for a flag, which he considered due to him after having been so long first captain to the admiral of the fleet, was refused, as was his application to be put on the half pay of his rank. Instead he was plainly told that he must either go to sea as a private captain or resign his commission. Unable, for financial reasons, to quit his profession, he accepted the command of the *Nassau* (70 guns) on 29 June 1702. In July he joined the fleet under Sir Cloudesley Shovell which, after looking for the French under Châteaurenault, went south towards Cape Finisterre. On 10 October Byng, having been separated from the fleet, fell in with Sir George Rooke, but was at once dispatched in search of Shovell, with orders for him to join Rooke with immediate effect. Knowing that the attack on Vigo was imminent, Rooke refused Byng's plea to stay and participate in the action. Though Byng made all haste to carry the orders to Shovell, he rejoined the fleet only on the evening of 12 October with an advance group of five ships and a fireship while the attack was in progress. At that point nothing remained but to complete the work of destruction, which he joined under the direction of Sir Stafford Fairborne. In the days following, Rooke employed Byng as an unofficial staff officer, sending him to post warships off Bayonne, serving as a liaison officer with the duke of Ormond, and supervising the re-embarkation of the troops. On Rooke's departure Byng was left with three ships to defend the rear.

On 1 March 1703 Byng was promoted rear-admiral of the red; he was sent out to the Mediterranean in the *Ranelagh* as third in command under Shovell. While there he was detached with a small squadron to Algiers, where, on 28 October, he succeeded in renewing the peace treaty which provided for the protection of English commerce. In November he returned to England, arriving in the channel just in time to feel some of the strength of the great storm, without sustaining any serious damage. In 1704, still in the *Ranelagh*, he commanded, as rear-admiral of the red squadron, in the fleet under Rooke in the Mediterranean. With the immediate command of the detachment engaged in the bombardment and capture of Gibraltar, and from his position in the centre of the line of battle, Byng played an important part in the battle of Malaga. Following his return home he was knighted by Queen Anne on 22 October 'as a testimony of her high approbation of his behaviour in the late action' (Laughton, 166). On 3 January 1705 he was advanced to the rank of vice-admiral of the blue, and in May he was elected MP in the second seat for Plymouth, which he held until raised to a peerage in 1721. In the summer of 1705 he commanded a squadron in the channel with his flag in the *Royal Anne* to defend trade, and later, in the Bay of Biscay, providing protection to the expedition under Shovell and Peterborough. Having become ill in late August, Byng passed his command to Sir John Jennings and went ashore. After his recovery he took up duties as commander-in-chief at Portsmouth. In March 1706 he sailed for Lisbon and the Mediterranean, where, under the command of Sir John Leake, he took part in the operations on the Spanish coast to prevent the French from recapturing Barcelona in April, bombarding Alicante on 20 June, capturing Ibiza and Majorca in September, and remaining at Lisbon with a squadron to protect trade during the winter. In January 1707 Byng briefly joined Shovell to assist in landing 7000 troops at Alicante; he then returned to Lisbon. After being joined by ten Dutch ships under Vice-Admiral Philip van der Goes, Byng sailed with twelve English ships to Alicante where, on 21 April, he received word of the defeat of the earl of Galway's allied force at Almanza. After supporting allied positions at Alicante, Valencia, and Denia, Byng sailed to Toulon as second in command to Shovell during the siege which took place between June and August 1707. On his homeward voyage he narrowly escaped being killed with Shovell off the Isles of Scilly in October 1707. In January of the following year Byng was promoted admiral of the blue, and appointed to command the squadron in the North Sea for the protection of the British coast against the threatened French invasion. On news that a French squadron with the Pretender had slipped out of Dunkirk, Byng's squadron put to sea in the midst of a gale on 21 March and sighted the French squadron under Forbin off the entrance of the Firth of Forth on 24 March; one ship, the *Salisbury*, was captured, while the remainder escaped to Dunkirk. In England the question was at once raised whether Byng had done all that he might. Finally the discontent subsided, and the House of Commons passed a vote of thanks to Prince George of Denmark, the lord high admiral, for his prompt response to the events of March. In the wake of the debate Byng was presented with the freedom of the city of Edinburgh. The queen offered to appoint him one of the prince's naval council. This, however, he declined as a supporter of the whig junta, thereby disappointing Godolphin's attempts to ameliorate the party conflict and increasing the aversion of the queen, the duke of Marlborough, and Marlborough's brother, George Churchill.

After returning to sea in May Byng cruised to prevent the juncture of the French Dunkirk and Brest squadrons. With General Earle he made plans for an amphibious invasion during the summer on the north coast of France, but after false starts he eventually landed the troops at Ostend and continued on to the Mediterranean. In October he carried the Queen of Portugal to Lisbon. After being promoted admiral of the white on 21 December 1708 he was commander-in-chief in the Mediterranean until returning to England in the autumn of 1709. In November his old chief Russell (now earl of Orford) was appointed first lord of the Admiralty. His influence was sufficient to overcome the court's prejudice against Byng, who was appointed a commissioner of the Admiralty. Although Orford's term of office lasted only ten months, Byng continued at the Admiralty until January 1714 and then, with Orford's reappointment in the following October after the accession of George I, returned and remained there until 30 September 1721. In these years John Macky described him as being 'a fair complexioned man' and 'one of the best sailors in England and a fine gentleman in everything else; of a good family and estate in Bedfordshire, understands all the several branches of the Navy thoroughly' (*Memoirs of the Secret Services*, 175). In 1715 he was appointed to command the fleet for the defence of the coast, and succeeded in stopping and preventing all supplies to the adherents of the Pretender, while working in close co-operation with the British ambassador in Paris, Lord Stair. In acknowledgement of his success the king created him a baronet on 15 November 1715, and gave him a diamond ring of considerable value. In 1717 the British government used the Görtz affair and the associated popular fear that Sweden was supporting a Jacobite invasion of Britain as the pretext to send Byng and his squadron to the Baltic. The real and more complex functions of the fleet were to control privateering activity against British trade and to stabilize northern Europe in a manner that would allow the allies to implement the treaty of Utrecht and to control Spanish aspirations. At the same time the British fleet indirectly supported the Hanoverian policy objectives of George I in trying to remove Russian troops from Mecklenberg and to obtain control of Bremen and Verden.

The Sicilian campaign, 1718–1720 On 14 March 1718 Byng was advanced to the rank of admiral of the fleet, and was, in pursuance of the objects of the pending Quadruple Alliance, sent to the Mediterranean in command of a fleet to prevent a Spanish invasion of Italy or Sicily. With his flag in the *Barfleur* he sailed from Spithead on 14 June, and on 31 July he anchored before Naples. He conferred with the viceroy, and received more exact intelligence of the movements of the Spaniards, who had just begun to besiege Messina. He sailed from Naples during the night of 5 August and arrived off the entrance of the strait of Messina three days later. From this position he wrote to the Spanish commander, proposing a two-month postponement of combat to allow their respective governments to attempt to conclude a lasting peace. The refusal of the offer and this flagrant rejection of the objectives of the Quadruple Alliance led Byng to engage the Spanish, even though war had not been declared.

Early on the morning of 9 August 1718 the British fleet entered the strait; before noon their advance ships had made out the Spaniards under Gaztañeta, drawn up in a line of battle. Byng followed the Spaniards as they moved away in a light north-easterly wind. He detached his four fastest ships to maintain contact with the Spanish during the following night. Next morning, when the British fleet was nearly up with the Spanish, the Spanish rear-admiral, the marqués de Mardi, separated from the main fleet with six ships of the line, and the galleys, fireships, and bomb-vessels, and stood in for the Sicilian shore. Byng ordered Captain George Walton in the *Canterbury*, with five other vessels, to pursue and to destroy them. Taking the remainder of the British fleet, Byng drew towards the main Spanish fleet and, demonstrating his tactical flexibility, ordered a general chase in a loose line-ahead formation, allowing some ships to be on one side of the Spanish, and others on the opposite side, and expecting his captains to engage individual ships of similar size. During a dramatic running engagement in the afternoon Byng's brother-in-law, Captain Streynsham Master in the *Superb* (60 guns), captured Gaztañeta and his flagship, *San Felipe el Reale* (74 guns). The encounters between Byng's fleet and the Spanish took place in a variety of engagements along the east coast of Sicily, extending south from the strait of Messina and to some 6 leagues east of Cape Passaro. In the final tally Byng had succeeded in capturing eleven ships and destroying three more of the original twenty-one Spanish ships. This was a remarkable success by any standard and a major blow to Spain's ambitions, putting an immediate end to her long-term plans for creating a wider European league against Britain and, for the immediate future, isolating the Spanish army in Sicily. Despite this, the Spanish government under Cardinal Alberoni declared war against the allies. During the following two years Byng remained in Mediterranean waters supporting the alliance. Finally, following Alberoni's dismissal, the new Spanish government began to come to terms.

Later career and final years, 1720–1733 In August 1720 the Spaniards evacuated Sicily and embarked for Barcelona. Byng, having convoyed the Piedmontese troops to Cagliari, acted as the British plenipotentiary at the conferences held there for settling the surrender of Sardinia to the duke of Savoy who, in acknowledgement of Byng's services in delivering him to his new lands in the *Blenheim*, presented him with his picture set in diamonds. On his return home in October 1729 he was appointed rear-admiral of Great Britain and treasurer of the navy; and in the following January he was sworn of the privy council. On 21 September 1721 he was raised to the peerage with the title Baron Byng of Southill, taking the name of the Bedfordshire estate he had purchased in 1693. On 27 May 1725 he was both created Viscount Torrington and invested one of the original knights companion of the Order of the Garter (installed on 17 June), when George I revived that order. Following the accession of George II Byng was appointed first lord of the Admiralty on 2 August 1727. In earlier years Admiral Russell had been a patron to both Byng and Robert Walpole. In his memoirs of Walpole's government Lord Hervey suggests that the prime minister had removed Byng's predecessor, Lord Berkeley, for political reasons and that Byng was 'pitched upon for this post not so much from desiring to show him favour as to embitter Lord Berkeley' (Hervey, 1.38). Byng held this office until his death from 'epidemical distemper' aged sixty-nine on 17 January 1733. He was buried at Southill, Bedfordshire, on 23 January. His wife survived him, dying on 1 April 1756 at the age of eighty-six.

The victory which Byng won off Cape Passaro, by its extraordinary completeness, gave him perhaps an exaggerated reputation as a naval commander. Nevertheless his uniform success in all his undertakings bears out Thomas Corbett's warm praise of a firm, straightforward, and impartial man who devoted all of his efforts to any service entrusted to him and who 'left nothing to fortune that could be accomplished by foresight and application' (Corbett, 32). John B. Hattendorf

Sources *Memoirs relating to the Lord Torrington*, ed. J. K. Laughton, CS, new ser., 46 (1889) • P. Le Fevre, 'Tangier, the navy and its connection with the Glorious Revolution, 1688', *Mariner's Mirror*, 73 (1987), 187–190 • P. Le Fevre, 'John Tyrrell, 1646–1692: a Restoration naval captain', *Mariner's Mirror*, 70 (1984), 149–60 • *The Byng papers: selected from the letters and papers of Admiral Sir George Byng, first Viscount Torrington, and of his son, Admiral the Hon. John Byng*, ed. B. Tunstall, 3 vols., Navy RS, 67–8, 70 (1930–32) • J. Ehrman, *The navy in the war of William III, 1689–1697* (1953) • E. B. Powley, *The naval side of King William's war* (1972) • J. D. Davies, *Gentlemen and tarpaulins: the officers and men of the Restoration navy* (1991) • W. E. May, 'The *Phoenix* in India, 1684–1687', *Mariner's Mirror*, 57 (1971), 193–202 • *The journal of Sir George Rooke, 1700–1704*, ed. J. B. Hattendorf, Navy RS [forthcoming] • *The Marlborough–Godolphin correspondence*, ed. H. L. Snyder, 3 vols. (1975) • J. B. Hattendorf, 'Byng: Passaro', *Great battles of the Royal Navy*, ed. E. Grove (1994) • J. B. Hattendorf, 'Admiral Sir George Byng and Cape Passaro', in *Guerres et paix, 1660–1815*, Service Historique de la Marine (Vincennes, 1987) • G. Byng, 'Victory at Cape Passaro, 1718', *British naval documents, 1204–1960*, ed. J. B. Hattendorf and others, Navy RS, 131 (1993), 360–62 • John, Lord Hervey, *Some materials towards memoirs of the reign of King George II*, ed. R. Sedgwick, 3 vols. (1931) • *Memoirs of the secret services of John Macky*, ed. A. R. (1733) • T. Corbett, *An account of the expedition of the British fleet to Sicily* (1739) • *DNB*

Archives BL, memoirs, Add. MS 31958 • NMM, letters • priv. coll., Wortham Park, Barnet, corresp. and family papers | Beds. & Luton ARS, letters to Sir John Osborne • CAC Cam., corresp. with Thomas Erle • Glos. RO, letters to Thomas Reynolds • NA Scot., letters to Lord Leven

Likenesses attrib. J. Davison, *c*.1725, NPG [*see illus.*] • J. Davison, oils, 1734, NMM • J. Faber, mezzotint (after G. Kneller), BM, NPG •

G. Kneller, oils, NMM • G. Kneller, oils, probably Wrotham Park, Barnet

Wealth at death left to eldest son: will, PRO, PROB 11/660 fols. 9–12

Byng, John (*bap.* 1704, *d.* 1757), naval officer, the fifth surviving son of the fifteen children of George *Byng, first Viscount Torrington (1663–1733), and Margaret Master (1670–1756), was born at Southill, Bedfordshire, where he was baptized on 29 October 1704. In March 1718 he went to sea under the care of his uncle, Captain Streynsham *Master of the *Superb*. The ship played a leading role in the battle off Cape Passaro and thus at fourteen John participated in his father's great victory. He then served in the *Orford*, *Newcastle*, *Nassau*, and *Torbay*, passing his lieutenant's examination on 31 December 1722. After service in the *Dover* he was promoted lieutenant of the *Solebay* on 20 June 1723 and moved to the *Superb* as second lieutenant in 1724.

From lieutenant to vice-admiral When the *Superb* was ordered to the West Indies Byng resigned (29 March 1726), but within a month he became fourth lieutenant of the *Burford*, in which he continued on the home station and at Cadiz where, on 26 May 1727, he was discharged to return to England. That summer his father became first lord of the Admiralty. On 8 August 1727 John was promoted captain of the *Gibraltar* (20 guns) and a year later he moved to the *Princess Louisa* (60 guns), serving in the Mediterranean in both. When the latter was paid off at Woolwich he was immediately appointed to the *Falmouth* (50 guns) and spent the next four years either at Port Mahon or in bringing money there from Lisbon to pay the garrison. Upon leaving the *Falmouth* in June 1735 he at last spent some time in England. His service had been profitable, comfortable, safe (the *Superb* joined Admiral Hosier's squadron), unchallenging, and uninterrupted. As the son of the most influential man in the navy Byng had got what he wanted.

Byng took command of the *Augusta* in June 1738, moved to the *Portland* in April 1739, and then went to the *Sunderland* (60 guns), in which during the autumn of 1740 he commanded a detachment of three ships that watched Cadiz. In April 1741 he requested assignment to escort the trade home 'to gett a better ship' (BL, Egerton MS 2529), and late in the year he was given the *Sutherland* (50 guns) in which, in 1742, he accompanied the fishing fleet to Newfoundland. After taking two prizes he arrived on 17 June to administer the governorship; not everyone was pleased by his honest rectitude. Soon after returning he was appointed to the *Captain* (70 guns) and he cruised in the Bay of Biscay in summer 1743 with two other ships under his command. He briefly commanded the *Winchester* before being given the *St George* (90 guns). She was assigned to the channel under Sir John Norris but also served in spring 1744 as Sir Charles Hardy's flagship in the squadron that saw the victualling convoy to Lisbon.

Byng's promotion to rear-admiral came on 8 August 1745. He was immediately sent to the frigate *Kinsale* to command a flotilla for keeping watch on the Flanders coast, and soon afterwards he was ordered to the east coast of Scotland with a small squadron for assisting the army against the Jacobite rising. In 1746 he served on the courts martial of Admirals Richard Lestock and Thomas Mathews, after which he was appointed second-in-command to Vice-Admiral Henry Medley in the Mediterranean. In replying to the first lord he accepted but said that he did not think himself equal to the task.

Although initially directed to go overland to Genoa, Byng went out in the *Superb* and joined Medley in mid-April 1747. Medley's main responsibility was to help Austrian forces in Italy, especially by denying to the French army the Riviera's coastal roads and waters for resupply. It helped that the Austrians had garrisoned the Lérins Islands and Byng was assigned to prevent their recapture by the French. Unlike his predecessor he took no offensive risks inshore to disturb the enemy's amphibious preparations, and he told Medley that it would be 'impossible' for his force to defend the islands, adding however: 'but you may depend I will do everything that lies in my power to protect them' (*Du Cane MSS*, 177). When a gale blew his ships briefly off station French troops crossed and conquered. Admiral Medley died on 5 August and Byng, already promoted vice-admiral, became commander-in-chief. He concentrated on continuing the Riviera blockade.

The peace of 1748 brought Byng home by October. Settled in his London house at 41 Hill Street, off Berkeley Square, with a small fortune from his flag share of prizes, he set about buying land near Barnet, Hertfordshire, to build a country house. He named it Wrotham Park (after the Kentish locale of the Byng family) and spent happy hours not only attending to the building project but also, beginning in 1751, in quiet company with a mistress. Byng was a shy man, gentlemanly but inclined to be haughty and off-putting. His circle of friends was unusually narrow for a naval officer and he never married. With Mrs Susannah Hickson (*d.* 1755), a widow of humble means, not young, he was clearly happy. In January 1751 he became MP for Rochester (he had been considered for this Admiralty seat in 1746 but was assigned to the Mediterranean instead).

His quiet comfort was ended by the pre-war hostilities of 1755. Byng was selected to take over command of the western squadron and hoisted his flag in the *Ramillies* (90 guns) at Spithead on 28 September. His orders were to arrest all French ships and crews and send them to an English port for retention. Cruising west of Ushant in that season was arduous, cold, and physically punishing, but Byng did his duty efficiently and without complaint, and did not elect to come in until terrible weather in mid-November 'almost crippled all the ships' (PRO, ADM 1/88, 19 Nov 1755). Back at Spithead on 23 November, he was pleased to see that the Admiralty had already ordered the squadron's return. Lord Anson, always mindful of the western squadron, must have taken favourable notice of his performance. Sadly, a few days after his return to London Mrs Hickson died.

The Minorca mission In March 1756 Byng was promoted admiral of the red; he sailed from Spithead on 6 April with ten ships of the line under orders to try to prevent the French from capturing Port Mahon. This mission was to end in his arrest, conviction by court martial, and death by firing squad.

From the outset Byng believed that he had been sent out too late with too little, and it was true. The Admiralty, guided by Lord Anson, had underestimated the strength of the Toulon squadron and refused to believe that the French would actually attack Minorca. Although Byng spent more than a week closing up his residences and getting to Portsmouth, their lordships did not criticize, and they gave low priority to getting his squadron manned until, rather desperately in the last days of March (there was further intelligence), they urged him to sail immediately. Even then, some fusiliers were assigned to his complements which, it was implied, should also be put ashore for garrisoning. Further intelligence soon made it obvious that additional ships were required, but six weeks passed before Rear-Admiral Thomas Broderick was ordered from Spithead with five.

Byng's passage to Gibraltar met with contrary winds and took almost a month. Upon arrival he took Commodore George Edgcumbe's ships (one of 60 guns, one of 50 guns, and four frigates) under his command. Edgcumbe, who had come from Port Mahon, told him that the French had landed a large army on Minorca. Byng carried explicit orders to transport a detachment from the Gibraltar garrison to Port Mahon if the latter were threatened, but General Thomas Fowke fed him with misinformation regarding the ability of St Philip's Castle to hold out and an army council of war concluded that the troops should not go. Knowing, however, that Byng's orders were clear, Fowke offered to let him take the detachment anyway. Fatefully, Byng declined the offer and wrote a letter (4 May 1756) to London explaining his decision: he had arrived too late; 700 more troops thrown into the fortress would 'only enable it to hold out a little longer' and would be pointlessly sacrificed; a far larger force was necessary to 'dislodge the French, or raise the siege'. He also mentioned: 'If I should fail in the relief of Port Mahon, I shall look on the security and protection of Gibraltar as my next object' (Tunstall, 84–5). A French attack on Gibraltar was clearly not possible, since all French forces in the Mediterranean were committed at Minorca. Fowke and his staff had deceived him outrageously. Yet Byng was disposed to be deceived. Upon reading his orders at Spithead on 1 April he had replied that although he would do all he could against the enemy 'if they should make an attempt in the island of Minorca' (he clearly understood his main mission), he would think himself 'most fortunate' to succeed (ibid., 53).

When Byng's letter from Gibraltar arrived in London on 31 May it was known via Paris that the French had landed. But it was also understood that St Philip's Castle was not easy to besiege and could probably hold out if adequately garrisoned. The news that Byng had sailed without the detachment was therefore extremely upsetting. Some ministers hoped that Byng would beat the French in a naval battle and save their reputations, but George II was sure that this would not happen. He reacted angrily to Byng's dispatch, saying, 'This man will not fight!' Three days later the ministers received a report, again from Paris, that a naval battle had been fought but without a British victory. Henry Fox, secretary of state, suspected the worst: 'I doubt not', he wrote to the duke of Devonshire, 'our first news will be that Byng is returned to Gibraltar, and that a council of war says he did wisely. The consternation, anger and shame of everybody here on this occasion is extreme' (Ilchester, 1.330). The ministers resolved immediately to supersede all the participating generals and admirals without awaiting Byng's report of the battle.

The twelfth article of war under which Byng was later tried for his life referred specifically to a naval engagement. The court found him guilty of the charge that

> he did withdraw or keep back, and did not do his utmost to take, seize, and destroy the ships of the French King, which it was his duty to have engaged, and to assist such of his Majesty's ships as were engaged in fight with the French ships, which it was his duty to have assisted.

Was this finding justified? The record of testimony is consistent on many points. On the morning of 20 May 1756 the two squadrons sighted and headed towards each other, thirteen British ships of the line against twelve French, but the French had heavier guns. With help from a wind shift Byng won the contest for the weather gauge. His ships had to reverse course individually to attack, and the flagship wound up in the rear, third from last. When he hoisted the signal to engage, the lead ships (Rear-Admiral Temple West's division) turned downwind and battled at close quarters, as Byng expected of them even though the rear, approaching the enemy line at an angle, was unable to participate. When the sixth ship of the van division, the *Intrepid*, turned down wind and began to engage, her foretop mast was soon brought down by enemy fire and she spun out of control. The witnesses did not fully agree on why the next ships in line failed to bypass her. There was a stoppage, and to avoid collisions Byng's flagship and others of the rear division backed their sails. When they finally moved in to engage in late afternoon, the French squadron turned downwind and sailed away. The marquis de la Galissonnière had handled his squadron with intelligence and skill. He ordered his ships to move forward after discharging their broadsides; they could thus maul the British van while mitigating their opponents' advantage in rapidity of fire.

Byng's plan of attack was advantageous in theory but precarious in practice. Tacking late and attempting an angled line of approach was bound to leave the ships of the rear at a distance when the van became engaged. Everything depended upon an uninterrupted advance, but disruption was a likely hazard, and Byng, having chosen to fight in two divisions rather than three, was not near the centre where he could readily deal with it. The plan was ill-advised, but not censurable. Byng's misconduct lay, rather, in his failure to take remedial action.

Observing the van hotly engaged and the rear's slow approach, Arthur Gardiner, Byng's flag captain, suggested that he turn the *Ramillies* downwind, remarking that the other ships of the rear would surely imitate. Byng replied that Admiral Mathews had been cashiered for doing that (a false recollection of the findings). In any case he could have solved the problem by temporarily lowering the line-ahead signal (Creswell, 102). Soon after came the stoppage. The admiral expected the captains in the centre to work around it: he gave no signals to direct them. And so, except for one ship, the rear division failed to engage. The 90-gun *Ramillies* fired uselessly, and the two ships behind her never fired at all. In the last five ships (counting the *Deptford* which Byng kept in the rear in reserve) the total number of killed and wounded was zero; in the ships ahead two captains were killed. A balladeer later made the most of this:

> West gallantly charged in the van, Sir; Without dismay or fear;
> But Byng who would not risk a man, Sir, Kept cautiously snug in the rear.
> Sing, sing, great Rear-Admiral Byng.
> (Tunstall, 192)

Byng claimed victory because the French had gone off, but after repairing battle damage he made no attempt to carry out his mission. He did not convey the hundred regimental recruits and officers who were aboard his ships to the sea gate of St Philip's Castle or even try to establish communication. Instead he drafted some questions and summoned a council of war. The questions were framed in such a way that the participating captains and army officers could readily discern the answers desired. Without any input from the garrison Byng and the council agreed that even if 'there were no French fleet cruising off Minorca', the British fleet could do nothing to help raise the siege. How eighteen officers could have allowed themselves to appear so destitute of strategic imagination is a puzzle. The council also decided that a second naval battle would result in British defeat and Gibraltar would be thus endangered. The squadron arrived at Gibraltar on 19 June. Henry Fox had guessed correctly.

Thomas Broderick's ships had arrived on 15 June 1756 and the admirals prepared to return to Minorca. Admiral Edward Hawke arrived on 3 July, however, with orders to supersede. He sailed for Minorca not knowing that General William Blakeney, his garrison exhausted and overwhelmed, had surrendered on 28 June. Meanwhile Byng was on passage home together with West and the army officers. They arrived on 26 July.

Arrest, trial, and execution News of the capitulation had come from France ten days earlier. Paris was as overjoyed as London was chagrined. Orders went forth to arrest Byng on arrival. Believing that he would be vindicated, he was slow to grasp the full measure of his peril. The Tower was considered, but confining him under guard in a small, rudely furnished upper room in Greenwich Hospital sufficed. The ministers could claim that they were protecting him from the mob, but anger motivated the decision to make him a prisoner. They knew that the public would hold them responsible for the loss of Minorca, and in fact public demands for an inquiry into their conduct proliferated, along with burnings of Byng in effigy. Minorca completely dominated politics. Unwilling to stand as defender of the ministry's conduct in the House of Commons, Fox resigned, and in mid-November the government fell. However, towards the end of the year there developed a counter-wave of sympathy for Byng. It was generally agreed that he had not been sent in time or with sufficient forces and that his arrest and confinement had been unnecessarily rude. But had he failed to do his duty? For six months a raging pamphlet war based on fragmentary information had debated the question. The public expected the court martial to provide a reliable answer.

It was convened on the *St George* at Portsmouth on 28 December 1756, Vice-Admiral Thomas Smith presiding. The charge, issued by the Admiralty, had two elements. First, in language patterned on the twelfth article of war, had Byng done 'his utmost' during the engagement? Second, had he, as ordered, done his utmost to assist the garrison? After ascertaining that Byng was blameless for any delays, the trial focused on the two charges. Most of the testimony concerned the sea battle, especially the reasons for the rear division's slim participation. Byng cross-examined the witnesses, often shrewdly, sometimes unwisely. He was able to expose some inconsistencies and interject some doubts, but despite the reluctance of some witnesses to speak candidly against him, he could not remove an impression that he had unnecessarily kept the rear at a distance. All through January 1757 news of the testimony was reported, sometimes in detail, by London newspapers. The biggest stir was made by General Blakeney, hailed as a hero for the gallant resistance of the Minorca garrison, when he exposed the fallacies of Byng's excuses for not opening communication with the fortress after the battle. The court heard evidence every day but Sunday for four weeks. On 27 January it found Byng guilty on both counts and he was sentenced to death.

Byng did not expect the death penalty, and the court did not want to pronounce it. The wording of the sentence seemed odd and questionable. Byng was exonerated of disaffection and cowardice (it was testified that he appeared cool and self-possessed during the battle). As for the third word employed by the twelfth article that could warrant the death penalty, negligence, the court did not use it. Nor did it say that he had committed errors of judgement; the phrase 'error of judgement' appeared only hypothetically in the plea for mercy which the court attached to the sentence. While the members had no doubt that Byng had repeatedly ignored explicit orders to try to assist the garrison, the articles of war did not cover that form of negligence. Although it appeared that he had not done 'his utmost' in the battle, the admirals and captains, no doubt mindful that battles could go awry, considered the mandatory punishment too severe. The omission of the word 'negligence' brought some scathing criticism, but was probably deliberate, leaving open an avenue for review. The accompanying plea to the Admiralty for mercy was unanimous.

Numerous intelligent and humane people, most notably Voltaire and Horace Walpole but also the French commanders-in-chief, earnestly tried to prevent Byng's execution. His sister, Sarah *Osborn, was likewise an active correspondent of the duke of Bedford and the lords of the Admiralty. A new government and Admiralty board were in place, and neither had any incentive to act vindictively. Admiral Smith did all he reasonably could to obtain mercy. At first success seemed likely: the duke of Newcastle, pitched from office by the uproar, was still popularly reviled and Lord Anson was criticized for poor strategic judgement. Yet there were serious obstacles. The court martial's evidence, made public, placed Byng's conduct in a very poor light. Although the sentence was controversial, the findings appeared justified. In early 1757 the debate moved away from the issue of whether Byng or the ministers had been the more negligent, and came to stress the unfairness of the death penalty and the counterclaim that fighting spirit needed the support of hard discipline (thus supplying the context for Voltaire's famous phrase, *pour encourager les autres*). In this climate of opinion William Pitt, secretary of state, was much criticized when he advocated mercy.

Meanwhile the Admiralty, under Earl Temple, threw the question of whether the sentence was legal to the courts; the judges found that it was. Since Byng was an MP, an effort could be mounted in the House of Commons to allow the members of the court martial to break the oath of silence. In consequence they were questioned by the House of Lords, but they had nothing to offer except that the death penalty was too severe. Another obstacle was the king. Clemency was in his hands, and George II considered Byng a coward, and said so. A noisy populace shared this view. When Pitt informed him that the House of Commons did not want Byng executed, the king responded that Pitt had taught him to look beyond it for the sense of his people.

At noon on 14 March 1757 on the quarterdeck of the *Monarque* in Portsmouth harbour, a blindfolded Admiral Byng signalled his readiness by dropping a handkerchief and was executed by a firing squad of six marines. Prior to and on that dreadful day he exhibited stoic bravery. What he lacked was the courage to strive. Even his sympathetic biographers have acknowledged his caution and passivity, and tendency to magnify difficulties. Such a man should not have been assigned to such a mission.

Self-centred and quick to blame others, Byng believed to the end that he had done 'his utmost' (though practically no one else in the navy did) and that he was 'a martyr to political persecution'—the bitter words of his epitaph on the family vault at Southill where he was buried. Charging him under the twelfth article was certainly in a broad sense politically motivated. Yet the persecution was not partisan. Lord Anson and those who approved his appointment had considered him a political ally. Anson's confidence in his capacity as an admiral was evidently not matched by Byng's self-belief in action. His conduct of the mission genuinely shocked the ministers who chose him, and not just because it blatantly exposed their own strategic misjudgements.

In the final days the admiral carefully drew up his will, which distributed over £16,000 in annuities plus silver plate and substantial real estate. Among the personal items was an ornamental French clock which he bequeathed to his right-hand man, Captain Augustus Hervey. His London house went to a nephew, John. Wrotham Park was bequeathed to George, fourth Viscount Torrington, and served as the family seat thereafter.

Reputation Byng's trial occurred during the flowering of the Enlightenment. His execution was denounced by élites at the time and has continued to be universally deplored. The application of the twelfth article was legal if severe; the puzzle is the failure to obtain mercy. It has sometimes been attributed to hidden pressure from the deposed ministers, but recent scholarship suggests that popular opinion in the 1750s was autonomous and powerful—and was what Pitt feared most. As C. D. Yonge observed in 1863, practically no one in the corps of naval officers or the governing élite, except the king, actually wanted Byng executed; the cruel result, he added, 'caused something more than justice to be done to his reputation' (C. D. Yonge, *History of the British Navy*, 1863, 1.236–42).

There has been no broad shift in the tide of opinion for or against Byng. Experts have agreed that the Admiralty, under Lord Anson, miscalculated the strategic situation egregiously and rather easily could have provided Byng with two or three more ships. Even John Campbell (*Lives of the British Admirals*, 1813) and Sir John Laughton (*DNB*), both of whom took the rare position that the death penalty was justified, acknowledged these points. General histories have commonly noted that the Newcastle administration cast Byng as a scapegoat to hide its own negligence. They have often left it at that, with the implication that Byng was simply a victim. Yet as H. W. Richmond showed in his introduction to *The Loss of Minorca* (still the best researched and most penetrating investigation of the strategic circumstances), there are ample grounds for indicting both the administration and the admiral. On the question of Byng's misconduct historical opinion has varied widely. At one extreme his timid decisions have been entirely excused by reference to circumstances and the inadequacy of his squadron (Beatson, 1.462–512; L. H. Gipson, *The Great War for Empire*, 1949; Pope). Criticisms of Byng's conduct of the battle have been generally mild, though the close analyses by Brian Tunstall and John Creswell convey sharp disapproval. Practically no one, however, has excused his decision to return to Gibraltar without attempting to communicate with St Philip's. It is broadly agreed, even by some writers sympathetic to Byng, that his mind was rigid and his spirit defeatist. John Charnock, carried away by detestation of the administration, went so far as to claim that the Admiralty knew that he was 'naturally incompetent to the task' and appointed him in order to bring about his disgrace (J. Charnock, *Biographia navalis*, 1794–8, 4.156, 178–9). The modern biography by Dudley Pope provides the best-informed personal portrait of the man, but its sympathetic pleading of Byng's case uses Augustus Hervey's journal uncritically and omits some awkward facts that may be found in Tunstall.

DANIEL A. BAUGH

Sources B. Tunstall, *Admiral Byng and the loss of Minorca* (1928) · D. Pope, *At twelve Mr. Byng was shot* (1962) · J. Creswell, *British admirals of the eighteenth century: tactics in battle* (1972) · *DNB* · R. Beatson, *Naval and military memoirs of Great Britain*, 2nd edn, 6 vols. (1804), vols. 1, 3 · H. W. Richmond, ed., *Papers relating to the loss of Minorca in 1756*, Navy RS, 42 (1913) · M. Peters, *Pitt and popularity: the patriot minister and London opinion during the Seven Years War* (1980) · *Read's Weekly Journal, or, British-Gazetteer* (1756–7) · *A collection of several pamphlets, very little known, some suppressed letters, and sundry detached pieces, published in the daily papers relative to the case of Admiral Byng* (1756) · *Impartial reflections on the case of Mr. Byng, as stated in an appeal to the people* (1756) · *The trial of the Honble. Admiral Byng, at a court-martial* (1757) [minutes of the testimony certified on 19 Jan 1757 by Thomas Cook for the use of Admiral Byng] · H. Walpole, *Memoirs of the reign of King George the Second*, ed. Lord Holland, 2nd edn, 2 (1847) · *Augustus Hervey's Journal*, ed. D. Erskine, 2nd edn (1954) · H. W. Richmond, *The navy in the war of 1739–48*, 3 vols. (1920) · letters from flag officers, 1755, PRO, ADM 1/88 · Earl of Ilchester [G. S. Holland Fox-Strangways], *Henry Fox, first Lord Holland, his family and relations*, 2 vols. (1920) · *Report on the manuscripts of Lady Du Cane*, HMC, 61 (1905) · *Correspondence of John, fourth duke of Bedford*, ed. J. Russell, 1 (1842) · J. S. Corbett, *England in the Seven Years' War: a study in combined strategy*, 2 vols. (1907) · M. Godfrey, 'Byng, John', *DCB*, vol. 3 · M. E. Matcham, *A forgotten John Russell* (1905) · 'Boscawen's letters to his wife, 1755–1756', ed. P. K. Kemp, *The naval miscellany*, ed. C. Lloyd, 4, Navy RS, 92 (1952), 163–256 · P. C. Yorke, *The life and correspondence of Philip Yorke, earl of Hardwicke*, 2 (1913) · J. C. D. Clark, *The dynamics of change: the crisis of the 1750s and English party systems* (1982)

Archives BL, MSS relating to expedition against the French Toulon fleet, Add. MS 31959 · NMM, corresp. · NRA, priv. coll., corresp., admiralty and family MSS | East Riding of Yorkshire Archives Service, Beverley, corresp. with Vice-Admiral Medley and J. Howe · Mount Stuart Trust, Isle of Bute, letters · NA Scot., letters to Lord Polwarth

Likenesses T. Hudson, oils, 1749, NMM · studio of T. Hudson, oils, NMM; repro. in Tunstall, *Admiral Byng*, facing p. 48 · T. Hudson, oils, Wrotham Park, Hertfordshire; repro. in Pope, *At twelve Mr. Byng was shot*, facing p. 256

Wealth at death over £16,000; plus real estate and personalty: Pope, *At twelve*, 320-2

Byng, John, fifth Viscount Torrington (1743–1813), diarist, was born on 18 February 1743, the younger son (there were no daughters) of George Byng, third Viscount Torrington (*bap.* 1701, *d.* 1750), of Southill, Bedfordshire, and his wife, Elizabeth (*d.* 1759), daughter of Lyonel Daniel of Clapham, Surrey. Both his parents died while he was still young. He was nephew to the unfortunate Admiral John Byng (1704–1757), who was executed in 1757. Byng followed his brother, George, to Westminster School, but was, as he wrote, primarily 'Train'd up to glory' (*Torrington Diaries*, 1.344), that is, to follow his grandfather, father, and uncle in some form of military or naval career. He was page of honour to George II; from January 1760 cornet of the Royal Horse Guards; from March 1762 captain of the 58th foot (a nominal appointment, this regiment then being in America); then, from August of that year, lieutenant and captain of the 1st foot guards (Grenadier Guards). He served with both horse and foot in Germany during the Seven Years' War, an experience to which he often subsequently referred.

In 1776 Byng was made lieutenant-colonel. Not being detached for service in America, he probably spent most of the next few years in London. Financial troubles marred these years: fear of arrest for debt probably motivated his flight to the continent in November 1777; his resignation from the army in May 1780 may likewise have been prompted by such troubles. He accepted minor administrative office under Lord North's ministry, then from 1782 to 1799 served as a commissioner of stamps. He succeeded his brother, George, as viscount on 14 December 1812, but held the title for only a few weeks before his own death.

In his lifetime an obscure figure (he was ignored by contemporary obituarists), Byng became known in the twentieth century through the publication of his *Diaries*, journals of horseback tours through England and Wales. Byng did not chronicle his earlier travels; it is known from the diary of William Windham that he and Byng toured the midlands and north in 1774. Only in 1780 was Byng 'first seized with this journalizing frenzy' (*Torrington Diaries*, 1.104). His writings fill twenty-four manuscript volumes, spanning the years 1781–94. Byng wrote partly to enhance and prolong his pleasure in 'tourism', but also to preserve details of 'the manners of our travelling, the rates of our provisions; and of castles, churches and houses' (ibid., 1.249). His diaries—particularly the manuscript originals, which are scattered with engraved prints (the picture postcards of the day)—do serve this function, but are most valuable as a record of individual sensibility. Byng pertinaciously sought out ruined castles and abbeys—relics, in his view, of an age in which spiritual and temporal lords had accepted duties of stewardship they had since abnegated. Though generally critical of his own era, Byng none the less extended qualified sympathy to developments that served ends he valued: to Methodism, inasmuch as it instilled 'wholesome morals' (ibid., 1.141), and to spreading industry, inasmuch as it provided employment, though he worried that, like religion, which had 'overstretch'd her power … and was blown up … the cotton trade … may crack!' (ibid., 3.114).

On 3 March 1767 Byng married Bridget (*d.* 1823), daughter of the deceased Commodore Arthur Forrest and his wife, Juliana, a notorious eccentric, whose company Byng shunned. The marriage produced five sons and eight daughters, one of whom died young. Three of the sons followed military or naval careers, with two attaining the rank of admiral. Their youngest son was known to Regency society by the sobriquet Poodle Byng.

Although sometimes morose and tetchy, particularly when subjected to the formalities and *longueurs* of polite society, or when contemplating his reduced fortunes, Byng had yet a fund of good spirits, and endeavoured 'to be pleased with the world, and content with its comforts' (*Torrington Diaries*, 1.205). He wrote of himself that he had a 'heart full of blood & quick of impression' (ibid., 1.115), was 'hasty of determination', and 'leaky of secrets' (ibid., 1.135). According to his wife, he had generally 'a pleased or lively look' (ibid., 1.xxxviii). John Byng died on 8 January 1813 at Tenterden Street, Hanover Square, London. JOANNA INNES, *rev.*

Sources R. W. Ketton-Cremer, *The early life and diaries of William Windham* (1930) • *The Torrington diaries: containing the tours through England and Wales of the Hon. John Byng (later Viscount Torrington) between the years 1781 and 1794*, ed. C. B. Andrews, 4 vols. (1934–8) • *Old Westminsters* • GEC, *Peerage*

Archives Bodl. Oxf., travel journals • Hants. RO, travel journal • Shakespeare Birthplace Trust RO, Stratford upon Avon, diary

Byng, John, first earl of Strafford (1772–1860), army officer, was born in Hill Street, Berkeley Square, London, the third son of the three sons and two daughters of George Byng (1735–1789) of Wrotham Park, Middlesex, and his wife, Anne, daughter of the Rt Hon. William Conolly of Castledown, Ireland, and Lady Anne, eldest daughter of Thomas Wentworth, earl of Strafford. After attending Westminster School, London (from September 1786), he entered the army on 30 September 1793 as ensign in the 33rd foot, and was promoted lieutenant on 1 December 1793 and captain on 24 May 1794. He served with the 33rd during the disastrous campaigns in Flanders and throughout the retreat to Bremen (1793–5), being wounded in the skirmish at Geldermalsen. Aide-de-camp to Major-General Richard Vyse in 1797, he then commanded the southern district of Ireland and was again wounded while suppressing the Irish uprising of 1798. On 20 June 1799 he became major in the 60th foot, and on 14 March 1800 lieutenant-colonel of the 29th.

Byng exchanged into the 3rd foot guards as captain and lieutenant-colonel on 4 August 1804, serving with the regiment in expeditions to Hanover (1805), Copenhagen (1807), and Walcheren (1809); during the Walcheren expedition, while in command of the grenadier battalion of the guards and a detachment of the 95th rifles, he captured more than a hundred enemy troops in one action. On 14 June 1804 he had married Mary Stevens Mackenzie (*d.* 1806), daughter of Peter Mackenzie of Grove House, Twickenham, Middlesex; they had one son, George Stevens Byng (1806–1886). He married, on 9 May 1809, his second wife, Marianne James (*d.* 1845), daughter of Sir Walter James James, bt. They had four children: William Frederick, Harriet Frances, Frances, and Caroline Frances.

On 25 July 1810 Byng was promoted colonel, and the following year he joined Viscount Wellington's army in Portugal. Warmly recommended to Wellington by the duke of York, in September 1811 he was appointed to command a brigade under Lieutenant-General Rowland Hill, retaining that post until the end of the Peninsular War. His brigade served with Hill's corps in Estremadura and Andalusia during 1812 and with Wellington's main force from 1813. It was hotly engaged at the battle of Vitoria on 21 June 1813 and attacked by Maréchal Soult at the pass of Roncesvalles in July, when Byng's stubborn resistance and fighting withdrawal towards Sorauren enabled Wellington to concentrate enough troops to beat the French. Byng was wounded during subsequent operations near Pamplona, and yet once more after crossing the River Nive to attack a fortified camp, where two horses were shot from under him. He subsequently fought to secure passage of the Nive, notably at Cambo, and lost another horse in a further encounter, after which he was

> permitted to bear as an honourable augmentation to his arms the colours of the 31st regiment, which he planted in the enemy's lines, as an especial mark in appreciation of the signal intrepidity and heroic valour displayed by him in the action fought at Mougerre, near Bayonne, on 18 Dec 1813. (*DNB*)

Major-General Byng (as he had been promoted on 4 June 1813) continued to lead his brigade on the right of the army throughout the advance across southern France, and he was present at the actions at Espellette and Garris, at the battle of Orthez, the storming of the camp of Aire, and the battle of Toulouse. At the conclusion of the war he was made KCB. He commanded the 2nd brigade of the first (or guards) division under Lieutenant-General Sir George Cooke at the battle of Waterloo, where he was prominent in the defence of Hougoumont. After the battle his brigade advanced into France, taking Péronne on the march and occupying the heights of Belle Ville and Montmartre in Paris.

Following withdrawal of the army of occupation from France, Byng saw no more active service. He was colonel of the York infantry volunteers (1815–16) and then, until its disbandment, of the 4th West India regiment (1816–19). In 1819 he received the command of the northern district. On 26 July 1822 he became colonel of the 2nd West India regiment, on 27 May 1825 was promoted lieutenant-general, and on 23 January 1828 received the colonelcy of the 29th foot. In 1828 he became commander-in-chief of the forces in Ireland and that year was also sworn of the Irish privy council (thereafter appearing in the *Army List* as 'Rt Hon.'). On 15 June 1832 he was made honorary governor of Londonderry and Culmore, having resigned his Irish command in 1831 to enter the House of Commons as MP for Poole. As one of the few distinguished generals who supported the Reform Bill of 1832 and was looked upon with favour by Lord Melbourne, he was created Baron Strafford of Harmondsworth on 12 May 1835, and earl of Strafford and Viscount Enfield on 18 September 1847. He had been made a knight of Maria Theresa of Austria and of St George of Russia after the battle of Waterloo, and appointed GCB in 1828 and GCH on 24 February 1831. On 23 November 1841 Lord Strafford was promoted general, on 15 August 1850 he succeeded the duke of Cambridge as colonel of the Coldstream Guards, and on 2 October 1855 he became a field marshal. He also received the thanks of parliament for his services in the Peninsular War and at Waterloo; a gold cross and one clasp for the battles of Vitoria, the Pyrenees, Nivelle, Nive, and Orthez; the silver war medal with one clasp for Toulouse; and the Waterloo medal. On 3 June 1860 he died at his residence, 44 Grosvenor Square, London. His son George Stevens Byng succeeded to his titles.

H. M. STEPHENS, *rev.* JOHN SWEETMAN

Sources *Army List* • Burke, *Peerage* (1887) • *The dispatches of … the duke of Wellington … from 1799 to 1818*, ed. J. Gurwood, new edn, 11–12 (1838) • E. Longford [E. H. Pakenham, countess of Longford], *Wellington*, 1: *The years of the sword* (1969) • J. Philippart, ed., *The royal* *military calendar*, 2 (1815) · *The Times* (4 June 1860), 12 · GEC, *Peerage* · Boase, *Mod. Eng. biog.* · *CGPLA Eng. & Wales* (1860)

Archives BL, corresp. with Sir Robert Peel, Add. MSS 40254–40391, *passim* · Lpool RO, letters to E. G. Stanley · PRO NIre., corresp. with marquess of Anglesey · Sheff. Arch., corresp. with Earl Fitzwilliam · W. Sussex RO, letters to duke of Richmond · Woburn Abbey, corresp. with duke of Bedford

Likenesses W. Salter, *c.*1834–1840, NPG · G. Hayter, group portrait, oils (*The House of Commons, 1833*), NPG · W. Salter, group portrait, oils (*The Waterloo banquet at Apsley House*), Apsley House, London, Wellington Museum · engraving, repro. in J. Saunders, *Portraits and memoirs of eminent living political reformers* (1840), 88

Wealth at death under £100,000: probate, 4 July 1860, *CGPLA Eng. & Wales*

Byng, Julian Hedworth George, Viscount Byng of Vimy (**1862–1935**), army officer, was born on 11 September 1862 at Wrotham Park, Barnet, Hertfordshire, the seventh son and youngest of the thirteen children of George Stevens Byng, second earl of Strafford (1806–1886), and of the four sons and three daughters born to his second wife, Harriet Elizabeth (*d.* 1892), younger daughter of Charles Compton Cavendish, first Baron Chesham. His grandfather, John *Byng, first earl of Strafford, had commanded a brigade at Waterloo and ended his career as a field marshal. His great-great-great-uncle was the unfortunate Admiral John Byng who was shot on his own quarterdeck, as Voltaire put it, 'pour encourager les autres'.

Julian Hedworth George Byng, Viscount Byng of Vimy (1862–1935), by Bassano, 1915

Early years and education Financial strictures caused Lord Strafford to impose a regime of strict frugality on his household. Most of Julian's clothes were cast-offs, luxuries unknown. He was educated at home (1867–74), then at Eton College (1874–8), where he was nicknamed Bungo and failed to progress beyond the lower fifth form. Unable to afford a regular army commission, he entered the army at seventeen through the 2nd Middlesex militia. He became an excellent horseman, shot, and cricketer, and developed a love of music and the theatre. Three years later the prince of Wales offered his old friend Strafford a place for Julian in his own regiment, the 10th Royal Hussars, an invitation which could not be refused. He was gazetted on 27 January 1883 and, in March, joined them at Lucknow. The 10th was a very expensive regiment, the youngest officer needing a private income of at least £600, most having twice that. Julian's tastes were modest, but he was popular and, by buying ponies cheaply, training them for polo, and selling at a profit, he managed on £200.

Early in 1884 the 10th hussars were on their way home when they were diverted to Suakin to suppress the rebellion in eastern Sudan. In a month-long campaign Byng took part in the historic charge at al-Teb (29 February) and had his horse killed under him at the fierce engagement at Tamai (13 March). He was mentioned in dispatches. He was fortunate in experiencing his first action so early in his career for it gave him both the confidence of personal experience of battle and a compelling incentive to study his profession. On 20 October 1886 he became adjutant of his regiment. Nine days later his father died, leaving him £3500. In his four years in the appointment Byng proved a superb adjutant who achieved much for the lasting welfare of his soldiers.

While stationed at Hounslow, Byng helped Lord Rowton investigate the living conditions of 'casual labourers' in the most squalid districts of London, which led to the establishment of 'Rowton houses' to provide decent, inexpensive lodgings. In the process he learned far more about how much of the population of Britain lived than was known by most politicians, let alone officers of the army. In 1894 he had graduated from the Staff College, Camberley, where he had helped Colonel G. F. R. Henderson compile his classic work, *Stonewall Jackson and the American Civil War* (1898). After three years as a squadron leader in his regiment, he was appointed deputy assistant adjutant-general (DAAG) of Aldershot command. He was promoted captain in 1889 and major in 1898.

South Africa, 1899–1902 Byng arrived in South Africa with General Sir Redvers Buller's headquarters on 9 November 1899, to be met with orders to raise and command a new regiment of colonial irregulars, the South African light horse. Tough, irreverent, and natural horsemen, his new troopers were far from being the disciplined and highly trained hussars he knew, but Byng recognized their value as a military asset. Readily adapting to their informal ways, he soon earned their respect. Helped by his sense of humour and a sure military instinct, he became a leader of irregular cavalry of the highest quality. In the fighting along the Tugela River, Winston Churchill acted as his galloper. Later he was employed in command of a column, then of a group of columns, until March 1902 when he returned to England. Byng received the brevet rank of lieutenant-colonel on 29 November 1900 and of colonel in February 1902, and was five times mentioned in dispatches.

On 30 April 1902 Byng married Marie Evelyn (1870–1949), only child of Sir Richard Charles Moreton of Church Crookham, Hampshire. At the war's end he was appointed to command the 10th hussars at Mhow in the central provinces of India. There he suffered two bitter disappointments. Badly treated miscarriages resulted in his wife's being unable to bear children. Then in a polo accident in January 1904, his right elbow was so badly broken and dislocated that it was feared he would have to leave the army. He returned to England and after months of painful treatment, was pronounced fit for service in the field.

In 1904 Byng formed the army's new school for cavalry at Netheravon which he commanded until 1905 when he was promoted to command the 2nd cavalry brigade at Canterbury. He was appointed CB in 1906. In 1907 he moved to the 1st cavalry brigade at Aldershot which he commanded until 1 April 1909 when he was promoted major-general and placed on half pay until October 1910 when he took command of the territorial East Anglian division. In the interim he was part-time editor of the *Cavalry Journal* and became the first district commissioner for north Essex for the Boy Scout movement, which he helped organize with characteristic thoroughness. For the first time Byng had a home of his own, Newtown Hall, at Dunmow in Essex, which was then something of a literary centre. He formed lasting friendships with London editors and the well-known writers who were his neighbours. He read extensively and welcomed the opportunity of broadening his already wide range of interests. In October 1912 Byng was appointed to command the force in Egypt. When war broke out in 1914 he was recalled to command the 3rd cavalry division.

1914–1918 In the first battle of Ypres Byng's division gave brilliant support to the 1st corps and was repeatedly called upon to restore ugly situations at short notice and in the most unfavourable conditions. Byng proved as cool, determined, and resourceful in difficult circumstances as he had been in South Africa. In March 1915 he was appointed KCMG and in May he took command of the cavalry corps in the temporary rank of lieutenant-general. Three months later he was sent to Gallipoli to command the 9th corps at Suvla. General Sir Ian Hamilton's request for Byng to command the landing force there had been refused, and now that the operation had gone disastrously wrong he was being sent to retrieve it. It was too late. He set out immediately to make his corps' position tenable and, within a week of arrival, began to study the problem of evacuation. He reasoned that the Gallipoli operations were yielding few strategic benefits, that the army must either drive on and seize its final objectives, for which they did not have the resources, or that the force should be withdrawn and used elsewhere. Alone of the senior commanders, he considered that withdrawal need not be costly provided it was carried out before more German help to the Turkish enemy arrived and before the weather broke. His optimism and enthusiasm were infectious and turned the outlook of other commanders from an acceptance of the inevitability of disaster to a belief in the possibility of success. The withdrawal, without casualties, was completely successful and Byng was appointed KCB (1916).

In February, after a brief spell in Egypt in the Suez Canal defences, Byng was sent to command the 17th corps in France. Three months later he was ordered to replace another British officer, Lieutenant-General Sir E. A. H. Alderson, as commander of the Canadian corps, no Canadian yet being ready for the appointment. Simultaneously he was promoted to the substantive rank of lieutenant-general for distinguished services in the field. Unlike most corps of the British expeditionary force (BEF), which were simply headquarters to which divisions were assigned as required, the Canadian corps was a cohesive force consisting permanently of its national divisions. Its commander controlled its administration and preparation for battle in a way not open to his counterparts in the British army. Within a week, on 2 June, Byng had to deal with near disaster when the Germans captured Mount Sorrel and Hill 62 which overlooked Ypres. Local counter-attacks failed, but on 11 June the lost ground was recaptured in an expensive counter-offensive.

Byng had an extraordinary gift for impressing the troops under his command with his friendly personality and sense of humour. He soon gained not only the confidence but the affection of the Canadian corps where every man came to recognize the tall figure in crumpled uniform and worn boots. Nowhere in the world at war was there such a large formation in which the links between commander and soldiers were so strong. The corps distinguished itself on the Somme, in the battle of Flers-Courcelette in mid-September, and at the end of the month in the Thiepval Ridge operations; but its greatest feat under Byng's command was the capture, in April 1917, of Vimy Ridge, the most dominant and tactically important feature on the whole of the western front.

In June of that year, Byng, although loath to leave his Canadians, was appointed to command the Third Army in succession to General Sir Edmund Allenby. Within days of his arrival he became absorbed in planning the most daring and original operation yet undertaken by the British on the western front, the Cambrai offensive. Conceived as a diversion to distract the enemy from the main British attack near Ypres, its objects were to capture the wooded heights above Bourlon and roll up the German front towards the Sensee marshes to the north; at the same time it was to thrust eastwards, capture Cambrai, and exploit in the direction of Valenciennes. The key elements were surprise, the use of a massive force of tanks to open gaps in the enemy wire, the employment of 'predicted fire' from massed artillery without preliminary registration, the use of aircraft to neutralize enemy batteries and interdict the battlefield, the swift breakthrough of the enemy defences by infantry, and the launch of cavalry divisions into the enemy rear areas. Planned to take place in October, the operation depended for its success on the Ypres offensive being in progress. In the event, the government ordered the reserves essential to the plan to be sent to Italy, and on 12 November Field Marshal Sir Douglas Haig halted the Ypres offensive but ordered the Cambrai operation to take place.

The first stage of the assault, launched on 20 November, was brilliantly successful, but serious setbacks occurred (including the last-minute arrival of German troops freed by the collapse of Russia), and the available reserves could not maintain the momentum. At the end of the month the Germans counter-attacked the salient created by the British advance. On the north they were held but they broke the southern flank and were only stopped by hurriedly organized counter-attacks.

As an operation Cambrai was a disappointment but it broke the mould of the accepted tactics of 1917. At that time there was no significant mobile force but cavalry: tanks were unreliable mechanically, too short in range, and too few in numbers. It is from Byng's attempt to exploit their potential in combination with other arms that Cambrai derives its influence on the history of warfare. Into a single operation, meticulously planned, he brought together the secret concentration of an overwhelming force of guns and armour, 'silent registration' by the artillery, the engagement of ground targets by the air force, deceptive measures, including simulated attacks and dummy tanks spread over a front of 30 miles, the breakthrough of the enemy's defences by tanks and infantry, the plan for a deep thrust into the enemy's rear by a mobile force and, above all, surprise. Notwithstanding the obvious technical limitations, it was the prototype of the wide-ranging battles of the Second World War.

The German offensive of March 1918 fell heavily upon the Third Army, though less so than on the Fifth on its right. The Third put up a stubborn resistance, lost relatively little ground, and smashed the offensive near Arras. Byng had, however, to make a rapid withdrawal, which got temporarily out of hand, from the remains of the Cambrai salient. That autumn the Third Army played a great part in the offensive which decided the issue of the war. Its first attack was launched on 21 August. By a series of heavy blows, in conjunction with the Fourth Army on its right and the First Army on its left, it drove the enemy back to the Hindenburg line and, on 27 September, broke that position. In the space of eighty days it advanced 60 miles—a fast pace for that war—won eighteen significant battles, and took 67,000 prisoners and 800 guns.

On only two subjects have Byng's judgement as a commander been brought into question: his aims in the battle of Cambrai and his delay in evacuating the Cambrai salient in March 1918. It has been suggested in the *History of the Great War* that in the former case he was unduly optimistic, refusing to modify an ambitious plan when it was found impossible to put at his disposal resources as large as originally intended because they had been used up at Ypres and in Italy. Yet Sir Douglas Haig, the commander-in-chief, approved Byng's plans for the attack at each stage of their development and was present with him at critical times during the operation. It was Haig who ordered the operation to take place when it did, and to continue when the hoped-for breakthrough was not achieved.

Byng's judgement may have been more questionable in the second case, but his conduct of the final offensive of 1918 established him as a field commander of the first rank. His was the largest of Britain's five field armies and he controlled its operations with a sureness of touch derived from four years of active operations. Its successes reflected his meticulous planning and a personal flair in which was combined an instinct for surprise and a faculty for forecasting the actions of the enemy. His willingness to break free from orthodoxy, to accept new weapons and concepts of operations, led to the plan for the Cambrai offensive which so influenced commanders in the Second World War. In 1919 Byng, who had been promoted general in 1917, was appointed GCB, raised to the peerage (August) as Baron Byng of Vimy, and received the thanks of parliament and a grant of £30,000. Other honours came his way. From Canada there was a commission as an honorary general (1920) and there were honorary doctorates from Cambridge (1919) and Oxford (1931). In March 1919 he was offered the southern command, but he requested retirement to make way for a younger man. While he was in Egypt in 1913 his wife had bought Thorpe Hall at Thorpe-le-Soken. There she created a beautiful home and a widely famed garden and Byng was able to enjoy his favourite sport of shooting. In the interest of his soldiers he took on the trying and delicate task of administering the United Services Fund.

Canada In June 1921 Byng was appointed governor-general of Canada where already he was widely popular. Yet even those who had hoped for the most from it were astonished by the success which he made of his mission. Well supported by his wife, he kept up the requisite state and entertained on a large scale, but was otherwise unconventional, mixing with people as had none of his predecessors. He travelled widely and developed a talent for making brief and telling speeches devoid of the platitudes too common on official occasions. The theme to which he constantly returned was the need for unity in the dominion and for eliminating the bitterness of political strife. In his last year there was a widespread desire that he should serve a second term, but this he would not consider.

In June 1926, shortly before he was due to return to England, Byng became involved in a painful political crisis. The prime minister, W. L. Mackenzie King, had in the previous September sought and obtained from the governor-general a dissolution of parliament on the understanding that, if after the election King met the Canadian House of Commons and subsequently was unable to carry on, the leader of the opposition should be given the chance to form a government. The general election which followed seriously weakened King's position, and he had since governed with his minority Liberal Party dependent on outside support. Now, having to face a vote of censure certain to go against him, King asked for a second dissolution. Byng refused it and called upon Arthur Meighen, leader of the Conservatives, the strongest party in the house, to form a government. In less than a week, having seen the censure motion passed, the new prime minister was defeated. Byng then granted Meighen a dissolution, and in the subsequent election the Liberals were victorious.

Though accused during the election of favouring Meighen over King, Byng had behaved with complete impartiality. He refused King's advice to dissolve parliament at a time when to do so would have prevented its voting on an outstanding motion censuring the government. He accepted Meighen's advice to dissolve parliament, after it had been shown that neither party could govern. Byng's last days in Canada were clouded by this episode but it was with affection and deep regret that the people of Canada said farewell to him.

Until King's second request for dissolution no prime minister in Britain or Canada had attempted to challenge the right of the crown to refuse unconstitutional advice. Byng's response to it confirmed that residual power was real and deterred similar situations from developing elsewhere in the Commonwealth. Byng contended that the governor-general should represent the crown, not the British government, and that the constitutional relationship between him and the prime minister of Canada was the same as that between the sovereign and the British prime minister. The Imperial Conference, held shortly after Byng's return to England in 1928, confirmed this principle.

Metropolitan Police In June 1928 Byng was asked by the home secretary, Sir William Joynson-Hicks, to become chief commissioner of the Metropolitan Police. There was a need at Scotland Yard for a leader of great character and prestige: the public was worried by apparent inefficiency and corruption within the police, and morale within the force was low. Byng tried to excuse himself on the grounds of age and indifferent health, but strong pressure was put upon him and he gave way. The appointment was vigorously attacked on class grounds by the Labour opposition in parliament—virulently by the left-wing press. Yet so effective was his leadership of the police that when, a year later, a Labour government took office, they refused to accept his offer of resignation, and assured him of their full confidence and support.

Byng's reforms were widespread and fundamental. He retired inefficient senior officers, tightened up discipline, instituted a system of promotion based on merit, and reorganized the structure of the force to correspond with the distribution of London's population. He reorganized the system of patrolling, abolishing the regular schedules of policemen's beats to which criminals became accustomed. He instituted police telephone boxes, greatly extended the use of police cars, and established a central information room to control them by radio. Yet his reforms were not resented in the force, over which he established as strong a hold as he had done over every other body of men he had commanded. Byng's health deteriorated towards the end of his term of office and he resigned in September 1931.

Assessment Byng had been appointed GCMG in August 1921 and advanced to a viscountcy in June 1926 but the award which gave him the greatest satisfaction was that of a field marshal's baton in October 1932. He died suddenly on 6 June 1935 at Thorpe Hall of an inoperable abdominal blockage, and was buried on 8 June at the church of Beaumont-cum-Moze in Essex which, as a devoted Anglican, he had regularly attended. He and his wife having had no children, Byng's peerage became extinct.

Byng had developed, through careful self-preparation and experience, from a somewhat shy young officer, avoiding when he could all society except that most congenial to him, to a public figure at home in any society and able to impress his personality on multitudes. He was one of the most intellectual of Britain's wartime commanders and his qualities of leadership were unquestionably high. Unlike the popular conception, his headquarters in the field was notoriously simple. He had a deep and natural empathy with his men, a genius for friendship, and many friends in all walks of life. Unlike other generals, he refused to write his memoirs—he ordered his papers to be destroyed on his death—or to criticize others, which may account for the lack of wide recognition, until recently, of his true worth. He never held independent command in the field, and on that basis he cannot be judged. On the other hand, beyond being thoroughly competent and personally inspiring, he was gifted with an open-mindedness and imagination which rose above the pervading orthodoxy of the First World War.

Byng's greatest weakness was a guileless belief in the integrity of mankind, of which some less scrupulous occasionally took advantage. But coupled with his massive integrity, it was the basis of the trust and devotion of his soldiers and the root of his reputation as a battlefield leader. CYRIL FALLS, *rev.* JEFFERY WILLIAMS

Sources J. Williams, *Byng of Vimy: general and governor general* (1983) [incl. extensive list of further sources] • J. E. Edmonds, ed., *Military operations, France and Belgium, 1914*, 2 vols., History of the Great War (1922) • C. F. Aspinall-Oglander, ed., *Military operations: Gallipoli*, 2, History of the Great War (1932) • G. W. L. Nicholson, *Canadian expeditionary force, 1914–1919: official history of the Canadian army in the First World War*, 2nd edn (1964) • E. Byng, *Up the stream of time* (1945) • E. A. Forsey, *The royal power of dissolution of parliament in the British commonwealth* (1943) • *CGPLA Eng. & Wales* (1935) • private information (2004) • Wrotham Park, Byng MSS • GEC, *Peerage*

Archives NRA, priv. coll., scrapbooks | HLRO, letters to R. D. Blumenfeld • LPL, letters to H. R. L. Sheppard • NRA, priv. coll., corresp. with Sir John Ewart | FILM BFI NFTVA, news footage • IWM FVA, actuality footage • IWM FVA, documentary footage • IWM FVA, news footage

Likenesses P. A. de Laszlo, oils, 1907, repro. in Williams, *Byng of Vimy* • Bassano, photograph, 1915, NPG [*see illus.*] • F. Dodd, charcoal and watercolour drawing, 1917, IWM • W. Stoneman, photograph, 1918–19, NPG • J. S. Sargent, group portrait, oils, 1922 (*General officers of World War I*), NPG; related sketch, NPG • B. Partridge, ink caricature, 1926, NPG • P. A. de Laszlo, oils, *c.*1933, NPG • P. A. de Laszlo, oils, 1933, NPG • F. O. Salisbury, oils, IWM • photographs, repro. in Williams, *Byng of Vimy* • photographs, IWM • photographs, NA Canada

Wealth at death £31,002 12*s.* 9*d.*: probate, 26 Oct 1935, *CGPLA Eng. & Wales*

Byng, Thomas (*d.* **1599**), civil lawyer and college head, was the second son of John Byng of Wrotham in Kent and his wife, Agnes, daughter of Robert Spencer. His elder brother, Robert, was the ancestor of the well-known naval and military family. Thomas Byng was admitted to Peterhouse, Cambridge, as a sizar in 1552, took his BA degree in 1555/6, being twentieth in the order of seniority, and became a fellow on 16 February 1558. He took his MA degree in 1559 and was a proctor of the university in 1564/5 and also in 1565/6. In August 1564 he came to prominence when he performed his philosophy act in the presence of Queen Elizabeth, arguing two theses in Latin: that monarchy was the best form of government and that frequent change of the laws was dangerous. He also contributed twelve Greek iambic dimeters to a volume of verses in Elizabeth's honour (CUL, Add. MS 8915, fol. 91). In 1565 he became public orator, responsible for the official correspondence of the university, and the following year he incorporated MA at Oxford on the occasion of a royal visit. Having received a royal licence dispensing him from having to give up his fellowship on receiving a living worth more than his fellowship, in 1567 he became prebendary of Strensall in York Minster.

In 1570 Byng took his LLD degree. In 1571 he was elected master of Clare College and in that year he married Katherine Randolph or Rendall (1553–1627); they had ten sons, including Andrew *Byng, Church of England clergyman and Hebraist, and two daughters. They lived in the manor house at Grantchester, which he leased from King's College. In 1572 (and again in 1578) he served as vice-chancellor of the university. Also in 1572 he became a member of Doctors' Commons and was admitted to practise as an advocate in the ecclesiastical courts. In 1574 he was appointed regius professor of civil law in the university. Although he wrote Greek and Latin verses and translations he contributed nothing to the literature of the civil law. As visitor of Christ's College he gave an opinion on the scope of a fellowship and gave another in a dispute between Doctors' Commons and Trinity Hall, which owned the Doctors' premises in London (both preserved in the manuscripts of the university library). He also sat as an assessor in the vice-chancellor's court, which followed the civil law. In July 1578 he was a member of a delegation which visited Queen Elizabeth at Audley End and he read a Latin oration in her presence. In 1590 he became one of the civilian masters in chancery. He was also a member of the commission of the peace for Cambridgeshire. He used a printed almanac to keep a diary (with the entries often in Greek); it shows him to have been a conscientious and systematic administrator.

In 1594 Byng resigned the regius chair but on 5 May of that year it was granted by letters patent to Byng and John Cowel, his eventual successor, 'or the longest liver of them'. In July 1595 he made a similar arrangement with Richard Cosin, under which they were both appointed to certain ecclesiastical judicial offices, with the survivor to enjoy them alone. On 24 July 1595 Byng became dean of peculiars of the province of Canterbury. On 3 November 1597 he succeeded Cosin as president of Doctors' Commons, and soon afterwards as dean of arches, the highest judicial office open to a civilian, but he was not able to enjoy these honours for long. By May 1598 he had resigned the presidency of Doctors' Commons and in December 1599 he died and was buried on 23 December in Hackney church, Middlesex. PETER STEIN

Sources T. A. Walker, *A biographical register of Peterhouse men*, 1 (1927) • Cooper, *Ath. Cantab.*, 2.279–80 • F. H. Stubbings, 'A Cambridge pocket diary, 1587–1592', *Transactions of the Cambridge Bibliographical Society*, 5 (1969–71), 191–202 • *Fasti Angl.* (Hardy) • G. D. Squibb, *Doctors' Commons: a history of the College of Advocates and Doctors of Law* (1977)

Archives Canterbury Cathedral Library, V.2.17–21 • CUL, MSS 1.40, 1.42, 2.22, 2.24, Add. 8915

Bynneman, Henry (*b.* in or before **1542**, *d.* **1583**), printer and bookseller, of unknown parentage, was apprenticed to the printer Richard Harrison on 24 June 1559. After Harrison's death in 1563 it is assumed that he worked with Harrison's former partner, the printer Reginald Wolfe, whose devices, ornaments, and initials Bynneman acquired after Wolfe's death in 1573. Freed as a stationer on 15 August 1566, Bynneman printed first in Paternoster Row at the sign of the Black Boy, but by 1567 had adopted his familiar sign of the Mermaid, moving to premises first in Knightrider Street (1568–75) and later in Thames Street near Baynard's Castle (1579–83). As well as his main printing house and shop he rented shops in St Paul's Churchyard, one of them run by his former apprentice Nicholas Ling also under the Mermaid sign. He became a liveryman of the Stationers' Company on 30 June 1578.

Archbishop Parker encouraged Bynneman in many ways, allowed him to open a shed at the north-west door of St Paul's, at the sign of the 'Three Wells', and in 1569 asked Burghley to allow Bynneman 'a privilege for Prynting two or 3 usual bokes for Grammarians, as *Therence*, *Virgile*, Tullys Office' (Bodl. Oxf., MS Ballard 62, p. 35). After Parker's death in 1575 Sir Christopher Hatton became Bynneman's patron: his arms are found among Bynneman's ornaments and at least twelve of Bynneman's books carried dedications to Hatton. Hatton's position as chancellor of Oxford may have helped Bynneman in his vigorous pursuit of printing patents. Despite his participation in a *c.*1577 complaint about privileges, Bynneman himself acquired several, including one for '*Dictionaries* in all tongues, all *Chronicles* and *histories* whatsoever' and for music books and ruled paper (Arber, *Regs. Stationers*, 1.116).

The financial burden of printing large works was to prove ruinous and Bynneman was at least twice associated with illegal printing, doubtless in an attempt to make a short-term profit. In 1580 he was called to the bar of the House of Commons for having published on behalf of Arthur Hall, MP for Grantham, a libel on Sir Robert Bell and others. Bynneman confessed to printing '80 or 90' copies because 'Mr. Hall promised to get him a Priviledge' and that he had been paid in 'Linnen-Cloth to the value of 6*l.* 13*s.* 4*d.* for Printing the said Book' (D'Ewes, 291–309). He was also implicated in Richard Day's piracy of John Day's

ABC with the Little Catechism (Oastler, 22–3). That the Stationers' Company was apprehensive about Bynneman's ambitions is clear from his last entry in the Stationers' register on 26 March 1583, which was made conditional on his choosing five other stationers as partners for his projected volumes of Aristotle, a Greek and Latin Homer, and a Greek New Testament (Arber, *Regs. Stationers*, 2.422).

Bynneman's business was one of the largest in London, with three presses in 1583. According to Plomer he was 'one of the few English printers of the sixteenth century whose work merits special notice' (Plomer, 226). He printed many notable works, such as the second part of Paynter's *Palace of Pleasure* (1567), Turberville's *Booke of Faulconrie* (1575), and Gascoigne's *A Hundreth Sundrie Flowers* (*c*.1573). In 1574 he began to print in folio, producing the first edition of Holinshed's *Chronicle* in 1577. In the later part of his career Bynneman looked to several other stationers (notably Ralph Newbery and Francis Coldocke) to share the costs of his projects, but eventually the financial risk proved too great. By June 1581 he was in debt to Richard Hutton, armourer, for £1000. Hutton began proceedings to recover the unpaid debt, but Bynneman's death in the parish of St Benedict, Paul's Wharf, London, on 15 April 1583 preceded the issue of a writ in May for his imprisonment and the seizure of his goods. Printing of the Greek, Latin, and English dictionary of Morelius, left incomplete on Bynneman's death, was continued and it appeared 'per assignationem Richardi Hutton'. Newbery and Denham obtained Bynneman's dictionary patent and completed several of his projected editions. A detailed inventory shows that Bynneman's estate was valued at £791 12*s*. 9*d*. at the time of his death, more than £600 of which was tied up in over 19,000 unsold books. His widow, Brigid, later married Charles Sledd, gentleman of Great Milton, Oxfordshire. His son Christopher was freed as a stationer in 1615 and died in March 1620.

MAUREEN BELL

Sources M. Eccles, 'Bynneman's books', *The Library*, 5th ser., 12 (1957), 81–92 • J. Barnard and M. Bell, 'The inventory of Henry Bynneman (1583): a preliminary survey', *Publishing History*, 29 (1991), 5–46 • H. R. Plomer, 'Henry Bynneman, printer, 1566–83', *The Library*, new ser., 9 (1908), 225–44 • Arber, *Regs. Stationers* • *STC*, *1475–1640* • S. D'Ewes, ed., *The journals of all the parliaments during the reign of Queen Elizabeth, both of the House of Lords and House of Commons* (1682) • 'London book trades: a biographical database, 1550–1830', Bodl. Oxf. [electronic database, held by M. L. Turner] • C. L. Oastler, *John Day, the Elizabethan printer* (1975) • F. B. Williams, *Index of dedications and commendatory verses in English books before 1641* (1962) • writ and inventory, PRO, statute staple proceedings, C152/36, 34 Eliz. [transcribed in Eccles] • administration, PRO, PROB 6/3, fol. 35*r*; PROB 6/3, fol. 66*r* • Bodl. Oxf., MS Ballard 62, fol. 35

Archives PRO, statute staple proceedings, C 152/36, 34 Eliz.

Wealth at death £791 12*s*. 9*d*.: Eccles, 'Bynneman's books'

Bynoe, Benjamin (1803–1865), ship's surgeon and naturalist, was born at Christ Church, Barbados, on 25 July 1803, the son of Samuel and Elizabeth Bynoe. Nothing is known of Bynoe's education and though he was sometimes styled MD there is no record that he obtained this qualification in the British Isles. However, Bynoe obtained his 'London diploma' on 18 March 1825 and on 20 May 1825 he became a member of the Royal College of Surgeons.

In September 1825 Bynoe passed for appointment as assistant surgeon, Royal Navy. Four weeks later he joined the surveying ship *Beagle*, on its voyage to South America. When the *Beagle*'s senior surgeon was invalided in July 1828, Bynoe was appointed acting surgeon. The *Beagle* surveyed Patagonia, Tierra del Fuego, and the Strait of Magellan. For three months in 1829 Bynoe joined a small party crewing the tender *Adelaide*; they surveyed the Magdalen and Barbara channels. Bynoe was also aboard the *Adelaide* during its survey of the Gulf of Penas. His name was given to two landmarks on that notoriously dangerous coast: Cape Bynoe (Bynoe Point) and Bynoe Island. They rejoined the *Beagle* at Port Famine in May 1830. By October Bynoe was on half-pay, lodging in the New Kent Road area of London.

On 5 July 1831 Bynoe qualified as a surgeon, but he found promotion elusive and rejoined the *Beagle* as assistant surgeon; they sailed in December 1831. Joining them on this voyage was Charles Darwin, sailing as private naturalist. Darwin profoundly influenced Bynoe, who subsequently became an ardent collector. In April 1832 the *Beagle*'s surgeon was invalided and Bynoe again became acting surgeon. The ship visited the coasts of South America; while at Valparaiso, Bynoe treated Darwin with calomel after he had become unwell, possibly with the illness which was to recur throughout his lifetime. They then travelled on to the Galápagos Islands, Polynesia, New Zealand, Australia, Mauritius, and the Cape; he returned to England via Brazil, and arrived at Falmouth in October 1836. After his return Bynoe's rank of surgeon was officially confirmed, and he was appointed surgeon of the *Beagle* in February 1837, on its voyage to survey the Australian coast. In September 1839 Captain Wickham named a coastal feature Bynoe harbour (Bynoe Bay). The Bynoe inlet and Bynoe River, on the Gulf of Carpentaria, commemorate Bynoe's skill as a surgeon, as it was here that he saved an officer's badly damaged foot. The *Beagle* reached England in September 1843. Bynoe married about this time and he and his wife Charlotte lived at various addresses near the Old Kent Road, London.

In early 1844 Bynoe was appointed surgeon superintendent of the convict ship *Blundell*, destined for Norfolk Island. Later he was appointed surgeon on the survey vessel *Fly*, travelling with John MacGillivray, the earl of Derby's private natural history collector on the ship's survey of the Great Barrier Reef and Torres Strait. During his absence Bynoe was elected a fellow of the Royal College of Surgeons. In March 1846 Bynoe joined the *Lord Auckland*, a convict transport to Hobart, but he was landed at the Cape of Good Hope with pneumonia and returned to England. Throughout the winter of 1846–7 Bynoe worked for his certificate proving that he had 'performed the capital operations of surgery on the dead body' (Keevil, 105). In February 1847 Bynoe was sent to Cork to aid victims of the potato famine, but he fell ill himself with dysentery and fever.

Bynoe returned to London in October 1847 and in succession joined the *Ocean*, the *Ganges*, and the *Wellington*; in 1850 he joined the *Monarch*, and in November 1851 the

Aboukir, a convict transport. Although in increasingly poor health, he joined the *Madagascar* in 1853. In 1860 he was appointed staff surgeon but he did not return to sea again; he was put on the retired list on 23 January 1863. Bynoe died at his home, 440 Old Kent Road, London, on 13 November 1865. He was survived by his wife.

Professionally, Bynoe was a ship's surgeon, but he was immortalized in geographical features and in the names of Australian plants and animals, notably the Acacia *Acacia bynoeana*, the Golden Whistler *Pachycephala melanura bynoei*, and the kangaroo *Halmaturus binoe*. Bynoe collected many natural history specimens; many still exist in museums. Of his birds and mammals, about twenty-five were new to science. CLEMENCY THORNE FISHER

Sources J. J. Keevil, 'Benjamin Bynoe, surgeon of the *Beagle*', *Journal of the History of Medicine and Allied Sciences*, 4 (1949), 90–111 · K. S. Thomson, *H. M. S. Beagle* (1995) · C. T. Fisher, 'The importance of early Victorian natural historians in the discovery and interpretation of the Australian fauna', PhD diss., CNAA, Liverpool Polytechnic, 1992, 477–8 · H. M. Whittell, *The literature of Australian birds: a history and a bibliography of Australian ornithology* (1954), 97 · C. Darwin, *Narrative of the surveying voyages of His Majesty's Ships Adventure and Beagle, 1826–1836*, 3 (1839) · *CGPLA Eng. & Wales* (1866)

Archives Academy of Natural Sciences, Philadelphia · NHM | PRO, ADM 101/1/1, 101/12/7

Wealth at death under £450: probate, 18 Jan 1866, *CGPLA Eng. & Wales*

Byrd, William (1542/3?–1623), composer, was born most probably in London between 15 November 1542 and 14 November 1543, one of seven children and the youngest son of Thomas Byrd (*fl.* 1520–1570) and his wife, Margery (*fl.* 1520–1570).

Origins and early years Byrd's family believed that their ancestors had resided at Ingatestone, Essex, until the 1400s, when the composer's great-great-grandfather had settled in London. Thomas Byrd's occupation cannot be established; he was not the gentleman of the Chapel Royal of that name in the 1540s and 1550s. William's birth date is based upon his own statement in his will that on 15 November 1622 he was 'in the 80th yeare of myne age', a detail uncommonly included in wills of that time. Alternatively, his birth date has been pushed back to as early as late 1539, based upon a more vaguely worded deposition, recorded by a court scribe on 2 October 1598, indicating his age as '58. Yeares or ther about' (Harley, 14).

Although William Byrd's elder brothers John and Simon were choirboys at St Paul's Cathedral, no surviving evidence attests to William's membership in that choir; however, the text of a petition to the court of exchequer, mentioned as having been seen *c.*1810–1820, noted that he was indeed a chorister of St Paul's in early 1554 (aged ten or eleven), and it would have been natural for him to have followed his elder brothers there. Anthony Wood's claim that Byrd had been 'bred up to musick under Tho. Tallis' (*DNB*) receives support from Ferdinando Richardson's reference in Byrd's and Tallis's *Cantiones sacrae* (1575) to Byrd as 'born to honour such a great teacher' (*The Byrd Edition*, 1.xxvi) and from Byrd's abiding, close relationship to the elder composer. Given Tallis's prominent position in the Chapel Royal, Byrd might have studied with him there as a choirboy, having been taken for service from St Paul's, where he was certainly no longer in the choir by October 1554.

Lincoln, 1563–1572 On 6 February 1563 the cathedral chapter at Lincoln granted the rectory of Hainton, Lincolnshire, to 'a certain William Byrd, zealous in the art of music' (Shaw, 'William Byrd of Lincoln', 54), presumably an inducement to Byrd to accept the position of organist and master of the choristers. The appointment officially began on 25 March 1563 with a salary of £13 6*s.* 8*d.* for the two posts, and a rent-free house. During his later Lincoln years Byrd resided at the spot now known as 6 Minster Yard. Lincoln payment records from his early years attest to intensified musical activities: organ repairs, trips to Newark and Louth in search of choirboys, and flurries of music copying. Byrd also bore some teaching responsibilities. Much of his church music for the prayer book services probably dates from this period, together with most of the earlier settings of Latin sacred texts and a few songs for solo voice and viol consort, as well as instrumental works for solo keyboard or viol consort.

On 14 September 1568 Byrd married Julian Birley of Lincolnshire at St Margaret's in the Close, where their first son, Christopher, was baptized on 18 November 1569. Their eldest daughter, Elizabeth, followed Christopher to the font at St Margaret's on 20 January 1572.

Music at the cathedral may have suffered during Byrd's later years there, when attitudes of protestant austerity increasingly predominated. The composer ran foul of the cathedral chapter in 1569: on 19 November his salary was sequestrated because of 'certain matters of objection to the same by the said lords of the chapter' (Shaw, 'William Byrd of Lincoln', 55). He incurred no financial loss, however, because the order was rescinded nine months later. The reason behind the chapter's action is unclear. Possibly Byrd's adherence to the old religion became more apparent to an intensifyingly vigilant and reform-minded clergy. Another chapter minute from September 1570 suggests that his elaborate performance style as organist might have caused the problem. He was instructed to restrict himself in future to giving the singers their pitches for the canticles at matins and evensong and to singing his part with the choir during the anthem. The chapter might also have frowned upon his increased absences. That his future patron John Petre paid 1*d.* 'To Byrdes boye' (Harley, 40) at the Middle Temple in January 1568 may suggest that the composer had been venturing to London, perhaps in hopes of preferment at court.

London, 1572–*c.*1577 The composer Robert Parsons's drowning in the River Trent at Newark early in 1572 provided Byrd with the opportunity to return to London, where he was sworn in as a gentleman of the Chapel Royal on 22 February. He may have wished to keep some hold on the Lincoln position. The following year the chapter resolved to pay him £3 6*s.* 8*d.* a year (the difference between his former salary and his successor's reduced salary) after 'certain noblemen and counsellors of the queen's highness had addressed to them their gracious letters on behalf and in favour of the said William Byrde' (Shaw, 'William Byrd of Lincoln', 58). In return Byrd was to provide 'the aforesaid cathedral church songs and divine services well set to music' (ibid.).

The Byrds may soon have taken up residence in Westminster. Mary Byrd was baptized at St Margaret's, Westminster, on 24 January 1574. Thomas Byrd was baptized there on 30 March 1576, with Thomas Tallis standing godfather; a twin brother, Edward, baptized simultaneously, may not have long survived, since no further reference to him has come to light. Another daughter, Rachel, seems to have been born about the time of the removal from Lincoln.

Although never so designated in the records of the Chapel Royal, Byrd and Tallis served as chapel organists and styled themselves accordingly on the title-page of the 1575 *Cantiones sacrae*, as Byrd continued to do in his later Latin music publications. In addition to establishing himself alongside Tallis at the centre of Chapel Royal musical activities, he quickly became involved in entrepreneurial schemes, such as the acquisition of property and the establishment of music printing in England, where that enterprise had scarcely existed previously. On 22 January 1575 Queen Elizabeth granted Byrd and Tallis the exclusive right to print any 'songe or songes in partes, either in English, Latine, Frenche, Italian, or other tongues that may serve for musicke either in Churche or chamber, or otherwise to be either plaid or soonge' (*The Byrd Edition*, 1.xxiv) for a period of twenty-one years. The monopoly extended to the printing of music-staff paper, while other booksellers were even forbidden to import or market music from abroad. To make their patent known and to honour their royal patron Tallis and Byrd inaugurated their monopoly later that year with *Cantiones, quae ab argumento sacrae vocantur* ('Songs which because of their Subject Matter are called Sacred'). These thirty-four Latin motets were printed by the Huguenot émigré Thomas Vautrollier.

This impressive inauguration of the monopoly had no immediate successors. In 1577 Tallis and Byrd lamented to the queen that the 'lycense for the printinge of musicke … hath fallen oute to oure greate losse and hinderaunce to the value of two hundred markes at the least' (*The Byrd Edition*, 1.viii). They had apparently overestimated England's incipient music market. Thomas Norton, in a protest against English printing monopolies dated 1586, observed that 'Bird and Tallys have musicke books with note which the complainantes confesse they would not print nor be furnished to print though there were no privilege' (ibid.). Byrd further complained that he had 'come into debt & greate necessitie' (Fellowes, 10) because his daily attendance at court prevented his teaching to supplement his salary. The queen did no more than make to the composers a grant in reversion for twenty-one years of manors and a clutch of tithes in five counties; for this they were to pay the exchequer £35 5*s*. 9*d*. per year, keeping for themselves any surplus they were able to extract.

Harlington, c.1577–1593 About 1577 the Byrds moved to the village of Harlington, Middlesex. The earliest evidence of their presence there is a list of recusants from the village, which includes 'The wife of William Bird one of the gent of her Majesties chappell' (Harley, 63). This is also the first documentation of the Byrds' espousal of the old religion. Byrd's wife, Julian, more obdurate in her resistance towards the new religion, was cited much more frequently than her husband, often with John Reason, a singing-man from Lincoln who had followed Byrd to London as a trusted family servant. In 1584 Reason was apprehended carrying letters from Byrd to Catholic sympathizers, together with 'one old prynted songe booke' (Harley, 73), possibly the 1575 *Cantiones sacrae*. He was repeatedly committed to prison for recusancy, where he died in the plague of 1603–4.

Byrd's Roman Catholic sympathies had become apparent to the authorities at least by 1581, when 'Wylliam Byrde of the Chappell At his house in the parish of Harlington in com. Midd.' appears in a catalogue of 'The places where certaine recusantes remove in and about the city of London or are to be com by uppon warninge' (Fellowes, 38–9). Concurrently he was listed among 'relievers of papistes' in the London area 'at the Lord Padgettes house Draighton' (ibid.), not far from the Byrds' new home at Harlington. Thomas, Lord Paget, shared not only Byrd's Catholic sympathies but also a keen interest in music, and may have provided him with an annuity in the 1580s. Letters to Paget suggest that Byrd criticized the compositional efforts of Paget and his circle (which included another Byrd patron, the earl of Worcester), and was indeed a 'reliever of papists'. He could be found amid those convened to meet the Jesuits Henry Garnet and Robert Southwell at Hurleyford, not far from Harlington, in July 1586.

Yet in spite of frequent charges for recusancy, assessment of apparently crippling fines, and even his excommunication in the 1590s, Byrd retained his post in the Chapel Royal and his family never felt the full severity of the recusancy laws, for his political allies interceded on his behalf. The controlment roll from the 1590s includes a note regarding Byrd, for example: 'process to cease by order of the Queen' (Mateer, 'William Byrd's Middlesex recusancy', 11). The attorney-general also intervened in support of the composer in 1589 and 1591.

Byrd did not exercise his music printing privilege again for a dozen years, by which time Tallis had died and his interest in the patent had passed to his godson Thomas Byrd. It was only in 1588, a few months after the death of the printer Vautrollier, that Byrd once more ventured into print. During the eight remaining years of Byrd's monopoly Thomas East, his assignee, brought out more than twenty music publications, thereby establishing England's modest music printing trade. The publication of Byrd's own works dominated the early stages of this music printing 'boom': four different collections appeared between 1588 and 1591, which brought together systematically the fruits of his musical labours during the highly productive 1580s. The first collection, *Psalmes, Sonets, & Songs of Sadness and Pietie* (1588), dedicated to Sir Christopher Hatton, sold sufficiently well for two further editions to be printed before the year was out, and a fourth as late as 1606–7. The thirty-five songs in five parts had the look of newfangled madrigals, but in fact belonged to the older English tradition of accompanied solo song, as Byrd explained in the preface: 'heere are divers songs, which being originally made for Instruments to expresse the harmonie, and one voyce to pronounce the dittie, are now framed in all parts for voyces to sing the same' (*Collected Works*, 12.xii).

The success of the *Psalmes* encouraged Byrd to bring out his *Songs of Sundrie Natures* in 1589, dedicated to Queen Elizabeth's first cousin Henry Carey, Lord Hunsdon. A second edition of this comparably successful collection was printed before the end of the year, and a further edition appeared as late as 1610. For this volume Byrd relied less on pre-existent songs—the title-page specifies that the works were 'lately made and composed into Musicke' (*Collected Works*, 13.vii)—and incorporated greater diversity, with music in three to six parts. It included not only a few old accompanied solo songs, now fully texted, but also partsongs, a song with its original viol accompaniment, carols, and 'Christ rising again from the dead', an impressively expansive consort anthem for solo voices and viols, alternating with full chorus.

Neither of these collections partook significantly of the Italian madrigal vogue sweeping England by the late 1580s. Only in his two madrigals (four- and six-part versions of 'This sweet and merry month of May') for Thomas Watson's *The First Sett, of Italian Madrigalls Englished* (1590) did Byrd embrace the madrigal idiom with much outward enthusiasm, thereby creating the earliest examples of native English madrigals. His true feelings about the style may be reflected in the final line of the madrigal text, however: 'take well in worth a simple toy' (*The Byrd Edition*, 16.43–5).

Byrd's dedication for the 1588 *Psalmes* had promised 'some other things of more depth and skill to folow these, which being not yet finished, are of divers expected and desired' (*Collected Works*, 12.xi). *Liber primus sacrarum cantionum* (1589), dedicated to the composer's long-time friend, patron, and fellow Roman Catholic Edward Somerset, earl of Worcester, consists of sixteen Latin motets in five parts, composed over the previous decade. *Liber secundus sacrarum cantionum* followed in 1591, dedicated to John, first Lord Lumley, and offering another twenty-one motets in six as well as five parts. These motets revealed Byrd as the first English composer to master thoroughly the flexibly imitative textures and intense textual expression associated with their continental counterparts, but still new to England. Concurrently he assembled much of his most significant keyboard music for compilation in a manuscript anthology. My Ladye Nevells Booke, copied in 1591 by John Baldwin, a singing-man of St George's Chapel, Windsor, and apparently corrected by Byrd himself, includes some forty-two pieces in various forms and styles, and has an impressive collection of pavan–galliard dance pairs as its centrepiece.

Among the most striking features of Byrd's music of the 1580s is the way it reflects his commitment to the strongly besieged old religion. His 1588 *Psalmes, Sonets, & Songs* included, for example, 'Why do I use paper, ink, and pen', verses commemorating the notorious execution of the priest Edmund Campion at Tyburn in 1581. More arresting still are the expressive settings of several motet texts about the plight of Jerusalem, the Egyptian or Babylonian captivity, martyrdom, or the coming of God, many of which were published in 1589 and 1591. These employ language that reappears in the letters of Roman Catholic martyrs, in their speeches from the scaffold, in the texts of published underground Catholic propaganda, and even on the title-pages of some of these publications.

Stondon Massey, 1593–1623 Between July 1593 and early 1595 Byrd moved his family to Stondon Place in the parish of Stondon Massey, Essex, the area where the family had originated, but also the home territory of another long-time friend and patron, Sir John Petre of Ingatestone, Essex. Byrd had had his eye on that part of the country since as early as 1574, when he had acquired the lease of Battyshall Manor, not far from Stondon Massey. By the mid-1580s his friendship with Petre had grown to the point where Byrd visited for extended periods, particularly at religious holidays. In the early seventeenth century he had a room of his own in the Petre household at Thorndon Hall. Byrd advised his patron on musical hiring, procured music for him, and regularly gave him and his wife two turkeys at Christmas.

The removal to Stondon Massey seems to have coincided with changes in Byrd's professional status. In 1592 John Bull was named in the Chapel Royal cheque book as organist. Though Byrd continued to be certified as a court resident for tax purposes, his signature does not occur among the gentlemen of the Chapel Royal who began to sign the cheque book more regularly after 1592, and he appears very rarely on lists of chapel members. He probably attended the funeral of Queen Elizabeth and the coronation of James I in 1603, and he definitely sang 'melodious songs' with the likes of Orlando Gibbons, Elway Bevin, William Lawes, and other gentlemen when James I dined at the Merchant Taylors' Hall in 1607 (Nichols, 2.139). But otherwise he is scarcely heard of at court.

Byrd's sizeable contribution to the musical repertory of the official Elizabethan liturgy had a lasting impact, however. He composed examples of virtually every type of service music, from the modest 'short' service, to the varied textures of the verse service, to the lavish and complex 'great' service. Because much of this music was eventually published in John Barnard's *First Book of Selected Church Musick* (1641), some of it was still performed long after his other works had been temporarily forgotten.

Having withdrawn into semi-retirement at Stondon, Byrd became part of the Roman Catholic community that Petre discreetly maintained in his country manors, where an irregular round of services took place and where priest holes can be seen to this day. The Byrds soon began to appear on recusancy lists at the quarter sessions and in the archidiaconal court of Essex, but Petre's influence on the jury probably shielded the family from severe reprisals.

Byrd seems also to have continued his dangerous flirtations with the Catholic underground and the Jesuits. In 1605 one Charles de Ligny, recently returned to France from Britain, described a musical evening involving the Jesuit Henry Garnet, other Jesuits and English gentlemen, and 'Mr. William Byrd, who played the organs and many other instruments' (Harley, 143). De Ligny was subsequently arrested and briefly imprisoned for possessing Byrd's recently published *Gradualia*.

The two volumes of *Gradualia* (1605–7) offer striking musical testimony to Byrd's links to the Catholic community, for they contain polyphonic settings of the propers (the texts that change from feast to feast) of the Roman Catholic mass. Concurrent with his removal to Stondon, Byrd had arranged for the printing of three settings of the mass ordinary (the unchanging liturgical texts), one for four voices in 1592–3, one for three voices in 1593–4, and one for five voices in 1594–5; second editions of the three- and four-part masses appeared about 1599. That the ordinary settings lacked identifying title-pages, dedicatees, and printer's devices and apparently were not registered with the Stationers' Company suggests surreptitious printing for use by Britain's Roman Catholics. Recusant enclaves such as Byrd's patrons the Pastons of Norfolk, known to have celebrated mass with music and processions around the garden, could well have employed Byrd's masses and *Gradualia* to adorn their liturgies.

The *Gradualia* were registered and published more openly. The first volume's title-page and dedication to Henry Howard, earl of Northampton, may have been added only when both sets were reissued in 1610, however. Volume 2 was dedicated to John Petre of Writtle, now Lord Petre, with the remark that the works 'have mostly proceded from your house … these little flowers, plucked as it were from your gardens and most rightfully due to you as tithes' (Kerman, *Masses and Motets*, 50). The publication was also more overt about its provision of the chief propers of the mass on the primary feasts of the Roman Catholic church year and for feasts of the Virgin Mary, as well as for some texts of the office. In both volumes these texts were set much more concisely than the 1589 and 1591 *Cantiones* and followed a complicated scheme whereby propers for different services that shared the same text or partial text employed a single music setting in the different contexts. The necessary transfer of a music setting from one feast to another was sometimes (but not always) indicated in the print with rubrics or special signs, a scheme which music scholars and performers sorted out only in the late twentieth century.

Although Byrd referred to *Gradualia* as his swan song, he ventured into print another three times. In 1611 his *Psalmes, Songs, and Sonnets*, dedicated to Francis Clifford, earl of Cumberland, was published by the assignee of William Barley, Thomas Snodham. In this collection, which Byrd described as 'like to be my last Travailes in this kind' and 'my last labours, for myne ultimum vale' (*The Byrd Edition*, 14.xx–xxi), he brought together solo songs with viol accompaniment, anthems for full chorus, consort anthems with viol accompaniment, partsongs in three to six parts, even the four-part version of his old madrigal 'This sweet and merry month of May' from 1590, and two highly imitative fantasias for consort that probably date back to the same period.

Shortly thereafter, *c.*1612–1613, Byrd joined John Bull and Orlando Gibbons in the ground-breaking keyboard publication *Parthenia*, to which he contributed pavans and galliards, with brief introductory preludes, the only representatives of his important body of keyboard music published during his lifetime. Finally, in 1614 he collaborated with twenty other composers in Sir William Leighton's *The Teares or Lamentacions of a Sorrowful Soule*, for which he provided four modest sacred partsongs.

Byrd's mention of 'my family's troubled affairs' (*The Byrd Edition*, 5.xxxvi) in the dedication to the first volume of *Gradualia* may refer not only to trials suffered because of his faith during his semi-retirement at Stondon, but also to his intense preoccupation with legal entanglements of a sort that were common throughout his life. Ever since the late 1570s he had been embroiled almost continuously in half a dozen different legal disputes over landholdings. The majority began in the 1590s; some went on for twenty years or more, generated an endless stream of legal documents (extensively excerpted in Fellowes and Harley), and reveal the composer as a determined, aggressive pursuer of his own interests, prepared even to resort to force if necessary. In the bitter, protracted dispute over Stondon Hall he claimed, for example, 'that yf he could not hould it by right, he would holde it by might' (Harley, 147).

Fellowes suggested that Byrd's wife, Julian, had died at Harlington and had been succeeded by a second wife named Ellen, whose name occurs in recusancy records between March 1600 and October 1607. This may have resulted from confusion with a recusant family servant, Ellen Barcroft, for Julian was still listed as the composer's wife in a document from April 1608 regarding the family's land disputes. She seems to have died before July 1609, and was buried at Stondon. Their elder son, Christopher, followed her in 1615. Their other son, Thomas, wandered widely from the family home. Apparently having studied for a time at one of the inns of court, he was admitted to the English College at Valladolid, Spain, in December 1596, on the recommendation of the Jesuit Henry Garnet. Thomas left the college, then returned, but was expelled in 1599, after which he appeared briefly the following year at the English College at Rome; he eventually came to reside in Drury Lane, London. Thomas must have achieved some distinction in music, for he was John Bull's substitute as music lecturer at Gresham College from 1601 to 1603.

Byrd probably passed his last years within the community at Ingatestone, without the company of Petre, who died in 1613. Byrd remained in contact with his other old patron, the earl of Worcester, at whose house in the Strand he still had a room when he drafted his will. The document was signed on 15 November 1622, some six months before his death on 4 July 1623. Byrd presumably was laid to rest, as his will had stipulated, 'in the parish of

Stondon … neare unto the place where my wife lyest buryed' (Fellowes, 246).

Reputation The prefatory materials to Byrd's *Cantiones sacrae* (1575) and *Gradualia* (vol. 2, 1607) refer to the composer in similar terms, as British music's 'parent', a characterization reaffirmed in the cheque book of the Chapel Royal at his death: 'a father of musicke' (*DNB*, 578). In Oxford, Christ Church, MSS 984–988, Robert Dow echoed other sentiments expressed from the 1575 *Cantiones*. Responding to Cicero's remark, 'I do not think you will find any [Englishman] skilled in either reading, writing, or music', Dow added, 'One man, Byrd, completely frees all the English from this reproach' (Boyd, 82). For Nicholas Yonge, Byrd was 'a great Maister of Musicke' (Boyd, 208); for John Baldwin, 'homo memorabilis' (Fellowes, 237); and for Henry Peacham, 'Our Phoenix' (Boyd, 83). Thus, Byrd and his contemporaries were aware of the innovative and singular quality of his art, and his role as a 'founding father' of Renaissance music in Britain. Thomas Morley and Thomas Tomkins both claimed Byrd as their teacher. John Bull, Peter Phillips, and Thomas Weelkes may have studied with him as well.

Byrd was the first Englishman to master fully the quintessential feature of continental Renaissance music, systematic but flexible imitative textures. In setting secular texts he avoided another commonplace of the late Renaissance, madrigalian word-painting, preferring instead the less demonstrative accompanied solo song—'his vein is not so much for leight Madrigals or Canzonets' (Boyd, 83), as Henry Peacham observed in 1622. Yet Byrd espoused the expressive Renaissance aesthetic with great conviction in setting Latin words. Although his Latin motets had no real successors in England, his generally reserved, syllabic, but frequently highly imitative music for the prayer book services remained in use for generations, and established the model for the more complex varieties of Jacobean church music. He was also central to the development of the verse anthem and verse service.

The only surviving likeness of William Byrd is a much reproduced engraving by G. Van der Gucht, preserved in the British Museum. It was based on a drawing by Nicola Francesco Haym, who intended to include it in a history of music, never published. A portrait of Tallis, reversed in the engraving process, appears on the same plate. The authenticity of both likenesses has long been questioned. CRAIG MONSON

Sources J. Harley, *William Byrd, gentleman of the Chapel Royal* (1997) [incl. complete work list] • *The Byrd edition*, ed. P. Brett, [17 vols.] (1976–) • *The collected works of William Byrd*, ed. E. H. Fellowes, 20 vols. (1937–50) • W. Byrd, *Keyboard music*, ed. A. Brown, Musica Britannica, 27–8 (1976) • R. Bowers, 'Music and liturgy to 1640', *A history of Lincoln Minster*, ed. D. Owen (1994), 47–76 • R. Turbet, *William Byrd, a guide to research* (1987) • R. Turbet, *Tudor music: a research and information guide; with an appendix updating 'William Byrd, a guide to research'* (1994) • J. Kerman, 'Byrd, William', *New Grove*, 2nd edn [incl. work list] • E. H. Fellowes, *William Byrd*, 2nd edn (1974) • W. Shaw, 'William Byrd of Lincoln', *Music and Letters*, 48 (1967), 52–9 • D. Mateer, 'William Byrd's Middlesex recusancy', *Music and Letters*, 78 (1997), 1–14 • D. Mateer, 'William Byrd, John Petre and Oxford, Bodleian MS Mus. Sch. e. 423', *Royal Musical Association Research Chronicle*, 29 (1996), 21–46 • M. C. Boyd, *Elizabethan music and musical criticism*, new edn (1974) • J. Kerman, *The masses and motets of William Byrd* (1981), vol. 1 of *The music of William Byrd* • *DNB* • J. Nichols, *The progresses, processions, and magnificent festivities of King James I, his royal consort, family and court*, 4 vols. (1828) • J. L. Smith, 'From "rights to copy" to "bibliographic ego": a new look at the last edition of Byrd's *Psalmes, Sonets & Songs*', *Music and Letters*, 80 (1999), 511–30 • C. Monson, 'Byrd, the Catholics, and the motet: the hearing reopened', *Hearing the motet*, ed. D. Pesce (1997), 348–74 • I. Payne, *The provision and practice of sacred music at Cambridge colleges and selected cathedrals, c.1547–c.1646* (1993) • H. W. Shaw, *The succession of organists of the Chapel Royal and the cathedrals of England and Wales from c.1538* (1991) • P. Clulow, 'Publication dates for Byrd's Latin masses', *Music and Letters*, 47 (1966), 1–9 • J. L. Jackman, 'Liturgical aspects of Byrd's *Gradualia*', *Musical Quarterly*, 49 (1963), 17–37 • O. W. Neighbour, *The consort and keyboard music of William Byrd* (1978), vol. 3 of *The music of William Byrd* • P. Brett, 'Edward Paston (1550–1630): a Norfolk gentleman and his musical collection', *Transactions of the Cambridge Bibliographical Society*, 4 (1964–8), 51–69 • will, proved 30 Oct 1623, PRO, PROB 11/142

Archives BL, MSS, Add. MSS • Bodl. Oxf. • Christ Church Oxf., MSS • Durham Cath. CL, MSS • Pembroke Cam., MSS • Peterhouse, Cambridge, MSS • Royal College of Music, MSS • Royal Music Library, MSS

Likenesses G. Vandergucht, engraving (after drawing by N. F. Haym, c.1729), BM • engraving (after earlier engraving); reproduction, BM

Wealth at death farm at Stondon Massey, Essex, with contents and woods, to widow of eldest son; contents of rooms in earl of Worcester's house in the Strand to his second son; £20 p.a. to eldest daughter: will, PRO, PROB 10, box 404; PRO, PROB 11/142, proved 30 Oct 1623; Harley, 391–3; Fellowes, 246–8

Byrd, William (1674–1744), landowner and diarist, was born on 28 March 1674 near the fall line of the James River, Virginia, the first of five children of William Byrd (1652–1704), colonial officer and planter, and Mary Horsmanden Filmer (1650–1699), a well-connected widow and daughter of Warham Horsmanden. When he died in 1704 Byrd's father, one of the wealthiest and most prominent citizens of Virginia, bequeathed to his son a fortune, high social position, and political prestige. At the tender age of two Byrd accompanied his mother to England to avoid the dangers occasioned by Bacon's rebellion. In 1681 he travelled alone to England to commence his education under the care of his grandfather, Warham Horsmanden, and his uncle, Daniel Horsmanden. For nine years he studied at Felsted grammar school in Essex; thereafter he was apprenticed to Byrd's English merchants, Perry and Lane, and served for a brief time in the Netherlands. In 1692 he entered the Middle Temple to read law and was appointed agent for Virginia by the house of burgesses. That same year, on the strength of his interest in natural history and his friendship with Sir Robert Southwell, he became a fellow of the Royal Society. He also became a close friend of Charles Boyle, later earl of Orrery. In 1695 he was admitted to the English bar; a year later he sought a position with the Board of Trade but was rejected. In 1696 he returned to Virginia as a polished gentleman with a taste for classical literature, an eye for fashion, a training in law, and a circle of distinguished friends among the English gentry and nobility. Immediately he was elected to the house of burgesses.

In 1697 Byrd went back to England, again as agent for the colony of Virginia. During all his services in this office

William Byrd (**1674–1744**), attrib. Hans Hysing, *c.*1725

he proved to be a most urbane and successful diplomat. Upon the death of his father in December 1704 he returned to Virginia and settled on the estate, Westover, that his father had purchased in 1688. In 1733 he laid plans to found two cities, Richmond and Petersburg, on prosperous plantations in his possession. About two years later he demolished his father's wood frame house at Westover and replaced it with a superb brick mansion that still stands. He continued in the Indian trade his father had begun, bought and sold tobacco, and imported supplies which he sold to his neighbours. Although he deplored the increase of black slaves in Virginia he had become part owner of a slave ship, the *William and Jane*, in 1697; later this ship was captured by a French privateer off the coast of Africa. During his lifetime he accumulated over 179,000 acres of land and was considered to be vastly wealthy. Nevertheless he sometimes made mistakes in business and was left short of ready cash. He was constantly hatching schemes, never brought to fruition, to relieve himself of temporary money problems.

Byrd also continued his careers in politics and public service. In 1706 he assumed the post of receiver-general of the royal revenues; ten years later, when he returned to England, he sold the post for £500. In 1709 he was appointed a member of the council of state, a powerful office that he retained for the rest of his life; in his last year he was president of the council, a post of high honour. Also in 1709 he unsuccessfully sought the governorships of Virginia and Maryland. As agent for Virginia from 1714 to 1722, he struggled with Lieutenant-Governor Alexander Spottswood, who wanted to change the way quitrents were collected in order to weaken the power of wealthy planters. Moreover Spottswood tried to establish courts of oyer and terminer to curtail the judicial powers of the council. Byrd opposed Spottswood's attempts to strengthen royal authority in Virginia, and Spottswood tried to have Byrd removed from the council. Eventually the two men reconciled their differences, with neither side winning a clear-cut victory. Subsequently Byrd attempted, without success, to become surveyor of customs for the southern district. In the military line he commanded the militias of Charles City and Henrico counties. In 1711 he mobilized these militias when a false alarm—that fourteen French men-of-war were threatening an invasion—swept Virginia.

In his later years Byrd lived quietly at Westover, enjoying his extensive library and his family. In 1706 he had married Lucy Parke, daughter of Daniel Parke, governor of the Leeward Islands. Although their relationship at times was stormy they had four children, two of whom survived infancy, before Lucy died of smallpox in 1716. Eight years later Byrd married Maria Taylor, daughter of Thomas Taylor of Kensington, London; they also had four children, all of whom grew to adulthood and had families. In 1728 Byrd led a party in surveying the Virginia–North Carolina boundary. From this experience came his *History of the Dividing Line Run in the Year 1728* (eventually edited by Edmund Ruffin and published in 1841) which permanently established his reputation as a man of letters. In 1736 he oversaw another survey that delineated the boundaries of the Northern Neck.

For years Byrd kept diaries, written in code, on an almost daily basis. The surviving diaries, covering the years 1709–12, 1717–21, and 1739–41, were 'translated' and published in the 1940s. Never intended to be made public, they reveal an extraordinary amount of information about Byrd's personal affairs, including his sexual life. They also throw light on the political and social doings of the Virginia aristocracy in the first half of the eighteenth century. The diaries also include the earliest reference to the game of cricket being played in the American colonies, involving no more than four players at a time and for a wager. Byrd died on 26 August 1744 at Westover and was buried there; his second wife survived him.

PAUL DAVID NELSON

Sources M. Tinling, ed., *The correspondence of the three William Byrds of Westover, Virginia, 1684–1776*, 2 vols. (1977) • *The writings of 'Colonel William Byrd of Westover in Virginia'*, ed. J. S. Bassett (1901) • P. Marambaud, *William Byrd of Westover, 1674–1744* (1971) • R. C. Beatty, *William Byrd of Westover* (1932) • A. Hatch, *The Byrds of Virginia* (1969) • L. B. Wright and M. Tinling, eds., *The secret diary of William Byrd of Westover, 1709–1712* (1941) • *The London diary, 1717–1721, and other writings [of] William Byrd of Virginia*, ed. L. B. Wright and M. Tinling (1958) • *Executive journals of the council of colonial Virginia*, 1, ed. H. R. McIlwaine (1925) • J. P. Greene, 'The opposition to Lieutenant Governor Alexander Spottswood, 1718', *Virginia Magazine of History and Biography*, 70 (1962), 35–42 • W. D. Houlette, 'The Byrd library', *Tyler's Quarterly Historical and Genealogical Magazine*, 16 (1934), 100–09 • L. B. Wright, *The first gentlemen of Virginia: intellectual qualities of the early colonial ruling class* (1940) • K. A. Lockridge, *The diary, and life, of William Byrd II of Virginia, 1674–1744* (1987) • M. B. Pritchard and V. L. Sites, *William Byrd II and his lost history* (1993)

Archives Hunt. L., diaries • University of North Carolina, Chapel Hill, diary and notebook • Virginia Historical Society, Richmond, diary, commonplace book, and letter-books
Likenesses oils, before 1705, Colonial Williamsburg Foundation, Williamsburg, Virginia • attrib. H. Hysing, oils, *c*.1725, Virginia Historical Society, Richmond [*see illus.*]

Byrde, John. *See* Turval, Jean l'Oiseau de (*d*. 1631), *under* Tuvell, Daniel (*d*. 1660).

Byres, James, of Tonley (1734–1817), antiquary and architect, was born on 7 May 1734 at Tonley, his family's estate in the parish of Tough, Aberdeenshire; he was the first of the seven children of Patrick Byres (*b*. 1713), laird of Tonley, and of his wife, Janet Moir (*d*. 1787). His father, a staunch Jacobite, escaped after the Jacobite rising of 1745 to France, where James was presumably educated. In 1758 he went to Rome. There he initially studied painting under Rafael Mengs, and in 1768 was elected as an *architetto* to the Accademia di San Luca, where the portrait of him in his academician's robes probably gave rise to the family tradition that he was a 'lay cardinal'. From 1764 he was the leading cicerone, or antiquarian guide, to the young aristocrats on the grand tour; he dealt in antiquities and art, and introduced potential clients to Italian and other painters. Among the latter were Pompeo Batoni, who painted a number of Scots, and Louis Ducros, whose classical scenes, purchased at Byres's suggestion by Sir Richard Colt Hoare, impressed J. M. W. Turner; the talented young Scottish artists he assisted in Rome included David Allan. Unlike many of his rivals, Byres belonged to more or less the same social class as his clients; intellectually, he was in touch with his contemporaries Piranesi and Winckelmann, and he corresponded with James Black and Joseph Hutton in Edinburgh. It is clear that his interest in the past was far from exclusively artistic, or commercial.

At an early stage in his antiquarian career Byres visited Tarquinia and inspected some of the painted Etruscan tombs there. This prompted the idea of compiling an illustrated account of them. In the event only some of the plates, engraved by Byres's associate Christopher Norton from drawings by the Polish painter Franciszek Smuglewicz, were finally published by Frank Howard as *Hypogaei, or, Sepulchral Caverns of Tarquinia* (1842). Byres's text was apparently never finished: the surviving notes grapple bravely with the nature of the evidence, the geology of the Mediterranean, the first inhabitants of Italy, and what he regarded as the Romans' barbarous suppression of Etruscan achievements.

Professionally, Byres contributed much to the formation of neo-classical taste in Britain. Personally, he was no less fascinated by the remote past. This is reflected in his tireless quest, confided to his private journal, for 'petrifications' (fossils) and volcanoes during a journey undertaken in 1766, ostensibly to introduce a certain Mr Wilbraham to the classical antiquities of south Italy and Sicily. A similar itinerary was followed three years later by Sir William Hamilton, with whom Byres corresponded about earthquakes, and to whom he sold the Barberini vase (later known as the Portland vase, now in the British

James Byres of Tonley (1734–1817), by John Bogle, pubd 1782

Museum). Byres's careful descriptions of geological phenomena and of excavated artefacts now readily identifiable as prehistoric vividly illustrate the first steps towards the recognition—in the following century—of the antiquity of man.

Contemporary descriptions of Byres's character are few, and not wholly positive: 'My guide was Mr Byers [*sic*], a Scotch antiquary of experience and taste; but in the daily labour of eighteen weeks the powers of attention were sometimes fatigued …', wrote Edward Gibbon (*Memoirs of my Life*, ed. B. Radice, 1984, 142). However, Gibbon also indicated that he had conceived *The Decline and Fall of the Roman Empire* shortly after beginning his course with Byres (in 1764), and that 'it was the view of Italy and Rome which determined the choice of the subject' (ibid., 143).

Byres left Rome in 1790, and spent the next twenty-seven years as laird of Tonley. His concern for the improvement of the estate and for the well-being of his numerous relatives was clearly exemplary. He died, unmarried, at Tonley on 3 September 1817. One of his few executed architectural projects, the free-standing domed temple that he designed as a mausoleum for his neighbour Miss Eliza Fraser of Castle Fraser, is the finest classical tomb in the north of Scotland. DAVID RIDGWAY

Sources B. Ford, 'James Byres: principal antiquarian for the English visitors to Rome', *Apollo*, 99 (1974), 446–61 • H. Gordon-Slade, 'James Byres of Tonley, 1734–1817: the Aberdeen years', *Deeside Field*, 19 (1987), 130–39 • D. Ridgway, 'James Byres and the ancient state of Italy: unpublished documents in Edinburgh', *Atti, secondo congresso internazionale Etrusco, Firenze, 1985*, 1 (1989), 213–29 • F. Howard, *Hypogaei, or, Sepulchral caverns of Tarquinia, the capital of antient Etruria by the late James Byres Esq., of Tonley Aberdeenshire, nearly forty years antiquarian resident at Rome prior to 1791* (1842) • A. J. M.

Gill, *The families of Moir and Byres* (1885) • *DNB* • J. Ingamells, ed., *A dictionary of British and Irish travellers in Italy, 1701–1800* (1997)

Archives NL Scot., 'Journal of my jaunt to Sicily in company with Mr Wilbraham', inv. n. MS 10339 • NL Scot., letters, MSS, and works • NL Scot., notes for his *History of the Etrurians* and other documents and letters, deposit 184 • NL Wales, unexecuted designs for Wynnstay

Likenesses attrib. A. Maron, oils, 1767, Accademia di San Luca, Rome • attrib. P. Wickstead, group portrait, oils, *c.*1773 (with group of Englishmen), Audley End House, Essex; version Springhill, Londonderry, Northern Ireland • Tassie, paste medallion, 1779, Scot. NPG • J. Bogle, mezzotint, pubd 1782, NPG [*see illus.*] • H. D. Hamilton, oils, Aberdeen • F. Smuglewicz, group portrait, oils (with family), Scot. NPG • F. Smuglewicz, group portrait, oils, Paul Mellon Centre, London, Brinsley Ford archive

Byrhtferth of Ramsey (*fl.* *c.*986–*c.*1016), Benedictine monk and scholar, was the author of a substantial corpus of writing, in both Latin and Old English. Very little is known of his life beyond what can be gleaned from incidental references in his writings.

Life The date of Byrhtferth's birth is unknown (it may conjecturally be placed *c.*970). He was probably given as an oblate to Ramsey Abbey (founded in 966), for he always speaks of Ramsey as his home in terms of warmth and gratitude. He was a young student, perhaps in his teens, when Ramsey housed the great Frankish scholar, Abbo of Fleury, for two years between 985 and 987. One of the most learned men of his time, Abbo helped to establish Ramsey as a prominent centre of scholarship in late tenth-century western Europe. He evidently brought with him to Ramsey a substantial collection of books, from which he taught such subjects as computus and prosody. He was also an accomplished prose stylist and hagiographer. Byrhtferth followed his master Abbo, to whom he always referred in terms of deep respect, in each of these fields, and probably succeeded Abbo as master of the Ramsey school. Beyond these few details, however, nothing is known of Byrhtferth's life, and he is best approached through his writings, in Latin and Old English, some (but not all) of which can be dated and placed in a chronological sequence.

Computistical works and glosses Perhaps Byrhtferth's earliest composition is a Latin computus, that is, a compilation consisting of arithmetical tables, formulas, and rules used in the calculation of movable Christian feasts, principally Easter. Before ordination all priests were required to demonstrate some knowledge of computistical reckoning; and, as schoolmaster at Ramsey, Byrhtferth was responsible for teaching computus not only to novices among the Ramsey monks later to be ordained, but also (as emerges from his *Enchiridion*) other ordinands from the diocese who were not monks but secular clerics. Byrhtferth's *Computus* (which has never been printed in its entirety) took over much material from an earlier one by Abbo; but in revising Abbo's work Byrhtferth added a number of items from earlier English computi (which, presumably, he regarded as more accessible than those in Abbo's work), as well as various items of his own, including a prefatory *Epilogus* (he wrongly understood the word *epilogus* to mean 'prologue'), an intricate diagram showing the harmony of the four elements, humours and seasons, a metrical calendar, and other miscellaneous tables and formulas. From various indications it is clear that Byrhtferth's *Computus* was being compiled during the years 988–96. The work is preserved in three twelfth-century English manuscripts (all of which have suffered some later interpolation and revision, although the outline of Byrhtferth's original work is clearly reconstructible), which show that it was found useful in the neighbouring fenland monasteries of Thorney and Peterborough, as well as at Winchcombe, Worcestershire, a house which had always enjoyed close links with Ramsey.

In the *Epilogus* Byrhtferth explained that the subject is best to be understood through study of Bede's scientific treatises (*De temporum ratione* and *De natura rerum*) as well as of the treatise on computus by Helperic of Auxerre. In a principal manuscript of Byrhtferth's *Computus* (Oxford, St John's College, MS 17), his work is followed by copies of these works of Bede and Helperic, which suggests that Byrhtferth assembled them as a sort of 'computistical miscellany'. The St John's manuscript carries extensive marginal glossing, some of which must, on stylistic grounds alone, derive from Byrhtferth himself. (None of this glossing has been printed.) It is interesting that one of the glosses to Bede's *De temporum ratione* includes a calculation on the *annus praesens* as 993, which squares well with the dating of 988–96 for Byrhtferth's *Computus*.

Another work by Byrhtferth which probably belongs to this early period of scholarly activity is the so-called Byrhtferth glosses. No manuscript of this survives. In his great edition of Bede published at Basel in 1563, Johannes Herwagen published alongside his texts of Bede's *De natura rerum* and *De temporum ratione* a series of what he called 'Brideferti glossae'. Although Byrhtferth's authorship of this work has been called in doubt, it was attributed to him by antiquaries such as John Bale, and it was arguably through the agency of Bale (who was in Basel 1554–9) that a copy reached Herwagen. In any event these Byrhtferth glosses are what might be described as a *collectaneum* or anthology of patristic quotations designed to amplify and elucidate the individual chapters of Bede's two works. They contain very little of Byrhtferth's own composition, but are an impressive witness to the breadth of his reading, and have many links with his other writings, notably the *Enchiridion*.

Computus is a difficult subject, and in an attempt to make his own computus more accessible to his students at Ramsey, Byrhtferth composed an introductory handbook, partly in Latin, partly in English, which he called his *Enchiridion*, and which he intended as a commentary on the various tables and diagrams in his Latin computus (many of which were reproduced, for sake of convenience, in the *Enchiridion*). From a calculation contained in the work, it is evident that he was composing his *Enchiridion* in 1011. In addition to computus, Byrhtferth's characteristic pedantry led him to include long digressions on other scholarly matters, such as metrical scansion, rhetorical terminology, weights and measures; the last section of the work (Part IV) is a self-contained Latin treatise on the arithmological significance of numbers, from one to one thousand. This is drawn from a wide range of patristic and Carolingian texts, many of which had already been excerpted in the Byrhtferth glosses, with which the *Enchiridion* is closely linked.

Historical and hagiographical works Byrhtferth modelled himself in many ways on his predecessor Bede; and as Bede's study of computus led him to chronography and the writing of history, so too did Byrhtferth's. One historical compilation which may confidently be attributed to Byrhtferth is the *Historia regum*, which is preserved as the earliest part of a work of the same name by the twelfth-century historian Symeon of Durham, who incorporated Byrhtferth's earlier work in his own. Byrhtferth's work covers the period from the earliest English kingdoms to the death of King Alfred; it is largely drawn from earlier works, including Byrhtferth's own *Passio SS. Æthelredi et Æthelberhti*, Bede's *De die judicii*, *Historia abbatum*, and *Historia ecclesiastica*; a set of annals for the years 732–802, evidently compiled at York and not otherwise extant; and Asser's life of Alfred. Byrhtferth may also have composed, as a sequel to his *Historia regum*, a history of tenth-century England up to his own day. This work has not survived, but it was demonstrably exploited by Byrhtferth himself in his life of St Oswald, by John of Worcester in his *Chronica chronicarum*, and by the anonymous twelfth-century compiler of the Ramsey *Liber benefactorum*.

Byrhtferth was also, like Bede, a productive hagiographer. His earliest essay in this genre was his *Passio SS. Æthelredi et Æthelberhti*, an account of two royal princes of Kent who were murdered, and whose remains were translated to Ramsey by the abbey's lay patron, Ealdorman Æthelwine, hence before 992. It is possible that Byrhtferth composed the work to accompany the translation; he subsequently incorporated it into his *Historia regum*. Some few years later, probably between 997 and 1002, he composed his life of St Oswald in commemoration of Oswald, the archbishop of York and founder of Ramsey Abbey, who had died in 992. Byrhtferth's life is a very substantial work, probably the longest surviving Anglo-Latin saint's life, and also one of the most historically valuable. It contains much information not found elsewhere about Oswald and his uncle Oda, archbishop of Canterbury from 941 to 958. However, Byrhtferth's intention was not to write history (he supplies no date anywhere in the work) but to glorify Archbishop Oswald as an icon of Benedictine monasticism. Byrhtferth's third saint's life, and probably his last composition (*c.*1016), is his life of St Ecgwine, an early eighth-century bishop of Worcester, who was the founder of Evesham Abbey. Unlike the life of St Oswald, where he was writing of a contemporary whom he had probably known, Byrhtferth had almost no information concerning Ecgwine beyond a (spurious) foundation charter and some deductions from place names of Evesham estates. He was therefore obliged to tease out his work by resort to arithmology and allegory, as well as pedantic digressions of various kinds.

Unlike Byrhtferth's other writings, which are clearly associable with Ramsey, the life of St Ecgwine is concerned with Evesham, and its final paragraph contains a direct address to the Evesham monks. Byrhtferth might simply have been fulfilling a commission from a closely associated monastery; but it is worth remembering that at the battle of 'Assandun' on 18 October 1016 several members of Edmund Ironside's defeated forces were Ramsey monks, including the bishop of Dorchester (Eadnoth) and the abbot of Ramsey (Wulfsige), both of whom were killed there. As a result of this opposition, the victor at 'Assandun', King Cnut, determined to suppress Ramsey, and was only dissuaded from so doing by the intercession of the abbot of Peterborough. It is possible that, in the turmoil which followed 'Assandun', Byrhtferth left his alma mater at the invitation of his colleague Ælfweard, a former monk of Ramsey who was then abbot of Evesham, and that he composed his life of St Ecgwine in response to this hospitality. But this can be no more than conjecture, and the date of Byrhtferth's death is unknown.

Assessment In spite of his pedantry and flair for ostentation, Byrhtferth was one of the most learned and prolific authors of the late Anglo-Saxon period. He was able to quote from a wide range of reading, including the poets (both classical and Christian) of the school curriculum, as well as the writings of many church fathers. His favourite author was Aldhelm, whose flamboyant prose style had an unfortunate influence on Byrhtferth, who was able to imitate the verbosity, but not the clear structure, of Aldhelm's sentences. As a result of his training with Abbo, Byrhtferth acquired some knowledge of the scientific curriculum (the quadrivium) which was then being taught in continental schools, but was unknown in England. In his range of interest and achievement, particularly in the fields of computus and historiography, Byrhtferth bears comparison with Bede, though he lacked his predecessor's clarity of thought and language.

MICHAEL LAPIDGE

Sources *Byrhtferth's Enchiridion*, ed. P. S. Baker and M. Lapidge, EETS, suppl. ser., 15 (1995) • *Byrhtferth of Ramsey: the lives of Oswald and Ecgwine*, ed. M. Lapidge [forthcoming] • M. Lapidge, 'Byrhtferth of Ramsey and the early sections of the *Historia regum* attributed to Symeon of Durham', *Anglo-Saxon England*, 10 (1982), 97–122 • W. D. Macray, ed., *Chronicon abbatiae Rameseiensis a saec. x usque ad an. circiter 1200*, Rolls Series, 83 (1886) • [Byrhtferth of Ramsey], 'Vita sancti Oswaldi auctore anonymo', *The historians of the church of York and its archbishops*, ed. J. Raine, 1, Rolls Series, 71 (1879), 399–475 • Symeon of Durham, *Opera*, 2.3–91 • *Opera Bedae venerabilis*, 8 vols. (1563) • M. Gorman, 'The glosses on Bede's *De temporum ratione* attributed to Byrhrferth of Ramsey', *Anglo-Saxon England*, 25 (1996), 209–33 • M. Lapidge, 'Byrhtferth and Oswald', *St Oswald at Worcester: life and influence*, ed. N. Brooks and C. Cubitt (1996), 64–83
Archives St John's College, Oxford, MS 17

Byrhtnoth [Brihtnoth] (*d.* **991**), magnate and soldier, was the hero of the battle of Maldon. His family origins are obscure, although his wealth, connections, and office imply noble birth. His name appears as Byrhtnoth in the poem *The Battle of Maldon*, which names Byrhthelm (Brihthelm) as his father. He had a brother, Brihtric, and a sister, whose son Wulfmær fought and died at his side at Maldon. Byrhtferth, his immediate predecessor as ealdorman of

Essex, may also have been a kinsman, but the evidence for this is circumstantial, amounting to little more than the similarity in names and their shared office. Byrhtnoth married Ælfflæd, the younger daughter of Ealdorman Ælfgar, possibly of Essex, some time before 951. If they had children, none survived into adulthood. He did, however, have a daughter, Leofflæd, with a previous wife or concubine. Byrhtnoth accumulated through inheritance, marriage, and royal patronage a large estate centred on Essex, Suffolk, and Cambridgeshire (where much of his patrimony lay). In all he possessed more than fifty separate holdings in ten shires. Through blood or marriage he was related to most of the men who ruled southern England. Even *Ælfhere of Mercia, his opponent during the so-called 'anti-monastic' crisis of 975, was a distant kinsman. Byrhtnoth was appointed ealdorman of Essex late in 956 and held that position until his death thirty-five years later. His authority extended beyond the boundaries of the modern county to Huntingdonshire and, possibly, Northamptonshire and the territory of the Five Boroughs.

Byrhtnoth played critical roles in the two main crises of the late tenth century: the struggle over the fate of monastic reform and the return of the vikings to England. He and Ealdorman Æthelwine of East Anglia, his ally and friend, were among the greatest lay supporters of the monastic revival initiated by Dunstan, Oswald, and Æthelwold. Both strenuously defended the monks and their endowments during the 'anti-monastic' reaction that broke out upon the death of King Edgar in 975, when a disputed succession gave disaffected nobles the opportunity to recover lands and family religious houses lost to the reformed monasteries. Byrhtferth of Ramsey, who wrote a highly partisan account of the conflict, singled Byrhtnoth out for special praise, depicting him as 'a religious and God fearing-man' (*English Historical Documents*, 1, no. 236) who stood steadfastly at the side of Ealdorman Æthelwine and his brothers in opposing the expulsion of the monks and the seizure of their property. Byrhtnoth was a generous patron and benefactor of Ely. In his will he left the abbey nine estates in Cambridgeshire and several others in Huntingdon, Norfolk, and Suffolk. He also gave land to several other religious houses, including Ramsey, Abingdon, Christ Church, Canterbury, and Mersea in Essex. The twelfth-century chronicles of Ely and Ramsey relate similar stories explaining how Ely won the ealdorman's special favour by providing hospitality and provisions to him and his army on their way to Maldon after the abbot of Ramsey had refused to do so. Although both accounts are riddled with historical errors, including misidentifications of the abbots, they may preserve a kernel of truth.

Byrhtnoth's lasting fame rests on the survival of a 325-line fragment of an Old English poem in alliterative verse celebrating the courage that he and his followers demonstrated in battle against a viking army near Maldon on 10 or 11 August 991. On the basis of topographical references in the poem, the battle site has been located across from Northey Island, near the confluence of the Blackwater River and Southey Creek. In the summer of 991 a large viking fleet of uncertain leadership (the rather muddled A text of the Anglo-Saxon Chronicle, s.a. 993, names Olaf Tryggvason) attacked and plundered the town of Ipswich and then sailed along the coast of Essex to Maldon. Here they were intercepted by Byrhtnoth at the head of an army consisting of his own household troops and the Essex *fyrd* (the local forces of the shire). The various recensions of the Anglo-Saxon Chronicle report only that the English were defeated and that Byrhtnoth died in the battle. The poem and a prose account in Byrhtferth's near-contemporary life of Oswald provide details of the battle that are colourful but of questionable reliability. According to the poem, Byrhtnoth, out of pride or excessive courage, permitted the vikings to cross a causeway so that the two armies could engage. (Byrhtnoth's decision to accept battle has been defended on strategic grounds; the alternative was to allow the vikings to slip away in their ships and ravage elsewhere.) The defeat of the English is attributed to the ealdorman's death and to the flight of a few cowardly men. But sturdy in battle despite his advanced age, eloquent in his speech, generous to his men, and loyal to his lord King Æthelred, Byrhtnoth inspired such devotion in his followers that most preferred to die avenging him than to seek safety in flight. The poem is among the fullest expressions of the heroic ideals of the Anglo-Saxon warrior aristocracy.

In 991 Byrhtnoth was King Æthelred II's senior ealdorman and, given the illness of Æthelwine, probably the most influential layman in England after the king. It was his death that made the battle of Maldon significant enough to receive notices in the surviving versions of the Anglo-Saxon Chronicle. The deaths of Byrhtnoth and, in the following year, Æthelwine signalled a changing of the guard in the political leadership of England. Contemporary chroniclers and modern historians alike have seen the battle as a turning point in the English response to this new round of viking invasions of England. Before Maldon the viking raids, which were sporadic and small-scale, were virtually ignored except by the locals who suffered their immediate effects. Byrhtnoth's shocking defeat brought home to Æthelred and his advisers the gravity of the situation and persuaded them of the wisdom of purchasing peace. The £10,000 with which the English bought off the raiders in 991 was only the first of many such payments.

The monks of Ely fetched Byrhtnoth's headless corpse from the battlefield and buried it in their abbey. Byrhtferth's characterization of him in the life of Oswald as 'tall of stature, standing above the rest' (*English Historical Documents*, 1, no. 236) is substantiated by measurements of his remains, which indicate that he was a little over 6 feet tall. Given that Byrhtnoth married before 951, he must have been in his sixties at the time of his death.

RICHARD ABELS

Sources D. Scragg, ed., *The battle of Maldon, AD 991* (1991) · J. Cooper, ed., *The battle of Maldon: fiction and fact* (1993) · *English historical documents*, 1, ed. D. Whitelock (1955), nos. 10, 236 · *ASC*, s.a.

991, texts A, C • C. Hart, 'The ealdordom of Essex', in C. Hart, *The Danelaw* (1992), 115–40 • E. O. Blake, ed., *Liber Eliensis*, CS, 3rd ser., 92 (1962) • D. Whitelock, ed. and trans., *Anglo-Saxon wills* (1930) • E. John, 'War and society in the tenth century: the Maldon campaign', *TRHS*, 5th ser., 27 (1977), 173–95 • S. Keynes, *An atlas of attestations in Anglo-Saxon charters, c.670–1066*, rev. (privately printed, Cambridge, 1996)

Byrhtnoth (*d.* **996**), abbot of Ely, spent his entire career in reformed Benedictine abbeys and was responsible for the refoundation of Ely Abbey after the depredations of the viking age. He was one of the original band of monks who had assembled under Æthelwold at Abingdon about 954, where he received a Benedictine training and education; and about 963, when his patron became the bishop of Winchester, he was appointed as the prior of the Old Minster. It has been suggested that he was the son of Byrhtferth and the first cousin of the better-known Byrhtnoth (*d.* 991), ealdorman of Essex. If so, these family connections with the southern Danelaw may have been a factor in his selection as the abbot of Ely in 970. King Edgar granted Byrhtnoth and the monks of Ely authority over the two royal hundreds of the Isle of Ely, which freed the abbey from unwanted diocesan and secular attention, and was the basis of its great immunity in the high middle ages.

Between *c.*970 and *c.*990 Byrhtnoth excelled in the acquisition of relics and land for the abbey. During the night of 8 July 974 he and a party of Ely monks stole the body of St Wihtburh from East Dereham in Norfolk. After placing the saint in their wagon, the monks drove for 20 miles to reach their waiting ship. Although the villagers discovered the theft, they could not stop the Ely ship with its naval armaments sailing past them as they stood armed on the river bank. Byrhtnoth's putative kinsman, Ealdorman Byrhtnoth, became a patron of the abbey, with the result that the monks acquired forty-five estates during the late tenth and early eleventh centuries. When purchasing an estate, Byrhtnoth took a careful interest in the livestock before paying out any cash; and when buying land for the monks, he drove a hard bargain at local assemblies. His boldness, business acumen, and family connections ensured that by the end of the tenth century the abbey regained the prosperity that it had enjoyed in the seventh, thereby laying the foundations for the community's elevation into a bishopric about a hundred years after Byrhtnoth's death. In the early twelfth century the Ely monks invented incidents in Byrhtnoth's life, claiming that he played a vital role in the Maldon campaign of 991, and that he was murdered while seeking to curb the witchcraft of Queen Æthelthryth. According to the *Liber Eliensis* Byrhtnoth died on 5 May 996 and was buried at Ely. His real achievement was to negotiate his way through the political landscape of the fenland shires for twenty-five years, ensuring that the Ely monks were not overshadowed by their neighbours at Ramsey Abbey.

A. F. Wareham

Sources E. O. Blake, ed., *Liber Eliensis*, CS, 3rd ser., 92 (1962) • *The life of St Æthelwold / Wulfstan of Winchester*, ed. M. Lapidge and M. Winterbottom, OMT (1991) • A. J. Robertson, ed. and trans., *Anglo-Saxon charters*, 2nd edn (1956)

Byrne family (*per.* **1765–1849**), engravers and painters, came to prominence with **William Byrne** (1743–1805), landscape engraver, who was born in London but studied for some time under his uncle, an engraver of arms in Birmingham, and, it is said, under F. G. Aliamet, who was in London between at least 1760 and 1765. At the age of twenty-two Byrne won a premium of 25 guineas from the Society of Arts for the *Villa Madama* (1765), after Richard Wilson. In the following year he exhibited *Carnarvon Castle*, also after Wilson, with the Society of Artists. Boydell employed him to engrave *Apollo Herdsman to King Admetus*, after Lauri, and *Flight into Egypt*, after Domenichino (1767). He had a letter sent to Johann Georg Wille in Paris asking whether, on the strength of an engraving that he enclosed, Wille would employ him. He arrived on Wille's doorstep on 10 October 1769, and the famous engraver noted: 'Il paroît fort doux; mais il ne sait pas un mot de françois, cela sera un peu gênant' ('He seems very sweet, but he does not know a word of French, which will be a little troublesome'; *Mémoires et journal*, 1.415). Byrne was back in England by May 1772. He became a fellow of the Incorporated Society of Artists and exhibited between 1766 and 1780.

Byrne set up as a specialist engraver and publisher of landscapes. With Thomas Hearne he launched *The Antiquities of Britain* in 1778, and he issued a smaller set of Hearne's designs, *Rural Sports*, from 1780. He published John Warwick Smith's *Views in Italy* and Joseph Farington's *Views of the Lakes* (1785–), as well as many other beautiful line-engravings of literary subjects designed by Hearne, and further magnificent topographical views. Such was his prosperity that in 1785 he insured the contents of his home at 79 Titchfield Street, Westminster, for £3000 (including £2500 cover for stock and goods in trust). By 1797, however, Farington reported that 'Byrne complained much of the difficulties of the Times, and said the war had made £2000 difference to him', mentioning that he and his wife had an annuity of £100 per annum and received another £150 from the Society of Dilettanti, 'but this was much less than his expenses' (Farington, *Diary*, 747). His pupils included Samuel Middiman and Johann Gottlieb Schumann, and Byrne also frequently collaborated with engravers trained by William Woollett, such as Benjamin Pouncy and William Ellis. *The Death of Captain Cook* and twenty views of Scottish scenery were published in 1807, after his death.

Byrne and his first wife, whose name is unknown, raised a family of artistic children: **Anne Frances Byrne** (1775–1837), Mary *Green (1776–1845) [*see under* Green, James (1771–1834)], **Letitia Byrne** (1779–1849), **Elizabeth Byrne** (*fl.* 1809–1849), and **John Byrne** (1786–1847). His second marriage, in July 1792, was to Marianne Francotte, governess to Lady Elizabeth Chichester, the daughter of Lord Donegal. Byrne died suddenly at his home in Titchfield Street on 24 September 1805 and was buried at St Pancras parish church. His neighbour Rigaud wrote to his son: 'though he had some oddities, he was a very quiet man, and leaves the name of having been great in his line of the Arts' (Rigaud, 116). Byrne's widow moved to Cleveland

Street; one sale of his prints took place on 12–14 May 1806 and another on 15 June 1808.

Anne Frances Byrne was taught by her father and became his assistant, etching for him and preparing his work. She also taught for a while, but soon turned to full-time practice as a painter of flowers and fruit; she exhibited a fruit piece at the Royal Academy in 1796, and only occasionally admitted a bird or insect into her work. Her flower studies were sometimes grouped in the manner of Dutch masters and were notable for their richness of colour. In 1805 she was elected the first female associate of the Society of Painters in Water Colours, and in 1821 she became a member. She was the first to break the society's initial ban on flower paintings, to which she remained faithful, exhibiting there regularly—apart from the 'oil invasion' of the years 1812–19, when the society permitted oil paintings to be shown. From 1805 Anne Frances lived at 55 Upper John Street, Fitzroy Square, Westminster. She retired in 1834 and died, unmarried, at her home in Cirencester Place on 2 January 1837. She was buried at Kensal Green cemetery.

Letitia Byrne was born on 24 November 1779 and was still a pupil of her father when she exhibited landscape views at the Royal Academy in 1799. In 1810 she etched the illustrations for *A Description of Tunbridge Wells*, and among other work entrusted to her were four views for James Hakewill's *History of Winchester* (1813). She also etched six plates from topographical and other drawings made by the late Revd William Warren Porter of St John's College, Oxford. From 1799 to 1848 she exhibited views in Derbyshire, Wales, and France. Letitia Byrne died at her home, 8 Weymouth Street, Marylebone, on 21 May 1849, and was buried at Kensal Green cemetery.

Elizabeth Byrne exhibited English and continental landscapes between 1838 and 1849, and produced six steel engravings for R. H. Shepherd's *Modern Athens*. She resided with her brother John, who began as an engraver assisting his father, then undertook on his own account plates for Wilde's *Cathedrals*. After his father's death he moved to 54 John Street. He contributed engravings in 1810–11 for Matthew Flinders's *Voyage to Terra Australis* (1814) and was drawing-master at Eton College, possibly about 1818 (an appointment which may have been connected with Letitia's *From Eton College Play-Fields*, exhibited in 1822). He then moved to landscape painting and was elected associate of the Society of Painters in Water Colours in 1827. After 1832 he travelled widely in France and Italy, but, apart from some subjects taken from Roman history, drew his subject matter mainly from the home counties and Wales. He visited the west country in 1844 and Yorkshire in 1845. He died on 11 March 1847 and was buried at Kensal Green cemetery.

TIMOTHY CLAYTON and ANITA MCCONNELL

Sources Mallalieu, *Watercolour artists*, 1.63–4 · *GM*, 1st ser., 75 (1805), 974, 1071 · *GM*, 1st ser., 62 (1792), 765 · F. Lugt, *Répertoire des catalogues de ventes publiques*, 1 (The Hague, 1938) · B. Hunnisett, *A dictionary of British steel engravers* (1980) · J. L. Roget, *A history of the 'Old Water-Colour' Society*, 2 vols. (1891) · S. F. D. Rigaud, 'Facts and recollections of the XVIIIth century in a memoir of John Francis Rigaud', ed. W. L. Pressly, *Walpole Society*, 50 (1984), 1–164 · GL, Sun Insurance Office, MS 11936, Sun Insurance, vol. 330, no. 508791 · Farington, *Diary* · D. Morris, *Thomas Hearne and his landscape* (1989) · *Mémoires et journal de Jean-Georges Wille*, ed. G. Duplessis, 2 vols. (1857) · parish register, St Mary Marylebone, LMA [marriage] · d. cert. [Letitia Byrne]

Byrne, Anne Frances (1775–1837). *See under* Byrne family (*per.* 1765–1849).

Byrne [O'Brien], **Charles** (1761–1783), giant, was born in Ireland, the son of an Irish father and a Scottish mother. He had at least one brother; none of his family was of particularly noteworthy size. Charles Byrne, however, was recorded as measuring 8 feet tall in August 1780, 2 inches more in 1782, and 8 feet 4 inches on his death in 1783. He travelled as part of an exhibition: physical abnormality was popular with showmen, and a number of Irish giants (some of them spurious, and usually called O'Brien, as was Byrne) are recorded in this period. In London he created a great sensation, and the Haymarket pantomime (18 August 1782) was entitled *Harlequin Teague, or, The Giant's Causeway* in reference to him. Byrne, a heavy drinker, died on 1 June 1783 at Cockspur Street, Charing Cross, shortly after converting most of his property into a banknote for £700 which was then stolen.

Byrne was apparently alarmed at the prospect of his corpse falling into the hands of 'the chirurgical fraternity' (*GM*, 53, 1783, 541), and gave instructions for his remains to be sunk in deep water; but the anatomist and collector John Hunter bribed the undertaker to the tune of some £500 and had the body stolen before it reached the sea. It was then promptly skeletonized and eventually placed on display in the Hunterian Museum. Thus, having been obliged to make an exhibit of himself in life, in death Byrne was made an exhibit by others, and has remained on view ever since. K. D. REYNOLDS

Sources *DNB* · *GM*, 1st ser., 53 (1783), 541 · *GM*, 1st ser., 54 (1784), 553 · Highfill, Burnim & Langhans, *BDA* · *N&Q*, 2nd ser., 11 (1861), 369, 396, 476 · *N&Q*, 2nd ser., 12 (1861), 59 · *N&Q*, 5th ser., 4 (1875), 132–3 · J. Kay, *A series of original portraits and caricature etchings … with biographical sketches and illustrative anecdotes*, ed. [H. Paton and others], new edn [3rd edn], 1 (1877), 10–11, 417 · R. Harris, *Death, dissection and the destitute* (1988)

Archives RCS Eng., Hunterian Museum, skeleton

Likenesses J. Kay, etchings, BM, NPG; repro. in Kay, *Original portraits and character etchings*, vol. 1 · T. Rowlandson, watercolour, RCS Eng.

Wealth at death recently robbed of £700 (virtually entire wealth)

Byrne [*née* King], **Charlotte** [*pseud.* Charlotte Dacre] (1782?–1825), writer, was the daughter of Jonathan King, born Jacob Rey (1753–1824), a moneylender and radical writer well known in London society. Her father divorced her mother, Deborah, *née* Lara, under Jewish law in 1785 in order to marry the dowager countess of Lanesborough. In 1798 Charlotte King published with her sister Sophia [*see* Fortnum, Sophia (*b.* 1781/2, *d.* in or after 1805)] a volume of Gothic verses, *Trifles of Helicon*, and dedicated it to her bankrupt father to show 'the education you have afforded us has not been totally lost'. The reappearance of poems from this volume in *Hours of Solitude* (1805), published under the pseudonym Charlotte Dacre, confirms the identity between Dacre and King; the pen-name was probably designed to suggest aristocratic connections. She also wrote verses for the *Morning Post* and *Morning Herald* under the name Rosa Matilda, perhaps after the demonic lover in Matthew Lewis's *The Monk* (1796); *Hours of Solitude* had for a frontispiece a darkly glamorous portrait of herself as Rosa Matilda. The poems, full of Gothic passions and imagery, briefly influenced Byron (*Hours of Idleness*, 1807) though in *English Bards and Scotch Reviewers* (1809, ll. 755–62) he would scorn 'the lovely ROSA's prose in masquerade'. Also in 1805 she published *The Confessions of the Nun of St. Omer*, a Gothic tale of sexual repression and misbehaviour. In the preface Dacre claims the book was written at the age of eighteen and left untouched for three years during journeys abroad. The *British Critic* for December 1805 (p. 671) called it 'a very fine, sentimental, and improbable story written in turgid and affected language … The moral, however, is good, for it teaches the mischief which arises from the neglect and violation of social duties.'

In the following year Dacre published *Zofloya, or, The Moor*. The corruption of the strong and sexually ruthless heroine Victoria, and her gradual enslavement to the charismatic Moorish servant Zofloya (later revealed to be Satan), is set against a sublime landscape of extreme and irrational forces. Ostensibly didactic in purpose, its evident taste for murderous horror shocked reviewers: the *Literary Journal* (June 1806, 631) thought the author had 'maggots in the brain'; the *Monthly Literary Recreations* (July 1806, 80) deplored the 'odious and indecent performance'. Its poetic character, psychological acuteness, and moral status were, however, praised voluminously in the *Morning Post* (17 May), the paper for which Dacre mostly wrote (she also bore the first of three children by its editor in this year). The book's influence on Shelley's perfervid Gothic fantasies *Zastrozzi* and *St. Irvyne* is well documented.

In 1807 Dacre continued her series of sexual case studies with *The Libertine*. Again the *Morning Post* defended its 'liberality of sentiment' and 'utmost purity of moral' against those (like the *Monthly Magazine*) who thought it 'prurient trash' (Jones, 245). Her last novel, *The Passions* (1811), tried, according to its preface, to expose 'the danger … of yielding to the guilty violence of the Passions, or of swerving, even in *thought*, from the sacred line of virtue'. Her sporadic newspaper verse of the next decade indicates a reactionary turn, and in 1822, she published the naïvely royalist *George the Fourth, a Poem*.

Charlotte's children with Nicholas Byrne (*d.* 1833), married owner and editor of the *Morning Post*, although born in 1806, 1807, and 1809, were not baptized until 8 June 1811 (at St Paul's, Covent Garden). On 1 July 1815 Byrne, now a widower, married 'Charlotte King spinster' at St James's, Westminster. She died on 7 November 1825, 'in Lancaster Place, after a long and painful illness, which her purity of heart and sublime greatness of soul enabled her patiently and piously to endure' (*The Times*, 9 Nov 1825). She was buried at St Mary's, Paddington, on 11 November. The register records her age as fifty-three, which would put her date of birth about 1772; this is probably a mistake, but if true then her statement about her age in the preface to *Hours of Solitude* underestimates it by a decade. PAUL BAINES

Sources A. H. Jones, *Ideas and innovations: best sellers of Jane Austen's age* (1986), 224–49 • A. Craciun, '"I hasten to be disembodied": Charlotte Dacre, the demon lover, and representations of the body', *European Romantic Review*, 6/1 (summer 1995), 75–97 • K. I. Michasiw, 'Introduction', *Zofloya, or, The Moor* (1997) • Blain, Clements & Grundy, *Feminist comp.*, 259–60 • W. S. Ward, *Literary reviews in British periodicals, 1798–1820: a bibliography*, 1 (1972), 233–4 • S. Knight-Roth, 'Charlotte Dacre and the Gothic tradition', PhD diss., Dalhousie University, 1972 • D. P. Varma, 'Introduction', *Zofloya, or, The Moor* (1974) • J. J. McGann, '"My brain is feminine": Byron and the poetry of deception', *Byron: Augustan and Romantic*, ed. A. Rutherford (1990), 26–51 • H. Herd, *Seven editors* (1955), 52–5 • B. R. Pollin, 'Byron, Poe, and Miss Matilda', *Names: Journal of the American Name Society*, 16 (1968), 390–414 • M. Summers, 'Byron's lovely Rosa', *Essays in Petto* (1928), 57–73 • C. Dacre, *Hours of solitude* (1805) • *The Times* (9 Nov 1825)

Likenesses R. Mackenzie, engraving (after A. Buck), repro. in Dacre, *Hours of solitude*, frontispiece

Byrne, Sir Edmund Widdrington (1844–1904), judge, was born at Islington, London, on 30 June 1844, the eldest son of Edmund Byrne of Whitehall Place, Westminster, solicitor, and his wife, Mary Elizabeth, *née* Cowell. He was educated at King's College, London, before entering as student at Lincoln's Inn on 5 November 1863. He was a pupil in the chambers of George Osborne Morgan and was called to the bar on 26 January 1867. His family's connections with solicitors gave him a large practice as a conveyancer and equity draftsman, while his powers of clear and concise statement in court put him among the leading juniors of the Chancery bar. On 13 August 1874 he married Henrietta Johnstone, daughter of James Gulland of Newton, of Wemyss, Fife; they had several children.

Byrne became queen's counsel in 1888 and a bencher of Lincoln's Inn in 1892. He attached himself to the court of Mr Justice Chitty where he and Robert Romer QC soon shared most of the work between them. A well-grounded lawyer and pleasant speaker, Byrne was an admirable leader in routine Chancery cases. He was at his best as advocate in a court of first instance. His appearances in the higher tribunals were rare, except in the Court of Appeal in cases in which he had appeared at earlier hearings.

In July 1892 Byrne won a parliamentary seat, the Walthamstow division of Essex, as a Conservative candidate. The Finance Act of 1894 and the abortive Employers' Liability Bill of 1895 gave him the opportunity to make many legally minded interventions in debate. Byrne quickly adapted to parliamentary life and he was referred to in the press as one of 'the busy bees'. In July 1895 he was again returned for Walthamstow with a largely increased majority.

On the promotion of Chitty to lord justice, Byrne was given the vacant judgeship in the Chancery Division (18 January 1897), and was duly knighted. On the bench he was painstaking, courteous, and patient, and his judgments, which included many patent cases, were nearly always affirmed upon appeal. Contemporary colleagues thought him overly scrupulous, however, and judged him too slow, morbidly conscientious, and reliant on authority, being particularly irritated by his falling behind in his cases.

Byrne died after a very short illness on 4 April 1904 at his home, 33 Lancaster Gate, Hyde Park, London. He was buried at Brookwood cemetery.

J. B. ATLAY, *rev.* HUGH MOONEY

Sources *The Times* (6 April 1905)
Likenesses E. Brock, portrait, priv. coll. • Spy [L. Ward], caricature, chromolithograph, NPG; repro. in *VF* (30 Jan 1896), pl. 664 • portrait, repro. in *ILN*, 110 (1897), 110 • portrait, repro. in *ILN*, 124 (1904), 522
Wealth at death £17,297 1*s.* 6*d.*: probate, 7 May 1904, *CGPLA Eng. & Wales*

Byrne, Elizabeth (*fl.* 1809–1849). *See under* Byrne family (*per.* 1765–1849).

Byrne, John (1786–1847). *See under* Byrne family (*per.* 1765–1849).

Byrne [*née* Busk], **Julia Clara** (1819–1894), author, was the second daughter and fourth child of the poet Hans *Busk (1772–1862) and his wife, Maria, daughter of Joseph Green. She was one of seven children; her elder brother, Hans *Busk (1815–1882), was a pioneer of the military volunteer movement, and her younger sister, Rachel Harriette *Busk (1831–1907), was a folklorist. Julia received a good, although rather conventional, private education at home: she learned several foreign and dead languages and practised miniature painting and sketching. On 28 April 1842 she married William Pitt Byrne (*d.* 1861), son of Nicholas Byrne (*d.* 1833) and founder and proprietor of the *Morning Post*. After their marriage William Byrne disengaged himself from his business concerns. The couple had one son and one daughter.

Contemporaries found Julia Byrne a sparkling conversationalist and a good correspondent, and the Byrnes' London home became a popular venue for social celebrities, including the poet Letitia Elizabeth Landon, the singer Giulia Grisi, and the eccentric naturalist and traveller Charles Waterton. One frequent visitor, Henry Edward Manning, viewed it as 'neutral ground', and relaxed in the company of Julia and her sister Rachel, revealing a lighter side to his personality. After his own conversion to Roman Catholicism in 1850 Manning succeeded in converting both women, Julia being received into the Catholic church in 1860; William Byrne, although sympathetic, was converted only on his deathbed.

Julia Byrne's first book, *A Glance behind the Grilles of the Religious Houses in France*, published in 1855, reflected her growing sympathy for Roman Catholicism. Published in the wake of the 'papal aggression' crisis of 1850, it purported to be the impressions of a Tractarian clergyman touring French conventual and monastic establishments. The Roman Catholic church was compared favourably, though not entirely uncritically, with the Church of England. The work was published anonymously, as were all of Byrne's publications, and an informed reviewer of a later work found her adoption of a protestant clergyman's persona 'plainly indefensible' (*Saturday Review*, 310). *The Athenaeum*'s critic, however, found the work interesting and impartial.

This early work was followed by *Flemish Interiors* (1856), an impressionistic travel book, which was succeeded by similar publications, including *Cosas de España, Illustrative of Spain and the Spaniards as they are* (2 vols., 1866) and *Pictures of Hungarian Life* (1869). Such works were sometimes illustrated by the author, and bore witness to Byrne's love of travel to rather unconventional destinations. *Undercurrents Overlooked* (2 vols., 1860) also revealed her cosmopolitan attitude: a Mayhewite examination of working-class life in London, it drew a questionable contrast between what the author saw as the wretched lives of the poor in the English capital and those of their more fortunate Parisian counterparts. Severely critical of contemporary treatment of the destitute and the insane, this work purported to be based on first-hand observation, a claim which was disputed by a critic in the *Saturday Review* (311) who questioned also 'the good taste and propriety of a lady attempting to discuss such questions at all'. Byrne produced other works addressing contemporary social issues with a comparative angle. *Gheel, the City of the Simple* (1869) considered Belgian mental-health provision, while *The Beggynhof, or, City of the Single* (1869) praised the Flemish religious order of the Beguines as a model for coping with the 'surplus women' problem. The latter work incidentally gave Byrne the opportunity to qualify her earlier enthusiasm for monasticism by condemning extravagant austerities and perpetual religious vows.

Byrne's later works were of less interest: *Curiosities of the Search Room: a Collection of Serious and Whimsical Wills* (1880) met with a very lukewarm response in *The Academy*, as the reviewer felt that the author had failed to exploit the access to interesting material afforded by the search room at Somerset House, relying instead on newspaper cuttings. *Gossip of the Century* (1892) was more appealing: although many of its court and society anecdotes were unoriginal, Byrne's wide acquaintance with many social, literary, and musical figures, both minor and major, lends the work some modern interest. After her death, her sister Rachel published a third and fourth volume of *Gossip* in 1898, under the alternative title *Social Hours with Celebrities*.

After a brief illness, Byrne died at her home, 16 Montagu Street, Portman Square, London, on 29 March 1894. Although extravagant, *The Athenaeum*'s eulogistic obituary, which opined that 'The grave has seldom closed over a woman of more versatile parts', rightly paid tribute to her varied talents. A frontispiece photograph in the first volume of *Social Hours* (1898) shows a tall, stylish, and handsome woman, with dark eyes and good features, and her biography exemplifies the fulfilment open to a well-connected and energetic middle-class woman within the apparent limitations of Victorian society.

ROSEMARY MITCHELL

Sources *The Athenaeum* (7 April 1894), 446–7 • Allibone, *Dict.* • J. C. Byrne, *Gossip of the century*, 2 vols. (1892) • J. C. Byrne, *Social hours with* *celebrities*, ed. R. H. Busk, 2 vols. (1898) • M. J. Peterson, *Family, love and work in the lives of Victorian gentlewomen* (1989), 156–7 • *Saturday Review*, 9 (1860), 310–12 • *The Athenaeum* (7 July 1855), 790 • E. S. Purcell, *Life of Cardinal Manning*, 2 (1896), 697 • *DNB*

Likenesses photograph, repro. in Byrne, *Social hours with celebrities*, vol. 1, frontispiece

Wealth at death £33,704 13*s*. 7*d*.: resworn probate, July 1894, *CGPLA Eng. & Wales*

Byrne, Letitia (1779–1849). *See under* Byrne family (*per*. 1765–1849).

Byrne, Miles (1780–1862), Irish revolutionary and officer in the French army, was born on 20 March 1780 at Monaseed on the borders between co. Wexford and co. Wicklow, the son of Patrick Byrne (*d*. 1796), a farmer, and Mary Graham. His family were Catholic petty gentry in a region that was marked by sectarian tensions. Byrne joined the United Irishmen in early 1797 and was heavily involved in the subsequent rising in Wexford in 1798. His *Memoirs* (1863) are the most authoritative source for the military history of the United Irish rising and reflect the insight gained through his later service in the French army.

Owing to his youth Byrne was not in the first rank of United Irish leaders; however, by the end of the uprising he commanded the remnants of the Monaseed corps of the insurgents. He was involved in all the major engagements: Oulart, Enniscorthy, Arklow, and Vinegar Hill. After that defeat he remained with the rebel forces that tried to break out into Kildare and eventually joined the guerrilla force led by Michael Dwyer and Joseph Holt. He remained in the Wicklow Mountains in hope of a French landing and after that hope evaporated, he took refuge in Dublin, where for some years he was employed as a clerk in a timber yard. His final participation in military and political affairs in Ireland was to be involved in planning Robert Emmet's abortive revolution in 1803. In the plan for the capture of Dublin Castle in July he was given command of the Wexford and Wicklow men. He subsequently travelled to France in an effort to rally support there by presenting Napoleon, then first consul, with a detailed report on the situation in Ireland.

The first volume of Byrne's *Memoirs*—edited by his widow, and published in three volumes at Paris in 1863—depicts the insurrection in Ireland in 1798 and its military failure. His analysis claims that the leaders of the uprising did not understand the nature of the warfare they were conducting: it was Byrne's own view that the uprising should have aimed to make the country ungovernable by spreading the unrest as widely and quickly as possible. Byrne's insight was to recognize the contrast between the efforts of Irish rebels in 1798 and the new kind of irregular warfare successfully conducted by the Spanish against Napoleon and the Greeks against the Turks in 1828. Byrne was to figure in both theatres, suppressing the Spanish and supporting the Greeks.

In December 1803 Miles Byrne was given a commission as a sub-lieutenant in the newly formed Irish legion of the French army. The legion was intended to provide the core of an invasion force for Ireland, but as that prospect receded it fought in Spain, Portugal, the Low Countries, and Germany. Byrne's own service was largely with the 2nd battalion of the legion in Spain, where he was promoted captain in 1808. The legion was disbanded in 1815, ending the long history of Irish forces in the French service. Byrne took out French citizenship in 1817, and was recalled from half pay only in 1828 when he served as a staff officer in the Morea campaign in support of Greek independence. He was promoted *chef de bataillon* of the 56th regiment in 1830 and retired in 1835. On 24 December that year he married Frances (known as Fanny) Horner at the chapel of the British embassy in Paris (*IGI*). His retirement was spent in Paris where 'his tall and to the last straight figure, thin bronzed face, and mobile yet keen features were … well known to frequenters of the avenue of the Champs-Elysées' (*DNB*). He died in the city on 24 January 1862, and was buried in the cemetery of Montmartre. His wife survived him. JAMES LIVESEY

Sources *Memoirs of Miles Byrne*, ed. F. Byrne, 3 vols. (1863) • T. Bartlett, 'Defence, counter-insurgency and rebellion: Ireland, 1793–1803', *A military history of Ireland*, ed. T. Bartlett and K. Jeffrey (1996), 247–93 • K. Whelan, 'The Catholic community in eighteenth-century county Wexford', *Endurance and emergence: Catholics in Ireland in the eighteenth century*, ed. T. Power and K. Whelan (1990), 129–70 • J. G. Gallaher, *Napoleon's Irish legion* (1993) • *DNB* • *IGI*

Archives Archives de Guerre, Vincennes, France, Personnel File No. 49, 404

Byrne, Oscar (1794/5–1867), ballet master, was the son of James Byrne (1756–1845), an actor and ballet master. He was brought up to be a dancer and for several years performed at various provincial theatres. His first appearance in London was in 1803 at Drury Lane Theatre in a ballet arranged by his father from *Ossian* called *Oscar and Elwina*, which had first been presented twelve years previously at Covent Garden. It is said that it is because of his father's success in this ballet that Byrne was called Oscar. Byrne also played his first part at Covent Garden in November 1803 as Cheerly in Prince Hoare's *Lock and Key*.

Much of Byrne's early life was passed abroad or in Ireland. He was in America for a long time, playing in New York and Philadelphia. There he met his future wife, Abigail, an actress and singer, who returned to England with her husband. In 1850 Charles Kean, during his memorable series of performances at the Princess's Theatre, engaged Byrne to arrange ballets for the principal revivals and for pantomimes. The most popular productions were *Actaeon and Diana* and *Old Harlequin's Fireside*. In 1862 Byrne went to Drury Lane, at that time under the management of Falconer and Chatterton, then moved on to the Haymarket and St James's Theatre (1864). His last engagement was at Her Majesty's Theatre in 1866, when Falconer produced his ill-starred drama *Oonah*. In his own line Byrne showed both invention and resource. He died rather suddenly at his home, 22 Islip Street, Kentish Town, London, on 4 September 1867 at the age of seventy-two, leaving his widow and seven children.

JOSEPH KNIGHT, *rev*. NILANJANA BANERJI

Sources Adams, *Drama* • *Era Almanack and Annual* (1868) • T. Gilliland, *The dramatic mirror, containing the history of the stage from the earliest period, to the present time*, 2 vols. (1808) • W. Oxberry, *Oxberry's*

dramatic chronology [n.d., c.1849] • T. A. Brown, *History of the American stage* (1870) • private information (1886) • *CGPLA Eng. & Wales* (1867)
Wealth at death under £8000: probate, 28 Sept 1867, *CGPLA Eng. & Wales*

Byrne, Roger William (1929–1958). *See under* Busby Babes (*act.* 1953–1958).

Byrne, William (1743–1805). *See under* Byrne family (*per.* 1765–1849).

Byrnes, Thomas Joseph (1860–1898), politician in Australia, born in Brisbane, Queensland, on 11 November 1860, was the son of Irish Roman Catholic immigrants, Patrick Byrnes (*d.* 1867), a farmer, and his wife, Anna, *née* Tighe. He was educated at the Bowen primary school, gained two state scholarships, and entered the Brisbane grammar school. After winning an exhibition tenable at any university in the empire, he studied arts and law at Melbourne University where he graduated BA in 1882 and LLB in 1884. He was called to the bar in Victoria in 1884, but returned to Queensland to practise. He quickly attained a leading position at the supreme court bar, and accepted a seat in the legislative council in August 1890, with the office of solicitor-general in the Griffith–McIlwraith ministry.

In the following year Byrnes made his reputation by the harsh manner in which he dealt with the troubles arising from the dispute between the new shearers' union and the pastoralists' association over the employment of non-union labour. Reports of incendiarism and physical violence alarmed the government, which sent a force of 'mounted infantry' to the disturbed districts, and Byrnes invoked an archaic British conspiracy act (6 Geo. IV, c.129) to imprison the strike leaders. In 1893, he was appointed attorney-general and moved to the legislative assembly, where the next year he strongly supported the draconian Peace Preservation Bill which allowed extensive powers of detention without trial; however, though enacted, the act for the moment was not enforced.

In 1897 Byrnes accompanied the premier, Sir Hugh Nelson, to England on the occasion of the queen's diamond jubilee and succeeded Nelson as premier in April 1898. His attitudes to the employment of the Pacific labourers (Kanakas) and to northern separation fluctuated over time and he lost interest in Australian federation, but as premier he subsidized immigration and encouraged development. He died, unmarried, from pneumonia and heart failure, following measles, at Brisbane on 27 September 1898, and after a state funeral was buried in Toowong cemetery, Brisbane, leaving an estate of £20,000. Statues to his memory put up in Warwick and Brisbane testify to his immediate popularity, as a representative of the possibility of successful self-betterment in a capitalist economy through intelligence and hard work; but the legend exaggerates an achievement necessarily limited by his early death, and overlooks his political tergiversations and the evidence of malpractice which later came to light.

E. I. CARLYLE, *rev.* A. G. L. SHAW

Sources R. Gill, 'Thomas Joseph Byrnes: the man and the legend', *Queensland political portraits, 1859–1952*, ed. D. J. Murphy and R. B. Joyce (1978), 177–91 • *AusDB*, 7.517–19 • S. Svensen, *The shearers' war* (1989) • C. A. Bernays, *Queensland politics during sixty years, 1859–1919* [1919]
Archives State Library of Queensland, South Brisbane, John Oxley Library, Palmer–McIlwraith MSS
Likenesses statue, Warwick, Queensland, Australia • statue, Brisbane, Queensland, Australia
Wealth at death £20,000 in Australia: *AusDB*

Byrnstan [St Byrnstan] (*d.* 934), bishop of Winchester, was probably a royal chaplain before his episcopal appointment and the mass priest who, with other members of the royal household, witnessed the freeing of a slave soon after Æthelstan became king. He was consecrated as bishop on 29 May 931 and died on 1 November 934 at Old Minster, Winchester, where he was presumably buried. The only acts of Byrnstan as bishop which have survived are his attestation of a few charters. He was remembered subsequently for his humility, charity, and piety; later writers thought that he had taken monastic vows but there is no contemporary evidence to support their claim. The main traditions about him are recorded by William of Malmesbury and include his serving the poor at table on feast days and his daily washing of their feet. He said masses for the souls of the dead every day and would walk in the minster cemeteries at night reciting psalms for their repose; on one occasion his *requiescunt in pace* was answered by voices from the graves adding 'Amen'. Byrnstan is said to have died while at prayer. His cult as a saint seems to have been largely developed through the sponsorship of Bishop Æthelwold to whom the saint is said to have appeared complaining angrily that in heaven he was honoured equally with Birinus and Swithun, but that he was not receiving the same respect in Winchester. His cult never became as widely observed as that of some of the other Winchester bishops who were regarded as saints.

BARBARA YORKE

Sources *Willelmi Malmesbiriensis monachi de gestis pontificum Anglorum libri quinque*, ed. N. E. S. A. Hamilton, Rolls Series, 52 (1870), 162–3 • M. A. O'Donovan, 'An interim revision of episcopal dates for the province of Canterbury, 850–950 [pt 2]', *Anglo-Saxon England*, 2 (1973), 91–113, esp. 110–11 • S. Keynes, 'King Athelstan's books', *Learning and literature in Anglo-Saxon England: studies presented to Peter Clemoes on the occasion of his sixty-fifth birthday*, ed. M. Lapidge and H. Gneuss (1985), 143–201 [esp. 185–9]

Byrom, Elizabeth [Beppy] (1722–1801), Jacobite sympathizer and diarist, was born on 1 January 1722 and baptized at the college church, Manchester, on 8 January. She was the eldest child of the three daughters and one son of John *Byrom (1692–1763), poet and creator of a system of shorthand, and his wife and cousin, Elizabeth (1700–1778), second daughter of Joseph Byrom (1660–1733) and his wife, Elizabeth (1675–1730). Elizabeth, commonly known as Beppy, was a beneficiary in the will of her grandfather, Joseph Byrom, which paid for her education and maintenance from the age of eleven; she was also a beneficiary of her uncle, Josiah Byrom (*d.* 1740). By the age of fourteen Beppy was undertaking the keeping of accounts with her younger brother, Edward (1724–1773), and she later became adept at the system of shorthand developed by John Byrom.

Like her father and her younger sister Dorothy (Dolly), Beppy Byrom was a firm supporter of the Jacobite cause. She is now best known for her diary in which, interspersed with details of domestic chores, she recorded the exploits of Charles Edward Stuart, the Young Pretender, during his stay in Manchester during the rising of 1745. Byrom began her diary on 14 August 1745 and wrote of her enthusiasm for Prince Charles's landing in Britain on 23 July. On 28 November she expressed her excitement at the arrival of the Jacobite highlanders in Manchester, when they settled their artillery on the land of her uncle, Edward Byrom, at Campfield. To signify her support for the Stuart cause, Beppy bought a gown in the Jacobite colours of blue and white, together with a pair of garters which had a loyal motto woven into a chequered pattern of red, yellow, and blue. On 29 November she records how, with other like-minded women, she sat up until late at the house of her aunt, Sarah Brearcliffe, drinking the prince's health.

On 30 November Byrom visited Salford Bridge to see Charles Edward ('I would not have missed it for a great deal of money'), and later that day was introduced to the prince and 'had the honour to kiss his hand' (Talon, 230–31). Following the retreat of the Jacobite troops from Derby on 6 December, the 23-year-old Beppy took the lead in collecting supplies for the eighteen highlanders left in the Manchester house of correction. Beppy's sister Dolly also collected money and food for the prisoners and visited them in gaol. Byrom evidently still cherished her Stuart sympathies in 1768, when the remaining Jacobites proclaimed the Young Pretender as Charles III; some time later she bought a blue-glazed teapot bearing the monogram 'C.R. III' alongside the white rose of Stuart.

On her father's death in September 1763 Byrom inherited £700 and a half-share of the income from property in Adswood and Hurdsfield, near Macclesfield; following her mother's death in December 1778 she was endowed with all of her father's right and interest in the family residence, Kersall Cell, Salford, where her manuscript diary was discovered. Byrom herself died, unmarried, in December 1801, aged seventy-nine.

JOYCE GOODMAN

Sources W. H. Thompson, *Bonnie Prince Charlie in Manchester: Beppie Byrom's diary —an eye witness account of Bonnie Prince Charlie in Manchester with illustrations and notes* (1954) • W. H. Thompson, ed., *The Byroms of Manchester: a unique collection of deeds and wills relating to a Manchester family and their home, the black and white building which still stands in the market place*, vol. 3 [n.d.] • J. Hancox, *The queen's chameleon: the life of John Byrom, a study in conflicting loyalties* (1994) • T. Swindells, *Manchester streets and Manchester men*, 1st ser. (1906) • L. H. Grindon, *Manchester banks and bankers: historical, biographical, and anecdotal*, 2nd edn (1878) • W. E. A. Axon, ed., *The annals of Manchester: a chronological record from the earliest times to the end of 1885* (1886) • H. Talon, *Selections from the journals and papers of John Byrom* (1950)
Archives Chetham's Library, Manchester

Byrom, John (1692–1763), poet and creator of a system of shorthand, was born on 29 February 1692 at Kersall Cell, Broughton, near Manchester, the second son of Edward Byrom (*d.* 1711), merchant, and his wife, Sarah Allen. The

John Byrom (1692–1763), by Dorning Rasbotham

Byrom family were well known in the district: the Byroms of Salford even had a coat of arms, 'arg. a chev. between three hedgehogs sable', on which Byrom wrote a poem, 'On the Author's Coat of Arms':

> Sharp on your Minds let pointed Virtues grow,
> That, without injuring, resist a Foe;

with the hedgehog as

> A foe to none, but ev'ry body's friend,
> And loth, altho' offended, to offend.
> (*Poems*)

Byrom was educated at school at Chester and then Merchant Taylors' School, London, and Trinity College, Cambridge (matriculated 6 July 1708; elected scholar, May 1709; BA, 1712; MA, 1715). He became a fellow of Trinity College at Michaelmas 1714 but subsequently lost his fellowship by declining to take holy orders. During his time at Trinity he contributed two papers to *The Spectator* (586 and 593) and wrote a pastoral, 'Colin and Phoebe', which appeared in *The Spectator* (605, 6 October 1714). The inspiration for Phoebe is said to have been Joanna (known as Jug), the charming eleven-year-old daughter of the master, Richard Bentley. Byrom subsequently studied medicine at Montpellier, signing one of his letters 'J. B., Dr. of Physic, January 17th 1718', but he stayed at Montpellier for such a short time (spring 1717 to May 1718) that the signature was almost certainly facetious (he subsequently declined an invitation to practise medicine in Manchester). Back in Cambridge in December 1718, he took the side of the master of Trinity in his dispute with the fellows: his pamphlet, *A Review of the Proceedings Against Dr Bentley*, was published anonymously in 1719. Byrom feared that 'our V. C.' would 'swallow me at a mouthfull' if he knew the author (Talon, 48).

On the death of Byrom's father in 1711, the estate and

family business passed to his elder brother, Edward. John, who married his cousin Elizabeth Byrom (1700–1778) on 14 February 1721, was in need of an income. He turned to the promotion of a system of shorthand which he had invented while at Cambridge, encouraged by Thomas Sharp, son of Archbishop John Sharp. The younger Sharp had been advised by his father to learn shorthand, but neither he nor Byrom liked the systems that were available. Byrom therefore returned to Cambridge in July 1723 with his *Proposals Printed May 27th, 1723, for Printing and Publishing a New Method of Shorthand*. He was elected a fellow of the Royal Society in March 1724, and contributed two papers on the subject of shorthand to its *Philosophical Transactions* (488).

Byrom's system became widely adopted, and was used by, among others, John and Charles Wesley, David Hartley, Horace Walpole, and prominent members of the aristocracy. For a number of years he spent much time in London, Cambridge, and Oxford, teaching pupils the art of shorthand. They paid 5 guineas, and were sworn to secrecy, becoming members of what Byrom, again perhaps facetiously, called his Societas Tachygraphica ('Speedwriting Society'). He built up a wide range of acquaintances in the course of promoting his system, until the death of his elder brother on 12 May 1740 put him in possession of the family property and relieved him of the need to teach it. He remained closely associated with it, however: he had printed new *Proposals* in 1739, and an act of parliament, passed on 5 May 1742, gave him the sole rights to the system for twenty-one years. It was finally made available to all by being published in its entirety in 1767 as *The Universal English Short-Hand*.

Byrom's politics, which were high church and mildly Jacobite, led him into controversy in 1727, when he appears to have opposed an address to the king from the Royal Society. But while he could be stubborn, and something of an enthusiast, he disliked fanaticism, and his poem 'On Clergymen Preaching Politics' shows a healthy contempt for vicar-of-Bray-like figures:

> Recall the Time from conquering William's Reign,
> And guess the Fruits of such a preaching Vein:
> How oft its Nonsense must have veer'd about,
> Just as the Politics were in or out:
> (*Poems*)

and, although he has been accused of being a Jacobite, he was lukewarm towards Charles Edward Stuart on his entry into Manchester in 1745. His daughter Elizabeth went to kiss the Young Pretender's hand, and reported with some amusement in her journal (30 November 1745) that 'my papa was fetched prisoner to do the same' (Talon, 231). It must have been at about this time that he wrote the epigram about Hanoverians and Jacobites:

> God bless the King! I mean the Faith's Defender.
> God bless—no harm in blessing—the Pretender!
> But who Pretender is, or who is King,
> God bless us all, that's quite another thing.
> (ibid.)

Byrom's scepticism about politics was counter-balanced by a deep seriousness about religion. He was particularly attached to William Law, whom he met in 1729. He bought a copy of Law's *Serious Call to a Devout and Holy Life* and became to some degree Law's disciple: Law's interest in the work of Jakob Boehme, and Law's advocacy of the spirit rather than the letter of doctrine, appealed to Byrom. Law, for his part, admired Byrom's versification of a passage from the *Serious Call* in his poem 'The Pond', about a man who, though he was always thirsty, took great care to put into his pond more water than he took out, and who finally drowned in it. Law later described Byrom as 'my dear Laureate, whom I love and esteem with all the truth of Christian fellowship' (*Private Journal*, 2.588). Byrom sided with Law against Warburton, the champion of literal evidence, so that Warburton thought him 'certainly a man of genius, plunged deep into the rankest fanaticism' and 'not malevolent, but mad' (ibid., Warburton to Hurd, 2 Jan 1752, 2.522). Byrom's enthusiasm is shown in his report of a conversation with Dr Joseph Butler, later bishop of Durham, in which 'the Dr. talked with much mildness and myself with too much impetuosity' and Byrom found himself wishing that he had some of Butler's temper and calmness, 'yet not quite, because I thought he was a little too little vigorous' (ibid., diary, 28 March 1737, 2.97, 99).

Although he knew the work of French writers such as Malebranche and Antoinette Bourignon, it seems unlikely that Byrom was responsible for the translation of the latter's hymns in an early Methodist hymn book, as has been suggested. In a letter to his son (26 April 1739) he mentions that John and Charles Wesley 'have both together printed a book of hymns, amongst which they have inserted two of Mrs Bourignon's' (*Private Journal*, 2.242). This suggests that Byrom himself had nothing to do with the book. John Wesley, for his part, noted of Byrom's poetry that 'he has all the wit and humour of Dr Swift, together with much more learning, deep and strong understanding, and, above all, a serious vein of piety' (*The Journal of the Revd. John Wesley*, ed. N. Curnock, 1909–16, 5.518). Wesley was not the only person to compare Byrom to Swift: the verses on the feud between Handel and Bononcini, written by Byrom in 1725 and containing the first use in the language of 'tweedle-dum' and 'tweedle-dee', were often attributed to Swift or Pope:

> Some say, compar'd to Bononcini,
> That Mynheer Handel's but a Ninny;
> Others aver, that he to Handel
> Is scarcely fit to hold a Candle.
> Strange all this difference should be
> 'Twixt Tweedle-dum and Tweedle-dee!
> (*Poems*)

Byrom had an extraordinary facility in verse: he wrote comic poems, such as 'A full and true account, of a horrid and barbarous robbery, committed on Epping forest, upon the body of the Cambridge coach', which has as its epigraph the mock-heroic *Arma virumque cano*; and he wrote many serious poems, in which he discusses matters of morality or religion, often with a skilful and light touch. He generally rhymed in couplets, discussing the relative merits of rhyme and blank verse in 'Thoughts on Rime and Blank Verse' and in 'An Epistle to a Friend, on the Art of English Poetry', and defending rhyme in 'A Defence of Rime'. The last-named was part of a friendly controversy between Byrom and Roger Comberbach, prothonotary of the palatinate of Chester and recorder of Macclesfield. Byrom was on the side of rhyme, as a rule, though he realized that it was

the Subject, in fine, in the Matter of Song
That makes a blank Verse or a Rime to be wrong.
(*Poems*)

His verse was often sharp and pithy, though his editor, A. W. Ward, thought, in a neat and telling phrase, that 'Byrom's foible in literature as well as in life was—if I may so describe it—a love of his dressing-gown rather late in the morning and rather early at night' (ibid., 1.xix).

The poems were collected, ten years after Byrom's death, in *Miscellaneous poems, by John Byrom, M.A., F.R.S., sometime fellow of Trinity College, Cambridge, and inventor of the universal English short-hand*, published in Manchester in 1773 (John Wesley was reading them hot from the press). The writer of the preface expressed the view that 'The Reader may be surprized perhaps to find in these Volumes so many learned, and critical Questions discussed in Verse. This is indeed a Singularity almost peculiar to our Author: but he had so accustomed himself to the Language of Poetry, that he always found it the easiest Way of expressing his Sentiments upon all Occasions.' The poetry thus ranges from the early pastoral in *The Spectator* and the 1726 poem *Tunbridgiale*, 'being a description of Tunbridge, in a letter to a friend in London', to a knotty discussion of theology in 'An epistle to a gentleman of the Temple, occasioned by two treatises, wherein the fall of Man is differently represented'. In *Enthusiasm: a Poetical Essay. In a Letter to a Friend in Town* (1752) Byrom suggests, in contradiction to the orthodox view of the time, that enthusiasm is not all bad—'Blame not Enthusiasm, if rightly bent'. True enthusiasm involves not wild fanaticism, but faith, hope, and the godlike mind:

In this Enthusiasm, advanc'd thus high,
Tis a true Christian Wish to live and die.
(*Poems*)

In similarly charitable mood Byrom attacks those who would denounce the clergy in 'An expostulation with a zealous sectarist, who inveighed in bitter terms against the clergy and church institutions':

No Sir: I cannot see to what good End
Such bitter words against the Clergy tend …
(ibid.)

During his own lifetime Byrom's best-known poem was probably 'A Divine Pastoral', his expansive version of the twenty-third psalm (it was included, for example, in Ash and Evans's *A Collection of Hymns Adapted to Public Worship*, 1781). The poem by which he is now most widely known is the magnificent Christmas hymn, 'Christians, awake, salute the happy morn'. It was a Christmas present to the poet's daughter Dolly, who, when asked what she would like for Christmas, had said (presumably knowing her father's pleasure in writing, and his skill) 'a poem'. It was written for Christmas 1749: most of its fifty-two lines were then divided into stanzas, and a tune was written for them by John Wainwright, organist of Stockport parish church, so that the hymn could be sung to the Byrom family at Christmas 1750. It is Byrom's verse at its finest: a reworking of Milton's 'Nativity Ode' in eighteenth-century terms, and with eighteenth-century diction: it is crisp and economical, a superb mixture of narrative and reflection, and it is a wonderful opening to a Christmas morning service. Although it is still found in modern hymn books, it is now sung less frequently.

Byrom had lived throughout his later years in Stockport. He died on 26 September 1763 after a long illness. Among his and Elizabeth's children was Elizabeth (Beppy) *Byrom, Jacobite sympathizer and diarist.

J. R. Watson

Sources *The private journal and literary remains of John Byrom*, ed. R. Parkinson, 2 vols. in 4 pts, Chetham Society, 32, 34, 40, 44 (1854–7) • H. Talon, *Selections from the journals and papers of John Byrom* (1950) • *The poems of John Byrom*, ed. A. W. Ward, 5 vols., Chetham Society, new ser., 29–30, 34–5, 70 (1894–1912) • J. E. Bailey, 'John Byrom's journal, letters, etc.', *Palatine Note-Book*, 2 (1882), 89–96; pubd separately (1882) • J. Byrom, *The universal English short-hand* (1767) • *The Spectator* (27 Aug 1714) • *The Spectator* (13 Sept 1714) • *The Spectator* (6 Oct 1714) • Venn, *Alum. Cant.*

Archives Chetham's Library, Manchester, corresp., papers, and material • JRL, family papers

Likenesses Topham, line engraving, pubd 1814 (after D. Rasbotham), NPG • D. Rasbotham, etching, NPG [*see illus.*] • engraving (as undergraduate), repro. in Talon, *Selections*, frontispiece

Byron. For this title name *see* individual entries under Byron; *see also* Noel, Anne Isabella, *suo jure* Baroness Wentworth, and Lady Byron (1792–1860).

Byron, (Augusta) Ada [*married name* (Augusta) Ada King, countess of Lovelace] (**1815–1852**), mathematician and computer pioneer, was born on 10 December 1815 at 13 Piccadilly Terrace, London, the only child of George Gordon Noel *Byron, sixth Baron Byron (1788–1824), poet, and his wife, Anne Isabella *Noel, *née* Milbanke, Lady Byron (1792–1860), daughter of Sir Ralph Milbanke Noel, bt. Soon after her birth and the subsequent celebrated break-up of her parents' marriage she became famous through the opening lines of canto three of Byron's poem *Childe Harold*:

Is thy face like thy mother's, my fair child!
Ada! sole daughter of my house and my heart?
When last I saw thy young blue eyes they smiled,
And then we parted—not as now we part, But with a hope.

Ada was brought up in the sole custody of her mother, who kept her out of the limelight. She was educated to be a mathematician and a scientist because her mother feared that she might turn out to be a poet like her father. A lonely but imaginative child, she was taught by a series of tutors (including the celebrated mathematician Augustus De Morgan) and at an early age was fascinated by mechanical things and toyed with the idea of designs for a flying machine powered by steam. When she was seventeen, in 1833, she met Charles Babbage, most likely through the natural philosopher Mary Somerville, a mutual acquaintance. Babbage showed Ada his first calculating engine, the difference engine, and her interest in mathematics was transformed from a duty to a joy. She

(Augusta) Ada Byron (1815–1852), by Margaret Sarah Carpenter, 1836

attended lectures about the engine, examined the blueprints, studied and taught mathematics, and became part of the same social circle as Babbage. They had many friends in common, in addition to De Morgan and Somerville, including Charles Dickens and Sir Charles Wheatstone.

Ada is best-known for her incisive notes and comments on Babbage's plans for an analytical engine. Because she was an independent (albeit enthusiastic) observer, and possessed a marked talent for conveying new and sometimes difficult concepts in limpid prose, her writings on this topic are much valued by historians. In November 1834 Babbage first shared with her his general idea for a new calculating engine that would not only have foresight but could act on that foresight. According to Lady Byron's diaries, Ada was touched by the 'universality of his ideas' (Toole, 69). In 1843 she translated a paper by General L. F. Menabrea, later to be prime minister of Italy, describing Babbage's main attempt to implement this notion, the projected analytical engine (which was to supersede the aborted difference engine but which was never built). She added extensive notes to Menabrea's paper which contain not only what is regarded as one of the earliest computer programs but also prescient comments about the future of such an engine, which have stood the test of time. Her correspondence with Babbage about the time that she was preparing this work for publication elaborates further on her idea of what would now be termed a program, and, moreover, places it in the context of its possible use. Thus on 10 July 1843 she suggested to him:

> I want to put in something about Bernoulli's Number, in one of my Notes, as an example of how an explicit function, may be worked out by the engine, without having been worked out by human head and hands first. (Toole, 198)

Though other instances of what might be regarded as a program of instructions for the engine to calculate numbers have been found, the Bernoulli numbers were a perfect choice of example with which to differentiate Babbage's analytical engine from all other calculating engines.

Ada's work was published in September 1843 in Taylor's *Scientific Memoirs* (vol. 3) as 'Sketch of the analytical engine invented by Charles Babbage esq. by L. F. Menabrea, of Turin, officier of the military engineers'. The translator and annotator is not identified on the title page, but each of her notes is individually signed AAL (Augusta Ada Lovelace). She asked penetrating questions about how the analytical engine might be applied, and hypothesized that if it could understand the relations of pitched sounds and the science of harmony 'the engine might compose elaborate and scientific pieces of music of any degree of complexity and extent' (*Scientific Memoirs*, 3, 1843, 694). She also saw the graphical potential of the analytical engine, and that by changing to a new medium, the punched card, scientific information would be seen in a new light. Thus, in a famous and influential metaphor, she wrote 'Analytical Engine *weaves algebraical patterns* just as the Jacquard loom weaves flowers and leaves' (ibid., 696).

Interestingly, Ada also saw the limits of such a technological innovation and described the tendency people have to 'first, *overrate* what we find to be … remarkable, and secondly, by a sort of natural reaction, to *undervalue* the true state of the case' (*Scientific Memoirs*, 3, 1843, 722). Her comment 'The Analytical Engine has no pretension whatever to originate anything' (ibid.) evokes and anticipates the heated debate between proponents of artificial intelligence and those who believe the human mind cannot be reduced to a machine.

On 8 July 1835 Ada married William King, eighth Baron King of Ockham (1805–1893), lord lieutenant of Surrey. He was created earl of Lovelace in 1838. They had two sons, Byron Noel (1836–1862) and Ralph Gordon (1839–1906), who were successively Baron Wentworth and second and third earl of Lovelace, and a daughter, Anne Isabella Noel *Blunt, an equestrian, who wrote *A Pilgrimage to Nejd* (1881) and was married to the poet Wilfrid Scawen Blunt.

After Ada, Lady Lovelace, wrote the 'Sketch' in 1843 her health, which was always fragile, became worse. Physicians prescribed laudanum, and many of the extensive letters she left were written under the influence of her illness and drugs. She hypothesized a 'calculus of the nervous system' (Toole, 296) but at the same time was sceptical of the claims of mesmerism's ability to cure tumours. Her social circle expanded to include not only Sir David Brewster and Michael Faraday but intellectual characters who were also great followers of the horse races, such as members of the Zetland family. She gambled and won on the horses, and gambled and lost, and was at the mercy, both emotionally and financially, of several of her gambling friends. According to the bank books, her involvement in gambling stopped in June of 1851 when she suffered severe haemorrhages. In a panic Lord Lovelace went for help to Lady Byron, only to be faced with Lady Byron's concern being Ada's gambling, not her health. Until Ada's tragic death, from cancer of the uterus, at 6 Great Cumberland Place, London, on 27 November 1852, she was in excruciating pain, bedridden, and, because of financial need, at the mercy of Lady Byron who took over the Lovelace household and prevented Babbage from seeing her daughter.

On 3 December 1852 Ada was buried (at her own request) next to her father in the parish church of St Mary Magdalene in Hucknall near Lord Byron's ancestral home at Newstead Abbey. In 1979 a computer software language, the official language of the United States department of defense, was named 'Ada' in her honour and in 1993 a blue plaque was erected at her home at 12 (formerly 10) St James's Square, London, in commemoration of her being a 'pioneer of the computer'.

BETTY ALEXANDRA TOOLE

Sources B. A. Toole, ed., *Ada, the enchantress of numbers* (1992) • A. Hyman, *Charles Babbage: pioneer of the computer* (1982) • *DNB* • GEC, *Peerage* • d. cert.

Archives Bodl. Oxf., corresp. and papers | BL, letters to Charles Babbage, Add. MSS 37189–37194 • Bodl. Oxf., corresp. with Mary Somerville and her family

Likenesses M. Carpenter, portrait, 1836, Gov. Art Coll. [*see illus.*] • A. E. Châlon, portrait, *c*.1838, BM

Wealth at death under £10,000: letters; bank books

Byron, Elizabeth. *See* Strutt, Elizabeth (*fl*. 1805–1863).

Byron, George Gordon Noel, sixth Baron Byron (1788–1824), poet, was born on 22 January 1788 at 16 (later 24) Holles Street, London, the son of Captain John Byron (1756–1791) and his second wife, Catherine, *née* Gordon (1765–1811). In the visitations of Nottingham of 1569 and 1615 the family pedigree begins with Sir Richard Byron, of Byron and Clayton in Lancashire, whose son Sir John Byron was rewarded for his services to Henry VIII with the possession of Newstead Abbey in Nottinghamshire. His descendant Sir John Byron was created Baron Byron of Rochdale by Charles I in 1643. The fourth Lord Byron, William (1669–1736), had three children, the second of whom was John, later Admiral *Byron (Foulweather Jack) (1723–1786), the poet's grandfather, whose adventures by land and sea were legendary. The admiral had three children, the eldest being Captain Byron (Mad Jack), the poet's father, whose profligacy was so great that he was eventually disinherited by his father. Resigning his commission in the guards by 1778, the handsome captain plunged into the fast world of London fashionable life. He seduced and in 1779 eventually married after her divorce Amelia

George Gordon Noel Byron, sixth Baron Byron (1788–1824), by Thomas Phillips, 1814

D'Arcy, marchioness of Carmarthen, later *suo jure* Baroness Conyers, with whom he had a daughter, Augusta Mary (1783–1851), Byron's half-sister who later played a central part in his life.

Deprived of his wife's income of £4000 a year by her death in January 1784, Captain Byron went to Bath in search of another rich wife, and settled on Catherine Gordon. She was one of the three surviving daughters of George Gordon, twelfth laird of Gight, Aberdeenshire, and his wife and second cousin, Catherine, daughter of Alexander Innes, sheriff-clerk and provost of Banff. Both her parents died during her infancy and Catherine was brought up near Banff by her grandmother Margaret Gordon, *née* Duff (1720–1801), known by the courtesy title of Lady Gight. From her grandmother Catherine inherited a love of books but she remained unsophisticated, emotional, and naïve. Also plump and plain, the twenty-year-old Catherine was quickly charmed by the dashing captain and they were married at St Michael's Church, Bath, on 13 May 1785.

By July the newly-weds had settled at Gight where, in no time at all, Captain Byron ran through most of the £23,000 Catherine had brought to their marriage. (Much would have been swallowed up by pre-existing debts.) In March 1786 they went through a second marriage ceremony and Captain Byron took on the family name of Gordon, both events relating to the need to sell the estate of Gight. In July 1787 Captain Byron fled from the Isle of Wight where, to avoid creditors, the couple had been living, to Paris. He was joined there the following September by Mrs Byron who was pregnant. In December she returned to London and rented rooms at 16 Holles Street, off Oxford Street, where Byron was born with a deformed right foot. Harassed by creditors, Byron's father was constantly on the move to remain one step ahead of the bailiffs. He was in Edinburgh on 26 January when he wrote to Mrs Byron's agent informing him that she had given birth to a son. Byron was baptized George Gordon Byron at the parish church of St Marylebone, St Marylebone Road, on 1 March (though 1788 was not in fact a leap year the date was mistakenly entered as 29 February) and his godfathers were named as George Gordon, fifth duke of Gordon, and Colonel Robert Duff of Fetteresso, Aberdeenshire. Byron's forebears on each side were, as he later observed, 'all meridian', and as time passed he constructed an increasingly imaginative relationship to his ancestry. He developed a pride in his lineage which on his father's side can be traced back to the time of William the Conqueror, and on his mother's side descends from James I of Scotland. The motto *Crede Byron* that appears over the family's arms was one to which Byron adhered throughout his life; it later adorned the ceremonial helmets that helped to define his role as a figurehead in the Greek War of Independence.

Childhood In March 1788 Mrs Byron received a settlement securing £4222 of her estate against creditors, and in summer 1789 settled with her son and his nurse Agnes Gray, a religious woman with strict Calvinist views, in a furnished apartment in Queen Street, Aberdeen. By August she had been joined by her husband who stayed with her intermittently until September 1790 when Captain Byron abandoned his wife and child and went to live with his sister Fanny (Frances) Leigh in Valenciennes where he died, possibly of consumption, on 2 August 1791 at thirty-five. He appointed his son 'Mr. George Gordon, heir of my real and personal estate, and charge[d] him to pay my debts, legacies, and funeral expenses' (Marchand, *Biography*, 1.32). As a small boy Byron was known as George Byron Gordon. Byron preserved a fond memory of his feckless and disgraceful father. He was not yet four when his father died, but according to Medwin he remembered him well, and traced his 'horror of matrimony' to the 'domestic broils' of his parents (ibid.). Despite everything, Mrs Byron was desolate when her husband died.

For his mother, who was doting, volatile, and capricious, Byron's feelings were deeper and more ambivalent. She was fiercely loyal, proud, and devoted to her son, who was as fiery as she. He grew up in an emotional world that swung between extremes of violence and tenderness. Fond of his nurse and doted on by his mother, Byron spent his formative years in a closed and intense emotional world, its effect heightened by his mother's straitened circumstances and the emotional and physical pain arising from his deformed foot. For this Mrs Byron sought advice from John Hunter, a London surgeon, but her finances prevented her from taking the boy south for treatment. Borrowing money, Mrs Byron moved to 64 Broad Street, a respectable address in Aberdeen new town, where she occupied the whole of the first floor which she furnished herself. At the age of five Byron was sent to the nearby school 'kept by a Mr *Bowers*—who was called "*Bodsy* Bowers" by reason of his dapperness.—It was a school for both sexes' (*Letters and Journals*, ed. Marchand, 8.107). After about a year he left ('I learned little there') and was instructed by a clergyman called Ross who taught him to read, and then by a young man called Paterson, 'the son of my Shoemaker—but a good Scholar … [and] a rigid Presbyterian also', who taught him Latin (ibid.). News reached Mrs Byron that William, grandson of the fifth Lord Byron, had been killed at the battle of Calvi in Corsica on 31 July 1794 and that her son, then aged six and a half, was heir presumptive to the Byron title and estates. Byron entered Aberdeen grammar school, where over the next four years he continued to study Latin, and in the afternoons attended Mr Duncan's writing school across the road. His passion for reading, which began with listening to his nurse's readings from the Old Testament and the Psalms and was fostered by his mother, took in 'Knolles, Cantemir, De Tod, Lady M. W. Montague, Hawkins's Translation from Mignot's History of the Turk, the Arabian Nights, all travels or histories, or books upon the East I could meet with … before I was *ten years old*' (Marchand, *Biography*, 1.38). 'When a boy I could never bear to read any Poetry whatever without disgust and reluctance' (ibid.). Visits during the school holidays to his great-grandmother Lady Gight at Banff, and to the Dee valley where he was taken to convalesce after an attack of scarlet fever in 1795 or 1796, introduced Byron to the splendours of highland scenery to which he formed a lifelong attachment, and which formed a sublime ideal in the landscape of his imagination. At Banff, or at her home near Aberdeen, he met his cousin, Mary Duff, 'my first of flames' (*Letters and Journals*, ed. Marchand, 3.210). Years later Byron recalled that 'my love for her was so violent, that I sometimes doubt if I have been really attached since … [she] still lives in my imagination' (ibid., 222). The intensity of his early reaction to Scottish scenery and of his attachment to Mary Duff fused with his imagination to create ideals that were seldom fully realized in later years. This set a pattern that established a vital creative source for the expression of melancholy to which Byron's letters and journals refer and that famously pervades much of his poetry. These boyhood visits to the country also provided opportunities to learn to swim, ride, and shoot, activities in which he later excelled.

On 21 May 1798 the old Lord Byron died and, at the age of ten, Byron inherited the title of sixth Baron Byron of Rochdale. Through her Aberdeen attorney, Alexander Crombie, Mrs Byron heard that John Hanson, a chancery solicitor in London, had agreed to act for the young heir. Hanson was to remain a lifelong friend and adviser to Byron. His first tasks were to make his charge a ward in chancery and to arrange the appointment of Frederick Howard, fifth earl of Carlisle, son of Admiral Byron's sister Isabella and first cousin of Byron's father, as Byron's legal guardian. Meanwhile, Mrs Byron applied to the chancellor for an allowance, sold her furniture, and at the end of August set forth, with Byron and his nurse May Gray (who had replaced her sister Agnes), for Newstead Abbey.

Both abbey and house were in a ruinous condition and the estate was heavily encumbered with debts. Other valuable properties in Rochdale had also been neglected by the old Lord Byron and would need to be recovered at law. After a brief stay at Newstead, when both mother and son were enchanted by its romantic aspect and by the family history it represented, Byron, accompanied by his nurse, went to stay in Nottingham with his great-aunt the Hon. Frances Byron, and afterwards lodged with a Mr Gill. His mother engaged a tutor and arranged for him to receive treatment for his foot; the last, however, caused Byron only pain and distress. In July 1799 he was taken to London where he met John Hanson who introduced him to his guardian and arranged for him to receive long-term treatment for his foot. At this time he also met his cousin the beautiful Margaret Parker ('she looked as if she had been made out of a rainbow'), and his passion for the thirteen-year-old gave rise to his 'first dash into poetry' in 1800. (For Byron's account of this see his *Letters and Journals*, ed. Marchand, 9.40.) Hanson engaged the boy's confidence sufficiently for Byron to unburden to him the sexual abuse to which he had been subjected by his nurse May Gray. She was dismissed but her treatment of the boy, combined with her Calvinist religious beliefs, gave him a permanent loathing of religious cant and hypocrisy and contributed to the complex range of attitudes he held towards women in adult life.

Youth In August 1799 Byron entered the school of a Dr Glennie, an Aberdonian, in Dulwich. During the holidays his time was divided between stays with the Hanson family at their home in Earl's Court and visits to his mother who took lodgings with a Mrs Massingberd at 16 Piccadilly. Hanson secured from the court of chancery £500 a year for Byron's education and his mother's annual pension of £300 was thereby reduced to £200. Medical treatment for Byron's foot amounted to £150 a year with 2 guineas per school visit by the physician. Byron refused to let his lameness prevent him from participating in any of the usual physical activities that schoolboys engage in, and on one occasion threw his leg brace into a pond. In April 1801 he entered Harrow School, where for the first time he mixed with boys of his own social rank. At first, however, the headmaster, Dr Joseph Drury, whose strategy with Byron was to lead this 'wild mountain colt' with a 'silken string', placed him under the individual tutorial guidance of his own son Henry Drury, an assistant master (Marchand, *Biography*, 1.66). B. W. Procter recalled that 'There were during his schooltime no symptoms of such a destiny. He was loud, even coarse, and very capable of a boy's vulgar enjoyments. He was then a rough, curly headed boy, and apparently nothing more' (Procter, 22). At Harrow 'P. Hunter, Curzon, Long and Tattersall were my principal friends. Clare, Dorset, Cs. Gordon, De Bath[e], Claridge and Jno. Wingfield, were my juniors and favourites, whom I spoilt by indulgence' (Moore, *Letters*, 21). Others included George John West, fifth Earl De La Warr (who, like Byron, succeeded to his title as a boy), and William Harness. 'My School friendships were with *me passions*' (*Letters and Journals*, ed. Marchand, 9.44). Though not homosexual, these friendships were intense and intimate, and Byron's patronizing of younger boys, a role he maintained in adult life, often led to small jealousies among his favourites.

At Christmas 1802 Henry Edward, nineteenth Baron Grey of Ruthin, a young man of twenty-three, had taken on the lease of Newstead at £50 a year for the remainder of Byron's minority. Mrs Byron took a house in the nearby town of Southwell, Burgage Manor, and in the following summer holidays Byron rode over to Newstead at the invitation of his tenant and lodged with the steward, Owen Mealey. From there he visited at Annesley Hall, Mary Chaworth whose father was descended from the William Chaworth killed by the 'Wicked' Lord Byron in a duel in 1765. In response to his passionate attachment to her, Mary flirted with Byron, but at seventeen (two years his senior) she was already engaged to marry John Musters, a neighbour. Regardless of this, Byron refused to return to school and instead rode over to Annesley where he moodily practised pistol shooting on the terrace. Agonized by a sharp rebuff from Mary, he went hunting and shooting on the Newstead estate with his tenant, but his stay ended abruptly in January 1804, probably following a sexual advance from Grey. Henceforth, Byron, deeply shocked, intended to 'ever consider [him] my most inveterate enemy', but later stated he would be happy 'to meet as friends' (*Letters and Journals*, ed. Marchand, 1.49–50, 168).

Byron returned to Harrow and by Easter 1804 he had begun to correspond with his half-sister, Augusta. His early letters to her illustrate his earnest desire to establish an affectionate friendship with 'a Friend to whom I can confide' (*Letters and Journals*, ed. Marchand, 1.45). At school, meanwhile, he was 'remarked for the extent and readiness of my *general* information' and capable of 'great sudden exertions—(such as thirty Greek Hexameters or forty Greek Hexameters) … but of few continuous drudgeries' and later acknowledged that 'my qualities were much more oratorical and martial than poetical' (ibid., 9.42). Following 'two or three scrapes' he was reprimanded by Henry Drury and stung by some comments from his brother Mark Drury into the ambitious realization that 'the way to riches to Greatness lies before me, I can, I will cut myself a path through the world or perish in the attempt' (ibid., 1.49). He enjoyed declaiming at speech-days and delighted in the headmaster's notice of his performance, but remained at odds with the established order and led a rebellion among the boys against the new headmaster, the Revd Dr George Butler (the 'Pomposus' of his satire 'On a Change of Masters at a Great Public School'). Though, during the holidays, his relationship with Mrs Byron became increasingly quarrelsome, he found a release in new friendships in Southwell, particularly with Elizabeth *Pigot and her brother John, who lived across the green from Burgage Manor. Five years older than he, Elizabeth formed a lively friendship with Byron that was sustained by a shared sense of satirical humour and a mutual interest in writing verse. Her first impression of Byron, as she later described him to Thomas Moore, was of 'a fat bashful boy, with his hair combed straight over his forehead' (Moore, 1.75). Friendship helped to make Byron's last year at Harrow enjoyable: he later recalled that 'I always *hated* Harrow till my last year and a half—but then I liked it' (*Letters and Journals*, ed. Marchand, 9.37).

'A college life' Recollecting his university education Byron wrote that:

> when I went up to Trinity, in 1805, at the age of seventeen and a half, I was miserable and untoward to a degree. I was wretched at leaving Harrow … wretched at going to Cambridge instead of Oxford (there were no rooms vacant at Christchurch); wretched from some private domestic circumstances of different kinds, and consequently about as unsocial as a wolf taken from the troop. (*Letters and Journals*, ed. Marchand, 7.230, 19 November 1820, to John Murray)

He nevertheless liked his '*Super*excellent Rooms' in the south-east corner of the great court at Trinity (known as Merton-hall corner), and soon wrote to Hargreaves Hanson (the son of his solicitor, who had been with him at Harrow) that 'college improves in everything but Learning, nobody here seems to look into an author ancient or modern if they can avoid it' (ibid., 1.80). To Hanson he had written with requests for '4 dozen of Wine, Port—Sherry—Claret, & Madeira, one Dozen of Each', and told him that he 'beg[an] to *admire* a College Life' (ibid., 78). His comment that 'my appearance in the Hall in my State Robes [on formal university occasions undergraduate noblemen wore an elaborately decorated gown] was *Superb*, but uncomfortable to my *Diffidence*' (ibid.) records the beginning of Byron's acute awareness of the impact of his public appearance, which later took on an importance far beyond the immediate social context, but at the same time reveals the self-consciousness of a newly matriculated freshman. During his first term Byron strengthened his friendship with Edward Noel Long who had come up with him from Harrow, and developed a 'violent, though *pure* passion' for a young chorister, John Edleston, the Thyrza of some of his early poems, who gave him a cornelian heart (ibid., 8.24). Though (as was usual among undergraduate noblemen) he rarely attended lectures, Byron widened his reading and pursued his enjoyment of swimming and riding. College dissipations, the refurbishment of his rooms, and the expense of keeping horses soon disposed of his allowance and, still a minor, in December he asked Augusta to stand guarantor to the first of the huge debts he contracted with moneylenders. These were arranged by his landlady in Piccadilly, Mrs Massingberd. To the alarm of his mother, Byron wrote to say that, having paid off his debts and with 'a few hundreds in ready Cash lying about me' he had decided not to return to college but to pass a couple of years abroad (ibid., 1.89). Instead, however, he lingered in London where he took lessons from the fashionable fencing master Henry Angelo, learned to box with 'Gentleman' John Jackson, went to the theatre, and sought sexual entertainment from a 'famous French entremetteuse' (*Letters and Journals*, ed. Prothero, 5.575). In April he returned to Cambridge, where at the end of term he was detained by the painting of a carriage he had recently acquired. His mounting debts deeply worried his mother and her anxiety further increased the tension in their volatile relationship. To escape from her scolding Byron sought refuge that summer in the home of Elizabeth Pigot where he began to compile a volume of his early poems. With Elizabeth's assistance he gathered together some of his sentimental verses with various school exercises and literary imitations and had them privately printed by John Ridge at Newark in a volume he called *Fugitive Pieces*. Many of the Southwell inhabitants were shocked by its inclusion of some stanzas 'To Mary'; according to the Revd John Becher, these were 'too warmly drawn' (Marchand, *Biography*, 1.97). Byron asked for the return of all copies of the work and, except for four, all were destroyed. Almost immediately he began preparing a revised collection of his poems for a new edition.

In August 1806, following a spectacular quarrel with 'Mrs. Byron furiosa' (Marchand, *Biography*, 1.92–3), Byron left Southwell in his carriage in the middle of the night, driving first to London and then on to visit Edward Long who was staying with his family in Littlehampton on the Sussex coast. He put up at a local inn and impressed Long's younger brother Henry, who left an account of Byron and Long's swimming feats which included diving off the high jetty into the river as the tide was racing out and being thus carried at speed far out to sea from where they swam back in a large semi-circle to the shore. Back at Southwell in September he went with John Pigot to visit Harrogate. There he was busy writing verse, and on the return journey dashed off a prologue to *The Wheel of Fortune*. Lack of funds prevented Byron from returning to Cambridge for the start of the new term and so he agreed to join in some private theatricals in Southwell, taking the part of Penruddock in George Cumberland's *Wheel of Fortune* and Tristram Fickle in J. T. Allingham's *The Weathercock*. Rehearsals for these brought him into contact with the 'Southwell Belles', with one of whom, Julia Leacroft, in a bid by the girl's family to entrap the young lord into marriage, he became briefly entangled.

Poems on Various Occasions, the revised collection of Byron's early poems, appeared in a private edition of about 100 copies in January 1807. For this he received many 'insipid Compliments' and for this reason appreciated the 'Critique' of William Bankes, a Trinity College friend, whom Byron later referred to as his 'collegiate pastor, and master and patron' who was also 'the father of all mischiefs' (*Letters and Journals*, ed. Marchand, 1.110 and n. 9). In April he wrote to Hanson that:

> I am grown very thin … so much so that people here think I am going, I have lost 18 LB in my weight, that is one Stone & 4 pounds since January … I shall continue my Exertions, having no other amusement, I wear *seven* waistcoats, & a great Coat, run & play at Cricket in this Dress, till quite exhausted by excessive perspiration, use the hot Bath daily. (ibid., 113–14)

A series of ten watercolour drawings by Elizabeth Pigot in her 'The Wonderful History of Lord Byron and his Dog' (dated 26 March 1807, Ransom HRC), a lively pastiche of *The Wonderful Adventure of Old Mother Hubbard and her Dog* (illustrated 2nd edn, 1805), provides a delightful illustration of Byron's Southwell activities. They show him playing cricket, listening to his dog Boatswain preaching from a pulpit the words 'Repent ye wicked, resist temptation', immersed up to his neck in a hot bath, seated at a table writing, and finally, being driven away in his carriage and four (some repr., Peach, figs. 6–9).

Following the publication of *Hours of Idleness*, his first published volume of poetry, Byron returned to Cambridge at the end of June 1807. From there he wrote several amusing letters to Elizabeth Pigot and informed her of his decision to 'reside *another year* at *Granta* as my Rooms &c. &c. are finished in *great Style*, several old friends *come up* again, & many *new* acquaintances made' (*Letters and Journals*, ed. Marchand, 1.124). These included John Cam *Hobhouse and Charles Skinner Matthews, young men with serious intellectual interests. Hobhouse became a lifelong and completely devoted friend. Matthews, who had occupied Byron's rooms in his absence, was mischievous, one of a 'band of profane scoffers' led by Bankes. It was to Matthews that Byron wrote from Falmouth with veiled allusion to intended homosexual encounters, both there and with 'exotics we expect to meet in Asia' (ibid., 1.206–7). From Gordon's Hotel, London, Byron wrote to Elizabeth Pigot that the copies of *Hours of Idleness* Ridge had sent to London had all sold and more were in demand. Though he wrote on 20 August from Cambridge to his old schoolfriend the earl of Clare that he was 'now setting off for the Highlands of Scotland' nothing further is known of his movements until he wrote again to Elizabeth from Cambridge on 26 October. Through Matthews and Hobhouse Byron met Scrope Berdmore *Davies, a fellow of King's College, and the slightly older Francis *Hodgson, former master of Eton College and resident tutor at King's. Davies was a dandy, a friend of Beau Brummell, and renowned for his play for high stakes at the London gaming tables.

With Hodgson, a noted classical scholar, Byron shared an interest in the poetry of Dryden and Pope. The intellectual and political interests and urbane, witty, and often facetious conversation of this sophisticated circle stimulated Byron to expand the range of his poetry and he began to develop his work in satire. He reviewed Wordsworth's *Poems* (2 vols., 1807) in *Monthly Literary Recreations*, began to write the satirical poem *English Bards and Scotch Reviewers* (1809), and joined the Cambridge Whig Club. Prevented by the rules from keeping his new bulldog, Smut, in college he bought a tame bear which, according to J. M. F. Wright, who was admitted to Trinity in 1813, he kept in the tower above his rooms (J. M. F. Wright, *Alma Mater, or, Seven Years at the University of Cambridge, by a Trinity Man*, 2 vols., 1827). When asked what he meant to do with him he replied that 'he should *sit* for *a Fellowship* … this answer delighted them not' (*Letters and Journals*, ed. Marchand, 1.136–7). The bear's fame long outlasted his residence at Trinity. Though praised in the *Critical Review*, *Hours of Idleness* was ridiculed by Hewson Clarke in *The Satirist* (October 1807), and Byron instructed Ridge to omit the preface in the second edition. But this agreeable life in college was short-lived. He left for the Christmas holidays in 1807 and did not return, except to visit his friends, until he went up for his MA in July 1808.

Life in London Early in 1808 Byron settled at Dorant's Hotel, London. Late in January he met his distant kinsman Robert Charles Dallas, a dull author who had written to Byron praising his poetry. Over thirty years older and lacking the liveliness of his other friends, Dallas assisted Byron in the publication of some of his poetry. Byron resumed friendships with several of his Harrow schoolfellows and, being reconciled with Henry Drury, paid several visits to Harrow. With Scrope Davies he dined, played at hazard, and, as he confessed to Hobhouse, was otherwise 'buried in an abyss of Sensuality' (*Letters and Journals*, ed. Marchand, 1.158). This did not prevent him from being devastated by an *ad hominem* attack in the *Edinburgh Review* which ridiculed the vanities of the author of the preface to *Hours of Idleness*. Appalled by this criticism from a whig journal, Byron believed that the review was written by its editor, Francis Jeffrey, though it was actually from the hand of the reformist lawyer and politician Henry Brougham, who incurred Byron's implacable hatred during his marital separation in 1816. Though he later affected nonchalance about the review, Hobhouse, to whom he wrote of it at the time, noted that 'he was very near destroying himself' (Marchand, *Biography*, 1.148).

This infamous review is important in the development of Byron's writing for two reasons. First, it led directly to the publication of his first major poem, *English Bards and Scotch Reviewers*, in 1809. Second, it exposed a number of contradictions which Byron experienced and registered in himself and in contemporary society. Towards the end of March 1808 he received copies of the new edition of *Hours of Idleness* entitled *Poems Original and Translated*, but was less sanguine in distributing them to friends. After visiting Cambridge to take his degree, he made a summer visit to Brighton accompanied by a young girl in male attire whom he introduced in society as his younger brother. He was joined there by Davies and Hobhouse, and the latter noticed a despondency in his friend that he attributed to exhausting involvements with women. Tiring of the solace offered by various 'nymphs' and 'cursedly dipped' for cash, Byron returned in September to Newstead following the departure of Lord Grey on the expiration of his lease in June.

Again enchanted by the Romantic, ruinous, appearance of the abbey, Byron resolved not to sell but to restore it. He made preparations to welcome his friends, the first of whom to arrive was Hobhouse. Together they rode and swam in the lake, as refurbishment of a few rooms went ahead. Byron worked on his satirical poem, but was thrown into despondency by the effect on his emotions of a meeting with Mary Chaworth, now Mrs Musters, and the death of his beloved Newfoundland dog Boatswain. He wrote a commemorative poem that was inscribed on an elaborate monument to Boatswain he had erected at Newstead. A plan he had formed earlier in the year to go abroad began to take hold of his imagination. Though he would not invite Mrs Byron to stay while he was in residence at Newstead, he wrote to inform her of his plans and to invite her to be chatelaine during his absence abroad. Lonely and bored after Hobhouse's departure, and with the approach of his twenty-first birthday, Byron left Newstead after the Christmas holidays for London. Before doing so he made provision for a young servant girl, Lucy, who was pregnant with his child.

On his arrival Byron contacted Dallas for assistance in finding a publisher for his satire, and wrote to his guardian for advice on taking his seat in the House of Lords. Lord Carlisle's cool reply, which informed him of procedural details but did not include an offer of a personal introduction, was a slight that wounded Byron deeply. It placed him in the unusual and humiliating position of having to prove his legitimacy to the chancellor before he could take his seat. Dallas settled with James Cawthorn to publish *English Bards*, which came out in mid-March, a few days after Byron took his seat to 'the left of the throne, on one of the benches usually occupied by the Lords in opposition' (Marchand, *Biography*, 1.170).

The production of *English Bards* was an act of enormous pretension for one who had barely reached his majority. Nevertheless, it forms the all but inevitable conclusion of the process which Byron had set in motion when he first issued *Fugitive Pieces*. The coy self-consciousness of this work led to the even more personal and self-conscious *Hours of Idleness*; this in turn produced Brougham's ridiculing notice, the impetus behind Byron's broad-ranging critique of English letters and culture. Byron's intention to attack on all fronts the contemporary literary scene (as signalled in his poem's title) is replicated in the poem's unsparing pursuit of Jacobins, and anti-Jacobins, the lake school (Wordsworth, Coleridge, and Southey), the Della Cruscans, sentimentalists and Gothic writers, romancers (for example, Scott), lyricists, and balladeers. The poem is quintessential Byron in that he includes himself in his charges of cultural degeneracy. 'I was born for opposition' Byron famously declared years later in *Don Juan*, a truth fully realized in this early work. The poem gained a measure of notoriety—it went through several editions between 1809 and 1811—but Byron did not stay to enjoy its success. Shortly after its publication he went abroad.

Byron's satire served to extend the social context in which he insisted on asserting and defining himself. In so doing, however, he was forced to confront British society in a much larger frame of reference, and to deal with several contradictions of which he had scarcely been aware. When he wrote his early poetry his closest circles and sympathies were reformist and whig. It was therefore a shock to find himself ridiculed in the *Edinburgh Review*. When he struck back he found his readiest weapons were often supplied by the *Anti-Jacobin* and by conservative literary voices like William Gifford. As a consequence, the most notable quality of the early satire is the peculiar and idiosyncratic nature of its social critique. Byron singles out a few individuals for praise and honour, but his attack is launched at British culture as a whole, where he is able to see no party, no class, no institution with which to identify. British culture is represented in a state of crisis, and Byron's is a voice crying in the wilderness.

With the publication of his satire Byron completed his preparations for leaving England. He entertained his friends Matthews, Hobhouse, James Wedderburn Webster, and probably Davies at Newstead where, dressed in monks' habits, they 'used to sit up late … drinking burgundy, claret, champagne and what not, out of the *skull-cup* [and] buffoon[ed] around the house, in our conventual garments' (*Letters and Journals*, ed. Marchand, 8.231). Hobhouse agreed to accompany Byron on his travels, and when Hanson's attempt to raise a loan of £6000 to pay for the journey failed to materialize in total, Davies loaned Byron £4800, recently won at the gaming tables. On board the Lisbon packet as it lay in Falmouth Roads on 30 June Byron fired off an exuberant farewell letter in verse:

> Huzza! Hodgson, we are going,
> Our embargo's off at last
> Favourable Breezes blowing
> Bend the canvass oer the mast,
> From aloft the signal's streaming
> Hark! The farewell gun is fired,
> Women screeching, Tars blaspheming,
> Tells us that our time's expired …
> (ibid., 1.211)

Grand tour This famous tour of the Iberian peninsula and the Turkish dominions in the Levant produced Byron's equally famous account of that journey: the first two cantos of *Childe Harold's Pilgrimage*, published after his return in July 1811. Here for the first time Byron projected his sense of social and cultural crisis to include the whole of Europe. The focus of his analysis is, of course, an English one, but his is an English view that transcended chauvinist, patriotic interpretations of European affairs which were current in England at the time. With this poem all the fundamental lines of Byron's thinking, if not his conclusions, are set in place. Byron often imagined for himself a reformist, if not a revolutionary political career, but his ironical, not to say cynical, view of society, its institutions, and its representatives made such an idea an impossible dream. An epigram he wrote in 1814 conveys Byron's social view with devastating clarity:

> 'Tis said Indifference marks the present time,
> Then hear the reason—though 'tis told in rhyme—
> A King who can't—a Prince of Wales who don't—
> Patriots who shan't, and Ministers who won't—
> What matters who are in or out of place
> The Mad—the Bad—the Useless—or the Base?
> (*Complete Poetical Works*, 3.91)

Byron's grand tour was full of incident and adventure. On 2 July 1809 he sailed from Falmouth with Hobhouse and three servants—his valet, William Fletcher (who stayed with him throughout), 'Old' Joe Murray, and the young Robert Rushton, of whom Byron was very fond. (Rushton is the second figure in the double portrait of Byron by George Sanders, 1807–8, in the Royal Collection. The image of Byron in this portrait, suggestive of his grand tour by its inclusion of a yacht moored at anchor before a background of wild, mountainous scenery, has since become a figurehead of Romanticism.) From Lisbon they rode across a peninsula still in the throes of political and military conflict. They went to Cintra, Seville, and Cadiz and thence sailed to Malta on the frigate *Hyperion*. At that point Murray and Rushton were sent home ('I would have taken him [Rushton] on but you *know boys* are not *safe* amongst the Turks'), and on 19 August 1809 Byron, Hobhouse, and Fletcher sailed in the packet for Sardinia, Sicily, and Malta, in the company of the traveller John Galt (*Letters and Journals*, ed. Marchand, 1.221–2). At Malta Byron had a brief affair with the celebrated Mrs Constance Spencer Smith, to whom he addressed several poems. He left Malta on the brig of war *Spider* and arrived in Prevesa, Albania, on 29 September. He went immediately to visit Ali Pasha at his court at Tepelene and was graciously received by the pasha: 'To me he was indeed a father, giving me letters, guards, & every possible accommodation'; 'he said he was certain I was a man of birth because I had small ears, curling hair, & little white hands, and expressed himself pleased with my appearance & garb' (ibid., 1.228). His travels through Albania were full of adventure, inimitably described in his letters, among the best in the English language, especially those to his mother, which are fully equal to the scenes and events he witnessed:

> I shall never forget the singular scene on entering Tepaleen at five in the afternoon as the Sun was going down, it brought to my recollection (with some change of *dress* however) Scott's description of Branksome Castle in his lay, & the feudal system.—The Albanians in their dresses (the most magnificent in the world, consisting of a long *white kilt*, gold worked cloak, crimson velvet gold laced jacket & waistcoat, silver mounted pistols & daggers,) the Tartars with their high caps, the Turks in their vast pelises & turbans, the soldiers & black slaves with the horses, the former stretched in groupes in an immense open gallery in front of the palace, the latter placed in a kind of cloister below it, two hundred steeds ready caparisoned to move in a moment, couriers entering or passing out with dispatches, the kettle drums beating, boys calling the hour from the minaret of the mosque, altogether with the singular appearance of the building itself, formed a new & delightful spectacle to a stranger. (ibid.)

Accompanied by a guard of Albanians, Byron went on to visit various sites in Arcanania and western Greece, including, in late November, the fateful Missolonghi. After a fortnight's sojourn in Patras he journeyed to Athens, where he arrived on Christmas day. There he was the guest of Tarsia Macri, widow of the English vice-consul, whose three daughters provided Byron with much entertainment throughout his stay. The eldest, Teresa, was celebrated by Byron in his famous lines on the 'Maid of Athens'. His principal passion, however, was for Greece herself and her antiquities. On 5 March 1810 he left Athens for Smyrna, Ephesus, Constantinople, and the Troad, taking with him a young boy, Nicolo Giraud. On 3 May he repeated Leander's legendary feat of swimming the Hellespont from Sestos to Abydos, and commemorated the event in some amusing verses. After visiting Constantinople he and Hobhouse separated, the latter sailing back to England and Byron proceeding on to Zea and thence back to Athens. It was at Athens that Byron was said to have met with the adventure, referred to in *The Giaour* (1813) and its notes, of saving a girl from being drowned in a sack. There is no doubt that some such event took place, but the part Byron played in her rescue remains unclear. His tour of Greece then took him to the Morea (the Peloponnese) where he contracted a dangerous fever at Patras. Returning to Athens he spent the winter of 1810–11 in a Capuchin convent. During his last months in Greece he met the traveller Lady Hester Stanhope, who later wrote that he 'had a great deal of vice in his looks' (*Memoirs*, 3.219).

When he left Piraeus for England in April 1811 on the transport ship *Hydra*, Byron took Nicolo with him and placed him in a school at Malta. Throughout his life Byron formed attachments to young boys. Though most perhaps were not homosexual, allusions in his letters indicate that he was bisexual. Hotly refuting Hobhouse's cryptic allegation, in a letter he wrote from Cadiz, of an 'unnatural', or homosexual, relationship with his servant Rushton, Byron nevertheless added to his reply from Malta: 'My fantastical adventures I reserve for you and Matthieu [Matthews] and a bottle of champagne' (*Letters and Journals*, ed. Marchand, 2.46; see also Peach, 30 and n. 23). Then a capital offence in England, homosexuality was not a subject to be discussed openly in correspondence. Also on board the *Hydra* was the last large shipment of marbles Lord Elgin was transporting to England, and, by an ironic coincidence, among Byron's numerous poetical manuscripts, his scathing satire on Elgin's work *The Curse of Minerva*. After spending a month in Malta to renew his liaison with Mrs Spencer Smith, Byron sailed for England on the frigate *Volage* and arrived in Portsmouth on 14 July 1811.

'Famous in my time' During his two years abroad Byron's financial problems had grown increasingly acute, as letters from Hanson and his mother had made him aware. Mrs Byron fought off creditors and bailiffs on her son's behalf, though he could hardly have been aware of the extent of her efforts and privations. In this her strong character was a formidable and effective defence. Worried about his affairs and weighed down by debt, shortly after his return Byron heard of the deaths of four of his close friends: Matthews, Edleston, Wingfield, and Hargreaves Hanson. In London he received news that his mother was seriously ill. She died at Newstead on 1 August before he arrived home. He diverted his grief by a new series of dissipations with servant girls at the abbey. Dallas attempted to revive him by urging him to publish the verse he had written on his tour abroad, especially the two cantos of *Childe Harold*. Byron showed little interest, as did the publishers to whom Dallas showed the manuscript. Cawthorn, who had published *English Bards*, which had gone through four editions, urged him to a fifth, but Byron held back and eventually suppressed the poem which had attacked some of his new friends, especially the poet Thomas Moore. Byron wanted to publish not the highly original *Childe Harold* but his imitation of Horace, *Hints from Horace*, which was set in type but not (then) published. Dallas persisted despite Byron's reluctance and the refusals of two publishers. He eventually prevailed and the first two cantos of *Childe Harold* were taken by John *Murray (1778–1820), who had an interest in travel literature. Attempts to persuade Byron to moderate the poem's misanthropy were unsuccessful. It appeared in March 1812 in a handsome quarto, sold out in three days, and overnight he became famous. As important a work in the history of Romanticism as Wordsworth and Coleridge's *Lyrical Ballads* (1805), *Childe Harold* marks the special character of Byron's poetry: it deliberately and completely transforms the Spenserian stanza just as *English Bards* began the process of death and rebirth that Byron forced on the English heroic couplet. Byron consumed an extraordinary range of European verse forms and forced them to bear his signature, to live again only, as it were, under his name and at his insistence.

Byron rapidly became the most brilliant star in the dazzling world of regency London. He was sought after at every society venue, elected to several exclusive clubs including the Alfred, the Cocoa Tree, and Watiers, and frequented the most fashionable London drawing-rooms, especially at Holland, Devonshire, and Melbourne houses. The dandies 'were always very civil' to Byron even 'though in general they disliked literary people' (*Letters and Journals*, ed. Marchand, 9.22). Literary friendships and acquaintances were soon formed, first with Moore, and then with Samuel Rogers, Sir Walter Scott, Coleridge, and Madame de Stäel. Fascinated by the theatre, he attended often and became friends with the tragedian Edmund Kean and many other actors and actresses, eventually becoming a member of the committee of the Drury Lane Theatre in 1815. He visited Leigh Hunt in prison, and twice spoke in the House of Lords on the side of reform, once in February 1812 to oppose the repressive legislation against the frame-makers in Nottingham, and once in April that year in support of Catholic emancipation. He was a member of the whig opposition, and his views grew increasingly radical until in 1814 he came under attack in the government papers. This hostility came to a head in 1815–16 in the campaign of vilification that surrounded the 'separation controversy' which drove Byron out of England forever.

Loves ... and marriage In 1812, however, the duchess of Devonshire recorded that '*Childe Harold* ... is on every table, and himself courted, visited, flattered and praised wherever he appears' (Foster, 375–6). She also noted Byron's 'handsome countenance ... animated and amusing conversation ... in short, he is really the only topic almost of every conversation—the men jealous of him, the women of each other' (ibid.). Over the next few years he formed a number of more or less intense and sometimes reckless liaisons, the most famous being with Lady Caroline *Lamb, wife of William Lamb (later second Viscount Melbourne). Shortly after meeting Byron in spring 1812 Caroline wrote in her diary '*That beautiful pale face is my fate*' (Marchand, 1.331). With her fashionably short blond hair and slim, boyish figure she did not immediately appeal to Byron, but what she lacked in 'roundness' she made up for in vitality and startling conversation. At the height of their affair he wrote to her describing her as 'a little volcano ... the cleverest most agreeable, absurd, amiable, perplexing, dangerous, fascinating little being that lives' (*Letters and Journals*, ed. Marchand, 2.170–71). But the boldness of her behaviour and reckless disregard for social conventions eventually alarmed and then bored Byron who turned instead to the more soothing 'autumnal charms' of Lady Oxford. Lady Caroline's famous diary description of Byron as 'Mad, bad and dangerous to know' is one that has been applied by several later commentators to herself. In autumn 1813 Lady Oxford, wife of Edward Harley, fifth earl of Oxford, whose children's varied paternity led to their being sometimes referred to after the famous collection of manuscripts in her husband's library as 'the Harleian miscellany', provided Byron with a calm refuge at Eywood, Herefordshire, away from Caroline's increasingly frantic attempts to see him. She encouraged his whig interests and Byron formed a plan to go abroad with the Oxfords the following summer.

In 1813 Annabella Milbanke (1792–1860) [*see* Noel, Anne Isabella, Lady Byron] opened a correspondence with Byron that was to culminate in their marriage in January 1815. In the same year Byron and his half-sister, Augusta, rediscovered each other. Since her marriage to Colonel George Leigh in 1807 Augusta had had little contact with Byron, but on meeting again they quickly became intimate friends. Although, as Leslie Marchand stated, 'the extant evidence that Byron had sexual relations with Augusta does not amount to *legal proof*', their relationship 'cannot be explained sensibly in any other terms' (Marchand, *Portrait*, 148n.) That Byron was the father of Augusta's daughter Medora (*b.* 1814) is a recurrent theme of speculation. With no other woman did Byron feel more at ease, more able to get on, as he put it in his 'Epistle to Augusta' (1816) 'without a mask'.

During this time Byron's poetry poured forth—in satire, in various lyric forms, but mostly in the sequence of remarkable narratives that began with *The Giaour* and *The Bride of Abydos* (1813) and culminated with *Parisina* and *The Siege of Corinth* (1815). These were the works that defined and perfected the Byronic hero, whose initial incarnation was Childe Harold. Brooding throughout nineteenth-century European literature, the Byronic figure—usually an aristocrat—embodied a culturally alienated anti-hero, bearing within a dark secret that seemed as threatening to others as to himself. The popularity of Byron's oriental tales, which were coded with political allegory and personal references, was unprecedented. Ten thousand copies of *The Corsair* (1814)—the complete edition—sold out on the day of publication. All were written '*con amore* and too much from existence' (*Letters and Journals*, ed. Marchand, 3.243). Murray, Byron's publisher and later friend, was growing rich from these successes and pressed Byron to accept payment for his poems. Despite his extreme financial difficulties Byron nobly refused. By 1814, however, he was so troubled by the severity of his debts that he accepted Murray's offer of £700 for the copyright of *Lara* which had just been published anonymously with

Rogers's *Jacqueline*. Henceforth Byron drove increasingly hard bargains for the copyright of his work.

The climax of these tumultuous years came with Byron's marriage, separation, and departure from England. In the midst of his affair with Lady Caroline Lamb he had told Lady Melbourne, who was his epistolary confidante, of his interest in her niece Annabella Milbanke: 'I never saw a woman I *esteemed* so much' (*Letters and Journals*, ed. Marchand, 2.195). Keen to put an end to the affair between Byron and her daughter-in-law, Lady Melbourne made discreet enquiries to Annabella about the qualities she would look for in a husband. Her cool, analytical reply was unpromising but Byron was not put off and sent her a proposal of marriage. Taken by surprise, but doubtless flattered, for Byron had piqued her interest, she sent him a refusal. This he regarded as a 'mutual escape.—That would have been but a *cold* collation, & I prefer hot suppers' (ibid., 2.246). She none the less encouraged Byron to maintain 'an acquaintance that does me honour and is capable of imparting so much rational pleasure' (Marchand, *Biography*, 1.370). In view of her interest in mathematics, but in retrospect, prophetically, Byron referred to her as the 'Princess of Parallelograms': 'her proceedings are quite rectangular, or rather we are two parallel lines prolonged to infinity side by side but never to meet' (*Letters and Journals*, ed. Marchand, 2.231).

Their correspondence continued into 1814 when Annabella let Byron know that she would be willing to consider another proposal of marriage. Just at this time his financial situation improved as a result of a legal settlement in his favour. In 1812 Thomas Claughton had reneged on his offer to purchase Newstead and then refused to pay the £25,000 penalty he incurred for so doing. When the matter was settled in 1814 Byron's interest in marriage cooled somewhat. Hesitating between a visit to Italy and a renewal of his offer of marriage he finally proposed again—and was accepted. A marriage settlement of about £60,000 was arranged with the addition of handsome prospects from Annabella's uncle Thomas Noel, second Viscount Wentworth. Byron went to Seaham, co. Durham, in November to stay with Annabella and her parents, Sir Ralph and Judith, Lady Milbanke, who were uneasy about the match. Byron and Annabella were married on 2 January 1815 and spent their 'treaclemoon' (as Byron later referred to their wedding holiday) at Sir Ralph's property, Halnaby Hall, in Yorkshire.

The next thirteen months brought home the realization on both sides that for all their good intentions and fondness for each other (Byron addressed letters to Annabella as 'dearest Duck' and 'Pip') they had each made an appalling error of judgement. On their return journey to London Byron took his bride to meet his half-sister, Augusta, at her home in Six Mile Bottom, near Newmarket. In conversation he made several innuendoes that alarmed both women. At their London home at 13 Piccadilly Terrace, leased from the duchess of Devonshire, Byron became moody and behaved erratically, sometimes wildly, and Annabella became fearful and apprehensive. He taunted her cruelly with tales of his profligate past, and had casual affairs with women, including the actress Susan Boyce. Still heavily encumbered with debt, Byron found no refuge from creditors and bailiffs in his marital home. Lady Byron, who had become pregnant in March, gave birth to a baby daughter, (Augusta) Ada [*see* Byron, (Augusta) Ada, countess of Lovelace] on 10 December 1815. The baby brought no respite to their domestic tension, and even Augusta Leigh, to whose appeals Byron was usually susceptible, was unable to relieve the black moods which nightly drove him out to the theatre and its green-room distractions. In early January 1816 Annabella decided that her husband was insane. She went through his private papers looking for evidence and began to plan a separation. Maintaining an appearance of affection, on 15 January she left with her child to visit her parents at Kirkby Mallory in Leicestershire. Byron never saw either of them again.

At the beginning of February Byron received a letter from Annabella's father (who had taken the name Noel on the death of Lord Wentworth the previous April) proposing that he agree to an amicable separation from his wife. Separation proceedings were undertaken, and afraid that Byron would claim custody of their child, Annabella determined to threaten Byron with infamous crimes. Her charge was inexplicit but rumours abounded. Byron was riven with tension and Augusta's fears of some terrible exposure were carefully nurtured by Annabella. Eventually his public and political enemies turned to the press to increase pressure on Byron and he was pilloried, much to Lady Byron's satisfaction. A deed of separation was signed on 15 April and Byron immediately left England, bitterly believing henceforward that he had been driven from his homeland.

Geneva Byron sailed from Dover to Ostend on 24 April 1816 seen off by his friends Hobhouse and Scrope Davies. He was accompanied by the physician Dr John Polidori, a Swiss named Berger, and two servants, Fletcher and Rushton. His equipage was elaborate and included a large Napoleonic coach with bed, library, and kitchen. He visited Waterloo and then travelled up the Rhine to Geneva where he settled in mid-June at the Villa Diodati on the south side of the lake. As he was travelling he had begun writing the third canto of *Childe Harold* on scraps of paper, and finished it during that summer. At Lake Geneva he met Shelley, Mary Shelley, and her stepsister Claire *Clairmont. Earlier in the spring Claire had besieged Byron in London and the association between the two poets that summer gave her the opportunity to come 'prancing to [him] at all hours', as the Shelleys had taken the Villa Montalègre just along the lake shore from the Villa Diodati (*Letters and Journals*, ed. Marchand, 5.162). Byron grew tired of her before she returned at the end of August with the Shelleys to England. There she gave birth to a daughter, (Clara) Allegra Biron ('to distinguish her from little Legitimacy'), in January 1817 (ibid., 6.7).

The summer had been glorious. Shelley and Byron had become good friends, to the annoyance of Byron's more conservative circle of friends at home. They toured the lake visiting places associated with Rousseau in *La nouvelle*

Héloïse, and spent much time together writing and talking. One evening in June the party gathered in Byron's villa to tell each other ghost stories, a famous occasion that inspired Mary Shelley to write *Frankenstein* and Byron to begin writing a vampire novel. When he abandoned it, Polidori took up the idea and wrote *The Vampyre*. Byron finished the third canto of *Childe Harold* and wrote *The Prisoner of Chillon* and many shorter poems, including 'Darkness' and 'Prometheus'. A visit from the Gothic novelist M. G. 'Monk' Lewis spurred his interest in the story of Faust and he began *Manfred* (finished the following spring), in which the character of the Byronic hero is exposed to a deeper level than is manifest in *Childe Harold*.

When Hobhouse and Davies arrived in August the three made a tour of the Bernese Oberland which Byron recorded in his stunning 'Alpine journal' written for Augusta. Elegant, intimate, precise, and with an uncanny tonal flexibility, the journal is typical of Byron's prose writing:

> Arrived at the Grindelwald—dined—mounted again & rode to the higher Glacier—twilight—but distinct—very fine Glacier—like a *frozen hurricane*—starlight—beautiful—but a devil of a path—never mind—got safe in—a little lightning—but the whole of the day as fine in point of weather—as the day on which Paradise was made.—Passed *whole woods of withered pines—all withered*—trunks stripped & barkless—branches lifeless—done by a single winter—their appearance reminded me of me & my family. (*Letters and Journals*, ed. Marchand, 5.102)

Venice Byron was making plans for Italy. Davies returned to England with Rushton, and Byron and Hobhouse set off together on 5 October and visited Milan before arriving in Venice. Captivated by the city which 'has always been (next to the East) the greenest island of my imagination … I like the gloomy gaiety of their gondolas—and the silence of their canals' (*Letters and Journals*, ed. Marchand, 5.129, 132), Byron took lodgings with the Segatis. He fell in love with Marianna Segati, writing to Augusta that 'we are one of the happiest—unlawful couples this side of the Alps' (ibid., 5.141). At about the same time Murray published the third canto of *Childe Harold* which Shelley had taken to him (together with other poems Byron had written in Switzerland) in manuscript. Byron improved his Italian (the 'soft bastard Latin' of which he wrote in *Beppo*) with Marianna and studied Armenian with Father Aucher at the monastery on the island of San Lazzaro. December saw the publication of *The Prisoner of Chillon and Other Poems*, and Hobhouse's departure for a tour of Italy with his brother and sister—he planned to meet Byron in Rome. Byron attended the *conversazioni* of the Countess Albrizzi, and feeling contented with his way of life he remained in Venice through the carnival, finally leaving for Rome via Arqua, Ferrara, Bologna, and Florence the following April. During the journey he began writing the autobiographical *Lament of Tasso*. At Rome he sat, at Hobhouse's request, to the Dane Bertel Thorvaldsen for a bust. The city 'delighted [him] beyond everything since Athens—& Constantinople' but he did not intend to remain long on this first visit, and by the end of May was back with Marianna in Venice (ibid., 5.219). He had begun to sketch the fourth canto of *Childe Harold*.

Now that he was selling his poetry—Murray had paid £2000 for the works that Shelley brought back from Lake Geneva—Byron's finances began to improve. When Newstead was sold to Major Thomas Wildman for £94,500 in November that year (1816) he was able to clear his debts and begin to live well in Italy. His financial situation continued to improve for he was able to reach very favourable terms with Murray for all his writings. On the death of his mother-in-law, Lady Judith Noel, in 1822 he received an additional £2500 per annum from the Wentworth estate, so that by the end of 1822 his total income came to about £6000 a year. On returning to Venice he took a six-month lease on the Villa Foscarini at La Mira where he settled down to write for the summer. He finished the draft of canto 4 of *Childe Harold* in late June, just before Hobhouse and Monk Lewis came to stay. During August the tranquillity of his affair with Marianna Segati (who was staying with him at the Villa Foscarini) ruptured when she heard of Byron's infatuation with the beautiful Margarita Cogni ('La Fornarina'), the wife of a baker. The complications of these amorous adventures form the source of much amusement in his letters home, but more importantly, they initiated a sequence of events that culminated in the writing of *Beppo* ('in two nights') early in October. Byron had read John Hookham Frere's *Whistlecraft* and, following *Beppo*, went on to study the Italian tradition of *ottava rima* serio-comic narrative medley poetry. This led him to translate the first canto of Pulci's *Morgante Maggiore* and, crucially, to begin his masterpiece *Don Juan*, the first canto of which was completed in September 1818.

Hobhouse left for England early in January 1818. Alone again, Byron plunged more deeply into the voluptuous life of Venice. From the *conversazioni* of the Countess Albrizzi he migrated to the more informal and literary parties of the Countess Marina Benzoni. In May he took on a three-year lease of the Palazzo Mocenigo on the Grand Canal in Venice, and shortly afterwards his natural daughter Allegra and her nurse Elise came to stay with him. (Desperately unhappy at giving up her daughter to Byron's care, Claire Clairmont was nevertheless bitterly aware that this would provide the child with a more socially secure future than to remain with her mother.) In August that year Byron placed Allegra in the care of his new friends, Richard Belgrave Hoppner, British consul at Venice, and his wife—his life at the Palazzo Mocenigo provided an unsuitable environment in which to care for a child. His household included fourteen servants, including Fletcher, his ferocious-looking gondolier, 'Tita' Falcieri, and Margarita Cogni, who acted as his 'housekeeper', as well as a menagerie of animals. Byron spent the summer indulging himself in food, conversation, and lovemaking. In August Claire and Shelley arrived in Venice. Allegra was sent to visit her mother at Este, and Byron and Shelley rode out on the Lido (an experience that was to form the basis of Shelley's poem 'Julian and Maddalo'). Though he gained in weight—Newton Hanson who brought out papers relating to the sale of Newstead for

Byron to sign recorded that 'Lord Byron could not have been more than 30, but he looked 40. His face had become pale, bloated and sallow' (Peach, 14)—Shelley thought he had 'changed into the liveliest, & happiest looking man I ever met' (letter to T. L. Peacock, 8 October 1818, *The Letters of Percy Bysshe Shelley*, ed. F. L. Jones, 1964, 2.483).

By November Byron had sent off the first canto of *Don Juan* to Murray. He was well aware that the work was as provocative as it was brilliant and he wanted to test the reactions of his publisher and his friends. To Moore he wrote 'It is called "Don Juan", and is meant to be a little quietly facetious upon every thing' (*Letters and Journals*, ed. Marchand, 6.67). The response from every quarter, including Hobhouse and his banker and urbane friend Douglas Kinnaird, was the same: unpublishable. Byron protested '*Don Juan* shall be an entire horse or none … I will not give way to all the Cant of Christendom', but to no avail, and early in 1819 seemed to acquiesce (ibid., 6.91). With the return of the carnival, however, Byron flared up against the timidity of Murray and his London circle. When his publisher wrote to beg him to continue with *Childe Harold* or some other similar 'work and subject worthy of you' Byron retorted 'you have so many "divine" poems, is it nothing to have written a *Human* one?' (ibid., 6.105). Threatening to find another publisher, Byron forced Murray's hand, and the first two cantos finally appeared, anonymously, and with some late and unauthorized expurgations, in July 1819. Murray also kept his name, as publisher, from the title-page of the handsome (and expensive) quarto volume, but this attempt to protect himself backfired badly for it left the work open to the maraudings of pirate printers who soon deluged the market with cheap reprints. Byron was more saleable than ever, in circumstances that promised scandal. Virginia Woolf described *Don Juan* as the most readable poem in the language, a view that few would gainsay. It is an opinion that can, however, obscure the poem's greatness. In English only *The Canterbury Tales* can compare in terms of stylistic brilliance, and no English poem—perhaps no novel—has aspired to, or achieved, such a comprehensive interpretative grasp of a period and a world. It is also the funniest poem in the language. To Kinnaird Byron wrote:

> As to 'Don Juan'—confess—confess—you dog—and be candid—that it is the sublime of *that there* sort of writing—it may be bawdy—but is it not good English?—it may be profligate—but is it not *life*, is it not *the thing*?—Could any man have written it—who has not lived in the world?—and tooled in a post-chaise? in a hackney-coach? in a Gondola? Against a wall? in a court carriage? in a vis a vis?—on a table?—and under it? (ibid., 6.252)

And he reassured Murray:

> D[on] Juan will be known by and bye for what it is intended a *satire* on *abuses* of the present *states* of Society—and not a eulogy of vice;—it may be now and then voluptuous—I can't help that. (ibid., 10.68)

Byron used *Don Juan* as a vehicle to survey and explain the historical import and meaning, as he saw it, of the years 1788–1824: that is to say, the meaning of one of the defining moments in English and European history.

While the struggle over *Don Juan* continued in the spring of 1819, Byron met the young and beautiful Countess Teresa Guiccioli (1799–1873) one early April evening at the Countess Benzoni's. They were immediately attracted to each other and discussed Dante, Petrarch, and Italian literature with equal enthusiasm. Byron was taken with her lack of 'bluestocking' seriousness and wrote of his passion for this 'Romagnuola Countess from Ravenna—who is nineteen years old & has a Count of fifty … What shall I do! I am in love, and tired of promiscuous concubinage' (*Letters and Journals*, ed. Marchand, 6.107–8). They met privately and plunged quickly into an intense, if highly sentimental, affair. After ten days or so Count Guiccioli left with his young wife for his palazzo in Ravenna. Following their departure on 18 April they travelled slowly, stopping at several of the count's houses on the way. Under the cover of her maid, Fanny Silvestrini, Teresa and Byron exchanged passionate love letters, though they were unable to make arrangements to see one another. Byron chafed under the uncertainties, which became more troubling when Teresa fell ill in May. She had been pregnant for several months and her illness precipitated a miscarriage. Unable to tolerate these strained circumstances Byron left Venice for Ravenna at the beginning of June and arrived on 10 June.

Ravenna Though Teresa had been seriously ill her health improved and soon she and Byron renewed their affair, cuckolding her husband even in his own house. Despite gossip about the lovers, Count Guiccioli maintained friendly relations with Byron. For his part, Byron became transfixed by contradictory feelings. His letters to England narrated his relations with Teresa in his inimitable prose, at once elegant and coarse: 'She is fair as Sunrise—and warm as Noon—we had but ten days—to manage all our little matters in beginning middle and end. & we managed them;—and I have done my duty—with the proper consummation' (*Letters and Journals*, ed. Marchand, 5.114). But he was deeply attached to his young *amorosa*. When the count left with his wife for Bologna early in August, Teresa commanded Byron to follow them. He obeyed and spent the next month fulfilling the role of *cavaliere servente*.

When Teresa suffered a relapse Byron offered to accompany her back to Venice and arrange medical attention. Count Guiccioli agreed and the lovers set off together, eventually settling into his house at La Mira. They spent the next two months more or less completely together, appearing little as Venetian society was scandalized by the openness of their affair. Teresa's father was concerned about her conduct and urged her to return to her husband. When Count Guiccioli arrived in Venice in October he demanded that his wife choose between himself and her lover, and when she chose Byron the affair reached a crisis. Byron persuaded Teresa to return with her husband to Ravenna, and she agreed only if he would follow. He did, late in December, as a consequence of a letter from Teresa's father whose opposition to the affair collapsed in the face of his daughter's unhappiness. Byron's decision to follow his mistress, however, might easily not have happened. Having grown restless and unsure of the stability of his own feelings, that autumn he began making plans to leave Italy. He toyed with various ideas—going to South America, buying a Greek island, or returning to England to join a revolution after the Peterloo massacre. But he hesitated, stopped by love, by inertia, and by circumstances including the sudden illness of his daughter Allegra. He completed the first instalment of his memoirs, begun the year before in Venice, and when Moore came on a short visit in October gave him the manuscript stipulating that it was only for posthumous publication. Notoriously, after his death the memoirs were burnt by a group of friends in a disastrous act of good intentions.

When Byron arrived in Ravenna he arranged to rent the upper floor of the Palazzo Guiccioli, and for several months this unusual arrangement superficially alleviated tension. Settling into a routine, Byron was writing at a remarkable rate. Two new cantos of *Don Juan* were completed as well as various other works, including his translation of the first canto of Pulci's *Morgante Maggiore* and *The Prophecy of Dante*. He also began the first of his dramas, *Marino Faliero*, which he completed in July, and by the end of the year had completed a fifth canto of his masterpiece. Count Guiccioli's acquiescence in the domestic arrangements came to an end in the spring, when he seems to have become threatening towards Byron. He had a reputation for ruthlessness and cruelty, and although Byron had never experienced this facet of the count's behaviour, he grew cautious. With the aid of Teresa's father, Count Ruggiero Gamba, and her brother Pietro, he moved to bring to an end the volatile situation. He was prepared to give up Teresa, but she would not give up Byron. When the Guicciolis' separation decree arrived in July, Teresa returned to her father's country house in Filetto. Byron placed Allegra in a villa nearby, an arrangement that allowed him easily to visit both his lover and his daughter. The Gamba household was relaxed and happy. Their staunch liberal politics and Pietro's passionate and active involvement in the secret revolutionary society of the Romagna, the Carbonari, reinvigorated Byron's political interests and drew him into a new set of less personal intensities. He began to spend more time at the Gamba house in Ravenna and reduced his visits to Teresa at Filetto. Unhappy in her country retreat, she moved back to her father's house in Ravenna in November. The end of the year 1820 saw Byron a nightly visitor to the Gamba household, deeply involved in love and politics.

The clashes between the Carbonari and the authorities brought severe counter-revolutionary measures, and the consequence was a series of set-backs for the insurgents. The Neapolitan revolution failed and the resistance movement in the Romagna collapsed, partly from internal problems. Byron became cynical with disappointment and began to think of pursuing his political ideals elsewhere, perhaps in Greece, where the struggle for independence had broken out in March 1821. His poetry at this time became a vehicle for interrogating and developing his ideas about love, society, politics, and culture. He wrote *Sardanapalus*, *The Two Foscari*, and *Cain* successively between January and July and published all three together in December 1821. *Cain* caused an immense furore and was vehemently attacked by religious and conservative writers. Between August and October he continued to produce important work, including 'The Vision of Judgement' and 'Heaven and Earth'. The last of his programmatic efforts to revive what he called a 'mental theatre' came in December 1821 and January 1822 when he began writing *Werner* and *The Deformed Transformed*.

Two crises precipitated out of this spiral of activity. The first was in July 1821 when Pietro Gamba was arrested while returning from the theatre. Together with about a thousand other families the Gambas were banished from the Romagna for their revolutionary activities. In these circumstances Count Guiccioli moved to recover his wife. Teresa fled to Florence where her father and brother had been given asylum. Byron was active in trying to persuade the government to repeal its order against the Gamba family, but the authorities also wanted to get rid of him and hoped that Byron would follow his friends. When Shelley arrived in August to visit Byron in Ravenna, Byron spoke of moving to Switzerland with the Gambas, but Shelley proposed instead that they all move to Pisa and stay in Italy. An important concern was the future of Allegra, whom Byron had placed in a convent at Bagnacavallo, near Ravenna, the previous spring. Shelley offered to find everyone accommodation in Pisa and Byron agreed. At the end of October he left Ravenna to join the Shelleys and the Gambas in Pisa. The move was exasperatingly difficult, complicated, as Shelley later wrote to T. L. Peacock, by the comical complexities of transporting 'Besides servants' Byron's 'ten horses, eight enormous dogs, three monkeys, five cats, an eagle, a crow, and a falcon … five peacocks, two guinea hens, and an Egyptian crane' (Marchand, *Biography*, 2.923).

The second crisis was literary. Byron's new writings, especially *Cain* and 'The Vision of Judgement', signalled his renewed determination to 'throw away the scabbard' as he wrote in his preface to *Don Juan*, cantos 7–8, and to engage in a serious intellectual war with the forces of reaction in England and Europe. He had stopped writing *Don Juan* at the request of Teresa, who found it too cynical, but in 1821 was making plans to resume work on the poem, which he did (secretly) in 1822, exactly at the moment the storm broke over *Cain* in England. His publisher and friend John Murray, cautious and conservative, was being drawn into embarrassing legal conflicts by his famous author. These had begun with the publication of the first two cantos of *Don Juan* and erupted again with *Cain*; others threatened with each new work Byron sent him. Murray had received 'The Vision of Judgement' but refused to publish it, and he procrastinated over other works such as 'The Blues'. He was beginning to find Byron's work intolerable and when he received the three new cantos of *Don Juan* in autumn 1822 he pronounced them 'outrageously shocking' and flatly refused to publish. The break at that point was complete and Murray turned the cantos over to John Hunt, brother of (James Henry) Leigh *Hunt, who henceforth served as Byron's publisher.

Pisa But 1822 brought other turbulent and even more painful events. In 1821 Southey had published his turgid apotheosis of George III, *A Vision of Judgement*, which carried a preface attacking Byron as the chief exponent of what Southey called 'the Satanic School' of poetry. Byron had immediately written his own 'Vision' in response. A few months later Byron read Southey's more personal attack printed in *The Courier* (5 January 1822), and when he also heard that Southey was spreading malicious gossip about him, he sent the poet laureate a challenge through his friend Kinnaird, who wisely did not deliver it. Shortly afterwards, late in March 1822, Byron and the whole 'Pisan circle' had a violent altercation with a contingent of government soldiers. Serious blows were exchanged and several arrests were made, though an uneasy settlement was finally reached. On 22 April came the terrible news that the five-year-old Allegra had died two days previously in the convent at Bagnacavallo. Her death was mourned by the whole circle in Pisa which, besides the Shelleys (with whom Allegra's mother, Claire Clairmont, then lived) and Byron, included an interesting, if also volatile, set of people. Among the residents and visitors were Edward and Jane Williams, E. J. Trelawny, Thomas Medwin, Captain John Hay, and (later) Leigh Hunt and his family.

Byron sought relief in his writing. He leased a house, the Villa Dupuy, in Montenero, near Leghorn, which at first was occupied by Trelawny and Captain Daniel Roberts who were overseeing the construction of two boats, a small sloop for Shelley (the *Don Juan*, which Shelley called the *Ariel*) and an elaborate schooner, complete with guns, for Byron (the *Bolivar*). Byron stayed at the villa from May until July while Leigh Hunt arrived with his family and moved into apartments in the Casa Lanfranchi, Byron's house in Pisa. Hunt was preparing to launch, with Shelley and Byron, a radical journal to be called (at Byron's suggestion) *The Liberal*. Byron's relations with the Hunts were strained, however, largely because, following his return, he found their children unruly and did not hesitate to complain. He later wrote to Mary Shelley that they were 'dirtier and more mischievous than Yahoos' (*Letters and Journals*, ed. Marchand, 10.11).

With the drowning of Shelley, Williams, and Charles Vivian in the Bay of Spezia on 8 July the 'Pisan circle' was broken. The news reached Byron at the Casa Lanfranchi on 11 July, and the bodies of Shelley and Williams were washed ashore on 16 July, near Viareggio. They were buried in the sand by the authorities on 18 July, but were exhumed and cremated on 15 August, at Mary Shelley's request, in a ceremony that has now become one of the legends of Romanticism. Byron was deeply affected and wrote to Moore:

> We have been burning the bodies of Shelley and Williams on the sea-shore, to render them fit for removal and regular interment. You can have no idea what an extraordinary effect such a funeral pile has, on a desolate shore, with mountains in the back-ground and the sea before, and the singular appearance the salt and frankincense gave to the flame. All of Shelley was consumed, except his *heart*, which would not take the flame, and is now preserved in spirits of wine. (*Letters and Journals*, ed. Marchand, 9.197)

Afterwards Byron swam out, in the midday sun, to his yacht the *Bolivar* and back, a distance of about 3 miles, and was badly sunburnt. 'But it is over,—and I have got a new skin, and am as glossy as a snake in a new suit' (ibid.). His letters home included eloquent tributes to Shelley whom he defended as 'the *best* and least selfish man I ever met' (ibid., 9.189–90). '*Shelley* is *truth* itself—and *honour* itself—notwithstanding his out-of-the-way notions about religion' (ibid., 8.132). Byron kept his promise to Hunt and contributed substantially to the four issues of the journal that were published from October 1822 to July 1823. The satirical 'Letter to my Grandmother's Review', 'The Vision of Judgement', 'The Blues', 'Heaven and Earth', and the *Morgante Maggiore* translation all first appeared in *The Liberal*. With Byron's agreement the modest profit went entirely to Hunt. Since the death of his mother-in-law, Lady Noel, in January 1822, Byron had taken the name Noel (and used the signature Noel Byron); his share in the Wentworth estate had increased further his by now substantial income.

Genoa Though famous for his travels, Byron was reluctant to move when he had found an agreeable place, and the Casa Lanfranchi was certainly to his taste. Events, however, made it impossible for him to stay, and so in September, after a brief visit from his old friend Hobhouse, he set off by boat for Genoa with Teresa, Trelawny, and the Hunts. He moved into the palatial Casa Saluzzo situated on a hill at Albaro, where it overlooked Genoa harbour. There he settled into a comfortable life with Teresa, writing and receiving visits from old friends such as James Wedderburn Webster, and new acquaintances including Lady Blessington. He continued writing *Don Juan* (cantos 10–16 were written between October 1822 and May 1823) and also wrote his last tale, *The Island*, and last formal satire, *The Age of Bronze*, a dark meditation on the post-Napoleonic condition of Europe. The arrival of the Blessington party in April 1823 enlivened his desultory existence with some brief, if trivial, pleasures, later described in Lady Blessington's *Conversations of Lord Byron* (1834). Events in London, however, were moving towards a point where they would have a decisive impact on the last year of Byron's life and initiate the movement that brought his spectacular career to its famous climax.

In February the London Greek Committee, established to promote the cause of Greek independence, held its first meeting and decided that Edward Blaquiere should go to Greece to see what practical help might be given. Hobhouse, one of the committee's organizers, suggested that Blaquiere should stop off in Genoa to sound out Byron's interest. Byron had been thinking about Greece ever since the war for independence had broken out, and Blaquiere's visit fired his determination to 'go up to the Levant in July, if the Greek provisional Government think that I could be of any use' (*Letters and Journals*, ed. Marchand, 10.142). In April he was formally elected to the committee which enthusiastically endorsed his plan to go to Greece. On hearing from Byron of his plans Teresa was distressed, the more so as her brother Pietro determined to accompany Byron, and feared the worst. Her distress made departure difficult, but Byron was set on his course. He wrote to Kinnaird asking him to consolidate as many of his assets as possible, and Kinnaird put together a sum of about £10,000 for expenses, which included a plan to equip a small fighting force that would serve directly under Byron's command. His knowledge of the campaigns of Napoleon, his own great hero, had given him an understanding of the need of the Greeks for a figurehead. Like Napoleon he understood the value of impressive visual propaganda and ordered several splendid uniforms including a fine Homeric helmet (Newstead Abbey collections). Beneath the display, however, he also recognized the force of will that underpinned the politics of Napoleon.

'That Greece might still be free' In mid-July Byron sailed for Greece aboard the *Hercules*. His party included Pietro Gamba, Trelawny, a young physician, Dr Francesco Bruno, Count Constantine Skilitzy (Schilizzi), who had asked for a passage to Greece, and five or six servants (including the faithful Fletcher, Tita, and his steward Lega Zambelli). Four of Byron's horses, two dogs (one of them Byron's Newfoundland Lyon), and other livestock took up the rest of the space. Byron's friend and banker in Genoa Charles Barry stayed behind to take care of his affairs in Italy while he was gone, for despite Teresa's fears, Byron's intention was to return. In the meantime, Teresa went to her father's house in Bologna.

Byron's original plan was to sail to Zante, but he decided instead on Cephalonia during a brief stopover in Leghorn where the party was joined by James Hamilton Browne, a Scot who had served in Ionia and was sympathetic to the revolutionary cause. They arrived at Argostoli, Cephalonia, on 2 August. Byron settled into quarters in Metaxata and sought information about the military and political situation from various English and Greeks. The British resident, Colonel Charles Napier, was especially helpful, as were George Finlay and Colonel Leicester Stanhope (who arrived slightly later). Byron quickly saw how vexed circumstances were because of the conflicts between different revolutionary leaders. As the representative of the London Greek Committee Byron had to proceed with caution, which irked Browne and Trelawny, who set out early in September on their own to join the Greek forces in the Morea. Byron remained in Cephalonia with Pietro Gamba multiplying his Greek contacts and assessing information he was gathering as a prelude to action. When Prince Alexander Mavrocordatos, who eventually became first president of independent Greece, moved to Missolonghi in December he invited Byron to join him and his forces. Byron decided that this was the right move and left shortly after Christmas to join the forces of western Greece. The short journey proved harrowing because their passage was intercepted by a Turkish vessel, and Byron was forced to seek shelter near Dragomestre. Arriving at Missolonghi on 4 January 1824 Byron met with a great reception. As he sailed into the harbour each ship in the Greek squadron fired a salute as his small vessel passed by.

Byron, eager for action and pleased with Mavrocordatos, undertook to support a force of 500 Suliote soldiers for a year. Plans were made for various expeditions including an assault on Lepanto to be led by Byron. But the Greeks were difficult to deal with, particularly the fiercely independent Suliotes, and Byron began to chafe under delays and complications that increased daily. His mood is captured in the memorable lines 'On this day I complete my thirty-sixth year', which he wrote on 22 January, thinking of the conflicting claims of love and war, and particularly of Loukas Chalandritsanos, the Greek boy he brought with him from Cephalonia. When the firemaster James Parry arrived in February with long-awaited and much needed supplies, Byron's enthusiasm for the cause revived, not least because of Parry's own energetic character.

In the midst of these changes of mood came an ominous incident. Conversing with Parry and others on the evening of 15 January, Byron collapsed in a violent convulsion. Though he slowly recovered, his constitution was severely weakened, and his spirits continued to be discouraged by the ineffectual state of the Greek military situation. The Lepanto expedition was abandoned and many of Byron's Suliote troops decided to leave. To Parry and Findlay, Byron despaired of ever being able to give practical help to the Greek cause. The weather was wet and the low-lying area of marshy land around Missolonghi did nothing to improve Byron's precarious state of health.

On the rainy morning of 10 April, after returning from a ride, Byron complained of pain and fever. His physicians attended him closely but he slipped into a decline. On 14 April he suffered bouts of delirium which became increasingly severe. By 16 April it was clear that he was dangerously ill and his room became the focus of a large and various group of worried friends, servants, and physicians. The next day Byron told one of his medical attendants that:

> Your efforts to preserve my life will be vain. Die I must: I feel it. Its loss I do not lament; for to terminate my wearisome existence I came to Greece.—My wealth, my abilities I devote to her cause.—Well: there is my life to her. (Marchand, *Biography*, 3.1224)

As he slipped in and out of consciousness over the next two days he talked of his sister Augusta and his daughter Ada and made provision for Tita and Loukas and others; and he rambled, as if he were in battle, fighting for Greece. Glimpsing Tita weeping at his bedside he smiled and said 'Oh questa è una bella scena' (ibid., 1225). It was his old servant, Fletcher, who heard his last words: 'I want to sleep now' (ibid.). A tremendous storm broke on the night Byron died.

The news of his death on the evening of 19 April was a heavy blow to the Greek forces, but it proved a turning point in their fortunes and helped them unite as they came together to honour a man who gave his life 'that Greece might still be free'. News of his death did not reach England until mid-May, but it shook the nation. Contrary to his wish to be buried in Greece, Byron's body was sent home to England where it arrived in the Thames estuary aboard the *Florida* on 29 June. Some wanted Byron buried in Westminster Abbey but the dean, Dr Ireland, refused.

Augusta, however, had determined that he should be buried in the family vault at Hucknall Torkard church near Newstead; after a lying in state for two days (on 9–10 July) a cortège of forty-seven carriages accompanied Byron's hearse out of London. Many were empty and had been sent out of courtesy to Hobhouse who wrote in his diary (12 July 1824) that 'He was buried like a nobleman—since we could not bury him as a poet' (Marchand, *Biography*, 3.1260). In an important sense, however, a new life began for Byron in 1824. No English writer except Shakespeare acquired greater fame or exercised more world influence.

'Pretensions to permanency' Images of Byron circulated widely during his lifetime and after his death rapidly became more widely distributed in Europe than those of any other individual except perhaps Napoleon. 'Lord Byron's head', wrote Scott's son-in-law J. G. Lockhart, 'is without doubt the finest in our time. It is better on the whole than either Napoleon's, or Goethe's, or Canova's or Wordsworth's' (Lockhart, 2.338). These images have been of central importance to the cultural transmission of his life and of Byronism more broadly conceived.

The most celebrated portraits are those by George *Sanders (mentioned above), whose Romanticized figure of Byron, based on the famous *Apollo Belvedere* (Vatican Museum, Rome), became widely known in the nineteenth century through its engraving by William Finden for Moore's *Life of Byron*; Richard *Westall (1813; NPG), whose portrait, painted shortly after he completed a series of illustrations for *Childe Harold*, cantos 1 and 2, depicts a pale, melancholic Byron, clearly identifiable with the narrative hero of the *Pilgrimage*; Thomas *Phillips (half-length, 1813; several versions, including one at Newstead Abbey; and in Albanian dress, 1814; Gov. Art Coll., HM embassy, Athens; half-length copy, NPG). Both Phillips's portraits were exhibited at the Royal Academy in 1814 and caused a sensation. The glamorous, exotic portrait in Albanian dress re-emerged via engravings after the original passed to Byron's daughter, Ada, in 1835, but it was not until the second half of the twentieth century when it entered a national collection that it acquired the status of a cultural icon. The American painter William Edward West, who painted Byron at Montenero in 1822 (versions in Scot. NPG and Harrow School), took a version of his portrait back to America and there painted more copies that helped to make this image one that became, through engravings, perhaps more familiar to American readers than those at home.

Of the two well-known busts of Byron that by Lorenzo Bartolini (1822; plaster model, Gipsoteca Bartoliniana, on loan to Pitti Palace, Florence; first marble version, the South African Library, Cape Town) Byron thought made him look like 'a superannuated Jesuit' (*Letters and Journals*, ed. Marchand, 9.214). (Byron had sat to Bartolini at the sculptor's request, and probably because he was intrigued to meet an artist who had served in Napoleon's army and to whom the emperor himself had sat for a bust.) The other, by Bertel Thorvaldsen (1817; plaster model, Thorvaldsens Museum, Copenhagen; first marble copy, Royal Collection), forms, in neo-classical terms, an ideal head, and its beauty recalls Scott's description of Byron's head as 'an alabaster vase lit from within' (Peach, 43). Thorvaldsen later sculpted the fine memorial statue of Byron in the handsome library, designed by Sir Christopher Wren, at Trinity College, Cambridge.

'As for fame and all that': posthumous reputation 'Famous in [his] time', Byron became a legend after his death. His influence on the art, music, and literature of the nineteenth century can scarcely be calculated, eclipsing even that of Sir Walter Scott. This influence is more notable perhaps in Europe and America than in England, however, partly because of the evangelical moralism that was gaining momentum even in Byron's lifetime and which went on to mould the Victorian ethos. Satire itself—Byron's stylistic signature—went out of fashion in the age of Victoria. Byron and his work thus reflect the contradictions within Victorian England—as the ambivalent responses of Carlyle, Tennyson, and Arnold to his work illustrate. The ambivalence is explicit in Carlyle's *Sartor Resartus* and in Arnold's famous essay on the poet; it is implicit—if unmistakable—in all Tennyson's poetry, perhaps especially in his *Maud*.

Middle-class Victorian moralism preserved for Byron a twentieth-century afterlife, as one may see in the scandalous event of 1924, the centenary of Byron's glorious death fighting for the freedom of Greece. A petition for a Byron memorial in Westminster Abbey was refused by Herbert Ryle, the dean at the time, despite the strong support of notable figures like Thomas Hardy, Rudyard Kipling, and three former prime ministers. 'The Abbey is not a mere literary Valhalla', Ryle declared: 'Byron, partly by his openly dissolute life and partly by the influence of licentious verse, earned a world-wide reputation for immorality among English-speaking people' (M. H. Fitzgerald, *Herbert Edward Ryle*, 1928, 321–2). Not until 1968 did Eric Abbott as dean at last endorse a petition from the Poetry Society for a memorial, for which a ceremony of dedication was held on 8 May 1969.

In the nineteenth century Byron's fame and influence flourished 'among English-speaking people', quite apart from those who were most responsible for perpetuating the official culture: that is to say, among the working classes, on one hand, and on the other hand among those who struggled against the growing power of the middle-class values of imperial Britain. Byron's uncompromising commitment to liberty of thought, word, and act made him a heroic figure to those who opposed the growth of the power of the state, not least among the Chartists during the 1830s and 1840s. The mid-century defeat of that movement marks a watershed in Byron's English afterlife. Whereas his name, his words, and his image were inspiring presences during the years of the Chartist struggle, afterwards Byron's contempt for the established order shaped him as the figure 'in the wilderness' that Blake had already recognized and addressed in 1822 in his brief prophetic work *The Death of Abel*. Byron's Romantic, aristocratic, and fiercely independent character thereafter made him an equivocal presence even among those, like the suffragists, who might have enlisted him in their causes. This was at least as true inside as outside the orbit of 'English-speaking people'. In the British labour movement, for example, Michael Foot's steady and passionate adherence to Byronic values has been the exception rather than the rule. From the middle of the twentieth century, however, Byron emerged once again as a figure of real inspiration in a broad social context. This signal change was clearly driven by the emergence of the gay rights movement, where the idea and ideal of heroism itself was finally stripped of its bourgeois trappings. In the domain of ideology the change was forecast in the remarkable work of G. Wilson Knight, whose writings in the 1930s (*The Christian Renaissance*, 1933, and *The Burning Oracle*, 1939) must now be seen as prophetic.

But if Victorian unease moulded the contradictions of Byron's fame in England and, in the twentieth century, 'among English-speaking people', a very different story emerges elsewhere. No fastidious moralism infects the majestic and clearly Byronic power of Emily Brontë's work, but in England she represents a band of angels who were following a different drummer—a heterogeneous group of libertarians, atheists, and activists for human and individual rights. That band largely mustered elsewhere: in America, for example, with authors like Poe and Melville, or on the continent among the host of Byron-influenced European writers, musicians, and artists from Goethe and Pushkin and Stendhal, Delacroix and Verdi, through Baudelaire, Berlioz, Wagner, Lautréamont, Nietzsche. In Britain Byron's impact remained strong in all Gothic writing as well as in the fiction of the 'silver fork' and dandy tradition, including Disraeli, Bulwer Lytton, and Thackeray (who abused Byron for his lack of 'sincerity'); within this group, Byronic appearance in dress and hairstyle was important. Disraeli secured Giovanni Falcieri ('Tita'), Byron's gondolier, as a family servant, and as prime minister in 1875 arranged for his widow to receive a pension. Most of Byron's nineteenth-century English inheritors, however, were marginal figures like Letitia Elizabeth Landon, John Clare, and Arthur Hugh Clough.

Celebrity and influence were always connected to the mythology of Byron's extraordinary life. Whether through admiration or disgust, Byron *in propria persona* was seen—is still correctly seen—as an essential figure in the written work, so 'biographical criticism' has established the framework for the reception and evaluation of his literary works. This begins with the first of the biographies, Thomas Moore's magnificent *Letters and Journals of Lord Byron, with Notices of his Life* (2 vols., 1830). Fascination with Byron spawned a host of subsequent biographies, many excellent, which show no sign of abatement. The standard life is Leslie *Marchand's magisterial *Byron: a Biography* (3 vols., 1957; rev. in 1 vol. as *Byron: a Portrait*, 1970).

As Britain consolidated her imperial power Byron's cultural status slowly shed its notoriety. A cultural ideology emerged, not least in the literary world, flowing through Arnold from sources in Wordsworth and Coleridge. Emphasizing formal and moral-thematic concerns and devaluing political, historical, and biographical issues, this tradition peaked in the mid-twentieth century. During that period, significant Byron scholarship was firmly located in textual, historical, and biographical areas. E. H. Coleridge's edition of the *Poetry* appeared together with R. E. Prothero's edition of *Letters and Journals* under the uniform title *The Works of Lord Byron* (12 vols., 1898–1904) and both superseded the great early edition of the prose and poetry edited by Thomas Moore and John Wright (17 vols., 1832–3). The new edition, which dominated Byron studies for more than fifty years, provoked and underwrote a series of key scholarly works.

Despite such scholarship, the early twentieth-century critical and interpretative lines of work left Byron at the margin of cultural and literary studies. This happened because Byron seemed an inappropriate writer for academic and pedagogical purposes. His influence remained strong largely in the genre work he so strongly marked—the Gothic—and in the writing of a few key cultural figures like Wilde and Joyce. The emergence of film as an artistic form—perhaps the major art form of the twentieth century—preserved Byron's influence and presence in some of its key genres: adventure, *film noir*, and the inexhaustible Gothic. Visual aspects of the Byronic combined with mood and tone to create in the 1950s and 1960s a strongly defined anti-heroic attitude or stance apparent in roles played by actors such as James Dean and Marlon Brando. Byronism made an impact, too, on the images assumed by some of the more outrageous rock stars of the 1960s. The fast rhythm and excesses of his life that became synonymous with Byron are now recognized as part of the pattern of celebrity. The continuing appeal of this glamorous aspect of Byronism reflects the intense cultural interest in the individuality of the self that lies at the heart of Romanticism. Byron's afterlife in popular culture was a crucial factor in his re-emergence after the Second World War in the high-cultural venue of post-modernism where parody, satire, wit, and an ethos of irony regained cultural authority.

Two scholarly events of 1957 mark the year as an epoch in the history of Byron's reception: the publication of Leslie Marchand's biography, and T. G. Steffan and W. W. Pratt's variorum edition of *Don Juan* (4 vols., 1957; rev. 1971). These two works stimulated and inspired, first, the complete re-editing of the works of Byron, and second, a massive re-evaluation of Byron's significance as a writer and cultural force. Marchand went on to re-edit *Byron's Letters and Journals* (12 vols., 1973–82; supp. vol., 1994); Jerome McGann edited *Lord Byron: the Complete Poetical Works* (7 vols., 1980–93); and Andrew Nicholson edited *Lord Byron: the Complete Miscellaneous Prose* (1991). After 1957 critical and interpretative Byron scholarship gained a new freedom through the emergent post-modern ethos. The studies by Robert Escarpit, *Lord Byron: un temperament littéraire* (2 vols., 1955–7), Paul West, *Byron and the Spoiler's Art* (1960), Andrew Rutherford, *Byron* (1961), and M. K. Joseph, *Byron the Poet* (1964) inaugurated a fertile period of critical work. The watershed came, however, in 1967–9 when Robert

F. Gleckner's *Byron and the Ruins of Paradise*, McGann's *Fiery Dust: Byron's Poetic Development*, and Michael Cooke's *The Blind Man Traces the Circle* appeared in successive years. These three books changed the landscape of Byron literary studies, and in their wake followed a trenchant period of critical exploration of the poetry.

Interest in visual representations of Byron was marked by Sir David Piper's chapter on 'Byron and the Romantic image' in *The Image of the Poet* (1982), which was followed by an entry for Byron in Richard Walker's catalogue *National Portrait Gallery, Regency Portraits* (2 vols., 1985). Annette Peach's comprehensive catalogue 'Portraits of Byron' was published in the *Walpole Society* (2000). Interest in Byron as a cultural phenomenon continues to stimulate interdisciplinary work among, for example, historians of art, fashion, and culture.

Biographical, critical, visual, and cultural approaches to Byron identify his pre-eminent status within English and European Romanticism. On a broader canvas they illuminate the vital energy and self-determination that define Byron's individuality as an iconic figure who gave his life in the cause of liberation. JEROME MCGANN

Sources L. A. Marchand, *Byron: a biography*, 3 vols. (1957); rev. in 1 vol. as *Byron: a portrait* (1970) • *Letters and journals of Lord Byron, with notices of his life*, ed. T. Moore, 2 vols. (1830) • *Lord Byron: the complete poetical works*, ed. J. J. McGann, 7 vols. (1980–93) • *Byron's letters and journals*, ed. L. A. Marchand, 12 vols. (1973–82); suppl. (1994) • *The works of Lord Byron: letters and journals*, ed. R. E. Prothero, 6 vols. (1898–1904) • GEC, *Peerage* • parish register, Marylebone, St Mary, 1 March 1788, LMA [baptism] • E. J. Lovell, ed., *His very self and voice* (1954) • E. J. Lovell, ed., *Medwin's conversations of Lord Byron* (1966) • I. Origo, *The last attachment* (1949) • *Lord Byron: the complete miscellaneous prose*, ed. A. Nicholson (1991) • *Lord Byron: poetry*, ed. E. H. Coleridge, 7 vols. (1898–1901) • S. C. Chew, *Byron in England* (1924); (1965) • E. J. Lovell, ed., *Lady Blessington's conversations of Lord Byron* (1969) • D. L. Moore, *The late Lord Byron* (1961); rev. (1976) • D. L. Moore, *Lord Byron: accounts rendered* (1974) • M. Elwin, *Lord Byron's wife* (1962) • M. Elwin, *The Noels and the Milbankes* (1967) • M. Elwin, *Lord Byron's family*, ed. P. Thompson (1975) • S. Hyman, 'Contemporary portraits of Byron', *Lord Byron and his contemporaries*, ed. C. E. Robinson (1982), 204–36 • A. Peach, 'Portraits of Byron', *Walpole Society*, 62 (2000), 1–144 • V. Foster, ed., *The two duchesses* (1898) • V. Walker, *The house of Byron*, rev. M. J. Howell (1988) • B. W. Procter [Barry Cornwall], *An autobiographical fragment and biographical notes*, ed. C. Patmore (1877) • *Memoirs of Lady Hester Stanhope*, ed. C. L. Meryon, 3 vols. (1845), vol. 3, p. 219 • [J. G. Lockhart], *Peter's letters to his kinsfolk*, 2nd edn, 3 vols. (1819), vol. 2, p. 338 • Ralph, earl of Lovelace, *Astarte* (1905); rev. edn (1921) • H. B. Stowe, *Lady Byron vindicated* (1870) • E. C. Mayne, *Lord Byron's correspondence* (1922) • T. J. Wise, *A bibliography of the writings … of Byron* (1933) • P. Quennell, *Byron: the years of fame* (1935) • P. Quennell, *Byron in Italy* (1941) • P. Quennell, *Byron: a self-portrait* (1950) • H. Nicholson, *Byron: the last journey* (1924) • D. N. Raymond, *The political career of Lord Byron* (1924) • J. Drinkwater, *The pilgrim of eternity* (1925) • C. du Bos, *Byron et le besoin de la fatalité* (1929) • W. J. Calvert, *Byron: Romantic paradox* (1925) • E. Boyd, *Don Juan* (1945) • F. L. Randolph, *Studies for a Byron bibliography* (1979) • D. L. Moore, *Ada, countess of Lovelace* (1977) • P. Gunn, *My dearest Augusta* (1968) • W. St Clair, *Lord Elgin and the marbles* (1967); new edn (1998) • W. St Clair, *That Greece might still be free* (1972) • R. F. Gleckner, *Critical essays on Lord Byron* (1991) • A. Levine and R. N. Keane, eds., *Rereading Byron* (1993) • C. E. Robinson, ed., *Lord Byron and his contemporaries* (1982) • M. Kelsall, *Byron's politics* (1987) • P. Graham, *Byron and regency England* (1990) • J. Christensen, *Lord Byron's strength* (1993) • J. Soderholm, *Fantasy, forgery, and the Byron legend* (1996) • J. McGann, *Byron and Romanticism* (2001) • G. Ridenour, *The style of 'Don Juan'* (1960) • A. Horn, *Byron's 'Don Juan' and the eighteenth-century English novel* (1962) • E. E. Bostetter, ed., *Twentieth-century interpretations of 'Don Juan'* (1969) • A. B. England, *Byron's 'Don Juan' and eighteenth-century literature* (1975) • J. McGann, *'Don Juan' in context* (1976) • A. Barton, *Byron: Don Juan* (1992) • O. J. Santucho, *George Gordon, Lord Byron: a comprehensive bibliography of secondary materials in English, 1807–1974* (1977) • C. T. Goode, *Lord Byron: a comprehensive, annotated research bibliography of secondary materials in English, 1973–1994* (1997)

Archives BL, accounts relating to Newstead Abbey and Rochdale Manor, Add. MS 62910 • BL, corresp. and papers relating to his separation from his wife • BL, deeds, Add. Ch 72100–72103 • BL, letters and notebooks, loan 70 • Bodl. Oxf., verse, papers, and corresp. • Harrow School, Middlesex, letters and memorabilia • Hunt. L., letters and literary MSS • John Murray, London, papers • King's School, Canterbury, pocket book • Morgan L., corresp., literary MSS, and papers • Ransom HRC, corresp., literary MSS, and papers • Yale U., Beinecke L., papers | BL, letters to John Hanson, Egerton MS 2611 • BL, corresp. with Lord Holland, Add. MS 51639 • BL, letters to John Cam Hobhouse and Douglas Kinnaird, Add. MS 42093 • BL, Ashley library • BL, corresp. with Lady Melbourne, Add. MS 45547 • BL, letters to John Murray • Bodl. Oxf., Lytton papers • Indiana University, Bloomington, Lilly Library, letters, papers, and drawings • NL Scot., letters to Edward Ellice • NYPL, Berg collection • RA, corresp. with Thomas Lawrence • UCL, letters to Samuel Rogers • V&A NAL, letters to Leigh Hunt

Likenesses E. Pigot, miniature, *c.*1807 (of Byron's right eye), priv. coll. • E. Pigot, ten watercolour drawings, 1807, Ransom HRC • G. Sanders, double portrait, oils, 1807–8 (with Robert Rushton), Royal Collection • G. Sanders, miniature, 1809, priv. coll. • G. Sanders, miniature, *c.*1812, priv. coll.; copy, priv. coll. • T. Phillips, oils, 1813, priv. coll.; versions, John Murray, City of Nottingham Museums, Newstead Abbey, and priv. coll. • R. Westall, oils, 1813, NPG; versions, Hughenden Manor, Buckinghamshire, NPG • T. Phillips, oils, 1814, Gov. Art Coll. [*see illus.*] • T. Phillips, oils, *c.*1835 (version of oils, 1814), NPG • G. H. Harlow, chalk drawing, *c.*1815, priv. coll. • J. Holmes, miniature, 1815–16; whereabouts unknown; copies, priv. coll. • B. Thorvaldsen, bust, plaster model, 1817, Thorvaldsens Museum, Copenhagen • B. Thorvaldsen, bust, first marble copy, 1817, Royal Collection • G. H. Harlow, chalk drawing, 1818, John Murray • L. Bartolini, bust, first marble copy, 1822, National Library of South Africa, Cape Town • L. Bartolini, bust, plaster model, 1822, Palazzo Pitti, Florence • W. E. West, oils, 1822, Scot. NPG; copy, Harrow School

Wealth at death approx. £100,000 with two settlements (marriage) of £64,000 and £16,000 reverting to Lady Byron and Ada Byron: *Byron's letters and journals*, ed. Marchand; Moore, *Lord Byron*

Byron, Henry James (1835–1884), playwright and actor, was born in Manchester on 8 January 1835. His father, Henry Byron (1804–1884), British consul in Port-au-Prince, Haiti, was second cousin to the poet Lord Byron. His mother, Elizabeth Josephine, was the daughter of Dr Bradley of Buxton, the last in a sequence of private tutors to whom her son's education was largely entrusted. A plan to enter him as a naval cadet in 1849 was vetoed by his father, and he was placed instead as an articled clerk to a London surgeon, Miles Morley of Cork Street, Burlington Gardens. The inability to settle, which characterized Byron's later life, was already evident, and after four years with Morley he severed family ties by becoming an actor. Between 1853 and 1857 he appeared without much success in provincial theatres from Colchester to Oldham, sometimes in the equally unsuccessful company of the struggling playwright T. W. (Tom) Robertson. On 4 January 1856 Byron married Martha Foulkes (1831/2–1876) of Ashfield, near Wrexham. He had already displayed some facility in the

Henry James Byron (1835–1884), by Lock & Whitfield, pubd 1878

writing of comic dialogue and monologue—his burlesque *Richard of the Lion Heart* opened at the Strand Theatre on 23 November 1857—but he made a further attempt to regularize his life by entering the Middle Temple on 14 January 1858. The turning point came three months later, when his *Fra diavolo travestie*, again at the Strand, proved a popular success. The aspiring barrister was quickly swallowed by the practising playwright who, over the next twenty-five years, would produce upwards of 150 dramatic pieces. The connection with the Strand, the favourite home of London burlesque under the management of William Swanborough and his daughter Ada, brought Byron into contact with Marie Wilton (later Lady Bancroft), whose playing of Pippo in his *The Maid and the Magpie* was the theatrical sensation of autumn 1858. Before the end of 1859 he had provided further burlesques and travesties for the Strand, the Olympic, and the Adelphi and the first of a sequence of Christmas pantomimes for the Princess's Theatre, *Jack the Giant Killer, or, Harlequin, King Arthur, and ye Knights of ye Round Table*.

Byron was now able to indulge in the masculine pleasures of London's clubland. He was a regular diner at the Albion in Drury Lane, a leading member of the Savage Club, and, in 1863, a founder member of the Arundel Club. At the Garrick Club too his table talk, like his burlesques and pantomimes, was based on wordplay. Even when the inspiration of Victorian 'nonsense' had faded, the pun remained, and Byron was the supreme punster of the late nineteenth-century theatre. The solemn Henry Morley, while deploring Byron's punning, acknowledged in him 'a true power of fun that makes itself felt by high and low' (*Journal of a London Playgoer*, 1866, 209). At its worst, the punning habit depends on mere aural coincidence; at its best, it can carry a double thrust of meaning and associative sound. Byron sank often to the first ('Your cattle swell the *cattle*-ogue of grief'), but could also earn his obligatory laughter ('It cuts you like a knife, don't it Nar-*scissors*?'). He once confessed to fellow diners in Birmingham: 'I have so trained myself to make them that I almost see the pun before I write the word that I want it to play upon' (Pemberton, *Sir Charles Wyndham*, 59). Only a few examples of his impromptu punning have survived in the published reminiscences of his friends. They are unremarkable, but they do tend to confirm claims that he was at pains never to give offence even to the most squeamish members of his audience. Byron was socially adept and well liked. Tall and slender, with meticulously parted hair, he was so fond of his luxurious moustache that he refused to shave it even when he returned to acting in 1869, an eccentricity pardoned by theatregoers, who probably recognized in it a silent assertion that he was more a writer than an actor.

Byron's association with the Strand Theatre lasted until the end of 1864. His *Cinderella* of 1860 introduced Buttoni, later naturalized as Buttons, and his 1861 *Aladdin, or, The Wonderful Scamp* saw the first stage appearance of the Widow Twankay, later further Anglicized as Twankey. During these years he also sold burlesques to the Adelphi, the Theatres Royal in both Drury Lane and the Haymarket, and the Princess's, as well as pantomimes to the Princess's, the St James's, and the Theatre Royal in Covent Garden. He supplemented his income by contributing comic pieces to newspapers and journals, notably to *Fun*, for many years the most effective rival to *Punch*. Byron was involved in the editing of the early issues of *Fun* from its first appearance on 21 September 1861, and was sole editor of the less successful *Comic News* (1863), *Wag* (1867), and *Mirth* (1877). *Paid in Full*, a three-volume novel, was published in 1865, but that year was more notable for Byron's first venture into theatre management. The money to convert an unfashionable theatre in Tottenham Street into the uniquely decorous Prince of Wales's was provided by Marie Wilton. Byron's plays were to be his share. For the opening on 15 April 1865 he wrote a burlesque of *La sonnambula*, but the partnership soon proved problematic. Byron, not unreasonably, had assumed that the Prince of Wales's was to be a new home for burlesque; Wilton, once in management, aimed higher. There were attempts at compromise. She agreed to stage three more burlesques by Byron, and he to write his first comedies, *War to the Knife* (10 June 1865) and *A Hundred Thousand Pounds* (5 May 1866). But in 1866, either before or because Byron had committed himself to the management of the Theatre Royal in Liverpool, the partnership was dissolved. Its finest achievement, for which much credit belongs to Byron, was the staging on 11 November 1865 of his old friend Tom Robertson's *Society*.

For a while, Byron, who, according to the actor J. H. Barnes, 'had a perfect mania for changing his places of residence' (*Forty Years on the Stage*, 23), turned his back on London. He undertook the management of two more Liverpool theatres, the Alexandra and the Amphitheatre, and wrote for them a burlesque, three pantomimes, and one of his more successful comedies, *Dearer than Life*, which opened at the Alexandra on 26 November 1867. Taking seriously what he had made his name by mocking, he staged at the Amphitheatre on 28 October 1867 his first and best melodrama, *The Lancashire Lass*. The management of three theatres had, however, overstretched Byron's resources. On 4 March 1868 he filed a petition for bankruptcy. The next few years were occupied with strenuous efforts to recover his position. *Dearer than Life* was triumphantly restaged at the Queen's Theatre in London in early 1868, with a cast including the popular comedian J. L. Toole and the comparatively unknown Henry Irving, who again starred at the Queen's in a revival of *The Lancashire Lass*. The theatre made money, but the playwright made little, even with his most ambitious comedy, *Cyril's Success*, which opened at the Globe on 28 November 1868. Before the establishment of a royalty system, playwrights had to be prolific to remain in pocket, and it was financial exigency that persuaded Byron to resume his acting career in a provincial tour of his own *Not such a Fool as he Looks*. Monocled and elegant as Sir Simon Simple, he made his London début in the play on 23 October 1869 at the very theatre where the run of *Cyril's Success* had just ended. A moderate actor, at his best in the timing of his own witty lines, Byron continued to appear, almost exclusively in his own plays, until his health failed in 1882. His son Henry and daughter Crede (punningly named after the Byron family motto, *Crede Byron*) also had brief and unimpressive acting careers.

Byron's popularity as a playwright outlasted his literary reputation. While the higher criticism was calling for the abandonment of dramatic stereotypes, Byron triumphantly depended on them. His comedy *Our Boys* began a record-breaking run of 1362 performances at the Vaudeville Theatre on 16 January 1875, two months before the staging of *Trial by Jury* brought Gilbert and Sullivan into association with Richard D'Oyly Carte. This, and not the contemporary strivings of the Ibsenites, was his world. His last major theatrical attachment was to John Hollingshead's Gaiety Theatre, for whose famous 'Gaiety Quartette' he provided tailor-made burlesque roles from 1876 to 1879. Whatever his private pain, in public he remained relaxed and humorous. When Irving assumed the management of the Lyceum in 1878 (Byron's own last venture into management had been at the Criterion in 1874 in short-lived partnership with E. P. Hingston), he received a letter from Byron: 'Now, old fellow, don't let management worry you—take things easily'. By then, Byron was showing symptoms of the consumption that caused his retirement in 1882 and his death on 11 April 1884. His first wife had died on 25 September 1876, and he was nursed in his last home, 6 Queen's Road, Clapham Park, London, by his second wife, Eleanor Mary, the daughter of Edward Joy, a lawyer, whom he had married on 17 October 1876, less than a month after Martha's death. Byron was buried in Brompton cemetery on 18 April 1884. PETER THOMSON

Sources *Plays by H. J. Byron*, ed. J. Davis (1984) · H. G. Hibbert, *A playgoer's memories* (1920) · J. H. Barnes, *Forty years on the stage* (1914) · [S. Bancroft and M. E. Bancroft], *Mr and Mrs Bancroft on and off the stage* (1888) · T. E. Pemberton, *The life and writings of T. W. Robertson* (1893) · T. E. Pemberton, *A memoir of Edward Askew Sothern*, 2nd edn (1889) · T. E. Pemberton, *Sir Charles Wyndham* (1904) · H. M. Walbrook, *A playgoer's wanderings* (1920) · *Dame Madge Kendal by herself*, ed. R. de Cordova (1933) · L. Irving, *Henry Irving: the actor and his world* [1951] · J. Hollingshead, *Gaiety chronicles* (1898) · H. Swears, *When all's said and done* (1937) · d. cert. · m. certs.

Archives Theatre Museum, London, letters

Likenesses Lock & Whitfield, woodburytype photograph, pubd 1878, NPG [*see illus.*] · H. C. Maguire, chromolithograph, NPG · E. Matthews & Sons, lithograph, NPG · caricature (as Sir Simon Simple), repro. in *The Hornet* (18 Sept 1872) · photograph, repro. in J. Hollingshead, *Good old Gaiety* (1903) · photograph, repro. in W. Macqueen-Pope, *Gaiety, theatre of enchantment* (1949) · prints, Harvard TC · wood-engraving, NPG; repro. in *Illustrated Review* (6 Dec 1873) · woodburytype photograph, NPG

Wealth at death £4783 4s. 10d.: probate, 12 May 1884, *CGPLA Eng. & Wales*

Byron, John, **first Baron Byron** (1598/9–1652), royalist army officer, was the eldest son and heir of Sir John Byron KB of Newstead Abbey, Nottinghamshire, who owned estates in that county and Lancashire and died on 28 September 1625. His mother was Anne Molyneux, daughter of Sir Richard Molyneux of Sefton, Lancashire, and his birth date may be surmised from the fact that he was fifteen years old in 1614. The following year Byron was admitted as a fellow-commoner at Trinity College, Cambridge, and was created MA in 1618.

Byron represented Nottingham in the parliaments of 1624 and 1625. He was created a knight of the Bath in the coronation honours of Charles I, and made a gentleman of the bedchamber. He sat for Nottinghamshire in the parliament of 1628–9, serving as its high sheriff in 1634. The brutal resolution of his character even in this period of early manhood was revealed in 1618 or 1619 upon the death of his sister Margaret, who had married Sir Thomas Hutchinson. He arrived to find the bereaved husband and other relatives prostrate with grief, and reacted by having his sister buried with the utmost speed, and without inviting Hutchinson and the others to attend. Byron himself became a widower in 1638, upon the death of his first wife, Cecilia, daughter of Thomas West, Lord De La Warr, and his wife, Cicely Shirley, and widow of Sir Francis Bindloss of Barwick.

Byron and his brothers were said to have been 'bred up in arms' (Hutchinson, 29), but it is not clear what this means in terms of actual military experience before he joined the royal army serving against the Scots in the disastrous war of 1640. Writing from Berwick on 24 September, he expressed unconditional support for the king, and referred to the Scots as 'vipers' (PRO, SP 16/468/27). It was doubtless this fervent loyalty which caused Charles to appoint him lieutenant of the Tower of London on 26 December 1641, as the political crisis in the capital moved towards its climax. On 12 January 1642 the Commons

John Byron, first Baron Byron (1598/9–1652), by William Dobson, *c*.1643

expressed a lack of confidence in him, and ordered that the Tower be blockaded by the City militia. Byron appeared in person twice before the Lords to plead his case, and they refused to concur in an address to the king to remove him until 8 February, when they gave in to continuing pressure from the Commons. Sir John felt that this, and the blockade, made his position impossible, and begged Charles to accept his resignation, which was done on 11 February.

This, however, merely freed Byron to serve his monarch in the field, and he subsequently joined the king at York. By 24 July he had been made colonel of a horse regiment in the army which Charles had decided to form, almost certainly the first cavalry unit to be commissioned for that force. Three of his brothers served under him, and three more elsewhere in the same army. The regiment was formed by 20 August, when it was with the king at his summons of Coventry, and was dispatched from there to secure Oxford, cutting its way through an enemy force at Brackley on the 28th. It reached Oxford on the evening of that day, 160 strong, and occupied the city until 10 September, when Byron withdrew in the face of an advancing parliamentarian army. On the following day both houses formally declared him a traitor.

Byron had evacuated Oxford taking with him a large convoy of money and plate, furnished by the university for the royal army now mustering at Shrewsbury. By 16 September he had reached Worcester, with a parliamentarian field force in pursuit, and decided to halt his exhausted men there and hold that city while appealing for help. The relief was provided on the 23rd by Prince Rupert, who routed the enemy advance guard at Powick Bridge and gave Sir John time to get his convoy clear. Having delivered it, Byron and his regiment rejoined the royal army, and at the battle of Edgehill on 23 October they were posted as the reserve for the right wing of royalist horse. As such, their duty was either to cover the flank of the royal foot, or to strike at that of the opposing infantry if it became exposed. They failed totally in both, for when the main royalist cavalry wing swept away the horsemen opposite them, Sir John's men galloped after the fleeing parliamentarian cavalry, leaving their own infantry vulnerable and playing some part in depriving the king of outright victory in the battle.

Between November 1642 and November 1643 the regiment spent most of its time quartered at various places in Oxfordshire, Berkshire, and Buckinghamshire. One of these was the mansion of the prominent parliamentarian Bulstrode Whitelocke, Fawley Court, where Byron explicitly forbade his troopers to plunder or cause damage, and was wantonly ignored. Twice in 1643 the regiment thinned badly because its members were disappointed of pay or loot. On the other hand, it saw action four times in the year, and on each occasion men and commander performed admirably. At Burford on 1 January 1643 they drove a band of local parliamentarians out of the town; a halberd blow laid open Byron's left cheek and left a prominent scar. On 6 May they routed another party of enemies at Bicester. Sir John was given command of the right wing of the cavalry force which destroyed Waller's army at Roundway Down on 13 July, and led it to the attack with distinction. At Newbury on 20 September he had charge of the equivalent wing of the royal army itself, and gained control of the hill which dominated that part of the battlefield after a long and bloody fight. His men were then too exhausted to push further, and so decisive victory was again missed.

Nantwich and Marston Moor For these services, Sir John was rewarded on 24 October 1643 with the title Baron Byron of Rochdale, and began angling for the office of governor to the prince of Wales. Rupert, however, obtained for him the different honour of an independent field command, to reconquer Lancashire and so pave the way for royalist reinforcements from Ireland which were due to land in the north-west. He had accepted the posting by 7 November, and was then hurried north with 1300 men to shore up a collapsing royalist position in Cheshire. By early December he had reached Chester to meet the soldiers from Ireland, and there on the 19th he was promoted to the rank of field marshal in Lancashire, Cheshire, and the six counties of north Wales, giving him control of the Irish regiments and all local forces. Although his instructions have not survived, they were fairly obviously to clear Lancashire and Cheshire of the enemy and then turn northward to meet an expected Scottish invasion. On 12 December he led 5000 men into the field, which broke the Cheshire parliamentarian army at Middlewich on the 26th and soon took every one of its garrisons except the main one at Nantwich, which was besieged from 10 January 1644. For the brutality which Byron showed at the storming of Barthomley church, where he exulted in the slaughter of the defenders, the enemy press dubbed him 'the Bloody Braggadocchio'.

Nantwich, however, was strongly held, and the siege rapidly thinned the royalist army, 500 being killed in an attempt to storm the defences on 18 January. On the 25th a relieving force of 4000 parliamentarians approached, under Sir Thomas Fairfax. Byron had just 3500 men left, divided by a river and with the garrison poised to attack their rear, but he apparently did not hesitate to engage Fairfax's forces. The result was a disaster from which only some royalist cavalry escaped. Byron fell back on Chester to secure the city, but was now effectively immobilized there while his victorious opponents reconquered most of the county. Pressure was taken off him only by the arrival of Rupert himself to command in the region in March, allowing Byron to venture out to re-establish superiority in western Cheshire and north-east Wales. In April he convinced both Rupert and the king that the former should resume the task of conquering the north-west, and Rupert was duly instructed to restore royalist dominance in Cheshire and Lancashire and then relieve York. On 18 May Byron's forces from Chester united with those of the prince at Whitchurch, Shropshire, and marched with them in the triumphant progress across Cheshire and Lancashire which culminated in the relief of York on 1 July. On the 2nd Byron found himself in the position of trust which he had held twice before, of commanding the right wing of cavalry in an army deployed for battle, as Rupert confronted the parliamentarians and Scots on Marston Moor.

The military dispositions were not, however, familiar. Rupert's right wing of horse was clearly outnumbered by the parliamentarian cavalry facing them. Byron was therefore apparently instructed to hold back his men when battle was joined, until the attacking enemy had been thinned by muskets and a field battery posted to catch them while crossing a ditch which divided the two forces. In the event, the attack took the royalists by surprise, and Byron allegedly forgot his orders and led forward his regiments to meet it in conventional fashion, blocking the fire of the battery and giving his own men the trouble of crossing the ditch. As a result they were swept away when struck by the superior enemy forces, causing the royalist right wing to disintegrate and thus condemning the entire army to defeat. This, at any rate, is what was claimed by Rupert and his friends, making Byron arguably the man who lost the king the battle and therefore the north of England, and cost him a good chance of outright victory in the war. It would certainly have been in character for him to have acted in this fashion; but he may simply have lost control of his men as at Edgehill, and it is by no means certain that Rupert's plan would ever have sufficed to counterbalance the numerical weakness of the whole wing.

Chester Rupert and Byron fled westward, reaching Chester on 25 July and settling there to recruit new forces. In August Byron gathered the northern royalist cavalry in Lancashire to attack the local parliamentarians, but the latter took them by surprise at Ormskirk on the 19th and routed them. This defeat lost the royalists control of most of that county once more, and Rupert went south with most of the remaining soldiers to rejoin the king, leaving Byron to hold Chester as its military governor. Almost at once he had to deal with a parliamentarian thrust into Wales, and rallied 3500 of the local forces to attack an enemy 3000 strong at Montgomery on 18 September. The odds were in his favour, but for some reason it was his men who broke after a hard fight, and only 100 escaped. The result was to give parliament control of central Wales.

This string of disasters left Chester increasingly encircled, and during the winter of 1644–5 Byron's main task was to hold the city. He did so by the obvious means of ensuring pay and supplies for the garrison, trying to keep open lines of communication and trade, and greatly strengthening the fortifications; but he also laid great emphasis on subjecting local government, which until 1644 had been vested in the corporation, to the strict control of himself and his officers. Inevitably this led to friction with civilian leaders, to compound that created by his growing financial demands upon the city. By November Chester was under blockade, and a sally in January was repulsed. Relief came in March, when Rupert made a sortie into the region, and in April the king formally confirmed Byron's commission to govern Chester, which had hitherto rested only on the authority of Rupert as regional commander. In April also the blockade of Chester was renewed, and once again the royal army provided relief, the king himself leading it into the region in May. Byron met it in Staffordshire on the 22nd, with the news that his enemies had retired, and urged Charles to deploy it in the north-west. Instead it turned eastward, to be destroyed at Naseby.

News of this catastrophe reached Byron at Chester, and he prepared for the full-scale siege of the city which now seemed inevitable. It opened on 19 September, with a surprise attack at dawn which overwhelmed the outer defences on the east side and enabled the attackers to bombard the walls themselves. Byron may be held ultimately responsible for this reverse, for he had extended the vital outer circuit of earthworks to contain most of the suburbs, which otherwise would have been burned to deny attackers cover. This saved him from worse unpopularity, but spread his line of defenders too thinly. The king brought up his remaining soldiers to the rescue, but they were defeated at Rowton Moor on the 23rd, and by 9 October the walls were breached in two places. Now, however, Byron showed his worth, for he had prepared defences behind each breach which turned them into death traps when the attackers stormed them. The city subsequently came under mortar fire, but he had equipped fire squads to extinguish the blazes caused by the shells. After this, the besiegers had no option other than to starve it out, and Byron's determination made this as protracted a process as possible. He repeatedly sent sorties against the enemy lines, and ostentatiously restricted himself to a diet of boiled wheat and spring water. Without hope of relief such heroics could only postpone surrender, and he made it on 2 February 1646.

Byron and his soldiers retired to Caernarfon, from which he set to work to turn north-west Wales into the final redoubt of his command. Unhappily, his contempt for civilians in general and for the Welsh in particular—clear in his dispatches—can only have enhanced the natural effects of war-weariness and defeatism to make the local population increasingly disaffected from him. In March the gentry of Anglesey rejected his authority, and gunmen tried to assassinate him as he crossed the Menai Strait to protest. Their rebellion left him helpless at Caernarfon, which came under siege by a parliamentarian invasion force in early May. Byron waited a month in the hope of aid from Ireland, and then on 4 June he gave up the town, his command, and the war, sailing away into exile.

Byron made his way, like many other defeated royalists, to the court of the queen at St Germain, and seems to have remained there, largely invisible, until the second civil war was planned early in 1648. His part in it was decided in March, when the prince of Wales, as royalist commander-in-chief, commissioned him anew to control royalist forces in north Wales, Cheshire, and Lancashire. Once again he was expected to prepare the way for an invading army that was expected to assist the king, but this time the force was from Scotland, coming down into the north-west. Byron was expected to take overall command of a series of royalist risings, commencing in north-west Wales, which would secure the region ahead of the Scottish advance. He duly made his journey from France to Anglesey in May, only to find the gentry there no more prepared to serve him than in 1646. He was compelled to withdraw, frustrated, to Dublin, from where he watched as the Welsh royalists rose under their own commanders and were crushed, together with all the other royalist insurgents of the summer, and the oncoming Scots. He now threw himself into supporting the lord lieutenant of Ireland, Ormond, in his talks to ally with the Irish confederate Catholics to assist the royalist cause. Byron had co-operated well with Ormond during his years at Chester, and in January 1649 he was able to carry the treaty with the confederates to the new king Charles II at The Hague, together with an invitation to proceed to Ireland to command the allied forces. Before he and the royal party had got further than Jersey, they received fresh news from Ormond, warning that so much of Ireland had already fallen to Cromwell's army that it was no longer wise to come there.

Byron now became one of those royalists who urged the king to make a fresh treaty with the Scottish covenanters, even at the cost of sacrificing traditional principles of their cause. The treaty was made at Breda in April 1650, but Byron himself did not accompany Charles to Scotland, either because he was unacceptable to the Scottish government or because he had residual qualms about serving it. Instead he attached himself to the household of the duke of York, who also remained on the continent, and journeyed with it between Paris, Brussels, and The Hague during the next two years; on 30 April 1651 he was formally appointed as its superintendent, because of the favour of the queen mother. There seems to have been little warmth between him and the royal duke, but his charge did return him to a military life, as he accompanied York on his first campaign with the French royal army. He died suddenly at Paris in early August 1652, the event being reported at the exiled royal court there on the 13th. Neither the cause of his demise, nor his place of burial, seem to be recorded.

Byron had been married a second time in 1644, to Eleanor Warburton (1626/7–1664), daughter of the prominent Cheshire royalist Robert Needham, Viscount Kilmorey, and his wife, Eleanor Gerard, *née* Dutton, and widow of another Cheshire gentleman, Peter Warburton of Arley. She was still only about seventeen at the time, having been eleven when first married in 1638, and survived Byron to die in September 1664. Both Byron's marriages were childless, and Byron's heir was his brother Richard.

A fine portrait of John Byron survives by the royalist painter William Dobson. It was made in about 1643, and shows a passionate and overbearing man of medium height, with rounded, swarthy features, black hair, and well-trimmed beard and moustache, the scar from Burford plainly visible. The image projected well bears out the man's positive qualities of courage, resolution, loyalty, energy, and aggression. The many letters and memoirs which survive from his hand also testify to his intelligence, impatience, enterprise, arrogance, brutality, and administrative efficiency. For all these, and when every allowance is made for misfortune, disadvantage, or misrepresentation, he still seems deficient in the career for which he is chiefly remembered, as a soldier. While he could clearly hold a position with the utmost determination and resource, in the field his single sense of tactics seems to have been to attack headlong, whatever the circumstances, and with the minimum of control over his men. As such, his part in the defeats and missed opportunities of the royalist cause, at both national and regional level, is likely to remain rather more memorable than his role in its successes. RONALD HUTTON

Sources Bodl. Oxf., MSS Clarendon 21–42 • Bodl. Oxf., MSS Carte 7–17 • R. Scrope and T. Monkhouse, eds., *State papers collected by Edward, earl of Clarendon*, 3 vols. (1767–86) • *The siege of Chester: Nathaniel Lancaster's narrative*, ed. J. Lewis (1982) • Bodl. Oxf., MS Rawl. B. 210 • Bodl. Oxf., MS Ashmole 832, fols. 191–4 • J. A. Atkinson, ed., *Tracts relating to the civil war in Cheshire, 1641–1659: including Sir George Booth's rising in that county*, Chetham Society, new ser., 65 (1909) • *Memoirs of Prince Rupert and the cavaliers including their private correspondence*, ed. E. Warburton, 3 vols. (1849), vols. 1–2 • J. Lowe, 'The campaign of the Irish royalist army in Cheshire, November 1643 – January 1644', *Transactions of the Historic Society of Lancashire and Cheshire*, 111 (1959), 47–76 • *The manuscripts of the duke of Hamilton*, HMC, 21 (1887) • L. Hutchinson, *Memoirs of the life of Colonel Hutchinson*, ed. J. Hutchinson (1806), 1–92 • PRO, SP 16/468/27 • Venn, *Alum. Cant.* • GEC, *Peerage*

Archives BL, MS account of first battle of Newbury; MS account of proceedings in Chester and parts adjacent • BL, letters, Add. MSS 18980–18982 • Bodl. Oxf., MS Clarendon 23; MS Clarendon 31 | Bodl. Oxf., corresp., MSS Carte 7–17

Likenesses W. Dobson, oils, *c.*1643, priv. coll. [*see illus.*] • S. De Wilde, etching, BM

Byron, John (1723–1786), naval officer, second son of William Byron, fourth Baron Byron (1669–1736), and his third wife, Frances (*d.* 1757), second daughter of William Berkeley, Baron Berkeley of Stratton, was born on 8 November 1723. He joined the navy in 1737 and served in the *Romney*. In 1740 he was appointed midshipman to the storeship *Wager*, one of the squadron under Commodore Anson bound for the Pacific. On 14 May 1741, after rounding Cape Horn, the *Wager* was wrecked on the southern coast of Chile. The survivors separated, Byron and a few others remaining with the captain. After undergoing considerable hardship they succeeded in reaching Valparaiso, and from here, in December 1744, they were permitted to return to Europe by a French ship, which carried them to Brest. They arrived in England in February 1746. Many years later, in 1768, Byron was to publish a *Narrative* of the struggle for survival after the shipwreck, and it supplied some hints for the shipwreck scene in *Don Juan*, by George *Byron, sixth Baron Byron, John Byron's grandson.

During his absence Byron had been promoted lieutenant; immediately on his arrival he was made commander, and on 30 December 1746 he was made captain and appointed to the frigate *Syren*. In August 1748 he married Sophia (*d.* 1790), daughter of John Trevanion of Carhays in Cornwall; they had two sons and seven daughters, of whom three died in infancy. After the peace Byron commanded the *St Albans*, one of the squadron patrolling the coast of Guinea; in 1753 he commanded the guardship *Augusta* at Plymouth; and in 1755 the *Vanguard*. In 1757 he commanded the *America* in Edward Hawke's futile expedition against Rochefort; he afterwards cruised with some success on the coast of France, and in the following year, still in the *America*, served in the fleet off Brest under George Anson. In 1760 he was sent to North America in command of the *Fame* and a small squadron to superintend the demolition of the fortifications of Louisbourg, and while the work was in progress had the opportunity of destroying a quantity of French shipping and stores in the Bay of Chaleur, including three small men-of-war. He returned to England in November, but continued in command of the *Fame* until the peace, being for the most part attached to the squadron before Brest.

Anson's circumnavigation of 1740–44 had had the effect of renewing British interest in the Pacific. In 1749 Lord Sandwich, first lord of the Admiralty, put forward a plan, probably suggested by Anson, to send British ships to the Falkland Islands and then into the Pacific. After reaching the Juan Fernandez Islands they were to head due west for 3000 miles across the ocean, searching for islands or other undiscovered land. The hope was to find a base from which Britain could break into Spanish trade in the Pacific. Preparations for this expedition were carried out openly and details soon reached the Spanish. They protested strongly and since the British government was at this time trying to negotiate a trade treaty with Spain, it decided to cancel the expedition to appease the Spanish.

After Lord Egmont became first lord of the Admiralty he decided in 1764 to carry out a modified version of the 1749 plan; his principal interest at this time was in securing British command of the Falkland Islands, which he regarded as controlling the southern gateway to the Pacific. Since the Spanish claimed ownership of the Falklands and would object to any revival of the 1749 plan, Egmont prepared the expedition in some secrecy. Only the Admiralty and George III knew its true aims, with most members of the government being kept in the dark.

Byron was chosen to command the expedition, which consisted of the frigate *Dolphin*, one of the first British warships with a copper-sheathed bottom, and the sloop *Tamar*. It was given out that Byron was going out to take command of the East India station, and would fly the broad pennant of a commodore in the *Dolphin*. Byron left England in July 1764, and took his ships to Brazil. Only when leaving Rio de Janeiro on 22 October did he reveal his secret orders to his men. The plan was that they would first go into the south Atlantic and search for Pepys's Island, and then to the Falkland Islands. After they had been claimed for Britain, Byron was to proceed into the Pacific, sail to New Albion (California), and then begin a search for the north-west passage, leading back to the Atlantic across the top of North America. If the passage could not be found Byron was to come home across the Pacific.

From Rio Byron went first to Port Desire in Patagonia. Here he met tall natives and noted their existence in his journal. When John Hawkesworth brought out a somewhat romanticized version of Byron's circumnavigation journal in 1773 he greatly exaggerated the size of these natives, and this led to much levity at Byron's expense concerning Patagonian giants. From Port Desire Byron headed out into the south Atlantic searching for Pepys's Island, which had been noted on earlier charts. When it became clear that the island did not exist Byron sailed for the Falklands.

In January 1765 Byron reached West Falkland and anchored at a place he named Port Egmont after the first lord. Byron then formally claimed the islands for George III, and explored along the north coasts of both West and East Falkland. His cursory inspection failed to find the French settlement which had recently been established at Berkeley Sound on East Falkland. For the rest of the decade Britain, France, and Spain would engage in a three-cornered dispute about the ownership of the Falklands. For the moment Byron left the islands and returned to Port Desire to meet a storeship that was bringing supplies for his ships.

Once resupplied Byron took his ships through the Strait of Magellan, but once in the Pacific in April 1765 he decided to ignore his orders to search for the north-west passage. Instead Byron intended to cross the Pacific following a track between the tropic of Capricorn and the equator. He was never censured for this clear breach of his written orders, possibly because it was a reversion to part of the 1749 plan. Byron intended to look for islands along this track, in particular the Solomon Islands and their fabled riches. These islands had been first discovered in the sixteenth century, but their exact position and extent had never been established.

In fact Byron found very few islands during his voyage across the Pacific, and none of importance. After finding several small islands in the Tuamotu group but being unable to anchor at them, Byron called them the Islands of Disappointment; some small islands found later were called the King George Islands; and another island found in the Gilbert group Byron named after himself. Byron narrowly missed sighting Tahiti, but he did claim to have seen signs which indicated the existence of a southern continent. At the end of July 1765 Byron's ships reached Tinian in the Marianas, which had been visited by Anson during his voyage, and then they set off on their homeward passage. On his arrival in England in May 1766 Byron was able to claim the fastest circumnavigation up to that time; his men were relatively untouched by scurvy, while the *Dolphin*'s copper-sheathed bottom survived the voyage in good condition, an important advance in naval technology. Byron's mention of signs of a southern continent encouraged the immediate preparation of another expedition to the Pacific, and Byron may have had a hand in preparing the instructions to its commander, Captain Wallis. He was specifically ordered to search for the southern continent, but it was to prove elusive. However, by following a track similar to Byron's, but further to the south, Wallis did discover Tahiti in 1767.

In January 1769 Byron was appointed governor of Newfoundland, an office he held for the next three years. On 31 March 1775 he was advanced to be rear-admiral, and on 29 January 1778 to vice-admiral. He was then ordered to go out to India as commander-in-chief, but these orders were countermanded in favour of his taking command of a squadron fitting out at Plymouth. The government believed a French fleet under Comte d'Estaing was soon to leave Toulon bound for North America. Byron's squadron was ordered to pursue d'Estaing and if possible bring his force to battle. Byron, in the *Princess Royal*, led his ships out into the Atlantic in June 1778 once it was known that d'Estaing was on his way to assist the American rebels. However, Byron lived up to his nickname, Foulweather Jack, when his squadron was scattered by gales. The damaged ships eventually collected at New York, but were in no state to put to sea again until October. D'Estaing was then at Boston and Byron set out for that port, only for his ships to be dispersed once more by gales. By December Byron knew that d'Estaing had gone to the West Indies. With ten ships of the line, Byron set off in pursuit, and promptly ran into further bad weather.

On 6 January 1779 Byron's storm-battered ships reached St Lucia, which had recently been captured by Admiral Samuel Barrington and General James Grant and successfully defended against d'Estaing. Since Byron's orders were to pursue d'Estaing wherever he went, the admiral at first tried to preserve a distinction between his ships and Barrington's Leeward Islands squadron. However, this soon proved unworkable, so Byron merged the two forces, with Barrington as his second in command. Byron and General Grant kept the fleet and the troops concentrated at St Lucia to watch d'Estaing's forces in Martinique. However, the governors of the neighbouring British islands complained that the admiral and the general were not using their superior forces either to recapture the lost island of Dominica or to attack French islands.

Byron's attention remained fixed on d'Estaing and he looked for an opportunity to bring the French fleet to battle. This determination may have led Byron into a rash move. In June 1779 he took the whole British fleet to leeward to St Kitts to cover the departure of the trade convoy to England. Since a couple of ships of the line and frigates would normally have been adequate for this task, Byron's movement may have been a feint to draw the French out in the hope of bringing them to battle as they went to attack a British island. If this was Byron's plan, it produced unfortunate results. After a small force from Martinique had captured St Vincent in late June, d'Estaing took his fleet and troops to attack Grenada, said to be the richest British island in the Caribbean after Jamaica. By the time Byron returned to St Lucia, Grenada had fallen, but he rushed to its relief believing it was still holding out.

On 6 July 1779 Byron's fleet was approaching Grenada when the admiral saw the French fleet coming out of the harbour of St George's in what appeared to be a state of confusion. Byron ordered a general chase, hoping his ships would come up with the French quickly and defeat them in detail. The admiral thought his fleet was still superior in numbers to that of d'Estaing, but it soon became clear that the French had been reinforced and now had twenty-five ships of the line while Byron had only twenty-one. Byron now ordered his ships into line of battle, but before this could be done three of the leading ships were badly damaged by enemy fire. Once both fleets had formed line, the battle became desultory, d'Estaing making little attempt to exploit his numerical superiority. Byron eventually withdrew, and was fortunate that his three crippled ships were not captured by the French. With battle and island both lost Byron withdrew to St Kitts. D'Estaing's fleet appeared off that island on 22 July and found the British fleet anchored in line of battle in Basseterre Roads. The French approached the British line as if to give battle, only to withdraw at the last moment. D'Estaing then took his fleet to leeward, planning eventually to return to North America, but Byron did not follow him. Instead the admiral left his own fleet and returned to England, partly because of ill health, but mainly to explain the loss of Grenada. Byron was not employed again during the American War of Independence.

It is said that, after the peace of 1783, Byron was offered the command in the Mediterranean, but declined it. He had thus no further employment, and died vice-admiral of the white on 10 April 1786. Subsequent assessments of Byron's career have dwelt on his lack of significant success as an explorer and his part in the loss of Grenada. Both elements, once explained in terms of Byron's lack of experience and inability to act under pressure, are now seen as the result of misfortune. Byron was survived by his wife, who died in 1790. Of his sons, the elder, John (1756–1791), known as Mad Jack, was the profligate father of George, sixth Baron Byron. Byron's second son, George Anson (1758–1793), captain of the frigate *Andromache*, provided Sir George Rodney with information of the French fleet's departure from Martinique on 8 April 1782 and thus contributed to the decisive victory in the battle of the Saints, off Dominica, four days later. Of Byron's three surviving daughters, Frances (*d.* 1823) married General Charles Leigh, Juliana Elizabeth (*d.* 1788) married her cousin, William Byron, and Augusta Barbara Charlotte (*d.* 1824) married Vice-Admiral Christopher Parker.

ALAN G. JAMIESON

Sources J. Byron, *The narrative of the Hon. John Byron containing an account of the great distresses suffered by himself and his companions* (1768) · *Byron's journal of his circumnavigation, 1764–1766*, ed. R. E. Gallagher, Hakluyt Society, 2nd ser., 122 (1964) · J. Charnock, ed., *Biographia navalis*, 5 (1797), 423–39 · P. Shankland, *Byron of the Wager* (1975) · A. G. Jamieson, 'The battle of Grenada and Caribbean strategy, 1779', *Naval history: the seventh symposium of the US Naval Academy* [1988], ed. W. B. Cogar and P. Sine (Wilmington, DE, 1988), 55–62 · A. L. Rowse, *The Byrons and the Trevanions* (1978) · J. Hawkesworth, ed., *An account of the voyages undertaken by the order of his present majesty … by Commodore Byron, Captain Wallis, Captain Carteret, and Captain Cook*, 3 vols. (1773) · N. A. M. Rodger, *The insatiable earl: a life of John Montagu, fourth earl of Sandwich* (1993) · D. Syrett, *The Royal Navy in American waters, 1775–1783* (1989) · P. Mackesy, *The war for America, 1775–1783* (1964) · G. Williams, *The great South Sea: English voyages and encounters, 1570–1750* (1997) · Burke, *Peerage* · *DNB* · R. Cock, 'Precursors of Cook: the voyages of the *Dolphin*, 1764–8', *Mariner's Mirror*, 85 (1999), 30–52

Archives Bodl. Oxf., corresp. and papers, incl. wife's · Bodl. Oxf., logbook · NMM, journal | PRO, letters to admiralty and Edward Hay, PRO 30/20

Likenesses J. Reynolds, oils, 1759, NMM · line print (*The nautical lover*), BM, NPG; repro. in *Town and Country Magazine* (1773)

Byron, Sir Nicholas (*bap.* **1596**, *d.* **1648**), royalist army officer, was baptized on 6 March 1596, the second son of Sir John Byron (*c.*1560–1623) of Newstead, Nottinghamshire, and his wife, Margaret (*bap.* 1559, *d.* 1623), daughter of Sir William Fitzwilliam of Milton, Northamptonshire. He was uncle to the royalist commander John *Byron, first Baron Byron of Rochdale.

Nicholas Byron was admitted to Emmanuel College, Cambridge, as a fellow-commoner in 1612 (he matriculated but apparently did not graduate), and to Lincoln's Inn in 1625. He was knighted in 1630, and created a DCL at Oxford in 1642. He married Sophia (*d.* 1654x57), daughter of Charles Lambert of Nijmegen, the Netherlands, governor of Breda, and had five children with her.

Byron's family originated from Lancashire, acquired Newstead Abbey at the dissolution of the monasteries, and by the seventeenth century had their main interests in Nottinghamshire. Nicholas received no major inheritance from his father. His principal property was the manor of Gaynes Park, near Epping, Essex, which came to him in reversion from his mother in 1634. He let the estate while he pursued a military career.

By the late 1630s Byron was captain of a company of foot in the regiment of English volunteers fighting against the Habsburgs in the Netherlands. He also assisted Charles I's sister, Elizabeth of Bohemia, carrying letters from her to the English court about the vexed question of how to achieve the restoration of her lands. In January 1639 Byron was made a colonel for the first bishops' war against Scotland. He occupied one of the islands outside Edinburgh with '1,500 good men, well commanded' (*CSP dom., 1639*, 233). But the English forces were never adequate. Later that year, as Charles tried to revive the failing enterprise, Byron joined the council of war and gave advice about military plans. He was appointed governor of Carlisle for the resumption of hostilities. But even the faithful Byron could not ignore the obstacles which the project faced. In June 1640 he returned empty-handed from a mission to collect coat and conduct money from Lincolnshire, and two months later he declined a similar task in Hertfordshire, complaining to Secretary Vane, 'The King says "send Byron to them, he will take order with them:" but Byron has no mind to be made a moon-calf, and advance the king's service nothing by it' (ibid., 1640, 617).

When the first civil war began Byron was immediately at the centre of the king's military organization. In August 1642 he took a detachment from the embryo royal army to bolster the cause in the east midlands by seizing munitions from local magazines. In the autumn, as the king's forces grew, three infantry brigades were formed, and Byron commanded the most prestigious: about 2000 men, including the king's life guard. His career amply bears out the tradition that Charles so valued his ability that 'in warlike engagements he would have him always near him' (Byron, 42).

At the battle of Edgehill on 23 October 1642 Byron's brigade constituted the left centre of the royalist infantry, and bore the brunt of the fighting. The cavalry led by his nephew John were initially successful but then disappeared from the field, and the parliamentarian horse launched a counter-attack. Byron's men repulsed the first assault, but the royalist right collapsed, and the whole weight of the opposing army fell upon Byron's brigade. This time they were driven back, the royal standard was briefly captured, and its bearer, Sir Edmund Verney, killed. Byron himself was slightly wounded. But the royalists retained the momentum to march towards London. Byron was also prominent at the first battle of Newbury on 20 September 1643. His brigade was detailed to support his nephew's cavalry in taking Round Hill, a vital artillery position. After furious fighting they were forced to retreat and take cover from the parliamentarian guns, and they never got more than a temporary foothold on their objective. The royalists had to withdraw to Oxford and the king's advance on London was halted.

Early in 1643 the king had made Byron colonel-general of Cheshire in response to the city of Chester's request for a military expert. Clarendon noted that Byron, 'being a person of great affability and dexterity as well as martial knowledge gave great life to the designs of the well affected there' (Clarendon, *Hist. rebellion*, 2.470). The city was safely secured, but it was a limited success, marred by feuding between Byron as military governor, the townsmen, and the local royalist gentry. Byron saw the weakness of divided authority and begged Prince Rupert that 'it will not be thought fit that I should be left … under the commands of the mayor and his regiment of citizens' (Morrill, 131). Lack of co-ordination frustrated attempts to exploit sequestration powers. The Cheshire committee reported that the scheme raised little money, partly because 'Sir Nicholas Byron claims some rents as his private perquisites' (Hutton, 91). The royalists never gained control of the area beyond Chester and failed to influence the wider conflict.

Byron recognized the narrow base of royalist support. In captured letters to Lord Capel in April 1643 he suggested that if their advance on London and Reading failed, they should retreat westwards, 'and not stay in the midst of an enemy to be surrounded on all sides'. They should fall back on Chester and Shrewsbury, 'where we may countenance such succour as may easily come out of Ireland' (*Portland MSS*, 2.713). At the end of 1643 this analysis was reflected in a systematic attempt by the king to strengthen his forces in Shropshire and Cheshire. However, Byron was to play little part in the ensuing campaigning. It is possible that he had already been superseded as governor of Chester even before he was captured by a parliamentarian force at Ellesmere, Shropshire, while escorting an armaments train from Shrewsbury to Chester. He was quickly exchanged, but was captured a second time when Shrewsbury fell to the parliamentarians on 22 February 1644. His wife tried unsuccessfully to arrange for his release in exchange for Edmund Ludlow, while his nephew Lord Byron was quite adamant when he protested to the parliamentarian commander Sir William Brereton that 'My uncle since his last imprisonment has not been in anyway engaged in his Majesty's army or service' (*Letter Books*, 1.365). Byron was paroled in April and exchanged in May; he appears to have played no further part in the war.

In March 1648 Gaynes Park was sequestered by the parliamentarians. Byron died later that year; his will was proved on 25 December. In 1657 Byron's surviving son, Ernestus, compounded for the estate, and was fined £99, at one tenth of its value. Later the same year he sold it for £3000. Ernestus inherited his father's royalism, and in July 1659 was imprisoned by the council of state for his suspected association with the plot to restore the king.

George Yerby

Sources Clarendon, *Hist. rebellion* • M. Byron, *The Byron chronicle* (1965) • V. Walker, Byron family pedigree, 1949, Notts. Arch., M 24/731 • S. Reid, *All the king's armies: a military history of the English civil war* (1998) • R. Hutton, *The royalist war effort, 1642–1646* (1982) • *The letter books of Sir William Brereton*, ed. R. N. Dore, 1, Lancashire and Cheshire RS, 123 (1984) • J. S. Morrill, *Cheshire, 1630–1660: county government and society during the English revolution* (1974) • *The memoirs of Edmund Ludlow*, ed. C. H. Firth, 2 vols. (1894), vol. 1 • *The diary of Bulstrode Whitelocke, 1605–1675*, ed. R. Spalding, British Academy, Records of Social and Economic History, new ser., 13 (1990) • *VCH Essex*, vol. 3 • *The manuscripts of his grace the duke of Rutland*, 4 vols., HMC, 24 (1888–1905), vol. 1 • *The manuscripts of his grace the duke of Portland*, 10 vols., HMC, 29 (1891–1931), vol. 2 • *CSP dom., 1635–43* • will, PRO, PROB 11/206, sig. 176 • M. A. E. Green, ed., *Calendar of the proceedings of the committee for compounding … 1643–1660*, 5 vols., PRO (1889–92) • G. W. Marshall, ed., *The visitations of the county of Nottingham in the years 1569 and 1614*, Harleian Society, 4 (1871) • Foster, *Alum. Oxon.* • Venn, *Alum. Cant.* • W. P. Baildon, ed., *The records of the Honorable Society of Lincoln's Inn: admissions*, 1 (1896) • A. Collins, *The peerage of England: containing a genealogical and historical account of all the peers of England* • W. A. Shaw, *The knights of England*, 2 (1906), 197

Wealth at death see M. A. E. Green, *Calendar of the proceedings of the committee for compounding*, vol. 5, p. 3245; *VCH Essex*, vol. 3, p. 267

Byron, Robert (1905–1941), traveller and writer on art, was born at Wembley, London, on 26 February 1905, the only son among three children of Eric Byron, civil engineer, and his wife, Margaret, daughter of William Robinson, of Southall Manor, Middlesex. He was educated at Eton College and at Merton College, Oxford, where he obtained a third class in modern history in 1925. At Eton Byron was active in the Society of Arts, where, according to his contemporary Harold Acton, he 'distinguished himself for his provocative tirades' (Acton, 92). The pair did not get on at school but became friends at Oxford, where they discovered a shared taste for Victoriana. Believing that it was not necessary 'to be solemn in order to be serious', they made humour 'one of their symbols' (ibid., 119), and were originators of the social milieu captured by Evelyn Waugh in *Brideshead Revisited*. At one particularly uproarious fancy dress party, staged by the Hypocrites' Club, Byron 'gave a hectic impersonation of the Widow of Windsor'. Few women were present on this occasion, which 'rumour transformed … into a shocking orgy' (ibid., 124). Soon afterwards the club was closed by the proctors.

Acton remembered being somewhat cowed by Byron's self-confidence at Oxford: 'He could not understand what prevented me from rushing into print when I expressed some casual opinion. He saw an article in everything' (Acton, 192). And Byron's first book emanated from his first travels, in 1925 to Greece, a country for which he had a passionate admiration and where, as a distant relative of Lord Byron, his name carried a particular resonance. *Europe in the Looking-Glass* (1926) was a high-spirited account of this undergraduate jaunt, and it was followed during the next four years by three ambitious studies in late Hellenism, of which *The Byzantine Achievement* (1929; repr. 1987) is the most satisfying.

In 1929 Byron travelled to India as special correspondent for the *Daily Express*, and in the next year made a brief journey into Tibet. The first literary result of these experiences was *An Essay on India* (1931) which, in the opinion of the viceroy, Lord Willingdon, contained the best brief statement of Indian political problems at that time. His Tibetan journey was recorded two years later in *First Russia, then Tibet*. A period of journalism in London was followed by a visit to Persia and Afghanistan during 1933 and 1934, an adventure which promoted the best of his books, *The Road to Oxiana* (1937). This may be described as an enquiry into the origins of Islamic art presented in the form of one of the most entertaining travel books of modern times. He wrote it in China during 1935 and 1936 after making the overland journey to the Far East through Russia. *The Road to Oxiana* was reprinted in 1981 with an introduction by Bruce Chatwin. Chatwin considered it 'a work of genius' which he personally elevated 'to the status of "sacred text"' (Chatwin, ix). But it was also an important book. In between the 'bravura passages' (ibid., xvi) Byron was expounding a serious thesis about the significance of Afghan influence on Persian civilization.

In 1936 Byron settled in London, where he found work as a public relations officer with the petroleum information bureau. He had become obsessed with the threat posed to European civilization by Nazism, and confessed to his friend Christopher Sykes: 'It's a queer unexpected situation to find that the only person talking sense in this country is Winston Churchill' (Sykes, 161). Byron visited Germany in 1937 and again in 1938, when he attended the Nuremberg rally 'to see the enemy' (ibid., 166). Each visit intensified his anger: 'I shall have warmonger put on my passport' (ibid., 163). He took 'the extremest imaginable anti-Munich view' (ibid., 168) and conducted a personal crusade against appeasement: he startled the diners at a London club by leaning across a table to ask a Chamberlainite member of parliament: 'Are you in German pay?' (ibid., 173).

The violence of his behaviour, though, earned Byron disapproval in high places and when war broke a first-rate appointment was denied him. Disappointed, he accepted work as a sub-editor in the overseas news department of the British Broadcasting Corporation. While on his way to Cairo as a special war correspondent for a group of English newspapers he was drowned by enemy action, when his ship was torpedoed off Stornoway on 24 February 1941. He was unmarried. He had greeted the war with characteristic levity when it finally came: 'Well, there's one thing to be thankful for: the post-war decadence ought to be even better than the last' (Sykes, 175).

Byron's writing showed continuous growth and even his lightest things, such as *How we Celebrate the Coronation* (1937), were written with all his energy and care. His development was very rapid and while still a young man he became, what he remained, the only writer of his time to convey a vivid idea of Byzantine art and civilization to the common reader. His first books sometimes erred on the side of massiveness of expression but his most considered and interesting performance, *The Road to Oxiana*, was written with such charm and verve that most contemporary readers did not recognize it as a serious and original contribution to Islamic studies. Paradoxically it was better appreciated by the specialists, for whom he had no liking, than by the unspecialized readers to whom it was addressed. He may be said to have anticipated views which later scholarship has adduced from fuller evidence than was then available.

Byron was

> moderately fat, short, with very fair hair, a penetrating rolling eye … and a voice whose quiet lazy intonations never concealed the abounding vitality behind it, and which, on sometimes small, and sometimes not easily detectable provocation, broke out into violent spatter of invective. (Sykes, 81–2)

He was of a polemical disposition and unfortunately he allowed this to leave blemishes on all his books, even his best. *The Byzantine Achievement* includes a bitter condemnation of the Roman Catholic church, and *An Essay on India* seven pages of vituperation directed at the 'anti-dominion' party in Britain in the 1930s. There is some disproportion in his work as a result, but the fault is compensated by the delight which goes with intense enthusiasm and mastery of style. Byron was the subject of the principal essay in Christopher Sykes's *Four Studies in Loyalty* (1946) and a selection of his letters to his mother was published in 1991, edited by his sister Lucy Butler.

C. H. Sykes, *rev.* Mark Pottle

Sources C. Sykes, *Four studies in loyalty* (1946) • H. Acton, *Memoirs of an aesthete* (1948) • personal knowledge (1959) • L. Butler, *Robert Byron: letters home* (1991) • B. Chatwin, introduction, in R. Byron, *The road to Oxiana* (1994)

Archives BL, corresp. with Macmillans, Add. MS 55229 • LPL, corresp. with John Douglas

Likenesses A. M. Daintrey, portrait; in possession of family, 1959

Byron, Sir Thomas (*c.*1610–1644), royalist army officer, was the fifth of the seven sons of Sir John Byron (*d.* 1625) of Newstead, Nottinghamshire, and his wife, Anne Molyneux, daughter of Sir Richard Molyneux of Sefton, Lancashire, and brother of John *Byron, first Baron Byron. Byron's family originated from Lancashire and acquired Newstead Abbey at the dissolution of the monasteries; by the seventeenth century they were established among the Nottinghamshire elite. Thomas married Catherine Braine (*d.* 1676), the daughter of Henry Braine, and they had two sons, Thomas and John, both of whom predeceased him in infancy.

Lucy Hutchinson, a family connection, noted that the Byron brothers were 'bred up in arms' and 'all passionately the King's' when civil war broke out (Hutchinson, 61). Byron fought at Edgehill in October 1642, was knighted, and was said to have had a degree conferred on him at Oxford in November. Later that month, as part of Prince Rupert's forces harrying the Thames valley, Byron and his brother John occupied Bulstrode Whitelocke's estate at Fawley Court. The undisciplined soldiers ransacked the house. But when Byron discovered Whitelocke's children hiding at a servant's farm, he treated them kindly, saying 'it were a barbarous thing to hurt the pretty, innocent children' (*Diary of Bulstrode Whitelocke*, 139).

Clarendon called Byron a 'gentleman of great courage and good conduct', and regarded him as the *de facto* commander of the prince of Wales's regiment, under the titular authority of the earl of Cumberland (Clarendon, *Hist. rebellion*, 2.476–7). He was mainly noted for his action at the battle of Hopton Heath on 19 March 1643. After the earl of Northampton had been killed leading a charge, Byron led another charge, which drove the remaining parliamentarian cavalry from the field and overran the enemy gun line. He was then forced to withdraw by a wound to his thigh. But the battered parliamentarians later withdrew completely, and the royalists' victory reinforced their hold on Stafford, and further consolidated their position in the midlands at the time.

Ironically Byron was killed by one of his own soldiers—a Captain Hurst, who attacked him because of a pay dispute as he left his lodgings in Oxford on 7 December 1643. Hurst was executed a week later, and Byron died of his chest wound on 5 February 1644. He was buried in Christ Church Cathedral, Oxford, four days later. His widow was buried on 11 February 1676, in Westminster Abbey.

GEORGE YERBY

Sources L. Hutchinson, *Memoirs of the life of Colonel Hutchinson*, ed. J. Sutherland (1973) • *The diary of Bulstrode Whitelocke, 1605–1675*, ed. R. Spalding, British Academy, Records of Social and Economic History, new ser., 13 (1990) • Clarendon, *Hist. rebellion* • M. Byron, *The Byron chronicle* (1965) • S. Reid, *All the king's armies* (1998) • *Thoroton's history of Nottinghamshire*, ed. J. Throsby, 3 vols. (1797) • Wood, *Ath. Oxon.* • *A collection of original letters and papers, concerning the affairs of England from the year 1641 to 1660. Found among the duke of Ormonde's papers*, ed. T. Carte, 1 (1739) • *The life, diary, and correspondence of Sir William Dugdale*, ed. W. Hamper (1827) • GEC, *Peerage*, new edn, vol. 2 • V. Walker, Byron family pedigree, 1949, Notts. Arch., M 24/731

Likenesses W. N. Gardiner, pen and wash drawing, AM Oxf.

Byrth, Thomas (1793–1849), Church of England clergyman and author, was the son of John Byrth, of Stoke Damerell, Devon, a man of Irish descent, who married Mary Hobling, a member of an old Cornish family. He was born at Plymouth Dock on 11 September 1793, and received his early education in that town and at Launceston, under Richard Cope LLD. For five years (1809–14) he served his apprenticeship to the Cookworthys, well-known chemists and druggists in the west of England, and during that period started, with other young men, the *Plymouth Magazine*, which expired with its sixth number on 19 November 1814. After this he passed some years as a schoolmaster, but in 1818 he matriculated from Magdalen Hall, Oxford. Hitherto he had been in sympathy with the Society of Friends, but on 21 October 1819 he was baptized into the Church of England at St Andrew's Church, Plymouth. He was ordained to the curacy of Diptford, near Totnes, in April 1823, remaining there until 1825, and took his degrees of BA and MA in the spring of 1826. After that he was at Oxford as a tutor, but this occupation ceased in 1827, when he became the incumbent of St James, Latchford, near Warrington. In the same year, on 19 June, he married Mary Kingdom, *née* Stewart; they had seven surviving children. In 1834 he was appointed to the more important and more lucrative rectory of Wallasey in Cheshire, where he died on Sunday night, 28 October 1849, having preached two sermons that day. After Byrth's death £4000 was collected for his widow and their seven children. She died on 20 February 1879, aged eighty. The west window of Wallasey church was filled with stained glass in Byrth's memory.

Byrth became BD on 17 October 1839 and took his degree of DD two days later. He was an evangelical in religion and a whig in politics. His scholarship was thorough, and he was possessed of poetic taste and antiquarian enthusiasm. He published many sermons and addresses, and was engaged in controversy with the Revd J. H. Thom on the unitarian interpretation of the New Testament. In 1848 he edited the sermons of the Revd Thomas Tattershall DD, incumbent of St Augustine's Church, Liverpool, and prefixed to them a memoir of the author. His own *Remains*, with a memoir by the Revd G. R. Moncreiff, was published in 1851, and a sermon on his death, preached by the Revd John Tobin in St John's Church, Liscard, on 4 November 1849, was published in the same year.

W. P. COURTNEY, *rev.* H. C. G. MATTHEW

Sources *GM*, 2nd ser., 33 (1850), 324 • *Remains of Thomas Byrth … with a memoir of his life by the Rev. G. R. Moncreiff* (1851) • G. Ormerod, *The history of the county palatine and city of Chester*, 2nd edn, ed. T. Helsby, 3 vols. (1882)

Bysshe, Sir Edward (*c.*1610–1679), herald and politician, was one of the seven children of Edward Bysshe MP (*d.* 1655), of Burstow, Surrey, and his wife, Mary, daughter of John Turner of Ham, Bletchingley, Surrey. The family had been at Burstow since the fifteenth century, and there his father, a successful lawyer in the court of wards, built their residence, Smallfield Place. In 1633, according to Wood, Bysshe attended Trinity College, Oxford, aged eighteen (Wood, *Ath. Oxon.*, 3.1218). He may be confused with his brother Thomas who matriculated from Trinity in 1634 aged nineteen. Bysshe entered Lincoln's Inn in 1627, and was called to the bar in 1634. In 1635 he gave his age as twenty-five (Comber, 65). On 5 November 1635 he married Margaret (*d.* 1698), daughter of John Greene, a judge of the sheriff's court and member of Lincoln's Inn. The marriage produced at least three sons.

On 3 November 1640 Bysshe entered parliament as the member for Bletchingley, succeeding his father. He aligned himself with the opposition, taking the covenant in February 1644. He served in two protectorate parliaments, representing Reigate in 1654 and Gatton in 1659. His political sympathies were nevertheless mixed. John Gibbon accused him of being 'imbued with the Presbyterian spirit' (Wagner, 257), yet he was implicated in conspiracy, claiming in 1651 that 'his father and he could have a 1,000 men in readinesse there upon the least opportunity' (*Portland MSS*, 1.582).

In 1641 and 1645 Bysshe was a member of parliamentary committees regulating the heralds. Consequently, the Commons appointed him Garter king of arms on 20 October 1646, and he supervised the earl of Essex's funeral shortly afterwards. In 1650 he received the additional office of Clarenceux. In these capacities he provided hospitality to scholars such as Dugdale and Dodsworth, who called him 'the Host on the Hill' (Wagner, 260).

Bysshe edited a collection of works on heraldry, *Nicolai Uptoni de studio militari, libri quatuor; Iohn. de Bado Aureo tractatus de armis; Henrici Spelmanni aspilogia* (1654). He also published three treatises on Brahmanism, *Palladius de gentibus Indiae et Bragmanibus; S. Ambrosius de moribus Brachmanorum; Anonymus de Bragmanibus* (1665; reissued 1668). Neither volume was of great scholarly merit, although the first made accessible two of the earliest known heraldic treatises and included illustrations of several seals.

At the Restoration, Bysshe failed to be returned as member for Bletchingley, and was ejected from the office of Garter king, which was given to the royalist Edward

Walker. He fought successfully to retain the office of Clarenceux. In 1661 he successfully recontested his parliamentary seat, and was knighted on 20 April. He subsequently renovated Smallfield Place, displaying the ancient arms of de la Bishe and quarterings which he had assumed in lieu of his family's traditional coat. This pretence led Walker to charge him with forgery and involved Bysshe in protracted litigation. In the 1660s Bysshe increasingly neglected his duties. Although a member of Parliament until his death, he was named to only seven committees. He undertook several visitations for the College of Arms, yet without the vigour of his contemporary Dugdale. He provided only the briefest accounts of each family, was lax about enforcing his rights as Clarenceux in the localities, and failed to finish the visitation returns. The college repeatedly ordered him to submit his paperwork without success, eventually appealing to the king and sequestering his fees. In 1677 the college appointed a deputy to finish the incomplete visitations in return for his fees, but Bysshe died before this took effect.

Despite receiving £100 for attending a parliamentary session, Bysshe was in debt. In November 1679 he sold his 'very choice library' (Wood, *Ath. Oxon.*, 3.1219), the contents recorded in *Bibliotheca Bissaeana* (1679). He died on 15 December 1679 in the parish of St Paul, Covent Garden, in London, and was buried at night at St Olave Jewry, where his wife's nephew was the minister.

Bysshe's failures in later life overshadowed his reputation as the herald who had preserved the records of the College of Arms and made them available for study during the interregnum. He was little mourned by the heralds, who had difficulty retrieving records from his widow. The earl marshal wrote: 'since I have for these many yeares without successe endevored his conversion to his duty and breatheren, and could never wash this blackamore into any other coler, I am I confesse very little moretifyed at his death' (Wagner, 295). John Aubrey denounced him as one who 'eat the Bread of Loyalists and accepted of a Pension … from the Sequestrators' (J. Aubrey, *Antiquities of Surrey*, 1718, 3.72). PETER SHERLOCK

Sources A. Wagner, *Heralds of England: a history of the office and College of Arms* (1967) • HoP, *Commons, 1660–90*, 1.760 • Wood, *Ath. Oxon.*, new edn, 3.1218–20 • J. Comber, *Sussex genealogies*, 3 vols. (1931–3), vol. 2, pp. 64–8 • *Le Neve's Pedigrees of the knights*, ed. G. W. Marshall, Harleian Society, 8 (1873) • *The manuscripts of his grace the duke of Portland*, 10 vols., HMC, 29 (1891–1931), vol. 1

Archives BL, corresp. and papers, Add. MS 22883 • Coll. Arms, visitation books and papers | BL, Add. MS 14284

Bysshe, Edward (*fl.* **1702–1714**), writer, was possibly the eldest son of Henry Bysshe of Buxted, Sussex, a barrister, and his wife, Anne James (*b.* 1660/61). If so, the poet Percy Bysshe Shelley was a distant cousin, as Edward Bysshe's great-grandmother was a direct ancestor of Shelley. Another possibility is that he was the eldest son of George Bysshe of Burstow, Surrey, and his wife, Sarah; he would then be nephew to Sir Edward Bysshe, Clarenceux king of arms. Bysshe styles himself 'Gent.' on title-pages and there was a strong concentration of Bysshe gentry in Sussex.

In 1702 Bysshe's *The Art of English Poetry* appeared. It consisted of three separately paginated sections: 'Rules for making English verse', 'A Dictionary of Rhymes', and 'A collection of the most natural, agreeable, & noble thoughts … that are to be found in the best English poets', this latter, by far the longest section, forming a dictionary of quotations arranged by theme. The rhyming dictionary was the first serious example of its kind. The dictionary of quotations, which Bysshe claims to have begun in 1692 at the suggestion of the earl of Lauderdale, and which drew heavily on Restoration poets, especially Dryden, was similarly innovative and influential, though Bysshe had models in pedagogic compilations such as Joshua Poole's *English Parnassus* (1657). Bysshe derived his 'Rules for making English verse' from a French model, Claude Lancelot's *Quatre traitez de poesies* (1663); despite forcing English verse to fit a strict syllabic system, the 'Rules' remained dominant in English prosodic theory for over a century.

Bysshe's *Art of Poetry* was heavily criticized for its mechanistic reductiveness, and as heavily used for its supreme convenience. Hogarth places a copy of the book on the desk of his *Distrest Poet* (1736), but Johnson, Goldsmith, and even Blake owned copies, and the majority of the poetry and drama quoted in Richardson's novels is drawn from Bysshe. New editions of the book were published in 1705, 1708, 1710, 1714, 1718, 1724, 1737, and 1762. Bysshe appears to have supervised the revisions at least as far as 1708; the 'Collection' in particular was greatly expanded. Bysshe published in 1714 another handbook, the *British Parnassus*, containing an alternative rhyming dictionary and commonplace book; this was less successful and it was passed off as volumes 3 and 4 of the *Art of Poetry* (1718).

Bysshe translated Xenophon's *Memorabilia* as *Memorable Things of Socrates* (1712, with a dedication to Lord Ashburnham dated London, 24 November 1711). His edition of *Original Letters Written to the Earl of Arlington by Sir Richard Bulstrode* (1712, dedicated to George, Lord Cardigan) suggests Jacobite sympathies; if his reference to Lauderdale is to Richard Maitland, the fourth earl, this would be confirmed, but his dedication of the *Art of Poetry* to Edmund Dunch, a well-known whig MP, stands against it, and the other dedications suggest mixed loyalties. He signalled his intention to publish Bulstrode's essays and other works, but when these appeared (edited by Bulstrode's son, in 1715 and 1721) he was apparently not involved, prompting the suggestion that he died before 1715.

PAUL BAINES

Sources A. D. Culler, 'Edward Bysshe and the poet's handbook', *Publications of the Modern Language Association of America*, 63 (1948), 858–85 • E. Bysshe, *The visitation of Sussex Anno Domini 1662*, ed. A. W. Hughes Clarke (1937), 20–22 • J. Comber, *Sussex genealogies*, 3 vols. (1931–3), vol. 2, p. 68 • P. B. Shelley, *The works in verse and prose*, ed. H. B. Forman, 8 vols. (1880), vol. 5, pp. xxxiv, xl • G. J. Armytage, ed., *A visitation of the county of Surrey, begun … 1662, finished … 1668*, Harleian Society, 60 (1910), 22–3 • M. E. Connaughton, 'Richardson's familiar quotations: *Clarissa* and Bysshe's *Art of English poetry*', *Philological Quarterly*, 60 (1981), 183–95 • P. Dixon, 'Edward Bysshe and Pope's *Shakespeare*', *N&Q*, 209 (1964), 292–3

Bythell, John Kenworthy (1840–1916), businessman, was born on 20 April 1840 at 83 Great Jackson Street, Hulme, Manchester, the son of James Bythell, a calenderer and maker-up employed in the city's shipping trade, and his wife, Sarah, *née* Southell. He joined the merchant firm of Gaddum & Co. and served from 1864 as resident partner in Bombay during the cotton boom induced by the American Civil War. There he acquired a thorough knowledge of the links between commerce, shipping, railways, and ports. He became a prime mover in the construction of the great harbour works of the port and was elected chairman of the Bombay chamber of commerce in 1872, returning home in 1875.

In 1886 Bythell became a founder member of the Manchester Ship Canal consultative committee and was converted by a study of the evidence from disbelief in the project to faith in its practicality. He agreed to join the board of the canal company if Daniel Adamson, the original promoter whose financial competence was now being questioned, ceased to be chairman. On 19 February 1887 Adamson resigned, and Bythell became a director, as well as chairman of the finance committee. On 20 July 1894 he was elected chairman in succession to Lord Egerton of Tatton (1832–1909). As such he became the first paid, resident, and full-time chief executive officer in the history of the company, which was the largest business firm in the region. Bythell assumed office six months after the opening of the canal to traffic and did so at a critical juncture in its affairs, created by the bitter opposition of Liverpool, by the formation of hostile shipping conferences, by the unanticipated reduction of railway rates, and by the lack of essential warehousing facilities. He averted bankruptcy by using the revenues generated by the Bridgwater Canal and by persuading Manchester corporation to levy from 1896 a special ship canal rate. He attracted trade by extending the port's facilities, by encouraging their use by means of a special 'promotional tariff', and by avoiding conflict with potential clients. Through negotiation with his friends among the Hindu merchants of Bombay he secured the conclusion of the vital contract of 29 December 1894 for the shipment of piece-goods direct from Manchester to Bombay. He extended the functions of the ship canal company far outside the normal range of a port authority. In particular he encouraged the formation of a clutch of companies intended to provide the necessary facilities and to attract traffic to the port, especially the Manchester Cotton Association (1894), the Manchester Ship Canal Warehousing Company Ltd (1895), and Manchester Liners Ltd (1898).

Bythell's talents were primarily those of a merchant, a financier, and a diplomat. His unresting activity helped to raise Manchester from the status of the sixteenth port of the kingdom in 1894 to that of the fourth in 1906. Manchester ranked second in the export of cotton yarn from 1894 and second in the export of piece-goods from 1895. It became the second largest importer of raw cotton from 1896 and the second largest importer of petroleum from 1903. Bythell established a permanent partnership with the local corporation in 1904 at the price of conceding to it a perpetual majority upon the board of directors. He was primarily responsible for the development of the Port of Manchester, translating a legal concept and an engineering achievement into a commercial reality. He shattered Liverpool's historic monopoly and crowned his career by paying a first dividend, for the year 1915, to his loyal ordinary shareholders.

John Kenworthy Bythell (1840–1916), by Thomas Edwin Mostyn

A Manchester Scot by origin, a Liberal in politics, and a Presbyterian in religion, Bythell devoted all his energies to business and lived entirely for the ship canal, becoming its 'second founder' (*Manchester Guardian*, 19 Aug 1916, 6). He did not become a director of other companies save as a representative of the canal company, serving from 1889 on the board of the Manchester chamber of commerce and from 1897 on that of the Manchester Dry Docks Company Ltd, established in 1891. He guided the destiny of the company for twenty-two years and retired in 1916, having throughout his life shunned all personal publicity and declined all national honours. His wife, Elizabeth, died in 1909, aged seventy-six. Bythell died at Fernhill, Singleton Road, Broughton, Salford, on 18 August 1916 and was buried at Kensal church, Salford, on 22 August.

D. A. FARNIE

Sources Minute books of the board of directors of the Manchester Ship Canal Co., 1887–1916 • Manchester Ship Canal Co., Reports of shareholders' meetings, 1894–1917 • D. A. Farnie, *The Manchester Ship Canal and the rise of the port of Manchester, 1894–1975* (1980) • D. A. Farnie, 'The Manchester Ship Canal, 1894–1913', *Trade and transport: essays in economic history in honour of T. S. William*, ed. W. H. Chaloner and B. M. Ratcliffe (1977), 173–213 • D. A. Farnie, 'Bythell, John Kenworthy', *DBB* • 'Mr. John K. Bythell', *Manchester Faces and Places*, 10 (1893–4), 56–7 • *Manchester City News* (19 Aug 1916), 6 • *Manchester Guardian* (19 Aug 1916) • *Manchester Guardian* (23 Aug 1916) •

P. M. Hodson, ed., *The Manchester Ship Canal: a guide to historical sources* (1985) • *CGPLA Eng. & Wales* (1916) • d. cert. [Elizabeth Bythell] • b. cert.

Archives Lancs. RO, J. W. G. Beaumont papers • Man. CL, Manchester Association of Importers and Exporters, minutes, 1908–16 • Man. CL, Manchester Cotton Association, minutes of the board, 1894–1917

Likenesses T. E. Mostyn, portrait, Man. City Gall. [*see illus.*] • Sarony, portrait, repro. in *Manchester Faces and Places*, 5 (April 1894), 57 • portrait, Peel Holdings Ltd; repro. in Farnie, *The Manchester Ship Canal and the rise of the port*, frontispiece • portrait, repro. in B. T. Leech, *History of the Manchester Ship Canal*, 2 (1907), 38

Wealth at death £18,563 0s. 11*d*.: probate, 20 Oct 1916, *CGPLA Eng. & Wales*

Bythner, Victorinus (*c*.1605–*c*.1670), grammarian and university teacher, was born at Głębowicach in the Sandomierz district of south-eastern Poland, one of several sons of Bartholomäus Bythner (1559/60–1629), a Catholic theologian of Calvinistic beliefs and the author of several influential works highly regarded by European Catholics and protestants alike. The Bythner family was evidently of German ancestry.

Bythner was 'blessed with a most admirable geny for the obtaining of the tongues' (Wood, *Ath. Oxon.*, 3.675). Undoubtedly his native linguistic facility was enhanced by his youthful exposure to languages spoken in central Europe and by his subsequent education in Germany and the Netherlands. In June 1629 Bythner matriculated at the University of Frankfurt an der Oder, and on 30 May 1632 he became a theology student at the University of Groningen, where, under the direction of Franciscus Gomerus, he refined his command of the Hebrew language and tutored another pupil of Gomerus, the precocious Jacobus Alting.

By 1635 Bythner was at Christ Church, Oxford, where he lectured on Hebrew in the great refectory before the outbreak of the civil war. A 'useful person' (Wood, *Ath. Oxon.*, 3.675), Bythner published five works for the benefit of his students, including *Nova et methodica institutio linguae Hebraeae & Chaldaeae* (1635), dedicated to his patrons, the churchmen of the Sandomierz region, Poland; *Praxis grammatica Hebraeae* (1635), dedicated to Sir Arthur Hesilrige and indicating his strong puritan sympathies; and the influential work known as his Hebrew grammar, *Lingua eruditorum … nova et methodica institutio linguae sanctae* (1638).

Bythner's life at Christ Church was disrupted by the civil war, during which, after the battle of Edgehill, Charles I and his army entered Oxford on 29 October 1642. The king took up his quarters in the college, and the army's animals were penned in the quadrangle. At or shortly after this time Bythner, who was no stranger to conflict and violence (in 1613 his father had been attacked by a group of Cracow students and severely injured), abandoned Oxford for Cambridge. His life and activities during the civil war and Commonwealth period are not well recorded. He lived in Cambridge, where his *Clavis linguae sanctae* (1648) was published, and in London, where he published his last work and *magnum opus*, *Lyra prophetica Davidis regis, sive, Analysis critico-practica psalmorum* (1650), a lexicon for the critical and grammatical study of the Hebrew psalter. Bythner returned to Oxford, however, for the accounts of Magdalen College record a payment of £1 to him in 1650 for unspecified (presumably teaching) services rendered.

About 1664 Bythner retired to Cornwall, where he 'practised physic … for some time, and concluded his last day' (Wood, *Ath. Oxon.*, 3.676). In Cornwall he remained in contact with other puritan scholars and tutored members of the Prideaux family near Padstow, perhaps the younger children of Edmund Prideaux of Place House, Padstow, sheriff of Cornwall in 1664. Among Prideaux's older children was Humphrey Prideaux, later dean of Norwich, who in 1691 was offered (but refused) the chair of oriental languages at Oxford. It has been assumed that Bythner died near Padstow about 1670; it has been stated, however, that he died at Deventer in the eastern Netherlands (Heurtebize).

'Bythner's grammatical works, though written in curiously faulty Latin, are models of lucid and compact arrangement, and continued long in use' (*DNB*). His Hebrew grammar (*Lingua eruditorum*) was edited by J. A. Hessey (*Institutio linguae sanctae*, 1853). *Lyra prophetica Davidis regis*, his best-known and most influential work, was twice published in the nineteenth century (at Edinburgh in 1818, and at Glasgow in 1823) and translated by Thomas Dee as *The Lyre of David, or, An Analysis of the Psalms* (Dublin, 1836; revised 1847 by Nathan Benmohel). PAGE LIFE

Sources Wood, *Ath. Oxon.*, new edn, 3.675–6, 923 • *Polski słownik biograficzny*, 3 (1937), 181–4 • E. Friedlaender, *Aeltere Universitäts-Matrikeln. I: Universität Frankfurt a. O.*, 3 vols. (1887–91); repr. (1965), vol. 1, p. 700 • P. C. Molhuysen and P. J. Blok, eds., *Nieuw Nederlandsch biografisch woordenboek*, 3 (Leiden, 1914), 191–2 • J. P. de Bie, J. Loosjes, and L. A. van Langeraad, eds., *Biographisch woordenboek van protestantsche godgeleerden in Nederland*, 1 (The Hague, 1919?), 119 • J. Mazerski, 'Victorinus Bythner', *N&Q*, 175 (1938), 135 • B. Heurtebize, 'Bythner, Victorinus', *Dictionnaire de la Bible*, ed. F. Vigoureux, 1 (1895) • W. D. Macray, *A register of the members of St Mary Magdalen College, Oxford*, 8 vols. (1894–1915), vol. 4, p. 7 • M. Feingold, 'Oriental studies', *Hist. U. Oxf.* 4: *17th-cent. Oxf.*, 449–503, esp. 460n, 463 • W. Orme, *Bibliotheca biblica* (1824), 72 • J. Michaud and L. G. Michaud, eds., *Biographie universelle ancienne et moderne*, 84 vols. (1811–62), vol. 4, p. 578 • [J. C. F. Hoefer], ed., *Nouvelle biographie générale*, 6 (1853), 146 • C. G. Jöcher, *Allgemeines Gelehrten-Lexicon*, 1 (1750); repr. (1960), 1528 • P. Gregg, *King Charles I* (1984), 369

Archives BL, autograph, Egerton MS 1324, fol. 106

Bywater, Ingram (1840–1914), Greek scholar, was born in Islington, London, on 27 June 1840, the only son of John Ingram Bywater (1812/13–1864), a customs clerk, and his wife, Emma, *née* Marshall (*d*. September 1903). He was educated at private schools, University College School, London (1853–6), King's College School, London, where he started Greek, and at Queen's College, Oxford, where he matriculated as a scholar in 1858.

As an undergraduate Bywater was the pupil of Jowett and Robinson Ellis, and the friend of Pater and Swinburne. He read and was influenced by Carlyle. His father generously supported his education, paying for private coaching by James Bryce and T. H. Green. He gained a first in classical moderations in 1860, and in *literae humaniores*

Ingram Bywater (1840–1914), by John Singer Sargent, 1901

in 1862 (BA 1862, MA 1865). In 1863 he was elected to an open fellowship at Exeter College. As a young fellow he became a close friend of Mark Pattison and his accomplished wife [*see* Dilke, Emilia Francis (1840–1904)]; they influenced his attitudes. With them Bywater travelled on the continent, visiting many libraries and museums. Pattison collected early printed books, and Bywater's Sunday visits to his lodgings were presumably partly devoted to bibliography. Pattison was also an uncompromising advocate of scholarship, who alleged that the atmosphere of Oxford was inimical to study: 'a Fellowship is the grave of learning'. Bywater's opinions were more moderate, and his manner of expression more conciliatory; but he stated that research was undervalued and undersupported at Oxford, and that the college tutorial system left too little time and initiative to the student or his teachers. He became a friend of William Morris and of Dilke, and was an early supporter of the Society for the Protection of Ancient Buildings (1877), who always lamented the effect in Oxford of the neo-Gothic revival.

During Bywater's twenty years as a tutor most of his time was spent teaching and on the studies for which he became famous. The publication in 1877 of his edition of the Fragments of Heraclitus won him an assured position in the world of European scholarship, and he was invited by the Prussian Academy of Sciences to edit the works of Priscianus Lydus (published 1886). He contributed to German journals and his relations with continental scholars, notably Professor Jacob Bernays, of Bonn, were cordial and fruitful. He travelled on the continent, but never visited Greece.

Charles Cannan used to say that though Bywater was doubtless an eminent Aristotelian, it was to be deplored that he had not become a bookseller, in which profession he must have been pre-eminent. Actually, he might have become librarian of the Bodleian. The curators, of whom Pattison was one, and Coxe, the veteran librarian, wanted him; and in 1879 he accepted, experimentally, the post of sub-librarian. He found the duties too irksome. He was expected routinely to read manuscripts and shrank from doing so: 'those who care for MSS. *per se* are usually dull dogs' (Jackson, 88). He resigned in 1880. He declined the headship of Exeter College, offered in 1887.

In 1884 Bywater was appointed to a new readership in Greek. On 19 August 1885 he married Charlotte (*d*. 17 Feb 1908), widow of Hans William Sotheby (*d*. 1874), formerly fellow of Exeter College, and daughter of Charles John Cornish of Salcombe Regis, from the well-known Devon family of Cornish; they had no children. She had ample means and varied accomplishments, literary and artistic. They lived in term-time at a 'very ordinary villa' (Jackson, 212) at 6 Norham Gardens, on the edge of the university parks, and in vacation at Mrs Bywater's London house, 93 Onslow Square, Kensington. This was Bywater's real home until his death; and there, with his wife's help, he gradually increased his remarkable collection of early classical books, on which he spent much.

In 1893 Jowett died, and Gladstone nominated Bywater, whose claims were supported by the testimony of German scholars, as regius professor of Greek. The popularizer and translator was thus succeeded by a scholar more purely scientific: Bywater's aim was 'the perfection of learning' (Jackson, 126). He occupied the chair until 1908. He continued to lecture, especially on Plato's *Republic* and Aristotle's *Poetics*. Those who believed college particularism or examination demands prevented the university from making the most of its professors noted that few undergraduates attended in the Schools lectures which formerly had crowded Exeter College hall.

Following his wife's death in 1908 Bywater resigned his professorship and retired to his London house. In 1909 he published the crowning labour of his Aristotelian studies, the monumental edition of the *Poetics*. Thereafter he undertook no large work of his own, but he continued to contribute occasional articles to the *Journal of Philology* (of which he had been an editor since 1879), and to help scholars by reading their proofs.

As an editor of Greek texts Bywater was the first of the English scholars of his generation. He had a wide familiarity with manuscripts, an unrivalled knowledge of the history of classical learning and the editorial art, and a fine sense of what he called the *Sprachgebrauch*. He added untiring industry and keen insight into the logical sequence of his author's thought. It has been objected to his interpretations of Aristotle that he was too much a grammarian and too little a philosopher; but this apparent limitation was due not to narrowness but to a considered scepticism. In the preface to the *Poetics* he reminds us 'that the very idea of a Theory of Art is modern, and that our present use of this term "Art" does not go further back than the age of Winckelmann and Goethe' (Jackson, 136). This was with oblique reference to the work on the *Poetics* of Samuel Henry Butcher, much of which Bywater regarded as irrelevant. In private he was more outspoken: 'You must not expect from me anything about fine art, for I don't think Aristotle said anything about it' (ibid., 136).

Scholars evaluating Bywater's published work have laid stress on the quality of its form, the laborious accuracy of his indexes, and the fine judgement which by a punctuation change clarified an obscure passage. But his editions of Heraclitus and Aristotle, and even the ampler commentary on the *Poetics*, reflect one side only of his vast learning and his catholic humanism. His profound veneration for Aristotle was untinged by superstition. His statement in 1914 to a *Morning Post* interviewer was characteristic: 'My chief works … have been on Aristotle, a philosopher who influences people to this day without their knowing it … It is astonishing how profound in some ways was Aristotle's knowledge of science' (Jackson, 199).

Much of Bywater's work was anonymous, and hardly known except to those who benefited by it. He was a delegate of Oxford University Press from 1879 until his death, and assiduous in reading manuscripts and proofs. His immense bibliographical knowledge and his practical wisdom were enough to assure him power and usefulness as a learned publisher; but on many scholarly enterprises he was not content to advise or to decide. He read with care the proofs of the Oxford Classical Texts, which he and Charles Cannan promoted, and guided the editors' critical methods. He contributed much to the *Oxford English Dictionary* that would otherwise hardly have been found.

Bywater was president of the Oxford Aristotelian Society from its inception in the early 1880s until he left Oxford in 1908. Members met in his rooms weekly during term and construed and discussed one of Aristotle's more important writings. The knowledge and the methods inculcated had far-reaching influence on philosophical studies in Oxford.

In university politics Bywater was a liberal and reformer. He wanted examinations reduced and did not favour compulsory Greek in universities. To national and international affairs his attitude was sceptical; his values were conservative—'the vulgar radicalism of my youth' was his own phrase—and he had no illusions. He considered liberalism destructive, disliked democracy—quoting Carlyle—and disliked the influence of the United States, which he considered 'the great breeding-ground of popular crazes' (Jackson, 187). He was long acquainted with Joseph Chamberlain—whom he referred to as Camerarius—and favoured tariff reform. He had learned much from Germans, and had done much to introduce German scientific methods into English scholarship; but in later years he deplored the growing chauvinism which prevented Germans from admitting that they could learn anything from an English book.

Bywater was an expert bibliophile, 'a prince among bibliophiles' (Jackson, 161). The collection he bequeathed to the Bodleian Library, which there bears his name, is much more than a collection of rare and beautiful books. It is, as he himself wrote, 'a conspectus in its limited way of the literature of learning from the age of Bessarion to that of the Elenisgonoi of Scaliger and Casaubon'; and it is also part of the work of a great humanist. He was generous in gifts of valuable books to individuals and institutions, and a benefactor of the Ashmolean Museum and Cambridge University Library. In his London home, surrounded by his books, Bywater was most himself. As one of his younger friends wrote:

> It was there that he was a great teacher. It was not merely that he was a master of his subject—and of one's own; but one felt powerfully the stimulus of a temperament from which what may be called the casual impurities of intellectual life—pedantry, hurry, irrelevance, pretentiousness, cleverness—had been purged away.

Admired as a great scholar, Bywater received honorary degrees from Cambridge, Dublin, and Durham, and foreign academic honours, and was one of the original fellows of the British Academy. He was of medium height with square shoulders, spoke with a 'never-to-be-forgotten lisp' (Jackson, 59), and smoked much, both a large pipe and cigars. He died at his home, 93 Onslow Square, London, on 17 December 1914, and was buried at Salcombe Regis, near Sidmouth, Devon, on 23 December.

R. W. CHAPMAN, *rev.* ROGER T. STEARN

Sources W. W. Jackson, *Ingram Bywater: the memoir of an Oxford scholar, 1840–1914* (1917) • Foster, *Alum. Oxon.* • *WWW, 1897–1915* • *Hist. U. Oxf.* 6: *19th-cent. Oxf.* • T. Orme, *University College School, London, alphabetical and chronological register for 1831–1891* (1892) • C. W. Boase, ed., *Registrum Collegii Exoniensis*, new edn, OHS, 27 (1894) • F. MacCarthy, *William Morris: a life for our time* (1994) • *CGPLA Eng. & Wales* (1915)

Archives Bodl. Oxf., corresp. and papers | Bodl. Oxf., letters to H. W. Garrod

Likenesses M. Beerbohm, caricature, drawing, *c.*1892, AM Oxf. • M. Beerbohm, caricature, drawing, *c.*1892, Merton Oxf. • J. S. Sargent, oils, 1901, Tate collection [*see illus.*] • W. Rothenstein, lithograph, BM

Wealth at death £11,004 5*s.* 11*d.*: probate, 29 March 1915, *CGPLA Eng. & Wales*

C. M. (*fl.* **1753**), supposed projector of the electric telegraph, is an illusory figure, the offspring of credulity and wishful thinking. In 1753 the *Scots Magazine* published a letter purporting to show how messages could be transmitted over a distance of some yards, by directing electric current to a sequence of wires, each representing a letter of the alphabet, enabling the equivalent letters to be read off at the far end. The letter, dated Renfrew, 1 February 1753, was signed C. M. At this date, however, electricity had already been transmitted over far longer distances than C. M. was so boldly proposing, for by 1748 William Watson had sent current along more than 2 miles of wire, and similar experiments were being made elsewhere. C. M. was not, it would seem, aware of progress in this field.

A century passed; in November 1853 the letter was

republished in the *Glasgow Reformers' Gazette* by a correspondent who urged that C. M.'s identity be investigated. There it caught the eye of Sir David Brewster and was republished at his desire in the *Glasgow Commonwealth* of 21 January 1854. Five years passed before a Mr Dick wrote claiming that C. M. was one Charles Marshall, of Well Meadows, Paisley. His reasons were slight: Marshall's name appeared on a list of residents in 1791 or thereabouts, and he recalled his mother speaking of a clever young man at Paisley who could make lightning speak and write against a wall. On this slender and untrustworthy support, those who should have known better built their insubstantial candidate. The letter was passed to Brewster who gave it a cursory glance and took Dick's probabilities as accredited fact. So the stamp of authority was impressed, and this identification was followed by the writer of an article entitled 'Electricity and the electric telegraph', published in the *Cornhill Magazine* in July 1860. This in turn drew a response from George Blair, published in *Notes and Queries* for 14 July 1860. Blair claimed to have spoken to Marshall's son, from whom he learned that although Marshall had been on the list seen by Dick, he was not the C. M. of the *Scots Magazine*. Meanwhile, six to eight months previously, an anonymous writer to the *Glasgow Herald* proclaimed C. M. to be Charles Morrison, born in Greenock, who resided for some time in Renfrew, and then emigrated to Virginia. The story was plausible, but though the writer was challenged to identify himself and name his authorities, he declined to do so. Blair noticed sufficient inconsistencies in his facts to judge the letter a hoax. When the matter was being debated in the 1850s, various office-holders and ancients of the parish of Renfrew sought to identify C. M., but without success. A similar enquiry launched in 1995 proved equally fruitless. C. M. eludes us still. ANITA MCCONNELL

Sources W. B. Ober, 'Charles Morrison, surgeon of Greenock and telegraph pioneer', *New York State Journal of Medicine*, 66 (1966), 769–70 • G. Blair, 'Charles Marshall not the inventor of the electric telegraph', *N&Q*, 2nd ser., 10 (1860), 22–3 • 'The electric telegraph', *North British Review*, 22 (1854–5), 545–91 • M. M. Gordon, *The home life of Sir David Brewster* (1869), 206 • C. M., 'An expeditious method of conveying intelligence by means of electricity', *Scots Magazine*, 15 (1753), 73–4

Cabanel, Rudolphe (1762/3–1839), engineer and theatre designer, was 'a native' of Aachen (some accounts say Liège) but lived in London for most of his life. Little is known of his family or his early years. His mother was probably Victoire Cabanel, a dancer. His father seems to have been an actor and pyrotechnist. 'Cabanell' senior and junior were billed at Astley's Royal Amphitheatre in 1789, one as performer, the other as machinist. A 'Cobonell and Son' were credited in 1804 as producers of a firework display for Astleys. Rudolphe's sisters Eliza and Harriot were dancers on the London stage.

Precisely how Cabanel obtained the technical training in stage mechanics, building construction, and architectural design that enabled him to pursue his career is not known. When Henry Holland rebuilt Drury Lane Theatre Royal in 1791–4, Cabanel modelled and built the stage, which he subsequently managed. It was elaborately equipped with machinery permitting all the elements of the scene to be changed simultaneously, with a minimum number of stage hands. He also designed machinery for the Birmingham Theatre in 1794 and 1814. By 1799, when he designed the stage and interior of the Royal Circus in Lambeth, he was establishing himself as an architect as well as a machinist. In 1802 he completely reconstructed the auditorium of Sadler's Wells and, in 1806, designed a new Royal Circus (later known as the Surrey Theatre), constructed under the supervision of another architect, James Donaldson the younger, to replace the earlier building, which had been destroyed by fire. When proposals were invited in 1811 for the rebuilding of Drury Lane (Holland's theatre having burnt down), Cabanel's designs were among those highly commended, but the commission went to Benjamin Dean Wyatt. In 1818 Cabanel designed the Royal Cobourg Theatre (the Old Vic), for which he also devised a great looking-glass curtain. Among his other inventions were a form of roof truss and patented designs for wheel and axle trees (1807) and machinery for raising water (1825).

Cabanel was a significant figure in the development of stage machinery in England. He died at his home, 2 Mount Gardens, Lambeth, on 4 February 1839, leaving a widow, Elizabeth. JOHN EARL

Sources *GM*, 2nd ser., 11 (1839), 329 • *Civil Engineer and Architect's Journal*, 3 (1839), 118 • [W. Papworth], ed., *The dictionary of architecture*, 11 vols. (1853–92) • Colvin, *Archs.* • Highfill, Burnim & Langhans, *BDA* • I. Darlington, *The parishes of St George the Martyr, Southwark, and St Mary, Newington*, Survey of London, 25 (1955), 57–8 • *The parish of St Mary, Lambeth*, 2 (1956), 37 • F. H. W. Sheppard, ed., *The Theatre Royal, Drury Lane, and the Royal Opera House, Covent Garden*, Survey of London, 35 (1970), 54–6, 22n • R. Leacroft, *Development of the English playhouse* (1973), 148 ff. • C. B. Hogan, 'An eighteenth-century prompter's notes', *Theatre Notebook*, 10 (1955–6), 37–44, esp. 40 • K. Burnim and P. Highfill, 'Alexander Johnston, machinist', *Theatre Notebook*, 23 (1968–9), 100–02, esp. 102 • D. Stroud, *Henry Holland: his life and architecture* (1966), 121 • D. Arundell, *The story of Sadler's Wells, 1683–1964* (1965), 64 • d. cert.

Cabbell, Benjamin Bond (1782/3–1874), politician and philanthropist, was born in Vere Street, Oxford Street, London, the third son of George Cabbell, apothecary, of Marylebone, Middlesex, and his wife, Mary, daughter of Thomas Bliss and niece of Nathaniel Bliss, astronomer royal (1762–4). He was educated at Westminster School, and matriculated from Oriel College, Oxford, on 19 June 1800, at the age of seventeen. He transferred to Exeter College on 25 February 1801, but left the university in 1803 without a degree. He was admitted to the Middle Temple on 4 April 1803 and called to the bar on 9 February 1816. He practised on the western circuit and at the Somersetshire sessions and in 1850 became a bencher of his inn. After unsuccessfully contesting St Albans in 1837 and again in February 1841, and Marylebone in August 1841, Cabbell entered parliament in August 1846. He was Conservative MP for St Albans from 1846 to July 1847, and for Boston from July 1847 until he retired in March 1857. His opposition to the Maynooth grant and his interest in reform of the 1834 poor law suggest mild tory paternalism.

Cabbell was elected a fellow of the Royal Society on 19 January 1837. He was a magistrate for Norfolk, Middlesex, and Westminster, deputy lieutenant of Middlesex in 1852, and sheriff of Norfolk in 1854. He was president of the City of London General Pension Society, vice-president of the Royal Literary Fund, treasurer to the Lock Hospital, and sub-treasurer to the Infant Orphan Asylum. He was also a freemason, serving as a trustee of the Royal Masonic Institution and as provincial grand master of the freemasons of Norfolk. He had a country house, Cromer Hall, in Norfolk, and was a generous benefactor to Cromer: he paid for a lifeboat for the town and donated a large piece of land for a cemetery. However, although he subscribed to a number of London charities, he allowed the buildings he owned in Marylebone to fall into disrepair because they were entailed on a nephew whom he disliked; these houses were regarded as a disgrace to the neighbourhood.

Cabbell was also known as an art patron: he became a member of the committee of the Artists' Benevolent Fund in 1824, and in 1827 helped to draw up the fund's application for a royal charter. Cabbell died unmarried at his London home, 39 Chapel Street, Edgware Road, on 9 December 1874. G. C. Boase, *rev.* Anne Pimlott Baker

Sources J. Pye, *Patronage of British art: an historical sketch* (1845), 58, 365 • H. A. C. Sturgess, ed., *Register of admissions to the Honourable Society of the Middle Temple, from the fifteenth century to the year 1944*, 3 vols. (1949) • *WWBMP*, vol. 1 • Foster, *Alum. Oxon.* • *Law Times* (19 Dec 1874) • *Solicitors' Journal*, 19 (1874–5), 128 • *CGPLA Eng. & Wales* (1874)
Archives Norfolk RO, papers
Likenesses B. P. Gibbon, etching, 1845 (after W. Mulready), BM • W. Mulready, pen-and-ink sketch, repro. in Pye, *Patronage of British art*, 358
Wealth at death under £100,000: probate, 23 Dec 1874, *CGPLA Eng. & Wales*

Cable, Ernest, Baron Cable (1859–1927), financier and industrialist, was born in Calcutta, India, on 1 December 1859, the only son of George Herbert Cable (1823–1876), a superintendent in the Indian customs and excise service, and his wife, Emily Maria *née* Pickersgill. He was considered too delicate to send to Britain to a public school, and was educated mainly at a private school at the hill station of Mussooree and then at Calcutta University.

Cable spent the whole of his career in the service of British agency houses, merchant partnerships that from the 1870s were changing to investment groups by acquiring controlling interests in industrial, transport, plantation, freehold estate, and other companies. After a period gaining experience with Ashburner & Co. and Lyall, Rennie & Co. of Calcutta, he became an assistant manager with Bird & Co., which had started in 1864 as labour contractors for loading and unloading railway trucks and ships. Bird's involvement with bulk cargoes (such as coal, timber, and jute) brought the company into contact with a variety of new industrial developments.

However, the firm was confronted with bad management in some of their major suppliers; and it was not long before the Birds partnership was appointed managing agents to bring the ailing companies back into profit. The firm's earliest project was the Barrakur Coal Co. in 1878, the second the Oriental Jute Manufacturing Co. in 1880. From these early successes it turned to the management of the Bull Patent Brick Co. (1882) and the Baragunda Copper Co. (1883).

This extension of Bird & Co. gathered further momentum after Cable became a partner in 1886, with the greatest growth in colliery companies, jute mills, and labour contracting. Not content to take control of existing enterprises, Cable floated new companies, first in jute (from 1893), then in coal (from 1898). In 1896 the partnership was already responsible, through the various companies it controlled, for employing about 15,000 people, with another 15,000 toiling for the firm at the ports and on the railways.

Two reasons have been suggested for Cable's outstanding achievements as an entrepreneur. He spent nearly all his young life in India and enjoyed happy relations with Indians long before there was much friendly association between expatriates and the indigenous population. The other reason was his financial acumen and the City of London connection he built. The London stock exchange showed only occasional interest in Indian investments, while the Indian population was long inured to hoarding bullion rather than investing capital, and in any event had little access to banks or the British business community. Bird & Co. floated the Investment and Finance Co. in Calcutta in 1896 in order to offer a safe investment for British savings. In addition, Cable's friendship with C. S. Cox in the City led to the formation of Bird, Cox, Hunt & Co. in London to float, finance, and underwrite new companies in India and Egypt. The General Trust and Investment Co. (1908) was another vehicle formed in India to support industrial development, notably of jute mills. The result was that the bulk of the capital employed in Bird & Co.'s multifarious enterprises came from the public rather than the partners, as was still the case with most other agency houses at the period.

The peak of Cable's achievement came in 1917, when he acquired a controlling interest in F. W. Heilgers & Co., a Calcutta agency house of German origin with strong interest in the paper industry (comprising three mills), coal (seven companies), and jute (two mills). The combined Bird and Heilgers operation was much the biggest in India at the time, controlling companies with a total capital of some £20 million and a revenue of £3 million, and employing directly or indirectly 100,000 people. There were more than 2000 shareholders in the coal companies and nearly 3000 in the jute mills.

Cable could not bring the Midas touch to all branches of business: Bird & Co. failed with tea gardens (1881–93) and, until 1906, with insurance agencies, both because of management problems. A venture in shipping wheat lost heavily (1904), apparently for want of experience to match Ralli Bros. and other local specialists. However, Cable was fortunate—or more likely skilful—in choosing able partners, both in Calcutta and in the City of London.

Cable played an active part in the Bengal chamber of

commerce, and for two years (1903–05) served as its president and representative on the viceroy's legislative council, where he warmly supported Lord Curzon's policies on commercial and industrial development. He was sheriff of Calcutta in 1905, and was knighted when the prince and princess of Wales toured India in 1906. By the First World War he was the senior partner in Bird & Co. and resident in the UK, though he made frequent voyages to Calcutta.

In 1888 Cable married Lilian Sarah, the daughter of Weston Joseph Sparkes of Dawlish. Their only son was killed in the First World War in 1915; there were also two daughters, one of whom married Edward Benthall of Calcutta, a partner in Bird & Co. He acquired a country house, Lindridge, near Bishopsteignton, Devon, as well as a house in London's Grosvenor Square. He was created Baron Cable of Ideford in 1921. Cable died at 9 Mandeville Place, Marylebone, London, on 28 March 1927.

S. D. CHAPMAN

Sources *The Times* (29 March 1927), 19 • *WWW* • G. Harrison, *Bird & Co. of Calcutta, 1864–1964* (1964) [privately printed] • 'Indian industrial commission: evidence', *Parl. papers* (1919), 18.869–905, Cmd 235 [evidence of W. A. Ironside; Bengal and the Central Provinces] • 'Royal commission on Indian finance', *Parl. papers* (1914), 19.511, Cd 7069; 20.709, Cd 7236; 20.965, Cd 7238 • S. D. Chapman, *Merchant enterprise in Britain: from the industrial revolution to World War I* (1992), ch. 8 • d. cert.

Archives SOUND BL OIOC, taped reminiscences of Sir Paul Benthall of Bird & Co., Calcutta

Wealth at death £214,715 15*s*. 8*d*.: probate, 17 Nov 1927, *CGPLA Eng. & Wales*

Cable, (Alice) Mildred (1878–1952), missionary and author, was born on 21 February 1878 in Sydenham Road, Guildford, the daughter of John Cable, master draper and sometime borough councillor and magistrate, and his wife, Eliza Kindred. From early youth she believed that she had a missionary vocation, and while still at Guildford Girls' High School she began training with the China Inland Mission. Confirmed in her intentions, she went to London to receive formal training as a pharmacist, taking courses which would be useful in her future endeavour including anatomy, surgery, and midwifery, and qualifying as MPS. Her plans were seriously threatened when the Boxer uprising in 1900 disrupted Chinese missionary work; and this was further compounded by the ending of a love affair, to which she only ever made one public reference, in the spiritual autobiography, *Something Happened* (1934), where, thirty-five years after the event, she described receiving news which made a 'goblin of the sun' and where 'the brightest things of life burnt themselves to ashes' (p. 75).

Despite these set-backs Cable left England for China in September 1901, as soon as it was safe for missionaries to return there. She was sent to Huozhou in Shanxi province, where she joined the veteran missionary Evangeline *French (1869–1960) in setting up a girls' school, which eventually developed into a women's teacher training college. They also campaigned against foot binding and were active in the rehabilitation of opium addicts. In 1907 they were joined by Francesca Law *French (1871–1960) [*see under* French, Evangeline], younger sister of Evangeline, and, as the Trio, they were to spend the rest of their lives together.

Cable was committed to the idea of an indigenous church, and sought to involve Chinese Christians in all areas of their mission. She believed that their work in Huozhou could be self-sustaining and that her skills might be more usefully exploited in areas still relatively untouched by the protestant missionary movement. It was with this intention that she gained permission to initiate a mission in north-west China. The Trio left Shanxi in June 1923 and arrived in Jiuquan in Gansu province in late 1924. After establishing a base and native church at Jiuquan they devoted the next thirteen years to travelling, by mule cart, across the trade routes of the Gobi Desert, 'gossiping the Gospel', as Cable described their method of proselytizing; leaving biblical tracts in hostelries, visiting country fairs, and disseminating their Christian message on a personal level by befriending local people.

It is for the Trio's work in this part of central Asia that they were to become widely known in missionary circles and also to the British public. While their numerous journeys across the Gobi Desert were motivated by their evangelical calling, the hardships and frequent dangers endured made them pioneer women travellers and explorers of this region, and they were the first British women to visit the city of Urumchi. Their work was frequently obstructed by growing political disturbance, and Cable's medical skills, which saved the life of Muslim warlord Ma Zhangying, proved a valuable passport to their own survival. She was recognized as a leading authority on the Gobi Desert, and her most famous book, of eponymous title, was published in 1942. It was in recognition of that expertise that she was awarded the Lawrence memorial medal by the Royal Central Asian Society in 1942, and, with the French sisters, the Livingstone memorial medal of the Royal Scottish Geographical Society in 1943.

Although Cable was the youngest of the Trio she soon established herself as its dominant partner. The numerous books published while they were in China and afterwards, though written with Francesca French, were largely Cable's work, and their tone and views more accurately reflect her own personality. Cable described herself as someone for whom faith was difficult, but she seemed not always to appreciate that this might also be true for the people among whom she evangelized. While generally appreciative of the various cultures in that part of China, she maintained a horror of all forms of idolatry, a prejudice which is reflected in her descriptions of Tibetan lamaism and, occasionally, in the methods of the mission's Roman Catholic rivals.

In 1936, as China collapsed into further political instability and Soviet influence increased in the north-west, the Trio were finally forced to leave. On their return to England, Cable immediately threw herself into the work of the British and Foreign Bible Society and, as its vice-president and chairman of the women's committee, it was to the service of this organization that she devoted the rest of her life. Cable and Francesca French toured England and Wales on the society's behalf and, in 1947, the Trio visited Australia, New Zealand, and India as part of their ongoing missionary project. In 1951 they were invited to Brazil by the Evangelical Union of South America, and Cable was enthusiastic about the future of the protestant church in that part of the world.

Cable was of medium height with hair, turned grey at a young age, scraped back in a bun, and dark rings around her eyes which made her look rather like a panda. She was generally seen as a formidable and rather intimidating personality, which earned her the nickname Napoleon among Bible Society activists. Her life was shared in total companionship with the French sisters and as a guardian to Eileen Guy, a Tibeto-Mongolian deaf mute adopted in Jiuquan in 1925. Cable died on 30 April 1952 at her London home, 13 Buckingham Mansions, West End Lane. She was cremated at Golders Green on 6 May. She bequeathed her estate to the French sisters and, after their deaths, to Eileen Guy. G. H. TIMMERMANS

Sources W. J. Platt, *Three women* (1964) • A. M. Cable and F. French, *Something happened* (1934) • B. McCredie, 'The wild, wild Gobi', 1994, SOAS, China Inland Mission Archive • P. East, 'Cart tracks across the Gobi', 1994, SOAS, China Inland Mission Archive • M. Cable and F. French, *The Gobi Desert* (1942) • private information (2004) • *DNB* • M. Warner, 'Introduction', in M. Cable and F. French, *The Gobi Desert* (1984), xi–xxi • W. C. Northcott, *Star over Gobi* (1957) • *CGPLA Eng. & Wales* (1952) • b. cert. • d. cert.

Archives British and Foreign Bible Society, Swindon, Wiltshire • CUL, British and Foreign Bible Society archive • Overseas Missionary Fellowship, Sevenoaks, Kent • SOAS, China Inland Mission archive

Likenesses double portrait, photograph, *c*.1925 (with E. Guy), priv. coll. • H. Wrightson, group portrait, photograph, *c*.1935, priv. coll. • E. O. Fearnley-Whittingstall, oils, 1953, British and Foreign Bible Society, London • H. Wrighton, group portrait, photograph, repro. in 'In town today (1)', *China Inland Mission notice of meeting* (1935) • group portrait, photograph, repro. in Platt, *Three women*, frontispiece • photograph, repro. in M. Cable and F. French, *Why not for the world?* (1952), frontispiece • photograph, repro. in M. Cable and F. French, *The story of Topsy* (1937), 16–17

Wealth at death £5807 15*s*. 0*d*.: probate, 28 July 1952, *CGPLA Eng. & Wales*

Cabot, John [Zuan Caboto] (*c*.**1451–1498**), navigator, was Italian by birth, the son of Julio Caboto (apparently of Genoese origin) and his wife, Mattea (who was Venetian). His parents were active in Venetian territories, and passed on their business and property dealings to John, their eldest son, when he was still young. Born about 1451, John Cabot was granted Venetian citizenship on 28 March 1476. His and his family's business have been traced in Venetian archives between 1482 and 1485. Nothing is known of his training as a merchant and navigator, but in 1497 he claimed to have been engaged in the Mediterranean spice trade, and even to have journeyed to Mecca. It is not known when or why he left Venice, but it is generally agreed that he is the John Cabot Montecalunya of Venice (the implications of the name Montecalunya have not been traced) who in 1492 was commissioned by King Ferdinand to design harbour works for the city of Valencia. These were finally abandoned early in 1493 for financial reasons.

Cabot was still in Valencia in April 1493, when Columbus passed through on his way to meet the Spanish sovereigns at Barcelona, and it has been plausibly argued that the two men met, and that Cabot was there inspired by transatlantic voyaging ambitions. Pedro de Ayála, a Spanish diplomat in England, in 1498 described him as 'another Genoese like Columbus who has been at Seville and at Lisbon seeking to obtain persons to aid him in his discovery' (Williamson, 228). If this is so, his navigational expertise may have indicated to him that a transatlantic passage in higher latitudes would be shorter than one in the lower ones traversed by Columbus. It was known in Spain that the men of Bristol were interested in transatlantic discoveries; it was believed (at least in the Basque country) that Bristol had made a transatlantic discovery before 1465, and there is evidence for their involvement in Atlantic exploration from 1480. Cabot's appearance in Bristol in 1494, or, more probably, in 1495, is thus not surprising.

Cabot arrived with his Venetian wife, Mattea, and his three sons, Lewis (Ludovico), Sebastian *Cabot, and Sancio, and was soon able to lease a house in St Nicholas Street. Bristol merchants were, above all, concerned to find a fishing ground to compensate for their exclusion from the Iceland cod fishery by the Hanseatic League. Cabot and his plans were readily accepted by the Bristol men and, through their influence in London, he contrived to gain access to royal circles. On 5 March 1496 Henry VII responded to a petition from Cabot by issuing letters patent to him and his sons, empowering them to sail freely in search of new lands to the east, west, and north (excluding Spanish claims to the south). They were to be lands hitherto unknown to Christians, and the Cabots were to hold them in the king's name and to have exclusive rights of access. A ship was ready at Bristol, probably by June, and Cabot set sail. It made some progress before an unruly crew, a shortage of provisions, and, above all, contrary winds, forced him to turn back, but the Bristol men had not lost faith in him and on May 20 1497 the *Matthew* of 50 tons, with Cabot and most probably his son Sebastian (aged about twelve), along with a Netherlander, a Genoese barber-surgeon, and about sixteen Bristol men, set sail on 20 May.

The main source for the voyage is a letter (probably of early January 1498) by John Jay (alias Hugh Say, a London mercer). It might seem that Jay had induced the master of the *Matthew* to give him a detailed account of the voyage, which he was relaying in outline to Columbus (the Grand Admiral) who was contemplating a further voyage. The ship took its bearings from Dursey Head, Kerry, and sailed with an east-north-east wind for thirty-five days, with only one storm shortly before sighting land on 24 June. A landing was made a little to the south and ceremonies of annexation held, together with the planting of banners for England, the papacy, and (perhaps) Venice. A precise landfall is not known, but it was probably either Cape Dégrat or Cape Bauld (about 51°35′ N) near the opening of the Strait of Belle Isle. Careful reckoning of latitude by sun and star sights appears to have brought them close to the latitude of Dursey Head after a dead reckoning voyage of 1800 miles (a reasonable estimate). Another landing was made not far away to the south but no people were seen, though 'a stick half a yard long pierced at both ends carved and painted with brasil [iron oxide]' was found, with other evidence of human presence, 'and by such signs they believe the land to be inhabited' (Williamson, 212).

The ship now sailed southwards in sight of land, at least reaching the southern tip of Newfoundland at Cape Race. Cabot then turned north again, since 'most of the land was discovered after turning back' (Williamson, 212), and capes, harbours, and islands were noted and named. Back at Cape Bauld or thereabouts, Cabot set sail on the same route with a strong westerly wind, probably on 20 July. They made a very fast passage, but because the sailors insisted that Cabot was sailing too far north, their first sighting of land was Cape Ushant, Brittany, on 4 August. They finally reached Bristol two days later. Rapidly, after celebrations, Cabot set out for London, had a quick audience with King Henry on 10 or 11 August, and received a reward of £10 for his enterprise, followed by a pension of £20 a year on 13 December. Day enclosed with his letter 'a copy of the land' (an unscaled sketch chart) which in altered state may (controversially) have provided the English coasts on the Juan de la Cosa map of 1500 (Museo Naval, Madrid), displaying English standards at five points and twenty-two names of locations, some distorted or illegible, but clearly English in origin. Three surviving letters record reactions to Cabot's return as seen from London. Lorenzo Pasqualigo, writing to his brothers in Venice, on 23 August alleged that Cabot equated the land of his discovery with that of 'the Great Khan' (over a century too late as a reference to China, where the Mongol khans had long since been replaced by Chinese emperors), and was flaunting himself as the Great Admiral. Raimondo da Soncino, the duke of Milan's ambassador in England, on 18 December wrote to his master, praising Cabot as 'of kindly wit and a most expert mariner' (Williamson, 209), and stating that he claimed to have a description of the world in a map (probably a Ptolemy) and also a globe. Cabot now recalled his part in the spice trade and said his next voyage would be to Cipango (Japan), farther to the east and near the equator. He also stressed the discovery of a massive fishing ground, which endeared him to the men of Bristol. Ayála stated on 25 July 1498 that Cabot's future plans would intrude on Spain's rightful sphere.

As early as August 1497 Pasqualigo said Cabot was boasting that the king would give him a fleet for his next voyage and criminals to found a colony on lands he would discover, and even Day expected this might happen. A second patent to Cabot, of 3 February 1498, empowering him to impress six ships, was not used. In fact Henry VII provided just one ship, which had belonged to Lancelot Thirkill, who with Thomas Bradley received a total of £113 8*s*. towards their preparations. This was all. She would go to Bristol and join three or four Bristol vessels for the voyage. London merchants ventured only 'small stokkys' in her, while Bristol men would lade their four small ships with 'slight and gross merchandise' such as cloth caps, laces, points, and other trifles. These ladings did not suggest that rich spice-selling people would be encountered. The little fleet left Bristol in May and had not been heard of by late September. However, Ayála reported on 25 July that he had learned that one vessel, damaged by a storm, had put into an Irish port, but that Cabot had continued on his way. This was the last that was ever heard of him or his ships, though one may have survived to return. In Bristol his pension was paid in 1498 and 1499, but the lease of his house was terminated at Michaelmas 1499, leaving Mattea and her children to the care of the city authorities. In 1512 or 1513 Polydore Vergil stated he had been lost at sea.

Cabot's enterprise in persisting in his deeply felt objective was admirable in its way, even if it was no more realistic than Columbus's original projects had been. He established that a substantial land mass did exist within reasonable sailing from Europe, and laid the way for the Bristol fishery (the first catches were brought home in 1502 and 1504), even if the Portuguese were already exploiting the area with much more substantial resources by the time the first fish reached Bristol. Little light is shed on his personality except from Soncino's passing reference, but he certainly had a strong character and a considerable capacity for imposing his views on king and merchants alike, and undoubted skill in navigation. That skill was commemorated at Bristol in 1897, the 400th anniversary of Cabot's first voyage, by the building of the Cabot Memorial Tower, a structure 105 feet high on the top of Brandon Hill. A century later Cabot's achievement was celebrated again, this time by the construction of a replica of the *Matthew*, which like its original successfully crossed the Atlantic to Newfoundland, and toured the east coast of the United States, before returning to its moorings in Bristol. DAVID B. QUINN

Sources J. A. Williamson, *The Cabot voyages and Bristol discovery under Henry VII*, Hakluyt Society, 2nd ser., 120 (1962) • R. Gallo, 'Intorno a Giovanni Caboto', *Atti della Accademia Nazionale dei Lincei*, 8th ser., 3 (1948), 209–20 • M. B. Gaibrois, 'Juan Caboto en España', *Revista de Indias*, 16 (1943), 607–27 • L. A. Vigneras, 'New light on the 1497 Cabot voyage to America', *Hispanic American Historical Review*, 36 (1956), 503–9 • L. A. Vigneras, 'The Cape Breton landfall: 1494 or 1497; note on a letter from John Day', *Canadian Historical Review*, 38 (1957), 219–28, esp. 219–22 • L.-A. Vigneras, 'État présent des études sur Jean Cabot', *Actas do congresso internacional de historia dos decobrimentos* [Lisbon 1961], 3 (1961), 655–68 • A. A. Ruddock, 'John Day of Bristol and the English voyages across the Atlantic before 1497', *GJ*, 132 (1966), 225–33 • A. A. Ruddock, 'The rehabilitation of Sebastian Cabot', *BIHR*, 47 (1974), 95–9 • S. E. Morison, *The European discovery of America: the northern voyages* (1971) • D. B. Quinn, A. M. Quinn, and S. Hillier, eds., *New American world: a documentary history of North America to 1612*, 1 (1979)

Wealth at death £20 p.a. pension: Williamson, *Cabot voyages*, 217

Cabot, Sebastian (*c*.1481/2–1557), explorer and cartographer, was the son of the explorer and navigator John *Cabot (*c*.1451–1498) and his wife, Mattea.

Origins and youth Neither the place nor the date of Cabot's birth is entirely certain. His father appears to have been of Genoese origin, but was a citizen of Venice when he first appears in the records. As a merchant, he moved himself and his family around, and between 1472 and 1495 was resident in Venice, Spain, and England. By 1484 (when he was in Venice) he had two sons, of whom Sebastian was the second. His wife also appears to have been Venetian. From this and other circumstantial evidence it has been concluded that Sebastian was born in Venice, and he is certainly described as a Venetian when he first appears in English records in 1496. Later in life he claimed to be a subject of the king of England, which could only have been by birth as his father was always recognized as Venetian, and he was never naturalized. He also confided to his friend Richard Eden that he had really been born in Bristol, and taken to Venice in his infancy, which was why he was usually taken for Venetian-born. By the time it was made (after 1548), this claim could have been a matter of convenience, or the defective memory of an old man, but it cannot be entirely refuted. He also described himself as a youth at the time of his father's Bristol voyage of 1497, although already well educated, which would be consistent with a birth date some time in 1481 or 1482, rather than the traditional date of 1472, which would have made him twenty-five.

Early career In response to a petition from John Cabot and his three sons, Henry VII issued letters patent in March 1496 for a voyage of discovery to the north-west, and empowered them to claim for the English crown any lands hitherto unknown to Christian princes. The seamen of Bristol already had some tradition of Atlantic exploration, and Bristol merchants were willing (up to a point) to invest in such a venture. In order to reinforce his own claim to anything that might be discovered, the king himself provided some modest support.

Cabot probably accompanied his father on this very small-scale expedition, which made a landfall in either Labrador or Nova Scotia. He thought that he had landed in China, and proposed to follow up his success with a larger venture in the following year. Further letters patent were granted to John Cabot alone in February 1498, to return to the scene of his earlier discoveries, and he set out with five ships during the summer. The fate of this voyage is completely unknown. As John makes no further appearance in the records he is usually supposed to have perished, along with his whole fleet. Reports that he was still living in Bristol some years later, and that at least one of his ships returned safely, have never been satisfactorily substantiated, and the former is intrinsically improbable.

Whatever his father's fate, Sebastian Cabot returned to, or remained in, Bristol, where he continued to function as a merchant. There were further Atlantic voyages from Bristol in the first decade of the sixteenth century, and a company to trade to the New Found Lands was set up in 1502, although it seems to have achieved little. Cabot is not mentioned in this connection, but may well have been involved. In 1505 he was the principal beneficiary of a new royal grant, which also awarded him a pension of £10 a year, in consideration of his services. What these may have been was not specified, but they were probably in Bristol rather than at sea, and may well have been in cartography and the study of navigation. In 1508 he managed to attract enough investment for a further voyage, and appears to have discovered the entrance to Hudson Bay, but the only tangible result was a further improvement in his own cartographical knowledge. It was later claimed that he had never visited Newfoundland, and represented it only by hearsay, but this was almost certainly either a mistake or a deliberate attempt to undermine his credibility. By 1512 he had acquired a considerable reputation, both as a seaman and as a cartographer, which suggests that he had made other voyages, because in 1497 he was little more than an apprentice and his solitary recorded voyage in 1508–9 seems a slender basis for such a reputation.

Spanish service In 1512 Henry VIII paid Cabot for making a 'carde', or map, of Gascony and Guyenne, but if he made any attempt to enter the royal service on a regular basis he failed. He accompanied the expeditionary force sent by Henry to that region later in the same year in support of Ferdinand, then the king's ally. When the force was withdrawn, Cabot remained behind, and entered Ferdinand's service as a cartographer. Some impression of the reputation that he had by then acquired can be gathered from the fact that he was immediately accorded the rank of captain, given a salary of 50,000 marevedis, and appointed to the council of the Indies. Once established in Seville, Cabot asked leave to go to England in order to arrange the removal of his household to Spain. This would suggest that he was already married, and possibly had been so for some time. On the other hand, the first reference to his wife by name (after 1512) calls her Catalina Medrano, which does not look like the Spanish version of an English name. Probably he had had regular business contacts with Spain, and found a wife there, while still resident in Bristol. This is supported by the fact that he had a daughter named Elizabeth when he removed to Spain, although her age is unknown. If he had so married, it would help to explain his decision to enter Ferdinand's service. In November 1515 he was one of the cartographers consulted about defining the rights of the Spanish crown in the Moluccas, but Ferdinand's death in the following year disrupted his career. He seems to have fallen foul of the powerful Cardinal Ximenes, regent for the young Charles I, and to have returned temporarily to England.

What happened next is a matter of some dispute. According to Richard Eden, Henry VIII engaged Cabot to lead another voyage westward, in company with 'Sir Thomas Perte', but the expedition was aborted by Perte's 'faynt herte'. It would have been out of character for Henry to have taken such an initiative, and in any case there was at that time no such person as Sir Thomas Perte. The man referred to seems to have been Thomas Sperte, an experienced sea captain, and later clerk comptroller of the navy, but not knighted until 1535. Cabot's own recollection, recorded much nearer to the time (in 1522) by Gasparo Contarini, is full of similar inconsistencies. According to Contarini, Cabot claimed to have been offered generous terms by Wolsey to lead such an expedition 'about three years' earlier, but had evaded the responsibility by claiming that he must seek the emperor's permission, and then by taking steps to ensure that such permission would not be granted. If, as seems to have been the case, Cabot was in England from 1517 to 1519, he can hardly have been in Charles's service, and the king of Spain was not elected emperor until June 1519, after Cabot had returned to Spain and been appointed pilot major (6 May). Either Cabot was deliberately confusing Contarini, or he paid a second visit to England in the latter part of 1519, and was understandably reluctant to be detained. If that was the case, then two voyages may well have been proposed, one in 1517 and one in late 1519, but it is certain that neither took place, and that Cabot did nothing in English service at that time. In 1521, when Henry and Charles were allies, Cabot was again in London, with his employer's permission, discussing the possibility of leading an English expedition, but nothing came of that idea either.

Cabot's work as pilot major seems to have been mainly that of a theoretician, rather than a practical seaman. In 1524 he represented the emperor in a conference at Badajoz, convened to make a further attempt to delimit Spanish and Portuguese spheres of influence. This confirmed the Moluccas to Spain and Brazil to Portugal. The following year he was appointed to lead what appears to have been a large and ambitious expedition to South America. Because he anticipated being away for some time, he asked that his salary should be paid to Catalina during his absence, as she would obviously have more need of it than he would. The expedition departed in April 1526, and lasted for a total of four years, during which Cabot appears to have visited the Amazon estuary and the surrounding lands, and to have founded a fort at San Salvador. If the purpose was to wrest the initiative from the Portuguese, then it failed completely, and when Cabot returned, he found himself in disgrace. He was imprisoned for about a year from August 1530 for mismanagement and abuse of his office during the expedition, and the council of the Indies then exiled him to Oran in north Africa for a further two years. It did not, however, deprive him of his office, and by June 1533 he was reinstated in Seville. What had happened to his family during this period of disfavour is not clear. Catalina was ill when he returned to Seville, and is not mentioned again, so she probably died then, or soon after. An unnamed daughter also died in the same year. By this time it was clearly recognized by the authorities, if not by Cabot himself, that his talent did not lie in command or administration, but in the technicalities of navigation and cartography.

Return to England Cabot became busy teaching navigation and examining pilots at the Casa de Contratación, making a few low-profile voyages, but not in command. It was in 1544 that he made his first major contribution to cartographic knowledge by drawing a superb *mappa mundi*, incorporating all the knowledge of the New World that had been acquired by Spanish, Portuguese, and English explorations up to that point. Some of this knowledge derived from his father's voyages, and may even have been firsthand. The original of this map disappeared in 1575, after the death of Juan de Ovando, president of the council of the Indies. By then three engravings had been taken, the first immediately after the drawing, the second in 1549, probably in Antwerp, and the third later in England. It formed the basis for the even more celebrated map of Abraham Ortelius, and was copied in a large number of modified versions. In many ways it was Cabot's most tangible memorial.

Cabot never lost touch with his English friends, and seems to have recruited a few to his South American expedition in 1526. After Henry VIII's death, in the summer of 1547, an opportunity arose for him to return to England on a regular basis. How this opportunity arose is not clear, but it is likely that it started with a change of priorities in London, and an invitation conveyed on behalf of John Dudley, Henry's last lord admiral, and now earl of Warwick. Cabot's position in Seville was prestigious and well rewarded, but he may have felt that the emperor's favour was not to be relied on. For whatever reason, he accepted the offer, and in October 1547 the privy council provided £100 to pay the costs of removing himself and his establishment. He appears to have returned to his old haunts in Bristol, and in January 1549 was granted an annuity of 200 marks, back-dated to Michaelmas 1548. This was not gratuitous, because he was already putting his vast knowledge and experience at the disposal of those both in Bristol and London who believed that England should expand her geographical and commercial horizons. The emperor was incensed, fearing the consequences of the disclosures that his former pilot major was uniquely placed to make, and in April 1549 demanded his return in no very diplomatic language.

There then followed a prolonged game of cat and mouse, which was to last for over five years. Charles refused to believe that Cabot was staying in England voluntarily, and Cabot himself repeatedly said that he wanted to be recalled to imperial service, and that he had important information to convey to the emperor. Protector Somerset started by informing the imperial ambassador that Cabot had been discharged from imperial service, even displaying a copy of the relevant letter, and that he was the king of England's subject, adding that he was free to return to Spain if he wished. In September 1549 the privy council provided another £100 for his 'conducion', presumably thinking that he was about to go back to Seville. However, Cabot was clearly telling the imperialists one thing, and the English something else, although the reason for this elaborate deception is obscure. Nor was Somerset consistent, sometimes saying that he was in the king's service (which Cabot denied—mendaciously, it would seem), and sometimes that he was an old man who had chosen to retire in the land of his birth. Meanwhile Cabot continued to be busy in London, persuading the merchants of the city and their friends in the council of the need to discover a new route to the Far East, around the north of Europe.

In June 1550 Cabot received £200 in reward from the king for these efforts, and secured an exemplification of the patent that he, his father, and his brothers had received from Henry VII in 1496. None of this suggests an urgent desire to leave the country. The emperor's representatives watched developments in London with mounting alarm, and in 1551 it was reported that Cabot was consulting with the French freebooter Jean Ribaut, who had sailed with him before. Finally, at the beginning of 1553, Cabot's efforts came to fruition, when a China Company was launched. The purpose of this was exploration and the discovery of new markets rather than immediate trade, and it was the first venture of its kind. Two hundred and forty shares were sold at £25 each, an unprecedented mobilization of capital which involved city merchants, courtiers, royal servants, and members of the privy council. The expected opposition of the Merchant Adventurers was weakened, partly by a crisis in the cloth trade with Antwerp, and partly by the clear evidence of royal support for the new venture. Several merchant adventurers also invested in the new company. Cabot was named as governor, and drew up the instructions; a charter was applied for. It was under the auspices of this company that Sir Hugh Willoughby and Richard Chancellor sailed in May 1553, in search of the 'north-east passage'.

English achievement Willoughby perished, with his entire company, on the Russian Arctic coast during the winter of 1553–4, but Chancellor made a landfall in northern Russia, and made his way to Moscow. Meanwhile Edward VI had died and Cabot's main English backer, John Dudley, had been executed for attempting to alter the succession. Between Willoughby's departure and Edward's death (with a timing that is as mysterious as the event itself), Cabot renewed his approaches to the imperial ambassador, and Charles again demanded his return. Once Mary had secured the throne, in the autumn of 1553, and Anglo-imperial relations had been transformed, permission for his departure was duly granted. It looks as though Cabot's bluff had been called by this unexpected move, because he did not go, pleading ill health. Charles's ambassador reported that the prospect of his leaving had created alarm in London, and later that the permission had been rescinded. In February 1555 Richard Chancellor's more or less accidental contact with Russia resulted finally in the grant of a charter to Cabot's China Company, but not under that name. The most immediate purpose was to exploit the privileges granted by Tsar Ivan IV, but trade much further afield was also looked for, and the full title of what was later to be known as the Muscovy or Russia Company was the 'Merchant Adventurers of England for the Discovery of Lands, Territories, Iles, Dominions and Seignories unknowen, and not before that late adventure or enterprise by sea or navigation commonly frequented'. Cabot was named as governor for life, and in November 1555 his annuity was renewed.

By this time Cabot was a well-established and extremely influential figure in London. Mary's (and even more Philip's) relations with the city were strained, but Cabot stopped claiming (or pretending) that he wanted to go back to Spain. The urgent information that he had wanted to convey to Charles in person, and which he eventually committed to writing instead, turned out to be a tip-off that the duke of Northumberland had been planning a raid on Peru in alliance with the French. This was obviously not the same information that he had wished to convey in 1549, and by the time he wrote it down Northumberland was dead, and there was not the faintest chance that the present English government would countenance any such scheme. Charles took the warning seriously, not because he feared the English, but because he feared the French. It is possible that it was the emperor's abdication in the autumn of 1555 that finally ended the inexplicable exchanges about Cabot's return to imperial service. The former pilot major may have been simply protecting his back while he got on with his new life, and there was no need to continue with that once Philip was in control. When the third Muscovy voyage departed in May 1556, the leader, Stephen Borough, wrote a vivid description of how Cabot (who had wanted to go on the voyage, but had been dissuaded) came to see them off, and gave the company 'great cheer' at the sign of the *Christopher*, dancing vigorously with the youthful crew and their friends.

Cabot died some time during the summer of 1557, at the age of about seventy-five or seventy-six. Neither the place nor the date of his death is known, but Richard Eden was with him, and recorded that he had claimed on his deathbed to know the secret of finding longitude by a divine revelation, 'But I think that the goode olde man, in that extreme age, somewhat doted' (Eden, preface). By the time that he died, the initiatives in which he had played such an important part were firmly established in England, and although it would be many years before a major part of English trade went beyond Europe, the whole mindset of commercial enterprise had changed.

Nothing is certainly known about Cabot's personal circumstances during the last ten years of his life. It seems that Catalina had died many years earlier, and there are no references to a second wife. If the daughter who died in 1533 was not Elizabeth, then she may have returned to England with him, possibly as a widow. An Elizabeth Cabot married one Robert Saddler in London in 1560, and another woman of the same name later married Henry Ostrich, who is known to have been the promoter of a voyage to Morocco. It is not certain that either of these women had any connection with the cartographer, and the original Elizabeth would have been nearly fifty by 1560, but the name was not a common one. Cabot was known and respected by navigators all over Europe, and it is doubtful if anyone without his combination of knowledge, prestige, and energy could have had the impact necessary to jolt the commercial community of London out of its accustomed habits of mind. That he did so gives this curiously ambivalent and international figure a unique place in English history. DAVID LOADES

Sources *LP Henry VIII* · *CSP Spain, 1550–58* · *APC* · R. Hakluyt, *The principall navigations, voiages and discoveries of the English nation*, 3 vols. in 2 (1589); facs. edn, Hakluyt Society, extra ser., 39 (1965) · *DNB* · J. A. Williamson, *The Cabot voyages and Bristol discovery under Henry VII*, Hakluyt Society, 2nd ser., 120 (1962) · D. B. Quinn, *England and the discovery of America* (1974) · P. McGrath, 'Bristol and America', *The Westward enterprise: English activities in Ireland, the Atlantic, and America, 1486–1650*, ed. K. R. Andrews, N. P. Canny, and P. E. H.

Hair (1978), 81–102 · patent rolls, PRO, C 66 · J. Taisnierus, *A very necessarie and profitable booke concerning navigation*, trans. R. Eden (c.1579)

Likenesses portrait, 18th cent. (after portrait attrib. Holbein), Ducal palace, Venice · J. Barry, group portrait, etching and line print, pubd 1791 (*The Thames, or, The triumph of navigation, with Sir Walter Raleigh, Sir Frances Drake, Sebastian Cabot, Captain James Cook, and Dr Charles Burney*; after oil painting, 1777–84), NG Ire. · engraving (after unknown portrait, c.1500–1599), repro. in S. Seyer, *Memoirs historical and topographical of Bristol and its neighbourhood: from the earliest period down to the present time* (1821–3)

Cabrol, Fernand-Michel (1855–1937). *See under* Farnborough scholars (*act.* 1896–1945).

Caccia, Harold Anthony, Baron Caccia (1905–1990), diplomatist, was born on 21 December 1905 in Pachmarhi, India, the only child of Anthony Mario Felix Caccia, of the Indian forest service, and his wife, Fanny Theodora, daughter of Azim Salvador Birch, of Erewhon and Oruamatua, New Zealand. Caccia's great-grandfather had fled to England from Lombardy as a political refugee in 1826. Caccia went to Eton College, where he was a popular all-rounder, and then to Trinity College, Oxford, where he gained a rugby blue and second-class honours in philosophy, politics, and economics (1927). In 1928 he won a Laming travelling fellowship from Queen's College, Oxford.

Caccia entered the Foreign Office in 1929 and was appointed third secretary at Peking (Beijing) in 1932. Also in that year he married Anne Catherine (Nancy), daughter of Sir George Lewis *Barstow, civil servant. He returned to London in 1935 as a second secretary and, from 1936, as assistant private secretary to the secretary of state until, in 1939, he was transferred to Athens. Driven from Athens in 1941, the Caccias with the embassy wives and children and some commandos, including Oliver Barstow, his wife's brother, had a perilous journey. Their ship was bombed en route to Crete, and Barstow was killed. They reached Crete in another small craft and a destroyer took them to Cairo. Caccia was appointed in 1943 to the staff of the resident minister in north Africa, Harold Macmillan, at Algiers. He soon moved to Italy as vice-president of the Allied Control Commission, and political adviser to General Harold Alexander. In 1944 he became the political adviser to the general officer commanding British land forces in Greece, and was in the embassy during the communist uprising in Athens in December 1944. Caccia was in his element in a military environment, and got on well with the allied commanders. In 1945 he became minister at the Athens embassy, before returning to the Foreign Office as chief clerk in 1949. In this post he was instrumental in putting into effect the administrative reforms which Anthony Eden had announced in 1943.

In 1950 Caccia went to Austria, then still under four-power administration, first as minister, then as British high commissioner, and finally as ambassador from 1951 to 1954. He was again in his element in Austria, *persona grata* to the allied military commanders and popular with the Austrian authorities. For relaxation he pursued chamois in the mountains. In 1956 he became British ambassador in Washington. After the Suez débâcle, communications between the two governments were virtually suspended. In spite of his earlier relationship with the US president, Caccia received a frosty reception. However, after Harold Macmillan became prime minister normal relations were rapidly restored, and there were no further crises during his mission. A major success was the resumption of full co-operation on atomic energy in 1958, and the relationship was further enhanced by an official visit by the queen. Caccia soon got back on excellent terms with the administration and became a respected and popular figure in the United States.

Harold Anthony Caccia, Baron Caccia (1905–1990), by Elliott & Fry, 1962

In 1962 Caccia became permanent under-secretary of state, and in 1964 head of the diplomatic service until his retirement in 1965. He was appointed CMG (1945), KCMG (1950), GCMG (1959), and GCVO (1961). In 1965 he was created a life peer as Baron Caccia. He took the arms of his Florentine ancestors.

From 1965 to 1977 Caccia was provost of Eton, and he also accepted many outside appointments in banking, finance, industry, and insurance. He was director of the National Westminster Bank, chairman of the Orion Bank, a director of the Foreign and Colonial Investment and European trusts, director of the Prudential, chairman of Standard Telephones and Cables and of ITT (UK) Ltd, and a member of the advisory council of Foseco Minsep plc. He was chairman of the Gabbitas Thring educational trust, a member of the advisory committee on public records, and chairman of the Marylebone Cricket Club. In 1969 he became first chancellor and then lord prior of the order of St John of Jerusalem. He was a regular attender at the House of Lords, where he sat on the cross benches, speaking mainly on foreign affairs. He was chairman of the Anglo-Austrian Society and became an honorary fellow of Trinity College, Oxford, in 1963, and of Queen's College, Oxford, in 1974.

In appearance Caccia was short, stocky, and bald with a fair complexion. He was forthright in speech and energetic in action, and he retained throughout his life a cheerful and light-hearted, almost boyish, manner, which concealed a serious and thoughtful disposition. He was a good administrator and universally popular in all that he undertook. He ended as he had begun, as a great all-rounder.

Caccia was happy in his family life and he and his wife were a devoted couple. They had two daughters and one son. But his latter years were saddened by the untimely death of his son, David, in 1983. Caccia died of cancer at his home, Aber-nant, Builth Wells, Brecknockshire, on 31 October 1990. SHERFIELD, *rev.*

Sources *The Times* (1 Nov 1990) • *WWW* • H. Macmillan, *Riding the storm, 1956–1959* (1971) [vol. 4 of autobiography] • private information (2004) • personal knowledge (2004) • *CGPLA Eng. & Wales* (1991)
Archives U. Birm. L., corresp. with Lord Avon
Likenesses Elliott & Fry, photograph, 1962, NPG [*see illus.*]
Wealth at death £234,388: probate, 19 Feb 1991, *CGPLA Eng. & Wales*

Cachepol, Walter (*d.* 1369), canon lawyer, came from the diocese of Hereford. When he was already an Oxford master of arts and a tonsured cleric, although not yet in minor orders, he was collated by Archbishop Islip on 6 January 1362 to the rectorship of Lyminge in Kent, a benefice he held until his death. Cachepol entered almost immediately into his course of studies in canon law, and received a *cum ex eo* licence on 27 August 1364 to hold for one year a benefice *in absentia* while studying at university. Proceeding through minor and major orders, he was ordained priest on 30 March 1366.

Cachepol's lectures provide a major source for our knowledge of the canon-law lecture hall in the medieval English universities. They form the core of the principal surviving collection of such university lectures (BL, Royal MS 9 E.viii). This collection contains the lectures of twenty Oxford canonists, yet carries as a heading for the table of contents 'Lectura Walteri Cachepole super decretales …', an indication of their substantial prominence. Twenty-six titles from the standard canon-law texts (*Decretals, Liber sextus, Clementines, Extravagantes* of John XXII) were treated in Cachepol's lectures (fols. 27–94*v*). Although not showing originality, his lectures can be taken as fairly representative of the type and quality of such scholastic acts and of canon-law studies generally in the second half of the fourteenth century.

Cachepol died, with apparent suddenness, at some time between 14 and 27 April 1369, while teaching at Oxford and in the midst of lecturing on the title 'De electione' of the *Liber sextus*. At that point a student wrote in his notes, *heu, cum hic moritur doctor Walterus Cachepol* ('when, alas, Dr Walter Cachepol died'; BL, Royal MS 9 E.viii, fol. 94*v*). His will, dated 14 April 1368, requesting burial in the parish church of St Magnus the Martyr, London, was proved on 27 April 1369. F. DONALD LOGAN

Sources Emden, *Oxf.* • C. Lutgens, 'The canonists of BL Royal MS 9 E.viii and canon law in the fourteenth century', PhD diss., University of Toronto, 1979 • BL, Royal MS 9 E.viii, fols. 27–94*v* • Register of William Whittlesey, archbishop of Canterbury, LPL, fols. 98*v*–99
Archives BL, Royal MS 9 E.viii, fols. 27–94*v*

Cadbury [*née* Taylor], **Dame Elizabeth Mary** (1858–1951), welfare worker and philanthropist, was born at 3 Elm Place, Peckham Rye, London, on 24 June 1858; she was born into one Quaker family and married into a second. One of ten children of John Taylor (*d.* 1894), a company director and stockbroker, and his wife, Mary Jane Cash (*d.* 1887), her family background was affluent. Her parents were active temperance crusaders, and enthusiasts for the adult education provided by mechanics' institutes. Elizabeth (or Elsie, as she was known) and her sister Margaret were educated privately in Germany, and Elizabeth then attended North London Collegiate School from 1874 to 1876 where Frances Mary Buss was the headmistress. In 1876 she passed the senior Cambridge examination in ten subjects, but did not enter higher education. As the second eldest of the ten children, in what was described as a 'large and boisterous family', Elizabeth taught her younger brothers and sisters. In her childhood and adolescence she loved music.

In the years after leaving school Elizabeth Taylor did social work in the London docks and in Paris. These activities, along with regular teaching in a Quaker Sunday school, show her religious and philanthropic energies. Her work in the London docks, where she started a boys' club in 1884 at the age of twenty-six, was a pioneering effort for a woman of her age, marital status, and class. She also used her musical talent to entertain seamen. Her Parisian experience from February to July 1885 was work with a protestant mission for the relief of victims of the Franco-Prussian War. From July 1885 she worked with women in the London slums.

In 1888 Elizabeth Taylor married George *Cadbury (1839–1922), a widower with five children. George and his brother Richard were the founders of the Bournville works, and they rebuilt the Cadbury family fortune. George Cadbury's first marriage was in 1872 to Mary Tylor, who died in 1887, and his second wife became stepmother to the five children—his biographer wrote that she did this with 'skill and passion'. The Cadburys had a further six children: Laurence John *Cadbury, born in 1889; George Norman, born in 1890; Elsie Dorothea (1892); Egbert (1893); Marion Janet (1894); and Ursula (1906). Laurence became, in his turn, chairman of Cadburys. Their family home until 1894 was Woodbrooke in Selly Oak, Birmingham, but in 1894 they moved to the Manor House, Northfield, Birmingham. They lived there together until

Dame Elizabeth Mary Cadbury (1858–1951), by Elliott & Fry, 1942

George's death in 1922, and Elizabeth continued to live there until her own death in 1951. In 1948, at the family gathering to celebrate her ninetieth birthday, there were 150 relatives, and at her death she left thirty-seven grandchildren and forty-nine great-grandchildren.

Elizabeth Cadbury's central work, apart from the rearing of eleven children, was in three spheres: Bournville Village, education and youth work, and the welfare of women. In all these arenas, her efforts were suffused with her Quaker faith. Although it is extremely hard to recreate the religious belief of past generations, commentators on Elizabeth Cadbury are unanimous in their judgement that her Quaker faith was strong, practical, and *active*: a faith producing practical activity in this world. These activities were grounded in the philanthropic capitalism of the Cadburys in Bournville, working to create a new type of community. The factory was already established at Bournville when George and Elizabeth Cadbury married, but the task of establishing the village was carried through by the couple together. The idea of housing at several price levels mixed together to avoid a one-class community was an original one in the 1890s. Unlike at Port Sunlight, houses at Bournville were not 'tied' accommodation, so people who left their jobs with Cadburys did not lose their homes, and non-employees were able to live in Bournville among the Cadbury workers. The pioneering nature of Bournville was publicly recognized by the British Association, who held their annual conference there in 1914 and 1950, and by a royal visit from George V and Queen Mary in 1919. The 200th house at Bournville was opened by Elizabeth Cadbury herself in 1951, and her last public appearance before her death was at the Bournville Village jubilee. She succeeded her husband in chairing the Bournville Village Trust. Her educational work in Bournville included the opening to women of the adult classes (started by George Cadbury) and the establishment of infant schools in 1910. In 1899 she founded an athletic club for young women in Bournville, which opened with a bicycle gymkhana in which both the Cadburys took part.

Elizabeth Cadbury was particularly concerned with disabled and sick children, and in 1909 opened the Woodland Hospital, which became the Royal Orthopaedic Hospital. Later she built The Beeches, to give holidays for children from the Birmingham slums. She chaired the Birmingham school medical service committee and worked energetically to provide medical inspection in schools. From 1941 to 1948 she was president of the United Hospital in Birmingham. Throughout her life she campaigned for the education and welfare of women. She was a convinced non-militant suffragist. The founder in 1898 of the Birmingham Union of Girls' Clubs, she was active in the YWCA and in the National Council for Women from 1896 to her death. In 1936, at the age of seventy-eight, she led the UK delegation to the World Congress of the International Council of Women which was held in Calcutta.

Elizabeth Cadbury was an active pacifist. She was the first chair of the Peace and International Relations Committee of the National Council of Women, established in 1914. In 1916 she was elected to the National Peace Council, becoming its treasurer and then its vice-president. Along with Lady Aberdeen, Millicent Fawcett, and Mrs Corbett Ashby, she pressed for the inclusion of women's issues in the agenda of the Congress of Versailles. She chaired the Peace and Arbitration Committee of the International Council of Women, and was an energetic supporter of the League of Nations Union. In the Second World War, she worked with Belgian refugees, and after that war continued her efforts with the International Council of Women.

In national politics Elizabeth Cadbury's sympathies were similar to those usually associated with Christian socialism, and she was a pillar of the Liberal Party. She was a Birmingham city councillor, for King's Norton ward, from 1919 to 1924, as a Liberal, losing her seat to a Conservative. Her political platform was a reformist one: municipal action in housing improvement, a school health service, and equality of opportunity. Among her political successes were her co-option to the Birmingham education committee in 1919, and her services as a magistrate from 1926.

For her public service Elizabeth Cadbury was made an OBE in 1918 and a DBE in 1934. The Belgian government honoured her in 1918 for her work with refugees, making her an officer of the order of the Crown, and she was decorated by Queen Elizabeth of the Belgians. The Red Cross organizations of Serbia, Greece, and Yugoslavia also made awards to her for her war work. The University of Birmingham made her an honorary MA in 1919 for her services to education and to the city.

Elizabeth Cadbury died at the Manor House, Northfield, Birmingham, on 4 December 1951, and was cremated in Birmingham on the 7th. SARA DELAMONT

Sources R. Scott, *Elizabeth Cadbury, 1858–1951* (1955) · 'Elizabeth Mary Cadbury, 1858–1951', *Bournville Works Magazine*, memorial no. (1951) · A. G. Gardiner, *Life of George Cadbury* (1923) · I. A. Williams, *The firm of Cadbury, 1831–1931* (1931) · D. Owen, *English philanthropy, 1660–1960* (1965) · *CGPLA Eng. & Wales* (1952)

Likenesses Elliott & Fry, photograph, 1942, NPG [*see illus.*]

Wealth at death £102,129 13*s*. 2*d*.: probate, 28 Feb 1952, *CGPLA Eng. & Wales*

Cadbury, George (1839–1922), confectionery manufacturer and social reformer, was born at Edgbaston, Birmingham, on 19 September 1839, the third son and fourth child of John *Cadbury (1801–1889), cocoa and chocolate manufacturer, and his wife, Candia (1805–1855), daughter of George Barrow, merchant and shipowner, of Lancaster. The Cadbury family, of west-country origin, had settled in Birmingham at the end of the eighteenth century. John Cadbury began as a tea and coffee dealer in 1824, and started to manufacture cocoa in 1831. The firm of Cadbury Brothers was established in 1847, when Benjamin Head Cadbury left the family drapery business to join his brother John. The Cadburys were long associated with the Society of Friends, and Quakerism was a powerful influence on the attitudes and actions of George Cadbury.

George Cadbury was educated at home and as a day-boy at Lean's Quaker school at Edgbaston. His mother, an ardent temperance worker, died in 1855, and soon afterwards his schooling ended. His original wish was to become a surgeon, but circumstances led him into commerce, and, in 1856, after a period of employment in the grocery business of Joseph Rowntree at York, he joined his father's cocoa factory in Bridge Street, Birmingham. His elder brother, Richard, had been at work there since 1850. John Cadbury's health failed after his wife's death, and the business declined to a position where its future was threatened. In April 1861 Richard and George, aged respectively twenty-five and twenty-one, took entire control. It was only after a hard struggle and great personal sacrifice on the part of the two young partners that in 1864 prosperity began to return. Richard had scientific and artistic interests, but George, it was said, channelled his energies into the creation of a strong business, which would reflect his religious ideals, his belief in thrift and hard work, worthy products, fair dealing, and good employment conditions.

The place of Cadbury Brothers as one of Victorian Britain's most notable businesses was achieved with the introduction of Cocoa Essence in 1866. Cadburys was the first British firm to employ the Van Heuten press, which removed excess oils from the cocoa bean; its use enabled the firm to manufacture a finer powder, in large quantities. At a time when parliamentary attacks were being levelled at adulterated foodstuffs, Cocoa Essence benefited from the absence of additives traditionally used to

George Cadbury (1839–1922), by Francis Dodd, *c*.1920–22

counteract the taste of the excess oils, and the new product was effectively packaged, branded, and advertised. What distinguished George Cadbury from his competitors was his willingness to introduce innovations, and, by 1910, his firm had replaced Frys of Bristol as the country's largest cocoa and chocolate manufacturer.

By 1879 the Bridge Street building was inadequate to the firm's needs, and the partners took the opportunity of making their greatest social and economic experiment—the moving of their works into the healthier rural surroundings of Bournville, 4 miles from Birmingham. Here, they improved factory layout and the efficiency of their operation, and they were able to expand their industrial welfare work, improving employment conditions and creating a model housing estate. Benefit schemes, including sick pay and pensions, were eventually introduced. The Bournville experiment in housing and town planning was George Cadbury's own. However, the success of the new factory made it likely that slum conditions would, if allowed, grow up in its neighbourhood. To avoid this, he bought, between the years 1893 and 1900, some 300 acres of adjoining land, on which he had built about 30 houses by the time he founded the independent Bournville Village Trust, in December 1900. The trust could own land anywhere in Great Britain, and even the Bournville estate was never intended by George Cadbury to be solely for the benefit of employees of his own business. By 1931 the capital of the trust had increased from £170,000 to over £500,000, and it held more than 1000 acres of land.

Cadbury married, in 1873, Mary (*d*. 1887), daughter of

Charles Tylor, writer and lecturer, of London; they had three sons and two daughters. After her death he married, in 1888, Elizabeth Mary *Cadbury (1858–1951), daughter of John Taylor, a member of the London stock exchange and director of various City companies; three sons and three daughters were born of the second marriage. The oldest son of George and Elizabeth was Laurence *Cadbury, who became managing director of Cadbury Brothers in 1919.

Richard Cadbury died in 1899, and Cadbury Brothers finally became a company, with George as its chairman. Innovation in product technology and marketing continued with the introduction of Cadbury's Dairy Milk in 1905 and Bournville cocoa in 1906. Under George's leadership, Cadbury Brothers had grown from an enterprise of 20 employees to one of about 8600.

An important part of George Cadbury's social work was the adult school movement. As a young man he had begun as a teacher in an adult school in Birmingham, and he continued to teach until the age of seventy-two, riding or, in his later years, bicycling into the city at six o'clock on Sunday mornings to take his Bible class. Hundreds of Birmingham men learned from him how to read and write. The resulting insight which he gained into working-class conditions inspired his interest in housing and factory reform. His love of the country led him to attach special importance to the provision of gardens for working-class houses.

Cadbury's other social activities were many, and were mostly concerned with giving practical form to the opinions he held. In 1901 he acquired a controlling interest in the *Daily News* in order to give voice to Liberal Party, nonconformist views in general, and to oppose the Second South African War in particular. He also owned four newspapers in the Birmingham district, and he took a leading part in the campaign against sweated labour. Cadbury died at his home, the Manor House, Northfield, Birmingham, on 24 October 1922, survived by his second wife.

I. A. Williams, *rev.* Robert Fitzgerald

Sources R. Fitzgerald, *Rowntree and the marketing revolution, 1862–1969* (1995) • I. A. Williams, *The firm of Cadbury* (1931) • A. G. Gardiner, *The life of George Cadbury* (1923) • D. J. Jeremy, *Capitalists and Christians: business leaders and the churches in Britain, 1900–1960* (1990) • D. J. Jeremy, ed., *Business and religion in Britain* (1988)

Archives Birm. CA, corresp.; corresp. and papers • Haverford College, Pennsylvania, Quaker collection, corresp. and papers • Labour History Archive and Study Centre, Manchester, letters and papers • Selly Manor Museum, letters | BL, letters to Lord Gladstone, Add. MSS 46057–46063 • BLPES, letters to A. G. Gardiner; corresp. with the Independent Labour Party | FILM BFI NFTVA, 'Solving the housing problem at Bournville', 1919

Likenesses F. Dodd, oils, *c.*1920–1922, Cadbury Schweppes Ltd, Birmingham [*see illus.*] • photographs, Cadbury Archives, Bournville

Wealth at death £1,071,099 13*s.* 8*d.*: probate, 5 Feb 1923, *CGPLA Eng. & Wales*

Cadbury, John (1801–1889), cocoa and chocolate manufacturer, was born on 12 August 1801, at 92 Bull Street, Birmingham, into a family of four generations of Quakers, the fifth child and third son in the family of five sons and five daughters of Richard Tapper Cadbury (1768–1860), draper, and his wife, Elizabeth, daughter of John Head of Ipswich. He was educated from 1810 to 1815 at Joseph Crosfield's Quaker school at Hartshill.

In 1816 Cadbury was apprenticed to John Cudworth, a Quaker, of the firm Broadhead and Cudworth, Leeds, to learn the retail tea trade. After six years his father sent him to work in the bonded tea house of Sanderson Fox in London, to broaden his experience. In 1824 he was given a sum of money, and was able to set up his own business as a tea dealer and coffee roaster at 93 Bull Street, Birmingham. On 9 March 1826 Cadbury married Priscilla Ann (1799–1828), daughter of John Dymond of Exeter, a draper and Quaker minister. She died two years later. In 1832 he married Candia (1805–1855), eldest daughter of George Barrow, merchant and shipping-fleet owner, of Lancaster. They had five sons and one daughter.

Cocoa powder for making an instant drink was first marketed about 1830. John Cadbury saw the potential for the product, and with his experience in roasting beans and preparing nib (crushed cocoa beans) for his shop, decided to open a factory. He purchased a former malthouse at Crooked Lane in 1831, and this is considered the founding date of the Cadbury manufacturing firm. During the first ten years he developed many new lines, and the earliest existing price list (1842) offered sixteen varieties of drinking chocolate and eleven cocoas. In 1846 he took his brother Benjamin (1798–1880) into partnership and changed the name of the firm to Cadbury Brothers, moving it in 1847 to larger premises at Bridge Street. In 1853 Cadbury Brothers were appointed cocoa manufacturers to Queen Victoria.

Convinced that there were practical solutions to the social evils of his day, Cadbury devoted himself particularly to the temperance movement. His campaigns for total abstinence were based on appeals to reason. The abstainer, he pointed out, could afford a good joint of beef on a Sunday. He was appointed to the Birmingham board of commissions in 1829 and in 1851 was chairman of the committee which steered through parliament the bill to transfer the board's powers to the elected council. He also served as an overseer and guardian of the poor (1830–41). He was prominent in the movement to replace 'climbing boys' with machines to sweep chimneys.

Cadbury's second wife, Candia, died from tuberculosis in 1855, and later that year Cadbury suffered a severe attack of rheumatic fever. This was a double blow from which he never fully recovered. The business declined seriously and in 1861 Cadbury retired, handing over to two of his sons, Richard and George *Cadbury. He died on 11 May 1889 at his home, 10 Harborne Road, Edgbaston, Birmingham, and was buried at Witton cemetery, Birmingham.

H. M. Davies, *rev.* Christine Clark

Sources J. F. Crosfield, *A history of the Cadbury family*, 1 (1985) • I. A. Williams, *The firm of Cadbury, 1831–1931* (1931) • H. C. Alexander, *Richard Cadbury of Birmingham* (1906) • T. Insull, *John Cadbury, 1801–1889* (privately printed, Birmingham, 1979) • *CGPLA Eng. & Wales* (1899)

Archives Birm. CL, MSS • RS Friends, Lond.

Likenesses photographs, RS Friends, Lond., Richard Cadbury's 'family book' · portrait, RS Friends, Lond., Richard Cadbury's 'family book' · portraits, repro. in W. A. Cadbury, *Family letters and portraits*, 2–4 (1910) · portraits, repro. in Crosfield, *History of the Cadbury family*, 1

Wealth at death £43,773: probate, 20 June 1889, *CGPLA Eng. & Wales*

Cadbury, Laurence John (1889–1982), chocolate and food manufacturer, was born at Woodbrook, Northfield, King's Norton, Birmingham, on 30 March 1889, the first son of George *Cadbury (1839–1922), chocolate and food manufacturer, and his second wife, Elizabeth Mary, *née* Taylor (1858–1951) [*see* Cadbury, Dame Elizabeth Mary]. He was educated at Leighton Park, Reading, a Quaker public school, and studied at Trinity College, Cambridge (1908–11), where he graduated with a degree in economics. As a young man his sporting interests included sculling, skiing, and motor racing. He then joined the family business in Birmingham, Cadbury Brothers, and three years later served in the Friends' Ambulance Unit in France; he was presented with the Croix de Guerre, as well as the Mons medal and the 1914 star. In 1919 he was appointed OBE, and was also appointed managing director of Cadbury Brothers and associated companies, with special responsibility for engineering, production, and factory development. It was a post he held for forty years.

Cadbury also oversaw wage and employment policies at the company. He actively supported the industry's National Joint Industrial Council, becoming a trustee of the firm's pension fund in 1920 and its chairman in 1932, a position he retained until his retirement. In 1921 he was appointed a director of the British Cocoa and Chocolate Company, the holding company which linked Cadburys and Frys until their formal merger in 1936; he was also active in the formation of overseas subsidiaries in Canada, Australia, Germany, New Zealand, Ireland, and South Africa between 1920 and 1937. On 10 November 1925 he married Joyce (*b*. 1905/6), the daughter of Lewis Oster Mathews, an estate agent of Birmingham; they had two daughters and four sons.

Cadbury was a key figure in the expansion of the family business during the inter-war years, and improvements in production and work organization underpinned marketing and strategic objectives which successfully exploited the firm's competitive advantages. In response to the depressed conditions and falling sales prices of the time, improvements in machinery and plant layout, mostly implemented between 1926 and 1932, increased productivity. The company additionally accrued the returns to scale which were to be found in the rising popularity of milk chocolate bars, and specifically Cadbury's Dairy Milk. Alongside new power plant and other innovations, automatic chocolate moulding machines were introduced in 1927; larger buildings were erected, including the cocoa block in 1929; and throughput was improved. The per unit labour and overhead costs of milk chocolate fell by 56 per cent between 1924 and 1936, and the continuous reduction in the sales price of Cadbury's Dairy Milk, beginning in 1920, reached in 1933 the level of '2oz for 2d', a competitive advantage that was turned into a famous advertising slogan. The brand was established as the industry's leader, and helped Cadburys achieve the powerful combination of efficiency, size, and consumer loyalty. Unrivalled positive cash flows created a virtuous circle of capital investment, heavy advertising, and price reductions. Output per employee grew significantly between 1922 and 1936; overall output even increased after 1928 and especially after 1933. Although the number of employees fell in the short term as a result of mechanization and enhanced factory organization, the upward trend in demand for confectionery had by 1934 restored employment levels at the company. In 1935 approximately 11,700 people worked for British Cocoa and Chocolate, making it the twenty-ninth largest manufacturing employer in Britain.

Laurence John Cadbury (1889–1982), by Elliott & Fry, 1949

During the Second World War parts of the main factory came under the control of the Ministry of Supply, and Cadbury chaired Bournville Utilities, which produced gas masks, aeroplane wings, petrol cans, and machine tools. He went with Lord Beaverbrook's mission to the USSR in 1941 as head of its economic section. In 1944 he succeeded his brother Edward as chairman of both Cadbury Brothers and British Cocoa and Chocolate; he resigned from the Cadbury board and as chairman of British Cocoa and Chocolate in 1959. He chaired the finance committee of the main company until 1962, when its ordinary shares were traded on the stock exchange for the first time, and he finally retired as a director of British Cocoa and Chocolate in 1964. From 1910 until 1978 Cadbury was a trustee of the Bournville Village Trust, which acquired responsibility for some 7000 dwellings, and he served as its chairman from 1954 to 1974. He was also a member of the University of Birmingham's council, which awarded him an honorary doctorate in law in 1970.

In 1922 Cadbury was appointed to the board of the Daily News Trust, established by his father to protect the independence of several Liberal, reforming newspapers, most of which were merged into a single title in 1930. He became its chairman in 1950, and between 1958 and 1967 he also served as a director of Tyne-Tees Television, part owned by the Daily News. In 1960 he was much criticized for secretly selling the *News Chronicle* to Associated Newspapers, owners of the Conservative-inclined *Daily Mail*, and for the subsequent loss of 3500 jobs. The circulation of the *News Chronicle* had declined for over a decade, and Cadbury was blamed for failing to appoint a successor more attuned to the requirements of modern journalism.

In the inter-war period, Laurence and Edward Cadbury had effected a business policy which established their chocolate manufacturing business as the industry leader; and, as company chairman, Laurence Cadbury oversaw the end of rationing and the expansion of demand in the 1950s. The next generation of directors, in the 1960s, responded to a new market and new marketing demands and sought to convert Cadburys into a global food and drinks enterprise. Although not a key player in this transformation, Cadbury did employ his expertise within the City of London to supervise the associated conversion to a public company. In 1969, the business merged to form Cadbury Schweppes.

Although deeply involved in the confectionery business and the Daily News Trust for most of his life, Cadbury showed little commitment to his family's Quaker connections. He became concerned chiefly with matters of economics and finance and with issues of population, and regularly offered his views and analysis in a range of journals. He was a director of the Bank of England in 1936–8 and from 1941 to 1961, and high sheriff of the county of London in 1947–8 and 1959–60. He acted as treasurer of the populations investigation committee for forty years (1936–76), and he also served as a trustee of the historic churches preservation committee. In contrast to his background, Cadbury in the post-war years tended to support Conservative policies, although he was neither interested in politics nor directly associated with any political party. Reserved by nature, he had no inclination to enter public life, preferring his home, family, and collections of antique furniture, guns, and books. He died at his home, The Davids, Hole Lane, Northfield, Birmingham, on 5 November 1982, survived by his wife. Their eldest son, Sir Adrian Cadbury, was chairman of Cadbury Schweppes from 1975 to 1989. ROBERT FITZGERALD

Sources *The Times* (9 Nov 1982), 12 • *The Times* (17 Nov 1982), 12 • *Bournville Works Magazine* (Dec 1959) • I. A. Williams, *The firm of Cadbury, 1831–1931* (1931) • Cadbury Bros., *Industrial record, 1919–39* (1944) • Cadbury Bros., *Industrial challenge* (1964) • R. Fitzgerald, *Rowntree and the marketing revolution, 1862–1969* (1995) • B. G. Murray, 'Cadbury, Laurence John', *DBB* • *WW* • b. cert. • m. cert. • d. cert.

Archives Cadbury Schweppes plc, Birmingham | Selly Manor Museum, Bournville, Birmingham

Likenesses Elliott & Fry, photograph, 1949, NPG [*see illus.*] • portrait, Cadbury Schweppes Ltd, Birmingham • portrait, repro. in Murray, 'Cadbury, Laurence John'

Wealth at death £1,046,801: probate, 30 Dec 1982, *CGPLA Eng. & Wales*

Caddell, Cecilia Mary (1814–1877), religious author, was born at Harbourstown, co. Meath, the daughter of Richard O'Farrel Caddell, of Harbourstown House, Balbriggan, co. Meath, and Paulina (*d.* 1856), daughter of Thomas Arthur, second Viscount Southwell. Through her father she was descended from an old Catholic family.

Although she was an invalid, Caddell became a relatively prolific author, specializing in hymns as well as religious and historical fiction written from a Catholic point of view. Initially she published in Dublin with James Duffy, but after 1856 with English publishers. Some of Caddell's work concentrated on the history of Roman Catholics in Ireland, for example *Nellie Netterville* (1867); a number—such as *Wild Times: a Tale of the Times of Queen Elizabeth* (1872)—carried strong anti-protestant overtones; others were directed at agnostics (for example, *Home and the Homeless*, 1858). Her most popular work was *Blind Agnese, or, Little Spouse of the Blessed Sacrament* (1856), which was translated into several languages. Since this work and several others were partly set on the continent it seems likely that she had visited France and Italy. Caddell also wrote some historical works, including *A History of the Missions in Japan and Paraguay* (1856), and a biography, *Hidden Saints: Life of Sœur Marie* (1869). She also contributed to Catholic periodicals, including the *Irish Monthly*. She died unmarried at Kingstown (Dún Laoghaire), co. Dublin, on 11 September 1877. She is not to be confused with C. M. Cadell, author of *Massenburg* (1825) and *The Reformer* (1832).

ROLF LOEBER and MAGDA STOUTHAMER-LOEBER

Sources *Irish Monthly Magazine*, 2 (1874), 332–5 • Blain, Clements & Grundy, *Feminist comp.* • S. J. Brown, *Ireland in fiction*, new edn (1919) • Burke, *Gen. Ire.* (1912) • D. J. O'Donoghue, *The poets of Ireland: a biographical dictionary with bibliographical particulars*, 1 vol. in 3 pts (1892–3) • *CGPLA Ire.* (1877)

Wealth at death under £8000: Irish probate, 1877, *CGPLA Ire.*

Caddick family (*per. c.*1740–*c.*1800), portrait painters, came to prominence with **William Caddick** (1719/20–1794). The events of his life and his paintings have often been confused with those of his sons, **Richard Caddick** (1748–1831) and **William Caddick** (1756–1784). Seven portraits by the family are in the Walker Art Gallery, Liverpool; of these two are definitely by the father and one is by Richard. Eleven more whose attributions are traditional but not always safe are known from reproductions (among these is a portrait of Thomas Bentley, the Liverpool-based partner of Josiah Wedgwood); a further handful are known only from early sources and exhibition records.

The elder William is said to have been the son of William Caddick, Liverpool mercer, but the fact that the artist spelt his name Caddock in early life casts doubt on this, and he may have been the son William born on 9 April

1719 to William Chadock, shoemaker (although at his death on 29 December 1794 his age was given as seventy-four). Later accounts state that Caddick studied alongside George Stubbs and the marine painter Richard Wright. Entries for October 1746 in a diary kept by Caddick's friend William Clarke, when both men were working in Chester, show that Caddick often saw Wright and was in contact with Stubbs. This diary, which provides a unique glimpse of Caddick's early life, chiefly describes a short trip Clarke and Caddick made to London in August 1746, when they visited artists' studios, including those of Hudson, Ramsay, and Rysbrack, bought prints, and enjoyed life on the town.

Caddick's first securely attributed work, a small portrait of Aaron Wood of the Burslem family of potters (who were related by marriage to the Wedgwoods), is traditionally dated to the following year. An undated portrait of Wood's sister Eliza (1724–1795), whom Caddick married about this time, was probably intended as its companion. The Caddicks and Woods apparently remained close. In 1768 Aaron Wood commissioned his nephew Richard Caddick to paint a portrait of his daughter Elizabeth; and about 1770 her younger brother Enoch was sent to Liverpool for three months to be instructed by all three Caddicks 'in the art of drawing, Perspective, Anatomy &c &c' (memorandum by Enoch Wood on the reverse of the portrait of Aaron Wood, Walker Art Gallery, Liverpool). A group portrait of about 1790 attributed to Richard Caddick in which items of pottery are prominent probably represents members of the two families. Liverpool's growth as a centre for the manufacture of pottery undoubtedly gained momentum from their connection.

William and Eliza had seven children, four boys and three girls, of whom Richard Caddick, born on 7 June 1748 at Old Hall Street, Liverpool, and baptized on 4 July at St Nicholas's Church, Liverpool, was probably the oldest. He and his brother William are the only two known to have reached maturity. If the statement by later local historians is true that Richard was a founder member of the first Society of Artists of Liverpool in 1769, his youthful reputation must have been considerable; but this may represent a confusion with his father, who the same sources say was elected president of the society when it was re-constituted shortly afterwards. A similar uncertainty exists over the authorship of the Caddicks' grandest work, the portrait of the Liverpool builder Joseph Brooks (1774). This chronic confusion, as well as the fact that almost always only one of the family is recorded in street directories, suggests that they operated virtually interchangeably as a family practice.

During the 1780s Richard probably lived away from Liverpool. The catalogue of the Society for Promoting Painting and Design in Liverpool's 1784 exhibition, at which he showed three portraits of gentlemen, describes him as 'visitor'; and he is absent from its exhibition of 1787 altogether. From 1790, however, he is recorded as portrait painter in Old Hall Street, Liverpool; this corresponds with his father's disappearance from the directories following his death on 29 December 1794. About this time, too, Richard married. He and his wife, Martha (who died aged sixty-five in 1829), had one daughter, also Martha, born in 1797. Richard evidently gave up painting altogether about 1800. Between 1805 and 1829 he is described in street directories as 'gentleman'. He died about 22 May 1831, leaving his daughter an estate valued at under £4000, and was buried on 27 May.

Of the younger William, born on 16 June 1756, and baptized in St Nicholas's Church, Liverpool, on 13 July, almost nothing is known. The register recording his death on 12 March 1784 describes him as portrait painter, but no work can be certainly ascribed to him. Probably, however, it was he rather than his father who sent *Portrait in the Character of Circe* to the Royal Academy in 1780, the only work exhibited by any member of the family in London. With the exception of this last work, all above-mentioned portraits that survive are in the Walker Art Gallery, Liverpool.

ALEX KIDSON

Sources M. Bennett, *Merseyside painters, people and places*, 2 vols. (1978), vol. 1, pp. 63–7 · 'British oils: Caddick', curatorial files, Walker Art Gallery, Liverpool · F. Falkner, *The Wood family of Burslem* (1912), 8, 21, 28, 32–9 · E. R. Dibdin, 'Liverpool art and artists in the eighteenth century', *Walpole Society*, 6 (1917–18), 59–91, esp. 69–71 · W. Clarke, diary, Aug–Oct 1746, Lpool RO, MS 920 ROS 612 · *IGI* · will, Lancs. RO [Richard Caddick] · parish register, Liverpool, St Nicholas, Lpool RO, 1 Jan 1785 [burial; William Caddick]

Wealth at death under £4000—Richard Caddick: will, Lancs. RO, 26 July 1816

Caddick, Richard (*bap.* **1741**, *d.* **1819**), Hebrew scholar, was baptized at the Unitarian New Meeting-House, Moor Street, Birmingham, the son of Job Caddick of Sedgley, Staffordshire, and his wife, Rebecca. He matriculated at St Edmund Hall, Oxford, on 21 October 1772 and graduated BA (5 June 1776) and MA (20 June 1799) at Christ Church.

In 1799 Caddick published *Hebrew Made Easy*, a small Hebrew grammar, which is very inaccurate and inconveniently arranged. An advertisement prefixed to this volume refers to Caddick's earlier edition of the gospels in Hebrew. The years 1799–1800 also saw the publication of his three-volume Hebrew New Testament, a corrected reprint of the translation published by William Robertson in 1641, which is substantially identical with Elias Hutter's 1599 version. Caddick's edition was simultaneously issued both separately and interleaved with the Authorized English translation. In 1805 it was reprinted, interleaved with the Greek and the Latin Vulgate texts as well as the English.

In 1802 Caddick published three sermons, 'True Christianity', 'Peace the Christian's happiness', and 'Counsel for Christians'. Three years later he issued proposals for printing by subscription a Hebrew and English edition of the Book of Common Prayer, an annotated edition of the Old and New testaments in Hebrew and English, and 'A volume of sermons preached in the parish churches in and about the cities of London and Westminster from 1780 to 1804'. It does not appear, however, that any of these works were actually published. During the last forty years of his life he resided in or near London—in Whitehall, at Islington, and at Caddicklodge, Fulham, where he died on 30 May 1819. The obituary in the *Gentleman's Magazine* gives Caddick the title of DD, though there is no record of his having received this degree from either Oxford or Cambridge universities.

HENRY BRADLEY, *rev.* PHILIP CARTER

Sources *GM*, 1st ser., 89/1 (1819), 587, 655 • Foster, *Alum. Oxon.* • *IGI*

Caddick, Richard (1748–1831). *See under* Caddick family (*per. c.*1740–*c.*1800).

Caddick, William (1719/20–1794). *See under* Caddick family (*per. c.*1740–*c.*1800).

Caddick, William (1756–1784). *See under* Caddick family (*per. c.*1740–*c.*1800).

Caddy, Florence (1820/21–1898), writer, was born according to her death certificate in London and according to the 1881 census in Penryn, Cornwall. She claimed to have been born into a low-church family and was educated privately, chiefly at Paris and Düsseldorf. In 1857 she married John Caddy who was born in North Petherwin, Devon, and who was some eleven years her junior. In the 1881 census he was described as a sawyer, but elsewhere she described him as Dr Caddy RN, retired. They had at least one daughter and lived in Cornwall before his death at an unknown date between 1881 and 1898. Mrs Caddy turned to writing during her husband's lifetime and in her first published work, *Household Organisation* (1877), her stress on economy and insistence that there was no work unfit for a lady probably point to her own straitened circumstances. She tried her hand at novel-writing with *Artist and Amateur* (3 vols., 1878) and *Adrian Bright* (3 vols., 1883) and revisited her earlier genre in *Lares and Penates* (1881), with its homilies and reflections. *Footsteps of Jeanne d'Arc* (1886) was an interesting experiment to assess 'the value of the geographical treatment of history' (p. 372), since she felt 'much might be gained by treating history geographically' (ibid., x). Her idea was to prepare by reading histories and biographies of Jeanne d'Arc, but to write as a traveller, visiting the places Jeanne had visited and writing with an immediacy that their common surroundings would bring. This commendable aim sadly resulted in a book that, although it avoided dullness, did not avoid superficiality. *Through the Fields with Linnaeus* (2 vols., 1887) followed a similar method, although Mrs Caddy seems to have followed her subject only to Småland in 1886. A reviewer's remark that 'Mrs Caddy has thoughts upon many things entirely unconnected with botany … and she expresses them as they arise' (*Spectator*, 60, 1218, cited in Allibone, *Dict.*) is unkind, as the book is not intended as pure biography, still less pure botany. However, the extracts from Linnaeus's diary that she commendably reproduced stand out from her prose for their conciseness, pertinence, and clarity. Mrs Caddy described Linnaeus's classification as a 'natural method' of classification, though his sexual system stands in contradistinction to Jussieu's natural system. She was sympathetic to the Scandinavians, but her observations lack penetration: visiting Småland, a region of Sweden from which poverty was to drive thousands to the United States, she remarked 'there appear to be no poor people' (F. Caddy, *Through the Fields with Linnaeus*, 1887, 1.5). *To Siam and Malaya* (1889) shows the same lack of curiosity and insight on Caddy's part about her trip in the duke of Sutherland's yacht *Sans peur*, on which she was engaged as geographer and naturalist, having previously sailed in the yacht to the Baltic. Caddy died at 38 Kenwyn Street, Truro, on 19 November 1898, having suffered from general paralysis for twelve years.

Mrs Caddy thought herself something of a scholar: there is no trace of irony in her statement of her appointment as botanist and naturalist to the trip to the Far East, and her prefaces stress the thoroughness of her preparatory research and the fresh insights she will give into her subjects' lives: yet if this learning was genuine, it is well masked in her books. The blend of biographical, topographical, and historical writing that characterizes her two most important works, *Jeanne d'Arc* and *Linnaeus*, was a well-established formula which had found a ready audience with a reading public that included an increasing number of actual or future tourists. She aimed higher than many such authors and travelled further than most, but never consistently rose above the trivial.

ELIZABETH BAIGENT

Sources Allibone, *Dict.* • d. cert. • census returns, 1881

Caddy [Cade], **Laurence** (*b.* 1557/8, *d.* in or after 1583), Roman Catholic seminarist, matriculated as a sizar from Trinity College, Cambridge, in 1577. On being converted to Rome he left the country and was admitted to the English College, Douai, on 11 June 1578. By 1579, when he was twenty-one, he was a student of logic at the English College at Rome but was dismissed soon afterwards. On his return to England he was arrested and, being unwilling to answer such questions as were put to him, was committed to the Tower. He regained his liberty in 1581 after making a public recantation at Paul's Cross. He later claimed that he feigned conformity in order to be able to be reunited with his parents without imperilling them.

John Aylmer, bishop of London, sent Caddy to Cambridge for a period of theological study. There he fell in with another former student from Rome, John Nichols, who had published several anti-Catholic pamphlets. As a result of his persuasion Nichols left the country, only to be arrested and imprisoned at Rouen. Caddy himself had left England for France by 1583 and, now penitent, sought to regain the favour of William Allen, though the latter regarded him as unstable and deranged. He wrote a palinode which was included in Allen's *True Report of the Late Apprehension and Imprisonment of John Nichols, Minister, at Roan* (1583) and, in a Latin translation, later incorporated in the 1588 edition of John Gibbons's *Concertatio ecclesiae catholicae in Anglia*. In it Caddy claimed to have been led astray by the devil, and took the credit for being instrumental in having had Nichols arrested and silenced. When last heard of in April 1583 he was said to have been preparing to enter a Carmelite friary in Paris.

G. MARTIN MURPHY

Sources [J. Gibbons and J. Fenn], *Concertatio ecclesiae catholicae in Anglia adversus Calvinopapistas et puritanos*, 2nd edn (1588), 234–8 · *The letters and memorials of William, Cardinal Allen (1532–1594)*, ed. T. F. Knox (1882), vol. 2 of *Records of the English Catholics under the penal laws* (1878–82), 177 · [W. Allen], *A true report of the late apprehension and imprisonment of John Nichols, minister, at Roan* (1583) · T. F. Knox and others, eds., *The first and second diaries of the English College, Douay* (1878) · Venn, *Alum. Cant.*, 1/1.279 · 'The memoirs of Father Robert Persons', ed. J. H. Pollen, *Miscellanea, II*, Catholic RS, 2 (1906), 12–218, esp. 34, 134 · W. Kelly, ed., *Liber ruber venerabilis collegii Anglorum de urbe*, 1, Catholic RS, 37 (1940) · L. Hicks, ed., *Letters and memorials of Father Robert Persons*, Catholic RS, 39 (1942), 115–17 · *Letters of William Allen and Richard Barret, 1572–1598*, ed. P. Renold, Catholic RS, 58 (1967), 44–5 · M. C. Questier, *Conversion, politics and religion in England, 1580–1625* (1996), 38, 158

Cade, John [Jack; *alias* John Mortimer; *called* the Captain of Kent] (*d.* **1450**), rebel leader, was believed by contemporary chroniclers and the royal administration to be Irish, but this may have been no more than a supposition based on Cade's adoption of the surname Mortimer (the Mortimers were a long-established line of Irish landowners, ancestors of the duke of York). There are no reliable details about his origins or livelihood, and some rumours about him were theatrical or lurid. Some said that he was a physician, John Aylmere, who had married a squire's daughter from Surrey and who was remembered for going about dressed in scarlet. According to the royal proclamation issued for his capture in the summer of 1450, he had worked in sorcery, was a former soldier who had fought at one time for enemy France, and was a murderer, who had fled the household of Sir Thomas Dacre in Sussex after killing a pregnant woman. A John Cade, yeoman, is recorded in royal accounts as fleeing the realm between December 1448 and December 1449, but whether he was, as the authorities believed, one and the same man as the rebel leader cannot be known. There is no corroboration of any of the other allegations made about him and certainly no evidence at all that he had any family ties with the aristocratic Mortimers. His decision to assume the name John Mortimer looks to have been a ploy to gain public support by the suggestion that he was connected to the duke of York, a magnate popularly regarded as neglected by the king and, moreover, one untainted by allegations of misgovernment. The authorities took the Mortimer name seriously. They issued Cade's pardon in this name in July 1450, and even as late as the winter of 1450–51, by which time he was recognized to be Cade, parliament attainted him under the name of Mortimer. The duke of York's enemies were later to try to implicate the duke as a moving figure behind Cade's rebellion, but this is unlikely to have been the case. Had he been so, he would surely not have waited until at least two months after the rising was over before returning to England from Ireland.

Fairly certain biographical details can be established for Cade only for the few months of the uprising's duration in 1450. He acted as leader first in Kent (whence his nickname the Captain of Kent), where the rising began, and then as spokesman for all the insurgents who rose up from Kent, Surrey, Sussex, Middlesex, and Essex. Accounts of these events suggest that he was someone from the lower ranks of society. Features of the rising further suggest that he had both intelligence and courage. He led a movement that began as a mass petition to the king, fuelled by righteous indignation about Henry VI's insolvent and corrupt administration. Written lists of grievances were drawn up which showed an awareness of maladministration at the national level by courtier favourites connected with the once highly influential duke of Suffolk, William de la Pole, as well as a clear understanding of county administration in Kent, and its perversion by grasping members of this court clique. Chief among them was Lord Saye, treasurer of England, warden of the Cinque Ports and constable of Dover Castle. At the national level, Suffolk's circle was widely regarded as responsible for the territorial losses in France. Since the summer of 1449 the French had surged into the English-held lands of northern France, and by the end of 1450 all Normandy, once the prize and pride of the king's father, Henry V, was lost. It was pointed out by the rebels in one of their petitions that the king could see that he had been ill advised because 'his londez ern lost, his marchundize is lost, his comyns destroyed, the see is lost, Fraunse his lost' (Griffiths, 636). Cade appears to have been supported to a significant degree by solid members of village society—the lesser gentry, yeomen, and husbandmen—a following which lost its discipline and order only upon entering London. This was no peasants' revolt concerned with conditions of servitude, though the events of 1381 were evidently in men's minds. These were men with a stake in society, who feared for the safety of their own property, faced both with perverters of law and taxation in their own counties and the northward advancing French.

Cade's role as leader seems to have been established early on in the rising, which began in Kent towards the end of May 1450, following the death of the much loathed duke of Suffolk off the coast of Kent when he was fleeing into exile by ship. A large rebel host moved westwards across Kent and by the second week of June was encamped on Blackheath, defending the site with ditches and stakes. Henry VI was alarmed enough to adjourn the parliament he was holding at Leicester and return to London. Messengers were sent to the rebel camp ordering the rebels home, followed by a reconnaissance group led by the earl of Northumberland to assess the strength and size of the host. Probably they found its dimensions sobering, as the king did not go to meet it. Rather, a delegation led by Archbishop Stafford and Cardinal Kemp was sent on his behalf to persuade the rebels to ask for a royal pardon. The attempt failed. When the king then marched against Blackheath with men and arms he found the camp abandoned: the rebels had decided to go home, perhaps loath to meet their king in battle. The rising might have ended there, but a posse of the king's men which rode on into Kent harrying the rebels was set upon by a group of them near Sevenoaks, and Sir Humphrey Stafford and his kinsman William Stafford were both killed. Cade was able to put on Sir Humphrey's armoured velvet jacket and his spurs. As news of the incident spread his followers began to gather themselves together again. A new sense of resolve was created among them, not only by the small military victory that had been scored over the king's forces but also by the news of random violence wrought upon villagers of western Kent over the following few days by members of the king's entourage. It was the sort of *chevauchée* the English visited upon the French.

It was at this point that a further development occurred which caused the rising to regain its momentum. Retainers of the king and his magnates in the area around Blackheath began to show signs of sympathy for the rebels' grievances. They threatened to join their ranks unless certain public traitors, that is, dishonest royal servants, were arrested. The notorious Lord Saye, Lord Dudley, Bishop Aiscough of Salisbury, Abbot Boulers of Gloucester, John Trevilian, John Say, and Thomas Daniel were among those they named. Some retainers ran riot around the capital and attacked the property of those they decried. This was all very alarming, coming from persons whose very function was loyalty to their lords. To calm the situation Henry authorized Lord Saye's arrest and had him placed in the Tower of London. He also removed himself, and in the last week of June fled to Kenilworth, a Lancastrian stronghold in the midlands. This was despite the appeals of the mayor of London for him to stay. A few days later, on 29 June, the insurgents returned to Blackheath. It may have been on this second encampment that the men of Kent were joined by insurgents from Surrey and Sussex. It was at about this time that a contingent of rebels from Essex gathered and approached Mile End. On 1 or 2 July Cade led his followers down from the heath into the more comfortable surrounds of Southwark. He installed himself at the White Hart. This placed the rebel host in the immediate vicinity of London Bridge which it crossed on 3 July after some resistance. That day and the following day a commission ordered by the king on 1 July gathered at the Guildhall to sit in judgment on some of the hated ministers and royal servants of whom the insurgents complained, including Lord Saye, who was taken to the standard in Cheapside for execution. Another similarly unpopular figure, William Crowmer, the sheriff of Kent, was among those executed.

These executions, so relished by the crowds of insurgents, were performed with at least a semblance of legal form. However, despite Cade's proclamations made upon entry into London that anyone committing acts of robbery would be put to death, once within the city walls the ranks of the rebels lost all sense of order. Robberies, murders, and burnings were rife, and even Cade himself fell to looting. By the evening of 5 July Londoners were determined to ensure that the captain and his rabble should have no further entry from the Southwark side into the city. They took to arms on the bridge and fought through the night until the rebels were defeated and they were able to bar the gateway at the bridge's entry. The following day a settlement was reached by a delegation of churchmen, the archbishops of Canterbury and York and the bishop of Winchester, who met Cade in St Margaret's Church, Southwark. They were presented with the rebels' petitions and offered free royal charters of pardon in return. The rising was over.

A large number, more than 3000 people, took a charter of pardon. Not all of these were rebels. They were inhabitants of the south-eastern counties who calculated that if a time of royal retribution were to come then a charter of pardon would serve them as a form of indemnity, irrespective of their own personal involvement in the rising. It is one of the most important changes in historians' understanding of the rising that the long list of persons enrolled as taking out a pardon on 6 and 7 July is no longer analysed and counted as a simple tally of those who rose. The list is far more complex than that, and includes even enemies of the insurgents. This change has meant that there is no certain way of saying precisely how many thousand people rose or who they were. The subject has to be treated more impressionistically and heads can no longer be counted.

Cade, laden with stolen valuables, tried to take refuge in Queenborough Castle on the north Kent coast but was refused entry by its keeper. He then turned south-westwards into Sussex; his booty was sent by barge down to Rochester, where it was to be transferred to a bigger vessel, but it was seized there by the authorities. They were now in pursuit. On 10 July Cade, under his own name, rather than as John Mortimer, was proclaimed a traitor and the enormous price of 1000 marks put on his head. Half that price was placed on the capture of his under-captains. Alexander Iden, the new sheriff of Kent, led the group who tracked down and took Cade at Heathfield in Sussex, wounding him in such a way that he did not survive the journey to London. He died on 12 or 13 July. The wife of the innkeeper of the White Hart in Southwark, on being shown his corpse, confirmed that it was Cade's, and so three days later it was given the proper treatment for a traitor and beheaded at Newgate. Cade's head was placed on London Bridge and his quarters sent to be displayed at Blackheath, Norwich, Salisbury, and Gloucester.

It was important for the authorities that evidence of Cade's destruction, and of that of his henchmen who were also rounded up, should be displayed around southern England and not only in London and Kent, as there were several eruptions of popular discontent in the south of the country during 1450. Two prominent members of the duke of Suffolk's circle met their deaths at the hands of angry mobs: Adam Moleyns, the bishop of Chichester, slaughtered in January at Portsmouth by unpaid soldiers long kept waiting to embark for France, and William Aiscough, the bishop of Salisbury, similarly murdered in June at Edington by men from surrounding Wiltshire villages, a county which had suffered from the slump in the cloth industry.

With the exception of a judicial commission, which visited the south-eastern counties, hearing indictments of past miscarriages of justice and the corrupt doings of the local officials of whom the rebels complained, Cade's petitions met with no direct success. Indirectly, his rising may well have aided the success in parliament in 1451 of a new act of resumption cancelling a large number of grants which the king had made in the past with undue generosity and partiality. Both Cade and the grievances he represented were remembered. Sporadic risings loyal to Cade's aims continued in the south-east for the next half-dozen years; it was even rumoured that Cade was still alive. Several of Cade's grievances were echoed by the Yorkist lords who revolted against Henry VI and who in 1461 placed Edward IV on the throne. That political turnabout in certain ways vindicated the anger expressed under Cade in 1450 when the south-east rose in indictment of Henry VI's regime. I. M. W. HARVEY

Sources J. S. Davies, ed., *An English chronicle of the reigns of Richard II, Henry IV, Henry V, and Henry VI*, CS, 64 (1856), 64–9 • 'William Gregory's chronicle of London', *The historical collections of a citizen of London in the fifteenth century*, ed. J. Gairdner, CS, new ser., 17 (1876), 55–239, esp. 189–95 • R. Flenley, ed., *Six town chronicles of England* (1911), 127–34, 153–7 • C. L. Kingsford, ed., *Chronicles of London* (1905), 158–62 • J. Gairdner, ed., *Three fifteenth-century chronicles*, CS, new ser., 28 (1880), 66–8 • 'John Benet's chronicle for the years 1400 to 1462', ed. G. L. Harriss, *Camden miscellany, XXIV*, CS, 4th ser., 9 (1972), 198–201 • R. A. Griffiths, *The reign of King Henry VI: the exercise of royal authority, 1422–1461* (1981) • I. M. W. Harvey, *Jack Cade's rebellion of 1450* (1991) • B. Wolffe, *Henry VI* (1981)

Cade, John (1734–1806), linen draper and antiquary, was born in January 1734 at Darlington, where he was educated at the free grammar school. He was employed by a wholesale linen draper in London; within a few years he was in charge of the counting-house, and subsequently became a partner at the Dublin branch. In 1775 he was sufficiently wealthy to retire from business, first to Durham and then to Gainford, where he occupied himself with antiquarian studies. He collected illustrations for a copy of Bishop Gibson's edition of William Camden's *Britannia*, and also supplied Richard Gough with many corrections for his edition. Some of his letters to Gough were published by John Nichols in his *Literary Anecdotes* (1815). Cade was not a member of the Society of Antiquaries, but he contributed several papers on Roman antiquities in co. Durham to their *Archaeologia*. In 1790 he suffered a stroke which left him bedridden for the rest of his life, and he died at Gainford on 10 December 1806; he was buried at Darlington. He never married.

T. F. HENDERSON, *rev.* J. A. MARCHAND

Sources Nichols, *Lit. anecdotes*, 8.313–28 • *GM*, 1st ser., 76 (1806), 1252

Cade, Laurence. *See* Caddy, Laurence (*b.* 1557/8, *d.* in or after 1583).

Cade, Rowena (1893–1983), founder of the Minack Theatre, Cornwall, was born at The Homestead, Spondon, Derbyshire, on 2 August 1893, the daughter of James Cade and his wife, Alice. Her father owned the town's cotton mill and the family had lived in the area for over three hundred years. Her great-great-grandfather was Joseph Wright, a well-known painter of the industrial revolution. She was the second of four children. Her consuming interest in theatre dated back to when, at the age of eight, she played Alice in a family production of *Through the Looking Glass*, though in other ways she was a tomboy, preferring tree-climbing and games. When she was nine the family moved to Cheltenham, as her uncle was headmaster of Cheltenham College junior school, and later she became what she described as an 'unwilling pupil' at Cheltenham Ladies' College. At the beginning of the First World War she was sent to Sir John Gilbey's estate at Elsenham to work in the remount stables, where she happily traded living in a fine great house for looking after herself in an old caravan. Her job was to select and break in horses to be sent out to France and Belgium for the cavalry.

Cade's father died during the war, the family was scattered, and the Cheltenham house sold. After moving around a good deal she and her mother finally went to Cornwall, and Rowena decided that she wanted to settle there. Shortly afterwards she bought the whole of the Minack headland, not far from Land's End, for just £100 and had Minack House built there, using local granite from a nearby quarry. The Cades had been used to making their own entertainment and throughout the 1920s they had put on a number of plays in the garden with family and friends, Rowena making and designing costumes. It was a more ambitious project, a production of *A Midsummer Night's Dream* in 1928, and its repeat a year later, that made her determined to provide a proper theatrical space. Below her garden was a natural amphitheatre and it was there that Cade set about creating the magnificent open-air Minack Theatre, on the cliffs above Porthcurno. She was assisted by her gardener, Billy Rawlings, and a local craftsman, Charles Thomas Angove. From the first the work was hard: terraces had to be cut for seating and it took months even to make a surface for a rough stage. The Minack Theatre became her all-consuming passion and she was to spend every working moment in it until almost the very end of her life. Charles Angove recalled her single-handedly carrying twelve 15 foot wooden beams that were washed up on the beach from the shore to the theatre, and local people remembered seeing her bringing sacks of sand on her back up the steep cliff path from the beach. No one who ever saw her at work could forget the spare, almost gaunt, figure with short silver hair and weather-beaten face, dressed in her uniform of jersey, knee breeches, thick socks, and boots, and almost always carrying a bucket of cement or concrete. The first production at the theatre was *The Tempest* in 1932, lit by batteries and car headlights. Regular productions followed right up until the Second World War, while the work of providing seating, a better playing area, and, eventually, a dressing-room continued, all the work being undertaken by Rowena Cade and her two assistants. The war put paid to any performances until 1944 when the film *Love Story* was filmed there. As soon as it was possible she worked unceasingly to make improvements, more seating, a car park, steps up from the beach, safety measures—as late as the 1960s getting from one side of the stage to the other over a deep inlet was hazardous to say the least. In 1966 Billy Rawlings died and Rowena inscribed his name on a seat, the only one which has this distinction, the others bearing the names of past productions.

From the two or three plays in a summer during the 1950s the season grew to sixteen weeks every year, with companies competing to play at the theatre, which now also boasts a proper lighting and sound box, better dressing rooms, a café, lavatories, and an exhibition centre. Since the Second World War almost every kind of play has been produced, from Shakespeare and the classics to modern comedy and musicals. Large-cast plays with a strong storyline and a good deal of action (such as Shakespeare) generally work best there, as more intimate and static drama is liable to disappear when performed against such a stunning natural background. From the outset Rowena Cade financed the theatre from her own pocket, and after several failed attempts to find a body willing to take over the upkeep of the theatre from her, she finally gave it to a specially formed charitable trust, the Minack Theatre Trust. She was still working in the theatre in 1976 when she was well over eighty, and before she died she bought a nearby bungalow and more land to provide theatre offices and a larger car park. She died peacefully at Minack House on 26 March 1983, and was buried on 30 March. Few twentieth-century women can have left so spectacular a physical memorial behind them. JUDITH COOK

Sources archive material, Minack Theatre Trust, Porthcurno, Cornwall • b. cert. • d. cert.

Wealth at death negligible; house, theatre, and money made over years before to Minack Theatre Trust

Cade, Salusbury (*c*.1660–1720), physician, was born in Kent and was educated as a foundation scholar at Lewisham grammar school. He entered Trinity College, Oxford, in July 1678 and graduated BA (1681), MA (1684), BM (1687), and DM (1691), having been admitted a licentiate of the Royal College of Physicians in 1688. Cade was elected a fellow of the college in 1694, and was censor in 1716 and 1719. He was appointed physician to St Bartholomew's Hospital, London, on 14 October 1708, and held the office until his death. He was the only member of the Royal College of Physicians nominated for the post under the terms of Baldwin Hamey's will ever to have been successful (Medvei and Thornton, 131). He lived at Greenwich, Kent, until he obtained this appointment, and from then in the Old Bailey.

A Latin letter of Cade's, dated 8 September 1716, on the treatment of smallpox, is printed in Robert Freind's edition of John Freind's *Works* (1733). It shows that Cade had considerable experience of the disease. He makes the interesting observation that he had never known a case of haematuria in smallpox to survive the sixteenth day from the eruption, and his remarks on treatment are worth while. The *Pharmacopoeia pauperum* of 1718 preserves a prescription of his for a powder to be taken internally for skin diseases. It was called Pulvis Aethiopicus, and consisted of one part of aethiopic mineral to two of crude antimony. Cade died on 22 December 1720.

NORMAN MOORE, *rev.* PATRICK WALLIS

Sources Foster, *Alum. Oxon.* • Munk, *Roll* • V. C. Medvei and J. L. Thornton, eds., *The royal hospital of Saint Bartholomew, 1123–1973* (1974)

Cade, Sir Stanford (1895–1973), surgeon, born on 22 March 1895 in Dvinsk, Russia, was one of five children and the youngest son of Samuel Kadinsky, a diamond merchant. Born Saloman Kadinsky, he changed his name to Stanford Cade by deed poll in 1924, having become naturalized British in 1920. Cade was sent to school in Brussels, Belgium, in 1903. He matriculated in 1913 and entered the University of Brussels as a medical student, in his eighteenth year. At the outbreak of the First World War in 1914 he joined the Belgian army as a private and served at the defence of Antwerp. Evacuated to the United Kingdom, Cade was unable to enlist in the British army because of his insufficient knowledge of English. However, he was given permission to take the first part of his conjoint medical examination in French. Having passed this successfully, he was admitted as a medical student to King's College, London, and then obtained an entrance scholarship to Westminster medical school for his clinical studies. He qualified MRCS, LRCP, in 1917, and also won the Bird prize and gold medal and the Chadwick prize.

After qualification Cade held a series of junior surgical appointments at Westminster Hospital, London, and obtained fellowship of the Royal College of Surgeons in 1923. He was deeply influenced by three surgeons on the Westminster staff: Walter Spencer, Arthur Evans, and Ernest Rock Carling. All three were particularly interested in the treatment of malignant disease, and this topic became fundamental in Cade's subsequent career. In 1924 Cade was appointed assistant surgeon and in 1937 full surgeon on the staff of Westminster Hospital, a position he held until 1960. In addition Cade served on the staffs of the Radium Institute and of Mount Vernon Hospital. Cade was one of the early pioneers of radiotherapy in Britain, obtaining the first supply of radium for his hospital from the Radium Institute in Paris. He published *Radium Treatment of Cancer* in 1929; his encyclopaedic *Malignant Disease and its Treatment by Radium* was published in four volumes between 1948 and 1952.

At the outbreak of the Second World War, Cade joined the medical branch of the Royal Air Force as a squadron leader; he reached the rank of air vice-marshal in 1946. He made a great contribution both to surgical organization and to the surgical care of pilots. His services were recognized by his appointment as CB in 1944 and KBE in 1946. He continued as honorary civilian consultant to the air force after the war until 1965. Cade also held numerous appointments of distinction. At the Royal College of Surgeons he served on council from 1949 to 1965; he was vice-president from 1959 to 1961; and he gave many eponymous lectures there, including three Hunterian lectures, the Bradshaw lecture in 1960, and the Hunterian oration in 1963. He held high offices in the British Empire Cancer Campaign and received numerous honorary diplomas, including fellowships of the American (1955), Edinburgh (1957), and Irish (1960) colleges of surgeons. He became MRCP (1941) and FRCP (1960).

In 1920 Cade had married Margaret Hester (1887–1951), daughter of William Agate, organist at Paisley Abbey, and a nurse at Westminster Hospital. Her death on 31 August 1951 of malignant malaria while in Africa was a profound tragedy. They had three daughters, one of whom, Irene, became a radiotherapist at St Mary's Hospital, Portsmouth.

Cade, who was small of stature, was an indefatigable worker, teacher, operative surgeon, diagnostician, and counsellor. He exuded energy, and after exhausting his surgical team he would frequently work in his office until two or three in the morning on his letters and publications. He was a brilliant lecturer and this was accentuated by his picturesque foreign accent, which he never lost. However, his command of English, both spoken and written, was superb. His excitable nature sometimes gave rise to outbursts which were misinterpreted as irascible, for he would not tolerate stupidity either in opinion or, more importantly, in action. To those who did their best for him, and to his patients, he proved a kind friend.

Cade's contributions to the treatment of cancer included his pioneer work on radium and radiotherapy, his concept of the team treatment of malignant disease, and his ground-breaking studies on adrenalectomy in the treatment of advanced cancer, the subject of his third Hunterian lecture, in 1954. His Wednesday tumour clinics at Westminster Hospital were crowded with patients from all over the country and indeed the world, and were attended by surgical visitors from many countries. His encyclopaedic knowledge of the management of cancer was matched by his skill at microscopic pathology.

After retirement Cade settled at Southsea, Hampshire, to be near his daughter Irene. He died at another of his residences, Wick Farm, Finchdean, Hampshire, of bronchopneumonia on 19 September 1973; he was cremated, and his ashes were scattered on the garden of remembrance, at Chichester crematorium. HAROLD ELLIS

Sources J. P. Ross and W. R. Le Fanu, *Lives of the fellows of the Royal College of Surgeons of England, 1965–1973* (1981) • *BMJ* (6 Oct 1973), 54–5 [with photograph] • *British Journal of Surgery*, 61 (1974), 239–40 • *The Lancet* (29 Sept 1973), 745–6 [incl. photograph] • private information (2004) • personal knowledge (2004) • *WWW*

Archives Wellcome L., patent records

Likenesses W. Stoneman, photograph, 1946, NPG • W. Bird, photograph, 1959, NPG • Oppenheimer, oils, RCS Eng. • photograph, RCS Eng. • photograph, repro. in *BMJ* • photograph, repro. in *The Lancet* (29 Sept 1973)

Wealth at death £70,594: probate, 2 Jan 1974, *CGPLA Eng. & Wales*

Cade, William (*d.* in or before **1166**), financier, is first noted in the early 1150s and was dead by 1166, when a note of his debts came to the exchequer. It shows that he was owed approximately £5000 by about 200 individuals. In just a few cases the bonds that lie behind these transactions have survived, and they show how his loans were arranged and secured. Cade occurs frequently in the early pipe rolls of Henry II's reign, where payments to him of about £5600 are recorded, in settlement of various loans that he had made to the crown. These records establish his importance (his operations were crucial to the establishment of the Angevin dynasty in England) but supply little by way of biographical information.

It is clear that Cade was a Fleming from St Omer: he had a house there, close connections with local monasteries, and members of his family have Flemish names. The names of his parents are not known, nor is that of his wife, but he had brothers Baldwin and Eustace, and sons Eustace and Ernulf. The latter gave to the hospitallers land in Stalisfield and Oare close to Faversham in Kent; and a descendant of the same name held a manor at Ospring, which was known as Cade's manor as late as the eighteenth century. Faversham was one of the main centres in England of the honour of Boulogne, which county lay against the border of western Flanders, whose mercantile centre was at St Omer. The supply of wool from England to Flanders provided the main economic link between the two areas; and it is not surprising to find a merchant financier with a base at each end of this trade.

The Flemings who surrounded King Stephen and sustained his cause were not popular in England, and the peace settlements of 1153 provided that they be sent home. William Cade, however, was clearly indispensable to the financial operations of the crown. The exchequer was still functioning, but in a limited and *ad hoc* way. Cade could provide for both the crown and its debtors credit and financial expertise. He was one of a select group, which included the justiciars Robert, earl of Leicester (*d.* 1168), and Richard de Lucy (*d.* 1179), and the treasurer Nigel, bishop of Ely (*d.* 1169), who provided continuity between the old and the new regimes. Cade was the man behind the men behind the scenes.

The evidence for Cade's operations suggests that they shared many of the characteristics of the better-known Italian merchant bankers of the late middle ages. It was a family firm. Cade was in partnership with his brother and son, and debts were repayable to any partner, in London or in St Omer. Careful arrangements were made to secure loans. The crown's credit was good, but still it needed to assign some regular revenue: thus Cade had the farm of Dover from 1154 (and presumably earlier) until 1161. Individuals might assign the income from specified lands to pay off their debts, pledge their own faith, and produce guarantors. The position of churchmen in such transactions caused some debate, and their giving security was forbidden in the constitutions of Clarendon of 1164. This was because of the element of usury involved. At times it was blatant, as when the sheriff of Hampshire, presumably in order to enable him to settle a debt at the exchequer, borrowed £61 12*s.* 8*d.*, paying 'for each pound 2*d.* in interest a week' (Jenkinson, 'A money-lender's bonds', no. 2). More often Cade exacted a bond for a sum larger than the amount of cash advanced.

Towards the end of his life Cade was being superseded by Jewish moneylenders, and as a Christian usurer he would come to appear as something of an anomaly after his death. He was, however, long remembered. About 1202 the canonist Robert de Courson (*d.* 1219) cited him as a man 'who became immensely rich through lending money to innumerable merchants throughout the world' (Haskins, 730), objecting that in his partnerships he shared the profits but kept the capital safe. Cade founded no dynasty, but in his day he was a major operator in what R. H. Tawney in 1958 called 'the ambiguous *demi-monde* between politics and business' (Tawney, 81).

EDMUND KING, *rev.*

Sources E. Amt, *The accession of Henry II in England* (1993) • H. G. Richardson, *The English Jewry under Angevin kings* (1960) • H. Jenkinson, 'A money-lender's bonds of the twelfth century', *Essays in history presented to Reginald Lane Poole*, ed. H. W. C. Davis (1927), 190–210 • H. Jenkinson, 'William Cade, a financier of the twelfth century', *EngHR*, 28 (1913), 209–27 • H. Jenkinson, 'William Cade', *EngHR*, 28 (1913), 731–2 • C. H. Haskins, 'William Cade', *EngHR*, 28 (1913), 730–31 • R. H. Tawney, *Business and politics under James I* (1958) • J. H. Round, 'The debtors of William Cade', *EngHR*, 28 (1913), 522–7

Wealth at death unknown, but at least £5000 in debts owed to him

Cadell family (*per.* c.1740–1934), coal and ironmasters, engineers and geologists, came to prominence with **William** [i] **Cadell** (1668–1728), who appeared in Haddington as a journeyman glazier in 1701, and became a burgess there in 1704 by right of his father-in-law.

Although his origins are unknown, Cadell was an able man, and by the time of his death was a well-to-do merchant. In 1701 he married Anna (1681–1743), daughter of James Hogg, a burgess of Haddington. They had three sons and one daughter, including **William** [ii] **Cadell** (*bap.* 1708, *d.* 1777), who was baptized at Haddington on 10 May 1708. William [i] Cadell died at Haddington on 20 May 1728.

Initially a merchant like his father, by the late 1740s William [ii] Cadell was also managing collieries near Tranent in East Lothian for the York Buildings Company (responsible for running forfeited Jacobite estates). It was probably as a mine manager that he was approached by John *Roebuck and Samuel *Garbett when they came to establish a sulphuric acid works at Prestonpans in 1749. Roebuck and Cadell both knew Alexander 'Jupiter' Carlyle (1722–1805), and may have met through him. On 20 July 1734 Cadell married Christeen (*b.* 1703), daughter of John Hog, a shipmaster at Prestonpans. They had three sons and three daughters. Their eldest son, **William** [iii] **Cadell** (*bap.* 1737, *d.* 1819), was born at Cockenzie, East Lothian, and baptized on 16 August 1737.

The works were a success; so when, nearly ten years later, the two Englishmen resolved to establish a modern ironworks in Scotland, they approached Cadell again. He and his eldest son, William [iii], joined Roebuck and Garbett, and each putting in £1500, provided a quarter of the founding capital of what was to become Carron Company.

Like his father, William [iii] Cadell was trained to the commerce of east-coast Scotland. His grand tour in 1755 took him to Göteborg, Copenhagen, and Stettin, and in 1759, when the Carron partnership was formed, he was considered able enough to be its first managing partner. The first of Carron's great furnaces went into blast on Boxing day 1760, the date which marks the start of the industrial revolution in Scotland. At the age of twenty-three, therefore, William [iii] Cadell found himself running a factory where advanced technology was allied to managerial problems of a complexity never before encountered in Scotland. By 1762 the firm employed 615 men and was thus many times the size of any other industrial undertaking in the country.

The Cadells were involved with the firm through the first ten exciting and precarious years of its existence, and were the only founding partners never to go bankrupt. William [iii] Cadell ceased to be manager in 1769, and went on to make a name for himself as a coal and ironmaster first at Cramond just outside Edinburgh, and then at Grange near Bo'ness. His father, William [ii] Cadell, died at Cockenzie on 31 March 1777.

Cramond was a group of small traditional mills on the River Almond, acquired by Carron Company, and it passed to the Cadells as part of the financial arrangements by which they extricated themselves from Carron. Until the end of the century it was a reasonably successful business. It exported a variety of goods, notably bar iron and barrel hoops to Europe and the West Indies. It was unusual as early as 1782 in having much of the mill-train and even the haft of the forge hammer made of iron, and it had the distinction of being the first ironworks in Scotland to produce steel commercially. It remained in the Cadell family until 1860. Grange was a small estate on the edge of the Forth over a good coal seam. The coal was mined profitably by the Cadells until nationalization in 1947, and the estate continued to be owned by the family.

William [iii] Cadell's other interests included the manufacture of high-quality paper at Auchendinny. This was a mill which had come to him through his marriage in 1773 to Katherine (*d.* 1797), daughter of Archibald Inglis of Auchendinny, with whom he had five sons and one daughter. In addition, Cadell became a founder partner in the Muirkirk and Clyde ironworks, both of which, like Carron, were still functioning in the twentieth century. By the end of his life Cadell had limited his interests to Cramond and Grange, but was characteristic of those simple hard-working merchants who wanted only to turn an honest penny, and on whose enterprise the early industrial development of Scotland was founded. William [iii] Cadell died on 17 September 1819.

William's younger brother **John Cadell** (*bap.* 1740, *d.* 1814) was a mine owner at Tranent. Baptized at Cockenzie on 2 May 1740, in 1772 he married Marie (1753–1841), daughter of John Buchan of Letham, East Lothian; they had eight sons and four daughters. John Cadell had the melancholy distinction of being the magistrate responsible for giving the orders to the militia that led to the 'massacre of Tranent' in 1797, at which eleven men were killed during a riot in protest against the Militia Act. He died at Cockenzie on 20 January 1814. Among John's sons, William [iv] Cadell (1773–1840) was briefly employed at Cramond before becoming treasurer of the Bank of Scotland, and Robert *Cadell (1788–1849) was Sir Walter Scott's publisher.

William [iii] Cadell's sons included William Archibald *Cadell (1775–1855), traveller, mathematician, and friend of Sir Joseph Banks. Later significant members of the family included William's grandson **Henry Cadell** (*bap.* 1812, *d.* 1888), a distinguished mining engineer. He was baptized on 21 May 1812 at Grange, Bo'ness, the son of James John Cadell and his wife, Isabella, daughter of Henry Moubray of Calderbank. He was one of the earliest to study and exploit the silting propensities of the Firth of Forth, and his purchase in 1868 of 86 acres of foreshore, which he started to reclaim by a process of silting and the use of pit waste, added considerably to the industrial possibilities of the area. A notable inventor, he also exhibited weighing equipment at the Great Exhibition of 1851. Henry Cadell married Martha (*d.* 1854), daughter of Robert Hislop, in 1841, and they had two sons and three daughters. He married again in 1859, his second wife being Jessie Gray (*d.* 1895), daughter of the Revd John McFarlane. There were a further four sons and three daughters from this marriage. Henry Cadell died at Grange on 8 January 1888.

Henry's son **Henry Moubray Cadell** (1860–1934), a geologist, was one of the earliest members of the geological survey of Scotland under Professor Archibald Geikie. Born on 30 May 1860 at Crawhill, Torphichen, West Lothian, he was the eldest child of Henry Cadell and his second wife, Jessie. He studied at Edinburgh University from 1876 to 1882, and then at the renowned mining school at Clausthal in Germany from 1882 to 1883. His discovery of the great thrust planes of Sutherland, his work on the shale fields of West Lothian, and his two major books, *The Story of the Forth* (1913) and *The Rocks of West Lothian* (1918), were pioneering studies. Henry Moubray Cadell married Elinor (1868–1945), daughter of David Simson of Bonaly, in 1889; they had one son and seven daughters. He died at Edinburgh on 10 April 1934.

Through their ironworks and collieries the Cadell family played a key role in inaugurating the industrial revolution in Scotland. During the later nineteenth and early twentieth centuries they continued to contribute to Scottish industrial and technological development, and, although no longer directly involved in manufacturing, members of the family still occupied the land first acquired for industrial purposes in the eighteenth century.

PATRICK CADELL

Sources NL Scot., Cadell MS Acc. 5381 · P. Cadell, *The iron mills at Cramond* (1973) · P. Cadell, 'The industrial associates of the Cadell family in the 18th century', *Scottish Genealogist*, 23 (1977), 69–76, 82–90 · R. H. Campbell, *Carron Company* (1961) · J. H. Stevenson, *The Cadells of Banton … being a chart of the descendants of William Cadell* (1890) · private information (2004) · tombstone, Haddington [William (i) Cadell] · tombstones, Carriden, West Lothian [Henry Cadell; Henry Moubray Cadell] · *CGPLA Eng. & Wales* (1934)

Archives NL Scot., family papers, Acc. 5381 | NA Scot., Carron papers

Likenesses H. Raeburn, portrait (William (iii) Cadell), priv. coll.

Wealth at death £41,818 17*s.* 7*d.*—Henry Cadell: confirmation, 31 May 1888, *CCI* · £151 6*s.* 6*d.*—Henry Cadell: additional estate, 9 Aug 1892, *CCI* · £40,880 7*s.* 4*d.*—Henry Moubray Cadell: confirmation, 27 Sept 1934, *CCI*

Cadell ab Arthfael (*d.* **942**), king of Gwent, was son of Arthfael ap Hywel of Gwent in south Wales. He ruled the kingdom of Gwent from perhaps about 916 until his death in 942. Little is known of his reign. He is mentioned twice in the Book of Llandaff as witness to charters granting land to Bishop Wulfrith of Llandaff possibly about 940–42; and he was killed by poison in 942, though it is not known who administered the poison. The relatively detailed account of Cadell's exploits in the so-called 'Gwentian' *Brut Aberpergwm*, an unreliable chronicle composed in the eighteenth century by the infamous Edward Williams, alias Iolo Morganwg, must be rejected as a later forgery.

DAVID E. THORNTON

Sources J. Williams ab Ithel, ed., *Annales Cambriae*, Rolls Series, 20 (1860) · T. Jones, ed. and trans., *Brenhinedd y Saesson, or, The kings of the Saxons* (1971) [another version of *Brut y tywysogyon*] · T. Jones, ed. and trans., *Brut y tywysogyon, or, The chronicle of the princes: Peniarth MS 20* (1952) · T. Jones, ed. and trans., *Brut y tywysogyon, or, The chronicle of the princes: Red Book of Hergest* (1955) · P. C. Bartrum, ed., *Early Welsh genealogical tracts* (1966) · J. G. Evans and J. Rhys, eds., *The text of the Book of Llan Dâv reproduced from the Gwysaney manuscript* (1893) · J. E. Lloyd, *A history of Wales from the earliest times to the Edwardian conquest*, 3rd edn, 2 vols. (1939); repr. (1988) · W. Davies, *An early Welsh microcosm: studies in the Llandaff charters* (1978) · O. Jones, E. Williams, and W. O. Pughe, eds., *The Myvyrian archaiology of Wales, collected out of ancient manuscripts*, new edn (1870)

Cadell ap Gruffudd (*d.* **1175**). *See under* Rhys ap Gruffudd (1131/2–1197).

Cadell ap Rhodri (*d.* **910**), king in Wales, was one of the sons of *Rhodri Mawr and Angharad ferch Feurig of Ceredigion. Although he is described as 'king' on his death in 910 and possibly had held that status since the demise of his father in 878, the exact location and extent of his 'kingdom' is not apparent. Later medieval accounts of the division of political power following Rhodri's death invariably credit Cadell with Deheubarth (probably here meaning south Wales in general), and one version claims he outlived his brothers and ruled the whole of Wales. Most of this is patently incorrect. Rhodri Mawr's authority never even extended over Dyfed which remained independent until 903–4 when it may have passed to Cadell's son *Hywel Dda. Cadell's longevity is incorrect also: the longest-surviving known brother was *Anarawd ap Rhodri (*d.* 916) of Gwynedd. Cadell is often allotted Ceredigion, which Rhodri had probably acquired in 872 through his wife, Angharad. His sons probably controlled this kingdom in the mid-880s when (according to Asser in his *Life of King Alfred*) they were able to launch attacks against Dyfed and Brycheiniog, no doubt using Ceredigion as a base for such raids. However, in 895 Anarawd is said to have attacked Ceredigion and Ystrad Tywi with English help. Some have suggested that it had passed into Scandinavian control by this point whereas others, maintaining Cadell held the kingdom, would see Anarawd's action as an attack on his brother. Anarawd had entered into an alliance with Alfred a few years before this raid and it is possible that Cadell had rejected their alliance, thereby inviting a hostile response from both parties. Cadell lived for a further fifteen years, whether as king of Ceredigion or of some other region. His death in

910 was, as far as can be determined, from natural causes. His sons were called Hywel Dda, Clydog, and Meurig; Hywel succeeded Cadell in the kingship.

DAVID E. THORNTON

Sources J. Williams ab Ithel, ed., *Annales Cambriae*, Rolls Series, 20 (1860) • T. Jones, ed. and trans., *Brenhinedd y Saesson, or, The kings of the Saxons* (1971) [another version of *Brut y tywysogyon*] • T. Jones, ed. and trans., *Brut y tywysogyon, or, The chronicle of the princes: Peniarth MS 20* (1952) • T. Jones, ed. and trans., *Brut y tywysogyon, or, The chronicle of the princes: Red Book of Hergest* (1955) • P. C. Bartrum, ed., *Early Welsh genealogical tracts* (1966) • *Asser's Life of King Alfred: together with the 'Annals of Saint Neots' erroneously ascribed to Asser*, ed. W. H. Stevenson (1904); repr. with a supplementary article by D. Whitelock (1959) • *Gir. Camb. opera*, vol. 6 • D. N. Dumville, 'The "six" sons of Rhodri Mawr: a problem in Asser's *Life of King Alfred*', *Cambridge Medieval Celtic Studies*, 4 (1982), 5–18 • J. E. Lloyd, *A history of Wales from the earliest times to the Edwardian conquest*, 3rd edn, 2 vols. (1939); repr. (1988)

Cadell Ddyrnllug (*fl.* 5th cent.), king of Powys, was the legendary ancestor of the later 'Cadelling' kings of early medieval Powys in north-east and east Wales; his epithet means 'gleaming hilt'. His parentage is unclear from the genealogical sources, though later genealogies (probably erroneously) render him grandson of the great Vortigern. Little genuine historical information is known about Cadell, and the account in a Latin life of St Germanus has the appearance of a dynastic origin-legend. According to this life, Cadell was a servant of one Benlli, the ruler of that region at the time of Germanus's visit(s) to Britain (428–9 and 445–6). He entertained the holy man in his household because Germanus had been refused an audience with Benlli. Germanus subsequently advised Cadell to remove himself and his sons from Benlli's fortress, and they were thus spared when the fortress and its tyrannical occupant were destroyed by fire from heaven through the holy man's intercession. Germanus then baptized Cadell and his sons and elevated them as kings, predicting that all subsequent rulers of Powys would be descended from Cadell. Cadell's son in the main genealogies is called Cadeyrn; later sources added Cyngen Glodrydd, Gwynnan, Iddig (Medig), and Tegid. The dynasty of Powys down to the middle of the ninth century was known as the Cadelling. That these later kings would be satisfied with an ancestor of such humble origins is an interesting sidelight on their attitude to their descent, as is the fact that the inscription on the so-called 'pillar of Elise' (or Eliseg), raised by Cyngen ap Cadell in the first half of the ninth century, makes no mention of him. However, the fragmentary nature of the text possibly accounts for this deficiency.

DAVID E. THORNTON

Sources P. C. Bartrum, ed., *Early Welsh genealogical tracts* (1966) • T. Mommsen, ed., *Chronica minora saec. IV. V. VI. VII.*, 3, MGH Auctores Antiquissimi, 13 (Berlin, 1898) • J. E. Lloyd, *A history of Wales from the earliest times to the Edwardian conquest*, 3rd edn, 2 vols. (1939); repr. (1988) • Nennius, *'British history' and 'The Welsh annals'*, ed. and trans. J. Morris (1980)

Cadell, Francis (1822–1879), riverine explorer and trader in Australia, was born on 9 February 1822 at Cockenzie, near Prestonpans, East Lothian, Scotland, the second son of Hew Francis Cadell, a mine owner and shipbuilder.

Francis Cadell (1822–1879), by unknown photographer

After education in Edinburgh and at Cuxhaven in Germany, he became a midshipman on the East Indiaman *Minerva* at the age of fourteen. The ship was sent to the First Anglo-Chinese War in 1839 and took some part in the siege of Canton (Guangzhou). In 1844, on the *Royal Sovereign*, Cadell visited European and South American ports and planned to explore the upper Amazon by canoe. But his plans came to nothing and in 1846 he travelled back to Scotland, where for a year he studied shipbuilding and the application of steam power to navigation at the yard of Robert Napier & Sons, Glasgow. By 1849 he was in Australia and tried unsuccessfully to raffle the *Royal Sovereign* in Adelaide and to sell it in Sydney. On his return to Scotland he had the *Queen of Sheba* built to his specifications, and in 1851–2 he sailed back to Adelaide through the Pacific. He then took over the *Cleopatra* and entered the Adelaide–Sydney coastal trade.

At this time there was great interest in the possibilities of steam navigation on the River Murray. Cadell and his agent and partner William Younghusband, a member of the South Australian legislative council, negotiated with the government and stood to receive £500 for taking a steamer through the mouth of the Murray, £1000 if this became one of the first steamers to negotiate the Murray from Goolwa to the Darling junction, and a further £1000 for continuing the service for twelve months. While Cadell had a wooden paddle-steamer built in Sydney, he travelled down the Murray from Swan Hill to Lake Alexandrina (over 1300 miles) in a canvas boat, crewed by Bendigo diggers, and concluded with an examination of the mouth of the Murray. On 16 August 1853 he took the new steamer, *Lady Augusta*, through the mouth and soon afterwards started up the Murray with the barge *Eureka*. His sixteen passengers included the governor, Sir Henry Fox Young, and Lady Augusta Young. It took until 17 September to reach Swan Hill. William Randell had already preceded them and gone further up the river, but it was Cadell's achievement which Governor Young honoured in having the commemorative gold medals struck. The South Australian government promised Cadell a further £4000 for additional services.

During the 1850s Cadell was an active trader along the Murray and its main tributaries. His firm, the River Murray Navigation Company, of which Younghusband was a partner, bought the steamer *Melbourne* and two more ships in parts from Glasgow and assembled them at Goolwa. One of them reached the town of Albury on 2 October 1855 (about 1740 miles). Other activities included clearing snags from the Murray and the Murrumbidgee in return for £2000 from the New South Wales government and a commission in 1857 from the South Australian government to supervise the building of a snagging boat. Cadell's company was dissolved that year, but he and one other continued trading, and extended their activities into all the tributaries, up the Murray and the Murrumbidgee to Gundagai, and, in 1854, up the Darling to Mount Murchison, near Wilcannia. On this last trip Cadell was accompanied by the then governor, Sir Richard Graves McDonnell: pioneering and networking went together. In 1859, too, he founded the port of Milang on Lake Alexandrina and planned the irrigation of the Yanko–Billabong area in New South Wales.

Although some settlers complained of Cadell's trading methods, others collected a testimonial fund of £1100 in April 1859. Unfortunately it was insufficient to offset the £6000 loss he and his partner sustained when the *Melbourne* was lost at the mouth of the Murray that November. Despite losses, which were estimated at £17,000 in 1860, Cadell continued to develop the Murray trade. He examined the La Trobe and Snowy rivers, but was also unsuccessful in obtaining finance from the government of Victoria to establish a steamer service from Melbourne to the Gippsland Lakes and the Snowy. In mid-1861 the business failed and the various river town stores, such as Menindee and Hay, ceased to operate. Cadell was forced to sell the *Albury* and the *Bogan*, and in 1863 he sold his remaining vessel, the *Wakool*, to the New Zealand government.

The following year Cadell was in charge of steam transport on the Waikato during the New Zealand wars. At the end of 1866 he was back in South Australia. He then undertook more snag removal on the Darling for the government of New South Wales and early in 1867 he was appointed by the South Australian government to lead an expedition to the Northern Territory, in order to select a site for the capital and an area for agricultural settlement. For nearly a year he investigated thoroughly the Roper, Liverpool, and Victoria rivers, Anson Bay, and Port Darwin, but his report in 1868 was ignored. Two years later he was whaling in New Zealand waters, then trading among Pacific island groups, and in 1873 he was trading on the northern coast of Australia. He was busily recruiting native labour for the pearling fleets in the mid-1870s, and there were allegations concerning the ill treatment of both pearlers and fishermen. In 1879 Cadell disappeared while either trading or recruiting in the Dutch East Indies, probably murdered off the Kei Islands on the schooner *Gem* by the cook's mate, who alleged he had not been paid for five years. According to this version of events, Cadell's body was still on board when the vessel was scuttled.

Opinions about, and even descriptions of, Cadell vary from 'pompous and bombastic' to considerate to a fault (*AusDB*). He was an unsuccessful businessman and accumulated neither property nor money. His real memorial lies in his riverine exploration of South Australia, New South Wales, and the Northern Territory: his name is commemorated by Cadell River in the Northern Territory and a small town on the River Murray in South Australia.

G. R. Henning

Sources J. Allen, *Journal of an experimental trip by the 'Lady Augusta' on the River Murray* (1853) • A. Kinloch, *The Murray River: being a journal of the Lady Augusta steamer from the Goolwa in South Australia to Gannewarra, above Swan Hill, Victoria* (1853) • A. G. Price, *Founders and pioneers of South Australia* (1929) • I. Mudie, *Riverboats* (1961) • *Votes and proceedings*, South Australia Legislative Assembly (1853), papers 78, 96; (1857–8), paper 64; (1860), paper 17; (1862), paper 239; (1866–7), paper 44; (1867), paper 188; (1868), paper 24 • *Votes and proceedings*, New South Wales Legislative Assembly (1858), papers 3, 685, 721; (1866), papers 2, 190 • *Votes and proceedings*, Victoria Legislative Assembly (1862–3), paper 2 (D42) • *The Examiner and Melbourne Weekly News* (8 Nov 1862) • *Adelaide Observer* (29 April 1866) • *Adelaide Observer* (27 Dec 1873) • *Adelaide Observer* (10 Oct 1874) • *Adelaide Observer* (20 March 1880) • *South Australian Register* (20 Sept 1879) • *The Register* [Adelaide] (25 Sept 1920) • *The Register* [Adelaide] (10 June 1927) • *The Argus* [Melbourne] (20 Aug 1879) • *The Argus* [Melbourne] (15 March 1880) • Mitchell L., NSW, Cadell MSS, FM4/1765 • State Library of South Australia, Adelaide, Mortlock Library of South Australiana, Cadell MSS • State Library of South Australia, Adelaide, Mortlock Library of South Australiana, A. Grenfell Price MSS • State Library of South Australia, Adelaide, Mortlock Library of South Australiana, I. Mudie MSS • I. Mudie, 'Cadell, Francis', *AusDB*, vol. 3 • S. Mullins, 'Australian pearl-shellers in the Moluccas: confrontation and compromise on a maritime frontier', *Great Circle*, 23/2 (2001), 3–23

Archives Mitchell L., NSW, FM4/1765 • State Library of South Australia, Adelaide, Mortlock Library of South Australiana | State Library of South Australia, Adelaide, Mortlock Library of South Australiana, I. Mudie MSS • State Library of South Australia, Adelaide, Mortlock Library of South Australiana, A. Grenfell Price MSS

Likenesses photograph, State Library of Victoria, Melbourne, La Trobe picture collection [*see illus.*]

Cadell, Francis Campbell Boileau (1883–1937). *See under* Scottish colourists (*act.* 1900–1935).

Cadell, Henry (*bap.* 1812, *d.* 1888). *See under* Cadell family (*per. c.*1740–1934).

Cadell, Henry Moubray (1860–1934). *See under* Cadell family (*per. c.*1740–1934).

Cadell [*née* Nash], **Jessie Ellen** (1844–1884), novelist and orientalist, was born at Devonshire Lodge, Pancras Vale, Hampstead Road, London, on 23 August 1844, the daughter of William Nash, a City merchant, and his wife, Emma, *née* Jell. Her father died while she was young, and her mother married General Liptrop, and she and Jessie went with him to India in 1859. On 2 February 1861 in Ferozepore Jessie married a 39-year-old Scot, Captain Henry Moubray Cadell of the Bengal artillery, with whom she had two sons. After time spent on the north-west frontier, they returned to Europe in 1864, living in the south of France and Algeria until Captain Cadell's death in 1867. Jessie

Cadell devoted herself to writing and to studying Persian, first in Edinburgh, where she cared for her mother-in-law, then from 1873 in London. From 1879 her health became increasingly frail, and she moved to Italy, living in Siena and Florence.

Jessie Cadell's writing sprang essentially from her personal experience. Her first novel, *Ida Craven* (1876), set in Peshawar in the early 1860s, depicts the way in which a very young woman comes to terms with marriage to a much older officer, the theme being resolved in a well-managed plot involving a campaign on the north-west frontier. British life in India is depicted in a lively and not uncritical manner; Jessie Cadell regretted British lack of sympathy for Indians, and the novel contains an affectionate portrait of a well-born Indian who, despite prejudice, is befriended and promoted by the heroine's husband. Jessie Cadell's second novel, *Worthy: a Study of Friendship*, written shortly before her death, was prepared for publication in 1895 by her son John. Set in Corsica, London, Edinburgh, and France, it again has a strong autobiographical element: the young widow of an Indian army officer struggles to bring up her son, immersing herself meanwhile in writing and academic study. Emotional relationships evolve through the Franco-Prussian War of 1870–71. The novel was felt to reflect the declining state of health in which the author wrote, and lacked the taut construction and pace of its predecessor.

Jessie Cadell's oriental studies began in Peshawar, where she first learned Persian. She continued her studies in Edinburgh, intending originally to write a history of India. However, on moving to London, she became immersed in the poetry of the Persian ʿUmar Khayyam, and collated manuscripts from libraries in England and Paris, with a view to publishing an authoritative edition of his *Rubaiyat*. Before her death she was also preparing a study of parallel lines of thought in Persian and European religious and mystical poetry, including the work of St Catherine of Siena. The only result of her researches published during her lifetime was 'The true Omar Khayam', published in *Fraser's Magazine* (May 1879), in which she defended ʿUmar Khayyam from the charge of irreligion, and maintained that Edward Fitzgerald's recent version of his poetry was a paraphrase rather than a translation. Her scholarship was praised by Bodenstedt in his own German translation in 1881. Following her death, Jessie Cadell's verse translation of one hundred and fifty authentic quatrains was published in 1899. Although her success as a poet was questioned, her faithfulness to the spirit of Khayyam was recognized: 'Her strong point is her sympathy with Omar which renders her more of a Persian than any of her competitors' (Garnett, xxix).

The Athenaeum recalled that Cadell 'was a brave, frank, true woman, bright and animated in the midst of sickness and trouble, disinterestedly attached to whatever was good and excellent, a devoted mother, a staunch and sympathising friend' (*Athenaeum*, 824); while the scholar Richard Garnett noted 'It would be difficult to find a more thoroughly sterling character, one whose gifts and accomplishments were more conscientiously and systematically made auxiliary to serious ends' (Garnett, viii). After many years of ill health she died on 17 June 1884 in Florence, where she was buried. ROSEMARY CARGILL RAZA

Sources R. Garnett, 'Introduction', *The Ruba'yat of Omar Khayam*, trans. H. M. Cadell (1899) · *The Athenaeum* (28 June 1884), 824 · J. E. Cadell, 'The true Omar Khayam', *Fraser's Magazine*, new ser., 19 (1879), 650–59 · b. cert.

Wealth at death £775 16*s*. 10*d*. gross; £526 8*s*. 2*d*. net after funeral expenses and deduction of debts: NA Scot.

Cadell, John (*bap.* 1740, *d.* 1814). *See under* Cadell family (*per. c.*1740–1934).

Cadell, Robert (1788–1849), bookseller and publisher, was born on 16 December 1788 at Cockenzie, East Lothian, Scotland, the fifth son of John *Cadell (*bap.* 1740, *d.* 1814) [*see under* Cadell family], a laird of Cockenzie, and his wife, Marie Buchan (1753–1841).

Robert Cadell is known for his professional and personal association with Sir Walter Scott, and for his enormously successful re-publication and promotion of that author's work. At about the age of nineteen, Cadell became a clerk in the publishing house of Archibald Constable & Co., of Edinburgh, Scott's publisher. In 1811, at the urging of his brother-in-law Robert Cathcart, himself in partnership with Constable, Cadell became a partner in the firm. On Cathcart's death after an illness in November 1812, Cadell was Constable's sole partner, an arrangement that lasted for ten years.

Cadell married Constable's daughter Elizabeth on 14 October 1817; her death on 16 July 1818 heralded frequent disagreements between the partners. Cadell was known as cautious and frugal, while Constable spent lavishly and made risky business decisions. Although they were very wary of Scott's business practices with James and John Ballantyne, Cadell especially, they did agree that the firm's connection to Walter Scott was valuable; Cadell, in his partner's absence, once offered £1000 for an unwritten drama, 'Halidon Hill'.

The partnership was further eroded when Cadell married Anne Fletcher Mylne (1796–1867) on 25 January 1821. The bankruptcy of Constable's London agents Hurst Robinson and the long-term effects of assisting in the prevention of the ruin of Ballantyne & Co., Scott's own publishing company with the Ballantynes, caused Archibald Constable & Co. to fall into receivership in January 1826. The partnership dissolved, Scott deciding to remain with Cadell. Scott's diary entry of 24 January 1825 remarks 'Constable without Cadell is like getting the clock without the pendulum, the one having the ingenuity, the other the caution of business' (Lockhart, *Life*).

Scott and Cadell united in purchasing the property in the novels, from *Waverley* to *Quentin Durward*, with a majority of the shares in the poetical works. They also determined to issue a uniform edition of the Waverley novels, with new prefaces and notes by the author. Scott and Cadell were able to purchase the copyrights for the below-market price of £8500. The publication of the 'author's edition' began in 1827, illustrated by J. M. W. Turner, and was highly successful. Cadell even persuaded Scott not to issue a fourth 'Malachi Malagrowther' letter against parliamentary reform, for fear that it might endanger the success of that edition of the novels.

Scott made his will in Cadell's house in Edinburgh, entrusting it to his keeping. Lockhart speaks of Cadell's 'delicate and watchful attention' to Scott during the writer's later years. He accompanied Scott on his final journey from London to Edinburgh and Abbotsford in July 1832. The balance of Scott's debts after his death amounted to £30,000, through his partnership with the failed Ballantyne firm. In 1833 Cadell ('very handsomely', says Lockhart) offered to liquidate this debt, advancing £30,000 to Scott's family in exchange for only the right to the profit from the copyrights until this new liability to himself was thus repaid.

Restricting operations almost exclusively to the publication of Scott's works, Cadell issued with great success an edition of the Waverley novels in forty-eight volumes, from 1830 to 1834. From 1842 to 1847 he published the lavishly illustrated Abbotsford edition in twelve volumes, which is said to have cost him £40,000. Additionally, Cadell supposedly sold 70,000 copies of an inexpensive 'people's edition'.

In 1847 the Scott family was still in debt to Cadell, as well as to other creditors of Scott's estate for money raised on the house and lands of Abbotsford. Cadell relieved the guardians of Sir Walter Scott's granddaughter of all liabilities to him and to the mortgage holders of Abbotsford, in exchange for the family's rights to Scott's works, seemingly along with the future profits of Lockhart's *Life of Scott*. Another stipulation was that Lockhart would produce for Cadell's firm an abridgement of that biography.

Cadell held considerable land and personal property, due nearly exclusively to his proposition to the Scott family and Lockhart. He died on 20 January 1849 at Ratho House, Midlothian. On 26 March 1851 the novels, prose, poetic works, and the *Life* by Lockhart were auctioned at the London Coffee House. The 'largest trade gathering that has ever been witnessed' assembled for the sale (Curwen, 1968, 139). Robert Darnton credits Robert Cadell with helping to define the role of the publisher through new marketing strategies (Darnton, 52). Lockhart characterizes him as 'a cool, inflexible specimen of the national character', and as 'one of the most acute men of business in existence' (*The Ballantyne-Humbug Handled*, 1839, 103).

FRANCIS ESPINASSE, *rev.* BARBARA A. CORNELIUS

Sources J. G. Lockhart, *Life of Sir Walter Scott* (1871) • Scottish Book Trade Index, NL Scot. • H. Curwen, *A history of booksellers, the old and the new* (1873); repr. with introduction by L. Shepard (1968) • J. T. Hillhouse, *The Waverley novels and their critics* (1968) • R. Darnton, *The forbidden best-sellers of pre-revolutionary France* (1996) • T. Constable, *Archibald Constable and his literary correspondents*, 3 vols. (1873) • Chambers, *Scots.* (1868–70), 1.386–8 [Archibald Constable] • Anderson, *Scot. nat.* • *The Athenaeum* (27 Jan 1849) • J. G. Lockhart, *The Ballantyne-humbug handled, a letter* (1839) • J. Millgate, *Scott's last edition* (1987) • J. Sutherland, *The life of Sir Walter Scott* (1995) • www.onthenet.com.au/~gmylne/mylne/thomasamylneofamylnefield_m.htm, 5 Aug 2002

Archives NL Scot., accounts, legal papers, corresp., and personal papers • NL Scot., corresp. and papers • NL Scot., letter-books and accounts | NL Scot., corresp. with Archibald Constable • NL Scot., corresp. with Basil Hall • NL Scot., letters to William Laidlaw • NL Scot., corresp. with Lord Macaulay • NL Scot., corresp. with Sir Walter Scott

Likenesses D. O. Hill and R. Adamson, photograph, 1843–8, NPG

Cadell, Thomas, the elder (1742–1802), bookseller, was born in Bristol and baptized on 12 November 1742, the son of William Cadell and his wife, Mary. On 7 March 1758 he was apprenticed by his father to the eminent London bookseller and publisher Andrew Millar, and eventually became Millar's partner in April 1765. When Millar retired two years later, Cadell took over the business altogether with the support of Millar's capable assistant Robert Lawless. Cadell was named one of Millar's executors at his death in 1768. Having established himself in his profession, Cadell shortly thereafter married the daughter of the Revd Thomas Jones on 1 April 1769.

In occasional partnership with William Strahan and later with Andrew Strahan, Cadell continued the business at 141 Strand, London, 'over against Catherine Street', as his imprint stated, for over twenty-five years. He published works by the foremost writers of the day and followed his predecessor's example in paying authors generously. Cadell and Strahan had a notable success with the publication of Gibbon's *Decline and Fall of the Roman Empire* (1776–88), for which Gibbon received close to two-thirds of the sales profits (Norton, 44–5). Other popular works included Mackenzie's *The Man of Feeling* (1771) and the poetry of Robert Burns, which Cadell began publishing in 1787. Praising the successful début of *Decline and Fall*, Hume wrote to Strahan in 1776 that 'There will no Books of Reputation now be printed in London but through your hands and Mr Cadel's' (*Letters of David Hume*, 2.313).

Nichols recalled that Cadell spoke of the letter *B* as having been particularly successful to him during his career, instancing Blackstone, Blair, Buchan, and Burns among the authors he published (Nichols, *Lit. anecdotes*, 9.667). To that list should be added Beattie, Fordyce, Hume, Johnson, William Robertson, Adam Smith, and Smollett. Cadell commented in a letter to Gibbon in 1787, 'I had rather risk my fortune with a few such Authors as Mr Gibbon, Dr Robertson, D Hume … than be the publisher of a hundred insipid publications' (BL, Add. MS 34886, fol. 151). Cadell's publication list also included books by Frances Brooke, Fanny Burney, Catharine Macaulay, and Hannah More. He published the novels of Charlotte Smith as well, until her radical views became too extreme, and in 1792 he declined to publish her novel *Desmond*.

Cadell was also the friend and publisher of Johnson and, along with Thomas Davies and Strahan, was delegated by a consortium of booksellers in spring 1777 'to wait upon Dr. Johnson, to solicit him to undertake the Lives', that is, the biographical prefaces to *The Works of the English Poets* (1779–81), a proposal that Johnson accepted on terms very agreeable to the booksellers (Boswell, *Life*, 3.111). Cadell published Johnson's political tracts of the 1770s and, along with Strahan, his *Journey to the Western Islands of Scotland* (1775). He later offered Johnson a substantial sum of

Thomas Cadell the elder (1742–1802), by Henry Hoppner Meyer (after W. Evans, after Sir William Beechey)

money for a volume of 'Devotional Exercises', but Johnson declined his proposal (Nichols, *Lit. anecdotes*, 2.552). After Johnson's death Cadell published *Prayers and Meditations* (1785), a volume edited from the manuscripts of his private devotions. He also published Mrs Piozzi's *Anecdotes of the Late Samuel Johnson* (1786) and paid her 500 guineas for her *Letters to Samuel Johnson* (1788).

Popular among his colleagues, Cadell was a founding member of the booksellers' dining club which met monthly at the Shakespeare tavern in Wych Street, Strand. On numerous occasions he joined other booksellers and printers in prosecuting Scottish and Irish printers who infringed their copyrights. Cadell's wife died in January 1786. Of their two children, his daughter married Dr Charles Lucas Eldridge, chaplain to King George III; his son, Thomas Cadell the younger [*see below*], succeeded in the family firm. On his retirement in 1793 Cadell turned the business over jointly to his son and to his assistant, William Davies.

Cadell remained active in public life during his retirement. He was made a governor of the Foundling Hospital in 1795, served as treasurer of the Asylum, and is said to have regularly attended chapel in one of the prisons. On 30 March 1798 he was unanimously elected alderman of Walbrook ward in the City of London, and served in the office of sheriff, 1800–01. He was master of the Stationers' Company in 1798–9, and a stockkeeper in 1800. He presented a painted glass window to the Stationers' Hall in 1802, which has since been replaced, although his portrait, by Sir William Beechey, still hangs in the company's hall. Cadell also commissioned from Beechey a portrait of his long-serving chief assistant Lawless to ornament his drawing-room. Cadell died at his house in Bloomsbury Place on 27 December 1802 from a sudden attack of an asthmatic complaint. Having acquired a fortune through his publishing business, he left a valuable estate with property in several counties and substantial legacies to his friends, including one to William Davies of £100.

Thomas Cadell the younger (1773–1836), bookseller, succeeded his father in the family business with William Davies as his partner. The firm operated as Cadell and Davies from 1793, although Davies is thought to have managed the business alone until a serious illness in 1813 prevented him from continuing. From that time until his own death in 1836, Cadell directed the affairs of the firm, having relocated the business from the Strand to his house in Charlotte Street, Fitzroy Square. Cadell had been admitted to the Stationers' Company in 1794, and was a member of the court in 1831. The position of the firm slipped somewhat in the nineteenth century; although still trying to uphold its former reputation for liberality to authors, Cadell and Davies undertook several expensive projects, including James Murphy's *Arabian Antiquities of Spain* (1815) and *British Gallery of Contemporary Portraits* (1822), which put a strain on the business's finances. Cadell married Sophia Elizabeth Smith, sister of the authors of *Rejected Addresses*, on 11 March 1802, and had a large family, including four daughters and a son, but none of his children carried on the family business, which was sold off after his death. Cadell died on 23 or 26 November 1836, at his residence in Charlotte Street, Fitzroy Square, leaving his family in comfortable circumstances. Sophia Elizabeth Cadell died on 11 May 1848.

CATHERINE DILLE

Sources Nichols, *Lit. anecdotes*, 2.552; 3.386–9; 6.441–3; 9.667 · Nichols, *Illustrations*, 8.510, 552 · *The letters of David Hume*, ed. J. Y. T. Greig, 2 (1932) · *Thraliana: the diary of Mrs. Hester Lynch Thrale (later Mrs. Piozzi), 1776–1809*, ed. K. C. Balderston, 2nd edn, 2 (1951), 694 · Boswell, *Life*, vol. 3 · T. Besterman, *The publishing firm of Cadell & Davies: select correspondence and accounts, 1793–1836* (1938) · J. Norton, *Bibliography of the works of Edward Gibbon* (1940), 44–5 · R. Myers, ed., *Records of the Stationers' Company, 1554–1920* [1984–6] [microfilm; with guide, *The Stationers' Company archive: an account of the records, 1554–1984* (1990)] · D. F. McKenzie, ed., *Stationers' Company apprentices*, [3]: *1701–1800* (1978), 63, 235 · *GM*, 1st ser., 72 (1802), 1173–222 · W. McDougall, 'Smugglers, reprinters and hot pursuers: the Irish–Scottish book trade and copyright prosecutions in the late eighteenth century', *The Stationers' Company and the book trade, 1550–1990*, ed. R. Myers and M. Harris, St Paul's Bibliographies (1997), 151–83 · *The letters of Edward Gibbon*, ed. J. E. Norton, 3 (1956) · R. H. Nichols and F. A. Wray, *The history of the Foundling Hospital* (1935) · will, PRO, PROB 11/1868, sig. 647 [Thomas Cadell the younger]

Archives Boston PL, corresp. · Duke U., Perkins L., corresp. and MSS · Harvard U. · NL Scot., corresp. and business MSS, MSS 1653–1655 · U. Edin. L., corresp., La ii 646–647 · U. Reading L., corresp. and business MSS | BL, letters to Gibbon, Add. MS 34886 · BL, corresp. with Strahan & Spottiswoode, Add. MSS 48902–48905 · Bodl. Oxf., letters to Kincaid & Bell · NA Scot., letters to A. Grant · NL Scot., corresp. with Blackwoods, MSS 4005–4714, *passim* · Yale U., Beinecke L., corresp. with W. Davies

Likenesses W. Beechey, portrait, *c*.1793, Stationers' Company, London · J. G. Walker, engraving, 1824 (after T. Stothard), BL, Add. MS 38730, fol. 296 · J. G. Walker, line engraving, pubd 1824 (after T. Stothard), NPG · H. H. Meyer, stipple (after W. Evans, after W. Beechey), BM, NPG [*see illus.*]

Wealth at death substantial; left property in several counties and substantial fortune: Besterman, *The publishing firm*, ix • substantial; Stationers' Company stock left to wife; value of business sold; Thomas Cadell: Besterman, *The publishing firm*, xii

Cadell, Thomas, the younger (1773–1836). *See under* Cadell, Thomas, the elder (1742–1802).

Cadell, William (1668–1728). *See under* Cadell family (*per.* c.1740–1934).

Cadell, William (*bap.* 1708, *d.* 1777). *See under* Cadell family (*per.* c.1740–1934).

Cadell, William (*bap.* 1737, *d.* 1819). *See under* Cadell family (*per.* c.1740–1934).

Cadell, William Archibald (1775–1855), traveller, was the eldest son of William *Cadell (*bap.* 1737, *d.* 1819) [*see under* Cadell family (*per.* c.1740–1934)], the original managing partner and one of the founders of the Carron ironworks, and his wife, Katherine (*d.* 1797), daughter of Archibald Inglis of Auchendinny, Edinburghshire, owner of a mill producing high-quality paper. He was born at his parents' house, Carron Park, near Falkirk, on 27 June 1775, one of five sons and one daughter born to the couple, and, after having been educated at Edinburgh University, became a member of the Faculty of Advocates in 1798. He did not practise, since he had private means and owned the estate of Banton, Stirlingshire, but spent his time in scientific and antiquarian research at home and abroad. His scientific interests, which were reflected in two papers, won him the friendship of Sir Joseph Banks, at whose suggestion Cadell was elected fellow of the Royal Society on 28 June 1810. He was also fellow of the Geological Society and of the Royal Society of Edinburgh, and a member of the Wernerian Natural History Society of Edinburgh. While travelling in Europe during the war with France, Cadell was taken prisoner in 1802, but escaped several years later by pretending to be a Frenchman, a feat which his knowledge of French enabled him to accomplish successfully. He returned to Scotland in 1809. Following a later journey he published *A Journey in Carniola, Italy, and France in the Years 1817, 1818* (2 vols., 1820), which contemporaries found reliable, if dry. Cadell died unmarried at Edinburgh on 19 February 1855. The family businesses of coal mining, and iron and paper manufacture gave him the means to study and travel, but his involvement in the businesses was confined to the investment of capital.

GORDON GOODWIN, *rev.* ELIZABETH BAIGENT

Sources private information (1886) • Boase, *Mod. Eng. biog.* • P. Cadell, *The iron mills at Cramond* (1973) • P. Cadell, 'The industrial associates of the Cadell family in the 18th century', *Scottish Genealogist*, 23 (1977), 69–76, 82–90 • R. H. Campbell, *Carron Company* (1961)

Archives NL Scot., corresp. and papers | NA Scot., Carron MSS • NA Scot., Dundas family MSS

Cademan, Sir Thomas (c.1590–1651), physician, born in Norfolk, matriculated as a pensioner from Trinity College, Cambridge, about 1601, and proceeded BA in 1606 and MA in 1609. He then studied abroad and took an MD in 1620 from Padua, where he studied with Roderigo Fonseca. The next year he established a practice in London. In 1626 he resided in Fetter Lane; two years later he was included by the JPs as a recusant of Westminster, and in 1637 he reportedly lived near St Martin-in-the-Fields.

In 1623 Cademan passed his examinations before the censors of the College of Physicians, and on 25 June was ordered to get incorporated into an English university, which he appears not to have done, thus inaugurating a strained relationship with the college. In 1616 the college had debated whether Catholics should be examined, since they were not supposed to be admitted; they named Cademan as a papist to the parliamentary commission of 1626. The year before they had fined him £20 for mistreating one of the earl of Hertford's servants, who eventually died. Cademan did not become a licentiate until 3 December 1630, and became a fellow on 22 December. He seems to have been inactive in the college for the better part of the next two decades. In 1649 he was chosen as anatomy lecturer, and on the appointed day he opened the doors to the hall and allowed in all sorts of servants, footmen, and rabble, and then delivered a poorly prepared lecture that angered Baldwin Hamey and other members. He became an elect on 25 June 1650, perhaps a sign that the college wanted to appeal to conservative sentiment after the execution of the king.

Cademan's Catholicism brought him to the attention of Henrietta Maria, who made him a royal physician in 1626. He signed himself *medicus regineus* after this, and his position at court led to influence and profit. Thus, on 19 November 1628 he and John Gifford certified that John St Johns, a recusant imprisoned in the New prison, was sick of the spleen and should be released. Similarly, on 24 May 1634 Thomas Reynolds, a secular priest, confined in Newgate for some years, petitioned for release, and appended a certificate from Cademan and others.

Cademan and Sir William Brouncker had a patent for distilling and brewing in a house at the back of St James's Park, and this patent, they noted in 1633, they had exercised for many years. By 1638 Cademan had obtained the assistance of Sir Theodore Turquet de Mayerne, the queen's favourite physician, and Cademan and Mayerne were made master and founder, respectively, of a new company incorporated as the Distillers of London. Cademan and Mayerne were directed to approve of a set of suitable rules for the making of strong waters and vinegars according to art, which the masters, warden, and assistants were to compose. The Society of Apothecaries, alarmed at this scheme, petitioned against it in September as infringing their monopoly. Mayerne, Brouncker, and Cademan replied to this petition, denying the statements made, and urging that the apothecaries should be admonished to confine their attention to their shops and their patients, and to speak in a more respectful fashion to the physicians. The undertaking proceeded, and in 1639 *The Distiller of London* was published 'to be a book of rules and directions concerning the distillation of strong waters and making vinegars' (*Distiller*, ii). A second edition of the *Distiller* with 'the Clavis to unlock the deepest secrets of that mysterious art' was issued in 1652.

Cademan was also physician to Francis Russell, fourth

earl of Bedford, and wrote an account of the earl's death entitled *The earl of Bedford's Passage to the Highest Court of Parliament, 9 May 1641, about Tenne a Clock in the Morning* (1641). There he argued that the earl 'died of too much of his bed, and not of the small-pox'. Cademan noted that Russell 'was so weary of his bed, as he feared it would be his grave', but was forbidden to rise by other unnamed physicians, to which the earl responded, 'well then I will die to observe the physitians'.

A manuscript of Cademan's, entitled 'De signis morborum tractatus, cura Thamae Clargicii', is in the library of the Royal Society of Medicine. A work of 1318 folios, all in a single hand, it is a treatise on medical semiology that catalogues the symptoms by which diseases could be recognized. Cademan obviously intended to publish the work, and in the dedication to Henrietta Maria he claimed to have been in the service of the queen for twenty or so years, which would date the manuscript to about 1646.

Cademan died on 2 May 1651. Information about his family is sketchy. In 1631 the privy council granted a pass for travel to the spa to Anne, described as the wife of Doctor Cademan. His son, Sir John Cademan, served Charles I as physician to the royalist army. BRIAN NANCE

Sources annals, RCP Lond. • BL, Sloane MSS, MS 2149 • 'De signis morborum tractatus', Royal Society of Medicine, London • *CSP dom.* • *APC, 1630–31*, 397 • T. Cademan, *The earl of Bedford's passage* (1641) • *The distiller of London* (1639) • *DNB* • Venn, *Alum. Cant.* • Munk, *Roll*

Archives Royal Society of Medicine, London, 'De signis morborum tractatus'

Cadfan [St Cadfan] (*supp. fl.* **6th cent.**), founder of a religious settlement, was the patron saint of Tywyn (Merioneth), Llangadfan (Montgomeryshire), and perhaps a monastery on Ynys Enlli (Bardsey Island); his feast day was celebrated on 1 November. There is no surviving life of Cadfan, but there is a twelfth-century poem by Llywelyn Fardd (to be distinguished from his thirteenth-century namesake) which is informative about the cult of the saint at Tywyn *c.*1150. The poem begins with a prayer to God of fitting eloquence; it thus acts as a confession before God of the virtues and miracles of Cadfan, but also as an act of praise, before both God and Cadfan, for the stalwart virtues of Morfran (*fl.* 1147), currently the abbot of Tywyn and patron of the poet. The poem thus binds together God, the saint, Cadfan, his church, Tywyn, and Morfran. The last is presented as a tough defender of the rights of his church, an abbot to whose sanctuary fighting men could flee, secure in the belief that the abbot was as good a fighter as they were.

Cadfan was believed to be from Brittany, and came to Wales in the company of other saints, notably Padarn and Tydecho. This was a device to justify an alliance between their churches, but it also detached the exile-saints from any close connection with local dynasties. His parents, apparently wholly legendary, are given as Eneas of Brittany and Gwen of Three Breasts. According to a vernacular life of St Llawddog, preserved only in a sixteenth-century manuscript, Cadfan bequeathed the church he had founded on Bardsey to Llawddog, although there was no kinship between them. Cadfan's association with Bardsey is commemorated by the twelfth-century poem, but it differs from the later life in several respects: it has a different form of the name, Lleuddad rather than Llawddog; it maintains that they were first cousins; and it claims that Cadfan remained as much the patron of the monastery on Bardsey as was Lleuddad. Suggestions that the poet was referring only to a spiritual kinship between the two saints are not, in the context of the poem, plausible. Since the reputation of Bardsey in the twelfth century was high, it is not surprising that Llywelyn Fardd should wish to safeguard Cadfan's role as founder and patron; it must, however, be remembered that his testimony is earlier by some centuries than that of the life.

T. M. CHARLES-EDWARDS

Sources P. C. Bartrum, ed., *Early Welsh genealogical tracts* (1966) • *Gwaith Llywelyn Fardd I ac eraill o feirdd y ddeuddegfed ganrif*, ed. K. A. Bramley and M. E. Owen (1994), no. 1, 9–32 • V. E. Nash-Williams, *The early Christian monuments of Wales* (1950), nos. 286–8 [no. 287 has been reconsidered by I. Williams, *The beginnings of Welsh poetry*, ed. R. Bromwich (1972), 25–40] • S. Baring-Gould and J. Fisher, *The lives of the British saints*, 4 vols., Honourable Society of Cymmrodorion, Cymmrodorion Record Series (1907–13) • E. R. Henken, *Traditions of the Welsh saints* (1987), no. 17 • E. R. Henken, *The Welsh saints: a study in patterned lives* (1991) • M. Richards, *Welsh administrative and territorial units* (1969)

Cadfan ab Iago (*fl. c.*616–*c.*625), king of Gwynedd, was son of Iago ap Beli of Gwynedd. Cadfan seems to have ruled the kingdom of Gwynedd in north-west Wales during the early decades of the seventh century. Few facts concerning his reign or the extent of his power are known, and the details recounted by Geoffrey of Monmouth in his *Historia regum Britanniae* and followed in later Welsh traditions should be rejected as unhistorical. Cadfan was of the traditional ruling line of Gwynedd, allegedly descended from Maelgwn Gwynedd of the previous century. Cadfan's father, Iago ap Beli, had died in the same year as (but not necessarily at) the battle of Chester, in 613 or 616, at which point Cadfan may have succeeded to the kingship. However, as Iago's death-notice has an ecclesiastical flavour (*dormitatio*) it is possible that he had retired from the kingship and that Cadfan had succeeded him earlier. Cadfan did not necessarily fight at the battle of Chester as ally of the unfortunate Selyf ap Cynan Garwyn, though the later genealogies claim that Cadfan's wife was Tandreg Ddu, Selyf's sister. Cadfan in turn may have been dead by the late 620s when his son, the famous *Cadwallon, was active politically. His memorial stone, which was probably raised by Cadwallon or his son *Cadwaladr, survives at the church of Llangadwaladr on Anglesey and describes Cadfan as 'the wisest and most renowned king of all kings'. However, it was Cadwallon who ultimately achieved greater fame for his struggles against the English. Cadfan is also credited in late sources with a daughter called Efeilian. DAVID E. THORNTON

Sources J. Williams ab Ithel, ed., *Annales Cambriae*, Rolls Series, 20 (1860) • T. Jones, ed. and trans., *Brenhinedd y Saesson, or, The kings of the Saxons* (1971) [another version of *Brut y tywysogyon*] • T. Jones, ed. and trans., *Brut y tywysogyon, or, The chronicle of the princes: Peniarth*

MS 20 (1952) · T. Jones, ed. and trans., *Brut y tywysogyon, or, The chronicle of the princes: Red Book of Hergest* (1955) · P. C. Bartrum, ed., *Early Welsh genealogical tracts* (1966) · V. E. Nash-Williams, *The early Christian monuments of Wales* (1950) · *The Historia regum Britannie of Geoffrey of Monmouth*, ed. N. Wright, 1: *Bern, Bürgerbibliothek, MS 568* (1985) · A. W. Wade-Evans, ed. and trans., *Vitae sanctorum Britanniae et genealogiae* (1944) · J. E. Lloyd, *A history of Wales from the earliest times to the Edwardian conquest*, 3rd edn, 2 vols. (1939); repr. (1988)

Cadman, John, first Baron Cadman (1877–1941), mining engineer and industrialist, was born on 7 September 1877 at The Villas, in the north Staffordshire mining village of Silverdale, the eldest son of James Cope Cadman (1851–1914) and his wife, Betty, *née* Keeling (*d.* 1924). His father was a mining surveyor and engineer and the general manager of the Silverdale Coal and Iron Works; later he became president of the Institution of Mining Engineers, in 1903. After local schooling, Cadman left Newcastle under Lyme high school at seventeen to become a pupil of his father. He attended local mining classes which the Staffordshire county technical education department had established for working miners. In 1896 Cadman won the council's first county mining scholarship, to study geology and mining at Armstrong College in Newcastle upon Tyne, then part of Durham College of Science, where he graduated BSc (first class) in 1899 and MSc in 1902; he was elected fellow of the Geological Society of London in 1900 and became DSc in 1908.

After graduation Cadman went to Silverdale as assistant general manager to his father. Then, after a period as a colliery agent in Durham, he moved to Scotland in 1902 as HM inspector of mines (east Scotland), before once more returning to Staffordshire as HM inspector in 1903. Here he was to show conspicuous bravery in mine rescue work, particularly at the Hamstead colliery disaster of March 1908. In September 1904 he was seconded as chief mining engineer for Trinidad and Tobago. Having previously encountered oil seeps in Staffordshire and the oil shales of Fife and Lothian, he was now introduced to the natural oil and bitumen of the asphalt lakes. From then on it was the oil industry to which he was to make such a major contribution, though he remained a loyal servant of the coal industry too. This posting also introduced Cadman to his future wife, Lilian Julia (*d.* 1963), daughter of John Harrigan, magistrate of Port of Spain, Trinidad. They married on 27 July 1907, and had two sons and two daughters.

In 1908, soon after his return to England, Cadman was appointed professor of mining at Birmingham University, where his main duties were to lecture on the mining of coal and metal ores. However, his interests in oil were already aroused and he gave courses on petroleum as soon as he took up his chair, when there were only about twenty students in the department. To demonstrate the vital role he saw for the emerging oil industry, in 1912 he set up the first undergraduate course in Britain on petroleum mining technology, leading to the new degree of bachelor of science (petroleum). Cadman drew initially on his oil experiences in England, Scotland, and Trinidad, but these were soon augmented by his introduction to oil in the Middle East in 1913. Cadman's desire to integrate the

John Cadman, first Baron Cadman (1877–1941), by Ivan Opffer, 1930

training of geologists, chemists, and engineers was furthered when Professor W. S. Boulton established a petroleum exploration course in the geology department, which Cadman's petroleum mining students could take for their final year.

These courses had been established in the face of much academic opposition; T. H. Holland (1868–1947), professor of geology at Manchester University, reported in 1913:

> I really cannot find one commendable feature in the latest and most flagrantly advertised of our now bewildering variety of university degrees, the 'B.Sc. (Petroleum Mining)', at Birmingham … It is unfair to entice young men into a blind alley, and saddle them with a freak title that will handicap every attempt that they make in after life to specialise in a recognised branch of technology. (Holland, 351–2)

In 1913 Cadman, appointed to the Admiralty commission on fuel oil under Admiral Sir Edmund Slade, visited the Persian oilfields to report on whether an assured supply of oil could be found there for the British navy, thus fulfilling the wishes of Admiral John Arbuthnot Fisher (1841–1920) to convert the engines of British navy ships to burn oil. The commission's report influenced Churchill's epoch making decision to adopt oil burning engines in the British fleet. It also dramatically changed the fortunes of the Anglo-Persian Oil Company (APOC), in which the government acquired a majority holding in 1914. Cadman also helped to organize the search for oil in Britain during the First World War, using imported American technology. Two of the sites chosen to drill for oil were in north Staffordshire. These attempts, to check the sources of the local oil seeps which he had long known, gave useful, if negative, lessons for the future. Cadman was made CMG in 1916.

Cadman was a founder member of the Institution of Petroleum Technologists, established in London in March 1914 to advance both the study of petroleum and British interests in the rapidly developing world of oil. Clashes of personality at the institution, amid crises over maintaining oil supplies to Britain and the empire during the First World War, disrupted the two academic petroleum courses available in Britain (that in London had started in 1913). When the war ended a major libel action resulted, which was won by Cadman. This, with the death of Sir Boverton Redwood amid the aftermath of war, caused the true significance of these developments to be forgotten.

During the First World War, Cadman emerged as the leading British authority on oil. He directed HM petroleum executive between 1917 and 1921 with conspicuous success. He was appointed KCMG in 1918 for this service. With the ending of war, he was appointed technical adviser on oil to the British government and, with much new diplomatic work demanding long absences from Birmingham, he resigned his chair there in 1920. In 1921 he was made technical adviser to APOC and moved to London. With typical energy, he collaborated with Standard Oil of America and encouraged American participation in the Turkish Petroleum Company. In this Cadman proved a fine diplomat and successful negotiator. He was largely responsible for stopping the aggressive and self-destructive oil policies then existing between Britain and the United States.

In 1923 Cadman became a managing director of APOC. Here he organized the better application of science to industry and to oil exploration, and he built up the research element of APOC's operations. Cadman was instrumental in encouraging the British Geological Survey's foray into geophysics, by giving it APOC advice and funds. These allowed survey officers to see first-hand the results of their geophysical work in the field in Persia. Cadman's management skills, helped by an unusual understanding of human nature, were appreciated by many in APOC, and 1925 saw him appointed deputy chairman; early in 1927 he became chairman, a post he retained until his death. These were remarkable appointments, with Cadman the first 'professor' scientist to become chairman of a British industrial company with a capital of tens of millions of pounds. He was rewarded by being made GCMG in 1929. He also played a vital role by acting as chairman in setting up the Iraq Petroleum Company and by devising a pipeline by which Iraqi oil could reach the Mediterranean.

Cadman fought any division of science into 'pure' or 'applied'. Alongside his pioneering role in the international oil industry, he showed his continuing vision in his involvements with the Bridgeman committee on television from 1935, which he later chaired. This was the first body to see the future significance of this new means of communication. Not content with this, in 1937 Cadman was asked to chair a government committee into the work of Imperial Airways and the future of international aviation transport. Cadman thus played a vital role in three of the most significant developments of the twentieth century. He was awarded several honorary degrees and became Lord Cadman in 1937, choosing to recall his mining birthplace as Baron Cadman of Silverdale. He was finally elected FRS in 1940.

Throughout his life Cadman was a devout Anglican, and he was appreciated for his friendliness, humour, and humanity. He enjoyed music and played the violin in his earlier years. He died from a stroke, at his home, Shenley Park, near Bletchley, Buckinghamshire, on 31 May 1941, aged sixty-three, worn out by further wartime work. He was buried at his birthplace, Silverdale, in the church of St Luke on 4 June. He had made an enormous and international contribution to the industry he had helped to create, making probably the greatest contribution to oil ever achieved by an individual Briton. He is honoured by the Cadman medals which are awarded by Birmingham University, the Institute of Petroleum, and the Institution of Mining Engineers, and by the Cadman memorial lectures of the Institute of Petroleum and the Royal Society of Arts. H. S. TORRENS

Sources J. Rowland and B. Cadman, *Ambassador for oil* (1960) • A. D. Cadman, *'Semper paratus': a biographical family heritage* (privately printed, 1970) • R. W. Ferrier, 'Cadman, John', *DBB* • F. E. Smith, *Obits. FRS*, 3 (1939–41), 915–28 • A. Beeby-Thompson, *Oil pioneer* (1961) • T. H. Holland, 'Presidential address', *Transactions of the Institution of Mining Engineers*, 46 (1914), 339–55 • R. W. Ferrier, *The history of the British Petroleum Company*, 1: *The developing years, 1901–1932* (1982) • J. H. Bamberg, *The history of the British Petroleum Company*, 2: *The Anglo-Iranian years, 1928–1954* (1994) • J. H. Bamberg, *The history of the British Petroleum Company*, 3: *British Petroleum and global oil, 1950-1975: the challenge of nationalism* (2000) • H. S. Torrens, '300 years of oil', *The British Association lectures* (1993), 4–8 • R. W. Ferrier, 'The early management organisation of British Petroleum and Sir John Cadman', *Management strategy and business development*, ed. L. Hannah (1976), 130–47 • parish register (baptisms), St Luke's Church, Silverdale, Staffordshire • *CGPLA Eng. & Wales* (1941) • *The Times* (12 Nov 1963)

Archives University of Wyoming, American Heritage Center | NA Scot., corresp. with Philip Ker • U. Birm. L., letters to Granville Bantock; corresp. with Oliver Lodge • U. Warwick Mod. RC, British Petroleum Archives

Likenesses I. Opffer, black chalk drawing, 1930, NPG [*see illus.*] • W. Stoneman, photograph, 1933, NPG • J. A. A. Berrie, oils, British Petroleum, London • photographs, repro. in Rowland and Cadman, *Ambassador for oil* • photographs, repro. in Ferrier, 'Cadman, John'

Wealth at death £234,748 10s. 4d.: probate, 12 Nov 1941, *CGPLA Eng. & Wales*

Cadoc the Wise. *See* Cadog (*fl.* 6th cent.).

Cadog [St Cadog, Cadoc, Cadfael, Cathmáel] (*fl.* **6th cent.**), founder and abbot of Llancarfan, and brother of St *Cynidr, is assigned a feast day on 24 January by the late eleventh- or early twelfth-century life by Lifris and by Welsh calendars. The life by Lifris is of unique length and richness of detail among Welsh lives of saints and it was reworked for a wider audience in the early twelfth century by *Caradog of Llancarfan. Cadog also appears in the Irish lives of Cainnech, probably dating to the eighth century, and Finnian, perhaps of the eleventh century but probably based on a lost life of around the ninth century. The role in which he appears in the Irish lives is that of a teacher of Irish saints who sought him out in Britain. In Lifris's life of Cadog the saint returns to Britain from Ireland, bringing with him Irish disciples. This return is then followed by a series of episodes, several of which have counterparts in the lives of Cainnech of Aghaboe and Finnian of Clonard. There is a parallel series of episodes in the life of Maedóc of Ferns, except that Maedóc is said to have studied with David rather than with Cadog. In this section of Lifris's life of Cadog, therefore, it is possible to gain some idea of the sources he may have used and the way he may have handled them. The picture is complicated, however, by the length of time involved: if the life of Cainnech is taken to be eighth-century, a version of the story would appear to have been in existence some three centuries before Lifris. Lifris himself attests a confraternity between Llancarfan and Clonard, and the material in the Latin life of Finnian suggests that this confraternity may have been in existence for a long time before Lifris wrote the life of Cadog. An interchange of hagiographical material, both written and oral, between Ireland and Wales is thus likely to go back well before the eleventh century. It cannot be said, therefore, that Lifris was working on an Irish text that has survived: his immediate sources are likely to have perished and they may have been Welsh rather than Irish. The general lesson to be drawn from the relationship of these texts is that Lifris was, at least in part, a reshaper of texts already in existence.

Lifris's life is followed in the manuscript that contains it by a *passio* (account of martyrdom) which says that Cadog's body was translated, while the saint was still alive, to Benevento in southern Italy. It also contains an angelic message instructing Cadog to appoint Elli as his successor at Llancarfan. When abbot, Elli is said to have visited Cadog at Benevento every year. Cadog was consecrated bishop of Benevento, died, and was enshrined, and a basilica was built over the shrine, where no Briton was allowed to enter for fear that someone from Llancarfan would attempt to steal the corporeal relics. The *passio* declares that more miracles were performed at the shrine than during the saint's lifetime, but the next text in the manuscript is in fact a collection of narrations of post-obit miracles performed in Glamorgan, of which the first recounts how the shrine of the saint and other relics were saved from raiding Danes and Englishmen. This collection ends with a doxology and a piece of verse naming Lifris, as if it were the end of the entire text. But it is then followed by Cadog's genealogies, by an account of the prebends of Llancarfan and the sharing of certain dues, by a brief narrative about the conversion of Cadog's father and mother to the religious life, and a declaration that the *familia* of Cadog was to receive the dues of food from churches built by his parents. The penultimate text in the dossier is a collection of charters, followed by an anecdote about Maelgwn, king of Gwynedd (*d.* 549), his demand for tribute, the killing of his tax gatherers, and the settlement subsequently made, very much to the advantage of Cadog. This is a version of an anecdote in the life (Lifris, chap. 23).

There is no full analysis of this dossier. While the collection itself may have been made in response to the threat posed to the community of Llancarfan by the Norman invasion, and the composition of Lifris's life may have been precipitated by the same threat, it seems unlikely that all the texts are of the same date. To take one example, the *passio* has been seen as an invention by Lifris designed to explain why Llancarfan did not have the body of Cadog; a marginal note in the Gotha manuscript of the life of Cadog by Caradog of Llancarfan has been cited, and records the tradition that Cadog's body lay at St David's. On this basis the Beneventan connection is seen as pure fiction, in a period when Normans were conquerors both in Glamorgan and in southern Italy. Yet the eighth-century life of Cainnech, in a passage which may form part of the material shared, in various proportions, with the lives of Cadog, Maedóc, and Finnian, has Cainnech going on pilgrimage to Rome, converting a cruel Italian king, and promising to be buried in Italy. God has to intervene to bring Cainnech back to Ireland, but, even so, he leaves behind a toe as a relic. This suggests that, whatever the degree of elaboration by Lifris, he was not responsible for inventing the entire story.

The story of Cadog and Benevento may have offered an explanation of why Llancarfan did not have the body of the saint, but it also enabled Lifris to depict a Cadog consecrated as bishop, even though he made no claim to episcopal rank on behalf of Llancarfan. One of the striking aspects of the life is that it hardly mentions Teilo, who was currently being adopted as the saint of Llandaff, except as one in a group of witnesses or judges, and even then, David is given precedence. Moreover, when a concern is shown to define the status of Cadog and Llancarfan *vis-à-vis* other principal saints and churches, the point of reference is David, not Teilo. At issue was the right to summon a synod, the usual way in which the early Irish and Welsh churches appear to have interpreted metropolitan rights. When David protested his unworthiness to the angel sent to instruct him to summon the synod, he declared that there was a worthier person in Glywysing (modern Glamorgan but often including Gwent), namely Cadog. The angel replied that Cadog would be no obstacle for he would soon be going on pilgrimage. When Cadog returned, no one was brave enough to tell him what had happened until Finnian was chosen by lot to reveal the news; Cadog was greatly incensed until an angel assuaged his anger with a short homily on brotherly forgiveness and a hefty bribe of extra privileges. So far as this story is concerned, therefore, Cadog was the principal saint of Glywysing, equal or even superior to David.

The story, with its twin themes of Cadog as *peregrinus*

('pilgrim-saint') and Cadog as defender of his own local standing in south Wales, typifies the life as a whole. One of its main concerns is to set out, in narrative form, the status or privilege (*braint*) of Cadog, similar to *Braint Teilo*, which was written at the same period and later copied into the Book of Llandaff. In advancing the case for this *braint* Lifris makes good use of Cadog's own worldly status, as son of *Gwynllyw, the eponymous king of Gwynllŵg, and as grandson on his father's side of Glywys, eponymous king of Glywysing, and on the side of his mother, Gwladus, of *Brychan, likewise eponymous king of Brycheiniog. Gwynllyw blesses Cadog as Isaac blessed Jacob, granting the cemetery of Llancarfan the right to bury the dead of Gwynllŵg, and reserving for Gwynllyw's own church (St Woolloos, Newport) only the burial of exiles and women who died in childbirth. In the cause of protecting and extending his powers of sanctuary, however, Cadog could also handle secular powers beyond Glywysing, beginning with Arthur, and going on to Maelgwn, king of Gwynedd, his son Rhun, and finishing with his maternal uncle, Rhain, king of Brycheiniog. Lifris's life of Cadog, very much like some of the charters in the Book of Llandaff, presents a picture of a church adept at bullying kings. It is also thoroughly aristocratic in outlook: the great saints of south Wales are themselves accounted noblemen, and when David professed in reply to the angel his inferiority to Cadog, he began by saying that 'he [Cadog] is by kindred much more worthy than I am' (Lifris, chap. 13). As a man of high birth and as a saint Cadog could handle both kings and popes. When Gildas took his melodious bell to Rome to give it to God and St Peter, having refused it to Cadog, the bell, once presented to the pope, gave out no sound. In reply to questioning by the pope Gildas explained that it had last rung in the guest house of Cadog, to which the pope replied: 'Some time ago I got to know the man you mention, for he came here as a pilgrim seven times, and three times to Jerusalem, to seek forgiveness for the souls of his parents and kinsmen' (Lifris, chap. 27). A man of royal birth, a friend of God and his saints, Cadog could, by much hard travelling, unite his local world with all Christendom.

T. M. CHARLES-EDWARDS

Sources Lifris, 'Vita sancti Cadoci', *Vitae sanctorum Britanniae et genealogiae*, ed. and trans. A. M. Wade-Evans (1944), 24–141 · 'Vie de Saint Cadoc par Caradoc de Llancarfan', ed. P. Grosjean, *Analecta Bollandiana*, 60 (1942), 35–67, esp. 45–67 · P. C. Bartrum, ed., *Early Welsh genealogical tracts* (1966) · W. W. Heist, ed., *Vitae sanctorum Hiberniae ex codice olim Salmanticensi nunc Bruxellensi*, Subsidia Hagiographica, 28 (Brussels, 1965), 82 · C. Brooke, *The church and the border in the central middle ages* (1986) · H. D. Emanuel, 'An analysis of the composition of the *Vita Cadoci*', *National Library of Wales Journal*, 7 (1951–2), 217–27 · *Gwaith Rhys Brydydd a Rhisiart ap Rhys*, ed. J. M. Williams and E. I. Rowlands (1976), nos. 6 and 7 · V. E. Nash-Williams, *The early Christian monuments of Wales* (1950), no. 204 · S. Baring-Gould and J. Fisher, *The lives of the British saints*, Honourable Society of Cymmrodorion, Cymmrodorion Record Series, 2 (1908), 14–42 · G. H. Doble, *St Cadoc in Cornwall and Brittany* (1937) · G. H. Doble, *The saints of Cornwall*, ed. D. Attwater, 4 vols. (1960–65) · G. H. Doble, *Lives of the Welsh saints*, ed. D. S. Evans (1971) · H. D. Emanuel, 'Beneventana civitas', *Journal of the Historical Society of the Church in Wales*, 3 (1953), 54–63 · E. R. Henken, *Traditions of the Welsh saints* (1987), no. 3 · E. R. Henken, *The Welsh saints: a study in patterned lives* (1991) · M. Richards, *Welsh administrative and territorial units* (1969)

Cadogan. *See also* Cadwgan.

Cadogan, Sir Alexander George Montagu (1884–1968), diplomatist, was born in London on 24 November 1884, the youngest child in the family of seven sons and two daughters of George Henry *Cadogan, fifth Earl Cadogan (1840–1915), a politician, and his first wife, Lady Beatrix Jane Craven (1844–1907), the fourth daughter of William Craven, second earl of Craven.

Education and early career Alec Cadogan grew up in surroundings of what can only be called grandeur. Life alternated between Chelsea House at the corner of Cadogan Square, a residence described by Harold Macmillan as 'a kind of baronial castle' (Macmillan, 30), and a family estate of 11,000 acres at Culford Hall, near Bury St Edmunds, Suffolk. However, the grandeur was tempered by strict routine and cultivation of a high sense of obligation. In 1897 Cadogan went to Eton College, to the house of A. C. Benson, an outstanding and versatile master in an outstanding Eton period. His all-round ability brought him to be captain of the Oppidans, president of the Eton Society, and an editor of the *Eton College Chronicle*. He also showed early signs of that satirical sense of humour that never left him nor ever descended into wounding sarcasm or bad taste. A. F. Scholfield, librarian of Cambridge University (1923–49), a contemporary of Cadogan, later recalled the pleasure with which the back row of sixth form awaited the next cartoon or caricature to be handed down from Cadogan further in front. He proceeded in 1903 to Balliol College, Oxford, where he obtained a second-class degree in history in 1906.

In October 1908 Cadogan headed the list in the examinations for the diplomatic service, and in the following January was posted as attaché to the embassy in Constantinople. In September 1910 he was granted an allowance for knowledge of Turkish and almost immediately afterwards was promoted third secretary. On 3 August 1912, shortly after returning to London, he married Lady Theodosia Louisa Augusta Acheson (*d.* 1977), the third daughter of Archibald Brabazon Sparrow Acheson, fourth earl of Gosford. Theo Cadogan was a lady of highly individual character who exercised great influence in family matters without intrusion into official business, and the marriage was extremely happy. They had one son, Ambrose (*b.* 1914), and three daughters, Patricia (*b.* 1916), Cynthia (*b.* 1918), and Gillian (*b.* 1922).

In April 1913 Cadogan was transferred to another grand embassy, in Vienna, where high society was obsessed with the measurement of social rank. However, this was not a completely wasted opportunity for further diplomatic education because the Balkans remained volatile, and there was no reluctance to give him responsibility. He was temporarily in charge at the embassy when news of the assassination of the heir to the Austro-Hungarian throne, Archduke Franz Ferdinand, came in from the consul at Sarajevo. The sequence of events that this precipitated led to Britain's declaration of war on Austria-Hungary on 12

Sir Alexander George Montagu Cadogan (1884–1968), by Walter Stoneman, 1941

August 1914, and two days later Cadogan returned to London.

The League of Nations, and China There followed a period of nearly twenty years in the Foreign Office. During this time Cadogan went steadily up the promotion ladder, and as private secretary from January 1919 to March 1920 to Cecil Harmsworth, parliamentary under-secretary of state for foreign affairs, he was in a position to observe political life closely. But his most important assignment, commencing in 1923, was as head of the small but influential League of Nations section, for which the permanent under-secretary, Sir Eyre Crowe, recommended him as 'the best man in the Office' (*The Times*, 17 July 1968). He accepted this task in the belief that the league itself and, above all, the pursuit of disarmament could lead to real and permanent results, and that, if it did not, nothing would prevent the rearmament of Germany. It meant long periods accompanying successive Foreign Office ministers to Geneva, but he thought their active involvement preferable to greater reliance on a permanent British representative. He was soon indispensable to them and was highly regarded by the league secretariat. He was made a CMG in June 1926 and promoted counsellor in December 1928.

In this uphill pioneering work at the League of Nations there were periods of progress under Sir Austen Chamberlain and Arthur Henderson. But the Japanese invasion of Manchuria in September 1931, a little over four months before the world disarmament conference convened in Geneva, was an irretrievable set-back. Cadogan, who was secretary-general of the large British delegation to this conference, was temporarily buoyed up by the fresh presentation of British disarmament policy in early 1933 provided by Anthony Eden. But once Hitler had assumed power in Germany, there was no further hope of reconciling German claims and French insistence on security—and Cadogan attached much weight to security. The task now seemed hopeless. Thus it was that in the late summer of 1933 Cadogan, who had resisted suggestions that he might become secretary-general of the League of Nations or high commissioner at Danzig, accepted the suggestion of the permanent under-secretary, Sir Robert Vansittart, that he should become minister in Beijing. He had been made a CB in June 1932, and in January 1934 was knighted KCMG and formally appointed to the China legation. He confided to his diary his pleasure at 'going 11,000 miles away' (*Diaries*, ed. Dilks, 8).

Cadogan established a good relationship with Chiang Kai-shek but could not escape the British Far Eastern dilemma of the time. This was how to protect Britain's important interests in China while striving to limit the military and political ambitions of Japan by keeping relationships with it as friendly as possible. Cadogan was not happy with the guidance on or offers of practical assistance for China that he received from home, and was forced to support a policy of playing for time. This meant recommending to the Chinese direct negotiations with the Japanese invaders and to his own government protest at only their more outrageous actions. In June 1935 his legation was upgraded to embassy status, and he was accordingly promoted ambassador.

Permanent under-secretary Early in 1936 Eden, now foreign secretary, invited Cadogan to return from China in order to become the senior deputy under-secretary in the Foreign Office. Surmising correctly 'that this post might carry the succession to Vansittart' (*Diaries*, ed. Dilks, 12), the colourful campaigner against Germany whom Eden was determined to oust, Cadogan accepted, taking up his post in October 1936. By now he was universally regarded as the perfect embodiment of the senior civil servant. He was not only intelligent, efficient, imperturbable, loyal, economical in language, and thoroughly conventional (to his detractors 'cold'), he was also 'sound' in judgement, reserved but not without charm, and possessed of an instinct for contacting the right person in the right way at the right time. In short, he would be a first-class assistant rather than a dangerous rival, and on 1 January 1938 he duly succeeded as permanent under-secretary. However, Cadogan's situation was rendered difficult by the retention of his predecessor (until the summer of 1941) as chief diplomatic adviser, a title that signified no authority but was not interpreted by Vansittart as disguising a sinecure. The two men were as different in outlook as in temperament, Vansittart seeing the worsening European situation with intellectual clarity, Cadogan seeing it without illusions but with a sensitive eye to what the country and its leaders would in fact be prepared to do. As a result, when

Eden resigned in February 1938 in protest at Chamberlain's attitude towards negotiations with Mussolini, Cadogan found himself more in agreement on this as on most other matters of foreign policy with the prime minister than with Eden.

In the trauma of Munich in September 1938 Cadogan took a characteristically middle position. He knew the Anglo-French weakness in defence, and, like the new foreign secretary, Lord Halifax, was reconciled to cutting Britain's losses in Europe's heartland in order to defend her interests more effectively around its perimeter. Thus he felt that great efforts should be made to reach a compromise with Hitler while concentrating on rearmament. But when at one moment it appeared that the British government might positively encourage Hitler to march into Czechoslovakia, he wrote a strong minute urging Halifax to try to dissuade Chamberlain from going as far as that; Halifax was persuaded—and successful. Cadogan was first and foremost of the *realpolitik* school of foreign policy, and had no illusions about the power of diplomacy unsupported by force. This sometimes brought him into conflict with younger colleagues in the Foreign Office, but he was not completely unsentimental.

By the time the Second World War broke out in 1939 Cadogan (who was promoted GCMG in January that year) enjoyed the complete confidence of Halifax. When Eden returned to the Foreign Office in 1940, this confidence was continued, if in a somewhat different mode, and he soon acquired that of Churchill. The pressures on Eden were huge even before he assumed leadership of the House of Commons in November 1942, and the chairmanship of the cabinet by the prime minister was notoriously—and increasingly—chaotic. It is thus hardly surprising that the dependence on Cadogan's advice and brisk execution of business was great, and that in April 1944 it was seriously rumoured that he was to be appointed foreign secretary. Throughout the war he was at the shoulders of both Churchill and Eden at the inter-allied conferences, and was frequently present at cabinet meetings after April 1940. Nor did he confine his non-deferential side entirely to his secret diary strewn with exclamation marks. At a critical moment in Moscow in August 1942, following an acerbic encounter between Churchill and Stalin, he told the prime minister flatly and repeatedly and with some effect that his attitude to the draft Soviet communiqué was wrong. 'I had never', observed Churchill's doctor, who was present at this encounter, 'seen anyone talk to the P.M. like this' (Lord Moran, *Winston Churchill: the Struggle for Survival*, 1966, 78). Cadogan was also required to devote considerable time in London to dealing with the representatives of exiled governments and difficult personalities such as de Gaulle. During the last years of the war he also had to cope with the amalgamation of the various branches of Britain's overseas representation and the Foreign Office in order to create the new combined foreign service, though he passionately hated discussion of administrative questions. The issue of reform in which he was most immediately interested was how to prevent the accumulation of mountains of red-labelled red boxes on his desk. It is as well that he had a robust constitution and that at the end of his impossibly long working day he was able, after having 'refreshed himself' (Butler, 37), to open his heart in his diary. He was promoted KCB in January 1941.

The United Nations From July 1945 Cadogan received from Ernest Bevin and Clement Attlee the same confidence accorded to him by Churchill. But in that year the Labour government, after debating whether to appoint a politician or a diplomatist as the first United Kingdom permanent representative at the headquarters of the United Nations (UN) in New York, appointed Cadogan. He would have preferred the Washington embassy. However, while he had a vast understanding of world affairs as a whole, he had little specialized knowledge of the United States. Moreover, he had extensive experience of the League of Nations, and in August–September 1944 had been the principal British delegate at the allied conference on world organization at Dumbarton Oaks, where his performance 'won him golden opinions in the United States' (*Diaries*, ed. Dilks, 669). Since he had also been prominent at the UN's charter-drafting conference at San Francisco in April–May 1945, he was clearly the safe choice, though some would have preferred a 'younger and more original man' (G. McDermott, *The Eden Legacy and the Decline of British Diplomacy*, 1969, 88). He left the Foreign Office in February 1946, and in the same year was sworn of the privy council. He had been permanent under-secretary for the unusually long period of eight years.

New York, to which Cadogan went when he was already sixty-two, and where he was allowed considerable latitude, was his final post. Despite his legendary antipathy to personal publicity, he adapted surprisingly well to conference diplomacy. He also displayed here an authority, in all senses of the word, which maintained at a time of relative material weakness the standing of the United Kingdom in the world organization, and so the post proved a worthy culmination to his diplomatic career. For all his quietly ironic humour, he was never a cynic, and continued to believe that, despite human frailty and incompetence, it was better to strive after workable international institutions than do nothing. His advice on the teething problems of the UN was often sought by other delegations and the secretariat. He remained in his post at New York until his retirement in June 1950. In the same year he was elected an honorary fellow of Balliol, and on 1 January 1951 he was given the Order of Merit, the first civil servant to receive this honour.

The BBC, and the Suez Canal Company Shortly after his retirement in 1950 Cadogan joined the boards of the National Provincial Bank and the Phoenix Assurance Company. However, this did not signal the end of his involvement in public affairs—far from it. In 1951 he accepted nomination as one of the three government directors of the Suez Canal Company, and in the following year Churchill appointed him chairman of the board of governors of the BBC. He had no liking for radio and television and took a poor view of the journalistic profession, but this did not matter unduly since he did not believe that the job required interference in daily administration. This suited his director-general, Sir Ian Jacob, for whom Cadogan had both liking and respect. Cadogan refused to take the BBC into the political battle over whether it should retain a monopoly over television, from which emerged in 1954 the Television Act and the Independent Television Authority. Nevertheless, he was sometimes less reticent with regard to the content and timing of the BBC's own programmes. His position at the BBC presented him with a conflict of interests when the Suez crisis broke in 1956, because of his role in the Suez Canal Company and his long and close connections with Anthony Eden, though it is not clear whether he acknowledged this. In January of that year Cadogan was also appointed chairman of the Commonwealth-American Current Affairs Unit, an offshoot of the English-Speaking Union and important vehicle of British cultural diplomacy.

Though he had no part in its planning and marked reservations about its execution, Cadogan strongly supported government policy during the Suez crisis. He also firmly opposed broadcasting that might disturb an imminent diplomatic conference or unsettle British troops on the eve of battle. It is not surprising, therefore, that at certain intervals, especially in the earlier stages of the crisis, Eden was able to exploit his position and personal relationship with Cadogan in order to secure favourable treatment for the government by the BBC. This led to pronounced unease at the corporation. Nevertheless, it is a mistake to believe either that Cadogan was solely responsible for the BBC's behaviour during Suez or that he was Eden's entirely pliable agent at Bush House. It is notable in particular that he actively and successfully resisted the government's attempt late in October to force it into line by threatening a 20 per cent cut in the funding of the external services. At the end of his term with the BBC and the Suez Canal Company in 1957 Cadogan retired completely from public life.

Assessment Cadogan was a man of outstanding professional skill and standards, of consistent calm, reticent about personal and family matters, and eschewing conventional affability. His naturally grave face, long in proportion to his height, made him at first sight a little forbidding unless one knew about the humorous corner to his mouth or provoked a sudden smile. As part of his professional equipment, he practised a truly prodigious self-control. Colleagues who worked close to him testified to a 'passion for work', in which some, but not all, found a trace of melancholy, alleviated in his last two years at the United Nations by an easing of the strains of recurring crisis. What all could agree is that he was, as one colleague put it, 'a most distinguished civil servant'. When younger he had been skilful at woodwork and oil painting; in later life he returned to the latter and added keenness for gardening and the open air. Throughout his life he played golf regularly, vehemently, and rather badly. He died in London on 9 July 1968, survived by his wife and their four children.

GORE-BOOTH, *rev.* G. R. BERRIDGE

Sources *The diaries of Sir Alexander Cadogan, 1938–1945*, ed. D. Dilks (1971) • H. Grisewood, *One thing at a time* (1968) • T. Shaw, 'Cadogan's last fling: Sir Alexander Cadogan, chairman of the board of governors of the BBC', *Whitehall and the Suez crisis*, ed. S. Kelly and A. Gorst (2000) • Lord Gladwyn, *The memoirs of Lord Gladwyn* (1972) • N. Rose, *Vansittart: study of a diplomat* (1978) • A. C. Temperley, *The whispering gallery of Europe* (1938) • *The Second World War diary of Hugh Dalton, 1940–1945*, ed. B. Pimlott (1986) • L. Woodward, *British foreign policy in the Second World War*, 1 (1970) • *The diplomatic diaries of Oliver Harvey, 1937–1940*, ed. J. Harvey (1970) • Lord Butler, *The art of memory: friends in perspective* (1982) • H. Macmillan, *Winds of change, 1914–1939* (1966) [vol. 1 of autobiography] • *The Times* (10 July 1968); (13 July 1968); (16–17 July 1968); (22 July 1968) • *WWW* • Burke, *Peerage* • *FO List* (–1951) • register, Eton • college register, Balliol Oxf. • personal knowledge (1981) • private information (1981)

Archives CAC Cam., diaries, corresp., and papers • PRO, corresp. and papers relating to China and Turkey, FO800/293–4, 896 | BL, corresp. with Lord Cecil, Add. MS 51089 • Bodl. Oxf., corresp. with Lord Monckton • Borth. Inst., corresp. with Lord Halifax • CUL, corresp. with Sir Samuel Hoare • U. Birm. L., corresp. with Lord Avon

Likenesses W. Stoneman, three photographs, 1934–53, NPG [*see illus.*] • photograph, 1946, repro. in *Diaries*, ed. Dilks, facing p. 597 • F. Eastman, portrait, priv. coll. • D. Grant, portrait, priv. coll. • photograph, repro. in *The Times* (10 July 1968)

Wealth at death £124,958: probate, 27 Nov 1968, *CGPLA Eng. & Wales*

Cadogan, Charles, second Baron Cadogan of Oakley (**1684/5–1776**). *See under* Cadogan, William, Earl Cadogan (1671/2–1726).

Cadogan, George Henry, fifth Earl Cadogan (**1840–1915**), politician, was born at Durham on 9 May 1840. He was the eldest son of Henry Charles Cadogan, the fourth earl (1812–1873), and his wife, Mary Sarah (1808–1873), daughter of Gerald Valerian Wellesley (prebendary of Durham and brother of the first duke of Wellington) and his wife, Emily Mary, *née* Sloane. He was educated at Eton College and at Christ Church, Oxford, and as a young man accompanied the prince of Wales on various tours at home and abroad. At the general election of 1868, as Viscount Chelsea, he stood unsuccessfully as a Conservative for Bury. He was elected for Bath in 1873, but in the same year went to the House of Lords as Earl Cadogan in consequence of his father's death. Disraeli made him under-secretary of state for war in 1875, and under-secretary for the colonies in 1878. During the second Salisbury administration (1886–1892) he was lord privy seal, and responsible for Irish business in the House of Lords. In the session of 1887 he introduced the Irish Land Act of that year, and in April he joined the cabinet. At this time he advised Queen Victoria with respect to her domestic affairs. For his political and other services he received the Garter in July 1891.

When the third Salisbury administration was formed (June 1895) Cadogan became lord lieutenant of Ireland with a seat in the cabinet. He was warmly interested in G. W. Balfour's Land Act of 1896, and pressed the Treasury until he obtained more liberal terms of purchase for Irish tenants than that department was at first inclined to allow. Afterwards he turned to the subject of Irish education. He appointed commissions to investigate intermediate education (1899) and university education (1901); and

George Henry Cadogan, fifth Earl Cadogan (1840–1915), by Barraud

he sponsored the act of 1899 which created a new department of agriculture, industries, and technical instruction for Ireland. He dealt quietly but firmly with the demonstrations which were stimulated in Ireland by the Second South African War. He was accused of weakness by *The Times* (1902), which drew an unfavourable and unfair contrast between his views and those of the chief secretary, George Wyndham, who had succeeded Gerald Balfour in 1900. But Cadogan enjoyed the full confidence of Lord Salisbury, by whom he was twice dissuaded from resigning. Though he was in favour of pacifying agrarian discontent by the concessions embodied in the Wyndham Land Bill of 1902, he consistently urged the cabinet to coerce disaffected areas and to proceed against seditious newspapers. He resigned in July 1902, at the same time as Lord Salisbury, and retired into private life.

Cadogan was one of those peers to gain spectacularly from urban property at the end of the century. In 1880 he owned about 800 acres in London, much of it in Chelsea, where he was lord of the manor. Against the trend, he extended his agricultural holdings, buying the Culford estate in Suffolk for £175,000 in 1890. In conjunction with Lord Iveagh he spent substantial sums on model dwellings for workmen and on other schemes of social betterment. In 1900 he was elected as the first mayor of Chelsea.

He married twice: first, in 1865, Lady Beatrix Jane Craven (1844–1907), daughter of the second earl of Craven and his wife, Emily Mary, *née* Walter; and second in 1911 at Florence his cousin, Countess Adèle Palagi, daughter of Count Neri Palagi and his wife, Olivia Georgiana, daughter of Sir George Cadogan, brother of the fourth earl. With his first wife he had seven sons (one of whom was Sir Alexander *Cadogan of the Foreign Office) and two daughters. He died at his home, Chelsea House, Cadogan Place, Chelsea, London on 6 March 1915.

H. W. C. DAVIS, *rev.* H. C. G. MATTHEW

Sources private information (1927, 2004) • GEC, *Peerage* • *WWW* • D. Cannadine, *Lords and landlords: the aristocracy and the towns, 1774–1967* (1980)

Archives HLRO | Bodl. Oxf., Disraeli MSS • Glos. RO, Hicks Beach MSS • HLRO, Ashbourne MSS • Kent Archives Office, Stanhope MSS • NA Scot., G. W. Balfour MSS • PRO NIre., E. Carson MSS

Likenesses print, 1907 (after H. J. Stock), NPG • Barraud, photograph, NPG [*see illus.*] • J. Brown, stipple (after photograph), BM; repro. in *Baily's Magazine* (1881) • F. Sargent, pencil drawing, NPG • Spy [L. Ward], caricature, repro. in *VF* (30 Nov 1887) • Spy [L. Ward], caricature, chromolithograph, NPG; repro. in *VF* (4 June 1881) • C. W. Walton, lithograph (after photograph by Bassano), NPG • portrait, repro. in *ILN*, 107 (1895), 5 • portrait, repro. in *ILN*, 117 (1900), 721 • portrait, repro. in *ILN*, 124 (1904)

Wealth at death £354,207 0s. 8d.: probate, 27 April 1915, *CGPLA Eng. & Wales*

Cadogan, Henry (1780–1813), army officer, was born in London on 26 February 1780, the eldest of six children from the second marriage of Charles Sloane, third Baron Cadogan and first Earl Cadogan (1728–1807), to Mary Churchill (1750–1811). After attending Eton College, on 9 August 1797 Cadogan became an ensign in the 18th (Royal Irish) foot, and advanced to lieutenant and captain in the 2nd (Coldstream) guards on 9 December 1799. After a brief spell on half pay, he purchased a majority in the 53rd foot on 8 December 1804, then a lieutenant-colonelcy in the 18th foot, his old regiment, on 22 August 1805. He went on half pay again, on 5 March 1807, and led a half-column of the light brigade in Lieutenant-General John Whitelock's disastrous expedition to capture Buenos Aires in July. Meanwhile, his father had died on 5 April 1807, leaving him an annuity of £700; and, on 7 January 1808, he returned to full pay as lieutenant-colonel in the 71st foot.

In March 1809 his sister Charlotte, the wife of Henry Wellesley, eloped with Henry, Lord Paget. Cadogan offered to 'sell out of the army in order entirely to devote himself to her protection' if she would leave Paget, but Charlotte demurred (Anglesey, 100). On 28 March Cadogan therefore demanded from Paget 'satisfaction for the injury done myself and my whole family by your conduct to my sister' (ibid., 101). The reply mollified Cadogan, but his brother George did subsequently fight an inconclusive duel with Paget.

As aide-de-camp to Sir Arthur Wellesley (later the duke of Wellington), Cadogan left Cork on 12 July 1809 for Portugal, where he liaised with the Spanish Captain-General Cuesta about allied co-operation, before rejoining Wellesley at Talavera on 27–8 July. He assumed command of 1/71st (now designated light infantry) on its arrival from Scotland and fought with the battalion at Sobral on 14 October. When the army advanced from the lines of Torres Vedras in 1810, he dramatically urged the 71st into battle at Fuentes d'Oñoro on 5 May with a cry of 'charge 'em down the Gallowgate' (Pearman, 123), took responsibility for defence of the village when its commander fell, and earned Wellington's formal approval for his actions. He received further praise at Arroyo dos Molinos on 28 October 1811, and he took part in successful actions under Lieutenant-General Sir Rowland Hill south-west of Madrid in 1812. On 21 June 1813, while leading the 71st on the heights of Puebla, near Vitoria, Cadogan was mortally wounded. At his request he was carried 'to the top of a neighbouring precipice, from whence he could have a birds-eye view of the whole of the approaching battle' (ibid., 130). He died shortly before 4 p.m. and was buried near the village of Sovejana de Álava the following day. Wellington wrote: 'He was an officer of the greatest zeal and promise and attached to his profession enthusiastically' (ibid., 129).

Monuments to Cadogan were erected in St Paul's Cathedral (by Francis Chantrey, for which the House of Commons voted £1575) and Chelsea parish church in London, and in Glasgow Cathedral. Aged thirty-three and unmarried, officially he died without issue, though in 1832 Wellington recommended to the commander-in-chief in India, Henry Carr, 'the son of the late Colonel Cadogan of the seventy-first regiment of foot' (Pearman, 132). In noting Henry Cadogan's death, the *Army List* (1814) shows him unequivocally as 'colonel', not 'lieutenant-colonel'.

JOHN SWEETMAN

Sources *Army List* • *The dispatches of … the duke of Wellington … from 1799 to 1818*, ed. J. Gurwood, 7–8, 10 (1837–8) • R. Pearman, *The Cadogans at war, 1783–1864* (1990) • Fortescue, *Brit. army*, vol. 5 • R. Cannon, ed., *Historical record of the seventy-first regiment, highland light infantry* (1852) • *Regimental records of the highland light infantry (old 71st and 74th)* (1914) • Marquess of Anglesey [G. C. H. V. Paget], *One-leg: the life and letters of Henry William Paget, first marquess of Anglesey* (1961) • Burke, *Peerage* (1887)

Archives BL, miscellaneous correspondence, 1843–62 | Som. ARS, letters to Sir William Jolliffe, 1857–9

Likenesses F. Chantrey, relief figure on monument, St Paul's Cathedral, London; repro. in Pearman, *The Cadogans at war*, 141 • painting (his death), AM, Oxford; repro. in Pearman, *The Cadogans at war*, 131 • portrait, repro. in Pearman, *The Cadogans at war*, 111

Cadogan, William (1601–1661), soldier and settler in Ireland, was born in Cardiff on 5 February 1601, the eldest son of Henry Cadogan of Llanbedr Felffre, Pembrokeshire, and Catherine, daughter of Thomas Stradling of St Donats Castle and Merthyr Mawr, Glamorgan. Although a Welshman by birth and upbringing, Cadogan pursued a career which was centred on Ireland, where he joined the secretariat of Sir Thomas Wentworth, the lord deputy, in 1636, and acquired property and a captain's commission in the Irish army soon afterwards. His election for Monaghan borough in the Irish parliament of 1640 was as a government place-man, but with the fall of Wentworth he joined the opposition, sitting on the committee which drew up charges against Sir George Radcliffe and other members of the regime in June 1641.

In the initial stages of the Irish rising Cadogan organized the defence of co. Meath and Drogheda, before moving to Dublin 'about his Majesty's special service' (*Ormonde MSS*, old ser., 2.16). He continued to support the king's commander, the marquess of Ormond, after the cessation of arms of 1643. By early 1645 Cadogan had been appointed deputy governor of Trim, co. Meath, where he tried to keep the peace between the rival protestant and Catholic troops based in the area. The strain soon began to tell, and in September 1645 he dismissed the cessation as a sham: 'every man is able to discern how the Irish, to gain time to provide themselves arms and ammunition, have played poltrons with a good king' (*Ormonde MSS*, old ser., 2.24–5). Despite his misgivings Cadogan remained loyal to Ormond until Dublin was handed over to the parliamentarians in June 1647, when he became commander of Trim under Michael Jones. He was promoted major in 1648, and showed great courage when Drogheda was captured by the Ormondists in July 1649. The arrival of Oliver Cromwell the following month marked the end of Cadogan's military career.

During the 1650s Cadogan worked with the surveyors in setting out confiscated lands, and he was elected MP for the combined constituency of Meath and co. Louth in the 1654 parliament. In the mid-1650s he stayed in London as an agent for those who (like himself) claimed pay arrears for their service in Ireland before 1649. In 1655 he purchased a further 411 acres in co. Meath from an English adventurer; in 1658 he served as sheriff for the county; and in 1659 he took command of its militia troop. On the Restoration, Cadogan continued to live in co. Meath, and was elected portreeve of Navan. He died at Trim on 14 March 1661 and was buried in Christ Church, Dublin. The surname of his wife, Elizabeth (*d.* 1665), is unknown. His eldest son, Henry, married Bridget, the daughter of Sir Hardress *Waller, and was the father of William *Cadogan, Earl Cadogan.

PATRICK LITTLE

Sources HoP, *Commons* [draft] • *The manuscripts of the marquis of Ormonde*, [old ser.], 3 vols., HMC, 36 (1895–1909), esp. vol. 2, pp. 1–113 • *Calendar of the manuscripts of the marquess of Ormonde*, new ser., 8 vols., HMC, 36 (1902–20) • *CSP Ire.*, *1633–60* • *Collins peerage of England: genealogical, biographical and historical*, ed. E. Brydges, 9 vols. (1812) • W. J. Smith, ed., *Herbert correspondence: the sixteenth and seventeenth century letters of the Herberts of Chirbury, Powis Castle and Dolguog* (1963) • K. S. Bottigheimer, *English money and Irish land* (1971) • *Report on the manuscripts of the earl of Egmont*, 2 vols. in 3, HMC, 63 (1905–9) • Bodl. Oxf., MS Firth c.5 • NA Ire., Ferguson MS 10 • S. Pender, ed., *A census of Ireland, circa 1659, with supplementary material from the poll money ordinances (1660–1661)* (1939) • *Calendar of the Clarendon state papers preserved in the Bodleian Library*, ed. O. Ogle and others, 5 vols. (1869–1970) • A. Vicars, *Prerogative wills in Ireland, 1536–1810* (1897) • R. Refaussé and C. Lennon, eds., *The registers of Christ Church Cathedral, Dublin* (1998), 92, 121

Archives NL Ire., papers

Cadogan, William, **Earl Cadogan** (1671/2–1726), army officer and diplomat, was born at Liscarton, co. Meath, the eldest son of Henry Cadogan (*d.* 1715), barrister, and his wife, Bridget, daughter of Sir Hardress Waller. His grandfather was Major William *Cadogan, governor of Trim. He entered Trinity College, Dublin, in 1687 at the age of fifteen, but took no degree.

Early career William Cadogan enlisted in the army of William III in 1689, and served in the rank of cornet at the battle of the Boyne in July that year, with Wynn's dragoons (subsequently known as Ross's, or the Royal Irish Dragoons, reformed as the 5th Royal Irish Lancers in 1858). He served under William III and Frederick, first duke of Schomberg, in the campaign in Ireland that followed, being present at the battle of Aughrim in 1690 and the subsequent capture of both Cork and Kinsale, where he made the acquaintance of John Churchill, earl and subsequently first duke of Marlborough. Cadogan went with his regiment to Flanders during the Nine Years' War (1688–97) and first saw active service under Marlborough there,

William Cadogan, Earl Cadogan (**1671/2–1726**), attrib. Louis Laguerre, *c.*1716

beginning a long professional association and close friendship.

In 1701 Cadogan went with Ross's dragoons to the Netherlands, as a part of the reinforcement of English and Irish troops sent there by William III just prior to the outbreak of the War of the Spanish Succession, following Louis XIV's seizure of the barrier towns in the Southern Netherlands. Cadogan was now a major and quartermaster for his regiment, and that year he was involved in preparations for the transporting to the Netherlands of Danish and Württemberg mercenary troops to join the allied army. When Marlborough assumed command of the allied army in the Low Countries in April 1702, he appointed Cadogan his quartermaster-general and, unofficially, his chief of staff and director of military intelligence, although these posts did not exist in the modern sense at that time. Cadogan very quickly gained the full trust of Marlborough, with his calm and efficient conduct of his duties, during the campaign to force the French Marshal Boufflers away from Maastricht towards Brabant. On 2 March 1703 Cadogan was appointed colonel of the 6th horse (subsequently known as Cadogan's or the 2nd Irish horse, the 5th dragoon guards). After his arrival in the Low Countries, Cadogan married about 1704 Margaretta (1675–1749), daughter of Willem Munter, counsellor of the court of Holland, and his wife, Margaret Tripp, of Amsterdam. There were two daughters of the marriage—Lady Sarah who subsequently married Charles *Lennox, second duke of Richmond, and Lady Margaretta who married Charles John Bentinck (1709–1779), fourth son of William Bentinck, first earl of Portland, the confidential adviser of William III.

During Marlborough's march up the River Rhine in the early summer of 1704, Cadogan was responsible for many of the highly complex logistical details of the movement. Considerable stockpiles of supplies had been gathered along the route, and much of the labour of the administration of these fell to Cadogan. On 2 July 1704, just prior to the storming of the Schellenberg Hill, Cadogan accompanied Marlborough on his close reconnaissance of the position, and his preparations for laying out the allied encampment on the banks of the River Wörnitz largely convinced the Bavarian commander that the allies would not attack the hill that day. Cadogan had his horse killed beneath him during the assault, and he is said to have been injured at this time. He accompanied Marlborough during the battle of Blenheim on 13 August 1704, and was then responsible for the movement back to the Low Countries, down the River Rhine on barges, of many of the weakened allied battalions, and their numerous prisoners. He simultaneously had to arrange the logistics of the movement of the allied army back towards the French frontier. Cadogan's value to Marlborough increased rapidly throughout this entire period. This was particularly so as the duke's close confidant and aide, the Dutch engineer officer Johan Goor, had been killed at the Schellenberg. On 24 August 1704 Cadogan was made brigadier-general, and he shortly afterwards received a Blenheim bounty of £273.

Confidant of Marlborough Cadogan's political career progressed simultaneously with his military activities. On 11 May 1705 he became MP for New Woodstock in Oxfordshire, probably on the nomination of Marlborough. He was returned for the same seat on five successive occasions.

On 17 July 1705 Cadogan was present with Marlborough at the forcing of the lines of Brabant and had an active part in the cavalry battle at Elixheim later that day when Caraman's Bavarian corps was routed. He was employed on various diplomatic missions during the following winter, and on 23 May 1706 he commanded the allied advance party that discovered Villeroy's French army deploying on the ridge at Ramillies. His urgent message brought Marlborough forward and committed the allies to battle. Later that day Marlborough sent Cadogan to recall the British infantry, under George Hamilton, first earl of Orkney, who were pressing home their attacks against the French at Offus. Heated words were exchanged between the two generals, as Orkney was unable to perceive that the British infantry would have been unduly exposed if they continued to advance. Rumours abounded that Cadogan's action was motivated by jealousy at Orkney's success on the right wing, but these were wholly unfounded.

Immediately after Ramillies, Cadogan was sent by Marlborough with a corps of cavalry and infantry to seize Ghent and Antwerp. This important task was accomplished with great skill, and on 1 June 1706 he was made major-general. Six weeks later Cadogan was taken prisoner by a French cavalry patrol while commanding a reconnaissance and foraging expedition near Tournai. Marlborough was alarmed at this loss but, chivalrously, the French promptly released Cadogan in an exchange of prisoners, as they were aware of the duke's high regard for his subordinate. At this time Cadogan was also appointed lieutenant at the Tower of London, in addition to his other duties.

During 1707 William Cadogan was appointed envoy-extraordinary and minister-plenipotentiary to the states general of the United Provinces, although he spent most of the year with Marlborough during the abortive campaigning in Flanders. In February 1708 Cadogan supervised the planned reinforcement of the army in Scotland with battalions from Flanders on rumours of an imminent French invasion. During the series of manoeuvres and marches that led to the battle of Oudenarde on 11 July 1708, Cadogan had command of the advance guard of the allied army. The taut discipline and well-measured control he exercised over the marching soldiers enabled his troops to surprise the French commander, the duke of Vendôme, firstly at Lessines on the River Dender, and then by crossing the River Scheldt at Eename near Oudenarde. The battle that this bold initiative brought on found Cadogan's detachment heavily outnumbered by the French forces in the immediate area, but he controlled the deployment of his troops with great skill, and ensured the security of the bridgehead over the river while Marlborough's main army marched to the scene. The eventual allied success was largely due to Cadogan's highly professional handling of these crucial opening stages of the battle for, although Marlborough and Prince Eugene of Savoy were present, the control of the troops at this point was entirely in his hands. During the lengthy siege of Lille during the summer and autumn that year, Cadogan was involved in the convoying of heavy ordnance from Ostend to the allied armies. On 1 January 1709 he became lieutenant-general, and was among the general officers of cavalry listed in the allied army in Flanders for that year.

During the siege of Menin in the spring of 1709, Marlborough dropped his glove while riding on a reconnaissance with Cadogan. Cadogan was requested to retrieve the garment, which was done without comment, although it would be more usual for an aide to do so. Later that evening the duke asked if he remembered the precise spot that the glove was dropped, and requested that he erect a siege battery there the following day. Cadogan replied that he had already given orders for the works to be commenced—he was well aware that the duke would not have had him undertake such a humble task without good reason.

On 11 September 1709 Cadogan accompanied Marlborough during the terrible fighting at the battle of Malplaquet, and he was sent afterwards as an envoy to arrange with the French for their numerous wounded to be cared for. Shortly afterwards, during the siege of Mons, Cadogan was shot and wounded in the neck, but he recovered soon afterwards. He then took a major part in Marlborough's campaigns during 1710 and 1711. During this period he was removed from his diplomatic duties at The Hague, as his close association with Marlborough told increasingly heavily against him in London, where criticism of the duke was mounting. Cadogan was active during the operations against Douai, and in the complex series of manoeuvres which led to the breaking of the lines of Non Plus Ultra at Arleux in August 1711. Cadogan also played a significant part in the huge siege operations which led to the fall of Bouchain on 13 September 1711.

Peace and diplomacy On Marlborough's dismissal as captain-general in December 1711, Cadogan remained with the allied army in Flanders in a temporary capacity, at his own request, and served as quartermaster-general under James Butler, second duke of Ormond, during the 1712 campaign. Ormond did not employ Cadogan fully as a field commander at this time, apparently on account of his connections with Marlborough. When Marlborough left England in November 1712, to go into exile in the Netherlands, Cadogan joined him there, after refusing to accompany the British troops returning to England. His prominent part in the warm welcome that Marlborough received on his arrival in the Netherlands brought particular censure from the tory government in London, and Cadogan was obliged to resign all those offices and appointments he still held. In December 1712 he sold the colonelcy of the Royal Irish Dragoons to Lieutenant-General George Kellum for £3000, and was removed as lieutenant at the Tower in 1713.

Cadogan had close contacts with the electoral court at Hanover, and in 1714 he returned to London just prior to the accession to the British throne of George I. He was appointed master of the robes by the new king, and to the colonelcy of the 2nd foot guards (Coldstream) on 11 August 1714. Despite allegations that he attempted to bribe the electors of Reading (which nearly brought about a riot in the town market square) Cadogan was returned as MP for New Woodstock, for the fifth successive time, that year. At this time he was also re-appointed to the posts of minister-plenipotentiary and envoy-extraordinary to the states general. Additionally, he became governor of the Isle of Wight on 31 August 1715. On 15 November 1715 he signed the crucial third barrier treaty for Britain on behalf of George I at The Hague, which secured foreign recognition of the validity of the Hanoverian succession to the British crown. During the Jacobite uprising in 1715, Cadogan sailed to Scotland with 6000 Dutch troops lent to Britain by the states general for the suppression of the rebellion. Claiming to be concerned at the apparent leniency towards the rebels of the commander in Scotland, John Campbell, second duke of Argyll, Marlborough, as commander-in-chief, had him recalled to London while Cadogan completed the operations throughout the highlands to suppress the uprising. Cadogan and Argyll were old antagonists from the Flanders campaigns where Argyll had been a severe critic both of Marlborough and of the duke's own close circle. Their opinion of Argyll's conduct at this time may, accordingly, be considered to be rather prejudiced.

Cadogan returned to London in May 1716, after handing over the command to Brigadier-General Joseph Sabine, an old comrade from the war in Flanders. On 21 June 1716 he was created Baron Cadogan of Reading, and he received the Order of the Thistle from George I on 29 June. Later that year he became high steward of Reading. On 4 January 1717 Cadogan signed the treaty of triple alliance between Britain, the Netherlands, and France on behalf of the king. He was sworn of the privy council in London on 17 March 1717, and on 12 July, after the duke of Marlborough had suffered a stroke, was appointed general of all the foot forces (infantry) of the crown.

Following this appointment Cadogan's relationship with the Marlboroughs, particularly with Sarah, duchess of Marlborough, deteriorated, partly over Cadogan's increasing political independence, but also over the investment of up to £50,000 which had been entrusted to him when Marlborough was preparing to go into exile in the Netherlands. Cadogan had, on his own initiative, lent the Dutch securities he had bought on Marlborough's behalf to Emperor Charles VI at double the interest. The Austrian investments fell in value; the duchess secured control of the original investment and transferred the money back to the Netherlands, insisting that the loss be made good, with interest. Eventually Cadogan, who was undoubtedly at fault, and may be suspected of speculating on his own behalf with Marlborough's money, was obliged to pay the shortfall at a considerable personal financial loss.

That was not the only time Cadogan's honesty was questioned. During 1717 he was accused in the House of Commons of embezzling funds allocated for the transportation of Dutch troops to Scotland in 1715. The charges were unfounded but he was acquitted by only a narrow majority of ten in the house. On 8 May 1718 he was created Earl Cadogan, Viscount Caversham, and Baron Cadogan of Oakley; the barony could be passed to his younger brother, Charles [*see below*], should Cadogan die leaving no son. His diplomatic duties in The Hague over the third barrier treaty continued, and in February 1720 he was sent to Vienna to confer with Charles VI over the final details of the treaty. Having gradually established his independence of Marlborough and having then allied himself with Charles Spencer, third earl of Sunderland, he was less well-favoured under the Walpole–Townshend ministry, although he did succeed to the post of master-general of the ordnance on the death of Marlborough in June 1722. Criticism that Cadogan was carelessly dressed and conducted himself loudly and improperly at Marlborough's funeral appears to be misplaced. He became colonel of the 1st foot guards on 18 June 1722, and was made a commissioner of the Royal Hospital, Chelsea. During a fresh Jacobite alarm that year Cadogan had command of an encampment of foot guards established in Hyde Park for the close protection of the king.

Cadogan died at his London home at Kensington Gravel Pits on 17 July 1726. His will contained generous bequests to his close family, and to his personal servants. At his own request Cadogan was buried privately at night in Henry VII's chapel in Westminster Abbey, on 21 July. His wife, Margaretta, survived him, living to October 1749 when she died at The Hague.

William Cadogan was large, heavily built, and bluff in manner. Bishop Francis Atterbury described him rather maliciously as a 'big, bad, bold, blustering, bloody, blundering booby' (*DNB*). His manner was often boisterous and loud and his dress ostentatious. He also had an unfortunate tendency to teasing levity that could give offence on occasions. However, Cadogan had enough diplomatic skill and courtesy to carry off many delicate and complex missions during the War of the Spanish Succession. He was equally valuable in the difficult period following the death of Queen Anne, when the Hanoverian hold on the throne of Great Britain was not secure. However, Cadogan's most significant achievement was as Marlborough's chief of staff. Hard-working and efficient, while he held the post he was utterly loyal to Marlborough, recognizing that his own rise to good fortune stemmed from the duke's appreciation of, and confidence in, his abilities. It has been occasionally suggested that Marlborough's victories were, in reality, the result of Cadogan's efforts. This is not the case, although Cadogan was undoubtedly a sound tactician as well as a diligent staff officer. His loyalty to Marlborough had its limits, but in seeking to profit from his position Cadogan was little different from most of his contemporaries.

Charles Cadogan, second Baron Cadogan of Oakley (1684/5–1776), army officer, younger brother of William Cadogan, began his military career in Heyman Rooke's foot guards in 1704. He became a cornet in the 5th dragoon guards in 1708, rising to lieutenant in 1709, and captain in 1712. He served with his regiment in Flanders during 1710 and 1711, and was present in Scotland during the Jacobite rising in 1715. In that year he was appointed captain and lieutenant-colonel of the 2nd foot guards. Elected as MP for Reading in 1716, he then represented Newport in the Isle of Wight from 1722 to 1726. He supported his brother's political allies in the Commons, and accompanied him to Vienna in 1720. He purchased the colonelcy of the 4th (King's Own) regiment of foot on 21 April 1719, retaining it until 19 June 1734, when he became colonel of the 6th dragoons (Inniskillings). On 25 April 1742 Cadogan was appointed colonel of the 2nd troop of Horse Guards (Life Guards). He was governor of Sheerness from 1749 to 1752, and of Gravesend and Tilbury from 1751 until his death. On 25 July 1717 Cadogan married Elizabeth (*d.* 1768), daughter of Sir Hans *Sloane, and they had one son, Charles, who became the heir to the Sloane estates in Chelsea, and was created Viscount Chelsea and Earl Cadogan on 27 December 1800.

Charles Cadogan became FRS on 30 November 1718 and was Sloane trustee of the British Museum from 1753 until his death. He died at his home in Bruton Street, London, on 24 September 1776, 'in the 92nd year of his age' (*GM*, 1st ser., 46, 1776, 436) and was buried on 30 September 1776 at Caversham, near his other residence, Caversham Park.

JAMES FALKNER

Sources *DNB* • *The letters and dispatches of John Churchill, first duke of Marlborough, from 1702 to 1712*, ed. G. Murray, 5 vols. (1845) • N. B. Leslie, *The succession of colonels of the British army from 1660 to the present day* (1974) • E. Cruickshanks, 'Cadogan, William', HoP, *Commons, 1715–54* • R. S. Lea, 'Cadogan, Charles', HoP, *Commons, 1715–54* • F. Harris, *A passion for government: the life of Sarah, duchess of Marlborough* (1991) • W. S. Churchill, *Marlborough: his life and times*, 2 vols. (1947) • A. Alison, *The military life of John, duke of Marlborough* (1848) • Fortescue, *Brit. army* • C. Dalton, ed., *English army lists and commission registers, 1661–1714*, 6 vols. (1892–1904) • D. Chandler, *Marlborough as military commander* (1973) • D. Green, *Sarah, duchess of Marlborough* (1967) • will, PRO, PROB 11/611, sig. 223 • G. M. Trevelyan, *England under Queen Anne*, 3 vols. (1930–34); repr. (1948) • *GM*, 1st ser., 46 (1776), 436

Archives BL, corresp. with Lord Raby, Add. MS 22196 • BL, corresp. mainly with Jean Robethon, Stowe MSS 225–231 • BL, corresp. with Lord Townshend, Egerton MS 3124 • BL, corresp. with Charles Whitworth, Add. MSS 37364–37387 • CAC Cam., corresp. with Thomas Erle • Hunt. L., corresp. with duke of Chandos • Suffolk RO, Ipswich, letters to William Leathes

Likenesses attrib. L. Laguerre, oils, *c*.1716, NPG [*see illus.*] • H. Hysing, oils, Goodwood, West Sussex • J. Simon, mezzotint (after L. Laguerre), BM, NPG

Wealth at death see will, PRO, PROB 11/611, sig. 223

Cadogan, William (1711–1797), physician, the son of Roger Cadogan and his wife, Jane Thomas, was born in Usk, Monmouthshire, and matriculated from Oriel College, Oxford, on 5 December 1727, aged sixteen. After graduating BA in 1731 he studied at Leiden, where he took the degree of MD in 1737. He was elected physician to the Bristol Royal Infirmary in 1747 and while resident in Bristol was elected in 1752 FRS. In 1747 he was elected a governor to the Foundling Hospital, and was made its physician in 1753, having moved to London. He took the degrees of MA, BM, and DM at Oxford in June 1755, became a fellow of the Royal College of Physicians in 1758, was four times a censor, and twice delivered the Harveian oration. Cadogan's works are his graduation thesis, *De nutritione, incremento, et decremento corporis* (1737); his two Harveian orations, 1764 and 1792; *An Essay on the Nursing and Management of Children* (1748); and *A Dissertation on the Gout and on All Chronic Diseases* (1771). His thesis is a statement of the current physiological opinions, and contains no original observation, and his Harveian orations are mere rhetorical exercises. His book on nursing was his most influential work, and went through ten editions in twenty-five years. His view that the new-born child should be put to the breast as early as possible so as to receive colostrum, although not novel, was put forward very positively, and was widely heeded, and thus marked a watershed in nursing practice. And his advice was prescient on the necessity of a physician's careful observation of the child so as to act on the very first signs of ill health, and then sensitively to monitor, and to react expeditiously to, each subsequent change. His sensible directions on the management of children were used as a guide in the Foundling Hospital. Cadogan's book on gout was widely read, and reached an eleventh edition within two years. It

William Cadogan (1711–1797), by Robert Edge Pine, 1769

was attacked by several of his medical contemporaries for the view that gout is not hereditary, and, in common with most chronic diseases, arises from indolence and intemperance, so that he advises a spare diet and as much exercise as possible. By challenging conventional wisdom in arguing that gout was bad for the constitution, and was not a hereditary disease, Cadogan was perceived to be challenging the hereditary principle not only in medicine but also in politics, and in doing so aroused the hostility of conservatives. Equally, his views on the mercenary nature of his fellow physicians in treating chronic diseases were also calculated to arouse hostility.

Cadogan was married three times: first to Frances Cochrane; second, on 2 August 1759, to Anne Spencer; and third, on 13 July 1772, to Miss Groen, 'a Dutch lady' (*GM*, 42.342), who died three months later. Cadogan died at his home in George Street, Hanover Square, London, on 26 February 1797, and was buried in the churchyard at Fulham, where he had a villa.

NORMAN MOORE, *rev.* ANNE DIGBY

Sources M. Rendle-Short and J. Rendle-Short, *The father of child care: life of William Cadogan* (1966) • J. Rendle-Short, 'William Cadogan, eighteenth century physician', *Medical History*, 4 (1960), 288–309 • J. Rendle-Short, 'Infant management in the eighteenth century with special reference to the work of William Cadogan', *Bulletin of the History of Medicine*, 34 (1960), 97–122 • R. Porter, 'Gout: framing and fantasizing disease', *Bulletin of the History of Medicine*, 68 (1994), 1–28 • A. Digby, *Making a medical living: doctors and patients in the English market for medicine, 1720–1911* (1994) • Munk, *Roll* • V. Fildes, *Breast, bottles and babies: a history of infant feeding* (1980) • Foster, *Alum. Oxon.* • *GM*, 1st ser., 22 (1752), 352 • *GM*, 1st ser., 42 (1772), 342, 496

Likenesses R. E. Pine, oils, 1769, RCP Lond. [*see illus.*] • W. Dickinson, mezzotint, 1772 (after R. E. Pine), Wellcome L.

Cadogan, William Bromley (1751–1797), religious writer, was born on 22 January 1751 in Bruton Street, London, the second son of Charles Sloane Cadogan, third Earl Cadogan (1728–1807), landowner, and his first wife, Frances Bromley (*d.* 1768), the only daughter of Henry Bromley, first Baron Montford. He began his education at Westminster School, then matriculated at Christ Church, Oxford, in 1769, whence he proceeded BA in 1773 and MA in 1776. Henry Bathurst, later second Earl Bathurst, who was at the time lord chancellor, presented him to the vicarage of St Giles, Reading, in 1774, when the previous evangelical vicar, William Talbot, died. Cadogan was then collated to the rectory of Chelsea in 1775, which was in his father's gift. In 1782 he married Mrs Bradshaw, formerly Graham (*d.* 1827), the widow of Captain Bradshaw, private secretary and aide-de-camp to General Vaughan. From his letters to her, it appears that their marriage was a happy one—he always addressed her as 'my dear life'; they had no children.

When Cadogan first arrived in the parish of St Giles, he had the reputation of being a haughty pastor and a stern opponent of Methodism; he threatened to sue proprietors who opened for business on Sundays, he dismissed his evangelical curate, and he castigated his parishioners for going to hear Methodist preachers. He proved, however, to be an attentive pastor and an earnest seeker of truth. John Wesley heard of his zeal, and sent him a set of his writings, but Cadogan responded by burning the books in his own kitchen, because he vowed that he would learn the truth from scripture alone. Some time during the first few years of his tenure at Reading, he fell under the influence of Mrs Talbot, the late vicar's wife. The Talbots had been close friends of the evangelical Calvinist William Romaine, rector of St Ann Blackfriars, and Romaine was careful to keep in touch with Mrs Talbot after her husband's death. Cadogan acknowledged her influence on him when he preached at her funeral in 1785. She was, he said, not only 'the best friend I ever had in my life, but … a Mother to me in love, in every good office, and in continual prayers for my person and ministry' (*The Love of Christ the Portion and Principle of the Children of God*, 1785, 6). Largely because of her encouragement and through his subsequent contact with William Romaine, Cadogan developed an evangelical fervour in his ministry. He offered to reinstate his old curate, who, however, declined, and began preaching extemporaneously on 'experimental' religion. By taking such an evangelical stand, he seems to have forfeited further preferment, despite the fact that he was respected by and an intimate of Robert Lowth, the bishop of London. He became very popular in Reading and Chelsea on account of his preaching and his cure of souls: his biographer, Richard Cecil, reported that he attracted large crowds to his services and that he garnered much respect because of his diligent care for his parishioners and his charity and benevolence to all.

Cadogan was, according to Cecil, a high-churchman and a Calvinist. He never could appreciate Wesley's Arminianism, which he complained was a system that was 'founded in ignorance, supported by pride' and would 'end in delusion' (Rogal). Although he resisted Wesley's influence, Romaine's influence was evidently potent: Cadogan remained very close to the rector of St Anne's for the rest of the latter's life. Romaine's letters indicate that he often went to Reading, and that he gave a Thursday evening lecture there with some regularity. Cadogan often officiated in Romaine's parish; he preached the funeral sermon when the latter died in 1795, and wrote a short biography of the rector, published in 1796. He had other evangelical friends—his letters indicate that he was well known to John Newton and Richard Cecil, and that he occasionally preached in the latter's parish—but none was as close as Romaine.

Cadogan published a number of individual sermons as well as collections of his works which demonstrate the attractive nature of his theology and the power of his preaching. In *Liberty and Equality: Two Sermons* (1792), for example, he gushes with emotion about the joy of salvation: true believers

> shall be ranging at large in the bright regions of eternal day, they shall be singing hallelujahs to the Lord God omnipotent, and rejoicing in Him who hath saved them with an everlasting salvation: in a word, for ever released from shame and sorrow, and for ever crowned with glory and righteousness, they are 'free indeed'. (pp. 25–6)

His florid language led the reviewer in the *Gentleman's Magazine* to call these two sermons 'nothing more nor less than the ranting effusions of methodistical orthodoxy' (*GM*, 63/1, 1793, 246). He produced a hymnal in a style very similar to that of his friend John Newton, entitled *Psalms and Hymns Collected by W. B. Cadogan* (1785), which was reprinted in 1787, 1793, and 1803. It was divided into two parts, as indicated by the title—psalms put to metre and hymns—and was full of effusive praise.

Cadogan died in Reading on 18 January 1797, aged forty-five, and was buried at St Giles's, Reading. A monument was erected to him in St Giles's, on which his 'mourning flock' expressed their admiration and respect for their late pastor because of his abilities, labour, and piety (*GM*, 67/2, 1797, 796). A few of his discourses and letters, together with a short memoir of his life, were published in Richard Cecil, *Discourses of the honourable and reverend William Bromley Cadogan, A.M. … to which are now added short observations on the Lord's prayer, and letters to several of his friends* (1798). J. S. Chamberlain

Sources R. Cecil, *Discourses of the honourable and reverend William Bromley Cadogan … to which are now added short observations on the Lord's prayer, and letters to several of his friends* (1798) • *GM*, 1st ser., 63 (1793), 246 • *GM*, 1st ser., 64 (1794), 1032 • *GM*, 1st ser., 65 (1795), 762–3 • *GM*, 1st ser., 67 (1797), 166 • *GM*, 1st ser., 67 (1797), 796 • S. J. Rogal, *A biographical dictionary of 18th century Methodism*, 1 (1997), 260 • D. B. Hindmarsh, *John Newton and the English evangelical tradition between the conversions of Wesley and Wilberforce* (1996) • L. Tyerman, *The life and times of the Rev. John Wesley*, 2nd edn, 3 (1872), 179 • J. Julian, ed., *A dictionary of hymnology*, rev. edn (1907), 333 • Allibone, *Dict.* • Foster, *Alum. Oxon.*

Cadoux, Cecil John (1883–1947), theologian, was born on 24 May 1883 in Smyrna, Turkey, the ninth child of William Henry Cadoux (1840–1899), merchant, and Emma Temple (1840–1887). His father's family was Huguenot in origin, and a grandfather and an uncle were Congregational ministers. The Cadoux family left Smyrna soon after Cecil John's birth and settled in south London. He attended Stamford House School, Croydon, and then St Dunstan's College, Catford (1894–1900), before beginning work as a civil servant at the Admiralty in 1902. For the succeeding nine and a half years he spent all his spare time leading Sunday school and Boy's Brigade classes attached to a Congregational church, and studying for a London University arts degree as an external student.

Having become convinced of a call to Christian ministry, Cadoux left the Admiralty and applied to Mansfield College, Oxford, where he was accepted as a student in 1911. Here he had a distinguished academic career and established lifelong friendships with his teachers W. B. Selbie and J. Vernon Bartlet. At the conclusion of his course he was accredited as a Congregational minister and appointed as a tutor at the college.

Cadoux was already a convinced pacifist when war broke out in 1914, and for the rest of his life he used all his intellectual skills to produce a rational defence of pacifism. He was among the founders of the Fellowship of Reconciliation in Cambridge in December 1914. His initial research explored the attitude of the early church to pagan society and the state, and resulted in the publication of his first book, *The Early Christian Attitude to War* (1919; reissued 1940, 1982), which long remained a classic work on the subject. He went to France with the Friends' Ambulance Unit for several months in 1915; after the introduction of conscription, he gave moral support to many young conscientious objectors. At the end of 1915 he married Marguerite Asplin (1889–1965), and they had two sons and two daughters.

In 1919 Cadoux was appointed professor (a courtesy title used by contemporary theological colleges) of New Testament studies at the Yorkshire United Independent College in Bradford, which prepared students for the Congregational ministry. During his fourteen years in Bradford he established his reputation as a scholar, not only writing numerous articles but also publishing two major works, *The early church and the world: a history of the Christian attitude to pagan society and the state down to the time of Constantine* (1925), which was a revised version of his London University DD thesis, and *Catholicism and Christianity: a Vindication of Progressive Protestantism* (1928), an exhaustive and vigorous defence of liberal protestantism as against the claims of the Roman Catholic church. He was well known in Yorkshire as a preacher who believed that the churches should offer firm moral leadership, and as an exacting teacher and lecturer with advanced views on biblical criticism.

In 1933 an opportunity arose for Cadoux to realize his ambition of returning to Oxford, when he was offered the post of Mackennal professor of church history and vice-principal at Mansfield College, Oxford. Here he remained until his death fourteen years later. He continued to take an active role in the life of local Congregational churches. At Mansfield he found himself out of sympathy with the direction of thought of many of his colleagues, especially the principal, Nathaniel Micklem. While Cadoux affirmed ever more strongly his liberal protestantism, particularly in *The Case for Evangelical Modernism* (1938), a growing number of Congregational theologians were influenced by the work of Karl Barth and Emil Brunner. In addition he differed from those of his colleagues who were involved in the negotiations for union with the Presbyterian Church of England, favouring mutual respect and co-operation between denominations rather than organic union. His position was set out in *The Congregational Way* (1946).

The outbreak of the Second World War forced Cadoux to reconsider his pacifism; the result was *Christian Pacifism Re-Examined* (1940), in which he reaffirmed his commitment to non-violence. He continued to pursue his interests in both New Testament studies and in history. The former led to the publication of *The Historic Mission of Jesus* (1941), and finally to his most widely read book, *The Life of Jesus*, published posthumously by Penguin Books in 1948. His interest in history resulted in the publication of the first of two projected volumes, *Ancient Smyrna* (1938) and, in the year of his death, *Philip of Spain and the Netherlands: an Essay on Moral Judgments in History* (1947).

At the time of his death Cadoux was considering a book on the human treatment of animals, a subject on which he felt strongly; from early adulthood to the end of his life he was a strict vegetarian. He died on 16 August 1947 at his home, 179 Woodstock Road, Oxford, after a long period of ill health. His funeral was held in Mansfield College chapel, and he was buried in Wolvercote cemetery, Oxford, on 19 August 1947. ELAINE KAYE

Sources Bodl. Oxf., MSS Cadoux · C. J. Cadoux diaries, priv. coll. · E. Kaye, *C. J. Cadoux: theologian, scholar and pacifist* (1988) · JCR and SCR minute books, Mansfield College, Oxford · private information (2004) [Cadoux family] · *Congregational Year Book* (1914–47) · *CGPLA Eng. & Wales* (1948)
Archives Bodl. Oxf., corresp. and papers
Likenesses Elliott & Fry, photograph, 1929, repro. in Kaye, *C. J. Cadoux*
Wealth at death £5899 14*s*. 8*d*.: probate, 28 Feb 1948, *CGPLA Eng. & Wales*

Cadroe. *See* Catroe (900/01–971).

Cadurcis, Robert de (*fl. c.*1160). *See under* Chaworth family (*per. c.*1160–*c.*1521).

Cadurcis, Thomas de (*fl. c.*1255). *See under* Chaworth family (*per. c.*1160–*c.*1521).

Cadurcis, William de (*fl. c.*1230). *See under* Chaworth family (*per. c.*1160–*c.*1521).

Cadvan. *See* Cadfan ab Iago (*fl. c.*616–*c.*625).

Cadwaladr ap Cadwallon [*called* Cadwaladr Fendigaid] (*d.* 664/682), king of Gwynedd, was son of *Cadwallon ap Cadfan of Gwynedd; the claim in late sources that his mother was a daughter of Pybba of Mercia is based on

Geoffrey of Monmouth and is probably unhistorical. Cadwaladr ruled Gwynedd in north-west Wales during the middle decades of the seventh century, but his precise regnal years are difficult to determine. His father, Cadwallon, was slain in 631 or 634 and according to the *Historia Brittonum* Cadwaladr ruled after him. However, the same text also states that the king of Gwynedd at the time of the battle of 'Winwaed' in 655 was Cadfael, nicknamed Cadomedd: he cannot be located in the genealogies of Gwynedd and later tradition regarded him as a usurper. Therefore Cadwaladr may not have succeeded his father immediately, but had done so on Cadfael's death at some point after 655. The termination of his own reign is also problematic. The Welsh chronicles state that Cadwaladr died of plague in 682, and other sources mention a mortality at about this time. However, the *Historia Brittonum* states that Cadwaladr succumbed to plague during the reign of Oswiu of Northumbria, thus before 671. Consequently, his demise is often attributed to the plague of 664, which is mentioned in both English and Irish sources.

No genuine deeds of Cadwaladr during his reign are known, but he is notable in a number of regards. His cognomen Bendigaid (lenited to Fendigaid) or 'the Blessed' may reflect his religious nature (he is allegedly founder of the church at Llangadwaladr on Anglesey, for example) or may refer to his function in later Welsh tradition as the last 'king of the Britons' and as messianic hero of the Welsh. The claim that he was the last king of the Britons and that his successors were merely princes, no doubt propagated by Geoffrey of Monmouth, perhaps stems from the fact that he is the last-named king of Gwynedd in the aforementioned *Historia Brittonum*. The legend, current as early as the tenth century, that he and Cynan Meriadoc of Brittany were messianic saviours of the Britons from English dominion may also stem from the structure of the *Historia*. Later sources claim that Cadwaladr was succeeded by his son Idwal Iwrch, but this is not certain.

DAVID E. THORNTON

Sources J. Williams ab Ithel, ed., *Annales Cambriae*, Rolls Series, 20 (1860) • T. Jones, ed. and trans., *Brenhinedd y Saesson, or, The kings of the Saxons* (1971) [another version of *Brut y tywysogyon*] • T. Jones, ed. and trans., *Brut y tywysogyon, or, The chronicle of the princes: Peniarth MS 20* (1952) • T. Jones, ed. and trans., *Brut y tywysogyon, or, The chronicle of the princes: Red Book of Hergest* (1955) • P. C. Bartrum, ed., *Early Welsh genealogical tracts* (1966) • *The Historia regum Britannie of Geoffrey of Monmouth*, ed. N. Wright, 1: *Bern, Bürgerbibliothek, MS 568* (1985) • Taliesin, *Armes Prydein / The prophecy of Britain*, ed. I. Williams, trans. R. Bromwich (1972) • J. E. Lloyd, *A history of Wales from the earliest times to the Edwardian conquest*, 3rd edn, 2 vols. (1939); repr. (1988) • D. N. Dumville, 'Brittany and "Armes Prydein Vawr"', *Études Celtiques*, 20 (1983), 145–59 • Nennius, *'British history' and 'The Welsh annals'*, ed. and trans. J. Morris (1980)

Cadwaladr ap Gruffudd (*d.* 1172). *See under* Owain Gwynedd (*d.* 1170).

Cadwaladr Cesail (*fl.* 1614–1626), poet, is said to have lived at the homestead of Y Gesail Gyfarch in Penmorfa, Eifionydd, and although there is no direct evidence for this, his name, and likewise his poetry, do suggest his close involvement not only with the family who occupied the property but also with this part of Caernarvonshire. About fifty pieces remain in various manuscripts (many safeguarded by that diligent local contemporary scribe, Wiliam Bodwrda), which can be classified as occasional verse, mostly *englynion* to minstrels and fellow poets such as Rhisiart Phylip, Ieuan Tew Ieuanc, Richard Hughes, footman to Elizabeth I, and Robert Peilin, harpist to James I; and as formal eulogy and elegy to families in Penmorfa and the immediate vicinity.

Cadwaladr composed one elegy to Elis Wyn of Y Gesail Gyfarch, and significantly, most of the other individuals addressed in his poems were related to that family either directly or through a complex web of marriage ties. The poet does not reveal the nature of his relationship with Wyn's family, but he implies that he was a nephew to Wyn's uncle, Owain Elis of Ystumllyn, the subject of another elegy, as was the latter's brother, Siôn Elis. Another family branch, established by one of Elis Wyn's great-great-grandfather's one of thirty or so children, also welcomed Cadwaladr. He sang to three of Sir John Wynn of Gwydir's sons; one died in St Lucas, Italy, in 1614.

Happily from the historian's viewpoint, but to the modern reader's dismay, Cadwaladr versifies in all his elegies the subject's year of death; likewise, the poems composed on the occasion of birth and marriage record the year of the event (in one case not only is the year of birth given but also the month, date, and time of day!). Seventeen such poems were composed between 1614 and 1626, and those other pieces which cannot be dated with the same precision would seem to belong to the same period.

A. CYNFAEL LAKE

Sources I. Foulkes, *Geirlyfr bywgraffiadol o enwogion Cymru* (1870) • *DWB* • M. Stephens, ed., *Cydymaith i lenyddiaeth Cymru*, rev. edn (1997) • R. Williams, *Enwogion Cymru: a biographical dictionary of eminent Welshmen* (1852)

Archives BL, MSS • Glamorgan RO, Cardiff, MSS • NL Wales, MSS

Cadwallador, Roger (1566/7–1610), Roman Catholic priest, was the eldest son of a well-to-do yeoman, John Cadwallador, and his wife, and was born at Stretton Sugwas, Herefordshire. He left for the English College of Douai, temporarily at Rheims, and was admitted in March 1590; on 21 September 1591 he was made a subdeacon, and was ordained deacon on 24 February 1592. In August of that year he left with three others to continue his studies at the English College, Valladolid, in Spain, where, in 1593, he was ordained priest. In October 1593 he returned to Herefordshire.

For sixteen years Cadwallador worked as a bilingual priest mainly in Herefordshire, but also in the neighbouring counties of Monmouthshire and Worcestershire. Challoner said of him

> that he deservedly gained the character of a pious, prudent and zealous missioner: and God was pleased to bless his labours with great success, in winning over many souls to Christ and his Church, especially among the poorer sort, for whose comfort and assistance he spared no pains night nor day. (Challoner, *Memoirs*)

He visited his flock on foot and said masses at various houses in the neighbourhood of Hereford, like Whitefield in Treville Parts and Stretton Court in his home village. In

1595 he was responsible for sending George Berington, a member of a recusant family associated with Winsley House and Wintercott, near Leominster, to Valladolid.

Cadwallador sided with the appellant priests, who sought to uphold the continuity of English Catholic institutions against what they considered a Jesuit dominated mission. He signed the appellants' protestation of allegiance to Elizabeth I of 31 January 1603 (their failed attempt to find an accommodation with the state on the matter of political allegiance), but, like other signatories, he repudiated James I's oath of allegiance, to the great delight of Father Robert Jones, superior of the English Jesuits and a fellow missioner in the Welsh marches.

Cadwallador was a notable Greek scholar, translating from Greek into English *The Ecclesiastical History of Theodoret* (published posthumously in 1612). He argued that Theodoret's evidence for the beliefs and practices of the early church demonstrated them to be 'that, which we Catholikes hold' as against the claims of Church of England apologists.

The activities of Cadwallador were irksome to the bishop of Hereford, Robert Bennet. In 1605 there was open resistance to the bishop's authority at Allensmore, and the subsequent inquiry concluded that Cadwallador was the fomentor of the disturbance. He escaped to Winsley House, Hope under Dinmore, to be with the Berington family. Eventually, on Easter Sunday 1610 Bishop Bennet had him arrested while he was saying mass in the home of a Catholic widow, Mrs Winifred Scoop, at Sutton Surgas, 8 miles outside Hereford. He was brought before the high sheriff and was transferred to the bishop, who committed him to Hereford gaol. As there was an epidemic raging at Hereford in 1610 he was forced to walk in chains with the assistance of a lad to Leominster gaol to be tried at the assizes there. Charged with being a priest ordained abroad he was found guilty, condemned as a traitor, and sentenced to be hanged, drawn, and quartered. On the day he was condemned to death Robert Jones visited him; he would later write an account of Cadwallador's imprisonment, trial, and death. Father John Stevens also visited him and was instructed to look after his flock. On 27 August 1610, together with Mr Powel, a lay Catholic prisoner, he was executed, and his head was placed on the Cross House in Broad Street. The church of St Ethelbert's in Leominster was built on the site where one of his quarters was displayed. Inside the church a chapel was dedicated to his memory as well as a stained glass window illustrating his execution. The Catholics in the southern marches were greatly encouraged by his martyrdom.

D. BEN REES

Sources *DWB* • N. C. Reeves, *The parish of Saint Ethelbert Leominster* (1998) • R. Challoner, *Memoirs of missionary priests*, ed. J. H. Pollen, rev. edn (1924), 299–306 • R. Challoner, *Martyrs to the Catholic faith: memoirs of missionary priests and other Catholics of both sexes that have suffered death in England on religous accounts from the year 1577 to 1684*, [new edn] (1878), 24–31 • Gillow, *Lit. biog. hist.*, 1.369–70 • D. Rogers, 'The English recusants: some mediaeval literary hints', *Recusant History*, 23 (1996–7), 483–507 • A. F. Allison and D. M. Rogers, eds., *The contemporary printed literature of the English Counter-Reformation between 1558 and 1640*, 2 (1994) • J. Bossy, *The English Catholic community, 1570–1850* (1975) • G. Anstruther, *The seminary priests*, 1 (1969), 61–2 • private information (2004) [Sue Hubbard, Herefs. RO]

Likenesses portrait (of Cadwallador?), English College of Valladolid; repro. in Reeves, *Parish of Saint Ethelbert Leominster*, 6

Cadwallon [Cædwalla] **ap Cadfan** (*d.* 634), king of Gwynedd, was the subject of two very different portraits. In Bede's *Historia ecclesiastica* he was 'the raging tyrant' and 'the unspeakable leader of the Britons' (Bede, *Hist. eccl.*, 3.1); in an early Welsh poem in his praise he was the champion of the Britons against their oppressor, Eadwine, king of Northumbria. Bede was probably working on material that already gave Cadwallon a pivotal role in Northumbrian history, since he refers to the year of Cadwallon's military dominance as the 'ill-omened year', a year which the framers of lists of Northumbrian kings had decided to attribute to the following king, Oswald. Because Cadwallon was for Bede so outstanding a royal villain, it is especially desirable to find some evidence that makes it possible to control his account.

According to the genealogies, Cadwallon's parents were *Cadfan ab Iago (*fl.* c.616–c.625), king of Gwynedd, and Tandreg Ddu, daughter of Cynan Garwyn. Cadfan is commemorated in an inscription at Llangadwaladr in Anglesey. The lettering of this inscription is half-uncial but with an uncial 'a'. Since it has been thought that the church of Llangadwaladr was founded by Cadwallon's son, *Cadwaladr (*d.* 664/682), it has been argued that the inscription may have been put up by Cadwaladr. The evidence for Cadwaladr's foundation of the church is, however, late and unreliable; it is likely to be merely an inference from the name. The likeliest interpretation is that the inscription in memory of Cadfan was put up by his son and successor, Cadwallon; the character of the inscription thus provides a clue to the son as much as to the father. Cadfan is praised with a series of superlatives more redolent of a late Roman emperor than a Welsh king; they recall the imperial links of the previous century betrayed by the Penmachno inscription, also from Gwynedd, with its consular dating. Yet one epithet, *sapientissimus* ('most wise'), has a more local resonance. *Sapiens* was the term regularly used by the Irish annals for ecclesiastical scholars of the highest degree of learning. Aldfrith, king of Northumbria, was *sapiens* in his obit in the annals of Ulster, and Bede called him *doctissimus* ('most learned'; Bede, *Hist. eccl.*, 4.26). In the sixth century an earlier king of Gwynedd, Maelgwn, was, for Gildas, as notable for his learning as for his vices. The inscription suggests that the royal line of Gwynedd retained the cultural aspirations of the previous century. In the sixth century British inscriptions continued to be in more or less skilful roman capitals. The Cadfan inscription demonstrates, however, a collapse in the distinction between inscriptional and book letter-forms: half-uncial, the book script, was now being used on stone. Whatever the aspirations of Cadwallon, the achievement was a culture edging away from the Roman past and becoming more ecclesiastically dominated.

None of this could be guessed from Bede's account. In the *Historia ecclesiastica* Cadwallon is a brutal and feared enemy, a man who not only killed Eadwine, the first Christian king of Northumbria, and his successors, Osric of Deira and Eanfrith of Bernicia, but also desired to exterminate the entire Northumbrian people. He had allied with the pagan leader, and later king, of the Mercians, Penda, against the Christian Eadwine, so demonstrating again that indifference to the Christian conversion of the English that, in Bede's eyes, damned the British people.

Bede and the Welsh poem agree on one crucial point: that Eadwine attacked Anglesey. This event may be the one recorded in the *Annales Cambriae* under the year 629, but here referring to the year before the battle of Hatfield, and thus to Bede's 632: 'The besieging of King Cadwallon in the island of *Glannauc*' (Priestholm, off Anglesey). For Bede the subjection of Anglesey and Man was the culmination of Eadwine's power over Britain. When Cadwallon allied with Penda, he was, again according to Bede, rebelling against Eadwine's rule. The result of this alliance was the battle of Hatfield (12 October 633), on the southern border of Northumbria; Cadwallon and Penda were, therefore, the aggressors. In the battle Eadwine and one of his sons were killed. The newly Christian king of Northumbria had been defeated and killed by a pagan Mercian and by a British king who, though a Christian, was:

> so barbarian in mind and habits that he did not even spare women or innocent children, but rather, with beastlike ferocity, brought everyone to a death by torments, and for a considerable time ravaged and laid waste their provinces; he was intending to eradicate the entire race of the English from within the bounds of Britain. (Bede, *Hist. eccl.*, 2.20)

Cadwallon, for Bede, exemplified to the most extreme degree the refusal of the Britons to pay any regard to the evangelization of the English or to their Christianity once they had been converted.

To judge by the Welsh poem, Eadwine's conquest of Anglesey had mainly consisted of ravaging, so that vengeance was no doubt taken. Bede's verdict may also reflect the recent nature of the Anglian conquest of much of what is now northern England and southern Scotland. It would not be in the least surprising if scattered English settlements in recently British territory, such as the kingdom of Elmet, conquered by Eadwine, had been largely wiped out after the battle of Hatfield. The 'ill-omened year' was marked not merely by 'the insane tyranny of the British king' (Bede, *Hist. eccl.*, 3.1) but also by the apostasy of Eadwine's immediate successors, his cousin Osric in Deira and Eanfrith son of Æthelfrith in Bernicia. Both Osric and Eanfrith were killed by Cadwallon in the course of 634: Osric was killed in a surprise British sortie, when he was besieging Cadwallon; Eanfrith was killed treacherously when he had gone to Cadwallon to ask for peace. For those reasons, Bede says, the year 634 was assigned to the next king, Oswald, by 'all those computing the reigns of the kings' (ibid.); and this is indeed what is found in the Northumbrian regnal lists in the Moore manuscript of Bede's *Historia ecclesiastica* and in the Anglian collection of English royal genealogies and king-lists.

There are two accounts of the battle of Denisesburna or Heavenfield (near Hexham) in which, in the autumn of 634, Cadwallon was killed by Oswald. The earlier is by Adomnán in his life of St Columba; the later by Bede. For both, Oswald achieved what was, in human terms, a surprising victory over greatly superior forces. Adomnán tells a story that he claims was told by Oswald to Ségéne, abbot of Iona, in the presence of Adomnán's informant and predecessor as abbot, Faílbe. Columba is said to have appeared in a vision to Oswald and to have declared that the Lord had granted to him that Oswald should triumph over his enemies. The story equates Oswald's reconquest of his homeland with Joshua's conquest of the Promised Land; and, having completed his account of the battle, Adomnán added the words 'the victor, returning from the battle, was afterwards ordained by God as the emperor of the whole of Britain' (*Adomnán's Life of Columba*, 1.1). Bede's story was at least influenced by traditions about the battle deriving from Wilfrid's foundation at Hexham; it formed part of a body of material about Oswald brought together in the course of Wilfrid's promotion of his cult. Not surprisingly, therefore, it says nothing about Columba. It may, instead, have been influenced by the association between Constantine, the first Christian emperor, and the cross: Oswald, the first Bernician ruler of all Northumbria to be a Christian, also fought with the cross as his standard. This connection may have then influenced the way in which Bede contrasted the *imperium* of Eadwine and Oswald with 'the insane tyranny' of Cadwallon. He was using late Roman political vocabulary, contrasting *imperium* with tyranny, in its Christian guise; he may also have been influenced by Gildas, who had similarly contrasted legitimate empire and British tyrants. What Cadwallon had briefly achieved was to expose the fragility of English power in northern Britain; and the Northumbrians never forgot their terror and never forgave the British king who had so frightened them. 'That ill-omened year', so Bede said, 'remains hateful to all good men even to this day' (Bede, *Hist. eccl.*, 3.1). T. M. CHARLES-EDWARDS

Sources V. E. Nash-Williams, *The early Christian monuments of Wales* (1950), no. 13 · *Adomnán's Life of Columba*, ed. and trans. A. O. Anderson and M. O. Anderson, rev. edn, rev. M. O. Anderson, OMT (1991) · Adomnán of Iona, *Life of St Columba*, ed. and trans. R. Sharpe (1995) · Bede, *Hist. eccl.*, 2.20; 3.1; 4.26 · R. G. Gruffydd, 'Canu Cadwallon ap Cadfan', *Astudiaethau ar yr Hengerdd / Studies in Old Welsh poetry*, ed. R. Bromwich and R. Brinley Jones (1978), 25–43 · E. Phillimore, ed., 'The *Annales Cambriae* and Old Welsh genealogies', *Y Cymmrodor*, 9 (1888), 141–83 [version A] · J. Williams ab Ithel, ed., *Annales Cambriae*, Rolls Series, 20 (1860) [B and C versions, with the A version] · T. Mommsen, ed., 'Historia Brittonum', *Chronica minora saec. IV. V. VI. VII.*, 3, MGH Auctores Antiquissimi, 13 (Berlin, 1898), 111–222, chaps. 63–4 · C. Stancliffe, 'Oswald, "Most Holy and Most Victorious King of the Northumbrians"', *Oswald: Northumbrian king to European saint*, ed. C. Stancliffe and E. Cambridge (1995), 33–83, esp. 46–53 · J. M. Wallace-Hadrill, *Bede's Ecclesiastical history of the English people: a historical commentary*, OMT (1988) · T. M. Charles-Edwards, 'Bede, the Irish and the Britons', *Celtica*, 15 (1983), 45–52 · P. C. Bartrum, ed., *Early Welsh genealogical tracts* (1966)

Cadwgan [Cadwgan of Llandefai] (*d.* **1241**), Cistercian monk and bishop of Bangor, appears in chronicles written at Tewkesbury and Worcester which, drawing upon a common source, record his name as Martin. In a brief and distorted account of his career, Gerald of Wales identified him as the son of an Irish father—scarcely a compliment from a fitz Gerald—and a Welsh mother. His father was said to have been a fervent and effective preacher in Welsh, his brother a monk at Caerleon. Cadwgan offended Gerald at Strata Florida when Gerald placed his books there for safety, only to find that he could not regain possession of them. It was a personal disaster for which he held Cadwgan responsible, and it coloured all that Gerald wrote about him; Cadwgan's lifelong interest in books may perhaps give some substance to Gerald's suspicions.

There seems to be no foundation for Gerald's claim that Cadwgan became abbot of Strata Florida, but some time after December 1202 he became abbot of Whitland. He claimed to be a kinsman of Llywelyn ab Iorwerth, prince of Gwynedd, and to have won his support. His election to Bangor rested almost entirely with King John, who took him into royal protection at the end of 1214, and who may have wished to gain Llywelyn's neutrality as he faced baronial unrest in England. He gave the canons of Bangor leave to elect their bishop and indicated that Cadwgan would be acceptable, and on 13 April 1215 he informed the archbishop of Canterbury that the abbot of Whitland had been elected. Cadwgan was consecrated by Archbishop Stephen Langton at Staines in Middlesex on 21 June 1215. His episcopate is sparsely recorded. On 12 November 1216, less than a month after the death of King John, he was at Bristol at the court of the young Henry III. In September 1221, Ragnvald, king of the Isles, surrendered the Isle of Man to be held in fee from the papacy, and his formal letter was attested by Bishop Cadwgan. After the peace of Montgomery, in October 1223, royal administrators found his assistance useful in an inquiry into the lands held by Llywelyn ab Iorwerth's supporters in Deheubarth. In 1234 Cadwgan made the gesture for which he is best remembered: he secured from Henry III a mandate to the justiciar of Ireland, ordering him to allow passage for the ship which the bishop sent to Ireland to collect corn for the poor of his diocese.

A charter issued to the Cistercians of Combermere, Cheshire, pointed towards the future: Cadwgan witnessed it as bishop of Bangor, monk, and abbot. In 1235 or 1236 he secured permission to resign his see and to become a monk at Dore Abbey. As Cadwgan, formerly bishop of Bangor, he made his profession to the abbot of Dore, renouncing all his possessions, and giving his books, horses, and other items to the abbey, while obliging it to pay his nephew, Cadwaladr, what the bishop owed him for his services. Gregory IX finally released him from his bishopric in 1236, and when he issued a mandate to the chapter to elect a new bishop, he instructed them to apply Cadwgan's goods, with the exception of his books and clothes, to the payment of the debts of the church.

Cadwgan was himself responsible for a number of books, written for a practical purpose, and combining a European scholastic tradition with a Welsh cultural tradition: a collection of homilies, a book called *Speculum Christianorum*, a tract on confession, a meditation on a verse from the Psalms (Psalm 17:7), and a collection of prayers. After resigning his bishopric he had five years at Dore, where he was not free from criticism. He was admonished at the general chapter of the order in 1239 for breaking silence and causing disturbance and dissension by the manner of his life. He died on 11 April 1241.

David Walker

Sources T. Jones, ed. and trans., *Brut y tywysogyon, or, The chronicle of the princes: Peniarth MS 20* (1952) • *Ann. mon.*, 1, 4 • *Gir. Camb. opera*, vol. 4 • *CPR, 1231–4* • H. S. Sweetman and G. F. Handcock, eds., *Calendar of documents relating to Ireland*, 5 vols., PRO (1875–86), vol. 1 • *CEPR letters*, vol. 1 • J. M. Canivez, ed., *Statuta capitulorum generalium ordinis Cisterciensis*, 2 (1934) • *The manuscripts of the earl of Westmorland*, HMC, 13 (1885); repr. (1906) • A. W. Haddan and W. Stubbs, eds., *Councils and ecclesiastical documents relating to Great Britain and Ireland*, 1 (1869) • T. Madox, *Formulare Anglicanum* (1702) • M. Richter, ed., *Canterbury professions*, CYS, 67 (1973) • R. R. Davies, *Conquest, coexistence, and change: Wales, 1063–1415*, History of Wales, 2 (1987) • E. B. Fryde and others, eds., *Handbook of British chronology*, 3rd edn, Royal Historical Society Guides and Handbooks, 2 (1986)

Cadwgan ap Bleddyn (*d.* 1111). *See under* Bleddyn ap Cynfyn (*d.* 1075).

Cædmon (*fl. c.*670), poet, is the earliest vernacular English poet whose name is known. Information about him is derived entirely from book 4, chapter 24, of Bede's *Historia ecclesiastica gentis Anglorum*, finished in 731. Cædmon lived at the time of St Hild's abbacy (657–80) of Streanaeshalch (Whitby). The name Cædmon is of Celtic origin, but not enough is known of name giving among the Anglo-Saxons for use as evidence of Celtic descent; Bede says English was Cædmon's own tongue. Bede's account of Cædmon's saintly life and death is reflected in John Wilson's pious compilation, *The English Martyrologe* (first included in its second edition, published at St Omer in 1640), which was treated in the Bollandist *Acta sanctorum* as providing authority for the veneration of Cædmon as a saint on 11 February. However, that is not supported by the calendar of the Benedictine abbey of Whitby (Bodl. Oxf., MS Rawl. liturg. b.1), in which local saints of the Anglo-Saxon era are specially honoured, but Cædmon is not included.

Bede relates how Cædmon came to utter his first song, 'Cædmon's Hymn' (forty-two words long), and judges that he gave to vernacular verse a sacred authority for expressing divine praise and sacred story. The account of Cædmon is to be read in the immediate context of Bede's account of St Hild. Her wisdom was accessible to all, ordinary people and kings and princes. Bede stresses the nobility of her rank, and Cædmon's humble status, as he advanced from being a monastery servant, a 'neatherd', to monkhood. His holy dying is related at length. Bede says:

> He used to compose godly and religious songs; thus, whatever he learned from the holy Scriptures by means of interpreters, he quickly turned into extremely delightful and moving poetry, in English, which was his own tongue … It is true that after him other Englishmen attempted to compose religious poems, but none could compare with him … He had lived in the secular habit until he was well advanced in years and had never learned any songs. Hence sometimes at a feast, for the sake of providing entertainment that they should all sing in turn, when he saw the harp approaching him, he would rise up in the middle of the feasting, go out, and return home.
>
> On one such occasion when he did so … in due time he … went to sleep, whereupon he dreamt that someone stood by

him, saluted him, and called him by name: 'Cædmon,' he said, 'sing me something.' Cædmon answered, 'I cannot sing; that is why I left the feast and came here because I could not sing.' Once again the speaker said, 'Nevertheless you must sing to me.' 'What must I sing?' said Cædmon. 'Sing,' he said, 'about the beginning of created things.' Thereupon Cædmon began to sing verses which he had never heard before in praise of God the Creator ... When he awoke, he remembered all that he had sung while asleep and soon added more verse in the same manner, praising God in fitting style.

In the morning he went to ... his master, telling him of the gift he had received, and he took him to the abbess. He was then bidden to describe his dream in the presence of a number of the more learned men and also to recite his song so that they might all examine him and decide upon the nature and origin of the gift of which he spoke; and it seemed clear to all of them that the Lord had granted him heavenly grace. They then read to him a passage of sacred history or doctrine, bidding him make a song out of it, if he could, in metrical form. He undertook the task and went away; on returning next morning he repeated the passage he had been given, which he had put into excellent verse. The abbess ... instructed him to renounce his secular habit and to take monastic vows. She and all her people received him into the community of the brothers and ordered that he should be instructed in the whole course of sacred history. He learned all he could by listening to them and then, memorizing it and ruminating over it ... he turned it into the most melodious verse; and it sounded so sweet as he recited it that his teachers became in turn his audience. He sang about the creation of the world, the origin of the human race, and the whole history of Genesis, of the departure of Israel from Egypt and the entry into the promised land and of many other of the stories taken from the sacred scriptures: of the incarnation, passion, and resurrection of the Lord, of His ascension into heaven, of the coming of the Holy Spirit and the teaching of the apostles. He also made songs about the terrors of future judgement, the horrors of the pains of hell, and the joys of the heavenly kingdom. In addition he composed many other songs about the divine mercies and judgements. (Bede, *Hist. eccl.*, 4.24)

The divine gift of song has been claimed by or for the first poets in many languages, and scholarly doubts in this miracle have been expressed. Yet Bede claims for Cædmon only that he, who had not previously shown any aptitude for verse or song of any kind, was given the art of sacred song in a dream, and that he was the first to use English for sacred poetry. By way of evidence Bede translates freely 'Cædmon's Hymn', and in some twenty manuscripts and in versions of the Old English translation of the *Historia* the poem itself is recorded, in Cædmon's Northumbrian and in later West Saxon. It is a typical piece of Old English alliterative poetry, using well the traditional devices of Anglo-Saxon verse, and adapting the heroic poetic diction to Christian use, for it is thought that the inherited verse of England before Cædmon was heroic, perhaps epic when long, perhaps in the form of lays when short, but none survives untouched by Christianity (or only in forms fragmentary and not necessarily early). The harp is not mentioned among Cædmon's new-found skills, though his fellow servants had sung their songs to the harp—secular songs, of a kind presumably not now known. Cædmon was not literate: memory played a great part in his verse composition, both in retaining what he was taught, and in retaining the poetry he himself composed from what he had learnt so that he in turn could deliver it and, according to the Old English translation of Bede's *Historia* (of *c.*900), dictate it to his teachers.

Bede says that 'after him other Englishmen attempted to compose religious poems, but none could compare with him'. One poetic manuscript has been associated with his name since the seventeenth century, 'the Cædmon manuscript' (Bodl. Oxf., MS Junius 11, *c.*1000). It contains substantial poetic paraphrases of the kind Bede says that Cædmon composed. Since being first edited by Francis Junius in 1655, they were ascribed to Cædmon, but are no longer regarded as his. In 1875 Eduard Sievers demonstrated that *Genesis*, lines 235–851, are not of a piece with the surrounding poem, but are a translation of a poem written in Old Saxon, the language of *Heliand*. Less than twenty years later, poetic fragments were found (in Vatican MS Palatinus latinus 1447) both of *Heliand* and of a hitherto unknown Old Saxon *Genesis*, lines 1–26 of the latter being the source of lines 790–817 of the Old English poem.

Soon after Cædmon's authorship was rejected for parts of *Genesis*, his authorship was rejected also for the other poems in the manuscript, because of variation in style, use of allegorical exegesis (nowhere extensive), and different textual transmission. These poems are Cædmonian only in that Old English biblical paraphrase was begun by Cædmon, and they form part of that tradition. It is thought possible that when Junius 11 was put together such poems were selected as recalling Cædmon's programme of verse composition according to Bede.

The connection with *Heliand* is no irrelevance when the Cædmonian tradition is considered. It seems likely that both *Heliand* and the Old Saxon *Genesis* resulted from Anglo-Saxon missionary activity on the continent, or from subsequent contacts, so that the influence of Cædmon was felt even beyond England, where he shaped the language of religious poetry for four hundred years, and gave to the vernacular a sacred authority for verse on many themes of divine praise and sacred story, religious alliterative poetry more varied and extensive than that in any other early Germanic language. E. G. STANLEY

Sources Bede, *Hist. eccl.*, 4.24 · T. Miller, ed., *The Old English version of Bede's ecclesiastical history of the English people*, 1/2; EETS, original ser., 96 (1891), 342–9 · T. Miller, ed., *The Old English version of Bede's ecclesiastical history of the English people*, 2/2; EETS, original ser., 112 (1898), 405–17 · F. C. Robinson and E. G. Stanley, eds., *Old English verse texts from many sources: a comprehensive collection*, Early English Manuscripts in Facsimile, 23 (1991), 2.1–21 · E. V. K. Dobbie, ed., *The manuscripts of Cædmon's 'Hymn' and Bede's 'Death song'* (1937) · F. Junius, ed., *Cædmonis monachi paraphrasis poetica Genesios ac praecipuarum sacrae paginae historiarum* (1655) · I. Gollancz, ed., *The Cædmon manuscript of Anglo-Saxon biblical poetry* (1927) · G. P. Krapp, ed., *The Junius manuscript*, The Anglo-Saxon Poetic Records, 1 (1931) · E. Sievers, *Der Heliand und die angelsächsiche Genesis* (1875) · K. Zangemeister and W. Braune, eds., 'Bruchstücke der altsächsischen Bibeldichtung aus der Bibliotheca Palatina', *Neue Heidelberger Jahrbücher*, 4 (1894), 205–94 · A. N. Doane, ed., *The Saxon Genesis: an edition of the West Saxon Genesis B and the Old Saxon Vatican Genesis* (1991) · K. Jackson, *The language and history of early Britain* (1953), 244

Cædwalla [Ceadwalla] (*c.***659–689**), king of the Gewisse, was the son of Cenbert, who is called king by the Anglo-Saxon Chronicle, which records his death under 661; they were descendants of *Ceawlin. Cædwalla (whose name is also spelt Ceadwalla in some sources) was probably born about 659, as the epitaph on his tomb gave his age at death as about thirty. He first appears in written records as an exiled prince who based himself in the Chilterns and the Weald. From these bases he brought together an army and invaded the kingdom of the South Saxons, killing its king Æthelwalh. Although Cædwalla was soon driven out by the *duces* Berhthun and Andhun, he was able not long afterwards to establish himself as king of his own people, in 685. He then began to pursue what appears to have been a new policy for the Gewisse, of conquest of the other Anglo-Saxon kingdoms south of the Thames. He had his revenge on the South Saxons when he killed Berhthun and placed the province under his own control. In 686 he attacked the Isle of Wight, which had been under South Saxon overlordship, and had its king Aruald and his two brothers put to death. In the same year he invaded Kent with his brother Mul who, it would appear from the evidence of a charter confirming land to the abbess of Thanet, was installed as king. In 687 the men of Kent burnt to death Mul and twelve companions. In revenge Cædwalla ravaged the province and may then have ruled it himself for a short time. Charter evidence suggests he also gained control of Surrey and may have been overlord of the East Saxon kings. Cædwalla's conquests seem to have involved not only regicide, but brutal treatment of the captured provinces. Ravaging of Kent, Sussex, and the Isle of Wight is recorded and Bede wrote of the South Saxons being reduced 'to a state of slavery' and of a major slaughter of the inhabitants of the Isle of Wight who were replaced by people from his own kingdom (Bede, *Hist. eccl.*, 4.15–16).

Bede does not condemn Cædwalla's actions and is more inclined to praise him for his generosity to the church and for bringing Christianity to the Isle of Wight, the last pagan stronghold; even Aruald's young brothers were quickly converted before their execution. Cædwalla's support for the church is all the more surprising as he had not himself been baptized as a Christian. However, when he had first invaded Sussex he had encountered the exiled Northumbrian bishop, Wilfrid, who had been serving as bishop of the South Saxons. He was so impressed that, in the words of Wilfrid's biographer, he asked the bishop 'to be his true father, to teach and help him, while he, on his side, promised him with a vow that he would be an obedient son' (Eddius Stephanus, chap. 42). When Cædwalla conquered the Isle of Wight he had apparently made a vow that if he was successful he would give a quarter of it and of the booty to the church. Accordingly, Wilfrid received 300 hides on the island, which he entrusted to his nephew Beornwine. Another influence on Cædwalla seems to have been Bishop Earconwald of London, who may have drafted the charter in which the king granted land to found a minster at Farnham in Surrey. The monastery of Barking, which had been founded by Earconwald's sister Æthelburh, received land at Battersea from Cædwalla, who is also known to have granted land in Kent to an Abbot Ecgwald, and, at the other end of his domain, to Aldhelm's monastery at Malmesbury.

The climax of Cædwalla's enthusiasm for Christianity came when he abdicated in 688 in order to travel to Rome to be baptized. This abdication after such a short and successful reign appears surprising and has been seen as a tribute to the charismatic powers of Bishop Wilfrid, but Bede records that Cædwalla had been severely wounded in his attack on the Isle of Wight and it is possible that when he set out for Rome he knew he did not have long to live. He was the first Anglo-Saxon king who is known to have travelled to Rome, and he was baptized there on 10 April 689, Easter Saturday, by Pope Sergius I and given the baptismal name of Peter. He died on 20 April and was buried the same day in St Peter's, wearing his baptismal robes. Bede reproduces the verse epitaph from his tomb, which may have been composed by Archbishop Crispus of Milan. The poem plays on the theme of renunciation of worldly wealth and power in favour of a heavenly kingdom, and begins:

> His high estate, wealth, kin, a mighty crown,
> His strongholds, chieftains, spoils, his own renown
> And that of all his sires, Cædwal forsook,
> Inspired by love of Heaven, that he might look,
> A pilgrim king, on Peter and his shrine.
> (Bede, *Hist. eccl.*, 5.7)

In the epitaph Cædwalla is described as *rex Saxonum* and that appears to have been his favoured designation. After he had established his dynasty as rulers of other Saxon peoples, they seem to have ceased to be known as kings of the Gewisse and instead became kings of the Saxons and, eventually, of the West Saxons. Cædwalla's reign may have been short, but it was decisive in extending the scope of West Saxon interests and his successor Ine was able to build upon his achievements. BARBARA YORKE

Sources *ASC*, s.a. 685–8 [texts A, E] · Bede, *Hist. eccl.*, 4.12, 15–16; 5.7 · *AS chart.*, S 10, 230–35 · E. Stephanus, *The life of Bishop Wilfrid*, ed. and trans. B. Colgrave (1927), chap. 42 · H. E. Walker, 'Bede and the Gewissae: the political evolution of the heptarchy and its nomenclature', *Cambridge Historical Journal*, 12 (1956), 174–86 · B. Yorke, *Wessex in the early middle ages* (1995)

Cædwalla ap Cadfan. *See* Cadwallon ap Cadfan (*d.* 634).

Caerfallwch. *See* Edwards, Thomas (1779–1858).

Caerleon, John (*d. c.***1482**). *See under* Siôn Cent (*fl.* 1400–1430).

Caerleon, Lewis (*d.* in or after **1495**), physician and astronomer, was a native of Wales. He is first recorded in 1465–6, when he was admitted bachelor of medicine of Cambridge University. The university fined him 20*s.* in 1466 for not fulfilling his commitment to lecture in medicine. According to a seventeenth-century biography of Rhys ap Thomas (*d.* 1525), Caerleon was tutor to that influential Welsh nobleman. The biography describes Caerleon as 'a man of readie witt, cleare judgment, and well redd in the liberall sciences, as having most of his breeding in Italie, in the universitie of Padua' (*Cambrian Register*, 83). No documentary evidence of his possible stay or education in Italy has been found. However, by 1481 he had been made MD by an English university.

Caerleon's medical practice led him to political intrigue. Among those who consulted him were Elizabeth Woodville (*d.* 1492), Edward IV's queen, Margaret Beaufort, countess of Richmond (*d.* 1509), and her son, Henry, who was to become Henry VII. After the *coup d'état* of Richard III, Lady Margaret sent Caerleon to sound out the queen dowager's position on Henry's claim to the throne. Elizabeth had taken sanctuary at Westminster, where she was under close guard, but as her personal physician Caerleon had unchallenged access to her. There is good reason to believe that he conducted the secret exchanges between Lady Margaret and the queen that resulted in the betrothal of Henry Tudor and Elizabeth of York (*d.* 1503). Caerleon's participation in the Tudor conspiracy came to an end when he was arrested and confined to the Tower of London, probably at the time of the bill of attainder against Lady Margaret in January 1484. He was still incarcerated in March 1485 and perhaps remained so until the battle of Bosworth Field on 22 August. The victorious faction rewarded one of its own: shortly after Henry VII's accession Caerleon received a pension of 40 marks a year for life which was soon increased to 60 marks. In 1488 he became a knight of the king's alms in St George's Chapel, Windsor, with the right of free residence in the outer ward of the castle. Caerleon served as physician to Elizabeth of York until at least 1494. The latest certain record of his existence is a letter from him to Thomas Stoke, dated 6 May 1495 (San Francisco, California State Library, MS 8, art. 4).

Despite being a physician, Caerleon had little concern for medical literature; he was rather an enthusiastic annotator, copyist, and writer of astronomical texts. He had a special interest in eclipses and during his imprisonment he occupied himself with the compilation of eclipse tables, which he had begun in 1482, based on the Alfonsine tables. He carried out involved calculations for the solar eclipses of 28 May 1481 and 16 March 1485. His scholarship is of historical significance because he collected works by earlier English astronomers, particularly those of Richard Wallingford (*d.* 1336), Simon Bredon (*d.* 1372), John Holbroke (*d.* 1437), John Killingworth (*d.* 1445), John Somer (*d.* *c.*1409), and John Walter (*d.* *c.*1412). Caerleon exposed these to a critical eye, commenting on technical aspects as well as matters of attribution. He doubted, for instance, that a set of 'universal tables' of oblique ascensions was correctly attributed to John Walter. A recent analysis of the tables suggests that Caerleon's scepticism was well founded. His copy of *Cum rerum motu* is the only extant rendition of that anonymous astrological treatise on the nativity of Henry VI (CUL, MS Ee.3.61, fols. 155*r*–171*r*); it is the single most informative text on political astrology in fifteenth-century England. In 1490 Caerleon presented an astronomical volume to the chained library of Merton College, Oxford. He also left copies of his eclipse tables to Oxford and Cambridge universities.

Lewis Caerleon has in the past been confused with Lewis Charlton, bishop of Hereford (*d.* 1369); and he is not to be identified with 'Master Lewis', a physician noted in royal accounts for 1510. KEITH SNEDEGAR

Sources Emden, *Cam.*, 116–17 · H. M. Carey, *Courting disaster: astrology at the English court and university in the later middle ages* (1992) · 'A short view of the long life of … Rice ap Thomas', *Cambrian Register*, 1 (1796), 49–144 · P. Kibre, 'Lewis of Caerleon, doctor of medicine, astronomer and mathematician (1494?)', *Isis*, 43 (1952), 100–08 · J. D. North, *Horoscopes and history* (1986)
Archives BL, Royal MS 12.G.i · BL, Sloane MS 1697 · California State Library, San Francisco, MS 8, art. 4 · CUL, MS Ee.3.61 · St John Cam., MS 41

Caer-went, Gregory of (*fl.* 1237), Benedictine monk and supposed chronicler, was responsible for at least some of the annals compiled at St Peter's, Gloucester, covering the period from the foundation of the abbey to 1290. These survive only in the form of extracts transcribed by the antiquary Laurence Nowell, probably in the mid-1560s, which are preserved in BL, Cotton MS Vespasian A.v, folios 195–203*v*. Gregory, who presumably took his name from Caer-went in Gwent, and may have been related to the infirmarer Richard of Caer-went and the prior Philip of Caer-went recorded in 1275 and 1284 respectively, is named in an entry under the year 1237, stating that he had received the monastic habit on 29 October, 'who wrote this book up to this point' (BL, Cotton MS Vespasian A.v, fol. 201). How far beyond this year he continued to write it is impossible to tell, but his absence from a full list of the Gloucester monks in 1284 suggests that he was dead by then. Nor can it be said with confidence that Gregory was the composer of annals in an authorial sense, as opposed to a scribe or editor working on pre-existing material—the word *scripsit* is neutral on the point.

The material written down by Gregory of Caer-went was doubtless one of the sources employed by Abbot Walter Froucester when he had the Gloucester Abbey chronicle refurbished at the end of the fourteenth century. But comparison shows that Froucester's redactor omitted much that he found in Gregory, and in particular discarded entries that had no immediate relevance to the fortunes of the abbey in the years around 1400. Grants of land and the doings of benefactors are included in both chronicles, but some of Gregory's entries were shortened and others were omitted altogether. Thus both sources record the death of Abbot Peter in 1114, but only Gregory adds that Peter died at Eynsham on 17 July on his way to meet the king, and that his benefactions to his monks included partitions in the dormitory. And other events in Gloucester and its vicinity, like the union of the Hereford houses of St Peter and St Guthlac in 1144, the death of the Gloucester monk Gregory in 1157, his holy activity attested by the many books written in his hand, and the disastrous consequences of floods and bad weather in 1258, when imported wines 'were acid and green as if they were English' (BL, Cotton MS Vespasian A.v, fol. 202), found no place in Froucester's annals. The surviving annals of Gregory of Caer-went provide a tantalizing glimpse of the kind of source which might lie behind a monastic chronicle, and of the way changes in outlook could dictate the latter's composition. HENRY SUMMERSON

Sources BL, Cotton MS Vespasian A.v, fols. 195–203*v* • W. H. Hart, ed., *Historia et cartularium monasterii Sancti Petri Gloucestriae*, 3 vols., Rolls Series, 33 (1863–7) • J. C. Russell, 'Dictionary of writers of thirteenth century England', *BIHR*, special suppl., 3 (1936) [whole issue], esp. 41 • R. Flower, 'Laurence Nowell and the discovery of England in Tudor times', *PBA*, 21 (1935), 46–73
Archives BL, Cotton MS Vespasian A.v, fols. 195–203*v*

Caesar [Gaius Julius Caesar] (**100–44 BC**), politician, author, and military commander, was born on 13 Quinctilis (July) 100 BC, probably at Rome, the son of Gaius Julius Caesar, a patrician of old but recently undistinguished family whose brother-in-law was Gaius Marius, and Aurelia, probably daughter of Lucius Aurelius Cotta (consul in 119 BC). He had two sisters, married to Quintus Pedius and to Marcus Atius Balbus of Aricia; the latter's grandson, adopted in Caesar's will, became the emperor Augustus.

Nothing is known of Caesar's education. He was twelve when his uncle Marius was driven into exile by Sulla's march on Rome, and thirteen at the time of Marius's vengeful return with Lucius Cornelius Cinna. When he was fifteen, his father died; the following year Caesar broke off his engagement to a girl from a wealthy equestrian family to marry Cinna's daughter Cornelia (*d.* 69 BC). In 82 BC Sulla returned victorious from the east; by now Marius and Cinna were both dead, and Caesar went into hiding. His relatives successfully pleaded for his life, but the dictator sourly commented 'There are many Mariuses in that boy' ('Life of Caesar'). Caesar left Rome to serve in Asia Minor, where he was decorated for bravery in the attack on Mytilene. He came back to Rome at the news of Sulla's death, and announced his arrival on the political scene with the prosecution (unsuccessful) of a senior senator for extortion. In 75 BC, sailing to Rhodes to study rhetoric, he was captured by pirates; on payment of the ransom, he raised a squadron to defeat them, and had them crucified.

Caesar's first public office was the elective military tribunate (probably in 72 BC); in 69 he was quaestor, serving in Spain; in 65, curule aedile. It was a period of revived hope for *popularis* politicians: the Sullan oligarchy had proved itself corrupt, and the people's tribunes had regained the powers of which Sulla had stripped them. Caesar advertised his allegiance by his funeral speech for his aunt Julia, widow of Marius, in 69 BC, and by restoring to public view, as aedile, the Marian trophies Sulla had pulled down. In 63 BC, though still a junior senator, and in competition with two distinguished ex-consuls, he got himself elected to the high office of *pontifex maximus*. He was thirty-seven, already a formidable politician, and no friend of the conservative 'establishment' in the senate.

After a stormy praetorship in 62 BC, Caesar's first military command came with his proconsulship of Further Spain, in campaigns against the Callaeci and Lusitani conducted with characteristic decisiveness and dash. He was granted the right to a triumph, which for most Romans was the height of ambition. Caesar chose to forgo it. He

Caesar (100–44 BC), head

wanted the consulship, and by entering the city to declare his candidacy he had to abandon his military command. His ambitions were not those of ordinary Romans. After the consulship there would be a greater command, one like those the people had conferred on Gnaeus Pompeius (Pompey the Great), whose triumph over the pirates and Mithridates, an affair of unprecedented splendour, had taken place in 61 BC.

'Caesar has the wind in his sails just now', wrote Cicero in June 60 BC (Cicero, *ad Atticum*, II.1.6). Certainly Caesar's enemies thought so, and did their best to prevent his election as consul, or to commit him in advance to a harmlessly administrative consular command (the forests and drove-roads of Italy). It was in vain: Caesar was elected consul for 59 BC, with the powerful backing of Pompey and Marcus Licinius Crassus, and, having swiftly neutralized his optimate colleague Marcus Calpurnius Bibulus, forced through a programme of land distribution in the teeth of furious conservative opposition.

The people's consul was rewarded with an extraordinary command (like those for Pompey in 67 and 66 BC) passed by a tribune's law in May 59 BC: he was to have Cisalpine Gaul and Illyricum (that is, northern Italy and the eastern coast of the Adriatic) for five years; Pompey subsequently got the senate to add Gallia Narbonensis (Provence). So the great campaigns of conquest, to rival Pompey's in Asia, would be either eastward or north-westward (in modern terms, either on the middle Danube or in France and Belgium) according to opportunity. As it turned out, the migration of the Helvetii took Caesar west and north. He left Rome as proconsul on or about 19 March 58 BC. When he next entered it, just over nine years later, it would be as an invader in a civil war.

As consul, Caesar's first act had been to make public the proceedings of the senate. As proconsul, he reported his campaigns to the Roman people in annual 'commentaries', which have been recognized ever since as masterpieces of military narrative. First (58 BC), the defeat of the Helvetii, and of Ariovistus's Germans; second (57), the defeat of the Nervii (a very close-run thing) and the conquest of the Belgic peoples; third (56), the conquest of Brittany and Aquitaine. In three years, Caesar had conquered to the ocean and the Rhine; now it was time to go beyond.

Again, Caesar kept his options open. The fourth *commentarius*, for 55 BC, reports the bridging of the Rhine and the punitive raid into Germany, and after that the preliminary expedition to Britain in late summer. Either of those could be repeated on a larger scale the following year, for his allies Pompey and Crassus were now consuls, and the people duly voted him a five-year extension to his command. Britain was the more glamorous option, an adventure beyond Ocean itself, and public opinion in Rome was excited about the conquest of this people at the very ends of the earth (*ultimi Britanni*, Catullus, 11.11f).

The show of force in September 55 BC was very nearly a disaster. Caesar's main cavalry force was unable to make the crossing; he had the greatest difficulty in getting his two legions disembarked (near Deal in Kent), against fierce opposition; four days after the landing a violent storm and high tides seriously damaged his transports; and when one of the legions was ambushed, only the last-minute arrival of reinforcements prevented its total defeat. In the end Caesar was glad to be able to get back to Gaul in his patched-up transports before the equinox.

For the main assault the following year Caesar ordered the building of large numbers of new transport ships, low in draught to be beached easily, and able to be worked by oars or sail. In the midsummer of 54 BC he set sail from Portus Itius (Boulogne) with five legions and 2000 cavalry, in an armada of 800 ships. Tides and currents made it an awkward crossing, and oars were needed to get the transports to the landing place, probably not far from the previous year's, though this time undefended. The British forces had withdrawn inland to higher ground; Caesar disembarked, left his ships at anchor, and marched inland the same night. His forces had crossed the Stour and captured a British defensive stronghold, probably Bigbury, when news came that a storm had driven the ships ashore, with great damage. Caesar had to return to the coast, organize repairs, send for replacements from Gaul, and bring the ships on shore behind a defensive fortification. In the meantime the Britons had put Cassivellaunus, the powerful king of the Catuvellauni, in command of their forces.

Resuming his advance through Cantium (Kent), after hard fighting against well-organized British cavalry and charioteers, Caesar forced a crossing of the Thames (possibly at Brentford) and eventually found Cassivellaunus's fortress and stormed it. Meanwhile, an attack on the base camp and Caesar's ships was successfully beaten off. Cassivellaunus asked for terms; Caesar accepted his surrender, demanded hostages and an annual tribute, and took his army back to Gaul.

On his return Caesar was told of the death of his only child, his beloved daughter, Julia, Pompey's wife, in childbirth in her early twenties. (Julia's mother, Caesar's first wife, Cornelia, had also died young; his second wife, Pompeia, was divorced in 62 BC, for not being 'above suspicion'; he then married Calpurnia, who outlived him—it was she who had bad dreams on the night before the ides of March.) He also found dangerous unrest in Gaul, which was why he had come back so quickly. It soon blew up into full-scale rebellion in the Belgic lands, with one Roman winter camp wiped out and another, under Cicero's brother Quintus, only narrowly saved from the same fate. One and a half legions, about 7000 men, were lost in the disaster.

It is not known where or when the fifth book of commentaries was written; Caesar was desperately occupied in the winter of 54–53 BC. But it contains, among other things, the first ever account of the geography and ethnography of Britain: 'The island is triangular in shape, with one side facing Gaul ... The second side faces westward, towards Spain' (Caesar, V.12–14). As Caesar's contemporary Catullus confirms (*ultima occidentis insula*, Catullus, 29.12), the Romans thought of Britain as in the far west, close to Spain. It was a fitting scene for a heroic epic, duly composed by Cicero from material supplied by his brother (Cicero, *Ad Q. fratrem*, II.14.2, 16.4, III.7.6). But now that adventure was over, as Quintus, after his narrow escape, knew better than most.

Caesar spent the next four years reconquering his conquests. The great pan-Gallic rebellion of Vercingetorix in 52 BC came very close to destroying his whole achievement, and him with it. His enemies in Rome took heart: Crassus was dead, Pompey could be seduced to their side as the protector of the republic. They were determined to destroy Caesar, and he was determined not to be destroyed. In January 49 BC he threw the dice in the air and marched into Italy.

With his battle-hardened army of veterans, Caesar fought his civil war against Pompey and the republicans all over the empire of Rome, and beyond: Spain in 49 BC, Thessaly in 48 (defeating Pompey at Pharsalus), Alexandria in 48–7 (where he probably wrote the three books of his *De bello civili* commentaries), Asia Minor in 47 ('I came, I saw, I conquered'), and above all north Africa in 46, where Marcus Porcius Cato, symbol of the old republic, killed himself after Caesar's victory at Utica. In September 46 BC, by the then calendar, Caesar at last held the great triumph that would outshine Pompey's of fifteen years before. He was now dictator for a ten-year term, with a formidable programme of projects of which the most lasting was the Julian calendar, introduced on 1 January 45 BC. But warfare still preoccupied him: first against Pompey's sons in

Spain, won only by a hair's breadth at the battle of Munda (March 45 BC), and then a planned campaign against the Parthians, to avenge Crassus. But by now his autocracy was openly regal, and deeply offensive to the senate. He was careless of his own security, trusting perhaps in the luck that had protected him for so long. The latest of his long line of mistresses was Cleopatra, queen of Egypt, now conspicuously living in Rome; in 44 BC he was made dictator for life; the month of his birth, Quinctilis, was renamed 'July'; a cult of Caesar, with his own priest (*flamen*), was instituted. It was too much. On 15 March he was murdered in the Curia Pompei in Rome by republican senators under the leadership of Cato's son-in-law Marcus Junius Brutus.

> The body lay where it fell, unworthily fouled with the blood of a man who had forced his way to the west as far as Britain and Ocean, and intended to force his way to the east against the empires of Parthia and India. (Nicolaus of Damascus, 95)

So Nicolaus of Damascus, writing about twenty years after the event, sums up the many-sided genius of Caesar in the way he would probably have wanted, as an imperial conqueror.

In 42 BC Caesar was deified. The heir to his name and fortune was his great-nephew Gaius Octavius, whom he adopted in his will as Gaius Julius Caesar Octavianus and who dedicated the temple of Divus Julius on 18 Sextilis (later 'August') 29 BC, immediately after his own triumph over Cleopatra's Egypt. The young Caesar 'Octavian' became Caesar Augustus, and thereafter Caesar's name became synonymous with imperial autocracy throughout the history of Europe.

Shakespeare's *Julius Caesar* was first performed in 1599 and has always been one of his most frequently performed plays. Shakespeare's source was Plutarch's *Lives* (written some 150 years after Caesar's death) in the translation by Sir Thomas North of 1579, or its reprint of 1595. Shakespeare's play deals with the final days and assassination of Caesar and shows no interest in his role as Britain's first invader. T. P. WISEMAN

Sources Caesar, *Bellum Gallicum*, ed. W. Hering (Leipzig, 1987) · Suetonius, *Divus Iulius*, ed. H. E. Butler and M. Cary (1927) · 'Life of Caesar', *Plutarch's Lives*, ed. and trans. B. Perrin, 7 (1919) · Cicero, *Cicero's Letters to Atticus*, ed. and trans. D. R. Shackleton Bailey, 7 vols. (1965–70) · Cicero, *Epistulae ad Quintum fratrem et M. Brutum*, ed. D. R. Shackleton Bailey (1980) · Catullus, *Carmina*, ed. R. A. B. Mynors, Oxford Classical Texts (1958) · Nicolaus of Damascus, 'Bios kaisaros', *Die Fragmente der griechischen Historiker*, ed. F. Jacoby (1961), 395–420 · M. Gelzer, *Caesar: politician and statesman*, trans. P. Needham (1968) [Ger. orig., *Caesar: der Politiker und Staatsman*, (Munich, 1921)] · J. A. Crook, A. Lintott, and E. Rawson, eds., *The Cambridge ancient history*, 2nd edn, 9 (1994), chaps. 6–11 · K. Welch and A. Powell, eds., *Julius Caesar as artful reporter: the war commentaries as political instruments* (1998) · T. R. Holmes, *Ancient Britain and the invasions of Julius Caesar* (1907), chaps. 6–7 · S. Weinstock, *Divus Julius* (1971) · W. Shakespeare, *Julius Caesar*, ed. A. Humphreys (1984) · J. Ripley, *'Julius Caesar' on stage in England and America, 1599–1973* (1980) · C. Meier, *Caesar*, trans. D. McLintock (1995) [Ger. orig., *Caesar* (Berlin, 1982)]

Likenesses coin, 44BC, repro. in A. Alföldi, *Antike Kunst*, 2 (1959), 27ff. · bust, Turin Museum, Turin, Italy · bust, Vatican Museum, Vatican City · bust, Museo Torlonia, Italy · head, BM [*see illus.*]

Caesar, Sir Charles (1590–1642), judge, was born in London on 27 January 1590, the third son of Sir Julius *Caesar (*bap.* 1558, *d.* 1636) and his first wife, Dorcas Lusher, *née* Martin (*d.* 1590). His older brother of the same name had died in infancy. Charles Howard, Lord Effingham, was godfather to the deceased child but was reluctant to repeat his office for the younger Charles lest it bring him bad fortune. Caesar matriculated at Magdalen College, Oxford, in 1602 but it was from All Souls College that he graduated BA in 1606, and proceeded MA and BCL in 1608. The king interceded on his behalf in 1605 when he sought a fellowship in All Souls but he was not admitted to the fellowship until 1607. He then studied law in Paris, where the English ambassador entrusted him with confidential correspondence about papal spies as an apparently safer course than using the diplomatic pouch. He returned to Oxford to receive the DCL in 1612.

Sir Julius Caesar lavished his attention on Charles, especially after the untimely death of his older brother Julius in 1607. Through his father's connections Caesar was accorded special admission to the Inner Temple in 1610 and after 1613 was associated with Doctors' Commons although he was not fully admitted until 1623. On 9 October 1613 he was knighted at Theobalds in the presence of the privy council. Ten days later he married his first wife, Anne, daughter of Sir Peter *Vanlore (*c.*1547–1627), a prominent member of the Dutch mercantile community in England. Through the patronage of Thomas Howard, Lord Bindon, Caesar sat in the 1614 parliament for Weymouth and Melcombe Regis, Dorset. That year Sir Julius purchased for his son the manor of Bennington, Hertfordshire, where he built a home that would be the seat of the Caesar family until the eighteenth century.

Caesar's legal career concentrated on ecclesiastical and admiralty law. He was admitted a master of chancery in 1615, his father being the master of the rolls, and he served on numerous admiralty and piracy commissions in London and Middlesex. He was a great favourite of his uncle, Henry *Caesar, dean of Ely, and through him he enjoyed favour among the ecclesiastical establishment. He earned high praise from Justice Davies when they returned from the western circuit in 1620. Davies wrote to his father that 'his discretion and sweetness of manners hath caused everyman to take care of his entertainment everywhere, which did deminish my care, but did encrease my love towards him' (BL, Add. MS 12504, fol. 99). After 1620 Caesar was frequently included in the high commission. Archbishop Abbot made him judge of the court of Audience and master of faculties for life. When Abbot was suspended in 1627, Caesar was one of the commissioners charged with exercising archiepiscopal jurisdiction.

Caesar's first wife, with whom he had had six children, died on 13 June 1625. The following year he married Jane, daughter of Sir Edward Barkham, a former lord mayor of London. They had nine children. In 1636 Caesar inherited from his uncle Henry Caesar, who died childless, money and land in Huntingdonshire, and from his father the bulk of Sir Julius's sizeable estate, which included extensive landholdings in Lincolnshire. In 1639 the death of Sir Dudley Digges, his father's successor as master of the rolls, vacated that office. Caesar prevailed in the heated competition for the post which followed, but at the cost of £15,000. None the less, by the end of his life he had amassed a considerable property holding in three counties and in London. He died from smallpox on 6 December 1642, at Bennington, where he was buried. One of his sons died several days later of the same disease, but two other sons and two daughters survived. Jane Caesar outlived her husband by nearly twenty years, dying on 18 June 1661. Throughout his life Caesar had enjoyed a reputation for charm and discretion but he was also criticized for being too malleable and perhaps corrupt. His epitaph spoke rather grandly of his being 'an equal distributor of unsuspected justice' (Lodge), but some contemporaries believed him a fool who was too easily manipulated by his colleagues in Doctors' Commons. L. M. Hill

Sources L. M. Hill, *Bench and bureaucracy: the public career of Sir Julius Caesar, 1580–1636* (1988) • B. P. Levack, *The civil lawyers in England, 1603–1641* (1973) • Sir Julius Caesar's curriculum vitae, BL, Add. MS 4160, fols. 18–23 • E. Lodge, *The life of Sir Julius Caesar … with memoirs of his family and descendants*, new edn (1827) • BL, Add. MS 12504, fol. 99 • BL, Add. MS 15208, fol. 177

Likenesses G. P. D. Harding, watercolour drawing, NPG; version, AM Oxf. • engraving, repro. in Lodge, *Life of Sir Julius Caesar*

Caesar, Charles (1673–1741), politician and Jacobite agent, was born in London on 21 November 1673, the eldest of four children of Sir Charles Caesar (1654–1694), politician, and Susanna (*d.* 1693), daughter and heir of Sir Thomas Bonfoy, a London merchant. He was descended from a prominent political family; both his great-great-grandfather Sir Julius Caesar and his great-grandfather Sir Charles Caesar had served as master of the rolls under James I and Charles I respectively. From 1 April 1689 to 1690 he was a fellow-commoner at St Catharine's College, Cambridge. He was admitted to the Middle Temple on 26 November 1690. In 1694 he inherited the family estate at Benington, Hertfordshire, worth £3500 p.a., and with it the family's 'country' party interest. In January 1701 he won Hertford borough, defeating Sir William Cowper, one of whose sons had been tried for the murder of a Quaker girl. Caesar was to receive the support of the Quakers in subsequent elections to 1737. He fought the borough seat eleven times, winning on nine occasions, and the county seat four times, winning twice. During the 1705 debate on the protestant succession Caesar accused Sidney Godolphin of a constant correspondence with the exiled Jacobite court during William's reign and was sent to the Tower.

On 24 November 1702 Caesar married Mary Freeman [**Mary Caesar** (*bap.* 1677, *d.* 1741)], garden designer, the daughter of Ralph Freeman (1625/6–1714) and Elizabeth Aubrey (1642/3–1720) of Aspenden, Hertfordshire, where she was baptized on 3 October 1677. Mary played an active part in the design of the gardens at Benington, where she built a shell-decorated grotto, details of which were recorded in the couple's letter-books.

Defeated in 1708, but re-elected in 1710, Caesar was asked by Harley to choose his favoured government office, but was then, against his wishes, made under-treasurer at the navy. Returned for Hertford borough in 1715 and 1722, he was unseated on petition by the committee of privileges. In 1716 he negotiated with the Swedish ambassador, Count Gyllenborg, for help in pursuing the Jacobite cause. Both Caesar and Gyllenborg were arrested in 1717 and imprisoned in the Tower, but 'nothing material … [was] found among Mr Caesar's papers' (*Stuart Papers*, 2.47), which makes Keith Feiling's description of him as 'hardly fit to manage a wine club' (Feiling, 19) as inappropriate as Sir John Plumb's 'rabid old Jacobite' (Plumb, 214). Following his release he acted as a peacemaker between Harley (now Lord Oxford) and Francis Atterbury, and in 1723 was active with Oxford in defending the bishop at his trial before the Lords. A triumvirate, Caesar and lords Wentworth and Orrery, managed Jacobite affairs after Atterbury's exile and Oxford's death in 1724. Caesar was trusted as a Jacobite agent until 1729, and the Stuart papers refer to his usefulness and loyalty.

Though bottom of the poll in the county election of 1722, Caesar defeated his tory brother-in-law Ralph Freeman in September 1727 with a large majority drawn from the Quakers, voters who lived in London, those voting for Hertfordshire towns, and the local gentry. The nature of Caesar's victory was such that a number of tories suspected him of moving towards the Walpole ministry. Deeply indebted on account of losses in the South Sea Bubble, the cost of electioneering, and the extravagance of a new house at Benington, burnt down before being occupied, Caesar was defeated by his former supporter William Plumer in 1734. He was then detained in debtors' prison, where he remained until April 1736, when at a county by-election 'the independent freeholders carried Mr Caesar's election at their own expense' (Turnor, 160).

Caesar appears to have enjoyed a happy marriage throughout his troubled political career. In 1730 he wrote to Mary of weeding her garden, adding 'how happy a loveing and beloved wife makes her husband' (Caesar MSS, letter-book F). The seven letter-books and her diary also reveal Mary to have acted as an election agent for her husband, corresponding with peers, literary figures, the clergy, and Hertfordshire voters. A passionate Jacobite sympathizer, for Mary there was scant difference between the tory and the Stuart cause of the 1720s. Such dedication led her to see, and expect, similar loyalties among family friends such as the former lord chancellor William, Earl Cowper, whose stance at the time of the Atterbury conspiracy is better understood as 'independent' whiggery.

Charles Caesar died at Benington, presumably in late March or early April 1741, and on 5 April was buried there, 'with as little expense as decency will admit' (HoP, *Commons, 1715–54*). His will, dated 19 August 1740, was a 'melancholy memorial of the ruin of the elder branch of this once flourishing family' (Clutterbuck, 2.285). He was survived by Mary, who died at Benington on 8 July 1741 and was buried there four days later. Their granddaughter,

Jane Caesar, married Sir Charles Cotterell Dormer of Rousham, Oxfordshire, and was responsible for moving there the family papers and portraits. LIONEL M. MUNBY

Sources L. M. Munby, *The common people are not nothing: conflict in religion and politics in Hertfordshire* (1995) • priv. coll., Caesar MSS • Mary Caesar's diary, BL, Add. MS 62558 • parish register, Aspenden, 1677–1702, Herts. ALS, D/P8/1/1 [baptism, marriage] • parish register, Benington, 1741, Herts. ALS, D/P18/1/2 [burials] • R. R. Sedgwick, 'Caesar, Charles', HoP, *Commons, 1715–54* • *The manuscripts of his grace the duke of Portland*, 10 vols., HMC, 29 (1891–1931), vol. 4, p. 154 • R. Clutterbuck, ed., *The history and antiquities of the county of Hertford*, 2 (1821), 285–7; 3 (1827), 347–8 • Venn, *Alum. Cant.*, 1/1.280 • K. Feiling, *The second tory party, 1714–1832*, new edn (1951) • J. H. Plumb, *Sir Robert Walpole*, 2 vols. (1956–60) • L. Turnor, *History of the ancient town and borough of Hertford* (1830) • private information (2004) [letter from registrar, Royal Arch.] • C. Jones, 'Jacobitism and the historian: the case of William, first Earl Cowper', *Albion*, 23 (1991), 681–97 • V. Rumbold, 'The Jacobite vision of Mary Caesar', *Women, writing, history, 1640-1740*, ed. I. Grundy and S. Wiseman (1992), 178–98 • L. M. Munby, 'Mary Caesar and her gardens at Bennington Place', *Garden making and the Freman family: a memoir of Hamels, 1713–1733*, ed. A. Rowe, Hertfordshire Record Publications, 17 (2001)

Archives BL, Mary Caesar, diary, Add. MS 62558 [Mary Caesar] • BL, account as treasurer of navy, Add. MS 34402 • priv. coll., letter-books, notes on the family in notebook, poll books | Herts. ALS, Hertford borough records, poll returns • Herts. ALS, Panshanger MSS D/EP

Likenesses portrait (of Charles Caesar?), repro. in E. Lodge, *Life of Sir Julius Caesar … with memoirs of his family and descendants* (Oct 1810)

Wealth at death left estates to be sold to pay debts: Clutterbuck, ed., *History and antiquities*, vol. 2, p. 285

Caesar, Henry Adelmare (1564/5–1636), dean of Ely, was probably born at his father's house in the Old Priory, St Helen, Bishopsgate, London, the fifth son of Cesare *Adelmare (*d.* 1569) [*see under* Caesar, Sir Julius], physician, and Margaret (or Margery) (*d.* 1586), daughter of Michael Perin; Julius *Caesar (*bap.* 1558, *d.* 1636) and Thomas *Caesar (1561–1610) were his elder brothers, and he had three known sisters. He grew up with close Roman Catholic connections, such as the family of Lord Montagu, his brother's godfather, and strong protestant ones, from the influence of his mother and stepfather, Michael *Lok.

Caesar went to Cambridge University, but when accused of being popishly inclined, travelled overseas for a few months without a licence, accompanied by an Italian godfather, and visited Rome. He then returned to Cambridge and recanted, with confirmation from Sir Francis Walsingham, and was able to obtain a presentation to the vicarage of Lostwithiel, Cornwall, to which he was instituted in December 1583. Here he was suspected of popery for wearing a cope, having books by Roman Catholic theologians, and expressing approval of practices such as fasting. He appeared at the quarter sessions in October 1584 for alleging that Sir Walter Mildmay had desired to see the spirit of Cardinal Pole and had done so, and was examined about whether he was a Roman Catholic. This he denied. In the atmosphere of panic against possible Roman Catholics engendered by the Throckmorton plot, he was further examined, sent to Sir Walter Mildmay for punishment rather than the Star Chamber, and required to apologize at the next sessions in Mildmay's shire. Measures were then taken in 1585 to deprive him, as unfit for the ministry, of his benefice.

Caesar next spent four years in Paris, perhaps in order to study at the university. He became well established among core recusant exiles and by December 1588 was reporting to Walsingham on the murky world of double-crossing agents, and on English priests there. His views had become very hostile to Roman Catholic priests:

> I could never come acquainted w[i]th Priest yet [tha]t would wish well either to his prince ore Country but usse villainouse word[es] against her, [and] [th]e [pre]sent estate. Yea suche woord[es] as are intollerable [and] with honest eares cannot, neither may abide to heare. (PRO, SP 15/30/120)

He pleaded that poverty prevented greater service. Walsingham responded by promising him a good reception in England, and Caesar returned in January 1589. He then studied theology in Oxford, taking his BD from Balliol in 1593, and his DD from St Edmund Hall in 1595. He was incorporated DD at Cambridge in 1597.

No doubt helped by the position of his brother Julius as master of requests, which involved attending the queen, Caesar became successively rector of St Christopher-le-Stocks, London, in 1596, and of Somersham, Huntingdonshire, from 1597. To the latter he added a prebend at Westminster Abbey between 1609 and 1625, the deanery of Ely in 1614, and the family living of Benington, Hertfordshire, in 1616. The last two he held with Somersham for the rest of his life.

As dean of Ely, Caesar was on good terms with Bishop Lancelot Andrewes, and took a keen interest in the cathedral music. John Amner, organist throughout his time, composed service settings, including a collection of morning and evening canticles, and settings of the Kyrie and the Credo, which are known as 'Caesar's'. As this very lovely work has versified words, he may have written them. It belongs to the polyphonic style which Amner adopted in response to the beauty of holiness movement, so clearly Caesar sympathized with it. He left endowments for the petty canons (which would include Amner), singing men, and choristers of the cathedral, as well as one for the 'chaunter' to commemorate benefactors. He also sought to encourage learning by endowments to Ely Free School, and for four scholarships from there to a college, leading on to two fellowships at a time: Jesus College, Cambridge, benefited.

Caesar never married, but enjoyed warm relationships with his siblings Sir Julius Caesar and Elizabeth Hunt, and intended very substantial legacies for Sir Julius and some nephews and nieces. His wealth was considerable: his endowment legacies alone were financed from over £2000 and others reached well over £1360. He died 'in his seventy-second year' on 27 June 1636, and was buried in Ely Cathedral, where an elaborate wall-plaque commemorated him. ELIZABETH ALLEN

Sources E. Lodge, *The life of Sir Julius Caesar … with memoirs of his family and descendants*, new edn (1827), 7, 10, 43–4 • *DNB* • PRO, SP 12/176/46, SP 15/30/120, SP 12/173/61 • will, PRO, PROB 11/172, fols. 53r–54r • R. B. Wernham, ed., *List and analysis of state papers, foreign*

series, Elizabeth I, 1 (1964), 302 · A. J. Greening, 'Amner, John', *New Grove* · W. E. Dickson, *A catalogue of ancient choral services and anthems, preserved … in the cathedral church of Ely* (1861), 13 · Devon RO, Chanter 21 MFC4/7/11 · memorial inscription, Ely Cathedral · W. B. Bannerman, ed., *The registers of St Helen's, Bishopsgate, London*, Harleian Society, register section, 31 (1904), 255

Likenesses effigy, wall plaque, Ely Cathedral · stipple, NPG

Caesar [*formerly* Adelmare], **Sir Julius** (*bap.* **1558**, *d.* **1636**), civil lawyer, was born in Tottenham, the eldest son of **Cesare Adelmare** (*d.* 1569) and Margery (or Margaret) Perient (or Perin). His father, known as Dr Adelmare or Dr Caesar, had been a subject of the republic of Venice. About 1550 he emigrated to England, where in 1557 he was granted naturalization with immunity from the taxation imposed on aliens; he was a graduate of the faculty of medicine at Padua and was admitted a fellow of the College of Physicians in 1554. He attended upon Queen Mary and later upon Queen Elizabeth and members of the court. He enjoyed the patronage and the protection of William Paulet, marquess of Winchester, who was one of Julius's godparents. When he sent a cure to William Cecil in 1563, Adelmare addressed him as his 'dominus and patronus'. He possessed houses in the close of St Helen, Bishopsgate, and in Tottenham, and held several leases granted by the queen. He had at least seven children: Julius; William, who was active as a merchant in the Mediterranean between 1586 and 1591, when he disappeared after a shipwreck; Sir Thomas *Caesar (1561–1610), who became a cursitor baron of the exchequer; Henry *Caesar (1564/5–1636), who became dean of Ely; Margaret, who married Nicholas Wright, of Gray's Inn; Anne, who married Damian Peck, also of Gray's Inn; and Elizabeth, who married John Hunt, a member of Doctors' Commons.

Julius was baptized on 10 February 1558 at the church of St Dunstan-in-the-East; his godparents were, besides Winchester, Henry Fitzalan, earl of Arundel, and the queen, represented by Lady Montague. A year after his father's death his mother married Michael Lok, a London merchant whose family had puritan sympathies. In a letter to William Cecil, Caesar referred to being in Burghley's service prior to 1578; possibly Burghley, as master of the wards, had taken up Julius's wardship himself and provided for his education in his household. Caesar graduated BA from Magdalen Hall, Oxford, in May 1575 and MA in February 1578, before pursuing a legal education at Clement's Inn. David Lewes, judge of the high court of admiralty, took an interest in him and encouraged further legal studies in France, where Caesar stayed between 1578 and 1581; he was awarded, allegedly in Paris, a licentiate's degree and a doctorate in law in April 1581. On 10 May 1581 he was admitted as an advocate in the *parlement* of Paris, perhaps an honorary mark of recognition at a time when France and England were negotiating an alliance. In 1580 he had been admitted to the Inner Temple.

Upon Caesar's return to London in 1581 Lewes further forwarded his career by naming him commissioner for piracy causes and commissary of the master of the royal hospital of St Katharine; years later, in 1596, he would accede to the mastership of the hospital. Shortly before

Sir Julius Caesar (*bap.* 1558, *d.* 1636), by Renold Elstrack

his death Lewes also intervened to ensure that Caesar successfully supplicated for a DCL in Oxford, a degree awarded on 3 March 1584. With Lewes's and Walsingham's support, and after an intervention of the queen on his behalf, the corporation of London awarded Caesar the freedom of the city and an extraordinary appointment as its civil-law counsel (11 June 1583); as a result he was admitted to his father-in-law's company, the Worshipful Company of Goldsmiths. In December 1583, again with Walsingham's help, he was commissioned as the bishop of London's commissary for Essex, Hertfordshire, and Middlesex. In 1584, following Lewes's death, Caesar, who had often acted as the judge's deputy in the court of admiralty, was asked by the lord admiral to act temporarily as the judge. In 1585 the queen named Caesar and Valentine Dale as joint commissioners for dealing with the high court of admiralty's business, awarding the former two-thirds of the fees and profits that would normally accrue to the judge. In November 1587 Caesar was awarded a commission for life as the sole judge, an office he held until 1606. In 1596 the queen awarded him an annual pension of £100.

Caesar continued to pursue other offices traditionally

open to civil lawyers. On 10 January 1591 he was sworn in as an extraordinary master in the court of requests, and in 1596 he was appointed an ordinary master. His involvement in that court prompted him to research its jurisdiction and to publish in 1597 a treatise on *The Ancient State, Authoritie, and Proceedings of the Court of Requests*. Shortly after Lewes's death in 1584 Walsingham's influence ensured that Caesar was made an extraordinary master in chancery; he became an ordinary master in October 1588. On 24 January 1591 Caesar was called to the bench of the Inner Temple; between 1593 and 1595 he presided over the society's parliaments with Edward Coke; in November 1593 he was elected treasurer, a post he held until 1595, when he was succeeded by Coke. In 1596 he made a gift of £300 to the inn, which went towards the erection of a block of chambers which were known until the eighteenth century as Caesar's Buildings. In recognition he was granted a life-chamber in the inn, and a right during his lifetime of up to six appointments at any time to the inn and to a chamber.

Caesar was knighted at Greenwich on 20 May 1603. His career as a judge was deflected between 1606 and 1614, when he was chancellor of the exchequer. His years at the exchequer were dominated by the government's attempts to work out a system which would ensure a substantial and permanent increase in the crown's regular income, and at the same time reduce its debt, and which culminated in the failed proposals of 1610 known as the 'Great Contract'. Caesar's approach consisted mainly in seeking specific improvements within the existing framework, which would have reduced costs and abuses and increased existing sources of income. Even measures such as these, however, were to a degree politically sensitive, because they often implied a more vigorous exercise of the king's prerogative. A memorandum Caesar wrote during the summer of 1610 was critical of the proposed contract, as it endeavoured to show that the king's finances could be balanced without it, and even without further aids from parliament. The repeated debates on the crown's prerogative he had witnessed in parliament made him fear that the contract would undermine the monarchy and the fundamental laws of the kingdom. After the project's failure and Salisbury's death, Caesar worked out more proposals which were calculated to balance the crown's receipts and issues within the existing means of the political system. Even after he had left the exchequer the government continued to draw occasionally upon his experience and expertise in the crown's finances; in 1619, after the dismissal of Suffolk as lord treasurer, Caesar was a member of the treasury commission. He also remained a privy councillor, having been sworn of the council in 1607.

In 1614 Caesar left the exchequer for the mastership of the rolls, a position he held until his death. As a privy councillor he contributed to the approval and enforcement of the Book of Orders in 1631. He was a member of the subcommittee which supervised its implementation in Hampshire, Wiltshire, Somerset, Dorset, Devon, and Cornwall, and his own copy of the Book of Orders, heavily annotated in his hand, testifies to his interest in the council's efforts to reorganize local administration. He was also an active member of the commission which in 1624 was responsible for drawing up a new statute for a colonial government in Virginia; while the reorganization reinforced the crown's public interest in the colony, there is evidence that Caesar also ensured that the interest of Captain John Martin, his first wife's brother and one of the founders of the colony, were taken into account. In 1629 the earl of Bedford, who was suspected with others of having circulated a pamphlet against parliament, was for a brief period assigned to be kept in custody at Caesar's house.

As a client of Charles Howard, Caesar sat in the Elizabethan parliaments as a member for Reigate (1589), Bletchingley (1593), and New Windsor (1597 and 1601). In the Jacobean parliaments he secured seats through court patronage (Westminster, 1607; Middlesex, 1614; Malden, 1620). He sat on committees considering the subsidy bill of 1593; bills on recusancy (1593); prohibition proceedings (1597); the organization of merchants and seamen (1597); maritime insurance (1601); criminal law (1601); the merger of the lordships of Eye and Dunsden to the manor of Sunning (1601); and the jurisdiction of the City of London over some precincts belonging to St Katharine's Hospital (1601).

Caesar married Dorcas Lusher on 26 February 1583; she was the daughter of Alderman Richard Martin and widow of Richard Lusher of the Inner Temple. From their marriage were born Dorcas, in 1584; two years later, a son, Charles, who died a few months after; Julius, in 1588; and Charles, in 1590. Their mother died in 1595, having given birth to another son, Richard, who survived for only a few weeks. Caesar married again the following year; his new wife, Alice, was the widow of John Dent, an alderman, who had left his estate to his wife and their two daughters. Caesar and Alice had three sons—John (*b.* 1597), Thomas (*b.* 1600), and Robert (*b.* 1602). Their marriage also brought Caesar the manor of Mitcham, Surrey, where he received the queen on 12 September 1598. Alice joined her husband in the foundation of a chapel in the Strand in 1613, which was consecrated the following year, shortly before her death. On 19 April 1615 Caesar married his third wife, Anne, *née* Woodhouse, widow of Henry Hogan and William Hungate, and granddaughter of Sir Nicholas Bacon; the ceremony took place in the Rolls Chapel, where Sir Francis Bacon, a long-time acquaintance of Caesar, gave the bride, his niece, away. No children were born from this third marriage. Caesar's daughter Dorcas died in 1608. The same year, during a brawl, his son Julius was killed by a fellow student in Padua. Sir Charles *Caesar (1590–1642) studied at Oxford before becoming a civil lawyer; he worked on ecclesiastical and admiralty causes, and served on several commissions and in chancery. John was educated at Eton and Magdalen College, Oxford. He accompanied King James on his visit to Scotland in 1617, where he was knighted. From his father he received or inherited lands in Hertfordshire. Thomas was educated at Oxford and Cambridge, where he proceeded to a doctorate and was praised by John Collins, provost of King's College. Robert was also educated at Oxford, was trained as a lawyer, and became one of the six clerks in chancery in 1636.

Caesar's involvement in commercial ventures and investments is partly documented. In 1583 he acquired a share in the Mineral and Battery Company, and in 1594 became one of the company's two governors; he took an active part in pursuing its legal interests and obtaining a new charter in 1604. He was also a member of the North-west Passage Company and of the French Company, and backed voyages of Thomas Cavendish and Sir Martin Frobisher. His landed interests were spread over Middlesex (a house in Hackney, on the corner of Humberton Street), Hertfordshire, Lincolnshire, Norfolk (a house in Bradenham, which belonged to his wife Anne), Essex (a house in Tremnall), and Kent. Although not mentioned in the inquisition post mortem taken at Hatfield, he had also been granted leases for estates in Staffordshire. The provisions of his will refer to his library and books.

Caesar died on 18 April 1636. He was buried the following day in St Helen, Bishopsgate, where he had installed a funeral monument of black marble, covered by a carved parchment-coloured stone in the form of a deed with a pendant seal, its ribbons cut and an inscription referring to the deceased's debt of mortality. His reputation as a lawyer has suffered from unsustained rumours questioning his legal abilities. From Caesar's extensive notes as a judge, he appears to have had a keen interest in counsels' technical arguments and in the complex civil and canon law authorities which supported such arguments. As in the case of many of his own opinions, memoranda, and writings, his notes do not reflect any particular ambition for original thinking. Documentary evidence, whether collected or drafted by himself, was of foremost importance to him, as witnessed by the vast collection of the Caesar papers, which are now to a large extent to be found in the Lansdowne papers and in the Additional Manuscripts of the British Library, and which often reflect in detail both his versatile professional occupations and his private life. In many cases, as with his research into the court of requests, the exchequer, chancery, or the privy council (a research which sometimes resulted in a more or less systematic treatise), his interest appears to have been prompted by the desire to establish, largely through an antiquarian study of the records, the jurisdiction, benefits, and liabilities of the offices he held, without aiming at any practical result other than buttressing or securing his own position. Recent scholarship has enhanced the appraisal of a successful careerist who relied on a complex network of patronage, but whose professional ambitions were encompassed by the offices traditionally accessible to civil lawyers before the civil war. In spite of these limitations, Caesar succeeded, through his offices, his marriages, and private dealings, in accumulating considerable wealth and furthering his children's careers. At the same time, his reputation for benefactions was well established, as illustrated by Fuller's reference to Caesar as 'a person of prodigious bounty to all of worth or want, so that he might seem to be almoner-general of the nation' (*DNB*). His reputation has suffered from the failure of the Great Contract, and the resulting controversy among historians whether his critical memorandum betrayed his patron Salisbury's trust. However, his career both before and after 1610 would suggest that he was seen by his superiors as a safe pair of hands for the crown offices with which he was entrusted. ALAIN WIJFFELS

Sources BL, Caesar papers, Lansdowne MSS • L. M. Hill, *Bench and bureaucracy: the public career of Sir Julius Caesar, 1580–1636* (1988) • PRO, HCA • PRO, state papers • E. Lodge, *The life of Sir Julius Caesar … with memoirs of his family and descendants*, new edn (1827) • *The ancient state, authoritie, and proceedings of the court of requests by Sir Julius Caesar*, ed. L. M. Hill (1975) • L. M. Hill, 'The admiralty circuit of 1591: some comments on the relations between central government and local interests', *HJ*, 14 (1971), 3–14 • L. M. Hill, 'Sir Julius Caesar's journal of Salisbury's first two months and twenty days as lord treasurer, 1608', *BIHR*, 45 (1972), 311–27 • A. Wijffels, 'Sir Julius Caesar's notes on admiralty cases: an alternative to judicial reporting?', *Law reporting in England*, ed. C. Stebbings (1995) • A. Wijffels, 'Julius Caesar's notes on the status of PoWs', *Revue d'Histoire de Droit* (1997), 349–72 • memorial, St Helen, Bishopsgate • inventory, PRO, CHAN 192/560/159 • will, PRO, PROB 11/170, sig. 34 [27 Feb 1636]

Archives BL, corresp. and papers, Add. MSS 6038, 5664, 11405–11406, 11574, 12496–12497, 12504, 14027, 34324, 36111–36113, 36767, 38170 • BL, corresp. and papers, Lansdowne MSS 123–174 • Bodl. Oxf., letters and papers • Bodl. Oxf., state and other papers • Hatfield House, Hertfordshire, letters and papers | Inner Temple, London, chancery suit against earl of Manchester and other material

Likenesses oils, 1597, Rousham Hall, Oxfordshire • R. Elstrack, line engraving, BM, NPG [*see illus.*]

Wealth at death wealthy: inventory, PRO, CHAN 192/560/159; will, PRO, PROB 11/170, sig. 34

Caesar, Julius (1656?–1712?), apothecary and composer, lived at Rochester. He was the author of three convivial catches which appeared in the sixth edition of *The Pleasant Musical Companion* (1720). He practised in Strood and Rochester, Kent, presumably with some success, for in 1711 he could charge a £50 premium to take on an apprentice (Wallis and Wallis, 97). Many of his prescriptions are preserved in Sloane MS 2815, having been copied from original MSS by Sir Hans Sloane. He was probably the same Julius Caesar who was the son of Joseph Caesar, a grandson of Dr Gerard Caesar of Canterbury, who is generally supposed to have been a grandson of Sir Thomas Caesar. This Julius Caesar died at Strood, aged fifty-five, on 29 April 1712. W. B. SQUIRE, *rev.* PATRICK WALLIS

Sources J. Hawkins, *A general history of the science and practice of music*, new edn, 2 (1853), 767 • E. Lodge, *The life of Sir Julius Caesar … with memoirs of his family and descendants*, new edn (1827) • P. J. Wallis and R. V. Wallis, *Eighteenth century medics*, 2nd edn (1988)

Archives BL, Sloane MS 2815

Caesar, Mary (*bap.* **1677**, *d.* **1741**). *See under* Caesar, Charles (1673–1741).

Caesar [*formerly* Adelmare], **Sir Thomas** (**1561–1610**), judge, was born in the parish of St Helen, Bishopsgate, London, the second son of Cesare *Adelmare (*d.* 1569) [*see under* Caesar, Sir Julius], court physician, and Margery (or Margaret) Perient (or Perin), and younger brother of Sir Julius *Caesar (*bap.* 1558, *d.* 1636). His father was sometimes known as Dr Caesar (the English form of his forename), from which his family took its surname. Thomas was educated at Merchant Taylors' School from 1570 to 1578 and entered the Inner Temple in 1581. Having been called to the bar in 1591, he practised law in London. He was married three times: first, in January 1589, to Susanna Longe, a widow, who died in 1590; his second wife was Anne, widow of Nicholas Beeston and daughter of George Lynn of Southwick, Northamptonshire, who also lived only a short time; on 18 January 1593 he married Susan, daughter of Sir William Ryder, haberdasher and later lord mayor of London, with whom he had three sons (including another Thomas) and five daughters.

Caesar engaged in various business enterprises connected with the cloth trade and in farming crown revenue. He was a client of George Clifford, third earl of Cumberland, with whom he sailed in 1601, and he sat as member for Appleby, a Clifford seat, in the 1601 parliament. His brother Sir Julius, master of requests, frequently called upon him to give legal advice in that court, and in 1603 appointed him surveyor of the royal hospital of St Katharine by the Tower. He became a bencher of his inn in 1607. In 1609 Caesar was appointed clock keeper to Prince Henry. The king had agreed in 1605 to appoint him exchequer baron but because the incumbent wished to preserve the reversion he was not admitted until 25 May 1610 and then only as cursitor baron. He was knighted on 25 June 1610 but he died a few weeks later, on 18 July at his house in Chancery Lane. He was intestate, and owned little more than a few parcels of land. Susan Caesar survived her husband. L. M. HILL

Sources L. M. Hill, *Bench and bureaucracy: the public career of Sir Julius Caesar, 1580–1636* (1988) • E. Lodge, *The life of Sir Julius Caesar … with memoirs of his family and descendants*, new edn (1827) • E. L. C. Mullins, 'Caesar, Thomas', HoP, *Commons, 1558–1603* • C. Jamison, *The history of the Royal Hospital of St Katharine by the Tower of London* (1952) • inquisition post mortem, PRO, CHAN 142/317/121 • *CSP dom., 1603–10*

Likenesses engraving, repro. in Lodge, *Life of Sir Julius Caesar* • stipple (after miniature), NPG

Caffin, Sir James Crawford (**1812–1883**), naval officer, third son of William Caffin of the Royal Laboratory, Woolwich, and his wife, Bethia, daughter of George Crawford, adjutant Royal Artillery, was born at Woolwich Common on 1 March 1812. He entered the navy in August 1824, and in 1827 was midshipman of the frigate *Cambrian* at Navarino, and when she was wrecked off Carabusa on 31 January 1828. In August 1831 he passed his examination, and in October 1834 was appointed to the *Excellent*, recently organized as a school of gunnery. He afterwards served for two years as gunnery-mate of the *Asia* in the Mediterranean, and on his promotion to lieutenant (28 June 1838) was again appointed to the *Excellent*, in which, with only a short break, he remained for the next three years.

Caffin was made commander on 7 March 1842, and after studying for some months at the Royal Naval College, Portsmouth, was appointed, with Lieutenant-Colonel Chalmer RA to investigate and report on the charlatan Samuel Alfred Warner's 'long range, invisible shells'; their report was unfavourable. In February 1845 he was one of a commission for experimenting on the relative merits of paddle and screw propulsion; their report paved the way for the general introduction of the screw propeller into the navy. On 11 October 1847 Caffin was advanced to post rank; in 1854 he commanded the *Penelope* in the Baltic, and was present at the capture of Bomarsund; and in 1855 he commanded the *Hastings* at the bombardment of Sveaborg, for which, with the other captains, he was made a CB on 5 July. On his return from the Baltic he was appointed director-general of naval ordnance, and vice-president of the ordnance select committee at the War Office. In 1858 he was appointed director of stores in the war department, an office which he held until 1868.

On his retirement Caffin was made a civil KCB (December 1868). He had previously (2 December 1865) attained his flag rank, but, not having served his time at sea, was placed on the retired list, on which he duly advanced to the higher ranks—vice-admiral on 2 November 1871 and admiral on 1 August 1877. He was also a magistrate for Kent. He lived at Blackheath, the leading light of a religious society of pronounced views, possibly Plymouth Brethren. He had married on 21 September 1843 Frances (Fanny) Brouncker (*d.* 1871), youngest daughter of William Atfield JP, of Cosham House, Hampshire; they had a daughter, Emily Burns, and a son, Crawford, a commander, RN, who was promoted for his services in the transport department during the Anglo-Zulu War. Caffin died at his home, Woodlawn, Vanbrugh Park Road, Blackheath, on 24 May 1883.

J. K. LAUGHTON, *rev.* ROGER MORRISS

Sources O'Byrne, *Naval biog. dict.* • *The Times* (26 May 1883), 12 • J. Marshall, *Royal naval biography*, 4 vols. (1823–35) [with 4 suppls.] • Boase, *Mod. Eng. biog.* • Kelly, *Handbk* • *CGPLA Eng. & Wales* (1883)

Wealth at death £7590 4*s.* 0*d.*: probate, 30 June 1883, *CGPLA Eng. & Wales*

Caffyn, Katharine Mannington [*née* Katharine Hunt; *pseud.* Iota] (**1852/3–1926**), novelist, was born at Waterloo House, co. Tipperary, daughter of William de Vere Hunt and Louisa Going. Educated at home by English and German governesses, she lived in the country until about twenty, when she moved to London, training at St Thomas's Hospital for a year for the National and Metropolitan Nursing Association. On 25 February 1879, when she was twenty-six, she married Stephen Mannington Caffyn (1851–1896), surgeon, writer, and inventor; they had one son. After their marriage she and her husband moved to Australia, where he held several medical posts.

When they returned to England in 1892, Caffyn began to publish under the pseudonym Iota, and established herself as a 'new woman' writer, one of a number of audible women engaged in the late nineteenth-century debates around femininity. *A Yellow Aster* (1894) was her most renowned novel; Gwen, locked into a loveless marriage, is awakened by pregnancy into womanhood: 'I am a woman at last, a full, complete, proper woman, and it is magnificent' (3.172). Like a number of other 'new woman' writers, notably Sarah Grand (Frances McFall), Caffyn came out firmly in favour of biological essentialism in *A Yellow Aster*. *Children of Circumstances* appeared the same year, followed by *A Comedy in Spasms* (1895); *A Quaker Grandmother* (1896);

Poor Max (1898); *Ann Mauleverer* (1899); *The Minx* (1900); *The Happiness of Jill* (1901); *He for God Only* (1903); *Patricia: a Mother* (1905); *Smoke in the Flame* (1907); *The Magic of May* (1908); *Whoso Breaketh an Hedge* (1909); *Mary Mirrielees* (1916); and several short stories. W. T. Stead, editor of the *Pall Mall Gazette*, and agitator for sexual reform, was inspired by *A Yellow Aster* to write:

> there is something powerful though revolting in the discovery of the fact that Gwen, who cannot bring herself even to touch her husband … has actually consented, as an experiment, to permit him to make her the mother of his child. … Gwen certainly seems to have lived up to her conception of her sex as 'the least part of a woman', when she regarded conjugal intercourse as a mere bagatelle compared with a voluntary touch of her husband's hand. (Stead, 70)

Stead, who in 1885 had purchased a thirteen-year-old girl for unlawful sex (to prove it could be done), found Iota insufficiently exercised by the sexual double standard: 'she is not enough of the Modern Woman to raise even a passing protest against the pre-nuptial immoralities of her hero' (ibid.).

Caffyn was a reluctant, contrary, and, at best, conservative feminist. Asked in 1898 by *The Ludgate* to comment on the progress of women in the previous six decades of Victoria's reign, she responded:

> our advance is palpable enough. We have more opinions than ever we had. We write more books, we paint more pictures. We sing more songs—we sing them louder. And yet through all these causes for gratulation there quivers a note of sadness. Women were made for leisure, and just a little for sauntering, and necessity with its inexorable brood drives us too hard. We are forgetting how to be idle, to pause, to rest tired eyes. We should have been given just a little more time in which to evolute ourselves into speech, and print, and action. (Brooke and others, 215)

There are suggestions in her later novels, however, that her attitude underwent a slow change, bringing it more in line with her character as a 'physical, hard-living woman', in whose fiction 'affairs of the horse as well as the heart frequently figure' (Sutherland, 320). Katharine Caffyn died on 6 February 1926. ANGELIQUE RICHARDSON

Sources m. cert. • *WWW* • E. F. Brooke, Iota, S. Grand, and G. Egerton, 'Women in the queen's reign: some notable opinions, illustrated with photographs', *The Ludgate* (1898), 213–17 • W. T. Stead, 'Book of the month: the novel of the modern woman', *Review of Reviews*, 10 (1894), 64–74 • J. Sutherland, *The Longman companion to Victorian fiction* (1988) • A. Richardson, *Love and eugenics in the late nineteenth century: rational reproduction and the new woman* (2003) • A. Richardson and C. Willis, eds., *The New Woman in fiction and in fact* (2000) • A. L. Ardis, *New Women, new novels: feminism and early modernism* (1990)

Archives Richmond Local Studies Library, London, letters to Douglas Sladen

Likenesses Elliott & Fry, photograph, repro. in Stead, 'Book of the month'

Caffyn, Matthew (*bap.* **1628**, *d.* **1714**), General Baptist minister, was baptized on 26 October 1628 at Horsham, Sussex, the seventh son of a yeoman farmer, Thomas Caffin (*d.* before 1653), and his wife, Elizabeth. Lord Onslow of Wisborough Green adopted Matthew as a companion for his only son, Richard, and sent the two boys to grammar school in Kent. In 1643, they went to All Souls College, Oxford, where Caffyn studied divinity but was expelled in 1645 for opposing infant baptism. He returned to Horsham and joined a General Baptist church at Southwater led by Samuel Lover, and became his assistant. After succeeding Lover as pastor, Caffyn made his livelihood as a farmer while evangelizing and planting churches throughout Kent, Sussex, and Surrey. Parliament gaoled him twice: first for unordained preaching and then for heresy apparently because of his opposition to infant baptism. Between imprisonments, on 8 February 1653 in the parish church of Westerham, Kent, Caffyn married Elizabeth Jeffery (*d.* 1693) of Westerham, who was related to, and probably the sister of, William Jeffery, Baptist minister of Orpington. That same year, the Caffyns settled at Pond Farm, Southwater, 3 miles from Horsham.

In 1654, Caffyn was a founding messenger of the general assembly of General Baptists. An excellent speaker, he earned a reputation as a skilful polemicist in debates with Anglican incumbents of Henfield and Waldron, several presbyterians, and leading Quakers. For this Baptists called him their 'battle-axe of Sussex' (Caffyn, 146–7). In June 1655, he debated with the Quaker leader George Fox in Bryan Wilkinson's house, Sedgwick Lodge, Horsham. This led to two more disputations that September with Thomas Lawson and John Slee, at the Quaker meeting-house in Crawley, Sussex, and at Caffyn's church. Caffyn challenged their views of Christ's second coming, the resurrection of the body, and the authority of scripture. Lawson, a former Anglican clergyman and baronet's son, started a pamphlet war, abusively attacking Caffyn in *An Untaught Teacher Witnessed Against* (1655). Caffyn responded with *The Deceived, and Deceiving, Quakers Discovered* (1656), to which William Jeffery appended challenges to Quaker eschatology. This drew a response from James Nayler in *The Light of Christ* (1656); George Fox also commented on it in his *Great Mistery* (1659). Caffyn renewed his charges in an appendix to *Faith in God's Promises* (1661), answered by Humphrey Woolrich's *One Warning More to the Baptists* (1661) and George Whitehead's *The Pernicious Way* (1662). Joseph Wright, a physician and Baptist minister from Maidstone, joined Caffyn's cause by publishing *A Testimony for the Son of Man* (1661).

By the Restoration, radical Mennonite views on Christology had influenced General Baptists in south-east England including Caffyn; Baptists in the northern association (the midlands), however, were firmly orthodox. When the general assembly composed their 'standard confession' in 1660 they made it broad enough to remain united for the sake of solidarity before the crown. Led by Caffyn and Thomas Monk, a messenger from Hertfordshire, they then appealed to Charles to allow the toleration he had promised in the declaration of Breda of that same year. Instead, persecution ensued, and Caffyn, Wright, and Monk were imprisoned. Caffyn was fined, his goods distrained, and gaoled three times variously in Horsham and Maidstone, while Elizabeth supported the family with her spinning-wheel. Between imprisonments (about 1666), he moved his growing family, with his elder brothers William and Richard, to a larger house at Broadbridge Farm, 2 miles from Horsham. Matthew and Elizabeth had nine children, who all lived to adulthood.

By 1670 the fragile solidarity of General Baptists was cracking. In 1673, Monk, suspecting Caffyn of heresy, published *A Cure for the Cankering Error of the New Eutychians*, which warned fellow Baptists against denying Christ's humanity. In June 1673, the general assembly denied Caffyn's request to censure Monk, but it refused to condemn Caffyn's teaching. It also postponed Richard Haines's appeal against Caffyn for getting him excommunicated: Caffyn charged Haines with covetousness for patenting a process to clean hop clover. Another pamphlet war ensued. In *New Lords, New Law* (1674), Haines accused Caffyn of usurping civil authority and holding suspect Christology; Caffyn responded with *Envy's Bitterness Corrected* (1674). Haines followed with *A Protestation Against Usurpation* and continued appealing to the general assembly, which finally ordered Caffyn to reinstate him (1680). Caffyn's parting shot in the exchange was *A Raging Wave Foming* (1675), in which he rejected Monk's and Haines's charges that he had denied both the full divinity and full humanity of Christ. Yet because he was unwilling to express himself in traditional trinitarian terminology, he left himself vulnerable to charges of doceticism and Arianism. His real discomfort was with the Athanasian creed; he preferred to describe the godhead in strictly scriptural terms, not 'unrevealed sublimities'.

In 1679, seeking common ground with Calvinists in the wake of the Popish Plot, Monk drafted 'an orthodox creed [confession]', which also firmly opposed the heresies Monk had identified in *A Cure*. Though fifty-four messengers and pastors, mainly from the midlands, signed this on 30 January 1679, Caffyn convinced the general assembly not to adopt it. At some time after Wright's release after a twenty-year imprisonment, probably in the mid-1680s, Caffyn confided to him about his scrupling the Athanasian creed. Wright revealed this to the assembly and twice tried to have Caffyn expelled. The majority acquitted Caffyn both times and censured Wright, who promptly withdrew. His leaving did not ameliorate the tension. In 1691 the assembly reaffirmed the broad confession of 1660, not Monk's 1679 version, and they wrote to the churches in Buckinghamshire who had absented themselves from the 1691 meeting, urging them to return to the next annual gathering. When William Smart of Wingrave asked the assembly to clarify its position on Christology, members denounced both Arianism and doceticism as heresies. After examining him, the assembly further exonerated Caffyn from holding either view. Three years later, when the northern association was blocked from raising the issue again, it withdrew, formed the general association under the leadership of Clement Hunt, and continued to appeal to the assembly for a hearing. This was granted for Whitsuntide 1700, when a committee of eight, including four complainants, conferred with Caffyn. They drew up a healing resolution that affirmed the humanity and divinity of Christ and the unity of the godhead but did not speculate about the nature of his flesh or the essence of the godhead. The assembly approved the report. Its action was likely influenced by *The Moderate Trinitarian* (1699), in which Daniel Allen, a member of the orthodox party, argued that differing views concerning the Trinity should not be a bar to communion. In essence, Allen defended the position Caffyn had taken in a disputation against three London ministers at Smarden in 1698. Before the next meeting of the assembly, Christopher Cooper challenged Allen in *The Vail Turn'd aside* (1701) and accused Caffyn of spreading Socinianism throughout Kent, Sussex, and London. At the assembly meeting of 1701, messengers from Northampton complained that Caffyn had not been properly tried, but the majority said his subscription to the committee's resolution was sufficient. With more churches steadily joining the general association, the assembly relented in 1704 and joined with the association in signing six articles of agreement, the first two affirming the orthodox view of the Trinity and the incarnation. Unorthodox preaching was to be suppressed, but not silent dissent. Temporarily Caffyn was isolated. But the next year the orthodox party overextended itself by demanding subscription to the articles as a condition for membership. The rupture was instant and complete: much of the old assembly withdrew, accusing the others of bad faith. Not until 1731 was the breach healed, when the two groups reunited on the six principles of Hebrews 6: 1–2 and Caffyn's view that disagreement about Christ's nature should not be a bar to communion.

After ministering at Southwater for over sixty years, Caffyn died at Broadbridge Heath and was buried on 10 June 1714 in the churchyard at Itchingfield, Sussex. He was succeeded as pastor by his son Matthew. JIM SPIVEY

Sources *DNB* • W. T. Whitley, *Minutes of the general assembly of the General Baptist Churches in England* (1909), xxii–xxiii, 30–32, 37–40, 43 • T. Crosby, *The history of the English Baptists, from the Reformation to the beginning of the reign of King George I*, 4 vols. (1738–40), vol. 3, pp. 116, 97–9, 280–85; vol. 4, pp. 328–42 • J. Caffyn, *Sussex believers, Baptist marriage in the 17th and 18th centuries* (1988) • B. R. White, 'Caffyn, Matthew', Greaves & Zaller, *BDBR*, 1.115–16 • F. Gregg, *Matthew Caffin* (1890) • A. H. J. Baines, 'The preface to the orthodox confession of 1679', *Baptist Quarterly*, 15 (1953–4), 62–74 • A. H. J. Baines, 'The signatories of the orthodox confession of 1679', *Baptist Quarterly*, 17 (1957–8), 35–42 • M. A. Lower, *The worthies of Sussex* (1865), 342–3 • A. Langley, 'Seventeenth-century Baptist disputations', *Transactions of the Baptist Historical Society*, 6 (1918–19), 216–43, esp. 230–32 • W. J. Collins, 'Some memorials of the Denby family', *Transactions of the Baptist Historical Society*, 5 (1916–17), 133–4 • 'Baptists in Kent', *Baptist Quarterly*, 2 (1924–5), 139

Cahill, Daniel William (1796–1864), Roman Catholic priest and public lecturer, was born on 28 November 1796 at Arless, in Queen's county, Ireland, the youngest of the three sons of Daniel Cahill (*c*.1754–1836), a civil engineer and allegedly a participant in the rebellion of 1798, and his wife, Catherine, youngest daughter of Oliver Brett of Seville. After attending Ferris Academy, Athy, Cahill studied in Carlow College in 1811–12 as a lay student, with the aim of joining the army as an engineer like his father, but on 24 October 1816 took up residence in St Patrick's College, Maynooth, being supported by his relative Dr Michael

Daniel William Cahill (1796–1864), by Maclure & Macdonald (after Leon Gluckman)

Corcoran, bishop of Kildare and Leighlin. He studied theology, natural philosophy, Hebrew, German, French, and Italian. After ordination to the priesthood in 1822 by Dr Thomas Doyle, bishop of Kildare and Leighlin, he entered the Dunboyne establishment of the college for further study of theology and ecclesiastical history. Doyle thought highly of him. He was appointed to a curacy at Leighlin Bridge, and in 1825 became professor of natural theology (also teaching mathematics and astronomy) in Carlow College, where he remained until 1834, when he established a school in Carlow. He also received a doctorate of divinity from Rome.

In 1827, with William Kinsella, bishop of Ossory, Cahill published a *Letter on the Subject of the New Reformation*, in response to a fresh attempt by protestants to convert Irish Catholics to protestantism. In 1835 he opened a school at Seafort House, Seapoint, Williamstown, near Dublin, later moved to Prospect House, Blackrock, but it failed in 1846, allegedly because of parents who could not pay their children's fees. He then edited the *Dublin Telegraph*. Of 'independent bearing, ardent temperament, striking countenance, and gigantic frame (of six feet five inches in stature)' (*Life, Letters and Lectures*, 1.1), he became a popular lecturer on political as well as scientific and theological issues, hoping to convince the rising generation 'of the hatred of England to the race, the liberty, and the religion of Irishmen' (D. Cahill, *Letters, Addressed to Several Members of the British Cabinet: and Speeches on Various Subjects*, 1856, vii). He addressed public letters to the Irish Catholic bishops and people, to Prince Albert, to protestant controversialists, and to leading British politicians, including Lord John Russell, the duke of Wellington, the earls of Derby and Carlisle, and Lord Palmerston. Russell's attack on the Catholic church in 1850, together with the great famine and other Irish grievances, created an audience for Cahill's talent for fiery nationalist rhetoric: he compared Russell with Milton's Satan, and informed Palmerston that he was 'the greatest and the most perfidious enemy the Catholic Church has ever had in ancient or modern times' (ibid., 458). His visit to Britain between 1851 and 1854 included appearances in Newcastle, Caernarfon, Cambridge, Glasgow, and Whitehaven. Irish Catholics presented him with a gold snuff box in Liverpool and a gold watch in St Helens.

Cahill's pseudo-scientific illustrations of transubstantiation distressed the English Catholic monthly *The Rambler*, conducted by Anglican converts to Catholicism (J. M. Capes, 'Dr Cahill's letter on transubstantiation', *The Rambler*, new ser., 1, 1854, 169–77). Cahill dismissed his opponents as 'a clique of converted parsons' and 'the three parsons of Portman Street' (Cahill, *Letters and Speeches*, 402). His political and religious militancy equally distressed the prudent Paul Cullen, archbishop of Dublin. 'He exercises no function—but goes about as lecturer' wrote Cullen of Cahill in 1852. 'His letters do great mischief to us. Perhaps he is paid by the Government for writing. It is by mere chance that he was not made vice President of Queen's College Cork. Sir Robt. Kane wd [*sic*] not act with a priest. I cannot but suspect that he is encouraged to write his nonsense in order to discredit the Catholics' (Larkin, 186). Cullen banned him from preaching in the Dublin archdiocese. John Henry Newman, as rector of the Catholic University in Dublin, considered him in 1853 for an annual lectureship in astronomy on the condition of his 'abstaining from politics and other Lecturing during his year'. But Newman was discouraged by a report via Robert Ornsby from Frederick Lucas, the editor of *The Tablet*, that Cahill 'was rather a quack … he lectured, not so much from real knowledge, as by having got up a subject, and treating it with clever manipulation' (*The Letters and Diaries of John Henry Newman*, ed. C. S. Dessain and others, 31 vols., 1961–77, 15.483–4).

Cahill was invited to the United States in 1853, and on 8 August delivered a farewell address in Dublin, but he deferred the journey, allegedly in part because of ill health. America was in the throes of Nativist agitation against Catholics, and in 1854 Newman sent Cullen a message from Archbishop Hughes of New York begging Cullen 'for God's sake to arrest the advent of the Revd Dr Cahill, whose presence here at this moment can have no other effect than that of betraying us into a worse position than what we now occupy' (*The Letters and Diaries of John Henry Newman*, ed. C. S. Dessain and others, 16.194). Cahill did not reach New York until 24 December 1859. He remained in America as a popular lecturer on a range of subjects and as a preacher for charitable causes, and in the following four and a half years is said to have raised $100,000. He died in the Carney Hospital in Boston on 28 October 1864, and, after embalming, his body was buried in Holyrood cemetery in the city. His dying wish, however, was to be buried in Ireland, and his name remained potent in death. Dr Cahill memorial committees in Ireland and America in 1885 arranged for the return of his body to

Dublin via New York as a series of great public demonstrations. The archbishops of Boston and New York celebrated solemn requiems in their cathedrals, and the coffin was then carried down a packed Fifth Avenue to the steamer *Wyoming*. There were further solemn requiems after its arrival in Ireland, in Queenstown, Cork, and Dublin, where on 9 March 1885 the confraternities and sodalities of the city, accompanied by the lord mayor, escorted the coffin to its final resting place in the O'Connell Circle in Glasnevin cemetery. SHERIDAN GILLEY

Sources *The life, letters, and lectures of Dr Cahill*, 1 (1886) • *Catholic directory, almanac, and registry, of Ireland, England, and Scotland* (1865), 412–15 • *The Lamp*, 2/25 (7 June 1851), 361 • *The Lamp*, 2/27 (21 June 1851), 392–3 • J. McEvoy, *Carlow College, 1793–1993* (1993), 264 • *The Tablet* (14 March 1885), 417–18 • E. Larkin, *The making of the Roman Catholic church in Ireland, 1850–1860* (1980) • W. J. Fitzpatrick, *The life, times, and correspondence of the Right Rev. Dr Doyle, bishop of Kildare and Leighlin*, 2 vols. (1861), vol. 1, p. 310; vol. 2, pp. 94, 184, 493

Likenesses Maclure & Macdonald, lithograph (after photograph by L. Gluckman), NPG [*see illus.*] • drawing, repro. in *The Lamp* (7 June 1851) • portrait, repro. in McEvoy, *Carlow College*

Caillard, Sir Vincent Henry Penalver (1856–1930), financier, was born in Kensington, London, on 23 October 1856, fifth child and eldest son of Camille Felix Désiré Caillard (1822–1898) of Wingfield House, Trowbridge, Wiltshire, who was at his death the longest serving county court judge, and his first wife, Emma Louisa (1827–1865), daughter of Vincent Stuckey Reynolds of Canonsgrove, Taunton. His maternal grandmother was first cousin to George Basevi and Benjamin Disraeli, earl of Beaconsfield. He had three brothers, one half-brother, and five sisters. He was educated at Eton College (1869–72) and the Royal Military Academy, Woolwich (1875), where he was a gold medallist. He was commissioned in the Royal Engineers in 1876.

During 1879–80 Caillard helped to delineate the new Balkan borders when, following defeat in the Russo-Turkish War, the Ottoman empire ceded independence to Serbia, Romania, and Montenegro. He served initially as an assistant commissioner on the Montenegrin frontier commission and was later sent on special missions to Epirus and Dulcigno. During 1882 he worked in the intelligence branch of the War Office before Sir Charles Dilke obtained his appointment to the headquarters staff of Sir Garnet Wolseley in Egypt.

It was possibly to Dilke's influence that Caillard owed his appointment in 1883 to succeed Edgar Vincent, afterwards Viscount D'Abernon, as financial representative of Britain, Belgium, and the Netherlands in Constantinople, alternating with French representatives as president of the council of administration of the Ottoman public debt. This body managed tobacco, silk, wine, and salt revenues in the interests of foreign creditors, and many higher administrative or financial questions were under its sanction. Caillard reorganized its administration and modernized its methods of sericulture and viticulture. In Constantinople he soon developed a taste for sinuous intrigue. He had a cosmopolitan outlook, was somewhat reserved in manner, and was inclined to overstretch himself. Admired by some for his tact, initiative, and ambition, he was also distrusted as meddlesome, self-seeking,

Sir Vincent Henry Penalver Caillard (1856–1930), by Elliott & Fry, pubd 1907–9

and unrealistic. In the late 1880s he headed a group seeking the concession to build the strategic Anatolian Railway, but his manoeuvres were over-elaborate, and the concession was jockeyed into German control partly as a result of his muddling.

In 1898, when Caillard's father died, he inherited his Wiltshire property, resigned from the Ottoman public debt, and was nominated by Ernest Cassel as a director of the National Bank of Egypt (1898–1908) and the armaments manufacturers Vickers. After becoming financial director of Vickers in 1906, he was a leading power in the strategy and management of one of Britain's most diversified and dynamic industrial combines. He travelled widely on its behalf, and was engaged in many international negotiations of byzantine complexity, notably for the erection of arsenals in Turkey and Russia (1913–14). The collapse of the company's internal accounting system during the wartime expansion of 1914–18, and its purchase of rolling-stock and electrical companies associated with Dudley Docker for inflated prices in 1918–19, were misfortunes for which Caillard was responsible. After a long decline, he was forced to retire from Vickers in 1927. He was a director of many associated companies, as well as the London, Chatham and Dover (1905–22) and other railways.

Caillard composed musical settings for the *Songs of Innocence* of William Blake and had other artistic interests. From the 1880s he professed strong anti-German sentiments and supported many patriotic causes. In 1885 he contributed articles on Albania, Bulgaria, and Turkish finance to the radical-imperialist *Fortnightly Review* (vols. 43 and 44), and his later articles in the *National Review*, particularly 'Industry and protection' in vol. 75 (1920), proved a decisive influence in the decision of Joseph Chamberlain to launch his protectionist campaign. As chairman of the tariff commission in 1904, as unsuccessful Conservative parliamentary candidate for Central Bradford in 1906, in articles, speeches, committees, and clubland cabals, at the Royal Colonial Institute and the Compatriots' Club, Caillard worked for imperial tariff preference and British world hegemony. He strove hard to assert the interests of large-scale manufacturing in British policy: in 1916 he joined Docker in founding the Federation of British Industries (of which he was president in 1919) and in the same year, together with other Vickers directors, he formed the London Imperialists (renamed the British Commonwealth Union), which tried to increase the influence of business leaders in parliamentary life. In the 1890s he privately corresponded on Turkish affairs with Lord Salisbury, and in 1917 he was an intermediary between David Lloyd George and Basil Zaharoff when the latter was entrusted with negotiations to bribe Turkish politicians with £10 million in gold to accept peace terms.

Caillard was knighted in 1896 and held several decorations. His name was suggested for a peerage by his country neighbour Walter Long in 1923. He married first, in 1881, his stepsister, Eliza Frances (1859–1926), sister of Sir John Hanham, ninth baronet, and daughter of Captain John Hanham, whose widow became Caillard's father's second wife. By this marriage Caillard had one son and one daughter. He married secondly, in 1927, Zoë Gertrude (1868–1935), widow of John Oakley Maund (*d.* 1902), rentier, and daughter of Robert Ellis Dudgeon, physician. Caillard died of pneumonia at 63 boulevard Victor Hugo, Neuilly-sur-Seine, Paris, on 18 March 1930, following an operation at the American Hospital in Paris, and was buried on 26 March at St Mary's Church, Wingfield.

RICHARD DAVENPORT-HINES

Sources R. P. T. Davenport-Hines, 'The Ottoman empire in decline: the business imperialism of Sir Vincent Caillard', *The City and the empire*, ed. R. V. Turrell and J. J. van Helten (1985), 118–34 · R. P. T. Davenport-Hines, *Dudley Docker: the life and times of a trade warrior* (1984) · C. Trebilcock, *The Vickers brothers* (1977) · D. Blaisdell, *European financial control in the Ottoman empire* (1929) · C. L. Smith, *The embassy of Sir William White at Constantinople, 1886–1891* (1957) · W. A. S. Hewins, *The apologia of an imperialist: forty years of empire policy*, 2 vols. (1929) · S. Leslie, *The Jerome connexion* (1964) · *The Times* (20 March 1930), 10g · *The Times* (27 March 1930), 17c · b. cert. · Burke, *Gen. GB* · *CGPLA Eng. & Wales* (1930)

Archives BLPES, letters to tariff commission · CUL, Vickers archives · PRO, Board of Trade MSS, BT 55/32/FFT 1 · PRO, Foreign Office MSS · U. Warwick Mod. RC, Federation of British Industries MSS | BL, Dilke MSS · Hatfield House, Hertfordshire, Salisbury MSS · HLRO, Lloyd George MSS · PRO NIre., Dufferin and Ava MSS · University of Sheffield, corresp. with W. A. S. Hewins · W. Sussex RO, Leo Maxse MSS · Wilts. & Swindon RO, Walter Long MSS

Likenesses photograph, 1896–9, repro. in R. P. T. Davenport-Hines, 'Vickers as a multinational', *British multinationals*, ed. G. Jones (1986), 58 · Elliott & Fry, photograph, pubd 1907–9, NPG [*see illus.*] · photograph, *c.*1914, repro. in Leslie, *Jerome connexion*, facing p. 55 · photograph, 1920–29, repro. in Hewins, *Apologia*, facing p. 48 · Spy [L. Ward], cartoon, chromolithograph, NPG; repro. in *DBB*, 1, 564 · oils, priv. coll. · photograph, repro. in Davenport-Hines, *Dudley Docker*, 111

Wealth at death £91,086 8*s.* 10*d.*: resworn probate, 28 July 1930, *CGPLA Eng. & Wales*

Caillaud, John (1726–1812), army officer in the East India Company, was born in Dublin on 5 February 1726 and baptized in the French (Huguenot) church in Peter Street on 16 February, the younger son and youngest of the three children of Ruben Caillaud (*d.* 1732), army officer, born in Charente but naturalized in 1699, and his wife, Marguerite. He joined Onslow's regiment (afterwards the 8th King's) in 1743. He was present at the engagement at Fontenoy and also took part in the actions against the Jacobite Young Pretender (Charles Edward Stuart) at Falkirk and Culloden in 1746. Appointed captain in the East India Company's Madras army in 1752, he sailed for India in the *Edgbaston* in December and arrived in June 1753. He was soon in skirmishes with the French near Trichinopoly, and in 1758 undertook a hazardous journey to Tanjore to secure mercenaries to reinforce the detachments harassing the French forces investing Madras. By January 1759 he was in command of a body of some 5000 sepoys and Europeans which was active in hindering the French siege.

At the instigation of Lord Clive, Caillaud was put in command of the Bengal army in November 1759 and promoted to lieutenant-colonel in January 1760. His forces repelled an incursion into Bihar by an army commanded by the Mughal emperor's eldest son, but a more contentious aspect of his service in Bengal was the part that he played in the events which preceded the replacement of the nawab of Bengal, Mir Jafar, by his son-in-law Mir Kasim. Twenty-eight years later (on 16 February 1788, the second day of his opening speech at Warren Hastings's impeachment) Edmund Burke, in attempting to discredit Hastings, alleged that Caillaud had been party to a plot to kill the Mughal crown prince by setting his seal, along with those of Mir Jafar and his son Miran, to a document which expressed that intent on 15 April 1760. Caillaud attempted to have the allegations, in what became known as the affair of the three seals, withdrawn or properly investigated. The bishop of Salisbury spoke on his behalf in the House of Lords.

Caillaud returned to Madras in 1761, where he became officiating commander-in-chief. Promoted brigadier-general on 8 July 1763, he was appointed substantive commander-in-chief in 1766. His troops occupied the Northern Circars without resistance in 1765, and on 12 November 1766 he concluded a treaty at Hyderabad by which the company, in return for a grant of the five Circars, agreed to provide conditional military assistance to Nizam Ali or to pay a tribute of nine lakhs each year that military assistance was not required. He returned to England in 1767 and settled down to the life of a country gentleman at Aston House, Aston Rowant, Oxfordshire, although he maintained a lively interest in company affairs and corresponded with Warren Hastings. In 1775 the Company granted him an annual pension of £200.

Caillaud had married Mary Pechell (1728–1808) in 1763; they had no children. According to Edward Mangin, whose mother was Caillaud's niece, he was 'a man of great fire of character, and personal spirit; not classically educated but extensively acquainted with books and possessed of strong natural talents' (Mangin, 621–2). He was also a David Garrick lookalike and in public was sometimes mistaken for the actor. He was made an honorary DCL by Oxford University in 1773, served as high sheriff for Oxfordshire in 1793, and was a colonel in the Oxfordshire militia. He died at Aston House in December 1812 and was buried in Aston Rowant. T. H. BOWYER

Sources *DNB* • H. D. Love, *Vestiges of old Madras, 1640–1800*, 4 vols. (1913), vol. 2 • V. C. P. Hodson, *List of officers of the Bengal army, 1758–1834*, 1 (1927) • J. Philippart, *East India military calendar*, 2 (1824), 57–9 • *The correspondence of Edmund Burke*, 6, ed. A. Cobban and R. A. Smith (1967), 243–6 • E. Mangin, 'List of names of French refugees', 1841, UCL, Huguenot Library, MS M22, repr. in *Proceedings of the Huguenot Society*, 26 (1997), 611–34 • T. P. Le Fanu, ed., *Registers of the French non-conformist churches of Lucy Lane and Peter Street, Dublin*, Huguenot Society Publications, 14 (1901), 75, 80 • T. P. Le Fanu and W. H. Manchee, eds., *Dublin and Portarlington veterans*, Huguenot Society Publications, 41 (1946), 24 • W. A. Shaw, ed., *Letters of denization and acts of naturalization for aliens in England and Ireland, 1603–1700*, Huguenot Society of London, 18 (1911), 248, 269 • *The writings and speeches of Edmund Burke*, ed. P. Langford, 6: *India: the launching of the Hastings impeachment, 1786–1788* (1991), 319–31 • R. Orme, *A history of the military transactions of the British nation in Indostan from the year 1745*, 4th edn, 3 vols (Madras, 1861) • J. Mill, *The history of British India*, 4th edn, 9 vols (1840), vol. 3 • K. Feiling, *Warren Hastings* (1954) • C. E. Lart, *Huguenot pedigrees*, vol. 2 (1928), 40

Archives BL OIOC, corresp. and MSS, MS Eur. Orme | BL, letters to W. Hastings, Add. MSS 29133–29183 • BL OIOC, Sutton Court MSS, letters to J. Carnac, MS Eur. F 128 • BL OIOC, Home misc. series, corresp. relating to India

Caillín mac Niataig (*fl.* **6th cent.**?). *See under* Meath, saints of (*act.* *c.*400–*c.*900).

Caimín (*d.* **644**?). *See under* Munster, saints of (*act.* *c.*450–*c.*700).

Cain, Rhys. *See* Rhys Cain (*c.*1540–1614).

Caine, Sir (Thomas Henry) Hall (**1853–1931**), novelist, was born on 14 May 1853 at 130 Bridgewater Street, Runcorn, Cheshire, the eldest of the six children of John Caine (*bap.* 1821, *d.* 1904), blacksmith, and Sarah (1829–1912), daughter of Ralph Hall of Liverpool and his wife, Mary. John Caine was born in the Isle of Man, and was working as a journeyman ship's smith in the Runcorn docks when his first child was born. Soon afterwards he took his family to the Toxteth area of Liverpool, where he lived for the rest of his life. Sarah Caine, a seamstress, was born in Whitehaven and went to Liverpool when her father, a stonemason, sought work there. Caine was educated at the Hope Street British Schools in Liverpool, becoming head boy in his final year. On leaving school in 1867, aged fourteen, with a talent for drawing, he was apprenticed to John Murray, an architect. He later maintained that he was an autodidact who owed his further education to the Liverpool Free Library, where he read voraciously. At the age of seventeen, after the death of his grandfather Ralph Hall in 1870, Caine suffered the first of the 'nervous collapses' which were to plague him for most of his life. He threw up his apprenticeship and fled to the Isle of Man, where as a child he had spent holidays with his maternal grandmother. She had died in 1866, however, so he went to stay with his aunt Catherine Teare and her husband James, who was the schoolmaster at Maughold. He stayed for over a year, helping with the school and taking over at a salary of £40 p.a. when his uncle died.

Sir (Thomas Henry) Hall Caine (1853–1931), by London Stereoscopic Co., *c.*1915

It was during this period that Caine encountered the writings of John Ruskin, who greatly influenced his political thinking. He returned to Liverpool and his architectural work in the spring of 1872, becoming an active member of the Ruskin Society. He later made Ruskin's acquaintance and visited him at Coniston. Caine also joined the Society for the Protection of Ancient Buildings, where he met William Morris. He began to write regularly both for the Liverpool papers and for journals such as *The Builder*. As a theatre critic he met the actor Henry Irving. When Bram Stoker joined Irving as manager at the Lyceum Theatre, he and Caine became devoted friends. Stoker dedicated his vampire novel *Dracula* to Hall Caine, although the form, 'To Hommy-Beg' (Manx for Little Tommy), kept it secret from the public for years.

Increasingly drawn to writing as a career, Caine resigned his job with John Murray and went to work for Bromleys, a firm of builders, as a draughtsman. At this time he helped to found the Liverpool Notes and Queries Society, which flourished. This and his journalistic work brought him to the notice of a number of influential people in Liverpool, and he began corresponding with several eminent literary men. A chance meeting on holiday in the Lake District introduced him to the poetry of Dante Gabriel Rossetti. Enthralled by Rossetti's work, he gave a lecture on it in January 1879, and when it was published he sent a copy to Rossetti, who replied in friendly manner. Much correspondence ensued before Caine was invited to Rossetti's Chelsea home in September 1880; in the following year he went to live there and remained until Rossetti's death in 1882. He idolized Rossetti and without doubt the poet was the most important influence on his life. Through Rossetti, Caine was introduced to the Pre-Raphaelite circle, and consequently to London literary and artistic society, making a number of good friends in the process, including Ford Madox Brown, William Sharp, Frederic Shields, and Theodore Watts (later Watts-Dunton), as well as Christina Rossetti.

In January 1882 Caine published an anthology, *Sonnets of Three Centuries*, and some months later produced *Recollections of Rossetti*, a tribute published in the same year. He remained in London, launched as an author and journalist. *Cobwebs of Criticism* appeared in 1883 and his first novel, *Shadow of a Crime*, in 1885, followed by *A Son of Hagar* (1886). He had hoped to be seen as a man of letters but the failure of his *Life of Coleridge* (1887) sent him back to fiction, and he produced his first commercial success with *The Deemster* (1887), a novel set on the Isle of Man in the eighteenth century, and centring on the redemption of a murderer condemned to exile in isolation for his crime. While the critics carped, Caine's readership grew, and the novel was adapted for the stage by Wilson Barrett as *Ben-my-chree*—Manx for 'Girl of my heart'.

In December 1882 Mary Alice Chandler (1869–1932) went to live with him; she was thirteen, which was at that time the age of consent. Their elder son, Ralph, was born in Hampstead, London, in 1884 and they were married secretly in Edinburgh on 3 September 1886. The ceremony was the Scottish one, by declaration before witnesses. They were living in Bexleyheath, Kent, at the time; they moved to Keswick in Cumberland in 1888. A second son, Derwent, was born there in 1891.

For forty years Caine travelled widely, visiting the places where he was to set several of his romances, from Iceland to Egypt, London to Rome. In 1892 he went to Berlin and the Russian frontier on behalf of the London Russo-Jewish Committee to investigate Jewish persecution. In 1895 he made the first of many visits to the USA and also went to Canada, where he negotiated with the government on behalf of the Society of Authors and the Foreign Office over a new copyright law.

Caine continued to write, eventually producing fifteen romantic novels, and he became astonishingly popular and famous. He was a powerful story-teller, using his novels, mostly based on the eternal love triangle, to propound his political and social ideals. *The Bondman* (1890) launched the publishing firm of Heinemann. Set in the Isle of Man and Iceland, it was an involved story of love and revenge, and was adapted and staged at the Drury Lane Theatre, London, in 1906, with Mrs Patrick Campbell as Greeba; it was filmed by Herbert Wilcox in 1929. *The Manxman* (1894) was an immediate success, and is probably Caine's best-known book. It was dramatized in two forms, first by Wilson Barrett and later by the author himself. It was filmed by the London Film Company in 1916, and again, by Alfred Hitchcock, in 1929. In a letter to Caine, Edmund Gosse wrote that it was 'a contribution to literature and the most fastidious critic would give in exchange for it a wilderness of that deciduous trash which our publishers call fiction' (Hall Caine archive).

The Christian (1897) was the first novel in Britain to sell 1 million copies. The central characters of Glory Quayle and John Storm are among Caine's best creations, although his frank treatment of sexuality worried some readers and critics. The play was first staged in the USA, to great acclaim, but did less well in London. *The Eternal City* (1901), set in Rome, sold even better, and was dramatized twice, filmed in 1915, and remade in 1923. *The White Prophet* (1909), however, immersed Caine in political controversy, as it expressed sympathy with the position of the Egyptian nationalists. *The Woman thou Gavest me* (1913) retrieved his reputation while at the same time causing the biggest furore of any of his novels because of its open-minded treatment of marriage and divorce; it made a popular film after the First World War. It is clear that many of his novels were well-suited for dramatic and cinematic adaptation; their sometimes improbable plots none the less made for good drama, particularly when shorn of their didactic element. Caine himself also wrote a number of original stage plays and film scripts.

As a youth Caine was a communist but later became a Christian socialist. Votes for women, marriage law reform, and workers' rights were some of the causes he championed. A member of the House of Keys from 1901 to 1908, he advocated nationalization of the Isle of Man's trains, trams, and ferries as well as the land. He had long supported the Liberals in England, but declined an invitation from Lloyd George to stand for the Westminster parliament.

Caine had met the prince of Wales through Irving's Beefsteak Club and remained on friendly terms when the prince became Edward VII. In 1905 and 1908 he edited 'gift books' for Queen Alexandra in aid of her charities but did not allow his name to appear other than as a contributor. In September 1914 he resumed his desk at the *Daily Telegraph* and wrote impassioned propaganda. He also edited *King Albert's Book* (Christmas 1914) to raise money for the *Telegraph's* Belgian fund, and a delighted King Albert created him an officer of the order of Leopold of Belgium. In 1918 the Belgian government presented him with his portrait painted by Alfred Jonniaux.

Caine returned to America in 1915 and 1916, speaking in the allied cause. In 1916 he joined Lord Robert Cecil at the Foreign Office to draft the document proposing a League of Nations after the war. The government invited him to write an epic propaganda film but the war ended before it was finished. In November 1917 he was offered a baronetcy but refused it, and soon afterwards he was made a KBE. Hating his forename, he insisted he should be known as Sir Hall, not Sir Thomas. Later he was made a Companion of Honour. His war work finished, he returned to fiction. *The Master of Man* (1921) was followed by *The Woman of Knockaloe* (1923), his last novel. Both were set in the Isle of Man, where he had made his home at Greeba Castle. For the centenary of Rossetti's birth he brought out a revised version of his *Recollections* (1928), dedicated to the memory of their friendship.

In appearance Caine was short, not more than 5 feet 4 inches tall, with red hair and beard and staring, slightly protuberant eyes. His hair receded while he was still young and with his pointed beard he bore a slight resemblance to the Stratford portrait of Shakespeare, a likeness he cultivated: if people did not remark on it he was apt to point it out. He could be charming though always serious but had a temper to match his hair. He had been born into the Church of England but his father joined the Myrtle Street Baptist Chapel when he was about seven years old. Caine, a deeply religious man who hoped to be remembered by his voluminous *Life of Christ* (published posthumously in 1937) returned to the Church of England as an adult. Hall Caine died at Greeba Castle on 31 August 1931, and was buried in Maughold churchyard, Isle of Man, on 4 September. His wife died six months later and was buried beside him. The handsome monument over their grave was designed by Archibald Knox. VIVIEN ALLEN

Sources V. Allen, *Hall Caine: portrait of a Victorian romancer* (1997) · H. Caine, *My story* (1908) · H. Caine, *Recollections of Dante Gabriel Rossetti* (1882); [another edn] (1928) · S. Norris, *Manx memories and movements* (1994) · S. Norris, *Two men of Manxland* (1948) · *The Times* (1 Sept 1931) · *Daily Telegraph* (1 Sept 1931) · C. F. Kenyon, *Hall Caine: the man and the novelist* (1901) · private information (2004) · b. cert. · memorial, Maughold churchyard, Isle of Man · Manx Museum and National Heritage, Douglas, Isle of Man, Hall Caine archive

Archives Georgetown University, Washington, DC, Lauinger Library, corresp. relating to business matters incl. film productions · Hunt. L., letters and literary MSS · Lpool RO, letters · Manx Museum and National Heritage, Douglas, Isle of Man, corresp. and papers; papers | BL, corresp. with Lord Northcliffe, Add. MS 62178 · BL, corresp. with George Bernard Shaw, Add. MS 50531 · BL, corresp. with Society of Authors, Add. MS 56678 · CAC Cam., letters to W. T. Stead · CUL, corresp. with Lord Hardinge · Elgar Birthplace Museum, letters to Sir Edward Elgar · GL, letters to Hodder and Stoughton and draft articles · Lpool RO, William Ralph Hall Caine archive · NL Scot., corresp. mostly with Lord Rosebery · NYPL, Berg collection, letters to his wife · Richmond Local Studies Library, London, corresp. with Douglas Sladen · TCD, letters to Edward Dowden · Theatre Museum, London, letters to lord chamberlain's licensee · U. Edin. L., letters to James Halliwell-Phillipps · U. Leeds, Brotherton L., letters to Sir E. W. Gosse · U. Leeds, Brotherton L., letters to Theodore Watts-Dunton · University of British Columbia, Angeli collection, corresp. with Dante Gabriel Rossetti [copies in Bodl. Oxf.] | FILM BFI NFTVA, news footage · IWM FVA

Likenesses H. Furniss, caricatures, pen-and-ink sketches, 1854–1925, NPG · F. Pegram, pen-and-ink drawing, 1893, Manx Museum and National Heritage, Douglas, Isle of Man · G. C. Beresford, photographs, 1904, NPG · London Stereoscopic Co., cabinet lithograph, *c*.1915, NPG [*see illus.*] · W. Tittle, lithograph, 1922, NPG · G. B. Cowen, photograph, NPG · W. and D. Downey, woodburytype photograph, repro. in W. Downey and D. Downey, *The cabinet portrait gallery*, 3 (1892) · E. T. R., pencil cartoon, Manx Museum and National Heritage, Douglas, Isle of Man; repro. in *Punch* (11 Sept 1907) · A. Jonniaux, oils; copy, Greeba Castle, Douglas, Isle of Man · R. E. Morrison, oils, Manx Museum and National Heritage, Douglas, Isle of Man · B. Partridge, caricature, watercolour study, NPG; repro. in *VF* (2 July 1896) · B. Partridge, cartoon, repro. in *Punch* (Oct 1926) · A. P. F. Ritchie, cigarette card, NPG · J. W. Swynnerton, bust, central library, Douglas, Isle of Man · Walery, photograph, NPG · photographs, postcards

Wealth at death £200,000: Central Registry and Deeds Office, Douglas, Isle of Man

Caine, Sir Michael Harris (1927–1999), businessman, was born at the Hollies Nursing Home, Welwyn Garden City, Hertfordshire, on 17 June 1927, the son of Sir Sydney *Caine (1902–1991), an official in the Colonial Office and a university administrator, and his wife, Muriel Ann Maud Harris (*d.* 1962). After a period in Hong Kong he was educated at Bedales School, Petersfield (1939–45), where he was head boy. Conscripted in 1945, Caine served in the navy and became a petty officer radar specialist. At Oxford, where he studied modern history at Lincoln College (1947–50), he was the centre of a small group including M. H. (Fredy) Fisher, later editor of the *Financial Times*. Thanks to his father, and his father's friends such as Lionel Robbins, he had grown away very early from the collectivism which was conventional in mid-twentieth-century Britain, and was already a convinced free-market libertarian.

It was a criticism of Oxford examining that this hard-working and impressive undergraduate received only a third-class degree. After Oxford, Caine spent a postgraduate year at George Washington University in Washington, DC. Through his father, he knew Jock Campbell, later Lord Campbell of Eskan, chairman of Booker Bros. McConnell, a British-based business with extensive investments in sugar plantations and trading businesses in the Caribbean, especially in British Guiana, and in central Africa. In 1952 he was recruited by Campbell to Booker, where he spent the whole of his working life, starting as a management trainee in London and British Guiana and retiring in 1993 as chairman. It was also in 1952 (on 30 August) that he married Janice Denise Mercer (*b.* 1928), with whom he had a son and a daughter.

Caine's rise in Booker was swift. He was a main board director by 1964 and became chief executive in 1975. He remained chief executive until 1984, and from 1979 combined that role with the chairmanship. His promotion coincided with significant change in Booker. Campbell had converted a traditional colonial business in British Guiana into one which treated its mainly Guyanese employees well, and developed their skills. He had done similarly with the Booker companies in Northern Rhodesia and Nyasaland. However, Campbell early recognized that, in the face of West Indian and African nationalism, Booker had to diversify away from being a tropically based company into a modern multinational. Caine was heavily preoccupied with Booker's attempts to diversify. The group's experience and connections in the developing world were used to move into engineering, rum marketing, retail shops, and wholesale warehouses, and latterly into food processing and manufacture. The new activities were in Britain and the USA. Not all new Booker investments were a success, but the success rate was high.

There were continued efforts to live with nationalism, both by sharing the ownership of Booker operations with governments in Africa, and by developing a worldwide agricultural consultancy business. Caine's business acumen, lateral thinking, and total lack of pretension and pomposity made him particularly successful. He had a special bond with Africa and Africans, and was trusted, respected, and liked throughout the continent. It was also a tribute to the good relationships Caine had retained that independent Guyana welcomed Booker Tate, the agricultural consultancy company jointly owned with Tate and Lyle, to manage the Booker sugar estates which had been nationalized.

The Booker prize for literature in English was not started by Caine, but he had ultimate responsibility for its becoming a national event. Booker had become the owner of several best-selling copyrights, and it had agreed to fund a literary prize. The first was awarded in 1969. Caine became chairman of the prize committee in 1972 and remained chairman until 1995. Over this period a modest prizegiving was transformed into a banquet at the London Guildhall, which was televised from 1980. It was the first literary prize in Britain to attract mass publicity. In a material sense it did not noticeably benefit Booker, but for Caine personally it was a cherished commitment.

The mechanism for awarding the prize was guided by Caine. There was a management committee which represented Booker and a range of national literary interests. The prize was for the year's best work in the English language. It had to be written by a Commonwealth or Irish citizen and published in the UK. Booker emphasis on the Commonwealth outside Britain declined, but Caine's did not, and nor did the proportion of Commonwealth prizewinners. He strongly influenced the management committee's annual choice for chairman of the judges and ensured a year-on-year balance in the background of the judges. While he took no part in the judging process, he read the short-listed novels, and always insisted that the aim was not to produce best-sellers but rather that 'some winners would be A level set books in 20 years' time' (*The Guardian*, 23 March 1999). His personal authority increased respect for the prize, because he valued literature so knowledgeably himself.

Caine had always loved the classical Russian novels, and as the Soviet Union crumbled he saw a chance to encourage enfranchised Russian writing with a substantial prize. This was very much his own initiative, pursued in Moscow without any knowledge of the language, and he succeeded in finding enough moral and financial support from Russian and other sources. The result was that in 1992 a Booker Russian prize was started, amid tremendous Russian media acclaim and controversy. It was a remarkable achievement, made possible by Caine's intelligence, humanity, determination, and connections.

Caine's reputation for incisive wisdom and imaginative thinking brought him many invitations to serve outside Booker. He was a member of the council of Bedford College as early as 1966, and education remained a particular interest. This combined well with his interest in the developing world. Among other appointments, he was chairman of the UK Council for Overseas Student Affairs, a member of the Commonwealth Scholarship Commission in the UK, and a member of the governing body of the Institute of Development Studies.

Caine's passion for Africa was reflected in his chairmanship of the Royal African Society and of the Africa Centre, but his greatest achievement was his chairmanship of the remarkable Africa '95 festival of the arts. He showed great skill and dedication in leading a disparate agglomeration of interests, and in ensuring the financial and cultural success of the enterprise. There were over sixty events in the UK and Africa, which included televised concerts and nationwide exhibitions. These created a new mass audience of millions for African music, art, dance, theatre, and poetry. During his last months he had also begun to plan a prize for African writing in English. A Caine prize for African writing was established in his memory.

Caine was very tall, gangling, and good-looking. He had a speech impediment which seemed only to add to his persuasive charm. He had a self-deprecating sense of humour and a total lack of self-importance. Wonderfully gifted himself, and a master of both detail and the wider picture, he could tolerate the fallibility of those whom he valued. At the same time he was intensely ambitious in promoting and transforming Booker. He was thoroughly convinced that capitalism is preferable to collectivism. This was connected with his great faith in human potential. He was a lifelong sceptic, with permanent Anglican instincts, and a devoted member of the Reform Club.

Michael and Janice Caine separated in 1983 and their marriage was dissolved on 16 March 1987. On 9 May 1987 Michael Caine married Emma Harriet Nicholson, later Baroness Nicholson of Winterbourne (*b*. 1941), MP. They became the guardians of an Iraqi war orphan. Michael Caine was knighted in 1988. He was admitted to a private hospital in January 1999 for an operation for bowel cancer. In the course of his aftercare a tracheotomy tube became dislodged, and lack of oxygen caused irreversible brain damage. He lingered for another month, and finally died on 20 March 1999 in St Thomas's Hospital, Lambeth. He was buried on 29 March at Winterbourne parish church, Berkshire. The coroner returned a verdict of misadventure; his widow, convinced that the under-regulation of private health-care facilities contributed to his death, used her position in the House of Lords to campaign for legislative changes to bring private hospitals into line with those in the National Health Service.

ARTHUR GREEN

Sources *The Times* (23 March 1999) · *Daily Telegraph* (23 March 1999) · *The Guardian* (23 March 1999) · *The Independent* (24 March 1999) · *WW* · private information (2004) [Janice Caine; Richard Caine; Amanda Caine; C. W. Kellaway; Mrs R. Fisher; H. R. Douglas; D. Taylor; C. Whitaker; M. Goff; Sir Peter Parker; Baroness Nicholson of Winterbourne] · personal knowledge (2004) · b. cert. · m. cert. [Emma Harriet Nicholson] · d. cert. · *The Times* (5 Dec 2000)
Archives priv. coll.

Likenesses bust, Bodl. Oxf.
Wealth at death £838,723: probate, 1999, *CGPLA Eng. & Wales*

Caine, Sir Sydney (1902–1991), colonial official and university administrator, was born on 27 June 1902 at 58 Gresham Road, Hendon, London, the son of Harry Edward Caine, railway clerk, and his wife, Jane Harker, *née* Buckley. He was educated at Harrow county school and the London School of Economics (LSE), obtaining a first-class honours degree in economics in 1922. He first became an assistant collector of taxes, then in 1926 passed the revived civil service competitive examination and entered the Colonial Office, where his understanding of fiscal administration was appreciated at a time when the department and the colonial governments were forced by worldwide recession to make cuts in expenditure. In 1929 he was appointed secretary to the West Indian sugar commission and five years after that secretary to the United Kingdom sugar industry inquiry committee, created to protect the economies and expand the markets of the sugar-producing British dependencies.

In 1937, when Hong Kong required a sounder economic structure, Caine was sent there as financial secretary. He reshaped the system of revenue collection and designed a number of fiscal reforms which, because of the Japanese invasion, could not be fully implemented until after the Second World War, when they formed the basis of the territory's subsequent prosperity. He enjoyed living in the Far East and the many intellectual challenges it presented.

Caine was recalled to the Colonial Office as an assistant secretary in 1940. There his wide understanding of the financial implications of radical economic and social changes in colonial administration intended by the first Colonial Development and Welfare Act was particularly valuable. He was soon seconded to the colonial supply liaison office in Washington, to handle economic and labour problems arising from the United States Lend-Lease Act. As a member of the Anglo-American Caribbean commission he was afforded in 1942 an opportunity to further the interests of the West Indies and help protect their constitutional advance while negotiating the terms of collaboration between Britain and America to defend that region during and immediately after the war. The scope of his work widened when that same year he returned to England as financial adviser to Oliver Stanley, the secretary of state for the colonies. In 1944 Stanley promoted him to assistant under-secretary of state and in 1947 Arthur Creech Jones promoted him to deputy under-secretary of state. As such, early in 1948 he led the discussion in Paris between French and British officials on closer economic co-operation between the colonies of the two countries, including the building of better communications between neighbouring territories. Later that year he presided over similar discussions with officials of the Belgian ministry for colonial affairs. Although he transferred to the Treasury as third secretary towards the end of the year, his work still had a strong connection with Britain's overseas possessions as, from 1949 to 1951, he led the United Kingdom Treasury and supply delegation in Washington and the World Bank mission to Ceylon.

Caine's career took a different direction in 1952 when he became vice-chancellor of the new University of Malaya. Once again radical innovations were required of him. Instead of one university site where the faculties covered the complete range of subjects, he oversaw the development and expansion of two branches of the university, and witnessed the creation of a third. In 1949 Raffles College had combined with King Edward VII's Medical College to form the basis of a university in Singapore. When Caine arrived in Malaya plans were under way for an expensive transfer to Johore, where a site had already been acquired by the government but not yet transferred to the university authorities. Caine, with the assistance of the then director of the London School of Economics, Sir Alexander Carr-Saunders, drew up a new plan for the Singapore University College to remain a centre for the arts, science, medicine, social science, education, and law, with a separate campus in Kuala Lumpur for teaching agriculture and engineering as well as the arts, science, and medicine. Already Nanyang University College had been hurriedly created for Chinese students who were not sufficiently fluent in English to qualify for places in the University of Malaya. It had a more technical leaning, resembling some American universities. In 1957 Malaya became an independent kingdom and Caine returned to England, having already set in motion the scheme for the branches of the University of Malaya to become separate universities by 1962. While there he had also acted as economic adviser to the chief minister of Singapore, helping to design long-term economic policies to foster the development of local industries, rapid expansion of the social services to the extent that could be supported financially by the colony, and a more even distribution of income. At the same time he was appointed chairman of the Caribbean fiscal commission, which drew up financially viable plans for the support of the administration of the short-lived Federation of the West Indies.

From 1957 to 1967 Caine was director of the London School of Economics, responsible for considerable expansion of its premises and for handling the notorious student protest at the announcement of Sir Walter Adams, principal of the University College of Rhodesia and Nyasaland, as his successor. Since 1965 Caine had himself served as governor of the Reserve Bank of Rhodesia, created by the British government after Ian Smith's unilateral declaration of independence to handle the external finances of the government of Rhodesia, including colonial administrators' pensions and students' fees. Caine regarded the LSE insurrection as a bid for student power, such as had begun the previous year at Berkeley in the United States, and believed it was fomented in the LSE by American agitators. He had been considering ways to give students a voice in the management of the school, and had sympathy with some of their demands. He exercised reason and firm resolution in dealing with the protesters, until the issue was settled in time for them to sit their final examinations and for him to retire on 30 September 1967.

In retirement, as well as writing several papers on financial matters (including one for the Institute of Economic Affairs advocating 'pay television') and educational principles, he produced one book on the foundation of the LSE and another on the purpose and prospects of British universities, over which he considered the government exercised too much control. As a practical expression of those views he became chairman of the planning board of the independent University of Buckingham, which opened in 1973. The latter was unusual in offering two-year degree courses, the academic year consisting of four, rather than three, long terms.

Caine was created CMG in 1945, KCMG in 1947, a grand officer of the order of Orange Nassau (Netherlands) in 1947, and commander of the order of Dannebrog (Denmark) in 1965. He served as a member of the Independent Television Authority from 1960 to 1967 (deputy chairman from 1964 to 1967); as a member of the International Institute of Educational Planning from 1963 to 1970; and as co-ordinator of the Indonesian Sugar Study from 1971 to 1972. He received honorary doctorates from the University of Malaya in 1956 and from the University of Buckingham in 1980.

Caine was a handsome man with a considerable presence. He was married three times: first on 15 August 1925 to Muriel Ann Maud (*d.* 1962), daughter of Abner Harris, of 18 Hervey Close, London; second on 23 March 1965 to Doris Winifred (1900/01–1973), daughter of Walter Folkard, of Forest Gate, London; and third in 1975 to Elizabeth Crane Bowyer, daughter of J. Crane Nicholls and widow of Sir Eric Bowyer (1902–1964). There was one son of his first marriage, Sir Michael *Caine (1927–1999), and two stepsons and two stepdaughters of his third marriage. Caine died on 2 January 1991; he was survived by his third wife, his son, and his stepchildren. A memorial service was held at St Clement Danes on 2 February 1991.

PATRICIA M. PUGH

Sources *The Times* (3 Jan 1991) · *The Independent* (4 Jan 1991) · *Times Higher Education Supplement* (21 July 1989) · *WWW* · Colonial office lists · J. Pemberton and J. Pemberton, *The university college at Buckingham: a first account of its conception, foundation, and early years* (1979) · b. cert. · m. cert. [Doris Folkard] · Burke, *Peerage* · *CGPLA Eng. & Wales* (1991)

Archives BLPES, papers relating to history of LSE; papers relating to Rhodesia | BLPES, corresp. relating to Royal Economic Society and with the editors of the *Economic Journal*

Likenesses E. Halliday, oils, 1967, London School of Economics · photograph, repro. in *The Times* (14 March 1956), 10d · photograph, repro. in *The Times* (4 Dec 1965), 8a · photograph, repro. in *The Times* (29 March 1967), 3 · photograph, repro. in *The Times* (17 Nov 1967), 3a · photograph, repro. in *The Times* (3 Jan 1991) · photograph, repro. in Pemberton and Pemberton, *The university college at Buckingham*, 19 · photograph, repro. in *The Independent* · photographs, London School of Economics, Caine collection

Wealth at death £320,266: probate, 28 May 1991, *CGPLA Eng. & Wales*

Caine, William Sproston (1842–1903), politician and temperance advocate, born at Egremont, Wallasey, Cheshire, on 26 March 1842, was the eldest surviving son of Nathaniel Caine JP (*d.* 1877), metal merchant, and his wife, Hannah (*d.* 1861), daughter of William Rushton of Liverpool.

William Sproston Caine (1842–1903), by Sir Benjamin Stone, 1901

Educated privately at Gibson's school, Egremont, and the Revd Richard Wall's school at Birkenhead, Caine entered his father's business at Egremont in 1861, and in 1864 was taken into partnership. He moved to Liverpool in 1871. Public affairs soon occupied much of his attention, and he retired from the firm in 1878. He retained, however, the directorship of the Hodbarrow Mining Co. Ltd, Millom, and he secured the controlling interest in the Shaw's Brow Iron Co., Liverpool, leaving the management of the concern in the hands of his partner, Arthur S. Cox. The collapse of this business in 1893 involved Caine in heavy liabilities, which he honourably discharged, but thenceforth his resources were largely devoted to paying off the mortgage which he raised to meet the firm's losses.

Caine's father was raised a Wesleyan but joined the Baptists on his marriage; Caine was brought up as a Baptist under the influence of Hugh Stowell *Brown, whose memorial volume he edited (1887). On 24 March 1868 he married Alice, Stowell Brown's daughter; they had two sons and three daughters. He developed early a bent for preaching and philanthropic work. In later life in London he was from 1884 to 1903 the lay pastor of a mission church known as the Wheatsheaf in Stockwell, south London, but he was largely preoccupied with the temperance movement, and at Liverpool he found his first scope for propagandist zeal. As president of the Liverpool Temperance and Band of Hope Union, he formed and became chairman of a Popular Control and License Reform Association, with a monthly organ, the *Liverpool Social Reformer*. In

1873 he was elected vice-president of the United Kingdom Alliance. He was also president of the Baptist Total Abstinence Society, the Congregational Temperance Society, the British Temperance League, and the National Temperance Federation.

In 1873 Caine first sought election to parliament, mainly with a view to enforcing his temperance views. He was in general agreement with the radical wing of the Liberal Party, and unsuccessfully contested Liverpool for the Liberals in both that and the next year. In 1880 he was returned as radical member for Scarborough, and without delay he urged on the House of Commons his advanced temperance opinions. In a maiden speech on 18 June 1880 he supported the successful motion of his friend, Sir Wilfrid Lawson, in favour of local option. Identifying himself with the extreme radical section of the party, he seconded Henry Labouchere's motion of dissent from Gladstone's proposal for a national monument to Lord Beaconsfield (12 May 1881). His activity was officially recognized by Gladstone on 17 November 1884 by his appointment as civil lord of the Admiralty in succession to Sir Thomas Brassey. Although he retained his seat at the necessary by-election, he was defeated in Tottenham at the general election of 1885. He soon, however, returned to the house as MP for Barrow in Furness at a by-election on 6 April 1886.

Caine declined to accept Gladstone's home-rule policy, and took an active part in organizing under Chamberlain's direction the dissentient Liberals into a new party of 'Liberal Unionists'. In the division on the second reading of Gladstone's Home Rule Bill (7 June) Caine and Henry Robert Brand (afterwards second Viscount Hampden) acted as tellers for the ninety-three Liberal Unionists, who brought down the government. The home-rulers gave the new party the sobriquet of the 'Brand of Caine'. At the ensuing general election Caine was again returned for Barrow, and was appointed chief Liberal Unionist whip. But his radical convictions and extreme temperance views, which were unaltered, soon rendered the alliance with the Conservatives distasteful. Although the scheme of G. J. Goschen in 1890 for compensating holders of extinguished public-house licences was modified under pressure from Caine, he marked his dislike of it not only by resigning his post of whip but by vacating his seat in the house. On seeking re-election at Barrow as an independent Liberal he was defeated. Within the same year he rejoined the Liberal fold, and in 1892 re-entered the house for East Bradford as a Gladstonian Liberal and voted for the 1893 Home Rule Bill. At the general election of 1895 he lost his seat, and only re-entered the house in 1900 as Liberal member for Camborne. In the interval he sat on Lord Peel's royal commission on the liquor-licensing laws (1896–9), and signed the minority report and the addendum in favour of direct local veto.

The native population of India also engaged Caine's sympathies, and he criticized severely British methods of government, especially the encouragement for fiscal purposes of the liquor and opium trade. In 1890 he visited India as a delegate to the Indian National Congress at Calcutta, and contributed to the *Pall Mall Gazette* a series of letters called 'Young India' which ably advocated large measures of self-government. He sat on the royal commission of 1895–6 on the administration of Indian expenditure, signing the minority report recommending a diminution of civil and military expenditure, and would, but for ill health, have sat on the opium commission.

Caine's activities exhausted his strength. A voyage to South America in 1902 failed to restore his health, and he died of heart failure on 17 March 1903 at his home, 42 Grosvenor Road, Westminster, London. He was buried in Brookwood cemetery, Woking. Caine was a puritan in politics and religion, whose moral courage and philanthropic instincts were superior to his intellectual gifts. Abrupt in manner, downright in speech, but of imperturbable good humour, he was dubbed by political associates the 'genial ruffian'. G. S. Woods, *rev.* H. C. G. Matthew

Sources J. Newton, *W. S. Caine* (1907) • *The Times* (18 March 1903) • Gladstone, *Diaries* • *The Athenaeum* (13 April 1907), 440 • B. Harrison, *Drink and the Victorians: the temperance question in England, 1815–1872* (1971)

Archives BL, corresp. with W. E. Gladstone, Add. MSS 44456–44788, *passim* • Bodl. Oxf., corresp. with Sir William Harcourt • U. Birm. L., special collections department, corresp. with J. Chamberlain

Likenesses B. Stone, two photographs, 1901, NPG [*see illus.*] • seven photographs, repro. in Newton, *W. S. Caine*

Wealth at death £2501 3*s.* 4*d.*: probate, 22 May 1903, *CGPLA Eng. & Wales*

Cainnech moccu Dálann (521/527–599/600). *See under* Munster, saints of (*act. c.*450–*c.*700).

Caird, Edward (1835–1908), philosopher and college head, was born on 23 March 1835 in Greenock. His father, John Caird (1787–1838), the partner and manager of a firm of engineers in Greenock and a deeply religious man, died while Edward was still an infant. His mother, Janet (1799–1889), the daughter of Roderick and Isabella Young of Paisley, raised her large family after her husband's early death, with the assistance of her extended family. Among Edward's brothers was John *Caird, theologian and principal of Glasgow University. Edward lived for much of his childhood with his aunt Jane Caird of Greenock. He was a delicate and retiring child; brought up by his aunt in religious and secluded surroundings, he displayed an interest in spiritual matters from an early age. He was first schooled at Greenock Academy, where he was taught by David Duff, later professor of church history at Edinburgh. Caird recalled: 'He was the first teacher that really awakened my mind' (Jones and Muirhead, 14).

Caird began studies at the University of Glasgow in the winter of 1850. He won prizes in Greek and Latin, ecclesiastical history, and divinity. At this time he also made several lasting friendships, most notably with John Nichol, later professor of English literature at Glasgow University. His university career, however, was punctuated by bouts of ill health. In the winter of 1856 he went to St Andrews with his aunt Jane to convalesce and to study divinity, and in the spring of 1857 he went to Perthshire to visit his

Edward Caird (1835–1908), by Thomas Annan, pubd 1871

brother John. He resumed studies in divinity at Glasgow later that year, although by this time he had decided not to enter the ministry and to pursue philosophical scholarship instead. He was already much influenced by the idealist bent of Carlyle and Goethe, for whom he developed a lifelong admiration.

Elected to a Snell exhibition in 1860, a scholarship which sent Scottish students to Oxford, Caird went up to Balliol College, where he found himself in the company of men such as Sir Courtney Ilbert—who was to gain fame as the law member of the viceroy's council in India—J. A. Symonds, and Thomas Case. But Caird at twenty-five was by this time rather older than many of the other students, and he tended to associate with the younger dons, notably the idealist philosopher T. H. Green. 'Caird and Green were kindred souls', observed J. L. Strachan-Davidson, a fellow student who later succeeded Caird as master of Balliol (Jones and Muirhead, 28). Caird was elected to the Old Mortality Club, which promoted the study of reform, in the company of Green, A. V. Dicey, John Nichol, James Bryce, and others. He was awarded the Pusey and Ellerton scholarship in Hebrew in 1861 and the Jenkyns exhibition in 1862. He earned a first class in the final classical school in the next year and was elected a tutor at Merton College in 1864.

In May 1866 Caird was unanimously elected professor of moral philosophy at Glasgow against a field of strong candidates. He was initially reluctant to stand because his friend Nichol was also a candidate and, as he wrote to Jowett, 'I would rather have no professorship while the world standeth than do anything unkind to Nichol' (Jones and Muirhead, 48). But Nichol withdrew in his friend's favour and Caird was pleased to return to Scotland to take up the joint work of lecturing and scholarship for which he was so well suited. A year later, on 8 May 1867, he married Caroline Frances (Fanny) Wylie of Carluke, Lanarkshire.

After twenty-seven years at Glasgow, in 1893 Caird was unanimously elected master of Balliol College. He was reluctant to leave Glasgow: 'I may say that nothing would have made me do it, except what has happened—a unanimous call to the College of Jowett and Green' (Bosanquet, 381). Upon his return to Balliol, he remarked to a friend: 'I shall have my hand on the heart of England' (Jones and Muirhead, 54). While he was less intimately connected to undergraduate life and more closely engaged in scholarship than his predecessor Benjamin Jowett, he was regarded as a very effective master. Like Jowett and T. H. Green, he regarded the task of the college as training students in the art of moral citizenship. As master, he continued to read and write philosophy: in this period he published *The Evolution of Religion* (1893) and, drawn by the emphasis in the Oxford curriculum on classical Greek philosophy to return to a study of Plato and Aristotle, he also published *The Evolution of Theology in the Greek Philosophy* (1904). But by 1907 his work was so hampered by a paralytic illness that he resigned the mastership of the college.

In the company of T. H. Green and F. H. Bradley, Caird led the revival of an idealist philosophy which became the most striking and powerful intellectual force in late nineteenth- and early twentieth-century Britain. His most significant contribution to this philosophical movement lay in his two works on Kant. In 1877 he published a critical account of the *Critique of Pure Reason*; this was followed in 1889 by a two-volume exposition of Kant's *Critique of Pure Reason*, *Critique of Practical Reason*, and *Critique of Judgement*. Caird's primary purpose was to demonstrate that, notwithstanding Kant's reputation for promoting dualism, the Kantian system was premised on a deep organic unity. Caird interpreted Kant freely, for he was convinced that Kant did not fully understand how consistently organic his own philosophical system actually was. Some critics regretted this radical reconstruction of Kant. But none the less, the volumes were widely regarded as authoritative, 'in many ways the culmination of the long English endeavour to assimilate Kant' (Pringle-Pattison, 278).

In 1883 Caird published a short study of Hegel: the first part was a biographical account, and the second a brief critical review of his philosophy. The comprehensive grasp of the development of philosophy in Germany which characterized his volumes on Kant was also demonstrated here. He paid special attention to Hegel's notion of a spiritual unity underlying superficial difference. He was also much interested in the resonance between Hegelian principles and Christianity. He read the Hegelian language of self-realization as essentially that of St Paul and St Augustine: the individual must relinquish an isolated life in order to live a spiritual or universal one. As a friend and contemporary philosopher, Bernard Bosanquet, commented: 'In Hegel … he found the nearest approach which any philosopher had made to the conception which he sought of a fully correlated concrete whole' (Bosanquet, 384). The highest expression of this unity he found in Christianity. For Caird, God was the absolute principle of unity.

The Evolution of Religion, initially delivered as the Gifford lectures at St Andrews between 1890 and 1892, is Caird's most explicitly constructive work. Here he sought to interpret Christianity along idealist principles and to weld together evolutionary ideas and theology by arguing that human history is an unfolding of a consciousness of the universal unity which underlies our experience. In a sense, Christianity was simply one of many expressions of this spiritual revelation; but Caird claimed a unique status for Christianity, more specifically for a thinking protestantism: it alone makes explicit in human consciousness the implicit idea of God or the Absolute. A modern and philosophical Christianity, Caird contended, also rightly admits the reality of evil but rather than lapsing into despair employs the idea of a timeless unity in which truth and good triumph over evil. While those of his contemporaries who leaned towards a materialist view of human experience were unconvinced, the book had a significant impact on others who had been searching for a rational account of spiritual experience, especially for those who, like Caird, were increasingly dissatisfied with the Calvinism in which they had been raised.

A contemporary of his regretted that Caird had devoted so much labour to the exposition of other philosophical systems, notably that of Kant, and suggested that he might have had a greater influence on his generation by working out an independent position. It is true that, with the exception of the work on religion, most of Caird's publications were interpretations of other philosophers. But like Green's these interpretative works indirectly formulated an alternative philosophical position. As Bosanquet explained, their critical interpretations were animated by the obligation to contest atomism and to demonstrate the underlying organic nature of human experience: 'we find in them throughout a peculiar lofty preoccupation or sense of spiritual duty', Bosanquet noted, which did not infuse the writings of even slightly younger idealists to the same extent (Bosanquet, 382). This commitment to revealing an all-pervasive organicism was linked to a strong communitarian strand which ran through Caird's work, most strongly expressed in the lay sermons which he delivered as master at Balliol College. He constantly returned to the twin themes of social unity and individual independence, depicting the barrenness of a society which does not seek harmony between social and individual ends. He called on students to renounce selfishness and to pursue the common good. Philosophical study and social duty could not be separated.

For Caird social duty meant engagement in a variety of reform causes. As a student at Glasgow he became involved in campaigns for free education, the extension of the franchise, and the rights of women. He was at the forefront of the long and arduous campaign to admit women to university classes and degrees at Glasgow. He was one of four professors to begin lecturing to university extension classes of women in 1868; he repeatedly argued the cause of women's education before the university senate; and he served on the governing body of Queen Mary College, a women's college, before and after its formal incorporation into the University of Glasgow. He was also much involved with other aspects of university reform, for example ending the restriction of the teaching of theology to established church members. He played an important role in the Women's Protective and Provident League, which had been founded in 1888 to improve the working conditions of women and children and which later became the Glasgow Council for Women's Trades. Caird worked energetically to improve the industrial position of women; he advocated that the Factory Acts include laundries. This invited one critic to complain that Caird was 'the principal teacher of what is called the new or sympathetic economy' (Jones and Muirhead, 118). Both Edward and Caroline Caird were instrumental in initiating the university settlement movement in Glasgow. Caird defended the philosophy of settlement: 'The general condition of the life of the poor could not be raised unless they were given the opportunities of social and intellectual progress and of contact with things that are beautiful' (Jones and Muirhead, 115). In keeping with this ideal, Edward and Caroline hosted evenings of entertainment, mainly music, once a fortnight at a house in the East End. Upon his return to Oxford as master of Balliol, Caird continued his support for university settlement by giving talks at Toynbee Hall. He also continued to crusade for extending university education to women: one of his first tasks as master was to open Balliol lectures to women students.

While aspects of contemporary socialism appealed strongly to him, Caird, like many of his contemporary idealists, regarded class difference as a necessary and constructive feature of modern society, on the grounds that each class had an appropriate function and place in the social organism. He regretted, however, class antagonism which stood in the way of a sense of national unity. For Caird, the nation was 'the greatest ethical unity to which our services are immediately owing' (E. Caird, *Lay Sermons and Addresses*, 1907, 80). He was convinced that 'it is only that ideal of social service that can really purify our lives' (ibid., 118). But the patriotism which Caird himself felt and which he attempted to encourage in Balliol students was in no sense a shallow jingoism or antithetical to a wider internationalism. He was opposed to the Second South African War, and accordingly to the university's conferring of an honorary degree on Cecil Rhodes; he supported the movement towards international federation.

Caird was distinguished by a prominent forehead, imposing mutton-chop whiskers, penetrating dark eyes, and a tall frame. His contemporaries recalled his sympathetic, gentle, and modest nature, which concealed great strength of will and conviction. A colleague remembered that, while at a meeting of the philosophical society at Oxford, Caird, then master of Balliol, commented favourably on all the speakers, save one. On this speaker, he was silent. For Caird this silence expressed an outspoken and forceful disagreement. He told a friend after the meeting that he 'was glad to get that shot' at the philosopher in question (Jones and Muirhead, 69).

Caird was one of the foremost British philosophers of the late nineteenth and early twentieth centuries. He was also an important figure in the liberal theology movement. His influential study of Kant gave vitality to the discussion of the philosopher, and of German philosophy more generally, in Britain. For decades it remained the most important work on Kant in the English language. His students filled the chairs of philosophy in American, British, and colonial universities, continuing to expound variations of Caird's philosophical idealism, even as idealism began to be superseded by logical positivism. Caird's contribution to philosophy was recognized by the conferring of the honorary degrees of LLD by St Andrews in 1883 and by Glasgow in 1894, DCL by Oxford in 1891, and DLitt by Cambridge in 1898 and the University of Wales in 1902. Portraits of Caird hang in Balliol College and Glasgow; a tablet in Balliol College chapel and a bronze medallion at Glasgow further commemorate his legacy. He was an original member of the British Academy and a member of the French Académie des Sciences Morales et Politiques. Edward Caird died in the evening of 1 November 1908 at his home, 12 Bardwell Road, Oxford, and was buried in St Sepulchre's cemetery, Oxford, beside T. H. Green and Benjamin Jowett. He was survived by his wife.

S. M. DEN OTTER

Sources H. Jones and J. H. Muirhead, *The life and philosophy of Edward Caird* (1921) · B. Bosanquet, 'Edward Caird, 1835–1908', *PBA*, [3] (1907–8), 379–86 · E. McTaggart, 'E. Caird, *The evolution of religion*', *Mind*, new ser., 2 (1893), 376–83 · A. S. Pringle-Pattison, 'E. Caird, *The critical philosophy of Immanuel Kant*', *Mind*, 15 (1890), 274–8 · *DNB* · private information (2004) [M. A. Moss]

Archives Balliol Oxf., corresp. and papers relating to him · Bodl. Oxf., notes on his lectures on logic · U. Glas., lecture notes | Balliol Oxf., corresp. with J. L. Strachan-Davidson · Bodl. Oxf., letters to Gilbert Murray · CUL, letters to May Crum · Merton Oxf., F. H. Bradley MSS · NL Scot., corresp. relating to Balliol College

Likenesses T. Annan, photograph, pubd 1871, NPG [*see illus.*] · G. Reid, oils, 1886, U. Glas. · J. Collier, oils, 1904, Balliol Oxf. · D. MacGill, tablet, 1910, U. Glas. · T. Annan, carte-de-visite, NPG · Spy [L. Ward], caricature, chromolithograph, NPG; repro. in *VF* (4 April 1895) · J. Stuart, wood-engraving (after photograph), NPG

Caird, George Bradford (1917–1984), biblical scholar, was born in Springfield, Wandsworth, on 19 July 1917, the youngest of three children and only son of George Caird, an engineer who was from Dundee but was then in London because of war work, and his wife, Esther Love Bradford. The family home was afterwards in Birmingham, where Caird attended King Edward's School (1929–36) and went on to Peterhouse, Cambridge. He took a first class in both parts of the classical tripos (1938 and 1939), with distinction in Greek and Latin verse. From Cambridge he went on to study for the Congregational ministry at Mansfield College, Oxford (1939–43), and at the same time did postgraduate research, for which he gained the degree of DPhil in 1944. From 1943 to 1946 he was minister of Highgate Congregational Church in London, and the instincts and styles of the preacher remained with him throughout his life. In 1945 he married Viola Mary (Mollie), daughter of Ezra Benjamin Newport, schoolmaster, of Reigate, and, after their move to Canada which soon followed, they had three sons (one of whom was John Caird, the theatre director) and one daughter. Caird never tired of talking of his children, all of whom came to be professionally noted, and of his grandchildren.

George Bradford Caird (1917–1984), by unknown photographer

Caird's career specifically as an academic scholar of the Bible began when he went to St Stephen's College, Edmonton, Alberta, an institution of the United Church of Canada, to teach Old Testament (1946–50). In 1950 he became the first professor of New Testament in the newly formed faculty of divinity at McGill University, Montreal, and he stayed there until 1959; in addition he was (1955–9) principal of the theological college of the United Church in Montreal. He greatly admired the United Church, which fitted well with his spiritual and theological tendencies. But Oxford was his spiritual home, and Mansfield and English Congregationalism drew him back: he became tutor in theology at Mansfield in 1959 and principal in 1970. His academic duties were complemented by service to the church: he was an observer at the Second Vatican Council and in 1975–6 was moderator of the general assembly of the recently formed United Reformed church.

In Oxford theology Caird's comprehensiveness of

scope, command of language and evidence, and deep theological emphasis, combined with his excellence as a lecturer, quickly established him as a central figure. He was appointed to a readership in 1969, and in 1977 became Dean Ireland's professor of the exegesis of holy scripture, a position which carried with it a professorial fellowship at Queen's College. As the senior person in New Testament studies in Oxford, Caird exercised a deep influence and was greatly admired by many of those who heard him.

Caird's books included: *The Truth of the Gospel* (1950), a general account of the whole range of Christian doctrine; a commentary on the books of Samuel in *The Interpreter's Bible* (1953); *The Apostolic Age* (1955); *Principalities and Powers* (1956); commentaries on St Luke (1963), on Revelation (1966), on Paul's letters from prison (1976); and *The Language and Imagery of the Bible* (1980), which received wide notice and was awarded the Collins Religious Book award in 1982. At the time of his death he was preparing a theology of the New Testament, which was afterwards completed by one of his pupils, L. D. Hurst, and published as *New Testament Theology* (1994). In addition, a volume of essays, intended as a Festschrift but appearing, sadly, as a memorial volume, was *The glory of Christ in the New Testament: studies in Christology in memory of George Bradford Caird*, edited by L. D. Hurst and N. T. Wright (1987). Among other scholarly achievements may be mentioned his work on the Septuagint—he was Grinfield lecturer on the Septuagint at Oxford for four years from 1961; his work as joint editor of the *Journal of Theological Studies*, from 1978; and his interest in biblical translation, as shown by his warm support for the *New English Bible*, for which he served on the Apocrypha panel from 1961.

Caird's academic distinction was recognized by honorary doctorates of divinity from St Stephen's College, Edmonton (1959), the diocesan (Anglican) college in Montreal (1959), and Aberdeen University (1966). In 1966 he also gained Oxford's own doctorate of divinity. In 1973 he was elected a fellow of the British Academy.

Caird's thinking combined a moderate criticism, a somewhat conservative theological position, and a strong sense for linguistic nuances and literary values. His handling of the Bible followed critical lines but rejected scepticism; he was judicious and fair but also quite combative in controversy, and his opposition to the work of Rudolf Bultmann was marked. He greatly emphasized the historical Jesus, while denying that the quest for him would lead away from theological values. Biblical authority was central in all his thinking, yet he completely rejected the fundamentalist understanding of scripture. Religion for him filled the whole of life and affected attitudes to sickness and health, life and death, peace and war (he was a committed pacifist), and such matters as the situation in South Africa. He particularly stressed the element of metaphor and myth in human talk about the divine, and thought that much distortion had arisen because interpreters had taken as literal expressions that were meant from the beginning to be literary figures.

Music was important to Caird, and he wrote several hymns, some of which were included in standard hymnals. Precision in language was central to his personality; he relaxed in joy among family and friends. In the year in which he would have retired from his chair, he suddenly died in his home, Brook Cottage, Bassett Road, Letcombe Regis, Oxfordshire, on 21 April 1984. He was survived by his wife. JAMES BARR, *rev.*

Sources J. Barr, 'George Bradford Caird, 1917–1984', *PBA*, 71 (1985), 493–521 · D. A. Sykes and H. Chadwick, *Mansfield College Magazine*, 186, 48–9, 50–54 · private information (1990) · *CGPLA Eng. & Wales* (1984)

Likenesses photograph, British Academy [*see illus.*]

Wealth at death under £40,000: probate, 25 July 1984, *CGPLA Eng. & Wales*

Caird, Sir James (1816–1892), agriculturist and writer, was the third son of James Caird of Stranraer, solicitor and procurator fiscal for Wigtownshire, and Isabella, daughter of Archibald McNeel of Stranraer. He was born at Stranraer on 10 June 1816, and was educated at the burgh school and Edinburgh high school. He entered Edinburgh University, but left after about a year without taking a degree and went to Northumberland to learn practical farming. After some twelve months in Northumberland he took over the management of a farm near Stranraer belonging to his uncle, Alexander McNeel, and also assisted in his uncle's law and banking business. In 1841 he took the lease of a farm at Baldoon on the earl of Galloway's estate near Wigtown, where he remained until 1860. He married Margaret, the only child of Captain John Henryson RE, on 15 February 1843; she died in 1863, having borne four sons and four daughters. On 6 April 1865 he married a forty-year-old widow, Elizabeth Jane Dickson, the daughter of Robert Dudgeon of Cleveland Square, London.

An ardent free-trader, Caird first attracted public notice in the controversy over the repeal of the corn laws. In 1849 he published a pamphlet, *High Farming under Liberal Covenants, the Best Substitute for Protection*, a study based on his own experience, to show that good farmers need have no fear of free trade. The work was widely read and ran into eight editions. Caird argued that the farmer's answer to the lower grain prices brought about by free trade was to produce more green crops for feeding dairy cows and fattening bullocks and sheep, as dairy produce and meat were less subject to foreign competition and benefited from the rising demand of increasing numbers of urban consumers. What he termed 'high farming' involved heavy applications of fertilizer to produce the higher yields that he had achieved on his own farm; it depended also on the landlord's provision of drainage and adequate buildings, so that the farmer could ascertain the most profitable combination of crops and livestock for his land.

The success of the pamphlet brought Caird to the notice of Peel, who in 1849 commissioned him to report on conditions in Ireland, then still recovering from the famine.

Sir James Caird (1816–1892), by Vincent Brooks, Day & Son, pubd 1881

Caird's report was subsequently enlarged into a book, *The Plantation System, or, The West of Ireland as a Field for Investment* (1850). This also made a considerable impression and encouraged interest in Irish land reform, resulting in substantial new investment there of English capital.

Following quickly on these two influential publications, Caird was engaged by *The Times* to carry out a systematic inquiry into the state of English agriculture, then depressed by the fall in grain prices which had occurred since 1846. Although Henry Colman had included a large section on England in his *European Agriculture and Rural Oeconomy from Personal Observation* (1846), Caird's investigation, published as a series of 'letters' in *The Times*, attracted much greater attention. His reports, covering the majority of English counties, appeared in 1852 as *English Agriculture in 1850–51* (repr. 1968). The work was also published in the United States, and was translated into French, German, and Swedish. Caird's background as a practical Scottish farmer enabled him to take a critical, independent view of English practices, and he was not afraid to express his conclusions in forthright terms. He noted many examples of inefficient farming as well as of advanced methods, and he also remarked that western pastoral districts were more profitable and produced higher rents than eastern arable ones. In particular, he attacked the landowners for failing to provide their tenants with adequate buildings, subsoil drainage, and long leases, and he advocated means of cheapening the transfer of land in order to permit the sale of encumbered estates to owners who had the resources to improve them with new investment.

In 1852, his name now very well known, Caird contested the parliamentary seat of the Wigtown burghs as a liberal conservative. He lost by the margin of only one vote, but was returned five years later for Dartmouth. In parliament he supported Lord Palmerston and was opposed to intervention in continental wars. His first speech, on 21 July 1857, was on his motion for leave to bring in a bill for the collection of agricultural statistics. This matter was one which had been discussed in parliament since 1835 but had always been put aside because of the difficulty of finding a suitable agency for the purpose. In 1854 statistics had been collected as an experiment in eleven counties, but no permanent organization had resulted. Caird pursued this question assiduously for his first nine years in parliament, and in 1865 a severe outbreak of rinderpest, together with the government policy of compulsory slaughter of infected cattle, drew attention to the importance of having reliable information on agricultural matters. It was agreed that statistics should be collected by the Inland Revenue and published by the Board of Trade, and the first complete agricultural statistics for Great Britain were collected in 1866.

In 1858 Caird made an extensive tour of Canada and the United States, and in 1859 he published the notes of his journey as *Prairie Farming in America, with Notes by the Way on Canada and the United States*. His observations on Canada provoked resentment there and gave rise to a pamphlet, published in Toronto, *Caird's Slanders on Canada Answered and Refuted* (1859). In his book Caird took the opportunity of emphasizing the advantages of emigration to British farmers. The United States, he pointed out, was now only a fortnight's journey away, and there, by contrast with Britain, the farmer could have his own land and reap the capital gains available from more intensive settlement and rising land values. At home, on the other hand, farmers faced rising rents and the uncertainties of foreign competition, which went far to offset the advantages of climate, field sports, and life under the British constitution.

In 1859, having opposed the government on its Conspiracy Bill and also on a bill for parliamentary reform, and having alienated his conservative English constituents by proposing a bill to assimilate the county franchise of Scotland to that of England, Caird decided not to contest his Dartmouth seat again. Instead, he stood for the Stirling burghs and was returned unopposed. He claimed support as a 'consistent Liberal' for proposing measures to reduce the cost of land transfer and for more economical administration of the Office of Woods and Forests. In 1860, after taking a prominent part in debates on the national fisheries, he was made a member of the fishery board. In that year he also relinquished his tenancy of Baldoon and bought the estate of Cassencarie (now Castle Cary), Creetown, which then became his home. In 1863 Caird became chairman of a royal commission to inquire into the conditions of the sea fisheries, and spent much time visiting eighty-six of the more important fishing ports. The commission's report of 1866 proved influential in subsequent legislation on the subject.

After the outbreak of the American Civil War in 1861 the growing scarcity of cotton led Caird to look for alternative sources of supply. In July 1863 he moved for a select committee to inquire into the possibility of increasing cotton imports from India, a motion supported by John Bright and Richard Cobden. The motion failed, but his initiative created a long-lasting friendship between Bright and Caird. Undeterred by the rebuff, Caird visited Algeria, Italy, and Sicily to ascertain their capacity for growing cotton, and for the remainder of his parliamentary career he continued to speak on subjects connected with agriculture, and occasionally on India and Ireland.

In June 1865 Caird vacated his parliamentary seat on his appointment as a member of the inclosure commission. This body was responsible for supervising the enclosure of land under the General Inclosure Act of 1845, and Caird remained in land administration for the rest of his life. The inclosure commission was renamed the land commission in 1882, and when in 1889 it became the land department of the newly formed Board of Agriculture, Caird became its director; he was in the same year sworn of the privy council. He remained active as a prominent member of the Royal Agricultural Society of England and of the Statistical Society, becoming president of the latter body in 1880. He published numerous articles in the journals of these societies, as well as pamphlets on food, American farming, the Irish land question, and India, where he had gone as a member of the commission appointed to inquire into the causes of the great Indian famine of 1876–7. He was appointed CB in 1869, and KCB in 1882, and was elected a fellow of the Royal Society in 1875.

As president of the economic section of the Social Science Congress held at Aberdeen in 1877 Caird gave an address entitled 'Food supply and the land question'. He developed this subject for an international agricultural congress held in Paris in the following year, and subsequently published it in both English and French as a book entitled *The Landed Interest and the Supply of Food* (1878). This work was in part a reflective sequel to his *High Farming* and *English Agriculture* of a quarter-century earlier.

Caird's extensive journeys in India in 1878–9 as a member of the famine commission resulted in accounts of his experiences which were published in *Nineteenth Century* in 1879. In 1884 these articles were published in an extended form as *India, the Land and the People*, which ran through three editions. In 1887 he contributed a review of the development of English farming since 1837 to a volume edited by T. H. Ward, *The Reign of Queen Victoria*. He subsequently revised this essay for the *Journal of the Royal Agricultural Society* of England on the occasion of the society's jubilee in 1890. His last contribution to the journal was in 1891, 'On the cost of wheat growing'. Meanwhile, he had received the honorary degree of LLD from the University of Edinburgh in its tercentenary year, 1884. He retired from the Board of Agriculture in December 1891, and died suddenly at his London home at 8 Queen's Gate Gardens on 9 February 1892.

Caird's approach to agricultural questions was always a practical one, for his own experience of farming continued after he gave up his Scottish farm, when he took an interest in a farm in the home counties managed by his son. He saw that the prosperity of British farming was bound up with the success of the British economy, and he believed that efficient farmers could survive the effects of mounting food imports by adapting to the changing character of the home market. He was critical of English landlords, however, believing them to be slow in helping their tenants with necessary land improvements and, particularly, in preferring customary 'tenant right' to the greater security provided by long leases. He saw farming as a business, and was always conscious of the importance of making the best use of the land. It was to this end that he campaigned for the collection of agricultural statistics and the cheaper transfer of land, and that his agricultural writings and his career in land administration were devoted.

G. E. Mingay

Sources C. S. Orwin and E. H. Whetham, *History of British agriculture, 1846–1914* (1964) • J. H. Clapham, *Economic history of modern Britain*, 2 (1932) • R. E. Prothero, *English farming past and present*, ed. D. Hall, 6th edn (1961) • G. E. Mingay, introduction, in J. Caird, *English agriculture in 1850–51*, 2nd edn (1968) • *Hansard 3* (1857–9), vols. 145–52 • *The Times* (11 Feb 1892) • b. cert. • m. cert. • index to old parochial registers of Scotland, NL Scot.

Archives BL OIOC, home misc. series, corresp. and papers relating to Indian famine commission | BL, letters to W. E. Gladstone, Add. MSS 44394–44497, *passim* • W. Sussex RO, corresp. with Richard Cobden

Likenesses V. Brooks, Day & Son, engraving, NPG; repro. in *Country Gentleman* (13 Aug 1881) [*see illus.*] • Tweedie, oils, Castle Cary, Creeton, Kirkcudbrightshire • photograph, NPG; repro. in *Review of Reviews* (1892?) • photogravure, Reform Club, Pall Mall, London, archives

Wealth at death £44,328 10s. 3d. in UK: probate, 12 April 1892, *CGPLA Eng. & Wales*

Caird, Sir James, of Glenfarquhar, baronet (1864–1954), shipowner, was born in Glasgow on 2 January 1864, the elder son in a family of six of James Caird, lawyer, and his wife, Mary Ann Hutcheson. Educated at Glasgow Academy, he joined the firm of William Graham & Co., East India merchants, in 1878. Eleven years later he went to London and in 1890 joined Turnbull, Martin & Co., managers of the Scottish Shire Line of steamships. By hard work and enterprise he prospered, and in twelve months was made manager. By 1903 he was sole partner and owner of the Scottish Shire Line, and in co-operation with the Houlder and Federal Lines he opened up the trade between the United Kingdom and the Antipodes. Early in 1916 he started a new shipyard at Chepstow to build standard ships quickly where enemy attacks could not interfere with production.

Overcoming immense difficulties, the venture succeeded so well that in 1917 the government stepped in and bought out Caird and his associates. Foreseeing the slump in shipping which would follow the end of the First World War, Caird in the same year sold to the Clan Line his interest in the Shire Line, and in Turnbull, Martin & Co. He remained a director of some twenty-five companies connected with shipping, shipbuilding, ship repairing, and allied industries, as well as being chairman of the Smithfield and Argentine Meat Company, in which he held a large block of founders' shares.

By then Caird was a comparatively rich man, and from the early 1920s he devoted a large part of his fortune to preserving British naval and shipping memorials, to which he became passionately devoted. In association with the Society for Nautical Research he provided most of the money needed to repair and restore HMS *Victory* (Nelson's flagship at Trafalgar, berthed at Portsmouth) with an initial sum of £50,000 to start the work and a further £15,000 to enable it to continue. In 1927 steps were being taken to found a national museum of the sea, a venture to which Caird gave his wholehearted and energetic support. Under the chairmanship of the seventh Earl Stanhope, and in association with the honorary secretary, Geoffrey Callender, of the Society for Nautical Research, a board of trustees, of whom Caird was one, was set up to found the new museum. The realization of this project became possible when the Royal Hospital school moved to Holbrook and the old school buildings at Greenwich, including the Queen's House, became vacant. Caird then guaranteed to meet the whole cost (amounting eventually to over £80,000) of converting the buildings. In addition, he began purchasing every available collection or individual item of maritime historical interest, including rare books, globes, atlases, instruments, and manuscripts. The Macpherson collection of sea pictures and the *Mercury* collection of ships' models were secured, and to these he added his own collections. During the second reading of the National Maritime Museum Bill in the House of Commons in June 1934 it was stated that the collections Caird had already offered to the nation were worth more than £300,000.

The new museum was opened by King George VI in April 1937 and Caird continued his never-flagging interest and support. In all, he gave more than £1.25 million to the museum. His account of the inception of the National Maritime Museum was published in *Syren and Shipping* (2 January 1935), under the title 'A museum in the making'. To the last, when he became too ill to take an active part, he continued to shower his gifts upon it. His name is perpetuated in the Caird Library and the Caird Entrance. A Caird medal has been awarded annually since 1984. The Caird Fund makes grants for maritime research and finances Caird fellowships. Nor were the museum and HMS *Victory* alone in benefiting from his generosity. The historic 74-gun ship of the line HMS *Implacable* (the last survivor of the enemy ships that fought at Trafalgar) was also saved by him in the years between the wars. She was sunk with naval honours in 1949, her timbers having deteriorated beyond repair. To museums and art galleries in his native Scotland he was a generous benefactor; and in the Second World War he provided the cost of a complete ambulance unit. To his parish church, St Mary's, Wimbledon, his gifts included a house for the curate and money for the new church spire.

Caird was stocky in stature, tough and wiry, with immense energy, a shrewd expression, a merry twinkle in his eye, and a delightful Scots voice. He was the kindliest of men, generous almost to a fault, but never making a show of his benefactions, shrouding his greatest gifts in secrecy, and never seeking any reward. He nevertheless loved to drive a hard bargain and could not bear to be 'had'; but he was always scrupulously fair and often gave more than was asked when he thought the seller might be in need, or even that a dealer was not taking sufficient profit.

Until his illness in 1949 Caird continued to attend his office in the City daily. He was extremely alert and had an excellent memory. He celebrated his eightieth birthday at his home in Scotland by bringing down a 'royal' after a long day's stalk, which many a younger man would have given up. It was this wonderful vitality and his simple way of living which endeared him so much to all around him at Glenfarquhar, Fordoun, where he dispensed quiet yet generous hospitality in which gillies, keepers, shepherds, and guests shared alike.

In 1928 Caird was created a baronet; and after the opening of the new museum in 1937 the prime minister wanted to submit his name for a peerage, but Caird refused, saying that he did not want reward for what he had done or for what he had given to the nation.

Caird married in 1894 Henrietta Anna (*d.* 1953), daughter of William Henry Stephens, architect, of Ardshane, Holywood, co. Down. They had one daughter but no son and on Caird's death at his home, Well House, Arthur Road, Wimbledon, Surrey, on 27 September 1954, the baronetcy became extinct.

F. G. G. CARR, *rev.* ANN SAVOURS

Sources J. Caird, 'A museum in the making', *Syren and Shipping* (2 Jan 1935) • private information (1971) • personal knowledge (1971) • G. P. B. Naish, *Forging ahead: an account of the work and aims of the Society for Nautical Research* (1948) • *National Maritime Museum catalogue* (1937) • *National Maritime Museum guide* (1947) • staff circular, NMM, HDP 17/72 • list of papers of the Society for Nautical Research held in MSS collection, April 1986, NMM

Archives NMM | NMM, Society for Nautical Research MSS, largely corresp. with Callender

Likenesses W. R. Dick, marble bust, 1937, NMM • photograph, NMM • photograph, repro. in Caird, 'Museum in the making'

Wealth at death £1,418,715 16*s.* 3*d.*: probate, 23 Oct 1954, *CGPLA Eng. & Wales*

Caird, Sir James Key, baronet (1837–1916), jute manufacturer and benefactor, was born on 7 January 1837, the eldest son of the five children of Edward Caird (1806–1889), linen manufacturer of Dundee, and his wife, Mary, *née* Key (*c.*1806–1843). Edward Caird had founded the business of Caird and Renny, later Caird & Co., linen merchants and manufacturers, and in 1832 he established the Ashton Jute Works at Hawkshill, Dundee. James is first recorded in connection with this factory in 1864, at which time it was operating 208 power looms, and employed some 350 people. About 1868, Edward retired to Finnart, Dunbartonshire, leaving James in control of a flourishing business, at a time of rising prosperity in the linen and jute trades. The opening up of the colonies created enormous demand for coarse canvas for tents and temporary housing, and for bags and sacks to transport produce. The Ashton works was rebuilt in 1876, and extended in 1887, and again in 1906–8. In addition, Caird & Co. purchased Craigie Mill, Arbroath Road, Dundee, in 1905. While not the largest in the Dundee area, Caird's mills were said to be the best equipped, and he was acknowledged locally as a technical innovator and an effective and benevolent manager. By the time of his death Caird was employing 2000 workers.

On 16 July 1873 Caird married Sophie (1844/5–1882), daughter of George Gray, a solicitor and banker of Bowerswell, Perthshire, and his wife, Sophia Margaret, *née* Jameson. Their one daughter died in early life, and Caird's wife died in 1882. He became a generous benefactor, his gifts totalling about £250,000, the greater part of this bestowed on the people of Dundee. His great interest in medical provision in the city was manifested in gifts to Dundee Royal Infirmary to found a women's and children's ward (1897) and an outpatient department (1909). In addition, he provided money for the foundation of a cancer hospital (1902) and the Springrove Home for Old Men (1911), and his donation of £5000 kept the Sidlaw Sanatorium open. He purchased Dens of Mains and adjacent land in 1912 and 1913 to be enjoyed as a public park, later named after him. He was created a baronet in the new year honours of 1913, and received the honorary degree of LLD from the University of St Andrews. He did not live to see the outcome of his largest donation, a gift of £100,000 in 1914 for the building of a new city hall in Dundee. George V laid the foundation stone in 1914, but construction was interrupted by war and it was opened by the prince of Wales on 11 December 1922. Sir James had a long-standing interest in science and was a life member of the British Association for the Advancement of Science (BAAS) from 1861. When the BAAS met in Dundee in 1867 he spoke on 'an iron comb for power looms'. When the association again met at Dundee in 1912 he made an unconditional gift of £10,000, which was distributed by the council to various worthy scientific projects. In 1913 he gave a further £1000 to be devoted to the study of radioactivity. £1000 went to the London Zoological Society, of which he was a member, for a new insect house, and the Royal Society received £5000 for physical research. As a known benefactor, he was approached in 1914 by Edward Shackleton, who was seeking support for his Antarctic expedition. Caird, who was a linguist and well-travelled, had no interest in polar exploration, but was impressed by Shackleton's determined search for financial backing. A few days after their meeting he sent a cheque for £24,000 with no conditions attached, expressing the hope that other wealthy backers would follow suit. The Caird coast, Weddell Sea, was named in his honour, as was the whaler in which Shackleton sailed from Elephant Island in Antarctica to South Georgia to obtain help for the stranded expedition.

In later life Caird was a recluse, playing no part in civic or public life. A well-built man, he wore a moustache and beard, somewhat in the manner of King Edward VII. He died on 9 March 1916 at his home, Belmont Castle, Meigle, Perthshire, and was buried at Dean cemetery, Edinburgh. His only close surviving relative was an elder sister, Mary Ann Maryat, who continued his benevolent work.

GRAHAM KING

Sources *Dundee Yearbook* (1916) • census returns for the Dundee area, 1841, 1851, 1861, 1871, 1881, 1891 • *Dundee Yearbook* (1837–8) • *Dundee Yearbook* (1842–3) • *Dundee Yearbook* (1845) • *Dundee Yearbook* (1846–7) • *Dundee Yearbook* (1850) • *Dundee Yearbook* (1853–4) • *Dundee Yearbook* (1856–7) • *Dundee Yearbook* (1858–9) • *Dundee Yearbook* (1864–5) • *Dundee Yearbook* (1867–8) • *Dundee Yearbook* (1869–70) • *Dundee Yearbook* (1872) • *Dundee Yearbook* (1874–5) • *Dundee Yearbook* (1876–1916), *passim* • *WWW*, 1916–28 • M. Watson, *Jute and flax mills of Dundee* (1990) • *The Times* (11 March 1916), 9b • *Report of the British Association for the Advancement of Science* (1917), xxiv • R. Huntford, *Shackleton* (1985), 376 • d. cert. • m. cert. • *CCI* (1916) • Burke, *Peerage*
Archives City of Dundee Museum and Art Galleries, principally Egyptology • Dundee City Archive and Record Centre, material relating to city buildings and Caird Hall | Dundee Central Library, papers, primarily relating to his sister Mrs Maryat
Likenesses D. Foggie, oils, *c*.1912, Caird Hall, Dundee
Wealth at death £751,989 3*s*. 5*d*.: confirmation, 26 July 1916, *CCI*

Caird, John (1820–1898), Church of Scotland minister, theologian, and university principal, was born on 15 December 1820 in Greenock, the eldest of seven sons of John Caird (*d*. 1838), marine engineer, and Janet Young (*d*. 1889) of Port Glasgow. His younger brother Edward *Caird (1835–1908), philosopher, became master of Balliol College, Oxford. John was educated at the Greenock grammar school until the age of fifteen, when he went to work in the office of his father's engineering firm. At his earnest request, his father allowed him to attend classes in mathematics and logic at Glasgow University in 1837–8, after which he returned to work in the family firm. In September 1838 his father died suddenly, and his firm was sold. Caird took a position in an uncle's chain-making firm, but, freed from the expectation that he would follow his father in business, he decided on a career in the ministry. He returned to Glasgow University in 1840 and proceeded through the arts and divinity curricula, gaining prizes in poetry, Hebrew, and Latin, and demonstrating a capacity for steady, orderly work. He graduated MA in 1845. In the same year he was licensed as a probationary minister in the Church of Scotland by the presbytery of Glasgow, and was ordained to the ministry of the parish of Newton upon Ayr on 18 September 1845.

Caird's talents were soon recognized, and on 6 May 1847 he was translated to the Edinburgh parish of Lady Yester's. There he experienced an extraordinary rise to fame as a vehement preacher of a practical, non-dogmatic religion. He had an arresting presence in the pulpit, with a slight physique, long, black hair, swarthy complexion, dark eyes, and powerful voice. For the young he held a particular fascination, and students were prominent among the crowds that packed into the church Sunday after Sunday. As one admirer later recalled, 'the fire of the eye, the rapidity of the gestures, the resonance of the voice, the sacred passion of the orator, were not to be withstood' (Caird, xlviii). The Church of Scotland, which had lost nearly half its membership and its most zealous clergymen at the Disruption of 1843, was in need of fresh talent, and many

John Caird (1820–1898), by Thomas Annan, pubd 1871

looked to Caird as a revitalizing force. Others, however, were less enthusiastic. Complaints about him spread: his doctrine, some said, was unsound; he placed too much emphasis on worldly morality; he did not preach Christ. The criticisms became too much for the sensitive young man, still in his twenties. In a state of emotional turmoil and physical exhaustion, Caird decided to withdraw from Edinburgh. In July 1849 he became minister of the quiet Perthshire parish of Errol.

Caird devoted himself to the ministry of his rural parish. He invested considerable effort in writing his sermons, striving for greater clarity of expression. He worked to enhance the beauty of worship and he founded a school for girls of the labouring classes. He avoided ecclesiastical politics and seldom attended presbytery meetings. He read widely, giving particular attention to the work of Thomas Carlyle, John Ruskin, the Oxford Tractarians, and German theologians, especially Schleiermacher. Above all, he recovered his emotional equilibrium. In 1855 he was again drawn to the public notice, when in October he preached before Queen Victoria at Balmoral. With eloquence and power, Caird proclaimed the unity and sanctity of all life, insisted that Christianity must infuse the business of this world, and summoned Christians to quiet, earnest labour under the shadow of eternity. Deeply moved—she wrote it was 'a most admirable and beautiful sermon … which kept one's attention riveted' (Victoria, 155)—the queen commanded that the sermon be published. Entitled *Religion in Common Life*, it went through several editions and was later described by A. P. Stanley, dean of Westminster Abbey, as 'the best single sermon in the language' (Caird, xxxii). On 7 December 1857 Victoria appointed Caird one of her chaplains-in-ordinary in Scotland, which he continued until 1856.

Caird had by now decided to return to an urban pastorate. On receiving offers to become minister of both the new Park Church in Glasgow and St George's Church in Edinburgh, he accepted the Park Church, and was translated there on 24 December 1857. As in Edinburgh in the late 1840s, his preaching in Glasgow attracted huge crowds. He was, however, now better prepared to confront controversy. His youthful vehemence had grown into a more restrained eloquence, a chastened, mature understanding of the world, and a deepened compassion for human suffering and frailty. Contributing to his increased confidence and self-control was his marriage, on 15 June 1858, to Isabella Riddle Glover (1832–1913), daughter of William Glover, minister of Greenside parish, Edinburgh. The marriage—there were no children—was a long and happy one.

During his years at the Park Church, Caird emerged as one of the leading figures in the broad-church movement in Scotland, a movement that contributed much to the mid-Victorian revival of the Church of Scotland. His preaching was characterized by a belief in the essential reasonableness of Christianity, a focus on the person of Jesus, a concentration on practical Christian morality over doctrinal distinctions, and a confidence that Christianity had nothing to fear from developments in science and historical scholarship. He was committed to liturgical reform, including the revival of ancient liturgies, and he worked to bring greater simplicity, reverence, and beauty to public worship. His social ethic included concern to improve conditions for the labouring classes. He recruited voluntary workers from his Park congregation for mission work in an impoverished urban district. Near the end of his life, when told that the Glasgow city council had refused to open a public park to working people on Sundays, he responded with characteristic emotion. 'Could they not', he asked, 'offer them *this* brief refuge from the wretchedness of their narrow and crowded and noisy and too often fireless hearths? Oh! the prejudice and bigotry of men!' (Jones, 12).

In 1860 the University of Glasgow awarded Caird a DD. In 1862 he was appointed professor of divinity at the University of Glasgow, and left the parish ministry. He approached his new position with some apprehension, suspecting rightly that his lectures would be scrutinized critically by those who adhered strictly to orthodox doctrinal standards. Caird devoted the same meticulous care to preparing his theological lectures as he did to his sermons. As a teacher, he endeavoured to promote a spirit of enquiry; he was concerned less to provide students with a set of doctrinal propositions to be accepted on authority, and more to give them principles which might guide their honest exploration of the Christian faith. Deeply influenced by the thought of Hegel, Caird placed emphasis on the progressive unfolding of Christian truth. Together with his brother Edward, professor of moral philosophy at Glasgow University from 1866 to 1893, Caird was a leading force in promoting Hegelian idealism in Scotland. He also championed religious toleration. He refused to censure unbelief as a moral or intellectual fault; rather, he emphasized the consolations and joys of the Christian faith as positive gifts which Christians should treasure and share with others. In 1866 he helped make it possible for students from nonconformist seminaries to gain a University of Glasgow BD through examination. In 1868 he successfully proposed that a Glasgow DD be conferred upon the eminent Scottish theologian John Macleod Campbell, who in 1831 had been deposed from the ministry of the Church of Scotland for heresy. In 1871 he helped to revive regular university chapel services, and invited members of different denominations to preach. He was, his brother later recalled, 'almost indifferent to the causes of disagreement between the main denominations into which the Christian church is divided' (Caird, xcvii).

When the principalship of Glasgow University became vacant early in 1873, the university senate unanimously petitioned the queen to appoint Caird to the vacancy, which she did on 7 March 1873. He immersed himself in the practical work of administering the university, providing steady academic leadership during a period that witnessed the appointment of a universities commission in 1876, the University Act of 1889, and the radical reorganization of the university system. He also campaigned publicly for extending full university privileges to women. In addition to his demanding administrative workload, he continued to preach several times each session in the university chapel and to address the students at the opening of each session. In 1880 he published his first major work, the *Introduction to the Philosophy of Religion*, based on the Croall lectures he delivered in Edinburgh. In 1888 he published a brief study of the ethics of Spinoza. He returned to the subject of theism with his Gifford lectures, which he delivered in 1890–91 and in 1896. They were published posthumously as *The Fundamental Ideas of Christianity* in 1899. These mature works were infused by Hegelian idealism and, while not original in their argument, they expressed Caird's characteristic commitment to a reasonable, inclusive Christianity. Caird suffered a stroke in 1896, and became seriously ill again in February 1898. He died of 'inflammatory illness' (probably pleurisy) on 30 July 1898 at his brother Colin's house, Dungourney, Newark Street, Greenock, and was buried in Greenock cemetery on 3 August. A liberal protestant, Caird was pre-eminently a preacher of a confident, consoling Christian faith, prepared to respond creatively to the challenges and opportunities of a progressive age.

STEWART J. BROWN

Sources E. Caird, 'Memoir of Principal Caird', in J. Caird, *The fundamental ideas of Christianity*, 2 vols. (1899), ix–cxli • C. L. Warr, *Principal Caird* (1926) • A. C. Cheyne, 'John Caird (1820–98): preacher, professor, principal', *Studies in Scottish church history* (1999), 165–83 • A. P. F. Sell, 'John Caird (1820–1898): apostle of continuity', *Defending and declaring the faith: some Scottish examples, 1860–1920* (1987), 64–88 • H. Jones, *Principal Caird: an address* (1898) • *Fasti Scot.*, new edn • Boase, *Mod. Eng. biog.* • W. I. Addison, *A roll of graduates of the University of Glasgow from 31st December 1727 to 31st December 1897* (1898) • Queen Victoria, *Leaves from the journal of our life in the highlands, from 1848 to 1861*, ed. A. Helps (1868)

Archives NL Scot., corresp. with Blackwoods • NL Scot., notes of sermons; scattered letters | Bodl. Oxf., letters to Gilbert Murray • U. Glas., corresp. and MSS relating to his principalship • U. Glas. L., special collections department, divinity lectures; letters; MS sermon

Likenesses T. Annan, photograph, pubd 1871, NPG [*see illus.*] • W. and T. Bonner, engraving, 1873 (after W. Bonner), Scot. NPG • J. E. Millais, oils, exh. RA 1881, U. Glas.

Wealth at death £11,604 7*s*. 3*d*.: confirmation, 22 Oct 1898, *CCI*

Caird [*née* Alison], **(Alice) Mona** (**1854–1932**), writer, was born on 24 May 1854 at 34 Pier Street, Ryde, Isle of Wight, to John Alison, an inventor from Midlothian, and Matilda Ann Jane, *née* Hector. As a child she wrote plays and stories. It seems that she spent part of her childhood in Australia and she uses this experience in her first novel, *Aunt Hetty*, published anonymously in 1877. On 19 December 1877 she married James Alexander Caird (*d.* 1921), son of Sir James Caird, at Christ Church, Paddington, London. The couple resided at Leyland, Arkwright Road, Hampstead, London, for the remainder of their forty-four-year marriage. Their only child, Alison James Caird, was born at Leyland on 22 March 1884.

At the beginning of her writing career, Caird briefly used the pseudonym G. Noel Hatton, but of the five novels she published between 1883 and 1915, *The Wings of Azrael* (1889), *A Romance of the Moors* (1891), and *The Daughters of Danaus* (1894; repr. 1989), published under her own name, have received the most attention from literary critics. In *A Romance of the Moors* she tells the story of Dick Coverdale and his lover, Bessie Saunders. The plot's catalyst involves Dick's meeting Mrs Margaret Ellwood, a widowed London artist who has lost her way on the moor, who introduces the two young people to the idea of independence. She advises Dick and Bessie to reject the traditional ideas about marriage and to marry when they are mature and able to act reasonably and responsibly. In the end Mrs Ellwood encourages Bessie to return to London with her where she can 'form other interests; that will bring [her] nearer to Dick, not take [her] farther away from him'. While this novel indicates that women's liberation can sometimes be accomplished peacefully, in *The Wings of Azrael* Caird has the main character, Victoria Sedley, murder her husband Philip to end a violent marriage. She escapes into the wilderness to avoid prosecution and she must reject her long-time lover, Harry Lancaster, to save him from a destructive association with her. The ideas expressed in these two novels, while poles apart in tone and action, reflect the positions on women's lives which Caird espoused in her non-fictional tracts and essays as well.

In 1897 Caird collected essays which previously had been published in the *North American Review*, the *Westminster Review*, the *Fortnightly Review*, and *Nineteenth Century* for her book *The Morality of Marriage and other Essays on the Status and Destiny of Women*. Her general ideas are focused on equality for women in marriage and for equal partnerships in the home which will 'bring us to the end of the patriarchal system' (*The Morality of Marriage*, 59) which she

(Alice) Mona Caird (1854–1932), by unknown engraver, pubd 1894 (after Hayman Selig Mendelssohn)

described as repressive both for men, who were trained to see only 'the woman's-sphere and woman's-responsibility condition of things' (ibid., 53), and for women, whose 'best qualities … will disappear' (ibid.) if they keep within such a system. Her essays are frequently derisive and she employs irony to make her points about the repressive order of society which cannot separate wives from other types of property. As a progressive thinker, Caird sought legal reforms in childcare and divorce which would improve women's social positions by removing the stigmas of irresponsibility and ignorance. Her views have been the subject of late twentieth-century feminist literary criticism concentrated on how she approached the issue of social change in her fiction and her essays. Her efforts earned her the label of 'feminist' in her lifetime and she has been described by John Sutherland as 'one of the most aggressive of the New Woman novelists' (Sutherland, 99). She was also active in the temperance movement, and was an outspoken antivivisectionist, publishing two works on the subject in 1894 and 1896.

Mona Caird died of colon cancer on 4 February 1932 at 34 Woronzow Road, St John's Wood, London, where she had moved some time after her husband's death. At her death her name is given as Henryson Caird, suggesting that her husband had taken this extra surname some time after their marriage. Her probate record indicates that she owned property, Cassencary, at Creetown, Kirkcudbrightshire, Scotland. BEVERLY E. SCHNELLER

Sources N. L. Manos, 'Caird, Mona Alison', *The 1890s: an encyclopedia of British literature, art, and culture*, ed. G. A. Cevasco (1993) · Allibone, *Dict.* · *New century handbook of English literature* · L. Pykett, 'The cause of women and the course of fiction', *Gender roles and sexuality in Victorian literature*, ed. C. Parker (1995), 128–42 · M. D. Stetz, 'Turning points: Mona Caird' and 'The future of the home', *Turn-of-the-Century*, 2/2 (winter 1985), 2–9 · J. Todd, ed., *British women writers: a critical reference guide* (1989) · Blain, Clements & Grundy, *Feminist comp.* · J. Sutherland, *The Longman companion to Victorian fiction* (1988) · b. cert. · m. cert. · d. cert. · b. cert. [Alison James Caird] · *CGPLA Eng. & Wales* (1932)

Likenesses engraving, pubd 1894 (after H. S. Mendelssohn), NPG [*see illus.*]

Wealth at death £8204 16*s*. 5*d*.: probate, 30 March 1932, *CGPLA Eng. & Wales*

Cairech Dergain (*d.* 577/9). *See under* Connacht, saints of (*act. c.*400–*c.*800).

Cairncross, Alexander (*c.*1637–1701), archbishop of Glasgow, was the son of George Cairncross (*d.* 1667), a dyer burgess of the Canongate, Edinburgh, and his wife, Christian Ogilvie (*d.* 1668). A tradition records that from financial necessity he followed his father's trade, but he graduated MA at Edinburgh on 26 July 1657, and was licensed by the bishop of Edinburgh on 31 October 1662. On 29 April 1663 he was elected to the second charge of Trinity parish, Edinburgh, where he remained, despite a call to Ayton on 13 October 1664, until translated to Dumfries some time before 30 August 1668. Nominated to the see of Brechin on 5 June 1684, at his consecration on about 12 August, Archbishop Alexander Burnet of St Andrews fell ill and died soon afterwards. Archbishop Arthur Ross succeeded Burnet, thereby allowing Cairncross's patron, William Douglas, first duke of Queensberry, to propel him into the vacant archbishopric of Glasgow. He was nominated on 6 December and installed on 25 December 1684.

As a privy councillor from 30 December, Cairncross served dutifully and supported action against presbyterian dissent. In 1685 he seems to have taken possession of a family estate of Balmashannar, Forfarshire. The next January, Ross thwarted Cairncross's intended protest against the first appearance in council of the chancellor, James Drummond, earl of Perth, as a Catholic convert. In February Perth tried to force a reluctant Cairncross to discipline Dr James Canaries for an anti-Catholic sermon, and was infuriated when Canaries later revealed that his archbishop had secretly supported his journey to London, where his sermon was published. With Queensberry's dismissal in February, Cairncross lost his patron, offered little resistance to the repeal of the penal laws, and became isolated during summer 1686 as Perth secured the dismissal of Bishop Bruce of Dunkeld and cowed the other bishops. Slighted by the removal of some responsibility for his archdiocese Cairncross was finally deprived of his see and his council place by royal instruction to the council, dated 13 January 1687.

Cairncross regarded as illegal this use of the prerogative without any stated accusation or canonical process. In March 1689 the convention of estates refused him redress, to the relief of his successor and adversary, John Paterson. Cairncross's potential role as leader of a Williamite episcopate dissolved with the abolition of bishops in July 1689, but even without prospects in Scotland he clung to the style of 'archbishop of Glasgow'. Claiming past rents, he secured £300 from Glasgow. On 22 March 1693, perhaps aided by Bishop Gilbert Burnet or the earl of Drumlanrig, he was nominated to the see of Raphoe, Ireland. He remained concerned for his deprived Scottish brethren and, bequeathing money for their support, on 14 May 1701 he died at Raphoe unmarried, and was buried in his cathedral. TRISTRAM CLARKE

Sources *Historical notices of Scotish affairs, selected from the manuscripts of Sir John Lauder of Fountainhall*, ed. D. Laing, 2 vols., Bannatyne Club, 87 (1848) · R. Keith and J. Spottiswoode, *An historical catalogue of the Scottish bishops, down to the year 1688*, new edn, ed. M. Russel [M. Russell] (1824) · W. L. Mathieson, *Politics and religion: a study in Scottish history from the Reformation to the revolution*, 2 vols. (1902) · G. Grub, *An ecclesiastical history of Scotland*, 4 vols. (1861), vol. 3 · E. B. Fryde and others, eds., *Handbook of British chronology*, 3rd edn, Royal Historical Society Guides and Handbooks, 2 (1986) · *The whole works of Sir James Ware concerning Ireland*, ed. and trans. W. Harris, rev. edn, 2 vols. in 3 (1764) · testimonial for James Williamson, 1691, Glos. RO, D3549/78a/G/19 · inventory of titles of Carnegie of Lour, 1542–1850, NA Scot., NRAS 244, item 48 · [A. F. Cairncross and B. L. Cairncross], *Cairncross: the history of a Scottish family* (privately printed, George, South Africa, 1959) · J. McUre, *A view of the city of Glasgow* (1736) · testament of George Cairncross, 1668, NA Scot., CC8/8/73, pp. 250–51 · *Fasti Scot.*, new edn, 7.324

Wealth at death £20 to parish poor of Raphoe; one tenth of remainder to distressed episcopal clergy in Scotland: *Whole works*, ed. Harris, vol. 1, p. 277

Cairncross, Sir Alexander Kirkland [Alec] (**1911–1998**), economist and public servant, was born on 11 February 1911 at Pine Cottage, Lesmahagow, Lanarkshire, Scotland, the third of four sons and the seventh of eight children of Alexander Kirkland Cairncross (*b.* 1865), draper and ironmonger, and his wife, Elizabeth Andrew Wishart (*b.* 1875), schoolteacher, both of them proudly Scottish. The spy John *Cairncross was his younger brother. He was educated first at Turfholm village school, where the majority of his schoolmates were the children of farmers and miners, and then moved to Hamilton Academy.

Sir Alexander Kirkland Cairncross (1911–1998), by Walter Bird, 1963

Young economist At seventeen Cairncross, holding two bursaries, went to Glasgow University, where he read economics with the vague intention of becoming an accountant. He had discarded this idea by his final year, and after gaining a first and winning a research studentship to Trinity College, Cambridge, in 1932, he went south. His three years at Cambridge were spent among giants of economics—J. M. Keynes, A. C. Pigou, Joan Robinson, Austin Robinson, Dennis Robertson, James Meade, and Richard Kahn—and he was a member of the Keynes 'circus'. Upon his departure in 1935 he was awarded only the second PhD in economics at Cambridge. His thesis, 'British home and foreign investment, 1870–1913', was not published until 1953, but it then rapidly became a classic in the field and earned Cairncross a satisfactory royalty income for many years.

In 1935 Cairncross returned to Glasgow University as a lecturer in economics, and this position, together with an additional lectureship at the West of Scotland Agricultural College, gave him a total annual income of nearly £600. This, he later noted, provided him with greater affluence than he enjoyed at any other period of his life. He worked for it, lecturing for up to seventeen hours a week and marking each year several hundred examination scripts and essays. A particular trial was teaching the principles of economics in forty lectures over ten weeks to classes of trainee accountants, who stumbled in at the end of long working days. Their exhaustion prevented many of them from understanding or even listening to his lectures, and in desperation he began to hand out one-page summaries of the points to be made in each lecture. These were so useful that he was asked to put them together as a textbook. In the end, he did write a textbook (but not one based on these notes), *Introduction to Economics*, but the war precluded its completion and publication until 1944. Its six editions provided the basic principles of economics for students during the 1950s and 1960s.

Wartime economist The Second World War propelled Cairncross into the government service, where he spent the subsequent decade. In January 1940 he joined a small group of professional economists in the war cabinet office under Lord Stamp, himself an eminent economist. A major task was to assemble and circulate series of digests of the secret statistics collected by government departments and official agencies. On the basis of these they tackled problems and proposed solutions. Cairncross concentrated on imports, stock building, shipping, and transport. In June 1941 he moved to the Board of Trade, where he continued to work on port capacity and reserves of factory and storage space. In November he made his final move, to the Ministry of Aircraft Production, where he remained until the end of the war.

Cairncross enjoyed the Ministry of Aircraft Production. Production needed to be planned, and planning required information; upon the basis of this information intelligent choices could be made. But imagination helped. Soon after his arrival at the ministry he discovered that there were 300 Wellington bombers on a beach in Blackpool which could not be used because they had no propellers;

thus for every two propellers added to output the RAF would gain an additional aircraft. He discovered that there were American propellers available, but they had the wrong size of blade. His solution? To fit British blades to American hubs. It is perhaps not surprising that by the end of the war he had become the director of programmes in the ministry.

Cairncross had also become a husband. In 1939 he met Mary Frances Glynn (1919–1998), an assistant housing estate manager and a member of a military and professional family, and they married on 29 May 1943. She married Alec, she claimed, because he was the one boyfriend who would willingly ride on the back of her BSA motorcycle. Her singular approach to problems charmed him. Once when wishing to use the family microscope to look at some cheese mites from France, she found that its lenses were covered with condensation. Rather than taking it apart and cleaning the lenses, she popped it into the oven.

In 1945 Cairncross went to Berlin for five months as Treasury representative in the negotiations with economists from the USA, France, the UK, and the USSR over the level of German reparations. Believing that Germany should be left with sufficient resources to sustain a reasonable standard of living, he argued vigorously with the other national representatives. The reparations plan was published in March 1946. By this time he had joined the magazine *The Economist* but he was spending so much time advising the government that he decided he might as well do it properly. He moved to the Board of Trade as economic adviser in 1946 and remained for three years, the period which saw the 'bonfire of controls' over trade and industry. He rounded off this period of government service by spending 1950 in Paris as director of the economics division of the Organization for European Economic Co-operation, the mediator between the USA and the European recipients of Marshall aid. Most memorable during this period was his work with Per Jacobsson of the Bank for International Settlements on a plan to deal with Germany's only post-war balance-of-payments crisis.

University professor In 1951 Cairncross returned to Glasgow University, with some relief, as professor of applied economics, and there established one of the UK's first research departments in the field. Much of the department's work focused on regional policies, particularly with regard to the Scottish economy. Yet during his ten years at Glasgow, Cairncross continued to spend a proportion of his time on national and international duties. During 1952–3 he was a member of the Phillips committee on old age, set up to look at the implications for public policy of the rising proportion of old people in the population. In 1954 he was invited by the World Bank to organize training for senior administrators from relatively undeveloped countries. From July 1955 to December 1956 he was in Washington setting up the Economic Development Institute, which over the years developed a cadre of economists trained in development economics to serve in third-world countries. Upon his return he was asked to serve on the Radcliffe committee on the working of the monetary system (1957–9), in his words 'the most important [committee] on which an economist could hope to serve' (Cairncross, *Living with the Century*, 204); much of the drafting of its report was his. He also served on the Crofters' Commission (1951–4) and the anthrax committee (1957–8), the latter out of a sense of duty rather than from knowledge or interest.

Civil servant In June 1961 Cairncross joined the Treasury as economic adviser and head of its economic section, a staff of about twelve professional economists. Until the Conservatives lost the general election in 1964, he observed (without approval) the 'dash for growth' led by the chancellor of the exchequer, Reginald Maudling, the outcome of which was the ferocious balance-of-payments crisis that greeted the newly elected Labour government. In professional terms this was a period of some difficulty for him. The prime minister, Harold Wilson, set up a Department of Economic Affairs, whose remit was to concentrate more on growth than the Treasury was prone to do. Cairncross's role as economic adviser was abolished without his being told, and he was offered a move to Washington as economic minister at the embassy. The problem was that Labour thought him tainted by having served as economic adviser to the Conservative government—an unfair judgement, since he was an established civil servant appointed on the basis of his professional skills as an applied economist. In the end he complained to the chancellor, James Callaghan, who then denied all knowledge of events and urged him to stay. He retained the title of director of the economic section and was made first head of the government economic service, in which post he increased the number of professional economists serving in government.

The subsequent three years were nerve-wracking. The theme was the weakness of sterling, and the question was whether to devalue. The prime minister and the chancellor were determined not to devalue, and at first Cairncross agreed. But gradually he changed his mind: he believed that measures had to be taken to deflate demand and/or to control imports, and when neither policy was adopted he came to see devaluation as inevitable. It fell to him on 2 November 1967 to confront the chancellor with the unwelcome news—unwelcome in particular since with the failure of his policy the chancellor would have to resign. Cairncross was appointed KCMG in 1967.

Oxford and retirement During 1967 Cairncross was invited to go to the new University of Kent as master of Keynes College, an invitation which he verbally accepted. However, there was no public announcement, and in the autumn St Peter's College, Oxford, asked him to allow his name to go forward for the mastership. He withdrew his acceptance of the Keynes College headship, and in December 1967 was elected master of St Peter's, a post he took up in January 1969 and held until 1978. He followed the advice of another economist who was head of house, Robert Hall, to devote half his time to college affairs and the other half to private or public purposes. He served on a number of public committees as well as holding professional posts, such as the presidencies of the Royal Economic Society, the British Association, and the Girls' Public Day School Trust. In 1971 he became chancellor of Glasgow University—'I doubt', he said, 'whether I ever had a prouder moment' (Cairncross, *Living with the Century*, 258); he resigned in 1996 when he reached eighty-five.

Cairncross never actually retired. His pleasure was in writing, and during his final decade and a half a stream of books and articles poured out. Many combined personal involvement and deep immersion in the archives: *Sterling in Decline: the Devaluations of 1931, 1949 and 1967* (1983, with Barry Eichengreen), *Years of Recovery: British Economic Policy, 1945–51* (1985), *The Price of War* (1986), *The Economic Section, 1939–61* (1989, with Nita Watts), and *Managing the British Economy in the 1960s* (1996). Although not a participant, he was an observer with strong opinions of the International Monetary Fund crisis of 1976, which resulted in *'Goodbye Great Britain': the 1976 IMF Crisis* (1992, with Kathleen Burk). For some years he ran a seminar on economic history at All Souls College, Oxford, and gave papers at home and abroad. He became a fellow of the British Academy in 1961.

Probably Cairncross's greatest source of pleasure was his family: Mary, his adored wife for fifty-five years, and his five children with their progeny. He also loved to travel, studying problems or advising governments (China, India, and Saudi Arabia were only three of his destinations). His friendships were international and covered all ages. Students thought he was wonderful, not least because he was entirely without 'side'. He was seemingly interested in everything, had great enthusiasm, and was blessed with physical and intellectual energy to match. He was generous with his time and his interest. He was, in the best sense, lovable.

Personally austere, Cairncross never took a taxi if he could take a bus, but best of all was to cycle. In October 1998 he fell off his bicycle near his home in Oxford; after undergoing surgery on his damaged hip, he developed pneumonia. His wife had died four months before; he clearly did not want to linger on without her, and died in the John Radcliffe Hospital, Oxford, two weeks later, on 21 October 1998. His death was greeted with universal regret, and by his friends with real grief. After a funeral service in St Peter's College on 6 November, he was cremated.

KATHLEEN BURK

Sources A. Cairncross, *Living with the century* (1998) • T. Wilson and B. Hopkin, *PBA*, 105 (2000), 339–61 • *The Independent* (23 Oct 1998) • *Daily Telegraph* (28 Oct 1998) • *The Guardian* (Oct 1998) • *The Scotsman* (28 Oct 1998) • *The Times* (26 Oct 1998) • H. McRae, *The Independent* (18 July 1998) [obit. of Mary Cairncross] • personal knowledge (2004) • A. Cairncross, *The price of war* (1986) • b. cert. • m. cert. • d. cert.

Archives BLPES, corresp. and papers relating to Royal Economic Society and *Economic Journal* • Bodl. Oxf., papers relating to career in the United Nations • U. Glas., Archives and Business Records Centre, corresp., lecture notes, and papers • U. Glas. L. | PRO, official papers

Likenesses W. Bird, photograph, 1963, NPG [*see illus.*] • photograph (as chancellor), U. Glas. • portrait, St Peter's College, Oxford • portraits, priv. coll.

Cairncross, John (1913–1995), spy, was born on 25 July 1913, at Pine Cottage, Lesmahagow, Lanarkshire, the youngest of four boys and four girls of Alexander Kirkland Cairncross (*b.* 1865), ironmonger, and his wife, Elizabeth Andrew Wishart (*b.* 1875), schoolteacher. Sir Alexander Kirkland *Cairncross (1911–1998), economist, was his elder brother. John Cairncross attended Lesmahagow village school before Hamilton Academy; at seventeen he won an open scholarship at Glasgow University, where his subjects were French and German; next he studied at the University of Paris, at the Sorbonne. In 1934 he succeeded George Painter as Bell exhibitioner at Trinity College, Cambridge, where he obtained his BA degree in two years. During 1935–6 he participated in communist meetings held at Cambridge, but later he insisted that he had been a fellow traveller rather than a party member; this is not universally accepted. Stuart Hampshire remembered him at this time: 'an absurd and rather untidy scholar, very bright and academic. He was socially from the lower rather than the higher, very talkative, sort of chaotic' (Carter, 189).

Cairncross passed top of his year in the civil service examinations of 1936 and was appointed to the Foreign Office on 14 October 1936. As his touchy and graceless manners made him unsuitable for a foreign posting he was transferred to the Treasury as an assistant principal on 1 October 1938. He suggested that his frank dislike of appeasement contributed to this move. In 1937, shortly after entering the Foreign Office, he was recruited to work for Soviet espionage in manoeuvres involving the Cambridge Marxist James Klugmann, Anthony Blunt, and Guy Burgess. Cairncross was largely inactive as an agent until after the Nazi attack on Russia in 1941.

In 1940 Cairncross was appointed private secretary to the chancellor of the duchy of Lancaster, Lord Hankey. Despite developing an affectionate admiration for Hankey, from June 1941 he transmitted cabinet papers and Foreign Office telegrams to his Soviet controller. Jack Hewit, the working-class lover of Blunt and Burgess, who knew Cairncross at this time, was unimpressed by him. 'He was a nobody; he was dull' (Carter, 265). Similarly Sir John Colville considered Cairncross 'very brilliant but very boring' (Penrose and Freeman, 370). During 1942 Cairncross was called up to the Royal Armoured Corps, but then, as a fluent German speaker, he was posted to the Government Code and Cypher School at Bletchley, and assigned to work on the Enigma decrypts. He was shocked to find that the Soviets were not trusted with Ultra intelligence obtained at Bletchley, and sought to remedy the situation. According to Russian intelligence archives Cairncross supplied 5832 documents between 1941 and 1945. The Soviets mistrusted his information until in February 1943 he supplied the original flimsy papers containing full intercepted details of the Germans' forthcoming summer offensive. As a result he decisively influenced the outcome of the battle of Kursk, Germany's final major attack on the eastern front. However, working night shifts, together with the strains of his duplicity, weakened his health, and in 1943, after a year at Bletchley, he engineered a transfer to the Secret Intelligence Service, where he joined the section responsible for counter-espionage abroad.

In 1945 Cairncross returned to the Treasury; both there, and during a brief secondment to the Ministry of Supply, his prickliness remained an obstacle to promotion. Later he denied that in this period he continued to supply the Soviets with information on NATO and other crucial matters, though his Soviet controller Yuri Modin has given a detailed contrary account. 'Cairncross was anti-social and a wretched hand at making friends', with 'a sizeable chip on his shoulder', according to Modin. 'I liked Cairncross best of all our London agents. He wasn't an easy man to deal with, but he was a profoundly decent one' (Modin, 107, 168). An unsigned but compromising memorandum was found in Burgess's flat, after his disappearance with Donald Maclean in 1951, written on the day that the Nazis marched into Prague (15 March 1939). Cairncross was identified as the memorandum's author, but when confronted by the British authorities he outsmarted his interrogators; after admitting to carelessness with official papers he was required to resign from the civil service in 1952. On 26 January 1951 Cairncross had married Gabriele Susanne (1914–1995), daughter of Sebastian Oppenheim, a retired Bristol merchant, from a Frankfurt Jewish family, but they were to separate during the 1960s.

Cairncross became Rome correspondent of *The Economist*, *The Observer*, and the Canadian Broadcasting Corporation. Subsequently he was employed by the United Nations at Geneva (1953–6), as chief editor (based in Bangkok) for the Economic Council for Asia and the Far East (1957–62), and he was among the Harvard group's advisers to Pakistan's Planning Commission (1962–3). He wrote three books on Molière, and translated into English verse seven plays by Racine (published in 1963 and 1967) as well as *La Fontaine fables* (1982). He also wrote a history of Christian sexual morality, *After Polygamy was Made a Sin* (1974).

Following Philby's defection MI5 resumed its hunt for Soviet spies, and in 1964 Cairncross made an extended, though possibly incomplete, confession. In subsequent years he continued co-operation with the British authorities. 'He was a clever, rather frail-looking Scotsman with a shock of red hair and a broad accent', according to one of his interrogators, Peter Wright, who found him 'engaging' (Wright, 281–2). Stella Rimington, who re-interrogated him during the 1970s, recalled 'a thin, grey, stooping figure … turning our conversations into intellectual sparring matches and … determined to … tell us no more than he had already admitted, which was nothing like the full story' (Rimington, 119–20). Following Margaret Thatcher's denunciation of Blunt in 1979, journalists established Cairncross's identity, and he endured frantic publicity. In 1982 he was convicted of smuggling currency across the Italian/Swiss border. There were further journalistic storms around his name, notably in 1990 when he had just settled at St Antonin du Var, Provence.

Cairncross, who was deaf in one ear, could seem unprepossessing: conceited, unpunctual, clumsy, untidily dressed, and a laboriously slow trencherman. His courage and self-sufficiency won the admiration, though, of Graham Greene. Despite suffering a stroke in 1993 he continued writing his self-exculpatory memoirs, which were posthumously published and are not wholly convincing. He returned to England in 1995, settling in a cottage in the Welsh marches, and a week after his wife's death, married on 8 September 1995 his long-term companion, Gayle Anne (*b*. 1952/3), an American opera singer and daughter of John Richmond Brinkerhoff, army officer. Following another stroke, he died of heart failure on 8 October 1995, at Longhope, Weston, Pembridge, near Leominster.

Richard Davenport-Hines

Sources J. Cairncross, *The Enigma spy* (1997) • M. Carter, *Anthony Blunt* (2001) • P. Wright, *Spycatcher* (1987) • S. Rimington, *Open secret* (2001) • Y. Modin, *My five Cambridge friends* (1994) • B. Penrose and S. Freeman, *Conspiracy of silence* (1986) • T. Bowyer, *The Independent* (10 Oct 1995) • *The Times* (11 Oct 1995) • R. Norton-Taylor, 'Outsider in a ring of spies', *The Guardian* (11 Oct 1995), 17 • b. cert. • m. certs. • d. cert.

Likenesses J. Murch, photograph, 1990, France Soir press agency; repro. in Modin, *My five Cambridge friends*, following p. 122 • photographs, repro. in Cairncross, *Enigma spy*

Wealth at death £145,000: probate, 1996, *CGPLA Eng. & Wales* (1996)

Cairncross, Robert (*d*. 1545), administrator and bishop of Ross, was related to the Cairncrosses of Colmslie, near Melrose. Nothing is known of his parentage or early life. Though not a graduate, he became a priest of Glasgow diocese and in 1521, witnessing a document in Edinburgh, was described as *capellanus* (chaplain). On 5 August 1527 he was inducted as provost of the collegiate church of Corstorphine, Edinburgh. Having earlier, during James V's minority, received a royal grant, he was made treasurer of the kingdom on 19 July 1528. On 5 September, when he received a grant from the lands of the disgraced Sir Archibald Douglas of Kilspindie, he was described as a royal chaplain, and on 6 November he was provided as abbot of Holyrood with the obligation of becoming an Augustinian canon regular.

Although removed from being treasurer in early 1529 on suspicion of dealing with the outlawed earl of Angus, Cairncross served in various financial capacities throughout the 1530s: as an auditor of exchequer, as clerk of the king's household expenses, as collector of churchmen's taxes, and then again as treasurer from 29 May 1537 to 8 February following. In addition he was a lord of session and a commissioner for holding parliament. Living in Edinburgh beside the royal palace made his holding public office convenient. Three children of his, John, Andrew, and Isabel, were legitimated in 1537.

On 12 November 1538 Cairncross made an indenture with the king, undertaking to resign Holyrood and so allow James to nominate his own infant son as commendator; in return he would receive the bishopric of Ross and a pension from Holyrood revenues. Nominated to Ross in December, Cairncross received papal provision on 14 April 1539, and then in March 1541 was nominated to Fearn Abbey as commendator. Despite the distance from

Edinburgh, he was again commissioner of parliament in 1541, and in March 1543, while attending Governor Arran's first parliament, he was appointed a lord of council. He resigned Fearn in 1545 in favour of a young kinsman, but retained the revenues for himself. On 30 November 1545 he died at his residence at Chanonry, Fortrose, and was buried in the cathedral there. He was more notable as an important crown official than as a churchman, and both at Holyrood and in Ross he alienated property to his Cairncross kinsmen. MARK DILWORTH

Sources [A. F. Cairncross and B. L. Cairncross], *Cairncross: the history of a Scottish family* (privately printed, George, South Africa, 1959), 41–5 • T. Thomson, 'List of protocol books', *Proceedings of the Society of Antiquaries of Scotland*, 2 (1854–7), 354–68 • J. Dowden, *The bishops of Scotland … prior to the Reformation*, ed. J. M. Thomson (1912), 225–6 • J. B. Paul, ed., *Compota thesaurariorum regum Scotorum / Accounts of the lord high treasurer of Scotland*, 6 (1905) • *APS*, 1424–1567 • J. M. Thomson and others, eds., *Registrum magni sigilli regum Scotorum / The register of the great seal of Scotland*, 11 vols. (1882–1914), vol. 3 • M. Dilworth, 'Fearn Abbey as a monastic institution', *Innes Review*, 51 (2000), 40–54 • M. Livingstone, D. Hay Fleming, and others, eds., *Registrum secreti sigilli regum Scotorum / The register of the privy seal of Scotland*, 2 (1921) • D. E. R. Watt, ed., *Fasti ecclesiae Scoticanae medii aevi ad annum 1638*, [2nd edn], Scottish RS, new ser., 1 (1969), 270, 348 • G. Burnett and others, eds., *The exchequer rolls of Scotland*, 15–16 (1895–7) • T. Thomson, ed., *A diurnal of remarkable occurrents that have passed within the country of Scotland*, Bannatyne Club, 43 (1833), 11, 13 • J. Cameron, *James V: the personal rule, 1528–1542*, ed. N. Macdougall (1998) • R. J. Adam, ed., *The calendar of Fearn: text and additions, 1471–1667*, Scottish History Society, 5th ser., 4 (1991) • J. Stuart, ed., *Records of the monastery of Kinloss*, Society of Antiquaries of Scotland, 9 (1872)

Cairnech (*fl.* **5th–early 6th cent.**). *See under* Meath, saints of (*act. c.*400–*c.*900).

Cairnes, David (**1645–1722**), politician, was born in co. Tyrone, Ireland, on 15 November 1645, the fourth son of John Cairnes, of Parsonstown, co. Tyrone, MP for Augher, and Jane Miller. He was admitted to the Middle Temple in 1668 and called to the bar at King's Inns in 1673. He owned land in Knockmany, co. Tyrone, and practised law in Londonderry, where he was elected burgess in 1680. He married, first, Margaret Edwards of Straw, co. Londonderry, with whom he had a son and a daughter, and second, Mary Barnes, with whom he had a daughter.

With Ireland on the brink of civil war, the lord deputy, the earl of Tyrconnell, ordered the earl of Antrim to garrison Londonderry with Catholic troops. Rumours were circulated that there was to be a general massacre of the protestants, and on 7 December 1688, as the first companies approached the city, a gang of armed apprentice boys seized the keys and locked the city gates on them. Several leading citizens, including the bishop of Derry, fearful of what this act of rebellion would provoke, tried without success to persuade the mob to let the garrison in.

> The multitude acted without the least publick countenance from any of considerable note, or figure in the town, till that afternoon came in David Cairns, Esq. who having received a full account of what was done, and their inducements thereunto, declared openly his approbation of it, commending their courage, and assuring them of his utmost assistance; and thereupon went round the walls, and to the gates, encouraging their guards and sentinels. (Hempton, 163)

His influence was such that he took command of the rebels and persuaded other members of the corporation to support the revolt. Two days later Colonel George Phillips, who was sent by Antrim to treat with him, was not only won over by Cairnes, but agreed to be the city's governor, although he only did so on the condition that Cairnes made a show of publicly threatening him with violence.

On 10 December 1688 Cairnes was chosen to travel to London to represent the city's plight to the Irish Society. Although he set sail the next day, storms forced him to return and he took part in the council meeting of 2 January 1689 which re-established the protestant corporation of Londonderry, removed by Tyrconnell. He reached London by the end of January, where he was granted an interview with William III. On 12 March he set out for Londonderry with a letter for the new governor, Robert Lundy, and instructions to get an exact account of the city's circumstances. On his arrival in Londonderry on 10 April he harangued a council of war and persuaded those present 'to stand by each other with our forces against the common enemy' (Hempton, 199). Within a week, and shortly after the arrival of King James's besieging army, he returned to London to report. While he was there, he appeared before the parliamentary committee of inquiry and gave hostile evidence against Lundy. About the same time he was attainted of high treason by the Jacobite parliament in Dublin.

Cairnes was entrusted with Major-General Kirke's orders to attempt an immediate relief of Londonderry, but on the way back to Ireland in early July he was chased by three French warships. To avoid capture he ran his ship aground on the north side of the Mull of Kintyre and fled overland to Campbeltown. He reached Kirke by the end of the month, after which a desperate but successful attempt was made on the boom across the River Foyle, and Londonderry was relieved.

After the war Cairnes was elected to the 1692 Irish parliament as a member for Londonderry City. He was re-elected in 1695, in which year he presented an unsuccessful petition for the compensation of those who had suffered losses during the siege. In his will he expressed disappointment that he and the people of Londonderry, whose

> services and sufferings that were of such high consequence to these kingdoms and so amply confessed by their parliaments, both of England and Ireland, come to be so strangely overlooked and neglected as they have been, reflects not a little shame on the honour of these nations, so that all the assurances I had should be buried in utter oblivion. (Graham, 314)

He died in 1722 in Londonderry and was buried in the cathedral churchyard there. PIERS WAUCHOPE

Sources J. Graham, ed., *Ireland preserved, or, The siege of Londonderry* (1841) • J. Hempton, ed., *The siege and history of Londonderry* (1861) • C. D. Milligan, *The siege of Londonderry* (1951) • H. C. Lawlor, *A history of the family of Cairnes or Cairns and its connections* (1906) • *The manuscripts of the duke of Hamilton*, HMC, 21 (1887), 182–3 • E. Keane, P. Beryl Phair, and T. U. Sadleir, eds., *King's Inns admission papers, 1607–1867*, IMC (1982)

Likenesses T. Jenkins, engraving (after C. Smith by G. Kneller), repro. in Graham, ed., *Ireland preserved*

Cairnes, John Elliot (1823–1875), economist, was born at Castle Bellingham, co. Louth, on 26 December 1823. He was the sixth child and eldest surviving son of William Cairnes (1787–1863) and his wife, Marianne Woolsey. His father was a partner in a brewery in Castle Bellingham, but two years after the son's birth went into business on his own account, taking over a brewery in Drogheda. When eight years old the boy was sent to a boarding-school at Kingstown, co. Dublin, and at fourteen or fifteen was placed with a clergyman named Hutton (probably the Revd William Pepperal Hutton) at Chester. Hutton thought him a dull boy, and told his father that he was unfit for higher education. He was therefore placed in his father's business at Drogheda, and stayed there three years, during which he learned some chemistry and became friendly with a young man named La Bart. La Bart's influence drew him for a time towards Calvinism, and the young men held prayer meetings together, while Cairnes also began to develop intellectual tastes, reading Gibbon and many other writers.

Gradually Cairnes took a dislike to business, and his desire to go to university led to a coolness with his father, which lasted for some years. His father, however, made him a small allowance which enabled him to study at Trinity College, Dublin, where he matriculated on 7 November 1842. He graduated as BA in 1848, and proceeded MA in 1854. He led a desultory life for some time, studying chemistry occasionally, but also engaging in journalism. He entered an engineer's office in Galway, where he became acquainted with William Nesbitt, a classical scholar who then was professor of Latin at Queen's College, Galway. Nesbitt turned his attention to political economy, and in 1854 Cairnes published his first contributions to that field, in the form of two papers read to the Dublin Statistical Society. On Nesbitt's advice, he competed in the examination for the Whately professorship of political economy in Trinity College, Dublin, in 1856, and was the successful candidate. He held the chair for the regular term of five years, but in 1859 he was also appointed professor of political economy and jurisprudence in Queen's College, Galway. He had been called to the Irish bar in 1857, but never seriously practised.

In 1860 Cairnes married Eliza Charlotte, daughter of George Henry Minto Alexander, a judge of the High Court at Banda, in the United Provinces of India, and sister of the wife of his great friend William Nesbitt. There were five children of the marriage, but only three survived infancy, among them William Elliot *Cairnes, army officer and military writer. Cairnes retained his post at Galway until

John Elliot Cairnes (1823–1875), by unknown photographer

1870, but discharged its duties through a deputy after he moved his residence to London in 1865.

In 1866 Cairnes was appointed professor of political economy in University College, London, but ill health forced him to resign this chair in 1872. He had injured a knee in a riding accident in 1860, and this led to inflammation of the joint; the symptoms of rheumatoid arthritis first manifested themselves here. A severe operation in 1868 gave him some relief, but he was in time left completely disabled by the disease. In 1870 he settled at Lee, near Blackheath, and two years later moved to Kidbrooke Park Road, Blackheath. Here he remained for the rest of his life, becoming by degrees a more helpless invalid, but never losing his cheerfulness or intellectual vigour. He was a near neighbour and warm friend of J. S. Mill, and was constantly visited also by Henry Fawcett and Leonard Courtney. He died at his home, Rasay, Kidbrooke Park Road, from the effects of his disease on 8 July 1875 and was buried four days later in Paddington old cemetery, Kilburn.

At the time of his death Cairnes was undoubtedly the leading economist in Britain. Having once found the work to which his abilities were best suited he quickly established a reputation in his chosen field. His first course of lectures as Whately professor dealt with 'The character and logical method of political economy'. Published under that title in 1857, and in a revised and enlarged second edition in 1875, they came to be accepted as the definitive statement of the methodology of classical economics, and as such remain a landmark in the history of the subject. Despite his confident assertion in these lectures that 'the economist starts with a knowledge of ultimate causes' so that for the discovery of the premisses of deductive analysis 'no elaborate process of induction is needed', Cairnes did not himself neglect the study of economic facts. Pre-eminently a theorist, he could yet employ his analytical skills to bring out the essence of a current problem with originality and clarity. Thus in the articles on the change in the value of gold which he published in *Fraser's Magazine* in 1858–60 he used only literary methods, but his predictions were subsequently verified by the conclusions which W. S. Jevons reached by statistical methods quite independently some years later. Cairnes gained a national, in fact an international, reputation when in 1862 he published *The Slave Power*. This book made such an impression both in Britain and America that a second, enlarged edition was called for in 1863; through its well-argued indictment of the economic and social system of the Confederate states it did much to influence public opinion in Britain towards support of the northern cause in the American Civil War.

Writing to his friend William Nesbitt on 28 May 1866, Cairnes admitted that 'a seat in Parliament has of course long been the object of my ambition' (National Library of Ireland, MS 8941). Financial considerations prevented him from realizing it, but his friendship with Mill and Fawcett enabled him indirectly to exert considerable influence on political decisions, particularly about Irish issues—in which his interest did not fade after his move to London. Of most significance here were his contributions to the discussions on the Irish land question in the 1860s. In these Cairnes moved from a moderate to a radical position, and his ideas had substantial influence on Mill's thinking. He held that state intervention to fix rents was not only necessitated by the conditions existing in Ireland but was also in line with the classical theory of rent, since a *laissez-faire* policy might not ensure that 'the limits set by "economic rent" shall … be observed in the actual rent which landlords obtain' (*Essays in Political Economy*, 1873, 198).

In this, as in every case, the analytical system which Cairnes applied to practical problems was the classical system as it had been set out in Mill's *Principles of Political Economy*; yet he did not merely accept Mill's doctrines, but developed them in important respects. His best-known contribution was to show that the principle of reciprocal demand, which Mill had stated for the case of international trade, was applicable also in domestic exchanges to explain the determination of normal values in cases such as those where non-competing groups existed in the supply of labour. However, as he himself wrote in the preface to his last book, *Some Leading Principles of Political Economy Newly Expounded* (1874), his purpose was 'to strengthen and add consistency' to the fabric constructed by Smith, Ricardo, Malthus, and Mill; and since in that work he defended the wages-fund doctrine after Mill had abandoned it, and showed himself unsympathetic towards Jevons's new approach to value theory it left a last, and lasting, impression of Cairnes as a very conservative political economist, which was not wholly deserved.

R. D. Collison Black

Sources *DNB* • H. C. Lawlor, *A history of the family of Cairnes or Cairns and its connections* (1906) • H. Fawcett, 'Professor Cairnes', *Fortnightly Review*, 24 (1875), 149–54 • *The Athenaeum* (17 July 1875), 83–5 • [L. Courtney], *The Times* (9 July 1875) • *The collected works of John Stuart Mill*, ed. J. M. Robson and others, 33 vols. (1963–91), vols. 3, 14, 15 • J. Weinberg, *John E. Cairnes and the American Civil War* (1970) • G. O'Brien, 'J. S. Mill and J. E. Cairnes', *Economica*, new ser., 10 (1943), 273–85 • T. A. Boylan and T. P. Foley, 'John Elliot Cairnes, J. S. Mill and Ireland', *Hermathena*, 135 (1983), 96–118 • T. E. Cliffe Leslie, 'Professor Cairnes', in T. E. Cliffe Leslie, *Essays in political and moral philosophy* (1879), 248–50

Archives NL Ire., MS 8940–8986 | BLPES, J. S. Mill MSS • Harvard U., Houghton L., Sarah Blake Shaw MSS • London School of Economics, Courtney collection [fifty-three letters] • NL Ire., R. McDonnell MSS

Likenesses portrait, *c.*1860, repro. in R. D. C. Black, *History of the Statistical and Social Inquiry Society of Ireland: centenary volume, 1847–1947* (1947), facing p. 76 • photograph, University College, Galway [*see illus.*] • portrait, repro. in *ILN*, 67 (1875) • portrait, repro. in *Graphic*, 11 (1875)

Wealth at death under £4000: probate, 7 Aug 1875, *CGPLA Eng. & Wales*

Cairnes, William Elliot (1862–1902), army officer and military writer, was born at Galway on 18 September 1862, to an old family of Scottish descent, the son of John Elliot *Cairnes (1823–1875), economist and professor at University College, London, and his wife, Eliza Charlotte, daughter of George Henry Minto Alexander. In 1872 Cairnes's father moved to Blackheath, having lived nearby since 1870; Cairnes attended Blackheath proprietary school, University College School (1877–9), and the International College, Spring Grove, Isleworth, a boarding-school emphasizing modern languages and science, which started with Cobdenite idealism but declined into indiscipline and violence.

Cairnes entered the army through the militia 'back door', presumably attending a crammer. He was commissioned lieutenant in the militia (Royal Irish Rifles) on 16 September 1882, became lieutenant 3rd dragoon guards on 14 May 1884, and was transferred to the South Staffordshire regiment on 21 May; he was moved to the Royal Irish Fusiliers on 16 July, and served with the 2nd battalion at several home stations. He married in June 1884 Mary (Mamie) Elizabeth, daughter of M. McClelland of Glendarragh, co. Londonderry; she was to survive her husband, with one daughter, Dorothy Elliot. Having been promoted captain on 21 May 1890, Cairnes was adjutant of the 1st volunteer battalion, Yorkshire light infantry, at Wakefield, from 31 March 1897 to 30 March 1902. This prevented his going to South Africa with his regiment, whose regular battalions both served in the Second South African War.

Cairnes's army career was undistinguished, with neither active service nor time at a staff college. In 1899 he was approaching middle age, and was stuck training part-time soldiers in a northern industrial town, while his fellow officers took their chances of distinction and dysentery. However, the Second South African War offered him new opportunity, as a part-time military journalist and writer. From November 1899 to April 1901 he was 'military correspondent' of George Newnes's prestigious, influential, but unprofitable Liberal evening paper, the *Westminster Gazette*, contributing daily articles on the war, considered among the best of their kind. The war aroused immense public and media interest, which, after the British blunders and defeats of 1899, turned to angry criticism and recrimination.

Cairnes responded with *An Absent-Minded War* (1900), published pseudonymously as a shilling cardback, its cover printed as if tied with red tape. The book was a polemical indictment of the 'system', the War Office—'that shrine of mediocrity and incompetence' (Cairnes, *Absent-Minded War*, 70)—, jobbery, the Staff College and its graduates, conspicuous uniforms and pipeclaying, and the failure to train and prepare for war. It alleged that there had been 'an army of lions led by ignoramuses' (ibid., 146), and criticized Buller, Warren, and other generals, but praised Roberts and Kitchener. It demanded army reforms for an 'up-to-date fighting machine' (ibid.). Much in it had been and was being asserted by others, and arguably it was the work of a resentful outsider. Yet it was vivid, sarcastic, quotable, and fitted the public mood, and because of it Cairnes became 'a well-known writer of books on military subjects' (*Annual Register*, 123). Controversial, it provoked a pseudonymous reply by a retired colonel, James Edward Goodwyn, *Unfounded Attacks on British Officers Made in 'An Absent-Minded War' … A Refutation* (1901), which, however, agreed with some of the criticisms in Cairnes's book. A German translation of the latter was published in 1903.

Cairnes's pseudonymous *Social Life in the British Army* (1900) was less polemical and more descriptive, and warned against admitting as officers men of lower social rank. His pseudonymous *The Army from within* (1901) repeated some of his earlier criticisms, his warning against socially inferior officers, and his call for reforms. It also warned against 'hedgerow' defence by civilian riflemen against invasion. With Roberts's reputation at its zenith, Cairnes published a eulogistic and derivative biography, *Lord Roberts as a Soldier in Peace and War* (1901), praising him as 'the greatest living soldier' (Cairnes, *Lord Roberts*, 331). Cairnes's *The Coming Waterloo* (1901) was in the genre of purposive future-war fiction which had flourished since George Tomkyns Chesney's *The Battle of Dorking* (1871). It described a war in 1903 in which Britain—her army decisively improved after the Second South African War—allied with Germany and Austria and defeated France and Russia. Its message was the need for army reform, the inconclusiveness of seapower, the dominance of infantry firepower, and the limited role of *arme blanche* cavalry. Cairnes's books earned 'widespread acclaim' (Spiers, *Late Victorian Army*, 308). He also contributed to the *National Review*, *Contemporary Review*, *Harper's Magazine*, and occasionally *The Times*. He was a clever draftsman, able to illustrate his articles, and he patented several inventions.

In April 1901 a committee on officer education and training was appointed, with Aretas Akers-Douglas (later Viscount Chilston) chairman and Cairnes secretary. In their report in March 1902 the committee stated that Cairnes's knowledge, tact, and ability had greatly facilitated their inquiry. Cairnes was also secretary to the military court of inquiry into the remount department. These duties and his writing taxed his strength. He died of pneumonia at 15 Bury Street, London, on 19 April 1902. His army career was undistinguished: his notable achievement was as a military writer at the time of the Second South African War. Through his writings he was among those who contributed to the army reforms during and after that war, and so to the quality of the British expeditionary force in 1914.

ROGER T. STEARN

Sources *DNB* • W. E. Cairnes, *An absent-minded war* (1900) • W. E. Cairnes, *Lord Roberts as a soldier in peace and war* (1901) • *Army List* (1902) • *WWW, 1897–1915* • *Hart's Army List* (1891) • *Annual Register* (1902), pt 2, pp. 122–3 • T. Orme, *University College School, London, alphabetical and chronological register for 1831–1891* (1892) • H. C. Lawlor, *A history of the family of Cairnes or Cairns and its connections* (1906) • E. M. Spiers, *The late Victorian army, 1868–1902* (1992) • E. M. Spiers, *The army and society, 1815–1914* (1980) • G. R. Searle, *The quest for national efficiency: a study in British politics and political thought, 1899–1914*, pbk edn (1990) • K. T. Surridge, *Managing the South African War, 1899–1902: politicians v. generals* (1998) • I. F. Clarke, *Voices prophesying war, 1763–1984*, new edn (1970) • S. E. Koss, *The rise and fall of the political press in Britain*, 2 (1984) • J. W. Kirby, *The history of the Blackheath proprietary school* (1933) • J. R. de S. Honey, *Tom Brown's universe: the development of the Victorian public school* (1977) • *VCH Middlesex*, vols. 1–2 • *CGPLA Eng. & Wales* (1902)

Wealth at death £426 13*s*. 6*d*. in England: Irish probate sealed in England, 20 June 1902, *CGPLA Eng. & Wales*

Cairns, David (1904–1992), Church of Scotland minister and theologian, was born on 11 June 1904 at the manse of Ayton, Berwickshire, the first of the two children of David Smith *Cairns (1862–1946), minister of the United Presbyterian church, and his wife, Helen Wilson Craw (*d*. 1910), daughter of a neighbouring farmer. In 1907 his father was appointed to the chair of systematic theology in the United Free Church college in Aberdeen, becoming moderator of the United Free church general assembly in 1923, and in 1929 principal of the college, where he taught until his retirement in 1937.

The younger David Cairns was schooled extensively, at Aberdeen grammar school (1912–16), at Merchiston Castle School, Edinburgh (1916–22), at Aberdeen University (1922–4), at Balliol College, Oxford (BA 1928), at Christ's College, Aberdeen (1928–31), and in postgraduate study at the University of Zürich (1931–2). A year as assistant minister of Govan Old Parish under the charismatic Revd George MacLeod was followed by ordination and induction to the charge of Bridge of Allan, Trinity, where he ministered until 1941, demitting upon commissioning into the royal army chaplain's department, in which he served until the end of the Second World War. In 1946–7 David Cairns was secretary to the Student Christian Movement at Oxford, whence he was appointed to the chair of practical theology at Christ's College, Aberdeen—a post which he held until his retirement in 1972. He received an honorary doctorate of divinity from Edinburgh University in 1953. On 16 December 1948 Cairns married Emily Rosemary Russell (*b.* 1920), daughter of Dr A. S. Russell of Christ Church, Oxford. They adopted a daughter in 1953 and a son in 1954.

David Cairns was the son of a highly distinguished churchman, theologian, and academic scholar, a father whom he revered. From an early stage in life he demonstrated the same intellectual aptitude and giftedness as his father had before him, gaining a first-class honours degree at Oxford and the clear commendation of his mentor there, Dr John MacMurray, who wrote to Cairns senior that 'David owes his First to himself more than to anyone for sheer hard work and sound self-reliant thinking' (private information). His early years as a minister prepared him well for what was to be his major life work in the academic world, continuing scholarly research in the fields of systematic and practical theology, for example in the translating of Emil Brunner's work, and in the production of numerous articles for a variety of journals. In his care for and preparation of candidates for the ordained ministry, principally though not exclusively for the Church of Scotland, David Cairns was a kindly mentor, meticulous in his work, possessed of a lively, sometimes sharp, sense of humour and motivated always by a deep pastoral sensitivity for his students.

In his later years Cairns was severely afflicted by arthritis and, despite suffering great physical discomfort, periodic surgery, and hospitalization, he was quite indomitable in his determination to continue with his work. He was an avid reader on all manner of subjects and, since his close association from Govan days with George MacLeod, founder of the Iona community, he maintained a lifelong concern for social, political, and theological subjects and, in particular, issues of justice, peace, and disarmament. A very gifted artist especially in watercolour, whose work was widely commended, he revelled in capturing the magnificent landscapes of Europe and Britain, travelling frequently while his health permitted, but continuing to find and give pleasure through painting, even in the latter years of confinement at home or in hospital. As was his family's custom, David Cairns corresponded voluminously. A deeply committed minister and churchman all his life, his faith was a continual pilgrimage of exploration even to the end, where a copy of his Greek New Testament, often accompanied by a volume of the Greek classics, was always to be found by his bed; and he would engage with visitors in deep theological discussion and debate, his mind and intellect still keen, and quite undimmed by age.

His own path of life was modelled on that of Cairns senior, with whom he maintained a close, affectionate, and highly intellectual correspondence until his father's death. He immersed himself totally in his work and he is remembered fondly, with respect and high regard by the successive generations of students at Christ's College. After a long period of increasing frailty, patiently borne, David Cairns died at Woodend Hospital, Aberdeen, on 17 October 1992. He was buried from Beechgrove parish church, Aberdeen, where he had given long and faithful service as a member of the kirk session. ALAN MAIN

Sources *Fasti Scot.*, new edn, vols. 9–11 • J. A. Lamb, ed., *The fasti of the United Free Church of Scotland, 1900–1929* (1956) • *David Cairns: an autobiography, some recollections of a long life, and selected letters*, ed. [D. Cairns and A. H. Cairns] (1950) • U. Aberdeen L., special libraries and archives, David Cairns MSS • personal knowledge (2004) • private information (2004) • *CCI* (1992)

Archives NL Scot., corresp. and papers, incl. diaries and literary MSS • U. Aberdeen L., family archival material, MS 3384 • U. Aberdeen L., special libraries and archives, personal and academic papers

Wealth at death £15,865.73: confirmation, 1992, *CCI*

Cairns, David Smith (1862–1946), theologian, was born on 8 November 1862 at Stichill in Roxburghshire, the third of four children of the Revd David Cairns, minister of the United Presbyterian church there, and his wife, Elisabeth, daughter of the Revd Dr David Smith, of Biggar. After his schooling at Ednam and the high school, Kelso, he took his arts degree at Edinburgh University and studied theology at the United Presbyterian College in Edinburgh, of which his uncle, the celebrated John *Cairns, was principal, spending one semester also at Marburg University, where he was influenced by the Ritschlian theologian Wilhelm Herrmann.

Cairns was ordained in 1895 and became minister of the United Presbyterian church at Ayton, Berwickshire. In 1901 he married Helen Wilson (*d.* 1910), daughter of Henry Hewat Craw, gentleman farmer, of West Foulden, Berwickshire. They had one daughter and one son, David *Cairns, later professor at Christ's College, Aberdeen. In 1907 Cairns became professor of systematic theology in the United Free Church college, Aberdeen, known after the church union of 1929 as Christ's College. He became principal in 1929 and taught at the college until he retired in 1937 and went to live in Edinburgh.

Cairns took an active part in the life of the church and in many public movements. He played an important role in the World Missionary Conference that met in Edinburgh in 1910, and also prepared its significant report, *The Missionary Message in Relation to Nonchristian Religions.* Cairns also actively supported the growth of the Student Christian Movement. In addition he made a number of lecture tours both in America and in the Far East: he delivered the Deems lectures in New York University and Lafayette College after the First World War, and the Russell lectures in Auburn Theological Seminary in 1923. In 1927 he lectured in China and Japan. In 1932 he delivered the Baird lectures, later published as *The Riddle of the World* (1937). This volume has been described as 'his maturest exercise in apologetics' (Needham, 117).

In 1923 Cairns was elected moderator of the general assembly of the United Free church of Scotland. He received the honorary degree of DD from the universities of Aberdeen (1909), Debrecen (Hungary, 1929), and Edinburgh (1933), and of LLD from St Andrews (1937) and Aberdeen (1938). In 1918 he was appointed OBE in recognition of work done for the troops during the war.

Cairns was above all a Christian apologist, interpreting the Christian faith to his age in the light of modern science and historical criticism. In his undergraduate days he had passed through a profound crisis of religious doubt, under which his health broke down, and he had to interrupt his studies for a period of foreign travel. At this time the poet Robert Browning became his main spiritual guide (as recorded in his autobiography, published in 1950). When his faith was restored he was committed to the lifelong enterprise of thinking it out and giving theological help to other questioners. This he did not only in a succession of theological works, but in many more personal contacts, for which his warm human sympathy well fitted him. His thought was dominated by the conviction, which found its most original expression in his most influential book, *The Faith that Rebels* (1928), that the universe is not a closed system but a purposive universe, in which nothing is impossible to God, and therefore nothing is impossible to a human faith which absolutely trusted him, as Jesus did. It was along this line that he interpreted the miracles, and closely connected with this was his interpretation of the kingdom of God and its victory in this world, including the victory over disease and suffering. Cairns died in Edinburgh on 27 July 1946.

D. M. BAILLIE, *rev.*

Sources D. Cairns, *An autobiography* (1950) • personal knowledge (1959) • private information (1959) • *WWW* • N. R. Needham, 'Cairns, David Smith', *DSCHT* • *CGPLA Eng. & Wales* (1947)
Archives NL Scot., corresp. • U. Aberdeen L., personal and academic papers
Likenesses I. G. Shields, oils, Christ's College, Aberdeen
Wealth at death confirmation, 1947, sealed • £12,514 11*s.* 4*d.*: confirmation, Scotland, 1946

Cairns, Hugh McCalmont, first Earl Cairns (1819–1885), lord chancellor, was born on 27 December 1819, the second son of William Cairns (*b.* 1789), sometime captain in the 47th foot, later of Parkmount, co. Antrim, and his first wife, Rosanna (*d.* 1822), daughter of Hugh Johnston of Belfast. A descendant of seventeenth-century Scots immigrants into Ulster, merchants and landowners long settled on the Parkmount property, the elder Cairns also had a town house in Belfast, where Hugh attended Belfast Academy before entering Trinity College, Dublin, in 1834, of which he became chancellor in 1867. An infant prodigy, who delivered a public lecture on chemistry at the age of eight, Hugh Cairns took a first in classics in 1838, and was willingly diverted to the law from the established church, for which his father had intended him. A law student in Dublin from 1839, he enrolled at Lincoln's Inn in 1841, moving to the Middle Temple in 1844, where he was called to the bar in the same year. He was to marry (on 9 May 1856) within the network of Ulster business and gentry families to which he belonged: his wife, Mary Harriet McNeile (*d.* 1919), was the daughter of John McNeile, to whom William Cairns sold Parkmount in 1857, and the niece of Hugh McNeile, the fervently anti-Catholic vicar of St Jude's, Liverpool, and later dean of Ripon. They had five sons and two daughters.

Hugh McCalmont Cairns, first Earl Cairns (1819–1885), by Lowes Cato Dickinson, exh. RA 1876

The law, religion, and politics, 1844–1867 Cairns's rise at the bar and in politics was rapid by any standards. He mastered initial nervousness about appearing in court and the physical weakness of a lifelong asthmatic. Persuaded by his pupil master, Richard Malins, to stay in England instead of returning to practise in Ireland, he had the financial support of his wealthy brother-in-law, with whom he lived in Eaton Place, Westminster. The tale was told of the unknown young barrister's luck in coming to the notice of a leading attorney, who ensured a flow of briefs for his protégé. While the story was true, Cairns's unusual powers of analysis and exposition were apparent from the start of his career; they ranked him with Richard Bethell (Lord Westbury) and Roundell Palmer (Lord Selborne) as one of the outstanding advocates of his generation. His manner and delivery were never particularly attractive: it was the common sense and directness of his arguments in the most involved cases that distinguished him. He was fortunate, too, in being a tory when that party was short of legal talent during its long years in the wilderness after 1832. His local connections secured him a seat in the Commons for Belfast at the 1852 election; he took silk four years later, and his practice was huge after Lord Derby made him solicitor-general in the minority government of 1858–9. He led for the successful respondent in the Windham case of 1861, when a mass of unsavoury evidence was deployed by both sides as his family sought to show that W. F. Windham, the squire of Felbrigg, was of unsound mind. A little later Cairns defended Lairds, the

Birkenhead shipbuilders, in the courts and in parliament against the Palmerston government's only partly effectual attempt to seize warships under construction for the south in the American Civil War. Cairns and Palmer, his Liberal opponent in those proceedings, collaborated in the important opinion they wrote for Edward Bouverie Pusey and others, confirming that Lord Westbury and a majority of the judicial committee of the privy council had acted within the law when they famously 'dismissed Hell with costs' in the *Essays and Reviews* case of 1863 (Holdsworth, *Eng. law*, 16.79).

Cairns was a devout low-churchman, whose evangelical piety, shared by his wife, ruled his personal life. Even as a barrister MP he began the day with an hour and a half studying the Bible before family prayers. He observed the sabbath strictly and taught in a Sunday school long after he had become a public figure. He was unmoved by the mockery of high society when he sat at the feet of the American revivalists Moody and Sankey. His churchmanship embraced co-operation with nonconformists, and his good works ranged from helping Thomas Barnardo with the orphanages to providing 'coffee palaces' in the unending Victorian struggle against intemperance. This puritanism had the limits common in his class: he was not a teetotaller; as a young man he rode to hounds once a week in the season, and in later years he rented shooting in the highlands every August. But his Scottish guests were expected to attend the Sunday services he organized in the house, at which, in the absence of a visiting clergyman, he preached himself; there was hymn-singing in the evenings.

If Cairns's austere protestantism, with its Ulster flavour, was more benign than critics alleged, his reputation as a partisan tory lightly concealed a modernizing Conservative. Like the Gladstonian and high-church Palmer, and often in conjunction with him, he was a determined law reformer, who by the early 1870s was ready to take on the inns of court and 'roll them all into a legal university. The public rights and privileges … they enjoy are amply sufficient to justify public interference and control' (Cairns to Selborne, 11 Oct 1872, Palmer, 1.50). As solicitor-general he took up the protracted attempt to simplify and register titles to land, but this technical initiative was overshadowed by his emergence as a formidable and versatile parliamentarian. The speech he delivered in the debate on the Indian province of Oudh in May 1858, when the ministry was still in some danger of falling after Lord Ellenborough's resignation from the India board, was the making of him politically. Another impressive performance on the tory Reform Bill in March 1859 emphasized his value to the party. His rise continued in opposition, and on the formation of Derby's next government in July 1866 he became attorney-general (and a privy councillor in November) on the understanding that he would succeed Lord Chelmsford on the woolsack when he could be spared from the Commons. Cairns was, however, reluctant to burden his heirs with a peerage not founded on a more substantial fortune than even his earnings at the bar had built up. He also shared the inclination of some tories and Liberals to form 'a moderate party' (*Diary of Gathorne Hardy*, 13–14, 14 and 20 June 1886) under the fourth marquess of Lansdowne, or someone equally acceptable, as an alternative to Derby and Disraeli, on the one hand, and Russell and Gladstone on the other.

In the debates on the Russell–Gladstone Reform Bill of 1866, Cairns's contribution to its defeat had been second only to Robert Lowe's, and his theme was similar. A working-class majority in the electorate must destroy the balance of classes on which the smooth working of the contemporary constitution depended: 'take a class as a class', he contended, '[and] they will act as members of my own or any other profession would do … in accordance with the overwhelming sense of their own interest' (*Hansard 3*, 182, 16 April 1866, 1474). As a politician Cairns was apt to talk in this utilitarian vein: after his reform speeches Disraeli said of him that with 'only a little heart and a little imagination he would have been by far the first man in the House of Commons' (Disraeli to Northcote, 14 Oct 1866, Monypenny & Buckle, 2.213). At that point his political life seemed to be over. Concern for his health drove him to take a vacant lord justiceship of appeal in October 1866 without the peerage he was offered. Sorely missed by ministers very conscious of their weakness, he was soon induced to enter the Lords and combine his judicial duties with active defence of the government and its bid to settle the question of parliamentary reform. Help from one of the rich men in his extended family enabled him to support the dignity of Baron Cairns of Garmoyle (27 February 1867) without undue anxiety for his children's prospects. Although he disliked the tory Reform Bill after it was shorn in the Commons of the safeguards that were to have accompanied household suffrage in the boroughs, he had to concede that the urban working class could no longer be substantially excluded from the political nation: 'it is safer to have the … force of that opinion inside rather than outside the legislative power' (*Hansard 3*, 188, 23 July 1867, 2007). His was a typical conversion following months of public discussion and demonstrations. He carried amendments to the bill: one, which ministers opposed, lifted the £10 lodger franchise to £15 and was subsequently reversed; another, to promote minority representation in large constituencies with three or more members, disappointed in practice.

Lord chancellor and lieutenant of Disraeli, 1868–1880 When Disraeli succeeded Derby as prime minister for less than a year (February–December 1868), he at once replaced Chelmsford with Cairns, who was again his lord chancellor in the majority administration of 1874–80. The relationship between the two men was not a simple one, for Cairns's loyalty was to the party rather than the leader. At the Burghley House gathering of tory notables in January 1872 it was he who suggested that Disraeli should be persuaded to retire from the leadership after the lost battles of the previous four years. On his side, Disraeli was not above making fun of the chancellor's religiosity to others. Cairns, as he confessed when he found himself unequal to leading the Lords in opposition, was by nature a lieutenant, lacking the political courage which in Disraeli compensated for much else (Cairns to Disraeli, 27 Sept 1869, Bodl. Oxf., MS Hughenden B/XX/Ca). It was nevertheless plain that the leader leant heavily on Cairns's judgement. He redrafted manifestos and summarized choices for colleagues who did not have his acute sense of the possible. He chaired the committee that watched over the tories' electoral triumph in 1874. If Disraeli never really liked him, and was a little jealous (*Selection from the Diaries of … Stanley*, 198, 4 March 1875), he could not have dispensed with this influential member of his cabinets, who was universally considered, politics apart, a great lord chancellor.

As chairman of the judicature commission in 1867–9 Cairns completed, though he was obliged to modify, Palmer's reform of appellate jurisdiction. His 1875 Land Transfer Act was a failure, largely because it was optional. The Conveyancing Acts (1881–2), the Married Women's Property Act, and the Settled Land Act (both 1882) were measures that he had set in train, and were enacted with his assistance by Lord Selborne, as Palmer became in 1872. All were major pieces of legislation, enacted in a spirit of constructive reform. By common consent Cairns excelled on the bench, bringing to his work the same grasp of principle and lucidity that marked him as a barrister. Among his judgments, those on company law, narrowing the scope of directors and promoters for malpractice, were significant additions to case law. Bryce, a political opponent, thought him the greatest of Victorian judges (Bryce, 193).

Cairns played a part in the tory response to the evolving Liberal policy on the Irish church and land questions between 1868 and 1870, and he was at the centre of the related and delicate problem of his party's leadership in the Lords. He seconded Disraeli's bid to check ritualism in the Church of England by statute in 1874. Last, but not least, he was prominent in cabinet discussions of the revived and increasingly worrying Eastern question in 1876–8. As an Ulster protestant he had little sympathy with Irish Catholic nationalism. More than any other of Disraeli's colleagues, he shaped the insufficiently flexible alternative to Gladstone's call for Anglican disestablishment in Ireland. While he was right in believing that the concession would not reconcile even moderate nationalists to British rule, he made it difficult for the tories to avoid being viewed as obscurantist by Liberal opinion in Britain when he refused to contemplate any but minor changes to the Irish establishment's position. After the 1868 election had been fought and lost mainly on the issue, he came badly out of the Lords' rearguard action against the Liberal bill to disestablish and partly disendow the church in Ireland. As their reluctant leader in the new parliament, most tory peers supported him in opposing the second reading: but enough of them went with Lord Salisbury, the future prime minister, to give the government a majority of thirty-three on the second reading. In committee Cairns amended the bill to add considerably to the amount left to the disestablished church, but pressure to avert a constitutional crisis forced him to settle for a fraction of what he had hoped to get. He acted without consulting his followers in the house, and his Liberal counterpart, Lord Granville, observed that his hand shook when they finally reached agreement (Granville to Gladstone, 4 Aug 1869, *Political Correspondence*, 1.42).

The explanation that Cairns circulated to the tory peers read embarrassingly like an admission of failure: he had had no choice but to close with the government's offer, conditional upon its prompt acceptance, and 'put an end to what was a violent, and was rapidly becoming a dangerous, strain upon the … relations of the two Houses' (Malmesbury, 660–61, 24 July 1869). The loss of face led him to resign his leadership; the tory majority in the Lords, he told Disraeli, should be led by someone who enjoyed the 'traditional and material weight' that he did not possess (Cairns to Disraeli, 27 Sept 1869, Bodl. Oxf., MS Hughenden B/XX/Ca). For different reasons Salisbury and the fifteenth earl of Derby, who had just succeeded his father, declined the post. The eventual successor, the sixth duke of Richmond, who had little to recommend him but his rank, relied on Cairns's advice. Between them the English magnate and the Ulster lawyer contrived to trim subsequent bills in the first Gladstone ministry's programme without provoking a dispute comparable to that of 1869. Cairns believed compensation for disturbance in the Irish Land Bill for 1870 was, 'disguise it as you will, … giving the landlord's property to the tenant' (Cairns to Hardy, 6 April 1870, Steele, 309): but he and Richmond sided with the government in getting it through essentially unchanged. The partnership with the duke continued into Disraeli's second administration, beginning with the legislation on ritualism in its first year. Richmond stood by Cairns when their high-church colleagues thought that in presenting the report of a cabinet committee the chancellor had 'so manipulated every proposition as to give it a different sense'. Salisbury, who had sat on the committee, interrupted him repeatedly, 'a curious scene' (Carnarvon diary, 9 May 1874, BL, Add. MS 60906). Already aware of the real danger that these tensions might break up the government, Cairns was instrumental in amending its Public Worship Regulation Bill going through the Lords to secure a viable compromise. Entrusting the trial of cases brought under its provisions to a lay judge took much of the heat out of litigation.

The Eastern question did split the government. At the outset Cairns's sympathies were with the Balkan Christians in revolt against Ottoman rule, while Disraeli—Lord Beaconsfield from August 1876—identified British interests with saving Turkey from Russia, the Christians' champion. Beaconsfield complained that 'Moody and Sankey', as he called the chancellor behind his back, was making common cause with the pro-Russian high-churchmen in the cabinet. 'When I explained to him', the prime minister recounted, 'that he had unintentionally lent himself to sacerdotal intrigue he turned quite pale' (Beaconsfield to Derby, 20 Dec 1876, Monypenny & Buckle, 2.968). In fact several months elapsed before Cairns shifted his ground, carrying Richmond with him. He became as strongly anti-

Russian as Beaconsfield, and critical of Derby, the foreign secretary, for his anxiety to keep Britain from being drawn into the Russo-Turkish conflict that broke out in 1877. In December that year Cairns was the prime ministerial emissary who visited Hatfield to further the detaching of Salisbury from the group of ministers opposed to war. For the last few weeks before Derby's resignation at the end of March 1878 Beaconsfield, Cairns, and Salisbury did their best to take the conduct of foreign policy out of his hands. Without the lord chancellor's assistance it is doubtful whether Beaconsfield could have got his way to the extent that he did in a divided cabinet. Cairns's facility with words was invaluable as the debate behind closed doors slowly moved in the desired direction. In parliament, too, he stood forth as the champion of Disraelian imperialism. His reward was the earldom conferred upon him (27 September 1878) after the Congress of Berlin and 'peace with honour' in the Near East.

Cairns and Salisbury, 1880–1885 Cairns's uncertain health often kept him away from the Lords after the tories returned to opposition in 1880. On Beaconfield's death in the following year there was some talk of him, once again, as tory leader in the house: but Salisbury was the clear favourite over Richmond, who would have liked to resume the post he had relinquished to the then prime minister in 1876. Furthermore, Salisbury also emerged as joint leader of the party with Sir Stafford Northcote in the Commons. Cairns and Richmond were uncomfortable with their new chief's use of the tory majority among the peers to challenge the Gladstonian domination of British politics. According to Salisbury's doctrine, the Lords had a constitutional right to reject bills not backed by a specific electoral mandate and to amend those that were, consistently with the principle of the legislation. Cairns urged a more realistic interpretation of what the peers might do. At a meeting of the 'shadow cabinet' in August 1881 he argued that the Lords should not try to block even 'questionable legislation' lacking a mandate, such as the 1881 Irish Land Bill they were then considering (Carnarvon diary, 15 Aug 1881, BL, Add. MS 60917). Next year he went further, and refused to support Salisbury on his amendments to another Irish land measure, the Arrears Bill: 'the House … would be beaten and humbled' (Cairns to Salisbury, 6 Aug 1882, Hatfield House, Salisbury MSS HHM/3/E). The recent recruit to the peerage wanted to husband the Lords' diminished prestige: Salisbury was suspected, with some reason, of being ready to see the house abolished rather than surviving to acquiesce in anything on which the Commons insisted. In successive sessions from 1881 to 1883 tory peers showed that they preferred following Cairns's caution to defying of Gladstone. Salisbury seemed to have achieved nothing, and Cairns raised his tactics with others in the party leadership in October 1883, which by implication, at least, threw doubt on his leader's future. The peers, he told Richmond afterwards, 'must not swagger over amendments as if they were going to stick to them' (P. Marsh, 29–30; Cairns to Richmond, 29 Oct 1883, W. Sussex RO, Goodwood MSS, 871).

Cairns was more apprehensive still when Salisbury held up the 1884 Reform Bill until there was agreement on the redistribution of seats. A trial of strength between the main components of 'a tempered and balanced institution … is a bad thing', he said, as, 'with much alarm', he worked to stave off a dissolution that would set the people against the peers (Cairns to Richmond, 2 Nov 1884, W. Sussex RO, Goodwood MSS, 872; Cairns to Salisbury, 13 Nov 1884, Hatfield House, Salisbury MSS, HHM/3/E). This time, however, Salisbury obtained the result he wanted from confrontation with the government. If, over several years he had only once allowed his 'pent up personal feeling' about Cairns's attitude to escape in their discussions, their different temperaments, party histories, and religious convictions made for uneasy co-operation at best (Carnarvon diary, 15 Aug 1881, BL, Add. MS 60917). Yet Cairns was fully in sympathy with Salisbury's charge that Gladstonian Liberalism was sapping Britain's imperial will. His parliamentary oratory, effective but seldom inspired, rose to unexpected heights in his denunciation of the treaty recognizing the Transvaal's virtual independence after the battle of Majuba. He pilloried the Gladstone government for their cumulative concessions to the Boer rebels—'the "Surrender's Progress" … almost worthy of the pencil of a Hogarth'—and looked forward grimly to a similar capitulation in Ireland (*Hansard* 3, 260, 21 March 1881, 259).

A man in the puritan mould Cairns is not easily classifiable by posterity a century after his death. His 'great hope', wrote Lord Shaftesbury, who knew him well, 'is the Second Coming of our blessed Lord' (C. M. Marsh, 56). There can be little doubt that his life centred on what was not, for him, a truth without much bearing on everyday concerns. He had undergone the classical experience of conversion for an evangelical: 'a *separate*, real, personal transaction between the individual and his Saviour' (ibid., 54). The consequences of that informed everything he did. Any suggestion in the cut and thrust of politics that he had been less than honest visibly upset him (Carnarvon diary, 9 May 1874, BL, Add. MS 60906). In the villa he built for himself at Bournemouth, rooms were reserved for workers in need of a holiday from two of the evangelical societies that enjoyed his active patronage: the Bible-Women and Nurses Association and the London City Mission. He reconciled his religion, his patriotism, and his economic beliefs in the time-honoured puritan fashion, seeing in the 'pioneers of commerce and civilization … the Anglo-Saxon race and mainly England … the bearers of … [a] wondrous revelation' (C. M. Marsh, 65).

In the law, Cairns won acceptance by his unquestioned distinction: in politics he remained an outsider. A leading article on his passing did not spare his 'limited sympathy with the feelings of ordinary English gentlemen … and lack of geniality … not atoned for by dialectical ability' (*The Times*, 3 April 1885). No biography, excepting a very slim volume by an evangelical contemporary, exists of this, in a real sense, unworldly man. It is difficult to think of a more incongruous associate for Disraeli; but he served his party and the state conscientiously and intelligently. He died at Lindisfarne, his Bournemouth home, of congestion of the lungs on 2 April 1885, and was buried on 8 April in the town's cemetery. His eldest surviving son, Arthur Cairns, Viscount Garmoyle (*d.* 1890), succeeded to the earldom. DAVID STEELE

Sources C. M. Marsh, *Brief memories of Hugh McCalmont, first Earl Cairns* (1885) • PRO, Cairns MSS, PRO 30/51 • *A selection from the diaries of Edward Henry Stanley, 15th earl of Derby (1826–93), between March 1869 and September 1878*, ed. J. R. Vincent, CS, 5th ser., 4 (1994) • *Disraeli, Derby and the conservative party: journals and memoirs of Edward Henry, Lord Stanley, 1849–1869*, ed. J. R. Vincent (1978) • W. F. Monypenny and G. E. Buckle, *The life of Benjamin Disraeli*, rev. G. E. Buckle, 2nd edn, 2 vols. (1929) • Holdsworth, *Eng. law*, vol. 16 • R. Shannon, *The age of Disraeli, 1868–1881: the rise of tory democracy* (1992) • R. Shannon, *The age of Salisbury, 1881–1902: unionism and empire* (1996) • Bodl. Oxf., Dep. Hughenden • R. Millman, *Britain and the Eastern question, 1875–1878* (1979) • P. Marsh, *The discipline of popular government: Lord Salisbury's domestic statecraft, 1881–1902* (1978) • W. Sussex RO, Goodwood MSS • Carnarvon diary, BL, Add. MSS 60906, 60917 • M. Cowling, *1867: Disraeli, Gladstone and revolution* (1967) • J. Bentley, *Ritualism and politics in Victorian Britain* (1978) • E. J. Feuchtwanger, *Disraeli, democracy and the tory party: conservative leadership and organization after the second Reform Bill* (1968) • A. Jones, *The politics of reform, 1884* (1972) • *The political correspondence of Mr Gladstone and Lord Granville, 1868–1876*, ed. A. Ramm, 2 vols., CS, 3rd ser., 81–2 (1952) • E. D. Steele, *Irish land and British politics: tenant-right and nationality, 1865–1870* (1974) • J. Bryce, *Studies in contemporary biography* (1903) • *The diary of Gathorne Hardy, later Lord Cranbrook, 1866–1892: political selections*, ed. N. E. Johnson (1981) • *Hansard 3* • J. H. Harris [third earl of Malmesbury], *Memoirs of an ex-minister: an autobiography*, new edn (1885) • GEC, *Peerage* • *Dod's Parliamentary Companion* • Hatfield House, Hertfordshire, Salisbury MSS • R. Palmer, first earl of Selborne, *Memorials. Part II: personal and political, 1865–1895*, ed. S. M. Palmer, 2 vols. (1898)

Archives PRO, corresp., PRO 30/51 | BL, corresp. with Lord Carnarvon, Add. MS 60768 • BL, corresp. with Lord Cross, Add. MS 51268 • BL, letters to Sir Stafford Northcote, Add. MS 50021 • Bodl. Oxf., corresp. with Lord Kimberley • Bodl. Oxf., letters to Benjamin Disraeli • Harrowby Manuscript Trust, Sandon, Staffordshire, corresp. with Lord Harrowby • Hatfield House, Hertfordshire, Salisbury MSS • Herts. ALS, corresp. with Lord Lytton • LPL, corresp. with Lord Selborne • LPL, corresp. with A. C. Tait • Lpool RO, corresp. with Lord Derby • Suffolk RO, Ipswich, letters to Lord Cranbrook • W. Sussex RO, Goodwood MSS • W. Sussex RO, letters to duke of Richmond

Likenesses J. J. E. Mayall, photographs, 1860–69, NPG • L. Dickinson, portrait, 1876, Hughenden Manor, Buckinghamshire • L. C. Dickinson, oils, exh. RA 1876, TCD [*see illus.*] • lithograph, 1877, BM • Lock & Whitfield, woodburytype, 1881, NPG • A. B. Joy, marble bust, 1888, law courts, London • A. B. Joy, marble bust, 1894, Lincoln's Inn, London • Ape [C. Pellegrini], chromolithograph cartoon, repro. in *VF* (31 July 1869) • W. Holl, stipple (after G. Richmond), BM • J. Philip, group portrait, oils (*House of Commons, 1860*), Palace of Westminster, London • D. J. Pound, line engraving (after photograph by J. J. E. Mayall), BM, NPG • F. Sargent, etching, NPG • G. J. Stodart, stipple and line (after photograph by E. Debenham), NPG • cartes-de-visite, NPG • prints, NPG

Wealth at death £148,168 14*s.*: probate, 3 July 1885, *CGPLA Eng. & Wales*

Cairns, Sir Hugh William Bell (1896–1952), neurosurgeon, was born on 26 June 1896 in Port Pirie, South Australia. His father, William Cairns (1868–1958), a carpenter and joiner, had emigrated from Glasgow in 1889 and married Amy Florence Bell (1867–1964), a local music teacher. In 1903 they moved to the small township of Riverton, where Hugh Cairns, their only child, had his early education before obtaining scholarships to the high school in Adelaide and the University of Adelaide. In May 1915, at the beginning of the fourth year of his medical course, he joined the Australian Army Medical Corps (AAMC) as a private and was posted to a general hospital on Lemnos during the Gallipoli campaign. He then returned to Adelaide to complete his medical studies, qualifying MB, BS in June 1917. Rejoining the AAMC as captain, he served in France until January 1919, and then entered Balliol College, Oxford, with a Rhodes scholarship. There he studied physiology under C. S. Sherrington, and anatomy, and rowed for the university in the 1920 boat race. House appointments followed at the Radcliffe Infirmary, Oxford, and at the London Hospital, where he became an assistant to Professor Turnbull in the pathology department. He passed the FRCS Eng. in November 1921; on 24 November he married Barbara Forster Smith (1908–1987), the youngest daughter of A. L. *Smith (1850–1924), master of Balliol; they had two sons and two daughters.

For the next three years Cairns worked as first assistant to several surgeons at the London Hospital and published original work in the genito-urinary field. He gave a Hunterian lecture in 1926 and was appointed honorary assistant surgeon to the London Hospital. Then, advised by the neurologist George Riddoch, he obtained a Rockefeller fellowship and spent a year in the USA, working under Harvey Cushing, the famous Boston neurosurgeon. On returning to the London, Cairns determined to specialize in neurosurgery, but remained responsible for some general surgical patients. A Medical Research Council Special Report summarizing Cushing's methods brought him recognition; and, together with Geoffrey Jefferson in Manchester and Norman Dott in Edinburgh, he helped to lay the foundations of modern British neurosurgery. In 1931 he joined the staff of the Maida Vale Hospital as a neurosurgeon, while continuing his work at the London Hospital where he became a full surgeon in June 1933 and then practised neurosurgery exclusively. He also had a part-time appointment at the National Hospital, Queen Square, and was a consultant to the Queen Alexandra Military Hospital, Millbank.

Cairns's reputation flowered. After a further visit to Cushing in 1935 he proposed plans for a medical school at Oxford. With the munificence of Lord Nuffield, and the support of Sir Farquhar Buzzard, and others, he provided much of the impetus that led the university to give its approval, and was appointed its first Nuffield professor of surgery in 1937. In April 1938 the department of neurological surgery was opened at the Radcliffe Infirmary; Cairns was awarded an honorary DM degree and became a fellow of Balliol.

Following the Munich agreement in September 1938, Cairns ordered supplies of those neurosurgical instruments that the army would require in the event of war and, with Charles Symonds and George Riddoch, organized a hospital for head injuries in St Hugh's College, Oxford. Its importance during the subsequent war was paramount; its archives were later deposited in St Hugh's College Library. According to Charles Symonds,

After Munich Cairns formed the idea of a special hospital for head injuries at Oxford and a project of this kind in his mind could not rest without action. As a planner he was supreme, nor did he ever hesitate to put his plans forward at the highest operative level. Thus in a very short time the war office decided to take over St Hugh's College as a hospital for head injuries. (Fraenkel, 140)

Cairns achieved the peak of his career during the Second World War. After a short time as an adviser to the Ministry of Health, he began work at the military hospital for head injuries based at St Hugh's, when it opened in February 1940. Beginning with 50 beds it eventually held 430 by the time of the invasion of Normandy. Among the hospital's staff were the neurologists D. Denny-Brown and W. Ritchie Russell, the pathologist Dorothy Russell, and the bacteriologist and bee-keeper G. T. 'Daddy' Western. St Hugh's became 'a bustling, keen, sort of place' (Fraenkel, 141), where Cairns was able to carry out research into the incidence of epilepsy after brain injury, the assessment of the psychological state of the brain-injured patient, and electroencephalography. Work was also carried out on the nature of concussion. The college gardens played an important part in helping patients to recuperate, and are discussed in Anthony Babbington's book *No Memorial* (1954), which offers a patient's view of St Hugh's.

In June 1940 Cairns was gazetted lieutenant, acting colonel RAMC, and later brigadier. In the same year he created the first of eight mobile neurosurgical units, to operate close to the action, and was also responsible for introducing specially designed crash helmets for army motor cyclists, thereby dramatically reducing their injuries. He set up rehabilitation centres for head-injured patients at Middleton Park, near Bicester, and Tusmore Park, and from at least 1943 worked with Howard Florey in assessing the value of penicillin in treating and preventing wound infection. Cairns was president of the section of neurology of the Royal Society of Medicine, and later presided over the Society of British Neurological Surgeons from 1945 to 1948, and the Association of Surgeons in 1947.

It had been Cairns's intention that the Oxford medical school should be a centre of excellence, where selected graduates would be trained in research. However, with the onset of war it developed as an undergraduate school. Nevertheless, Cairns always hoped that his original idea might eventually be adopted. Teaching was always one of his prime concerns, and many of the next generation of neurosurgeons were trained by him according to the principles laid down by Cushing.

Cairns was knighted (KBE) in June 1946. He was closely involved in post-war planning, on which he left his mark. He became the first Sims travelling professor of the Royal College of Surgeons in 1948 and lectured in New Zealand, Australia, and southern Africa. His association with Florey stimulated an interest in the treatment of infections of the central nervous system, particularly tuberculous meningitis, which occupied his attention for the rest of his life. He was also interested in the surgery of mental illness and the physiology of consciousness. Important work was being produced in these fields, when a lymphosarcoma of the caecum brought about his untimely death in the Radcliffe Infirmary, Oxford, at the age of fifty-six, on 18 July 1952. Four days later he was buried at Holywell church, Oxford, following a funeral service at the university church of St Mary. Memorial services were held at St Mary's, Oxford, and St Philip's, London Hospital.

A handsome, rather tense man, Cairns possessed enormous energy and charm, and a tremendous drive that supported his ambition and ideas. He had a gift for attracting loyal and able co-workers, whom he led with imagination, sparing neither himself nor them, striving hard for whatever he wanted. His devotion to music and literature was stimulated and supported by Lady Cairns, who survived her husband. The Cairns Library at the John Radcliffe Hospital, Oxford, is named after him. PETER H. SCHURR

Sources G. J. Fraenkel, *Hugh Cairns* (1991) • G. Jefferson, 'Memories of Hugh Cairns', *Journal of Neurology, Neurosurgery and Psychiatry*, 22 (1959), 155–66 [contains a bibliography of Cairns's writings.] • J. B. Pennybacker, 'Sir Hugh William Bell Cairns', *Neurosurgical giants: feet of clay and iron*, ed. P. C. Bucy (1991), 255–61 • J. B. Pennybacker, *Surgical Neurology*, 4 (1975), 347–50 • C. P. Symonds, 'Tria juncta in uno', *The 6th Sir Hugh Cairns memorial lecture: Society of British Neurological Surgeons* (1970) • R. H. O. B. Robinson and W. R. Le Fanu, *Lives of the fellows of the Royal College of Surgeons of England, 1952–1964* (1970), 61–5 • *The Lancet* (26 July 1952), 202–3 • P. H. Schurr, 'The Cairns tradition', 12th Sir Hugh Cairns memorial lecture, 1988, *Journal of Neurology, Neurosurgery and Psychiatry*, 53 (1990), 188–93 • G. Jefferson, 'Sir Hugh Cairns, KBE, DM, FRCS', *Journal of Neurosurgery*, 10 (1953), 87–9 • P. H. Schurr, 'Sir Hugh Cairns, KBE, MD, FRCS (1896–1952)', *Journal of Medical Biography*, 1 (1993), 202–6 • H. Cairns, 'Neurosurgery in the British army, 1939–45', *British Journal of Surgery* [war suppl.], 1 (1947), 9–26 • *CGPLA Eng. & Wales* (1952) • *DNB*

Archives Cairns Memorial Library, Oxford • Flinders University, Adelaide, Australia | Cairns Family Archive

Likenesses W. Stoneman, photograph, 1947, NPG • photographs, U. Oxf., Nuffield department of surgery • photographs, Cairns Memorial Library, Oxford • photographs, Society of British Neurological Surgeons, Oxford

Wealth at death £22,102 12*s*. 3*d*.: probate, 16 Oct 1952, *CGPLA Eng. & Wales*

Cairns, John (1818–1892), minister of the United Presbyterian church and theologian, was born on 23 August 1818 at Ayton Hill, Berwickshire, the third of eight children of John Cairns (1790?–1841), shepherd, and his wife, Alison Murray (1788?–1860). Cairns was raised in the strict but loving environment provided by his godly parents within the tradition of Presbyterian dissent: the family belonged to its largest branch, the United Secession church. He received his early education at Ayton and later at the parish school at Cockburnspath, whose learned schoolmaster, John McGregor, had qualified in theology at St Andrews. When Cairns had to leave school at age thirteen to assist his father at herding, McGregor diligently tutored him for three years part-time in a broad range of classical studies in preparation for university. In 1834 he entered the University of Edinburgh, where he excelled in every academic discipline. He was a favourite student of Sir William Hamilton, the celebrated philosopher and professor of logic. Another of his professors, John Wilson—better known under his pen-name of Christopher North—wrote that among all his many hundreds of students, Cairns was unsurpassed in terms of academic brilliance, strength of character, and future promise (MacEwen, 71–2). In April of 1841 Cairns received his MA, standing first in classics and philosophy, and sharing first in mathematics.

While many of his professors and friends urged upon him an academic or literary career, Cairns resolved to respond to what he regarded as the highest of callings—that of the ministry of the gospel of Christ. Accordingly, in August 1840 he entered upon the study of theology at the Secession Church Divinity Hall, where, under the influence of professors Robert Balmer and John Brown in particular, he continued his brilliant career as a student. Since at this period the theology curriculum called for only two months of full-time intramural study annually (extending for five years), students could arrange to pursue other avenues for theological enrichment for the rest of the year. From the autumn of 1843 Cairns took the opportunity to spend a year on the continent, travelling widely and studying in Berlin, where he took classes in philosophy and theology, and so thoroughly mastered German that he was invited to remain as an instructor the next year.

On his return to Scotland, the 1844 autumn session concluded Cairns's studies. On 5 February 1845 he was licensed by Edinburgh presbytery and on 6 August of that year was ordained and inducted into the charge of Golden Square Secession Church in Berwick upon Tweed. Here he was to remain as minister for thirty-one years, until he took up his appointment in 1876 as a full-time professor at the United Presbyterian Divinity Hall in Edinburgh. (He served as a professor at the hall from 1867, but, as was the practice for all professors at the time, he lectured for the two-month autumn session only and therefore retained his pastoral charge.) In 1879 Cairns became principal of the hall, an office he held until shortly before his death in 1892. Cairns never married: his biographer notes that when he was thirty-one his marriage proposal to a young woman was declined (MacEwen, 338). From 1856 to the end of his life his housekeeper was his sister Janet.

From the beginning of his ministry in Berwick, Cairns set himself a rigorous work schedule which was to be the mark of his whole life. A large and vigorous man requiring only five or six hours of sleep, he crowded into each long day a major component of reading, academic study and writing, sermon preparation, and pastoral visitation. In his thirty-one years in Berwick he never failed to fulfil a commitment to visit each year every home in his congregation of over 700 members. Cairns was noted for his phenomenal powers of memory: on one occasion, when asked, he was able to give the names of every child in his congregation. Although he wrote out his 45–50-minute sermons in full, he was able by reading them through—usually only once—to deliver them verbatim without further reference to his manuscript. In spite of his commanding intellect, his vast wealth of learning, and his scholarly yet animated preaching style (several churches claimed that their pulpit lamps had been demolished by his arm swings), he exhibited a remarkable humility of character and indifference to the prevailing social distinctions of the time.

Two years after his ordination, in 1847, the union took place between the United Secession church and the Relief church to form the United Presbyterian church, a union of which Cairns very much approved. Within a few years, although he was still in his early thirties, Cairns had come to be recognized within his denomination as its most eminent theologian and church leader, and had gained a formidable reputation in the wider church both in Britain and on the continent. Having mastered the German language as a student, Cairns continued to immerse himself in German modes of thought, becoming familiar with the emerging forms of biblical criticism, Hegelian philosophy, and the various schools of German theology. Over the years, he was the author of numerous scholarly articles on German theology and philosophy—from his 1856 article on Kant in the *Encyclopaedia Britannica* (8th edn) to his exhaustive study of recent German theology in 1889 (MacEwen, 744). However, Cairns never embraced the more radical forms of German thought, although, no doubt, such thought played a large part in moderating his, and through him his church's, traditional Calvinist confessional orthodoxy. Cairns's departure from such orthodoxy is reflected in his qualified support of the evangelistic campaigns of Moody and Sankey. Although he acknowledged the concerns about the emotional appeals and 'altar calls' during the campaign services (MacEwen, 721), he was impressed by the strong evangelical note of grace and free offer of salvation which counteracted the hyper-Calvinist doctrine of predestination and limited atonement which marked the old orthodoxy.

Early in his ministry Cairns came to prize evangelical catholicity more than reformed confessionalism. Consequently, during the atonement controversy of the 1840s in his church, he sided with those who favoured a softening of the traditional doctrine of a limited atonement. Later in the century he guided the United Presbyterian church in modifying subscription to the Calvinist orthodoxy of the Westminster confession by means of the landmark 1879 Declaratory Act. From 1863 to 1873 he laboured hard to promote the union of his church with the Free Church, only to see the effort fail. Cairns was a proponent of disestablishment and, in later years, total abstinence. He took an active role in the Pan-Presbyterian Alliance and the Evangelical Alliance. At the latter's meeting in Berlin in 1857 he gave a widely acclaimed address in German on behalf of all English-speaking delegates. In 1872 he was elected moderator of the United Presbyterian synod, and at the 1884 tercentenary celebrations of Edinburgh University he was among a select few chosen to receive the doctor of laws degree.

During his years in Berwick, Cairns was offered several professorial chairs in Scotland, England, and Canada, as well as the position of principal of Edinburgh University in 1859, a year after it bestowed on him the honorary DD degree. He also received numerous calls to prestigious city congregations in both Scotland and England. In connection with a vacancy in an Edinburgh charge in 1864, he was sent one memorial signed by several hundred students at the university. On the same occasion another memorial urging him to come to Edinburgh, signed by three judges of the court of session, the lord advocate, the principal, and seven professors at the university, among numerous others, referred to 'his great intellectual gifts and powers, his deep and wide scholarship, his mastery of the literature of modern unbelief, and the commanding simplicity and godly sincerity of his personal character and public teaching' (MacEwen, 470). Yet in spite of this acclaim there were those, especially later in his life, who made the critical observation that while other theologians were embroiled in controversy over Darwin and evolution, Cairns spent his energy learning new languages—Arabic, Assyrian, Dutch, and Spanish; and that this saintly man, whose personal faith and deep convictions seem never to have been tested or shaken, failed to grasp and experience the depth of religious doubt and the widespread scepticism of his age (*Principal Cairns*, 88–9).

Whatever validity there may have been to such criticisms, there can be no doubt that in his time this much loved man had a vast influence on the Scottish church and people. That his influence did not appear to last long into the new century may be explained in part by the legacy of his writings. Although vast in number and scope (most are listed in MacEwen, 789–90), they were overwhelmingly pamphlets, church reports, and serial articles rather than weighty monographs. He did write the biography of his former professor: *Memoir of John Brown D.D.* (1860), and his Cunningham lectures were published in 1881 as *Unbelief in the Eighteenth Century*. However, Cairns during his lifetime was known not for his writings but as a captivating preacher, a learned scholar and teacher, an outstanding church statesman, and a humble servant of Christ. In 1891 Cairns's health began to fail, and he was unable to teach the autumn session. On 12 March 1892 he died in his home at 10 Spence Street, Edinburgh, and was buried on 17 March in Echo Bank (later renamed Newington) cemetery, Edinburgh. DONALD C. SMITH

Sources A. R. MacEwen, *Life and letters of John Cairns D.D., LL.D.* (1895) · J. Cairns, *Principal Cairns* (1903) · *DNB* · W. R. Nicoll, 'Dr John Cairns', *Princes of the church* (1921), 85–92 · *David Cairns: an autobiography, some recollections of a long life, and selected letters*, ed. [D. Cairns and A. H. Cairns] (1950) · D. Woodside, *The soul of a Scottish church: the contribution of the United Presbyterian church to Scottish life and religion* (1918) · D. Cairns, 'John Cairns', *Fathers of the kirk*, ed. R. S. Wright (1960), 204–13

Archives NL Scot., corresp.; travel diaries | NL Scot., letters to Alexander Campbell Fraser

Likenesses J. Edgar, portrait, 1862, Scot. NPG · W. E. Lockhart, portrait, *c*.1888, Lockhart Memorial Church, Edinburgh · W. Noll, engraving (after J. Edgar), Scot. NPG · bust, priv. coll. · photograph, repro. in MacEwen, *Life and letters*, frontispiece · portrait, Scot. NPG

Wealth at death £9818 7*s*. 11*d*.: confirmation, 2 April 1892, *CCI*

Cairns, William (*d*. 1848), philosopher, studied at the University of Glasgow. He graduated MA in 1802 and received an LLD in 1838. After entering the Antiburgher Secession Hall in 1800, he was ordained minister of the Secession church at Johnshaven, Kincardineshire, in March 1808. He resigned in October 1815 in order to take up a position as professor of logic, belles-lettres, and rhetoric at the Belfast Institution, where he remained until his death in Belfast on 21 April 1848.

As is evident from his *Outlines of Lectures on Logic and Belles-Lettres*, published in Belfast in 1829, Cairns belonged very much to the Scottish common-sense school of philosophy. His major work was his *Treatise on Moral Freedom*, published in London in 1844, in which he examines the relationship between judgement and moral responsibility. Cairns attempts to refute the arguments of necessitarians such as Jonathan Edwards by arguing that the relationship between motive and will is not one of cause and effect. Starting from an examination of the question of whether we can be held morally responsible for our opinions, Cairns suggests that the process of willing must include an element of judgement in which the relative importance of motives for the individual subject is compared. For Cairns, if this intellectual component in volition is granted, then the will must be allowed to be self-originating. Postulating this intellectual basis for the decisions of the will allows Cairns to come to the theologically orthodox conclusion that human moral freedom is not incompatible with divine fore-knowledge. GAVIN BUDGE

Sources *DNB* · W. Cairns, *Outlines of lectures on logic and belles-lettres* (1829) · W. Cairns, *Treatise on moral freedom* (1844) · W. I. Addison, *A roll of graduates of the University of Glasgow from 31st December 1727 to 31st December 1897* (1898)

Likenesses miniature, Belfast Museum

Caistor, Richard (*d*. 1420), priest and supposed theologian, is said to have come from near Norwich, possibly from the village of Caister St Edmund. Sometimes he was styled master but there is no clear evidence that he studied at a university. Probably by 1385 he had been tonsured as a cleric. He was vicar of Sedgeford near Bishop's Lynn from 1397 to 1402, and vicar of St Stephen's parish in Norwich from 1402 until his death, presentation to both benefices being made by the prior and monks of the cathedral priory of Norwich. In both parishes he was, as vicar, the parish priest. Margery Kempe provides a glowing portrait of him as vicar of St Stephen's. He was, she indicates, a generous and apostolic parish priest, and a noted and effective preacher. He acted as her confessor in Norwich and supported her against her critics, including the officials of the bishop. Books on the ten commandments, the beatitudes, and the meditations of St Bernard, and also some homilies, were attributed to him. His only extant work, however, is the hymn 'Jesu, lord, that madest me', which seems to have been very popular, surviving in numerous manuscripts (though eight of its twelve stanzas come from an earlier poem).

Caistor's will, made probably within a few days of his death, is remarkable, especially for a man who had been incumbent for eighteen years of one of the most valuable livings in Norwich. It is very brief: it contains no requests for masses and prayers to be said for his soul: and he wanted his wealth—whose value was not specified—

apart from £10 that was to be spent on buying two antiphonaries for his church, to be given to the poor, with preference being given to those of his parish, on the grounds that 'the goods of the church, according to canon law, belong to the poor' (Tanner, 232–3). Following his death in 1420, perhaps on 29 March, his reputation for holiness developed into a minor cult. Margery Kempe went to pray at his grave in St Stephen's Church, to thank him for the recovery of a friend from sickness: between 1429 and 1500 a number of bequests were left in wills for people to make pilgrimages to his grave, or for offerings to be left at it. He appears to have been a radical and evangelical priest, one in a succession as vicars of St Stephen's parish, though Bale's claim that he was an enthusiastic Wycliffite, albeit a secret one, seems unfounded. NORMAN P. TANNER

Sources D. Harford, 'Richard of Caister, and his metrical prayer', *Norfolk Archaeology*, 17 (1908–10), 221–44 • *The book of Margery Kempe*, ed. S. B. Meech and H. E. Allen, EETS, 212 (1940) • N. P. Tanner, *The church in late medieval Norwich, 1370–1532* (1984) • Bale, *Cat.* • C. F. Brown, ed., *Religious lyrics of the XVth century* (1939) • J. Pits, *Relationum historicarum de rebus Anglicis*, ed. [W. Bishop] (Paris, 1619) • C. Brown and R. H. Robbins, *The index of Middle English verse* (1943), no. 1727 • R. H. Robbins and J. L. Cutler, *Supplement to the index of Middle English verse* (1965), no. 1727

Wealth at death over £10: Tanner, *The church*; 232–3

Caithness. For this title name *see* Harald Maddadson, earl of Caithness and earl of Orkney (1133/4–1206); Macheth, Hvarflod, countess of Orkney and Caithness (*fl.* 1196) [*see under* Macheth family (*per. c.*1124–1215)]; Magnus, earl of Caithness and earl of Orkney (*c.*1290–1320/21); Stewart, David, first earl of Strathearn and first earl of Caithness (*b.* in or after 1357?, *d.* 1386?); Stewart, Walter, earl of Atholl, first earl of Caithness, and earl of Strathearn (early 1360s–1437); Crichton, George, of that ilk, earl of Caithness (*d.* 1454) [*see under* Crichton, William, of that ilk, first Lord Crichton (*d.* 1453)]; Sinclair, William, third earl of Orkney and first earl of Caithness (*b.* after 1407, *d.* 1480) [*see under* Sinclair family]; Sinclair, George, fourth earl of Caithness (*b.* in or before 1527, *d.* 1582); Sinclair, George, fifth earl of Caithness (1566/7–1643); Sinclair, James, fourteenth earl of Caithness (1821–1881); Sinclair, Marie, countess of Caithness (1830–1895) [*see under* Sinclair, James, fourteenth earl of Caithness (1821–1881)].

Caius, John. *See* Kay, John (*fl. c.*1482).

Caius, John (1510–1573), scholar and physician, was born at Norwich on 6 October 1510, the son of Robert Caius and Alice, *née* Wode or Woda. The English form of his name is variously given in archival records but was probably Keys or Kees.

Study in Cambridge and Italy After school in Norwich alongside the equally precocious William Framingham he entered Gonville Hall, Cambridge, on 12 September 1529, a sober student of theology, heavily influenced by the ideas of Erasmus, one of whose works he translated into English and another he epitomized. A talented linguist, Caius studied Hebrew and translated some patristic Greek texts into Latin for his friends. In November 1533 he was appointed principal of Physwick's Hall, and on 6 December he was elected a fellow of Gonville Hall. When his interests began to turn to medicine is unclear—Gonville Hall already numbered several eminent physicians among its members, notably the royal physician, Sir William Butts—but in 1539 Caius left Cambridge for Italy.

Padua, where Caius studied medicine, was the leading medical university of Europe, and its most celebrated professor, Johannes Baptista Montanus, enjoyed a European reputation as a medical humanist. He believed that by a return to the texts and principles of the Greek physician Galen modern medicine could be purified of erroneous and dangerous medieval misunderstandings, and by following the method of healing laid down by Galen diagnosis and treatment could be made more precise and effective. At the same time the rediscovery of the classical Greek texts in botany, zoology, and anatomy had brought about a resurgence of interest in these practical subjects, as scholars strove to relate the evidence of their texts to what they could see around them. At Padua the brilliant young Vesalius had been appointed in 1537 to teach anatomy, and with him Caius shared a house as well as an interest in Galenic manuscripts of anatomy. From his teachers Caius gained a passionate attachment to Galen which dominated his medical life. Into the volumes of his copy of the 1538 Galen, bought perhaps at Basel on his outward journey (now Eton College, Fc. 2, 6–8), he copied innumerable notes, comments, emendations, as well as readings from manuscripts inspected over almost twenty years. By correcting the Greek text on philological principles or by proper translation, he believed, apparent errors of Galen could be removed, and the accusations of his detractors, including, after 1542, Vesalius, answered.

In Padua, after graduating on 13 May 1541, Caius lectured for a while on Aristotle's logic in Greek, before moving to study with Matteo Corti at Pisa and embarking on a tour of libraries in Italy, collecting and copying Greek manuscripts of ancient medicine and philosophy. In 1544, on his way home, he published at Basel an edition of seven Galenic texts, *Libri aliquot Graeci*, some for the first time in Greek, and his *De methodo medendi*, ostensibly his own summary of the method of healing, but deriving, with little or no acknowledgement, verbatim from the lectures of Montanus. Of his activities on his immediate return to England little is certain. He left Cambridge in September 1545, and by the end of 1546, at the request of Henry VIII, he had begun a series of anatomical demonstrations for the London Barber–Surgeons that lasted for twenty years. In 1547 he was elected fellow of the College of Physicians of London, serving as a member of its council from 1551 until his death.

Physician in London Like Caius's teachers at Padua, the leading members of the college were staunch Galenists: Edward Wotton and John Clement, a Norfolk man and Caius's model, had been involved in the 1525 Venetian *editio princeps* of Galen, and several others, like George Owen, owned Greek manuscripts, which in the earlier 1550s Caius was reading. The college was also concerned to impose the new Galenism not only on London physicians but throughout England. The accession of Mary and the return of Cardinal Pole (whom Caius and many other members had known in Padua), John Clement, and other exiles, saw a revival in the college's fortunes and ambitions. Caius was elected president annually from 1555 until 1560, again in 1562 and 1563, and finally in 1571, but it was under Mary that he and his colleagues tried to impose their writ most firmly. The college statutes were revised to reflect both the latest humanist medicine and the college's desire to place its model of medical practice at the apex of medical practice even beyond London. The statutes were approved by parliament, and Pole's support ensured the acquiescence of the universities, albeit temporarily. But after Mary's death, despite Caius's continued attempts to assert its authority, the college met with scant success in controlling medical practice in the metropolis. Elizabethan magnates could easily protect their favourites from the wrath of the college, and the tiny number of fellows and licentiates (never more than twenty-five), while appropriate for an Italian town, could attend only a small élite of patients in the burgeoning capital, let alone beyond it.

Caius became extremely wealthy as a London physician, mainly to the court and city; although he seems to have attended Elizabeth I in 1564 his name does not appear in the royal household accounts, and the story of his dismissal from court in 1568 for popery is far from proven. His generosity to the College of Physicians (including the refurbishment of the tomb of its founder, Thomas Linacre, in St Paul's Cathedral) was exceeded only by that to his old Cambridge college. In 1557 he set in train plans for its massive enlargement, in personnel as well as in buildings. On 4 September 1557 a royal charter converted Gonville Hall into its refoundation as Gonville and Caius College. By March 1558 he had transferred to it his manors of Croxley, Hertfordshire, and Burnham Wyndhams and Runcton Holme, Norfolk, which he had purchased for £1033 12*s*. 6*d*. In gratitude he was allowed to incorporate his Padua MD at a university ceremony on 26 March 1558. Nine months later, on 24 January 1559, Caius was elected master of his college.

Master of Caius Although Caius felt that he was returning to a home filled with strangers, his first years as master bloomed with promise. New buildings, including the symbolic and Italianate gates of humility, virtue, and honour, were erected with an eye to hygiene as well as beauty; the fellowship and student numbers expanded. But Caius was not at his best with the young; he lamented the decline in student behaviour from the days of his youth, and there were vigorous protests against his autocratic rule, and accusations of atheism in 1565–6. In an Elizabethan Cambridge that was becoming more puritan and Calvinist his college stood out increasingly for its religious conservatism. Caius's own religious views remained firmly Erasmian; he had Catholic friends, notably John Clement, and he looked back to the last years of Henry VIII as the golden age. He hoarded the vestments, mass books, and other medieval treasures of his college even as his friend Archbishop Parker was calling in such relics of the past from other colleges. His college statutes, with their prayers for the dead, preserve the atmosphere of a medieval chantry in a notionally protestant chapel. His own, at times curious, behaviour, his ownership of at least one magical manuscript (BL, Add. MS 36674), and his overt lack of sympathy with puritanism (although he seems to have kept on friendly terms with certain individuals, like Bishop Parkhurst of Norwich, whose theological views he did not share) allowed his opponents the chance to accuse him of popery and preposterous government. In 1572, at the insistence of Archbishop Sandys, the university authorities ransacked his room, burning and smashing what they could find. The old man retired, sick and worn out, to London, where his stomach ailment grew worse. On a brief return in June 1573 he handed over his mastership to Thomas Legge before returning to his house near St Bartholomew's Hospital, where he died on 29 July 1573.

In his will, printed in *The Works of John Caius* (1912), Caius left his extensive library and, save for a few legacies, all his property to his college, enjoining it to repair the tomb of Linacre and to erect an appropriate tomb for him (Caius) in the college chapel. The latter can be seen today. It bears two inscriptions: 'vivit post funera virtus' ('virtue lives beyond the grave'), and the lapidary 'fui Caius' ('I was Caius').

Writings Of Caius's early theological writings nothing is known save what he himself reports, especially in his *De libris suis* (London, 1570). He published four volumes containing editions and translations of his beloved Galen; *Galeni libri aliquot* (dedicated to Butts, Basel, 1544); *De sanitate tuenda* (dedicated to Edward VI, Basel, 1549); *Opera aliquot et versiones* (dedicated to Cardinal Granvelle, Louvain, 1556); and a collection of minor works (Basel, 1557?) dedicated to Thomas Wendy and others. His annotations confirm his plan to correct and translate many more Galenic texts, and to enlarge his commentary on Galen's *Anatomical Procedures*, included in the Basel 1544 collection, with further defences of Galen against Vesalius (see his own copy, CUL, Adv. d. 3, 1), but none was brought to fruition. As a translator he is lucid and accurate, but his Greek editions are more enthusiastic than scholarly. None the less, his annotations contain much important information on manuscripts or annotations now lost, and often have readings superior to those in more modern standard editions.

Caius was a learned, intelligent, if not always scrupulous Galenist. His *De methodo medendi*, he claimed, had the merit of bringing the new, humanist Galenism to public attention—its real author, Montanus, was outraged at the plagiarism, but Caius reprinted the book in the Louvain collection of 1556. His work on the English sweat of 1551 is in Latin in the Louvain *Opera aliquot*, and was reprinted in London, 1721; Berlin, 1833; and Jena, 1847. In English as *A Boke or Counseil … Againste … the Sweate* (London, 1552) it was reprinted in London, 1844, and Jena, 1847. The book shows a shrewd and careful observer, eager to introduce the latest Italian ideas to England. The description of symptoms and spread of the disease are remarkably detailed, and Caius provided lengthy prescriptions for both therapy and prophylaxis, all according to the principles of Galen. Both versions are vigorously written, but, typically, suffer from long and extremely irrelevant digressions on, for example, Newcastle collieries (Latin, 73) or his own early life and writings (English, 5–9). None the less, they provide the best account of the sweating sickness, and were appreciated in Italy and as far afield as the court of the Ottoman sultan.

Caius's annotations in his books at Eton and Cambridge show how much he was determined to introduce the new Galenic anatomy into England, but of the details of his teaching little save the plaudits of some of his audience survives. It is clear that he, like Galen, saw anatomy as fundamental to medicine, and he made provision in his college statutes for an annual anatomy to be carried out in Cambridge, a procedure that may have influenced the young William Harvey, a later scholar of Gonville and Caius. But he resolutely refused to follow Vesalius in his claims that Galen was an animal anatomist, collecting passages which showed that Galen had, at least at times, dissected or looked at a human corpse. Since Galen himself claimed near infallibility, any errors in his human anatomy as it reached Caius must be the result of others' errors.

At the end of his life Caius turned to more antiquarian pursuits, albeit occasioned by (and occasioning) contemporary controversies. His *De pronunciatione Graecae et Latinae linguae* (1574) was an attempt to reimpose an older pronunciation than that introduced into Cambridge in the 1550s, and contains interesting comments on the pronunciation of the two languages by European scholars he had met or had read and the modern Greek community in Venice, as well as evidence drawn from his study of manuscripts. Far less successful are his *De antiquitate Cantabrigiensis academiae* (1568) and his *Historia Cantabrigiensis academiae* (1574). Encouraged by Archbishop Parker to reply to the *Assertio* of Thomas Caius of Oxford that his university was the older, Caius poured out a mass of information, good, bad, and irrelevant, to reclaim the pre-eminence for Cambridge. Some of his sources can be identified, and show the considerable extent of his knowledge of Cambridge libraries and archives, but the result lacks judgement. He also contributed large sections to the *Annals* of his own college and of the College of Physicians (in part transcribed in *Works*). His zeal for the past is manifest also in his own library and in the records of his friendship with his fellow antiquarian, Archbishop Parker, whose protection may have prevented further trouble for him in the 1560s.

James I, when offered a copy of *De antiquitate* is said by Thomas Fuller to have demanded instead a copy of Caius's *De canibus* (1570). This book, along with its accompanying *De rariorum animalium et stirpium historia*, shows Caius at his most attractive, and even humorous. Caius was in part inspired to work on natural history by Conrad Gesner, the great Swiss naturalist and physician, to whose *Historia animalium* Caius contributed entries and plates. Gesner, to whom Caius dedicates some moving pages in *De libris suis*, was a fellow Galenist, equally concerned to expand on the truths of the past by incorporating new information on the natural world. Caius provided him with abundant information, drawn from his travels around England, the royal zoos, and even folklore, which show how good and accurate an observer he was even of tiny details. The tinker's cur is described with as much care as a greyhound, the fish of Yarmouth with precision given to a white raven or an exotic civet. The humble puffin kept by Caius in his own house is as absorbing (and as difficult) a pet as a Barbary ape. In reporting on these creatures Caius is not only being an up-to-date, serious, and scholarly naturalist, familiar both with texts and with practical observation; he is also contributing to the European community of scholars, with whom he may well have felt more at home than with the unruly young of Elizabethan Cambridge.

Certainly, Caius's zoological interests add a certain humanity to the severe portrait of a short man with a long beard and a squeaky voice, somewhat pompous and addicted to ceremonial, at times autocratic and overbearing. Even his friends were constrained to remark on some of his eccentric personal habits, and his name, his profession and his oddity were immortalized by Shakespeare in the *Merry Wives of Windsor*, even if the nationality of that Dr Caius was French. But, although his writings are now little read, what he did for his Cambridge college and for the College of Physicians is still deservedly remembered by his successors today. VIVIAN NUTTON

Sources J. O. Halliwell, *The life of St. Katherine … and … the magical manuscript of Dr. Caius* (1848) · Munk, *Roll* · *The works of John Caius, MD … with a memoir of his life*, ed. J. Venn (1912) · Venn, *Alum. Cant.* · C. E. Raven, *English naturalists from Neckam to Ray: a study of the making of the modern world* (1947) · G. Clark and A. M. Cooke, *A history of the Royal College of Physicians of London*, 1 (1964) · P. Grierson, 'John Caius' library', *Biographical history of Gonville and Caius College*, ed. J. Venn and others, 7: *Admissions from 1957 to 1962* (1978), 516 · C. Webster, ed., *Health, medicine and mortality in the sixteenth century* (1979) · H. D. Isaacs, 'European influences on medicine', *Mashriq: proceedings of the Manchester East Mediterranean seminar: 1977–78* (1980), 27–8 · V. Nutton, 'Conrad Gesner and the English naturalists', *Medical History*, 29 (1985), 93–7 · C. N. L. Brooke, *A history of Gonville and Caius College* (1985) · V. Nutton, *John Caius and the manuscripts of Galen* (1987) · CUL, Adv. d.3, 1

Archives CUL · Eton · Gon. & Caius Cam. · RCP Lond.

Likenesses oils, 1563, Gon. & Caius Cam. · Passe, line engraving, BM; repro. in H. Holland, *Herōologia* (1620) · woodcut, repro. in J. Caius, *Ioannis Caii Britanni Opera aliquot et versiones* (Louvain, 1556)

Wealth at death over £513 7*s*. 10*d*.—incl. £241 handed over to his executor for payment for land for his college: *The works*, ed. Venn, 45–6; 59–72

Caius [Kay, Key], **Thomas** (*c*.**1505–1572**), antiquary and college head, was born *c*.1505, on the evidence of his university career. His family origins are uncertain, although Anthony Wood thought he was born in Lincolnshire of Yorkshire heritage. His family name was Kay or Key, but no relationship has been traced to the two Tudor scholars named John Kay who also adopted Caius as a neo-classical surname.

Caius matriculated at Oxford *c*.1522 and was elected to an All Souls fellowship in 1525. He was admitted BA in 1526 and proceeded MA in 1531. As an undergraduate he embraced the new humanist curriculum, studying Latin and Greek grammar, rhetoric, and some natural philosophy. He may have followed the public Greek lectures of Thomas Lupset (1520–23) and Juan Luis Vives (1523–4). In

1527 Caius published a translation of three sermons by the humanist Bishop John Longland, including the one preached in 1525 at the cornerstone ceremony for Thomas Wolsey's Cardinal College. Caius's literary skill was well respected. He translated Erasmus's *Paraphrase* of St Mark's gospel into English at the request of Queen Katherine Parr and George Owen (the king's physician), and John Leland praised Caius's Latin epigrams. He is credited by Wood with translations from Greek into Latin of Aristotle, Euripides, and Isocrates, and his library contained books on medieval theology and British history.

Caius spent his life in Oxford, first as one of the minority of artists at All Souls and, from 1561, as master of University College (by royal presentation). He served the university in several capacities in the late 1520s (including supervisor of ale and keeper of several chests). His 1532 election as registrar, a lucrative post, further indicates his stature, although he was ousted as registrar by convocation in 1552 for negligence. After the vote Caius stormed from the room and hit in the face Henry Walshe MA, whom the vice-chancellor had ordered to restrain him. The vice-chancellor sent Caius to prison until he agreed, the next day, to apologize to convocation and pay a large fine.

Caius's religious convictions are unrecorded. His possession of medieval theology books supports Wood's contention that he was not a reformer, but Caius survived the Henrician, Edwardian, Marian, and Elizabethan changes with no apparent ill effects. It is not clear when he was ordained, but he received several benefices under Edward VI and Elizabeth: master of Ewelme Hospital (1549); rector of Steeple Langford, Wiltshire (1551); rector of Newington, Oxfordshire (1559); canon of Salisbury and prebendary of Stratton (1560); rector of Tredington, Wiltshire (1563). His non-residence was unusual but not unique, as college presidents and fellows were exempted from residence by decrees of Canterbury convocation in 1529 and 1536. He never married.

Caius is best-known for his writings defending Oxford's claim to greater antiquity than Cambridge. He was prompted by a speech made in 1564 by Cambridge's orator to the visiting Queen Elizabeth claiming that Cambridge had been founded by King Cantaber, a contemporary of the Trojans. Caius replied with the *Assertio antiquitatis Oxoniensis academiae* in 1566, refuting Cambridge's claims with the equally mythological view that Oxford was founded by King Alfred, who imported international scholars and settled them at University College. To buttress his claims Caius draws on the varied witnesses of Geoffrey of Monmouth, the fourteenth-century philosopher Walter Burley, Polydore Vergil, George Lily, and especially his friend John Leland.

Caius circulated his work at first in two manuscripts. In 1568 John Caius, the eponymous Cambridge college founder, published the *Assertio* as an appendix to his own *De antiquitate Cantabrigiensis academiae libri duo*, his refutation of the *Assertio* renewing the case for Cambridge's claims. Thomas Caius replied with his *Examen judicii Cantabrigiensis*, which also circulated in manuscript and was later published by Thomas Hearne in 1730 as *Vindiciae antiquitatis academiae Oxoniensis contra Johannen Caium Cantabrigiensem*.

Caius died in 1572. In his will, drawn up on 8 May, he bequeathed a number of his books to All Souls. No books are mentioned in an inventory of his possessions which was made at the same time, but the latter gives a detailed picture of the domestic furnishings of an early Elizabethan master's lodge, and also sheds light on Caius's own interests and tastes. He had thirty-six pictures, mostly portraits, a mixed bag that included Erasmus, Queen Elizabeth, the 'Grand Turk' and the 'King of the Moors', Calvin, Beza, Plato, Aristotle, and Pope Pius V. His sixteen maps are unusual for their time, and show Caius's lively interest in geography and exploration. There were two by Mercator, one by Ortelius, and individual maps including representations of Iceland and Egypt. Geography was not part of the sixteenth-century Oxford curriculum, although its study by individual scholars increased during Caius's lifetime. Caius was buried in the north aisle of the church of St Peter-in-the-East, Oxford on 20 May.

DAMIAN R. LEADER

Sources Emden, *Oxf.*, 4.325–6, 723 • Wood, *Ath. Oxon.*, new edn, 1.397–400 • T. Caius, *Vindiciae antiquitatis academiae Oxoniensis*, ed. T. Hearne (1730) • *Reg. Oxf.*, vols. 1–2 • *Hist. U. Oxf.* 3: *Colleg. univ.* • W. T. Mitchell, ed., *Epistolae academicae, 1508–1596*, OHS, new ser., 26 (1980) • H. E. Salter, ed., *Mediaeval archives of the University of Oxford*, 2, OHS, 73 (1921) • U. Oxf., archives, registers GG, H, and inventories K–L • Bodl. Oxf., MSS dd All Souls College, b. 30

Archives Bodl. Oxf., MSS dd All Souls College, b. 30 • U. Oxf., archives, registers GG, H, and inventories K–L

Wealth at death library, maps, globes, pictures, and furnishings of University College master's lodge: U. Oxf., archives, register GG, fol. 219*v* and inventories K–L; *Hist. U. Oxf.* 3: *Colleg. univ.*

Calah, John (**1757/8–1798**), organist and composer, succeeded John Jackson as organist of the parish church and master of the song school at Newark-on-Trent in December 1781. He remained there until he was appointed organist and master of the choristers at Peterborough Cathedral on 28 June 1785. He composed some insignificant church music, and died at Peterborough on 4 August 1798, at the age of forty, and was buried in the New Building of the cathedral on 8 August.

W. B. SQUIRE, *rev.* K. D. REYNOLDS

Sources *GM*, 1st ser., 68 (1798), 728 • J. A. F. Maitland, 'Calah, John', Grove, *Dict. mus.* (1927)

Calamy, Benjamin (*bap.* **1646**, *d.* **1685/6**), Church of England clergyman, was baptized at St Mary Aldermanbury, London, on 11 February 1646, the second surviving son of Edmund *Calamy (1600–1666) and the eldest son with his second wife, Anne Leaver (*d.* in or before 1675). Benjamin came from a nonconforming family: his father, elder half-brother Edmund *Calamy (*bap.* 1634, *d.* 1685), and nephew Edmund *Calamy (1671–1732) were all dissenting ministers, while his mother was also a presbyterian. Benjamin attended St Paul's School, London, before his admission to Sidney Sussex College, Cambridge, on 9 May 1661. He migrated to St Catharine's College, where he was elected a fellow, graduating BA in 1664 and proceeding MA in 1668. After the Restoration, his father and elder brother were ejected from their livings, but Benjamin and his younger

Benjamin Calamy (*bap.* 1646, *d.* 1685/6), by Michael Vandergucht, pubd 1690

brother James conformed. Despite this, Benjamin stayed on amiable terms with his family and was ordained by the bishop of Ely in December 1668. Among his pupils at Cambridge were James Bonnell and probably Offspring Blackall, both close friends of James Calamy. Later Bonnell became accountant-general of Ireland, and when Blackall became bishop of Exeter, he made James a prebendary.

While in Cambridge, Benjamin Calamy formed important political ties in London, where he preached before the lord mayor on 13 July 1673 a sermon which was printed, and befriended George Jeffreys, a resident of Aldermanbury and at that point in his judicial career common serjeant and recorder of London. On 25 April 1677, with Jeffreys's help, Calamy succeeded Simon Ford as curate of St Mary Aldermanbury, the very living from which his father had been ejected, and the parish where his brother Edmund lived. Calamy's next printed work was his edition of six of Robert Needham's sermons (1679), and he himself was an eloquent pulpiteer, much in demand. His excellent learning, fluid rhetoric, and penetrating insights transported his hearers and caught the eye of Charles II, who made him a king's chaplain-in-ordinary. In 1680 he proceeded DD and in or after the following year married Mary, daughter of the physician Thomas Tymme. Calamy's star was rising: he continued to preach regularly before the lord mayor and was so favoured at court that his prospects of ecclesiastical preferment were excellent. This was due partly to his growing reputation as a polemicist intent on recovering dissenters. His familiarity with *Cases of Conscience* by the Elizabethan puritan William Perkins also influenced him greatly. In 1683 he published two works about dissenters' consciences at the very time when the Rye House Plot renewed suspicions about sedition in nonconformist conventicles. His *Some Considerations about the Case of Scandal* tried to reach dissenters who did not object to the Anglican liturgy but would not conform because they might 'scandalize' others who scrupled those rites. He argued that no one should absent the parish church for fear of offending 'weak brethren'.

The more important work, dedicated to Jeffreys, was *A Discourse about a Scrupulous Conscience*, a sermon on Luke 11: 41 which Calamy had preached to enthusiastic responses in his parish and at Bow church. This targeted dissenters who opposed the Anglican liturgy. Quoting from Richard Baxter and his own father, Calamy argued that all church problems stemmed from forsaking parish churches: this led to factionalism and the need to root out needless scruples, to bridle 'skittish Consciences' before they undermined both church and state. Calamy wrote with a flourish, confident that, with Jeffreys, now lord chief justice, behind him, no one would dare answer his challenge. He wrote that if dissenters would objectively examine the issues, Anglicans surely would win the day. The Baptist schoolmaster Thomas Delaune, taking this as an invitation to respond, wrote *A Plea for the Nonconformists* (1683), which powerfully argued their reasons for separation. Delaune's book was confiscated, and he was committed to Newgate prison on charges of sedition and libel against the king. Claiming to be there simply because he had obeyed Calamy's call, Delaune implored Calamy three times to intercede. Not being a party to the indictment, Calamy answered that it was not his concern. Delaune published his letters and upbraided Calamy for not answering *A Plea* or even visiting him in prison. Delaune was arraigned with 'Mr. Ralphson', really Jeremiah Marsden, a dissenting minister with a history of sedition. Delaune's book was burnt, and when he could not pay his £100 fine, he and his family languished to death in prison. Later, Calamy's nephew claimed his uncle tried to get Delaune released, and this failure greatly troubled him. If so, he failed probably because the hardline Jeffreys judged the case. Daniel Defoe reprinted *A Plea* with his own preface, which laid the blame on Calamy. Defoe's numerous editions ran well into the nineteenth century, making Delaune a martyr and Calamy's name odious to dissenters. Yet Calamy was rewarded. In 1683 the dean of St Paul's gave him the vicarage of St Lawrence Jewry, with St Mary Magdalen, Milk Street, annexed.

Calamy was a strong supporter of the court party. In a sermon before the lord mayor (30 September 1683), he waxed eloquent on one of its key principles—passive obedience. Holding nothing back, he called the Rye House Plot a black conspiracy by men with 'blind Zeal' who must suffer the 'utmost Vengeance' (B. Calamy, *A Sermon*

Preached before … the Lord Mayor … the 30th of September, 1683, 1683, 9, 5). As a token of his growing favour, on John Wells's death Calamy was granted the prebend of Harleston in St Paul's (18 June 1685). Then, ironically, his own parishioner and close friend, the whig Alderman Henry Cornish, was arrested on the false charge of conspiracy. Really this was retribution for his role in uncovering the supposed 'popish plot'. Calamy stood by his friend. He ministered to him in prison and risked royal disfavour by speaking on his behalf at the trial. In contrast to his treatment of Delaune, he importunately and repeatedly pleaded with Jeffreys to intercede for Cornish. Profoundly affected by Cornish's execution on 23 October 1685, Calamy became very depressed. This was probably a factor that hastened his death after he contracted pleurisy barely two months later. He was buried on 7 January 1686 at St Lawrence Jewry. His co-prebendary, William Sherlock, preached the funeral, and his parishioners gave a generous gift to his widow, Mary. Apart from *A Discourse* and *Some Considerations*, all his printed works were sermons. In 1687 his brother James published thirteen of them in a volume that ran into seven editions.

JIM SPIVEY

Sources E. Calamy, *An historical account of my own life, with some reflections on the times I have lived in, 1671–1731*, ed. J. T. Rutt, 2 vols. (1829), vol. 1, pp. 57–63 • Venn, *Alum. Cant.* • *DNB* • *Calamy rev.* • W. Sherlock, *A sermon preached at the funeral of … Benj. Calamy* (1686) • T. Delaune, *A narrative of the sufferings of Thomas Delaune, for writing, printing and publishing a late book, called, A PLEA FOR THE NONCONFORMISTS, with some modest reflections thereon, directed to Doctor Calamy, in obedience to whose call, that work was undertaken* (1684) • J. Granger, *A biographical history of England, from Egbert the Great to the revolution*, 4th edn, 4 vols. (1804), vol. 3 • A. Kippis, *Biographica Britannia*, 5 vols. (1778–93), vol. 3 • S. Knight, *The life of Dr John Colet* (1724) • J. Ivimey, *A brief history of the dissenters* (1827) • T. Crosby, *The history of the English Baptists, from the Reformation to the beginning of the reign of King George I*, 4 vols. (1738–40), vol. 2 • W. B. Bannerman, ed., *The registers of St Mary the Virgin, Aldermanbury, London*, 1, Harleian Society, register section, 61 (1931)

Likenesses M. Vandergucht, line engraving (after oil portrait), BM, NPG; repro. in B. Calamy, *Sermons preached upon several occasions*, ed. [J. Calamy] (1690) [*see illus.*] • oils, St Catharine's College, Cambridge

Calamy, Edmund (1600–1666), clergyman and ejected minister, was born in 1600 and baptized on 24 February at St Thomas the Apostle, London, the only son of George Calamy, tradesman and citizen of Walbrook, London, who came from Guernsey, and whose family tradition held that he was an exiled Huguenot from Normandy; his mother may have been Frances Warner, who married George at St Thomas's on 11 August 1594. Edmund was enrolled in 1613 at the Merchant Taylors' School, London, and on 4 July 1616 admitted as a scholar to Pembroke College, Cambridge. He graduated BA in 1620 and proceeded MA in 1623. His resistance to Arminianism kept him from a permanent fellowship, but he was made a Fellow *tanquam socius* in 1625.

Soon after this appointment Calamy was taken by the moderate Calvinist Nicholas Felton, bishop of Ely, as his family chaplain, and was presented the vicarage of St Mary, Swaffham Prior, Cambridgeshire, on 6 March 1626.

Edmund Calamy (1600–1666), by James Caldwall, pubd 1775 (after William Dobson?)

Living in Felton's household, where there were other puritans, Calamy was guided in his intensive biblical and theological studies by the bishop. Following Felton's death on 5 October 1626, the next year Calamy resigned the living at Swaffham Prior; he spent the next decade as lecturer at Bury St Edmunds, Suffolk, preaching three times a week. He was licensed to preach in the diocese of Norwich on 18 June 1629 and proceeded BD in 1632. By 1634 he had married Mary, daughter of Robert Snelling of Ipswich; their son, Edmund *Calamy (*bap.* 1634, *d.* 1685) was born at Bury, and baptized there on 16 April that year; they also had a daughter, Mary. The register of St James, Bury, also records the baptism of a Jeremy Calamy, son of Edmund and Amy, on 1 November 1638, but nothing more is known of him or his mother.

Calamy's puritan leanings intensified. He later recalled that he had refused to bow to the altar or read the Book of Sports, and had preached against the Laudian innovations, although the conformist apologist Laurence Womock taunted him in *Sober Sadness* (1643) for his compliance with regulations on clerical dress and ceremony. Cited by Bishop Matthew Wren's commissioners and forced to read set prayers in 1636, Calamy resigned the lectureship at Bury St Edmunds and accepted the offer of the rectory of Rochford, Essex, from the prominent puritan peer Robert Rich, earl of Warwick, with whom he retained a long personal connection, often sharing his closet in private prayer, and whose funeral sermon he preached in 1658. At Rochford he suffered poor health, and surrendered to a dizziness that prevented him from ever again climbing up into a pulpit; thereafter he always preached from a reading desk.

London minister in the 1640s Within three weeks of the death on 4 May 1639 of John Stoughton, Calamy was elected to succeed him as perpetual curate of St Mary Aldermanbury, London. In July he was incorporated BD at Oxford, and he was admitted to the living on 26 October. His departure from Rochford signalled the beginning of an extremely active career in London politics, and marked his rise to leadership in the presbyterian and civic community. Aldermanbury was a parish with a strongly puritan tradition and with many wealthy merchants and prominent civic leaders in its membership. When the earl of Warwick went to London in 1640, he requested a pew in the Aldermanbury church. The minister's stipend, at £160 a year, may have been the highest in London at that time, and in November 1642 sixty-four of Aldermanbury's inhabitants contributed £924 to the parliament—one of the largest contributions of all the London parishes.

On his arrival Calamy became embroiled in controversy over the episcopacy and resistance to the 'etcetera oath'. Along with other puritan leaders he accompanied Sir Robert Harley in presenting to the Commons on 23 January 1641 the 'Ministers' petition and remonstrance' with nearly 1000 signatures advocating a root and branch reform of church government. His first entrance into print was a response to Bishop Joseph Hall, in the form of *An Answer to a Booke Entituled an Humble Remonstrance … Written by Smectymnuus* (1641). Authorship was shared between Stephen Marshall, Edmund Calamy, Thomas Young, Matthew Newcomen (who in 1640 had married Calamy's sister-in-law Hannah Snelling), and William Spurstowe, who had been meeting regularly at Calamy's house since the calling of parliament, and whose initials formed the acronym for the *nom de plume*. This controversial work, with its appeal for the primitive episcopacy of the early church, was defended in a sonnet as well as in five anti-episcopal tracts by John Milton.

Calamy had now become, by Anthony Wood's judgement, 'a great evangelist of the new way, [who] encouraged the people to rebellion' (Wood, *Ath. Oxon.*, 3rd edn, 1813–20, 3.682). In March 1641 he and Marshall were invited by the Lords' committee for innovations to consider the possibility of comprehension, and in the course of discussions they met Hall, but Calamy was probably already then in collusion with Scottish presbyterian ministers. Irresolvable conflict was emerging between those who later became presbyterians and Independents, but in November 1641 clergy of both persuasions met at Calamy's house, a choice of rendezvous which signalled his prominence in the ministerial community, to work on a unified front in parliament's reform of episcopacy and treatment of the sectaries. The ensuing agreement, signed by Calamy (for the presbyterians) and Philip Nye (for the Independents), while it did not heal the real rifts that later emerged fully in the Westminster assembly, declared that neither side would dispute against the other. At a special fast on 22 December prompted by the Irish rising, Calamy and Marshall preached before the Commons. Calamy's sermon, *Englands Looking-Glasse* (1642), earned him the approbation of the Commons, who issued a massive almsdish, bearing his arms and the inscription, 'This is the Gift of the House of Commons to Edmund Calamy, B.D., 1641'. The sermon was so popular it reached five editions, and it urged the burial of all superstitious ceremonies 'in the grave of oblivion', the calling of a national synod of ministers (a position that had been included in the grand remonstrance to the king in November 1641), and the sending of preachers into the dark corners of the land. When the Long Parliament instituted its programme of regular monthly preaching early in 1642, Calamy and Marshall gave the inaugural sermons on 23 February at St Margaret's, Westminster. Calamy was a friend to the parliamentarian diarist Sir Simonds D'Ewes. With the outbreak of the civil war in late 1642 Charles I had Calamy, Marshall, Hugh Peter, and Henry Burton indicted for high treason early in 1643. Calamy, favouring the war, was elected a London representative in the Westminster assembly on 25 April 1642.

Calamy was involved in the transformation of Sion College in London into a gathering place of presbyterian clergy during the Westminster assembly; he later served as junior dean of the college in 1644 and senior dean in 1649, and became its president in 1650. In April 1643, along with Henry Roborough, he was elected assistant to the newly elected president, Andrew Janaway of All Hallows. All the Smectymnuuans were nominated in the ordinance of 12 June 1643 as members of the Westminster assembly of divines, where Calamy took the solemn league and covenant together with the rest. In a sermon to the Lords three days later, published as *The Noble-Mans Patterne* (1643), he insisted that the attack on the prelates was not a prelude to abolishing the distinction between the nobility and the common people.

Civil war, interregnum and Restoration During the 1640s Calamy remained a popular and outspoken preacher. When he gave his weekly lectures, sixty or more coaches could often be seen outside his church (Calamy, *Abridgement*, 2.5). In the civil war period he remained constant to the duties of his own parish, but also looked to national concerns, speaking at the Guildhall in favour of raising a City loan to subsidize the Scottish army on 6 October 1643; later that same year he was designated by parliament as collector of donations to transport children from Ireland and England to New England. On 4 October 1644 parliament appointed him, with others, to examine and ordain ministers. In a Christmas sermon in December 1644 he urged maintaining loyalty to the solemn league and covenant in the period of crisis over negotiations with Charles I at Uxbridge. He served on a special commission for trial of witches in Suffolk in 1645. An opponent of toleration, he was appointed a licenser for books of divinity on 14 June 1643, with his first imprimatur appearing on *The Souldiers Pocket Bible* published by Giles Calvert and entered 27 July 1643. Calamy's licensing hand is in evidence up until 1658. Though ever a moderate Calvinist, his hostility to sectaries is in evidence in his 1645 controversy with the Independent lecturer Henry Burton. Calamy had Burton locked out of the church in 1645 for fear his separatist principles would lure souls away, and he published pamphlets in reply to Burton's protests. On 20 October 1645 Calamy was appointed by parliament as trier, responsible for the approbation of elders, in the sixth classis of the London province, an appointment renewed on 26 September 1646 and again on 29 August 1648. His assistant at St Mary Aldermanbury from 1643 to 1648 was his fellow Smectymnuuan, Matthew Newcomen. By the mid-1640s Calamy had married Anne Leaver (*d.* in or before 1675), a presbyterian from Lancashire. Their eldest child, Benjamin *Calamy (*bap.* 1646, *d.* 1685/6) was baptized on 11 February 1646, and five others, Anne, Susanna, Elizabeth, James, and John, were baptized at St Mary between 1647 and 1658.

A leader in the assembly, Calamy participated in a number of its significant debates, including the discussion of marriage in 1644 where he categorized the rite as a civil ordinance; his committee work ranged from printing to the problem of absenteeism in the assembly. He served on committees dealing with fasting and, with Newcomen, William Seaman, Sedgwick, John Dury, Thomas Temple, and others, was appointed to a committee in February 1646 that examined the subject of Christian liberty. The chapter on the Lord's supper in the Westminster confession of faith was the responsibility of Calamy, Cornelius Burgess, and Jeremiah Whitaker; he also prepared the preface to the shorter catechism. He was appointed on 14 September 1643 to chair the committee concerned with antinomianism and in May 1645 to the committee to deal with the preaching of antinomians and other sectaries. He remained loyal to the solemn league, preaching for its renewal in a sermon to the lord mayor, aldermen, and common council in January 1646. When in the summer of 1647 turbulence erupted in London after the end of the first civil war, Calamy signed a petition urging London City leaders to negotiate with the New Model Army. With other presbyterian leaders he opposed Pride's Purge on 6 December 1648, preaching openly against it on 17 December. On 11 January 1649 he was dispatched, along with Marshall and others, to consult with Fairfax, critical of the army's actions. Regarding the trial of Charles as a violation of both scripture and constitution, Calamy was among fifty-eight ministers who signed *A Vindication of the Ministers of the Gospel in, and about London*, calling for the people to be loyal to the solemn league and covenant. Though this effort was a failure, Calamy was one of a group of ministers who went to St James's on 30 January to offer the king their services on his day of execution.

Deeply troubled by the regicide Calamy, however, continued his ministerial responsibilities, and his service to presbyterians was recognized when he was named president of Sion College, London, in 1650. He also continued to license books, with a higher number of titles than in any other period under his imprimatur in the years 1652–4. On 2 May 1651, following the discovery of a conspiracy in London that sought to restore the MPs secluded in Pride's Purge, as well as the monarchy, prominent presbyterian clergy including Christopher Love, Thomas Case, and William Jenkyn, Calamy's cosignatories of the *Vindication*, were arrested. Love was condemned to death and executed on 22 August and, although Calamy's involvement in the plot is not clear, with Simeon Ashe and Thomas Manton he attended Love on the scaffold and preached on Love's funeral (*A Sermon Preached … at Aldermanbury*, 1651). In the following years he edited several of Love's works for posthumous publication.

Two years later Calamy opposed the dissolution of the Rump, condemning Oliver Cromwell's action as unlawful, unpopular, and impractical. Although his grandson Edmund *Calamy (1671–1732), the famous biographical historian of nonconformity, insisted his grandfather 'kept himself as private as he could' (*Calamy rev.*, 97), under the protectorate the elder Calamy was active in supporting John Dury's mission to the continent to promote an evangelical protestant alliance in April 1654, and was appointed by the council of state in May 1654, along with a multi-denominational group of ministers, including Independents, Baptists, and Fifth Monarchists, as a treasurer to receive funds to assist persecuted protestants in Piedmont. Calamy willingly co-operated with religious radicals in these ventures, and may have developed a more tolerant attitude towards sectaries at this time, even in 1655 interceding on behalf of the exiled Socinian John Biddle. In 1657 he was invited to consult with Cromwell concerning Cromwell's assumption of the crown, and reportedly replied to Cromwell's face that the proposal was illegal and impractical, 'Oh it is against the Voice of the Nation; there will be Nine in Ten against you', according to Henry Neville, a member of the council of state (Greaves & Zaller, *BDBR*, 38). The first edition of Calamy's very popular collection of five sermons, *The Godly Mans Ark*, appeared in 1657; by 1683 it had gone through eight editions.

In the period following Oliver Cromwell's death on 3 September 1658, Calamy and other presbyterian ministers gave their support to Richard Cromwell and the restored Long Parliament, preaching before the House of Commons in January 1658, and urging congregationalists and presbyterians to unify. However, Calamy soon began to turn his mind toward the return of monarchy, seeking accommodation with royalists, and in January 1660 he was courted both by representatives of Sir Edward Hyde and by General George Monck's emissaries. Monck announced support for a presbyterian polity, and subsequently appointed Calamy as one of his chaplains; he received the Lord's supper at Calamy's hands. Edmund Ludlow recalls seeing Calamy and others conferring with Monck at his home on 13 February 1660. Following the return of secluded members of parliament on 21 February, Calamy and Manton were selected to preach a thanksgiving celebrating their return. When the newly elected Convention Parliament met on 25 April 1660, Calamy, John Gauden, and Richard Baxter were selected to preach to the Commons on the next fast, 30 April, the day before the king was voted home. On 11 May Calamy, with John

Reynolds, Manton, Thomas Case, Spurstowe, and others, left England for the Netherlands to consult with Charles II, presenting a letter signed by more than eighty ministers at Sion College, expressing a willingness to accept a modified episcopacy. They left apparently satisfied that Charles intended presbyterian comprehension in a national church.

Upon Charles's arrival in England, he appointed ten presbyterians, among them Calamy, as his chaplains-in-ordinary. Calamy and others also met the king in June at the earl of Manchester's house. However, Henry Sampson, historian of dissent, was told an anecdote that revealed Calamy's uneasiness, and disapproval of Monck's dissolving parliament before a church settlement had been achieved. Having Monck as his auditor on a sacrament day shortly after the Restoration, Calamy made the remark, 'Some men will betray three kingdoms for filthy lucre's sake', adding emphasis by flinging 'his handkerchiefe (as he was wont to move it up & down) towards the Generals pew' (BL, Add. MS 4460, fols. 59*v*–60). In July 1660 trouble erupted in his parish as nine parishioners refused to pay Calamy for his services, and one Mrs Gilburd, widow, had the lock on her pew door removed. Calamy only preached once in his royal position, on 12 August at Whitehall on the text 'To whom much is given, of him much is required', and Samuel Pepys reported that Calamy 'was very officious with his three reverences [*sic*] to the King, as others do' (Pepys, 1.220). Calamy worked with presbyterian leaders to urge the king towards greater accommodation and to procure parliamentary legislation, efforts rewarded when Charles offered him the bishopric of Coventry and Lichfield, which he took some time in considering, and, as John Tillotson recounted to Thomas Birch, declined because of his wife's insistence. At the Savoy conference (April–July 1661), convened to revise the liturgy in such a way as to satisfy both presbyterians and advocates of episcopacy, Calamy drafted major proposals for reform, but the conference broke up without having achieved its goals. Although on 2 May 1661 he was elected by the London clergy to sit in convocation, Bishop Gilbert Sheldon rejected him.

After uniformity On 19 May 1662 Charles accepted the Act of Uniformity, signalling the failure of comprehension, and though Calamy, Manton, William Bates, and several others petitioned the king on 27 August for dispensations, these were to no avail. Calamy's farewell sermon on 2 Samuel 24: 14 was preached to his congregation at St Mary Aldermanbury on 17 August, even though he received his quarterly pay of £50 up until Michaelmas. John Tillotson was elected as his successor on 16 December 1662 but declined to serve. After the St Bartholomew's day ejection, Calamy did preach there on 28 December, allegedly when the serving minister failed to appear, a sermon on 1 Samuel 4: 13 published as *Eli Trembling for Fear of the Ark* (1652). Fearing that 'the ark of God was lost, and the glory was departed from Israel', Calamy made many topical allusions to this period of enforced silencing: 'when the ark of God is taken, then the Ministers of Christ are driven into corners', he warned; 'where false Religion comes in at one door, the true Religion goes out at the other'. Since on 26 December (two days earlier) Charles had issued a declaration of indulgence, nonconformist hopes had been raised, and Calamy himself may have used this occasion to test the resolve of those supporting uniformity. His subsequent arrest and imprisonment on 6 January 1663 in Newgate became a *cause célèbre* for tolerationists, as Richard Baxter reported, 'many daily flocking to visit him' in prison (*Reliquiae Baxterianae*, 2.386). Contemporary newsbooks gave comment, and the proceedings of the trial were presented in a pamphlet, *Master Edmund Calamies Leading Case* (1663); there was also rebuttal by the conformist Laurence Womock. Calamy was the first of the nonconformists to suffer imprisonment due to the act, and there was a burst of pamphleteering in response. In competing satirical poems the presbyterian humorist Robert Wild praised Calamy, while Hudibras complained that:

> Tis He who taught the *Pulpit* and the *Press*
> To mask *Rebellion* in a *Gospel-dress*.

Baxter interceded with the king to obtain a release, and it was granted on 13 January 1663 on the ground that Calamy had preached 'with the privity of several lords of the Council, and not in contempt of law' (*CSP dom.*, *1663–4*, 10). The Commons on 19 February referred it to a committee to inquire further, and addressed the king against toleration.

Calamy's public role did not end with the Act of Uniformity. Subsequently he reputedly preached every Sunday after evening service in his home, where he was also reported to hold fasts, and he also participated in conventicles which met at the house of Samuel Bayly, who had married his eldest daughter, Mary, in 1657. He was also involved in channelling money to support needy ejected nonconformist ministers, and maintained links with exiles in the Netherlands. After the great fire Calamy was driven through the City of London in a coach; this reportedly broke his heart:

> seeing the desolate Condition of so flourishing a City, for which he had so great an Affection, his tender Spirit receiv'd such Impressions as he could never wear off. he went home, and never came out of his Chamber more; but dy'd within a Month. (Calamy, *Abridgement*, 187)

Following his death at Enfield on 29 October, Calamy was buried in the burned ruins of his old church, St Mary Aldermanbury, on 6 November 1666. Robert Wild's epitaph, *On the Death of Mr Calamy*, commented:

> how have we known him captivate a throng.
> And made a Sermon twenty-thousand strong.

Baxter noted that Calamy 'was much valued and followed by the *London* ministers, as their Guide; and many frequently met at his House' (*Reliquiae Baxterianae*, 2.229).

Calamy's will, dated 4 October 1666, and proved on 14 November, reveals that he owned property in Kent and Suffolk as well as his house in St Nicholas Lane, London. He was survived by his wife, whose will was proved in 1675, and by most of his children. Of the three sons who followed him into the ministry, Edmund was ejected in

1662 but Benjamin and James, who had a Bedfordshire living, conformed. Of his daughters, Anne Calamy married Henry Asgill at St Mary Aldermanbury on 4 February 1663, Susanna married Francis Ives at Hackney in 1670, Elizabeth married John Reynolds of St Giles Cripplegate, merchant, in 1673, and Rebecca (whose baptism record seems lost) married John Marryon on 4 October 1677 at St Mary Aldermanbury. A minister whose commitment to national reform was lifelong, Calamy is an emblem for the old dissenting presbyterianism which sought political solutions to national religious problems. His sermons and other works continued to be published long after his death. SHARON ACHINSTEIN

Sources R. L. Greaves, *Saints and rebels: seven nonconformists in Stuart England* (1985) • *Calamy rev.*, 97–8 • Greaves & Zaller, *BDBR* • G. R. Abernathy, *The English presbyterians and the Stuart restoration, 1648–1663* (1965) • E. Calamy, ed., *An abridgement of Mr. Baxter's history of his life and times, with an account of the ministers, &c., who were ejected after the Restauration of King Charles II*, 2nd edn, 2 vols. (1713) • E. Calamy, *An historical account of my own life, with some reflections on the times I have lived in, 1671–1731*, ed. J. T. Rutt, 2nd edn, 2 vols. (1830) • *Reliquiae Baxterianae, or, Mr Richard Baxter's narrative of the most memorable passages of his life and times*, ed. M. Sylvester, 1 vol. in 3 pts (1696) • G. E. B. Eyre, ed., *A transcript of the registers of the Worshipful Company of Stationers from 1640 to 1708*, 3 vols. (1913–14) • W. S. Barker, *Puritan profiles* (1996) • J. T. Cliffe, *The puritan gentry: the great puritan families of early Stuart England* (1984) • P. C. Carter, *The history of the church and parish of St. Mary the Virgin, Aldermanbury* (1913) • R. Wild, *Poem upon the imprisonment of Mr. Calamy* (1662) • *CSP dom.*, 1663–4 • Pepys, *Diary* • *Saints memorials, or, Words fitly spoken* (1674) • *The memoirs of Edmund Ludlow*, ed. C. H. Firth, 2 vols. (1894) • *IGI* • T. Webster, *Godly clergy in early Stuart England: the Caroline puritan movement, c.1620–1643* (1997)

Archives Worcester College, Oxford, sermons

Likenesses engraving, 1667, repro. in E. Calamy, *The godly man's ark, or, City of refuge in the day of his distress*, 5th edn (1667), frontispiece • engraving, 1674, repro. in *Saints memorials*, frontispiece • J. Caldwall, engraving, pubd 1775 (after W. Dobson?), NPG [*see illus.*] • Mackenzie, portrait, 1802, repro. in E. Calamy, *The nonconformist's memorial*, ed. S. Palmer, 2nd edn, 1 (1802), i • R. White, line engraving, BM, NPG

Wealth at death property in Kent and Suffolk; house in St Nicholas Lane, London; also silver basin and ewer: *Calamy rev.*, 97–8

Calamy, Edmund (*bap.* 1634, *d.* 1685), clergyman and ejected minister, was the eldest son of Edmund *Calamy the elder (1600–1666) and his first wife, Mary Snelling of Ipswich. He was born at Bury St Edmunds and baptized there on 16 April 1634. From St Paul's School in London, Edmund Calamy the younger entered Sidney Sussex College, Cambridge, as a pensioner in 1652. After graduating BA in 1655 he transferred to Pembroke College where he proceeded MA in 1658. In his will he described himself as 'sometime fellow of Pembroke Hall', though the college's records do not confirm this. On 10 November 1658 he was ordained, along with Samuel Borfet and Richard Roberts, at Moreton, Essex, by seven local ministers. Having preached for some months at Moreton, he obtained the living in April 1659 following the death of the incumbent, Samuel Hoard, from the trustees of the late earl of Warwick—the earl of Manchester, John, Lord Robartes, Sir Gilbert Gerrard, and three clergymen, Simeon Ashe, Anthony Tuckney, and Calamy's father.

Although Calamy initially welcomed the Restoration and contributed generously to the king's exchequer in 1661, he could not conform under the Act of Uniformity and was ejected in 1662. He retired to his father's house in London until 1665 when he left the city during the plague to serve as chaplain to Sir Samuel Barnardiston at Brightwell Hall near Ipswich. he was back in London the next year when his father died. In 1669 he was preaching privately to a few friends and relations in a hired house in Aldermanbury. Following the king's declaration of indulgence he took out a licence on 2 April 1672, and ministered to a small congregation at Curriers' Hall, Cripplegate. Even after this liberty was withdrawn he continued to preach unmolested for nearly a decade. In both 1681 and 1683, however, the government issued warrants against him for holding conventicles. Though never imprisoned, he was 'forced to disguise himself and skulk in private holes and corners, and frequently change his lodgings' (Calamy, *Own Life*, 1.88).

In 1669 Calamy married Mary (*d.* 1715), the eldest daughter of Joshua Gearing, a retired London merchant then living at Tooting, Surrey. The couple had four daughters, Sarah, Hannah, Phebe, and Elizabeth, and one son, Edmund *Calamy (1671–1732), the Presbyterian pastor and historian of nonconformity. Calamy could never be persuaded to publish, and while his son attributed this to modesty, others were less charitable, concluding him a man of small abilities. One critic, John Newte, the vicar of Tiverton, Devon, related gleefully that Calamy had admitted to his father that he 'understood but little' of academic learning, and desired 'to know nothing save Jesus Christ and him crucified', to which the elder Calamy allegedly retorted that he was 'fit for nothing but a conventicle' (Bodl. Oxf., MS Walker C. 2, fol. 441). Newte's tale was most likely spurious, and certainly malicious, but even Calamy's son celebrated his father's moderation rather than his preaching or scholarship. Calamy cultivated close relations with members of the established church, including Anthony Walker, who had helped ordain him, and Richard Kidder, the future bishop of Bath and Wells. At least, according to his son, he also remained on excellent terms, despite their professional differences, with his half-brother, the high-flying Anglican Benjamin *Calamy. This commitment to moderation was Calamy's chief legacy to his more famous son.

Calamy had been declining 'in a consumptive way' (Calamy, *Own Life*, 1.126) for several years, and had lately been afflicted with 'asthmatical fitts' (PRO, PROB 11/380, fol. 142), when he died suddenly in May 1685 while visiting a member of his congregation, Edward Haynes FRS of Totteridge, Hertfordshire. He was buried near his father beneath the pulpit of St Mary Aldermanbury. He asked that no funeral sermon be preached and that no gifts be distributed to the mourners except sprigs of rosemary, hoping his friends would attend purely out of love and respect for him. From his father he had inherited a considerable estate, enabling him to provide £250 to each of his daughters and £300 to his son. He also left Edmund his library, 'if he be bred a scholar', and a silver basin which the House of Commons had given his father in 1641 (PRO,

PROB 11/380, fol. 142). His widow died in March 1715 at Bath, where she had been visiting with her 'intimate' friend Lady Levet (Calamy, *Own Life*, 2.309–10). She too was interred in Aldermanbury.

ALEXANDER GORDON, *rev.* JIM BENEDICT

Sources E. Calamy, *An historical account of my own life, with some reflections on the times I have lived in, 1671–1731*, ed. J. T. Rutt, 1 (1829), 52–89, 126; 2 (1829), 309–10, 342 • *Calamy rev.*, 98 • W. Wilson, *The history and antiquities of the dissenting churches and meeting houses in London, Westminster and Southwark*, 4 vols. (1808–14), vol. 1, pp. 306–8 • H. Smith, *The ecclesiastical history of Essex under the Long Parliament and Commonwealth* [1933], 325, 335, 365 • E. Calamy, ed., *An abridgement of Mr. Baxter's history of his life and times, with an account of the ministers, &c., who were ejected after the Restauration of King Charles II*, 2nd edn, 2 vols. (1713), vol. 2, p. 301 • E. Calamy, *A continuation of the account of the ministers … who were ejected and silenced after the Restoration in 1660*, 2 vols. (1727), vol. 1, pp. 461–4 • PRO, PROB 11/380, sig. 69, fols. 142–3 • PRO, PROB 11/381, fols. 447–9 • abstract of the will of Calamy's widow Mary, DWL, MS 38.59, 191 • abstract of the wills of Calamy's father and his step-mother, DWL, MS 38. 59, 179–82 • Bodl. Oxf., MS Walker C2, fol. 441 • J. T. Spivey, 'Middle way men, Edmund Calamy and the crises of moderate nonconformity, 1688–1732', DPhil diss., U. Oxf., 1986, 110–34 • *CSP dom.*, *1680–81*, pp. 592, 613 • T. W. Davids, *Annals of evangelical nonconformity in Essex* (1863), 427–9 • D. L. Wykes, 'Manchester College at York (1803–1840): its intellectual and cultural contribution', *Yorkshire Archaeological Journal*, 63 (1991), 207–18, 5 • Venn, *Alum. Cant.* • E. Calamy IV, letter to Thomas Birch, 1742, BL, Add. MS 4302, fol. 24

Wealth at death £1300 to his five children, also lands to widow: will, PRO, PROB 11/380, sig. 69

Calamy, Edmund (1671–1732), Presbyterian minister and historian, was born on 5 April 1671 in the parish of St Mary Aldermanbury, London, the only son of Edmund *Calamy (*bap.* 1634, *d.* 1685), former rector of Moreton, Essex, and Mary (*d.* 1715), daughter of Joshua Gearing of Tooting, merchant, and the grandson of Edmund *Calamy (1600–1666). He was therefore the son and grandson of ejected ministers. Calamy was conscious of his pedigree: 'I count it my Honour to be descended on ye side both of Father & Mother' from the 'Old Puritans' of Elizabeth and James I's reigns (Bodl. Oxf., MS Eng. hist. c.237, fol. 64*r*).

Education Calamy was educated for the ministry from an early age. Taught his catechism and to read by his mother, he was sent to be publicly catechized at Dyers' Hall by Thomas Lye (1621–1684), who in turn had instructed his mother. He was a sickly child and was attended by Dr Henry Sampson, who was later to assist Calamy with his account of the ejected ministers. He was sent first to Mr Nelson's school kept in the vestry of St Alfege, where he learnt little, and then to Mr Yewel's school at Epsom, Surrey, for the benefit of the air, where his health rather than his learning improved. About 1676 he was sent to Robert Tatnal's school in Winchester Street, London, where he made better progress, remaining until he was the senior scholar. In 1682 he entered Thomas Doolittle's academy, but because of his age he studied only grammar. When Doolittle was forced by renewed persecution to move his academy to Battersea in 1683, Calamy transferred to Thomas Walton's school in Bethnal Green, which was shortly afterwards broken up. With the death of his father in 1685, he was sent on the advice of his uncle

Edmund Calamy (1671–1732), by George Vertue, pubd 1722

Benjamin to Merchant Taylors' School, where his fellow pupils included William Dawes, later archbishop of York, and Hugh Boulter, later archbishop of Armagh.

After leaving school Calamy spent a few months with Walton, his former schoolmaster, reading Greek in preparation for entering on university studies. He was invited by Charles Morton, who had been forced to give up his academy by renewed persecution, to accompany him to America. Although he was inclined to accept, his mother would not consent, and in 1686 he entered Samuel Cradock's academy at Wickhambrook, Suffolk, where he remained for two years studying philosophy. He received private tuition in Greek from a fellow student, Timothy Goodwin, afterwards archbishop of Cashel. He then returned to study for a few months under Doolittle, who at the time was living in Clerkenwell, before accepting the advice of John Howe and a number of other ministers to study at Utrecht. He sailed for the Netherlands in the middle of March 1688. At Utrecht he attended both public and private lectures, studying philosophy under Gerard de Vries, divinity under Hermann Witsius and Melchior Leydekker, Roman antiquities and history under Joannes Georgius Graevius, civil law with Willem van der Meulen, and philosophy and astronomy with Jan Luyts. He also visited Leiden, where he heard lectures by Jacobus Gronovius and Friedrich Spanheim. Quick to make friends, he made several who proved valuable to him in later life. He attended the same class as Charles Spencer, afterwards third earl of Sunderland and secretary of state under Queen Anne, and became very friendly with Spencer's tutor, Charles Trinmell, later bishop of Winchester. He also formed a friendship with William Carstares, who was in the Netherlands in 1691 looking for suitable candidates to fill university chairs in Scotland.

Ministerial career Calamy returned to London in May 1691. He met Richard Baxter for the first time shortly before the latter's death. Baxter preached 'with great freedom about another world, like one that had been there, and was come as a sort of an express from thence to make a report concerning it' (Calamy, *Life*, 2.220–21). Soon after midsummer Calamy set out for Oxford with the intention of studying the arguments for and against conformity in order to determine his own position. Helped by letters of introduction from Graevius, Calamy was openly received within the university and admitted to the Bodleian Library. He was particularly friendly with Joshua Oldfield, Presbyterian minister in Oxford, and was 'almost at his house as one of his domestics' (ibid., 2.224). Against his own judgement, Calamy was encouraged by Oldfield to begin preaching before he was twenty-one. After reluctantly supplying for Oldfield, he was pressed to preaching at other places in the neighbourhood of Oxford, most frequently at Bicester for the elderly Henry Cornish, and on one occasion at Caversfield 'in the public church in the afternoon' (ibid., 2.301). He declined an invitation to become minister at Andover.

Calamy returned to London in 1692 and preached frequently about the City, waiting until 'Providence opened a way to some fixed and settled work' (Calamy, *Life*, 2.310). Within a short time he was invited to become assistant to John Weekes at Bristol. Having agreed to a trial, he received a similar invitation from Matthew Sylvester's congregation at Meeting-House Court, Blackfriars. At Bristol he was offered a house, £100 a year, and a horse's keep, but he refused as a result of his mother's opposition, she being unwilling that he should live at such a distance from her. He accepted the call to Blackfriars with only 'the prospect of bare 40l. a-year', lodging in Hoxton Square with Thomas Reynolds, Howe's assistant. Having determined on the ministry, Calamy and Reynolds thought it proper they should be ordained, seeking, if possible, a public ordination, the first in London among dissenters since the Act of Uniformity. They consulted Howe, who initially encouraged them warmly, but because of the Happy Union, a formal accommodation between Presbyterians and Independents, he strongly urged them to invite Matthew Mead, an Independent, to preach. Calamy was reluctant to involve Mead, for he and Reynolds were anxious to be 'ordained ministers of the Catholic Church, without any confinement to particular flocks, or any one denomination' (ibid., 2.341), and did not want 'any narrow, confining, cramping notions' (ibid., 2.342). Mead, though willing to comply on these terms, declined 'fearful that some would be offended' (ibid., 2.343). Howe, after consulting Lord Somers, refused to take part unless the ordinations took place in private. William Bates, minister at Hackney, though he encouraged Calamy, declined for personal reasons to assist. After much difficulty Calamy persuaded five ejected ministers and Daniel Williams to take part. On 22 June 1694 Calamy and Reynolds and five other candidates, after being strictly examined in philosophy and divinity and each defending a question, were ordained in Samuel Annesley's meeting-house between the hours of ten and six. Calamy was later to admit to John Fox of Plymouth that he never undertook legally to qualify himself as a dissenting minister by subscribing the doctrinal articles of the Church of England as required by the Toleration Act.

In 1695 Daniel Williams, grateful to Calamy for his help in obtaining an important witness, made him his assistant at Hand Alley with £60 a year. With the meeting at Blackfriars no longer able to support two ministers, Calamy accepted at midsummer. On 19 December 1695 he married Mary (*d.* 1713), daughter of Michael Watts (*c.*1636–1708), cloth merchant and haberdasher. When Williams made an extended visit to Ireland in 1700, he left Calamy in charge of his congregation for several months, but Calamy refused an invitation to become to become joint pastor. In October 1702 Calamy was chosen one of the Tuesday lecturers at Salters' Hall to replace Nathaniel Taylor. Attempts to invite Calamy to be Taylor's successor as minister to the congregation at Salters' Hall were thwarted by Sir David Hamilton, who vehemently opposed the idea. Calamy remained as Williams's assistant until June 1703, when, after refusing several other offers, he accepted the unanimous invitation to become minister at Tothill Street, Westminster, following Vincent Alsop's death.

Biographer In 1702 Calamy published his *Abridgment of Mr Baxter's Narrative*. The work grew out of his experience as Matthew Sylvester's assistant and the latter's failings as the editor of Baxter's autobiographical narrative. Sylvester had finally published *Reliquiae Baxterianae*, an ill-digested volume of 800 folio pages, in 1696 after little effective editing. Calamy prepared the index and received a copy of the work from the publishers for his pains. Unfortunately, such an unmanageable volume was of little service to the dissenting cause. Calamy was therefore encouraged to undertake a new edition involving the abridgement and rearrangement of the original text to create a more manageable and coherent work. As well as reorganizing the material and dividing the volume into chapters, he recast Baxter's narrative in the third person to form a general history of dissent, and continued the narrative from 1684 to the end of Baxter's life in 1691. It was Calamy's list of the silenced ministers with 'the Characters and Works of many of them', forming the celebrated ninth chapter and accounting for over two-fifths of the volume, that established his reputation. The *Abridgment* was published at a critical juncture in the history of dissent. The whole work was intended as a popular statement and defence of nonconformity against the high-church attack on dissent and toleration.

Its publication provoked a storm, and 'for some Years there was scarce a Pamphlet came out on the Church side, in which I had not the Honour of being referr'd to in the invective Part of it' (Calamy, *Abridgement*, 2nd edn, 1713, preface). The most celebrated rejoinder to Calamy's account of the ejected ministers was John Walker's *Sufferings of the Clergy* (1714), valuable in its own right, but so long delayed that Calamy republished the *Abridgment* first in 1713. In the second edition the narrative of Baxter's life was left largely unaltered, though two additional chapters took the history down to the passing of the Occasional Conformity Act in 1711. But the ninth chapter, greatly enlarged and revised, and essentially a new edition, was issued as a separate volume, the *Account of many others of those worthy ministers who were ejected after the restauration of King Charles the Second*, amounting to over 850 pages. A further two volumes totalling another 1000 pages and containing corrections and additional information on the ejected ministers, the *Continuation of the Account*, were issued in 1727. The different editions of Calamy's work make it cumbersome to use. A new edition was published by Samuel Palmer in 1775 (rev. edn, 1777–8; 2nd edn, 3 vols., 1802). His *Nonconformist's Memorial* condensed Calamy's four volumes into two, gathering together the scattered biographies in Calamy's different editions, but it is an unreliable work with many misprints and errors. Calamy's original work is to be preferred. Unfortunately the *Nonconformist's Memorial* is more widely used and often erroneously attributed to Calamy. A. G. Matthews's outstanding biographical index, *Calamy revised* (1934), corrects and verifies Calamy's identification of the ejected ministers and provides the essential reference work for the historian.

Calamy's account of the ejected ministers was based on the work of other historians, most notably Henry Sampson, and he was assisted in collecting his lives by many local correspondents. Nevertheless the scale of his achievement in completing such an enormous project was extraordinary: over 2000 pages recording the lives and characters of the ejected ministers from every part of the country. Moreover the main revisions of the accounts of individual ministers were achieved when he was preoccupied with his duties as the minister of a leading London congregation and at a time when he was also the chief apologist for moderate nonconformity. He agreed to read Robert Wodrow's manuscript for his *History of the Sufferings of the Church of Scotland*, but Wodrow complained in March 1720 that 'the Doctor's multiplicity of affairs would not permit him to do any thing' in this matter (*Correspondence of the Rev. Robert Wodrow*, 2.519).

Champion of nonconformity Calamy, as a result of his growing reputation from his writings in defence of nonconformity, undertook an increasingly important role in the public affairs of the dissenters. In 1702, during the debate on the first Occasional Conformity Bill, with Benjamin Robinson he represented the position of the dissenters to Gilbert Burnet with some success. In 1709, at the invitation of his friend Carstares and with a pass from the secretary of state, Lord Sunderland, he travelled to Scotland for his health and out of curiosity, but also to establish a correspondence on behalf of English dissent with the ministers there following the union with Scotland. He attended the general assembly of the Church of Scotland at Edinburgh as an honoured guest, but he considered some of their proceedings 'the Inquisition revived' (Calamy, *Life*, 2.156). He preached in the New Church, and met and dined with a wide circle of leading figures, including the high commissioner. He relished the claret of his hosts more than their church government. He was made a free burgess of Edinburgh; and accepted, though he would have declined but for fear of causing offence, honorary MA (22 April) and DD (2 May) degrees from the University of Edinburgh. He subsequently accepted honorary DD degrees from King's College, Aberdeen (9 May), and Glasgow (17 May). In May 1713, shortly after the death of his first wife, he made a similar journey through the west of England for 'health and diversion' (ibid., 2.262), though to advise, in part, on the appointment of James Peirce as minister of James's Meeting, Exeter. He preached before the Exeter assembly and at each of the towns where he stayed, 'I never went a journey, in which I worked harder, or fared better' (ibid., 2.266).

Calamy was to use his considerable political skills and personal contacts on behalf of dissent. In 1714 he prevented an ill-judged address to Queen Anne by dissenters following the passing of the Schism Act. He intervened with Stanhope in 1717 to obtain the payment of compensation promised by the government for the destruction of the dissenting meeting-houses in 1715. In 1724 he also assisted Joseph Boyse in obtaining the royal bounty for nonconformist ministers in southern as well as northern Ireland.

> He understood the value of backstairs influence and the use of a silver key. But he was at his best when confronted with able men in church and state, and seldom failed to make them feel the strength of the case of dissent. (*DNB*)

He took Daniel Williams's place as the leading Presbyterian minister after the latter's death in 1716, often heading the body of ministers making loyal addresses to the throne. He was one of the original managers of the *regium donum*, was a member of the Presbyterian Fund Board from 1703 until his death, and was named by Williams as a trustee of his charity, later Dr Williams's Trust. Calamy helped to raise a subscription among wealthy London dissenters to enable a building to be erected for the library in Red Cross Street, Williams's own provisions being inadequate. Calamy preached the first sermon to ministers at Dr Williams's Library on 28 October 1731.

In 1707 Calamy's congregation was seriously disturbed by the French Prophets, led by John Lacy, who had earlier been very active in securing Calamy's election as minister. Calamy preached a series of lectures, which he later condensed into two discourses and delivered at the Salters' Hall Tuesday lecture. They were afterwards published as *A Caveat Against New Prophets* (1708), and a copy was presented to Queen Anne, who expressed her thanks for 'the service … done the public by appearing against the new prophets' (p. 100). Calamy was also consulted indirectly by Godolphin and Harley on the question of whether to prosecute the prophets for blasphemy. Despite efforts by both parties to engage him on their side, he stood aloof from the Salters' Hall debate which convulsed dissent in 1719. Although he claimed he was afterwards able to remain friendly with both parties, he undoubtedly lost credit. Both Rutt and Gordon suggested that Calamy's refusal was explained by his failure as a minister to subscribe to the necessary declarations under the Toleration Act, but Calamy himself stated that he believed the breach was unavoidable and he could see no good in attending. In 1721, after considerable difficulties in finding a site, his congregation built a new meeting-house in Long Ditch (now Princes Street). Calamy was a Baxterian in theology, firmly adhering to the middle way throughout his life. William Harris told Calamy's successor at Westminster, Samuel Say, that 'Dr Calamy was bred in the Middle Way, and his whole preaching was in that strain. He never troubled them with Predestination' (DWL, MS 12.107, 144). Dudley Ryder heard Calamy at Hackney in April 1716 and thought 'He preached very well, but he has a stiff, affecting manner of delivery, though a good voice and the delivery pretty good' (*Diary of Dudley Ryder*, 224).

Although Calamy is best remembered as the historian of the ejected ministers, he published over thirty other works between the publication of the *Abridgment* (1702) and the *Continuation of the Account* (1727). Many were single sermons, but they included his *Defence of Moderate Non-Conformity*, perhaps his most influential work. Issued in three parts between 1703 and 1705 in response to John Ollyffe's *Defence of Ministerial Conformity* (1702) and Benjamin Hoadly's *Reasonableness of Conformity* (1703), and answered in turn by Hoadly's *Serious Admonition* (1703) and *Defence of Episcopal Ordination* (1705), it helped to confirm in their dissent a number of young men who were in suspense between conformity and nonconformity. The most important of his remaining works were *Inspiration of the Holy Writings* (1710), dedicated by permission to Queen Anne, and *Thirteen Sermons Concerning the Doctrine of the Trinity* (1722), dedicated to George I, who received Calamy 'very graciously' when he came to present it and granted him a royal bounty of £50 (Calamy, *Life*, 2.446). Calamy kept the papers relating to the ejected ministers 'ready to be produc'd if there should be occasion' (Calamy, *Abridgement*, 2.xxv), but with the death of his great-grandson in 1870 they were apparently lost. Of his original manuscripts, only a copy of his autobiography and his commonplace book appear to have survived. The loss of his archive is incalculable. The autobiography, 'An historical account of my own life, with some reflections on the times I have lived in', used by Kippis in 1784, was edited by John Towill Rutt in two volumes (1829; 2nd edn with index 1830). It provides the main details about Calamy's life and contemporaries, but is itself a valuable source.

Final years Following the death of Calamy's first wife in 1713 he married Mary Jones, niece of Adam Cardonnel, secretary to the first duke of Marlborough, on 14 February 1716; she survived him. He had thirteen children, but only six survived him, four of them, including his eldest son, Edmund *Calamy (1698–1755), from his first marriage. In the summer of 1729 he spent ten weeks at Scarborough taking the waters. In February 1732, in poor health, he visited Bath, but returned home having experienced little benefit. He died in London on 3 June, and was buried at St Mary Aldermanbury on 9 June 1732.

Calamy's considerable reputation rests on his account of the ejected ministers, which has achieved the status of a nonconformist classic, though largely as a result of Samuel Palmer's *Nonconformist's Memorial*. The enduring appeal and indeed influence of Calamy's account is evident. Even modern historians continue to see early dissent very largely in terms of the sufferings of the ejected clergy. As a biographer he was responsible for rescuing many details and even the names of ejected ministers which would otherwise have been lost. Among his contemporaries he provided vital political leadership during a challenging period for dissent. DAVID L. WYKES

Sources E. Calamy, *An historical account of my own life, with some reflections on the times I have lived in, 1671–1731*, ed. J. T. Rutt, 2nd edn, 2 vols. (1830) · 'An historical account of my own life, with some reflections on the times I have lived in', BL, Add. MSS 50958, 50959 · D. L. Wykes, *To revive the memory of some excellent men: Edmund Calamy and the early historians of nonconformity* (1997) [Friends of Dr Williams's Library fiftieth lecture] · D. L. Wykes, '"To let the Memory of these Men Dye is injurious to Posterity": Edmund Calamy's *Account* of the ejected ministers', *The church retrospective*, ed. T. S. Freeman, SCH, 33 (1997), 379–92 · *Calamy rev.* · A. Gordon, 'Calamy as a biographer', *Transactions of the Congregational Historical Society*, 6 (1914), 233–47 · D. Mayo, *A funeral sermon occasioned by the much lamented death of the late reverend and learned Edmund Calamy, D.D. who departed this life, June 3, 1732. Preached at Westminster, June 11, 1732* (1732) · W. Wilson, *The history and antiquities of the dissenting churches and meeting houses in London, Westminster and Southwark*, 4 vols. (1808–14), vol. 2, pp. 135, 212; vol. 4, pp. 69ff. · A. Gordon, ed., *Freedom after ejection: a review (1690–1692) of presbyterian and congregational nonconformity in England and Wales* (1917), 228 · E. Calamy, letter to [R. Thoresby], 29 Jan 1701/2, Bodl. Oxf., MS Eng. hist. c. 237, fol. 64*r* · W. Harris, London, letter to S. Say, 20 April 1734, DWL, Say MS 12.107 (144) · E. Calamy, literary commonplace book, Bodl. Oxf., MS Eng. hist. d. 90 · *The correspondence of the Rev. Robert Wodrow*, ed. T. M'Crie, 3 vols., Wodrow Society, [3] (1842–3), vol. 2, pp. 431, 435, 519–20; vol. 3, pp. 169, 174 · 'Memoirs of himself, by Mr John Fox … with biographical sketches of some of his contemporaries; and some unpublished letters [pt 2]', *Monthly Repository*, 16 (1821), 193–200, esp. 194 · *The diary of Dudley Ryder, 1715–1716*, ed. W. Matthews (1939), 224 · *The nonconformist's memorial … originally written by … Edmund Calamy*, ed. S. Palmer, 2 vols. (1775); [3rd edn], 3 vols. (1802–3) · *DNB* · *GM*, 1st ser., 2 (1732), 826 · parish register, St Mary Aldermanbury, London, 9 June 1732, burial

Archives BL, MS autobiography, Add. MSS 50958–50959 [copy] · BL, MS copies of sermons and notes for sermons, P64 · BL, sermon notes, Harley MS 3753 · Bodl. Oxf., notes and diary

Likenesses G. Vertue, engraving (after unknown artist), BM, NPG; repro. in E. Calamy, *Thirteen sermons concerning the doctrine of the Trinity* (1722), frontispiece [*see illus.*] · mezzotint (after J. Richardson)

Calamy, Edmund (1698–1755), Presbyterian minister, was born at London on 17 August 1698, the eldest son of Edmund *Calamy (1671–1732), Presbyterian minister and the biographer of the ejected ministers, and his first wife, Mary (*d.* 1713), daughter of Michael Watts. He was educated at Westminster School before entering Edinburgh University in 1714, whence he graduated MA on 15 June 1717. On graduation he presented twelve theological works written by his father and other members of the family to the university library. He then studied at Leiden University, which he entered on 29 September 1717. He first assisted his father, and in 1723 was chosen with a number of other younger ministers to preach a Tuesday lecture at the Old Jewry. In 1726, to the disappointment of his father, who had hoped for 'the satisfaction and comfort' of his son's 'assistance and help for the remaining part of my life' (Calamy, 2.489), he was chosen as assistant to Benjamin Grosvenor at Crosby Square, London, in succession to Clark Oldisworth. He received a bachelor of divinity degree from King's College, Aberdeen, on 16 February 1738.

On 11 March 1739 Calamy married Bethia Biscoe. He was a trustee of Dr Williams's Trust from 1740 until his death and a member of the Presbyterian Board from 1739 until 1748. His widow gave £100 to the fund in 1758. When Grosvenor resigned in 1749 Calamy also retired from preaching, living in retirement in St John's Square, Clerkenwell. He died on 13 June 1755 in poor health, having 'preach'd only occasionally for some Years past' and was buried on 17 June at St Mary Aldermanbury, London, being 'interred among his Ancestors' (*Whitehall Evening Post*, 17–19 June 1755). Walter Wilson described him as 'a learned and ingenious man, of great worth, and much respected in his day' (Wilson, 1.354), but he never matched his father for ability or reputation. A younger brother, Adam Calamy, was an early contributor to the *Gentleman's Magazine*, writing chiefly on polemical theology and civil liberty under the pseudonym 'A Consistent Protestant'.

Edmund's son, also Edmund, was born on 18 May 1743, and entered Warrington Academy as a divinity student in 1761, but moved to Emmanuel College, Cambridge, in September 1763 and turned to the law. He was admitted to Lincoln's Inn on 29 January 1765, though in later years he practised mainly in conveyancing. He was a member of the Presbyterian Board from 1787 and until 1804, and a trustee of Dr Williams's Trust from 1784 until 1812, when he retired to Devon. He died on 12 May 1816 at Alphington near Exeter, and was buried at Gulliford, near Lympstone, Devon. He and his wife, Hester, daughter of the Revd Michael Pope (1709–1788), whom he had married on 26 May 1774, had two sons: Edmund (*d.* 27 Aug 1850) and Michael Calamy, who was the last of the male line and lived a very secluded life at Exeter in a house full of family papers and books. Michael Calamy was educated for the ministry at Wymondley and under John Jervis, the Presbyterian minister at Lympstone. He was apparently never ordained and held no pastoral charge, though in 1817, when he was recommended as a candidate for the vacant pulpit at Mill Hill Unitarian Chapel, Leeds, he was preaching occasionally to Unitarian congregations in Exeter, Topsham, and elsewhere in Devon. He died unmarried on 3 January 1870, aged eighty-five, at 4 Barrington Crescent, Exeter. With his death the papers of his great-grandfather, which had probably survived largely intact, were lost.

DAVID L. WYKES

Sources E. Calamy, *An historical account of my own life, with some reflections on the times I have lived in, 1671–1731*, ed. J. T. Rutt, 2nd edn, 2 (1830), 145, 307, 489 • W. Wilson, *The history and antiquities of the dissenting churches and meeting houses in London, Westminster and Southwark*, 4 vols. (1808–14), vol. 1, p. 354; vol. 4, p. 89 • W. D. Jeremy, *The Presbyterian Fund and Dr Daniel Williams's Trust* (1885), 135, 171–2 • *Whitehall Evening Post* (17–19 June 1755) • *GM*, 1st ser., 25 (1755), 284 • Venn, *Alum. Cant.*, 2/1.489 • E. Peacock, *Index to English speaking students who have graduated at Leyden University* (1883), 16 • Presbyterian Fund Board minutes, DWL, MS OD 69, p. 289 (8 Oct 1739), vol. 3, 8 Oct 1722–3 June 1751; vol. 5, 6 Jan 1752–2 June 1760, MS OD 72, p. 147 (6 Nov 1758); vol. 7, 5 Oct 1772–2 May 1796, MS OD 74, p. 374 (3 Jan 1787); vol. 8, 3 Oct 1796–4 March 1811, MS OD 75, p. 146 (3 Dec 1804) • *Monthly Repository*, 11 (1816), 300 • H. J. McLachlan, 'Mill Hill, Leeds, and a ministerial appointment, 1817', *Transactions of the Unitarian Historical Society*, 10/1 (1951), 26–9 • J. Manning, Exeter, to Joshua Wilson, esq., Highbury Place, Islington, 6 March 1820, DWL, New College collection, L54/4/65 • R. Thomas, 'Lapsus Calamy', *Transactions of the Unitarian Historical Society*, 13 (1966), 168–71 • *The Inquirer* (8 Jan 1870), 31 • *The Inquirer* (15 Jan 1870), 46 • *DNB*

Likenesses portraits, priv. coll.

Calandrini, Cesar (1595–1665), Reformed minister, was born in Stade, in Germany, on 6 February 1595, the son of Giovanni Calandrini (*b. c.*1542, *d.* after 1607) and his first wife, Marie, daughter of Jean de Maistres, a wealthy Antwerp merchant. His father, who belonged to an influential Calvinist family of Italian origin, had fled Lucca in 1567 because of his Reformed faith, and lived subsequently in France, Antwerp, Germany, and then London. There, during the first years of James I's reign, Calandrini senior founded an influential merchant banking house with his son-in-law, Philip Burlamachi. Cesar appears to have been destined for a clerical career from the start. In May 1612 he matriculated at the Academy of Geneva and later attended the Calvinist Academy of Saumur. In April 1616 he was admitted as a reader to the Bodleian Library in Oxford, and he matriculated in theology at the University of Leiden on 7 November 1616. In Leiden he met his lifelong friend and correspondent, the Dutch poet and diplomat, Constantijn Huygens.

In late 1617 Calandrini became a trainee minister in the French church in London and in March 1618 he was ordained by the joint body of ministers from the Dutch and French churches. Their support and the backing of the apostate archbishop of Spalato, Marco Antonio de Dominis, secured Calandrini the appointment of minister to the Italian Reformed church in London. Initially, Calandrini was on excellent terms with his mentor, de Dominis, lodging with him at the Savoy Hospital. Later, after Calandrini had attended the Synod of Dort and finished his studies in theology under John Prideaux at Exeter College, Oxford, from where he graduated BD on 18 July 1620, he found it increasingly difficult to reconcile his Calvinism with de Dominis's Catholic syncretism. Before the archbishop left England for Rome he apparently denounced Calandrini to James I as a dangerous puritan. That he was a hardline Calvinist is corroborated by Anthony Wood, who described him as 'a puritanical theologist' (Wood, 1.393).

Shortly before he received his BD, Calandrini was instituted on 20 June 1620 at the rectory of Stapleford Abbots in Essex. In August 1621 he married Elizabeth Harderet, a granddaughter of Robert *Le Macon (*d.* 1611), who had been minister of the London French church. It was probably through the patronage of John Prideaux that he came into contact with James Ussher, later archbishop of Armagh, whom he assisted in his scholarly activities during the latter's three-year stay in London. He became closely involved in Ussher's great protestant scheme, the *Bibliotheca theologica*, accompanying him to Ireland. Not until the collapse of Ussher's project in 1626 did Calandrini live in Stapleford Abbots.

Calandrini corresponded with an impressive number of leading European Calvinists, and among his English correspondents were such leading puritan divines as Herbert Palmer, John Davenport, Stephen Marshall, Thomas Gataker, Hugh Peters, and Cornelius Burgess. In 1639 he was appointed minister to the Dutch church in London, thus becoming a colleague of his stepbrother, Ambrosius Regemorter. Calandrini's excellent contacts with leading puritans such as William Kiffin and Sidrach Simpson helped to ease many of the difficulties the Dutch community in London faced during the turbulent 1640s. As the son of a protestant immigrant, and a pivotal figure in the international Calvinist republic of letters, Calandrini remained actively involved in relief work for European co-religionists until his death from the plague in London on 26 September 1665; he was buried a day later. He left at least one son, Lewis Calandrine, who had been ejected from the rectory of Stapleford Abbots in 1662.

Ole Peter Grell, *rev.*

Sources O. P. Grell, *Dutch Calvinists in early Stuart London: the Dutch church in Austin Friars, 1603–1642* (1989) • O. P. Grell, *Calvinist exiles in Tudor and Stuart England* (1996) • A. G. H. Bachrach, *Sir Constantine Huygens and Britain* (1962) • Wood, *Ath. Oxon.: Fasti* (1815), 393–4 • *Calamy rev.*, 98

Calcott, Wellins (*bap.* **1726**), religious writer and freemason, was a native of Shropshire and was baptized at St Chad's, Shrewsbury, on 27 January 1726, the son of Matthew Calcott, a member of the town corporation. All that is known of Calcott's life is taken from his *Collection of Thoughts, Moral and Divine* (1756), which suggests that he was prompted to write by a reversal of fortune. His *Collection* was reprinted several times; it appends a long list of subscribers, who included John Wilkes MP.

In 1769 Calcott published the influential *Candid disquisition of the principles and practices of the most ancient and honourable Society of Free and Accepted Masons*, in which he argues that freemasonry promotes every social and moral virtue. He dedicated this work to Henry Somerset, duke of Beaufort, and it was reprinted in 1847 by Dr George Oliver. It is not known where or when Calcott died.

C. W. Sutton, *rev.* Emma Major

Sources W. Calcott, *A collection of thoughts, moral and divine* (1756), preface • *ESTC* • *N&Q*, 4th ser., 2 (1868), 9 • G. Oliver, *Golden remains of the early masonic writers*, 5 vols. (1847–50), 2.1847 • G. Oliver, *Revelations of a square* (1855), 118 • *Temperance Spectator* (1866), 181 • *IGI*

Calcraft, Sir Granby Thomas (**1767?–1820**), army officer, was the younger (illegitimate) son of John *Calcraft (*bap.* 1726, *d.* 1772) of Rempstone Hall in the Isle of Purbeck, politician, and the actress Mrs Elizabeth Bride; John *Calcraft (1765–1831) was his elder brother. He was educated at Harrow School (1775), and Eton College (1778–9). He entered the army as a cornet in the 15th light dragoons in March 1788, and was promoted lieutenant in 1793. His regiment having been ordered to join the force under the duke of York in Flanders, he served at the battle of Famars, the siege of Valenciennes, and, in April 1794, the affair of Villers-en-Cauchies, where 160 troopers of the 15th light dragoons and 112 Austrian hussars stemmed an advance by the enemy and saved the Austrian emperor's life. All eight officers of the 15th present were knighted, and received the order of Maria Theresa from Emperor Leopold. In the same month Calcraft was promoted captain. His regiment was frequently engaged throughout the disastrous retreat of the following winter.

In 1799 Calcraft accompanied, as aide-de-camp, Major-General Lord Paget, who commanded the cavalry brigade, in the expedition to The Helder. He was wounded at the second battle of Alkmaer on 1 October, and was for his services promoted major into the 25th light dragoons in December 1799. In 1800 he exchanged into the 3rd dragoon guards, of which he became lieutenant-colonel on 25 December; he commanded them until his promotion to major-general in 1813. In May 1807 he was elected whig MP for Wareham, Dorset, on his brother's interest, but resigned his seat in April 1808, and was ordered to the Peninsula soon afterwards.

The 3rd were at once brigaded with the 4th dragoon guards, under the command of Henry Fane, as the heavy brigade, which was engaged in the battle of Talavera. General Fane fell ill, and Calcraft replaced him until the arrival of George de Grey in May 1810. The brigade was frequently engaged during the retreat on Torres Vedras, and again in the pursuit of Masséna in March 1811. After the action of Foz d'Aronce, the brigade served on the left bank of the Tagus under Marshal Beresford. Calcraft, who had been promoted colonel for his services on 25 July 1810, was engaged at the head of his regiment at Campo Mayor, where he begged to be allowed to help the 13th light dragoons. He participated in both Lumley's charge at Los Santos on 16 April 1811 and the battle of Albuera. In January 1812 the heavy brigade, which was again temporarily under the command of Calcraft, assisted in covering the siege of Ciudad Rodrigo; and when Wellington besieged Badajoz, it was left with General Graham's division to watch Marmont. After Salamanca the cavalry division distinguished itself in the affair of Llera on 11 June 1812, when General Lallemand's cavalry were defeated; in General Slade's report the 'conspicuous gallantry' of Calcraft was specially mentioned (*Supplementary Despatches*, 7.348). The brigade was then engaged in covering Hill's retreat from Madrid, and in December 1812 Calcraft was made a knight of the Portuguese order of the Tower and

Sword. On 4 June 1813 he was promoted major-general, and left the Peninsula after four years' continuous and distinguished service.

Calcraft was relatively neglected in later years. His political opinions were obnoxious to the tory ministry, whose jobbery was repeatedly attacked by his brother, at (it was believed) Calcraft's instigation. In 1813 he was appointed to the command of a brigade in England, and in 1814 received a gold medal for the battle of Talavera. In 1814 he relinquished his staff appointment, and retired, a disappointed man, believing his services inadequately recognized. He died, unmarried, at Bath on 20 August 1820: reportedly 'gout in the stomach was the immediate cause of his sudden death' (*GM*, 282).

H. M. STEPHENS, *rev.* DAVID GATES

Sources HoP, *Commons* • *Supplementary despatches (correspondence) and memoranda of Field Marshal Arthur, duke of Wellington*, ed. A. R. Wellesley, second duke of Wellington, 15 vols. (1858–72), vol. 7, p. 348 • R. Cannon, ed., *Historical record of the third, or prince of Wales' regiment of dragoon guards* (1838) • J. Philippart, ed., *The royal military calendar*, 3rd edn, 5 vols. (1820) • *GM*, 1st ser., 90/2 (1820), 282 • D. Gates, *The Spanish ulcer: a history of the Peninsular War* (1986) • A. B. Rodger, *The war of the second coalition: 1798–1801, a strategic commentary* (1964)

Calcraft, John, the elder (*bap.* **1726**, *d.* **1772**), politician, baptized on 4 September 1726, was the first son of John Calcraft of Grantham, Lincolnshire, and his wife, Christian Bursbie. His father, an attorney, was town clerk of Grantham and the duke of Rutland's election agent for the borough. After being educated in Leicester, in 1745 Calcraft became a clerk in the pay office through the influence of Rutland's eldest son, the marquess of Granby. He was also deputy paymaster to Cumberland's army from 25 November 1745 to 15 March 1747. However, his astounding rise into wealth and power was due to the patronage of the unscrupulous Henry Fox, to whom he was in some unspecified way related. Possibly he was a cousin, but some contemporary writers insinuated that he was Fox's natural son. There were other mysteries in his personal life: in 1744 he married Bridget, whose surname is unknown, but he separated from her soon afterwards and kept her existence secret. He later lived with the actress George Anne *Bellamy (1731?–1788), with whom he had several children, but after repeatedly paying the debts arising from her extravagant habits he dismissed her with a pension. The letter to him which was advertised for publication in October 1767, but afterwards suppressed, was printed in 1785, with an address to the public (*An Apology for the Life of George Anne Bellamy*, 1785, 5.87–144). In his final years he consorted with another actress, Mrs Elizabeth Bride; they had four sons and one daughter, of whom the eldest son, John *Calcraft the younger (1765–1831), also pursued a political career. Another son, Sir Granby Thomas *Calcraft, became an army officer.

Fox secured Calcraft a clerkship in the war office (1747–56) and the lucrative posts of paymaster of widows' pensions (1757–62) and deputy commissary of musters (1756–63). He was also involved in the rebuilding of the Horse Guards and held contracts for delivering coal to Gibraltar. Fox reposed implicit trust in his young protégé: he made him the medium in his communications with the chiefs of the army and appointed him agent for as many regiments as he could. Calcraft increasingly concentrated on these agencies and by 1762 held fifty-seven, which comprised about half of the regiments in the army. This effectively made him quasi-banker and contractor for the forces, and his official knowledge was of the greatest utility. On 3 December 1764, following his decision to retire from such business, the *Public Advertiser* estimated that it had netted him £500,000. He 'riots in the plunder of an army', was Junius's later expressive phrase.

By April 1763, when Calcraft was talked of as a possible Irish peer, an irreparable breach had developed between him and Fox, now Lord Holland, over ministerial changes and the pay office. In August 1763 his growing connections with Shelburne led to his involvement in attempts to form a new government, but he was unable to reconcile the elder Pitt with the duke of Bedford. On 24 November 1763 Shelburne and his parliamentary followers opposed Grenville's administration over Wilkes, and Calcraft was consequently ejected from his post as deputy commissary of musters.

Calcraft now harboured parliamentary ambitions. In December 1765 he contested Rochester against Grey Cooper, but was narrowly defeated, probably through Cooper's influence as secretary to the Treasury. A month later he was negotiating in his native Grantham, but in April 1766 was returned by Shelburne for Calne. In 1768 he was returned with government support for Rochester, which he continued to represent until his death. He calculated that Pitt had the best future of any of the party leaders and thus worked hard to promote his interests for a return to power. In 1768 he helped to effect a reconciliation between Chatham and Lord Temple, and he tried, though with less success, to connect Henry Conway with them. In January 1770 he was largely responsible for persuading Granby, who had become indebted to him for considerable loans, to resign. Throughout this period Calcraft acted as Chatham's eyes and ears in parliament and wrote him regular political reports. Encouraged by Chatham, now his near neighbour in Kent, Calcraft also participated in the petitioning movement over the Middlesex election: he spoke at the Buckinghamshire meeting in September 1769, signing that county's petition as well as that of Aylesbury, was active in Essex, and stirred up Kent despite the determined opposition of many of the local gentry.

Calcraft made large purchases of property over the years. In particular, he acquired the estates of Rempstone, Dorset, in 1757, Ingress, Kent, in 1760, and Wareham, Dorset, in 1767. By the early 1770s he was reported to possess estate worth £10,000 per annum. This gave him considerable borough influence, most particularly at Wareham, where he had gradually purchased the chief part of the town. He had also ingratiated himself with the proprietors of the chief London newspapers, and had won over to his side many of the leading members of the London corporation. His activity was now thrown into the cause of the 'liberty of the subject and parliamentary reform', and together with Philip Francis, the reputed author of the *Letters of Junius*, whom he had patronized previously, he exerted himself in the task of forcing Chatham into power. In October 1771 Calcraft was one of Junius's principal targets, but this may have been a blind to divert suspicion of the authorship of the letters from Francis.

Calcraft had aspirations of acquiring an English peerage and he coveted the title of earl of Ormond, but in April 1772 he was seized by a fatal illness. On 21 August following he wrote optimistically to Chatham that he was recovering and planned to winter at Naples, but two days later, on 23 August 1772, he died at Ingress. He was buried at St Mary's, Wareham. The chief heir of his will, dated 9 July 1771, was John Calcraft, his eldest son with Elizabeth Bride, and provision was made for all his other surviving illegitimate offspring. Philip Francis, whom Calcraft desired to be returned to parliament for Wareham, also received £1000 in cash, and provision was made for Francis's wife in the event that she was widowed with less than £300 a year. Having outlived him, Calcraft's estranged wife, Bridget, made a successful claim against his estate.

W. P. Courtney, *rev.* Patrick Woodland

Sources L. B. Namier, 'Calcraft, John', HoP, *Commons* • J. Parkes and H. Merivale, *Memoirs of Sir Philip Francis*, 2 vols. (1867) • *Correspondence of William Pitt, earl of Chatham*, ed. W. S. Taylor and J. H. Pringle, 4 vols. (1838–40) • *The letters of Horace Walpole, earl of Orford*, ed. P. Cunningham, 9 vols. (1857–9) • H. Walpole, *Memoirs of the reign of King George the Second*, ed. Lord Holland [H. R. Fox], 2 vols. (1846) • H. Walpole, *Memoirs of the reign of King George the Third*, ed. G. F. R. Barker, 4 vols. (1894) • G. A. Bellamy, *An apology for the life of George Anne Bellamy*, ed. [A. Bicknell], 3rd edn, 6 vols. (1785) • J. Hutchins, *The history and antiquities of the county of Dorset*, 3rd edn, ed. W. Shipp and J. W. Hodson, 4 vols. (1861–74) • *The poetical works of Charles Churchill*, ed. W. Tooke, [rev. edn], 2 vols. (1871) • *Correspondence of John, fourth duke of Bedford*, ed. J. Russell, 3 vols. (1842–6) • *The Grenville papers: being the correspondence of Richard Grenville … and … George Grenville*, ed. W. J. Smith, 4 vols. (1852–3) • F. G. Stephens and M. D. George, eds., *Catalogue of prints and drawings in the British Museum, division 1: political and personal satires*, 3 (1877), p. 171, nos. 2247–8; pp. 1184–5, no. 3659; 4 (1883), p. 588, no. 4357; p. 593, no. 4360; pp. 608–10, no. 4375 • G. Rudé, *Wilkes and liberty: a social study of 1763 to 1774* (1962) • *DNB*

Archives BL, Add. MSS 17493–17496, 51899 • Dorset RO • NA Canada, agency account books [microfilmed] • NAM, regimental ledger | BL, Chatham MSS • BL, Holland MSS • BL, Tyrawley MSS • Bodl. Oxf., Shelburne MSS [microfilm] • Duke U., Perkins L., Almon MSS • NL Scot., letters to Lord Charles Hay • NRA Scotland, priv. coll., Loudon MSS • PRO, Amherst MSS • PRO, Chatham MSS

Likenesses line engraving, NPG • monument (including Calcraft?), St Mary's, Wareham

Wealth at death estates worth over £10,000 p.a.; some reckoned him worth £300,000 in 1760s; large legacies in will: Namier, 'Calcraft, John'

Calcraft, John, the younger (**1765–1831**), politician, was the first illegitimate son of John *Calcraft, the elder (*bap.* 1726, *d.* 1772), also a politician, and Elizabeth Bride, an actress. Sir Granby Thomas *Calcraft was his younger brother. He was born on 16 October 1765, and was educated at Harrow, from 1774, and at Eton, 1778–9. Under his late father's influence, he soon entered upon political life and followed him in his attachment to the theatre and loose living. Before he was twenty-one he was returned for the family borough of Wareham in Dorset (15 July 1786), and sat for it until the dissolution in 1790. On 5 March 1790, he married Elizabeth, third daughter and coheiress of Sir Thomas Pym Hales (*d.* 1773) of Bekesbourne, Kent. They had two sons and three daughters before her death, aged forty-five, on 2 July 1815. For ten years after 1790, Calcraft by choice stayed out of parliament, but on a casual vacancy was again elected for Wareham (16 June 1800), retaining his seat until 1806. At this time he was a member of the Whig Club and a personal friend of the prince of Wales, his attachment being shown by his (unsuccessful) motion in March 1803 for a select committee to inquire into the prince's pecuniary embarrassments. In the Grenville administration of 1806 Fox secured for Calcraft the post of clerk of the ordnance, and he acquired considerable reputation as an administrator. At the general election in that year he was returned for the city of Rochester, defeating Admiral Sir Sidney Smith both at the polling booth and before the election committee of the House of Commons. He sat for Rochester until 1818, when he was again returned for Wareham, which he represented until 1831.

Calcraft was a prominent and early reformer of the liquor trade. He opposed excessive government expenditure and in 1816 advocated reducing the army estimates. In 1819 he was on the select committee on the Bank of England. He supported Tierney as leader of the whigs in 1818. In 1828 Wellington offered him the paymaster-generalship in his brief administration; he at first declined, but later accepted. He was sworn of the privy council on 16 June 1828. In 1831 he spoke against the Reform Bill on 4 March but, after a last-minute conversion, voted for its second reading, when it was carried by one vote on 22 March. Subsequently, in a rumbustious election, he contested and carried the county of Dorset as a reformer. Under the reproaches of the tories, with whom he had co-operated from 1828 to 1830, his mind became unhinged, and he committed suicide at Whitehall Place, London, on 11 September 1831. Ellenborough noted: 'Calcraft has cut his throat because he thought both Tories & Whigs despised him. He was right' (Aspinall, 128). On 17 September he was buried in the chancel vault of St James's Church, Piccadilly, and at a later date a monument was erected to his memory in St Mary's, Wareham.

W. P. Courtney, *rev.* H. C. G. Matthew

Sources *GM*, 1st ser., 60 (1790) • *GM*, 1st ser., 85/2 (1815) • HoP, *Commons* • A. Aspinall, ed., *Three early nineteenth-century diaries* (1952) [extracts from Le Marchant, E. J. Littleton, Baron Hatherton, and E. Law, earl of Ellenborough] • M. Brock, *The Great Reform Act* (1973)

Likenesses J. Posselwhite, stipple, pubd 1825 (after A. Wivell), BM, NPG • C. Turner, mezzotint, pubd 1826 (after J. Lonsdale), BM, NPG • line engraving, NPG

Calcraft, William (**1800–1879**), hangman, was born at Baddow, near Chelmsford. He was a cobbler by trade and had once been a nightwatchman at Reid's brewery in Clerkenwell. He then hawked meat pies around the streets, and particularly around Newgate, where he became known to the execution staff and to the hangman, John

Foxen or Foxton. This led to his employment at Newgate, flogging juvenile offenders at 10s. a week. In an emergency during 1828 he was sent to Lincoln, where he put two men to death. When Foxen died on 14 February 1829 Calcraft was appointed his successor and sworn in on 4 April 1829. His wage was 1 guinea a week, with an extra guinea per capita for each execution and an allowance for cats-o'-nine-tails and birch rods. Later he was to receive £10 for each execution, and increased his income by the sale of ropes and belongings of the victims. He was engaged to ply his trade all over the country and was particularly busy in the 1860s with public executions. Among those he executed were François Courvoisier (1840), Marie and Frederick Manning (1849), and James Rush (1849). Reasonably enough, he became nervous when asked to hang Fenians, as he had received a number of threats. An act of parliament restricted executions to private locations, and the last public execution took place outside Newgate on 26 May 1868.

In 1869 Calcraft was summonsed for refusing to come to the assistance of his mother, Sarah, who was a pauper in a workhouse at Hatfield Peveril, near Chelmsford, Calcraft saying that he had a brother and sister who should also be made to help and that he had three children of his own to support. No record of his marriage has been found. Calcraft's last official act was the hanging of James Godwin on 25 May 1874. He was, protestingly, obliged to retire, and received a City of London pension of 1 guinea a week. Having once been a genial man who took pleasure in breeding rabbits, by the age of seventy he was described as surly and sinister-looking, with long hair and beard, in scruffy black attire and a fob chain. He wore a tall hat and walked with a slouching gait. He died at Poole Street, Hoxton, on 13 December 1879.

Calcraft was the most famous hangman of the century, and held his post for forty-five years. None the less, he seems to have been particularly incompetent at his job, clumsy, bungling, and notoriously unable to calculate the correct length of rope required for each individual hanging; he frequently had to rush below the scaffold to pull on his victim's legs to hasten death.

G. C. Boase, *rev.* J. Gilliland

Sources B. Bailey, *Hangmen of England* (1989) • Ward, *Men of the reign* • *Daily Telegraph* (17 Dec 1879), 5a • J. Hancock, *The groans of the gallows* (1846) • Boase, *Mod. Eng. biog.* • *The life and recollections of Calcraft* (1880)

Caldecote. For this title name *see* Inskip, Thomas Walker Hobart, first Viscount Caldecote (1876–1947); Inskip, Robert Andrew, second Viscount Caldecote (1917–1999).

Caldecotes, Joan (*fl.* 1417). *See under* Women in trade and industry in York (*act. c.*1300–*c.*1500).

Caldecott, Sir Andrew (1884–1951), colonial governor, was born at Boxley, Kent, on 26 October 1884, the eldest son of the Revd Andrew Caldecott and his wife, Isobel, daughter of the Revd Stenning Johnson. He was educated at Uppingham and at Exeter College, Oxford, of which he was a scholar and later, in 1948, an honorary fellow. He was awarded a third class in classical honour moderations

Sir Andrew Caldecott (1884–1951), by Walter Stoneman, 1937

and, in 1907, a second class in *literae humaniores*. In that year he joined the Malayan civil service and between then and 1935 he held a variety of posts including acting controller of labour, under-secretary Straits Settlements, commissioner of lands Federated Malay States, secretary for postal affairs, acting British resident Negri Sembilan and then Perak, British resident Selangor, chief secretary to government Federated Malay States, and colonial secretary Straits Settlements. In 1934 he was appointed officer administering the government of the Straits Settlements and high commissioner for the Malay states. In 1924–5 he had been Malayan commissioner at the British Empire Exhibition. The sympathy and understanding which accompanied his great administrative ability, and his wise and tactful handling of racial issues, earned him exceptional respect and popularity.

In 1935 Caldecott was appointed governor of Hong Kong where he was equally popular, and he was also knighted. When in 1937 he was offered the governorship of Ceylon, strong representations were made for him to remain in Hong Kong. However, Caldecott was clearly sent to Ceylon to smooth the way for further advance at a time when agitation for constitutional reform was intense. In November 1937 he was instructed to sound opinion and to recommend amendments to the constitution. His 'reforms dispatch' of June 1938 was written with a vigour and directness unusual in official documents: it led to prolonged discussion in the state council, but to no general agreement, the basic difficulty, as always, being the question of minority representation. The outbreak of war halted consideration of constitutional advance, but Caldecott was convinced that if Ceylon's war effort were to be maintained a positive approach was required. On his recommendation the British government in 1941, and again in 1943, promised a commission on constitutional reform as soon as the war ended; and a commission was in fact appointed in 1944, the year in which Caldecott retired.

In the meantime Caldecott set himself out to be a constitutional governor, an objective misunderstood by certain sections of the European community which failed to see, with his clarity, that early self-government was inevitable. His aims were more clearly appreciated by the local politicians, such as D. S. Senanayake and J. R. Jayewardene, and he soon earned their respect and confidence. That Ceylon remained stable during the critical war years was largely due to his leadership. The sudden appointment, after the fall of Malaya, of Admiral Sir Geoffrey Layton as commander-in-chief in place of the governor, nearly led to Caldecott's resignation; happily this step was not taken and the two men, temperamentally so different, worked harmoniously together to the great benefit of Ceylon. With Caldecott's consent King's Pavilion (the governor's house in Kandy) was taken over by Mountbatten when he was appointed supreme allied commander, south-east Asia command. This proved to be an ideal arrangement since Mountbatten had chosen Peradeniya, only a few miles away, as his headquarters in Ceylon.

A brilliant, far-sighted administrator, but withal warm-hearted and with a quick intelligence tempered by a human sympathy and understanding, Caldecott was ideally suited for the task of helping to transform empire into Commonwealth. Ceylon owed to him much of her trouble-free progress towards the independence which she attained in 1948. His contribution to the development of the Commonwealth, and in particular of Britain's overseas services, continued after his retirement. Early in 1947, after failing to convince the Colonial Office of the necessity to create a colonial administrative service centrally controlled and hence able to make a positive contribution to the development of colonies achieving home rule, he resigned from the colonial service appointments board to which he had been appointed on retirement. A letter of his to *The Times* in June 1947 gave widespread publicity to the urgent need for a true unification of the colonial service and for a central control over its cadre and rate of recruitment as each colony progressed along the road to self-government. It is fair to say that the creation of HM overseas civil service with effect from 1 October 1954—such a vital step in the smooth progress from colonies to independence—owed much to the stand taken by such a respected former colonial governor as Caldecott.

Artistically gifted, Caldecott painted, was a skilled pianist, had a happy talent for light verse, and in his Malayan days wrote several witty burlesques; he published two books of uneasy stories: *Not Exactly Ghosts* (1947) and *Fires Burn Blue* (1948). He was twice married: first, in 1918, to Olive Mary (*d.* 1943), daughter of John Robert Innes, of the Malayan civil service, with whom he had a daughter and a son; and second, in 1946, to Evelyn May, widow of Dr J. Robertson and daughter of Canon H. Palmer.

Caldecott was appointed CBE in 1926 and CMG in 1932, and was advanced to KCMG in 1937 and GCMG in 1941. He was made a knight of grace of St John of Jerusalem in 1936 and was awarded the Silver Wolf in 1943 for his services to scouting. He died on 14 July 1951 at his home, Pierpoint, Itchenor, Sussex. An unconventional portrait of him by David Paynter, the Ceylon artist, was presented by Caldecott to Queen's House, Colombo. A memorial window, commissioned by his widow, was installed in Itchenor church. JOHN O'REGAN, *rev.*

Sources *The Times* (16 July 1951) • *Ceylon Daily News* (16 July 1951) • private information (1971) • K. M. De Silva and H. Wriggins, *J. R. Jayewardene of Sri Lanka* (1988) • *WWW* • *British Malaya* (Aug 1951) • *CGPLA Eng. & Wales* (1951) • personal knowledge (1971, 2004)
Archives Bodl. RH, corresp. with John W. H. O'Regan
Likenesses W. Stoneman, photograph, 1937, NPG [*see illus.*] • J. Napper, portrait, priv. coll. • D. Paynter, portrait, Queen's House, Colombo, Sri Lanka
Wealth at death £40,489 3*s*. 2*d*.: probate, 10 Oct 1951

Caldecott, John (1800–1849), astronomer, is believed to have trained as an architect, but no details are known of his origin, background, or education. He was married, but by 1829 was living apart from his wife, whose given name was Selina. Caldecott left England for India, probably in 1829, to take up a post as commercial agent at Alleppey for the Travancore government. He shared an interest in astronomy, in which he was self-taught, with General Stuart Fraser, British government representative at Trivandrum, and through Fraser was introduced in 1832 to Rama Vurmah, maharaja of Travancore. The maharaja was a cultured man who had been educated in England and admired European scientific ideas. He engaged Caldecott as his astronomer, responsible for the design and establishment of an observatory at Trivandrum, the building of which was completed in 1837. Operations began using Caldecott's own portable but substantial instruments, with the help of an Indian assistant who had been trained by T. G. Taylor, astronomer at the East India Company's Madras observatory.

While the observatory was under construction Caldecott and Taylor undertook a magnetic survey of southern India, through which the magnetic equator passed, using second-hand instruments from previous surveys. The unsatisfactory outcome of this survey was in part due, as they discovered, to defective instruments, but probably also to geological effects unrecognized at the time.

In December 1838 Caldecott sailed for England to procure apparatus from the leading makers. He ordered a transit instrument and an equatorial telescope from Dollond, mural circles of 5 ft diameter from Troughton and Simms and from Thomas Jones, a clock from Dent, and various other items. While in London he became aware of plans for a worldwide network of magnetic observatories, and obtained the raja's consent to buy a set of magnetic instruments from Grubb of Dublin to match those being provided for the other British and East India Company observatories. He sailed from England in the autumn of

1840, pausing at Cadiz to visit the Spanish naval observatory at San Fernando, and then the Cairo observatory, reaching Trivandrum in April 1841 a few days after the arrival of the magnetic instruments which he had ordered. A magnetic and meteorological observatory was constructed that year and a new building for the 7 ft equatorial telescope went up in 1842. Taylor helped with the erection of the two mural circles. Caldecott also corresponded with the Scottish scientist J. D. Forbes who was actively promoting experiments to measure deep-soil temperatures, following those made in France; he obtained from Adie of Edinburgh a set of thermometers 3, 6, and 12 French feet in length so that readings would be comparable with the French results. They were put into the ground near the observatory and the results, which were not extensive as one of the thermometers was soon broken, were communicated to the British Association.

Though not officially part of the international magnetic observatories network, Caldecott assiduously met the same demanding schedule of observations, which he returned to Edward Sabine at the Royal Society. Isolated, overworked, and harassed by the 'narrow-minded jealous fool of a Resident' (Caldecott to Sabine, 12 Jan 1842, RS Sa.270)—this was General Cullen, who had replaced the amiable former resident, Foster—and receiving no acknowledgement of his flow of observations and correspondence, he wrote bitterly to Sabine:

> you have such little idea of all I have to contend with … to keep scientific matters going here, or I am sure you would be inclined to give me a helping hand … rather than a silence now maintained for 12 months since I first commenced operations. (Caldecott to Sabine, 16 April 1842, RS Sa.268)

His reward was a batch of letters which had been delayed in transit, including one in which Sabine complained about the excess postage which Caldecott's observations had incurred. Caldecott was even more frustrated when the first abstracts published in England ignored the data from Trivandrum (which Sabine may well have considered less reliable than that from the nearby and official Madras observatory). He went to England in 1846 to seek the help of some scientific society to publish his observations, but in vain. He returned to Travancore in 1847; the raja undertook to publish the data and Caldecott was preparing this when he was taken ill. In January 1849 he travelled to Bombay and into the hills, seeking relief. In October he suffered a seizure, recovered, but fell ill on 8 December and was found dead on the morning of 17 December 1849. He left instructions in his will that his wife should be maintained for her lifetime; his effects were then sold, his estate, as he had requested, divided equally between his two brothers.

Caldecott's enthusiasm was no substitute for professional training. His results were never published. His successor at the observatory, John Allan Broun, found that the astronomical apparatus had not been properly installed, nor its errors determined. The Indian assistants, less than scrupulous about their observations in Broun's day, had probably grown lax during Caldecott's absences.

Anita McConnell

Sources *Bombay Times* (2 Jan 1850), 4–5 · J. A. Broun, 'Trivandrum observatory, a history and description', *Madras Journal of Literature and Science*, 6 (1837) · J. Caldecott, correspondence with E. Sabine, RS, Sa. 258–76 · J. Caldecott, correspondence with H. Lloyd, RS, Te.2.111 · will, BL OIOC, L/Ag/34/29/250, fols. 21–23 · *Annual Register* (1849), 299 · J. Caldecott, 'Notice accompanying a series of meteorological observations made at Trevandrum', *Report of the British Association for the Advancement of Science* (1840), sections 28–30

Caldecott, Randolph (1846–1886), artist and book illustrator, was born at 150 Bridge Street, Chester, on 22 March 1846, the son of John Caldecott, a hatter and tailor who was also a pioneer of modern accounting, and his wife, Mary Dinah Brookes. He was educated at King Henry VIII School, Chester, where he won a prize for drawing and, despite bouts of rheumatic fever, rose to become head boy. Among his early accomplishments was a talent for caricature and for carving animals in wood. His father, however, intended him for a financial career and in 1861 arranged a position for him in the Whitchurch and Ellesmere Bank in Whitchurch, Shropshire. He did well there and in 1867 was transferred to the Manchester and Salford Bank in Manchester.

Though he was careful and numerate, banking had never been Caldecott's first love. He continued to draw, and was ideally placed when employed in the quiet country town of Whitchurch to observe rural subjects with his keen, attentive eye. He lodged on a farm in these years, and travelled the county to visit farmers, landworkers, and landowners who were the bank's clients. It was from these experiences that Caldecott's knowledge of the forms and behaviour of animals, and of the manners of country people, first reached maturity. He paid particular attention to domestic and agricultural detail, such as furniture, costume, implements, and rural architecture, assimilating a depth and richness of subject matter both in his notebooks and his memory. He took part in fox-hunting, and his experience as a rider and huntsman gave him yet more insight into country practices, which found vivid expression in his later work.

After he moved to Manchester, Caldecott's discontent with banking evolved into action to get himself out of it. He joined the Brasenose Club, a centre of Manchester's cultural life, and over the years 1868–72 submitted drawings to the local weeklies *Will o' the Wisp* and *The Sphinx*, many of which were published. He sketched within the city, fascinated by local detail, the comic and the grotesque together, and attended evening classes at Manchester School of Art. Having been given an introduction to the Manchester-born painter Thomas Armstrong, later director of the South Kensington Museum and then living in London, Caldecott took his advice and began to send drawings to London publishers. Armstrong showed Caldecott's work to authors and publishers, including Henry Blackburn, who, from 1871, began to buy them for publication in his magazine *London Society*. In 1872 Caldecott gave up banking and moved to London to pursue a career as an artist. That year he briefly joined the Slade School to study life drawing under Sir E. J. Poynter, but his

Randolph Caldecott (1846–1886), self-portrait, 1884

central activity was as a news reporter, finding a rich vein of subject matter in the House of Commons, the law courts, the theatre, and public lectures.

Caldecott's wry, anecdotal humour, combined with his characteristically economical use of line, soon brought him an eager following among publishers and readers. His graphic manner—spare, simple lines and forms set onto wide areas of white paper—translated well into wood engraving, and later photo-etching on zinc blocks, and contrasted happily with denser passages of type. This was a calculated and thoroughly considered style, of which he wrote: 'The art of leaving out is a science. The fewer the lines, the less error committed' (Blackburn, 126). Caldecott settled in a studio at 46 Great Russell Street, Bloomsbury, and gradually widened his outlets in working for *Punch*, *The Graphic*, and the *Illustrated London News*. Though becoming successful as an illustrator and a journalist, Caldecott did not neglect his youthful talent for animal sculpture, and in 1873 he worked in the Chelsea studio of the expatriate French sculptor Jules Dalou. In exchange for English lessons, Dalou gave Caldecott modelling tuition, encouraging him to study animals from life, in the London streets, the zoo, and the South Kensington and British museums. Among Caldecott's animal sculpture is the bronze relief *Horse Fair in Brittany* (exh. RA, 1876), inspired by the Elgin marbles, and gilt capitals of birds in the Arab Hall, Leighton House, London, commissioned by the artist Frederick Leighton, in 1880. From observations of animals and birds in London, Caldecott painted and exhibited decorative schemes and murals, an early example being panels for the dining-room of Bank Hall, near Buxton, Derbyshire (1873).

Caldecott's sunny and cheerful personality endeared him to artists and publishers alike. His obituarist wrote:

> The handsome lad carried his own recommendation. With light brown hair falling with a ripple over his brow, blue-grey eyes shaded by long lashes, sweet and mobile mouth, tall and well made, he joined to these physical advantages a gay humour and a charming disposition. No wonder then that he was a general favourite. (*Manchester Quarterly*, July 1886)

Henry Blackburn encouraged Caldecott to broaden his range as an artist, and the two men travelled in France, Germany, Austria, and Italy together to collect material for collaborative books and articles. In the first of these, *The Hartz Mountains* (1873), Blackburn published twenty-seven of Caldecott's drawings. Other patrons in London included Captain Frederick Marryat, of whose book *Frank Mildmay* (1873) Caldecott was the sole illustrator, and the authors Juliana Horatia Ewing and Mrs Frederick Locker.

Caldecott found professional success and security when he illustrated Washington Irving's *Old Christmas* (1875) with 120 line drawings, and subsequently Irving's *Bracebridge Hall* (1877) with a similar number of illustrations. These books were early examples of 'gift books', publications made to a higher standard of printing, decoration, binding, and tooling than was the commercial norm. They were bought for family libraries by members of the increasingly affluent and numerous middle and upper classes in Britain, and kept for display as much as for reading. Caldecott found himself on a rising wave of demand for such publications, and had the talent and assiduity to help satisfy the market. He also had financial acumen, a product of his years in the bank, and a faith in his own work, preferring to take royalties rather than a fee. The printer Edmund Evans recalled that Caldecott 'wished to share the speculation—said he would make the drawings—if they sold and paid he would be paid, but was content to bear the loss if they did not sell, and not be paid' (S. E. Mayer, *A Treasury of the Great Children's Book Illustrators*, 1983, 98).

When colour lithographic printing developed in the 1870s to become technically and commercially viable for the mass production of books, Caldecott's talents were on hand to take his own art forward into colour printing with *John Gilpin* (1878) and *The House that Jack Built* (1878). These were the first of his long series of Caldecott's Picture Books published by Routledge under the innovative direction of Edmund Evans, and selling in great numbers. The series continued in popularity with titles such as *Babes in the Wood* (1879), *The Three Jovial Huntsmen* (1880), and *Ride a Cock Horse* (1884).

The careers of two almost exact contemporaries of Caldecott, Walter Crane and Kate Greenaway, likewise took advantage of the changes in printing techniques, and it is instructive to consider these three artists together. Whereas Greenaway had a childish, rather simpering and fey approach to her texts, and Crane was in tune with contemporary aestheticism, Caldecott touched a nerve of realism and truth in his illustrations. His horses smell, his mud sticks, and while his drawings are appealing and childlike, they are always truthful as to detail. He does, however, share with Greenaway a tendency to set his subjects in a nostalgic late eighteenth-century world, the period in which much of rural Shropshire and Cheshire appeared fixed during his childhood and youth.

Among the many sources for Caldecott's art are the wood engravings of Thomas Bewick and James Cooper, the latter having been instrumental in obtaining the early commission for Caldecott to illustrate Washington Irving. Other influences, which reflect his historicizing tendency, include the works of Thomas Gainsborough, George Morland, and Thomas Rowlandson. In his own century some of his more informal work reflects, none too palely, the compositions and rural sympathies of painters such as Stanhope Forbes and George Clausen. His illustrations were greatly admired by the painters Vincent Van Gogh and Paul Gauguin, and his influence is visible in, variously, the illustrations of Beatrix Potter, Arthur Rackham, Hugh Thomson and the Brocks, E. H. Shepherd, and Robert Lawson, the illustrator of *The Story of Ferdinand* (1937). With Walter Crane, a lifelong friend, he developed the practice of unifying the design of children's books, making them interesting and amusing by decoration and layout from the front cover to the back.

Caldecott was elected a member of the Institute of Painters in Water Colours (1882). He exhibited in the institute's galleries in 1883 and 1885, at the Royal Academy (1876, 1878, and 1882), and at the Grosvenor Gallery (1878). In 1879 he bought a house at Kemsing, near Sevenoaks, Kent. He met and on 18 March 1880 married a Kentish woman, Marian Harriet, daughter of Frederick William Brind, a merchant. The couple had no children. The poor health that had dogged Caldecott's childhood affected him throughout his life, but he tended to play down his condition and continued to work at a prodigious pace. One unidentified friend remarked: 'The quality and quantity of his work done manfully for years under these painful conditions was heroic, and to the anxious enquiries of friends he was always "quite well", although unable to mount two flights of stairs' (*DNB*).

Caldecott was well rewarded financially for his work. His earnings enabled him to travel, and he and his wife spent winters in the south of France or Italy. In the autumn of 1885 the couple travelled to the United States, where he engaged himself in studies of American life and manners for *The Graphic*. Weakened by a long transatlantic crossing, however, he died, aged thirty-nine, in St Augustine, Florida, on 12 February 1886. There are memorials to him in Chester Cathedral and Westminster Abbey, the latter designed by Alfred Gilbert. JAMES HAMILTON

Sources H. Blackburn, *Randolph Caldecott: a personal memoir of his early art career* (1886); new edn (1890) · R. K. Engen, *Randolph Caldecott, 'lord of the nursery'* (1976) · M. G. Davies, *Randolph Caldecott* (1946) · M. Hutchins, *Yours pictorially: illustrated letters of Randolph Caldecott* (1976) · R. K. Engen, *Randolph Caldecott: a Christmas exhibition of the work of the Victorian book illustrator* (1977) [exhibition catalogue, Man. City Gall., 13 Dec 1977 – 28 Jan 1978] · N. Finlay, *Randolph Caldecott: a checklist of the Caroline Miller Parker collection, Houghton Library, Harvard* (1986) · B. Alderson, *Sing a song for sixpence: the English picture book tradition and Randolph Caldecott* (1986) · *Manchester Quarterly* (July 1886) · *Manchester Courier* (16 Feb 1886)

Archives Harvard U., Houghton L., corresp., sketchbooks, etc. | Ches. & Chester ALSS, letters to Stapleton Caldecott · Harvard U., Houghton L., letters to Frederick Locker-Lampson · Sheff. Arch., corresp. with Julia Ewing · V&A, letters to John Nunnerly

Likenesses R. Caldecott, self-portrait, oils, 1884, Aberdeen Art Gallery [*see illus.*]

Wealth at death £4594 19*s*. 3*d*.: probate, 9 June 1886, *CGPLA Eng. & Wales*

Caldecott, Thomas (*bap.* 1744, *d.* 1833), barrister and literary editor, was born in Rugby and baptized on 13 April 1744, the eldest of three sons of William Caldecott of Rugby and his first wife, Elizabeth, daughter of the Revd Peter Senhouse, of Linton, Herefordshire. He entered Rugby School in 1750 and then Winchester College, where he was a scholar from 1757 to 1762. He matriculated at New College, Oxford, on 19 February 1763 and after the customary two-year probationary period was elected fellow on 17 February 1765. He was admitted to the Middle Temple on 29 May 1767, graduated BCL from Oxford on 24 October 1770, and was called to the bar on 8 February 1771. A member of the Oxford circuit, he continued Sir James Burrow's *Decisions upon Orders of Justices* with texts of court cases entitled *Reports of Cases Relative to the Duty and Office of a Justice of the Peace*, issued in three parts in 1786, 1789, and 1800, and enlarging the original plan to answer questions that related 'not only to the system of the poor laws, but also to the general jurisdiction of the justice of the peace … and to include all such cases, as relate to that office in general' ('Preface'). In 1787 he was appointed steward for life of the New College estates. He was not only active in the estate and financial business of the college but, as indicated in a letter of 5 March 1795 written from the college, was clearly instrumental in promoting the designs by Sir Joshua Reynolds for a window in the chapel. On 10 June 1803 he became a bencher of the Middle Temple, prestigiously a reader for autumn 1807, and treasurer for the year 1814.

In addition to his legal activities and flourishing practice, Caldecott was an avid book collector and editor of Shakespeare. The sale of his 'Exceedingly Curious Collection of Books, Illustrative of Early English Literature', held at Sothebys from 9 to 14 December 1833, consisted of 1499 lots and fetched a total of £1210 6*s*. 6*d*. Drawn mainly from the seventeenth and eighteenth centuries, but also quite a few from the sixteenth and some from the nineteenth, the books and manuscripts included a large number of choice items, among which one, *A Treatyse how the Hye Fader of Heuen Sendeth Dethe … in Maner of a Morall Playe*, sold for a notable £32 10*s*. Also offered were three imperfect copies of the first folio edition of Shakespeare's plays (1623) and a second folio of 1632, erroneously called 'Third'. On 11 April 1833 the Bodleian Library, Oxford, received from him a volume (now Malone 886) containing first editions of Shakespeare's *Venus and Adonis* (1594), *The Rape of Lucrece* (1594), *The Sonnets* (1609) with *A Lover's Complaint*, as well as later quartos, a 1627 *Venus and Adonis* (Malone 890), a *Lucrece* of 1616, and one of 1655 (Malone

892 and 899). Caldecott's library must have been considerable; childless, he bequeathed his music books, in print and manuscript, to his nephew Edward James, and all his other books, maps, and papers to William James.

Caldecott's literary interests were not limited to passive collecting. For one thing, his extensive manuscript notes in two editions of Milton's *Poems upon Several Occasions* and Isaac Reed's variorum edition of Shakespeare (1813)—all in the British Library—are proof enough of his intellectual engagement. For another, he must have been involved in the literary wrangles of the day, as may be adduced from his being considered, albeit without evidence, a joint author of Samuel Ireland's defence of his son's forgeries in the pamphlet *Mr. Ireland's Vindication of his Conduct* (1796). Above all, his independent, richly annotated, and controversial (in its dependence on the first folio as copytext) *'Hamlet', and 'As You Like It': a Specimen of a New Edition of Shakespeare*, which appeared in 1819, 1820, and was revised in 1832, together with his copious manuscript notes and additions in the copies in the British Library, demonstrates his assiduous devotion to serious scholarship. Only 'ill health and a growing infirmity of many years', as Caldecott says in the preface to the 1832 edition, 'which terminated in total blindness' (Caldecott, x), prevented him from further work with the abundance of material he had collected over the years. He managed, however, to produce *Sacred Songs*, a selection of hymns without music, in 1832.

Caldecott was prominent enough to appear in John Nichols's *Illustrations of the Literary History of the Eighteenth Century* in letters of 1803 to Bishop Percy enclosing the unpublished part of Thomas Warton's *History of English Poetry* and from Thomas Dromore, both defending 'honest' Warton against the attacks of 'poor mad' Joseph Ritson (Nichols, *Illustrations* 8.373). In the three-part description of the sale of Caldecott's library, Thomas Frognall Dibdin gives a portrait of the ageing Caldecott:

> His figure and manner were at once striking. Extreme shortness of vision induced him always to carry a glass, which, in the studied absence of spectacles, was placed close to his eye. His head was slightly bent on one side during the use of this glass; and he seemed to be as lively and intent upon 'men and things' before him as the youngest in the room. His critical epithets upon the old school of Shakespeare-commentators, were unsparing and vituperative; especially upon Steevens and Malone, denoting the former to be 'an ass,' and the latter 'a fool'. (*GM*, 59)

Caldecott was benevolent as well: in his will he remembered his relatives generously, not forgetting his gardener, and showing concern for the well-being of his old horses.

Caldecott died on 25 May 1833 in Dartford, Kent, his home for many years after the death of his wife, Charlotta Poole (*d.* 1790?), whom he had married on 27 October 1789. He was buried in Linton on 4 June 1833.

Marvin Spevack

Sources *GM*, 2nd ser., 1 (1834), 59–61, 194–6, 284–6 · Nichols, *Illustrations*, 8.372–4 · Burke, *Gen. GB* (1836) · private information · *DNB* · parish register (baptism), 13 April 1744, Rugby · Foster, *Alum. Oxon.* · F. L. Colvile, *The worthies of Warwickshire who lived between 1500 and 1800* [1870] · parish register (burial), 4 June 1833, Linton, Herefordshire · T. Caldecott, preface, in *'Hamlet', and 'As you like it': a specimen of a new edition of Shakespeare*, ed. T. Caldecott (1832)
Archives BL, MS editions and annotations
Wealth at death approx. £17,000 in bequests; also books, papers, maps: will, 1833

Calder, Fanny Louisa (1838–1923), promoter of education in domestic subjects, was born on 26 March 1838, at 26 Rodney Street, Liverpool, the youngest of the eleven children of James Calder and his wife, Jane Elizabeth Mitchell. Her father was a cotton merchant and the family had lived in South Carolina for many years before settling in Liverpool about 1835.

A devout Anglican, in youth Fanny followed a common pattern of women's voluntary work, Sunday school teaching, and running a Bible class for mothers. While working with the poor she formulated the philanthropic enterprise that was to become her life's work. 'In my early days of social work … I soon learnt that the too evident degraded condition of the women and girls … was not from poverty in the main, but from absolute ignorance of the essential methods of "making a home"' ('The F. L. Calder College of Domestic Science', F. L. Calder College archives). Aged thirty-six, she formed a committee of like-minded women to organize cookery teaching in Liverpool, and for the next fifty years single-mindedly promulgated the systematic teaching of domestic skills to women and girls.

The Ladies Committee formed in 1874, of which she remained honorary secretary until her death, inaugurated the Liverpool School of Cookery in the following year by running classes at St George's Hall, Liverpool, with the aim of training educated women to teach cookery around the city and beyond. Miss Calder was soon convinced that teaching adults would not herald improvements in the conditions of the poor. She persuaded local elementary board- and church-school managers to support her experimental schemes of instruction and allow the teaching of cookery to girls. The school's staff and members of the committee ran demonstration and practice classes in all types of cookery. The unrealized hope was that the income from classes attended by wealthy women would subsidize the training of teachers and the direct work with children.

In parallel Miss Calder began the task of persuading local and national education authorities to support the teaching. She worked with her Ladies Committee at the school, and with the founders of similar schools throughout England and Scotland, to promote the training of women who would provide practical programmes of instruction in the growing elementary school system. With representatives of the Yorkshire, Edinburgh, and Glasgow schools of cookery she founded the Northern Union of Training Schools of Cookery in 1876. This organization issued teaching diplomas, and worked to standardize instruction and to persuade the education department to develop the teaching. 'There was a great deal of difficulty in persuading educationalists that the duties of home life could be systematised and organised as practical science', she recalled (Calder, 318). The education code of 1882 admitted practical cookery as a grant-earning subject. After continual pressure from Miss Calder and others in the domestic subjects movement, laundry work was added to the code in 1890, and the 1880s and 1890s saw the steady growth of practical domestic training in schools.

Miss Calder was instrumental in founding the movement's first national organization, the Association of Teachers of Domestic Science in 1897. This organization furthered the work of popularizing and professionalizing domestic subjects, and by 1914 had more than 1300 members. The Liverpool school remained in the forefront, and in 1898 the duchess of York became its patron. In 1903, in recognition of her work, Miss Calder was invited to join the new Liverpool education committee. A tall and striking woman, she was nevertheless unassuming and reserved. She attended committee meetings conscientiously, but rarely spoke. Yet in her propagandizing of cookery teaching she noted, 'I visited many cities and villages, explaining possibilities to large gatherings of ladies and gentlemen interested in the welfare of the people. … In fact I missionised the subject' ('The F. L. Calder College of Domestic Science', F. L. Calder College archives). She also wrote articles and letters about her mission, promoted the distribution of cheap cookery books produced at the school, and co-authored with E. E. Mann, head cookery teacher at the school, what was probably the first laundry work teaching manual, *A Teachers' Manual of Elementary Laundry Work* (1891).

Miss Calder's efforts to develop national regulation of the training of teachers of domestic subjects met with less success, and the Liverpool school, like others, continued to be privately funded until the first decades of the twentieth century. Not surprisingly, therefore, much of Miss Calder's energies were devoted to the financial and curriculum management of the school, and she doggedly pursued benefactors to ensure the expansion of its work. Development was expensive, however, and reluctantly in 1920, unable to continue to subsidize the Liverpool school from the private purses of her committee, she requested Liverpool education authority to continue the work. In her honour the school was renamed the F. L. Calder College of Domestic Science.

While Millicent Garrett Fawcett believed that the 'new born zeal for needlework and cookery … has arisen mainly as an offshoot of the "women's rights" movement' (M. G. Fawcett, 'The future of Englishwomen: a reply', *Nineteenth Century*, 4, 1878, 354), late twentieth-century historians have disputed the significance of the domestic subjects movement. The place of domestic ideology and work in women's lives is a contentious issue. Fanny Louisa Calder's contemporaries, however, acknowledged her personal and local achievements for women's education when, in 1913, Liverpool University conferred upon her the degree of MA *honoris causa* in education. Her life has a wider significance as that of one of the many single, mid-Victorian, middle-class, philanthropically inspired women who worked in education with a zealous and often crusading commitment to raise the status of women's household work. In 1892 Florence Nightingale wrote to her, 'Good speed to your great work—Saint of the Laundry, Cooking and Health' (F. Nightingale to Fanny Calder, 21 Nov 1892, copy in F. L. Calder College archives). Fanny Calder died at her home, 49 Canning Street, Liverpool, on 6 June 1923, and was buried at Smithdown Road cemetery in Liverpool. ANNMARIE TURNBULL

Sources M. E. Scott, *The history of F. L. Calder College of Domestic Science, 1875–1965* (1967) • A. Turnbull, 'Women, education and domesticity: a study of the domestic subjects movement, 1870–1914', PhD diss., Polytechnic of the South Bank, 1983 • A. Turnbull, 'An isolated missionary: the domestic subjects teacher in England, 1870–1914', *Women's History Review*, 3 (1994), 81–100 • miscellaneous papers, Liverpool John Moores University, F. L. Calder College archives • H. Sillitoe, *A history of the teaching of domestic subjects* (1933) • F. L. Calder, 'The growth and development of domestic science', *Women's mission: a series of congress papers on the philanthropic work of women*, ed. Baroness Burdett-Coutts [A. G. Bourdett-Coutts] (1893), 317–22 • b. cert. • d. cert.

Archives Liverpool John Moores University, F. L. Calder College archives • U. Warwick Mod. RC, Association of Teachers of Domestic Subjects MSS

Likenesses three photographs, 1913, Liverpool John Moores University • W. L. Stevenson, oils, 1959, Liverpool John Moores University • photograph (as a young woman), Liverpool John Moores University

Wealth at death £11,471 1s. 0d.: probate, 20 July 1923, *CGPLA Eng. & Wales*

Calder, Sir James Charles (1869–1962), distiller, was born on 28 December 1869 in Alloa, Scotland, the younger son of James Calder, a timber merchant and brewer, and his wife, Cecilia, *née* Mackenzie, the daughter of an Edinburgh market gardener. Calder was educated at Perth Academy and St Benedict's College, Fort Augustus. In 1886 he joined his father's brewing business and in 1889 he was appointed manager of Bo'ness distillery, purchased by his father in 1873 from A. and J. Vannan. Originally a pot still (malt whisky) distillery, it was enlarged and converted (in 1876) to a patent still (grain whisky) distillery with an output of 870,000 gallons. In conjunction with Glenfoyle distillery, acquired by his father in 1880, this allowed the family's interests to straddle malt and grain whisky. Bo'ness also made yeast and Calder increased production and built up a sizeable business through Calder's Yeast Company as yeast proved an important source of revenue following the collapse of the grain distillers' cartel (the United Kingdom Distillers' Association) in 1888. Calder was made a partner in James Calder & Co. in 1890 and a director when the firm adopted limited liability status in 1892.

Calder's main interest was in blended whisky (mixtures of malt and grain whiskies) where demand was expanding rapidly. Distillers sought access to this fast growing trade while blenders sought security of supply, and in 1895 James Calder became a partner in the Leith blending firm of Alexander and MacDonald. In the boom of the 1890s Alexander and MacDonald built a pot still distillery, Stronachie distillery at Forgandenny, Perthshire. When demand for whisky declined after 1900, Alexander and MacDonald were forced to reorganize and James Calder &

Co. acquired control of Stronachie distillery. In the controversy over blending Calder appeared as a witness at the royal commission on whisky in 1908, arguing for a definition of whisky which would include both pot and patent still products, a view confirmed by the commission.

The decline in whisky drinking prompted an amalgamation movement. James Calder & Co. were wooed by the 'big three' blenders (James Buchanan & Co., John Dewar & Sons, and John Walker & Sons), who were interested in obtaining an alternative source of supply to the Distillers Company Ltd (DCL), and by DCL which saw Calders as a means of further consolidating control of yeast and spirit production. James Calder participated in merger talks with the 'big three' in 1910 and was one of the few participants to emphasize managerial problems. These convinced him that independence was better and that it made more sense 'to remain on good terms with the DCL … and aim in the future at a larger affair' (J. Calder to A. J. Cameron, 14 Sept 1910, John Dewar & Sons, original amalgamation papers, United Distillers archive). Nevertheless Calder co-operated in fixing prices and restricting output during the pre-war years.

The pace of the merger movement hastened with the anti-drink campaign during the First World War and the Immature Spirits Act of 1915 which exacerbated the shortage of mature whisky stocks. In 1919 Alexander and MacDonald combined with two other blending firms, William Williams & Son of Aberdeen and Greenlees Brothers of London, to form MacDonald, Greenlees and Williams (Distillers) Ltd with Calder as chairman. With his extensive knowledge of the trade, Calder's advice was sought by distillers who were contemplating reconstruction schemes. In 1922 he advised the owners of Balmenach distillery and became chairman of the reconstructed company. After his father's death in 1917, he chaired the family timber business and during the war held the posts of deputy timber controller (1917–19) and timber controller (1920) at the Board of Trade. For this service he was made CBE in 1920 and received a knighthood in 1921.

When DCL's plans for a post-war cartel embracing all patent distilleries proved abortive, amalgamation discussions with Calder were resumed. Calders had acquired control of a second patent still distillery, Gartloch, in 1907 and the possibility of the firm entering the DCL offered DCL control over all Scottish patent still distilling capacity except for the North British distillery whose unique, 'co-operative' constitution shielded it from take-over. Unknown to Calder, DCL and the 'big three' blenders had agreed in April 1918 that neither party would enter into negotiations with Calder & Co. without securing the other party's consent. In effect Calders' future had been decided well before August 1921 when provisional agreement was reached between DCL and Calder. Finalized eight months later, it provided for the transfer of properties, plant, and working stock to DCL in exchange for 20,000 DCL ordinary shares (some six per cent of DCL's ordinary share capital), and a seat on DCL's board. Calder proved a tough and skilful negotiator, retaining ownership of the mature whisky stocks which were the firm's most valuable asset given the post-war shortage. Calder's Yeast Company was sold to the United Yeast Company at the same time.

When Calder joined DCL the company was desperately trying to develop new activities to replace the declining spirit market. Calder's wide business interests assisted this process. While visiting his timber interests in the Black Forest, for example, Calder heard of the 'Prodor' and 'Goldschmidt' processes for hydrolysing cellulose. This led to DCL, and Calder on a personal basis, investing in the British Bergius Syndicate which tried to develop the oil-from-coal (hydrogenation of coal) process. Calder retained his seat on DCL's board following the 'big amalgamation' in 1925, when Buchanan–Dewar and Walkers were acquired by DCL, and was active in the management. In December 1925 he brought MacDonald, Greenlees and Williams into DCL. In 1926–7 he was part of a DCL delegation investigating the production of potable spirit in Australia. This was in response to Australian import duty on Scotch whisky and the delegation recommended that DCL should build a distillery at Corio Bay, Geelong. Calder's none too compelling argument was that 'if Australian whisky was going to supplant Scotch then the company may as well supply it' (Distillers Company Ltd, annual general meeting, 15 July 1927). In fact the investment proved unprofitable because Australia was severely affected by the international depression and merchants were unable to mature stocks of whisky.

Calder was a member of DCL's technical and research committee from 1925 to 1935, a period which saw the creation of a research laboratory at Great Burgh and an increased recruitment of scientists. When DCL formalized its management structure in 1935 Calder was appointed to the powerful management committee with responsibility for industrial alcohol, yeast, malt extract, methylated spirit, the works department, and the gin trade in the USA. As a senior director he represented DCL in several important negotiations including the attempt to prevent the Commercial Solvents Corporation invading the British solvents market, the initial discussions with ICI which culminated in the DCL–ICI agreement, and the abortive project with Union Carbide for oil-cracking. His most enduring contribution was probably the gin trade in the USA for it gave DCL a firm foothold in the liquor trade following the repeal of prohibition. It also brought Calder into contact with Joseph Kennedy, reformed bootlegger and head of Somerset Importers, one of DCL's most successful distributors. He acted as host to Joseph Kennedy and the young John Kennedy when they toured Scotland during Joseph Kennedy's period of office as ambassador to Britain. Calder retired from the management committee in December 1940 and from the board in July 1941.

Calder also had extensive interests in brewing and forestry. He was a director of several brewing firms including the family brewing firm, though his younger brother, John, played the more active part. Calder owned sawmills in the north of Scotland and plantations in Germany and the United States. During the Second World War he was appointed director of home timber production (1940–41).

Calder held a number of public offices, being a justice of

the peace for Kinross-shire and a deputy lieutenant of the county from 1930. He owned estates at Ledlanet, Milnathort, and Lyndford Hall, Norfolk. His leisure activities included golf, shooting, and fishing, and he was chairman of the syndicate which owned the Grimersta River in Lewis. He married Mildred Louise, daughter of Colonel R. A. Manners, the Royal Scots, in 1904. They had no children. Lady Calder died in 1936; Sir James died of cerebral thrombosis, on 22 August 1962, at Ledlanet, Milnathort, aged ninety-two, and was buried at Lyndford Hall, Norfolk. RONALD B. WEIR

Sources *DCL Gazette* (1925), 138 • R. B. Weir, *The history of the Distillers Company, 1877–1939* (1995) • R. B. Weir, 'Calder, Sir James Charles', *DSBB* • *WWW* • d. cert.

Archives United Distillers archive, Leven, Fife

Calder, James Traill (1794–1864), local historian, was born on 18 October 1794 at Olrig, near Castletown, Caithness, the son of George Calder, gardener to James Traill of Ratter, and his wife, Janet Reid. Calder lost the use of one of his limbs at the age of four. He was educated in the parish schools of Olrig and Dunnet; he was briefly a tutor and then in November 1814 entered Edinburgh University, where, despite his time being interrupted by a spell of school teaching at Canisbay he won prizes in logic and philosophy.

Calder settled in Canisbay as a schoolteacher, and also wrote occasionally for the *Inverness Courier*. His satirical poem *Macroary* caused a local sensation. In 1842 he published at Wick *Sketches from John o'Groat's in Prose and Verse*, with an interesting chapter on 'Ancient superstitions and customs in Caithness'. In 1846 he published *The Soldier's Bride* and in 1849 *St Mary's Fair and other Poems*. In the 1850s he retired from school teaching to write poetry and local history. His verses were collected as *Poems from John o'Groat's* (1856). His *Sketch of the Civil and Traditional History of Caithness from the Tenth Century* (1861) remains a standard work. Calder was a defendant in print of the Church of Scotland. He died at the house of his brother Peter, Elwick Bank, Shapinsay, Orkney on 14 January 1864. In 1900, on the instigation of John Horne, a statue to his memory was raised in Wick. H. C. G. MATTHEW

Sources J. T. Calder, 'Memoir', *Sketch of the civil and traditional history of Caithness*, 2nd edn (1887), xiv–xvii • *Orkney Herald* (19 Jan 1864) • D. Omand, ed., *The new Caithness book* (1989) • old parish register, Olrig

Calder, John (1733–1815), author, was a native of Aberdeen, where he was educated at Marischal College. At an early period he obtained the patronage of the duke of Northumberland, who employed him as private literary secretary both at Alnwick Castle and in London. Subsequently (1773–5) he was appointed deputy librarian at the library bequeathed by Dr Williams for the special use of nonconforming clergy, and he also officiated as a dissenting minister at a meeting-house near the Tower. On resigning this charge he declined to exercise for the future any part of the ministerial function. In 1772 he published a sermon on the value of charity, for the benefit of the children educated at the charity school in Gravel Lane, Southwark, London.

When a new edition of *Chambers's cyclopaedia* was proposed, Calder was engaged as editor, by a group of booksellers in 1773. In 1776 the proprietors became anxious about the length and quality of his contributions and set about replacing him. Calder appealed to Samuel Johnson, who wrote forcibly to the printer, Archibald Hamilton, on his behalf (13 February 1776). Admitting that Calder had behaved with 'an improper degree of turbulence and impatience', he urged that he be allowed to continue as his prolixity was not the 'result of inability' but of 'superfluous diligence' (Boswell, *Life*, 2.294). Even so, Calder was sacked in favour of Dr Abraham Rees.

In the same year, 1776, Calder drew up a plan of a periodical work called *The Selector* (November 1776–January 1777), contributing a number of articles to the early issues. He also proposed to establish a *Foreign Intelligencer*. While at Alnwick he made the acquaintance of Thomas Percy, afterwards bishop of Dromore, whom he assisted in preparing a new edition of *The Tatler*, *The Spectator*, and *The Guardian*, with notes and illustrations. When Calder moved to London, the materials collected by Percy passed into his hands, and were afterwards used in various editions of these works by Calder's friend John Nichols. His annotations appeared in *The Tatler* (6 vols., 1786), *The Guardian* (2 vols., 1789), and *The Spectator* (8 vols., 1789). In 1787 he translated from the French Pierre François le Courayer's *A Declaration of his Last Sentiments on the Different Doctrines of Religion*, to which he prefixed a memoir of le Courayer. He also contributed to Andrew Kippis's new edition of *Biographia Britannica* (1778–93) an elaborate article on the Courten family. About 1789 he moved from Furnival's Inn to Croydon, Surrey, where he formed an intimacy with Dr Apthorp, contributing materials on his life for inclusion in Nichols's *Literary Anecdotes*.

Calder was twice married. On 24 January 1789 he married his second wife, Martha Huddleston, daughter of John Green of Croydon. During his lifetime he formed an extensive library, especially of classical and numismatic works, and also possessed a large cabinet of Greek and Roman coins. His last years were spent at Lisson Grove, Marylebone, Middlesex, where he died on 10 June 1815. His remains were interred by his widow on 17 June in her family vault at Sanderstead in Surrey.

T. F. HENDERSON, *rev.* MICHAEL HARRIS

Sources Nichols, *Illustrations*, 4.799–848 • Nichols, *Lit. anecdotes*, vol. 6 • *GM*, 1st ser., 85/1 (1815), 564 • Boswell, *Life* • *The letters of Samuel Johnson*, ed. B. Redford, 5 vols. (1992–4)

Archives BL • Yale U., Beinecke L., letters and papers relating to dispute with *Chambers's cyclopaedia*; notebook | Bodl. Oxf., letters to John Bower Nichols

Calder, Peter Ritchie, Baron Ritchie-Calder (1906–1982), author and journalist, was born on 1 July 1906 at 6 Newmonthill, Forfar, Forfarshire, the youngest in the family of one daughter and three sons of David Lindsay Calder, linen worker (later works manager), and his wife, Georgina, daughter of John Ritchie, master mason. He was educated at Forfar Academy, which he left at the age of sixteen.

Peter Ritchie Calder, Baron Ritchie-Calder (1906–1982), by Walter Bird, 1966

Calder began his career in 1922 as a police court reporter with the *Dundee Courier*. He then worked with the D. C. Thomson Press before joining the *Daily News* (1926–30), the *Daily Chronicle* (1930), and the *Daily Herald* (1930–41). During these years his range of interests broadened considerably. Politically he was, and always remained, a dedicated socialist and member of the Labour Party, and the social problems and political strife of the inter-war years provided many subjects for perceptive record and comment. In 1927 he married Mabel Jane Forbes, daughter of David McKail, a physician, of Glasgow; they had three sons and two daughters.

A chance assignment to cover a science story opened up a completely new field for Calder. He realized that application of new scientific knowledge could powerfully augment the conventional approach to social problems. A timely stimulus to this new interest was provided by acquaintanceship—which grew into close and lasting friendship—with John Boyd Orr, who was making a name for himself in the field of animal and human nutrition. Seeing malnutrition as a global problem, Calder devoted much effort to publicizing Boyd Orr's ideas and activities. This he did not only through his own newspaper connections but also through documentary films, then establishing themselves as a powerful means of influencing public opinion. Boyd Orr's book *Food, Health and Income* was published in 1936 and Calder played an important part in producing a film version entitled *Enough to Eat?*

The outbreak of the Second World War inevitably diverted much of Calder's activity into other fields. During the blitz his vivid reports helped to make the world aware that temporarily the front line of the war was in London. In 1941 he was appointed to the political warfare executive of the Foreign Office, a service for which he was appointed CBE in 1945. One of his first tasks during this time was to assist, with Boyd Orr, in the production of a film, *World of Plenty*, to show the world how Britain was using food sent from the USA.

The immediate post-war years were very favourable to the resumption of Calder's career, initially as science editor of the *News Chronicle* (1945–56) and as a member of the editorial staff of the *New Statesman*. The new Labour government was committed to a radical programme of social reform in which a key element was to be the harnessing of science to national needs. On a wider front, the newly created agencies of the United Nations sought to achieve similar ends internationally. In recording and promoting all these activities he found himself involved to an extent that severely taxed even his seemingly boundless enthusiasm and energy. He clearly understood that progress could be made only if public opinion was informed and favourable.

Despite the euphoric view of science created by great wartime achievements such as atomic energy, radar, and penicillin, the post-war media paid little more than lip-service to science. To help to alleviate this, Calder took a leading role in establishing the Association of British Science Writers, of which he was the first chairman (1949–55), and in which he always took great pride. In 1960 he was awarded the Kalinga award for science writing.

After the war Calder undertook many assignments for United Nations agencies, often on the initiative of Boyd Orr, who became the first director-general of the Food and Agriculture Organization and invited him to attend the famine conference in Washington (1946) as a special adviser. He went on arduous missions to study the utilization of human resources in north Africa, Congo (1960), and south-east Asia (1962).

Calder's exceptional knowledge of international affairs led the University of Edinburgh to appoint him to the Montague Burton professorship of international relations (1961–7). This was a remarkable tribute to a man who had had no formal higher education. His fluent and easy manner, and varied reminiscences, appealed to the students. The appointment opened many academic doors and he was awarded honorary doctorates by the Open University (1975) and York University in Ontario, Canada (1976). He was senior fellow at the Center for the Study of Democratic Institutions, Santa Barbara, California, USA (1972–5).

Calder was passionately devoted to the cause of peace, particularly in the post-war years when there was so much uncertainty about where atomic weapons would ultimately take us. He was president of the British Peace Council and a leader of the Campaign for Nuclear Disarmament. He wrote a number of books on scientific, medical, and environmental topics for a general audience, including histories of the World Health Organization (1958) and the Weizmann Institute (1959). In 1966 he was created a life peer as Baron Ritchie-Calder of Balmashannar and three years later was made chairman of the Metrication Board, retiring in 1972. He died on 31 January 1982 at the Western General Hospital, Edinburgh.

TREVOR I. WILLIAMS, *rev.*

Sources *The Times* (2 Feb 1982) • *The Times* (6 Feb 1982) • *The Times* (12 Feb 1982) • *WWW* • personal knowledge (1990)
Archives FILM BFI NFTVA, performance footage | SOUND BL NSA, performance recording
Likenesses W. Bird, photograph, 1966, NPG [*see illus.*]

Calder, Robert (1659/60–1723), Scottish Episcopal clergyman and writer, was a native of Moray and a near relative of Sir James Calder of Muirton (*d.* 1711). After matriculating at King's College, Aberdeen, in 1674, aged fourteen, he graduated MA in 1678. In 1684 he was ordained by Bishop Paterson of Edinburgh, and later became minister of the parish of Nenthorn, Berwickshire. On 3 September 1689 he was deprived by the privy council for neither reading their 13 April proclamation of William and Mary as sovereigns, nor praying for the new monarchs.

After briefly returning to Moray, Calder settled in Edinburgh as a nonjuring minister and propagandist. At an unknown date he married a teacher, Grace Toward. Following a search of the papers of his correspondent, Dr Alexander Monro, in March 1693 Calder was questioned by the Scottish privy council, which deduced that he was a 'great traffiquer' (register of acta, 4 March 1693) in composing and publishing pamphlets against the established church and the government. He admitted writing, in 1691, a manifesto against oppressions and free quarterings, and for the restoration of episcopacy. The government sought his life for treason, but as it could not be proved that he had divulged the manifesto to others he was released in January 1694.

In August 1694 Calder assisted at the ordination of James Greenshields in Edinburgh. Subsequently he preached on the necessity of liturgical worship in several places, moving on when banished by the authorities. He claimed that the privy council twice summoned him from Aberdeen. In 1697 he was at Fochabers, and at Elgin from about 1704 he acted with other clergy despite repeated measures by the civil and church authorities. On 17 April 1706 the privy council ordered the suppression of the meeting-houses there and at Keith, where he also ministered.

Although known for his forthright anti-presbyterian pamphlets, Calder is not now credited with *Scotch Presbyterian Eloquence* (1693). After writing *Schola sepulchri* (1701), a work on mortality, he mainly published polemics in which he repeatedly expounded the superiority of the episcopalians' claims to scriptural and historical authority for their government and worship, for example in *The Lawfulness and Expediency of Set Forms of Prayer* (1705). During his abusive controversy with John Anderson, minister of Dumbarton in 1710–13, he advertised a paper proving that his adversary was 'one of the grossest Lyers that ever put Pen to Paper' (Calder, *Nail*, 4). The presbyterians vilified 'Curate Calder' as a drunken hack writer, but William Carstares showed him charity.

In 1711–12 Calder promoted the adoption in the highlands of John Richardson's Irish translation of the Book of Common Prayer, trained Gaelic speakers for deacon's orders, and may himself have used the prayer book with one of them in his meeting-house in Todrig's Wynd, Edinburgh. That year he was instrumental in the reprinting of the Scottish liturgy of 1637 at the expense of the earl of Winton, in whose chapel at Tranent he also officiated between about 1712 and 1716. He did not qualify himself for the toleration granted in 1712, maintaining a stiff Jacobite position in 1713 when some nonjurors agreed to pray for Queen Anne. In 1716 he was among the nonjuring clergy barred from ministering for having officiated illegally in Edinburgh. He continued to promote the liturgy, and in 1723 resisted the bishops' prohibition of certain liturgical usages. He died at Edinburgh on 18 or 28 May 1723, and was buried in Greyfriars churchyard.

TRISTRAM CLARKE

Sources *Fasti Scot.*, new edn, vol. 2 • J. B. Craven, *History of the episcopal church in the diocese of Moray* (1889) • register of acta of privy council, 1693–1706, NA Scot., PC 1/48 and 53 • J. Greenshields, letter to Arthur Charlett, 1711–12, Bodl. Oxf., MS Ballard 36 • R. Calder, *Schola sepulchri: the school of the grave* (1701) • R. Calder, *The nail struck to the head* (1712) • letters and papers concerning Calder, NA Scot., CH 12/12 • P. Hopkins, *Glencoe and the end of the highland war* (1986) • *Diary of Alexander Jaffray*, ed. J. Barclay, 3rd edn (1856) • W. Christie, notes on Calder, *c.*1899–1923, University of Dundee, Brechin Diocesan Library MS Br. MS. 3. DC/95–6 • W. R. McLeod and V. B. McLeod, *Anglo-Scottish tracts, 1701–1714: a descriptive checklist* (1979) • records of high court of justiciary, 1716, NA Scot., JC 3/7, JC 7/8, JC 26/D/91 • P. J. Anderson, ed., *Roll of alumni in arts of the University and King's College of Aberdeen, 1596–1860* (1900) • [J. Anderson], *Curat Calder whipt* (1712)
Archives NL Scot., poems attributed to subject, 1703, 1710, MS 17799; Wodrow Quarto XXVIII • U. Edin., a satire on Sir James Steuart of Goodtrees, 1702, MS La. III. 611/9

Calder, Sir Robert, baronet (1744/5–1818), naval officer, was the second son of Sir James Calder, third baronet, and Alice, daughter of Admiral Robert Hughes. His father, a descendant of the Calders of Muirtown, Moray, had settled in Kent; in 1761 Sir James was appointed gentleman-usher of the privy chamber to the queen by the prime minister, Lord Bute.

In 1759 Calder entered the navy on the *Chesterfield*, with Captain Herbert Sawyer, whom he followed to the *Active*, and thus participated in the capture of the Spanish register-ship *Hermione* on 21 May 1762, probably the richest prize on record, even a midshipman's share amounting to £1800. His passing certificate, dated 2 June 1762, described Calder as appearing to be twenty years old, though he was then only seventeen. On 31 August of that year he was made lieutenant. In 1779 he was promoted commander and on 27 August 1780 he was advanced to the rank of post captain. In May 1779 he had married Amelia, daughter of John Michell of Bayfield, Norfolk; the couple had no children.

During the next three years Calder successively commanded the *Buffalo*, *Diana*, and *Thalia*, all on the home station. The *Thalia* was paid off at the peace, and he had no further employment until the outbreak of the French Revolutionary Wars, when he was appointed to the *Theseus* (74 guns) for service in the channel. In 1796, when Sir John Jervis (later earl of St Vincent) was appointed commander-in-chief in the Mediterranean, Calder was appointed captain of the fleet, and served in that capacity at the battle of Cape St Vincent, after which he carried home the admiral's dispatches, and was knighted on 3 March 1797. Calder was held in high regard by St Vincent.

On 22 August 1798 Calder was made a baronet, and on 14 February 1799 he was advanced to the rank of rear-admiral. In 1800 he hoisted his flag on the *Prince of Wales* (98 guns), in the Channel Fleet, then commanded by St Vincent; and in February 1801 he was detached in pursuit of a French squadron, which slipped down the coast into the Mediterranean, while Calder, with seven ships of the line and three frigates, followed an imaginary chase to the West Indies. It was only at Jamaica that he learned his mistake, and he did not rejoin the fleet until June. He was advanced to the rank of vice-admiral, on 23 April 1804, and shortly afterwards hoisted his flag, again in the *Prince of Wales*, in which he joined the fleet off Brest, under Admiral Sir William Cornwallis. In the following February he was detached off Ferrol, with five sail of the line, to keep watch over a Franco-Spanish squadron of ten ships ready for sea, and two more fitting. These, however, would not be tempted out, although Calder, notwithstanding occasional reinforcements, had never more than nine ships of the line under his command. It was not until 15 July 1805 that he was joined by the squadron from off Rochefort, bringing his numbers up to fifteen ships, with which he was ordered to stretch out to the westward of Cape Finisterre, in order to intercept the combined fleet of France and Spain which was making for Ferrol and reinforcements on its return from the West Indies. It was understood that this consisted of sixteen ships, but when Calder fell in with it on 22 July he found it had twenty.

Notwithstanding these disadvantages, compounded by poor weather and the fact that the British fleet was to leeward, Calder succeeded in bringing the enemies' fleet to action, and in cutting off and capturing two of the Spanish ships. This was an important victory, and Calder was rightly commended for it. The next day was clear; but though the combined fleet had still the advantage of the wind, the allied commander Villeneuve conceived that his instructions forbade him to fight except under compulsion, while Calder was anxious to secure his prizes, and to cover the *Windsor Castle*, which had sustained severe damage. Above all he recognized the danger of his position if the fifteen ships in Ferrol and the five in Rochefort should come out and join the fleet with Villeneuve. By holding his ground Calder denied the enemy the chance to concentrate. On 24 July the hostile fleets lost sight of each other. Villeneuve headed south and on 26 July the combined fleet put into Vigo, whence Villeneuve slipped round to Ferrol, which Calder had temporarily left open. When on 9 August Calder, with a squadron again reduced to nine ships, arrived off Ferrol, he found the French and Spanish in vastly superior force, and on the point of putting to sea. His orders authorized him to retire when in the presence of such unequal numbers, which he accordingly did, joining Cornwallis off Brest to deny the French any opportunity to combine their fleets in the western approaches.

As Calder had expected, Villeneuve, with twenty-nine ships of the line, did put to sea on the evening of 9 August with the intention of carrying out his instructions and making the English Channel. On 13 August, his fleet having finally assembled, the French commander, realizing his chance had gone, sailed for Cadiz, where he arrived on 21 August. His retreat has been generally and erroneously attributed to the result of the action of 22 July, with which, in point of fact, it had very little connection. More pertinently the constant attention of the British ensured that he was watched at every turn, and his messages captured. By this time Villeneuve was a broken man.

On 30 August Calder, with a large part of the Brest fleet, joined Vice-Admiral Cuthbert Collingwood off Cadiz, and while cruising off that port he learned that his conduct on 23 and 24 July had been severely commented on in England. He immediately wrote to apply for a court martial. The Admiralty had, independently, given Nelson orders to send Calder home for trial. Nelson arrived off Cadiz on 28 September, and sent Calder back in his own ship. Nelson wrote:

> I may be thought wrong as an officer … in not insisting on Sir Robert Calder's quitting the *Prince of Wales* for the *Dreadnought*, and for parting with a gun ship, but I trust that I shall be considered to have done right as a man and to a brother officer in affliction; my heart could not stand it, and so the thing must rest. (*Dispatches and Letters*, 7.56)

Calder accordingly sailed a few days before the battle of Trafalgar. The court did not assemble until 23 December, and on 26 December found that Calder in his conduct on 23 and 24 July had been guilty of an error in judgement, and sentenced him to be severely reprimanded. This was the end of his seagoing career; he never served afloat again, though he rose by seniority to the rank of admiral on 31 July 1810. Between 1810 and 1812 he served as commander-in-chief at Plymouth. He was made KCB in April 1815.

Calder died on 31 August 1818 at his home, The Holt, near Bishop's Waltham, Hampshire, and was survived by his wife. Calder was a fine officer of solid merit; it was his misfortune to be judged by a new standard, set at Trafalgar by the peerless Nelson, and not that which had applied throughout his career. His title became extinct at his death. J. K. LAUGHTON, *rev.* ANDREW LAMBERT

Sources J. S. Corbett, *The campaign of Trafalgar* (1910) • *Letters and papers of Charles, Lord Barham*, ed. J. K. Laughton, 1, Navy RS, 32 (1907), 38–9 • *Letters of … the earl of St Vincent, whilst the first lord of the admiralty, 1801–1804*, ed. D. B. Smith, 2 vols., Navy RS, 55, 61 (1922–7) • *GM*, 1st ser., 88/2 (1818), 380 • *GM*, 1st ser., 89/1 (1819), 382 • *Minutes of the proceedings at a court martial assembled … for the trial of Sir Robert Calder* (1806) • W. James, *The naval history of Great Britain, from the declaration of war by France in 1793, to the accession of George IV*, [5th edn], 6 vols. (1859–60), vol. 3, pp. 356–79 • *The dispatches and letters of Vice-Admiral Lord Viscount Nelson*, ed. N. H. Nicolas, 7 vols. (1844–6)

Archives BL, orders and memoranda rel. to Mediterranean, Add. MS 40741 | BL, letters to Lord Nelson, Add. MSS 34904–34907 · Princeton University, letters, incl. to William Budge · Yale U., letters to Thomas Coutts · St Vincent MS

Likenesses L. F. Abbott, oils, *c*.1790, National Gallery of Art, Washington, DC · L. F. Abbott, oils, *c*.1798, NMM · H. R. Cook, stipple, pubd 1807, NPG · Worthington and Parker, group portrait, line engraving (*Commemoration of the 14th February 1797*), BM, NPG

Wealth at death under £30,000: *GM*, 89/1, 382

Calderbank, James (1770–1821), Benedictine monk, was born on 16 April 1770 in Liverpool; his father's details are not known, but his mother's maiden name was probably Brewer. He entered the English monastery of St Laurence's at Dieulouard in Lorraine in 1787, where he received some ecclesiastical education and where he made his profession in 1792 and was ordained priest on 21 December 1793. The monks of St Laurence's, dispossessed by the French Revolution and finding a permanent home at Ampleforth, Yorkshire, only in 1804, sought temporary refuge at Trier in Germany, at Acton Burnell in Shropshire, and elsewhere. Calderbank remained with the community until, after a short period at Woolton in Lancashire with his uncle and fellow monk Dom Bede Brewer (1742–1822), president-general of the English Benedictines from 1799 to 1822, he began his pastoral ministry. He was at Bath (1800–05, and again during 1809–17, the last three years as incumbent), at Weston Underwood, Buckinghamshire (1805–6), at the Portuguese Chapel, London (1806–8), and at Seel Street, Liverpool (1808–9).

Calderbank was secretary of the general chapter of the English Benedictine congregation from 1802 to 1814, and secretary to his uncle, the president-general, from 1802 to 1810. He was honoured with the title of cathedral prior of Peterborough in 1810. In 1814 he published *Observations in a series of letters in answer to certain questions relating to various subjects of religion, proposed by a clergyman of the established church to a Catholic convert*, in which he showed himself a gentle controversialist hoping 'that no divisions among men, even on the subject of religion itself, can go to justify even a momentary departure, either from the tender duties of charity, or from the rules of politeness and good breeding' (J. Calderbank, *Observations*, 1814, vi). Calderbank spent his last years in his native county, first at Crosby and then at Woolton, where he died on 9 April 1821. He was buried at St Peter's, Seel Street, Liverpool, and a memorial tablet was erected to his honour in the Bath chapel (which later became a masonic hall in Pierrepoint Street), a building acquired for the Bath Catholics while he was assistant priest in 1809. Athanasius Allanson (1804–1876), the English Benedictine annalist, rather a stern judge, says that Calderbank was 'noted for his good sense and correct judgment' (Allanson, fol. 131), much needed qualities in a time of crisis among the English Benedictines, who had lost most of their continental safe houses by 1815. DOMINIC AIDAN BELLENGER

Sources A. Allanson, 'Biography of the English Benedictines', 1850, Downside Abbey [2 vols.], vol. 2 · T. B. Snow, *Obit book of the English Benedictines from 1600 to 1912*, rev. H. N. Birt (privately printed, Edinburgh, 1913), 132 · *DNB* · J. A. Williams, ed., *Post-Reformation Catholicism in Bath*, 1, Catholic RS, 65 (1975), 83n.

Likenesses oils, Ampleforth Abbey, Yorkshire

Wealth at death monk; great benefactor of Ampleforth: Allanson, *Biography*

Calderbank, Leonard (1809–1864), Roman Catholic priest, nephew of James *Calderbank, and son of Richard and Jane Calderbank, was born on 3 June 1809 at Standish, near Wigan, in Lancashire. He was educated first at a school in his native village, and afterwards became a student at Ampleforth College in Yorkshire. In December 1829 he went from Ampleforth to Prior Park College, near Bath. A few years later Calderbank went to complete his theological studies at the English College at Rome, where, on 11 November 1832, he was ordained to the priesthood.

On his return to England in 1833 Calderbank was immediately appointed to missions in the western district, working successively at Trelawney, Tawstock, Weobley, Poole, and Cannington. In April 1839 he was appointed chaplain to the Convent of the Immaculate Conception, in Sion House, at Spetisbury, near Blandford, in Dorset. On 9 November 1849 he was recalled to Prior Park by Bishop Hendren, then vicar apostolic of the western district. For nearly a year he held at Prior Park the double position of vice-president and professor of theology at St Paul's College. On 9 October 1850 he was again sent on mission, this time being put in charge of the Catholic congregation at St Peter's, Gloucester. Not long afterwards he was installed as canon by the bishop of the newly established diocese of Clifton. As missionary rector at Gloucester he worked zealously in the erection of a new church and presbytery. The church was formally opened in March 1860. Calderbank, who died suddenly of heart disease on 24 June 1864 at Gloucester, may be justly regarded as the founding father of one of the more important Catholic missions in the new diocese.

CHARLES KENT, *rev.* J. A. HARDING

Sources *Gloucester Journal* (25 June 1864) · *Gloucester Journal* (2 July 1864) · G. Oliver, *Collections illustrating the history of the Catholic religion in the counties of Cornwall, Devon, Dorset, Somerset, Wilts, and Gloucester* (1857), 258 · register of clergy (diocese of Clifton), Clifton Roman Catholic diocese, Bristol, archives · J. N. Langston, 'The Catholic mission in Gloucester and its resident priests', bound typescript, City of Gloucester Library

Archives Clifton Roman Catholic diocese, Bristol, archives

Wealth at death under £450: probate, 21 Dec 1864, *CGPLA Eng. & Wales*

Calderon, George Leslie (1868–1915), playwright, was born in St John's Wood, London, on 2 December 1868, the fifth son of the painter Philip Hermogenes *Calderon, RA (1833–1898) and his wife, Clara Marianne, daughter of James Payne Storey. He was educated at Rugby School and at Trinity College, Oxford, where he gained a second in classics in 1891. He was called to the bar in 1894, but turned to literature and journalism for support. Calderon spent the years 1895–7 at St Petersburg, and he returned with a profound knowledge of Russian and a lasting bent towards Slavonic studies. In November 1900 he married Katharine, widow of his college friend Archibald Ripley, and daughter of John Hamilton, of Brown Hall, co. Donegal. The couple lived at Hampstead, and had no children.

From 1900 to 1903 Calderon held the post of specialist in Slavonic literature on the library staff of the British Museum. During this period he wrote two stories in a vein of ironic extravaganza, *Downy V. Green* (1902) and *Dwala* (1904). In 1906 he spent several months in the South Seas, writing a collection of impressions called *Tahiti by Tihoti*, eventually published in 1921.

Calderon was best known as a dramatist, and his first play, *The Fountain*, was produced by the Stage Society in 1909; it was followed by *The Little Stone House* (1911), *Revolt* (1912), and a few shorter pieces. Two volumes of his collected plays were published posthumously in 1922 by Grant Richards. Among these plays, in strong contrast with the rest, is a tragedy in blank verse, *Cromwell: Mall o' Monks*.

Calderon's gift as a dramatist inhered in a quick eye for modern character, and a remarkable command of vivid and expressive dialogue. Calderon's plays were carefully designed for the conditions of the stage, and it was perhaps an accident that none of them had a popular success. Nevertheless, *The Times* wrote of his death as 'the heaviest blow which struck the English drama during the war'.

Calderon's work was always to some extent hampered by his great versatility. He was primarily a man of letters; but he might equally have been a scholar, a publicist, an adventurer. He was an exceptional linguist, translating Chekhov's *The Cherry Orchard* and *The Seagull* into English for publication in 1912. He also took an active and enterprising part in various public affairs, and was especially known as the secretary and passionate campaigner for The Men's League for Opposing Women's Suffrage, whose arguments he promoted in lecture tours and in his book *Woman in Relation to the State* (1908).

On the outbreak of war in 1914 Calderon was determined, in spite of his age, to reach the fighting line. He went to France as an interpreter, was wounded in the first battle of Ypres, and in May 1915 was sent, with a commission in the Oxfordshire and Buckinghamshire light infantry, to the Dardanelles, where he was attached to the King's Own Scottish Borderers. He was reported wounded and missing in the action of 4 June 1915, and was afterwards presumed killed on that date.

PERCY LUBBOCK, *rev.* KATHERINE MULLIN

Sources P. Lubbock, *George Calderon: a sketch from memory* (1921) • *Memorials of Rugbeians who fell in the Great War*, Rugby School, 2 (privately printed, Rugby, 1916) • J. Foster, *Oxford men, 1880–1892: with a record of their schools, honours, and degrees* (1893) • *WWW*, *1897–1915* • *Location register of twentieth-century English literary manuscripts and letters*, BL, 1 (1988)

Archives UCL, Sturge Moore MSS

Likenesses F. Hollyer, photograph, repro. in Lubbock, *George Calderon*, frontispiece

Calderon, Philip Hermogenes (1833–1898), historical genre painter, was born on 3 May 1833 in Poitiers, France. His mother, Margueritte Chapelle, was French and his father, the Revd Juan Calderón, was Spanish, from the area of La Mancha, and was descended from the famous playwright Pedro Calderón. Juan Calderón trained first for the priesthood, but on becoming a protestant he left for France; in 1845 he moved to London, where he was appointed minister to the Spanish Reform church and professor of Spanish literature at King's College. Philip Calderon, who became a naturalized British subject in 1873, was first educated by his father before studying with a civil engineer. In 1850 he enrolled in the recently founded art school of James Matthews Leigh in Newman Street, London; there he met Stacy Marks, who was to become a lifelong friend. In 1851–2 he was in Paris at the atelier of François-Édouard Picot, who emphasized drawing and provided him with a foundation in draughtsmanship that was to stay with him all his life. On returning to London, Calderon continued his studies at Leigh's school, while developing his sense of colour by participating in students' days at the National Gallery, working from paintings by Veronese and Rubens. He exhibited his first work at the Royal Academy, *By the Waters of Babylon* (Tate collection) in 1853.

Calderon's father died in 1854, leaving his widow with little money; even though she remarried two years later, Calderon continued to support her financially for the rest of his life. Over the next few years he painted mainly portraits, few of which are now identifiable. He continued to produce portraits throughout his career, especially of women and children, for example *The Ambush: Portraits of the Wife and Children of J. H. S. Cotton, Esq.* (1879) and *Mrs Henry Fellows* (1884). Having exhibited *Broken Vows* (Tate collection) at the Royal Academy in 1857, he showed there almost every year thereafter until his death. This painting, showing a young woman betrayed, was his first public success and was engraved by William Henry Simmons. Calderon's reputation grew quickly with such paintings as *The Gaoler's Daughter* and *Flora Macdonald's Farewell to Charles Edward* (exh. RA, 1858) and later *La demande en mariage* and *Liberating Prisoners on the Young Heir's Birthday*, both exhibited in 1861; for this last work he was awarded the silver medal of the Society of Arts.

It was at this time that Calderon became a central figure in the St John's Wood clique, an association of young artists, including Marks, many of whom had studied at Leigh's school, who met every Saturday to hold informal sketching classes and enjoy each other's company in games; Calderon, who was nicknamed the Fiend, specialized in overly dramatic singing. Most of this group were very successful in these years, becoming members of the Royal Academy. But if they had any shared interests, beyond such sociability, it was in a form of historical painting, which the critic Tom Taylor described as representing 'the home life of past times'. Among these were works such as Calderon's *Lord: thy Will be Done* (Yale U. CBA), exhibited at the Royal Academy in 1855, which showed a widow grieving for her husband who had been killed in the Crimean War, the more dramatic *The British Embassy in Paris on the Night of the Massacre of St Bartholomew* (exh. RA, 1863), and, in a more peaceful key, *Drink to me Only with thine Eyes*, shown at the Fraser Gallery in 1863. On 9 August 1860 Calderon married Clara Marianne, the daughter of James Payne Storey and the sister of G. A. Storey, another member of the group; they had two daughters and six sons, the third of whom, William Frank Calderon (1865–1943), became a well-known painter specializing in subjects of animals, and the fifth, George Leslie *Calderon (1868–1915), a playwright.

In the years immediately after his marriage, Calderon achieved considerable financial and critical success. In 1864 he was elected an associate of the Royal Academy and in 1867 a full academician. In that same year he exhibited *Her most High, Noble, and Puissant Grace* (Leeds City Art Gallery) at the Universal Exhibition in Paris, for which he won a gold medal, the only one given to an English artist. The painting was bought by J. G. Morris, an important collector of contemporary English paintings, for £1000. He had a number of loyal collectors, among them Baron Albert Grant, Charles Matthews, and George Holt of Liverpool. A group of his works was given in 1886 to the Kunsthalle in Hamburg by G. C. Schwabe, a noted collector of English pictures, including *In the Cloisters at Arles*, *Sighing his Soul into his Lady's Face*, *La gloire de Dijon*, and portraits of Mr and Mrs Schwabe. In summer 1867 Calderon rented Hever Castle, Kent, where he was joined by other members of the St John's Wood clique, who used many of the interiors of the castle for their historical paintings, especially those on subjects from Tudor and Stuart history. Calderon was very sociable, and among his large circle of friends were members of the Pre-Raphaelite circle, G. F. Watts, who did a portrait of him, and many literary figures, notably George Du Maurier, Anthony Trollope, and Charles Dickens. In 1873 Calderon received a medal in Vienna, and a few years later he was also made a knight of the Légion d'honneur. In 1882 he travelled to Venice with his friend G. A. Storey. But in the mid-1880s the St John's Wood clique began to break up, in part on account of the deaths of two members, Fred Walker in 1875 and D. W. Wynfield in 1887, and in part from the fact that many of the artists had moved from that part of London, making social contacts more difficult. His income also began to drop, forcing him to leave Weston Lodge, the grand mansion that he owned in St John's Wood, for a smaller house in the country, near Steadham in Kent. In 1887 he was appointed keeper of the Royal Academy, which gave him a new place of residence but much less time for his own work, since he took his new responsibilities as a teacher very seriously.

Calderon's last important easel painting was *The Reconciliation of St Elizabeth of Hungary* (Tate collection), exhibited in 1891, a subject taken from the poem of Charles Kingsley entitled 'The Saint's Tragedy', published in 1872. This, in its depiction of the saint, in her abjection, naked and kneeling before the altar, caused great offence in Roman Catholic circles. Another notable work of his later years was a group of decorative subjects, painted for Sir John Aird, a rich builder, at his house at 14 Hyde Park Terrace. But Calderon began to suffer more from ill health, and on 30 April 1898, after a protracted illness, he died at home at Burlington House, Piccadilly, survived by his wife. He was buried four days later at Kensal Green cemetery. A number of Calderon's works are in the Tate collection, the Walker Art Gallery, Liverpool, and Salford Museum and Art Gallery. DAVID CAST

Sources W. W. Fenn, *Some modern artists and their work*, ed. W. Meynell (1883), 235–9 · G. A. Storey, 'Philip Hermogenes Calderon', *Magazine of Art*, 22 (1897–8), 446–52 · Graves, *RA exhibitors*, 1 (1905), 375–6 · B. Hillier, 'The St John's Wood clique', *Apollo*, 79 (1964), 490–95 · S. Casteras, 'The unsettled hearth: P. H. Calderon's "Lord: thy will be done" and the problematics of women in Victorian interiors', *Reframing the Pre-Raphaelites*, ed. E. Harding (1996), 149–72 · m. cert.

Archives priv. coll., studio notebook

Likenesses D. W. Wynfield, photographs, *c.*1862–1864, NPG · G. F. Watts, oils, 1871, Watts Gallery, Compton, Surrey · G. Reid, oils, 1881, Aberdeen Art Gallery · H. J. Brooks, group portrait, oils (*Private view of the Old Masters Exhibition*), NPG · G. Grenville Marton, group portrait, watercolour (*Conversazione at the Royal Academy*), NPG · Lock & Whitfield, woodburytype, NPG; repro. in T. Cooper, *Men of mark: a gallery of contemporary portraits* (1882) · R. W. Robinson, photograph, NPG; repro. in *Members and associates of the Royal Academy of Arts, 1891* (1891) · J. & C. Watkins, cartes-de-visite, NPG · H. T. Wells, group portrait, oils (*Friends at Yewden*), Hamburger Kunsthalle, Hamburg

Wealth at death £6168 7*s.* 1*d.*: probate, 25 May 1898, *CGPLA Eng. & Wales*

Calderón de la Barca, Frances Erskine Inglis [Fanny] (1804–1882), author, was born in Edinburgh on 23 December 1804, the fifth of the ten children of William Inglis, a writer to the signet, of Queen Street and Middleton Hall, and his wife, Jane, the daughter of James Stern of Kilbogie, a distiller. Her father was prominent in Edinburgh society, but his speculations bankrupted him in 1828. He took refuge in Normandy, with his family, and died at Le Havre in 1830. His daughter Frances, whose thorough education had included sojourns abroad, first took to writing in these straitened circumstances, and produced the novels *Gertrude: a Tale of the Sixteenth Century* (2 vols., 1830) and *The Affianced One* (3 vols., 1832). After her father's death the family moved to Boston, Massachusetts, and the widow opened a school for young ladies. On 24 September 1838 Fanny, as Frances was known, married Angel Calderón de la Barca (1790–1861), since 1835 Spanish minister to the United States. Though the bearer of a famous name, her husband was not rich, and depended on his career as a diplomat and politician of the *moderado* liberal tendency. He was born in Buenos Aires. It is possible that the couple met through their friendship with the Boston historian and Hispanist William Hickling Prescott. The marriage was childless but clearly affectionate.

In 1839 Calderón de la Barca was named first Spanish minister to independent Mexico. Fanny's journal in Mexico, published as a series of letters dated 27 October 1839 to 27 February 1842, appeared at the end of that year as *Life in Mexico, during a Residence of Two Years in that Country*, the work by which she is principally remembered and which remains the best-known foreigner's description of early republican Mexico. Published with the support of Prescott, who enlisted the help of Charles Dickens for the English edition, it was in general well received by Anglo-Saxon readers, though one reviewer doubted that it was genuine. It did not please many Mexicans; they with justice likened the author to Frances Trollope, whose *Domestic Manners of the Americans* had appeared in 1832.

Life in Mexico is a somewhat relentlessly picturesque account of Mexican scenes, society, and politics, which may explain that one reviewer's reservations about its authenticity; Fanny Calderón's strong visual sense gives a record that is the literary equivalent of that left by the contemporary Romantic artists who visited Mexico, such as Carl Nebel and Johann Moritz Rugendas. None the less it contains penetrating sketches of many of the principal figures of the time, Santa Anna, Bustamante, Victoria, Alamán, and many others, of the society of Mexico City, particularly its religious institutions and observances and the situation of women, and records a number of excursions to the provinces. Both Fanny Calderón and her husband were assiduous providers of documentation and information to Prescott; her descriptions of Mexican scenery served him in writing his *Conquest of Mexico*, which appeared in 1843.

Prefaced by Prescott, *Life in Mexico* was given the form of letters, presumably written to him, but, as is established in the 1966 edition by Howard T. Fisher and Marion Hall Fisher, it was in reality based extensively on the author's journal, of which two out of the original three manuscript volumes survive (priv. coll.), containing many expurgated passages. The complete text is not only more critical of many aspects of Mexican life—filth, insects, corruption, ignorance, bombast, 'horrid Mexican fruit'—but is also more penetrating, understanding, and affectionate. The restored parts show a capacity for reflection not so apparent in the other editions, which merely reprint the text of 1842.

From Mexico the Calderóns returned to Europe via Cuba and Boston. Calderón, an amiable and effective diplomat, was once again named envoy to Washington in 1844, an appointment both welcomed. In 1853 he became foreign minister in the brief and disastrous administration of the Conde de San Luis, which in July 1854 was overthrown by Espartero and O'Donnell. This brought to an end a decade of *moderado* rule amid scenes of violence in the capital. Calderón had to leave Spain in disguise, and Fanny followed him to Paris. In 1856 she published both her translation of D. Bartoli's *History of the Life and Institute of St Ignatius Loyola*—she had become a Roman Catholic in 1847—and also anonymously *The Attaché in Madrid, or, Sketches of the Court of Isabella II*, her version of the *pronunciamiento* of 1854. Though it does not rival her Mexican work, it is lively and level-headed, despite being a courtier's book.

The Calderóns returned to Spain in 1856. On the death of her husband in 1861, Fanny retired to a convent, but was promptly appointed governess to the Infanta Isabella. She was made a *marquesa* in her own right by the restored Alfonso XII in 1876, and died in the royal palace in Madrid on 6 February 1882. MALCOLM DEAS

Sources *Life in Mexico: the letters of Fanny Calderón de la Barca*, ed. H. T. Fisher and M. H. Fisher (1966) • *The correspondence of William Hickling Prescott, 1833–1847*, ed. R. Wolcott (1925) • *Prescott: unpublished letters to Gayangos in the library of the Hispanic Society of America*, ed. C. L. Penney (1927) • F. Calderón de la Barca, *La vida en Mexico*, ed. F. Teixidor, 2 vols. (1959)

Archives priv. coll. | Hispanic Society of America Library, New York, Gayangos MSS • Mass. Hist. Soc., Prescott MSS

Likenesses photograph (after oil painting), repro. in Fisher and Fisher, eds., *Life in Mexico*

Calderwood, David (*c.*1575–1650), Church of Scotland minister and historian, was the second son of William Calderwood (*d. c.*1605) of Dalkeith, near Edinburgh. He was educated first at the grammar school and then at the University of Edinburgh (under the regency of Charles Ferme, later minister of Fraserburgh), graduating on 12 August 1593. He was registered as an expectant minister in November 1597 by the presbytery of Edinburgh, where he attended the weekly exercise regularly between May 1598 and April 1601.

Early career In December 1604 Calderwood was appointed minister of Crailing, near Jedburgh, Roxburghshire. By his appointment Calderwood became the parish minister of William Cranston (Lord Cranston from 1609, and a member of the privy council from 1611) and his wife, Sarah, whom Calderwood later remembered affectionately as 'a mother, in effect' (*Scots peerage*, 2.593; Calderwood, 7.275).

From the outset of his career as a minister Calderwood was resolutely opposed to the attempts of James VI to reintroduce episcopacy into the Church of Scotland. He voted against the imposition of a constant moderator on the presbytery of Jedburgh in 1606, and courted further controversy when he and two other ministers, George Johnston of Ancrum and John Boyle of Eckford, resisted an episcopal visitation by James Law, bishop of Orkney, in 1608. The trio openly protested against the jurisdiction of the bishop, penning a declinator to that effect, for which offence they were deprived of the right to attend church courts, and confined within the limits of their respective parishes.

The intransigence of the crown, together with legislation passed by the Glasgow assembly of 1610, served only to harden Calderwood's attitude towards royal policy. In particular, he objected that—by the 'Act of Glasgow'—all power had been removed from the presbytery, leaving 'nothing but a weeklie meeting of brethren for exercise in doctrine' (Wodrow MS 76/2, fol. 25*v*). The minister was also highly critical of legislation regarding the altered constitution of the synod, and urged ministers to boycott that court, since 'none hath jurisdiction [there] but onlie the bishop' (ibid.). Despite his continued opposition the interdict on the minister's movements was lifted in March 1613. Nevertheless Calderwood refused thereafter to attend either presbytery or synod while the courts remained subject to episcopal jurisdiction.

Under such circumstances a clash with the king's new bishops became inevitable. In June 1617 Calderwood co-wrote a 'protestatioun' against the king's intention to assume full powers, 'with the advice of bishops and archbishops', to 'make ecclesiasticall lawes' (Wodrow MS 76/1, fol. 1*v*). By July he had been hauled before the court of high commission at St Andrews. Yet the cause of Calderwood's ultimate downfall was not his connection with the offending petition (a charge which the minister was able to refute), but his principled stand against episcopal domination of presbyteries and synods. Indeed, it was a fact that the minister—more than three years after his initial pardon—remained a 'refractar' who had 'servit no ordour, [and had] neither repaired to presbyteries nor synods, and [was] nowayes conforme' (ibid., fol. 2*r*). Seizing the opportunity to turn the minister's presbyterian principles to his own advantage the king ordered Calderwood to attend the courts of the kirk. On Calderwood's obstinate refusal he was deprived of his ministry and banished from the kingdom.

Having failed to comply with the order to depart 'furth of his Majesties dominions' (an act which the minister blamed on the weather), Calderwood was pronounced a 'rebel' (Wodrow MS 42, fols. 163*r*–164*r*). Thereafter he spent many months 'lurking in a secrete chamber appointed for him at the house of Sarah Cranston' (Wells, 111) in Jedburgh, or in hiding at Edinburgh. During this period the minister produced a rare autobiographical tract which detailed the 'Trew relatioun of my tryall before the High Commissioun, and my troubles following thereupon' (Wodrow MS 76/1). It was written out of fear that the official record might misrepresent his words and conduct—both during and after the trial—to the presbyterian faithful. Calderwood's experiences at the hands of king and bishops during his trial also prompted him to write his additional 'Remarks on the high commission' in 1618, thus offering the earliest known critique of the judicial power and processes of the latter court in its Scottish context. In 1619 he wrote the notorious pamphlet *Perth Assemblie*, noting elsewhere that—as a result of the conclusions of that meeting—'the kirk [would] be brought to consent to English discipline' (Maidment, 602–3). Amid the subsequent furore the minister fled the country.

Exile Calderwood's enforced sojourn in the Netherlands from 1619 to 1625 heralded his most prolific period as an author. The sheer volume of production during this period is made all the more remarkable because he often wrote two versions of a selected text, the one a shorter polemic—in English—for popular consumption and the other a longer and deductive Latin text for the scholar. For example, Calderwood's *Perth Assemblie* of 1619 was the forerunner of his masterly *Parasynagma Perthense et juramentum ecclesiae Scoticanae* in 1620, while his *Altar of Damascus, or, The patern of the English heirarchie … obtruded upon the Kirke of Scotland* (1621) was merely the prelude to his magisterial *Altare Damascenum* (1623).

It was not that the authorities were unaware of the vast potential of the minister's pen, since his patron, Lord Cranston, informed the king bluntly in 1617 that if Calderwood were exiled 'he will doe more hurt by his writings than all he is worth' (Wells, 114). To make matters worse Calderwood had departed Scotland 'with his purse well filled by the wives of Edinburgh' (ibid.). The money funded a flood of propaganda which included the *Speech of the Kirk of Scotland to her Beloved Children* in 1620. By 1622 the crown was sufficiently concerned to encourage rumours of the minister's death, and promoted a disingenuous tract by Patrick Scot, *Calderwood's Recantation*. This 'unworthie pamphlet', published in London in the latter year, purported to be the minister's dying testament. Somewhat begrudgingly Calderwood found time to write an extensive 'Answere … to the tripartite discourse of Scot', refuting the claims contained therein and reassuring the faithful of Edinburgh that he was 'yit alive to bear witnes against such knaverie' (Wodrow MS 76/3, fol. 37*r*). As if to prove the point Calderwood renewed his assault upon religious innovation with three further works, including an *Exhortation of the Particular Kirks in Scotland to their Sister Kirk in Edinburgh*, all of which were on the streets of the Scottish capital in 1624.

In all likelihood Calderwood lived in Amsterdam while in the Netherlands. The city was home to the exiled English puritan John Paget, and the two men struck up a lifelong friendship during this period. It was rumoured that the minister 'had bothe the keepinge and sellinge of [his own] bookes', and that he lived at the 'printer's house' in Amsterdam. Here, he was 'kept close amongst those of his owen profession [presbyterians]', so that none but the most trusted sympathizers could gain access to his person (Maidment, 387). He returned to his native country soon after the death of James VI in 1625.

Historian Contrary to popular belief it is unlikely that Calderwood collected the documentation for his history of the reformed kirk after his return there. Rather, it is probable that much of the material was already to hand in 1614, at which date he launched his first attack on episcopalian historiography. As 'Confutation of the dikaiologie' of William Cowper, bishop of Galloway, while conceding that 'ther wes Bishops' in the 'first age' of the reformed church, it argued that they had been subject to the general assembly and not the crown. In any case (the minister continued), the general assembly 'abbrogat the office' in 1581, and thereafter presbyterianism was 'practisid, suorne and subscryved' in Scotland until its overthrow in 1610 (Wodrow MS 76/2). Thus the 'Confutation' constitutes the earliest known exposition of Calderwood's interpretation of the history of the kirk from 1560 to 1610.

Following his return to Scotland about 1625 Calderwood moved to Jedburgh, where he collated and extended his impressive collection of histories, diaries, scrolls, acts of parliament, and other official documents. In its entirety, the record 'comprehendeth an history [of the kirk] from the beginning of King James the Fifth to the death of King James the Sixth' (BL, Add. MSS 4734–4736). The collection's 3136 pages (about two thirds of which have since been lost) were intended only as a personal work of reference, which was to be used in his continuing literary battle against crown policy regarding the kirk. As a consequence the irreplaceable contents were jealously guarded by the author, who went to the length of compiling a second work 'contracted and digested in better order' as insurance against accident or discovery by the authorities. This second digest, of 2013 pages, constituted a 'Historie of the Kirk of Scotland, beginning at Mr Patrik Hammiltoun, and ending with the Death of James Sixt' (BL, Add. MSS 4737–4739), and was probably complete by 1630.

From this latter work Calderwood produced a third and final digest of 838 pages, eventually published as *The True*

History of the Church of Scotland. It was this version which the 'author desireth onlie to be communicat to the use and benefite of others' (Calderwood, vi–vii). The conclusion that it was complete 'in or soon after the year 1631' (ibid., x) is, however, open to question. If the minister had completed the work during this period then it was a well-kept secret. The diarist Robert Baillie hoped that the 'Lord [would] strengthen and encourage [Calderwood] to write the Historie of our Church' in 1646: and in 1648 the general assembly spent an entire 'session … on encouraging Mr David Calderwood to perfyte his Church story' (*Letters and Journals of Robert Baillie*, 2.374, 384; 3.60). This last comment, coupled with the fact that the assembly paid Calderwood £800 Scots to assist his efforts in the latter year, appears to suggest that the work remained under preparation. In any event, the *True History* was not published until 1678, almost three decades after the minister's death.

Covenanter In 1636 David Calderwood published *A Re-Examination of the Five Articles*, amid persistent rumour that Charles I was about to enforce the infamous prayer book upon Scotland. The work was probably printed in Amsterdam at the instigation of John Paget, who was instrumental in obtaining printing facilities for Scottish presbyterian manuscripts in the 1630s, including those of Samuel Rutherford. In concert with other preparations for widespread demonstrations against crown policy, the publication of the *Re-Examination* was a deliberate attempt to raise presbyterian tempers as the country moved towards revolution.

Following the riot at Edinburgh on 23 July 1637 Calderwood worked closely with the architect of the covenanting revolution, Archibald Johnston of Wariston. The two men co-operated in refuting the claims of those who opposed the cause, and were the dual authors of *Ane Answere to Mr J. Forbes of Corse his Peaceable Warning [Against the Covenant]* in 1638. The partnership continued throughout the Glasgow assembly of the same year, at which episcopacy was abjured. As Baillie noted, the 'Moderator [Johnston of Wariston] caused read some papers … of Mr D. Calderwood's penning, who lived all the time of the Assembly privily beside the Moderators chamber, and furthered what he could by his studies all our proceedings' (*Letters and Journals of Robert Baillie*, 1.138).

Later life and character Powerful as a controversialist, Calderwood does not seem either to have been attractive as a speaker or to have had a particularly winning manner. In 1641 he obtained the charge of Pencaitland in Haddingtonshire, at which time Baillie recorded that his 'utterance [was] unpleasant' and his carriage arrogant (Thomson, xxxi). Nevertheless the diarist's assessment that Calderwood was not well suited to the pastoral ministry may reflect personal tensions between the two men. In the 1640s Baillie was keen to reach an accommodation with English puritanism, an attitude that clashed with Calderwood's essential nationalism in matters of public worship. As a member of the committee on the directory of public worship in 1643 (for example), Calderwood fought in vain for the retention of the singing of the doxology at the end of psalms. When defeated on the issue the minister—then almost seventy years of age—gained consolation from the fact that he would soon sing it again in heaven.

Little is known of Calderwood's activities during the late 1640s (although he continued to attend meetings of the general assembly until 1649), and it is probable, as noted above, that he spent his last years perfecting his *True History* of the kirk. Whatever the case, by 23 October 1650 Calderwood had retired to Jedburgh, where he lay 'seik in bodie but whole and perfyte in memorie' ('Testament', in Calderwood, 8.xvii). He died there six days later, on 29 October. He had never married. His estate was valued (26 December 1651) at £1816 Scots, and his extensive library, which filled at least fourteen kists, was bequeathed to his 'nephewes and nyce' (ibid., xviii). It was probably Johnston of Wariston who ensured that 'ane coffer' of especially valuable 'wryts and work' of the minister's authorship was deposited in Edinburgh Castle for safekeeping (ibid.; *Diary*, 1650–54, 165). The special relationship enjoyed by the two men was not ended by Calderwood's death, as Wariston used the store of information to further debate on matters of religious and political controversy throughout the 1650s.

On 29 January 1765 William Calderwood of Polton presented the manuscripts of the minister's history to the British Museum. Other collections of papers were given to Robert Wodrow, and (following Wodrow's death) were purchased by the Faculty of Advocates at Edinburgh in 1792. The value of Calderwood's collected works to students of the Scottish kirk is encapsulated in Baillie's enduring portrait of Calderwood as 'that living magazine of [Scotland's] whole Ecclesiastick History' (Mullan, 22).

VAUGHAN T. WELLS

Sources NL Scot., Wodrow MSS 42, 76 · histories, BL, Add. MSS 4734–4739 · D. Calderwood, *The history of the Kirk of Scotland*, ed. T. Thomson and D. Laing, 8 vols., Wodrow Society, 7 (1842–9) · *The letters and journals of Robert Baillie*, ed. D. Laing, 3 vols. (1841–2) · *Diary of Sir Archibald Johnston of Wariston*, 1, ed. G. M. Paul, Scottish History Society, 61 (1911) · *Diary of Sir Archibald Johnston of Wariston*, 2, ed. D. H. Fleming, Scottish History Society, 2nd ser., 18 (1919) · *Diary of Sir Archibald Johnston of Wariston*, 3, ed. J. D. Ogilvie, Scottish History Society, 3rd ser., 34 (1940) · *CSP dom.*, 1611–18 · J. Maidment, ed., *Letters and state papers during the reign of King James the Sixth*, Abbotsford Club, 13 (1838) · A. MacDonald, 'David Calderwood: the not so hidden years, 1590–1604', *SHR*, 74 (1995), 1, 197 · V. T. Wells, 'The origins of covenanting thought and resistance, *c*.1580–1638', PhD diss., University of Stirling, 1997 · *Scots peerage*, vol. 8 · T. Thomson, 'Mr David Calderwood', in D. Calderwood, *History of the Kirk of Scotland*, ed. T. Thomson and D. Laing, 8 vols., Wodrow Society, 5/8 (1849), xv–xix · J. Howie, 'David Calderwood', in J. Howie, *The Scots worthies*, ed. W. H. Carlaw, [new edn] (1870) · G. Donaldson and R. S. Morpeth, *Who's who in Scottish history*, pbk edn (1996) · D. G. Mullan, *Scottish puritanism, 1590–1638* (2000) · *Fasti Scot.*, new edn, vols. 2, 6 · *DNB*

Archives BL, histories, Add. MSS 4734–4739 | NL Scot., Wodrow MSS

Wealth at death £1816 Scots: testament, Calderwood, *History*, vol. 8

Calderwood, Henry (1808?–1865), missionary and government official, was born in Peebles, the son of Henry Calderwood (1772/3?–1842), and his wife, Elizabeth *née* Mudie (1773/4?–1835), members of the Secession church. He was educated at Edinburgh University and entered the Divinity Hall of the United Secession church in Glasgow in 1828; after his first ministry in Orkney, he was ordained minister of a United Secession congregation in Kendal, Westmorland, on 28 May 1834. He was married on 10 April 1838 at Windermere to Mary Elizabeth Taylor (*c*.1812–1892); they were to have five sons and a daughter. Following his appointment to the South African mission of the London Missionary Society, the couple arrived in Cape Town on 17 September 1838 with another missionary, Richard Birt.

Calderwood initially supplied for Dr John Philip in Cape Town but in March 1839 he travelled east to establish a new station on the Kat River at Blinkwater, on the colonial side of the frontier. Very soon he was proficient enough in Xhosa to preach in it, as well as in Dutch, the language by which he could reach the Khoi-Khoi (Hottentots). In 1845 he moved to Birklands (later Healdtown), in Kaffraria, where he established a new station from which he was compelled to withdraw on the outbreak of war in 1846, together with a group of converts known as Calderwood's Kaffirs. The destruction of his mission premises left him discouraged to the point that he would have left South Africa altogether had he not been dissuaded by Sir Peregrine Maitland, who in 1846 appointed him commissioner for the Gaika (Ngqika) tribes. Calderwood then resigned his missionary connection, but he remained an active minister, a member of the Kaffrarian Presbytery of the Free Church of Scotland, a keen collaborator with the missionaries at Lovedale, and the founder of a church at Alice.

In 1848 Calderwood was appointed civil commissioner and resident magistrate in the new division of Victoria East. He was charged with settling Fingoes (Mfengu), who had assisted the military during the recent war, along the border from Alice to the sea. His scheme for establishing Fingo locations was imaginative and involved the allocation of individual plots in return for annual quit-rents, the use of native headmen and European superintendents, and the encouragement of cultivation and other improvements through prizes. Sir Harry Smith, one of a succession of governors with whom Calderwood had good relations, welcomed his scheme. In 1853 Calderwood prepared a report for Sir George Cathcart on Fingo education, and in 1854 he was appointed chairman of the Native Improvement Board. At the time of the 'Fingo panic' in 1854, when there were fears that the Mfengu would join forces with other Xhosa tribes in rebellion, Calderwood was asked by Lieutenant-Governor C. H. Darling to enquire into the state of the Mfengu. In January 1855 he submitted his valuable *Final Report on Fingo Locations*, which much impressed Colonial Office officials.

Unlike many of his missionary contemporaries Calderwood saw his ministry as being directed as much towards the white population of the Cape as the indigenous tribes. His commitment to the development of the native population was sincere, but he considered that their civilization was best advanced by a continued influx of European migrants. He had considerable dealings with the Xhosa chief Maqoma, though he could not be said to have influenced him. Calderwood's health was poor in later years; there is reference to it in his *Caffres and Caffre Missions* (1858), written while on furlough in Britain. He appears to have continued in his official duties until a few months before his death. After a series of paralytic strokes he died on 31 May 1865 at his residence on Settlers Hill, Grahamstown, where he was buried on 3 June.

LIONEL ALEXANDER RITCHIE

Sources H. Calderwood, *Caffres and Caffre missions* (1858) · *The Journal* [Grahamstown] (2 June 1865) · *The Journal* [Grahamstown] (12 June 1865) · *The Missionary Magazine and Chronicle* (1838–46) · *DSAB*, 1.148–9 · *Register of LMS missionaries* · A. E. Du Toit, 'The Cape frontier: a study of native policy with special reference to the years 1847–1866', *Archives year book for South African history*, 1 (1954) · R. H. W. Shepherd, *Lovedale, South Africa* (1940) · E. H. Brookes, *The history of native policy in South Africa* (1927) · W. Govan, *Memorials of the missionary career of … J. Laing* (1875), 354–6 · W. Mackelvie, *Annals and statistics of the United Presbyterian church*, ed. W. Blair and D. Young (1873), 482 · *DSCHT* · *IGI*
Archives SOAS, Council for World Mission archives

Calderwood, Henry (1830–1897), philosopher, was born on 10 May 1830 at Turnbull's House in the High Street in Peebles, where his forefathers had lived for generations. He was the son of William Calderwood and his wife, Elizabeth Mitchell, and had three brothers and a sister. He was baptized in the East United Presbyterian Church (later the Leckie Memorial Church), Peebles. In his boyhood his parents moved to Edinburgh, where his father became a corn merchant, and he received his early education at the Royal High School, Edinburgh. He studied at the University of Edinburgh (1847–50?) with a view to the ministry. He concentrated chiefly on philosophy, and he came second in Sir William Hamilton's prize list in 1847. In the logic class in 1850 his name appears next to that of John Veitch. He entered the Divinity Hall of the United Presbyterian church in 1851, and was licensed to preach by the presbytery of Edinburgh in January 1856.

In 1854, while still a student, Calderwood published *The Philosophy of the Infinite*. This work is an early marker of Calderwood's tendency in philosophy, which was to defend the Scottish doctrine of common sense against the agnosticism which he considered to have been implied by the work of Sir William Hamilton and later against the threat of a Darwinian-inspired agnosticism. In opposition to Hamilton, who taught that though we must believe in God we can have no knowledge of his nature, Calderwood maintained that a partial and ever-extending intuitive knowledge of God is possible for man, and that faith in him implies knowledge. It was generally acknowledged that in the essence of the contention at least the pupil had scored against his professor, and the learning, courage, and logical acumen of the young author at once made him a respected philosopher.

On 16 September 1856 Calderwood was ordained minister of Greyfriars Church, Glasgow, in succession to David

King. By his clear incisive preaching and his efficient pastoral work Calderwood led the church successfully, and when he left it after twelve years' ministry it was compact, well organized, and prosperous. Calderwood threw himself heartily into many political and religious movements intended to benefit his fellow citizens, especially the lower classes of Glasgow. There was scarcely an organization of a philanthropic nature in the city that did not receive his support, and when he later left Glasgow for Edinburgh he received a public testimonial from the citizens in token of their appreciation of his services. He married Anne Hulton Leadbetter, daughter of Thomas Leadbetter of Alderbank, Bothwell, in March 1857.

In 1861 Calderwood was elected examiner in philosophy to the University of Glasgow. That university conferred upon him the degree of LLD in 1865. In 1866, pending the appointment of a successor to William Fleming and the introduction of Professor Edward Caird, afterwards master of Balliol College, Oxford, he conducted the moral philosophy classes in Glasgow.

In 1868 Calderwood was appointed to the chair of moral philosophy in the University of Edinburgh. His systematic teaching was on the lines of the Scottish philosophy and against all Hegelian and agnostic tendencies. In 1872 he published his *Handbook of Moral Philosophy*, in which the intuitionalism of his earlier work is applied to the sphere of ethics. He discusses all current ethical positions and attacks naturalism and hedonism. The absolute law and aim of conduct is stated to be not happiness or pleasure but the full use of our talents to the fulfilment of their natural purposes. The book was popular in Britain and America. It went through numerous editions and through it Calderwood came during the 1870s to be regarded as a major representative of intuitionalism. The newer evolutionary science then rising into prominence engaged his attention, and he tried to discover and explain the bearings of physiological science on man's mental and moral nature. He made a close study of the physiology of the brain and nervous system. In three works—*The Relations of Mind and Brain* (1879), *The Relations of Science and Religion* (1881), and *Evolution and Man's Place in Nature* (1893)—Calderwood tried to prove that the primary function of the brain is to serve not as an organ of thought, but as an organ of sensory-motor activity. He believed it to be demonstrated by physiology that the direct dependence of mind on brain was confined to the sensory-motor functions, the dependence of the higher forms of mental activity being on the other hand only indirect. He endeavoured to establish the thesis that man's intellectual and spiritual life is not the product of natural evolution, but necessitates the assumption of a transcendent intelligence as its creative cause.

Calderwood was an able teacher. His students gained an extremely high proportion of the Ferguson scholarships in philosophy, open to all the Scottish universities. But, besides his work as a professor, he took an active interest in political, philanthropic, educational, and religious matters in Edinburgh. He was an active supporter of women's suffrage and of the provision of higher education for women. He gave lectures on moral philosophy for the Edinburgh Association for the University Education of Women and served on its executive committee. Between 1869 and 1874 he was extensively involved in the battle to obtain women's admission as medical students. In 1892, when Scottish universities were empowered to accept women, he successfully urged that Edinburgh University should make use of this power.

In 1869 Calderwood was elected a fellow of the Royal Society of Edinburgh. He was the first chairman of the Edinburgh school board, elected in 1873, and on his retirement from the post in 1877 he received an address from the public school teachers of the city. He was repeatedly asked to stand as a candidate for parliament for the southern division of Edinburgh, and was at the time of his death chairman of the North and East of Scotland Liberal Unionist association, having relinquished Gladstonian Liberalism. In 1870 he was elected a ruling elder in Morningside United Presbyterian Church, Edinburgh, and until his death was seldom absent from the annual meetings of synod. He sat on the mission board of his church for three terms of four years, and in 1880 he was elected moderator of synod. Issues such as temperance reform, Presbyterian union, and foreign missions received his advocacy. For some years he was editor of the *United Presbyterian Magazine*. He received the freedom of Peebles, his native town, in 1877. In 1897 he was presented with a handsome testimonial by the residents and visitors at Carr Bridge, Inverness-shire, for conducting religious services during several holiday seasons. Calderwood died at his home, Craigrowan, 7 Napier Road, Merchiston, Edinburgh, on 19 November 1897 and was buried in the Morningside United Presbyterian Church. His son William Leadbetter Calderwood (1865–1950), became inspector of salmon fisheries for Scotland. T. B. JOHNSTONE, *rev.* C. A. CREFFIELD

Sources W. C. Calderwood and D. Woodside, *The life of Henry Calderwood* (1900) • R. Metz, *A hundred years of British philosophy*, ed. J. H. Muirhead, trans. J. W. Harvey (1938) [Ger. orig., *Die philophischen Strömungen der Gegenwart in Grossbritannien* (1935)] • personal knowledge (1901) • A. L. Drummond and J. Bulloch, *The church in late Victorian Scotland* (1978)

Archives U. Edin. L., lecture notes

Likenesses G. Reid, portrait, 1897 • W. Hole, etching, NPG; repro. in W. Hole, *Quasi cursores* (1884) • photograph, repro. in Calderwood and Woodside, *Life of Henry Calderwood*

Wealth at death £3757 18*s*. 5*d*.: confirmation, 13 Jan 1898, *CCI*

Calderwood [*née* Steuart], **Margaret** (1715–1774), diarist and traveller, was the eldest daughter of Sir James Steuart of Goodtrees and Coltness, baronet (1681–1727), solicitor-general for Scotland, whose father was Sir James *Stewart of Goodtrees (1635–1713), and his wife, Anne (*d.* 1736), daughter of Sir Hew *Dalrymple, Lord North Berwick. Her sister Agnes was the mother of the lord advocate Henry Erskine and the lord chancellor Thomas Erskine.

On 30 March 1735 Margaret married Thomas Calderwood (*d.* 1773/4) of Polton near Edinburgh, the son of Sir William *Calderwood, Lord Polton. He was an easy-going man who later entrusted the care of his estate to his wife.

Margaret Calderwood (1715–1774), by Allan Ramsay, 1734–5

He was a good linguist and fond of books, presenting the manuscript original of David Calderwood's *History of the Church of Scotland* to the British Museum. Mrs Calderwood was encouraged to travel by the prolonged exile of her brother Sir James Steuart. Steuart had fled to the continent following his involvement with the 1745 Jacobite rising. He seems not to have taken arms but was in Edinburgh when Prince Charles Edward captured it. His wife, Lady Frances Wemyss, was dangerously ill with smallpox, and he was surrounded by Jacobite friends and relatives. Consequently his name appeared on a list of traitors. By 1756 he was living in the Southern Netherlands. Mrs Calderwood decided to visit him as part of a tour that would benefit her sons William and James; travelling with them were her husband and their servants Peggy Rainy and John Rattray. Her journals and letters started on her departure from Polton on 3 June 1756 and continued until her return, probably in February 1757. The family travelled by road to London and crossed from Harwich to Helvoetsluys. They then progressed to Rotterdam, Delft, The Hague, Haarlem, and Amsterdam. After moving through Antwerp to Liège, Mrs Calderwood was reunited with her brother. After a visit to Spa, the party went on to Brussels. In Brussels in the winter of 1756, clearly knowing her correspondence would be circulated among her friends, she compiled her letters and journals into 'volumes' which she sent by messengers to Scotland. They concern everyday life rather than gossip or conversations. Dialogue enlivened descriptions of occurrences on the journey. Alexander Fergusson, editor of the 1884 edition of the letters and journals, wrote that the only significant material he expunged was Mrs Calderwood's bitter comments on Roman Catholic ritual. He excused this on the basis that she was only one generation removed from the horrors of the 'killing time' in which her grandfather had suffered.

During her journey, Mrs Calderwood recorded many general features of eighteenth-century life such as dress, agriculture, cheesemaking, land tenure, conveyances by road and water, currency, housing, water supply, bleaching, fuel, coal mining, religion, and education. The diaries also contain many specific incidents, including an encounter with a highwayman, a religious dispute, a meeting with a Hungarian princess at a ball, discussion of a nun's profession, and Mr Calderwood's loss of the guidebook. Sir James Steuart was pardoned in 1771 and returned with his wife to their estate of Coltness, Lanarkshire, in 1773.

Margaret Calderwood died in 1774, shortly after her husband. The Polton estate passed to their son Lieutenant-Colonel William Calderwood (*d.* 1787) and then to their daughter Anne, mother of Sir Philip Charles Henderson Calderwood *Durham. Another daughter, Margaret, died unmarried. STUART W. McDONALD

Sources A. Fergusson, *Letters and journals of Mrs Calderwood of Polton: from England, Holland and the Low Countries in 1756* (1884) · *DNB* · J. Dennistoun, ed., *The Coltness collections, MDCVIII–MDCCCXL*, Maitland Club, [58] (1842) · m. reg. Scot.
Archives U. Edin., Steuart of Coltness MSS, corresp. and diaries
Likenesses A. Ramsay, portrait, 1734–5, Arniston House, Gorebridge, Scotland [*see illus.*] · Chambers, portrait; formerly at Polton, 1884

Calderwood, Sir William, Lord Polton (*bap.* 1660?, *d.* 1733), judge, was baptized at Dalkeith, Edinburghshire, probably on 23 December 1660, the sixth of nine sons of Alexander Calderwood, baillie of Dalkeith, and his wife, Janet Moffet. He was admitted advocate at the Scottish bar in July 1687. He was made deputy sheriff of the county of Edinburgh in 1688, and was knighted in 1706. Calderwood served as clerk of the Faculty of Advocates in 1690, and was its treasurer in 1694–95. He succeeded Sir William Anstruther as an ordinary lord of session in 1711, and was at the same time nominated a lord of justiciary, taking his title from Polton, an estate in Edinburghshire which he had recently purchased. On 13 March 1701 he had married Susanna, daughter of John Scott of Malleny. His second marriage, in July 1706, to Margaret Leirmont, produced two sons and two daughters; a third marriage, to Alice (or Alison) Walker, widow of Walter Scott, which took place on 20 April 1721, was childless. Describing her father-in-law, Margaret, wife of Thomas Calderwood, wrote that he:

> lived to a great age, had been all his life employed in the law; was long Sheriff of the county, and related to many of the families, and connected in friendship with most of the people of the greatest fortune … an upright judicious dispassionate man, and never interfered in politics, which in his time had run very high. (Dennistoun, 394)

He died on 7 August 1733.

T. F. HENDERSON, *rev.* ANITA MCCONNELL

Sources G. Brunton and D. Haig, *An historical account of the senators of the college of justice, from its institution in MDXXXII* (1832), 492 • J. Dennistoun, ed., *The Coltness collections, MDCVIII–MDCCCXL*, Maitland Club, [58] (1842) • F. J. Grant, ed., *The Faculty of Advocates in Scotland, 1532–1943*, Scottish RS, 145 (1944) • *IGI*
Likenesses attrib. J. B. Medina, oils, Arniston House, Midlothian

Caldicott, Alfred James (1842–1897), organist and composer, was the eldest son of William Caldicott, a hop merchant of Worcester and a musical amateur, and was born at Worcester on 26 November 1842. In 1851 he became a choirboy in the cathedral, and he later rose to be the leading treble. At the age of fourteen his voice broke and he was articled to William Done, the cathedral organist. He remained at Worcester, acting as assistant to Done, until 1863, when he entered the Leipzig conservatory to complete his studies.

In 1865 Caldicott returned to Worcester and became organist at St Stephen's and honorary organist to the corporation. He spent twelve years in routine work, teaching, playing the organ, and conducting the Worcester Musical Society, which he had established. In 1878 he graduated MusB at Cambridge. In the same year he made his first notable success as a composer, when his humorous glee 'Humpty Dumpty' won a prize from the Manchester Glee Society. This success was followed by another, 'Jack and Jill', in the same year. In 1879 his serious glee 'Winter Days' won the prize offered by the Huddersfield Glee and Madrigal Union. He was then commissioned to compose an oratorio for the Worcester festival. The resulting *The Widow of Nain*, for which he wrote both words and music, was conducted by Caldicott in Worcester Cathedral on 12 September 1881.

In 1882 Caldicott left Worcester for Torquay, but a few months later settled in London. He then began to compose operettas for Thomas German Reed, the first being *Treasure Trove*, performed in 1883. Reed produced twelve others, including *A Moss Rose Rent* (1883), *Old Knockles* (1884), *In Cupid's Court* (1885), *A United Pair* (1886), *The Bosun's Mate* (1888), and *Tally Ho!* (1890). After a brief appointment as conductor at the Albert Palace, Battersea Park, in 1885, Caldicott conducted at the Prince of Wales's Theatre, where two further operettas, *All Abroad* and *John Smith*, commissioned by Carl Rosa, were performed in 1889–90. He went to the United States in 1890 as conductor of Agnes Huntingdon's light opera company. After his return to England in 1891 he was appointed a professor at the Royal College of Music and the Guildhall School of Music, but he resigned these posts the following year on being appointed principal of the London College of Music. He also became conductor at the Comedy Theatre in 1893.

The most notable of Caldicott's several operettas were *A Fishy Case* (1885) and *The Girton Girl and the Milkmaid* (1893). He also wrote nearly a hundred songs and numerous cantatas, of which the songs 'Unless' (1883) and 'Two Spoons' and the cantatas *The Queen of May* (1884) and *A Rhine Legend* (1882) were particularly popular among his contemporaries. He married the niece of Sir Richard Mayne, the Metropolitan Police commissioner, herself a soprano, and they had three sons and a daughter. Overworked and suffering from mental exhaustion, Caldicott died at the Barnwood House Institution, near Gloucester, on 24 October 1897. HENRY DAVEY, *rev.* JAMES J. NOTT

Sources *MT*, 38 (1897), 842 • *Musical Herald* (Nov 1897) • Brown & Stratton, *Brit. mus.* • Boase, *Mod. Eng. biog.* • A. T. C. Pratt, ed., *People of the period: being a collection of the biographies of upwards of six thousand living celebrities*, 2 vols. (1897) • J. D. Champlin, ed., *Cyclopedia of music and musicians*, 3 vols. (1888–90) • private information (1901)
Likenesses portrait, repro. in *Musical Herald* (Nov 1897)
Wealth at death £580: probate, 21 Dec 1897, *CGPLA Eng. & Wales*

Caldwall, James (*b.* 1739, *d.* in or after 1819?), engraver, born in London, was a pupil of John Keyse Sherwin. Like many of his contemporaries, he used a combined technique of engraving and etching. Samuel Redgrave and Michael Bryan considered him a good draughtsman and a brilliant engraver. He was known mainly for his portraits, such as that of Sarah Siddons (and her son) in *Isabella*, after William Hamilton (1783). He also engraved genre and fancy pictures, and a military subject, *The engagement between the Quebec frigate, Captain George Farmer, and the surveillante frigate, Monsieur Couëdic*, after George Carter in 1782. He probably contributed plates to G. W. Anderson's edition of James Cook's *Voyages* (1784–6) and John Boydell's *Shakspeare Gallery* (1789), and between 1768 and 1780 he exhibited one work at the Society of Artists and twenty-nine at the Free Society of Artists. The latest of his engravings is dated 1783, but, according to Redgrave, he survived his brother John Caldwall, a portrait and miniature painter, who was born about 1738 in London or in Scotland and died in Scotland in February 1819. An advertisement for an engraving by Caldwall of Sarah Siddons, after William Hamilton, appeared in *The Times* on 30 January 1792, and gave his address as Angel Court, Great Windmill Street, Piccadilly.
W. C. MONKHOUSE, *rev.* ANNE PUETZ

Sources Redgrave, *Artists* • G. Meissner, ed., *Allgemeines Künstlerlexikon: die bildenden Künstler aller Zeiten und Völker*, [new edn], 15, ed. W. Baumberger and others (1997), 572 • Bryan, *Painters* (1886–9) • T. Clayton, *The English print, 1688–1802* (1997), 224, 277 • W. H. Friedman, *Boydell's Shakespeare Gallery* (1976), 258, 261, 266 • *Engraved Brit. ports.*, 4.100; 6.56–7 • Bénézit, *Dict.*, 3rd edn • M. H. Grant, *A dictionary of British etchers* (1952) • Graves, *Soc. Artists* • [K. H. von Heinecken], *Dictionnaire des artistes dont nous avons des estampes*, 4 vols. (Leipzig, 1778–90) • *The Times* (30 Jan 1792)
Archives Herbert Art Gallery and Museum, Coventry, works

Caldwall, Richard (*c.*1515–1584), physician, was born in Staffordshire. He was educated at Brasenose College, Oxford, graduating BA on 20 July 1533, and MA on 12 March 1538. He became a fellow there, but later moved to Christ Church. He took his BM, and was admitted to practise in 1552, and gained his DM on 29 July 1555. He was present at the trial of Archbishop Cranmer in September 1555. Caldwall was admitted a fellow of the College of Physicians on 22 December 1559, was made a censor the same day, and went on to be censor again in 1560, 1561, and 1564. He was elected president in 1570.

Together with Lord Lumley, Caldwall founded the Lumleian lecture in the College of Physicians, and endowed it with £40 per annum. In return, the college paid £100 to renovate its rooms and make more space for his lectures.

Only one work of Caldwall's was published, and that posthumously, with the imprint E. Caldwall. This was the *Tables of Surgery* (1585), a translation of a Latin version by the Florentine physician Horatius Morus of the surgical work of Jean Tagault: it was a surgical text laid out in the form of a series of structured tables.

Caldwall died in 1584, and was buried in St Benet Paul's Wharf. William Camden described his tomb—an elaborate work in later Renaissance style, with many panels and borders, and adorned with surgical instruments. After Caldwall's death five hundred copies of *Tables of Surgery* were presented by his executors to the Company of Barber-Surgeons for their apprentices' use.

SARAH BAKEWELL

Sources Munk, *Roll* • Foster, *Alum. Oxon.* • G. Lewis, 'The faculty of medicine', *Hist. U. Oxf.* 3: *Colleg. univ.*, 213–56, esp. 229, 233, 238, 243, 245 • Emden, *Oxf.* • will, PRO, PROB 11/67, sig. 31

Archives BL, tables of surgery, Sloane MS 759

Wealth at death left a number of bequests; owned land in Staffordshire

Caldwell, Sir Alexander (1763–1839), army officer in the East India Company, was born on 1 February 1763, a younger son of William Caldwell (1710–1802) and his third wife, Isabella, daughter of Alexander Clark of Inverness. Alexander was nominated a cadet in the Bengal artillery in 1782, and on 3 April 1783, after a year's study at Woolwich, was appointed lieutenant-fireworker, and soon after arrived at Calcutta. After some garrison duty there he was ordered to Dacca in 1787 in command of a brigade of four 6-pounders, but was sent home on sick leave in 1789.

Caldwell again studied at Woolwich, and after being promoted a lieutenant in November 1790 returned to India in 1791. In 1792 he was made commandant of the artillery at Midnapore, and in the following year he was present at the capture of Pondicherry. From 1794 to 1796 he commanded the artillery at Dinapore and Cawnpore, and on 7 January 1796 he was promoted captain. In 1798 he was nominated to command the artillery of the force which, under the command of Colonel Hyndman and the superintendence of John Malcolm, conquered and disbanded the powerful army trained for the service of the nizam of Hyderabad by M. Raymond. After this service he proceeded with the nizam's contingent, which was placed under the command of Colonel Arthur Wellesley, and took part in the last Anglo-Mysore war.

In 1800 Caldwell returned to Calcutta, and from 1802 to 1806 was aide-de-camp to Major-General George Green there, and was employed in instructing the cadets for the Bengal artillery on their arrival from England. (The cadets were no longer permitted to receive their professional education at Woolwich.) In 1806 Caldwell came to England on sick leave; in 1807 he was promoted major, and in 1810 returned to Calcutta. In February 1811 he was appointed to command the artillery, consisting of detachments from the Royal, Bengal, and Madras artillery, which accompanied the expedition under Sir Samuel Auchmuty to Java, and was instrumental in the capture of Batavia. He was then prostrated with fever, but nevertheless insisted on reporting himself fit and was present at the battle and the storming of the lines of Cornelis on 26 August, when his services were specially noticed in General Auchmuty's dispatch.

Caldwell was promoted lieutenant-colonel on 1 March 1812. In July 1812 he commanded the artillery at Agra in the operations against Zaman Shah, and was thanked in general orders for his conduct. In 1815 he again came to England on sick leave, and on 3 February 1817 was appointed CB. In 1819 he returned to India for the last time, and in 1821 retired from active service.

In 1829 Caldwell was promoted colonel and in 1837 major-general, and in the latter year he was also made a KCB. In 1838, when the court of directors was asked to nominate three distinguished officers of their army to be made extra GCBs on the occasion of the coronation of Queen Victoria, Caldwell was one of those selected. Caldwell was twice married: first to Ann Miller (*d.* 1836), and secondly to Elizabeth (*d.* 1891), second daughter of E. W. Shepheard of Great Russell Street, London. She later married Colonel Le Blanc. Caldwell died at his house in Upper Berkeley Street, London, on 6 December 1839.

H. M. STEPHENS, *rev.* JAMES LUNT

Sources F. W. Stubbs, ed., *History of the organization, equipment, and war services of the regiment of Bengal artillery*, 3 vols. (1877–95) • *United Service Journal*, 1 (1840), 247–8 • *GM*, 2nd ser., 13 (1840) • B. P. Hughes, *The Bengal horse artillery, 1800–1861* (1971) • W. Thorn, *Memoir of the conquest of Java* (1815) • Fortescue, *Brit. army*, vols. 4, 7, 11 • Sir W. Thorn, *A memoir of Major General Sir R. R. Gillespie, knight commander of the most honourable order of the Bath, &c* (1816) • V. C. P. Hodson, *List of officers of the Bengal army, 1758–1834*, 1 (1927) • C. E. Buckland, *Dictionary of Indian biography* (1906)

Caldwell, Andrew (1733–1808), barrister and connoisseur of architecture, was born on 19 December 1733, the eldest of the ten children of Charles Caldwell (1707–1776), solicitor to the commissioners of revenue in Ireland, and his wife, Elizabeth (1709–1792), daughter of Benjamin Heywood, merchant, of Drogheda, and his wife, Ann Graham. He attended Glasgow University between 1751 and 1754 but chose not to graduate and was admitted to the Middle Temple in December 1752 while still at university. He began his law studies with his father in Dublin before proceeding to London, and in Michaelmas term 1760 he was called to the Irish bar.

Caldwell's wealth allowed him to practise law when it suited him and to devote time to his public and private interests. He was of a literary disposition and loved the fine arts, especially architecture, his favourite architect being William Chambers. He is reputed to have written the important 'Observations on architecture' published anonymously in *Freeman's Journal* between December 1768 and February 1769. Caldwell was also a distinguished bibliophile and his library reflected his eclectic range of interests. His literary friends in Ireland included James Caulfeild, first earl of Charlemont, Joseph Cooper Walker, and Thomas Percy, bishop of Dromore; outside Ireland his circle included Edmund Malone and Charlotte Smith, and

Andrew Caldwell (1733–1808), by Robert Woodburn, 1793

he was known and liked by Lady Eleanor Butler and Sarah Ponsonby, the 'ladies of Llangollen'.

Caldwell never made the grand tour but he did visit the Netherlands in the summer of 1773. Two years later he was made guardian to his orphaned nephew George *Cockburn (who later had a distinguished military career) and left his family home in Henry Street, Dublin, for his nephew's house, 10 Cavendish Row, Rutland Square East, and later for his own at 12 Cavendish Row. On the death of his father in 1776 he inherited a considerable estate, including Newgrange, in co. Meath, and succeeded him as agent for William Ponsonby, second earl of Bessborough. He was MP for Knocktopher from 1776 to 1783 and for Downpatrick from 1783 to 1790, following the Ponsonby interest. He was unusual among members of the Irish Commons in that he was a presbyterian and attended the Strand Street meeting-house.

Caldwell's public responsibilities included service on the Dublin paving board. In 1783 he was appointed a commissioner for planning the town of New Geneva, near Passage East in co. Waterford, intended as a settlement for entrepreneurial Swiss immigrants. From 1784 until his death he was an active member of the wide streets commission. He became a member of the Royal Irish Academy shortly after its foundation in 1785. A longstanding member of the Dublin Society, he was an enthusiastic amateur botanist. One of his best friends was James Smith, the first president of the Linnean Society, of which Caldwell was made a fellow in 1796. He was involved in the purchase of land for the botanic garden at Glasnevin, co. Dublin. Caldwell was also knowledgeable about painting and promoted young artists; his close friend Alexander Mangin, who died in 1802, bequeathed his entire collection of prints and drawings to him.

Shortly before his death Caldwell wrote a memoir of his family, which his brother the admiral Sir Benjamin *Caldwell added to and subsequently published. Small of stature, with an unusually long nose, Andrew Caldwell was a cultivated man who commanded the respect and affection of his friends and of the female members of his family but whose relationship with his brothers was uneasy. He died on 2 July 1808, unmarried, at Shanganagh, near Bray, co. Wicklow, the house of his nephew George Cockburn, and was buried on 4 July in the family plot in Glasnevin parish churchyard, adjacent to the tomb of Dr Patrick Delany. JANE A. MEREDITH

Sources priv. coll., Caldwell MSS • *GM*, 1st ser., 78 (1808), 661, 746 • *Monthly Magazine*, 26 (Sept 1808) • A. Caldwell and B. Caldwell, *Caldwell family* (privately printed, 1817?) • *Dublin directory* (1762–1808) • E. McParland, 'The wide streets commissioners', *Quarterly Bulletin of the Irish Georgian Society*, 15 (1972), 18–26 • Unitarian Church, St Stephen's Green, Dublin, Presbyterian/Unitarian Archive • *Public Register, or, Freeman's Journal* (Dec 1768–Feb 1769) • Burke, *Gen. Ire.* • James Smith, correspondence, Linn. Soc. • H. A. C. Sturgess, ed., *Register of admissions to the Honourable Society of the Middle Temple, from the fifteenth century to the year 1944*, 1 (1949), 345 • E. C. Nelson and E. M. McCracken, *The brightest jewel: a history of the National Botanic Gardens, Glasnevin, Dublin* (1987), 33–4, 36 • F. G. Hall, *The Bank of Ireland, 1783–1946*, ed. G. O'Brien (1949), 458–9, 512 • record of burials in Glasnevin churchyard, Representative Church Body

Archives NG Ire., prints and drawings • priv. coll. | Dublin City Archive, paving board and wide streets commission minute books • Linn. Soc., corresp. with Sir James Smith • NAM, corresp. with Sir George Cockburn • Unitarian Church, St Stephen's Green, Dublin, Presbyterian/Unitarian MSS

Likenesses R. Woodburn, oils, 1793, NG Ire. [*see illus.*]

Wealth at death cash assets of £13,609 16*s*. 9*d*. before payment of legacies and outstanding debts; sale of his house (12 Cavendish Row), £2800: Caldwell MSS, priv. coll.

Caldwell, Sir Benjamin (1739–1820), naval officer and politician, was born in Liverpool on 31 January 1739, the third son of Charles Caldwell (1707–1776), solicitor to the customs in Dublin, and Elizabeth Heywood (1709–1792). Andrew *Caldwell was his eldest brother. In 1754 Benjamin Caldwell entered the Royal Academy at Portsmouth, and two years later he joined the *Isis* (50 guns). In March 1759 he transferred to the *Namur*, bearing Admiral Edward Boscawen's flag, and he served in her at the defeat of Clue's squadron in Lagos Bay on 18–19 August, and afterwards in Admiral Edward Hawke's crushing defeat of Admiral Hubert de Brienne, comte de Conflans in Quiberon Bay on 20 November.

From 1760 to 1762 Caldwell was a lieutenant of the *Achilles* (60 guns) and after commanding the sloop *Martin* for three years he was made captain of the frigate *Milford*. He afterwards commanded the *Rose* (24 guns), and from 1775 to 1779 the *Emerald* (32 guns), on the North American station; on 25 December he took command of the *Hannibal* (50 guns), and at the start of 1781 he moved into the *Agamemnon* (64 guns). During the summer and autumn the *Agamemnon* was in the Channel Fleet under Vice-Admiral George Darby, and in December she was one of the small squadron with Rear-Admiral Richard Kempenfelt in the

Bay of Biscay. Following Kempenfelt's engagement of Guichen's squadron off Ushant on 12 December, the *Agamemnon* was detached to pick up any stragglers of the scattered French convoy, and succeeded in capturing five more to add to Kempenfelt's initial haul of twenty. Caldwell returned to England in time to sail with Sir George Rodney for the West Indies, where he had a significant share in the battle of the Saints (12 April 1782). He remained on the North America and West Indies station until the peace, when the *Agamemnon* was paid off in May 1783. On 7 June 1784 Caldwell married Charlotte, daughter of Admiral Henry *Osborn, with whom he had a son, Charles Andrew.

Caldwell was MP for Knocktopher in the Irish House of Commons (1776–83), and for Harristown (1783–90). In 1787 he commanded the *Alcide* (74 guns) for a short time in the Dutch armament, and for a few months during the Spanish armament of 1790 he commanded the *Berwick* (74 guns). On 1 February 1793 he became rear-admiral of the white, and towards the close of the year he hoisted his flag in the *Cumberland* (74 guns) in the fleet under Lord Howe. In April of the following year he became rear-admiral of the red, and transferred his flag to the *Impregnable* (98 guns), still in Lord Howe's fleet, before taking part in the battle of 1 June 1794, in which the *Impregnable* had thirty-one men killed or wounded. Caldwell, with many other senior officers, was nevertheless left unmentioned in the official dispatches of Lord Howe. In consequence the gold medal was withheld from him, as it was from the other flag officers and captains who had not been specially mentioned; and though it was very quickly perceived that Howe had committed a serious blunder, and that the Admiralty had acquiesced in this affront to several deserving officers, the error went unrectified. Of those passed over for honours, only Cuthbert Collingwood later had it in his power to force the Admiralty to acknowledge their mistake.

On 4 July 1794 Caldwell was advanced to vice-admiral of the blue, and in the following September he was sent out to the Leeward Islands, with his flag in the *Majestic* (74 guns), to join Sir John Jervis. Jervis shortly afterwards returned to England, leaving Caldwell as commander-in-chief. However, in the following June, he was superseded by Sir John Laforey. As Caldwell's rank entitled him to the command, he was apparently led to believe that Laforey's appointment was a continuation of the same insult which had deprived him of the gold medal. He returned to England in the frigate *Blanche*, and neither applied for nor accepted any further appointment. His advancement to the rank of admiral on 14 February 1799 came as matter of course by seniority. His name was markedly omitted from the honours conferred at the end of the war, and it was not until after the death of George III that, in May 1820, he received a tardy acknowledgement of his services by being nominated an extra GCB. Caldwell died at his son's house, near Basingstoke, in November 1820. His wife survived him. J. K. LAUGHTON, *rev.* P. L. C. WEBB

Sources 'Biographical memoir of Benjamin Caldwell', *Naval Chronicle*, 11 (1804), 1–9 · J. Charnock, ed., *Biographia navalis*, 6 (1798) · J. Ralfe, *The naval biography of Great Britain*, 1 (1828) · *GM*, 1st ser., 90/2 (1820), 565 · D. Syrett and R. L. DiNardo, *The commissioned sea officers of the Royal Navy, 1660–1815*, rev. edn, Occasional Publications of the Navy RS, 1 (1994)

Archives NMM, logbooks, notebooks, corresp., and papers · Surrey HC, bank book | PRO, letters to Lord Rodney, 30/20/21/3 · Sheff. Arch., corresp. with Earl Fitzwilliam

Likenesses R. Horne, oils, 1784, NMM · Bartolozzi, Landseer, Ryder, and Stow, group portrait, line engraving, pubd 1803 (*Commemoration of the victory of June 1st 1794*; after *Naval Victories* by R. Smirke), BM, NPG · W. Ridley, print, 1804, NMM · Ridley, stipple, pubd 1804, NPG · attrib. S. Medley, oils, NMM

Caldwell, Hume (1735–1762), army officer in the Austrian service, was born in Castle Caldwell, co. Fermanagh, Ireland, the third son of the eight children of Sir John Caldwell, second baronet (*d.* 1744), landowner, and Ann, eldest daughter of the Revd John Trench, dean of Raphoe, and his wife, Anne Warburton. The possibility that he may have been an illegitimate child of a Catholic tenant, who later received money, has been questioned by recent historians.

Caldwell entered the Austrian army at the age of fifteen, thus following the example of his elder brother, Sir James Caldwell (*d.* 1784), who was created count of Milan by Maria Theresa. While stationed at Prague he accidentally set fire to the furniture in his lodgings, and his landlord applied to have his pay sequestrated to pay for the damage. The brothers of the Irish Franciscan convent came to his aid on account of the kindness with which his father had treated his Catholic neighbours. Caldwell served with honour during the Seven Years' War. Although he had enlisted as a common soldier, he soon rose to the rank of lieutenant through the influence of his brother, the count of Milan. Shortly after the battle of Prague he obtained the command of a company of grenadiers in the combined army of Charles of Lorraine and Marshal Daune which besieged Breslau in the autumn of 1757. In search of further advancement he volunteered his unit for harassing the Prussians as they crossed the mountains on their way to besiege Olmütz. This part in the Austrian success in destroying a large Prussian convoy at the battle of Domstädtl earned him promotion to major and the cross of the order of Maria Theresa from the empress queen. His greatest exploit was at the sudden attack on the fortress of Schweidnitz, in Silesia, by General Loudon on 30 September 1761, when he led the stormers of the garden fort and carried it in a quarter of an hour, for which he was specially mentioned in Loudon's dispatches. He died aged twenty-seven on 19 August 1762 at Schweidnitz from a wound received during a sortie from the fortress, when it was being besieged by Frederick the Great. Maria Theresa never forgot Caldwell's services; in 1766, when his brother was passing through Vienna, she gave him a magnificently enamelled gold box to present to his mother, the dowager Lady Caldwell.

H. M. STEPHENS, *rev.* ROSEMARY RICHEY

Sources J. B. Cunningham, *A history of Castle Caldwell and its families* (1980) · Burke, *Peerage* (1837) · R. von Liliencron and others, eds., *Allgemeine deutsche Biographie*, 56 vols. (Leipzig, 1875–1912)

Archives BM, King's MS

Caldwell, Sir James Lillyman (1770–1863), army officer in the East India Company, born at Greenwich on 22 November 1770, was the son of Major Arthur Caldwell (*d.* 26 Jan 1786) of the Bengal Engineers, who died at Benares, and his wife, Elizabeth Weed (*d.* 30 Dec 1832) of Greenwich, Kent. He was the nephew of General Sir Alexander Caldwell of the Bengal artillery. He entered the East India Company service as a cadet in 1788, and received a commission as ensign in the Madras engineers on 27 July 1789. He was promoted lieutenant on 2 December 1792, and, successively, captain-lieutenant (8 January 1796), captain (12 August 1802), major (1 January 1806), lieutenant-colonel (26 September 1811), lieutenant-colonel commandant (1 May 1824), colonel (20 May 1825), major-general (10 January 1837), lieutenant-general (9 November 1846), and general (20 June 1854).

Early in 1791 Caldwell joined the force under Lord Cornwallis for the campaign against Tipu Sultan in Mysore. He was present at the attack by Colonel Floyd on Tipu's camp in front of Bangalore on 6 March, and took part in the successful assault of the *pettah* of Bangalore on the following day, when the British loss was heavy. He served throughout the siege of Bangalore (8–20 March) and, despite having been wounded in the trenches, entered the breach with the storming party on 21 March. He was present at the battle of Arakere, when Tipu was defeated by Cornwallis, on 14 May, and was with the advanced brigade on 15 July at the capture of Usur. He served as an engineer at the siege of Rayakottai and of five other strong forts during the same month. On 17 September he assisted in the capture of Raymanghur, and took part in the surprise and capture of the *pettah* of Nandidroog on 22 September, and in the siege of Nandidroog from 27 September to 18 October, when he mounted the breach with the storming party at its capture. On 29 November he accompanied the chief engineer, Lieutenant-Colonel Patrick Ross, to the siege of the strong hill fort of Savanadrug, and climbed to the breach and entered with the storming party on 21 December.

On 6 February 1792 Caldwell was engaged in the night attack under Cornwallis on Tipu's entrenched camp in front of Seringapatam, and served through the siege of that town which immediately followed, until 22 February, when he was wounded in the trenches. After the capitulation and treaty of peace with Tipu on 19 March he returned to Madras.

In 1794 Caldwell went to the Northern Circars with Michael Topping, who went to India as an astronomer and was employed on public works, to investigate and report upon proposals for the improvement of that part of the country. He constructed various public works until 1799, when he took part under General Harris in the final campaign against Tipu. He was present at the action of Malavalli on 27 March and at the second siege of Seringapatam in April, when he commanded the 3rd brigade of engineers. He led the ladder party in the successful assault on 4 May. He was twice wounded, once in the trenches, and again with the forlorn hope at the top of the breach, when he was shot and rolled down into the ditch. He was mentioned in dispatches, and received the medal for Seringapatam and a pension for his wounds.

On his recovery Caldwell resumed his civil duties, and was engaged for the next ten years on important public works. At the end of August 1810 he sailed with Sir John Abercromby in the frigate *Ceylon* as chief engineer in the expedition against Mauritius. On 18 September they met the French warship *Venus*, off St Denis, Réunion, and after action, in which both vessels were dismasted, the *Ceylon* was compelled to surrender to the French sloop *Victor*, which came to the assistance of the *Venus*. Next morning, however, Commodore Rowley, arriving in the *Boadicea*, retook the *Ceylon* and also picked up the *Venus*. The expedition assembled at Rodriguez in November, and on the 29th landed at Mauritius. Next day the French were defeated, and on 2 December the island surrendered. Caldwell was thanked in general orders and mentioned in dispatches.

Caldwell returned to Madras in January 1811, and in March was appointed to the engineer charge of the centre division of the Madras army. In 1812 he repaired and reconstructed the fortress of Seringapatam. In 1813 he was appointed special surveyor of fortresses. In June 1815 he was made a CB, military division. In 1816 he was appointed acting chief engineer of Madras and a commissioner for the restoration of the French settlements on the Malabar and Coromandel coasts. Eight years later he became lieutenant-colonel commandant of his corps. He retired from the active list in 1837 and was made a KCB on 10 March. After returning home that year he lived chiefly at his house, 19 place Vendôme, Paris, until his wife's death, when he bought a house, Beachlands, on the Isle of Wight, and lived partly there and partly at his London house in Portland Place. He was made a GCB in August 1848. In the earlier part of his life he was a skilled watercolourist, and painted many Indian landscapes.

In India, in 1796, Caldwell had married Jeanne Baptiste, widow of Captain Charles Johnston of the Madras army, and daughter of Jean Maillard of Dôle, Franche-Comté; they had a son, Arthur James (1799–1843), major 2nd (Queen's) dragoon guards, who had no children, and a daughter, Elizabeth Maria (1797–1870), who married, in 1815, Edward Richard Sullivan (1791–1823) of the Madras civil service, third son of Sir Richard Sullivan, first baronet, of Thames Ditton, and had at least one child. Caldwell died at his residence, Beachlands, Ryde, Isle of Wight, on 28 June 1863. R. H. Vetch, *rev.* Roger T. Stearn

Sources BL OIOC · *GM*, 3rd ser., 15 (1863) · H. M. Vibart, *The military history of the Madras engineers and pioneers*, 2 vols. (1881–3) · J. Welsh, *Military reminiscences*, 2 vols. (1830) · *Annual Register* (1811) · private information (1901) · V. C. P. Hodson, *List of officers of the Bengal army, 1758–1834*, 3 (1946) · T. A. Heathcote, *The military in British India: the development of British land forces in south Asia, 1600–1947* (1995) · P. Lawson, *The East India Company* (1993) · Boase, *Mod. Eng. biog.*

Archives Royal Engineers, Chatham, Kent, papers relating to works in India · Royal Engineers Museum, Chatham, Kent, reports on Indian rivers, canals, etc.

Likenesses crayon, repro. in Vibart, *Military history*, 1, frontispiece • portrait, Kitchener barracks, royal engineers, Chatham
Wealth at death under £120,000: probate, 28 Aug 1863, *CGPLA Eng. & Wales*

Caldwell [*alias* Fenwick], **John** (1628–1679), Jesuit, was born in co. Durham of protestant parents who disowned him when, on his arriving at mature age, he embraced the Roman Catholic faith. He studied humanities at the English College at St Omer from 1654 to 1656 and entered the Society of Jesus at Watten on 28 September 1656. He studied philosophy and theology at the Jesuit college at Liège from 1657 to 1664. Having completed his studies he was ordained priest in 1664 and was procurator or agent at the English College, St Omer, from 1665 to 1672. He returned to Watten in 1672, was made a professed father in 1673 and was sent to England in the same year. He used the alias John Fenwick. He lived in London at the College of St Ignatius (1674–9) and also acted as procurator of St Omer's College. In the fourth year of his ministerial labours he was summoned, on the information of Titus Oates, to appear before the privy council, and was committed to Newgate. After suffering a long and painful confinement he was tried for high treason with Father Ireland, but as the evidence was insufficient, he was remanded back to prison. He was arraigned a second time at the Old Bailey on 13 June 1679, together with four other Jesuit fathers. Oates and Dugdale were witnesses against them, and in accordance with the direction of Chief Justice Scroggs the jury found the prisoners guilty. They suffered death at Tyburn on 20 June 1679. Caldwell's remains were buried in the churchyard of St Giles-in-the-Fields. An account of *The tryals and condemnation … for high treason, in conspiring the death of the king, the subversion of the government and protestant religion* of the five Jesuits was published in 1679 and an account of their final protestations and devotions was published as *A Remonstrance of Piety and Innocence* in 1683. Caldwell was beatified by Pope Pius XI on 15 December 1929 with other victims of the Popish Plot.

THOMPSON COOPER, *rev.* RUTH JORDAN

John Caldwell (1628–1679), by Martin Bouché, pubd 1683

Sources G. Holt, *The English Jesuits, 1650–1829: a biographical dictionary*, Catholic RS, 70 (1984) • R. Challoner, *Memoirs of missionary priests*, ed. J. H. Pollen, rev. edn (1924) • G. Holt, *St Omers and Bruges colleges, 1593–1773: a biographical dictionary*, Catholic RS, 69 (1979) • J. Warner, *The history of English persecution of Catholics and the presbyterian plot*, ed. T. A. Birrell, trans. J. Bligh, 2 vols., Catholic RS, 47–8 (1953) • H. Chadwick, *St Omers to Stonyhurst* (1962) • D. A. Bellenger, ed., *English and Welsh priests, 1558–1800* (1984) • Gillow, *Lit. biog. hist.*, 1.373–4 • *Engraved Brit. ports.*, 2.204; 5.75 • J. Kenyon, *The Popish Plot* (1972)

Likenesses M. Bouché, line engraving, BM, NPG; repro. in M. Tanner, *Brevis relatio* (1683) [*see illus.*] • engraving (Titus Oates standing in pillory, 1685), BM

Caldwell, Robert (1814–1891), missionary and orientalist, was born near Belfast, Ulster, on 7 May 1814, into an impoverished family. He began working at the age of nine, after his family moved to Glasgow. Largely self-educated, at fifteen he went to live with his elder brother in Dublin, where he studied art (1829–33). A religious crisis seems to have prompted his return to Glasgow, where he became active in a Congregational church. When a scholarship to Balliol College, Oxford, was invalidated on the discovery of his being born in Ireland, he applied to the London Missionary Society (LMS) and was sent to Glasgow University for further training. There he came under the influence of the Greek professor, Sir Daniel Keyte Standford, whose pioneering research intensified Caldwell's love for comparative philology. Standford also encouraged critical theology and promoted the merits of Anglicanism.

Following graduation (with distinction), ordination as a Congregational minister, and commissioning into missionary service, Caldwell embarked on the *Mary Ann*. The ship was also carrying the renowned Telugu scholar of the Madras civil service, Charles Philip Brown, who aided Caldwell's linguistic learning. Caldwell landed in Madras on 8 January 1838, and devoted the next three years to mastering Tamil. During this time he became acquainted with the Scottish missionary John Anderson (1805–1855). Whether Anderson played a role in Caldwell's decision to leave the LMS for the Society for the Propagation of the Gospel (SPG) is not clear. A number of Madras missionaries at that time took the 'Canterbury trail' into high-church (Puseyite) conformity. In 1841, after concluding that the Church of England was the least unchristian option, Caldwell journeyed up to Ootacamund, in the Nilagiri hills, and was ordained by George Trevor Spencer, bishop of Madras. Spencer was concerned about open rebellion against Anglicanism among Tamil congregations in the south which had been under the wing of the Society for the Promotion of Christian Knowledge (SPCK). Caldwell responded to this concern. By December 1841, after stopping to visit the aged John Caspar Kohlhoff at Tanjore, he established himself in Tinnevelly country. He settled at Idayankudi, or 'shepherd's abode', and remained there for the next fifty years. He took especial pains to contact older missionaries such as Augustus Friedrich Caemmerer jun., at Nazareth, and George Heyne, at Mudalur, both India-born German missionaries for the SPCK who had trained at Bishop's College, Calcutta.

Caldwell's primary task was to restore the loyalty of congregations which had been alienated by the Rhenius affair. Rhenius, a gifted, highly charismatic, and popular German missionary of the Church Missionary Society (CMS), had been summarily dismissed for not conforming to Anglican modes of 'apostolic succession' in ordaining Tamil Christians. The event had caused deep resentment and led to a schism. Tamil evangelical (protestant) congregations dated from the 1770s and 1780s, when two disciples of the great Friedrich Schwartz of Tanjore—Satyanathan Pillai and Clarinda (a Christian Brahman widow)—had gone to Palamcottai and when Satyanathan and David Sundaranandam had initiated a mass movement of conversions among the *shanar* or *nadar* peoples of the area. This movement, rising in the 1790s had, in the wake of severe persecution, led to a process of doubling and redoubling numbers of converts in every decade thereafter, bringing many thousands of people into local churches. Rhenius had built upon foundations of the old royal Danish system of education (also of Hallé in Germany), first introduced into Tranquebar in 1706, into Tanjore as early as 1731, and into Tinnevelly in 1783. Expanded and strengthened by Rhenius, hundreds of village schools had begun to provide training in literacy and science for girls and women, as well as for boys and men, often before baptism. Spectacular results had brought revolutionary changes to many villages, occasionally accompanied by violent reactions from landed gentry. Caldwell's work, in short, was to win back Tamil congregations and regain control of village schools. His work was made easier after March 1844, when he married Eliza Mault (*d.* 1899), eldest daughter of Charles Mault, LMS missionary in the south of Travancore. Eliza, like Rhenius's wife also India-born, strengthened the effectiveness of educational work for women. She ran a boarding-school for girls and, like her predecessor, encouraged home-making, lacemaking, and income-producing crafts, which enabled Tamil Christian women to achieve greater personal, social, and financial independence.

However, like his contemporary George Uglow Pope, Caldwell became much more widely known as an orientalist than as a missionary. His scholarly contributions to the understanding of Tamil culture were eventually to become wide-ranging and profound. His first book, *The Tinnevelly shanars: a sketch of their religion and their moral conditions and characteristics as a caste* (1849 and 1850), landed him in such trouble with local Tamil Christians that he was never completely able to extricate himself from its consequences. The work was an ethnographic description of the community out of which the vast majority of Tinnevelly Christians had come. However accurate or valuable his conclusions might or might not have been, especially for later generations of historians, he offended the prominent and upwardly mobile members of the community, Christian and non-Christian alike. As members of this community had become progressively more respectable, they had shunned designation by the defiling expletive *shanar*—a term deemed so unmentionable as not to be spoken in polite discourse—and instead proudly called themselves *nadars* ('lords'). *Nadars* objected to any suggestion that their roots were less noble than those of the Aryans. They sent petitions to the SPG and to the archbishop of Canterbury, venting their outrage at the notion that their lineage or occupations were as low or polluting as the term implied. Caldwell, even though he later withdrew the book, and despite becoming a bishop, was never forgiven.

In Europe and other parts of India, on the other hand, Caldwell's reputation soared. He became widely known, especially for his *Comparative Grammar of the Dravidian, or South Indian Family of Languages* (1856). This work, subsequently revised and enlarged, established his reputation as a leading orientalist of his day. It remains a standard authority and is still in print. Caldwell was the first to argue that south India's four main languages—Tamil, Telugu, Kannada, and Malayalam—had 'a common origin' and were 'a separate family', altogether distinct from the Aryan family of languages. The implications of his theory were far-reaching. By arguing that these 'Dravidian' languages of the south were different from those derived from Sanskrit, that their cultures, societies, and polities had existed prior to the arrival of Brahmans in the south, and that intrinsic differences in physical anthropology, religion, and social structures were attributes of such distinctions, Caldwell can be seen as having laid the foundations for the strongly anti-Brahman cultural and political movements which followed.

No less significant were Caldwell's other scholarly contributions. *A political and general history of the district of Tinnevelly, in the presidency of Madras, from the earliest period to its cession to the English government in 1801* (1881), drawn from archaeological, epigraphic, and literary sources, was perhaps his most comprehensive single work. He also published *Lectures on the Tinnevelly Mission* (1857), *Records of the Early History of the Tinnevelly Mission* (1881), and *On reserve in communicating religious instruction to non-Christians in mission schools of India* (1881). Posthumously his *Reminiscences of Bishop Caldwell* (1894) were edited and published by his son-in-law, the Revd J. L. Wyatt. During his career Caldwell also published a number of smaller works—lectures, sermons, scholarly contributions to the *Indian Antiquary*, and more popular articles. These reflect both his wider-ranging interests and the depth of his command of literary resources, public and private. At the same time, even while in the process of producing these works, Caldwell continued to discover and to make public many collections of rare manuscripts. Finally he assisted in making revisions in the Tamil Book of Common Prayer (in 1842 and 1872), the Tamil hymn-book (in collaboration with Edward Sargent), and the Tamil Bible (from 1858 to 1869), working with both the Madras branches of the British and Foreign Bible Society and the Christian Literature Society in these enterprises.

Caldwell's piety and scholarship eventually led to his nomination for bishop. However, when the decision to create a separate bishopric for Tinnevelly was made, both Caldwell and Sargent were put forward for the position (no Indian Christian then being thought to qualify). The double nomination caused complications: each candidate represented a different constituency in Tinnevelly and a different missionary society—Caldwell the SPG, and Sargent the CMS—and had a different and incompatible cultural ethos and ecclesiology. Only after passage of the Colonial Clergy Act of 1874 were both people finally consecrated, in Calcutta on 11 March 1877, each becoming an assistant bishop. Neither appointment was satisfactory: both men were ageing and could not travel very far; and each, in his own way, was becoming increasingly rigid. Moreover, as the number of European missionaries steadily began to decline, the Tinnevelly (native Indian) church council became restive and determined to gain greater autonomy. Bitter memories of the Rhenius schism had never been erased. Tamil Christians connected to the SPG and the CMS had been divided by that tragic event, so neither side could forget what the other had done. This situation persisted even though the two bishops remained on good terms. The final amalgamation of the two branches into a single diocesan structure did not occur until after the death of Sargent in October 1887, when Caldwell, who since 1881 had been preoccupied with building a theological school in Tuticorin, was persuaded to retire.

Caldwell's final years were spent in the hill station of Kodaikanal, where he had erected St Peter's Church many years earlier. It was there that he died on 28 August 1891. His body was returned to Idayankudi and buried under the altar of the magnificent church building which his people had constructed. Eliza Caldwell, his widow, stayed on in Kodaikanal, remaining until her death on 18 June 1899. Her body was then returned to the plains to lie beside that of her husband. At least one daughter, married to J. L. Wyatt of the SPG, continued in missionary service. Portraits and photographs of Caldwell with his distinctively long and flowing white beard can be found where he served and in books about his work. His statue was placed on the esplanade in Madras, erected by the DMK government, as a tribute to his manifold contributions to the culture and to the peoples of Tamil Nadu.

ROBERT ERIC FRYKENBERG

Sources A. P. Appasawmy, *A history of the CMS in Tinnevelly* (1923) • K. N. Arooran, *Tamil renaissance and Dravidian nationalism, 1905–1944* (1980), viii, 300 • E. Chatterton, *A history of the Church of England in India, since the early days of the East India Company* (1924) • M. E. Gibbs, *The Anglican church in India, 1600–1970* (1972) • H. Grafe, *Tamilnadu in the nineteenth and twentieth centuries* (1982), vol. 4, pt 2 of *History of Christianity in India* (1982–) • J. Hough, *History of Christianity in India*, 5 vols. (1845), vols. 4, 5 • S. Neill, *A history of Christianity in India, 1707–1858* (1985) • C. F. Pascoe, *Two hundred years of the SPG*, rev. edn, 2 vols. (1901) • T. T. Perowne, *A memoir of the Rev. Thomas Gajetan Ragland … missionary of the Church Missionary Society in north Tinnevelly, south India* (1861), viii, 356 • G. Pettitt, *Narrative of the affairs of the Tinnevelly mission* (1836) • G. Pettitt, *An account of the Palamcottah mission church* (1844) • G. Pettitt, *The Tinnevelly mission of the Church Missionary Society* (1851) • J. Rhenius, ed., *Memoirs of the Rev. C. T. E. Rhenius, comprising extracts from his journal and correspondence, with details of missionary proceedings in south India* (1841) • J. A. Richey, ed., *Selections from the educational records* (1922), pt 2: 1840–59 • J. Richter, *Die deutsche Mission in Südindien* (1902) • J. Richter, *The history of missions in India* (1906) • H. Sharp, *Selections from the educational records* (1920), pt 1, 1811–39; pt 2, 1839ff • J. A. Sharrock, *South Indian missions* (1910) • M. A. Sherring, *The history of protestant missions in India, from their commencement in 1706 to 1871*, rev. edn (1884) • S. T. [S. Tucker], *South Indian sketches … in letters to a young friend*, 2 vols. (1842–3)
Archives Bodl. RH, SPG MSS • Holy Trinity Church, Marylebone Road, London, SPCK MSS • U. Birm. L., CMS MSS

Caledfryn. *See* Williams, William (1801–1869).

Calenius, Walter. *See* Oxford, Walter of (*d.* in or before 1151?).

Caleto, John de. *See* Caux, John de (*c*.1205–1263).

Caley, George (1770–1829), farrier and botanist, was born on 10 June 1770 in Craven, Yorkshire, the oldest son of William Caley, horse dealer, and Martha Norbury. His parents were married in Manchester in February 1770 but moved to Yorkshire before Caley's birth. After several years, they moved to Middleton, Lancashire. Caley attended Manchester Free Grammar School between the ages of eight and twelve, learning some Latin and a smattering of arithmetic, before starting work as a stable-boy. Coming across prescriptions for treating horse diseases, Caley searched for the herbs required in these recipes: this sparked off his interest in plants, which he was unable to satisfy until he came across William Withering's *Botanical Arrangement* (1787–92), a work to which Caley himself contributed information by the fourth edition of 1801.

After studying the Linnaean classification laid out in Withering's book, Caley began botanizing with companions such as James Crowther and John Dewhurst. Lacking their flexibility of time, he abandoned farriery work for weaving, but had to reverse his decision when trade slumped. Again he turned to books and studied Linnaeus's works. He developed a strong desire to travel as a botanical collector and in 1795 he wrote directly to Sir Joseph Banks to ask about possible opportunities. Banks, impressed by Caley's botanical discoveries, responded by placing him in London botanic gardens for the necessary training to become a government collector. However, after two years, Caley found this discipline unbearable and in early 1798 returned to Manchester. His belief that he had been let down with regard to a travelling post was dispelled when, in November, an unexpected vacancy on a voyage to New South Wales prompted Banks to employ Caley as his personal collector at 15*s*. a week.

Caley arrived in New South Wales in 1800 and established himself in Parramatta. He immediately began to make collections aided by two convicts assigned to him but also seeking help and information from Aborigines. In 1805 he practically adopted a fifteen-year-old Aborigine boy called Moowat'tin, whose ability to climb trees to collect fruits and blossoms allowed Caley's detailed study of eucalypts. Caley's obvious sympathy with Aborigines resulted in clashes with some settlers, which, as with his criticism of governors King and Bligh over the running of the colony, often required Banks's conciliatory intervention.

Caley botanized with Robert Brown, who visited Australia from 1802 to 1805, and Caley's botanical skills were acknowledged in Brown's *Prodromus florae Novae Hollandiae* (1810) and later works on Australian flora. Claims that Brown's work eclipsed that of Caley must be offset against the celebrity Caley achieved by being acknowledged in published work. Although he always named his specimens, Caley lacked the ability to publish precise scientific descriptions and his expertise was embodied in his extensive collections. Towards the end of Brown's visit, Caley turned his attention mainly to exploration; his 1804 attempt to cross the Blue Mountains is now commemorated on a plaque on Mount Banks.

In 1809 Caley was relieved to be released from Banks's service with an annuity of £50. He returned to England in 1810 with the authoritarian governor of New South Wales, William Bligh, to act as a witness in the court martial against George Johnston whose deposition and imprisonment of Bligh in 1808 had been reported by Caley in detailed letters to Banks. Controversially, Caley brought Moowat'tin to England, only to see him shipped home the following year. While in London for the trial, Caley frequently visited Banks and other leading botanists before sending his collections to Manchester. He turned down Aylmer Bourke Lambert's offer to become curator of his London herbarium and, although dismayed by changes in Lancashire, settled in Chadderton.

Caley re-established old friendships and, via the network of botanical meetings held in pubs, made new friends such as Edward Hobson. He prepared Australian plant collections for sale to Lambert and Benjamin Delessert. The tedium of cleaning specimens, ill health, unrest in Lancashire, and the climate, all contributed to Caley's gloomy conclusion that his collection was a millstone round his neck, and his longing to return to New South Wales. In 1813 Caley began stuffing his bird skins with the intention of exhibiting them. This was a failure but Caley sold several of the best skins to Lord Stanley and the remainder, together with specimens of quadrupeds and reptiles, were bought by the Linnean Society.

In 1815 Banks and Brown recommended Caley, albeit with some misgivings about his status, as superintendent of the St Vincent Botanical Garden. While Caley fulfilled their expectations in improving the garden, particularly in cultivating nutmegs, cinnamon, and cloves, his disdain for the British society on the island proved disastrous. Appearing to flaunt his lack of gentility, he lost the goodwill of those willing to help to protect the garden against encroachers and thieves. As in New South Wales, Caley applied strict moral standards to judge whether his social superiors were worthy of respect. Especially critical of the governor, Caley was soon locked in quarrels over the running of the garden. He wished to resign in 1818 but was not released from his duties until December 1822.

In 1800, Caley had, as a servant of Banks, requested permission to marry Mrs Wise, widow of a weaver sent out by the British government to New South Wales. Before Banks's irritated reply arrived, Caley changed his mind and he and Mrs Wise lived in adjoining cottages in Parramatta and did not marry, possibly to ensure that the widow would get free passage back to England as part of her late husband's agreement with the government. Mrs Wise eventually married Caley in England between 1811 and 1816 and she and her daughter accompanied him to St Vincent. Caley's opinion of St Vincent as 'the most nasty place I ever lived', expressed in a letter to Banks on 27 August 1816 (Dawson Turner correspondence, 19, 303–11, Botany Library, Natural History Museum), was compounded by his wife's illness and her death in 1818 as well as his own poor health and failing eyesight.

In 1823 Caley settled at 5 Upper Moscow Cottages, Bayswater, London, with his stepdaughter, Sally Wise. In London, Caley spent the remainder of his life building up a library and reading his books, free from the quarrels that so marked his career. He died at his Bayswater home on 23 May 1829 after a painful illness and was buried at St George's Fields, off the Bayswater Road, a burial-ground belonging to St George's, Hanover Square, London. Judged harshly by many, Caley was always appreciated by his patron Banks, although even he admitted in a letter to Philip Gidley King of 29 August 1804, that, had Caley 'been born a Gentleman, he would have been shot long ago in a Duel' (Dawson Turner correspondence, 15, 73–8, Botany Library, Natural History Museum). ANNE SECORD

Sources J. B. Webb, *George Caley: nineteenth century naturalist* (1995) • *Magazine of Natural History*, 2 (1829), 310–12 • W. Withering, 'Further notice of the late Mr George Carey', *Magazine of Natural History*, 3 (1830), 226–32 • J. E. B. Currey, ed., *Reflections on the colony of New South Wales: George Caley* (1966) • A. Secord, 'Science in the pub: artisan botanists in early nineteenth-century Lancashire', *History of Science*, 32 (1994), 269–315 • A. Secord, 'Corresponding interests: artisans and gentlemen in nineteenth-century natural history', *British Journal for the History of Science*, 27 (1994), 383–408 • H. B. Carter, *Sir Joseph Banks, 1743–1820* (1988), 358–60, 436–8 • J. Cash, *Where there's a will there's a way! or, Science in the cottage* (1873), 21–40

Archives NHM, botanical notebooks, journals of tours in New South Wales • RBG Kew • UCL, travel diary | BL, Robert Brown corresp. • Mitchell L., NSW, Banks MSS • NHM, letters to Joseph Banks • NHM, Robert Brown corresp.

Wealth at death approx. £1480; plus some 'residue' sufficient to be shared by his four brothers: will, Webb, *George Caley*, 159

Caley, John (*bap.* **1760**, *d.* **1834**), antiquary, baptized at St Botolph without Bishopsgate, London, on 27 April 1760, was the eldest son of John Caley, a grocer in Bishopsgate Street, and his wife, Margaret. From an early age he was a keen antiquarian, and in the pursuit of his interests, met

Thomas Astle, keeper of the records, by whose influence he was placed in the record office in the Tower. Here he quickly became known as a skilful decipherer of early manuscripts, and his promotion was rapid. In 1787 he received from Lord William Bentinck, as clerk of the pipe, the keepership of the records in the augmentation office; and in 1818, on the death of George Rose, he was appointed keeper of the records in the ancient treasury at Westminster, formerly the chapter house of the abbey. Meanwhile he had entered himself at Gray's Inn, on 11 January 1786, but he never proceeded to the bar. When the first record commission was nominated in 1801, Caley was appointed secretary, an office which he continued to hold until the dissolution of the commission in March 1831. A special office, that of subcommissioner, to superintend the arranging, repairing, and binding of records, was subsequently created for him, for which he received a salary of £500 a year, in addition to retaining his two lucrative keeperships.

To Caley's influence were attributed many of the scandals which brought the commission into such ill repute. Much was left to his discretion, a situation which he turned to his own benefit. Sir Henry Cole, William Illingworth, and others testified that, owing to Caley's systematic neglect of duty, records were poorly arranged and bound, with frequent errors in lettering and dates. His binding of the Domesday Book in 1819 has been justifiably criticized for its tightness. He also removed valuable seals from many conventual leases, cartae antiquae, and Scottish records, ostensibly to arrange the documents in volumes, but actually in order to copy them and take casts to add to his collection at his house in Spa Fields, Clerkenwell. Here he also stored, greatly to their injury, many of the important manuscripts entrusted to him. Applicants for historical documents had to apply at Caley's house, to which papers were brought in bags by his footman. The length of time before the right document was produced, and the cost of searches, were arbitrary. Caley entirely excluded the public from the record offices themselves, the contents of which were kept in a state of disorder, the only clue to them being the indexes in Caley's own house. No access was allowed to the indexes, nor to any records except those sent to Spa Fields for examination.

As a subcommissioner Caley became a joint editor of fourteen of the works undertaken by the commission. He also printed, at the request of Thomas Burgess, the bishop of the diocese, several copies of the *Ecclesiastical Survey of the Possessions, &c., of the Bishop of St. David's* (1812). In the following year, 1813, he agreed, in conjunction with Bulkeley Bandinel and Sir Henry Ellis, to prepare a new edition of Dugdale's *Monasticon* (6 vols., 1817–30), but he did little more than supply documents. Caley was elected a fellow of the Society of Antiquaries of London in March 1786, and contributed several papers to *Archaeologia*, notably 'On the origin of the Jews in England'. He was also a fellow of the Royal and Linnean societies, and a member of the Society of Arts.

Caley died at his house in Exmouth Street, Spa Fields, on 28 April 1834. His library, rich in topography and collections of reports and searches made by him as a legal antiquary during a period of fifty years, was sold by Evans on 22 July 1834; thirty-nine lots were purchased by Sir Thomas Phillipps. His large collection of drawings and impressions of seals was offered for sale by Thomas Thorpe the same year. Several of his manuscripts were acquired much later by the British Museum.

GORDON GOODWIN, *rev.* BERNARD NURSE

Sources *GM*, 1st ser., 57 (1787), 1033 · *GM*, 1st ser., 88/1 (1818), 367 · *GM*, 2nd ser., 2 (1834), 320–21 · J. D. Cantwell, *The Public Record Office, 1838–1958* (1991) · 'Select committee on … the record commission: minutes of evidence and appendix', *Parl. papers* (1836), vol. 16, no. 429 · J. Foster, *The register of admissions to Gray's Inn, 1521–1889, together with the register of marriages in Gray's Inn chapel, 1695–1754* (privately printed, London, 1889) · *N&Q*, 8 (1853), 104 · *N&Q*, 2nd ser., 11 (1861), 233–4 · Nichols, *Illustrations*, vol. 8 · baptism register, GL, MS 4517/2 · T. Thorpe, *Catalogue of beautiful drawings of ancient seals* (c.1834) · T. Thorpe, *Catalogue … of fifteen hundred impressions from ancient seals … collected by the late J. Caley* (1834) [copy in V&A NAL]

Archives Bath Central Library, MS collections relating to Somerset · Birm. CL, legal cases; papers; reports; searches · BL, indexes; notes; official corresp.; papers, Add. MSS 21316–21328, 21344–21345, 24692, 24711, 24723–24734, 35335, 44938; Add. Ch 70861 · BL, letters and reports relating to Derbyshire tithes, Add. MSS 6673–6675, *passim* · Bodl. Oxf., collections for a feudal history of Buckinghamshire; corresp. and notes relating to the feudal history of Oxfordshire; index of inquisitions post mortem for Buckinghamshire, temp Henry III–Edward IV; index of places mentioned in Harley MSS · Cardiff Central Library, collections relating to Welsh and English counties; index to public records and calendar of chantry certificates · CUL, indexes to Cambridgeshire documents in augmentation office; papers · Devon RO, corresp. and reports relating to endowments, tithes, etc., in Devon · Essex RO, Chelmsford, extracts from records in the Tower · JRL, indexes to grants in augmentation office · Leics. RO, collections for a feudal history of Leicestershire · Man. CL, Manchester Archives and Local Studies, place name index to duchy of Lancaster fee farm rolls, etc. · Norfolk RO, lists and indexes to public records relating to confiscation of land at Reformation · Suffolk RO, Ipswich, feudal collections relating to Suffolk · Tyne and Wear Archive Service, Newcastle upon Tyne, tithe papers for Northumberland | BL, corresp. with Sir Henry Ellis, Add. MS 6363 · BL, corresp. with Lord Redesdale, Add. MS 36650 · Bodl. Oxf., letters to Sir Thomas Phillipps · NL Scot., calendar of records in Westminster chapter house, presented by William Illingworth

Calfhill, James (1529/30–1570), Church of England clergyman, was born in Edinburgh. Nothing is known of his parentage, but he reminded Sir William Cecil that he was cousin to Toby Matthew, future archbishop of York, whom he had persuaded to take orders despite his parents' opposition. He also described himself as 'brought up in Eton for five years together and thence removed, as many other Cambridge men, to the King's new erection in Oxford' (Lansdowne MS 12, fol. 88*r*). A student of Christ Church from 1548, he supplicated for his BA in early 1549 and for his MA in early 1552. That year he contributed a Latin poem to the volume mourning the deaths of the boy-dukes of Suffolk, Henry and Charles Brandon, and is perhaps more likely than Nicholas Kervile to have been the 'Master Cavyll' to whom verse-legends in *The Mirror for Magistrates*, written during Edward VI's reign and published in 1559, have been attributed.

Not known to have gone abroad during Mary I's reign, Calfhill may have lived quietly in West Horsley, Surrey. After Princess Elizabeth's release from the Tower in May 1554, but before her enforced removal to Woodstock, he contrived a meeting with her at Hanworth, Middlesex, during which he pledged his loyalty. Later that year he wrote Latin verses in response to those composed by John White, bishop of Lincoln, celebrating Queen Mary's marriage. Thereafter he translated the Wisdom of Solomon into Latin verse as *Sapientiae Solomonis liber carmine redditus*. Its dedication to Elizabeth, dated at Horsley (*Horsleae*) on 16 April (15 *Kal. Maii*) 1559, records the details of their meeting at Hanworth. The holograph survives in the Royal Collection (BL, Royal MS 2 D ii).

Calfhill was ordained deacon by Edmund Grindal, bishop of London, on 13 January 1560, giving his age as thirty, and priest on the following 19 June. Thereafter his rise was among the most meteoric of the first Elizabethan decade. Having returned to Christ Church as one of the leaders of the reforming party in Oxford, he was granted letters patent as canon of the second prebend on 25 July 1560, and was also appointed subdean. On 11 January 1561, probably at his instigation, the chapter solemnly reburied the remains of Peter Martyr's widow, Catherine (*d.* 1553), whose body had been disinterred on the orders of Cardinal Pole. Calfhill composed for the occasion *De Katherinae nuper uxoris D. Petri Martyris effossae exhumatione*, printed by John Day with the subtitle 'Carmina, cum praefatione'. This act of homage 'symbolized, perhaps, the reinstatement of the university's link with the continental reformed churches' (Dent, 32).

Preaching at Paul's Cross a few days later Calfhill lamented the decayed state of the university, 'yet under the papistical yoke'. John Foxe's admiring correspondent recorded that his eloquence 'moved a number of tears' (BL, Harleian MS 416, fol. 176*v*). That same month, with Laurence Humphrey and twenty others, Calfhill petitioned Lord Robert Dudley to persuade Elizabeth to bestow the deanery of Christ Church on Thomas Sampson rather than upon Francis Babington. After Sampson's installation in September the chapter assented to the destruction of all images remaining in the cathedral.

The sermon (*concio*) which, in preparation for the degree of BD, Calfhill delivered on 1 December 1561 on the text 'Let a man so account of us as of the ministers of Christ and stewards of the mysteries of God' (1 Corinthians 13: 1) is preserved at Corpus Christi College, Oxford (MS 257). He proceeded BD eleven days later and thereafter found rapid promotion within the diocese of London. Bishop Grindal collated him rector of the city parish of St Andrew by the Wardrobe on 16 May 1562. On 4 October following he was instituted prebendary of Pancratius in St Paul's, which carried with it the office of penitentiary. The appointment was made at Elizabeth's prerogative since his predecessor, William Alley, had been elevated to the bishopric of Exeter.

Calfhill's radicalism was expressed forcibly in the convocation of 1562–3, where he had the disposal of three votes as proctor for the Oxford chapter, for the clergy of Oxford diocese, and for the clergy of London. He was one of thirty-four members who put their names to seven articles aimed at the drastic curtailment of the ceremonies and vestments prescribed by the 1559 prayer book. Six more moderate articles were debated instead, Calfhill casting his three votes in favour of them, but when other proxy votes were counted their adoption was rejected by a majority of one.

On 18 February 1564 Calfhill succeeded Francis Babington as Oxford's Lady Margaret professor of divinity. In July 1564 Walter Haddon informed Archbishop Matthew Parker, without disclosing the subject matter, that a sermon he had preached before the queen had caused great offence. It may have played its part in launching the vestiarian controversy of the following two years, essentially the product of Parker's mounting hostility towards the Oxford leaders and their resistance to the ceremonies. On 20 March 1565 Sampson, Humphrey, and Calfhill were among twenty leading hierarchs who respectfully requested Parker and the ecclesiastical commissioners not to press them to wear the prescribed vestments.

That year Calfhill published his only work in English, *An Aunswere to the 'Treatise of the Crosse'* (by John Martial), in which he argued that ceremonies which had no scriptural authority should be severely restricted. Yet on 16 July 1565 Grindal collated Calfhill archdeacon of Colchester, while on the following 4 August Parker collated him to one of his Essex peculiars, the rectory of Bocking. Thus there may be truth in the tradition that, far from being as offended as Haddon by his court sermon of 1564, Elizabeth expressly requested his promotion. Perhaps she never forgot their fugitive meeting at Hanworth in 1554.

Despite the fact that Parker was moving towards confrontation with the clergy of the city of London, Calfhill preached against the vestments at Paul's Cross as late as 10 February 1566, asserting that the church should ultimately be tried by the scriptures, 'and not the scriptures by the church' (Bodl. Oxf., MS Tanner 50, fol. 41*v*). Eight days later he proceeded DTh at Oxford.

On 26 March Parker summoned the London city clergy to Lambeth and suspended thirty-seven who refused the canonical vestments. It has been assumed that since Calfhill retained his city living and his prebend he must have conformed, but it is more likely that as archdeacon of Colchester he was discreetly excused attendance, or else was not penalized for his refusal. In May 1566, with the bailiffs, justices, and aldermen, he presided over a tribunal for the punishment of fornication 'unique in Colchester's history' (Byford, 165): never before had the borough authorities and the archdeacon acted jointly to promote the reformation of morals. Altogether the borough court books suggest that the bailiffs and the archdeacon's court worked closely together during Calfhill's tenure.

Back in Oxford by the late summer of 1566, Calfhill was one of those who organized Elizabeth's official visit to the university, writing congratulatory Latin verses to Sir William Cecil and a (lost) Latin tragedy, *Progne*, which was performed before the queen on 7 September. He again served as subdean of Christ Church in 1567–8. In the latter year he preached in Bristol Cathedral what Bishop Richard Cheyney of Gloucester (who held Bristol *in commendam*) called 'two sermons or rather invectives', parading his trenchant Calvinism, deriding the bishop's old-fashioned 'free will' views, and refusing to communicate or dine with Cheyney afterwards (SP 12/48/11).

On 24 January 1569 Calfhill was instituted to the rectory of West Horsley on the presentation of Edward, Lord Clinton. Coming to court at Leicester's bidding later that year on behalf of Toby Matthew, Calfhill applied to Cecil for the provostship of King's College, Cambridge. That post had already been earmarked for Roger Goad, but in the summer of 1570 Calfhill was selected for the bishopric of Worcester in succession to Edwin Sandys, resigning his prebend at Christ Church by 19 July. No *congé d'élire* was ever issued for his election since, scarcely forty, he died suddenly at the rectory, Bocking, Essex. Letters of administration for his estate were granted on 21 August to his widow, Margaret. He was buried at Bocking the next day.

The legend that Calfhill was dean of Bocking, the archbishop of Canterbury's commissary in Essex and Suffolk, derives from Anthony Wood's memoir in which, unaware of the distinction between the two offices, he described Calfhill as 'dean or rector'. The dean of Bocking from about 1560 until his death in 1571 was Thomas Cole, archdeacon of Essex. BRETT USHER

Sources Wood, *Ath. Oxon.*, new edn, 1.377–80 • Cooper, *Ath. Cantab.*, 1.285–7 • Venn, *Alum. Cant.*, 1/1.282 • Foster, *Alum. Oxon.* • C. M. Dent, *Protestant reformers in Elizabethan Oxford* (1983) • M. Byford, 'The price of protestantism: assessing the impact of religious change on Elizabethan Essex: the cases of Heydon and Colchester, 1558–1594', DPhil diss., U. Oxf., 1988 • J. Nichols, *The progresses and public processions of Queen Elizabeth*, new edn, 3 vols. (1823) • *Correspondence of Matthew Parker*, ed. J. Bruce and T. T. Perowne, Parker Society, 42 (1853) • register of Edmund Grindal, GL, MS 9531/13 • *Registrum Matthei Parker, diocesis Cantuariensis*, AD 1559–1575, ed. W. H. Frere and E. M. Thompson, 3 vols., CYS, 35–6, 39 (1928–33) [correcting dates for rectory of Bocking found in Richard Newcourt, *Repertorium* (1708–10)] • GL, MS 9535/1, fols. 84*r*, 92*r* [ordination] • BL, Lansdowne MS 12, fol. 88*r* • BL, Harleian MS 416, fol. 176*v* • Bodl. Oxf., MS Tanner 50, fol. 41*v* • state papers domestic, Elizabeth I, PRO, SP 12/48/11

Archives Essex RO, Chelmsford, records of archdeaconry of Colchester, series D/ACV, D/ACA, etc.

Calgacus [Galgacus] (*fl.* c.AD 83/4), chieftain in Caledonia, was the British war leader whom Tacitus represents as exhorting the confederate host which opposed a Roman army under Cn. Julius Agricola at the battle of 'Mons Graupius'. The site of this conflict, in which upwards of (reportedly) 30,000 native troops united to defend Caledonia (that is, eastern Scotland north of the Forth–Clyde isthmus), only to be routed by a numerically inferior force, has yet to be identified with certainty; but it is unlikely to lie further south than the north-east end of Strathmore, and could possibly adjoin the distinctively peaked massif of Bennachie, between the rivers Don and Urie in Aberdeenshire, on the line of march indicated by a series of large temporary camps datable to the late first century. The place name 'Graupius' (the best reading in Tacitus, *Agricola*, 29) may be derived from Celtic *Craup*, related to modern Welsh *crwb*, 'a hump', but whether such a term is appropriate to Bennachie is debatable. The battle, which formed the decisive climax of Agricola's governorship (AD 77/8–83/4), appears to have broken resistance to Rome in the north for almost two decades, inaugurating a military occupation of most of what is now lowland Scotland whose effectiveness, until early in the next century, was constricted only by the availability of manpower.

Calgacus is the earliest of only four named personages to figure in the history of Roman Scotland, and significantly, like the others, he bore a recognizably Celtic name, the equivalent of Calgaich, meaning 'swordsman' or 'swordbearer'—an element occasionally found in Irish Gaelic place names. Whether this represents a personal name, or a title, cannot be determined, but, for the leader of warriors whose main strength lay in their skill at wielding the long slashing swords of which Tacitus writes, either would have been highly appropriate. Unfortunately, these weapons were no more effective against the short stabbing-swords of their Roman opponents than the claymores of Jacobite clansmen were against Hanoverian bayonets and musket-fire at the comparably decisive battle of Culloden.

Of Calgacus's status no more is known than that of all the chieftains (*duces*) present at the battle, he was 'the foremost in courage and the noblest in birth' (Tacitus, 29), but the words put into his mouth by Tacitus identify him as supreme commander. Beyond that, his pre-battle speech largely reflects sentiments moulded in contemporary schools of rhetoric in Rome: similar expressions of defiance and condemnation of the *pax Romana* are attributed by Julius Caesar to Critognatus at Alesia in 52 BC, and by Tacitus to the German leader Arminius in AD 16. Calgacus, of whom no more is heard, may have fallen, with many of his followers, on the field of battle. G. S. MAXWELL

Sources Tacitus, *De vita Agricolae*, ed. R. M. Ogilvie and I. Richmond (1967) • W. S. Hanson, *Agricola and the conquest of the north* (1987) • G. S. Maxwell, *A battle lost: Romans and Caledonians at 'Mons Graupius'* (1990) • R. G. Collingwood and R. P. Wright, eds., *The Roman inscriptions of Britain*, 1 (1965) • A. L. F. Rivet and C. Smith, *The place names of Roman Britain* (1979)

Calhoun, Patrick (1727–1796), politician and landowner in America, was born in Donegal into a family of Scottish origin. He emigrated to Pennsylvania with his family in 1733, and several years later they moved to the western part of Virginia about 15 miles from the North Carolina line. After the defeat of Major-General Edward Braddock near Fort Duquesne, this settlement was broken up by the American Indians and, on Calhoun's advice, the family moved to the district of the sixty nine on the frontier of south-western South Carolina. Further fighting between the settlers and the Cherokee, on whose land they encroached, resulted in a number of deaths among Calhoun's family, including that of his mother, Catherine Montgomery Calhoun, in 1760. Many settlers, among them Calhoun, left the region as a result of the Cherokee attacks. On the conclusion of peace in 1763 he and others returned.

Calhoun was then appointed to command the regulator

movement, a body of rangers for the defence of the frontiers, in which he displayed great intrepidity and skill. He was the first member of the provincial congress elected from the upper county of the state, and campaigned for fairer representation of this region in the colony's government. In 1791 he was elected to the state senate, of which, with the intermission of a single term, he remained a member until his death.

In 1770 Calhoun married Martha Caldwell, also of Scots-Irish descent and then resident in Charlotte county, Virginia. The couple had three children, one of whom, John Caldwell Calhoun, became vice-president of the United States. During the American War of Independence Patrick Calhoun was an active supporter of the revolutionary cause, yet his avoidance of bitter factional politics meant that he was spared the hardships endured by other family members. At the conclusion of the war Calhoun was one of the wealthiest farmers, as well as one of the first slave owners in the up-country region. He died in 1796.

T. F. Henderson, *rev.* Philip Carter

Sources W. Allen, *An American biographical and historical dictionary*, 2nd edn (1832) • J. Niven, 'Calhoun, John Caldwell', *ANB* • J. Niven, *John C. Calhoun and the price of union* (1988) • I. H. Bartlett, *John C. Calhoun* (1993)
Likenesses portrait, repro. in Bartlett, *John C. Calhoun*, 29

Calico Jack. *See* Rackam, John (*d.* 1720).

Calkin, James (1786–1862), organist and music teacher, the son of Joseph and Mary Calkin, was born in London on 19 September 1786. He attended Dr Burrow's school in Soho Square, learned to play the violin under his brother Joseph (1781–1846), a violinist and cellist who was taught by Thomas Lyon and Paolo Spagnoletti, and later studied under Lyon and William Crotch. In 1823 he became one of the earliest members and directors of the Philharmonic Society, and in the same year his string quartet, dedicated to and played by Nicholas Mori, was performed at the British Concerts. On the consecration of the Regent Square Church, Gray's Inn Road, Calkin was appointed organist, a post he held for thirty years. In 1846 his madrigal 'When Chloris weeps' gained a prize from the Western Madrigal Society. His long, uneventful life was devoted almost entirely to teaching, in which he acquired a considerable reputation as a successful master, particularly as a professor at the London Academy of Music. He also taught his younger brother William (1791–1849), who became the organist of the parish church at Arundel, Sussex, and was appointed organist for the county of Sussex by the duke of Richmond. Besides teaching, Calkin played the cello at the Philharmonic Society's concerts, at the Royal Italian Opera, and at leading provincial festivals. His compositions comprise an overture and symphony for orchestra, string quartets, a large quantity of piano music, and sixteen books of organ voluntaries. His organ transcriptions from the works of Mendelssohn were much admired.

Calkin died at 12 Oakley Square, Camden Town, London, on 18 January 1862. He was survived by four sons, all of whom were musicians. James Joseph Calkin (1813–1868) became a violinist; Joseph Calkin (1816–1874) was a tenor who sang under the name of Tennielli; John Baptiste *Calkin (1827–1905), an organist and composer, was the best known; and George Calkin (1829–1911) was a cellist and organist.

Nilanjana Banerji

Sources *New Grove* • Brown & Stratton, *Brit. mus.* • D. Baptie, *A handbook of musical biography* (1883) • *Musical Directory*

Calkin, John Baptiste (1827–1905), organist and composer, born in London on 16 March 1827, was the third son of the organist and teacher James *Calkin (1786–1862). Reared in a musical atmosphere, he studied under his father, and when aged only nineteen was appointed organist, precentor, and choirmaster of St Columba's College, Rathfarnham, near Dublin, in succession to Edwin George Monk. St Columba's College was a school mainly for the boys of the upper classes and for candidates for the ministry of the Anglican church; music and the Irish language were prominent features in the curriculum. From 1846 to 1853 Calkin zealously maintained a high standard of choral music at St Columba's and began exploring his own powers of composition. From 1853 to 1863 he was organist and choirmaster of Woburn Chapel, London; from 1863 to 1868 organist of Camden Road Chapel; and from 1870 to 1884 organist at St Thomas's Church, Elm Road, Camden Town. In 1883 he became professor at the Guildhall School of Music under Thomas Henry Weist-Hill, and subsequently devoted himself to teaching and composing. He was on the council of Trinity College, London, a member of the Philharmonic Society (1862), and a fellow of the Royal College of Organists, incorporated in 1893.

As a composer, Calkin tried his hand at many forms, but his sacred music is best known, especially his morning and evening services in B♭, G, and D, his Te Deum in D, and a Magnificat in F. He wrote various pieces for the organ, including numerous transcriptions, and he scored many string arrangements. Many of his anthems and hymn tunes gained an enduring popularity, while his setting of 'Fling out the Banner' (by Bishop G. W. Doane) became well known in America and the colonies, and was included in the Canadian *Book of Common Praise*, edited by Sir George Martin in 1909. His 'Agape' was composed specially for the *Church Hymnary* of Scotland in 1871, to the words 'Jesu, most loving God', and was inserted in the *Church Hymnal* of Ireland in 1874.

Calkin died at 37 Hornsey Rise Gardens, Crouch End, London, on 15 April 1905, and was buried in Highgate cemetery.

W. H. G. Flood, *rev.* Nilanjana Banerji

Sources Brown & Stratton, *Brit. mus.* • *New Grove* • W. Cowan and J. Love, *The music of the church hymnary and the psalter in metre* (1901) • *MT*, 46 (1905), 317
Wealth at death £479 3*s.* 2*d.*: probate, 4 May 1905, *CGPLA Eng. & Wales*

Call, Sir John, first baronet (1732–1801), East India Company servant and military engineer, was born on 30 June 1732 at Fenny Park, near Tiverton, Devon, the son of John Call (1704–1766) of Prestacott in Launcells, Cornwall, and his wife, Jane, daughter of John Mill of Shernick Farm in Launcells. He was educated in Tiverton and also Somerton, Somerset, and then left England for India. In 1751 he was employed on the coast of Coromandel as an assistant to Benjamin Robins, the mathematician who had been appointed engineer-general of the East India Company's settlements. Call, who had the rank of writer, remained on the coast after Robins died in July 1751, and held the post of sub-engineer at Fort St David. The rivalry between the French under Dupleix and the British led by Clive gave Call the opportunity to display his skills as a military engineer, and the directors of the company were impressed by accounts of his abilities. A friend described him to the historian Robert Orme as 'a very worthy as well as very ingenious young man; possessing much knowledge, adorned with great modesty' (Hill, 235). He remained at Fort St David, becoming assistant engineer to the presidency, which was based at Fort St George, Madras.

In 1757 Call was appointed chief engineer to the presidency and consequently moved to Fort St George. He also became captain of the newly formed corps of engineers. The Seven Years' War revived the Anglo-French struggle in southern India. Once again Call's skills were put to the test, notably during the French siege of Fort St George between 1758 and 1759, which ended in success for the British. He also took part in the siege of Karikal which ended in April 1760 and that of Pondicherry, which fell in January 1761, marking the end of French power in India. Call kept journals of the operations he was involved in, and copies were made by Orme, who described the events in his *History of the Military Transactions of the British Nation in Indostan* (2 vols., 1763), which included prints of drawings by Call.

By 1765 Call was a member of the council at Fort St George, and in that year was appointed to the rank of colonel. The war against Haidar Ali of Mysore between 1767 and 1769 and the conduct of company servants at Madras provoked criticism and blame from the directors and others from which Call himself was not immune. In common with others he had made loans to the nawab of Arcot. In January 1770 Call resigned from the company's service and returned to England, 'bringing with him an ample fortune, which might have been much larger' (*GM*, 369).

In England Call, in common with other nabobs, acquired an estate. Soon after his arrival he made purchases at Whiteford, near Callington, in Cornwall, and his presence in the county was underlined by his serving as high sheriff between 1771 and 1772. Callington returned two MPs, but Call's interest was not sufficient at first to give him significant influence there and it was not until 1784 that he was elected for the borough. Call, who also acted on behalf of another nabob, Paul Benfield, in the electoral affairs of Shaftesbury, in Dorset, remained an MP until his death and supported William Pitt. There is no record of his having spoken in the House of Commons until 1792 and he apparently made only a few contributions thereafter. He acted as an agent for the creditors of the nawab of Arcot and played a prominent role in negotiating a favourable settlement for them with Pitt's administration in 1784. In addition to these activities he began an investigation into crown lands in 1782 and served as one of the commissioners appointed by act of parliament in 1786 to inquire into the management of the woods, forests, and land revenues of the crown. Between 1787 and 1793 the commissioners produced seventeen reports and one special report to the House of Lords. Call was also treasurer for the board of agriculture, which presented him with a medal, between 1794 and 1800 and he produced an abstract of births and burials for that board in 1800. On 28 July 1791 he was created a baronet.

Call maintained an interest in Indian affairs following his return to England, but also developed views on other subjects, such as the transportation of criminals and trading opportunities. These he communicated to the government. He designed a prison for Cornwall which was built at Bodmin, had interests in copper smelting and plate glass manufacture, and founded in 1785 the banking firm of Pybus's, Call, Grant & Co. His intellectual pursuits were reflected in his election to fellowships of the Royal Society and the Society of Antiquaries in 1775 and 1785 respectively. The latter were informed in 1785 that he possessed some drawings of Indian deities on the island of Elephanta. Call had married Philadelphia Batty (*d.* 1822), third daughter and coheir of William Batty MD, on 28 March 1772 and had two sons and four daughters. Blind towards the end of his life, he died of apoplexy on 7 March 1801 at his home in Old Burlington Street, London, and was buried at Lee in Kent one week later. D. L. PRIOR

Sources East India Company records, BL OIOC · BL OIOC, MS Eur. Orme · BL, Warren Hastings MSS · BL, Arthur Young MSS · *Reports of commissioners appointed to enquire into the management of the woods, forests and land revenues of the crown* (1787–93) · HoP, *Commons, 1754–90* · HoP, *Commons, 1790–1820* · S. C. Hill, ed., *Catalogue of manuscripts in European languages belonging to the library of the India Office*, 2/1: *The Orme collection* (1916) · J. M. Holzman, *The nabobs in England* (1926) · *GM*, 1st ser., 71 (1801), 282, 369 · *A complete parochial history of the county of Cornwall*, 4 vols. (1867–72) · F. H. Hart, *History of Lee and its neighbourhood* (1882) · Burke, *Peerage* (1889) · GEC, *Baronetage*

Archives BL OIOC, letters to Paul Benfield and Nathaniel Wraxall, MS Eur. C 307 · BL OIOC, Clive MSS · BL OIOC, corresp. and journals, MSS Eur. Orme · BL OIOC, narrative of French attack, MS Eur. E 1 [copy] · BL OIOC, Home misc. Series, corresp. and papers relating to India · NRA, priv. coll., letters to Lord Shelburne · PRO, letters to William Pitt, PRO 30/8

Likenesses oils, Royal Engineers, Chatham, Kent

Callaghan, Sir George Astley (1852–1920), naval officer, was born in London on 21 December 1852, the third son of Captain Frederic Marcus Callaghan JP, of Lotabeg, co. Cork, and his wife, Georgina Frances, daughter of Captain James Hodgson, of the East India Company. He entered the Royal Navy in January 1866 on the *Britannia*, and was promoted sub-lieutenant in April 1872, lieutenant in 1875. His first appointment as lieutenant was to the *Ruby*, East India station. During this commission one of the ship's boats capsized in the Irrawady, and Callaghan earned Admiralty commendation by his gallant conduct, which saved the lives of several of the crew. He married in 1876

Sir George Astley Callaghan (1852–1920), by Walter Stoneman, 1918

Edith Saumarez, daughter of the Revd Frederick Grosvenor, rector of Dunkerton, Bath. They had one son and three daughters.

In 1880 Callaghan returned to Britain to qualify in gunnery, and was afterwards on the staff of the port gunnery schools. In 1885 he was again appointed to the *Ruby*, this time as first and gunnery lieutenant on the South American station. He was promoted commander in 1887, and in 1888 was appointed to the *Bellerophon*, the North American station flagship, in which he returned home in 1892. That year he was given the command of the *Alacrity*, yacht of the commander-in-chief, China station, and he was promoted captain in 1894.

From then on Callaghan's rise was rapid. He served for three years (1894–7) as naval adviser to the inspector-general of fortifications at the War Office. In July 1897 he took command of the *Hermione*, first in the channel squadron and later on the China station, where he remained until 1901, having been given command of the *Endymion*, a first-class cruiser, in 1899. The Boxer uprising broke that year. Admiral Sir Edward Hobart Seymour was then commander-in-chief on the China station; and, on the decision of the powers to intervene, brigades were landed from various ships to relieve the legations in Peking (Beijing). This was found impracticable with the small force available, and Seymour returned to Tientsin (Tianjin). The following month a combined naval and military relief force was formed under Lieutenant-General Sir Alfred Gaselee. Callaghan was given the command of the British naval brigade which, after severe fighting and much hardship from the heat, succeeded in entering Peking in time to relieve the legations. He was mentioned in dispatches and received the CB (1900).

After commanding the *Edgar* in manoeuvres as senior officer of the cruisers, Callaghan was appointed to the *Caesar*, first-class battleship, on the Mediterranean station, at the time when Sir John Fisher was commander-in-chief. He returned in 1903 to be captain of Portsmouth Dockyard. This shore service lasted only one year, as, by his own request, he was sent again to sea so that his last year as captain should be spent in familiarizing himself with the most recent developments in the fleet. He commanded the *Prince of Wales* in the Mediterranean during 1904–5 and was at this time also made aide-de-camp to the king.

In July 1905 Callaghan was promoted rear-admiral, and hoisted his flag in the *Illustrious* as rear-admiral in the Channel Fleet in 1906. From then he was in uninterrupted command afloat for eight years. The years immediately preceding the First World War were a time of strenuous activity in the navy. Fisher was carrying out his reforms and redistributions, shifting the centre of power from the Mediterranean, and forming new fleets in home waters. Callaghan was to play an important part in these schemes from the outset. In 1907 he was given the command of the new 5th cruiser squadron, the 'tip of the spear' as it was designated, hoisting his flag in the *Leviathan*, and afterwards transferring it to the newly built *Shannon*. Having spent eighteen strenuous months in bringing his squadron up to high efficiency, Callaghan hoisted his flag in the *Duncan* as second in command of the Mediterranean station (1908). During this command he was created KCVO (1909) and was also made grand officer of the Crown of Italy for his services in connection with the Messina earthquake. He became vice-admiral in 1910 and, on returning to home waters, immediately hoisted his flag in the *King Edward VII*, commanding the 2nd division of the Home Fleet. The next year he was made commander-in-chief, Home Fleets, with the acting rank of admiral. He retained this great command, of the largest naval fighting force which, up to that time, had ever acted under one flag, during the three years of incessant preparation for war, his appointment being extended in December 1913 for the further period of one year. Recognizing the impossibility of controlling such a large fleet by signals from his flagship Callaghan began to decentralize the command of his fleet, giving permission to his squadron commanders to act within general instructions. He was awarded the GCVO after the inspection of the fleet by King George V at Weymouth in 1912, and the grand cordon of the Légion d'honneur on President Poincaré's official visit to the fleet in 1913.

In July 1914 Callaghan was in command of the mobilized naval forces at Portsmouth on the occasion of another royal inspection, when 460 ships assembled under his flag. This great fleet was about to disperse when the European situation became critical. Callaghan was summoned to the Admiralty, while the fleet meanwhile left for Scapa Flow. At the Admiralty the disposition of the fleet and the plan of operations in the event of war were discussed with him. Sir John Rushworth (later Earl) Jellicoe had already been appointed to succeed Callaghan in December, when the latter's extension of command would be completed, and Callaghan welcomed the intimation that Sir John should immediately act as his second in command. But, after Callaghan had gone north, Winston Churchill and Prince Louis of Battenberg, the first sea lord, decided that, if war broke out, Jellicoe should at once take over the supreme command; they doubted that Callaghan's physical strength would stand the immense strain. Although he was sixty-two, however, he had shown no signs of ill health, unlike Jellicoe. Even if Jellicoe were the better man, the removal of so experienced and able an officer at the outbreak of war was an unnecessary risk. He should, in all conscience, have been left in command for the remainder of his term, saving Jellicoe much anxiety, and completing his education in fleet command. However, when Jellicoe left London for the fleet at Scapa Flow, he was given sealed instructions directing him to take over the command. Soon after midnight on 3–4 August, when war was certain, telegrams were sent to both admirals informing them of the decisions and instructing Callaghan to haul down his flag and hand over the command. Much sympathy was felt throughout the fleet for Callaghan, and protests were made by all the principal admirals who had served under him, and by Jellicoe himself. This last reflected a friendship of long standing, and mutual respect. Callaghan was loved by all who served under him. It was a bitter disappointment to Callaghan not to command in war the fleet to which he had devoted his energies and abilities for so long, and his departure saddened all those under his command. Although it was not his fortune to wield the weapon which he had brought to so fine an edge, he could at least lay it down knowing it was ready and in place to meet and repulse any enemy attack. Callaghan was immediately appointed for special service at the Admiralty and also first and principal naval aide-de-camp to the king. This was followed on 1 January 1915 by his appointment as commander-in-chief at the Nore, a post which he held until March 1918. He received the GCB in 1916, and in April 1917 he was promoted admiral of the fleet and flew his flag as such for one year, a unique record.

When Callaghan hauled down his flag in March 1918, he had completed fifty-two years' service, of which only eleven had been spent in shore posts, and for the last twelve years he had kept his flag flying continuously, except for the few months at the beginning of the war. He was essentially a sea officer, with a remarkable knowledge, formed by continual and exceptional experience, of tactics and gunnery, and of cruiser and destroyer operations. His appreciation of new technology was very much of an 'empirical' nature. His fairness, judgement, common sense, equable temperament, modesty, and charm of manner, apart from his great fleet knowledge, rendered him a fine commander-in-chief. His successor in command of the Grand Fleet, Jellicoe, on many public occasions testified to the efficient state of the fleet when Callaghan was so abruptly replaced. After his naval service was ended, Callaghan was in 1919 appointed by the king Bath king of arms, and he officiated at the historic chapter of the Order of the Bath held in Westminster Abbey in the spring of 1920.

Callaghan died at 11 Cadogan Court, Chelsea, on 23 November 1920 at the age of sixty-eight, and had a public funeral in Westminster Abbey. He was survived by his wife. Considered by all his contemporaries to be an outstanding fleet commander, Callaghan had a very human side that earned the love and loyalty of all those who served under him. He was an officer of high accomplishment in all branches of the service. He was able to rise above the jealousies and feuds of the Fisher era to play a vital role in building the fleet up to wartime efficiency. His supersession at the outbreak of war in 1914 denied him the opportunity to achieve greatness.

V. W. Baddeley, *rev.* Andrew Lambert

Sources A. J. Marder, *From the Dreadnought to Scapa Flow: the Royal Navy in the Fisher era, 1904–1919*, 5 vols. (1961–70), vol. 1 • A. Gordon, *The rules of the game: Jutland and British naval command* (1996) • R. S. Churchill, ed., *Winston S. Churchill*, companion vol. 2/3 (1969) • S. W. Roskill, *Admiral of the fleet Earl Beatty: the last naval hero, an intimate biography* (1980) • *Fear God and dread nought: the correspondence of Admiral of the Fleet Lord Fisher of Kilverstone*, ed. A. J. Marder, 2 (1956) • J. T. Sumida, *In defence of naval supremacy: finance, technology and British naval policy, 1889–1914* (1989) • W. E. Goodenough, *A rough record* (1943) • *CGPLA Eng. & Wales* (1920)

Likenesses W. Stoneman, photograph, 1918, NPG [*see illus.*] • portrait, repro. in Marder, *From the Dreadnought to Scapa Flow*, vol. 1, p. 219

Wealth at death £11,990 5*s*. 6*d*.: probate, 21 July 1921, *CGPLA Eng. & Wales*

Callan [*née* Hughes], **Margaret** (*c*.**1817**–*c*.**1883**), Irish nationalist, was born about 1817 in Newry, co. Down, one of the six daughters and five sons of Philip Hughes, a merchant in Newry, and his wife, Susanna, the daughter of Patrick Gavan, a gentleman farmer of Aughabog, co. Monaghan, and Judith MacMahon of Oriel. Susanna's sister was Anne Duffy, the mother of Charles Gavan *Duffy. Following Philip Hughes's death, in 1835 Margaret and her mother opened the Whitehall Boarding and Day School for Young Ladies in Blackrock, Dublin, where she taught until she married the physician John B. Callan. It was through her cousin (and later also brother-in-law) Charles Gavan Duffy that Margaret, her sister Susan (later Susan Duffy), and her brother Terence MacMahon Hughes became involved in the Young Ireland movement. Margaret Callan wrote articles for *The Nation*, but, since they were published anonymously, only two can be clearly attributed to her: 'A day at Versailles' and 'A day in Paris', which appeared on 29 July and 9 September 1843 respectively. These travel reports were most likely the first lengthy writings by a woman in *The Nation*. In them, Callan emphasized the benefits of Irish self-government and encouraged the Irish to show the same national pride as the French. She also pointed out that many French people thought highly of Daniel O'Connell's policies, thus stressing the support for repeal of the union abroad.

In 1846, under the pseudonym Thornton MacMahon, Callan edited *The Casket of Irish Pearls*, a collection of works of Irish writers for the Library of Ireland series. In the introduction she urged the Irish people to gain knowledge and self-respect through education, so that ignorance and bigotry could be overcome. She strongly attacked the English policy of divide and conquer in Ireland and appealed to all Irish factions to unite and obtain self-government by peaceful means. Callan praised Irish nationalism as a unifying ideology for all classes and creeds. Her writings show her as a very educated and sophisticated woman.

When in 1848 many Young Ireland leaders were arrested, Callan, together with Jane Francesca Elgee, continued the publication of *The Nation* until the office was raided on 29 July. Duffy describes the incident as follows:

> Before the number issued the police were sent to seize and carry off the type, the manuscripts, and the proofs. When they took possession of the establishment they found a lady in the editor's room, and the journal ready to be issued. The manuscript of the number on which they had laid their hands consisted in a large degree of articles in two handwritings, both of them plainly feminine. … The courageous woman found in control of the Nation office was Margaret Callan, my sister-in-law … (Duffy, *Four Years*, 681)

After the failed rebellion in Tipperary, Callan kept in contact with many Young Irelanders. She is known to have also attended the trial of Duffy on 10 April 1849, in which he was finally acquitted. In 1856 the Callans followed the Duffys in emigrating to Victoria, Australia. Nothing else is known about Margaret's life there, but from Duffy's correspondence it can be inferred that she remained interested in the Irish political situation and that she kept up an active correspondence with writers and politicians. It is also likely that she continued writing, since she encouraged other female Young Irelanders to do likewise. She died in Melbourne, Australia, about 1883.

BRIGITTE ANTON

Sources B. Anton, 'Northern voices: Ulsterwomen in the Young Ireland movement', *Coming into the light: the work, politics and religion of women in Ulster*, ed. J. Holmes and D. Urquhart (1994), 60–92 · 'The women of Young Ireland', *c*.1920x29, NL Ire., MS 10,906 · C. G. Duffy, *Four years of Irish history, 1845–1849: a sequel to 'Young Ireland'* (1883) · C. G. Duffy, *My life in two hemispheres*, 1 (1898); facs. edn (Shannon, 1969) · *Irish Press* (12 Sept 1945), suppl. · Newry Catholic Church records, PRO NIre., MIC ID 26 · C. Pearl, *The three lives of Gavan Duffy* (1979) · 'More about "Mary" of the *Nation*', *Irish Monthly*, 36 (1908), 69–83 · R. J. Hayes, ed., *Manuscript sources for the history of Irish civilisation*, 1 (1965) · R. J. Hayes, ed., *Manuscript sources for the history of Irish civilisation: first supplement, 1965–1975*, 1 (1979) · R. J. Hayes, ed., *Sources for the history of Irish civilisation: articles in Irish periodicals*, 1 (1970) · 'Queries and answers', *Irish Book Lover*, 5 (1913–14), 201, 220 · advertisement for Whitehall School, *The Nation* [Dublin], 5 (1846), 209 · advertisement for Whitehall School, *The Nation* [Dublin], 5 (1847), 433 · *The commercial directory of Ireland, Scotland, and the four most northern counties of England for 1820–21 & 22* (1820) · T. Bradshaw, *The general directory of Newry, Armagh … for 1820* (1819); repr. (1984) · *MacCabe's Directory of Newry, Warrenpoint, and Rosstrevor, Drogheda* (1830)

Likenesses photograph (in old age), repro. in *Irish Press*, suppl.; priv. coll.

Callan, Nicholas Joseph (1799–1864), Roman Catholic priest and physicist, was born on 20 December 1799 at Darver in the parish of Dromiskin, co. Louth, Ireland, into a well-to-do Roman Catholic family, the fifth child and third son of Donnchadh Beag or Wee Denis Callan (*c*.1745–1813), possibly a farmer, and his wife, Margaret Smith. Little is known about Callan's preparatory schooling but he later attended the academy at Dundalk run by the Presbyterian minister William Neilson. He took the name Joseph on confirmation. Callan prepared for the priesthood at Navan Seminary before entering St Patrick's College, Maynooth, on 26 August 1816. There the first three years were devoted to literature and science—in his third year he excelled in experimental philosophy or physics; the latter three years formed his theological studies. These concluded with his election to the Dunboyne Establishment—the postgraduate institution of the college. In theological studies he was exposed to influences of Gallicanism. At the end of the academic year 1823–4 he headed the premium list and was first in theology, canon law, and ecclesiastical history. He was ordained subdeacon in 1822, deacon on 23 May 1823, and priest, one day later. On completion of his postgraduate studies in 1824 Callan was chosen to assist the Revd Michael Blake in re-establishing the Collegio Irlandese in Rome; there he attended lectures at the Sapienza University and prepared for a doctorate in divinity, conferred on 13 April 1826. On 15 September 1826 he succeeded to the chair of natural philosophy at Maynooth which he occupied until his death. He paid little further attention to theological scholarship.

As professor Callan strove to raise standards in physics; he wrote an introductory textbook *Electricity and Galvanism* (1832) and brought out a new and enlarged edition of a textbook on geometry. In his life as a scientist two periods can be identified, one of outstanding activity and achievement as a young professor, and another of consolidation and development in his later years. Perhaps inspired by the knowledge of the work of Galvani and Volta gained during his stay in Rome, Callan became a pioneer in the investigation of electricity and electromagnetism; he made important contributions in developing and improving electromagnets and coils, electric motors for traction, batteries, and electric lighting. In developing electromagnets (1836–8) Callan followed up the work of Sturgeon in England and of Joseph Henry in America. With coils joined in series he recognized that the intensity of the shocks experienced depended on the rapidity of the break in the primary and he developed a device called a repeater, for rapid interruption using the escapement mechanism of a clock. He found that shocks were augmented when the circuits were separated. He discovered the principle of the step-up transformer and the induction coil, a replica of which he sent to Sturgeon, who demonstrated it in August 1837 to the Electrical Society. Employing primary coils of thick copper wire insulated with tape and secondary coils of very great lengths of fine iron wire coated with a mixture of beeswax and guttapercha, he obtained powerful spark discharges. Callan devised a motor using electromagnets for excitation and powered by batteries and he conducted experiments with a view to producing electric railway locomotion. He envisaged an electric railway from Dublin to Kingstown (later Dunlaoghaire) and designed an engine to propel a carriage and load, but practical difficulties led to the demise of the project.

Callan modified the Wollaston cell by placing the zinc plates in copper containers without glass or porcelain vessels. In 1836 he described a very large battery containing 20 square zinc plates with about 140 litres of acid. He proceeded to improve two-fluid cells working in succession with the Poggendorff, Daniel, Grove, and Bunsen cells. He developed a new two liquid cast-iron voltaic battery, and converted his original Wollaston battery into a cast-iron one; using the zinc plates of the former he constructed 577 cells, obtaining what was probably the world's largest battery. Subsequently these cells were manufactured commercially at the Adelaide Gallery in London. His work on the cast-iron battery also led to the discovery that cast iron treated with nitric acid became resistant to weathering and he was granted a patent (2340 of 1853) for this process. He experimented with limelighting and electric arc lighting for application in lighthouses, for which he also devised a special single-fluid battery. He developed a type of tangent galvanometer which later found commercial application as did some other findings, for example in the design of lightning conductors. Of particular significance was his discovery (published in 1863) of the point plate valve or rectifier.

Callan was active in the Roman Catholic publication movement that opposed the activities of evangelical proselytizing societies in Ireland, especially in the 1840s, the decade of the great famine. Over several years he devoted nearly all his leisure time to producing English versions of the popular devotional works of St Alphonsus Liguori, at least sixteen of which were published between 1842 and 1850; a book of meditations by Callan chiefly for ecclesiastics, entitled *Selva* (1844), also enjoyed popularity. At the time of the famine Callan donated all of his professorial salary for relief. Whereas a considerable number of his instruments have been preserved, the corpus of his published research papers is small, consisting of nineteen mostly short papers in William Sturgeon's *Annals of Electricity*, the *Philosophical Magazine*, the *Proceedings of the Royal Irish Academy*, and the *British Association Report* for 1857.

Callan's researches were financed largely from private or family means. Most of his apparatus was made by himself with the help of local tradesmen or blacksmiths. He was seen by many as an eccentric and was the subject of anecdote. In his later years he sought recognition for his earlier discoveries: at the Dublin meeting of the British Association in 1857, where his work was honoured, he upheld his priority claim as inventor of the induction coil.

Callan, who was small in stature, suffered from high blood pressure and he was twice relieved of his duties and sent to convalesce on the continent, in 1849 and in 1850–51. On 2 January 1864 he suffered a stroke in the college chapel and died at Maynooth on 14 January at 8 p.m. His possessions, consisting of books, furniture, prints, and wine, and a share in property inherited from his late sister Catherine, were willed to the college library, to charity, or to his superiors and professors of the college. A Celtic cross and headstone were erected about forty years after his death on his grave in the college cemetery.

James G. O'Hara

Sources P. J. McLaughlin, *Nicholas Callan: priest-scientist, 1799–1864* (1965) · M. T. Casey, 'Nicholas Callan: priest, professor and scientist', *Physics Education*, 17 (1982), 224–34 · R. C. Mollan and J. Upton, *St Patrick's College, Maynooth: the scientific apparatus of Nicholas Callan* (1994) · N. H. de V. Heathcote, 'N. J. Callan, inventor of the induction coil', *Annals of Science*, 21 (1965), 145–67 · P. J. McLaughlin, 'Some Irish contemporaries of Faraday and Henry', *Proceedings of the Royal Irish Academy*, 64A (1964–6), 17–35 · P. J. McLaughlin, 'Prelections of Nicholas Callan', *Irish Astronomical Journal*, 6 (1963–4), 249–52 · A. J. Webb, 'Callan, Nicholas', *A compendium of Irish biography* (1878)

Archives St Patrick's College, Maynooth, Ireland, MSS and scientific apparatus

Likenesses engraving, repro. in McLaughlin, *Nicholas Callan* · photograph, repro. in Mollan and Upton, *St Patrick's College, Maynooth* · photograph, repro. in McLaughlin, 'Some Irish contemporaries of Faraday and Henry'

Wealth at death books, furniture, prints, wine, and share in property left by sister: will, McLaughlin, *Nicholas Callan*, 107

Callanan, Jeremiah John (1795–1829), poet, was born in Ballinhassig, just outside Cork, where his father practised medicine. Ballinhassig was at the time Irish-speaking, and he grew up in an area rich in Gaelic culture. He was educated locally, then at Cobh, co. Cork, before going to St Patrick's College, Maynooth, to study for the Catholic priesthood. He left without taking holy orders, and moved to Trinity College, Dublin, which by then admitted Catholics to its rolls, and he won a prize there for a poem on the famous Greek soldier-scholar Alexander. He left Trinity, enlisted in the army, and sailed to the Isle of Wight, but implored his Cork friends to buy him out, and he returned to his native city. He taught for a time at the school run by William Maginn, and he joined The Hermitage, an artistic club, where Cork literati would meet—among them John Windele, Thomas Crofton Croker, and Maginn himself. Calling themselves The Anchorites, they were interested in Irish archaeology and folklore.

Callanan submitted a number of translations from the Irish to *Blackwood's Magazine*, encouraged by Maginn, who was now contributing to this journal. Among these versions, remarkable for their energy and clarity, and for deploying Gaelic song metres to create arresting prosodic effects, were 'The Dirge of O'Sullivan Beare' and 'O say, my brown drimin', two pieces of marked anti-English sentiment. Inspired by the example of Thomas Moore and his success with *Irish Melodies* (1808–24), Callanan hoped to emulate this achievement with a series of *Munster Melodies*, based on original fieldwork in west Cork and co. Kerry. He spent much time in the countryside, perhaps gathering material; little survives, apart from transcripts of some remains made by John Windele and preserved in the Royal Irish Academy. *Blackwood's* published his best poem, 'The Outlaw of Loch Lene' in 1828, a loose adaptation of a love song 'Muna bé an t-ól', which is also a song of regret for over-indulgence in drink. Callanan, perhaps because of his own dependence on alcohol, makes of this amalgam of originality and folk-tradition one of the finest Irish poems in English before Yeats:

O many a day have I made good ale in the glen,
That came not of stream, or malt, like the brewing of men.

Callanan's most sustained work was a longer poem, after the model of Byron, entitled *The Recluse of Inchydoney* (1830). The 'Recluse' is leaving Ireland, driven into exile by a despair induced by the 'Saxon yoke' of English oppression, and a mood of melancholy blackens into a bitter attack on foreign rule and protestantism. Inchydoney is in west Cork, as is Gougane Barra, a place invoked with great affection in the poem of that title.

Callanan fell in love with Alicia Fisher, a Methodist, but they drifted apart, she refusing to convert to Catholicism. Callanan was, by this time, suffering from tuberculosis. He accepted an offer to act as tutor in an Irish household in Lisbon, hoping the climate would improve his condition, but he weakened further, and died on 19 September 1829. Towards the end he cultivated a special devotion to the Virgin Mary. Callanan's body of work is small, but it is intense and extremely powerful. His influence on Yeats was deep and lasting. Yeats made extensive use of the long, flexible, floating line, loosely stressed, a rhythmic pulse he found in the verse of Callanan and Thomas Moore. Callanan's metrics were more open than those Moore employed, his imagery more unpredictable. Yeats learned much from Callanan's open and gapped rhythms, and from his urgent and surprising images. The poems were collected after his death in *The Recluse of Inchydoney and other Poems* (1830). His name among his confreres in The Hermitage was Dr Mac Slatt (Son of the Stick). His 'Literary remains', assembled in manuscript form by Windele and held in the Royal Irish Academy, include some material in Callanan's own hand. ROBERT WELCH

Sources R. Welch, *A history of verse translation from the Irish, 1789–1897* (1988)
Archives Royal Irish Acad., 'Literary remains of Jeremiah J. Callanan', collected and compiled by John Fitzpatrick Fitzthos Windele of Blain's Castle, Cork, 1847, MS 12.1.13

Callander, John (*b.* in or after **1721**, *d.* **1789**), antiquary, was the son of James Callander (*d.* 1725), advocate, of Craigforth, Stirlingshire, and Catherine Mackenzie, who married on 21 September 1721. His father was descended from James VI's master smith in Scotland, John Callander, who purchased Craigforth from the earls of Livingston and Callander about 1603; his mother was the daughter of Sir Kenneth Mackenzie, third baronet, of Cromarty, and Ann Campbell. Callander passed advocate at the Scottish bar, being admitted into the Faculty of Advocates on 15 June 1743, but never obtained a practice, and seems to have devoted his leisure chiefly to classical pursuits. On 26 November 1743 he married at Gargunnock, near Stirling, Mary (*d.* 1802), daughter of Sir James Livingston of Westquarter; they had seventeen children.

In April 1781 Callander was elected a fellow of the Society of Antiquaries of Scotland, to which he presented five volumes of manuscripts entitled 'Spicilegia antiquitatis Graecae, sive, Ex veteribus poetis deperdita fragmenta'. At the same time he presented nine volumes of manuscript annotations on Milton's *Paradise Lost*, volume 1 of which had been published in 1750. In 1766–8 he brought out in three volumes, *Terra Australis cognita, or, Voyages to the southern hemisphere during the sixteenth, seventeenth, and eighteenth centuries*, which was partly translated from the French of M. de Brosses. In 1779 he published an essay on a literal English translation of St Paul's letter to the Ephesians, in which he gave a complete representation in English of the Greek idiom. Unfortunately this extended to the order of the words, with the result that it was all but incomprehensible. Furthermore, notes he added to the work were all in Greek. *Two Ancient Scottish Poems, the Gaberlunzie Man, and Christ's Kirk on the Green* (1782) included helpful notes for those unfamiliar with the Scottish language, but many of Callander's etymological remarks have been considered unsound. This edition was intended as a preliminary to 'a Scots-Gothic glossary', which he promised would establish the structure, etymology, and real meaning of the Scottish language based on 'Principles so totally different from Those of Skinner, Junius, Lye, Ruddiman etc' (NL Scot., Adv. MS 29.3.8), but Callander seems not to have persisted with this project. He projected a variety of other works, including *Bibliotheca septentrionalis*, of which he printed a specimen in 1778, and a *History of the Ancient Music of Scotland*, for which he printed 'Proposals' in 1781. Besides antiquarian research, his main interest was music and he was a keen violinist.

In his later years Callander became very reclusive and saw little company. He appears to have suffered from a religiously grounded depression, which made him unsociable. He died in his sixties at Craigforth on 14 September 1789; he was survived by his wife, who died on 18 October 1802. Their eldest son, James, assumed the name Campbell [*see* Campbell, James (1745–1831)].

In March 1818 an article on Callander's edition of book 1 of Milton's *Paradise Lost* appeared in *Blackwood's Magazine*, in which it was shown that many of his notes had been taken without acknowledgement from Patrick Hume's edition, published by Jacob Tonson in 1695. On account of this article, a committee of the Society of Antiquaries of Scotland was appointed to examine Callander's manuscript notes on Milton in their possession. In a paper presented to the society by David Laing on 27 March 1826 it was reported that, though only a small proportion of Callander's notes were borrowed from Hume, his obligations to him were not sufficiently acknowledged.

T. F. HENDERSON, *rev.* ALEXANDER DU TOIT

Sources Chambers, *Scots.* (1855) • F. J. Grant, ed., *The Faculty of Advocates in Scotland, 1532–1943*, Scottish RS, 145 (1944), 27 • *Letters from Thomas Percy … John Callander … David Herd, and others, to George Paton*, ed. J. Maidment (1830) • *Scots Magazine*, 51 (1789), 466 • *Blackwood*, 4 (1818–19), 658–62 • *Transactions of the Society of Antiquaries of Scotland*, 3 (1831), 83–91 • Burke, *Gen. GB* (1886) • W. Orme, *Bibliotheca biblica* (1824), 73–4 • GEC, *Baronetage*
Archives NL Scot., antiquaries • NL Scot., notes on Greek poets and Milton • U. Edin. L., financial and legal documents | NL Scot.,

letters to G. Paton • U. Edin., notes refuting William Lauder's charges against Milton

Callard, Sir (Eric) John [Jack] (**1913–1998**), engineer and industrialist, was born on 15 March 1913 at 162 Union Street, Torquay, Devon, the son of Frank Callard, master baker and confectioner, and his wife, Ada Mary, *née* Fawkes. He had a brother and a sister, and the family lived over their father's shop. Callard later claimed that a career which was to take him to the chairmanship of Britain's largest industrial company was set in motion by a boyhood encounter with a Methodist minister, who advised: 'Train to be a chemical engineer and you will earn £1000 a year' (Callard). Educated at Queen's College, Taunton, he took a first-class degree in mechanical engineering at St John's College, Cambridge. Then, after a brief stint as a student apprentice at the large Vickers Armstrong shipyard at Barrow in Furness, he joined the chief engineer's department of Britain's industrial flagship, Imperial Chemical Industries (ICI), at its major centre at Billingham on Teesside. On 9 April 1938 Jack Callard married Pauline Mary Pengelly (*b.* 1914/15), daughter of Charles Pengelly, Methodist minister. They had three daughters.

During the Second World War Callard was seconded to the Ministry of Aircraft Production's factory at Heysham, which produced aviation fuel. Then he briefly returned to Billingham before being appointed deputy chief engineer of ICI's paints division at Slough in 1947. Paint was not one of the company's principal operations, although ironically it became the only significant original component to survive within ICI by the end of the century. But it gave Callard a chance to move up the management tree—he became chairman in 1959—and to gain notice as part of the team which broke with tradition and company policy in marketing the company's Dulux brand directly to the consumer, with huge success as a result of the do-it-yourself revolution.

It was, however, as engineering director that Callard was selected for the ICI board in 1964. With Britain outside the European Common Market, ICI was one of only a handful of major British companies to grasp the importance of investing on the European mainland. Taking over as chairman of ICI Europa, the company's European operation, in 1965, Callard quickly and presciently moved its headquarters out of the UK to Brussels. Soon ICI was selling more in Europe than in the UK. Callard became recognized as a safe pair of hands: judicious, modest, with an aversion to personal publicity, fair-minded, an archetypal pipe-smoker. As one colleague put it, he was 'one of the world's gentlemen. A very good administrator—but not a vast amount of imagination' (private information).

In 1971 Callard became chairman of ICI (the first engineer to reach that position) in preference to his fellow deputy chairman, Michael Clapham. ICI was still struggling to secure the returns from its 'dash for growth' in the 1960s. Profits, margins, and share price were all falling back and Callard's calm management style was preferred to the more adventurous views of Clapham, who was also heavily involved with the Confederation of British Industry.

Sir (Eric) John Callard (1913–1998), by unknown photographer, 1972

Callard delivered on the immediate concerns. He announced his intention of making ICI 'a lean and profit-hungry giant' (*Daily Telegraph*, 30 Sept 1998), and at a time of huge unrest in British industry and increasing alarm about inflation he almost doubled profits between 1972 and 1974 while forcing through rationalizations. He energetically expanded the company's export business, making ICI Britain's largest exporter.

Nevertheless, surrounded by a board overwhelmingly drawn from the heavy chemical divisions, Callard was deaf to suggestions that the company should take major steps away from those roots and look to new technologies and pharmaceuticals. He was unimaginative at implementing the company's major strategic step-out, concluded at the start of his chairmanship: its move into North American manufacture through acquiring Atlas Chemicals and its Stuart Pharmaceuticals subsidiary. Instead of using it as a bridgehead for change, ICI tried to replicate its traditional asset-base against established rivals in the ruthlessly competitive American marketplace. It paid the price: an opportunity for fundamental change was missed.

Callard was a Conservative and a vigorous foe of Labour's plans for extending state ownership, pointedly directed against ICI in recurrent policy proposals to take over a leading company in each of the major sectors of the economy. He attacked high taxation and price controls even though his old colleague Michael Clapham was negotiating them with the Heath government for the CBI. Although a believer in industrial participation, he and the combative Sir Barrie Heath of Guest, Keen and Nettlefolds walked out of Labour's Bullock inquiry into industrial democracy, believing it rigged to ensure a recommendation for statutory worker-directors.

Callard was knighted in 1974 a year before his retirement from ICI, after which he joined the board of British Home Stores; he served as chairman from 1976 to 1982 during a difficult trading period. He was a keen supporter of management education, and was on the council of the Institute of Management Education and the Manchester University Business School and a governor of the London Business School. An enthusiastic rugby player and golfer in his youth, he was greatly taken by the Lake District in his early career. He retired to Crookwath Cottage, High Row, Dockray, Penrith, where he enjoyed flyfishing, fell-walking, and successfully cultivating his high-altitude garden. He died of heart disease at 8 The Orchard, The Croft, Fairford, Gloucestershire, on 21 September 1998. He was survived by his wife and their three daughters.

MARTIN ADENEY

Sources *Daily Telegraph* (30 Sept 1998) · D. Callard, 'Sir Jack Callard', *The Guardian* (3 Oct 1998) · *The Times* (15 Oct 1998) · *WWW* · private information (2004) · b. cert. · m. cert. · d. cert.

Likenesses photograph, 1971, repro. in *Daily Telegraph* · photograph, 1972, News International Syndication, London [*see illus.*] · J. Mendoza, oils, ICI headquarters, Manchester Square, London · photograph, repro. in Callard, 'Sir Jack Callard' · photographs, Times Photo Library

Callaway, Charles (1838–1915), geologist, was born at 2 Stratton Street, Bristol, on 9 March 1838, the son of Lemuel Callaway, accountant, and his wife, Jane Williams. After schooling in Bristol and Cheltenham, he enrolled in 1859 at Cheshunt College, intending to becoming a Congregationalist minister, and during his studies he received support from the Castle Green Chapel, Bristol. In addition to the college curriculum in theology, Callaway sat for examinations at London University, where he took philosophy (BA, 1862) and philosophy and political economy (MA, 1863). His youthful interest in fossils, which he had collected from the nearby Lower Oolite, eventually led to two further London degrees—a BSc in geology (first-class hons., 1872) and DSc in geology and physical geography (1878). His results were consistently excellent in all subjects except theology.

After leaving Cheshunt in 1864 Callaway was called in 1865 to a pastorate in Kirkby Stephen, Westmorland, where he remained until 1868. He ministered at Wellington, Shropshire, from October 1869 until mid-1871, when he went to Bradford, to work as a librarian and museum curator. The noted American geologist James Hall met Callaway in 1872, and invited him to work at the New York State Museum at Albany. Callaway learned much palaeontology during his American sojourn (1873–4), though he later specialized in Archaean geology. After returning to England Callaway became curator of the Sheffield public museum, but felt obliged to resign in 1876 because of disagreements with one of the management committee. Following treatment in Malvern for a 'nervous illness', Callaway returned to Wellington, where, on 29 June 1876, he married Hannah Maria Clark (*b.* 1832/3), a music teacher at Hiatt's Ladies' College there, of which her sister was principal. Hannah was a widow, and daughter of John Keay, boot manufacturer. On marrying, Callaway left the ministry and taught English, history, and science part-time at the college, thus having opportunity for geological researches. These were chiefly focused on the ancient rocks of Shropshire, Anglesey, the Malverns, and Scotland's north-west highlands.

Callaway studied particularly the rocks of the Wrekin area near Wellington. By 1873 he had discovered fossils near Shineton; they were apparently Upper Cambrian, but the government survey had mapped the rocks in which they occurred as Caradoc Sandstone (Silurian). (The Shineton Shales were later regarded as Ordovician, but this system was not proposed until 1879.) If the Shales were Upper Cambrian, the underlying Wrekin Quartzite was plausibly Lower Cambrian, and since this unit lapped round the volcanic ashes of the Wrekin, the hill was arguably Precambrian (Archaean). This interpretation differed from the survey's, which regarded the Wrekin's igneous rocks as intrusive, and the Quartzite as baked Caradoc Sandstone. Thus Callaway joined a group of amateur geologists, dubbed 'the Archaeans', who took issue with several survey interpretations, and argued for the existence of a number of Precambrian sites in England and Wales. The observations and interpretations near Wellington were paralleled in the Malverns and also extended to rocks near Church Stretton, where Callaway introduced the term 'Uriconian' for one of the claimed local Precambrian units.

Callaway's most significant work was in the north-west highlands of Scotland, where he challenged the interpretation of the structure long held by Roderick Murchison (1792–1871) and Archibald Geikie (1835–1924). Callaway mapped around Ullapool, Durness, and Eriboll in 1880–82 and established the geometrical and temporal sequence of a series of anticlinally folded rocks near Eriboll, thereby contributing significantly towards unravelling the geological structure of the district. His findings were confirmed and extended by Charles Lapworth, who invoked the idea of low-angle reverse faulting, and the formation of schists as a result of compression and movement. Callaway later applied such ideas to Anglesey geology. He also considered the problems of stratigraphic work in unfossiliferous Precambrian rocks, putting forward the idea that observers should make lithological comparisons and look for evidence provided by included pebbles. Study of anticlinal structures could yield information about stratigraphic sequences. Callaway proposed some 'long-distance' correlations—for example between the various claimed Precambrian sites in Britain, and even between British and American units. Besides his work on ancient rocks, Callaway assembled a substantial fossil collection, was regarded as an authority on American brachiopods, and studied local archaeology.

Callaway retired in 1898 and moved to Cheltenham, where he founded and was first president of the Cheltenham Ethical Society. In his later years he became a militant agnostic, writing for the *Agnostic Annual* and serving on the editorial board of the Rationalist Press. He died of prostate cancer at his home, 16 Montpellier Villas, Cheltenham, on 29 September 1915, and was buried without religious ceremony in Wellington cemetery. His indifferent undergraduate results in theology, as compared with excellent marks in science and philosophy, perhaps suggest that he was never a fully committed Christian.

David Oldroyd

Sources L. Richardson, *Geological Magazine*, new ser., 6th decade, 2 (1915), 525–8 • D. R. Oldroyd, 'The Archaean controversy in Britain: pt 2', *Annals of Science*, 49 (1992), 401–60 • D. R. Oldroyd, 'The Archaean controversy in Britain: pt 3—the rocks of Anglesey and Caernarvonshire', *Annals of Science*, 50 (1993), 523–84 • D. R. Oldroyd, 'The Archaean controversy in Britain: pt 4', *Annals of Science*, 51 (1994), 571–92 • A. S. Woodward, *Quarterly Journal of the Geological Society*, 72 (1916), lvii • *Shrewsbury Chronicle* (1 Oct 1915) • *Shrewsbury Chronicle* (8 Oct 1915) • D. R. Oldroyd, *The highlands controversy: constructing geological knowledge through fieldwork in nineteenth-century Britain* (1990) • E. Elliot, *History of Congregationalism in Shropshire* (1898) • *The Hiatt College, Wellington, Salop, 1847–1947* [n.d.] • J. M. Clarke, *James Hall of Albany: geologist and palaeontologist, 1811–1898* (1923) • b. cert. • d. cert. • m. cert. • private information (2004) • T. Whitehead, *History of the dales congregational churches* (1930), 274
Archives Sheffield City Museum • U. Birm. L.
Likenesses photograph, repro. in Richardson, *Geological Magazine*, facing p. 525
Wealth at death £930 3*s*. 2*d*.: probate, 28 Dec 1915, *CGPLA Eng. & Wales*

Callaway, Henry (1817–1890), bishop of St John's, Kaffraria, in Cape Colony, was born at Lymington, Hampshire, on 17 January 1817, the eleventh child of James Callaway, an exciseman, formerly a bootmaker, and of his wife, the daughter of a farmer at Minehead. His parents moved to Southampton shortly after his birth, then to London, and finally to Crediton, where his father was appointed supervisor of excise. Callaway was educated at Crediton grammar school, and in May 1833 he went to Heavitree as assistant teacher in a small school. The headmaster, William Dymond, was a Quaker, and Callaway inclined to his opinions. In 1835 he went to Wellington as private tutor in a Quaker family, and in the spring of 1837, impressed by the lively Quaker teaching on the work of the Holy Spirit, he was admitted a member of the Society of Friends.

In April 1839 Callaway entered the service of Cornelius Hanbury, a chemist at Southampton who later became his literary executor, but soon afterwards he moved to London as surgeon's assistant at Tottenham to E. C. May, a former acquaintance. Early in 1841 he began studying at St Bartholomew's Hospital; he was licensed by the Royal College of Surgeons in July 1842 and by the Society of Apothecaries in April 1844. He took rooms in Bishopsgate Street in the summer of 1844, and in a short time succeeded in making a fair practice. On 14 October 1845 he married another Quaker, Ann, daughter of James Chalk. Both their children died shortly after birth. Callaway also held posts at the Red Lion Square (later Soho Square) Hospital, St Bartholomew's, and the Farringdon General Dispensary, and about 1848 he took a house in Finsbury Circus. During this period he wrote a religious work, *Immediate Revelation* (1841), and *A Memoir of James Parnell* (1846), but he was increasingly beset by religious doubts and difficulties. The onset of tuberculosis compelled him to sell his practice, worth about £1000 a year, in the summer of 1852, and in October he moved to southern France; soon afterwards he left the Society of Friends. On 12 August 1853 he graduated MD at King's College, Aberdeen, having resolved to practise as a physician.

With returning health, however, Callaway was increasingly attracted by the idea of mission work, and at the beginning of 1854 he wrote to John William Colenso, bishop of Natal, offering his services. He was accepted by the Society for the Propagation of the Gospel, and ordained deacon in Norwich Cathedral on 13 August 1854. On 26 August he and his wife left England in the *Lady of the Lake*, and they reached Durban on 5 December. After Christmas they moved to Pietermaritzburg, where Callaway remained in charge of the nearby mission church at Ekukanyeni. On 23 September 1855 he was ordained priest, and on 14 October St Andrew's Church was opened, and he was placed in charge. At the beginning of 1858 he obtained a grant of land from government beyond the Umkomanzi River, and settled at a vacated Dutch farm on the Insunguze, which he named Spring Vale. At this settlement he began the work among the local people which made his name a household word in south Africa. In 1868, when Robert Gray, bishop of Cape Town, consecrated William Kenneth Macrorie bishop of Natal, in place of Colenso, Callaway after some hesitation resolved to support Macrorie, though he had held himself aloof from the Colenso controversy and had not participated in the election of his successor.

From the beginning of his residence at Spring Vale, Callaway studied African beliefs, traditions, and customs. In 1868 he published *Nursery Tales, Traditions, and Histories of the Zulus*, a valuable contribution to folklore, which was printed at Spring Vale. Between 1868 and 1870 he published his greatest work, *The Religious System of the Amazulu*, which appeared in four parts: *The Tradition of Creation*; *Amatonga, or, Ancestor Worship*; *Diviners*; and *Medical Magic and Witchcraft*. The last part was not completed. The depth of Callaway's anthropological research led him into the field of comparative religion, to which he contributed *A Fragment of Comparative Religion* (1874) and *On the Religious Sentiment among the Tribes of South Africa* (1876), as well as other studies published in *Folk-Lore*, a monthly anthropological journal produced in Cape Town. Callaway's work in philology and translation was equally distinguished. In 1871 he published *Incwadi yamahhubo: the Book of Psalms* (1871), to be followed by *Incwadi yokukeleka yabantu abakmitu … the Book of Common Prayer* (1882). Additionally the first complete translation of the Bible into Zulu, which appeared in 1883, was largely his work.

In December 1871 the south African bishops petitioned the Scottish Episcopal church to establish a bishopric in Kaffraria, and on All Saints' day 1873 Callaway was consecrated missionary bishop of St John's, Kaffraria, at St Paul's Episcopal Church, Edinburgh. On 2 June 1874 he received the honorary degree of DD from the University of Oxford in recognition of his anthropological and philological work, and on 25 August he returned to south Africa. In 1876 the headquarters of the diocese moved to Umtata. In 1877 war broke out, and Umtata was fortified by the directions of the governor, Sir Bartle Frere. After the conclusion of the war an important advance was made in regard to African education, which Callaway had especially at heart, through the foundation of St John's Theological College at Umtata in June 1879. It is a mark of Callaway's greatness as a bishop that St John's was a diocese in which African tribal culture was given positive support, and African abilities were recognized and encouraged.

The failure of Callaway's health caused the consecration of Bransby Key on 12 August 1873 as coadjutor bishop, and in June 1886 Callaway himself resigned the bishopric. He returned to England in May 1887 and settled at Ottery St Mary in Devon in 1888. Stricken by paralysis in 1889 he died at his home at Woodcote, Ottery, on 26 March 1890, survived by his wife. He was buried in Ottery churchyard on 31 March; among the mourners present was Dr E. B. Taylor, reader in anthropology in the University of Oxford. E. I. CARLYLE, *rev.* CLARE BROWN

Sources M. S. Benham, *Henry Callaway: a memoir* (1896) • M. Blunden, 'The Anglican clergy and the politics of southern Africa, 1888–1909', DPhil diss., U. Oxf., 1980 • *DSAB* • P. B. Hinchliff, *The Anglican church in South Africa* (1963) • *The Times* (29 March 1890), 11f • *The Athenaeum* (12 April 1890), 471 • m. cert. • d. cert. • *CGPLA Eng. & Wales* (1890)

Archives UCL, Archives of the Folklore Society, MSS of *Religious System of the Amazulu* | RHBod., SPG archives, E series

Wealth at death £4627 12s. 2d.: probate, 9 June 1890, *CGPLA Eng. & Wales*

Sir Augustus Wall Callcott (1770–1844), by Sir Edwin Landseer, 1833

Callcott, Sir Augustus Wall (1770–1844), painter, was born on 20 February 1770, the son of Thomas Callcott, builder of the then-rustic hamlet of Kensington Gravel Pits, and his second wife, Charlotte, *née* Wall. He was first intended for a musical career in the footsteps of his elder brother, the glee composer and organist John Wall *Callcott (1766–1821), and spent six years in the choir at Westminster Abbey. He entered the Royal Academy Schools in 1797, and also studied with the portrait painter John Hoppner. His first exhibits were portraits, but by the turn of the century he was specializing in landscape in watercolour and oil; this soon won him admiration and commissions from important patrons such as Edward, Viscount Lascelles, also an early patron of Turner.

Unlike Turner, Callcott eschewed topographical work and drawing for the engraver, preferring to develop a landscape style based on the Dutch tradition and the rustic landscapes of Gainsborough, and later on the classical style of Claude. His concern for imaginative or literary concepts of landscape, rather than for study of nature, was reflected in his membership, in 1801, of the Sketching Society (also known as 'the Brothers'), which met to invent watercolour compositions on set themes, but he soon decided to concentrate on oil painting. His initial appeal for patrons and connoisseurs like Sir John Leicester or Richard Payne Knight was based on a style and picturesque subject matter that appeared to promise a distinct alternative to the emerging genius of Turner. Leicester bought *The Water Mill* (priv. coll.), a richly picturesque upright composition, from the Royal Academy in 1805; it was the first of Callcott's pictures to win wide critical acclaim, as well as the subject of a notable single-plate mezzotint by Charles Turner, and marked out a landscape territory of its own. However, in two marine compositions exhibited the following year, *Sea-Coast, with Figures Bargaining for Fish* and *Calm, with Figures: Shrimping* (both priv. coll.), Callcott moved much closer to Turner, and in these and subsequent pastoral landscape and marine subjects the two artists could be seen progressing along parallel if not identical lines, especially in their joint investigation of qualities of light and atmosphere. The cool and luminous palette developed by both artists led to their being jointly attacked by the conservative connoisseur Sir George Beaumont as 'white painters', but was much appreciated by other collectors and by colleagues, who elected Callcott associate of the Royal Academy in 1806 and Royal Academician in 1810.

By 1813 and 1814 Callcott was both a celebrated and a controversial figure. In both these years he was sufficiently stung by Beaumont's criticism to absent himself from the Royal Academy exhibitions. He also campaigned aggressively among colleagues against the influence Beaumont and other connoisseurs claimed upon artists and on the public taste as directors of the British Institution, which threatened to rival the Royal Academy by its exhibitions of living artists as well as of old masters. His involvement in two infamous, spoof *catalogues raisonnés* of the institution's exhibitions in 1815 and 1816—which certainly embodied his views—has been often suspected but never proved. If his opinions reflected a radical streak, this was perhaps influenced by his family's earlier associations with the London Corresponding Society, and for much of his life his grander patrons came from whig rather than tory circles; with other members of his family he had long been a protégé of the Holland family in Kensington, and his later clients included Lord William Russell and the prime minister, Earl Grey. On the other hand he was an increasingly sincere admirer of the Dutch old masters; their pictures, lent to the institution's exhibition in 1815, had provoked the first *catalogue* and their work underpinned his most famous pictures, a series of 'tranquil marines' of English and continental harbour and river scenes best represented by his masterpiece, *Entrance to the Pool of London* (priv. coll.), shown in 1816. While Turner declared that he would have valued the picture at 1000 guineas, and his atmospheric lighting continued to be matched in Callcott's work, his increasingly bold and extravagant handling and brilliant colour were not, and Callcott's characteristically meticulous execution and more sober palette now emerged as more acceptable options for many collectors, contributing to his metamorphosis into a quintessential establishment artist. Furthermore, it was not until 1819 that Callcott began charging prices commensurate with his friend's.

Callcott's later years were both dominated, and somewhat eclipsed, by his wife, the writer and traveller Maria Graham (1785–1842) [*see* Callcott, Maria], whom he married as her second husband on 20 February 1827. A forceful bluestocking, she turned their Kensington house into one of London's most stimulating cultural salons, attracting an international circle of visitors. She also encouraged Callcott, who had so far visited Paris only in 1815, to travel; an extended honeymoon tour of Italy and Germany in 1827–8 introduced the couple to leading continental artists and provided the opportunity for art-historical study, especially of the early Renaissance. They met such pioneers of art history as Sulpiz and Melchior Boisserée, Carlo Lasinio and Georg von Dillis, and Maria's journals describe their experiences and express her own trenchant and original opinions—which on such matters as Flemish or Italian 'Primitives' or the work of the contemporary German Nazarenes were often ahead of their time—while engravings after Callcott's drawings accompanied her *Description of the Chapel of the Annunziata dell'Arena, or Giotto's Chapel, in Padua* (1835), a harbinger of other historical works the couple seem to have planned together. A scheme for an ambitious history of art was abandoned, however, owing to Maria's failing health; her tuberculosis worsened with the rupture of a blood vessel in 1831, and her remaining years were spent as an invalid. Nevertheless, Callcott was able to put his new-found connoisseurship to good use on the board of the government schools of design (from 1836) and on the National Gallery's purchasing committee (from 1841), for the benefit of younger friends such as Charles Eastlake and William Dyce, and eventually, as surveyor of the queen's pictures (from 1843). His interest in early art and in modern German painting accorded well with Prince Albert's taste, but the appointment came too late for him to be a very active or influential member of the household. He was knighted in 1837.

Meanwhile, Callcott's other activities, together with caring for his wife, had for some time curtailed his painting. His output declined in volume, and his pictures became generally smaller and, increasingly, formulaic; he continued to paint marines and, recalling his honeymoon travels as well as the art of Claude, Italian landscapes, and he experimented with newly fashionable subjects of narrative genre. His *Raphael and the Fornarina*, exhibited in 1837, and *Milton Dictating to his Daughters*, shown in 1840—both lost but the former also the subject of a popular print, engraved by Lumb Stocks for the Art Union of London in 1843—took him into those other current preoccupations, artistic historicism and the costume piece. He was unsuccessful in the election for president of the Royal Academy on the death of Sir Thomas Lawrence in 1830. Yet his personal prestige and—in his later years at least—notably charming and diplomatic manner ensured that his work continued to be much sought after in his lifetime, and his private displays of his works glittering social occasions. But soon after his death these very attributes began to count against him, suggesting that his reputation had been founded on the manners of a courtier rather than on the more substantial and original achievements of his earlier years, which became for some time forgotten and obscured by his later and lesser work. Callcott died on 25 November 1844 at his lifelong home in The Mall, Kensington Gravel Pits, London, and was buried in Kensal Green cemetery. He was the subject of a retrospective at the British Institution in 1845, and selections of his later work were shown again at the Manchester Art Treasures and International exhibitions of 1857 and 1862, and at the Royal Academy in 1875. The most complete graphic record of his work is the collection of lithographs published by T. C. Dibdin in 1847. Callcott was commercially and socially one of the most successful artists of the early nineteenth century, considered in his lifetime as a serious rival if not as actually superior to his close friend Turner, and a much more familiar figure in the more urbane quarters of London society. DAVID BLAYNEY BROWN

Sources D. B. Brown, *Augustus Wall Callcott* (1981) [exhibition catalogue, Tate Gallery, London] · J. C. Dafforne, *Pictures by Sir Augustus Wall Callcott, R.A., with a biographical memoir* (1876) · T. C. Dibdin, *Sir*

Augustus Wall Callcott's Italian and English landscapes, lithographed by T. C. Dibdin (1847) • J. C. Horsley, *Recollections of a Royal Academician*, ed. M. E. Helps (1903) • *The journal of Maria, Lady Callcott, 1827–8*, ed. C. Lloyd and D. B. Brown (1981) • R. Redgrave and S. Redgrave, *A century of painters of the British school* (1890) • Callcott family papers, Bodl. Oxf., MSS Eng. [incl. 'Fragments of a family history written by Sir Augustus Wall Callcott R.A. a few years before his death in 1844'; his journal, July 1805, and Paris journal, 1815; his 'Dictionary of anecdotes', notes on pictorial technique, and catalogue of his works; and the travel journals of Maria Callcott] • W. Horsley, 'Memoir of Dr Callcott', in J. W. Callcott, *A collection of glees, canons and catches*, 1 (1824), 1–19 • d. cert. • will, PRO, PROB 11/2022, sig. 627 • *DNB*

Archives Bodl. Oxf., papers • Courtauld Inst., papers • Royal Arch., corresp.

Likenesses P. Williams, pencil drawing, *c.*1825, BM • K. Vogel von Vogelstein, pencil and chalk drawing, 1827, Kupferstich-Kabinett, Dresden • F. Chantrey, pencil drawing, *c.*1830, NPG • J. Linnell, oils, 1831, Yale U. CBA • E. Landseer, oils, 1833, NPG [*see illus.*]

Wealth at death left all property incl. 'books plate pictures drawings prints and china and also all and every sum and sums of money', to niece Sophia: will, PRO, PROB 11/2022, sig. 627

Callcott, John Wall (1766–1821), composer and music teacher, was born on 20 November 1766 at The Mall, Kensington Gravel Pits, London, the son of Thomas Callcott, builder, and his second wife, Charlotte, *née* Wall; his brother was the painter Sir Augustus Wall *Callcott. From the age of seven John Callcott was a pupil at a school near his home run by William Young, where he was said to have been a brilliant student of the classics, Hebrew, and philosophy. He was obliged to leave at the age of twelve because of family circumstances and was subsequently self-taught.

Callcott's early musical education, from 1778, was with Henry Whitney, organist of Kensington parish church. His father bought a spinet for him in 1779, and he later took up the clarinet and the oboe. In 1780 he wrote music for a Christmas play at Young's school. In 1782, through his attendance at Westminster Abbey, he became acquainted with Benjamin Cooke and Samuel Arnold, who encouraged him to enter the musical profession. From 1782 he occasionally played in the orchestra of the Academy of Ancient Music as a 'supernumerary hautboy', and sang in the chorus of the oratorio concerts at Drury Lane Theatre. In 1783, on the recommendation of Thomas Attwood, he became deputy organist under Rheinhold of St George the Martyr, Queen Square, Bloomsbury, a post he held until 1785.

Most of Callcott's early compositions were glees. For much of the 1780s he dominated the annual Catch Club competitions, gaining fame for the number of his entries which won gold medals and notoriety for the single-mindedness of his approach to the competition. His first glee, 'O sovereign of the willing soul', which he entered in 1784, was unsuccessful, but he won three out of the four prizes in 1785, and two prizes in each of the two following years. In 1787 he submitted no fewer than 120 entries, and the club subsequently passed a resolution limiting the number of entries by any competitor to twelve. Offended by this change in the rules, Callcott refused to compete in 1788, but he entered again in 1789 and won all four prizes.

John Wall Callcott (1766–1821), by Frederick Christian Lewis senior, pubd 1824 (after Sir Augustus Wall Callcott)

Between 1790 and 1793, after which the competition was abolished altogether, he entered each year and won a further nine prizes.

Callcott took the Oxford BMus degree on 4 July 1785. In 1787 he was involved with Arnold in the formation of the Glee Club. On 2 November 1788 he was elected to membership of the Royal Society of Musicians. In 1789 he was appointed joint organist with C. S. Evans of St Paul's, Covent Garden. In 1793 he was appointed organist to the Asylum for Female Orphans in Lambeth, a post which he held until 1802, when he resigned it to his future son-in-law and memorialist William *Horsley. On 18 June 1800 he took the Oxford DMus degree.

Callcott married Elizabeth Mary Hutchins at St Paul's, Covent Garden, on 14 July 1791. They had eleven children, all of whom had Hutchins as their second forename. Elizabeth (1793–1875), their eldest daughter, married Horsley in 1813. Sophia (*b.* 1794) was a piano teacher and organist of St Mary Abbots, Kensington. William Hutchins *Callcott was a prolific composer, organist, and teacher of music. **Maria Hutchins Callcott** (1798–1859) was the author of a number of 'improving' works, most of them published by the SPCK. They included *The Singer's Alphabet* (1849), *Daily Charity* and *The Power of Meekness* (both 1853), and *A Few Household Hints, and Lessons of Conduct for Female Servants* (1856). She died of liver disease on 3 April 1859 at 10 Campden Grove, Kensington, London.

As he grew older, Callcott's interests increasingly turned from composition to questions of theory. His interest developed through his friendship with Marmaduke Overend, organist of Isleworth. On Overend's death in

1790 Callcott bought all his manuscripts, including all his compositions and the manuscript writings on harmony of William Boyce, which Overend had acquired after Boyce's death in 1779. Callcott's ambitious plans for a comprehensive dictionary of music, for which he issued a prospectus in 1797 but which he never completed, involved him in many years of study of theoretical writings and mathematical and philosophical treatises relating to music, all undertaken in addition to his heavy teaching and other commitments. He also worked on an alphabetical dictionary of composers, which he was able to complete only as far as the letter O. Work on these projects ceased in 1808, when Callcott suffered a breakdown, but Horsley in his *Memoir* doubted if he would in any case ever have completed them, remarking that 'habit had rendered the accumulation of materials a pleasing task for him, but he always appeared to shrink from the labour of arranging them' (Horsley, 11).

Callcott's activities around the turn of the century were many and varied. About 1799 he published *The Sentences, Psalms, Hymns, and Anthems, as Sung at the Asylum Chapel* and in 1801, anonymously, an elementary English grammar and dictionary, *The Way to Speak Well, Made Easy for Youth*. In 1802 he wrote the anthem 'I heard a voice from heaven', which was sung at the funeral of Samuel Arnold on 29 October; soon afterwards he applied unsuccessfully for Arnold's post as composer to George III. In 1806, 'thinking that the public would be led to expect something from him, on the Theory of Music' (Horsley, 10), he published his *Musical Grammar*. This became his best-known work, and went into two further editions in 1809 and 1817, the first revised by Samuel Wesley and the second by Horsley; it broke no new ground in its approach or contents, but was a valuable instruction manual on harmony and counterpoint and continued to be used for many years. He also found time to be active in the local militia: he had taken a commission in the Kensington volunteer corps in 1795, and in 1801 founded a military band, buying instruments, composing, compiling, and arranging the music, and teaching the musicians.

In early 1808 Callcott began to give a course of lectures on music at the Royal Institution. In April that year, however, he suffered a serious nervous collapse, possibly brought on by overwork, and on 30 May he was admitted to the asylum of Dr Joseph Mason Cox (1763–1818) at Fishponds, near Bristol. By 1813 he had recovered sufficiently to resume some of his former activities, but he gave up any plans to complete his dictionary of music. He suffered another collapse in 1816 and was once more confined to the Fishponds Asylum, where he spent the remaining years of his life. He died there on 15 May 1821, and was buried in Kensington churchyard on 23 May.

Callcott's significance is twofold: as one of the greatest and most prolific English glee composers, and as a musical theorist. In addition, as is clear from all contemporary accounts, he was held in high esteem and regarded with great affection by all who knew him. The benefit concert organized by his professional colleagues on 7 April 1809 was so well supported that it had to be moved from the Hanover Square Rooms to the King's Theatre; on this occasion nearly 4000 tickets were sold, and 1500 guineas were raised for Callcott's family. Further well-supported benefit concerts were held on 22 February 1813 and 3 May 1819. Three years after his death a lavish three-volume selection of his principal vocal works was published by subscription by Horsley for the benefit of his widow and family. The subscription list, headed by the duke of Cambridge and the duchess of Gloucester, included over 360 names, bearing witness to the strength of Callcott's continuing posthumous reputation. PHILIP OLLESON

Sources W. Horsley, 'Memoir of Dr Callcott', in J. W. Callcott, *A collection of glees, canons and catches*, 1 (1824), 1–19 · 'Memoir of Dr Callcott', *Quarterly Musical Magazine and Review*, 3 (1820), 404–5 · 'Memoir of Dr Callcott', *The Harmonicon*, 9 (1831), 53–5 · Callcott notebooks and MSS, BL, Add. MSS 27646–27693 · *Recollections of R. J. S. Stevens: an organist in Georgian London*, ed. M. Argent (1992) · J. C. Kassler, *The science of music in Britain, 1714–1830: a catalogue of writings, lectures, and inventions*, 1 (1979), 149–62 · D. Baptie, *Sketches of the English glee composers: historical, biographical and critical (from about 1735–1866)* [1896] · *Mendelssohn and his friends in Kensington: letters from Fanny and Sophy Horsley, written 1833–36*, ed. R. B. Gotch (1934) · H. T. Phillips, 'The history of the old private lunatic asylum at Fishponds, Bristol, 1740–1859', MSc diss., University of Bristol, 1973 · d. cert. [Maria Hutchins Callcott]

Archives BL, Add. MSS 27633–27693 · Bodl. Oxf. · Glasgow UL, Euing Music Collection

Likenesses A. W. Callcott, stipple, pubd 1824 (after F. C. Lewis), BM, NPG · A. W. Callcott, portrait · F. C. Lewis senior, stipple (after A. W. Callcott), BM, NPG; repro. in J. W. Callcott, *A collection of glees, canons and catches*, ed. W. Horsley, 3 vols. (1824) [*see illus.*] · H. Meyer, stipple, BM; repro. in Highfill, Burnim & Langhans, *BDA*

Wealth at death under £4000—Maria Hutchins Callcott: probate, 1 June 1859, *CGPLA Eng. & Wales*

Callcott [*née* Dundas; *other married name* Graham], **Maria, Lady Callcott** (**1785–1842**), traveller and author, was born on 19 July 1785 at Papcastle, near Cockermouth in Cumberland, the eldest of the four children of George Dundas, a naval officer, and his wife, Miss Thomson or Thompson, a Virginian brought up in Liverpool.

Childhood and education, 1785–1807 Soon after her birth, Maria Dundas's father took an appointment with the revenue service, and the family moved to Douglas on the Isle of Man. When Maria was about six the family moved to Wallasey in Cheshire. She was taught to read and write by her mother and the local curate, and had a happy childhood, gardening, riding her highland pony, and visiting lighthouses, bridges, and canals with her father. In 1793 she was sent to a school at the Manor House in Drayton, near Oxford. She was a passionate child and something of a tomboy—she later recalled that she 'narrowly escaped becoming a slattern for life' (Gotch, 33)—but she was an enthusiastic student, learning Latin, French, Italian, botany, history, geography, English literature, music, and drawing. This last subject was taught by William Delamotte, who encouraged her interest in the fine arts by making her read Joshua Reynolds's *Discourses* and Edmund Burke's treatise on the picturesque and the sublime. In the holidays she stayed with the family of her uncle Sir

Maria Callcott, Lady Callcott (1785–1842), by Sir Thomas Lawrence, 1819

David Dundas in Richmond: here she met French émigrés and a range of London cultural celebrities.

Maria Dundas's teachers, the Misses Bright, belonged to the circle of Sir Horace Walpole, and when Maria reached eighteen they found her an appointment as teaching assistant to Barbara Seton, a cousin of the Misses Berry, who was starting a school in Bideford. After six months there Maria Dundas was taken to Edinburgh by her father to stay with the family of her uncle, James Dundas, clerk to the signet. Here she met leading lights of the Scottish Enlightenment, including Dugald Stewart and John Playfair. However, she became ill with tuberculosis (which eventually killed her) and was sent south to London. Here she spent the winter of 1806–7 as an invalid, using her enforced leisure to read books ranging from Gibbon to Dante.

Travels in India, Europe, and South America, 1808–1825 In December 1808 Maria Dundas boarded the HMS *Cornelia* with her sister, her younger brother, and her father, who had been appointed to the commission of the navy in Bombay. She kept a journal of the voyage, which records her pleasure in tasting her first banana, reading Froissart's *Chronicles*, learning Persian, drawing (many of these sketches are now in the British Museum), and teaching the four youngest midshipmen. Among the passengers was Lieutenant Thomas Graham, with whom she fell in love while they were reading together the somewhat unromantic works of Tacitus and Dugald Stewart's *Philosophy of the Human Mind*. They were engaged when the ship docked in Bombay in May 1809, and were married on 9 December 1809.

Over the next two years Maria Graham travelled fairly widely in south and east India, sometimes with her husband, staying in Madras, Calcutta, and Ceylon, and developing a keen interest in Indian culture, religion, and antiquities. After her return to England in February 1811 she seems to have lived in London, where she became acquainted with the Murrays. They were not, however, the publishers of her *Journal of a Residence in India* (1812), a work intended to perform the 'humble but useful office' of supplementing more learned and specialized accounts of the continent (preface, iv). Covering everything from flora and wildlife to Parsi theology and the daily routine of the Madras lady, it is a lively account of her stay in India, and includes extensive descriptions and illustrations of her visits to the cave temples of Elephanta, Carli, and Canary, and the ancient city of Maliaballipooram. In this work and her subsequent *Letters from India* (1814) she became a popular exponent of the scholarly work of orientalists such as Sir William Jones, explaining and celebrating Hindu culture and achievements and attempting to put them within the context of the ancient world and European culture: she compares suttee, for instance, to ancient Greek customs. Although not uncritical of the Indian way of life, she was appreciative and open-minded: an approach which was to become increasingly less apparent as evangelicalism and utilitarianism impacted on attitudes to India in the 1830s and 1840s.

By February 1815 Maria Graham was living in Edinburgh; by December 1815 she was at Broughty Ferry in Forfarshire. Between household duties—such as making black puddings—and attacks of tuberculosis, she continued to read widely, admiring Byron and Scott. She continued to study, completing *Memoirs of the Wars of the French in Spain* (1815), translated from an original by De Rocca, and teaching herself Icelandic. She spent most of 1817 in London, and in September 1818 sailed on the HMS *Ganymede* with her husband to Italy. They arrived in December in Naples, and in early 1819 reached Rome, where they stayed for at least a year. Here they formed a close friendship with the painter Charles Eastlake, who introduced them to a circle of artists including John Jackson and Turner, and accompanied them on a visit to the village of Poli, in the Lazio region east of Rome. In 1820 Maria Graham published her journal of this three-month excursion, which described the economy, agriculture, people, and customs of this area, as well as the exploits of local brigands who eventually drove the party back to Tivoli and then Rome.

In the same year Maria Graham also published *Memoirs of the Life of Nicholas Poussin*, which has been described as 'both a scholarly and a pioneering work' (Lloyd and Brown, in Callcott, *The Journal of Maria Lady Callcott*, 2). It was the first monograph in English on this artist. Although the content draws heavily on Lanzi's earlier life and the art criticism is highly dependent on Reynolds's *Discourses* and Henry Fuseli's *Lectures*, it is nevertheless a comprehensive consideration of his work, which carefully identifies the geographical locations, patrons, originals, and copies of his paintings.

The Grahams were back in England in 1820, but in July 1821 they sailed for South America on the *Doris*. Once again Maria Graham kept a journal, this time recording her impressions of Madeira and Tenerife. In the autumn they arrived at Olinda in Brazil, which was in a state of revolution against the royalist government of Luiz de Rego. She was fascinated by the flora and fauna, but appalled by the slave market at Bahia (San Salvador) and the political disturbances in the streets, although she was firmly on the side of the independence movement. In December the Grahams reached Rio de Janeiro; in March they sailed for Valparaiso in Chile. Thomas Graham died at sea on 9 April 1822.

After docking at Valparaiso, Maria Graham buried her husband and took a house to recover from her grief. She was no recluse, though, exploring her surroundings, making friends with her Chilean neighbours, and attending religious festivals. Lord Cochrane, the Scottish mercenary in charge of the Brazilian and Chilean fleets, and the crew of the *Doris* were highly attentive. It was while staying at Cochrane's house in Quintero in November 1822 that she experienced an earthquake. Her account of its effects was published in the *Transactions* of the London Geological Society in 1823. Charles Lyell, in his *Principles of Geology* (1830), drew on her evidence to support his argument that earthquakes caused land elevation; G. B. Greenough, president of the society, subsequently attacked both the theory and Mrs Graham's account of the 1822 earthquake, leading her to reply publicly in a pamphlet in 1835. A further earthquake of that year—observed by Charles Darwin—led to her vindication of her report (although contemporary explanations of the exact causes of elevation were all mistaken).

In January 1823 Mrs Graham sailed for Rio de Janeiro, where she stayed until October. She nursed a sick cousin, attended the opera and the state opening of the legislative assembly, explored the surroundings in the company of a Mr Dampier, and read Brazilian history in the public library. In October she was appointed governess to Donna Maria, daughter of the emperor of Brazil. She briefly returned to England before taking up her appointment, and while there prepared her journals for publication: they appeared in two instalments in 1824.

Second marriage and the continent, 1826–1828 By May 1826 Maria Graham had returned to England, where she supported herself by writing articles and acting as a reader for John Murray. She began by editing a travel book on the Sandwich Islands written by the crew of the HMS *Blonde*. By autumn 1826 she had moved from her lodgings in Park Street to 8 High Row, Kensington Gravel Pits. This address was close to The Mall there, where the landscape painter Augustus Wall *Callcott (1770–1844) lived; she was probably already engaged to him by this time. They were married on 20 February 1827, and in May set out on a honeymoon on the continent, travelling through Germany, Bavaria, Austria, Italy, and France.

Both the Callcotts took notes of their travels, and Maria Callcott's journal of the excursion has been edited and published in microfiche form. It shows her usual lively interest in scenery and local customs—Frankfurt shops, for instance, she found sadly inferior to British—but the major focus of the journal is on works of art. Maria Callcott exhibited an extraordinarily wide and growing appreciation of continental paintings, and especially for Netherlandish, German, and Italian artists working before the Renaissance—she praised artists as various as Memling, Holbein, Lorenzetti, Caravaggio, and Altichiero. This understanding was owed partly to the Callcotts' contacts in the course of the tour: they met not only Nazarene artists such as Gotzenberger and K. C. Voger, but also pioneering curators and connoisseurs such as Sulpiz and Melchior Boisserée in Munich, and Carlo Lasinio in Pisa.

Maria Callcott's interest in the Italian primitives bore fruit in a publication of 1835, a *Description of the Chapel of the Annunziata dell'Arena, or Giotto's Chapel, in Padua*. Illustrated copiously by her husband, it was the first publication in English on this fourteenth-century artist, who was to be assigned a key role by nineteenth-century art historians in the prelude to the Renaissance. In addition she is held to have influenced the taste of Charles Eastlake and through him that of his wife: in the 1850s and 1860s the Eastlakes were responsible for the purchase of an impressive number of early Italian and northern European paintings for the National Gallery.

Kensington years, 1828–1842 After returning to London in mid-1828 Maria Callcott resumed her work for Murray, apparently working on a translation of a book on Turkish history and writing a textbook, *A Short History of Spain* (1828). This was originally intended to be modelled on Mrs Markham's enormously popular *History of England*—also published by Murray—but despite the inclusion of similar wood-engravings as illustrations Mrs Callcott did not employ the framing device of a mother narrating history to her children, nor did she include their subsequent questions and conversation.

In 1831, Maria Callcott burst a blood vessel and became a permanent invalid. Her social life was much curtailed, but nevertheless remained active: her visitors included the wit Sydney Smith, Maria Edgeworth, the art collector Samuel Rogers, the Hallam family, Joanne Baillie, Sarah Austin, and Jane Marcet. Her closest friend, however, was the Hon. Caroline Fox, with whom she shared political, religious, and leisure interests. In *A Century of British Painters* (1866) Richard and Samuel Redgrave gave an evocative description of the 'quaint, picturesque, and irregular room' in which the Callcotts, surrounded by dogs and rare plants (no doubt evidence of Mrs Callcott's continuing botanical studies), received their visitor: apparently, she 'mostly supported the conversation … [being] somewhat imperious in her state chamber; the painter being more of a silent listener, until some incident of travel, some question of art, roused him up to earnest interest or wise remark' (Redgrave and Redgrave, 376).

Maria Callcott's most famous book was *Little Arthur's History of England* (1835). She adopted a relaxed approach to writing this best-selling textbook, telling Caroline Fox that she intended to write from memory, only subsequently reading sources and correcting her text. The result was a great popular success, and the only nineteenth-century textbook history to rival Mrs Markham's *History of England*: it went through seventy editions—some 80,000 copies—in the course of a century. A reader later recalled that it 'read like a delightful story … we gained a fair idea of the flow of events and the stories of leading people without boredom' (M. V. Hughes, *A London Child of the 1870s*, 1977 edn, 42). Part of its long-standing popularity can be attributed to its anticipation of Victorian developments: *Little Arthur's History* reflected a more romantic, patriotic, and nationalist approach to the English past than its more domestic predecessors, which had emphasized private rather than public virtues.

A rather more weighty work, *Essays towards a History of Painting* (1836), was possibly written in collaboration with Callcott's husband. A wide-ranging consideration of the early history of painting in the ancient world, with separate sections on the classification of paintings and the materials used, it showed extensive knowledge of appropriate sources in classical literature and drew heavily on her tour of the continent in 1827–8. Other works published in later life reflected Maria Callcott's interest in botany. In 1841 she published *The Little Bracken-Burners, a Tale; and Little Mary's Four Saturdays*, two tiresome tales which reflected her wide knowledge of plants and the medicinal, social, and religious lore relating to them. In 1842 her *Scriptural Herbal* followed.

Death and assessment By the early 1840s Lady Callcott—as she had become in 1837, when her husband was knighted—had become extremely ill. She died at her home in The Mall, Kensington Gravel Pits, on 21 November 1842, and was buried at Kensal Green cemetery; Callcott survived her by only two years. She left no children by either marriage, but had greatly enjoyed the company of Callcott's great-nieces—the sisters of the painter J. C. Horsley—in her later years.

Lady Callcott was clearly a vivid personality: unconventional, occasionally irascible (increasingly so as her health declined), bookish, but lively, humane, and interested in everything and everybody. Her portraits—the most famous of which was painted in 1819 by Thomas Lawrence—show a handsome, shrewd-looking, dark-eyed, and curly-haired woman sporting a turban (it has been suggested that this perennial headdress was worn to conceal a childhood injury, when she fell backwards into a fireplace). Her travel books have been described as 'stiff with history and politics' and 'rather impersonal' (Robinson, 45), but they brim with details about local customs, flora and fauna, and people, as well as drier matters; they make her one of the most significant travel writers of the early nineteenth century. Her contribution to the development of art criticism and history is still more important: Francis Haskell has praised her as 'a remarkable woman who deserves a place in any account of early nineteenth-century taste', one whose response to art was 'exceptional in its range and perception' (*Rediscoveries in Art*, 1976, 91). However, it is likely that she will continue to be best known for one of her slightest works—the classic history textbook, *Little Arthur's History of England*. ROSEMARY MITCHELL

Sources R. B. Gotch, *Maria, Lady Callcott: the creator of 'Little Arthur'* (1937) • *The captain's wife: the South American journals of Maria Graham, 1821–23*, ed. E. Mavor (1993) • M. Graham, *Journal of a residence in India* (1812) • *The journal of Maria, Lady Callcott, 1827–8*, ed. C. Lloyd and D. B. Brown (1981) • M. Graham, *Three months passed in the mountains east of Rome during the year 1819* (1820) • R. A. Mitchell, *Picturing the past: English history in text and image, 1830–1870* (2000) • R. A. Raza, 'British women writers on India between the mid-eighteenth century and 1857', DPhil diss., U. Oxf., 1998 • C. Lloyd, 'Lady Callcott's honeymoon, 1827–8: art-historical reflections in Germany and Italy', *Taste and travel in the nineteenth century*, ed. C. Richardson and G. Smith (2000) • M. Kölbl-Ebert, 'Observing Oregeny: Maria Graham's account of the earthquake in Chile in 1822', *Episodes*, 22/1 (1999), 36–40, 45–58 • R. Redgrave and S. Redgrave, *A century of British painters* (1866); (1981) • J. Robinson, *Wayward women: a guide to women travellers* (1990) • C. R. Sherman and A. M. Holcomb, *Women as interpretators of the visual arts, 1820–1979* (1981)

Archives Biblioteca Nacional, Rio de Janeiro, Brazilian journal [facs. in BL, MS Facs 512] • Bodl. Oxf., papers incl. journals, travel diaries, memoirs, and other biographical papers • John Murray, London • RA, notes on art and other subjects | BL, corresp. with Caroline Fox, Add. MSS 51962–51964 • BL, corresp. with third Lord Holland, Add. MSS 51838–51839 • Bodl. Oxf., letters to Mary Somerville • Borth. Inst., letters to Mary Ponsonby, Countess Grey • NL Scot., letters to family members • NL Scot., letters to William Gordon Mackenzie

Likenesses C. Eastlake, chalk drawing, 1818, BM • T. Lawrence, oil sketch, 1819, NPG [*see illus.*] • C. Eastlake, sketch, 1819–20, BM • A. Callcott, oils, *c*.1830, Gov. Art Coll. • J. C. Horsley, portrait, *c*.1830–1839; known to be in the possession of Lady Whitelegg in 1937 • D. Wilkie, oil sketch, *c*.1830–1839, repro. in F. Haskell, *Rediscoveries in art* (1976), 91; formerly at P. and D. Colnaghi & Co., London, in 1976 • C. Philips, chalk drawing, BM

Callcott, Maria Hutchins (1798–1859). *See under* Callcott, John Wall (1766–1821).

Callcott, William Hutchins (1807–1882), composer, was the son of Dr John Wall *Callcott (1766–1821), composer and singer, and his wife, Elizabeth Mary Hutchins, and nephew of Sir Augustus Wall *Callcott, RA (1770–1844), painter and singer. He was born on 28 September 1807 in Kensington, London, and baptized there on 24 October 1807. As a child he received some instruction in music from his father, and later continued his studies under his brother-in-law, William Horsley. He then began to teach in London and became organist of the new district chapel in Addison Road, Kensington, and of St Barnabas's Church. On 4 July 1830 he was elected as a member of the Royal Society of Musicians. In 1836 he published an abridged version of his father's *A Musical Grammar*, in 1840 a collection of psalm and hymn tunes for Bickersteth's *Christian Psalmody*, and in 1843 *The Child's Own Singing Book*. In this last work he was assisted by his wife, Maria, who also wrote several religious stories. In 1851 Callcott published *Remarks on the Royal Albert Piano* (exhibited at the International Exhibition), and in 1859 *A Few Facts on the Life of Handel*. He also composed several songs, glees, and anthems, but his name is known principally for his arrangements and transcriptions for the piano, which amount to several hundred pieces. He was for some years organist of Ely Place Chapel. In the latter part of his life he suffered much from ill health. He died at 1 Campden House Road, Kensington, on 4 August 1882, and was buried on the 9th at Kensal Green.

Callcott's son William Robert Stuart Callcott (1852–1886) showed great promise as an organist and musician, but died young in the spring of 1886.

W. B. SQUIRE, *rev.* DAVID J. GOLBY

Sources Highfill, Burnim & Langhans, *BDA* [John Wall Callcott] · *MT*, 23 (1882), 503 · D. Baptie, *A handbook of musical biography* (1883); facs. repr. (1986) · *Monthly Musical Record*, 12 (1882), 212 · *Musical Standard* (3 Feb 1883) · Brown & Stratton, *Brit. mus.*

Wealth at death £14,954 5s. 10d.: resworn probate, April 1883, *CGPLA Eng. & Wales* (1882)

Calle, Margery (*c.*1450–*c.*1479). *See under* Paston family (*per. c.*1420–1504).

Callendar. For this title name *see* Livingston, James, first earl of Callendar (*d.* 1674).

Callendar, Hugh Longbourne (1863–1930), physicist, was born on 18 April 1863 at Hatherop, Gloucestershire, the eldest son of Hugh Callendar, rector of Hatherop, and his wife, Anne (Annie) Cecilia Longbourne. From Marlborough College, where he ranked top in classics and mathematics and excelled at sports, he entered Trinity College, Cambridge, in 1882, obtaining a first class in the classical tripos in his second year and graduating as sixteenth wrangler in 1885. Later that year he arrived at the Cavendish Laboratory, then under J. J. Thomson, having done no serious reading in physics and lacking practical laboratory experience. Nevertheless Thomson considered that he was capable of experimental research and the accurate measurement of electrical resistance was selected as a suitable subject. Callendar's thesis on platinum thermometry was accepted, and he was elected a fellow of Trinity in 1886.

The importance of Callendar's thesis led swiftly to its publication, 'On the practical measurements of temperature: experiments made at the Cavendish Laboratory, Cambridge' (*PTRS*, 1887, 161–230), and determined one of the two major lines of Callendar's subsequent work, the other being on the properties of steam. He was appointed professor of physics at Royal Holloway College, Englefield Green, in 1888, and in 1893 to the chair of physics at McGill University, Montreal, where he was in charge of the new Macdonald physics building. There Callendar found suitable apparatus on which he could pursue his plans for high-precision work based on electrical measures. He also studied engineering problems connected with steam turbines, and with John Thomas Nicolson determined the temperature of steam expansion behind a piston. In collaboration with Professor Howard Turner Barnes he began the study of the calorimetric properties of water. On 17 May 1894 he married Victoria Mary, eldest daughter of Alexander Stewart of Saundersfoot, Pembrokeshire. They had three sons and a daughter. In June that year he was elected fellow of the Royal Society. On leaving McGill his place was taken by Ernest Rutherford. Callendar returned to England in 1898 as Quain professor of physics at University College, London. In 1902 he succeeded Sir Arthur Rücker as professor of physics at the Royal College of Science, London, incorporated into the Imperial College of Science and Technology in 1907, where he remained until his death.

Building on the work in 1861 of Ernst Werner von Siemens, Callendar developed the platinum resistance thermometer to the point where it provided a standard for the establishment of the thermometric scale. Platinum thermometers were appreciated in the laboratory where they were superior to the air thermometers in use hitherto, and they were also welcomed by engineers as convenient and practicable means of regulating heat in industrial operations. Among other inventions made in connection with his researches Callendar devised in 1887 an extremely accurate compensation bridge; the original, constructed in 1893, was used throughout his researches on steam. An important paper, 'Thermodynamic properties of gases and vapours deduced from a modified form of the Joule-Thomson equation' (*PRS*, 67, 1900, 266–86) formed the basis of his subsequent work on steam, for in it he stated all the thermodynamic properties of steam by means of consistent thermodynamic formulae, leading to the formulation of his steam equation and the publication of his *Callendar Steam Tables* (1915, 1922, 1927), giving the properties of steam up to and beyond the critical pressure. He also published *The Properties of Steam* (1920). Callendar took part in the first International Steam Tables Conference, held in London in 1929 to co-ordinate research work in various countries. In 1899 Lord Rayleigh's committee of electrical standards accepted Callendar's proposals for a standard scale of temperature based on the platinum thermometer, and it continues to be relied on for temperatures between the boiling point of liquid oxygen (−182.97 °C) and the melting point of antimony (630.5 °C).

Among his other projects Callendar directed and carried out, sometimes with collaborators, research on the specific heat of gases, the osmotic pressure of solutions (1908), the absolute expansion of mercury (1911), and the boiling point of sulphur (1890 and 1912). For the Air Ministry he investigated dopes and detonation (1925 and 1926), and in 1926, a keen motorist himself, he published on the cause of knock in petrol engines and the effects of anti-knock additives to petrol. In a completely different field he published *A Manual of Cursive Shorthand* (1889), which came into fairly general use in some of the British colonies, and *A System of Phonetic Spelling Adapted to English* (1890).

Callendar received many awards and honours, among them the Watt medal of the Institution of Civil Engineers (1898), the Rumford medal of the Royal Society (1906), and the Hawksley gold medal of the Institution of Mechanical Engineers (1915). He was president of the Physical Society of London in 1910, and their first Duddell memorial medallist in 1924. He was president of section A of the British Association in 1912 and was made CBE in 1920. Callendar's early passion for sport remained with him; when too old for tennis he enjoyed watching his wife and children play in tournaments. He was an excellent teacher and his dignified kindliness endeared him to his students. He died at 11 Grange Park, Ealing, London, on 21 January 1930. He was survived by his wife. ANITA MCCONNELL

Sources S. W. J. S., *PRS*, 134A (1931–2), xviii–xxvi • J. J. Thomson, *Recollections and reflections* (1936) • *DSB* • L. E. Upcott, *The Times* (31 Jan 1930), 199 • Y. Gingras, *Physics and the rise of scientific research in Canada*, trans. P. Keating (1991) • *Engineering* (24 Jan 1930), 115–17 • *Nature*, 125 (1930), 173–4 • W. E. K. Middleton, *A history of the thermometer and its use in meteorology* [1966] • b. cert. • m. cert. • d. cert.
Wealth at death £8154 12s. 4d.: probate, 11 March 1930, *CGPLA Eng. & Wales*

Callender, Sir Geoffrey Arthur Romaine (1875–1946), naval historian and museum director, was born at Didsbury, Manchester, on 25 November 1875, the elder son of Arthur William Callender, cotton mill owner, and his wife, Agnes Louisa, daughter of the Revd George Stephen Woodgate, vicar of Pembury, Kent. Educated in Oxford at St Edward's School and at Merton College, he was placed in the second class of the honours list in modern history in 1897. He was appointed in January 1905 to the new Royal Naval College, Osborne, where he embraced the study of naval history with characteristic enthusiasm. Finding no textbook suitable for naval cadets, he instantly set about producing his *Sea Kings of Britain* (3 vols., 1907–11). He became head of the history and English department in January 1913, and thereafter the navy and its history were the guiding interests of his life.

In 1921 Callender moved to the Royal Naval College, Dartmouth, as head of the history department there, but he did not remain long. Experience gleaned from the First World War showed that a study of history was essential at all levels of naval education: a chair of history was therefore established in London at the Royal Naval College, Greenwich, where a staff college and a war college were also being formed. Callender was appointed first occupant in 1922 and it was there that he published his best-known work, *The Naval Side of British History* (1924). Meanwhile (1921–4), the Society for Nautical Research was conducting its campaign to save HMS *Victory*. Callender was already that body's honorary secretary and treasurer—a dual post which he held continuously from 1920 until his death—and he was largely responsible for the successful outcome of the campaign.

Callender now embarked on his dearest project: the foundation of a museum which would assemble under one roof the priceless naval and maritime treasures of Britain. The co-operation of the Society for Nautical Research and beneficent sympathizers like Sir James Caird secured in 1928 the acquisition for the nation of the magnificent Macpherson collection of naval and nautical prints, to form, with the pictures and models already at the college, the nucleus of the new museum. The ideal site was Inigo Jones's Queen's House at Greenwich, then occupied by the Royal Hospital school; and on the latter's migrating to Holbrook, the last difficulty was overcome. The National Maritime Museum Act was passed in 1934 and Callender became, as of right, the first director. Into the immense task of restoring the Queen's House, preparing the galleries, assembling the exhibits, and arranging them he threw his whole energy, and the museum was opened by George VI on 27 April 1937. Callender was knighted in the following year and spent the rest of his life improving and adding to the collections. He died, suddenly, but fittingly, in the museum on 6 November 1946. He was unmarried. Callender was a man of exceptional personality, a born conversationalist, and a brilliant lecturer, respected and beloved by several generations of naval officers, and possessed of an encyclopaedic knowledge of nautical antiquities.

MICHAEL LEWIS, *rev.* H. C. G. MATTHEW

Sources *WWW* • personal knowledge (1959) • private information (1959) • *CGPLA Eng. & Wales* (1947)
Archives NMM, letters to various persons
Likenesses W. Stoneman, photograph, 1944, NPG • D. S. Ewart, oils, 1945, NMM
Wealth at death £31,777 11s. 2d.: administration, 19 Aug 1947

Callender, George William (1830–1878), surgeon, son of Richard Boucher Callender, solicitor, was born at Clifton, Bristol, Gloucestershire, on 24 June 1830, and was educated at Bishop's College, Bristol. He then began his medical career by studying with his uncle, Dr Lancaster of Clifton, before entering St Bartholomew's Hospital, London, as a student in 1849. In 1852 he gained his membership of the Royal College of Surgeons and three years later he gained his fellowship of the college. In July 1854 he became registrar and demonstrator of morbid anatomy at St Bartholomew's Hospital. Throughout his career he maintained a keen interest in anatomy, knowledge of which he regarded as the foundation of a surgeon's skill.

In 1861, after several years as house surgeon, he was elected assistant surgeon. Ten years later he became full surgeon to the hospital on the resignation of Sir James Paget. In 1873 he was appointed lecturer in surgery at the hospital. He shared the teaching of surgery with his friend and colleague William Savory.

In 1869 Callender published a paper, entitled 'Development of the bones of the face in man', in the *Philosophical Transactions* of the Royal Society, which secured his election as fellow of the Royal Society in 1871. This paper outlined the development of the premaxilla and maxilla bone in the human face. The premaxilla is apparently absent in the human skull, though it exists in many other mammals. Callender studied the position and shape of both bones in a number of human foetuses and concluded that the premaxilla, which is present in the facial structure of the foetus, becomes covered by part of the maxilla. He suggested that the two bones become completely fused before birth.

Callender published on many other anatomical subjects, including the development of the thyroid and the formation of the human subaxial arches. In 1863 a book on the anatomy of the hip appeared. Callender also contributed to many journals, including *Medico-Chirurgical Transactions*, *Transactions of the Clinical Society*, *Transactions of the Pathological Society*, and *St Bartholomew's Hospital Reports*.

Callender was not an innovative surgeon but was known for his neat and dextrous operations. Like his colleagues Howard Marsh and William Savory at St Bartholomew's, he was openly suspicious of Joseph Lister's antiseptic methods. He supported Savory's public opposition to Lister. However, he was committed to the principles of cleanliness in operating theatres and surgical wards. He took a holistic view in caring for his patients, stressing the value of good diet, rest, and careful nursing. By this system of patient management and by controlling post-operative infections he succeeded in dramatically reducing surgical mortality.

Callender lived in Queen Anne Street, London, and was married with several children. He was beginning to establish a large practice when he began to suffer from Bright's disease, from which he died on 20 October 1878. His death took place at sea on his way back from a holiday in the United States; travelling had exacerbated his illness. Callender had been treated with great kindness and respect by colleagues in the United States, in part at least because of his achievements as a distinguished British surgeon. He was buried at Kensal Green on 29 October 1878.

NORMAN MOORE, *rev.* STELLA BUTLER

Sources *St Bartholomew's Hospital Reports*, 15 (1879), xli–xlviii · J. Dobson, 'George William Callender: pioneers of osteogeny', *The Journal of Bone and Joint Surgery*, 31, B (1949), 127–9 · V. G. Plarr, *Plarr's Lives of the fellows of the Royal College of Surgeons of England*, rev. D'A. Power, 1 (1930), 187–8 · personal knowledge (1886) · Venn, *Alum. Cant.* [Richard Clement Callender] · *DNB*

Likenesses portrait, St Bartholomew's Hospital, London

Wealth at death under £3000: probate, 17 Nov 1879, *CGPLA Eng. & Wales*

Callender, James Thomson (1758–1803), political writer and radical, was born in Scotland, the son of a tobacconist, though further details of his early years are obscure. The poet James Thomson may have been a relative. Callender was raised as a Presbyterian of the strongly Calvinist variety, possibly in Stirling, and received a classical education. He first came to the attention of Edinburgh literary society in 1782 on publication of his *Deformities of Samuel Johnson*, a crude, vindictive and slashing assault on the work of the great lexicographer which included hints of a latent Scottish nationalism. *A Critical Review of the Works of Dr. Samuel Johnson*, published in 1783, was repetitive and less well received. Unable to secure the patronage necessary for a literary career, Callender spent the next seven years as a clerk in the Edinburgh sasine (conveyancing) office, also qualifying as a messenger-at-arms. During this period he married, though his wife's identify is unknown; the couple had four children, at least one of whom died at a young age. He also developed a strong misanthropic streak, caused, no doubt, by the world's failure to recognize his talents.

Callender's government career ended in dismissal in 1790, following his leadership of a long-running but unsuccessful revolt among the writing clerks against their superior, Andrew Steele, whom they accused of administrative corruption. Thereafter Callender became obsessed with the evils of 'old corruption', which he first attacked in a pamphlet, *An Impartial Account of the Excise*, on behalf of the big Edinburgh brewers, in 1789. Callender was kept from poverty by the liberal but eccentric judge Francis, Lord Gardenstone, who helped him obtain regular employment as a messenger-at-arms and welcomed him into his circle of young poets and writers. Here Callender's increasingly radical political views evolved in a milieu of youthful high spirits, eroticism, and satirical verse. *Miscellanies in Prose and Verse* (1792), to which he contributed prolifically, and which received some good reviews, was the product of Gardenstone's circle.

In February 1792 Callender published in the Edinburgh *Bee* the first of eight parts of what was to become a very successful pamphlet, *The Political Progress of Britain*. As an inflammatory critique of imperialism, war, and corruption, with a strong Scottish nationalist flavour, Callender's work rivalled Thomas Paine's in its radicalism. It sold well, although not in the numbers of the *Rights of Man*. At the same time Callender joined the Edinburgh Friends of the People, becoming a drinking companion of Thomas Muir but siding usually with the more militant radicals. In December 1792 he represented the Canongate no. 1 branch of the society at the Edinburgh convention, where he supported resolutions favouring Scottish nationalist sentiment, which his writings had done much to promote. Within a month of the convention, however, Callender was forced into exile, first to Dublin, then to Philadelphia, after the Scottish authorities, anxious to arrest the seditious author of *Political Progress*, persuaded Gardenstone to incriminate him.

In the United States Callender worked as a journalist and congressional reporter for the *Philadelphia Gazette*, quickly gaining notoriety for his partisan reports favouring Thomas Jefferson's Republican Party. Throughout the 1790s he wrote, with many other exiled British radicals, as a militant propagandist, anonymously attacking President Washington and other prominent Federalists in the strongly Republican newspaper, the Philadelphia *Aurora*, and crossing quills with the equally notorious expatriate British pamphleteer, William Cobbett. In this battle of 'billingsgate', Cobbett, who dubbed him 'Newgate Callender', was the victor.

Callender also published ten political pamphlets in the United States, the most sensational of which, *The History of the United States for 1796*, destroyed Alexander Hamilton's public career by exposing his illicit affair with Maria Reynolds. Shortly after the death of his wife in 1798, Callender, now in dire poverty and drinking heavily, was forced by a campaign of Federalist harassment to flee Philadelphia to Virginia, where, with the support of Jefferson, he continued his writings in favour of radical democracy. In June 1800 he was imprisoned for six months under the sedition law for his anti-Federalist pamphlet *The Prospect before Us*. He was seen by the more radical Jeffersonians as a political martyr, but on his release he found that his exertions in support of Jefferson's successful presidential election campaign were not to be rewarded. He was left isolated and bitter by Jefferson's policy of political consensus, which required the jettisoning of immoderate Republican militants. In partnership with Henry Pace, a Federalist, Callender established the *Richmond Recorder*, which he used to expose the petty vices of the Virginia aristocracy and to attack Jefferson's administration. He remained, however, a radical republican and idiosyncratic democrat, but when in September 1802 he heard that his former colleagues in Philadelphia were spreading rumours about his marriage, Callender retaliated by publishing the gossip, which had been circulating among the Virginia gentry, about Jefferson's relationship with his slave, Sally Hemings.

This was to be Callender's final scoop. He was shunned and scorned by all, beaten in public by an outraged lawyer, and again gaoled for several days as a martyr for a free press. His newspaper lost circulation and he fell into penury. He drowned in the James River at Richmond in the early hours of 17 July 1803, probably having committed suicide, for he left a letter in which he expressed remorse for some of his excesses, although he did not apologize to Jefferson, nor did he renounce his extreme politics. The democratic legacy he might have left remained obscured by the misanthropic outpourings from his vitriolic pen.

MICHAEL DUREY

Sources M. Durey, *'With the hammer of truth': James Thomson Callender and America's early national heroes* (1990) · M. Durey, 'Callender, James Thomson', *ANB* · C. A. Jellison, 'That scoundrel Callender', *Virginia Magazine of History and Biography*, 64 (1959), 295–306 · A. Gordon-Reed, *Thomas Jefferson and Sally Hemings: an American controversy* (1997) · R. N. Rosenfeld, *American Aurora: a democratic republican returns* (1997) · M. Durey, *Transatlantic radicals and the early American republic* (1997) · P. Ross, *The Scot in America* (1896), 354
Archives L. Cong., Washington DC, Thomas Jefferson MSS
Wealth at death virtually nothing: Virginia newspapers

Callender, John (1706–1748), Baptist minister and historian in America, was born on 7 June 1706 in Boston, Massachusetts, the first of the four children of John Callender (1674–1742), shopkeeper, and his wife, Priscilla (1680–1716), daughter of John Ballard of Lynn, Massachusetts, and his wife, Rebecca. A precocious student, Callender entered Harvard College on a scholarship at the age of thirteen and, as a scholar of erudition, he authored the first serious history of Rhode Island. His historical significance lies in his successful efforts to promote amicable relations between New England's Baptist and Congregational churches.

At the time of Callender's birth the puritans of Massachusetts and Connecticut still regarded Baptists as dangerous radicals who threatened the New England way of life. His grandfather Ellis Callender (1666–1726) and his uncle Elisha Callender (1692–1738) had both served as ministers of Boston's first Baptist church and had begun the process of legitimizing the Baptists' place in New England. In particular Elisha Callender, the first Baptist known to have graduated from Harvard (1710), used his warm personal relationship with New England's puritan leaders to bridge the gap between dissent and orthodoxy. Increase and Cotton Mather attended his ordination in 1718—an extraordinary gesture of approval and support. The significance of the sermon Cotton Mather preached, 'Good Men United', was lost on no one.

Thus John Callender's career as peacemaker continued an unusual family tradition. After receiving his AB in 1724 and his AM in 1726 Callender briefly taught at a school in Swansea, the site of the first Baptist church in Massachusetts. From 1728 to 1730 he preached to the Swansea Baptists on an occasional basis but then declined their offer of a permanent position; he confessed to friends that he did not enjoy life in a small village. Callender left Swansea to practise medicine in Newport, Rhode Island, which had a cosmopolitan society more congenial to his tastes, and in October 1731 he was ordained as pastor of Newport's Baptist church. After his uncle Elisha died in 1738 Callender became New England's best-known Baptist and also developed a reputation as one of its most urbane gentlemen and scholars. He cultivated friendships with noted Congregational ministers (particularly Samuel Mather, son of Cotton Mather); he was a voice of moderation within New England's Baptist community, which was becoming increasingly militant; and he published a sermon that took the remarkably ecumenical position that pious non-Baptists should be allowed communion in a Baptist church.

The publication of his *Historical Discourse on the Civil and Religious Affairs of the Colony of Rhode Island and Providence* (1739) cemented Callender's place in New England history. Initially presented as a lecture to the Society for Promoting Virtue and Knowledge by a Free Conversation, an intellectual club in Newport, the *Historical Discourse* was expanded into a full-length study of Rhode Island's first century. A monument to accuracy and restraint, Callender's history defended the conduct of Rhode Island's early founders, who had been regarded as rogues and heretics by the leaders of Massachusetts who had exiled them, but his conciliatory tone softened the fight between puritans and dissenters into a conflict of conscience on both sides. Isaac Backus, who wrote the first general history of the Baptists in New England in 1777, relied heavily on Callender's work and on his research notes.

Callender married Elizabeth Hardin (1712–1770) of Swansea on 15 February 1730 and they had nine children. An adviser to the governments of Newport and the colony of Rhode Island on law, education, and external relations, Callender exemplified the ideal of the cultivated public citizen and was a gentleman of the Enlightenment as well as a model of Reformation piety. Having been in poor health for much of his life he died prematurely, on 26 January 1748, and was mourned throughout New England. He was buried in the common burial-ground of Newport.

BRUCE C. DANIELS

Sources C. K. Shipton, 'Callender, John', *Sibley's Harvard graduates: biographical sketches of those who attended Harvard College*, 7 (1945), 150–55 · W. Joyce, 'Callender, John', *ANB* · R. Elton, 'Memoir of the Rev. John Callender', *Collections of the Rhode Island Historical Society*, 4 (1843), 9–25 · W. G. McLoughlin, *Soul liberty: the Baptists' struggle in New England, 1630–1833* (1991) · *The diary of Isaac Backus*, ed. W. G. McLoughlin, 3 vols. (1979) · E. Woodworth Barnes, 'Descendants of Ellis Callender of Boston', *New England Historical and Genealogical Register*, 144 (1990), 195–210

Archives Rhode Island Historical Society, Providence, MSS | Yale U., Isaac Backus MSS, MSS and research notes
Likenesses R. Fete, oils, Rhode Island Historical Society, Providence

Callender, Sir Thomas Octavius (1855–1938), electrical engineer, was born on 9 April 1855 at Clydeview, Partick, Lanarkshire, Scotland, the eldest of the ten children (five boys and five girls) of William Ormiston Callender (1827–1908), a commission merchant, and his wife, Jean, *née* Marshall, the daughter of a Greenock tanner, whom he had married in 1854. In 1859 the family moved to Hammersmith, London, a decision most likely prompted by the collapse of the Western Bank of Glasgow, which resulted in Thomas's grandfather losing all his money. After some years, Thomas's father, then an agent for a number of Scottish textile mills, established the connection that was to make Callenders pioneers in the manufacture and laying of cables worldwide.

Thomas was sent to school in Boulogne but returned to London to continue his education at the outbreak of the Franco-Prussian War in 1870. In that same year his father returned from Switzerland after visiting the asphalt deposits at Val de Travers, and set up Callender and Amos to act as agents for the Val de Travers Company of Neuchâtel to import asphalt for the extensive road-making schemes that were taking place in the City of London. In 1877, in the wake of this successful venture, William Callender obtained an interest in the import of bitumen from Trinidad for road-making and other waterproofing purposes, and decided it would be timely to take on his two eldest sons, Thomas and William, to form the firm of Callender & Sons for the refining of bitumen and for asphalt paving. The company's first offices were at 150 Leadenhall Street, London, with a small refinery at Millwall, where the bitumen was landed. Thomas Callender quickly realized that importing unrefined bitumen halfway across the world was costly and a potential drag on the efficiency of the company, and he arranged that all impurities be eliminated at source. This undoubtedly contributed to the growing success of the company, which was developing numerous overseas road-making contracts. While on a business trip to St Petersburg in 1880, Callender was hugely impressed by the opera house, which was lit by Jablochoff candles, a primitive form of electric lighting. This, together with the simultaneous discovery of the incandescent lamp by Edison and Swan, persuaded Callender of the need to turn the business towards the production of large-capacity insulated cables if the revolution in electric lighting was to be exploited. His younger brother William had already successfully produced vulcanized bitumen (VB); the waterproofing and insulant technology was therefore already familiar to the company, and this prompted the elder William Callender to patent the new material in 1881, in order to begin tests on the production of insulated wire at their new factory on a 4.5 acre site in Erith, Kent.

In 1882 Callender's Bitumen Telegraph and Waterproof Company was formed to finance the development of VB, with the original firm continuing alongside, providing the management for a further two years. Although the new company had only minimal experience of telegraph cables, it nevertheless managed to secure the services of Sir Samuel Canning of the Telegraph Construction and Maintenance Company, who had successfully laid the Atlantic telegraph cables in 1866, to make good any disadvantage. Over the following fourteen years the business of consolidating successes was due in large part to Callender's vision, his business acumen, and his indefatigable search for fresh orders, both at home and overseas. His skills, though, were not confined simply to commercial matters, for in the early 1880s he had invented the Callender solid system, whereby cables were laid in wooden troughs and embedded in bitumen, a development which was later used extensively for the laying of mains cables.

The period between 1882 and the eventual reorganization of the company in 1896 saw the development of most of Callenders' pioneering projects. The management of the Erith works became Callender's responsibility, and under his direction many important early contracts were secured. The company supplied the VB cables for the electric lighting of the new law courts in the Strand and for the Covent Garden Opera House in 1883, as well as mains cables for the growing number of electricity supply companies. In 1891 the firm introduced an underground electric haulage system at the Abercannaid colliery, Merthyr, and in the same year received its first tramways order. It was also closely associated with the first electrified underground railway. By the late 1880s it was becoming clear that the company's activities required a much broader financial base to accommodate the increased demand for electric power. In 1896 the firm of Callender's Cable and Construction Company was created and within two years the number of contracts had grown from thirty-one to seventy, and total sales over the same period had increased from £95,764 to £296,946. With Callender as managing director (a position he held until his death), the company was well placed to profit from the huge expansion of the many applications of the electricity industry, from the early days of electric lighting to the creation of the national grid following the 1926 Electricity (Supply) Act. Indeed, the national grid was to provide Callenders with valuable business during the lean years of the depression.

The number of overseas contracts increased dramatically in the period following reorganization, and in February 1904 the first of a number of major cabling projects was undertaken in India for electricity supply and tramways. India was to become one of Callenders' most important markets, and Callender, eager to maintain personal contact with important operations wherever possible, proposed setting up permanent headquarters there. At home the company undertook the electrification of London's metropolitan tramways, a seven-year scheme, which was completed in 1909. The General Post Office, meanwhile, was in the process of negotiating large telephone cable contracts, and the first of many large orders was placed with Callenders in 1913. The years 1914–18 were given over to the war effort, and orders from the

Admiralty went some way to compensate for the interruption to Callenders' usual supply lines from Trinidad.

Callender was knighted in June 1918, and he continued to play a very active part in the management of the company over the following two decades. Even when in poor physical health he remained alert to all business opportunities. In 1930 he began discussions with the directors of British Insulated Cables on prospects for closer co-operation between the two companies, but it was not until June 1945 that the Callender board met for the last time before British Insulated Callender Cables began operations as a truly international company.

Callender was a JP for the county of Kent, a member of the Institution of Electrical Engineers, and a director of a number of power companies. He died at his home, Bidborough Court, Bidborough, Tunbridge Wells, Kent, on 2 December 1938, surviving his wife, Bessie Emmeline, *née* Pinnock, whom he had married on 19 March 1885, by just six months. He was buried on 8 December at Erith cemetery, and a memorial service was held at St Clement Danes, Strand. His estate was shared between his only child, Thomas Ormiston Callender (1896–1941), and other members of his family. BARBARA TROMPETER

Sources R. M. Morgan, *Callender's, 1882–1945* (1982) • *The Times* (5 Dec 1938) • *The Times* (9–10 Dec 1938) • *WWW* • d. cert. • b. cert.
Archives Callenders cables from 1882 [company only]
Likenesses oils, 1932?, British Insulated Callender Cables Group, London
Wealth at death £383,276 15*s*. 9*d*.: probate, 3 May 1939, *CGPLA Eng. & Wales*

Callender, William Romaine (1825–1876), cotton spinner and politician, was born on 2 June 1825 at 7 Nelson Street, Chorlton Row, Manchester, the elder son of William Romaine Callender (1794–1872), merchant and calico printer, and his first wife, Hannah, the daughter of Samuel Pope from Exeter, probably a solicitor.

The Callenders were an ancient Scottish family, while the Romaines were of Huguenot origin, William Romaine (1714–1795), Callender's great-uncle, having been a noted Calvinistic Anglican divine. Callender's father, after apprenticeship to a Birmingham draper, was by 1825 a partner in the expanding Manchester firm of Kershaw, Leese and Callender. He left this firm in 1836 and, after several more partnerships, set up Callender & Sons, merchants and manufacturers, with his sons William Romaine Callender (from 1847) and Samuel Pope Callender as partners. This became one of Manchester's leading cotton spinners and merchants, acquiring in 1862 the mills of Thomas Bazley in Water Street, Manchester, and the Dean mills, Halliwell, Bolton.

The latter village community provided an ideal setting for Callender to put into practice his paternalist beliefs, as he attempted to revive its mutual improvement society and regularly addressed his workers on the values of literacy and self-help. Callender also invested, with Thomas Hughes among others, in the co-operative Cobden memorial mills in 1866, and in the late 1860s the family firm had purchased and modernized the Jackson Street Spinning Company of the philanthropic tory Robert Barnes. In 1849 Callender married Hannah, the only daughter of John Mayson JP of Manchester. Of their three sons and two daughters, the eldest son, Arthur William, Wykehamist, cotton spinner and insurance agent, was the father of the naval historian Sir Geoffrey Callender.

Callender's early death was to leave his business ventures in a parlous state, but his originality lay in his articulate rejection, in several influential pamphlets, of the creed of the cotton masters which his father, a stalwart Liberal nonconformist supporter of the Anti-Corn Law League, typified. For already by 1850 Callender, identifying himself with Manchester's strong tory–Anglican élite, was a critic of Cobdenite panaceas, doubting the ability of free trade to create new markets abroad for British goods, and urging the importance of home demand. He also discounted the ethical optimism of the league, emphasizing, in the manner of earlier evangelicals, the dependence of prosperity on morality in commerce.

Callender became a leading Manchester churchman and sought to rebuild local Conservatism on the pillars of church defence and working-class welfare. Unlike many employers, he defended, even lauded, trade unions and shorter hours. He was also a stalwart advocate of popular education, ready to insist that it should be compulsory and free, and of temperance, for, with his fellow Manchester tory Hugh Birley, he was one of the few tory supporters of the United Kingdom Alliance (led by his cousin Samuel Pope). Callender became the linchpin for the organizational rebuilding of the Conservative Party in south-east Lancashire in the 1850s, and sought a full place within it for the working classes.

Callender's anti-Liberalism took him in some strange directions (including financial succour to the former Chartist, Ernest Jones), but he became the most influential of the Lancashire employers, who in the late 1860s not only ensured the revitalization of the tory party locally, but also gave it a growing voice within the national party. Callender acted as Benjamin Disraeli's host on his famous Manchester visit of 1872 and influenced significantly the social legislation of the Conservative government, having become MP for Manchester in 1874. A leading and original exemplar of grassroots tory democracy, he would have been rewarded for his important contribution to the Disraelian Conservative Party with a baronetcy but for his unexpected death.

Balding, but heavily sideburned, Callender was a familiar, kindly, energetic, and popular figure in Manchester, occupying the usual array of positions for a provincial notable, JP for Salford, JP and deputy lieutenant for Lancashire, a director of the Manchester chamber of commerce, a captain in the volunteers, a member of the Union of the Institutes of Lancashire and Cheshire, a member of the Manchester school board from 1870 to 1873, and, succeeding J. A. Nicholls, honorary secretary of the Manchester Athenaeum. He was also prominent in the freemasons locally and nationally. His personal interests may be gleaned from his fellowship of the Society of Arts, travel in Palestine and Spain, and his collection of fine porcelain.

Callender, suffering from rheumatic neuralgia, and nervous prostration, died at 27 Eversfield Place, St Leonards, Sussex, on 22 January 1876, and was buried on 29 January at St John's, Heaton Mersey, his coffin accompanied by a mile-long cortège from his home, Mauldeth Hall, Burnage, Manchester (until 1872, the episcopal palace of Bishop James Fraser). He was survived by his wife. His untimely death belied his career and beliefs, for following the deaths of his father and brother in 1872 it was claimed that Callender had retained in the firm large sums due to the latter's heirs. This precipitated a complicated family legal dispute (resolved only in 1889), as a result of which the mills were closed in August 1877, the workforce was dispersed, and Barrow Bridge, the erstwhile model community, was soon known as Lancashire's 'deserted village'. A. C. Howe

Sources biographical cuttings, Man. CL • *Manchester Courier* (24 Jan 1876) • *Manchester Courier* (31 Jan 1876) • *Manchester City News* (18 Feb 1865) [Callender, Sons and Co.] • D. O'Connor, *Barrow Bridge, Bolton, Dean Mills estate: a Victorian model achievement* (1972) • P. Smith, *Disraelian Conservatism and social reform* (1967) • H. J. Hanham, *Elections and party management: politics in the time of Disraeli and Gladstone* (1959) • P. Joyce, *Work, society and politics* (1980) • *Callender v. Callender*, PRO, Records of the high courts of justice • A. Howe, *The cotton masters, 1830–1860* (1984) • *CGPLA Eng. & Wales* (1876)

Archives PRO, *Callender v. Callender*, J4/284, 285; J54/55; PL 31/190; PL 31/191 | Bodl. Oxf., Disraeli papers

Likenesses portraits, Man. CL

Wealth at death under £80,000: probate, 18 March 1876, *CGPLA Eng. & Wales*

Callis, Robert (*c*.1577–1642), barrister, was the younger son of Robert Callis of Great Hale, Lincolnshire, yeoman. He entered Gray's Inn in 1596 and was called to the bar in 1601. In spite of his modest beginnings Callis became a highly successful practitioner both locally and at Westminster. In 1604 he served as counsel to Sir Edward Dymock in his feud with Henry, second earl of Lincoln. During a special session arranged by the earl, Callis offended the peer when he alleged (correctly) that the jury had been packed with Lincoln's supporters. During his subsequent examination in Star Chamber the earl was unapologetic and expressed open contempt for Callis's humble yeomanry origins.

In 1609 and 1610 Callis represented his relatives from Little Hale (probably his elder brother William) in a dispute over common rights in the fen with other villagers and residents of Swineshead. Also in 1610 he represented the yeoman of Wilsford in their fight against an enclosure scheme of Sir Edward Carr. He became deputy recorder of Lincoln in 1612 but was soon forced to leave the post with the downfall of his patron, George Anton. Also during the reign of James he wrote *The Case and Argument Against Sir Ignoramus of Cambridg*, subsequently published in 1648. This tract, based on a reading at Staple Inn in Lent 1616, was a response to George Ruggle's Latin play *Ignoramus*, performed before James I at Cambridge in March 1615. In reply to Ruggle's satire of common lawyers Callis offered a satirical reading on the laws governing ecclesiastical benefices ridiculing the dealings of Sir Ignoramus, a fictionalized corrupt cleric. This controversy also influenced John Selden to begin work on his famous *History of Tithes* (1618).

During his career Callis also served as a justice of the peace and, most notably, as commissioner of sewers for the county of Lincolnshire. He became a bencher of his inn in 1622 and in August 1622 delivered a reading that was subsequently published in 1647 as *The reading of that famous and learned gentleman, Robert Callis esq.; sergeant at law, upon the statute of 23 H. 8. cap. 5. of sewers*. Although particularly concerned with the commissioners of sewers, the tract had broader significance as a work of jurisprudence. Callis argued that, although the 'bare words' of the statute provided only for the maintenance of existing defences against the sea, the laws of the sewers were 'of great and urgent necessity and use for the good of the whole Commonwealth of the Realm' (Callis, *Of Sewers*, 71). Accordingly he argued that the statute should be constructed according to its equity, empowering commissioners to provide for new engines and defences against the sea. He also defended the status of the court of sewers as a court of record empowered to fine, imprison, and offer a variety of legal remedies. Considering his legal justification for the construction of new defences it is unsurprising that Callis later became a supporter of the earl of Lindsey's 'Lindsey level' drainage scheme. In April 1627 Charles I created him serjeant-at-law although his judicial activities appear to have remained confined to the locality. He married Esher (or Hester; *fl.* 1580–1640), daughter of William Fitzwilliam of Mablethorpe, Lincolnshire. He is known to have acquired a farm at Dalderby and to have owned houses, closes, and other freehold lands in and around the city of Lincoln and its suburbs. The exact date of his death is not known, but he apparently died in good circumstances leaving in his will, probated on 16 May 1642, a portion of £1500 to his daughter and 10*s*. to the poor in every parish of Lincoln. He bequeathed his law books to the library of Gray's Inn. D. A. Orr

Sources *DNB* • Baker, *Serjeants*, 183, 363–4, 503 • W. R. Prest, *The rise of the barristers: a social history of the English bar, 1590–1640* (1986), 68, 111, 348 • W. R. Prest, *The inns of court under Elizabeth I and the early Stuarts, 1590–1640* (1972), 209–10 • C. Holmes, *Seventeenth-century Lincolnshire*, History of Lincolnshire, 7 (1980), 48–50 • R. Callis, *The case and argument against Sir Ignoramus of Cambridg* (1648) • R. Callis, *The reading of that famous and learned gentleman, Robert Callis esq.; sergeant at law, upon the statute of 23 H. 8. cap. 5. of sewers: as it was delivered by him at Grays-Inn, in August, 1622* (1647) • 'The Bill of Sewers with a new proviso', *Statutes at large*, ed. O. Ruffhead, 2 (1763), 163–7 [cap. 5] • F. S. Boas, 'University plays', *The drama to 1642* [part 2] (1910), vol. 6 of *The Cambridge history of English literature*, ed. A. W. Ward and A. R. Waller (1907–27); repr. (1932) • A. Cromartie, 'The constitutionalist revolution: the transformation of political culture in early Stuart England', *Past and Present*, 163 (1999), 91–2 • H. C. Darby, *The draining of the fens*, 2nd edn (1956); repr. (1968), 48, 62 • L. Stone, *The crisis of the aristocracy, 1558–1641*, abridged edn (1967), 104

Callow, John (1822–1878), marine painter and drawing-master, was born on 19 July 1822 in St Pancras, London, son of Robert Callow (*b.* 1786), a London carpenter, and his wife, Elizabeth, both of whom died in 1848. His childhood ambition was to be a sailor but in 1835 his elder brother

William *Callow (1812–1908), who was then living in Paris and exhibiting paintings at the Salon, persuaded him to come to Paris to study under his supervision. In this way John Callow became affiliated to the Anglo-French school of artists, whose members followed in the wake of Richard Parkes Bonington. He began his studies by copying paintings in the Musée du Louvre. He returned to England in 1843 or 1844 and began to exhibit his work in London and elsewhere; between 1844 and 1856 he exhibited a small number of oil paintings at the Royal Academy and the British Institution. He also exhibited a larger number of works at the Royal Hibernian Academy, but his main exhibition venues were the New Society of Painters in Water Colours, where he exhibited twenty-eight works, all marine paintings, between 1845 and 1847, and the Society of Painters in Water Colours, where he had exhibited 345 (counting only full-sized works) by the time of his death. He was a member of the new society from 1845 to 1848 and became an associate of the old society in 1849, retaining his association until his death. Besides his exhibited works, he produced a large number of illustrations in sepia and watercolour for school books published by the Irish educationist Vere Foster.

In July 1855 Callow was appointed junior professor of drawing at Addiscombe College. Unlike his senior colleague, Aaron Penley, he was not popular with the cadets, who regarded him as 'a jaundiced, saturnine character with no good humour or geniality about him' (Vibart, 212). Following the closure of the college in 1861 he was appointed additional landscape drawing-master at the Royal Military Academy, Woolwich. He resigned this position in 1865 to concentrate on private teaching but in 1875 became a professor at Queen's College, London, the girls' public school where all the teachers were men; he held this post until his death. Callow married Rebecca Searle on 15 February 1864; they had several children, of whom the eldest, John Robert, was thirteen when their father died of tuberculosis on 25 April 1878 at his home, 35 Lewisham High Road, Deptford, London.

Callow's style of painting was formed on that of William, his master and elder brother, though he treated a different range of subjects. Skilled in giving colour and depth to representations of water and sky, he was uncomfortable with figures. It is probable that the necessity of devoting much of his time to teaching impeded the development of his talents. His brother's works have always been more highly valued than his by art collectors and no public gallery holds a large number of his paintings. The most substantial collection (four watercolours) is in the National Gallery of Ireland, Dublin. A. R. PENNIE

Sources J. L. Roget, *A history of the 'Old Water-Colour' Society*, 2 (1891) • W. Callow, *William Callow, RWS, FRGS: an autobiography*, ed. H. M. Cundall (1908) • G. Meissner, ed., *Allgemeines Künstlerlexikon: die bildenden Künstler aller Zeiten und Völker*, [new edn, 34 vols.] (Leipzig and Munich, 1983–) • H. M. Vibart, *Addiscombe: its heroes and men of note* (1894) • Graves, *RA exhibitors* • Graves, *Brit. Inst.* • A. M. Stewart and C. de Courcy, eds., *Royal Hibernian Academy of Arts: index of exhibitors and their works, 1826–1979*, 1 (1985) • H. D. Buchanan-Dunlop, *Records of the Royal Military Academy, 1741–1892*, 2nd edn (1892) • b. cert. • m. cert. • d. cert. • Bénézit, *Dict.*, 3rd edn • E. Kaye, *A history of Queen's College, London, 1848–1972* (1972) • M. McNeill, *Vere Foster, 1819–1900* (1971) • J. Reynolds, *William Callow, R.W.S.* (1980) • *CGPLA Eng. & Wales* (1878) • parish records, Greenwich St Alphege, LMA, P78/ ALF 004, 377, ALF 006, 273 • index of deaths, General Register Office for England, 10/1848–12/1848

Likenesses possibly by F. F. Cotton, sepia print, 1860, NPG • Elliott & Fry, carte-de-visite, NPG

Wealth at death under £3000: probate, 30 May 1878, *CGPLA Eng. & Wales*

Callow, William (1812–1908), watercolour painter, was born in Greenwich, Kent, on 28 July 1812, elder son of Robert Callow (1786–1848), a master builder, and his wife, Elizabeth (*d.* 1848). John *Callow was his younger brother. William Callow showed an early talent for drawing and at the age of eleven was tinting prints for the engraver Theodore Fielding at his Newman Street studio, which was near to the Callow home in Tottenham Place, Camden Town, London. In 1825 Callow was formally articled to Fielding as a pupil in engraving and watercolour painting. Copley Fielding, future president of the Society of Painters in Water Colours, recognized potential in the young student and gave him advice and encouragement.

In 1829 Callow was sent to work with Newton Fielding in Paris and was at once enchanted with France, where the essential pattern of his career evolved. In Paris he met Thomas Shotter Boys, from whom he assimilated a method of calligraphic brush strokes and a liking for picturesque city scenes. There was also a received influence from R. P. Bonington, whose luminous use of wash is reflected in the style of Boys. By 1833 Callow was independent of the Fieldings and established in his own atelier. He enjoyed a growing reputation as a watercolourist, and his studio attracted a flourishing circle of pupils, including members of the French aristocracy. The success of *Vue du pont de Richmond*, exhibited at the Paris Salon in 1834, led to Callow being asked to give lessons in watercolour painting to the family of King Louis Philippe. His daughter, Princess Clémentine, was a pupil of Callow for seven years and became a lifelong friend.

Callow's range of subject matter was broadened by a series of long walking tours through France, Germany, and Switzerland (1835–40). These were chronicled in detailed diary entries which appear in his posthumously published autobiography. Many finished watercolours were based on sketches made at this time.

In 1838 Copley Fielding strongly supported the election of Callow as an associate of the Society of Painters in Water Colours, although his work was virtually unknown in England. He was awarded a gold medal at the Paris Salon in 1840, but in the following year gave up an established career in France and returned to London, where he purchased 20 Charlotte Street (later Hallam Street), near Regent's Park, in 1842. Callow's watercolours proved to be an immediate success in England and he soon gathered another group of well-connected pupils, including two future viceroys of India and members of the Rothschild family. He was a tall, handsome man, with an air of French courtliness and a real love of teaching which made him one of the best-known drawing masters of the day.

William Callow (1812–1908), by Edward Robert Hughes

In 1843 the duke of Devonshire commissioned two watercolours from Callow as a gift for Queen Victoria, *Chatsworth, the Garden Front* and *The Great Conservatory*, which are now in the Royal Collection at Windsor Castle (where in 1829 Robert Callow had superintended some building work). Callow was elected a full member of the Society of Painters in Water Colours in 1848 and was presented to Queen Victoria and Prince Albert at the 1852 exhibition and again in 1860. Prince Albert acquired two watercolours, of which *The Bay of Naples, Early Morning* (1852) was later engraved in the *Art Journal* in a series entitled 'The Royal Pictures' (Jan 1856, 16). Callow had first visited Italy in 1840, after which Italian scenes, particularly of Venice, were among his most popular subjects. An art critic in *The Athenaeum* commented: 'Mr. Callow is beyond average in his clever, highly tinted architectural sketches' (1488, 3 May 1856, 559). Over fifty years of extensive travel is reflected in his continental street scenes of tall façades and bustling crowds, but tours of the British Isles are also represented, often in breezy coastal subjects, with shipping.

On 2 July 1846 Callow married one of his fashionable pupils, Harriet Anne Smart (1818–1883), niece of the prominent musician Sir George Smart. The couple shared cultural interests: William delighted in music and Harriet was a talented amateur artist. As her health was delicate, the Callows moved out of London in 1855 to Great Missenden, Buckinghamshire. There they built a large house, named The Firs, although Callow retained premises in London until he finally gave up teaching in 1882. He exhibited 1400 works with the Society of Painters in Water Colours (which became the Royal Society after 1881) and was a trustee (1861 to 1876) and secretary from 1866 to 1870. He painted some pictures in oils, mostly for exhibition at the Royal Academy, including *Porta della Carta, Venice* (exh. 1854). He also showed with the British Institution and the Royal Liverpool Academy. Callow never deviated from traditional watercolour methods, in spite of a trend for experimentation, but some original purity of colour and clarity of line was lost in later over-elaboration. A convoluted monogram (which can be misread as CW) was used by Callow for a period in the mid-1830s, but W. Callow or Wm. Callow in back-sloping script is his most characteristic signature.

In 1863 Princess Clémentine (by then duchess of Saxe-Coburg and Gotha) arranged for Callow to sketch at some of the German castles, including Rosenau, near Coburg. Queen Victoria was staying there at the time and received Callow in the garden, much admiring his work. He gave several lessons to the crown princess of Prussia during this tour and was entertained as a guest at Potsdam palace, where he again taught the princess in 1874.

Harriet Callow died on 30 June 1883. Only six months later, on 8 January 1884, Callow, aged seventy-one, married Mary Louisa Jefferay (1857–1937), aged twenty-seven, daughter of a harness maker from Wendover, Buckinghamshire. There were no children of either marriage, but the second was one of special contentment. On his ninetieth birthday Callow was presented with a congratulatory address from the Royal Society of Painters in Water Colours, illuminated by the painter E. R. Hughes, a close friend, who always referred to Callow as 'the Maestro'. By now his sight was failing, but work from earlier portfolios continued to sell and a highly praised retrospective exhibition was mounted at the Leicester Galleries in 1907. A review in *The Studio* declared that 'Mr. Callow has faithfully upheld the best tradition of the old British School of watercolour painting' (1907, 142). He was now the oldest living British artist, but retained remarkable stamina, walking 5 miles a day, until just before his death at The Firs, from pleurisy, following influenza, aged ninety-five, on 20 February 1908. The obituary in *The Times* paid tribute to a celebrated artist who had progressed from boy apprentice to friend of royalty. A memorial plaque to Callow was placed in the church of St Peter and St Paul, Great Missenden, in the churchyard of which he had been buried on 25 February 1908.

Two watercolours were donated to the Tate Gallery, London, in 1909, which purchased twenty-six of Callow's continental sketches in 1912. These spanned thirty years of his career, from *Belfry Tower, Ghent* (1844) to *Old Street, Prague* (1874). The Victoria and Albert Museum has thirty-three examples of his work, including *Market Place, Frankfurt* and *Leaning Towers, Bologna*. This prolific watercolour painter is represented in over sixty public collections, including the Musée du Château de Versailles.

JAN REYNOLDS

Sources W. Callow, *William Callow, RWS, FRGS: an autobiography*, ed. H. M. Cundall (1908) • J. Reynolds, *William Callow* (1980) • J. Reynolds, 'William Callow, RWS', *Old Water-Colour Society's Club*, 56 (1981), 31–46 • *William Callow* (1987) [catalogue, Albany Gallery, London] • *The Times* (24 Feb 1908), 7 • 'Studio-talk', *The Studio*, 42 (1907–8), 136–60, esp. 142 • M. Hardie, *Water-colour painting in Britain*, ed. D. Snelgrove, J. Mayne, and B. Taylor, 2nd edn, 3: *The Victorian period* [1968], 51–4 • *DNB* • private information (2004)
Likenesses W. Coles, photograph (aged 86), repro. in Cundall, ed., *William Callow*, frontispiece • Elliott & Fry, carte-de-visite, NPG • E. R. Hughes, pastel drawing, NPG [*see illus.*] • watercolour (as a young man), NPG; repro. in Reynolds, *William Callow*, pl. 101
Wealth at death £60: probate, 14 March 1908, *CGPLA Eng. & Wales*

Callwell, Sir Charles Edward (1859–1928), army officer and writer, was born on 2 April 1859 in London, the only son of Henry Callwell of Lismoyne, Ballycastle, co. Antrim, and his wife, Maud, fourth daughter of James Martin, of Ross, Connemara. He was educated at home by a German governess, at Haileybury College (1871–6), and at the Royal Military Academy (1876–7), Woolwich. In January 1878 he was commissioned second lieutenant, Royal Field Artillery. After a short course for new officers at Woolwich and Shoeburyness, he travelled to India on HMS *Serapis*. In March 1879 he joined F battery of the 3rd brigade stationed at Dinapore. He was later attached to 10/11 heavy battery, in which he served during the closing stages of the Second Anglo-Afghan War, when he marched through the Khyber Pass to join the Kabul field force. Following his return to India he enjoyed five months' medical leave in Kashmir, before rejoining F battery at Dinapore. Shortly afterwards this battery was ordered to south Africa: it landed at Durban in January 1881, just in time to take part in the final operations of the First South African War. Callwell returned to Britain in December 1881.

While stationed at Woolwich and then after being transferred to Aldershot, he began regularly contributing articles to the service press, notably the *Proceedings of the Royal Artillery Institution*, on a range of military issues, as well as preparing for the Staff College examination. In 1883 he returned to India with A/1 battery and was again stationed at Dinapore. In 1884 he passed comfortably first the entrance examination for the Staff College, Camberley, held at Jutogh, while still a subaltern. In the autumn of 1884 Callwell returned home and for the next two years studied at Camberley. While there he was promoted captain in March 1886 and later that year was awarded the gold medal for the Royal United Service Institution prize essay competition, with an essay on the lessons learned from British colonial campaigns since 1865. This established his reputation as a military theorist and was later translated into Italian.

After the course Callwell was briefly posted to the garrison artillery at Portsmouth before being attached to an infantry and later a cavalry unit at Aldershot. He attended as an observer Italian army manoeuvres near Reggio. In October 1887 he was posted as staff captain to the intelligence branch of the War Office in London, as a result of

Sir Charles Edward Callwell (1859–1928), by unknown photographer

his extensive knowledge of foreign languages and countries; there he was appointed deputy assistant adjutant-general. He joined section E, responsible for Austria-Hungary, the Balkans, Turkey, Egypt, and independent African states. Callwell proved highly successful and served in this post until September 1892, making several tours to Turkey, Greece, Algeria, and Morocco, and in Europe, to gather information. He returned to the garrison artillery at Sheerness before being appointed a year later brigade major of artillery to the western district at Devonport. In March 1896 he was promoted major and that year published *Small Wars: their Principles and Practice*, which became a standard text and firmly established his reputation as the army's foremost expert on colonial warfare, and was also translated into French. At the end of the year he was posted to Malta in charge of a garrison artillery company on coastal defence. Following the outbreak of the Graeco-Turkish War in 1897 he was attached as a military observer to the Greek army in the Near East while on leave, and was present at the battle of Domokos. He published *The Effect of Maritime Command on Land Campaigns since Waterloo* (1897) and *Tactics of Today* (1900).

Following the disasters of 'black week' during the Second South African War, Callwell's company was sent in December 1899 to south Africa, where it was reorganized as a heavy battery. Callwell led his battery in Natal in support of operations under Sir Redvers Buller along the Tugela River, which led to the relief of Ladysmith on 28

February 1900, and then with the Natal army that crossed the Drakensbergs into the Transvaal. Callwell was promoted brevet lieutenant-colonel in November 1900 and on 31 July 1901 was given command of a mobile column, operating under Sir John French, hunting down elusive, widely scattered Boer commandos in the western Transvaal and Cape Colony. He was not particularly successful in this role, and fell foul of Sir John French after letting a Boer commando under Van Deventer escape at Brand Kraal. Despite this setback, he remained a column commander until the war ended in 1902. When he returned to Britain he was stationed briefly at Cork and Dover in 1902–3, while also serving on a committee of senior officers to select a new heavy gun for the Royal Artillery. He was then appointed a deputy assistant quartermaster-general in the mobilization branch of the War Office, in the strategical section dealing with the British empire and general questions of imperial defence that he first served in and then led. In October 1904 he was promoted brevet colonel, made substantive shortly afterwards, and was created CB in 1907. He continued writing on military affairs and produced *Military Operations and Maritime Preponderance* (1905), on joint operations between the army and the Royal Navy, and *The Tactics of Home Defence* (1908). Following the end of this War Office appointment in 1907, Callwell went on half pay and worked for the *Morning Post*. After being passed over for promotion by several contemporaries and being offered only minor staff appointments, a piqued Callwell finally retired from active service later in the summer of 1909. He turned to writing as full-time employment, specializing in military affairs and military history. He wrote articles, short stories, and books—including humorous parodies of life in the army and of War Office routine—in various periodicals, including the *Cornhill Magazine* and *Blackwood's Magazine*. These were later published in *Service Yarns and Memories* (1912). Callwell's more serious published work during this period included a didactic account of the 1897–8 Tirah campaign, *Tirah, 1897* (1911).

Following the outbreak of war in August 1914, Callwell was recalled to active service and was appointed, with the temporary rank of major-general, to the influential post of director of military operations and intelligence at the War Office. With few trained and experienced staff officers remaining at the War Office, this was a particularly arduous appointment, and involved working closely with Lord Kitchener. Callwell was unwilling, however, to challenge the views of the overbearing new secretary of state for war, who misunderstood the role of the general staff and was reluctant to make full use of it. Instead, Callwell kept quiet and largely acquiesced in Kitchener's proposals. Perhaps most notably he did not actively seek an opportunity to put forward his personal views opposing a naval action at the Dardanelles, an operation he had studied in considerable detail in the intelligence department before the outbreak of war, and deferred instead to Kitchener's view. Despite his strong scepticism, Callwell was heavily involved in planning the Dardanelles campaign, for whose failure he was in small part to blame. Later Callwell drafted the memorandum that formed the formal basis for the recommendations of the new chief of the Imperial General Staff that Gallipoli should be evacuated. In December 1915 Callwell refused an offer from Sir Douglas Haig to be his military secretary. Callwell remained at the War Office until January 1916, when, following the appointment of Sir William Robertson as chief of the Imperial General Staff, the general staff underwent complete reorganization. Callwell was replaced when his post was split into two and new appointments were made for both positions.

Callwell was sent on two special missions to Russia in January–February and March–May 1916 to discuss the supply of munitions and other issues concerned with Russian co-operation in the war. Following his return to Britain in the autumn of 1916, he served on the War Office's Russian purchasing committee, served in the Ministry of Munitions as an adviser on the supply of munitions to Russia and then other various entente armies, and finally sat on the Milner committee. In May–June 1917 he very briefly stood in for the deputy chief of the Imperial General Staff, was promoted substantive major-general, and created a KCB for his services.

Callwell returned to his previous career as a journalist and writer following the end of the First World War. His post-war work included *The Dardanelles* (1919), *The Life of Sir Stanley Maude* (1920), and two humorous autobiographical volumes covering his early career and military service between 1914 and 1918. In March 1921 he was awarded the Chesney medal of the Royal United Service Institution for his services to military literature and continued until his death writing for various military periodicals, most notably the *Journal of the Royal Artillery*. His later work included editing the autobiography of General Sir O'Moore Creagh and the memoirs of Sir Hugh MacCalmont and writing a tendentious two-volume biography (1920) of Sir Henry Wilson, whom he had known as a friend since boyhood. His last writing project was a history of the Royal Artillery, written in co-operation with Major-General Sir John Headlam, which appeared in 1937. Callwell died, unmarried, on 16 May 1928 at the Queen Alexandra Military Hospital, Millbank, London.

Callwell was an accomplished linguist, a skilled intelligence officer, and a prolific writer of quality on a wide range of military affairs and on military history throughout his career. He acquired a reputation as a skilled theorist and, predominantly, as a staff officer. His only period of field command, however, was in south Africa, where he was not particularly successful. It was this failure and his passion for military writing that perhaps led to his being passed over and his early retirement from the army in 1909. Indeed, Callwell may well have been his own worst enemy by being indiscreet, having a sharp tongue, and writing parodies of military life and service at the War Office. Throughout his life, writing for the service press and military literature occupied a large part of Callwell's attention and he was perhaps more accomplished as a theorist than as a soldier. His *Military Operations and Maritime*

Preponderance: their Relations and Interdependence was arguably the best study of joint warfare ever written. It is for his *Small Wars: their Principles and Practice*, however, that Callwell is best remembered. It remained a standard textbook on the subject for the British army up to the Second World War and, in the view of several historians, established his credentials as the founding father of modern counter-insurgency. T. R. MOREMAN

Sources C. E. Callwell, *Stray recollections*, 2 vols. (1923) • C. E. Callwell, *Experiences of a dug-out, 1914–18* (1920) • *The Times* (17 May 1928) • C. Gray, 'Introduction', in C. E. Callwell, *Military operations and maritime preponderance* (1996) • *DNB* • *RA Regimental News* (June 1928) • T. G. Fergusson, *British military intelligence, 1870–1914* (1984) • T. R. Moreman, *The army in India and the development of frontier warfare, 1849–1947* (1998) • T. R. Mockaitis, *British counterinsurgency, 1919–1960* (1990) • L. S. Milford, *Haileybury register, 1862–1910* (1910) • *Hart's Army List* (1891) • *CGPLA Eng. & Wales* (1928)

Archives Berks. RO, letters to Lord Glyn, D/EGI • King's Lond., Liddell Hart C., Hamilton MSS • PRO, letters to Lord Kitchener, WO159; PRO30/57

Likenesses photograph, NAM • photograph, NPG [*see illus.*] • portrait, repro. in Callwell, *Stray recollections*, frontispiece

Wealth at death £8884 1*s*.: probate, 25 June 1928, *CGPLA Eng. & Wales*

Calman, Melville [Mel] (**1931–1994**), cartoonist and illustrator, was born on 19 May 1931 at 64 Linthorpe Road, Stamford Hill, London, the youngest of the three children of Clement Calman, timber merchant, and his wife, Anna. His parents were Russian-Jewish immigrants, his father from Odessa and his mother from Lithuania, who came to England about 1912.

Mel Calman experienced the start of the German blitz on London in 1940, and as it intensified was sent with his sister Lydia to the outskirts of Cambridge. He was awarded a scholarship to the Perse School, Cambridge, where he felt estranged as a Jew; he attributed much of his subsequent depression to the trauma of his schooldays. Failing in his first ambition—to read English at Cambridge University—he returned to London in 1949 intending to study journalism, but finding the course full he enrolled, *faute de mieux*, at the Borough Polytechnic Art School to study illustration. There he was made aware of his deficiencies as a draughtsman, but managed to pass his examinations and went on to study at Goldsmiths' College, and at St Martin's School of Art (1951–4) where with Len Deighton he edited the school magazine. During this time he developed a passion for films and jazz.

After four years of art schools and with an aversion to exercise, Calman found life in the army during his two years of national service pointless and unpleasant. He became a sergeant in the army education corps because a private room went with the job. A number of his cartoons were published in the magazine *Soldier*.

Demobilized in 1956, Calman hoped to become a freelance cartoonist and illustrator. The art editor of *Punch* was not encouraging: 'I rather doubt' he wrote 'if "cartooning" (as it is generally called) is really your line. Neither drawings nor ideas measure up to the standard required here, I'm afraid' (Calman, *What else do you do?*, 8). So he found a job as assistant to a designer of corporate 'house styles' where the importance of good lettering and design

Melville Calman (1931–1994), by Stephen Hyde, 1986

was impressed upon him. On 29 August 1957 he married Patricia (Pat) McNeill, then assistant art editor of *Woman* magazine. They had two daughters; the elder, Stephanie, became a writer and broadcaster.

Calman wrote, 'I cannot remember ever deciding to become a cartoonist: I seem to have slid into it in the way that some criminals say they slid onto the wrong side of the law' (Calman, *What else do you do?*, 10). He began to find his métier in 1958 when he started to supply small humorous drawings to illustrate the 'William Hickey' gossip column in the *Daily Express*. Over the next five years he progressed into drawing humorous vignettes for several other columns but left the *Express* because he saw no real prospects on a newspaper that already employed Giles and Osbert Lancaster.

Through the Telephone Directory with Mel Calman, a book of humorous drawings, was published in 1962, the first of more than twenty collections. In that year too he started to draw pocket cartoons for the *Sunday Telegraph* and his *alter ego*, a little man with an oversized nose and a gift for angst-ridden aphorism, emerged. In the following year he did a stint as resident cartoonist on the BBC television programme *Tonight*. Later in the decade he moved to the *Observer*, then to the *Sunday Times*, designed many advertisements (most notably for Shell), illustrated *Town* and *Nova* magazines, and wrote the first of three short plays for Radios 3 and 4.

By the time Calman started to draw pocket cartoons for *The Times* in 1979 his style was formed. He had absorbed early influences—Thurber, Steinberg, and Feiffer—and now organized his tiny space so as to provide an instantly recognizable image. The joke was hand-lettered in soft pencil and the naked figures were reduced to a few curves, indicating facial expression and body language, on the principle that less is more. It was a technique he had evolved, with great intelligence, to disguise the shortcomings of his draughtsmanship.

Although topical cartoons for *The Times*, four days a week for fifteen years, accounted for much of Calman's output, they were not his forte. He was most celebrated for his worries: about health, death, God, achievement, morality, and women. Above all women, as in the cartoons syndicated throughout the United States, 1976–82, under the title 'Men and Women' and republished for the British market in collections. For these worries, the little man, like his creator, often consulted a doctor or a psychiatrist, giving rise to some of the most penetrating jokes. 'What are the symptoms of happiness, Doctor?' asks the patient, and on another occasion, 'Do you have something for the HUMAN CONDITION?' In the battle of the sexes the little man generally came off worse and was driven to declarations like 'It's only you that's incompatible!' The humour was introspective, self-deprecating, and cerebral, in the Jewish tradition.

Calman became an art dealer in 1970 partly to provide the artist Karen Elizabeth Usborne, who became his second wife on 8 June 1973 (they parted in 1982), with a studio. The Workshop in Lamb's Conduit Street (later called the Cartoon Gallery and moved to Museum Street) uniquely at the time specialized in the work of cartoonists and, besides being an encouragement to them, was a godsend for collectors.

Calman's contacts with cartoonists and interest in comic art (he was an avid collector) led to his becoming in 1989 the co-founder of the Cartoon Art Trust, the aim of which was to establish a national museum of cartoon art. He devoted energy and imagination to the trust's affairs, and it now holds a small collection of his drawings.

Calman was 5 feet 6 inches tall, bearded, and stylishly dressed. His friend Michael Palin wrote, 'his morose appearance was so at odds with his inquisitive wit that I used to wonder if he practised looking miserable because he thought it suited him better' (Calman, *A Little Light Worrying*, 9). This appearance, together with his depressiveness (he listed his recreations in *Who's Who* as 'brooding and worrying') and taciturnity with strangers earned him the nickname of Dismal Mel. On the other hand with friends and people he respected he was, if not always even-tempered, lovable and, as Palin put it, 'seriously funny'. He was a popular member of the Garrick and Groucho clubs.

From 1984, when he had suffered a minor heart attack, Calman had been obliged to look after his health. On 10 February 1994 he went to the Empire cinema, Leicester Square, with his partner for the previous ten years, the novelist Deborah Moggach. A short way into the film he had a coronary thrombosis and died. His last words, addressed to some talkative people in the row behind, were 'Would you shut up, please.' He was buried on 15 February in the cemetery of the London United Synagogue at Waltham Abbey. SIMON HENEAGE

Sources M. Calman, *What else do you do?* (1986) · M. Calman, *A little light worrying* (1997) [sel. and introduced by C. Calman with a preface by M. Palin] · *A collection of Calmans* (1996) [exhibition catalogue] · *The Times* (12 Feb 1994) · *The Independent* (12 Feb 1994) · *Daily Telegraph* (14 Feb 1994) · *The Guardian* (12 Feb 1994) · *Sunday Times* (13 Feb 1994) · *The Penguin Calman* (1968) · *The new Penguin Calman* (1977) · *Humour from Shell: Shell advertising art, 1928–1963* (1991), 7–11 [exhibition catalogue, Oriel 31, Davies Memorial Gallery, Newtown, Powys] · P. Maddocks, *How to be a super cartoonist* (1985) · M. Bryant and S. Heneage, eds., *Dictionary of British cartoonists and caricaturists, 1730–1980* (1994) · m. cert. [Patricia McNeill] · m. cert. [Karen Elizabeth Usborne]

Likenesses S. Hyde, photograph, 1986, NPG [*see illus.*] · photograph, *c.*1990, repro. in *Collection of Calmans* · photograph, 1990, repro. in *Fusion* (spring 1990) · M. Kehoe, photograph, 1994, repro. in *Daily Express* (6 Feb 1994)

Wealth at death £373,775: probate, 30 Sept 1994, *CGPLA Eng. & Wales*

Calman, William Thomas (1871–1952), zoologist, was born at 94 Nethergate, Dundee, on 29 December 1871, the only son and elder child of Thomas Calman (*d.* 1877), a music teacher blind from childhood, and his wife, Agnes Beatts Maclean. His father's family had been in the shipping trade and were originally from the Anstruther district of Fife. A timid lad with no aptitude for games, Calman became an ardent amateur microscopist and student of pond life while still at Dundee high school, where his scientific interests were encouraged by Frank Young. At sixteen Calman was apprenticed in the Caledonian Insurance Company but was advised, when his term ended four years later, that his stammer made him unsuitable for the work. Meanwhile he had become an active member of the Dundee Working Men's Field Club and joined the Dundee Naturalists' Society, over which he was to preside in 1944. There he met the young professor of natural history at Dundee, D'Arcy Wentworth Thompson (whose notice he subsequently contributed to the *Dictionary of National Biography*), whose timely offer of a job as laboratory assistant was eagerly accepted since it enabled Calman to attend classes at University College, Dundee, without payment of fees. He graduated BSc with distinction in botany, physiology, and zoology in 1895. He also found time to learn several foreign languages and assisted with the classification of a large and varied assortment of animals obtained from all parts of the world for the departmental museum. He became interested chiefly, though by no means exclusively, in the crustaceans and published several scientific papers. One of these, which was soon to become a classic, was read before the Royal Society of Edinburgh just before he graduated. He was next appointed assistant lecturer and demonstrator in the natural history department, a post he held until 1903, obtaining his DSc in 1900. He was an excellent teacher and during Thompson's absences abroad was responsible for all the work of the department. In later years he served as external examiner to many universities.

An invitation in 1901 to write the volume on the Crustacea for *A Treatise on Zoology* edited by Ray Lankester marked another turning-point in Calman's career. In 1903 he moved to London to take up a temporary post at the British Museum (Natural History) and the following year he was placed in charge of the Crustacea and Pycnogonida, where he worked on specimens of these groups brought back by the *Siboga* expedition (1899–1900), the British Antarctic *Terra Nova* expedition (1910), and the *John Murray* expedition (1933–4). In addition to his official duties he compiled the Arachnida and Crustacea parts of the *Zoological Record* for many years. On 28 March 1906 Calman married Alice Jean, daughter of James Donaldson, timber merchant, of Tayport, Fife. She was one of the first women graduates in medicine of St Andrews and in due course their son and daughter both entered the medical profession.

In 1921, the year in which he was elected FRS, Calman became deputy keeper of the department of zoology at the museum, and in 1927 he succeeded Tate Regan as keeper, a post which he held until his retirement in 1936. As a curator he kept the collections under his care in excellent order, while from 1904 onwards, until administrative duties claimed most of his time, he produced a steady stream of scientific papers of the highest order and became the leading carcinologist of his time. To a remarkably retentive memory was added a gift for winnowing the significant from masses of detail. The *Treatise* volume, which specialists regard as his masterpiece, was published in 1909 and remained throughout the century as the best introduction to the subject. Much of interest which was unsuited to a textbook was included in his more popular book, *The Life of Crustacea* (1911). In 1919 he published a report on marine boring animals injurious to submerged structures in the museum's economic series, ahead of his report for a committee of the Institution of Civil Engineers.

Calman took a prominent part in scientific activities outside the museum. He was a member of the board of studies of London University and served on the council of the Royal Society from 1933 to 1935. He was president of the Quekett Microscopical Club (1927–9) and of the zoology section at the Bristol meeting of the British Association in 1930. As secretary of the Ray Society (1919–46) he edited its monographs. He was zoological secretary of the Linnean Society (1923–8), president (1934–7), and received its gold medal (1949). He was appointed CB in 1935 and made an honorary LLD of St Andrews and an honorary FRS (Edinburgh) in 1937.

Somewhat below average height, Calman was a rather sedate, modest, kind, and sociable man, with a delightful sense of humour. His early appreciation of English literature gave him an unusual command of words and purity of style which were enhanced by the slight hesitancy of speech which replaced his stammer. He was impatient with inaccuracy in any form and as editor and administrator he set a very high standard. But this was no more than he always demanded of himself and his strictness was tempered by his kindly common sense. If he sometimes treated his younger colleagues with benign ferocity he taught them many things besides zoology.

Three years after his retirement Calman moved to Tayport and during the war years he was a part-time lecturer in zoology at St Andrews and Dundee. A series of lectures delivered to his students, *The Classification of Animals*, was published in 1949. Following a serious illness he returned to London and died at Woodcote Grove House, his home at Carshalton, Surrey, on 29 September 1952.

Isabella Gordon, *rev.* Anita McConnell

Sources H. G. Cannon, *Obits. FRS*, 8 (1952–3), 355–72 • I. Gordon, *Proceedings of the Linnean Society of London*, 165th session (1952–3), 83–7 • I. W. Gordon, 'Dr W. T. Calman', *Nature*, 170 (1952), 780–81 • *The Times* (1 Oct 1952) • *The Times* (17 Oct 1952), 8c • private information (1971) • personal knowledge (1971) • b. cert. • m. cert. • d. cert. • *CGPLA Eng. & Wales* (1952)

Likenesses W. T. Mornington, lithograph, 1936, NHM • photograph, repro. in *Obits. FRS*, facing p. 355

Wealth at death £1042 15*s*. 6*d*.: administration with will, 4 Nov 1952, *CGPLA Eng. & Wales*

Calthorpe, Augustus Cholmondeley Gough-, sixth Baron Calthorpe (1829–1910), agriculturist, was born at Elvetham, Hampshire, on 8 November 1829, the third son in the family of four sons and six daughters of Frederick Gough Calthorpe, fourth Baron Calthorpe (1790–1868), and Lady Charlotte Sophia (1795–1865), eldest daughter of Henry Charles Somerset, sixth duke of Beaufort. The family was descended from Sir Henry Gough (*d.* 1774), first baronet, of Edgbaston, whose heir Henry, from his second marriage, to Barbara, daughter and heir of Reynolds Calthorpe of Elvetham, succeeded in 1788 to the Elvetham estates; taking the surname of Calthorpe, Henry was created Baron Calthorpe on 15 June 1796. Augustus was educated at Harrow School from 1845 to 1847 and matriculated at Merton College, Oxford, on 23 February 1848; he graduated BA in 1851, and proceeded MA in 1855. On the 22 July 1869 he married Maud Augusta Louisa (*b.* 1850, *d.* in or after 1912), youngest daughter of the Hon. Octavius Duncombe, seventh son of the first Lord Feversham. They had one son, Walter, and four daughters.

Calthorpe's main interests were sport, agriculture, and the duties of a county magistrate. He lived on family property at Perry Hall, Staffordshire, serving as high sheriff of that county in 1881. At the general election of 1880 he stood with Major Fred Burnaby as Conservative candidate for the undivided borough of Birmingham, near which a part of the family estates lay; he was defeated, and Philip Henry Muntz, John Bright, and Joseph Chamberlain were returned. On the death on 26 June 1893 of his eldest brother, Frederick, fifth baron (1826–1893), who was unmarried (his second brother, George, had died unmarried in 1843), he succeeded to the peerage as sixth baron. On the family estates at Elvetham he established in 1900 what was to become a famous herd of pedigree shorthorn cattle, as well as Southdown sheep and Berkshire pigs.

In 1894 Calthorpe made over to Birmingham corporation the freehold of the nearby Calthorpe Park, which his father had created in 1857, and he took much interest in the development of the new Birmingham University. In 1900 he and his only son, Walter (1873–1906), presented about 28 acres of land, valued at £20,000 for the site of the university buildings, and in 1907 he gave another site, immediately adjacent, of nearly 20 acres, of the estimated value of £15,000, for a private recreation ground for the students. He died after a short illness at his London residence at 38 Grosvenor Square on 22 July 1910, survived by his wife; he was buried at Elvetham on 27 July, after cremation at Golders Green. On his death, his only son, Walter, having predeceased him, he was succeeded in the title by his next brother, Lieutenant-General Sir Somerset John Gough-Calthorpe (1831–1912).

ERNEST CLARKE, *rev.* JOHN MARTIN

Sources *The Times* (23 July 1910) · *The Times* (28 July 1910) · J. H. Stogdon, ed., *The Harrow School register, 1845–1925*, 4th edn, 2 vols. (1925) · Foster, *Alum. Oxon.* · GEC, *Peerage* · *CGPLA Eng. & Wales* (1910) · d. cert.

Archives Hants. RO

Wealth at death £177,393 2*s*. 3*d*.: probate, 28 Sept 1910, *CGPLA Eng. & Wales*

Calthorpe [Calthrope], **Sir Charles** (*d.* **1616**), judge, was a younger son of Sir Francis Calthorpe of Hempstead and Ingham in Norfolk and his wife, Elizabeth, daughter of Ralph Berney of Gunton. He entered Lincoln's Inn in 1560 and delivered readings in Furnival's Inn which were published two years later. In 1569 he was called to the bar and became a parliamentary member for Eye in 1572. He was elected a member of the bench of his inn in 1582. On 22 June 1584 he was appointed attorney-general of Ireland, and was confirmed in this office by letters patent on 19 April 1603.

Throughout the 1580s and 1590s Calthorpe served as a member of several commissions in Connaught, Munster, and Thomond, overseeing civil and military government, surveying and shiring Gaelic countries and attainted lands, compounding fixed rents, and adjudicating on civil and ecclesiastical causes. In December 1586 he initiated proceedings to sue the archbishop of Dublin and other clergy for outstanding payments of first fruits. In late January 1587 he notified Burghley that as a result of his efforts the queen had recovered £4000 in outstanding arrears. He was rewarded with a salary increase and the town of Mallow was assigned to him, though he set little value on the latter. In mid-March Geoffrey Fenton sharply criticized the slow progress of reform in Munster, claiming that this stemmed in part from Calthorpe's being 'short of that learning and judgement which his place requireth' and his being 'rather a pleaser of the lord deputy than careful to the public service'. He was also suspected for being 'too much addicted to the Irishry' (*CSP Ire.*, *1586–8*, 282). Calthorpe was in England in August and September 1587 but had returned to Ireland by early October.

In July 1588 Calthorpe was again criticized severely as he allegedly 'wanteth law and cannot speak' and 'is so linked in with the lawyers that he dare not speak' (*CSP Ire.*, *1588–92*, 310). In February 1590 Sir William Fitzwilliam instigated a conspiracy against Perrot and his supporters. In late March Calthorpe was appointed a commissioner by the English privy council to investigate Perrot's involvement in the alleged conspiracy. However, the manner in which he conducted the inquiry aroused the suspicion of the privy council and resulted in his temporary suspension from the attorneyship, though he continued to receive his salary. While out of royal favour during the period 1590–92 he resided at Kilsallaghan near Dublin. He was set to stand trial in the castle chamber for being implicated in the plot, but Perrot's death in September 1592 caused the trial to be abandoned.

On 18 November 1592 the privy council ordered the restoration of Calthorpe to the attorneyship on the grounds that 'his offence proceeded of negligence and not of any undutiful affection' (*APC*, 23.312). He was appointed commissioner to implement the Acts of Supremacy and Uniformity in November of the following year. In January 1594 he refused to assume the vacant post of chief justice of Munster on the grounds of his own unfitness and his wife Winifred's ill health. Winifred, daughter of Antonio Toto of Florence, sergeant-painter to Henry VIII, was Calthorpe's first wife. She died childless on 1 August 1605. In autumn 1597 Calthorpe sought the office of chief justice of the common pleas but terminated his suit upon his discovery that the salary was to be reduced. On 24 March 1604 he was knighted.

As attorney-general Calthorpe earned an annual salary of £159 6*s*. 8*d*. On 29 May 1606 he was promoted by patent to the position of puisne judge in the court of common pleas. Although pleased at his promotion Calthorpe was disappointed by his salary which amounted to only half that of the office of attorney-general. Sir Arthur Chichester undertook to supplement Calthorpe's income and, as a result, in 1609 his annual income amounted to £200. In spring 1607 he served as justice of assize in Kildare, but in June 1611 he was described as 'an old weak man, unable to serve' (*CSP Ire.*, *1611–14*, 79). He died on 6 January 1616 and was buried in Christ Church, Dublin. His second wife, Dorothy, daughter of John Deane of London, died later the same year.

MARY ANN LYONS

Sources J. S. Brewer and W. Bullen, eds., *Calendar of the Carew manuscripts*, 2: *1575–1588*, PRO (1868) · J. S. Brewer and W. Bullen, eds., *Calendar of the Carew manuscripts*, 6: *Miscellaneous papers*, PRO (1873) · *CSP Ire.* · E. Keane, P. Beryl Phair, and T. U. Sadleir, eds., *King's Inns admission papers, 1607–1867*, IMC (1982) · *APC*, *1587–93* · *Report on the manuscripts of the late Reginald Rawdon Hastings*, 4 vols., HMC, 78 (1928–47), vol. 4 · *Calendar of the manuscripts of the most hon. the marquess of Salisbury*, 18, HMC, 9 (1940) · T. W. Moody, F. X. Martin, and F. J. Byrne, eds., *Maps, genealogies, lists: a companion to Irish history, part 2* (1984) · R. Lascelles, ed., *Liber munerum publicorum Hiberniae … or, The establishments of Ireland*, 2 vols. [1824–30], pt 2 · J. Morrin, ed., *Calendar of the patent and close rolls of chancery in Ireland, of the reigns of Henry VIII, Edward VI, Mary, and Elizabeth*, 2 (1862) · *Calendar of the Irish patent rolls of James I* (before 1830); facs. edn as *Irish patent rolls of James I* (1966) · F. E. Ball, *The judges in Ireland, 1221–1921*, 1 (1926) · J. O'Hart, *Irish pedigrees, or, The origin and stem of the Irish nation*, American edn, 2 vols. (New York, 1915) · C. J. Smyth, *Chronicle of the law officers of Ireland* (1839) · J. Haydn, *The book of dignities: containing rolls of the official personages of the British empire* (1851) · H. Morgan, *Tyrone's rebellion: the outbreak of the Nine Years' War in Tudor Ireland*, Royal Historical Society Studies in History, 67 (1993) · V. Treadwell, 'Sir John Perrot and the Irish parliament of 1585–6', *Proceedings of the Royal Irish Academy*, 85C (1985), 259–308 · J. Ohlmeyer and É. Ó Ciardha, eds., *The Irish statute staple books, 1596–1687* (1998) · 'Calendar of fiants, Henry VIII to Elizabeth', *Report of the Deputy Keeper of the Public Records in Ireland*, 7–22 (1875–90), appxs · HoP, *Commons*, *1558–1603*

Calthorpe, Sir Henry (**1586–1637**), lawyer, was born at Cockthorpe, Norfolk, the home of his father, Sir James Calthorpe, and his wife, Barbara, daughter of John Bacon of Hesset, Suffolk. The second or third son of a family of eight sons and six daughters, Henry graduated BA at Trinity College, Cambridge, in 1605, entered the Middle Temple in 1607, and was called to the bar there in 1616. Although he inherited a considerable landed estate on his father's death in 1615, he must have been from his earliest days a particularly assiduous attender of hearings in Westminster Hall. The first case in his vast, but unpublished, three-volume collection of law reports (BL, Hargrave MSS 385, 386, 387 (index); Add. MS 9787) is dated Michaelmas 1611, and the last is from 1635. In addition to a few very brief personal and political notes, the reports include cases from exchequer chamber, chancery, and the court of wards as well as from king's bench and common pleas, and Calthorpe also extracted some of the most important cases, including some of his own arguments, into a further two volumes (BL, Hargrave MSS 35 and 36).

Shortly after the marriage of Charles I to Henrietta Maria in 1625, Calthorpe became solicitor-general to the queen, after whom he and his wife, Dorothy, daughter and heir of Edward Humphrey, named one of their own children. In 1627 he was appointed by the judges to act as counsel for Sir John Corbet, one of the 'five knights' who applied to the king's bench for a writ of habeas corpus after being imprisoned for refusing to contribute to the forced loan. He was the last of the lawyers to speak for the defendants; his (unsuccessful) argument, which he illustrated with numerous citations, was that there was a weight of precedents proving that those imprisoned by order of the king and council should be set free if the charges were either unspecified or insufficiently precise. In the spring of 1630 Calthorpe also acted as counsel for Benjamin Valentine, one of the members of the House of Commons who held down the speaker in his chair on the dissolution of parliament in 1629, arguing that, since the offence was committed in parliament, only the House of Commons could punish it.

Along with several of the other notable lawyers with whom he acted in the later 1620s, Calthorpe seemed set to prosper under the 'personal rule' of Charles I. He was appointed recorder of London in 1635 at the special request of the king, but he did not hold the post for long since he resigned it upon being made attorney of the court of wards and liveries in the following January. Knighted shortly afterwards, he was also made a bencher of the Middle Temple, and designated reader for Michaelmas 1636. Although it is unclear from the records of the inn whether or not the reading was ever delivered, his lengthy and highly technical lecture on the Statute of Concealments (21 James I c. 2) survives among his papers.

A rich man, with a house at Ampton in Suffolk as well as one in London, Calthorpe died suddenly in August 1637. He bequeathed marriage portions of £2000 each to his daughters, but only one of his ten children, James, survived into adulthood. The diarist and judge Sir Richard Hutton described Calthorpe as learned, able, honest, and experienced; beloved in his life and lamented after his death. *The liberties, usages, and customes of the City of London; confirmed by especial acts of parliament … also, divers ample and most beneficiall charters … collected by Sir Henry Calthrop …*, which was published in 1642, does not appear to have been an original collection, and probably has little to do with the reputed author. *Reports of speciall cases touching severall customs and liberties of the City of London, collected by Sir H. Calthrop … whereunto is annexed divers ancient customes, and usages of the said City of London …*, which was first published in 1655 and reprinted in 1670, is more likely to be authentic, and is a useful collection of material on legal and administrative issues peculiar to early modern London.

CHRISTOPHER W. BROOKS

Sources *DNB* • *State trials*, vol. 3 • C. T. Martin, ed., *Minutes of parliament of the Middle Temple*, 4 vols. (1904–5) • *The diary of Sir Richard Hutton, 1614–1639*, ed. W. R. Prest, SeldS, suppl. ser., 9 (1991) • W. R. Prest, *The rise of the barristers: a social history of the English bar, 1590–1640* (1986) • law reports, BL, Hargrave MSS 35, 36, 385–387; Add. MS 9787 • will, PRO, PROB 11/175, fols. 103ff. • V. Pearl, *London and the outbreak of the puritan revolution: city government and national politics, 1625–1643* (1961) • *Reports of speciall cases touching severall customs and liberties of the City of London, collected by Sir H. Calthrop … whereunto is annexed divers ancient customes, and usages of the said City of London …* (1655) [repr. 1670]

Archives BL, law reports, Hargrave MSS 35, 36, 385–387; Add. MSS 9787

Wealth at death wealthy, but unspecified; £2000 in marriage portions to each of two daughters; extensive land holdings: will, PRO, PROB 11/175, fols. 103ff.

Calthorpe, Sir Somerset Arthur Gough (1864–1937), naval officer, was born in London on 23 December 1864, the second son of Lieutenant-General Somerset John Gough Calthorpe, seventh Baron Calthorpe (1831–1912), and his wife, Eliza Maria (*d.* 1919), daughter of Captain Frederick Chamier RN, and widow of Captain Frederick Crewe. He entered the navy as a cadet at the Royal Naval College, Dartmouth, in 1878 and was promoted to lieutenant in 1886. In 1895 Calthorpe served in naval brigades landed for punitive expeditions on first the west and later the east coast of Africa and was specially promoted to commander for his services on 1 January 1896. In 1900 Calthorpe married Annie Euphemia (*d.* 1952), daughter of Robert Dunsmuir of Victoria, British Columbia. They had no children.

Calthorpe was promoted to captain in 1902 and was naval attaché to Russia, Norway, and Sweden from 1902 to 1905, a period including the Russo-Japanese War, during which he concentrated on Russia. Calthorpe returned to command the armoured cruiser *Roxburgh* and later the battleship *Hindustan*. He was captain of the fleet and commodore first class to Admiral Sir William May in the Home Fleet (1909–10), and was promoted rear-admiral in 1911. He was then rear-admiral in the 1st battle squadron (1912–13), with his flag in the dreadnought *St Vincent*, and in 1912 was also an assessor on the wrecks commission inquiry into the loss of the *Titanic* and a member of the Board of Trade committee investigating methods of stowing, launching, and propelling ships' boats.

On the outbreak of the First World War Calthorpe was rear- and then vice-admiral commanding the 2nd cruiser squadron (1914–16), with his flag in the armoured cruiser *Shannon*. He left the Grand Fleet in 1916 shortly before the battle of Jutland to become second sea lord. In December

Sir Somerset Arthur Gough Calthorpe (1864–1937), by Walter Stoneman, 1925

1916 he was appointed admiral commanding coastguard and reserves. Calthorpe had until this date a worthy but certainly not a spectacular career and both inside and outside the navy there was a certain amount of surprise when in August 1917 he was named commander-in-chief of British forces in the Mediterranean. He has been described as 'conscientious and hard-working, a good all-round officer who held no aces' (Marder, 2.13). Moreover, his past experience as an attaché and his Mediterranean command undoubtedly benefited from his fluency in French, the result of spending part of his boyhood in France.

The British had actually left command in the Mediterranean to the French at the beginning of the war anticipating that the decisive naval battle would be fought in northern waters. This proved to be an untenable situation after the German submarine campaign began in earnest. There were simply too many British interests in the Mediterranean to leave it to the French and Italians, whose anti-submarine resources and methods proved woefully inadequate. The British of necessity shouldered the greater portion of the anti-submarine war in the Mediterranean and in 1917 the position of British Mediterranean commander-in-chief was revived, subject to the overall authority of the French commander-in-chief, at the time Vice-Admiral Gauchet. The latter, however, was preoccupied with the French battle fleet at Corfu guarding the entrance of the Adriatic against a sortie by the Austrian fleet. His control was increasingly more theoretical than real. Calthorpe's command was essentially shore based, its most important feature presiding over an inter-allied commission in Malta established to co-ordinate the campaign against submarines. The British with the greatest resources and shipping interests played the leading role although allied co-operation was less than perfect, the French and Italians having a tendency to follow their own interests. Nevertheless an elaborate convoy organization was gradually established and losses to submarines were brought down to acceptable levels, although always painful. Calthorpe, relatively modest and unassuming and reportedly a bit unsure of himself at first, had difficulty establishing his authority over the various British commands extending from the Aegean to Gibraltar as the local commanders-in-chief had become used to a good deal of independence. But Calthorpe gradually grew tougher and more assertive. In late 1917 he nearly made a major error of judgement suggesting he did not really understand the dynamics of the convoy system. Discouraged by persistently high losses, he considered strengthening the Otranto barrage at the expense of convoy escorts. This would have been a waste of resources for the barrage was ineffective, but fortunately these proposals were blocked by convoy advocates at the Admiralty.

In the spring of 1918 the collapse of Russia created the danger that the Germans would gain possession of the Russian Black sea Fleet and French battleships were shifted to the Aegean giving a French admiral local command. This situation was unacceptable to the British government once Turkey seemed on the verge of collapse in the autumn of 1918 and Calthorpe was ordered to proceed to the Aegean and take personal command, reinforced by two dreadnoughts detached from the Grand Fleet. Consequently it was Calthorpe who, rigidly excluding the French from the proceedings, negotiated the armistice with the Turks signed at Mudros on 30 October. On 12 November Calthorpe, flying his flag in the dreadnought *Superb*, led the allied fleets through the Dardanelles to anchor off Constantinople the next day. Calthorpe was now, in addition to his naval duties, appointed British high commissioner at Constantinople responsible to the Foreign Office rather than the Admiralty. In this dual capacity for nine months he faced an incredibly complicated situation that included the Russian civil war and allied intervention in the Black Sea, allied rivalries over the remains of the Ottoman empire and the resurgence of Turkish nationalism. He was now at the height of his powers and proved to be a tough and shrewd negotiator who earned the appreciation of the Foreign Office by the time he relinquished his command in July 1919. The Foreign Office praised his clear political and economic reports on provinces outside of the allied occupation and his good relations with his allied colleagues.

Calthorpe was commander-in-chief, Portsmouth, from 1920 to 1923, and was first and principal aide-de-camp to George V from 1924 to 1925. He was also the first British naval representative on the permanent armaments commission of the League of Nations. Calthorpe, promoted to admiral of the fleet in 1925, was placed on the retired list in 1930. He was awarded a number of British and foreign decorations; he was appointed KCB (1916), GCMG (1918), and GCB (1922). He died on 27 July 1937 at his home, Woodlands Vale, Ryde, Isle of Wight.

Calthorpe was fated never to command a squadron or fleet in action. Nevertheless, when thrust into a position of great responsibility he performed far better than anticipated, particularly in confronting the diplomatic and political issues that went with his command.

PAUL G. HALPERN

Sources P. G. Halpern, *The naval war in the Mediterranean, 1914–1918* (1987) • P. G. Halpern, ed., *The Royal Navy in the Mediterranean, 1915–1918* (1987) • A. J. Marder, *From the Dreadnought to Scapa Flow: the Royal Navy in the Fisher era, 1904–1919*, 5 vols. (1961–70) • Burke, *Peerage* • *WWW, 1929–40* • *The Times* (28 July 1937) • *The Royal Navy list, or, Who's who in the navy* (1915) • *Navy List* (1928) • R. Burmester, 'An appreciation', *The Times* (30 July 1937) • Walford, *County families* (1920) • Admiralty [ADM 137] and Foreign Office [FO 371] documents: Foreign Office to Calthorpe, 30 Aug 1919, PRO, ADM 137/1768, fols. 216–17
Archives Naval Library, London, J. H. Godfrey MSS • PRO, letters of proceedings, reports, ADM 137 series
Likenesses P. Connard, oils, 1919, IWM • W. Stoneman, photograph, 1925, NPG [*see illus.*]
Wealth at death £151,753 4*s*. 0*d*.: probate, 25 Oct 1937, *CGPLA Eng. & Wales*

Calthrope, Sir Charles. *See* Calthorpe, Sir Charles (*d*. 1616).

Calveley, Sir Hugh (*d*. 1394), military commander, was the son of David Calveley of Lea in Cheshire and his first wife, Joan.

Military apprenticeship Calveley served his military apprenticeship in the war of succession in Brittany (1341–64), in which the English supported the partisans of John de Montfort (*d*. 1345) against those of the French claimant to the duchy, Charles de Blois. In this war he was closely associated with another Cheshire soldier of fortune, Sir Robert Knolles, and on the French side, the Breton Bertrand du Guesclin, later constable of France, and he may have been a brother-in-arms of both men. He is first mentioned among the forces that laid siege to La Roche-Derrien under the king's lieutenant and captain-general in the duchy, Sir Thomas Dagworth, in 1346. In the guerrilla warfare that increasingly characterized the scene in Brittany, he was twice taken prisoner, first in 1351 among the combatants in the battle of the Thirty, and again in 1354 when, as one of the captains of the garrison town of Bécherel, he was captured beneath the walls of the neighbouring town of Montmuran. He may have been in charge of a contingent of archers in the first battle of the prince's army at Poitiers, and in the ensuing years he was able to command a substantial body of men-at-arms and archers in a war increasingly outside English royal control: with the Navarrese forces in Normandy in 1358–9, in the Auvergne in the latter year, and in the Loire provinces. Following the conclusion of peace between England and France at Brétigny (8 May 1360), he continued to operate on his own account, taking du Guesclin prisoner in a combat on the bridge of Juigné-sur-Sarthe towards the end of that year or early in 1361. In 1362 he commanded a contingent of men-at-arms in the army of Pedro of Castile, who supported Mohammed V, the deposed Moorish king of Granada, in his war against Abu Saïd. Returning to France, in January 1363 a royal order was put out for his arrest for violations against the Anglo-French peace; but at the beginning of May he was again in Brittany, where he led a contingent of forces sent to the relief of Bécherel, and in the following year he was present at the battle of Auray (29 September 1364), which brought an end to the succession dispute, and provided him with a substantial lump sum and a life annuity for his services to John de Montfort's son and heir, the new duke, John (*d*. 1399). He returned once again to fighting on his own account, but in November following, another royal order was issued forbidding him to make war in France, ostensibly in Navarrese service.

Career in Spain The years that followed until 1369 were the most important in Calveley's life. During the course of 1365, as part of a more general plan to rid France of the independent companies whose numbers were swollen by the demobilization of troops that followed the Breton settlement and the fragile accommodation between the kings of France and Navarre, Charles V recruited du Guesclin to lead into Spain those forces occupying towns and fortresses in Normandy, Brittany, the Chartrain, and the Loire provinces, and Calveley was engaged as one of du Guesclin's subordinate commanders in respect of the English and other forces in those provinces over which he could use his influence. With the blessing of the pope and the emperor, in league with the king of France, the expedition took on the aspect of a crusade against the Moors of Granada; but as it emerged that the troops under du Guesclin's command were intended, first, to support Enrique da Trastamara's bid to dethrone Enrique's half-brother, England's ally Pedro of Castile, and, second, to assist Pedro IV, king of Aragon, to recover territories occupied by Castile on the Aragonese frontiers, Edward III ordered Calveley and other English captains in France to prevent English troops from entering Spain. The orders, issued on 6 December 1365, were too late to stem the flow of English troops, which arrived around Barcelona before Christmas, and the general concentration of the allied forces around Saragossa where, on 16 February 1366, du Guesclin and Calveley drew up a contract in the English diplomatic form of an indenture of war. By the terms of this agreement the two captains joined forces for the campaign in Castile and Granada, agreed the terms of pay for Calveley and the forces under his command, provided for the division of their profits of war (three-quarters to du Guesclin and one-quarter to Calveley), including the grants already made to du Guesclin by Pedro IV, notably the towns of Borja and Magallon on the Aragonese–Castilian frontier near Saragossa, and the valleys of Elda and Novelda in the kingdom of Valencia, which were still to be secured in the forthcoming campaign. The only exception to this division was the kingdom of Granada, over which Trastamara had already made certain undertakings to du Guesclin, and which, if conquered, was to be retained by him, with the exception of the fortified places of the

Moorish king of Benamarin to the north of the Strait of Gibraltar, which were to be awarded to Calveley. A further significant clause provided that Calveley could abandon the campaign if Edward III or any of his sons required him to do so, or if they or the constable of Aquitaine, Sir John Chandos, intervened in the war in Castile or Granada.

The companies under Calveley's command—1000 combatants of an army of 10,000–12,000—spearheaded the attack up the Ebro valley in the direction of Logroño which opened the campaign and speedily established Trastamara's position. On 28 March Trastamara entered Burgos and on the following day was crowned at Las Huelgas. By way of reward for his services Calveley was granted the ancient town of Carrión in Palencia, which was erected into a county, thus making him count of Carrión. Before the end of May Enrique's army had pushed south to encircle and take both Toledo and Seville which, like Burgos, were abandoned by Pedro, who had fled the realm by the beginning of June. Although the new king disbanded the greater part of his forces at this juncture, it was not until 2 January 1367 that he formally discontinued the service of the contingents under the direct command of du Guesclin and Calveley, some 1000–1500 lances in all. On the same day du Guesclin released Calveley from all the terms of their indenture, thereby facilitating Calveley's capture of Miranda de Arga and Puente la Reina in Navarre within the following two weeks, which was intended, it seems, to protect the frontiers of that kingdom from a new Franco-Aragonese invasion and thereby facilitate the invasion of Castile by Edward, the Black Prince. In the following year Calveley began a long pursuit, through the Aragonese court, of du Guesclin's debts to him.

Following the prince's intervention, Calveley's forces were placed in the van of the army, commanded by John of Gaunt, duke of Lancaster, together with the contingents of the Great Companies under the banner of Sir John Chandos. In an initial encounter near Ariñez in March they suffered a serious mauling in a night raid by Enrique's brother, Don Tello, perhaps in revenge for his abandoning the Trastamaran cause; but Calveley himself was not injured and took part in the battle of Nájera (3 April 1367). Thereafter he played a significant, if somewhat equivocal, role as a mediator between Pedro IV of Aragon and the prince, acting as an independent adviser to the king, while technically representing the prince, and taking advantage of his position to secure further rewards from Pedro IV. These were already substantial. While his forces were assembled at Saragossa in February 1366, he had been granted the service of twenty armed galleys for a crusade against the enemies of the faith for a period of four months following the conclusion of the Castilian campaign, which were clearly intended to secure the coveted fortresses in Granada; a perpetual pension of 2000 gold florins; the rank of a baron of Aragon; and the promise of a castle in the kingdom of Valencia. These grants were in part realized in August 1367, when he was awarded the town of Elda, together with the castle and town of Mola, situated in the south of the kingdom of Valencia. Calveley remained in Aragon when the Black Prince returned to Aquitaine during the second half of that month, and there is every evidence that he was building for a future life there. In June 1368 he married Constança, one of the ladies attached to the queen of Aragon's household, the daughter of a Sicilian baron, Bonifacio d'Aragón. The match brought him extensive rights and jurisdiction in the barony and castellany of Cervellón, just outside Barcelona. Together with certain rights that Pedro IV had previously retained in the Valencian territories granted to him in the previous year, the entire dowry had a value of some 40,000 libra of Barcelona. In the following two months he acquired the castle and place of Aspe, as part of a grant that doubled his pension, and disposed of certain annuities that he held in the principality of Aquitaine, which allowed him to purchase the town and valley of Novelda, hitherto granted to his comrade-in-arms, Sir Matthew Gournay. His combined possessions in the kingdom of Valencia thus gave him considerable interests on the Castilian and Granadian frontiers, which alone would have sufficed to detain him in Spain indefinitely. Events dictated otherwise.

Later campaigns With the renewal of the war with France, in the spring of 1369 the Black Prince recalled Calveley to Aquitaine, where he was given command of an army drawn from his own forces and several contingents of the Great Companies brought down from Normandy, which together conducted a destructive raid into the territories of the count of Armagnac and the seigneur d'Albret. Towards the end of the year they took part in a raid into Anjou under the earl of Pembroke, occupying Les Ponts-de-Cé and the abbey of St Maur which, together with a number of other places occupied around Angers, hemmed in the town from the north and south, with the intention of keeping communications open between the English garrisons in Aquitaine and those in Brittany and Normandy. Thereafter Calveley's fortunes were in large measure dictated by the wider decline in England's military position. With the breakup of the army commanded by Sir Robert Knolles at the end of his disastrous campaign in 1370, he avoided confronting du Guesclin at Pontvallain (4 December 1370) and the engagements that followed it, when the remaining contingents of the Great Companies were either defeated or dispersed by the constable's forces. Retreating to St Maur, which had been heavily fortified, he shortly afterwards negotiated its evacuation for a very considerable sum with his old comrade-in-arms. After the prince's return to England in January 1371 Calveley's services were primarily engaged by John of Gaunt, who first retained him in Aquitaine in that year, and with a more substantial retinue in July 1372 for a projected expedition to Aquitaine and Spain. When this was cancelled, he joined him in the expedition to relieve Thouars with a much smaller retinue, which was marooned for a month off the Norman and Breton coasts by contrary winds. In 1373 he commanded a contingent in the duke's impressive but largely ineffectual 'great march', at the outset of which his retinue once again suffered some serious casualties in an ambush by the captain of Ribemont. Appointed the duke's marshal, on his arrival in Aquitaine at the end of the year he established a base of operations in the Dordogne valley and lingered a while in Quercy. By August 1374 he was in command of the important town of La Réole, up the River Garonne some 40 miles from Bordeaux, and conducted a heroic defence of the castle, vigorously besieged by the duke of Anjou, but had to surrender it on 8 September, when no relieving force had materialized.

Returning to England following the conclusion of a truce with France and her allies in the summer of 1375, Calveley was appointed captain of Calais (1375–8), admiral of the fleet to the west (1379–80), captain of Brest (1379–81), along with Sir Thomas Percy, and of Cherbourg (1382). Although he does not appear to have taken up the captaincy of Cherbourg, and his wardenship of the Channel Islands (1375–94) seems largely to have been delegated, at least during the first ten years, these appointments derived from a new military strategy, outlined in parliament by Sir Richard Scrope in 1378: to defend England at sea, and through bases down the French Atlantic seaboard, from which the enemy could also be attacked in their own lands. It was formulated in response to the renewed military activity following the expiry of the truce in June 1377, and to Franco-Castilian naval attacks on the south coast of England, and Calveley played a significant role. From Calais he conducted two notable raids: on Boulogne, where his forces captured a large number of ships, burnt part of the town, and returned with considerable booty; and on Étaples, during a fair, where the French merchants produced rich pickings. He also recovered a number of the castles around Calais surrendered or taken by the French, notably Ouderwyk and Mark, and that of Ardres, which was razed to the ground after the captain had been captured and sent to England for his treachery. When crossing to Brittany early in 1379, Calveley and Percy took seven merchant ships and a man-of-war, which they sent on to Bristol. Rather more important was an engagement that took place in August of that year, when they were providing a naval escort for the return of John de Montfort, duke of Brittany, to his duchy. Following an attack on the duke's transport vessels, a flotilla of French and Castilian galleys, armed with cannons, attempted to prevent their departure. The battle was fierce and the outcome would probably have been disastrous but for Calveley's valiance and determination. In December, when an expeditionary force was being sent to the duke's assistance under Sir John Arundel, almost the entire fleet was wiped out in a storm, and Calveley narrowly escaped with his life by clinging to some of the wreckage. Having rebuilt his retinue following this disaster, in the summer of 1380 he commanded a contingent of 200 men-at-arms and 200 archers in the vanguard of the earl of Buckingham's expedition from Calais across northern France to the outskirts of Rheims, before it turned south into Champagne and descended the Loire valley into Brittany. Three years later he took part in another ill-fated expedition—the bishop of Norwich's 'crusade' to Flanders—which was doomed from the outset by fatal delays and a lack of any firm direction or clear-cut objectives. Calveley came out of it well enough, his military counsels having largely been ignored, having taken no part in the bribes to surrender Bourbourg, and having had no alternative but to acquiesce in the evacuation of Gravelines against overwhelming odds. It was his last campaign.

Retirement from active service Following the invasion scare of 1385–6, and the advent of a further period of truce, Calveley's military services were no longer required. He was thus able to give some time to affairs in the Channel Islands, served twice as knight of the shire for Rutland (October–December 1385 and January–March 1390), and occupied himself with charitable pursuits at home. Although a large part of the profits of his service in Spain appear to have eluded him—in the 1390s he, and after him his nephew John, were still pursuing claims of 300,000 francs in the Aragonese court—it would seem that he was a moderately wealthy man. His paternal estate of Lea had devolved upon him on the death of his father's second wife, Mabel, in 1361. He enjoyed a life annuity of 200 marks from the Black Prince. In 1378 he had acquired the manors of Steventon in Berkshire and Westbury in Wiltshire from the priory of Ste Marie de Pré near Rouen, and in 1385 he had a grant of the royal manor of Shotwick in Cheshire. In March 1387 he secured a royal licence to appropriate the rectory of Bunbury, near Tarporley, Cheshire, which he had purchased, for the foundation of a college with a master and six chaplains. Work on it was already in progress in the previous year, and doubtless completed before his death on 23 April 1394, which may have occurred in Guernsey. Whether or not he was buried at Bunbury, his effigy, in complete armour, may still be seen in the chancel of his college on one of the finest altar tombs in the country. Around the tomb chest are traces of the arms of the founder, interspersed with those of Sir Robert Knolles. Their appearance together may allude to their family or a military relationship, or derive from the possible erection of the tomb by Calveley's old comrade-in-arms. Stow's statement that the two men, together with Sir John Hawkwood, founded a hospital in Rome in 1380, is of doubtful authenticity.

Calveley was physically a large man, of great personal strength and courage, undoubtedly an able soldier, and one who could command the loyalty of his men; but, sometimes impulsive, he lacked the cool calculation of Hawkwood and Knolles. He was estranged from his wife, who continued to reside on their estates in Valencia until the spring of 1380, despite Calveley's repeated requests for her to join him. A year later, when she was cohabiting with Pedro IV's son Juan, their marriage, which was childless, had effectively broken up. Following Calveley's death the custody of his lands and tenements in England was granted, during the minority of his great-nephew David, to his second nephew, John, but on David's death the estate passed to his second great-nephew, also called Hugh. KENNETH FOWLER

Sources *Chroniques de J. Froissart*, ed. S. Luce and others, 15 vols. (Paris, 1869–1975) • *Œuvres de Froissart: chroniques*, ed. K. de Lettenhove, 25 vols. (Brussels, 1867–77) • *Thomae Walsingham, quondam monachi S. Albani, historia Anglicana*, ed. H. T. Riley, 2 vols., pt 1 of

Chronica monasterii S. Albani, Rolls Series, 28 (1863–4) · [T. Walsingham], *Chronicon Angliae, ab anno Domini 1328 usque ad annum 1388*, ed. E. M. Thompson, Rolls Series, 64 (1874) · L. C. Hector and B. F. Harvey, eds. and trans., *The Westminster chronicle, 1381–1394*, OMT (1982) · A. Molinier and E. Molinier, eds., *Chronique normande du XIVe siècle*, Société de l'Histoire de France (1882) · S. Luce, ed., *Chronique des quatre premiers Valois, 1327–1393* (Paris, 1862) · G. de Saint-André, *Chronique de Bertrand du Guesclin, par Cuvelier, trouvère due XIVeme siècle*, ed. E. Charrière, 2 vols. (Paris, 1839) · V. H. Galbraith, ed., *The Anonimalle chronicle, 1333 to 1381* (1927); repr. with corrections (1970) · *Scalacronica: the reigns of Edward I, Edward II and Edward III as recorded by Sir Thomas Gray*, trans. H. Maxwell (1907) · Rymer, *Foedera*, new edn · *Chancery records* · J. Stow and E. Howes, *Annales, or, A generall chronicle of England … unto the end of this present yeere, 1631* (1631) · K. A. Fowler, *The great companies* (2001), vol. 1 of *Medieval mercenaries* (2001–) · K. A. Fowler, 'Deux entrepreneurs militaires au XIVe siècle: Bertrand du Guesclin et Sir Hugh Calveley', in *Le combattant au moyen âge*, Société des Historiens Médiévistes de l'Enseignement Supérieur Public ([Saint-Herblain], 1991), 243–56 · K. A. Fowler, 'The wages of war: the mercenaries of the Great Companies', *Viajeros, perigrinos, mercaderes en el Occidente medieval* [Estella 1991] (Pamplona, 1992), 217–44 · J. C. Bridge, 'Two Cheshire soldiers of fortune of the XIV century: Sir Hugh Calveley and Sir Robert Knolles', *Journal of the Architectural, Archaeological, and Historic Society for the County and City of Chester and North Wales*, new ser., 14 (1908), 112–65 · S. Luce, *Histoire de Bertrand du Guesclin et de son époque* (1876) · K. A. Fowler, 'L'emploi des mercenaires par les pouvoirs ibériques et l'intervention militaire anglaise en Espagne (vers 1361–vers 1379)', *Realidad e imagines del poder: España a fines de la edad media*, ed. A. Rucquoi (Valladolid, 1988), 23–55 · K. A. Fowler, 'Les finances et la discipline dans les armées anglaises en France au XIVe siècle', *Les Cahiers Vernonnais*, 4 (1964), 55–84 · C. Blair, 'The effigy and tomb of Sir Hugh Calveley', *Bunbury papers*, ed. M. H. Ridgway, 4 (1951), 1–16 · K. A. Fowler, 'News from the front: letters and despatches of the fourteenth century', *Guerre et société en France, en Angleterre et en Bourgogne, XIVe–XVe siècle*, ed. P. Contamine, C. Giry Deloison, and M. H. Keen (Lille, 1991), 63–92 · R. Delachenal, *Histoire de Charles V*, 5 vols. (Paris, 1909–31) · P. E. Russell, *The English intervention in Spain and Portugal in the time of Edward III and Richard II* (1955)

Likenesses alabaster effigy on monument, *c.*1390–1410, Bunbury Church, near Tarporley, Cheshire; repro. in Blair, 'The effigy and tomb of Sir Hugh Calveley' · C. A. Stothard, Indian ink drawing (after effigy), BM; repro. in C. A. Stothard, *The monumental effigies of Great Britain*, 12 pts (1817–32), pl. 98, 99

Wealth at death moderately wealthy; owned various estates and was able to found a collegiate church

Calver, Edward (*bap.* 1598?), poet, may have been the Edward Calver, the son of John Calver, who was baptized on 1 May 1598 at Wilby, Suffolk. Very little is known of his life beyond information contained in his books. It is averred that he was a relation of Bernard Calver (or Calvert) of Andover, who sailed from Southwark to Calais and back in a day on 17 July 1620. Calver's two published volumes of poetry from 1641, before the outbreak of the English civil war, reveal a meagre talent dedicated towards unremarkable moral themes. These are interlinked and have the same title: *Passion and Discretion, in Youth and Age*. One is a short work, providing brief verse meditations on engravings from 1635 by Peter Stent, entitled *The Foure Ages of Man*. The other volume is considerably longer, and does not contain the engravings. Calver's sympathies appear to have been parliamentarian: the dedicatees and addressees of his verse include the earl of Manchester and Thomas, Lord Fairfax, both major commanders of the parliamentary forces. But his verse is not strictly partisan: he praises parliament and parliamentarian leaders for restoring peace and national unity, yet nowhere does he attack the king or the royalists. Indeed, *Calver's Royall Vision* (11 October 1648) looks forward to a restored monarchy. This was no doubt the poem mentioned by William Heveningham in his letter to Sir John Potts of 4 September, requesting that Calver join Potts's retinue so that he could present his poem in person to the imprisoned Charles I on the Isle of Wight. Heveningham describes his friend Calver as 'very well affected to the Parliament and the Poeticall'. Calver's civil war poetry is prophetic, often referring to particular visionary experiences, and it looks forward to a reconstituted and reinvigorated body politic. In these respects his verse is like that of another parliamentarian, George Wither, but Calver was neither as prolific nor as successful. Another theme is the poet's need to find a patron who will listen. Calver may be the 'Mr. Calver', the addressee of a manuscript English translation of an allegory in Traiano Boccalini's *De Ragguali di Parnaso* (1612–13) concerned with ensuring that the 'learned and virtuous might safely reach the favour of princes'. In so far as he sought to address the great at significant junctures in time, Calver's sentiments were often either ill-judged or cruelly exposed by contingencies: his praise of parliament for achieving peace in 1642 predates most if not all of the fighting in the civil war, and his address to the king predates the regicide by just four months. This he seems to have realized. In calling on Fairfax to lead an army of pacification to Ireland in 1649 (it was Cromwell who finally led the force), he apologized for the embarrassment his vision of restored monarchy might have caused:

> knowing dreams and visions of such kinde
> Are much uncertaine … O leave the sequel, and do passe it over
> To time, which only can events discover.
> (*Englands Fortresse*, 1649, 5)

NIGEL SMITH

Sources *IGI* · *DNB*

Calverley [*formerly* Blayds], **Charles Stuart** (1831–1884), poet and lawyer, was born on 22 December 1831 at Martley in Worcestershire. His father, the Revd Henry Blayds (1794–1874?), was a descendant of the ancient Yorkshire family of Calverley, and his mother, Elizabeth, was the daughter of Thomas Meade of Chatley, Somerset.

Blayds, after being educated at home by private tutors (1836–46) and for three months in 1846 at Marlborough College, was on 9 September of that year admitted at Harrow School, where he became famous for athletic feats, especially in jumping, and for his extraordinary ability to memorize books of the *Iliad* at short notice. His facility in writing Latin verse won him a scholarship to Balliol College, Oxford, in 1850. There he won the chancellor's prize in 1851 for a Latin poem, which confirmed his high academic standing. However, he was sent down in January 1852 for disciplinary offences involving excessive drunkenness and the illicit keeping of dogs in his rooms. In the following October he entered Christ's College, Cambridge, having changed his name from Blayds to Calverley to evade the disgrace following him from Oxford. He won the Craven scholarship in 1854, the Camden medal in 1853 and 1855, the Browne medal (Greek ode) in 1855, and the members' prize for a Latin essay in 1856, graduating second class in the classical tripos that year. Two years later he was elected a fellow of Christ's. His academic success was the more remarkable because his inherent laziness and love of socializing prevented him from studying regularly. His friends had to drag him out of bed by force, or lock him in his rooms to ensure that he concentrated on his work. He made friends with many prominent members of his college, including professors John Robert Seeley, Walter William Skeat, and John Hales, Walter Besant, and Dr Robert Liveing. His parodies and other humorous verses were well known among fellow students by the time of the publication of *Verses and Translations* in 1862. This collection of gently parodic poems concentrated upon a comfortable and leisured upper-middle-class world and became extremely popular. In 1894 a fourteenth edition was published, and the book was issued as a Pocket Book Classic twenty years after his death. *The Athenaeum* wished that 'some of our prolific small poets would write as good poetry in earnest as Mr Calverley does in play' (Allibone, *Dict.*).

Calverley resigned his fellowship and began to study law shortly before his marriage to his first cousin Ellen Calverley of Oulton, Yorkshire, in 1863. He was called to the bar as a member of the Inner Temple in 1865 and joined the northern circuit. Over the next five years he and his wife had three children, Harold, Evelyn, and John, though Evelyn died in infancy in 1868.

In the winter of 1866–7 Calverley fell on his head while skating at Oulton Hall and received a concussion of the brain. The injury was neglected at the time, and symptoms soon developed which forced him to abandon his legal profession. In 1869 he published a scholarly translation of Theocritus, but the result of his injuries was a gradual incapacitation for all serious work, though he continued to write light verse. In 1872 the success of *Verses and Translations* was repeated in its sequel, *Fly Leaves*, which sold 18,000 copies by 1890. Like *Verses and Translations*, the second volume combined academic scholarship with witty verse, and his parodies were acclaimed as having 'only been equalled by the *Rejected Addresses* [by James and Horatio Smith, 1812]' (Sanders). The collection was particularly notorious for its skilful parody of Robert Browning's 'The Ring and the Book', which Calverley 'rewrote' as 'The Cock and the Bull'. *Fly Leaves* was to mark the end of his literary career.

After a long period of ill health and depression Calverley died of Bright's disease at his home, 17 Devonshire Terrace, Hyde Park, London, on 17 February 1884 and was buried at Folkestone cemetery, Kent. He was survived by his wife and two sons. His *Complete Works* were published in 1885 and reissued in 1896 and 1901.

LESLIE STEPHEN, *rev.* KATHERINE MULLIN

Sources Boase, *Mod. Eng. biog.* • Ward, *Men of the reign* • W. D. Adams, 'Calverley, Charles Stuart', *Dictionary of English literature*, rev. edn [1879–80] • Allibone, *Dict.* • L. C. Sanders, *Celebrities of the century: being a dictionary of men and women of the nineteenth century* (1887) • H. D. Spear, ed., *The poems of C. S. Calverley* (1950) • *The Athenaeum* (23 March 1872), 364 • *The Times* (20 Feb 1884) • P. Scott, 'C. S. Calverley', *Victorian poets after 1850*, ed. W. E. Fredeman and I. B. Nadel, DLitB, 35 (1985), 29–33 • W. J. Sendall, 'Memoir', in *Literary remains of Charles Stuart Calverley* (1885) • J. Payn, *Some literary recollections* (1884), 180–84 • *CGPLA Eng. & Wales* (1884) • Venn, *Alum. Cant.*

Archives Christ's College, Cambridge • University of Toronto | Harvard U., Houghton L., letters to Frederick Locker-Lampson

Likenesses G. J. Stodart, stipple, NPG • mezzotint, Christ's College, Cambridge

Wealth at death £11,988 3*s.* 9*d.*: probate, 26 March 1884, *CGPLA Eng. & Wales*

Calverley, Henry (1604–1661). *See under* Calverley, Walter (*d.* 1605).

Calverley, Walter (*d.* 1605), murderer, was the eldest son and heir of William *Calverley (*d.* 1572), writer, and his wife, Katharine, daughter of John Thorneholme of Haysthorpe, Yorkshire. His family were recusant landowners of Calverley, West Riding of Yorkshire, where he was probably born. While still a child, he lost his father. Under the terms of William Calverley's will, his son became a ward to a relative of William Brooke, tenth Baron Cobham, and inherited the family lands at Calverley as well as titles to the manors of Pudsey and Burley in Wharfedale, along with other lands in Bayley, Tarsley, Ecclesall Bierlow, Bolton in Bradfordale, and Seacroft, all in the West Riding. On 5 May 1579 he entered the University of Cambridge as a scholar of Clare College alongside his brother William. Both matriculated as pensioners on 1 October 1579. Walter left Cambridge without gaining a degree and spent his youth in riotous living.

Calverley was already betrothed to the daughter of a local landowner when, at the will of his guardian, he married Philippa (*d.* after 1605), daughter of Sir John Brooke and his wife, Alice, and niece of Lord Cobham, at London. His neighbours asserted that by this union 'he had made a new bargain, knit a new marriage knot'. However, Calverley's marriage was not happy and, according to his contemporaries, he sought solace in 'excesse, rioting, … diceing, drinking, revelling, and it is feared other things' (Whitaker, 221, 224). He and his wife withdrew to Calverley Hall. He spent excessively and had to mortgage his estates and spend his wife's dowry as a result. The Calverleys had three sons, William (1600/01–1605), Walter (1603–1605), and Henry [*see below*]. Ultimately, their father's squandering proved to be fatal; his excesses caused his bankruptcy and his lands were confiscated by creditors. His younger brother William had stood surety for his estate and was arrested as a result. On 23 April 1605, on hearing the news and presumably in confusion, 'frantic from strong liquors, jealousy, or embarrassed circumstances, or from all these causes united', Calverley murdered his two elder sons and attempted to kill his wife and youngest son. The day after the murders he was arrested by two local JPs, Sir John Savile and Sir Thomas Blande, and was committed to Wakefield gaol. There he made a statement that he had intended to kill his sons 'for the whole space of two years past' as he believed that the 'said children were not of him begotten' (Whitaker, 219, 228–9).

In order to save his estate from forfeiture he refused to plead his cause, and was sentenced and executed by being pressed to death at York Castle on 5 August 1605. He was buried at St Mary's Church, Castlegate, in York. A witness of the execution, Roger Dodsworth, asserted that Calverley had been in holy orders, which is highly unlikely. His estates escaped forfeiture and his widow married Sir Thomas Burton of Stokerston, Leicestershire.

Calverley's social status, and the fact that the victims were children, made the case notorious and sparked off a series of sensational literary works. His story was published immediately by a local writer, Nathaniel Butter, on 12 June and 24 August. In 1605 George Wilkins dramatized the events in his *Miseries of Enforced Marriage*. That year, the London printer Thomas Pavyer also published the story, as a ballad, under the title *A ballad of lamentable murder done in Yorkshire, by a gentleman upon two of his owne children, sore wounding his wyfe and nurse*. In 1608 this ballad was rewritten and published as *A Yorkshire Tragedie: not so New as Lamentable and True, Written by W. Shakespeare*. Two successive reprints, in 1608 and 1619, associated Shakespeare's name with the otherwise mediocre play. The work is included in the 1664 and 1685 folio editions of Shakespeare's works.

Henry Calverley (1604–1661), landowner, inherited his father's estates, although they were heavily encumbered with debt. A fervent royalist, he suffered substantially during the Commonwealth when his estates, then worth £1455, were sequestrated. The last Calverley to live at the family home, he married twice: his first wife was Elizabeth, daughter of John Moore of Grantham, Lincolnshire, and his second was Joyce, daughter of Sir Walter Pye. With them, he had four children, of whom the eldest, Walter, was later knighted by Charles II in recognition of his father's loyalty. His second son, John, was a barrister at Gray's Inn, while his remaining two children, Esther and Henry, died in early childhood. Henry Calverley died on new year's day, 1661. J. ANDREAS LÖWE

Sources Venn, *Alum. Cant.* • Cooper, *Ath. Cantab.*, vol. 3 • J. Burke, *The romance of the aristocracy, or, Anecdotes and records of distinguished families* (1855) • T. D. Whitaker, *Loidis and Elmete, or, An attempt to illustrate the districts described in those works by Bede* (1816) • J. Stow, *The annals of England, untill 1592* (1631) • *DNB*

Archives BL, commonplace book, Add. MS 27419 [Henry Calverley]

Calverley, William (*d.* 1572), writer, was born early in the sixteenth century in Yorkshire, the eldest of the three sons of Walter Calverley and Anne Danby, daughter of Sir Christopher Danby of Farnley. It seems that he participated in the Pilgrimage of Grace in the north of England, and his name is found in a muster of Lord Darcy's men taken in 1536. Calverley was imprisoned in the Tower of London for his part in the uprising, and there wrote *A Dyalogue Bitwene the Playntife and the Defendaunt*, a verse dialogue in which the eponymous plaintiff is made to admit to his errors, and to attest to the justice of his punishment, and which concludes with a warning to those who counsel rebellion against the crown:

From yll counsayle fast loke thou flee
For that hath brought many to mischaunce.

Calverley was released from the Tower in 1537, and was enjoying a prominent place in the Yorkshire community as early as 1539, where he is listed in a local muster roll as constable. In 1540 he was apparently granted the wardship and marriage of his relation, Anne Calverley, although he married Katherine Thorneholme, daughter of John Thorneholme of Haysthorpe. He died in 1572, and according to the visitation of Yorkshire of 1665–6 had six children, including the murderer Walter *Calverley (*d.* 1605). CHRISTOPHER BURLINSON

Sources J. Liedl, 'The penitent pilgrim: William Calverley and the Pilgrimage of Grace', *Sixteenth Century Journal*, 25 (1994), 585–94 • *LP Henry VIII* • W. Dugdale, *The visitation of the county of Yorke*, ed. R. Davies and G. J. Armytage, SurtS, 36 (1859) • C. B. Norcliffe, ed., *The visitation of Yorkshire in the years 1563 and 1564*, Harleian Society, 16 (1881) • *STC, 1475–1640*

Calvert, Adelaide Helen (*bap.* 1836, *d.* 1921). *See under* Calvert, Charles Alexander (1828–1879).

Calvert, Albert Frederick (1872?–1946), traveller and author, was the son of John Frederick (Fred) Calvert, a mining engineer, and his wife, Grace Easley. There is doubt about the date and place of his birth. Some sources make him Australian, born in New South Wales on 20 July 1869, a date consistent with Calvert's own claim to have written about Western Australia in 1889, when he would have been twenty, and a statement in *Vanity Fair* (no. 635, November 1895) that 'he was born in New South Wales some seven and twenty years ago'. On the other hand none of the 190 laudatory fragments of reviews to ten of his books, appended to *My Fourth Tour in Western Australia* (1897), refers to him as an Australian, when they had every occasion to do so. On a birth certificate his birth was registered as having taken place at St Pancras, Kentish Town, London, on 20 July 1872. His grandfather, John Calvert (1814–1897), a goldmining expert, was mainly responsible for his upbringing.

In the 1890s Calvert achieved eminence as an authority on Australia, on the basis of his expeditions, and the accounts he wrote of them and of other aspects of Australian life and mores. In April 1890, partly in the company of his grandfather and perhaps his father, he set out from London under the auspices of the General Exploration Company on his first gold-seeking trip to Australia. It was unsuccessful, and a second expedition, sponsored by the same body, spanned spring 1891 and summer 1892 and encompassed a route of about 500 miles into the north-west of Western Australia. Subsequently he incorporated a detour to the pearl fisheries, described in his *Pearls: their Origin and Formation* (1892). For his third 'tour' his destination was again Roebourne, Western Australia. He set out in December 1892, on this occasion financed by the British Australian Exploration Company, inspecting mines in the goldfields. On his return to London Calvert founded the *Western Australian Review*, with the avowed intention of 'promoting the interests' of that colony, and published *Western Australia: its History and Progress* (1894) and *The Exploration of Australia* (2 vols., 1895; 2nd edn, 1901). Simultaneously he was involved in floating mining enterprises on the stock exchange, acting as managing director for two, and as consultant for others. On 28 March 1894, in Kentish Town, he married Florence, daughter of James Holcombe, solicitor; they had five sons, one of whom, probably the eldest, was killed in action in France in 1915. Calvert was now at the apex of his business career, and was a celebrity.

Before undertaking his next expedition Calvert was guest at a farewell dinner given in his honour by the lord mayor of London in October 1895. His ensuing publication, *My Fourth Tour in Western Australia* (1897), listed the fellowships that he held at that time, including those of the Royal Geographical Society, the Geological Society of Edinburgh, the Scottish Geographical Society, the Geographical Society of Australia, the Royal Society of Australia, the Colonial Institute, and the Imperial Institute. The profuse illustrations, comprising photographs and sketches by the artist Walker Hodgson together with a special map of the western region, were a hallmark of his publications. In 1898 this period of prestige and prosperity came to an end when he sued for bankruptcy, claiming losses on his journal in London and the failure of certain Western Australian mining companies as the causes. His speculative investments in goldmining enterprises appear to have ceased at this time, when the whole course of his life changed.

For the next twenty or so years Calvert turned his attention primarily to Spain and to things Spanish. Within ten years he became such an expert on Spain that he was made a knight grand cross of the royal order of Isabel the Catholic, and made commander of the royal order of Alfonso XII. These honours superseded all others and he used them after his name on most of his publications after 1909. He was the self-styled 'editor' of the Spanish Series which was to consist of nineteen volumes brought out between 1907 and 1921. They were published by John Lane at the Bodley Head, were uniformly bound in distinctive crimson cloth with gilt decoration, and were characterized by an unvarying presentation: a historical or background survey of the city or subject under discussion, followed by the plates, normally photographic and invariably exceeding by far the quantity of pages taken up by the text. At the turn of the twentieth century, and before 1903, he travelled extensively throughout the Peninsula, establishing a large number of 'contacts' in the process. Before launching his Spanish Series he tested the water with *Impressions of Spain* (1903), the first of his publications on that country. This is a perceptive and informed account, with a sensitive appraisal of Spanish character, and an extensive final section on mining in the Peninsula. *The Alhambra* (1906) and its companion volume, *Moorish Remains in Spain* (1906), dedicated to Alfonso XIII, are book productions of the highest quality, embellished with an abundance of colour plates drawn from nineteenth-century works on the architectural legacy of Islam in Spain, notably by Owen Jones, to whose masterpiece on the design of the Alhambra Calvert's publications are particularly indebted. Also noteworthy are his volumes on the painters Murillo (1907), Velázquez, written in collaboration with C. Gasquoine Hartley (1908), and Goya (with 612 'reproductions', also 1908), as well as *The Life of Cervantes* (1905). This last study is subtitled 'the tercentenary edition' to commemorate the year of publication of the first part of *Don Quijote*, and is a spirited biography.

All Calvert's works on Spain were written in London, with the preface indicating his home address of Royston, Eton Avenue, Hampstead (or, occasionally, Swiss Cottage), and many are dedicated to Spanish grandees of his acquaintance, notably the marqués de Villalobar, minister for Spain in London. The majority of Calvert's books on Spanish topics were published before the outbreak of the First World War. Subsequently his only work on a Spanish subject appears to have been *The Spanish Royal Tapestries* (1921), the last in the series.

In 1902 Calvert had contributed to the controversy on the authorship of Shakespeare's works with *Bacon and Shakespeare*, an erudite coverage of the theories and an impassioned defence of Shakespeare's authorship, with appropriate illustrations, including a reproduction of the singular 'wheel' 'used by Dr Owen in deciphering Sir Francis Bacon's cipher writings'. That he never entirely neglected his training as a mineralogist is testified by his *Nigeria and its Tin Fields* (1910)—'compiled in haste, but care has been taken to verify the facts'. A second edition was published in 1912, followed by the substantial *Nigerian Mining Manual* (1913). There is no evidence that he visited Nigeria nor that he ever went to Brazil, the location for his *Mineral Resources of Minas Geraes (Brazil)* (1915), for which he stated that he 'searched official records and read all the available literature that has been published on the subject in English, French, and Portuguese'. He also consulted 'geologists and mining men' who had been to Brazil, and clearly set great store by his sources in his quest to provide as full and up-to-date a picture as possible. He also had an interest in salt, which led to his *Salt in Cheshire* (1915), to his political study *A History of the Salt Union* (1913), and his *Salt and the Salt Industry* for Pitman's series Common Commodities and Industries, published after the First World War. Before 1918 he brought out five books on German African colonies, a subject he investigated in depth, and the product of political concerns at the time. A freemason since 1894 he was renowned as an authority on the history of freemasonry, some sixteen publications on the subject being attributed to him, including *The Grand Lodge of England, 1717–1917* (1917). His last publication of note demonstrated another aspect of his versatility: *Daffodil Growing for Pleasure and Profit* (1929). This consists of eighteen chapters by Calvert, an equal number by sundry authors, and photographs of over two hundred classes of daffodil. The inclusion of two photographs of 'daffodils growing in one of R. F. Calvert's fields at Coverack, Cornwall' suggests that the Calvert mentioned might have been a relation, perhaps one of his four surviving sons.

In 1923 Calvert was involved in a curious lawsuit in which he did not give evidence; damages of £10,000 were awarded against him and in favour of a sister of the tsar of Russia who had implicated him in scheming to deprive her of the proceeds from the sale of her jewels. The tone of the proceedings suggests that he was no longer a person of note, and that his earlier reputation had not been durable. Thirty petitions of bankruptcy had been filed against him, the last in 1921, but he had never been 'adjudicated bankrupt'. After 1929 little is known of his life. Seemingly there were no further publications, and there is some evidence that he received assistance from the masons before his death, at Archway Hospital, Islington, London, on 27 June 1946. His wife survived him. Part of his notable collection of masonic material was acquired for the Lady Lever Art Gallery, Port Sunlight, Cheshire, before 1926. There has been a revival of interest in Calvert's 'Australian' years, while his substantial contribution to Hispanism is awaiting reassessment. RICHARD HITCHCOCK

Sources G. Blackburn, *Calvert's golden west* (1997) • P. Orssich, *Albert F. Calvert (1872–1946)* (1997) [book catalogue] • *AusDB* • J. G. Hill, *Leaves from the Calvert papers* (1893) • *The Times* (18 April 1923)
Likenesses Spy [L. Ward], repro. in *VF*, no. 635 (Nov 1895)

Calvert, Benedict Leonard, **fourth Baron Baltimore** (**1679–1715**), colonial proprietor, was born on 21 March 1679, probably at Woodcote Park in Epsom, Surrey, the second but first surviving son of Charles Calvert, third Baron Baltimore (1637–1715), and his second wife, Jane (*d.* 1701), the widow of Henry Irwell and daughter of Nicholas Lows. On 2 January 1699 Benedict married Charlotte (1678–1721), daughter of Edward Henry Lee, first earl of Lichfield, and Lady Charlotte Fitzroy (1664–1718), illegitimate daughter of Charles II. Their children included Charles *Calvert, fifth Baron Baltimore (1699–1751), and Benedict Leonard *Calvert (1700–1732).

Benedict's career was dedicated to winning back his family's proprietorship over Maryland, which his father had lost in 1689 owing to his connections, inferred and actual, with James II; Baltimore had also been named in the plot of Titus Oates and was associated with the Lancashire plot of 1694. Though not arrested, he was outlawed by the Wexford grand jury in 1691, a judgment soon reversed by the king. Calvert worked hard to shed his family's associations with the house of Stuart. He sold Woodstock Park, which he gained by marriage, to Queen Anne for a gift to John Churchill, first duke of Marlborough; it subsequently became the site of Blenheim Palace, built to celebrate Marlborough's military victory at Blindheim. By 1705 Calvert was separated from his wife, and eight years later he renounced Roman Catholicism, being confirmed in the Church of England in 1713. The obstacle of his former religion removed, he served as the MP for Harwich from 1714 until his death. Following his father's death on 21 February 1715, Benedict succeeded to the barony and regained Maryland for the Calverts. However, his success was short-lived. He died less than two months later on 16 April 1715, and was buried on 2 May at his family estate of Woodcote Park. TROY O. BICKHAM

Sources GEC, *Peerage*, 1.393–5 • A. E. Yentsch, *A Chesapeake family and their slaves: a study in historical archaeology* (1994) • R. B. M. Bibbins, *The beginnings of Maryland in England and America* (1934) • A. C. Land, *Colonial Maryland: a history* (1981) • J. G. Morris, *The lords Baltimore* (1874)
Archives Maryland Historical Society, Baltimore, papers
Wealth at death owned substantial estates in England as well as most of Maryland

Calvert, Benedict Leonard (1700–1732), colonial governor, was born on 20 September 1700 at his mother's ancestral home, Ditchley Park, Oxfordshire, the second son of Benedict Leonard *Calvert, fourth Baron Baltimore (1679–1715), and his wife, Charlotte (1678–1721), daughter of Edward Henry Lee, first earl of Lichfield, and Lady Charlotte Fitzroy, illegitimate daughter of Charles II. The Calverts were the hereditary proprietors of Maryland, having been granted nearly absolute powers by the Maryland charter in 1632; however, the proprietary rights of this Roman Catholic family had been taken away in the wake of the revolution of 1688. Calvert was thus born into a wealthy but troubled family. During his childhood the family suffered further divisions: first when his mother and father separated in 1705 and soon afterwards when his father attempted to regain the family's proprietorship by renouncing Catholicism (1713) and aligning himself with Queen Anne—much to the irritation of Charles, third Baron Baltimore. Calvert, like his six siblings, was extremely well educated, attending the English Jesuit school at St Omer until his father withdrew him and his brothers in favour of the Church of England school at Weston about 1713. In 1716 he entered Christ Church, Oxford, where he developed an interest in antiquities which he pursued further during a three-year grand tour starting in 1723.

Calvert's father succeeded in regaining the proprietorship after the third baron's death in February 1715, only to die two months later. This left Calvert and his slightly older brother, Charles *Calvert, fifth Baron Baltimore (1699–1751), with the monumental task of reasserting the family's influence over Maryland once they came of age. The first step was to send Charles *Calvert (formerly Lazenby Calvert), probably the illegitimate son of the third baron, to Maryland as the governor. Dissatisfied with Charles's progress in settling the ambitions of the lower house of the colony's general assembly, which had grown increasingly assertive and independent during the Calverts' long absence, the fifth Baron Baltimore sent out Benedict—who had recently returned from the grand tour—as colonial governor.

Calvert did not flourish in Maryland. Prone to illness even in the best of climates, he suffered in the Maryland heat, falling ill almost the moment he arrived in Annapolis in March 1727. Nevertheless, he worked hard to complete his obligations to make the Maryland venture as profitable as possible for his family. Like his predecessor he faced opposition from the lower house of the general assembly; Calvert's acquiescence to their demands, such as when he signed an act limiting tobacco production, were, moreover, rejected by Lord Baltimore who refused to grant his assent. Ill health and political troubles also prevented Calvert from pursuing his antiquarian passions and making a lasting mark on the colony. His greatest contribution was his astute observations sent to his older brother, which allowed Baltimore to deal so successfully and decisively with the colonists during his visit in 1732. Calvert's younger brother Edward Henry Calvert (1701–

1730) arrived in January 1729 to assist him, but the 'seasonal' sickness struck the new arrival almost immediately. Edward died seventeen months later. Calvert finally found relief with the arrival of his replacement, Samuel Ogle, on 2 December 1731, but this aid came too late. Calvert died at sea during his passage home on 1 June 1732. Not having married, he left one-third of his estate to the King William School in Annapolis.

TROY O. BICKHAM

Sources GEC, *Peerage*, 1.393–5 • A. E. Yentsch, *A Chesapeake family and their slaves: a study in historical archaeology* (1994) • A. C. Land, *Colonial Maryland: a history* (1981) • J. G. Morris, *The lords Baltimore* (1874) • E. C. Papenfuse and others, *A biographical dictionary of the Maryland legislature, 1635–1789* (1979), 1.185–6 • C. A. Barker, *The background of the revolution in Maryland* (1990)

Archives Maryland Historical Society, Baltimore, family papers

Likenesses F. Brerewood, oils, *c.*1726, Baltimore Museum of Art, Maryland

Wealth at death £315 11*s.* 5*d.* sterling; £325 16*s.* 9*d.* current money, one slave: Papenfuse and others, *Biographical dictionary*, 86

Calvert, Caroline Louisa Waring. *See* Atkinson, (Caroline) Louisa Waring (1834–1872).

Calvert, Cecil, **second Baron Baltimore** (**1605–1675**), colonial promoter, was born on 8 August 1605, probably in Kent, and baptized on 2 March 1606, the son of George *Calvert, first Baron Baltimore (1579/80–1632), statesman, and his first wife, Anne (1579–1622), the daughter of George Mynne of Hertingfordbury. George Calvert, a protégé of Sir Robert Cecil, after whom he named his eldest son, was a member of the privy council and principal secretary of state in the reign of James I. He resigned his office in November 1624, but was retained on the council when he announced his family's conversion to Roman Catholicism.

Cecil matriculated from Trinity College, Oxford, on 16 July 1621 but did not proceed to a degree. A year before his father's conversion Cecil journeyed to Rome and made his own avowal of Catholicism. In 1628 he married Anne, the Catholic daughter of Thomas *Arundell, first Baron Arundell of Wardour, and became even more firmly identified with the Catholic faction. They had at least five children, including two sons, the elder of whom died in infancy.

Cecil Calvert shared his father's interest in the New World and was actively involved in his effort to establish a colony. When the charter to Maryland sought by George Calvert passed the great seal on 20 June 1632, Cecil Calvert was named the grantee since his father had died earlier in the year and Cecil had inherited the barony. The charter granted Calvert palatinate powers over a domain of almost 7 million acres that had once belonged to Virginia. Disputes with that Chesapeake neighbour would trouble the new Lord Baltimore for the remainder of his life. He was himself forced to remain in England to defend his interests and never settled in his colony, appointing in his stead first his brother Leonard *Calvert and then his second son, Charles, to the post of governor.

Although concerned like his father to offer relief to Catholics, Calvert was also motivated by the desire for profit that characterized most colonial promoters. The

Cecil Calvert, second Baron Baltimore (1605–1675), by Abraham Blooteling, 1657

manuscript *Account of the Colony of the Lord Baron of Baltimore* (1633), written by the Revd Andrew White and edited by Calvert, was a promotional piece that enthused about the natural blessings of the region. Calvert sought to attract large investors to whom he would grant large manors in the expectation that they would then bring indentured servants with them to work the land.

Vulnerable to the attacks of his enemies because of his religion, Calvert said little about the role of Catholics in the colony and urged them to maintain a low profile. He worked to prevent the Jesuits from acquiring land and influence. Though he supported their spiritual ministry, he believed their efforts to be divisive in the colony and he came close to expelling them in 1642. In 1643 he invited New England settlers to move to Maryland, and in 1648 and 1649 he encouraged disgruntled Virginia puritans to settle there, hoping these moves and the appointment of a protestant governor and council would avoid action against his colony by the English parliament. Through his instructions he was partly responsible for the 1649 Maryland Act of Toleration, which was the earliest legislation in the English-speaking world that explicitly guaranteed toleration to all Christians. These efforts did not, however, prevent parliament from appointing commissioners to take control of the colony in 1652. Oliver Cromwell, however, restored Calvert's proprietary rights in 1658.

Calvert's last years as proprietor were troubled by growing political, religious, and economic divisions within Maryland. He responded with policies that restricted the franchise and gave the governor power to manipulate the composition of the lower legislative house. These in turn prompted greater resistance, and eventually a successful uprising against the proprietary in 1689.

Calvert died on 30 November 1675 in London, and was buried at St Giles-in-the-Fields, Middlesex. He was succeeded in the barony by his second son, Charles.

FRANCIS J. BREMER

Sources W. H. Browne, *George Calvert and Cecilius Calvert* (1890) • D. B. Quinn, ed., *Early Maryland in a wider world* (1982) • D. W. Jordan, *Foundations of representative government in Maryland, 1632–1715* (1987) • J. D. Krugler, 'Lord Baltimore, Roman Catholics, and toleration', *Catholic Historical Review*, 65 (1979), 49–75
Archives Maryland Historical Society, Baltimore, MSS | Enoch Pratt Free Library, Baltimore, Hugh Hampton MSS • PRO, Colonial office papers, 5th ser. • Sheffield Central Library, Wentworth MSS
Likenesses A. Blooteling, engraving, 1657, NPG [*see illus.*]
Wealth at death substantial, was proprietor of Maryland, which gave family substantial landholding in America in addition to wealth amassed in England

Calvert [*formerly* Lazenby Calvert]**, Charles** (*c.*1688–1734), army officer and colonial governor, may have been the illegitimate son of Charles Calvert, third Baron Baltimore (1637–1715), proprietor of Maryland. The reasons for his former name Lazenby are uncertain, but most likely it indicates a connection with the Lazenbys of Yorkshire. By the time he entered the Grenadier Guards as an ensign in 1709 he had dropped the name Lazenby, choosing to associate himself solely with the Calverts, who appear to have supported his military career by purchasing his commissions.

In February 1720 Calvert, now a captain, was appointed governor of Maryland by the privy council on the advice of Francis North, second Baron Guilford, guardian of Charles *Calvert, fifth Baron Baltimore. In the wake of the revolution of 1688 the third baron, a Roman Catholic, had lost the Calverts' proprietary rights which were restored only upon his death in 1715 when his Anglican son succeeded to the barony. Charles's appointment as governor was intended to reassert the Calvert presence in the colony, which had increasingly come under the influence of an independently minded general assembly. As governor Calvert worked hard to block the aspirations of the emerging 'country' party, led by Thomas Bordley and Daniel Dulany, which sought to diminish the proprietor's authority. In order to pass controversial acts, particularly those regulating the colony's all-important tobacco production, Calvert called legislative sessions during the start of planting season when most assemblymen, who were planters, were unable to leave their farms. Such measures worked temporarily but by the mid-1720s the government had ground to a halt, as governor and his appointed council battled the lower assembly. In March 1727 Calvert was replaced by Benedict Leonard *Calvert (1700–1732), Lord Baltimore's younger brother. Calvert's disappointment was soothed with proprietary appointments to a number of lucrative posts, which included surveyor-general of the western shore (1726–34) and commissary-general (1727–8 and 1729–34).

Calvert's position as one of the wealthiest men in the colony was further ensured by his marriage on 21 November 1722 to Rebecca (1705/6–1735), the sole heir and daughter of John Gerard, a wealthy and recently deceased planter. Calvert died in Maryland on 2 February 1734 and was survived by Rebecca, who died in March of the following year, and by their two daughters, Anne and Elizabeth.

TROY O. BICKHAM

Sources A. E. Yentsch, *A Chesapeake family and their slaves: a study in historical archaeology* (1994) • A. C. Land, *Colonial Maryland: a history* (1981) • J. G. Morris, *The lords Baltimore* (1874) • E. C. Papenfuse and others, eds., *A biographical dictionary of the Maryland legislature, 1635–1789* (1979), 1.188
Archives Maryland Historical Society, Baltimore, family papers
Likenesses J. Wollaston, oils, Baltimore Museum of Art
Wealth at death £151 3*s*. 11*d*. gold; £1288 18*s*. sterling; £2245 15*s*. 10*d*. current money; 1962 acres and warrant for 5000 more acres: Papenfuse and others, eds., *Biographical dictionary*

Calvert, Charles, fifth Baron Baltimore (**1699–1751**), colonial proprietor and politician, was born on 29 September 1699, probably at his family estate, Woodcote Park in Epsom, Surrey, the eldest son of Benedict Leonard *Calvert, fourth Baron Baltimore (1679–1715), and his wife, Charlotte (1678–1721), daughter of Edward Henry Lee, first earl of Lichfield, and Lady Charlotte Fitzroy (1664–1718), illegitimate daughter of Charles II. Since 1632 the Calverts had been the hereditary proprietors of Maryland with near absolute powers granted by the Maryland charter. However, the proprietorship was lost following the revolution of 1688 in view of the Calverts' Roman Catholicism and alleged sympathy for James II. Charles's father spent much of his life shedding his Stuart ties in the hope of regaining the proprietorship. His renunciation of Roman Catholicism in 1713 and confirmation in the Church of England removed the final obstacle. On the death of Charles's grandfather Charles Calvert, third Baron Baltimore, on 21 February 1715, the proprietorship was returned to the family. The success of Charles's father was short-lived, however, as he died less than two months later.

Aged fifteen, Charles Calvert now inherited the barony and the proprietorship. During his minority, Baltimore's guardian, Francis North, second Baron Guilford, acted as proprietor on Charles's behalf. Upon coming of age Baltimore made it clear that he had no intention of being an idle proprietor. Facing him, however, was a monumental task of reasserting his authority over a colony that had grown steadily independent in the Calverts' absence. The lower house of the Maryland assembly had steadily eroded the authority of the executive, and its members would not be brought to heal without a struggle. Baltimore's first action was to reassert the physical presence of the Calverts by sending family members to the colony as governors. The first, in 1720, was Charles *Calvert (formerly Charles Lazenby Calvert), who was probably the third baron's illegitimate son. Seven years later he sent his younger brother, Benedict Leonard *Calvert (1700–1732). Baltimore followed this up with a personal visit in December 1732—the first by a Calvert proprietor since 1684—which, though lasting only seven months, had a profound impact. With the aid of his younger brother's detailed reports, Baltimore was well aware of the economic and political problems facing Maryland, and he was prepared to exercise his authority to resolve them. He assented to the general assembly's paper-currency bill, which had previously been a point of contention but had since become a rather popular measure. However, signs of co-operation ended there. Baltimore rejected the assembly's 'equivalency bill', which continued the practice of negating quitrents owed to the proprietor in favour of a duty on tobacco. Typically, equivalency acts had proved pragmatic, because the proprietor lacked the manpower to collect the quitrents, but Baltimore solved this by creating a new bureaucracy and increasing quitrents by 250 per cent to fund it. He then set fees and salaries of proprietary officials that were not dependent on the general assembly's approval and were independent of further reform. In addition, he undercut opposition in the lower house by bringing its leader and his traditional opponent, Daniel Dulany, on side with bribes in the form of appointments to key lucrative posts in the colony. Baltimore's visit had mixed consequences for the Calverts' control of Maryland. Making his officers and their salaries independent of the general assembly ensured his patronage remained a powerful independent tool. Equally this and his other actions ensured the long-term polarization of Maryland politics as the lower house and the proprietor became pitted in a battle of wills. Political stagnation ensued, making the approval of even the simplest bills a painful process.

At home in Britain, Baltimore was active socially and politically. On 20 July 1730 he had married Mary (*d.* 1770), daughter of the financier Sir Theodore *Janssen, first baronet, with whom he had two sons and three daughters. He also had an illegitimate son, Benedict (born Swingate, but he later took the name Calvert), who was born before his marriage to Mary. In addition to his proprietorship he held court appointments, including the post of gentleman of the bedchamber to the prince of Wales (1731–7), and, an expert on naval matters, was a lord of the Admiralty from 1741 to his death; from December 1731 he was also a fellow of the Royal Society. In 1734 he was elected MP for St Germans, which he represented as a supporter of Prince Frederick's opposition until 1741 when he became member for Surrey. For a brief period in the late 1740s he led the opposition party but in Horace Walpole's opinion 'was not capable of leading a party' despite his being 'the best and honestest man in the world' (Walpole, *Corr.*, 17.173). Baltimore died on 24 April 1751 and was buried at Erith, Kent. His widow died nineteen years later at Chaillot, near Paris, and he was succeeded to the barony by his only legitimate son, Frederick *Calvert (1732–1771).

TROY O. BICKHAM

Sources GEC, *Peerage*, new edn, 1.393–5 • A. E. Yentsch, *A Chesapeake family and their slaves: a study in historical archaeology* (1994) • R. B. M. Bibbins, *The beginnings of Maryland in England and America* (1934) • A. C. Land, *Colonial Maryland: a history* (1981) • J. G. Morris, *The lords Baltimore* (1874) • G. A. Stiverson, 'Calvert, Charles', *ANB* • R. R. Sedgwick, 'Calvert, Charles', HoP, *Commons, 1715–54* • Walpole, *Corr.*
Archives Maryland Historical Society, Baltimore, papers
Wealth at death enormous; owned much of Maryland as well as substantial estates in England

Calvert, Charles (1754–1797). *See under* Calvert, Charles (1785–1852).

Calvert, Charles (1785–1852), landscape painter, born at Glossop Hall, Derbyshire, on 23 September 1785, was the eldest son of **Charles Calvert** (1754–1797), land agent, and his wife, Elizabeth Holliday (1751/2–1842). His father was agent of the duke of Norfolk's estate in Derbyshire and an amateur artist. Charles Calvert senior died on 13 June 1797 and was buried in St Mary's churchyard, Manchester. Calvert began business as a cotton merchant in Manchester, having been apprenticed to the cotton trade, but abandoned commerce for art and became a landscape painter. He was instrumental in the foundation of the Manchester Royal Institution (which later became Manchester City Art Gallery) and gained the Heywood gold medal (awarded to local artists) for a landscape in oil, and the Heywood silver medal for a landscape in watercolour. The *Manchester Courier* reported in 1828 that, of local artists, Calvert's paintings were the most consistently sold. He was not well known outside his region, however, and exhibited only two works in London, one of which, at the British Institution in 1825, was entitled *Near Rustom, Cheshire*.

Calvert devoted much of his time to teaching, and spent the remainder painting in the Lake District. Although confined to his bed in later years, he continued to paint landscapes from memory. He died at Bowness, Westmorland, on 26 February 1852, and was buried there. Examples of his work are in the Victoria and Albert Museum, London, and Manchester City Galleries.

Charles Calvert's brothers included Frederick Baltimore *Calvert (1793–1877), actor and lecturer on elocution, George *Calvert (1794–1825), surgeon, Henry Calvert (1785–*c.*1869), sporting and animal painter, and Michael Pease Calvert, painter. He was father-in-law to the portrait painter William *Bradley (1801–1857).

In the *Dictionary of National Biography* **Raisley Calvert** (*bap.* 1773, *d.* 1795), friend and benefactor of William Wordsworth, is incorrectly described as Charles Calvert's younger brother. Raisley Calvert was baptized on 16 September 1773, the younger son of Raisley Calvert senior (1728/9–1791), steward of the duke of Norfolk's estate at Greystoke Castle, near Penrith, Cumberland. His elder brother was William Calvert (1771–1829), who was at school with Wordsworth at Hawkshead, Lancashire, where he later became schoolmaster. On the death of his father, William Calvert became a man of independent means, inheriting, with other property, the estate of Bowness on the east shore of Bassenthwaite, near Keswick. Raisley Calvert inherited from his father several farms near Keswick, the income from which was held in trust until he attained his majority in 1794. He was admitted to Magdalene College, Cambridge, on 14 February 1793, where he became friends with Wordsworth, but left soon afterwards with a resolve to educate himself by travel on the continent. Though described in the *Dictionary of National Biography* as a sculptor, no evidence has come to light of any works sculpted by Raisley Calvert. On falling ill with consumption, he returned to the Lake District, where he died at Penrith after 7 January 1795, when Dorothy Wordsworth mentioned that he was 'barely alive' (*Letters of William and Dorothy Wordsworth*, 139). He was buried on 12 January. In his will, signed on 23 October 1794, Raisley Calvert left £900 to Wordsworth. The poet subsequently wrote a sonnet, 'To the Memory of Raisley Calvert', and later mentioned him in lines 349–67 of the thirteenth book of *The Prelude*:

A Youth (he bore
The name of Calvert.
(lines 349–50)

W. E. A. Axon, *rev.* L. R. Houliston

Sources *Art Journal*, 14 (1852), 150 • S. Urbans, *GM*, 2nd ser., 37 (1852), 630 • T. Fawcett, *The rise of English provincial art: artist, patron and institution outside London, 1800–1830* (1974) • G. Meissner, ed., *Allgemeines Künstlerlexikon: die bildenden Künstler aller Zeiten und Völker*, [new edn, 34 vols.] (Leipzig and Munich, 1983–) • M. Hall, *The artists of Cumbria* (1979) • D. Child, *Painters in the northern counties of England and Wales* (1994) • Bryan, *Painters* (1903–5) • Redgrave, *Artists* • Mallalieu, *Watercolour artists* • M. H. Grant, *A chronological history of the old English landscape painters*, rev. edn, 8 vols. (1957–61) • *IGI* • H. M. Cundall, *A history of British water colour painting* (1908), 193 • *The letters of William and Dorothy Wordsworth*, ed. E. De Selincourt, 2nd edn, rev. C. L. Shaver, M. Moorman, and A. G. Hill, 8 vols. (1967–93), vol. 2, pp. 81, 97, 126n., 139–40 • W. Wordsworth, *Poems, in two volumes, and other poems, 1800–1807*, ed. J. Curtis (1983), 151–2
Archives Manchester Local Studies Archive Service, Manchester, letters to Royal Manchester Institution

Calvert, Charles Alexander (1828–1879), actor and theatre manager, was born in London on 28 February 1828, the son of William Henry Calvert (*d.* 1857), a silk merchant, who claimed descent from George Calvert, the first Lord Baltimore. A. W. Ward's assertion (*DNB*) that Calvert attended King's College School is not substantiated by that institution's records; his education was undoubtedly affected by reverses in his father's business, as was his aspiration to take holy orders in the Church of England. Calvert's father was a man of deep but unconventional piety, who had his son 'baptized into no less than four different denominations' (Calvert, 18). As a young man Charles was drawn to the works of Emanuel Swedenborg, as a result of which he felt that he could no longer accept the tenets of the Church of England. In later life he found a religious refuge in Unitarianism. Having abandoned the idea of a religious vocation, he was articled to a solicitor, but gave up the law in favour of commerce and became a traveller for a company dealing chiefly in straw hats.

Early theatrical career Calvert's interest in the theatre was awakened by Samuel Phelps, whose performances at Sadler's Wells he attended, as he did W. C. Macready's farewell London seasons. He entered the theatrical profession in 1852 and gained early experience in Weymouth (with E. A. Sothern), in Southampton (where he met his future wife, Adelaide Biddles [*see below*]), and in south Wales. He made his London début, as Leonardo, prince of Mantua, in Sheridan Knowles's *The Wife* (24 September 1855) at the

Charles Alexander Calvert (1828–1879), by William Keith, *c.*1860 [as Caliban in *The Tempest*]

Surrey Theatre under the managers Richard Shepherd and William Creswick, who aspired to emulate, south of the river, Phelps's regime at Sadler's Wells. The repertory was varied, including melodrama, Shakespeare, and an adaptation of Henry Mayhew's *London Labour and London Poor* by J. B. Johnstone, entitled *How we Live in the World of London* (March 1856). On 31 August 1856 Calvert married Adelaide Biddles at St Mary's Church, Lambeth, after which she joined the Surrey company. In April 1857 Calvert used an inheritance of £500 to establish the Allied Metropolitan Dramatic Company, whose touring venues included Southampton and Manchester. The venture was not a financial success, and in the autumn of 1858 the Calverts returned to the Surrey, but not before Charles had gained his first experience of management and established contacts in the city to which he was to devote the greater part of his professional life—Manchester.

In the autumn of 1859 Calvert was engaged by the legendary John Knowles at the Theatre Royal, Manchester; he impressed as an actor (alternating Othello and Iago with David H. Jones), but it was in his capacity as stage manager that he made the greatest mark. Undeterred by Knowles's penny-pinching regime, Calvert staged *Hamlet* (November 1859) with Scandinavian-style costumes (refashioned from the wardrobe), graphic scenery (painted over old stock), atmospheric lighting, and extensive use of music. The result was hailed as a triumph. Calvert's relationship with Knowles was never easy and he spent periods in Newcastle and Glasgow; he also wrote a number of plays, of which *Rube the Showman* was the most successful, but his industriousness combined with his highly strung temperament resulted in the first of the nervous illnesses from which he was to suffer for the rest of his life.

Productions of Shakespeare To a man of Calvert's intelligence and social awareness, the opportunities afforded by the expansion and growing wealth of Manchester must have been clearly apparent. Fortunately, a group of local businessmen launched an enterprise well suited to Calvert's aspirations, and in the autumn of 1864 he became manager of the new Prince's Theatre. The nature of Calvert's involvement in the Prince's fluctuated (for a time he held a significant financial stake), but essentially between 1864 and 1875 the architect Edward Salomon's beautiful and intimate theatre provided Calvert with the base for a management which was unrivalled in the provinces and not consistently matched in the metropolis. The cornerstone of Calvert's achievement was Shakespeare—from the opening production of *The Tempest* (15 October 1864) to *Much Ado about Nothing* (13 February 1865), *A Midsummer Night's Dream* (2 September 1865), *Antony and Cleopatra* (10 September 1866), *The Winter's Tale* (8 September 1869), *Richard III* (31 January 1870), *Timon of Athens* (6 March 1871), *The Merchant of Venice* (18 August 1871), *Henry V* (16 September 1872), *Twelfth Night* (8 September 1873), and *Henry IV Part 2* (28 September 1874). Although it was Samuel Phelps whose work had fired Calvert's interest in the theatre (he appeared in two of Calvert's revivals, *Twelfth Night* and *Henry IV Part 2*), Charles Kean was a stronger influence. Calvert fully subscribed to Kean's antiquarianism and the place in the theatre of the allied arts of painting (the Telbins, the Gordons, and the Grieves provided scenery) and music (Clay, Macfarren, and Sullivan composed settings and background music). Several of Calvert's published acting editions reveal his indebtedness to Kean, but they also show an awareness of textual scholarship. Beddoes Peacock recalled Calvert's scrutiny of the Folio text, and in A. W. Ward, successively professor of history and English literature and language and principal of Owens College, Manchester, Calvert had recourse to a scholar of dramatic literature. The monumental task of mounting these revivals meant that Calvert's own performances were often under-prepared, but his capacity for original interpretation was evident in his sympathetic Shylock and reflective Henry V. The production of *Henry V* was bought by the New York managers Jarrett and Palmer—as *Richard III* had been—and Calvert supervised the staging at Booth's Theatre in February 1875 with George Rignold in the title role.

Calvert's management of the Prince's was also characterized by revivals of Byron (*The Two Foscari*, *Manfred*, and *Sardanapalus*, the last also being bought by Jarrett and Palmer) and the annual pantomimes, upon which he lavished the same attention as he did on his Shakespearian revivals. Despite his own incursion into playwriting Calvert did little to encourage new plays. At the Theatre Royal he had encouraged the youthful talent of Henry Irving, and the Prince's was renowned as a nursery for aspiring actors, including Frank Archer, A. W. Pinero, Johnston Forbes-Robertson, Pauline Markham, Teresa Furtado, Fanny Brough, Kate Bishop, Nelly Moore, and Rose Coghlan. Just how much individual attention these performers received from Calvert is a matter of dispute, but the experience of working with a man endowed with such idealism, integrity, and imagination stood them in good stead in their later careers.

Calvert departed the Prince's Theatre in 1875. He achieved one further major Shakespearian revival—*Henry VIII* at the Theatre Royal, Manchester (28 September 1877)—but his plans to stage *Henry VI* and *Coriolanus* remained unrealized, as did his involvement in a Shakespeare Memorial Theatre and Colonel J. H. Mapleson's Grand Opera House—both in London. The remaining years of Calvert's life were spent touring the provinces with his own company in a repertory which still included Shakespeare alongside other less worthy offerings. He succumbed to a terminal bout of nervous prostration in Glasgow in April 1879 and died, aged fifty-two, in Fulham on 12 June 1879. The high esteem in which Calvert was held by his profession and the public was manifested in two ways. An estimated 50,000 people lined the route of his funeral procession through the streets of Manchester to Brooklands cemetery, where the liberal-minded Congregational minister Edwin Paxton Hood presided over the service, as a result of which he incurred the disfavour of his congregation at the Alexander Street Chapel. On 1 and 2 October two memorial (benefit) performances of *As You Like It* were played at the Theatre Royal, Manchester, with a combined cast of amateurs and professionals, led on 2 October by Helen Faucit as Rosalind. Calvert left a widow, five sons, and two daughters. In his address, spoken before the performances, H. M. Acton wrote

> But none who Calvert knew
> Will doubt his place amongst the foremost few.

As an actor, though his physical advantages were few, Calvert had stage presence and a good voice. Above all he brought a sharp intelligence to his interpretations, especially of Shakespearian roles. As a manager 'his place amongst the foremost few' is assured. Calvert's Shakespearian revivals were not merely stepping-stones between the eras of Phelps–Kean and Irving, but they stand proud in their own right, equal to comparison with what was to come and what had gone before.

Other acting Calverts Calvert's widow, **Adelaide Helen Calvert** (*bap.* 1836, *d.* 1921), actress, was born in Loughborough, the eldest of the four daughters of James Biddles, then a tobacconist, soon to be an actor and entertainer, and his first wife, Ann Maria. Adelaide was baptized at All Saints' Church, Loughborough, on 1 April 1836. At the age of six she was established as 'an infant prodigy' in the stock company (that of Mr Harvey operating in Weymouth, Guernsey, and Exeter) of which her parents were members. She appeared with Henry Betty, son of the 'Infant Roscius', and Charles and Ellen Kean. Following the death of their mother, Adelaide and her sister Clara were sent to a boarding-school in Nottingham, but when their father took over the management of the Bower Saloon in October 1845 they rejoined him (and his second wife) and were soon appearing on stage. In a varied repertory Adelaide undertook roles in melodrama, Shakespeare, and pantomime; she also became the pupil of the celebrated clown Richard Flexmore, a neighbour in Hercules Buildings, Lambeth. In October 1851 her drama *Amy Lawrence: a Tale of an Old Man's Love* (adapted from a story serialized in the *London Journal of Science and Art*) was successfully staged at the Bower with the author in the title role.

In August 1853 Biddles secured engagements for both Adelaide and Clara with E. Holmes at the Theatre Royal, Southampton, where the company included Mary Seyton (Mary E. Braddon, the novelist) and Charles Calvert, Adelaide's future husband. Adelaide achieved further success with *Amy Lawrence*, wrote and appeared in *Minnegray the Gipsy Girl*, and was acclaimed as Ophelia and Juliet. The sisters were recalled in the summer of 1854 to the Bower Saloon, where their acting impressed Thomas Barry and was the major inducement for Barry to contract the whole Biddles family for the new Boston Theatre, of which he was the manager. Following a prolonged and stormy voyage, during which Adelaide exercised her literary talents, writing poetry and short stories, the Biddleses arrived in the New World in the autumn of 1854. Adelaide swiftly proved her worth, appearing with Edwin Forrest, who coached her as Calanthe in *Damon and Pythias*, and as Lady Percy to James Hackett's Falstaff in *Henry IV*. Adelaide remained in Boston for the 1855–6 season, adding to her laurels as Hero and Black-eyed Susan, but Calvert was still pressing his suit and she returned to England for their marriage, at St Mary's Church, Lambeth, on 31 August 1856. Adelaide joined her husband at the Surrey Theatre, where her performance as Juliet won plaudits from *The Times* (18 December 1856): 'a commanding yet delicate figure, a distinct but not unfeminine voice, and a profusion of raven hair … In the traditional business of the character she is thoroughly versed, and … she manifests an amount of genuine feeling that may obtain for her a position more generally recognised than that which she at present holds.'

Adelaide's 'delicate figure' soon swelled with the first (Leonard) of eight children (of whom seven survived) but she resolutely pursued her acting career, appearing not only with her husband, but also, in Brighton in October 1860, with Ira Aldridge (the 'Negro Tragedian'), as Lavinia, in his singular adaptation of *Titus Andronicus*. By then Charles was in Manchester, and when he assumed the management of the Prince's Theatre in 1864 Adelaide supported him not only on stage, but also in the management. Family responsibilities and the perennial dearth of roles for actresses of middle years somewhat curtailed her appearances for a time, but she played Miranda, Beatrice, Cleopatra (with thrilling power in the final act), Hermione, Queen Elizabeth in *Richard III*, and Chorus in *Henry V* in Calvert's revivals and was also admired as Portia (*The Merchant of Venice*) and Queen Katharine. She repeated Chorus in the opening weeks (February 1875) of *Henry V* in New York, before which she visited her sister Clara (who had married Thomas Barry, forty years her senior) in Boston.

At the time of Charles Calvert's last illness in April 1879 Adelaide was appearing, as Gertrude to Barry Sullivan's Hamlet, at the opening of the Shakespeare Memorial Theatre in Stratford upon Avon. Once she was widowed, the pursuit of her career was a financial imperative. In October 1881 she embarked on a forty-week tour of the United States with Edwin Booth, playing Emilia, Goneril, and Gertrude; back in England—in 1883—she appeared with Adelaide Ristori, partnering the Italian actress as Queen Elizabeth in Schiller's *Mary Stuart*. Further visits to America followed with Mary Anderson (1885–6 and 1888) and with Lillie Langtry (1886), but Adelaide's opportunities were limited to relatively minor roles.

Adelaide Calvert was reconciling herself to imminent retirement when very much by chance, in April 1894, came what Shaw described as the 'rise from utter extinction' (*Bernard Shaw and Mrs Patrick Campbell: their Correspondence*, ed. A. Dent, 1952, 264) with the role of Catherine Petkoff in *Arms and the Man*. This revived her career for a further fifteen years, during which she appeared, principally in the West End, in a succession of contemporary plays (by F. C. Burnand, Captain Marshall, H. A. Jones, R. C. Carton, Maugham) and classic revivals. Her Mrs Malaprop in *The Rivals* (March 1900), her Mrs Heidleberg in *The Clandestine Marriage* (March 1903)—both with Cyril Maude at the Haymarket—and her Mrs Hardcastle in *She Stoops to Conquer* (first in New York and then at the Waldorf Theatre with Maude in February 1906) were hailed as definitive performances in the finest tradition of comedy character acting. Adelaide joined Beerbohm Tree's company for *Henry VIII* at His Majesty's to play An Old Lady in September 1910, and in June 1911 she took her place alongside Madge Kendal and Ellen Terry in the coronation gala performance. In that year she published her memoirs, *Sixty-Eight Years on the Stage*, in which she recounted her remarkable career and reflected upon the changes, principally its 'gentrification', in her profession. From infant prodigy in an 1840s stock company to *grande dame* at the 1911 coronation gala, from Juliet to Mrs Malaprop, Adelaide Calvert had achieved distinction in every age of her lengthy career. She died, after forty-two years of widowhood, in Barnes on 20 September 1921.

Louis Calvert (1859–1923), actor, the third son of Charles and Adelaide Calvert, was born in Manchester on 25 November 1859. He was educated at Dr Ernest Adams's academy in Manchester, where he showed an early inclination towards acting, and in Germany. Although Charles Calvert discouraged his children from taking up the theatre as a career, Louis, like his brothers Leonard, William,

Alexander, and Cecil, followed in his parents' footsteps on to the stage. Louis made his début in Natal in 1878 and proceeded to Australia before returning to England in 1880. During the following decade he gained varied experience with Sarah Thorne at Margate, with Henry Irving at the Lyceum, and with Lillie Langtry in America.

By the mid-1890s Calvert was concentrating on Shakespeare and earning a reputation as both an actor and a producer. He was a finely articulated Mark Antony in Frank Benson's *Julius Caesar*. For the Manchester committee of the Independent Theatre he staged an Elizabethan-style production of *Richard II* (February 1895), to which his work for Richard Flanagan at the Queen's Theatre in the same city (*Henry IV Part 1*, February 1896; *Antony and Cleopatra*, February 1897) was—in its Saxe-Meiningen style of archaeological naturalism—a marked contrast. It was this style of production which commended Calvert to Beerbohm Tree initially as co-producer of *Henry IV Part 1* at the Haymarket (May 1896) and in the same capacity with *Julius Caesar* at Her Majesty's in January 1898. Calvert's performances as Casca, Cardinal Pandulf (*King John*, September 1899), Flute (January 1900), and Dogberry were noted for his ability to deliver dialogue with freshness and clarity. Of Calvert's Dogberry Shaw wrote: 'To Mr Calvert it [the dialogue] is as natural as his native speech; he makes it clear, expressive and vivid without the least preoccupation' ('The dying tongue of Great Elizabeth', *Saturday Review*, 11 Feb 1905).

By 1905 Calvert had already created the role of Broadbent in Shaw's *John Bull's other Island* under the Vedrenne–Barker management at the Court Theatre (November 1904). A hard taskmaster, Shaw recognized Calvert's ability to give just the right emphasis and accentuation down to the minutest inflection. In May 1905 Calvert played the Waiter in *You Never can Tell*, but it was his creation of the role of Andrew Undershaft in *Major Barbara* (Court Theatre, 28 November 1905) that posed the greatest challenge to the partnership between author and actor. Shaw likened the role to playing a trombone; Calvert certainly had the volume, and under Shaw's tutelage he gradually mastered the structure of the long speeches and their infinite nuances. In his manual *Problems of the Actor* (1919), Calvert acknowledged his debt to Shaw and upheld the virtues of traditional—by then often damned as declamatory—elocution which, he maintained, was not incompatible with the appearance of naturalism.

With numerous relatives in the United States (seventy-two in Chicago alone), Calvert was a regular visitor. In 1909 he was engaged as stage-manager of the recently constructed New Theatre in New York, an ambitious venture modelled on the state theatres of Europe, but without their subsidies. Calvert's brief was to supervise, and appear in, productions of plays from the English repertory, particularly Shakespeare. The task was a difficult one with mixed casts of English and American actors, the latter with little experience of classical acting. The opening production of *Antony and Cleopatra* (in November 1909) foundered under monumental sets and the egos of E. H. Sothern and Julia Marlowe in the title roles; *Twelfth Night* (January 1910) was lacklustre, but with *The Winter's Tale* (March 1910) Calvert combined ensemble acting with an Elizabethan-style setting in a production which prefigured Granville Barker's at the Savoy Theatre, London, in 1912. The repertory seasons at the New Theatre survived for less than two years, but Calvert spent most of the remainder of his life in America, establishing himself as a respected teacher of acting in several universities and academies. Calvert was twice married, first to Rose Roberts, an actress, and secondly to Violet Fenton, also an actress, with whom he had two daughters, Ray (Beatrice) and Patricia. He died at his home, 321, West 55th Street, New York, on 18 July 1923. James Agate's verdict was 'Calvert was not only a fine actor, but the cause whereby fine acting is in others' (*Sunday Times*, 22 July 1923).

RICHARD FOULKES

Sources Mrs Charles Calvert, *Sixty-eight years on the stage* (1911) · R. Foulkes, *The Calverts: actors of some importance* (1992) · A. Darbyshire, *An architect's experiences: professional, artistic, and theatrical* (1897) · A. Darbyshire, *The art of the Victorian stage* (1907) · R. Foulkes, ed., *British theatre in the 1890s* (1992) · *The Era* (1852–1923) · *Era Almanack and Annual* (1868–70) · J. Parker, ed., *Who's who in the theatre*, 10th edn (1947) · *Who's who in the theatre*, various edns · B. Hunt, ed., *The green room book, or, Who's who on the stage* (1906) · *Shakespeare Survey*, 41 (1989) · *Theatre Research International*, 18/3 (autumn 1993) · m. cert. · d. cert. · *CGPLA Eng. & Wales* (1879) · parish registers, Leics. RO [Adelaide Helen Calvert] · WWT, 1947 [Adelaide Helen Calvert]

Archives BL · Folger · Harvard TC · Man. CL, Arts Library · Man. CL, Manchester Archives and Local Studies · Schubert archive, New York · Shakespeare Birthplace Trust RO, Stratford upon Avon · Theatre Museum, London

Likenesses W. Keith, photograph, *c.*1860 (as Caliban in *The Tempest*), Theatre Museum, London [*see illus.*] · photographs, repro. in Calvert, *Sixty-eight years* · photographs, Man. CL · photographs, Mander and McKevenson (Theatre) Coll. · photographs, repro. in Foulkes, *The Calverts* · prints, Harvard TC

Wealth at death under £5000: probate, 11 July 1879, *CGPLA Eng. & Wales* · £2281 2s. 6d.—Adelaide Helen Calvert: probate, 15 Nov 1921, *CGPLA Eng. & Wales*

Calvert, Edward (1799–1883), artist, was born at Appledore, Devon, on 22 September 1799, the elder son of Rowland Edward Calvert (*c.*1750–1813), an army officer, and his wife, Katherine, *née* Rider. He was baptized privately at Appledore, and about two years afterwards was received into the church at Poltimore, by the Revd R. W. Bampfylde. His father's health deteriorated, so the family moved further west to the more salubrious St Winow, near Lostwithiel on the Fowey estuary, Cornwall. Here Calvert indulged his love of boats and sailing, once rowing alone to a fishing fleet some miles from shore. His formal education began at Bodmin grammar school, but when he was fifteen, he entered the navy as a midshipman. He served on several ships, and was present at the eight-hour bombardment of Algiers in 1816, during which his closest friend, Midshipman Jardine, was killed.

During Calvert's service, the Mediterranean Fleet visited the Aegean, where Greek classicism fired his imagination, moving him to make copious notes and sketches. These impressed the midshipmen's instructor, Herr Runker, a German, who put his cabin at Calvert's disposal for study. Calvert was later disillusioned with naval

Edward Calvert (1799–1883), by unknown artist

life and left the service on 30 October 1820. Thereafter, he settled in Plymouth where he received lessons from Ambrose Bowden Johns (1776–1858), a painter of dreamy landscapes, and from Thomas (or James) Ball (*fl.* 1817–1835), an enthusiastic classicist, who set Calvert to draw from antique casts. Little of Calvert's work from this time survives; he destroyed what displeased him, and much early work undoubtedly disappeared in this way. One brilliant little watercolour remains: *A Primitive City* (1822; British Museum, London), measuring 2¾ x 4 in. Its sensitive line and gem-like colour afford a foretaste of his minutely detailed little engravings.

In Plymouth, Calvert lodged with a Mrs Glyddons, in Tavistock Street. A family from Brixton lodged in the same house, and Calvert fell in love with one of the daughters, Mary Bennell (1805–1869). They married in 1824, and moved to London, taking lodgings in Arundel Street near St Clement Danes Church; later they stayed with Mary's parents at Claremont Lodge, Brixton; then from 1826 to 1832 they lived at 17 Russell Street, Brixton. During this time Calvert attended the drawing and life schools of the Royal Academy, which he first entered as a probationer on 31 March 1825.

Calvert had independent means, and wishing to dispose of some shares, consulted a stockbroker, John Giles (1810–1880); the conversation turned to art, and Giles mentioned his cousin the artist Samuel Palmer, who was the leading figure of a group of earnest young men, mostly artists, who had gathered around William Blake in his old age. Styling themselves the 'Ancients', they worked for a few years creating work of visionary intensity, and reinforcing one another's artistic and religious beliefs. Giles, though not an artist, was an enthusiastic member of the group. Soon after learning of the Ancients from Giles, Calvert met the painter George Richmond, another Ancient, who introduced him to Palmer and the others, whom he joined at times at their rural retreat at Shoreham, in Kent.

Blake's direct influence was greater on Calvert's work than on that of any other Ancient. In Calvert's little engravings made from 1827 to 1831, many details are traceable directly to Blake's illustrations for Robert John Thornton's *Virgil for Schools* (1821); but Calvert's designs are mingled also with the spirit of what he called 'Pan and the rustic deities, elemental natures' (Calvert, *Memoir*, 97). This is especially apparent in his wood-engraving *The Cyder Feast* (1828) and in the lithograph *Ideal Pastoral Life* (1829). Elsewhere details are inspired by classical gems and statuary: such are the women's figures in the line engraving *The Bride* (1828) and the wood-engraving *The Chamber Idyll* (1831). In these works, some no bigger than a visiting card, Calvert took engraving to its limits. Originally several of them had Christian inscriptions, but Calvert's paganism overtook his Christian beliefs, and he removed them wherever possible.

Calvert's rejection of fine engraving has never been satisfactorily explained, but after 1831 he abandoned it completely. Instead he turned to painting—mainly in oil—dreamy classical pastorals. Their quality varies: in some, where his treatment resembles that of his friend, William Etty (1787–1849), it is firmly controlled and convincing; elsewhere it is misty and insubstantial. In 1832 the Calverts moved to Park Place, Paddington. In 1851 they moved to Hampton Court, where they remained three years, then to Park Road Villas, Dalston, until about 1856, after which they moved to two consecutive addresses in Hackney: Frampton House, Wells Road, and finally, 11 Darnley Road. Mary Calvert bore six children, but later became an invalid, staying for periods between 1852 and 1855 on the south coast. She died on 12 March 1869, aged sixty-four.

In 1844 Calvert revisited Greece. From then until 1855 he wrote much on art: typical are studies of individual painters from Tintoretto to Ingres, and a lack-lustre investigation of a musical theory of colour. A selection of these works was printed in his son's *Memoir* (1893). In appearance, Calvert was sturdy, always unmistakably a sailor, with nautical white trousers. In old age, he had white hair and beard and retained limpid blue eyes. He died at his home, aged eighty-three after two days' illness on 14 July 1883, and was buried in Abney Park cemetery, Stoke Newington. There are works by Calvert in the British Museum and the Victoria and Albert Museum, London; the Yale Center for British Art, New Haven, Connecticut; and the Ashmolean Museum, Oxford. RAYMOND LISTER

Sources S. Calvert, *A memoir of Edward Calvert, artist* (1893) · *The letters of Samuel Palmer*, ed. R. Lister, 2 vols. (1974) · R. Lister, *Edward Calvert* (1962) · A. H. Palmer, *The life and letters of Samuel Palmer* (1892); repr. (1972) · *CGPLA Eng. & Wales* (1883) · G. E. Bentley, jun. and others, *Essays on the Blake followers* (1983) · R. Lister, *Beulah to Byzantium* (1965) · S. M. Bennett, *Prints by the Blake followers* (1981) · J. Viscomi, *Prints by William Blake and his followers* (1983) · R. Lister, 'Calvert's "Lady and the rooks" and Cornish scenes', *Blake Newsletter*, 10/1 (1976), 34 · R. Lister, *Samuel Palmer and 'the ancients'* (1984) [exhibition catalogue, FM Cam., 9 Oct–16 Dec 1984] · R. Lister, introduction, in E. Calvert, *Edward Calvert: eleven engravings* [1966] · R. Lister, '"The Ancients" and the classics', *Studies in Romanticism*, 15/3 (1976), 395–404

Likenesses photograph, *c.*1883, repro. in Calvert, *Memoir of Edward Calvert*, frontispiece · drawing?, priv. coll.; copyprint, NPG [*see illus.*]

Wealth at death £1124 6s. 10d.: probate, 2 Aug 1883, *CGPLA Eng. & Wales*

Calvert, Elizabeth (*d.* 1675?), bookseller, was the wife of Giles *Calvert (*bap.* 1612, *d.* 1663) and sister-in-law of the Quaker Martha *Simmonds. The Calverts' shop at the Black Spread Eagle at the west end of St Paul's Churchyard, London, was a major source of radical and Quaker publications during the periods of the civil war and Commonwealth. After the Restoration Elizabeth Calvert carried on the trade in republican, nonconformist, and oppositional literature. Of the Calverts' three surviving children, Elizabeth (*b.* 1639), Nathaniel (*b.* 1643), and Giles (*b.* 1653), the two sons were also booksellers.

After the Restoration, when Giles and other male stationers were under constant pressure from the government for oppositional publications, Elizabeth Calvert took a central role in arranging the printing and distribution of radical pamphlets. In 1661 while her husband was imprisoned she 'went on with the Prodigies' (that is, the 'signs and wonders' pamphlet, *Eniautos terastios mirabilis annus*), the very text which had led to Giles's incarceration (L'Estrange, *Truth and Loyalty*, 57). After the 'Confederate knot' of male stationers had been broken up by deaths and imprisonments, she and other book-trade wives and widows (Hannah Allen, Joan Dover (later Darby), and Ann(a) Brewster) carried on the surreptitious trade in anti-monarchy texts (L'Estrange, *Considerations*, 6). Elizabeth was arrested twice (in 1661 and 1663) before Giles's death in August 1663. In October of that year their son Nathaniel was freed as a stationer by his uncle, the bookseller George Calvert, and presumably joined his mother in the business. Several warrants for the arrest of Elizabeth, her maid Elizabeth Evans, her apprentice Mathias Stephenson, and her son Nathaniel were issued during 1662–3 in connection with the printer John Twyn's trial for treason, and Elizabeth was questioned about the printing of *Mene tekel, or, A Treatise of the Execution of Justice* and the *Speeches and Prayers* of the regicides. Committed to prison on 2 February 1664, she petitioned for her discharge to nurse Nathaniel, who after his own release from prison had become 'dangerously sick' (PRO, SP 29/95/98). Her request was refused, and a second petition shows that her release on 8 April came too late: Nathaniel was 'ever since fryday morning dead and is yett unburied' (PRO, SP 29/96/64).

Despite repeated imprisonments, deaths, consequent debts, and the destruction of her shop in the great fire of 1666, Calvert persisted in her trade, continuing to publish both openly and surreptitiously. She was apparently unmolested for her publication of works by nonconformists, Independents, and Quakers such as Richard Steele, John Owen, Benjamin Agas, Francis Howgill, and Thomas Wilson. Other publications, however, attracted harassment from the Stationers' Company and, more frequently, from Roger L'Estrange, the surveyor of the press, who was well aware that her distribution network stretched far beyond London. Both Richard Moone, a former apprentice of Giles's who had moved to Bristol, and Moone's wife, Susannah, were caught in possession of books sent by Elizabeth Calvert, and her pamphlets reached at least as far north as Flintshire and Carlisle. Although her name appears in only twenty-seven imprints she is known to have been responsible for many more 'seditious' works, including tracts about the great fire such as *A True and Faithfull Account* (1667), Benjamin Keach's *A Trumpet Blown in Sion* (edition now lost), John Wilson's *Nehushtan* (1668), and Andrew Marvell's *Directions to a Painter* (1668). After the destruction by fire of her shop she moved to Duck Lane, returning to St Paul's Churchyard in 1669. Her secret press in Southwark had been discovered and broken up the previous year, but she continued her illegal trade. Early in 1670 she supplied the printer Samuel Simmons with the copy of Dyer's *Christ's Famous Titles*, which was interrupted and seized while at the press, and in December she was indicted for her publication in 1668 of *Directions to a Painter*. After her trial in March 1671 she absconded and pursuit of her fine seems to have been dropped. Circumstantial evidence suggests that she may have been protected by the earl of Carlisle, whose secretary was Andrew Marvell.

After the trial Calvert's trade seems to have been largely in old stock which had survived the great fire, in reprints, and a few new works of inoffensive character. One of her few secular works, William Rabisha's *The Whole Body of Cookery*, appeared in 1673. But assumptions that she turned to more innocuous publishing in her last years are belied by the survival of a warrant for her arrest in January 1674. Her offence is not stated, but it may have been in connection with the publication of the pamphlet *Verbum sapienti*. In February 1674 she bound the last of her four apprentices, on 19 October she made her will, and she died probably in early 1675, her will being proved on 5 February 1675. The 1675 edition of Rabisha's cookery book has, uniquely, the imprint 'for E. C. And are to be sold by Francis SMITH, at the Elephant and Castle near the Royal Exchange in Cornhill', presumably a posthumous title-page. The residue of her estate, after debts, was left to her only surviving son, Giles. Although he is described as 'bookseller' of the City of London, there is no evidence that he was active in the trade or that he carried on the business at the Black Spread Eagle.

Although Giles and Elizabeth had earlier been sympathetic to Quakers, there seems to have been a rift after the James Nayler incident of 1656, in which Giles's sister Martha had played a central part. After 1656 the Calverts published few Quaker works, and Elizabeth seems to have been regarded by Quakers as an enemy. In a letter of 1671 Ellis Hookes, clerk to London Friends, associates 'Jesebell; Giles Calverts wife' with a group of apostates and 'Ranters' including Robert Rich, John Pennyman, and Mary Boreman (Ellis Hookes to Margaret Fell Fox, 21 Oct 1671, Swarthmore MS, I.57). The best indication of her religious beliefs, however, is that in her will Elizabeth asked to be 'decently buryed amongst the Baptists' (PRO, PROB 11/347, sig. 12).

MAUREEN BELL

Sources M. Bell, 'Elizabeth Calvert and the "confederates"', *Publishing History*, 32 (1992), 5–49 • M. Bell, '"Her Usual Practices": the later career of Elizabeth Calvert, 1664–75', *Publishing History*, 35

(1994), 5–64 · E. C. Thomas, 'A purveyor of soul-poysons: an analysis of the career of Giles Calvert, a publisher and bookseller in mid-seventeenth century London', PhD diss., La Trobe University, 1999 · A. E. Terry, 'Giles Calvert, mid-seventeenth-century English bookseller and publisher', MA diss., Columbia University, 1937 · PRO, State papers · RS Friends, Lond., Swarthmore papers · files and minute books of gaol delivery, oyer and terminer and peace, CLRO, London sessions · R. L'Estrange, *Truth and loyalty vindicated* (1662) · R. L'Estrange, *Considerations and proposals in order to the regulation of the press* (1663) · PRO, SP 29/95/98; SP 29/96/64 · will, PRO, PROB 11/347, sig. 12 · will, PRO, PROB 11/312 [Giles Calvert], sig. 106 · *IGI*

Calvert, Frank (1828–1908), archaeologist, was born on 3 September 1828 at strada Zecca, Valletta, Malta, the youngest of seven children of James Calvert (1778–1852), civil servant and grain merchant, and his wife, Louisa Ann (1792–1867), daughter of John and Mary Campbell Lander.

Educated in Valletta until the age of sixteen Calvert moved, in 1845, to the Dardanelles, where his uncle Charles Lander was British consul. The family engaged in a number of agricultural and commercial ventures in the Troad, with Frank's brother Frederick, who took over as British consul in 1846, playing the leading role. Frank assisted in these enterprises but spent much of his free time developing an unrivalled expertise in the topography of the Troad, through exploration, avid reading, and small-scale excavations. Between 1859 and 1865 he published a series of six articles in the *Archaeological Journal*; he was clearly preparing himself to tackle the problem of the location of Homeric Troy. Most contemporary scholars regarded Pınarbaşı/Ballı Dağ, at the south end of the plain of Troy, as the most likely candidate but Charles Maclaren, who stayed with the Calverts in 1847, had championed Hisarlık, 4 miles further north.

Trial excavations on Ballı Dağ persuaded Calvert that Troy was not located there. Between 1863 and 1865 he dug four small trenches on the eastern part of Hisarlık, which he had purchased in 1855. By October 1863 he had uncovered part of the temple of Athena and was convinced that Homeric Troy lay underneath. In a letter to Charles Newton of the British Museum he proposed that the museum sponsor large-scale excavations and offered to donate all finds and the site itself to the museum, provided that he be given direction of the excavations. This generous proposal was not accepted, however, apparently because Frederick Calvert was at that time implicated in a major insurance fraud scandal.

When Heinrich Schliemann was leaving the Troad in August 1868, after disappointing soundings at Pınarbaşı/Ballı Dağ, Calvert suggested that he excavate at Hisarlık; despite later claims Schliemann appears not to have realized, in 1868, that Hisarlık was a possible site of Troy. During Schliemann's early excavations at Hisarlık (1870–73), Calvert provided expert advice and ready assistance in countless practical matters, but Schliemann shamelessly cheated him out of a fair price for the Helios metope in 1872 and for inscriptions in 1873. Calvert's perceptive observation, in 1873, that the strata so far excavated were either far earlier or far later than the Trojan War, angered Schliemann, who ridiculed Calvert in *Troy and its Remains* (1875) and misrepresented the extent of his 1863–5 excavations at Hisarlık.

In 1874 Calvert succeeded his brother James as US consular agent at the Dardanelles, an unsalaried post which he held until his death. Relations with Schliemann remained cool for some years but improved when Schliemann resumed work at Hisarlık in 1878 and 1879. Calvert allowed Schliemann to excavate on his own land; in return Schliemann funded Calvert's excavation (1879–80) of Hanay Tepe, then held to be another possible site of Troy. Calvert's account of his careful excavations forms an appendix to Schliemann's *Ilios* (1881). Throughout his life Calvert acted as host and guide to scholars visiting the Troad; he also had a sophisticated knowledge of the region's geology and botany, on which scholars, such as Rudolf Virchow, gratefully drew.

Over the years Calvert accumulated an important collection of antiquities from various sites in the Troad. Parts of this collection are now in the British Museum, at Boston, and at Worcester, Massachusetts. The bulk, however, was donated to the Çanakkale Museum.

Calvert's view, that the stratum held by Schliemann to be that of Homeric Troy (Troy II) was too early, was vindicated in the 1890s, when Dörpfeld acknowledged that the recently discovered Troy VI level was a much more likely candidate. On 12 August 1908 Calvert died, unmarried, either at Calvert Mansion, Çanakkale, or at the family farm, Thymbra, at Akça Köy; he was buried a few days later in the consular cemetery Çanak at Çanakkale.

David A. Traill

Sources S. H. Allen, *Finding the walls of Troy: Frank Calvert and Heinrich Schliemann at Hisarlik* (1999) · M. Robinson, 'Schliemann's silent partner: Frank Calvert (1828–1908), pioneer, scholar, survivor', privately distributed book-length typescript, 1997 · D. A. Traill, *Schliemann of Troy: treasure and deceit* (1995) · M. Robinson, 'Pioneer, scholar and victim: an appreciation of Frank Calvert', *Anatolian Studies*, 44 (1994), 153–68 · M. Robinson, 'Frank Calvert and the discovery of Troia', *Studia Troica*, 5 (1995), 323–41

Archives National Archives Research Administration, Washington, DC, US consular agency, Dardanelles, vols. 1–14, RG 84 · National Archives Research Administration, Washington, DC, US consulate general, Constantinople, RG 84 · National Archives Research Administration, Washington, DC, US legation to Turkey, vols. 287 and 288 · PRO, Foreign Office records | Akademie der Wissenschaften, Berlin, Virchow archive · American School of Classical Studies, Athens, Gennadius Library, Schliemann archive · BM, department of Greek and Roman antiquities, Newton archive · Mitchell L., Glas., Glasgow City Archives, William Simpson collection

Likenesses F. H. Bacon, photographs, 1892, repro. in Allen, *Finding the walls of Troy*, 406

Calvert, Frederick, sixth Baron Baltimore (1732–1771), author and libertine, was the eldest son of Charles *Calvert, fifth Baron Baltimore (1699–1751), and Mary Janssen (*d.* 1770), daughter of Sir Theodore *Janssen. His father's title was Irish but Frederick was born in England on 6 February 1732; he was educated at Eton College. On 9 March 1753 he married Lady Diana Egerton (1732–1758), youngest daughter of the duke of Bridgewater, but separated from her three years later on account of his rakish ways. Calvert's subsequent life is noteworthy in part for scholarship, but more infamously for his libertinism. He was the author of *Tour in the East in the Years 1763 and 1764*, which Lord Orford thought 'no more deserved to be published than his bills on the road for the post-horses' (*Catalogue of the Royal and Noble Authors*, 5.278). His debauched lifestyle was also the subject of much critical comment, and in 1768 he was charged with raping Sarah Woodcock, a London milliner, at his country house at Epsom. Lurid details of the case, which was tried at Kingston assizes on 26 March 1768, were discussed in numerous pamphlets. With sufficient evidence to prove Woodcock's earlier complicity, he was eventually acquitted, but left England after the trial. In the following year he printed at Augsburg ten copies of *Gaudia poetica Latina, Anglica, et Gallica lingua composita*, praised by Linnaeus, to whom the study was dedicated, as an 'immortal work' (Morris, 57). *Caelestes et inferi*, published in Venice, followed two years later. Described by Thomas Carlyle as 'something of a fool, to judge by the face of him in portraits, and by some of his doings in the world' (ibid., 59), Baltimore was one of several noblemen vilified as examples of aristocratic vice in an age eager to celebrate the virtues of sentimental domesticity. He died in Naples on 14 September 1771, 'one of those worn-out beings, a hipped Englishman, who had lost all moral and physical taste' according to J. J. Winckelmann (ibid., 58–9). Before being interred in the family vault at Epsom, his body lay in state at the Exeter Exchange, the Strand, London; such was his unpopularity that, on its removal, the room was plundered by an angry crowd. Baltimore died without a legitimate heir, and the title became extinct at his death.

T. F. HENDERSON, *rev.* DAVID TURNER

Sources W. Shugg, 'The baron and the milliner: Lord Baltimore's rape trial as a mirror of class tension in mid-Georgian London', *Maryland Historical Magazine*, 83 (1988), 310–30 • GEC, *Peerage* • J. G. Morris, *The lords Baltimore* (1874) • *A catalogue of the royal and noble authors of England, Scotland and Ireland … by the late Horatio Walpole*, ed. T. Park, 5 (1806), 278–82 • J. Gurney, *The trial of Frederick Calvert* (1768) • *Memoirs of the seraglio of the bashaw of Merryland, by a discarded sultana* (1768) • *GM*, 1st ser., 42 (1772), 44 • *GM*, 1st ser., 38 (1768), 80–88

Archives Maryland Historical Society, Baltimore, MSS

Likenesses J. L. Tietz, oils, *c*.1762, Enoch Pratt Free Library, Baltimore; repro. in Shugg, 'The baron and the milliner', 311 • J. Miller, stipple and line engraving, NPG • engraving, repro. in *Catalogue of the royal and noble authors*, ed. Park

Calvert, Frederick Baltimore (1793–1877), actor and lecturer on elocution, was one of the eight children of Charles *Calvert (1754–1797) [*see under* Calvert, Charles (1785–1852)], an amateur painter and steward to the duke of Norfolk at Glossop Hall, Derbyshire, and his wife, Elizabeth Holliday (1751/2–1842). Charles *Calvert (1785–1852) and George *Calvert (1794–1825) were among his brothers. Frederick was born on 10 April 1793 at Glossop Hall and entered Manchester School on 12 January 1804. From there he was sent to the Roman Catholic college at Old Hall Green, Hertfordshire, with a view to entering the priesthood; but he took to the stage, and at the peak of his career alternated leading parts with the elder Kean, W. C. Macready, and the elder Vandenhoff. In 1818 he married a Miss Percy of Whitby, who predeceased him about 1866, after the couple had had numerous children.

In 1824 Calvert published *A Defence of the Drama*, which had an extensive circulation, and was read by John Fawcett to the members of the Theatrical Fund at their annual dinner in that year. In 1829 he became elocutionary lecturer of King's College, Aberdeen, and gave lectures on oratory, poetry, and other literary subjects in various English towns. Afterwards he went to America, where he lectured on the English poets, and on returning to England gave evening lectures on what he had seen during his visit to the Western hemisphere. About 1846 he was appointed master of English language and literature at the Edinburgh Academy. In the winter of 1847–8 he gave readings of the English poets in connection with the Edinburgh Philosophical Institution. Some years later he became lecturer on elocution to the free church colleges of Edinburgh and Glasgow. He was a man of great literary refinement, and had an extensive acquaintance with the literature of Greece and Rome as well as with that of England and France. He revised *Principles of Elocution*, by T. Ewing (1852; second edition, 1870), wrote *A letter to the Very Rev. Dean Ramsay, Edinburgh, on the art of reading and preaching distinctly* (1869), translated the *De oratore* of Cicero (1870), and composed *An Ode to Shakespeare*. Calvert died on 21 April 1877 at his residence, 2 West Newington, Edinburgh. Of his seven surviving children, two sons and five daughters, his youngest son, Michael Talbot Calvert, made a name for himself as an actor, performing in tragedies at Drury Lane under the stage name of Henry Talbot.

G. C. BOASE, *rev.* NILANJANA BANERJI

Sources J. F. Smith, ed., *The admission register of the Manchester School, with some notes of the more distinguished scholars*, 3 vols. in 4 pts, Chetham Society, 69, 73, 93, 94 (1866–74) • *The Era* (6 May 1877) • *Era Almanack and Annual* (1879)

Wealth at death £1268 13*s*. 9*d*.: confirmation, 1 June 1877, *CCI*

Calvert, Frederick Crace- (1819–1873), industrial and analytical chemist, was born on 14 November 1819 in London, into a military family. Nothing is known of his early education; at the age of sixteen he went to France to study chemistry. During his time there he studied under Gerardin at Rouen and was employed at the chemical company of Robiquet, Boyveau, and Pelletier. Between 1841 and 1846 he was assistant to the celebrated chemist Michel-Eugène Chevreul at the Gobelins dye works and the Musée d'Histoire Naturelle, and at the museum gained valuable experience in biological studies. While in France, he also published his first papers in applied chemistry, writing on alkaloids, brewing, lead, indigo, and animal carbon.

In 1846 Crace-Calvert returned to England to establish himself as a chemist in Manchester. There he became one of a small group of scientists, then emerging as professionals, who promoted the benefits of applying science to industry and public health. Supporting himself initially by public teaching and as a consultant to manufacturing businesses, Crace-Calvert became a first-class propagandist for applied chemistry. Soon after his arrival he was appointed honorary professor at the Manchester Royal Institution. He also taught at the Pine Street school of medicine and his close association with Manchester physicians is evident in much of his biological and sanitary studies. His contributions to manufacturing were often connected with the Lancashire cotton industry and included investigations into bleaching, dyeing, and mildew.

Crace-Calvert's election to fellowship of the Royal Society in 1859 reflected a broad range of scientific contributions. By this time he was particularly recognized for his studies on phenol (then more widely known as carbolic acid), a product that straddled his interests in dyeing and sanitary science. In the early 1850s Crace-Calvert had not only used phenol to prevent fermentation of tannin extracts and thus extend their useful life in the dyeing industry, but he had also encouraged its employment in taxidermy and in preserving cadavers for dissection. By 1857 his search for a 'cheap and practical process for obtaining carbolic acid in considerable quantity' (Calvert, 'Carbolic acid') for use in the production of dyes (for example picric acid and rosolic acid) was coming to fruition.

In 1859 Crace-Calvert founded a manufacturing company bearing his name which developed an international market for phenol and phenol-based products. It was Crace-Calvert's pure phenol that fostered Joseph Lister's far-reaching work on antiseptic surgery—Lister used phenol to destroy micro-organisms associated with post-operative infections. Lister's work was first published in 1867, but even before then Crace-Calvert had been to the forefront in promoting sanitary and medical uses of phenol, as a disinfectant for sewage and in the management of sloughing wounds, foetid ulcers, and diarrhoea.

Crace-Calvert was also interested in the vigorous, widely publicized British debates on spontaneous generation of micro-organisms. He had long accepted the germ theory of putrefaction and its association with certain disease conditions and repudiated spontaneous generation in his *On Protoplasmic Life* (1871). In further papers he examined the temperatures required to kill bacteria and reported on the comparative effects of germicides. These studies contributed both to the general acceptance of the germ theory of disease and to the development of the emerging science of microbiology.

Of average height, Crace-Calvert was known for his effusive, somewhat argumentative nature, tempered with a friendly disposition. In 1873 he went to Vienna as a juror at the international exhibition. While there he contracted typhoid, which led to his death at his home, Clayton Vale House, Newton Heath, near Manchester, on 24 October 1873. He was survived by his wife, Jeanne Françoise Clemence Crace-Calvert. J. K. Crellin

Sources *Annual Register* (1873), pt 2, p. 151 • *Journal of the Society of Arts*, 21 (1872–3), 919 • *Nature*, 9 (1873–4), 16 • *Pharmaceutical Journal and Transactions*, 3rd ser., 4 (1873–4), 377 • *Proceedings of the Literary and Philosophical Society of Manchester*, 13 (1873–4), 158–9 • *DNB* • J. K. Crellin, 'Spontaneous generation and the serum theory (1860–1880): the controversy in Britain and the work of F. Crace Calvert', MSc diss., U. Lond., 1965 • R. H. Kargon, *Science in Victorian Manchester* (1977) • F. C. Calvert, 'On protoplasmic life', *PRS*, 19 (1870–71), 468–72 • *Catalogue of scientific papers*, Royal Society, 2 (1868), 80–81 • *Catalogue of scientific papers*, Royal Society, 7 (1877), 451–2 • F. C. Calvert, 'On the manufacture and properties of carbolic acid', *The Lancet*, 2 (1867), 733–4 • *CGPLA Eng. & Wales* (1874) • election certificate, RS

Archives RS, MSS • UCL, MSS

Likenesses photograph, repro. in Crellin, 'Spontaneous generation and the serum theory'

Wealth at death under £8000: administration with will, 12 March 1874, *CGPLA Eng. & Wales*

Calvert, George, first Baron Baltimore (1579/80–1632), courtier and colonist in America, was born in Kiplin in Catterick parish, Yorkshire, the son of Leonard Calvert (*b. c.*1550) and Alica Crosland (*d.* early 1580s). He was descended from a Roman Catholic family that had been in Yorkshire for generations; members of the family had been prosecuted in 1580 for their failure to conform. In 1592 authorities determined that the tutor with whom George studied used a 'popish primer' (H. Aveling, *Northern Catholics: the Catholic Recusants of the North Riding of Yorkshire, 1558–1790*, 1966, 176–7). Under the penalty of law, father and son conformed to the established church. After two years of study with a protestant tutor, the fourteen-year-old Calvert matriculated in 1594 at Trinity College, Oxford. He signed the subscription book, attesting to his support of the established church, on 12 July 1594. The 'Oxford experience confirmed his acceptance of the doctrines of the Church of England' (Foster, 53). He studied foreign languages and proved to be an able student, graduating BA in February 1597. In August 1598 he went to London, where he studied law at Lincoln's Inn for three years.

In 1601 Calvert travelled to the continent, returning in April 1603 with a packet from Paris for Sir Robert Cecil, the secretary of state who had recently mediated the accession of James I to the English throne. He entered Cecil's service as one of his secretaries. He married Anne Mynne (1579–1622) in London at the church of St Peter Cornhill on 22 November 1604; they had twelve children. He named his eldest son Cecil *Calvert, after Robert Cecil, who served as a godfather. His diligence and painstaking attention to detail led to a succession of lesser offices and sinecures. He attended James I at Oxford University in August 1605 and was among those who received an honorary MA. On 10 July 1606 the king granted him the office of clerk of the crown in the province of Connaught and county of Clare in Ireland, and in 1609 James appointed him one of the clerks of the signet office. Through the influence of Cecil (created earl of Salisbury in 1605) he served briefly for Bossiney in parliament, being elected in October 1609. The king appointed Calvert one of the clerks of the privy council in July 1610. That same year Salisbury dispatched him on an extended trip to the continent (August 1610–March 1611), where he visited ambassadors and gathered intelligence. He received an appointment as joint commissary of Ireland in 1611. As he accumulated capital, he invested in both the Virginia Company of London and the East India Company. Later

George Calvert, first Baron Baltimore (1579/80–1632), by Daniel Mytens, 1627

the East India Company allowed him to add £600 to his adventure of £1000.

After Salisbury's death in 1612 Calvert's advancement at court continued. Even before his patron's death he had worked closely with the king, researching and translating material for a book refuting the Dutch theologian Conrad Vorstius. In the absence of a secretary of state, in June 1613 the king delegated foreign correspondence to a few trusted individuals and Calvert took responsibility for the Spanish correspondence, sharing the Italian correspondence with a colleague. He travelled to Ireland in 1613 as part of a royal commission to investigate the grievances of Irish Catholics. James dispatched him to the Palatinate in 1615 to handle a number of sensitive matters involving his daughter Elizabeth, who was married to Frederick, the elector palatine. Always prudent, Calvert continued to diversify his investments. He acquired Danby Wiske manor, located about 5 miles east of his birthplace, in 1616. His cautious and diligent nature, to say nothing of his loyal service, marked him as a man well suited for James's style of leadership. James knighted him on 29 September 1617, and in February 1619 named him as secretary of state and appointed him to the privy council. Fearing he had been advanced beyond his status, his initial reaction was that he was not worthy 'to sit in that place, so lately possessed by his noble lord and master'. He assumed he owed his appointment to the marquess of Buckingham, the royal favourite, and presented Buckingham with an expensive jewel. Buckingham refused it and informed Calvert that his appointment was entirely the king's doing. On 2 May 1620 the king showed further favour by granting Calvert a yearly pension of £1000.

The knowledge that Buckingham was not well disposed towards him meant that Calvert had to be careful not to overreach his station. As secretary of state he was aware that he did not formulate foreign or domestic policies but administered decisions made at a level to which he could not aspire. This left him dependent on and loyal to a lethargic monarch who envisaged that England could play the role of peacemaker in Europe through an alliance with Spain. Although Calvert corresponded with ambassadors throughout the western world, the negotiations to marry the prince of Wales to the Spanish infanta Maria consumed his time. Ending the war in Europe through a negotiated settlement with the Spanish proved an elusive goal. To succeed with the Spanish, James had to ameliorate the condition of his Catholic subjects, a delicate domestic issue.

When the king called for parliamentary elections in 1620, Calvert stood for election in Yorkshire. Long absent from the county, he won a closely contested election only through the intervention of his friend and fellow candidate Sir Thomas Wentworth. Together they worked to foster Wentworth's interests at court and Calvert's influence in Yorkshire. As one of the king's men, Calvert became a lightning rod for those in the House of Commons who opposed the king's Spanish and religious policies. He was suspected of communicating intelligence of their proceedings to the king, to the detriment of the leading members. The secretary, however, served as the king's spokesman without enjoying the full confidence of the king and his closest advisers. The Venetian ambassador reported that there were matters about which Calvert 'scarcely knows anything'. The French ambassador, who extolled Calvert's virtues, judged him 'entirely without authority or influence' (*CSP Venice*, *1621–3*, 133; Tilliers to Puysieulse, 15 Nov 1621, PRO, SP 31/3/55). Although he worked tirelessly on the king's behalf, the Commons were too fearful of an increasing Catholic influence and too suspicious of Spanish intentions to meet the king's needs.

Calvert acquired title to land in Newfoundland (1620) and Ireland (1622) and secured appointments to the Council for New England (1622) and the council of the north (1623). In Yorkshire he built (1622–5) a country house, Kiplin Hall, 'designed on the scale to fit his own recently expanded resources' (C. B. Schulz, *Kiplin Hall and its Families: a History*, 1994, 4). With the Spanish negotiations deadlocked by mid-1623, Buckingham and Charles, in disguise and without the secretary's knowledge, ventured to Spain to break the impasse. This misguided mission ended in a humiliating failure. The royal pair returned in October 1623 without the princess and with treaties they were determined to break. Their calculated anti-Spanish posturing eventually led to war with Spain and sealed Calvert's fate as a courtier. Infighting over the king's Spanish policy put Calvert in a difficult position. His persistent support for the Spanish match annoyed Buckingham and led to his further isolation at court. He was the MP for Oxford University in the parliament that met in 1624 but had a greatly diminished role.

Out of favour, Calvert concluded that he must resign his office on the best possible terms and took the necessary steps to reconcile himself to Buckingham. At the same time he resolved the issue of his religious commitments. During the course of the marriage negotiations he had become inextricably associated with the Spanish and Roman Catholic causes. Some later incorrectly charged that he had been a Catholic at the time of his appointment or converted during the Spanish negotiations. No contemporary left any statement questioning his conformity at the time of his appointment or for the years he served as secretary of state, and the official records of marriage, baptism, and burial testify to his conformity. Whatever his inner feelings, he conformed as long as he served as secretary of state. Calvert's contemporaries appropriately attributed his resignation to Buckingham's hostility and to the general purge of all who favoured the discredited Spanish policy James had pursued. They did not attribute it to his change of religion. His conversion to Roman Catholicism, which took place in October or November 1624, freed him spiritually. But before resigning, he engaged in hard-nosed bargaining to avoid the appearance that he had left in disgrace. The king allowed him to sell the secretary's office for £3000. More importantly, the king retained him as a privy councillor and rewarded him for his loyal service by creating him Baron Baltimore in Ireland and reissuing the grant to his estates in Ireland without the restrictive anti-Catholic clauses. Baltimore did not see his conversion as having a detrimental effect on his plans. Indeed, his outward behaviour changed. After February 1625 he acted audaciously and with confidence in pursuing his new interests. James's death in March scuttled his plans to continue as a privy councillor and to have at least a nominal role in court politics. The new king refused Catholics a role in mourning his father and ordered all councillors to take the oath of allegiance. Baltimore boldly refused and resigned his position on the privy council. Soon after, probably fleeing another outbreak of plague, he moved his family to Ireland.

Lord Baltimore's resignation, subsequent conversion, wealth, and status permitted him to devote himself to developing his investments by expanding the king's dominions in North America. On 7 April 1623 he received a charter for the province of Avalon, in Newfoundland, where he had established a colony as early as 1621. War with Spain prevented him from sailing to Avalon in 1626 and led to his summons to court early in February 1627 to consult about the peace negotiations with Spain. While there he secured a renewal of his 1621 grant of the duties on silk imports. His July 1627 visit to Avalon convinced him that his investment could be salvaged. A year later he and his second wife, Joan (*d.* 1630), whom he had married about three years earlier possibly in a Catholic ceremony in Ireland and with whom he had one son, Philip, their family, and a predominantly Catholic contingent of colonists journeyed to Avalon with the intention of reviving the colony. He lamented that 'I came to builde, and sett, and sowe, but I am falne to fighting with Frenchmen' (Baltimore to the duke of Buckingham, 25 Aug 1628, Cell, 279). This, along with the harsh climate, disease, and intermittent religious squabbling, led him to sail to Virginia, where he hoped to establish a new enterprise. Before leaving the colony, on which he invested more than £20,000, he petitioned the king for a grant of land there in order to continue his work 'to further the best I may the enlarging your Majesties empire in this part of the world' (Baltimore to King Charles, 19 Aug 1629, Cell, 296). But the Virginians did not welcome the former secretary, who had been involved in the legal proceedings that voided their charter in 1624, and when Baltimore refused the oaths of supremacy and allegiance, authorities ordered him to depart the colony. By 1630 a determined Baltimore was in London seeking a grant from the king for a tract of land along the Chesapeake Bay. Aided by his two closest friends, Wentworth and Sir Francis Cottington, who were by this time in the king's good graces, and in the face of determined opposition from supporters of the defunct Virginia Company, Baltimore pursued his goal. The government supported the Catholic Baltimore's new enterprise because it fostered the interests of the English nation. Baltimore died in London on 15 April 1632, shortly before the Maryland charter passed the great seal. To his eldest son, Cecil, who served as his secretary after 1630, he bequeathed his goal of establishing a prosperous colony where all Christians were free to worship according to the dictates of conscience. Baltimore was buried at St Dunstan-in-the-West, London. He was preceded in death by both wives, Anne in 1622 and Joan in 1630. JOHN D. KRUGLER

Sources J. D. Krugler, *English and Catholic: the lords Baltimore in the seventeenth century* [forthcoming] • J. W. Foster, *George Calvert: the early years* (1983) • *CSP dom., 1603–25* • *CSP Venice* • W. Notestein, F. H. Relf, and H. Simpson, eds., *Commons debates, 1621*, 7 vols. (1935) • *The letters of John Chamberlain*, ed. N. E. McClure, 2 vols. (1939) • *Report on the manuscripts of the marquis of Downshire*, 6 vols. in 7, HMC, 75 (1924–95) • G. T. Cell, ed., *Newfoundland discovered: English attempts at colonisation, 1610–1630*, Hakluyt Society, new ser., 160 (1982) • T. Hughes, *History of the Society of Jesus in North America, colonial and federal*, 2 vols. (1908–17) • J. D. Krugler, 'Sir George Calvert's resignation as secretary of state and the founding of Maryland', *Maryland Historical Magazine*, 68 (1973), 239–54 • J. D. Krugler, '"The face of a protestant and the heart of a Papist": a re-examination of Sir George Calvert's conversion to Roman Catholicism', *Journal of Church and State*, 20 (1978), 507–31 • L. Codignola, *The coldest harbour of the land: Simon Stock and Lord Baltimore's colony in Newfoundland, 1621–1649*, trans. A. Weston (1988)

Archives Maryland Historical Society, Baltimore, Maryland, papers | BL, corresp. with Sir W. Aston, Add. MSS 36444–36446 • BL, corresp. with Lord Doncaster, Egerton MSS 2592–2595 • CKS, letters to Lionel Cranfield • PRO, state papers 63 (Ireland), 77 (Flanders), 78 (France), 81 (German states), 84 (Holland), 94 (Spain) • Sheffield City Libraries, Sheffield, Strafford papers

Likenesses D. Mytens, oils, 1625, Enoch Pratt Free Library, Baltimore • D. Mytens, oils, 1627, priv. coll. [*see illus.*] • D. Mytens, oils, second version, 1627, Gorhambury, Herts. • J. Caldwall, line engraving, BM, NPG; repro. in T. Pennant, *The journey from Chester to London* (1782) • P. Oliver, miniature, Walters Art Gallery, Baltimore • pen-and-ink drawing (after engraving), NPG

Calvert, George (1794–1825), surgeon, was one of the eight children of Charles *Calvert (1754–1797) [*see under* Calvert, Charles (1785–1852)], the duke of Norfolk's agent at Glossop Hall, Derbyshire, and his wife, Elizabeth Holliday (1751/2–1842). Among his brothers were Charles *Calvert (1785–1852) and Frederick Baltimore *Calvert (1793–1877). After his father's death the family settled in Manchester, which had been their winter place of residence; George attended Manchester grammar school and later served an apprenticeship at the Public Infirmary (Royal Infirmary). He qualified LSA and MRCS in 1816. He was awarded the Jacksonian prize of the Royal College of Surgeons in three successive years for his essays 'On diseases of the rectum' (1822), 'On fungus haematodes' (1823), and 'On *tic douloureux*' (1824). The first of these was expanded and published in 1824 as *A Practical Treatise on Haemorrhoids*. He seems to have spent some time in foreign travel. The *Practical Treatise* refers to observations made in France, Italy, Poland, Greece, and Turkey. Also in 1824 Calvert provided stylistic assistance for Constant Coffyn's *General Anatomy*, a translation of the work by M. F. X. Bichat. Calvert died at his home, 68 Lamb's Conduit Street, London, on 14 July 1825, aged thirty. JOHN SYMONS

Sources *GM*, 1st ser., 95/2 (1825), 92, 475 • *The Times* (16 July 1825) • J. F. Smith, ed., *The admission register of the Manchester School, with some notes of the more distinguished scholars*, 2, Chetham Society, 73 (1868), 236–7; 3/1, Chetham Society, 93 (1874), 21–2

Calvert, Giles (*bap.* 1612, *d.* 1663), bookseller, was baptized on 20 December 1612 in the parish of Meare, Somerset, the eldest son of George Calvert (*d.* 1628), vicar there since 1601. Soon after his preferment George Calvert was charged in an ecclesiastical court with not observing the order of service prescribed in the Book of Common Prayer and with preaching over-long sermons. On 30 June 1628 Giles Calvert was bound apprentice to William Lugger (*d.* 1658), citizen and stationer of London, for the term of nine years. For some unknown reason Calvert's indentures were cancelled and on 11 January 1632 he was apprenticed for the term of seven years to Joseph Hunscott (*d.* 1660), who was also the master of his younger brother, George Calvert (1620–1691). On 25 January 1639 Giles was made free of the Stationers' Company.

Shortly after gaining his freedom Calvert married Elizabeth *Calvert (*d.* 1675?), whose maiden name is unknown. The couple settled in the parish of St Nicholas Cole Abbey, London, where their first child, Elizabeth (*d.* 1646), was baptized on 15 March 1640; their other children were Nathaniel (1643–1664), John (*d.* 1648), a stillborn (1651), and Giles (*b.* 1653, *d.* in or after 1674). On 4 March 1641 'Calvert a book binder' was questioned by a committee of the House of Lords concerning the publication of Richard Overton's unlicensed pamphlet *A Dreame, or, Nevves from Hell*, issued that year. Although he refused to identify the man who supplied him with the copy, no further action seems to have been taken against Calvert. Thereafter Calvert entered several publications into the Stationers' register. In 1642 he published *Napiers narration, or, An Epitome of his booke on the Revelation* and William Carter's *Israels Peace with God, Beniamines Overthrow*. The following year he published two works by Joseph Caryl (one in partnership with John Rothwell), *The Souldiers Pocket Bible* and *The Pathway to Peace*.

In 1644 Calvert signed the Stationers' Company petition to the House of Commons protesting at the 'monopolies' held by royal patent to print English bibles and 'sundry Bookes of generall use' (*Stationers' Company*, Stationers' Hall, London, liber A: letter-book of the Stationers' Company, fol. 149*r*). That year he published one tract by Joseph Caryl and sold two titles by John Saltmarsh. He also took on Gregory Moule, an apprentice who had been turned over to him by Joseph Hunscott. By late May 1644 Calvert was occupying a tenement at the sign of the Black-Spread-Eagle at the west end of St Paul's Cathedral in the parish of St Gregory by Paul's. Situated on the busy street leading from Ludgate Hill to the cathedral, Calvert's premises consisted of a cellar, a shop with a street frontage, four rooms above the shop, and a little yard behind the property where the privy and the stairs leading up into the house were located. This well-known address was to become a lodging, meeting-place, postal address, and distribution point for radicals and their printed literature. Indeed 'Lame' Giles Calvert was to gain a reputation as a purveyor of 'soul-poysons', for example in Thomas Hall's *Vindicae literarum* (quoted in R. Baxter, *The Worcester-Shire Petition to the Parliament for the Ministry of England Defended*, 1653, 39), his shop branded 'That forge of the Devill, from whence so many blasphemous, lying, scandalous Pamphlets … have spread over the Land, to the great dishonour of the Nation' (T. Hall, *Vindicae literarum*, 1654, 215).

On 27 March 1646 'One *Calvert* a Sectary' (T. Edwards, *Gangraena*, 1646, 2.9) was examined before the lord mayor of London concerning the publication of Richard Overton's anti-monarchical *The last warning to all the inhabitants of London*. Calvert was subsequently brought before the bar of the House of Lords, but, unlike the printer and bookseller William Larner and his two servants, escaped imprisonment. Thereafter Calvert's publishing activities continued unabated. In 1646 he issued or sold thirty-seven known new titles, including two numbers (20–27 October and 27 October–12 November) of the newsbook *The Military Actions of Europe*, as well as works by Robert Bacon, Henry Burton, Thomas Collier, Benjamin Coxe, William Dell, Henry Lawrence, Hugh Peters, and William Walwyn. A similar picture emerges for 1647. That year Calvert issued or sold thirty-one known new titles, including works by Mary Cary, Nicholas Cowling, William Erbury, Francis Freeman, Paul Hobson, and Joseph Salmon.

On 12 April 1647 Calvert, having paid £20, was admitted into the livery of the Stationers' Company. On 17 December he was nominated for the lowest and most undesirable ward office, that of scavenger. In March 1648 Calvert and Adam Haughton, a London merchant, purchased a parcel of former bishops' lands in the manor of Thorfield,

Gloucestershire, for £410 15*s*. 10*d*. At the same time Calvert continued to publish, issuing or selling thirty-two known new titles in 1648, including works by John Lewin, Isaac Penington, Henry Pinnell, William Sedgwick, Joshua Sprigge, John Warr, Valentin Weigel, Robert Wilkinson, and Gerrard Winstanley.

By January 1649 Calvert's widespread network of contacts included a group called 'My one flesh'. Abiezer Coppe appeared 'in a most dreadful manner' before members of 'My one flesh' and it was to this conventicle that Calvert directed the itinerant preacher Lawrence Clarkson. Calvert was also prolific in 1649, issuing or selling sixty-one known new titles including one number of the newsbook the *Irish Monthly Mercury* (ending 21 December), as well as works by Thomas Banaster, Jacob Böhme, Ellis Bradshaw, Thomas Butler, Peter Chamberlen, John Cooke, Abiezer Coppe, Richard Coppin, Henry Danvers, J[ohn] F[ile?], Joseph Heming, John Lilburne, Richard Mercer, Henrick Niclaes, M[ary] P[ordage?], Robert Purnell, William Rabisha, and William Sheppard. Significantly Calvert also published in partnership with John Partridge, Rapha Harford, and George Whittington *A petition from his excellency Thomas Lord Fairfax and the general councel of officers of the army … concerning the draught of An agreement of the people* (20 January 1649). Calvert, moreover, issued a parliamentary act (23 February 1649), suggesting that he may have had friends both in the army and parliament.

In 1650 Calvert issued or sold twenty-five known new titles, including works by Samuel Eaton, John Fry, Henry Halhead, John Horn, Samuel Loveday, William Potter, Nicholas Rust, and Theaurau John Tany. Calvert was also believed to have printed Lawrence Clarkson's 'impious and blasphemous' book *A single eye all light, no darkness* (*JHC*, 6.474). While Clarkson was questioned by a parliamentary committee and subsequently sentenced by the House of Commons 'to be kept to Labour for one Month; and from that Time to be banished out of this Commonwealth' (ibid., 6.475), no action seems to have been taken against Calvert. In 1651 he issued or sold twenty-seven known new titles; these included works by Noah Biggs, Abraham Boune, William Bray, Christopher Cob, Charles Hotham, Edward Hyde, John Jackson, Joseph Mede, and Thomas Tillam. Again, in 1652 Calvert issued or sold twenty-five known new titles, including works by James Cranford, John Graunt, Henry Haggar, Simon Henden, Thomas Larkham, and Roger Williams.

On 2 June 1652 Giles Calvert and George Poole, clockmaker, came upon bail before the sessions held for the Newgate gaol delivery, and were committed. Although the reasons for Calvert's confinement are unknown he does not appear to have remained long in Newgate, for on 11 October 1652 he freed his apprentice Richard Moone (*d.* 1663). In May 1653 Calvert, his former apprentice Thomas Brewster (*d.* 1664), and Henry Hills (*d.* 1689) were appointed printers to the new council of state that had been established on 29 April 1653. Calvert appears to have held this position until early August 1653. Afterwards Hills continued in the post alone.

In 1653 Calvert began publishing Quaker writings including works by Christopher Atkinson, Samuel Buttivant, Richard Farnworth, George Fox, and James Nayler. Of the fifty-two known new titles issued or sold by Calvert that year, fourteen were by Quaker authors. In 1654 Calvert issued or sold thirty-eight known new titles. Of these, thirty were by Quaker authors, representing 47 per cent of all known Quaker publications that year. By the end of 1654 several Quakers had also entrusted Calvert with forwarding their letters. This trust was reciprocated with the loans that Calvert gave to Quakers newly arrived in London. In January 1655 a group of over two hundred Quakers, including James Nayler and George Fox, gathered for a 'General Meeting' at Swannington, Leicestershire. Also present were 'many Ranters' including Jacob Bothumley, as well as 'other professors' and Baptists (*Journal of George Fox*, ed. J. Nickalls, 1986, 182). It was said that the Quakers had 'a printer with them', later identified as 'Giles Calvert of London, who stay'd with them eight or nine dayes, and is now gone up to London with two or three queere of paper written to be putt into print' (Thurloe, *State papers*, 3.116).

Calvert issued or sold seventy-five known new titles in 1655. Of the fifty-seven new texts by Quaker authors, perhaps fifteen or more derived from manuscripts he had collected at Swannington. Some of this new stock was seized on Oliver Cromwell's orders in February 1655 and taken to Westminster for examination.

On 4 July that year Calvert came to a London Quaker meeting with George Fox. Afterwards Alexander Parker and James Nayler 'passed downe' to Calvert's, where they found him 'exceeding tender and loving towards us' (I. Ross, *Margaret Fell, Mother of Quakerism*, 1949, 116). Calvert remained a 'Loving frend' (RS Friends, Lond., Swarthmore MS 3.30) of the Quakers throughout 1655 and for some time afterwards, as he continued to publish their writings, forward their letters, and supply them with credit and printed books. On 19 April 1656 Stephen Bowtell, a deputy of the commission for regulating of printing, presented information against Calvert for selling Edward Burrough's *A Trumpet of the Lord Sounded out of Sion* (1656), a work thought to be 'scandalous and prejudiciall to the Comonwealth' (Thurloe, *State papers*, 4.717). For issuing this and some other books 'reflexive upon the present Government' Calvert was ordered to appear before the council of state on 6 May 1656 (*CSP dom.*, 1655–6, 308). In December 1656 Calvert was one of eighty-seven signatories to a petition for remitting the remaining part of James Nayler's punishment. One of Nayler's followers was Calvert's sister, Martha *Simmonds (*bap.* 1624, *d.* 1665), and by the end of 1658 her husband, Thomas Simmonds, had replaced Calvert as the leading Quaker publisher.

In 1660 Calvert served as second renter warden of the Stationers' Company. The following year he chose to pay a £24 fine on demand rather than serve again. About November 1660 Calvert published in partnership with Thomas Brewster and Livewell Chapman a seditious book, *The Speeches and Prayers of some of the Late King's Judges*. On 29 June 1661 Calvert was examined before the secretary of state, Sir Edward Nicholas, concerning the publication of

A Phoenix, or, The Solemn League and Covenant. Calvert was committed prisoner to the Gatehouse, Westminster, by order of Secretary Nicholas. During Calvert's confinement his wife, Elizabeth, carried on his business, completing the publication of *ENIAYTOS TEPASTIOS mirabilis annus, or, The year of prodigies and wonders*.

Giles Calvert was released with the adjournment of parliament on 30 July 1661 and by October had gone into hiding outside London, apparently fearing arrest for debt. On 21 December a warrant was issued to release Elizabeth Calvert on her bond of £500. By March 1662 Giles appears to have returned to London. On 8 May 1662 he entered into two bonds with John Harris of Carmarthen and Walter Lloyd. Thereafter he was imprisoned for distributing seditious books. On 27 November 1662 he was released on his bond of £500. His freedom was to be short-lived. On 16 December 1662, four days after a warrant for imprisoning him in the Tower had been executed, Calvert was committed to Newgate for dangerous and seditious practices by order of the secretary of state, Sir Henry Bennet. The same day Elizabeth Calvert entered into an obligation to surrender herself to one of the king's messengers. Giles was probably released at some time in January 1663, whereupon he appears to have continued selling 'many sedicious books' (N. Penney, ed., *Extracts from State Papers Relating to Friends, 1654 to 1672*, 1913, 168). On 29 June 1663 Elizabeth Calvert was again committed to the Gatehouse for delivering unlawful books. Following the intercession of the earl of Carlisle and a bond of £600 for her good behaviour she was released on 24 July 1663. On 11 August that year Giles Calvert drew up his will. No doubt debilitated by his periods of imprisonment he died before 28 August. He had issued or sold either individually or in partnership 475 known different publications, of which about 200 were by Quaker authors. ARIEL HESSAYON

Sources A. Hessayon, *'Gold tried in the fire': the prophet Theaurau John Tany and the puritan revolution* [forthcoming] • M. K. Peters, 'Quaker pamphleteering and the development of the Quaker movement, 1652–1656', PhD diss., U. Cam., 1996, 80–86 • A. E. Terry, 'Giles Calvert, mid-seventeenth-century English bookseller and publisher', MA diss., Columbia University, 1937 • A. E. Terry, 'Giles Calvert's publishing career', *Journal of the Friends' Historical Society*, 35 (1938), 45–9 • E. Thomas, 'A purveyor of soul-poysons: an analysis of the career of Giles Calvert, a publisher and bookseller in mid-seventeenth century London', PhD diss., La Trobe University, 1999

Calvert, Sir Harry, first baronet (*bap.* **1763**, *d.* **1826**), army officer, baptized in March 1763, was the eldest son of Peter Calvert (*d.* 1810) of Hampton Court, Middlesex, a partner in a brewing firm, and his wife, Mary, daughter of Thomas Reeve MD. He was educated at Harrow School, and left it probably in 1778. On 24 April 1778 he was commissioned into the 23rd foot (Royal Welch Fusiliers) as second lieutenant. He left Chatham, Kent, on 26 March 1779 to join his regiment at New York, where he became a first lieutenant on 2 October. He served with the regiment at the siege of Charleston, South Carolina, and throughout the subsequent campaigns under Lieutenant-General Lord Cornwallis, being present at the English surrender at Yorktown, Virginia, on 19 October 1781. Calvert remained a prisoner of war in America from 1781 until the peace of Versailles in 1783, returned to England with his regiment early in 1784, and then received permission to spend the remainder of the year travelling in Europe. On 26 October 1785 he purchased a company in the 100th, a reduced regiment on half pay, transferring to the 23rd as a captain on 23 November. He served with it at home until he exchanged into the Coldstream Guards as lieutenant and captain on 19 February 1790.

In February 1793 Calvert embarked for the Netherlands with his battalion, forming part of the brigade of guards under Major-General Gerard Lake. After the arrival of the troops before Tournai, he was appointed aide-de-camp to the duke of York, in which capacity he took part in the principal engagements during the campaigns of 1793–4. Meanwhile, he had advanced to brevet major on 1 July 1793, and to captain and lieutenant-colonel in the Coldstream Guards and brevet lieutenant-colonel in the army on 25 December of the same year. He returned home with the duke of York in December 1794 and was dispatched in April 1795 on a confidential mission to Brunswick and Berlin, to induce Friedrich Wilhelm II of Prussia to take the initiative in placing the duke of Brunswick at the head of the allied armies. Calvert was promoted colonel on 26 January 1797 and appointed deputy adjutant-general at headquarters. He became adjutant-general of the forces on 9 January 1799 and lieutenant-colonel of the 63rd foot on 27 January, while holding this staff appointment. On 8 June 1799 he married the second daughter of Thomas Hammersley of Pall Mall, London, and niece of Mr Greenwood of the firm of Cox and Greenwood, army agents. He and his wife, who died in 1806, had two sons, including Sir Harry *Verney, politician, and three daughters.

Calvert was made colonel of the 5th West India regiment on 6 August 1800 and was promoted major-general on 25 September 1803. On 8 February 1806 he transferred to the colonelcy of the 14th foot, which during the latter part of the Napoleonic wars had the unusual number of three battalions and was therefore dubbed Calvert's Entire; its county title was altered from Bedfordshire to Buckinghamshire at his request. In 1818 Calvert, who had become lieutenant-general on 25 July 1810, and who had been made a GCB in 1815 and a GCH in 1817, received a baronetcy in recognition of his services. He was appointed lieutenant-governor of Chelsea Hospital, London, on 19 February 1820, with an annual salary of £400, and attained the rank of general on 19 July 1821.

Rumour alleged that Calvert's advancement to the post of adjutant-general, which he left on 25 March 1820, was partly due to the fact that the duke of York was under heavy obligations to Cox & Co. Whether or not this was true, the appointment was justified by the results, as during his long tenure Calvert proved himself a true soldier's friend and implemented many valuable improvements in the administration and discipline of the army. Among these were the better organization of the medical department and army hospitals, and of the chaplains' department; the introduction of regimental schools; the development of the military colleges at High Wycombe and

Marlow, later merged in the Royal Military College at Sandhurst; the founding of the Royal Military Asylum for Soldiers' Orphans, better known as the Duke of York's School; and various other measures for the benefit of the service. He bequeathed one specific item of lasting, administrative interest. In October 1815, as adjutant-general, he signed a general order in which a specimen pay-book for the possibly mythical private Thomas Atkins from Odiham, Hampshire, appeared. 'Tommy Atkins' thus entered military folklore. One of his immediate subordinates wrote of him, long afterwards:

> Such was the kindness of his look and demeanour, and courtesy of his manner, that it was impossible to offer him any disrespect, and with whatever sentiments a gentleman might have approached him, he could only retire with those of regard and esteem.

Calvert died suddenly of apoplexy on 3 September 1826 at Claydon Hall, Middle Claydon, Buckinghamshire, where he was on a visit with his family. He was buried at West Claydon (Steeple Claydon), where the church spire was erected as a memorial to him. His son, the second baronet, took the name of Verney instead of Calvert on succeeding to the Verney estates. Calvert's journals and letters during the campaigns in Flanders, together with memoranda relating to his Berlin mission and to the early nineteenth-century anti-invasion measures of the United Kingdom, were published by his son as *Journals and Correspondence of Sir H. Calvert, Bart.* (1853).

H. M. Chichester, *rev.* John Sweetman

Sources *Army List* • A. D. L. Cary, S. McCance, and others, eds., *Regimental records of the Royal Welch Fusiliers (late the 23rd foot)*, 7 vols. (1921–), vol. 1 • M. Glover, *That astonishing infantry: three hundred years of the history of the Royal Welch Fusiliers* (1989) • Hertfordshire genealogies

Archives priv. coll. | BL, letters to William Windham, etc., Add. MSS 37874–37888 • Morgan L., Murray-Pulteney MSS • NA Scot., Hope MSS • NAM, Nugent MSS • priv. coll., letters to Rt Hon. Richard Ryder • Royal Military Academy, Sandhurst, Le Marchant MSS • U. Durham L., Grey MSS • U. Nott. L., Cavendish-Bentinck MSS

Likenesses T. Phillips, oils, 1825, Claydon House, Buckinghamshire

Calvert, James (*bap.* 1631, *d.* **1698**), nonconformist minister, was baptized at Allhallows Pavement, York, on 23 May 1631, the eldest son and second of the nine children of Robert Calvert, merchant and sheriff of York, and his wife, Judith Taylor. He was named after his grandfather, James Calvert. His uncle was Thomas *Calvert (1605/6–1679), the York presbyterian minister and Hebraist in whose footsteps Calvert would follow. Calvert was admitted pensioner at Clare College, Cambridge, on 9 June 1646. He graduated BA in 1650 and proceeded MA in 1653. He was appointed vicar of Boynton, Yorkshire, on 20 July 1652, curate of Kirkdale on 30 May 1654, and vicar of Topcliffe on 12 March 1656, from which post he had resigned by 26 March 1661, when his successor was installed. After his resignation Calvert may have supported himself through commerce: he was identified as a 'merchant' when he was admitted to the freedom of the city of York in 1664. According to Calamy, Calvert 'lived privately but not idly; for he studied hard' (Calamy, *Abridgement*, 2.472). He was licensed to preach as a presbyterian at his house in York on 25 July 1672.

Calvert was a moderate presbyterian who maintained good relations with some Anglicans, including his cousin Thomas Harrison, a fellow of Sidney Sussex College, Cambridge, to whom Calvert left most of his library of books and manuscripts. Calvert's one publication, *Napthali* (1672), a Latin work on the ten tribes of Israel and the conversion of the Jews, was dedicated to the bishop of Chester, John Wilkins. He waited on Wilkins in company with another York presbyterian minister, Peter Williams, at Scarborough-Spaw, when Wilkins received them cordially and expressed hopes for religious comprehension. A letter Calvert addressed to the Anglican Hebraist Dr John Lightfoot in August 1669 asked for assistance in interpreting the prophecy of Ezekiel. Calvert's interpretation of Ezekiel 48 differed from mainstream Christian and Jewish prophetic interpretation in that he believed that the division of the Holy Land among the twelve tribes was a literal description of the situation after the end of the Babylonian captivity rather than an apocalyptic prophecy or an allegory. Thus, the supposedly 'lost' ten tribes were not lost at all—they had long ago returned to the Holy Land, either with the two tribes of Benjamin and Judah at the end of the Babylonian captivity or shortly thereafter, and presumably had simply been reabsorbed into the Jewish people.

Despite Calvert's friendships with individual Anglicans and the entreaties of conformists who admired his learning, he refused to conform because he continued to object to some aspects of the Anglican liturgy and because it would have required an episcopal reordination. About 1675 Calvert became a chaplain to Sir Thomas Strickland of Boynton, whose sons he also tutored. Calvert was not usually politically active but while at Boynton he became mixed up in the aftermath of the Rye House plot. Along with another member of Strickland's household, the gardener Marmaduke Baine, Calvert went to Bridlington in late June 1683 to arrange a boat to the Netherlands for the plotter Sir John Cochrane of Ochiltree and his son. Cochrane was the husband of Sir Thomas Strickland's sister. Calvert was charged with treason for the action and briefly imprisoned in York Castle, but the charge seems to have come to nothing. Sir Thomas Strickland seems to have approved of Calvert's actions—in his will written that August he left him £20.

Later Calvert moved to Hull, and afterwards became chaplain to Sir William Middleton, bt, of Belsay Castle, Northumberland, and tutor to Middleton's only son, John. Calvert died at Belsay Castle in December 1698, 'an ingenious and pious man, of a meek and quiet temper' (Calamy, *Abridgement*, 2.472).

William E. Burns

Sources *Calamy rev.* • *Register of the freemen of the City of York from the city records, vol. 2, 1559–1759* (1900) • *CSP dom., 1671–2* • *IGI* • J. T. Cliffe, *The puritan gentry besieged, 1650–1700* (1993) • Venn, *Alum. Cant.* • *The whole works of the Rev. John Lightfoot*, ed. J. R. Pitman, 13 vols. (1822–5) • E. Calamy, ed., *An abridgement of Mr. Baxter's history of his life and* *times, with an account of the ministers, &c., who were ejected after the Restauration of King Charles II*, 2nd edn, 2 vols. (1713)

Calvert, James Snowden (1825–1884), explorer in Australia, was born on 13 July 1825, at Otley, Yorkshire, the son of William Calvert, leather manufacturer, and his wife, Ann Coates. He was educated at Liverpool, Manchester, Birmingham, and London, where his family successively moved. Having friends in New South Wales, Calvert and his brother William decided to go out there. Sailing in September 1841, Calvert made a lasting friendship with Dr Ludwig Leichhardt, the explorer, who was a fellow passenger. The ship arrived in Sydney in February 1842 and Calvert engaged in desultory employment before meeting Leichhardt again and agreeing to accompany him on his first expedition. Somewhat ill-prepared, the party left the Darling Downs, west of Brisbane, in September 1844 and reached Port Essington, 3000 miles away on the north-west coast, in December 1845, although Calvert was seriously injured by Aborigines and another man was killed. Leichhardt recognized the value of Calvert's easy temperament to the difficult expedition.

Calvert made no further expeditions but became manager of Cavan station, near Yass, and a JP. He developed a keen interest in botany and had botanical entries at exhibitions in London and Paris. At the London Exhibition of 1862 he was awarded a silver medal for his collection of Australian paper-making materials. On 11 March 1869 at Oldbury, near Berrima, Calvert married (Caroline) Louisa Waring *Atkinson (1834–1872), who shared his keen interest in botany. After her sudden death he led a retired life. He died in Sydney on 22 July 1884, and was survived by his only daughter, Dr Louise Cash.

H. M. Chichester, *rev.* Elizabeth Baigent

Sources *The letters of F. W. Ludwig Leichhardt*, ed. M. Aurousseau, 3 vols. (1968) • F. W. L. Leichhardt, *Journal of an overland journey* (1847) • A. H. Chisholm, *Strange new world* (1955) • A. H. Chisholm, 'Calvert, James Snowden', *AusDB*, vol. 3 • E. Connell, *The mystery of Ludwig Leichhardt* (1980) • D. Bunce, *Travels with Dr. Leichhardt* (1979)

Calvert, Leonard (1610?–1647), colonial governor, was the second son of George *Calvert, first Baron Baltimore (1579/80–1632), and Anne Mynne (1579–1622), and the brother of Cecil (Cecilius) *Calvert, second Baron Baltimore (1605–1675). Charles I granted Maryland, named to honour his French Catholic wife, Henrietta Maria, to Cecil Calvert on 20 June 1632. Cecil entrusted its government to his younger brother Leonard, who had experienced the rigours of colonization with their father in Newfoundland in 1628–9. The Catholic Calverts sought to recoup the family fortune that had been depleted in Newfoundland while creating a society in which people of diverse religious commitments, but especially English Catholics, could enjoy religious freedom and prosper. On 13 November 1633 Baltimore prepared 'Instructions' to his brother and the councillors who were to assist him. The majority of the approximately 140 colonists who sailed on 22 November were protestant servants, and Baltimore instructed the Catholic leaders to deal equitably with the protestants. He ordered them to 'cause all Acts of Romane Catholique Religion to be done as privately as may be', and to 'instruct all Roman Catholiques to be silent upon all Occasions of discourse concerning matters of Religion' (Hall, 16).

Leonard Calvert and the colonists arrived in the Chesapeake in late February 1634. They took possession of Baltimore's territory, in the king's name, on 25 March and celebrated a mass. Calvert negotiated with the American Indians for land along St George's River they were about to abandon and renamed the site St Mary's. He worked hard to implement his brother's objectives but all too frequently conflict and turmoil resulted. The Calverts hoped to exploit the lucrative beaver fur trade with the Indians but were thwarted by Virginian William Claiborne, who in 1631 established an outpost on Kent Island at the head of Chesapeake Bay. Calvert's attempts to establish jurisdiction led to sporadic warfare that continued until he led a small force to the island in 1638 to subdue it. He enforced Baltimore's religious policy when he adjudicated an incident in favour of some protestant servants who had been forbidden by their Catholic overseer to read aloud from a book of puritan sermons. He attempted to maintain his brother's prerogatives as proprietor in the face of increasing opposition from Catholic and protestant freemen in the assembly, but failed to prevent them from seizing the right to initiate legislation. His loyalty to his brother conflicted with his deference to members of the Society of Jesus who came in 1634 to bring Christianity to the Native Americans. His inability to control the missionaries, who not only accepted land directly from the Indians but demanded privileges enjoyed by the clergy in Catholic countries, led to a sharp rebuke from his brother.

In April 1643 Calvert sailed to England, where he found parliamentarian forces waging war against the king and his supporters. During his absence Richard Ingle, a tobacco merchant who had traded with Maryland tobacco planters for years but now sailed under parliamentarian authority, spoke ill of the king. The provincial court on 18 January 1644 issued a warrant for his arrest for high treason, but Ingle escaped, and returned determined to avenge himself. When the governor returned in September 1644, he carried a commission from the king that authorized him to seize all ships and property of all in 'actual rebellion' against the king. The impecunious Calverts sought to profit from their loyalty, but Ingle's rebellion against their authority in Maryland prevented the governor from executing the commission. Calvert lacked the requisite forces needed to battle Ingle and fled to Virginia. Ingle plundered the colony, singling out the houses of prominent Catholics, and returned to England to broadcast the Calverts' support of 'the Popish and Romish Religion' and the royalist cause (Browne and others, 1.270, 3.165). In 1646, with a force of Marylanders and mercenary Virginians, Calvert returned, dispersed the remaining rebels, and re-established proprietary authority. Shortly before his death in St Mary's on 9 June 1647 he designated the Catholic Thomas Greene as his successor and named Margaret Brent as his sole executrix. He may have married in a Catholic ceremony while in England in 1643–4. William and Anne Calvert, who claimed to be his children, emigrated to Maryland in the 1660s.

JOHN D. KRUGLER

Sources W. H. Browne and others, eds., *Archives of Maryland* (1883–) · T. Hughes, *History of the Society of Jesus in North America, colonial and federal*, 2 vols. (1908–17) · C. C. Hall, ed., *Narratives of early Maryland, 1633–1684* (1910) · J. D. Krugler, *English and Catholic: the lords Baltimore in the seventeenth century* [forthcoming] · *The Calvert papers*, 3 vols., Maryland Historical Society (1889–99) · R. R. Menard, 'Economy and society in early colonial Maryland', PhD diss., University of Iowa, 1975 · D. W. Jordan, *Foundations of representative government in Maryland, 1632–1715* (1987) · E. C. Papenfuse and others, eds., *A biographical dictionary of the Maryland legislature, 1635–1789*, 2 vols. (1979–85) · J. D. Krugler, 'Lord Baltimore, Roman Catholics, and toleration', *Catholic Historical Review*, 65 (1979), 49–75 · G. T. Cell, ed., *Newfoundland discovered: English attempts at colonisation, 1610–1630*, Hakluyt Society, new ser., 160 (1982) · T. M. Coakley, 'George Calvert and Newfoundland: "the sad face of winter"', *Maryland Historical Magazine*, 71 (1976), 1–18

Wealth at death in debt; patents on certificates for approx. 9000 acres: Browne and others, eds., *Archives of Maryland*, 4.320–21, 388–9; Papenfuse and others, *Biographical dictionary*, 1.190

Calvert, Louis (1859–1923). *See under* Calvert, Charles Alexander (1828–1879).

Calvert, Michael (*bap.* **1770**, *d.* **1862**), topographer, son of Richard and Barbara Calvert, was born in Knaresborough, Yorkshire, and baptized at the parish church on 2 February 1770. By profession a chemist, he filled the office of churchwarden in 1808 and 1809 and in the latter year repaired the chancel of the church. Among other local concerns in which Calvert took an interest was the restoration of Knaresborough spa, a mild sulphur spring on the Harrogate road. He attended a public meeting on 4 March 1822 to discuss the rebuilding of the spa, and was secretary and treasurer of the Knaresborough spa trust from that year until 1849. Through the trust's efforts the pump room was rebuilt in 1822, and in 1828 the baths were erected. In 1823 Calvert published *An Account of the Knaresborough Spaw* [*sic*], and in 1844 *The history of Knaresborough, comprising an accurate and detailed account of the castle, the forest, and the several townships included in the said parish*. He died on 3 December 1862 at York Place, Knaresborough, the town where he had spent all his life.

C. W. SUTTON, *rev.* JOANNE POTIER

Sources M. Calvert, *The History of Knaresborough* (1844), 97 · W. Boyne, *The Yorkshire library* (1869), 142 · Boase, *Mod. Eng. biog.* · W. Grainge, *The history and topography of Harrogate and the forest of Knaresborough* (1871) · private information (1886) · d. cert.

Wealth at death under £600: probate, 7 May 1863, *CGPLA Eng. & Wales*

Calvert, (James) Michael (**1913–1998**), army officer, was born on 6 March 1913 in Rohtak, near Delhi, India, the youngest son in the family of four sons and two daughters of Hubert Calvert (1875–1961), an officer of the Indian Civil Service, and his wife, Oclanis, daughter of Edward O'Brien, also of the Indian Civil Service. His father was then serving as a deputy commissioner in the Punjab; he later rose to become acting governor of the Punjab, before retiring in 1933. Calvert was educated at Bradfield School (1926–31) and the Royal Military Academy, Woolwich

(James) Michael Calvert (1913–1998), by unknown photographer

(1931–3), before being commissioned a second lieutenant in the Royal Engineers in 1933. From 1933 to 1935 he read mechanical sciences at St John's College, Cambridge, where he was a swimming blue. Later he was the army's middleweight boxing champion.

A dedicated professional, Calvert eschewed normal social activity, and devoted himself to studying the art of war. His postings took him to Hong Kong and then to Shanghai, where he saw at first hand the brutality and expertise of the Japanese army. Back in England as adjutant of a London Royal Engineers' battalion, in 1939 he volunteered for the fifth battalion, the Scots Guards, who were then preparing to fight for the Finns against the Russians. Following the outbreak of the Second World War he fought in northern Norway, blowing up bridges before the advancing Germans. He then joined the first commando training centre at Lochailort, as an explosives expert. From there he was posted to Australia with Spencer Chapman, to set up a training centre for the Australian independent companies (commandos).

Posted to Burma, Calvert met Orde Wingate. After the British retreat from Burma, Wingate sent for Calvert, and together they set up and trained the Chindits, to carry out Wingate's idea of 'long-range penetration' behind the Japanese lines in Burma. This revolutionary concept of establishing substantial units behind enemy lines, supplied entirely by air, was tried out in the first Chindit expedition of February 1943, in which Calvert was outstandingly the most successful column commander. After the expedition returned—despite casualties of one third—Wingate was hailed as a brilliant new leader, and was called to Downing Street by Churchill. He convinced Churchill, as well as the joint chiefs of staff at the Quebec conference, of the efficacy of long-range penetration. The Americans eagerly backed a 'Limey' leader who really wanted to fight the Japanese, and Wingate returned to Delhi as a major-general with the American air commando to support a Chindit expedition several brigades strong. Calvert, meanwhile, was appointed DSO for his part in the expedition.

Against the bitter opposition of general headquarters, Delhi, Calvert and Wingate prepared the Chindits for Operation Thursday. The plan was for three brigades of Chindits to fly in to the area of Indaw, behind the Japanese lines, to disrupt their supplies and communications, just when the British Fourteenth Army, the American Chinese forces under Lieutenant-General Joseph W. Stilwell, and the main Chinese armies under Chiang Kai-shek, all attacked. In fact none of these attacks took place, but the Chindits were given their chance when the Japanese attacked Imphal and Kohima. Calvert, now a brigadier at the early age of thirty-one, led 77 brigade to establish a stronghold at 'White City', in March 1944. This was a brilliant success, and Calvert's stronghold drove off every attack by several Japanese divisions. Shortly afterwards Wingate was killed in an air crash, and under his weak successor the Chindits were transferred to the command of 'Vinegar Joe' Stilwell, whose paranoid dislike of 'Limeys' was to cost the lives of many Chindits. Their role as guerrilla troops—unsupported by tanks or artillery—was to move swiftly, attack, and then disperse. Instead, Stilwell ordered them to attack Mogaung, a heavily fortified town. In carrying out this order Calvert showed his superb leadership qualities, and, despite appalling casualties, the Chindits captured the town. Calvert received the American Silver Star, and was recommended for the VC by his three battalion commanders, but received nothing from a grudging British military establishment.

Calvert was invalided home in late 1944, but was fit enough to be given command of the Special Air Service (SAS) in succession to Brigadier R. W. McLeod in March 1945, serving with it in the Netherlands and north-west Germany in the dying months of the war. For this he received both the French and the Belgian Croix de Guerre. After attending Staff College, in 1950 he established the Malayan Scouts SAS to fight communist insurgents, but this was not a success, and he was invalided home on medical grounds. Immediately afterwards he was posted to Soltau in north Germany.

By this time Calvert was suffering from a cocktail of tropical diseases, was drinking heavily, and certainly behaved indiscreetly. In 1951 he was court-martialled for indecency with German youths. He protested his innocence, but was convicted and dismissed from the army. This catastrophe led to ten years in Australia, as an alcoholic and almost as a down and out, but by 1960 he had recovered sufficiently to return to England, where he largely overcame his alcoholism, and obtained a salaried post as an engineer with the Greater London council. His main interest still lay in guerrilla warfare and military history. He then took unwise advice, and gave up his post to follow a career as a writer. This condemned him to a lifetime of penury. He gained a temporary post at Manchester University in 1971, and was a successful military commentator, but a major work on guerrilla warfare was never completed.

In 1997 Calvert's biography, *Mad Mike*, by David Rooney, contained dramatic evidence that the court martial verdict was unjust. Two by now respected men in Soltau, who had been witnesses at the court martial, swore that the British military police had pressurized them to present evidence against Calvert as a homosexual. In spite of this evidence, an appeal, supported by more than one MP, was rejected. On 26 November 1998 Calvert, who had been called 'the bravest of the brave', died in penury at the Star and Garter Home, Richmond, Surrey, his character still unjustly besmirched. He was cremated at Amersham on 2 December. He was unmarried. DAVID ROONEY

Sources D. Rooney, *Mad Mike: the life of Brigadier Michael Calvert* (1997) • M. Calvert, *Prisoners of hope* (1952) • M. Calvert, *Fighting mad* (1964) • *The Times* (28 Nov 1998) • *The Independent* (2 Dec 1998) • *The Guardian* (18 Dec 1998) • *WWW*, 1961–70 • personal knowledge (2004) • private information (2004)
Archives IWM, papers relating to service with royal engineers, Chindit, and on terrorism | FILM IWM | SOUND IWM
Likenesses photograph, 1944, IWM; repro. in *The Guardian* • photograph, *c.*1945, repro. in *The Independent* • photograph, News International Syndication, London [*see illus.*]

Calvert, Raisley (*bap.* 1773, *d.* 1795). *See under* Calvert, Charles (1785–1852).

Calvert, Thomas (1605/6–1679), clergyman and ejected minister, and author, son of James Calvert of St Crux, York, baker, was educated at schools in York and Coxwold, Yorkshire, before being admitted to Sidney Sussex College, Cambridge, in 1622. Having graduated BA in 1626 he was ordained deacon at York as curate of Holme on the Wolds, Yorkshire, in September that year, and priest the following February. He proceeded MA in 1629.

Calvert became chaplain to Sir Thomas Burdett of Foremark, Derbyshire, and also in 1632 vicar of Burton Agnes in the East Riding of Yorkshire, and then from 1638 vicar of Holy Trinity, King's Court, York. In the household of Burdett and his wife, Jane, he encountered others, including Lady Burdett, who shared his literary interests. When she died he preached her funeral sermon on 24 March 1637, and with Sir George Gresley, John Newdigate, and others composed epitaphs and elegies on the occasion. It was not until after the appearance of his *Heart-Salve for the Wounded Soule* (1647) and *The Blessed Jew of Marocco* (1648)—the latter a translation of Rabbi Samuel's testimony, to which Calvert added numerous annotations and an account of Jewish tribulations since the death of Christ—that he was persuaded to publish the funeral sermon, with the accompanying compositions, as *The Wearie Soule's Wish, or, The Dove's Wings* (1650). In a dedication to Lady Burdett's son, Sir Francis, Calvert revealed that he felt its sentiments—the desirability of escape from an evil world by prayer, an innocent heart, and finally death—to be even more apposite than thirteen years earlier: 'we are now from a Kingdome turned into a Common-weale, and our sins are ready to turne that into Common-woe'.

None the less Calvert, a believer in a national church

and an opponent of separatism, prospered during the 1650s. Continuing at Holy Trinity he worked harmoniously with Sir Thomas Fairfax's chaplain, Edward Bowles, a minister at York Minster, where Calvert held one of the four lectureships, and his preaching was highly regarded by the city corporation. Two more sermons were published, *Mel caeli … or, The Prophet Isaiah's Crucifix* (1657) and *The Wise Merchant, or, The Peerless Pearl* (1660), and he acted as assistant to commissions for the West and North ridings in 1654 and the East Riding in 1657. He had married in 1640 Elizabeth Becke (*b.* 1615/16) of St Cuthbert's, York, and the extravagance of their merchant son, John, caused him great concern, but he found a spiritual heir in his nephew James Calvert, vicar of Topcliffe until the Restoration, who shared his moderate nonconformity.

In 1662 Calvert was ejected from his living, and subsequently banished from York by the Five Mile Act, gaining asylum at the house of Ursula, Lady Barwick, near Tadcaster. Later he returned to York where he lived quietly until he died, aged seventy-three. He was buried in All Saints', Pavement, on 18 April 1679. CLAIRE CROSS

Sources [J. Hunter], ed., *Letters of eminent men, addressed to Ralph Thoresby*, 1 (1832), 404–8 [letter from Timothy Hodgson, 1702] • *The nonconformist's memorial … originally written by … Edmund Calamy*, ed. S. Palmer, 2 (1775) • *Calamy rev.* • Venn, *Alum. Cant.* • R. Marchant, *The puritans and the church courts in the diocese of York, 1560–1642* (1960) • C. Cross, 'Achieving the millennium: the church in York during the Commonwealth', *The province of York*, ed. G. J. Cuming, SCH, 4 (1967), 122–42 • *BL cat.* • Wing, *STC* • T. M. Fisher, ed., *The parish register of All Saints' Church, Pavement, in the city of York*, 1: 1554–1690 (1935), 12, 154

Calvert [*formerly* Jackson], **Thomas** (1775?–1840), Church of England clergyman, was born at Newsham, near Preston. His father, whose name was Jackson, sent him to Clitheroe Free Grammar School, of which the master was the learned Revd Thomas Wilson BD. He entered St John's College, Cambridge, in 1793 and was fourth wrangler. He was BA in 1797, MA in 1800, BD in 1807, and DD in 1823. He took his DD in the name of Calvert, which he assumed by royal licence on 30 April 1817, following the death of a friend belonging to an old Lancashire family who, although not a relative, left him a large fortune. He was able to buy the estate of Woodplumpton, St Michael's-on-Wyre, though he usually lived at Ardwick, near Manchester. He was fellow of his college in 1798, tutor in 1814, and Norrisian professor of divinity from 1815 to 1824, in which year he resigned the post of Lady Margaret's preacher, which he had held since 1819. On 24 September 1824 he married Juliana, daughter of Sir Charles Watson of Wratting Park, Cambridgeshire; they had three sons. Having been appointed king's preacher at Whitehall, he attracted the attention and admiration of Lord Liverpool, who appointed him to the rectory of Wilmslow. Although the crown claimed the patronage, it was ultimately decided that the right was vested in the ancient and recusant family of the Traffords of Trafford. Calvert had his consolation in the college living of Holme, Yorkshire, in 1822, and in the wardenship, from March 1823, of the collegiate church of Manchester, conferred unsolicited on the recommendation of his patron, Lord Liverpool. He was installed on 8 March 1823.

Calvert's many theological works include the sermons *The Disinterested and Benevolent Character of Christianity* (1819), *The Rich and Poor Shown to be of God's Appointment and Equally the Objects of his Regard* (1820), *Infidelity Unmasked* (1831), *An Established Church the Best Means of Providing for the Care of a Christian Community* (1834), and *On the Duty of Bridling the Tongue* (1840). This last was written for a volume made up of contributions by thirty-nine divines towards a fund for St Andrew's Schools, Manchester. Calvert was constitutionally diffident, and did not take much part in public affairs except in his opposition to Catholic emancipation. His serene manners and gentle deportment made him very popular. He died after a short illness at Ardwick on 4 June 1840; at his funeral the coffin was followed to its resting-place by the whole body of the Manchester clergy. W. E. A. AXON, *rev.* H. C. G. MATTHEW

Sources Venn, *Alum. Cant.* • F. R. Raines, *The rectors of Manchester, and the wardens of the collegiate church of that town*, ed. [J. E. Bailey], 2 vols., Chetham Society, new ser., 5–6 (1885) • T. Baker, *History of the college of St John the Evangelist, Cambridge*, ed. J. E. B. Mayor, 2 vols. (1869)

Archives Blackburn District Central Library, Whittaker MSS

Calvert, Thomas Christopher [Kit] (1903–1984), businessman and philanthropist, was born on 26 April 1903 at Burtersett, Wensleydale, Yorkshire, the oldest of the three sons of John Edward Calvert (1877–1946), quarryman, and his wife, Rose, *née* Fothergill (1878–1966). Both his parents were natives of the Yorkshire dales. He was educated at Hawes elementary school, but left at the age of twelve and began his working life in farm service at Colby Hall, Askrigg. A motorcycle accident prevented him from doing hard manual work. He then found a job at Hawes auction mart but left when a request for a wage increase from 18*s.* to £1 a week was refused. He was already showing a fighting spirit.

Calvert married Jenny Horn (*d.* 1976), a daleswoman, in 1931. Their early married life coincided with a period of trade depression. Kit and his brother Robert kept cattle and sheep on rented land. Milk was produced for a cheese factory inaugurated by Edward Chapman in 1897 which was now suffering from poor trading conditions. When the milk producers were no longer being paid and the dairy faced closure, the newly established Milk Marketing Board offered milk contracts. When the upper-dale farmers were told that milk would no longer be used for local cheesemaking, however, Calvert called a meeting in Hawes town hall, in 1935, and the dalesmen formed their own company with a capital of £1085. Calvert, who had put £200 into the scheme, was appointed managing director. Over the next years, he used his vast knowledge of Wensleydale cheese production successfully to promote dales cheese. In 1953 he built a new creamery in Hawes, on a spacious site beside the road to Gayle. To his regret, it had by now become commercially expedient to exchange the cheese's traditional linen bandage for a polythene wrapping. He introduced the 'baby Wensleydale', a 1 lb

Thomas Christopher [Kit] **Calvert** (**1903–1984**), by Barbara Drew

cheese which the average household might buy weekly. About 50,000 such cheeses were sold in the first year; production rose to 250,000 per year by the 1960s. The Milk Marketing Board purchased Wensleydale Creamery for £500,000 in 1966 but persuaded Calvert to continue to run it. In 1967 he retired.

Calvert had long collected second-hand books about the Yorkshire dales. In 1965 he gave the best of them, with an estimated value of almost £3000, to the Wensleydale county modern school. He then quietly set about restocking his empty shelves. For over twenty-five years, from 1951, Kit's single-room bookshop in the main street at Hawes was the talk of the town. It was a cal-oil (gossiping place) on market days. Some 5000 books, set haphazardly on floor-to-ceiling shelves, were available at 2*s*. for a hardback, 1*s*. for a less substantial work. If there was no one in attendance money was left in a box, in a chapel collecting plate, or, at one point, in a tin designed to hold Oxo cubes. For a time John Mason, a retired railwayman, looked after the bookshop, describing it on a framed card as 'The University of Hawes' and himself as 'bursar'. Mason died in 1975 at the age of ninety-two. Calvert said of his bookshop: 'If it makes my bacca [tobacco] money, and covers the cost of a drop or two of petrol, I'm satisfied.'

Calvert was an authentic dalesman and full of character. He often reverted to local dialect. His grizzle-grey hair did not frequently have a comb drawn through it. He wore comfortable rather than fashionable clothes. He smoked black twist using a clay pipe, as had the farmers and lead-miners of old. A devout Christian, he was deacon and secretary of Hawes Congregational Chapel, and a preacher in the homely yet forceful dales manner. His translation of passages from the Bible into the dialect of his native district included, from St John's gospel, chapter 21, the conversation between Jesus and his disciples, who had no luck when fishing: 'He called out: "Lads, hey ye caught owt?" They shouted back: "Nowt!" So he said: "Kest yer net over t'reet side ev t'booat an' ye'll git a catch"' (*The Dalesman*, May 1953, 89).

Calvert transformed a tract of land near his home into a well-equipped children's playground. When, in February 1977, his services to dales life and the cheese industry were acknowledged by his appointment as MBE, and he received the medal at Buckingham Palace, he was accompanied by his daughter Florence and granddaughter Pauline. He died in Hawes on 4 January 1984. Four days later, on a Sunday, he was interred at the roadside cemetery on the Burtersett side of Hawes, the coffin having been transported on a cart pulled by Dolly, his favourite pony. The Wensleydale Creamery at Hawes continued to flourish, and was the subject of a management buy-out in 1992. A portrait of Calvert, languidly applying a match to his clay pipe, adorned every 500 gram packet of 'real Wensleydale' cheese. W. R. MITCHELL

Sources personal knowledge (2004) · private information (2004) [Florence Garnett] · *The Dalesman*
Likenesses B. Drew, drawing, Wensleydale Museum, Hawes [*see illus.*] · photograph, repro. in *The Dalesman* (Dec 1976)
Wealth at death £120,144: probate, 27 Feb 1984, *CGPLA Eng. & Wales*

Cam, Helen Maud (**1885–1968**), historian, the fourth of the nine children of the Revd William Herbert Cam and his wife, Katherine, daughter of George Erving Scott, was born at Abingdon, Berkshire, on 22 August 1885. Her early life was spent there and at Birchanger, Essex, where her father became rector when he retired from the headmastership of Roysse's Grammar School in Abingdon. She and three sisters were educated at home by their parents, an education which she delightfully described in a broadcast talk, 'Eating and drinking Greek', in 1964. With this grounding she won a scholarship in 1904 to Royal Holloway College, London, and gained a first in history (1907). In 1908 a fellowship in history took her for a year to Bryn Mawr College in the United States, where she worked on Anglo-Saxon and Frankish studies; the results were presented as a thesis for the MA degree at London University in 1909, and published in 1912 as *Local Government in Francia and England, 768–1034*.

For three years Helen Cam taught with great success at Cheltenham Ladies' College and in 1912 returned to Royal Holloway, first as assistant lecturer until 1919, then as staff lecturer. In 1921 she went to Girton College, Cambridge, where she became successively Pfeiffer research fellow (until 1926), fellow, and lecturer in history for the college, and for the university from 1929; she was also director of studies in history and law, and vice-mistress from 1944. In 1948 she left one Cambridge for the other on appointment as the first Zemurray Radcliffe professor at Harvard. This chair she held for six years with much enjoyment, greatly appreciated by the academic world of Harvard and other centres of medieval study in the United States. Retirement in 1954 brought increased opportunity to research, write, and lecture, as well as to contribute to historical

Helen Maud Cam (1885–1968), by Ramsey & Muspratt

studies as a member of councils of learned societies, especially as president of the International Commission for the History of Representative and Parliamentary Institutions from 1949 to 1960—in which capacity she was described as 'a great abbess'. She was editing the records of the eyre of London of 1321 for the Selden Society up to the time of her death, and a memoir by Professor S. F. C. Milsom, who completed the edition and saw the volumes through the press, gives a vivid picture of her at eighty-two, as enthralled by her subject as if she had been fifty years younger.

When Helen Cam began historical research the principal interests of the great teachers of the day and of the immediate past were constitutional, legal, and administrative. To Stubbs, Maitland, and Vinogradoff she gave a lifetime's allegiance. With the exception of the paper 'Suitors and *scabini*' read at Warsaw in 1933, her published work after 1912 was confined to English history, but was enriched by her continual contact with continental scholars and their work.

After the publication in the *English Historical Review* of a surprising short article, 'The legend of the incendiary birds' (1916), she produced an impressive series of articles and books on counties and boroughs based on the hundred rolls, with which her name will always be especially connected, on the *quo warranto* rolls, and on the records of the general eyres. Her appreciation of the importance of topography as a key to some local problems was illustrated by the subtitle of the first group of her collected papers, *Liberties and Communities in Medieval England: collected studies in administration and topography* (1944). Her feeling for the continuity of English institutions was brilliantly expounded in the John Coffin lecture of 1960, 'What of the middle ages is alive in England to-day?' Her second collection, *Law Finders and Law Makers in Medieval England* (1962), included her inaugural lecture at Harvard in 1948, in which she reviewed the study of medieval history at the time, surveying also the contribution of Harvard's first professor of medieval history, Henry Adams, and the graduate school he founded, with tributes to and reminiscences of the historians who had been her teachers, guides, and colleagues.

As a teacher Helen Cam herself gave her pupils contact with a great range of learning and an interest in them as marked as in the subjects of her own studies. As one said, 'Judgement might be severe but it was impersonal: no-one was more ready to respect the personalities of students.' To those past their undergraduate days and to those who consulted her she gave unstinted help in their fields of research.

Nor were her interests and sympathies solely academic. A lecture to which she went as a student, impelled thereto by a tutor rather than of her own volition, converted her to the cause of women's suffrage though not to its militancy. She was also much concerned with the YWCA, and the provision of education for women who had to start earning their living after very limited schooling, and she gave every possible help to the residential centre which later became Hillcroft College, in conjunction with her contemporary at Royal Holloway, Miss Fanny Street. For some years she contributed a monthly page on novels, plays, and questions of the day to *The Torch*, a paper for those beginning to make increasing use of the free libraries. She was also an active member of the Cambridge Labour Party and Trades Council.

Helen Cam had always greatly enjoyed historical novels, considering them a 'standing reminder that history is about human beings', and lectures on them resulted in the pamphlet *Historical Novels* (1961). Nothing roused her wrath more than the attempted whitewashing of certain historical characters, especially Richard III. Among her other recreations was watercolour sketching, in which she had considerable talent. She is described in her thirties, as 'of serious and matronly mien', and during vacations spent at Oxford (whither, to Keble Road, her parents retired in 1926) she was to be seen in the Bodleian, 'sitting squarely by a window' in one of the carrels in Duke Humfrey's Library:

> sharp eyes, sharp nose, heavy eyebrows—intent on her books, looking like a broody hen in a nesting box, placid and comfortable, but ready to peck if the occasion demanded. Some of her best articles must have been hatched there.

Helen Cam was a woman who by her learning, integrity, and warmth of personality contributed much to any group of which she was a member. Her importance as a historian was recognized by election to the British Academy in 1945, in which year she was the first woman to deliver the Raleigh lecture of the academy. She also received honorary doctorates at Smith College, Mount Holyoke College, the University of North Carolina, and, in 1962, Oxford; she became an honorary fellow of Somerville College in 1964. She was one of the first women to join the council of the Selden Society, of which she was vice-president in 1962–5. In 1958 she became a vice-president of the Royal Historical Society, and in 1963 honorary vice-president; she was also a corresponding fellow of the Medieval Academy of Arts and Sciences. Her work for the International Commission for the History of Representative and Parliamentary Institutions was commemorated by the *Album Helen Maud Cam* (1960), two volumes presented to her for her seventy-fifth birthday, containing essays by scholars of many nations, a bibliography of her works to 1957, and an appreciation by an American colleague, Professor Caroline Robbins. Her public as well as her historical services were recognized by her appointment as CBE in 1957. She died in hospital at Orpington, Kent, on 9 February 1968. KATHLEEN MAJOR, *rev.*

Sources *The Times* (12 Feb 1968) · Girton Cam., Cam MSS · C. R. Cheney, 'Helen Maud Cam, 1885–1968', *PBA*, 55 (1969), 293–310 · *Album Helen Maud Cam* (1960) · J. Sondheimer, *Girton Review* (1969) [centenary number] · G. Constable, *Harvard University Gazette* (Dec 1968) · personal knowledge (1981) · private information (1981) · *CGPLA Eng. & Wales* (1968)

Archives Girton Cam., corresp., lectures, papers, and research notes · Royal Holloway College, Egham, Surrey, corresp. and papers, incl. historical articles | SOUND BBC, 'Eating and drinking Greek' [1964]

Likenesses M. Osborne, pencil drawing, 1948, Girton Cam. · Ramsey & Muspratt, photograph, Girton Cam. [*see illus.*] · photograph, repro. in Cheney, 'Helen Maud Cam'

Wealth at death £19,579: probate, 12 June 1968, *CGPLA Eng. & Wales*

Cambell, Sir James (*c.*1570–1642), merchant, born in London, was the eldest son of Sir Thomas Cambell (*d.* 1614) and his wife, Alice Bright. The Cambell family, originally from Scotland, moved to London in the previous generation from Foulsham, Norfolk. Sir Thomas had a successful commercial and civic career in London, and was very active in the fifteen-year period at the end of his life: knighted in 1603, he served as alderman of Bridge Without, Bread Street, and Coleman Street between 1599 and 1614, as sheriff in 1600, and as lord mayor in 1609; he was also the master of the Ironmongers' Company in 1604 and 1613 and the second governor of the East India Company in 1602. We know little of James's early training, despite his father's prominence. After Sir Thomas died in February 1614, his eldest son was to emulate his career in almost every particular; but the positions James took in his public career were often at variance with his strict, if private, Calvinist observances.

In the Cambell family, the continued participation in or connection with the London élite was not limited to James but extended to many of Sir Thomas's ten children. Robert Cambell, the second son, served as sheriff in 1630, as master of the Ironmongers' Company in 1631, then for seven years as alderman of Farringdon Without and Bridge Without. Three of the six daughters married prominent merchants: Abigail married Anthony Abdy, who was sheriff and the long-time deputy governor of the Levant Company; Hester married Sir John Gore, who became lord mayor in 1624; and Mary married Sir Christopher Clitherow, whose career rivalled, or even excelled, those of her father and elder brother. The group was bound by ties of commercial interest, civic affairs, and family.

James Cambell concentrated early in his career on the northern European trades where his father had first made his mark; for instance, in 1567 he was trading goods primarily in Rouen, but also in Antwerp and Danzig. Information about his commercial transactions and principal areas of investment is scanty at best, but it is possible to infer his active interest in the trade to France and in exports of wool to northern Europe from the eminent positions he held in the companies which controlled these trades. He became governor of the French Company and of the Merchants of the Staple. His commercial vision was not limited to north-western Europe, however. His father's period of prominence in the East India Company just after 1600 first brought Cambell into contact with the charter members of that company. Probably beginning with the second joint stock in 1617, he made substantial investments, and easily surpassed the £2000 minimum requirement to serve on the committee of directors, which he did for fifteen years (1622–9, 1631–4, 1635–40). In addition, Cambell was a member of the Eastland Company, became one of the founding members of the Spanish Company in 1604, and five years later invested in the venture to colonize Virginia. Connections between the different companies could be especially important, as, for example, when he joined a group of Eastland merchants in 1633, including his brother-in-law Sir Christopher Clitherow, in purchasing pepper from the East India Company for sale in the Baltic. In his sizeable accumulation of wealth, Cambell probably benefited as much from a frugal household, for which he was well known, as from his commercial connections in the City or from adept commercial strategies.

After twenty-five years of largely commercial pursuits, Cambell entered civic politics. Initially, just after his father's death in 1614, he had declined to serve as sheriff, but five years later, at the age of fifty, he accepted when again elected. While serving in that capacity he was elected in 1620 to be alderman for Billingsgate ward. He then served for seventeen years as alderman for Lime Street ward, from May 1625 until his death early in 1642. For sixteen years, beginning in 1626, he was president of St Thomas's Hospital in Southwark. He served three terms, in 1615, 1623, and 1631, as master of the Ironmongers' Company, and in 1631 he became a colonel in the trained bands. His services to the ironmongers were commemorated in a portrait of Cambell the company commissioned in 1640 from Edward Cocke. It now hangs in the banqueting room of Ironmongers' Hall and shows Cambell as an aged man with a white beard and hair, wearing a grey cloak with a rich crimson under-vest, a gold chain, and a ruff.

The high point of Cambell's career was his election in 1629, at the age of fifty-nine, to be lord mayor. Thomas

Dekker wrote the inaugural pageant for a fee, paid by the ironmongers, of £180. The title *London's Tempe, or, The Field of Happiness*, according to Dekker, played on the mayor-elect's name of 'Campe-bell or *Le Beau Champe*, or fair and glorious field' (*Dramatic Works*, vol. 4). During his tenure of office Cambell worked most importantly to mitigate the effects of excessive early rains by distributing adequate supplies of food in the capital. Supplementary sales of grain during summer reduced the City's holdings to 1500 lasts. His service in this and other matters while lord mayor was recognized with a knighthood in May 1630.

After the death of his brother-in-law Sir John Gore in December 1636, Cambell succeeded him as senior alderman, or father of the City, and passed the last years of his civic life in that position. Strongly supportive of the royal government in matters of public policy, he participated in several *ad hoc* committees, including a notorious one designed to stem the prevalent criticism of 'popish soap' made by monopoly producers (among whom were several Catholics). He also participated in a committee which assessed the value of houses abutting St Paul's Cathedral; as part of the restoration of the cathedral initiated by Archbishop William Laud, they were to be demolished and their owners recompensed. In 1641, in the last year of his life, Cambell lent £500 to the government for putting down the Irish rising.

Cambell's most remarkable act was to be revealed in his will. After his death, in London on 5 January 1642, he was, like his father, buried in the parish church of St Olave Jewry. Having signed a marriage agreement with his Dutch wife, Rachel, he was not obliged by the custom of London to give her one-third of the estate, and he settled on her their principal residence in Throgmorton Street and £10,000. Having no children of his own, he gave the largest single bequest, £2500 and property in Glastonbury, Somerset, to Sir James Cambell, the son of his brother Robert. To other specified individuals he gave small to moderate gifts totalling £11,000. What was so unusual, however, was the magnitude of his other public and philanthropic bequests.

Some of these bequests exceeded the largesse that normally accompanied the mnemonic perpetuation of London's leading citizens. He bequeathed money, to begin with, for four dinners to be held in his honour at the Ironmongers' Company, at the French Company, by the governors of the London hospitals, and by the gentlemen of the artillery; he gave £100 so that his fellow parishioners could erect a monument in his honour in the church of St Olave Jewry; and he directed £200 to be disbursed to beggars at his funeral. His gifts also extended to assisting those who were financially vulnerable or otherwise subject to misfortune. Cambell bequeathed very considerable sums to London hospitals: £1500 to enlarge St Thomas's Hospital, and £1000 divided between Christ's, Bridewell, St Bartholomew's, and Bethlem. In addition to the usual bequests to the poor of the four parishes to which he had some connection, he gave moneys to establish funds for debtors and vagrants, specifically £1000 to release small debtors from prison and £2000 to Bridewell Hospital to help vagrants obtain employment. To help with ongoing efforts to purchase the freedom of Englishmen and -women who had been captured and enslaved by Algerians, Tunisians, and Tripolitans, Cambell contributed £1000, enough by contemporary estimates to secure the release of a hundred people. He directed other assistance amounting to £500 towards impoverished ministers, £667 to establish a free school in Barking, Essex, and a fund of £1300 towards assisting young members of the Ironmongers' Company with loans in the early part of their careers.

The will also reveals a continuation of Cambell's attempts to maintain an equilibrium between the public demands of civic affairs and the possible implications of his private beliefs. In his eulogy, Edward Browne, Cambell's secretary and a pamphleteer, called attention to the fervency of these beliefs. Together with his wife, Cambell steadfastly applied in his household the principles of the Calvinist writers William Perkins and Richard Greenham and a steady regimen of prayer. Following from a desire to help others with similar religious views, he bequeathed £100 to assist Dutch and French immigrants and £40 to a 'silenced minister' identified as 'Mr Smith'. At the same time his bequests reflect the public schemes of the government of the day, in particular the project initiated by Laud to restore St Paul's Cathedral, in which Cambell had not only assisted during his life but to which he bequeathed £1000, a great deal more than other leading figures of the City contributed. Attempts by parliament to have this money redesignated to the effort to put down the Irish rising were firmly rebuffed by the executors, Sir James Cambell and Sir Thomas Abdy.

A final provision established an extraordinary fund of £10,000 to be distributed by the executors towards the philanthropic causes of their choice. Browne petitioned the king for confirmation of this provision out of fear that Cambell and Abdy would find a clandestine means to circumvent it. His petition was to result in the intervention of Charles, who confirmed the terms of the will, although we know nothing of the subsequent distribution of this money. All told, Cambell bequeathed £48,967 6*s.* 8*d.*, excluding property, and approximately half of this sum went to charity. Nearly a century later, in his new edition of John Stow's *Survey of London*, John Strype included the significant provisions of the will as a singular example of philanthropic generosity.

SIDNEY LEE, *rev.* TREVOR DICKIE

Sources V. Pearl, *London and the outbreak of the puritan revolution: city government and national politics, 1625–1643* (1961) • R. Brenner, *Merchants and revolution: commercial change, political conflict, and London's overseas traders, 1550–1653* (1993) • J. Nicholl, *Some account of the Worshipful Company of Ironmongers* (1851) • J. Stow, *A survey of the cities of London and Westminster and the borough of Southwark*, ed. J. Strype, new edn, 2 vols. (1720) • E. Browne, *A rare paterne of justice and mercy* (1642) • *CSP dom.*, *1629–31; 1633–4; 1639* • T. K. Rabb, *Enterprise and empire: merchant and gentry investment in the expansion of England, 1575–1630* (1967) • A. B. Beaven, ed., *The aldermen of the City of London, temp. Henry III–[1912]*, 2 vols. (1908–13) • E. B. Sainsbury, ed., *A calendar of the court minutes … of the East India Company*, [1]: *1635–1639* (1907) • K. N. Chaudhuri, *The English East India Company: the study of an early English joint-stock company* (1965) • *The dramatic works of*

Thomas Dekker, ed. R. H. Shepherd, 4 (1873) · B. Dietz, ed., *The port and trade of early Elizabethan London: documents*, London RS, 8 (1972) · H. R. Trevor-Roper, *Archbishop Laud, 1573–1645* (1940) · H. Stevens, ed., *The dawn of British trade to the East Indies as recorded in the court minutes of the East India Company, 1599–1603* (1886) · will, PRO, PROB 11/188, sig. 1642

Likenesses E. Cocke, oils, *c.*1640, Ironmongers' Hall, London · G. Glover, line print, BM; repro. in E. Browne, *A rare paterne of justice and mercy* (1642), frontispiece

Wealth at death over £50,000—bequeathed £48,967 6*s.* 8*d.*; house in Throgmorton Street and property in Glastonbury, Somerset: Stow, *A survey of the cities*

Cambridge. For this title name *see* Richard, earl of Cambridge (1385–1415); Adolphus Frederick, Prince, first duke of Cambridge (1774–1850); George, Prince, second duke of Cambridge (1819–1904).

Cambridge [*married name* Cross]**, Ada** (**1844–1926**), novelist and poet, was born at Wiggenhall St Germans, Norfolk, on 21 November 1844, the second child and eldest daughter of Henry Cambridge (*b.* 1815), a gentleman farmer, and his wife, Thomasine (*b.* 1819/20), daughter of William Charles Emerson or Emmerson, a medical practitioner. Her early childhood (of which she provides a nostalgic reminiscence in *The Retrospect*, 1912) was spent at Thorpland and Downham Market in Norfolk, but about 1859 the family's straitened finances forced them to move first to Great Yarmouth, where Henry Cambridge became a commercial traveller, and shortly afterwards to Egremont Street in Ely, where Ada Cambridge resided until her marriage. She was patchily educated by a series of governesses, but she was a voracious reader and by the age of twenty-five she had published three religious novelettes and two collections of hymns.

On 25 April 1870 Cambridge married the Revd George Frederick Cross (1844–1917), the son of an Ely grocer and a recent graduate of St Augustine's College, Canterbury, where he had trained for the colonial ministry. The couple sailed for Australia on 28 May, and for the next forty years Cambridge accompanied her husband to a succession of parishes in Victoria: Wangaratta (1870–72), Yackandandah (1872–4), Ballan (1874–7), Coleraine (1877–83), Sandhurst (Bendigo; 1883–5); Beechworth (1885–93), and Williamstown (1893–1909). During the first decade of this unsettled, often harsh, existence (which is somewhat blandly chronicled in the autobiographical *Thirty Years in Australia*, 1903) she gave birth to five children: Arthur Stuart (1871–1876), Edith Constance (1873–1874), Vera Lyon (*b.* 1876), Hugh (1878–1902), and Kenneth Stuart (1880–1967). In order to help support this growing family, she resumed her writing career as early as 1871. Many of the longer works of fiction she produced with businesslike regularity from 1875 onwards were serialized in *The Australasian* and other magazines before being revised for book publication in Britain (and later the United States), and her sometimes formulaic romance narratives, enlivened by sharply observed and often contrasted sketches of contemporary British and Australian life, enjoyed steady sales. Of her eighteen novels which appeared in book form (others remained unrevised in periodicals), the best are probably *A Marked Man* (1890), *The Three Miss Kings* (1891), *Not All in Vain* (1892), *Fidelis* (1895), and the wittily subversive *Materfamilias* (1898), in all of which she sought to adapt romantic conventions to the exploration of such controversial issues as the decline of religious faith, the social position of women, and the politics of the family. Some of these questions also form the subject matter of her verse, and the poems collected in *Unspoken Thoughts* (1887) articulate uncompromisingly her loss of Christian belief and her reservations about the limiting conditions of marriage.

Following Cross's retirement from the active ministry in 1909, the couple returned to England in 1912 and settled in Cambridge. In 1917, however, after her husband's death, Ada Cambridge returned to Australia and lived in Melbourne at 8 Union Street, Malvern. Despite financial hardship and a series of strokes, she remained fiercely independent until her death from heart failure on 19 July 1926 at Seymour Road, Elsternwick, Melbourne. She was buried in Brighton cemetery in Melbourne.

Although Cambridge's writings enjoyed a high reputation among Australian reviewers in the last decades of the nineteenth century, her failure to comply with the ruggedly masculine ethos of the 'Bush nationalists' and their critical acolytes ensured posthumous neglect until her retrieval by feminist scholars in the 1970s. Her work is uneven in quality, but at its best her ironic, sceptical intelligence enables her to transcend her political conservatism and sometimes outrageous snobbery (when she learned, during the First World War, that a soldier was to be billeted on her, she stipulated firmly that he must be a 'gentleman') and to test the social, sexual, and intellectual boundaries of her surrounding culture.

ROBERT DINGLEY

Sources M. Bradstock and L. Wakeling, *Rattling the orthodoxies: a life of Ada Cambridge* (1991) · A. Tate, *Ada Cambridge: her life and work, 1844–1926* (1991) · A. Cambridge, *Thirty years in Australia* (1903) · A. Cambridge, *The retrospect* (1912) · P. Barton, 'Ada Cambridge: writing for her life', *A bright and fiery troop: Australian women writers of the nineteenth century*, ed. D. Adelaide (1988), 133–50 · E. Morrison, 'Editor's introduction', in A. Cambridge, *A woman's friendship* (1988), xiii–lvii · R. Beilby and C. Hadgraft, *Ada Cambridge, Tasma, and Rosa Praed* (1979)

Archives University of Queensland, Fryer Library, Cross family MSS | Mitchell L., NSW, Angus and Robertson MSS · State Library of Victoria, Melbourne, La Trobe manuscript collection

Likenesses photograph, *c.*1880, State Library of Victoria, Melbourne, Australia; repro. in Barton, 'Ada Cambridge' · photograph, *c.*1886, University of Queensland, Fryer Library, Cross family MSS; repro. in Tate, *Ada Cambridge* · photograph, *c.*1888, University of Queensland, Fryer Library, Cross family MSS; repro. in Tate, *Ada Cambridge* · photograph, *c.*1920, University of Queensland, Fryer Library, Cross family MSS; repro. in Tate, *Ada Cambridge*

Cambridge, Alexander Augustus Frederick William Alfred George, earl of Athlone [*formerly* Prince Alexander of Teck] (**1874–1957**), army officer and governor-general of South Africa, was born at Kensington Palace on 14 April 1874, the third son of Princess *Mary Adelaide

Wilhelmina Elizabeth (1833–1897) and Francis, duke of Teck (1837–1900), and brother of the future Queen *Mary. Originally styled his serene highness, Prince Alexander of Teck, he was known to his family as Alge. In 1917, in accordance with policy, he relinquished his titles and the name of Teck, and took the family name of Cambridge and the title of earl of Athlone.

Prince Alexander was educated at Eton College and Sandhurst, was commissioned second lieutenant in the 7th hussars in 1894, joined his regiment in India, and thereafter received his promotion in the normal way. He served in the Matabele (Ndebele) campaign of 1896–7 and was mentioned in dispatches. He transferred to the Inniskilling dragoons in order to be able to serve in the Second South African War, during which he was mentioned again in dispatches and appointed to the DSO. He was spoken of as a capable and enterprising officer and a cheerful comrade, ever willing to endure and to share with his troops the discomforts of a nomad campaign.

On 10 February 1904 Prince Alexander married Princess *Alice Mary Victoria Augusta Pauline (1883–1981), daughter of Queen Victoria's fourth son, Prince *Leopold, duke of Albany. On this occasion he was appointed GCVO. Their first child, May Helen Emma, was born in 1906; in the following year they had a son, Rupert Alexander George Augustus, later Viscount Trematon, who died as the result of a motor accident in 1928. A second son, Maurice Francis George, died in 1910 before he was six months old.

The prince joined the Royal Horse Guards in 1904. In 1911, at the request of George V, he transferred to the 2nd Life Guards with the rank of major. At the coronation he was appointed GCB. In 1914 he was nominated governor-general of Canada but did not take up the appointment owing to the outbreak of war, in which he served as a lieutenant-colonel in the Life Guards. Later he joined the staff as general staff officer grade 2 and was attached to the British military mission to the Belgian army. He was promoted general staff officer 1 with the rank of brigadier-general in 1915 and received Belgian, French, and Russian decorations. He was twice mentioned in dispatches and in 1918 he joined the general headquarters staff.

After the war Athlone (as he had become) retired from the army, and took an active interest in national and social work. A man of compassion, he was especially attracted to the work of institutions connected with the relief of human suffering. He had been chairman of the Middlesex Hospital since 1910, and in 1921 the minister of health appointed him chairman of a committee composed of the foremost doctors and surgeons of the day to investigate the needs of medical practitioners. Under his enthusiastic guidance the Athlone committee produced a comprehensive report which recommended the appropriation of substantial sums from public funds to finance the establishment of a postgraduate medical school (to be associated with the University of London and existing medical institutions) to promote postgraduate instruction and medical research. The work thus initiated by the Athlone committee was carried on by committees presided over by Neville Chamberlain and Arthur Greenwood. The Postgraduate School, subsequently attached to the Hammersmith Hospital, became one of the most famous institutions of its kind. Athlone took a special interest and pride in the school, which he visited frequently in later years.

Athlone was closely identified also with the promotion of education. He was chancellor of the University of London (1932–55), taking office at a difficult time in the development of the university under its new statutes. He was an honorary bencher of the Middle Temple, a fellow of the Royal Society, vice-president of the Royal Academy of Music, an honorary fellow of the Royal College of Surgeons, and a knight grand cross of the order of St John of Jerusalem.

In 1923 Athlone was appointed governor-general of the Union of South Africa, and high commissioner, being appointed GCMG and promoted to the rank of major-general. He arrived in South Africa in time to open parliament in January 1924. Shortly afterwards J. B. M. Hertzog succeeded J. C. Smuts as prime minister. A difficult period followed. Racial antagonism between the British and the Afrikaners was inflamed by a Nationalist proposal to adopt a new flag for the union, omitting anything symbolic of the British connection. Athlone worked quietly behind the scenes to secure the inclusion of the union flag in the white central panel. His speech at the unveiling of this compromise flag in Cape Town did much to soothe and reconcile animosities. His frequent tours in the provinces enhanced his prestige and popularity and did much to bring the two white communities closer together. His patience, courtesy, and tact won the trust and esteem of the political leaders of all parties. He was appointed KG in 1928 in recognition of his services and his term of office was extended at the request of the government.

At the conclusion of his very successful term of office, Athlone was sworn of the privy council in 1931 and appointed governor and constable of Windsor Castle. He and Princess Alice took up residence at Brantridge Park and afterwards transferred to Kensington Palace, which they decorated with trophies of their big-game hunting expeditions and paintings of African landscapes by local artists whom they had patronized and encouraged during their tour of duty. They continued their interest in South African affairs and personalities and resumed their social activities in England. Queen Mary and her brother had always been close companions and regular correspondents. After George V recovered from his serious illness he expressed the wish that Lord Athlone should, for family reasons, remain in England.

In 1940 George VI showed his uncle a telegram from W. L. Mackenzie King, asking if he might submit Athlone's name for the governor-generalship of Canada. Greatly as he appreciated the compliment, Athlone thought a younger man should be appointed, but the king persuaded him to accept for a period of two years. In the event he served the full term of five years. He entered upon his new duties with his usual enthusiasm and took a keen interest in efforts to establish in the dominion various military training schemes and factories for the production of war materials. He travelled extensively at all seasons of the year to attend troop reviews and encourage munition workers. In addition he and Princess Alice were always ready to entertain members of official missions, including those of President Roosevelt and Winston Churchill, and they offered open hospitality to royalty and other distinguished exiles from allied countries under German occupation. Although Athlone had occasional differences with Mackenzie King, he had a natural gift for getting on with people and their personal relations always remained very friendly. Athlone's unsuccessful efforts to reconcile differences between the prime minister and his defence minister, J. L. Ralston, were a disappointment to him.

Those who knew Athlone intimately and worked with him would agree that kindness was his outstanding characteristic. Yet, like many kind people, he had a quick temper which subsided as rapidly as it flared up. His military training had endowed him with an eye for detail and a keen perception of the manners and peculiarities of others upon which he liked to exercise his quizzical sense of humour. He gave the impression that he modelled his conduct on the precepts of Polonius—especially those relating to manners and deportment. His dress was meticulous but never 'expressed in fancy'. He had an exact sense of symmetry and tidiness and would often adjust ornaments and pictures. His memory for names and faces was quite extraordinary and he was a good judge of character. In public affairs he was tolerant and strove to induce others to modify fixed or extreme opinions before giving expression to his own. His natural tact and intellectual modesty enabled him to impress his counsel upon ministers without provoking opposition or appearing to intrude upon their constitutional prerogatives. His command over the loyalty and affection of his staff was exceptional, and he delighted in renewing friendships with them in later years. At the conclusion of his term of office in Canada in 1946 he and Princess Alice made time to stay in Trinidad with their former secretary in South Africa. On his return to England Athlone resumed his interest in national affairs. In 1936 he had been appointed grand master of the Order of St Michael and St George, an order associated especially with the dominions, colonial, and foreign services. In that office he presided over the last tributes paid to many of Britain's most distinguished sons. On his death at Kensington Palace, on 16 January 1957, he received in his turn the homage of members of the order who, like himself, had faithfully and diligently served their country. The peerage became extinct.

BEDE CLIFFORD, *rev.*

Sources Princess Alice, countess of Athlone, *For my grandchildren* (1966) · personal knowledge (1971) · private information (1971) · J. Pope-Hennessy, *Queen Mary* (1959) · K. Rose, *King George V* (1983)
Archives IWM, papers relating to British military mission with Belgian army | Bodl. RH, letters to Sir Edward Garraway · NL Scot., letters to H. P. Macmillan | FILM BFI NFTVA, news footage

Likenesses L. Tuxen, group portrait, oils, 1893 (*Marriage of King George V and Queen Mary*), Royal Collection · L. Tuxen, group portrait, oils, 1896 (*Marriage of Princess Maud and Prince Charles of Denmark*), Royal Collection · A. Broom, two photographs, *c.*1911–1912, NPG · A. Broom, group portrait, photograph, *c.*1914, NPG · W. Stoneman, three photographs, 1919–46, NPG · F. O. Salisbury, group portrait, oils, 1922 (wedding group of Princess Mary), Harewood House, West Yorkshire · F. O. Salisbury, group portrait, oils, 1922 (wedding group of Princess Mary), Royal Collection · F. Hodge, oils, 1937, Middlesex Hospital, London, Athlone House · A. John, oils, 1941, U. Lond. · H. Carr, portrait, 1948, Government House, Ottawa, Canada · J. Gunn, oils, 1955, Vintners' Hall, London · H. de T. Glazebrook, portrait, Kensington Palace, London · N. Hepple, portrait, Kensington Palace, London · Spy [L. Ward], lithograph cartoon, NPG; repro. in *VF* (9 Dec 1908) · photographs, Royal Collection

Wealth at death £36,005 9*s.* 7*d.*: probate, 5 April 1957, *CGPLA Eng. & Wales*

Cambridge, Alice (1762–1829), preacher, was born on 1 January 1762 in Bandon, co. Cork, the daughter of a Church of Ireland father and a Presbyterian mother (*d.* 1780). According to a fragment of autobiography, her father was a convivial man, whose love of company 'led him from his God, and kept him from making his own home and family as comfortable as they should be'. Her mother, on the other hand, was 'of a meek and quiet spirit and … of a very sweet and peaceable demeanour' (*Memoir*, 3). She was educated locally, but left school early despite a 'wish to learn, and … a degree of capacity' (ibid., 5). She was brought up in the Church of Ireland, but, following the death of her mother in 1780, began to attend meetings at the Methodist preaching-house in Bandon, and shortly afterwards joined the society. Resolving to dedicate herself to the pursuit of holiness and to the promotion of Methodism, she broke off her engagement to a young man, 'having no other fault to find … but that his mind did not bend heavenward; that indeed was enough' (ibid., 24).

Having begun her missionary career privately among friends and neighbours, Cambridge went on to speak at Methodist meetings in Bandon, Kinsale, Youghal, and other towns in Munster. Her eloquence, coupled with the novelty of female preaching, made a powerful impact on her hearers and attracted many new converts. Nevertheless, there were some within the movement who opposed her right to speak in public, declaring female preaching to be contrary to Christian teaching and practice. In response to such objections, Cambridge appealed to John Wesley, who counselled discretion and against any 'appearance of pride or magnifying yourself', but defended her right to preach: conscience, he wrote, 'will not permit you to be silent when God commands you to speak' (*Memoir*, 39). Following Wesley's death, however, and as Methodism became increasingly institutionalized, hostility to women preachers intensified. In 1802 the Methodist conference outlawed female preaching, and Cambridge herself was excluded from the society. She continued to preach, but resisted suggestions that she establish a breakaway organization. As she told a correspondent in 1814, 'I love Wesleyan Methodists, and Methodism' (*Memoir*, 55), and she regretted the disputes which resulted in a number of splits within the movement. In 1811 she herself was readmitted to the society by a special resolution of the Methodist conference.

About 1800 Cambridge moved to Dublin, where she worked for some years as a shop assistant before setting up business in Cork in 1809. During these years she held frequent public meetings, and from 1813 devoted herself entirely to preaching. In 1813–14 she visited Longford, co. Westmeath, Roscommon, and King's county; in 1815 she spoke in Cork, the west, and the midlands, and later that year made the first of several visits to Ulster. This was the area in which she was to enjoy her greatest success: describing her experience there in 1816, she reported that 'in Lurgan, I had to go to a field, where it was judged that eight or ten thousand were assembled to hear … Yesterday, and on one day in the preceding week, I had to speak in the open air also: I think I may say with truth, that at each time, thousands assembled, and God was with us' (*Memoir*, 60–61).

Cambridge spent most of the years 1818–20 in the north and west of Ireland and in Dublin. Despite a serious illness in 1820, she continued to tour and to preach, but a relapse forced her to curtail her activities. In 1823 she paid a final visit to Bandon and spoke in Kinsale and Nenagh. In the following year she visited Dublin for the last time, before retiring to Nenagh, where she spent her final years, holding regular meetings in her house and addressing the local congregation on alternate Sundays. Following a further attack of illness in 1827, her physical and mental health deteriorated sharply. She died in Nenagh on her sixty-seventh birthday, 1 January 1829, and was buried in the graveyard there. ROSEMARY RAUGHTER

Sources *Memoir of Miss A. Cambridge*, ed. J. J. McGregor (1832) · C. H. Crookshank, *Memorable women of Irish Methodism in the last century* (1882) · C. H. Crookshank, *History of Methodism in Ireland*, 1–2 (1885–6) · D. Hempton and M. Hill, 'Women and protestant minorities in 18th-century Ireland', *Women in early modern Ireland*, ed. M. MacCurtain and M. O'Dowd (1991), 197–211 · D. Hempton and M. Hill, *Evangelical protestantism in Ulster society, 1740–1890* (1992)
Likenesses engraving, repro. in *Memoir*, ed. McGregor

Cambridge [Cantebrig], **Sir John** (*d.* **1335**), justice, was the son of William Combe of Cambridge and Matilda, daughter of Robert Whitesmith also of Cambridge. First mentioned as the recipient of land jointly with his mother in July 1293, he began to acquire land in his own right from 1296. He was MP for Cambridgeshire in 1320 and regularly thereafter until 1327. He is first named as a serjeant in Michaelmas 1309, and was king's serjeant, 1328–9. He was a justice on eyre for Northamptonshire and Bedfordshire, 1329–30, and on 22 October 1330 was made a knight *tanquam banerettus*, with a grant for his robes of investiture out of the king's wardrobe. On 18 January 1331 he was made a justice of the common pleas, along with Robert Malberthorpe and John Inge, and received a new patent on 30 January 1334. He was one of the justices commissioned for the abortive Kent eyre of 1333–4. No fines were levied before him after Michaelmas term 1334.

John Cambridge married Joan, daughter and heir of John Dunning and Agnes Gogging and widow of Henry *piscator*, who brought him substantial land in Cambridge. In 1314/15 he was assessed as one of the wealthiest inhabitants of Cambridge, and in 1311 was alderman of St Mary's Guild. He died in 1335 and was buried in St Mary by the Market, Cambridge. He willed his capital messuage, the Stone Hall in St Michael's parish, to St Mary's Guild. It was subsequently transferred to Corpus Christi College, which acquired the rest of his lands from his son Thomas after the latter's death in 1361.

J. A. HAMILTON, *rev.* ROSEMARY HORROX

Sources Baker, *Serjeants* · M. Bateson, ed., *Cambridge gild records*, Cambridge Antiquarian RS, 39 (1903) · *Return of the name of every member of the lower house, 1213–1874*, 2 vols. (1878) · cartulary of John de Cantebrig, CCC Cam. · D. Crook, *Records of the general eyre*, Public Record Office Handbooks, 20 (1982) · *CIPM*, 7, no. 650
Archives CCC Cam.

Cambridge, Richard Owen (1717–1802), poet and essayist, was born in London on 14 February 1717, the son of Nathaniel Cambridge (*bap.* 1685) and Meriel Owen (*bap.* 1689), originally from Presteigne, Radnorshire. Nathaniel Cambridge came from a Gloucestershire family: being a younger son, he was bred to business as a London merchant trading with Turkey, but retired to Whitminster, near the River Severn, south of Gloucester, before his death in late 1725 or January 1726. His widow remarried, whereupon her brother, a rich, retired lawyer named Richard Owen, became largely responsible for her son's upbringing.

At some date between 1728 and 1732 Richard Cambridge entered Eton College, where he 'distinguished himself rather by facility than application' (*DNB*). He was admitted to Lincoln's Inn on 10 April 1734 and shortly afterwards entered St John's College, Oxford, as a gentleman commoner, matriculating on 22 May 1735. He took no degree, but he contributed a faintly Spenserian pastiche to an Oxford collection of congratulatory poems on the marriage of Frederick, prince of Wales (1736).

On 18 June 1740 Cambridge married Mary (1716/17–1806), daughter of George and Mary Trenchard of Woolveton, Dorset, and granddaughter of Sir John Trenchard, one-time secretary of state to William III; over the next sixteen years three boys and three girls were born. The young couple lived first at Whitminster, where, among other country pursuits, Cambridge speared fish with arrows, improved the landscape, made a grotto, canalized a stretch of the River Frome, and designed boats, including a catamaran (one of the earliest on English waters). Archery, grotto, and catamaran all appear in his Spenserian parody *Archimage* (published posthumously). On the death of his uncle in January 1748 Cambridge inherited a large fortune and adopted the name of Owen in addition to his own surname. For two years the Cambridges divided their time between Whitminster and London, but in 1751 they settled in Twickenham and bought a fine villa beside the Thames, near Richmond Bridge.

Cambridge's *The Scribleriad: an Heroic Poem in Six Books*, mostly written at Whitminster, was published in six parts between January and April 1751; a preface, notes, and index were added to the second edition (1752, actually

Richard Owen Cambridge (**1717–1802**), by Charles Bestland, pubd 1803 (after Ozias Humphry)

December 1751). This work was conceived as a sequel to the Pope–Arbuthnot *Memoirs of Martinus Scriblerus*, ridiculing pedants, antiquaries, scientists, and travellers. Its references to aerial combat, submarines, and electricity have caught the attention of a few modern readers, but an unremitting bookishness blunts its satiric point. Cambridge wrote other parodies and light occasional verse, much of it in octosyllabic couplets, but, apart from six poems printed between 1752 and 1758, separately and/or in Dodsley's *Collection of Poems*, volume 6, all these pieces remained unpublished during his lifetime.

Between 1753 and 1756 Cambridge wrote twenty-one genial rambling essays in Edward Moore's weekly periodical *The World*, doing so as an act of charity to Moore, who depended on this journal for the support of his family. When *The World* ended Cambridge dabbled in contemporary history, but his *Account of the War in India between the English and French on the Coast of Coromandel from the Year 1750 to the Year 1760* (1761) is a mere compilation. After this, he lived for more than forty years and published only three short pieces in journals.

At Twickenham Cambridge played host to a wide circle of friends and acquaintances, including actors, admirals, aristocrats, artists, and many literary figures. In Boswell's *Life of Johnson*, for instance, there is a vivid account on 18 April 1775 of a select dinner party of Johnson, Gibbon, Reynolds, Boswell, and James (Hermes) Harris at Cambridge's Twickenham villa. The host's observation of Boswell's methods prompted him later to commission the well-known satirical engraving of Johnson's ghost admonishing Boswell for '[dealing] in Remnants of Remnants,/Like a Maker of Pincushions', first published in Cambridge's *Works* (1803). Cambridge is very frequently mentioned in the letters of his former schoolfellow Horace Walpole. By all accounts he was good-natured and well-liked, though his friends laughed at his dedication to the collection and dissemination of news and gossip, a practice that led Gibbon to call him 'the Cambridge Mail'.

Writing of himself aged thirty-two, Cambridge refers to:

> My body light, my figure slim,
> My mind dispos'd to mirth and whim.
> (*Works*, 66)

A half-length portrait by Ozias Humphry shows Cambridge aged about sixty, still fairly slim, with refined features, a long Roman nose, and faintly sardonic expression (*Works*, frontispiece). Cambridge died of old age on 17 September 1802 and was buried six days later at Twickenham. His widow died on 5 September 1806 and was buried beside him. His *Works*, edited by his youngest son, George Owen Cambridge (1756–1841), published in 1803, included over forty hitherto unpublished poems and a memoir; more unpublished poems remain among his many manuscripts in the British Library. JAMES SAMBROOK

Sources R. D. Altick, *Richard Owen Cambridge: belated Augustan* (1941) • *Works of Richard Owen Cambridge, with an account of his life*, ed. G. D. Cambridge (1803) • Walpole, *Corr.*, vols. 11–12, 15, 28–9, 32–4, 35, 42 • *The journals and letters of Fanny Burney (Madame D'Arblay)*, ed. J. Hemlow and others, 12 vols. (1972–84), vols. 1–4 • Boswell, *Life* • *IGI* • Foster, *Alum. Oxon.* • W. P. Baildon, ed., *The records of the Honorable Society of Lincoln's Inn: admissions*, 1 (1896) • R. A. Austen-Leigh, ed., *Eton College lists, 1678–1790* (1907) • Burke, *Gen. GB* (1852) • H. D. Weinbrot, 'Johnson's *Dictionary* and *The World*: the papers of Lord Chesterfield and Richard Owen Cambridge', *Philological Quarterly*, 50 (1971), 663–9 • M. R. Brownell, '*Dr Johnson's ghost*: genesis of a satirical engraving', *Huntington Library Quarterly*, 50 (1987), 339–57 • F. C. Hodgson, 'Richard Owen Cambridge', *Thames-side in the past* (1913) • A. Dobson, 'Cambridge the everything', *Eighteenth century vignettes: third series* (1896), 179–205 • R. S. Cobbett, *Memorials of Twickenham* (1872)

Archives BL, corresp., Add. MSS 4302, 22976, 29173, 29176, 29192, 33090, 35633, 35639, 35643, 37726, 37728 • BL, corresp., Egerton MS 3698 | Beds. & Luton ARS, letters to Marchioness Grey and Countess de Grey, L 30/9–11 • BL, letters to Lord Hardwicke and others, Add. MSS 35606–35623 • Bodl. Oxf., corresp. with Thomas Edwards

Likenesses engraving, 1781 (after O. Humphry), Bodl. Oxf. • E. Finden, stipple, pubd 1835 (after O. Humphry), BM • C. Bestland, stipple (after O. Humphry), BM, NPG; repro. in *Works*, frontispiece [*see illus.*]

Wealth at death estates in Gloucestershire, Radnor, London, and Twickenham; plate, jewels, and valuable pictures; £410 p.a. of annuities: will, 17 April 1797

Camden. For this title name *see* Pratt, Charles, first Earl Camden (1714–1794); Pratt, John Jeffreys, first Marquess Camden (1759–1840).

Camden, William (**1551–1623**), historian and herald, was born on 2 May 1551 at the Old Bailey, London, the son of Sampson Camden and his wife, Elizabeth Curwen. Sampson, originally from Lichfield, had settled in London as a painter–stainer, a profession which made a lasting

William Camden (1551–1623), by unknown artist, 1622–3

impression on his son and which William later commemorated through a gift of plate made to the company in his father's name. His maternal grandfather, Giles Curwen of Poulton Hall, Lancashire, came from the Curwen family in Workington, Cumberland, according to Camden himself, descended anciently from the earls of Northumberland and reputedly connected to Katherine Parr. Camden was very much the denizen of London and its Reformation institutions. He attended Christ's Hospital, a school for orphaned and poor children established by Edward VI in 1552 under the Chantries Act. This was a large school occupying the massive structure of the Greyfriars and in which nearly 400 children were educated. How long he attended is not known, but in 1563 Camden was afflicted with plague and removed to Islington, after which he attended St Paul's School, where the humanist agenda for educational reform of the founder, John Colet, remained strong under the leadership of Alexander Nowell, dean of St Paul's, and John Cooke, the school's headmaster. While at St Paul's Camden seems to have developed a taste for antiquities, and no doubt he also made contacts in the literary and political world that would shape his future.

Years at Oxford After several years at St Paul's School, heavily influenced by close associates of Sir William Cecil, Camden began a long, complex, often troubled relationship with the University of Oxford, one that continued until the end of his life, when he established the Camden professorship in history. He went to Oxford in 1566, when the earl of Leicester was celebrating his appointment as chancellor with a grand reception for Elizabeth. It was a time of intense religious controversy in which the university authorities often supported extreme puritan positions. At Oxford he benefited from the community of like-minded scholars and a university in which new areas of study, including geography and science, flourished alongside traditions of dramatic and musical performance. But he was also the victim of the religious power struggles within the university. According to Wood the impecunious Camden entered Magdalen College as a chorister, reflecting his lifelong passion for music. His mentor was Dr Thomas Cooper, an outspoken opponent of Leicester and of the radical puritans whom the earl supported. When Camden failed to get a fellowship, the first of many disappointments in the university, he entered Broadgates Hall and the household of Dr Thornton, where by Wood's account he remained for three years; from there he followed his patron to Christ Church, which had become a centre for new areas of study. In Dr Thornton's household Camden began his acquaintance with Philip Sidney and others with antiquarian interests, like George and Richard Carew. In his *Britannia* Camden speaks with affection and gratitude for Sidney's encouragement of him and his work. The serious thinking about the relations between poetry, myth, and history that pervades Sidney's *Defense of Poesie*, Camden's *Britannia*, and Edmund Spenser's *The Faerie Queene*, must have begun for Camden during these years at Oxford, if it had not already begun at St Paul's.

Rich as the intellectual experience at Oxford seems to have been, and attached to the university as Camden became, his record there was chequered, his ambitions thwarted, and his achievements overlooked. In 1569 he again met disappointment when political and religious controversy led to his being passed over for a fellowship at All Souls College for 'defending the Religion established', as he says in a letter to James Ussher in 1618 (*Epistolae*, no. 195). A religious conservative comfortable with the settlement devised by Elizabeth and Burghley, Camden seems to have been caught in the powerful puritan and Roman Catholic rivalries that developed during these years. In 1570 he petitioned for his bachelor's degree, having 'spent four years in study of logic' (Wood, *Ath. Oxon.*, 2.340); apparently unsuccessful he left the university in 1571, no degree in hand. Having the degree from Oxford was important for a man of Camden's station and he again petitioned for it in 1574, this time successfully, although Wood states that he 'did not compleat it by determination in School-street' (ibid.). He displayed his academic ambitions again in 1588, when after the success of the *Britannia* he petitioned for the MA degree. Wood relates that on the basis of having spent the equivalent of sixteen years 'from the time he had taken the degree of bachelor, in the study of philosophy and other liberal arts' Camden asked that the degree be conferred and the requirement that he deliver 'three solemn lectures' be waived (ibid., 2.341). The degree was approved conditionally, on the understanding that he would stand at the next convocation, which he apparently did not do. In 1613, when Camden was in Oxford for the funeral of Thomas Bodley, the university convocation eventually did offer him his MA degree, and he dismissed it as 'being then too late to gain any benefit or honour thereby' (ibid., 2.343). Camden's determination over so many years to obtain due recognition from Oxford authorities and his establishment of a professorship in his own name suggest his strong interest in the academic life and also his involvement in and vulnerability to the controversies of the time. Camden was attracted to and found success in institutional contexts, but he never managed to secure his desired place in Oxford, and came to see academic life as beset with controversy.

Westminster School At twenty Camden left Oxford with no known financial resources, patron, or position. For four years the record is silent on how this young man with no publications and no degree occupied himself. Unsubstantiated tradition has him travelling Britain, perhaps under the patronage of Gabriel Goodman, dean of Westminster, in search of antiquities and topographical and historical material that found its way into the *Britannia*. The economic and social realities of his time were such as to make Camden in large measure the product of cultural institutions, and his disappearance during these years between known institutional affiliations is in itself interesting.

Camden's appointment in 1575 as second master at Westminster School returns him to the public landscape. He spent twenty-two years at the school that was emerging as academically one of the most prestigious in the kingdom, taking the place once held by St Paul's. He contributed significantly to its distinction, first as second master for eighteen years, with a yearly salary of £10, and then as headmaster from 1593 to 1597, with a salary of £20. During this time of stability not only was he an effective educator and administrator, but he also travelled, collected material for and wrote the *Britannia*, brought it through its first four enlarged editions, and compiled a Greek grammar.

Camden's move to Westminster from Christ Church, Oxford, is not itself surprising; the institutions had formal links that enabled several Westminster students to go each year to Christ Church. He joined a school and a chapter that had close ties with the intellectual community of St Paul's, and that were deeply imbued with the political, scholarly, and religious vision of William Cecil, now Lord Burghley. Dean Goodman had been a prebendary at St Paul's, served as Burghley's chaplain, and maintained a close friendship with him, finally acting as his executor. Camden was second master to headmaster Edward Grant, a long-time friend and associate of Burghley's and colleague and apologist for Roger Ascham, whose *Scholemaster* imagines a humanist 'academy' presided over by Burghley. In 1576 Grant published Ascham's letters, and in this volume Camden made his literary début, publishing an encomiastic elegy, 'In doctissimi viri Rogeri Aschami laudem sylva'. The chapter at Westminster was something like the academy envisioned by Ascham: John Stow describes it as organized around the dean and twelve prebendaries, and likens it to a school of theology. William Cecil was appointed steward of Westminster at this time, and presided over the chapter and the school. Although by statute the school was independent of the ecclesiastical body, they shared precious space and buildings in the congested abbey close, and many personnel served both institutions, with prebendaries sometimes assisting with instruction in the school. Camden's position as second master thus brought with it the advantage of involvement in a close, homogeneous community of scholars and political and religious thinkers and officers. Quite aside from his work at the school this group and its steward exerted an enormous influence on Camden's intellectual and personal development, as is apparent in his major publications, most of which were initially inspired by or dedicated to Lord Burghley.

Westminster School's prominence during the later Elizabethan decades was part of an important socio-economic shift from London to Westminster. The old school had been newly re-established by Burghley; the centrality of Greek to its curriculum was affirmed at a time when the language was disappearing from its rival institutions; it too had deeply rooted musical and dramatic traditions that went back to its early headmasters and instructors. Its unique curriculum combined classical Greek and Latin models complemented by instruction in grammar and rhetoric that drew heavily on material from the catechism and liturgy of the Church of England to form an Elizabethan humanism different from its Henrician predecessor. Lessons in the classroom found their social applications for the students in the practice of state and church in the adjoining buildings of the abbey, parliament, and Westminster Palace. For the twenty-two years that he taught there Camden disseminated a secular education that served the broad objectives of the religious settlement of 1559. Judging from this and from the respect that he commanded among men such as Ben Jonson (who had been his pupil) and John Donne, his particular form of protestant pedagogy appealed to individuals who felt the need to reconcile their Roman Catholicism with the reformed religion of England. Indeed the several encomia that Ben Jonson addressed to William Camden, particularly epigram 14, convey the affection and respect that he inspired, along with his undogmatic learning and a Christian humanism which seems to have provided an intellectual common ground for his students.

Starting the *Britannia* The stability of his life at Westminster enabled Camden to do the research and travel necessary for writing the *Britannia*, and to establish a name for himself early in his time there, before he had published anything besides some encomiastic poetry. In 1576 he inherited his father's property in Staffordshire which provided him with additional financial security. As early as 1577 he came to the attention of the great geographer Abraham Ortelius, then travelling in England, who encouraged Camden in his national enterprise, and whose work provided him with a model for topographical and historical writing. Further encouraged and supported by Dean Gabriel Goodman and his nephew Godfrey Goodman, Camden travelled extensively in pursuit of topographical and antiquarian information: in 1578 through

Suffolk and Norfolk, and in 1582 to Yorkshire and Lancashire. Working with a knowledge of the current continental methods and the example and friendship of English scholars such as Alexander Nowell, William Lambarde, his schoolmate Richard Carew, and others, he developed his own approach to empirical research into topographical and historical study through travel, archival scholarship, and the use of original documents, along with the deployment of linguistic and philological evidence and artefacts for interpreting historical and cultural events.

As his work advanced Camden's reputation spread, well before the eventual publication of the *Britannia* in 1586. Scholars from across Europe, both protestant and Roman Catholic, included a meeting with Camden on their itinerary when they came to England. Geographers such as Gerardus Mercator, lawyers such as Alberico Gentili, scholars and poets such as the Hungarian Parmenius, and statesmen such as Barnabé Brisson, president of the *parlement* of Paris, sought Camden's company, advice, or views. His work for the *Britannia*, then, was conducted in the field, through study and collaboration, and through research into original sources, both printed and manuscript.

Publication of the *Britannia* Much anticipated, the *Britannia* made its début on 2 May 1586, Camden's thirty-fifth birthday; the squat octavo volume was dedicated to Lord Burghley. Of Camden's published work the *Britannia* has had the greatest and most lasting impact. It received immediate recognition when it appeared, and its successive, enlarged editions of 1587, 1590, 1594, 1600 (dedicated to Queen Elizabeth) and 1607 (dedicated to King James) and its English translation of 1610 by Philemon Holland attest to its popularity. A contemporary translation by Richard Knolles, once in Camden's possession, survives in manuscript in the Bodleian Library as MS Ashmole 849. It was also published in Frankfurt in 1590 and 1610. Throughout the decades after its first appearance Camden continued to revise the text and experiment with the work's format and apparatus, and he worked closely with Holland on the 1610 translation. In spite of the author's collaboration, however, the translation is often inaccurate and takes liberties with the material, and for this reason is regarded as inferior to Edmund Gibson's translation of 1695. By 1607, the year of its last Latin edition in Camden's lifetime, published in folio and containing an index, maps by Saxton and Norden, and engravings of coins, monuments, and topographical sites, it had evolved into an impressive and editorially sophisticated work of scholarship. It continued to be edited and translated during the eighteenth and early nineteenth centuries, the major editions being those of Gibson in 1695 and 1722, and Richard Gough in 1786 and 1806.

The *Britannia* had an enormous and lasting impact on multidisciplinary historical writing, and was also of the highest importance as a cultural icon affecting the national self-image. Like most works of exceptional originality and influence the *Britannia* is not the unique or unheralded achievement that some have professed it to be. Rather it culminates, consolidates, and transforms much of the newest work in different historical genres, and draws on traditions that made its achievement both recognizable and strikingly new.

Not a history, the *Britannia* attempts (in the words of Gibson's translation of Camden's preface) 'to restore Britain to Antiquity, and Antiquity to Britain'—the charge that Camden says was given to him by the 'great Restorer of old Geography', Ortelius himself. It does so by attempting to document the ancient pre-Roman British past using every kind of primary historical evidence imaginable, whether written records, inscriptions, literary remains, material both historical and mythological, or testimony drawn from the physical landscape. In his use of non-literary evidence Camden was a leading figure in his generation, and his work in numismatics and his recognition of the existence of coinage in pre-Roman Britain has been described as 'of pioneering importance' (Piggott, 204). Recognizing the imperfection of the written record, particularly the scarcity of genuine British material, Camden looks to multiple kinds of evidence to push the record as far back as possible and to trace continuities through the different periods of British history. Histories of the different peoples who settled Britain supplement the chorographical description of the country. In the process of tracing Britain's cultural diversity, Camden was also a major force in discrediting the Brutus myth that had long dominated perceptions of British origins.

This emphasis on primary materials and philological information marks Camden's divergence from the rhetorical historical writing characteristic of the middle ages and early Renaissance, as does the extensive use of material culture (such as coins, shards, and inscriptions) which contributed to the advancement of the discipline of antiquarian study at this time. Indeed, the publication history of Camden's *Britannia* coincides almost perfectly with the formation and activities of the Society of Antiquaries, whose weekly meetings at Derby House must have prepared the way for Camden's eventual appointment as Clarenceux king of arms. At those weekly meetings members of the society delivered papers on topics often directly related to the *Britannia*, and Camden himself presented on numerous topics; many of these papers were published by Thomas Hearne as *A Collection of Curious Discourses* (1720, expanded edition 1771). The *Britannia*, the investigations of the Society of Antiquaries, and the work of others among Camden's contemporaries helped to transform historical thinking and writing by moving away from a providential view of events toward a more scientific methodology and an interest in material and cultural history.

In a similar way Camden's overriding organization of the *Britannia* combines tradition and innovation, and builds on current intellectual developments. His chorographical description of Britain had its classical models in such works as Pausanias's *Description of Greece*, but the genre enjoyed a revival during the Renaissance with the emergence of national and regional self-consciousness, particularly in states which embraced the Reformation. The chorography, which uses the physical configuration of the land as the organizing principle for description, allows the landscape to present its own political and cultural destiny. Description of distinguishing features on the physical landscape such as mountains, rivers, and splendid buildings or ruins, as well as of the people and their language, customs, and laws, provided a vehicle for patriotic national and regional self-definition at a time when nation states were proclaiming their identity internationally. In England the revival of the genre was directly linked to Henrician reform by John Leland, whose fragmentary unpublished *Itinerary*, written between 1535 and 1543 and dedicated to Henry VIII, was the prototype for Camden's county-by-county chorography. Camden reputedly gave John Stow an annuity of £8 for his autograph transcription of Leland's *Itinerary*. Several of Camden's contemporaries experimented with a similar chorographic form, including William Harrison, author of *The Description of Britain* (1577); Camden's Oxford schoolmate Richard Carew, whose *Survey of Cornwall* was written at this time (and published in 1602); and his friend the distinguished lawyer William Lambarde, who published his *Perambulation of Kent* in 1576 and pressed Camden to complete a description of all the British counties. In its refined later and fully illustrated editions the *Britannia* brought to its peak the work being done by these contemporaries. It quickly became a model for a new kind of literature of national self-consciousness that brought together a number of different genres, methodologies, and materials.

The wide acclaim given to the *Britannia* solidified the respect and support that Camden received. In 1587, just after its first edition, he was appointed keeper of the Westminster School and chapter library, which no doubt assisted him in his researches, and also brought him an additional 20s. p.a. He continued to travel in search of material for revisions and corrections to the work: in 1588, with Gabriel Goodman's assistance, he went to Oxford and Ilfracombe, in 1590 he travelled to Wales with Francis Godwin, in 1596 to Salisbury, Wells, and Oxford, and in 1600 to Carlisle with Robert Cotton. On 3 February 1589, just after Camden's visit to Oxford, Bishop John Piers collated him to the prebend of Ilfracombe in Salisbury Cathedral. Although a layman Camden accepted the benefice and retained it until his death. It was also on the Oxford tour of 1588, enjoying Goodman's patronage and still savouring the success of the *Britannia*, that Camden again sought recognition from Oxford and supplicated the university for the degree of MA. And again his hopes were dashed and his request denied. It would be another twenty-five years before the university, on its own initiative, would recognize Camden's achievement.

Headmaster of Westminster Other recognition, however, did ensue from the success of the *Britannia*. According to the Westminster chapter book for 2 December 1591 (fol. 222*v*), while Camden was still second master he was granted the lease of 'a litle tenement in the close for the tearme of his life'—an exceptional honour considering his rank and the very limited private accommodation in the close. When Edward Grant stepped down as headmaster in 1593 Camden assumed that office, which he held for four years. This distinction was followed in 1594 by the granting of his request that for his lifetime he be allowed to take his 'diet … at the Dean and prebends table' (BL, Add. MS 36294, fol. 24), thus ensuring his place in the company of political and religious leaders situated in Westminster.

During his years as headmaster Camden combined his teaching, administrative, and literary activities with travelling to collect material on arms, antiquities, monuments, and other kinds of evidence that he brought into the broad scope of antiquarian study. Much of what he gathered survives in manuscript form in the Bodleian and British libraries. Early in his term he compiled his instructional material for the study of Greek, and in 1595 published the *Institutio Graecae grammatices compendiaria in usum regiae scholae Westmonasteriensis*, which became the standard Greek grammar in Britain for over a century. Like so much of his work it reflects his ability to draw on and advance his humanist models, in this case Lily's authorized Latin grammar, and the Greek grammar that his predecessor, Edward Grant, had used in the school.

Over his twenty-two years at Westminster Camden helped with the reinvigoration of the school by his mentor Lord Burghley. He helped transform its curriculum and revitalize the study of Greek, he organized the library and its contents, and he advanced the unstated but unmistakable mission to serve the religious goals of the Elizabethan settlement. The physical setting of the school embodied its unique role within the Elizabethan capital. Sharing the buildings of the church and chapter complex, adjoining the house of parliament and facing the old Westminster Palace, Westminster School negotiated the influences of church and state, monarch and shared government, under the watchful stewardship of William Cecil. Himself a product of the institutionalized forces of Elizabethan reform Camden helped to further them during his time there. Indeed, from a letter that he wrote to James Ussher, the future archbishop of Armagh, in 1618 it is clear that he saw his mission at the school as linked to the particular, tolerant episcopal vision of Elizabeth and Burghley:

> At my coming to *Westminster* I took the like Oath, where … God so blessed my labours that now the bishops of *London*, *Durham*, and *St. Asaph*, to say nothing of persons employed now in eminent place abroad, and many of especial note at home of all degrees, do acknowledge themselves to have been my Scholars—yea, I brought there to church divers gentlemen of Ireland, as *Walshes*, *Nugents*, *O'Raily*, *Shees* … and others bred Popishly and so affected. (*Epistolae*, no. 195)

In turn the school and chapter community meant much to him personally. He sang in the choir, kept his tenement in the close and took his meals there even after he left the school, and gave money for improvements to the school; throughout his life, moreover, he maintained a close friendship with his former pupil Robert Cotton, whose house abutted the walls of the school, and who developed his magnificent library in collaboration with Camden.

During his four years as headmaster Camden's health, always frail, began to deteriorate and travel was increasingly difficult. In 1592 he was beset by a quartan ague and passed blood; his health remained poor for a long time. In his 'Memorabilia' or autobiographical notes (published in Smith's *Epistolae* of 1691) he records being freed of the ague only in 1594. In 1597, after his travel to Salisbury and Oxford, he was afflicted by 'a most dangerous sickness' and taken into the house of one Cuthbert Line, whose wife was able to cure him. From about this time for the remainder of his life Camden was plagued by intermittent but severe illnesses. It was also at this time that he wearied of the demanding life of schoolteacher and headmaster and expressed interest in seeking other opportunities. He writes of having been offered the position of master of requests, which he refused. In 1597 the office of Clarenceux king of arms, one of the three principal offices in the College of Arms, became vacant at the death of Richard Lee. Apparently without Camden seeking it Fulke Greville, biographer and friend of Sir Philip Sidney, recommended to the queen that Camden be appointed to the position. To satisfy the conditions of office Camden was made Richmond herald on 22 October 1597, and was then installed as Clarenceux next day in a ceremony conducted by Lord Burghley.

Clarenceux king of arms The three kings of arms are the senior heralds in the College of Arms. Answerable to the earl marshal, they are the arbiters on matters of arms throughout the realm, and in Elizabethan England their influence and power were considerable. They sat in attendance at court, presided over tournaments, public processions, noble marriages and funerals; they granted arms and approved genealogies, determined on matters of title and degree, and had authority to confiscate any armigerous images that were determined to be false, inaccurate, or unauthorized. Each king of arms was responsible for a specific region; according to Camden's grant Clarenceux's area included the regions south of the Trent to the south, west, and east. The heralds, pursuivants, and other officers of arms held more restricted authority and limited prerogatives than the kings of arms.

Normally the position of king of arms was filled through promotion from within the college, and no doubt Camden's appointment with virtually no previous formal links with the college produced resentment. The only surviving record of this, however, is provided by the bitter and continuous attacks made on Camden by Ralph Brooke, York herald; it may be that Camden's supporters were powerful enough to silence more cautious opponents or perhaps his popularity was such that there was no resistance beside Brooke's. If Camden's appointment was unconventional it had a logic and a purposefulness that reveal much about him, his work, and how he was perceived by his mentors. Through his father and his own ties with the painters-stainers, he would have been very familiar with the people and activities of the College of Arms, notwithstanding increasingly strained relations between the groups. Camden's leadership in the Society of Antiquaries would also have involved him with the heralds. The society met at Derby House, the college's residence, there were heralds among its membership, and many of the discussion topics addressed matters central to their work, such as the origin of titles, the use of arms, and the office of earl marshal. While not trained in the mysteries of arms Camden had used genealogical material of the heralds in the *Britannia*. Indeed, as a historian and topographical writer he used material and cultural artefacts in a way very close to the work of the heralds. Camden's work and his appointment to the College of Arms brought together groups and areas of activity and intellectual enquiry that had previously been separate, and helped to precipitate changes in historical, antiquarian, and heraldic research and writing.

Camden's appointment was purposeful in other ways as well, and it is telling that William Cecil was annoyed that it was Greville and not he who had proposed Camden, although he was mollified when he learned that Camden had not solicited the post. With Camden as Clarenceux, Burghley's interests and his concerns for order and procedure were firmly represented in the college just when the increasingly volatile Essex had been appointed earl marshal. The College of Arms was in disarray and badly needed the kind of thoughtful and orderly leadership that Camden provided. His grant from Elizabeth accorded him unusually broad powers which were reaffirmed even more emphatically by James I on 4 August 1604. After Camden's taking office the chapter resumed regular meetings, began to keep orderly records, and established procedures for dealing with the vitriolic exchanges and occasional peculation that had become associated with the college. Through the discourses of the Society of Antiquaries many of the fundamentals on which heralds' activities were built were re-examined and given new and clearer meaning. While the broils among the heralds certainly continued throughout Camden's life, from 1597 the college became an increasingly well-ordered community. From the work of the heralds, the redefinition of their activities, the theoretical and antiquarian discourses on issues relating to titles, the earl marshal's office, parliament, and other topics, and the fuller scholarly and historical writing of men like John Selden, Francis Thynne, John Doderidge, Robert Cotton, and Camden himself, there emerged an ample body of work documenting, re-examining, and at times redefining the political and power structures of Britain.

The quarrel with Brooke If these were the large-scale fruits of Camden's new career they were not won easily or without controversy, most of it generated by his arch-enemy, Ralph Brooke. Brooke seemed first to have taken offence at Camden's incursions into genealogical matters in the *Britannia*, possibly even before its author became Clarenceux: in his attack of 1599 on Camden in *A discoverie of certaine errours published in print in the much commended Britannia, 1594*, focusing on the fourth edition, he addressed him as 'maister Camden' without reference to his heraldic office. This may, however, simply represent Brooke's refusal to acknowledge Camden as a fellow herald. The history of Brooke's attack on Camden provides a revealing insight into the volatile, competitive, abusive, and sometimes even dangerous world of patronage, public ideas, and publication in the period. Brooke's charges against Camden were many. The schoolmaster, he wrote with sarcasm, blundered foolishly into the erudite realm of arms without proper training, making numerous errors in heraldic matters, making bastards and misalliances through his mistakes in genealogy. He repeatedly accused Camden of plagiarizing the work of Clarenceux Cooke and John Leland's unpublished *Itinerary*, which was in fact a model in form for the *Britannia*. Camden had used and acknowledged Leland's work, although not to Brooke's satisfaction. A glance at the undeveloped notes of the *Itinerary* and comparable sections of the *Britannia* soon shows how Camden was able to benefit from the manuscript material and yet wholly transform it. In the matter of genealogical errors Brooke's allegations were at times correct. Camden replied to Brooke's charges in an address 'Ad lectorem' in the fifth edition of the *Britannia* of 1600, conceding some mistakes, blaming his sources in the papers of Clarenceux Cooke for others, and emphasizing that his primary interest was not arms or great families. In the address to the reader Camden provided an autobiographical sketch that gave a broad picture of the influences on and his intentions for the *Britannia*, one that put the discussion of heraldry in its proper perspective.

Brooke was unremitting both in sowing discord among the heralds and in making personal attacks on Camden. Over the next twenty years he prepared a *Second Discoverie of Errors*, particularizing more flaws in Camden's work. Presenting himself as Camden's senior in matters of arms, as an 'auncient Herauld' who had professed arms 'almost these fourty yeares' (*Brooke's Errors*, 3, 6), and casting himself as the humble, wronged party, he affected indignation at Camden's arrogance and presented him as aloof, snide, and pretentious; Camden was described as spurning his offers of assistance, 'not accompting them worthy his thankes or acceptation' (ibid., 4); he mocked Camden's use of Latin while he used unadorned English in the interests of England's nobility; Camden, like a struck 'cuttle-fish' 'thinkes to hide and shift' in the 'Inke of his Rhetorike' (ibid., 6). When among colleagues Brooke, 'a poore unrespected freinde' (ibid.), was slighted, while Camden, in 'the heat and height of his spirit' (ibid.) at table talk, was admired. In recalling these indignities and characterizing his rival Brooke described how, just before going to press, the printing of the first *Discoverie of Errours* had been interrupted by 'friends' (ibid.) of Camden, and the final copy damaged and left incomplete as a result.

Invoking its patriotic intent Brooke dedicated the *Second Discoverie of Errors* to King James, but it remained unpublished for over 100 years: John Anstis, Garter, published the manuscript and Camden's responses to Brooke in 1723. If Brooke had hoped to take advantage of political changes between Elizabeth and James he miscalculated the Stuart monarch's relationship to his nobility and to Camden, to whom James had extended extraordinary privileges as Clarenceux. He also underestimated his contemporaries' affection for Camden. In 1619, when Brooke published *A Catalogue and Succession of … Kings*, another volume on arms written at the expense of his peers, and was completing his *Second Discoverie* against Camden, Augustine Vincent, rouge dragon pursuivant, parodying Brooke's title and fault-finding methodology, published *A discoverie of errours in the first edition of the catalogue of nobility, published by Raphe Brooke, York herald, 1619*. Vincent's folio is two-pronged: an attack on Brooke and a vindication of Camden. A younger herald who had acted as the latter's deputy, Vincent levelled an intellectual battery upon his opponent. A significant portion of his work consists of epistles from eminent scholars attacking Brooke's heraldry, his personality, and his scholarship, and praising Camden. Cleverly, Vincent had Brooke's own publisher, William Jaggard, write against his author; major national figures who had observed Brooke over the years, including John Selden, registered their disgust, and many of the heralds made themselves heard at last. In the records of Renaissance letters, after the Marprelate controversy of the late 1580s, there are few literary exchanges that are as heated and full of animus as this between Brooke, Camden, and Vincent. Vincent's carefully argued and very public defence, however, attests to how much this debate contributed to the increased professionalization and methodological refinement not only of heraldry and genealogy, but also of closely related areas of study including historical and antiquarian writing of many sorts. As at Westminster School and chapter, so in the College of Arms did Camden help to reorganize the institution and broaden the intellectual debate at its centre.

Miscellaneous writings, 1600–1607 The College of Arms provided a professional and financial base for Camden from 1597 until the end of his life, but intellectually he worked in a number of interconnected circles. Derby House was home for many of the heralds and may also have been home for Camden, although we know that he kept his lodging and table privileges at Westminster, near to Robert Cotton, and in 1609 he acquired a house in Chislehurst, close to London. His literary work under James radiated outwards, retaining its links with Westminster, the *Britannia*, and the patriotic intent that informs all of his work, but becoming more focused. From summer to December 1600 he travelled extensively with Robert Cotton to Carlisle and the north, his last major journey, and in the same year he published the fifth edition of the *Britannia*, containing new material and also his reply to Brooke. The year 1600 also saw the appearance of a work that in certain ways resembles the perambulatory design of the *Britannia* and also shows classical and medieval influences, but which is none the less a strikingly unusual publication for Reformation Britain of 1600. Camden's *Reges, reginae, nobiles et alii in ecclesia collegiata B. Petri Westmonasterii sepulti*, published anonymously, is a guided tour of the secular monuments adorning the abbey church interior, including images of kings, queens, and nobility. Resembling medieval Roman Catholic travel literature in genre, and running counter to the iconoclastic inclinations of puritan reformers, it combines the methods and interests of the herald and antiquarian. This unusual work was popular enough to appear in two expanded editions, in 1603 and in 1606.

On his return from the north in 1601 Camden was incapacitated by fever and retired to the home of his lifelong friend the musician William Heather. His writing from this point on was increasingly based on his library work rather than on firsthand travel. In 1603, with the outbreak of plague in London, he withdrew to Robert Cotton's house in Connington, Huntingdonshire. That year saw the publication in Frankfurt of his *Anglica, Normannica, Hibernica, Cambrica, a veteribus scripta*. Dedicated to Fulke Greville this is a collection of early manuscript chronicles that Camden had used for his preliminary study of the history of the different regions and peoples of Britain. It represents a significant contribution to the establishment of medieval texts. In editing the chronicles of the middle ages so as to purge them of the scribal errors made in earlier times Camden placed himself in the company of an older generation of humanist scholars led by Matthew Parker, who had committed themselves to preserving documents relating to Britain's past. Asser's life of Alfred, edited by Parker himself and modified by Camden, was used by Cotton for a genealogy of King James and as support for James's proposed union of England and Scotland, prefigured in Alfred's uniting the kingdoms of the heptarchy under his rule. However, Camden included within the chronicle of Asser an account of King Alfred's supposed foundation of the University of Oxford which proved to be a forgery (possibly the work of Sir Henry Savile). The original manuscript has since been lost, but whatever the reason for Camden's printing it the blunder caused a certain amount of embarrassment for a man whose scholarship and integrity were now legendary.

The year 1605 produced another volume of material gathered from Camden's and Robert Cotton's libraries, the *Remaines of a Greater Worke Concerning Britain*. Camden did not put his name to it, identifying himself only by the final letter of each name, as M. N., but he dedicated it to Robert Cotton, suggesting his own ambivalence about a book that consisted of (as he wrote in the 'Epistle Dedicatorie') 'the rude rubble and out-cast rubbish … of a greater and more serious worke'. If the *Remaines* is an ungainly, seemingly shapeless collection, it is also frequently witty and wise, and richly varied. Bringing together Camden's interest in literature and language, and social and cultural history, including both popular and high culture, the *Remaines* contains a wealth of material. Moreover, as a collection it reflects the unusual moment in the emergence of early modern Britain when the artefacts of the vernacular culture were coming to be valued in new ways. With the first historically organized anthology of medieval poetry, a historical and comparative study of the English language, collections of names and their meanings, of (in the words of one of the chapter headings) 'grave speeches, and wittie apothogemes', and of epitaphs, it can be seen as a popular spin-off from its more expensive and serious historical mother lode, the *Britannia*. With two additional, enlarged editions in his own lifetime, seven throughout the seventeenth century, and several reprints thereafter, the *Remaines* remained a popular and useful work.

With the ever expanding impact of the *Britannia*, his close relationship with Robert Cotton, and his visibility as Clarenceux king of arms, Camden became an increasingly public figure. His international correspondents increased during these years; an epistolary friendship with the French minister and social historian Jacques-Auguste De Thou commenced in 1606, and he maintained regular correspondence with political and intellectual figures across Europe, including Casper Dorn, Janus Gruterus, Peter Puteanus, and Justus Lipsius. After the Gunpowder Plot in 1605 Camden was asked to provide a Latin translation of the subsequent trial. His *Actio in Henricum Garnetum, Societatis Jesuiticae in Anglia superiorem*, which appeared in 1607, was probably intended for the international readership interested in England's handling of the Roman Catholic threat, and he was no doubt selected for the task because he could handle such matters with tact and integrity. It may also be work that he undertook during a long sedentary period following a serious fall from his horse in September 1607, which laid him up until the following summer, when he was able to attend the funeral of his friend John Fortescue in July 1608. It was also during this time that he further expanded the format and content of the *Britannia* for its first folio edition in 1607.

The History of Elizabeth In his autobiographical notes for 1608 Camden records the beginning of his next major literary project, one with important political implications. Once begun, the *Annales rerum Anglicarum, et Hibernicarum, regnante Elizabetha*, or the *History of Elizabeth*, occupied him for more than seven years. The work was interrupted by sickness, other literary projects, and his duties as Clarenceux. Even as he began work on the *Annales* he was taken seriously ill, on his birthday, 2 May 1609. On that day, he tells us in his autobiographical notes, he was again taken in by William Heather and was attended by the physician John Gifford of New College, Oxford. There he remained until August, when he went to Chislehurst, and he convalesced there until October.

That Camden should write the first biography of Elizabeth is in many ways appropriate. Because he had been educated in institutions shaped by Elizabeth's own conception of reform, nurtured by a network of institutional and personal patrons close to her and embodying her religious, political, and humanist vision, Camden's interpenetrating personal and professional lives were 'authored' by Elizabeth, while Burghley was his symbolic father. Burghley first asked Camden to undertake the project in the late 1590s, providing him with private papers of his own and 'Rolls, Memorials, and Records' from the queen's own archives. His access to private papers as well as to Cotton's library, and his closeness to Burghley and other members of her court, gave Camden a privileged perspective on her reign. With considerable reluctance he agreed to the project, although greatly daunted by what in his epistle to the reader he describes as the 'piles and heaps' of material available to him. After Elizabeth's death he put it aside hoping that someone else better suited to the job would take it on, but by 1608 the task seemed inescapable. Camden's suitability for the project had not diminished, although it was more problematic. As Clarenceux he was a servant to the king, who was personally interested in how Camden would represent his mother, Mary, queen of Scots. Indeed his return to the project coincided with the publication of De Thou's *Universal History*, with its critical account of Mary. The international community was particularly interested in the English account of the Scottish queen, and De Thou had asked Camden how he might represent her life and the circumstances of her death more favourably. Political sensitivities surrounding the treatment of Mary greatly influenced Camden's work on the *Annales*. James himself pressed Camden to proceed with the biography, hoping for a more positive representation of his mother than that presented by De Thou, and asked Camden to prepare a separate account of events in Scotland during his mother's reign, which seems to survive among the published *Epistolae* in the form of 'Animadversiones in Jac. Aug. Thuani Historiam, in qua res Scoticae memorantur'.

Camden worked on the *Annales* with Cotton's help, and evidently shared information with De Thou up to 1613 and 1615. Afraid that a pirated edition was going to be printed at the king's request he completed the first three books of the biography, covering the years up to 1589, and hastened it into print in 1615, dedicating the work to his collaborator, Robert Cotton, whose library was indispensable to the project. His prefatory address to Truth is an acknowledgement of the sensitivity of the project. He continued to work on the *Annales* for the next two years, completing it in 1617. It is clear that Camden felt strongly the difficulty of his position throughout the preparation, writing, and publication of the first part, and when he completed the second part he sent the manuscript to Pierre Dupuy in Leiden with instructions that it should not be published until after his death. All the more likely, then, that Camden felt unable to write candidly in the first part of the work. In spite of his instructions to Dupuy, Camden seems to have bowed to further royal pressure to publish part two, but only in Latin. As he wrote to the king, 'As I do not dislike, that they should be published in my life-time, so I do not desire that they should be set forth in *English* untill after my death, knowing how unjust capers the unlearned Readers are' (*Epistolae*, no. 287). Part two of the *Annales*, comprising its fourth book, was eventually published posthumously in Latin at Leiden in 1625, appearing in London in 1627.

The *Annales*, or the *History of Elizabeth*, was also a long-awaited success. Not only did it contain the material of international political intrigue, but it commemorated Elizabeth and her court at a time when literary tastes were enjoying a revival of things Elizabethan. The first part was translated into English in 1625 by Abraham Darcie, from the 1624 French edition of Pierre de Bellegent. Its elaborate frontispiece reflects the nostalgic cult of Elizabeth that was served by the biography. The fourth book was soon translated (1629), and the entire work became available in Latin and English editions. Camden's organization of the *Annales* in chronicle form is itself interestingly old-fashioned, and in part influenced by De Thou's *Universal History*. The form tends to underplay Elizabeth's involvement in national affairs and defuse political controversy. Camden's historical method is here consistent with his other work in its effort to remain objective: he works closely from primary documents, quotes extensively, and recognizes the complexity of secular forces shaping human affairs. While generally successful in maintaining a disinterested tone the work occasionally betrays the author's personal feelings, as in his critical treatment of the earl of Leicester. Many of the papers that Camden used in compiling the history as well as numerous manuscript drafts of portions of the *Annales* survive among the Cotton manuscripts in the British Library (Faustina F. i–x).

Throughout his career, alike in his major works—the *Britannia* and the *Annales*—and in establishing his Oxford lectureship in civil history, Camden explicitly avoided matters of ecclesiastical controversy. However, during the years in which he worked on the history of Elizabeth and remained active as Clarenceux he was sometimes drawn into arenas of public policy or debate. In 1610, for example, Dr Matthew Sutcliffe, dean of Exeter, received royal approval for the establishment of Chelsea College, conceived in the tradition of an Italian academy but having as its primary objective the development of anti-Catholic arguments and policy. King James nominated Sutcliffe as provost and there were to be seventeen fellows and two historians, Camden being one of the latter; his appointment was dated 10 May 1610. Polemical as the college's goals were, in its patriotic and political mission, and also in some of its membership, it converged with those of the Society of Antiquaries; there is no record of activity by the college, however, and the initiative soon foundered.

To the end of his life Camden continued to work in his capacity of unofficial court chronicler and historian: he kept detailed notes on domestic and international events during James's reign that could later be expanded into a chronicle history like that for Elizabeth. According to Wood, at Camden's death his 'friend' John Hacket, later bishop of Lichfield, 'did privately convey [the manuscript of the Jacobean "Annals"] out of the library' (Wood, *Ath. Oxon.*, 2.347); it eventually found its way to Trinity College Library, Cambridge, and was printed in Thomas Smith's 1691 edition of Camden's epistles.

Last years and death By 1618, weary and in poor health, Camden had sought some respite from his duties in retirement at his house in Chislehurst, as he wrote to James Ussher in that year: 'being retired into the country for the recovery of my tender health … I purposed to sequester myself from worldly business and cogitations' (*Epistolae*, no. 195). But his life among the heralds allowed him no rest. Ralph Brooke renewed his attacks with the preparation of a *Second Discoverie of Errors* commenting on the *Britannia*, and then in 1619 with the publication of *A catalogue and succession of the kings, princes, dukes, marquesses, earles, and viscounts of this realme of England*. On 19 February Brooke sent Camden a copy of the *Catalogue and Succession*, soliciting his views, and on 25 February, six days later, he returned it to Brooke, its 268 folio pages heavily annotated with corrections. In the meantime Camden's use of deputies to carry out his county visitations was being challenged by his fellow kings of arms, and it was necessary for him to invoke the special privileges that James conferred on him, granting him extraordinary powers and authority, including unlimited use of deputies.

From February until August 1619 Camden was again seriously ill; in February he coughed and vomited so much blood that, according to Wood, 'he was left in a manner dead and deprived of all sense', and was again placed in the care of Dr Gifford (Wood, *Ath. Oxon.*, 2.343). When possible during these years he attended court functions, as he recorded in his 'Memorabilia': he was present in February 1621, for instance, when Sir Francis Bacon was created Viscount St Albans, and in the following June at the rare ceremonial degradation from his knighthood of the monopolies commissioner Sir Francis Michell. Judging from the partition books, however, Camden's attendance at official court or College of Arms functions was infrequent and this caused concern among his colleagues about the office of Clarenceux. Yet infirm as he apparently was after further illness in 1621 he held tenaciously to his position and authority when there were concerted efforts by Norroy and Garter to remove him from office. As late as 1623 his fellow kings of arms attempted to replace him in office by going directly to the earl marshal without consulting Camden himself. When he learned that he was to be offered £600 and an annuity of 100 marks to relinquish his post, he was deeply shocked and pained, and in October 1623 he wrote a plaintive letter to Robert Cotton requesting his direct intervention with the king.

During the last years of his life Camden directed his creative energies toward a final project that would stand as a capstone to his lifetime accomplishments and a vindication of his frustrated academic career at Oxford. After considerable correspondence and planning, in 1620 he succeeded in establishing by deed the terms for the first lectureship in civil history at the University of Oxford, thus formalizing his own contributions to the secular study of history and helping to broaden the curriculum at the university. He endowed the chair from the rents from property at Bexley, Kent, that he had acquired from Sir John Spilman, jeweller to King James, for this purpose. In his will he assigned the income of £400 p.a. to William Heather and his heirs for ninety-nine years, from which the very generous stipend of £140 was to be paid for the history professorship. In providing so large a salary Camden no doubt recalled his own meagre pay at Westminster and wanted the person occupying the chair in his name not to be subject to the financial pressures that forced him from the university half a century before. After making enquiries about suitable contenders for the professorship Camden received a request from Degory Wheare to be considered for the position. Camden and Wheare had apparently not previously met or corresponded. In 1622 Camden appointed Wheare as the first Camden professor of history and, as prescribed by the benefactor, he delivered a lecture on Lucius Annaeus Florus and the method of writing and studying history. During that year Camden was himself declared a public benefactor of the university. Shortly afterwards, on 7 June, Camden again fell seriously ill: the last entry in his 'Memorabilia' was made on this day, recording a sleepless night and grave sickness. Nevertheless he continued to make notes on state affairs for his *Annales* until August 1623. On the 18th he recorded falling from a chair and being temporarily paralysed, and then taken with illness. He died at Chislehurst on 9 November 1623 in his seventy-third year.

Camden's body was moved to his house at Westminster. His funeral certificate relates that on 19 November his remains were taken in state to the abbey, and describes the procession in some detail. His entourage was stately beyond his rank and testifies to the respect and affection that he inspired. Led by twenty-six poor men in gowns, it was followed by 'gentlemen in cloaks … esquires, then knights', with Sir Henry Bourchier, Sir Francis Lee, Sir Robert Cotton, William Heather, and Dr Christopher Sutton nearest the hearse. Next came the members of the College of Arms (except Ralph Brooke), who carried Camden's arms and a velvet pall with the king's arms; Garter and Norroy accompanied the body. Following the hearse were 'dyvers noblemen' including the lord keeper (Bishop John Williams), the earl of Leicester, numerous bishops, 'and many more barons, knights, esquires, and gentlemen' (Ellis, xi–xii). The prebendaries and other officers and attendants of the chapter met the body and escorted it to the nave. Dr Sutton, a prebendary of Westminster, delivered the funeral sermon. The social microcosm reflected in this stately and diverse procession is typical of the funerals of royalty or peers—it resembles the long roll depicting Elizabeth's funeral procession attributed to Camden himself (BL, Add. MS 5408)—but very much less so for a man of Camden's rank. With his death the University of Oxford, too, at last paid him homage: Zouch Townley, deputy orator for the university, and Degory Wheare, Camden professor of history, delivered eulogies on Camden; these were published in 1624 in a collection of elegies entitled *Camdeni insignia*.

Memorials and legacies Appropriately, though coincidentally, the immediate sepulchral neighbours to Camden's place of rest in the south aisle were the scholar Isaac Casaubon and the poet Geoffrey Chaucer, placing his monument, like his writings, between scholarly research and the poetic imagination; ironically and yet also aptly, his epitaph testifies to the fallibility of historical evidence by incorrectly recording his age as seventy-four, rather than seventy-two. His white marble effigy represents his head and bust, with an arm resting on the *Britannia*. The monument was defaced later in the century, with damage to the nose, arm, and book. One account, preserved by Thomas Smith, reports that this was perpetrated by a young man indignant at Camden's mention of his family, but another attributes the damage to cavaliers who entered the abbey to vandalize the hearse of the earl of

Essex and there 'used the like uncivil deportment' towards Camden's monument (Stanley, 290).

In his later years Camden lived a financially secure, even prosperous life, befitting a member of the Elizabethan 'middling sort'. His life as educator and herald gave him a fair degree of financial independence—enough to purchase the estate at Bexley. Throughout his professional life he retained the coveted if non-negotiable privilege of accommodation and board in Westminster, together with his prebend of Ilfracombe. The bulk of his disposable estate comprised the revenues of the manor at Bexley, which he took care to settle before his death. He also had a small inheritance in Staffordshire, as well as a sizeable library that was inextricably linked with Robert Cotton's. In dedicating most of his fortune to the establishment of a history lectureship Camden placed himself modestly in the tradition of educational benefactors such as those who paved the way for him and his studies at St Paul's. His will, proved on 10 November 1623, reflected the various cultural traditions which had influenced Camden's life and moulded his identity. His legacies recognized ties to extended family members, to his profession and colleagues, and to friends; most were largely symbolic. His abiding filial ties to the Painter–Stainers were underscored by his gift of money to purchase plate in his own and his father's memory. His gifts to that company and to the Cordwainers, and to individuals associated with them, suggests a deeply felt connection that is not documented in the details of his daily life. His greatest monetary gift, of £100, was made to his 'cousin' John Wyatt, 'painter'; other apparently distant family members were remembered in small bequests: to 'Camden of London a silkman ten pounds', to 'Giles Nicholson of Poulton in Lancashire … twentye pounds', £2 each to three godchildren, and small gifts as well for servants. Perhaps out of his love of music, perhaps from the sense of social obligation developed from his untitled but distinguished social station, or perhaps from a religious concern to see that his soul was accompanied on its passage by song and music if not prayer (since intercessory prayers were banned by the Chantries Acts), Camden left bequests for the 'singing men of the collegiate church of Westminster', the bell-ringers and the choristers.

Most of Camden's gifts were to friends and individuals associated with his professional and public life. The first named beneficiary was also the first in rank, Fulke Greville, 'Lord Brooke, Chancellor of the Exchequer who preferred me gratis to my office a peece of plate of ten pounds'. Others included John Chamberlain, Peter Manwood, John Selden, Thomas Allen of Gloucester Hall, Oxford, and Janus Gruterus, 'librarie Keeper to the Prince Palatin Elector at Hidelberge': all men of different stations and professions, and reminders that public and private realms were still inseparable during this period. Receiving special mention in his will was Sir Robert Cotton, former student and close friend and collaborator; their relationship went back over forty years. Camden's bequest to Cotton suggests the extent to which their lives and work overlapped over the years: 'As for my books and papers', Camden wrote, Cotton should have first view to retrieve whatever had been borrowed from him; then, he bequeathed to him 'all my imprinted bookes and manuscripts except such as concerne Arms and Heraldrie', including ancient seals, which he left to the office of Clarenceux. He named William Heather executor of his will, and Cotton and John Wise as overseers of his estate.

Influence and legacy Camden's intellectual and literary legacy to his own and succeeding generations has been considerable. His work and friendship exerted both direct and indirect influence on writers and historians and helped transform the methods of historical enquiry and the forms and genres of their work. He had a profound interest in imaginary literature as well as in the many different forms of non-fiction writing, and he had exceptionally strong ties with the literary world, including such men as Sidney, Spenser, Jonson, Drayton, and William Browne. Camden exerted a powerful influence on Edmund Spenser, acknowledged by the latter in *The Ruines of Time*, where he apostrophizes

> Cambden, the nourice of antiquitie
> And lanterne unto late succeeding age.
> (*Works of Edmund Spenser*, vol. 5, ll. 168–9)

Camden's friendship with Ben Jonson speaks volumes about Camden the man and writer: a sharper contrast than that between the unbuttoned self-assertive playwright and the sober, self-effacing scholar can hardly be imagined. According to tradition Camden sponsored Jonson's attendance at Westminster School, and while it is not known how long Jonson persevered there, Camden's influence was long and deep. In epigram 14, and other acknowledgements of his debt to Camden, Jonson praises him in high, humanistic terms as a poet, teacher, historian, and even playwright. Himself a poet, in the *Britannia* Camden shows an acute awareness of the creative tension that can exist between the literary and historical imagination, and he interweaves his own and others' verse within the historical and descriptive prose as different means of representing 'truth'. His 'De connubio Tamae et Isis', interspersed throughout the *Britannia*, is an extended poetic celebration of the marriage of the two rivers, and combines mythological, historical, and topographical elements; in it he attempts to transcend the shortcomings of the historical record and to find a higher order of expression. He draws on classical models and also on that of his predecessor, John Leland, and helps transform topographical and historical writing in prose and verse. Camden's verses outside the *Britannia* are essentially occasional in character, either elegiac or encomiastic; his complete poems were collected by George B. Johnson in 1975.

Camden's importance and contributions have been assured by the enduring place enjoyed by the *Britannia* and by the *Annales rerum Anglicarum, et Hibernicarum, regnante Elizabetha* or *History of Elizabeth*. Their combination of tradition and formal innovation, and their strong reliance on primary sources made them effective models of up-to-date historical writing. Relatedly, Camden's influence on the course of antiquarian study was considerable and has still to be fully explored. It goes beyond his actual writings and extends to the ways in which historians value the material objects of the past, and how they are used to understand cultural history. In addition to the *Britannia* his essays on antiquarian subjects, most of which were apparently prepared for the Society of Antiquaries, are perceptive historical studies and offer important glimpses into his methodology. The full extent of Camden's involvement in the intellectual, political, and international affairs of his generation also goes beyond his published writing and the professional offices that he held. A fuller measure of this involvement can be gathered from his correspondence, a significant part of which is collected in Thomas Smith's edition, *V. cl. Gulielmi Camdeni et illustrium virorum ad G. Camdenum epistolae* (1691), which also contains a reasonably full Latin life of Camden.

In addition to the marble bust of Camden in Westminster Abbey there are many likenesses of him that have made his serious, scholarly countenance a familiar one. According to Smith, Camden agreed to have his portrait painted at the request of Peiresc. Three portraits were completed by the distinguished Dutch artist Marcus Gheeraerts. One, once in the possession of Degory Wheare, is in the Bodleian Library, and the second, which belonged to Robert Cotton, is in the National Portrait Gallery. A contemporary deathbed portrait by an unknown artist is reported to have passed into the collection of the first earl of Clarendon. Numerous early engraved portraits of Camden survive, including one by J. T. de Bry, for Boissard's *Bibliotheca, sive, Thesaurus virtutis et gloriae* (1628), another that was used in the 1637 edition of the *Remaines*, published by G. Humble, and another by W. Marshall for the 1648 edition of Fuller's *Holy State*.

WYMAN H. HERENDEEN

Sources *V. cl. Gulielmi Camdeni et illustrium virorum ad G. Camdenum epistolae*, ed. T. Smith (1691) [incl. Camden's 'Memorabilia', or autobiographical notes] • W. Camden, *Britannia: or, A chorographical description of Britain and Ireland together with the adjacent islands*, ed. and trans. E. Gibson, 2 vols. (1753) • T. Hearne, ed., *A collection of curious discourses written by eminent antiquarians*, rev. T. Ayloffe, 2 vols. (1771) • Wood, *Ath. Oxon.*, new edn, 2.339–50 • A. Wagner, *Heralds of England: a history of the office and College of Arms* (1967) • *Brooke's errors of Camden … with Camden's reply*, ed. J. Anstis (1723) • W. H. Herendeen, *From landscape to literature: the river and the myth of geography* (1986) • W. H. Herendeen, '"Wanton discourse and the engines of Time": William Camden—historian among poets-historical', *Renaissance rereadings: intertext and context*, ed. M. C. Horowitz, A. J. Cruz, and W. A. Furman (1989), 142–56 • W. H. Herendeen, 'William Camden: historian, herald, and antiquary', *Studies in Philology*, 85 (1988), 192–210 • W. H. Herendeen, '"Like a circle bounded in itself": Jonson, Camden, and the strategies of praise', *Journal of Medieval and Renaissance Studies*, 11 (1981), 137–67 • F. S. Fussner, *The historical revolution: English historical writing and thought, 1580–1640* (1962) • F. J. Levy, 'The making of Camden's *Britannia*', *Bibliothèque d'Humanisme et Renaissance*, 26 (1964), 76–97 • P. Beal, *Index of English literary manuscripts*, ed. P. J. Croft and others, 1/1 (1980) • S. Piggott, 'William Camden and the *Britannia*', *PBA*, 37 (1951), 199–217 • M. Powicke, 'William Camden', *Essays and Studies by Members of the English Association*, new ser., 1 (1948), 67–84 • H. Trevor-Roper, *Queen Elizabeth's first historian: William Camden and the beginnings of English 'civil history'* (1971) • *DNB* • R. D. Dunn, ed., *Remains concerning Britain* (1984) • W. Camden, *The history of the most renowned and victorious Princess Elizabeth*, [new edn], ed. W. T. MacCaffrey (1970) • G. B. Johnston, 'Poems by William Camden, with notes and translations from the Latin', *Studies in Philology*, 72 (1975) • T. D. Kendrick, *British antiquity* (1950), 143–65 • D. R. Woolf, *The idea of history in early Stuart England* (1990) • J. Evans, *A history of the Society of Antiquaries* (1956) • C. E. Wright, 'The Elizabethan Society of Antiquaries and the formation of the Cottonian Library', *The English library before 1700*, ed. F. Wormald and C. E. Wright (1958), 177–97 • R. L. DeMolen, 'The library of William Camden', *Proceedings of the American Philosophical Society*, 128 (1984), 327–409 • K. Sharpe, *Sir Robert Cotton, 1586–1631: history and politics in early modern England* (1979) • M. Noble, *A history of the College of Arms* (1805) • *Reg. Oxf.*, 2/1.10–11 • M. Eccles, 'Brief lives: Tudor and Stuart authors', *Studies in Philology*, 79 (1982) [special issue] • will, PRO, PROB 11/142, fols. 351v–352r • Westminster Abbey Muniments, Westminster chapter book, 1591, Westminster Abbey muniment room • H. Ellis, ed., *The visitation of the county of Huntingdon … 1613*, CS, 43 (1849) • A. P. Stanley, *Historical memorials of Westminster Abbey*, 2nd edn (1868) • D. C. Douglas, *English scholars, 1660–1730*, 2nd edn (1951) • *The works of Edmund Spenser*, ed. E. Greenlaw and others, 11 vols. (1932–57), vol. 5 [*The ruines of time*] • W. Rockett, '*Britannia*, Ralph Brooke, and the representation of privilege in Elizabethan England', *Renaissance Quarterly*, 53 (2000), 474–99

Archives BL, Add. MS 5408 • BL, corresp. and literary MSS, Cotton MSS Cleo. E i., Julius F. vi and xi, Faustina E. i and v, Faustina F. i–ix, Titus F. vii–ix, Titus B. viii, Vespasian E. viii • BL, draft letters and MSS, Add. MS 36294 • Westminster Abbey, Muniments, portions of Camden's library • Yale U., Beinecke L., commonplace book, MS 370 | Bodl. Oxf., MS C.7.2, Ashmole MSS 846, 849, Douce 68, MS Rawl. B.70, Smith MSS 1, 2, 18, 19, 74, 85 • NL Scot., Scottish genealogy MSS

Likenesses M. Gheeraerts, oils, 1609, Bodl. Oxf.; version, NPG • oils, 1622–3, Worcester College, Oxford [*see illus.*] • R. Gaywood, prints, 1661, BM, NPG; repro. in S. Morgan, *The sphere of gentry* (1661) • J. T. de Bry, portrait, repro. in J. J. Boissard, *Bibliotheca, sive, Thesaurus virtutis et gloriae*, 5 vols. (Frankfurt, 1628) • W. Marshall, portrait, repro. in T. Fuller, *The Holy state*, 2nd edn (1648) • J. Payne?, portrait, repro. in W. Camden, *Remaines concerning Britaine* (1637) • marble effigy, Westminster Abbey

Wealth at death over £300 in gifts and cash bequests: will, PRO, PROB 11/142, fols. 351v–352r • property at Bexley, Kent, brought rental of £400 p.a.

Camden Town Group (*act.* **1911–1913**) was a society of sixteen artists: Walter Bayes [*see below*], Robert *Bevan, Malcolm Drummond [*see below*], Harold *Gilman, Charles *Ginner, Spencer *Gore, James Dickson *Innes, Augustus *John, Henry *Lamb, (Percy) Wyndham *Lewis, Maxwell Gordon Lightfoot [*see below*], James Bolivar *Manson, Lucien *Pissarro, William Ratcliffe [*see below*], Walter *Sickert, and John Doman Turner [*see below*]. Duncan *Grant was elected to replace Lightfoot after the latter's death in September 1911. The group held only three exhibitions, in June 1911, December 1911, and December 1912, all at the Carfax Gallery in fashionable St James's. By the end of 1913 it had ceased to exist as an independent entity.

Background history The Camden Town Group was nurtured by a number of painters who regularly attended the informal Saturday afternoon gatherings hosted by Walter Sickert at 19 Fitzroy Street, London. In spring 1907 the first floor at this address (to the south of more run-down Camden Town) had been jointly rented by Sickert and seven of his colleagues, among whom were Gore and Gilman. The eight founder members of what came to be known as the Fitzroy Street Group, together with disciples, pupils, and colleagues, met weekly to display their work to each other and to a small band of patrons while discussing art and its politics in London. Other painters were soon drawn to join the group, including more future members of the Camden Town Group: Pissarro in autumn 1907, Bayes and Bevan in 1908, and Ginner in 1910.

The district of Camden Town in north-west London also lent its name to the style of painting nurtured between 1907 and 1911 within the Fitzroy Street Group. The pictures were domestic in scale: 'mostly little pictures for little patrons' (L. F. Fergusson and W. Lewis, *Harold Gilman*, 1919, 19). An unmistakable Sickert-inspired vocabulary of favourite themes was established: nudes on a bed or at their toilet, informal portraits of friends and coster models in shabby bedsitter interiors, mantelpiece still-lifes of cluttered bric-à-brac, landscapes of commonplace London streets, squares, and gardens (not all of the Camden Town neighbourhood), and landscapes studied on visits to the country and abroad. Every theme was treated with objective perceptual honesty. The surface of 'Camden Town' paintings was typically constructed from a mosaic of crusty touches of high-keyed colours, often dominated by violets and greens. Because Lucien Pissarro (son of the great French impressionist Camille Pissarro), through advocacy and example, influenced his Fitzroy Street colleagues to adopt this handling, it is interpreted as a late and temperate English flowering of French impressionism. As a style, Camden Town painting outlived the group by some five years, kept alive in the studios of the many pupils and disciples of Sickert and Gilman.

By the end of 1910 the gatherings at 19 Fitzroy Street attracted an extensive circle of painters drawn there through a network of friendships and professional relationships. Work by several of the group's younger and less well-known members had begun to breach the conservatism of the New English Art Club (NEAC) jury. Then during the winter of 1910–11 Roger *Fry staged his exhibition 'Manet and the Post-Impressionists' at the Grafton Gallery. The figureheads of the art world united to condemn the exhibition as an outrage. The old guard of the NEAC were among the most hostile, and it became obvious that the tolerance recently displayed towards the mildly progressive art of Fitzroy Street and its allies would be abruptly withdrawn. This revived antagonism was the main impetus behind the creation of the Camden Town Group.

The chief topic of discussion among members and satellites of Fitzroy Street early in 1911 was this rift with the NEAC. The relative merits of capturing control of its jury or setting up a rival exhibiting society were hotly debated. Ginner told the story of how, dining together at Gatti's, he, Sickert, Bevan, Gore, and Gilman decided to create a new society. Discussion continued at Fitzroy Street and over dinner at the Criterion, when it was decided whom to invite as members. Gilman, strongly supported by Sickert, insisted that the group should exclude women. Ginner recorded that they wished to create a limited circle of those painters whom they considered to be the best and most promising of the day. A restaurant in Golden Square was the setting for a plenary meeting where Gore was elected president and J. B. Manson, recently introduced to the Fitzroy Street circle by Lucien Pissarro, was elected secretary. Bayes recorded that the name of the group was bestowed by Sickert because Camden Town 'had been so watered with his tears that something important must sooner or later spring from its soil' (*Saturday Review*, 25 Jan 1930).

New recruits **Walter John Bayes** (1869–1956), born in north-west London on 31 May 1869, was the son of Alfred Walter Bayes (1832–1909), a painter and etcher, and his wife, Emily Ann, *née* Fielden (*fl.* *c.*1840–*c.*1910). His younger brother was the sculptor Gilbert *Bayes, and his sister Jessie Bayes (1878–1970) was also a painter. Following his early education at a Quaker school in Saffron Walden, Essex, and University College School, London, he had been drawn into the Fitzroy Street circle in 1908 when the scale and competence of the decorative paintings he had submitted to the first exhibition of the non-jury Allied Artists' Association (AAA) caught Sickert's attention. Despite having had work accepted for exhibition at the Royal Academy since his student days at Westminster School of Art (1900–02), Bayes had enjoyed little commercial success. His rhythmic sense of composition, his gift for synthesis and simplification, and his idiosyncratic humour won admiration from critics but scant attention from collectors. He was equally at home working on a huge scale—for example, his commissioned war paintings (IWM)—or a small—such as his direct oil sketches of figures, often his wife, Kitty (he married Katherine Teller in 1904), and one or other of their two sons on the beach (public collections with good examples include the Graves Art Gallery, Sheffield, and the art galleries of Aberdeen, Bradford, and Bury). He earned his living as an art critic (at this period of *The Athenaeum*) and in later life as a distinguished teacher (he was headmaster of the Westminster School of Art, 1918–34, and of the Lancaster School of Arts and Crafts, 1944–9). He died at his home, 54 Fitzjohn's Avenue, Hampstead, on 21 January 1956.

Just as Sickert introduced Bayes to Fitzroy Street because he liked his work, so recruitment to the Camden Town Group was unsystematic, guided more by personal preference than communal ideology. Wyndham Lewis, his style already touched by the angularity of cubism, was introduced by Gilman or Gore, both of whom he had known since his days at the Slade School of Fine Art. Henry Lamb, a neighbour in Fitzroy Street, and Augustus John, already an artist of wide prestige and repute, sometimes joined the circle at Fitzroy Street on Saturday afternoons. John's membership of the Camden Town Group was a gesture of endorsement rather than personal involvement in the collective effort. The two slight sketches of Wales he sent to the first exhibition were unlikely to divert attention from his lesser-known colleagues. Lamb, on the other hand, treated the Camden Town Group exhibitions as a useful means of widening the audience for his art.

John's Welsh compatriot, James Dickson Innes (1887–1914), was another irregular visitor to the Saturday afternoon gatherings. Innes was born in Llanelli on 27 February 1887. He studied at the Slade School from 1906 to 1908 and had his work accepted for exhibition at the NEAC from 1907 onwards. He travelled extensively. From 1910 to 1912 he frequently returned, sometimes with John, to their native Wales, where both created intense and colourful small-scale landscapes (most public collections in the United Kingdom have paintings by Innes, the greatest number being in the National Museum and Gallery of Wales, Cardiff). Many of Innes's paintings featured Mount Arenig, the personification of his unrequited love for Euphemia Lamb (the ubiquitous *femme fatale* and wife of Henry Lamb). He is said to have buried her letters in a silver casket on its summit. His fragile connection with the Fitzroy Street and Camden Town groups was severed in 1912 when deteriorating health led him to seek the sun in southern Spain and in north Africa and the Canary Islands. He died in Kent of consumption on 22 August 1914.

According to Bayes, it was Gore who proposed the precocious draughtsman **Maxwell Gordon Lightfoot** (1886–1911). Lightfoot, born in Granby Street, Liverpool, on 19 July 1886, was the son of William Henry Lightfoot (1852/3–1898), an insurance agent, commercial traveller, and pawnbroker, and his wife, Maxwell Gordon Lindsay (1858/9–1946). After studying at Chester Art School (1901–2) and taking evening classes at Sandon Studios, Liverpool (1905–7), Lightfoot moved to London in 1907 to continue his studies, until December 1909, at the Slade School. During his time there he carried off many of the most coveted prizes. His refined technique, exquisite sense of tone, tender sentiment, and fastidious temperament would have set him apart from most contemporary cliques. The inspiration of the two tender figure paintings (*Mother and Child* and *Boy with a Hoop, Frank*, both priv. coll.) contributed by Lightfoot to the first exhibition of the Camden Town Group in June 1911 was removed from the twentieth century: *Frank* harked back through Whistler to Velázquez; the tondo *Mother and Child* had its roots in fifteenth-century Florence. Both paintings stood out as totally different from anything else in the show. Lightfoot regretted joining the Camden Town Group and resigned immediately after the exhibition. On 27 September 1911, aged twenty-five, he cut his throat and died at his home, 13 Fitzroy Road, Primrose Hill.

The art of Lewis, Bayes, Lightfoot, Lamb, John, and Innes was barely touched by association with the Camden Town and Fitzroy Street groups. However, communion with the inner core of Camden Town painters was the mainspring of the artistic development of two other new recruits, Drummond and Ratcliffe.

It is thought that Ginner supported Sickert's proposal of **Malcolm Cyril Drummond** (1880–1945). The son of Arthur Hislop Drummond and his wife, Anna Harriup, *née* Dodsworth, Drummond was born on 24 May 1880 at the vicarage in Boyne Hill, near Maidenhead, Berkshire, where his father was a canon of the Church of England. Drummond did not immediately choose painting as his career. After leaving the Oratory School, Birmingham, where he converted to Roman Catholicism, he read history at Christ Church, Oxford (1898–1902), then spent a year in Yorkshire training as an estate agent before studying at the Slade School (1903–7). In 1906 he married Zina Lilias Ogilvie, herself an artist and illustrator, with whom he shared a deep love of music. He was Sickert's pupil from 1908 to 1910 at the Westminster School of Art, in 1909 at his private etching class, and in 1910 at Rowlandson House. By 1910 paintings such as *Brompton Oratory* (exh. 1910; Arts Council of England) demonstrate his sophisticated grasp of form, colour, and design. His most innovative work was done during the Camden Town period, and his finest paintings were exhibited at the three Camden Town Group exhibitions, beginning with *Paddington Station* exhibited in June 1911, when it was much praised by the critics. He was a founder member of the London Group (1913) and its treasurer in 1921. During the war he worked in the War Office and later taught at the Westminster School of Art (1925–31). Following the death of his wife in 1931, he left London and settled in Moulsford, Berkshire. In 1934 he married Margaret Triquet Browning. He died at his home, Grange Cottage, Moulsford, on 10 April 1945, having been totally blind since 1943.

William Whitehead Ratcliffe (1870–1955) was proposed by Gilman. The son of Zachariah Johnson Ratcliffe, a mill worker, and his wife, Kezia, *née* Harness, a draper, Ratcliffe was born in Clenchwarton, near King's Lynn, Norfolk, on 6 October 1870 and grew up in Manchester. He went to evening classes at the Manchester School of Art, where he was influenced by the teaching of Walter Crane, an arts and crafts designer and illustrator. In 1894 he went to London to work as a wallpaper pattern designer, and in 1906 moved to the new garden city of Letchworth. When in 1908 Gilman moved to the same road in Letchworth as Ratcliffe, the two became friends. In 1910 Gilman persuaded Ratcliffe to abandon his work as a commercial designer in Letchworth to live as a full-time painter in London, where he briefly attended the Slade.

Membership of the Camden Town Group gave Ratcliffe, a shy and diminutive man (he was under 5 feet tall), the self-confidence to produce paintings at once distinguished and original. His controlled use of broken brushwork and high-keyed colour to support a taut design structure is seen at its best in his views of London, for example, *Clarence Gardens* (Tate collection), shown at the AAA and Camden Town Group exhibitions in 1912, and in the landscapes he painted on a visit to Sweden in 1913. Figures played but an incidental role in his paintings, even in *The Coffee House, East Finchley* of 1914 (Southampton City Art Gallery), which brilliantly captures the dingy respectability of a suburban café. Ratcliffe exhibited *The Coffee House* with the London Group in 1919, the year in which Gilman, its president, had died. The main body of Ratcliffe's work thereafter was watercolours and wood-engravings. Unencumbered by possessions, he led a peripatetic life, staying with friends and family. When he died, unmarried, at 24

Hayes Crescent, Golders Green, London, on 6 January 1955 he was barely remembered, despite the one-man show held at the Roland, Browse, and Delbanco Gallery in London in 1946 and another in Letchworth Art Gallery in 1954. After his death his brother, the journalist S. K. Ratcliffe, gave some of his better paintings to various provincial art galleries; the residue of his studio went to Letchworth.

Gore proposed his pupil **John Doman Turner** (1872/3–1938), who worked in pencil, charcoal, chalk, and watercolour, but not in oils. The son of Edmund Turner, a builder, Turner had married Frances Elizabeth, the daughter of George Birch, a carpenter, in Norwich on 25 November 1893, when his address was recorded as 61 Kings Road, Peckham. He lived most of his adult life—certainly from 1900 onwards—in Streatham, where he earned his living as a stockbroker's clerk. He was deaf. These facts, together with his unusual training as an artist through a sequence of some thirty letters from Gore offering constructive criticism on the drawings Turner sent to him over the period 1908–13, suggest he was an amateur. So he was in the literal sense, but the quality of his work and his dedication were professional (Southampton City Art Gallery and the University of Hull own drawings by Turner). His extant drawings of Ilfracombe, Tenby, Walberswick, Eastbourne, and Folkestone probably reflect holidays in these seaside towns. In London he studied contemporary life, including theatre and music-hall interiors and fairground scenes on Mitcham Common. After the death of Gore in March 1914, Turner rarely exhibited his work. He died from pneumonia at his home, 63 Downton Avenue, Streatham, on 3 January 1938.

Camden Town Group exhibitions Once a finite membership of sixteen was achieved, Sickert persuaded Arthur Clifton of the Carfax Gallery in Bury Street, St James's, to lend his basement premises in June 1911 for their first exhibition. Each of the members was entitled to show four works, to be hung together rather than mixed on the walls. In fact at the first exhibition only fifty-five instead of sixty-four pictures were shown; Innes did not exhibit, while Lamb with three and Lewis and John with two pictures each did not take their full quota. Sickert's four contributions included two related figure subjects given the Camden Town murder title—probably for publicity reasons. Lewis contributed two angular pen-and-ink drawings of a man's head which excited much derision. Otherwise, there was little to offend the critics: fresh urban and rural landscapes, Camden Town figures in interiors, two cab-yard scenes by Bevan, two music-halls by Gore. John's presence was reassuring, and every critic could recognize the qualities of design and draughtsmanship and the technical fluency of Lightfoot and Lamb.

The second exhibition of the group was held at the Carfax Gallery in December 1911, when fifty-three pictures were shown. Duncan Grant, elected to replace Lightfoot, contributed one picture; John did not exhibit; Bayes and Lewis with three pictures each and Lamb with two explain the shortfall. At a meeting attended by all members except Grant, Innes, and John, the idea of expanding the group was first debated but finally voted down. However, a motion that new and larger premises be sought for their exhibitions was carried unanimously and effectively delayed active consideration of their next exhibition, which did not take place until December 1912.

At the third and last Camden Town Group exhibition, held yet again at the Carfax Gallery because larger premises had not been found, thirteen of the sixteen members showed a total of forty-five pictures. Grant, John, and Innes abstained. Each, having closer artistic and commercial allegiances to rival societies and galleries, had exhibited only once with the group. Their absence meant that the overall character of the paintings on view was more cohesive than in 1911. Only Bayes, Lamb, and Lewis remained to represent styles developed outside the influence of the original nucleus of Fitzroy Street painters. The year between shows had allowed time for the talents of less experienced exhibitors to mature, and this third exhibition included Drummond's *St James's Park* (Southampton City Art Gallery) and Ratcliffe's *Clarence Gardens* (Tate collection). Ginner also showed a painting of central London, *Piccadilly Circus* (Tate collection), one of his earliest brilliantly coloured and tautly constructed cityscapes. Bevan showed his first London horse-sale paintings. Three artists exhibiting with the Camden Town Group—Lewis, Lamb, and Gore—were also invited by Roger Fry to contribute to his second post-impressionist exhibition at the Grafton Gallery, which opened in October 1912 and was extended in December, thus overlapping the Carfax Gallery offering. The coincidence of these two exhibitions tended to polarize their respective characters in the eyes of critics and public. The viability of the Camden Town Group was threatened when it was relegated to a neutral position between the radicalism of Fry's selection and the conservatism of the NEAC.

During 1913, as in 1912, Arthur Clifton continued to sponsor the work of individual members of the Camden Town Group by offering them separate exhibitions at the Carfax Gallery. The gatherings chaired by Sickert at 19 Fitzroy Street remained a focus where members of the Camden Town Group were joined by visitors drawn from a wider compass. Some—for instance, Jacob *Epstein in April 1913—became members of the parent society. Radical art politics were in a state of constant flux during this year as rival factions formed, overlapped, and re-formed. In the autumn, when the Fitzroy Street Group reassembled after a summer recess to face decisions about expansion of the Camden Town Group, it was resolved that a new society be formed by amalgamating the two groups. Thus was the more broadly based London Group born.

The Camden Town Group has no clear death date: it petered out after less than three years' independent existence. Its last gesture as a corporate body was to respond to the invitation to select an exhibition of 'English Post-Impressionists, Cubists and Others' held at the Brighton Art Gallery from December 1913 until January 1914.

Significance The Camden Town Group brought together a group of painters each in his own way gifted with a desire to explore and to innovate within the boundaries of figurative art. At a time of unprecedented ferment in the arts, when all the traditional canons were being cast aside, Sickert and his colleagues negotiated a path between the ultimately sterile working of tired styles from the past and the wilder shores of experimentation to which technically and intellectually they were not willing to respond. The lasting achievement of the Fitzroy Street Group and its Camden Town satellite was not to shelter a belated flowering of English impressionism but to offer a milieu where iconoclasm was not demanded as a proof of modernity, where the patient effort to present objective records of urban life was not anachronistic, and where the craft of painting was respected. Over twenty years later, when the jazz and the machine ages had passed, the Euston Road School drew inspiration from its north-west London forebears. The legacy endures. WENDY BARON

Sources W. Baron, *Perfect moderns: a history of the Camden Town Group* (2000) • W. Bayes, 'The Camden Town Group', *Saturday Review* (25 Jan 1930) • C. Ginner, 'The Camden Town Group', *The Studio*, 130 (1945), 129–36 • F. Rutter, *Since I was twenty-five* (1927) • M. Easton, '"Camden Town" into "London": some intimate glimpses of the transition and its artists, 1911–1914', *Art in Britain, 1890–1940* (1967), appendix [exhibition catalogue, University of Hull, 1967] • G. Engert, *Maxwell Gordon Lightfoot* (1972) [exhibition catalogue, Walker Art Gallery, Liverpool, 1972] • *Spencer Gore and his circle with special focus on John Doman Turner* (1996) [exhibition catalogue, Piano Nobile, Richmond, 1996–7] • C. Haenlein, *Malcolm Drummond, 1880–1945* (1974) [exhibition catalogue, Maltzahn Gallery, London, 1974] • J. Marjoram, introduction, *William Ratcliffe* (1982) [exhibition catalogue, Letchworth Museum and Art Gallery, 1982] • d. cert. [Walter John Bayes] • d. cert. [Maxwell Gordon Lightfoot] • b. cert. [Malcolm Cyril Drummond] • d. cert. [Malcolm Cyril Drummond] • m. cert. [John Doman Turner] • d. cert. [John Doman Turner] • b. cert. [William Whitehead Ratcliffe] • d. cert. [William Whitehead Ratcliffe]

Archives AM Oxf., corresp. with J. B. Manson [Lucien Pissarro] • priv. coll., letters to J. Doman Turner [S. F. Gore] • priv. coll., letters [A. Rutherston] • Tate collection, letters to Nan Hudson and Ethel Sands [Walter Sickert] • U. Glas. L., letters to D. S. MacColl [Walter John Bayes]

Camelford. For this title name *see* Pitt, Thomas, first Baron Camelford (1737–1793); Pitt, Thomas, second Baron Camelford (1775–1804).

Cameron, Sir Alan, of Erracht (1750–1828), army officer, the eldest of the six children of Ewen Cameron of Erracht (1711?–1780?), leaseholder and farmer, and his wife, Marsali Maclean of Drimnin (*d.* 1795?), a designer of regimental tartan, was born at Erracht, Lochaber. He was educated at Inverness Academy and at King's College, Aberdeen University (1761–5). In 1772 he killed a man in a duel and had to leave Scotland. After reaching America he settled in the department of Indian affairs; during this period he fathered an illegitimate child, Adam Cameron (*c.*1772–1841). In 1775 he was commissioned in a provincial regiment, but was taken prisoner when on his way to raise men for the loyalist cause. He was imprisoned by the rebels for nearly two years in Philadelphia gaol, and while attempting to escape fell from the roof and broke both ankles. In 1778, still crippled, he sailed to Britain and was put on half pay. In London, on 16 September 1779, he married Ann Phillips (1765–1795), whose father, Nathaniel Phillips, was a wealthy Jamaican planter.

On 17 August 1793 the war office issued a letter of service authorizing Cameron to raise a highland regiment, of which he was to be major commandant. Although he was given no allowance to pay bounties and his officers came mainly from the half-pay list, he recruited his regiment to full establishment; most of the men came from Lochaber and north Argyll. The regiment was passed as fit for service at Stirling on 3 January 1794 and designated the 79th regiment of foot (or Cameronian Volunteers). Shortly afterwards Cameron was authorized to augment the 79th to a war establishment of 1000 men and was gazetted lieutenant-colonel commandant. He and the 79th served the winter of 1794–5 in the Low Countries and Westphalia. In July 1795 an attempt was made to draft men from the 79th into other regiments, but Cameron defeated the move after a fiery interview with the commander-in-chief, the duke of York. The regiment was ordered to the West Indies instead and by 1797 had suffered such severe losses from disease that the rank and file were drafted into the Royal Highlanders.

Cameron returned to Scotland with the cadre of the 79th and within a few months had recruited his regiment up to strength. In 1799 he took the 79th to the Netherlands. The regiment distinguished itself in the attack at Egmont op Zee, although Cameron was twice wounded. Having recruited his regiment to establishment again, he commanded it in Pulteney's expedition to Ferrol before joining Sir Ralph Abercromby's army for the landing in Egypt in 1801. On 1 January 1804 he was gazetted colonel in the army and colonel of the 79th and was authorized to raise a second battalion. From 1806 the 79th was redesignated the 79th Cameron Highlanders. In Lord Cathcart's expedition to Denmark in 1807 Cameron commanded a highland brigade formed from the 1st battalions of the 79th and the 92nd, and on 7 September he was appointed commandant of Copenhagen. In 1808 he again commanded this brigade in Sir John Moore's expedition to Sweden, and he retained the appointment of brigadier-general under Moore in Portugal. Having handed over command of the 79th to his eldest son, Lieutenant-Colonel Phillips Cameron, he remained as commandant of Lisbon. After Wellesley's return to the Peninsula in April 1809 he was relieved in Lisbon and formed the stragglers and convalescents of Moore's army into a fighting formation. At the battle of Talavera he commanded a brigade, comprising the 1/61st foot, the 2nd/83rd foot, and a company of the 5/60th rifles, in Sherbrooke's 1st division, which held an important position in the right centre of Wellesley's line. As the French columns advanced he exercised rigid fire control, and the devastating effect of his volley halted Sebastiani's division and allowed his own brigade to drive the French back, halting only because the flanking brigades had recklessly advanced too far. Cameron had two horses shot under him.

On 5 April 1810 Cameron suffered a personal loss when his youngest son, Captain Ewen Cameron of the 79th, who had served as his father's aide-de-camp at Talavera, died of fever, aged twenty-one. Despite suffering from rheumatism and arthritis, Cameron was present at the battle of Busaco on 27 September 1810 as a major-general. Although not wounded, he was injured during the night withdrawal when his horse stumbled and came down, and he retired in November 1810. His eldest son, Lieutenant-Colonel Phillips Cameron, was fatally wounded on 5 May 1811 while commanding the 79th at the battle of Fuentes d'Oñoro. After his return to London Cameron kept open house, but visitors were not quite the same as campaigns, and the letters telling of casualties hit him hard. He was made KCB on 3 January 1815. At Waterloo the 79th earned particular praise from Wellington, but at a terrible cost, losing 456 killed or wounded, including thirty-two officers. After the battle Cameron went to Brussels to see the casualties of the 79th. It was a matter of pride that his regiment had finished the day under the command of the senior unwounded officer, his nephew Lieutenant Alexander Cameron. On 12 August 1819 Cameron was promoted lieutenant-general. He died at Holcrofts, Parson's Green, Fulham, on 9 March 1828, and was buried in St Marylebone burial-ground, but his grave is no longer identifiable.

LORAINE MACLEAN OF DOCHGARROCH

Sources L. Maclean, *Indomitable colonel* (1986) • priv. coll., Alan Cameron MSS • memorial of Alan Cameron, PRO, Audit Office, 12–56 • *Historical records of the queen's own Cameron highlanders*, 7 vols. (1909–75) • *DNB*

Archives NRA, priv. coll., MSS and corresp. • PRO, Audit Office, memorial • Queen's Own Highlanders Regimental Museum, Fort George, Inverness-shire

Likenesses oils, Fort George, Highland • silhouette, Fort George, Highland

Cameron, Alexander (1747–1828), vicar apostolic of the lowland district, was born at Auchindryne, Braemar, Aberdeenshire, on 28 July 1747, the son of James Cameron and Marjory Mackintosh. He first studied at the Lowland seminary at Scalan, in Glenlivet, then entered the Scots College, Rome, on 22 December 1764. On his return to Scotland in 1772 he was appointed to the mission of Strathaven. On 23 January 1781 he became rector of the Scots College, Valladolid. He remained in Spain until 1802, though he was nominated titular bishop of Maximianopolis in Palaestina and coadjutor to Bishop Hay after Bishop John Geddes's resignation in 1797. He was consecrated at Madrid on 28 October of the following year. On Bishop Hay's resignation in 1805 Cameron, now resident in Edinburgh, succeeded as vicar apostolic of the lowland district. He resigned his vicarial functions in 1825 and died at Edinburgh on 7 February 1828. He was buried there in St Mary's Church, on which occasion the funeral service of the Roman Catholic church was publicly performed with the proper ceremonial for the first time in Scotland since the Reformation.

THOMPSON COOPER, *rev.* CLOTILDE PRUNIER

Sources J. Darragh, *The Catholic hierarchy of Scotland: a biographical list, 1653–1985* (1986) • J. F. S. Gordon, *Ecclesiastical chronicle for Scotland, 1–2: Scotichronicon* (1875) • W. J. Anderson, ed., 'The college for the lowland district of Scotland at Scalan and Aquhorties: registers and documents', *Innes Review*, 14 (1963), 89–212 • W. J. Anderson, 'The autobiographical notes of Bishop John Geddes', *Innes Review*, 18 (1967), 36–57

Archives Scottish Catholic Archives, Edinburgh, accounts; corresp.; papers

Likenesses W. Nicholson, etching, BM, NPG • portrait, Blairs College; repro. in Gordon, *Scotichronicon* (1867), following p. 459

Cameron, Sir Alexander (1781–1850), army officer, a younger son of Alexander Cameron of Inverailort, Argyll, and his wife, the daughter of Alexander M'Donald of Achtrichan, was born at Inverailort. On 22 October 1797 he received a commission as ensign in the Breadalbane fencibles, and in 1799 he volunteered to serve with the 92nd highlanders in the expedition to The Helder, and received an ensigncy. In 1800, when the rifle brigade, then known as the corps of riflemen and afterwards as the 95th regiment, was raised, Cameron volunteered, and was promoted lieutenant on 6 September 1800. In the same year he was at the battle of Copenhagen, and in 1801 he volunteered to serve with his former regiment, the 92nd, in Egypt, and was severely wounded in the arm and side in the battle of 13 March.

Cameron then returned to England, rejoined the rifles, and was trained in the camp at Shorncliffe by Sir John Moore, who secured his promotion to the rank of captain on 6 May 1805. He served with his battalion in Lord Cathcart's expedition to Hanover in 1805, and in the expedition to Denmark, and was present at the action of Kjöge.

In 1808 Cameron was ordered to Portugal with Anstruther's brigade, and was present at the battle of Vimeiro. During Moore's retreat he was continually engaged with the rest of the reserve. He especially distinguished himself at the action of Cacabelos and the battle of Corunna, at both of which he commanded two companies of his battalion. In May 1809 he was again ordered to Portugal, and on reaching Lisbon his battalion was brigaded, with the 43rd and 52nd, into the celebrated light brigade, under Robert Craufurd, which made its famous forced march in July, and joined the main army the day after the battle of Talavera.

From January to June 1810 Craufurd's advanced position on the Coa was one of extreme danger, and Cameron distinguished himself in many emergencies, and in the action on 24 June 1810 held the bridge with two companies against the French army until Major Macleod of the 43rd came to his assistance. In the retreat on Busaco he commanded the rear companies of the light brigade, which covered the retreat. He commanded the outposts during the time when Masséna remained at Santarem, and in the pursuit after Masséna he succeeded to the command of the left wing of the rifles, after the fall of Major Stuart at Foz d'Aronce, and twice led it into action, at Casal Nova and at Sabugal.

The light brigade had during the occupation of the lines of Torres Vedras become the light division by the addition of two regiments of Portuguese *caçadores*, and as a wing of the rifles was attached to each brigade, Cameron's command was of proportionate importance, and he was specially recommended by Lord Wellington for a brevet majority, to which he was promoted on 30 May 1811. He was also at the sieges of Almeida, Ciudad Rodrigo, and

Badajoz, and at the battle of Fuentes de Oñoro. He received a brevet lieutenant-colonelcy and the vacant regimental majority on 27 April and 14 May 1812. He then succeeded to the command of the 1st battalion, which was again united on the 2nd battalion rifles joining the division, and became a model to the whole army. This battalion he commanded at the battle of Salamanca, and in the advance to Madrid, and with it covered Hill's retreat along the left bank of the Tagus. He had the disappointment of being superseded in his command of the battalion by the arrival of Lieutenant-Colonel Norcott in May 1813, and so was present at the battle of Vitoria only as a regimental major, where he was so severely wounded that he had to return to England.

Towards the close of 1813 Cameron was selected for the command of a provisional battalion of rifles, which was sent to Flanders to serve in Sir Thomas Graham's expedition, and he commanded it at Merxem (when he was thanked in the general orders and mentioned in dispatches) and before Antwerp. At the conclusion of peace he received a gold medal and two clasps, and was made CB.

When war resumed in 1815, Cameron accompanied the 1st battalion rifles to Belgium as regimental major, and commanded the light companies of Kempt's brigade of Picton's division at Quatre Bras and his battalion at the battle of Waterloo, when he was wounded in the throat. He saw no more service.

In 1818 Cameron married the only daughter of C. M'Donnell of Barisdale. In October 1815 he was made a knight of the Russian order of St Anne, and in 1830 was promoted colonel. Appointed deputy governor of St Mawes, in 1832, he was promoted major-general and made a KCB in 1838. He received the colonelcy of the 74th regiment in 1846. On 26 July 1850 Cameron died at his seat, Inverailort, in Argyll. He was one of the best officers of light troops ever trained by Moore and employed by Wellington, which is high praise indeed.

H. M. STEPHENS, *rev.* JAMES LUNT

Sources J. Philippart, ed., *The royal military calendar*, 3 vols. (1815–16) • W. Cope, *The history of the rifle brigade* (1877) • J. Weller, *Wellington in the Peninsula, 1808–1814*, new edn (1992) • J. Paget, *Wellington's Peninsular War* (1990) • *GM*, 2nd ser., 34 (1850), 437

Archives Highland Council archive, corresp. and papers

Cameron, Alexander Anthony (1877–1951), athlete, was born at Lochtreig Head, Kilmonivaig, in the district of Lochaber, Inverness-shire, on 1 April 1877, the son of Donald Cameron, shepherd, and his wife, Mary McMillan. His father was quite a small man, but his mother's McMillan line were famous for their physique, and Alexander grew to a weight of 17 stone, standing 6 feet 1 inch. Renowned later for his devoted attachment to his native Lochaber, he was for a time in youth a policeman in Partick (Glasgow), but he found a more distinguished way of alleviating rural indigence when he became a star of the highland games circuit. A product of nineteenth-century 'invention of tradition', the highland games developed as centres where local landowners (increasingly, non-Scottish) flaunted their kilts, their tartan-clad retinues, and their noteworthy acquaintance while hard-headed, thick-thewed men of the people earned useful prize money. The first great games star was Donald Dinnie, who was still winning prizes in special competitions as late as 1910, when he was aged over seventy.

In the early twentieth century Cameron was firmly installed as successor to Dinnie and G. H. Johnstone as 'Champion Heavy of Scotland'. He set new records in such events as hammer throwing, weightlifting, caber tossing, putting the stone, and the distinctive highland 'standing jump', where his record of 4 feet 11 inches still stood at the time of his death. He was undisputed champion from 1903 to 1914. By this time the games had standardized forms and rules and were regulated by judges and stewards. In 1910 51,000 spectators attended the Cowal gathering, so that prize money on offer of £160 might seem meagre—and indeed, Cameron himself led an athletes' strike for higher prizes at the Turriff games.

English impresarios were greatly interested in 'strong men', and Cameron accepted the lure of high wages. He toured as far as Australia (1904) and Russia. But unlike Dinnie he could not settle for footlights and 'gee-whiz' promotions. It is part of Cameron's legend that when George Hackenschmidt, 'the Russian Lion'—who thought him, after a wrestling match, the strongest man he had ever handled—made him an especially good offer to tour with his team, Cameron took time to think it over. Pressing him again, Hackenschmidt said, 'You'll be going, I take it?' 'Aye, I'll be going', replied Cameron, adjusting (it is said) his bowler hat, 'back to Lochaber' (Webster, 88).

Cameron, who remained unmarried, was nicknamed the Mighty Muccomber (or Mucomir) after the name of his home farm. After the First World War had cut his dominance short, he displayed his disinterested love of the games as a popular judge. Not long before he died, he was chatting happily in Gaelic to athletes at the Glenfinnan games. He collapsed fatally on 18 September 1951, while cutting grass in front of his cottage on the Letterfinlay estate at Spean Bridge, Inverness-shire. In his heyday, he had rarely trained, except by swinging a scythe day after day. He was buried at Blarour cemetery, Spean Bridge.

ANGUS CALDER

Sources D. Webster, *Scottish highland games* (1973) • G. Jarvie, *Highland games: the making of the myth* (1991) • *Inverness Courier* (21 Sept 1951) • I. Colquhoun and H. Machell, eds., *Highland gatherings* (1927) • b. cert. • d. cert.

Likenesses photograph, repro. in Colquhoun and Machell, eds., *Highland gatherings*

Wealth at death £2351 5*s.* 11*d.*: confirmation, 7 Nov 1951, *CCI*

Cameron, Archibald (1707–1753), physician and Jacobite conspirator, was the fourth son of John Cameron (*c.*1663–1748), laird of Lochiel, and his wife, Isabel, daughter of Alexander Campbell of Lochnell, and the younger brother of Donald *Cameron of Lochiel, who took a prominent part in the Jacobite rising of 1745. Archibald Cameron was originally intended for the bar but preferred medicine to the law. After completing his studies at Edinburgh University and in Paris, he settled at Lochaber among his own clan. There he devoted his time to the general welfare of the people, sustaining them both financially and medically. He married Jean (*d.* in or after 1753), daughter of Archibald Cameron of Dungallon, and they had seven children. In the 'Forty-Five he was present with his clan and he described his involvement as arising not from choice 'but from compulsion of kindred'. During the rising he held the rank of captain and placed his medical skill at the disposal of his people.

After the defeat of the highlanders at Culloden on 16 April 1746, Cameron took an active part in concealing Prince Charles, remaining in constant communication with him. While the prince was in a hiding place known as the 'cage' at Benalder (Forbes, 3.41–2), Cameron sent information to him of the arrival of two vessels to carry him and his friends to France. After escaping with the party of which his brother was a member, Cameron was appointed physician and captain in Albany's regiment, a regiment in which his brother had been appointed colonel. On his brother's death in 1748 he took up a similar position in Ogilvie's regiment.

In 1752 Cameron became involved in one of the many impractical schemes devised in the 1750s for the restoration of the Stuarts. The scheme, which had been concocted by Alexander Murray, brother of Patrick Murray, fifth Lord Elibank, involved the fomenting of a rising in Scotland to coincide with a coup in London initiated by assaults on St James's and the Tower. There were also rumours that Frederick the Great of Prussia had promised 15,000 men to aid the invasion of England by Jacobites (Walpole, *Corr.*, 20.373). This was no more than a rumour, as it was unlikely that Frederick's resentment against England created by debts in Silesia and ill treatment of his merchant navy would be translated into military support for a cause so quixotic as a Stuart restoration. The plot was abandoned in November 1752 when the conspirators became aware of their betrayal to the government by Alaistair Macdonald of Glengarry (Pickle the Spy) who, while posing as a participant in the plot, had been sending dispatches to London giving detailed information about the scheme. When he travelled to Scotland in 1753 Cameron was taken up by a party of Lord George Beauclerk's regiment at Glenbucket after information had been received at the garrison at Inversnaid that he was in the neighbourhood.

After a short period of imprisonment at Edinburgh Castle, Cameron was sent to London. Notwithstanding clear evidence of his involvement in the so-called Elibank plot, Cameron was arraigned before the court of king's bench upon the act of attainder passed in 1746 against him and others for their involvement in the rising of 1745 and sentenced to be hanged, drawn, and quartered. Despite the desperate efforts of his wife to save him by petitioning the king and leading members of the aristocracy, the sentence was carried out on 7 June 1753. Cameron bore himself with great composure and it was said that 'He met the last great enemy with as much intrepidity and as much decency as even the great Balmerino' (Forbes, 3.130). Cameron was attended on the scaffold by a nonjuring clergyman, the Revd James Falconar, who, according to Horace Walpole, was 'not content with seeing the Doctor hanged, [but] let down the top of the landau for the better convenience of seeing him disembowelled!' (Walpole, *Corr.*, 20.384). Cameron's execution led Samuel Johnson, when on a visit to the novelist Samuel Richardson, to vilify George II 'as one who, upon all occasions, is unrelenting and barbarous' (Boswell, *Life*, 1.147).

A number of theories have been advanced to explain Cameron's execution for his part in the 'Forty-Five so long after that rising had been subdued (see, for example, Walter Scott, *Redgauntlet*, 1832, introduction). However, the most likely explanation for the government's conduct is probably twofold: first that it was inspired by the anxiety of the Pelhams not to reveal their spy, Alaistair Macdonald, as the source of their information; second, that it sprang from a wish not to upset the financial markets at a time when Henry Pelham, prime minister and chancellor of the exchequer, was trying to simplify government finance by means of consolidated annuities. This scheme involved the difficult operation of converting the national debt to a lower rate of interest, and Pelham's scheme would have been jeopardized had the City of London believed the country to be on the verge of yet another Jacobite rising (Beatty, 46–50). To Cameron himself the government's accusing him of complicity in the plot of 1752 was simply 'to cover the Cruelty of murdering me at [such a] Distance of Time from the passing of [the act of attainder]' (BL, Add. MS 32732, fol. 47v). ROGER TURNER

Sources *The life of Dr Archibald Cameron* (1753), 2, 3, 29 · Walpole, *Corr.*, 20.373, 384 · J. L. Beatty, 'Henry Pelham and the execution of Archibald Cameron', *SHR*, 41 (1962), 46–50 · W. Scott, *Redgauntlet* (1832), introduction · R. Forbes, *The lyon in mourning, or, A collection of speeches, letters, journals … relative to … Prince Charles Edward Stuart*, ed. H. Paton, 3, Scottish History Society, 22 (1896), 41–2, 130 · Boswell, *Life*, 1.145–7 · *State trials*, 19.733–46 · BL, Add. MS 32732, fols. 5, 47r, 47v · F. J. McLynn, *Charles Edward Stuart: a tragedy in many acts* (1988); repr. (1991) · BL, Add. MS 35887, fol. 31

Likenesses mezzotint, BM · mezzotint, repro. in *Life of Dr Archibald Cameron*, frontispiece

Cameron, Basil George (1884–1975), conductor, was born Basil George Cameron Hindenberg at 34 Waylen Street, Reading, on 18 August 1884, the son of Frederick Clementz Hindenberg, a piano tuner, and his wife, Elize Helena Sherman. He was educated at Tiverton grammar school. After a period at York, where Cameron studied the violin with Editha Knocker and theory with Tertius Noble, he attended the Berlin Hochschule für Musik between 1902 and 1906. From Berlin Cameron moved to London and joined the Queen's Hall Orchestra in 1908. He gained valuable early experience as a professional violinist: arguing that British audiences preferred foreign musicians to those from the United Kingdom, he continued to perform as Hindenberg until the outbreak of war in 1914.

Appointed conductor of the Torquay Municipal Orchestra in 1912, Cameron was determined that his band of twenty-five players would present interesting and challenging programmes. By including the works of Stravinsky and Delius at his concerts, he both challenged and educated his audiences, and with his festivals devoted to the music of Wagner and Strauss, in 1913 and 1914 respectively, he raised the profile of the orchestra. For these he increased his ensemble to seventy players; engaged prominent instrumentalists, like Eugene Goossens (violin) and Aubrey Brain (horn), to supplement the festival orchestras; and invited Thomas Beecham, Henry J. Wood, and Percy Pitt to share the conducting. But the orchestra did not survive the First World War and, having adopted Cameron as his surname in 1914, he served with the 13th (Kensington) battalion, the London regiment, during the hostilities. He rose to the rank of lieutenant and was wounded in action.

After demobilization Cameron directed the Regent Cinema Orchestra of Brighton. In 1923 he was appointed conductor of the Hastings Municipal Orchestra, and in 1924 he accepted a similar post at Harrogate. Performing with limited musical forces to audiences from contrasting backgrounds, Cameron programmed accordingly: for his seaside concerts, he arranged classical symphonies for his orchestra of twenty-one players, and at the Yorkshire spa, with its affluent and educated clientele, he performed works from music's cutting edge. The Harrogate concerts included the first English performance of G. F. Malipiero's symphonic fragments from *San Francesco d'Assisi* in 1927 and, in 1929, an all-British festival where the music of Frederick Delius, Arnold Bax, Peter Warlock, Henry Balfour Gardiner, Joseph Holbrooke, and W. Y. Hurlstone was heard. Cameron's success in the provinces soon attracted the interest of London managers, and on 26 January 1928 he made his Queen's Hall début. Performing for the Royal Philharmonic Society, he directed a programme of works by Joachim, Bax, Elgar, Beethoven, Delius, and Malipiero. The concert was a success, and he was invited to perform with the society again on 31 January 1929. After concerts with it in 1930 and 1931 he conducted regularly for the organization from 1941.

By the late 1920s Cameron's reputation had spread to North America. In 1930 he left his posts at Hastings and Harrogate and was appointed music director of the San Francisco Symphony Orchestra, a position that he shared with Issay Dobroven. A champion of British music, Cameron gave the first performance of Bax's symphony no. 4 at San Francisco. But the greater part of his American period was spent in Seattle: from 14 November 1932 to 28 February 1938 he was music director of the Seattle Symphony Orchestra. Working with an orchestra whose members were openly hostile, and whose loyalties were to their previous conductor, Cameron found his abilities tested to the full. But his easy-going manner soon helped to create a satisfactory working environment that continued throughout the rest of his tenure. And having gained the orchestra's trust he instigated a series of reforms and innovations: on 30 November 1933 he conducted the orchestra's first broadcast concert; in 1935, he toured the Pacific north-west with the ensemble; he programmed a series of 'pop' concerts, attracting new listeners; he increased the size of the orchestra and the number of concerts given each season; and he ensured increased financial security for the players.

After returning to Great Britain in 1938 Cameron was engaged to conduct opera at Covent Garden and, on 5 June 1939, directed a performance of Wagner's *Tristan und Isolde* for an indisposed Sir Thomas Beecham. A gifted concert conductor, Cameron had little or no experience of working in the theatre. He had difficulty imparting his ideas to the singers and handled the mechanics of the work badly. Nevertheless, he continued to perform with the company on tour. Though he failed at Covent Garden, his abilities as an orchestral conductor remained his greatest asset. In 1938 he was suggested as a possible permanent conductor of the Hallé Orchestra of Manchester, an ensemble that he later visited regularly. But it was his work at the Henry Wood Promenade Concerts that secured his reputation in Britain. Sir Henry appreciated Cameron's strengths and drew upon them accordingly; he accepted him as associate conductor from 1941. With an interest in modern music, Cameron was an ideal conductor for the Proms. His passion for new and interesting works never faltered, and during his twenty-four years with the series he directed a number of first performances, including those of E. J. Moeran's serenade in G (2 September 1948) and Alan Bush's violin concerto (25 August 1949). But with the appointment of William Glock as the BBC's controller of music in 1959, Cameron began to fall from favour, and, with an administration that encouraged the use of younger musicians, his position became increasingly tenuous. He retired from the Proms in 1964, the year of his eightieth birthday.

Modern listeners often undervalue Cameron's standing as an executant. While his discography is not substantial, the list of orchestras with whom he worked is impressive. He directed concerts with most of the major British ensembles and led performances with the Berlin Philharmonic, Amsterdam Concertgebouw, Los Angeles Philharmonic, Czech Philharmonic, and Budapest Symphony orchestras. Though he was never a charismatic figure, fellow musicians admired his podium manner, his skills as an interpreter, and his quiet professionalism. Appointed CBE in 1957, Cameron died unmarried at the Glendaph Nursing Home, Kingsland, Leominster, Herefordshire, on 26 June 1975. RAYMOND HOLDEN

Sources *WWW, 1941–50, 1929–1940* · *WWW, 1981–90, 1971–80* · Grove, *Dict. mus.* (1954) · R. W. Clarke, *The Royal Albert Hall* (1958) · Grove, *Dict. mus.* (1927) · D. Cox, *The Henry Wood Proms* (1980) · C. Ehrlich, *First philharmonic: a history of the Royal Philharmonic Society* (1995) · R. Elkin, *Queen's Hall, 1893–1941* [1944] · R. Elkin, *Royal Philharmonic: the annals of the Royal Philharmonic Society* (1946) · H. Foss and N. Goodwin, *London Symphony Orchestra* (1954) · A. Jacobs, *Henry J. Wood, maker of the proms* (1994) · M. Kennedy, *The Hallé tradition: a century of music* (1960) · P. Muck, *Einhundert Jahre Berliner Philharmonisches Orchester* (Tutzing, 1982) · *The Times* (28 June 1975) · J. Pike, *Torquay, the place and the people: a centenary history* (1992) · *Who's who in music*, 3rd edn (1950) · *Baker's biographical dictionary of musicians*, rev. N. Slonimsky, 8th edn (1992) · *New Grove* · *CGPLA Eng. & Wales* (1975) · b. cert. · d. cert. · J. R. Thackrah, *The Royal Albert Hall* (1983) · K. Young, *Music's great days in the spas and watering places* (1968)

Archives Kensington Central Library, MSS and music scores | SOUND BL NSA

Likenesses E. Kapp, drawing, 1943, Barber Institute of Fine Arts, Birmingham · photograph, *c.*1966, NPG

Wealth at death £5005: probate, 1975, *CGPLA Eng. & Wales*

Cameron [*née* Sharp], **Caroline Emily Lovett** (1844–1921), novelist, was born at Walthamstow on 15 June 1844, the daughter of Granvill Sharp, a successful merchant, who died before she was born, and his wife, Ann Elizabeth, *née* Hill. She was educated first at a Putney boarding-school, then in Paris. In 1874 Caroline Emily married Henry William Lovett Cameron, parliamentary agent to the Treasury; they had two sons. Her brother-in-law was the famous explorer and author of boys' adventure novels Verney Lovett Cameron (1844–1894). Three years after her marriage she published her first novel, *Juliet's Guardian* (1877), in serialized form in the journal *Belgravia*. Recounting the romance between Juliet Blair, a young girl of seventeen, and her older guardian, Colonel Fleming, this novel received good reviews, initiating a large career output of forty-five novels at the rate of about two a year.

In her own day Caroline Emily was classed among the second-rank novelists, with 'some half-dozen lady authors', according to her publisher William Tinsley, although he goes on to state that she 'should have top place for always better diction, and perhaps as a rule more homely sentiment' (Tinsley). The titles of her many novels display this homely sentiment: *Deceivers Ever* (1878), *Poor Wisdom's Chance* (1880), *Worth Winning* (1882), *Pure Gold* (1885), *A Lost Wife* (1889), *Weak Woman* (1892), *A Bad Lot* (1895), and *Devil's Apples* (1898). Her best-known novel, *In a Grass Country* (1885), emulates the hunting novels of G. Whyte-Melville. A reviewer in 1885 described Cameron's typical plot as: 'beautiful women and handsome men, all misunderstanding each other, tormenting and tempting each other, dying of broken hearts and blood vessels' (Sutherland, 102).

Like many writers of popular women's fiction, however, Cameron received attention in the twentieth century for the radical views on sexual relations sometimes expressed in her works. For example, *A Sister's Sin* (1893) sympathetically depicts the plight of a woman made pregnant by a man who abandons her so that he may not cross his mother's will. *The Man who Didn't* (1895) participates in the cultural conversation on the 'new woman' begun by Grant Allen's *The Woman who Did* (1890) and continued by Victoria Cross's *The Woman who Didn't* (1895). Cameron's contribution to this conversation advocates marriage reform and the governmental maintenance of children. Although she lived well into the twentieth century, Cameron stopped publishing fiction at the turn of the century. She died on 4 August 1921 at Millbrook House, Shepperton. BONNIE J. ROBINSON

Sources Blain, Clements & Grundy, *Feminist comp.* • S. Kemp, C. Mitchell, and D. Trotter, *Edwardian fiction: an Oxford companion* (1997) • J. Sutherland, *The Longman companion to Victorian fiction* (1988) • *WWW* • W. Tinsley, *Random recollections of an old publisher*, 2 vols. (1900) • R. L. Wolff, *Nineteenth-century fiction: a bibliographical catalogue based on the collection formed by Robert Lee Wolff*, 5 vols. (1981–6) • b. cert. • d. cert.

Wealth at death probate, 1921 • £9340 7s. 9d.: administration, 1922

Cameron, Charles (1745–1812), architect, was born on 1 June 1745, at Bolton Street, London, the son of Walter Cameron (*d.* after 1780), master carpenter and speculative builder, and his wife, Hannah. His grandfather Archibald Cameron came from Edinburgh, and Cameron may have been distantly related to the Cameron of Lochiel family. It is certain that the architect's father was closely connected to one of the main figures of the Jacobite rising of 1745, Dr Archibald Cameron, whom he visited in prison before his execution in 1753. It is likely that Walter Cameron took care in London of Dr Cameron's wife and his son Charles, probably named—as was Walter's own son—after the Pretender, before they emigrated to the continent.

In 1760 Charles Cameron was apprenticed to his father in the Carpenters' Company, but about 1764 he developed different interests: an album of 100 drawings consists of remarkable images of vases, plates, and silverwork in a variety of styles (although towards the end of the album his taste for classical antiquity was clearly increasing). It was probably the talent of the young draughtsman that attracted the attention of the architect Isaac Ware. Ware was planning a new edition of Lord Burlington's *Fabbriche antiche* (*c*.1732), a book of engravings from the drawings of Palladio, mostly of Roman baths. After Ware's death in 1766, Cameron wanted to go to Italy, in order to update the drawings of the ancient monuments. Altering the character of the book, he made it a model of Enlightenment scholarship, with an extensive commentary and a strong neo-classical bias. After arriving in Rome in 1768, Cameron spent less than a year there. He may have met Charles Louis Clérisseau, the French architectural draughtsman and one of the leading figures in the neo-classical movement, but it is more likely that he learned of his works later, when Clérisseau travelled to England in 1771. Certainly Cameron socialized with Jacobites in Rome and they helped him to obtain permission from the Vatican for the excavation of the baths of Titus. In the book of another Charles Cameron—possibly the son of Dr Archibald Cameron—*Memori per le belle arti* (1785), the activity of the young architect investigating the Roman thermae is described with sympathy.

Charles Cameron returned to England in 1769, and published his book in folio under the title *The baths of the Romans explained and illustrated, with the restorations of Palladio corrected and improved*, with English and French texts, in 1772. Two other editions were issued in 1774 and 1775, but the book did not bring success to the author in spite of the dedication to Lord Bute and other efforts to obtain patronage. During these years Cameron produced his only known architectural work in Britain: drawings for the decoration of Jervoise Clarke's house in Hanover Square, London, built by Cameron's father in 1770–74. In 1774 Cameron applied for a district surveyorship in Middlesex, but did not attend the interview. About this time his financial troubles began: in 1775–6 his father was put into the Fleet prison for debts, and Charles lost the family fortune and his own belongings (including his 1500 books). His father was still in the Fleet when the architect left for Russia.

Cameron arrived in St Petersburg in 1778, in response to an invitation from the Russian court. Catherine the Great had been planning to build a Roman bath in her summer residence, Tsarskoye Selo, for several years, an idea suggested by Clérisseau. However, his design, based on the thermae of Diocletian, was too large and the empress looked for a specialist to build a smaller and more private bath for her. Cameron was clearly the best-qualified architect in Europe for the task, although it is likely that Catherine's Scottish physician John Rogerson may have proposed his compatriot. The empress proudly proclaimed Cameron to be a Jacobite and a nephew of Jenny Cameron, 'the Pretender's Diana'.

Cameron held a unique position among his Russian contemporaries: he was officially the private architect to the empress and worked only for her and the heir to the throne, the Grand Duke Paul. In 1779–96 he worked at the palace and gardens of Tsarskoye Selo, near St Petersburg. There he created between 1779 and 1786: the private apartments; the Roman thermae, including the cold bath; the Agate Pavilion, decorated with precious stones; a hanging garden; a ramp; and a colonnaded gallery, which was named after him. At the same time he completed the Chinese ensemble in the park, the largest in eighteenth-century Europe. He designed and built the model town of Sofia as part of the landscaping of the park, and constructed there the monumental cathedral of St Sophia. The town united Tsarskoye Selo and Paul's residence, Pavlovsk; here, in 1782–6, Cameron built the palace and several garden pavilions (including the famous Temple of Friendship) and created the 1000 hectare landscape park.

On Catherine's death in 1796, Paul I—hostile to the memory of his mother—dismissed her beloved architect Cameron. After the emperor's murder, however, Cameron returned to Pavlovsk to design garden pavilions for the Dowager Empress Maria, among them his masterpiece the Three Graces. About 1800 he may have made designs for the Baturin palace in Ukraine for Count Kirill Rasumovsky; another Scottish architect, Adam Menelaws, was also involved in this project. It seems that Cameron never left St Petersburg and did not visit Moscow, Ukraine, or the Crimea; his design for a triumphal arch, displayed by J. L. Bond in the Royal Academy in 1793 as 'to be erected in the Crimea', must be the one built at Tsarskoye Selo to celebrate the conquest of the Crimea.

In 1803 Alexander I appointed Cameron to the important post of the architect-in-chief of the admiralty. The next three years were a period of intensive, mostly technical work. In 1806 he left this post to resume his role as the emperor's private architect. In 1784 Cameron had married Catherine Busch (*d.* 1817), daughter of the British head gardener of Tsarskoye Selo. He died at his home, Ingeneering Castle, St Petersburg, on 26 March 1812. The main collections of his drawings are in the Hermitage and the Academy of Fine Arts museums, the library of the Institute of Railway Engineers in St Petersburg, the Museum of Pavlovsk, and the Museum of Architecture in Moscow.

Cameron was the leader of the neo-classical architectural movement in Russia: he was the first to introduce the Greek revival style, using the publications of James Stuart and Nicholas Revett, while the dome of the cathedral of St Sophia was the earliest example of the Byzantine revival style in Russia. Cameron also encouraged the Chinese taste in Russia, inspired by the work of Sir William Chambers. Most importantly, he combined an enthusiasm for the archaeology of antiquity with a firm grasp of English Palladianism, both of which are apparent in the palace at Pavlovsk, which became the model for the country residences of the Russian gentry. Similarly, his park in Pavlovsk established in Russia landscape gardening in the style of Capability Brown: it is considered to be the best one in the country. In fact, Cameron created the 'language' of the architecture of the Russian Enlightenment which expressed the spirit of the epoch of Catherine the Great: his buildings became symbols of this period in Russian literature. DIMITRY SHVIDKOVSKY

Sources D. Shvidkovsky, *The empress and the architect* (1996) • T. Talbot Rice, *Charles Cameron* (1967) • I. Rae, *Charles Cameron: architect to the court of Russia* (1971) • A. Cross, 'Cameron's Scottish workmen', *Scottish Slavonic Review*, 10 (spring 1988), 51–74 • *Catalogue d'une bibliothèque précieuse … provenant de la succession de feu Mr Ch. Cameron* (Paris, 1812)

Archives Museum of Architecture, Moscow • Pushkin Museum of Fine Arts, Moscow

Likenesses A. Orlovsky, group portrait, pencil, 1809 (A), Russian Museum, St Petersburg, Russia • A. Orlovsky, pencil, 1809, Russian Museum, St Petersburg, Russia

Cameron, Sir Charles, first baronet (1841–1924), politician and newspaper proprietor, was born in Dublin on 18 December 1841, the eldest son of John Cameron (1804–1873), a newspaper proprietor of Glasgow and Dublin, and his wife, Ellen (*d.* 1846), daughter of Alexander Galloway. He was educated at Madras College, St Andrews, before going to Trinity College, Dublin, graduating BA in 1862. He studied medicine in Dublin, graduating MB in 1862, and was gold medallist of the Pathological Society of Dublin. He went on to study at medical schools in Paris, Berlin, and Vienna, taking the degrees of MD and MA at Dublin in 1865, though he never practised medicine. He also studied law, graduating LLB and LLD in 1871. In 1869 he married Frances Caroline (*d.* 1899), daughter of William Macauley MD.

In 1864 Cameron became sole proprietor and editor (until 1874) of the *North British Daily Mail*, which had been established by his father in 1847. The first Glasgow daily newspaper, it outlasted many competitors and settled into a rivalry with the less politically advanced *Glasgow Herald*. Under Charles Cameron the tone of the paper became markedly more radical. He was particularly concerned with social issues and much space was given over to analyses of problems such as the drink trade, conditions in prisons and lunatic asylums, and prostitution. Another important theme in the *North British Daily Mail* was the attempt to expose municipal corruption in connection with the City Improvement Trust, which sought to clear and improve slum areas.

Sir Charles Cameron, first baronet (1841–1924), by Bassano, 1899

At the general election of February 1874 Cameron entered parliament as an MP for Glasgow, one of five Liberals who contested the three-member seat. He benefited from the organizational power of the temperance movement which, together with an energetic leafleting campaign, helped to secure his return. The election stimulated the formation of the Glasgow Liberal Association. Glasgow became established as the centre of radical Liberalism in Scotland, enjoying its greatest moment at the general election of November 1885, when Liberals won all seven of the new constituencies in the city. When the Liberal Party divided over home rule in 1886 Cameron remained loyal to Gladstone, and the *North British Daily Mail* overcame initial caution to become steadily more supportive of home rule for Ireland. Cameron remained the MP for Glasgow College division until he was defeated in July 1895. Although he represented Glasgow Bridgeton from February 1897 until his retirement in 1900, his political career largely ended in 1895 with the demise of the issues which he had championed.

As an MP Cameron has been regarded as a 'faddist', and it is certainly true that he was interested in a host of single-issue campaigns. He was remarkably successful at carrying private members' bills on a range of subjects including liquor licensing (1876), the Scottish marriage laws (1878), the abolition of imprisonment for debt in Scotland (1880), the conferring of the municipal franchise on women in Scotland, and the adoption of the sixpenny telegram. Through his interest in public health he took part in the proceedings of the Social Science Association and the British Medical Association, publishing a treatise entitled *The Cholera Microbe* (1884).

After 1880 Cameron's career was dominated by the crofter issue and Scottish church disestablishment. He had chaired the meeting of the Federation of Celtic Societies in Glasgow in 1881 and in his address to the delegates he placed particular emphasis on the crofter question. This was before the issue gained widespread publicity from the events in Skye in 1882 and 1883. One of the earliest parliamentary supporters of the crofters, Cameron lent his support in 1882 to Donald Horne MacFarlane's motion for a royal commission on the crofter question. Along with MacFarlane, he was disappointed with the crofters bills of 1885 and 1886, regarding as 'illusory' the notion that the 1886 bill could provide a settlement of the highland land question. He bemoaned the fact that the bills did not deal with deer forests or make any attempt to alleviate the plight of the landless cottars. After the passage of the act he kept up a barrage of criticism of the Conservative government's resort to military expeditions to quell highland land agitation. This issue received considerable space in the *North British Daily Mail* and Cameron published a pamphlet on the subject in 1886.

The second issue which absorbed Cameron was the campaign for Scottish church disestablishment. After the Conservatives had abolished patronage in the Church of Scotland in 1874 this became an extremely divisive issue in Scottish politics. The Free Church divided over the issue after 1874, with a constitutional wing, adhering to the ideal of aiming for a purified establishment, being opposed by a group of outright disestablishers. There was also a strong voluntary group, mostly located in the United Presbyterian church, which dated from 1847 and which had always been opposed to the notion of establishment. Cameron's support for disestablishment did not endear him to highland opinion, which was strongly constitutional. The Liberal leadership feared the divisive nature of this issue and Gladstone was concerned about the likely impact on the Church of England. Cameron attempted to counter leadership caution with a series of motions in the House of Commons in March 1886, June 1888, May 1890, and May 1892. He also introduced two Scottish disestablishment bills to the House of Commons, in April 1894 and March 1895; both passed first readings but made no further progress. The disestablishment campaign ended with the Liberal defeat in 1895.

Cameron was created a baronet on 7 August 1893 and was deputy lieutenant of the city of Glasgow in 1894. He was a member of the royal commission on liquor licensing laws, chaired by Viscount Peel (1896–9). Following the death of his first wife, in 1900 he married Blanche (*d.* 1954), daughter of Arthur Perman, and settled in Surrey. He had one daughter from his first marriage and one son and one daughter from his second. Cameron died at his home, Braeside, Englefield Green, Surrey, on 2 October 1924.

EWEN A. CAMERON

Sources I. G. C. Hutchison, *A political history of Scotland, 1832–1924* (1986) • I. G. C. Hutchison, 'Politics and society in mid-Victorian Glasgow, 1846–1886', PhD diss., U. Edin., 1975 • J. G. Kellas, 'The liberal party and the Scottish church disestablishment crisis', *EngHR*, 79 (1964), 31–46 • I. M. M. MacPhail, *The crofters' war* (1989) • *Glasgow Herald* (4 Oct 1924) • *Men and women of the time* (1899) • Burke, *Peerage* • *CGPLA Eng. & Wales* (1924)

Likenesses Bassano, photograph, 1899, NPG [*see illus.*] • J. Henderson, portrait

Wealth at death £11,101 12*s.* 6*d.*: probate, 13 Dec 1924, *CGPLA Eng. & Wales*

Cameron, Sir Charles Alexander (1830–1921), public health officer, was born on 16 July 1830 at Dublin, one of three children of Ewen Cameron (1787–1846), soldier, and Belinda, daughter of John Smith of co. Cavan. He was educated privately in Dublin and Guernsey, where his family lived in 1844–5. He studied medicine in Dublin and chemistry in Germany under Baron Liebig and was appointed professor to the Dublin Chemical Society at the age of twenty-three. As he noted himself, in one of his very few self-deprecatory observations, this was a pretentious title to give to the teacher of an unchartered private society. Cameron also lectured on chemistry and physics in three of Dublin's flourishing mid-nineteenth-century medical schools: Peter Street, Dr Steevens's, and the Ledwich. On 16 October 1862, at St Mary's Church, Donnybrook, Dublin, Cameron married Lucie Frances (*d.* 1883), only daughter of John Macnamara, solicitor, of Dublin. They had six sons and two daughters.

Cameron obtained his first medical qualification, the licence of the King and Queen's College of Physicians in Ireland (subsequently the Royal College of Physicians of Ireland), in 1868, and he later became a member and honorary fellow of that body. He was awarded the fellowship of the Royal College of Surgeons in Ireland in 1874 and obtained a diploma in public health from Cambridge University three years later. Cameron was elected to the chair of hygiene in the Royal College of Surgeons in Ireland in 1868 and to the professorship of chemistry in 1875, and held both appointments until his ninetieth year.

Cameron's most important work was in the area of public health. In 1862, he began his long connection with the municipal administration of Dublin when he was appointed public analyst. A few years later, he became medical officer of health and held this office until his death more than fifty years later. During this half-century of revolutionary change, Cameron played a key role in improving the living conditions of the Dublin poor. He was knighted in 1885 in recognition of his services to public health and was elevated to the companionship of the Bath in January 1899. He was awarded an honorary MD degree by the Royal University of Ireland in October 1896 and in September 1910 his work was publicly acknowledged by Dublin corporation when he was made an honorary freeman of the city, the capital's highest civic honour.

Cameron was closely associated with the Royal College of Surgeons in Ireland for many years and was elected president in 1885–6. He published a monumental history of the college in 1886 and a revised, extended edition thirty years later. Cameron could rightly claim that this work was 'practically a history of Irish medicine and institutions from the earliest ages' but, as one critic noted, his literary abilities did not match his industry. The same can be said of his tedious, octogenarian reminiscences and his factually inconsistent autobiography, which were published in 1913 and 1920 respectively. Cameron was on much firmer ground with the professional publications of a career spanning almost seventy years. Several monographs and scores of articles in the leading British and Irish medical, sanitary, and scientific journals are testimony to his intellectual curiosity, prolificacy, and versatility. In addition he produced a booklet on Irish freemasonry, a guide to the Dublin Zoological Gardens, and a volume of German poetry in translation. His unpublished writings include his diaries for the years 1880–1916, which are in the archives of the Royal College of Surgeons in Ireland.

Cameron was a Renaissance figure, interested alike in the scientific and the literary. He was, variously, theatre critic for the *Irish Times*, and joint owner, editor, and contributor to the *Agricultural Review*. A great socializer, he was at home in the clubs, drawing rooms, and salons of Dublin and London. He was a striking figure, full-bearded, and of imposing stature, a feature which may have owed something to his interest in gastronomy and fine wines. Witty, urbane, and gregarious, he was acquainted with singers and theatre folk, aristocrats, and members of the royal family. Cameron's politics were unionist and he subscribed to the tenets of the Church of Ireland. He was initiated into freemasonry on 22 December 1858 and was elected deputy grand master of the grand lodge of Ireland in 1911. He was also deputy grand master of the great priory of Ireland and sovereign grand commander of the supreme council 33rd degree, ancient and accepted rite for Ireland.

Cameron's last official assignment, at the age of eighty-six, was to inspect and report on the camp and buildings at Fron-goch, north Wales, where hundreds of participants in the 1916 rising were interned. He appeared 'immensely old' to the youthful prisoners but, one of them recorded, 'his sharp intelligent face and keen piercing eyes gave indications of a mental alertness and acumen far beyond the ordinary' (Widdess, ix). Although the next five years took their inevitable physical toll, Cameron retained his full mental faculties to the very end. He died at his home, 27 Raglan Road, Dublin, on 27 February 1921 and was buried alongside his wife at Mount Jerome cemetery, Dublin, on 2 March. His gross assets at the time of his death were £11,126 12*s.* 2*d.* LAURENCE M. GEARY

Sources C. A. Cameron, *Autobiography* [1920] • C. A. Cameron, *Reminiscences* (1913) • *Irish Times* (28 Feb 1921) • *Medical Press* (9 March 1921) • *The Lancet* (5 March 1921) • *BMJ* (12 March 1921) • J. D. H. Widdess, *The Royal College of Surgeons in Ireland and its medical school, 1784–1984*, 3rd edn (1984) • C. A. Cameron, *List of works and of the more important original papers* [n.d.] • *Irish Times* (3 March 1921)

Archives Royal College of Surgeons in Ireland, Dublin, diaries; newspaper cuttings relating to Dublin Chemical Society and Cameron's activities; scrap-album

Likenesses L. Stephens, chalk, 1869?, Royal College of Surgeons in Ireland, Dublin • T. Farrell, bust, 1893, Royal College of Surgeons in Ireland, Dublin • S. C. Smith, oils, Freemasons' Hall, Dublin • photograph, repro. in Cameron, *Reminiscences*, 108

Wealth at death £11,126 12*s*. 2*d*.: Oath of Executor, Dublin, NA Ire.

Cameron, Charles Duncan (*d*. 1870), army officer and diplomatist, was the son of Colonel Charles Cameron, 3rd Buffs, who had served in the Peninsular War. He entered the army by purchase as ensign in the 45th foot on 19 May 1846, serving the regiment until July 1851. He was attached to the native levies during the Cape Frontier War of 1846–7. After his retirement from the 45th, he settled in Natal where he was employed by the lieutenant-governor, Benjamin Chilley Pine, as an envoy to the Zulu country, and where he also acted as magistrate in the Klip River district of Natal. He commanded the African irregulars sent from Natal to the Cape Colony overland during the war of 1851–2. When war broke out with Russia he was appointed to the staff of Sir Fenwick Williams, her majesty's commissioner with the Turkish army, receiving the local rank of captain in Turkey. He was placed in command of the fortifications which were being constructed at Erzurum, and after the fall of Kars was detached on special service to Trebizond until September 1856. For his military services he received the Cape Frontier and Turkish war medals, and the Turkish medal for Kars. He passed a civil service examination and obtained an honorary certificate on 16 June 1858; in the same year he was also elected a fellow of the Royal Geographical Society and in April was appointed vice-consul at Redout Kale. He was posted to Poti in 1859.

Cameron was appointed British consul in Abyssinia in 1860 and left for his new station, with its residence at Massawa, in November 1861, arriving there on 9 January 1862. In the same year, he accompanied the duke of Saxe-Coburg and Gotha during a visit to the interior. Cameron afterwards left Massawa for Gondar, to deliver to Emperor Tewodros of Abyssinia a royal letter and presents from Queen Victoria, and arrived on 23 June 1862. Cameron had visited the rival Sudanese provinces on the way, and Tewodros, disappointed that the British had not supported him against Egypt and the Ottoman empire, became suspicious. He imprisoned Cameron, on the charge of interfering with the internal politics of the kingdom, from 4 January 1864 until 12 March 1866, when he was handed over to Hormuzd Rassam, an assistant political agent at Aden, who had been sent on a special mission to Abyssinia to obtain his release. He was reimprisoned by Tewodros, together with Rassam and others, at Amba Magdala from 13 April 1866 until the appearance of the British army at Magdala on 11 April 1868, when all the prisoners were released. Cameron returned to England in July 1868, where he retired on a pension of £350 per annum. He died at Geneva on 30 May 1870. His account of his imprisonment and the Abyssinian expedition, together with related correspondence, has been preserved in the parliamentary papers for 1868–9.

H. M. CHICHESTER, *rev.* LYNN MILNE

Sources H. M. Hozier, *The British expedition to Abyssinia* (1869) • 'Report from Consul Cameron respecting his imprisonment in Abyssinia', *Parl. papers* (1868–9), 63.713–34, no. 4089 • *Journal of the Royal Geographical Society*, 41 (1871), cliii • J. E. Flint, ed., *The Cambridge history of Africa from c.1790 to c.1870* (1976), vol. 5 of *The Cambridge history of Africa*, ed. J. D. Fage and R. Oliver (1975–86) • J. F. Ade Ajayi, ed., *Africa in the nineteenth century until the 1880s* (1989), vol. 6 of *General history of Africa* (1981–93) • Boase, *Mod. Eng. biog.*

Archives RGS, corresp. and notes on the Caucasus

Cameron, Charles Hay (1795–1880), jurist, was born on 11 February 1795, the son of Charles Cameron, partner in Harley, Cameron & Co., bankers, civil commissioner of Malta (1801–32), and governor of the Bahamas (1804–20), and his wife, Lady Margaret Hay (1769–1832), daughter of James, fifteenth earl of Erroll. His grandfather, Donald Cameron, banker, of Valentines, Essex, high sheriff of Essex in 1791, was the younger son of Dr Archibald *Cameron (1707–1753), physician and Jacobite. Charles Hay Cameron erected a monument to his great-grandfather in the Savoy Chapel, London. It was injured by a fire in 1864, when Charles Lloyd Norman, Cameron's son-in-law, replaced it by a painted window. Cameron was educated at Eton College from 1811 and was admitted to Lincoln's Inn on 7 February 1815; he was called to the bar on 16 June 1820. He could recite from memory much Homer and Virgil, and was considered cultured and well read. His friend Sir Henry Taylor described him as 'an accomplished scholar and a gentleman of great literary and general knowledge' (Hill, 44). He was a Benthamite, and ultimately among the last such.

In 1823 Lieutenant-Colonel (later Sir) William Macbean George Colebrooke (1787–1870) was appointed a commissioner of inquiry into the Eastern Colonies, and he went to Ceylon. The lawyer appointed to assist him with judicial and legal matters soon left, and Cameron was appointed to the vacancy on 23 August 1829, landing in Ceylon on 26 March 1830. Colebrooke investigated various aspects of government, and Cameron the judicial system and related matters; they agreed on the desirability of reform. The commissioners were deeply resented by the conservative governor, Sir Edward Barnes. They left Ceylon on 14 February 1831. Cameron substantially accepted criticisms of the existing system and his judicial report (dated 31 January 1832) recommended a uniform system for the entire island, ending the distinct jurisdiction over Europeans in civil cases; it recommended also that control of local courts be moved from the governor to the supreme court, whose appellate jurisdiction should be extended. The secretary of state for the colonies received favourably the commission's reports, and in February 1832 a new charter was issued reorganizing the Ceylon courts. As the result of Cameron's proposals, John Stuart Mill wrote in 1838, Ceylon was the only country with a judicial system

> constructed on the best conceptions of philosophic jurists—a system in which, without any servile deference to the authority of Bentham, the principal improvements made in the theory of the subject by that great man have been, with due consideration of local circumstances, adopted and carried into practice. (Clive, 438–9)

Charles Hay Cameron (1795–1880), by Julia Margaret Cameron, 1871

Cameron greatly liked Ceylon, and later purchased coffee estates there in the Dimbula and Dikoya valleys.

Back in England, Cameron was a commissioner for inquiring into charities, and wrote a report on the operation of the poor laws (April 1833, published 1834) in which he refused to distinguish between the deserving and undeserving poor, claiming he could find no legally satisfactory way to do so. In 1833 and 1834 he was on the committee of the Society for the Diffusion of Useful Knowledge, and in 1835 published an attack on duelling.

Bentham and Benthamites wanted the reform and codification of Indian law. Thomas Babington Macaulay, not a Benthamite but largely agreeing with Benthamite legal reform, was law member of the governor-general's council from 1834 to 1838, and from 1835 headed a new law commission to reform and codify Indian law. Because, according to J. S. Mill, of his Ceylon judicial reforms, Cameron was appointed a member and worked under Macaulay on the Indian penal code. Cameron agreed with Macaulay on the principles of the code, and Macaulay thought highly of and praised Cameron's work, and valued his friendship and conversation. Cameron and his colleagues were also members of a committee on prison discipline; their essentially Benthamite report, published in 1838, was 'a classic of its kind' (Stokes, 217). Cameron was also, on Macaulay's recommendation, a member of the General Committee of Public Instruction, agreeing with Macaulay's Anglicist education policy and working to Anglicize and improve Indian education. However, Cameron's health broke down and he was incapacitated for the latter part of 1836, and went on sick leave to the Cape of Good Hope.

Cameron had previously been married. At the Cape he met Julia Margaret Pattle [*see* Cameron, Julia Margaret (1815–1879)], daughter of James Pattle and his wife, Adeline, *née* de l'Étang. They married in Calcutta on 1 February 1838, Cameron settling 100,000 rupees on her; they had five sons and one daughter. By marriage Cameron was subsequently related to H. A. L. Fisher, admiral of the fleet Sir William Fisher, Vanessa Bell, and Virginia Woolf.

Cameron resumed his Indian legal work, replacing Macaulay as chairman of the law commission. In 1843 he was appointed fourth or low member of the governor-general's council, and became president of the Council of Education for Bengal. During the governor-generalship of Lord Hardinge, who was not accompanied by his wife, Mrs Cameron became the leading Calcutta hostess. Hardinge wrote of Cameron in 1845, 'he is well meaning, a gt. friend of Macaulay's', describing him as 'my *Benthamite* member of council' (*Letters of … Hardinge*, 96, 113). Macaulay's draft penal code, published in 1837, had been referred by Lord Auckland (governor-general, 1835–41) to the *Sadr* and supreme court judges of the three presidencies and they made many comments, which Cameron answered in two extensive reports (July 1846, June 1847). Despite his recommendation that the code should be passed into law, the Indian government delayed doing so until after he had left India. He also continued his work for Indian education, and contributed to the establishment of the University of Calcutta. Before he retired and left for England, a public meeting of Indians was held in Calcutta in February 1848, thanking him for his services to the 'moral and educational improvement of the native community' (Hopkinson, 47).

In 1848 Cameron retired to England, though he made periodic visits to his Ceylon estates. In 1850 and 1853 he published tracts advocating more rights and opportunities for Indians. He was considered for colonial governorships. In June 1861, when Cameron was considered for the Cape, Sir Henry Taylor wrote a testimonial asserting that he was 'a man of far higher intellectual power than any likely to be his competitor' (Hopkinson, 91). The duke of Newcastle, colonial secretary from 1859 to 1864 and fellow old Etonian, considered him for the governorship of Ceylon, but Cameron's friends advised against it because of his age and health, and the offer was not made. Cameron and his family lived at Tunbridge Wells, East Sheen, Putney, and from 1860 at Dimbola (named after his Ceylon estate), Freshwater, Isle of Wight, near Tennyson's home. They knew some of the leading writers and artists including Carlyle, Tennyson, Browning, Millais, and Watts. Carlyle wrote, 'Cameron has snow-white hair, a sleek small red face, lively little black eyes, and no *chin* to speak of' (Hill, 45). He affected long hair and a long beard—Tennyson called it a 'beard dipt in moonlight' (ibid., 97)—posed in a blue caftan, and declaimed classical Greek in his garden. He often went to bed, possibly from poor health, hypochondria, or to withdraw from his forceful if adoring wife—she said of him to a visitor, 'Behold the most beautiful old man on earth' (Gernsheim, 42)—and her guests. In 1863 she began her photography. He encouraged her—she wrote that he 'watched every picture with delight' (ibid., 18) and he posed for her as Merlin and as Lear (with Alice Liddell as Cordelia). She took several portraits of him.

Cameron decided to live his last years in Ceylon, partly because four of his five sons were there. In October 1875 he and his wife sailed for Ceylon with, among their luggage, two coffins. They resided at Kalutara, where in 1877 Marianne North visited them: she wrote that Cameron was 'perfectly happy' (*Recollections of a Happy Life*, 314). Mrs Cameron died on 26 January 1879. Cameron died on 8 May 1880 at Glencairn estate, Newara Elluja, Dikoya valley, Ceylon, and was buried next to his wife at St Mary's churchyard, Bagawantalawa, Dikoya. He had enjoyed a career of modest distinction and been praised by contemporaries. Since his death, however, and especially since 1948, his reputation has been eclipsed by that of his wife, and he has been remembered primarily as the husband and photographic model of Julia Margaret Cameron. LESLIE STEPHEN, *rev.* ROGER T. STEARN

Sources *The Academy* (26 June 1880), 474 • *Autobiography of Henry Taylor, 1800–1875*, 2 (1885) • A. Mackenzie, *History of the Camerons* (1884) • private information (1886) [from the family] • G. C. Mendis, ed., *The Colebrooke–Cameron papers*, 1 (1956) • Burke, *Gen. GB* (1937) • J. L. Clive, *Thomas Babington Macaulay: the shaping of the historian* (1973) • G. O. Trevelyan, *The life and letters of Lord Macaulay*, [rev. edn], 2 vols. (1908) • C. R. De Silva, *Ceylon under the British occupation, 1795–1833*, 1 (1941) • E. Stokes, *The English utilitarians and India* (1959) • H. E. C. Stapylton, *The Eton school lists, from 1791 to 1850*, 2nd edn (1864) • W. P. Baildon, ed., *The records of the Honorable Society of Lincoln's Inn: admissions*, 2 (1896) • B. Hill, *Julia Margaret Cameron: a Victorian family portrait* (1973) • H. Gernsheim, *Julia Margaret Cameron: her life and photographic work* (1975) • A. Hopkinson, *Julia Margaret Cameron* (1986) • *The letters of the first Viscount Hardinge of Lahore … 1844–1847*, ed. B. S. Singh, CS, 4th ser., 32 (1986) • M. Weaver, *Julia Margaret Cameron, 1815–1879* (1984) • M. Harker, *Julia Margaret Cameron* (1983) • G. Ovenden, ed., *A Victorian album: Julia Margaret Cameron and her circle* (1975) • *Recollections of a happy life: being the autobiography of Marianne North*, ed. Mrs J. A. Symonds, 1 (1892) • L. A. Mills, *Ceylon under British rule, 1795–1932* (1933) • P. Spear, *The Oxford history of modern India, 1740–1947* (1965) • W. Menski, *Indian legal systems past and present* (1997)

Archives BL, corresp. of him and his wife with George Broadfoot, Add. MS 40127 • CKS, letters to his daughter, Julia Norman • LUL, letters from him and his family to Lord Overstone, MS 804 • PRO, corresp. with Lord Ellenborough, PRO 30/12

Likenesses W. Drummond, lithograph, pubd 1836, BM, NPG • J. M. Cameron, photograph, 1871, priv. coll.; copyprint, NPG [*see illus.*] • J. M. Cameron, photograph, NPG

Wealth at death under £600: probate, 11 Dec 1880, *CGPLA Eng. & Wales*

Cameron [*née* Wales-Almy]**, Charlotte** (1872/3–1946), traveller and author, was born in Portsmouth, the daughter of Jacob Wales-Almy (*d.* in or before 1901), a captain in the Royal Navy. Nothing is known of her upbringing and early life. She was married to Major Donald Cameron (*d.* in or before 1901) of the 42nd Highlanders. After being widowed, she married again, aged twenty-eight, on 29 May 1901; her second husband was Auguste Ernest George Jacquemard de Landresse (*b.* 1872/3), gentleman, son of Seraphin Jacquemard de Landresse, gentleman, but this union may have been short-lived for she did not use her second husband's name.

By the time of her election to fellowship of the Royal Geographical Society in 1913 (when she was among the second cohort of women members), Cameron, who was living at 36 Carlton Hill, London, had been twice around the world. She had also published a travel account, *A Woman's Winter in South America* (1911), with a further volume, *A Woman's Winter in Africa: a 26,000 Mile Journey* (1913), in the press. Her two novels—*A Passion in Morocco* (1911) and *A Durbar Bride* (1912)—were based on her travels, including her time in India (1911), when she acted as foreign correspondent for the *Ladies Pictorial* and other periodicals. She was also a member of the Lyceum Club (where she was vice-president of the geographical circle), the Author's Society, the Society of Women Journalists, and she was a fellow of the Colonial Institute and fellow of the Royal Empire Society.

During the First World War Cameron travelled throughout the United States (1917–18) giving lectures in support of the allied cause. After the war she was awarded the OBE. She travelled over 250,000 miles between 1910 and 1925, largely by sea and railway, taking in Alaska and the Yukon (1919), Australasia and the Pacific (1921–2 and 1922–3), and Mexico (1924), each resulting in a travel account: *A Cheechako in Alaska and Yukon* (1920), *Two Years in Southern Seas* (1923), *Wanderings in South-Eastern Seas* (1924), and *Mexico in Revolution* (1925). She wrote three further novels and continued to travel in the 1930s, but did not publish any further travel accounts. An avid collector of local curios and souvenirs, she presented a collection of indigenous handicraft to Liverpool Museum (1938) and a further collection of oriental items to the Royal Scottish Museum in Edinburgh (1945). Latterly she was resident at the Hyde Park Hotel, Knightsbridge. She died at 95 Howards Lane, Putney, London, on 9 December 1946.

Cameron was a keen proponent of the British empire. In *Two Years in Southern Seas* she chronicled the virtues of colonial expansion and the work of colonialists, including a brief hagiography of Thomas Stamford Raffles and British oil drilling in Miri. Her outlook reflected a genre of her time, particularly in Anglocentric cultural and social judgements of race. However, her admiration for Prince Yumar's physique in her novel of 1911 (albeit that his character has been modified by an Oxford education) and her praise of the sultan of Jahore and admiration of 'native grace and beauty' (Cameron, *Wanderings*, 47) suggest that her attitudes were not uniform, but were cut across by class and individual experience. Similar complexity can be seen in her horror of British vulnerability to the threat of German expansion in the Americas (1911) and her appreciation of the kindnesses she received from Germans living in and travelling around Africa (1913). Other recurring themes in her books are the rights of women, harsh penal codes (including Britain's record in Tasmania), and the refrain of 'East is East, and West is West'.

Cameron was described by an obituarist as a 'woman explorer' (*The Times*, 11 Dec 1946), but could arguably be considered more of a sightseer or globetrotter, 'determined to get to the end of the beaten track but never off it' (Robinson). Critics appreciated her practical advice on travelling and her lively style, but were intolerant when this became gushing or melodramatic and, in the case of her African travels, included her *alter ego*, the 'imp of travel' who added 'his' own comments to the text. While her novels were credited with accurate settings in foreign countries, her travel writing is often pedestrian, including well-known information and secondhand accounts.

In her later work Cameron moved away from cataloguing hotel bills and attempts to include historical and political context to places visited (although not always accurate), as well as geographical information on matters such as trade and population, including her own photographic record. Cameron adopted for herself the late nineteenth- and early twentieth-century discourse of intrepid adventurer: 'Travel has been my comrade, Adventure my inspiration, Accomplishment my recompense' (Cameron, *Wanderings*), crediting herself with the bloodline of military, naval, and pioneer ancestors. However, she coupled this self-image with that of vulnerable woman alone, obliged by ill health to travel. She did experience a dramatic exit from revolutionary war-torn Mexico, for example, but for the most part her travels were perhaps more socially brave in setting out for six months at a time without a companion. In doing so she transgressed class and gender expectations, but in other respects her travel was socially (and racially) circumscribed, travelling by established means of public transport and largely confined to European contacts along the way. Her work is of value not only for its insight into the colonial outlook of the time but also as a social exploration of the places she visited and the people she met, albeit largely via a network of European colonial ports and expatriates. AVRIL M. C. MADDRELL

Sources *WWW*, *1941–50* • J. Robinson, *Wayward women: a guide to women travellers* (1990) • certificate of candidate for election, 1913, RGS • B. P. Kanner, *Two hundred years of British women's autobiographies: a reference guide and reader* (1997) • C. Cameron, *A passion in Morocco* (1911) • C. Cameron, *A woman's winter in South America* (1911) • C. Cameron, *A woman's winter in Africa: a 26,000 mile journey* (1913) • C. Cameron, *Wanderings in south-eastern seas* (1924) • C. Cameron, *Mexico in revolution* (1925) • m. cert. • d. cert. • *CGPLA Eng. & Wales* (1947)
Archives RGS, certificate of candidate for election
Likenesses photographs, repro. in Cameron, *Woman's winter in South America*
Wealth at death £20,464 5*s*. 10*d*.: probate, 1947

Cameron, Sir David Young (1865–1945), painter and etcher, was born on 28 June 1865 at 1 Queen's Terrace, Glasgow, the fourth of the nine children and elder surviving son of the Revd Robert Cameron (1825–1898), minister of Cambridge Street United Presbyterian Church in Glasgow, and his wife, Margaret Johnston (*bap.* 1839, *d.* 1924), elder daughter of Donald Robertson, a surgeon in Perth, and his wife, Jessie. Cameron inherited his artistic ability from his mother, who was a talented amateur watercolourist, as did his younger sister Katharine *Cameron (1874–1965), a watercolourist and etcher. From 1874 to 1881 he attended Glasgow Academy. In his final year he began classes at the Glasgow School of Art, which he continued when he began work as a clerk in a Glasgow iron

Sir David Young Cameron (1865–1945), by unknown photographer

foundry. After two years he left Glasgow for Perth, where he spent a further period working in the law office of his great-uncle David Hepburn. However, he loathed office work. In 1884 he finally decided to become a painter, despite his father's cool response to the idea, and enrolled at the Trustees' Academy in Edinburgh, where he remained until 1887. His fellow students included William Miller Frazer, George Denholm Armour, Charles Mackie, James Pryde, and William Walls. In 1886 he exhibited for the first time at the Royal Scottish Academy and the Glasgow Institute of the Fine Arts. On 30 April 1896 he married Jeanie Ure (1871–1931), the eldest of the three daughters of Robert Maclaurin, a partner in Archibald Orr Ewing & Co., and his wife, Margaret Anderson. They had no children.

Cameron first came to prominence as an etcher. In 1887 George Stevenson, himself a talented amateur etcher and friend of the noted etcher Francis Seymour Haden, saw by chance some of Cameron's sketches, persuaded him to take up etching, and helped him to etch his first plates. Subsequently Cameron produced about 520 etchings and dry-points—principally architectural subjects and landscapes—in a career which spanned forty-five years, becoming with fellow Scots Muirhead Bone and James McBey one of the foremost British etchers of the etching revival of 1880–1930. On the strength of his print *A Perthshire Village* (1888) he was elected an associate of the Society of Painter-Etchers in 1889 at the age of twenty-three, becoming a fellow six years later. He exhibited with the society each year until 1903, when he resigned along with

William Strang in protest at its decision to admit reproductions to its exhibitions. Cameron held his first one-man show in the galleries of Van Baerle in Glasgow in 1891. Four years later he had his first exhibition in the United States, in the New York gallery of Frederick Keppel & Co. He was awarded medals for etching at expositions in Chicago (1893), Brussels and Dresden (1897), Paris (1900), and Munich (1905). His achievement as one of the foremost etchers of his day was recognized in 1911, when he was made an associate engraver of the Royal Academy. Five years later he was elected an associate painter, the only person to have achieved this double distinction. His prints were issued in small editions, averaging fifty impressions, almost invariably printed by Cameron himself. This led collectors in Britain and the United States to vie with each other to acquire his later prints, and resulted in relatively high prices at auction during the 'etching mania' of the 1920s. No plates were executed between 1918 and 1922, when he was busy completing his work as a war artist for the Canadian War Memorials Fund (1917–19). In 1932 he executed his last plate, *The Broken Crucifix*, seen by many as a poignant reminder of his wife's suffering before her death from cancer on 17 November 1931. They were a devoted couple; although he survived her by nearly fourteen years, he never got over her death.

Cameron did not display the immediate brilliance which characterized the work of Bone and McBey. It took several years of steady development for him to reach a position of mastery in terms of technique and composition. His early etchings, which include the Paisley Set (1887) and the Clyde Set (1889), are little more than views, somewhat lacking in individuality of expression but occasionally displaying a hint of what was to come. 1892 marks a greater maturity, evidenced by several etchings in the North Holland Set and *A Rembrandt Farm*, which signals his lifelong admiration of the great Dutch master. Other early influences were Maxime Lalanne, Haden, Whistler, and the French etcher Charles Meryon.

From 1892, when he visited the Netherlands with the Glasgow photographer James Craig Annan, to the winter of 1908–9, when he visited Egypt, Cameron travelled regularly on the continent. Often his travels were followed by the issue of a set of etchings. The North Holland Set (1892) was followed by the North Italian Set (1896), the Paris Set (1904), and the Belgian Set (1907). The London Set was issued in 1900, following a move to London in 1898. However, after a year the Camerons returned to Scotland, to Kippen, Stirlingshire, where they built a house, Dun Eaglais, in which they lived for the rest of their lives.

Cameron developed great skill in the depiction of architectural subjects, conveying not only the beauty of a building but also something of its history and 'soul'. A master of detail and mood, of light and shadow, his notable plates include *Newgate* (1899), *Siena* (1900), *Place Plumereau, Tours* (1903), and *Thermae of Caracalla* (1923). He executed several atmospheric church interiors, such as *St Laumer, Blois* (1903) and *Notre Dame, Dinant* (1907) and culminating in *The Five Sisters, York Minster* (1907), arguably his finest print. He had an acute sense of design in terms of structure, tone, and balance, which is particularly evident in his landscapes. Fine early examples include *Landscape with Trees* (1892), *A Border Tower* (1894), and *The Meuse* (1907). From 1911 onward he produced a series of plates depicting the Scottish landscape, for which he is rightly renowned. They are noted for their simple design and wonderful quality of line, exemplified by prints such as the masterly *Ben Ledi* (1911), *Ben Lomond* (1923), and *Balquhidder* (1931).

In his painting in oil and watercolours Cameron executed mainly figure subjects and portraits until 1900. Stylistically they have an affinity with the later decorative phase of the Glasgow Boys or with Hague school painters such as Matthijs Maris. However, he was never entirely happy in his representation of the human form. Some of his figure paintings, such as his portrait *Dorothy Maude Kay* (1898, priv. coll.), and his busy harbour scenes, are successful, but others are less so. In 1899 the London dealer Colnaghi mounted an ambitious one-man exhibition, but it was not as successful as Cameron might have wished. Henceforth he concentrated on architectural subjects and landscapes.

During the first decade of the twentieth century Cameron's subjects were drawn from the landscapes and townscapes of the continent as well as from Scotland. *Early Spring in Tuscany* (c.1901), *Dark Angers* (1903, Manchester City Galleries), *Glencaple* (1905, National Gallery of Scotland, Edinburgh), *Nightfall, Luxor* (1909, Walker Art Gallery, Liverpool), *Craigievar* (1909, Aberdeen Art Gallery), *The Marble Quarry, Iona* (1909, Cartwright Hall, Bradford), and *Old Paris* (c.1910, priv. coll., London) are some fine examples. From 1910 to about 1916 he concentrated on Scottish landscape. By 1910 he had developed an individual landscape style, which was to change little over the next thirty-five years, though his palette went through a number of phases, ranging from sombre browns, greys, and black to unrestrained blue, plum, pink, gold, and red. He used a strong line to build up the structure of a landscape and accentuated mass and tonal relationships. He tended to eliminate everything trivial or inconsequential, which gave many of his landscapes an austere beauty. His intense love and feeling for Scotland and its scenery are immediately apparent in works such as *The Boddin, Angus* (c.1911, priv. coll., London), *Cir Mhor* (1912, Glasgow Art Gallery and Museum), *The Hill of the Winds* (c.1913, National Gallery of Scotland, Edinburgh), and *Balquhidder* (c.1916, Laing Art Gallery, Newcastle upon Tyne). About 1916 Cameron began a series of architectural studies, including several powerful church interiors, exemplified by *Café Leroux* (1918, priv. coll.), *Durham* (1920, Royal Academy), and *The Baths of Caracalla* (1924, Harris Museum and Art Gallery, Preston). His work as a war artist includes *The Battlefield of Ypres* (1919, Imperial War Museum, London), *Bailleul* (c.1919, Central Museum and Art Gallery, Dundee), and *A Garment of War* (c.1926, City Art Centre, Edinburgh).

In the 1920s and 1930s D. Y., as Cameron preferred to be called, was one of the best-known painters in England as well as Scotland. His work received great critical acclaim and was acquired by many public galleries in Britain and abroad. He was an academician of both the Royal Scottish

Academy (1918) and the Royal Academy (1920), a member of the Scottish (1906) and English (1915) watercolour societies and the International Society (1901), and a founder member of the Society of Twelve (1904).

Following a heart attack in August 1921, Cameron went to the south of France to recuperate. Influenced by the region's intensity of light, he produced on this and subsequent visits a body of work—imbued with the most vibrant colour he had used thus far—which must rank among his best. Typical examples are *La rue Annette* (c.1922, National Gallery of Scotland, Edinburgh), *Barlou* (c.1922, priv. coll.), and *En Provence* (c.1926, National Gallery of Scotland). This use of rich colour was continued in his later Scottish landscapes, of which *Wilds of Assynt* (1936, Perth Museum and Art Gallery) is a fine example. At times he appears guilty of exaggeration, but, to those who know the Scottish highlands well, reality bears out his extraordinary vision of colour and setting.

In the latter part of his career Cameron's importance and influence in British art circles extended far beyond the boundaries of the studio. Between 1919 and 1945 he was associated with the British School at Rome, which he visited several times in the 1920s. In 1925 the speaker of the House of Commons asked him to choose and lead a group of eight painters for the decoration of St Stephen's Hall at Westminster. He played a similar role from 1927 to 1938 when the Bank of England was rebuilt. He served as a member of the Royal Fine Arts Commission and was a trustee of the Tate Gallery (1920–27) and the National Galleries of Scotland (1920–45). He was knighted in 1924 and in 1933 was appointed the king's painter and limner in Scotland. He received honorary degrees from the universities of Glasgow (1911), Manchester (1923), Cambridge (1928), and St Andrews (1936).

Cameron was a squarish man of under medium height with blond hair and blue eyes. He did not look like an artist; his upbringing as a son of the manse was reflected in his preference for dark clothes. He was a man of firm convictions. The church was a very important element throughout his life and had a considerable influence on his art, especially in his later years. He was just as eloquent in his ardent appeals for a greater recognition of the arts by the Church of Scotland as he was in the interest of fine art. He gave advice to individual congregations on the redecoration of their churches and with Lady Cameron gave much time and many of their collected treasures and essential funding towards the renovation and decoration of their own church at Kippen. He also advised on the design of war memorials following the First World War. At the age of eighty, still carrying banners for art and for the church, he died of a heart attack on 16 September 1945, shortly after delivering a lecture, 'Beauty and worship', at St John's Kirk in Perth. Three days later he was buried beside Lady Cameron in the churchyard outside Kippen, overlooking his beloved Ben Ledi, which he painted many times.

Cameron was not a trailblazer, but neither was he an imitator. Allied to superb draughtsmanship and technique, he had an individual conception and style, to which he remained true throughout his life. Many of his oils are impressive in their power and drama. However, it is in his watercolours—fresh and spontaneous, rarely mannered or laboured—and in his etchings and drypoints that his true ability can be seen. W. N. SMITH

Sources W. Smith, *David Young Cameron: the visions of the hills* (1992) • F. Rinder, *D. Y. Cameron: an illustrated catalogue of his etchings and dry-points, 1887–1932*, 2nd edn (1932) • A. M. Hind, *The etchings of D. Y. Cameron* (1924) • A. A. Auld, *Sir D. Y. Cameron, 1865–1945: centenary exhibition* (1965) [exhibition catalogue, Scottish Arts Council, Edinburgh, Nov 1965] • J. L. Caw, 'Sir D. Y. Cameron', *Old Water-Colour Society's Club*, 27 (1949), 1–10 • M. C. Salaman, ed., *Sir D. Y. Cameron* (1925), vol. 7 of *Modern masters of etching* (1924–32) • M. C. Salaman, ed., *Sir D. Y. Cameron* (1932), vol. 33 of *Modern masters of etching* (1924–32) • H. J. L. Wright, *The etchings and drypoints of Sir D. Y. Cameron*, Print Collectors' Club (1947) • General Register Office for Scotland, Edinburgh • NL Scot., Cameron MSS, Acc. 8950, MS 8887, fols. 215–19 • Bank of England, London • British School at Rome

Archives Bank of England, London, corresp. and MSS • British School at Rome, Rome, corresp. and MSS • NL Scot., corresp.; diaries; papers; sketchbooks, Acc. 8950; MS 8887, fols. 215–19 | HLRO, corresp. and papers relating to St Stephen's Hall • NL Scot., corresp. mainly with A. E. Borthwick • NL Scot., letters to James Connell & Sons • NL Scot., letters to Frost and Reed • NL Scot., letters to Seton Gordon • NL Scot., letters to Sir George Henschel • U. Glas. L., special collections department, letters to D. S. MacColl

Likenesses K. Cameron, pencil, 1922, Scot. NPG • F. Dodd, etching, Flemings, London; repro. in Smith, *David Young Cameron*, frontispiece • A. K. Lawrence, oils, Scot. NPG • P. H. Portsmouth, bronze bust, City Art Centre, Edinburgh • photograph, NPG [*see illus.*]

Wealth at death £64,374 1*s*. 5*d*.: confirmation, 5 Dec 1945, *CCI*

Cameron, Donald, of Lochiel (*c*.1700–1748), chief of clan Cameron and Jacobite army officer, was born at Achnacarry House in Lochaber, the son of John Cameron of Lochiel (*c*.1663–1748) and Isabel, daughter of Alexander Campbell of Lochnell; Archibald *Cameron was his younger brother. His father, like his grandfather, Sir Ewen *Cameron, was an active supporter of the Jacobite cause, and in 1716 was created Lord Lochiel in the Jacobite peerage. He was involved in the abortive rising of 1708 and led his clan in its successor of 1715, after which he went into lifelong exile. Donald soon after assumed chiefship of the Cameron, and from then on was generally known as Lochiel. In 1729 he married Ann (*d*. 1761), the daughter of another (Jacobite) Campbell laird, Sir James Campbell of Auchinbreck; they had three sons and four daughters. The years that followed the collapse of the 'Fifteen had seen the nadir of hopes for a Jacobite restoration, though Lochiel in 1729 took on the role of secret agent for James III (James Francis Edward Stuart) in the highlands, while John Murray of Broughton, a clever Peeblesshire laird, took the corresponding role for the Scottish lowlands. However, the outbreak of hostilities between Great Britain and France in the early 1740s raised Jacobite hopes, Lochiel being one of the Scottish chiefs who undertook to raise 20,000 troops in James's interest if France would assist.

The cancellation of the French invasion attempt in 1744 had the consequence of resolving Prince Charles Edward Stuart, who had been involved in the abortive invasion, to make an attempt on Britain through the highlands, unaided if necessary, in 1745. Lochiel, now at the head of the conspiracy, recognized that a rising without French support could not succeed, and sought by smuggled messages to persuade the prince not to leave France. His despair on hearing of the prince's imminent arrival was alleviated by Murray, who persuaded Lochiel that honour demanded he raise his clan in support of Charles Edward. If duty was the main motive, other issues may also have been part of Lochiel's considerations. The Camerons were notoriously touchy about jibes from their clan Donald neighbours for their poor showing at the battle of Sheriffmuir in 1715. His own financial insecurity may also have played a part, James having insisted that the clan be kept at a war strength far above what Lochiel's estate could sustain. (This, too, had frustrated Lochiel's genuine attempts to be an 'improving' laird.)

When, two months later, the prince landed in the west highlands, Lochiel had wavered, but fatefully he agreed to meet Charles Edward and was persuaded to support the proposed invasion. Lochiel's own account of events shows that he was, in reality, playing for time in the hope that the prince, recognizing how little support there was for him, would return to France. The prince, however, outsmarted him, sending his frigate back to France, thus leaving no line of escape for himself and placing total reliance for his protection on the Camerons. When the Jacobite standard was raised at Glenfinnan on 19 August 1745, it was the presence of Lochiel and his clan regiment which effectively guaranteed that the rising went ahead. Lochiel, who had never had any military training, now showed himself to be an excellent regimental commander. From the outset he kept a firm control of his Camerons, and it was on account of his daring initiative that Edinburgh was captured. At the Jacobite victory at the battle of Prestonpans against a government force supported by guns and cavalry, Lochiel distinguished himself, leading the attack and then showing a humane concern for the wounded prisoners. He was now made governor of Edinburgh, insisting there be no reprisals against the whigs, while he led in person the blockade of the castle.

The capture of Edinburgh proved to be the limit of Lochiel's ambitions. In the prince's council he argued strongly against an invasion of England, and for the adoption of a defensive strategy supported from France against the British army. At the crucial debate at Derby, Lochiel's voice was strongly for abandonment of the advance on London now it was seen that it must fail. On the army's return to Scotland, he ensured that the city of Glasgow was not punished for its Hanoverian loyalties, as some in the army wanted. Wounded at the victorious battle of Falkirk in January 1746, in the subsequent retreat to the north he took his clan to the siege of Fort William, which still held out for George II.

Lochiel now showed a sharper side to his character, threatening 'my pretended Campbell friends' with the hanging of prisoners if Campbell reprisals against Jacobite clansmen in the west highlands continued. He abandoned the siege of Fort William in early April when a summons came from Charles Edward, now at Inverness, to rejoin him there. It was proof of Lochiel's firm grip on his clan regiment that, when others did not, he should have been able to join the prince in time to confront the duke of Cumberland's advance on Inverness.

At the disastrous battle of Culloden on 16 April 1746, Lochiel's Camerons fought bravely and lost about half their number. Again, Lochiel was wounded, this time severely. After escaping the field of battle he was borne on horseback to his house at Achnacarry. Following the excesses on the battlefield, which he had sanctioned, the duke of Cumberland promised the clansmen no further retribution if they would detach themselves from their chiefs and hand in their arms. At the same time, by Lochiel's own account, he offered the Cameron chief the prospect of terms if he and the other chiefs would surrender. Lochiel rejected this olive branch (if such it was), believing that the prince (who at that time was thought to have escaped to France) would return with French troops to support his cause. At the same time he sought to rally the clans of the west highlands. When word of this reached Cumberland he ordered the stamping out of further Jacobite resistance by 'fire and sword', particularly in Lochaber. In the resultant mayhem, Jacobite resistance ended; but, at enormous risk to himself, Lochiel now sought unsuccessfully to answer the prince's plea for help by bringing him over to the mainland from the Hebrides. By midsummer Lochiel had found refuge with his Jacobite cousin Cluny Macpherson on the slopes of Ben Alder. There he was joined by the prince at the very beginning of September, and from there, after a few days, he and Charles Edward made their way to the west coast, to two big privateering frigates which had arrived on a rescue attempt from France.

Returned to France by early October the prince at once set to press Louis XV to mount a major cross-channel invasion. Louis's reply was to suggest a much more limited initiative, landing 6000 French troops in the west highlands. Charles Edward, to his credit, rejected this proposal for which Lochiel was enthusiastic. Lochiel's motives were, however, highly personal: to return to his country for a resumption of the rising or to die in the attempt was, as he told James at Rome, the only way for him to honour hundreds of his fallen clansmen. Later in 1747 Lochiel accepted Louis's offer of the Régiment d'Albanie in the French army, but he died 'of an apoplexy' on 26 October 1748 at Bergues, in Flanders.

No portrait of Lochiel has survived. Ever since his death was marked in the whiggish *Scots Magazine* by sympathetic verse by a former adversary, his lasting reputation has been of a man whose humanity—he came to be known as the Gentle Lochiel—matched both his courage and his loyalty to the Stuarts, and whose high sense of honour, prevailing over the certainty of disaster it invited, gave his story lasting significance. There is, however, the old Lochaber saying about this unusually fair-haired Cameron chief, that 'it will be a sad day for Lochaber when there is next a fair-haired Lochiel!' JOHN SIBBALD GIBSON

Sources J. S. Gibson, *Lochiel of the '45: the Jacobite chief and the prince* (1994) • D. Cameron, 'Mémoire d'un Écossais', 1747, Archives of the Ministère des Affaires Etrangères, Paris, MD Angleterre, vol. 82, fols. 216–21 • 'On the death of Lochiel', *Scots Magazine*, 10 (1748), 586–7 • *Memorials of John Murray of Broughton*, ed. R. F. Bell, Scottish History Society, 27 (1898) • W. B. Blakie, *Origins of the 'Forty-Five* (1915) • J. Stewart, *The Camerons: a history of clan Cameron* (1974) • J. L. Campbell, ed., *Highland songs of the Forty-Five* (1984) • NA Scot., RD3/154 • *Inventorie of the charters etc. of the family of Cameron of Locheill* • Windsor, Stuart MSS

Archives Achnacarry, Lochiel MSS • NL Scot., accounts and letters | NL Scot., letters to William MacGregor • Royal Arch., Cumberland MSS

Cameron, Donald (*c*.1810–1868), highland bagpipe player and teacher, was born probably at Contin near Strathpeffer in eastern Ross and Cromarty, one of three sons of Colin Cameron (*c*.1770–1862), a farmer, and his wife, Mary Cameron (*c*.1777–1865), also a farmer. On 9 December 1841 he married Margaret Mackenzie (1818–1877), known as Maggie Cameron, a housemaid from Kilmorack near Beauly and later the dedicatee of one of the finest piping strathspeys. They had three sons, Colin Cameron (1843–1916), Alexander Cameron (1848–1923), and Keith William Cameron (1855–1899), each famous in his own right as a player and teacher of the highland bagpipe.

Nothing is known of Donald Cameron's formal schooling, but in piping he had distinguished teachers, including Donald Mór MacLennan of Moy, John Bàn MacKenzie, and Kenneth MacRae. He was also a friend and pupil of Queen Victoria's piper, Angus MacKay. Cameron worked as personal piper to various northern lairds before being engaged by Keith Stewart-MacKenzie of Seaforth at Brahan Castle near Dingwall from 1849 until his death. He taught several leading players of the following generation, including, as well as his own sons, J. F. Farquharson, Alexander MacLennan, Donald MacKay (the younger, nephew of Angus MacKay), and Alexander MacDonald (father of John MacDonald of Inverness).

Donald Cameron was the leading competitive piper of his generation, winning the prize pipe at Inverness in 1843; the prize pipe at Edinburgh in 1844; and gold medals at Inverness in 1849, 1850, and 1859. He also won the new Champion of Champions contest sponsored by the Club of True Highlanders and held at Inverness in 1867. While he spent his working life as a professional piper in a traditional setting, Donald Cameron lived at a time of rapid change. It is said that he would not even consider taking on a pupil who could not think in Gaelic; but within half a century of his death professional piping was dominated by Scots and English speakers and Glasgow was described as the centre of the piping world. The competition circuit in which he achieved such renown was itself of recent growth, having begun in 1781 with the Highland Society of London contests at the Falkirk Trysts, later transferred to Edinburgh. As highland games developed from the 1820s onwards, major new events emerged, including the Northern Meeting at Inverness and the Argyllshire Gathering at Oban. A new kind of professional ascendancy became possible, founded upon success in competition.

While Cameron's contemporaries acknowledged him as the leading representative of 'the true MacCruimen style' in piobaireachd (Donaldson, *The Highland Pipe*, 243), he also made a contribution to the rapidly expanding competition repertory in *ceòl beag*, the light music of the pipe: his 'Lord Breadalbane's March', later known as 'Highland Wedding', was one of the earliest fully developed competition marches and remains a classic. Trips to the Edinburgh competitions brought Cameron into contact with the pipe music editor and publisher Donald MacDonald (1767–1840) and access to his extensive manuscript collection. MacDonald was in the forefront of the movement to translate piobaireachd into staff notation, and Donald Cameron and his sons were to play an important part in this process. In 1853 Cameron started his own manuscript collection, which was taken up and completed by his son Colin. It contains some eighty tunes and is one of the most important Victorian sources. Colin Cameron probably intended to publish this, but he was anticipated by *Ross's Collection* (1869), edited by William Ross, Angus MacKay's successor as piper to Queen Victoria, which contained the earliest published versions of many of the classic tunes. Although he lived in relative seclusion as piper to the duke of Fife at Mar Lodge, near Braemar, and competed seldom (prize pipe, Inverness, 1861; gold medal, Inverness, 1865), Colin Cameron dominated the world of late Victorian piping. He made important contributions to David Glen's *Ancient Piobaireachd* (1880–1907) and C. S. Thomason's *Ceol Mor* (1900), and was regarded by contemporaries as the greatest living authority on piobaireachd. His brother Alexander (prize pipe, Inverness, 1867; gold medal, Inverness, 1870), also enjoyed a high reputation as a player and teacher. While serving as piper to the marquess of Huntly at Aboyne, he taught John MacDougall Gillies (1855–1925), who in turn became a leading exponent of the art.

The idea of a distinctive 'Cameron school', including Donald, his brother Sandy (1821–1871) (prize pipe, Inverness, 1846; gold medal, Inverness, 1862), and Donald's sons and their pupils, is frequently encountered in the twentieth-century literature; but the evidence suggests that they had a wide variety of individual styles. This characteristic range of musical choice contracted significantly during the twentieth century, however. In 1911 Alexander Cameron gave three weeks of basic instruction to Archibald Campbell (1877–1963), a gentleman amateur from a landed family of Kilberry in Argyll. Campbell went on to edit the bulk of the *Piobaireachd Society Collection* (15 vols., 1925–) and the *Kilberry Book of Ceol Mor* (1948), which, owing to the society's social power, were the only piobaireachd sources available in print for much of the twentieth century and provided the set scores for all the important competitions. Although frequently claiming to represent the style of the Cameron family, and in particular of Alexander Cameron and John MacDougall Gillies, Campbell published what were effectively his own arrangements, making many silent changes to his sources. Campbell's work was described in 1949 by John MacDonald of Inverness (the leading player and teacher of the first half of the twentieth century, and himself a pupil of Alexander Cameron) as marking the demise of piobaireachd as an idiomatic form. The manuscript of Donald and Colin Cameron is an important record of their playing style, but by the end of the twentieth century it remained unpublished and virtually unknown.

Donald Cameron died at his home, Seaforth Cottage, Maryburgh, near Dingwall, on 7 January 1868, and was conveyed to his parents' grave in the churchyard at the High Kirk of Inverness by a large company of pipers.

WILLIAM DONALDSON

Sources W. Donaldson, *The highland pipe and Scottish society, 1750–1950* (2000) · B. Mackenzie, *Piping traditions of the north of Scotland* (1998) · A. Fairrie, *The Northern Meeting, 1788–1988* (1988) · C. Cameron, 'Piobaireachd MS', 1853–69, NL Scot., MS 3745 · J. Campbell, *Highland bagpipe makers* (2001) · D. MacDonald, 'A select collection of the ancient music of Caledonia, called piobaireachd', NL Scot., MS 1680 · D. Glen, *A collection of ancient piobaireachd or highland bagpipe music* (1880–1907) · C. S. Thomason, *A collection of piobaireachd, as played on the great highland bagpipe: ceol mor* (1900) · A. Campbell, ed., *Piobaireachd Society Collection*, 2–9 (1928–58) · A. Campbell, ed., *Kilberry book of ceol mor* (1948) · A. Campbell, 'A page of old time piping', *Oban Times* (1 May 1948) [pt 1] · W. Donaldson, '18 tunes: an exploration of piobaireachd', www.piperanddrummer.com [*Piper and Drummer* online]
Archives NL Scot., piobaireachd manuscript
Likenesses photograph, repro. in Mackenzie, *Piping traditions* · photographs, repro. in Thomason, *Collection of piobaireachd*

Cameron, Sir Donald Charles (1872–1948), colonial governor, was born in British Guiana on 3 June 1872, the second son of Donald Charles Cameron, a sugar planter of Plantation Blankenberg and later of Georgetown, Demerara, and his wife, Mary Emily, daughter of Richard Brassington of Dublin. His mother died when he was a boy, and his father marrying again, Cameron was sent to England and later attended Rathmines School in Dublin, where he remained until he was eighteen. Unusually for one who rose so high in the ranks of the colonial service, he had no university or college education, and his sometime colleague Sir Philip Mitchell used to say he was largely self-educated.

Cameron returned to British Guiana and began his career modestly enough in 1890 as a clerk in the inland revenue department. His ability soon earned him promotion to private secretary to the governor, then in 1900 to secretary and clerk to both the executive and legislative councils. In the following year he became principal clerk to the secretariat, under the acting governor, Sir Cavendish Boyle. Cameron's marriage to Gertrude, daughter of Duncan Gittens, a sugar planter of Barbados, took place in 1903. They had a son. When Boyle was appointed governor of Mauritius in 1904, Cameron followed him there in the same year as assistant colonial secretary. Boyle clearly thought well of him and he was acting colonial secretary on various occasions. His outspokenness caused him to run into some trouble with local opinion: in a council of government meeting he made some critical remarks about a section of the Mauritian public service. A protest motion in the council caused a public demonstration, and the elected members of the council requested the secretary of state to remove him. The governor agreed to Cameron's offer to go on leave so as not to embarrass the administration. Thus he left rather under a cloud, the only negative episode in an otherwise brilliant career.

Sir Donald Charles Cameron (1872–1948), by Walter Stoneman, 1932

Cameron's next appointment, as assistant colonial secretary of the protectorate of Southern Nigeria in 1908, was something of a demotion. His ability soon showed through, however, and he acted as provincial commissioner on various occasions, and in 1912 twice acted as colonial secretary of Southern Nigeria. This was the time when Sir Frederick Lugard was bringing about the very important step of amalgamating the divisions of north and south administrations, as governor-general of Nigeria. He was a strong advocate of the practice of indirect rule, whereby the traditional rulers and native authorities were left with a considerable degree of autonomy in the day-to-day administration of their people, while colonial officers were intended to be advisers for the most part. Cameron became an ardent disciple of Lugard in this respect, and enthusiastically developed this policy in both Nigeria and Tanganyika. However, he was disappointed to be only made central secretary, a post which he thought gave him insufficient status, given his abilities and strong ambition. He became critical of Lugard's *ad hoc* methods and unwillingness to deputize. The situation changed for the better in 1919 when Sir Hugh Clifford became governor and Cameron enjoyed a period of close collaboration with him. They reorganized the central administrative system including its functions, staffing, and salaries, and Cameron's work was recognized when he was appointed chief secretary to the government and knighted in 1923. On the three occasions when Clifford was away, Cameron acted as governor.

The good record Cameron had built up was rewarded in

1924 when he was appointed governor and commander-in-chief of Tanganyika, arriving there in 1925. The former territory of German East Africa had been awarded to Britain by the League of Nations under mandate in 1922, but little development had taken place before Cameron took over. In developing indirect rule further, he gave the chiefs wide powers of administration, jurisdiction, and control of their own budgets, but at the same time he believed in firm central control of the main policy decision making process. Aware that indirect rule through chiefs might produce a static society, he also respected the terms of the mandate which stressed the need for social progress, education, and training for eventual self-determination. Thus he encouraged rapid growth in the education system through government schools and state-aided mission schools, and he supported the founding of Tabora School for the sons of chiefs, which became the leading secondary school, at which many future African leaders of Tanganyika received their education.

Cameron created a new post of secretary for native affairs, which he filled successively with two very able men—Charles Dundas and later Philip Mitchell. They were to travel round the country and Cameron himself believed in travel as a way not only to gain knowledge of the people but also to 'show' himself as governor (in full dress uniform) and talk to them—a habit which gained him great popularity and respect. He established a legislative council in 1926 with twenty-three members, either officials or nominated members. British settlers and Indians were in it, though no Africans as yet, because Cameron considered their English insufficient. He believed in gradually building up a sense of responsibility in the native authorities, but distrusted ideas for more advanced ideas of democracy and 'exotic' devices such as the ballot box. Instead he wanted the growing African educated élite to gain experience first in the advisory councils of the chiefs—a policy which critics might say ignored the possibility that the élite might become impatient with the methods of traditional rule. His creation of an African civil service, however, provided at least one outlet for them.

Cameron successfully built up the economy of the country, improving harbour facilities, and extending the main railway from Tabora to Mwanza on the shore of Lake Victoria, to benefit the central and north-west districts. He established a labour department, abolished forced labour and manual porterage, and refused to give priority to European settlement, insisting that the mandate stressed the paramountcy of African interests. New crops were encouraged, and Cameron resisted pressure from settlers to ban Africans from growing coffee. However, he warned against too much dependence on cash crops and took care not to press Africans to grow more than they wished. When he left in 1931 revenues had been increased by 83 per cent, recurrent expenditure by 53 per cent, and there was a healthy government surplus. In addition, Tanganyika had purchased five aeroplanes in 1930 for survey work—the first colonial or mandated territory to do so.

Cameron was less happy in his relationship with Kenya colony, the Uganda protectorate, and indeed with the Colonial Office. During his governorship he had to defend Tanganyika from the mounting pressure for 'closer union' of these territories of British East Africa, and also possibly including central Africa. Cameron always maintained that Tanganyika, as a mandated territory, differed from Kenya or Uganda. This angered Sir Edward Grigg, governor of Kenya, and also the Colonial Office, which tended to treat Cameron as a colonial governor like any other. But Grigg, along with Lord Delamere, the influential Kenya settler, and the colonial secretary Leopold Amery envisaged a settler-dominated group of territories on the Kenya model. Cameron argued that this was entirely against African interests in Tanganyika as laid down in the mandate, and if it came to that he would resign on this issue.

When the first conference of governors was held in Nairobi, Cameron attended very reluctantly and left early, holding that its decisions would not be binding on Tanganyika. Later he was particularly annoyed at Kenyan opposition to his proposal to extend the railway to Mwanza, as it was argued that this would detract from the profits of the Kenya–Uganda railway. It was partly a clash of personalities between Grigg and Cameron. When Amery called another governors' conference in London to press for closer union, Cameron again stood against it, and Amery sent out the Hilton Young commission in 1927 to inquire further into it. In the following year Cameron was again called to London to discuss their report, and he refused to support the type of union proposed. He utilized the support he had long enjoyed from the Labour Party, and they, and indeed some Conservatives and Liberals, joined him in opposing it. When the Labour government took power, another inquiry was sent to sound out opinions, but this time, apparently at Cameron's suggestion, it was a joint committee of both houses of parliament. This meant of course that it included some strong supporters for his view, and their recommendation was that there was no general agreement on closer union. Thus, for the time being at least, the matter was dropped.

In 1931 Cameron was appointed governor and commander-in-chief of Nigeria. At that time Nigeria faced many difficulties. Taxation and other grievances had caused riots, especially the women's riots of 1929 in the east, causing many deaths. In the west Yoruba chiefs had been given new and greater powers than they had traditionally wielded, while in Lagos the growing educated élite—many of them university trained—were becoming increasingly impatient with the frustrations of indirect rule through traditional rulers. In the legislative council Herbert Macauley's National Democratic Party held all the elected seats and could be a political force. Cameron still favoured indirect rule but perceived that in the north the ruling emirs were almost heads of states within a state, and they were supported in this demeanour by the British officers there who tended to resent Cameron's efforts to exert some overall control from Lagos. Above all, the world depression was having serious effects, forcing Cameron to make severe cuts in staffing and budgets.

In his short governorship of four years, however, Cameron achieved much. By 1934 the prices of groundnuts and palm oil, the major exports, had starting rising again and he managed to balance the budget. Because of his ruthless economies in managing the revenues he could claim that, by 1935, 30 per cent of the revenue was spent on education and social services—goals dear to his heart. By introducing new native authority and native courts ordinances he reformed and refined the indirect rule system, to be more flexible and adaptable to modern Western methods and the advances of technology. In the north, Cameron may have been biased against the rulers and their officers, and according to some, relations were not good, but he tried to introduce measured reforms. He tried to curb their separatist tendencies, and in particular, to free non-Muslims and followers of traditional African religions, of whom there were many in the north, from Muslim domination. He encouraged new developments in this region by increasing the power of technical departments in Lagos. In 1933 he appointed his ally in these policies, G. S. Browne, to be the new chief commissioner—not lieutenant-governor, as he abolished this grander title. Further, he sought to reduce the entrenched position of the northern officers by ruling that no officer could serve more than three consecutive tours in one province. However, Cameron did not have time to grapple with the problems of Northern Nigeria, which remained troublesome for many years to come.

In 1935 his wife's illness forced Cameron to retire to England. Although he still took much interest in colonial affairs, for a former governor with such a reputation for administrative ability he was not used very much by the Colonial Office: he served as a member of the Colonial Office education advisory committee, and was vice-chairman of the governing body of the Imperial College of Tropical Agriculture. In 1939 he published his autobiography under the curious title *My Tanganyika Service and some Nigeria*, suggesting that his real pride lay in his work in Tanganyika, where he indeed achieved much. The dominant theme of the book was his concern for African interests, and his total conviction that indirect rule through native authorities was the key to peaceful and purposeful colonial rule. Though he referred to the possible conflicts of interest between traditional chiefs and younger generations of educated Africans, he did not think this issue really serious. However, as governor he was popular with the masses and his departure from Tanganyika was regretted; scores of chiefs came all the way to Dar es Salaam to say goodbye. Julius Nyerere was an admirer, and said in a speech to the United Nations that all the British governors except Cameron had administered the country as if it were a colony and exploited the fear instilled into people by the Germans.

In appearance Cameron was tall and upstanding, with dark hair, and he had a magisterial and commanding presence. He was an indefatigable worker and expected the same level of commitment from his subordinates. A brilliant administrator, he could at the same time be aloof, brusque, abrasive, with a caustic wit that earned him some enemies. Above all, however, there was universal recognition that he had at heart the best interests of the peoples he governed. His only child, Geoffrey Valentine Cameron, who became legal secretary to the government of Malta, perished in an aircraft which disappeared at sea in May 1941. Towards the end of his life Cameron suffered from increasing blindness. He was appointed CMG in 1918, KBE in 1923, KCMG in 1926, and GCMG in 1932, and received the honorary degree of LLD from Cambridge University in 1937. He died at his home, 21 Grosvenor Court, Sloane Street, London, on 8 January 1948.

OLIVER FURLEY

Sources D. Cameron, *My Tanganyika service and some Nigeria* (1939) • H. M. Gailey, *Sir Donald Cameron, colonial governor* (1974) • J. Listowel, *The making of Tanganyika* (1965) • R. Heussler, *British Tanganyika* (1971) • R. Heussler, *The British in Northern Nigeria* (1968) • I. F. Nicolson, *The administration of Nigeria, 1900–1960* (1969) • Lord Altrincham, *Kenya's opportunity: memories, hopes and ideas* (1955) • J. F. Ajayi and M. Crowder, *History of west Africa*, 2 (1974) • V. Harlow, E. M. Chilver, and A. Smith, eds., *History of East Africa*, 2 (1965) • *DNB* • K. Ingham, *A history of East Africa* (1962) • J. Iliffe, *A modern history of Tanganyika* (1979) • *The Times* (10 Jan 1948) • *The Times* (16 Jan 1948) • *The Times* (20 Jan 1948) • *CGPLA Eng. & Wales* (1948) • J. White, *Central administration in Nigeria, 1914–48* (1981) • P. Mitchell, *African afterthoughts* (1954) • *WWW, 1941–50*

Archives Bodl. RH, corresp. with Lord Lugard; corresp. with J. H. Oldham | FILM IWM FVA, actuality footage

Likenesses W. Stoneman, photograph, 1932, NPG [*see illus.*] • group portrait, photograph, repro. in Altrincham, *Kenya's opportunity* • photograph, repro. in Listowel, *Making of Tanganyika*

Wealth at death £18,541 15s. od.: probate, 19 Aug 1948, *CGPLA Eng. & Wales*

Cameron, Sir Duncan Alexander (1808–1888), army officer, was born on 19 December 1808, the only son of Sir John *Cameron (1773–1844) and his wife, *née* Brock. He joined the Royal Highlanders (Black Watch) as ensign on 8 April 1825. He became lieutenant on 15 August 1826, captain on 21 June 1833, major on 23 August 1839, and lieutenant-colonel on 5 September 1843. On the outbreak of the Crimean War he obtained the local rank in Turkey of brigadier. He commanded the 42nd at Alma on 20 September 1854 and the Highland brigade at Balaklava on 26 September, and took part in the siege of Sevastopol and in the assault on the Redan on 18 June 1855. He was mentioned in dispatches, made an officer of the Légion d'honneur, and was awarded the Mejidiye (third class) and the CB. On 5 October 1855 he received the local rank of major-general in Turkey, and on 24 July 1856 the same local rank in Britain. On 25 March 1859 he was promoted major-general, and in 1860 appointed commander-in-chief in Scotland.

The War Office, dissatisfied with the progress of the war in New Zealand, promoted Cameron (local) lieutenant-general on 23 January 1861 and sent him to New Zealand to replace Major-General Thomas Simpson Pratt. Cameron arrived in March, at the conclusion of the war. Eager for war, he supported the intention of the governor, Thomas Gore Browne, to invade Waikatu and crush the Maori King movement. However in mid-1861 Browne was replaced by George Grey and the invasion cancelled. Grey and Cameron had an uneasy, fluctuating relationship. On 4 June

1863, responding to an attack on British troops, Cameron successfully attacked Katikara in Taranaki. On 12 July the invasion finally began: Cameron intended to force the Maori to a decisive battle and so quickly end the war and Maori independence. The British won a minor victory at Koheroa (17 July)—when Cameron's bravery was such that he was recommended for the Victoria Cross—and on 20 November Cameron captured the *pa* (fortified position) at Rangiriri, by unscrupulous use of a flag of truce. He was rewarded by the KCB (20 February 1864). On 20–21 February, in what James Belich has called his 'greatest military achievement' (*DNZB*, 1.66), Cameron outflanked the Kingite Paterangi line and captured the entire district, thereby seriously weakening the King movement. In April he moved his force east from the Waikato basin to attack the Gate Pa: the assault (29 April) failed. Cameron had failed to achieve his decisive victory. In the first half of 1865 he invaded South Taranaki slowly and cautiously: Maori people called him 'the lame seagull'. He won victories at Nukumaru (24–5 January) and Te Ngaio (13 March) but refused to attack the strong *pa* at Werdroa, which led to the breakdown of relations with Grey. Cameron had already (7 February 1865) sent in his resignation, and he left New Zealand on 1 August. His conduct was approved by the War Office.

Although in 1865 Cameron criticized the war as caused by settler demand for Maori land, and criticized colonial ministers, this attitude seems to have come late, apparently with his frustration at failure to achieve decisive victory. His military reputation in New Zealand was long low, but in the late twentieth century James Belich proposed a more favourable, revisionist evolution. According to Belich:

> A good tactician, a very good strategist, and a superb organiser, he [Cameron] was the best European commander to serve in New Zealand, and among the best of Victorian generals … it was Duncan Cameron at Paterangi … who sounded the death-knell of Maori independence. (*DNZB*, 1.66)

On 9 September 1863 Cameron was nominated colonel of the 42nd, and in 1867 he served on the royal commission on military education. He became lieutenant-general on 1 January 1868 and on 5 December 1874 general. He was commandant of the Royal Military College, Sandhurst, from 1868 to 1875. On 24 May 1873 he was made GCB. Cameron married at Kew, on 10 September 1873, Louisa Flora (*d.* 5 May 1875), fourth daughter of Andrew Maclean, deputy inspector-general of the Royal Military College; they had no children. He died at his home, Cambridge House, Kidbrooke Park Road, Blackheath, on 8 June 1888.

JAMES LUNT

Sources *The Times* (12 June 1888) • *DNZB*, vol. 1 • Foster, *Alum. Oxon.* • A. Mackenzie, *History of the Camerons* (1884), 413–14 • P. Mennell, *The dictionary of Australasian biography* (1892) • W. L. Rees and L. Rees, *Life and times of Sir George Grey* (1892) • A. W. Kinglake, *The invasion of the Crimea*, 8 vols. (1863–87) • Fortescue, *Brit. army*, vol. 13 • T. W. Gudgeon, *Reminiscences of the war in New Zealand* (1879) • Boase, *Mod. Eng. biog.*

Wealth at death £2495 15*s.* 1*d.*: probate, 30 July 1888, *CGPLA Eng. & Wales*

Cameron, Elizabeth Jane [*pseud.* Jane Duncan] (**1910–1976**), novelist, was born on 10 March 1910 in Renton, Dunbartonshire, the first of three children of Duncan Cameron (1878–1951), policeman, and Jessie Sandison (1882–1920), later called Janet. Her childhood was spent near Glasgow, her holidays at her grandparents' Black Isle croft. After some years at Lenzie Academy she went on to the University of Glasgow, where she received an honours MA in literature in 1930. She then worked as a secretary, and served (1939–45) as a Women's Auxiliary Air Force photographic intelligence officer. In 1948 she and Alexander Clapperton (1910–1958), engineer, moved to Jamaica as a married couple, despite the fact that he never divorced his first wife. When he died, Duncan returned to Jemimaville, near Cromarty, Ross-shire.

Jane Duncan had secretly written and burned manuscripts for years. To her astonishment, in 1958–9, Macmillan accepted seven of her novels. They published all nineteen Reachfar novels, the Jean quartet (four novels published under the pseudonym Janet Sandison), eight children's books, and an autobiography, *Letter from Reachfar* (1975).

Duncan walked with an erect carriage, clothed her tall slenderness in tailored tweeds, and wore her hair in a bun. A caring, private person, initially austere, she had a warm smile, gentle brown eyes, and a soft 'Inverness' voice. Raised a Presbyterian, she belonged to no church, believing simply in love as salvation and hate as evil. Eminently practical, she wrote with pen and paper, an old atlas as backboard on her lap, reweaving every shred of experience, celebrating the extraordinariness of the ordinary.

The *My Friend* (Reachfar) novels are set in Scotland, England, and Jamaica. They explore the mysteries of friendship and change, with the remembered croft, Reachfar, as symbol of value. A vanished highland life is evoked idyllically in *The Miss Boyds* (1959), and darkly in *Flora* (1962), but Duncan's range and complexity are remarkable, as seen in the witty *Muriel* (1959), the tragic *Macleans* (1967), the meditative *Hungry Generation* (1968), and the intimate *Sashie* (1972).

Jane Duncan died of coronary thrombosis on 20 October 1976, at her home, the Old Store, Jemimaville. She was buried in nearby Kirkmichael churchyard, Balblair.

FRANCIS RUSSELL HART and LORENA LAING HART

Sources J. Duncan, *Letter from Reachfar* (1975) • personal knowledge (2004) • L. L. Hart and F. R. Hart, 'Jane Duncan: the homecoming of imagination', *A history of Scottish women's writing*, ed. D. Gifford and D. McMillan (1997), 468–80 • private information (2004) • F. R. Hart, *The Scottish novel: a critical survey* (1978), 375–91

Archives priv. coll., MSS | FILM *Tonight*, BBC (6 March 1959), interview of Jane Duncan | SOUND *Highland novelists*, BBC Radio (June 1972), interview of Jane Duncan by Ian Grimble

Likenesses photograph, 1945, repro. in Duncan, *Letter from Reachfar* • photograph (as a young woman), repro. in Duncan, *Letter from Reachfar* • photograph, repro. in Duncan, *Letter from Reachfar*, jacket • photograph, repro. in *The Scotsman* (17 Nov 1979)

Cameron, Sir Ewen, of Lochiel (**1629–1719**), clan chief, was born at his maternal grandfather's seat, Kilchurn

Sir Ewen Cameron of Lochiel (1629–1719), by unknown artist

Castle, in February 1629, the son of John McAllan Cameron and Margaret, eldest daughter of Sir Robert Campbell of Glenfalloch (afterwards of Glenorchy). Immediately recognizable to many, owing to the production of the Jacobite *Memoir*, as the premier example of lifelong loyalty to the house of Stuart, Lochiel's actual life involved degrees of ambiguity characteristic of highland allegiances. His loyalty to the royal dynasty often conflicted with his clan's needs and with his family ties to the Campbells. Clan Cameron remained firmly protestant and disliked the survival and revival of Roman Catholicism in the highlands.

Early years Left fatherless while still an infant, Ewen's upbringing was under the control of his grandfather, clan chief fifteenth in descent from John Ochtery, who had established the family's prominence during a distinguished career in the service of kings Robert I and David II. Following highland custom Ewen spent the first years of his life under the care of his foster father, MacMartin of Letterfinlay, who was leader of clan Cameron's second most important family. In 1640 Archibald Campbell, marquess of Argyll, replaced the marquess of Huntly as the clan's feudal superior and Ewen's grandfather had the lands of the Camerons transferred from Inverness-shire to the shire of Argyll, of which the marquess was the chief judicial official. As part of the arrangement, when Ewen was twelve Argyll became his foster father. He attended the parish school at Inveraray, where he showed some academic inclinations. The marquess intended that he should study at Oxford, but the civil turmoil of the 1640s prevented his proceeding any further south than Berwick.

Cameron's first public act occurred in 1642 when with other heritors he petitioned for new ministers in Kilmonivaig and Kilmallie. He often accompanied Argyll; for instance, on 10 August 1645 they were together in Dollar Castle, the marquess's lowland stronghold. While Argyll was attending the parliament held at St Andrews in September 1646, Cameron met Sir Robert Spottiswoode, former secretary of state for Scotland and a royalist prisoner in the castle. Reputedly, this interview changed his life, making him sympathetic to the royalist cause. With his grandfather's death, he became chief and that December, after a petition from the Cameron leaders, Argyll permitted Lochiel to return to his clan.

Highland politics, 1648–1660 The political turbulence of the period, as well as the clan's interest, directly affected Lochiel's career. In April 1648 the engager parliament, recognizing his local prominence, named him to the committee of war for Inverness-shire. In the following February the kirk party parliament nominated him as one of the colonels of foot for the shire of Argyll. Late that month he received orders from the committee for dispatches to join Dougal Campbell of Inverawe in marching to Inverness to aid Lieutenant-General David Leslie in crushing royalist uprisings. It is uncertain if he intended to comply: his first biographer, John Drummond/MacGregor, would have suppressed any evidence that he did since it would have been impossible to explain away in such a supposedly firm adherent of the Stuarts. Following the news of the execution of the ultra-royalist James Graham, marquess of Montrose, Lochiel seemingly became a devotee of his memory. However, his first known military action tears at the fabric of his royalist reputation. On 20 December 1650 the Scottish parliament commissioned him as colonel of a clan regiment to fight the English Commonwealth army, which by then controlled much of Scotland south of the Forth. In spring 1651 he levied 1000 men but failed (unlike clans living further north) to join the army at Stirling. Instead he used his regiment for financial gain. First he despoiled the lands of Aeneas MacDonald of Glengarry (a Roman Catholic royalist), who owed him feu duties for some of his lands. Next the regiment marched on another Roman Catholic royalist, MacDonald of Keppoch, and ravaged his lands because of arrears in mortgage interest payments. With the MacDonalds brought to financial obedience, Lochiel returned home and disbanded the unit.

Lochiel gradually slipped into the royalist orbit of western highland clans. In October 1652 he was not covered by Argyll's submission to the English. On 30 December Charles II recognized his local prominence by naming him to a council of war in Scotland and as a colonel in the royalist uprising. Lochiel moved slowly to join the latter. In October 1653 Argyll had convinced him not to join the earl of Glencairn's rising and Lochiel was in any case working on keeping the Mackenzies quiet, but by December he had cast aside his reluctance, joining Glencairn. His first order, to be implemented in collaboration with his old enemy Glengarry, was to apprehend the independent royalist Archibald Campbell, Lord Lorne, Argyll's heir. In June 1654 the English general George Monck burnt the clan lands as punishment for the clan's actions. When, during the ensuing uprising, an English officer cornered him at Achdalieu, Lochiel bit out his throat. Despite his royalist actions, he remained at odds with Glengarry, who appointed a rendezvous on 25 November to revive the rebellion. Although personally inclined to support it, Lochiel could not bring out his clan. In December he was lurking on the bounds of Lochaber with only forty men.

Three months later, with the rebellion in tatters, Monck began playing the remaining royalists against each other. He offered Lochiel a low security payment or land taken from Glengarry, if he brought in his rival. On 17 May 1655 Lochiel submitted and received one of the better deals the English gave to their former enemies. In exchange for a bond of £12,000 Scots, he received security of his estates, the right of his clansmen to bear arms, the remission of cess to September 1654, responsibility for controlling robbers in his clan, freedom from prosecution for old thefts, satisfaction to his uncle Donald for losses caused by the Inverlochy garrison, and an advantageous deal regarding lands owned by William Mackintosh of Torcastle. The deal illustrates Lochiel's pattern of self-interested activity. Since 1637 the chiefs of the Camerons had obstructed Torcastle's legitimate efforts to evict them from Glenloy and Locharkaig in Lochaber, ignoring all legal judgments against them. Monck allowed Lochiel to retain possession, and arbitrarily reduced the rent arrears owed by him. In a dispute with the royalist earl of Atholl, Monck appointed himself, Argyll, and Colonel William Brayne to determine what minimal sum Lochiel would pay to end the matter. Owing to Glengarry's intransigent royalism, Monck also permitted Lochiel to encroach upon Glengarry's lands, which gained him 7500 merks in rent. Lochiel's submission brought him the further benefit that highland men with no relation to his clan acknowledged him as chief in order to carry weapons.

Lochiel's efforts to maintain his good standing with the English through the ruthless pursuit of thieves brought him, in October 1656, authority over public order in all of Lochaber. From that time (through 1688) the governments in Edinburgh relied upon Lochiel to suppress crime in the south-west highlands. On 5 October 1658 he attended the proclamation of Richard Cromwell at Inverlochy in the company of the garrison commander, his friend Colonel John Hill. The act was hardly coincidental, because the Camerons profited by selling timber, fuel, and supplies to the English garrisons, and when Hill later evacuated the post at Inverlochy, he gave Lochiel the keys to it as a token of respect. Just under a year later Lochiel signed Monck's engagement to live peaceably. In November 1659 the general ordered him to pursue Glengarry Macdonells who had committed theft, with authority to attack their chief, if he assisted them.

Financial and political difficulties, 1660–1685 In 1660 Lochiel accompanied Monck to London, where he gained a taste for court life. His first wife, Mary, daughter of Sir Donald MacDonald, first baronet and eighth baron of Sleat, Skye, had died childless. His second wife was Isabel, eldest daughter of Sir Lachlan Maclean of Duart (*d.* 1672). They had three sons (of whom the eldest, John, was born about 1663) and four daughters.

Lochiel joined the ultra-royalist faction of John Middleton, first earl of Middleton, and again abandoned Lorne (claimant to the earldom of Argyll after his father's execution). In 1661 he was twice introduced at court, where he was again in April 1662. He returned north by mid-June when he received protection from creditors to conduct business in Edinburgh. Despite his support of Middleton's regime, parliament ruled against him in the dispute with Lauchlan Mackintosh of Torcastle on 5 July. Two months later the marquess of Huntly was recognized as his feudal superior, much to his chagrin. The feud with Torcastle continued to his disadvantage with the privy council issuing letters of fire and sword against him for non-compliance with the 1662 judgment. His prevarication paid off, however, since the replacement of Middleton by John Maitland, second earl of Lauderdale, allowed Lorne to succeed as marquess of Argyll and Lochiel to make peace in 1664 with both Argyll and the earl of Moray. With the Campbells unwilling to attack their ally, and clan Chattan in disarray, the letters of fire and sword remained a dead issue. Instead Lochiel negotiated with Torcastle, agreeing to buy the lands but later reneging. In 1665 the earl of Rothes attempted to negotiate a settlement, but Lochiel prepared for victory by cultivating dissension within the clan Chattan. Refusing to accept Rothes's suggestion that he sell the lands for £48,000 Scots, Torcastle marched on Lochaber with 1500 men. Lochiel responded by levying 900 Camerons, and by persuading 300 Glencoe MacDonalds and the MacGregors to join him. As the two forces faced each other at River Arkaig, John Campbell the younger of Glenorchy (Lochiel's first cousin) and Argyll's bailie arrived to arbitrate accompanied by 200–300 men. Torcastle accepted the sale for 25 per cent less than he demanded, but the deal was far worse for him than that. As Lochiel had neither money nor credit (two months earlier the council had recorded his debt of 3000 merks to Cornet John Davidson on Skye alone), Argyll advanced him the money in order to gain the feudal superiority over the lands. However, the earl's finances were in a poor state, too, and he managed to make only one payment to Torcastle. On 20 September, Lochiel and Torcastle ritually exchanged swords, ending a 360-year feud over the lands for which the former had never paid any rent. The dispute failed to deter Lochiel's appetite for such illegal land transactions, since he granted leases and wadsets in Rannoch on lands belonging to Alexander Robertson of Struan. On 22 November 1666 the privy council fined him 1000 merks for non-appearance in Struan's complaint. For the moment, however, that matter had no ill consequences.

Within the clan affairs were not entirely in Lochiel's favour, for in 1663 MacMartin of Letterfinlay had entered into a bond of manrent with his rival Glengarry (now Lord Macdonnell). On 15 January 1669 the council noted that

Lochiel, with other Camerons and MacDonalds of Keppoch, had assailed government officials collecting public arrears in the marquess of Huntly's Inverness-shire lands, and authorized the earl of Moray to apprehend him. Just a month later Lochiel appeared before the council and gave in a bond of peace. Between June and August he was cited to make an annual appearance before the council and to arrange for a bond of caution regarding his clan's behaviour. On 24 August he responded to the allegations relative to his attack on the tax gatherers, and complained against the Mackintoshes for raiding his lands when he was last in Edinburgh. His clan continued to behave belligerently, being involved in a fight at Inverlochy in autumn 1670 with the MacDonalds of Glengarry, following which the council ordered him to maintain good order.

Lochiel's differences with other landowners continued. In 1671 a dispute of which the details are uncertain arose between him and Donald MacDonald of Moidart. From 26 February to 6 March 1672 he was imprisoned in Edinburgh Castle as a result of his problems with Struan. The financial implications of his illegal grants of Struan's Rannoch lands forced him to post a bond of caution of 5000 merks and to pay an annual rent of £24. Yet despite his somewhat dubious reputation the council named him in June 1674 as a commissioner of excise for Argyll. From 1674 to 1682 he was one of the equivocating parties in the dispute between the earl of Argyll and the Macleans. In September 1674 and July 1675 the privy council named him with the Campbells in the commission of fire and sword against the Macleans, a reflection of his now reinvigorated personal ties to the earl of Argyll. For instance, in May 1675 he contracted with the earl to provide fifty men to fight the Macleans. However, that September, in exchange for a pension from the Macleans of 1420 merks per annum and the chance to plunder Campbell territory, Lochiel formally switched sides. That October he plundered Campbell lands, but purposely dispersed his force with a false night alarm so his clansmen could return home with their plunder and without seeing action. His service on Mull in the following year created a controversy with his allies when his men plundered their lands.

The death in 1676 of Lochiel's second wife, and his subsequent marriage to Jean, daughter of Colonel David Barclay of Urie, caused a weakening of ties to the Macleans, but he remained on bad terms with Argyll. The earl complained to the council about Lochiel, Lord Macdonnell, and the Macleans on 13 July. The council appointed the earl of Seaforth and Viscount Aboyne to examine the matter for Argyll. On 23 November Lochiel appeared before the council to answer the charges, but without result. A week later he failed to appear before the council for sending 1000 Camerons, MacDonalds, and Macleans to Mull in August–September 1675, and was put to the horn. On 16 January 1677 the council issued another judgment against him in the dispute—this time for robbery of John Campbell of Airds and his tenants in October 1675. As a sign of the complexity of highland affairs, the council appointed the recently outlawed Lochiel to assist the marquess of Huntly in suppressing Lochaber disorders in September 1677. As late as 21 February 1678 the council was still pursuing him for actions in 1675—in that instance reimbursement for the plundering of Alexander Campbell of Lochnell. Eight months later Argyll regained his allegiance by cancelling a debt of 40,000 merks. The Macleans remarked, 'Ewen has lost his God, but the Earl his money' (Hopkins, 64). That December Lochiel joined Lord Neil Campbell (the earl's brother) with 400 Camerons to attack the mainland Macleans. He remained an ally of Argyll until the defeat of the Macleans.

Lochiel's financial entanglement with the earl exposed him to the latter's creditors when his affairs were settled in 1682, following his temporary exile for refusing the Test Act. However, James, duke of York and regent in Scotland, knighted Lochiel (known to the royal brothers as 'the king of thieves'; Prebble, 67), and gave him feudal independence from Argyll in that year. Meanwhile, with 400–500 Camerons, Lochiel had attacked soldiers gathering tax arrears in Inverlochy. The council proceeded against him for that act until 4 January 1683 when it ruled he was not a principal in the case, but he paid the £1200 fine of his clansmen for the act, gaining their freedom. The central government continued to rely upon him for maintenance of public order, naming him to the commission for securing the highlands in August 1682. On 27 October, as a member of the Crieff justice court, he took the Test Act, accepting royal supremacy in religious matters. In June and August 1683 he sat on the courts in Kinachlader, Rannoch, and Achallander for trying highland cases.

Unfortunately, Lochiel's finances were unravelling owing to demands by Argyll's creditors for debts of over 5000 merks. His third wife's brother seemed to offer the chance to escape their grip. Robert Barclay, a Quaker, obtained a royal charter for a Scottish colony in New Jersey. Lochiel acquired lands there and considered emigrating in 1683–5. Although he remained in Scotland he partnered Lord Neil Campbell as an East Jersey proprietor in 1685, and held lands there until his death. He also speculated in New England real estate. At home he wanted Inverlochy to develop as a commercial centre for the cattle, grain, and timber trades; a garrison there actually offered him financial benefits. In 1684 he tried, but failed, to gain his son John a charter for his Scottish lands. Late November found him successfully pursued in the privy council for his illegal activities on Struan's Rannoch lands. Fearing a landing by Argyll, on 30 December the council ordered him to raise 200 men in the event of one and to secure Dunstaffnage Castle.

Royal patronage, 1685–1688 Following a royal grant of feudal superiority over Lochiel's lands to the duke of Gordon in January 1685, some time in the winter or spring he travelled to London to negotiate with the king to become a tenant-in-chief/royal vassal. He persuaded James VII of his case, but had to leave in May before a charter was promulgated. The failure of settling the matter caused friction with Gordon in the coming years, but Argyll's rising was the first concern of the government. On 11 May the council ordered Lochiel to rendezvous his twenty men with the earl of Atholl at Inverlochy. He joined the earl in June with

300 men, amid rumours that he planned to desert the royal cause. On 9 June he stirred dissension in the royalist camp by opposing Atholl's plan. Then with 200 Camerons he attacked some of the Perthshire gentry in the army. Atholl drew up the army to attack the highlanders and seize Lochiel, but relented when he decided it was an accident. The failure of Lochiel, with 600 Camerons and Macleans, to capture Argyll on 15 June led critics to call him treacherous and incompetent, but the next day he captured Colin Campbell of Ellangreg and his son Duncan. Afterwards, save for forty to fifty men, the Camerons broke up into plundering parties, for which the privy council criticized him in October.

Lochiel journeyed to Edinburgh, where he faulted Atholl's generalship. The rumours of his pro-Argyll inclinations resurfaced, and he travelled to London to rescue his reputation—a difficult task because in August Lord Charles Campbell, a son of Argyll, said that Lochiel had kept a secret correspondence with his father. Perhaps these rumours explain the king's failure to honour his promise of direct royal vassalage to Lochiel. On 15 June 1686 and in January 1687 parliament and the crown confirmed Gordon's feudal superiority over him. In late February 1687 the duke pursued him for 20 merks annual feu duty for lands in Mamore and Lochaber (formerly held of Argyll), but Lochiel disputed the claim. On 30 July the king wrote that he had promised Lochiel to be a tenant-in-chief, but that Gordon had been made his superior, and urged that the dispute be settled. Intriguingly, the letter only reached Scotland on 9 December. Just five days later Gordon again pressed his claims for feudal arrears. In spring 1688 a compromise settlement was reached. On 21 May the king made Lochiel a vassal of the duke at a feu duty of 4 merks per every 1000 merks valuation and no military service, but discharged him of the debts he owed to the now dead Argyll. On 2 June he was excused the arrears owing to Gordon; furthermore, he was released from technical forfeiture as a vassal of Argyll (a route by which the duke had tried to impose himself upon the Camerons). He was now answerable only to the king or privy council. The king augmented his lands with a grant of Sunart and Ardnamurchan.

While Lochiel was in London his clan assisted MacDonald of Keppoch to fight the Mackintoshes at Mulroy—the last major clan battle. As a result of the Camerons' actions, on his return to Scotland their chief hid in the Edinburgh Tolbooth to escape arrest for their breach of public order. As a precautionary move against a landing by the titular earl of Argyll, in November he received orders to keep his clansmen in the shire. His status was elevated on 12 November by receiving a warrant of bailery (jurisdiction). Thus the Restoration period ended with Lochiel enjoying the favour of the government—a position similar to that he had at the conclusion of the interregnum.

Jacobitism and survival, 1689–1719 From 1689 Lochiel's Jacobitism hampered his ability to augment his and his clan's fortunes. Upon hearing of the flight of his patron, James VII, he began organizing a highland alliance for the exiled king. In March 1689 in Dunblane his son-in-law Alexander Drummond/MacGregor of Balhadie informed John Graham, Viscount Dundee, of his efforts, but they were temporarily halted by the reappointment of Lochiel's old friend Colonel Hill to command the garrison at Inverlochy (then renamed Fort William). Dundee raised the Jacobite standard on 16 April, and in May Lochiel led 600 men of his clan with 400 MacGregors, Cowals, Gibbons/MacGibbons, and Macnabs of the Lennox out; and was the first to reach Dundee's rendezvous at Dalcomera on the River Lochy on 16 May. None the less, as late as 1 June, Lochiel allowed his clan to sell food to the Fort William garrison.

This did not apparently undermine Lochiel's position within Dundee's army. He successfully opposed the latter's plan to train the highlanders to fight on the continental model and received command of the army's second battle. On 11 July, Dundee stayed at Lochiel's seat of Achnacarry; a week later the Scottish estates proclaimed him and his son John traitors. He signed a letter on 17 August with other Jacobites scorning William's blandishments. On 27 July he advised Dundee to attack General William Mackay of Scourie at Killiecrankie, but his clan lost 120 men in the encounter. Afterwards Lochiel departed for home leaving his son John in command. On 27 August, six days after the Jacobite defeat at Dunkeld, Lochiel met eleven other chiefs at Blair Castle and promised 200 men for the rising. In mid-February 1690 he persuaded the chiefs to fight on until released by James VII. In June he took the field with 200 men, but no other Jacobite joined him. A Royal Navy landing party captured his home in punishment for his rebellion. Although from the spring rumours developed of his willingness to submit, the estates still forfeited Lochiel and John on 13 June. By midsummer Lochiel was again permitting his people to sell food to Fort William and urging caution to the Jacobites. His enthusiasm for the cause continued to deteriorate and by 3 June 1691 he had decided to allow the Camerons to submit to the Williamite government; within three weeks most had. Lochiel then revived his interest in the garrison as an engine for economic development and encouraged the clan to build sawmills and corn mills near it.

Although Lochiel distrusted his cousin John Campbell, now earl of Breadalbane, he supported his negotiations with the other chiefs. However, to protect his reputation he waited until 28 December (when he had James's permission) to leave for Inveraray to swear the oath of submission. He then joined Breadalbane in London, where he was presented to King William on 19 January 1692. His subsequent failure to assist with the toppling of Breadalbane led to his arrest and imprisonment in the Edinburgh Tolbooth in June 1695. In 1696 he returned to Argyll's favour and managed to settle the dispute with the Campbells over Sunart and Ardnamurchan. With his mature sons serving in William's army, he settled his estate on his heir, John, reserving the life rent to himself. Also in 1696 he plotted with Simon Fraser (later Lord Lovat) before the latter's attempted abduction of the Lovat heiress. Following imprisonment in 1697 during an invasion scare, Lochiel slipped into obscurity for six years.

In 1703 both the London government and Jacobites counted Lochiel and his 400 clansmen as their supporters. That year he met Stewart of Appin and the chief of the MacGregors at Drummond Castle as part of Simon Fraser's mission to enlist support for the Jacobite cause. In 1704–5 he was listed, with the captain of Clanranald, Macdonell of Glengarry, MacDonald of Glencoe, and Maclean of Duart, as a Jacobite. None the less, the Scottish estates appointed him a commissioner of supply for Argyll in August 1705. In mid-1707 Colonel Hooke, a Jacobite agent, reported that the presence of a garrison at Fort William tempered Lochiel's enthusiasm for the cause, and equally dampened that of Appin, Glencoe, and MacDonald of Keppoch. During the French invasion scare in 1708 Lochiel was held a prisoner at the fort (16 April to 13 May at least), but his age and infirmity relieved him from being taken to London. In May 1711 Jacobite agent Captain John Ogilvie noted 'Sir Evan Cameron—an old cunning man, very brave but old', who held command of the Lovat Frasers under charge from their exiled chief, and led 2000 men 'great robbers of the low countries' (*Portland MSS*, 10.369). Following the death of Queen Anne, Lochiel joined with Macleod of Dunvegan, MacDonald of Sleat, Chisholm of Comar, Duart, and Glengarry in signing a loyal address to King George. Campbell of Fonab delayed his and Appin's alliance with the Jacobite earl of Mar in 1715. Towards the end of his life Lochiel allowed his son John to lead the clan. Owing to his earlier demission of the estate, government attempts to forfeit him in 1716 failed. He died at Achnacarry from a fever in February 1719 in his ninetieth year. John Cameron, who in 1716 had been created Lord Lochiel in the Jacobite peerage, and who died in 1748, was the father of Donald *Cameron of Lochiel (*c.*1700–1748) and of Archibald *Cameron (1707–1753).

EDWARD M. FURGOL

Sources *APS* · *Reg. PCS*, 2nd ser. · *Reg. PCS*, 3rd ser. · A. I. Macinnes, *Clanship, commerce and the house of Stewart, 1603–1788* (1996) · D. Stevenson, *Alasdair MacColla and the highland problem in the 17th century* (1980) · E. M. Furgol, *A regimental history of the covenanting armies, 1639–1651* (1990) · F. D. Dow, *Cromwellian Scotland, 1651–1660* (1979) · P. Hopkins, *Glencoe and the end of the Highland war* (1986) · C. H. Firth, ed., *Scotland and the Commonwealth: letters and papers relating to the military government of Scotland, from August 1651 to December 1653*, Scottish History Society, 18 (1895) · C. H. Firth, ed., *Scotland and the protectorate: letters and papers relating to the military government of Scotland from January 1654 to June 1659*, Scottish History Society, 31 (1899) · J. Philip, *The Grameid*, ed. A. D. Murdoch, Scottish History Society, 1st ser., 3 (1888) · *Correspondence of Colonel N. Hooke*, ed. W. D. Macray, 2 vols., Roxburghe Club, 92, 95 (1870–71) · *The manuscripts of the House of Lords*, new ser., 12 vols. (1900–77), vol. 8 · *The manuscripts of his grace the duke of Portland*, 10 vols., HMC, 29 (1891–1931), vol. 10 · D. Stevenson, ed., *The government of Scotland under the covenanters*, Scottish History Society, 4th ser., 18 (1982) · W. H. L. Melville, ed., *Leven and Melville papers: letters and state papers chiefly addressed to George, earl of Melville … 1689–1691*, Bannatyne Club, 77 (1843) · *Historical notices of Scotish affairs, selected from the manuscripts of Sir John Lauder of Fountainhall*, ed. D. Laing, 2, Bannatyne Club, 87 (1848) · *Memoirs of Sir Ewen Cameron of Locheill*, ed. J. Macknight, Abbotsford Club, 24 (1842) · E. J. Cowan, *Montrose for covenant and king* (1977) · J. Buchan, *Montrose* (1928) · C. S. Terry, *John Graham of Claverhouse, Viscount Dundee, 1648–1689* (1905) · B. Lenman, *The Jacobite risings in Britain, 1689–1746* (1980) · C. Sinclair-Stevenson, *Inglorious rebellion: the Jacobite risings of 1708, 1715 and 1719* (1971) · J. Prebble, *Glencoe* (1966) · B. Lenman, 'The highland aristocracy and North America, 1603–1784', *The 17th century in the highlands*, ed. L. Maclean (1986) · F. Adam, *The clans, septs and regiments of the Scottish highlands*, rev. T. Innes, 8th edn (1970) · J. S. Gibson, *Playing the Scottish card: the Franco-Jacobite invasion of 1708* (1988) · *DNB*

Archives NL Scot., letters, accounts, and receipts | Blair Castle, Atholl MS, Breadalbane MSS, Clanrandald MSS · NA Scot., Breadalbane and Argyll MSS

Likenesses oils, Scot. NPG [*see illus.*]

Cameron, George Poulett (1805/6–1882), army officer in the East India Company, was the son of Commander Robert Cameron RN, who perished with the greater part of his crew under the batteries of Fort St Andero (Santander), on the north coast of Spain, on 22 January 1807. He was appointed a cadet of infantry at Madras in 1821, and in 1824 and 1825 served as adjutant of a light field battalion under Lieutenant-General Sir C. Deacon in the southern Maratha country. He returned to England in 1831, and shortly afterwards joined the expedition to Portugal organized by Don Pedro to recover the throne for his daughter, Maria. Cameron was attached to the staff of Field Marshal the duke of Terceira, under whose command he distinguished himself in two actions fought on 4 March and 5 July 1833, receiving special commendation on the second occasion for having remained at his post after being severely wounded.

A few years later Cameron was sent on special service to Persia, and was employed with the Persian army in 1836, 1837, and 1838, commanding the garrison of Tabriz. On leaving Persia in 1838 he visited the Russian garrisons in Circassia. In 1842 he held for a short time the appointment of political agent at the titular court of the nawab of Arcot. In 1843 he was created a CB, having previously received from the government of Portugal the order of the Tower and Sword, and from that of Persia the order of the Lion and Sun. After serving for a time in the quartermaster-general's department in the Madras presidency, he was transferred, in consequence of ill health, to the invalid establishment. Subsequently, in 1856, he was commandant of the Nilgiri hills: his duties were principally civil.

Having retired from the service of the East India Company early in 1858, Cameron was with the Austrian army in the Italian campaign of the following year. He published *Personal Adventures and Excursions in Georgia, Circassia, and Russia* (2 vols., 1848) and *The Romance of Military Life, being Souvenirs Connected with Thirty Years' Service* (1853). He died at Cheltenham on 12 February 1882.

A. J. ARBUTHNOT, *rev.* JAMES LUNT

Sources *Annual Register* (1882) · G. P. Cameron, *Personal adventures and excursions in Georgia, Circassia, and Russia*, 2 vols. (1848) · G. P. Cameron, *The romance of military life, being souvenirs connected with thirty years service*, 2 vols. (1853) · W. J. Wilson, ed., *History of the Madras army*, 5 vols. (1882–9) · C. E. Buckland, *Dictionary of Indian biography* (1906) · Boase, *Mod. Eng. biog.*

Wealth at death £2001 12s. 2d.: probate, 27 March 1882, *CGPLA Eng. & Wales*

Cameron, Hugh [Eobhan Camshran, Eobhan na Pillie] (1705?–1817), miller, was a native of Breadalbane, Perthshire. The origin of the epithet in his Gaelic name Eobhan na Pillie is obscure. He served his apprenticeship in Crieff and settled at Shiain of Lawers, where he built the first lint mill in the highlands, and introduced spinning-wheels and jackreels and taught their use. Cameron played a prominent role in introducing, adapting, and disseminating the new technology of the most important and most heavily government-sponsored industry in eighteenth-century Scotland, and it is significant that, enjoying this position, he was a native speaker of Gaelic. He worked in the Gaidhealtachd, the mainland highlands of Perthshire and counties of Inverness, Ross, Caithness, and Sutherland, where he is said to have constructed more than eighty mills, nearly all the lint mills in that area. He also designed the first barley-shelling mills in the highlands. At his home at Shiain he ran lint, barley, meal, and spinning mills off one water-wheel concurrently and under one roof. His lint mill at Invervar survives and has been restored.

A convivial man, Cameron made his house the local meeting-place for ceilidhs; a song, 'Moladh di Eobhan Camashran muilleir lin', was composed in his honour by the bard Mac a Ghlastrich. He died in penury at the reputed age of 112, on 15 April 1817.

T. F. Henderson, *rev.* Monica Clough

Sources *Perthshire Courier* (24 April 1817) • *Scots Magazine and Edinburgh Literary Miscellany*, 79 (1817), 585–6 • Anderson, *Scot. nat.* • A. Stewart, *A highland parish, or, The history of Fortingall* (1928) • W. A. Gillies, *In famed Breadalbane* (1938) • A. H. Millar, ed., *A selection of Scottish forfeited estates papers*, Scottish History Society, 57 (1909) • J. Christie, *The antiquity of Aberfeldy* (1906) • A. S. Cowper, ed., *Linen in the highlands, 1753–1762* (1969)

Wealth at death 'died in great poverty': obituary

Cameron, Sir James Clark (1905–1991), general practitioner and medical administrator, was born on 8 April 1905 at Bridge of Earn, Perthshire, Scotland, the only son and elder child of Malcolm Clark Cameron (1872–1917), police officer, and his wife, Grace (1879–1963), seamstress, daughter of James Clark and his wife, Isabella, *née* MacArthur of Aberfeldy. The family had roots in Rannoch, Perthshire.

Early experiences as doctor and prisoner of war Cameron was educated at Glencarse School, Acharn School (near Kenmore), Breadalbane Academy, and Perth Academy. Leaving school in 1923 he took a gap year working in a pharmacy, an experience which persuaded him to study medicine. He then attended University College, Dundee (then part of St Andrews University), graduating MB and ChB in 1929. This was followed by a hospital residency in Arbroath.

Like many of Scotland's medical graduates Cameron migrated south after qualification. Settling in general practice in Croydon in 1931 he proved a popular doctor and soon opened a second surgery in his home, near Wallington. This early expansion in a flourishing London suburb no doubt prompted his subsequent advice to aspiring general practitioners, quoted by a local colleague Trevor Silver: 'Always count the chimney pots before setting up your plate' (Silver, 1131). On 25 February 1933 he married Irene Ferguson (1905–1986), daughter of Arthur Ferguson of Perth, an Edinburgh graduate who, until her death, provided staunch support. He was deeply attached to her and to their three children: Hamish, who became a consultant child psychiatrist; Sheila, who became a QC; and Jennifer, who became a magistrate.

Cameron's group practice in Wallington remained his professional base for forty-five years, and throughout his post-war career in medico-politics he maintained this strong clinical foundation, holding large Saturday surgeries to compensate for the hours spent in weekday committees. He kept close links with local colleagues, successfully chairing the south-west London and Surrey local medical committee. A firm believer in democracy, Cameron practised it assiduously throughout two decades of representing doctors. Indeed, his chairmanship of local and national committees was sometimes marked by a surfeit of democracy as he allowed fractious colleagues to talk themselves out in his pursuit of an agreed solution to a controversial problem. On occasions he displayed a Nelsonian disregard for an inquorate meeting, and some of his most effective work was done when subsequently socializing late into the night with committee members after formal proceedings had ended.

Cameron had joined the Officers' Training Corps at university, and in 1939 was commissioned into the Territorial Army. By the spring of 1940 he was a battalion medical officer in the King's Royal Rifle Brigade. His unit was deployed to hold Calais against the advancing Germans, to give time for the British expeditionary force's evacuation to England from nearby Dunkirk. His gallantry in this fierce battle, during which, under fire, he amputated a wounded soldier's forearm with a rusty hacksaw, earned him a mention in dispatches. He was, inevitably, captured and sent to Stalag Luft 21 in Germany. There, as well as caring for many nationalities in the prison's hospital, he worked hard to maintain prisoners' morale, organizing camp shows, taking church services, learning German, and negotiating on the prisoners' behalf with the camp authorities. Such was his command of German and ability to represent prisoners' interests that on one occasion the authorities locked him up as a suspected spy. In October 1944 he was moved to a camp in Poland with American prisoners of war. From there he wrote home: 'Everyone is very optimistic … but I have given up prophesying' (private information, J. Isaacs). This was an understandable sentiment after five years of incarceration.

Cameron later remained reticent about his wartime experiences, which ended with his leading a gruelling trek of fellow prisoners to Odessa after their release by the Russian army. Certainly, the years in camps coloured the remainder of his life, although fortunately his natural affability, gregariousness, and common sense survived intact. He kept in touch with former comrades, but an enduring hatred of his captors was manifest over twenty years later when he refused to enter a car hired to take him to negotiations in Whitehall because it was a Mercedes. A positive outcome of his camp experiences was his abiding support for the Red Cross, with which he had worked when organizing the repatriation of sick prisoners. Back in general practice he regularly lectured Red Cross volunteers, and in 1958 was awarded the organization's badge of honour and was made a life member.

Negotiator for the British Medical Association As well as great stamina Cameron had a well disguised inner toughness, products, no doubt, of his strict Presbyterian upbringing and the war. These traits were coupled with a shrewd intelligence, an unusual empathy with people, a remarkable memory, and the ability to identify the sentence that mattered in a mass of text. It was no surprise that he became a skilful negotiator as well as an effective family doctor. One quirk for such a successful medico-politician was a reluctance to put pen to paper: listening and talking were his strengths. He could, however, be an uncompromising opponent of anyone he believed had let him down; nor did he suffer fools gladly, though his kindness to friends and to the British Medical Association (BMA) staff was legendary.

A champion of principles he held dear, Cameron's belief in and deep anxieties about general practice in the National Health Service (NHS) prompted his entry into medico-politics in the early years of the service. 'I came back from five years in a prisoner of war camp to find general practice in a mess and my gut feeling was that it was a branch of medicine with no future' (Macpherson, 26). It was Cameron's determination to help revive general practice—for the benefit of patients as well as doctors—rather than any desire for personal aggrandizement that motivated his medico-political activities.

In 1956 Cameron was elected to the BMA's general medical services committee, which represented nearly all family doctors via a network of active local committees, and on 19 March 1964—when still relatively unknown outside the BMA—he was elected its chairman. A modest man, he was as surprised as many others when he beat the two fancied, high-profile candidates in what was an unexpected election for the chair. The committee's previous chairman, A. B. Davies, had resigned following an angry national conference of representatives of general practitioners (GPs) which had castigated the committee's proposed evidence for a pay rise to the doctors' and dentists' independent pay review body. As someone who epitomized the value of patients having a personal doctor, Cameron was to prove an ideal leader for Britain's family doctors. In the period after his election he judged the main hope for general practice to be with the government-initiated Fraser inquiry. This was, however, overtaken by events in February 1965, when the review body recommended 'such a tiny pay award that GPs exploded' (Timmins, 220). Cameron's abilities were tested to their limits at local and national meetings where he and his committee colleagues struggled to channel doctors' anger into a constructive policy.

The task was formidable. As well as having to persuade a financially beleaguered government to accept potentially expensive reforms, Cameron had to combat militant rival GP organizations and unite general practitioners, many of whom hankered nostalgically for pre-NHS practice and fees for items of service in place of remuneration based on patient list size—a change that the government deemed non-negotiable. As general medical services committee chairman, however, Cameron was determined also to improve standards of training and practice, a necessary quid pro quo for better pay and conditions of service. Furthermore, more well qualified recruits were needed urgently to offset a debilitating loss of disillusioned, experienced doctors from the NHS. The level of anger among family doctors was such that in February 1965 the BMA decided to collect GPs' undated resignations from the NHS, for possible use later. An overwhelming majority responded and, whatever personal reservations Cameron may have had about industrial action by doctors, he recognized the *realpolitik* of the situation. As the committee chairman he had both to placate alarmed consultants' leaders, fearful that hospitals would be overwhelmed, and to persuade an angry minister of health, Kenneth Robinson, to stay at the negotiating table.

Drawing on many professional and governmental sources, including ideas from the progressive Royal College of General Practitioners (of which he was later elected an honorary fellow) and the Medical Practitioners Union, Cameron and his negotiating team of elected GPs and BMA secretariat staff set out to turn the crisis to the advantage of patients and doctors. He never pretended to be an original thinker, but he could spot a good idea, and he had the leadership qualities to weld a group of informed, independent, often prickly individuals into an effective team. The negotiators' proposals, *A Charter for the Family Doctor Service*, hammered out during a hectic weekend in Brighton in February 1965, were the basis of negotiations with the government. Robinson, the minister of health and the son of a family doctor, recognized the parlous state of general practice and the risk this posed for the NHS, and saw in Cameron someone with whom he could deal. Their mutual empathy—and willingness to communicate informally to test their respective positions—contributed to resolving the crisis. Indeed, Cameron sometimes had more trouble with militants in the profession than with the minister and his civil service team. Interestingly, Robinson admitted privately many years later that the net loss of 600 GPs from the NHS in 1963–4 worried him more than the threat of mass resignations or the BMA's attempt to launch an insurance-based scheme for general practice. For his part Cameron saw the resignation threat as being as much a safety valve for the profession as a credible weapon in negotiations.

Cameron, 'a dead straight but artful Scot' (Timmins, 220), handled acrimonious professional meetings and intense negotiations with skill, courtesy, and determination. 'When rarely and deliberately, he was terse, the result was dramatically effective' (Gullick). Certainly, when necessary he faced down the profession's militants, and on one occasion refused to accept a ministerial letter. Many months of tense and complex negotiations finally resulted in 1966 in Cameron and Robinson agreeing a vastly improved contract. Timmins later wrote: 'The deal not only stopped the rot. It produced a renaissance in general practice' (Timmins, 223). Cameron would surely have been proud of this judgement.

After the agreement was implemented Cameron wanted to resign as chairman of the general medical services committee, but members asked him to stay on. So, despite illness, he led Britain's GPs for ten years, until a serious operation obliged him to resign in 1974. During that time he contributed greatly to the development of postgraduate education for family doctors. GPs honoured him by naming a charity for GPs and their families after him. The money came from a government-held practice compensation fund set up in 1948, and his memory of a ministerial chance remark, made seven years earlier, secured the return of the money to the profession. The committee made him its only life member on his retirement. He was appointed CBE in 1974, and in 1975 the BMA awarded him its gold medal for distinguished merit.

Chairman of the BMA council In 1971 Cameron had failed by one vote to get elected chairman of the BMA council. The defeat hit him hard, even though the result may have been in part because the previous chairman had been a general practitioner, and members wanted a consultant. Restored to health by 1976 he was elected to the chair of the BMA council in that year, serving until 1979, the year in which he was knighted for services to medicine.

Cameron's three years as council chairman were not as memorable as his time with the general medical services committee. The NHS was, with difficulty, trying to cope with the consequences of reorganization, a lack of resources, and rising militancy among its staff, including senior and junior doctors. Cameron wanted fundamental change in the NHS to prevent its recurring crises. He did not, however, have the empathy with the diverse medical groupings on the council that he had enjoyed with his GP colleagues on the general medical services committee. In any case the medico-political issues were complex and messy, without the intense focus of the GP contract crisis. They were not susceptible to fundamental solutions, at least not under the existing Labour administration. In addition, the BMA secretariat, upon whom Cameron had relied heavily during the 1960s, was under strain, struggling to respond to BMA members' 'union' needs without damaging the association's professional role. Organizational reform was not the chairman's forte, and the intraprofessional stresses within the association taxed even his patience: late-night convivial socializing was no longer the effective problem-solver that it had been in the 1960s. Indeed, it was on occasions counterproductive. Even so, he presided over a reorientation of the BMA's activities that strengthened its regional services to individual members, a necessary response to the challenge of an NHS that had moved from being an administered service to a managed one. He was also active in promoting the interests of GPs in the European Community as a member of the advisory committee on medical training of the European Commission from 1976 to 1982.

Medico-politically, Cameron's time as council chairman could best be described as a holding operation. But this in no way detracted from his pivotal contribution to the renaissance of general practice. Had that rescue operation failed it was probable that the NHS itself would have failed. Ironically, in his final speech to the BMA's annual meeting in June 1979, Cameron warned of the failing state of the NHS: 'It suffers from chronic underfinancing … an overblown administration … bad personnel management and … poor industrial relations. … So far none of these fundamental problems have been realistically tackled' (*BMJ*, 1979/2, 1803). At the previous annual meeting he had declared his belief that 'if the care of the patient is to be paramount—and that after all is what the NHS is about—then the doctor's authority in all matters affecting the patient's welfare must be recognised and his clinical judgement accepted'. Aneurin Bevan had set out, Cameron said, 'to provide the facilities and the circumstances in which doctors could exercise their skills for the benefit of the patient. The basic concept has become corrupted' (*BMJ*, 1978/2, 297). It was to be further corrupted during the remaining years of Cameron's life, when he observed the radical policies of successive Conservative governments converting patients into customers, with clinical priorities too often being subordinated to management and accounting objectives. Such a cultural change was anathema to him.

Cameron retired from clinical practice in 1977. After his wife's death in 1986 he moved to a flat in Haven Green, Ealing. He died of leukaemia at the Royal Marsden Hospital, London, on 22 October 1991. He was cremated six days later and his ashes were interred in the family grave at Aberfeldy. Had this complex, friendly, caring man—the archetypal family doctor—survived the decade, he would surely have grieved to see his family doctors' charter crushed by the management mills of the NHS internal market. GORDON MACPHERSON

Sources T. Silver, *BMJ* (2 Nov 1991), 1131 · A. Neave, *The flames of Calais* (1974), 129 · G. Macpherson, 'Reviving the fortunes of general practice: James Cameron and Kenneth Robinson', *BMJ* (5 July 1982), 26 · *BMJ*, suppl. (1964), 115–28 · *BMJ*, suppl. (1964), 109–12 · *BMJ*, suppl. (1965), 51 · N. Timmins, *The five giants: a biography of the welfare state* (1995) · D. Gullick, *BMJ* (2 Nov 1991), 1130–31 · J. C. Cameron, 'What to do with the ailing giant of the NHS', *BMJ* (30 June 1979), 1803 [opening speech to the BMA's annual representative meeting, 25/6/1979] · J. C. Cameron, 'Government's priorities fundamentally mistaken', *BMJ* (22 July 1978), 296–7 [opening speech to the BMA's annual representative meeting, 11/7/1978] · 'Royal commission on the national health service', *Parl. papers* (1979–80), p. 355, Cmnd 7615 · memorial service address, British Medical Association Archives, London · personal knowledge (2004) · private information (2004) · *WWW*, 1991–5 · *The Times* (26 Oct 1991) · *The Independent* (24 Oct 1991)

Archives British Medical Association Archives, London

Likenesses L. Boden, oils, British Medical Association, London · photograph, repro. in *The Independent* · photograph (after oil portrait), repro. in *The Times*

Wealth at death £376,037: probate, 20 Feb 1992, *CGPLA Eng. & Wales*

Cameron, (Mark) James Walter (1911–1985), journalist and author, was born in Battersea, London, on 17 June 1911, the elder son (there were no daughters) of William Ernest Cameron, barrister and novelist, and his wife, Margaret Douglas Robertson. His Scottish links always remained unshaken. His grandfather was a highland divine, whose Gaelic ecclesiastical writings won him local renown, and his father was a lawyer turned author under the name Mark Allerton. He was educated, on his own testimony, 'erratically, at a variety of small schools, mostly in France', and then started real work, filling paste pots, at the age of sixteen for 15s. a week, in the offices of D. C. Thomson's *Red Star Weekly* in Dundee.

Escaping to the *Scottish Daily Express* in 1938, Cameron was able to afford to marry his first love, Eleanor (Elma) Mara Murray (*b.* 1913/14), an artist. She was the daughter of George John Murray, a surgeon of Dundee. It was an idyllic but cruelly brief affair, cut short by her death in childbirth in 1940. A daughter was born. Turned down for the armed forces because of 'organic cardiac disease', Cameron moved in 1939 to the *Daily Express* in Fleet Street, subbing other people's copy. He met Elizabeth O'Conor working in the art room of the newspaper, and they were married at the Chelsea register office, London, on 25 November 1943. She was the daughter of Stanley Punshon Marris, a retired clergyman, and the former wife of Denis Armor O'Conor, with whom she had a son. She was also to have a son with Cameron.

As the war ended, Cameron stumbled on his real trade. One assignment sent him to India at the moment of the independence negotiations; he started to comprehend the moral impetus behind the Asian and the worldwide revolt against imperialism. He had Jawaharlal Nehru and M. K. Gandhi for his tutors. Another assignment took him to Bikini when the American atomic bomb was exploded; his allegiance to the Campaign for Nuclear Disarmament, launched much later, was born in that forgotten summer of 1946. A third assignment took him to expose the brutality and corruption of Syngman Rhee's regime in South Korea. And back at home he chose his own allies with some delicacy. When the *Evening Standard* engaged in what he justly believed to be a shameful slur against the Labour minister, E. John St Loe Strachey, in 1950, he resigned from the Beaverbrook newspapers altogether, and when Edward Hulton, the owner of *Picture Post*, fired its talented editor, H. T. Hopkinson, for daring to attempt to publish Cameron's Korean dispatches, he resigned again in sympathy (1951).

Soon thereafter Cameron's genius flowed in the truly great and truly Liberal *News Chronicle* of those times. Many contributed to the triumph: Sir Gerald Barry, his editor; Tom Baistow, his foreign editor; and Vicky, the cartoonist, soon to become the closest friend of all. His passion and his wit and his readiness to fit every incident into the worldwide scene were all part of his charm. His matchless integrity was part of it too, and yet he could wear his armour without a hint of pride or piety. He could raise journalism to the highest level of literature, like a Swift or a Hazlitt.

But the Liberal hour did not last; the Liberal financiers killed off the *News Chronicle* in 1960. Other wars, requiring investigation, had broken out, and Cameron could turn to other instruments than his pen. To persuade the world that the North Vietnamese were made of flesh and blood, in 1965 he staked all the fortune he had not got, and all his precious time and energy, to get in and out of Hanoi with a camera crew. His film, *Western Eyewitness*, was shown on BBC television and was also bought by several overseas stations.

Most of Cameron's journalistic accomplishments were recited in what he called his 'experiment in biography', *Point of Departure*, published in 1967. Another title, *An Indian Summer*, which appeared in October 1974, offered even more enticing prospects. After the dissolution of his previous marriage in 1969, in January 1971 he married Moneesha Sarkar, airline receptionist, the daughter of Kandrachanda Ayuppa Appachod, coffee planter. She had a daughter and a son from a previous marriage. She took him on honeymoon to her native land, which ended in a car crash. A bundle of skin, bones, wood, and wire was somehow trans-shipped back to London and there stuck

(Mark) **James Walter Cameron** (1911–1985), by Paul Joyce, 1975

together by the National Health Service and Cameron's wife.

All such accidents, susceptibilities, memories, and broken hopes and dreams were woven together into a single thread in *An Indian Summer*. It is a book about ancient and modern India, brave, beautiful, astringent, withering, and, just occasionally, savage; an Anglo-Indian classic fit to take its place beside *A Passage to India* by E. M. Forster. Cameron was appointed CBE in 1979. In 1965 he won the Granada journalist of the year award. He had honorary degrees from the universities of Lancaster (DLitt, 1970), Bradford (LLD, 1977), and Essex (DUniv 1978). He died at his London home, 3 Eton College Road, Chalk Farm, on 26 January 1985. MICHAEL FOOT, *rev.*

Sources *The Times* (28 Jan 1985) · *The Times* (8 Feb 1985) · personal knowledge (1990) · *CGPLA Eng. & Wales* (1986) · J. Cameron, *Point of departure* (1967) · J. Cameron, *An Indian summer* (1974)
Archives FILM BFI NFTVA, current affairs footage · BFI NFTVA, documentary footage · BFI NFTVA, performance footage | SOUND BL NSA, *Tribute to James Cameron*, 9274/01R1 TR2, R2TR2 · BL NSA, documentary recording · BL NSA, performance recording · BL NSA, recorded talks
Likenesses photographs, 1950–68, Hult. Arch. · P. Joyce, photograph, 1975, NPG [*see illus.*]
Wealth at death under £40,000: administration with will, 7 Feb 1986, *CGPLA Eng. & Wales*

Cameron, John (*d.* 1446), administrator and bishop of Glasgow, was the first of the great political bishops of fifteenth-century Scotland who combined their episcopal duties with extensive royal service in ecclesiastical and secular politics. His origins are uncertain, though his surname may point to a birthplace in a settlement of that name either near Edinburgh or south of St Andrews. He was educated at the new University of St Andrews, becoming a licentiate in canon law in 1420. Between 1420 and 1427 he experienced a speedy rise in the church, thanks to a series of secular patrons. In particular, during the early 1420s he was in the service of the Black Douglas family, and by 1423 he was the secretary of the fourth earl of Douglas's son, Archibald, earl of Wigtown, the future fifth earl (*d.* 1439). This brought Cameron rewards in the form of a number of lucrative benefices in the areas of Douglas lands and influence, the most important of which was the provostry of the Douglas-founded collegiate church of Lincluden near Dumfries.

The co-operation of Wigtown with James I when the latter returned from exile in early 1424 opened a route into royal service for Cameron and a number of other followers of the Black Douglases. Out of this group, which included James Douglas of Balvenie (*d.* 1443), Wigtown's uncle, and William Fowlis, the future keeper of the privy seal and archdeacon of St Andrews, it was Cameron who enjoyed the fastest access to major royal patronage. By early 1425 he was the king's first secretary, and on the death of the king's chief ecclesiastical minister, William Lauder, bishop of Glasgow, in 1425, James I clearly looked to Cameron as a replacement. He was quickly elected by the Glasgow chapter, but found his appointment blocked by Pope Martin V, who claimed the right to provide the bishop. It was only in April 1426 that, following an embassy to Rome, Martin provided Cameron to the see. Until the end of his career, though, his interests made him a royal servant and suspect to the papacy. During the disputed election he had remained a major royal councillor as keeper of the great seal, and his appointment as chancellor came swiftly after his confirmation as bishop.

From 1427 until 1432 Cameron was a regular member of the king's council and was employed in diplomacy with England and France, but throughout the reign his principal role was as James's chief agent in royal attempts to control the Scottish church. Statutes of 1427 and 1428 gave him power to limit clerical access to the Roman court. This association with laws 'against ecclesiastical liberty' brought the bishop under renewed papal criticism and led to his being cited for failure to pay his common services to Rome. The king may have used Cameron to soak up the papal hostility which his policies aroused, and the bishop had still not paid his services in 1431, though he made an agreed part payment in 1432. He also came under personal attack in Rome from a number of Scottish churchmen at the curia. Chief among these was William Croyser, the papal candidate for the archdeaconry of Teviotdale, another former Douglas servant whose animosity towards Cameron may have stemmed from his own comparatively slow promotion.

From 1432 Cameron's pursuit of his master's ecclesiastical goals was centred on the Council of Basel. He crossed to the continent in late 1433 and was incorporated into the council in February 1434, along with a group of other Scottish churchmen. For the next three years he was active in defence of the king's policies before the council and Pope Eugenius IV, especially against the attacks of William Croyser, now also at Basel. In accordance with the king's refusal to commit himself to either party in the schism, Cameron visited Pope Eugenius in Florence in 1435. Any reconciliation there was short-lived. Cameron had returned to Basel from the curia and may have paid a visit to Scotland in late 1435. The pope concluded that Cameron was an obstacle to his relations with James, and in the summer of 1436 he forbade the bishop to return to Scotland while he dispatched a nuncio to the king.

Cameron remained an exile in Bruges until after the assassination of King James on 21 February 1437. By April he was back in Scotland and installed as chancellor on the council of regency for the young James II, which was headed by Queen Joan. His presence alongside other former Douglas adherents in the government may have aided the transfer of power from the queen to his old employer, Archibald, fifth earl of Douglas, in June 1437. Cameron could no longer count on the prominence enjoyed during the reign of James I, however, and in May 1439 Douglas replaced him as chancellor with William Crichton, another servant of James I with Douglas connections. Though briefly on the royal council in 1440, Cameron was effectively eclipsed by other ex-Douglas servants who clearly had no love for the bishop; his position may have been weakened by the 'Black Dinner' and execution of the sixth earl of Douglas on 24 November. In 1441 he came under attack from the king's new councillors, probably led by James Douglas of Balvenie, now seventh earl of Douglas. Named a 'son of perdition' and accused of conspiring against the king, Cameron managed to survive any attempts to deprive him of his bishopric, but his influence was gone. He died on Christmas eve 1446 at Glasgow Castle.

While he was above all a political churchman and spent the majority of his time on the king's business, Cameron was also an able diocesan bishop. He undertook measures to limit absenteeism in the cathedral chapter and in 1432, perhaps in connection with his imminent departure for Basel, issued a code of statutes for the government of Glasgow Cathedral and had inventories made of the cathedral treasury and library. He was obviously a man of talents which were quickly recognized by both the Douglases and the king. These talents and his promotion seem to have made him enemies who were concerned to bring about his downfall. M. H. Brown

Sources E. W. M. Balfour-Melville, *James I, king of Scots, 1406–1437* (1936) • R. K. Hannay, 'James I, Bishop Cameron and the papacy', *SHR*, 15 (1917–18), 190–200 • J. H. Burns, 'Scottish churchmen and the Council of Basle, pt 1', *Innes Review*, 13 (1962), 3–53 • C. Innes, ed., *Registrum episcopatus Glasguensis*, 2 vols., Bannatyne Club, 75 (1843); also pubd as 2 vols., Maitland Club, 61 (1843) • J. M. Thomson and others, eds., *Registrum magni sigilli regum Scotorum / The register of the great seal of Scotland*, 11 vols. (1882–1914), vol. 2 • C. McGladdery, *James II* (1990) • M. Brown, *James I* (1994)

Cameron, John (1579/80–1625), Reformed minister and theologian, was born in Glasgow; nothing certain is known of his parents except that his father was a burgess of the city. In 1595 he entered the University of Glasgow at the age of fifteen to study arts and philosophy and supported himself through the four-year course by performing menial tasks in return for a bursary of 25 marks. In 1599 he took the degree of MA, graduating first in his year, and was immediately appointed professor in Greek. Despite agreeing to serve in the post for six years, he left for reasons unknown after only one year and went abroad to Bordeaux.

Theological formation At Bordeaux Cameron became a member of the local Huguenot community, one of whose two pastors was his countryman Gilbert Primrose. Presumably through Primrose's patronage, he was quickly appointed to teach Latin and Greek at the protestant college of Bergerac. Again he served for only a year, for in the autumn of 1601 he became professor of philosophy at the protestant academy of Sedan. After two years he returned to Bordeaux and early in 1604 he was given a four-year scholarship by the protestant church there to train for the ministry. He spent one year at Paris, two at Geneva, and one at Heidelberg, acting at the same time as tutor to two of the sons of Suffret de Calignon, one of the protestant councillors of King Henri IV of France. In April 1608, in Heidelberg, Cameron seems to have written and defended a set of theses entitled 'De triplici Dei cum homine foedere'. Later printed in his posthumous collected works, these contain the first signs of his originality as a Reformed theologian. In its traditional form, covenant theology identified two covenants, one prelapsarian of nature and the other postlapsarian of grace, the second divided into the dispensations of the Old and New testaments. Cameron controversially insisted that the old and new covenants were different in kind, and that the only covenant of grace was God's promise to man in return for faith in the fullness of Christ's sacrifice.

Later in 1608 Cameron returned to Bordeaux and was appointed as second pastor to the Huguenot congregation on the death of Primrose's colleague Renaud. He seems to have kept himself relatively aloof from his flock, and when he married for the first time on 1 March 1611 he eschewed a local bride in favour of Suzanne Bernardin (*c*.1594–1624), daughter of a rich protestant from Tonneins on the upper Garonne. In the early, uneventful years of his ministry Cameron began to develop the distinctive salvation theology with which his name is associated. In a series of letters dated 1610 to 1612 addressed to Louis Cappel, a young theology student at Saumur, he rejected the orthodox Calvinist belief promoted by Beza that Christ died only for the elect and adumbrated what became known as the doctrine of hypothetical universalism. According to Cameron, as God was a merciful judge Christ still died for all, even if only the elect were ultimately saved.

Theological and civil disputes Since the letters remained unpublished until his death, Cameron's rejection of Beza's theology only became public knowledge later in his career. Almost immediately, however, he found himself publicly at odds with the French Calvinist establishment over another theological issue. In 1612 the national synod of Privas outlawed the doctrine of the Herborn Calvinist Johann Fischer or Piscator that only Christ's death, not his perfect life, was required as satisfaction for human sin. When, on two separate occasions, Cameron refused to swear allegiance to the synod's ruling he became a suspect figure to many Reformed ministers. However, he quickly repaired the breach by staunchly defending the French Reformed church against its Catholic critics in *Discours apologétique pour ceux de la religion réformée au jugement de Dieu* (Bergerac, 1614). Republished under a different title in 1627 and translated into English the following year, the work showed for the first time in print his abilities as a biblical scholar. Then in a public dispute at Bordeaux early in 1615 he worsted the Sorbonne theologian Parent who had been called to the city by Cardinal-Archbishop de Sourdis to attack the Reformation in a series of Lenten sermons. In the ensuing flurry of pamphlets Cameron once more demonstrated his talents as a polemicist.

Having thereby angered the city's ecclesiastical establishment, Cameron proceeded in subsequent years to antagonize the civil authorities. In late 1615, during the rebellion of the prince de Condé against the regency government, Cameron and Primrose shut the Huguenot church in protest against the Bordeaux authorities' disarming of local protestants. The local *parlement*, egged on by disgruntled members of the congregation who complained that their pastors were foreign subversives, judged the decision provocative and on 5 January 1616 ordered services to be resumed. Both pastors refused to obey and withdrew from the city, Cameron to his wife's home town of Tonneins, where rebel troops were based. It was eighteen months before he returned, by which time he had had written a vituperative Latin pamphlet against one of his Huguenot opponents, the lawyer Saint-Ange, denying the charge of high treason. On returning to Bordeaux in June 1617, Cameron and Primrose had Saint-Ange excommunicated, which only antagonized the *parlement* the more and resulted in Cameron's being fined. A month later he was in trouble again. Having ministered at the execution of two Huguenot pirate captains condemned by the high court to be broken on the wheel, he published a moving account of their last moments, which the furious *parlement* by a decree of 24 July ordered to be burned by the hangman. By then Cameron must have been *persona non grata* in Bordeaux, all the more that the year 1617 also saw him publish at La Rochelle another significant defence of the Reformed religion, noted for its historical and critical approach. Entitled *Traicté auquel sont examinez les prejugez de ceux de l'église romaine contre la religion réformée*, it appeared in an English version in 1626.

In the light of events at Bordeaux it is not surprising that Cameron applied the following year for a chair of theology at Saumur. Having demonstrated his superiority as a linguist, exegete, and debater before the appointing committee, he was admitted on 22 August 1618. He held the chair for the next three years, giving three to four lectures per week on the most difficult passages of the New Testament and presiding over weekly private and monthly theological disputations. He also gave regular and lengthy sermons, including a series published in 1624 on chapter 6 of St John's gospel.

Shortly after Cameron took up his post representatives of the different Calvinist churches met at Dort and condemned the salvation theology of the Leiden professor, Arminius (*d.* 1609). Like Cameron, Arminius and his followers believed that Christ died for all men, but they rejected traditional Calvinist teaching much more fully than the Scottish theologian by arguing that the individual could reject the gift of faith and that faith, once given, could be lost. For the rest of his life Cameron repeatedly insisted that he accepted the Dort decrees and argued rightly that his own theory of hypothetical universalism, which he had publicly aired in obtaining his chair, was never condemned by the delegates. As an earnest of his orthodoxy he defended the Dort line in a debate at L'Isle, near Orléans, with one of the leading French supporters of Arminius, Daniel Tilenus, in April 1620 (at Tilenus's request). Cameron's account of the debate, published at Leiden as *Amica collatio de gratia et voluntatis humanae concursu in vocatione* (1622), did not appear with the blessing of the Leiden theology faculty, for the professors objected to Cameron's idiosyncratic description of the way in which God ineluctably bestowed on the sinner the grace to believe. Cameron refused to accept the traditional Calvinist explanation that God illuminated the mind and physically moved the individual will and argued instead that God had merely to convince the intellect through a moral persuasion and the will would automatically come into line. Critics in Leiden, however, thought that this was too close to the Arminian theology Cameron was attacking.

English and Scottish sojourn, 1621–1623 Cameron's teaching at Saumur came to an abrupt end in the spring of 1621. Sections of the French protestant community were again in rebellion and Cameron's patron, the governor of Saumur, Duplessis-Mornay, was relieved of his post by the crown on 17 May. Fearing moves against the academy, Cameron and Cappel, now the professor of Hebrew, fled to Paris. By late September Cameron had left France and settled in London, where he was permitted by the bishop of London to preach to the French refugee church and at the Austin Friars. During the autumn he seems to have come to the attention of Matthew Wren, later bishop of Ely, who recommended him to the king as sound on episcopacy. James, at that moment seeking to impose the 1617 articles of Perth on the University of Glasgow, appointed Cameron principal and professor of theology at the Scottish university in the wake of the resignation of Robert Boyd of Trochrig. He probably did not leave for Scotland immediately, however, as his son was born in London on 10 May 1622.

From the time Cameron arrived in Glasgow his stay was marred by conflict. Even before he arrived in the city he seems to have had to write a letter to the king on the advice of Archbishop James Law emphasizing his support for divine-right monarchy after he had been libelled by Tilenus as a subversive. In post he nailed his colours firmly to the royalist mast by insisting from 6 January 1623 that a fidelity and supremacy oath be taken by all university officials and by framing class prayers to be said every morning and evening that included the names of the king and the royal family. According to the then professor of philosophy, Robert Blair, Cameron compounded his royalism and episcopalianism by promoting Arminian doctrines in theological disputations. However implausible the accusation, rumour of his unorthodoxy was rife and Cameron's stay was not a happy one. Although he forced his chief opponent, Blair, to resign, he himself taught for only one session (November 1622–March 1623). By early summer he was back in London, where he took part in a theological dispute at the English court over the divine responsibility for sin.

Final years and legacy In July Cameron was once more in Paris. There on 2 August 1623 he immediately gave the lie to his Glasgow critics by defending the Dort decrees in a dispute with the Arminian Courcelles, minister of Amiens. Cameron hoped to be restored to his Saumur professorship. In September 1623 the national synod of Charenton accepted his request but his reappointment was stopped by the king, who was suspicious of the number of foreign protestants holding posts in France. Cameron, however, still returned to Saumur, buoyed up by a gratuity of 1000 livres voted by the synod, and in October began to give private lectures. The following spring Louis XIII relented. Although Cameron was not restored to his original chair he was permitted to take up the vacant professorship in theology at the protestant academy of Montauban. Again his stay was destined to be short and unhappy. In March 1624 his wife died and his son died the same year; on 26 February 1625 he married Jeanne de Thomas, daughter of a barrister. His ideological enemies continued to hound him. In December 1624 a pamphlet appeared written by the Dutch Arminian, Simon Episcopius, accusing him of Pelagianism and Manicheism, and Cameron was forced to reply with yet another account of his theology. Above all, he became involved in a conflict within the town's Huguenot community, which had split into two groups over the legitimacy of using violence to secure its religious rights. Cameron was firmly on the side of non-resistance. Brawls between the two parties were common and on 13 May 1625 Cameron was badly injured in attempting to break up a riot. He never fully recovered and died on 27 November 1625. His eldest daughter from his first marriage, Joanna, predeceased him, but he was survived by his other daughters, Elizabeth and Susannah.

Cameron's legacy was mixed. Initially the French Calvinist establishment gave its imprimatur to his theology by ordering that his Saumur lectures and an edition of his collected works (printed and manuscript) be published. The first appeared in three volumes at Saumur in 1626–8; the second in a single folio volume at Geneva in 1642. However, the honeymoon period was short. While at Saumur Cameron's memory was permanently idolized, and his friend Louis Cappel not only helped edit the official version of his works but also published an independent selection of Cameron's sermons and biblical commentaries, *Myrothecium evangelicum* (1632), with a fulsome obituary, professors in the other French protestant academies were soon far less enthusiastic. As Cameron's Saumur pupils, especially Moïse Amyraut, further refined and developed his critique of orthodox Calvinism, hardline Calvinists became alarmed. Their suspicions were only strengthened when one of Cameron's intimate friends and pupils, Théophile Brachet de la Milletière, converted to Catholicism and claimed that his professor had aimed to reconcile Geneva and Rome. By the mid-seventeenth century many French Calvinists shared the view of Pierre du Moulin, professor of theology at Sedan, that Cameron was a heretic. This judgment has been repeated almost to the present day in histories of Calvinist theology. It is only since the 1960s that commentators have viewed Cameron as an original and creative humanist scholar, anxious to rescue Calvin from Beza's scholastic excess. The Scottish theologian placed careful biblical exegesis before system-building and anticipated the historicist and critical approach to the scriptures and the church fathers of later more radical exegetes such as Richard Simon.

L. W. B. Brockliss

Sources G. Bonet-Maury, 'John Cameron: a Scottish protestant theologian in France', *SHR*, 7 (1909–10), 325–45 • H. M. B. Reid, *The divinity principals in the University of Glasgow, 1545–1654* (1917), chap. 5 • F. Laplanche, *Orthodoxie et prédication: l'œuvre d'Amyraut et la querelle de la grâce universelle* (Paris, 1965), chap. 4 • B. G. Armstrong, *Calvinism and the Amyraut heresy: protestant scholasticism and humanism in seventeenth-century France* (1969), 6–12, 31–70 • A. H. Swinne, *John Cameron, Philosoph und Theologe (1579–1625): bibliographisch-kritische Analyse der Hand und Druckschriften sowie der Cameron-Literatur*, 2nd edn (1972) • R. Wodrow, 'Collections on the life of Mr John Cameron, minister at Bordeaux, professor of divinity at Saumur, principal of the College of Glasgow and professor of divinity at Montauban', in R. Wodrow, *Collections upon the lives of the reformers and most eminent ministers of the Church of Scotland*, ed. W. J. Duncan, 2/2, Maitland Club, 32 (1848), 2/2.81–229

Likenesses J. Scougall, portrait (after portrait: now probably lost)

Cameron, John (1725–1799), minister of the Presbyterian General Synod of Ulster, was born near Edinburgh. He was apprenticed to an Edinburgh bookseller and afterwards studied at Edinburgh University, where he was awarded the degree of MA. He belonged to the Reformed Presbyterians or 'covenanters' and was admitted as a probationer to that body.

About 1750 Cameron and a fellow probationer, Thomas Cuthbertson, went to the north of Ireland as missionaries. For some years Cameron itinerated in various parts of Ulster as an outdoor preacher, or mountain man, as such preachers were commonly called. He was a skilled public speaker and attracted considerable audiences. In 1753 or 1754 there was a division in the Presbyterian congregation of Bushmills, co. Antrim, part adhering to their minister, John Logue, and part forming a new congregation at Dunluce. The Dunluce congregation offered Cameron the position of minister provided he leave the covenanters and join the regular Presbyterian body, the presbytery of Route, and submit himself to preaching trials preliminary to ordination. The invitation contained the names of 137 members of the congregation and was dated 24 April 1755. Cameron agreed to these conditions and on 3 June was ordained as minister of Dunluce, having distinguished himself in the course of his trials as an extemporary preacher.

At Dunluce Cameron proved to be an able preacher and an assiduous pastor, but he soon abandoned his orthodox opinions after reading Dr John Taylor's *Scriptural Doctrine of Original Sin* and adopted Arianism. He was later to progress beyond Arianism into anti-Trinitarianism. Had his religious views been widely known at the time it is doubtful whether he would have been invited in 1768 to become moderator of the synod of Ulster. His year in office was marked by the resumption, for the first time since 1726, of a dialogue between the synod and the breakaway presbytery of Antrim.

Cameron, a man of liberal views and cultivated understanding, also turned his attention to science. Being in need of a parish schoolmaster, he took into his house Robert Hamilton (1749–1830), the promising son of a neighbouring weaver, trained him for his work, and introduced him to the study of anatomy. Together Cameron and Hamilton amused themselves investigating animal physiology. Hamilton afterwards became a physician of some distinction at Ipswich, and showed his gratitude to Cameron by dedicating to him *The Duties of a Regimental Surgeon* (2 vols., 1788).

Cameron is best remembered for his literary output. His first published work, *The Policy of Satan to Destroy the Christian Religion*, appeared anonymously in 1767. In this he outlined his opposition to the enforcement of creeds and confessions by the protestant churches. This was the theme to which he returned in several subsequent works, such as *The Catholic Christian* (1769), which was to lead to a two-year literary dispute with the Revd Benjamin McDowell of Ballykelly. His year as moderator of the synod of Ulster saw the publication of *The Messiah*, a prose epic in nine books. The book was republished in Dublin in 1811 and continued to attract attention throughout the nineteenth century. It has been described as a work of 'creative power, imagination and even genius' (Witherow, 125). A paper by Cameron rejecting the doctrine of the resurrection of the body was published by Joseph Priestley in the *Theological Repository* for 1771, and led to a correspondence between Priestley and Cameron and to the placement of Cameron's son, William, as a button-maker in Birmingham. Among Cameron's other works were *Doctrines of Orthodoxy* (1782) and the posthumously published *The Doctrine of the Holy Scriptures* (1828), in which he presented his anti-Trinitarian views and which contained a preface by the Revd Arthur Nelson of Kilmore. In addition to his published works he produced carefully elaborated and written sermons which he lent to his neighbouring colleagues and which led in turn to the claim that on occasions Cameron preached 'to half a dozen congregations on the same day' (ibid., 129).

Cameron died on 31 December 1799 at Park, in co. Londonderry, and was buried in the parish churchyard of Dunluce, a picturesque spot on the road between Portrush and the Giant's Causeway. A striking elegy on his grave was written by the Revd George Hill, a former librarian of Queen's College, Belfast. Cameron was married and, besides his son, left a daughter, who was married to John Boyd of Dunluce.

ALEXANDER GORDON, *rev.* M. J. MERCER

Sources T. Witherow, *Historical and literary memorials of presbyterianism in Ireland, 1731–1800* (1880) • J. S. Reid and W. D. Killen, *History of the Presbyterian church in Ireland*, new edn, 3 (1867) • *Monthly Repository* (1831) • private information (2004) [D. L. Wykes]

Cameron, John (1771–1815), army officer, was born at Inverscadale on Linnha Loch, Argyll, on 16 August 1771, one of the six children of Sir Ewen Cameron, first baronet (1738?–1828) of Inverscadale (afterwards of Fassiefern, Argyll), and his first wife, Lucy Campbell of Balwardine. Nursed by the wife of a family retainer, whose son, Ewen McMillan, was his foster brother and faithful attendant through life, young Cameron grew up in close sympathy with the traditions and associations of his home and people, who looked to his father as the representative head of the clan in the enforced absence of the chief of Lochiel. He was educated partly at the grammar school at Fort William, but mainly by private tuition. Later he studied at University and King's College, Aberdeen. He was articled to a writer to the signet at Edinburgh, James Fraser of Gorthleck, but after the outbreak of war with France, at his special request, a commission was procured for him,

John Cameron (1771–1815), by Charles Turner, pubd 1815

and he entered the army as an ensign, reputedly in the 26th (Cameronian) regiment, on 12 April 1793, and advanced to a lieutenancy in Captain Campbell's independent highland company, which was embodied with the 93rd foot. His father helped to raise the 100th foot, soon renamed the 92nd, Gordon Highlanders, in which John Cameron secured a company, on 13 February 1794, as one of the new regiment's original officers, serving with it in Corsica and at Gibraltar from 1795 to 1797, and in the south of Ireland in 1798. There he is said to have lost his heart to a young Irish lady at Kilkenny, but the match was broken off in accordance with his father's wishes.

The next year saw Cameron with the duke of York's expedition to the Helder peninsula, from where he wrote to his father that, on 2 October 1799, among sandhills near Bergen, a 'battle raged with great fury' (Gardyne, 69), in which he suffered 'a slight wound in the knee' (ibid., 70). During the action, his foster brother broke ranks to stalk a Frenchman, lost part of his ear in the process, but received scant sympathy from Cameron: 'You well deserved it, Ewen, for leaving your place' (ibid., 72). He was with the regiment at the occupation of Isle Houat, on the coast of Brittany, off Cadiz in 1800, and went with it to Egypt, where he wrote home 'from a hole in the sand' (ibid., 88), was wounded at the battle of Alexandria, on 21 March 1801, and received the gold medal given by the Ottoman Porte for the campaign. He became a major in the regiment on 5 April 1801, and commanded a detachment of the 92nd in Nelson's funeral procession. A brevet lieutenant-colonel on 25 April 1808, he was appointed lieutenant-colonel of the new 2nd battalion on 23 June 1808. Cameron rejoined the 1st battalion in March 1809, and led it in the Walcheren campaign that year. After Walcheren, he wrote that 'I am so wedded to these poor fellows, that I cannot leave them, in their present state' (ibid., 179). He ordered that breakfast messes be established in the regiment and, when once again on campaign, petitioned the government for a special 'tear and wear of tartan' allowance. The Gordons were ordered to Portugal in 1810 while he was grouse shooting in Scotland, and he spent £36 to hurry south by coach from Inverness: 'I arrived here at five o'clock this morning', he recorded on reaching London. 'I had an outside and inside place on the mail, and by changing with Ewen [McMillan] stage by stage, we made it out without stopping at York' (ibid., 190 n.). But they missed the troop ship and finally caught up with the regiment on 20 October at Torres Vedras. Cameron then led the 92nd with distinction, particularly at Fuentes d'Oñoro, on 5 May 1811; at Arroyo dos Molinos, on 28 October 1811, where his middle finger was shattered; at Almaraz, on 19 May 1812; and at Vitoria, on 21 June 1813, where he sternly reminded his men to 'be steady and sure', calling the piper to play 'The Camerons' Gathering' (ibid., 248), and he later received a medal for taking command of a brigade, when Colonel Cadogan fell. He led the regiment, too, at the passage of Maya, on 13 July 1813; at the battle of the Nive between 9 and 13 December 1813, during the latter having his dead horse roll on him and being commended for his leadership by Lieutenant-General Sir William Stewart; at the passage of the Gave at Arriverette, on 17 February 1814; and at the capture of Aire, on 2 March 1814, where he earned Lieutenant-General Sir Rowland Hill's formal approbation.

At the close of the Peninsular War, Cameron was awarded the Portuguese order of the Tower and Sword. Although promoted colonel, on 4 June 1814, Cameron led the 92nd in Flanders the following year, attending the duchess of Richmond's ball on 15 June 1815 and riding at the regiment's head when it marched south from Brussels at dawn the next morning, with Lieutenant-General Sir Thomas Picton's 5th division, to reinforce Quatre-Bras. Late in the afternoon, having repelled several cavalry attacks from behind a bank immediately left of the crossroads, the 92nd charged French infantry advancing along the Charleroi road, and Cameron was mortally wounded by a sniper in the upper storey of a wayside house. He was carried to the rear on a cart, and died near the village of Waterloo that night. His last words, in highland dialect, were: 'I trust my dear country will think I have done enough; I hope she will think I have served her faithfully' (Gardyne, 358). He was buried beside the Ghent road, during the great storm of the 17th, by private Ewen McMillan, who had followed his fortunes from the first day he joined the service, James Gordon, the regimental paymaster, a close personal friend, and a few soldiers of the regiment whose wounds prevented their taking their places in the ranks. At the request of the family, however, Cameron's remains were disinterred soon afterwards, brought home in a man-of-war, and, in the presence of 3000 highlanders, were laid in Kilmallie churchyard, where a tall obelisk, bearing an inscription by Sir Walter Scott, marks the site of his grave. Another monument to him and other highlanders killed during the French wars was erected at Kintara. In 1817, a baronetcy was conferred on Ewen Cameron of Fassiefern, in recognition of the distinguished military services of his late son. Known as Fassiefern by his men, Cameron had commanded a battalion since 1806. When he died a pocket book, listing the names and details of all those who joined the regiment with him in 1794, was found in his possession. A strict disciplinarian, he insisted on clean accoutrements and dealt severely with drunkenness. John Downie, a veteran highlander, recalled that he was 'a splendid soldier [who] made us do our duty … his only fault, his reckless bravery' (Gardyne, 358). Apart from showing a keen interest in his men's welfare, he actively supported the development of highland music, especially the bagpipes.

H. M. Chichester, *rev.* John Sweetman

Sources *Army List* • C. G. Gardyne, *The life of a regiment: the history of the Gordon Highlanders from its formation in 1794 to 1816*, 2 vols. (1901) • *The dispatches of … the duke of Wellington … from 1799 to 1818*, ed. J. Gurwood, 7: *Peninsula, 1790–1813* (1837) • *The dispatches of … the duke of Wellington … from 1799 to 1815*, ed. J. Gurwood, 12: *France and the Low Countries, 1814–1815* (1838) • *DNB* • Burke, *Gen. GB* • R. Cannon, ed., *Historical record of the ninety-second regiment, originally termed 'the Gordon highlanders' and numbered the hundredth regiment* (1851) • W. F. P. Napier, *History of the war in the Peninsula and in the south of France*, 6 vols. (1828–40) • H. T. Siborne, ed., *Waterloo letters* (1891) • C. Dulton, *The Waterloo Roll Call* (1971)

Likenesses C. Turner, print, pubd 1815, BM, AM Oxf. [*see illus.*] • lithograph (after engraving by C. Turner, 1815), repro. in A. Clerk, *Memoir of Colonel John Cameron* (1858)

Cameron, Sir John (1773–1844), army officer, born on 3 January 1773, was the second son of John Cameron of Calchenna, and nephew of John Cameron of Caltort, the head of a branch of clan Cameron, and a descendant of Lochiel. He was educated at Eton College, and on 25 April 1787 received his first commission as an ensign in the 43rd regiment. On 30 September 1790 he was promoted lieutenant, and on 11 July 1794 captain in the 43rd.

In 1793 the 43rd regiment participated in Sir Charles Grey's expedition to the West Indies. Cameron was present at the capture of the islands of Martinique, St Lucia, and Guadeloupe, and was especially distinguished at the storming of Fort Fleur d'Épée on Guadeloupe, where he won his captaincy. In 1794 Grey returned to England, in the belief that his West Indian conquests were safe. The 43rd, which had been so reduced by sickness that Cameron, though only a junior captain, commanded it, formed part of the garrison of the Berville camp under Brigadier-General Graham, who had been left in charge of Guadeloupe. Victor Hugues, the commissary of the French republic in the West Indies, then organized an army out of the defeated French soldiers, the slaves, and the Caribs, reconquered St Lucia, and in the autumn of 1794 attacked Guadeloupe. His first assault on the Berville camp on 30 September was unsuccessful, but on 4 October the camp was captured, and Cameron was wounded and taken prisoner. He remained in France as a prisoner of war more than two years, but in 1797 he was exchanged and immediately rejoined the 43rd in the West Indies. He remained there until 1800, when he was promoted major, and brought the 43rd home after it had suffered terrible losses from disease. When stationed in Guernsey in 1803, he married Miss Brock, the eldest daughter of Henry Brock of Belmont, Guernsey, and niece of the first Lord de Saumarez. They had one son, Sir Duncan Alexander *Cameron (1808–1888), who served in the Crimean and New Zealand wars and was governor of the Royal Military College at Sandhurst, Berkshire.

On 28 May 1807 Cameron was appointed lieutenant-colonel of the 7th West India regiment, and on 5 September of that year transferred to the 9th regiment. In July 1808 he sailed for Portugal with the expedition under Sir Arthur Wellesley and the 9th and 29th were brigaded together as the 3rd brigade under Brigadier-General Catlin Craufurd. This brigade bore the brunt of the battle of Roliça, attacking the strong position of Laborde, where Colonel Stewart, of the 2nd battalion of the 9th, was killed. Cameron succeeded to the command of the 9th. He served with it at the battle of Vimeiro, in the advance to Salamanca, and in the disastrous retreat to Corunna, and then returned to England at its head.

From July to September 1809 Cameron commanded the 1st battalion in the Walcheren expedition in the Netherlands, and in March 1810 he returned to Portugal at the head of the 2nd battalion of the 9th, which he commanded until the end of the Peninsular War. At the battle of Busaco on 27 September 1810 he was particularly distinguished; the picked regiments of General Reynier's *corps d'armée* had driven in the right of the 3rd division and established themselves in the very heart of the British position. General Leith ordered up his 1st brigade to drive off the enemy, but the ground was too rugged for them to advance. 'Meanwhile', according to Sir William Napier:

> Colonel Cameron, informed by a staff officer of the critical state of affairs, formed the 9th regiment in line under a violent fire, and, without returning a single shot, ran in upon and drove the grenadiers from the rocks with irresistible bravery, plying them with a destructive musketry as long as they could be reached, and yet with excellent discipline refraining from pursuit, lest the crest of the position should be again lost, for the mountain was so rugged that it was impossible to judge clearly of the general state of the action. (Napier, chap. 7, bk 11)

Cameron afterwards commanded his regiment at the battle of Fuentes d' Oñoro, the siege of Badajoz, the battle of Salamanca, the encounter with the French rearguard at Osma on 18 June 1813, and the battle of Vitoria, on all of which occasions it formed a part of the 2nd brigade of the 5th division under General Leith. At the siege of San Sebastian the 9th captured the convent of San Bartolomé on 17 July 1813, when Cameron was wounded. It was engaged in the attempt of 25 July to storm San Sebastian, and in the successful assault of 31 August, when Cameron was again wounded. During the siege operations the 9th lost two-thirds of its officers and three-quarters of its soldiers. The loss of the regiment in 1813 exceeded that of any other in the Peninsula, amounting to 41 officers and 646 men killed and wounded.

In the invasion of France, as in the advance upon Vitoria, the 5th division formed the extreme left of the army. The 9th led the division across the River Bidassoa and in the attack on the French position, in the battle of the Nivelle, and in the fiercely contested battles of 9, 10, and 11 December before Bayonne, which are known as the battle of the Nive. In these three days the 9th lost 300 men. On 10 December it was completely surrounded, but broke out towards the main army and took 400 prisoners. On the 11th Cameron had his horse killed under him when reconnoitring the village of Anglet.

Cameron was not present at the battles of Orthez and Toulouse in February and April 1814, but was engaged until the end of the war in Sir John Hope's operations before Bayonne. On the conclusion of peace he received many rewards. On 4 June 1814 he was promoted colonel, and in January 1815 he was one of the first KCBs. He was also made a knight of the Tower and Sword of Portugal and received a gold cross with three clasps in commemoration of the six battles and one siege at which he had commanded his regiment.

In 1814 Cameron commanded his regiment in Canada, where he acted as brigadier-general and commandant of the garrison of Kingston, Upper Canada, until 1815, when he commanded a brigade in the army of occupation in France. On 19 July 1821 he was promoted major-general and commanded the western district from 1823 to 1833, when he was appointed colonel of the 9th regiment, which he had so long commanded. He had been colonel of the 93rd in 1832–3, and was lieutenant-governor of Plymouth from 1823 to 1835. On 10 January 1837 he was promoted lieutenant-general; and on 23 November 1844 he died at Guernsey.

H. M. Stephens, *rev.* Stewart M. Fraser

Sources *Supplementary despatches (correspondence) and memoranda of Field Marshal Arthur, duke of Wellington*, ed. A. R. Wellesley, second duke of Wellington, 15 vols. (1858–72) · J. Philippart, ed., *The royal military calendar*, 3 (1816), 205–6 · W. F. P. Napier, *History of the war in the Peninsula and in the south of France*, 3 vols. (1878) · C. W. C. Oman, *A history of the Peninsular War*, 7 vols. (1902–30); repr. (1995–7) · *GM*, 2nd ser., 23 (1845) · private information (1886) · Boase, *Mod. Eng. biog.* · R. Cannon, ed., *Historical record of the ninth, or the east Norfolk regiment of foot* (1848) · T. C. W. Blanning, *The French revolutionary wars, 1787–1802* (1996)

Archives Royal Norfolk Regiment Museum, Norwich

Cameron, Sir John [Jock], **Lord Cameron** (**1900–1996**), judge, was born on 8 February 1900 in Edinburgh, the son of John Cameron, solicitor at the Supreme Court, and his wife, Wilhelmina Louise Wilson. Known as Jock, he was educated at Edinburgh Academy from 1911 to 1917; in his final year he was dux (top classical scholar). Notably well read, Cameron won prizes, mainly in classics, and was active in the debating society. The First World War interrupted his passage to university and in 1917, after a brief period as a private in the Edinburgh University OTC, he served in the Royal Navy, taking part in a minor Baltic campaign as a probationary midshipman on destroyers.

In 1919 Cameron entered Edinburgh University and obtained an MA degree in classics and history. Subsequently he gained an LLB degree with distinction, and was

Sir John Cameron, Lord Cameron (1900–1996), by Alberto Morrocco, 1974

admitted to the Faculty of Advocates in 1924. Specializing in criminal work, he served as advocate-depute, the equivalent in Scotland of a crown prosecutor, from 1929 until 1936, the year in which he became a king's counsel. Cameron showed great skill with civil and criminal juries, and cross-examined witnesses with 'deceptive art', the phrase used by Lord John Wheatley, later lord justice clerk, who was devilling for Cameron at the time. On one occasion in the 1930s, when capital punishment was still common in Scotland, Cameron was defending in a murder trial and asked the key prosecution witness in a kindly tone what happened to people convicted of murder. The witness replied, with the smile of a simpleton, that he thought they would get the tawse—the strap used in Scottish schools. The point was made. The court fell silent. Cameron's client was acquitted.

In 1927 Cameron married Eileen Dorothea (*d.* 1943), daughter of H. M. Burrell; they had two daughters and a son, Kenneth (later Lord Cameron of Lochbroom, lord advocate in Margaret Thatcher's government from 1984 to 1989, and a judge like his father). In the late 1930s Cameron came increasingly to detest Hitler and fascism. In 1938 he signed up for the Royal Naval Volunteer Supplementary Reserve, in which he served during the Second World War. In 1940 he was in charge of one of the last craft to escape from Dunkirk before the Germans arrived, and manoeuvred his coastal motor boat, which carried a full load of prominent generals, at full speed astern through a narrow channel. He was mentioned in dispatches for this exploit and in 1944, as a lieutenant-commander, was awarded the DSC for his 'gallantry, skill, and determination and undaunted devotion to duty' during the allied landings in Normandy.

Cameron's wife died in 1943 while he was at sea, and on 4 November 1944 he married her friend Iris Eunice (*b.* 1913/14), daughter of Eric Alfred Henry of the India and Burma imperial police, and widow of Lambert C. Shepherd. They enjoyed an exceptionally happy marriage for the remainder of his life.

On demobilization in 1945 Cameron was appointed sheriff of Inverness, Elgin, and Nairn, and from 1946 to 1948 he held the successor sheriffdom of Inverness, Elgin, Moray, Nairn, and Ross and Cromarty. Having been elected by his contemporaries dean of the Faculty of Advocates (leader of the Scottish bar) in 1948, he was knighted in 1954 and in 1955 appointed a senator of the college of justice and a lord of session. He presided over some of the most high-profile trials of the day, including that of Peter Manuel—an armed robber convicted in 1958 of killing seven people—whom he sentenced to death.

Alongside his work on the bench, Cameron was extremely active in public service. On leaving the navy he became chairman of the legal aid committee in Scotland; he was involved in numerous industrial inquiries, including the feasibility of the dock labour scheme in 1948. He chaired a three-man commission into the rioting in Northern Ireland in 1969, which found many of the Catholic grievances justified. His service as chairman of the Highlands and Islands Development Consultative Council was part of a lifelong interest in the north-west of Scotland, where his ancestors originated. In 1978 he was appointed a knight of the Thistle, probably the first serving judge to receive that honour.

The sea remained among Cameron's many interests—he was honorary commodore of the Forth Yacht Club—but he also supported the arts in Scotland, as a member of the Edinburgh festival council, chairman of the Edinburgh Concert Society, and a supporter of Edinburgh music and theatre. He was an amateur artist and a collector of pictures. A large, impressive figure, Cameron was a sociable man with 'swept-back hair and a face full of character' (*Daily Telegraph*). He had many friends and a reputation for hospitality and good humour: 'He sang songs, enjoyed mimicking his stuffier colleagues, and relished intelligent conversation and the exchange of ideas' (ibid.). While chairing the committee on the law of contempt, which had been set up in June 1971, Cameron recounted the story of how an egg had been thrown at Vice-Chancellor Mallins. 'He is said to have remarked that he presumed it was intended for his brother Bacon, who was sitting in an adjoining court' (*The Independent*). He died on 30 May 1996 at his home, 28 Moray Place, Edinburgh; he was survived by his second wife. TAM DALYELL

Sources *Daily Telegraph* (7 June 1996) · *The Times* (6 June 1996) · *The Independent* (5 June 1996) · *WWW* · personal knowledge (2004) · private information (2004) · *CCI* (1996) · Lord Hunter, 'The Honourable Lord Cameron (10–17) KT, DSC, QC', *The Academical*, no. 5 [n.d.], 17–19 · m. cert. [Iris Eunice Shepherd] · d. cert.

Likenesses A. Morrocco, portrait, 1974, U. Edin., Old College [*see illus.*] · photograph, repro. in *The Independent*

Wealth at death £559,584.11, Scotland: confirmation, 29 July 1996, *CCI*

Cameron, John Alexander (*d.* 1885), journalist, was descended from the Camerons of Kinlochiel, in Argyll, and was born at Inverness, where he was a bank clerk. He went to India, and was employed by a mercantile firm in Bombay. He contributed to the *Bombay Gazette*, and was for some time acting editor, when on the outbreak of the Anglo-Afghan War in 1878 he was appointed special correspondent, and accompanied Roberts's Kurram field force. When in late 1879 the war broke out afresh, he became correspondent of the London *Standard*. Joining the column under General Robert Phayrer, sent to the relief of Kandahar, he was the first to ride with the news of Roberts's victory outside Kandahar (1 September 1880) to the nearest telegraph post, beating competitors by a day and a half. After returning to Kandahar he went to the battlefield of Maiwand (the British disaster on 27 July 1880), and his description of it established his reputation as one of the most graphic correspondents. On the outbreak of the First South African War (December 1880) he crossed from Bombay to Natal, arriving long before the correspondents from England. He witnessed the battles of Laing's Nek (28 January 1881), Ingogo (7 February 1881), and Majuba Hill (27 February 1881), when he was taken prisoner but released as a non-combatant. On the following day he interviewed the Boer commander, Petrus Jacobus Joubert, and sent a famous report on the battle. With the help of his friend Melton Prior, he scooped his rivals in reporting that peace had been agreed. Sharing the anger at the Gladstone government's Transvaal retrocession, at Newcastle, Natal, Cameron helped burn an effigy of Gladstone.

Cameron returned to England, but on the news of the riots in Alexandria (June 1882) left for Egypt, and was aboard Sir Frederick Seymour's flagship *Invincible* at the bombardment of the Alexandria fortifications. He afterwards continued with the British troops throughout the Egyptian campaign until their arrival in Cairo. After a short interval he left for Madagascar, and filed reports which attracted much attention. As the French delayed their attack on the island, he crossed the Pacific to Melbourne in Australia. From there he went to Tonkin, and was present at the engagement in which the French failed to carry the Black Flags' defences. British correspondents being forbidden to remain with the French forces, he left for home. He was on his way when Osman Digna's forces began to threaten Suakin, in the Sudan; on reaching Suez he immediately took ship for that port. When Valentine Baker's force was routed by the Mahdists at Trinkitat (4 February 1884) he narrowly escaped with his life, then stayed at Suakin. He accompanied Sir James Graham's force in its advance on Tokar, and witnessed the battles of al-Teb and Tamanieb. After a short stay in England he went again for *The Standard*, to report the Gordon relief expedition in 1884. Wolseley, maybe wrongly, considered him cowardly, and wrote in his journal that Cameron 'always runs away if he by accident finds his body in any danger' (Preston, 95). He accompanied Sir Herbert Stewart's desert column, and on 19 January 1885 was in the British square at Gubat, near Metemmah, when the Mahdists attacked. As he sat between camels, eating sardines and biscuits, Cameron was shot dead. He was buried with the other British dead at Abu Kru near Metemmah. He was survived by his widowed mother, Christina Cameron.

'Of little more than the middle height, his frame was well knit and very powerful' (Watson, 199). Vigorous, competitive, truculent, taciturn but outspoken and rough-mannered, Cameron was a successful war correspondent.

T. F. HENDERSON, *rev.* ROGER T. STEARN

Sources *The Standard* (27 Jan 1885) • *ILN* (7 Feb 1885) • J. Lehmann, *The First Boer War* (1972); repr. (1985) • *In relief of Gordon: Lord Wolseley's campaign journal of the Khartoum relief expedition, 1884–1885*, ed. A. Preston (1967) • M. Prior, *Campaigns of a war correspondent*, ed. S. L. Bensusan (1912) • J. Symons, *England's pride: the story of the Gordon relief expedition* (1965) • R. Furneaux, *News of war* (1964) • B. Robson, *Fuzzy-wuzzy: the campaigns in the eastern Sudan, 1884–85* (1993) • Boase, *Mod. Eng. biog.* • P. Hodgson, *The war illustrators* (1977) • A. Watson, *The Savage Club* (1907) • *CGPLA Eng. & Wales* (1885)

Wealth at death £1062 10s.: probate, 13 March 1885, *CGPLA Eng. & Wales*

Cameron [*née* Pattle], **Julia Margaret** (1815–1879), photographer, was born at Garden Reach, Calcutta, India, on 11 June 1815, fourth of the ten children (of whom seven, all daughters, survived to adulthood) of James Pattle (1775–1845) and his wife, Adeline de l'Étang (1793?–1845). Her mother was from a family of French aristocrats; her father had risen through the East India Company to hold a number of important legal and administrative positions; according to some (disputed) accounts he was a colourful and heavy-drinking character. The Pattle family was prominent in Anglo-Indian society, but Julia Pattle and her sisters spent much of their childhood in France and England, receiving an informal and unconventional education, chiefly with their French grandmother in Versailles. An affectionate, eccentric, and often oppressively generous woman, Julia Pattle was considered the one plain sister among a family of celebrated beauties. All seven sisters were noted for their unorthodox behaviour and dress. Julia and her sister Sara (later Sara Prinsep) were also known for intervening in other people's lives in an often intrusive and overbearing fashion. The term 'Pattledom' was coined, probably by the novelist William Makepeace Thackeray (Hill, 19), to describe both the closeness of the Pattle sisters and their domineering tendencies.

In 1835, after a series of illnesses, Julia Pattle was sent to southern Africa to convalesce, and it was there that she met the scientist John Herschel. An astronomer, he was also a pioneer of the chemistry of photography, still an embryonic process at this time. He became not only a lifelong friend but also her main guide and critic when she later took up photography. He was to sit for some of her finest portraits, and her most famous album, the Herschel Album (now in the National Museum of Photography, Film, and Television, Bradford), is dedicated to him. It was on this trip to southern Africa, too, that she met her future husband, Charles Hay *Cameron (1795–1880); they married in Calcutta on 1 February 1838. Of their six children—a daughter and five sons—Henry Herschel Hay Cameron, the youngest son, also became a photographer. They remained happily married until Julia Margaret Cameron's

Julia Margaret Cameron (1815–1879), by Henry Herschel Hay Cameron, 1870

death in 1879, for, although twenty years her senior, her husband outlived her by a year. Charles Cameron regarded his wife's eccentricities and excesses with a degree of tolerance which itself bordered on the eccentric. He was a Benthamite liberal reformer, a classical scholar, a jurist, and (between 1843 and 1848) the legal member of the Council of India; his published work includes *Address to parliament on the duties of Great Britain to India in respect of the education of the natives, and their official employment* (1853). Mrs Cameron was sympathetic to her husband's humanitarian, if paternalistic, principles, though her own good causes were motivated by a simpler sense of compassion, her most notable charitable achievement being the organization of the Calcutta relief fund for the Irish potato famine of 1845, which raised £14,000.

Mrs Cameron was a noted conversationalist; during the 1840s she was effectively the first lady of Anglo-Indian society, acting as organizer and hostess of the social engagements of the governor-general, Lord Henry Hardinge. Even in this role, however, she reputedly demonstrated her unconventionality with her readiness to include Indians—albeit those whom she perceived as respectable and educated—on her guest list. She also wrote some undistinguished poetry, and in 1847 published a translation of Gottfried Bürger's Gothic ballad *Lenore*, illustrated with woodcuts by Daniel Maclise.

Charles Cameron retired in 1848, and the family then settled in England, though Cameron himself continued to make periodic visits to his estates in Ceylon. Until 1860 they lived in south-east England, moving several times, usually to be near friends for whom Mrs Cameron had conceived a particular affection. She was a frequent visitor to Little Holland House, the Kensington home of Sara and Thoby Prinsep, her sister and brother-in-law; here Sara had formed a salon which in some respects foreshadowed the Bloomsbury circle—in familial terms as well as artistic and intellectual ones, for Julia's niece and one of her favourite models, Julia Jackson, became the mother of the novelist Virginia Woolf and the painter Vanessa Bell, through her second marriage, to Leslie Stephen, the first editor of the *Dictionary of National Biography*. Woolf's comic play *Freshwater* (1923?) parodies Cameron and her circle; but, together with Roger Fry, Woolf was also responsible for the first major book on Cameron's work, *Victorian Photographs of Famous Men and Fair Women* (1926).

At Little Holland House, Cameron met many of the people whom she photographed: guests included Thackeray, Robert Browning, John Ruskin, Dante Gabriel Rossetti, James Abbott McNeill Whistler, and, most significantly, Alfred Tennyson and the painter G. F. Watts (who came to visit the Prinseps and stayed for more than twenty years). Tennyson, a reluctant model, was persuaded to sit for her on many occasions: her best-known portrait of him shows him in profile, swathed in a cloak, with a book in his hand. It was a favourite of his, and he famously called it *The Dirty Monk* (Royal Photographic Society collection, National Museum of Photography, Film, and Television, Bradford, C5: 2055/1). In addition to sitting for Julia Margaret Cameron, Watts and Tennyson also influenced her work significantly, both in her conception of art and in the inspiration for many of her subjects. In 1860 her friendship with Tennyson had prompted her to move to Freshwater, on the Isle of Wight; she took the house next to his, which she called Dimbola, after one of her husband's estates in Ceylon. The hen house at Dimbola became her first studio when she took up photography in 1863, after her daughter, Julia, gave her a set of photographic equipment. Her photographic career effectively covers a period of just over ten years, until 1875; she apparently took very few photographs after she moved to Ceylon.

Cameron had no formal technical training, and her style and technique derived largely from a combination of aesthetic instinct and trial and error. Some of her contemporaries criticized her refusal to 'retouch' her work to remove blemishes, and they regarded her use of soft focus as a simple inability to focus the camera correctly. However, she did not lack professional guidance: she turned to Herschel for technical advice and aesthetic criticism, and is known to have been on good terms with her fellow photographer O. G. Rejlander. Her relationship with Charles Dodgson (Lewis Carroll) was less friendly, and they disagreed professionally over the issue of focus. In a letter to Herschel she defended herself against her critics, denying that anyone had the right to say what focus was legitimate.

In 1864 Cameron took the photograph which she called *My First Success* (National Portrait Gallery, London), a portrait of a child named Annie Philpot. It already shows the basis of her mature style—the large portrait head, devoid of the props and backdrops typical of the period. The image was taken using only daylight, which Cameron learned thereafter to manipulate using a system of roller blinds; exposures might last up to six minutes. She did not enlarge her photographs, but printed directly off large negatives. (From 1866 she used a camera which took photographic plates measuring 12 inches by 15.) In her own eyes, her most important photographs were probably her illustrations for Tennyson's *Idylls of the King*, which she began in 1874, following up the volume in 1875 with further illustrations of Tennyson's poems. However, these have appealed less to later tastes, and she has come to be most highly regarded for her portrait photographs, particularly those of the eminent men of her day. Her best work was produced about 1867 and is typified by such powerful images as her portraits of Thomas Carlyle (Royal Photographic Society collection, National Museum of Photography, Film, and Television, Bradford, C3: 2029 and 2505), and of Herschel, particularly *The Astronomer* (the Herschel Album, National Museum of Photography, Film and Television, Bradford). Many of her photographs include an element of costume—often a simple cloak for the men, covering their Victorian dress and giving them a timeless quality. Women sitters are frequently depicted with covered head as madonnas or with flowing hair as magdalens. The more elaborate use of costume and props in her Arthurian tableaux, however, contributes significantly to their stiff and stilted appearance in the eyes of later viewers.

Julia Margaret Cameron was most deeply influenced by the old masters: compositional parallels have been traced between some of her images and paintings by Raphael and Rembrandt and others, and Titian and Rembrandt have both been seen to influence her dramatic use of light and shade. Parallels can also be drawn between some of her photographs and Pre-Raphaelite works, but of all the painters who were her contemporaries, she was closest in her artistic ideals and the ethos of her work to G. F. Watts. His belief that 'Painting is poetry, made manifest by Science' (Howard, 17) equally describes Cameron's attitude towards photography. In *Annals of my Glass House* (1874), an unfinished account of her photographic career (published posthumously in 1889), she explained the spirit and intention of her work with reference to her photographs of Carlyle: 'When I have had such men before my camera, my whole soul has endeavoured to do its duty towards them in recording faithfully the greatness of the inner as well as the features of the outer man'. She described such photographs as 'the embodiment of a prayer' (Weaver, 157).

Julia Margaret Cameron was not the only Victorian woman photographer, but for most others, however enthusiastic, photography was primarily a means of creating a family record. Although her images are often deeply informed by her feelings for her sitter, they go far beyond the personal to epitomize particular qualities or essences—typically, genius in men and beauty in women. Mike Weaver, in a key work of Cameron scholarship, published in 1984, has placed Cameron's conception of genius and beauty within a specifically Christian framework, as indicative of the sublime and the sacred. The simple and profound spiritual certainty underlying her work, and the function of the large, iconic, individual portrait head in expressing this, is made particularly clear if one compares her photographs with those of her contemporary Lady Clementina Hawarden. Hawarden's work was often exhibited in the same shows as Cameron's, and, like Cameron, she was a photographer for whom the portrayal of loved ones was not a simple matter of the personal and familial. Her mature photographs, almost exclusively featuring young women often depicted in pairs, or reflected in a mirror, are frequently expressive of a deep ambiguity and anxiety which has no parallel in Cameron's work.

Cameron was concerned to be taken seriously and to earn an income from her work. In 1864 she was elected to the Photographic Society of London, and she showed work at its annual exhibitions. In November 1865 she organized her first solo exhibition, hiring the gallery of the printsellers P. and D. Colnaghi in London, with whom she also entered into an arrangement for the printing and sale of her photographs; a similar arrangement was made with the Autotype Company for mass reproduction. She exhibited regularly in Europe, winning a bronze medal in Berlin in 1865 and a gold medal in 1866, and there was a strong demand for her prints.

Despite her professional success, Cameron and her husband emigrated to Ceylon in October 1875. Financial worries may have contributed to the decision, along with the weakening of their family ties with England: their daughter, Julia, had died in childbirth in 1873, and four of their five sons were living in Ceylon. Charles Cameron regarded it as his spiritual home, and wished to die there; Julia Margaret Cameron's feelings about the move are less clear. It effectively meant the end of her career: the climate of Ceylon intensified the difficulties of early photographic processes, and chemicals and other materials must have been hard to come by. She died on 26 January 1879 at the Glencairn estate, Newara Elluja, Dikoya valley, Ceylon, and was buried in the churchyard in the valley between Colombo and Galle.

Apart from the publication of Woolf and Fry's book in 1926, Julia Margaret Cameron's work was largely forgotten for many years. In the 1940s Helmut Gernsheim, a researcher in photography, saw a number of her photographs on the walls of the waiting-room at Brockenhurst railway station in Hampshire. (In a typically eccentric gesture, Cameron had presented them to the station in 1871, to mark her reunion there with one of her sons after a separation of four years.) The subsequent research of Gernsheim and his wife, Alison, culminated in a book, first published in 1948, which was instrumental in re-establishing Cameron's status as one of the most important photographers not only of the Victorian period but in the whole history of the medium. Collections of her work are in the National Museum of Photography, Film, and Television, Bradford; the Victoria and Albert Museum, London; the J. Paul Getty Museum, Brentwood, California; and the

Gernsheim Collection, University of Texas at Austin. Dimbola Lodge at Freshwater Bay, Isle of Wight, was opened in the 1990s as a museum by the Julia Margaret Cameron Trust. HELEN BARLOW

Sources A. Hopkinson, *Julia Margaret Cameron* (1986) • M. Harker, *Julia Margaret Cameron* (1983) • B. Hill, *Julia Margaret Cameron: a Victorian family portrait* (1973) • M. Weaver, *Julia Margaret Cameron, 1815–1879* (1984) • J. Howard, *Whisper of the muse: the world of Julia Margaret Cameron* (1990) [exhibition catalogue, P. & D. Colnaghi & Co. Ltd, London] • H. Gernsheim, *Julia Margaret Cameron: her life and photographic work*, 2nd edn (1975) • C. Ford, *The Cameron collection: an album of photographs by Julia Margaret Cameron presented to Sir John Herschel* (1975) • J. M. Cameron, *Victorian photographs of famous men and fair women*, ed. V. Woolf and R. Fry, rev. T. Powell (1973) • G. Ovenden, ed., *A Victorian album: Julia Margaret Cameron and her circle* (1975) • V. Woolf, *Freshwater: a comedy*, ed. L. P. Ruotolo (1976) • *CGPLA Eng. & Wales* (1881) • *DNB*

Archives National Museum of Photography, Film and Television, Bradford, Royal Photographic Society collection | Bodl. Oxf., corresp. with Sir Henry Taylor • CKS, letters to daughter, Julia Norman, and son-in-law, C. L. Norman • RS, corresp. with J. F. W. Herschel

Likenesses G. F. Watts, oils, 1850?–1852, NPG • G. F. Watts, pencil drawing, *c.*1852, priv. coll.; repro. in Howard, *Whisper of the muse*, 85 • Lord Somers, photograph, *c.*1860, NPG • H. H. H. Cameron, albumen print, 1870, NPG [*see illus.*] • H. H. H. Cameron, albumen print, 1875?, National Museum of Photography, Film and Television, Bradford, Royal Photographic Society collection; repro. in Howard, *Whisper of the muse*, 6 • H. H. H. Cameron, photograph, V&A • double portrait, photograph (with her daughter, Julia), priv. coll.; repro. in Hopkinson, *Julia Margaret Cameron*, frontispiece • photograph, NPG

Wealth at death £5940: probate, 25 Aug 1881, *CGPLA Eng. & Wales*

Cameron, Katharine (1874–1965), watercolour painter and etcher, was born on 26 February 1874 at 16 Sardinia Terrace, Hillhead, Glasgow, the eighth of the nine children of Robert Cameron (1825–1898), minister of Cambridge Street United Presbyterian Church in Glasgow, and his wife, Margaret Johnston (*bap.* 1839, *d.* 1924), elder daughter of Donald Robertson, a surgeon in Perth, and his wife, Jessie. Although she was baptized Catherine, she spelt her name Katharine, signing her paintings K. Cameron or KC. She was a younger sister of the distinguished painter and etcher Sir David Young *Cameron. Both inherited their artistic ability from their mother, a talented amateur watercolourist.

Cameron attended the Glasgow School of Art intermittently from 1889 to 1901, which was then under the inspired direction of Francis Newbery. She was a member of a small circle of female students who called themselves The Immortals. Other members included the sisters Margaret and Frances Macdonald, the former marrying the architect Charles Rennie Mackintosh, a fellow student of Cameron in the early 1890s. In 1902 she studied at the Académie Colarossi in Paris.

Apart from her etching, Cameron worked exclusively in watercolour. By the age of twenty she had achieved considerable maturity in terms of technique and composition. In 1897 she was elected a member of the Royal Scottish Society of Painters in Watercolour, then a remarkable achievement for a woman of twenty-two. Her

Katharine Cameron (1874–1965), by unknown photographer, 1931 [detail]

early paintings are predominantly flower pieces. However, inspired by the Celtic revival and by the work of Edward Burne-Jones, Dante Gabriel Rossetti, and the Hague school painter Matthijs Maris, whom she met on several occasions, she also executed a number of romantic figure studies, illustrating characters or incidents from Scottish ballads and folklore. Landscapes feature in her work after 1900. She had the same love of the highlands as her brother, always striving to capture their magical beauty.

In 1902 Cameron illustrated a book for children titled *In Fairyland*, the first of a number of such commissions. Her watercolour illustrations are varied and colourful, but are—with a few exceptions—unremarkable. She had little real commitment to illustration. What inspired her most was painting flowers; at her best her work is exemplary, combining acute observation with a sensitive painterly technique.

Cameron began etching in 1898, but did not take it up seriously until 1911, when her first set of eight etchings of flowers was published. She went on to etch about seventy-three plates over the next twenty-five years. The majority are of flowers and/or insects, the remainder being landscapes. They are characterized by a strong, yet sensitive line. She was elected an associate of the Royal Society of

Painter-Etchers and Engravers in 1920, becoming a fellow in 1964.

A prolific artist, Cameron painted with barely diminished vigour into her eighties. She was an assiduous exhibitor throughout her life, showing for the first time at the Royal Glasgow Institute in 1891 at the age of seventeen. She had a joint exhibition with her brother in London in 1897 and held the first of many solo exhibitions in 1900.

On 17 April 1928 Cameron married, as his second wife, the collector **Arthur Kay** (1861–1939), whom she had known for many years. He was born at 11 Whittingham Villas, Studley Road, Clapham Road, London, on 11 November 1861, the son of John Robert Kay, a merchant, and his wife, Eliza Perks. Kay joined his father on the board of Arthur & Co. Ltd, the major Glasgow wholesale warehousing firm, in 1887. Educated at Rossall School and Glasgow University, he was a very cultured man with a wide range of interests. A true connoisseur and a discriminating collector, he devoted the whole of his leisure time to art for almost sixty years. He was one of the first in Britain to recognize the true worth of the impressionists, at one time owning Degas's *L'absinthe* (Louvre Museum, Paris). He died at his home, 11 Regent Terrace, Edinburgh, on 1 January 1939.

In her younger days Cameron was petite, pretty, and vivacious, but she became rather stout in later life. She was noted for her distinctive clothes. Friends remembered her as a kind person who was very supportive of young artists. She died at 3 Marshall Crescent, Edinburgh, on 21 August 1965 after a fall. W. N. SMITH

Sources W. Smith, *D. Y. Cameron: the visions of the hills* (1992) • J. Burkhauser, ed., *The Glasgow girls: women in art and design, 1880–1920* (1990) • T. J. Honeyman, 'Katharine Cameron', *Scottish Field* (Oct 1959), 26–8 • A. Kay, *Treasure trove in art* (1939) • L. Annand, 'Katharine Cameron', *Glasgow Herald* (6 March 1959) • C. Clark, 'Arthur Kay', *Scottish Art Review*, 13/1 (1971), 25–8 • J. H. Hanson, 'The landscapes and flower pictures of Miss Katharine Cameron ARE, RSW', *Walker's Monthly* (April 1930) • 'Katharine Cameron', *Scots Bulletin and Pictorial* (18 Oct 1919) • H. C. Marillier, 'The romantic water-colours of Miss Cameron', *Art Journal*, new ser., 20 (1900), 148–9 • H. Wright, 'The etchings of Katherine Cameron', *International Studio*, 75 (1922), 401 • G. E. Todd, *Who's who in Glasgow in 1909* (1909) • b. cert. (Katharine Cameron) • m. cert. • b. cert. (Arthur Kay) • d. cert. (Arthur Kay) • d. cert. (Katharine Cameron)

Archives NL Scot., MSS

Likenesses J. Gunn, oils, 1930, Scot. NPG • photograph, 1931, NL Scot. [*see illus.*] • photographs, NL Scot., Cameron MSS

Cameron [*née* Butt], **Lucy Lyttelton** [*known as* Mrs Cameron] **(1781–1858)**, children's author, was born on 29 April 1781 in Stanford-on-Teme, Worcestershire, daughter of George *Butt (1741–1795), vicar of Stanford-on-Teme, and his wife, Martha Sherwood (*d.* 1817), daughter of a London silk merchant. The youngest of three children, she took her name from her godmother, Lady Lucy Fortescue Lyttelton, daughter of the first Lord Lyttelton and wife of Earl Mountnorris.

In 1787 Lord Foley appointed George Butt vicar of Kidderminster where, under the supervision of her parents, Lucy Lyttleton Butt's education began a year later with Latin, extending to French, Italian, and Greek. In 1792 she was sent to the Abbey School in Reading, which she attended until 1797. About 1794 the family returned to Stanford parsonage; one year later, on 30 September 1795, George Butt died there, and shortly afterwards the family moved to Bridgnorth.

From her earliest years Lucy Lyttelton Butt had the advantage of constant exposure to a highly literary and intellectual society. Her father was among the close friends of Anna Seward, 'the Swan of Lichfield', a factor that possibly played a significant part in his daughter's own career as a writer, which began in 1798 with the writing of *The History of Margaret Whyte*.

On 12 June 1806 Lucy Lyttelton Butt married the Revd Charles Richard Cameron (1781–1865) of Christ Church, Oxford, the eldest son of Dr Cameron, physician at Worcester; they had a large family. Through her husband Mrs Cameron met Gerrard Andrewes (1750–1825), dean of Canterbury and rector of St James's, Piccadilly, whose rectory was the meeting place for much of London society. There she met Elizabeth Carter and Humphry Davy. While visiting Bristol Mrs Cameron was introduced to Hannah More, Mary Anne Galton (later Mrs Schimmelpenninck), and other members of the literary coteries of London.

Mrs Cameron's acquaintances included writers for children with whom she was soon to be ranked. Although overshadowed at the time by the works of her sister, Mary Martha *Sherwood, Mrs Cameron's narrative tracts, such as the *Two Lambs*, written in 1803 but not published until 1827, effected similar changes in children's religious literature of the period. With its concern for the individual's life, background, and sentiments, their work replaced the earlier eighteenth-century moral tracts that concentrated not upon the individual but upon society and the individual's duties within it. Works such as Mrs Cameron's *Margaret Whyte* (1799) and her sister's *History of Little Henry and his Bearer* (1814) both have, according to Margaret Nancy Cutt, a quality of detail and expression that anticipates Victorian fiction for children. After starting to compose penny books for children in 1816, Mrs Cameron continued to write rapidly, completing one of her books, *The Raven and the Dove* (1817), in only four hours. This book, together with others such as *The Caskets* (1820), *Memoirs of Emma and her Nurse* (2nd edn, 1821), *Marten and his Two Little Scholars at a Sunday School* (1827), and *The Faithful Little Girl* (1823), and those of Mrs Sherwood, became for the children of the time a natural part not only of each Sunday but of childhood itself. By the 1870s, however, Mrs Cameron's works, including *Addresses to Children on the Beatitudes* (1828), *Englishwomen* (1841), and *The Farmer's Daughter* (1843), like those of Mrs Sherwood and Hannah More, were no longer circulated beyond the confines of the Sunday school.

Beyond her writing Mrs Cameron's life was the busy one of a clergyman's wife. Shortly after her marriage her husband was appointed to a church in Donnington Wood in the parish of Lilleshall, Shropshire, recently built on the estate of Lord Stafford for the colliers of the district; the Camerons lived in Snedshill. Mrs Cameron's mother died in 1817; the death of her sister-in-law, Mrs Butt, followed shortly after in 1818. Her brother, Marten Butt, unable to cope with the shock of his wife's death, became ill, and found himself unable to look after their children; Mrs Sherwood took charge of his four sons and Mrs Cameron, already caring for her own children, most of whom died before her, took in his three daughters. That summer, in 1818, Isaac Hawkins Browne MP, a close friend of Mrs Cameron's father, died leaving a legacy of £50 a year for life to Mrs Cameron.

In 1831 Charles Cameron accepted a cure at Swaby near Alford in Lincolnshire, but continued to live with his family in Snedshill, serving his old parish as curate until 1836. They then moved to Louth and finally, on the completion of the rectory, settled at Swaby in 1839. In 1856, while visiting the Lakes, Mrs Cameron was caught in a storm on Ullswater and caught a cold from which she never recovered. She died at Swaby rectory on 6 September 1858 and was buried in the churchyard there. JOANNE POTIER

Sources Boase, *Mod. Eng. biog.* • L. L. Cameron, *The life of Mrs. Cameron*, ed. [C. Cameron], rev. G. T. Cameron, 2nd edn [1873] • F. J. H. Darton, ed., *The life and times of Mrs. Sherwood (1775–1851)* (1910) • M. N. Cutt, *Ministering angels: a study of nineteenth-century evangelical writing for children* (1979) • M. N. Cutt, *Mrs Sherwood and her books for children* (1974) • G. Avery, *Childhood's pattern: a study of the heroes and heroines of children's fiction, 1770–1950* (1975) • N. Royde-Smith, *The state of mind of Mrs Sherwood: a study* (1946) • Allibone, *Dict.*

Likenesses engraving, repro. in Cameron, *Life of Mrs. Cameron*, frontispiece

Cameron, Neil (1854–1932), Free Presbyterian Church of Scotland minister, was born on 26 August 1854 at Kilninver, Argyll, son of James Cameron, then ploughman on the farm at Kilninver, and his wife, Flora Macdiarmid. He played a significant part in the formation of the Free Presbyterian Church of Scotland and became its most prominent and influential minister. His early years were spent at Kilninver, at Lochaweside, where his father served as grieve on the farm of Cladich (*c.*1858–*c.*1864), and at Ardnamurchan, where for four years he attended the parish school of Kilchoan. On leaving school he worked as a shepherd. About the age of fourteen he began to experience deep spiritual struggles and he frequently resorted, when in the hills, to a copy of the New Testament which he carried with him. Dissatisfaction with the preaching to which he was exposed in the Church of Scotland (his familial denomination), on the ground of its inadequate attention to the biblical basics of sin and salvation, eventually led to his leaving that church when about twenty years old. Initial prejudice against the Free Church was sufficiently removed to enable him to join that denomination. His spiritual conflicts culminated, in April 1879, in a conversion experience and he became a communicant member of the Free Church at Acharacle where from 1880 he attended worship.

Contact with the preachers who came to the preaching station at Acharacle, combined with his reading of the secular and religious press, convinced Cameron of the increasing departure of the Free Church, particularly in the lowlands, from the Bible and the theology of the Westminster confession of faith. Having experienced a call to the ministry he embarked on what would be an eleven-year period of preparatory study. A year at Onich's public school (1885–6) was followed by study at Edinburgh University (1886–91) and at New College, Edinburgh (1891–2). During this period Cameron became a leader among a group of students who strongly supported constitutionalist opposition to moves within the Free Church to have a declaratory act passed by its general assembly. Such an act would allow for qualified, rather than full, subscription to the Westminster confession of faith by office-bearers and Cameron believed that the result would be the accommodation of theological liberalism within the Free Church.

When a declaratory act was passed by a large majority in 1892 Cameron urged the need for secession from a body which, he believed, now constitutionally tolerated error. He travelled widely in the highlands in support of this cause. Although still a student he played an important part in the formation and organization of the new, seceding Free Presbyterian denomination of 1893 whose first two ministers were Donald Macfarlane and Donald Macdonald. Cameron's theological studies were completed at Glasgow University's Divinity Hall.

Called to the newly formed St Jude's Free Presbyterian congregation in Glasgow, Cameron was ordained and inducted to this charge on 9 January 1896. Widely regarded as an unusually solemn and searching preacher, he conducted services five times each week in his congregation. Throughout his ministry he played a leading role in his church. Deeply interested in its witness overseas (for example, in Canada), he served as convenor of the foreign mission committee from its inception, visiting the church's expanding South African mission in 1921. He vigorously opposed attempts to bring closer together his own denomination and the post-1900 Free Church (which had rescinded the declaratory act) and his motions in opposition to this, as in connection with most other matters, regularly carried at synod (the Free Presbyterian Church's supreme court).

Cameron's influence on the future course of the Free Presbyterian church, with its distinctive stress on the need for absolute continuity and its total resistance to any change in the denomination's doctrinal position and form of worship, was great. He died, unmarried, on 9 March 1932 in Glasgow (where his address was 216 West Regent Street) and was buried in Cathcart cemetery, Glasgow, two days later. ANGUS MORRISON

Sources D. Beaton, *Memoir etc. of Rev. Neil Cameron* (1932) • A. MacPherson, ed., *History of the Free Presbyterian Church of Scotland, 1893–1970* [n.d.] • N. Cameron, *Ministers and men of the Free Presbyterian Church*, ed. R. Middleton (1993) • D. Ansdall, *The people of the great faith: the highland church, 1690–1900* (1998) • *CCI* (1932) • J. L. MacLeod, *The second disruption: the Free Church in Victorian Scotland and the origins of the Free Presbyterian church* (2000)

Wealth at death £3947 18*s.* 10*d.*: confirmation, 7 July 1932, *CCI*

Cameron, Neil, **Baron Cameron of Balhousie** (1920–1985), air force officer, was born in Perth on 8 July 1920, the only son and younger child of Neil Cameron, an inspector of the poor, and his wife, Isabella Stewart. His father died in the year he was born and he and his sister were brought up by his mother and grandfather in Perth. Having attended Perth Academy he worked in the Royal

Bank of Scotland. After joining the Royal Air Force Volunteer Reserve in May 1939 he was called up on the outbreak of war and qualified as a pilot. He joined 17 squadron towards the end of the battle of Britain, was commissioned in 1941, flew in Russia with 151 wing, and in 1942–3 served with the desert air force in 213 squadron. In 1944–5, now a squadron leader, he commanded 258 squadron and flew Hurricanes and Thunderbolts in Burma, earning the DFC (1944) and DSO (1945) for his outstanding leadership.

Having been awarded a permanent commission after the war, Cameron instructed at the School of Air Support, Old Sarum, and attended the Staff College. He married, in 1947, Patricia Louise, the daughter of Major Edward Asprey, a civil engineer; they had a son and daughter. In 1949 he went to the Air Ministry, where he became seriously ill with subacute bacterial endocarditis. He was never again allowed a full flying category, making his eventual rise to the top of the RAF particularly remarkable. A spell instructing at the Staff College (1953–6) enabled him to deepen his thinking and begin writing about air power, and he saw something of the academic world while commanding London University air squadron (1956–8). He then served as personal staff officer to the chief of the air staff (1958–60), commanded RAF Abingdon (1960–62), attended the Imperial Defence College (1963), went to the supreme headquarters of the allied powers in Europe (1964), and in 1965—now an air commodore—became assistant commandant at Cranwell. There ensued four years in the Ministry of Defence working in Denis Healey's programme evaluation group and as assistant chief of staff (policy), when he showed the ability to take an overall defence view but in the process aroused suspicions among his single-service contemporaries, and he subsequently saw little chance of further advancement. Nevertheless after serving at headquarters air support command and RAF Germany he was promoted to air marshal in 1973 to become air officer commanding 46 group. Ten months later he became air member for personnel, where—at a time of major cuts in RAF strength—he combined his essential humanity with the ability to take hard decisions, notably in the matter of redundancy.

Cameron became chief of the air staff (CAS) in 1976 but had hardly had time to make much impression before the sudden death of Sir Andrew Humphrey led to his service as chief of the defence staff (CDS; 1977–9) and marshal of the Royal Air Force (1977). As CAS he had already emphasized the need for better communication within the RAF and deeper thinking about air power, and as CDS he was determined to argue the defence case in public debate; he held strong views on what he saw as a dangerous growth in Soviet military power, and his much publicized reference in China to the Russians as 'an enemy' led to their calling him 'a drunken hare' and to a minor political storm at home. Of the domestic issues he faced the most difficult was service pay, where he led his colleagues in confronting the government and winning the battle for the military salary.

After handing over as CDS in 1979 Cameron was appointed principal of King's College, London, in August 1980, giving him the opportunity to show his leadership qualities in the academic environment that had eluded him in his youth. Here, despite failing health, he played a major part in the restructuring of London University and in particular the merger between King's, Chelsea, and Queen Elizabeth colleges. He was created a life peer in 1983 and a knight of the Thistle the same year. He had been appointed CBE (1967), CB (1971), KCB (1975), and GCB (1976). He received an honorary LLD degree from Dundee in 1981.

Cameron's many wider interests included the RAF rugby football union, the RAF Club, the RAF Museum, the Trident Trust, and the British Atlantic committee, and underlying all else was a deep Christian faith rooted in his experience when ill in the 1950s and quietly but sincerely demonstrated through his support for St Clement Danes and organizations such as the Officers' Christian Union. A man of great honesty, integrity, and forthrightness, who was widely respected, he saw no difficulty in combining a firm military stance based on a belief in nuclear deterrence with his strongly held Christian convictions. He died in the Middlesex Hospital on 29 January 1985.

HENRY A. PROBERT, *rev.*

Sources N. Cameron, *In the midst of things* (1986) • record of service, ministry of defence, air historical branch • *The Times* (30 Jan 1985) • *The Times* (6 Feb 1985) • personal knowledge (1990) • *CGPLA Eng. & Wales* (1985)

Archives Royal Air Force Museum, Hendon, MSS | SOUND IWM SA, recorded lecture

Likenesses photograph, 1978 (with General Francesco Cavalera), Hult. Arch.

Wealth at death £13,277: probate, 28 Feb 1985, *CGPLA Eng. & Wales*

Cameron, Richard (*d.* 1680), covenanter field preacher, was the eldest son of Allan Cameron and Margaret Paterson. He spent his early childhood on the family estate at Fordell near Leuchars, Fife, and may have attended the grammar school in St Andrews. He entered St Salvator's College, St Andrews, on 5 March 1662 and graduated MA on 22 July 1665.

Pecuniary problems compelled Cameron's parents to sell their property and move to Falkland, and Cameron himself transferred there after completing his education. He was appointed schoolmaster of Falkland burgh school, in the winter of 1669–70, and also became a precentor in the parish church there. Cameron was soon greatly influenced by the field preacher John Welwood, who forcefully condemned the indulgence initiated by the government in an attempt to comprehend moderate covenanters within the national church, as a capitulation to Erastianism. By April 1675 he was charged by the local stewarty court, along with other members of his family, for attending conventicles. He resigned his post and accompanied his family to Edinburgh. In the autumn of that year he was appointed private chaplain to the house of Sir William Scott of Harden. However, he was soon dismissed for his refusal to attend a church service conducted by a minister who had accepted the indulgence.

In June 1677 Cameron became chaplain to Lady Douglas of Cavers near Hawick, who shared his covenanting and presbyterian convictions. In March 1678 he was licensed to preach by the nonconformist presbyterian ministers John Welsh, Gabriel Semple, David Williamson, and Thomas Douglas, in the house of Henry Hall at Haugh-Head in Teviotdale. As a preacher he very quickly drew large followings in the borders, the south-west, and into Clydesdale. By August, however, he had been summoned before an ecclesiastical tribunal in Edinburgh; it admonished him for preaching vehemently against, and for advocating separation from, the indulged ministers. By November he had been formally indicted on the same charge.

In May 1679 Cameron sailed to the Netherlands to seek advice and counsel from the influential presbyterian exiles Robert MacWard and John Brown of Wamphrey. He was ordained in the Scottish church in Rotterdam soon afterwards by MacWard, Brown, and Jacob Koelman of Sluiss in Flanders, to the consternation and reproach of the non-complying churchmen in Scotland. He returned to Scotland in early autumn 1679 and proceeded to preach and minister to large and enthusiastic crowds in the south and west. However, partly because of the severity of the reprisals and the clampdown against those who remained wholly committed to covenanting and presbyterian principles in the wake of Bothwell Bridge, only Donald Cargill and Thomas Douglas initially supported his new offensive to resume field preaching. In spite of the real danger posed to those attending conventicles, Cameron continued to attract large crowds. His gift as an experiential preacher can be gleaned in six of his sermons which were published by John Howie as *A Collection of Lectures and Sermons* (1779), reissued in 1880 entitled *Sermons in Time of Persecution in Scotland*. Similarly, *The Lion of the Covenant* (M. Grant, 1997) contains many extracts from his extant sermons.

In order to promote the covenanters' cause and defend it from government propaganda, Cameron and his supporters drew up 'The declaration and testimony of the true presbyterian, anti-prelatic, anti-Erastian, persecuted party in Scotland', which they fixed to the mercat cross in the town of Sanquhar on 22 June 1680. In it they renounced their allegiance to Charles II, repudiating:

> [his] perjury and breach of covenant both to God and His Kirk, and usurpation of His Crown and royal prerogatives therein, and many other breaches in matters ecclesiastic, and by tyranny and breach of the very *leges regnandi* in matters civil. (Grant, 240)

The declaration went on to name Charles as a 'tyrant and usurper'. In consequence a reward of 5000 merks was offered for Cameron's apprehension and an indemnity was passed for anyone who happened to 'kill or mutilate' him or any of his followers (*Reg. PCS*, 6.482–5). On 22 July 1680 government troops under the command of Andrew Bruce of Earlshall located and engaged Cameron and some of his followers at Ayrsmoss near Muirkirk in Ayrshire. Cameron, along with eight other covenanters, was killed in the fighting that ensued. On the orders of the privy council his head and hands were removed from his corpse and taken to Edinburgh, where his head was fixed to the Netherbow gate. His body was interred, along with those who fell in battle with him, close to the site where he died. A. S. WAYNE PEARCE

Sources M. Grant, *The lion of the covenant: the story of Richard Cameron* (1997) • *DSCHT*, 124–5 • R. Wodrow, *The history of the sufferings of the Church of Scotland from the Restoration to the revolution*, ed. R. Burns, 2 (1840); 3 (1840) • *DNB* • I. B. Cowan, *The Scottish covenanters, 1660–1688* (1976) • *Reg. PCS*, 3rd ser., vol. 6 • J. Howie, *Biographia Scoticana, or, A brief historical account … of the most eminent Scots worthies*, 3rd edn (1796), 421–9 • P. Walker and A. Shields, *Biographia Presbyteriana*, ed. J. Stevenson, 1 (1827), 191–207
Archives NL Scot., Wodrow MSS

Cameron, Sir (Gordon) Roy (1899–1966), pathologist, was born at Echuca, Victoria, Australia, on 30 June 1899, the son of George Cameron, a Methodist preacher from South Australia, and his wife, Emily Pascoe, who had emigrated from Cornwall with her parents at the age of eleven. Cameron was their elder child—his younger brother died in infancy—and because his father, like most Methodist preachers, went on circuit, Cameron was brought up mainly by the women of the family.

All Cameron's early schooling was in the state schools of the villages: Mitiamo, Lancefield, Dunkeld, and finally Kyneton, where he lived from 1911 to 1917, and where he was able to read extensively and to listen to music. From 1913 to 1917 he did his compulsory military training, and reached the rank of second lieutenant. The teaching at Kyneton was mediocre, but he managed to obtain a senior scholarship and a major scholarship at Queen's College, Melbourne University, which he joined in February 1916.

Cameron had already decided on medicine, but it was not easy to make up for his ignorance of physics and chemistry, and he did only fairly well until his fourth year; in 1922 he graduated MB BS with second-class honours. After hearing Sir Harry Allen lecture on pathology he had decided on this as his subject, and after a year as resident medical officer at Melbourne Hospital, during which he did some research work in the pathology of pancreatitis, Cameron was appointed Stewart lecturer in pathology in the university department, where he pioneered experimental work by setting up a small animal house and a colony of guinea-pigs.

Early in 1925 Cameron was invited by C. H. Kellaway to succeed F. M. Burnet as his first assistant and deputy director of Walter and Eliza Hall Institute in Melbourne. Two years later he went on leave to work under Ludwig Aschoff in Freiburg im Breisgau and later under A. E. Boycott in University College Hospital medical school, London. It was intended that he should in time return to Melbourne to succeed Allen as professor, but when his time was up, he found, to his great consternation, that he did not wish to return. Encouraged by his father, he went to live with Boycott's chief technician, Fred Crew, who, with his wife, Alice, looked after him until he died.

Cameron became Graham scholar in pathology in 1928 and was Beit fellow from 1930 to 1933. After a rather unhappy year as pathologist at Queen Mary's Hospital, Stratford, London, he returned to University College medical school as reader in morbid anatomy (1934). In 1937, after Boycott's retirement, he was appointed professor, and in 1946 director of the Graham department, both of which posts he held until he retired in 1964. During the Second World War he was seconded to the Chemical Defence Experimental Establishment at Porton, Wiltshire.

Over the years Cameron received many honours and was always in demand for work. From 1935 to 1955 he was an assistant editor of the *Journal of Pathology and Bacteriology* under Matthew Stewart. In 1941 he became an honorary FRCP. He was elected FRS in 1946, served on its council in 1948–9, and was one of its royal medallists in 1960. He became honorary LLD of Edinburgh in 1956 and of Melbourne in 1962. He received the gold medal of the Graham Research Fund and the Crawford Mollison research prize of the British Medical Association in Australia, and was honorary member of many pathological societies. From 1947 to 1956 he was a member of the Agricultural Research Council and from 1952 to 1956 a member of the Medical Research Council. He was knighted in 1957. But the honour which gave him the greatest pleasure was undoubtedly his unanimous election in 1962 to be founder president of the College of Pathologists.

Cameron's research work covered a very wide field, but he is most likely to be remembered for his work on the pathology of liver disease and of oedema of the lung, and for his willingness to encourage those who could bring biochemical concepts into pathology. By working out the pathological changes in the liver associated with poisoning by pure substances he was able to provide others with tools that would produce well-defined limited lesions in the liver, and thus to show how biliary obstruction, liver necrosis, vascular changes, and poisons affected it. Though not a biochemist, he had little difficulty in understanding biochemical concepts, and gave every help to those who wished to introduce them. Similar comment applies to his work on pulmonary oedema; he introduced new methods of producing it, and made a number of valuable suggestions to account for its development and for the remarkable species specific response to some lung irritants. He was in the main an experimental pathologist, according to some neither particularly expert nor interested in morbid anatomy. In practice, however, he used anything that came to hand—casual findings at necropsy, the results of surgery, intended or unintended, accidental experimental results, morbid anatomy—to stimulate experimental inquiry.

Cameron was universally regarded as an honest, kindly man, whose judgements were based on wide learning, vast experience, and natural impartiality. He had a sparkling sense of humour and took the greatest delight in human absurdity. He loved music, was a good pianist, and a goodish mathematician; he had a profound knowledge of the history of the Renaissance popes, and of the Renaissance in Italy—a country he greatly loved. From his early years he liked walking, even mountaineering. In politics he was a benevolent Conservative, with considerable attachment to the idea of the British empire. This conservatism he brought into his work, mainly by working with the simplest available techniques, and refusing, sometimes perhaps unreasonably, to buy apparatus by which newer techniques might have been introduced. The vast amount that he did with these simple means is perhaps his best justification.

In his early days Cameron's lectures and papers were rather heavy; later he became a brilliant lecturer, whose papers were models of clarity and conciseness. He was the author of several books, notably *The Pathology of the Cell* (1952). Cameron, who never married, died in the Memorial Hospital, Finchley, London, of heart disease on 7 October 1966. C. L. Oakley, *rev.*

Sources C. L. Oakley, *Memoirs FRS*, 14 (1968), 83–116 • personal knowledge (1981) • private information (1981) • *CGPLA Eng. & Wales* (1966) • *AusDB* • W. R. Merrington, *University College Hospital and its medical school: a history* (1976) • *WWW*

Archives Royal College of Pathologists, London, papers • U. Oxf., Wellcome Unit for the History of Medicine • UCL, corresp. and papers • Wellcome L., papers | Bodl. Oxf., corresp. with Sir R. A. Peters

Likenesses R. B. Claughton, bust, Royal College of Pathologists; copy, University College Hospital medical school, London

Wealth at death £57,314: probate, 23 Nov 1966, *CGPLA Eng. & Wales*

Cameron, Una May (1904–1987), mountaineer, was born at Rutherford House, West Linton, Peeblesshire, Scotland, on 6 May 1904, one of twin girls, the daughter of Ewen Cameron, landed proprietor, and his wife, Jeanie Dewar. The family was Scottish by descent, and its fortune was based on whisky. In adulthood this wealth enabled Una to indulge her passion for ski touring, mountaineering, and travel. She was educated in Montreux, Switzerland, at Cheltenham Ladies' College, and at the Central School of Arts and Crafts in London. While at art college in Rome she was able to cultivate her interest in climbing. After several seasons in the western Alps, the Julian Alps, and the Dolomites, in 1929 she gained membership of the Ladies' Alpine Club with a list of classic alpine climbs to her credit.

The 1930s was a decade of varied activity and high achievement for Una Cameron. She ski toured in the Canadian Rockies and the Alps, and climbed all year round in locations as diverse as the English Lake District and east Africa. In 1932 with Édouard Bareux and Élisée Croux, the Courmayeur guides with whom she climbed and travelled almost exclusively, she went to Kazbek, Russia, to pursue new challenges in the Caucasus. The journey and their ascents of three peaks and five unnamed rock towers, all presumed to be firsts, yielded her only published work, *A Good Line* (1932). This reveals something of Cameron's forthright and witty character through its description of a journey made in the days when visas were difficult to obtain and local people rarely encountered travellers from the West. Officials and peasants alike were intrigued enough by her androgynous appearance to render their reactions to it worthy of mention. Indeed, she did cut a remarkable figure: tall, heavily built, and with hair cut short, she often donned trousers as everyday attire when it was uncommon for women to do so.

Courmayeur became the adopted home of Cameron, who was fluent in Italian and French. She supported the local Waldensian church and had the Villa Cameron built there, above La Palud. Thus, able to explore the south side of Mont Blanc at her leisure, between 1933 and 1939 she traversed the mountain in most ways possible. Notably, she and Dora de Beer became the first British women to make a complete ascent of Peuteret Ridge in 1935. Cameron is also remembered for her ascents of the Innominata Ridge (1934), the Sentinelle Rouge (1935), the Route Major (1938), and the Brenva Ridge (1939), also in the Mont Blanc range. Further afield, during a trip to Ruwenzori, Africa, in 1938 she became the first woman to climb Nelion and Batian, the two peaks of Mount Kenya.

After the Second World War Cameron largely replaced climbing activity with travel. When in Courmayeur, friends benefited from her hospitality, contacts, and extensive local knowledge, rather than her company in the mountains. She could undoubtedly have cut a higher public profile for herself in the context of her climbing achievements, but she never chose to use her successes as a means to any end other than that of personal fulfilment. She was a lifelong member of the Ladies' Alpine Club and one of its most prominent, on account of her outstanding climbing record in the 1930s and her editorship of, and artistic contributions to, its journal. In 1957 she was given due recognition when elected president of the club in its jubilee year. Her obituarist summed up the essence of her lifestyle and character: 'She was privileged, and she knew it—but what matters is the enterprising uses she made of her money and leisure, and the way she shared with others the pleasures they made possible' (Adam Smith, 326). Her later years were spent in the Hamilton House Nursing Home, West Street, Buckingham, where she died, unmarried, on 15 October 1987. CAROL A. OSBORNE

Sources J. Adam Smith, *Alpine Journal*, 93 (1988–9), 323–6 • U. Cameron, *A good line* (1932) • U. Cameron, application form to the Ladies' Alpine Club, 1929, Alpine Club Library, London, G25 • U. Cameron, climbing list, Ladies' Alpine Club, 1929–39, Alpine Club Library, London, G25 • b. cert. • d. cert.

Archives NL Scot., climbing diaries

Likenesses C. D. Milner, photograph, 1953, repro. in *Alpine Journal*, illus. 91

Wealth at death £676,436: probate, 11 Dec 1987, *CGPLA Eng. & Wales*

Cameron, Verney Lovett (1844–1894), explorer in Africa, was born on 1 July 1844 at Radipole, Weymouth, Dorset, one of eight children—and the third of five sons—of the Revd Jonathan Henry Lovett Cameron (1807–1888) MA of Trinity College, Cambridge, and vicar of Radipole and his wife, Frances (*d.* 1893), the daughter of Francis Sapte of Cadicote Lodge, Welwyn, Hertfordshire. Although it has been written (Foran, 24) that he and his other family members used a hyphenated version of their name—Lovett-Cameron—after 1855, the explorer's writings and published use of his name do not confirm this.

Cameron received his early education at Bourton, Somerset, before, in August 1857, he joined the Royal Navy and

Verney Lovett Cameron (1844–1894), by Maull & Fox, *c.*1870

was assigned to the training ship *Illustrious*. He had a successful, if unremarkable, early career in the navy, spending nearly four years in the Mediterranean and off the Syrian coast, being promoted midshipman in June 1860, and being sent to the West Indian squadron late in 1861. He was in New Orleans when it fell to Union troops in the American Civil War, after which he was reassigned to the channel squadron, and in August 1863 was promoted sub-lieutenant. In October 1865 he was promoted lieutenant, and in 1867–8 saw eight months' service in the Red Sea on HMS *Star*, during the British punitive expedition against Emperor Theodore of Abyssinia, for which he earned a service medal. He then served some three years on *Star* and HMS *Briton* as part of the British attempt to curb the Arab slave trade that was centred in Zanzibar. It was during this period that he began to learn Swahili and that his appetite was whetted for the exploration of central Africa.

When *Star* was relieved on the east African station about 1870, Cameron was appointed to the steam reserve at Sheerness, from where he began an active campaign to convince the Royal Geographical Society (RGS) to send him as part of a search expedition to find David Livingstone in central Africa. He was not chosen to participate on the expedition under L. S. Dawson that the RGS eventually sent, but the news that Henry Morton Stanley had found Livingstone caused that expedition to be abandoned even before it left Bagamoyo, on the east African coast. This proved a boon to Cameron, who, after continuing to offer his services to the RGS, was finally selected to lead a further expedition to find Livingstone—then thought to be somewhere south of Lake Bangweolo—and thereafter to give the explorer any relief required and to assist him in completing his discoveries. Cameron proved physically well suited to lead the expedition that he called the Livingstone East Coast Expedition. Although a little less than medium height, he was wiry, hardy, and surprisingly strong for his size. His remarkable stamina and persistence also stood him in good stead.

Cameron and his close friend Dr W. E. Dillon left England on 30 November 1872 and were joined in Aden by Lieutenant Cecil Murphy. Having arrived in Zanzibar in early 1873, they met numerous problems in their attempts to organize the expedition, owing in part to the mistaken assumptions of the locals that they were part of the anti-slavery mission of Sir H. Bartle Frere, which arrived in Zanzibar at the same time, and in part to the hiring as headman of Mbarak Mombée (known widely as Sidi Bombay), who previously had served Richard Francis Burton and John Hanning Speke, but who proved extremely inefficient. The party was also soon joined by a fourth European, Robert Moffatt, Livingstone's nephew.

The expedition left Zanzibar on 2 February 1873, but it did not leave Kikoga, a village only 15 miles from Bagamoyo—the town that was the traditional starting point for Arab trading and slaving caravans—until almost two months later. Despite various set-backs, such as Moffatt's death in May, the party made progress in fits and starts, and reached the settlement of Kwiharah in Unyanyembe country—having traversed approximately 550 miles—in early August. There, however, all three of the Europeans went down with severe fever; as well as suffering from malaria, Cameron was stricken blind for six weeks. In late October 1873, still in Kwiharah, Cameron and his party were joined by the small retinue of Livingstone's followers bearing the explorer's body back to the coast. Dillon and Murphy decided to return to Bagamoyo with Livingstone's body, while Cameron, despite continuing poor health, proceeded to Ujiji to find Livingstone's journals. He was again delayed shortly after his departure when he received the unexpected news that Dillon, while delirious, had grabbed a gun and killed himself.

It took Cameron almost three more months finally to reach Ujiji and Lake Tanganyika, which he first saw on 18 February 1874. Once there, he spent almost two months carefully exploring the previously uninvestigated southern extremity of the lake. His investigations convinced him that Lake Tanganyika could have nothing to do with the source of the Nile, because, of the ninety-seven rivers that he found, all but one, the Lukuga, flowed into the lake rather than out of it; the Lukuga flowed directly west towards the Lualaba. After his return to Ujiji in May 1874, Cameron sent Livingstone's papers and his own journals back to the east coast, and proceeded westwards. He reached the Lualaba and the settlement at Nyangwe in early August, and attempted unsuccessfully to purchase canoes to follow the Lualaba north in order to confirm his belief that it became part of the Congo (as was later proven by Stanley).

Several weeks after Cameron arrived in Nyangwe, the famous Arab trader Hamed ibn Hamed, known in the west as Tippu Tib, also arrived there. Tippu Tib convinced Cameron that the northern route he desired to follow would be impassable, and suggested he turn south and find a passage through Portuguese territory. His advice appears to have been more of an attempt to divert Cameron from Arab territory than to help him. Nevertheless, Cameron travelled south in the company of Tippu Tib, and soon reached the Arab base camp near the Lomami River. He had hoped to cross the Lomami and to reach the mysterious Lake Sankorra, but he found the route closed due to tribal wars, so he slowly continued south, and eventually met up with the slaver José António Alvez near Kilembe, the chief settlement of Urua. Cameron accepted Alvez's offer of help in getting to Bihé, a settlement some 240 miles from the coast, but this turned into a painfully slow business, punctuated with long stops enforced by local rulers, such as Kasongo of Urua. Cameron spent much of this time plotting elevations and recording the flow of rivers. However, he did once show imperial aspirations, when, on 28 December 1874, he declared a British protectorate over the Congo basin, a declaration which the Foreign Office later declined to approve.

Cameron and Alvez ultimately travelled along the watershed between the Congo and the Zambezi, and reached Bihé in early October 1875. Cameron then pushed on at full speed towards the Pacific Ocean, but the weather and the cumulative effects of disease and weariness proved too much for his men. When still 126 miles from the coast, Cameron decided that he had to make a forced march to the coast with just a few comrades to fetch help for his party. This was successfully completed on 7 November 1875, when he reached Katombora. The night of his arrival, however, blood began to flow from his mouth, he became unable to swallow, and clots in his throat began to choke him. He was hurried to nearby Benguela for treatment by the resident medical officer, who recognized extreme symptoms of scurvy and nursed him back to health.

Cameron's journey made him the first European to cross Africa from east to west. It also showed him to be a humanitarian traveller in a time when other explorers, such as Stanley, frequently used firepower to obtain their objectives. Indeed, Cameron, unlike most of his contemporaries, had no taste even for big-game hunting, except to feed his men. He also proved an enlightened and detailed observer, and although he was not in the rank of Burton as observer or writer, he showed a good ear for language and solid ethnographic abilities.

After recovering his health, Cameron returned to England to a hero's welcome. His humble, self-effacing manner immediately endeared him to the British public. He was created a companion of the Bath, was specially promoted to the rank of commander in the Royal Navy, was given an honorary DCL by Oxford University, and was awarded a gold medal by the RGS. In 1876 he was selected by the British government to attend the Brussels Conference on Africa. *Across Africa* (1877), his tale of his African adventures, became a popular and acclaimed work.

Following his return home Cameron returned to regular naval duty, but the routine soon bored him, and in 1878–9 he journeyed from Turkey to India. In *Our Future Highway to India* (1880), he described his travels and argued for a railway from the Mediterranean to India that did not follow the course of the Euphrates River. The book made little impact, however, and Cameron turned his attentions back to Africa.

In 1881–2, Cameron joined Burton on a mission to west Africa. The two explorers examined the interior of the Gold Coast, searching for evidence of its gold-producing potential. Cameron also plotted the course of the Ankobrah River, and together they sent back to Kew 151 plants native to the Gold Coast. In 1883 their book *To the Gold Coast for Gold* was published and Cameron retired from the active list of the Royal Navy. On 2 June 1885 he married Amy Mona Reid (*d.* 1929), the daughter of William Bristowe Morris of Kingston, Jamaica. The couple had no children, and, in the ensuing years, they both spent a great deal of time writing books. Cameron's first boys' book, *Jack Hooper*, appeared in 1885, and he wrote at least another six in the next three years.

Cameron spent the following years involved with a number of companies, the goals of which were the future development, management, and commercialization of Africa; these included the Central African and Zoutpansberg Exploration Company and the Companhia da Zambesia, an Anglo-Portuguese concern for the development of the resources of the Zambezi valley.

In 1892 Cameron retired from the Royal Navy with the rank of captain on the retired list. Although still extremely active, he spent much time at his country house—The Lodge, Soulbury, near Leighton Buzzard, Buckinghamshire. On Easter Monday, 26 March 1894, he was returning home from a day's hunting when he was thrown from his horse and landed on his head. He died within several hours from brain damage. He was buried on 30 March at the parish church at Shoreham, Kent, where his father had been rector, and where his triumphant homecoming in 1876 had been recorded in a painting by Charles Cope. B. A. Riffenburgh

Sources V. L. Cameron, *Across Africa*, 2 vols. (1877) • W. R. Foran, *African odyssey: the life of Verney Lovett-Cameron* (1937) • V. L. Cameron, journal, April–Sept 1875, RGS • J. R. Hooker, 'Verney Lovett Cameron: a sailor in central Africa', *Africa and its explorers*, ed. R. I. Rotberg (1970) • J. A. Casada, 'Verney Lovett Cameron: a centenary appreciation', *GJ*, 141 (1975), 203–15 • V. L. Cameron, *Our future highway to India*, 2 vols. (1880) • *The Times* (28 March 1894) • *Daily Telegraph* (28 March 1894) • *The Standard* (28 March 1894) • F. McLynn, *Hearts of darkness: the European exploration of Africa* (1992) • *DNB* • *CGPLA Eng. & Wales* (1894)

Archives NL Scot., corresp., journals, and papers • RGS, corresp. and papers relating to Livingstone relief expedition, and notes • University of Cape Town Library, Cape Town, diary of expedition to Guinea

Likenesses Maull & Fox, photograph, *c.*1870, RGS [*see illus.*] • C. Cope, portrait, 1876, Church of SS Peter and Paul, Shoreham, Kent • memorial window, 1905, St John's Church, Mortimer Common, Berkshire • Lock & Whitfield, woodburytype photograph, NPG; repro. in T. Cooper, *Men of mark: a gallery of contemporary portraits* (*c.*1878) • Maull & Co., carte-de-visite, NPG • Spy [L. Ward], caricature, chromolithograph, NPG; repro. in *VF* (15 July 1876) • photograph, repro. in Foran, *African odyssey* • photograph, Time Life, Inc.; repro. in McLynn, *Hearts of darkness* [formerly priv. coll.] • photograph, repro. in Casada, 'Verney Lovett Cameron' • wood-engravings, NPG; repro. in *ILN*

Wealth at death £3615 10*s.* 8*d.*: probate, 29 May 1894, *CGPLA Eng. & Wales*

Cameron, Violet [*real name* Violet Lydia Thompson] (**1862–1919**), actress, was born on 7 December 1862. The birth of a Violet Lydia Thompson, at 38 Argyle Street, St Pancras, London, the daughter of William Melfington Thompson, linen merchant, and his wife, Mary Josephine, *née* Brougham, was registered for that date, though on her marriage certificate Violet gave her father's name as Frederick Thompson. She was the niece of the celebrated actress and dancer Lydia *Thompson, who, with her husband Alexander Henderson, manager of the Comedy Theatre, played a major part in her upbringing. Violet made her stage début on 10 April 1871 as Karl in a revival of Dion Boucicault's *Faust and Marguerite*, with the veteran actor Samuel Phelps, at the Princess's Theatre. Such was her success that she obtained a three-year engagement for children's parts in the Drury Lane pantomime. In 1876 Miss Cameron (her stage name) appeared as Perdita in *The Winter's Tale* in Liverpool, but when later asked why she did not 'go in' for Shakespeare she replied, 'Oh, when one has a voice, I suppose it pays to cultivate that talent', recognizing that big salaries were then paid for 'opera bouffe' (*The Era*, 26 Aug 1893). In addition to her vocal gifts Violet Cameron was blessed with extremely blond hair, a fine figure, and of course the support of Lydia Thompson, with whom she appeared in burlesque and opera bouffe at the Folly (subsequently Toole's) Theatre. In 1878 she triumphed at the Folly as Germaine in *Les cloches de Corneville* by Henry Brougham Farnie and R. Reece, and she acknowledged her debt to Farnie, who, in his capacity as stage manager, helped her to 'work up' these pieces.

It was at the Gaiety Theatre on 14 October 1882 that Violet Cameron scored a tremendous personal success in the dual role of Gretchen and Alice in Farnie's treatment of Robert Planquette's light opera *Rip Van Winkle*. The cast included Fred Leslie, Frederick Storey, W. S. Penley, and Lionel Brough. Following further success in *Falka* in October 1883 Cameron left the stage. On 20 September 1884, at the register office in the district of St George, Hanover Square, she married David de Bensaude, a native Moroccan of Spanish descent and a tea taster by trade. They had one child, probably born in 1885. In that year Cameron reappeared on stage with Lionel Brough in Audran's *La mascotte*, the play with which Alexander Henderson opened the Comedy Theatre: it enjoyed an enormous success and established opera bouffe at the Comedy for some time.

In 1886 Cameron and her husband were befriended by Hugh Cecil *Lowther, fifth earl of Lonsdale (1857–1944), who offered to finance their plan to take a theatre company to America that autumn. Lonsdale was an old acquaintance of Cameron's and the attention that he paid to her soon aroused the resentment and suspicion of her husband. In July 1886 she sought a judicial separation from Bensaude on the grounds of his violent and threatening language, while he in turn sought a divorce on the ground of her alleged adultery with Lonsdale. On 30 July there was an altercation between the two men at Newcastle, and Lonsdale was fined for assault. The following month the weekly paper *The Umpire* published an interview with Lonsdale that, in the words of the judge who presided over the subsequent libel case, depicted Bensaude as 'a thief, a liar, and a drunkard, and as having sponged on his wife's earnings and pawned her jewellery' (*The Times*, 23 May 1887). Bensaude won damages for this 'atrocious' libel.

In these fraught circumstances the planned American tour went ahead, with Lonsdale in attendance as business manager. The production of the musical plays *Kenilworth* and *The Commodore* was judged a success, but further scandalous stories about Bensaude, Cameron, and Lonsdale crossed the Atlantic and appeared in the British press. Husband and wife were by now totally estranged and in July 1887 the parties reached an agreement whereby Bensaude signed a separation deed and withdrew divorce proceedings in return for a settlement of £750. He soon renounced this agreement, however, after discovering that in May 1887 his wife had given birth to a daughter, of whom Lord Lonsdale was the father. Cameron's counsel subsequently admitted that there had after all been 'immoral relations' between the actress and the earl, but it was also claimed that Bensaude had known of all of the circumstances, including the illegitimate child, before signing the separation deed, and that he was motivated purely by money (*The Times*, 17 Nov 1887). The scandal obliged Lonsdale to leave London for a time—in February 1888 he set off on a lengthy expedition to the Canadian Arctic—while Bensaude, who was prevented by the courts from further confronting his wife, faded into a background of indigence, living in rented rooms in London. He died some time before his wife, whom he never divorced.

The scandal seems hardly to have affected Cameron's career. On her return from America, she performed in Alfred Cellier's comic opera *The Sultan of Mocha* at the Strand Theatre (21 September 1887). This was followed by several successes culminating in Alan-a-Dale in *Maid Marian* at the Prince of Wales (5 February 1891), after which she left the stage for two years. Asked whether she preferred appearing as a boy or a girl Cameron replied emphatically the latter, explaining that 'it was Mr Farnie who used to insist on casting her for boys' parts, because he thought she was rarely gifted therefor in figure and deportment', a view from which her many admirers did not dissent (*The Era*, 26 Aug 1893). In 1893 Violet Cameron caught public taste in *Morocco Bound*, a musical farce by Arthur Branscombe which enjoyed great success at the Shaftesbury Theatre (13 April). Thereafter her stage appearances were few. She returned to Drury Lane in January 1901 to take over as principal boy in *Jack and the Beanstalk* making 'a comely figure in her handsome costumes … all she does in a part, that cannot be said to help her much, bears the mark of refinement, and her singing is as bright and cultural as ever' (*The Stage*, 30 Oct 1919).

Violet Cameron's last performance was as the Abbess (Mother Superior) in Henry Hamilton's and Paul Potter's musical play *The School Girl* at the Prince of Wales's Theatre (9 May 1903). She died after a short illness at Holindale, Madeira Avenue, Worthing, Sussex, on 25 October 1919, and was buried on 30 October at Broadwater cemetery, Worthing. Though only fifty-six when she died, she had long since departed from the London stage: she was admiringly recalled by a diminishing few who had witnessed her brilliant though intermittent career in comic opera and opera bouffe. RICHARD FOULKES

Sources *The Era* (26 Aug 1893) · *The Era* (29 Oct 1919) · *The Era*, 83/4, 223 · *The Stage* (30 Oct 1919) · *The Times* (12 Aug 1886) · *The Times* (4 Oct 1886) · *The Times* (31 March 1887) · *The Times* (20 May 1887) · *The Times* (21 May 1887) · *The Times* (23 May 1887) · *The Times* (9 Aug 1887) · *The Times* (15 Sept 1887) · *The Times* (22 Sept 1887) · *The Times* (17 Nov 1887) · *The Times* (24 Dec 1887) · *The Times* (25 Feb 1888) · *The Times* (27 Oct 1919) · *The Times* (28 Oct 1919) · B. Hunt, ed., *The green room book, or, Who's who on the stage* (1906) · J. Parker, ed., *Who's who in the theatre*, 10th edn (1947) · W. Macqueen-Pope, *An indiscreet guide to theatreland* (1947) · W. Macqueen-Pope, *Ghosts and greasepaint: a story of the days that were* (1951) · W. Macqueen-Pope, *Carriages at eleven: the story of Edwardian theatre* (1974) · W. Macqueen-Pope, *Gaiety: theatre of enchantment* (1949) · *Financial Times* (18 Nov 1989) · L. Dawson, *Lonsdale: the authorised life of Hugh Lowther, fifth Earl of Lonsdale* (1946) · T. W. Herringshaw, *Prominent men and women of the day* (1888) · b. cert. · m. cert. · d. cert.

Likenesses portrait, Bodl. Oxf., Harding Mus. R 432; repro. in F. Keston, *Somebody that I like better* (1886) · portrait, Bodl. Oxf., Harding Mus. R 433; repro. in R. Planquette, *Yea or Nay* (1885?)

Cameron, William (1751–1811), poet, was educated at Marischal College, Aberdeen, where he was a pupil of James Beattie, with whom he later continued to correspond. Having been licensed a preacher of the Church of Scotland, he was ordained minister of the parish of Kirknewton, Edinburghshire, on 17 August 1786. On 14 September 1788 he married Agnes Montgomery of Irvine (1764–1837), with whom he had a daughter.

In 1780 Cameron published anonymously *Poems on Various Occasions*. To celebrate the restoration of the forfeited estates in the highlands in 1784 he wrote 'As o'er the highland hills I hied', which was included in James Johnson's *Scots Musical Museum*, to the tune of 'The Haughs o' Cromdale'. Along with Revd John Logan and Dr John Morrison, he assisted in preparing the collection of 'Paraphrases' from scripture for the use of the Church of Scotland, and he himself wrote Paraphrases XIV and XVII. His other publications are a sermon, 'The abuse of civil and religious liberty' (1793), 'Ode on Lochiel's Birthday' (1796), 'A review of the French Revolution' (1802), and the account of the parish of Kirknewton in Sinclair's *Statistical Account of Scotland*. *Poems on Several Occasions* was published posthumously in 1813. Cameron died on 17 November 1811. His wife survived him. T. F. HENDERSON, *rev.* SARAH COUPER

Sources *Fasti Scot.*, 1.143–4 · C. Rogers, *The modern Scottish minstrel, or, The songs of Scotland of the past half-century*, 1 (1855), 34–8 · W. Forbes, *An account of the life and writings of James Beattie*, 1 (1806), 375 · *Scots Magazine and Edinburgh Literary Miscellany*, 74 (1812), 79 · Anderson, *Scot. nat.* · *IGI*

Camidge, John (*bap.* 1734, *d.* 1803), organist and composer, was baptized on 8 December 1734 at Holy Trinity, Goodramgate, York, the youngest of the seven children of Robert Camidge (*bap.* 1689, *d.* 1773), bricklayer, and his wife, Ann, *née* Haigh (*d.* 1752). His parents were both from York. He received his early musical education from James Nares, probably as a chorister in York Minster. In the early 1750s he sang in concerts in the assembly rooms, York, and was paid by York Minster for copying music. It is supposed that he had lessons in London from Greene and Handel some time before 1755, when he was appointed organist at Doncaster parish church. A similar appointment followed almost immediately at York Minster, where he commenced his duties on 31 January 1756, remaining in office until his resignation on 11 November 1799. He married Elizabeth Walshaw (*c.*1723–1793) on 17 October 1756 and they had seven children, of whom the fifth, Matthew *Camidge, succeeded him as organist of York Minster. Elizabeth died on 21 February 1793 and just over a year later, on 4 June 1794, John Camidge married Jane Mills (*c.*1751–1837). He died on 25 April 1803 and was buried on 28 April at St Olave's, York; his second wife survived him by almost thirty-four years.

Camidge was also organist at St Michael-le-Belfrey, York, and a regular performer in the annual concert series given in the assembly rooms, York, from the autumn of 1756 until the spring of 1789, probably exclusively as a soloist in organ concertos but perhaps as a keyboard continuo player also. In addition he was a violinist: in 1766 he led the band in a concert in York; in 1769 he was the leader in a performance of *Messiah* at nearby Tadcaster; and on three occasions between 1771 and 1775 a Mr Camidge, almost certainly John Camidge, led the band at the York theatre in performances of *An Ode upon Dedicating a Building to Shakespeare* (the music by Arne). He was the founder of the York Musical Society, a gentleman's club (and not to be confused with the later choral society of the same name), some time in the 1760s. His *Six Easy Lessons for the Harpsichord* were published in York in 1763 and later reprinted in London; two of his songs were also published. He composed several anthems which remain, incomplete, in manuscript, and for the York theatre a song entitled 'The Wicked Wits' and a choral ode, *The Rival Queens*, both of which are now lost. DAVID GRIFFITHS

Sources A. Ford, 'Camidge', *Die Musik in Geschichte und Gegenwart*, ed. F. Blume (Kassel and Basel, 1949–86) · D. Griffiths, *'A musical place of the first quality': a history of institutional music-making in York, c.1550–1990* (1994) · D. Griffiths, 'Music in the 18th-century York theatre', *York Historian*, 15 (1998), 37–52 · *York Courant* (19 Aug 1755) · *York Courant* (4 March 1793) · *York Courant* (9 June 1794) · *York Courant* (2 May 1803) · D. Griffiths, ed., *A catalogue of the music manuscripts in York Minster Library* (1981) · Publications of the Yorkshire Parish Register Society [vols. 11, *St Michael-le-Belfrey, York*; 36, *St Martin, Coney Street, York*; 41, *Holy Trinity, Goodramgate, York*] · York Minster Library, archives of the dean and chapter of York Minster, chapter acts, H9/1 and H 9/3; St Peter's account, E2 (23) · parish register, Borth. Inst., St Olave's, York

Likenesses attrib. W. Staveley, pastel, York City Art Gallery; repro. in R. Rose, *The history of the York Musical Society and the York Choral Society* (1948) · miniature on snuff box, repro. in Griffiths, *A musical place*, 140 · oils, York Minster, Camera Cantorum; repro. in J. S. Smith, *A musical pilgrimage in Yorkshire* (1928), facing p. 146

Wealth at death see will, 6 Sept 1796, Borth. Inst., prerogative court of York, probate registers, 148, fol. 48

Camidge, John, the younger (1790–1859), organist and composer, born in York, was the son of Matthew *Camidge (*bap.* 1764, *d.* 1844) and his wife, Mary, *née* Shaw (*c.*1764–1835), and the grandson of John *Camidge the elder (*bap.* 1734, *d.* 1803). He received his musical education from his father. In 1812 he graduated MusB at Cambridge, and in 1819 took his doctor's degree. In 1828 he published a volume of his own *Cathedral Music* (a new edition appeared *c.*1830), and he also adapted much classical music for use in the Anglican service; but he was known principally as an accomplished performer. From his youth he played on the organ at York Minster, and was retained at a high salary by the dean and chapter as assistant to his father. After the fire in the cathedral in 1829, Camidge devoted much attention to the planning and specification of the magnificent new organ, which for many years was one of the finest in the world. Following his father's retirement, he was appointed organist of the cathedral (15 October 1842), a post he held until his death. However, the last occasion on which he presided at the organ was on 28 November 1848 (1850 according to the *Musical World*), when he was suddenly seized with paralysis and lost the use of his right hand. He died at his home in Gray's Court, Chapter House Street, York, on 21 September 1859.

Camidge had one daughter and three sons, Charles, John, and Thomas Simpson (1828–1912). John and Thomas Simpson followed their father's profession. The latter, having acted as his father's deputy following his paralysis, went on to become organist of Hexham Abbey. His elder brother John briefly took over the post at York until Edwin George Monk was appointed in 1859. John Camidge (1853–1939), a son of T. S. Camidge, was organist of Beverley Minster from 1876 until his death—the fifth generation in which the family produced an organist.

W. B. SQUIRE, *rev.* DAVID J. GOLBY

Sources *Musical World* (1 Oct 1859), 634 · N. Temperley, 'Camidge', *New Grove* · A. P. Purey-Cust, *Organs and organists of York minster* (1899) · *GM*, 2nd ser., 26 (1846), 92 · private information (1886) · *CGPLA Eng. & Wales* (1860)

Likenesses W. Etty, oils, *c.*1820–1821, FM Cam.

Wealth at death under £2000: resworn probate, Aug 1860, *CGPLA Eng. & Wales*

Camidge, Matthew (*bap.* 1764, *d.* 1844), organist and composer, was baptized at Holy Trinity, Goodramgate, York, on 25 May 1764, the fifth of the seven children of John *Camidge (*bap.* 1734, *d.* 1803), organist and composer, and his first wife, Elizabeth (*c.*1723–1793), daughter of Matthew Walshaw. At an early age Matthew became a chorister of the Chapel Royal, where he was taught by his father's old master, James Nares. Following his return from London, Matthew Camidge settled permanently in

York, where on 3 September 1789 he married Mary Shaw (*c*.1764–1835), the daughter of a local musician. They had three sons and two daughters; two of the sons took orders and became respectively vicar of Wakefield, and chaplain at Moscow and Kronstadt, and the third, John *Camidge the younger, succeeded his father as organist of York Minster following the latter's resignation on 8 October 1842. Matthew Camidge died on 23 October 1844 at the age of eighty, and was buried at St Olave's, York, on 25 October.

After isolated appearances as a keyboard player in York at the Theatre Royal (in 1777 and 1781) and at the assembly rooms (in 1780), Matthew performed regularly at the latter venue from 1784 until 1822. Until 1788 he was the soloist in piano concertos and thereafter, almost exclusively, in organ concertos; his *Six Concertos for the Organ or Grand Piano forte* (*c*.1815), by which he is today remembered, were probably first performed as organ concertos in the assembly room concerts. In these compositions he 'endeavoured to imitate the particular style of music which has been so long admired, namely that of Handel & Corelli' (preface), by which admission he hoped to escape the critics' censure.

Camidge and John Ashley jointly promoted in 1791 the first musical festival held in York Minster. In the four great festivals held there between 1823 and 1835 he was an assistant conductor in the first three and choral conductor in the last. On the resignation of his father, John Camidge, as organist of York Minster on 11 November 1799, Matthew was appointed his successor, a post he held until his resignation in 1842. Following his father's death Matthew Camidge also became organist of St Michael-le-Belfrey, York, for which church he had published *c*.1800 *A Musical Companion to the Psalms* (of which second and third editions followed *c*.1808 and 1825 respectively). He also published some keyboard music, *Instructions for the Piano forte or Harpsichord*, some songs, and a collection of church music entitled *Cathedral Music* (1806). DAVID GRIFFITHS

Sources A. Ford, 'Camidge', *Die Musik in Geschichte und Gegenwart*, ed. F. Blume (Kassel and Basel, 1949–86) • D. Griffiths, *'A musical place of the first quality': a history of institutional music-making in York, c.1550–1990* (1994) • N. Temperley, *Jonathan Gray and church music in York, 1770–1840* (1977) • N. Temperley, 'Camidge', *New Grove* • D. Griffiths, 'Music in the 18th-century York theatre', *York Historian*, 15 (1998), 37–52 • *York Courant* (1784–1822) • *York Herald* (26 Oct 1844) • Publications of the Yorkshire Parish Register Society [vols. 11, *St Michael-le-Belfrey, York*; 36, *St Martin, Coney Street, York*; 41, *Holy Trinity, Goodramgate, York*] • H. W. Shaw, *The succession of organists of the Chapel Royal and the cathedrals of England and Wales from c.1538* (1991) • parish register, Borth. Inst., St Olave's, York • York Minster library, archives of the dean and chapter of York Minster, chapter acts, H 9/3 and H 10/2

Likenesses oils, York Minster, Camera Cantorum; repro. in J. S. Smith, *A musical pilgrimage in Yorkshire* (1928), facing p. 146

Wealth at death see will, 20 Jan 1831, Borth. Inst., prerogative court of York, probate register, 210, fol. 347v

Camm [*née* Newby; *other married name* Audland], **Anne (1627–1705)**, Quaker preacher, was born in August 1627, the daughter of Richard Newby of Kendal; she was baptized there on 28 October 1627. Westmorland was to remain her home in later life: she lived at Crosslands, Preston Patrick, during her first marriage, then at Camsgill during her second. She came from a 'respectable' family and received an education 'in those branches of learning suitable for her sex' (Evans and Evans, 1.473). At the age of thirteen years she was sent to London to her aunt and lived there for several years, associating with puritans. On her return to Kendal she became attached to a group of Seekers, where she met and married John *Audland (*c*.1630–1664), a linen draper, about 1650. Both Anne and her husband were 'convinced' in 1652 upon hearing George Fox preach.

During her first marriage, Anne Audland travelled around the country disseminating the Quaker message. She was imprisoned at Auckland, Durham, for preaching on market day and continued to do so from her prison window. With her future mother-in-law, Mabel Camm, she travelled widely through Yorkshire, Derbyshire, Leicestershire, and Oxfordshire. In Banbury she was responsible for the 'convincement' of many, but encountered some hostility there. At the assizes in 1653 she was accused of saying that 'God did not live' (Evans and Evans, 1.475). She outlined this episode in her work of 1655, *A True Declaration of the Suffering of the Innocent*, and denied blasphemy by referring to Jeremiah 5:2, 'And though they say, the Lord liveth, surely they swear falsely' (Audland, 1). Acquitted of blasphemy by the judge but found guilty of misdemeanour by the jury, Anne was imprisoned for several months and lived in appalling conditions until her release in 1656. Anne then stayed in Banbury to campaign for the release of her fellow Quaker Jane Waugh, and then travelled to Bristol before visiting George Fox in Launceston gaol.

Anne Audland was widowed in 1664 and in her testimony to John she declared 'How exceeding dear and kindly affectionate husband he was to me … I believe few ever enjoyed a greater blessing in a husband, than I in him' ('Testimony'). She gave birth to their son just two weeks after her husband's death.

In 1666 Anne married Thomas *Camm (1640/41–1708), who was almost fourteen years younger than his wife, yet they enjoyed a marriage of almost forty years' duration in 'the utmost harmony and affection' (Evans and Evans, 1.476). They had a daughter Mary (later Moore) and another, Sarah, who died from smallpox and fever in 1682 at the age of almost nine years, an event lamented by both parents in *The Admirable and Glorious Appearance of the Eternal God in and through a Child* (1684).

During her second marriage, Anne Camm travelled much less, occasionally accompanying her husband when he was released from his many years of imprisonment, but otherwise she '[supplied] his place … in his family and business' (Evans and Evans, 1.476). Like many Quaker women of the first generation, she settled down to the tasks of establishing women's meetings for administrative purposes. In 1675 Anne and other women from Kendal monthly meeting wrote to the women's Box Meeting at London alarmed at the opposition to women's meetings. They were no doubt referring to a group of breakaway Quakers led by John Wilkinson and John Story, who, among other issues, were aggrieved at George Fox's establishment of meetings for women.

Anne Camm's character seems to have been a quiet one. 'It was her manner often to retire alone … exercising herself in fervent prayer' (Tomkins, 207–8). At meetings 'she was not forward', but 'was a good example to her sex, for without extenuating impulse and concern it was rare for her to preach in large meetings' (ibid., 208).

The years after Anne Camm's second marriage perhaps serve to highlight the degree to which Quakerism, and the role which women played within the movement, had changed. No longer the travelling prophetess, she stayed at home and expressed her ministry in a different way. Anne Camm died on 30 September 1705 at the age of seventy-eight years, and was buried on 3 October.

CAROLINE L. LEACHMAN

Sources W. Evans and T. Evans, eds., *The Friends' Library*, 14 vols. (1837–50), vol. 1 • J. Tomkins, *Piety promoted … the third part* (1706) • A. Audland, *A true declaration of the suffering of the innocent…* (1655) • 'The testimony of Ann Camm concerning John Audland', *The memory of the righteous revived*, ed. T. Camm and C. Marshall (1689) • C. Trevett, 'Anne Camm and the vanishing Quaker prophets', *Quaker Studies*, 3 (1988), 82–110 • J. Smith, ed., *A descriptive catalogue of Friends' books*, 1 (1867) • *IGI* • parish registers of Kendal

Archives RS Friends, Lond., A. R. Barclay MSS • RS Friends, Lond., Box meeting MSS • RS Friends, Lond., Caton MSS • RS Friends, Lond., Robson MSS • RS Friends, Lond., Swarthmore MSS

Camm, John (1605–1657), Quaker preacher, was born at Camsgill, near Kendal, Westmorland. His parentage and education were of 'honest' and 'good report' and 'as good as any of that degree in that part of the country' ('Thomas Camm's Testimony'). A soldier in the parliamentary army during the civil wars, Camm was a man of property, being a successful yeoman. He no doubt had good prospects, for his son Thomas described him as having 'great concerns and dealings' in 'worldly matters' (ibid.). From early on, he had an interest in religious matters and associated with those 'that were the most strict and upright' (ibid.). He left the national church and may have been a presbyterian in Kendal by 1646, and later perhaps a Grindletonian, before joining the large gathering of Westmorland Seekers.

By 1641 he had married Mabel (1605?–1692), later the wife of the Quaker Gervase Benson, and they had a number of children, two of whom are known, Thomas and Ruth. The latter, however, died before her second birthday in 1656.

Camm's son, Thomas *Camm, described his father as a man 'of noble spirit, and exceeding grave in his carriage and deportment, profound in judgement, and of quick discerning' ('Thomas Camm's Testimony'). Charles Marshall, a contemporary, noted how Camm was 'full of zeal and fervency in the gospel'. However, Camm suffered from a weak constitution and consumption with the result that his son frequently had to assist him.

Camm was 'convinced' by George Fox during the latter's visit to Westmorland in 1652, when he spoke at a meeting of Seekers from Westmorland, Lancashire, and Yorkshire, and spent some time at Camm's home. Camm's ministry took him into the northern counties and the Scottish borders and then to London with his fellow Quaker Francis Howgill, where they 'were two of the first that published the message of truth in that city' ('Thomas Camm's Testimony'). Part of the reason for travelling to the capital in 1654 was to see Oliver Cromwell to speak of their concern for the law which punished those who interrupted ministers. The meeting was not a success, for Camm later wrote twice to Cromwell exhorting him to remove the laws upon religion, but to no avail. He outlined his concerns in his two tracts of 1654, *This was the Word of the Lord* and *Some Particulars Concerning the Law.*

Camm travelled to Oxford in 1654, where he 'convinced' Thomas Loe, who would later be responsible for the conversion of William Penn. Some time was spent at Bristol with John Audland where, according to Camm's son Thomas, 'many hundreds were by the word and testimony of truth by them published convinced' ('Thomas Camm's Testimony'). They held their first large public meeting in a local field, since those in attendance numbered around 1500. Other meetings followed, before they moved on to Gloucestershire, Wales, Hereford, Shrewsbury, Chester, and a brief respite in Kendal with their families. On their return to Bristol, Camm and Audland encountered some hostility. They were assaulted by a group of apprentices while passing over Bristol Bridge to a meeting in Brislington, Somerset, but saved by a Friend who took them into his house. A warrant was issued for Camm and others including James Nayler and George Fox on the false information that the Friends were Franciscan friars, though nothing came of this and Camm was never brought before the magistrates.

Camm fell ill shortly after this episode, about March 1655, and was nursed by his wife, Mabel, in Bristol. Camm experienced a number of bouts of illness, in-between which he made several further visits to such places as London, Gloucestershire, and Warwickshire, and spent twelve days appointing meetings with George Fox before returning to Bristol in November 1655. Camm returned to Camsgill in March 1656; he travelled a little more but died in Camsgill on 10 January 1657, in much pain from consumption, and was buried at the Birkrigg Park Friends' burial-ground, Westmorland.

CAROLINE L. LEACHMAN

Sources 'Thomas Camm's testimony concerning John Camm and John Audland', *The memory of the righteous revived*, ed. T. Camm and C. Marshall (1689) • C. W. Horle, 'John Camm: profile of a Quaker minister during the interregnum', *Quaker History*, 70 (1981), 69–83; 71 (1982), 3–15 • W. Evans and T. Evans, eds., *The Friends' Library*, 14 vols. (1837–50), vol. 5 • J. Tomkins and J. Field, *Piety promoted … in five parts* (1721) • C. Marshall, 'A testimony to the glorious…', *The memory of the righteous revived*, ed. T. Camm and C. Marshall (1689) • J. Smith, ed., *A descriptive catalogue of Friends' books*, 1 (1867) • 'Dictionary of Quaker biography', RS Friends, Lond. [card index]

Archives RS Friends, Lond., letter-book of John Audland and John Camm | RS Friends, Lond., A. R. Barclay MSS • RS Friends, Lond., Caton MSS • RS Friends, Lond., portfolio MSS • RS Friends, Lond., Robson MSS • RS Friends, Lond., Swarthmore MSS

Camm, Sir Sydney (1893–1966), aircraft designer, was born in Windsor on 5 August 1893, the eldest of twelve children of Frederick Camm, journeyman carpenter and joiner, and his wife, Mary Smith. At the Royal Free School at Windsor his interest in aviation was awakened at an early age through the construction of elementary flying models. Soon after he left school Camm became an apprentice woodworker, helped to set up the Windsor Model Aeroplane Club, and became its secretary at the age of nineteen. Stimulated by his efforts, the club rapidly progressed from models to the design and building of a man-carrying glider which flew in December 1912. It was followed by a powered aircraft project, and Camm's leading role in these activities was cut short only by the outbreak of war in 1914.

With his knowledge of practical woodworking and theoretical aerodynamics Camm had no difficulty in joining the Martinsyde aeroplane company at Brooklands. There he remained throughout the war, rising through the practical working levels to first minor and then major design tasks on Martinsyde aircraft. It was during this period that he learned his profession, taking every opportunity to study and write articles about all available types of British and captured enemy aircraft. Thus, when he was elected an associate fellow of the Royal Aeronautical Society in 1918, he was able to describe himself as a technical journalist.

After the war, Martinsyde declined from lack of orders and closed in 1921. G. H. Handasyde continued as an independent designer and took on Camm as his assistant, and together they designed an advanced glider. R. P. Raynham, the Martinsyde test pilot, took Camm with him as mechanic when he competed in the first king's cup race in 1922 with a Martinsyde F4.

In the same year Raynham joined the Hawker Engineering Company at Kingston upon Thames and when Camm's work with Handasyde finished, in 1923, he followed his friend into this famous firm, in which he was to work with the greatest distinction for the next forty-three years. He was already an expert in detail design and practical workmanship, and much preoccupied with the aeronautical virtues of simplicity, symmetry, and lightness. He joined as a senior draughtsman; such was his ability that he became chief designer only two years later. At this period aircraft could still be designed and built cheaply and quickly, and Camm was charged with the supervision of the design of a light biplane, the Cygnet. This remarkable little two-seater won many light aircraft competitions in 1925 and 1926, and clearly showed his gifts for imaginative conception, excellence of detail, and careful weight control. Camm was directed, from 1925 onwards, to the development of future military types. He produced two biplane aircraft, the Heron in 1925, which used metal for the main structure, and the Hornbill in 1926, the basic design from which his future bomber and fighter types were developed.

In 1928 the emergence of the Hawker Hart day bomber with a Rolls-Royce Kestrel engine produced the first characteristically Camm aircraft. It was notable for grace, balance of design, and the complete integration of the engine within the aircraft, contrasting strongly with most contemporary aeroplanes whose engines often appeared to have been added as an afterthought. The Hart was adopted by the Royal Air Force, and with its variants the Hind, Audax, Osprey, and Nimrod was also sold to a large number of foreign air forces, so that finally some 3000 were built. A single-seater redesign of the Hart produced a high performance fighter named the Fury, which was similarly sold all over the world and is widely held to have been the most beautiful biplane ever flown. The Hart and Fury put Hawker back on the map.

The Supermarine and Gloster companies were engaged in producing the monoplanes associated with the Schneider Trophy, but Hawkers had not been drawn in. Camm, and Hawkers, decided, however, that the firm's future lay in the construction of fast fighter aircraft. By 1933 Camm realized that he could go no further with biplane designs, and he began the study of a fighter monoplane to be built round the new Rolls-Royce Merlin. In 1934 the Air Ministry issued specification F. 36/34 for a monoplane eight-gun fighter, and the new Hawker design was thereafter produced to this specification, in close co-operation with the ministry's operational requirements branch. It was named the Hurricane.

This was the first monoplane fighter supplied to the Royal Air Force, 100 m.p.h. faster than anything previously flown, and it went into production under the shadow of impending war. This urgency caused Camm to allow some compromises in design which he would not otherwise have permitted, but the aircraft was fast, manoeuvrable, and sturdy. It was in full production by the outbreak of war in 1939 and formed the major part of the strength of Fighter Command during the battle of Britain, so earning the major credit in the winning of that decisive battle. Hurricanes also fought in Europe, Africa, Burma, and over the oceans, first armed with eight machine-guns, later carrying bombs, rockets, and cannons. Some thousands were supplied to Russia, and a total of some 14,500 were finally built. As for the pilots of Fighter Command, 1940 provided Camm's finest hour. He was made CBE in 1941, prompting the *News Chronicle* to hail him as the man who saved Britain. By the outbreak of war Camm was already well into the design of the Hurricane's successor, the Typhoon. When the Normandy invasion was launched in 1944 Typhoon fighter–bombers were present in large quantities, and Camm, driving himself and his team relentlessly through years of continual and intensive work, was producing the Tempest. This very powerful fighter, derived from the Typhoon and itself the parent of the Sea Fury, achieved the ultimate in the exploitation of propeller-driven monoplanes; indeed, the Tempest and Sea Fury were so fast and robust that they served on until the fifties, well into the jet era.

The advent of the jet engine in 1942 was a powerful stimulant to a designer with Camm's special interests, and before the war was over his team was directed on to studies using the new engine. Others were ahead of him, and owing to the post-war relaxation his new jet-driven design was not needed until 1948, when the navy ordered it for carrier work and named it the Sea Hawk. This too was a successful project for peacetime military sales, 500 being built and supplied to a number of navies. The well-marked line of his design progress was continued with its successor, the Hunter. In this aircraft Camm pushed performance to the limit possible with subsonic aircraft, and once more he brought forth an outstanding machine, carrying all the distinctive marks of his design genius. Two thousand were built and sold, in 1953 it gained the world air speed record, and the Hunter was still in operational service twenty years after its first flight.

Camm's next logical step was to design a supersonic fighter, and this he did in a number of variants, but owing to chance and government policy none were built, a denial which he resented greatly. Instead, he embarked on studies with Bristol Siddeley Engines of a possible combination of a special engine and airframe, which would give the flying characteristics of a high-performance fighter together with the landing and take-off of a helicopter. This concept, VTOL (vertical take-off and landing), permitted a number of different solutions, but the gifted Bristol Siddeley engine designer, Stanley George Hooker, favoured a single engine with vectored thrust, giving the ability to swivel the thrust of the engine downwards under the control of the pilot. Such a system required a completely new control system based on reaction jets, for that phase of flight in which the aircraft had insufficient speed for normal control. It is a proof of Camm's persistent character in design that, though revolutionary in concept, the resulting fighter looked much like the others of its line. However, it added a completely new dimension to military aviation, releasing aircraft from the prepared bases on which they had always been at their most vulnerable and bringing them nearer to the areas where they needed to fight. Such a radical step took much time to evolve, mainly owing to timidity by the customers, and its development exercised him from 1958 until his death.

As an aircraft designer Camm was pre-eminent during the exciting early years of aviation. Circumstances placed him in a position in which, by his undoubted design genius, he made a major contribution to the outcome of one of the great battles of history. He worked so hard for most of his life that, though not without other interests, his history is inseparable from the aircraft projects he fathered and carried through. He was a tall, lean man, of quick speech and mercurial disposition. As his success and prestige grew, the same self-confidence which displayed his signature on each one of his aircraft showed also in a growing intolerance of questioning or opposition. He fiercely resented criticism of any of his projects, and persistent overwork brought this quality at times to the borderline of eccentricity, although his angriest outbursts, after a subsequent period of brooding solitude, might be succeeded by a reasonable assimilation of the criticism into his own opinion. He drove his staff hard, and his opinions of officialdom were more often than not unprintable. However, although not himself a pilot, Camm was always sympathetic to those who had to test and fly his aircraft. In an era when individual design was possible he could be regarded as one of the last of the great individual designers, whose personality and name could never be submerged in any committee or project team.

Camm was elected a fellow of the Royal Aeronautical Society in 1932, received the society's gold medal in 1958, served as president in 1954–5, and was elected honorary fellow in 1961. From 1951 to 1953 he was chairman of the technical board of the Society of British Aircraft Constructors. He was knighted in 1953. He received a number of foreign professional honours, of which the chief was the Daniel Guggenheim medal, which he received in 1965. He was elected to the board of Hawker Siddeley Aviation in 1935 and served until his death while playing golf at Richmond, Surrey, on 12 March 1966. His home was at Thames Ditton. He was survived by his wife, Hilda Rose Starnes, whom he married in 1915 and who died in 1977, and by one daughter. In 1984, on the occasion of Camm's investment in the International Hall of Aerospace Fame at San Diego, California (where he was then only the seventh Briton to be thus honoured), his daughter spoke of the father she had known: 'To the world at large he was a reticent figure, austere and reserved—a perfectionist in his profession. In private he had a well-developed sense of humour and derived great enjoyment from reading Damon Runyon and Evelyn Waugh's novels' (Fozard, *Aeronautical Journal*, 144). His tastes in music were conventional and apart from a passion for golf, he enjoyed the simple pleasures of life. PETER WYKEHAM, *rev.*

Sources *The Times* (14 March 1966), 12e • *The Times* (30 March 1966), 12c • J. W. Fozard, 'Camm's engine legacy', *Aeroplane Monthly*, 20 (1922), (1) 18–23, (3) 56–9 • J. W. Fozard, ed., *Sydney Camm and the Hurricane: perspectives on the master fighter designer and his finest achievement* (1991) • J. W. Fozard, 'Jubilees in design and development: some comments on change over the period of Camm's work and influence', *Aeronautical Journal*, 92 (1988), 127–44 • personal knowledge (1981) • private information (1981) • *News Chronicle* (18 Feb 1941) • probate • *The Engineer* (18 March 1966), 420 • *Journal of the Royal Aeronautical Society*, 70 (1966), 749–56

Likenesses F. Eastman, oils, *c.*1954–1955, Royal Aeronautical Society, London • photograph, repro. in *The Times* (14 March 1966) • photograph, repro. in *Royal Aeronautical Society Journal* • photographs, repro. in *News Chronicle* • portrait, International Hall of Aerospace Fame, San Diego, California

Wealth at death £67,614: probate, 4 May 1966, *CGPLA Eng. & Wales*

Camm, Thomas (1640/41–1708), Quaker preacher and writer, was born at Camsgill, Preston Patrick, Westmorland, the son of John *Camm (1605–1657), a yeoman, and his wife, Mabel (1605?–1692), themselves both Quakers. He received a good education at the hands of his father, whose 'tender care' said Camm, 'was great for the education of me, and the rest of his children' ('Thomas Camm's testimony'). He was brought up in the Quaker faith, and at an early age became a Quaker minister and travelled widely to spread the message; he wrote a number of Quaker works.

Camm suffered imprisonment and other forms of persecution in the Quaker cause. In 1660 he was incarcerated in Lancashire for refusing the oath of allegiance, and again in 1674 at Kendal for three years after being sued for small tithes and oblations. Following this, Camm spent six years in Appleby gaol, most likely for some offence against the Conventicle Act. In addition there were numerous distraints upon his goods, one of the harshest being for preaching at a meeting at Ackmonthwaite in 1678, for which he lost nine head of cattle and fifty-five sheep, worth over £31. Later in Westmorland, in 1690, he paid over £20 relating to tithes of corn.

Thomas married Anne Audland, *née* Newby (1627–1705) [*see* Camm, Anne] in 1666, and they had two daughters, Mary (later Moore) and Sarah, who died of smallpox and fever at the age of almost nine, an event which was commemorated in a joint work with his wife entitled *The Admirable and Glorious Appearance of the Eternal God in and through a Child* (1684).

Thomas Camm became involved in the Wilkinson–Story Separation (a breakaway group within the Quaker movement), and wrote against William Rogers and John Story, two of the principal protagonists. In 1684 he wrote *The Line of Truth and True Judgement* in response to a pro-Wilkinson– Story pamphlet (*The Memory of that Servant of God John Story Revived*, 1683), and accused its authors in his epistle to the reader of 'bitter and ungodly false reflections against Friends', which he claimed were an attempt to 'stir up persecution against us, and to render truth odious' (Camm, *Line of Truth*, 'To the Reader', sig. B). It seems that Camm had actually for a time flirted with separation, for he wrote a testimony against himself in 1677, which is in the Kendal monthly minute book.

Camm's output of Quaker writings was reasonably large and included, in addition to those listed above, 'Thomas Camm's testimony concerning John Camm and John Audland', in *The Memory of the Righteous Revived* (1689), and a 'Testimony concerning Margaret Fox' (written in 1706). In *A testimony to the fulfilling promise of God relating to such women, who through the pouring out of God's spirit upon them, are become prophetesses* (1689), Camm gave examples of biblical prophetesses such as Miriam and Deborah in support of a Quaker female ministry. In three later works, *An Old Apostate Justly Exposed* (1698), *Truth Prevailing with Reason* (1706), and *A Lying Tongue Reproved* (1708), he defended Quakerism against the criticisms of Henry Winder, who claimed to have once been a Quaker; Camm defended Quaker doctrines and denied the existence of discord within the movement.

In terms of character, Thomas had a 'kind and gentle disposition' and was a man of 'great humility' (Evans and Evans, *Friends' Library*, 1.480; Evans and Evans, *Piety Promoted*, 1.397). He continued his travels into old age, his last one being into Yorkshire, Lancashire, and his home county of Westmorland. Thomas Camm died at Eldworth, Yorkshire, on 13 January 1708, aged sixty-seven, after suffering from a condition which left him unable to eat due to the ensuing pain and incapable of sleep. He was buried at the Quaker burial-ground, Park End, Preston Patrick, three days later. CAROLINE L. LEACHMAN

Sources W. Evans and T. Evans, eds., *The Friends' Library*, 14 vols. (1837–50), vol. 1 • W. Evans and T. Evans, eds., *Piety promoted*, 4 vols. (1854), vol. 1 • J. Besse, *A collection of the sufferings of the people called Quakers*, 2 vols. (1753) • T. Camm, *The line of truth and true judgement* (1684) • 'Thomas Camm's testimony concerning John Camm and John Audland', *The memory of the righteous revived*, ed. T. Camm and C. Marshall (1689) • W. C. Braithwaite, *The second period of Quakerism* (1919); 2nd edn, ed. H. J. Cadbury (1961); repr. (1979) • J. Smith, ed., *A descriptive catalogue of Friends' books*, 1 (1867) • 'Dictionary of Quaker biography', RS Friends, Lond. [card index] • J. Tomkins and J. Field, *Piety promoted … in five parts* (1721)

Archives RS Friends, Lond., Robson MSS • RS Friends, Lond., Bristol MSS • RS Friends, Lond., portfolio MSS • RS Friends, Lond., Spence MSS • RS Friends, Lond., Gibson MSS

Cammell, Charles (1810–1879), steelmaker, was born on 8 January 1810 in Sculcoates, Hull, the fourth son of George Cammell, a shipmaster with Scottish connections, and his wife, Hannah (*d.* 1825). A self-made man, he was apprenticed to a local ironmonger before moving to Sheffield in 1830, where he joined the steel and tool firm of Ibbotson Brothers. Like John Brown, Cammell made his mark as a salesman—a career in which he demonstrated great ability. A crisis in the American market, however, led Cammell in 1837 to start his own business, with the help of Thomas and Henry Johnson (the former the head bookkeeper from Ibbotsons). Johnson, Cammell & Co., based in Furnival Street, made and merchanted tool steel and files, though by the 1840s the firm was becoming increasingly involved with the expanding market for heavy steel goods, such as railway materials. In 1845 Cammell moved his operations from the centre of Sheffield to the Don valley, where he erected the Cyclops works.

By 1855 Cammell's early partners had either died or retired and the company became Charles Cammell & Co. However, from 1846 Cammell was helped by George Wilson (1829–1885), a scientifically trained Scot, who was to become an important influence at the company. Under the two men—Cammell the salesman and Wilson the works manager—the firm expanded rapidly in the 1850s and 1860s, exploiting new tonnage steel technologies, especially the Bessemer process. Cammell followed John Brown's lead by installing Bessemer converters for steel rail production in 1861, with the firm supplying not only the British market, but also America, Canada, and South America.

In 1864—in another parallel move to Brown—Cammells became a limited liability company, with a paid-up capital of £800,000. Charles Cammell (who was paid £200,000 for the goodwill) became the chairman, with George Wilson as managing director. The company employed over 3000 workers and, alongside Browns, was the largest steelworks in Sheffield. It continued to grow through the 1870s, when such was the demand for rails that the Cammell steelworks, despite major plant extensions at Grimesthorpe, had difficulty in producing enough ingots to feed its mills. This demand, combined with orders for armour-plate—which Cammells began rolling in 1863—resulted in the company expanding outside Sheffield. Having already extended its Bessemer operations by taking over a works at Penistone, Cammells purchased the Oaks colliery in 1874 to gain access to the rich Barnsley coal seam. Charles Cammell and his board were also shareholders and directors in the Wilson–Cammell Patent Wheel Company Ltd, built in 1873 at Dronfield to further exploit the market for steel rails.

To what extent was Cammell personally responsible for this success? According to one reporter, Cammell 'used often to say that Sheffield owed much to him'—though the same report quickly added that his success was 'almost as much due to those associated with him as to himself. He possessed in special degree the power of finding out those who could assist him in his work, and of attaching them to himself' (*Sheffield and Rotherham Independent*, 14 Jan 1879). Chief among these was George Wilson, the managing director between 1864 and 1885. Cammell was chairman until his death and usually attended board and annual company meetings; however, it is clear that after 1864 Wilson was the driving force.

Outside his business, Cammell was a gentrified industrialist. On 23 October 1845 he married a widow, Marianne Wright, daughter of Thomas Rollinson; they had six sons and one daughter. In 1851 he purchased the Norton Hall estate on the southern outskirts of Sheffield, and eventually became lord of the manor of Norton. He also owned the Brookfield Hall estate at Hathersage in Derbyshire and Ditcham Park in Hampshire. Although Cammell served as a JP and Conservative member of the Sheffield council, he eschewed public life and does not appear to have had any philanthropic interests.

Cammell died at 7 Southwick Crescent, London, on 12 January 1879 and was buried five days later at Hathersage church. He was survived by his wife. One of his sons, Bernard, later took a seat on the board of the Cammell company. GEOFFREY TWEEDALE

Sources P. Nunn, 'Cammell, Charles', *DBB* • *Sheffield Daily Telegraph* (14 Jan 1879) • *Sheffield and Rotherham Independent* (14 Jan 1879) • G. Tweedale, *Steel city: entrepreneurship, strategy, and technology in Sheffield, 1743–1993* (1995) • J. Austin and M. Ford, *Steel town: Dronfield and Wilson Cammell, 1873–1883* (1983) • J. H. Stainton, *The making of Sheffield* (1924) • W. Odom, *Hallamshire worthies* (1926) • *Charles Cammell & Co Ltd* (1900) • m. cert. • *CGPLA Eng. & Wales* (1879)
Archives Birkenhead Town Hall, Birkenhead, Cammell-Laird MSS
Likenesses oils, Birkenhead Town Hall
Wealth at death under £250,000: probate, 21 Feb 1879, *CGPLA Eng. & Wales*

Cammell, Donald Seton (1934–1996), film-maker, was born on 17 January 1934 at the Outlook Tower, Castle Hill, Edinburgh, the son of Charles Richard Cammell (*b.* 1890), author, and his second wife, Iona Katherine Lamont Macdonald (*b.* 1903/4), daughter of David Macdonald, medical practitioner, and his wife, Anne Jane, *née* Cameron. Charles Cammell had inherited a large fortune from the Cammell Laird shipbuilding company and was able to devote himself to writing. He later became acquainted with the notorious Aleister Crowley, publishing his biography in 1951. Cammell's father was later to observe that: 'There is something "fey" about Donald's personality, which my wife believes to be due to the fact that a Highland friend of ours … immediately after Donald's birth, took him in her arms and sung to him Hebridean faery-songs' (Cammell, 87). Cammell also showed an early gift for drawing and possessed so clear an idea of perspective that the artist John Duncan, a family friend, maintained that it proved that he had learned the skill in a previous incarnation. Cammell's artistic talent was such that his father had exhibited his work at the Royal Drawing Society from the age of eight. During the early years of the Second World War, Cammell and his brother David (*b.* 1937) lived in the highlands of Scotland, Cammell attending a preparatory school in Fort Augustus. However, in the winter of 1942–3 homesickness resulted in his returning to London, where the family had moved in 1935. He then attended Shrewsbury House School, near Thames Ditton, and Westminster School, before moving to the Byam Shaw School of Art from where, in 1954, he won a scholarship to the Royal Academy. Two years earlier he had travelled in Italy, where he received lessons from Pietro Annigoni.

On returning to London, Cammell set himself up as a portrait painter in studios at Flood Street, Chelsea. His 1953 portrait of the marquess of Dufferin and Ava was judged society portrait of the year. Cammell was also enjoying a busy social life as part of the 'Chelsea set', a mixture of public schoolboys and débutantes who indulged their tastes for parties and sexual excess, and who had a fascination with working-class crime and violence. There was nothing particularly new in this; members of the British upper classes had long been excited by being close, but not too close, to working-class criminality. In Cammell's case this fascination was an integral part of his major artistic achievement: the film *Performance*. Another key element of the film, sex, is also crucial to understanding Cammell. Extremely handsome, Cammell had no difficulty in attracting a series of beautiful women to his studio; he also developed a taste for threesomes. On 30 August 1954 he married the actress Mary Antippas (formerly Maria Mastrantones; *b.* 1927/8), a divorcee, and daughter of Anthony Antippas, a company secretary. The marriage, which produced a son, soon ended. Cammell then left London and headed for New York; he never resided permanently in Britain again.

It appears that Cammell had become disenchanted with life as a society portraitist and was looking to adopt other approaches to art. During the late 1950s he met Deborah Dixon, a Texan model, with whom he travelled to Paris in the early 1960s. There he again took up figurative painting, although he now eschewed formal society portraits for something a little more flexible. However, by the mid-1960s his disillusionment with painting was such that he abandoned it for a new medium: film. His first script was for *The Touchables* (1968); he then went on to write the original script for *Duffy* (1968), a crime film starring James Coburn as an American hippie who assists two brothers to rob their father. The films, as envisaged by Cammell, contained elements of violence, sex, and rock music, but his vision never made it to the screen. Cammell's experiences with both *The Touchables* and *Duffy* were distinctly unhappy. The directors of both films delivered finished products totally at odds with Cammell's original ideas. Indeed, his dissatisfaction with *Duffy* became so intense that he was eventually thrown off the set. It was apparent that what Cammell craved was control, and the only way he could achieve this was by directing his next project himself. He began shooting in the summer of 1968.

Performance, which Cammell co-directed with Nicolas Roeg, is the tale of a gangster, Chas Devlin (played by Edward Fox), who is on the run from some of his associates and hides out in the home of reclusive rock star Turner (Mick Jagger) and his entourage. The key themes of the film—sexuality, class, violence, and identity—are explored as a fusion occurs between the world of East End crime and a flourishing youth culture, exemplified by rock music. The film also contains a liberal amount of references to magic and eastern mysticism. *Performance* was soon recognized as a minor classic, and the filming of it became surrounded by myths of the excesses said to have taken place on set and by stories of the tensions that developed between the actors. The charming but manipulative Cammell encouraged these tensions in the belief that they would produce a more truthful performance. When Warner Bros. executives saw Cammell's original version of the film, they were horrified. The copious amounts of sex, violence, and drug-taking, not to mention the sight of dirty bathwater in one scene, was too much for them, and they insisted that the film be edited in Los Angeles. *Performance* was released, to a mixed reaction, in the USA in the summer of 1970 and, to good reviews, in Britain in January 1971.

What really should have been only the beginning of a successful career for Cammell as a director was, in truth, its pinnacle. The remainder of his career was taken up with battles with studios, and littered with abandoned projects. His only other films were *Demon Seed* (1977), *White of the Eye* (1986), and *Wild Side* (1995), none of which approached the success of *Performance*. Nevertheless *Performance* alone was both a key film of the 1960s and a landmark in British cinema. Many film-makers more prolific than Cammell would have been happy with these achievements. He had been commissioned to direct another film when, on 24 April 1996, he shot himself through the head at the home he shared with his second wife, China, at Lookout Mountain, Hollywood. Cammell, who had for some time been interested in suicide, aimed the shot so that death would not be instantaneous, but painless and pleasurable. He remained conscious for some forty-five minutes, during which time he asked for a mirror with which he might view his death. Among his last words were: 'Can you see the picture of Borges now?', a reference to the death of Turner in *Performance*, this too the result of a gunshot to the head. MICHAEL BEVAN

Sources C. MacCabe, *Performance* (1998) • 'Donald Cammell: the ultimate performance', 1998 [documentary film, directed by Kevin Macdonald and Mark Cousins] • C. R. Cammell, *Castles in the air: a memoir* (1952) • T. D. Mathews, 'Shoot to kill', *The Guardian* (1 May 1998) • K. Macdonald, *The Observer* (3 May 1998) • b. cert. • m. cert. • m. cert. [Charles Richard Cammell and Iona Katherine Lamont Macdonald] • J. Savage, 'Tuning into wonders', *Sight and Sound*, new ser., 5/9 (1995), 24–5

Archives FILM BFI NFTVA, 'Donald Cammell: the ultimate performance', BBC 2, 17 May 1998

Likenesses photographs, repro. in MacCabe, *Performance*

Camocke, George (*c.*1666–1732), Jacobite naval officer and officer in the Spanish service, was the son of one of the Camocks of Ballymoney, co. Antrim (formerly of Layer Marney, Essex), and Mary Arney (1643–1699) of Ixworth, Suffolk. He entered the navy about 1682 and was promoted lieutenant in 1690 'for boarding a cat that was laden with masts for his majesty's ships, then riding at Cow and Calf in Norway, with a French privateer of 12 guns lashed on board her, which ship I brought safe to England' (Camocke to Admiralty, 5 Sept 1699, PRO, ADM 1/1588). He was second lieutenant of the *Lion* at the battle of Barfleur, and commanded her boats during the subsequent burning of the French ships at La Hogue: he claimed to have personally set fire to a three-decker and to have been wounded in so doing. On 13 March 1693 he became first lieutenant of the *Loyal Merchant*, part of Sir George Rooke's Mediterranean Fleet, and on 14 June 1695 he took command of the *Owner's Goodwill*, one of the 'machine vessels' developed by the Dutchman Meesters. In her he took part in the abortive attack on Dunkirk on 1 August 1695. Camocke moved shortly afterwards to command the brigantine *Intelligence*, before taking part in several bombardments of Calais, but when she was paid off in December 1697 he found himself unemployed. In May and June 1699 he wrote a series of letters to the Admiralty, setting out his services and requesting employment, and though he was appointed lieutenant of a Portsmouth guardship on 28 June, the ship was not commissioned, and he begged that 'after serving his Majesty all my life, I may not have my bread to seek in another service' (5 Sept 1699, PRO, ADM 1/1588). Camocke's request was answered almost immediately with the command of the sloop *Bonetta*, serving on the Irish coast. He moved to the *Speedwell*, on the same station, on 6 June 1702, when he attained post rank, and remained in her for eight years, successfully cruising against French privateers.

Camocke took command of the *Monck* (60 guns), still on the Irish station, in May 1711, and took her out to the Mediterranean in February 1713. Early the following year he received an order from Sir John Jennings, the flag-officer commanding, to go to Port Mahon to embark some soldiers for England. Instead Camocke transported some Spanish troops from Palermo to Alicante, and when he did finally embark the soldiers at Mahon he made unauthorized visits to Cadiz and Lisbon on his way home. He was suspended on Queen Anne's orders pending a court martial, but in a letter to the Admiralty from Hornchurch, Essex, on 18 January 1715 he declined the opportunity of clearing himself at such a court, claiming the late queen had approved his conduct and leaving the matter for the Admiralty to settle. Their response was to strike him off the list of captains. Despite his assertion in his letter that he wished 'to show my zeal for his majesty King George's service' (PRO, ADM 1/1596), Camocke's effective dismissal drove him to Jacobitism. He was heavily involved in the naval preparations for the 1715 rising, commanding the ship which made two attempts to bring over his old patron, the duke of Ormond, and on 17 October 1715 he received a commission from James Stuart, the Pretender, as admiral of the White squadron. In the following years Camocke was one of the main naval advisers to the Jacobite government-in-exile, putting forward a number of schemes of varying degrees of plausibility.

In May 1718 Camocke was appointed a rear-admiral in the Spanish fleet, hoisting his flag on 29 May aboard the *San Ferdinand* as commander-in-chief of a squadron at Barcelona. The appointment was seen as a way of encouraging desertions from the British fleet, and Camocke claimed he had held secret talks with its admiral, George Byng, but such hopes were dashed at Cape Passaro on 31 July when Byng smashed the Spanish fleet. Camocke escaped to Messina and lay there over the winter of 1718–19 with five Spanish ships, continuing his efforts to win over British officers, from Byng downwards, in letters containing offers of money and peerages if they would defect. In January 1719 Camocke attempted to run the blockade of Messina in the *San Juanico*, but the *Royal Oak* captured her on 26 January, and he narrowly escaped by boat to Catania, leaving behind all his papers (including his admiral's commission from James III). In February he transported James Edward from Italy to Spain. Camocke was censured by the Spanish for their losses in the attempted invasion of Britain in 1719, a project for which they believed he was partly responsible, but in 1722 he was involved in negotiations with King Frederick of Sweden for 12,000 Swedish troops to assist the Jacobites. Despite Ormond's efforts on his behalf Camocke continued to be out of favour in Spain and was banished to Ceuta, where he was said to have lived in great poverty. He later returned to Spain before moving to France, where he died at Rouen on 3 June 1732. In 1733 his widow, Jane (*née* Morgan), proved a will which he had made in 1699, leaving his lands in Ixworth to her. She died in Dublin in 1735.

Camocke's adherence to Jacobitism seems to have been based on opportunism following his dismissal from the navy, and was possibly also a consequence of Ormond's decision to support the Old Pretender. His entry into the Spanish service was also consistent with a career which had always shown an awareness of opportunities abroad: in 1712 he claimed to have been offered a flag post in the Russian navy, in 1715 in the Swedish. However, his career also reveals him to have been impetuous, arrogant, overconfident of his own abilities, and forever advocating the wildest schemes: James Edward found him blunt and untrustworthy, and one of the Old Pretender's advisers 'wished his moderation in temper were equal to his fidelity' (*Stuart Papers*, 6.302). J. D. Davies

Sources PRO, ADM MSS 1/1588; 1/1596 • *Calendar of the Stuart papers belonging to his majesty the king, preserved at Windsor Castle*, 7 vols., HMC, 56 (1902–23) • F. O. Fisher, *Memoirs of the Camacs of county Down*, 1 (1897) • PRO, PROB 11/658, fol. 146 [Camocke's will] • H. McDonnell, 'Irishmen in the Stuart navy, 1660–90', *Irish Sword*, 16 (1985–6), 94–5 • captains' services, NMM, MS ser-136 • *The Byng papers: selected from the letters and papers of Admiral Sir George Byng, first Viscount Torrington, and of his son, Admiral the Hon. John Byng*, ed. B. Tunstall, 3 vols., Navy RS, 67–8, 70 (1930–32) • *Pattee Byng's journal, 1718–1720*, ed. J. L. Cranmer-Byng, Navy RS, 88 (1950) • duke of Ormond's letterbook, 1718–19, BL, Add. MS 33950 • E. W. H. Fyers, 'The story of the machine vessels', *Mariner's Mirror*, 11 (1925), 50–90

Archives PRO, Admiralty papers • Royal Arch., Stuart MSS

Wealth at death land inherited from his mother, in Ixworth, Suffolk: will, PRO, PROB 11/658, fol. 146 • died in poverty: Fisher, *Memoirs*; *DNB*

Camoys, Thomas, Baron Camoys (*c.*1350–1420/21), administrator and soldier, was the son of John Camoys and heir of his uncle Thomas, Lord Camoys. The uncle died on 11 April 1372, and his lands were given to the heir on 12 October. Camoys served with the retinue of his kinsman William, Lord Latimer, in a French expedition in 1380 and was knighted by the earl of Buckingham. In 1383, now allied with the more royalist courtiers, Camoys was elected member of parliament for Surrey, but was disqualified, ostensibly because he was a banneret, who 'used not to be elected knights of the shire' (*CClR, 1381–1385*, 398–9). Thereafter Camoys was summoned as baron to parliament and to the Scottish expedition of 1385. The next year his uncle's widow died, and he inherited her dower lands, notably the manor of Trotton, Sussex, re-enfeoffed to him on 1 April 1386.

When the lords appellant purged Richard II's friends in 1387–8, Camoys was compelled to abjure the court. After the king regained power in 1389, Camoys headed the Sussex peace commission (15 July 1389). Further, on 1 March 1390, he was granted a yearly fair at his manor of Broadwater in lieu of a fee, and in 1392 King Richard granted Camoys forfeited land in Surrey. None the less Camoys appeared with the king's opponents the earl of Arundel (his Sussex neighbour), the earl's brother Thomas, and Thomas (I) Mowbray in receiving a quitclaim on 18 February 1397. Despite this, in November 1397, after the destruction of the lords appellant in parliament, Camoys appeared again on a Sussex peace commission now dominated by Richard II's allies.

Otherwise Lord Camoys received little from Richard II, and when Richard was deposed he attended Henry IV's first parliament, gaining a regrant of a forest, and a grant of the castle of Portchester to himself and his son Richard, who was knighted by King Henry at his coronation. Unlike some whom Henry favoured Camoys remained loyal to him for the next few years, serving on commissions in Surrey, Sussex, and Southampton to array soldiers, muster sailors, and suppress treasonous rumours (1400–04). On a more personal level he also escorted Henry's new queen, Joan, from Brittany to England in June 1403. He was accused of conniving at a French naval attack on the king but acquitted in October 1406 and served with the king's half-brother, Henry Beaufort, bishop of Winchester, as an envoy to France in 1406.

For the rest of Henry IV's reign Camoys had local duties, but when Henry V prepared to invade France, Camoys attended the council on 16 April 1415 to plan the invasion. Just before the embarkation Camoys was appointed on 31 July to the commission which condemned the earl of

Thomas Camoys, Baron Camoys (*c*.1350–1420/21), memorial brass [with his wife, Elizabeth]

Cambridge and Lord Scrope of Masham for the 'Southampton plot'. In the invasion itself Camoys led twenty-four lances and sixty-nine archers. He commanded the rearguard, which was on the left of the English line at Agincourt. His success that day was rewarded with the Garter on 23 April 1416. On 7 April he had been among those who welcomed Emperor Sigismund at Rochester, and in October he attended the negotiations for the treaty with Burgundy at Calais. Thereafter he served on many commissions in the next few years (1416–20) to array and muster men and borrow money for the wars, or to deal with Sussex criminals, such as Frere Tuck, on 9 February 1417. He also served as trier of petitions in parliament (October 1419) while many lords were in France.

By 1 May 1417 Camoys's second wife, Elizabeth Mortimer, widow of Henry Percy (Hotspur), whom he had probably married after June 1406 (*CPR*, *1405–8*, 232–3), was dead. He himself died on 28 March 1420 or 1421, a date wrongly given as 28 March 1419 on the brass of himself and his wife in the parish church in Trotton, Sussex, where he may also have commissioned wall-paintings. His elder son, Richard, predeceased him, leaving a grandson Hugh as heir, but Thomas Camoys's second son, Roger, seneschal of Guyenne, was also called Lord Camoys. Thomas Camoys was more an organizer of war than a warrior, but his work at Agincourt earned him his place in history.

John L. Leland

Sources *Chancery records* • N. H. Nicolas, *History of the battle of Agincourt*, 2nd edn (1832); facs. edn (1970) • F. Taylor and J. S. Roskell, eds. and trans., *Gesta Henrici quinti / The deeds of Henry the Fifth*, OMT (1975) • GEC, *Peerage* • PRO • Rymer, *Foedera*, 3rd edn, vols. 3–4 • J. H. Wylie, *History of England under Henry the Fourth*, 4 vols. (1884–98); repr. (New York, 1969) • J. H. Wylie and W. T. Waugh, eds., *The reign of Henry the Fifth*, 3 (1929) • C. L. Kingsford, *Chronicle of London* (1905) • A. Goodman, *The loyal conspiracy: the lords appellant under Richard II* (1971) • F. Devon, ed. and trans., *Issues of the exchequer: being payments made out of his majesty's revenue, from King Henry III to King Henry VI inclusive*, RC (1837) • G. L. Harriss, *Cardinal Beaufort: a study of Lancastrian ascendancy and decline* (1988) • J. Rosenthal, *Patriarchy and families of privilege in fifteenth century England* (1991) • C. Allmand, *Henry V* (1992) • *VCH Sussex*, vol. 4 • C. Hibbert, *Agincourt*, 2nd edn (1978)

Likenesses memorial brass, Trotton, Sussex [*see illus.*]

Wealth at death see GEC, *Peerage*; *VCH Sussex*; inquisition post mortem, PRO

Campbell family (*per. c.*1300–1453), nobility, was important in the history of the western highlands, and especially Argyll, in the fourteenth and fifteenth centuries. Recorded from about the middle of the thirteenth century, the family first came to prominence in the person of **Sir Neil Campbell** (*d.* 1315?), who was noted for his active military and political support for the cause of King Robert I in the period after February 1306. He was later identified by John Barbour as one of the small band which accompanied Robert during his desperate flight from English and Scottish foes in the winter of 1306–7, and contemporary evidence seems to confirm that he was in the king's personal entourage at this time, in particular the band into which he entered about 1308, along with Thomas Hay and Alexander Seton, to defend to the death their king and the liberty of the realm. In 1309 and 1314, moreover, he represented Robert in negotiations with the English crown. Sir Neil's loyal service resulted in a number of gains for his family and kinsmen at the expense of King Robert's enemies in the west, most notably the Macdougall lords of Argyll.

The most striking confirmation of the closeness of the links between Campbell and the king came in the form of Sir Neil's prestigious marriage with Robert's sister Mary Bruce, which took place either just before Mary was captured by the English in 1306 or, more probably, following her release in 1312. Shortly after Bannockburn (24 June 1314) Sir Neil, his spouse, and their son John received a grant of the earldom and other lands which had belonged to David Strathbogie, tenth earl of Atholl. Then, on 10 February 1315, Colin Campbell, who was filially Sir Neil's eldest son, was granted his father's lands of Lochawe and Ardskeodnish in free barony. Sir Neil was probably still alive when the charter was issued, but seems to have died shortly afterwards; since Colin may have been technically illegitimate, the Lochawe charter was probably intended to ensure his succession to the lands and Campbell chieftainship. The name of Colin's mother is unknown. His father was, however, apparently married to Alice, one of the two daughters and coheirs of Sir Reginald Crawford, about 1302–3, after he and his brother Donald had allegedly abducted Alice and her sister. If the marriage took place it cannot be shown to have produced any children, and had in any case ended no later than 1312–14, when Sir Neil married Mary Bruce.

Their son **John Campbell**, earl of Atholl (*d.* 1333),

shared King Robert's favour with his parents. Besides the earldom of Atholl he also received a third of the annual rents due to the crown from the burgh of Dundee and from the royal barony of Inverbervie. He adopted the title of earl of Atholl some time after 1323, but his career was cut short by his death at the battle of Halidon Hill on 19 July 1333. There were no children of his marriage to Joanna Menteith, daughter of Sir John Menteith of Rursky and widow of Malise, seventh earl of Strathearn, and consequently the main line of the Campbells of Lochawe continued through his nephews, Dougall and **Gill-Easbuig** [Gillespic] **Campbell** (*d.* 1385x7), the sons of John's half-brother Colin, who probably died about 1323. Colin's early death seems to have resulted in a redistribution of his estates among his kinsmen, with the lordship of Ardskeodnish passing to another branch of the family rather than descending to Dougall and Gill-Easbuig. By 4 July 1342 Dougall was dead and his lands, which had been forfeited to the crown, probably for supporting Edward Balliol, were granted by David II to his younger brother. In a long career, Gill-Easbuig presided over a dramatic expansion of Campbell lordship, especially in mid-Argyll, Cowal, and the Firth of Clyde. By 1369 he had acquired the lordships of Craignish, Melfort, and Strachur, as well as extensive estates in Cowal and Arran. Many of these territorial advances resulted from his close political relationship with the overlord of Cowal, Robert the Steward, who became king as Robert II in 1371.

On 24 May 1382 the growing influence of the Campbell chief and his family in Argyll was confirmed when Robert II granted Gill-Easbuig Campbell and his son and heir a heritable royal lieutenancy in mid-Argyll which effectively covered the territory between the lordships of Lorn and Knapdale. Gill-Easbuig was apparently still alive on 1 June 1385, but seems to have died within two years. His only known wife was Isabella Lamont, the mother of his son and successor, **Colin Campbell** (*d.* 1412/13). Perhaps the most significant aspect of the latter's chieftainship was his marriage to Mariota Campbell, the daughter and heir of John Campbell, lord of Ardskeodnish, under a dispensation granted on 16 January 1366. Through this match the lordships of the Ardskeodnish Campbells, including Ardskeodnish and Glenorchy, were united to those of the Lochawe family. By 1395 Colin was confident enough of his regional power to use the style 'lord of Argyll', a long-established title which had connotations of provincial overlordship.

Colin Campbell died between 18 June 1412 and 19 January 1413. He left a number of children from his marriage to Mariota (although only Duncan [*see below*], his son and successor, can be positively identified as a product of this match) and also had a number of sons from other relationships. **Duncan Campbell**, first Lord Campbell (*d.* 1453), had succeeded his father as lord of Lochawe by 19 January 1413. His career was initially enhanced by his marriage (probably in the 1390s) to Marjory Stewart, daughter of Robert, duke of Albany. In 1424–5, however, the Albany Stewarts and their allies came under political attack from King James I. Duncan Campbell had been one of the men chosen in 1423 to go to England as surety for the payment of the king's ransom, and he was still in England in May 1425 when his brother-in-law Murdoch, duke of Albany, his cousins, Murdoch's sons, and his uncle Duncan, earl of Lennox, were all executed. After his return to Scotland, Campbell worked hard to win back the favour of the king and was noted for his service to James at the siege of Roxburgh Castle in 1436–7. After the king's assassination in February 1437 Campbell identified himself with the interests of the king's widow, Queen Joan Beaufort and her infant son, James II. A rich man—in 1423 his annual revenue was estimated at 1500 merks—in Argyll he presided over a substantial building programme which resulted in the construction of a major centre for the exercise of secular lordship at Inveraray on Loch Fyne, and the endowment (4 August 1442) of a new ecclesiastical and religious focus for the family in the form of a secular college at Kilmun in Cowal.

Duncan Campbell was knighted before 1430, and by 10 August 1440 (and perhaps as early as 1437) he had been granted, or had simply adopted, the parliamentary peerage title Lord Campbell. He was still alive in February 1453, but seems to have died shortly afterwards. He was buried in the collegiate kirk of Kilmun. He was twice married. His marriage to Marjory Stewart probably produced two sons. The elder was Gillespic, who seems to have died *c.*1432 (and certainly before March 1440). Gillespic's son Colin *Campbell eventually succeeded his grandfather as chief of clan Campbell, lord of Lochawe and Lord Campbell, and went on to become first earl of Argyll. The second son born to Duncan and Marjory was Colin, first of Glenorchy and progenitor of the Breadalbane family, although some accounts claim that Colin was a son of Duncan's second wife. The latter was Margaret Stewart, daughter of Sir John Stewart of Ardgowan, an illegitimate son of King Robert III. The marriage produced a number of children, including at least three sons, Neil, Duncan, and Gillespic, who founded important cadet branches.

S. I. Boardman

Sources charters, U. Glas., department of history, Argyll transcripts • G. W. S. Barrow and others, eds., *Regesta regum Scottorum*, 5–6, ed. A. A. M. Duncan and B. Webster (1982–8) • J. Barbour, *The Bruce*, ed. A. A. M. Duncan (1997) • *CDS*, vols. 2, 3 • *APS*, *1124–1567* • NA Scot., Register House charters, RH6 • W. Robertson, ed., *An index, drawn up about the year 1629, of many records of charters* (1798) • W. R. Childs and J. Taylor, eds., *The Anonimalle Chronicle, 1307 to 1334: from Brotherton collection MS 29*, Yorkshire Archaeological Society, 147 (1991) • J. M. Thomson and others, eds., *Registrum magni sigilli regum Scotorum / The register of the great seal of Scotland*, 11 vols. (1882–1914), vols. 1–2 • A. Theiner, *Vetera monumenta Hibernorum et Scotorum historiam illustrantia* (Rome, 1864) • G. W. S. Barrow, *Robert Bruce and the community of the realm of Scotland*, 3rd edn (1988) • S. I. Boardman, *The early Stewart kings: Robert II and Robert III, 1371–1406* (1996) • R. Nicholson, *Scotland: the later middle ages* (1974), vol. 2 of *The Edinburgh history of Scotland*, ed. G. Donaldson (1965–75) • A. Grant, *Independence and nationhood: Scotland, 1306–1469* (1984) • *Inventories of the royal commission on the ancient and historical mounments of Scotland: Argyll*, 2: *Lorn* (1975) • *Argyll: an inventory of the ancient monuments*, Royal Commission on the Ancient and Historical Monuments of Scotland, 6: *Mid Argyll and Cowal* (1984)

Archives NA Scot., Breadalbane muniments, charters, GD 112 • U. Glas., department of history, Argyll transcripts, charters

Likenesses R. Johnson, wash drawing (Duncan Campbell; after German painter), Scot. NPG

Campbell family of Cawdor (*per.* 1511–1821), highland chiefs, landowners, and politicians, provide a rare example of a Campbell family based some distance from Argyll which until the end of the seventeenth century, following the pattern of the clan, remained closely associated with its chief and his affairs. The family was founded by the marriage in 1511 of **Sir John Campbell of Cawdor** (*d.* 1546), third son of Archibald *Campbell, second earl of Argyll (*d.* 1513), to Muriel (1498–*c.*1575), daughter of John Calder (*d.* 1498) and heir of her grandfather's modest but fertile lands near Nairn and Inverness, known as the thanedom of Calder or Cawdor; famously abducted as an infant after her father's death, Muriel was brought up in Argyll. A thane was a pre-Norman district ruler, and although in 1476 Calder had been granted the liberties and privileges of a barony, Muriel almost a century later was still describing her lands as the thanedom and barony of Cawdor. The earl of Argyll saw these lands as a useful outpost from which to further Campbell interests in the north. In spite of his wife's inheritance, however, which was unsuccessfully disputed by her Calder uncles, Sir John maintained his links with the west and wove a web of alliances among the clans there. One of his sisters had married Lachlan Maclean of Duart, who exposed her below high tide on 'Lady's rock' near Duart, whence she was rescued and taken home to Inveraray. Sir John took his revenge with a party of fourteen men on 10 November 1523, when he broke into a house in Edinburgh 'under silence of night' and murdered Duart in his bed. For this he received a remission in 1524. Family tradition suggests that only after this did Sir John make his home in the north, in a castle previously built or extended and fortified by the Calders in 1454–5, and begin to make alliances with his neighbours, extend his possessions, and encourage his younger sons to found families there. He died in spring 1546.

Sir John was followed by Archibald (*d.* 1551), the eldest of his five sons, who died just five years later. Muriel, who seems to have been a redoubtable lady, survived until about 1575. Archibald, who in 1545 married Isabel Grant of Frenchie, was succeeded by his eldest son, **John Campbell of Cawdor** (*d.* 1592), for whom his uncle John Campbell, prior of Ardchattan and later bishop of the Isles, acted as tutor. In 1575 John married Mary, daughter of William Keith, fourth Earl Marischal, and younger sister of Agnes Keith, widow of the regent Moray and now married to Colin *Campbell (*c.*1542–1584), and mother of his heir. This marriage led Cawdor once more firmly into the Argyll circle. On his death in 1584 Colin left a nine-year-old son, over whose upbringing there arose much (uncharacteristic) trouble among the Campbell gentry. Cawdor was nominated by the late earl as one of the six curators and, along with Sir James Campbell of Ardkinglass and Neil Campbell, bishop of Argyll, one of three principals. In a bond dated 1586 between Cawdor and Campbell of Lochnell on the subject of the custody and management of the young seventh earl, there is a reference to 'the abuse of thais quhilk keipis my lord of Argyllis body' (Innes, 188). They were clearly trying to reduce the influence of Ardkinglass, who was, however, supported by the powerful Duncan Campbell of Glenorchy. There was already a close link between the earls of Moray and Argyll owing to their strong protestant background and family relationship, and Cawdor was also involved with Moray over his lands in the north, where there was great rivalry between Moray and the earl of Huntly. Cawdor, with the earls of Atholl and Moray, was part of a group who in 1590 formed an offensive and defensive alliance apparently directed against Huntly. In the same year the young earl of Argyll, now aged fourteen, chose his own nine curators, of whom once again Cawdor was a principal, with Campbell of Lochnell in place of Ardkinglass. A widespread plot led to a contract by which seven signatories, including Huntly and Campbell of Glenorchy, aimed 'to cut of and slay' Argyll, his brother Colin, Moray, and Campbell of Cawdor (Macphail, 184). Accordingly on 4 February 1592 Cawdor, while sitting by the fire in a house at Knipoch near Oban, was killed by three or four shots fired from 'ane long hagbit' (ibid., 154). John Campbell of Ardkinglass, who had succeeded his father in 1591, had been easily persuaded by Glenorchy to arrange this, and it was he who confessed to implication in the murder. Three days later came the better-known assassination of the 'bonnie earl of Moray' at Donibristle by Huntly. Argyll and his brother survived.

The aftermath of the murders left chaos in the north and the highlands were said to be like a huge harp of which it was impossible to touch one string without setting the others jangling. But the Campbells managed to restore clan unity, in the pursuit of which in 1601 **Sir John Campbell of Cawdor** (*d. c.*1642), son and heir of the murdered laird, married Jean, daughter of Sir Duncan Campbell of Glenorchy. Meanwhile various branches of the clan Donald were afflicted by internal strife, which they were unable to bring under control; one who was to benefit from this was Donald Campbell, natural son of the murdered Cawdor. He became involved in northern affairs through marriage with Jean Campbell, widow of Angus Mackintosh the younger of Torcastle and mother of the young heir who succeeded as chief in 1606 and to whom Donald was curator. Donald Campbell also kept a close interest in the west and later acquired Macdonald lands in Ardnamurchan, including the castle of Mingary, and also parts of Appin with the spectacular Castle Stalker on its rock in Loch Linnhe.

The rifts in the clan Donald also provided the background for the younger Cawdor's greatest acquisition. For a brief period after 1519 Sir John Campbell had undertaken the administration of the MacIan lands on Islay, but the interest of his great-grandson Sir John in that fertile island revived through the marriage of his sister Margaret to Sir John Macdonald of Dunyvaig, whose family held most of it in the 1590s. Turmoil among the island clans resulted in rebellion in 1614 and Cawdor, backed by Argyll and the privy council, was ordered to lead an expedition to

Islay, where he took the castles of Dunyvaig and Lochgorme. In 1615 he arranged to buy the forfeited Macdonald lands from Argyll for sums which proved to be so large—his debts were said at one point to have amounted to 100,000 merks—that he had to sell silver and some land in the north to raise the money, and later generations are said to have regretted the purchase. Cawdor devolved Islay to his son John Campbell (*d.* 1654), who was declared insane in 1639 during his father's lifetime and whose affairs until his death were managed first by Cawdor's brother Colin Campbell of Ardersier (*d. c.*1642) and then by a younger brother, George Campbell. An attempt was made to develop Islay by settling friends and supporters there and by trying to raise profits from the island, including an attempt to 'drawe in Inglische men to Ila boithe for the fisching and leid myneis' (Innes, 250) and by building up a large cattle trade.

Sir Hugh Campbell of Cawdor (*c.*1639–1716), the son of Colin Campbell of Ardersier and his wife, Elizabeth, daughter of David Brodie of Brodie, succeeded to the family estates in 1654. In 1660 he was made the ward of the earl of Lauderdale. In 1661, soon after coming of age, he was elected to the Scottish parliament as MP for Nairnshire, for which he continued to sit until 1693. In January 1662 he was contracted to marry Lady Henrietta Stewart, daughter of James, fourth earl of Moray, and the niece of Lauderdale's wife. They had four sons and four daughters. Sir Hugh was active in Scottish politics throughout the Restoration period. He did not join Argyll's rebellion in 1685, but supported the revolution of 1688–9 and was appointed to the Scottish privy council in May 1689. Some suspected his loyalty given the marriage in March 1689 of his second son, Archibald, to the daughter of Duncan Macpherson of Cluny, a Jacobite, and he was suspected of providing Viscount Dundee with information on council deliberations. During the first session of the 1690 parliament he was a member of the Club opposition, and he failed to attend the second session of 1690. He was not reappointed to the privy council in March 1692, but he was excepted from pardon in James II's proclamation of April 1692. He relinquished his seat in parliament to his son, Alexander, in 1693, probably owing to ill health. In 1704 he published his *Essay on the Lord's Prayer*, which advocated the use of the Lord's prayer in public worship. The suppression of his letters to the general assembly on this issue led to the publication of his correspondence with the moderators of the general assembly when the *Essay* was republished in 1709. Sir Hugh was an opponent of the union of 1707, believing that 'a federal union and free trading would certainly be an advantage' (Innes, 405). He condoned the mobilization of Cawdor men for the Pretender (James Edward Stuart) on 19 September 1715, delegating his authority to his grandson, Duncan Campbell, son of Sir Archibald Campbell of Cluny. His death on 11 March 1716 may have prevented the forfeiture of his estates. He was buried on 29 March.

Sir Hugh Campbell's eldest son, **Sir Alexander Campbell the younger of Cawdor** (*d.* 1697), predeceased his father. After matriculating at King's College, Aberdeen, in 1677, Alexander travelled abroad to France and possibly to Italy. In September 1688 he was contracted to marry Elizabeth (*d.* 1714), daughter of Sir John Lort, second baronet, of Stackpole Court, Pembrokeshire, and Lady Susannah Holles. They had two sons—the elder, Gilbert, died in 1711—and two daughters, one of whom, Susannah, married in 1718 Sir James Campbell, fifth baronet. Alexander sat for Nairnshire in the Scottish parliament in 1693–5, but died shortly after, on 27 August 1697. In 1698 his wife, Lady Campbell, succeeded her brother, Sir Gilbert Lort, third baronet, to the family's Welsh estates. Henceforth, the Campbells of Cawdor ceased to be merely Scottish landowners (with lands primarily in eastern Inverness-shire and Nairnshire, with control also of the islands of Islay and Jura), and became more British in their orientation with extensive interests in Wales. Indeed, there seems to have been some hostility to the Scots within the Lort family, Lady Lort's will making bequests contingent on her grandsons not marrying North Britons. Lady Campbell resided in England with her affairs closely watched over by her brother's friend, Edward Harley, brother of Robert, earl of Oxford from 1711.

Sir Hugh Campbell was succeeded by his grandson **John Campbell of Cawdor** (1695–1777), and given his grandfather's actions in 1715 it was perhaps rather fortuitous that John had spent most of his childhood in England and Wales and avoided any real taint of Jacobitism. John was educated in England, entering Lincoln's Inn in London in 1708 and Clare College, Cambridge, in 1711. John succeeded his mother in 1714 and his grandfather in 1716. His actions in the personal, commercial, and political spheres reveal just how far he had moved beyond the traditional concerns and agendas of a highland laird. Following his father's example he married, on 30 April 1726, Mary (*d.* in or before 1777), daughter of Lewis Pryse of Gogerddan, Cardiganshire; they had three sons and three daughters. This new Welsh connection gave John access to coal-rich estates and enabled him, in 1727, to sell the islands of Islay and Jura to the family's major creditor, Daniel Campbell of Shawfield, for £12,000. Initially John Campbell was MP for Pembrokeshire from 1727 to 1747, though in the election of 1734 he was returned for both the Welsh county and Nairnshire, the first MP since the union to be elected simultaneously north and south of the border. Despite his family's Jacobite antecedents, John was very much a supporter of first Robert Walpole, then the Pelhams (to whom he was related through his maternal grandmother), and above all Henry Fox. His political loyalty resulted in his appointment as a lord of the Admiralty from 1736 to 1742, and then as a lord of the treasury from June 1746 until the parliamentary election of 1754. In 1747, unsure of his electoral prospects in Wales, John had fallen back on his family's traditional power base in Nairnshire, where his hereditary sheriffdom was to be valued at £2000 under the terms of the Jurisdictions Act. Having held Nairnshire from 1747 to 1754 and with the approval of Henry Pelham and the third duke of Argyll, he sat as MP for the Inverness-shire burghs from 1754 to 1761, defeating the strong challenge mounted by Sir Alexander Grant. During the political upheavals of 1755–7, Campbell was very much opposed to the prospect of William Pitt the elder's becoming a leading figure in government. Although he was persuaded by his political ally Henry Fox to sit as MP for Corfe Castle from December 1762 to 1768, he took a much less active role after his return to the Commons. He died on 6 September 1777.

From as early as the 1761 election, leadership of the family interest had effectively devolved upon John Campbell's first son, **Pryse Campbell of Cawdor** (1727–1768), politician. Having matriculated at Clare College, Cambridge, in 1745, Pryse married on 20 September 1752 Sarah (1726–1767), daughter and heir of Sir Edmund Bacon, sixth baronet, of Garboldisham, Norfolk; they had four sons and three daughters. Initially Pryse seemed destined for a successful political career, not least because, unlike his father, he was a strong supporter of Pitt the elder. In 1754 he was returned as MP for Inverness-shire with the co-operation of Argyll, who, though supportive of the political pretensions of Simon Fraser of Lovat, believed that the erstwhile Jacobite's re-entry into county politics was premature and would certainly offend sensibilities in London. Competition with the Lovat interest remained, however. Clearly aware that Fraser's acquisition of a Highland regiment in January 1757 heightened his political credibility with Inverness-shire voters, Pryse refused to assist in the recruitment process; but it was his support for the Irish Cattle Importation Act during February and March 1759 that deeply damaged his relationship with his constituents. By February 1761 Argyll had made it clear he would oppose reselection of Pryse for Inverness-shire, with the result that the latter, with the support of the earl of Bute, stood for and won the Nairnshire seat. Having been created a lord of treasury in August 1766 and re-elected to parliament on 4 December 1766, he still faced the fact that under the Scottish electoral system Nairnshire would not be represented at the next election. He switched to his Welsh interest and was elected for the Cardigan Boroughs on 24 March 1768, but died on 14 December of the same year.

His first son, **John Pryse Campbell**, first Baron Cawdor of Castlemartin (1755–1821), politician and army officer, was born on 24 April 1755. He studied first at Eton College (1763–7), before entering Clare College, Cambridge, in 1772. Although he was brought up in Wales and England and knew little of Scotland, his political career commenced north of the border when he sat as MP for Nairnshire from 18 April 1777 until May 1780, when he vacated his seat to take over the Cardigan Boroughs seat vacated by Thomas Johnes. He was then returned for Cardigan Boroughs at the 1780 general election, and thereafter he held the now traditional Welsh seat of the Cawdor family until 1796. A strong supporter of Lord North, he helped to recruit the 75th regiment from south Wales in 1777, and voted against the peace preliminaries in early 1783. Although he was initially neutral on the administration of William Pitt the younger, Campbell's marriage on 28 July 1789 to Lady Isabella Caroline Howard (1771–1848), daughter of Frederick, fifth earl of Carlisle, not only demonstrated the family's final integration into the British landed élite, but also hastened Campbell's drift into opposition circles. He voted for the repeal of the Test Act in Scotland and became associated with the moderate Portland whigs. By March 1794, however, as the scale and scope of the conflict with the French intensified, Campbell, along with the rest of Portland's parliamentary interest, joined Pitt's administration. The posts held by Campbell during this period give some indication of how far the family's horizons were now dominated by their Welsh, as opposed to Scottish, interests. Governor of Milford Haven from 1780 until his death, Campbell was commissioned as a captain in the Castlemartin yeomanry from 1794 to 1802 and captain in the Pembrokeshire Volunteers in 1803, as well as lieutenant-colonel-commandant of the Royal Carmarthenshire militia from 1798 and brevet colonel from 1799 to 1821. In his capacity as an officer of the Castlemartin yeomanry Campbell was to gain the distinction of being largely responsible for repulsing the attempted French landings in Pembrokeshire in 1797. His demonstrable loyalty had in fact already been rewarded when, on 21 June 1796, he was created Baron Cawdor of Castlemartin. His local influence in Wales was confirmed in 1808 when he became mayor of Carmarthen, a position enhanced by his reputation as an improving landlord. He died at Great Pulteney Street, Bath, on 1 June 1821, and was buried in the town's abbey eight days later.

Mirroring their political development, the Campbell family's commercial concerns during the eighteenth century had focused increasingly on their valuable Welsh estates. By 1789 John Pryse Campbell had an income of £11,000–12,000 per annum. In political terms, however, the connection with the north of Scotland remained strong. A survey of Inverness-shire in 1788 revealed that Campbell held 7 votes of a total of 103; in Nairnshire, meanwhile, the family retained 8 votes out of a total of 20. Moreover, although they were increasingly absentee landlords, the family continued to direct commercial developments on their Scottish estates. During the period from the later 1710s until his death in 1744, another of Sir Hugh's grandsons, Sir Archibald Campbell of Cluny, managed the estate. He initiated various improvements, not least by creating an impressive oak plantation in and around Castle Cawdor during the 1730s. A year after his death an attempt was made to ensure protection for Cawdor tenantry by subscribing to the cattle watch of Ewan Macpherson of Cluny. Later a Welsh factor, Valentine White, was appointed to oversee the estate; he planted large amounts of hedgerow for enclosures and had created a series of planned crofts at Ardersier by the time John Campbell of Cawdor died in 1777. Improvements continued under John Pryse Campbell, with the opening up of marl pits for liming, as well as the abolition of feudal obligations upon the tenantry by the early 1790s. Perhaps only the continuing lack of systematic enclosures in the parish of Cawdor, noted by Sinclair's *Statistical Account*, reveals something of the estate-management drift that was a consequence of the family's evolution from highland lairds to gentry with British political and commercial interests.

ANDREW MACKILLOP, JEAN MUNRO, and R. W. MUNRO

Sources [C. Innes], ed., *The Book of the thanes of Cawdor, 1236–1742: a series of papers selected from the charter room at Cawdor*, Spalding Club, 30 (1859) • E. J. Cowan, 'Clanship, kinship and the Campbell acquisition of Islay', *SHR*, 58 (1979), 132–57 • D. Gregory, *The history of the western highlands and the isles of Scotland* (1836) • A. Campbell of Airds, *The life and troubled times of Sir Donald Campbell of Ardnamurchan*, Society of West Highland and Island Historical Research (1992) • J. R. N. Macphail, ed., 'The murder of the laird of Calder', *Highland papers*, 1, 141–94, Scottish History Society, 2nd ser., 5 (1914) • J. Goodare, *State and society in early modern Scotland* (1999) • M. D. Young, ed., *The parliaments of Scotland: burgh and shire commissioners*, 1 (1992), 93–5 • *Scots peerage* • H. Campbell, *An essay on the Lord's prayer* (1704) • H. Campbell, *A collection of letters, relative to an essay upon the Lord's prayer which was printed, anno. 1704, and now reprinted anno. 1709* • P. Hopkins, *Glencoe and the end of the highland war* (1986) • *IGI* • *CSP dom., 1689–92* • P. D. G. Thomas, *Politics in eighteenth-century Wales* (1998) • P. W. J. Riley, *King William and the Scottish politicians* (1979) • R. Steele, *Tudor and Stuart proclamations, 1485–1714*, 2.445 • will of Lady Susannah Lort, PRO, PROB 11/515, fol. 160 • will of Sir Gilbert Lort, third baronet, PRO, PROB 11/448, fol. 226 • will of Gilbert Campbell, PRO, PROB 11/521, fol. 208

Archives Carmarthenshire Archive Service, Carmarthen, corresp., diaries, and papers [John Campbell, first Baron Cawdor] • Cawdor Castle, Inverness-shire, MSS | BL, letters to Lord Hardwicke and duke of Newcastle [John Campbell (1695–1777)] • MHS Oxf., corresp. with W. Smith [John Campbell, first Baron Cawdor] • NL Wales, general MS/1352 • priv. coll., corresp. relating to Nairnshire elections [John Campbell, first Baron Cawdor]

Campbell family of Glenorchy (*per.* 1432–1631), nobility, formed the principal cadet branch of clan Campbell and in the early modern period constituted one of the most successful Scottish noble houses. They entered the peerage, as earls of Breadalbane, in 1681, exploiting a mixture of highland and lowland techniques to ensure their rise to prominence, as they came to dominate the central highlands of Scotland.

Colin Campbell of Glenorchy (*c.*1395–1475) was the younger son of Duncan *Campbell of Lochawe (*d.* 1453), first Lord Campbell, of the main branch of that clan, subsequently earls of Argyll [*see under* Campbell family (*per. c.*1300–1453)]; his mother was Duncan's first wife, Marjory Stewart. Colin's long and important career established the family's fortunes and demonstrated many of the characteristics that brought success for subsequent generations: the acquisition of land; advantageous marriages; a leading role within clan Campbell; a long life; and an adult male successor. In 1432 his father established Colin in northern Argyll by granting him the lands and lordship of Glenorchy, which became the new branch's territorial designation. Colin's marital career was complex. His first wife was Mariota, daughter of Walter Stewart of Lennox, and on her death he contracted a marriage with Janet Borthwick, Lady Dalkeith. This was conveniently annulled on 7 May 1449, a couple of months after he had married Janet Stewart, eldest daughter and coheir of John, Lord Lorne, with whom he had two sons. Through her Colin received a third of the substantial lordship of

Sir Duncan Campbell of Glenorchy (1551x4–1631), by unknown artist, 1601

Lorn, thereby providing the family with strategically important territory in northern Argyll. He subsequently married Margaret (*d.* in or before 1467), daughter of Robert Robertson of Strowan, and then Margaret, daughter of Luke Stirling of Keir, who bore him three more sons, the youngest of whom founded the Lawers branch. As tutor (guardian) to his great-nephew, the first earl of Argyll, Colin became a major power within clan Campbell during the middle of the fifteenth century, building Inveraray Castle for the earl and Kilchurn (also known as Glenorchy) Castle for himself. He was much travelled, with his reputed three visits to Rome providing his by-name 'Black Colin of Rome' (Cailean Dubh na Roimh). He probably fought the Turks in Rhodes alongside the knights hospitallers of St John; by tradition he was protected during the fighting by the Glenorchy charm stone (now in the National Museum of Scotland). He died in 1475 at Strathfillan, where he had built a tower, and was buried at Kilmartin, in Argyll.

Colin's son **Duncan Campbell of Glenorchy** (*c.*1443–1513) had an equally long career, during which he made major territorial acquisitions in the Breadalbane region, in particular securing the strategically vital holdings of the Isle of Loch Tay at the west end of that loch and Finlarig at its east end. He married twice; his first wife was Margaret Douglas, daughter of the fourth earl of Angus, with whom he had four sons and three daughters, and the second was Margaret (*d.* 1554), daughter of Sir John Moncrieff of that ilk, who bore him another son. Duncan's considerable literary and artistic skills placed him at the centre of the Gaelic literary circle which included the Fortingall MacGregors who compiled *The Book of the Dean of Lismore* and allowed Campbell to contribute nine humorous and bawdy poems to that Gaelic collection. For many years he worked closely with his cousin, the second earl of Argyll, and when both were killed at the battle of Flodden (9 September 1513) they were buried side by side at Kilmun, Argyll.

Colin Campbell of Glenorchy (*c.*1468–1523), the third laird, was a mature forty-five years of age when he inherited after Flodden. He had married Marjory Stewart (*d.* 1524), daughter of the earl of Atholl, and they had three sons, all of whom succeeded him as laird of Glenorchy. His ten-year tenure settled the family's estates and witnessed a symbolic shift away from the Campbell heartland of Argyll and Glenorchy into Perthshire and a new base in Breadalbane. Colin built a chapel to the Blessed Virgin Mary at Finlarig and when he died, on 8 August 1523, he was buried there, as were all his successors. The deaths of the two older of his three sons, the fourth laird, Duncan Campbell (*c.*1486–1536), and the fifth laird, John Campbell (*c.*1496–1550), without male heirs threatened the dynasty's survival. Duncan had married Elizabeth, daughter of Sir John Colquhoun of Luss, producing no surviving children. John's wife, Marion Edmonstone of Duntreath, bore him two daughters. Although they retained the lands their predecessors had obtained and the fifth laird accumulated considerable wealth, the lordship stagnated during the 1530s and 1540s.

The fortunes of the Campbell lordship were revitalized by the dynamism and longevity of Colin's third son, the sixth laird, **Colin Campbell of Glenorchy** (1499–1583), known as Grey Colin (Cailean Liath) from his long white hair and beard. Before his succession in 1550 he had married Margaret, widow of Patrick Graham and daughter of Alexander Stewart, bishop of Moray, and had two daughters. On 28 January 1551 he married his second wife, Katherine Ruthven, daughter of William *Ruthven, second Lord Ruthven. This alliance brought a crucial connection to the important burgh of Perth, dominated by the Ruthvens, and to eastern Perthshire. Of even greater importance, it provided Colin with additional influential contacts at the royal court. The couple had eight surviving children, four of whom were sons, thus successfully re-establishing the dynastic line. Colin was a keen advocate of the protestant cause, trying unsuccessfully to persuade John Knox to remain in Scotland in May 1556, supplying troops during the crisis of 1559–60 and attending the Reformation Parliament of August 1560. Many of the first generation of protestant ministers within the Breadalbane region had been members of his household and were supported by him.

Colin Campbell's tenure as laird was dominated by his feud with the MacGregors. During the previous century the two clans had been partners and allies in their joint expansion eastwards from the adjacent Argyll lands of Glenorchy and Glen Strae across the Drumalban range into Glen Lyon and the entire Breadalbane region. Relations deteriorated rapidly after Colin's succession, when he adopted a tough policy during the minority of Gregor Roy, the MacGregor chief. From 1562 the feud degenerated into raiding and open warfare. In 1569 Gregor Roy was captured and on 7 April 1570, having presided at the trial, Colin personally executed him, an event commemorated by Gregor's wife, Marion Campbell of Glenlyon, in a famous Gaelic lullaby. Although a settlement was patched up the following autumn, the feud later re-emerged, continuing even after the proscription of the very name of MacGregor by the Scottish privy council in April 1603. In the long run the Campbells of Glenorchy, aided by support from their fellow clansmen and the government, reduced clan Gregor to 'children of the mist'. The feud did not hinder Grey Colin making major additions to his land holdings and increasing his control upon his estates. He built one new castle at the east end of Loch Tay at Balloch (now Taymouth Castle at Kenmore) and another at Edinample on Loch Earn and also renovated Kilchurn and his town house at Perth. He died at Balloch on 11 April 1583.

Grey Colin's eldest son and heir, **Sir Duncan Campbell of Glenorchy**, first baronet (1551x4–1631), variously known as Black Duncan of the Cowl (Donnachadh Dubh a' Churraic) or Black Duncan of the Castles, was laird for forty-eight years. He was knighted in 1590 and became baronet of Nova Scotia in 1625. A ruthless man, he was prepared to use fair means and foul to increase his dominance within his region and his clan and to amass greater wealth. By squeezing out the existing proprietors, he bought or obtained legal rights over much of the land which separated existing holdings, thereby tightening his grip upon a vast swathe of territory, from the Lorn coast in the west to Strathtay in the east. During the minority of the seventh earl of Argyll, Duncan even attempted to seize control of clan Campbell. In 1592 John Campbell of Cawdor was murdered and there was an attempt to poison the seventh earl. Although deeply implicated, Duncan avoided serious punishment for his part in these murky plots which were linked to the bitter national feud between the earls of Huntly and Moray. In 1596 as part of a grand reconciliation within clan Campbell, Argyll demonstrated his trust by sending his son and heir to be fostered by Duncan. When repeating the arrangement for his own heir, the marquess of Argyll later recalled how happy had been his time as Glenorchy's foster son. Better relations with his clan chief did not prevent Duncan quarrelling with his own cadet branch, the Campbells of Lawers, in part over the final stages of the MacGregor feud. In 1601 Duncan was imprisoned in Edinburgh Castle and secured his freedom only by paying 40,000 merks (£26,666 Scots) and spending time on the continent until things were more settled at home. He recovered royal favour, not least by being so co-operative to the royal huntsmen who came to Breadalbane seeking the white hind which had captivated James VI's imagination. When Duncan died at Balloch on 23 June 1631 his achievements were celebrated in a Gaelic elegy, and also in the family history commissioned by his son known as *The Black Book of Taymouth*. He had married twice: his first wife was Jean or Janet Stewart (*d*. 1593), daughter of the fourth earl of Atholl; and then in 1597 he married Elizabeth Sinclair (*d*. 1654). He had at least eleven children from his first marriage and seven from his second, amply ensuring the continuation of his line.

During the tenure of the first seven lairds, the Glenorchy family's rise was the most spectacular example of the general success of clan Campbell and it owed much to the strength of their wider kindred. It was achieved by a combination of efficiency and ruthlessness. The Glenorchys' massive expansion of their territorial base, through warfare, the acquisition and exploitation of feudal rights, and by land purchases, enabled them to build up their power and wealth and establish cadet branches. They managed their estates with great, sometimes harsh, determination but also with imagination, being willing to innovate by planting parks and woodland and investing in saltpans. To add to their security, they undertook an extensive programme of castle building which helped them control the key routes running between the southern highlands and the lowlands. They bound the people of the Breadalbane region to them by the extensive use of bonds of manrent and alliances with other highland clans. They secured their social and political position at national and regional levels by the adroit use of marriage strategies and through their patronage of both the Gaelic learned orders and lowland professionals and artists. Apart from the danger point in 1550, the dynastic line was kept secure by large families and adult lairds with long tenures providing continuity and stability. By 1631 the house of Glenorchy's extensive landholdings within Argyll and Perthshire had brought it control over the frontier zones between the central highlands and the lowlands, guaranteeing them power, wealth, and a national political profile. JANE E. A. DAWSON

Sources J. Dawson, ed., *Clan Campbell letters, 1559–83*, Scottish History Society, 5th ser., 10 (1997) • C. Innes, ed., *The black book of Taymouth*, Bannatyne Club, 100 (1855) • NA Scot., Breadalbane collection, GD112 • W. A. Gillies, *In famed Breadalbane*, 2nd edn (1980) • M. MacGregor, 'A political history of the MacGregors before 1571', PhD diss., U. Edin., 1989 • A. Campbell of Airds, *A history of clan Campbell*, 1, 2 (2000–02) • K. M. Brown, *Noble society in Scotland* (2000) • *Scots peerage*, vol. 2

Archives Inveraray Castle, Argyll MSS • NA Scot., Breadalbane collection, GD112

Likenesses oils on panel, 1601 (Sir Duncan Campbell of Glenorchy), Scot. NPG [*see illus.*] • oils, 1619 (Sir Duncan Campbell of Glenorchy), Scot. NPG • portraits, repro. in Innes, ed., *Black book of Taymouth*

Campbell, Lady Agnes (*d*. in or after **1590**), noblewoman, was the second daughter and fifth child of Colin *Campbell, third earl of Argyll (*d*. 1529), landowner and administrator, and his wife, Janet Gordon. She was educated at the Scottish court, learning English and French. In 1545 she married James *MacDonald of Dunyvaig and the Glens (*d*. 1565), chieftain, head of MacDonald south, and had sons Archibald, Angus, and Donnell Gorm, and daughters Katherine and Finola [*see below*]. On 2 May 1565 Agnes's husband and his brother Sorley Boy were defeated by Shane O'Neill at Glenshesk and James died as a prisoner of Shane in August of that year. The position of Lady Agnes is well described by the historian J. M. Hill:

> Whether she possessed surpassing personal charm we know not but she could command the services of multitudinous redshanks … never was widow, therefore, more interesting in the eyes of Ulster lords than Lady Cantyre [Kintyre] and more than one Ulsterman sought her hand. (Hill, *Fire and Sword*, 148–9)

The killing of Shane O'Neill by the MacDonalds in June 1567 was followed by an apparent rapprochement between Sorley Boy and Shane's successor, Turlough Luineach *O'Neill (*c*.1530–1595). Turlough Luineach looked to Archibald *Campbell, fifth earl of Argyll, for aid and it came in February 1568 in the form of an offer of marriage with his aunt, Lady Agnes.

Government military activity in Ulster and the dilatoriness of Argyll in supplying redshanks (highland Scottish mercenary infantry serving the Irish chieftains) for an Ulster incursion combined to delay the marriage until 1569. Before that, however, Argyll had come up with a new approach to his aunt's nuptials, suggesting to Sir Henry Sidney, lord deputy of Ireland, that Agnes would marry an Irish chief chosen by Elizabeth I if the queen would make a grant to her and her sons of the territory of the Glens of Antrim. This was unlikely to find favour with Sorley Boy who had sought a grant of the area for himself. In any event, before either Argyll or Sidney could further elaborate upon the scheme, Turlough Luineach and Lady Agnes married, with Captain William Piers reporting from Carrickfergus, co. Antrim, on 5 August that the lady had brought over 1000 redshanks with her into Ulster, while Sir William Fitzwilliam, vice-treasurer and lord justice, noted that they had spent fourteen days in celebration on Rathlin Island in Antrim. From this marriage Lady Agnes had one son, Art.

Lady Agnes's actions suggest that she felt her interests and those of her sons were best advanced by Turlough Luineach's success. Although Sorley Boy encouraged him to invade the English pale in 1569, Turlough Luineach did little more than keep the English busy while forcing agreements upon several Ulster chiefs and accruing considerable plunder to himself. In December 1569 Sidney wrote that Turlough Luineach was about to 'sunder' from his wife. This may have been wishful thinking for although by April 1570 Agnes was in Scotland, it was to procure redshanks on Turlough Luineach's behalf. The following year she was in Scotland again, intent on the same task but this time followed by Sorley Boy, apparently to prevent her augmenting her husband's forces. On 20 January 1571 Turlough Luineach came to an agreement with the government which, if it conferred no special advantage upon himself, at least left Sorley Boy no better off.

In December 1572, as an English colonization project

threatened Ulster, Lady Agnes departed to Scotland with a large number of redshanks in her train. Again, the government placed its trust in 'discord' between husband and wife, but Lady Agnes seems simply to have exchanged some of her husband's forces for fresh men. Certainly, Turlough Luineach substantially increased his Scottish forces from early 1573, continuing to hold these at full strength as Walter Devereux, first earl of Essex, attempted to support the colonists. In May 1574 Sir Brian mac Phelim O'Neill, chief of the rival O'Neills of Clandeboye, surrendered Clandeboye to the queen's forces but Essex admitted in October that Turlough Luineach's strength remained intact. Following the attack on Rathlin in July 1575 and Essex's withdrawal from Ulster, Sorley Boy and Lord Deputy Sidney reached an agreement in October 1575 which included the revocation of a number of colonist grants and recognized Sorley's claim to the Glens. It remained to be seen to what degree Sorley Boy could enforce this provision against the counter-claims of Lady Agnes and her sons. Turlough Luineach had meanwhile succeeded in enhancing his position by skilfully measured shows of strength which ultimately cost him little and in this process the efforts of Lady Agnes in Argyll had been invaluable.

Turlough Luineach regularly employed Lady Agnes as his delegate in meetings with government officials; from 1575 this was even more frequent. This ploy enabled him to distance himself from negotiations, rendering escape from agreements all the more easy should he deem it necessary. In June 1575 he sent his wife to treat with Essex, extracting considerable land grants and permission to refuse to meet any governor against his will. In November Turlough Luineach and Lady Agnes both met Sidney. He offered to submit to Sidney in return for an earldom and lands promised by Essex, while Lady Agnes requested recognition of the claims of her sons to the Glens. Her demeanour was noted by one of the officials: 'She is a very nobell wysse woman and as dutifully uses herself to further the Queenes service as if she weare a naturall borne subiecte' (PRO, SP 63/53/69). Despite Sidney's demands, Lady Agnes continued to organize the dispatch of Scottish mercenaries to Turlough Luineach and it is clear that the lord deputy considered her an important political figure in her own right, and no mere cipher of her husband. This view was shared in 1579 by his colleagues, Sir William Drury, lord justice, and Sir William Gerard, lord chancellor. In September 1579 Turlough Luineach refused to deal with the queen's representatives save in the presence of his wife.

Lady Agnes's diplomatic skills and military connections continued to be indispensable to Turlough Luineach throughout the 1580s. Though no longer young, she still travelled regularly to Scotland to ensure that support there was continuously maintained. A letter by Arthur, fourteenth Baron Grey of Wilton, lord deputy, during his encampment at the River Blackwater in August 1580 described vividly the skill of husband and wife as joint negotiators. He got an agreement but could neither commend the 'surety of it nor honer', nor had he secured the rebel William Nugent who had fled to Turlough Luineach for protection (PRO, SP 63/85.5). As she pressed her husband's interests, Lady Agnes continued to support those of her sons. By 1575, she believed Sorley Boy to be a serious threat to them and in January 1577 induced Turlough Luineach to decline negotiation with Sidney until he should agree to 'repel the Scots' and assist her sons in their ambitions to become chiefs in Antrim. Articles were signed in the autumn of 1584 between Sir John Perrot, lord deputy, and the Irish privy council, and Lady Agnes's younger son Donell Gorm for a grant of the former Bisset lands in the Glens, followed by a similar agreement with her son Angus in August 1585. In 1586 Turlough Luineach employed Lady Agnes to represent him in talks with Perrot. In 1587 she travelled to Scotland to calm an outbreak of hostilities between her son Angus and MacLean of Duart. In March 1588 she went to Edinburgh to plead for Angus before James VI and at the end of that year was again to be found negotiating on behalf of Turlough Luineach. In Scotland once more in April 1590, she subsequently disappears from state records and died soon after.

Finola MacDonald (*d.* in or after 1610), noblewoman, was the second daughter of James MacDonald and Agnes Campbell. In 1569 she married Hugh Manus O'Donnell of Tyrconnell (*d.* 1593), chieftain, sometimes known as the elder, son of Hugh O'Donnell. With him she had a son, Hugh, and a daughter, Nuala. As sister of MacDonald of Dunyvaig, she could bring Scottish mercenaries to the service of her husband and, like her mother, frequently negotiated on her husband's behalf. Michael O'Cleary, in his *Life of Red Hugh*, described Finola as 'much praised for her womanly qualities, with the heart of a hero and soul of a soldier' (p. 39). The historian C. Falls, however, observed that 'she exhibited a savagery of which no trace can be found in the record of her mother' (Falls, 82). She was credited with arranging the murder in 1588 of Hugh O'Gallagher, who had been implicated in the killing of her cousin, Alexander MacSorley. Later, considering that the O'Donnell castle at Donegal could act as a bridgehead for entry by English forces into O'Donnell country, Finola ordered the structure to be burnt. She showed a singular ruthlessness in advancing the causes of her son, Red Hugh O'Donnell, apparently ordering the death of Hugh, son of former chief Calvagh, to clear the way for her son to succeed to the chieftainship. In September 1590, while Red Hugh was a prisoner at Dublin Castle, Donnell, a son of Finola's husband by an earlier liaison, was killed at Derrylahan by Finola's forces. After Red Hugh's succession, as he was engaged in the Nine Years' War (1594–1603), he used his mother to speak for him in Scotland. During the war, Red Hugh's kinsman, Niall Garbh O'Donnell, deserted to the English side. After the flight of the earls of Tyrone and Tyrconnell from Ireland in September 1607, Finola contrived Niall Garbh's arrest for rebellion in 1609; he was incarcerated in the Tower of London where he died in 1626. Finola died some time after 1610.

HELEN COBURN WALSHE

Sources state papers Ireland, Elizabeth I, PRO, SP 63 series • *CSP Ire.* • G. Hill, *An historical account of the MacDonnells of Antrim* (1873) • G. A. Hayes-McCoy, *Scots mercenary forces in Ireland (1565–1603)* (1937) • C. Falls, *Elizabeth's Irish wars* (1950) • *Michael O'Cleary's Life of Red Hugh O'Donnell*, ed. P. Walsh, 2 pts (Dublin, 1948–57), • *AFM* • R. Bagwell, *Ireland under the Tudors*, 3 vols. (1885–90) • C. Brady, 'The killing of Shane O'Neill', *Irish Sword*, 15 (1982–3) • H. Morgan, 'The colonial venture of Sir Thomas Smith in Ulster, 1571–1575', *HJ*, 28 (1985), 261–78 • J. M. Hill, *Fire and sword: Sorley Boy MacDonnell and the rise of Clan Ian Mor* (1993) • J. E. A. Dawson, 'The fifth earl of Argyle, Gaelic lordship and political power in sixteenth-century Scotland', *SHR*, 67 (1988), 1–27 • *Scots peerage*, vol. 1

Wealth at death jointure in Kintyre

Campbell [*married names* Anderson, Telfer], **Agnes** (**1637–1716**), printer and book merchant, was born in Edinburgh in August 1637 and baptized there on 1 September 1637, the third daughter of James Campbell, a merchant of Edinburgh, formerly from Cumnock in Ayrshire, and Issobell, daughter of John Orr, merchant of Edinburgh. Agnes Campbell's sisters Beatrix and Jean were married respectively to the Edinburgh bookseller Archibald Hislop and to the Edinburgh goldsmith William Law, whose son John was the financial innovator responsible for the French economic crisis known as the Mississippi Bubble. In 1676 on the death of her husband, Andrew Anderson, Agnes succeeded as king's printer and printer to the burgh and university of Edinburgh; she generally used the imprint 'Heirs of Andrew Anderson'. Latterly she adopted the name Lady Roseburn after acquiring the lands of Roseburn, Dalry, to the north-west of Edinburgh.

Andrew Anderson (*c.*1635–1676) was a son of the printer George Anderson and Isobel Aitcheson. George, famous as printer to the revolutionary Glasgow general assembly of 1638, was burgh and college printer for Edinburgh (1637–8), and first printer to the burgh of Glasgow (1638–47). He had died by November 1647, but his widow continued the business, first in Glasgow (1648), and then in Edinburgh (1649–53), at which point Andrew Anderson began running the press, which now took his name for its imprint. On 26 June 1656 he married Agnes. After returning to Glasgow (where he lived 1657–61), Anderson finally settled his family and press in Edinburgh in May 1661, and he was in 1663 appointed burgh and university printer on the death of Gideon Lithgow (*fl.* 1645–1662), at which time he became a burgess of the burgh by right of his wife, Agnes. He took advantage of the withdrawal from Edinburgh by the London Society of Stationers to purchase his appointment as king's printer in 1671, and the forty-one year patent was ratified by parliament in September 1672. Andrew and his partners were given unprecedented and controversial supervisory powers over the Scottish press; this began a period of trade dispute and litigation. However, in spite of his monopoly privileges, Anderson was heavily in debt at his death in Edinburgh on 1 June 1676.

Thereafter, in spite of a shaky start, Agnes Campbell developed her press until it was the largest in Scotland in the early modern period. Even in 1678 she had no fewer than sixteen apprentices. As royal printer she was exempt from import and export customs and excise dues. She traded widely in books and paper, taking advantage of these exemptions, and she acted as moneylender to numerous book traders in England, Ireland, and throughout Scotland. Competitors in Aberdeen, Glasgow, and Edinburgh protested repeatedly against her extensive monopoly rights, and in 1681 persuaded the privy council to reduce her privileges to those of her husband's predecessors. None the less, she was a dogged and generally successful litigant throughout her career and she was able to restrict the liberties of competitors and especially her major rival in Edinburgh, James Watson the younger (*fl.* 1695–1722). Unfortunately for Campbell, she lost the most complex book-patent dispute of the time, which began in 1711. With her patent due to expire in 1712 she was unable to defeat Watson in the court of session when a new gift granted to Watson, the Jacobite printer Robert Freebairn (*fl.* 1701–1747), and the English royal printer John Basket clashed with an alternative patent to Campbell, Freebairn, and Basket. George I did his best to confuse matters, but finally in 1718 the House of Lords confirmed Watson's rights and by 1726 the Anderson press had closed and the family were in financial difficulties.

Agnes Campbell's political and religious inclinations were establishment orientated. Hers was, nevertheless, the largest Presbyterian press in Edinburgh for her city competitors, Watson and Freebairn, were inclined to Episcopalian and Jacobite sympathies. In *A brief reply to the letter from Edinburgh relating to the case of Mrs. Anderson, her majesty's printer in Scotland* (1712) she smeared Watson as a 'papist' and Freebairn as an educated drunk, but her motives were entirely personal and commercial, not idealistic. In fact, she was briefly censured by the revolution government in 1690 for being slow to take the oath of allegiance to William and Mary, her priority being, for the benefit of her press, to ensure she backed the winning side. Thereafter her long campaign to become printer to the general assembly, which lasted over two decades, ensured she took every opportunity to support Presbyterianism, though in a moderate manner acceptable in a government appointee. At last in 1712 she was appointed printer to the Church of Scotland.

Historians' assessments of Agnes Campbell's personality have been too dependent on the bitter reflections of James Watson. The 'wicked widow' caricature emanates from Watson's disgust that a printer of such poor quality possessed the royal patent and also from his view that her extensive monopoly, and ruthless exploitation of it, gave 'the Art of printing a dead Stroke' and 'damp'd all ingenious Attempts of advancing it' (Watson, 11–12). Certainly Campbell protected her rights, restricted competitors, used the courts, printed propaganda, and produced counterfeit editions to undermine other licence holders, although her behaviour was typical not unique. One unbiased contemporary, Sir John Lauder of Fountainhall, simply stated that Mrs Anderson printed 'poor books' and that her patent involved 'exorbitant clauses' (*Historical Notices*, 2.866; 1.393). Yet Campbell is remarkable for her business success, if not for the quality of her printing. She was not merely a successful woman in the masculine world of commerce, but she became uniquely wealthy for a commercial woman in Scotland who had not inherited substantial means. The value of her inheritance lay in the potential of her position and monopolies, and her subsequent rise was testament to her business acumen.

Campbell's marriage to Andrew Anderson brought them at least eight children. Unfortunately, James, the only son to survive into adulthood, died in 1693, just when he was beginning to engage in the family business. On 22 March 1681 she married Patrick Telfer, Edinburgh merchant and widower. There were no children—in fact the couple were estranged by the 1690s and she rarely used her second married name. When Agnes died, her book and paper businesses, including a large papermill established in 1706 at Valleyfield on the Esk waters of Penicuik, fell to her daughters and her sons-in-law. She acquired various properties in and around Edinburgh, some of which were tenements rented to members of the city's legal profession. The lands of Roseburn were acquired in 1704 and her further properties at Coats in Edinburgh and Cowdenknowes, Berwickshire, were acquired in 1710 and 1711 respectively. Her will and testament survive and at her death her estate was valued at £78,000 Scots, a very large sum in Scottish terms. Agnes died in Edinburgh on 24 July 1716, and was buried at Greyfriars churchyard there three days later. A. J. MANN

Sources register of testaments, Edinburgh, NA Scot., CC 8/8/75; 86; 112.1 • C. B. B. Watson, ed., *Roll of Edinburgh burgesses and guild-brethren, 1406–1700*, Scottish RS, 59 (1929), 31, 94 • Edinburgh old parish register, register house, NA Scot., OPR.685.1 • Edinburgh marriages, 111 • Glasgow burgh records, printed ser., vols. 1 and 2 • Edinburgh burgh records, printed ser., vols. 9–13 • J. Fairley, *Agnes Campbell, Lady Roseburn* (1925) • registers of the privy council, 3rd printed ser., vols. 4–15 • J. Watson, *The history of the art of printing* (1713), 10–24 • *Historical notices of Scotish affairs, selected from the manuscripts of Sir John Lauder of Fountainhall*, ed. D. Laing, 1, Bannatyne Club, 87 (1848), 311, 393; 2, Bannatyne Club, 87 (1848), 464–5, 866 • J. Lauder, ed., *The decisions of the lords of council and session*, 2 vols. (1759–61), vol. 1, pp. 104, 188–9, 205, 270, 273, 496; vol. 2, pp. 13–14 • court of session papers, production and processes, NA Scot., CS.29. box 443 and 436.1 (Mackenzies) • *JHL*, 11 (1660–66), 609–10 • *APS*, *1670–86*, 206–7; *1689–95*, 269 • A. Mann, 'Book commerce, litigation and the art of monopoly: the case of Agnes Campbell, royal printer, 1676–1712', *Scottish Economic and Social History*, 18/2 (1998), 132–56

Wealth at death £78,000 Scots; also paper stock: will, proved 1717, register of testaments, Edinburgh, NA Scot., CC 8/8/86

Campbell, Alexander, of Carco (*d.* 1608), bishop of Brechin, was a younger son of Sir John Campbell of Ardkinglas in Argyll, and brother to James Campbell of Ardkinglas, comptroller during the minority of James VI. In May 1566, while still apparently a minor, he received the bishopric of Brechin, described as 'now vacant', in a privy seal grant from Queen Mary, with power to dispose of both spiritual and temporal property. This is supposed to have been obtained through the offices of Archibald Campbell, fifth earl of Argyll, and Alexander is said then to have alienated most of the property to the earl, 'retaining for his successors scarce so much as would be a moderate competency for a minister in Brechin' (Keith, 166). In May 1567 Campbell was given licence to go abroad, but he was still in Scotland in July 1569 when he attended a convention of the estates at Perth as bishop (the first time he was so designated) and there he voted against granting Mary a divorce from Bothwell. He eventually left Scotland, displaying his protestant credentials by being recorded as 'in Genewy at the scullis' in January 1574 (Kirk, *Thirds of Benefices*, 387–8). He was travelling with his tutor Andrew Polwart, who was instrumental in persuading Andrew Melville to return to Scotland, and he thus travelled back with Melville through France, then via London, and arrived at Edinburgh in July.

Thereafter Campbell acted for a time as a minister in Brechin, though without a specific charge. He attended general assemblies as bishop of Brechin, and at the assembly held at Edinburgh in March 1575 he formally complained against the bishop of Dunkeld, who had accused him of having given out pensions from the bishopric. Instead of citing his 1566 grant, however, he claimed to have been 'pressed … against his will' by the late earl of Argyll (Thomson, 1.315). He was still very young, and the assembly ordered that he should be instructed in his duties as bishop by John Erskine of Dun, the superintendent for Angus and the Mearns. Nevertheless, in July 1580 the assembly at Dundee summoned him to the next assembly to answer various questions, and his failure to comply led to a reissue of the summons. In 1582 the assembly ordered the presbytery of the Mearns to proceed against him on a number of charges, but nothing further is known of the case and he is not mentioned in the records of assemblies after 1583. Campbell regularly attended parliaments and conventions of the estates until 1607, often associated with the earl of Argyll, and was regularly appointed to parliament's drafting body, the committee of articles. He did not appear on a privy council sederunt until December 1597, and only twice after that. On the last of these occasions, in April 1602, the council was meeting at Brechin for local judicial business. Bizarrely, Campbell was denounced rebel, for failure to conform to a horning for debt, by the very council on which he was himself sitting!

Campbell married twice. His first wife was Margaret Bethune, daughter of the laird of Circlet, and his second was Helen Clephane, who survived him along with two daughters and a son. He resigned his see on 22 April 1607 and retired to 'his place of Carco' in the parish of Kinclaven, Perthshire, where he died in February 1608.

ALAN R. MACDONALD

Sources *Fasti Scot.*, new edn, vol. 7 • T. Thomson, ed., *Acts and proceedings of the general assemblies of the Kirk of Scotland*, 3 pts, Bannatyne Club, 81 (1839–45) • R. Keith and J. Spottiswoode, *An historical catalogue of the Scottish bishops, down to the year 1688*, new edn, ed. M. Russel [M. Russell] (1824) • *The autobiography and diary of Mr James Melvill*, ed. R. Pitcairn, Wodrow Society (1842) • T. M'Crie, *The life of Andrew Melville*, 2nd edn, 2 vols. (1824) • P. Chalmers, J. I. Chalmers, and C. Innes, eds., *Registrum episcopatus Brechinensis*, 2 vols., Bannatyne Club, 102 (1856) • *Reg. PCS*, 1st ser. • *APS*, *1424–1625* • J. Kirk, ed., *The books of assumption of the thirds of benefices: Scottish ecclesiastical rentals at the Reformation* (1995) • Edinburgh commissary court register of testaments, NA Scot., CC8/8/44 • J. Kirk, *Patterns of reform: continuity and change in the Reformation kirk* (1989)

Wealth at death £868 Scots: NA Scot., Edinburgh commissary court records, register of testaments, NA Scot., CC8/8/44, 24 June 1608

Campbell, Sir Alexander, the younger, of Cawdor (*d.* **1697**). *See under* Campbell family of Cawdor (*per.* 1511–1821).

Campbell, Alexander, of Fonab and Monzie (*c.***1660–1724**), army officer, born in Perthshire, was the second but eldest surviving son of Robert Campbell, minister of Moulin, who had bought the Fonab estate, and his wife, Jean, second daughter of Duncan Menzies of Weem. His grandfather was Archibald Campbell of Lagvinshoch and Monzie, son of Sir Duncan Campbell of Glenorchy, a powerful member of the clan Campbell élite. There is no record of his early life or education but we know from his tombstone at Edinample (no longer extant) that he was in Belgium in 1690 as a member of the earl of Argyll's regiment of foot. In 1693 he is recorded as receiving a commission as captain in the same regiment, and is known to have been in Flanders in 1695, and in Holland in 1697, before being reduced to half pay the following year.

Some time between 1692 and 1699, having inherited his father's estate, Alexander Campbell, known as Fonab, married his cousin Susan Menzies of Weem, widow of Lord Neil Campbell of Ardmaddie, with whom he had a daughter, Jean. It was at this period in his life that he established himself as a hero in a time of national outrage and humiliation. In October 1699 he was appointed a counsellor of the Company of Scotland Trading to Africa and the Indies—a company which Scots investors hoped would challenge the English trade monopoly and revive the depressed Scottish economy by establishing Scotland's own trading colony in the Americas. He immediately proceeded to New Caledonia, Panama, to help establish the second expedition by defending it against Spanish attack. Arriving in New Caledonia on 2 February 1700, and hearing of the proposed Spanish attack on the colony by both land and sea, three days later, Fonab, along with Lieutenant Robert Turnbull, 200 Scotsmen, and sixty native Indians marched through almost impenetrable forests, jungle, and swamps to confront the Spaniards at Toubacanti. Although greatly outnumbered, and despite being wounded in the shoulder, Fonab led the Scots to victory thanks to his leadership and courage. Notwithstanding this moment of glory, misfortune continued to dog the colonists, and New Caledonia was shortly afterwards abandoned by the Scots. Fonab returned to Scotland in July 1700 where he was honoured as a national hero. The Company of Scotland commissioned a gold medal to be struck for him with the company's arms on the obverse, and a classical figure leading an attack upon the Spanish stockade on the reverse. In addition, his coat of arms was overlaid by that of the Company of Scotland, the only person to receive this distinction.

Fonab continued his career as a soldier. He was appointed captain of an independent company of foot for preserving the peace in the highlands in July 1701. He was a commissioner of supply in 1702 and 1704, and one of the duke of Argyll's five dependants who managed his estates in Scotland. He was appointed a brevet lieutenant-colonel in 1703. At the time of the Jacobite rising of 1715 Fonab is listed as a freeholder and heritor of Argyll; as a protestant and a member of the clan Campbell, he fought on the government side to support the Hanoverian succession. His dislike of fighting fellow Scots and neighbouring clansmen led to his part in the 'Fifteen being misconstrued by the earl of Ilay as displaying conflicting loyalties.

On 1 March 1719, his first wife having died, Fonab married Mary Home, daughter of Sir John Home of Blackadder, and with her had three children. He died on 16 September 1724 and was buried at Kilmun, Argyll. His son and heir by his second marriage, Robert, later removed Fonab's remains to Edinample on Loch Earn, Perthshire, where he erected a tombstone; his widow was still living in 1739. LINDA G. FRYER

Sources Marchioness of Tullibardine [K. M. Stewart-Murray, duchess of Atholl], ed., *A military history of Perthshire, 1660–1902*, 2 vols. (1908), 43–7, 372–6 • A. Nisbet, *A system of heraldry speculative and practical*, 1 (1722), 199–201, pl. 6 • H. Campbell, Campbell genealogies, Lyon Office, Edinburgh, 1.126 • G. P. Insh, *The Company of Scotland trading to Africa and the Indies* (1932), 184–97 • J. H. Burton, ed., *The Darien papers*, Bannatyne Club, 90 (1849), 176 • J. B. Paul, ed., *An ordinary of arms contained in the public register of all arms & bearings in Scotland* (1893) • *Scots peerage* • F. Borland, *Memoirs of Darien giving a short description of the countrey, with an account of the attempts of the Company of Scotland, to settle a colonie in that place … written mainly in the year 1700, while the author was in the American region* (1715), 59–60 • D. Campbell, ed., *The clan Campbell: abstracts relating Campbells from various sources*, 2nd edn (1916), 4.311 • Inveraray Castle archives, Inveraray, Argyll, service of Campbell officers, Alexander folder; miscellaneous bundles, letters and lists from 1704, bundle 146/13; from 1715, bundle 45/11, 79/3, 91/184, and 156/1 • testament and inventory of goods and gear of Alexander Campbell of Fonab, 4/10/1739, NA Scot., register of testaments, CC8.8.102 • Dumfries House, Cumnock, Ayrshire, Bute archives, Loudoun and Rowallan deeds, letters written in 1715, bundle A546/344 /389/392/394/396 and /399 • Hunt. L., Loudoun Scottish Collection, letter boxes, LO 7859, 8304, 11308

Archives Hunt. L., Loudon Scottish collection, letter boxes LO 7859, 8304, 11308 • Inveraray Castle, Argyll, archives, service of Campbell officers, letters, lists, etc., bundles 146/13, 45/11, 79/3, 91/184, 156/1 • NA Scot., testament and inventory of goods and gear of Alexander Campbell of Fonab, 4/10/1739, register of testaments | Dumfries House, Cumnock, Ayrshire, Bute archives, Loudoun and Rowallan deeds, letters, bundle A546/344/389/392/394/396 & /399

Likenesses oils, *c.*1700, repro. in Insh, *The Company of Scotland trading to Africa and the Indies*, facing p. 201; formerly at Dunstaffnage Castle, Connell, Argyll; destroyed by fire • negative (after portrait), Scot. NPG

Wealth at death invested £15 in Copartnery of Freemen Burgesses of the Royal Burrows for Carrying on a Fishing Trade: NA Scot., register of testaments, CC8.8.102, fols. 222–3

Campbell, Sir Alexander, first baronet (**1760–1824**), army officer, was born on 20 August 1760, the fourth son of John Campbell of Baleed, Perthshire, of a branch of the Breadalbane Campbells, and his wife, Isabella, daughter of John Campbell of Barcaldine. He entered the army by purchasing an ensign's commission in the 1/1st (Royal) regiment on 1 November 1776, became a lieutenant in the same regiment on 25 December 1778, and then became a captain (by purchase) in the newly raised 97th foot on 13

April 1780. He embarked with the 97th as a marine officer on board the Channel Fleet under Vice-Admiral George Darby in September 1780, was at the first relief of Gibraltar in May 1781, and afterwards again served as a marine in Hyde Parker's fleet at the battle of the Dogger Bank on 5 August 1781. In March 1782 the 97th foot returned to Gibraltar, to reinforce the garrison, whence it eventually returned after the end of the 'great siege' in July 1783 and was disbanded at Hilsea barracks on 23 September. Campbell was placed on half pay. In 1783 he married Olympia Elizabeth Morshead (*d.* 24 Dec 1794), eldest daughter of William Morshead of Cartuther, Cornwall, and sister of Sir John Morshead, baronet, of Trenant Park, Cornwall. They had three daughters (Olympia, Charlotte, and Amelia) and two sons, both of whom predeceased him. In 1787 four new regiments were raised specifically for service in India and Campbell was appointed a captain in the 74th (Argyll) highlanders with effect from 25 December 1787, and in 1793 went to India. He was promoted lieutenant-colonel of the regiment on 4 December 1795, and commanded it with distinction at the storming of Srirangapatnam on 4 May 1799. He held important commands in southern India, finally succeeding Sir Arthur Wellesley (later duke of Wellington) as governor of Srirangapatnam in 1805. He left India at the end of 1807.

On his return to the United Kingdom in 1808 Campbell was initially appointed a brigadier-general and placed on the staff in Ireland; then in January 1809 he went to Portugal as a brigade commander. Slightly wounded by grapeshot in the thigh at Talavera on 28 July 1809, while temporarily commanding the 4th division, he briefly returned home on sick leave and was appointed colonel of a penal unit incongruously called the York light infantry volunteers. Returning to the Peninsula in January 1810, he was promoted major-general on 25 July and transferred to the command of the new 6th division. He commanded the division at Fuentes d'Oñoro on 5 May 1811, but poor health compelled him to return home in December 1811. So he was fortuitously placed to stand proxy for Wellington at the latter's installation as a knight of the Bath and as such was himself knighted in 1812. On 9 March 1812 he was nominated commander-in-chief of the forces on the Indian Ocean islands of Mauritius and Bourbon, with the local rank of lieutenant-general, and he served there from January 1813 to August 1816. He was promoted substantive lieutenant-general on 4 June 1814. On 6 May 1815 he was created a baronet, and transferred to the more prestigious colonelcy of the 80th foot on 28 December 1815. On 6 December 1820 he was appointed commander-in-chief of the king's and East India Company's troops in the Madras presidency. He married, secondly, Elizabeth Anne (*d.* 20 Jan 1870), daughter of the Revd Thomas Pemberton; they had a son who died in infancy and a daughter, Flora Elizabeth (*b.* 1824). On 3 July 1821 Campbell obtained a renewed patent to the baronetcy, extending the limitation to his grandson, Alexander Cockburn, and after him to the male issue of his second daughter Isabella, Lady Malcolm. Campbell died on 11 December 1824 at Madras and was buried there. His elder son, Lieutenant John Morshead Campbell, was killed in action at Assaye in 1804, and the younger, Major Allan William Campbell, was fatally wounded at Sorauren, while temporarily attached to the Portuguese army, and died at Pamplona on 9 October 1813. He was succeeded by his grandson Alexander Thomas Cockburn, who in 1825 took the additional surname Campbell (making Cockburn-Campbell) and he and his descendants resided in Australia. STUART REID

Sources *GM*, 1st ser., 95/1 (1825), 564–7 · J. Philippart, ed., *The royal military calendar*, 3rd edn, 5 vols. (1820) · Burke, *Peerage* (1967) [see under Cockburn-Campbell of Gartsford] · D. Stewart, *Sketches of the character, manners, and present state of the highlanders of Scotland: with details of the military service of the highland regiments*, 2 vols. (1822) · *Army List* (1777–1825) · C. W. C. Oman, *A history of the Peninsular War*, 7 vols. (1902–30) · will, PRO, PROB 11/1701 · P. Griffith, 'The life of Sir Charles Oman', *Modern studies of the war in Spain and Portugal, 1808–1814*, ed. P. Griffith (1999), vol. 9 of C. W. C. Oman, *A history of the Peninsular War* (1902–99) · R. Muir, *Britain and the defeat of Napoleon, 1807–1815* (1996)

Wealth at death over £10,000: will, proved 21 Jan 1825

Campbell, Alexander (1764–1824), composer and writer, born on 22 February 1764 at Tombea, Loch Lubnaig, Perthshire, and first educated at the school in Callander, was the second son of a carpenter who moved to Edinburgh, where he died when Alexander was eleven years old. The family was supported by John (*d.* 1795), the eldest son, who was precentor at the Canongate church and a friend of Burns. The two brothers were pupils of the castrato G. F. Tenducci, then teaching in Edinburgh, who helped to establish them both as musicians. Campbell was appointed organist to an episcopalian chapel in the neighbourhood of Nicolson Street. He also gave lessons in harpsichord and singing. Among his pupils were Walter Scott and his brothers, but the lads had no taste for the subject and the master had no patience. The result was that 'our neighbour, Lady Cunningham, sent to beg the boys might not all be flogged precisely at the same hour, as, though she had no doubt the punishment was deserved, the noise of the concord was really dreadful' (Lockhart, chap. 1). While a teacher Campbell published *Twelve Songs Set to Music* (1785?). These are of mixed quality, but his settings of 'The Mad Song' from Henry Mackenzie's *The Man of Feeling*, and 'An Address to the Nightingale' from James Beattie's *The Hermit* are of historical as well as musical interest; and Oliver Goldsmith's 'When Lovely Woman Stoops to Folly' inspired from Campbell a song which is still in the repertory. About this time he became engaged in a quarrel with the caricaturist John Kay, whom he ridiculed in a sketch. This procured him a place in Kay's *Portraits*, where he is represented turning a hand-organ while asses bray, a dog howls, a bagpipe is blown, and a saw is sharpened as an accompaniment (vol. 2, print 204).

Campbell married twice at a comparatively early age. His second wife was the widow of Ranald Macdonald of Keppoch. An attempt to change profession from music to medicine appears to have failed, as did a financially disastrous venture into farming. About the same time he wrote *Odes and Miscellaneous Poems, by a Student of Medicine at the University of Edinburgh* (1796), and also published some drawings of highland scenery. Campbell's next work was

An Introduction to the History of Poetry in Scotland (1798). This contains a collection of Scottish songs; it was illustrated by David Allen, and dedicated to Henry Fuseli. It is written in a curiously stilted style, but contains much information about contemporary poets and poetasters and stoutly argues for the authenticity of James Macpherson's Ossian. Campbell then produced *A Journey from Edinburgh through Parts of North Britain* (n.d. [1816]), which he also illustrated. This is an interesting and even valuable picture of the state of many parts of the country at the beginning of the century. It was followed by *The Grampians Desolate, a Poem in Six Books* (1804). More than half of this work, which is without literary merit, consists of notes. Its object was to call attention to the 'deplorable condition' of the highlands, brought about by the introduction of sheep-farming, and is an interesting and early protest against the rural depopulation of the highlands. After some interval there appeared *Albyn's anthology, or, A select collection of the melodies and vocal poetry of Scotland, peculiar to Scotland and the Isles, hitherto unpublished* (2 vols., 1816 and 1818). Campbell had projected this work since 1790, but it was not until Henry Mackenzie, Walter Scott (who obtained the prince regent's acceptance of the dedication of the book), and other Edinburgh men of note gave him their help that the project was carried out. A grant was obtained from the Highland Society, and the author travelled between 1100 and 1200 miles in collecting materials. The publication was a success, though a projected third volume never appeared. The work is important on several counts: as an early example of Gaelic texts published with the music; for its inclusion of piobaireachd songs; and for its information and comments on early publications of Scottish music. It is also noteworthy for Campbell's publication and claim to authorship of the tune later made famous by Robert Tannahill's verses 'Gloomy winter's noo awa''. It is this tune which forms the substance of Michael Nyman's score for the film *The Piano* (1992), which earned an Oscar for its music. Campbell's claim has been disputed; but though his tune resembles an older traditional melody, there is sufficient change of character in it for Campbell to deserve the credit.

In the last years of his life Campbell fell into great poverty, and obtained his living chiefly by copying manuscripts for his old pupil Scott, though 'even from his patron he would take no more than he thought his services as a transcriber fairly earned'. At Abbotsford Campbell was known as the 'Dunnie-wassail'. He died from an attack of apoplexy on 15 May 1824 at his lodgings, 1 Adam Street, Edinburgh. His manuscripts were sold 'under judicial authority'. Among them was a tragedy, which was never published.

Campbell was a warm-hearted and accomplished, though somewhat unpractical, man. An obituary notice of him in the *Edinburgh Weekly Journal* says that, though his acquirements were considerable, 'they did not reach that point of perfection which the public demand of those who expect to derive bread from the practice of the fine arts'. FRANCIS WATT, *rev.* JOHN PURSER

Sources Anderson, *Scot. nat.*, 576–7 • H. G. Farmer, *A history of music in Scotland* (1947), 260–61, 339–40 • J. G. Lockhart, *Memoirs of the life of Sir Walter Scott*, 7 vols. (1837–8) • *Edinburgh Weekly Journal* (May 1824) • Chambers, *Scots.*, rev. T. Thomson (1875) • J. Kay, 'Portraits', BL, Department of Prints and Drawings
Archives NL Scot., chronological notes • U. Edin. L., special collections division, corresp. and papers | NL Scot., corresp. with Archibald Constable • U. Glas., Farmer MSS | SOUND Scottish Music Information Centre [recording of 'When lovely woman stoops to folly']
Likenesses J. Kay, etching, BM

Campbell, Alexander (1788–1866), a founder of the Disciples of Christ or Churches of Christ, was born on 12 September 1788 near Ballymena, co. Antrim, the eldest of the ten children of Thomas Campbell (1763–1854), an Anti-Burgher Seceder Presbyterian minister, and his wife, Jane Corneigle. He was educated at the elementary school in Market Hill and then at his uncles' academy in Newry, completing his education under his father, who had become minister of a church in Ahorey, co. Armagh, in 1798. His father introduced him to Locke's *Letter Concerning Toleration* and *Essay on Human Understanding* at an early date. In 1805 he became assistant in the academy in Rich Hill, which his father had opened to supplement his income. Thomas Campbell was criticized by the Anti-Burgher synod for joining the committee of the Evangelical Society of Ulster, and his work for the union of the Anti-Burgher and Burgher synods and for the independence of the Irish synod from Scotland was unsuccessful. His health began to fail, and Alexander joined with other friends and neighbours in persuading him to emigrate to the USA in 1807.

In October 1808 the rest of the Campbell family sailed from Londonderry for America, but were shipwrecked off the Isle of Islay. They spent the winter of 1808–9 in Glasgow, where Alexander attended classes at the university. He also met Greville Ewing, a Scottish Congregational minister, who persuaded him of the merits of Independent church order and the weekly celebration of the Lord's Supper, and Robert and James Haldane, who had initiated a movement for itinerant preaching in Scotland.

On 3 August 1809 the family left Glasgow for America, arriving in New York on 29 September, and joined Thomas at Washington, in south-western Pennsylvania. Thomas had been censured by the Associate Synod of North America for admitting non-Seceders to communion, and had withdrawn from their fellowship in May 1809. On 17 August, twenty-one people formed the Christian Association of Washington as an agency for the restoration of the unity of the church on the basis of the New Testament, and in September Thomas Campbell wrote his *Declaration and Address* to explain the principles of the new body. On 4 May 1811 the association constituted itself a church, and adopted congregational church government and the weekly celebration of the Lord's Supper. Thomas was chosen elder and Alexander licensed to preach the gospel. A meeting-house was built at Brush Run, and Alexander Campbell was ordained to the ministry there on 1 January 1812.

Campbell had married Margaret Brown (*d.* 1827), only

Alexander Campbell (1788–1866), by unknown photographer, 1858

daughter of John Brown, a local carpenter and millwright, on 2 March 1811. When their first child, Jane, was born on 13 March 1812 Campbell studied the biblical basis for infant baptism and concluded that the immersion of believers was the only scriptural baptism. On 12 June 1812 Campbell and his wife, his father, mother, and sister were immersed in Buffalo Creek by a Baptist preacher, Matthias Luce, and most of the Brush Run congregation were subsequently baptized as believers. In 1815 the congregation joined the Redstone Baptist Association, and shortly after that his father-in-law gave Campbell the family farm, which became the basis for his subsequent financial independence.

Campbell's association with the Baptists lasted until 1830. In his *Sermon on the Law* of 1816 he denied that it was necessary to preach the law in order to prepare people to receive the gospel. In 1820 and 1823 he held public debates on baptism with John Walker, a Secession minister, and W. L. Maccalla, a Kentucky Presbyterian. These debates made his reputation as a public controversialist, and led to later debates in 1829 with Robert Owen on the evidences of Christianity, in 1837 with Bishop John Purcell of Cincinnati on Roman Catholicism, and in 1843 with N. L. Rice on baptism, conversion and sanctification, and the place of creeds as terms of communion. In 1823 he also began his career as an editor, with the publication of the monthly *Christian Baptist*, through which he sought to persuade Baptists to accept his views on church order and baptism, and in particular that baptism for the remission of sins was essential to salvation.

Thus far Campbell's movement, the Disciples, or Churches, of Christ, had concentrated mainly on theological controversy and had not attracted a large following. This began to change in 1827 when Walter Scott was appointed an itinerant preacher in the Western Reserve, and the Disciples began to benefit from the westward movement of the frontier. In 1832 they united with Barton W. Stone's (1772–1844) Christian Connection in Kentucky and the south, a revival movement with Presbyterian roots and a concern for the unity of all Christians on the basis of primitive Christianity. The decade which followed was one of rapid expansion. Campbell had started a new magazine in 1830, the *Millennial Harbinger*, with a milder tone and a broader programme, which he edited until 1865. He believed that by a 'restoration of the ancient order of things' it would be possible to unite all Christians on the basis of the New Testament: thus he regarded his movement as a harbinger of the millennium, which would precede the personal coming of Christ. Furthermore he believed that by avoiding theological speculation (and in particular the use of non-scriptural terms) agreement could be reached on the facts of the gospel, which included not only the death and resurrection of Christ but also faith, repentance, baptism, remission of sins, reception of the Holy Spirit, sanctification, the resurrection, and eternal life. Here his debt to Locke was apparent. These themes were expounded in *Christianity Restored* (1835), subsequently revised as *The Christian System* (1839).

On 2 March 1840 Campbell was granted a charter by the Virginia state legislature for Bethany College, which he built near his home. He became its president, and a faculty of professors in arts and sciences was established. It opened on 1 November 1841, and was the first liberal arts college in western Virginia.

From May to October 1847 Campbell visited Great Britain. He spoke in most of the leading towns where Churches of Christ had been established from the mid-1830s, including Liverpool, Manchester, Nottingham, Leicester, and London. During his visit to Edinburgh the Scottish Anti-Slavery Society accused him of being a defender of slavery. His response led to a charge of libel, but he preferred to spend ten days in prison rather than give a bail bond, before the case was dismissed on appeal. He also revisited Ireland before presiding at the second conference of the British Churches of Christ at Chester on 1 October.

In the 1850s Campbell continued his writing and preaching, and after the fire of 1857 was involved in raising money for the rebuilding of Bethany College, modelled architecturally on the old buildings of the University of Glasgow. His final years were saddened by the civil war and he died at Bethany, West Virginia, on 4 March 1866, where he was buried in the family graveyard. His second wife, Selina Huntington Bakewell, whom he had married on 31 July 1828 after the death of his first wife on 22 October 1827, survived him, dying on 28 June 1897. Campbell was about 6 feet tall, with a full head of dark hair which turned white in later years. In 1874, within ten years of Campbell's death, the Disciples of Christ had 400,000 members; by 1900 there were over a million and they had become a permanent part of the international religious scene. DAVID M. THOMPSON

Sources R. Richardson, *Memoirs of Alexander Campbell*, 2 vols. (1870) • S. Campbell, *Home life and reminiscences of Alexander Campbell* (1882) • J. M. Seale, ed., *Lectures in honor of the Alexander Campbell bicentennial* (1988) • R. F. West, *Alexander Campbell and natural religion* (1948) • L. G. McAllister, *Thomas Campbell, man of the book* (1954) • W. H. Cramblet, *The Christian Church (Disciples of Christ) in West Virginia* (1971) • H. L. Lunger, *The political ethics of Alexander Campbell* (1954) • D. R. Lindley, *Apostle of freedom* (1957)

Archives Bethany College, West Virginia | Disciples of Christ Historical Society, Nashville, Tennessee

Likenesses photograph, 1858, Bethany College, West Virginia [*see illus.*] • portrait, priv. coll.

Wealth at death family legacies plus $15,000 to Bethany College and for support of preaching

Campbell, Alexander (1796–1870), Owenite socialist and journalist, was born near the point of Skipness, in Kintyre, Argyll. He was apprenticed as a joiner in Glasgow and set up his own business, which he pursued with some success. He was influenced early in his life by the ideas of Robert Owen and became involved with the ill-fated Orbiston community established by Archibald Hamilton and Abram Combe in 1825. When that disintegrated in 1828, Campbell, having made himself liable for some of its debts, was imprisoned in Hamilton gaol.

After release Campbell's enthusiasm for Owenite socialism led him to take part in the establishment of the first co-operative society in Glasgow (1829) and an associated bazaar (1830) where exchanges took place on the basis of labour equivalents; the ultimate aim was to secure the capital necessary for the formation of a co-operative community. He also published *An Address on the Progress of the Co-operative System* (1831), which, he was to argue, envisioned the 'Rochdale pioneer' idea of a dividend on purchases from co-operative stores.

It was in the early 1830s too that Campbell, like many Owenites, became involved with an increasingly militant trade unionism. In the autumn of 1831 he was instrumental in establishing a general union, the Glasgow and West of Scotland Association for the Protection of Labour (which became the General Union of Glasgow). He was also, on occasion, referred to as secretary of an embryonic trades council, the Glasgow United Committee of Trades, which had been established in 1830. It is possible too that he edited its newspaper, the *Herald to the Trades Advocate* (September 1830 – May 1831), one of the liveliest of the unstamped papers of the period.

It was his involvement with the unstamped press which led to Campbell's prosecution in the court of exchequer in Edinburgh in the summer of 1834. He was found guilty and although not immediately imprisoned was gaoled for seven weeks shortly afterwards for non-payment of the resulting fines and expenses. An account of this is provided in his *Trial and Self-Defence of A. Campbell* (1835).

In the late 1830s Campbell was associated with the political agitation which resulted from working-class frustration following the passage of the 1832 Reform Act. He was also involved with the mass demonstrations against the Poor Law Amendment Act (1834) and with a committee of trades delegates created in 1837 to help the leaders of the Cotton Spinners' Union arrested in the strike of that year. Most importantly, in 1838 he was appointed by the Association of All Classes of All Nations as a 'social missionary' to preach the Owenite gospel. This he did for the next two years, taking part in many public debates and earning the encomium 'Owen's principal Scottish disciple' (Marwick, 11). It was during this proselytizing period that Campbell came to be profoundly influenced by the ascetic transcendentalism and Pestalozzian educational principles of James Pierrepont Greaves, two volumes of whose letters and manuscripts Campbell was to publish in November 1843.

In 1848 Campbell became editor of the *Spirit of the Age* and in addition ran the Canadian Land and Railway Investment Association (also supported by Robert Owen), which aimed to promote working-class investment in railway developments in New Brunswick. In 1856, after a period in Oxford earlier in the decade, he returned to Glasgow and became editor of a paper, the *Weekly Chronicle*, concerned with trade union affairs. This subsequently became the *Glasgow Sentinel*, of which Campbell was the industrial reporter. Journalistic activity was once more combined with support for co-operation and, in particular, for producer co-operatives such as the West of Scotland Painting Company (1860). However, Campbell was involved, too, in a conference (April 1864) concerned with co-operative wholesaling, which ultimately led to the formation in September 1868 of the Scottish Co-operative Wholesale Society.

As in the 1830s, all this was combined with trade union activity, with Campbell assisting in the re-creation of the Glasgow Trades Council (1858), a body which campaigned, with Campbell's active support, for the repeal of the master and servant laws. It was in connection with this agitation that a national conference of trade union delegates took place in May 1864 (Campbell attending as one of the Glasgow representatives), which some subsequent commentators have seen as presaging the first Trades' Union Congress of 1868 (Webb and Webb, 235). Campbell died at his home, 11 North Coburg Street, Glasgow, on 10 February 1870, and was buried four days later in the city's southern necropolis. He was married with six children, but very little is known about his family life.

NOEL THOMPSON

Sources W. H. Marwick, *The life of Alexander Campbell* (1964) • W. H. Fraser, *Alexander Campbell and the search for socialism* (1996) • J. F. C. Harrison, *Robert Owen and the Owenites in Britain and America: the quest for the new moral world* (1969) • J. A. Flanagan, *Wholesale co-operation in Scotland: the fruits of fifty years' efforts, 1868–1918* (1920) • G. J. Holyoake, *The history of co-operation*, 2 (1906), 36–7 • G. D. H. Cole, *Attempts at general union: a study of British trade union history, 1818–1834* (1953) • S. J. Webb, B. P. Webb, and R. A. Peddie, *The history of trade unionism* (1894) • A. Cullen, *Adventures in socialism, New Lanark establishment and Orbiston community* (1910) • F. Podmore, *Robert Owen: a biography*, 2 vols. (1906) • G. D. H. Cole, *The life of Robert Owen*, 2nd edn (1930) • W. Maxwell, *The history of co-operation in Scotland* (1910) • D. Simon, 'Master and servant', *Democracy and the Labour movement*, ed. J. Saville (1954) • J. Saville, 'Campbell, Alexander', *DLB*, vol. 1

Archives Co-operative Union Library, Holyoake House, Manchester, Robert Owen corresp.
Likenesses J. K. Hunter, portrait, Co-operative Union, Glasgow

Campbell, Sir Alexander (1822–1892), lawyer and politician in Canada, born in Hedon, near Kingston upon Hull, Yorkshire, on 9 March 1822, was the son of James Campbell, a physician of Scottish parentage, and his wife, Lavinia Scatcherd. After living for some time in Yorkshire, in 1823 the family emigrated to Lower Canada. The Campbells lived in Montreal until 1832, then in Lachine, Quebec, until 1836, and then in Kingston, Upper Canada. Alexander Campbell was educated first by the Presbyterian minister at Lachine, then, with his brother Charles, in the Roman Catholic seminary of St Hyacinthe, and finally at Kingston grammar school. He began to study law in Kingston, and in 1839 became the second student articled to John A. Macdonald. He was called to the bar in 1843 and was thereupon taken into partnership by Macdonald. In 1856 he became queen's counsel and a bencher of the Law Society. Four years later he was appointed dean of the faculty of law in Queen's University, Kingston.

Campbell's first public office was that of alderman of Victoria ward, Kingston (1851–2). In 1856 Canada began to elect legislative councillors, and Campbell, standing for the district of Cataraqui, which included Kingston and the county of Frontenac, was returned by a large majority in 1858. He was then offered, but declined, a seat in the Macdonald–Cartier cabinet. In February 1863 he became speaker of the legislative council in succession to Sir Allan Napier Macnab and performed the duties of the office for about a year, when he entered the Macdonald–Taché administration as commissioner of crown lands. He held the same position in the coalition of 1864, the principal object of which was to bring about confederation. He took part in both the Charlottetown and Quebec conferences. In March 1865 he submitted the resolutions in favour of the Canadian federation to the council, and secured their passage by a large vote.

During 1866–7, when the governor-general and the leading members of the ministry were at the Westminster conference, Campbell stayed in Canada as minister in charge. At the inauguration of the dominion, on 1 July 1867, he was sworn of the privy council of Canada, and became the first postmaster-general, a portfolio which he held for the next six years. Summoned to the senate on 23 October 1867, he remained there for twenty years, acting, while the Conservative Party was in power, as government leader in that body. In 1870 he undertook a special mission to England to discuss Canadian import duties, which were then in dispute between England and the United States, and were dealt with by the Washington treaty of 1870. A new department of the interior and the office of superintendent of Indian affairs were created in 1872 and given to Campbell, but his incumbency was brief. In November of that year the ministry resigned. With the fall of the government, Campbell had time to pursue interests other than law and politics. He became very active in business and served as a director or officer of a series of firms, including the Isolated Risk Fire Insurance Company, the Kingston and Pembroke Railway, the London and Canadian Loan and Agency Company, the Intercolonial Express Company, and the Toronto branch of the Consolidated Bank.

From 1873 to 1878 Campbell led the Conservative opposition in the senate and took a very active part against the Mackenzie administration, particularly with regard to its Pacific Railway policy. After Macdonald returned to power in 1878, Campbell was appointed in succession receiver-general (8 November 1878), postmaster-general (20 May 1879), minister of militia (16 January 1880), postmaster-general (8 November 1880), and minister of justice (20 May 1881); he held the office of postmaster-general once again from 25 September 1885 to 26 January 1887. In each post he proved a painstaking administrator.

Campbell's most important department was that of justice. In exercising the dominion supervision over local legislation, a power inherited from the Colonial Office, Campbell was considered to take an unduly narrow view of the powers of the provincial legislatures as they were defined under the British North America Act. Two of his decisions aroused much public excitement. One was the disallowance on three occasions (in 1881, 1882, and 1883) of a railway measure by which the provincial legislature of Manitoba sought independent connection with the United States system. The province ultimately secured its end, for which the Canadian Pacific Railway Company was compensated. The second was when the legislature of British Columbia levied certain fines on the immigration of the Chinese. Campbell disallowed the act on imperial as well as on dominion grounds (1883). A later dispatch from Lord Derby (31 May 1884) asserted that similar legislation in Australia did not involve imperial interests. The legislature of British Columbia thereupon re-enacted the statute, which came into operation in 1885.

It is almost certainly the case that Campbell's most important political function was in the field of Conservative Party management. He managed several of Macdonald's campaigns in Kingston and intervened in numerous other ridings between the Ottawa River and Toronto. He encouraged candidates and offered advice, raised campaign funds, disciplined insufficiently partisan civil servants, convinced men of their duty to work in campaigns, appealed to religious leaders, and attempted to restrain factionalism. It is clear why Senator John Hamilton referred, in a letter of 2 August 1872 to Campbell, to those elections 'which you manipulate in Kingston' (John Hamilton to Alexander Campbell, 2 Aug 1872, Campbell MSS, Archives of Ontario, Toronto).

The honour of KCMG was bestowed on Campbell on 24 May 1879. In 1885 he married Georgina Frederica Locke, the daughter of Thomas Sandwith of Beverley in Yorkshire. They had two sons and three daughters. On 1 June 1887 Campbell was appointed lieutenant-governor of Ontario. He died on 24 May 1892, just before the expiry of his term, at Government House in Toronto, and was buried in Kingston with public honours.

T. B. Browning, *rev.* Donald Swainson

Sources *In memoriam: Sir Alexander Campbell* [1892] • M. K. Christie, 'Sir Alexander Campbell', MA diss., University of Toronto, 1950 • D. Swainson, 'Alexander Campbell: general manager of the conservative party (eastern Toronto section)', *Historic Kingston*, 17 (1969), 78–92 • J. O. Cote, ed., *Political appointments and elections in the province of Canada, from 1841 to 1865* (1866) • N. O. Cote, ed., *Political appointments, parliaments and the judicial bench in the dominion of Canada, 1867–1895* (1896) • A. Campbell, *Speeches on divers occasions* (1885) • *Parliamentary debates on the subject of the confederation of the British North American provinces* (1865); repr. (Ottawa, 1951) • *Senate debates, 1871–1887* • J. Pope, *Memoirs of the Right Honourable Sir John Alexander Macdonald*, 2 vols. (1894) • H. J. Morgan, ed., *The Canadian parliamentary companion*, 11 vols. (1862–76) • J. C. Dent, *The last forty years: Canada since the union of 1841*, 2 vols. (1881) • D. G. Creighton, *John A. Macdonald*, 2 vols. (Toronto, 1952–5) • *DNB* • *DCB*, vol. 12 • private information (2004)

Archives Public Archives of Ontario, Toronto | NA Canada, Macdonald MSS

Campbell, Alexander Hume, second earl of Marchmont (**1675–1740**), politician, was born Alexander Hume, the third and eldest surviving son of Sir Patrick *Hume (1641–1724) of Polwarth, first earl of Marchmont, politician and landowner, and Grizel, daughter of Sir Thomas Ker of Cavers. The family were staunch whigs and Presbyterians and were exiled to the Netherlands after the Rye House plot of 1683. They returned with William of Orange at the revolution. Hume spent two or three years at the University of Utrecht, where he studied civil law. It was his intention to follow the legal profession, and on 25 July 1696 he was admitted to the Faculty of Advocates. On 29 July 1697 he married Margaret (*d.* 1722), heir of Sir George Campbell of Cessnock, Ayrshire, whereupon he changed his name to Campbell; the couple had four sons and four daughters. He was knighted as Sir Alexander Campbell of Cessnock in 1697.

Campbell was parliamentary commissioner for Kirkwall, 1698–1702. On 16 October 1704 he was appointed an ordinary lord of session, in the place of Sir Colin Campbell, Lord Aberuchill, and took his seat on the bench on 7 November as Lord Cessnock. In April 1706 he was elected as one of the commissioners for Berwickshire, and sat in the last Scottish parliament, which met for its final session in the following October. He zealously supported the Union, and took an active share in the work of the subcommittee to which the articles of the Union were referred. When in 1709 his eldest brother, Lord Polwarth, died, he assumed his title.

In 1712 Polwarth went to Hanover, where his correspondence with the electoral family was the means of contradicting the eagerly circulated report that the elector was indifferent to the succession to the British throne. In 1714 he resigned his seat on the bench in favour of his younger brother, Sir Andrew Hume of Kimmerghame. He was made lord lieutenant of Berwickshire in 1715, and at the Jacobite rising raised 400 of the Berwickshire militia for the Hanoverian side.

In May 1716 Polwarth was appointed envoy-extraordinary and in 1720 ambassador-extraordinary to the court of Copenhagen, where he remained until the spring of 1721. From December 1716 to 1733 he held the office of lord clerk register of Scotland, and from 1722 to 1725 was one of the British ambassadors to the Congress of Cambrai. On his father's death on 1 August 1724 he succeeded to the earldom and changed his surname to Hume Campbell. On 10 March 1725, at Cambrai, Lord Whitworth invested him with the Order of the Thistle. In 1726 he was sworn of the privy council of Great Britain and in 1727 was elected one of the Scottish representative peers. From 1728 until his death he was a governor of the Bank of Scotland. In 1733, with other Scottish nobles, he joined the 'patriot' opposition to Sir Robert Walpole's excise scheme, hoping to overthrow Ilay's management of Scotland by joining forces with English critics of the scheme.

Although the bill was dropped, its opponents were not forgotten by Walpole, and in May 1733 Marchmont was dismissed from his office of lord clerk register. The following year he was not re-elected as a representative peer. He took an active part in the attempt to incriminate the government for interference in the election of the Scottish peers, which, however, was not successful. He died in London on 27 February 1740, aged sixty-four, and was buried on 17 March in Canongate churchyard, Edinburgh. He was succeeded by his third son, Hugh Hume *Campbell (1708–1794), through whom the barony of Polwarth descended to Hugh Scott of Harden.

G. F. R. Barker, *rev.* Mairianna Birkeland

Sources GEC, *Peerage* • R. M. Sunter, *Patronage and politics in Scotland, 1707–1832* (1986) • W. Ferguson, *Scotland: 1689 to the present* (1968); pbk edn (1978) • R. Wodrow, *Analecta, or, Materials for a history of remarkable providences, mostly relating to Scotch ministers and Christians*, ed. [M. Leishman], 4 vols., Maitland Club, 60 (1842–3) • G. Donaldson and R. S. Morpeth, *A dictionary of Scottish history* (1977) • *Report on the manuscripts of Lord Polwarth*, 5 vols., HMC, 67 (1911–61) • 'Characters of the late and present earls of Marchmont', *Scots Magazine*, 2 (1740), 94, 99–101

Archives BL, register of letters, Add. MS 37993 • NA Scot., corresp. and papers | BL, corresp. with Charles Whitworth, Add. MSS 37364–37397 • NRA Scotland, letters to William Hall • NRA Scotland, priv. coll., letters to Lady Grizell Baillie

Likenesses oils, Scot. NPG

Campbell, Alexander Hume (**1708–1760**). *See under* Campbell, Hugh Hume, third earl of Marchmont (1708–1794).

Campbell, Alison (*d.* **1608**), minister's wife, was the daughter of an Ayrshire laird, James Campbell of Stevenston (*fl.* 1542–1581). Soon after the Reformation (1560) she married, at some date after August 1560, William Kirkpatrick (*d.* 1577), former monk of Kilwinning Abbey, Ayrshire, and first minister of Kilwinning. Both families had connections with others in Ayrshire protestant circles in the 1550s: the Campbells with those of the earls of Glencairn and the Campbells of Loudoun, and the Kirkpatricks with leading families in the burgh of Ayr where a reformed church took shape in the late 1550s. William Kirkpatrick was sufficiently familiar with protestant doctrine to be made a minister, not simply a reader, by March 1563.

At a time when the circumstances of first-generation families in protestant manses varied considerably, the Kirkpatricks were comfortable financially. The manse itself may have been makeshift, comprising the minister's former monk's chamber (communal monastic living having died out) and that of a colleague at the Greenfoot of Kilwinning, virtually within the abbey precincts. There Alison reared her three children Martha, Marion, and William, at one point boarding out a child with a family in the town of Kilwinning. She and her husband had a substantial income, however, although like similar incomes it had to be collected twice a year from the tenants and parishioners of Kilwinning. It consisted of an annual pension worth 20 bolls of grain, 12 stones of cheese, and £20 in money, granted to Alison and her husband in 1567 by the commendator (non-elected head) of Kilwinning Abbey, Gavin Hamilton of Raploch; the minister's stipend worth £100 a year, drawn from the parish teinds (tithes); and the liferent of his former monk's portion, to which all Scottish former monks continued to be entitled. The minister and his wife also leased his former monk's yard (garden) and cultivated and kept stock on the parish glebe. Their household furnishings valued at £240 compare with those of middle-ranking lairds, the kind of family from which Alison came. When the minister died in 1577 Alison was made joint executor with her father and brother. Plans were made to send her son, William, to university, funded by the sale of his father's books.

In marrying twice more Alison gave up her pioneering role of minister's wife and instead married two small proprietors. First Neil Montgomery, brother of the laird of Smithston (a branch of the earl of Eglinton's family), and, second, another Neil Montgomery, proprietor of the Greenfoot of Kilwinning. In 1581 she petitioned the privy council for tax exemption for the commendator's pension, of which she held the liferent. Her second husband died in 1591 'at the dwelling place of Doucathill', a house on the lands of her brother George Campbell of Stevenston where they may have gone to live (Edinburgh register of testaments, NA Scot., CC 8/8/23, fol. 22*v*). She moved back to Kilwinning on her third marriage, to the Greenfoot, where she had first set up house thirty years before and where she lived until her death on 23 August 1608.

Alison's testament provides a vignette of the growing settlement of Kilwinning at the turn of the seventeenth century and of the pattern of her own housekeeping. She continued to farm some land, paying labourers to cultivate it for her. She paid a woman to tend her garden. She had considerable quantities of bleached and unbleached linen in the house probably spun at home and woven locally. She bought from merchants in the neighbouring royal burgh of Irvine but used the services of a shoemaker, tailor, smith, baker, maltster, and flesher (butcher) in Kilwinning, as well as local fishermen and those who carried coal. She had one man and two women servants. One witness of her will was Mr Alexander Wreitton, schoolmaster and son of the second minister of Kilwinning. She was survived by her third husband (*d.* 1623) and by the two daughters of her first marriage; it is not known whether they were married. Her son, William, appears to have predeceased her.

MARGARET H. B. SANDERSON

Sources NA Scot., Edinburgh commissary court records, register of testaments, CC8/8/45, 18 July 1609; CC8/8/23, fol. 22*v*; CC9/7/19, 25 Oct 1623; CC8/8/9, fol. 265 • *Reg. PCS*, 1st ser., 3.409 • register of abbreviates of feu charters of kirklands, NA Scot., E14/2, fol. 54 • H. Paton, *Ayrshire* (1913–22), vol. 5 of *The clan Campbell* • particular register of sasines for Ayrshire, 24 Oct 1605, NA Scot. • J. M. Thomson and others, eds., *Registrum magni sigilli regum Scotorum / The register of the great seal of Scotland*, 11 vols. (1882–1914), vol. 3 • M. H. B. Sanderson, *Ayrshire and the Reformation* (1997)

Archives NA Scot., Edinburgh commissary court records, register of testaments

Wealth at death £1577 Scots: NA Scot., Edinburgh commissary court records, register of testaments, CC8/8/45, 18 July 1609

Campbell, Amabel Hume- [*née* Lady Amabel Yorke], ***suo jure*** **Countess De Grey (1751–1833)**, political writer, was born on 22 January 1751, the first of the two children of Philip *Yorke, second earl of Hardwicke (1720–1790), and his wife, Jemima *Yorke, *née* Campbell, *suo jure* Marchioness Grey and Baroness Lucas of Crudwell (1722–1797). Amabel grew up in the intense political and intellectual atmosphere of her parents' homes at Wrest Park, Bedfordshire, and St James's Square, Westminster. She was educated at home, and quickly became a voracious reader; her mother's friend, the scholar Catherine Talbot, said of her that, aged five, she 'has no joy but in books, and of those will not read little idle stories such as were first given to her, but picks out for herself. Her knowledge in geography and English history is astonishing' (Godber, 61). Horace Walpole later wrote that her sister, Mary, 'behaved like a human creature, and not like her sister or a college-tutor' (Walpole, *Corr.*, 33.242).

On 16 July 1772, at St James's, Westminster, Amabel married Alexander Hume-Campbell, Lord Polwarth (1750–1781), eldest surviving son of Hugh *Campbell, third earl of Marchmont, and his second wife, Elizabeth Crompton. It appears to have been a love match. Polwarth was interested in books but was a keen hunter too and also established a model farm on the Bedfordshire estate to which Amabel was coheir. In 1776 he was created Baron Hume of Berwick. In 1777 his health began to fail, and after a long decline he died on 9 March 1781. In her diary, kept from 1769 to 1827, Amabel mourned the loss of 'the friend & protector I had hop'd for' (diary, 9 March 1781, W. Yorks. AS, Acc 2299). She never married again, and in 1792 lamented that the death of an uncle 'contributes to throw me … still more & more out of the company of gentlemen' (ibid., 3 Dec 1792). She divided her time between Wrest Park in Bedfordshire, London, and (from 1791) her villa on Putney Heath, with London usually accounting for about half the year. On the death of her mother in 1797 she inherited the family houses at Wrest Park and 4 St James's Square, and the title Baroness Lucas of Crudwell. In 1816 she was created Countess De Grey of Wrest, Bedfordshire.

Amabel's diary and her correspondence reveal an intense interest in politics. It was a matter of lifelong frustration that, being a woman, she could not be elected to the Commons or, later, take her place in the House of Lords. She told her mother on 21 November 1775 that 'if I were in Parliament' she would certainly have voted for the Rockingham party's amendments to the Militia Bill (Bedfordshire and Luton Archives and Record Service, L30/9/60/69), and in 1811 she wrote:

Amabel Hume-Campbell, *suo jure* Countess De Grey (1751–1833), by unknown artist, *c.*1776

> I can only flutter & beat against the wires of my large gilded cage in St. James Square whilst I embody in my reveries an imaginary Marquis de Grey speaking in Parliament. But alas! when I wake from my day-dreams, I find out that my poor Marquis (with my soul in a manly form) would probably have had a bullet in the thorax … long ago for the vehemence of his speeches. (Bedfordshire and Luton Archives and Record Service, L30/24/68)

She described herself as 'an old English Whig' (A. Hume-Campbell, *An Historical Essay on … France*, 1797, 344), and her views were dominated by a desire not to upset the *status quo*. She noted that 'most Reformers, though their cause may be good, yet are dangerous from their rash & impracticable notions' (diary, 11 July 1792, W. Yorks. AS, Acc 2299).

In 1792 Amabel wrote *An Historical Sketch of the French Revolution from its Commencement to the Year 1792*, recording:

> It was conveyed by Mrs Barker's means, so privately to Mr. Debrett, that I flatter myself it never can be trac'd to me … there are some crises so important to society that the weakest individual is authorised to take a part. (diary, 1 June 1792, W. Yorks. AS, Acc 2299)

Other writers had failed to provide 'a concise historical statement of the principal facts, and of the constitutional questions and disputes which led to that awful and unparalleled event' (*Historical Sketch*, 1–2). She largely endorsed Burke's sentiments, but chided him for supporting the American revolution, of which the French Revolution was the 'natural offspring' (ibid.).

In 1796 Amabel wrote *An historical essay on the ambition and conquests of France, with some remarks on the French Revolution*, published in 1797, also anonymously. Her intention was 'to consider its [the French Revolution's] external relations with the other nations of Europe, and trace its remote connections with past events' (back to the fifteenth century). The Revolution was 'one means of attaining … that aim of universal empire, so often the terror of Europe' (pp. 1–2). Debrett also accepted a pamphlet she described as 'an appeal to the People of Britain', and 'desir'd that the unknown author would send any other work to him' (diary, 31 Dec 1797, W. Yorks. AS, Acc 2299). No other crisis provoked her to write until the assassination of Spencer Perceval in 1812, when she discussed the possibility of a pamphlet directly with John Hatchard. She died on 4 March 1833 at St James's Square, Westminster, and was buried at Flitton, Bedfordshire. She was succeeded in her titles and estates by her nephew Thomas Philip de Grey. DORIAN GERHOLD

Sources diary (27 vols.), 1769–1827, W. Yorks. AS, Leeds, Acc 2299 · GEC, *Peerage* · J. Godber, *The Marchioness Grey of Wrest Park*, Bedfordshire Historical RS, 47 (1968) · Wrest Park papers, Beds. & Luton ARS, L30

Archives Beds. & Luton ARS, corresp. · W. Yorks. AS, Leeds, diary, Acc 2299

Likenesses portrait, *c.*1776, NPG [*see illus.*] · portrait, repro. in Godber, *Marchioness Grey*, pl. IV; priv. coll.

Wealth at death under £60,000: PRO, death duty registers, IR 26/1316, fol. 250

Campbell, Archibald, second earl of Argyll (*d.* 1513), magnate, was the eldest son and heir of Colin *Campbell, first earl of Argyll (*d.* 1493), and Isabel (*d.* 1510), eldest daughter of John Stewart, third Lord Lorne. He probably followed his father during the rebellions of 1488–90, at first in opposition to James III and then in support of James IV. Consequently he received a royal grant of the lands of Auchintorlie in Dunbartonshire in free barony on 3 July 1489, and was able to succeed his father as earl on 10 May 1493. Thereafter he would continue his father's career in acting both as a leading Gaelic magnate and as a key player in royal government and at court.

Argyll's inherited political and regional influence was initially undermined by the assumption of the chancellorship by Archibald Douglas, fifth earl of Angus, in January 1493, and by the forfeiture to the crown of the MacDonald lordship of the Isles in May–June 1493 (the heir to which, Donald Dubh, was Argyll's nephew and captive). The forfeiture was enforced by a royal expedition to Dunstaffnage in Lorne, Argyll, in August 1493 when James IV (with Angus) confirmed MacDonald grants to the islesmen; Argyll was absent from this expedition and from the royal council in 1493–5.

But following James IV's assertion of his independent authority Argyll became master of the king's household (24 March 1495), a regular royal council member, and a lord of council in civil causes. As bailie of the royal lordship of Cowal and keeper of Dunoon Castle, Argyll, he accompanied James IV's expedition to Ardnamurchan, Argyll, in May 1495, and his renewed influence at court probably precipitated a more coercive crown policy towards the former lordship of the Isles. As a lord of council he helped to pass an act on 26 April 1496 decreeing that royal summonses issued in the former lordship should be enforced by clan chiefs, failing which chiefs would be prosecuted. In 1499 Sir John MacDonald of Dunyvaig, former lord of the Isles, and his sons were executed in Edinburgh. In August of that year Argyll was made sheriff, justiciar, coroner, bailie, and chamberlain of the royal lordship of Knapdale and keeper of Tarbert Castle, Argyll. By 25 April 1500 he had a three-year commission of lieutenancy over the former lordship of the Isles, excepting Kintyre and Islay, with powers to set lands in lordship, make and enforce statutes in the king's name, execute or pardon rebels, and besiege castles.

Yet the king appears to have been reluctant to give too much power to any one magnate, and especially to Argyll. James IV made three further expeditions to the Isles himself, and in August 1501 appointed Alexander Gordon, third earl of Huntly (*d.* 1524), as lieutenant over the former lordship of the Isles north of the Mounth and in Lochaber, without limit of time. If this points to distrust of Argyll's ability to control the Isles, it was justified by the rebellion there which followed the liberation about October 1501 of Donald Dubh, the MacDonald heir, from Argyll's Innis Chonnell Castle, possibly by Argyll's brother-in-law Torquil MacLeod of Lewis. Argyll may have been unwilling to act against the rebellion when the crown favoured Huntly. In March 1504 the lords of council indicated that Argyll's failure to do justice in Lorne and Argyll might result in his regality ayre being undertaken instead by king and council at Perth.

But as James IV's concerns turned to England and the continent, co-operation became essential, and Argyll's lieutenancy was renewed in 1506. He received royal grants of lands in Dunbartonshire (24 April 1509) and Inverness-shire (14 October 1510), and confirmation of free barony in Argyll (13 August 1511), and he served as a truce conservator in the borders (from 26 July 1512) and a regular exchequer auditor. None the less, he does not seem to have regained the level of influence at court enjoyed by his father.

Argyll married Elizabeth Stewart, eldest daughter of John *Stewart, Lord Darnley and tenth earl of Lennox (*d.* 1495), and they had four sons, including Donald *Campbell, abbot of Coupar Angus, and eight daughters. His eldest son, Colin *Campbell, who succeeded as third earl, married Janet, the earl of Huntly's daughter; his sons-in-law included John, fourth Lord Erskine, Gilbert, second earl of Cassillis, John Stewart, second earl of Atholl, and Lachlan MacLean of Duart. His third son, Sir John *Campbell (*d.* 1546) founded the Campbell family of Cawdor [*see under* Campbell family of Cawdor (*per.* 1511–1821)]. Argyll was killed at the battle of Flodden, on 9 September 1513, commanding the men of the Gael on the right of James IV's host with his brother-in-law Matthew Stewart, eleventh earl of Lennox. He was buried at Kilmun collegiate church in Cowal. MICHAEL A. PENMAN

Sources J. M. Thomson and others, eds., *Registrum magni sigilli regum Scotorum / The register of the great seal of Scotland*, 11 vols. (1882–1914) • J. R. N. Macphail, ed., 'Ane accompt of the genealogie of the Campbells', *Highland papers*, 2, Scottish History Society, 2nd ser., 12 (1916), 72–111 • G. Burnett and others, eds., *The exchequer rolls of Scotland*, 6–12 (1883–9) • T. Dickson and J. B. Paul, eds., *Compota thesaurariorum regum Scotorum / Accounts of the lord high treasurer of Scotland*, 1–4 (1877–1902) • [T. Thomson] and others, eds., *The acts of the lords of council in civil causes, 1478–1503*, 3 vols. (1839–1993) • [T. Thomson], ed., *The acts of the lords auditors of causes and complaints*, AD *1466–*AD *1494*, RC, 40 (1839) • *APS*, *1424–1567* • S. Boardman, *Campbell lordship* [forthcoming] • *Scots peerage* • *CDS*, vol. 4 • C. M. MacDonald, *The history of Argyll* (1950) • 'Notes on the genealogy of the earls of Argyll and their descendants', 1709, NL Scot., Adv. MS 34.6.24, fol. 65 • NA Scot., GD 1/177 (1477–1662); GD 1/180 (1390–1693); GD 1/205 (1492–1862) • Lennox charters, NA Scot.
Archives Inveraray Castle, muniments

Campbell, Archibald, fourth earl of Argyll (1498–1558), magnate, was the eldest son of Colin *Campbell, third earl of Argyll (*d.* 1529), and Lady Janet Gordon, daughter of the third earl of Huntly. He was known as Archibald Roy Oig because he was redheaded and to distinguish him from the older Archibald Campbell, his grandfather the second earl. He married Lady Helen Hamilton (*d.* in or before 1541), daughter of the first earl of Arran, in 1529, and their son, Archibald *Campbell (1538–1573), became the fifth earl. After his first wife's death Argyll married on 21 April 1541 Lady Margaret Graham (*d.* in or before 1545), daughter of the third earl of Menteith, at the priory of Inchmahome on the Lake of Menteith. Their three children were Colin *Campbell (*c.*1542–1584), who became the sixth earl, Margaret, and Janet. His third wife, whom he married on 12 December 1545 in Dunblane Cathedral, was Katherine MacLean (*d.* 1588), daughter of Hector Mòr MacLean of Duart; they had no children. In addition, the earl fathered several illegitimate offspring.

As earl of Argyll, Archibald Campbell was one of the leading noblemen in the kingdom. His power rested upon his extensive lands in the lowlands as well as in Argyll and the western highlands. Previous earls had ensured that Campbell control extended into the isles, undermining the hegemony of the forfeited MacDonalds, lords of the Isles. The fourth earl succeeded his father in early October 1529 and was immediately confirmed in the major hereditary offices of justice-general of Scotland and master of the royal household. It was a critical juncture, with the Western Isles in rebellion. James V had ordered the third earl to suppress the uprising shortly before the latter died, but in 1530 the king decided to lead the campaign in person. However, after substantial preparations the military expedition was not needed because Alexander MacDonald of Dunyvaig submitted in March 1531. Having secured his remission for the rebellion, MacDonald sought to turn the tables upon the new earl, charging him with acting without a full commission. Although Argyll had to justify himself at the council and find sureties for good behaviour, he was not imprisoned and retained royal favour. Nevertheless, James V had undoubtedly snubbed Argyll, and he attempted to balance Campbell power in the highlands by favouring MacDonald of Islay and MacLean of Duart. The fourth earl remained a loyal servant of the crown, however, and for the rest of the reign was actively involved in royal government. He witnessed many charters under the great seal, accompanied the king when James acted against border malefactors in 1535, and as justiciar presided over the trials for treason of the master of Forbes (1537) and Sir James Hamilton of Finnart (1540). The king appointed Argyll his regent for the duration of the projected secret trip to France of July 1536. When this failed, and James V sailed openly in September to marry his bride, he took the earl with him as a bodyguard against possible English attacks during the voyage.

Argyll was generously rewarded for his services in France and the highlands. During 1540–41 the king reconfirmed the earl's lands, and in 1542 his heir, the master of Argyll, was infefted with the earldom and its hereditary offices, thereby remitting the crown's feudal casualties. James's purchase from Argyll of the inheritance of Maclain of Ardnamurchan in 1541 for the substantial sum of £5000 Scots was a further indication of royal favour and generosity.

Argyll was named as a member of the regency council after James V's early death in 1542. In the subsequent struggle for power he supported Cardinal David Beaton. In so doing he opposed his brother-in-law, the earl of Arran, and the projected marriage between the young Mary, queen of Scots, and the future Edward VI. During the 'rough wooing' he campaigned against the English and was rewarded by the French king in July 1548 by a pension and membership of the order of St Michel. In 1544 the earl of Lennox with English help attacked Argyll's territories all along the Firth of Clyde. The fourth earl also benefited considerably from Lennox's forfeiture the following year, acquiring lands and influence on the southern and eastern borders of his earldom. Argyll was a major supplier of troops for the Scottish armies, bringing 12,000 highlanders to fight in 1542 and 4000 archers to the battle of Pinkie in September 1547. Two years later his contacts with the Irish Gaelic chiefs made him the lynchpin of an ambitious French plan to create a major diversion for the English by provoking an Irish uprising.

During the latter part of his life Argyll was an unwavering supporter of religious reform. He provided a protestant education for his children and employed the reformer John Carswell, later superintendent of Argyll and bishop of the Isles, within his household. It is not clear precisely when Argyll converted, though the early seventeenth-century family history suggests it may have been as early as the visit to France in 1536. When John Knox came to Castle Campbell, the earl's main lowland residence, during his tour of Scotland in 1555–6, he preached there and, according to local tradition, administered a reformed communion. Argyll, his son and successor, and several leading Campbell lairds tried unsuccessfully to persuade Knox to remain in Scotland under their protection.

Henceforth Argyll and his heir took the lead in pushing forward a reforming programme. The earl headed the signatories on the first band of the lords of the congregation on 3 December 1557, which gave the first open declaration of support for the protestant cause. In the subsequent campaign to implement local reformations based upon noble households, Argyll encouraged and protected his own chaplain, John Grant or Douglas, to preach reforming ideas, even at the royal court. In March 1558 such overt encouragement for reform provoked his brother-in-law John Hamilton, archbishop of St Andrews, to urge the earl to be more circumspect about promoting heresy. Argyll flatly refused to hand over Douglas on a heresy charge and countered by making a ringing declaration of his personal faith. Although planning a complete reformation, his ill health prevented him from realizing his dream—as the seventeenth-century family history comments: 'David resolved to build the Temple, yet the Lord would have it done by Solomon' (Campbell, 7). On his deathbed in the middle of November 1558 Argyll commanded his son to continue the fight for protestantism. He died aged sixty at Dunoon and was buried in the family mausoleum at Kilmun on the Holy Loch. JANE E. A. DAWSON

Sources *Scots peerage*, 1.338–40 · A. Campbell, ed., *Records of Argyll* (1885) · N. D. Campbell, tenth duke of Argyll, Argyll transcripts, Inveraray Castle, Argyll · A. Macdonald, ed., *Letters of the Argyll family*, Maitland Club, 50 (1839) · *John Knox's History of the Reformation in Scotland*, ed. W. C. Dickinson, 2 vols. (1949) · *Reg. PCS*, 1st ser. · *CSP Scot.*, *1547–63* · *The Scottish correspondence of Mary of Lorraine*, ed. A. I. Cameron, Scottish History Society, 3rd ser., 10 (1927) · J. Cameron, *James V: the personal rule, 1528–1542*, ed. N. Macdougall (1998) · J. Wormald, *Lords and men in Scotland* (1985) · J. M. Thomson and others, eds., *Registrum magni sigilli regum Scotorum / The register of the great seal of Scotland*, 11 vols. (1882–1914), vols. 3–4 · M. Livingstone, D. Hay Fleming, and others, eds., *Registrum secreti sigilli regum Scotorum / The register of the privy seal of Scotland*, 2–5 (1921–57) · J. Dawson, 'Clan, kin and kirk: the Campbells and the Scottish Reformation', *The education of a Christian society*, ed. N. S. Amos, A. Pettegree, and H. von Nierop (1999), 211–42

Archives Inveraray Castle, Argyll, MSS and transcripts | NA Scot., Breadalbane collection, GD112

Campbell, Archibald, fifth earl of Argyll (1538–1573), magnate and protestant reformer, was the eldest son of Archibald *Campbell, fourth earl of Argyll (1498–1558), and his first wife, Lady Helen Hamilton (*d.* in or before 1541), daughter of the first earl of Arran. He was fostered as a child by Colin Campbell of Ardkinglas and his wife, Matilda Montgomery.

The context of greatness The earldom of Argyll made Archibald Campbell a leading Scottish noble, third in order of precedence after the duke of Châtelherault and the earl of Huntly. This status was evident in his possession of the hereditary offices of justice-general of Scotland and master of the royal household, while at the end of his life he was made chancellor, the most prestigious crown office. His extensive power base enabled the earl to play a prominent role in Scottish politics and to exert influence within Ireland and England. The earl dominated the west highlands and islands, where Campbell power had been established by his predecessors who had secured wide swathes of land and consolidated their influence through the clan structure and a comprehensive network of dependants. As the pre-eminent highland chief, he commanded military and naval forces to rival the crown's. He drew additional strength from his lowland estates and his full integration into the Scottish aristocracy. Such a range and depth of resources made him the most powerful magnate in the British Isles. The Campbells' involvement in national political life and their loyalty to the crown helped Scottish monarchs feel confident about their control of such an extensive highland domain.

Since the Gaelic world straddled the north channel,

Argyll was in regular contact with Ireland, especially through the thriving mercenary trade which carried highland soldiers to fight in Irish wars. By contrast his links with England rested upon a shared protestant faith which he believed should unite the two kingdoms of the British mainland in a common purpose. During the fifteen years (1558–73) he was earl, the relationships between Britain's three polities were transformed. Scotland adopted protestantism and became an ally of its old enemy England, while the English struggled to conquer Ireland. The fifth earl had a significant influence upon these changes within the British Isles.

The commitment to protestantism and the involvement in Scottish and British politics apparent throughout Campbell's career were established during his formative years. While still a teenager Lord Lorne—the courtesy title of the master or heir of Argyll—had demonstrated his fitness to be the next clan chief by leading a military expedition to northern Ireland in 1555. In the struggle for control over Tyrconnell (Donegal) he helped Calvagh O'Donnell defeat his father, Manus. This gave the future earl firsthand experience of warfare in Ulster and knowledge of northern Irish personalities and politics which were vital during the next two decades. A year earlier, in April 1554, he had married Lady Jane Stewart (*d.* 1588), the natural daughter of James V and Elizabeth Beaton of Creich. As brother-in-law to Mary, queen of Scots, he became a member of the royal circle and, when the queen returned to her kingdom, part of the intimate family group of blood relatives she gathered around her. Unfortunately, Argyll's own marriage was childless and unhappy, with extended separations and finally an acrimonious divorce. The earl did have several illegitimate children, Colin, born in 1557 or 1558, and, a decade or so later, three children from a liaison with Jean Campbell of Cawdor—Jane and Elspeth and another son, also called Colin.

Proponent of religious reform The fourth earl was an early convert to protestantism and employed in his household the reformers John Grant or Douglas (a former friar) and John Carswell, later superintendent of Argyll and bishop of the Isles. Under Carswell's direction the young Argyll developed both the firm religious conviction which remained throughout his life and a deep friendship with his mentor. Together the two men would establish the protestant kirk in the highlands in the decade following the Reformation. Lorne's enthusiasm for the evangelical cause was channelled into action after he heard a sermon by John Knox at Calder House in Haddingtonshire during the winter of 1555–6. While the preacher was visiting Castle Campbell, the family's main lowland residence, Lorne and other leading Campbells attempted unsuccessfully to persuade Knox to remain in Scotland rather than return to Geneva. From this period Lorne and his father emerged as the pre-eminent noble supporters of ecclesiastical reform. He signed the letter inviting Knox back to his native country in 1557, and at the end of that year was the youngest nobleman to put his name to the first band of the lords of the congregation, containing the first open declaration of support for protestantism in Scotland. This deep and enduring commitment to the Reformation was reinforced by his father's deathbed injunction 'to study to set forward the public and true preaching of the Evangel of Jesus Christ and to suppress all superstition and idolatry' (*Knox's History*, 1.138–9).

When only twenty, Lorne succeeded to the earldom on the fourth earl's death in mid-November 1558. In a parliament later that month he was selected with his close friend Lord James Stewart, later earl of Moray, to carry the honours of Scotland to France. These were to be presented to the dauphin, the husband of Mary, queen of Scots, who had been granted the Scottish crown matrimonial. The mission was postponed because the religious situation in Scotland had become increasingly unstable. Argyll and other nobles had seized the initiative by introducing limited local reforms and protecting protestant preaching. In May 1559 Knox's fiery sermon in Perth provided the flashpoint for an uprising which developed into the wars of the congregation. Argyll was present at the initial iconoclastic riot though shortly afterwards he joined Mary of Guise, the regent, in an attempt to negotiate a settlement. When their attempts foundered, Argyll and Lord James rejoined their co-religionists and became the two most important leaders of the 'lords of the congregation'. One of their first actions was to 'cleanse' St Andrews and introduce protestant worship there on 11 June 1559.

In addition to providing military and political leadership, Argyll contributed in two vital ways to the uprising's ultimate success. Drawing upon his highland power base, the fifth earl furnished the majority of the Scottish soldiers fighting for the congregation. He also provided the crucial incentive which helped persuade the English queen to send military and naval reinforcements to Scotland. In the treaty of Berwick of February 1560 between England and the Scottish lords, Argyll promised substantial help to the Tudor government in its efforts to control Ulster.

The wars of the congregation came to an end with Mary of Guise's death. Although they were on opposite sides in the conflict, the regent had summoned Argyll and other magnates in June 1560 and was reconciled to them on her deathbed. The English negotiator for the subsequent peace treaty was Sir William Cecil, Elizabeth I's secretary. During Cecil's stay in Edinburgh he and Argyll became firm friends and together devised a new British policy encompassing all three kingdoms. In July 1560 they agreed the terms of the earl's help in northern Ireland where his extensive co-operation became part of the English plan for the subjugation of Ulster.

Owing to the suspicions of the earl of Sussex, the lord lieutenant in Ireland, Argyll's military assistance was never requested, but until 1565 he used his influence with his Ulster clients and allies, the MacDonalds of Antrim and the O'Donnells of Tyrconnell, to persuade them to work with the Dublin government. He also assisted the English against their main enemy, Shane O'Neill of Tyrone. After 1565, however, Argyll's Irish policies were reversed because he felt that Queen Elizabeth had betrayed him and his Scottish friends, and he subsequently directed his efforts towards consolidating the position of his dependants, especially the MacDonalds, and using the Irish situation as a bargaining counter in his negotiations on Scottish affairs with London. Argyll's later policies in Ireland helped ensure that Ulster would be the last and most difficult province of the kingdom to be brought under English control.

The treaty of Edinburgh in July 1560 had guaranteed the victory of the congregation within Scotland. The Scottish parliament which met in August was steered by Argyll, Lord James, and William Maitland of Lethington into passing acts against papal authority and Roman Catholic worship. Thus during 1559–60 a new protestant kirk had been established in Scotland, with Argyll being particularly active destroying 'idolatrous' images in churches and monasteries and demolishing friaries.

Relations with Queen Mary François II's death in December 1560 and the return of his young widow, Mary, queen of Scots, caused a major shift in Scottish politics. Argyll had sent his brother Colin *Campbell, the future sixth earl, on a special embassy to the queen to assure her of his loyalty and goodwill. On Mary's arrival in her native land she appointed to her council the triumvirate of Argyll, Lord James, and Maitland of Lethington, who had governed Scotland since the regent's death. For the next four years they were her principal advisers and ensured the continuation of protestant and Anglophile policies. While Argyll and Lord James allowed the queen to retain her private mass, they forcibly disrupted the Catholic service conducted in the Chapel Royal in her absence. Knox remained on good terms with the earl, despite his vigorous objections to any celebration of the mass. The preacher also distrusted the warm personal relationship Argyll had developed with Mary. However, this did not prevent him co-operating with the queen during 1563 in achieving a temporary reconciliation between the earl and his estranged wife.

Argyll's political and personal co-operation with Mary was threatened first by the return of Matthew Stewart, thirteenth earl of Lennox, to Scotland in September 1564 and then by that of his son, Henry, Lord Darnley, in February 1565. Both the Campbells and the Hamiltons, Argyll's maternal kin, had profited greatly from Lennox's exile, which had lasted since 1544. Argyll was willing to accept a settlement with his regional rivals provided it guaranteed stability and maintained the English alliance and support for the kirk. However, these were threatened when Mary decided to marry Darnley in defiance of Elizabeth I. Argyll and Lord James, now earl of Moray, believed the marriage to Darnley, whose religious allegiance was ambiguous at best, also posed a threat to the kirk. Unwilling to accept the queen's choice of husband, the two men lost royal favour and were manoeuvred into open rebellion. In the chaseabout raid of summer and autumn 1565, the queen forced most of the rebels into exile in England. The earl retreated to his impregnable heartland, but could only watch his allies flee across the border. Elizabeth's failure to send help to Scotland made a profound impression upon Argyll. From the end of 1565 his attitude towards his erstwhile allies changed. In subsequent years he might co-operate with the English but the old friendship and belief in a common cause was gone. This new attitude was most evident in Ireland where the withdrawal of Argyll's co-operation and his assistance to the Gaelic chiefs of Ulster created profound problems for the Dublin administration which persisted until the end of the century.

Owing to the inherent strength of his position, Argyll was able to make his own peace with Mary. After Riccio's murder on 9 March 1566 and the consequent realignment within Scottish politics, many of the former rebels were welcomed back to court. The fifth earl was showered with favours, including being allocated the chamber next to the queen's during her confinement for the birth of her son, the future James VI. Argyll was also a member of the regency council which was named in case Mary died in childbirth.

The breakdown of the queen's relationship with her husband in 1566 combined with Darnley's unpleasant character and capricious behaviour to create a serious political problem. As Mary's counsellor and friend, the earl had discussed possible solutions with the queen's other advisers—it was to this end that he took part in the 'Craigmillar conference' at the end of November which featured so prominently in later propaganda. The extent of his involvement in Darnley's killing is unclear, but he accompanied the queen when she visited her husband on 9 February 1567, the night of his assassination, and as justice-general he presided at the trial on 12 April which acquitted the earl of Bothwell of the murder. In the turmoil of the next few months, however, with the queen's abduction and marriage to Bothwell, Argyll was beset by uncertainty. Despite Mary's personal pleas to support her third husband, the earl eventually joined the confederate lords against the royal couple.

Argyll accepted the need to imprison the queen after her surrender at the battle of Carberry, outside Edinburgh, on 15 June 1567, but he would not countenance her deposition. His loyalty to the monarchy and to Mary herself meant he could not accept the abdication the queen had been forced to make on 24 July. He left the confederate lords and refused to attend the young king's coronation on the 29th. The nature of Mary's position was a crucial issue in the breach between Argyll and his long-standing friend Moray, who had returned to Scotland to become regent for the infant James VI. Argyll became one of the leaders of the queen's party, but with Mary imprisoned in Lochleven Castle, he felt obliged to reach an accommodation with Moray. However, as soon as the queen escaped, she appointed the earl as her lieutenant-general. Although he commanded her forces at Langside on 13 May 1568, at the start of the battle he was taken seriously ill, possibly suffering a mild stroke or heart attack. The sudden loss of the commander contributed to the disastrous defeat of the queen's forces and Mary's precipitate flight from the battlefield which carried her in panic across the Solway Firth and into England.

Peacemaker Having recovered from his illness, Argyll faced an impossible dilemma as leader of the queen's party in Scotland. Mary's fate now lay in the hands of Elizabeth I. Whatever might be achieved by her Scottish supporters, their actions alone could not guarantee their queen's release from confinement in England. The earl was not directly involved in Mary's first 'trial', which took place in the autumn and winter of 1568, but its inconclusive outcome provoked a propaganda campaign within Scotland. It brought accusations of complicity in Darnley's murder against Argyll and Huntly who issued a joint refutation of their guilt. Rather than the propaganda or military campaigns, it was pressure from his own clan council which finally persuaded the earl to acknowledge Moray's regency in 1569.

The regent's assassination on 23 January 1570 once again plunged Scotland into civil strife. Although it had been planned and carried out by Argyll's Hamilton kinsmen, it is unlikely that the earl knew of the plot. Events were further confused by the arrival of the fugitive northern earls after the collapse of their rising in England. Their flight into Scotland provided the excuse for an English army commanded by the earl of Sussex to come to aid the king's party. Throughout 1570 Argyll was involved in a complex series of negotiations, interspersed with warfare, between the different Scottish factions, Sussex, Elizabeth I, and from her English prison, Queen Mary. By the end of the year a disillusioned Argyll had realized that Mary's restoration was impossible. Believing that the English government was using her plight to impose control over Scotland, he concluded that this external threat was a greater danger to the kingdom than recognizing Regent Lennox's authority. In the summer of 1571 Argyll abandoned the queen's party and settled with Lennox. Writing to his uncle, the duke of Châtelherault, on 13 August, he justified his decision by describing Mary's position: she 'continews under the power of the Quene of England, out of this realme, quhair she may not do nathing aither for this cuntrie or for hir self, but according to the pleasure of them that now she is thrall unto' (*CSP Scot.*, 3.645).

Having joined the king's supporters, Argyll saw his role as that of a peacemaker and sought to reconcile his former allies. Although it was difficult to overcome their sense of betrayal, by the spring of 1573 he had persuaded most of the queen's party to accept the final settlement in the pacification of Perth. The defiant remnant, based in Edinburgh Castle, were taken by siege, with the earl contributing troops and artillery. The successive regents (Lennox, Mar, and Morton) have usually been credited with ending the civil wars, yet they could not have achieved the reconciliations of 1571–3 without Argyll's help. The fifth earl's death a few months later has obscured his substantial contribution to the stabilization of the kingdom.

Argyll's personal settlement with the king's party had been on favourable terms, reflecting the immense strength of the Campbell power base and his own record of standing above the most bitter feuding. When Regent Mar, his old friend, died on 28 October 1572 Argyll was proposed as a successor but he gave his support to Morton. The new regent acknowledged the debt by making Argyll chancellor on 12 January 1573. During the final months of his life the fifth earl was active in government becoming Morton's 'right hand both abroad and at home' (*CSP Scot.*, 4.545).

Family and clan affairs The extended fighting in which the earl had been involved from the wars of the congregation to the civil wars had placed strains upon his substantial, but not inexhaustible, resources. The financial burden upon his own estates and clan was considerable. An anonymous family historian writing in the 1630s commented that to cover his debts the fifth earl had been forced to mortgage his lands, sell its produce cheaply, and tax his clansmen. Despite these measures, Campbell power and loyalty remained strong and Argyll's control over the west highlands and islands firm. Unlike his successors, the earl was on good terms with his powerful Hebridean neighbours, clan Donald, and re-established the southern branch after its crushing defeat in 1565 in Antrim. But although he preferred to persuade his fellow Gaels, Argyll did occasionally resort to force, as in the Campbell feud with the MacGregors which continued for most of his tenure of the earldom.

Argyll's personal religious commitment was evident in his enthusiastic support for protestantism throughout the highlands. He provided his former tutor and friend John Carswell with the military protection, substantial resources, and constant encouragement needed to enable him to fulfil his duties as superintendent of Argyll and first protestant bishop of the Isles. In addition his patronage allowed Carswell to translate into Gaelic the kirk's new liturgy, the Book of Common Order. When published in 1567 with a fulsome dedication to Argyll, it was the first book to be printed in Gaelic. It had a deep and enduring impact upon highland protestantism and upon the Gaelic language. Unfortunately, neither man lived long enough to complete a Gaelic Bible, the second stage of the translation project. The earl utilized his own and other Campbell households to offer additional support to protestant preachers and ministers, thereby supplementing the kirk's formal organization and resources which were stretched so thinly in the highlands. His clear lead and personal example helped ensure that clan Campbell became firmly identified with protestantism and the clan's influence greatly assisted the introduction of the new faith throughout the highland region.

In his later years Argyll's life was dominated by his marital problems. The final separation came in August 1567 when the countess left the Campbell castle of Dunoon. She then rejected the earl's offer of a speedy, uncontested divorce. Her half-brother Moray was also bitterly opposed to divorce, further poisoning his deteriorating relationship with Argyll. The earl's position was complicated by wanting to remarry so that he could father a legitimate heir. Having tried a variety of courts and different approaches, on 23 June 1573 Argyll obtained a divorce from the Edinburgh commissary court, the first in post-Reformation Scotland on grounds of separation. In the first week of August Argyll married Jean Cunningham (*d.*

1584?), daughter of the earl of Glencairn. A posthumous son was born nine months later, but died at birth.

Within six weeks of his second marriage and while travelling through Argyll, the fifth earl died unexpectedly. On 12 September 1573 he stayed at Barbreck and, though well on retiring to bed, was dead before morning. His death was ascribed to the 'stone', a generic term for internal disorders, from which he had suffered in previous years. His half-brother Colin succeeded him as earl. Argyll was buried alongside his predecessors in the family mausoleum at the church of Kilmun on the Holy Loch. No portraits of him have survived, but he was described by contemporaries as a very tall, handsome man, with brown hair and a fair complexion.

British statesman Argyll had been active in three main spheres: within the Gaelic worlds of the western highlands and islands and in northern Ireland; in Scottish national politics; and in the international diplomacy of the British Isles. In mid-sixteenth century Britain he enjoyed the unique position of being powerful enough to influence events in all three kingdoms. When he became earl, he consciously drew upon that position to formulate a British policy and to co-operate with Sir William Cecil and the English government to implement it. Although he later abandoned these grandiose schemes, he remained committed to viewing politics within the wider British perspective. Despite living before the creation of an embryonic British state in 1603, Argyll can be regarded as one of the first truly 'British' politicians.

The earl's untimely death has led to an undervaluation of his contribution to sixteenth-century politics within Scotland and in the wider British context. As he was only too aware, his policies had not been particularly successful. He did not achieve the idealistic vision of a protestant Britain which had seemed possible in 1560. His Scottish career was overshadowed by the civil wars, with his leadership of the queen's party being discounted because of his defection in 1571. The propaganda image of inconstancy and vacillation has endured. It highlighted his limited skill in the game of political bargaining and the lack of a driving ambition for individual success. However, in the two areas which were central to his own interests, Argyll's legacy was considerable. He made a major contribution to the establishment of protestantism within Scotland, especially in the highlands. Similarly, his remarkable British perspective ensured that future chiefs and the Campbell clan would operate upon the wider British stage and play an extremely active part in Scottish and British politics during succeeding centuries.

JANE E. A. DAWSON

Sources *Scots peerage*, 1.338–44 • A. Macdonald, ed., *Letters of the Argyll family*, Maitland Club, 50 (1839) • A. Campbell, ed., *Records of Argyll* (1885) • J. E. A. Dawson, *The politics of religion in the age of Mary, queen of Scots: the earl of Argyll and the struggle for Britain and Ireland* (2002) • *CSP Scot.*, 1547–81 • *CSP Ire.*, 1509–73 • *John Knox's History of the Reformation in Scotland*, ed. W. C. Dickinson, 2 vols. (1949) • D. Calderwood, *The history of the Kirk of Scotland*, ed. T. Thomson and D. Laing, 8 vols., Wodrow Society, 7 (1842–9), vols. 1–3 • R. Keith, *History of the affairs of church and state in Scotland from the beginning of the Reformation to the year 1568*, ed. J. P. Lawson and C. J. Lyon, Spottiswoode Society, 1 (1844) • N. D. Campbell, tenth duke of Argyll, Argyll transcripts, Inveraray Castle, Argyll [photocopy in department of Scottish History, University of Glasgow] • J. E. A. Dawson, 'The fifth earl of Argyle, Gaelic lordship and political power in sixteenth-century Scotland', *SHR*, 67 (1988), 1–27 • *Campbell letters, 1559–83*, ed. J. Dawson, Scottish History Society, 5th ser., 10 (2000) • *CSP for.*, 1572–4 • NA Scot., CC8/2/6, fol. 121*v*

Archives priv. coll., MSS and transcripts | NA Scot., Breadalbane collection, GD 112 • NA Scot., letters, mainly to Campbells of Glenorchy, GD 112/39 • PRO, state papers Irish, SP 63 • PRO, state papers Scottish, SP 51–2

Wealth at death £2012 4*s*.—incl. £1006 2*s*. 'deadis part': NA Scot., CC 8/8/4, fols. 160*v*–161*r* in Macdonald, ed., *Letters to the Argyll family*, 59–60

Campbell, Archibald, seventh earl of Argyll (1575/6–1638), magnate and politician, was the elder surviving son of Colin *Campbell, sixth earl of Argyll (*c*.1542–1584), and his second wife, Lady Annas or Agnes (*d*. 1588), eldest daughter of William Keith, fourth Earl Marischal. He was only about eight years of age when his father died on 10 September 1584 after a long period of infirmity. This loss created a power vacuum at the very heart of the clan, and led to rivalry, internal dissension, and a bitter feud that threatened to split the Campbells apart and to end the child's life. A council of guardians, comprising his mother and six kinsmen, had been appointed for his protection, but they soon quarrelled and one of their number, Archibald Campbell of Lochnell, 'a dark and ambitious spirit' (Anderson, *Scot. nat.*, vol. 1, pt 2, p. 553), set his own sights upon gaining the earldom. To this end, he forged an alliance with George Gordon, sixth earl of Huntly, and arranged for another of Argyll's guardians, Campbell of Calder, to be murdered. Since none of the conspirators was ever brought to justice and his mother died in 1588, young Argyll grew up in an atmosphere of profound insecurity. In order to provide both an heir and a much needed return to stability for the clan, he was married on 24 July 1592 to Lady Anne (1574–1607), fifth daughter of William Douglas, sixth earl of Morton. Having already entered the world of adult politics, carrying the sword of state at the opening of the Scottish parliament in May 1592, Argyll led a raid deep into Huntly's lands, burning and looting, in revenge for the murder that year of his ally James Stewart, second earl of Moray. However, in 1594 he fell ill at Stirling and hovered between life and death for several days. It was widely rumoured that Campbell of Lochnell had bribed his servants to poison Argyll, but there is no hard evidence to substantiate these dramatic claims.

Having made a full recovery, Argyll was an ideal candidate to prosecute the war against the rebel Huntly and the Roman Catholic earls. Armed with a lieutenancy from the king, he raised a force of some 6000 men and outstripped the rest of the royal army in search of his quarry. Unfortunately, he failed to take Ruthven Castle and was routed ignominiously on 3 October at the battle of Glenlivat by a far smaller, but better trained, body of rebel troops. Once again it was widely believed that Campbell of Lochnell had been responsible for major troop defections before and during the battle and that he had struck a bargain with Huntly in order to guarantee the defeat of his own

Archibald Campbell, seventh earl of Argyll (1575/6–1638), by unknown artist

side and Argyll's death. If this was Lochnell's plan, then it failed spectacularly as it was he and not Argyll who was scythed down in the initial artillery bombardment of the royalist positions. As his highlanders fled the field Argyll determined to die in action rather than follow suit, but his friends forcibly dragged him, distraught and tearful, away from the battle and escorted him to the safety of the king's encampment at Dundee. Recovered from the debris left behind by Argyll's army was the black and yellow standard of the Campbells, which was paraded in triumph before Huntly and hung—to taunt his foe—from the battlements of his castle at Strathbogie. If Argyll's reputation and sense of honour had been dealt a rough blow by this débâcle, then worse was to come at the hands of his own sovereign. James VI seems to have been pleased by the humbling of this over-mighty lord and shortly afterwards joked, upon seeing Argyll entering the Abbey Close at Holyrood, that he had been sent home and taught a lesson by Huntly, as though he was the poorest of his subjects.

Argyll immediately embarked upon a cycle of fresh raids upon Huntly's tenants, but he had earned the antipathy and suspicion of the king to such an extent that his depredations were cut short by his arrest and confinement to Edinburgh Castle on the orders of James VI. However, he was still useful and his imprisonment was short-lived. Released in the summer of 1595, he was used again in order to subjugate Huntly's lands by use of fire and the sword. The rule of James VI was hallmarked by the policy of entrusting the settlement of the highlands to feudal magnates and of setting one clan against the other in bouts of internecine, but relatively low-level, warfare and raiding. Argyll, however, chose to employ a mixture of approaches in order to extend his own patrimony: negotiating where possible, and forging formal bonds with other clan chiefs, but also countenancing extreme violence when this method failed. The success of these stratagems relied primarily upon the force of his own personality and the strength of the central government to keep him firmly in check. It was Argyll's good fortune that, until his physical exhaustion and spectacular fall from grace in the late 1610s, his exceptional personal toughness and astute grasp of *realpolitik* ensured the continual expansion of Campbell power and territorial influence.

To this end, Argyll was prepared to allow the king to broker a reconciliation between himself and Huntly in February 1603. Having previously made use of the MacGregors in order to exact private vengeance against the Colquhouns and other troublesome clans, he now joined with Huntly in order to destroy his former allies. He promised the chief of the MacGregors safe passage and an audience with the king, but instead betrayed him and on 18 January 1604 conveyed him into the hands of the executioner at Edinburgh. Between 1608 and 1610 Argyll and Huntly were repeatedly unleashed in what became campaigns of virtual extermination against the MacGregor clan. In 1611 Argyll was given full powers against them, including the right to levy swingeing fines on their property, with 77.5% of the profits going to his private purse, and the rest going to the crown.

By virtue of a royal charter of 1599 Argyll had been ceded authority—previously held by the MacDonalds as lords of the Isles—over the Kintyre peninsula and the Sudreys. However, this grant was not enforceable, and the MacDonalds bitterly resisted any incursion into their private fiefdom by the settlers and land agents of clan Campbell. In 1609 Argyll set about constructing a major new stronghold at Lochhead, which subsequently became known as Campbeltown, but it was not until 1614 that he made an inroad onto the peninsula of Kintyre and launched an invasion against the Isle of Islay, with the explicit objective of wresting the control of those domains from Sir James MacDonald. The struggle dragged on into the winter of 1614–15, with final subjugation of the MacDonalds occurring in 1617. After this success Argyll's grant to the whole of Kintyre was ratified by both the king and the Scottish parliament, and the lowland plantation, comparable to its counterpart in Ulster, went on in earnest.

Argyll had become highly favoured by the court, and between campaigns had spent at least some time in London. His first wife having died on 3 May 1607, at St Botolph without Bishopsgate on 30 November 1610 he married an English Roman Catholic, Anne (*d.* 1635), one of the daughters and eventual coheirs of Sir William Cornwallis of Brome, Suffolk. This brought him increasingly into contact with members of the Jesuit order and profoundly altered his religious sympathies. In 1617 he attended James VI and I upon his return visit to Scotland, but Argyll's willingness on 8 June to partake of the communion at Holyrood according to the Anglican, rather than the Scottish, rite aroused controversy in the kirk and solicited much adverse comment. Henceforth, religion would be the guiding motif of Argyll's career. However, it was the crippling debt that had mounted since his father's death and had been exacerbated by his own constant pursuit of warfare which led to Argyll's sudden and unexpected breach with the king.

Under the pretext of going to take the waters at Spa, in order to restore his failing health, in 1618 Argyll and his wife took ship for the continent. Once he had landed, however, Argyll announced in spectacular style his formal conversion to Roman Catholicism and took service with the Spanish army in Flanders. That November his commission to travel abroad was revoked by the governments of both England and Scotland 'in respect of his professed Poprie abroad' (*Reg. PCS*, 1st ser., 11.467–8) and on 16 February 1619 he was proclaimed a traitor to the state on the steps of the Mercat Cross in Edinburgh.

Though his proscription was revoked on 22 November 1621, Argyll preferred to remain in the service of Spain, consorting with his former enemies among the MacDonalds and attempting in spring 1622 to raise 4000 English and Scots to serve in a projected invasion of Ireland. However, though he could find officers to serve under him few private soldiers were forthcoming and the project was abandoned. By the summer of 1626 it was reported that he had dismissed a Roman Catholic rising in Scotland as 'a folly and madness that they could never bring to pass' (*CSP dom.*, 1625–6, 392); he appears to have been casting about for a means of reaching an accommodation with the new Stuart monarch. Certainly, the passing of James VI and I and the accession of Charles I eased a rapprochement and ensured Argyll's safe passage home.

After returning in November 1627, Argyll chose to abandon his Scottish estates and to settle instead in a house in Drury Lane, London. Years later the earl of Clarendon argued that the reason for this lay in Argyll's deteriorating relationship with his son and heir Archibald *Campbell, Lord Lorne, later marquess of Argyll (1605x7–1661), and that the earl was prevented from disinheriting his disobedient and insolent boy only by the timely intercession of Charles I. However, this would appear to be a verdict formed by hindsight and the desire to blacken the name of a proud and bold covenanter. Lord Lorne had already come into his inheritance shortly before, and probably because of, his father's remarriage in 1610, with the whole of Argyll's property being irrevocably conveyed to him, except for a significant sum paid out to the earl as a liferent. In 1631 Argyll even renounced this sinecure and gave up everything but the title relating to his estates. Reduced to no more than a cipher, with his political significance at an end, he was widowed again on 12 January 1635 and quietly eked out his last years in London, dying at Drury Lane in 1638, between 9 October, when his will was drawn up, and 29 November, when it was proved.

JOHN CALLOW

Sources Clarendon, *Hist. rebellion*, vol. 1 • Anderson, *Scot. nat.*, vol. 1, pt 2 • J. Willcock, *The great marquess: the life and times of Archibald, 8th earl and 1st (and only) marquess of Argyll* (1903) • *The house of Argyll and the collateral branches of the clan Campbell* (1871) • *Maccalein's raid: a legend of Kintyre* (1862) • *Reg. PCS*, 2nd ser. • *Reg. PCS*, 1st ser., vol. 14 • R. Douglas, *The peerage of Scotland* (1764) • GEC, *Peerage* • G. Donaldson, *Scotland: James V to James VII* (1971) • J. Wormald, *Court, kirk and community: Scotland, 1470–1625* (1981) • G. G. Simpson, ed., *The Scottish soldier abroad, 1247–1967* (1992) • J. Wormald, ed., *Scotland revisited* (1991)

Archives NA Scot., letters to the Campbells of Glenorchy, GD112/39

Likenesses oils, Drummond Castle, Tayside region • two oils, priv. coll. [*see illus.*]

Wealth at death had already made over most of estates, *c.*1610: will, GL, MS 9171/27, fols. 525*r*–525*v*

Campbell, Archibald, marquess of Argyll (1605x7–1661), nobleman and politician, was born between August 1605 and April 1607, the son of Archibald *Campbell, seventh earl of Argyll (1575/6–1638), and his first wife, Lady Anne Douglas (1574–1607), daughter of William *Douglas, sixth earl of Morton. His mother died while he was still an infant and his father virtually resigned the responsibilities of his earldom, transferring possession of his hereditary estates to his son (who took the courtesy title Lord Lorne until his father's death), though retaining his right to their revenues for life. In 1610 his father married a Roman Catholic, Anne Cornwallis (*d.* 1635), and in 1618 he converted to that faith and entered the service of Spain. As a result his title was forfeited in 1619 and, as the young Lord Lorne stated when appealing to advice from kinsmen, ruin threatened: 'I am obliged to succour both my father and the house of my expectation' (I. Innes, ed., *Thanes of Cawdor*, 1859, 246).

Early years Argyll's title was restored in 1621, but he did not return to Britain until 1627 and then lived quietly in England. Thus Lorne, in effect, took over his 'house of expectation'—the great Argyll inheritance—and struggled to satisfy a father who had deserted both him and his religion, yet denounced him from afar for insufficient filial respect. After his father's forfeiture his cousin, William *Douglas, seventh earl of Morton, was appointed Lorne's guardian, and Lorne later acknowledged the 'goodness and cair' of Morton since his birth, and his 'prudence and fatherly counsaills in my grittist difficulties' (Willcock, 355, 356). His education was entrusted to Robert Barclay (later provost of Irvine), and on 15 January 1622 he matriculated at St Leonard's College in the University of St Andrews. There he won the silver medal awarded for archery in 1623, but as was usual for those of his status he left without taking a degree, and by 1626 he was involved in public

Archibald Campbell, marquess of Argyll (1605x7–1661), by David Scougall

affairs, playing a role in suppressing disorder in the west highlands and Isles. He visited court in 1626 and in August that year he married Lady Margaret Douglas (1610–1678), Morton's daughter. Archibald *Campbell (1629–1685), politician and clan leader, was their son.

Lorne, now approaching the age of majority, fought to reduce the great burden of debt on the Argyll estates, but he was hindered by his father's granting Kintyre and Jura, recent family acquisitions, to James Campbell (*bap.* 1611, *d.* 1645), his son by his second marriage, who in February 1626 was created Lord Kintyre. The affair instilled 'bitter feelings of injury and humiliation' in Lorne (Willcock, 20). Though he resolved that 'I shall do nothing unworthie of a christian and a nobill man' he was angered by court favour to his half-brother in the dispute, and complained of being neglected and treated with contempt, threatening 'I will rather chose to be free abroad then ane sleave at hom' (ibid., 356, 359). Another blow to his attempts to revive his family's fortunes and power came in 1628, when Charles I insisted on his resigning, in his own name and his father's, the hereditary office of justice-general of Scotland, though he was allowed to retain jurisdiction over Argyll and the Isles. Admission to the Scottish privy council on 12 June 1628, however, indicated recognition of his status as a leading figure in Scotland, even if he had not yet the title of earl. In 1631, perhaps under pressure from the king, the old earl surrendered his rights to the revenues of the Argyll estates to his son, evidently in return for an annuity. Many years later the earl of Clarendon alleged that the old earl warned the king against favour to his son:

> Sir, I must know this young man better than you can do: you have brought me low, that you may raise him; which I doubt you will live to repent; for he is a man of craft, subtlety, and falsehood, and can love no man; and if ever he finds it in his power to do you mischief, he will be sure to do it. (Clarendon, *Hist. rebellion*, 1.169)

Argyll certainly regarded Lorne as an undutiful son, but the story is too neatly prophetic to be credible.

Lorne pursued his ambitions with determination and success. In Kintyre he 'reduced his half-brother from substantial landowner to absentee pensioner' (Macinnes, 75) by questioning his rights, buying church lands in Kintyre, and purchasing the rights to debts Lord Kintyre had incurred through mortgages. By 1634 Kintyre acknowledged that in effect Lorne was managing his estates, and his attempt to sell Kintyre and Jura to the earl of Antrim (representative of the MacDonalds to whom the lands had formerly belonged) failed when Lorne persuaded the king to forbid the sale; in 1636 rights to the disputed lands were transferred to Lorne's young son, thus officially recognizing his control of them.

Elsewhere Lorne used his financial skills to bring new areas under Campbell control, buying up rights to debts of the MacDonalds of Sleat and the MacLeans of Duart and using his hold over them to acquire feudal superiority over their lands. The MacDougalls of Dunollie and Stewarts of Appin also suffered losses of land and autonomy as Lorne manipulated feudal superiorities to his advantage. A more speculative enterprise saw Lorne gain the rights to an unknown island supposed to lie beyond the Hebrides, but a ship sent to find this new Campbell possession failed to locate it. Though his father was still nominal chief, by the later 1630s Lorne had consolidated and extended the west-highland regional empire of the Campbells. The price he paid was widespread hostility and unease on the part of those who lost former power or felt threatened: 'political reaction to the territorial ambitions of Clan Campbell was the most important polarising factor within Gaeldom [in the years] prior to the outbreak of the Scottish civil war' (Macinnes, 95).

Public affairs in the 1630s Lorne's role in national affairs remained limited, but in 1629 Charles I (in anticipation of a visit to Scotland) appointed him hereditary master of the household in place of his father, and in 1634 he was admitted as an extraordinary lord of the court of session. At a time when tension was growing in Scotland over innovations in church government and worship being introduced by the king, Lorne made his position clear through his support for those punished for nonconformity. When Samuel Rutherford was banished to Aberdeen in 1636 Lorne did all he could to have the sentence overturned, and in 1637 he paid a fine imposed on the laird of Earlston by the bishop of Galloway and sought to have his sentence of banishment cancelled. He raised the matter in council, and 'in high passion' accused the bishop of lying on the issue, which 'he and all the nobles takes it for a very pert affront done to their estate' (*Letters … Baillie*, 1.16). But the story that after the incident Lorne convened with leading nobles and others to discuss the pride and avarice of the bishops, who were seeking to rule the country (Spalding, 1.78–9) is no more than rumour.

When resistance to the king's policies began in July 1637 with the prayer book riots in Edinburgh there can be no doubt that Lorne sympathized with the movement. He hated the king's religious policies, despised the bishops, and feared they were excluding the nobility from civil power—and grievances over his treatment in the matters of Kintyre and the justice-generalship years before may have still rankled. Yet he failed to act. His refusal to commit himself may have been due to a cautious waiting to see how successful resistance was, but as the most powerful noble in the country he must have been aware that his decision might be crucial to the outcome of the struggle, and have seen it as his role to stand above the fray, able to act as a mediator seeking the trust of both sides as opinions polarized. A further complication was that his father still lived. Had Lorne been inclined to join those who were denounced as rebels for resistance to royal policy, he may have feared that the king might rescind in favour of his father the grants that gave him control of his estates, and drag the old earl out of retirement to form a rival focus for Campbell loyalties.

Lorne therefore continued to take his seat on the privy council as it struggled unsuccessfully to suppress resistance. After the national covenant was signed in February 1638 he was one of the councillors sent for by Charles I for consultations, but covenanters, who knew his sympathy for them, worried about what would happen: 'we tremble for Lorne, that the King either persuade him to goe his way' or detain him at court, so he went 'against the heart of many his friends' (*Letters … Baillie*, 1.65, 70). At court he had an hour-and-a-half meeting with Charles, and having sought permission 'had verie frie conference' with him. But, typically, Lorne's account of what he said 'was so generall and ambiguous, that I culd not knowe his meaning' as the covenanter earl of Loudoun recorded, but 'I am confident Lorne shall stand fast, and not be moved with all their temptationis' (ibid., 1.465). It is possible that the king had considered sending Lorne to Scotland as his commissioner to negotiate an end to conflict there. If so, Lorne's outspokenness when they met dissuaded him, and the marquess of Hamilton was sent north instead. Rumour said that Lorne's father urged the king to prevent him from returning home as 'he would wynd him a pirn' (do him mischief) (Guthry, 36) there, but, as in other cases, Charles showed himself ready to trust people who he knew disagreed with him, counting on their loyalty.

At first such continued trust in Lorne seemed justified. He helped Hamilton in his negotiations, and when the king put forward a rival to the national covenant, the 'king's covenant', Lorne signed it along with other councillors on 22 September 1638. But preliminary preparations for military intervention in Scotland were already being made while the negotiations continued, and part of the king's strategy was as much anti-Campbell as royalist. The earl of Antrim proposed raising his men in Ulster and invading Scotland through Argyllshire. His aim was to be rewarded with former MacDonald territory now in Campbell hands, above all Kintyre and Jura. Encouraged by this, MacDonald and other anti-Campbell clans within the highlands now also began to declare their willingness to fight for the king—though Charles was warned that they would fight out of 'splen to Lorne' rather than loyalty to the crown (Gardiner, *Hamilton*, 11). Lorne was thus faced with the fact that, in spite of his loyalty to the king, if the Scottish crisis came to war the king would probably sanction a major attack on his lands. Therefore in the summer of 1638 he began military preparations on his estates to guard against attack. Then, at last, in October or November, his father died, freeing him of a burden that had embarrassed and constrained him for most of his life.

Emergence as a leader Hopes of a compromise settlement rested on a general assembly of the Church of Scotland, which met in Glasgow in November. Hamilton presided as king's commissioner, and the new earl of Argyll accompanied him as one of six councillors acting as his assessors. It soon became clear that the assembly was determined to go far further in reform than the king would agree, and on 28 November Hamilton dissolved it in the king's name and withdrew, but before he did so Argyll rose and spoke. 'His voice was low, his speeche he addressed to the covenanters' (J. Gordon, 1.171–2). He indicated that he believed the assembly was still lawful in spite of Hamilton's action, and that he was now himself committed to the covenanting cause. The assembly, continuing to sit in Hamilton's absence, welcomed him, granting him the right to sit and speak though not to vote. However, in the confusion of the moment many failed to understand what was happening, believing that Argyll's action had official approval:

> No one thing did confirme [us, in our resolution to continue to meet] so much as Argyle's presence; not only the man was the far most powerfull subject in our kingdome, but also at this time being in good grace with the King and the Commissioner, we could not conceave bot his stay with us was with the allowance of both. (*Letters … Baillie*, 1.146)

Thus Argyll's continued presence was seen as giving the assembly a semblance of legitimacy, his being there covertly sanctioned by the king in the hope he could moderate the assembly's actions. And, to a degree, Argyll did play this role. When a sermon seemed to question the king's powers, Argyll immediately gave 'a grave admonition to let authoritie alone' (*Letters … Baillie*, 1.146). Members must speak respectfully of the king and royal prerogative, for the king would be more likely to be influenced by modesty than arrogance. The assembly obeyed. Only gradually did it realize that both Hamilton and the king were wholehearted in denouncing Argyll's action, which indeed became 'the greatest ground of all the wrath his Majestie has since kythed [displayed] towards him'. But the news that it 'was the equitie of our cause' that had made Argyll stay, and that he did so 'to the extreame hazard of his head' strengthened the morale of the assembly (ibid., 1.146).

Hamilton's analysis of the situation for the king reflects his indignation at Argyll's action being initially regarded as semi-official. Argyll was 'the only man now called up as a true patriot, a loyal subject, a faithful counsellor, and above all, rightly set for the preservation of the purity of religion. And truly, Sir, he takes it upon him'. Hamilton added grimly: 'He must be well looked to; for it fears me, he will prove the dangerousest man in the State. He is so far from favouring episcopal government, that with all his soul he wishes it totally abolished' (Yorke, 2.115). At the close of the assembly Argyll gave a speech explaining his slowness in joining the covenanters: 'he was alwayes sett ther waye, but had delayd to professe it, so long as he fownde his close carriadge might be adventageouse to ther cause' (J. Gordon, 2.172). Now matters had reached the point at which he had to come into the open, or prove a knave. The royalist retort was naturally that his conduct had already proved him a knave.

It seems that for reasons known to himself Argyll did not actually sign the national covenant until April 1639, but his status and reputation meant that he was now regarded as the outstanding noble leader of the covenanting movement. War was approaching, and Argyll was given command of the west coast, to guard against landings from Ireland, and occupied Hamilton's island of Arran and the MacDonald outpost of Colonsay. He also contributed to suppressing royalist opposition in north-east Scotland. His men, led by the earl of Montrose, occupied Aberdeen in April 1639, while Argyll himself ravaged the Airlie estates. When the main covenanter army assembled on the borders to face the threat from England, Argyll moved to command troops in the Stirling area, ready to deal with further trouble in the north or from Ireland. However, once it became clear that the king was going to negotiate rather than fight he moved to the camp on the borders. He took no direct part in the negotiations that led to the treaty of Berwick, preferring to work behind the scenes, but after the agreement was signed he and others went to kiss the king's hand, though not surprisingly they 'were bot coldlie welcomed' (*Letters … Baillie*, 1.220). The pacification immediately became the subject of controversy and bitter recriminations, and when Charles summoned many leading covenanter nobles to Berwick for discussion Argyll was among those who chose not to go.

Political crisis, 1639–1641 With widespread belief that the king would make a new attempt to conquer Scotland in 1640, controversy emerged about what the covenanters were seeking to achieve. They had begun by simply demanding redress of grievances, but some were moving towards believing that it was necessary to limit permanently the powers of a hostile monarch. The issue was forced into the open by the abolition of episcopacy. The fourteen bishops had formed a solid core of support for the crown in parliament, and when parliament met late in 1639 the earl of Montrose urged that the king be allowed to appoint fourteen laymen to replace them. Argyll opposed this, insisting that no replacement be made, with parliament reformed instead by doubling the voting power of the commissioners of the shires and declaring them a separate estate (rather than forming a single estate with the nobility) to replace the bishops. He got his way, and from this point growing rivalry between him and Montrose was visible, with a clash in personalities between the flamboyant and daring Montrose and the careful and pious Argyll intensifying political differences.

Constitutional crisis came to centre on the issue of whether to hold a meeting of parliament due on 2 June 1640 without the king's permission. Discussion among the covenanter leaders of political theories justifying resistance to kings went as far as ideas asserting the right of subjects to depose them—but this was expressed in abstract terms, care being taken not to apply them directly to the current situation. Parliament duly met, and passed acts changing its membership and asserting its powers in ways which destroyed royal control of the institution. Argyll and those who wanted royal power drastically limited had won. Attention then switched to preparations for war. There was evidently discussion of appointing Argyll 'dictator', or perhaps appointing several regional dictators, these being, in the old Roman meaning of the word, individuals given sweeping powers for a short period to deal with an emergency, in this case war. The idea was dropped, but rumours of it helped fuel growing fears that Argyll aimed at becoming ruler of Scotland. It was noticed that when a committee of estates was appointed to govern the country in June 1640 he was not made a member, even though 'all saw that he was *major potestas* [the great power]' (J. Gordon, 3.182). It may be that Argyll was being typically cautious, wishing to remain in the background, but his absence from the committee could also be interpreted as indicating that he was regarded as standing, in an almost kingly way, above the estates of the realm.

Argyll was appointed to lead forces against potential enemies in Atholl, Mar, Rannoch, the Braes of Angus, Lochaber, and Badenoch, a huge sweep of the central highlands. Montrose, previously chosen to command in Angus and Forfar, was thus partially displaced. The commission allowed Argyll to combine public duty with private gain, for the marquess of Huntly had assigned him Badenoch and Lochaber as security for unpaid debts, and he now had an opportunity to take forceful possession of them. His march through the highlands, 'playing *rex* [king]' (J. Gordon, 3.200) with about 4000 men (late June to early August) met with little resistance. At Ford of Lyon he met with the earl of Atholl and other notables, and in trying to persuade them to join the covenanters talked, in the abstract, of thinkers who believed that kings could be deposed or their power limited by subjects. One of those present, John Stewart the younger of Ladywell, later told Montrose that he had gone further, and spoken of deposing Charles. This was probably untrue, but was powerful ammunition for those who feared Argyll's ambition.

Argyll's determination to assert his power provoked a clash of wills with Montrose when his campaign brought him to the house of Airlie. Wishing, out of friendship, for the Ogilvies of Airlie to be spared the harsh treatment royalists could expect from Argyll, Montrose garrisoned Airlie in name of the covenanters. Argyll saw this as a challenge both to his military jurisdiction and to the effective deterrence of royalist activity, and he therefore ejected Montrose's men and had the house burnt. Harshness against enemies, in Argyll's eyes, would prevent future trouble: '*Quod mortui non mordent*' ('dead men don't bite') was alleged to be an aphorism he favoured (J. Gordon, 3.166). But he knew such harshness would not meet with universal approval, and in ordering the burning of another of the earl of Airlie's houses he wrote 'you neid not to latt know that ye have directions from me to fyir it' (*Sixth Report*, HMC, 616).

At some time in August those covenanter nobles opposed to Argyll's domination sought to organize themselves, binding themselves together by signing the Cumbernauld bond. Its wording was obscure, but its message that there was a danger to the covenanting cause through 'the particular and indirect practiking of a few' (Stevenson, *Scottish Revolution*, 207) hinted at fear that the movement was changing from one demanding limited reforms in religion to one seeking constitutional revolution and the aggrandizement of Argyll. However, the band at first remained secret, and when the covenanters' army invaded the north of England on 20 August Montrose played a leading part, while Argyll continued ensuring the security of the north, Dumbarton Castle surrendering to him on 27 August. He then moved to Edinburgh, where he secured the surrender of the castle on 15 September. The king was again forced to negotiate, accepting the humiliating treaty of Ripon (26 October), whereby the Scots would continue to occupy the north of England until the king summoned the English parliament to raise taxes to pay their army. Neither at Ripon, nor in subsequent negotiations in London, was Argyll present. In November the existence of the Cumbernauld bond became known, revealing Montrose's challenge to Argyll's position, but by this time Montrose had despaired of creating an effective anti-Argyll alliance within the covenanting movement, and turned to working with the king, sending him an account of Argyll's alleged treasonous statements at the Ford of Lyon. Rumours of Montrose's allegations soon spread, and when questioned he cited Ladywell, who duly swore that Argyll had said Charles would be deposed. Argyll hotly denied this, and after a few days Ladywell partly retracted, saying Argyll had only discussed deposing kings in general terms, and he also revealed that Montrose and a small group of friends had been secretly negotiating with the king. On 11 June 'the Plotters' were arrested and on 28 July Ladywell was executed for causing dissension between king and subjects by his false accusations of Argyll.

Thus by the time Charles I reached Edinburgh in August 1641 to ratify a peace settlement, Argyll had removed Montrose from the scene and demonstrated the ruthless punishment that awaited those who made allegations against him. However, though the king was prepared to concede virtually all the covenanters demanded, and heap gifts on their leaders, in order to free himself to deal with the growing crisis to his authority in England posed by parliament there, there proved to be limits to the favours he would bestow on Argyll. The covenanters demanded that he be appointed to the most prestigious office of state, the lord chancellorship, but Charles refused to accept this, proposing Morton for the office instead. This, he may have hoped, would embarrass Argyll, Morton being his father-in-law and former tutor, but Argyll showed no hesitation in denouncing him furiously as old, decrepit, practically bankrupt, and (being a royalist) a deserter of his country. Eventually the covenanters agreed to compromise, with the earl of Loudoun becoming chancellor. Though a close kinsman and ally of Argyll, he was less obnoxious personally in the king's eyes.

Arguments on the issue had increased tension in Edinburgh, and early in October it became known that some royalist officers had planned to seize, and perhaps kill, Argyll, Hamilton (who many royalists thought guilty of betraying the king's interests), and Hamilton's brother, the earl of Lanark. The three men fled from Edinburgh and Charles was forced to agree to an investigation, but before it could reach any conclusions news arrived of the Irish Roman Catholic rising in Ulster, forcing the king to make new concessions in order to reach a Scottish settlement. When he returned to England in November he left effective power in Scotland in the hands of a number of committees dominated by covenanter members, with Argyll's pre-eminence among them intact. As part of the settlement the latter received a marquessate, an annual pension of £1000 sterling, and the properties of the abolished bishoprics of the Isles and Argyll. Since he had joined the covenanters three years before, the man already then considered the most powerful noble in Scotland had grown hugely in power and property.

The solemn league and covenant and civil war Though Argyll's position in Scotland had been consolidated, threats loomed from developments elsewhere in Britain. The most immediate came from Ireland. The Irish rising threatened the future of the Scottish-dominated protestant settlement in Ulster, and its loss to Irish Catholic forces would pose a strategic threat to Scotland as a whole, and most particularly to Argyll. He already feared the continuing ambitions of the marquess of Antrim to seize former MacDonald lands in the highlands from him, and there were fears that the Irish might support such a project. Thus when the Scots, early in 1642, agreed to send an army of 10,000 men to Ulster, Argyll agreed to contribute a regiment of 1000 men under Sir Duncan Campbell of Auchinbreck. By May 1642 this force was occupying much of Antrim's land in north-east Ulster, but by this time attention in Scotland was switching to England and the drift towards civil war there.

Rival requests for Scottish military help from both sides led to rival shows of strength in Scotland. When a council meeting was due to consider the matter in December 1642, so many royalists gathered in Edinburgh that 'there was a great rumour raised of a wicked designe on Argyle's persone' (*Letters … Baillie*, 2.43), and his supporters hastened to the capital to protect him. In the struggle to decide on reaction to the English civil war, Argyll was constantly at the head of manoeuvrings aimed at aiding parliament, his skills in persuasion and manipulation proving crucial. When the privy council inclined towards helping the royalists he managed to get agreement that, in such a crisis, the council should meet jointly to debate the issue with two of the committees set up in November 1641, the committee for common burdens and the conservators of the peace, in which the covenanters held solid majorities. Some thought the three bodies were to meet jointly simply to consult, and that they would vote separately, but Argyll insisted they should vote together as a single body, thus ensuring a covenanting majority. He and his colleagues then persuaded the meeting that it had power to summon a convention of estates (a parliament in all but name) without consulting the king.

When the convention met (22 June 1643) the rival interests were led by Hamilton and Argyll. The majority of the nobility supported Hamilton and helping the king in England, but they were outweighed by the strong support Argyll had among the shire commissioners and burgesses. Negotiations were opened with representatives of the English parliament, and on 26 August the convention agreed to send an army into England, paid for by parliament there, in return for a promise to establish presbyterianism in England. As this army assembled on the borders, however, Argyll had to deal with a regional problem, for at the end of 1643 a force of about 300 Irish Catholics and MacDonald exiles, led by Alasdair MacColla, carried out a raid on the Western Isles to try to reclaim Colonsay and other MacDonald lands. The covenanters appointed Argyll king's lieutenant to suppress the rebels, freeing the shires of Argyll, Dumbarton, and Bute from other levies so he could raise men there. Not until June 1644 were MacColla and his surviving men driven back to Ireland.

Argyll himself had joined the Scots army which had entered England in January 1644, but in April he was recalled to deal with a half-hearted rising by the royalists of the north-east, led by Huntly. At Argyll's approach the royalists dispersed, and he occupied Aberdeen on 2 May. He now hoped to turn his attention back to the English war, being appointed one of the Scottish commissioners who were to stay in London to liaise with the English parliament. However, he was diverted by a new royalist rising in Scotland. Alasdair MacColla had returned to the western highlands with nearly 2000 Irish troops, and put himself under the command of Montrose to fight in the king's name. Argyll was commissioned to act against them, but his task was seen as a fairly minor one, as after their previous successes against royalists the covenanters had become over-confident. In fact Montrose took the initiative, and defeated hastily gathered covenanter levies at Tippermuir (1 September) before moving north to scatter the north-eastern covenanters at Aberdeen (16 September). By the time Argyll reached Aberdeen on 18 September, Montrose had moved on, and Argyll delayed for several days before setting off in pursuit. This, in retrospect, was seen as the first evidence of his alleged cowardice, but as it was not clear what Montrose's intentions were, indecision was understandable. When Argyll did set off in pursuit, Montrose led him a bewildering march through Atholl and Badenoch, then back into Aberdeenshire. Near Fyvie Argyll finally caught up with his enemy, but he failed to press his advantage and Montrose escaped. Calculating that further pursuit was likely to be equally fruitless, luring the covenanters into dancing to Montrose's tune, Argyll decided that it would be better to move south to Perth to block the strategic outlet to the lowlands through Atholl. As Montrose did indeed end up back in Atholl, Argyll's decision was justified, but again to those covenanters frustrated by lack of victory it seemed that he was reluctant to engage with the enemy, and he resigned his commission as commander in Scotland, being assigned instead to command the forces in the west highlands and Isles. However, instead of sidelining Argyll this put him at the centre of the action, as Montrose's men, more interested in killing Campbells than helping the king, persuaded him to undertake a winter campaign in Argyll.

Taken by surprise, as he was not expecting campaigning to begin again until spring, Argyll was forced into humiliating flight to Dumbarton as Montrose approached Inveraray Castle. He quickly recovered and with his own highlanders and lowland reinforcements was soon again in pursuit of Montrose, but was surprised at Inverlochy on 2 February 1645 after Montrose had switched abruptly from retreat to advance. The outcome was the bloodiest defeat the clan Campbell had ever suffered, but Argyll himself took no part in the battle. Incapacitated by a dislocated shoulder (about which his enemies had doubts), he had been persuaded to retire to his galley, and the Campbells were commanded by Auchinbreck, who had been withdrawn with Argyll's regiment from Ireland. Argyll was rowed away as his clansmen were slaughtered. His reputation never fully recovered, and his presence at Montrose's culminating victory, at Kilsyth on 15 August, did little to help. Major-General William Baillie was in command, but already knew he was to be replaced for past failures, and his army was accompanied by Argyll and other members of the committee of estates. Baillie resented their presence, being on particularly bad terms with Argyll. When Argyll asked him, as commander-in-chief, what was to be done, Baillie answered that he would do as they directed, as he was treated with contempt. This squabbling of politicians and soldiers proved disastrous. At Kilsyth Argyll and his colleagues urged Baillie to fight, but when he took up a position facing Montrose they suggested moving to another one. Baillie, in a sulky abdication of responsibility, began the move, and Montrose took advantage of the confusion to attack and overwhelm his men.

Argyll's flight from Kilsyth took him to Newcastle, for though the covenanters now had no army left in Scotland they still had an army in England at their disposal. Troops were hastened home, Argyll accompanying them, and just a month after Kilsyth, Montrose was routed at Philiphaugh, and his rising collapsed from major threat to mere nuisance. In 1646 he agreed to go into exile, but it was to take two years of further fighting in the west highlands before Argyll gained full control of his vast estates. Such was the devastation, Argyll stated, that for many years he collected no rents in the shire of Argyll. He provided for some of his destitute clansmen by authorizing them to plunder royalist estates: he himself was granted Huntly's forfeited estates, and some of Montrose's, and payment of large sums in compensation of his losses was ordered, but his claim to be by far the most powerful man in Scotland in terms of the armed men he could raise was shattered.

Some time after Inverlochy, Argyll had sent the remnants of his regiment in the Scottish army in Ireland back to Ulster, but early in 1646 he went there to divert it back to Scotland to use it in a campaign to reconquer Islay and Kintyre from the Irish and MacDonalds. While he was in Ulster news reached him that Charles I, to escape advancing parliamentarian armies, had surrendered to the Scottish army in England. He hastened to Newcastle, and kissed the king's hand there on 29 May. On 15 June he set off for London to take part in the complex negotiations for a peace settlement which would be acceptable to king, Scottish covenanters, and English parliamentarians. Many Scots were desperate for some sort of settlement with the king, but Argyll led those who insisted that peace must be according to the terms of the solemn league and covenant, meaning that presbyterianism must be imposed in England, something neither Charles nor parliament would accept. The king judged Argyll 'very civil and cunning, but his journey to London will show whether he be altered or not (if he be, it must be for the better), being gone with much professions of doing much for my service' (*Charles I in 1646*, 49). On 25 June committees of both houses of the English parliament met with the Scottish commissioners to discuss parliament's proposed terms for a settlement. These were vague about English church government, and in a speech Argyll denounced 'lawless liberty' which would promote heresies and argued for a settlement according to the covenant—which to him meant presbyterianism—but acknowledged that care must be taken 'that we persecute not piety and peaceable men'. On political issues, he urged that the two kingdoms, so closely allied, should be amalgamated, and that monarchy be maintained, though regulated as 'The safety of the people is the supreme law' (Willcock, 193–4). On these bases, the Scots would accept the terms parliament proposed to submit to the king.

Charles's refusal to accept them in the months that followed deeply split the covenanting movement, with many swinging towards a royalist stance and insisting that the Scottish army stay in England until a settlement was reached, or be allowed to come to Scotland, while Argyll led those who argued that to support Charles in this way, when he had refused the concessions demanded, would mean war with England and betray the covenant. Argyll prevailed, and the Scottish army left England in February 1647, leaving the king to fall into the hands of parliament. Up to the last minute Argyll battled to try to find a way in which 'his Majesty might both get and give satisfaction'. He knew the king had come to regard him as his enemy, but urged that he would be more happy to see the king 'preserve himself' than 'men that flater him most' (Laing, 1.203–4).

Having lost the battle to win the king, Argyll turned to protecting his position in Scotland. It was proposed that the army which had returned from England should be kept in arms, but Argyll feared that, with the drift towards royalism among officers and nobles continuing, it would eventually be used to help the king before he made adequate concessions, and therefore insisted (ostensibly on grounds of expense) that it be reduced to a 'new model' of about 7000 men, chosen for their support for him; they would be used to reconquer those parts of the highlands still in rebel hands—mainly his own estates.

The engagement Argyll had, for the moment, won the political battle in Scotland, but leaving the king in England increased sympathy for him, and the fight to reverse the decision became increasingly bitter. 'I can hardlie expres … the difficulties sum men ar put to, to carie on business her[e]; many being so weak, others so full of by ways and malice to men who heave served thair countrie … with faithfulness' he wrote in March of the difficulties facing him, though he still hoped that the king would 'grant the desyrs of his subjects as the best cure under God that I know for himself or ous' (Laing, 1.212). By this time most of the nobility had rallied under Hamilton in opposition, and Argyll maintained his domination only through the support of lesser men and the presbyterian ministers, and through a tactical difficulty that deterred his opponents from pressing for immediate intervention in England—the fact that the force that would undertake such action, the Scottish army, had now been remodelled to ensure its loyalty to Argyll.

Argyll marched to the west highlands with the army in May 1647, not returning to Edinburgh until August. The success of the military campaign, meaning he could now at last control his own estates again, might in some ways seem to restore his credibility, but it enabled his opponents to demand the army's disbandment and at the committee of estates on 15 October Argyll thwarted them by only a single vote. Moreover, on the central issue of fresh negotiations with the king he lost control, and the engagement treaty was signed in December, binding the Scots to intervene in England to help Charles without, in Argyll's eyes, adequate concessions from him. Argyll denounced this as likely to lead to a war which would ruin both kingdoms, and the church supported him, but the engagers now had an unshakeable majority in the committee and the Scottish parliament. There was talk of the Scottish army copying the English one—by purging parliament of Argyll's opponents—but it proved divided, and many of its officers were won over to the engagement. The bitterness of factional debate provoked the earl of Crawford-Lindsay and Argyll to arrange a duel: that the parties agreed to settle the matter by written statements led to renewed charges of cowardice against Argyll, and to his accepting censure from the church for agreeing to take part.

Unable to prevent the invasion of England, Argyll withdrew to Inveraray, but on news of the destruction of the engager army by Oliver Cromwell at Preston in August he gathered together some of his forces; however they were surprised, and were scattered near Stirling on 12 September by the remnants of the engagers' army. None the less, negotiations for the engagers' surrender continued, and Argyll hurried south to persuade the advancing Cromwell not to bring his army into Scotland, meeting him first on 21 September. He was unsuccessful, and only after the engagers had finally surrendered and a new anti-engager regime had given assurances of friendship with England, and that supporters of the engagement would be excluded from public life, did Cromwell withdraw from Scotland, on 7 October.

Kirk party to royalist revival Argyll was the dominant figure in the new 'kirk party' regime but, as its name suggests, it was a regime dependent on the church, which had opposed the engagement from the start. Much of the country's traditional élite, including most of the nobility, were now formally excluded from power as having been engagers, and hatred of Argyll personally was widespread. In the past he had been glad to co-operate with the church and had drawn much of his power from its support, but now, with more radical ministers in the ascendant, he increasingly found his need for its support forcing him into policies he opposed. At first, however, he and the kirk acted together, concentrating on consolidating their hold on power by purging engagers, but the major issue remained that of the monarchy. The English were determined to bring Charles I to trial, and Argyll sent messengers to the exiled prince of Wales, urging him to come to Scotland so that he and the kirk party could combine to help his father. This move was based on genuine belief that a political settlement must be founded on monarchy, but also, no doubt, on the calculation that if he brought the young prince to Scotland and he proved pliable, this would greatly strengthen Argyll's own position. The execution of the king in January 1649 was met with universal horror in Scotland, and the exiled prince of Wales was immediately proclaimed king (of England and Ireland as well as Scotland) in Edinburgh, but Charles I's death also increased the bitterness of political divisions in Scotland. Many blamed the new regime, set up with the help of Cromwell's armies, for permitting the execution to take place, and rumours circulated that haunted Argyll for the rest of his life: that in his talks with Cromwell the previous autumn he had agreed that the king should die.

The fact that the Scots had proclaimed Charles II king of England made war with the new Commonwealth regime there almost inevitable, but it was delayed by Cromwell's first undertaking the conquest of Ireland. Attempts to reach agreement with the new king in 1649 failed, but in January 1650 Charles wrote to Argyll and the kirk asking for new negotiations, while at the same time putting pressure on the regime by encouraging Montrose to return to Scotland and instigate a new royalist rising. On 29 April Scottish commissioners, desperate to reach a settlement when faced by threats from Cromwell in the south and Montrose in the north, issued an invitation to Charles to come to Scotland, which he accepted. In fact, two days before this Montrose's army had been routed and dispersed at Carbisdale. On 18 May Argyll was an onlooker as Montrose, in a cart driven by the hangman, was paraded through the streets of Edinburgh, where he was executed on 21 May. Argyll took no part in the decision that the death sentence should be carried out, a forbearance that Montrose's son repaid in 1661 by abstaining from voting for Argyll's execution. There can be no doubt, however, that he believed that Montrose deserved to die, but he may have thought the execution inexpedient at a time when he was trying to reach an agreement with the king. Argyll commented on Montrose's composure on the scaffold, but turned that to his disadvantage: 'he got sum resolution after he cam[e] her[e], how to goe out of this world, but nothing at all how to enter in ane other, not so muche as once humbling himself to pray at all on the scaffold' (Laing, 2.262).

Charles II landed in northern Scotland on 24 May, and wrote to Argyll assuring him of his friendship, evidently hoping that if he had Argyll's support it would be possible to resist the kirk party's endless demands for more concessions from him. But Argyll proved powerless. His resolution that the removal of the king's 'malignant' friends from court should be delayed was defeated in parliament, at which he was 'exceedingly unsatisfied' (Stevenson, *Revolution and Counter-Revolution*, 171). The landing of the king provoked Cromwell into invasion in July, but the more zealous of the kirk party insisted on thorough purging of the army to remove the ungodly, in spite of Argyll's opposition. The king, excluded from power, might be virtually the prisoner of Argyll, whose son Lord Lorne commanded the life guard, but Argyll in turn was captive of the kirk party. By the end of August it was being reported that he had told the king to be patient: for the moment it was necessary to please the madmen, but once he invaded England he would have greater freedom.

The disastrous defeat at Dunbar on 3 September discredited the kirk party and its power rapidly dwindled, but this made Argyll's position even worse, for the need to resist invasion led to an irresistible royalist revival. The king at first reassured him, promising on 24 September to make him a duke, a knight of the Garter, and a gentleman of the bedchamber and 'I doe further promis him to hearken to his counsels' (Willcock, 253). When restored in England he would ensure that Argyll was paid the £40,000 sterling due to him for expenses incurred in public service. Argyll would have been justified in suspecting that this was too good to be true, for on 3 October the royalists, supported by Charles, attempted a coup d'état. This failed, but emphasized that Argyll and the kirk party would have to make concessions if their regime was to survive. By the end of 1650 what soon became a flood of royalists began to join the army and take up office in government. Struggling to maintain his position, Argyll proposed (or perhaps supported a proposal made by others) that the king marry his daughter, but Charles won delay by urging that he needed to consult his mother on the matter. On 1 January 1651 when Charles was crowned king at Scone, Argyll placed the crown on his head and installed him on his throne. None the less, power was slipping away from the kingmaker, as royalists took power in a country crumbling before Cromwell. When it was decided to invade England to try to win support there and divert Cromwell from Scotland, Argyll refused to take part, and as at the time of the engagement retired to the highlands. In his eyes, an invasion for the cause of the covenant would have been justified, one simply undertaken to restore royal power was not.

Commonwealth and protectorate After the invasion collapsed at the battle of Worcester in September Argyll accepted completion of the Cromwellian conquest of Scotland as inevitable. He sought to negotiate with General George Monck, now in command of the English army in Scotland, to allow some sort of Scottish regime to continue to exist, but when he met English commissioners at Dumbarton on 18 March 1652 his ideas were rejected. 'He solicites hard and sends letter after letter, and one messenger after another, useing all the means he can … to obtaine some singular act of favour' (Firth, *Scotland and Commonwealth*, xxii). Exasperated by this, Major-General Richard Deane (who had succeeded Monck) marched on Inveraray, and Argyll hastily declared acceptance of the authority of the English parliament and the terms for a union of England and Scotland that it had offered. In an agreement signed on 19 August 1652 he undertook to live peacefully under the new government, and do all he could to ensure that his family and dependants did the same, so long as this did not hinder his 'good endeavours for the establishing religion according to his conscience' (ibid., 48–9).

However a new threat to Argyll's position soon appeared, for when in 1653 the royalists under the earl of Glencairn began a rising in the highlands they not only had the support of anti-Campbell clans but of Argyll's own son, Lorne, who had become a committed royalist. He sought by pleas and threats to deter his son, calling down God's judgment against disobedient children—'you are a crosse (I may say a curse) to your father and heavinesse to your mother … I shall remayne your loving father' (Firth, *Scotland and Commonwealth*, 167)—but to no avail. As a further humiliation Argyll had to admit to the English authorities that there was no point in his even attempting to oppose a royalist advance into Kintyre as the country people would not resist his son. In 1654 he asked for an English garrison to be established in Argyll to 'keep it from his son's violence'. Baillie noted that 'The people's great hatred lyes on him above any other, and whatever befalls him, few does pittie it'; adding that 'at this very time his state is very staggering', since the marquess was likely to be ruined by debt (*Letters … Baillie*, 3.288). Moreover, the English naturally suspected that Argyll secretly supported his son, and to persuade them of his loyalty to the regime he was forced into actively helping it rather than merely submitting to it. When in November 1654 he ventured into the lowlands to denounce his son to General Monck he found himself insulted by his creditors and branded in the streets as 'a fals traitour' (J. Nicoll, *Diary*, 1836, 295). Lorne's surrender to the English in August 1655 removed one embarrassment, but the two men remained bitterly estranged. Late in 1655 Argyll visited London to kiss the protector's hand and get his agreement of 1652 with Deane ratified, but was shocked in December to be arrested for debt at the instance of the dowager duchess of Dirleton; he evidently was not released until February 1656. However, in March he secured ratification of his submission of 1652 and a grant of £3000 sterling a year from Scottish excise duties towards payment of debts he had incurred under the covenanters. He remained in London until 1657, and is twice recorded visiting John Evelyn, amusing him by his ignorance of ornithology: he 'tooke the Turtle-Doves for Owles' (Evelyn, *Diary*, 3.175).

Argyll's willingness to help the English by supplying intelligence and raising men to fight (with English pay) against the royalists at first won him English trust and favour, but in the later 1650s doubts emerged as to his loyalty. After Oliver Cromwell's death in September 1658 he began to seek a role for himself in public affairs, urging that all those elected to sit for Scottish constituencies in Protector Richard Cromwell's parliament should be Scots. He was himself elected to sit in the Commons for Aberdeenshire, though General Monck protested that 'truly I thinke in his Heart there is noe man in the three Nations does more dissaffect the English Interest than hee' (Firth, *Scotland and Protectorate*, 411).

Trial and execution On news of the restoration of Charles II, Argyll, perhaps influenced by his son's advice, went to court. For a man many thought a coward it was a bold action. On 8 July 1660 he appeared in the outer chamber in Whitehall Palace and asked for permission to see the king to kiss hands, 'thinking that he had been in no worse favour than the other noblemen who had been engag'd in the same party' (Mackenzie, 13). But the king sent Sir Edward Walter, the Garter king-at-arms, to arrest him on charges of treason, and in spite of his indignant demands to be allowed to see the king he was taken to the Tower. On 7 December he was sent by sea to Leith, and then confined in Edinburgh Castle. His trial before parliament began on 13 February 1661, with the many charges of treason against him ranging through his actions in the 1640s and 1650s, and including complicity in the execution of Charles I. While also giving answers to specific charges, his defence relied mainly on two general arguments: first, that since the Scottish parliament had passed an act of indemnity, ratified by Charles II, in 1651 he could not be convicted for any actions previous to that date, and second, that in his compliance with the English during their occupation he was acting under necessity, and did no more than virtually all Scots. Through Lorne's intervention with the king, parliament was instructed to accept the first point, and (if Gilbert Burnet's account can be relied on) Charles also ordered that at the end of the trial no sentence was to be passed until the records of the trial had been scrutinized by the king. But, it is said, his commissioner the earl of Middleton, who presided in parliament, protested that this indicated distrust of parliament. The king then cancelled the order that sentence be delayed.

Attention now passed to Argyll's complicity in regicide (in spite of the 1651 indemnity) and his actions under English rule. The charge of complicity was pressed hard by the prosecution, but he was cleared for lack of evidence. On his relations with the English regime, it was stressed that he had been one of the last Scots to submit, and that he had never expressed approval of their government. His failure to join the royalist rising led by Glencairn, and subsequently by Middleton, was not culpable in law as neither had specifically summoned him to serve the king. It was admitted that he had been present in 1657 at a proclamation in Edinburgh of Oliver Cromwell as lord protector, but this had been accidental—he had gone to Edinburgh at Monck's request on other business. His attendance at Richard Cromwell's parliament was explained by the need to protect Scotland's interests. When parliament moved to debate on whether Argyll's conduct in the 1650s amounted to treason there seemed, remarkably, a chance that the most hated man in the country might be acquitted. Argyll's bearing in court had influenced even some of his enemies, but far more influential was the force of the argument that Argyll had done no more than many others—including most members of parliament. If in the case of Argyll they judged that this was treason, then they themselves were open to prosecution on the same charge. Middleton, in his zeal to have Argyll convicted of complicity in Charles I's death, himself drew attention to this. When a member said Argyll was no more guilty than most others, he savagely replied, 'we are all of us, or most, guilty, and the King may pitch on any he pleases to take his examples' (Willcock, 319). Middleton's intention was to terrify men into voting to condemn Argyll to avoid being picked on, but it took little thought to realize that the safest thing to do would be to acquit him.

However, the debate was interrupted by a messenger who 'knockt most rudely at the Parliament door' (Mackenzie, 39) and produced letters which had been sent by Argyll to Colonel Robert Lilburne and George Monck, commanders-in-chief in Scotland, in 1653–4. In spite of the fact that formal presentation of evidence had been completed, Middleton allowed the letters to be admitted, and they provided clear evidence that Argyll had not only submitted to the English but had been active in supplying intelligence of royalist plans and movements and otherwise assisting English military action. Whether this evidence, that Argyll had gone far further than other members of parliament in compliance, swung the balance of his judges against him cannot be known, but it clearly increased the majority who proceeded to vote for his condemnation. On 25 May 1661 he was sentenced to be beheaded two days later—moves to have him hanged, as Montrose had been, and thus die in a manner unfitting a noble, were rejected. Argyll's response was to observe he had put the crown on the king's head (in 1651) and hoped God would now give him a crown of glory. 'The Parliament seem'd much affected with this great revolution of fortune, and his own carriage, which drew tears from his very enemies' (Mackenzie, 40).

George Mackenzie, one of Argyll's advocates, noted:

> I remember that I having told him, a little before his death, that the people believ'd he was a coward and expected he would die timorously, he said to me he would not die as a Roman, braving death, but he would die as a Christian without being affrighted. (Mackenzie, 47)

Here, surely, he was thinking of his reaction to Montrose's death, and his belief that he had not died as a Christian should. On the scaffold on 27 May he observed 'I resolve to disappoint many; for I came here not to justify myself, but the Lord who is holy', adding that 'I entered not upon the work of reformation with any design of advantage for myself, or prejudice to the King and his government' (Mackenzie, 41). In his speech he repeatedly emphasized that he had had no part in Charles I's death, for though formally cleared of that charge he feared many still thought him guilty of it. He then coolly moved on to social-religious analysis. Three sorts of people made up most of the population. The profane ('I hear assuredly, that drinking, whoring, and swearing, were never more common, and never more countenanced than now' was his comment on Restoration libertinism), those 'not openly profane' who did not care whether the church 'sink or swim', and the truly godly. 'That I am look'd on as a friend of reformation, it is my glory' and men must decide whether to 'sin, or suffer'. Sinners would not suffer as he did, he asserted, indicating the maiden, the beheading machine on the scaffold, but in eternity 'when I shall be singing, they shall be howling' (Mackenzie, 43–5). He spoke 'to the people without any commotion and with his ordinary gestures' (ibid., 47) but some observers, on the lookout for fear, thought he spoke for too long, fiddling with the buttons on his doublet before finally taking it off, and then delaying further for a final declaration of his innocence concerning the death of Charles I, before laying his head on the block. His body was taken to Kilmun in Argyll for burial; his head, after being put on public display, followed in 1664.

Caution and conviction To presbyterians Argyll's execution made him a martyr for the godly cause. 'Whatever had been his escapes [lapses] and complying with the usurpers, he was a man that ever owned the good cause and the work of reformation of religion, and lived devoutly himself, always keeping a good order in his family' (R. Blair, *The Life of Mr Robert Blair*, ed. T. McCrie, 1848, 38). But to royalists he was the object of intense hatred, the man primarily to blame for the Scottish actions during the civil wars and central to the downfall of Charles I. Clarendon accused him of 'inveterate malice' towards Charles I (Clarendon, *Hist. rebellion*, 4.5), but Argyll was driven rather by principle and ambition, compelled to push himself into a dominant position in Scotland through conviction that his status (as representing a great noble family) justified it and the will of God required it. His joining the covenanters in 1638 grew out of his conviction that royal power must be checked both to protect the Church of Scotland and his own inheritance. His sudden emergence from concentration on regional affairs to asserting himself as a major national figure surprised some. The royalist Patrick Gordon thought he was, as if by:

> inchantment, turned out of his oun nature, and changed from his laborious disposition and caire of worldlie thrift to

> ane ambitious desyre of supreame and absolut rule, which he might weell hope for, being the most eminent and greatest among them [the covenanters].

Once involved in rebellion, on this interpretation, he found he could not escape from it safely so pressed ahead and allowed his best qualities to be overruled by 'Machewilles prince, which, by his practisses in the most part … he seemed perfectly to haue studied' (P. Gordon, 56). In fact, he showed no hesitation or regrets, moving from relative obscurity to political dominance in Scotland with confidence, for his social status was recognized and his piety widely respected. The single-minded commitment he had shown in advancing the house of Argyll was now redirected to national affairs with a characteristic mixture of boldness and self-effacing caution.

In his personal behaviour the influence of Argyll's high birth was modified by this piety. He devoted many hours to private prayer and family worship, studiously avoided ostentation, and showed himself prepared to listen to those far below him in rank if they shared his religious convictions. Though he could display fierce anger he was generally 'of a homely carriage, gentle, mild, and effable, gratious and courteous to speak too', and had:

> suche plaine and homely aspect, as he seemed rather inclyned to simplicitie then any wayes tented with a loftie and unsatiable ambition, though he proved the deepest statesman, the most craftie, subtill, and over-reacheing politician, that this age could produce. (P. Gordon, 56–7)

That he was fairly short in stature, slight in figure, and suffered from a squint added to the deceptively low-key impression he often gave. This simplicity of manner proved one of the keys to his success, for during most of the 1640s he was more dependent on the support of men of lower rank—parish ministers, gentry, and burgesses—than on his fellow noblemen. The claim that he was 'the statesman who had given over Scotland to the rule of the middle classes' (Gardiner, 1.353) has some truth in it if 'classes' is accepted as meaning 'ranks'. It was Argyll who pushed for the establishing of the shire commissioners in parliament as a separate estate with double their former voting power in 1640, believing that they were more likely to stand firm in promoting the 'godly' policies he stood for than were his colleagues of the titled nobility. He was proved correct. By 1643 he was reliant on burgh and shire votes in pushing through the solemn league and covenant against the opposition of most of the nobility, and after being forced from power by the noble-dominated engagers he only recovered it by excluding most of the nobility from parliament. But he then found that the shire and burgh commissioners on whom he was reliant were taking leadership from the ministers of the kirk rather than from him. He was no longer master but victim, caught between the 'middle class' kirk party on one side, and royalist revival on the other.

For a man who was at the centre of Scottish affairs for a decade, Argyll is surprisingly elusive, often choosing to work behind the scenes while others stood in the limelight. Military glory, of the sort Montrose valued, was evidently to Argyll unacceptably pagan and presumptuous (though perhaps not least because he found it unattainable). His own political skills were widely perceived as being based on unattractive qualities of craftiness and dissembling. In his own mind he acted honourably to advance the cause, but he was a master of words, clever in persuading, manipulating, and misleading, meaning one thing but deliberately using words which conveyed another to the unwary listener. Thus late in 1646 he assured Charles I that, if he was allowed to go to London to negotiate with the English parliament, he would make sure that the king's security would be guaranteed and he would be treated honourably. But the king was later informed that Argyll had remarked that what he had said was consistent with the king's being 'put into prison provided he be served by persons on their knees' (Fotheringham, 1.350; Willcock, 217).

Gilbert Burnet wrote that Argyll was:

> a solemn sort of man, grave and sober, free of all scandalous vices, of an invincible calmness, and a pretender to high degrees of piety: but he was a deep dissembler, and a great oppressor in all his private dealings, and he was noted for a defect in his courage on all occasions when danger met him. This had one of its usual effects on him, for he was cruel in cold blood. (*Bishop Burnet's History*, 1.149)

Cruelty, in that Argyll favoured harshness as a productive policy, showed little mercy to his enemies, and fully matched the brutality of his opponents in the bitter highland war of the mid-1640s, is a charge that sticks. So too is financial oppression, for in saving and seeking to advance both the house of Argyll and the covenant he was often in debt and ruthless in his financial dealings. But the charge of physical cowardice is harder to justify, and perhaps gets repeated because it can then be neatly contrasted with the heroism of Montrose. The accusation rests partly on his flights after military defeats, but though such defeats suggest a lack of military skill they do not prove cowardice. As to his conduct at Inverlochy in 1645, whether or not his arm was disabled, his Campbell kin insisted that he removed himself from danger—though it may be true that he accepted that his leading position in the causes for which he was fighting (Campbells and covenants) was such that to risk his life in battle would be folly. As to his conduct in the abortive duel with Crawford-Lindsay in 1648, it is not clear which party first proposed not fighting, and Argyll's willingness to avoid conflict was perhaps not so much the result of fear of physical harm but of spiritual dangers: duelling was ungodly. If this analysis seems over-charitable, it cannot be denied that at the end of his life he proved courageous, in boldly going to court instead of retreating into the highlands, and in his conduct at his trial and on the scaffold. Those who had come to believe in the stories of his cowardice were startled—and disappointed.

In politics as opposed to military affairs Argyll may have been devious in tactics, but he was courageous in the way that he proved unswerving in the cause of the covenants once he had committed himself. Even in 1651 he refused to flow with the royalist tide and, while his acceptance of Cromwellian rule was self-serving in that it saved him from ruin, it is probable also that he believed English puritan rule, however obnoxious, was less damaging to the cause of God than royalist victory would have been. His invocation on the scaffold of his enemies suffering eternal torment in hell may be unattractive, but there is no doubt of the strength of his religious beliefs. His speech on the scaffold reflects the depth of his convictions: for once the cautious politician spoke out. But hopes that the *Instructions to a Son by the Marquis of Argyle. Written in the Time of his Confinement*, published in London in 1661, might shed further light on his beliefs are disappointed on realization that the work is spurious, a conventional tract of advice to children crudely edited to make it appear to be by Argyll.

DAVID STEVENSON

Sources J. Willcock, *The great marquess: life and times of Archibald, 8th earl, and 1st (and only) marquess of Argyll (1607–1661)* (1903) • *DNB* • GEC, *Peerage* • A. I. Macinnes, *Clanship, commerce, and the house of Stuart, 1603–1788* (1996) • E. J. Cowan, 'The political ideas of a covenanting leader: Archibald Campbell, marquis of Argyll 1607–1661', *Scots and Britons: Scottish political thought and the union of 1603*, ed. R. A. Mason (1994), 241–61 • Clarendon, *Hist. rebellion* • *The letters and journals of Robert Baillie*, ed. D. Laing, 3 vols. (1841–2) • J. Spalding, *Memorialls of the trubles in Scotland and in England, AD 1624 – AD 1645*, ed. J. Stuart, 2 vols., Spalding Club, [21, 23] (1850–51) • P. Gordon, *A short abridgement of Britane's distemper*, ed. J. Dunn, Spalding Club, 10 (1844) • J. Gordon, *History of Scots affairs from 1637–1641*, ed. J. Robertson and G. Grub, 3 vols., Spalding Club, 1, 3, 5 (1841) • *Bishop Burnet's History* • *Correspondence of Sir Robert Kerr, first earl of Ancram, and his son William, third earl of Lothian*, ed. D. Laing, 2 vols., Roxburghe Club, 100 (1875) • G. Mackenzie, *Memoirs of the affairs of Scotland* (1821) • D. Stevenson, *The Scottish revolution, 1637–44: the triumph of the covenanters* (1973) • D. Stevenson, *Revolution and counter-revolution in Scotland, 1644–1651*, Royal Historical Society Studies in History, 4 (1977) • *CSP dom., 1625–61* • *Reg. PCS*, 2nd ser., vols. 1–8 • *Calendar of the Clarendon state papers preserved in the Bodleian Library*, ed. O. Ogle and others, 5 vols. (1869–1970) • C. H. Firth, ed., *Scotland and the Commonwealth: letters and papers relating to the military government of Scotland, from August 1651 to December 1653*, Scottish History Society, 18 (1895) • C. H. Firth, ed., *Scotland and the protectorate: letters and papers relating to the military government of Scotland from January 1654 to June 1659*, Scottish History Society, 31 (1899) • *Fourth report*, HMC, 3 (1874) • *Sixth report*, HMC, 5 (1877–8) • *State trials* • P. Yorke [earl of Hardwicke], ed., *Miscellaneous state papers, 1501–1726*, 2 vols. (1778) • *Charles I in 1646: letters of King Charles the first to Queen Henrietta Maria*, ed. J. Bruce, CS, 63 (1856) • [J. Hamilton, duke of Hamilton], *The Hamilton papers: being selections from original letters … relating to … 1638–1650*, ed. S. R. Gardiner, CS, new ser., 27 (1880) • S. R. Gardiner, *History of the Commonwealth and protectorate, 1649–1656*, new edn, 4 vols. (1903) • J. G. Fotheringham, ed., *The diplomatic correspondence of Jean de Montereul and the brothers de Bellièvre: French ambassadors in England and Scotland, 1645–1648*, 2 vols., Scottish History Society, 29–30 (1898–9) • *The memoirs of Henry Guthry, late bishop*, 2nd edn (1747)

Archives Inveraray Castle, Argyll • NL Scot., corresp. and MSS • NRA Scotland, priv. coll., accounts relating to army for Ireland | NA Scot., letters to Campbells of Glenorchy

Likenesses L. Schuneman, oils, *c.*1632, Buccleuch estates, Selkirk; repro. in Willcock, *Great marquess* • D. Scougall, oils, Scot. NPG [*see illus.*] • oils (after D. Scougall, *c.*1650), NPG

Campbell, Archibald, ninth earl of Argyll (1629–1685), politician and clan leader, was born on 26 February 1629 at Newbattle Abbey, Edinburghshire, the son of Archibald *Campbell, Lord Lorne and later eighth earl and marquess of Argyll (1605x7–1661), and his wife, Lady Margaret (1610–1678), daughter of William *Douglas, earl of Morton (1582–1648). At the age of four he was, in accordance with Gaelic tradition, fostered with a kinsman, Sir Colin Campbell of Glenorchy, living mainly at Balloch, Perthshire. After his father had inherited the earldom in 1638 he was known by the courtesy title Lord Lorne, and he returned to his family at Inveraray Castle in 1639. He was sent to the University of Glasgow in 1642, but he did not graduate.

The emergence of a royalist Being the son of the dominant figure in the covenanting regime which had seized power in Scotland through rebellion against Charles I, it was thought appropriate that when Lorne was sent abroad to continue his studies he, his friends, and followers should have the protection of letters of commendation from the Scottish parliament, and these were issued under the great seal in the king's name (January 1647). Lorne's travels in France and Italy lasted until late in 1649, and it was perhaps in this period that his royalist sympathies began to emerge. Some time after the execution of Charles I in January 1649 he wrote (presumably to someone accompanying the exiled Stuart court) expressing his dismay at Charles II's harsh opinions of Argyll. His father, he urged, was a loyal subject, and a well-wisher to the dynasty. But Lorne then proceeded to distance himself from his father and from events in Scotland by asserting that if his father was disloyal he would not support him. For two years he had heard so little from Scotland that he had seldom even heard of 'the state of my parents health' (Firth, *Commonwealth*, xlvii).

Lorne returned to Scotland in late 1649, and completion of his education was followed by marriage, on 13 May 1650, to Lady Mary, daughter of James Stuart, earl of Moray. He had been given a place in March on the committee of estates, which ruled Scotland in the name of the absentee Charles II, and after the king and covenanters reached agreement and Charles went to Scotland, Lorne was commissioned (6 August) by him to be captain of his foot life guard. As the king's guards were chosen for their dedication to the covenanting cause, Lorne's task was as much to supervise his movements and contacts with royalists as to protect him, and the story that Lorne refused to accept a commission from parliament and insisted on one from the king himself is dubious—parliament was not sitting at the time. How Lorne treated the king he was guarding depends on whether the much later account of a friend or an enemy is believed. The earl of Clarendon claimed Lorne 'had so strict a care of him [the king] both night and day that he could not go any whither without his leave' (Clarendon, *Hist. rebellion*, 5.149), and that he 'had treated his majesty with that rudeness and barbarity, that he was much more odious to him than his father' (E. Hyde, *Life of Edward, Earl of Clarendon*, 3 vols., 1827, 2.277). Gilbert Burnet said the opposite: Lorne 'made his court more dextrously' to Charles than his father did, allowed access to the king to all men he wished to see, 'and was in all respects not only faithful but zealous' (*Burnet's History*, 1.106). Probably, in view of the commitment to the king that Lorne was soon to show, Burnet comes closer to the truth than the vindictive Clarendon, though, as with many other Scots, Lorne's attachment to the king may have grown after the disastrous defeat by Cromwell at the battle of Dunbar (3 September 1650) which discredited the extreme kirk party covenanters. As for the king himself, at a time when his eagerness for Argyll's support led him to consider the idea that he should marry Argyll's daughter, he no doubt sought good relations with Lorne.

When Argyll's influence in Scotland collapsed and Charles embarked on his 1651 invasion of England, Lorne followed his father in refusing to have anything to do with the venture, but when, after its failure, the English moved towards the completion of the conquest of Scotland and Argyll accepted their rule, Lorne refused to submit. Early in 1653, when preparations were being made for a royalist rising in the highlands, it was reported that 'he hath been without the meerest shadow of complyance of any kind [with the English] most invincibly constant and faithfull to your Majesty's service and interests' (Firth, *Commonwealth*, 134). His father warned him that if he joined the royalists, then 'let all the curse and judgements pronounced in God's word against disobedient children to parents come upon you' (Firth, *Commonwealth*, 167), but Lorne refused to listen and joined the royalists in July. It has been argued that Lorne's royalism was a matter of collusion between father and son, designed to ensure that whichever side won there would be a Campbell leader to protect family interests, but such suspicions seem unfounded. None the less, they meant that Lorne met with distrust from the other leaders of the rising, who were already deeply divided among themselves. Many of the highland royalists sought not just the restoration of the king but also the downfall of the Campbells, and obviously for them co-operation with whatever forces Lorne raised from his clan was difficult. Lorne himself was never a tactful man and was determined that his high rank be acknowledged. He soon quarrelled with the earl of Glencairn, appointed commander-in-chief by Charles II, and other senior officers. In September, Lorne and Lord Kenmure commanded several hundred royalist troops camped in Menteith, west of Stirling, but they were forced to retire west into Argyll by English forces. Argyll made little attempt to hinder his son's recruiting activities, and most of the population sympathized with Lorne, but it was known that some lowlanders recently settled in Kintyre were hostile to the royalist cause. Lorne and Kenmure therefore advanced against them, forcing them to submit after some skirmishing. On their return to join Glencairn in Badenoch squabbling again broke out among the royalist commanders, culminating in Lorne fleeing in October to escape arrest.

It was hoped that the arrival of Lieutenant-General John Middleton in February 1654 to take over command from Glencairn might restore some unity among the royalists, but if anything the quarrels intensified. Lorne continued active in Argyll but was as much concerned with cattle raiding to support his men as with action against the English, and though in September he captured a ship laden with English supplies for Inveraray Castle, this provoked his father for the first time into joining the English in military action against him. English advances led most royalists to accept that they had no hope of success, and by late 1654 many were negotiating terms of surrender. Middleton urged Lorne to follow suit, writing to him on 31 March 1655 to 'loose no tyme in taking such course' for the good of himself, his family, and his estate, and praising his conduct during the rising (Willcock, 72–3). On 17 May terms were agreed, with Lorne undertaking to live peaceably under the government of Cromwell as lord protector, and to find £5000 sterling of 'good Lowland security' to do so. But ill feeling between him and his father continued to make 'both their lives bitter and uncomfortable for them; and the great burthen of debt puts their verie house in a hazard to ruine' (*Letters … Baillie*, 3.288).

Moreover, the regime remained deeply suspicious of

Archibald Campbell, ninth earl of Argyll (1629–1685), by unknown artist, 1660s [with his first wife, Lady Mary Stuart]

Lorne, and intelligence reports, though seldom reliable, suggested he was involved in plans for a new royalist rising, and his continued 'insubmissiveness' to his father (Willcock, 76) also indicated that he was not reconciled to royalist failure. In early 1657 it was resolved to smoke out closet royalists by imposing on suspects an oath renouncing allegiance to the Stuarts and specifically accepting the protectorate. Lorne refused the oath, and was imprisoned in Edinburgh Castle. But the suggestion that he was so dangerous a threat that he should be moved to a prison in England was not acted upon, and by March 1658 the conditions in which he was held were sufficiently relaxed for him to be 'playing at the bullets' with an officer of the castle garrison (Willcock, 80). The game involved throwing cannon balls, and almost had a fatal ending. One of the officer's shots, ricocheting off a stone, struck Lorne on the head, knocking him unconscious for some hours. After being trepanned he recovered, but it was said the incident left him with a tendency to irritability and a lifelong need to sleep for at least an hour every afternoon. He was released in July 1659, on £10,000 sterling security for good behaviour, and moved to Bog of Gight (Gordon) Castle, on the estates of the first marquess of Huntly which had been forfeited and awarded to Argyll. He agreed not to travel more than 25 miles from the castle, and to return to prison after twelve months, but in the event the collapse of the protectorate and the restoration of monarchy cancelled such obligations.

Forfeiture and recovery After Charles II's arrival in England in May 1660 Lorne hastened to London and was well received by the king, but his father, who followed him, was arrested and sent back to Scotland to be tried for treason. In due course Argyll was condemned and his titles and estates forfeited, and he was beheaded on 27 May 1661. Lorne had been consistent in support of his father during the trial but, given the credentials as a royalist he had acquired during the 1650s, Charles II and his Scottish secretary, the earl of Lauderdale, favoured a restoration of his family's titles and lands. Campbell power in the western highlands had long been seen as a bulwark of government control, and, in spite of the marquess of Argyll's treason, arguments of expediency doubtless suggested that retaining it would be far less disruptive than destroying it. But counter-arguments were also strong. It had been demonstrated in the 1640s that Campbell strength was a threat to the crown, and the many royalists who had suffered under Campbell domination of Scotland in the 1640s wanted revenge and compensation out of the family estates. Further, the family's huge debts could only be paid if the family property was dispersed. Intrigue at court over who should benefit from the fall of Argyll was intense, and the hopes of the wronged, of those owed money, and of the simply greedy would all be strengthened if Lorne shared his father's fate. A pretext was found in a letter from Lorne which was intercepted, in which he expressed hope that the king would see through 'the tricks' of his enemies in the Scottish parliament, and revealed that he had found an English nobleman who, for a bribe of £1000 sterling, would persuade the earl of Clarendon, lord chancellor of England, to abandon his hostility to Lorne (Willcock, 119). Parliament seized upon this to accuse Lorne of leasing-making, the crime (punishable by death) of causing dissension between the king and his subjects, and requested that he be arrested and sent to Scotland for trial. Charles, who believed Lorne indiscreet but not guilty of any crime, agreed to the trial, though Lorne was allowed to return to Scotland voluntarily rather that have the indignity of being arrested. On his appearance before parliament on 17 July 1662, however, he was committed to Edinburgh Castle. In his defence, he pleaded that in writing the words for which he was being tried he had been reacting to gross provocation, and that he had not sought to harm anyone but simply to defend himself from malicious lies. None the less, he was condemned to death, sentence being pronounced on 26 August. The king had ordered that any sentence should not be carried out until he had been consulted, but parliament sought to prevent his intervening to pardon Lorne by passing an act forbidding anyone to urge the king to favour the children of attainted persons.

The vindictiveness of the Scottish parliament in harrying Lorne was orchestrated by his commander in 1654–5, Middleton, now earl of Middleton and the king's commissioner in parliament. He headed the most vengeful of the royalists, more royalist than the king himself, but his determination to destroy Lorne was also driven by the hope of getting a generous grant from the forfeited Campbell estates. However, Middleton's disruptive policies soon led to his dismissal, and one of the first results of his fall was the release of Lorne from imprisonment on 15 June 1663. On 16 October the title of earl of Argyll was restored to him along with most of his father's estates, though his father's title of marquess was withheld. Political rehabilitation was completed by the new earl's admission to the Scottish privy council on 9 June 1664 and by his restoration to the hereditary sheriffship of Argyll in 1666. The estates not returned were intended to pay off the earl's debts, but in reality they only satisfied a fraction of his creditors. Moreover, Argyll was made accountable not only for his father's and his own debts, but also, as an added burden, for all the debts of the Huntly estates, although they had been returned to the Gordons. By one account 'this was the true occasion of all the hardship that [Argyll] was afterwards put on which raised such a clamour against him' (*Supplement to Burnet's History*, 6). Altogether he owed almost £600,000 Scots (£50,0000 sterling), and much of his time and energy in the years that followed were devoted to using all means available to keep his creditors at bay and to squeeze payment out of those who were in debt to him. In this he was much assisted not only by his rank but also by his positions as sheriff and hereditary justice-general of Argyll and the Isles, and by his remaining a close ally of Lauderdale, who was emerging as the king's chief Scottish minister. In his fight for financial survival, forced on him by the terms his restoration, Argyll quickly won an evil reputation for being harsh and unscrupulous, using his public offices in his own interests and exploiting the financial and other difficulties of neighbours. In particular, he sought to extend Campbell influence far beyond its former bounds by manipulating the indebtedness (both to him and to the state) of the clan Maclean. From 1665 to 1680 he also sought to restore his family fortunes by attempting to salvage the treasure which had supposedly sunk with a Spanish Armada galleon near Tobermory. However, the earl also found time at Inveraray to concern himself with the planting of trees and the development of gardens round his castle, and, with his wife, to supervise the lives of their six children who survived infancy. She died in childbirth in May 1668, and he paid her a heartfelt tribute:

> I need not tell you what an excellent persone shee was, nor what a comforter to me in all my troubles, a supporter of my spirite, a discreete adviser, a pleasant yokfellow, without repining or grudging, and never troublesome … and a serious, diligent, constant seeker of God. (Willcock, 156)

Argyll was also active in public affairs, working closely with Lauderdale, but hatred of his family and memory of his father's career meant that he was constantly the subject of suspicion. Thus when in 1666 he raised men to oppose the Pentland rising of presbyterian dissidents, James Sharp, the archbishop of St Andrews, feared that he intended to join rather than suppress the rebels. Argyll himself stated that though he had been brought up under presbyterianism, he had been influenced by experience abroad to believe that details of church government were not so important as many Scots believed them to be. At heart he had some sympathy for moderate dissidents who faced persecution, but like many others of his generation he believed that obedience to the king in matters of church government was essential to maintain order. After the 1666 rising had been crushed he stated that preachers who had been involved 'deserve torture' (*Letters from … Argyll to … Lauderdale*, 56), and that all who refused a sweeping oath never to rise in arms should be 'without hesitation transplanted' (*Laing MSS*, 1.356), though it may be suspected that in mouthing such hard-line sentiments Argyll was to some extent seeking to allay suspicion of his being sympathetic to rebels. His second marriage, to Lady Anne or Anna *Mackenzie, dowager countess of Balcarres (*c.*1621–1707), clearly indicates that presbyterian inclinations were no bar to his affections. Her first husband, Alexander Lindsay, earl of Balcarres (1618–1659), had been strongly royalist but staunchly presbyterian, and she herself was well known for similar views. She had befriended and supported Argyll during his imprisonment in 1662–3, and though Lauderdale opposed the union, Argyll, 'being engag'd in an amour' (Mackenzie, 181) rather than a marriage of convenience, went ahead and the marriage took place on 28 January 1670.

Loyalty to the regime brought reward when Lauderdale went to Scotland as king's commissioner to parliament in 1669. There had been many delays in finalizing the details of Argyll's 1663 restoration to titles, lands, and offices, and his enemies made a determined effort to prevent its ratification by parliament. But Lauderdale's bullying manner subdued protests over the matter, and indeed he insisted that even voting on the matter would be inappropriate: ratification was a matter for the king alone. It was rumoured, however, that Lauderdale pushed through the measure to maintain his own credibility (he having been the main proponent of restoring Argyll) rather than through continuing friendship, and that he swore 'that he should never own [uphold] Argyll for the future' (Mackenzie, 179). Argyll also fell out temporarily with one of Lauderdale's closest allies, the earl of Tweeddale, who opposed Argyll's confirmation as justice-general of Argyll and the Isles. Argyll, 'who was naturally violent … burst out into passionate railings against Tweeddale' (Mackenzie, 180).

Turning his attention back to his financial affairs, Argyll intensified his campaign to have debts due to him—and taxes due to government—paid. Judgment had been obtained in the court of session against the Macleans of Duart. In 1674 Argyll raised about 2000 of his own men and occupied Mull. The Macleans submitted, but again payment failed to follow, and a new expedition to the island was organized in 1675, this time supported by some government troops. However, the earl's fleet was scattered by storms before it sailed, and resistance was strengthened when other highland enemies of the Campbells supported the Macleans, though Duart Castle was occupied by the government forces. A visit to Edinburgh failed to gain the privy council's support for his plans, and on proceeding to London he was referred back to Scotland, where the case was judged by three members of the council. Hearings began in June 1676, but judgment in Argyll's favour only came a year later, after all attempts to reach a compromise settlement had failed. Again enforcement had to rely on invasion: three companies of regular soldiers were assigned to Argyll as reinforcements, and Mull had effectively passed into his possession by the end of 1678. Sporadic resistance to Campbell expansion continued, though Argyll was again able to secure government support by claiming (on the basis that some of his Macdonald opponents were Catholics) that he was fighting popish rebels. The supposed Popish Plot in England having caused panic, service in suppressing their supposed machinations in Scotland was most welcome.

When the 'highland host' was assembled in late 1678 to overawe religious dissidents from the opposite end of the religious spectrum, the presbyterians in the south-west, no contribution from Argyll was ordered, indicating that he was regarded as fully occupied in dealing with the 'popish' rebels in the highlands. Thus when the disarming of all Scottish Catholics was ordered, he was commissioned to enforce the order against the Macleans and Macdonalds (12 April 1679). However, the defeat of a government force by the dissident presbyterians at the battle of Drumclog (1 June) changed the regime's priorities, and Argyll was ordered to march his men south to deal with this new threat. In the event the rising was suppressed without his help.

Forfeiture and ruin The Catholicism of James, duke of York, Charles II's brother and the heir to the throne, having made him a political embarrassment in England, he was sent to Scotland as king's commissioner in 1679. On arrival he took his seat on the privy council without taking the oath of allegiance which denounced Catholicism. Argyll was one of five councillors who protested. They were overruled but, according to Gilbert Burnet, James decided that Argyll's power was dangerously great and it 'was necessary for him either to gain or to ruin' Argyll to avoid trouble in the future in Scotland (*Burnet's History*, 2.303). Thus there was no deep-laid plan on James's part to destroy Argyll, but rather a recognition that his position and family background made him a key figure in Scottish politics. If he could be relied on, his support would be a major asset, but any opposition from him would need to be dealt with sharply to prevent him becoming a figurehead for protestant backlash against favour to Catholics. Argyll was shown the benefits that enjoying continued favour would bring him. James's plans for pacifying the highlands included making Argyll one of four king's lieutenants in the region, and when in the 1681 parliament Argyll again came under fierce attack over his unscrupulous judicial and financial activities, and the legality of his 1663 restoration was again questioned, James made no attempt to support his enemies. Perhaps this led to overconfidence on Argyll's part at a time when he should have realized that he was becoming politically isolated. For twenty years the support of Lauderdale had been central to his success in resisting his enemies, and in 1678 he had shown his commitment to their alliance by a double marriage: Argyll's eldest son had married Lauderdale's stepdaughter, and his daughter had married Lauderdale's nephew. But Lauderdale's influence had then already been in decline, and by 1681 it had vanished.

The story that James had visited Argyll in February 1681 and told him he would be 'the greatest man in Scotland' if he would change 'the worst of religions for the best' (Willcock, 249) is not implausible in the light of the pressure that James put on others to convert to Catholicism, but it was not refusal to convert but Argyll's opposition to one of James's key policies that brought about his downfall. By the Test Act it was proposed to impose on all office-holders an oath that attempted to reconcile the inconciliable in pursuit of James's determination to make the legitimacy of his right to succeed to the throne unassailable. On the one hand the act demanded that signatories swore that they were, and would always remain, protestants and would defend the protestant church, on the other that they accepted the absolute power of the king and would obey him in all things—which obviously could mean obeying a Catholic king pursuing pro-Catholic policies. Argyll refused to vote on the act in parliament, taking a prominent part in arguing that the oath was unnecessary, and, as John Paterson, bishop of Edinburgh, put it (Willcock, 254), he 'fired the kiln' of fear about the oath's purpose by stressing that it was being proposed that James himself should be exempted from it.

By leading opposition to the Test Act, Argyll both drew upon himself the hostility of the regime and revived the hopes of personal enemies and rivals. It was proposed that there should be a commission of inquiry to review his right to the offices he held and to force him to pay his creditors, this clearly being intended to make him think about the consequences of his conduct. James overruled Argyll's protests, and though he at first agreed that he might go to court to plead his case, this was then made conditional on his first taking the Test Act oath. Argyll's submission would be an important propaganda victory, and as a further warning he lost office as an extraordinary lord of session (a post he had held since 1674). The Test Act specified that all office-holders should swear the oath by 1 January 1682, but it was ordered that Argyll should take it immediately. An interview with James led to heated argument, intensifying the crisis. Argyll appeared before James and the privy council on 3 November 1681 and took the oath, but he also made a statement explaining that he only took the oath 'as far as it is consistent with itself and the Protestant religion'. This made a mockery of the test oath, the swearing of it a nonsense. Yet, remarkably, at first the significance of Argyll's 'explanation' was not noticed by James and the council. It was only after the meeting ended that it was realized how damaging it was. However, it was possible for James to recover from this set-back because though Argyll had now taken the oath in his capacity as a councillor, he was also due to take it as a commissioner of the Treasury. He was therefore summoned to swear again on 4 November. Argyll saw the trap, and though he insisted on his explanation he sought to avoid repeating it by saying simply that he now swore 'as before' (Willcock, 262). But James demanded that he explain what he meant by giving the full explanation, and handing in a written copy. This he did. He was then warned that his action would have severe consequences, and on 8 November the council ordered his imprisonment in Edinburgh Castle and his trial for leasing-making, perjury, and treason. The embarrassing fact that the council had originally accepted Argyll's explanation without question was now explained as being owing to the fact that he had spoken in so low a voice that he had not been properly heard.

James had evidently hoped, up to the last minute, to force Argyll to withdraw his explanation, thus breaking opposition to the oath. He wrote of Argyll's second taking of the oath that he had 'spoiled all again' (*Burnet's History*, 2.317n). The earl's stubbornness now meant that he had provided an example of resistance rather than submission, and if the oath was not to be discredited severe punishment was necessary to deter others. Trial before the court of justiciary began on 12 December with Argyll protesting his lifelong loyalty to the crown, and his defence pleading that the actions and words attributed to him were not criminal, let alone treasonous. The judges ruled that the libel (accusation) was relevant, and the case was submitted to a jury which found him guilty of leasing-making and treason. On the orders of the king no sentence was to be passed until he was consulted, but the widespread belief was that the usual sentence for these crimes—execution and forfeiture—would be imposed. Argyll acted accordingly, escaping from Edinburgh Castle on 20 December 1681 with the help of his stepdaughter Sophia Lindsay, the success of his disguise as a page no doubt being helped by his short stature. Meanwhile it had been pointed out to the king that lack of sentence meant the legal process against Argyll was technically incomplete, and he had therefore agreed that sentence should be pronounced, though stressing that it must not be put into effect until he had further considered the matter. His orders arrived on 22 December, and the sentence of death and forfeiture was pronounced the following day. The sentence, imposed for a verbal attempt to stand up for protestantism, caused widespread shock, and it was commented that if James (who was blamed for the trial) could treat subjects so harshly when merely heir to the throne, he would be a hard master when he became king. The earl of Halifax is said to have told the king 'that he knew not the Scots law, but by the law of England that Explanation could not hang his dog' (Lauder, *Historical Observes*, 55). Lauder of Fountainhall, one of Argyll's lawyers, was also horrified to see Scots law used in this way, and attributed the determination to destroy Argyll to his being 'overrun by the violent malice of his enemies', to which the regime had only given way when he 'appeared to be a valiant assertor of the Protestant interest', though he accepted that there was justice in the hatred Argyll's oppressed creditors had for him (Lauder, *Historical Observes*, 54).

Helped by presbyterian sympathizers, Argyll made his way to London. The anonymity of the large city was attractive to the fugitive, but the decision not to flee abroad immediately suggests that he still hoped to find some solution to his problems. Possibly he had a lingering hope that he could find someone to approach the king on his behalf. But any such hope must have been slight, for to the crime of showing up the absurdity of a key official policy had been added his escape, a further mockery of royal authority. Moreover, the widespread reaction against the condemning of him to death on what was seen as a trumped up charge meant that he was already being depicted as a presbyterian—indeed general protestant—hero. The mantle of his father, which he had spent his life trying to escape, was insistently draping itself around his shoulders, and a pardon for him would have been seen as indicating a weakening of the policy of guaranteeing James's right to the throne. Yet the story that King Charles made sure that no real attempt was made to track Argyll down in London may be true. He was already ruined, and actually executing him held the danger of making him a martyr.

Argyll's real hopes for the future therefore came to lie in collaboration with extreme English whig politicians, whose prolonged attempts to have James excluded from the succession to the throne had recently failed. Some of the most committed were now plotting to prevent a Catholic succession by force, and Argyll met secretly with one of their leaders, the earl of Shaftesbury, during the summer of 1682, and with Lord Granard, who planned a rising in Ireland. Reports that Argyll was now actively involved in treason led to the renewal of attempts to trace and arrest him, and in the autumn of 1682 he fled to the Netherlands to join the Scottish and English exiles gathering there. In June 1683 the Rye House plot (to assassinate Charles and James) was exposed, and evidence emerged that Argyll had proposed to lead a rising in Scotland, and had asked for a subsidy of £30,000 sterling and 1000 cavalry to undertake this, though he later accepted reduced totals of £10,000 sterling and six or seven hundred horse.

After the death of King Charles and the accession of King James in February 1685 Argyll moved from Friesland, where he had been living (near Leeuwarden, according to tradition), to Rotterdam, and then to Amsterdam, where he had a series of meetings with Scottish exiles. Their talks were stormy. Most of these men were committed to constitutional reform in Britain, reducing royal power, whereas Argyll was a staunch royalist who had had no qualms about supporting absolute monarchy. His interests lay in the restoration of own position and the protection of protestantism, and he tended to see the rebellion he proposed to lead as traditional assertion of the rights of a feudal magnate against a king who had failed to recognize his rights. His fellow exiles he saw not so much as comrades as underlings who should accept his leadership and obey. He showed himself determined on action, 'very forward without delay to take shipping for Scotland', having already purchased arms and a frigate (Hume, 12), but his lack of forethought was extraordinary. The general assumption among exiles was that a landing by Argyll in Scotland would be co-ordinated with an English expedition by the duke of Monmouth (Charles II's illegitimate son and the figurehead of the plotters). The idea evidently surprised Argyll, and in 'tart expressions' he showed his jealousy of the duke (Hume, 12). On the Scottish gentry, led by Sir Patrick Hume of Polwarth, refusing to contemplate rebellion without co-operation with Monmouth, 'the Erle was high, peremptory, and passionate … and parted in that temper' (Hume, 17), though he quickly reconciled himself to the idea. Further trouble was caused by his assumption that he would be general of the expedition, whereas constitutionalists among the exiles insisted that it must be made clear that he was acting not just for himself and against Catholicism, but in the name of the nation. 'Argyll now fancied Scotland was his own, and was very insolent in all his discourses with the other gentlemen, who really thought his brain turned' (*Supplement to Burnet's History*, 156). None the less, he agreed to the formation of a council of gentlemen for managing war against King James in the name of protestant religion and the liberties of the British kingdoms, and this council then formally chose Argyll as general.

In military matters as in political ones Argyll found himself at odds with his fellow conspirators. The extent of his ambition was to raise his supporters in the west highlands, presenting a threat to the regime that would prevent Scottish troops being sent south against the army Monmouth would land in England. He seems to have had no thought of what sort of settlement would follow success—except that it would restore his own fortunes and protestantism. Many urged that his landing would be most effective if it took place in the western lowlands, to encourage the dissidents there to rise in arms, but Argyll saw himself as a chief who would first raise his clansmen in arms, and vehemently asserted that he could muster five or six thousand men in the highlands if he landed there. The claim was, rightly, greeted with scepticism, but he got his way. By Argyll's own account he had spent much of his time in exile in prayer and meditation. Whatever their merits, they were not the best preparation for a military adventure requiring daring, clear-headedness, and decision.

Argyll had been supported in the Netherlands by contributions sent from Scotland by sympathizers, and a donation approaching £10,000 sterling from a rich English widow in the Netherlands provided most of the finance for the tiny expeditionary force he assembled. About 300 men in three ships sailed at the beginning of May. After touching at Orkney—thus giving the regime advance warning of his approach and allowing it to assemble troops to oppose him—he sailed for Argyll. Arriving at Tobermory on 11 May, the earl had the 'fiery cross', the traditional summons to his men to rise in arms, sent out, but it quickly became clear that the thousands of eager clansmen Argyll had expected were not flocking to his standard. The countryside had been ravaged by government forces under the marquess of Atholl after the earl's 1681 forfeiture, and Atholl had now returned to enforce loyalty. Moving slowly south, delayed by contrary winds, Argyll's original force of 300 men had at most only doubled by the time he reached Kintyre, where he expected the support of lowland protestant settlers. At Campbeltown on 20 May he issued a proclamation detailing the oppressions of government in Scotland since 1660, the risks to protestantism of a Catholic king, and the unjust treatment of himself and his father. But while this might stir up indignation, it was not designed to steel men to commit themselves to rebellion, for although the intention to overthrow King James was clear, no indication was given of what would happen after that. The following day a declaration to his own vassals rebutted claims that his rebellion was motivated by desire to further his personal interests, as all he sought was peaceful possession of what he and his father had enjoyed before forfeiture—which amounted to admitting rather than refuting the charge that he was acting for selfish reasons—and to uphold protestantism. In a speech he explicitly argued that James had forfeited his right to the throne by becoming a Catholic, but again offered no alternative.

Meanwhile the earl and his council squabbled bitterly about military priorities, a matter which should have been settled before the expedition sailed. Argyll remained committed to raising a strong army in the highlands before thinking about intervening in the western lowlands, but the council tended to favour an immediate move to raise the dissidents there. But when a rendezvous at Tarbet produced over a thousand clansmen, Argyll proposed to advance to recover the Campbell heartland around Inveraray from Atholl's troops, arguing that the rest of his clan would be unwilling to march into the lowlands until this was done. After several changes of mind he moved instead to the island of Bute. The campaign was now well on its way to collapse. Moving back to the mainland, Argyll began to construct a fort on Eilean Dearg, while marching some of his men north to attempt to take Inveraray Castle after all. This failing, he changed his mind yet again, resolving to march on the lowlands, but, in a way which could now be recognized as typical, delayed in the hope that more men would join him. With the arrival of English naval ships the garrison he had left at Eilean Dearg fled, leaving arms and other stores landed there to the enemy. Even his standard, proclaiming (comprehensively though clumsily) 'For God and Religion against Poperie, Tyrrany, Arbitrary Government, and Erastianisme' (Lauder, *Historical Observes*, 177), fell into enemy hands. After blundering through Dunbartonshire as his force disintegrated, Argyll crossed the Clyde into Renfrewshire, hoping to find help from lowland dissidents. When this failed to materialize the officers and men who remained scattered. Argyll disguised himself and, armed with three loaded pistols, attempted to make his way back to the highlands, but on trying to cross the Clyde at Inchinnan the bedraggled fugitive was arrested as a suspect by John Riddel, a weaver, and his identity revealed. The ignominy of the manner of his capture, in view of his status and the expectations of others, must have been as clear to him as it was to observers: the 'dulnesse and sillinesse of the manner of his taking is very od' for 'every on reputed Argile waliant and witty' (Lauder, *Historical Observes*, 186).

On 12 June, for the third time in his life, Argyll was imprisoned in Edinburgh Castle. Under the sentence of death passed against him in 1681 it had been specified that the implementation of the sentence was a matter to be determined by the king, and on 29 June a letter was received by the privy council from James ordering that the earl be executed within three days. Argyll seems to have been bewildered by his failure, having put his faith in providence, the righteousness of his cause, and the facile argument that as the government had been oppressive the people were bound to join him in revolt. He complained bitterly that 'the generality [of the people] have perverted their way' in failing to rise in arms with him, while his fellow rebels had been 'not governable' (Wodrow, 4.298). There is truth in that, but he failed to see that he had shown himself totally unfit to govern. 'It seemeth, the Lord thought me not fit to be an instrument of his work' he concluded (Wodrow, 4.301). He proceeded to write his own epitaph, complaining that he had failed 'More by friend's fraud' than enemy action, but expressing confidence that the cause he had fought for would triumph, while he himself was about to 'enter endless glory' (Wodrow, 4.307).

A painting by E. M. Ward (1854), *The Last Sleep of Argyll*, was commissioned for the Commons corridor at Westminster, commemorating the fact that on 30 June 1685, shortly before he was to be taken to execution, the earl was found peacefully sleeping. The incident had come to be interpreted as demonstrating his remarkable serenity in the face of death, the fact that he had had to sleep for a time each day since his accident in 1658 being overlooked.

Legend also stressed his composure by claiming that when he mounted the scaffold he noted that the Maiden (the Scottish beheading machine) was set up unevenly, whereupon he took out a ruler, measured it, and had it properly adjusted, but a contemporary recorded that in fact he was 'somewhat appaled' at the sight of the device and had his eyes bound before he approached it (Lauder, *Historical Observes*, 193). He made a short speech, largely composed of biblical quotations about suffering meekly endured but ending with a denunciation of oppression and popery. He may too have at last made it clear that he was specifically committed to presbyterianism by declaring his 'heart-hatred of popery, prelacy, and all superstition whatsoever' (Wodrow, 4.306), though this may be myth. As his head fell, his body, in a macabre spasm, jumped upright on its feet, spouting blood 'like a cascade or jette d'eau' before being held down by the executioners (Lauder, *Historical Observes*, 194). His head, like that of his father before him, was displayed on a spike on the top of Edinburgh Tolbooth, while his body was buried at Newbattle Abbey, where he had been born. The head was reunited with the body in 1689 when his eldest son, Archibald *Campbell (*d.* 1703), was restored as tenth earl, and in 1704 they were taken to his family's burial place at Kilmun.

Reputation In terms of the immediate political situation King James's order for the execution of Argyll without a new trial made sense. Monmouth had landed in England and had proclaimed himself king. It was a time when swift and exemplary action against a leader of a rebellion was needed. But just a week after Argyll's death Monmouth was defeated and captured, and the precipitate execution quickly became damaging to the regime. Few had supported Argyll, and most accepted that he deserved death for rebellion against the crown. But he had never been tried for rebellion, being executed under his 1681 conviction relating to the test oath. The sentence had been seen as grotesque in relation to his offence, the result of a show trial designed to deter others from standing up for protestant interests. By executing him under it, it became possible to depict Argyll as having died not for rebellion, but for having made a peaceful and discreet protest against the Catholic menace to protestantism. Thus, in the eyes of many, Argyll became a martyr. Then, with James's overthrow in the 1688–9 revolution, use of armed force to overthrow a Catholic monarch was vindicated. Argyll's rebellion could now be hailed as a gallant forerunner of the 'glorious revolution'.

While Argyll in death became a hero to presbyterians, others pointed out his defects in life. Gilbert Burnet commented that he 'had not behaved himself in his prosperity like a man that thought he might at some time or another need the affections of his people' (*Supplement to Burnet's History*, 158), assuming in 1685 that he would have his clan's support in a crisis though he had never sought to ensure his men's loyalty. Fountainhall remarked that his death could be seen as divine judgment for his 'cruall oppression' of creditors, but, he added: 'He had all his life been the ludibrium [plaything] and tennis ball of fortune' (Lauder, *Historical Observes*, 184, 194), suggesting that Argyll's life had been shaped by events outside his control. To some extent this was true: being the son of 'the great marquess' brought him many enemies. Yet through his royalism in the 1650s he had chosen his own path, and from 1660 to 1681 he fought a long and successful battle for the survival of himself and his family. Given the strength of enmity towards him, his conduct seems well judged—defending his interests, retaining royal favour, and playing in full the political role to which his status entitled him, but never seeking political power in a way that would rouse fears of his ambition. Only on one matter was he potentially vulnerable—his commitment to protestantism and resistance to growing Catholic influence. At first, at least, his resistance was not specifically presbyterian: for thirty years he showed himself willing to accept episcopalianism. Even during his 1685 rebellion, which relied on presbyterians for support, his declarations at first avoided mentioning the issue of church government, and his refusal to put his fortunes in the hands of the presbyterians of the south-west contributed to his failure. Yet his bringing ruin upon himself over the Test Act in 1681 indicates the strength of his protestant convictions.

Though successful up to 1681, Argyll was not well liked. He was short-tempered, and never sought popularity. Perhaps he accepted that his family's past meant that he could never have it, and his struggle for financial survival made ruthlessness in asserting his rights essential. The preparations for the 1685 rebellion show a man used to assertion and obedience who found it hard to adjust to cicumstances in which he had to negotiate with lesser men and seek to win their support. While such inflexibility might have been predictable, his indecision once the rebellion began contrasts strongly with his previous career. He knew what he had to do, but was at a loss as to how to do it, relying too much on divine providence. Fountainhall suggests a degree of eccentricity in his behaviour: 'Tho Argile was very witty in knacks, yet it was observed, he hes never been very solid sen [since] his trepanning of his scull [in 1658] … he was so conceitty he had neir 20 severall pockets, some very secret, in his coat and breeches' (Lauder, *Historical Observes*, 195). None the less, Fountainhall was bewildered by Argyll's conduct in 1685, for he 'had alwayes the reputation of sence and reason' (Lauder, *Historical Observes*, 166). John Evelyn, who had met Argyll in 1662, had thought 'he seem'd a man of parts' (Evelyn, *Diary*, 3.318). In personal appearance Argyll was noted mainly for being short. In 1685 an astrologer's prediction that 'a little Highlandman' would triumph was taken to refer to him (Hume, 18), and he once wryly referred to himself as the shortest officer in his regiment. To the exasperated duke of York in 1681 he was 'that little Lord' (Willcock, 274), yet perhaps the clash between the two men in 1681 was in part owing to the fact that they had something in common, an inflexibility—or determination to adhere to principle—that led both to disaster.

David Stevenson

Sources J. Willcock, *A Scots earl in covenanting times: being life and times of Archibald, 9th earl of Argyll (1629–1685)* (1907) • *DNB* • GEC, *Peerage* • *Scots peerage* • *Reg. PCS*, 3rd ser., vols. 1–10 • J. Lauder, *Historical observes of memorable occurrents in church and state, from October 1680 to April 1686*, ed. A. Urquhart and D. Laing, Bannatyne Club, 66 (1840) • *Historical notices of Scotish affairs, selected from the manuscripts of Sir John Lauder of Fountainhall*, ed. D. Laing, 2 vols., Bannatyne Club, 87 (1848) • *Calendar of the Clarendon state papers preserved in the Bodleian Library*, ed. O. Ogle and others, 5 vols. (1869–1970) • *Fourth report*, HMC, 3 (1874) • *Sixth report*, HMC, 5 (1877–8) • A. Lang, *Sir George Mackenzie* (1909) • P. Hume of Polwarth, 'A narrative of the events which occurred in the enterprize of the earl of Argyl, in 1685', in G. Rose, *Observations on the historical works of … Charles James Fox* (1809) • R. Wodrow, *The history of the sufferings of the Church of Scotland from the Restoration to the revolution*, ed. R. Burns, 4 vols. (1828–30) • *Journal of the Hon. John Erskine of Carnock*, ed. W. Macleod, Scottish History Society, 14 (1893) • C. H. Firth, ed., *Scotland and the Commonwealth: letters and papers relating to the military government of Scotland, from August 1651 to December 1653*, Scottish History Society, 18 (1895) • C. H. Firth, ed., *Scotland and the protectorate: letters and papers relating to the military government of Scotland from January 1654 to June 1659*, Scottish History Society, 31 (1899) • Clarendon, *Hist. rebellion* • *Letters from Archibald, the earl of Argyll, to John, duke of Lauderdale*, ed. G. Sinclair and C. K. Sharpe (1829) • G. Mackenzie, *Memoirs of the affairs of Scotland* (1821) • *Bishop Burnet's History of his own time: with the suppressed passages of the first volume*, ed. M. J. Routh, 6 vols. (1823) • *A supplement to Burnet's History of my own time*, ed. H. C. Foxcroft (1902) • *The letters and journals of Robert Baillie*, ed. D. Laing, 3 vols. (1841–2) • F. D. Dow, *Cromwellian Scotland, 1651–1660* (1979) • A. I. Macinnes, *Clanship, commerce, and the house of Stuart, 1603–1788* (1996) • J. Maidment, ed., *Argyll papers, 1640–1723* (1834) • *Report of the Laing manuscripts*, 1, HMC, 72 (1914)

Archives BL, papers relating to his preparations for invasion of Scotland, Add. MS 41822 • Buckminster Park, Grantham, corresp. • Inveraray Castle, Argyll, Argyll MSS • LUL, authorization to seize contraband beef • NL Scot., corresp. and papers | BL, letters to Charles II, duke of Lauderdale, etc., Add. MSS 23118–23138, 23245–23247, *passim* • NL Scot., letters to duke of Lauderdale

Likenesses double portrait, oils, 1660–69, NPG [*see illus.*] • attrib. L. Schuneman, oils, *c.*1670, Scot. NPG • attrib. D. Loggan, miniature, oils, *c.*1680, Scot. NPG • R. Arondeaux, silver medal, Scot. NPG • Goupil & Co., photogravure (after E. M. Ward), NPG • A. Haelwegh, line engraving (after unknown artist), BM, NPG • oils, Scot. NPG • oils, Bowhill, Scottish Borders

Campbell, Archibald, first duke of Argyll (*d.* **1703**), nobleman and politician, was the eldest son of Archibald *Campbell, ninth earl of Argyll (1629–1685), and his first wife, Lady Mary Stuart (*d.* 1668), eldest daughter of James Stuart, fourth earl of Moray; his parents married in 1650. He was styled Lord Lorne—improperly so after the forfeiture of his father in 1681—until he took his seat as earl of Argyll on 14 March 1689 at the convention in Edinburgh that became a parliament on 5 June; on the latter day his father's forfeiture was rescinded. On 12 March 1678 Lorne married Elizabeth (*bap.* 1659, *d.* 1735), daughter of Sir Lionel Talmash or Tollemache, bt (1624–1669), of Helmingham, Suffolk, and Elizabeth *Murray, countess of Dysart and duchess of Lauderdale (*bap.* 1626, *d.* 1698). This marriage was resonant of the dangerous times in which Lorne lived: for Argyll it was an important means to negate a possible threat to his financial and political survival from the duchess of Lauderdale, who at that time had a political understanding with the marquess of Atholl, one of his enemies.

Lorne's acute instinct for self-preservation came to the fore when Argyll embarked upon rebellion against James VII and II in 1685. Lorne, in London, placed himself at James's mercy and offered to serve against his father. Thus he survived, although not in favour at court. Living in London in 'extreme want' (Lindsay, xxii) he obtained a pension of £800 sterling a year from James, it is said, through the intercession of Colin Lindsay, earl of Balcarres, his stepbrother; the circumstances under which Lorne lost his previous pension of £1250 granted out of the Argyll estates after his father's forfeiture are unclear. Lorne also 'turn'd Papist', nominally, to improve his position. The Jacobite George Lockhart of Carnwath, a friend of Lorne's sons, later observed that Lorne remained, notwithstanding, 'the darling of the Presbyterians' in Scotland as representative of 'a family that suffer'd for the cause (as they termed it) and of great power in the country' (Lockhart, 1.63). Sir James Montgomerie of Skelmorlie borrowed a large sum to bring Lorne to the Netherlands in late 1688 in support of William of Orange, a judicious move from Lorne's point of view. He was in the entourage, therefore, that accompanied William to England.

Both Montgomerie and the newly confirmed earl of Argyll were in the delegation of three who went to London to offer the Scottish crown to William and Mary. Argyll administered the coronation oath on 11 May 1689. He was, however, not in the first rank of Scottish politicians in the years immediately following the revolution. Strongly influenced for a time by the politically frustrated Montgomerie (*d.* 1694) he was a member of the group, the Club, organized by Montgomerie in opposition to William's ministers. Argyll was associated with the Montgomerie plot of 1690 but emerged unscathed. More critical than any baleful early association with Montgomerie in impeding Argyll's progress as a politician was his indolence in applying himself to business. Less damaging, ultimately, was his intemperate self-seeking attitude, which defined him as one of the most destructive magnate influences in those unsettled times. Having become, in 1694, an extraordinary lord of session (a position he held until his death), in 1695–6 he acquired an unexpected enthusiasm for the national political fray, entering it with grim and ruthless determination. He allied with another ambitious and frustrated magnate, William Douglas, first duke of Queensberry, in a push for power. In 1696, with Argyll as a lord of the Scottish Treasury and successor to Queensberry as colonel of the Scots horse guards, they joined a reconstructed court interest, one that William and his advisers hoped would achieve an accommodation in the presbyterian–episcopalian religious divide. The true driving force in Scottish national politics at the time, the conflict of magnate interests, remained, however, inside and outside the ministry. Above all there was polarization in the administration between the Queensberry–Argyll alliance on the one hand and John Murray, earl of Tullibardine (first duke of Atholl, 1703) and his supporters on the other. Tullibardine was forced out in 1698. Created duke of Argyll on 23 June 1701, that summer Argyll himself broke with Queensberry, whose dominant role he resented. Before and after William's death Argyll was engaged in setting up his own group from discontented elements in the court party.

Although Argyll was at the centre of Scottish parliamentary politics for only the last few years of his life, his impact on Scottish society was great in his contribution—not entirely of his own volition—to the rejection of the revolution settlement by a significant part of highland society. General Hugh Mackay (*d.* 1692) referred to the combination, in 1689,

> of severals of the Highland clans for their mutual defence, being afraid of the rising fortune and apparent favour of the Earle of Argyle, under the present government, who had considerable pretensions upon their estates, besides, that some of them had part of his estate in possession, by a gift of the late King, under whose reign the Earls father had been forfeited. (Mackay, 6)

The clans' fear turned out to be justified by Argyll's subsequent behaviour. It was no less justified by the carve-up of the forfeited Argyll estates that had taken place under Charles II. For example, from 1683 voracious enemies of the family including Atholl and the earl of Perth had bought up huge Argyll debts to qualify, as creditors, to have Argyll lands wadsetted or mortgaged to them. This followed a decision by Charles to make irreversible the forfeiture of the estates, other than such tenures as provided for the ninth earl's children. The tenth earl of Argyll's part in subduing the highlands is popularly associated with the role of detachments of his regiment (formed 1689–90) in the massacre of Glencoe on the night of 13 February 1692, although he was not present there nor were the troops under his orders. A fairer representation of his behaviour after the revolution was the implacable pursuit and breaking by military and other means, over a period of years, of his family's most bitter longstanding enemies in the west, the Macleans.

From 1696 Argyll and his wife were separated. The duchess, a strong and determined personality, had homes and farms at Duddingston near Edinburgh and Limecraigs, Campbeltown, Kintyre. Most of the Argyll estates in Kintyre had been conveyed to her under her marriage contract countersigned, no doubt through the Lauderdale influence, by Charles II. Argyll set up home at Chirton, near North Shields, Northumberland, in his later years with Margaret (Peggie) Allison and had a yacht berthed at North Shields to make travel easy. He was a keen follower of the turf and was a racehorse owner.

Argyll died at Chirton in September 1703. He had been seriously ill for some time, a symptom being black jaundice. However, stab wounds received in a brawl in a brothel were the more immediate cause of his death. His sons John *Campbell (1680–1743) and Archibald *Campbell (1682–1761) succeeded successively as second and third dukes of Argyll to an estate that was not in thriving condition. This could in part be attributed to the consequences of the forfeitures of Argyll's father and grandfather. George Lockhart was not so charitable in his views: Argyll, he said, was

> in outward appearance a good-natur'd, civil, and modest gentleman; but his actions were quite otherwise, being capable of the worst things to promote his interest, and altogether addicted to a lewd profligate life: he was not cut out for business, only applying himself to it in so far as it tended to secure his Court interest and politicks, from whence he got great sums of money to lavish upon his pleasures. (Lockhart, 1.62)

John S. Shaw

Sources P. Hopkins, *Glencoe and the end of the highland war* (1986) • P. W. J. Riley, *King William and the Scottish politicians* (1979) • *State papers and letters addressed to William Carstares*, ed. J. M'Cormick (1774) • [J. Maidment], ed., *The Argyle papers* (1834) • C. Lindsay [earl of Balcarres], *Memoirs touching the revolution in Scotland*, ed. A. W. C. Lindsay [earl of Crawford and Balcarres], Bannatyne Club (1841) • H. Mackay, *Memoirs of the war carried on in Scotland and Ireland*, ed. J. M. Hog and others, Bannatyne Club, 45 (1833) • G. Lockhart, *The Lockhart papers: containing memoirs and commentaries upon the affairs of Scotland from 1702 to 1715*, 2 vols. (1817) • *The manuscripts of his grace the duke of Portland*, 10 vols., HMC, 29 (1891–1931), vol. 4 • J. Willcock, *A Scots earl in covenanting times: being life and times of Archibald, 9th earl of Argyll (1629–1685)* (1907) • *Scots peerage* • *DNB*

Archives NA Scot., executorship papers • NL Scot., corresp. and papers • NL Scot., Adv. MSS 29.35.5 | NA Scot., corresp.

Likenesses attrib. W. Aikman, oils, Inveraray Castle, Strathclyde • M. Beale, oils, Bowhill (Buccleuch estates), Selkirk • N. Maes, oils, Inveraray Castle, Strathclyde • J. B. Medina, group portrait, oils (with two sons), Inveraray Castle, Strathclyde

Campbell, Archibald (*c.*1669–1744), Scottish Episcopal bishop, was the second son of Lord Neil *Campbell (*c.*1630–1692), second son of Archibald *Campbell, marquess of Argyll (1605x7–1661), and of Lady Vere Ker, third daughter of the third earl of Lothian. According to Samuel Johnson, he participated in the uprising of his uncle, the ninth earl of Argyll, in 1685. Taken prisoner on its failure, he accepted exile in Surinam as a condition of clemency. On his return he showed great zeal for episcopacy and monarchy. Formerly an ardent whig he later, said Johnson, 'kept better company, and became a Tory' (*Boswell's Journal*, 354–5). Ordained a priest in London, at the revolution in 1688 he adhered to the nonjurors. He was more than once apprehended in the reign of William III, and once after the accession of George I. Associated with Johnson's high-church tory circle in London, he was an intimate friend of the leading nonjurors George Hickes and Robert Nelson. Johnson described him as 'a man of letters, but injudicious; and very curious and inquisitive, but credulous' (ibid.). Owing to Hickes's concern for continuance of the English nonjuring episcopal succession, but also because of his rank, Campbell was consecrated a bishop at Dundee on 25 August 1711 by the Scottish bishops Alexander Rose, Robert Douglas, and John Falconer. However, his continued residence in London meant Campbell could be of little direct assistance to the struggling Scottish Episcopalians. The chevalier's agent in Scotland, George Lockhart of Carnwath, was hostile to Campbell's leadership in the Scottish Episcopal church, disliking him personally and believing Campbell's advocacy of diocesan episcopacy made the church less amenable to Jacobite political control.

Some time before 1716 Campbell made the acquaintance of Arsenius, the metropolitan of Thebais, who was in England seeking financial aid for the impoverished patriarch of Alexandria. With some of the nonjuring clergy Campbell entered into negotiations for a union with the

Eastern Orthodox church. The proposal eventually foundered when Archbishop Wake of Canterbury informed the Orthodox church of the schismatic nature of the nonjurors. In 1721 Campbell visited Scotland with a view to engendering support for the diocesan party, as opposed to the majority of bishops who upheld the government of the Scottish Episcopal church by the bishops acting as a college. The diocesan party among the bishops and clergy opposed royal appointments and control through a college of bishops because they believed the perilous situation of Episcopalians in Scotland necessitated greater local control of the church, a view supported by their nonjuring theology of a divine-right episcopacy. The result of this visit was that on 10 May 1721 Campbell was chosen by the clergy of Aberdeen as their diocesan bishop. This election to a diocese was not approved of by the bishops, who ratified Campbell's election only on condition he undertook to propagate no new doctrine or usage not sanctioned by the canons of the church. This condition reflected the college bishops' struggle with the diocesan party which was complicated by the latter's advocacy of some ancient liturgical usages unprecedented in the Scottish Episcopal church. Campbell refused to comply and the bishops withheld their approval. Characteristically intransigent, Campbell held himself to be validly elected, but continued to reside in London. While there his major contribution to his Scottish co-religionists was in assisting the implementation of a fund for the support of poorer Episcopalian clergy. Eventually the conflict between Campbell and the other bishops was resolved when he agreed in 1724 to resign his diocese in favour of Bishop James Gadderar.

Aside from his diocesan and liturgical views, Campbell's major contribution to nonjuring theology came in his idiosyncratic advocacy of an intermediate state for the souls of the faithful departed in *The Doctrine of the Middle State between Death and the Resurrection* (1721). He was also the author of *Queries to the Presbyterians of Scotland* (1702) and *A Query Turned into an Argument in Favour of Episcopacy* (1703). In his later years he formed a separate nonjuring communion distinct from that of the Sancroftian line and, against the counsel of his episcopal colleagues in Scotland, he took the exceptional step of an episcopal consecration by himself. This Campbell line of nonjurors gained a slight footing in the west of England before dying out in the nineteenth century. Campbell succeeded, somehow, in obtaining possession of the registers of the Church of Scotland from the Reformation to 1590. In 1737 he presented them to Sion College, London, for preservation. Several endeavours were made by the general assembly of the Church of Scotland to obtain their restoration, but Campbell's implacable opposition to Presbyterianism had made it a condition that they should not be given up until episcopacy should again be established in Scotland. Having been borrowed by the Commons, they perished in the fire which destroyed the houses of parliament in 1834. Campbell died in London on 16 June 1744.

ROWAN STRONG

Sources *DNB* · *Boswell's journal of a tour to the Hebrides with Samuel Johnson*, ed. F. A. Pottle and C. H. Bennett (1936) · T. Stephen, *The history of the Church of Scotland*, 4 vols. (1843–5), vol. 4 · J. Skinner, *An ecclesiastical history of Scotland*, 2 vols. (1788) · G. Grub, *An ecclesiastical history of Scotland*, 4 vols. (1861) · H. R. Sefton, 'The Scottish bishops and Archbishop Arsenius', *The Orthodox churches and the West*, ed. D. Baker, SCH, 13 (1976), 239–46 · J. P. Lawson, *History of the Scottish Episcopal church* (1843) · R. Keith and J. Spottiswoode, *An historical catalogue of the Scottish bishops, down to the year 1688*, new edn, ed. M. Russel [M. Russell] (1824), 530–31

Archives LPL, corresp. [copies] | NA Scot., Episcopal Church MSS

Campbell, Archibald, **third duke of Argyll** (1682–1761), politician, was born at Ham House, Petersham, Surrey, in June 1682, the second son of Archibald *Campbell, tenth earl and first duke of Argyll (*d.* 1703), and his wife, Elizabeth (*d.* 1735), eldest daughter of Sir Lionel Talmash (Tollemache) of Helmingham, Suffolk, and Elizabeth *Murray, countess of Dysart, later duchess of Lauderdale. His elder brother was John *Campbell, second duke of Argyll from 1703. Little is known of his early life. His parents separated in 1696.

Education and early career Campbell was educated at Eton College and later attended classes at the University of Glasgow in 1698. From Glasgow he was sent to Utrecht, to read civil law, and he probably accompanied his elder brother on a European tour with their tutor, Alexander Cunningham, in 1699 and 1700. After his father received the dukedom of Argyll in 1701 from William III, he abandoned his legal studies to follow his brother in a military career, and obtained the colonelcy of the 36th regiment of foot as well as the governorship of Dumbarton Castle. In 1705 he joined his brother's mission to Scotland to secure a treaty of union between that country's parliament and England as royal commissioner in the Scottish parliamentary session of 1705. It was at this time that he met John Law, the son of an Edinburgh goldsmith, who would so influence his economic thought over the rest of his career. Lord Archibald, as he then was known, was appointed lord high treasurer of Scotland by Queen Anne at this time, allowing him to vote in the Scottish parliament, although as the office was in commission it carried no direct administrative duties. He received his baptism into what became a lifelong career as a parliamentary politician in the most difficult of circumstances. Lord Archibald was then twenty-three. His elder brother, colonel of a Scottish regiment serving in the Low Countries with Marlborough, was only two years his senior. Somehow his brother was able to secure a vote in the Scottish parliament to leave the nomination of the commissioners to represent the Scottish parliament in renewed union negotiations to the queen, moved by the principal leader of the opposition, the duke of Hamilton. In 1706 Lord Archibald was nominated one of the Scottish commissioners by Anne and on 19 October he was created earl of Ilay (the spelling used at the time for what has since become known as the Isle of Islay), Lord Oransay, Dunoon and Arrose, with limitation to heirs-male of his body.

The earl of Mar reported at the time (*Mar and Kellie MSS*, 303–4) that the title originally chosen for the earldom was

Archibald Campbell, third duke of Argyll (1682–1761), by Allan Ramsay, 1749

Dundee, which was abandoned in the face of indignant protest by the duke of Montrose, a kinsman of the Jacobite commander John Graham of Claverhouse, Viscount Dundee, angry that a Campbell should take a title associated with that of his own family, and also a political rival of the brothers. The scholarly barb contained in the choice of the title was much in accord with Lord Archibald's later career. He passed into history as Lord Ilay, his exact role in the union negotiations unknown, but his close knowledge of their content informing all of his subsequent career of over five decades in British public life.

Ilay became one of the sixteen representative peers elected by the nobility of Scotland after the treaty of union was accepted to represent them in the House of Lords at Westminster. He was to be returned as one of these peers at every election for the rest of his life with the exception of the British parliament of 1713–15, the reasons for which are discussed below. As his brother's political influence continued to grow, so Ilay secured additional political offices as Argyll sought military preferment in pursuit of his increasing rivalry with the duke of Marlborough. In 1708 he was admitted one of the four extraordinary lords of the court of session, Scotland's supreme civil court, in succession to his brother. These 'extraordinary' seats on the court were abolished during Ilay's lifetime as allowing members of the nobility too much freedom to influence Scotland's highest court. Ilay, as third duke of Argyll in succession to his brother after 1743, was one of the last Scottish peers to have the privilege.

In 1711 Queen Anne appointed Ilay to another judicial post, that of lord justice-general of the court of justiciary in Scotland, the head of the country's highest criminal court. This court consisted of five ordinary 'lords', or judges, and a lord justice clerk as their presiding officer, all drawn from the court of session bench and receiving additional salaries for their justiciary work. The lord justice-general, however, like an extraordinary lord of session, had the right to sit with the court of justiciary (as well as a salary of £2000 on the Scottish civil list which survived the union). Ilay would exercise this right at key moments in Scottish history over the next five decades, to controversial effect, most notably in the Appin murder trial of 1752 (see below). He was sworn of the privy council in 1711.

Whig politician Like his brother, Ilay became an opponent of the tory administration and a committed Hanoverian by 1715. It is from this period that Ilay and his brother acquired their reputation in English politics as cynical political operators, intent only on their own gain. It is clear, however, that they were aware of the national aspect of their political activity within a newly created British state in which English political parties would always be dominant. 'I was always of the opinion,' Ilay wrote to William Carstares in 1710, that:

> it was obviously our interest not to mingle ourselves too much with the factions here [Westminster], I mean as Scotchmen, for it being very plain that no party here has our country much at heart, the exasperating any side here might at some conjuncture or other, draw both upon us, and crush us at once. (McCormick, 786–7)

This was to be their experience during the period 1710–13, when the tory ministry led by Robert Harley endeavoured to deal with Scottish affairs by encouraging Scottish tories, who were Jacobites to a man, to co-operate with Ilay and his brother. The earl of Mar and Ilay worked together on ministerial business relating to Scotland in 1710, and Ilay gained his place as lord justice-general and membership of the privy council.

Ilay aspired to succeed the duke of Queensberry as secretary of state for Scotland after the latter's death in 1711, but instead Harley (who became earl of Oxford in May 1711) did nothing, attempting to balance the political influence of the duke of Argyll (which Ilay represented), the duke of Hamilton, and the earl of Mar. Argyll had been sent to Spain as ambassador-extraordinary and commander-in-chief in 1711, Hamilton died in a duel in 1712, and by the time Argyll returned to London from his mission abroad in 1712 it was clear that Oxford preferred dealing with the earl of Mar in Scottish affairs rather than Argyll and Ilay. Mar did not have the power base in Scotland possessed by the Campbells, and was more dependent on Oxford's goodwill at the Treasury. By August 1713 he was secretary of state for Scotland, as Ilay and his brother emerged as opponents of English tory attempts in parliament to vote the extension of the malt tax to Scotland (deferred under the terms of the treaty of union until the end of the war against France). Early in 1713 Oxford had offered Ilay 'a job, albeit a rather dubious one, on a mission of some kind to Turkey' (Riley, 240, citing *Portland MSS*, 5.265). Although Ilay replied offering continued support if Oxford would provide some encouragement, this was abandoned over the malt tax. In 1713 the Jacobite MP George Lockhart of Carnwath wrote to an unknown correspondent:

> Argyle and Ilay roar and exclaim bloodily against the Union, and seem very positive that the Whig Lords woud join to dissolve if our peers would help in the mean time to stop the ministry. There are [those] here who say the 2 brothers, finding that their Court [interest] decays, are making this noise and opposition to force the ministry into their ways. If it be so I shall be sorry for it, but as yet I can't but think they propose what seems the most effectuall way. (*Letters of George Lockhart*, 80)

Whatever his motives, Ilay was reported to Oxford as in league with opposition whigs in Scotland, and as a result lost his place in the ministry's list of nominations of Scottish representative peers.

Of course this all changed with the death of Queen Anne and the accession of the Hanoverian George I, with whose cause Ilay and his brother had become identified after 1713. Ilay not only returned to the House of Lords as a representative peer in 1715, he was given the place of lord clerk register, responsible for the records of Scotland, in addition to his life appointment as lord justice-general. He and his brother subsequently were at the centre of Hanoverian resistance to the Jacobite rising of 1715 in Scotland. Ilay went to Argyll to repel Jacobite attempts to take the family seat at Inveraray, and was able later to join his brother with the Campbell militia at the battle of Sheriffmuir in central Scotland, where he was wounded. Yet success in defending the Hanoverian settlement in Scotland during the rising also prompted jealousy in England and the duke of Argyll decided to return to London in February 1716, presumably with Ilay. By July a jealous king, observing the second duke of Argyll's growing influence with his son, Prince George, abruptly removed Argyll and Ilay from all the offices they held under the crown, which meant that Ilay lost his place as lord clerk register, held at the king's pleasure, but not his legal appointment as lord justice-general, which was for life.

In view of the mixed fortunes of the Campbell brothers in the whirlpool of British high politics from 1710 to 1716—when they were in, then out, then in, then out again—it is perhaps not surprising that Ilay, the lawyer and politician to his brother's soldier and statesman, should in 1716 have expressed a less than idealistic view of politics to his brother-in-law the second earl of Bute:

> we always judge for ourselves without any prejudice of any side farther than honour and interest joined oblige us … thus Politics is a continuall petty war and game, and as at all other games, we will sometimes win and sometimes loose, and he that plays best and has the best stock has the best chance … It is enough that we can maintain an interest with some of both sides without giving up anything we must and ought to maintain, and if I can save myself or my friends by being thought a Mahometan by a Turk, I'l never decline it. (Ferguson, 137–8)

The period from 1716 to 1721 was one of mixed political fortunes for Ilay and his brother. This reflected the instability among the English whig political party, divided as it was between the earls of Stanhope and Sunderland on the one side, and Lord Townshend and Robert Walpole on the other, the latter two of whom left office in 1717. Although Townshend and Walpole never fully trusted Ilay and his brother, their political opponents had forged a close alliance with those who opposed Ilay and his brother in Scotland, known as the 'Squadrone', a political name first used at the time of the treaty of union negotiations for a group of whig independents in Scotland. Their leader after 1716 was the earl of Roxburghe, created secretary of state for Scotland after Ilay's and Argyll's dismissal and later raised to a dukedom. This left Townshend and Walpole as natural political partners of Ilay and Argyll.

A Walpolean whig All four men were heavily involved in the South Sea Bubble of financial speculation, which also involved the prince of Wales, and Ilay had close links with John Law, the Scottish banker at the centre of the French Mississippi Company whose success had led to the establishment of the South Sea Company in London. One of Law's biographers records the 'well-authenticated anecdote' that

> the then Earl of Ilay, going to wait upon Mr Law by appointment, found the antichambers filled with many of the highest quality in France; but being, by special orders, admitted into his private apartments, beheld the great man writing what, from the number and rank of those left to wait his leisure, he naturally concluded to be dispatches of the utmost consequence. Upon mentioning these surmises to his old friend, it was with no small surprise his Lordship learned that he was only writing to his gardener at Lauriston to plant cabbages on a particular spot. (Wood, *Memoirs*, 55)

From the published letters of Ilay to Henrietta, countess of Suffolk, close friend of his brother and himself, it is clear that Ilay was involved in financial speculation relating to Law's Compagnie d'Occident in France. The editor of these volumes, John Croker, claimed in a note that Ilay had been responsible for the reissue of one of Law's earlier Scottish works on paper currency in London in 1719, with 'an encomiastic preface from the pen of his lordship' (*Letters*, ed. Croker, 1.43 n. 4). There is a very favourable advertisement for Law published as 'The bookseller to the reader' in the 1720 London edition of Law's *Money and Trade Considered* which includes the quotation from Cicero identified by Croker as part of Ilay's preface. If Ilay and his brother lost in their financial speculations at this time, they survived with the basis of their fortunes intact, and the experience seems in particular to have forged a link between Ilay and Robert Walpole in which the former could represent the political influence of his elder brother and negotiate between Walpole and Argyll. In 1721 the king made Ilay lord privy seal in Scotland, a substantial civil list post of greater financial value than that of lord clerk register which Ilay had lost in 1716. During the parliamentary elections of 1722 Walpole supported Ilay and his brother in all disputed elections, which resulted in their having significant influence over two-thirds of the forty-five Scottish MPs in the House of Commons. Those Scottish whigs of the Squadrone party who opposed the Argyll interest had become too closely identified with Walpole's political rivals in London, particularly the king's favourite, Lord Carteret.

Walpole did not intend to support Ilay and his brother unreservedly in Scottish affairs, merely to give them the upper hand in their contest with their fellow whigs in return for support for his policies, which after 1722 included a Treasury inquiry into customs fraud in Scotland. He was able to achieve a degree of success in his endeavours by working with Ilay and the Argyll interest, who would not oppose the dismissal of so many customs officers in the Glasgow region, where they had been appointed on the recommendation originally of the Squadrone's duke of Montrose. This enabled Walpole to present Treasury action as positive to English tobacco merchants who claimed that customs irregularities had given the Scots an unfair advantage in this trade. Then Walpole, again under pressure of English opinion, decided to extend the malt tax to Scotland in 1725, albeit at a lower rate than that levied in England. Those who had threatened to dissolve the union in 1713 on this issue had included Ilay and Argyll. In 1725 they supported Walpole, on the grounds that payment at a lower rate recognized the argument of Scotland's relative poverty within the kingdom of Great Britain. The Squadrone Scottish whigs, however, confident of their ability to strike a telling blow against what had become known as the 'Argathelian' interest in Scotland, opposed the ministry. They won popular recognition in Scotland as patriotic defenders of national interest, but brought down upon themselves the full wrath of Walpole, determined to demonstrate to English opinion that the government's writ ran in Scotland. Robert Dundas of Arniston was sacked as lord advocate, the chief legal officer of the crown in Scotland, because he would not support the tax. He was a prominent Squadrone whig and was encouraged by the secretary of state for Scotland, the duke of Roxburghe.

Riots broke out in Glasgow on 24 June, directed at the home of the MP for the Glasgow district of burghs, Daniel Campbell of Shawfield, a member of the Argathelian interest. The new lord advocate, Duncan Forbes of Culloden, was also an Argathelian, and he exerted himself to preserve government authority by using troops and threatening legal action against the magistrates of Glasgow and Edinburgh if they did not act in support of the government. Ilay hurried from London to join Forbes in Scotland, where as lord justice-general and extraordinary lord of session he made clear that he expected the Scottish high courts of justiciary and session to support the government with their authority. By 24 August the duke of Roxburghe was given leave by the king (then in Hanover) to retire from his place as secretary of state. The vacancy was not filled. There is evidence that Ilay was again disappointed by this decision, as he had been in 1711 on the death of the duke of Queensberry. The Scottish privy council consisting of the Scottish officers of state had been abolished by parliament in 1708, leaving the offices such as keeper of the privy seal available as sinecures, no longer involving direct administrative responsibility. As these offices were associated with the former Scottish privy council, there was an expectation in Scotland that those who held them exercised influence in public life and policy. Ilay reported from Scotland to the duke of Newcastle as responsible secretary of state, and although Walpole at the Treasury accepted many of Ilay's recommendations, he made occasional appointments in favour of the Squadrone to demonstrate that government in London, not Ilay, controlled Scottish affairs.

Ilay had, however, secured a young protégé in 1724, Andrew Fletcher, nephew of the famous Scottish patriot of the same name, whom he had appointed to the court of session as Lord Milton. He wrote to Milton that in politics, 'alls a game', and 'in the main good cards never lose at the long run … though I am very far away from thinking that any consolation maxims are necessary for me at present, I leave that to my enemies' (NL Scot., Saltoun papers, MS 16529, 6 Feb 1724). With Milton as his constant correspondent, Ilay subsequently became associated with Scottish government under the Walpole ministry for the next fifteen years. He did so as representative of his brother's Argathelian interest, in which he shared on grounds of kinship as well as his close association with his brother. His brother had no interest in the day-to-day business of politics and patronage, however, which fell to Ilay, who also demonstrated a greater ability to develop a good working relationship with Walpole. At the time of the unpopular attempt to pass an excise bill increasing that tax in 1733, Ilay was one of four close associates who escorted Walpole out of the House of Commons after he had postponed the bill, braving a waiting mob (Plumb, 2.270). Walpole in retirement made it clear that he continued to regard Ilay as one of his principal supporters in his public career, according to a memoir left by Henry Etough.

Scotland's financier The efforts Ilay made after 1725 to effect a political settlement in Scotland had prompted a major attempt at securing government investment in the Scottish economy in the aftermath of the restoration of law and order. This included obtaining Walpole's agreement to the completion of the terms of the treaty of union eighteen years previously, which Ilay had helped to negotiate. Under article twenty of the treaty an 'Equivalent' of £398,085 10s. had been promised to compensate Scotland for assuming part of the burden of the national debt of England, for accepting higher rates of taxation on the English model, for compensation for losses which occurred through recoinage, and for many other purposes, and had included the stipulation that:

> two thousand pounds per annum for the space of seven years shall be applied towards Encouraging and Promoting the Manufacture of coarse Wool within these shires which produce the Wool … and afterwards the same shall be wholly applied towards the Encouraging and Promoting the Fisheries and such other Manufactures and Improvements in Scotland as may most conduce to the general Good of the United Kingdom.

This had never been paid, and when George II succeeded as king in 1727 Ilay was with Walpole's support able to obtain a new commission from the crown for what was entitled the 'Commissioners and Trustees for Improving Fisheries and Manufactures in Scotland' to disburse the annual sum promised under the treaty of Union, a further parliamentary grant made in 1718 through Ilay's influence, and any income arising from the provision in the act extending the malt tax into Scotland (12 Geo. I c.4) that any funds in excess of £20,000 annually from the tax were to be applied for the encouragement of manufactures in Scotland. Ilay had argued for reinvestment in the underdeveloped economy of Scotland in return for co-operation in improving the level of administration and revenue collection there. The new commission soon became known as the 'board of trustees', and as the commissioners were unpaid its activities were chiefly directed by Ilay's agent Lord Milton towards encouraging development of linen manufactures in Scotland.

Ilay also used his influence with Walpole to obtain a royal charter for a new Royal Bank of Scotland after the accession of George II in 1727, giving Scotland two chartered banks and thus departing significantly from the model of banking pursued by the Bank of England. The influence of John Law's ideas can be detected, and the new bank also grew out of the financial provisions of article twenty of the treaty of union. After the treaty of union the now British Treasury in London had been unable to provide the entire £398,085 10*s*. of the Equivalent in cash and instead issued Equivalent debentures with a promise of future payment. In 1724 Ilay had helped pass an act of parliament which incorporated those holding these debentures into an 'Equivalent Company', with a capital of approximately £250,000 (£170,000 of which by that time was held by financiers in London). It was the royal charter granted to this company in 1724 which created the Royal Bank of Scotland, in which £111,347 of Equivalent stock was invested in return for yearly perpetual interest from the Treasury of £5010. The income for the new board of trustees in Scotland was also deposited in the bank, as was government tax revenue in Scotland before annual remission to the Treasury in London. Thus out of article twenty of the treaty of union and the ideas of John Law, Ilay with his brother's backing created a new financial institution in Scotland that would give backing to his political interests but also contribute to the creation of a unique post-union Scottish system of banking based on the issue of paper currency which, despite some financial crises, would act as a powerful engine of Scottish economic development in the eighteenth century. In the twentieth century the Royal Bank of Scotland used Allan Ramsay's portrait of Ilay on all their notes, although arguably he acted as a disciple of John Law in the foundation of the bank.

Although Ilay's economic programme promised much, its immediate effects in Scotland were small. His efforts to assert the authority of civil government over the Church of Scotland attracted immediate opposition and led by 1733 to the secession of ministers opposing his policies, particularly on the issue of church patronage. This was the legal right to appoint parish ministers as a property right either by the crown or local landowners without reference to the clergy of the church or its heritors and elders. To Ilay this was part of the rule of law and a safeguard against the return to the sectarian violence of seventeenth-century Scotland. To his opponents, however, it was another example of him extending the power of an increasingly unpopular regime over another Scottish institution and undermining its civic independence. His influence over the Scottish burghs, particularly Edinburgh and Glasgow as the most important, and over the Scottish colleges, was viewed by some in the same light, although there is evidence that development of the burghs and the colleges into cities and universities was part of his programme of economic and social development for the country.

In the elections of 1733 Ilay helped Walpole repel a strong electoral challenge by working for the return of MPs and Scottish representative peers who would support the government. There was talk of trying to impeach Ilay for corrupt practices, but instead Ilay received the office of keeper of the great seal of Scotland, held before the union by the lord chancellor of Scotland. The lesser office of lord privy seal he ceded to his ally the second duke of Atholl. The Squadrone whigs feared obliteration. 'The whole nomination of sheriffs seems to be little more than a list of sons, sons-in-law, and alliances of those gentlemen whom the D[uke] of A[rgyll] has thought fit to place upon the bench,' wrote Andrew Mitchell to Robert Dundas (Ferguson, 143). Although the lord advocate, Duncan Forbes, was more loyal to Ilay's brother, he and Lord Milton in Edinburgh helped create a formidable administrative interest through which Ilay could extend the influence of the ministry and its policies.

In 1736 the Porteous riot in Edinburgh created a crisis which tested the limits of Scottish loyalty to the Walpole regime and in the process split the Argathelian party in Scotland. The execution of the captain of the Edinburgh town guard, John Porteous, by an anonymous mob after his men had fired on a crowd gathered at the execution of a smuggler shook Scottish government to its foundations, as Porteous had been taken from the Edinburgh tolbooth by a crowd determined that he should die before the crown could pardon him. Ilay consented to punitive measures proposed by Walpole to allay English opinion, unaware of how high feeling in Scotland ran against any reprisals. By September 1736 he was in Edinburgh to conduct personally an investigation into the outrage, but had to return to London in December 1736 empty handed. By March 1737 Ilay was trying to stop reprisals in parliament, writing to Milton that 'the House and indeed vast numbers of people here are so exasperated at the Edinburgh mob that whatever is proposed however violent and unjust is popular; and it is impossible to judge what effect this violence may have'. Ilay abstained in the House of Lords on the vote for the bill punishing Scotland while his brother voted against. All the Scottish MPs in the House of Commons with one exception (Philip Anstruther) voted against. This brought about a final break between Ilay and his brother Argyll, who went into opposition, although he was not dismissed from all his offices until 1740. Ilay held on to office, although he wrote to Milton in July that 'the Duke of Newcastle comes here today but I hardly think we can ever do business with him sincerely again however I will look on and watch the game as it shall lie' (Scott, 426). Milton replied by the end of the year that his efforts to persuade Scottish MPs to attend parliament had been fruitless:

> The Country (say they) has been ill used, Lord Ilay no better and his friends continue to be dispised. And though they are told if it had not been for Sir R, we should have been worse used, this has little Effect; They say, it is the same thing, both to the Country and them whether it proceeded from want of Inclination or Power in those upon whose protection they depended. (ibid., 432)

Third duke of Argyll At the election of 1741 in Scotland Ilay and his brother worked to different purposes, Ilay attempting to hold support for Walpole and the ministry while Argyll enthusiastically supported efforts to return MPs and Scottish representative peers opposed to it. It was the only election between the Union and the Reform Act of 1832 lost by the government in Scotland, and as a result Walpole lost power in the following session of parliament. Walpole's English supporters suspected Ilay of treachery, but subsequent research has disproved this (Scott, 442–5). Ilay did not lose the offices of state he held following Walpole's defeat, but the office of secretary of state for Scotland was revived in 1742 for John Hay, marquess of Tweeddale, who held office until his resignation in early 1746 at the time of the last Jacobite rising in Scotland. In the meantime Ilay's brother died, leaving four daughters, none of whom could succeed to the Scottish dukedom. Thus within a year of Walpole's loss of office Ilay, at the age of sixty-one, was transformed from younger son dependent on the income of government office for most of his wealth, to one of the largest territorial magnates in Scotland. It changed his life. He wrote to Lord Milton:

> I am now too old and have too great a stake to wish to set myself up again as a Cock to be thrown at, and farther I have not health and constitution and I shall not have time on account of my private affairs, and my amusements to enter into any political scheme that required application, attendance or bustling, and every year at my age I must expect to be less capable of it! (Murdoch, *People Above*, 34)

Nevertheless the accession to the most prestigious dukedom in Scotland, when taken with his previous political career, ensured that his public status remained high in Scotland. A public reception he gave in Edinburgh in 1744 was attended by all the leading judges, lawyers, and civil servants in the city, much to the disgust of his political opponents.

With the sudden and embarrassing outbreak of Jacobite support in Scotland in 1745, however, this changed. Argyll (as he now was as third duke) left Inveraray for Edinburgh, and after consulting Lord Milton departed for London to try to exert influence with the ministry, remembering that his brother's exertions against the Jacobites in 1715 had left the way open for his enemies in London to misrepresent his actions as those of an overmighty subject. Horace Walpole's accusation in his *Memoirs* that this was the result of cowardice is repeated occasionally, but Argyll understood that without informed advice in London the ministry's response to the rising would be hopelessly incompetent, as proved to be the case. Duncan Forbes, lord president of the court of session, and Lord Milton led government efforts in Scotland itself until the arrival in Scotland of the duke of Cumberland in late winter 1745–6.

Although Argyll's advice was taken in some instances, regarding the raising of militia in the country for example, his general influence was limited and his actions seen as an attempt to protect vested interests that had failed to prevent rebellion by being either sympathetic to Jacobitism or incompetent. He refused to appear in Scotland until after the elections of 1747 on the ground that he had no influence, although the portrait of him in his robes as lord justice-general painted by Allan Ramsay by order of the magistrates of Glasgow in 1749 contains an elaborate visual pun on the basis of loyalty and disloyalty in Scotland reflecting his own sense of the ebb and flow of fortune in politics. Ramsay painted him holding a volume containing the defence of his own great-grandfather Archibald Campbell, marquess of Argyll, against a charge of treason before the very justiciary court he headed eighty-seven years later as lord justice-general. Back in London his speech to the House of Lords on Hardwicke's bill to abolish heritable jurisdictions in Scotland provoked scorn from Scottish whigs who had opposed him, such as Andrew Mitchell. Argyll argued that the survival of heritable jurisdictions was not a sign of the primitive state of Scottish institutions but had been necessary in former times as a defence against Stuart absolutism. In fact heritable jurisdictions had nothing to do with the rising in 1745, although Argyll emerged as the largest beneficiary of the compensation paid by the government at their abolition. His opponents ascribed this to his influence of the court of session, his admirers pointed to the ambitious programme of redevelopment upon which he embarked at Inveraray Castle and town partly financed by these funds from the British Treasury. Feudal jurisdictions literally became the means of financing modern improvement which set an example of reinvention and redevelopment for the rest of the country as the immediate reprisals for Jacobite action faded away and a younger generation of Scottish landowners and professionals emerged determined to modernize their country.

Appin murder trial and later political career In this period Argyll acquired a degree of infamy for his intervention in the Appin murder trial, using his privilege as lord justice-general to sit with the ordinary lords of justiciary on circuit at Inveraray in their trial of James Stewart of the Glen for the murder of Colin Campbell of Glenure in 1752. Argyll's speech to the court had little to say about the murder itself and much to say about what he termed 'those barbarous cruelties and lawless oppressions practiced in the Highlands during several centuries' and that 'this murder has been visibly the effect and consequence of the late rebellion' (Mackay, 290–91). It was a harsh judgement, and the proceedings can be described as close to judicial murder rather than legal justice. Campbell's murder jeopardized Argyll's efforts to obtain a parliamentary act in effect nationalizing the Jacobite estates confiscated from rebel chiefs after the '45 for the purposes of improvement and redevelopment. Until 1752 factors like the murdered Campbell had administered the estates and collected the rents due to the crown, but the act of 1752 provided for the establishment of a commission very like that established as the board of trustees in 1727, with a remit to ensure that the estates were farmed in the most efficient manner possible, that the inhabitants be encouraged to undertake manufactures, and that any profits arising be employed for further economic development. Opponents of the bill in London alleged that it rewarded the Scots for rebellion, and the duke of Bedford in the House of Lords argued that Argyll was protecting Jacobites who held government offices in Scotland, and demanded an investigation. Argyll did not reply directly, he wrote to Milton, 'that I might have been engaged in an altercation with one too much above me', as he knew the duke of Cumberland supported Bedford's complaints. As a result Milton was forced to cancel a journey to London to discuss the administration of the annexed estates with the ministers, although the bill did become law. Whether the ministry led by Henry Pelham and his brother the duke of Newcastle would retain any interest in implementing the act remained an open question at the time, and after Pelham's death his brother Newcastle attempted to appoint opponents of Argyll to the board to avoid further accusations of Jacobite influence in parliament. This was the political context of the Appin murder trial, which will remain at the centre of any portrayal of Argyll as a man capable of putting policy over justice.

Newcastle's efforts to govern Scotland without direct dependence on Argyll were short-lived. By July 1755 Thomas Hay, Lord Dupplin, at the Treasury wrote to one of Newcastle's principal supporters on the board of annexed estates, James Ogilvy, Lord Deskford:

> in the distribution of offices in Scotland the Duke of Newcastle has showed and is determined to show an impartial regard to merit and the friends of the government … At the same time I think that the Duke of Argyll from his rank, his property, his abilities, his experience in business and his extensive connections must and will always claim a great deal of regard and attention … Though it might be an error in policy to carry on the affairs of Scotland entirely *by* one hand yet to carry on the business of government *with* the Duke of Argyll will in my poor opinion be wise, prudent, and necessary. I do not know whether I explain myself clearly, but to my own comprehension the distinction is obvious. There is a great difference between entire submission and proper regard. (Murdoch, *People Above*, 46–7)

By this time Argyll's political credit had been renewed through the emergence of his nephew John *Stuart, third earl of Bute, as an influence in the household of the young prince of Wales (later George III). Bute had sided with the second duke of Argyll when he broke with the Walpole ministry in 1737, and had never been on close terms with his uncle the third duke, but in October 1755 Newcastle wrote that the king wanted him to use Argyll 'to get *a certain Lord of his country*.' Negotiations continued into 1756, which led to the involvement of Attorney-General William Murray, erroneously reported in the *Dictionary of National Biography* as being employed by Newcastle in Scottish management at this time. Ironically, these negotiations brought Argyll into meaningful contact for the first time with William Pitt, and when Newcastle had to resign the Treasury to accommodate Pitt's accession to office as war broke out with France, it was Argyll who provided Pitt with the idea of raising Highland regiments for service in America. The result was an autumnal season of ministerial influence for the ageing politician. Pitt needed troops, and Argyll was given commissions to distribute to officers of two projected regiments. 'Some of the John Bulls cannot believe that such a body of men could be raised in so short a space,' Argyll's secretary reported to Lord Milton (Murdoch, *People Above*, 49).

It was Argyll's nephew who was the rising star, however, which led to some clashes in 1759 and 1760 over electoral matters in Scotland as Bute began to use his new-found influence on behalf of younger candidates who would not have found favour with Argyll. But the death of George II in October 1760 put paid to any real confrontation, as Bute was the new king's favourite and Argyll knew from long experience the futility of opposing the will of a politician who had more influence with the king. Yet because Bute had no interest in Scottish affairs and because Argyll was his uncle it was possible for the old man, by now in his seventy-ninth year, to continue to exercise significant influence on Scottish affairs.

Argyll (Ilay as he then was) had married Mary, daughter of Major Walter Whitfield, sometime paymaster of marines and MP, on 19 January 1713, but they separated early in the marriage. She had died on 1 September 1723, and was buried as Lady Iley at Kensington on 7 September 1723. By his will dated 14 August 1760 he left his English property to Mrs Anne Williams (*d.* 1762), otherwise Shireburn, of Whittondean, Middlesex, and of Marlborough Street, London; she died on 1 June 1762. Argyll himself had died on 15 April of the previous year, quietly passing away at home in London just before he was to leave for Scotland to attend the election of Scottish representative peers. He was buried at Inveraray in the following month.

Argyll's will also named Anne Williams's son, William Williams, commanding a company of the 3rd foot guards, who had been appointed auditor of excise in Scotland (4 January 1739), and died on 1 April 1786. Williams's widow died at Whittondean on 19 February 1799. They had a son, Archibald, 'to whom Mr. [William] Coxe expresses his acknowledgement for the papers of his grandfather Archibald Duke of Argyll, in which he found several original letters of Sir Robert Walpole' (Wood, *Scots peerage*, 1.115). Coxe's volumes on Walpole were published in 1798. The existence and location of Argyll's papers has since been unknown and they are presumed lost. The dukedom of Argyll passed to his cousin John Campbell of Mamore, who became fourth duke of Argyll.

Reputation Argyll is best known as a politician and as the personification of unionist Scotland in the first half century after union; indeed, the print of Ramsay's 1749 portrait was the most common in Scottish households of the eighteenth century (Nenadic, 179–80), but this misses much of significance in his career. He was a genuine scholar with particular expertise in the classics, as his letter of advice to his young nephew James Stuart Mackenzie demonstrates. It was written in 1738 while Mackenzie was a student in the Netherlands, and sets a stern standard of scholarship including history, classics, civil law, and mathematics (Bute papers, Mount Stuart, Isle of Bute). He collected one of the largest private libraries in western Europe, a catalogue of which was published in 1758 by the Foulis Press of Glasgow under the title *Catalogue librorum A.C.D.A.* His London home became known as 'the library', and he was a trustee of the British Museum from 1753 until his death. He took an interest in Scottish university appointments over his whole career, although despite references to the contrary he never formally served as chancellor of either of the colleges which later became the University of Aberdeen (Schweizer, 160–1, 175 nn.66 and 67). He promoted polite secular scholarship at the expense of the presbyterian theology with which his family had previously been identified. He was a scientist, who constructed laboratories at some of his residences, as well as an amateur mathematician, although he never produced work of real importance to these disciplines. His work as a botanist may have had more lasting importance. He was a keen player of whist, with which he used to make many analogies to politics. In the light of his patronage of Francis Hutcheson at Glasgow as well as many other professionals in Scotland he might be termed the father of what has become known as the Scottish Enlightenment of the eighteenth century, although there were those in Scotland who at his death described him as the father of his country, reluctant to acquire 'personal importance … by exasperating the misfortunes of a country' (Murdoch, *People Above*, 101–2; Schweizer, 127, 143).

ALEXANDER MURDOCH

Sources R. Douglas, *The peerage of Scotland* (1764) • R. Douglas, *The peerage of Scotland*, 2nd edn, ed. J. P. Wood, 2 vols. (1813) • *Scots peerage* • GEC, *Peerage* • *State papers and letters addressed to William Carstares*, ed. J. M'Cormick (1774) • P. W. J. Riley, *The English ministers and Scotland, 1707–1727* (1964) • R. Scott, 'The politics and administration of Scotland, 1725–48', PhD diss., U. Edin., 1982 • I. G. Lindsay and M. Cosh, *Inveraray and the dukes of Argyll* (1973) • A. Murdoch, *'The people above': politics and administration in mid-eighteenth-century Scotland* (1980) • J. S. Shaw, *The management of Scottish society, 1707–1764: power, nobles, lawyers, Edinburgh agents and English influences* (1983) • private information (2004) [R. L. Emerson] • D. N. Mackay, ed., *Trial of James Stuart* (1907) • Archibald Campbell, earl of Ilay, to James Stuart Mackenzie, 29 Sept 1738, Mount Stuart Trust, Isle of Bute, Bute MSS • *Catalogue librorum A.C.D.A.* (1758) • G. Lockhart, *Memoirs concerning the affairs of Scotland* (1714) • *Letters of George Lockhart of Carnwath, 1698–1732*, ed. D. Szechi, Scottish History Society, 5th ser., 2 (1989) • *Report on the manuscripts of the earl of Mar and Kellie*, HMC, 60 (1904) • *Letters to and from Henrietta countess of Suffolk*, ed. J. W. Croker, 2 vols. (1824) • J. P. Wood, *Memoirs of the life of John Law of Lauriston* (1824) • K. W. Schweizer, ed., *Lord Bute: essays in re-interpretation* (1988) • A. Smart, *Allan Ramsay: painter, essayist, and man of the Enlightenment* (1992) • A. Smart, *Allan Ramsay: a complete catalogue of his paintings*, ed. J. Ingamells (1999) • S. Nenadic, 'Enlightenment in Scotland and its popular passion for portraits', *British Journal for Eighteenth-Century Studies*, 21 (1998) • W. Ferguson, *Scotland: 1689 to the present* (1968) • J. Law, *Money and trade consider'd; with a proposal for supplying the nation with money*, 2nd edn (1720) • R. Saville, *Bank of Scotland: a history, 1695–1995* (1996) • J. H. Plumb, *Sir Robert Walpole*, 2 vols. (1956–60) • J. B. Owen, *The rise of the Pelhams* (1957) • A. Murdoch, 'Management or semi-independence?', www.ihrinfo.ac.uk/projects/elec/sem19.html

Archives NL Scot., medical recipe book • NRA Scotland, priv. coll., corresp. and papers | BL, corresp. with duke of Newcastle, Add. MSS 32688–33055 • Hunt. L., letters to earl of Louden • NA Scot., corresp. with Archibald Campbell of Stonefield; corresp. with earl of Marchmont • NL Scot., corresp. with John Campbell; Saltoun papers; letters to Lord Timwald • U. Nott. L., corresp. with Henry Pelham

Likenesses W. Aikman, oils, *c*.1715, Royal Collection • W. Aikman, portrait, *c*.1743, Parliament House, Edinburgh • R. Cooper, mezzotint, *c*.1743, Scot. NPG • J. Faber, mezzotint, pubd 1744 (after A. Ramsay), BM, NPG • A. Ramsay, oils, 1748, Inveraray Castle, Strathclyde region • J. Faber junior, mezzotint, 1749 (after A. Ramsay), BM, NPG • A. Ramsay, oils, 1749, Art Gallery and Museum, Glasgow [*see illus.*] • attrib. A. Ramsay, oils, *c*.1758, Scot. NPG • Medina, group portrait, Inveraray Castle, Strathclyde region

Campbell, Archibald (1691–1756), Church of Scotland minister and theologian, was born in Edinburgh on 24 July 1691 and baptized at Canongate church on 4 August, the son of Archibald Campbell (*fl.* 1645–1701), a merchant and brewer, and Christian, *née* Campbell (*fl.* 1650–1700). His father was related to the Campbells who held the estate of Succoth, near Inveraray. His education, at Edinburgh (1706?–1711) and Glasgow (1712?–1718) universities, was 'free and without any tincture of bigotry' (A. Campbell, *The Authenticity of the Gospel History*, 2 vols., 1759, 1. vi); at Glasgow he was much influenced by John Simson, professor of divinity, whose maxim was that reason is the basis of theology. Campbell was ordained in 1718 to the linked parishes of Larbert and Dunipace in Stirlingshire, and on 31 March 1723 he married Christian (*bap.* 1701), the daughter of John Watson, an Edinburgh merchant.

Campbell wrote what would be his most important work, *An Enquiry into the Original of Moral Virtue*, after reading Bernard Mandeville's *Fable of the Bees*, which described vice as essential to human nature. Campbell controverted Mandeville's theory by arguing that moral virtue was 'self-love or the desire for happiness' (Campbell, *Enquiry*, xv). In 1726 he entrusted the publication of the manuscript to Alexander Innes, preacher-assistant at St Margaret's, Westminster, but Innes published it under his own name in 1728 as *Arete-logia, or, An Enquiry into the Original of Moral Virtue*. When Campbell went to London in 1730 with his *Discourse Proving that the Apostles were no Enthusiasts*, he made Innes 'tremble in his shoes' (*DNB*) but did not prosecute. He merely stated in the 'Advertisement' to the *Discourse* that he was the author of the *Enquiry* and that in 1728 it had been published in Dr Innes's name. In 1731 Campbell became professor of divinity and church history at the University of St Andrews, and in 1733 he republished the *Enquiry*. Since he had been vilified in pamphlets that had accepted Innes's authorship, he decided to make Innes's duplicity public in the preface to the 1733 edition of the *Enquiry*. Campbell's thesis that moral virtue is to be located in demonstrable human experience was unacceptable in the contemporary climate of the Church of Scotland, which held the Calvinist doctrine of total depravity. He also held controversial views about the nature of authority. Regarding the education of divinity students, he believed that:

> submission to authority in matters of knowledge particularly of religion, whether natural or revealed, is a gross abuse and perversion of the gifts of God and a base prostitution of our noblest faculties … scholastick Divinity is most unworthy a generous mind and highly unbecoming a preacher of the Gospel. (Campbell, *Enquiry*, preface, xx–xxii)

To broaden their intellectual outlook, he required his students to read widely in classical philosophy.

By this time Campbell's opinions had begun to alarm the committee for purity of doctrine of the Church of Scotland. He was accused of having taught in the *Enquiry* that man was unable, by his own nature, to find out God; that the law of nature was sufficient to guide rational minds to happiness; and that self-love was the principle and motive of all virtuous and religious actions. Moreover he was criticized for having written in his *Discourse* that the apostles had regarded Christ as an impostor between his death and Pentecost. Campbell published these criticisms with a rebuttal in 1735, and the committee in its *Report* of 1736 more or less accepted his explanations apart from the last charge, and demanded that he abstain from speaking incautiously on this subject. Campbell was angry; he believed that the committee had twisted his words. In his next publication, *The Necessity of Revelation* (1739), he forestalled further criticism by asserting that 'in order to introduce natural religion among mankind, supernatural revelation is indispensably necessary' (Campbell, *The Necessity of Revelation*, 4). He died at his estate of Boarhill, near St Andrews, on 24 April 1756, and his widow published his *Authenticity of Gospel History* in 1759. The eldest of their twelve children, Archibald *Campbell (*bap.* 1724, *d.* 1780), was the author of the satire *Lexiphanes* (1767). MARGARET BATTY

Sources A. Moncrieff, *An enquiry into the principle, rule, and end of moral actions, wherein the scheme of selfish-love, laid down by Mr Archibald Campbell … is examined* (1735) • *General Assembly of the Church of Scotland*, Act x (1736) • *General Assembly of the Church of Scotland*, Act v (1737) • J. M'Kerrow, *History of the Secession church*, rev. edn (1841), 98–9 • D. Irving, *Lives of Scotish writers*, 2 (1850), 325–6 • *DNB* • *Fasti Scot.* • D. Laing, ed., *A catalogue of the graduates … of the University of Edinburgh*, Bannatyne Club, 106 (1858), 186 • J. D. Marwick, ed., *Extracts from the records of the burgh of Edinburgh*, AD *1403–1589*, [1–4], Scottish Burgh RS, 2–5 (1869–82)

Archives NA Scot., corresp. • NL Scot., MSS • NRA, priv. coll., corresp. and papers | BL, corresp. with Lord Hardwicke, Add. MSS 35446–35588, *passim*

Campbell, Archibald (*bap.* **1724**, *d.* **1780**), satirist, was baptized on 27 February 1724 in Larbert, Stirlingshire, the son of Archibald *Campbell (1691–1756), minister of Larbert and afterwards professor of church history at St Mary's College, St Andrews, and Christian (*bap.* 1701), daughter of John Watson, merchant of Edinburgh.

Campbell's father entertained 'sanguine hopes' for him, but 'this did not hinder his son Archibald from becoming a professed infidel' (*Scotland and Scotsmen*, 1.268). He clearly had a good education in the classical authors, an interest he maintained: 'I have been all my lifetime very little conversant with authors that can be called modern' (Campbell, 3).

At some point in his youth Campbell went to sea, and in 1761 was appointed purser in the navy. (The story that in 1745 the young William Falconer (1732–1769) was his servant and pupil is not true.) Long has a different version: Campbell 'had been labouring for the London booksellers as a translator' before venturing to sea (Long, 89).

Campbell describes his sea life as 'wandering and unsettled' (Campbell, xxviii). But about 1764 'in one of our American colonies', the generosity of an unnamed friend enabled him 'to resume long-interrupted and well-nigh forgotten studies' (ibid., xxvii). The result was the composition of two satirical prose works: *Lexiphanes; a Dialogue: Imitated from Lucian … being an attempt to restore the English tongue to its ancient purity* and *The Sale of Authors, a Dialogue, in Imitation of Lucian's 'Sale of Philosophers'*. Attempts to publish at the time of writing having failed, both were published anonymously in London in March and June 1767 respectively. The preface to *Lexiphanes* alludes to other imitations of Lucian, but these have not survived. In 1767 Campbell announced his intention 'to leave this country, to which I may never return' (ibid., xxxi). This intention was fulfilled, and he was living in Kingston, Jamaica, at the end of his life.

Lexiphanes is a lengthy satire attacking Johnson ('this great unlick'd Cub') for both his pedantic language and his dictionary-making. In the dialogue Lexiphanes (Johnson) first holds forth with great length and pomposity, and then is purged by vomiting of his excessive language by a critic and two physicians. It enjoyed some popularity; three further editions appeared (1767, 1774, 1783), and it was itself imitated. In *The Sale of Authors* fashionable writers of the day are sold at knock-down prices to grumbling booksellers. It contains the first printed appearance of the story about Gray's escaping from his college rooms in his shirt by a rope-ladder when undergraduates raised a false fire alarm (though Campbell gave the tale less credence than some later writers have done). Both works are written with spirit, wit, learning, and elegance.

Campbell appears to have had an unappealing personality, and an acerbic wit. Dismissed by Boswell as 'a Scotch purser in the Navy' (Boswell, *Life*, 2.44), he attracted harsher judgements from others, Johnson's other biographer Hawkins, for example: 'Campbell, who as well for the malignancy of his heart as his terrific countenance, was called horrible Campbell' (Hawkins, 347). According to Ramsay: 'His morals were as bad as his principles, so that he died wretched and unlamented' (*Scotland and Scotsmen*, 1.268). Campbell died on 10 December 1780, and was buried in Kingston parish churchyard.

WILLIAM R. JONES

Sources A. Campbell, dedication and preface, *Lexiphanes* (1767) • *Scotland and Scotsmen in the eighteenth century: from the MSS of John Ramsay, esq., of Ochtertyre*, ed. A. Allardyce, 1 (1888), 268n. • R. B. Langwill, 'An anonymous author', *Scottish Notes and Queries*, 5 (1891–

2), 136 • W. H. Long, 'The journal of a naval surgeon', *Naval yarns: letters and anecdotes, comprising accounts of sea fights and wrecks, actions with pirates and privateers etc from 1616 to 1831* (1899), 89–91 • Admiralty warrant books, PRO, Ad 6/19, 371 • *DNB* • Boswell, *Life*, 2.44 • J. Hawkins, *The life of Samuel Johnson, LL.D.*, 2nd edn (1787), 347 • *IGI*

Campbell, Sir Archibald (1739–1791), army officer and colonial governor, was born on 21 August 1739 and baptized on 25 August at Inveraray, Argyll, the second son of James Campbell (1706–1760), commissary of the western isles of Scotland and chamberlain to the duke of Argyll, and his wife, Elizabeth Fisher of Durren. He was educated at Glasgow University and at the Royal Military Academy, Woolwich. Having been commissioned in the corps of engineers of the king's army in 1758, during the Seven Years' War he served in the expeditions to the coast of France and the West Indies, at Guadeloupe, Dominica, Martinique, St Lucia, and Grenada (not, as many accounts have it, at Quebec). He was afterwards approached by Venice and by Portugal to join their services. In 1768 he was seconded to the East India Company as chief engineer in Bengal, where he reported on the Bombay fortifications, reorganized the defences of Fort William, and supervised the dismantling of the French fort at Chandernagore under the terms of the peace treaty. As a private venture, with Colonel Henry Watson, he built the docks and shipyards at Kidderpore, south of Fort William (he sold his interest to Watson shortly after returning to Britain in 1773), and made a fortune trading in silk.

In 1773 Campbell purchased Inverneill in Argyll; nearby Knap and Taynish were added to his estate by the end of the decade. He was elected MP for Stirling burghs in 1774, at great expense, and represented that constituency between 1774 and 1780, and again from 1789 until 1791. James Boswell acted as his legal adviser. Campbell was a supporter of the administration, but appears to have been little involved in politics.

In November 1775 Campbell raised the 71st regiment of highlanders, and with it sailed from Greenock to Boston in May 1776. He arrived in Boston harbour in June, unaware that the city had already fallen to the Americans. He surrendered and was imprisoned in Concord gaol in degrading conditions in retaliation for British ill treatment of captured American officers; strong protests to George Washington improved his conditions, but he remained a prisoner until he was exchanged for Ethan Allan and six other men in May 1778. He resumed his command, and led eight battalions of infantry to reconquer Georgia. After landing at Savannah at the end of December 1778 he achieved his objectives within three months. He then resigned the command to General Augustine Prevost and returned to Britain and popular acclaim.

On 7 July 1779 Campbell married Amelia (*d.* 1813), the daughter of the portraitist Allan *Ramsay. They had no children. In 1780 he was appointed lieutenant-governor of Jamaica, with the rank of brigadier-general and the command of the British troops on the island, which he refused to allow the governor, John Dalling, to use in expeditions against Nicaragua and Curaçao. Dalling was recalled in 1782 and Campbell was appointed governor of Jamaica in his place. He successfully reorganized the island's defences. He was appointed general of the line in November 1783 and returned to Britain in August 1784. On 30 September 1785 he was appointed KB for his services. Friendship with Henry Dundas led to his appointment as governor of Madras in the same year, and he arrived in India in April 1786. In addition to being one of the most highly regarded military engineers of his time, Campbell was also an able administrator; he devoted much energy to the civil institutions of Madras, and he concluded a treaty with the nawab of Arcot for the settlement of the nawab's debts. This last was strongly criticized by the directors of the East India Company, and, offended and in poor health, Campbell resigned in June 1789.

Campbell did not long survive his return to Scotland: he caught a severe cold in 1790, and, although he recuperated in Bath, he died at his house in Upper Grosvenor Street, London, on 31 March 1791. He was buried in Westminster Abbey, leaving his fortune and Inverneill estates to his elder brother, Sir James Campbell (1737–1805). His younger brother, Duncan Campbell (1742–1822), succeeded him at Taynish, chronicled the family history, and wrote the manuscript account of Sir Archibald's career on which this life is largely based. J. L. Campbell

Sources priv. coll., Campbell of Inverneill MSS • HoP, *Commons* • bap. reg. Scot. • E. W. C. Sandes, *The military engineer in India*, 2 vols. (1933–5) • H. D. Love, *Vestiges of old Madras, 1640–1800*, 4 vols. (1913) • *Journal of an expedition against the rebels of Georgia in North America under the orders of Archibald Campbell, Esquire*, ed. C. Campbell (1981)

Archives BL, memoir on the military state of Jamaica, King's MS 214 • BL OIOC, corresp. and papers relating to India, home misc. series • NA Scot., corresp.; letter-books and papers relating to Madras • NAM, department of film and sound, memoir on Jamaica • National Library of Jamaica, Kingston, memoir on Jamaica • NRA Scotland, priv. coll., corresp. and papers • PRO, corresp., PRO 30/55 | NL Scot., corresp. with Henry Dundas • PRO, corresp. with Lord Cornwallis, PRO 30/11 • Yale U., Beinecke L., corresp. with James Boswell

Likenesses G. Romney, portrait, 1790–92, National Gallery of Art, Washington, DC; repro. in Sandes, *Military engineer* • D. Orme, stipple, pubd 1794 (after Smart, 1788), NPG • three plaster medallions, 1797? (after J. Tassie), Scot. NPG • T. Kettle, portrait, Government House, Madras, India

Campbell, Sir Archibald, first baronet (1769–1843), army officer, son of Captain Archibald Campbell, and grandson of Duncan Campbell of Milntown, in Glen Lyon, Perthshire, was born on 12 March 1769. He entered the army on 28 December 1787 as an ensign in the 77th regiment, having obtained his commission by raising twenty men, and sailed for India in the spring of 1788. He joined the army in the Bombay presidency under the command of Sir Robert Abercromby at Cannanore, and served with that western division throughout the campaigns of 1790, 1791, and 1792, and was present at the first siege of Seringapatam, by Lord Cornwallis, in 1792. In 1791, during the campaign, he was promoted lieutenant and made adjutant of his regiment. He served at the capture of Cochin in 1795 and of the Dutch factories in Ceylon in 1796. In 1799, on the outbreak of the Fourth Anglo-Mysore War, he was appointed brigade major to the European brigade of the Bombay division, which advanced from the Malabar coast, and was present at the battle of Seddesvara and the fall of Seringapatam. For his services he was promoted captain into the 67th regiment, and at once exchanged into the 88th foot (Connaught Rangers), in order to remain in India, but his health broke down and he had to return to Britain. Wellesley had, however, observed Campbell's bravery at Seringapatam, and his usefulness as a staff officer, and he was therefore made brigade major in the southern district, and on 14 September 1804 promoted major into the 6th battalion of reserve, then stationed in Guernsey. On its reduction in 1805 he was transferred to the 71st (Highland light infantry), and for the next three years commanded the 2nd battalion in Scotland and Ireland. In June 1808 he joined the 1st battalion of his regiment under Denis Pack, and served at the battles of Roliça and Vimeiro, and throughout Sir John Moore's advance into Spain and his retreat on Corunna.

In 1809 Campbell was, on Wellesley's recommendation, one of the officers selected to accompany Marshal Beresford to Portugal to assist him in his task of reorganizing the Portuguese army, and was promoted lieutenant-colonel on 16 February 1809. He commanded the 6th Portuguese regiment to Beresford's high approval; as colonel he was present at the battle of Busaco, and, in 1811, as brigadier-general commanding the 6th and 18th Portuguese regiments was engaged at Arroyo Molinos and in the battle of Albuera. In 1813 Campbell received the Portuguese order of the Tower and Sword, and his brigade was ordered to form part of an independent Portuguese division under the command of Major-General John Hamilton, attached to General Hill's corps. Under Hill, Campbell was present at the battles of Vitoria, the Pyrenees, the Nivelle (when he was mentioned in dispatches), and the Nive, and was afterwards attached to Sir John Hope's corps before Bayonne, where he remained until the end of the war. On the declaration of peace he received a gold cross and one clasp for the battles of Albuera, Vitoria, the Pyrenees, the Nivelle, and the Nive, was knighted, promoted colonel in the army on 4 June 1814, and made an aide-de-camp to the prince regent, and in January 1815 he was made a KCB. In 1816 he was made a Portuguese major-general, and commanded the division at Lisbon. In 1820, during the absence of Lord Beresford, he offered to put down the rising at Oporto, but his services were declined; he at once resigned his Portuguese commission and returned to Britain.

On arriving in Britain, Campbell was, in 1821, appointed lieutenant-colonel of the 38th regiment, which he joined at the Cape and took to India, where he was stationed at Berhampore. He was soon after nominated to command the expedition against the Burmese. He arrived at Rangoon in May 1824 at the head of 11,500 men, including four British regiments, and at once took Rangoon. His first attack on the great Shwedagon pagoda at Kemmendine, near Rangoon, was repulsed with loss on 3 June, and he had to take the command in person; under his personal directions the pagoda was stormed on 10 June 1824. In July he detached a force, under Colonel H. F. Smith CB, to Pegu, which stormed the pagoda at Syriam on 4 August; the heavy rains then put an end to further operations, and caused much disease among the troops. He wrote urgently for reinforcements during the winter months of 1824–5, for in November 1824 he was besieged in Rangoon by the ablest Burmese chief, Maha Bundoola. He was joined by the 47th regiment and by two brigades of sepoys, and after storming the stockade of Kokein on 16 December he left Rangoon on 11 February 1825 and marched along the banks of the Irrawaddy towards Prome, accompanied by about forty gunboats under Commodore Chads and Captain Marryat. On 7 March the advanced brigades, under Brigadier-General Cotton, were utterly defeated in an attack on the stockades of Danubyu, but Campbell at once moved to the front, and directed a fresh attack on 1 April which was entirely successful, and Maha Bundoola was killed. Campbell entered Prome on 5 May 1825 and established his headquarters there for the rainy season; he again lost at least a seventh of his forces between May and September. Towards the close of the rainy season Campbell—who had been promoted major-general on 27 May 1825 for his services—prepared to advance from Prome on Ava (at that time the capital of Burma), when Burmese envoys came into Prome and asked for terms. Campbell, who had been specially entrusted by Lord Amherst with the political as well as the military conduct of the campaign, announced that peace would be granted only on terms which were rejected, and Campbell again advanced. An assault upon the stockades of Wetthigan failed, and Brigadier-General Macdowall was killed on 16 November, but Campbell was again able to make up for the failures of his subordinates by storming the stockades on 26 November. On his approach towards the capital the king of Burma sent envoys to his camp once more, and a truce was made on 26 December. Campbell soon discovered that the negotiations were intended only to gain time, and therefore continued his advance on 2 January. By storming Melloon, the last fortified place on the way to Ava, he so frightened the king that he accepted the terms offered, and signed a treaty of peace at Yandabo on 26 February 1826. The successful termination of this war was received with enthusiasm in Britain and India. Campbell was made a GCB on 26 December 1826, voted a gold medal and an income of £1000 a year by the court of directors, and thanked by the governor-general, Lord Amherst. For three years after his success he governed the ceded provinces of Burma, and acted as civil commissioner to the courts of Burma and Siam, but in 1829 returned to Britain in ill health.

Campbell was received with great acclaim on his arrival; on 30 September 1831 he was created a baronet, and on 14 November he was granted special arms, and the motto 'Ava' by royal licence. From 1831 to 1837 he was lieutenant-governor of New Brunswick, and in 1837 was nominated to command-in-chief in Canada if Sir John Colborne left the colony. In 1838 he was promoted lieutenant-general. He was colonel of the 95th regiment from 1829 to 1834, of the 77th from 1834 to 1840, and of the 62nd from 1840; in August 1839 he was appointed commander-in-chief at

Bombay, but refused the appointment from ill health. He married Helen, daughter of Sir John Macdonald of Garth; their son was General Sir John *Campbell, second baronet (1807–1855). Campbell died on 6 October 1843.

H. M. Stephens, *rev.* Roger T. Stearn

Sources J. Philippart, ed., *The royal military calendar*, 3 vols. (1815–16) • *The dispatches of … the duke of Wellington … from 1799 to 1818*, ed. J. Gurwood, 13 vols. in 12 (1834–9) • *Colburn's United Service Magazine* (1843) • H. H. Wilson, *Documents illustrative of the Burmese war* (1827) • Major Snodgrass [J. J. Snodgrass], *Narrative of the Burmese war* (1827) • H. Havelock, *Memoir of the three campaigns of Major-General Sir Archibald Campbell's army in Ava* (1828) • F. B. Doveton, *Reminiscences of the Burmese War, in 1824–5–6* (1852) • D. Gates, *The Spanish ulcer: a history of the Peninsular War* (1986) • R. Muir, *Britain and the defeat of Napoleon, 1807–1815* (1996) • H. V. Livermore, *A new history of Portugal* (1976) • G. Bruce, *The Burma Wars, 1824–1886* (1973) • T. A. Heathcote, *The military in British India: the development of British land forces in south Asia, 1600–1947* (1995)

Archives BL OIOC, corresp. as commander-in-chief, Burma, home misc. series • NA Canada, corresp. as lieutenant-governor of New Brunswick • National War Museum of Scotland, Edinburgh, corresp. and papers • New Brunswick Museum, Saint John, dispatches | BL OIOC, letters to Lord Amherst, MS Eur. F 140 • BL OIOC, letters to Sir Thomas Munro, MS Eur. F 151

Likenesses J. Cochran, stipple, 1833 (after J. Wood), BM, NPG; repro. in W. Jerdan, *National portrait gallery of illustrations of eminent personages* (1830–34)

Campbell, Archibald (1877–1963), editor of highland bagpipe music and lawyer, was born on 18 January 1877, the youngest among the three sons of John Campbell, laird of Kilberry in Argyll. He was educated at Harrow School and Pembroke College, Cambridge. After entering the Indian Civil Service in 1900, he became assistant commissioner of the Punjab in 1901 and a judge of the high court in 1921. On 12 December 1905 he married Violet (1878/9–1949), youngest daughter of Sir Cecil *Beadon, lieutenant-governor of Bengal. They had three sons and one daughter.

Campbell began to learn piping in 1897 and took lessons from Angus MacRae, John MacColl, and John MacDougall Gillies. But most of his knowledge of piobaireachd came from six weeks of instruction from John MacDonald of Inverness and Alexander Cameron the younger in 1905 and 1911 when home on leave from India. In 1903, along with his brothers John and Angus, he helped found the Piobaireachd Society of Scotland, which was dedicated to the promotion and preservation of the classical music of the pipe. Membership was restricted to gentlemen enthusiasts, whose collective wealth and social power quickly made the society important. It provided judges for the major events, nominated lists of set tunes for competition, published scores for these edited by its members, and employed leading pipers to teach them; under an agreement with the War Office in 1909 it became responsible for training senior pipers in the army. Campbell himself acted as a senior judge and was keen to foster the society's links with the army.

After retiring in 1927 Campbell became lecturer in Indian law at Cambridge University (1929–41) and secretary of the music committee of the Piobaireachd Society of Scotland, which had just begun to publish its influential second series (15 vols., from 1925). Although the society always spoke of its 'editors', implying collective responsibility, Campbell was sole editor of volumes 2–9, which contained the core of the competition repertory. His volumes gave a complete score for each tune in staff notation and in the Nether Lorn *canntaireachd* vocables, with accompanying notes discussing alternative settings and some of their differences from the preferred text. The apparatus suggested scrupulous scholarship and accuracy, and indeed his arrangements were published by the society as the authentic stylings of great traditional musicians. But Campbell intervened freely, although silently, in the sources. He removed instructions to repeat parts, added movements not present in the originals, reduced varied conventional movements to standardized single forms, and exaggeratedly prolonged note values. Although he had ready access to expert advice from leading players on how to set the music he seldom followed this. By 1938 senior members of the music committee proposed abandoning his work as 'most flagrantly wrong' (Donaldson, *The Highland Pipe*, 396). Campbell's only surviving teacher, John MacDonald of Inverness, wrote that 'our ancient and traditional music, with all its beautiful and melodious airs and sentiment, has passed into the wrong hands, and it will take a long time, if ever, before it can be restored to its original standard' (ibid., 397). Campbell went on to describe volume 8 (1939) as his last, and the second series was allowed to go temporarily out of print.

But during the war years Campbell consolidated his position, and in 1948 the Piobaireachd Society of Scotland published his personal anthology *The Kilberry Book of Ceol Mor* containing 114 tunes prefixed by a historical and textual 'Introduction'. The scores showed further corruption of time values, reflecting Campbell's belief that 'slowness is a characteristic of Highland music' (Campbell, *Kilberry Book*, 6) and his preference for 'heavy' rather than 'tuny' pieces (MacNeill and Richardson, 112–15). The introduction gave a sketch of the leading piping families, presenting the MacCrimmons as the source of all authenticity. It stated that piping had been saved by the army and the highland societies of London and Scotland and that the piobaireachd tradition had ended with Angus MacKay. Although little evidence was offered for many key points, Campbell's essay became the standard source of conventional wisdom during the second half of the twentieth century.

By 1950 'Archie Kilberry' had established himself as the leading authority on piobaireachd. His scores remained fixed texts for all competitions, and later editors of the Piobaireachd Society of Scotland faithfully followed his style. This changed the way in which the music was perceived, as pipers, whose light-music repertories demonstrated vigorous musicality, gradually came to believe that piobaireachd was distinguished by a strange distortion or even absence of melody. Some sought purity of idiom in orally transmitted teaching; but this too had been influenced by the society's texts. As the older published and manuscript sources, which were accurate and musically reliable, had become scarce and little-known, proper access to traditional styles became difficult. By the 1990s three generations of pipers had gained their status from playing Campbell's scores, which continued to be presented as the stylings of master musicians like the MacCrimmons, MacKays, and Camerons. The worldwide expansion of piping in the post-war period made the *Kilberry Book* 'the biggest selling piobaireachd book ever produced' (Campbell, *Story*, 53/5, 22).

Campbell's main achievement was the creation of an instrumental structure which ensured that performance, teaching, publishing, and career opportunity took place within a context defined by his editorial work. By 2000 broadcasting and the state education system had also been brought within the nexus of a society whose legitimacy had become inseparable from that of Campbell himself.

Archibald Campbell died on 24 April 1963 at his home, 1D The Mansions, Earls Court Road, Kensington, London.

WILLIAM DONALDSON

Sources W. Donaldson, *The highland pipe and Scottish society, 1750–1950* (2000) • W. Donaldson, '"Entirely at the pleasure of the performer": a further exploration of piobaireachd', www.piperanddrummer.com, 2001–2 • A. Campbell, ed., *The Kilberry book of ceol mor*, 2nd edn (1953) • NL Scot., Piobaireachd Society MS Acc. 9103 • A. Campbell, piobaireachd research papers, *c.*1903–1963, NL Scot., MSS 22098–22117 • NL Scot., Seton Gordon MSS Acc. 5640, 7451 • *Oban Times* [miscellaneous dates] • S. MacNeill and F. Richardson, *Piobaireachd and its interpretation* (1987) • J. Campbell, 'The story of the Kilberry book of ceol mor', *Piping Times*, 53/3, 13–19; 53/4, 17–23; 53/5, 13–22 • J. Campbell, ed., *Side lights on the Kilberry book of ceol mor* (1984) • *Some letters of Archibald Campbell of Kilberry 1935–1949*, ed. J. H. Shone (1980) • D. Henderson, 'Update on the history of the society', *Proceedings of the Piobaireachd Society Conference* (1996), 1–9 • m. cert. • d. cert.

Archives NL Scot., piobaireachd research papers, MSS 22098–22117 | NL Scot., papers of the Piobaireachd Society of Scotland, Acc. 9103

Likenesses double portrait, photograph (with his son James), repro. in *Piping Times*, 19 • photograph, repro. in *Piping Times*, cover • photograph (in his judge's robes), repro. in *The Voice*, 29/1 (spring 2000), 23 • photographs, repro. in Shone, ed., *Letters of Archibald Campbell*, 6, 46

Wealth at death see sealed confirmation, 13 Aug 1963, *CGPLA Eng. & Wales*

Campbell, Archibald Bruce (1881–1966), broadcaster, was born on 21 January 1881 at 178 Albert Road, Peckham, London, one of the children of Hugh Campbell and his wife, Caroline Mary Southern. His father had been a captain in the Royal Navy, but became a schoolmaster after converting to Christianity. He started a mission in south London when Campbell was a child; his mother was also a devout Christian. Little is known about his childhood, other than that he attended a grammar school in Southwark, and two schools run by naval coaches in Portsmouth. After failing the entrance examination for the Royal Navy he went to Canada, where he worked at a number of jobs, including an expedition to the Peace river county in northern Canada to survey timber for the Canadian government, returning to England after three years. He failed the medical examination for the merchant navy but got a job as an assistant purser with the Orient Line, spending the years before the First World War on passenger liners.

At the outbreak of war Campbell, who held a commission in the Royal Naval Volunteer Reserve, was called up, and spent the war years serving as paymaster-commander of HMS *Otranto*, an armed merchant cruiser patrolling in the south Atlantic. He was the senior surviving officer when the *Otranto* sank, with the loss of several hundred lives, after a collision with a troopship in fog off the island of Islay, in October 1918. After demobilization in December 1920 he decided to leave the sea.

After trying his hand at schoolteaching Campbell decided to become a publisher. A. B. Campbell & Co., with its office in London, published magazines, including *Health for All*, *Handicrafts*, and the *Stamp Magazine*, and survived until its premises were destroyed in a bombing raid in 1941. Many of the periodicals closed down during the depression, and, hoping for a new source of income, Campbell first approached the BBC in 1933, but it was not until 25 August 1935 that he made his first radio broadcast, 'The last voyage of the *Otranto*'. Following the success of this talk, he was invited to give further informal talks on his adventures at sea in the *Men Talking* and *Young Ideas* series, and later in *The World Goes By*. These were to be given without a script, seen as one-way conversations in front of the microphone. Campbell proved a natural broadcaster: 'he really is a brilliant broadcaster … he has the true sailor's flow of words' (memo from Moray McClaren, 20 April 1936, BBC WAC), and Stuart Hibberd, presenter of *Men Talking*, wrote in his diary in October 1935 that Campbell had an unrivalled collection of sailors' yarns, 'spun not by the yard but by the mile' (Hibberd, 119). He made his first television broadcast in December 1936.

Commander Campbell became a national figure as one of the original members of the panel of *The Brains Trust*, one of the most popular radio series during the war, first broadcast on 1 January 1940 as *Any Questions*. The original idea, conceived by the producer, Howard Thomas, was to bring the forces into contact with the best brains of the day, in an informal and entertaining way. The brains were those of the philosopher C. E. M. Joad and the zoologist Julian Huxley, and Campbell's role was to act as a link between the intellectuals and the listeners. Listeners were invited to send in questions, which were put to the team by the question master, Donald McCullough. Campbell drew on his own experiences in answering the questions, and his 'When I was in Patagonia' became a catchphrase. Although there were those in the BBC who questioned the value of his contribution, Campbell was enormously popular with the public, which liked his direct and commonsense approach and regarded him as a personal friend. He realized that if he could not understand what Joad and Huxley were saying, nor could most of the listeners, and he felt entitled to ask the intellectuals to explain themselves more clearly. His post-bag was full of letters from listeners taking his side in disputes with the other members of the team. He made over 200 appearances on the programme between 1941 and 1946, and later claimed that he was dropped because of a remark that he had made during a discussion on the Bikini atomic bomb tests, in which he suggested that scientists instead of animals should be sent to Bikini.

During the Second World War, while continuing to broadcast, Campbell was attached to the eastern command welfare station, working closely with Sir William Hornell, the welfare director, and travelled all over England talking to the troops. During the preparations for the Normandy landings, he visited units on the south coast to talk to them about the work of the merchant navy, which would be transporting them across the English Channel. Campbell was twice married. Nothing is known about his first wife, but on 30 March 1942 (as a widower), he married a secretary, May Evelyn (*b.* 1900/01), former wife of Charles George Plowman Prevost, and daughter of Harry Frederick Webb, accountant.

After the war Campbell broadcast for the BBC for a few more years until 1953. For *Children's Hour* he gave a series of talks, *The Old Sea Chest*, in which he brought out curiosities he had collected on his travels; and in 1952 he made a series, *Commander Campbell Talking*, for *Woman's Hour*. In 1956 he also had his own series on Independent Television, *Calling on Campbell*, in which he told his seafaring yarns. Although he was invited by the BBC to talk again in 1958, his last broadcast was in February 1959, on the *Today* programme.

Campbell's many books for adults and children included *My Adventurous Life on Land and Sea* (1937), *The Battle of the Plate* (1940), *Into the Straight* (1950), *Salute the Red Duster* (1952), about the merchant navy during the Second World War, *Customs and Traditions of the Royal Navy* (1956), and *Queer Shipmates* (1962). He published a second volume of memoirs, *When I was in Patagonia* (1953), having written the first, *With the Corners Off*, in 1937. But he found it difficult to make a living through his writing, and as late as 1963, when he was in his eighties, he was still writing to the BBC with suggestions for talks. His play, *The Million to One Chance* (1933), based on the mystery of the *Marie Celeste*, which had been performed in Australia and South Africa in 1934, was adapted by him for radio and broadcast in 1964. Campbell died in a London nursing home, Twyford Abbey, Ealing, on 11 April 1966. He was survived by his second wife. ANNE PIMLOTT BAKER

Sources A. B. Campbell, *With the corners off* (1937) · A. B. Campbell, *When I was in Patagonia* (1953) · BBC WAC · H. Thomas, *Britain's Brains Trust* (1944) · H. Thomas, *With an independent air* (1977), chap. 5, 69–93 · H. Thomas, ed., *The Brains Trust book* [1942] · A. Briggs, *The history of broadcasting in the United Kingdom*, 3 (1970), xxxx · J. Huxley, *Memories*, 1 (1970), 251 · C. E. M. Joad, 'The Brains Trust: a retrospect', *New Statesman* (27 May 1944) · S. Hibberd, *This is—London* (1950), 119 · *The Times* (14 April 1966) · b. cert. · m. cert., 1942 · d. cert.

Archives BBC WAC, articles | SOUND BL NSA

Likenesses group photograph, 1943 (original Brains Trust team), repro. in Thomas, *Britain's Brains Trust*, frontispiece · A. B. Campbell, photograph, repro. in A. B. Campbell, *Into the straight* (1950), frontispiece · photograph, repro. in Campbell, *With the corners off*, frontispiece

Campbell [*formerly* Douglas], **Archibald Campbell, first Baron Blythswood** (1835–1908), politician and physicist,

Archibald Campbell Campbell, first Baron Blythswood (1835–1908), by James Russell & Sons, 1887

was born in Florence on 22 February 1835, the eldest of the nine children of Archibald Douglas (1809–1868), laird of Mains, and his wife, Caroline Agnes, the daughter of Mungo Dick of Pitkerro. Campbell's name at birth was Archibald Campbell Douglas. His father claimed descent from the Scottish noble families of both Campbell and Douglas and in 1838 he changed his name to Campbell on succeeding his cousin, Archibald Campbell, as laird of Blythswood, Renfrewshire; his eldest son thus became Archibald Campbell Campbell.

Campbell was educated privately for an army career. At the age of sixteen he joined the 79th highlanders, transferring to the Scots guards in the following year. He fought in the Crimea, where he was badly wounded, and reached the rank of lieutenant-colonel before retiring from the army on the death of his father in 1868. While still in the army he married Augusta Clementina, the daughter of the wealthy Liberal peer Lord Carrington (1796–1868), on 7 July 1864. Campbell assumed his patrimony as laird of Blythswood, in the vicinity of Glasgow, in time to participate in the general election of 1868, in which he stood as the unsuccessful Conservative candidate for Paisley.

An enthusiast for Conservative causes, especially tariff reform, Campbell and his wife, Augusta, were both active in spreading the Conservative faith in Scotland, participating in the foundation of the Conservative Association and the Conservative Club in Glasgow, and in the extension of the Primrose League in Scotland. He first entered parliament after winning Renfrewshire in a by-election in 1873, losing his seat in the general election the following year. He was made a baronet in 1880, having failed to regain his seat in the general election of that year. On the division of the county he succeeded in being elected for West Renfrewshire in 1885 and remained in the Commons until the defeat of the Conservatives in 1892, when he was raised to the peerage in Salisbury's resignation honours list.

Lord Blythswood was a notable amateur scientist. Using his ample private resources he established an extensive private laboratory at his home, Blythswood House, Renfrew. In the conduct of his experiments he had the benefit of the detailed advice and guidance of the professor of natural philosophy at Glasgow, Lord Kelvin, who, as a leading Liberal Unionist in the west of Scotland, was also a political ally. Between 1892 and 1905 Blythswood Laboratory, as it was known, was a location for experiments into many areas at the frontier of physics including cathode rays, X-rays, spectroscopy, and radioactivity. In 1900 Blythswood recruited a young physicist, Herbert Stanley Allen (1873–1954), to take control of his laboratory. After Allen left to take up a teaching position in London in 1905, the laboratory was frequently used for engineering experiments by a Whitworth Scholar, Walter Scoble.

Blythswood's forte was the construction of large machines. The most notable of these was a Wimshurst electrical machine with 128 plates, about ten times the size of the larger models available on the market. In 1896, a few months after Röntgen's discovery of X-rays was announced, Blythswood claimed that with this machine he had managed to produce X-ray photographs without passing the electricity through a partial vacuum, a quite remarkable result. The credibility of his claim was aided by the cautious support of Lord Kelvin. Another important Blythswood machine was a sophisticated dividing engine for ruling diffraction gratings. He worked on the perfection of this for many years; it was later inherited by the National Physical Laboratory. In the last few years of his life Blythswood was much occupied with aerodynamics; 'his kites were a subject of wonder and awe to the rural population of Renfrewshire' (*The Times*) and his laboratory was used to conduct experiments into the efficiency of aerial propellers.

Blythswood's political style was described as 'bluff and uncompromising' (*The Times*). He commanded the Renfrewshire militia from 1874 and was appointed aide-de-camp to Queen Victoria on retiring this command in 1894. The queen had stayed at Blythswood House during her official visit to Glasgow in 1888. His main recreation, other than science, was angling. Elected president of the Philosophical Society of Glasgow for 1898–1901, he rarely attended their meetings but his 'agency and influence' (Minutes, 320) gained for them the right to call themselves the Royal Philosophical Society of Glasgow.

Blythswood was elected FRS the year before his death. He died of heart failure at Blythswood House on 8 July 1908, and was buried at Inchinnan, near Glasgow, on 11 July. He left no children. He was survived by his wife, and was succeeded to the peerage by his brother, the Revd Sholto Douglas Campbell Douglas. The last Lord Blythswood, the seventh baron, died in 1940 at the age of twenty-one, while serving in the Scots Guards.

T. E. James, *rev.* Joseph Gross

Sources *The Times* (9 July 1908) · *Nature*, 78 (1908), 301–2 · D. C. Savage, 'Scottish politics, 1885–1886', *SHR*, 40 (1961), 118–35 · Lord Blythswood [A. C. Campbell], 'The new actinic rays', *Nature*, 53 (1895–6), 340 · Lord Blythswood [A. C. Campbell], 'On the Röntgen X-rays', *Proceedings of the Philosophical Society of Glasgow*, 27 (1895–6), 156–64, esp. 160–61 · Lord Kelvin [W. Thomson], 'On the generation of longitudinal waves in ether', *PRS*, 59 (1895–6), 270–73 · W. Wilson, *Memoirs FRS*, 1 (1955), 5–10 [obit. of H. S. Allen] · W. A. Scoble, 'The strength and behaviour of ductile materials under combined stress', *London, Edinburgh, and Dublin Philosophical Magazine*, 6th ser., 12 (1906), 533–47 · G. L'E. Turner, *Nineteenth-century scientific instruments* (1983) · W. A. Scoble, 'Some anchored tests of aerial propellers', *Engineering* (25 Dec 1908), 843–5 · *Annual Report* [National Physical Laboratory] (1908) · minutes of meeting, *Proceedings of the Royal Philosophical Society of Glasgow*, 33 (1901), 318–20 · GEC, *Peerage*

Archives SML, Blythswood ruling engine, artifact · Strathclyde Regional Archives, family and estate papers, Blythswood

Likenesses J. Russell & Sons, photograph, 1887, NPG [*see illus.*] · portrait, repro. in *Proceedings of the Philosophical Society of Glasgow* (1908–9), frontispiece · portrait, Conservative Club, Glasgow

Wealth at death £89,119 17*s.* 3*d.*: confirmation, 26 Dec 1908, *CCI*

Campbell [*née* Elvery], **Beatrice Moss**, **Lady Glenavy** [*known as* Beatrice Glenavy] (**1883–1970**), artist, was born in the suburbs of Dublin, the second of the seven children of (John) William Elvery, merchant, and Mary Teresa Moss (*d.* 1925), sculptor and music teacher. Her mother was the youngest of seven surviving children, out of fourteen, of Dr William Moss of Kilternan, co. Dublin, and Teresa, *née* Richardson, of Kilgobbin, in the same county. Beatrice was the niece of Phoebe *Traquair (1852–1936), a versatile artist of the Edinburgh arts and crafts movement. Clever, enquiring, strong-willed, and dramatically attractive, with a mane of red hair that inspired her fellow artists, she inherited the artistic talents of her mother's family from an early age. Music, literature, and nature study also featured prominently in a happy, companionable, and imaginative childhood. Early examples of her precocious talent for modelling can be seen in romantically illustrative pokerwork panels (1902–3), small clay figures, and plaster-relief panels of mothers with children or babies and other allegorical subjects. Those few cast in bronze included a lectern angel (1904), with carved wooden embellishments by her mother, in their local church, Tullow, Carrickmines, and sporting trophies cast by the Dublin silversmiths West & Co. Her talents were soon recognized at the Dublin Metropolitan School of Art (at which she later tutored), where she studied from the age of thirteen, between 1896 and 1905, and won the first studentship for modelling, under the distinguished sculptor John Hughes, as well as scholarships and prizes that took her to the National Art Training School, South Kensington (Edouard Lanteri's classes), and to the Académie Colarossi, Paris. Her sculpture, which won the annual Taylor competition at the Royal Dublin Society between 1900 and 1908, was singled out at the 1904 Arts and Crafts Society of Ireland exhibition in Dublin. With that society she also exhibited graphic illustrations printed by Elizabeth Yeats's Cuala Press, and stained-glass panels made at Sarah Purser's co-operative workshop, An Túr Gloine (The Tower of Glass), in Dublin. Between 1904 and 1911, as a member of this studio, she designed and made twenty-six remarkably fine, original windows in a fundamentally English arts and crafts idiom for churches all over Ireland, primarily to support her modest income from painting, drawing, illustrating, and teaching.

Despite her instinctive skill in working imaginatively in this medium and her central role in Dublin's lively artistic, musical, and literary circles during the peak of the cultural renaissance, by 1910 Beatrice Elvery wanted to pursue her success as a painter with, for example, the Young Irish Artists. She left for London to study with Henry Tonks at the Slade School of Fine Art, and two years later, in August 1912, married Gordon Campbell (1885–1963), a barrister actively involved in politics, theatre, and literature, and the son of the Irish lord chancellor. In London their many literary and artistic friends included Mark Gertler, D. H. Lawrence, Katherine Mansfield, and George Bernard Shaw. Beatrice returned to Ireland as often as possible throughout the First World War and continued to draw book illustrations for Irish publications. In 1918, despite her husband's brilliant career at the London bar, they returned to Dublin with two small children at a politically explosive, seminal period in Irish politics. Because of his official position in the free state government they lived under siege in the Dublin outskirts during the civil war, during which most of Beatrice's work was destroyed. Exhilarated by having to start again from scratch, although also out of financial necessity, she began painting furniture, and portraits in a pointillist idiom, as well as continuing to design Cuala Press hand-coloured prints and cards and exhibiting with the Society of Dublin Painters and the Royal Hibernian Academy. She had first shown at the academy in 1902 and continued to do so more or less annually until 1969, being elected a Royal Hibernian academician in 1934. Once her youngest child, born in 1924, was old enough not to need her constant attention she resumed painting in oil and tempera on canvas, bringing her love of the theatre to her fanciful stage-set fantasies of departing sailors and their lasses languishing beneath trees at the water's edge, and Staffordshire china ornaments offset by beribboned flowers and memorabilia in sylvan settings.

Her husband became second Baron Glenavy in 1931. He predeceased her in 1963 and Lady Glenavy died on 21 May 1970 at her home in co. Dublin—Rockall, Ballygihen Avenue, Sandycove—and was buried in Dublin's Mount Jerome cemetery. Paintings by Beatrice, Lady Glenavy, are in the Hugh Lane Gallery, Dublin; the Ulster Museum, Belfast; and public galleries in Drogheda, Cork, and Limerick. NICOLA GORDON BOWE

Sources B. Glenavy, *Today we will only gossip* (1964) · N. Gordon Bowe, 'The art of Beatrice Glenavy (1883–1970)', *Irish Arts Review Yearbook*, 11 (1995), 169–75 · N. Gordon Bowe and E. S. Cumming, *The arts and crafts movements in Dublin and Edinburgh* (1998) · N. Gordon Bowe, D. Caron, and M. Wynne, *Gazetteer of Irish stained glass* (Dublin, 1998) · M. Reynolds, ed., *The Elvery family: a memory* (Cape Town, 1991) · A. Denson, *John Hughes, sculptor, 1865–1941: a documentary* (1969) · N. Gordon Bowe, 'Women and the arts and crafts revival in Ireland, c.1886–1930', *Irish women artists: from the eighteenth century to the present day* (1987) [exhibition catalogue, NG Ire., the Douglas Hyde Gallery, TCD, and the Hugh Lane Municipal Gallery of Modern Art, Dublin, July–Aug 1987] · P. Boylan, *All cultivated people: a history of the United Arts Club* (1988) · N. Gordon Bowe, 'Symbolism in turn-of-the-century Irish art', *GPA Irish Arts Review Yearbook*, 6 (1989–90), 133–44 · P. Larmour, *The arts and crafts movement in Ireland* (1992) · J. Turpin, *A school of art in Dublin since the eighteenth century: a history of the National College of Art and Design* (1995) · *CGPLA Eng. & Wales* (1970)

Archives TCD, scrapbooks and MSS; family corresp. and papers | National Gallery of South Africa, Cape Town, Elvery family collection, paintings, letters

Likenesses J. Hughes, plaster relief, *c*.1900, priv. coll.; repro. in Denson, *John Hughes* · W. Orpen, oils, 1909, priv. coll.; repro. in A. Hobart and M. Hobart, *Celtic splendour: an exhibition of Irish paintings and drawings, 1850–1950* (1985) [exhibition catalogue, Pyms Gallery, London, 24 April–25 May 1985] · O. Sheppard, marble relief, 1909, St Stephen's Green, Dublin · B. M. Glenavy, self-portraits, caricatures, repro. in Reynolds, ed., *Elvery family*

Wealth at death £1658: probate, 7 Sept 1970, *CGPLA Éire*

Campbell [*née* Tanner], **Beatrice Stella** [*performing name* Mrs Patrick Campbell] (**1865–1940**), actress, was born on 9 February 1865 in Forest House, Kensington, London, the sixth and youngest child of John Tanner (1831–1893), the son of a wealthy army contractor to the British East India Company, and of his wife, Maria Luigia Giovanna Romanini (1835–1908), daughter of Count Angelo Romanini, an Italian political exile. The young Stella was educated in Brighton, Hampstead, and Paris. Although she attended the Guildhall School of Music and won a scholarship, she did not keep up her studies. In 1884, pregnant with her first child, Beo, Stella eloped and was secretly married to the young Patrick Campbell (1864–1900). In 1886 they had a second child, Stella, who also had a career on the stage (although much against the wishes of her mother). Given that the couple were in desperate financial straits, Patrick Campbell, known as Pat, sought employment overseas and left for Australia, subsequently moving on to South Africa, where he worked for mining companies. Although he stayed in contact with his wife and family, the money he was able to send home was not enough to support Stella and the two children. The experience of performing with the amateur Anomalies Dramatic Club gave Stella the idea of taking up acting professionally as a way of supporting herself and the two children.

Stella chose her husband's name for her stage name, and made her professional début as Mrs Patrick Campbell in 1888 at the Alexandra Theatre, Liverpool, in R. Buchanan's and H. Vezin's *Bachelors*. Engagements with Millicent Bandmann-Palmer's company and with Ben Greet's Woodland Players (where her most successful role was as Rosalind in *As You Like It*) were to follow. In contrast to the open-air Shakespeare she played with Greet, Stella's early professional London work was in melodrama at the Adelphi, under the management of the Gattis, where she was contracted to play in R. Sims's and R. Buchanan's *The*

Trumpet Call. It was while playing at the Adelphi in 1893 in Sims's and Buchanan's melodrama *The Black Domino*, that she was 'discovered' by Florence Alexander and Graham Robertson as a possible contender for the title role in Arthur Wing Pinero's *The Second Mrs Tanqueray*. Pinero was making arrangements for the play's production at the St James's Theatre, managed by George Alexander, but was finding it difficult to cast an actress to play Paula Tanqueray, a woman with a past. When seen at the Adelphi, Stella was recovering from an almost fatal illness (typhoid fever), but her dark Italian looks, and her natural paleness and fragility heightened by the illness, were thought suited to the appearance of Paula: a woman who tries desperately, but hopelessly, to begin a new, respectable life. No sooner had Pinero agreed terms with Mrs Campbell, than the Gattis, who had been looking to release her, refused to let her go. The part was then given to Elizabeth Robins, who graciously backed down when the Gattis revised their decision, thereby allowing Mrs Campbell to accept the role which would bring her overnight fame.

Mrs Campbell's performance in *The Second Mrs Tanqueray*, which opened at the St James's Theatre on 27 May 1893, was arguably the highlight of her career. Reviewers compared her favourably to the star actresses: to Eleanora Duse (who had been playing in London shortly before *The Second Mrs Tanqueray*) and to Sarah Bernhardt. Typical of the lavish response to her performance was a comment from the reviewer for the *Daily Chronicle* that 'she showed a genius which gives her from this time forth an enviable place on the English stage' (29 May 1893, 3). Among the many commentators, Kate Terry Gielgud described Mrs Campbell as 'tall and slight and dark, not pretty but attractive, the type of face that excites curiosity: and she has nervous, characteristic hands. There is a tinge of commonness about her though, which helps the part to a certain extent' (*A Victorian Playgoer*, 1980, 10–11). Solomon J. Solomon painted her in the role of Paula Tanqueray; Aubrey Beardsley captured her as Paula in a pencil portrait for the first volume of the *Yellow Book*. However, playing the role of a woman with a past also brought her notoriety. As Mrs Campbell comments in her autobiography 'many people held the attitude—"She could not play Mrs. Tanqueray as she does if she did not know something of that kind of life"' (Campbell, 82).

After *The Second Mrs Tanqueray*, Mrs Campbell appeared as the barmaid Dulcie Larondie in Arthur Jones's *The Masqueraders* (1894)—a part which she did not care for and in which she did not excel. The degree of her antipathy was evidenced by the way in which she surrendered the part to Evelyn Millard, some few months after the production opened. Nor did a further woman with a past role—Kate Cloud in C. Haddon Chambers's *John-a-Dreams* (1894)—repeat the success of her Paula Tanqueray. 1894 was a more significant year in terms of her personal rather than professional life: her husband returned from abroad, penniless and in poor health. Even if she had wanted to, Mrs Campbell was unable to give up her acting career with her two children and now a husband to support.

Mrs Campbell's next major success came in 1895 in another of Pinero's plays, *The Notorious Mrs Ebbsmith*, in which she played Agnes Ebbsmith, a 'new woman' with unconventional views on marriage. Although radical in terms of its anti-marriage views, the drama was ultimately conservative in its treatment of Agnes who repents of her radicalism and returns to religion. The play was 'notorious' for its 'Bible burning' scene of the close of act III, in which Agnes throws her Bible onto the fire and then, regretting her action, pulls it out of the flames. Although a supporter of the new drama—Mrs Campbell appeared, for example, at the Avenue as the Ratwife in Ibsen's *Little Eyolf* (November 1896) in a series of matinées organized by

Beatrice Stella Campbell [Mrs Patrick Campbell] (**1865–1940**), by Frederick Hollyer, *c.*1895

Elizabeth Robins, and outbid Janet Achurch to take the lead as Rita Allmers in a commercial production of the play the following month—she needed commercial star vehicles, such as the eponymous heroine in V. Sardou's *Fédora* (made famous by Duse and Bernhardt), which she played at the Haymarket in May 1895.

In the summer of 1895 Mrs Campbell agreed generous terms with the actor-manager Johnston Forbes-Robertson and played Juliet to his Romeo (Lyceum, September 1895) for which she received rather mixed reviews. Their partnership continued over the next five years (both on and off the stage), the two appearing opposite each other in plays such as François Coppée's *For the Crown* (*Pour la couronne*) (February 1896), and *Magda*, a translation of Herman Sudermann's *Heimat* (June 1896)—a failure with both critics and audiences, and taken off in favour of R. B. Sheridan's *The School for Scandal*, with Stella as Lady Teazle. She played Lady Hamilton to Forbes-Robertson's Nelson in R. Home's *Nelson's Enchantress* (February 1897), a success for her, but a failure for him. After a period of illness, Mrs Campbell returned to the stage to play Ophelia to Forbes-Robertson's Hamlet (September 1897). This time their fortunes were reversed: Forbes-Robertson was praised for his Hamlet, while Mrs Campbell was heavily criticized for her playing of Ophelia, whom she chose to interpret as genuinely mad. The pattern continued: Forbes-Robertson angered Mrs Campbell because of his reluctance to stage Maeterlinck's *Pelléas et Mélisande* (June 1898), a production which delighted Mrs Campbell and the critics, while she was hostile to his choice of *Macbeth* (1898), widely admonished as a failure. The two agreed to separate and in 1899 Mrs Campbell arranged to tour with her own company. They were reunited in September 1899 in Chester Baily Fernald's Japanese play, *The Moonlight Blossom*, but on rather different terms: this was Mrs Patrick's management venture, not Forbes-Robertson's. The production was neither a critical, nor a financial success, and the two severed their professional and personal lives completely. In April 1900 her husband was killed in fighting in South Africa during the Second South African War.

Mrs Campbell continued in management, but at a smaller theatre, the Royalty, where productions included Louis N. Parker's *The Sacrament of Judas*, *Mrs Jordan*, George Fleming's *The Fantasticks*, *Mr and Mrs Daventry* (controversial because based on a scenario by Oscar Wilde), and revivals of *Pelléas et Mélisande*, *The Notorious Mrs Ebbsmith*, and *Magda*, which she played to much greater critical acclaim than in the original production. In 1901, in order to support her own extravagant lifestyle and family, Mrs Campbell undertook the first of several American tours, in between which she tried to find new plays to perform in England. During the first decade of the twentieth century, she appeared in the work of several internationally acclaimed playwrights, including Björnstjerne Björnson (*Beyond Human Power*, November 1901), Henrik Ibsen (*Hedda Gabler*, March 1907), W. B. Yeats (*Deirdre*, November 1908), and Eugène Brieux (*False Gods*, *La foi*, September 1909). Yet she was more popular (and financially successful) in plays such as Sardou's *La sorcière* (October 1904), or revivals of *The Second Mrs Tanqueray*.

One of Mrs Campbell's own passions was Maeterlinck's *Pelléas et Mélisande*, and in 1904 she appeared in a revival of the play with Sarah Bernhardt playing in *travesti* as Pelléas. As Bernhardt did not speak English, Mrs Campbell played her Mélisande in French. For this production Mrs Campbell wore the shimmering gold dress—nicknamed the 'gold umbrella case'—which she had worn in the original 1898 production and which had been designed by Edward Burne-Jones. Bernhardt, in tunic, chain mail, and tights, appeared as the young prince, although in reality she was a woman of sixty, while her princess was approaching forty. This caused one critic, Max Beerbohm, who had so admired Mrs Campbell's performance in the original production, to stay away (Peters, 249–50), and another, a Dublin critic, to complain during the subsequent 1905 tour of the production that the two actresses were old enough to know better (Campbell, 139). Beerbohm's reluctance to see the two stars playing opposite each other deprived him of a performance which other critics responded to with enthusiasm.

On 6 April 1914 Mrs Campbell married again. Her second husband was the recently divorced George Cornwallis-West (1874–1951), previously married to Jennie Churchill. They were married just days before Mrs Campbell opened in G. B. Shaw's *Pygmalion* at His Majesty's, in which she played Eliza Doolittle to Herbert Beerbohm Tree's Professor Higgins. Mrs Campbell was hugely successful as Eliza: 'I invented a Cockney accent and created a human Eliza', she wrote later (*DNB*). She and Shaw had known each other well for some time and they kept up an enduring, although tempestuous relationship. She used his letters in an autobiography published in 1922; and a fuller volume of their correspondence was published in 1952 after Shaw's death. Mrs Campbell was less fortunate in her marriage, which lasted barely six years: Cornwallis-West deserted her in December 1919, leaving behind huge debts. During the 1920s she appeared far less on the London stage. Her roles included George Sand in Philip Moeller's *Madame Sand* (Duke of York's, June 1920), and appearances in Ibsen's *Hedda Gabler* (1922), *Ghosts* (1928), and *John Gabriel Borkman* (1928). In 1929 she appeared for the last time at the Royalty, the theatre which she had previously managed, in a production of G. B. Stern's *The Matriarch*. In the 1930s she continued to tour America and had a relatively uneventful career in Hollywood. The close of the decade found her in France, first staying in Paris, then travelling south to Pau where she died of bronchial and pulmonary infection on 9 April 1940 and was later buried.

During her lifetime critics were divided over how 'great' an actress she was. For some she was the English Bernhardt, while others felt she did not take her art seriously enough. James Agate listed her as one of 'six great actresses, and six only', whom he saw during his lifetime: 'Bernhardt, Réjane, *Mrs.* Kendal, Ellen Terry, Duse and Mrs. Patrick Campbell' (Peters, 468). Modern theatre scholarship has focused on the significance of her career in relation to gender issues: on her work as an actress who was not afraid to play roles deemed socially unconventional or radical for their time, and as a woman who tried for an independent career as an actress-manager.

ELAINE ASTON

Sources M. Peters, *Mrs Pat: the life of Mrs Patrick Campbell* (1984) · A. Dent, *Mrs Patrick Campbell* (1961) · B. S. Campbell, *My life and some letters* (1922) · I. Clarke, 'Making Mrs Ebbsmith notorious: Mrs Patrick Campbell as Agnes Ebbsmith', *Women and theatre: occasional papers*, 1 (1992), 48–62 · B. Elliott, 'New and not so "new women" on the London stage: Aubrey Beardsley's *Yellow Book* images of Mrs Patrick Campbell and Réjane', *Victorian Studies*, 31 (1987–8), 33–57 · J. Dawick, 'The "first" Mrs Tanqueray: Pinero's scandalous play in rehearsal and production', *New Theatre Quarterly*, 9/35 (autumn 1979), 77–93 · *Bernard Shaw and Mrs Patrick Campbell: their correspondence*, ed. A. Dent (1952) · J. Parker, ed., *Who's who in the theatre*, 5th edn (1925) · *DNB*

Archives priv. coll., Tanner collection, family corresp. · Theatre Museum, London, letters · U. Birm., commonplace book · University of Chicago, corresp. and papers | BL, letters to George Bernard Shaw, Add. MS 50531 · BL, corresp. with Sir Arthur Wing Pinero, Add. MS 45982 · Bodl. Oxf., letters to Lewis Harcourt · Bodl. Oxf., letters to members of the Lewis family · Bodl. Oxf., letters to Gilbert Murray · Cornell University, Burgunder Shaw collection, unpublished memoir · Museum of London, Enthoven collection, Mrs Campbell's prompt books (annotated)

Likenesses S. J. Solomon, oils, 1893, repro. in Peters, *Mrs Pat* · A. Beardsley, pencil drawing, 1894, repro. in Elliott, 'New and not so "new women"' · F. Hollyer, photograph, *c.*1895, V&A [*see illus.*] · Biograph, photograph, *c.*1901, NPG · C. Shannon, oils, 1907, Tate collection · C. Beaton, photograph, 1938, NPG · G. C. Beresford, photographs, NPG · J. S. Eland, oils, Garr. Club · Violet, duchess of Rutland, lithograph, NPG · photographs, NPG

Wealth at death possessions sold after death to pay debts

Campbell, Charles Macfie (1876–1943), psychiatrist, was born at 1 Glengyle Terrace, Edinburgh, on 8 September 1876, the son of Daniel Campbell, a banker, and Eliza Lawson McLaren. Following attendance at George Watson's Boys' College in Edinburgh, Campbell matriculated at Edinburgh University in 1893, the year also of a brief first visit to the United States. He obtained the degrees of MA in 1897, BSc in 1900, and, in 1902, MB and ChB. During these years he spent two summers travelling abroad, visiting Paris in 1896 and Germany in 1897. In 1903 Campbell began specializing in neurology and psychiatry, after spells in Paris at the Bicetre (September 1902–April 1903) under Pierre Marie, also attending Babinski's clinic, and Heidelberg (April–September 1903) at Nissl's laboratory and taking courses with the eminent Emil Kraepelin and other leading figures such as Erb, Hoffmann, and Von Hippel. On his return to Scotland he obtained a residency at the Royal Edinburgh Hospital for Mental and Nervous Diseases under Alexander N. Bruce before moving in 1904 to the United States, where he spent three years at the New York State Hospital's Pathological (later Psychiatric) Institute under Adolf Meyer, rising from intern to assistant physician. Campbell spent 1907–8 in Scotland as assistant physician to Clouston at Morningside in Edinburgh, and on 3 June 1908 he married another doctor, Jessie Deans Rankin (*b.* 1879/80) of Glasgow, the daughter of William Rankin, a Cork merchant, and his wife, Annie *née* McNicoll. His future, however, lay in the United States, to which he emigrated permanently in 1908 (obtaining American citizenship in 1918).

Campbell held a succession of increasingly important posts. Following spells at the Psychiatric Institution, Ward Island (New York), an instructorship in psychiatry at Cornell medical school (1909), and two years at Bloomingdale Hospital, White Plains (New York), he resumed his links with Meyer at the Phipps Clinic, Johns Hopkins University medical school, where he was associate director and became professor of psychiatry in 1913, having obtained his MD degree from Edinburgh with a thesis entitled 'Focal symptoms in general paralysis' (1911). In 1920 he succeeded E. E. Southard in the prestigious linked posts of professor of psychiatry at Harvard medical school and medical director of the Boston Psychopathic Hospital, in which he remained until his death.

Primarily a practising physician and teacher, Campbell was not an especially prolific author, most of his seventy-odd publications being relatively short journal papers or chapter contributions to textbooks, but what he did produce was influential and significant in the American psychiatric community. Following Meyer's influence his approach was, from early on, marked by a concern for understanding the patient within his or her total life context rather than simply as a medical case. Although never a psychoanalyst, Campbell discussed Freud's ideas in such papers as 'Psychological mechanisms with special reference to wish fulfilment' (1908), 'The role of psychoanalysis in psychiatry' (1911), and 'The application of psychoanalysis to insanity' (1912). Another paper, 'The mechanism of some cases of manic-depressive excitement' (1914), has been considered the 'first American declaration of the importance of psychological and situational factors in cases of affective disorder' (Solam, 440)—delivering a message reinforced, in relation to children, in 'The psychopathologist and his responsibility' (1919).

Campbell increasingly saw psychiatry as being in an especially privileged position from which to analyse and diagnose the problems of society as a whole (his 1937 presidential address to the American Psychiatric Association being virtually a manifesto to this effect). Thus he became particularly interested in child delinquency—the psychiatric treatment of which he pioneered. In two book-length publications (collections of lectures), *Human Personality and the Environment* (1934) and *Destiny and Disease in Mental Disorders* (1936), he again argued that understanding mental illness demanded a dynamic analysis of patients' full social and environmental circumstances, warning against over-reliance on diagnostic terms. He was therefore interested in contemporary psychological work on personality (and had used association tests during his time at Bloomingdale). In 1932 he co-edited *Problems of Personality* (a Festschrift for Morton Prince) with psychologists such as William McDougall and H. S. Langfeld. From his eminent position Campbell strove to maintain a balanced mid-position in relation to the diverse and contending theories and approaches to mental illness of the early twentieth century. This did not however signify a passive eclecticism but rather a strong and centred personal ethical commitment to obtaining the broadest grasp possible of the human condition and constructively applying this. Campbell had planned to write a book on schizophrenia during his retirement but died from a heart attack on 7 August 1943, just a few days prior to his retirement date.

The praises sung by Campbell's obituarists appear genuinely to exceed the genre's hagiographic conventions. Professionally, the depth of his knowledge of the lives of his individual patients and sympathy for them was seemingly awesome, while his social conviviality, wit, ethical integrity, and self-reliance are constantly stressed. He was clearly an attractive figure with more than a touch of personal charisma. His historical significance lies primarily in how he used his influential position within American psychiatry to keep open the lines of communication between different schools of thought and counteract overly physiological and reductionist conceptions of mental illness, his own interests shifting away from strict neurology after 1911. Within psychiatry he shared the more environmentalist orientations and concerns of contemporary psychologists, and insisted on psychiatry's obligations to engage wider social issues and remain involved with society at large. Campbell was a member of numerous scientific societies and official committees. His wife, with whom he had three daughters and a son, predeceased him. GRAHAM RICHARDS

Sources H. C. Solam, *American Journal of Psychiatry*, 100 (1943), 438–41 • D. V. Henderson, *American Journal of Psychiatry*, 100 (1943), 441–2 • W. L. Russell, 'Charles Macfie Campbell: a biographical sketch', *American Journal of Psychiatry*, 94 (1937), 15–18 • C. M. Campbell, 'Presidential address: 93rd annual meeting of the American Psychiatric Association: perspectives in psychiatry', *American Journal of Psychiatry*, 94 (1937), 1–14 • *BMJ* (28 Aug 1943), 284 • *The Lancet* (4 Sept 1943), 306 • J. M. Harkness, 'Campbell, Charles Macfie', *ANB* • b. cert. • m. cert.

Likenesses photograph, repro. in Campbell, 'Presidential address'

Campbell, Colen, of Boghole and Urchany (1676–1729), architect, was born on 15 June 1676, the eldest of four children of Donald Campbell (*d.* 1680), laird of Boghole and Urchany (just south-east of the castle of his uncle Sir Hugh Campbell of Cawdor, Nairnshire), and of his wife, Elizabeth (*d.* 1719), daughter of Sir Robert Innes of Muirton, Morayshire.

Early years Nothing is known of Campbell's upbringing until he appears in Edinburgh about 1700; he may have been the owner of this common Scottish name who graduated from Edinburgh University in 1695. Thereafter he certainly trained as a lawyer and in 1702 performed so well in examinations that it was reported that his examiners considered him to have been 'the best civilian that past since the Revolutione' (Innes, 397–8). He looked after his uncle's affairs in the capital: as a correspondent wrote to Sir Hugh, 'your nevoy … being so inteligent and a wittnes to all that is done heir amongst us in Parliament can give you a better account of them then I can writt' (ibid., 399).

In the years following the Act of Union Campbell reinvented himself as an architect in England. The process of his transformation is barely documented, but his first building, Shawfield Mansion, Glasgow (dem. 1792), was described as 'new builded' in August 1712; so when he delivered designs of churches to the commission for the building of fifty new churches in June of that year in London, he was probably acting on his own account. Campbell may have been indebted for some architectural training to the well-known Scottish architect James Smith: in a collection of Campbell's drawings rediscovered in the 1960s several drawings by Smith were found, some of which, including one intended for Sir Hugh Campbell of Cawdor, were probably in Campbell's possession by 1712. In applying for a post in 1715, Campbell stated that he had travelled abroad to study architecture, but no further details are known.

The establishment of his reputation Campbell owed to a prestigious commission for a grand house just outside London, and to the publication of an extraordinarily widely distributed book of engravings of British architecture. The house—Wanstead, Essex, first designed in 1712 for Sir Richard Child (later Viscount Castlemaine) and demolished in 1822—was a significant indicator of changing taste: with its grand projecting portico of Corinthian columns and chaste decoration to walls and windows, it marked the return to a simpler, more classical manner of ornament than had been the fashion in the previous decade, typified by Vanbrugh's Castle Howard (1700) and Blenheim Palace (1705).

Vitruvius Britannicus By taking part in the making of a lavishly illustrated book, Campbell established a method of self-promotion for an aspiring architect which was to last the century. *Vitruvius Britannicus*, a record of the principal private and public British buildings of the time, was prepared by a group of booksellers active in the print trade during 1714. At a fairly late stage in the preparation of this costly enterprise they appear to have employed Campbell to give a more up-to-date and specifically architectural slant to volumes which would otherwise have been of a more conventionally topographical character. Campbell was presented as the author on the title-page; he probably wrote the introduction as well as the brief text which accompanied the plates for each building. Most importantly, he was able to include many of his own (mostly unexecuted) designs. Published in May 1715, the first volume of *Vitruvius Britannicus* decisively shaped the development of classical architecture in eighteenth-century England. Campbell's intervention betrayed his own hesitant and immature understanding of Palladianism. His 'New Designs' were dedicated to politicians identified as either interested or powerful enough to advance the cause of the new architecture and they reveal a bookish knowledge of Palladio's work, but his borrowings drew on a significantly wider range of the architect's works than that which was to become the austere canon of subsequent neo-Palladians. Some of his designs were straight compilations from illustrations in Palladio's *I quattro libri dell'architettura* (1570), while others were developed from drawings by James Smith. The text of his introduction was a powerful statement of pride in the achievement of British architects, a call to order against the extravagance of Italian baroque architecture for which the example of Palladio, mediated by Inigo Jones, was the ideal corrective. A second volume, intended at the outset, appeared in 1717, and a third was added in 1725. By then the work boasted an impressive list of 692 subscribers, headed by five members of the royal family, indicating a degree of popularity reached by few books of comparable scale. As may be expected in a book which focused on aristocratic houses, the lists show a higher proportion of noble subscribers, and a smaller proportion of artisans, mainly from the building trades, than was the case in the more specifically architectural books which followed the lead of *Vitruvius Britannicus*.

Major commissions However significant for Campbell's long-term reputation, and to his finances, the publication of *Vitruvius Britannicus* did not transform his architectural career overnight. Official posts were in the possession of the older generation, such as Wren and Vanbrugh, and private commissions arrived only slowly. Legal connections may have accounted for his first opportunity in London, the Rolls House, Chancery Lane, in 1717, but an important chance came in 1718 with his involvement in the transformation of Burlington House, Piccadilly, for Richard Boyle, third earl of Burlington, who was just then beginning his serious and lifelong study of Palladian architecture. For the court front, Campbell depended upon Palladio's Palazzo Iseppo de' Porti, Vicenza, which he had used for a design in *Vitruvius Britannicus*, but for the garden front he developed an astylar form which was more original and influential. The contacts between the fledgeling connoisseur and the architect eighteen years his senior are barely documented, but Campbell was involved in the beginnings of the development of Burlington's Westminster estate. Here his group of four town houses shows an abstraction of the complex vocabulary of Palladianism to the bareness of an ordinary street house. This suggests Campbell's awareness of the growing sophistication of Burlington's Palladianism, while his flattering description of the 'Bagnio' built at Chiswick in 1717, as 'the first essay of his Lordship's happy invention' (*Vitruvius Britannicus*, 3, 1725, 8) may indicate a measure of collaboration.

While still in Scotland, Campbell had tried to secure the royal office of master of work. During 1718 he joined in the attempt of the ambitious William Benson (1682–1754), influential among the king's German advisers if nowhere else, to take over the English office of works by ousting Wren and effectively privatizing the maintenance of the royal palaces. For a brief ten months from September 1718 Campbell was chief clerk and deputy surveyor, but the collapse of this rash and controversial venture ruined his chances of official recognition and yielded nothing beyond involvement in the design of a small suite at Kensington Palace. In the sharply polarized politics of the Hanoverian family it is not surprising that within months of this reversal Campbell was appointed as architect to George, prince of Wales. The post was unpaid, and resulted only in unimportant maintenance work for the prince at Leicester House, but it did offer opportunities for patronage among the young aristocratic followers of the prince which he was not slow to exploit. On the death of Vanbrugh in March 1726 he succeeded to the surveyorship at Greenwich Hospital, an appointment worth £200 a year.

If Campbell did not make a distinguished career in the official hierarchies of the early eighteenth-century building world, his significance as an architect is greater in terms of what he built even than through the influence of *Vitruvius Britannicus*. The bulk of his work as an architect was commissioned in the years 1718–26. He was not prolific, but appears to have been conscientious in attending upon distant works in Norfolk, or in the North Riding of Yorkshire; a client in the latter county paid tribute to his 'skill & judgement superior to his Contemporaries' (W. Robinson to T. Robinson, 28 Oct 1720, Leeds City Archive Service, Vyner MSS 13827). His change of country and career, as well as the fiasco at the office of works, did not assist the creation of a consistent group of patrons such as his rival James Gibbs enjoyed. The young Lord Burlington and aristocratic followers of the prince of Wales sought his services, as did members of the Child and Hoare banking families, settling to landed ease. Campbell's contacts with the City of London can be traced through his sponsor William Benson or Stamp Brooksbank of Hackney, or John Aislabie, for whom or for whose family he built in Surrey, Buckinghamshire, and Yorkshire, and possibly also in Grosvenor Square. Much of Campbell's patronage can be traced through family contacts, such as the link between William Benson and Henry Hoare of Stourhead, or between John Aislabie of Studley Royal, Yorkshire and Waverley, Surrey, Sir William Robinson of Baldersby, Yorkshire, and Edmund Waller of Hall Barn, Buckinghamshire. Political affiliation seems to have been less indicative: Sir Richard Child, for whom he designed Wanstead, was a tory in 1713, but as the growing security of whig government after the accession of George I in 1714 led to a building boom in the 1720s, most subsequent patrons were more or less actively whig. Campbell had used the dedications of the plates of *Vitruvius Britannicus* to bring himself to the attention of politicians but only in the case of Robert Walpole may this have been successful, for he was to play some role in the development of the design of Houghton in the years after 1722, although he had to see his elevations altered, probably by James Gibbs, and the interior finished by William Kent.

Of the works of Campbell's maturity, the most significant may be described as 'villas'. In the 1720s this term suggested an Italian, even accurately Palladian, character for the small house which several of Campbell's houses exemplified. In some cases the houses as built were in reality substantial country houses with offices attached, although when illustrating Newby (now Baldersby, Yorkshire) in *Vitruvius Britannicus*, Campbell took care to show it as an isolated cubical block, without dependencies. At Newby, and at Stourhead, Wiltshire, begun around 1720, and the later Waverley, Surrey (*c.*1724), Campbell adapted Palladian designs to the needs of his clients, while also illustrating his growing understanding of his models. The tripartite façade, with one window bay on each side of a centre often carrying an attached or free-standing portico, was to be an influential model of the small house for the rest of the century. Campbell's dependence on Palladio was not restricted to adjusting façades, for these houses often borrowed plans, including not only the layout but the use of careful proportions in the ordering of rooms. Most remarkable of these smaller houses was Mereworth, Kent (*c*.1720–25): here Campbell took up Palladio's Villa Rotonda design, which had earlier interested James Smith, and adapted its plan to English use with minimal alteration to the exterior. Its design acted as a prelude to Lord Burlington's Chiswick House (1725–9), where antique, Palladian, and other sources are synthesized with far greater inventiveness.

Later years, death, and reputation As a young man Campbell was described as lacking an 'opulent fortune in the world' (A. Campbell to H. Campbell, 26 Oct 1709, Cawdor Castle, Cawdor MSS); but by 1726 he had leased a house of his own design in Great Burlington Street and another in Brook Street in the fashionable Grosvenor estate, while living in a third. After being taken ill suddenly in August 1729, he died on 13 September in Brook Street and was buried in the south cloister of Westminster Abbey on 16 September 1729. After his death it was said that he had made 'much money' (Wodrow, 107–8), of which the reported figure of £12,000 may only represent a third share. This was contested between his sister Henrietta and her husband, the Revd John Grant, of Auchinleck, and Jane Bubb, alias Campbell, his maidservant, with whom he had been living for a long time before January 1721, when he made his will (Proceedings of John and Henrietta Grant against Jane Bubb, alias Campbell, Bodl. Oxf., MS Rawl. D. 923 (34)). Jane Bubb died in February 1738; there do not appear to have been any children from her liaison with Campbell. In 1762 his destitute nephew Colen Grant hoped to use his uncle's name in a petition to the earl of Bute.

At the time of his death Campbell had begun to publish a new English translation of Palladio's *I quattro libri dell'architettura*, of which the first book appeared in May 1728. This was intended by the publisher to replace Nicholas Dubois's inexact versions published by Giacomo Leoni in 1715–20, and to restore the original plates. Campbell based his revision on the French translation by Roland Fréart, whose architectural doctrines had influenced his criticism of current architecture in the introduction to *Vitruvius Britannicus*. With it he published 'Five curious plates of Doors, Windows and Chimneypieces' taken from his recent work.

Campbell's reputation was soon eclipsed by the achievements of Lord Burlington. He was perhaps lucky to avoid immortality as a named victim of Alexander Pope, who regarded as excessive the architect's estimate for building a house on the Burlington estate in 1718. To Horace Walpole he merely had 'fewer faults, but not more imagination' than James Gibbs (Walpole, 47). By the early nineteenth century he had disappeared in a void between 'the time of Vanbrugh, until Lord Burlington introduced a better style' (Stuart and Revett, xxvii). In the 1840s Joseph Gwilt felt that, although his 'talents were not of a very high order', buildings such as Wanstead could entitle him to be considered 'an artist of merit' (Gwilt, 221); even then, more credit was given for the publication of *Vitruvius Britannicus*—of which Lord Burlington was described as the 'original projector and patron'—than for any of his buildings. It was not until the discovery of a large collection of his drawings in 1966 that a fuller idea of Campbell's strengths and weaknesses as a designer became possible, while re-examination of *Vitruvius Britannicus*, by which he was principally known to contemporaries, lessens his participation in its origin and redefines the relation between his published plates and the buildings themselves. Sources cast little light on his personality and only one supposed portrait, in the plaster decoration of Compton Place, Sussex, is now known.

Although he had no pupils, Campbell worked from about 1724 with Roger Morris on commissions connected with the entourage of the prince of Wales. Marble Hill, Twickenham, of *c*.1724, built for Henrietta Howard, mistress of the prince of Wales, was a particularly influential restatement of the villa type which Campbell had developed, and he may have made some contribution to this design usually attributed to Morris and Henry Herbert, later ninth earl of Pembroke. T. P. Connor

Sources Colvin, *Archs.* • [C. Innes], ed., *The Book of the thanes of Cawdor, 1236–1742: a series of papers selected from the charter room at Cawdor*, Spalding Club, 30 (1859) • J. Harris, ed., *Catalogue of the drawings collection of the Royal Institute of British Architects: Colen Campbell* (1973) • E. Harris and N. Savage, *British architectural books and writers, 1556–1785* (1990) • G. L. M. Goodfellow, 'Colen Campbell', *ArchR*, 140 (1966), 145–6 • G. L. M. Goodfellow, 'Colen Campbell's last years', *Burlington Magazine*, 111 (1969), 185–91 • H. E. Stutchbury, *The architecture of Colen Campbell* (1967) • G. Worsley, *Classical architecture in Britain: the heroic age* (1994) • T. P. Connor, 'Colen Campbell as architect to the prince of Wales', *Architectural History*, 22 (1979), 64–71 • H. Walpole, *Anecdotes of painting in England … collected by the late George Vertue, and now digested and published*, 4 (1771, [1780]) • proceedings of John and Henrietta Grant against Jane Bubb, alias Campbell, Bodl. Oxf., MS Rawl. D. 923 (34) • R. Wodrow, *Analecta, or, Materials for a history of remarkable providences, mostly relating to Scotch ministers and Christians*, ed. [M. Leishman], 4, Maitland Club, 60 (1843) • *The antiquities of Athens: measured and delineated by James Stuart … and Nicholas Revett*, ed. J. Woods, 4 (1816) • J. Gwilt, *The encyclopaedia of architecture*, rev. edn, rev. W. Papworth (1867) • W. Robinson to T. Robinson, 28 Oct 1720, W. Yorks. AS, Leeds, Vyner papers, 13827 • A. Campbell to H. Campbell, 26 Oct 1709, Cawdor Castle, Nairnshire, Cawdor MSS • C. Hussey, *English country houses: early Georgian, 1715–1760* (1955)

Archives Cawdor Castle, Nairnshire, Cawdor MSS • Col. U., Rare Book and Manuscript Library, letters to Richard Arundell • W. Sussex RO, Goodwood MSS • W. Yorks. AS, Leeds, Vyner papers

Likenesses plaster relief (of Campbell?), Compton Place, Eastbourne, Sussex

Wealth at death 32 Great Burlington Street, London, 50 years' lease: will, PRO, PROB 11/632, sig. 243 • 76 and 78 Brook Street, London; allegedly left £12,000 as a third share of estate: Wodrow, *Analecta*, 107–8

Campbell, Colin (*d.* 1412/13). *See under* Campbell family (*per.* *c*.1300–1453).

Campbell, Colin, of Glenorchy (*c*.1395–1475). *See under* Campbell family of Glenorchy (*per.* 1432–1631).

Campbell [McGillespic], **Colin, first earl of Argyll** (*d.* **1493**), magnate, was the only son of Gillespic Campbell, first son of Sir Duncan *Campbell of Lochawe (created Lord Campbell in 1445) [*see under* Campbell family (*per.* *c.*1300–1453)]; Colin's mother was Gillespic's first wife, Elizabeth, daughter of John, third Lord Somerville of Carnwath. His father was dead by 1440, and it was his grandfather whom Colin succeeded *c.*1453 as chief of the Campbell kindred, before he had attained his majority. Under the guardianship of his uncle, Sir Colin Campbell of Glenorchy, he married Isabel (*d.* 1510), eldest of the three heiresses of John Stewart, third Lord Lorne, before May 1466; by February 1467 the marriage had brought him the resignation of the younger heiresses' lands in Perthshire and Fife. On 30 November 1469 he exchanged the barony of Innermeath for Walter Stewart's lordship of Lorne, adjoining Argyll, and he assumed the title of Lord Lorne after 17 April 1470.

Campbell was made earl of Argyll in 1457–8—significantly the only territorial earldom created by James II—a promotion which reflected his potential importance as a crown agent in the west, bordering on the troublesome MacDonald lordship of the Isles, and after 1460 he was a regular member of the royal council. In 1462, with Robert, Lord Boyd, he served as justiciar south of the Forth, continuing alone after Boyd's forfeiture in 1469. He was a truce commissioner in the borders in 1463 and in the following year joined a royal expedition to bring the lordship of the Isles under royal control. From 29 March 1464 Argyll was master of the king's household (until about October 1482) and a regular parliamentarian and lord of council in civil causes. In February 1473 he formally became bailie of the royal lordship of Cowal and keeper of Dunoon Castle, positions he had occupied in the 1460s as sheriff of Argyll, and in 1474 he was among the ambassadors to England who negotiated a marriage alliance with Edward IV. His burgh of Inveraray was erected into a free barony on 8 May 1474. On 4 December 1475 he received a commission of lieutenancy over Argyll, Lorne, and Menteith, as part of the proceedings against John MacDonald, lord of the Isles, who forfeited the earldom of Ross on 10 July 1476. One consequence of this was that on 26 February 1481 Argyll received a grant of lands in Knapdale and keepership of Castle Sween, Argyll.

In the crisis of 1482, however, Argyll supported the imprisonment of James III. His motives are uncertain, but he sought primarily to preserve his own political influence. Nevertheless, he was excluded from court and government by his rivals among the rebels, and on 7 August 1483, together with Sir Duncan Campbell of Glenorchy, he received a remission under the great seal from James III for his part in the revolt. Argyll's rehabilitation was necessary for James III's recovery of power. By 6 September 1483 he was chancellor, the first Gaelic lay magnate to be so appointed, and in 1484 he visited France as one of the commissioners to renew the auld alliance, before going on to Nottingham to conclude a truce and marriage alliances with Richard III.

Argyll then fell out of James III's favour and shortly after William Elphinstone, bishop of Aberdeen (*d.* 1514), was made chancellor (by 21 February 1488) Argyll joined the rebellion raised against the king in the name of Prince James. He was among those given a safe conduct to visit England in May 1488, but appears to have fought against James III at Sauchieburn, as on 17 June 1488 he helped to audit James III's treasure at Edinburgh Castle, five days after the king's death. Argyll resumed the chancellorship under James IV, and received from him the lands of Rosneath, Dunbartonshire, on 21 December 1491 and permission to rename Gloom Castle, his Stirlingshire residence, Castle Campbell. But his influence at court declined in his final years, and he played a low-key role on the royalist side against the rebellion in the Lennox of 1489–90.

Argyll died on 10 May 1493 and was buried in his family's collegiate church in Kilmun, Cowal. He had been an important patron of Gaelic poetry (which he also wrote) and music. He had used all available means—patronage, diplomacy, litigation, and force—to advance Campbell power in western Scotland, and his determination to extend his authority is further demonstrated by his detention *c.*1490 of his own grandson, Donald Dubh, son of Angus Og and heir to the MacDonald lordship of the Isles until its forfeiture in May–June 1493. He and his wife, Isabel, had eight children: Archibald *Campbell, who succeeded him as second earl of Argyll; Thomas, ancestor of the Campbells of Lundie, Angus; Marion, who married George, Lord Seton (*d.* 1507); Isabel, who married William, master of Drummond; Helen, who married Hugh Montgomery of Eglintoun; Elizabeth, who married John, second Lord Oliphant; Mary, who married Angus, bastard of John MacDonald of the Isles; and Catherine, who married Torquil MacLeod of Lewis. Argyll also had an illegitimate son, Sir John *Campbell of Lundie (*d.* 1562), administrator and ambassador. MICHAEL A. PENMAN

Sources J. M. Thomson and others, eds., *Registrum magni sigilli regum Scotorum / The register of the great seal of Scotland*, 11 vols. (1882–1914), vol. 2 · J. R. N. Macphail, ed., 'Ane accompt of the genealogie of the Campbells', *Highland papers*, 2, Scottish History Society, 2nd ser., 12 (1916), 72–111 · G. Burnett and others, eds., *The exchequer rolls of Scotland*, 6–12 (1883–9) · T. Dickson and J. B. Paul, eds., *Compota thesaurariorum regum Scotorum / Accounts of the lord high treasurer of Scotland*, 1–4 (1877–1902) · [T. Thomson] and others, eds., *The acts of the lords of council in civil causes, 1478–1503*, 3 vols. (1839–1993) · [T. Thomson], ed., *The acts of the lords auditors of causes and complaints*, AD 1466–AD 1494, RC, 40 (1839) · *APS*, *1424–1567* · *Scots peerage* · S. Boardman, *Campbell lordship* [forthcoming] · N. Macdougall, *James III: a political study* (1982) · N. Macdougall, *James IV* (1989) · *CDS*, vol. 4 · *Poems from the book of the dean of Lismore*, ed. E. C. Quiggin and J. Fraser (1937) · 'Notes on the genealogy of the earls of Argyll and their descendants', 1709, NL Scot., Adv. MS 34.6.24, fol. 65
Archives Inveraray Castle · NA Scot., GD 1/177 (1477–1662); GD 1/180 (1390–1693), GD 1/205 (1492–1862)

Campbell, Colin, of Glenorchy (*c.*1468–1523). *See under* Campbell family of Glenorchy (*per.* 1432–1631).

Campbell, Colin, third earl of Argyll (*d.* **1529**), magnate, was the eldest son of Archibald *Campbell, second earl of Argyll (*d.* 1513), and Lady Elizabeth Stewart, daughter of the tenth earl of Lennox. He was known as Colin of Carrick, probably after the place he was fostered, and was also called Lumpy Brow, from the wrinkling of his forehead when he became angry. Despite this nickname Argyll's anger did not affect his judgement and he was a notably level-headed politician. He was said to be very popular with his contemporaries and possessed a 'strong, invincible courage' (Campbell, 7), a vital attribute for the most important military commander of his day.

Colin Campbell had married Lady Janet Gordon, daughter of the third earl of Huntly, some time before 1498, when their son Archibald *Campbell, the future fourth earl, was born. Their other sons were John (Gorm) Campbell of Lochnell, and Alexander, who became dean of Moray. Their daughters were Elizabeth, who married James Stewart, earl of Moray, an illegitimate son of James IV, and Agnes *Campbell (*d.* in or after 1590), who subsequently played an important role in Irish politics as the wife of James MacDonald of Dunyvaig and then of Turlough Luineach O'Neill of Tyrone.

The third earl succeeded his father when the latter was killed at the battle of Flodden on 9 September 1513. He was immediately confronted by an uprising in the highlands led by Donald MacDonald of Lochalsh. During the minority of James V, Argyll became the dominant figure in the western highlands and the Western Isles, building upon his predecessors' efforts to extend Campbell power within that region, especially after the forfeiture of the MacDonald lords of the Isles in 1493 and the disintegration of their dominant position. Because clan Campbell relied heavily upon feudal superiorities and judicial authority to increase its territorial control, the third earl's appointment in 1514 as justice-general of Scotland, the highest criminal law officer of the kingdom, was extremely significant. The office was held by Argyll until his death, when it passed to his son, and was to remain in the possession of the earls of Argyll until 1628.

Within the highlands Argyll acquired increasingly broad-ranging royal commissions, culminating in his appointment in 1517 as lieutenant for the whole of the western highlands and islands. Although willing to employ force, he preferred conciliation and negotiation, seeking to tie the leading highland chiefs to him through marriage alliances and making extensive use of bonds of manrent. Kinship did not always bring harmony, as when Lachlan MacLean of Duart unsuccessfully attempted to drown his wife, who was Argyll's sister, thereby provoking John Campbell of Cawdor, the earl's younger brother, to kill Lachlan in 1523.

Argyll served the crown while remaining above the factional strife of James's minority; as the later family history comments, he was 'ever adhering to the authoritie, although the times were dangerous and his tentations [*sic*] very many' (Campbell, 7). However, when the king freed himself from the control of the earl of Angus in 1528, the third earl played a central role in James's escape. This reinforced James's deep trust and reliance upon Argyll, which lasted until the earl's death. Appointed lieutenant of Lothian, Merse, and Teviotdale on 24 November 1528, the earl led the military expedition against the Douglas strongholds, which forced Angus to flee to England in the following May. As a reward Argyll was granted the barony of Abernethy, the only part of the Angus regality to pass out of crown hands.

With Argyll conducting a campaign in the borders during 1528–9, an uprising broke out in the highlands, where the MacDonalds of Dunyvaig and the MacLeans of Duart raided Campbell lands. The MacLeans sought revenge for the murder of Lachlan, their chief, while the MacDonalds believed that their hold upon their recently recovered Kintyre lands was threatened. In his capacity as chamberlain of Kintyre, Argyll had been ordered to abandon his conciliatory approach and concentrate instead upon improving crown revenues. The rigorous collection of royal rents had probably led to the eviction of some crown tenants. To counter the raiding a military campaign was suggested in August 1529 by Cawdor and the following month the king and council ordered Argyll, who had again been made lieutenant of the west, to execute his brother's plan. However, the earl's illness and death soon afterwards meant that this task was left to his successor.

Although depicted as 'a man of great action and a valiant captain' (MacPhail, 2.100), the third earl was also a close friend and patron of the humanist scholar Hector Boece and was able to secure a number of important volumes from the Iona Abbey library to help him with his *Scotorum historia*. During the autumn of 1529, with his health failing, Argyll completed the transfer to his heir (begun in 1526) of his remaining lands and offices. The charter they both purport to have signed on 4 November is clearly incorrectly dated, because the earl had died at Inveraray in the first part of October. He was buried in the family mausoleum at Kilmun, on the Holy Loch, Argyll.

JANE E. A. DAWSON

Sources *Scots peerage*, 1.337–8 • A. Campbell, ed., *Records of Argyll* (1885) • N. D. Campbell, tenth duke of Argyll, Argyll transcripts, Inveraray Castle, Argyll • J. R. N. Macphail, ed., 'Ane accompt of the genealogie of the Campbells', *Highland papers*, 2, Scottish History Society, 2nd ser., 12 (1916), 72–111 • J. M. Thomson and others, eds., *Registrum magni sigilli regum Scotorum / The register of the great seal of Scotland*, 11 vols. (1882–1914), vol. 3 • *LP Henry VIII*, vols. 1–4 • J. Cameron, *James V: the personal rule, 1528–1542*, ed. N. Macdougall (1998) • J. Wormald, *Lords and men in Scotland* (1985) • R. K. Hannay, ed., *Acts of the lords of council in public affairs, 1501–1554* (1932) • C. N. Innes, ed., *Origines parochiales Scotiae*, 2/1, Bannatyne Club, 97 (1854) • N. MacLean-Bristol, *Warriors and priests: the history of the Clan MacLean, 1300–1570* (1995) • *Fourth report*, HMC, 3 (1874)

Archives priv. coll., MSS and transcripts | BL, Cotton MSS, letters to Thomas Wolsey, etc. • NA Scot., Breadalbane collection, GD112

Campbell, Colin, of Glenorchy (1499–1583). *See under* Campbell family of Glenorchy (*per.* 1432–1631).

Campbell, Colin, sixth earl of Argyll (*c.*1542–1584), magnate, was the second son of Archibald *Campbell, fourth earl of Argyll (1498–1558), and his second wife, Lady Margaret Graham (*d.* in or before 1545), daughter of the third earl of Menteith. Following Gaelic tradition he was probably fostered with his maternal kin, thereby acquiring the name Cailean Teach or Tealach, meaning Colin from Menteith. He was described as tall with a fair complexion, though no portrait has survived. Before becoming earl he was also known as Campbell of Boquhan, from his Stirlingshire lands, and appeared destined to found a Campbell cadet family in the Menteith region, following his family's established strategy of territorial expansion. He played little part in national politics prior to the serious illness of his elder half-brother the fifth earl in the autumn of 1571, though he had carried the latter's messages of loyalty to Mary, queen of Scots, in 1561 shortly before her return from France.

Colin Campbell's position changed during the winter of 1571–2 when he was formally recognized as Lord Lorne, the heir apparent to the earldom, and invested with its major landholdings and offices. Henceforth he played a prominent role both in clan affairs and national politics. His rising importance was reflected in his advantageous second marriage. His first wife, Lady Janet Stewart, daughter of the first Lord Methven, had died without issue. In January 1572 he married the beautiful, resourceful, and determined Lady Annas or Agnes Keith (*d.* 1588), widow of Regent Moray and daughter of the Earl Marischal. One contemporary unkindly commented that the sixth earl was 'weak in judgement and overmuch led by his wife' (Rogers, 35). They had three surviving children, Archibald *Campbell, the future seventh earl, Colin of Lundie, and Anna, who did not marry.

On 12 September 1573 Archibald *Campbell, the fifth earl of Argyll, died suddenly at the age of thirty-five. Colin succeeded to the earldom, and the following summer made an extended judicial progress through Argyll, pacifying feuds and hanging malefactors. In addition he ensured that the region's churches were properly manned and financed and were conducting protestant worship according to John Carswell's Gaelic translation of the Book of Common Order. This reflected the firm commitment to protestantism which he had imbibed from his father and brother. In his will the sixth earl sought to perpetuate the family's religious tradition, admonishing his wife and other guardians to raise his heir so that Archibald would never swerve nor shrink back 'from the treu religion of Jesus Cryst professit and prechit within this realme bot … sett forward the samin to the uttermost of [his and] thair poweris in all places, speciallie within the boundis of Argyll and Lorne' (Macdonald, 68).

Argyll's protracted and bitter feud with Regent Morton dominated his eleven years as earl and drew him into the factional struggles of the court. The first serious dispute between the two men arose over the custody of some of the jewels of Mary, queen of Scots, then in the possession of Argyll's wife. Although Morton demanded their return, the countess refused, declaring they were surety for payment of government expenses incurred during his regency by Moray, her first husband. Before surrendering the jewels, she wanted those debts paid, thus protecting the inheritance of the daughters of her first marriage. Rejecting compromise, Morton outlawed Argyll and his wife in February 1574. After the intervention of Elizabeth I, to whom the countess appealed, the deadlock was broken and the jewels handed back in March 1575 on promises of future recompense.

Thereafter Argyll interpreted all Morton's actions as hostile interference, especially where highland affairs were concerned. He had a narrower political perspective than the fifth earl, being less involved in Irish politics and Anglo-Scottish relations. He also lacked his brother's conciliatory skills and became embroiled in a series of highland feuds which provoked the unwelcome attention of the regent and the privy council. His bad relations with Lachlan MacLean of Duart and the latter's uncle John destroyed the traditional friendship existing between the MacLeans and the Campbells and destabilized the southern highlands and islands. Argyll also made enemies in the north, such as John MacDonald of Skye, Donald MacDonald of Glengarry, and Lachlan Mackintosh of Dunachton, the captain of the Chattan clan.

Argyll's most significant feud, however, was with the earl of Atholl. He had initially demanded that an earlier judicial commission granted to Atholl be revoked since it interfered with his own hereditary jurisdiction as Scotland's justice-general. By 1576 the raiding between the two earls' dependants had spread throughout the central highlands. When Argyll ignored the council's summons he was outlawed and Morton planned a military campaign against him. Meanwhile Atholl, believing the regent was deliberately exploiting the feud for his own benefit, settled with Argyll. The two earls and their supporters at court succeeded in removing Morton from power in 1578. On 17 August 1579 the sixth earl became chancellor, an office which he felt should have been his six years earlier when the fifth earl died. Despite his appointment as lieutenant of the west march in 1580, the sixth earl's relations with Morton remained uneasy during the ex-regent's partial rehabilitation, and in 1581 Argyll supported the prosecution and execution of Morton. Initially in favour of the Ruthven raid, which captured the young James VI in 1582, Argyll later became an opponent of its leader, the earl of Gowrie, and in 1584 approved his execution.

By the beginning of that year Argyll's health was deteriorating and he was unable to travel to Europe in search of a cure. He died at Darnaway Castle, Moray, on 10 September 1584, still in his early forties, and was buried in the family mausoleum at Kilmun on the Holy Loch, Argyll. His elder son was only about eight years old and the resulting political vacuum inaugurated a ruthless power struggle within the Campbell clan, causing severe disruption within the highlands and adding to the strife at court. The sixth earl's drive for justice too often became an excessive concern for his own jurisdictional authority, and he made many enemies, particularly in the highlands, which contributed towards the region's instability in the decade following Argyll's death. For a man praised in a later family history as modest and just, this was an unfortunate legacy. JANE E. A. DAWSON

Sources *Scots peerage*, 1.344–6 • A. Campbell, ed., *Records of Argyll* (1885) • A. Macdonald, ed., *Letters of the Argyll family*, Maitland Club, 50 (1839) • N. D. Campbell, tenth duke of Argyll, Argyll transcripts, Inveraray Castle, Argyll • A. Hay, *Estimate of the Scottish nobility during the minority of James the Sixth*, ed. C. Rogers, Grampian Club (1873) • *Reg. PCS*, 1st ser., vols. 2–3 • *CSP Scot.*, 1574–81 • G. R. Hewitt,

Scotland under Morton, 1572–80 (1982) • J. Dawson, ed., *Campbell letters, 1559–83*, 5th ser., Scottish History Society, 10 (2000) • G. Donaldson, *All the queen's men* (1983) • K. M. Brown, *Bloodfeud in Scotland, 1573–1625* (1986) • N. MacLean-Bristol, *Murder under trust: the crimes and death of Sir Lachlan Mor MacLean of Duart, 1558–98* (1999)

Archives priv. coll., MSS and transcripts | NA Scot., Breadalbane collection, GD112

Wealth at death total of the inventory was £3066 13*s*. 4*d*.; the 'deadis part', £1022 3*s*. 5*d*.: Macdonald, ed., *Letters to the Argyll family*, 61–70

Campbell, Colin, of Achnaba (1644–1726), Church of Scotland minister, was the son of Patrick Campbell (known as Patrick Dubh Beg; 1592–1678) of Invergeldie in Perthshire, and Bethia (*d*. in or after 1711), daughter of Patrick Murray of Ochtertyre, Perthshire. He was educated at St Salvator's College, St Andrews University, where he was in attendance by 1658 and graduated MA on 27 July 1661. John Gregorson, a descendant of Campbell's who donated many of his papers to Edinburgh University Library in 1827, believed that he then went to one of the English universities as companion or tutor to his relative, Robert, later Sir Robert Campbell of Glenorchy, but there is no other indication of this.

Campbell is described as an 'expectant' in the records of the presbytery of Lorn in 1666, was on trial for his licence in February and May 1667, and admitted as minister of Ardchattan and Muckairn on 27 November. In the following year he became presbytery clerk, an office which he performed to everyone's satisfaction, and to which he was continually reappointed until his death. He evidently performed his duties as minister of the gospel with great distinction too, except for one brief period when he was suspended for pre-nuptial intercourse. He was suspended on 12 January 1676 and early efforts to reinstate him, in March, were prevented at the request of the laird of Calder, Sir Hugh Campbell, father of the bride-to-be. The laird's opposition continued until 10 June 1676 when an act of synod noted Colin's 'satisfaction to the Church for the scandal', and certification of his lawful marriage to the laird's daughter, Mary (*d*. in or before 1702), in that year. It was also noted that Colin showed real remorse, and that he and his new wife were now in an indigent state 'through want of ordinances'. The bishop and synod unanimously reinstalled him 'into his former office, place and cure, as if the former occasion of his suspension had never been', on 25 June 1676 (Edinburgh University Library, MS 3099.1, fol. 4).

After the revolution of 1688 Campbell conformed to the civil government, subscribing on 7 June 1694 to the presbyterianism restored by the synod of Argyll, and was received into communion on the following day. It is said that after this time he travelled frequently to Morvern, Ardnamurchan, and the island of Mull to preach to the inhabitants of these remote parts. During these times he and his wife raised a family of four sons. Patrick, the oldest, continued to live on the family farm at Achnaba, Benderloch. Donald inherited his father's love of, and aptitude for, mathematics, and reportedly (by John Gregorson again) turned down a chair at one of the English universities, preferring to stay in his homeland. The third son, John, became a schoolteacher in Craignish, and the fourth, Dr Alexander Campbell, became a noted antiquary. Mary evidently died some time before March 1702, since Colin on the second of that month married the twice-widowed Margaret Campbell, daughter of Colin Campbell of Blarantibbert.

A learned and cultured man, Campbell left substantial manuscript remains. These show a wide interest in classical, literary, linguistic, medical, occult, and antiquarian matters, and include occasional pieces on Scottish history and politics. In 1689, writing as 'a lover of peace', he sent 'Ane assertione of the lawfulness of episcopall government and the expediency of continueing it in this present juncture' (Edinburgh University Library, MS 3099.11) to Professor David Gregory at Edinburgh University. Gregory replied that those to whom he had shown it had been 'wonderfully pleased with it', and he expressed confidence that it would easily find a publisher if liberty of printing should once again be tolerated (Gregory to Campbell, 5 June 1690, Edinburgh University Library, MS 3099.11). Instead, some five years later, Campbell is recorded subscribing to the synod of Argyll and accepting that presbyterian government is 'fully agreeable to the Apostolic pattern held out in the Word of God' (Edinburgh University Library, MS 3099.1, fol. 6).

By far the most extensive aspects of Campbell's papers are those devoted to religion and those concerned with natural philosophy and especially mathematics. The religious papers include not only notes for his sermons and a very long—but unfortunately scarcely legible—series of expositions of scripture, but also notes on the catechism made in 1658 while he was a student, a manuscript copy of *The Tree of Christian Faith* by Jakob Boehme, and various other theological pieces. The most significant of these are 'A demonstration of the existence of God against atheists', an exercise in rationalist natural theology, and 'Of the Trinity of persons in the unity of essence', a rationalist defence of Trinitarianism. In 1875 these were printed for private circulation by some of his admirers.

Campbell's mathematical papers have not yet been properly assessed but there can be no doubt that he was an impressive mathematician. He corresponded on mathematical matters with David Gregory in Edinburgh and, later, Oxford, James Gregory in St Andrews, and the younger James Gregory in Edinburgh, as well as George Cheyne, Archibald Pitcairne, John Craig, Colin McLaurin, George Sinclair, and others. Evident from the letters are Campbell's competence in 'quadrature of the parabolick space answering to another diameter than the axis'; 'the inverse Method of Fluxions', which would now be called integral calculus; a method of measuring the surface of solids 'made by the rotation of curve lines around their Axes' (letter from John Craig, 26 Jan 1707/8, Edinburgh University Library, MS 3099.8); and a method of reducing equations into series (Campbell to David Gregory, 14 Jan 1685, Edinburgh University Library, MS 3099.11). There is also a treatise on sundials, and various astronomical pieces. Campbell's descendant John Gregorson reported that he also corresponded with Isaac Newton but that the letters went missing before Campbell's papers came into his possession. Accordingly, he provides the names of three reliable witnesses who told him they had seen these letters (*New Statistical Account*, vol. 7. 488n.). However, no letters from Campbell to Newton have ever been found either, so some doubt must remain about the truth of this supposed correspondence. It has been reported that Newton said of Campbell in a letter to David Gregory, 'I see that were he among us he would make children of us all' (*Fasti Scot.*, 4.81), but this cannot be found in the letters to Gregory published in Newton's correspondence. If Campbell was not known to Newton himself, his work and worth as a mathematician were well known to a number who were close to Newton. John Craig, in particular, expressed a belief that Campbell had techniques 'which would make us all asham'd of our little performances' (Craig to Campbell, 26 January 1707/8, Edinburgh University Library, MS 3099.8). Described by one of his biographers as 'one of the most distinguished ministers ever in the Synod' (Edinburgh University Library, MS 3099.1, fol. 8), Campbell's worth was recognized some time before his death, on 13 March 1726, when he was designated 'Father of the Church'. JOHN HENRY

Sources *The new statistical account of Scotland*, 7 (1845) • *Fasti Scot.*, new edn, 4.81 • 'Life of the Reverend Colin Campbell', U. Edin. L., MS 3099.1 • U. Edin. L., Colin Campbell MSS, MSS 3096–3101 • C. Ó'Baoill, 'Gaelic manuscripts in the Colin Campbell collection', *Scottish Gaelic Studies*, 14/1 (1983), 83–99 • *The correspondence of Isaac Newton*, ed. H. W. Turnbull and others, 7 vols. (1959–77), vols. 2, 3
Archives U. Edin. L., corresp. and papers
Wealth at death feudal properties called Coullandalloch and Scoull; Achnaba Farm: *Fasti Scot.*

Campbell, Colin, of Kilberry (1721/2–1798), army officer, was born probably at Kilberry, Argyll, the eldest son of Dugald Campbell of Kilberry (*d.* 1733) and his wife, Elizabeth, daughter of another Dugald Campbell of Kilberry. The family had held Kilberry since the early seventeenth century. He was a lieutenant in the Earl of Loudoun's Highlanders in 1746, was captain in the 4th King's Own regiment in 1756, and raised and commanded the 10th regiment of highlanders in 1760. In 1761 he became a major in the 100th foot. He became notorious for his fatal assault on another officer, Captain John McKaarg, while stationed at the island of Martinique in 1762. The dispute reportedly originated at Jersey, where Campbell, then major-commandant of the 100th foot, was obliged to take the payment of McKaarg's company out of his hands, owing to the latter's financial difficulties. Following the regiment's arrival at Martinique, McKaarg vilified Campbell, who demanded an explanation in writing. McKaarg replied in a curt letter. Campbell immediately went to McKaarg's tent armed with a bayonet and a small-sword, and demanded satisfaction. McKaarg, having a broadsword only, tried to evade a meeting. Campbell struck him several times with his sword. McKaarg was compelled by Campbell to beg for his life, and immediately died. He had received eleven wounds, two of which were mortal. Campbell was arrested, and on 6 April 1762 was tried for murder by a general court martial held at Fort Royal. He tried to prove that McKaarg had fallen in a fair duel. On 14 April the court adjudged Campbell to be cashiered, and declared him incapable of serving the crown in any military employment.

Pending consideration of the sentence by George III, Campbell escaped from the island. Owing to some informalities the proceedings were not confirmed, but he was dismissed from the army. On his return to England, Campbell presented a memorial to the secretary-at-war, charging Major-General Robert Monckton, who commanded on Martinique, 'with many wrongs and deliberate acts of oppression'. A general court martial was consequently held at the judge advocate-general's office at the Horse Guards, London, in April 1764, and Monckton was honourably acquitted. The relatives of Captain McKaarg brought an action of assythment against Campbell, and ultimately damages of £200 were awarded to them. Campbell chiefly resided in Edinburgh, where he attracted notice by his foppery, and was well known as an antiquated old beau. In the summer he visited Buxton and the other fashionable watering places. He married Catherine Glass, daughter and heiress of Edward Glass; they had no children. He died at Edinburgh on 15 January 1798, and his estate at Kilberry descended to his kinsman John Campbell of Knockbuy.

G. F. R. BARKER, *rev.* ROGER T. STEARN

Sources J. Kay, *A series of original portraits and caricature etchings … with biographical sketches and illustrative anecdotes*, ed. [H. Paton and others], new edn [3rd edn], 2 (1877), 5–7 • *Proceedings of a general court-martial held at Fort Royal, in the island of Martinico, … upon the tryal of Major Commandant Colin Campbell* (1763) • *The case of Colin Campbell esq., late major-commandant of His Majesty's 100th regiment* (1763) • *Proceedings of a general court-martial held at the judge-advocate's office for a trial of a charge preferred by Colin Campbell, esq., against the Hon. Major-General Monckton, 1764* (1764) • A. N. Gilbert, 'Law and honour among eighteenth-century British army officers', *HJ*, 19 (1976), 75–85 • *GM*, 1st ser., 68 (1798), 88 • Burke, *Gen. GB* (1937)
Likenesses J. Kay, engraving, repro. in Kay, *A series of original portraits and caricature etchings*

Campbell, Colin (1754–1814), army officer, was the second son of John Campbell of the Citadel, reputedly descended from the noble house of Breadalbane, deputy keeper of the great seal of Scotland, and cashier of the Royal Bank of Scotland. He entered the army as an ensign in the 71st regiment in March 1771, and was promoted lieutenant in 1774. He accompanied the 71st to America, and was promoted captain in 1778 and major into the 6th on 19 March 1783. While stationed in New York he married Mary (*d.* 1832), eldest daughter of Colonel Guy Johnstone—who lost most of his property for remaining an active loyalist—and his wife, Mary, daughter of Sir William *Johnson, first baronet (1715?–1774). Campbell and his wife had six sons and five daughters.

In 1786 the 6th regiment was ordered to Nova Scotia, and remained there until the outbreak of the war with France in 1793, when it formed part of Sir Charles Grey's expedition to the West Indies, and distinguished itself at the capture of Martinique (March 1794), St Lucia (April), and Guadeloupe (April) but suffered losses from malaria and other diseases. Campbell was promoted lieutenant-colonel of the 6th on 29 April 1795, and returned with them from the West Indies in July. They went to Warwickshire to recruit. In February 1796 he went with his regiment to Ireland, where he served until 1803, and gained his reputation. Throughout 1798 he successfully suppressed rebellion in his area, making it a rule never to separate his companies. He was at the battle of Vinegar Hill, co. Wexford (21 July 1798), and the defeat of General Joseph Humbert's French invasion force. On 1 January 1798 Campbell was promoted colonel, and on 1 January 1805 he was promoted major-general and given command of the Limerick district.

From August 1810 Campbell was lieutenant-governor of Gibraltar. Prince Edward, duke of Kent and Strathearn (1767–1820), was still nominally governor, but had been recalled in March 1803 after his suppression of the December 1802 mutiny there, and until his death Gibraltar was ruled by successive lieutenant-governors. Campbell was lieutenant-governor through most of the Peninsular War (1807–14), and took an active and energetic role in it. During Soult's occupation of Andalusia Campbell insisted on keeping Gibraltar well garrisoned, despite Wellington's repeated requisitions. He insisted on regarding Tarifa (21 miles south-west of Gibraltar) as part of his Gibraltar command, maintaining a British garrison there, and thus deprived Soult of a port through which he might have imported supplies. He assisted the armies and guerrillas in Spain with supplies, despite repeated hindrances from the Spanish junta and even Wellington, who later did him full justice. He sent artillery and engineer officers to help the Spanish. He supported General Lord Blayney's unsuccessful attack on Fuengirola and General Thomas Graham's Barossa operation (March 1811). In December 1811, when Leval attacked Tarifa and the British commander Colonel John Skerrett wanted to abandon the town, Campbell was furious and ordered the removal of the boats in which the garrison might have withdrawn: Tarifa held. Sir William Napier in volume 10 of his *History of the War in the Peninsula* wrote conclusively on the importance of Campbell's work. He was colonel of the 5th garrison battalion from 1808 to 1812, and of the 55th foot from October 1812 until his death. He was promoted lieutenant-general on 4 June 1811, and died, after severe illness, at Gibraltar on 2 April 1814. Had he lived longer he would have been made a baronet. His son Colonel Guy *Campbell (1786–1849), who commanded the 6th, his father's old regiment, at Waterloo, was created a baronet on 22 May 1815, with remainder to the heirs male of General Colin Campbell, in recognition of his father's eminent services. H. M. STEPHENS, *rev.* ROGER T. STEARN

Sources W. F. P. Napier, *History of the war in the Peninsula and in the south of France*, new edn, 6 vols. (1853) · *The dispatches of … the duke of Wellington … from 1799 to 1818*, ed. J. Gurwood, 13 vols. in 12 (1834–9) · *Supplementary despatches (correspondence) and memoranda of Field Marshal Arthur, duke of Wellington*, ed. A. R. Wellesley, second duke of Wellington, 15 vols. (1858–72), vols. 1–11 · R. Cannon, ed., *Historical record of the sixth, or royal first Warwickshire regiment of foot* (1839) · Burke, *Peerage* (1967) · C. W. C. Oman, *A history of the Peninsular War*, 4 (1911) · *Army List* (1811) · *Army List* (1813) · J. Haydn, *The book of dignities: containing rolls of the official personages of the British empire* (1851) · T. Pakenham, *The year of liberty: the history of the great Irish rebellion of 1798* (1992) · T. W. Moody and others, eds., *A new history of Ireland*, 4: *Eighteenth-century Ireland, 1691–1800* (1986) · M. Harvey, *Gibraltar* (1996) · E. R. Kenyon, *Gibraltar: under Moor, Spaniard and Briton* (1938) · M. Duffy, *Soldiers, sugar, and sea power: the British expeditions to the West Indies and the war against revolutionary France* (1987) · R. Muir, *Britain and the defeat of Napoleon, 1807–1815* (1996) · P. Griffith, 'The life of Sir Charles Oman', *Modern studies of the war in Spain and Portugal, 1808–1814*, ed. P. Griffith (1999), vol. 9 of C. W. C. Oman, *A history of the Peninsular War* (1902–99) · A. J. Guy, ed., *The road to Waterloo: the British army and the struggle against revolutionary and Napoleonic France, 1793–1815* (1990)

Archives U. Nott. L., letters to Lord William Bentinck

Campbell, Sir Colin (1776–1847), army officer and colonial governor, was the fifth son of John Campbell of Melfort, and his wife, Colina, daughter of John Campbell of Auchalader, Perthshire. From boyhood he showed a daring disposition, and in 1792, at the age of sixteen, ran away from Perth Academy, and boarded a ship bound for the West Indies. He was met in the fruit market at Kingston, Jamaica, by his brother Patrick Campbell, then serving on the *Blonde*, who brought him home. His parents accepted his wishes, and in 1793 he became a midshipman on board an East Indiaman and made several voyages.

In February 1795 Campbell became a lieutenant in the 3rd battalion of the Breadalbane fencibles, then commanded by his uncle. On 3 October 1799 he entered a West India regiment as ensign, and in 1800 acted as brigade-major on the island of St Vincent. On 21 August 1801 Campbell was commissioned lieutenant in the 35th regiment, and at once exchanged into the 78th or Ross-shire Buffs, which was then stationed in India. He joined it at Poona, accompanied Wellesley's advance against Maharaja Sindhia and the raja of Nagpur, and so greatly distinguished himself by leading the flank companies at the storming of the pettah or inner fortress of Ahmednagar on 8 August 1803 that Wellesley at once appointed him brigade-major. As such he served at the battles of Assaye, where he was severely wounded and had two horses killed under him, Argaon, and at the storming of Gawilgarh. On leaving India, Wellesley strongly recommended Campbell to Lord Wellesley, who made him his aide-de-camp, and to Lake, who, on 9 January 1805, gave him a company in the 75th highlanders. He returned to England with Lord Wellesley in 1806, and Sir Arthur Wellesley asked that he be appointed brigade-major to his brigade, then stationed at Hastings.

As brigade-major Campbell accompanied Wellesley to Hanover and to Denmark, where his conduct at the battle of Kioge was conspicuous. In 1808 Sir Arthur Wellesley appointed him his senior aide-de-camp, when he took command of the expeditionary force destined for Portugal, and sent him home with the dispatches announcing the victory at Roliça on 17 August. Campbell, however, disembarked, and was present at Vimeiro. Sir Harry Burrard then gave him the Vimeiro dispatch, and Campbell was promoted brevet major in the army on 2 September 1808, and major of the 70th on 15 December 1808. On the same day he was appointed an assistant adjutant-general to a division of the reinforcements intended for the Peninsula. He was present at the passage of the Douro, at Talavera, and at Busaco, and was promoted brevet lieutenant-colonel on 3 May 1810. He was frequently engaged during the pursuit of Masséna and was present at Fuentes d'Oñoro. Campbell obtained the post of assistant quartermaster-general at the headquarters of the army in the Peninsula, at Wellington's request, in the spring of 1812, and acted in that capacity until the end of the Peninsular War, reputedly easing Wellington's relations with the quartermaster-general, George Murray. Wellington so valued Campbell that he fought with the Horse Guards to retain him. Campbell was present at the storming of Badajoz, and in nine general actions, for which he received a cross and six clasps.

On 4 June 1814 Campbell was promoted brevet colonel in the army, and on 25 July was made a captain and lieutenant-colonel in the Coldstream Guards. He was also appointed assistant quartermaster-general at the Horse Guards, and made a KCB, and a knight of the Tower and Sword of Portugal. In 1815 he was attached to Wellington's staff, as commandant at headquarters, and was present at the battle of Waterloo; he held the post throughout Wellington's residence at Paris, from 1815 to 1818. He then exchanged his company in the guards for the lieutenant-colonelcy of the 65th, which he held until he was promoted major-general in 1825. He held the command of the southern district for some years.

Campbell was lieutenant-governor of Tobago (1828), and of Portsmouth (1828–35), and in 1833 was appointed lieutenant-governor of Nova Scotia. In November 1840 he was promoted governor of Ceylon, where he remained from September 1839 until June 1847. It was during his tenure in the latter post that the duke of Wellington, to whose friendship he owed much, wrote to him: 'We are both growing old; God knows if we shall ever meet again. Happen what may, I shall never forget our first meeting under the walls of Ahmednuggur.'

Campbell had married early in life the eldest daughter (*d.* 1838) of Henry Harnden; they had three sons and three daughters. He was colonel 99th foot from 1834 to 1836, and 72nd foot from 1836 until his death. In June 1847 he returned to England, and on 13 June he died, at King Street, St James's, London; he was buried in the church of St James's, Piccadilly, London.

H. M. STEPHENS, *rev.* STEWART M. FRASER

Sources *GM*, 2nd ser., 28 (1847) • M. O. Campbell, *A memorial history of the Campbells of Melfort* (1882) • C. W. C. Oman, *A history of the Peninsular War*, 1–3 (1902–8); repr. (1995–6) • private information (1886) • S. G. P. Ward, *Wellington's headquarters: a study of the administrative problems in the Peninsula, 1809–14* (1957) • P. Moon, *The British conquest and dominion of India* (1989)

Archives NA Canada | priv. coll., Somerset MSS

Likenesses T. Heaphy, pencil and watercolour drawing, 1813, NPG • R. Dighton, drawing, pubd 1827, BM • R. Dighton, watercolour drawing, Scot. NPG • W. Salter, group portrait, oils (*Waterloo banquet at Apsley House*), Apsley House, London, Wellington Museum • W. Salter, oils, NPG

Campbell [*formerly* Macliver], **Colin**, **Baron Clyde** (**1792–1863**), army officer, born Macliver, the eldest son of John

Colin Campbell, Baron Clyde (1792–1863), by Roger Fenton, 1855

Macliver (*d.* 22 December 1858, aged ninety-two), a carpenter in Glasgow—whose father's Ardnave estate was forfeited following the Jacobite rising of 1745—and his wife, Agnes, *née* Campbell, of the Campbells of Islay, was born at John Street, Glasgow, on 20 October 1792. His mother died when he was a boy, and her brother, Colonel John Campbell, paid for Colin's education. He attended Glasgow high school and Gosport military academy. In 1807 Colonel Campbell took him to the duke of York as candidate for a commission. The duke assumed he was 'another of the clan' and his name was entered as Campbell, which he thenceforth used.

Peninsular War, 1808–1813 On 26 May 1808 Campbell was appointed ensign in the 9th regiment and sailed with the 2nd battalion, under Lieutenant-Colonel John Cameron, for Portugal, with the expedition under Sir Arthur Wellesley. He was first under fire at the battle of Roliça, was at Vimeiro, and served with the 9th in Sir John Moore's advance to Salamanca and the retreat to Corunna. He served with the 1st battalion of the 9th in the disastrous 1809 Walcheren expedition, when he was attacked by fever which troubled him for the rest of his life, and in 1810 joined the 2nd battalion at Gibraltar. He had been promoted lieutenant on 28 January 1809, and commanded the two flank companies of the 9th in the battle of Barossa, where his bravery attracted the notice of General Graham, afterwards Lord Lynedoch, who never forgot him. He was then attached by Lieutenant-General Colin Campbell to the Spanish army under Ballesteros, and served with it until December 1811, when he rejoined the 2nd battalion of the 9th in time for the defence of Tarifa.

In January 1813 he joined the 1st battalion under his old chief, Colonel John Cameron. The 9th formed part of Graham's corps, in which Campbell served at the battle of Vitoria and the siege of San Sebastian. On 17 July 1813 Campbell led the right wing of the 9th in the attack on the fortified convent of San Bartholomé, and was mentioned in dispatches, and on 25 July he led the forlorn hope in the unsuccessful attempt to storm the fortress itself, and was twice wounded. For his bravery Campbell was recommended for promotion by Sir Thomas Graham, and on 9 November 1813 he was promoted to a company without purchase in the 60th rifles. Before he left the 9th Campbell again distinguished himself. He left his quarters in San Sebastian before his wounds were healed or the doctors gave him permission, and led the night attack of the 9th on the batteries on the French side of the Bidassoa after fording the river, and was again seriously wounded. Colonel Cameron reprimanded him for leaving his quarters without leave, but did not report his disobedience. His wounds and his promotion necessitated his leaving the army, and he reached England in December 1813, when he was awarded a pension of £100 a year for his wounds and ordered to join the 7th battalion 60th rifles in Nova Scotia.

Colonies and China, 1813–1846 Campbell had fought his way to captain in five years; it was nearly thirty before he became colonel. He spent 1815 and 1816 on the Riviera on leave, and joined the 5th battalion 60th rifles at Gibraltar in November 1816. In 1818 he was transferred to the 21st regiment (Royal Scots Fusiliers), which he joined at Barbados in April 1819. In 1821 he went on the staff as aide-de-camp to General Murray, governor of British Guiana, and as brigade-major to the troops at Demerara, and was continued such by Sir Benjamin D'Urban, who succeeded Murray in 1823. In 1825 an opportunity occurred for him to purchase his majority, and a generous friend in Barbados lent him most of the required sum; the rest he borrowed from his agents. On 26 November 1825 he was promoted major, and in the following year resigned his staff appointment and returned to England. His bravery at San Sebastian had gained him powerful friends at headquarters—his former commanders, Sir John Cameron and Lord Lynedoch, never forgot him, while Sir Henry Hardinge and Lord Fitzroy Somerset remembered his services—and on 26 October 1832 he was promoted to an unattached lieutenant-colonelcy on payment of £1300, kindly provided by a maternal relative. Out of his scanty pay he managed to support his family, and meanwhile continued to request command of a regiment. In 1832 he observed the French siege of Antwerp, sending back valuable reports. At last, in 1835, he was appointed lieutenant-colonel of the 9th, on condition he at once exchange to the 98th, of which he assumed command on its return from the Cape in 1837. He commanded that regiment in the north of England during the Chartist disturbances, trained them in street fighting, and won praise from the general commanding the northern district, Sir Charles Napier.

In 1841 Campbell was ordered to China with the 98th to reinforce the army there under Sir Hugh Gough. He reached Hong Kong on 2 June 1842, joined Gough's army in north China, and was attached to Lord Saltoun's brigade. He covered the attack on Chinkiang (Zhenjiang), and co-operated in the march on Nanking (Nanjing). At the peace the 98th, reduced by fever, was ordered to Hong Kong, where Campbell commanded the troops. He was most favourably mentioned in dispatches by the general, who had known him in the Peninsula, was appointed aide-de-camp to the queen and promoted colonel (23 December 1842), and was made a CB (24 December 1842). In January 1844 he was made a brigadier-general, and took over the command of the brigade in Chushan. He remained there until 25 July 1846, and reached Calcutta on 24 October 1846 with the 98th.

India, 1847–1853 Soon after his arrival in India, in January 1847, Campbell was appointed to command the brigade at Lahore, and there made the acquaintance of Sir Henry Lawrence, the commissioner, whose intimate friend he became. With the insurrection of Moolraj and the siege of Multan, Campbell advocated prompt measures, and was bitterly disappointed when he was not allowed to serve in the relief of the besieged fortress. At the close of the year he was appointed to command a division by Lord Gough, and offered the post of adjutant-general to the forces, which he refused owing to his desire to return to England on the conclusion of the war. His services in the Second Anglo-Sikh War were notable: he covered the rout of the cavalry at Ramnagar, and by a forward movement prevented the Sikhs from following up their first success at Chilianwala. He commanded the right wing and the pursuit at the crowning victory of Gujrat. He commanded a brigade in Major-General Sir Walter Gilbert's pursuit of the Afghans, and afterwards received command of the brigade at Rawalpindi and of the frontier division stationed at Peshawar. After the Second Anglo-Sikh War he was made a KCB on 5 June 1849.

For most of his life Campbell, who supported his father and his beloved spinster sister Alicia, was relatively poor and had to live frugally. However, his Anglo-Sikh War prize money made him 'easier in his circumstances' (Shadwell, 1.238). Campbell seems then to have wanted to retire and return to Britain, for he was able to save his family from any privation. 'I am growing old and only fit for retirement', he wrote in his journal on 20 October 1849 (ibid., 1.239). The requests of Lord Dalhousie and Sir Charles Napier, however, persuaded him to remain, and he spent three years in the difficult work of the frontier. In February 1850 he cleared the Kohat Pass of the tribesmen who were occupying it, with a loss of nineteen killed and seventy-four wounded. In February 1852 he advanced in command of a force of two guns and 260 *sowars* against the Momands, and decisively defeated Sadut Khan, their leader, at Panj Pao on 15 April. In March he was ordered to punish the Swat tribes and advanced into the mountains with more than 2500 men and seven guns, and after able operations and several engagements defeated over 6000 of them at Iskakote on 18 May 1852. He wanted to follow up his victory, but the government refused to allow him to use the 22nd regiment, and he had to return to Peshawar with his object unattained on 1 June, and resigned his command on 25 July. In March 1853 he reached England after twelve years away, went on half pay, and took a year's holiday visiting his many friends, including his 'fellow-criminal', Sir Charles Napier.

Crimean War, 1854–1856 On 11 February 1854 Lord Hardinge, the commander-in-chief, offered Campbell the command of one of the two brigades intended for the East. Campbell accepted, but by the time he reached Turkey the intended division had grown into an army, and he commanded the 2nd (Highland) brigade of the 1st division, under the inexperienced but royal duke of Cambridge, consisting of the 42nd, 79th, and 93rd highlanders. On 20 June 1854, while at Varna, he was promoted major-general. 'This rank', he wrote in his journal, 'has arrived at a period of life when the small additional income which it carries with it is the only circumstance connected with the promotion in which I take any interest' (Shadwell, 1.319). At the head of his brigade he landed in the Crimea, and fought at the Alma. He led his brigade against the redoubt which had been retaken by the Russians after being captured by the light division, and with his highlanders in line defeated the last compact columns of the Russians. His horse had been shot under him, and he had won the victory, but the only reward he asked was permission to wear the highland bonnet instead of the cocked hat of a general officer.

When the army camped before Sevastopol, Campbell was appointed commandant at Balaklava, the crucial British harbour and base. At home his services were recognized by his being made colonel of the 67th regiment on 24 October 1854. On 25 October a large Russian force under General Liprandi attempted to attack Balaklava. Campbell's small force was heavily outnumbered. He placed his only British infantry regiment, the 93rd highlanders, in line to meet the advancing Russian cavalry. As some of the highlanders edged forward he shouted, '93rd! 93rd! Damn all that eagerness!' (Barthorp, 43). They drove off the Russians, saving the British base. William Howard Russell of *The Times* described the 93rd as 'that thin red streak tipped with a line of steel' (Lambert and Badsey, 110)—later much repeated as the 'thin red line'. Campbell was not engaged at Inkerman. In December 1854 he took command of the 1st division (guards and Highland brigades) when Cambridge returned to England, encamped them around Balaklava, and continued to command at Balaklava and to do all he could for the troops during the terrible winter. He received repeated thanks from Lord Raglan, at whose request he did not press for command of the Kerch expedition in May 1855, and he was made a GCB on 5 July 1855. Amid the Crimean failures Campbell's own reputation was enhanced. Following the death of Raglan, who considered Campbell too excitable, in June 1855, and again after Sir James Simpson's resignation in September 1855, Palmerston wanted Campbell appointed commander-in-chief in the Crimea, but lacked necessary cabinet support. There was controversy in the press as to his succeeding Raglan: *The Times* opposed it. On 16 June 1855 he led the 1st division up to the front, and commanded the reserve at the storming of the Redan on 8 September. But his position had become invidious. Lord Panmure, the war secretary, first proposed that he should be governor of Malta, and then that he should serve under Codrington, his junior, who had never seen battle until the Alma. This was too much for Campbell, and on 3 November he left the Crimea on leave. Interviews with the queen, however, softened his resentment, and on 4 June 1856 he was promoted lieutenant-general, and again went to the Crimea to command of a corps under Codrington. The latter would not organize the corps, and Campbell commanded the Highland division for only a month and then returned to England. He was awarded the Légion d'honneur, the order of St Maurice and St Lazarus, and the Mejidiye. He received a sword of honour from Glasgow and an Oxford honorary DCL (June 1857).

Campbell, whose own career had been so hampered by the purchase system, gave evidence to the 1856 royal commission on the purchase and sale of commissions. He criticized the system as unfair to meritorious officers and harmful to the army, and favoured selection by merit. In July 1856 he assumed command of the south-eastern district, and in September was appointed inspector-general of infantry. In December 1856 he went to Berlin to deliver to the prince of Prussia (later Kaiser Wilhelm I) the grand cross of the Bath.

Indian mutiny and after, 1856–1860 In March 1857 Campbell was offered command of the expedition then forming for China, which he refused. On 11 July arrived the news of the outbreak of the Indian mutiny and the death of General Anson, the commander-in-chief in India. That day Lord Panmure offered Campbell the command-in-chief. He accepted, and started next day for India. He arrived at Calcutta in August, and heard at once the news of the recovery of Delhi by Major-General Archdale Wilson, and of Havelock's capture of Cawnpore, and his preparations for the first relief of Lucknow. Campbell hurried to Cawnpore the troops intended for the China expedition, which Lord Elgin had wisely sent to Calcutta, and assembled there also picked troops from the army which had taken Delhi. After two months of hard work organizing the troops and clearing Lower Bengal, he took command of the army at the Alambagh, and, leaving General C. A. Windham to hold Cawnpore, started on 9 November with 4700 men and 32 guns to save the British (under Outram and Havelock) at Lucknow. His force, largely European troops—and including the 93rd and Captain William Peel's naval brigade—reached Lucknow, stormed the *sikandarabagh* (16 November), then broke through to Outram and Havelock in the residency. Campbell evacuated the Lucknow garrison and its many dependants (11–23 November), leaving a force under Outram holding the Alambagh, 3 miles south of Lucknow. On 30 November Campbell reached Cawnpore and sent the rescued on steamers to Calcutta. Meanwhile his success had been endangered by Tantia Topi's defeat of Windham in front of Cawnpore (26–8 November), but he arrived in time to prevent further disaster; on 6 December he attacked and decisively defeated Tantia Topi, and established his headquarters there. The winter months abounded in minor operations. Campbell decided that a thorough defeat of the mutineers in Oudh must be the first major step towards re-establishing British rule. By March 1858 he had assembled 25,000 men for this purpose, and then began his campaign. After ten days' hard fighting he finally recaptured Lucknow on 19 March, and then by a series of operations in Oudh and Rohilkhand pacified—with the usual executions and reprisals—the north of India by May. He then paused in his own personal exertions from ill health; but it was because of his careful organization that Sir Hugh Rose was able to muster an adequate army for the campaign in central India, and because of his planning that the campaign was finally successful.

In India grand strategy was decided, partly on political grounds, by Lord Canning, the governor-general. Influenced by his Crimean experience and wanting to reduce casualties, Campbell's conduct of operations was thorough, cautious, and so relatively slow. Nicknamed Old Kuberdar ('take care') and Sir Crawling Camel, he was criticized by some officers—and later by Sir John Fortescue—as too cautious and slow. Concerned at British casualties from sunstroke, in 1858 he ordered that shakos be replaced by sun helmets. As Lord Roberts wrote, 'there was a feeling throughout the army that Sir Colin was inclined to favour Highlanders unduly' (Roberts, 213). At Lucknow he ordered Colonel Ewart of the 93rd, 'Bring on the tartan! Let my own lads at them!' (Hibbert, *Great Mutiny*, 340). Campbell made some mistakes: for example, his preventing Outram cutting off the mutineers' retreat after their defeat at Lucknow in March 1858, and his appointment of the notoriously bungling Brigadier-General R. Walpole to command in Rohilkhand. Nevertheless, overall Campbell was a successful commander. The mutiny further enhanced his reputation, and also enriched him by prize money. On 14 May 1858 he was promoted general; on 15 January 1858 he was made colonel of his favourite 93rd highlanders. In late 1858 and early 1859 there was indiscipline among the East India Company's European troops over their transfer to the queen's service. Campbell sympathized with their grievances and advised concession and that the men 'be liberally dealt with' (Maclagan, 243). Initially he was over-ruled, then government policy changed and the crisis ended. Following this 'white mutiny' he told Canning, 'henceforth it will be dangerous to the State to maintain a European local army' (Shadwell, 2.419), and he opposed the establishment of such a force. In June 1861, on the foundation of the order, he was made KSI, and on 3 July 1858 he was made Baron Clyde of Clydesdale. His health was failing, and so on 4 June 1860 he left India.

Last years, 1860–1863 One of the last acts of the East India Company was to vote Campbell a pension of £2000 a year; in July 1860 he was appointed colonel of the Coldstream Guards, and on 9 November 1862 field marshal. In December 1860 he was presented with the freedom of the City of London; in 1861 he officially attended the Prussian manoeuvres, and in April 1862 he commanded at the Easter Volunteer review at Brighton.

Campbell was about 5 feet 9 inches tall, well built, with broad shoulders, keen eyes, a high forehead, and curly brown, later grey, hair: 'a very remarkable looking man, lionlike in appearance' (GEC, *Peerage*). Liked by his troops, he was charming and, Lady Canning wrote, 'very amiable and cheerful, an endless talker and *raconteur*' (Maclagan, 123). Yet he was also excitable, and sometimes bad tempered and enraged. Wolseley wrote of him in India, 'contorted with anger … round and round he went, shaking his fist and screaming at the top of his voice' (Hibbert, *Great Mutiny*, 336). In late 1861 he was much weakened by serious illness. Following further illness he died, unmarried, at the residence of his friends Major-General and Mrs Henry Eyre, Government House, Chatham, Kent, on 14 August 1863, and was buried on 22 August in Westminster Abbey; his peerage became extinct. Statues of him were erected in London and Glasgow. Brave, dutiful, and modest, 'war-bred Sir Colin' (Shadwell, 2.480) had risen slowly by military merit—as his grave inscription stated, 'by his own deserts' (ibid., 2.478)—in an army still dominated by privilege, patronage, and money. He was, if arguably not brilliant nor a great general—Sir Owen Burne wrote that he 'was not a heaven-born leader, nor was he gifted with much military genius' (Burne, 52–3)—a competent and successful commander. To contemporaries he was a great soldier, who had saved the British empire in India.

H. M. Stephens, *rev.* Roger T. Stearn

Sources L. Shadwell, *The life of Colin Campbell*, 2 vols. (1881) • O. T. Burne, *Clyde and Strathnairn* (1891) • J. M. Roy, *'Old Take Care': the story of Field Marshal Sir Colin Campbell, Lord Clyde* (1985) • B. Watson, *The great Indian mutiny: Colin Campbell and the campaign at Lucknow* (1991) • C. Hibbert, *The great mutiny, India, 1857* (1978); repr. (1980) • GEC, *Peerage* • A. D. Lambert, *The Crimean War: British grand strategy, 1853–56* (1990) • C. Hibbert, *The destruction of Lord Raglan* (1963) • T. A. Heathcote, *The military in British India: the development of British land forces in south Asia, 1600–1947* (1995) • M. Maclagan, *'Clemency' Canning* (1962) • A. Lambert and S. Badsey, *The war correspondents: the Crimean War* (1994) • Lord Roberts [F. S. Roberts], *Forty-one years in India*, 31st edn (1900) • G. B. Malleson, *The Indian mutiny of 1857*, 4th edn (1892) • A. Bruce, *The purchase system in the British army, 1660–1871*, Royal Historical Society Studies in History, 20 (1980) • *GM*, 3rd ser., 15 (1863) • M. Barthorp, *Heroes of the Crimea: the battles of Balaclava and Inkerman* (1991)

Archives BL OIOC, MSS relating to Indian mutiny, MS Eur. C 124 | BL, corresp. with Lt-Colonel H. Bruce, Add. MS 43996 • BL OIOC, letters to John Lawrence, MS Eur. F 90 • BL OIOC, letters to Sir William Gomm, MS Eur. D 626 • Lpool RO, letters to Lord Stanley • NAM, corresp. with Lord Raglan • PRO, letters to Charles Napier, 30/64 • PRO NIre., letters to Lord Gosford • Wellcome L., post-mortem and report on last illness by Thomas Longmore

Likenesses J. W. Pieneman, oils, 1821, Apsley House, London, Wellington Museum • J. W. Pieneman, group portrait, oils, 1824 (*The battle of Waterloo*), Rijksmuseum, Amsterdam • R. Fenton, photograph, 1855, NPG [*see illus.*] • G. G. Adams, plaster busts, *c*.1855–1861, NPG; Scot. NPG • H. W. Phillips, oils, *c*.1856, Art Gallery and Museum, Glasgow • T. J. Barker, group portrait, oils, 1857 (*Relief of Lucknow*; after sketches by E. Lundgren), Art Gallery and Museum, Glasgow • F. Beato, photograph, 1857–8 (with W. R. Mansfield), NAM • T. J. Barker, oils, 1860, Scot. NPG • F. Grant, pen, ink, and watercolour drawing, *c*.1860, NPG • M. Noble, group portrait, marble relief, 1866, Westminster Abbey, London • J. H. Foley, bronze statue, *c.*1868, George's Square, Glasgow · C. Marochetti, statue on memorial, Waterloo Place, London · H. Watkins, carte-de-visite, NPG · T. B. Wirgman, pencil drawing (with Lord Sandhurst), Scot. NPG · photograph, Royal Collection

Wealth at death under £100,000: resworn probate, Oct 1867, *CGPLA Eng. & Wales* (1863)

Campbell, Lord Colin (1853–1895). *See under* Campbell, George Douglas, eighth duke of Argyll in the peerage of Scotland, and first duke of Argyll in the peerage of the United Kingdom (1823–1900).

Campbell, Daniel (1671/2–1753), merchant and politician, was the third son of the covenanter captain Walter Campbell of Skipness. After being apprenticed to a Glasgow merchant, he sailed to New England in 1692 as part owner of a cargo, and spent the next two years trading on the Atlantic coast and in the Caribbean. At his return he married into another important Glasgow merchant family and carried on a trade to North America, Africa, and nearer home in Europe. He also began to make money by lending to impecunious lairds on the security of their estates, and acted as a kind of unofficial banker to his kinsman the first duke of Argyll. So successful was he that in 1706 he purchased the estate of Shawfield, just outside Glasgow, where he built an imposing mansion. A political client of the Argylls, he represented Inveraray on the family interest in the Scottish parliament from 1702 until the Union, and received a customs appointment (as collector of Port Glasgow) through his patron's influence. As one of the commissioners who signed the treaty, he sat in the first parliament of Great Britain (1707–8), and after the Hanoverian succession represented the Glasgow burghs from 1716 to 1734, being elected with Argyll's assistance.

In 1725 Campbell voted for the imposition of the malt tax in Scotland, and on this account became a particular target of popular protest against the tax. In Glasgow the mob, after taking possession of the city and obstructing the officers of excise from carrying out their duty, proceeded to the Shawfield mansion and completely demolished the interior. In due course Campbell received £9000 from the city as compensation. Soon afterwards he sold Shawfield and purchased the island of Islay. By this time his wealth was making him increasingly independent-minded. The second duke of Argyll eventually retaliated after several provocations, and dropped him as his nominee for Glasgow in the 1734 election. Contrary to Campbell's boasts, he did not find an alternative seat 'on his own legs'. He died on 8 June 1753, aged eighty-two. His first marriage, to Margaret Leckie in 1695, produced three sons and three daughters; his second, on 4 April 1714 to Catherine, the daughter of Henry Erskine, third Lord Cardross, and the widow of Sir William Denholm, bt, of Westshields, one daughter.

T. F. HENDERSON, *rev.* D. W. HAYTON

Sources M. D. Young, ed., *The parliaments of Scotland: burgh and shire commissioners*, 1 (1992), 100–01 · J. M. Simpson, 'Campbell, Daniel', HoP, *Commons, 1715–54* · HoP, *Commons, 1690–1715* [draft] · R. Wodrow, *Analecta, or, Materials for a history of remarkable providences, mostly relating to Scotch ministers and Christians*, ed. [M. Leishman], 4, Maitland Club, 60 (1843), 68, 171 · R. M. Sunter, *Patronage and politics in Scotland, 1707–1832* (1986), 199–209

Archives Mitchell L., Glas., business and legal papers | NA Scot., Hamilton MSS · NA Scot., Montrose MSS

Campbell, Sir David (1889–1978), physician, was born at Patna, Ayrshire, on 6 May 1889, the son of Agnes Smith Campbell, a seamstress. He was educated, by scholarships throughout, at Ayr Academy and at Glasgow University, where he graduated BSc and MA with honours in 1911 and MB ChB with honours in 1916, the most distinguished graduate of his year. He served as captain and then acting major in the Royal Army Medical Corps from 1916 to 1919 and in France in 1918 was awarded the MC as an immediate decoration in the field. On demobilization he returned to Glasgow as assistant to the renowned Professor Ralph Stockman in materia medica and therapeutics and in 1921 became Pollok lecturer in materia medica and pharmacology. On 4 August the same year Campbell married Margaret (*b.* 1890/91), a schoolteacher, daughter of Alexander Lyle, head teacher at Kerse near Grangemouth, and his wife, Isabella Paterson. Campbell often said that this was by far the best thing he had ever done. There were no children. In 1924 he took his MD with honours with a thesis on rheumatoid arthritis, winning the coveted Bellahouston gold medal. He spent 1925–6 as Rockefeller medical fellow at Johns Hopkins University, and in 1928 published *A Handbook of Therapeutics*, a great advance in its time on most preceding textbooks in the subject. During this period he was physician to out-patients (1920–29) and later assistant physician (1929–30) to the Western Infirmary, Glasgow.

The phase of major public achievement in Campbell's career opened with his appointment to the regius chair of materia medica in Aberdeen in 1930. Within two years he was dean of the faculty, a post he held for twenty-seven years until his retirement in 1959. He found the Aberdeen school in an early stage of outward-looking reform, and accelerated the process immensely. His shrewdness, pawky humour, tight mental discipline, nice judicial sense, and firmness with opposition made him a formidable chairman and administrator. Several major and beneficial appointments were largely to his credit, notably those of James Learmonth in surgery, Dugald Baird in obstetrics, and John Stirling Young in pathology. He put his influence behind the creation of an imaginative medical complex on the spacious heights of Foresterhill, to include the clinical and related departments of the university and soon to become the envy of many other medical schools. At the same time he ran an efficient department and was a conscientious and approachable teacher: his lecture notes, meticulously written out as they were meant to be read, with nicely judged classical allusion and quotation, bear witness to a medical scholarliness regrettably all but dead. His lectures on tea, tobacco, and alcohol are particularly remembered.

In 1936 Campbell joined the General Medical Council as representative of Aberdeen University and in 1949 became its president, serving also as chairman of its disciplinary committee. The challenges he met there on a larger scale were similar to those he had faced earlier in Aberdeen, and the same qualities again served him well.

Those post-war years were a time of radical and potentially stressful change for medical education and practice, and a more volatile personality than Campbell's might have served these causes less well than he did. He resigned from the council in 1961.

Campbell was knighted in 1953. He received the honorary degree of LLD from the universities of Glasgow, Liverpool, Dublin, and Aberdeen and of DCL from Durham. He was a fellow of the Royal Society of Edinburgh and of the royal colleges of physicians of London and of Glasgow.

In his long retirement Campbell was a kenspeckle figure often seen on the Aberdeen golf links and occasionally in the medical school. He excelled in golf and also in billiards: he is believed in Aberdeen to have been billiards champion of the Athenaeum. For many years he organized, with the flair and efficiency once devoted to more serious things, an annual golf competition for which he was the handicapper, later presenting the Ashley Mackintosh cup to the winners at the annual dinner of the Aberdeen Medico-Chirurgical Society; year by year the company waited affectionately for the well-known references in his presentation speech, not only to the competition but to settled convictions of Campbell himself—rabbits and tigers in handicapping, and the best of all arrangements being a committee of one, with powers.

Campbell died from cardiac failure at his home, 252 North Deeside Road, Milltimber, Peterculter, Aberdeenshire, on 30 May 1978. Lady Campbell survived him.

WILLIAM WALKER, *rev.*

Sources private information (1986) • personal knowledge (1986) • b. cert. • m. cert. • d. cert. • *The Times* (15 June 1978) • *WWW*
Likenesses A. Morrocco, portrait, Council Chamber of the General Medical Council
Wealth at death £41,065.99: confirmation, 26 Oct 1978, *CCI*

Campbell, David Robb (1874/5–1934), labour leader, was born in Belfast, the son of an insurance agent. The family was protestant; his father belonged to the Orange order. Educated in Belfast, Davy, as he was known, also went into insurance. He developed an interest in trade unionism and became the secretary of the life assurance agents' association in the city. As such, he won a seat in 1906 on the Belfast Trades Council, the focus of the labour movement in northern Ireland, and served as its president from 1909. He married, and he and his wife, Sarah Mary, had at least one son.

Unlike many union colleagues, David Campbell was an ideological socialist, and engaged in the Independent Labour Party (ILP) and the Belfast Socialist Society. The Belfast ILP, dominated by William Walker until 1911, identified with the British Labour Party and co-operated only gingerly with the Dublin-based labour movement, which inclined to Irish nationalism. Campbell, however, seemed happy to work with the Irish Trade Union Congress (ITUC), of which he was president in 1911 and treasurer from 1912 to 1918. The divergence between Walker and Campbell grew sharper as Irish home rule became a serious possibility after 1910. Radical socialists like Campbell feared that a surge of popular Unionism among protestant working men could engulf the labour movement in Belfast and divert it from the business of class politics unless it maintained a distinct identity. He joined the local branch of James Connolly's Socialist Party of Ireland (SPI) in 1910.

When Connolly, the most influential Irish socialist, settled in Belfast in 1911, his aim was to wean northern labour away from Unionism and towards all-Ireland institutions. One of his most valuable allies proved to be Campbell, who reckoned home rule inevitable. In the ensuing controversy Labour unionists were undermined by the British Labour Party's home rule sympathies. Campbell attended Connolly's Socialist Unity conference in Dublin at Easter 1912, when the non-Unionist segment of the ILP merged with the SPI to form a new Independent Labour Party of Ireland or ILP(I). His support also helped Connolly induce the ITUC to raise a political levy and restyle itself the Irish Trade Union Congress and Labour Party (ITUC&LP). Campbell and his comrades, Thomas Johnson and Danny McDevitt, carried the Belfast Trades Council with them in endorsing the ITUC&LP—but only because Unionists were deserting the council in droves.

Campbell deplored the mass expulsion of Catholic workers from the Belfast shipyards and engineering factories in July 1912 and gave assistance to the Expelled Workers' Committee. In his view sectarian violence was incited by tories, who conspired to fragment the working class: loyalists were dupes of the bourgeois Carson. The anti-war ILP(I) ceased to operate in Belfast in 1914. Martial law in the south after the Easter rising (1916) temporarily meant that Johnson and Campbell led the ITUC&LP by default. They went to London to urge Lloyd George to free gaoled trade union leaders and counsel him against partition. In April 1918 they infuriated Ulster protestants by opposing conscription. To Campbell's anger, the Irish Labour Party and Trade Union Congress (ILP&TUC, previously ITUC&LP) stood aside in December 1918 in favour of Sinn Féin at the general election.

Campbell fell back on the Belfast Labour Party (organized by the Trades Council). Having held no seats on the Belfast corporation since 1911, Labour managed to take thirteen out of sixty in the municipal elections of 15 January 1920—due largely to the one-off use of proportional representation. Councillor D. R. Campbell was leader of the Labour group. Further mass expulsions of Catholic workers in July led him to join Sinn Féin councillors in calling a special meeting of the corporation to demand reinstatement. Loyalists now branded Labour the cat's paw of republicanism. Campbell tried to cancel the meeting, but the Unionist mayor decided to proceed on 31 July 1920, despite the public galleries being packed with aggressive loyalists, some waving guns. When the Labour councillors failed to appear, their credibility was lost. The party barely survived the political polarization which attended the intense sectarian strife of 1920–22. Socialism might assert the primacy of class politics; Ulster workers had other priorities.

While remaining involved with the ILP&TUC, Campbell entered a new career as a barrister, but felt aggrieved when trade unions refused to entrust him with their law-suits. He died at his home, 11 Kimberley Street, Belfast, on 14 January 1934, aged fifty-nine. His wife survived him.

PETER COLLINS

Sources H. Patterson, *Class conflict and sectarianism: the protestant working class and the Belfast labour movement, 1868–1920* (1980) • A. Morgan, *Labour and partition: the Belfast working class 1905–1923* (1991) • A. Mitchell, *Labour in Irish politics, 1890–1930* (1974) • G. S. Walker, *The politics of frustration: Harry Midgley and the failure of Labour in Northern Ireland* (1985) • d. cert. • *CGPLA NIre.* (1934)
Wealth at death £79 9s. 6d.: probate, 24 April 1934, *CGPLA NIre.*

Campbell, Donald (*d.* 1562), abbot of Coupar Angus, was the fourth son of Archibald *Campbell, second earl of Argyll (*d.* 1513), and his wife, Elizabeth Stewart. He matriculated at St Salvator's College, St Andrews, in 1522. As a graduate and a clerk in Argyll diocese, he was presented to the abbacy of Coupar Angus on 25 May 1525. Parliament ratified his presentation on 14 June 1526 and the abbey was entrusted to him for eight months and then *in titulum* with the requirement he take the vows and habit, otherwise the abbacy would be considered vacant. He visited France and was naturalized there in May 1530. Yet he took his seat in parliament from 1532. In May 1533 he was appointed commissioner of the chapter-general of the Cistercians for visiting Scottish houses of the order for five years; but he dilapidated the patrimony of his own abbacy in favour of kinsmen and friends. He was present in France again in 1536, gained appointment as a senator of the college of justice in July 1541, became a lord of the articles in the parliaments of March and December 1543, and a member of the privy council in June 1545. He sided with Cardinal Beaton in 1543 in opposing English demands for the custody of the infant Mary, queen of Scots.

In 1546 Campbell sought a passport for a year and was expected in Rome. Supported by Governor Arran, he gained the temporality of the bishopric of Dunkeld in 1547 and again in 1549 but failed to obtain papal provision as bishop. His hopes of acquiring the archbishopric of Glasgow were also deflected. In 1549 he attended the provincial council of the Scottish church, summoned to effect internal reform, but was absent in France in 1551 and stayed there until Whitsun 1552. In 1554 he became keeper of the privy seal, a position he held until his death, and was nominated for the bishopric of Brechin perhaps as early as December 1557, but yet again failed to secure papal provision. In April 1558 he attended the burning of the protestant martyr Walter Milne (or Mill) at St Andrews. By May 1559 he had decided to 'put on secular weed' (*CSP Scot.*, *1547–63*, 212) and agreed to the request of the protestant lords of the congregation to reform his monastery by burning all images and altars, prohibiting the mass, and removing monastic habits, and also to support the congregation in parliament. He duly attended the Reformation Parliament of 1560 which annulled papal authority, prohibited the celebration of the mass, and approved a protestant confession of faith. Campbell died between 16 and 20 December 1562. Several of his bastard sons were legitimated.

JAMES KIRK

Sources *APS*, *1424–1567* • J. M. Anderson, ed., *Early records of the University of St Andrews*, Scottish History Society, 3rd ser., 8 (1926) • *The letters of James V*, ed. R. K. Hannay and D. Hay (1954) • C. Rogers, ed., *Rental book of the Cistercian abbey of Coupar Angus*, 2 vols., Grampian Club, 17 (1879–80) • J. M. Thomson and others, eds., *Registrum magni sigilli regum Scotorum / The register of the great seal of Scotland*, 11 vols. (1882–1914), vols. 3–4 • M. Livingstone, D. Hay Fleming, and others, eds., *Registrum secreti sigilli regum Scotorum / The register of the privy seal of Scotland*, 1–5 (1908–57) • *Scots peerage*, 1.336 • G. Brunton and D. Haig, *An historical account of the senators of the college of justice, from its institution in MDXXXII* (1832) • *LP Henry VIII*, vols. 18–21 • *CSP Scot.*, *1547–63* • H. Paton, ed., *The clan Campbell*, 8 vols. (1913–22) • N. D. Campbell, 'Two papers from the Argyll charter chest', *SHR*, 21 (1923–4), 140–43 • D. E. R. Watt, ed., *Fasti ecclesiae Scoticanae medii aevi ad annum 1638*, [2nd edn], Scottish RS, new ser., 1 (1969) • J. Dowden, *The bishops of Scotland … prior to the Reformation*, ed. J. M. Thomson (1912)

Campbell, Donald, of Duchernan (1665–1722), Church of Scotland minister, only son of Patrick Campbell of Quoycrook (*d.* 1705) and his wife, Helen Bayne, was born at Quoycrook, Halkirk parish, Caithness, on 1 August 1665. He graduated MA at King's College, Aberdeen, on 15 July 1686, and may thereafter have studied divinity at Edinburgh. On 31 December 1691 he was ordained minister of the parish of Glassary in Argyll, where his family originated, being descended from the Mac-Ivor Campbells of Lergachonzie. He remained there as minister for the rest of his life, declining an opportunity to return to Caithness when he received a call to the parish of Watten there in 1699.

In June 1692 Campbell married Jean, daughter of Patrick Campbell of Torblaren, minister of Glenary. They had five daughters, who all married in the county, and two sons, the elder of whom, James, afterwards became minister of Kilbrandon. When his father died Campbell sold the Caithness property. The family had previously acquired the estate of Duchernan in Glassary, and they were henceforth known as Campbells of Duchernan until 1800, when the estate passed into other hands owing to the financial difficulties of Campbell's grandson Duncan, who died in that year. The manse of Glassary was chiefly constructed at Campbell's expense, using money inherited from his father-in-law. It was one of the first manses in Argyll, and was remarkable for its numerous windows.

Campbell took an active, supervisory role in church affairs, being one of the trustees appointed to manage the public funds of the synod of Argyll. From 1716 onwards, however, he was crippled by gout and had to be carried to the church to preach on Sundays. He was the author of *Sacramental Meditations on the Sufferings and Death of Christ*, published in Edinburgh in 1698, which was based on Gaelic sermons preached to his Glassary congregation. These went through many editions, including a Gaelic one published in 1800. Campbell wrote several other devotional works. He died at his home at the manse, Glassary, on 28 March 1722.

ALEXANDER DU TOIT

Sources *Fasti Scot.*, new edn, 4.6–8 • *N&Q*, 3rd ser., 6 (1864), 171–2 • *Edinburgh Christian Instructor*, 4th ser., 1 (1838), 111–16, 568–9 • 'Abstracts of entries relating to Campbells in the sheriff court books of Argyll at Inveraray', *The clan Campbell: abstracts from the Campbell collection formed by Sir Duncan Campbell*, ed. H. Paton, 1 (1913), 14, 50, 52, 68, 75, 106, 116, 123, 140, 146, 156 • C. Innes, ed.,

Fasti Aberdonenses … 1494–1854, Spalding Club, 26 (1854), xxxiv, 531 · L. R. Timperley, ed., *A directory of landownership in Scotland, c.1770*, Scottish RS, new ser., 5 (1976), 32 · G. H. Johnston, *The heraldry of the Campbells*, 2 vols. (1920), 2.76

Wealth at death Duchernan estate valued at £13 10s. od. p.a., 1751: Timperley, ed., *Directory*

Campbell, Donald (1751–1804), army officer and travel writer, of Barbreck, Argyll, is best known for his *A journey over land to India … by Donald Campbell of Barbreck, who formerly commanded a regiment of cavalry in the service of the nabob of the Carnatic: in a series of letters to his son* (1795). The son in question was Frederick William *Campbell (1782–1846), who was born to Campbell and his wife, Mary, illegitimate daughter of Lord Frederick Campbell (1729–1816). The journey was made by way of Belgium, Tyrol, Venice, Alexandria, Aleppo, Diyarbakır, Mosul, Baghdad, Bushehr, Bombay, and Goa, all of which places and others are described in the work. Campbell was shipwrecked in the Indian Ocean, and imprisoned by Haider Ali of Mysore, but subsequently released. The book enjoyed much popularity. A new edition appeared in 1796, and an abridged version was published in the same year as *Narrative of Adventures*, and a sixth edition was reached in 1808. The third part of the travels, relating to the shipwreck and imprisonment of the writer, was published as a chapbook, *Shipwreck and Captivity of D. C.* (1800?). Campbell also published a *Letter to the Marquis of Lorn on the Present Times* in 1798, in which he protested against party factions in connection with the war with France. He died at Hutton in Essex on 5 June 1804.

STANLEY LANE-POOLE, *rev.* ELIZABETH BAIGENT

Sources *GM*, 1st ser., 74 (1804), 600 · Burke, *Peerage* (1939) · D. Campbell, *A journey over land to India* (1795)

Campbell, Donald Malcolm (1921–1967), land and water speed record-holder, was born on 23 March 1921 at Canbury, Kingston Hill, Surrey, the only son and younger child of Sir Malcolm *Campbell (1885–1948), racing motorist, and his second wife, Dorothy Evelyn, daughter of Major William Whittall. He left Uppingham School in 1937, following rheumatic fever, to serve with a Lloyd's underwriting firm. Invalided from the RAF in 1940, having been rejected for flying training, he spent a frustrating war as a special constable. In the late 1940s he invested in the Kine Engineering Company of Redhill, where he became managing director and fifty per cent shareholder. Always involved in his father's ventures, he decided after Sir Malcolm's death in 1948 to defend his water title, set in 1939 at 141.74 m.p.h., using his father's boat. Only after unsuccessful attempts in 1949, 1950, and 1951 did he seek and find funds for a new boat, called, like all his cars and boats, *Bluebird*. With this all-metal hydroplane, powered by two Metro-Vickers Beryll jet engines, he regained the record on Ullswater on 23 July 1955 at 202.32, raising this on six successive occasions, ultimately to 276.33 m.p.h. on Lake Dumbleyoung, Australia, on 31 December 1964.

In September 1960 Campbell turned to the land record. Driving a *Bluebird*, newly designed by Kenneth and Lewis Norris, using a Bristol-Siddeley Proteus jet engine, he sustained a hairline skull fracture in a crash at 365 m.p.h.

Donald Malcolm Campbell (1921–1967), by Peter Keen, 1956

while assaulting the land record of 394.2 m.p.h., set by John Cobb in 1947. Three years later, another new *Bluebird* was prevented from going for the record by floods at Lake Eyre, Australia, a delay which brought much criticism of Campbell from his backers, led by Sir Alfred Owen. But the following July Campbell returned to cover the measured kilometre at an average speed of 403.1 m.p.h. for the two runs, becoming the first person to take a shaft-driven vehicle over 400 m.p.h. and to break both land and water speed records in the same year. The next year the American Craig Breedlove took a jet-propelled car over the distance at 600 m.p.h. At the time of his death Campbell was unsuccessfully seeking backers for a jet-driven car to go through the sound barrier.

Campbell now turned back to the water. In 1966 a more powerful Bristol-Siddeley Orpheus jet engine with a 5000 lb thrust was fitted to *Bluebird*, intended to take the record over 300 m.p.h. After two months of frustrating delay, caused by bad weather and technical difficulties which reduced public interest and renewed public criticism, Campbell finally made his attempt on Coniston on 4 January 1967. On the outward run he achieved 297 m.p.h. Returning even faster to get his average over 300 m.p.h., Campbell's fears were confirmed: at this speed the bow lifted, and the boat somersaulted and plunged into the lake. The remains of Campbell's boat were located in 2000 and removed from the water in March 2001. His body was recovered from the lake in May 2001 and, after a funeral at St Andrew's Church, Coniston, was buried in the parish churchyard. In October 2002 an inquest returned a verdict of accidental death.

Though a trained engineer, an enthusiastic and effective advocate of his own cause, courageous and deeply patriotic, Campbell was not an easy man. He seemed driven to defend and challenge his father's achievement, but his enthusiasms were too boyish and his concerns overshadowed by the public shift in interest to the achievements of space scientists and astronauts. Campbell's crusade became uninteresting and irrelevant to the New World and advertisers were finding more rewarding ventures for sponsorship. He lived into a world which had outgrown him. He was appointed CBE in 1957.

Campbell married three times: on 8 September 1945, Daphne Margaret Harvey Harvey (*b.* 1923/4), daughter of William Calvert, engineer (marriage dissolved 1952); in 1952, Dorothy, daughter of Amos McKegg of Palmerston North, New Zealand (marriage dissolved 1957); in 1958, Antoinette Maria (Tonia Bern, the cabaret singer), daughter of Antoine Joseph Bern of Belgium. His third wife survived him. He had a daughter, Georgina, born in 1946.

H. G. PITT, *rev.*

Sources *The Times* (5 Jan 1967) • D. Campbell and A. W. Mitchell, *Into the water barrier* (1955) • A. Knowles, *With Campbell at Coniston* (1967) • A. Knowles and D. Campbell, *Donald Campbell C.B.E.* (1969) • D. A. de S. Young-James, *Donald Campbell: an informal biography* (1968) • L. Villa and T. Gray, *The record-breakers: Sir Malcolm and Donald Campbell* (1969) • b. cert. • m. cert. [Daphne Margaret Harvey Harvey] • *CGPLA Eng. & Wales* (1967) • *The Times* (26 Oct 2002)
Archives FILM BFI NFTVA, documentary footage • BFI NFTVA, news footage • BFI NFTVA, *Record breakers*, 1955 • BFI NFTVA, *This week*, 4 Jan 1967 | SOUND BL NSA, documentary recording
Likenesses photographs, *c.*1927–1967, Hult. Arch. • P. Keen, photograph, 1956, NPG [*see illus.*] • photographs, repro. in Knowles and Campbell, *Donald Campbell* • portrait, NPG
Wealth at death £38,066: probate, 15 June 1967, *CGPLA Eng. & Wales*

Campbell, Dorothea Primrose (1792–1863), poet and novelist, was born on 4 May 1792 in the Shetland Islands (perhaps at Laxfirth), the eldest of the many children of Duncan Campbell, a surgeon, and Elizabeth Campbell. Her grandfather had left the family heavily indebted. At sixteen, after her father's death, she approached the Inverness publisher J. Young, timidly hoping to make money from her poems. Young published her first volume, *Poems* (1811), by subscription, for her sole benefit. The title page bears her full name and a couplet from James Thomson. The poems are remarkably accomplished for her age, encompassing imaginary and actual material and celebrating local scenery and legends. Francis Jeffrey found much promise and originality in them. Campbell's expressed attitudes to Shetland are ambivalent: there is on the one hand delight and pride, on the other a longing for wider horizons.

A teacher by 1812, Campbell opened her own school at Lerwick in 1813. In 1816 she published a second edition of *Poems*, dedicated to Sir Walter Scott, with whom she corresponded. This work reflects a new melancholy, dwelling on death, on farewell to childhood scenes, and on insults heaped on poverty. She reprinted most of her earlier poems, identifying 'To the Evening Star' as written in 1803. Her subscription list ranges from London to Lerwick; Scott took four copies. Her introduction mentions her father's misfortunes and early death, but the publisher's bankruptcy dashed any hopes of profit. Campbell kept teaching after her own school foundered as a result of her illness and her mother's opium addiction.

For Campbell's last known publishing venture she assumed an air of proud indifference. Her novel, *Harley Radington: a Tale*, was published in 1821 by A. K. Newman; her payment consisted of twenty free copies. She drew both on canonical authors such as Chaucer, Shakespeare, and Goldsmith, and on recent, little-known women writers whose experience paralleled her own: the Scotswoman and teacher Anne Bannerman, the Englishwoman and traveller Eliza Fay, and Margaret Chalmers, who preceded Campbell as a distinguished Shetland poet admired by Scott, and who shared many of her subscribers.

Campbell's novel is a 'national tale' which deserves consideration with those of Scott and others. She supplied it with footnotes and a glossary on the life, customs, and superstitions of Zetland (Shetland), where most of it is set. Her narrator, Harley, grows up in fashionable London, not knowing (though clues are dropped) that his mother is a 'female adventurer' whose humble Shetland origins are her guilty secret. The rest of the plot is upstaged by his exploration of his roots, rendered colourfully and humorously during his period of dumbfounded revulsion, lyrically as he discovers a wider Shetland life of landscape, culture, and economic problems. Campbell's accounts of folk customs and beliefs—such as women raising a storm to wreck a ship—are particularly striking.

Newman thought well enough of *Harley Radington* to promise Campbell cash for another novel. It seems she never wrote this, though she may have contributed to magazines. She impressed the Methodist preacher and scholar Adam Clarke when he visited Shetland in 1826, and remained his correspondent.

Campbell's earnings from teaching paid for a younger brother's education and supported her mother's old age, but she could never save a penny. In 1841 she was invited to England by descendants of Clarke, who then went bankrupt and could not employ her according to promise. She applied for jobs first as teacher, then as matron of a public institution, as housekeeper, or 'even' as 'Sister in one of the Hospitals', but English employers looked askance at her age and origins. In 1844 she had not worked for a year and was destitute in London. She applied for help to the Royal Literary Fund: humbly, on grounds of need, though her referees, Jeffrey and the traveller and medical writer James Copland, stressed her literary merit. A grant of £30 enabled her to take up a teaching job at Sevenoaks, Kent. She died on 6 January 1863 at an Aged Governesses' Asylum in Kentish Town, London.

ISOBEL GRUNDY

Sources Royal Literary Fund, London, MS 1093 • NL Scot., MSS 3278, fol. 102; 3888, fol. 20; 3890, fols. 89, 208, 261 • D. P. Campbell, *Poems* (1816) [insert in BL copy, BL 11645.bbb.41]
Archives Royal Literary Fund, MS 1093 | NL Scot., Scott MSS

Campbell [*married names* Hurd, Howe], **Dorothy Iona** (1883–1945), golfer, was born on 24 March 1883 at 1 Carlton Terrace, Edinburgh, the daughter of William Campbell, a metal merchant, and his wife, Emily Mary Tipper. Her father was a native of Edinburgh, but her mother was born in England and they were married in London in 1861. She had several older siblings, all of whom were born in Edinburgh.

Dorothy Campbell learned to play golf at North Berwick, about 20 miles east of Edinburgh, under the instruction of the renowned Ben Sayers. She is reported as stating that she began playing at the age of ten and won her first medal when she was twelve. In 1897 the British ladies' championship came to Scotland for the first time and Dorothy's older sister reached the quarter-final stage. The Campbells did not venture out of Scotland to compete in subsequent years, so Dorothy's début in championship golf was at the age of twenty. In June 1903 she played in the inaugural Scottish ladies' close championship at St Andrews and reached the semi-finals. In May 1904 the British championship was played at the Scottish links of Troon. Dorothy represented Scotland for the first time in the preceding matches against England and Ireland, beating both her opponents. She then advanced to the semi-finals of the championship, where she was defeated by Lottie Dod, the eventual winner.

On 25 May 1905 at Cromer in Norfolk, Dorothy Campbell took part in the historic first international between the British Isles and America, which inspired the eventual establishment of the biennial Curtis cup matches, and she contributed to the overall victory of the home side. This match was followed by the ladies' internationals between England, Ireland, and Scotland, in which she again won both matches. Then in the British championship she won the preliminary stroke competition and again reached the semi-finals. After returning home, she took her first Scottish title with a nineteenth-hole victory over the holder, Molly Graham, on her home course of North Berwick.

In 1906 Campbell made her third appearance in the semi-finals of the British championship and retained her Scottish crown. In 1907 her form early in the season boded well. She took first place on both days of the Ranelagh stroke-play tournament in April, leading Scotland to victory in the international division. However, a bout of influenza the week before the British championship meeting forced her withdrawal from the ladies' internationals and ruled her out of contention for the championship. Nevertheless, she subsequently managed to reach the final of the Scottish close, though she lost the title to Frances Teacher.

The British championship was held at St Andrews in May 1908 and Dorothy Campbell contested the final against her fellow Scottish international Maud Titterton. They attracted a gallery of several thousand spectators, including the famous open champion Old Tom Morris, who died two days after the final. In adverse weather conditions which made the course almost unplayable Titterton squared the match on the final hole and won the championship on the nineteenth. Campbell went on to take the Scottish close title for a third time.

1909 was a pivotal year in Dorothy Campbell's career. In May at Birkdale she led Scotland to victory in the ladies' internationals before taking the British championship title for the first time, at the age of twenty-six. She then contested her fifth consecutive Scottish close final, losing 3 and 1 to Elsie Kyle. In the autumn she crossed the Atlantic to compete in the US ladies' championship at the Merion cricket club, Philadelphia. In the final she defeated Nonna Barlow to become the first player to win the two most important titles in ladies' golf, the British and US championships. After this achievement she settled in Canada, taking up residence in Hamilton, Ontario.

As a result of her move Campbell was unable to defend her British title in 1910. However, in that year she won the first of three consecutive Canadian ladies' championships in Toronto before travelling to Chicago, where she successfully defended her US title, also winning the preliminary stroke-play event. In 1911, accompanied by four North American golfers, she sailed from New York to Glasgow on board the *Caledonia* to take part in the British championship at Portrush in Ireland. Just days after her arrival she lined up for Scotland in the ladies' internationals, but lost both matches, to May Ross (*née* Hezlet) of Ireland and Cecil Leitch of England. However, her form evidently improved over the next few days, as she advanced through the championship to defeat Violet Hezlet, a local player, by 3 and 2 in the final, confirming her status as the best female golfer in the world. Though she retained the Canadian title later that year, she lost at the semi-final stage of the US championship to Margaret Curtis by 4 and 3.

After winning her third and final Canadian title in 1912, Campbell married J. V. Hurd on 11 February 1913. She went to live in Pittsburgh and her golfing career took second place to motherhood. However, she managed some notable performances in the late 1910s. In 1916 she won the preliminary stroke-play event at the US championship, and two years later at Pinehurst, North Carolina, she took the North and South championship, an important event in the American golfing calendar. She won the North and South for a second time in 1920 and reached the final of the US championship, where she was defeated by the defending champion, Alexa Stirling. A third win in the North and South came in 1921, when it is said that during the final she twice holed out from 40 yards using a goose-necked mashie she called Thomas.

In or about 1923 Mrs Hurd moved to Philadelphia and joined the Merion cricket club, where she had won her first US title. At about this time she recognized that her style of golf, with no wrist movement, a two-fisted grip, and a broad swing, was somewhat out of date. While it produced a straight but short shot, those using more modern techniques were gaining more length. Under the guidance of the professional at Merion, George Sayers, son of her old mentor at North Berwick, she adopted the Vardon grip and greater hand action. In September 1924, at the Rhode Island country club, she put her new style into action to remarkable effect, winning her third US championship. At the age of forty-one she became the oldest winner in the championship's history, a record that still stood at the end of the twentieth century.

Dorothy Campbell Hurd visited the British Isles in 1928, played on the Scottish international team for the first time since 1911, and reached the quarter-finals of the British championship. After returning home she made her last appearance in the semi-finals of the US championship at Hot Springs, Virginia. On her last competitive visit to Britain in 1930 she again lined up for Scotland in the ladies' internationals, winning two matches by 7 and 6 and losing the third by one hole. She later married Edward Howe. She died tragically on 20 March 1945 when she fell underneath an express train as it left Yemassee, South Carolina. She had been staying over the winter at the Tidalholm guest house in Beaufort, South Carolina, and had planned to take the train for New York. A funeral service and cremation took place at Ardsley, New York, on 24 March.

Dorothy Campbell was the first woman golfer to score major victories on both sides of the Atlantic and thus the first to make a truly international impact on the game. Her two British, three US, and three Canadian titles, won before the advent of women's professional golf, secure her position among the greatest female players in the history of the sport. In 1978 she was inducted into the World Golf Hall of Fame, and in 1991 her name was added to the Canadian Golf Hall of Fame. PAUL GORRY

Sources *The Times* (24 March 1945) • *Beaufort Times* (29 March 1945) • *Beaufort Gazette* (30 March 1945) • b. cert. • census returns, 1881 • *Irish Times* (11 May 1911) • M. Hezlet, *Ladies' golf* (1907) • D. Seaton, 'Campbell wins amateur double', www.north-berwick.co.uk/campbell.html, Jan 2001 • *Burke's Who's who in sport* (1922) • *USGA record book, 1895–1959* (Far Hills, New Jersey, 1960) • www.wgv.com [World Golf Hall of Fame profile], Jan 2001

Campbell, Duncan, **first Lord Campbell** (*d.* **1453**). *See under* Campbell family (*per.* *c.*1300–1453).

Campbell, Duncan, of Glenorchy (*c.***1443–1513**). *See under* Campbell family of Glenorchy (*per.* 1432–1631).

Campbell, Sir Duncan, of Glenorchy, **first baronet** (**1551x4–1631**). *See under* Campbell family of Glenorchy (*per.* 1432–1631).

Campbell, Duncan (*c.***1680–1730**), soothsayer, was born in Lapland, the son of Archibald Campbell, seaman, and his wife, an eminent Laplander whom he met after being shipwrecked there. Following the death of his mother, Campbell returned to Scotland with his father. Being deaf and mute he received instruction in reading from a 'learned divine of the University of Glasgow' (Defoe, 33), and having already demonstrated remarkable gifts of prophecy went to London in 1694, where his predictions soon caught the attention of fashionable society. Notwithstanding the large sums he obtained from those who consulted him, Campbell ran up large debts. To escape his creditors he went to Rotterdam, where he enlisted as a soldier. On returning after a few years to London, he read a wealthy young widow's fortune in his own favour, and, having taken a house in Monmouth Street, he found himself a greater centre of attraction than ever. *The Tatler* revealed that 'all his visitants come to him full of expectations, and pay his own rate for the interpretations they

Duncan Campbell (*c.***1680–1730**), by Michael Vandergucht, pubd 1720 (after Thomas Hill)

put upon his shrugs and nods' (Bond, *Tatler*, 2.121). According to *The Spectator*:

> every one has heard of the famous conjuror who, according to the opinion of the vulgar, has studied himself dumb. Be that as it will, the blind Tiresias was not more famous in Greece than this dumb artist has been for some years last past in the cities of London and Westminster. (Bond, *Spectator*, 4.512)

Among those whom Campbell seems to have particularly impressed was Daniel Defoe, who in 1720 published *The History of the Life and Adventures of Mr Duncan Campbell*, the first of several pamphlet accounts of Campbell's life and remarkable predictions. Defoe was also the author of the third section of *Mr Campbell's Pacquet* (1720) and may well have written *A Spy upon the Conjuror* (1724), which is also attributed to Eliza Haywood. About one-third of this pamphlet consists of letters, purportedly written by Campbell's clients, many of whom sought his advice on problems relating to courtship and marital relations. Defoe's *The Dumb Projector* appeared in 1725 and his original life, which had already passed through several editions, was republished in 1728 as *The Supernatural Philosopher*. Like other persons of eminence, Campbell succeeded in obtaining the notice of royalty. The *Daily Post* of 4 May 1720 reported that 'Last Monday Mr. Campbell, the deaf and dumb gentleman—introduced by Colonel Carr—kissed the king's hand, and presented to his majesty "The History of his Life and Adventures", which was by his majesty most graciously received' (Lee, 1.323).

By 1726 Campbell appears to have become a vendor of miraculous medicines. He published *The Friendly Daemon*, in which he gave an account of how, on the advice of his good genius, he had been cured of a long illness by use of the loadstone. A postscript informed readers that at 'Dr. Campbell's house, in Buckingham Court, over against Old Man's Coffee House, at Charing Cross, they may be readily furnished with his "Pulvis Miraculosus", and finest sort of Egyptian loadstones' (Wilson, 3.484). According to Defoe, Campbell was married, although no further details of his wife are known; he died after a severe illness in 1730. A further account of his life, *Secret Memoirs of the Late Mr Duncan Campbell*, appeared in 1732. Among the subscribers to the volume were the duke of Argyll and other members of the nobility. T. F. HENDERSON, *rev.* DAVID TURNER

Sources [D. Defoe], *The history of the life and adventures of Mr Duncan Campbell* (1720) • D. Campbell, *Secret memoirs of the late Mr Duncan Campbell, the famous deaf and dumb gentleman* (1732) • R. Steele and J. Addison, *The Spectator*, ed. D. Bond, 5 vols. (1965) • D. F. Bond, ed., *The Tatler*, 3 vols. (1987) • *Daniel Defoe: his life, and recently discovered writings*, ed. W. Lee, 3 vols. (1869) • W. Wilson, *Memoirs of the life and times of Daniel De Foe: containing a review of his writings, and his opinion on a variety of important matters, civil and ecclesiastical*, 3 vols. (1830) • J. Caulfield, *Portraits, memoirs, and characters, of remarkable persons, from the revolution in 1688 to the end of the reign of George II*, 4 vols. (1819–20) • [D. Campbell], *The friendly daemon, or, The generous apparition* (1726)

Likenesses Price, line engraving (after T. Hill), BM; repro. in Campbell, *Secret memoirs* • M. Vandergucht, line engraving (after T. Hill), BM, NPG; repro. in [Defoe], *History of the life and adventures of Mr Duncan Campbell* [*see illus.*] • engraving, repro. in Caulfield, *Portraits, memoirs, and characters*, vol. 2

Campbell, Eila Muriel Joice (1915–1994), university teacher and historian of cartography, was born on 31 December 1915 at Ropley, Hampshire, the eldest child of Walter Howard Claude Campbell (1894–1958), poultry farmer, and his wife, Lillian Muriel, *née* Locke (1884–1979). After military service Walter Campbell endeavoured to set up as a shopkeeper, with mixed success. A son, Peter, was born in 1926. From Bournemouth high school, Campbell studied at the diocesan teacher training college at Brighton from 1934 to 1936, and on qualifying taught at various girls' schools. Her lifelong association with Birkbeck College, which offered evening and weekend courses for people in employment, began in 1938 when she enrolled in the geography department under Professor Eva Taylor (1879–1966). On obtaining her BA in 1941, Campbell became a part-time assistant in the department while still a full-time schoolteacher, during the difficult wartime years. In 1945 she was appointed assistant lecturer, rising in 1948 to lecturer. She gained her MA with distinction in 1947.

During her time at Birkbeck, Campbell taught all aspects of human, regional, and physical geography, took her students on sometimes strenuous field trips, and introduced them to what had become her own enthusiasm: the histories of exploration and cartography. Her interest in the origins of settlement in wooded country, as she imagined Britain had been, led her to secure a research fellowship offered by the New Zealand Federation of University Women. In 1949 she sailed to New Zealand, where she held a visiting lectureship at Victoria University College, Wellington, and in the course of her research toured both islands, returning home via Fiji in 1950.

In her progress up the academic ladder at Birkbeck, then a college of the federal London University, Campbell followed in the wake of the much respected Eva Taylor, but none the less had to combat the hostility shown to intelligent and capable women. In 1963 she was appointed reader at London University, in respect of her Birkbeck post, but was unsuccessful when in 1965 she applied for a professorship at Bedford College, London. After spending the academic year 1965/6 as visiting professor in historical geography at Mickiewicz University, Posnan, Poland, she secured in 1970 the position of professor of geography and head of department at Birkbeck, which she held until 1981 when she became emeritus professor. She dealt competently—if on occasion undemocratically—with course planning, academic administration, and editorial work, and her participation in many societies carried her several times around the world and brought her a great many close friends. Campbell's beaming smile can be seen in many group photographs taken at congresses and other meetings over the years, often in the company of Helen Wallis (1924–1995), map librarian at the British Library, with whom she shared many interests.

Under Campbell's administration several undergraduate courses concerned with aspects of historical geography were introduced at Birkbeck. As an examiner in colleges of education she realized the need for teachers to be able to expand their geographical knowledge, and to this end she initiated taught masters' degrees, introducing the MSc in geography of the USA in 1966 and the MSc in historical geography in 1970.

Campbell was a co-editor, working under Henry Clifford Derby the series editor, for the *Domesday Geography of South-East England* (1962), which involved her in the analysis of the original folios, but her innovative work did not receive the acknowledgement it deserved. She contributed sixteen biographical articles to the fourteenth edition of the *Encyclopaedia Britannica* (1961–7). She also wrote school textbooks and spoke at numerous conferences, but published few scholarly articles, expending much of her time and effort on *Imago Mundi*, the leading international journal for the history of cartography, with which she was associated for forty-eight years. She was recruited to this by its editor, Leo Bagrow, who from his Amsterdam base expected Campbell to solicit and edit papers for this journal, while treating her very much as a hired help. Campbell endured this indignity, eventually took her place on the editorial board, and, on the retirement in 1972 of both editor and publisher, took over the editorship, which she held until her death.

Campbell joined most of the societies that covered her disciplines, where possible taking out life membership and generally serving on their councils, at which she was accustomed to dispense perceptive if acerbic comments and nuggets of wisdom. The Charles Close Society, concerned with the history of the Ordnance Survey, met in her department; she was a founder member in 1963 of the British Cartographic Society, a member of the Society of Women Geographers, of the Hakluyt Society (for the history of exploration), of the Society for Nautical Research, and of the Royal Geographical Society, receiving the Murchison award in 1979 for her distinguished service on its library and maps committee. She also served on numerous academic and administrative bodies. She served on the British National Committee for Geography and for six years chaired the Royal Society sub-committee for geography.

In addition to her extremely busy professional life, Campbell cared for her mother who lived with her from 1951 until her death at the age of ninety-five. She maintained a close relationship with her brother, and the three spent most holidays together. In the last decade of her life Campbell, a short and dumpy figure with poor sight, suffered various accidents and a mugging, each of which left her with cracked bones and other damage. She nevertheless continued travelling abroad and attending meetings until she was taken into a nursing home shortly before her death, in the Wellington Hospital, 27 Circus Road, St John's Wood, London, on 12 July 1994. At a celebration of her life, held at the Royal Geographic Society on 16 November 1994, those who had been her students recalled Campbell's concern for their academic progress, while those who knew her in the course of society or administrative business spoke warmly of her devotion and energy to each cause that she supported; all mentioned her indomitable character and her generous and friendly nature. ANITA MCCONNELL

Sources S. Tyacke, ed., *A celebration of the life and work of Eila M. J. Campbell, 1915–1994* (privately issued, 1994) • C. D. Smith and P. Barber, *Imago Mundi*, 47 (1995), 7–12 • Y. Hodson, *Sheetlines*, 41 (1994), 2 • P. Lawrence, *Cartographic Journal*, 31 (1994), 141–2 • W. R. Mead, 'Professor Eila Campbell', *The Independent* (26 July 1994), 11a • H. Wallis, 'Eila Muriel Joice Campbell, 1915–1994', *GJ*, 160 (1994), 361 • private information (2004) [P. Campbell] • personal knowledge (2004) • d. cert. • b. cert. • *CGPLA Eng. & Wales* (1994)
Archives BL
Wealth at death £350,230: probate, 5 Dec 1994, *CGPLA Eng. & Wales*

Elizabeth Campbell [Gunning], **duchess of Argyll and** *suo jure* **Baroness Hamilton of Hameldon** (*bap.* **1733**, *d.* **1790**), by Sir Joshua Reynolds, 1758–9

Campbell [*née* Gunning], **Elizabeth**, **duchess of Argyll and** ***suo jure*** **Baroness Hamilton of Hameldon** [*other married name* Elizabeth Hamilton, duchess of Hamilton and Brandon] (*bap.* **1733**, *d.* **1790**), courtier, was probably born at Hemingford Grey, Huntingdonshire, and was probably baptized there on 7 December 1733, the second of five daughters of Colonel John Gunning of Castle Coote, Roscommon, Ireland, and his wife, Bridget, daughter of Theobald Bourke, sixth Viscount Bourke of Mayo. Her early years were spent at Hemingford Grey, but when she was seven her parents decided to move back to Ireland, settling at Abbeytown, Roscommon. Both Elizabeth and her elder sister, Maria Gunning [*see* Coventry, Maria], came to be regarded as beauties while still in their teens, and their mother resolved to find them wealthy husbands. She took them across to England and introduced them to society at the Huntingdon assembly, where they created a sensation.

The following year Mrs Gunning persuaded William Stanhope, first earl of Harrington, lord lieutenant of Ireland, to grant her a pension, and on the proceeds she and the two girls went to London, where they made even more of a stir. Horace Walpole commented, 'I think there being *two* so handsome and both such perfect figures is their chief excellence' (Bleackley, 21). Maria, fair-haired with pink and white cheeks, was sparkling and vivacious. Elizabeth, tall and statuesque, had dark auburn hair and was quiet and gentle. Their very lack of sophistication merely enhanced their charm. Soon they were surrounded by eligible young noblemen who flirted with them but did not make them any offers, for the girls had no dowries.

Undeterred, their mother in July 1750 took them to Windsor, where George Coventry, Viscount Deerhurst, the son and heir of William, fifth earl of Coventry, fell in love with Maria. Back in London, Elizabeth met James Hamilton, sixth duke of Hamilton (1724–1758), at a masquerade on 16 January 1752. Handsome but tubercular, intelligent and fond of literature but an inveterate gambler, engaging in manner but a heavy drinker, the duke was instantly attracted. According to one contemporary, 'He was very debauched in bad women's company but among ladies he was one of the politest and best-behaved men in Great Britain' (Bleackley, 37). A month later the sisters attended a great ball held by Philip Stanhope, fourth earl of Chesterfield. Maria shimmered in gold and spangles while Elizabeth was demure in a plain Quaker dress.

The duke proposed to her that evening and she accepted. Two nights later he took her to a chapel in Curzon Street where the Revd Alexander Keith performed clandestine marriages. The duke had forgotten to bring a ring, and so he married Elizabeth in the early hours of 14 February 1752 with a bed-curtain ring hastily fetched from his house. A few days later Maria became the wife of Lord Deerhurst, now earl of Coventry.

The duke carried Elizabeth triumphantly back to Scotland, and they spent the summer at Hamilton Palace, his ancestral home near Glasgow. In the autumn they moved to the palace of Holyroodhouse, where the duke had apartments as hereditary keeper. Their first child was born there on 26 January 1753, a daughter whom they named Elizabeth. Dividing their time between Edinburgh and Hamilton, they were at the centre of Scottish society, entertaining such notable guests as Colonel James Wolfe and Oliver Goldsmith. Elizabeth gave birth to a son and heir on 18 February 1755. The baby was baptized George James, his godfather being George II. A second son, Douglas, was born the following year. The duke then moved his little family to London.

Although he was only thirty-three and, since his marriage, a reformed character, the duke's already fragile health had been ruined by his former dissipation. Visiting Anthony Keck, his aunt's husband, at Great Tew, Oxfordshire, early in 1758, he caught a chill when out hunting and died on 18 January. Elizabeth was left a widow at twenty-four with three young children. Devoted as she had been to her husband, she was soon besieged by suitors and the following year was rumoured to be engaged to Francis Egerton, third duke of Bridgewater. Nothing came of the relationship: the duke never married and allegedly would not even have women servants attend him. Elizabeth meanwhile fell deeply in love with 'Handsome Jack Campbell' (1723–1806), a kind-hearted professional soldier whose father, John Campbell of Mamore, was heir to Archibald, third duke of Argyll. They were married on 3 March 1759. Campbell was posted to Ireland that summer and Elizabeth went with him, but they were there for only a month when he was promoted to major-general and given command of the Argyll fencibles.

The following year George III inherited the throne and in 1761 married Princess Charlotte of Mecklenburg-Strelitz. Chosen as one of her ladies of the bedchamber, Elizabeth was sent to Germany to escort her to England. She attended the royal wedding on 8 September and remained in London for the coronation before going to Bristol, where the hot wells were recommended for chest ailments. Her sister Maria was dying of tuberculosis, and she too was showing signs of the disease. However, on 31 March 1762 she gave birth safely to the first child of her second family, a daughter named Augusta.

Elizabeth was slow to recover from the birth, and her anxious husband decided to take her to Italy for the winter. They travelled by way of Aix-la-Chapelle, where she took the waters, and felt so much better that they went no further. While they were abroad, her father-in-law succeeded his cousin as duke of Argyll, and Elizabeth and her husband became marquess and marchioness of Lorne, although she was still known as dowager duchess of Hamilton. That same year Lorne was appointed commander-in-chief of the royal forces in Scotland and Elizabeth gave birth to their first son.

A significant event of a less pleasing nature had been preoccupying Elizabeth ever since 21 July 1761, when Archibald, duke of Douglas, died. He had married a middle-aged lady late in life and had no children, and for many years it was assumed that his nearest relative in the male line of the Douglas family, Elizabeth's first husband, would inherit most of his titles and the Douglas estates. However, the duke of Douglas's sister, Lady Jane, eloped to France with a penniless adventurer, Colonel John Steuart, when she was nearly fifty. To everyone's astonishment she reappeared some months later, announcing that she had given birth to twins. One baby had died, but the other, Archibald, had survived, and she said that he was her brother's rightful heir.

The old duke at first had refused to believe that the child was hers, but his energetic wife, Margaret Douglas of Mains, known as Duchess Peggy, supported Lady Jane. Time passed, Lady Jane died, and on the death of the duke himself Duchess Peggy sprang into action. Within weeks Archibald was served heir to her dead husband and put in possession of the estates. Elizabeth was highly indignant. Her son George James, who had inherited many of the Douglas titles but not the lands, was now the Hamilton claimant, and his legal representatives immediately raised several actions against Archibald and his curators in the court of session in Edinburgh. The subsequent lawsuit, the celebrated Douglas cause, dragged on for years. All the eminent Scottish lawyers of the day were involved, hundreds of witnesses were heard, both Elizabeth and Duchess Peggy personally visited France to look for evidence, and public interest was overwhelming. In 1766 it was said that debts to the value of £100,000 had been placed on the outcome. The pleadings which began that summer are believed to have been the longest ever heard in a court of justice until that time. At last, on 7 July, the judges pronounced in favour of the duke of Hamilton. A week later Elizabeth gave birth to a stillborn child.

Elizabeth's health was causing grave concern and, apart from the worry of the Douglas cause, she was finding her duties as lady-in-waiting distinctly trying. Queen Charlotte had been pleased with everything when she first came to England, but George III was a great admirer of Elizabeth and his wife soon grew jealous, making the duchess's life at court difficult. If she had hoped that the Douglas cause had reached its triumphant conclusion she was disappointed, for Archibald Steuart's representatives now appealed to the House of Lords and the business of gathering and sifting evidence started all over again.

In March 1768 Elizabeth was much praised by her friends when she resolutely refused to illuminate Argyll House in London during the Wilkes riots despite the mob battering at her doors and demanding that she do so. The hearings in the Douglas cause began that autumn, shortly after Elizabeth gave birth to another son, and to her consternation the Lords overturned the court of session decision and found in favour of Archibald. There was great rejoicing in Scotland, for he had been the public favourite, and the Edinburgh mob smashed the windows of the judges who had supported the duke of Hamilton and plundered the Hamilton apartments in the palace of Holyroodhouse.

Elizabeth was bitterly disappointed for her handsome, sweet-natured, clever elder son. The following spring her husband took George James and his younger brother to Scotland for a holiday, while Elizabeth stayed at court to attend a baptism. When she joined them later, she found George lying seriously ill with a fever in a Glasgow inn. When he could be moved, she took him to Hamilton Palace and summoned the best doctors from Edinburgh, for he was still pitifully weak. Under their care he recovered a little, but he then lost the use of his limbs and died, serene and uncomplaining, on 7 July. He was only fourteen. Elizabeth was heartbroken, and her husband took her away to one of his own houses at Rosneath.

In 1770 Lorne inherited his father's titles and Elizabeth became duchess of Argyll. She now divided her time between London, where she was still a lady-in-waiting, and Inveraray Castle in Argyll, the duke of Argyll's principal seat. James Boswell and Samuel Johnson visited her there in 1773. She did not like Boswell, who had been involved in the Douglas cause on the opposite side, but she did enjoy meeting Dr Johnson. Her family was growing up now, and in 1774 she celebrated the marriage of Lady Betty, her daughter by the duke of Hamilton, to Edward Smith Stanley, twelfth earl of Derby. The following year, at the age of forty-one, she had her last child, a daughter, Charlotte.

On 14 May 1776 Elizabeth's services at court were rewarded when she was created Baroness Hamilton of Hameldon. She was by then greatly taken up with her eldest surviving son, Douglas, eighth duke of Hamilton, worrying about his health and his behaviour. Like his father he was charming but feckless, and she was thrown into a panic when he raised a regiment in 1778 and spoke of going to America. She managed to dissuade him, and hoped that he would settle down with his sensible wife, Elizabeth Anne Burrell, whom he married that year, but he began an affair with Frances Montgomerie (*née* Twisden), countess of Eglinton. Once again Elizabeth had to intervene and persuaded him to break off the relationship, but this did not prevent an embarrassing divorce case in 1788 in which the countess was divorced on grounds of adultery with the duke.

Elizabeth's winters were always spent in Italy now and she made friends there with Nelson's mistress Emma, Lady Hamilton. However, tuberculosis, long suspected, was taking its toll. She resigned her position as lady-in-waiting in 1784 and when she returned to London from Italy in 1790 people were shocked at her emaciated appearance. She insisted that she was feeling better, but they could see that she was dying. Her distraught husband kept watch by her bedside at Argyll House, Argyll Street, until, on 20 December 1790, she sent him from the room and slipped away quietly in her sleep. He took her body back to Scotland and buried her in the Argyll tomb in Kilmun church on 16 January 1791.

Elizabeth Gunning lived at a time when a woman was usually defined by her husband's career and social position, and she has been best remembered as the wife of two dukes and the mother of three. Her two Hamilton sons were successively seventh and eighth dukes of Hamilton and Brandon, and her eldest son by John Campbell eventually became sixth duke of Argyll. There was much more to Elizabeth than that, however. She was a figure of real significance in the household of Queen Charlotte, and the award of the peerage in her own right not only recognized this fact but was a unique achievement for a girl who had grown up as an impoverished member of the Irish gentry. Admired for her beauty and her sweet nature, she also possessed a strength of character which took her far beyond even her mother's aspirations for her and brought her into the first rank of society.

ROSALIND K. MARSHALL

Sources H. Bleackley, *The story of a beautiful duchess* (1908) • *Scots peerage*, 4.383; 1.387 • R. Douglas, *The peerage of Scotland*, 2nd edn, ed. J. P. Wood, 1 (1813), 119, 723 • GEC, *Peerage*, new edn, 1.209–10; 6.270–71 • *DNB* • Lennoxlove, East Lothian, archives of the duke of Hamilton • Duke of Argyll, ed., *Intimate society letters of the eighteenth century*, 2 vols. [1910], vol. 1, pp. 138, 144, 215, 303, 307; vol. 2, pp. 330–34 • [W. Mure], ed., *Selections from the family papers preserved at Caldwell*, pt 2, vol. 2, Maitland Club, 71 (1854), 146 • *Scots Magazine*, 28 (1766), 389 • *Scots Magazine*, 31 (1769), 109, 335, 389–90 • P. Fitzgerald, *Lady Jean: the romance of the great Douglas cause* (1904) • R. K. Marshall, *Women in Scotland, 1660–1780* (1976), 47–9 • R. W. Jones, '"Such strange unwonted softness to excuse": judgement and indulgence in Sir Joshua Reynolds's portrait of Elizabeth Gunning, duchess of Hamilton and Argyll', *Oxford Art Journal*, 18/1 (1995), 29–43

Archives Inveraray Castle, Argyll • Lennoxlove, East Lothian

Likenesses F. Cotes, pastel drawing, 1751, NPG • G. Hamilton, oils, *c.*1752–1755, Holyroodhouse, Edinburgh • R. Houston, group portrait, mezzotint, pubd 1756 (*The three Gunning sisters*), BM • J. Reynolds, oils, 1758–9, Lady Lever Art Gallery, Port Sunlight [*see illus.*] • G. Hamilton, oils, 1760, Lady Lever Art Gallery, Port Sunlight • F. H. Drouais, oils, 1763, Inveraray Castle, Argyll • F. Cotes, oils, 1767, Inveraray Castle, Argyll • G. Hamilton, oils, priv. coll. • G. Hamilton, two oil paintings, Scot. NPG • R. Houston, mezzotint (after F. Cotes), BM, NPG • C. Read, pastel drawing, Inveraray Castle, Argyll

Campbell, Lord Frederick (1729–1816), politician, born on 20 June 1729, was the fourth but second surviving son of Colonel John Campbell of Mamore, later fourth duke of Argyll (*c.*1693–1770), and his wife, Mary (*d.* 1736), daughter of John Bellenden, second Lord Bellenden. John Campbell, fifth duke of Argyll, was his brother. He was educated at Westminster School and at Christ Church, Oxford, and called to the bar in 1754. Elected to parliament in 1761, he sat as member for Glasgow burghs from 1761 to 1780 and for Argyll from 1781 to 1799.

According to Horace Walpole, 'no connexion or obligation could stand against the eagerness with which [Campbell] pursued immediate fortune. Nothing else weighed with him, except the inveteracy of national prejudice'

(Walpole, 1.406). Early support for Bute was rewarded in 1762 with a life grant of the feu duties of Islay. Having shifted to the Bedford party, Campbell was sworn of the privy council and appointed keeper of the privy seal of Scotland in May 1765, but soon followed Grenville and Bedford into opposition. Under Chatham he was appointed chief secretary of Ireland in August 1767, retaining this office until December 1768, shortly after appointment as lord clerk register of Scotland. Later association with Pitt and Dundas brought him appointment to the Board of Trade (1786–1801), the vice-treasurership of Ireland (1787–93), and membership of the Board of Control for India (1790–93). He was also rector of Glasgow University (1772–3), and treasurer of the Middle Temple (1803).

Campbell's initial appointment as lord clerk register, on 2 November 1766, was followed on 25 February 1777 by a new commission for life. He carried through the project for a new repository for the public records of Scotland initiated by his predecessor, James Douglas, fourteenth earl of Morton, but on a much grander scale, with Robert Adam as architect. He laid the foundation stone on 27 June 1774 but funds ran out and General Register House did not open until 1788. The building contains a statue of George III sculpted by Campbell's niece Anne Damer. Campbell was fortunate in having as deputy keepers Alexander and William Robertson who suggested improvements in record keeping that were incorporated in the Public Records (Scotland) Act of 1809, and he actively supported their efforts to recover Scottish records from England. Within Scotland the case of *Campbell* v. *Stuart* (1795) identified the clerk register as rightful custodian of all records, the custody of which was not otherwise provided for. Though the appointment of Thomas Thomson to the new post of deputy clerk register in 1806 reduced the clerk register to a more passive role, Campbell considered it 'the greatest honour I have in my life to have done that duty forty years altogether … There is not a transaction which I am not aware of' (Select committee, first report, 32–3). Thomson's reports to him provide a detailed commentary on the work of the Register House in the last ten years of Campbell's life.

Campbell's father bought for him the small estate of Ardencaple, in Argyll, and made over the family seat, Combe Bank, near Sevenoaks, Kent, his main residence from 1770 to 1813. He married, on 28 March 1769, Mary, sister of Sir William Meredith of Henbury, Cheshire, and widow of Laurence Shirley, fourth Earl Ferrers. She died on 25 June 1807 following an accident at Combe Bank. His two daughters, Mary and Jane, are said to have been illegitimate.

Even in his fifties Campbell:

> retained all the graces he had inherited from his mother. His figure united symmetry with elegance, and his manners, noble, yet soft, dignified, yet devoid of any pride or affectation, conciliated all who approached him. Devoid of shining talents, he nevertheless wanted not either ability or elegance in a certain degree, both which were under the control of reason and temper. (Wraxall, 1.246)

He died at his house in Queen Street, Mayfair, Westminster, on 8 June 1816, 'still elegant and distinguished even in decay' (Wraxall, 1.247), and was buried in the family vault at Sundridge church, Kent. ATHOL MURRAY

Sources HoP, *Commons, 1754–90* · HoP, *Commons, 1790–1820* · *Scots peerage*, 1.384–5 · A. L. Murray, 'The lord clerk register', *SHR*, 53 (1974), 124–56 · H. Walpole, *Memoirs of the reign of King George the Third*, ed. D. Le Marchant, 1 (1845) · N. W. Wraxall, *Posthumous memoirs of his own time*, 2nd edn, 1 (1836) · 'Select committee on sinecure offices: first report', *Parl. papers* (1810), 2.591, no. 362 · E. Hasted, *The history and topographical survey of the county of Kent*, 2nd edn, 3 (1797); facs. repr. (1972) · C. Russell, *Three generations of fascinating women* (1904), 91–4 · *DNB* · GEC, *Peerage*, new edn, 1.209; 5.337

Archives BL, charters · NA Scot., official corresp., SRO 8 | BL, letters to R. M. Keith, Add. MSS 35505–35536, *passim* · BL OIOC, letters to Lord Amherst, MS Eur. F 140

Likenesses oils, in or after 1765, Inveraray Castle, Strathclyde · T. Gainsborough, oils, 1786, repro. in Russell, *Three generations of fascinating women*, 94; formerly at Inveraray Castle, Strathclyde · H. Raeburn, oils, *c*.1810, General Register House, Edinburgh · H. Raeburn, oils, 1814, NA Scot. · T. Lawrence, oils, 1815, Brooks's Club, London, Society of Dilettanti · J. Stow, line print, pubd 1817 (after H. Edridge, 1812), BM; NPG · G. Dupont, mezzotint (after T. Gainsborough), BM · T. Lawrence, oils; formerly at St James's Club, London, 1958 · plaster replica (after J. Henning), Scot. NPG

Wealth at death £10,900 in legacies: will, PRO, PROB 11/1582, sig. 357

Campbell, Frederick Archibald Vaughan, **third Earl Cawdor** (**1847–1911**), politician and railway administrator, was born on 13 February 1847 at St Leonard's Hill, Windsor, the eldest child of John Frederick Vaughan Campbell, second Earl Cawdor (1817–1898) and his first wife, Sarah, daughter of the Hon. Henry Compton-Cavendish. He had two brothers and four sisters. The elder of his brothers, Ronald George Elidor, Coldstream Guards, was killed in a skirmish with Zulu near Isandlwana in March 1879. Until he inherited the earldom he was known as Viscount Emlyn. His family was descended from a cadet branch of the ducal house of Argyll which had in the early nineteenth century acquired the extensive west Wales estates of the Vaughan family, earls of Carbery. The family seats were Golden Grove, Carmarthenshire; Stackpole Court, Pembrokeshire; and Cawdor Castle, Nairn.

Emlyn was educated at Eton College and Christ Church, Oxford. He sat in parliament as Conservative MP for Carmarthenshire from 1874 to 1885. Between 1885 and 1898, when he succeeded his father, as third Earl Cawdor, he made several unsuccessful attempts to return to the Commons (West Carmarthenshire, 1885; South Manchester, 1892; Wiltshire, Cricklade division, 1898). In parliament he was active on Welsh topics, most notably as a member of the Aberdare committee (1880–81), set up by Gladstone to examine the state of intermediate and higher education in Wales. The committee's work was recognized in the establishment of university colleges in Cardiff (1883) and Bangor (1884), and in the ground-breaking Welsh Intermediate Education Act of 1889. Outside parliament, Emlyn was an ecclesiastical commissioner for England (1880), and a magistrate and deputy lieutenant for Carmarthenshire and Pembrokeshire as well as for Inverness-shire. He was lord lieutenant of Pembrokeshire in 1896. He commanded the Carmarthenshire militia and became

Frederick Archibald Vaughan Campbell, third Earl Cawdor (1847–1911), by Elliott & Fry

its honorary colonel. He joined the Royal Agricultural Society in 1863, served on its council from 1882, and was its president in 1901; he was a member of the Carlton Club and the Travellers' Club.

In 1868 Emlyn married Edith Georgiana Turnor, of Stoke Rochford, Lincolnshire. They had thirteen children, ten of whom survived their father.

Railway director In 1890 Emlyn became a director of the Great Western Railway and a year later deputy chairman. From July 1895 to March 1905 he was chairman, and in this role presided over a significant period of growth and restructuring in the company's activities. The radical change from broad to standard gauge, undertaken by his predecessor, F. G. Saunders, made possible the numerous reforming measures introduced during his tenure of office, measures whose aim was to maximize growth as well as efficiency; most significant was the laying of new lines, including a direct route to south Wales in 1903. The improvements destroyed the legend of the GWR as the 'Great Way Round'.

Cawdor's success as chairman of the GWR owed less to any extensive experience of the railway business than to innate management qualities. He was quick to spot a good idea, and imaginative and determined in pursuing its implementation. He was a persuasive advocate and a good manager of people. In 1903 Joseph Chamberlain referred to his reputation as 'the best chairman now living'. Such qualities had helped the GWR to become increasingly competitive and profitable by 1905. They had also led Cawdor to be considered for the post of war minister in the Conservative government of A. J. Balfour in 1903. In the event he was not called on, but in March 1905 he was offered and accepted the post of first lord of the Admiralty in succession to Lord Selborne.

The explanation for the appointment of Cawdor, an aristocratic businessman who had not sat in the Commons for twenty years and who had never held government, let alone cabinet, office, lies only partly in the lack of administrative talent in the Balfour ministry. It reflects also an Edwardian interest in bringing 'non-political' businessmen and methods to bear on national problems. Thus, confronted after the Second South African War by the imperative need for rationalizing and cutting the cost of the empire's defences, Balfour looked outside parliamentary circles for reformist talent.

At the Admiralty Although as a landed aristocrat and a former MP Cawdor was scarcely a technocratic outsider, his low political profile and managerial acumen made him an imaginative choice. So too did his complete lack of a background in naval matters. In the event his tenure as first lord lasted just nine months (March–December 1905), a period marred by poor health and frequent absences. His stewardship of the Admiralty won him contemporary plaudits. His *Times* obituary compared him with Charles Middleton, Baron Barham, a hundred years earlier. He too had gone to the Admiralty with no previous experience of government, had had a comparably brief tenure (May 1805 – February 1806), and had nevertheless left a mark on the navy. As had been the case at the GWR, however, Cawdor's achievement was less a matter of launching constructive ideas of his own than of developing and supporting those of others. He arrived at the Admiralty as the naval 'revolution' launched by Lord Selborne and Admiral Sir John Fisher in 1902 was reaching its height. 1905 saw the redistribution of the fleet on home waters, the scrapping of 147 obsolete vessels, and the adoption of the dreadnought design of capital ship. Fisher's gospel of the synergy of economy and efficiency found a receptive audience in the former railway chairman. Cawdor backed Fisher's policy and secured his extension in the office of first sea lord to 1910. During five years of intense and frequently bitter debate over Fisher's reforms from 1905 to 1910, Cawdor never wavered in his support, even though at times highly critical of Fisher's excesses and even though his stance won him enemies in his own party.

On 30 November 1905 a 'statement of admiralty policy' was issued, immediately known as the 'Cawdor memorandum', which committed the Admiralty to the future construction of four dreadnoughts a year. It was to become the focal point of the party-political debate over the navy in the years 1906–9, with the Liberal government seeking to justify, and the Unionist opposition to prevent, its abandonment. Cawdor played a crucial role in prosecuting the Unionist attack, both in the annual set-piece parliamentary debates over the navy estimates and on public platforms, particularly in 1909–10 when the navy became a prominent election issue. He proved himself an effective debater in public, while in private he worked closely and amicably with Balfour to formulate opposition policy and tactics.

Unionist politics Although Cawdor was primarily associated with naval questions after 1906, he also made an important contribution to Unionist education policy and constitutional reform. On both issues he represented the opposition in inter-party conferences convened to resolve a political impasse caused by the rejection of Liberal legislation by the Unionist-dominated House of Lords—on education in December 1906 and on the Lords' veto in June 1910. Cawdor's role on the former occasion reflected his background on the subject (namely the Aberdare committee), as much as his prominence on the Unionist benches. In 1910, however, his role alongside Balfour, Lord Lansdowne, and Austen Chamberlain as Unionist representative in the constitutional conference, reflected not only an identification with the cause of Lords' reform, but also the fact that he had by that time achieved a leading role in the party. By 1910 he was *de facto* if not formal deputy to Lansdowne, leader of the Unionists in the upper house, a considerable achievement for a man whose ministerial career had spanned a mere nine months. Even if account is taken of the fact that the Edwardian House of Lords was a far less testing arena than the Commons, Cawdor's rise was impressive. It occasioned little critical or sceptical contemporary comment, a sign of both his widely acknowledged abilities and a disarming personality.

Death Cawdor died at 9 John Street, Mayfair, on 8 February 1911, aged sixty-three, of pneumonia following a short illness. He was buried in Stackpole church, Pembrokeshire. A memorial service at Holy Trinity, Brompton, was attended by the prime minister, Asquith, and many politicians and peers. 'Few men of his generation enjoyed so general an esteem', observed Sir Almeric Fitzroy. He was succeeded by his eldest son, Hugh Frederick Vaughan, Viscount Emlyn. RHODRI WILLIAMS

Sources GEC, *Peerage* • *DWB* • Burke, *Peerage* • Burke, *Gen. GB* • *Dod's Parliamentary Companion* (1875–85) • A. Fitzroy, *Memoirs*, 2 vols. [1925] • F. Booker, *The Great Western Railway: a new history* (1977) • R. Williams, *Defending the empire: the conservative party and British defence policy, 1899–1915* (1991) • K. O. Morgan, *Rebirth of a nation: Wales, 1880–1980* (1981) • J. D. Fair, *British interparty conferences* (1980) • *The Times* (9 Feb 1911), 11

Archives Carmarthenshire RO, papers, mainly as first lord • NMM, Naval Historical Library, naval papers | Balliol Oxf., corresp. with Sir Robert Morier • BL, corresp. with Arthur James Balfour, Add. MS 49709, *passim* • CAC Cam., corresp. with Reginald McKenna • NL Wales, letters to Johnes family

Likenesses Elliott & Fry, photograph, NPG [*see illus.*] • pen-and-ink drawing (after F. Dicksee), Traveller's Club, London

Wealth at death £633,328 10*s*. 8*d*.: probate, 22 April 1911, *CGPLA Eng. & Wales*

Campbell, Frederick William (1782–1846), genealogist, was the eldest son of Donald *Campbell (1751–1804), of Barbreck, and his wife, Mary Campbell, daughter of Lord Frederick Campbell. He was born on 4 January 1782, and became a captain in the 1st regiment of guards. Some time after succeeding his father in 1804, he sold the estate in Argyll, retaining only the superiority to connect him with the county, and took up his residence at Birkfield Lodge, near Ipswich, Suffolk. He was a magistrate and deputy lieutenant of the county. In 1830 he printed privately at Ipswich a work entitled *A Letter to Mrs Campbell of Barbreck, Containing an Account of the Campbells of Barbreck*. He married, first Jessie Aspasia (*d*. 1812), daughter of Wade Toby Caulfeild of Raheenduff, Queen's county; second, her half-sister, Emma Ashwell Caulfeild (*d*. 1817); and third, on 21 February 1820, Sophia, daughter of Sir Edward Winnington, bt, MP, with whom he had one daughter. He died in 1846. T. F. HENDERSON, *rev*. MYFANWY LLOYD

Sources Burke, *Gen. GB* (1846) • Burke, *Peerage* (1879) • T. Cooper, *A new biographical dictionary: containing concise notices of eminent persons of all ages and countries* (1873)

Campbell, Sir George, of Cessnock (*fl*. 1671–1704), conspirator, was the eldest of four sons of Sir Hugh *Campbell (*d*. 1686) and his wife, Elizabeth, younger daughter and coheir of George Campbell, master of Loudoun. In 1665 he married Lady Anna McMurran (McMoran, McMouran), heir of a Fife estate, with whom he had five children. As substantial contributors to the parish kirk at Galston, Ayrshire, Sir George and his father petitioned the privy council in December 1671 for seats proportional to their contributions. Like his father, Sir George refused to sign a bond pledging not to support conventicles, for which he was outlawed in February 1678. Accused of aiding the covenanter ministers Donald Cargill and John Welsh, the Campbells denied the charge and were absolved. Sir George and his father reputedly provided 400 lances to the Bothwell Bridge rebels in the spring of 1679.

Three years later the Campbells became involved with other supporters of the earl of Argyll in discussions about a possible insurrection. On 28 April 1682 Alexander Monro of Bearcrofts wrote to Sir George Campbell about a plan to establish a Scottish colony; originally the intent had been to situate it in New York, but the focus was now on Carolina. Sir John Cochrane and Sir George were invited to London to participate in negotiations with the earl of Shaftesbury. By August they had reached an agreement and obtained King Charles's approval (15 August), probably because he shared Hamilton's belief that the colony would attract Scottish dissidents. Argyll was also in London, meeting secretly with Shaftesbury, apparently seeking funds to support a rebellion in Scotland. Sir George and his father were probably working with Argyll by this time. In late January or early February 1683 the duke of Monmouth, Algernon Sidney, John Hampden, and their fellow conspirators sent Aaron Smith to Scotland to invite the Campbells, Cochrane, Monro, and other Argyll supporters to London to explore the possibility of joint insurrections. The Scots arrived in April and May on the pretext of discussing the Carolina colony. Sir George conferred with the plotter Robert Ferguson, and both Campbells met with William Carstares, one of Argyll's agents, who was himself in contact with Ferguson. Distrustful of the English, the Campbells opposed an alliance with Monmouth. Argyll's supporters were still trying to raise money when the government learned of the Rye House plotting. The tangled skein of conspiracies soon led to the Campbells, who were arrested on 26 June.

Taken to Scotland with his father in September, Sir George Campbell remained in prison without trial until 1685, when he and his father were charged in the Scottish parliament with complicity in plotting an insurrection. After they threw themselves on King James's mercy, he spared their lives, though their estates were annexed and entrusted to Viscount Melfort. Released from prison with his father in August 1685, Sir George was reconfined in October after Cochrane confessed. He was liberated again in January 1686. Following the revolution of 1688, Sir George was appointed justice clerk with a pension of £400 p.a. (December 1689), commissioner of the excise in Ayrshire (January 1690), and sheriff of Ayrshire (June 1690). As a member of the privy council he attended fifty-six meetings in 1690, but only sixteen the following year owing to ill health. Secretary of state James Johnston forced his resignation as justice clerk in 1693. Sir George was again appointed to the privy council in 1696 and 1698. Although parliament had restored his estate in 1690, he was heavily in debt by the late 1690s. His date of death is uncertain: possibly in 1704, though he may still have been alive as late as 1710. No sons survived him; his daughter and heir, Margaret, married in 1697 Alexander Hume, later Alexander Hume *Campbell, second earl of Marchmont, to whom she carried the paternal estate in 1729.

RICHARD L. GREAVES

Sources *Reg. PCS*, 3rd ser. • *State trials*, 10.919–88 • state MSS, PRO, 29/425, 427–429, 432–433, 435–436, 438 • *CSP dom.*, *1689–90*; *1698–1700* • R. L. Greaves, *Secrets of the kingdom: British radicals from the Popish Plot to the revolution of 1688–89* (1992) • *The manuscripts of the duke of Roxburghe*, HMC, 34 (1894) • Burke, *Gen. GB* (1937) • NA Scot., PA 7/12, 6 (no. 1) [depositions of Sir Hugh and Sir George Campbell] • *Letters, illustrative of public affairs in Scotland, addressed by contemporary statesmen to George, earl of Aberdeen* (1851) • *The manuscripts of his grace the duke of Buccleuch and Queensberry … preserved at Drumlanrig Castle*, 2 vols., HMC, 44 (1897–1903) • U. Edin. L., MS La.II.89 • *CSP col.*, vols. 5, 7, 9–12 • *Index to the general register of sasines, 1701–1720*, Scottish Record Office, 3 (1917) • R. Wodrow, *The history of the sufferings of the Church of Scotland from the Restauration to the revolution*, 2 (1722), 379–85 • P. Karsten, 'Plotters and proprietors, 1682–83', *The Historian*, 38 (1975–6), 474–84

Archives Scot. RO, MSS, PA 7/12, p. 6 (no. 1)

Wealth at death apparently died in substantial debt: *CSP dom.*, *1699–1700*, 205

Campbell, George (1719–1796), Church of Scotland minister and college head, was born on 25 December 1719 in Aberdeen, the fifth of six children of Colin Campbell (1678–1728), a Church of Scotland minister, and Margaret Walker (*d.* 1747), daughter of a prominent Aberdeen merchant. He was educated at Aberdeen grammar school (1729–34) and at Marischal College (1734–8), where he learned Greek from Thomas Blackwell the younger, a noted classical scholar, and mathematics from John Stewart, a Newtonian popularizer. After graduating MA he was apprenticed to George Turnbull, a writer to the signet in Edinburgh, but in 1741 abandoned his legal education in favour of divinity. He studied briefly in Edinburgh under John Gowdie, and then returned to Aberdeen's Divinity Hall, where he was taught by Robert Pollock and John

George Campbell (1719–1796), by Caroline Watson, pubd 1798 (after John Bogle)

Lumsden. During this time he helped found the Theological Club, a student society which promoted polite conversation and encouraged the practice of preaching. He was licensed to preach by the presbytery of Aberdeen on 11 June 1746, and was later called to the parish of Banchory-Ternan in Aberdeenshire, receiving ordination in the Church of Scotland on 2 June 1748. Campbell remained in this country parish for nine years, during which time he began the private studies that would form the foundation of his scholarly career. His first published sermon, based on a synod address, appeared in 1752 as *The Character of a Minister of the Gospel as a Teacher and Pattern*, summarizing both his creed and his conception of the pastoral office. On 26 June 1755 he married Grace Farquharson (*d.* 1793), daughter of Harry Farquharson, an Episcopalian Jacobite who had died at Culloden for the Young Pretender. Their marriage was, by all accounts, a happy one; they had no children.

Campbell returned to Aberdeen on 23 June 1757, was translated to the city's second charge, and lived there for the rest of his life. When the principalship of Marischal College fell vacant in 1759 he was persuaded to apply to his kinsman, the third duke of Argyll, who managed Scottish affairs for the crown, and was rewarded with the office in August. On 1 October 1761 he received the degree of doctor of divinity from King's College in Old Aberdeen. In addition to the office of principal, Campbell was given Marischal's divinity chair by the Aberdeen town council on 26 June 1771, and was simultaneously translated to Greyfriars' Chapel, a living traditionally associated with the divinity chair but which demanded no parochial duties apart from a weekly sermon. Campbell's divinity lectures, which are preserved both in manuscript and in print, concentrated on biblical criticism, ecclesiastical history, and pulpit eloquence, but avoided controversial doctrine. He instructed his students that they were to teach themselves doctrine from their own studies of scripture. His weekly sermons, which have not survived, were noted for their biblical exegesis and practical piety. Campbell became a highly respected figure in the Church of Scotland's annual general assembly, and was remembered for his persuasive orations, though he always declined the office of moderator.

Campbell was an original member of the Aberdeen Philosophical Society, popularly known as the Wise Club, which was founded in January 1758 and survived until March 1773. The society was Aberdeen's leading intellectual body and the nursery of Scottish common-sense philosophy. Its fifteen members included Thomas Reid, James Beattie, and Alexander Gerard. As the society's purpose was explicitly philosophical Campbell shaped his formal discourses on eloquence and rhetoric to appeal to the group's common interests. But the questions he posed for the society's discussions reflected the entire range of his enlightened interests, including such topics as natural history, education, language, law, civil liberty, optics, animal husbandry, and the nature of pity. Campbell also developed a keen interest in botany, surveying the surrounding countryside and collecting plant samples, many of which are still preserved in the University of Aberdeen's herbarium.

The members of the Aberdeen Philosophical Society paid particular attention to the philosophy of David Hume, whose sceptical writings provoked many of their most famous works. This concern is particularly evident in Campbell's *A Dissertation on Miracles* (1762), which was based on a sermon delivered before the synod of Aberdeen in October 1760. In his essay 'Of miracles' (1748) Hume had categorically rejected all testimonial claims concerning miraculous events as inherently unbelievable. Campbell employed common-sense principles to demonstrate that the positive testimony of a reliable witness is superior even to the indirect body of evidence supporting the laws of nature, which are themselves founded on human testimony. Nevertheless, he concluded that only the early Christian miracles were founded on the testimony of reliable and unbiased witnesses, unlike modern Catholic claims. Contemporary audiences tended to agree with Campbell and concluded that he had decisively defeated Hume. The *Dissertation on Miracles* was frequently reprinted during the next eighty years, and was translated into several continental languages, establishing Campbell's reputation as one of Christianity's leading apologists.

Campbell was also concerned to defend the character of Christianity from its own extreme adherents. In his sermon *The Spirit of the Gospel a Spirit neither of Superstition nor of Enthusiasm* (1771) he attacked ritualistic and sacramental forms of religious adherence in favour of a charitable and reforming conception of Christianity. This latitudinarian stance provoked considerable controversy, and was attacked in print both by the nonjuring Scottish Episcopalian William Abernethy Drummond, and by the Roman Catholic priest George Hay. Campbell's apologetic strategy was continued in other sermons, notably *The Success of the First Publishers of the Gospel a Proof of its Truth* (1777), which argued the truth of Christianity from its historical successes, and *The Happy Influence of Religion on Civil Society* (1779), which upheld the common eighteenth-century thesis that religious belief is an indispensable pillar of civil society.

Campbell's discourses before the Aberdeen Philosophical Society were eventually expanded and published as *The Philosophy of Rhetoric* (1776). This work laid out classical rules of persuasion while recognizing that a living language must always adapt its standards of usage to suit contemporary needs. Campbell cited only the most famous authors to exemplify the typical flaws of modern stylists. But the *Rhetoric* was also philosophical, in keeping with the Scottish Enlightenment's broad intention to create an empirical science of man. Campbell sought to ground rhetorical theory in human nature itself, explaining the efficacy of the classically established ends of discourse with reference to the newly discovered faculties of the mind. The *Rhetoric* contains the bulk of Campbell's formal philosophy, including important treatments of the nature and types of evidence, and of the significance of the faculty of memory to human knowledge. Although generally well received by contemporary critics, *The Philosophy of Rhetoric* did not become a best-seller until the nineteenth century, when it was established as a standard text in the American college curriculum.

Campbell did not concern himself with political events until the outbreak of the American War of Independence. In December 1776 he preached a fast day sermon soon published as *The Nature, Extent, and Importance, of the Duty of Allegiance* (1777). It argued that rebellion is both contrary to scripture and unreasonable, but that the misguided Americans must be allowed the freedom to discover the errors of republicanism. This apparently unique combination of arguments not only failed to persuade wayward Americans but set him apart from the typical extremes of contemporary Scottish opinion. Campbell likewise found himself at odds with his compatriots during the No Popery affair (1778–80), when the government in Westminster attempted to repeal the civil disabilities in place against Scottish Catholics. Together with William Robertson he championed Catholic relief during the debates of the 1778 general assembly, and later published a pamphlet entitled *An Address to the People of Scotland, upon the Alarms that have been Raised in Regard to Popery* (1779). Campbell argued that persecution in any form is both morally wrong and counter-productive, and that Scottish Catholics threatened neither national security nor the established church. But his moderate tone proved ineffective against the overwhelming and sometimes violent protestant resistance to Catholic emancipation. Although this particular relief attempt failed, in 1792 Campbell successfully lobbied to lift similar legal disabilities from nonjuring Scottish Episcopalians.

Through all these years Campbell had diligently pursued his own critical and historical studies of scripture. These researches were finally published in 1789 as *The Four Gospels, Translated from the Greek, with Preliminary Dissertations, and Notes Critical and Explanatory*, acknowledged by contemporaries to be his scholarly masterpiece. This massive work contained fresh translations of the canonical gospels with extensive critical notes, as well as historical discussions of the nature and method of translating ancient terms and documents. Campbell believed that the critical arts constituted a vital foundation of rational and pious Christianity. Nevertheless, the bulky scholarship proved too much for popular sales and only the translations themselves were widely reprinted. Undaunted, Campbell continued to prepare new works for the press, focusing primarily on controversial issues relating to the history and character of the early church. He augmented his earlier strictures on the intolerant and superstitious nature of Catholicism with considerable historical detail, and also attacked the authoritarian tendencies evident in some protestant churches. Although most of these late works remain unpublished, the manuscripts can be found in Aberdeen University Library.

Campbell's final years were complicated first by serious illness in January 1791 and then by the death of his wife on 16 February 1793. He gradually withdrew from his public commitments, finally resigning the chair of divinity and the principalship in June and July 1795, and retiring on a crown pension of £300 a year. He died in Aberdeen on 6 April 1796, after suffering a debilitating stroke, and was buried in St Nicholas's churchyard in Aberdeen on 17 April. William Laurence Brown, Campbell's successor in both university posts, preached the funeral sermon, which was published as *The Death of the Righteous Precious in the Sight of God* (1796). The main beneficiary of Campbell's estate, worth at least £1550 sterling, was his wife's niece, Ann Farquharson, who had lived in the Campbell household for many years.

Campbell's divinity lectures were published in three posthumous instalments. The first, prepared for the press by Campbell, was entitled *Lectures on Ecclesiastical History* (2 vols., 1800), and included an important biographical account by G. S. Keith. The lectures presented a thematic rather than a narrative view of the inexorable corruption of the church, employing the principles of human nature to explain the rise of the episcopal hierarchy and the temporary triumph of the power-hungry Roman see. In outward form Campbell's arguments bore a striking resemblance to Edward Gibbon's more famous narrative, though without the latter's ironic intent. They provoked the ire of Episcopalian high-churchmen, who answered in several book-length rebuttals. The second and third instalments of Campbell's lecture series, *Lectures on Systematic Theology and Pulpit Eloquence* (1807) and *Lectures on the Pastoral Character* (1811), were collected and edited by Campbell's friend James Fraser of Drumoak. Although they did not generate controversy, they did illuminate the apologetic and religious character of Campbell's entire body of work, summarizing his lifelong pedagogical commitment to the themes of toleration, moderation, pastoral care, and scholarly precision.

During his lifetime, and for the half-century following his death, Campbell was remembered primarily as a Christian apologist and biblical scholar. Since the middle of the nineteenth century, however, his apologetic reputation declined while the fame of the one work which was not reprinted in his own lifetime, *The Philosophy of Rhetoric*, rose dramatically. Reprinted at least forty-five times it was elevated by later scholars to the status of a seminal text bridging classical and modern conceptions of rhetoric.

JEFFREY M. SUDERMAN

Sources J. M. Suderman, *Orthodoxy and enlightenment: George Campbell in the eighteenth century* (Montreal, 2001) · *Fasti Scot.*, new edn, vols. 6, 7 · G. S. Keith, 'Some account of the life and writings of Dr George Campbell', in G. Campbell, *Lectures on ecclesiastical history*, 2 vols. (1800), 1.v–lix · H. L. Ulman, ed., *The minutes of the Aberdeen Philosophical Society, 1758–1773* (1990) · L. F. Bitzer, introduction, in G. Campbell, *The philosophy of rhetoric*, 2nd edn (1988) · P. J. Anderson, ed., *Officers and graduates of University and King's College, Aberdeen, MVD–MDCCCLX*, New Spalding Club, 11 (1893) · will, NA Scot., CC1/6/60 · *IGI*

Archives NRA Scotland, priv. coll., corresp. · U. Aberdeen L., special libraries and archives

Likenesses C. Watson, stipple, pubd 1798 (after stipple by J. Bogle), BM, NPG [*see illus.*] · A. Robertson, oils, Trinity Hall, Aberdeen · watercolour, Scot. NPG

Wealth at death approx. £1550: copy of will, NA Scot., CC 1/6/60

Campbell, George (*bap.* 1761, *d.* 1817), poet, was born at Kilmarnock, and baptized there on 28 February 1761, the son of John Campbell and his wife, Janet, *née* Parker. His father died when he was still very young, and he was brought up under the care of his mother, who earned a living by winding yarn for the carpet works. Apprenticed to a shoemaker, Campbell made use of his scant leisure hours to educate himself, in order to enter the University of Glasgow. While a student in Glasgow he published in 1787 *Poems on Several Occasions*, which was printed at the press in Kilmarnock from which in the preceding year the first edition of the poems of Robert Burns had been issued. Campbell's poems, chiefly of a moral or didactic kind, are not written in dialect. Although commonplace in thought, the versification is easy and flowing. Campbell was ordained minister of the Secession church of Stockbridge, Midlothian, on 19 August 1794 at about the same time as he married a young woman of Kilmarnock. He remained in his charge until his death from consumption on 23 November 1817. In the year before his death he had published at Edinburgh *Sermons on Interesting Subjects*.

T. F. HENDERSON, *rev.* JAMES HOW

Sources J. Paterson, *The contemporaries of Burns and the more recent poets of Ayrshire* (1840) · Anderson, *Scot. nat.* · Irving, *Scots.* · Allibone, *Dict.* · W. Mackelvie, *Annals and statistics of the United Presbyterian church*, ed. W. Blair and D. Young (1873), 106 · *IGI*

Campbell, Sir George (1824–1892), administrator in India and author, was the eldest son of Sir George Campbell (*d.* 1854) of Edenwood, Fife, laird, and Margaret (*d.* 1873), daughter of Andrew Christie of Ferrybank. Knighted in 1833 for his services in preserving the peace in Fife during the reform riots, the elder Sir George, brother of John

Sir George Campbell (1824–1892), by unknown photographer

*Campbell, first Baron Campbell, had retired from the East India Company's medical service. The younger Sir George was, at the age of eight, sent to the Edinburgh Academy. After two years there he spent three at Madras College, St Andrews, followed by two sessions at St Andrews University, before family connections obtained a nomination for the East India Company. At Haileybury, over the next two years, his principal subjects were political economy and law. He left for India in September 1842 with his two brothers, Charles and John Scarlett Campbell, who also entered the Bengal civil service.

Early career in India Starting in June 1843 as assistant magistrate and collector at Budaun, Rohilkhand, in the North-Western Provinces, George Campbell was promoted to be joint magistrate of Moradabad in 1845. He soon began to study land tenures, and to confirm his knowledge by inquiries among the villagers. In May 1846 he was given temporary charge of Kaithal and Ladwa, the latter district being newly annexed from the Sikhs, and remained in the Cis-Sutlej territory for five years. After he had settled Ladwa—that is, established a record of rights as a basis of land taxation—he was dispatched to the Wadni district, between Ludhiana and Ferozepore. He then carried out the annexation of the Nabha and Kapurthala territories and the occupation and settlement of Aliwal; and, sent back to Kaithal and Ladwa, did good service in finding supplies and transport for the troops in the Second Anglo-Sikh War.

Early in 1849 Campbell contributed to the *Mofussilite*, a well-known Indian paper, a series of letters signed 'Economist', which attracted attention in official circles. They urged the annexation of the Punjab, but opposed the extension of British rule beyond the line of the Indus. After the annexation, he was promoted to the district of Ludhiana, and was also charged with the suppression of thuggee (the operations of a confederacy of professional assassins) and banditry across the Punjab. In January 1851, owing to ill health, he left Calcutta for Europe on long furlough. He had become 'in heart almost a Punjaubee', an admirer of John Lawrence, and his subsequent career made him a leading figure in the energetic 'Punjab school' of British Indian administrators, who saw themselves, especially in agrarian questions, as 'looking to the happiness and welfare of the masses' (Campbell, 2.5, 1.68). During his three years' absence from India, Campbell was called to the English bar from the Inner Temple in 1854. He gave evidence before the Commons select committee which examined the East India Company's record before its charter was renewed in 1853. His *Modern India* (1852) was another contribution to the defence of his employers. He also issued *India as it May Be* (1853), a long pamphlet advocating the reforms he thought necessary.

Now married, on 2 February 1854, to Laetitia, daughter of Thomas Gowan Vibart, of the Bengal civil service, with whom he had several children, Campbell returned to India with his wife in June that year. He went back to the North-Western Provinces as magistrate and collector of Azamgarh to the north of Benares. Early in 1855 he was made commissioner of customs for northern India and acted as assistant to John Russell Colvin, the lieutenant-governor. Later in the year he became commissioner of the Cis-Sutlej states, 'the appointment of all others … I most coveted' (Campbell, 1.176). Nominally under Lawrence, he held in reality an almost independent position. His policy was to leave the princely states alone so long as they were well governed. In March 1857 he was offered the secretaryship to the government of the North-Western Provinces, but the mutiny prevented him from taking up the appointment. Incidents of arson traceable to discontented sepoys had already occurred at Ambala, and in an interview at Simla shortly before the outbreak with General Anson (then commander-in-chief in India) Campbell impressed their importance upon him, aware of spreading contacts between native regiments. Unable to reach his new post at Agra, he remained at Ambala, sending *The Times* a series of letters on the course of the mutiny, over the signature of 'A Civilian'. Among the first to enter Delhi after its capture in September, he joined the column pursuing the mutineers, as provisional civil commissioner, and was at the relief of Agra. During the chase he rode ahead and accidentally captured three of the rebels' guns, whose crews believed he was leading a body of cavalry.

At Lucknow and Calcutta After a short stay at Agra he accompanied Sir Hope Grant's force to the first relief of Lucknow in October, and was soon afterwards ordered to Benares as adviser to John Peter Grant in that region. In a final letter to *The Times*, signed 'Judex', Campbell insisted upon the absence of concerted action among the Muslims, widely blamed for the rebellion, and declared that he could find no proof that white women had been tortured and raped before being put to death. He left Benares for Calcutta at the end of November 1857, and was employed by Lord Canning to write an account of the mutiny for the home authorities, to which Campbell added a recommendation to reorganize the North-Western Provinces on the Punjab system. For him the rising was nothing like a national revolt: he found its inspiration in 'a kind of military trades unionism' and in panic fears for both Hinduism and Islam at the hands of their reforming rulers (Campbell, 1.213–15).

After the second relief of Lucknow, Campbell was ordered there as judicial and also, briefly, financial commissioner in Oudh with charge for a time of the Lucknow district, where he restored order and had custody of the Oudh royal family. He did not always agree with the policy of Lord Canning. In his annual report for 1861 and subsequently he argued for continued protection of tenant right in Oudh in accordance with British Indian practice, taking on official superiors influenced by the 'aristocratic reaction' after the mutiny in favour of large landholders. The resulting controversy became acute. Although Sir John Lawrence, as viceroy from 1864, supported Campbell, their views did not prevail in the Oudh Rent Act of 1868 but were substantially adopted in 1886. In 1862 he introduced into Oudh the new Indian codes of civil and criminal procedure and the penal code, and in the same year Lord Elgin made him a judge of the newly constituted high court of Bengal. His judicial duties, confined almost entirely to appeals, were not heavy, and Lawrence employed him to inquire into the judicial system of the North-Western Provinces. His recommendations were the foundation on which a high court for those provinces was established in 1865. A succession of legal publications included collected papers on native law and custom, and a compendium of British legislation, *The Law Applicable to the Non-Regulation Provinces of India* (1863).

While at Calcutta, Campbell devoted much time to his favourite study of ethnology. He brought out *The Ethnology of India*, a special number of the *Journal of the Asiatic Society of Bengal* (1866), in which he reviewed the influence of race and caste on the failure of 'proper local nationalities' to emerge in the subcontinent. That year he travelled privately in China, and came away thinking, 'we have no right to assume that we are always right and the Chinese always wrong' (Campbell, 2.140). The humane outlook pervading these amateur researches was evident in his next important task, along with the robust approach characteristic of the 'Punjab school'. He headed a commission to report upon the causes of the Orissa famine, the most serious in Bengal since 1770, and the response of the local administrators. The report of 1867 was unfavourable to Bengal officialdom. It recommended better communications, increased expenditure on irrigation, and greater security of tenure for cultivators. Campbell himself was entrusted with a supplementary report on previous famines, and on structural changes needed to contain this periodic scourge; in the spring of 1867 he visited London to collect material at the India Office. He and his commission registered a powerful protest against the unintelligent application of the 'driest political economy' which they held partly responsibly for the mortality in Orissa (ibid., 2.156).

Later appointments On his return in the autumn he was appointed chief commissioner of the Central Provinces, where in his own words he went to work 'in new broom style'; but in 1868 his health broke down and he went to England on long furlough. In those two years Campbell stood for Dunbartonshire as a 'good Radical', withdrawing before the poll, and twice visited Ireland to study the land question. He published *The Irish Land* (1869), in which he contended for the legitimacy of the Irish custom of tenant right, hitherto almost entirely ignored in law. It was to this little book, wrote John Morley, that Gladstone owed the ruling idea of his first Irish Land Act in 1870 (Steele, 107) and its successor in 1881. He contributed an essay on India to the Cobden Club volume *Systems of Land Tenure* (1870), intended to put the imminent Irish legislation in a wider context. He was created DCL of Oxford on 22 June 1870 at the instance of the chancellor, Lord Salisbury, who admired his work on the famine commission. Somewhat unexpectedly he was offered the lieutenant-governorship of Bengal at the end of the year. Lord Mayo, then viceroy, sympathized with his reforming views: Campbell was appointed to carry out changes he had recommended in the supplemental Orissa report. He had the help as secretary of Charles Bernard, and of his own brother, Charles Campbell. The influence of Sir John Strachey in Mayo's council also stood him in good stead. One of the most important measures of Campbell's administration was the District Road Cess Act (1871), an early result of the decentralization of Indian finance introduced by the central government. That measure was successful in spite of both official and popular opposition. The systematic collection and publication of statistics were organized, and the first census of Bengal taken in 1871. Campbell also paid particular attention to education. He extended the village school system fostered by Sir John Peter Grant and established competitive examinations for the admission of Indians into the lower levels of government service. His preference for technical rather than legal and literary education encountered vigorous criticism from educated Bengalis and had to be modified.

During Campbell's term of office a successful frontier expedition was conducted against the Lushais, and the Garo Hills district, then unexplored, was annexed. While Campbell deprecated in general prosecution for press offences, he held an entirely free press to be inconsistent with government in the East, and strongly urged Mayo's successor, Lord Northbrook, to legislate against 'the unbridled licence' of vernacular newspapers (Moulton, 268). After the assassination of Lord Mayo, the acting viceroy, Francis, Lord Napier and Ettrick, continued the support for Campbell's reforms, but Northbrook, 'an extremely conservative Whig', was uneasy at the pace set and vetoed his Municipalities Bill, a well-intentioned measure, unpopular by reason of the increased local taxation it imposed (Campbell, 2.279, 285–8). In dealing with the Bengal famine of 1873–4, however, there was no serious disagreement between viceroy and lieutenant-governor, with the notable exception of the refusal to sanction Campbell's proposed prohibition of the export of rice from Bengal. He successfully directed the system of relief by public works and advances to cultivators, with the assistance of Richard Temple, who succeeded him as lieutenant-governor. In the latter's opinion he knew more of the realities of famine than any officer then in India, and his advice had great weight with the commission appointed after the south Indian famine of 1876–7.

Final years and writings Created KCSI in 1873, Campbell finally left India in April 1874, partly on account of bad health, but partly because he felt that he did not enjoy the full confidence of the central government. Named a member of the Council of India in London, he soon gave up the appointment to enter parliament, bringing to an end an official career in which ability and force of character sustained an unusual independence in one post after another. There is a vivid sketch of Campbell in the diary of a cabinet minister with Indian interests and experience, the fifteenth earl of Derby: 'In look, voice and manner, he resembles an American rather than an Englishman: nervous, eager and excitable: evidently a man marked out for action of a revolutionary kind' (diary, 4 Aug 1876, Derby MSS, Lpool RO). President of the economy and trade section at the Social Science Congress held at Glasgow in the autumn of 1874, he was elected for Kirkcaldy as a Liberal in the following April, and sat for that constituency until his death, specializing in overseas questions. Yet his failure as a politician was complete. The retired proconsul's discordant tones and self-importance—the subject of covert mockery in official Bengal—incurred open derision at Westminster, where he spoke, or tried to speak, far too often. He was 'positively and literally hooted as I have never heard a man hooted in the House of Commons', wrote H. W. Lucy (*Diary of Two Parliaments*, 198).

Campbell retained a great interest in the welfare of non-European peoples. In the autumn of 1878 he went to the United States to study the relationships between ethnic groups and published *Black and White: the Outcome of a Visit to the United States* (1879). A restless desire to inform himself and others produced *A Handy Book on the Eastern Question* (1876), a pamphlet, *The Afghan Frontier* (1879), and a volume entitled *The British Empire* (1887). He continued to write on ethnological subjects in the *Quarterly Ethnological Journal* and the *Journal of the Asiatic Society of Bengal*, and in 1874 edited for the Bengal Secretariat Press *Specimens of the Languages of India, including those of the Aboriginal Tribes of Bengal, the Central Provinces, and the Eastern Frontier*. At the time of his death he was in Egypt, writing his Indian memoirs.

Campbell died at the Continental Hotel, Cairo, from the effects of influenza, on 18 February 1892, and was buried in the British protestant cemetery there.

His *Memoirs of my Indian Career* (1893) reasserted his interpretation of the mutiny against that of Sir John W. Kaye and G. B. Malleson in their history of the rising. It is still a valuable source for agrarian policy and famine relief in the years when Campbell was in a position to influence both. The man emerges clearly from these recollections: authoritarian, paternalist, tireless in his enthusiasms. A perceptive critic allowed that his 'insatiable desire for change' was, on the whole, good for conservatively administered Bengal, if the haste of their introduction worked against some of his reforms (Beames, 199–202). Though not in the first rank of Indian administrators, Campbell's reputation is solidly based on his concern for the well-being of the peasant and his zeal for improvement generally.

G. LE G. NORGATE, *rev.* DAVID STEELE

Sources G. Campbell, *Memoirs of my Indian career*, ed. C. Bernard, 2 vols. (1893) · T. R. Metcalf, *The aftermath of revolt: India, 1857–1870* (1965) · P. H. M. van den Dungen, *The Punjab tradition: influence and authority in nineteenth-century India* (1972) · E. C. Moulton, *Lord Northbrook's Indian administration, 1872–1876* (1968) · J. Beames, *Memoirs of a Bengal civilian* (1961) · E. D. Steele, *Irish land and British politics: tenant-right and nationality, 1865–1870* (1974) · B. M. Bhatia, *Famines in India: a study in some aspects of the economic history of India, 1860–1945* (1963) · H. W. Lucy, *A diary of two parliaments*, 2 vols. (1885–6) · H. W. Lucy, *A diary of the Salisbury parliament, 1886–1892* (1892) · *The Times* (19 Feb 1892)

Archives BL OIOC, letters received and diaries, MS Eur. E 349 · NL Scot., diaries; journals · NRA Scotland | BL, corresp. with Florence Nightingale, Add. MSS 45803–45805 · BL OIOC, Lawrence MSS · BL OIOC, Northbrook MSS · BL OIOC, letters to Sir Richard Temple, MS Eur. F 86 · CUL, corresp. with Lord Mayo · NRA Scotland, priv. coll., letters to duke of Argyll

Likenesses group portrait, photograph, 1874, BL OIOC · Spy [L. Ward], chromolithograph cartoon, 1878, NPG; repro. in *VF* (21 Sept 1878) · photograph, repro. in Campbell, *Memoirs*, vol. 1, frontispiece [*see illus.*]

Wealth at death £41,200 2*s*. 2*d*. in UK: probate, 12 May 1892, *CGPLA Eng. & Wales*

Campbell, George Douglas, eighth duke of Argyll in the peerage of Scotland, and first duke of Argyll in the peerage of the United Kingdom (1823–1900), politician and scientist, was the second son of John Douglas Edward Henry Campbell (1777–1847) and his second wife, Joan, daughter and heir of John and Helen Glassel of Longniddry, East Lothian. He was born on 30 April 1823 at his parents' residence, Ardencaple Castle, Dunbartonshire, where he was brought up. His mother, who had been orphaned early and brought up by Anne Grant of Laggan, died in 1828, when he was five years old. His father became a recluse, but from 1831 George Campbell had a stepmother: his father's third wife, Anne, widow of Dr George Cunningham Menteath of Glasgow, who had been his mother's physician at the time of her death following childbirth. Anne died a Roman Catholic in 1874.

Education and early public work George Campbell was not reared to be a duke, for he had an elder brother, John, and his father, an MP until 1822, would succeed to the title only if his married brother had no heir. George Campbell was educated by private tutors: initially Church of Scotland ministers, then J. S. Howson (1816–1885), later dean of Chester. A confident boy, his lonely education made him self-reliant and accustomed to forming his opinions in isolation and with little discussion, a disadvantage when

George Douglas Campbell, eighth duke of Argyll in the peerage of Scotland, and first duke of Argyll in the peerage of the United Kingdom (1823–1900), by George Frederic Watts, *c.*1860

he entered the collegiate world of cabinet-level politics. He was a poet and a competent artist. He was powerfully influenced in youth by his observation of highland wildlife and he early developed a lifelong interest in ornithology and geology. He briefly attended lectures, including those of James David Forbes (1809–1868), at Edinburgh University in 1841 until poor health prevented his continuing them. He was influenced by Forbes's theories of glaciation and perhaps also by his passion for controversy.

In 1837 Campbell's elder brother died, and in 1839 his uncle, the sixth duke, died childless, his father thus becoming seventh duke of Argyll. George Campbell's status was thus transformed as he became marquess of Lorne and heir to the dukedom. The new duke, despite being perhaps the largest owner of church patronage in Scotland, sympathized with the claims of the Church of Scotland in the prolonged dispute over lay patronage which led to the Disruption of 1843. Lorne helped him prepare bills for the House of Lords on the subject and published anonymously *Letter to the Peers from a Peer's Son* (1842) on the dispute, its authorship soon being generally known. Lorne's view was that Lord Aberdeen, dangerously influenced by John Hope, was failing to prevent unnecessary disruption. Lorne did not approve of the secession from the established church, of which he continued to be a member, but he believed Scotland had been poorly treated by parliament. His study of the matter is set out in *Presbytery Examined: an Essay on the Ecclesiastical History of Scotland since the Reformation* (1848), which was reviewed by W. E. Gladstone in the *Quarterly Review* (December 1848) sympathetically with respect to the abilities, though not the arguments, of its author. Lorne believed that the church establishment in Scotland was the best representation of Scottish character, an effective balance between legitimate religious freedom and the dangers of private judgement (though he was influenced in his social thought by the evangelical theology of Thomas Chalmers, the leader of the disrupters). He deplored the Disruption and the self-righteousness of those who individually claimed the direct sanction of God for their opinions. In the heated religious atmosphere of Scotland in the half century after 1840, this moderate position, consistently enunciated by the head of one of Scotland's foremost families, was of some importance.

Marriage, succession as duke, and political rise On 31 July 1844 Lorne married Lady Elizabeth (*d.* 1878), eldest daughter of George Granville Leveson-Gower, second duke of Sutherland, and his wife, Harriet Elizabeth Georgiana Leveson-*Gower, thus further uniting two of the largest landowning families in Scotland. His mother-in-law, Duchess Harriet, was mistress of the robes and a leading political hostess, and played an important part in managing Lorne's entry into public life. Among their twelve children was the philanthropist Lady Victoria *Campbell.

The eighth duke of Argyll, as Lorne became on his father's death on 25 April 1847, was as a youth a Pittite (from reading the younger Pitt's speeches in his father's library) and by the early 1840s saw himself as a follower of Sir Robert Peel. He was irritated by Lord John Russell and the whigs and thought their views on free trade feeble. Argyll quickly established himself in Westminster politics, and especially as an orator by his maiden speech in May 1848 supporting the removal of Jewish disabilities. With one of the great ducal names, and his strong voice and striking red hair, he was courted by each of the political parties. After a speech in the Lords in 1850, Lord Stanley noted that he was

> the youngest peer who takes part in public affairs: he has some talent, more confidence, a diminutive figure, an affected style of dress, with long red hair loose over his shoulders, and a deep sonorous voice, capable of great rhetorical power. There is nothing to prevent this young man rising to a very high position except his too visible arrogance and conceit. … Brougham … clapped him on the back, with a 'well crowed, little Highland cock!', which the Duke did not appear to like. (*Disraeli, Derby and the Conservative Party*, 17–18)

By that year, at the age of twenty-seven, he was already well known, and in 1851 was elected FRS and chancellor of the University of St Andrews. His rise was confirmed in December 1852 when he became lord privy seal in Lord Aberdeen's coalition government, with the especial task of defending the government in the predominantly tory House of Lords, but with no departmental responsibilities.

Argyll was thus in cabinet but not really in office, a position repeated for much of his political career. This was due partly to his weak health, partly to his always vehemently expressed opinions, which were comparable to those of Lord John Russell in their angularity. Colleagues were wary of Argyll, though admiring his ability and combativeness. Argyll served on the cabinet committee to assist Gladstone on aspects of the 1853 budget but otherwise played little direct part in the extensive reforms of the coalition cabinet. He reminded his colleagues of the '*drift* of circumstances' by which Britain was becoming the ally of Turkey in the Near East crisis; but as war approached he vigorously, if anonymously, defended the cabinet's position in 'The diplomatic history of the Eastern question', *Edinburgh Review* (July 1854). When Aberdeen resigned, in January 1855, Argyll continued as lord privy seal in Palmerston's government, and did not resign from it with Gladstone and the Peelites in February 1855. He thus distanced himself from the Peelite group, with which he had become loosely associated. In December 1855 he transferred to the postmaster-generalship, a post he held until the government fell in February 1858. From June 1859, when Palmerston returned to office, until June 1866, when Russell's government resigned, Argyll was again lord privy seal; during 1860 he managed the Post Office while Lord Elgin was on a special mission to China. At the Post Office Argyll had the advantage of the support of Sir Rowland Hill; by his own admission he deferred on almost every occasion to Hill's energy and judgement in what was a period of considerable expansion of postal activities.

Like the Sutherland family with which he was by marriage associated, Argyll was a strong sympathizer with the anti-slavery movement in the USA and a strong opponent of the Confederate secessionists. For several years before the civil war began he corresponded with anti-slavers, and he met Harriet Beecher Stowe during her London visits. In cabinet he was, with Lord John Russell, the strongest opponent of sympathy or assistance being given to the Confederacy, his position being publicly stated in a strong speech in Edinburgh on 1 April 1863. He consistently opposed the cabinet's willingness to allow the gunship *Alabama* (built in England and sold to the Confederacy) to use British ports, arguing that she should have been detained and that manufacture of ironclad ships for sale to the South should have been prohibited.

Secretary of state for India, 1868–1874 Argyll had long been interested in India and had on occasion spoken for the government in the Lords on that subject. He had published several articles in the *Edinburgh Review* on the mutiny and its governmental aftermath (later collected as *India under Dalhousie and Canning* 1865). When Gladstone formed his first government in December 1868, he appointed Argyll secretary of state for India. Argyll held the office—his only major departmental post—until the ministry resigned in February 1874. Argyll took office when the secretaryship had been strengthened in its authority by the quiet work of Sir Charles Wood and the imperial tone of Argyll's immediate predecessor, Lord Cranborne. Argyll's tone sounded similarly imperious and he soon had the reputation of being something of an autocrat, but while emphasizing the general authority of the home government over the viceroy and the Indian government, he was in practice ready to work towards agreements. Having been in Palmerston's cabinet during the Indian mutiny, he was reluctant to relinquish any imperial authority in India. He saw the advancement of Indians in the Indian Civil Service as destabilizing and in April 1869 he cancelled the plans for a scholarship scheme with the comment, 'it is one of our first duties towards the people of India to guard the safety of our own dominions. For this purpose, we must proceed gradually, employing only such Natives as we can trust' (dispatch, 8 April 1869, Williams, 311). But his view of security in India did not require territorial expansion into Persia or the northwest. His policy in the Persian Gulf was 'no interference where it can possibly be avoided', except to prevent piracy and protect trade (memorandum, 11 Dec 1868; ibid., 204). He therefore quashed the demands of those wanting a 'forward policy' towards Russian expansion in central Asia, and later coined the word 'Mervousness' to describe those fretting over the Russian advance towards the city of Merv. Argyll thus brought no especial reforming zeal to the India Office. From the government's viewpoint, a ministry often overstretched was happy to have one area of its responsibility quiescent, and no attempt was made to urge reform upon Argyll.

Argyll was active in cabinet beyond his departmental brief. He expressed extensive reservations in 1869–70 about Gladstone's proposed legislation on Irish land. Though his departure to Inveraray to be with his sick wife removed him from London at the critical moment, he had some success in modifying the bill. He was also active in Scottish education, introducing a bill in February 1869 into the Lords, the predecessor of what became the important act of 1872 which he saw through the Lords. However, Argyll did not have the full trust of his prime minister, who saw him as gifted, but erratic. Thus, when the viceroy of India, Lord Mayo, was assassinated in February 1872, it was on Lord Granville, the foreign secretary, that Gladstone chiefly relied when discussing a successor; Lord Northbrook was appointed despite Argyll's prolonged objections. Argyll left office in February 1874 without regret: 'Politically, too, there are many compensations to me, as I am not a Radical, and many of the extreme joints of our tail had been wagging too much' (Argyll to Northbrook, 13 Feb 1874, *Autobiography*, 2.289). Despite this, Argyll soon found himself working with the radicals on the Eastern question and in opposing what he saw as the Conservative government's imperialistic initiatives.

Argyll was, with Gladstone, the most prominent survivor of the cabinet which had fought the Crimean War for the integrity of the Ottoman empire. He believed that Russia in that war had received and had registered a strong caution. Argyll blamed the Porte for its failure to reform internally since 1856 and for its brutal suppression of dissident Christians in the Balkans. He was also confident that Russia, in supporting the cause of the Balkan Christians when the British government stood aside, would not go too far in her dismemberment of 'Turkey in

Europe'. Argyll spoke vehemently in the Lords and on public platforms against the government's conduct of the Eastern question in 1876–8, and he also charged it with mishandling 'Afghan affairs' in 1879–80. He was an important representative of anti-Conservative opinion at court. In 1879 he published *The Eastern Question* in two volumes, of which *The Afghan Question from 1841 to 1878* (1879) was a substantial extract. Argyll was thus seen, slightly improbably, as a leading anti-Conservative critic when the government was defeated at the general election in 1880, even though he disapproved of the radicalism of Gladstone's Midlothian campaign and hoped Lord Granville would be the new prime minister.

Estates and Scotland Argyll's title and estates made him the dominant personality in the western highlands. He owned about 175,000 acres. Though the family was traditionally whig in politics, and Argyll was often described as a whig, he had none of the English whigs' veneration for prescriptive rights. 'No delusion', he wrote, 'can be greater than the common popular superstition that the clansmen under the Celtic system enjoyed rights and sources of wealth which they lost when that system was superseded and eventually destroyed' (*Unseen Foundations*, 265). For Argyll, the decisive moment in Scottish history was the change from clan-based customary society to a 'universal recognition of legally acknowledged rights', embodied in a strong law sustained by the monarchy (ibid., 272). His relationship with his tenantry was thus businesslike, rather than paternal, and this conditioned his view of land law generally, which, chiefly but not uniquely in relationship to Ireland, involved him in frequent political controversy, since many Liberals from the late 1860s took a more sympathetic view of customary rights. Even so, he wore full highland dress at dinner when in Scotland and liked to be referred to as the MacCailein-Mòr ('Son of the great Colin'), the traditional title of the head of the clan Campbell.

Argyll was from the first a notably vigorous landowner. During his father's dukedom he took much responsibility for the estates, which had been badly mismanaged in the 1820s and 1830s, the sixth duke having lost about £2 million. He superintended the heavily encumbered Argyll estates' response to the great famine which began in 1846, in which year and afterwards he was with the duke of Sutherland an early and effective sponsor of assisted emigration (especially from the Ross of Mull and the island of Tiree which he owned) as an alternative to clearance by default. Eviction was used to encourage emigration in a process which became known as compulsory emigration. 'I wish', the duke wrote on 5 May 1851, 'to send out those whom we would be obliged to feed if they stayed at home; to get rid of that class is *the object*' (Devine, *Clanship*, 190). The social costs were high, but the changes resulted in the long run in a more stable estate economy. The great Campbell diaspora in North America was in part the consequence of these efforts. Argyll calculated that between 1847 and 1897 he spent over £554,000 on the improvement of his estates (*Autobiography*, 2.551). He described his policy in *Essay on the Commercial Principles Applicable for the Hire of Land*, a pamphlet for the Cobden Club (1877), and in *Crofts and Farms in the Hebrides* (1883). A notable action was his gift in 1899 of the abbey church of Iona, with other ecclesiastical buildings on the island, to the Church of Scotland.

Argyll played an important part in the public life of Scotland. He was chancellor of the University of St Andrews from 1851 until his death, and was rector of Glasgow University in 1854–6. In 1856 he became a knight of the Thistle. He was president of the Royal Society of Edinburgh (1860–64) and of the Highland and Agricultural Society of Scotland (1862–6). His Liberal Unionism reflected an important tendency among the Scottish propertied classes. Even so, Argyll's influence in Scotland was less marked than might have been expected from his eminent position. He lacked Lord Rosebery's ability to associate the Scottish Liberal aristocracy with the wider culture of Scottish Liberalism and its nationalistic tendency.

Argyll's English contacts quickly brought visitors to Argyllshire. In 1847 Queen Victoria appeared unexpectedly at Inveraray by yacht and a welcome had to be swiftly manufactured. Inveraray became something of a highland political and cultural centre, though never matching Dunrobin, the Sutherlands' great house. The Argylls had five sons and seven daughters, the duchess's poor health causing her to leave much of the upbringing to the father. When in England, where the chief family house was Argyll Lodge in west London, Argyll and his family were frequently in the company of Duchess Harriet, often weekending with the Sutherlands and the Gladstones at Cliveden, where high society engaged in theological debate. At Inveraray the duke began the day punctually, for he was fussy about time, with prayers and Bible reading at the breakfast table. Close links with the court through Duchess Harriet were confirmed by the marriage of Argyll's eldest son, John Douglas Sutherland *Campbell, Lord Lorne, to Victoria and Albert's daughter Princess *Louise in March 1871. In 1879, when Lorne was governor-general of Canada, Argyll visited him there and also made a short visit to the USA.

Houses, wives, and children Argyll's life was disrupted in the later 1870s. On 12 October 1877 a fire at Inveraray Castle destroyed the centre of the house. Argyll had made few alterations to the castle (and later prevented the railway reaching the adjacent town), though he had earlier considered turning Roger Morris's Gothic castle into a Scottish-baronial extravaganza. Fortunately, he did not take advantage of the fire to do so, but employed Anthony Salvin to restore the building, though adding an extra floor and high-pitched conical roofs. He suffered a further blow on 25 May 1878 by the death of the duchess, at the dinner table in London when sitting next to Gladstone. On 17 August 1881 Argyll married again; his new wife was Amelia Maria, daughter of Thomas Legh *Claughton, bishop of St Albans, and his wife, Julia Susanna; she was the widow of Colonel Archibald Henry Augustus Anson. She died at Inveraray on 4 January 1894 and was buried at Cannes next to her first husband. Argyll's third wife was

Ina Erskine (*d.* 1925), daughter of Archibald McNeill of Colonsay, whom he married on 30 July 1895. She was an extra lady of the bedchamber. Argyll's second and third marriages were childless.

Argyll's second and third wives brought calm to balance the disconcerting effect of two of his children's marriages. Lorne's marriage to Princess Louise was a source of some awkwardness in Argyll's relations with the queen, as Lorne and Louise soon led partially separate lives, though never formally separating. Even more problematic was the impetuous marriage in 1881 of his fifth son, **Lord Colin Campbell** (1853–1895), city director and politician, who was Liberal MP for Argyllshire, to Gertrude Elizabeth, daughter of Edmond Maghlin Blood [*see* Campbell, Gertrude Elizabeth]. Argyll refused to recognize the engagement and handled the marriage unsympathetically. It ended in 1886 in the longest divorce case in English history, with both husband and wife petitioning the court. Argyll left the courtroom abruptly when his son was accused of having syphilis, but gave evidence for him on 6 December, clearly embarrassed and in a moral world he barely comprehended. Argyll's daughters fared more happily than those two of their brothers. Lady Edith (*d.* 1913) married the duke of Northumberland; Lady Frances married Eustace Balfour, brother of the prime minister [*see* Balfour, Lady Frances]; Lady Mary Emma (*d.* 1947) married Edward Carr Glyn, bishop of Peterborough.

Argyll and science Argyll had an abiding fascination with causation and morphology in nature, especially with respect to ornithology and geology; and in his later years he related his views to human society and government. His writings on science and society were characterized by a confidence which was impatient of understanding other opinions and arguments. His scientific writings, especially, became intemperate, relying increasingly on point scoring. On the island of Mull his tenant found fossilized leaves intercalated among basalt lava. Argyll announced the discovery—one of considerable importance in the geological discoveries of the day—to the British Association in 1850. Edward Forbes found the deposit to be of early Tertiary age. Argyll's paper to the Geological Society 'On Tertiary leaf-beds in the Isle of Mull' in 1851 made a considerable impact, and his description influenced subsequent work in Britain on Tertiary volcanic action. Argyll was a cataclysmal geologist, believing in a primeval convulsion, and he believed that local glaciers and floating ice accounted for geological markings, rather than a general glaciation submerging the mountainous areas of Britain. This position he defended in a long series of vehement papers against evolving contemporary geological opinion. Argyll has been termed a 'Christian Darwinist' (Moore, 306–7). He believed that there might have been several creations and, following Richard Owen, he focused on individual organisms, each of which he believed contained a 'plan' and through which the complexities of development could be examined and understood (ibid., 221–2). He believed in a special creation of the human body and soul and argued that palaeontological evidence conclusively denied 'any change whatever in the specific characters of Man since the oldest Human Being was born' and that 'all scientific evidence' favoured the derivation of mankind from a 'single pair' from which present-day humans had degenerated rather than progressively evolved (Argyll, *Primeval Man*, 1869, and *Unity of Nature*, 1884; cited in Moore, 231–2). Any progress that might be perceived was planned and directed by 'mind'. He thus denied a general and interrelated process of evolution, and clashed both with Darwin and with T. H. Huxley, emerging as one of the most combative of the defenders of the orthodoxies for the 1840s.

Argyll made a substantial attempt to integrate his scientific and social thought. He believed in 'the great natural law, which in all societies, has recognised the security of individual possession as the test of national prosperity and independence, even as it is the foundation of their organic life' (*Unseen Foundations*, 136). But this law could not be imposed, and must develop naturally, for the organic parts of society 'like the atoms in chemistry, are dynamic', each with its own function, fully pursuing that function only when untrammelled (ibid., 174). Consequently, he was a strong individualist, opposing the introduction of limited liability in 1856 and still defending his opposition in the 1890s, and also continuing to deplore—as in his article 'Christian socialising', *Nineteenth Century*, 36 (1894)—any national welfare system, even in the moderate form of the nineteenth-century workhouse network. He may be seen as one of the last leading remnants of Thomas Chalmers's moral individualism.

Argyll's intellectual output—unusual for a duke—was one of the most thoroughgoing attempts of the second half of his century to defend a Christian (or at any rate deistic) individualist position. His *Unseen Foundations of Society: an Examination of the Fallacies and Failure of Economic Science due to Neglected Elements* (1893)—his most substantial theoretical work—was a significant attempt to link his scientific position to social and political analysis, while denigrating the limitations of the Ricardian school of political economy, which limitations he also emphasized in *Application of the Historical Method to Economic Science* (1894).

In cabinet again, resignation, and final years Argyll became lord privy seal in Gladstone's second government, formed in April 1880. Though again associated with Liberalism during the Eastern question campaign, he approached most of the policies of the government with scepticism or hostility. He disliked the idea of evolution towards radicalism, and he quarrelled with its Irish policy on historical, political, and intellectual grounds (though, unusually among the landowners hostile to Liberal proposals, he owned no land in Ireland). Since Ireland was the predominant question of the government's early years, he was soon in conflict with it, first offering his resignation on 14 June 1880 on the proposal to give compensation to a tenant for disturbance.

When in the autumn of 1880 Gladstone began planning the Land Act of 1881, Argyll began a bombardment of correspondence, especially opposing a right of 'free sale' of land by tenants. Gladstone kept Argyll within the cabinet by encouraging him in this prolonged correspondence, but on 31 March 1881 Argyll resigned, making a statement of his reasons to the Lords on 8 April. He never again held office. Increasingly disabled by gout, which sometimes diminished, though it could not quell, his ability to write, he enjoyed emancipation from the restrictions of office and spoke and wrote much on public affairs. In 1884 he played some part as an intermediary between Gladstone and Salisbury after the Lords rejected the Representation of the People Bill, but he condemned the Liberal government's handling of Sudanese policy in 1884–5. In 1885–6 he was a vehement opponent of the Liberal cabinet's home-rule proposals, which he saw as an evil concession and a dangerous precedent, especially for Scotland. During that crisis he was sometimes thought of as a possible prime minister of a coalition government of tories and Liberal Unionists, and in July 1886 the queen considered, but quickly dropped, the notion of asking him to attempt to form a government. Argyll campaigned against home rule in print and on the platform. He developed his opinions on government and society in *Scotland as it Was and as it Is* (2 vols., 1887), *The New British Constitution and its Master Builders* (1888), and *Irish Nationalism: an Appeal to History* (1893). Ironically, his intellectual position was not greatly different from Gladstone's: their quarrel was more about means than ends.

Though in most respects estranged from the Liberal Party, Argyll's cautions about imperial expansion and his mistrust of Turkey—repeated in *Our Responsibilities for Turkey: Facts and Memories of Forty Years* (1896)—maintained some links with that party in the 1890s, and he was associated with the protests against atrocities in Armenia in 1895–6. His Liberal Unionism was confined to Irish policy and opposition to government intervention. It was Salisbury, however, who granted him a further dukedom, also of Argyll, in 1892.

In 1897 Argyll began his autobiography, reaching 1857 by his death. It is the best autobiography by a Victorian cabinet minister. He was unable to act as one of Gladstone's pallbearers in 1898, publicly explaining that this was not the consequence of their political differences (*The Times*, 27 May 1898). He continued to paint, to write poems on theological and ornithological subjects—his *Burdens of Belief and other Poems* (1894) is characteristic of his later compositions—and to study the habits of birds. One of his poems was included in the second series of Palgrave's *Golden Treasury*. Argyll died at Inveraray Castle on 24 April 1900 and was buried in the family grave at Kilmun on the Holy Loch. His widow, the third duchess, who died on 24 December 1925, edited his autobiography and added a biography with a thorough bibliography (2 vols., 1906) to cover the rest of a complex and interesting life, which has, unfortunately, been little studied since.

H. C. G. MATTHEW

Sources *George Douglas, 8th duke of Argyll, 1823–1900: autobiography and memoirs*, ed. I. E. Campbell, 2 vols. (1906) • G. D. Campbell, *The unseen foundations of society* (1893) • F. Balfour, *Ne obliviscaris: dinna forget*, 2 vols. [1930] • I. G. Lindsay and M. Cosh, *Inveraray and the dukes of Argyll* (1973) • T. M. Devine, *The great highland famine* (1988) • T. M. Devine, *Clanship to crofters' war: the social transformation of the Scottish highlands* (1994) • J. L. Duthie, 'Pressure from within: the "forward" group in the India Office during Gladstone's first ministry', *Journal of Asian History*, 15 (1981), 36–72 • S. N. Singh, *The secretary of state for India and his council* (1962) • D. Williams, *The India Office, 1858–1869* (1983) • A. P. Kaminsky, *The India Office, 1880–1910* (1986) • J. R. Moore, *The post-Darwinian controversies* (1979) • B. Hilton, *The age of atonement: the influence of evangelicalism on social and economic thought, 1795–1865* (1988) • Gladstone, *Diaries* • G. H. Fleming, *Victorian 'sex goddess': Lady Colin Campbell*, pbk edn (1990) • E. Longford, *Victoria RI* (1964) • *Disraeli, Derby and the conservative party: journals and memoirs of Edward Henry, Lord Stanley, 1849–1869*, ed. J. R. Vincent (1978) • A. B. Cooke and J. Vincent, *The governing passion: cabinet government and party politics in Britain, 1885–86* (1974) • GEC, *Peerage* • Boase, *Mod. Eng. biog.* • N. C. Gillespie, 'The duke of Argyll, evolutionary anthropology, and the art of scientific controversy', *Isis*, 68 (1977), 40–54 • J. W. Mason, 'The duke of Argyll and the land question in late nineteenth-century Britain', *Victorian Studies*, 21 (1977–8), 149–70

Archives NL Scot., corresp.; letters to his son and daughter-in-law • NRA Scotland, priv. coll., Inveraray Castle, Argyll, corresp. and papers | BL, corresp. with Lord Aberdeen, Add. MS 43199 • BL, corresp. with Arthur James Balfour, Add. MS 49800, *passim* • BL, Disraeli MSS • BL, corresp. with W. E. Gladstone, Add. MSS 44098–44106, 46227–46229 • BL, letters to Sir A. Paget, Add. MS 48404B • BL, corresp. with Lord Stanmore, Add. MS 49209 • BL OIOC, letters to Sir Owen Tudor Burne, MS Eur. D 951 • BL OIOC, letters to Sir Mountstuart Grant Duff, MS Eur. F 234 • BL OIOC, corresp. with Lord Northbrook • BL OIOC, corresp. with Sir Philip Wodehouse, MS Eur. D 726 • Bodl. Oxf., letters to Sir Henry Wentworth Acland • Bodl. Oxf., corresp. with Lord Clarendon • Bodl. Oxf., letters to Lord Kimberley • Bodl. Oxf., corresp. with Friedrich Max Müller • Borth. Inst., corresp. with Lord Halifax • Bucks. RLSS, letters to duke of Somerset • Chatsworth House, Derbyshire, letters to Lord Hartington • CKS, letters to Edward Stanhope • CUL, corresp. with Lord Kelvin • CUL, corresp. with Lord Mayo • Keele University Library, letters to Sneyd family • LPL, corresp. with Lord Selborne • LPL, corresp. with A. C. Tait • Mitchell L., Glas., Glasgow City Archives, letters to Smith family • NA Scot., letters to Lord Lothian • NA Scot., letters to Lord Panmure • NHM, letters to Albert C. L. G. Gunther • NHM, corresp. with Richard Owen and William Clift • NHM, corresp. with George Charles Wallich • NL Scot., letters to J. S. Blackie • PRO, corresp. with Lord Cardwell, PRO 30/48 • PRO, corresp. with Lord Granville, PRO 30/29 • PRO, corresp. with Lord John Russell, PRO 30/22 • PRO NIre., corresp. with Lord Dufferin • St Deiniol's Library, corresp. with W. E. Gladstone and Catherine Gladstone • Staffs. RO, corresp. with duke of Sutherland and Lord Stafford • U. Birm. L., special collections department, corresp. with Joseph Chamberlain • U. Durham L., archives and special collections, letters to third Earl Grey • U. Edin. L., special collections division, letters to Sir Charles Lyell • U. Nott. L., department of manuscripts and special collections, letters to John Denison • U. Nott. L., department of manuscripts and special collections, letters to duke of Newcastle • U. Southampton L., letters to Lord Palmerston • U. St Andr. L., corresp. with James Forbes • UCL, corresp. with Sir Edwin Chadwick • Harrowby Manuscript Trust, letters to Lord Harrowby

Likenesses L. Macdonald, marble bust, 1844, Inveraray Castle, Argyll • J. Watson-Gordon, oils, exh. RA 1851, Inveraray Castle, Argyll • J. R. Swinton, drawing, 1852, Inveraray Castle, Argyll • W. Brodie, bust, 1855, Dunrobin Castle, Sutherland • G. F. Watts, oils, *c.*1860, NPG [*see illus.*] • G. Richmond, drawing, 1861?, Inveraray Castle, Argyll • H. von Angeli, oils, exh. 1878, Inveraray Castle, Argyll; copy, H. Koberwein-Terrell, 1892, Royal Collection • G. P. Jacomb Hood, oils, 1890, Inveraray Castle, Argyll • S. P. Hall, pencil, 1893, NPG • F. S. Baden Powell, silhouette, 1895, NPG • G. Frampton, marble bust, 1905, Palace of Westminster, London • G. Frampton, recumbent effigy, exh. 1908, Iona Cathedral • Ape [C. Pellegrini], chromolithograph, repro. in *VF* (17 April 1869) • Elliott & Fry, photograph, NPG · J. Gilbert, group portrait, pencil and wash (*The coalition ministry, 1854*), NPG · S. P. Hall, oils, Inveraray Castle, Argyll · W. Holl, stipple (after drawing by by G. Richmond), BM, NPG · Princess Louise, oils, Inveraray Castle, Argyll · J. Pettie, oils, Scot. NPG · cartes-de-visite, NPG · oils, U. St Andr. · woodburytype, NPG

Wealth at death £92,158 2*s.* 7*d.*: confirmation, 9 Aug 1900, *CCI* · £1850—Colin Campbell: confirmation, 11 Jan 1896, *CCI*

Campbell [*née* Blood], **Gertrude Elizabeth** [Lady Colin Campbell] (**1857–1911**), art critic and journalist, was the second daughter and third of the four children of Edmond Maghlin Blood (1815–1891) of Brickhill, co. Clare, and his wife, Mary Anne (1814/15–1899), daughter of Thomas Fergusson of Leixlip, co. Kildare. She spent most of her childhood in Italy, which provided the setting for her popular children's book, *Topo*, published in 1878 under the name G. E. Brunefille, with illustrations by Kate Greenaway; her first published work was a travel article in *Cassell's Family Magazine*, 'My real Turkish bath: a lady's experience in Egypt' (1, 1874–5, 82–3).

While visiting friends in Scotland in September 1880, she met Lord Colin *Campbell (1853–1895) [*see under* Campbell, George Douglas, eighth duke of Argyll], the youngest son of George Douglas *Campbell, eighth duke of Argyll. Two days later he proposed marriage and was accepted. The marriage was delayed by the disapproval of his family and by his ill health, but took place on 21 July 1881 at the Chapel Royal in London. The marriage rapidly failed, and in August 1883 Lady Colin sued for a judicial separation on grounds of cruelty, which was granted the following March. Two years later, the Campbells engaged in one of the most sensational divorce cases of the century: Lady Colin offered her husband's infidelity and cruelty (she alleged that he knowingly infected her with syphilis) as grounds; Lord Colin's counter-petition alleged that Lady Colin had committed adultery with at least four named men: Lord Blandford, Eyre Massey Shaw (the head of the London Fire Brigade), Tom Bird (a surgeon), and (General) Sir William Butler. The jury decided that no adultery had been committed on either side and no divorce was obtained; but Lady Colin's reputation had been destroyed: one newspaper described her as having 'the unbridled lust of a Messalina and the indelicate readiness of a common harlot' (Fleming, 1–2). Even Lady Colin's apparently virtuous activities in helping in an East End soup kitchen, performing at charity concerts, and teaching factory girls in evening classes had been made to bear an unsavoury interpretation.

It is difficult to resist the temptation to view Lady Colin's entire career through the prism of this divorce case, the perspective of the only modern account of her life. And yet she was much more than a sexually compromised and socially disgraced woman. Indeed, the extent to which she lived beyond the prescribed roles of woman and wife was used against her in the trial, but it is for these transgressions, not sexual ones, that she should be remembered.

Lady Colin's precocious literary talents were to be turned to good account all her life. In October 1883 she submitted her first article to the editor of the *Saturday Review*, and thereafter became one of their staff writers,

Gertrude Elizabeth Campbell [Lady Colin Campbell] (**1857–1911**), by Giovanni Boldini, *c.*1897

producing up to three articles a week on a wide range on topics, from science and literature to political economy; she frequently reviewed books written in Italian, French, German, and Spanish. In 1886 she published a series of her *Saturday Review* essays as *A Book of the Running Brook and of Still Waters*, in part natural history and in part tract promoting the development of commercial inland fisheries to provide 'an immense increase in the supply of cheap and wholesome food for the nation' (p. 129). Her only novel, *Darrell Blake* (1889), which enjoyed considerable vogue (not merely because of the notoriety of its author), drew on her personal knowledge of journalism in its setting, while its plot—the destruction of the happiness of the newspaper editor principally through his seduction by the scheming aristocrat Lady Alma Vereker—demonstrated that Lady Colin (like Harriet Vane) would not be cowed by public notoriety into a show of 'proper feeling'.

She wrote for a number of periodicals, including the *Pall Mall Gazette*, especially on art, music, literature, and travel, and in 1889 became art editor of *The World*, the first woman editor on a London paper not exclusively aimed at a female readership. She retained this connection until 1903. As 'Q.E.D.' she wrote a weekly column 'In the picture galleries' for *The World*, and as Vera Tsaritsyn a series of travel articles, which were subsequently published as *A*

Woman's Walks: Studies in Colour Abroad and at Home (1903). In 1894 she founded a weekly review, *The Realm*, but it folded in December 1895. She became the editor of the *Ladies' Field* in 1901, remaining with that paper for two years.

Much of Lady Colin's journalistic career was based on her connections with the Victorian art world, and it seems likely (in the absence of detailed research as yet) that it is here that her importance lies; it has been suggested that she 'perform[ed] for the visual arts what her colleague George Bernard Shaw was doing for music' (Fleming, 243). She exhibited her own works a number of times at the Society of Women Artists, and in November 1886, at the height of the divorce case, her small landscape, *Thalassa*, was exhibited at the Society of British Artists' show in Suffolk Street, an exhibition which also included her portrait by the society's president, J. M. Whistler, *Harmony in White and Ivory* (now lost). She also turned her hand to drama, writing a one-act play, *Bud and Blossom*, performed at Terry's Theatre in the West End, and co-writing with Clothilde Graves a full-length melodrama, *St Martin's Summer*, which was played in London by William and Madge Kendal. Her circle included Oscar Wilde, Arthur Sullivan, Elizabeth Thompson (Lady Butler, in whose studio she regularly worked), and Paolo Tosti, who was her singing teacher (Lady Colin had a rich contralto voice, and frequently appeared at charity concerts). Her place in such circles after the trial has yet to be established, but the range of her interests gave her an enviable measure of authority in her chosen fields.

In 1893 appeared *Etiquette and Good Society*, edited and revised by Lady Colin Campbell. The work was immensely successful, 92,000 copies having been issued by 1911. Such success was intensely ironic, as by the time of its appearance the author had been excluded from 'good society' for thirteen years. Broadly conventional in the advice she offered, Lady Colin took the opportunity to pour scorn on the idea that labour was demeaning to a lady; she told an interviewer in 1902 that 'Work is the justification of living at all, the rent we are bound to pay to Nature for the actual space we occupy in the world' (Bertouche, 561). Lady Colin took her own injunctions to heart, until forced into retirement by the onset of rheumatoid arthritis in 1903. By 1906 she was wheelchair-bound and increasingly reclusive. She died at her home, 67 Carlisle Mansions, Carlisle Place, London, on 1 November 1911 from the effects of her disease, and was cremated at Golders Green. At her request, her portrait painted by Giovanni Boldini about 1897 was given to the National Portrait Gallery.

Lady Colin Campbell defined a lady as one who would 'never try, by any means, to appear other than she really is' (*Etiquette*, 1893, 18); the social ostracism engendered by her notoriety gave Lady Colin the freedom to be who she 'really was'. K. D. Reynolds

Sources G. H. Fleming, *Victorian 'sex goddess': Lady Colin Campbell*, pbk edn (1990) • Baroness de Bertouche, 'Lady Colin Campbell', *Crampton's Magazine*, 19 (1902), 559–63 • *The cabinet portrait gallery*, 4 (1893), 76 • Burke, *Gen. Ire.* • R. Dorment and M. F. MacDonald, *James McNeill Whistler* (1994) • J. Johnson and A. Greutzner, *The dictionary of British artists, 1880–1940* (1976), vol. 5 of *Dictionary of British art* • Wood, *Vic. painters*, 3rd edn • A. Sebba, *Battling for news: the rise of the woman reporter* (1994) • J. Sutherland, *The Longman companion to Victorian fiction* (1988) • m. cert. • d. cert. • will

Likenesses J. M. Whistler, portrait, 1886; lost • G. Boldini, oils, *c.*1897, NPG [*see illus.*] • W. & D. Downey, woodburytype photograph, NPG; repro. in W. Downey and D. Downey, *The cabinet portrait gallery*, 4 (1893), 76

Wealth at death £470 10s. 6*d.*: probate, 16 Nov 1911, *CGPLA Eng. & Wales*

Campbell, Gill-Easbuig (*d.* 1385x7). *See under* Campbell family (*per. c.*1300–1453).

Campbell, Gordon (1886–1953), naval officer, was born at Upper Norwood, London, on 6 January 1886, ninth son and thirteenth of the sixteen children of Colonel Frederick Campbell and his wife, Emilie, daughter of Donald Maclaine of Lochbuie. Educated at Dulwich College, he passed into the *Britannia* as a naval cadet in 1900. He was promoted lieutenant in 1907 and at the outbreak of the First World War he was commanding a destroyer on channel escort duties. In 1911 he married Mary Jeanne, daughter of Henry V. S. Davids, of Hillier House, Guildford; they had one son and one daughter.

Early in 1915 as part of the anti-submarine measures a number of tramp steamers were converted into decoy ships with naval crews and concealed guns. Campbell volunteered for these 'mystery' or Q-ships, and became the most brilliant exponent of this hazardous form of warfare. To outward appearance harmless merchantmen, the Q-ships offered themselves as targets in U-boat infested waters. After their existence became known and enemy submarine captains more wary, Campbell deliberately allowed his vessel to be torpedoed, remaining on board with his hidden gunners, after part of the crew had 'abandoned ship', waiting for the submarine to close her victim. Using these tactics he sank three of the eleven German submarines destroyed by Q-ships, for which actions he won the VC, was appointed to the DSO with two bars, and attained promotion to captain in 1917 at the early age of thirty-one. He also received the thanks of the war cabinet, was awarded the Croix de Guerre, and appointed chevalier of the Légion d'honneur. More than seventy decorations, including four Victoria crosses, were awarded to officers and men of the three Q-ships he commanded.

Campbell's last Q-ships action typified his outstanding courage and that of the crews he inspired. On 8 August 1917 his decoy ship *Dunraven* was attacked with gunfire by a surfaced U-boat which started a fierce fire on board. After torpedoing the *Dunraven* the submarine continued to shell her while Campbell and his gunners remained at their posts in the burning vessel, with ammunition exploding about them, waiting for the U-boat to come within range, but she finally made off without doing so. Later the *Dunraven* sank while in tow.

After the loss of the *Dunraven* Campbell served as flag captain to the commander-in-chief, coast of Ireland patrol, in charge of all anti-submarine operations in the Irish Sea.

After the war Campbell commanded successively the

cadet training cruiser *Cumberland* and the boys' training establishment *Impregnable*, and subsequently served as captain in charge of Simonstown Dockyard. In 1920, in recognition of his distinguished war service, he was elected a younger brother of Trinity House. His last seagoing appointment was in command of the battle cruiser *Tiger* from 1925 to 1927. In April 1928 he was retired as rear-admiral, his indifferent medical record since the end of the war undoubtedly contributing to this early retirement. He was promoted vice-admiral on the retired list in 1932.

Campbell then turned to writing and lecturing. His first book, *My Mystery Ships* (1928), told the story of his exploits in Q-ships, and he delivered many lectures on the subject in the United Kingdom, Canada, and the United States, proving a fluent and popular speaker. His autobiography, *Number Thirteen*, appeared in 1932; between 1933 and 1938 he produced a number of other works, mostly short historical accounts of various sea actions, also adventure stories for boys; and (with I. O. Evans) he published a textbook on flags (1950).

When the National Government was formed to deal with the economic crisis in 1931, Campbell, although not politically minded, decided to stand as a National candidate for Burnley where he sensationally defeated the Labour member Arthur Henderson, former foreign secretary. A staunch supporter of Baldwin and the League of Nations, Campbell was popular with his constituents and spoke often in the house. In the general election of 1935 he stood again as Liberal–National candidate but was defeated by the Labour contender.

At the outbreak of the Second World War Campbell was specially commissioned by Winston Churchill to requisition and fit out a number of decoy merchantmen with the object of repeating the earlier *ruse de guerre* of the Q-ships. Although under his direction the vessels were well armed and brilliantly disguised they met with no success, and after a few months the scheme was abandoned. Campbell was then appointed resident naval officer, Padstow, responsible for naval defences in that area. In appearance the traditional bluff, ruddy-faced sailor, he nevertheless continued to be dogged by ill health aggravated by the strain of his Q-ship experiences, and was finally forced to retire from active naval service in 1943. Campbell died at the West Middlesex Hospital, Hounslow, London, on 3 October 1953. He was the uncle of Lorne Maclaine *Campbell (1902–1991), who was also awarded the Victoria Cross. A. C. HAMPSHIRE, *rev.*

Sources G. Campbell, *Number thirteen* (1932) • *The Times* (6 Oct 1953) • *WWW* • private information (1971) • *CGPLA Eng. & Wales* (1954)
Likenesses F. Dodd, charcoal and watercolour, 1917, IWM
Wealth at death £1446 16*s.* 6*d.*: probate, 29 Jan 1954, *CGPLA Eng. & Wales*

Campbell, Sir Guy, first baronet (1786–1849), army officer, eldest son of Lieutenant-General Colin *Campbell (1754–1814) and his wife, Mary, eldest daughter of Colonel Guy Johnstone, an American loyalist, was born on 22 January 1786. He joined the 6th regiment as an ensign in 1795, and was promoted lieutenant on 4 April 1796. He was present at all his father's engagements during the Irish rising of 1798, and then accompanied the regiment to Canada in 1803, being promoted captain on 14 September 1804. He was present at the battles of Roliça and Vimeiro, and throughout Sir John Moore's advance into Spain and retreat to Corunna.

On 1 April 1813 Campbell was promoted major, and again accompanied his regiment to the Peninsula, and after the battle of Vitoria, where the colonel was severely wounded, he succeeded to the command of the regiment. The 6th regiment formed part of Barnes's brigade of the 7th division, and after fighting in the battle of the Pyrenees or Sorauren performed its greatest feat at Echalar on 2 August, when it defeated Clausel's division, more than six thousand strong. Campbell was severely wounded and strongly recommended for promotion, and was accordingly promoted lieutenant-colonel by brevet on 26 August 1813. At the end of the war he received a gold medal for the battle of the Pyrenees and was made a CB, and on 22 May 1815 was created a baronet in recognition of the important services rendered by his father, with remainder to the heirs of Lieutenant-General Colin Campbell. He rejoined his regiment in 1815, and was attached to the staff at the battle of Waterloo; he went on half pay in 1816.

On 17 January 1817 Campbell married Frances Elizabeth, eldest daughter of Montagu Burgoyne of Marks Hall. She died on 8 May 1818, leaving a daughter. On 21 November 1820 he married Pamela, eldest daughter of Lord Edward FitzGerald. She died on 25 November 1869 having borne four sons, one of whom died in infancy. In 1830 he was appointed deputy quartermaster-general in Ireland, a post which he held until his promotion to major-general in 1841, when he received command of the Athlone district. In 1848 he was appointed colonel of the 3rd West India regiment. Campbell died, after a long and painful illness, at Kingstown, near Dublin, on 25 January 1849, and was buried on 1 February in the cemetery by the Royal Barracks, Dublin. H. M. STEPHENS, *rev.* JAMES LUNT

Sources *Hart's Army List* • J. Philippart, ed., *The royal military calendar*, 3 vols. (1815–16) • *GM*, 2nd ser., 31 (1849), 426 • Burke, *Peerage*
Archives NAM | Bodl. Oxf., Napier MSS

Campbell, Harriette (1817–1841), novelist, daughter of Robert Campbell, was born at Stirling in August 1817. According to her obituary in the *Literary Gazette* she not only started writing while still very young but, despite poor health, 'had read almost all the best authors' in English as well as a number of French and Italian writers before she was twelve. Her first published articles, 'Legends of the lochs and glens', appeared in *Bentley's Miscellany* and were inspired by regular summer visits to the Scottish highlands with her family; other papers of hers appeared in the *Monthly Magazine*. Her first novel, *The Only Daughter*, finished in 1837 when she was twenty, was published in 1839. It was favourably received but, according to the *Gentleman's Magazine*, it was her second novel, *The Cardinal Virtues, or, Morals and Manners Connected* (1841), which 'place[d] her at once in the foremost rank of female writers' (*GM*). She spent the winter of 1839–40 in London, where she 'won all hearts' by her 'vivacity and charm' (ibid.), but her health broke down, and she was sent to the continent to attempt to recover in a warmer climate. She travelled no farther than Switzerland, however, and died at Lafarre, near Montreux, on 15 February 1841 following two severe attacks of influenza. She was buried in the cemetery of Petit Saccovex, near Geneva. Campbell's third novel, *Katherine Randolph, or, Self-Devotion*, was published posthumously in 1842, with a preface by G. R. Gleig; and *The Only Daughter* was reissued under the same editorship in the *Railway Library* in 1859.

JENNETT HUMPHREYS, *rev.* PAM PERKINS

Sources *GM*, 2nd ser., 15 (1841), 544 · *Literary Gazette* (13 March 1841), 170–71

Herbert Campbell (1844–1904), by unknown photographer

Campbell, Herbert [*real name* Herbert Edward Story] (**1844–1904**), music-hall performer, was born on 22 December 1844 at 16 Hamilton Street, Kennington, Surrey, the son of Henry George Story, smith, and his wife, Hannah Fisher. Little is known of his early life beyond the agitation which resulted whenever Henry Story attended his firm's annual outing. This 'excellent husband and devoted father' would return full of gin and cockles and bash the furniture to bits with a poker, with Mrs Story yelling murder, the children screaming—'and household bread at a shilling a quartern' (Booth, 115). The domestic observation and philosophical tag-line reflected Campbell's comic style.

Herbert Story started work as a messenger at *The Sun*, and made his first stage appearance at a teetotal hall in Clerkenwell, London, 'singing for ginger-beer and buns' (Thorn). He became a fan of Raynor's Original Christy Minstrels and, while working at a Woolwich gun factory, formed his own 'amateur nigger band' (*The Era*, 22 Sept 1888). During the 1860s he became a professional 'bone corner'—the bone-playing minstrel at the end of the row. After a disastrous booking in Oxford, Campbell (as he had now become) had to walk back to London. He later joined the minstrel performers Harmon and Elston but, finding his talents undervalued, abandoned burnt cork and gave his first solo performance at the Raglan Music-Hall, south London, at £3 a week. On 20 April 1867 he married Elizabeth Ann Mills (1848/9–1884), of Hoxton, London, and struggled to establish himself without a blacked-up face. Finally his cockney style caught on and in 1871 he made his first pantomime appearance in *King Winter* at the Theatre Royal, Liverpool. He was re-engaged the following year, but soon became a favourite with London pantomime audiences at the Grecian Theatre, Shoreditch.

In 1882 Augustus Harris (Druriolanus), the lessee of the Theatre Royal, Drury Lane, set Campbell on an uninterrupted run of pantomime success there that was to last until his death twenty-two years later. From 1889 he was joined every year by Dan Leno, and their partnership became the most celebrated in pantomime history. Its appeal owed much to their contrasting styles. Leno was small and whimsical with quicksilver movements, Campbell a 19 stone colossus with a voice like 'a powerful accordeon which some miracle-worker had got into tune' (Shaw). Beerbohm thought of Campbell as 'the offspring of some mystical union between beef and thunder' and took French visitors to see him 'as a liberal education in the character of this island' (Beerbohm). He often played a greedy boy or matron of a certain age, his enormous frame alternately filling blouse and breeches or an outsize frock. His only surviving film appearance shows him in the former guise guzzling a pudding, his broad features alight with gluttony. Campbell's accent was lustily cockney—Shaw begged him to stop pronouncing 'slave' as 'slive' in *Aladdin* (Shaw)—and his humour was 'rich, broad and pleasantly devoid of subtlety', but he had an 'extraordinary capacity for thinking out new moves for the nose, lips and eyes to portray all the human emotions without uttering a word' (*The Era*, 23 July 1904). Some critics felt music-hall was corrupting pantomime but the public regarded the Drury Lane spectaculars as the pinnacle of Christmas entertainment (even when the two stars took a few nights to polish their improvisations).

In his solo career Campbell bridged the old order and the new, having seen the halls with their presiding chairmen give way to palatial variety houses. True to the earlier style, he based his act on comic songs; only Marie Lloyd had more in her repertoire (Kilgarriff, 140–42). On the four records Campbell made late in life he is the cockney John Bull, but he showed his satirical streak in a parody of the song 'We don't want to fight' (which gave 'jingoism' to the language). In place of the bellicose original he declared he would 'let the Russians have Constantinople'. In 'The Great McNoodle' he lampooned Sir John McDougall, a London county councillor who opposed music-hall, while the song 'In my fust 'usband's time' mocked the aesthetic movement:

For we didn't think an old cracked pot intense,
Nor an old blue plate sublime.

Popular sentiment came in for caustic treatment when he turned 'The Miner's Dream of Home' into a family horror-story:

My pa was boozing nightly,
And my mother was shifting the gin,
And the lodger was taking the old girl out,
And the old man in.

Campbell's own domestic arrangements were unconventional. Mrs Campbell having died in 1884, he lived as man and wife with an actress who had been Rose Wiltshire (*c*.1858–1891). After her death a third 'Mrs Campbell', in reality (Ellen) Maud Bartram, a licensee, became his companion until he died. Campbell was president of the Music Hall Sick Fund, vice-president of the Music Hall Artistes' Railway Association, and a freemason. In 1898 he, Leno, and two fellow comedians built the Granville Theatre, in Fulham. At the opening Campbell said that when he should go off 'to Peckham Rye' (die) there would now be something to keep his memory green (Read, 225). The quartet ran three other halls but lost money against stiff competition from bigger proprietors. Fond of company, Campbell always referred to his favoured glass of whisky as 'a cup of tea' (Randle, 178). By 1904 he was considering retirement when, after another triumph in *Humpty-Dumpty*, he and Leno died within months of each other. Campbell's stentorian tones were the indirect cause of his death. As he alighted from his brougham, his instructions to the coachman startled the horse, which reared and knocked him over. A bruised leg became ulcerous, causing septicaemia, and he died on 19 July from a brain haemorrhage, at 28 Quadrant Road, Islington. He was fifty-nine. At his funeral three days later the route to Abney Park cemetery, Stoke Newington, was lined by so many mourners that traffic had to be diverted. 'Much we marvelled at him,' wrote Beerbohm, 'yet marvelling, much loved him' (Beerbohm). The irregular home life became public when his 'will' was contested in 1905. Claiming that Campbell had signed the original in the billiard-room of the Royal Music-Hall, Holborn, and then lost it, a commission agent produced a draft leaving the assets (£4477) to Maud Bartram and her niece. Campbell's relatives disputed the story, but the judge ruled that he would not have left his companion unprovided for. JAMES HOGG

Sources 'Herbert Campbell's start', *The Era* (22 Sept 1888) · 'Death of Herbert Campbell', *The Era* (23 July 1904) · G. Thorn, 'Mr Herbert Campbell passing away', *Islington Daily Gazette and North London Tribune* (18 July 1904) · M. Beerbohm, 'The last of the "Lions Comiques"', *Morning Leader* (21 July 1904) · L. Fergusson, *Old time music hall comedians* (1949) · H. Randle, *Harry Randle, old time comedian, by himself* (1930) · J. B. Booth, *'"Master" and men: Pink 'Un yesterdays'* (1926) · M. Kilgarriff, *Sing us one of the old songs* (1998) · G. B. Shaw, *Saturday Review*, 83 (1897), 87–9 · 'Herbert Campbell's will', *The Era* (29 July 1905) · J. Read, *Empires, hippodromes and palaces* (1985) · *The Stage* (21 July 1904) · b. cert.

Archives Theatre Museum, London, photographs and cuttings | FILM BFI NFTVA, performance footage | SOUND BL NSA, performance recordings

Likenesses photograph, NPG [*see illus.*]

Wealth at death £4477 10*s*. 8*d*.: probate, 28 Sept 1905, *CGPLA Eng. & Wales*

Campbell, (William) Howard (1859–1910), missionary and entomologist, was born in Londonderry on 20 September 1859, eldest of the nine children of Thomas Callender Campbell, businessman and lay Christian worker. Known to his family as Howard, he was an avid collector of insects and with his six brothers built up a nationally famous collection of Irish moths and butterflies. He was educated at the Academical Institution, Londonderry, and at Edinburgh University, where he studied first arts (MA, 1880), and afterwards, with a view to becoming a missionary, divinity (BD, 1882). He was a keen cricketer and he played rugby for the university; although not tall, he had a wiry, athletic frame and ran very fast.

On 12 September 1884 Campbell was ordained by the London Missionary Society (LMS) at Londonderry's Congregational church, and soon after he departed for the district of Cuddapah in south India. He was later joined by his fiancée, Elizabeth (Lizzie) Nevin (*b*. 1858), daughter of David Boyd of Drukendult, Ballymoney, co. Antrim, whom he married at Madras on 7 December 1885.

For seventeen years Campbell worked among the low-caste and 'untouchable' villagers of the Cuddapah plains, preaching a vigorous Christian socialism which attacked caste and economic inequalities head-on. His socialist sympathies were well known; he was a member of the Independent Labour Party and claimed Keir Hardie as a friend. Nevertheless, he also fully backed imperialism, arguing that no one could rule India as well as the British did.

Campbell's colleagues rated him as an excellent preacher and marvelled at his boundless energy which, even with a punishing itinerating schedule, enabled him to amass an internationally significant collection of Indian moths, between sixty and seventy species of which were new to science. He was credited with founding scores of churches and schools and he wrote several texts which became standard works in Indian theological colleges, three of which were: *Grounds for Belief in a Personal God* (1893); *Christian Evidences* (1898); and *Christian Theology* (1905).

About 1901, and initially against his will, Campbell was transferred to the LMS's training institution at Gooty. He was already an examiner in philosophy to Madras University and at Gooty he proved to be an excellent teacher and administrator, as well as a fine cricket coach. His skills in Telugu soon attracted the attention of the Madras government and, at their order and with Veerasalingam Pantalu, he revised C. P. Brown's *Telegu–English Dictionary* (1906) and A. H. Arden's *Progressive Telegu Grammar* (1905). He also served on the committee to revise the Telugu Bible between 1898 and 1903. Campbell was an enthusiastic advocate of union between the Congregationalist, Presbyterian, and Baptist missions, and in 1908 he rejoiced at the creation of the United Church of South India, which brought 150,000 protestants under one ecclesiastical umbrella.

In 1909 Campbell was appointed head of the new Union Theological College at Bangalore, but he was forced to return home by an attack of sprue. His condition worsening, he moved for the winter to Bordighera in the Italian riviera, where he died, aged fifty, on 18 February 1910. He was buried in the local English cemetery, which overlooked the Mediterranean. His wife and four sons survived him, one of whom, Samuel Burnside Boyd Campbell (1889–1971), won twelve international rugby caps.

C. H. IRWIN, *rev.* KATHERINE PRIOR

Sources *Chronicle of the London Missionary Society*, 75/887 (1910), 73–4 · M. Lawson, *Howard Campbell* (1926) · *British Weekly* (24 Feb 1910), 584 · ecclesiastical records, BL OIOC, N/11/6, 1235 · K. Newmann, *Dictionary of Ulster biography* (1993) [for son] · *CGPLA Ire.* (1910)

Archives SOAS, Council for World Mission archives, official correspondence

Likenesses photograph, repro. in *Chronicle of the London Missionary Society*

Wealth at death £1194 17*s*. 8*d*.: probate, 26 May 1910, *CGPLA Ire.*

Campbell, Sir Hugh, of Cessnock (*d.* **1686**), covenanter and conspirator, was the son of George Campbell of Cessnock and his first wife, Agnes Cunninghame (*d.* 1609). At his father's death on 27 May 1630 Hugh inherited land at Cessnock and Galston, and shortly thereafter he was knighted. He married, by a contract dated 14 October 1625, Elizabeth Campbell (*b.* after *c*.1605), younger daughter and coheir of George Campbell, master of Loudoun (*d.* 1612), and his wife, Jean, daughter of John Fleming, earl of Wigtown. Sir Hugh and his wife had four sons, the eldest of whom was Sir George *Campbell (*fl.* 1671–1704). Sir Hugh later married Jean Mure, with whom he had a daughter, Sarah.

Sir Hugh Campbell signed a petition opposing the Book of Common Prayer in 1637, served as MP for Ayr from 1639, and was sheriff of Ayrshire from 20 January 1642 until ill health forced his resignation on 24 January 1643. Appointed lord of the session and justice clerk in 1649, he declined both offices. Regarded as a radical, he sat on various parliamentary committees in 1649–50, including the committee of estates and the committee for dispatches. He was a leading proponent of the legislation of July 1649 shifting some of the financial burden for the army to the eastern shires for equitable purposes. Campbell was a member of the commission of the Kirk appointed on 4 August 1649. An opponent of the Commonwealth, in October 1650 he subscribed to the remonstrance that opposed giving power to Charles II until he denounced the house of Stuart's sins. In 1651, however, Sir Hugh signed a bond renouncing the remonstrance after parliament condemned it. Four years later the earl of Loudoun and Lord Mauchline commissioned him to provide bonds to George Monck for their peaceful behaviour.

Following the Restoration, Sir Hugh and others were fined large sums in December 1661 to compensate the earl of Queensberry for damages sustained from Scottish troops in 1650; Campbell's portion was £1566 13*s*. 4*d*. Scots. He was deemed sufficiently trustworthy in January 1662 to help oversee the demolition of the citadel at Ayr, but he was incarcerated from September 1665 to December 1667 as a perceived threat to the regime. He was released on the king's instructions after posting a bond of £1000 (Scots). A year later he was named a highway commissioner, and in July 1672 an excise commissioner for Ayrshire. He narrowly escaped assassination by a subordinate in early 1673.

With Sir John Cochrane and two others, Sir Hugh Campbell petitioned the council in November 1677 to provide toleration for presbyterian ministers. When the government attempted to suppress conventicles by requiring heritors to sign bonds, Sir Hugh refused and was outlawed in February 1678. As part of its campaign to intimidate covenanters in March 1678, the council garrisoned sixty troopers in his house, and the following year it charged him and other commissioners with failure to levy rates to support garrisons in Ayrshire. Sir Hugh's chaplain, James Brown, was holding conventicles in Ayr in 1679. The government suspected Campbell of assisting the covenanting ministers Donald Cargill and John Welsh, but it had no solid evidence. Although Sir Hugh and others denounced the Bothwell Bridge rebels on 28 April 1679, he apparently changed his mind, for he and Sir George reportedly provided 400 lances to the insurgents.

In 1682 the Campbells were exploring the possibilities for an insurrection in Scotland with Cochrane, Robert Baillie of Jerviswood, and others. This group was in communication with the earl of Argyll and was probably involved with his abortive attempt to smuggle weapons from the Netherlands into Scotland. The covenanter lawyer James Stewart provided William Carstares and Abraham Holmes, both Argyll allies, with a code that included ciphers for the Campbells, and coded references to the Campbells appear in the earl's correspondence. In early 1683 Monmouth, Lord William Russell, and their fellow conspirators sent Aaron Smith to Scotland to invite key dissidents to London for discussions about co-ordinated uprisings. The Campbells, Cochrane, Baillie, and others arrived in April and May, ostensibly to discuss the Carolina project, which the colony's proprietors, including Shaftesbury, had initiated in the spring of 1682 to encourage immigrants from Scotland and England. Dissident Scots, including the Campbells and Cochrane, saw Carolina as a refuge from persecution. Both Campbells consulted with Carstares, who was raising money for Argyll's intended insurrection in Scotland. Following the disclosure of the Rye House plotting, the Campbells were arrested in London on 26 June. On 16 August the Scottish privy council ordered the king's advocate to prosecute them for treason, and in November they were taken to Edinburgh. Sir Hugh was tried on 24–27 March 1684 on charges that he had aided the Bothwell rebels. Although he was acquitted, he remained in prison.

In the aftermath of the Argyll rebellion, the Scottish parliament charged Sir Hugh Campbell with conspiring to launch an insurrection. After throwing himself on the king's mercy in June 1685 his life was spared, though the crown annexed his estate and placed it in Viscount Melfort's care. Released from prison in August, Campbell was recommitted in October following Cochrane's confession. Freed once more in January 1686, he and Sir George soon illegally took possession of their Cessnock estate, for which they were summoned before the privy council in August and warned to stay away from it. Sir Hugh died in Edinburgh on 20 September 1686 and was buried in the city's Greyfriars churchyard three days later.

RICHARD L. GREAVES

Sources *Reg. PCS*, 2nd ser., vols. 5–8 • *Reg. PCS*, 3rd ser., vols. 1–12 • *State trials*, 10.919–88 • PRO, State MSS, 29/397, 425, 427–9, 432–3, 435–6 • PRO, State MSS, 44, entry books 56, 335 • *State papers and letters addressed to William Carstares*, ed. J. M'Cormick (1774) • NA Scot., PA 7/12, p. 6 (no. 1) • *The manuscripts of the duke of Roxburghe*, HMC, 34 (1894) • R. L. Greaves, *Secrets of the kingdom: British radicals from the Popish Plot to the revolution of 1688–89* (1992) • Burke, *Gen. GB* (1837) • J. R. Young, *The Scottish parliament, 1639–1661: a political and constitutional analysis* (1996) • U. Edin. L., MS La.2.89 • D. Stevenson, *Revolution and counter-revolution in Scotland, 1644–1651*, Royal Historical Society Studies in History, 4 (1977) • Burke, *Gen. GB* (1937) • *Journal of the Hon. John Erskine of Carnock*, ed. W. Macleod, Scottish History Society, 14 (1893) • GEC, *Peerage*, new edn, vol. 8

Archives NA Scot., MS PA 7/12, p. 6 (no. 1)

Campbell, Sir Hugh, of Cawdor (*c.*1639–1716). *See under* Campbell family of Cawdor (*per.* 1511–1821).

Campbell, Hugh, third earl of Loudoun (*c.*1673–1731), politician, grandson of John *Campbell, first earl of Loudoun, landowner, and eldest son of James, second earl (*d.* 1684), and Lady Margaret Montgomerie (*d.* in or before 1686), second daughter of Hugh, seventh earl of Eglinton, was probably born at Loudoun, Ayrshire. He held the title Lord Mauchline until he succeeded his father, who had refused to sign the bond for religious conformity for the heritors of Ayrshire in 1677, and was eventually cited for treason as a result; he died in exile at Leiden in 1684. In November 1688, while a student at Glasgow University, Loudoun was involved in a student riot in which effigies of the pope and archbishops were burned.

Loudoun first attended parliament on 8 September 1696, and was sworn of the privy council in April 1697. Through the influence of Archibald, tenth earl and first duke of Argyll, he was appointed extraordinary lord of session, and took his seat on 7 February 1699. Argyll, in a letter to William Carstares dated Edinburgh, 27 September 1698, thus recommended Loudoun: 'Pray, let not E. Melville's unreasonable pretending to the vacant gown make you slack as to E. Loudon, who, though a younger man, is an older and more noted presbyterian than he. Loudon has it in his blood' (McCormick, 451); this was a reference to the family's strong covenanting connections. In this post Loudoun 'behaved to all men's satisfaction, studying to understand the laws and constitution of the kingdom, and determine accordingly … He had nothing in his nature that was cruel and revengeful, was affable, courteous and just' (*'Scotland's Ruine'*, 99). He retained the office until his death. On 6 April 1700 he married his cousin Lady Margaret Dalrymple (*c.*1684–1779) at Kirkhiston. She was the third daughter of John, first earl of Stair [*see* Dalrymple, Sir John], and Elizabeth Dundas, heir of Sir John Dundas, and was a very accomplished woman.

After the accession of Queen Anne, Loudoun was again sworn of the Scottish privy council, and from 1702 to 1704 he served as one of the commissioners of the Scottish Treasury. In 1704 he was appointed joint secretary of state with William, third marquess of Annandale, and afterwards with John, sixth earl of Mar. This appointment enraged Annandale, who was alarmed at Stair's growing influence over Argyll. In March 1706 Loudoun was made one of the Scottish commissioners for the Union, and on 10 August was invested at Windsor with the Order of the Thistle. From 1707 the position of joint secretary of state was crucial to the smooth implementation of the Union and carried wide responsibilities. Loudoun became indispensable to the court interest, and was 'elected', by the system of court lists, as one of the sixteen representative Scottish peers at each election from 1708 until his death.

The office of secretary being temporarily suspended (it was not abolished until 1746), Loudoun was appointed keeper of the great seal of Scotland on 25 May 1708 at a salary of £1000 p.a., and in the same year was sworn of the privy council of Great Britain. In addition to his salary the queen granted him a pension of £2000 a year. In 1713 he was deprived of the office of keeper of the great seal for refusing to comply with some of the measures of the tory administration. On the accession of George I he was again sworn a privy councillor, and in 1715 appointed lord lieutenant of Ayrshire. He served as a volunteer under John, second duke of Argyll, at the battle of Sheriffmuir.

Disaster struck when, according to Wodrow, Loudoun lost a great deal of money in the South Sea Company and was bailed out by the earl of Ilay. In 1722, 1725, 1726, 1728, 1730, and 1731 he was lord high commissioner at the general assembly of the Church of Scotland, for which he received £1000 p.a. (most of which went to Ilay); he obtained a further pension in 1727 of £2000 a year for life. He died on 20 November 1731 in low estate. He was survived by his wife, his son, John *Campbell (1705–1782), who succeeded to the title, and two daughters, Elizabeth and Margaret. The countess lived on for many years at Sorn Castle in Ayrshire, where she interested herself in agricultural improvements, particularly tree planting. After a short illness she died on 3 April 1779, aged ninety-four.

G. F. R. BARKER, *rev.* MAIRIANNA BIRKELAND

Sources GEC, *Peerage* • R. Wodrow, *The history of the sufferings of the Church of Scotland from the Restauration to the revolution*, 2 vols. (1721–2) • *State papers and letters addressed to William Carstares*, ed. J. M'Cormick (1774) • *'Scotland's ruine': Lockhart of Carnwath's memoirs of the union*, ed. D. Szechi, Association of Scottish Literary Studies, 25 (1995) • R. Wodrow, *Analecta, or, Materials for a history of remarkable providences, mostly relating to Scotch ministers and Christians*, ed. [M. Leishman], 4 vols., Maitland Club, 60 (1842–3) • P. W. J. Riley, *The English ministers and Scotland, 1707–1727* (1964) • P. W. J. Riley, *King William and the Scottish politicians* (1979) • W. Ferguson, *Scotland: 1689 to the present* (1968); pbk edn (1978)

Archives Hunt. L., corresp. and papers • Mount Stuart Trust archive, corresp. and papers | NA Scot., letters to Lord Leven • NA Scot., letters to duke of Montrose

Wealth at death 'low'; lost much in South Sea Bubble: Wodrow, *Analecta*, 297

Campbell, Hugh Hume, third earl of Marchmont (1708–1794), politician, was born on 15 February 1708 in Canongate, Edinburgh, the third son (an elder twin) of the nine children of Alexander Hume *Campbell, second earl of Marchmont (1675–1740), and his wife, Margaret (*d.* 1722), second daughter and heir of Sir George Campbell of

Cessnock, lord justice clerk. The second earl changed his surname on inheriting his wife's estates in 1704. His family, the Humes of Polwarth, in Berwickshire, were descended from the Homes of Wedderburn and began their participation in national affairs during the last quarter of the fifteenth century. It was Hugh's grandfather Patrick *Hume, the first earl (1641–1724), lord chancellor of Scotland and confidant of William III, who laid the foundations which were to establish the family as the dominant landed interest in Berwickshire by the time of Hugh's succession to the title. He and his twin brother, the politician **Alexander Hume Campbell** (1708–1760), who were often mistaken for each other throughout their lives because of their almost identical looks, were both originally destined for the law, their father's profession, and like him they completed their education in the Netherlands at Utrecht and Franeker. After the death of his grandfather, the first earl, on 1 August 1724, Hugh was known as Lord Polwarth, his father's second title. He became the third earl of Marchmont on his father's death on 27 February 1740.

Hugh Hume Campbell married his first wife, Anne (*d.* 1747), daughter of Sir Thomas Western of London, on 1 May 1731; the couple had one son, Patrick, who died in childhood, and three daughters. Anne died on 9 May 1747 and Marchmont married Elizabeth (1730x32–1797), daughter of Windmill Crompton, a bankrupt Cheapside linen draper, on 30 January 1748. He was completely captivated by her stunning beauty on seeing her at the theatre one evening, and after a meeting with her father the next day he proposed to her then and there and the marriage took place three weeks later. According to the philosopher David Hume, writing to James Oswald of Dunnikier, on 29 January 1748:

> Lord Marchmont has had the most extraordinary adventure in the world. About three weeks ago he was at the play, where he espied in one of the boxes a fair virgin, whose looks, airs, and manners had such a powerful and undisguised affect upon him, as was visible by every bystander. His raptures were so undisguised, his looks so expressive of passion, his inquiries so earnest, that every person took note of it … The fair nymph herself was about sixteen or seventeen … But could you ever expect the ambitious, the severe, the bustling, the impetuous, the violent Marchmont, of becoming so tender and gentle a swain—an Artamenes—an Oroondates! (Greig, 1.110)

With Elizabeth Crompton, Marchmont had one son, Alexander, Lord Polwarth, who was born in London on 30 July 1750. He married Lady Annabella Yorke, eldest daughter of the second earl of Hardwicke and the Marchioness Grey (16 July 1772), was created Baron Hume of Berwick in 1776, and died at Wrest, Bedfordshire, on 9 March 1781.

Hugh Hume Campbell and his twin brother, Alexander, both entered politics at the same time; the 1734 general election saw him returned for the town of Berwick, while his brother was elected to represent the county. This election also marked the effective end of his father's active political career, Sir Robert Walpole having deprived him of all his political offices in the previous year to ensure that he was not re-elected as one of the sixteen representative peers of Scotland. The second earl's implacable opposition to Walpole, on account of his treatment of Scotland through the earl of Ilay, was continued by his sons to the extent that they were both driven to support the tories in opposition, thus forsaking the traditional family allegiances. Hugh Hume Campbell, sitting as Lord Polwarth, rapidly established a reputation for political sagacity and adroitness with his attacks on Walpole, to the point where he became acknowledged as one of the leaders of the opposition. Tobias Smollett, referring to his first appearance in the debates of the House of Commons, describes him as a 'nobleman of elegant parts, keen penetration, and uncommon sagacity, who spoke with all the fluency and fervour of elocution' (Warrender, 97).

After his father's death in 1740 and his accession to the earldom, Marchmont was effectively cast into the political wilderness, at the same time as his great friend Sir William Wyndham died, leaving the opposition severely weakened. Alexander Pope wrote to Marchmont on 29 February 1740: 'If God had not given this nation to perdition, he would not have removed from its service the men whose capacity and integrity alone could have saved it' (*Polwarth MSS*, vol. 5). Marchmont's diaries kept during this period, together with the substantial correspondence with his friends, particularly Lord Bolingbroke, indicate an endless quest to serve in government following Walpole's fall in 1742. His attempts to achieve this, particularly through Lord Chesterfield and the Pelham brothers, appear to have been frustrated by Ilay (now third duke of Argyll), who exerted a virtual monopoly over positions in Scotland. It was not until 1747 that Marchmont was at last rewarded with the minor office of first lord of police, though without a seat in the Lords such an appointment was of little value. His position improved in 1750 when he was elected one of the sixteen representative peers of Scotland, and his brother was made lord clerk register for life, a post normally reserved for a member of the nobility. By now, however, many of those active in Marchmont's earlier political life had moved on and he was never to play a decisive role in this sphere. His twin brother, Alexander, died relatively young, on 19 July 1760, thus depriving him of an invaluable associate in the Commons. Even so in 1764 he was made keeper of the great seal of Scotland (the highest Scottish office in the gift of the crown), in which capacity he achieved something of a reputation as an elder statesman.

The earls of Marchmont had always been the staunchest supporters of the union between England and Scotland, and Hugh Hume Campbell was no exception. In 1745 he sent a large quantity of arms from Marchmont to Berwick for its defence against the Jacobites, and was with difficulty dissuaded from raising a regiment to fight the Young Pretender. Always an enthusiastic supporter of the duke of Cumberland in his measures to suppress dissent in the highlands, he seems to have acquiesced readily to the act abolishing hereditable jurisdictions in 1747, by which he himself gained £300 in compensation for the regality of Marchmont.

From his position as pre-eminent landowner in Berwickshire and his control of the distribution of all local patronage, Marchmont's decision to field his son-in-law, Sir John Paterson of Eccles, bt, as candidate for the 1780 election remains a baffling one, given the unsavoury character and reputation Sir John enjoyed locally. His grandson by his youngest daughter, Anne—Hugh Scott of Harden—with the backing of Marchmont's son, Lord Polwarth, decided to contest the seat, thus incurring his grandfather's undying enmity. Scott won the seat, but at great cost, Henry Dundas effectively engineering its subsequent loss in 1784 (and the destruction of the Marchmont interest); furthermore Scott was cut out of his grandfather's will, thus forfeiting the Marchmont inheritance, being able only to establish a claim to the Polwarth title in the Scots peerage in 1838. Scott attempted reconciliations with the third earl, but all were rebuffed; Lady Marchmont wrote: 'I am obliged to write the following in my lord's own words. Lord Marchmont said his conduct is not owing to any mis-representation, and that he owes it to his own character to persevere in his behaviour' (Scott of Harden papers, GD 157 2319/1).

Relations between Marchmont and Lord Polwarth were likewise embittered and after the latter's death in 1781 Marchmont cut off Polwarth's allowance to his widow almost immediately. From 1784, the last year he served as a representative peer, the third earl had the greater part of his magnificent library sent from Marchmont to his house at Hemel Hempstead. He died there on 10 January 1794, having possibly composed his own epitaph:

Here lies all that is corruptible of
Hugh earl of Marchmont
Who in the House of Commons
Or in the House of Lords
Never spoke one word (unless provoked)
Or gave one vote
Upon any personal motive.
(Marchmont papers, GD158/2553)

Marchmont was acknowledged one of the leading agricultural improvers of his time, and he devoted considerable energies to enhancing and extending his Berwickshire estates. His greatest monument is Marchmont House, begun in 1750 and finished ten years later, which exhibits some of the finest plasterwork of the period in Scotland. Marchmont was an intimate of Alexander Pope and Sarah, duchess of Marlborough, and an executor for both. He was widely read and an expert on horsemanship, on which he wrote a manual. His abilities and interests covered a wide range, but were only fully rewarded in the private rather than the public field.

IAN MAITLAND HUME

Sources *DNB* • G. H. Rose, *A selection from the papers of the earls of Marchmont*, 3 vols. (1831), vols. 1–2 • [J. M. M. Warrender], *Marchmont and the Humes of Polwarth* (1894) • R. M. Sunter, *Patronage and politics in Scotland, 1707–1832* (1986) • *Report on the manuscripts of Lord Polwarth*, 5, HMC, 67 (1961) • *Scots peerage* • G. F. C. Hepburne Scott, 'Marchmont correspondence relating to the '45', *Miscellany … V*, Scottish History Society, 3rd ser., 21 (1933), 315–51 • J. S. Shaw, *The management of Scottish society, 1707–1764: power, nobles, lawyers, Edinburgh agents and English influences* (1983) • M. Fry, *The Dundas despotism* (1992) • A. Murdoch, *'The people above': politics and administration in mid-eighteenth-century Scotland* (1980) • NA Scot., Scott of Harden papers, GD157/2247–2956 • NA Scot., Marchmont papers, GD158/2514–2682 • Marchmont journals, stock and work books, NA Scot., GD1/648–651 • E. Haden-Guest, 'Hume Campbell, Alexander', HoP, *Commons, 1754–90* • GEC, *Peerage* • *The letters of David Hume*, ed. J. Y. T. Greig, 2 vols. (1932)

Archives BL, papers relating to Scottish peerage, Add. MS 42780 • NA Scot., corresp. and papers • NL Scot., corresp. • U. Reading, Rural History Centre, estate papers • V&A NAL, household accounts | Beds. & Luton ARS, letters to Lord Polwarth • BL, corresp. with Lord Hardwicke, Add. MSS 35447–35449 • BL, corresp. with duke of Newcastle, etc., Add. MSS 32712–32922, 33055, *passim* • NA Scot., letters to William Hall; corresp. with David Hume; letters to Walter Scott of Harden • NL Scot., letters to George Rose • NRA Scotland, priv. coll., corresp. with James Pringle

Likenesses P. Falconet, oils, 1769, Scot. NPG • double portrait, oils (aged four with Alexander Hume), Harden House, Roxburghshire • marble bust, Mellerstain House, Berwickshire • marble bust, Stowe, Buckinghamshire

Wealth at death 20,900 acres; income from rents and bonds; payments still being made on purchase of Hume barony • goods at Marchmont House valued at £1381: inventory, 1794 • house in Hemel Hempstead; library and plate

Campbell, Sir Ilay, of Succoth, first baronet (1734–1823), judge and politician, was born in Edinburgh on 23 August 1734, the eldest of four sons of Archibald Campbell of Succoth (*d.* 1790), a principal clerk of session and writer to the signet, and his wife, Helen (*d.* 1767), the only daughter of John Wallace of Elderslie, Renfrewshire. The family originated on both sides in the west of Scotland, its seat of Succoth lying in Dunbartonshire, but by the mid-eighteenth century it had become as firmly ensconced in the legal world of Edinburgh: Campbell was related to several other judges, including Henry Home, Lord Kames.

Campbell was educated at Mundell's School, Edinburgh, and entered Glasgow University in 1751, but did not take a degree. He was admitted an advocate on 11 January 1757, soon building up a large practice at the bar. On 14 November 1766 he married Susan Mary, the daughter of Archibald Murray (*d.* 1773) of Murrayfield, Edinburghshire, and his wife, Jean Hay (*d.* 1758), and sister of Alexander *Murray, Lord Henderland. They had two sons and six daughters. In his profession, Campbell excelled for clarity and concision at the written pleadings which then formed the staple of proceedings in the Scottish courts, but if he had to plead orally he was nervous, involved, and tedious. Like other rising stars of his generation he won renown in the Douglas cause, the action which, over ten years and amid intense public interest, settled the succession to the vast estates of the extinct dukedom of Douglas. In 1769 he formed part of the winning team of advocates which, at the final stage, pleaded the appeal of Archibald Douglas to the House of Lords. Campbell himself was first to bring the news to Edinburgh. On arrival he cast aside his usual impassive demeanour to cry 'Douglas for ever!' to the waiting mob, which drew his carriage in triumph up the High Street to his father's house at James Court. By 1774 Boswell said he was earning £1600 p.a. His dry, ineffective manner and low, dull voice must have concealed some

Sir Ilay Campbell of Succoth, first baronet (1734–1823), by Charles Turner, pubd 1822 (after John Partridge, exh. RA 1821)

taste for jollity because about this time he became a crony of the notoriously convivial rising man in Scottish politics, Henry Dundas, who also proved the key to his further advancement. Dundas had Campbell made solicitor-general in March 1783 in succession to Alexander Murray of Henderland. Almost immediately the coalition of Lord North and Charles James Fox took power and dismissed many of the existing Scottish establishment, including Dundas and Campbell. When the coalition fell at the end of the year both moved straight back into office, Campbell as lord advocate. At the general election of 1784 he was chosen MP for the Glasgow burghs. He cultivated links with the city, with the university in particular, where he was made doctor of laws in 1784 and was rector from 1799 to 1801.

Campbell's lack of presence was satirized in an epigram by Robert Burns after a visit to the court of session in 1787:

> He clench'd his pamphlets in his fist,
> He quoted and he hinted,
> Till in a declamation-mist,
> His argument, he tint it:
> He gaped for't, he graped for't,
> He fand it was awa, man:
> But what his common sense came short,
> He eked out wi law, man.
> (*Poetical Works*, 273)

Nor did Campbell always do better with the routine Scottish political business Dundas devolved on him. His first major piece of legislation was the Diminishing Bill of 1785. He proposed to cut the auld fifteen, the traditional number of judges in the court of session, but to raise their salaries, thus reforming the court without cost to the exchequer. He hoped to improve the quality of the bench by making it more lucrative for the abler advocates, who could earn more in private practice. But he failed to take into account that this might be held to alter the terms of the union of 1707 between Scotland and England, which had guaranteed the form and status of the court. His halting attempt to give the bill a first reading aroused furious opposition in the House of Commons, fuelled in Scotland by public meetings and other agitation. Eventually he was forced to back down and ask the Treasury for money to increase the judges' salaries without diminishing their number.

Campbell was active in the Commons as a defender of Scottish interests, for example opposing the duties on printed linens in 1784, and arguing for delay in the debates on Irish commerce in February 1785 until Scottish representations could be heard. He supported parliamentary reform in April 1785.

In 1789 the presidency of the court of session became vacant by the death of Sir Thomas Miller, Lord Glenlee. Dundas was offered but declined it, recommending Campbell instead. Campbell took his seat as Lord President Succoth on 14 November. The two decades he spent as president covered a period of economic and political upheaval which brought a steeply rising volume of civil litigation, and on the criminal side controversial prosecutions of radicals supporting French revolutionary ideas. During August 1794 Campbell presided in person over the trials for high treason of David Downie and Robert Watt, sentencing the latter to death. But it was the increase in civil business that at last made reform of the Scottish legal system inescapable. Henry Cockburn wrote of Campbell's part in this:

> As a lawyer, and in every department of the science, he was inferior to none of his brethren in depth or learning, and was greatly superior to them all in a genuine and liberal taste for the law's improvement. Of all the old judges he was the only one whose mind was thoroughly opened to the comprehension of modern mercantile jurisprudence.
> (*Memorials … by Henry Cockburn*, 94)

After long debate and further abortive attempts at legislation, a measure was agreed in 1807–8 which split the court of session into two divisions, one of first instance and the other appellate. Campbell presided over the final meeting of the auld fifteen on 11 July 1808, then resigned. On 17 September he was created a baronet. In retirement he continued to work on legal reform, especially the proposal for juries in civil causes, and resumed an earlier interest in collecting decisions of the court of session. He resided at his estate of Garscube, Dunbartonshire, where he was active in the affairs of the county. He died on 28 March 1823, at Garscube. His wife had predeceased him. His eldest son, Archibald (1769–1846), had followed in his father's footsteps and been appointed to the bench as Lord Succoth in 1809. His second son, Alexander (1771–1799), became a writer to the signet. His fourth daughter, Susan, married Craufurd Tait of Harviestown, Clackmannanshire, and their youngest son, Archibald Campbell *Tait, became archbishop of Canterbury in 1868.

MICHAEL FRY

Sources G. W. T. Omond, *The lord advocates of Scotland from the close of the fifteenth century to the passing of the Reform Bill*, 2 vols. (1883) • M. Fry, *The Dundas despotism* (1992) • *Memorials of his time, by Henry Cockburn* (1856) • *The complete poetical works of Robert Burns, 1759–1796*, ed. J. A. Mackay, rev. edn (1993) • G. Brunton and D. Haig, *An historical account of the senators of the college of justice of Scotland, from its institution in 1532* (1849) • *DNB* • W. I. Addison, *A roll of graduates of the University of Glasgow from 31st December 1727 to 31st December 1897* (1898), 91 • E. Haden-Guest, 'Campbell, Ilay', HoP, *Commons*, 1754–90 • Burke, *Peerage* (1970) • *GM*, 1st ser., 93/1 (1823), 569 • Irving, *Scots*.

Archives Mitchell L., Glas., corresp. and papers • NL Scot., papers | NA Scot., corresp. with Lord Melville etc. • NL Scot., corresp. mainly with Archibald Campbell Colquhoun • NRA, priv. coll., letters to Sir John Sinclair

Likenesses C. Turner, engraving, pubd 1822 (after J. Partridge, exh. RA 1821), AM Oxf. [*see illus.*] • J. Kay, caricature, etching, NPG; repro. in J. Kay, *A series of original portraits and caricature etchings … with biographical sketches and illustrative anecdotes*, ed. [H. Paton and others], new edn [3rd edn], 2 vols. in 4 (1877) • J. Partridge, oils, Parliament Hall, Edinburgh

Campbell, Sir James, of Lawers (*c.*1680–1745), army officer, was the third son of James Campbell, second earl of Loudoun (*d.* 1684), and his wife, Lady Margaret Montgomerie (*d.* before 22 Feb 1686), second daughter of the seventh earl of Eglinton. He entered the army as lieutenant in the Scots foot guards in September 1693 and was promoted to captain in July 1699. This commission was renewed in 1702 when he joined the Royal Scots Fusiliers, with whom he fought at Blenheim. In August 1706 he was made lieutenant-colonel of the 2nd Royal North British Dragoons (later the Scots Greys), whom he commanded at Oudenarde and at the hard fought battle of Malplaquet, on 11 September 1709, where he greatly distinguished himself.

At 1.30 p.m. the bulk of the allied cavalry were proceeding in column to form on the plain in front of Malplaquet. In the van the Scots Greys, led by Campbell (together with the Royal Irish Dragoons), met the full force of a pre-emptive charge by the French household cavalry under the command of Marshal Boufflers. Forced back by superior numbers, the Scots Greys rallied quickly and were led by Campbell in a series of desperate charges which succeeded in repulsing the French attack. This respite allowed the full deployment of the allied cavalry for a concerted attack upon the French lines which ultimately forced the French to withdraw from the field.

Campbell continued to serve at the head of the Scots Greys until the treaty of Utrecht (1713), and then threw himself, with his brother, Hugh *Campbell, third earl of Loudoun, ardently into politics as a warm supporter of the Hanoverian succession. He was made colonel of the 9th foot in 1715, and of the Scots Greys in 1717. On 29 March 1720 Campbell married Lady Jean Boyle, eldest daughter of David Boyle, first earl of Glasgow, and his second wife, Jean Fairlie. They had a son, James Mure-Campbell, fifth earl of Loudoun (1726–1786), and at least one daughter, called Margaret or Elizabeth. Jean died at Lawers on 19 December 1729 and was buried at Kilmarnock on 26 December.

When George II came to the throne, he showed his appreciation of military gallantry by appointing Campbell groom of his bedchamber, and in 1738 he was made governor and constable of Edinburgh Castle. Campbell was promoted brigadier-general in 1735, and major-general in 1739. He was MP for Ayrshire between 1727 and 1741, through the influence of his brother. His defeat in 1741 was at the hands of an anti-Walpole candidate backed by John Campbell, second duke of Argyll. The long period of peace maintained by Walpole prevented Campbell from seeing service for twenty-eight years, but in 1742, when war was again declared against France, he was promoted lieutenant-general and accompanied the king to Germany as general commanding the cavalry. At its head he charged the *maison du roi*, or household troops of France, at the battle of Dettingen on 16 June 1743, and was invested a knight of the Bath before the whole army on the field of battle, by George II. He continued to command the cavalry after the king returned to England until the battle of Fontenoy on 30 April 1745. During this battle he headed many unsuccessful charges against the army of Marshal Saxe, but towards the close of the day his leg was carried off by a cannon-ball; he died while being put into a litter, and was buried at Brussels.

H. M. STEPHENS, *rev.* JONATHAN SPAIN

Sources C. Dalton, ed., *English army lists and commission registers, 1661–1714*, 6 (1904) • R. R. Sedgwick, 'Campbell, Hon. James', HoP, *Commons, 1715–54* • D. Chandler, *Marlborough as military commander* (1973), 264–5 • *Scots peerage*, vol. 5 • F. Maurice, *The history of the Scots guards, from the creation of the regiment to the eve of the Great War*, 2 (1934), 295 • *GM*, 1st ser., 15 (1745), 276 • E. Almack, *History of the 2nd dragoons, royal Scots greys* (1908) • Burke, *Peerage* (1999) • GEC, *Peerage*

Archives Hunt. L., letters to earl of Loudoun • Mount Stuart Trust archive, corresp. with Loudoun and others • NL Scot., corresp. with earl of Loudoun

Likenesses oils, Scot. NPG

Campbell [*formerly* Callander], **James** (1745–1831), army officer, was born on 21 October 1745 at Ardkinglas, Argyll, the eldest son of John *Callander (*b.* in or after 1721, *d.* 1789) of Craigforth and Mary (*c.*1720–*c.*1802), daughter of Sir James Livingstone of Glentirran. He was educated at the high school of Edinburgh (1753–7), and afterwards by a private tutor (1757–8). In 1759 he joined the 51st regiment as ensign, and served in the Seven Years' War and then in Minorca and Ireland.

In 1769 Callander married the first of his four wives, Christiana Forbes (*d.* 1771), with whom he had two children. In the year after her death he married Henrietta Dutens (*d.* 1772); the couple had one daughter. On 22 August 1777 he married Elizabeth Helena MacDonnell (*d.* 1797), daughter of the earl of Antrim; the marriage produced five children, two sons and three daughters.

In 1789 Callander returned to Craigforth; in 1792 his cousin Sir Alexander Campbell of Ardkinglas had him arrested for debt. This, and other financial problems, made him return to Europe, where he was inspector-general of troops at Naples under Sir John Acton. By his own account, he went to the Ionian Islands at the request of Lord Nelson to confirm the inhabitants in their attachment to the British cause; in fact his actions had no official sanction. He remained there until the peace of Amiens in 1802, and then travelled extensively in the Middle East. On succeeding to the estate of his cousin in 1810 he adopted the name of Campbell; the baronetcy ended with his cousin but he nevertheless used the title baronet.

At this time Campbell lived in Paris, where he met a German woman, Lina Talina Sassen, with whom he had a daughter about 1813. Being detained by the order of Napoleon, he is supposed by Anderson to have sent her as his commissioner to Scotland, designating her in the power of attorney with which he furnished her as his 'beloved wife'. On his return to Scotland he declined to recognize the relationship, and she raised an action against him in the court of session, when, though the marriage was found not proven, she was awarded a sum of £300 per annum. On appeal to the House of Lords the award was withheld, and she spent the rest of her life in actions against him, being allowed to sue *in forma pauperis*. On 3 February 1815 Campbell married for a fourth time; his new wife was a Miss Descot (*b. c.*1796) and they had four children, one son and three daughters. Campbell died in May 1831. T. F. HENDERSON, *rev.* ALEXANDER DU TOIT

Sources J. Campbell, *Memoirs of James Campbell of Ardkinglas*, 2 vols. (1832) • Burke, *Gen. GB* • Anderson, *Scot. nat.* • *The journal of Sir Walter Scott*, 2 vols. (1890–91) • W. D. Wrigley, *The diplomatic significance of Ionian neutrality, 1821–31* (1988) • G. B. Livingston, *The Livingstons of Callander and their principal cadets* (1920)

Likenesses stipple, BM, NPG; repro. in Campbell, *Memoirs*

Wealth at death £3000 p.a. from Ardkinglas estate • £15,000 to go to children from third marriage after death: Campbell, *Memoirs*

Campbell, Sir James, baronet (1763–1819), army officer, was the eldest son of Sir James Campbell of Inverneil (1737–1805) and his wife, Jean (*d.* 1805), daughter of John Campbell of Askomíl, Argyll. His father, who was knighted in 1788, was hereditary usher of the white rod for Scotland and MP for Stirling burghs from 1780 to 1789. The younger James Campbell received his commission as ensign in the 1st regiment or Royal Scots on 19 July 1780, was promoted lieutenant into the 94th regiment on 5 December 1781, and at once exchanged into the 60th or American regiment, with which he served during the last two campaigns of the American War of Independence. On the conclusion of peace he was promoted captain in the 71st regiment on 6 March 1783. He transferred to the 73rd on 6 June 1787, which he joined in India, acting as aide-de-camp to his uncle Sir Archibald *Campbell (1739–1791). After exchanging into the 19th Dragoons Campbell served in the 1790, 1791, and 1792 campaigns of Lord Cornwallis against Tippoo Sahib.

On 1 March 1794 Campbell was promoted major; he then returned to England, and on 17 November was appointed lieutenant-colonel of the Cheshire fencibles. He served in the Channel Islands and in Ireland until 1800, when he was appointed assistant adjutant-general at the Horse Guards; on 1 January 1801 he was promoted brevet colonel and on 16 January 1804 lieutenant-colonel of the 61st regiment. In 1805 he was appointed adjutant-general of the force destined for the Mediterranean under Sir James Craig. He served there until 1813, being absent only during the battle of Maida, and winning the confidence of all the generals who commanded in Sicily. On 17 September 1810 General Cavaignac managed to transport 3500 men across the Strait of Messina; he had one battalion posted on the cliffs, and the others disembarking, when Campbell, attacking with the 21st, repelled the disembarking battalions, and forced those already landed to surrender. Forty-three officers and over 800 men were captured, with a loss to the British regiment of only three men wounded. During his tenure of office in the Mediterranean Campbell was promoted major-general on 25 April 1808, and lieutenant-general on 4 June 1813. In 1814 he was ordered to take possession of the Ionian Islands. The French governor refused to surrender control until Campbell threatened to open fire. He remained in the Ionian Islands as governor and commander of the forces until 1816, when Sir Thomas Maitland was appointed lord high commissioner. A French writer alleged that Campbell had acted despotically, abolishing the university, the academy, and the press established by the French.

Campbell returned to England in 1816, was made GCH in 1817, and baronet on 3 October 1818. He died on 5 June 1819, and was buried in Westminster Abbey on 19 June. As he left no children, the baronetcy of Campbell of Inverneil became extinct.

H. M. STEPHENS, *rev.* STEWART M. FRASER

Sources J. Philippart, ed., *The royal military calendar*, 1 (1815) • J. Foster, *Members of parliament, Scotland … 1357–1882*, 2nd edn (privately printed, London, 1882) • H. Bunbury, *Narratives of some passages in the great war with France (1799–1810)*, [new edn] (1927) • *GM*, 2nd ser., 3 (1835) • R. Muir, *Britain and the defeat of Napoleon, 1807–1815* (1996)

Archives NRA Scotland, priv. coll. | BL, corresp. with Sir William A'Court, Add. MS 41534 • Hunt. L., letters to Grenville family • NAM, Gordon MSS • Nottingham UL, Cavendish-Bentinck MSS

Likenesses C. Turner, mezzotint, pubd 1815 (after H. Thomson), BM

Campbell, Sir James (1773?–1835), army officer and colonial governor, entered the army as an ensign in the 1st Royal regiment of foot, and was promoted lieutenant on 20 March 1794 in the same regiment, and captain in the 42nd highlanders or Black Watch on 6 September 1794. Campbell joined the 42nd at Gibraltar, and was engaged in the capture of Minorca by Lieutenant-General the Hon. Sir Charles Stuart in 1798. On 3 January 1799 he was promoted major into the Argyll fencibles, then stationed in Ireland; but on 7 April 1802 he exchanged for a captaincy in the 94th regiment, which he joined at Madras in September 1802, and with which he remained continuously until obliged to leave by wounds received at the battle of Vitoria in 1813.

Campbell first served in the Second Anglo-Maratha War under Major-General the Hon. Arthur Wellesley, whose force he joined at Trichinopoly in January 1803, after a forced march of 984 miles. He distinguished himself throughout the war. He was thanked for his services at the battle of Argaon, and he led the centre attack on the fortress of Gawilgarh, where, heading the stormers of the inner fort, he was again mentioned in dispatches. He forced the enemy's outposts and batteries at Chandur, and for a short period towards the end of the war commanded a brigade. He was rewarded by being allowed batta for the rank of major, to which he had been promoted on 4 July 1803, though the information did not reach India until the war was over. The order was dated 29 August 1804, and he was promoted lieutenant-colonel on 27 October. In October 1807 the men of the 94th were drafted into other regiments, and the officers and headquarters under Campbell returned to England, where they were stationed in Jersey.

By vigorous recruiting, the regiment soon restored its numbers, and in January 1810 was ordered to Portugal, and from there to Cadiz. Campbell commanded a brigade at Cadiz, and for some time the garrison, but was ordered again to Lisbon in September 1810, when the 94th was brigaded with the 1st brigade of the 3rd division under Picton. As senior colonel, Campbell assumed command of the brigade until the arrival of Major-General the Hon. Charles Colville on 14 October 1810. Under him the 94th served in all the engagements in the pursuit after Masséna, and at the battle of Fuentes d'Oñoro.

In December 1811, when Colville took command of the 4th division, Campbell again assumed command of the brigade, which he held at the storming of Ciudad Rodrigo, and the siege of Badajoz. There, owing to Picton's and Kempt's injuries, he commanded the 3rd division, which took the castle and thus the city. Campbell also commanded the 3rd division at the battle of Salamanca, where he was wounded, and did not again surrender the command of the brigade to General Colville until June 1813. At the battle of Vitoria he commanded only his own regiment; he was very severely wounded early in the action, and had in consequence to return to England.

Campbell's wound prevented him from seeing further service, but he received some rewards for his long service. He was promoted colonel on 4 June 1813, made a CB and a knight of the Tower and Sword in 1814, and received a gold cross and one clasp for Fuentes d'Oñoro, Ciudad Rodrigo, Badajoz, Salamanca, and Vitoria. A regulation had been made on the extension of the Order of the Bath in January 1815, that only officers with a cross and two clasps should be made KCB, which excluded Campbell. However, both Wellington and Bathurst believed this rule to be unfair, since it excluded such men as Campbell, and included many who had only been present and scarcely engaged in a greater number of battles. In a letter dated 28 February 1815 Lord Bathurst, the secretary of state, proposed to make five distinguished officers, headed by Colonel Campbell KCB. This, however, was not done, and he was not made a KCB until 3 December 1822.

On 18 March 1817 Campbell married Lady Dorothea Cuffe, younger daughter of Otway Cuffe, first earl of Desart, and on 12 August 1819 he was promoted major-general; from 1825 to 1833 he was governor of Grenada. In 1831 he was appointed colonel of the 94th, and in 1834 colonel of the 74th. He died in Paris on 6 May 1835.

H. M. STEPHENS, *rev.* STEWART M. FRASER

Sources J. Philippart, ed., *The royal military calendar*, 3rd edn, 5 vols. (1820) • A. R. Wellesley, second duke of Wellington, *Despatches, correspondence, and memoranda of Field Marshal Arthur, duke of Wellington, K.G.: in continuation of the former series*, 8 vols. (1867–80) • *Supplementary despatches (correspondence) and memoranda of Field Marshal Arthur, duke of Wellington*, ed. A. R. Wellesley, second duke of Wellington, 15 vols. (1858–72) • *GM*, 2nd ser., 4 (1835), 90 • C. W. C. Oman, *A history of the Peninsular War*, 7 vols. (1902–30); repr. (1995–7) • HoP, *Commons* • P. Moon, *The British conquest and dominion of India* (1989) • R. Muir, *Britain and the defeat of Napoleon, 1807–1815* (1996)

Campbell, James Duncan (1833–1907), customs official, was born on 9 February 1833 at 7 Warriston Crescent, Edinburgh, the first child of Major Robert Campbell (1799–1874), of Craignish, Argyll, an officer in the 46th regiment, and his first wife, Louisa, *née* Baillie (*d.* 1870). After studying at Cheltenham College (from Easter 1844 to October 1850), at Boulogne, and at university in Paris (1851–2) and Heidelberg (1853) Campbell worked briefly at his uncle's firm in Calcutta from 1853 to 1854. After his uncle's death, the then somewhat aimless young man returned to Britain contemplating the army and the Indian Civil Service as careers. Eventually, however, he joined the British Civil Service, where he spent six years in the Treasury and Audit Office from 1856 to 1862. Campbell was by now seen as something of a high-flyer, and was appointed secretary to the chief of the Treasury; he was also a prominent member of the volunteer movement, and musketry-inspector to the Civil Service Volunteers.

The Treasury's rising star was poached by the nascent Chinese maritime customs service in 1862. This service was born in the chaos of the Taiping uprising in China (1850–65), at a time when the breakdown of effective Chinese administration in Shanghai threatened to undo the system of Sino-foreign trade and diplomacy founded on the treaty of Nanjing (1842). Foreign inspectors were appointed to oversee the collection of customs dues from foreign traders for the Chinese authorities. This 'Shanghai system' grew into a national service which, despite being an arm of the Chinese state, was controlled and staffed by foreign personnel. In this way China used foreign experts to mediate with foreign traders, and—effectively—to lobby and negotiate for China in the new world of state-to-state diplomacy that Chinese officials were entering after the mid-century wars with Britain and France. The service became in time the prime revenue-collection service of the Chinese state and the security on which foreign loans were raised. Its first inspector-general, Horatio Nelson Lay, was appointed in May 1859 to establish the service at all treaty ports, and Campbell was appointed by Lay as chief secretary and auditor; he sailed for China in March 1863.

Lay's was, however, a false start for the service, and it was effectively refounded after his dismissal in November 1863, by a firmer hand. Ulsterman Sir Robert Hart (1835–1911) had been Lay's deputy since 1860, and he took over the service and controlled it until his death. Lay was arrogant, and attempted to assume powers well beyond those acceptable to the Chinese. Hart was an altogether smoother figure; although he ruled the service like an autocrat he subordinated himself properly to Chinese control. Campbell had been taken on to help establish an accounting system for the service but after 1870 he found himself mostly based in Britain on various missions, and Hart decided that it would be more useful to have him formally based in London as non-resident secretary from 1873 onwards.

If the Chinese maritime customs service developed around the figure of Hart in Peking (Beijing)—and Hart became a dominant and dominating figure in Sino-British relations—it would certainly have been a very different organization without the effort and dedication of Campbell in London. Campbell was a hard-working man of solidly fixed habits, who in later life looked very much like—and was often taken for—Lord Salisbury. He established the London office in 1874—which was funded by quarterly subventions from the customs administration in Peking—and it became the nursery for some of the service's finest recruits. It also served as the examination centre for the service, as its supply department, and as an information bureau. The London office, at 8 Storey's Gate, also facilitated the visit of Chinese embassies, such as that of Guo Songtao in 1877–8, and at times rivalled the Chinese legation as the arm of the Chinese government in London. However, Hart was always careful to make sure that Campbell remained his own private representative and that he acquired no official diplomatic office (such as a consulship). Campbell also negotiated with Jules Ferry the 1885 peace treaty which ended the Franco-Chinese War of 1884–5, and the Sino-Portuguese commercial treaty of 1887, the 'protocol of Lisbon', which fixed the status of Macau (Macao). More importantly, in many ways he was Robert Hart's personal fixer in London. His duties ranged from negotiating with the Foreign Office on behalf of the service, to supplying Hart with new shoes and suits, violin music, and instruments for the brass band he formed in Peking to provide entertainment at soirées, or disbursing handouts to Hart's 'wards'—the three children of Sir Robert's liaison with a Chinese woman, Ayaou, who were educated and then worked in Britain before emigrating to Canada. Campbell became best-known not for his own contribution to the activities of the customs service, but rather for his absence from China and as Sir Robert Hart's London muse and London agent. Though the two men met in person only two or three times their correspondence was full and vigorous, lasting from 1868 to 1907 and affording an invaluable guide to the life and thoughts of that important and enigmatic figure, Hart, and also to the development of the service.

Campbell had married in Brighton, on 22 September 1870, Ellen Mary Lewis, daughter of T. R. Lewis, and they had five sons and two daughters. He never revisited China after 1870 and never met Hart after 1878. Campbell's eldest son, James Baillie Campbell, joined the service—its administrative ethos and structures were well-oiled by nepotism—but he died of typhoid in Peking in 1892 within a year of arriving in China. That year provided a further blow when Campbell lost some £80,000 in the Colman and May collapse. The customs service aside, the main preoccupation of Campbell's later years was attempting to prove himself the rightful heir to the Craignish succession.

Campbell died at his home, 18 Clanricarde Gardens, Hyde Park, London, on 3 December 1907, following complications after a bowel operation, and was buried on 6 December in Kensal Green cemetery, London. Hart lasted little longer in China and in 1908 left for England, where he died three years later. Campbell was much honoured over the years—as CMG (1885), as commander of the Légion d'honneur and of the Portuguese order of the Conception, and as a member of the imperial order of the Double Dragon—but Hart stole all the glory for the successes of the customs service, as was his wont. Campbell deserves much credit, however, for his contributions to the development of one of China's most important and influential modern institutions. ROBERT BICKERS

Sources R. R. Campbell, *James Duncan Campbell: a memoir by his son* (1970) • *The I.G. in Peking: letters of Sir Robert Hart, Chinese maritime customs, 1868–1907*, ed. J. K. Fairbank, K. F. Bruner, and E. M. Matheson, 2 vols. (1975) • S. F. Wright, *Hart and the Chinese customs* (1950) • *The Times* (5 Dec 1907) • *Archives of China's imperial maritime customs: confidential correspondence between Robert Hart and James Duncan Campbell, 1874–1907*, ed. Chen Xiafei and Han Rongfang, 4 vols. (1990–93) • E. S. Skirving, ed., *Cheltenham College register, 1841–1927* (1928) • *WWW, 1897–1915* • Kelly, *Handbk* (1891) • *The Times* (4 Dec 1907)

Archives NL Wales, corresp. with Lord Rendel • SOAS, corresp. with Sir Robert Hart

Likenesses photograph, 1870, Harvard-Yenching Library, Cambridge, Massachusetts, Drew collection • photograph, 1900, Queen's University, Belfast, Hart collection

Campbell, James Dykes (1838–1895), biographer of Samuel Taylor Coleridge, was born on 2 November 1838 at Port Glasgow, Inverclyde, the second son of Peter Campbell (*d.* 1854) and Jean, *née* Dykes, daughter of James Dykes. Dykes was the business partner of James Campbell's grandfather Duncan Campbell, a shipwright.

Campbell was educated from the age of six at the burgh school at Port Glasgow. In 1852 he joined a merchant's office and from 1854 he was employed at Cochrane & Co., Glasgow, manufacturers of Verreville pottery. He spent his leisure hours on literary pursuits. He was sent to Canada by his employers in 1860, and during his two-year stay he made many friends in literary circles, including the theologian Edwin Hatch.

A collector of editions of Tennyson, Campbell privately printed in 1862 a book of selected poems that the poet had afterwards suppressed, as well as a list of alterations made in the pieces he had retained in later editions. Tennyson obtained an injunction preventing further publication by a London publisher.

On his return to Glasgow, Campbell went into business for himself, but continued to pursue his literary interests. When he found original manuscripts for three of Addison's *Spectator* essays, he collected them in a pamphlet entitled *Some Portions of Spectator Papers* and privately printed 250 copies in 1864.

In 1867, after a trip to Bombay, Campbell joined a mercantile firm in Mauritius and in 1873 became a partner of Ireland, Fraser & Co. On 13 November 1875 he married Mary Sophia, daughter of General F. R. Chesney, who held command on the island; they had no children. In 1878 Campbell and his wife travelled to Europe, and in particular visited the Lake District, where they paid homage to both Wordsworth and Coleridge. By 1881 Campbell was able to retire and returned to a flat in Kensington, where his congenial literary friendships and activities, including the honorary secretaryship of the newly founded Browning Society, occupied him.

Having collected materials and published notes in *The Athenaeum* on Coleridge's life, Campbell produced his biographical introduction to the *Poetical Works*, edited by E. H. Coleridge (1893). This was published separately in the following year as *Samuel Taylor Coleridge: a Narrative of the Events of his Life*. 'There is an ever-lengthening array of estimates of Coleridge as a poet and philosopher', Campbell noted; what is wanting is a 'plain and, so far as possible, accurate narrative' (S. T. Coleridge, *Poetical Works*, ed. E. H. Coleridge, 1893, v–vi). He provided just this, tempering with irony Coleridge's own exaggerations and sifting the tales told by others. The biography by H. T. Traill in the English Men of Letters series (1884) presented the romantic view of Coleridge as having but a few marvellous years before his gifts abandoned him in 1803. Campbell gave Traill credit for his factual account of the poet's career as a journalist, and incorporated it in the array of materials he drew together from unpublished letters and various testimonies of Coleridge's associates. But he gave a different shape to the life: 'A brief dawn of unsurpassed promise and achievement'; 'a trouble' as of 'clouds and weeping rain'; then, a long summer evening's work done by 'the setting sun's pathetic light'. Such was 'Coleridge's day, the after-glow of which is still in the sky' (J. D. Campbell, *Samuel Taylor Coleridge: a Narrative of the Events of his Life*, 1894). This is far closer to the late-twentieth-century view established by the editing of the mature works of Coleridge's last decade. Though animated by a comprehensive and eloquent spirit of goodwill towards his subject, there is no hint of the philosophical or critical intellect in Campbell; he left that for the many others who built on his solid foundations.

Mary Campbell's ill health prompted the couple to move to St Leonards in 1889. Financial difficulties and the deaths of a number of close friends put a great strain on Campbell, and early in 1895 he and his wife moved to Tunbridge Wells, where he died at Walton Lodge, 9 Beulah Road, on 1 June 1895. He was buried in the churchyard of nearby Frant. He was survived by his wife.

A second edition of Campbell's Coleridge biography was issued in 1896 and included a memoir of the author by Leslie Stephen. *Coleridge's Poems*, a facsimile reproduction of the proofs and selected manuscripts, appeared in 1899, with a preface and notes by W. Hale White.

SIDNEY LEE, *rev.* ELINOR SHAFFER

Sources J. D. Campbell, *Samuel Taylor Coleridge, a narrative of the events of his life*, 2nd edn (1896) [with a memoir of the author by L. Stephen] · *The Athenaeum* (8 June 1895) · *The Times* (6 June 1895) · *ILN* (8 June 1895) · *CGPLA Eng. & Wales* (1895) · d. cert.

Archives University of Toronto, Victoria University, papers · Wordsworth Trust, Dove Cottage, Grasmere, notes | BL, letters to W. C. Hazlitt, Add. MS 38905 · BL, corresp. with Macmillans, Add. MS 55044 · Bodl. Oxf., letters to Bertram Dobell · Morgan L., letters to William Angus Knight · Trinity Cam., letters to W. Aldis Wright · U. Leeds, Brotherton L., letters to Clement Shorter

Wealth at death £5552 3*s.* 10*d.*: resworn probate, March/April 1896, *CGPLA Eng. & Wales* (1895)

Campbell, James Henry Mussen, first Baron Glenavy (**1851–1931**), lawyer and politician, was born at Terenure, Dublin, on 4 April 1851, the youngest son of William Mussen Campbell, a Dublin policeman, and his wife, Delia, daughter of Henry Francis Graham Poole, of Newtown Abbey, co. Kildare. He was educated at Kingstown, co. Dublin, and at Trinity College, Dublin, where he won a classical scholarship and was a senior moderator in both classics and history. He won the college historical society's gold medal for oratory and obtained his BA in 1874.

Campbell was called to the Irish bar in 1878 and rapidly became a leading junior on the north-eastern circuit. His skilful oratory won him the praise of distinguished advocates, including T. M. Healy (1855–1931), Edward Carson (1854–1935), and Seymour Bushe. He took silk in 1892 and was made a bencher of King's Inns in 1894. He was called to the English bar by Gray's Inn in 1899, and became a bencher in 1901 and KC in 1906, but did not practise much in England. In 1884 he married Emily MacCullagh (*d.* 1939), daughter of John MacCullagh, resident magistrate, of Newry, co. Down. They had three sons, the youngest of whom was killed in the First World War, and one daughter.

Like most Irish barristers of the time, Campbell was a politician. He became prominent as a Unionist. Elected to parliament for the St Stephen's Green division of Dublin at a by-election in 1898, he lost this seat to the nationalists in 1900. In 1903, at another by-election, he was returned as one of the two members for Dublin University, Carson having been the other member since 1892. Campbell held this seat until he was raised to the bench in 1916. He was solicitor-general for Ireland from 1901 to 1905 and attorney-general for a short time in December 1905. He was sworn of the Irish privy council in 1905.

During the home rule controversy of 1912–14 Campbell, deeply involved in the Ulster Unionist movement, was a member of Carson's provisional government. He was reappointed attorney-general in April 1916 a few days before the Sinn Féin rising. In December 1916 he was made lord chief justice of Ireland. He was created a baronet in 1917 and in June 1918 was appointed lord chancellor of Ireland. In the last scramble for office before the setting up of the Irish Free State in 1921 he was induced to retire in favour of Sir John Ross (1853–1935), and was raised to the peerage as Baron Glenavy of Milltown, co. Dublin.

Campbell's experience as potential rebel in the Ulster provisional government and as attorney-general after the rising of 1916 had considerably modified his views on home rule. As head of the Irish judiciary from 1918 to 1921, while the country was in active rebellion, he had come to see that a change was inevitable. Accordingly, when the Irish Free State was established he accepted the new regime and was made a member of its first senate; he was elected chairman in 1922. With his Unionist background, he was an unlikely choice for chairman and his dominance may have stunted the senate's independence. He was even known to adjourn the house to suit his own convenience. W. B. Yeats, a fellow senator, described him as 'handsome, watchful, vigorous, dominating, courteous, he seemed like some figure from an historical painting'. In 1928 he did not seek re-election.

Glenavy was a convinced member of the Church of Ireland and served on its synod. He was also a keen golfer and bridge player. He died at his residence, Glenavy, Milltown, co. Dublin, on 22 March 1931, and was succeeded as second baron by his eldest son, Charles Henry Gordon (*b.* 1885). A portrait by Sir William Orpen was left to Gray's Inn, and another, by Leo Whelan, to Glenavy's son.

DIARMID COFFEY, *rev.* SINÉAD AGNEW

Sources Burke, *Peerage* • F. E. Ball, *The judges in Ireland, 1221–1921*, 2 vols. (1926) • *The Times* (23 March 1931) • private information (1949) • personal knowledge (1949) • *CGPLA NIre.* (1931)

Archives HLRO, Law MSS • NL Ire., letters to John Middleton Murry • PRO NIre., Carson MSS

Likenesses W. Orpen, oils, 1922, Gray's Inn, London • L. Whelan, portrait, priv. coll.

Wealth at death £68 15*s.*: probate, 9 Sept 1931, *CGPLA NIre.* • £99,490 5*s.* 5*d.* effects in England: probate, 10 June 1931, *CGPLA Eng. & Wales*

Campbell, James Joseph [*pseud.* Ultach] **(1910–1979)**, scholar and educationist, was born on 8 March 1910 at 237 New Lodge Road, Belfast, the second (and eldest surviving) of the five children of James Campbell (*c.*1862–1930) and his second wife, Bridget McTeggart (1878–1959). His father was a hairdresser and spirit grocer who learned to read in later life. Campbell showed himself academically gifted. After secondary education at St Malachy's College, Belfast, he became a foundation entrance scholar of Queen's University, Belfast, in 1927, and obtained a first-class degree in classics in 1930. He taught classics, mainly at St Malachy's College, until 1950 and then joined the staff of St Joseph's College of Education, Belfast. In 1969 he became director of the Institute of Education at Queen's University, retiring in 1976. He had made an admirable contribution to co-ordinating work by the very separate Belfast colleges of education, and to bringing about a large increase of in-service training for teachers.

Campbell had many literary and public interests. Between 1946 and 1948 he was editor of the *Irish Bookman*. He edited two texts of Cicero for schools, and wrote *Legends of Ireland* (1955). He wrote extensively on Irish education. During a long-standing connection with the BBC in Belfast (especially in schools broadcasting) he wrote many radio scripts—his 'Dove on the Water', about St Columba, was particularly worth remembering. During the 1950s and 1960s he was a lively member, and ultimately chairman, of a Northern Ireland radio series called *Any Questions*. In 1960 he published *Television in Ireland*.

Campbell played an important part in the post-1945 entry of Roman Catholics (to which church he belonged) into Northern Ireland's public life. He was active in many social causes, but particularly involved in work for Queen's University, an institution he loved, and where he was ultimately chairman of convocation. Never a party politician, he often represented moderate Roman Catholic opinion. In 1969 he served with Sir John Biggart on Lord Cameron's penetrating inquiry into the disturbances in 1968–9.

In later life Campbell's temperament was balanced and cautious. Few of his friends, and none of his children, knew that during the Second World War he had published a well-known polemic, *Orange Terror* (1943), under the pseudonym Ultach. The article arose from his experiences of protestant violence and institutional anti-Catholicism as a child and a young man. But even when he wrote it his objective was not only to better the position of Roman Catholics, but ultimately to remove inter-community bitterness.

Campbell was a Christian humanist by temperament and conviction. For a decade after the Second Vatican Council he read the scriptures, Sunday after Sunday, at St Brigid's Church, Belfast, readings the more impressive because of his expertise in biblical Greek. Throughout the post-war period he had been an outstanding exponent of better community relations in Northern Ireland. It was his fate that in 1969, after threats from both republicans and loyalists, he had to move from his home in Clifton Park Avenue, Belfast.

On 27 June 1934 Campbell married Josephine Kerr (1911–1980). They had six children: five sons and a daughter. Their children remembered him perpetually working: sitting behind a desk, speaking on the telephone in English, Irish, and Latin, addressed as James by his family and oldest friends, as Seamus by Irish-speaking and other Irish-oriented friends, and as J. J. by his academic, media, and newer friends. Thanks to his father's training he was an expert hairdresser and used to cut all his children's hair. Parties meant music (Campbell liked to play the fiddle), stories, and Irish dancing. James Joseph Campbell died on 18 September 1979, at 3 Cross Avenue, Marlborough Park, Belfast. He was buried at Milltown cemetery. His wife survived him for only a few months. ARTHUR GREEN

Sources private information (2004) [Mrs Josephine Mount] • personal knowledge (2004) • *Belfast Telegraph* (19 Sept 1979) • *Irish News and Belfast Morning News* (19 Sept 1979) • Ultach [J. J. Campbell], *Orange terror* (1943)

Wealth at death £6275.67: probate, 22 Jan 1980, *CGPLA NIre.*

Campbell, Sir James Macnabb (1846–1903), administrator in India and ethnologist, born at Partick, Lanarkshire, on 4 October 1846, was the son of John McLeod *Campbell (1800–1872), Church of Scotland minister and theologian, and his wife, Mary Campbell. His brother Donald (*d.* 1909) was rector of Oakford, Devon, and rural dean of Tiverton. Two other brothers lived with him in Bombay, John McLeod (*d.* 1888) being a member of the Bombay civil service, and Robert Story a merchant.

Campbell was educated at Glasgow, first at the academy

and then at the university, graduating MA in 1866, with the highest honours in logic, philosophy, and English literature. Having passed the Indian Civil Service examination in 1867, he went to Bombay presidency in November 1869, and served as an assistant collector. Soon reputed for his interest in the history and customs of the people, he was in June 1873 entrusted with the compilation of the provincial *Gazetteer* of Bombay, though simultaneously having other duties. From April to August 1877 he was on famine work in the Kaladgi district; and from April 1880 until late 1881 he was successively municipal commissioner of Bombay, under-secretary to government in the political, judicial, and educational departments, and collector of Bombay. Yet to the *Gazetteer* he devoted every spare moment. By August 1884 the statistical accounts alone occupied twenty-seven volumes averaging 500 pages each. The government, while then terminating Campbell's formal appointment as compiler, eulogized his work as 'a record as complete perhaps as ever was produced on behalf of any government'. But in 1889 and again in 1892 the secretary of state for India urged the Bombay government to extend the gazetteer series to include volumes on the history of the Bombay presidency and on the town and island of Bombay, and suggested that this work should be entrusted to Campbell. As a result, five additional volumes (in nine parts) were published between 1893 and 1901, four of them written by Campbell himself. Campbell was made CIE in January 1885, and while home on his first furlough that year was created honorary DCL of Glasgow University. Campbell completed his *Bombay Gazetteer* at the close of 1901, when it consisted of twenty-six volumes embracing thirty-four sections; he himself wrote much in those dealing with ethnology. In 1904 R. E. Enthoven, his former assistant in Bombay, added an index volume, and brought up to date some of Campbell's earlier statistics, while in 1910 S. M. Edwards added three new volumes on the history of the city and island of Bombay.

After serving as collector of various districts, Campbell was from November 1891 stationed at Bombay as collector of land revenue, customs, and opium. He rendered valuable service during the cow protection riots of 1893 and contributed valuable help, as a member of a confidential preliminary committee, in formulating the scheme which led to the passage of the City of Bombay Improvement Act 1898.

Campbell was recalled from furlough early in 1897 to aid in measures against the great outbreak of plague; and in June 1897 he succeeded General Sir William Gatacre as chairman of a new and independent plague committee at Bombay. The committee's compulsory measures of sanitation had provoked rioting and the murder on 22 June 1897 of two British officers on plague duty in Poona, W. C. Rand and C. E. Ayerst. The difficulties of the situation were soon multiplied by the appearance of famine in the countryside and the return to Bombay of thousands of refugees. Campbell's resourcefulness and popular repute—he was nicknamed the Murani Collector-Sahib (the collector with the divinely lighted face)—greatly improved the public attitude and encouraged voluntary co-operation in inspection and other work. Largely under his influence, in June 1898 the plague committee was disbanded and the administration was restored to the municipality.

In June 1897 Campbell was made KCIE, and on 29 April 1898 he left Bombay in broken health, resigning, on the expiry of his furlough, in April 1900. The Bombay government on 14 February 1902 republished its earlier resolution of appreciation of his work and character and ordered it to be printed after the title-page of the first volume of the gazetteer and in every issue. Residing with his brother Robert at his father's old home, Achnashie, Rosneath, Dunbartonshire, he found his main recreation in gardening. He died unmarried at Achnashie on 26 May 1903, and was buried in Rosneath churchyard beside his parents. A memorial tablet on the ruined wall of the old church, in which his father had often preached when minister of the adjoining parish of Row, pays tribute to 'the noble example set by him during the great plague in Bombay, which led to his premature and deeply lamented death'. His friends also founded a gold medal, conferred triennially by the Bombay branch of the Royal Asiatic Society, for the best original work on Indian folklore, history, or ethnology. The first medal was presented on 1 March 1909 to A. M. Stein, the explorer, for his *Ancient Khotan*. Subsequent recipients were among the most distinguished scholars in these fields.

Campbell collected much material on Indian history and folklore. Apart from his gazetteer, he published the history of Mandu, the former capital of the Muslim kingdom of Malwa, in the *Journal of the Bombay Branch, Royal Asiatic Society* (19, 1895–7, 154–201); 'The bharwad jang, or, shepherds' wedding', in the *Journal of the Anthropological Society of Bombay* (4, 1895–7, 40–74); and *Saint Sophia in Ramazan* (2nd edn, 1897). One of his hobbies was the study of spirit-scaring, and some of the materials he collected on this subject were published under the title 'Notes on the spirit basis of belief and custom', in various issues of the *Indian Antiquary* (23–30, 1894–1901).

In compiling the *Bombay Gazetteer* Campbell displayed both unremitting energy over a period of nearly thirty years, and great tact in revising and where necessary recasting the many contributions that were made by British and Indian collaborators. The gazetteers were originally intended as sources of information for British district officials; in time they became invaluable reference sources for scholars interested in India.

Campbell was a contemporary of Sir Denzil Ibbetson (1847–1908), Vincent Smith (1848–1920), and Sir Herbert Hope Risley (1851–1911), who, like him, were both administrators and scholars. Campbell was a sympathetic and generous man. In the last decade of his service he was at the centre of the intellectual life of Bombay and brought together at his hospitable table at the Byculla Club and his residence at Breach Candy men of all occupations and professions in congenial company.

F. H. Brown, *rev.* Peter Harnetty

Sources J. M. Campbell, ed., *Gazetteer of the Bombay presidency*, 27 vols. (1877–1904) • *Times of India* (30 April 1898) • *Times of India* (12 April 1902) • *Times of India* (3 June 1903) • *Times of India* (2 March 1909) • J. F. Fleet, 'Sir James Macnabb Campbell', *Journal of the Royal Asiatic Society of Great Britain and Ireland* (1903), 651–4 • Lord Sandhurst and others, 'The Campbell memorial gold medal', *Journal of the Royal Asiatic Society of Great Britain and Ireland* (1916), 577–80 • R. E. Enthoven and others, 'Presentation of the Campbell memorial gold medal', *Journal of the Royal Asiatic Society of Great Britain and Ireland* (1924), 526–32 • H. Scholberg, *The district gazetteers of British India* (1970) • S. B. Chaudhuri, *History of the gazetteers of India* (1964) • V. Purohit, 'Gazetteers as records of the Indian bourgeoisification process', *Indian Archives*, 30 (1981), 32–58 • Honours papers, 1859–1947, BL OIOC, L/P&S/15, 275 • *Selections from despatches addressed to the several governments in India … 1858–1936*, 28 (1880); 32 (1889); 36 (1893) • *Journal of the Bombay Branch of the Royal Asiatic Society*, 22 (1905–7), lxi–lxv [foundation of the Campbell memorial medal] • *Report of the Bombay Presidency Committee on the Plague in Bombay, 1897–1898*, 2 vols. (1898) [chaired by Sir James Macnabb Campbell] • 'Plague commission, 1898–99', *Parl. papers* (1902), 72.223, Cd 810 • *The Times* (2 June 1903)

Wealth at death £5113 19*s*. 2*d*.: confirmation, 21 July 1903, *CCI*

Campbell, Jane. *See* Gordon, Jane, Viscountess Kenmure (*d*. 1675).

Campbell [*née* Black], **Janet** [Jessie] (**1827–1907**), promoter of higher education for women in Scotland, was born in Cross-Arthurlie, Renfrewshire, on 26 March 1827, the eldest child of James Black (1799?–1831) of Cross-Arthurlie, the owner of a bleaching business, and his wife, Eliza Taylor (1803?–1859) of Balgray House, Newton Mearns, Renfrewshire. One brother, Charles, died in 1832 and the other, James (1831?–1853), died in Trinidad, West Indies. On 21 April 1846 she married James Campbell (1823–1902) of Tullichewan, Dunbartonshire, a merchant and a principal of the firm of J. and W. Campbell & Co., warehousemen (wholesale drapers), Ingram Street, Glasgow; they had five children, three daughters and two sons. Her husband was a cousin of Henry Campbell-Bannerman. Staunch members of the Free Church of Scotland, they attended Alexandria North United Free Church.

Jessie Campbell was described as a lady with great intellectual gifts who identified herself with the various movements, social and intellectual, in which her husband was interested, such as the poor, education, and music. However, the movement for the higher education of women was her own cause. She recognized the need of women for education beyond school age, and desired to obtain for them educational advantages similar to those offered by universities to men. In 1868 she proposed that lectures for women be given by professors of Glasgow University. The first to respond were John Young, professor of natural history, Edward Caird (moral philosophy), John Nichol (English literature), and Robert Grant (astronomy). These lectures, given in the university and in the corporation galleries, were very successful and continued until 1877, when the Glasgow Association for the Higher Education of Women was formed to offer women opportunities of study at university level. Jessie Campbell became vice-president of the new association and Janet Galloway its honorary secretary. Lecture courses were offered with tutorial classes, set written work, and examinations. With Jessie Campbell at the helm the association thrived. It offered an ever-increasing range of courses while continuing to petition for the equal entry of women into Scottish universities.

In 1883 the association was incorporated as Queen Margaret College, and Jessie Campbell became its vice-president and chaired its executive committee. The new college required a building and secure financial resources, tasks which she took on with relish. She persuaded an old friend, Isabella Elder, to purchase North Park House for the college, and was the main fund-raiser of the £20,000 endowment fund, appealing to the wealthy merchants and industrialists of Glasgow. Queen Margaret College, which was the only college for the higher education of women in Scotland, amalgamated with Glasgow University in 1892 after the Scottish universities commissioners issued an ordinance empowering Scottish universities to make provision for the instruction and graduation of women. Affiliation with Glasgow University had always been one of the aims of Queen Margaret College, but following its dissolution Jessie Campbell led an action to ensure that women retained some share in the management of the women's department of the university, which the college became. The issue was sidelined, and in 1893 Mrs Campbell retired from active involvement in the higher education of women in Scotland. Glasgow University awarded her an honorary LLD in 1901 in recognition of her pioneering work. She contributed an article, 'The rise of the higher education of women movement in Glasgow', to *The book of the jubilee: in commemoration of the ninth jubilee of the University of Glasgow, 1451–1901* (1901). Jessie Campbell died at her home at Broomley, Alexandria, Dunbartonshire, on 10 February 1907, and was buried four days later in the family vault at Alexandria cemetery.

LESLEY M. RICHMOND

Sources records, U. Glas., Archives and Business Records Centre, Glasgow Association for the Higher Education of Women • U. Glas., Archives and Business Records Centre, Queen Margaret College archives • *Glasgow Herald* (14 Feb 1907), 6 • *Glasgow Herald* (15 Feb 1907), 12 • D. Murray, *Miss Janet Galloway and the higher education of women in Glasgow* (1914) • parish records (baptism), Neilston, Cross-Arthurlie, Renfrewshire, OPR 572, vol. 4, p. 220 • Burke, *Gen. GB* • *PO Directories*

Archives U. Glas., Archives and Business Records Centre, Glasgow Association for the Higher Education of Women • U. Glas., Archives and Business Records Centre, Queen Margaret College archives | U. Glas., Court MSS

Likenesses Lafayette, photograph, 1890–99, U. Glas. • Maclure, Macdonald & Co., photograph, 1890–99, U. Glas. • H. R. Annan, photograph, 1901, U. Glas. • Warneuke, photograph, 1901, U. Glas.

Wealth at death £3237: confirmation, 7 May 1907, *CCI*

Campbell, Dame Janet Mary (**1877–1954**), medical officer, was born in Brighton on 5 March 1877, the daughter of George Campbell, bank manager, and his wife, Mary Letitia Rowe. She attended Brighton high school and later went to Germany for some months; there she acquired a good knowledge of the language, which served her when she attended a postgraduate course in Vienna. After graduating MB in London in 1901 at the London School of Medicine for Women, Campbell took her MD and MS degrees in 1904 and 1905, a remarkable achievement.

There followed house appointments in London at the Royal Free Hospital followed by the position of senior medical officer at the Belgrave Hospital for Children, a post eagerly sought by women graduates since at that time it was one of the few London hospitals to employ them.

Janet Campbell was a member of the Medical Women's Federation and eventually became its president. At one time she was closely associated with Dartford Physical Training College, first as honorary secretary and afterwards for a time as chairman. As a result of the Second South African War, public interest in the concern for national physique had been aroused and under the Education Act of 1902 school medical officers were appointed by some education authorities. An interdepartmental committee appointed in 1903 recommended, after extensive inquiries, among other measures the introduction of systematic medical inspection of children in elementary schools. In 1904 Campbell became an assistant school medical officer in the London school medical service, where she came under the stimulating influence of James Kerr, the 'father' of school hygiene and author of *The Fundamentals of School Health* (1926). She went on to join the Board of Education as its first full-time woman medical officer in 1907.

The high rate of infant mortality was another issue giving concern to the public and to local authorities, and in 1919, when the Ministry of Health was formed with Sir George Newman as chief medical officer, Campbell was appointed senior medical officer in charge of maternity and child welfare. At the same time she retained her connection with the Board of Education as chief woman adviser. She gave her time and her energies wholeheartedly to the organization of a vigorous and progressive scheme for the welfare of mothers and children. During the First World War, in addition to her specialized work her services had been at the disposal of government and international committees; she later became a medical member of the war cabinet committee on women in industry, and from 1930 to 1936 served on the health committee of the League of Nations.

In 1917 Campbell wrote a valuable and influential report for the Carnegie United Kingdom Trust on the physical welfare of mothers and children. She also produced official reports on the recruitment and training of midwives and on the teaching of obstetrics and gynaecology in medical schools. In 1924 her well-known report on maternal mortality was published. She was appointed DBE, and Durham University made her an honorary doctor of hygiene in the same year. Her reports from 1923 to 1932 on the protection of motherhood, on neonatal and infant mortality, and on the maternity services all had an important influence on administrative reforms and helped in large part to reduce the mortality and morbidity rates of women and children.

In 1934 Dame Janet Campbell married Michael Heseltine (1886–1952), registrar of the General Medical Council and the son of the Revd Ernest Heseltine. Under the rules of the civil service she had to give up her office, but her influence on the public health services of the whole country as they affected women and children was nevertheless profound. She was the great pioneer of maternity and child welfare services and as such was universally acknowledged. It was not only the charming and rather diffident manner of this tall, good-looking, well-dressed woman which attracted the admiration and respect of those who came into contact with her. Her clear-thinking brain and her sound knowledge of her subject enabled her to grasp essentials quickly so that her wise, considered opinion and advice were sought by local authorities, medical officers, and hospitals throughout the country and by organizations far beyond the confines of the United Kingdom.

Dame Janet was a very good horsewoman and riding gave her special pleasure, as did walking and physical exercise, which probably accounted for her upright carriage. Gardening was a favourite hobby and when she lived outside London she grew a wonderful display of roses. She had always taken a keen interest in current affairs and in the politics of the day, and she was a JP for both Surrey and Gloucestershire. She loved a good play and had a lifelong interest in modern literature and in the world around her. Towards the end of her life she lived with her two cousins in Chelsea. After a long and painful illness, when she was in a nursing home, she died on 27 September 1954 at 12 Hornsey Lane, Upper Holloway, London. MARGARET HOGARTH, *rev.*

Sources *BMJ* (9 Oct 1954), 874–5 • *The Lancet* (9 Oct 1954) • private information (1971) • personal knowledge (1971) • *WWW* • *CGPLA Eng. & Wales* (1954) • *WWW*, 1951–60 [Michael Heseltine] • *The Times* (29 Sept 1954)

Wealth at death £37,606 17*s*. 10*d*.: probate, 19 Nov 1954, *CGPLA Eng. & Wales*

Campbell [*née* Callander], **Janey Sevilla** [Lady Archibald Campbell] (**1846–1923**), theatre producer, was born on 18 March 1846, probably at Craigforth House, Stirlingshire, the third daughter of James Henry Callander of Ardkinglas and Craigforth (1804–1851) and his first wife, Jane Plumer (1818–1846), daughter of David Montagu Erskine, second Baron Erskine. Janey Callander was orphaned at four, after the death within four years of her mother, stepmother, and father. She became a ward of George Douglas *Campbell, eighth duke of Argyll (a relative of her stepmother), and was brought up at the family seat, Inveraray Castle, Argyll, and at Argyll Lodge, Kensington. On 12 January 1869, at St George's, Campden Hill, Kensington, she married the duke's second son, Lord Archibald Campbell (1846–1913), and moved with him to Salem Villa, Grassendale, Liverpool. They returned to London, probably in 1871, and had two children, Niall Diarmid (1872–1949), who became tenth duke of Argyll in 1914, and Elspeth Angela (1873–1942). From as early as 1871 Janey and her husband—who became a junior partner in Coutts Bank, a position that did not trespass too severely on his leisure time—were keen ice-skaters, pursuing their enthusiasm at the Welsh Harp Reservoir and later at the Prince's skating club in London. They also shared an interest in the occult and in west highland lore, on which both published a number of periodical articles. She was also a keen cyclist. Her most substantial publication was *Rainbow Music* (1886), which asserts that there are harmonic analogies between music and colour, a view in which she was influenced by her friend the painter James McNeill Whistler. In 1882–3 'poor old Jimmy Whistler' (letter of Lord Archibald Campbell to Sir Joseph Noël Paton, NL Scot.) had painted several portraits of Lady Archibald, one of which, known as *La dame au brodequin jaune* (now in the Philadelphia Museum of Art), survives: her family disdained it 'with the delicate remark that it represented a street walker encouraging a shy follower with a backward glance' (letter of W. Graham Robertson, quoted in R. Dorment and M. F. MacDonald, eds., *James McNeill Whistler*, exhibition catalogue, Tate Gallery, London, 1994, 211).

But the enduring reputation of Lady Archie (as she was usually called) rests on her production of 'pastoral plays' at various locations around London in the 1880s. These plays were perhaps inspired by a report in *The World* of three open-air performances of scenes from *Romeo and Juliet* staged at Cadgwith, Cornwall, in the summer of 1880, starring two leading actors of the age, Helena Modjeska and Johnston Forbes-Robertson. In 1882 Lord and Lady Archibald acquired Coombe Hill Farm near Kingston upon Thames, and it was in the wooded grounds of the neighbouring hydropathic establishment that she staged and starred in the first three of six open-air theatrical productions between 1884 and 1888. These attracted much press attention and visits from the prince of Wales, and set a trend for open-air theatre that lasted beyond the end of the century. In these she collaborated with the architect Edward William Godwin, who had served as a historical consultant on several stage productions since the mid-1870s. In July 1884 they staged three performances of (appropriately) the forest scene from Shakespeare's *As You Like It*, with Janey Campbell playing the part of Orlando. These were repeated in May 1885, and in June and July 1885 they performed Godwin's adaptation of John Fletcher's *The Faithfull Shepherdesse* seven times. In July 1886, this time in Cannizaro Woods at Wimbledon, they staged three performances of *Fair Rosamund*, Godwin's adaptation of Tennyson's *Becket*, with Lady Archibald as Rosamund. In August 1888, after Godwin's death, the French émigré artist Theodore Roussel drew a pastel portrait and an etching of her as Pierrot in Théodore de Banville's play *Le baiser*, also produced in Cannizaro Woods. In 1899 she wrote, produced, and starred in a play based on the border ballad *Tam-Lin*, at the Theatre Royal, Edinburgh, and in 1907 she starred in her own dramatized monologue of W. B. Yeats's poem *Cap and Bells* at the Berkeley Theatre, Glasgow.

Janey Campbell was renowned for her beauty—'the Moon-Lady, the Grey Lady, the beautiful wraith with her beryl eyes' (Holland and Hart-Davis, 174)—and her eccentric ideas about personal adornment—in the summer she 'wore a large, round straw hat with an upturned rim, around which a tiny monkey incessantly ran, and where he slept' (Wake, 205). Her ideas on home decoration were also the acme of aesthetic taste: 'One day, deciding that she wished to live "under the sea", she draped the sitting room with a coloured fish net from which dangled shells of mother of pearl, silver fish and green seaweed.' At her London home in the 1880s, 14 Beaufort Gardens, her 'pink and brown drawing room, painted all over with large white birds, hung with hundreds of gilt palm leaves … every candle … carefully shaded by a green butterfly, and the room … very dark' did not meet with the approval of Disraeli, who opined that 'great nobles have great houses to receive the world in and not such hugger-mugger as I had to endure' (Wake, 206). Lady Archibald Campbell died, after ten years of widowhood, at Coombe Hill Farm on 15 July 1923, aged seventy-seven, and was buried near her parents at Cairndow churchyard, Inveraray, on 20 July 1923, close to the ancestral home at Ardkinglas.

AILEEN REID

Sources F. Baldwin, 'E. W. Godwin and design for the theater', *E. W. Godwin: aesthetic movement architect and designer*, ed. S. W. Soros (1999) • J. Wake, *Princess Louise: Queen Victoria's unconventional daughter* (1988) • J. Stokes, *Resistible theatres* (1972) • L. Lambourne, 'Edward William Godwin (1833–1886): aesthetic polymath', *E. W. Godwin: aesthetic movement architect and designer*, ed. S. W. Soros (1999) [exhibition catalogue, Bard Graduate Center, New York, Nov 1999–Feb 2000] • C. Arbuthnott, 'E. W. Godwin as an antiquary', *E. W. Godwin: aesthetic movement architect and designer*, ed. S. W. Soros (1999) • *The faithfull shepherdesse, by John Fletcher, adapted and arranged in three acts for the open air*, ed. E. W. Godwin (1885) • F. P. Baldwin, 'Victorian artists and stage design, 1870–1905', PhD diss., Courtauld Inst., 1991 • *WWW, 1916–28* • J. Parker, ed., *The green room book, or, Who's who on the stage* (1907) • *The Times* (17 July 1923) • m. cert. • d. cert. • theatre reviews (1884–5) [*The Stage*; *National Review*, 3–6; *Illustrated Sporting and Dramatic News*; *New York Mirror*; *VF*; *The Era*; *Society*; *ILN*; *Whitehall Review*; *Dramatic Review*; *The Observer*; *Pall Mall Gazette*; *Truth*; *Topical Times*] • J. Foster, *Members of parliament, Scotland … 1357–1882*, 2nd edn (privately printed, London, 1882) • E. Robins Pennell and J. Pennell, *The life of James McNeill Whistler*, 2 vols. (1908) • *The complete letters of Oscar Wilde*, ed. M. Holland and R. Hart-Davis (2000) • F. C. Wills, *W. G. Wills: dramatist and painter* (1898) • A. Soudar, 'E. W. Godwin and the visual theatre of the Victorians', MA diss., U. Reading, 1977 • F. Rutter, *Theodore Roussel* (1926) • P. Armytage, *By the clock of St James's* (1927) • D. Harbron, *The conscious stone: the life of Edward William Godwin* (1949) • Brown & Stratton, *Brit. mus.* • O. Ebel, *Women composers: a biographical handbook of woman's work in music*, 3rd edn (1913) • J. H. Callander, diaries for 1832–6, 1838–41, 1849–51, NL Scot., Acc. 8496 • A. Campbell, letters, U. Glas. L., Whistler archive • V&A NAL, Godwin papers [9 boxes of uncatalogued papers, esp. boxes 3, 5, and 7] • A. Campbell, letters to J. Noël Paton, 1879–85, NL Scot., Noël Paton MS Acc. 9133, no. 8 • MS copy of *Rainbow music*, V&A NAL, Godwin papers • BL, Watts-Dunton MSS, Add. MS 70267, fols. 29, 32–35v [letters from Lady Archibald Campbell] • BL, T. H. S. Escott MSS, Add. MS 58776, fols. 135–142v [letters from Lady Archibald Campbell] • letters of Lord and Lady Campbell, marquess of Lorne, and A. Callander, NL Scot., Blackwood MSS 4452–4656, *passim* • A. Campbell, album of caricatures, letters etc., NL Scot., MS 7195, fols. 10–33

Archives Inveraray Castle, Argyllshire, Argyll MSS • NL Scot., diaries of James Henry Callander of Ardkinglas and Craigforth, Acc. 8496 • NL Scot., Noël Paton letters, Acc. 9133, no. 8 • Theatre Museum, London, E. W. Godwin papers

Likenesses J. Whistler, portrait, 1882–3, Philadelphia Museum of Art • T. Roussel, etching, 1888 • T. Roussel, portrait, 1888

Campbell, John, earl of Atholl (*d.* **1333**). *See under* Campbell family (*per.* *c.*1300–1453).

Campbell, Sir John, of Cawdor (*d.* **1546**). *See under* Campbell family of Cawdor (*per.* 1511–1821).

Campbell, Sir John, of Lundie (*d.* **1562**), administrator and ambassador, was an illegitimate son of Colin *Campbell, first earl of Argyll (*d.* 1493). Although nothing is known of his early life, the title of master identifies him with the John Campbell who graduated master of arts at St Andrews in November 1507. He is said to have served the crown from about 1500, but the earliest extant references (1513–16) seem to connect him with John Stewart, duke of Albany, governor for James V. Albany appointed him lord treasurer on 22 January 1517, and granted him legitimation on 24 May. Gavin Douglas later denounced the appointment as that of 'ane bastard bribour quhilk had not v s. worth of goode of his aune' (*LP Henry VIII*, 3/2, no. 1898, corrected from MS). On 28 March 1517 Albany granted him Thornton in Haddingtonshire, forfeited by Alexander, third Lord Home; this was restored to Home's brother and successor in 1522, but by 1525 Campbell had acquired from Lord Lyle the lands of Lundie. He is said to have built a new castle there and helped to establish a Campbell presence in the region. Also in 1517, between 12 May and 12 September, Campbell married Isabel Gray (*d.* in or before 1553), daughter of Andrew *Gray, second Lord Gray [*see under* Gray, Andrew, first Lord Gray], and widow successively of Sir James Scrymgeour of Dudhope (*d.* *c.*1503) and Adam Crichton of Ruthven (*d.* *c.*1516). Their son John Campbell later succeeded him as laird of Lundie; two other sons, both also called John, had been legitimated with their father in 1517.

During this period Douglas alleged that Campbell and Robert Barton, the comptroller, had involved James V in debts of £12,000 Scots, leaving him badly clothed. In fact both were out of pocket. As early as August 1517 Campbell required protection from creditors and by May 1525 his official debts amounted to nearly £4000 Scots. Although the council agreed on 9 March 1526 that he should retain office until sums owing to him were repaid, he was replaced on 24 June by the master of Glencairn.

Campbell was knighted in 1529 shortly before being sent to Flanders, ostensibly to seek renewal of the privileges of Scottish merchants but also to explore alliance with the emperor and the possible marriage of James to his sister, the queen of Hungary. He was to enquire of her manners and 'wesy hir persone' but not to conclude it until James had taken counsel (*LP Henry VIII*, 4, pt. 1, appendix 239). Meanwhile James assured Henry VIII that it was not likely that he would send so mean a man as Campbell to conclude an alliance. In 1531 Campbell returned to Flanders for renewal of the old treaties between the houses of Burgundy and Scotland.

Having been a lord of session since 1517 Campbell was appointed in May 1532 a senator of the new college of justice. He also served as justice-depute in criminal trials from 1531 to 1553. In May 1533 he was made captain-general of all the footbands of Scotland. During the remainder of James V's reign he undertook further diplomatic missions, to Emperor Charles V in 1540–41, and several to England, as relations with Henry VIII deteriorated. After the king's death he sided with Beaton and Mary of Guise, whom he served as master of the household in 1543. In April 1544 the regent Arran sent him as ambassador to the French king. He appears to have retired from the privy council in 1553. Mary of Guise named him as an executor of her testament, but on 8 October 1560, Mary, queen of Scots, wrote forbidding him to act, while commending the 'guid affectioun and faithfull dewite' he had shown to her predecessors 'ane thre scor yeris syne and mare' (NA Scot., CS1/2, fol. 15).

Campbell sat in the court of session until July 1562, but on 12 November he was excused as sick and by 22 December he was dead. A man of wide intellectual interests ranging from botany to history, he was acknowledged by Hector Boece for the help he gave him in writing his history, which included taking books from Iona to Aberdeen.

Athol Murray

Sources G. Brunton and D. Haig, *An historical account of the senators of the college of justice, from its institution in MDXXXII* (1832) · *LP Henry VIII* · R. K. Hannay, ed., *Acts of the lords of council in public affairs, 1501–1554* (1932) · J. B. Paul, ed., *Compota thesaurariorum regum Scotorum / Accounts of the lord high treasurer of Scotland*, 4–11 (1902–16) · M. Livingstone, D. Hay Fleming, and others, eds., *Registrum secreti sigilli regum Scotorum / The register of the privy seal of Scotland*, 1–5 (1908–57) · *The Scottish correspondence of Mary of Lorraine*, ed. A. I. Cameron, Scottish History Society, 3rd ser., 10 (1927) · G. Burnett and others, eds., *The exchequer rolls of Scotland*, 14–19 (1893–8) · J. M. Thomson and others, eds., *Registrum magni sigilli regum Scotorum / The register of the great seal of Scotland*, 11 vols. (1882–1914), vols. 3–4 · books of sederunt, NA Scot., CS1/2 · *Scots peerage* · A. I. Dunlop, ed., *Acta facultatis artium universitatis Sanctiandree, 1413–1588*, 2 vols., Scottish History Society, 3rd ser., 54–5 (1964) · A. J. Warden, *Angus or Forfarshire: the land and people*, 5 vols. (1880–85), vol. 4 · E. J. Cowan, 'The Angus Campbells and the origins of the Campbell–Ogilvie feud', *Scottish Studies*, 25 (1981), 25–38

Wealth at death left lands to son

Campbell, John, of Cawdor (*d.* **1592**). *See under* Campbell family of Cawdor (*per.* 1511–1821).

Campbell, Sir John, of Cawdor (*d.* *c.***1642**). *See under* Campbell family of Cawdor (*per.* 1511–1821).

Campbell, John, first earl of Loudoun (**1598–1662**), lord chancellor of Scotland, was the eldest son of Sir James Campbell of Lawers and his wife, Jean, daughter of James Colvill, first Lord Colvill of Culros. He probably travelled abroad before he married (by March 1620) Margaret (*b.* *c.*1605), daughter of George Campbell, master of Loudoun, who had died in 1612. Margaret was heir to her grandfather Hugh Campbell, first Lord Loudoun (*d.* 1622), and in or before 1619 he resigned his peerage in favour of her husband. The transaction had evidently not been officially recognized by the time of Hugh's death in December 1622, but thereafter John Campbell was recognized as second Lord Loudoun and inherited the Loudoun estates in Ayrshire.

Royal favour and disfavour In November 1626 a meeting of nobles and gentry in Edinburgh drew up a petition to Charles I complaining of the harshness of some of the

John Campbell, first earl of Loudoun (1598–1662), by Abraham Simon, 1645

conditions of his proposed act of revocation, which threatened the rights of those who had acquired former church lands. Loudoun was one of a delegation of three young nobles chosen to present the petition to the king. Charles at first forbade them to approach the court, and on 14 December 'storm'd at ther petition', as of 'too heigh a straine for subiects and petitioners' (*Historical Works of Balfour*, 2.153), but on their apology he received them and won them over with promises and favours. Over the next few years Loudoun was active as a commissioner for the settlement of teinds (tithes) in Scotland, and earned sufficient royal favour for the king, prior to visiting Scotland, to sign a patent creating him earl of Loudoun (12 May 1633). However, in the Scottish parliament Loudoun supported those opposed to the king's religious policies, in particular objecting to an act allowing the king to prescribe the dress of the clergy, which would free him to introduce elaborate vestments on the English model. Charles immediately retaliated. The grant of Loudoun's earldom had not yet passed through the chancery, and the king had the process stopped and the grant suspended, though not cancelled. The message was clearly that if Loudoun wished to be an earl he would have to conform. In the event his path to promotion was to be very different.

Early covenanting years When open defiance of the king's religious policies emerged in July 1637 action began with popular demonstrations, which were then supported by supplications from ministers of the Church of Scotland. Only then did dissident nobles join in. The process was in part at least planned, and it is likely that Loudoun was closely involved in this. He was present at the first gathering of nobles and gentry in Edinburgh on 20 September 1637, and from then on was one of a handful of noble and other leaders who planned the political strategy of the covenanters and negotiated with representatives of the king and privy council. On 21 December he presented the dissidents' supplications to the Scottish privy council and 'in ane eloquent speache declared opinly the causes' of the grievances and fears of the Scots. At issue were 'bothe the weillfaire of the churche and commonwealthe, our condition of lyffe, our libertey and fortoune in this transitorey worlde, and the aeternall happines in the lyffe to come' (*Historical Works of Balfour*, 2.240–41). All these were threatened by enforcing innovations in religion, for subjects had to choose between being declared rebels and abandoning true religion. Loudoun spoke again on 27 and 28 February 1638 at meetings of ministers and of gentry in preparation for the signing of the national covenant, stressing the need for unity if they were to defeat enemies who relied on their divisions. He placed great stress on the legality of the covenanters' actions—but also argued that, as 'Lawes ar supposed to be made in favours of the whole natione, and for the good of all subjects', if three-quarters of subjects were prejudiced by a law they could justly abstain from obeying it until parliament met (Rothes, 77). In November and December 1638 he was a prominent figure in the general assembly in Glasgow which reformed the church in defiance of the king, and in June 1639 he was one of the commissioners who negotiated the treaty of Berwick, ending the first bishops' war.

After an abortive session of the Scottish parliament Loudoun was one of two men commissioned late in 1639 to hold talks with the king in London, but Charles refused to see them. When Loudoun and others returned to London in March 1640 talks began, but the Scots commissioners were arrested on 11 April. A copy of a letter the covenanters had sent to Louis XIII of France asking for support had been discovered and was regarded as treasonable, and though the other Scots were quickly released, Loudoun, as one of the signatories of the letter, was sent to the Tower of London. His wife stoutly told the Scottish parliament that it should not let 'loveing apprehensions' or 'compasionat consideratione' of her husband's sufferings and danger restrain it from acting for the good of church and country (*APS*, 5.266). As a new war approached it is said that it was decided that Loudoun should be executed, but the marquess of Hamilton intervened, persuading the king that it would be counterproductive. Charles therefore ordered Loudoun's release, something which was 'never understood' (*Clarendon State Papers*, 1.188–9). In fact Loudoun had promised to try to persuade the covenanters to disband their army. In the event he instead accompanied the Scots army that marched into England, and was present at its victory at Newburn (28 July). As in 1639 he was conspicuous in the negotiations which led to a truce with the king at the treaty of Ripon (28 July) and were then continued in London.

Lord chancellor When Charles came to Scotland in 1641 his political problems in England forced him into a settlement which gave many leading covenanters high office. The covenanters had agreed that Loudoun should be treasurer, but Charles 'declared him chancellour, against both his own mind and his friends' (*Letters … Baillie*, 1.390). In terms of precedence chancellor was the superior office, but income from it was relatively low, so Loudoun was consoled with a pension of £1000 sterling a year—and, in the end, was also made first commissioner of the Treasury when agreement could not be reached on a single office holder. On the day he was sworn in as chancellor, 2 October, the 1633 grant of his earldom was at last passed.

In the years that followed Loudoun continued at the heart of the Scottish regime. In April 1642 he was sent to Charles to offer Scots mediation in his growing quarrel with the English parliament—an offer which was, not surprisingly, refused—and he led a further mission designed to help end what was now civil war in England in January to April 1643. When the king refused to summon parliament in Scotland, Loudoun, as chancellor, took a lead in summoning a meeting of a convention of estates in June 1643 to decide how Scotland should react to the English war. When the privy council sought to reassure the king by promising that the convention would not raise armed forces Loudoun signed the act as president of the council, but declared that he had 'reasouned, voiced [voted] and protested aganis [against]' this (Stevenson, *Scottish Revolution*, 269). In due course the convention showed its agreement with his protest by allying itself with the English parliament by the solemn league and covenant of September 1643 and raising an army to aid parliament against the king. Predictably Loudoun was one of the Scots commissioners sent to London under the new alliance, becoming a member of the committee of both kingdoms there, and acting as one of the Scots observers who attended the Westminster assembly as it attempted reform of the Church of England. In February 1645 he led the Scots commissioners who took part in the unsuccessful treaty of Uxbridge aimed at ending the English civil war, being notable for arguing 'with much passion against bishops, of the mischieve they had done in all ages' including causing Britain's civil wars (Hyde, 3.483).

Robert Baillie, one of those whose early doubts about the covenanting movement had been removed by Loudoun's persuasive tongue, wrote of his 'divine eloquence' in the Westminster assembly (*Letters … Baillie*, 2.237) when arguing in favour of presbyterianism, and in November 1645 Baillie opposed Loudoun's pleas to be allowed to return to Scotland to help to deal with the aftermath of Montrose's royalist victories of 1644–5 and to see to his private affairs. There was, urged Baillie, 'no man of our nation, either for abilities, or credite with this people [the English] so fitt for these great things, as the Chancellour' (ibid., 2.325). Loudoun did manage a brief return to Scotland, but was back in London in March 1646. In May, after the defeated king surrendered to the Scottish army in England, Loudoun led attempts to force him to make concessions demanded by the English parliament, even though they were more radical than Loudoun himself would have wished. He bluntly warned the king in Newcastle in July, 'if your Majesty lose England by your willfulness, you will not be permitted to come and reign in Scotland' (Stevenson, *Revolution and Counter-Revolution*, 72). The covenanters were well aware that Charles was trying to divide his enemies, and their determination to prevent this led them to abandon him to the English when their army withdrew from England in January 1647.

From engagement to kirk party The failure to reach agreement with the king left 'The good Chancellour … distempered with griefe' (*Letters … Baillie*, 2.402), and in the months that followed the Scottish alliance with the English parliament that Loudoun had worked hard to maintain disintegrated in controversy over terms for a peace settlement. Eventually many covenanters swung towards the belief that a satisfactory peace was now most likely to be achieved through working with the king. In August Loudoun was again sent to talk with the king, though he was worried that this move towards making concessions to Charles would be exploited by royalists for their own ends. Compromise, he observed, might give neither God nor Caesar his dues. Talks took place at Hampton Court in October and subsequently in Carisbrooke Castle. Loudoun was torn as how to act, fearing (30 November) that Charles 'will not come the length he should so it will be hard to Resolve what should be next … I must confes I never hade so many difficulties as at this time' (Stevenson, *Revolution and Counter-Revolution*, 96). His fellow commissioners, the earls of Lauderdale and Lanark, inclined to favour the king more than he did, and on 26 December he joined them in signing the engagement, pledging Scottish military help for the king in return for concessions from him that had previously been considered inadequate by the Scots.

The engagement led to major political realignments in Scotland. Moderate covenanters joined with royalists to support the treaty, while the church and its lay allies bitterly opposed it, becoming known as the kirk party. Loudoun soon began to repent his support for the engagement. When the Scottish parliament made its first moves towards military action—by considering seizing Berwick—his doubts about the course of events resurfaced, and when he, as president of parliament, signed the act he stated that he did so 'as seruant of the hous, not as his oune opinion' (Stevenson, *Revolution and Counter-Revolution*, 102). In June, when parliament refused even to consider concessions offered by the English parliament to prevent a war, Loudoun finally broke with the engagers and retired to his home.

Loudoun thus avoided involvement in the engagers' disastrous invasion of England, and indeed he was active in organizing the Whiggamore raid whereby forces raised by supporters of the kirk party seized power from the engagers. The new civil regime imposed no penalty on him for his part in the early phases of the engagement, but the church was harder to satisfy, forcing him into public repentance in St Giles's in Edinburgh on 14 March 1649. Moreover, though he remained chancellor he was no longer fully trusted. For a decade he had been the leading negotiator between Charles I and the covenanters, but he was excluded from the 1649 and 1650 negotiations with the exiled Charles II, and in February 1650 'manney basse and eueill rumors were vented abroad of the Lord Chanceler; amongest maney, ther was one anent a woman that had borne him a chylde' (*Historical Works of Balfour*, 4.2–3). Loudoun maintained that such stories were spread by his enemies to discredit him, and his loyalty to the kirk party soon renewed his credibility. After Charles II arrived in Scotland in June 1650 Loudoun's office as chancellor made it appropriate that he be used in formal approaches to the king, and in August he took the lead in forcing on Charles a humiliating declaration repenting his family's sins. He also supported the kirk party in purging the army of those considered insufficiently godly to fight the Cromwellian English, and on 16 August, as purging was taking place, Loudoun was present and 'haraggued to them [the soldiers] for their incouragment', stressing the need for discipline in battle, whether in pursuit or defence (*Diary of Sir Archibald Johnston*, ed. Fleming, 20). In the face of a massive defeat at Dunbar (3 September) and the loss of Edinburgh to the English, the kirk party regime began to crumble, but Loudoun continued to support its losing battle to exclude royalists from power. By mid-1651, however, power had passed into royalist hands. Loudoun's life was further complicated by renewed allegations about his private life. He was summoned before the presbytery of the army in June to answer a charge of adultery with the wife of one Major Johnston. 'The Lord pity and give mercy to that miserable unclean man', prayed Archibald Johnston of Wariston (*Diary of Sir Archibald Johnston*, ed. Fleming, 93), worried that his friendship with the accused might tarnish his own reputation. Mercy—the Lord's or not—took the form of the swift collapse of resistance to English conquest, for in the confusion the case against Loudoun was abandoned.

Under English rule After Charles II led the disastrous invasion of England that was to end in calamity at the battle of Worcester (3 September 1651), and further English advance in Scotland, Loudoun as chancellor strove for months to preserve a vestige of an independent Scottish regime. He managed to assemble a skeleton committee of estates at Killin on Loch Tay on 10 September. It retreated successively to Dumbarton, Rosneath, and finally to Rothesay on the Isle of Bute (15 October), from which it hopefully summoned parliament to meet at Finlarig (near Killin) on 15 November. When Loudoun kept the tryst at Finlarig, however, three nobles were the only other members of parliament present, and he finally accepted that it was pointless to pretend to constitute a government.

Protected by his kinsman the marquess of Argyll, Loudoun remained in the west highlands, and though late in 1652 he came to Edinburgh with Argyll for talks with the English, he refused to make a formal submission, and was lectured to by the tiresome Johnston of Wariston about his political errors and 'personal uncleannesses' (*Diary of Sir Archibald Johnston*, ed. Fleming, 185). Argyll made his peace with the English, but Loudoun's continued defiance led to his estates being forfeited in 1654. In November, when Argyll's son Lord Lorne joined royalists in revolt in the highlands, it was reported that Loudoun 'rambles alongis with him' (Nicoll, 140). Only in March 1655 did he finally agree to live peaceably under English rule, and his estates were returned. On the restoration of monarchy in 1660 he was allowed to resign the chancellorship, to spare him the humiliation of being dismissed, and the following year he was fined £12,000 Scots (£1000 sterling) for his past support of the covenanters. Courageously he spoke out in parliament in defence of Argyll, on trial for treason in having submitted to English rule, developing the argument that in past centuries it had become customary, and indeed unavoidable, for Scots to submit to invaders and usurpers, but this had not previously been regarded as meriting subsequent punishment. In the prevailing atmosphere, however, there was no hope of acquittal, and Argyll was executed. The trial was the last opportunity that Loudoun had to exercise his talents as a public speaker, and he died in Edinburgh on 15 March 1662, his body being taken home to Loudoun for burial. His wife survived him.

Character Clarendon later wrote that Loudoun had been 'the principal manager of the rebellion' in Scotland (Hyde, 1.414), but he was never that in the public eye. In the first months of rebellion in 1637–8 the earls of Rothes and Montrose were the leaders with the highest profiles, and even before Montrose moved towards support for the king (1639–40) and Rothes died (1640), the earl of Argyll had superseded them as the dominant figure in the covenanting movement. The supremacy of Argyll strengthened Loudoun's position in that he was a kinsman of the Campbell chief, and he was content to be in the shadow of the head of his kin. None the less, though Loudoun never developed a strong individual image like Rothes, Montrose, or Argyll, he was constantly close to their shoulders, advising and planning. His skills as a negotiator and as an eloquent and persuasive public speaker were fully recognized and exploited. In dealing with the king and the English parliament he was the covenanting regime's leading diplomat for a decade, but in the messy aftermath of the English civil war he moved first towards working with royalists, then sharply back towards support for the more extreme covenanters. In view of the evidence that he was uncertain about the 1647 engagement from the start, the fact that he opposed it after he returned to Scotland (and was confronted with the arguments of Argyll and the church against it) hardly requires further explanation. Clarendon alleged that Loudoun, 'obnoxious for his loose and vicious life, which was notorious' (Hyde, 4.321), was blackmailed into changing sides by the threat of exposure and public disgrace, but this allegation receives no support from other sources, and may be based on confusion with the later (1650 and 1651) stories about Loudoun's sex life. The reliability of these tales is hard to judge. While Loudoun was not a person of notable outward piety like Argyll and Johnston of Wariston (and indeed his own wife, who prayed and corresponded with Wariston), there is no reason to doubt the sincerity of his commitment to presbyterianism and the covenants. That he may have failed in matters of sex to live up to strict ideals hardly makes him unusual.

DAVID STEVENSON

Sources *DNB* • GEC, *Peerage* • *Scots peerage* • D. Stevenson, *The Scottish revolution, 1637–44: the triumph of the covenanters* (1973) • D. Stevenson, *Revolution and counter-revolution in Scotland, 1644–1651*,

Royal Historical Society Studies in History, 4 (1977) • John, earl of Rothes, *A relation of proceedings concerning the affairs of the Kirk of Scotland*, Bannatyne Club, 37 (1830) • *Calendar of the Clarendon state papers preserved in the Bodleian Library*, ed. O. Ogle and others, 5 vols. (1869–1970) • *The letters and journals of Robert Baillie*, ed. D. Laing, 3 vols. (1841–2) • G. Crawfurd, *The lives and characters, of the officers of the crown, and of the state in Scotland* (1726) • J. Nicoll, *A diary of public transactions and other occurrences, chiefly in Scotland, from January 1650 to June 1667*, ed. D. Laing, Bannatyne Club, 52 (1836) • C. H. Firth, ed., *Scotland and the Commonwealth: letters and papers relating to the military government of Scotland, from August 1651 to December 1653*, Scottish History Society, 18 (1895) • C. H. Firth, ed., *Scotland and the protectorate: letters and papers relating to the military government of Scotland from January 1654 to June 1659*, Scottish History Society, 31 (1899) • Clarendon, *Hist. rebellion*, 4.45 • *The historical works of Sir James Balfour*, ed. J. Haig, 4 vols. (1824–5) • 'Fragment of the diary of Sir Archibald Johnston, Lord Wariston, 1639', ed. G. M. Paul, *Wariston's diary and other papers*, Scottish History Society, 26 (1896), 1–98 • *Diary of Sir Archibald Johnston of Wariston*, 1, ed. G. M. Paul, Scottish History Society, 61 (1911) • *Diary of Sir Archibald Johnston of Wariston*, 2, ed. D. H. Fleming, Scottish History Society, 2nd ser., 18 (1919) • *Diary of Sir Archibald Johnston of Wariston*, 3, ed. J. D. Ogilvie, Scottish History Society, 3rd ser., 34 (1940) • *APS*

Likenesses A. Simon, silver medal, 1645, BM [*see illus.*] • stipple (after G. Jamesone), BM, NPG

Campbell, John [*called* Iain Glas], **first earl of Breadalbane and Holland (1634–1717)**, magnate and politician, was born on 29 May 1634 at Stronmillochan, Glenorchy, Argyll, the eldest son of Sir John Campbell of Glenorchy, fourth baronet (*d.* 1686), and his first wife, Mary (*d.* 1653), daughter of William *Graham, first earl of Airth and Menteith. The Campbells of Glenorchy were the most important cadet family of clan Campbell, with major estates in Argyll and Perthshire and a main residence eventually at Balloch (later Taymouth) Castle on Loch Tay. They were traditionally ruthless expansionists, often at odds with the main Argyll line, and John Campbell's great-grandfather Sir Duncan *Campbell (*d.* 1631) [*see under* Campbell family of Glenorchy] had a deservedly sinister reputation which probably affected Campbell himself.

Youth and early career The head of the Glenorchy family in Campbell's youth was Sir Duncan's son Sir Robert Campbell (*d.* 1657), who took the covenanting side in the civil wars. Their castles could not save their estates from devastation or the slaughter of fighting men by the royalists, particularly Montrose on his winter advance into Argyll in 1644, and the family fell deep into debt. Providing for many children increased their difficulties. Sir Robert had eight sons and nine daughters while his heir, Sir John, married three times and had twelve sons and fifteen daughters, nearly all of whom reached adulthood. Through their marriages John Campbell acquired an extensive cousinage and wide influence in the west highlands.

During the earl of Glencairn's rising of 1653–5 young John Campbell assisted General George Monck against the royalists, including his cousin Archibald Campbell, future ninth earl of Argyll. While on a visit to London to seek a reward from Oliver Cromwell he married, at St Andrew by the Wardrobe on 17 December 1657, Lady Mary

John Campbell, first earl of Breadalbane and Holland (1634–1717), by Sir John Baptiste de Medina

Rich (*d.* 1666), daughter of Henry *Rich, first earl of Holland (*bap.* 1590, *d.* 1649), with a £5000 dowry. They had two sons, Duncan (*c.*1660–1727) and John (1662–1752), before she died on 8 February 1666.

At the Restoration Campbell was unscathed, partly through Glencairn's own favour. In 1660 he took informal control of the family estates. It was as Glenorchy that he was a member for Argyll in the parliaments of 1661–3 and 1669–74. Locally a JP he gained reputation in assisting the ninth earl of Argyll to settle Argyll, and in averting a clan battle and negotiating a compromise in 1665 between his cousin Sir Ewen Cameron of Lochiel and the laird of Mackintosh. However he had a decade-long dispute with his father, who claimed that he intended to cheat his siblings of their rights. Sir John's letters show admiration for his son's abilities but great distrust of his honesty, a combination many others would echo. To Sir John's unease Glenorchy followed a high-risk general strategy of large-scale expansion of the family estates, taking on in the process further massive debts and constant draining lawsuits. Total ruin threatened if any major decision went wrong. On existing estates he reinvested much of his income in steelbow (sharecropping) agreements in agriculture and sawmills to bring about higher productivity and diversity. Glenorchy was apparently an aggressive neighbour, a stance which later strengthened the suspicions after the massacre of Glencoe. There was, however, no blanket hostility between his family and clan Donald: the chiefs of Keppoch, despite civil war bloodshed, remained friends and dependants. Relations with the Glencoe Macdonalds, both notorious for cattle raiding and providers of cattle watches, were more ambiguous, but in the 1660s Glenorchy temporarily leased Glencoe from Argyll, and partly paid the fines for the inhabitants' robberies.

Earldom of Caithness and highland conflicts, 1669–1685 Hemmed in locally, for significant expansion Glenorchy looked to Caithness, where George Sinclair, sixth earl of Caithness, married since 1657 to Argyll's sister Mary (or Marie) Campbell but childless, was at odds with most of the Sinclair gentry. Originally sent there by the privy council in 1669 to pursue the earl's main recent Sinclair adviser for murder, Glenorchy found the couple threatened with dispossession by a creditor, the leading Edinburgh lawyer Sir Robert Sinclair of Longformacus. By loaning (borrowed) money to Caithnesses, on 8 October 1672 Glenorchy obtained a conveyance of his estates and title on promise to pay part of his debts (then over a million merks Scots). Initially this device was intended mainly to bring Sir Robert to terms, but when the latter attempted instead to ruin the Caithnesses they were driven closer to Glenorchy, with whom they lived. In 1676 Caithness died and Glenorchy, taking over his lands, illegally seized also those of the next heir, George Sinclair of Keiss. By bribing the duchess of Lauderdale with £2000 sterling, half cash, half a bond (and thereby straining his finances permanently), he had Charles II create him, on 28 June 1677, 'upon gross and false misrepresentations' (*APS*, 8.368), earl of Caithness, Viscount Breadalbane, and Lord St Clair of Berriedale and Glenorchie. He was to assume the Sinclair name and arms.

The patent allowed Caithness to name his younger son as his successor. Whether his elder son, Duncan (now styled Lord Sinclair, later Lord Ormelie), was actually simple minded, or his father merely considered him too backward and weak to head the family, he was eventually disinherited in 1686, living under supervision on a 2000 merk annuity. His brother, John, was always their father's workhorse. The patent contained so many subsidiary titles because Caithness intended to divide not only his estates but the peerage. On 7 April 1678 he married Mary, the widowed countess of Caithness (*b.* after 1634, *d.* 1699), becoming Argyll's brother-in-law. By the contract (which halved her existing jointure, 12,000 merks Scots a year, for his lifetime) their eldest son was to have most of the Argyll and Perthshire lands, the Breadalbane and Glenorchy titles, and the Campbell name, while the Caithness estates would be John's main patrimony. Their only son, Colin Campbell 'of Ardmaddie', was born the following year.

Caithness had been appointed to the privy council in August 1676. From 1674 he had assisted Argyll (though not uncritically) in his legally backed aggressive foreclosure on the estates of the infant Maclean chief, Sir John Maclean of Duart. Early in 1678 Caithness led the most disorderly contingent in the Highland Host sent to quarter on the south-western presbyterians. That September Argyll and he were ordered to raise two independent highland companies, commanded by local lairds, to suppress west highland cattle-raiding. In practice Argyll commandeered them for his campaign against the Macleans. In May–June 1679 his aggression provoked a large Macdonald and Maclean force to advance through Argyll. Caithness's negotiations with them averted a full-scale clan battle, but Argyll then ignored his agreements with them and overran Mull. If Caithness was the author of a mid-1670s plan among his papers, for a stewartry of Lochaber created by buying out private claims, its proposal of keeping a thousand local highlanders ready to suppress trouble foreshadowed his later great design.

Meanwhile the Sinclairs, led by the rightful heir, had from 1677 become increasingly rebellious against Campbell rule in Caithness. By 1680 they were destroying the earl's castles. That June, Caithness led a force of 500 Campbells north to subdue them, amid official warnings to act moderately. George Sinclair's followers, though fewer, had cannon and lowland contempt for highlanders. Caithness avoided a fight while advancing to Wick but when he marched away the Sinclairs attacked his force at nearby Allt-nam-Mearlach, on 13 July 1680, and the Campbells turned, charged, and, despite his efforts, slaughtered a hundred men.

Lauderdale's fall left Caithness vulnerable. The next year James, duke of York, abolished the Campbell highland companies and favoured rightful heirs. George Sinclair entered the parliament of 1681 without challenge as earl of Caithness, and recovered the Keiss estate. In compensation, on 13 August, Glenorchy was created, with the 1677 precedency, earl of Breadalbane ('Earl of Brea D'Albane and Holland, Viscount of Tay and Paintland, Lord Glenurchy, Benderaloch, Ormelie, and Weick') with freedom to name either Duncan or John his successor. He still intended to divide not only his estates but his earldom between his sons John (Holland) and Colin (Breadalbane). However, Argyll's unexpected fall and condemnation for treason that autumn left Breadalbane, and clan Campbell, dangerously exposed and vulnerable—a lesson he remembered during later differences with that family—and his creditors prevented his attending the council for a year. Early in 1683 Breadalbane and his subordinates were charged with treason for actions in Caithness, and his council colleagues prepared to divide his estates there after forfeiture, but John Murray, first marquess of Atholl, protected him, and on 10 August Charles II issued a full pardon. In December Breadalbane joined the successful justiciary commission against highland robbery.

Somehow Breadalbane arranged a marriage (by contract of 16 April 1685) between his son John and Lady Frances Cavendish (1660–1691), second daughter of the magnate Henry Cavendish, second duke of Newcastle. On 17 July Breadalbane nominated John (henceforward known as Lord Glenorchy) as heir to all his titles and his main estates. Colin was instead to inherit £7000 sterling. Meanwhile, in May, Breadalbane raised 300 men and, with other loyal Campbells, joined John Murray, marquess of Atholl, lord lieutenant of Argyll, in putting down Argyll's Campbell rising. This prevented a proposed parliamentary act to ban the clan name but Breadalbane's intelligent strategic advice destroyed Atholl's friendship for him. Immediately afterwards he proposed his lifelong great design. In its original form a plaided fusilier regiment was to be raised from several highland clans, with auxiliaries making up more than 4000 men. He of course would be colonel, gaining both a salary and political dominance in the highlands. But the scheme fell with his new patron, the first duke of Queensberry, that winter.

Jacobitism, highland negotiations, and Glencoe None the less Breadalbane's importance on the privy council had grown by 1688. During William's invasion he played a leading role in first raising and then disbanding the militia. He and three other councillors signed the warrant which authorized the Holyrood riot of 10 December 1688, and he was sent to London to explain it to King James. Finding on his arrival that James had fled, Breadalbane had an audience with William and signed the Scottish nobles' address of 10 January 1689 asking him to rule Scotland until a convention met; but, he claimed, dissenting from the methods employed, he returned home, even though recommended to William as the fittest man for chancellor. In Edinburgh during the convention he avoided sitting and in April retreated finally to Kilchurn on Loch Awe, his strongest castle. Meanwhile he wrote to James in Ireland promising support, and suggesting the restoration of the tenth earl of Argyll. His most trusted subordinates in his Jacobite and later political intrigues were his Edinburgh writer (solicitor), Colin Campbell of Carwhin, and his main chamberlain, Alexander Campbell of Barcaldine.

Breadalbane kept a constant secret correspondence with John Graham, Viscount Dundee, during his rising, and was of particular assistance to him in managing the highlanders. By July 1689—as the 'History of part of the late earl of Breadalbane's life' (NA Scot., GD 112/43/22, first drafted in 1695 for a Williamite audience) revealed—Breadalbane, although crippled by gout, planned to raise 1600 men from Argyll and Perthshire. Dundee's one surviving letter to him, of 20 July, shows that the plot was serious and that Breadalbane was still firmly urging James to restore the earl of Argyll, despite Dundee's insinuations that, without Argyll, Breadalbane might induce all the Campbells to follow him. However, Dundee's victory and death at Killiecrankie on 29 July transformed the situation and Breadalbane's claim that the Jacobite chiefs and nobles formally offered him the command afterwards is not confirmed by their surviving letters. Within a month the Jacobite army had been defeated at Dunkeld and dispersed for the winter. Even before Dunkeld, Breadalbane had appealed to Sir John Dalrymple for the government's protection. Like other Jacobite peers, on 9 September he took the oaths under a proclamation of indemnity.

This naturally made Breadalbane suspect in the Jacobite camp. In October mixed parties from the rebel clans, including Macdonalds of Glencoe, burnt his castle of Achallader, a potential government garrison, and ravaged Glenlyon, where one had been established, disabling the laird Robert Campbell from redeeming estates extorted from him by Atholl. Several historians have assumed that this made Breadalbane seek vengeance on MacIain, chief of Glencoe. However, he knew that the raiders were acting on orders, and blamed the government for planting garrisons; to Carwhin he praised MacIain's moderation towards Campbells on a November raid. During the winter, while smoothing disputes between overt Jacobite clans and crypto-Jacobite Campbells, he became in practice neutral.

In the context of factional manoeuvring Sir John Dalrymple ensured that in March 1690 Breadalbane was among nobles employed by the government to persuade clan chiefs to submit on payment of money, but he demanded £5000 for the purpose, and visibly acted in bad faith. He and other leading crypto-Jacobite nobles entered parliament in April as part of the Montgomery plot, an alliance with Sir James Montgomery's disaffected faction of the 'club' opposition to restore King James through parliament, but this fell apart after 3 May owing to internal dissensions. Breadalbane started negotiations with the Jacobite chiefs, disrupting promising existing initiatives by Viscount Tarbat's agent, Colonel John Hill, and sought a cessation of arms which would give them time to recover from a recent defeat at Cromdale and receive help from James in Ireland. When Major-General Mackay refused in early June to delay the campaign further Breadalbane rode to Chester to ask William, who was *en route* for Ireland, to extend the cessation and perhaps also to confess dealings with Montgomery, but he arrived too late. Breadalbane retreated to Kilchurn again for the rest of 1690, during which Mackay crushed the last attempts to expand the rebellion. Suspicion of Breadalbane's double dealing and Jacobite plotting remained to haunt his future negotiations.

In the winter of 1690–91 Dalrymple, now second secretary of state, assembled a faction of episcopalian nobles, mainly ex-Jacobites, with whom to supplant the earl of Melville's presbyterians in power. This required co-ordinated effort and a speedy pacification of the highlands by Breadalbane. Although rumours of a French invasion in April 1691 made Breadalbane and other nobles temporarily waver, he appreciated that the rising had failed and was prepared to co-operate. He revived his scheme of 1685, proposing a highland militia 3000–4000 strong, drawn largely from ex-Jacobite clans and with himself as its paid commander, which would secure the highlands for William. Although this plan necessarily remained secret he showed his commitment by rebuilding Kilchurn Castle from late 1690 onwards, incorporating barrack blocks (actually completed long afterwards) even though this would encourage the fate he dreaded most, government seizure for a garrison.

As always, family finances deeply affected Breadalbane's public career. On 4 February 1691 Lady Glenorchy's death a few months before that of her father, of whom she would have been a coheir, robbed him of a much needed injection of cash. Ruin was avoided only by large-scale land sales, the 'Caithness bargains', which threatened the countess's jointure and Colin's inheritance, provoking a violent marital quarrel. Meanwhile

Glenorchy insisted on a belated two-year grand tour. Needing profitable office Breadalbane followed his episcopalian colleagues to London, where he received a pardon for treason on 2 May 1691. The invasion rumour again led William and Mary to authorize him to negotiate with the highland chiefs for their submission, in return for the buying out of hostile feudal superiorities over them with £12,000 sterling promised from the English Treasury. In June 1691 supported by Lochiel, he held talks at Achallader with the Jacobite commander Major-General Buchan, and the chiefs, still defiant when most ordinary clansmen had submitted. Despite a violent quarrel over stolen cattle with MacIain of Glencoe, who said later that he feared no man so much, Breadalbane obtained for MacIain £150 and a pardon, promised in the general agreement at Achallader on 30 June. Under this, there would be a cessation of arms—eventually extended to 1 January 1692. In the interim Breadalbane would obtain William's confirmation for payment of the £12,000 in buying out superiorities, and the chiefs and clans would submit to the government and be pardoned for actions during the war. The allocation of the money inevitably provoked grumbling and suspicion that Breadalbane had embezzled some; in fact, driven by larger ambitions, he had not even covered expenses. In secret verbal articles Breadalbane let Buchan send messengers to ask James's permission to submit and promised to join a rising if William refused the settlement—a mere penalty clause, he later argued.

Accidents and delays obliged Breadalbane to follow William to Flanders, where the settlement was confirmed on 17 August 1691; meanwhile it unravelled behind him. The presbyterian majority on the privy council, wishing to prevent a success which would bring their rivals to power, infringed the cessation. Breadalbane's promise to the chiefs that Fort William would be demolished alienated its governor, Colonel John Hill, who reversed his conciliatory policies. Argyll and Atholl, incongruous fellow conspirators in Montgomery's revived Jacobite intrigues, helped sabotage the settlement. Atholl in particular alienated Macdonell of Glengarry from it. A forger turned Breadalbane's verbal promises into formal written 'private articles', misdated 2 July. Through various agents, opponents of the cessation appealed both to the chiefs' vanity, arguing that it was dishonourable to submit to the upstart Breadalbane, and to their greed, promising larger sums if they would repudiate the agreement and discredit him. The major chiefs were taken in, increasingly boasting of their Jacobite determination while secretly expecting large Williamite rewards upon verbal promises from their traditional presbyterian enemies.

Breadalbane, returning in September, found his agreement collapsing and a message just arrived from King James forbidding surrender. Suppressing this he sent a messenger, Duncan Menzies, to insist that James must allow it; then, collecting the £12,000, he left for the highlands to resume negotiations. Only Tarbat gave him assistance. Finally, in November 1691, after a month's boycott, he met the chiefs, but his enemies' increasingly extravagant promises tempted his main supporters, Sir John Maclean and even Lochiel, into defecting.

The surrender of Jacobite Ireland had hardened the government's attitudes. Dalrymple had now attained the power he sought, but he was furious with the highlanders, particularly the Catholic Macdonalds. Breadalbane's attempts to moderate or deflect his rage failed: Dalrymple, for instance, took his cryptic hint about his planned militia as a 'scheme for mauling' the highlanders, making an example of any who refused to take the oath of allegiance to William and Mary (Dalrymple, 2.3rd pagination.216). Breadalbane delayed near the highlands into December 1691 in the hope that the chiefs would belatedly return to sanity, even though this jeopardized his chance of office. He had departed when, at the end of the month, the Jacobite chiefs rushed to submit—less because Menzies had finally brought King James's permission than because the winter campaign they had disbelieved in was upon them. MacIain of Glencoe was one of several who took the oaths after the deadline.

Breadalbane, in London, circulated the first news of the submissions, but with little hope of results for himself or the chiefs. As Lochiel and other chiefs went to London, Breadalbane tried, unsuccessfully, to have the money distributed. In February 1692 he presented his scheme for a highland militia to William. The former Jacobite contingents listed included Glencoe men, under their new superior Stewart of Ardsheal. The scheme depended on the fiction of the highlanders' instant transfer of loyalty: news of the massacre in Glencoe on 13 February, committed by troops under his cousin Robert Campbell of Glenlyon, shattered it. For several reasons Breadalbane was almost the only person at court who openly denounced the massacre, but his anxiety to demonstrate his innocence only strengthened assumptions that he was guilty. His attempt to revive the agreement with the chiefs failed, and he had to return the £12,000, though allowed £2000 expenses for Achallader. The famous tradition that he said: 'My lord, the Highlands are quiet: the money is spent: and this is the best way of accounting among friends' (Dalrymple, 2.3rd pagination 221) is groundless.

The episcopalian ministry and the Glencoe inquiry Having largely failed in his mission, in March 1692 Breadalbane had to be content with membership of the privy council and the Scottish Treasury commission in the new ministry, which mixed episcopalians and presbyterians, but he showed his religious loyalties (and highland disrespect for the law) by a lifelong refusal to let any presbyterian clerics displace the nonjuring episcopalians on his estates. He was confident enough in 1693 to buy Netherlorne, Argyll, the estate of his late brother-in-law Lord Neil Campbell, for £20,000 Scots and a promise to pay Lord Neil's debts—assuming yet more financial commitments he could not meet. He was suspected of dubious profits from his Treasury position.

Invasion threats, wartime financial deficits, and presbyterian attacks organized by Secretary James Johnstone put the episcopalian ministry on the political defensive from the start. Breadalbane's frequent attempts to have William's 1691 indemnity observed towards highlanders attracted abuse from both sides, though it finally won Hill's friendship. A highland justiciary commission which he drafted in 1692 was dropped as giving him too much power; he was a leading figure in one set up in February 1694, where he and Atholl's son Lord Murray disputed what the indemnity meant.

Breadalbane kept occasional contacts with the Jacobite court, but was seen there as too influenced by Dalrymple to be trustworthy. The episcopalian faction briefly rallied during disputes over church matters in early 1694, but Johnstone's new alliance with Lord Chancellor Tweeddale further reduced Dalrymple's influence that year. Breadalbane apparently planned to become the episcopalians' political leader. He arranged Glenorchy's second marriage, on 23 May 1695 to Henrietta, daughter of Sir Edward Villiers and sister of William's mistress Elizabeth Villiers. For her £8000 sterling portion, intended to endow Breadalbane's son Colin, she was to receive £1000 a year jointure; her family's court connections would redress the balance.

As a result of the political machinations of Secretary Johnstone, on 10 June 1695 the parliamentary commission of inquiry into the massacre of Glencoe made a surprise accusation of treason against Breadalbane based on the Achallader 'private articles' and Glengarry's perjured claim that they were genuine. Despite repeated evidence, often from his former enemies, that the government had discounted them, small parliamentary majorities voted to prosecute Breadalbane for treason and to imprison him in Edinburgh Castle. He especially blamed Lord Murray, a leading commissioner, for his plight. The commission was convinced of Breadalbane's complicity in the massacre, but unexpectedly could not prove it. Breadalbane, rather than following repeated advice to resign and confess, prepared a fighting defence, with Tarbat's assistance, and was reconciled to Argyll, who defended him despite Johnstone's threats of a treason charge. Johnstone and Tweeddale persisted in their attempts to bring Breadalbane to trial. Ignoring William's known wishes, and a specific order presented on 1 October, Tweeddale kept Breadalbane imprisoned all autumn. By the time he was released on 23 December 1695, and went to London, deaths had eviscerated the episcopalian faction and the Glencoe inquiry had discredited Dalrymple. In early January 1696 William, bowing to realities, dismissed both Dalrymple and Breadalbane, though uproar over their Scottish East India Company Act also brought down Johnstone and Tweeddale soon afterwards.

Old age and the 'Fifteen In March 1696 Breadalbane returned to the highlands, where he remained politically inactive for several years. Glenorchy temporarily led the family, subscribing £2000 to the Scottish East India Company and receiving a £200 pension from 1699. Breadalbane apparently feared that the parliamentarians (now the opposition), who had repeatedly defied the king's orders in order to attack him in 1695, might now deny the validity of his pardon and imprison him again, and sulked because Argyll and the second duke of Queensberry, having become chief ministers, had not recalled him to office. However, repaying the latter for their assistance in 1695 he attended the stormy parliamentary session of 1700–01 to support the court party. An attempt in 1703 by Tarbat (now earl of Cromarty) to bring him back into politics failed. He did not attend the parliament of 1703–7 or vote on the union. The rumour that he had received a marquessate, which provoked John Macky's hostile 'character' and prophecy 'It is odds, if he live long enough, but he is a *Duke*' (*Memoirs of the Secret Services*, 199), was groundless.

Another longer-lasting reason for seclusion was fear of arrest for debt. The famine years of the late 1690s further damaged the family's credit. Colin Campbell's portion was still unsecured and the attendant worry contributed to the countess's death in December 1699. In 1703 it seemed that only a further major 'Caithness bargain', selling almost all remaining lands there, could avert ruin; but Breadalbane opposed the destruction of the evidence of his greatest triumph. He often proposed that the whole family should settle in Caithness for several years, freeing the Argyll and Perthshire rents to pay off debts, but only the Glenorchys did so, for fairly short periods. A tailzie (entail) of the estates on Lord Glenorchy of 13 December 1704 theoretically left Breadalbane only a liferenter with £500 a year, but his continued involvement in estate business, often to Lord Glenorchy's financial disadvantage, created a permanent breach between them. Breadalbane had always been a patron of Rob Roy Macgregor (who took the name Campbell in compliment to him) in his early careers as organizer of a watch and cattle dealer. After Rob Roy was bankrupted and outlawed in 1712 Breadalbane gave him tacks of land and, to Glenorchy's disgust, a minor estate judicial post.

The entail freed Breadalbane to take part in Jacobite conspiracy with less fear of harming the family. He was in the confidence of James Drummond, Lord Drummond, the Jacobite court's chief agent in the highlands, but he received Simon Fraser, Lord Lovat (of whose government contacts he knew), on his 1703 mission very lukewarmly, saying 'That he was too old to turn Papist … and that he would not meddle, for he was resolved to serve the Queen and her Government' (Glendaruel's confession, *JHL*, 17.405–6). Nevertheless Lovat and Lord Drummond's circle agreed on offering him the command of any Jacobite rising: an exaggerated version of his role in 1689 was widely believed. Breadalbane later became more active in Jacobitism, but, largely immobilized by gout and age, used as his chief agent Sir John Maclean's half-brother Colin Campbell of Glendaruel. Glendaruel's dubious role in Lovat's 'Scots plot' ensured that Breadalbane also was widely distrusted.

Colonel Nathaniel Hooke, organizing support in 1707 for a French invasion, found Breadalbane enthusiastic, though too cautious to sign, like others, a letter to Louis XIV. A year later, just before the attempt, another agent found him apparently ready. He was particularly valued because a high proportion of the duke of Argyll's Campbell tenants were expected to follow, or at worst be neutralized by, him. He inconspicuously prepared his own men, reviewing them secretly at fairs. In 1707 he was finally reconciled with Lord Murray, now first duke of Atholl, whom anti-union nationalism had temporarily driven into Jacobitism. Breadalbane's duties in the proposed 1708 rising would have included, congenially, attacking Fort William; but in March, during the invasion attempt, the government ordered his arrest. On the certificate of a Perth doctor and surgeon and the local minister that he was too ill to travel he was left under house arrest at Taymouth.

Simultaneously, Breadalbane's son Colin Campbell of Ardmaddie died of consumption at Kensington on 31 March 1708. In the early 1700s Breadalbane had taken as mistress Mildred Littler (*d.* 1746), housekeeper at Taymouth. About 1712 he married her morganatically to legitimate their daughter Lady Mary Campbell (*d.* 1725), who married Archibald Cockburn the younger of Langton.

Solicitations for his vote in the 1708 election of the sixteen Scottish representative peers brought Breadalbane back towards parliamentary politics; Glenorchy stood unsuccessfully for the Commons. In the 1710 general election, under a new tory ministry, Breadalbane sought to be chosen himself, at first supported by Atholl. His concern became still stronger after Lord Treasurer Robert Harley, earl of Oxford, adopted a rival method for controlling the highland clans, pensions paid via the minor chief Robert Stewart of Appin. Breadalbane and his agents tried to discredit Stewart and perhaps to resurrect his own scheme. His Jacobitism was becoming more overt. At the 1713 general election he helped to organize a slate of candidates committed to the dissolution of the union, until an order from James Stuart, the Old Pretender, forbade this, but his influence by this time was such that the reluctant ministers had to allow his election. However, he was the last representative peer to reach London, arriving only in April 1714. In the Lords he provided an opening for the duke of Buckinghamshire to report his eyewitness knowledge of the Pretender's birth.

On Anne's death Breadalbane, assuming that an English rising was prepared, organized at Kilchurn Castle a Jacobite conference, which sent messengers urging James to come immediately. When George I succeeded peacefully it was (to James's bewilderment) Breadalbane, through Glendaruel, who organized the address to him from the highland clans which the earl of Mar was to present. When the king refused to receive it he prepared for a Jacobite rising. In September 1715, summoned to Edinburgh to surrender by the government, he procured certificates from the same doctor and minister as in 1708 that he was helplessly sick at Taymouth, but immediately journeyed to consult the earl of Mar at Logierait. Barcaldine was sent in a vain attempt to gain his submission. He promised Mar, and received money for, two regiments, each 600 strong, to be raised in Argyll and Perthshire. While the two intended Campbell leaders of the Argyll rising panicked at the last minute and submitted, two regiments from Breadalbane's Perthshire estates, only 400 in all, urged forward by him from Finlarig, joined the Jacobite advance into Argyll. The disappointing numbers, after so many years' preparation, made cynics like Mar and the master of Sinclair suspect Breadalbane of deliberate treachery. However, Breadalbane was old, and had alienated some tenants by arbitrary harshness. Lord Glenorchy, who was pro-Hanoverian, was in Caithness during the rising of 1715, but his wife and agents sabotaged his father's schemes. Traditional political balancing within Scottish noble families here reflected the genuine internal division.

The master of Sinclair gives the most vivid picture of Breadalbane, visiting Mar's camp at Perth in late October.

> He was the merriest grave man I ever saw, … mockt the whole, and had a way of laughing inwardlie that was very perceptible … He told some of the pollitticiens … that it was a shame to them to be idle at Perth, … and since they did not fight, he advised them to get a printing press. (Sinclair, 186)

Mar, not seeing the oblique warning, sent for one. At Sheriffmuir on 13 November Breadalbane's men under John Campbell of Glenlyon fought on the victorious Jacobite right wing, and broke a government regiment. Breadalbane had met Mar again at Drummond Castle the night before, and, according to his servant Campbell of Kenloch, witnessed the battle, but returned home, sick from the journey, just afterwards, and most of his men likewise abandoned the Jacobite army. The pro-government Alexander Campbell of Fonab, under earlier secret collusive agreements with Lady Glenorchy and her husband's chamberlain, captured Kilchurn and Finlarig in December. Having briefly planned to raise his men again on news of James's landing, Breadalbane surrendered himself to Fonab at Taymouth on 27 February 1716. He remained under house arrest there until he died on 18 or 19 March 1717. He was buried on 28 March, presumably at Finlarig.

John Campbell, Lord Glenorchy, also summoned to surrender at Edinburgh in 1715, but cut off in Caithness by the rebellion, was briefly imprisoned in Edinburgh Castle early in 1716, but cleared himself fully and succeeded without trouble as second earl of Breadalbane. He broke off strong youthful contacts with Glendaruel and other exiled Jacobites on making a whig marriage in 1718. (Yet a passive Jacobitism among his Perthshire tenants was still significant in 1745.) The second earl's public career was entirely Hanoverian, but undistinguished. He was lord lieutenant of Perthshire from 1725 until his death, a whig representative peer from 1736 to 1747, and chief justice in eyre south of Trent from 1746. The many hostile traditions about 'Old Rag', hinted at by Sir Walter Scott, related to his private life. He spent his last years mainly in apartments in Holyrood Palace, remaining there during the Jacobite occupation in 1745, and died there on 23 February 1752. One son reached adulthood, John *Campbell, third earl of Breadalbane (*bap.* 1696, *d.* 1782); so did two daughters, of whom Lady Henrietta was a lady-in-waiting to George II's daughters.

Conclusion A portrait of the first earl in 1676 shows a strong, determined face, with none of the apparent exhaustion in the better-known one of 1696. 'He is of a fair Complexion, has the Gravity of a *Spaniard*', wrote John Macky. However, although there is some truth in the characterization that he was 'as cunning as a *Fox*, wise as a *Serpent*, but as slippery as an *Eel*: No Government can trust him but where his own private Interest is in View' (*Memoirs of the Secret Services*, 199), Macky's worst accusations against him merely reflect the continuing fury of Johnstone's faction over Breadalbane's defiance in 1695. Like many Scottish contemporaries with diverse interregnum careers he took the Restoration settlement, an independent Scotland, a Stuart monarch, a dominant aristocracy, and the episcopalian church as the norm to which his loyalties reverted whenever self-interest did not direct him otherwise, although as his shifts of practical allegiance in 1690–91 and both ways in 1714 showed, he and they were powerless when it did. Despite three English aristocratic marriages by him and his son he never developed from a Scottish into a British politician, though he would have needed to do so if his plan to head the Scottish ministry in 1695 had succeeded. Otherwise any prolonged residence in England was simply too expensive. The family's existing debts, and his gambler's policy of further expanding the estates and their burdens, particularly the only half successful seizure of Caithness, created constant financial crises which dominated his whole private and public career. With unfortunate consequences for the intrigues into which his private and public policies led him, his violent temper (which so alarmed MacIain of Glencoe) often produced quarrels with his second wife, his son, and others, and it grew worse in his old age, undermining in advance his last great gamble: involvement in the 1715 rebellion.

Breadalbane was publicly and privately a fairly unscrupulous intriguer. Yet, ironically, the events leading to the massacre of Glencoe, for which he is notorious, were probably the most creditable part of a long and dubious career. He had the intelligence to form a creative policy which, through the proposed highland militia, linked his selfish interests to a genuine pacification, paid for by England, benefiting Scotland and the highlands, and permanently settling several clan conflicts. In contrast his political enemies' irresponsible, purely destructive intrigues set the original course which led to the massacre. Deserted by the major chiefs and his episcopalian allies, Breadalbane risked his chance of office in the hope of a last-minute settlement, and afterwards tried persistently amid general hostility to have the spirit of the pacification observed.

While in most respects successful, Breadalbane was basically unlucky at the crises of his career. His one attempt to become head of Scotland's government was crushed by enemies who committed technical treason to destroy his faction. Twice he prepared to take the risk of committing himself to promising Jacobite risings; Dundee's death and Mar's incompetence brought them to nothing. He consistently negotiated to avert needless large-scale highland bloodshed, but commanded at the bloodiest post-Restoration clan battle and was wrongly blamed for the period's most treacherous massacre.

PAUL HOPKINS

Sources NA Scot., Breadalbane papers, GD112 • B. L. H. Horn, catalogue of the Breadalbane papers, NA Scot., GD112 • *Scots peerage* • P. A. Hopkins, *Glencoe and the end of the highland war*, rev. edn (1998) • Leven and Melville papers, NA Scot., GD26 • W. H. L. Melville, ed., *Leven and Melville papers: letters and state papers chiefly addressed to George, earl of Melville … 1689–1691*, Bannatyne Club, 77 (1843) • NA Scot., Campbell of Barcaldine papers, GD170 • J. Dalrymple, *Memoirs of Great Britain and Ireland*, 3 vols. (1771–8) • Dumfries House, Cumnock, Ayrshire, marquess of Bute's manuscripts, bundle A517 • W. A. Gillies, *In famed Breadalbane* (1938) • J. J. H. H. Stewart-Murray, seventh duke of Atholl, *Chronicles of the Atholl and Tullibardine families*, 5 vols. (privately printed, Edinburgh, 1908) • duke of Atholl's manuscripts, Blair Castle, Perthshire • GEC, *Peerage*, new edn • *APS* • *Report on the manuscripts of Allan George Finch*, 5 vols., HMC, 71 (1913–2003) • J. Sinclair, *Memoirs of the insurrection in Scotland in 1715*, ed. W. Scott (1858) • *CSP dom.* • C. Innes, ed., *The black book of Taymouth* (1865) • W. Fraser, ed., *The earls of Cromartie, their kindred, country and correspondence*, 2 vols. (1879) • J. Prebble, *Glencoe, the story of the massacre* (1966) • H. Mackay, *Memoirs of the war carried on in Scotland and Ireland, 1689–1691*, ed. J. M. Hog, P. F. Tytler, and A. Urquhart (1833) • *Memoirs of the secret services of John Macky*, ed. A. R. (1733) • *JHL*, 17 (1701–4) • C. Lindsay [earl of Balcarres], *Memoirs touching the revolution in Scotland*, ed. A. W. C. Lindsay [earl of Crawford and Balcarres], Bannatyne Club (1841) • review of T. B. Macaulay, *A history of England*, vols. 3–4, *EdinR*, 105 (1857), 142–80, esp. 172–9 • *Calendar of the Stuart papers belonging to his majesty the king, preserved at Windsor Castle*, 7 vols., HMC, 56 (1902–23) • NA Scot., John Macgregor collection, GD50 • BL, Lauderdale papers, Add. MSS 23125, 23135 • *The manuscripts of his grace the duke of Portland*, 10 vols., HMC, 29 (1891–1931) • PRO, Scottish state papers, Jan–Feb 1716, SP 54/11 • J. Macpherson, ed., *Original papers, containing the secret history of Great Britain*, 2 vols. (1775) • *Correspondence of Colonel N. Hooke*, ed. W. D. Macray, 2 vols., Roxburghe Club, 92, 95 (1870–71) • D. Szechi, *Jacobitism and tory politics, 1710–14* (1984) • duke of Buccleuch and Queensberry's papers, Drumlanrig Castle, Dumfriesshire • P. W. J. Riley, *The English ministers and Scotland* (1964) • [D. Campbell], *The lairds of Glenlyon* (1886) • J. Baynes, *The Jacobite rising of 1715* (1970) • A. Campbell, *A history of the clan Campbell, volume one: from origins to Flodden* (2000) • N. Hooke, *The secret history of Colonel Hooke's negotiations in Scotland in favour of the Pretender, in 1707* (1760) • M. D. Young, ed., *The parliaments of Scotland: burgh and shire commissioners*, 2 vols. (1992–3) • R. M. Gibson, ed., *The real Rob Roy* (1995) • NL Scot., Argyll MS 975 • *The manuscripts of J. Eliot Hodgkin … of Richmond, Surrey*, HMC, 39 (1897) • A. I. Macinnes, *Clanship, commerce and the house of Stewart* (1996) • P. Rae, *The history of the late rebellion* (1718) • spy's report [1715], NL Scot., MS 874, fols. 520–21 • *Calendar of the Stuart papers belonging to his majesty the king, preserved at Windsor Castle*, 7 vols., HMC, 56 (1902–23), vols. 3–7 • J. H. Burton and D. Laing, eds., *Jacobite correspondence of the Atholl family* (1840)

Archives NA Scot., corresp. and papers • NL Scot., corresp. and papers • NRA Scotland, priv. coll., letters • U. Glas. L., household book | BL, letters to duke of Lauderdale and duchess of Lauderdale, Add. MSS 23135–23138, 23246–23250, *passim* • Blair Castle, Perthshire, Atholl papers • Buckminster House, Grantham, Lincolnshire, Lauderdale papers • Doune Park, Perthshire, Moray manuscripts • Drumlanrig Castle, Dumfriesshire, Queensberry papers • Dumfries House, Cumnock, Ayrshire, Bute papers, letters, bundle A517 • Hunt. L., letters to earl of Loudon • Leics. RO, corresp. with earl of Nottingham • NA Scot., Campbell of Barcaldine papers • NA Scot., Cromartie papers • NA Scot., Leven & Melville papers • NA Scot., John Macgregor collection • NL Scot., Argyll papers, MS 975 • NRA Scotland, priv. coll., corresp. of factors on family matters • U. Nott. L., letters to Lord Portland

Likenesses attrib. G. Scougal, oils, 1676, priv. coll. • J. Medina the younger, portrait, 1729 (after oil copy attrib. G. Scougal; copy) • J. B. de Medina, oils, Scot. NPG [*see illus.*] • J. B. de Medina, oils, priv. coll. • attrib. G. Scougal (copy of 1676 portrait, with older face), priv. coll. • portrait, priv. coll.

Wealth at death huge estates in Perthshire, Argyll, and to a lesser extent Caithness; balanced by ruinously vast debts

Campbell, John, **second duke of Argyll and duke of Greenwich** (1680–1743), army officer and politician, was born on 10 October 1680, according to the inscription on his memorial at Westminster Abbey. His place of birth was Ham House, Petersham, Surrey, the residence of his maternal grandmother. He was the eldest son of Archibald *Campbell, tenth earl and first duke of Argyll (*d.* 1703), and his wife, Elizabeth (*d.* 1735), eldest daughter of Sir Lionel Talmash (Tollemache) of Helmingham, Suffolk, and Elizabeth, countess of Dysart in her own right, and, by her second marriage, countess and later duchess of Lauderdale.

Early military and political career Campbell was tutored by Walter Campbell of Dunloskin, afterwards minister of Dunoon, and by John Anderson, later minister of Dumbarton, who completed his career at the Glasgow North-West parish formed in 1718. The portrait by John Medina of Lord Lorne (as Campbell was then styled) with his father and his brother Lord Archibald *Campbell, later third duke of Argyll (J. Holloway, *Patrons and Painters: Art in Scotland, 1650–1760*, 1989), gives an indication of the military ambitions of his father, who in 1694 persuaded William III to commission his fourteen-year-old son as colonel of the regiment raised by the Argyll family for the king's service after his acceptance of the crown of Scotland in 1689. Lorne was 'likewise to be Captain of a Company in the same Regiment' (Dickson, 22). The regiment had been involved in black deeds at Glencoe in February 1692 but was on its way to the Low Countries for service in William's war against France. Before Lord Lorne joined them he was placed under the supervision of a third tutor, Alexander Cunningham, who had accompanied William and the tenth earl of Argyll from the Netherlands to England in 1688 and acquired a position of trust with both. Cunningham tutored Lorne and his brother in the classics, and until the separation of their parents in 1696. Cunningham then took Lorne to join his regiment on the continent; he wrote to William Carstares from Bruges, after news of the treaty of Ryswick had reached him, that:

> My Lord Argyle has not yet written anything concerning his son; he was gone from this place to his regiment before I came here, which I was glad of for I know his Lieutenant-Colonel will take care of him. He is mightily concerned for his regiment. Everybody tells him it will be broken. (McCormick, 360)

Lorne was right to be concerned, for the regiment was disbanded: Cunningham subsequently took him on a European tour in 1699–1700, during which they visited Paris and Rome. In 1701 Lorne's father was raised to a dukedom in the peerage of Scotland by William, thus marking the completion of a remarkable resurgence in the family's fortunes.

With the renewal of war between Britain and France in

John Campbell, second duke of Argyll and duke of Greenwich (1680–1743), by William Aikman, pubd *c.*1720–25

1702 Lorne once more turned to his military career, and became involved in Marlborough's campaigns in the Low Countries. He was active in the campaign of 1702, at the head of the 10th regiment of foot. During the winter of 1702–3 he was in Hanover, before his return to the war, but he was recalled to London and Scotland by his father's death on 25 September 1703. His father's friend the king had already died, and had been succeeded by his sister-in-law Anne in March 1702; but the new second duke of Argyll was given command of his father's regiment of Scots horse guards and sworn of the privy council, in succession to his father. Six months later he was invested with the Order of the Thistle. There was some delay in making him an extraordinary lord of session, due to his youth and lack of legal training, but these objections were overcome by the time that the new duke found himself called upon, at the age of twenty-five, to take a leading role in determining the future of his ancestral nation. The Scottish parliament elected on the accession of Anne refused to follow the lead of the English parliament in determining the succession to the throne of Scotland, using the issue as a means of drawing attention to problems of government in Scotland, which had grown worse during William's reign. In desperation the English court turned to Argyll, who demanded a high price: promotion to general and an English peerage. He got the first before meeting the Scots parliament in 1705; the second would become his eventual reward. Argyll distrusted the older Scots court politicians, such as the duke of Queensberry, but really he distrusted all politicians and, having inherited his father's place as head of one of the largest aristocratic interests in Scotland, he behaved almost as a monarch in his own right, threatening to resign as lord high commissioner if his recommendations were not accepted. It was a defining moment in his life. The court had no one else to turn to in dealing with the recalcitrant Scots parliament, despite the queen's feeling that:

> it grates my soul to take a man into my service that has not only betrayed us, but tricked me several times, one that has been obnoxious to his own countrymen these many years and one that I can never be convinced can be of any use. ('Letters from Queen Anne to Godolphin', ed. G. Davies, *SHR*, 19, 1922, 191–2)

Argyll was certainly obnoxious to Scots court politicians, although it is clear from contemporary accounts that he exuded a quasi-monarchical quality that persuaded many that this young man of great family and certain purpose held the key to the future of the country. 'Argyll's commissionership was conducted on military lines with a heavy emphasis on discipline' (Ferguson, *Scotland's Relations with England*, 227). He was:

> indifferent to the political outcome. Whatever the ultimate result (settlement of the succession, an incorporating union, a federal union, or even continued deadlock), he simply meant to win a personal campaign in parliament, reap the rewards of victory, and move on to where the real glory was, with the army in Flanders. (ibid.)

Argyll's Jacobite contemporary and childhood playmate George Lockhart of Carnwath wrote a sketch of Argyll's character published in 1714 (*Memorials Concerning the Affairs of Scotland*, 132–3) which has often been quoted and reflects many other contemporary accounts in its balance of criticism and grudging admiration. Argyll was not a reasonable man but he was someone who could win his way by making a grand gesture, whether it was in persuading his audience to risk their lives on a battlefield or risk their future by surrendering the political sovereignty of their nation. Lockhart wrote that Argyll:

> was not, strictly speaking, a Man of sound Understanding and Judgement; for all his natural Endowments were sullied with too much Impetuosity, Passion, and Positiveness, and his Sense rather lay in a sudden Flash of Wit, than a solid Conception and Reflexion … He was extremely forward in effecting what he aimed at and designed, which he owned and promoted above Board, being altogether free of the least Share of Dissimulation, and his Word so sacred, that one might assuredly depend on it. His Head ran more upon the Camp, than the Court; and it would appear Nature had dressed him up accordingly, being altogether incapable of the servile Dependency, and flattering Insinuations requisite in the last, and endowed with that cheerful, lively Temper, and personal Valour, esteemed and necessary in the other. (ibid.)

Evidence of this character can be found in Argyll's conduct in the Scots parliament of 1705, where he appears to have persuaded the obvious leader of the opposition, the duke of Hamilton, to move that the Scots commissioners to negotiate the union would be chosen by the queen rather than by parliament. It was a key victory, but Argyll had promised Hamilton that he would be appointed one of the commissioners; when the queen denied this appointment Argyll refused to continue as lord high commissioner in 1706. He did obtain his English peerage, as earl of Greenwich, on 26 November 1705 and his brother Lord Archibald became one of the union commissioners (as did Lockhart, despite his Jacobitism). A year later, after completion of the union negotiations but before their acceptance by the Scots parliament, Argyll was made major-general and his brother a peer of Scotland, as earl of Ilay. His future Jacobite opponent the earl of Mar, at that time supporting the court in working for union, wrote that Argyll had some reason to insist on this:

> for his being a peer of England himself, he will not have a vote in choosing his peers for Scotland who are to sit in the Parliament of Britain, and it's fit for him to have one of his family to take [care] of his interests here in that case. (Dickson, 102)

In all manner of Scottish politics Argyll's plan was to delegate to his younger brother, in whose favour he resigned his place as extraordinary lord of the court of session while he pursued fame on the field of battle.

From 1708 to 1710 Argyll acted as one of Marlborough's principal generals in his wars, acquiring a reputation for bravery if not conspicuous military talent. Marlborough encouraged him and supported his being sworn of the British privy council in 1708, his promotion to lieutenant-general in 1709, and the awarding to him of the Order of the Garter on 22 December 1710, which increased his sense of importance to the point that he felt that he was the equal of Marlborough himself. This led to a quite public and bitter break between the two even before Argyll had received the Garter; according to Jonathan Swift's well-known report, when Argyll was consulted about refusing Marlborough's demand that he be made general for life, he offered to return to Flanders and seize Marlborough if there was any threat of disloyalty on account of refusal. Marlborough wrote to his wife on 25 March 1710: 'I cannot have a worse opinion of any body than I have of the duke of Argyle, but what is past cannot be helped' (Coxe, 3.136 and n., 165).

The making of a whig politician His rivalry with Marlborough sent Argyll back to London to pursue his interests at court, where his brother Lord Ilay entered the service of the new first minister, Robert Harley, in managing Scottish politics while Argyll struck public poses at court. On 25 December 1710 he attended the queen in full costume as a knight of the Garter while she received visitors at St James's Palace. Argyll had supported censure of the whig ministry for failures in the war effort in Spain. In the spring of 1711 he was sent to Catalonia as ambassador-extraordinary to Charles III, claimant to the Spanish throne, and as commander-in-chief of the British forces in that kingdom, having been promoted to full general. His campaign was not distinguished by its success, the duke claiming lack of supply from Britain, the ministry keeping its own council while it pursued private peace negotiations with France. By November 1712 Argyll had evacuated his army from Barcelona for Minorca, where he was appointed governor, and promptly surrendered his responsibilities to a deputy while he set out to return to court once again.

In London, Argyll found his brother discontented at

being sidelined in Scots affairs and joined with him in opposition to the attempted extension of the malt tax to Scotland, deferred until time of peace under the terms of the treaty of Union. This included supporting the Scottish MPs in their motion to dissolve the treaty of Union brought before the House of Lords by the earl of Seafield on 1 June 1713, which failed narrowly. Argyll, speaking as an English peer through his title of earl of Greenwich, admitted that he had been a leading advocate of union but argued that the protestant succession could best be secured by other means, and that from a Scottish perspective union had not brought any benefit to that former kingdom. For this and other expressions of opposition he was dismissed from his command of the Scots horse guards, the governments of Edinburgh Castle and Minorca, and the command of the army in Scotland on 4 March 1714, as intrigue thickened over the succession to the queen as she entered her final illness. Though many accounts emphasize Argyll's role in ensuring that the privy council safeguarded the Hanoverian succession, this has been somewhat exaggerated (Shaw, 54); yet the common currency of these accounts indicates how completely Argyll, by 1714, was identified with such a succession, despite his earlier flirtation with the tories.

With the arrival of George I from Hanover all changed again for Argyll, who was restored to his offices. His former ally and colleague the earl of Mar did not fare so well at court and soon raised the Stuart standard in Scotland in rebellion, capitalizing on continued Scottish discontent with the union. For Argyll it was another call to the colours in defence of what he had done so much to create ten years before and had questioned so recently in 1713. He took up command in Scotland, centralized the small number of available troops at Stirling to keep the rebels in the north, and later foiled an attempt to take Edinburgh by a Jacobite detachment, sent over the Forth estuary to take advantage of Argyll's immobility at Stirling. Hearing of the threat Argyll mounted some foot soldiers on commandeered horses, took what dragoons he had, and—by repute—reached the West Port of Edinburgh just as the Jacobites approached the Nether Bow gate at the opposite end of the city. In November he advanced from Stirling, aware that after much delay the numerically superior Jacobite army at Perth was moving against him. At Sheriffmuir, near Dunblane, both armies blundered into each other but Argyll managed to hold his force together while the superior Jacobite army retreated towards Perth. It was no Blenheim or Malplaquet, but Argyll had prevented the Jacobites from reaching the central lowlands of Scotland and saved the Hanoverian cause in that country and by extension in Britain. Not everyone saw his actions in quite so admiring a light. General Cadogan, an old rival of Argyll's, arrived with a force of Dutch troops after the battle and was quick to accuse Argyll of lack of zeal against the rebels, writing to Marlborough on 4 February 1716:

> the duke of Argyle grows so intolerable uneasy, that it is almost impossible to live with him any longer; he is enraged at the success of this expedition, though he and his creatures attribute to themselves the honour of it. (Coxe, 3.612)

Argyll left the army to the command of Cadogan after it had reached Aberdeen. He was fêted at Edinburgh on his way south but met with a less enthusiastic reception at court. Apparently he gravitated towards the English-speaking prince of Wales rather than the king, and in a telling phrase 'fell first victim to the curious domestic relationships of the Guelf family' (Ferguson, *Scotland: 1689 to the Present*, 139). He lost his restored governorship of Minorca, the lord lieutenancy of Surrey (where he lived in his splendid house at Sudbrook), and the command of Scotland in 1716.

Brother and landowner Britain was now entering a long period of peace, although this was not evident to contemporaries, and Argyll was a man of war. His brother the earl of Ilay took the lead in politics and law; nevertheless Argyll, by privilege of his English peerage, was a frequent and influential speaker in the House of Lords. As ministerial rivalry in London increased between 1717 and 1721 Argyll, with his brother's help, found his way back to favour. He was appointed lord steward of the household on 6 February 1719 and on 27 April achieved what he had hoped for since 1707: he was created duke of Greenwich in the peerage of Great Britain. There has never been a systematic study of Argyll's role in the House of Lords, but clearly he played to a public such as the private gentleman who left £500 towards erecting his memorial at Westminster Abbey and those who read and believed the poetic tributes of Alexander Pope and other poets circulating at the time. Yet with the emergence of Sir Robert Walpole as leading figure in the ministry Argyll's pomp and circumstance began to lose influence to his younger brother Lord Ilay's political dexterity (or subservience). Though Argyll supported extension of the malt tax to Scotland at a lower rate than that levied in England in 1725, he was less energetic than his brother in ensuring that it was collected. It appears to be about this time that friction began to increase between the duke and his brother. Their grand-niece recorded a subsequent family tradition whereby Ilay recalled 'I wanted to discuss such an affair with my brother but all went wrong. I saw the Tollemache blood beginning to rise, so I e'en quitted the field' (Stuart, 16). Lord Hervey recorded that when the brothers were not on speaking terms they could still co-operate in what in Scotland became known as the Argathelian interest: 'by the means of a Mr. Stewart [identified by John Simpson as the MP William Steuart of Orkney] (who went between them), a Scotch gentleman, an adroit fellow and a common friend to them both, they acted as much in concert as if they had been the most intimate and most cordial friends' (Simpson, 65, quoting Hervey, *Memoirs of the Reign of George the Second*, 2 vols., 1848, 1.336). Lady Louisa Stuart, daughter of the third earl of Bute, for whom both brothers acted as guardian after the death of his father, recalled that 'when he was a boy under their joint direction, he could remember occasions where (non-intercourse chancing to prevail) all arrangements respecting him were to be made by letter' (Stuart, 15).

Argyll has been described as 'too much the monarch in the west Highlands to make a good courtier in London' (Ferguson, *Scotland: 1689 to the Present*, 145) yet he seldom visited his highland estates and in the 1730s embarked on an ambitious programme of commercialization by letting out farms to competitive tender, which seriously disrupted the operation of the estate (Cregeen, 13–17). There was a regal or at least vice-regal aspect to his public mien that many Scots and non-Scots resented but that others were willing to accept in pursuit of their own ends or those that they associated with their country's. In 1729 Robert Wodrow recorded an encounter between the duke and the magistrates of Glasgow, in which 'they lamented that the town for some time had been under his Grace's frouns, which they wished to have removed. The Duke said, he had no reason to take rubs and affronts upon his family and name well.' Upon protesting that they had opposed Campbell of Shawfield politically as an MP but not the Argathelian interest the magistrates appealed 'to the Laird of Blythswood [a Campbell], standing by his Grace … The Duke seemed struck with this, and said "Colin was it so?" He said it was. "Then," said the Duke, "never man was more abused than I have been."' He subsequently insisted on taking a memorial that had been prepared regarding the burgh's grievances himself, and some time later the magistrates were invited to Edinburgh to discuss its contents with Lord Ilay, who promised his support in attempting to remedy them (Wodrow, 4, 74–5).

Opposition to Walpole Argyll sympathized with the opposition to Walpole's excise tax but largely followed his brother in supporting the ministry. He was restored in 1733 as colonel of the Royal Horse Guards, a regiment that he had lost in 1717, and on 14 January 1736 he was promoted to the rank of field marshal. The aftermath of the famous Porteous riot of 1736 in Edinburgh, however, led him to break with the ministry over its attempts to appease the crown by obtaining punitive legislation directed at Edinburgh and the Church of Scotland. Argyll proclaimed his disinterest: 'I never was a minister, and I never will be one … and I thank God I had always too great a value for those few abilities which nature has given to me, to employ them in doing any drudgery' (Douglas, *Peerage of Scotland*, ed. Wood, 1.110). He claimed that the legislation was in breach of the treaty of Union, as he had in 1713 against the malt tax:

> I was in the Parliament of Scotland when that Part of the Treaty of Union relating to the Privileges of the Royal Boroughs [*sic*] was settled; and … they were not alterable by any subsequent Parliament of Great Britain. … The Nation of Scotland in all the Proceedings at that Time treated with England as an independent and free People; and as that Treaty, My Lords, had no other Guarantee for the due Performance of its Articles, but the Faith and Honour of a British Parliament, it would be both unjust and ungenerous should this House agree to any Proceedings that has a tendency to infringe it. (Campbell, 313)

Argyll blamed the riot on 'a few fanatical Preachers lately started up in that Country, who by their Sermons, and other Ways, instill into the Minds of the Vulgar and Ignorant such Enthusiastical Notions as are inconsistent with all Government' (ibid., 317).

While his brother Ilay remained loyal to the regime Argyll set himself at the head of opposition to Walpole's government in Scotland in particular. He wrote to his nephew James Stuart Mackenzie in January 1741, regarding family differences in politics, that 'tho your Relations differ in Publick affairs they live in civility with one another', yet he was quite clear about how deep these differences were:

> My Brother, Ilay, wants to make all his friends Tools to Walpole because he finds his ends in so doing your Brother Bute & I would have all Our friends Independent of Walpole & all Other Ministers Whatsoever, My Brother Ilay prefers his places to all other Considerations, friendship Honour Relation gratitude & Service to his Country seem at present to have no weight with him. (Bute MSS)

The Walpole ministry lost the election of 1741 in Scotland, the only election between the union and the Reform Act of 1832 in which a ministry did not win a majority of Scottish MPs and representative peers. As a result Walpole could not cling to his majority in the House of Commons and Argyll became central in opposition efforts to replace him. When the king sent for William Pulteney to begin discussions on ministerial change he told him: 'I rather chose to come to you, because I knew your aim was only directed against my minister, but I did not know but the Duke of Argyll wanted to be King himself' (Owen, 92, citing BL, Add. MS 18915, fol. 28). Argyll was convinced that party distinction had to end and that the only way to do this was to admit members of the opposition associated with the tory party to office. He failed utterly to convince the king and as a result resigned in March 1742 the offices that he had received in the previous month, including that of commander of the forces in England and Scotland, something to which he had aspired since at least 1715. He intended retirement, and this decision was confirmed emphatically when he received a letter from the Jacobite James VIII and III in June expressing admiration for his role in the downfall of Walpole. Shaken at the thought that he might be accused of treason Argyll communicated the letter to the privy council and very likely promised the king, in a subsequent audience, to refrain from all future opposition. His public career was over. The most sensitive assessment of his career has noted that 'it is hard not to sympathize with a man so evidently designed for a brilliant part, yet eternally at odds with the script, with his fellow players, and with himself' (Simpson, 57).

Argyll was twice married. His first wife was Mary (*d.* 1717), daughter of John Brown and niece of Sir Charles Duncombe, sometime lord mayor of London. They married on 30 December 1701 and soon separated; Mary died on 16 January 1717 and was buried at Westminster Abbey on 19 January. Argyll married second Jane (*d.* 1767), daughter of Thomas Warburton of Winnington, Cheshire, formerly a maid of honour to Queen Anne and to Caroline, princess of Wales. They married on 6 June 1717 and so sealed a love match. They had five daughters, four of whom lived to adulthood, among them Lady Mary *Coke, letter writer and noblewoman. As adults the daughters were known for their 'loud shrill voice common to the four, which gained them a variety of nicknames, such as the Screaming Sisterhood, the Bawling Campbells, and so forth' (Stuart, 43). Argyll's eldest daughter, Caroline [*see* Townshend, Caroline (1717–1794)], married Francis, earl of Dalkeith, eldest son of the second duke of Buccleuch, on 2 October 1742. Argyll died on 4 October 1743 at Sudbrook, having suffered a debilitating paralysis that had affected him in the final months of his political activity, and was buried at Westminster Abbey on 15 October. He left to Caroline his property acquired in his own right, Caroline Park, near Edinburgh, at what today is called Granton; Adderbury in Oxfordshire; and Sudbrook in Surrey. His English and British titles became extinct. The Argyll dukedom passed to his younger brother, Archibald, previously earl of Ilay, who became third duke.

ALEXANDER MURDOCH

Sources R. Douglas, *The peerage of Scotland* (1764) • R. Douglas, *The peerage of Scotland*, 2nd edn, ed. J. P. Wood, 2 vols. (1813) • R. Campbell, *The life of the most illustrious prince, John, duke of Argyle and Greenwich* (1745) • P. Dickson, *Red John of the battles* (1973) • L. Stuart, *Some account of John, duke of Argyll, and his family* (privately printed, 1863) • GEC, *Peerage*, new edn • [G. Lockhart], *Memorials concerning the affairs of Scotland* (1714) • W. Coxe, *Memoirs of John, duke of Marlborough, with his original correspondence*, 3 vols. (1818–19) • *State papers and letters addressed to William Carstares*, ed. J. M'Cormick (1774) • *The manuscripts of his grace the duke of Portland*, 10 vols., HMC, 29 (1891–1931), vols. 4–5 • letters from John, second duke of Argyll, to James Stuart Mackenzie, Mount Stuart Trust, Isle of Bute, Bute MSS • J. M. Simpson, 'Who steered the gravy train, 1707–1766?', *Scotland in the age of improvement*, ed. N. T. Phillipson and R. Mitchison (1970), 47–72; repr. (1996) • W. Ferguson, *Scotland's relations with England: a survey to 1707* (1977); repr. (1994) • R. Wodrow, *Analecta, or, Materials for a history of remarkable providences, mostly relating to Scotch ministers and Christians*, ed. [M. Leishman], 4 vols., Maitland Club, 60 (1842–3) • *The Marlborough–Godolphin correspondence*, ed. H. L. Snyder, 3 (1975) • [C. Fleming], *Remarks upon the life of John duke of Argyle in a letter to Robert Campbell, Esq.* (1745) • E. Cregeen, 'The changing role of the house of Argyll in the Scottish highlands', *Scotland in the age of improvement*, ed. N. T. Phillipson and R. Mitchison (1970), 5–23; repr. (1996) • *Correspondence of Colonel N. Hooke*, ed. W. D. Macray, 2 vols., Roxburghe Club, 92, 95 (1870–71) • W. Ferguson, *Scotland: 1689 to the present* (1968) • *Letters of George Lockhart of Carnwath, 1698–1732*, ed. D. Szechi, Scottish History Society, 5th ser., 2 (1989) • J. H. Plumb, *Sir Robert Walpole*, 2 vols. (1956–60) • J. B. Owen, *The rise of the Pelhams* (1957) • J. Stuart Shaw, *The political history of eighteenth-century Scotland* (1999)

Archives Beds. & Luton ARS, letter-books • CUL, letter-book • NL Scot., corresp. and papers | BL, letters to Lord Strafford, Add. MS 22221 • Hunt. L., letters to earl of Loudon • NL Scot., letters to Lord Godolphin • NRA, priv. coll., letters relating to Jacobite rebellion

Likenesses J. de Medina, oils, *c*.1692, Inveraray Castle • J. Closterman, oils, 1704, Melbourne Hall, Derbyshire • R. Williams, mezzotint, 1704 (after J. Closterman), BM, NPG • G. Kneller, oils, 1717, priv. coll. • C. F. Zincke, enamel miniature, 1719, Scot. NPG • W. Aikman, oils, pubd *c*.1720–1725, NPG [*see illus.*] • J. Houbraken, line engraving, 1735 (after W. Aikman), BM, NPG • T. Bardwell, oils, 1740, NPG • J. Faber, mezzotint, 1740 (after A. Ramsay), BM, NPG • J. A. Dassier, bronze medal, 1743, Scot. NPG • L. Roubiliac, monument, 1748, Westminster Abbey, London; terracotta model, V&A • W. Aikman, oils, second version, Royal Collection • B. Cole, engraving, repro. in Campbell, *Life* • A. Ramsay, oils, Inveraray Castle • J. Simon, mezzotint (after W. Aikman), BM, NPG • T. Woolnoth, mezzotint (after W. Gush), NPG

Campbell, John, of Cawdor (**1695–1777**). *See under* Campbell family of Cawdor (*per.* 1511–1821).

Campbell, John, third earl of Breadalbane and Holland (*bap.* **1696**, *d.* **1782**), politician, was baptized at the Chapel Royal, London, on 10 March 1696, the son of John, second earl of Breadalbane (1662–1752), politician and landowner, and Henrietta, second daughter of Sir Edward Villiers and Elizabeth *Villiers, countess of Orkney, mistress of William III; Edward *Villiers, first earl of Jersey, was his mother's brother. On 13 October 1711 he matriculated at Christ Church, Oxford, where he showed considerable academic talent and a zeal for study; he was later created DCL by the university (29 January 1756). On 20 February 1718 he married Lady Amabel Grey (*d.* 1727), daughter of Henry Grey, duke of Kent, and Jemima Crewe. The marriage produced one son, who died in infancy, and one daughter, Jemima (1722–1797) [*see* Yorke, Jemima], who later succeeded her maternal grandfather to become Marchioness Grey.

In 1720 Campbell was appointed envoy-extraordinary and minister-plenipotentiary to the court of Denmark, where he remained until March 1729. While in Copenhagen he was invested with the Order of the Bath at its revival in May 1725 and styled Lord Glenorchy. After the death of his wife in March 1727 he was married on 23 January 1730 to Arabella Pershall (1702/3–1762), daughter of John Pershall and Charlotte Colepeper. They had two sons: George, who died in infancy, and John, Viscount Glenorchy (1738–1771), who was married to Willielma Campbell, Viscountess Glenorchy. In December 1731 he became ambassador to Russia.

In 1727 and 1734 Glenorchy was elected MP for the borough of Saltash, and between 1741 and 1746 he represented Orford. He gave his support to Sir Robert Walpole's administration, and in May 1741 his abilities were recognized by his appointment as one of the lords of the Admiralty, an office that he held until the dissolution of Walpole's government in 1742. In 1745 he was nominated master of the king's jewel office. In February 1752 he succeeded his father as earl of Breadalbane; in July of that year he was chosen as a representative peer for Scotland and sat in the Lords (1752–68 and 1774–80). He was appointed lord chief justice in the eyre south of the Trent in 1756, an office he held until October 1765. He was keeper of the privy seal of Scotland (1765–6), was sworn of the privy council in May 1766, and was appointed vice-admiral of Scotland on 26 October 1776. He died at Holyroodhouse, Edinburgh, on 26 January 1782. With no direct male heir to inherit the title, the peerage and estates passed to the Campbells of Carwhin.

T. F. HENDERSON, *rev.* JANET SORENSEN

Sources E. Cruickshanks, 'Campbell, John', HoP, *Commons* • A. Valentine, *The British establishment, 1760–1784: an eighteenth-*

John Campbell, third earl of Breadalbane and Holland (*bap.* 1696, *d.* 1782), by Jeremiah Davison, 1730

century biographical dictionary, 2 vols. (1970) • *British diplomatic instructions, 1689–1789*, 3: *Denmark*, ed. J. F. Chance, CS, 3rd ser., 36 (1926) • PRO, FO x.1.8 • GEC, *Peerage*

Archives NA Scot., corresp. and papers; legal business; various contracts and family affairs | Beds. & Luton ARS, letters to his father-in-law, Henry Grey, duke of Kent, and to his daughter, Jemima, Marchioness Grey • BL, corresp. with earls of Hardwicke, etc., Add. MSS 35431, 35450–35451, *passim* • BL, corresp. with Lord Whitworth, etc., Add. MSS 37384–37396, *passim* • NA Scot., letters to John Campbell of Barcaldine • NA Scot., corresp. with Lord Polwarth • NL Scot., corresp. with duke of Argyll

Likenesses C. Jervas, oils, 1708, Scot. NPG • J. Davison, portrait, 1730, Scot. NPG [*see illus.*] • portrait (after A. Ramsay), Dunrobin Castle, Sutherland

Campbell, John (*c*.1703–1777), banker and businessman, was held by contemporaries to be an illegitimate son of Colin Campbell of Ardmaddy, younger son of the first earl of Breadalbane (1634–1717). Later testimonies suggest that Colin Campbell married Grizel Douglas against the earl's wishes, and that all evidence of this legal marriage was later destroyed, and with it, the claim of John Campbell's descendants to the earldom. After his father's death, John was raised in the Breadalbane household at Finlarig in the Perthshire highlands. In 1718 he was apprenticed to Colin Kirk, writer to the signet, for three years.

In 1727, through the influence of John, second earl of Breadalbane, Campbell joined the newly established Royal Bank of Scotland in Edinburgh, where he began in the accountant's office. He was appointed assistant secretary in 1732 and second cashier in 1734, succeeding to the post of chief cashier in July 1745, the office he was to hold throughout his banking career. On the approach of Charles Edward Stuart's highland army in September 1745, the bank, under its deputy governor, Lord Milton, a pillar of the Hanoverian establishment in Scotland, sent its reserves of specie and banknotes to Edinburgh Castle to keep them out of Jacobite hands. However, after Edinburgh was taken and Charles Edward Stuart secured his victory at the battle of Prestonpans, a large number of Royal Bank of Scotland notes—many from Glasgow—came into the possession of the prince's staff. His secretary, John Murray of Broughton, presented these to the bank and demanded that Campbell exchange them for guineas, if necessary by bringing the reserves down from the castle. If this were not done, said Murray, the houses of bank directors and officials would be 'distressed'.

By now Lord Milton and most of the bank's directors had fled, and Campbell and the two remaining directors, without much demur, agreed to Murray's demand. Although the castle was by now under siege by the highland army, they succeeded in gaining entrance to it, and informed Lieutenant-General Guest and General Preston, the castle's deputy governor, that they wanted access to the bank reserves deposited there, as Campbell put it, 'to do some business'. He and his party then brought down from the castle the reserves of specie and, that evening, exchanged over £3000 of coin for banknotes with Murray's representative. As Royal Bank of Scotland notes came into Jacobite hands in the remaining weeks of Jacobite occupation of Edinburgh, similar transactions more than doubled the amount exchanged, to £6700. It was a considerable help to the highland army, as it prepared for the invasion of England, to have all this added to its war chest.

The seemingly weak-kneed response to Murray's demands and the apparent hoodwinking of General Preston raise questions about the motives of Campbell and his colleagues, so obviously at variance with the wishes of Lord Milton; it is also inconceivable that General Preston, resolute Hanoverian that he was, would have allowed the Royal Bank's reserves to leave the castle, had he known their ultimate destination. Perhaps Campbell was Jacobite at heart. The Breadalbane Campbells, unlike the Argyll Campbells, had been strongly Jacobite in the rising of 1715, though in 1745 Lord Glenorchy, the second earl's heir, was a determined whig. It may have been that Campbell, in the absence of Lord Milton, was responding to the wishes of the aged second earl, his uncle, the clan chief, and an erstwhile Jacobite, who remained at Holyroodhouse throughout the six weeks of the occupation, and whose Hanoverian loyalties were suspect.

Curiously, when Hanoverian rule returned to Edinburgh in November 1745, though Lord Milton made clear his disapproval of what had been done, there were no active recriminations by him against Campbell and his directors. It may have been that the risk of embarrassment to the Royal Bank, to Lord Milton himself, and possibly to the second earl of Breadalbane was considered too great to allow disclosure. Campbell seems to have maintained the view that he had done nothing more than he was legally obliged to do. (A contrary view would be to question whether Murray in treasonable defiance of King George's rule could claim the protection of his laws.)

In 1728 Campbell had married Jean Kirk (*née* Stirling), a widow, who died in 1739. Campbell's second marriage took place in Edinburgh in the early part of 1751, to Anna Caroline, eldest daughter of James Campbell of Tofts, and they had seven sons and eight daughters. His second son, Colin, fought in the American War of Independence and became governor of Gibraltar. Initially Campbell resided in Newbank House, which belonged to the bank, in Newbank Close, off the High Street; later he moved to Restalrig, outside the city. After his second marriage, he moved to a more fashionable area, acquiring a house in the Citadel, Leith. Duncan Bàn Macintyre, himself something of a Jacobite, composed, probably in the 1760s, a long eulogy in Gaelic verse in Campbell's honour, extolling his demeanour, hospitality, and attachment to all things highland. A portrait of 1749, in the possession of the Royal Bank of Scotland, shows him (despite the recent prohibition of the wearing of tartan) in highland dress and fully armed.

Although he held a position of power and influence in the Royal Bank, Campbell's duties were not full-time. He acted as the Scottish representative of the Equivalent Company, which had close links with the bank, and had been set up in 1724 to dispense the pecuniary 'equivalent' paid to Scotland after the Act of Union. He acted as agent to the second earl of Breadalbane and his son, Lord Glenorchy, and for other highland gentry, keeping their personal accounts, and performing business and personal service for them in Edinburgh. He was a partner in the Marble and Slate Company of Netherlorn, and was involved in the management of a coalmining company and the Edinburgh Sugar House.

John Campbell's long reign at the Royal Bank coincided with the years of vigorous expansion, during which the Scottish banking system became the most developed in Europe. He died at Edinburgh in January 1777. *The Diary of John Campbell: a Scottish Banker and the Forty-Five* published by the Royal Bank of Scotland in 1995 reproduces Campbell's diary in full for the crucial months of 1745. Long excerpts from the diary for these months had been published without much accompanying comment in the *Miscellany of the Scottish History Society* (1893) but little attention was paid to their implication, least of all by Neil Munro in his *History of the Royal Bank of Scotland, 1727–1927*, though Walter Biggar Blaikie, in his article on Prince Charles Edward Stuart in the *Book of the Old Edinburgh Club* for 1909, did raise an eyebrow at Campbell's 'grotesque' action.

JOHN SIBBALD GIBSON

Sources *The diary of John Campbell: a Scottish banker and the forty-five*, ed. A. Turton (1995) · 'Leaves from the diary of John Campbell, an Edinburgh banker in 1745', ed. H. Paton, *Miscellany … I*, Scottish History Society, 15 (1893), 511–12 · N. Munro, *History of the Royal Bank of Scotland, 1727–1927* (1928) · W. B. Blaikie, 'Edinburgh at the time of the occupation of Prince Charles', *Book of the Old Edinburgh Club*, 2 (1909), 1–60 · W. Scott, *The tales of a grandfather* (1828), chap. 79 · J. Fergusson, *Argyll in the '45* (1951), appx · S. G. Checkland, *Scottish banking: a history, 1695–1973* (1975) · W. A. Gillies, *In famed Breadalbane* (1938) · *Scots Magazine*, 39 (1777), 55

Archives Royal Bank of Scotland, London

Likenesses oils, 1749, Royal Bank of Scotland, Edinburgh

Campbell, John, fourth earl of Loudoun (1705–1782), army officer, was born at Loudoun Castle, Galston, Ayrshire, on 5 May 1705, the only son of Hugh *Campbell, third earl of Loudoun (*c.*1673–1731), and his wife, Lady Margaret (*c.*1684–1779), the daughter of John Dalrymple, first earl of Stair. He was a conscientious, but conspicuously unlucky, professional soldier. He entered the Royal Scots Greys as a cornet in 1727 and by 1737 had risen to captain, with the army rank of lieutenant-colonel, in the 3rd foot guards. Having succeeded to the title in 1731, he was elected in 1734 as a Scottish representative peer; the resulting patronage gained him the governorship of Stirling Castle in 1741. In 1743 he campaigned in Flanders, and following the battle of Dettingen was appointed aide-de-camp to George II.

As a confirmed whig, Loudoun played an active pro-government role during the Jacobite rising of 1745 and raised a regiment of loyal highlanders. Elements of this unit were captured at Prestonpans, where Loudoun served as adjutant-general to the commander-in-chief in Scotland, Sir John Cope. He escaped amid the ensuing rout, and in October sailed north with arms and funds. After arriving at Inverness he took command of troops raised by Lord President Duncan Forbes, so helping to maintain the government's position in the northern highlands. On 3 December he marched from Inverness 'in a very severe frost' to supply the blockaded post of Fort Augustus (*Scots Magazine*, 1745, 589). In February 1746 he sought to end the rebellion by attempting to capture Prince Charles Edward Stuart at Moy Hall, near Ruthven. The night march terminated in farce after five quick-thinking Jacobites succeeded in panicking Loudoun's column of 1500 men by giving the impression, through much loud shouting, of being a large ambushing force. The 'rout of Moy' prompted desertions among Loudoun's forces, leading to the abandonment of Inverness. Loudoun was himself obliged to retreat to the Black Isle, and from thence to Skye. While his discomfiture disappointed government hopes of a rendezvous with the duke of Cumberland, it is clear that his presence had none the less limited the spread of rebellion; indeed, Loudoun had 'kept all that part of Scotland in awe, prevented numbers from joining the rebels, and greatly impeded all their measures' (*London Magazine*, 1757, 504). During the notorious punitive operations in the highlands after Culloden he earned a reputation for humanity and honourable conduct towards surrendering rebels.

In 1749 Loudoun became colonel of the 30th foot, in 1755 he was promoted major-general, and in January 1756 he accepted the position of commander-in-chief of the forces in North America. The post was proffered by Cumberland, as captain-general, with the backing of Halifax and Fox; in consequence Loudoun's fortunes were to be linked closely with those of his royal patron. Loudoun was simultaneously appointed to the sinecure of governor-

John Campbell, fourth earl of Loudoun (1705–1782), by Allan Ramsay, 1747

general of Virginia and created colonel-in-chief of the 60th foot, or Royal American regiment, which was being raised in the colonies. Because of administrative delays he did not arrive in New York until 23 July—too late to prevent Montcalm's destruction of the vulnerable frontier post of Oswego. His commission called for the unstinting support and co-operation of the colonial governments in the war against Canada, but his efforts to impose this theoretical authority were to prompt increasing friction. With the reputation of British regular soldiers at low ebb, an army composed of locally raised provincial troops initially refused to recognize Loudoun's authority; his tactful handling of this situation, however, coupled with a monopoly upon munitions, defused the potential crisis. Loudoun's subsequent relations with the colonial authorities proved less happy. Faced with disunity and a failure to lend whole-hearted support to Britain's war effort, he responded with a hot-tempered insistence upon his authority—a stance that prompted the provincial assemblies to fear the imposition of military rule. His troubled command coincided with an era of defeat, and his attempt to capture the stronghold of Louisbourg on Cape Breton Island in 1757 ended in ignominious failure on account of an inability to secure local naval superiority. While the bulk of Loudoun's redcoats remained gathered at Halifax, Nova Scotia, Montcalm took the opportunity to destroy Fort William Henry on the New York frontier. Discredited by such disasters, which stemmed partly from Pitt's interference in his original plans, Loudoun was recalled in December 1757 and replaced by Major-General James Abercromby. The lack of military progress during his tenure as commander-in-chief in America led traditional narrative historians to regard him as the very epitome of the frosty and incompetent British officer; more recently, scholars have sought to rehabilitate his reputation by emphasizing his role in creating the administrative and logistical basis for ultimate victory over Canada.

In 1762, after Spain intervened in the Seven Years' War, Loudoun was appointed second in command to the British forces in Portugal. Upon the resignation of Lord Tyrawley that June he assumed command of the British troops in the Peninsula, contributing to the rebuff of a Franco-Spanish invasion. As in America, Loudoun's relations with the civilian authorities were tense. He was created governor of Edinburgh Castle in 1763 and became colonel of the 3rd foot guards and attained the rank of general in April 1770. A keen botanist, he improved his Ayrshire estates through systematic and scientific planting and encouraged the building of roads and bridges. The Royal Society elected him a fellow in 1738. Loudoun died, a bachelor, at Loudoun Castle on 27 April 1782 and was succeeded by his cousin. STEPHEN BRUMWELL

Sources S. Pargellis, *Lord Loudoun in North America* (1933) • S. Pargellis, ed., *Military affairs in North America, 1748–1765: selected documents from the Cumberland papers in Windsor Castle* (1936) • T. Mante, *The history of the late war in North America and the islands of the West Indies, including the campaigns of MDCCLXIII and MDCCLXIV against his majesty's Indian enemies* (1772) • *Correspondence of William Pitt, when secretary of state, with colonial governors and military and naval commissioners in America*, ed. G. S. Kimball, 2 vols. (1906); repr. (1969) • F. J. McLynn, *Charles Edward Stuart: a tragedy in many acts* (1988) • L. H. Gipson, *The British empire before the American revolution*, 6: *The great war for the empire: the years of defeat, 1754–1757* (1946) • L. H. Gipson, *The British empire before the American revolution*, 7: *The great war for the empire: the victorious years, 1758–1760* (1949) • *Scots Magazine*, 7 (1745), 589 • *London Magazine*, 26 (1757), 504 • *GM*, 1st ser., 52 (1782), 262 • *Army List* • *The papers of Sir William Johnson*, ed. J. Sullivan and others, 14 vols. (1921–65) • *DNB* • *DAB* • *DCB*, vol. 3

Archives BL, corresp. and papers, Add. MSS 44063–44084 • Hunt. L., corresp. and papers • Mount Stuart Trust Archive, Isle of Bute, corresp. and papers • NL Scot., corresp. and papers • NRA Scotland, priv. coll., letter-book and notebooks | BL, Bourquet MSS • BL, Newcastle MSS • BL, letters to Lord Tyrawley, Add. MS 23635 • NAM, letters to George Townshend • NL Scot., corresp. with duke of Argyll • PRO, War Office MSS/Colonial Office MSS • Royal Arch., Cumberland MSS • Warks. CRO, corresp. with earl of Denbigh

Likenesses A. Ramsay, oils, 1747; Christies, 3 July 1996, lot 120 [*see illus.*] • A. Ramsay, oils, *c*.1750, Scot. NPG • J. Faber the younger, line engraving, pubd 1755 (after A. Ramsay), BM • J. Faber, engraving, repro. in *London Magazine*, 504

Campbell, John (1708–1775), historian, was born in Edinburgh on 8 March 1708, the fourth son of Robert Campbell of Glenlyon and his wife, Elizabeth Smith of Windsor. His father was related to the Campbells of Breadalbane and his mother to the poet Edmund Waller. At the age of five his mother took him to live in Windsor, where his education was entrusted to his uncle. Intended for the legal profession, he was placed as a clerk with an attorney but he had little interest in the law and spent most of his time reading history and literature. His first known publication, *The Military History of Prince Eugene and the Duke of Marlborough*, appeared anonymously in 1736. Shortly afterwards he married, on 23 May 1738, Elizabeth Vobe (*bap.* 1711), daughter of Benjamin Vobe and Mary Matthews of Leominster, Herefordshire. They had seven children but only one, Mary (1742–1778), survived her father; she married John Grant of Lovat on 22 August 1763.

Campbell's first successful work was *The Travels and Adventures of Edward Brown* (2 vols., 1739), a fictitious yet partly autobiographical account of the topography, history, natural products, political conditions, manners, and customs of the countries visited on a journey to the Levant. His *Memoirs of the Duke of Ripperda* appeared at the same time and was republished in 1740 and *c.*1744. The success of these early works led to an invitation to contribute to the celebrated *Universal History* (7 vols., 1736–44), compiled by John Swinton, George Sale, and others. The exact scale of his contribution is not clear. Andrew Kippis claimed he had written the cosmogony but Samuel Johnson attributed this to Sale and credited Campbell as author of the history of the Persians and the Byzantine empire. While engaged on this work Campbell published in 1741 his *Concise History of Spanish America* (2nd edn, 1756). His reputation as a historian was further enhanced by the publication of *The Lives of the British Admirals and other Eminent British Seamen* (4 vols., 1742, 1744), which proved to be one of his most popular works: it passed through three editions in his lifetime and was translated into German. After his death it swelled into eight volumes when continued first by John Berkenhout and then by Redhill York. In total six editions were published. However, an article in the *United Services Journal* for 1842–3 heavily criticized the work, exposing the blunders and absurdities but attributing most of the blame for these to the revisers for failing to detect the original errors.

In 1743 Campbell published his most curious work, *Hermippus redivivus, or, The Sage's Triumph over Old Age and the Grave*. He claimed that this was a *jeu d'esprit* based on the *Hermippus redivivus* by the German physician Dr John Cohausen, who had claimed that life could be prolonged to 115 years by breathing the breath of healthy young women. However, many took him seriously. Campbell returned to more familiar territory with a revised edition of John Harris's *Navigantium atque itinerantium bibliotheca, or, A Compleat Collection of Voyages and Travels*, published in 1744. His edition contained important new material on all the great seamen and explorers from Christopher Columbus to Lord Anson. He also contributed to the first edition of the *Biographia Britannica* and according to Kippis it was largely his articles, signed E and X, which gave the work its reputation as 'a most valuable repository of historical and literary knowledge' (Kippis, 3.211). In his articles Campbell displayed a striking impartiality on questions of religious and political controversy. However later critics found his articles too panegyric and apologetic with the result that they tended to 'almost conceal the true features of the character under a glare of brilliant varnish' (Aikin, 2.449).

Campbell's most celebrated work was probably *The Present State of Europe* (1750), which began as a series of contributions to the periodical *The Museum* and went through six editions in his lifetime. It consists of summaries of the history of the leading European states with analyses and insights into the conduct of their domestic and foreign policies. It was this work which gave Campbell a European reputation and later brought him to the attention of Catherine the Great, who presented him with her portrait in 1774 as a token of her esteem. The University of Glasgow rewarded him with the degree of LLD in 1754. Campbell's next literary undertaking was to write for the continuation of the *Universal History* into modern times. He contributed articles on the European settlements in the East Indies and the histories of Spain, Portugal, France, and Navarre from the dark ages to 1656.

In 1763 Campbell was commissioned by Lord Bute to write a vindication of the peace of Paris, published in *Candid and Impartial Considerations on the Nature of the Sugar Trade*, in which he demonstrated the potential value of the French West Indian islands acquired by Britain in the treaty of Paris. It was doubtless as a reward for this pamphlet that Campbell was appointed the king's agent for the province of Georgia in 1765. His last great work was his *Political Survey of Britain* (2 vols., 1774). It contained a prodigious amount of information on the economic life, trade, industry, transport, and agriculture of the country, but did not prove to be the success Campbell had anticipated. Sales of the book progressed very slowly. Furthermore the accuracy of much of his information was questionable and many of his arguments appeared ill-founded. According to Dr Johnson this poor reception of the *Survey* hastened Campbell's death. Campbell was also the author of numerous minor works on such subjects as the Dutch herring fishing industry off the coast of Scotland; the probability of man reaching the north pole; and travel through the Scottish highlands. By the end of his life Campbell had become a wealthy and well-liked man. Johnson described him as 'the richest author that ever grazed the common of literature' (Boswell, *Life*, 1.418n.). His Sunday soirées at his house in Bloomsbury were attended by 'great numbers of persons of the first eminence for success in literature' (ibid.). Johnson thought well of him and praised the usefulness of his knowledge. However, when Boswell reported that Campbell had once claimed to have drunk thirteen bottles of port at a sitting, Johnson replied that while Campbell never lied in print 'you could not entirely depend on anything he told you in conversation' (ibid., 3.243–4).

Campbell's health began to worsen noticeably in 1774. According to Kippis his last illness 'was a decline, the consequence of a life devoted to literary study' (Kippis, 3.214). He died at his home in Queen Square, Ormond Street, London, on 28 December 1775 and was buried on 4 January

1776 in the new burying-ground behind the Foundling Hospital. A monument to his memory was erected in the neighbouring church of St George the Martyr.

FRANCIS ESPINASSE, *rev.* M. J. MERCER

Sources A. Kippis and others, eds., *Biographia Britannica, or, The lives of the most eminent persons who have flourished in Great Britain and Ireland*, 2nd edn, 3 (1784), 209–15 · Boswell, *Life*, 1.417–18; 2.216, 427–8, 447; 3.243–4; 4.99 · *GM*, 1st ser., 13 (1743), 279–80 · *GM*, 1st ser., 54 (1784), 892 · *GM*, 1st ser., 55 (1785), 969 · Allibone, *Dict.* · J. Aikin and others, *General biography, or, Lives, critical and historical of the most eminent persons*, 10 vols. (1799–1815), vol. 2, pp. 448–50 · Chambers, *Scots.* (1855) · H. J. Rose, *A new general biographical dictionary*, ed. H. J. Rose and T. Wright, 12 vols. (1853) · A. Chalmers, ed., *The general biographical dictionary*, new edn, 8 (1813), 151–9 · *IGI*
Archives U. Edin. L., papers | BL, corresp. with first Lord Holland, Add. MS 51407 · BL, corresp. with earl of Liverpool, Add. MSS 38201–38208, 38457

Campbell, John (*b.* in or before **1720**, *d.* **1790**), naval officer, was born in the parish of Kirkbean, near Dumfries, where his father, John Campbell (*d.* 1733), was minister. At an early age he was bound apprentice to the master of a coasting vessel, and is said to have entered the navy by offering himself in exchange for the mate of that vessel, who had been pressed. After serving for three years in the *Blenheim*, *Torbay*, and *Russell* he was, in 1740, appointed to the *Centurion*, in which he sailed round the world with Commodore George Anson; he joined as a midshipman, was promoted master's mate in a vacancy not long after sailing, and was advanced to master after the engagement with the galleon *Manila* in 1743. During this voyage he began a lifelong friendship with Augustus Keppel, then a young midshipman.

In January 1745, on his return home, Campbell passed the examination for lieutenant and, through Anson's interest, soon obtained command of a sloop. In November 1747 he was advanced to a post captain's command in the frigate *Bellona* which he commanded with success until the peace in 1748. In 1749 he was appointed commander of a proposed expedition to the Pacific by the sloop *Porcupine* and the *Raven*, but this voyage was aborted for political reasons. An alternative expedition to the north-west and north-east passages in the Atlantic also came to nothing. He afterwards commanded the *Mermaid*, the *Prince* (90 guns), and in 1757 the *Essex* (64 guns) in the Bay of Biscay under Hawke. In 1758, when Anson temporarily succeeded Admiral Edward Hawke in command of the fleet off Brest, Campbell was Anson's flag captain in the *Royal George*. He afterwards returned to the *Essex*, which he commanded in the blockade of Brest under Hawke through the summer and autumn of 1759, but when in November Hawke moved his flag to the *Royal George*, Campbell was appointed his flag captain, and served in that capacity in the decisive battle of Quiberon Bay on 20 November 1759. Hawke sent Campbell to England in the frigate *Vengeance*—a six-day voyage beginning on 24 November—with the great news of the victory; and it was Campbell, accompanied by Lord Anson—his old captain in the *Centurion* and now first lord of the Admiralty—who delivered the good news to the king.

Campbell first became directly involved with the development of astronomical navigation about 1747. According to Wales he was the first person to use a Hadley quadrant for actually measuring, 'for his own amusement', the angular distance between the moon and fixed stars (Wales, xxxiv). He showed his results to the astronomer royal, James Bradley, who found them to correspond exactly with their true distance in the heavens, and the two men, in company at Greenwich, subsequently made frequent observations of the moon's distance from the sun and stars, and also that of stars from one another. It was not, therefore, surprising that in 1756 Bradley should suggest to the board of longitude (with Anson in the chair) that the Admiralty should be asked to direct Campbell to give a sea trial to Tobias Mayer's new lunar tables and circular repeating instrument. This he did successfully when in command of the *Essex* within sight of the French coast, 'though they [the observations] were not taken with all the advantages that might have attended them, had I been alone; for I was all the cruise in company with an admiral whose motions I was obliged to follow' (Bradley, 493). These trials—and Campbell himself—were to have a profound influence on marine navigation in the next 250 years. Comparing Mayer's new circular repeating instrument with the common wooden Hadley octant in observing lunar distances, he found the former was far too heavy and the latter was far more satisfactory even though it could only measure angles up to 90° and, with its wooden frame, was not always stable enough. He therefore suggested that the Hadley octant be modified so that the arc was extended from 45° to 60° (to allow the measurement of arcs up to 120°) and that the instrument should be made of brass rather than wood. In 1759 John Bird was commissioned by the board of longitude to make such an instrument, a sextant of 8 inches radius with a brass frame, one-third of the weight of the equivalent Mayer circle, a prototype of the marine sextant still used today. This was, according to Cotter, 'the first sextant and it is to John Campbell that every subsequent navigator owed a debt of gratitude for his single (but significant, nevertheless) suggestion' (Cotter, 139).

In 1760 Campbell was appointed to the *Dorsetshire* (70 guns), which he commanded on the home station and in the Mediterranean until the peace in 1763. Having been admitted a fellow of the Royal Society on 24 May 1764, he was one of those asked by the board of longitude to perform calculations in connection with the results of the 1764 second sea trial (to Barbados) of John Harrison's prizewinning longitude watch; and he was one of the Royal Society's visitors of the Royal Observatory in March 1765. He was appointed to the yacht *Mary* about 1764 and later moved to the *Royal Charlotte*, in which he remained until promoted to rear-admiral of the blue on 23 January 1778. Two months later he was chosen by his old friend, Admiral Keppel, commanding the Channel Fleet, to be captain of the fleet in the *Victory*—effectively chief of staff. He held that office throughout the rest of the year, taking a very important part in the battle of Ushant on 27 July. Despite the fact that he was warmly recommended to the king by Lord Sandwich, the first lord, Campbell was offered no further employment until April 1782, when Keppel succeeded Sandwich as first lord, and appointed Campbell, now a vice-admiral of the white, governor and commander-in-chief of Newfoundland; Campbell sailed there in the *Portland* (50 guns) on 17 June 1782. He held this post for four years, returning to England periodically. In 1784 and 1785, at the request of count de Brühl, he arranged trials of the first chronometer of Thomas Mudge, on passage to and from England and in Newfoundland, borrowing an achromatic telescope from the board of longitude to ascertain the longitude of Newfoundland in 1785–6. He died at his house in Charles Street, Berkeley Square, London, on 16 December 1790; he was married but no details of his wife are known. 'He was, undoubtedly, a very great naval character; being a man of undaunted courage, almost unrivalled as a seaman, and, among seamen, perhaps wholly so, as an Astronomer and Navigator. His integrity was unimpeachable' (*GM*, 100).

DEREK HOWSE

Sources *DNB* • B. Somerville, *Commodore Anson's voyage* (1934) • D. Syrett and R. L. DiNardo, *The commissioned sea officers of the Royal Navy, 1660–1815*, rev. edn, Occasional Publications of the Navy RS, 1 (1994) • A. Frost and G. Williams, 'The beginnings of Britain's exploration of the Pacific Ocean in the eighteenth century', *Mariner's Mirror*, 83 (1997), 410–18 • BL, Add. MS 35606, fols. 312–13 • W. Wales, ed., *The original astronomical observations, made in the course of a voyage towards the south pole, and round the world, in his majesty's ships the Resolution and Adventure, in the years MDCCLXXII, MDCCLXXIII, MDCCLXXIV, and MDCCLXXV, by William Wales … and Mr. William Bayly, etc.* (1777), xxxiv–xxxvii • *Miscellaneous works and correspondence of the Rev. James Bradley*, ed. [S. P. Rigaud] (1832) • board of longitude minutes, 1756–64, CUL, MS RGO 14/5 • C. H. Cotter, *A history of the navigator's sextant* (1983) • records, RS, II, 279, 1764 • *The correspondence of King George the Third from 1760 to December 1783*, ed. J. Fortescue, 4 (1928), 308 • H. Rollman, 'Richard Edwards, John Campbell, and the proclamation of religious liberty in eighteenth-century Newfoundland', *Newfoundland Quarterly*, 80/2 (1984), 4–12 • 'Report of the select committee of the House of Commons to whom it was referred to consider of the report which was made from the committee to whom the petition of Thomas Mudge, watch-maker, was referred', *JHC*, 48 (1792–3), 877–920, esp. 917–18 • CUL, RGO 14/6 [borrowing telescope], 80 ff. • *GM*, 1st ser., 61 (1791), 100

Archives BL, comparative observations on the accuracy of chronometers, Add. MS 30822, fols. 53–60

Likenesses portrait, Royal Ontario Museum, Toronto; repro. in Cotter, *History*, 138

Campbell, John (1753–1784), soldier, was born on 7 December 1753 at Levenside House, near Dumbarton, the second of seven sons of John Campbell, Lord Stonefield (*d.* 1801), a lord of session and of justiciary in Scotland, and his wife, Lady Grace Stuart (*d.* 1783), daughter of James Stuart, second earl of Bute. Educated at the high school, Edinburgh, he entered the army as an ensign in the 37th foot on 25 June 1771 and was promoted lieutenant in the 7th fusiliers on 9 May 1774. Campbell then served in America and was captured at Fort St Johns, Canada, in 1775. After his exchange he joined the 71st foot, or Fraser's Highlanders, as a captain in December 1775 and the 74th highlanders as a major in December 1777.

Campbell returned to England in 1780 and early the following year exchanged into the 100th regiment, or Seaforth Highlanders, as a major (lieutenant-colonel, February 1781), in command of which regiment he landed at Bombay on 26 January 1782. After his departure from England his transfer had been effected into the 2nd battalion 42nd regiment, or Black Watch, and on hearing the news he assumed its command. Thereafter he was involved in the Second Anglo-Mysore War against Haidar Ali and his son Tipu Sultan. The fort at Anantapur on the Malabar coast was stormed by forces under Campbell's command early in 1783 but further progress was hampered by the misconduct of Brigadier-General Mathews, the supreme commander, who was suspended from the service in May. As Mathews's successor was absent Campbell took charge of the army but was almost immediately besieged by Tipu, with overwhelming force, at Mangalore. Campbell's epic defence, which began on 23 May 1783, continued until 23 January 1784 and was marked by severe hardships. By the time he was forced to capitulate, the garrison had been reduced from 1883 men fit for duty to 856, but they marched out with the honours of war and kept their liberty. Campbell was exhausted by his exertions and died of a consumption at Bombay on 23 March 1784.

H. M. STEPHENS, *rev.* D. L. PRIOR

Sources J. Spens, *Memoir of the life and character of the late Lieut.-Colonel John Campbell* (1836) • *Scots peerage* • Burke, *Peerage* (1967) • C. A. Bayly, *Indian society and the making of the British empire* (1988), vol. 2/1 of *The new Cambridge history of India*, ed. G. Johnson

Campbell, John (1766–1840), Congregational minister and missions activist in Africa, was born at The Cowgate, Edinburgh, and was educated at the Royal High School (*c.*1772–*c.*1778), where he was a classmate of Sir Walter Scott. Both his parents died in his early childhood, and he was brought up by his mother's brother. Under the influence of his family's piety, he became a deeply religious young man who served as session clerk in College Street Relief Church from 1785 to 1795. Until her death Campbell had a regular correspondence with his spiritual guide, Lady Leven, but he was troubled by bouts of deep unhappiness until he came under the influence of the Independent evangelists James and Robert Haldane. One of their closest associates, the young Campbell was in 1793 a founder of the Religious Tract Society of Scotland, which preceded the London society by six years. He was also influential in the creation of Magdalene societies in both Edinburgh and Glasgow, and worked with James Haldane in his campaign to set up Sunday schools in areas they felt were neglected by the kirk. Unlike their English counterparts these provided religious instruction alone, since the majority of Scottish children attended school during the week. This campaign led Haldane and Campbell into lay preaching and the establishment of independent congregations in these same areas.

In 1801 Campbell felt a call to the ministry; he trained at Grenville Ewing's seminary in Glasgow and was called to Kingsland Independent Chapel, London, where he was ordained in 1804. The move to England was partly a result of his desire to be close to the circles which dominated the

John Campbell (**1766–1840**), by Thomas Hodgetts, pubd 1819 (after John Renton)

growing network of evangelical benevolent societies, but it was also a means of escaping the bitter divisions which had developed in Scotland around the Haldanes. His keen interest in the abolition of slavery had led to friendship with leading evangelical abolitionists such as John Newton, Charles Grant, Zachary Macaulay, and Wilberforce. Abolitionism and overseas mission were closely associated, and in 1805 Campbell became a director of the London Missionary Society (LMS). He was also one of the founders of the British and Foreign Bible Society and played a role in aiding street women in London, all while undertaking a preaching tour in Scotland every summer from 1804 until 1812. At Kingsland he expanded his output of books for children and young people and founded an evangelical magazine for young people entitled the *Youth's Magazine*, which he edited throughout the rest of his working life.

Africa had fascinated Campbell since his youth, and in 1812 the LMS sent him there to restore good relations between the missionaries and the governor, Sir John Cradock (in which he was successful), and to survey the work of the society. He covered over 5000 kilometres by ox-wagon, travelling where few Europeans had gone before. North of the Orange River, he met the Griqua of Adam Kok, with their missionary John Anderson. He was so impressed with this nascent Christian state that, on his return to London, he had minted for it a set of decimal coins, the first autonomous coinage in southern Africa. Back in London in 1814 Campbell wrote his *Travels in South Africa*, which was published the next year and rapidly went through three editions. Very soon after settling back into his pastoral and editorial work he was called again to go to Africa. In 1819 he and a fellow director of the LMS, John Philip, were sent to reorganize the work of the society in South Africa; Philip was to stay on as resident director after he and Campbell had completed their work. On his return to London, Campbell published, in 1822, two new volumes of *Travels in Africa*, which contained one of the most accurate maps of southern Africa yet produced. Almost to the end of his life he was in regular demand to speak at missionary rallies. Beside his *Travels*, his one other substantial work was *African Light Thrown on a Selection of Scripture* (1835). He died unmarried on 4 April 1840 in London.

ANDREW C. ROSS

Sources R. Philip, *The life, times and missionary enterprises of the Rev John Campbell* (1841) • W. G. Blaikie, *John Campbell, founder of the Tract Society of Scotland: an address on 9th June, 1886 at the opening of its new premises* (1886) • R. Ross, *Adam Kok's Griquas: a study in the development of stratification in South Africa* (1976) • *DNB*

Archives NL Scot., correspondence | SOAS, London Missionary Society archives

Likenesses T. Hodgetts, mezzotint, pubd 1819 (after J. Renton), BM, NPG [*see illus.*] • Thomson, stipple, pubd 1821 (after J. Partridge), NPG • H. Meyer, stipple (after W. T. Strutt), BM, NPG • drawing, repro. in Philip, *Life, times and missionary enterprises*, frontispiece

Campbell, John, **first Baron Campbell of St Andrews** (**1779–1861**), lord chancellor, was born on 15 September 1779 next to the Bell Inn in Cupar, Fife, where his father, George (1747–1824), was a minister of the Church of Scotland for fifty-one years. His mother, Magdalene, the daughter of John Hallyburton, died in 1793, when he was thirteen and a student at St Andrews (*Life*, ed. Hardcastle, 1.7). Throughout his life he remained close to his family, especially to his father and his older brother George, later Sir George Campbell of Edenwood. His precocious success at St Andrews (he was eleven when he entered and four years later had completed the arts curriculum) was due to his professed determination to excel. His attitude to his homeland was always ambivalent. On the one hand he proudly proclaimed his descent from the second earl of Argyll, who fell at Flodden, and Robert, duke of Albany, regent of Scotland; he also acquired an estate, Hartrigge, in Roxburghshire, which he loved to visit, although he 'could not endure to reside in the country permanently' (ibid., 2.330), and was buried in Jedburgh Abbey. On the other hand, he tried unsuccessfully to cultivate an English accent, regarded his Scottish education as inferior to that of Oxbridge contemporaries, and preferred the English to the Presbyterian burial service.

Early years in London Campbell was destined for the ministry. But three years of theology, Hebrew, and exercise sermons at St Mary's College at St Andrews failed to exorcize his worldly ambition. In 1798 he accepted a tutorship in London and within eighteen months was writing not very tactfully to his father—tact was never his forte—expressing his 'horror of inaction' which would be his fate as a 'country minister' (*Life*, ed. Hardcastle, 1.44). His father reluctantly agreed to his plan of studying law, which he saw as the path to worldly success. Campbell never doubted that he would succeed at the English bar, even

John Campbell, first Baron Campbell of St Andrews (1779–1861), by Thomas Woolnoth, *c*.1851

though he knew that he would have to find other ways of supporting himself in his early years. Through his Scottish acquaintances he became a reporter successively for *The Oracle* and the *Morning Chronicle*, then the whig mouthpiece, reviewing books, translating French newspapers, writing dramatic criticism, and reporting House of Commons debates and the business of the king's bench. He did not lament his lack of shorthand, since shorthand writers 'attend to words without entering the thoughts of the speaker' (ibid., 1.106). But he concealed his journalism from fellow students; with them he was careful 'in sinking the reporter and concealing [his] apprehensions' (ibid., 1.122). He resigned from the *Morning Chronicle* because his 'literary fame' had 'reached the ears' of one or two of them; his mind was then 'relieved from an oppressive sense of degradation' (ibid., 1.177).

The law reporter Law reporting was more respectable and in 1809 Campbell began the first of four volumes of *Nisi prius Reports* of the decisions of Lord Ellenborough. Judgments of the royal courts *in banc* had an ancient pedigree. But, with the exception of the rightly maligned reports of Espinasse (1793–1807) and the more accurate reports of Peake (1790–1812), there were no reports of civil trials. Campbell realized that the Napoleonic war, with the attendant continental blockade, would generate novel commercial litigation and that the reporting of Ellenborough's king's bench decisions would find a ready market. The volumes, covering the years 1808–16, were welcomed and praised by some later judges, like Lord Cranworth, for their accuracy and conciseness (*Williams* v. *Bayley*, 1866). But Maule J., admittedly no admirer of Campbell's (see Ballantine, 141), condemned them as dangerous precedents because they contained 'too short statements of the case' (J. W. Wallace, *The Reporters*, 4th edn, 1882, 542n.). In one respect Campbell was a less than honest reporter for he kept a drawer marked 'Bad Law' into which he threw all the cases which seemed to him 'improperly ruled'. Campbell's *Nisi prius Reports* were innovative in a more admirable sense. He recognized that pleadings and facts

> must often be imperfect, and may sometimes be inaccurate, and consequently subjoined the names of the attorneys on both sides; anyone who doubted the accuracy of the report could then inspect the briefs in the case to verify the report. (Campbell, *Nisi prius Reports*, 1.4n.)

Practice at the bar On 3 November 1800 Campbell entered Lincoln's Inn, 'the most expensive society, but the most respectable' (*Life*, ed. Hardcastle, 1.60), and so began a long legal apprenticeship. The formal qualifications for call to the bar were that a student's name must have been on the books for five years, the keeping of twelve legal terms, and the performance of exercises, which consisted of reading a few lines written down by the inn's butler. Campbell was one of the few who diligently attended the courts, sitting in the box set aside for students in the king's bench and 'writing out the cases' (ibid., 1.61, 70). Students were self-taught, although many would attach themselves for a year or more to a special pleader. The foremost of these was William Tidd, whose pupil Campbell became in 1804, helped by an introduction from Sir James Macintosh. The business of a special pleader, who was not a barrister, was to draw up all the written proceedings in a suit at law. In a letter to his father Campbell wrote contemptuously of the idleness of most of Tidd's pupils who only disputed such matters as the latest fashions of dress. Campbell occasionally relaxed over a half pint of cider in the Cider Club, where he delighted in the company of an inebriated Richard Porson. He was one of Tidd's industrious pupils, whose number included Copley (Lord Lyndhurst), Pepys (Lord Cottenham), and Denman (Lord Denman); they met weekly at Tidd's debating society to discuss juridical questions. Tidd appreciated Campbell's industry and treated him generously, paying him £100 a year as his devil (assistant). This financial support and the subventions of his brother, George, now in Calcutta, enabled him to build up a 'respectable law library' and to meet the cost (£120) of his call to the bar on 15 November 1806.

Not surprisingly Campbell's early years were frustratingly slow. He occupied himself by preparing the second edition of Watson's *Treatise on the Law of Partnership* (1807), although his name does not appear on the title-page, and the *Nisi prius Reports*. After three years of little reward he abandoned the home for the Oxford circuit. His ambition, ability, and energy, combined with the professional contacts with attorneys made through Tidd and the reputation of his *Reports*, ensured his eventual success. In 1811 he could write to his father, 'It is no bounce that I had more business last term in the Court of King's Bench than any man of my standing' (*Life*, ed. Hardcastle, 1.270). In that year he earned over £948 and five years later his professional income was £3000. In 1822 he claimed that, 'For junior business I am now the first, without a rival' (ibid., 1.409). He achieved this professional success even though he feared that he had initially incurred the enmity of the cantankerous Lord Ellenborough. A pugnacious advocate, he dreaded but did not succumb to Ellenborough's 'interruptions and rudeness' (ibid., 1.311). But he lost no clients. As he learned to be less aggressive, Ellenborough treated him with greater consideration (ibid., 1.311, 332). Campbell was not subtle. His mind was analytical and powerful; intelligence coupled with diligence and mastery of detail made him a formidable and sought after advocate (Hanworth, 112). Bagehot said that, like Macaulay, he had

> the Scotch faculties in perfection. He reduces legal matters to a sound broad principle better than any man who is now a judge. He has a steady, comprehensive, abstract, distinct consistency, which elaborates a formula and adheres to a formula; and it is this which has raised him from a plain—a very plain—Scotch lawyer to be Chief Justice of England. (Bagehot, 2.30)

Despite Campbell's domination of the junior bar Eldon denied him a silk gown and it was not until Copley became lord chancellor as Lord Lyndhurst (1827) that he became a king's counsel. It is not surprising that many contemporaries at the bar disliked him. 'His selfishness, desperate eagerness to push to the front and perpetual air of calculation … leave an unpleasant taste behind' (Atlay, 2.143). But despite his belief that there was a systematic conspiracy among leaders to depress juniors, his 'inward confidence' never left him. He wrote to his brother in 1824,

> I think I am in every way a match for Pollock, and as to Brougham and Denman, I shall improve in eloquence more than they will in law, and by and by I do not think that there will be any great inequality between us. (*Life*, ed. Hardcastle, 1.423)

Society and marriage Campbell's success gave him greater social confidence. He discreetly took dancing lessons and became a member of Brooks's, the whig stronghold. He was as determined in the pursuit of love as in the quest for professional success. Mary Elizabeth Scarlett (*d.* 1860), daughter of James Scarlett, the future Lord Abinger, won his heart. But he did not immediately win hers. Characteristically, he persevered, and on 8 September 1821 they were married. It was a most happy marriage. They had seven children, three sons and four daughters, to whom they were devoted. 'Geniality and tenderness distinguished [Campbell's] private life and made him beloved by all who knew him' (*Life*, ed. Hardcastle, preface). This was a side of Campbell which few outside his family saw.

Early interest in law reform Campbell was a committed but conservative whig, frequently upbraiding his brother for his more radical views. He confessed to him, 'What I should like above all things would be to be in the House of Commons; to bring in Bills for the improvement of the law' (*Life*, ed. Hardcastle, 1.465–6). His profound interest in law reform was an abiding one. As a consequence of Brougham's great speech in 1828 two commissions were appointed, one to inquire into common-law procedure and the other to inquire into the arcane law of real property, in particular, into the forms of transferring title. Sugden was the obvious choice as the chairman of the real property commission, but he declined. To Campbell's surprise he was then invited to chair it. He was the only common lawyer among the eight commissioners. Novel challenges never deterred Campbell, and he 'set to work systematically *ab ovo*' (ibid., 1.458). He wrote the introduction to the first report and that part of it which dealt with 'prescription and the statutes of limitation'; although still a busy practitioner, he read every case from the medieval period downwards, the relevant Roman civil law and the law of modern continental nations, and the law of the American states—a demonstration of his fearsome industry and application. The first report was published in 1829, the other three reports over the next three years. But Campbell had 'only the general superintendence' over these. The second report which proposed a general register of deeds and instruments relating to land was dear to Campbell's heart, but the proposal was not implemented in his lifetime. The other recommendations of the commissioners were adopted.

Entry into the House of Commons Campbell's first attempt to enter the House of Commons was for the notoriously corrupt borough of Stafford in 1826. He contributed to his defeat by declaiming against bribery (*Life*, ed. Hardcastle, 1.458), but was elected for the same borough at the general election after George IV's death (1830) (ibid., 1.474–5). Campbell viewed the prospect of electoral reform coolly. In October 1830 he told his brother that while he supported more members for the great towns and the reform of Scottish representation it was his view that 'You cannot generally alter the right of voting without a complete *bouleversement*, and making the House of Commons too strong for the other branches of the Legislature' (ibid., 1.478). He was a 'decided enemy to Ballot', which 'could not at all check undue influence, except in as far as it promoted falsehood and hypocrisy' (ibid., 1.503). With the enlargement of the franchise, 'there will be more corruption than ever at such a place as Stafford' (ibid., 1.514). Reform of the law against bribery and corruption was more essential. On 25 August 1831 Campbell spoke in the house for the first time on a motion to establish a general register of deeds affecting real property. The hour-long speech was not greeted with wild applause and the motion was eventually defeated by the 'most influential class in the country', the country attorneys, who won the support of Lord Grey (ibid., 2.3, 12).

Campbell played little part in the tumultuous reform debates in the Commons, partly to avoid 'direct collision' with Scarlett, his father-in-law, who had gone over to the tories (*Life*, ed. Hardcastle, 2.4), but his letters and autobiography provide a colourful picture of the debates in both houses. He was 'quite appalled' by the terms of the proposed Reform Bill of 1831 when it was first introduced (ibid., 1.504). On reflection and possibly influenced by his brother's more radical views, he concluded that it was not revolutionary, but a mere restoration of the constitution—very much an old whig view—and he claimed that it was his vote which ensured its second reading. He was much relieved that it was enacted without the creation of new peers for he doubted whether a numerous creation could be 'considered a constitutional proceeding, and can only be defended as a *coup d'état* to ward off greater evils' (ibid., 2.12).

Law officer In 1832 Brougham (now lord chancellor) plotted to make Campbell the attorney-general rather than Sir William Horne, whom Brougham thought incompetent; but the plan was aborted when Baron Bayley refused to resign immediately from the exchequer to make way for Horne. The result was that, in November, Horne became the attorney with Campbell as solicitor-general. A month later Campbell was re-elected as the member for Dudley in the reformed parliament and rejoiced that the election was accompanied by neither drunkenness nor bribery. Campbell was dismayed that the cabinet immediately decided to introduce the Irish Coercion Bill, a measure which, in his view, contained 'very obnoxious clauses' (*Life*, ed. Hardcastle, 2.27). He unsuccessfully sought to mitigate its severity, and avoided speaking in debate on its principle. But in committee he was compelled to defend it, alienating O'Connell, who denounced him as 'a tool of the "base and bloody Whigs"' (ibid., 2.29, 33–4).

In contrast, several law reform statutes, drafted by the real property commissioners and enacted in 1833, passed quietly, under Campbell's guidance, through an indifferent House of Commons, 'without one single syllable being altered in any of them' (*Life*, ed. Hardcastle, 2.29). These included statutes of limitations; for the abolition of fines and recoveries; to render freehold and copyhold estates assets for the payment of simple contract debts; for regulating the law relating to dower (a widow's life estate in half of her deceased husband's realty); and to allow brothers and sisters of the half blood to succeed one another. These were not the only law reform statutes enacted while Campbell was a law officer. Others included the Municipal Corporations Act of 1835 which obliged the new councils to establish watch committees to appoint constables; the Prisoners' Counsel Act of 1837, bitterly opposed by twelve of the fifteen judges, which allowed counsel for a person accused of felony to address the jury and the accused to inspect and take copies of any depositions against him; and the Wills Act of 1837, which prescribed the same formalities necessary for the validity of wills disposing of real and personal property. However, the 'opposition of tradesmen and moneylenders' frustrated his attempt to abolish imprisonment for non-payment of ordinary debts; the statute of 1838 only abolished imprisonment as a means of securing the defendant's attendance in court. Campbell's Land Registration Bill once again foundered.

In 1834 Horne, who had been seen infrequently in the house and whose parliamentary responsibilities had consequently fallen on Campbell, was ousted from office. Campbell succeeded him, '[grieving] on every account to see him thus sacrificed, even if it were by his own caprice' (*Life*, ed. Hardcastle, 2.41). Some claimed that Campbell had instigated his departure; although he was never shy in pressing his claim to office, there is no evidence to substantiate that allegation. Because of this promotion the 'absurd law' (ibid.) required him to vacate his seat, and to his chagrin he lost Dudley when he offered himself for re-election in 1834. It was three months before he returned to the house when he was elected to represent Edinburgh; and 'plain John Campbell' represented that city until he was ennobled in 1841.

Leach, the master of the rolls, died in 1834. Grey was anxious that Campbell should remain in the house. So, to his irritation, Campbell was passed over and the solicitor-general, Pepys, was appointed in Leach's place. Brougham partially placated him with the explanation that a common lawyer could not be appointed to the rolls when the lord chancellor was also a common lawyer. Campbell was content to protest, and urged that the appointment should not be seen as a precedent. His reaction was not as temperate when he was passed over a second time two years later when Pepys became lord chancellor and Bickersteth master of the rolls. He claimed that he had an 'unquestionable right' (*Life*, ed. Hardcastle, 2.77) to the rolls, and went to Melbourne in high dudgeon with a letter of resignation in his pocket. Melbourne flattered him, saying that his services as attorney-general were indispensable, and offered to raise his wife to the peerage. Campbell convinced himself that the elevation of his wife as Baroness Stratheden of Cupar would remove any notion of his being slighted, and so he stayed. Pollock was, however, among those who believed that Campbell had been 'bought off' and that the law officers and the profession had been insulted. He wrote, contemptuously, that Campbell had failed to 'distinguish between what you have done and agreeing to accept for your wife a valuable diamond necklace' (Hanworth, 205). However, this rebuff did lead Campbell to contemplate taking a puisne judgeship in 1838 and 1839 (he had refused one in 1830), but he was again persuaded not to abandon the government. During his parliamentary years his strong constitution enabled him to carry a crushing burden of work, frequently making do with two or three hours of sleep a night. '[A] man', he wrote,

> cannot take a portion of business and no more. He must play the whole game or give it up entirely. Then my station in the House of the Commons depends very much on my station at the bar. Many, there, look with foolish respect to an eminent counsel. (*Life*, ed. Hardcastle, 1.503)

When he was over seventy Mrs Beecher Stowe described him as a 'man of most dignified and imposing appearance. Tall with a large frame, a fine forehead, and strongly marked features' (Manson, 137). Fitzjames Stephens was also 'overpowered with admiration at his appearance. He was thick set as a navvy and hard as nails, still full of vigour at the age of 76' (Atlay, 2.199). As early as 1833 Campbell's practice at the bar was 'nearly equal' to Scarlett's, with whom he had some 'rather unpleasant collisions'

(*Life*, ed. Hardcastle, 2.31). He claimed that the fault lay with his father-in-law, who expected the same deference professionally as he did in private life; in contrast, Campbell behaved 'with great moderation and forbearance' (ibid.). After Scarlett became chief baron (1834) Campbell was the undoubted leader of the bar. He was learned in the law, hard-working, and had a way with juries. 'To get a verdict, the way is not to consider how your speech will read when reported, but to watch the jury, and to push any advantage you may make, disregarding irregularities and repetitions' (ibid., 2.89). Later, as a judge, he was equally adept in controlling his juries. He was never quite as sensitive to the mood of the House of Commons—few lawyers are—but the house listened to him with respect.

Writings and biographies Campbell's first significant literary foray was the ponderous *Speeches of Lord Campbell* (1842). They include his defence of the prime minister, Lord Melbourne, who had been accused by George Norton of criminal conversation with his wife, Caroline. It was the *cause célèbre* of 1836. The evidence was transparently thin and the jury did not hesitate before returning a verdict for the defendant. Campbell was buoyant and after the verdict returned to the House of Commons to cheers of praise and relief. But the publication of the speech six years later was condemned as insensitive, as it would revive painful memories for Mrs Norton and her family (*Law Magazine*, 341). The *Speeches* also contain Campbell's argument in *Stockdale* v. *Hansard* in 1839, over which he laboured during two summer vacations and which scrupulously examined the history and boundaries of parliamentary privilege and concluded that each house of parliament is a judge of its own privileges. Campbell was much put out when the court of king's bench, presided over by Denman, held that the existence of a privilege claimed by a house was a matter of law for the courts and was not determined by a resolution of that house. Campbell unreasonably castigated Denman's judgment as 'ill-considered and intemperate' (*Life*, ed. Hardcastle, 2.113), condemning him 'for his vain desire of putting himself forward as a champion of people's rights, with a view of obtaining popular applause' (J. Arnould, *Memoir of Thomas, First Lord Denman*, 2.51–2). It was effectively reversed by the Parliamentary Papers Act of 1840. Denman never forgave Campbell for this bad-tempered, public attack.

By 1841 the Melbourne administration was tired. A dissolution was resolved upon. Melbourne offered Campbell the Irish lord chancellorship. Plunket reluctantly resigned; Campbell was appointed and raised to the peerage as Baron Campbell of St Andrews. The appointment was unpopular with the Irish bar and seen as a political job. The fall of the whigs was imminent, so Campbell waived his right to a pension of £4000 a year. His tenure as lord chancellor was a mere six weeks.

With the return to power in 1841 of Peel and the 'new' Conservative Party, Campbell found himself with no judicial appointment and unable to return to the bar. He occupied his years out of office largely with writing his *Lives of the Lord Chancellors* and *Lives of the Chief Justices*. But he was not politically quiescent, boring Brougham with his ponderous speeches in the House of Lords. He remained the standard-bearer of law reform. Two statutes, the Libel Act of 1843 (making truth a defence in criminal cases if the publication was for the public benefit, and, in a civil action, allowing a plea in mitigation of liability that the libel was inserted without malice and negligence on the part of the newspaper owner) and the Fatal Accidents Act of 1846 (an action for wrongful death by the deceased's representatives), are still known as Lord Campbell's Acts.

Lord chief justice of England In 1846 the whigs were unexpectedly returned and Campbell was made chancellor of the duchy of Lancaster, with a seat in the cabinet; he wanted to return to Ireland but the cabinet concluded that the Irish chancellorship should be held by an Irishman. He claimed that he did the work, both in the Lords and in the cabinet, of the lord chancellor, Cottenham, who cared only for his court of chancery. In 1849 the lord chief justice, Denman, had a number of paralytic seizures. It became evident that he was unlikely to resume his judicial duties. The prime minister, Russell, assured Campbell that the office would be his. But Denman, who still smarted from Campbell's censure of his judgment in *Stockdale* v. *Hansard*, was reluctant to resign if Campbell was to succeed him. The succession became public knowledge and was publicly debated, *The Spectator* suggesting that Campbell was seeking to assassinate Denman by spreading ill-founded stories about his ill health. Campbell complained that he was 'assailed by a storm of flippancy, scurrility, and falsehood' (*Life*, ed. Hardcastle, 2.271). After months of uncertainty, heightened by the whig administration's tiny majority, Denman resigned in March 1850, and at the age of seventy Campbell became lord chief justice. He held this office until 1859. Even as chief justice he participated in the debates of the House of Lords, particularly on legal issues. He joined Lyndhurst in opposing the Wensleydale life peerage, presided over the committee whose report was the basis of the Divorce and Matrimonial Act of 1857, and was the progenitor of the Obscene Publications Act of 1857.

Lord chancellor In 1859 the Liberal Party regained power. Despite Bethell's protests Palmerston offered the great seal to Campbell. Campbell was in his eightieth year, but still vigorous. Apart from his chairmanship of the real property commissioners and his six weeks in Ireland he had no experience of the procedure and doctrine of the court of chancery. Campbell accepted the offer with alacrity, and remained on the woolsack until his death. He was undeterred by the challenge.

> To qualify [myself], during the vacation I looked over all the equity decisions during the last ten years … I did not meet any case which I did not understand, or on which, after hearing it well argued, I could not have given a satisfactory judgment. (*Life*, ed. Hardcastle, 2.383)

His prophecy that he had 'no hope of being quoted as a great Equity authority' (ibid.) proved correct; but he cleared most of the arrears, deciding 'off-hand' many cases which came before him. His judicial patronage was scrupulous and courageous, as demonstrated by his appointment of Blackburn as a judge of the king's bench, 'the fittest man in Westminster Hall, although wearing a stuff gown' (ibid., 2.372).

Reputation as a judge As a judge Campbell's reputation is built upon the thirteen volumes of cases reported by Adolphus and Ellis and by Ellis and Blackburn when he was chief justice of the queen's bench. His judgments are distinguished by a profound knowledge of the unreformed common law; very few of his decisions were reversed and some continue to be cited as authoritative. In court his irascibility sorely tried the patience of some senior counsel. Serjeant Ballantine accused him of a lack of compassion: 'he crushed where he ought to have striven to raise' (Ballantine, 124). The *Dictionary of Eminent Scotsmen* declared that 'while Denman possessed a noble and commanding presence which compelled respect, Lord Campbell was neither dignified in appearance nor eloquent in speech'. Yet the bar respected him, and would have endorsed Holdsworth's opinion that he was one of the greatest common lawyers of the age of reform (1833–75; Holdsworth, *Eng. law*, 429).

Literary reputation Campbell is best remembered for his legal biographies. The first series of the *Lives of the Lord Chancellors* (to 1689) appeared in 1845, the second (to 1806) a year later, and the third (to 1827) in 1847, seven volumes in all. A final volume on Lyndhurst and Brougham was not published until after the death of the author and his subjects. The three volumes of *Lives of the Chief Justices*, a more modest work, were published in 1847, 1849, and 1857 respectively. The *Lives*, over 6000 pages, written in a short time-span, were an extraordinary achievement. But his *Shakespeare's Legal Acquirements Considered*, which was derivative, attracted hostile criticism.

The *Lives of the Lord Chancellors* offer the best evidence of Campbell's merits and failings as an author. They were immediately popular with royalty, politicians, judges, and members of the bar. Posterity has been less kind. Macdonell described them as 'the most censurable publications in our literature' (*DNB*, 8.383); Wetherell said that they added a new sting to death (Brougham, 3.435). Campbell is a good story teller who enlivens the pages with entertaining anecdotes. Macaulay described the *Lives* as a 'most amusing book' (Macaulay to Frances Macaulay, 2 March 1850, *Letters of T. B. Macaulay*, ed. T. Pinney, 6 vols., 1974–81, 5.96). Its pages are 'the repository of a vast mass of tradition, legal and general' (Atlay, 2.184–5). Campbell's legal memory rivalled that of Lyndhurst and Brougham. One of the judges on his first circuit had been called to the bar in 1762, and as a young student he had seen and heard both Thurlow and Kenyon (ibid.). Some of his portraits are vivid and acute characterizations, drawn in a style which Holdsworth described as 'colloquial and ungrammatical' but not 'without its charm' (Holdsworth, *Eng. law*, 417). But Campbell was no historian. He rarely used primary sources and treated manuscript letters and gossip with the same authority. Frequently he plagiarized. There are egregious factual errors, often the product of malice.

Final assessment Brougham and Lyndhurst were much cleverer and quicker witted than Campbell, and 'delighted to play on his weaknesses and render him ludicrous' (*The Athenaeum*, 30 Jan 1869, 66). 'His personality seemed to rouse all the spirit of mischief in Lyndhurst, and on Brougham he acted like a red handkerchief to a bull' (Atlay, 2.209). 'Self-satisfaction carried [him] unscathed through the ordeal' (ibid., 2.210), but clearly the taunts rankled. Campbell's vignettes of these lord chancellors led Chief Baron Pollock to condemn Campbell, the biographer, as '*base and contemptible*. The truth is Campbell was neither *honorable* nor even *honest*' (Hanworth, 203). Campbell was maladroit and tactless, lacking 'taste and refinement' (C. C. F. Greville, *A Journal of the Reign of Queen Victoria*, 3, 1887, 327). Many were astonished to read, in his life of Eldon, his prediction that 'the world may decide that I have finished my biographical labours without forfeiting my claim to impartiality' (Campbell, *Lives of the Lord Chancellors*, 3rd edn, 1848, 7.696). Thin-skinned and insensitive, he quarrelled with many of his contemporaries, Lyndhurst, Brougham, Denman, Bethell, Parke, and his vice-chancellors; and, having quarrelled, he rarely forgave (Brougham, 3.434–5). His aggressive self-confidence and unconcealed ambition were unattractive. Always determined to reach the top of his profession Campbell quite shamelessly pressed his claims to office. So, in 1834 he irritated Brougham, the chancellor, by writing over his head to the prime minister, Grey, to 'state … with *manly sincerity* the disappointment' he felt at not succeeding Baron Bayley. Campbell lacked dignity and gravitas (ibid., 3.343–5).

Campbell's warts are all too evident. But they cannot detract from his great service as a law officer, chief justice and lord chancellor, legislator and law reformer. He could, moreover, be generous, as his moving tributes to Follett (Atlay, 190) and Denman (*Life*, ed. Hardcastle, 2.265) demonstrate. But his affection was largely reserved for his family. He felt keenly the deaths of his father and brother, and never recovered from the death of his wife in 1860. 'I never expect', he wrote, 'an hour of real happiness in this world, notwithstanding all the devoted and never-ceasing solicitude to comfort me of all my children' (ibid., 2.393).

On 22 June 1861 Campbell sat in court, attended a cabinet meeting, and in the evening gave a large dinner party. The following day a servant found him dead in his armchair at his home, Stratheden House, Knightsbridge. His petition against a lingering illness had been felicitously heard. He was buried at Jedburgh Abbey on 29 June.

Gareth H. Jones and Vivienne Jones

Sources *Life of John, Lord Campbell, lord high chancellor of Great Britain*, ed. Mrs Hardcastle, 2 vols. (1881) • Holdsworth, *Eng. law*, vol. 15 • J. B. Atlay, *The Victorian chancellors*, 2 vols. (1906–8) • E. Manson, *Builders of our law during the reign of Queen Victoria*, 2nd edn (1904) • W. Bagehot, *Literary studies*, ed. R. H. Hutton, new edn (1905) • Chambers, *Scots*. (1835) • Lord Hanworth [E. M. P. Hanworth], *Lord Chief Baron Pollock: a memoir* (1929) • W. Ballantine, *Some experiences of a barrister's life*, 3rd edn, 2 vols. (1882) • H. P. Brougham, *The life and times of Henry, Lord Brougham*, ed. W. Brougham, 3 vols. (1871) • *The*

Times (24 June 1861) • *Solicitors' Journal*, 5 (1860–61), 598–600 • *Law Times* (29 June 1861) • *Law Magazine*, 27 (1842) [various speeches]
Archives NRA Scotland, priv. coll., corresp. and papers | Cornwall RO, letters to Walter Coulson • NL Scot., letters to James Browne • NL Scot., corresp. with John Lee • PRO, corresp. with Lord Russell, PRO 30/22 • U. Durham L., letters to third Earl Grey • U. Southampton L., corresp. with Lord Palmerston
Likenesses J. Steell, marble bust, 1843, Scot. NPG • F. Grant, oils, 1850, NPG • T. Woolnoth, oils, *c*.1851, NPG [*see illus.*] • G. F. Watts, oils, *c*.1860, Palace of Westminster, London • J. Doyle, three caricatures, BM • G. Hayter, group portrait, oils (*The House of Commons, 1833*), NPG • D. Wilkie, group portrait, oils (*The first council of Queen Victoria, 1837*), Royal Collection • T. Woolnoth, study, Scot. NPG • photographs, NPG • portrait, oils, Scot. NPG
Wealth at death £120,000: probate, 25 July 1861, *CGPLA Eng. & Wales*

Campbell, Sir John (1780–1863), army officer in the Portuguese service, was born at Chatham Dockyard, Chatham, Kent, at the official residence of his father, William Campbell, commissioner of the Navy Board, and his wife, who was the daughter of Major Pitcairn of the Royal Marines, who died in 1775 at the battle of Bunker Hill during the American War of Independence. After attending Harrow School, in 1800 he obtained a cornetcy in the 7th hussars (Queen's Own light dragoons), in which he was promoted lieutenant in 1801 and captain in 1806. He served as brigade major on the staff of General Robert Craufurd's force in the attack on Buenos Aires in 1807. In 1808 he went to the Peninsula, where he fought at Sahagun and Benavente under Lord Paget. He returned to Portugal on the cavalry staff in 1809 and was transferred, as lieutenant-colonel, to the Portuguese cavalry under Marshal Beresford.

Campbell was a distinguished cavalry officer who served under Rowland Hill and Lowry Cole in the later years of the Peninsular War. The duke of Wellington commended his services, as later did the historian Charles Oman. In the later years of the war, as allied strength grew in the Peninsula, Campbell operated near Hill's position around the River Guadiana. During the allied advance into France, his Portuguese brigade fought well. At the peace of 1814 he accepted an offer to remain in Portugal, and for the next six years was actively engaged in the organization of the Portuguese forces. On 9 March 1815 he was created a knight bachelor in the United Kingdom, and also in 1815 a knight of the Tower and Sword of Portugal. In the following year he married Doña Maria Brigida de Faria e Lacerda of Lisbon. In 1820 he obtained the rank of major-general in the Portuguese army, and was also colonel of the 4th cavalry and deputy quartermaster-general.

When the liberal movement to install a constitutional government began, Campbell resigned from the Portuguese service and returned to England. Since he had retained his rank of brevet lieutenant-colonel in the British army, to which he had been advanced in 1812, he was appointed lieutenant-colonel of the 75th foot, which rank he held from 1820 to 1824, when he retired by the sale of his commission. Although absent from Portugal, he had corresponded regularly with the absolutist party there, and when Dom Miguel seized the throne, he was summoned to his aid and appointed major-general; on 5 October 1825 he was made knight commander of the Tower and Sword. He worked as zealously for his patron as did Sir Charles Napier for the opposing party of Doña Maria de Gloria, but unsuccessfully. His efforts to raise a naval force in the United Kingdom failed, though his opponents, the constitutionalists, had more success in raising support, evading the provisions of the Foreign Enlistment Act. When he actually took the field against the constitutionalists at Oporto, he accomplished nothing worthy of his old reputation as a dashing cavalry officer. When Dom Miguel acknowledged defeat, Campbell returned to England and retired from public life. He lived quietly and almost forgotten in London, where in 1842 he married his second wife, Harriet Maria Meadows, widow of Major-General Sir Alexander Dickson, adjutant-general Royal Artillery. He died at his residence, 51 Charles Street, Berkeley Square, London, on 19 December 1863, in his eighty-fourth year.

H. M. CHICHESTER, *rev.* GORDON L. TEFFETELLER

Sources Fortescue, *Brit. army* • *GM*, 3rd ser., 16 (1864), 389–90 • W. F. P. Napier, *History of the war in the Peninsula and in the south of France, from the year 1807 to the year 1814*, new edn, 6 vols. (1877–82) • C. W. C. Oman, *A history of the Peninsular War*, 7 vols. (1902–30) • A. I. Shand, *Wellington's lieutenants* (1902) • *The dispatches of … the duke of Wellington … from 1799 to 1818*, ed. J. Gurwood, 13 vols. in 12 (1834–9) • *Supplementary despatches (correspondence) and memoranda of Field Marshal Arthur, duke of Wellington*, ed. A. R. Wellesley, second duke of Wellington, 15 vols. (1858–72) • Boase, *Mod. Eng. biog.* • *Dod's Peerage* (1858) • *CGPLA Eng. & Wales* (1864)
Likenesses C. Baugniet, lithograph, BM • C. Baugniet, lithograph (with Lady Campbell), BM
Wealth at death under £10,000: resworn probate, March 1864, *CGPLA Eng. & Wales*

Campbell, John (1795–1867), Congregational minister and journal editor, only child of Alexander Campbell, surgeon, was born on 5 October 1795 at Kirriemuir, Forfarshire. He was educated at local schools then went to sea, but he deserted his ship at Fakenham, Norfolk, and walked home. He then worked as a blacksmith in Dundee. After an evangelical conversion in 1815 he secured private tuition and entered the University of St Andrews in October 1817; in 1819 he migrated to the University of Glasgow. For about a year he renounced Calvinism and joined the Methodists, becoming so enthusiastic an itinerant evangelist that he was disciplined by his new denomination. He then became an ardent Congregationalist. In 1823, at the end of his studies, his open-air preaching resulted in the formation of a church at Kilmarnock. He was ordained in February 1827 by Ralph Wardlaw (1779–1853) and Greville Ewing (1767–1841). On 24 January 1827, at Kilmarnock, he married Agnes Crichton, a schoolteacher from Irvine. They had four sons and three daughters.

During visits to London, Campbell attracted the attention of Matthew Wilks (1749–1829), who nominated him to be his successor as minister of Tabernacle, Moorfields, and Tottenham Court Chapel. He was minister there until 1848 when an affliction to his voice and the attractions of journalism led him to resign. Since 1829 he had contributed to the *Eclectic Review* (though no articles have yet been firmly attributed to him) and *The Patriot*, of which he became joint proprietor with Josiah Pratt (1768–1844). In

1844 he was invited by the Congregational Union to edit the monthly *Christian Witness* and in autumn 1845 he became editor also of the *Christian's Penny Magazine*. At the invitation of Thomas Challis, chairman of the managers of *The Patriot* and later lord mayor of London, he undertook in 1848 to edit the weekly *British Banner*. After disagreement with the proprietors he resigned in 1856, but immediately launched the *British Standard*, which he edited until his retirement in 1866. He was one of the most successful nonconformist editors of his age. The *Christian Witness* achieved a steady circulation of 31,000, and the *Christian's Penny Magazine* a surprising 100,000.

Campbell revelled in controversy. His two churches were proprietary chapels and he took legal action to transform them into independent churches. He came to national prominence in his campaign against the monopoly on Bible printing in 1840–41. He was an extremely pugnacious journalist and no person or institution was safe from his attacks. He severely criticized the Evangelical Alliance and the Anti-State Church Association, and the Roman Catholic church was a constant target. Above all he was, in his own words, 'ever on the watch tower as to every appearance of heresy', and 'heresy' meant deviation from Calvinist orthodoxy. It was this enthusiasm that led him to condemn in unmeasured terms the lack of evangelical content in the poems published by Thomas Toke Lynch in his book *The Rivulet* (1855). The resulting controversy all but destroyed the Congregational Union, and led to the union's resolution to cease direct sponsorship of the *Christian Witness* and the *Christian's Penny Magazine*. Campbell's literary methods were rumbustious, truculent, and often crude, but excellent for circulation.

Campbell's wife died of apoplexy in November 1857. On 13 January 1866 at All Saints' Church, St John's Wood, he married his second wife, Emma Anna Fontaine, daughter of James Bacon, and widow of William Fontaine (1811–1854) of Hoxton. She survived him. He died at his home, Manor House, St John's Wood Park, on 26 March 1867 and was buried at Abney Park cemetery. Campbell's numerous books are undistinguished but they reveal his passionate interest in foreign missions and biography. In 1842 he published a biography of John Williams 'of Erromanga' (1796–1839), in 1844 one of David Nasmith (1799–1839), and in 1860 one of John Angell James (1785–1859).

R. Tudur Jones

Sources R. Ferguson and A. Morton Brown, *Life and labours of John Campbell, DD* (1867) • A. Peel, *These hundred years: a history of the Congregational Union of England and Wales, 1831–1931* (1931) • H. S. Skeats, *History of the free churches of England, 1688–1891*, later edn, ed. C. S. Miall [1891] • *The Times* (27 March 1867) • J. Waddington, *Congregational history*, 5 (1880) • W. White, *Memoir of Thomas T. Lynch* (1874) • *Christian Witness* (1854), 574–6

Likenesses J. Brown, engraving (after photograph), repro. in Ferguson and Morton Brown, *Life and labours of John Campbell* • Mr Gush, oils • W. Gush, mezzotint (after T. Woolnoth), NPG • T. Woolnoth, mezzotint (after W. Gush), NPG • photograph (as a young man), repro. in Peel, *These hundred years*

Wealth at death under £3000: probate, 27 April 1867, *CGPLA Eng. & Wales*

Campbell, John, second marquess of Breadalbane (1796–1862), politician and courtier, known in his younger days as Lord Glenorchy, and, after his father's elevation to the marquessate in 1831, as earl of Ormelie, was born at Dundee on 26 October 1796. He was the son of John, fourth earl and first marquess of Breadalbane (1762–1834), and his wife, Mary (*d.* 1845), daughter of David Gavin. After attending Eton College, he represented Okehampton from 1820 to 1826 (as Lord Glenorchy). From 1832 (after a brilliant electoral campaign) until 1834 he represented Perthshire as a whig, then being styled Lord Ormelie. He had married on 23 November 1821, at Mellerstain, Eliza (*d.* 28 Aug 1861), eldest daughter of the late George Baillie of Jerviswood, and sister of the tenth earl of Haddington; they had no children.

On 29 March 1834, on the death of his father, Campbell succeeded to the marquessate and became a member of the House of Lords. He held the office of lord chamberlain from 1848 to 1852, and again from 1853 to 1858. From 1840 to 1842 he was lord rector of the University of Glasgow. His wife was a lady of the bedchamber from January until July 1839. During the controversy between the Church of Scotland and the civil courts Breadalbane was conspicuous for his earnest advocacy of the 'non-intrusion' cause. In that connection he was by far the most outstanding man among the laity. Though not a great speaker, he advocated the cause in the House of Lords, as well as in public meetings, and when the Free Church was set up in Scotland in 1843, he joined it and was one of its most munificent supporters. In 1840 he led the opposition in the House of Lords to the earl of Aberdeen's bill on the church question, and, though defeated, contributed significantly towards the withdrawal of the bill by its author soon afterwards.

Breadalbane was an energetic supporter of the volunteers and an enthusiastic freemason (being grand master of the freemasons, 1824–6), and was president of the Scottish Society of Antiquaries in 1852–62. He was a lavish bibliophile. He was governor of the Bank of Scotland in 1861–2. He was also KT, FRS, and president of the Literary Association of the Friends of Poland. Despite his evangelicalism, he enjoyed ornate architecture and employed James Gillespie Graham (1777–1855) from 1834 to expand and Gothicize his already vast seat, Taymouth Castle. Breadalbane's books were housed in a splendid new library. From 7 to 10 September 1842, Queen Victoria stayed at the castle during her first Scottish visit; she revisited it incognito in 1866, so much did she enjoy the visit. Breadalbane wore highland dress; 'it seemed as if a great chieftain in olden feudal times was receiving his sovereign', the queen noted (*Journal*, 24). Breadalbane kept American buffaloes at Taymouth. He died while on holiday at the Hôtel Beau Rivage, Ouchy, near Lausanne, Switzerland, on 8 November 1862, his British titles becoming extinct and his Scottish title (earl of Breadalbane) passing to his fourth cousin once removed, John Alexander Gavin Campbell (*d.* 1922).

W. G. Blaikie, *rev.* H. C. G. Matthew

Sources W. Chalmers, *In memoriam: Lord Breadalbane* (1862?) • GEC, *Peerage* • *GM*, 3rd ser., 13 (1862), 779–80 • R. Buchanan, *The ten*

years' conflict, 2 vols. (1849) • *The Witness* (Oct 1862) • A. Rowan, 'Taymouth Castle, Perthshire', *Country Life*, 136 (1964), 978–81 • Queen Victoria, *Leaves from the journal of our life in the highlands*, ed. A. Helps (1868)
Archives NA Scot., corresp. and papers • NL Scot., corresp. and papers • NRA Scotland, priv. coll., corresp. and papers | BL OIOC, letters to Lord Tweeddale • Hunt. L., corresp. with Grenville family • NA Scot., letters to second Lord Panmure • W. Sussex RO, letters to duke of Richmond
Likenesses G. Hayter, portrait, 1834, NPG • G. Harvey, group portrait, oils, Scot. NPG • G. Hayter, group portrait, oils (*The House of Commons, 1833*), NPG • B. Thorvaldsen, bust, Thorvaldsen Museum, Copenhagen, Denmark
Wealth at death £374,230 4*s*. 2*d*.: confirmation, 26 June 1863, NA Scot., SC 49/31/75, p. 1148

Campbell, Sir John (1802–1878), army officer in the East India Company, was born at Kingsburgh in the island of Skye, the eldest son of John Campbell (1771–1827) of Lochend, Argyll, and Annabella, daughter of John Campbell of Melfort. He was commissioned ensign in the 19th regiment in 1819, but he entered the East India Company's service in 1820, and on 5 April was appointed a lieutenant in the 41st Madras native infantry, and was stationed in various cantonments in the Madras presidency until his promotion to the rank of captain in 1830. In 1834 his regiment was ordered to quell an insurrection among the hill peoples in the province of Kimedy in Orissa, and on the death of Major Barclay, Campbell commanded the regiment with great success. His knowledge of Orissa caused him to be again employed in the Goomsur War of 1836–7, and at the end of this war he was placed in civil charge of the Gonds, or hill people of Orissa, with special instructions to suppress human sacrifice and female infanticide.

Campbell soon obtained a notable control over them, and, without resorting once to the use of troops, managed to save the lives of hundreds of destined victims by a consistent policy of expelling from the hills all refractory village headmen and by refusing to trust to native agents. In 1842 he accompanied his former regiment, the 41st Madras native infantry, to China as senior major, and for his services there he was promoted lieutenant-colonel and made a CB in December 1842. After his return to Madras he commanded his regiment in cantonments for five years.

Meanwhile the Gonds were not prospering under his successor in Orissa, Captain Macpherson, who had entirely changed Campbell's policy, and preferred to rely upon the influence of their headmen, whom he recalled to their villages; in one of them, named Sam Bye, a particular foe of Campbell's, he placed special confidence. Disturbances broke out, and in 1847 Campbell was ordered to supersede Captain Macpherson and to take up his previous appointment. He at once resumed his old system of government, the headmen and Sam Bye were again expelled, and he ruled the Gonds in his former absolute fashion. In 1849 he had to go to the Cape for his health for two years; in 1853 he was promoted colonel, and in 1855, when he was on the eve of obtaining his colonel's allowances, he finally resigned his appointment, and returned to Scotland after an absence of thirty-six years.

Campbell took up his residence at Edinburgh, and on 28 November 1859 he was promoted major-general. In 1861 he published, for private circulation, a narrative of his operations in Orissa, which was so appreciated that in 1864 he published his *Personal Narrative*, in which he deplored Macpherson's 'mistakes in judgment'. His book was immediately followed by one by Macpherson's brother, who vigorously contested many of Campbell's statements. The controversy created some excitement, and drew such attention to Campbell's services that he was made a KCSI in 1869. In 1867 he was promoted lieutenant-general, and in 1872 general. He was married and had a son. He died at his residence, 1 Hampton Terrace, Edinburgh, on 21 April 1878.

H. M. Stephens, *rev.* James Lunt

Sources M.O.C., *The Campbells of Melfort* (1882) • J. Campbell, *Narrative by Major-General John Campbell of his operations in the hill tracts of Orissa for the suppression of human sacrifices and female infanticide* (privately printed, 1861) • J. Campbell, *A personal narrative of thirteen years' service amongst the wild tribes of Khondistan for the suppression of human sacrifice* (1864) • W. Macpherson, ed., *Memorials of service in India from the correspondence of the late Major Samuel Charters Macpherson, CB* (1865) • W. W. Hunter, *Orissa* (1827) • P. Woodruff [P. Mason], *The men who ruled India*, 1: *The founders* (1953), 248–53 • Boase, *Mod. Eng. biog.* • C. E. Buckland, *Dictionary of Indian biography* (1906)
Wealth at death £54,794 4*s*. 7*d*.: probate, 13 June 1878, *CCI*

Campbell, Sir John, second baronet (1807–1855), army officer, was born on 14 April 1807, the only son of Lieutenant-General Sir Archibald *Campbell of Ava, first baronet (1769–1843), and Helen (*d*. 12 Oct 1848), daughter of John Macdonald of Garth, Perthshire. He entered the army in 1821 as an ensign in the 38th regiment, which his father commanded, and joined it in India. He served as aide-de-camp to his father throughout the First Anglo-Burmese War, and on 1 July 1824 he was promoted lieutenant, without purchase, and in 1826 thanked by the governor-general in council. On 11 July 1826 he was promoted to a company, and remained in Burma in a civil capacity until 1829, when he returned to England and joined the depot of his regiment. From 1831 to 1837 Campbell was aide-de-camp to his father when lieutenant-governor of New Brunswick, and in the latter year purchased the majority of his regiment.

In 1840 Campbell purchased the lieutenant-colonelcy of the 38th, and commanded it in the Mediterranean, the West Indies, and Nova Scotia, until, as a keen and successful regimental officer, he was selected to command a brigade in the expeditionary force intended for the East in 1854. He married on 21 July 1841 Helen Margaret (*d*. 6 May 1883), only child of Colonel John Crowe EICS; they had five sons and three daughters. In October 1843 he succeeded to the baronetcy. On 11 November 1851 he was promoted colonel by brevet, and on 24 March 1854 was posted to the command of the 2nd brigade of the 3rd division under Major-General Sir Richard England, with the rank of brigadier-general. With his brigade he was at the Alma and Inkerman, and on 12 December 1854 he was promoted major-general.

After Inkerman, as the senior brigadier-general Campbell temporarily commanded the 4th division. On 7 June 1855 he was superseded by Lieutenant-General Bentinck, and on hearing of the intended assault upon the Redan he volunteered to lead the detachments of the 4th division to the attack. On 18 June he displayed 'a courage amounting to rashness', for after sending away his aides-de-camp, Captain Hume and Captain Snodgrass, he rushed out of the trenches with a few followers, and fell at once while cheering on his men. In *The Gazette* of 5 July it was announced that had he survived he would have been made a KCB. He was buried on Cathcart's Hill in the Crimea.

H. M. STEPHENS, *rev.* JAMES LUNT

Sources H. H. Wilson, *Documents illustrative of the Burmese war* (1827) • Major Snodgrass [J. J. Snodgrass], *Narrative of the Burmese war* (1827) • Fortescue, *Brit. army*, vols. 11, 13 • A. W. Kinglake, *The invasion of the Crimea*, [new edn], 9 vols. (1877–88) • C. Hibbert, *The destruction of Lord Raglan* [1961] • *GM*, 2nd ser., 44 (1855) • Boase, *Mod. Eng. biog.* • Burke, *Peerage* • W. H. Russell, *The British expedition to the Crimea* (1858)

Likenesses engraving, repro. in *ILN*, 17 (1855), 373

Campbell, John Charles [Jock] (1894–1942), army officer, was born at Thurso, Caithness, on 10 January 1894, the second child and only son of Daniel Alexander Campbell, later in business in India, and his wife, Marion, daughter of Donald MacKay, sheep farmer, of Skelpick, Sutherland. He was educated at Sedbergh School, and on the first day of war in 1914 he enlisted in the Honourable Artillery Company. In July 1915 he was commissioned second lieutenant from the Royal Military Academy, Woolwich. He joined the British expeditionary force (BEF) in August, was wounded in February and May 1916, and in September was sent back to England, but returned to the front in August 1917. At the end of the war he was serving in France as a captain in the Royal Horse Artillery and had been awarded the MC.

Between the wars Campbell made his mark as a riding instructor at Woolwich and later at Weedon, Northamptonshire, with a reputation of being an ideal regimental officer and a first-class horseman. He was fond of all animals and devoted to horses. An excellent polo player, he was in all three Royal Artillery teams which won the inter-regimental polo cup, and for some years was probably unsurpassed in the shires as a heavyweight rider to hounds. On 12 September 1922 Campbell married Rosamond Elizabeth Rhodes (*b.* 1901/2), daughter of William Rhodes JP and great-niece of Cecil Rhodes. They had two daughters.

The outbreak of war in 1939 found him a major in command of C battery, 4th regiment, Royal Horse Artillery, in Egypt. In July 1940 he succeeded to the command of his regiment, and when in September the Italian advance began, he soon distinguished himself by the boldness and judgement with which he handled his guns in a series of rearguard actions while commanding alternately the 4th and 3rd regiments. During this period he organized and

John Charles Campbell (1894–1942), by unknown photographer [detail]

led a number of mobile columns, consisting of a few guns and escort, against the Italian communications, and when used against the Germans these were nicknamed, after him, 'Jock columns'. For this service he was appointed to the DSO. During the long advance to Benghazi in which, for his work on 14 December 1940, he received a bar to the DSO, Campbell displayed the same dash and enterprise, and during the subsequent retreat to Sollum he rendered marked service.

The climax of Campbell's career came in the autumn of 1941 when, on 3 September, he was appointed to the command of the 7th support group with the rank of brigadier. His handling of the group during the two most critical days of the battle of Sidi Rezegh (21 and 22 November) became an epic of the war. When almost surrounded by superior forces, Campbell showed great bravery. Three times he led tank forces against the advancing enemy, guiding his troops from his open car with a blue handkerchief, and three times he helped personally in the service of the guns at critical moments of the battle. Though wounded, he refused to be evacuated. For this work he was awarded the VC.

The following February Campbell was appointed to command the 7th armoured division with the rank of major-general, but on 26 February 1942 he was killed in a motor accident at Halfaya Pass, Egypt. There is a memorial to him at Sedbergh School.

ALFRED BURNE, *rev.* K. D. REYNOLDS

Sources *Army List* • R. Farran, *Winged dagger* (1948) • J. A. I. Agar-Hamilton and L. C. F. Turner, *The Sidi Rezeg battles, 1941* (1957) • personal knowledge (1959) • m. cert.
Archives IWM, diaries
Likenesses photograph, IWM [*see illus.*]
Wealth at death £24,540 14*s*. 4*d*.: probate, 20 July 1943, *CGPLA Eng. & Wales*

Campbell, John Francis, of Islay (1821?–1885), folklorist, was born in Edinburgh probably on 29 December 1821, the eldest son of Walter Frederick Campbell of Islay (1798–1855), MP for Argyllshire, and his first wife, Lady Eleanor Charteris (1796–1832), eldest daughter of Francis Charteris, seventh earl of Wemyss. John Francis would have succeeded as laird of Islay were it not for the enormous debt of £800,000 incurred by his father on improvements to the island. Creditors forced the sale of Islay and the family left in 1847. After his father's death John Francis was known as Campbell of Islay, even though the island was no longer in the family's possession. He was educated at Eton College and at the University of Edinburgh, and in May 1851 was called to the bar by the Inner Temple. In 1854 Campbell was appointed private secretary to his cousin, George, eighth duke of Argyll, and he later held several government posts including that of secretary to the Coal Commission.

Campbell devoted much of his time to collecting folklore, particularly in the Western Isles. As a native he spoke Gaelic fluently, so could build up a strong rapport with the indigenous population. In this manner he collected a large number of traditional folk-tales, which he published under the title *Popular Tales of the West Highlands Orally Collected, with a Translation* (4 vols., 1860–62). Campbell was also a keen observer of nature, and devoted much attention to geology and meteorology; particularly worthy of mention is a two-volume work published in 1865 entitled *Frost and Fire, Natural Engines, Toolmarks and Chips, with Sketches taken at Home and Abroad by a Traveller.* A reliable scientific method for recording sunshine hours occupied Campbell's mind for many years, the culmination of his efforts coming in 1883 when he published a book entitled *Thermography.* Campbell died at Cannes on 17 February 1885, and was buried there. He was survived by his widow, Katherine Isabella. Although a natural scientific curiosity was evident throughout his life, it is as a collector of Gaelic oral tradition that he is perhaps best remembered.

JAMES A. PRATT

Sources J. Mackechnie, 'Introduction', 'John Francis Campbell (Iain Og Ile) and his place in the literary history of the highlands', *The Dewar manuscripts*, ed. J. Mackechnie (1963), 17–56 • R. M. Dorson, *The British folklorists: a history* (1968), 392–418 • F. G. Thompson, 'John Francis Campbell', *Transactions of the Gaelic Society of Inverness*, 54 (1984–6), 1–57 • A. Nutt, 'The Campbell of Islay MSS, at the Advocates Library, Edinburgh', *Folk-Lore*, 1 (1890), 369–81 • M. A. Mackay, 'Here I am in another world: John Francis Campbell and Tiree', *Scottish Studies*, 32 (1993), 119–24 • F. Thompson, 'J. F. Campbell: Victorian polymath', *Lamp-lighter and storyteller* (1985), 7–9 [exhibition catalogue, NL Scot.] • I. F. Maciver, 'The John Campbell of Islay papers', *Quarto* [NL Scot. newsletter], 6 (1999), 3 • J. Foster, *Members of parliament, Scotland … 1357–1882*, 2nd edn (privately printed, London, 1882) • *Scots peerage* • W. Donaldson, *The highland pipe and Scottish society, 1750–1950* (2000) • *ILN* (28 Feb 1885) • *ILN* (21 March 1885) • *The Athenaeum* (1885), 250 • *The Academy*, 27 (1885), 151 • Burke, *Gen. GB*
Archives NL Scot., genealogical papers • NL Scot., geological and folklore notes • NL Scot., papers, Adv. MSS 50.1.1–51.2.7 | JRL, Bromley Davenport MSS • NL Scot., letters to John Stuart Blackie
Likenesses A. Campbell, drawings, repro. in *Dewar manuscripts*, ed. Mackechnie; priv. coll. • crayon drawing, repro. in *Dewar manuscripts*, ed. Mackechnie; priv. coll. • engraving (after C. Laurie, 1848), repro. in *Dewar manuscripts*, ed. Mackechnie • engraving (after photograph by Maull & Fox of Piccadilly), repro. in *ILN* (21 March 1885)
Wealth at death £52,456 11*s*. 5*d*.: will, 1 April 1885, *CGPLA Eng. & Wales*

Campbell, John George Edward Henry Douglas Sutherland, marquess of Lorne and ninth duke of Argyll (1845–1914), governor-general of Canada, was born on 6 August 1845 at Stafford House, London, the eldest son of George Douglas *Campbell, marquess of Lorne (1823–1900), and his wife, Lady Elizabeth Georgiana Sutherland-Leveson-Gower (*d.* 1878), the daughter of the second duke of Sutherland. Young Campbell, known in his family as Ian, assumed the courtesy title of marquess of Lorne in 1847 at the succession of his father as eighth duke of Argyll. He went to Eton College, and briefly to St Andrews University, where he supported the admission of women to lectures. After a year's tutoring in classics he proceeded to Trinity College, Cambridge, though his intellectual interests were more in science, history, and modern languages. He visited Jamaica in 1866, and spent a season at the University of Berlin, then another in Italy, all with the approval of his father, who felt Lorne's education was better served by travel than by Cambridge. His first book, *A Trip to the Tropics and Home through America*, was published in 1867.

Lorne represented Argyll in the House of Commons as a Liberal from 1868 to 1878. He made little mark in the house, and was chiefly occupied as private secretary to his father, whom W. E. Gladstone had appointed as secretary of state for India. Lorne had a flirtation with Gladstone's daughter Mary, but in 1870 events took a different turn. Not since 1515 had an English princess married within Great Britain; Queen Victoria now had a British husband in mind for her fourth and most attractive daughter, Princess Louise Caroline Alberta (1848–1939). In September 1870 five young British aristocrats were successively invited to Balmoral, with Lorne among them. The queen apparently liked everything about him except his nasal voice, a result of his having taken a cricket ball in the face while at Eton (he was, according to Vicary Gibbs's admirably concise physical description in the *Complete Peerage*, 'short, stout, with yellow hair, regular features, good complexion'), and he and Louise were married on 21 March 1871 at St George's Chapel, Windsor. Lorne refused a dukedom, and they went to live in Kensington Palace, with a country retreat near Tunbridge Wells, Kent. They had no children; after a few years this state of affairs gave rise to rumours that Lorne had homosexual inclinations. This is a view that some modern historians have been inclined to support, though it may simply have been that Louise was

John George Edward Henry Douglas Sutherland Campbell, marquess of Lorne and ninth duke of Argyll (1845–1914), by George Washington Wilson

unable to have children. Their marriage endured, and Louise was devastated at his death, but it appears that she sought a separation in the mid-1880s, and the couple spent long periods apart, celebrating their silver wedding separately.

In 1878 Lorne was appointed governor-general of Canada by Disraeli. He was a good choice; flexible, perspicacious, and sensitive, he became perhaps the most Canadian of all the British governor-generals, enjoying the climate of the new world, if not always the vagaries of its politics. In 1879 he was involved in controversy over Luc Letellier, the lieutenant-governor of Quebec, the dismissal of whom was desired by the Conservative federal government led by Sir John A. Macdonald. Lorne had opposed this, but, under instruction from the Colonial Office, acquiesced. This incident did not prevent Macdonald from describing the governor-general as 'a right good fellow, and a good Canadian' (*DNB*). In correspondence, Lorne put the word 'home' in quotation marks—an indication perhaps of his preference for Canada over Britain, but Princess Louise found life there less congenial. She was injured in a sleigh accident in February 1880 and returned to England. Lorne joined Louise for the winter of 1881–2, which he found dank and unhealthy compared with the Canadian winter, with its 'bright light and the dry and beautiful snow with its sapphire coloured shadows' (Lorne to Emma MacNeill, 29 Dec 1881, Lorne papers, National Archives of Canada).

Lorne was largely responsible for the creation in 1880 of the Royal Canadian Academy of Arts, which was followed in 1882 by the establishment of the Royal Society of Canada, which encompassed the English and French literary and scientific traditions. In 1881 he made a two-month expedition across the western Canadian prairies, at a time when the Canadian Pacific Railway was just being built. The expedition—of some seventy-seven men and ninety-six horses—left the railhead at Portage la Prairie, Manitoba, on 6 August. Lorne was tremendously impressed with the agricultural potential of the whole region, and overwhelmed with its beauty—especially at Fort Calgary, where mountains glittering with snow suddenly block the whole western horizon. His *Canadian Pictures Drawn with Pen and Pencil* (1884–5) was inspired by the trip, a good example of his artistic talent and flair for publicity.

In September 1882 Lorne took Louise to British Columbia, where both enjoyed the scenery and the climate; a mixture, as Lorne put it, of 'Scotland and Heaven' (Campbell, 56). The political consequences of their residence among the British Columbians were much improved relations between Victoria and the federal government in Ottawa. They returned east via the southern United States, with Louise wintering in Bermuda. She returned to Canada in April 1883, by which time Lorne had concluded that he should resign the post; he did so reluctantly, telling Macdonald that, for his own part, he would 'like to stay here all my days' (letter, 10 April 1883, John A. Macdonald papers, vol. 83, National Archives of Canada).

The furtherance of Lorne's career as an imperial administrator was stymied by Queen Victoria's desire to have Louise close by her: in 1900 he refused the governor-generalship of Australia. He immersed himself instead in the management of his Scottish estates and in authorship; his prolific output included a biography of Palmerston (1892), a pamphlet advocating imperial federation, and many travelogues and memoirs inspired by his stint in Canada, including *Yesterday and Today in Canada* (1910). In 1901 he published *V.R.I.: Her Life and Empire*, a lively and popular biography of Queen Victoria, and in 1907 his two-volume autobiography, *Passages from the Past*. He tried unsuccessfully for re-election to the House of Commons in 1885 (for Hampstead, as a Liberal) and 1892 (for Bradford Central, as a Liberal Unionist). He was eventually successful in 1895 as a Liberal Unionist for Manchester South; his estrangement from the Gladstonian Liberal Party was another point of difference with his wife, who was a supporter of Irish home rule. He became ninth duke of Argyll on the death of his father on 24 April 1900 but continued to be widely known by his courtesy title.

By this time Louise's enthusiasm for physical fitness had begun to show to her benefit; Lorne, by contrast, was content with a sedentary existence and was showing signs of eccentricity. Once, to his private amusement, he accepted the award of an order of the Black Eagle from the visiting

German Kaiser while wearing his dressing gown. In 1906 the couple travelled to Egypt, which Lorne disliked; his sister Frances observed that 'his heart is always in Canada' (Balfour, 2.414). After 1910 Lorne's health declined; he suffered from senility, and when visiting the Isle of Wight in April 1914 was struck with pneumonia. He died from this illness at Kent House, Cowes, on 2 May. After a memorial service in Westminster Abbey on 8 May, he was buried in the ancient family burial-ground at Kilmun, Argyll, on 15 May. He was succeeded in his titles by his nephew; his wife died on 3 December 1939.

Lorne was primarily a traveller and dilettante, whose greatest pleasures were literature and the great outdoors. It might be argued that his talents lacked focus; certainly the volume of his publications was not conducive to their overall quality or longevity. As governor-general of Canada, for which he is now best remembered, he was, however, generally regarded as a success. P. B. WAITE

Sources NA Canada, Lord Lorne MSS · NA Canada, Sir John A. Macdonald collection, political papers, MG26-A, vols. 80–83 · W. S. MacNutt, *Days of Lorne* (1955) · R. M. Stamp, *Royal rebels: Princess Louise and the marquis of Lorne* (1988) · D. G. Creighton, *John A. Macdonald: the old chieftain* (1955) · F. Balfour, *Ne obliviscaris: dinna forget*, 2 vols. (1930) · P. B. Waite, *Arduous destiny: Canada, 1874–1896* (1971) · J. Campbell, *Yesterday and today in Canada* (1910) · D. Duff, *The life story of H. R. H. Princess Louise, duchess of Argyll* (1940) · E. Longford, *Darling Loosey* (1991) · P. B. Waite, 'Campbell, John George Edward Henry Douglas Sutherland, marquess of Lorne and 9th duke of Argyll', *DCB*, vol. 14 · GEC, *Peerage*

Archives NA Canada, corresp. and papers · NRA, priv. coll., corresp. and papers | Berks. RO, corresp. with R. G. C. Glyn · BL, corresp. with W. E. Gladstone, Add. MSS 44416–44515, *passim* · BL, corresp. with Macmillans, Add. MS 55007 · Bodl. Oxf., corresp. with Sir William Harcourt · CUL, letters to H. A. Doubleday · Glos. RO, corresp. with Sir Michael Hicks Beach · Harrowby Manuscript Trust, Sandon Hall, Staffordshire, corresp. with earl of Harrowby · LPL, letters to A. C. Tait · NA Canada, Macdonald MSS · NL Scot., corresp. incl. with Lord Rosebery · NRA, priv. coll., corresp. with Sir John Ewart · Public Archives of Ontario, Toronto, corresp. with William Kirby

Likenesses W. H. Mate, stipple and line engraving, pubd 1855 (after W. S. Hernick), NPG · Ape [C. Pellegrini], watercolour caricature, 1870, NPG; repro. in *VF* (19 Nov 1870) · Count Gleichen, marble bust, exh. RA 1871, Inveraray Castle, Argyll and Bute · J. M. Barclay, oils, *c.*1872, Inveraray Castle, Argyll and Bute · H. von Angeli, oils, 1875, Royal Collection · photograph, *c.*1879, NA Canada, C-13227 · photograph, *c.*1881, NA Canada, C-5650 · J. E. Millais, oils, *c.*1884, National Gallery of Canada, Ottawa · B. Stone, photograph, 1898, NPG · S. P. Hale, oils, 1910, Inveraray Castle, Argyll and Bute · W. & D. Downey, carte-de-visite, NPG · Elliott & Fry, carte-de-visite, NPG; related photograph, NPG · Count Gleichen, pencil study, Royal Collection · S. P. Hale, group portrait, oils (*Marriage of Princess Louise and the marquess of Lorne, 1871*), Royal Collection · London Stereoscopic Co., carte-de-visite, NPG · London Stereoscopic Co., photograph, NPG · T. Rodger, carte-de-visite, NPG · Stuart of Glasgow, carte-de-visite (as young man), NPG · G. W. Wilson, carte-de-visite, NPG [*see illus.*] · pen-and-ink drawing, NPG · photograph, Royal Collection; repro. in Longford, *Darling Loosey*, 119

Wealth at death no information: R. M. Stamp, *Royal rebels: Princess Louise and the marquis of Lorne* (1988); *CGPLA Eng. & Wales* (1914) [no value given]

Campbell, John Lorne, of Canna (1906–1996), scholar of Scottish Gaelic folklore, was born in Edinburgh on 1 October 1906, the eldest son of Colonel Duncan Campbell, laird of Inverneill, Argyll, and his wife, Ethel, *née* Harriet, from New Jersey, USA. He was educated at Cargilfield School (near Edinburgh), Rugby School, and St John's College, Oxford. At Oxford he studied rural economy, graduating in 1929 and receiving a diploma in rural economy in 1930, but he also took up Gaelic studies under the guidance of John Fraser, then professor of Celtic at Jesus College. He had first become attracted to Gaelic on hearing young islanders speaking it in Oban, when he was in his teens. Rural economy and Gaelic studies were to be the twin interests of his working life.

Campbell's interests were quickly translated into action and publication. His *Highland Songs of the Forty-Five* was published in 1933, with full translations of thirty-two songs and poems by twelve eighteenth-century authors. In his preface he expressed his great indebtedness to John Fraser. A reprint, including corrections and additions, was published by the Scottish Gaelic Texts Society in 1984. In 1933 he went to Barra, in the southern Hebrides, where he met Compton Mackenzie. They set up the Sea League the same year, campaigning for strict fishing limits to protect local fishermen and fish stocks, and issuing *The Sea Leaguer*, a news-sheet for fishermen which included some Gaelic articles.

In 1934, while working on another book, *The Book of Barra*, with Compton Mackenzie, Campbell met Margaret Fay Shaw, the youngest daughter of Henry Clay Shaw, of Glenshaw, Pennsylvania. After studying piano in New York, London, and Paris, she had worked on recording songs and stories, and taking photographs, in South Uist from 1929 to 1935. They were married in Glasgow on 15 June 1935, with the service in Gaelic. There were no children. They both visited Nova Scotia soon after their marriage, and this began a long association with the Gaelic colonies in Canada, and collection of Gaelic songs from these communities. Margaret Fay Shaw published her *Folksongs and Folklore of South Uist* in 1955, with a second edition in 1977.

After three years together in Barra they bought the island of Canna, off the Inverness-shire coast, in 1938 (for £9000), and lived there thereafter, developing farming and cattle rearing, and encouraging and protecting the native community. Campbell became known as Fear Chanaidh (the laird of Canna), but his was a benevolent lairdship. At Canna House he and Margaret built up a formidable library and collection of Gaelic recordings and highland photographs. In 1981 they gave the island of Canna to the National Trust for Scotland, and subsequently arranged for their archive to be retained and protected at Canna House.

Campbell continued to take a close interest in environmental and community issues, and in conservation. In 1939 he collaborated with Sir Alexander MacEwen to produce *Act Now for the Highlands and Islands*, which included the suggestion of a highland development board. Another special interest was in collecting butterflies, and he pursued this both in Canna and in Italy, where he and his wife went for holidays over many years. They also visited Canada and the USA regularly. Over the years he was a voluminous correspondent: a passing remark in a letter could often trigger a two-page response.

Campbell's range of publications was wide, including *Gaelic in Scottish Education and Life* (1950), *Father Allan McDonald of Eriskay, 1859–1905* (1954), the Barra stories of John Macpherson, postmaster at Northbay, in *Tales from Barra Told by the Coddy* (1960), *The Furrow Behind Me*, the translated autobiography of the Hebridean crofter Angus MacLellan (1962), *Bàrdachd Mhgr Ailein air a deasachadh*, Father Allan's Gaelic verse (1965), *A Collection of Highland Rites and Customs* (1975), and some joint publications, including, with Derick Thomson, *Edward Lhuyd in the Scottish Highlands, 1699–1700* (1963), and, with Trevor H. Hall, *Strange Things: the Enquiry by the Society for Psychical Research into Second Sight in the Scottish Highlands* (1968). In 1984 he published *Canna: the Story of a Hebridean Island*, with revised editions in 1986 and 1994. There was also a continuous flow of articles in periodicals, on historical and literary topics, including several on the poetry of Alasdair Mac Mhaighstir Alasdair.

This wide range of publications contributed greatly to the understanding of highland life and history, but there can be little doubt that Campbell's most enduring life work was on Gaelic song as preserved in the oral tradition. He became deeply involved in this study in his Barra years, with the added stimulus of his wife's collecting work in South Uist, and this interest extended to the Gaelic colonies in Nova Scotia. Campbell converted to Catholicism at some point in the late 1930s, and had a tendency to concentrate on songs collected in Catholic areas, especially South Uist and Barra. With Francis Collinson he edited the three-volume *Hebridean Folksongs: a Collection of Waulking Songs made by Donald MacCormick in Kilphedir in South Uist in the Year 1893* (1969, 1977, 1981), and in 1990 he published *Songs Remembered in Exile*. The latter was a collection of traditional Gaelic songs from Nova Scotia, recorded in Cape Breton and Antigonish county in 1937; the tunes had mostly been transcribed by Séamus Ennis, a noted Irish collector of folk song. Campbell's work on folk song helped greatly to define the body of surviving work, particularly from the Catholic Hebrides and Nova Scotia, and especially in oral versions recorded in the nineteenth and twentieth centuries.

Campbell died on 25 April 1996 while he and his wife were on holiday near Fiesole, Florence, Italy, and staying in a nunnery in which there were Gaelic-speaking nuns. He had been awarded honorary degrees by the universities of Glasgow, Oxford, and St Francis Xavier in Antigonish, and had been made an OBE in 1990.

DERICK S. THOMSON

Sources personal knowledge (2004) • private information (2004) • *The Times* (1 May 1996) • *The Independent* (2 May 1996) • *Daily Telegraph* (8 May 1996) • M. F. Shaw, *From the Alleghenies to the Hebrides: an autobiography* (1993) • C. Mackenzie, *My life and times*, 10 vols. (1963–71)

Archives Canna House, Canna, archive | NL Scot., letters to Francis M. Collinson | FILM BFI NFTVA | SOUND BL NSA • BL NSA, 'Islanders', B4897/02 • BL NSA, other sound recording (field recordings, 1938) • Canna House, Canna

Likenesses photograph, repro. in *The Times* • photograph, repro. in *The Independent* • photograph, repro. in *Daily Telegraph* • photographs, repro. in Shaw, *From the Alleghenies to the Hebrides*

Wealth at death £227,607.86: confirmation, 11 Sept 1996, NA Scot., SC/CO 946/125

Campbell, John McLeod (1800–1872), Church of Scotland minister and theologian, was born on 4 May 1800 at Ardmaddy House, near Kilninver, the eldest son of the Revd Donald Campbell and his wife, Mary MacLeod of Raasay (*c*.1767–1806). Donald Campbell, the minister for Kilninver and Kilmeford, Argyll, was educated at King's College, Aberdeen. Following the death of his wife in 1806 he assumed the care and education of his children, fostering a relationship of mutual respect and affection that proved significant for the younger Campbell's theological development. Through his mother, John was related to the Macleods of Morvern, a dynasty of Scottish ministers.

John McLeod Campbell matriculated in 1811 at Glasgow University, having received from his father a good introduction to academic discipline and classical languages. His course in arts and divinity took nine years, after which he attended Edinburgh University, receiving his licence to preach from the presbytery of Lorn in 1821, and preaching his first sermon as a licentiate, in Gaelic, in his father's church at Kilninver. He continued to study in Edinburgh for a further four years.

In 1825 Campbell was presented by the duke of Argyll to the parish church of Rhu, near Glasgow, on the banks of the Gare Loch. During his first two years of ministry he attracted relatively little attention. Campbell came, however, to believe and preach that 'assurance is of the essence of faith', meaning that the essence of Christian faith lies in each believer's assurance of God's love for him individually. This teaching implied what theologians of the time called 'unlimited atonement', the doctrine that Christ's atonement is sufficient for all humanity, and not only for the elect. Both views were held, by many Scottish ministers, to be inconsistent with the doctrinal position of the Westminster confession, which Church of Scotland ministers were required to hold.

In 1829 petitions were sent from a small group of parishioners to the presbytery of Dumbarton objecting to Campbell's doctrine. The presbytery initially declined to act on these petitions. However, in 1830 a formal petition was presented by a larger group within the Rhu parish, charging Campbell with heresy. Although a second petition in favour of Campbell was also submitted to the presbytery, it was set aside, and the presbytery initiated a sequence of actions, beginning with a presbyterial visitation to the Rhu parish, which culminated in Campbell's trial for heresy before the presbytery of Dumbarton, a judicial process that stretched from the autumn of 1830 until March 1831. Having been found guilty, Campbell appealed to the synod of Glasgow and Ayr, before which he appeared in April 1831. The verdict of the presbytery was upheld both by the synod and, finally, by the general assembly.

Following his deposition from the ministry Campbell

John McLeod Campbell (1800–1872), by Charles Henry Jeens, pubd 1877

lived with his father at Kilninver for two years, preaching in the western highlands, before settling in Glasgow. During these years Campbell continued his friendship with Edward Irving, though he rejected Irving's invitation to join the schismatic Catholic Apostolic church which he had founded in London. As is evident in his correspondence, Campbell enjoyed friendships with many of the leading churchmen of his time, including Thomas Erskine of Linlathen, Norman MacLeod, A. J. Scott, and F. D. Maurice, despite the fact that he ministered for most of his life in a small chapel in Glasgow—as he said, as a 'nobody' to whom the pulpits of the national church remained closed. Campbell continued in this work, without pay, from 1833 to 1859, unwilling either to resign from active pastoral ministry or to found a sect of his own. In 1838 he married Mary, the daughter of John Campbell of Ardnahua, Kilninver; one of their children was Sir James Macnabb *Campbell, administrator in India and ethnologist.

Campbell emerged as a leading theologian of the Victorian era, publishing in 1851 *Christ, the Bread of Life*, a brief study of holy communion (a revised second edition appeared in 1869). Campbell considered the book a protestant answer to the Roman Catholic doctrine of transubstantiation and addressed his arguments to those protestants he feared might be drawn to Catholicism by the example of John Henry Newman. In 1856 Campbell wrote his most important work, *The Nature of the Atonement*, regarded by the theologian James Denney as the only theological classic that Scotland has produced. Campbell's mature theological ideas were given full play in this book, as he opposed what he described as the 'older Calvinism' of John Owen and Jonathan Edwards. In place of their legal or forensic conception of the atonement, which stressed humanity's offence against the honour of the divine judge, Campbell, drawing on the writings of Martin Luther, developed a filial understanding of atonement, in which God was conceived of as a loving father seeking to restore his lost children to sonship. The key theological concepts of this imaginative book include the 'vicarious penitence' of Christ and the 'retrospective' and 'prospective aspects' of the atonement. Campbell's thought was considered controversial in his time, though he understood it to represent an orthodox, contemporary restatement of Christian doctrine. In 1862 he wrote *Thoughts on Revelation* in response to *Essays and Reviews* (1860). Campbell conceived of his book as an answer particularly to questions regarding the inspiration of Christian scripture and the relation of inspiration to revelation.

By 1859 Campbell's health was such that he was compelled to retire from public ministry. The University of Glasgow gave him an honorary DD in 1868. Two years later a group of church leaders from across Scotland presented him with a testimonial in recognition of his labours as a theologian. Campbell died at Rosneath of a prostatic abscess on 27 February 1872, and was buried at the old church in Rosneath. MICHAEL JINKINS

Sources J. M. Campbell, *Memorials*, ed. D. Campbell, 2 vols. (1877) · J. M. Campbell, *Sermons and lectures*, 2 vols. (1832) · *The whole proceedings before the presbytery of Dumbarton and synod of Glasgow and Ayr in the case of the Rev. John M'Leod Campbell* (1831) · G. M. Tuttle, *So rich a soil: John McLeod Campbell on Christian atonement* (1986) · J. B. Torrance, 'The contribution of John McLeod Campbell to Scottish theology', *Scottish Journal of Theology*, 26 (1973), 295–311 · E. G. Bewkes, *Legacy of a Christian mind: John McLeod Campbell* (1937) · M. Jinkins, *A comparative study in the theology of atonement in Jonathan Edwards and John McLeod Campbell* (1993) · M. Jinkins, *Love is of the essence: an introduction to the theology of John McLeod Campbell* (1993) · J. C. Goodloe, 'John McLeod Campbell, the atonement, and the transformation of the religious consciousness', PhD diss., University of Chicago, 1987 · B. A. Gerrish, *Tradition and the modern world: reformed theology in the nineteenth century* [1978] · G. Turnbull, 'John McLeod Campbell: his life, times and contemporaries', 1994, Edinburgh · J. B. Torrance, 'Introduction', in J. M. Campbell, *The nature of atonement* (1996) · T. F. Torrance, *Scottish theology: from John Knox to John McLeod Campbell* (1996) · L. van Dyk, *The desire of divine love: John Mcleod Campbell's doctrine of the atonement* (1995)

Archives Mitchell L., Glas., Glasgow City Archives, corresp. [copies] · Scottish Regional Archives · U. Edin., New Coll. L., corresp. | BL, corresp. with Macmillans, Add. MS 55112

Likenesses C. H. Jeens, stipple, pubd 1877, BM, NPG [*see illus.*]

Campbell, John Middleton [Jock], **Baron Campbell of Eskan (1912–1994)**, businessman, was born on 8 August 1912 at 22 Queen's Gate Gardens, Kensington, London, the eldest in the family of four sons and one daughter of (Colin) Algernon Campbell, banker, merchant, and sugar plantation owner, and his wife, Mary Charlotte Gladys Barrington. He was educated at Eton College and Exeter College, Oxford. In his early teens he contracted polio, which left him with a permanently weakened left arm.

John Middleton Campbell, Baron Campbell of Eskan (1912–1994), by Godfrey Argent, 1969

Despite this he became a scratch golf player, a wily tennis player (he played at Wimbledon), and a skilful croquet and ping-pong player. His period of illness at home was also the basis of his wide-ranging and voracious reading.

Jock Campbell said that he 'was born with a silver sugar spoon in my mouth' (*The Independent*). It was thus the more remarkable that he emerged to be an innovative business leader with a deep and fundamental concern for social justice and overseas development, as well as becoming a Labour member of the House of Lords. He was probably the most notable socialist businessman of his day.

After leaving university without taking his degree, Campbell joined the family firm, Curtis Campbell, which owned two sugar estates and factories in British Guiana and trading interests in Northern Rhodesia and Nyasaland. He first visited British Guiana in 1934 as a junior partner in the family firm. It was a formative and sobering experience: 'I was profoundly shocked by what I found: the dereliction of the sugar estates and factories, the awful housing of labourers, the racial problems, the arrogance of the Plantocracy.'

On 8 January 1938 Campbell married Barbara Noel Roffey (*b.* 1914/15), the daughter of Leslie Arden Roffey, tea planter. They had two sons and two daughters before they were divorced in 1948. The following year, on 7 May 1949, he married Phyllis Jacqueline Gilmour Taylor, *née* Boyd (1904/5–1983).

In 1939 Curtis Campbell merged with the larger plantation-owning, shipping, and trading business of Booker Brothers and McConnell. During the Second World War, Campbell served in the economic section of the Colonial Office, but by 1945 he had taken over effective management of the combined business, and in 1952 he became chairman. Under Campbell's leadership Booker was one of very few British companies to evolve successfully from the ownership of colonial plantations to become a modern international business.

Campbell's liberal and enlightened business views began to take effect in the late 1940s and 1950s. In British Guiana, Booker controlled 80 per cent of the sugar industry and was involved in a range of activities, including the production of rum, shopkeeping, and drug manufacturing. The country was often referred to as Booker's Guiana. Conscious of his family history (the Campbell involvement went back to slave-owning times), Campbell transformed management skills and attitudes, invested in sugar processing and agricultural technology, improved workers' housing and health facilities (achieving among other things the eradication of malaria), and generally raised the standards of working conditions and remuneration. He initiated constructive dialogue between the company and the government before and after the country's independence in 1966.

One of Campbell's greatest achievements during this period was the establishment of the Commonwealth sugar agreement, of which he was the principal architect and which provided a secure, protected, and reasonably remunerative market for raw sugar from Commonwealth producers for refining in the UK. Later Campbell took the lead in consolidating these arrangements within the Lomé Convention of 1975, which gave sugar producers in Africa, the Caribbean, and the Pacific region preferential access to the European market.

In London, Campbell recognized the dangers of Booker's overdependence on businesses in British Guiana and the need to diversify both geographically and by asset type. He initiated a programme of what he termed 'hedgebuilding', with further investments in the UK, Canada, and central Africa. One of the more eccentric of these was the purchase of a 51 per cent interest in the literary copyright of the novels of his friend Ian Fleming; this transaction was devised over a game of golf. Even more profitable was the subsequent purchase of Agatha Christie's literary copyright. The success of these investments was such that in 1967 Booker established the eponymous literary prize.

In the 1950s Campbell articulated a business philosophy which would not be out of place thirty years later but was revolutionary in its time. In articles and speeches he declared that a business had a fourfold responsibility: to its employees, to its customers, to the communities in which it operated, and to its shareholders. His emphasis on people was dominant: 'People are more important than ships, shops and sugar estates' (Caine). His favourite quotation was from Pasternak's *Dr Zhivago*: Strelnikov, caught in the ebb and flow of the Russian Revolution, realized 'in order to do good to others he needed, besides the principles that filled his mind, an unprincipled heart—the kind of heart that knows of no general causes but only of particular ones and knows the greatness of small actions'. Understanding the importance of small causes and appreciating the greatness of small actions was important to Campbell.

Knighted in 1957, Campbell retired from Booker in 1967 at the age of fifty-five. He was created a life peer, as Baron Campbell of Eskan, by Harold Wilson in 1966. An active Labour peer, he relished the anomalies of the House of Lords; 'The only justification of the Lords is its irrationality: once you try to make it rational, you satisfy no one', he said (A. Jay, ed., *Oxford Dictionary of Political Quotations*, 2001).

From 1967 to 1983 he served as the first chairman of Milton Keynes Development Corporation, overseeing the successful creation of the new town and attracting to it the Open University. He was also chairman of the *New Statesman* from 1964 to 1977. He was an active member of the Community Relations Commission (deputy chairman in 1968), he was a director of London Weekend Television from 1967 to 1974, and in 1969 he had ambitions to chair the Commonwealth Development Corporation (of which he was a director) but was frustrated by Harold Wilson's need to find a safe haven for one of his less successful cabinet ministers.

Campbell delighted in his family and friends, whom he entertained with jokes, puns, puzzles, and riddles, as well as with backgammon and other more strenuous sporting activities which he almost invariably won. He died at his home, Lawers, Crocker End, Nettlebed, Oxfordshire, on 26 December 1994. Two days before he died he had finished all three crosswords in *The Independent* by 10.30, promptly ringing the paper to ask if it was a record.

JONATHAN F. TAYLOR

Sources *The Times* (28 Dec 1994) · *The Times* (23 March 1995) · *The Scotsman* (31 Dec 1994) · *The Independent* (4 Jan 1995) · *WWW* · personal knowledge (2004) · private information (2004) · b. cert. · m. certs. · d. cert. · M. H. Caine, 'Campbell, John Middleton', *DBB*
Likenesses G. Argent, photograph, 1969, NPG [*see illus.*] · photograph, repro. in *The Scotsman* · photograph, repro. in *The Independent* · photographs, repro. in *The Times* (28 Dec 1994)
Wealth at death £435,107: probate, 13 Sept 1995, *CGPLA Eng. & Wales*

Campbell, John Pryse (1755–1821). *See under* Campbell family of Cawdor (*per.* 1511–1821).

Campbell, John Ross (1894–1969), political organizer and newspaper editor, was born on 15 October 1894 at 39 Lady Lane, Paisley, Renfrewshire, to Scottish working-class parents, John Campbell and Mary, *née* Stevenson. His father was a journeyman slater. Educated at an elementary school in Paisley, he started work at fourteen as an apprentice grocer's assistant. He joined the British Socialist Party in 1912 and soon became known as 'the Boy', publicly propagating Marxist ideas. In 1914, as a reservist, he was posted to the Clydeside section of the Royal Naval division and served throughout the war. Wounded at Gallipoli, he was permanently disabled at the battle of the Somme, where he was awarded the Military Medal for conspicuous bravery.

On his return to Scotland in 1918, Campbell played a leading part in the Clyde Workers' Committee movement, editing its weekly paper, *The Worker*, from 1921 to 1924. He joined the Communist Party of Great Britain on its foundation in 1920 and in 1923 was elected to its central executive committee, on which he served until his retirement in 1965. He also sat on the party's political committee for most of those years. Among the party posts which he held were head of its industrial department in the 1920s, and *Daily Worker* foreign editor (1932–4), assistant editor (1937–8, 1939, and 1942–9), and editor (1939 and 1949–59). He was elected to the executive committee of

John Ross Campbell (1894–1969), by unknown photographer, 1956

the Communist International at its sixth (1928) and seventh (1935) congresses.

Campbell moved to London in 1924, becoming acting editor of the Communist Party's *Workers' Weekly*. He rose to national prominence in the Campbell case of that year, when on 5 August he was charged with incitement to mutiny for having published on 25 July an appeal to soldiers not to fire on striking workers. The article was actually written by Harry Pollitt. Under widespread labour movement pressure the Labour attorney-general, Sir Patrick Hastings, dropped the case, pointing in particular to Campbell's 'exceptional gallantry' in the war. This led on 8 October to the defeat of the minority MacDonald government by a combined Liberal and Conservative Commons confidence vote against it.

The next year, on 25 November, Campbell was sentenced to six months' imprisonment after being tried under the same act with eleven other Communist leaders. He conducted his own closely reasoned political and legal defence. He was released on 10 April 1926 in time to play an active part in Scotland in the general strike of 1926.

Campbell clashed with the Communist International on two major issues. In February 1928 at the Comintern's ninth executive plenum, he argued cogently against Moscow's demand for all-out opposition to the Labour Party. When this sectarian 'new line' was implemented he formally accepted it, but worked with Harry Pollitt to check its worst effects on communist influence in the trade unions. Their flexible approach here would pay increasing dividends in coming years. When war came in 1939, Campbell—alongside Pollitt and William Gallacher—argued with great force and logic against the Comintern's instruction to oppose it (King and Matthews). Outvoted and under great pressure, he subsequently rationalized the Comintern's position and publicly confessed to error in having opposed it. Later he believed his stand against the Moscow line had been correct.

Campbell liked to stress that his socialist convictions were rooted in the Scottish revolutionary Marxist movement, which he had joined before Russia's October revolution. Nevertheless, although standing out among Communist leaders for his independent-mindedness, he was strongly influenced and constrained by Stalinism during much of his political life. This is strikingly shown in his book *Soviet Policy and its Critics* (1939), which devoted two long chapters to a defence of the Moscow trials of 1936–8, which he recognized after 1956 to be unsustainable. It was also reflected in the 'divided nature' he revealed in confronting demands for fuller and more critical debate from many members of his *Daily Worker* staff in 1956–7 following Khrushchov's revelations about Stalin (Macleod, 191). Opinions differ on how far his stay in Moscow in 1938–9 had made him aware of Stalin's mass repression of innocent people.

While he remained a communist, Campbell's outlook evolved considerably in his last years. Whereas, for instance, in 1956 he had defended Soviet military intervention in Hungary, in 1968 he condemned the invasion of Czechoslovakia. As a Marxist economic specialist chairing his executive's economic subcommittee, he became increasingly cautious in his analyses, insisting on the basis of bitter experience that 'our Committee now makes no predictions'.

Campbell was a friendly but tough-minded Scot. His rather mournful face belied his ready wit and pawky humour. He and his wife, Sarah Marie Carlin, *née* O'Donnell, were married from 1920 until her death in 1965. He acted as father to five stepchildren and two daughters. He lived on a London council estate and ate with staff and printworkers in the *Daily Worker* canteen. A widely read and cultured worker-intellectual, he wrote over two dozen books and pamphlets and innumerable articles in his distinctive, sprawling handwriting. He was a recognized authority on Robert Burns, whose poems he recited in his strong Scottish accent. His humanity, selflessness, and down-to-earth intelligence led to his enjoying widespread popularity and affection, even among many who disagreed with him politically. He died on 18 September 1969 at the Middlesex Hospital, London, and was cremated on 23 September at Golders Green crematorium.

MONTY JOHNSTONE

Sources *Communist policy in Great Britain: the report of the British commission of the ninth plenum of the Comintern*, Communist party of Great Britain (1928) · *The communist party on trial: J. R. Campbell's defence* [n.d., 1925?] · Communist Party of Great Britain Congress reports, 1920s–1960s [esp. 14th (1937) congress, with Campbell's report on industrial and trade union work] · F. King and G. Matthews, eds., *About turn: the British communist party and the Second World War* (1990) · A. Macleod, *The death of Uncle Joe* (1997) · *WWW, 1961–70* · Communist Party of Great Britain and Communist International biographical material · personal knowledge (2004) · *Morning Star* (19 Sept 1969) · *Morning Star* (20 Sept 1969) · *The Times* (20 Sept 1969) · *Tribune* (26 Sept 1969) · *Sunday Worker* (25 Oct 1925) · W. Campbell, *Villi the clown* (1981)

Archives Labour History Archive and Study Centre, Manchester, communist party archive, corresp., speeches, and writings

Likenesses photograph, 1956, Hult. Arch. [*see illus.*]

Wealth at death £2113: probate, 21 Nov 1969, *CGPLA Eng. & Wales*

Campbell, Judith (1857–1893). *See under* Knock, visionaries of (*act.* 1879).

Campbell, Katherine, countess of Crawford (*d.* 1578), noblewoman, was the eldest daughter of Sir John *Campbell (*d.* 1546), first knight of Calder [*see under* Campbell family of Cawdor], and Muriel (1498/9–1573x5), heir of Cawdor. She married first, before 1 October 1539, James Ogilvy (*d.* 1547), master of Ogilvy and heir to Airlie. They had five children, three sons and two daughters. When the master was killed at Pinkie on 10 September 1547, Katherine became tutrix to the children, including her son James *Ogilvy, fifth Lord Ogilvy.

Katherine subsequently married David Lindsay of Edzell, ninth earl of Crawford (*d.* 1558), no later than 12 November 1550, when she was infeft in a conjunct fee of the barony of Ferne. They had seven children, five sons and two daughters. Their eldest son was David *Lindsay of Glenesk, who became heir to Edzell but not to Crawford—the latter title reverted to the direct line on the death of the ninth earl on 20 September 1558. Another son was John *Lindsay of Balcarres.

The countess of Crawford was appointed tutrix and sole guardian to the children of her second marriage, and until her offspring reached maturity she managed the affairs of the heirs to both Airlie and Edzell. Her widow's terce became the subject of extended litigation between her and the tenth earl, and was not settled until 1563. Katherine did not marry again, but the English ambassador Randolph noted in a letter of 1565 that she was a very eligible widow whose fortunes in yet another marriage were being considered by her kinsman, the fifth earl of Argyll.

Katherine maintained a close working relationship with Donald Campbell, Cistercian abbot of Coupar and curator of her eldest son, James Ogilvy of Airlie. The contents of Coupar Abbey were entrusted to her care by Campbell when his house was purged of 'Idolis and Imagis and tubernacuilis' in 1559 (Bardgett, 73). On Donald's death in 1562 the goods and gear of the abbey (except the commend) were granted to the earl of Argyll, who in taking up his gift removed from Katherine's possession some gold coins and rings bequeathed to her personally by the late abbot. Katherine spent four years in litigation trying to recover these items.

After 1560, and more so after 1567, the countess of Crawford found her loyalties divided in the aftermath of the religious reformation and in the political turmoil that followed Queen Mary's abdication. She was not only the tutrix of a major house but a widow with the interests of many children to uphold. The eldest sons of each marriage, James, Lord Ogilvy, and David Lindsay of Glenesk, followed the earl of Crawford into the queen's party during the 1560s. The two daughters of her Ogilvy marriage, however, married into the protestant families of Erskine of Dun and Ogilvy of Inverquharity. The two eldest sons of her marriage to David Lindsay of Edzell were sent to the University of Paris in the mid-1560s under the tutelage of the protestant James Lawson. Their education in France was a condition of Dame Katherine's purchase of the tack of the kirk of Menmure, to which her second (Lindsay) son, John, was collated in 1565. Her interest in their education and her expenses are documented in letters between Lawson and herself.

Katherine's religious opinions after 1560 are difficult to ascertain. She hosted Queen Mary overnight at Edzell in August 1562, and alluded to having attended the court of the queen regent in the 1550s, but Donald Campbell's adherence to the congregation probably brought her into the protestant camp. She maintained a close relationship with John Erskine of Dun, the superintendent of Angus and the Mearns, who borrowed money from her in 1571, and her testament suggests that she had greater confidence in her younger sons, who served the kirk, than she had in the elder two.

The letters from James Lawson and other extant documents, in the Crawford manuscripts and elsewhere, reveal Dame Katherine as a capable individual and administrator. She fought for her rights and for the protection of her interests in the courts. She dealt with merchants, negotiated contracts, and loaned money, ensuring the security of each contract by having it registered in the books of council. She kept around her a very loyal group of servants who carried out her wishes, wrote and witnessed her business, and provided advice when necessary. In April 1570 she made an agreement with her old antagonist the tenth earl of Crawford, whereby David Lindsay of Glenesk would marry the earl's daughter Helen without tocher. This arrangement finally brought to rest a long-standing dispute between the earl and the heirs of Edzell.

The countess of Crawford dictated her latterwill, without pious sentiment, at the castle of Brechin on 10 August 1578. She died there on 1 October following, and was buried at Edzell later the same month.

MARY BLACK VERSCHUUR

Sources F. D. Bardgett, *Scotland reformed: the Reformation in Angus and the Mearns* (1989) • D. E. Easson, ed., *Charters of the abbey of Coupar-Angus*, 2, Scottish History Society, 3rd ser., 41 (1947) • Lord Lindsay [A. W. C. Lindsay, earl of Crawford], *Lives of the Lindsays*, 2nd edn, 3 vols (1858), vol. 1 • *Scots peerage*, vol. 1 • *Scots peerage*, vol. 3 • *CSP for.*, 1560–61 • M. Livingstone, D. Hay Fleming, and others, eds., *Registrum secreti sigilli regum Scotorum / The register of the privy seal of Scotland*, 1–6 (1908–63) • *Reg. PCS*, 1st ser., vol. 1 • J. M. Thomson and others, eds., *Registrum magni sigilli regum Scotorum / The register of the great seal of Scotland*, 11 vols. (1882–1914), vols. 3–5 • W. Fraser, *History of the Carnegies, earls of Southesk, and of their kindred*, 2 vols. (1867) • sheriff court book of Perth, NA Scot., SC49/1 • commissary of Edinburgh, register of testaments, NA Scot., CC8/8 • [C. Innes], ed., *The Book of the thanes of Cawdor, 1236–1742: a series of papers selected from the charter room at Cawdor*, Spalding Club, 30 (1859)

Archives NA Scot., Airlie Muniments • NL Scot., Crawford Muniments

Wealth at death £7807 13*s*. 4*d*.—free gear; debts deducted: confirmation, NA Scot., CC8/8/7

Campbell, Lewis (1830–1908), classical scholar, was born on 3 September 1830 at Howard Place, Edinburgh, the elder son of Captain Robert Campbell RN, who was related to the Campbells of Kirnan, Argyll, and his wife, Eliza Constantia, eldest daughter of Richard Pryce of Gunley, Montgomeryshire. His father died in 1832 and in 1844 his mother married her second husband, Colonel Morrieson. Campbell was educated at Edinburgh Academy, where he was a close friend of the physicist James Clerk Maxwell, and at Glasgow University (1846–9), where he was taught Latin by William Ramsay and Greek by Edward Lushington. Campbell then went to Oxford in 1849, taking up, in preference to a scholarship at Trinity, the Snell exhibition from Glasgow, tenable at Balliol College. There he met Benjamin Jowett, who was to be the major influence on his life and his work both in theology and philosophy. After graduating with first-class honours in classics Campbell spent a brief period (1856–8) as fellow and tutor at Queen's College. He resigned his fellowship on his marriage on 11 May 1858 to Frances Pitt (Fanny), daughter of Thomas Andrews, serjeant-at-law.

Campbell was ordained deacon in 1857 and priest in 1858, spending five years of active ministry as vicar of Milford, Hampshire, a Queen's College living. In 1863 he was appointed professor of Greek at the University of St Andrews in succession to William Young Sellar who became professor of humanity at Edinburgh University. In 1875 he was an unsuccessful candidate for the Greek chair at Glasgow, to which Richard Claverhouse Jebb, ten years his junior, was appointed. The honorary LLD Campbell received from Glasgow in 1875 must have seemed a poor consolation. Then student numbers at St Andrews declined alarmingly, until in 1876 there were a mere 130 students in the entire university, which was threatened with extinction. When the Universities (Scotland) Act of 1889 addressed the situation, certain of its new provisions were perceived by Campbell as inimical to his subject and to academic standards. After a prolonged period of ill health in 1891–2, he resigned his chair. The Campbells soon made Alassio on the Italian riviera their winter home. Campbell's years of retirement were marked by further honours (including DLitt Oxon. in 1903) and continued professional activity, from the Gifford lectures at St Andrews in 1894–5 (published in 1898 as *Religion in Greek Literature*) to a lecture delivered shortly before his death entitled *The Religious Element in Plato* to a Congress of Religions at Oxford in September 1908.

Campbell had been appointed to the chair at St Andrews in recognition of his work on Plato, and for some time he continued to concentrate on Plato's philosophy: his *Theaetetus* of 1861 went into a second edition in 1883; in 1867 his edition of the *Sophistes* and *Politicus* appeared (dedicated to the senatus of the university); and in 1894 he edited the *Republic* with Jowett. Campbell pioneered the application of stylometry, a sophisticated examination of

Lewis Campbell (1830–1908), by George Charles Beresford, 1904

vocabulary, grammar, and sentence structure, to the question of Plato's chronological development. This innovatory and imaginative work was little appreciated at the time and continental scholars, failing to observe Campbell's results, later received more credit for proceeding on similar lines.

The second area in which Campbell made a lasting contribution to scholarship was tragedy, especially Sophocles. His edition of Sophocles came out in two volumes, the first (*Oedipus tyrannus*, *Oedipus Coloneus*, *Antigone*), with a fulsome tribute to Jowett, in 1871, with a second edition in 1879; and the second in 1881. Jebb's celebrated Sophocles, which came to overshadow Campbell's, was not begun until 1880, the first part appearing in 1883. Campbell's insights on language (especially in the long 'Essay on the language of Sophocles', prefaced to his first volume), on lyric metre, on the textual tradition, and on dramatic and staging questions are particularly valuable. Campbell's third main scholarly enterprise was again original in conception: verse translation allied with comparative literature. He published translations of Sophocles (1883) and of Aeschylus (1890) in blank verse and lyric metres, and also a *Guide to Greek Tragedy* (1891), and a comparative work on tragic method, *Tragic Drama in Aeschylus, Sophocles and Shakespeare* (1904). Gilbert Murray followed Campbell's translations of Aeschylus and Sophocles with translations of Euripides which were staged and much more widely read, despite being less economical and less faithful to sense and metrical structure. Campbell's more general work included a volume on Plato's *Republic* for the Home and School Library (1902); and one on Sophocles (1897) for the Classical Writers series.

Campbell remained a lifelong proponent of liberal ecumenical views, expressed not only in sermons, such as those collected in *The Christian Ideal* (1877), but also in correspondence, lectures, and essays. His *On the Nationalisation of the Old English Universities* (1901) was a restatement of the liberal cause of freeing the ancient universities from denominational restrictions. Loyalty to his early associates was apparent in his extensive biographical and editorial work: with William Garnett he produced a life of Clerk Maxwell (1882); with Evelyn Abbott the biography of Jowett (1897) and editions of his writings and correspondence (1899); extracts from Jowett's work on Plato (1902) and his theological essays (1906); and editions of the poems of his father's cousin Thomas Campbell (1904).

Campbell's unassuming character comes over in much of his work, especially his replies to Jebb in *Paralipomena Sophoclea* (1907). He is described by his younger contemporary John Burnet as sensitive, nervous, and excitable (*DNB*). His lifestyle was mildly bohemian; he founded the students' Shakespearian society, dramatic society, and gymnastic club; and himself participated in their activities. He was an advocate of higher education for women and was closely involved in the foundation of St Leonard's School for Girls, being chairman of the school council from 1886 to 1903. Campbell died at Brissago, Lake Maggiore, near Locarno, Switzerland, on the return journey from Oxford to his home at Alassio, on 25 October 1908. He was survived by his wife; they had no children. There are memorial tablets at the English cemetery, Locarno, where he was buried, and at St John's Church, Alassio, and the chapels of St Andrews and Balliol. E. M. CRAIK

Sources F. P. Campbell, *Memorials in verse and prose of Lewis Campbell* (1914) • E. M. Craik, 'Lewis Campbell', *19th century classical scholarship*, ed. H. D. Jocelyn (1996) • L. Huxley, 'Lewis Campbell', *Cornhill Magazine*, [3rd] ser., 25 (1908), 812–21 • *DNB* • U. St Andr. L., Campbell MSS • P. G. Naiditch, *A. E. Housman at University College, London: the election of 1892* (1988), 239 • *CGPLA Eng. & Wales* (1908)
Archives U. St Andr. | Balliol Oxf., Evelyn Abbott MSS • Balliol Oxf., Benjamin Jowett MSS • Bodl. Oxf., Gilbert Murray MSS
Likenesses M. O. Roty, medal, 1893, U. St Andr.; repro. in Campbell, *Memorials in verse and prose* • G. C. Beresford, photograph, 1904, NPG [*see illus.*] • A. Lenyon, oils, U. St Andr.; repro. in Campbell, *Memorials in verse and prose* • photograph, U. St Andr. L.
Wealth at death £3999 3*s*. 10*d*.: probate, 14 Nov 1908, *CGPLA Eng. & Wales*

Campbell, Lorne Maclaine, of Airds (1902–1991), army officer and wine merchant, was born at The Airds, Argyll, Scotland, on 22 July 1902, the eldest of the three sons of Colonel (Ian) Maxwell Campbell of Airds (1870–1954), army officer and wine merchant, and his wife, Hilda Mary, *née* Wade. He came from a family steeped in military service: he was the eleventh, with one exception, in a line of army officers. His great-great-grandfather had raised the grenadier company of the 98th, later the 91st, Argyll and Sutherland Highlanders. His father served with the 8th battalion Argyll and Sutherland Highlanders throughout the First World War, commanding it as a Territorial Army unit thereafter. His uncle Vice-Admiral Gordon *Campbell won the VC in 1917 for sinking a U-boat from a badly damaged Q-ship; he was later Conservative MP for Burnley from 1931 to 1935.

Campbell was educated at Dulwich College, where he was captain of school in 1920–21. From there he went as a postmaster (scholar) to Merton College, Oxford. He excelled in sports, and was awarded a half-blue for athletics. He missed a rugby blue through injury. He graduated with a second in *literae humaniores* in 1925. Meanwhile he had joined the 8th battalion Argyll and Sutherland Highlanders (then under his father's command) as a Territorial Army officer, in 1921. After leaving Oxford he joined the family firm of wine shippers. It was said of him that 'he had the finest palate for wine in Britain' (*The Independent*). On 27 December 1935 he married (Amy) Muriel Jordan Campbell (1905–1950), only daughter and second of the four children of Alastair Magnus Campbell of Auchendarroch. They had two sons.

By the outbreak of the Second World War, Campbell was second-in-command of the 8th battalion Argyll and Sutherland Highlanders. The battalion was sent to France in 51st Highland division as part of the British expeditionary force. When the Germans launched their blitzkrieg in May 1940, the 51st were ordered to move across France to recapture the Somme bridgeheads from the Germans, but the overwhelming success of the German army on all fronts made this task impracticable. The Argylls, with the rest of 51st division, were ordered to make their way to Le Havre and, under French command, launch counter-attacks. Conflicting orders in the face of a relentless German onslaught led to much confusion. Nevertheless Campbell managed to reach Le Havre with two companies of his highlanders, without losing a single man. The rest of 51st division were taken prisoner at St Valéry-en-Caux. Campbell was awarded a DSO for his conduct during the campaign.

Evacuated from Le Havre, Campbell was given command of the 7th/10th battalion in the newly formed 51st Highland division, which he took to north Africa to fight in the western desert. He was awarded a bar to his DSO at the battle of El Alamein in October–November 1942. When the British Eighth Army advanced to Tunisia, his battalion was given the task of crossing an enemy minefield and an anti-tank ditch at Wadi Akarit in order to form a bridgehead. After forming up in darkness and traversing an offshoot of the wadi (a dry, rocky watercourse) in order to attack, they accomplished their objective and took 600 prisoners. The following day Campbell's position was under constant heavy bombardment but, although wounded in the neck by shrapnel, he inspired his men to such an extent that all attacks were repulsed and the bridgehead held. Exposed in full view of the enemy he rallied his men and, although painfully wounded, he stood in the open to direct the fight under close fire from German infantry. His VC citation concluded with the words: 'It is the opinion of the Army Council that in all the long and glorious annals of the British Army the conduct of this officer has seldom been equalled and never surpassed' (*The Independent*).

In 1943 Campbell was promoted brigadier, and was given command of the 13th infantry brigade, which he then led through Sicily, the Anzio landings, and much of the Italian campaign. During the absence of the general officer commanding, he commanded 5th division for several weeks. He was then posted to the British army staff in Washington (1944–5), where he was made an officer of the US Legion of Merit. At the end of the war he was sent to Germany on an official mission to report on the possibilities of establishing the Boy Scout movement there, to replace the unwholesome ideology of the Hitler youth movement. He had always been an enthusiast for scouting, although later he declined the offer of high office in the organization.

Following demobilization Campbell returned to the wine trade, becoming a liveryman of the Vintners' Company, and eventually its master. He served on the committees selecting wine for the royal cellars and for official hospitality, and was instrumental in setting up the qualification 'master of wine'. For his services on official bodies he was made an OBE in 1968.

Although much of his life had been lived in Amersham, Buckinghamshire, Campbell's final years were spent in Scotland, where his recreations were fishing and gardening. An exceptionally modest man, he declined prestigious appointments and the possibility of a seat in parliament. He was religious, gentle, sociable, and unselfish. A fellow officer described him as the 'nicest man in Scotland' (*The Independent*). He died at the Royal Victoria Hospital, Edinburgh, on 25 May 1991, of bronchopneumonia. He was survived by his two sons, his wife, Muriel, having predeceased him in 1950. A memorial service was held on 21 June 1991 at Canongate Kirk, Edinburgh.

PHILIP WARNER

Sources A. D. Malcolm, *History of the Argyll and Sutherland highlanders, 8th battalion, 1939–47* (1949) • P. J. R. Mileham, *Fighting highlanders* (1993) • D. Sutherland, *The Argyll and Sutherland highlanders* (1969) • *The Times* (29 May 1991) • *The Independent* (30 July 1991) • D. Lang, memorial service address, 21 June 1991 • *WWW, 1991–5* • Burke, *Gen. GB* • *The register of the Victoria cross*, 3rd edn (1997) • d. cert. • private information (2004)

Likenesses photograph, repro. in *The Times* • photograph, repro. in *The Independent*

Wealth at death £453,041.19: confirmation, 1991, *CCI*

Campbell, Sir Malcolm (1885–1948), holder of land and water speed records, was born on 11 March 1885 at Chislehurst, Kent, the only son and elder of two children of William Campbell (*d.* 1920), diamond merchant, of Cheapside, and his wife, Ada Westerton. He was educated at a preparatory school near Guildford, and then at Uppingham School, but left at the age of sixteen to continue his studies—primarily to become a fluent linguist—in France and Germany. It was in Germany that he began a lifelong eagerness to test himself, and machines, to see how fast he could go. His first sporting pursuit was bicycle racing; as a youth he was fined 30*s.* for driving a pedal cycle at 27 m.p.h. 'to the confusion and terror of two elderly ladies'.

He graduated from racing bicycles to taking part in motor cycle trials and earned three gold medals in the London–Edinburgh trials of 1906, 1907, and 1908.

In 1906, aged twenty-one, Campbell became an underwriting member of Lloyd's and acquired the financial resources to develop his racing enthusiasms. He spotted the market for insuring newspapers against libel actions and built up a good and profitable business. He was a pioneer of aviation; as an innovative designer and engineer his aerial advances were more significant than those achieved in his land and sea speed quests. In 1909 he built a monoplane following a blueprint of his own that borrowed from the successful 'Blériot XI' aeroplane. The plane, built in a disused barn in a strawberry field, flew in a straight line—then crashed. Campbell's career was punctuated by a series of near disasters and spectacular crashes, as he literally drove himself to the limits of physical and technological performance. In an interview quoted in the *New York Times* of 2 January 1949, he observed, 'If I break my neck then I'm unlucky. It's just a great adventure.'

In 1910 Campbell immersed himself in the Brooklands motor track racing subculture. His first racing car was a Peugeot called 'The Flapper' after a successful racehorse. However, his Flapper vehicles did not perform well. In 1912 he started using the moniker *Blue Bird* for his racing cars, inspired by the play of that name by Maurice Maeterlinck, and he continued to use that name as a lucky talisman for the rest of his life. During a 1912 Brooklands race he brushed with death as *Blue Bird* (a 1906 Darracq) lost wheels, swerved, and nearly flipped over. Such was his skill and presence of mind that he steered the shuddering, clanking *Blue Bird* to a fourth place finish. Before the First World War he drove Lion Peugeot, Renault, Schneider, Sunbeam, Charron, and Gregoire cars, as well as Darracqs. He embarked on the first of his three marriages on 19 July 1913, when he married Marjorie Dagmar Knott (*b.* 1892/3), daughter of Henry Raglan Knott, gentleman. They separated and the marriage was dissolved.

At the outbreak of the First World War, Campbell enlisted as a motor cycle rider and was commissioned in the West Kent regiment. He was transferred to the Royal Flying Corps, where he was a ferry pilot and then a flying instructor. On demobilization, with the rank of captain and an MBE, he returned to Lloyd's and also established a motor car dealership. In March 1920 he married Dorothy Evelyn, daughter of Major William Whittall, with whom he had a son (Donald Malcolm *Campbell) and a daughter. Recalling his impulsive temperament and his string of affairs during their twenty-year marriage, Dorothy Campbell thought him 'quite unfitted for the role of husband and family man' (*Malcolm Campbell: the Man as I Knew Him*, 1951, 222). Motor-racing continued to be his chief interest and in the post-war years he won over 400 trophies, including the 200 mile race at Brooklands in 1927 and 1928, and the Boulogne grand prix in 1927, driving a variety of cars, including a 7.6 litre GP Peugeot, a collection of Talbots (1.5 to 4.5 litre), an Austro-Daimler, and a 5 litre Sunbeam.

Always spurred on by an energetic fascination to test himself and his newest racing gadget, Campbell decided in 1922 to make a bid for the land speed record and took on

Sir Malcolm Campbell (1885–1948), by unknown photographer [in *Blue Bird*]

Leo Villa as his racing mechanic. His first attempt, driving a 350 horse power Sunbeam at Saltburn in 1922, was unsuccessful, and this was followed by two failures at the international speed trial meetings at Fanöe, Denmark, in 1923 and 1924. Later in 1924 (on 25 September), however, driving the same vehicle at Pendine (Pen-tywyn) Sands, Carmarthenshire, he set a record of 146.16 m.p.h., and in the following year (21 July 1925) at Pendine became the first person to travel at over 150 m.p.h., setting a new record of 150.87 m.p.h.

From 1926 the rivalry between Campbell and Henry Segrave in turn established Britain at the forefront of land speed record attempts. Driving a new Napier-Campbell *Blue Bird*, Campbell pushed the record to 174.88 at Pendine on 4 February 1927, but at the end of March Segrave beat him to break the 200 m.p.h. barrier. Campbell responded by rebuilding *Blue Bird* and recording 206.95 m.p.h. at Daytona Beach, Florida, on 19 February 1928. This was subsequently broken by the American Ray Keech and then by Segrave. Campbell made an attempt to beat Segrave's record at Verneuk Pan, South Africa, in May 1929, but this proved a costly failure.

Campbell finally overhauled Segrave's record at Daytona on 5 February 1931, when he reached 231.4 m.p.h. in a rebuilt *Blue Bird*. On his triumphal return to London he received a knighthood. Successive attempts at Daytona pushed the record to 253.97 (24 February 1932), 272.46 (22 February 1933), and 276.88 (7 March 1935). Propelled by a Rolls-Royce 'R' engine, delivering 2350 brake horse power, he achieved his ninth and last land speed record on 3 September 1935 at Bonneville Salt Flats, Utah, where he became the first driver to exceed 300 m.p.h. with a speed of 301.13 m.p.h. His achievements were later (1940) recognized when he was awarded the trophy founded in memory of Segrave.

On his return from Daytona, Campbell, who believed that rearmament in the face of the German threat had become an urgent necessity, regarded it as his patriotic duty to enter politics. At the general election held in November 1935 he stood as a Conservative for the Deptford constituency but was beaten by the Labour candidate. As well as writing a number of books on motoring, and an account of his expedition in 1926 to the Cocos Islands in (fruitless) search of buried pirate treasure, he was motoring correspondent of *The Field* and the *Daily Mail*.

In the late 1930s Campbell took to the water with a *Blue Bird* motor boat designed by F. W. Cooper, powered by a Rolls-Royce aero engine. At Lake Maggiore, Switzerland, he set successive records of 126.33 m.p.h. and 129.5 m.p.h. in September 1937, achieving 130.93 at Halwill, Switzerland, in July 1938. In August 1939 he achieved his last record, 141.74 m.p.h., at Coniston Water.

During the early part of the Second World War, Campbell commanded a motor cycle unit and served for the remainder on the staff of combined operations, though he was frustrated not to be allowed to serve abroad with his regiment. After his second marriage was dissolved in 1940, he married on 16 August 1945 Betty Nicory (*b.* 1905/6), the divorced wife of Clement Nicory, and daughter of Sir John Humphery, company director. They separated within weeks and were divorced a year later. Campbell died at his home, Little Gatton, Reigate, Surrey, on 31 December 1948. His son succeeded him as a land and water speed record breaker.

SCOTT A. G. M. CRAWFORD

Sources *DNB* • J. W. Day, *Speed: the authentic life of Sir Malcolm Campbell* (1931) • M. Campbell, *My thirty years of speed* (1949) • M. Campbell, *Speed on wheels* (1949) • L. Villa and T. Gray, *Two record breakers: Sir Malcolm and Donald Campbell* (1969) • *The Times* (3 Jan 1949), 6 • *The Times* (7 Jan 1949), 7 • *The Times* (8 Jan 1949), 6 • m. certs. [Marjorie Knott, Betty Nicory] • *New York Times* (2 Jan 1949), 60 • *Chicago Tribune* (2 Jan 1949), pt 2, p. 4 • G. N. Georgano, ed., *The encyclopaedia of motor sport* (1971), 183–4 • P. Drackett, *Like father like son: the story of Malcolm and Donald Campbell* (1969) • C. Posthumus, *Land speed record* (1971)

Archives FILM BFI NFTVA, 'Bluebird's 206.9 mph', Topical Budget, 23 Feb 1928 • BFI NFTVA, 'Carmarthenshire: fastest car dash in history', Topical Budget, 24 Jan 1927 • BFI NFTVA, documentary footage • BFI NFTVA, 'Florida—world's speed record broken', *Pathé gazette*, 3 Feb 1931 • BFI NFTVA, home footage • BFI NFTVA, news footage • BFI NFTVA, *Record breakers*, 1955

Likenesses photographs, 1912–47, Hult. Arch. • H. A. Stermann, bronze mask, *c.*1935, NPG • photograph (in *Blue Bird*), NPG [*see illus.*]

Wealth at death £175,580 4*s.* 8*d.*: probate, 19 March 1949, *CGPLA Eng. & Wales*

Campbell, Margaret Gabrielle Vere. *See* Long, Margaret Gabrielle Vere (1885–1952).

Campbell, Sir Neil (*d.* 1315?). *See under* Campbell family (*per. c.*1300–1453).

Campbell, Neil (*d.* 1613?), bishop of Argyll, appears to have been the son of Alexander Macpherson of the Carnassarie Campbells, the surname meaning 'son of the parson', although the combination of a common surname and paucity of records makes certain identification difficult. One Mr Neil Campbell was recorded as parson of Kilmartin in Argyll and chanter of the cathedral of Lismore in 1574. It was probably he who, after the death of James Hamilton (1580), became bishop of Argyll, although he retained his parochial charge. He was commonly styled 'Mr', indicating a university education, and he may be identified with the Nigellus Campbell who graduated MA (1575) from the University of St Andrews. In March 1588 the privy council appointed him to examine witnesses in a civil dispute and in the following year he was named as responsible for Argyll in a privy council commission against Catholic missionaries. In that year he attended the general assembly, at Edinburgh in August, when the moderator, Patrick Galloway, chose him to be one of his assessors, the assembly's business committee.

Campbell was married to Christian, daughter of John *Carswell (*d.* 1572), superintendent of Argyll, bishop of the Isles, and Campbell's predecessor at Kilmartin. They had a number of children: John, named as the bishop's son and heir in a great seal charter of March 1603, succeeded him as bishop in 1608, although he does not seem ever to have been ordained; Neil, perhaps to be identified with the son of the rector of Kilmartin legitimated under the great seal in 1585, became bishop of the Isles (1633–8); Colin, named in the same legitimation; Alexander; Donald, who succeeded his father as minister at Kilmartin; and a daughter whose name is not known. In December 1606 Neil Campbell was appointed constant moderator of the presbytery of Argyll and he was last recorded as bishop in January 1608. He must have resigned his see before 1 June of that year, the date his son received provision from the crown. He died about five years later, probably in January 1613. ALAN R. MACDONALD

Sources *Fasti Scot.*, new edn • D. E. R. Watt, ed., *Fasti ecclesiae Scoticanae medii aevi ad annum 1638*, [2nd edn], Scottish RS, new ser., 1 (1969) • *Reg. PCS*, 1st ser. • T. Thomson, ed., *Acts and proceedings of the general assemblies of the Kirk of Scotland*, 3 pts, Bannatyne Club, 81 (1839–45) • J. M. Thomson and others, eds., *Registrum magni sigilli regum Scotorum / The register of the great seal of Scotland*, 11 vols. (1882–1914) • M. Livingstone, D. Hay Fleming, and others, eds., *Registrum secreti sigilli regum Scotorum / The register of the privy seal of Scotland*, 4 (1952) • A. I. Dunlop, ed., *Acta facultatis artium universitatis Sanctiandree, 1413–1588*, 2, Scottish History Society, 3rd ser., 55 (1964), 444

Campbell, Lord Neil, of Ardmaddie (*c.*1630–1692), colonial speculator, was the second of six children of Archibald *Campbell, marquess of Argyll (1605x7–1661), and his wife, Lady Margaret (1610–1678), second daughter of William Douglas, seventh earl of Morton; his parents lived mainly at Inveraray, Argyll. He was the younger brother of Archibald *Campbell, ninth earl of Argyll (*d.* 1685). It is likely that Lord Neil's formal education began at home, but in 1645 he attended classes at the University of Glasgow. From 1647 to 1649, he and his elder brother made a grand tour of France and Italy. Notwithstanding their father's political ascendancy as covenanter leader during the civil wars of the 1640s, and his political accommodation with Cromwell during the interregnum, there is little extant documentation highlighting Lord Neil's political stance or activities during this period. When, after the restoration of Charles II in 1660, Argyll was indicted for high treason, Lord Neil travelled to London to deal with his father's affairs, but was unable to prevent his execution in May 1661. On 23 January 1668 Lord Neil married his cousin Lady Vere Ker (1649–1674), third daughter of the third earl of Lothian. The couple had two sons, the younger of whom was the Scottish episcopal bishop Archibald *Campbell, and three daughters; it is likely that they spent most of their short married life at Ardmaddie Castle, Argyll.

During the following decade, Lord Neil assisted his brother in the ongoing feud between the Campbell and Gillean clans by leading two invasions on Maclean lands in Mull. As staunch presbyterians and covenanters, both Lord Neil and his brother opposed Charles II's enforced return to episcopacy. Events, centring on the earl's reservations in signing the Test Act, conspired to precipitate Argyll's forfeiture and flight to Holland in 1681, and in consequence, to Lord Neil being constantly under suspicion. To provide himself with a transatlantic refuge if the political situation in Scotland became too dangerous, and to shore up his dwindling wealth, Lord Neil participated in colonial ventures in the Americas. First he became a leading undertaker of the little-known Carolina Company, a company set up in 1681 to break into the Anglo-American trade by establishing a colony at Port Royal on the Ashley River, South Carolina; and second, he became an active participator and fractioner in the infant colony of East New Jersey set up by Robert Barclay of Ury. Along with his business partner, Robert Blackwood, an Edinburgh merchant, Lord Neil invested £1100 sterling in transporting servants and goods to East New Jersey, and in buying 8000 acres of land on the Rariton River and a 12-acre site and two plots by the sound in the colony's capital, Perth Amboy.

In 1685, possibly in March, Lord Neil married his second wife, Susan, eldest daughter of Sir Alexander Menzies of Weem; they had four children. On his brother's return from exile and rebellion against the Stuart monarchy in August 1685, Lord Neil was held under bond in Edinburgh, but was subsequently allowed to sail for East New Jersey. The following year he became the colony's third deputy governor. However, in 1687 he requested the council's permission to resign his position and return to Scotland, where he took up the post of governor of Dumbarton Castle, though he lived mainly at Nether Lorn, Argyll. Despite his colonial ventures and the income from his extensive estates in Lorne and Kintyre, Lord Neil was in considerable debt when he died in April 1692. He was buried on 11 April in Greyfriars churchyard, Edinburgh. By a disposition, dated 8 July 1693, his eldest son and heir, Charles, made over all his inheritance to the earl of Breadalbane for £20,000 Scots (£1666 sterling) and relief of all debts and claims against Lord Neil. LINDA G. FRYER

Sources J. Willcock, *The great marquess* (1903), 315, 344 • *Scots peerage* • L. G. Fryer, 'Documents relating to the formation of the Carolina Company in Scotland, 1682', *South Carolina Historical Magazine*, 99 (1998), 110–34 • L. G. Fryer, 'Robert Barclay of Ury and East New Jersey', *Northern Scotland*, 15 (1995), 1–17 • R. Douglas, *The peerage of Scotland*, 2nd edn, ed. J. P. Wood, 1 (1813), 100 • A. I. Macinnes, *Clanship, commerce, and the house of Stuart, 1603–1788* (1996), 147, 158 • I. M. M. McPhail, *Dumbarton Castle* (1979), 126–9 • J. Willcock, *A Scots earl in covenanting times: being life and times of Archibald, 9th earl of Argyll (1629–1685)* (1907) • NA Scot., John McGregor MSS, GD50/186/65/1, 2, 6 • NA Scot., Breadalbane muniments, GD 112/9/1/3/36–8 • Inveraray Castle Archives, Inveraray, Argyll, Argyll letters [fol. 85] • Inveraray Castle Archives, Inveraray, Argyll, bundles 18/1, 54/330

Archives NA Scot., 'Double instructiones given by Lord Neill Campbell and Mr Robert Blackwood to Mr James Campbell', GD50/186/65/1 • NA Scot., 'Instructions', Lord Neil Campbell to Mr Robert Blackwood, GD50/186/65/2 • NA Scot., John McGregor MSS, 'Accompt My Lord Neal Campbell to Mr Rob't Blackwood 1690', GD50/186/65/6 • NA Scot., 'Memorial about Nether Lorn', GD112/9/1/3/36 • NA Scot., 'List of Lord Neil's debts', GD112/9/1/3/37, Breadalbane muniments | Inveraray Castle, Argyll, 'The heads or minuit of a contract betuix Archibald Marquis of Argyll for himself and taking burden on him for Lord Neill Campbell his second lawful sonne', London, bundle 18/1 • Inveraray Castle, Argyll, 'Ane list of armes', 'The disarming of Mull', bundle 54/330 • Inveraray Castle, Argyll, 'Petition for the tutor', 20 Oct 1685, Argyll letters, MS on fol. 85 • NA Scot., Breadalbane muniments, 'Memorandum anent the rents of the estate of Nether Lorne Cropts 1692 and 93, and how they were disposed of, with some notes anent the rents and debts of that estate March 1698', GD112/9/1/3/38

Likenesses oils, Scot. NPG

Wealth at death in considerable debt; debts of *c.*£20,000 Scots in 1693: *Scots peerage*, vol. 1, p. 360 • debts totalling £59,906 7*s*. Scots in 1701: 'List of Lord Neil's debts', 1701, GD 112/9/1/3/37, Breadalbane muniments, NA Scot.

Campbell, Neil (1678–1761), university principal and Church of Scotland minister, was the son of Major John Campbell of Glenaray and his wife, Jean Campbell of Pennymore. His mother later married the Revd Patrick Campbell (1633–1700) of Glenaray, after which Neil was educated at home, and then apparently completed his divinity studies at the University of Glasgow (1693?–1697?). He was licensed to preach on 21 June 1701 by the presbytery of Inveraray. On 9 September 1702 he became minister of Kilmallie, an onerous position because the parish was the largest geographically in Scotland. In 1705 he married Henreta Campbell (*d.* 1767?) and they subsequently had ten children, four of whom survived into adulthood. Campbell's health deteriorated because of the gruelling travel involved in fulfilling his clerical duties, and in July 1709 he seized the opportunity to transfer to the living of Rosneath in Dunbartonshire, which was controlled by his kinsman John Campbell, second duke of Argyll. Thanks to Argyll he was presented to the parish of Renfrew by the crown on 15 November 1715, and assumed his post on 18 July 1716.

Having pursued a modestly successful career in the kirk, Campbell rose to prominence in Scotland in December 1727, when Argyll and his brother Archibald, Lord Ilay, prevailed upon George II to choose him as the principal of Glasgow University, following the death of Principal John Stirling. He was formally admitted on 8 February 1728, and was immediately embroiled in the controversy surrounding John Simson, the Glasgow professor of divinity, who was then being investigated for suspected Arianism by a committee of the general assembly of the Church of Scotland. Campbell tried to defend his colleague before the assembly primarily because he wanted to protect the university from external interference in its affairs, but in May 1728 the assembly suspended Simson from his duties, and a year later prohibited him from preaching and teaching. Campbell was forced to take over the divinity class, and he lectured, without remuneration, until Simson died in 1740. Despite his defeat in the Simson affair, Campbell remained closely involved with the business of the general assembly in the 1730s and 1740s. He was elected moderator in 1732 and 1737, and his political connections at court gained him an appointment as royal chaplain on 31 January 1734.

Within the university, Campbell faced a number of challenges. He repeatedly locked horns with the professor of moral philosophy, Francis Hutcheson, whose polite form of presbyterianism was anathema to those with evangelical leanings like Campbell. The Glasgow faculty was also fractured along political lines, and Campbell was hard pressed to manage his colleagues on behalf of his Argathelian masters. Despite these divisions the college flourished under his guidance, and he pushed for a number of improvements in the teaching of science and medicine. However, a paralytic attack he suffered in 1753 undermined his control over the university, and his power continued to wane until his death in Glasgow on 22 June 1761.

PAUL WOOD

Sources J. Warrick, *The moderators of the Church of Scotland from 1690 to 1740* (1913) • *Fasti Scot.*, new edn • R. Wodrow, *Analecta, or, Materials for a history of remarkable providences, mostly relating to Scotch ministers and Christians*, ed. [M. Leishman], 4 vols., Maitland Club, 60 (1842–3) • *The correspondence of the Rev. Robert Wodrow*, ed. T. M'Crie, 3 vols., Wodrow Society, [3] (1842–3) • C. Innes, ed., *Munimenta alme Universitatis Glasguensis / Records of the University of Glasgow from its foundation till 1727*, 1–3, Maitland Club, 72 (1854) • J. Coutts, *A history of the University of Glasgow* (1909) • R. L. Emerson, 'Politics and the Glasgow professors, 1690–1800', *The Glasgow Enlightenment*, ed. A. Hook and R. B. Sher (1995), 21–39 • *Glasgow Journal* (18–25 June 1761)

Campbell, Sir Neil (1776–1827), army officer and colonial governor, second son of Captain Neil Campbell of Duntroon, was born on 1 May 1776. He was commissioned ensign in the 6th West India regiment on 2 April 1797, and exchanged into the 67th regiment on 29 October 1798. He was for a time the commanding officer in the Caicos Islands or Turks Islands, and was publicly thanked by the inhabitants. On 23 August 1799 he purchased a lieutenancy in the 57th, and in 1800 returned to England and volunteered to join the 95th, afterwards the Rifle brigade, on its first formation. He purchased his company on 4 June 1801, and proved himself an able officer of light troops. His speed in running was reputedly remarkable, and a story is told by Sir William Napier of his beating even Sir John Moore, with whom he was a great favourite, in a race at Shorncliffe.

From February 1802 to September 1803, Campbell was at the Royal Military College, Marlow, and on leaving was appointed assistant quartermaster-general for the southern district. He purchased a majority in the 43rd on 24 January 1805, which he exchanged for a majority in the 54th on 20 February 1806. After two years in Jamaica with the 54th, he returned to England, became lieutenant-colonel on 20 August 1808, and was sent to the West Indies as deputy adjutant-general. As such he was at the capture of Martinique in January 1809, of the Saintes Islands in April 1809, and of Guadeloupe in January 1810. That year he returned to England, and was posted to Portugal with strong letters of recommendation to Marshal Beresford, who appointed him colonel of the 16th Portuguese infantry, one of the regiments of Pack's brigade, in April 1811. In January 1813, after serving at Ciudad Rodrigo and Salamanca, he returned to England on sick leave, and was then sent to join Lord Cathcart, British minister at the Russian court, and military commissioner with the Russian army in Poland. Campbell was attached by him to Wittgenstein's column, with which he remained, almost continuously, until the entry of the allies into Paris on 31 March 1814. Campbell took every opportunity of fighting. In the battle of Fère-Champenoise, fought on 24 March 1814, he led a Russian cavalry charge, and in the mêlée was mistaken for a French officer and severely wounded by a Cossack. He was strongly recommended by Lord Cathcart to Lord Castlereagh, and selected as British commissioner to accompany Napoleon to Elba.

Campbell was promoted colonel on 4 June 1814, made a knight of three Russian orders, appointed CB in 1815, and knighted by patent on 2 October. He accompanied Napoleon to Elba with orders from Lord Castlereagh that he was not to act as his gaoler, but rather to put the former emperor in possession of the island of which he was to be the sovereign prince. Campbell had further instructions as to the settlement of Italy, which clearly showed Lord Castlereagh's intention that he should not remain in Elba longer than he thought necessary. At Napoleon's request, however, Campbell promised to make Elba his headquarters until the conclusion of the Congress of Vienna, and it was the supposed presence of the British colonel there which put the British naval captains off their guard, and enabled Napoleon to escape so easily. It was during one of Campbell's frequent visits to Italy, from 17 to 28 February 1815, that Napoleon escaped. Many people at the time believed that Campbell was bribed, but the ministry declared that his behaviour had been satisfactory, and even continued his powers in Italy.

In this capacity, however, Campbell met with an unexpected rebuff from Lord Exmouth and, returning home, joined the 54th, in which he still held the regimental rank of major, in the Southern Netherlands. With it he served at Waterloo, and afterwards headed the column of attack on the Valenciennes gate of Cambrai. During the occupation of France, from 1815 to 1818, he commanded the Hanseatic Legion, which consisted of 3000 volunteers from the free cities of Hamburg, Bremen, and Lübeck, and afterwards made a short visit to Africa to see if it were possible to discover any traces of Mungo Park.

On 29 May 1825 Campbell was promoted major-general, and applied for a staff appointment. The first which fell vacant was the governorship of Sierra Leone, where the previous governor, Major-General Sir Charles Turner, had died of fever (apparently malaria) at Government House on 7 March 1826, after little more than a year in office; begged not to take it by his family, Campbell rejected their fears, and reached Freetown in May 1826. Sierra Leone was a controversial and corrupt colony, called by *The Times* 'a costly grave for British subjects' (Fyfe, 165). Campbell was an energetic governor who vigorously attempted both to reduce expenditure and to improve the colony. He drained the Freetown streets with deep gutters (into which horses and pedestrians fell at night), attempted to suppress jobbery and regularize land tenures, replaced recaptives' supplies by temporary money payments, and in defiance of orders followed an expansionist policy. He sent copious dispatches back to London. Apparently insecure and haunted by Bonaparte's escape—a friend wrote of his 'anxious, zealous—I may add *fidgetty*—disposition' (Fyfe, 162), he distrusted his second-in-command, Lieutenant-Colonel Dixon Denham (chief superintendent of the Liberated African Department), and other subordinates. He was in conflict with missionaries, merchants, officials, Freetown property owners, chiefs, and the navy (which he loathed). His doctor in England had warned him against over-exciting himself in Sierra Leone. He disregarded warnings and insisted that the country was perfectly healthy. In August 1827 dispatches arrived from the Colonial Office disapproving of almost all his actions. Disappointment apparently exacerbated a fever (seemingly malaria), and within ten days he had died at Government House, Freetown, on 14 August 1827.

H. M. STEPHENS, *rev.* STEWART M. FRASER

Sources N. Campbell, *Napoleon at Fontainebleau and Elba* (1869) · C. W. C. Oman, *A history of the Peninsular War*, 1–3 (1902–8); repr. (1995–6) · R. Muir, *Britain and the defeat of Napoleon, 1807–1815* (1996) · *GM*, 1st ser., 96/1 (1826) · C. Fyfe, *A history of Sierra Leone* (1962); repr. (1993) · J. Peterson, *Province of freedom: a history of Sierra Leone, 1787–1870* (1969) · C. P. Foray, *A historical dictionary of Sierra Leone* (1977)

Archives NL Scot.

Likenesses E. Pingret, oils, 1819, NAM

Campbell, Norman Robert (1880–1949), physicist and philosopher, was born on 7 March 1880 at 19 Westbourne Terrace, Kensington, London, the third son of William Middleton Campbell of Camis-Esken, Helensburgh, Dunbartonshire, a sugar merchant, and his wife, Edith Agneta Bevan. He was educated at Eton College where he was a king's scholar, Tomline prizeman in 1897, and captain of school 1898–9. Later in 1899 he went to Trinity College, Cambridge, becoming a scholar in 1902 and graduating in the natural sciences tripos in the same year. He was elected a fellow of Trinity in 1904, gaining the ScD in 1912.

Campbell joined the Cavendish Laboratory, Cambridge, under J. J. Thomson, working on spontaneous ionization of gases. With others he diagnosed penetrating radiation as the cause of the phenomenon and he and A. Wood detected and recorded a diurnal periodicity in its intensity.

In 1906 Campbell attempted to establish whether all metals were radioactive to some degree, verifying first that the radioactivity of a compound can be calculated from that of its constituent elements. This enabled him, again with A. Wood, to investigate for the first time the radioactivity of the reactive alkali metals, experimenting on their stable salts. They rapidly found that potassium and rubidium salts appeared to be more active than any substance previously tried which did not contain one of the well recognized radioactive elements such as radium ('The radioactivity of the alkali metals', *Proceedings of the Cambridge Philosophical Society*, 14, 1908, 15–21). Over the next two years Campbell established the activity of potassium and rubidium beyond doubt and showed that, while less intrinsically active than rubidium, the rays from potassium were exceptionally penetrating ('The radioactivity of potassium, with special reference to solutions of its salts', ibid., 557–67; 'The radioactivity of rubidium', *Proceedings of the Cambridge Philosophical Society*, 15, 1909, 11–12).

In 1910 Campbell applied to join W. H. Bragg's group at Leeds, studying X-ray ionization, on an honorary basis. He embarked on a study of the characteristics of secondary radiation. In 1912 his position at Leeds was formalized by the creation of an honorary research fellowship especially for him. While in Leeds, Campbell met Edith Utley Sowerbutts (1881–1948), a neighbour who taught science at Leeds Girls' High School. They married on 25 March 1912. Although she was the daughter of a Methodist minister, John Crompton Sowerbutts, Campbell, throughout his life, refused to have anything to do with formal religion.

During the First World War, Campbell left Leeds for the National Physical Laboratory, where he joined the department of electrotechnics and photometry under Clifford Paterson. In 1916 the Osram Lamp Works recruited Paterson to establish a research laboratory after the end of the war. Paterson in turn recruited Campbell as one of the first members of research staff at what became the General Electric Company (GEC) Research Laboratory. Before joining the laboratory in 1919, however, the Campbells, who were childless, adopted two babies, a boy and a girl, and retreated to Kettlewell in Yorkshire for nine months to adapt to family life. While here, out of reach of libraries or other sources of reference, Campbell wrote his most influential book, *Physics, the Elements* (1920).

Campbell remained at the GEC laboratories for twenty-five years, establishing long-standing friendships with H. Ward and C. Smithells. He conducted research on the clean-up of gases in the electric discharge, photoelectric photometry, and the standardization and theory of photoelectric cells on which he wrote a book with Dorothy Ritchie. At the end of his career, together with his colleagues V. J. Francis and E. G. James, he returned to the problem of noise in receiving systems for which he had laid the foundations while still at the Cavendish. Campbell avoided a prominent role in administration, but was responsible for running the patent department through most of the Second World War.

Soon after losing their son, torpedoed on service in the Mediterranean in 1941, the Campbells retired, in March 1944, to East Chaldon in Dorset. Two months later a stray bomb destroyed the house and most of their possessions. Campbell, who was buried in mud, was virtually unharmed but Edith was severely injured. Four years later, following her death in 1948, Campbell went to live with their daughter and grandchildren in Nottingham. He died on 18 May 1949 in Nottingham General Hospital and was cremated at Nottingham crematorium.

Campbell was described by his daughter as friendly and enthusiastic and by a contemporary as 'a man of the highest principles, [who] once convinced he was right was uncompromising in his attitude in ethical and scientific discussion' (*Nature*). He was slight in build and had a stammer which prevented his being a successful lecturer. His chief hobbies were walking and climbing and he is said to have climbed every Scottish peak over 2000 feet. Later, when ill health prevented walking, he amused himself with crosswords and chess.

Campbell's scientific work amounted to eighty-eight papers and nine books, and he counted himself as an experimental physicist. But his major influence was as a philosopher of science, contributing to the logic of theory construction and the principles of physical measurement. Campbell was unusual among J. J. Thomson's students in responding to the spirit of fundamental criticism which was revolutionizing pure mathematics at the time. He was also highly aware of the implications for physics of the change, then taking place, from mathematically trained to experimentally trained physicists. In his first book, *Modern Electrical Theory* (1907), he distinguished between the older style physics of the mathematicians and the new physics of the experimentalists. The mathematical physicists had believed that all phenomena were ultimately to be explained in terms of the ether which obeyed the laws of Newtonian dynamics, the mathematical logic of which guaranteed consistency and legitimated the use of unobservable entities, such as atoms, in deductive theories. Campbell, though, rejected the idea of a stationary ether, because it played no useful heuristic role for the experimenter, and developed a theory which foreshadowed aspects of Einstein's theory of relativity.

This adoption of an experimental approach left Campbell with a problem: he required a consistent epistemological underpinning for his belief that theoretical entities were meaningful only if they related directly to measurable quantities. Influenced by the writings of Mach and Poincaré, Campbell first set out his views in *The Principles of Electricity* (1912), followed in 1920 by his major work, *Physics, the Elements*. He emphasized the role of analogy in physical theorizing and introduced the idea of a 'dictionary' which defined the meaning of theoretical ideas. In *The Principles of Measurement and Calculation* (1928) he subsequently defined how measurement related to concepts such as mass.

Campbell was relatively exceptional in attempting to formulate a philosophy which described his experience of the actual practice of science. According to G. Buchdahl:

> By 1960 many of his doctrines concerning the nature of physical theories had become incorporated in the teaching of the philosophical classrooms … whilst to a superficial view [these doctrines] may appear as no more than a series of heuristic proposals, none the less they were meant at the same time to have the force of a *logical* conclusion; and yet when regarded in the light of Campbell's intellectual development, they were just as clearly motivated by his touching respect for the opinions of J. J. Thomson and his continuing regard for the ideas of Michael Faraday. (Buchdahl, 151)

Isobel Falconer

Sources *Nature*, 164 (1949), 14 · private information (2004) · A. Warwick, 'Cambridge mathematics and Cavendish physics: Cunningham, Campbell and Einstein's relativity, 1905–1911', Part 2, *Studies in the History and Philosophy of Science*, 24 (1993), 1–25 · G. Buchdahl, 'Theory construction: the work of Norman Robert Campbell', *Isis*, 55 (1964), 151–62 · *Annual Report* [University of Leeds] (1909–17) · *Calendar* [University of Leeds] (1912–18) · minutes of Senate and Council, 1912, U. Leeds · C. C. Paterson, *A confidential history of the research laboratories* (1945) · R. Clayton and J. Algar, eds., *A scientist's war: the war diary of Sir Clifford Paterson* (1991) · *The Eton register*, 6 (privately printed, Eton, 1910) · N. R. Campbell, preface, *Physics, the elements* (1920) · I. Hacking, *Scientific revolutions* (1981) · GEC-Marconi Research Centre, Chelmsford, Essex, GEC archives · b. cert. · b. cert. [Edith Utley Sowerbutts] · m. cert. · d. cert. · d. cert. [Edith Utley Campbell] · *CGPLA Eng. & Wales* (1949)

Likenesses group photographs, 1902–9, U. Cam., Cavendish Laboratory · group photograph, 1923, GEC Research Laboratory · photograph, 1940, priv. coll. · two photographs, 1943–7, priv. coll.
Wealth at death £21,198 3s. 6d.: probate, 17 Aug 1949, *CGPLA Eng. & Wales*

Campbell, Sir Patrick (1773–1841), naval officer, was a son of Colonel John Campbell of Melfort in Argyllshire, and his wife, Colina, daughter of John Campbell of Auchalader; he was elder brother of Lieutenant-General Sir Colin *Campbell (1776–1847). He was made lieutenant on 25 September 1794, and commander on 4 September 1797.

In 1799 Campbell was appointed to the sloop *Dart*, an experimental vessel designed by Sir Samuel Bentham, carrying a formidable armament of thirty 32-pounder carronades. On the night of 7 July 1800 the *Dart*, with two gunbrigs and four fireships, was sent into Dunkirk to attempt the destruction of four large French frigates. The *Dart* ran close alongside one, the *Désirée* (38 guns), fired a double-shotted broadside, carried her by boarding, and brought her out over the shoals. The other frigates evaded the fireships by running themselves ashore, and were afloat again the next day; but the capture of the *Désirée* was evidence of success, which seemed the more remarkable as the *Dart* was rated as a sloop, and her exceptional armament was not generally known. The achievement won Campbell his post rank (11 July) and his immediate appointment to the frigate *Ariadne*.

In September 1803 Campbell was appointed to the *Doris*, which on 12 January 1805 struck on a rock in Quiberon Bay, and had to be abandoned and burnt a few days later, the officers and men being received on board the *Tonnant* (80 guns, Captain W. H. Jervis). On joining Admiral Cornwallis off Brest on 26 January, the boat in which the two captains were going on board the flagship was swamped; Jervis was drowned, but Campbell was rescued.

In 1807 and following years Campbell commanded the frigate *Unité* in the Adriatic; in 1811 he was moved into the *Leviathan* (74 guns), also in the Mediterranean. He was nominated a CB in June 1815, and had no further service until 1824, when he commanded the *Ganges* on the home station. In March 1827 he commissioned the *Ocean* for the Mediterranean, but manning a ship then took many months, and he had not joined the fleet when Navarino was fought. The *Ocean* was paid off in the spring of 1830, and on 22 July Campbell attained the rank of rear-admiral. From 1834 to 1837 he was commander-in-chief at the Cape of Good Hope, with his flag in the frigate *Thalia*.

Campbell was made a KCB on 12 April 1836, became a vice-admiral on 28 June 1838, and died at Leamington Spa, Warwickshire, on 13 October 1841. He had married in 1825 Margaret, daughter of Captain Andrew Wauchope of Niddrie, and they had two sons: the elder, Patrick John, was by 1886 a major-general in the Royal Horse Artillery; the younger, Colin, as a lieutenant, commanded the gunboat *Opossum* in China from 1857 to 1859, was captain of the *Bombay* when she was burnt at Montevideo on 14 December 1864, and died at sea on board the *Ariadne* in 1869.

J. K. Laughton, *rev.* Roger Morriss

Sources J. Marshall, *Royal naval biography*, 3/2 (1832), 290 · personal knowledge (1886) · O'Byrne, *Naval biog. dict.* · *GM*, 2nd ser., 15 (1841), 542–3
Archives NRA Scotland, priv. coll., letters to Sir Charles Adams

Campbell, Mrs Patrick. *See* Campbell, Beatrice Stella (1865–1940).

Campbell, Patrick Gordon, third Baron Glenavy (1913–1980), journalist, was born at 21 Great Denmark Street, Dublin, on 6 June 1913, the eldest of the three children of Charles Henry Gordon Campbell, second Baron Glenavy (1885–1963), later governor of the Bank of Ireland, and his wife, Beatrice Moss Elvery, distinguished painter, and daughter of William Elvery, businessman, of Rothbury, Foxrock, co. Dublin. Campbell spent the first nine years of his life in London until the family returned to Dublin. As both his father and his grandfather, James Henry Mussen Campbell (1851–1931), lord chancellor of Ireland under the union and later chairman of the Irish Free State, were supporters of the pro-treaty party, they were marked for IRA reprisals during 'the troubles'; on Christmas eve 1922 the family was roused at gunpoint and herded out on to the lawn where they watched their home being set on fire.

Campbell was stimulated by the artistic interests of his parents who were part of circles which included Samuel Beckett, Elizabeth Bowen, and J. B. Priestley. His father himself had a novel admired by D. H. Lawrence and Katherine Mansfield. As a child Campbell was already tall and gangling (his knees knocked together so hard, he was to recall, that they were severely bruised) and he developed a sometimes paralysing stammer. His time at Crawley's preparatory school, Castle Park in Dublin, Rossall School, and briefly at Pembroke College, Oxford, was undistinguished. When he went down from Oxford after four terms without taking a degree his father did his best to launch him in business, without success. For two years he was an apprentice for an electrical firm in Munich. He left for Paris after being attacked for mocking the Nazi anthem. As a last resort his father sent him with an introduction to Robert Maire Smyllie, the Falstaffian but shrewd editor of the *Irish Times*. Smyllie tested him out by sending him to do a piece on a visit to the Dublin Zoo; it appeared unchanged the following day; and after a spell learning to type and failing to learn shorthand, Patrick Campbell was finally launched on his successful career with Smyllie nurturing Campbell's gift for prose.

Smyllie pursued a policy of sending his more promising recruits on a round of jobs: Campbell was briefly a feature writer, leader writer, literary editor, film critic, and parliamentary sketch writer, his mordant humour at the expense of some members of the Dáil establishing his reputation with readers. The *Irish Times* was one of the most respected English language newspapers, but after three years Campbell felt Dublin was becoming too small. He left for Fleet Street to work for Lord Beaverbrook, who had known and admired his grandfather. He failed to make an impression at either the *Daily Express* or the *Evening Standard*, and when the Second World War broke out he returned to Ireland where, as Smyllie declined to take him back, he struggled to establish himself as a writer and joined the Irish marine service, in which he stayed until 1944. It was a difficult decision, as many Irish were joining the British forces. Certainly after the war Campbell felt uncomfortable that he missed 'a fearful experience that millions of other people endured and some others failed to survive' (including his sister Elizabeth who was killed in an air raid in London). On 7 August 1941 Campbell married Sylvia Alfreda Willoughby-Lee, a secretary for the *Daily Mirror*, and daughter of Captain Kenneth Willoughby-Lee MC, of Muizenberg, South Africa. In 1944 Smyllie relented, and offered Campbell the job of writing 'An Irishman's diary', a popular column which he had to produce five days a week. The column provided the format he followed for the rest of his life: 'a situation with a beginning, a middle and an end—almost a short story—with myself right in the middle of it' (Campbell).

By 1947 Campbell felt sufficiently confident to return to Fleet Street to do a weekly column for the *Sunday Dispatch*, a paper which Smyllie abhorred. It proved to be very popular, as did the monthly article he wrote for the magazine *Lilliput* from 1947 to 1953. The more literary and distinguished *Lilliput* began to assume greater importance in Campbell's life. Here he built up his reputation as a humorist and was compared favourably with essayists James Thurber and Stephen Leacock. His best work from this period can be found in *Patrick Campbell's Omnibus* (1954).

But the *Lilliput* job put a strain on Campbell's already faltering marriage. In 1947 he was divorced and on 6 August 1949 he married Cherry Margaret Lowson Lawson, daughter of Major George Lowson Monro, of the Indian army. By the time of their marriage she had charged her name to Campbell by deed poll. They settled in Dolphin Square, London, where Brigid, his only child, was born. During this period Campbell also became a film writer for the Rank Organization, then at the height of its film production era, and he was employed as an 'additional dialogue writer' for Pinewood Studios. He also made his mark in gatherings such as the Thursday Club.

Agreeable though the life was, it did Campbell's writing no good; this became, as he admitted, mechanical. One by one he lost his regular jobs. But after a shaky spell which culminated in the end of his second marriage in divorce, a series of entertaining recollections of past episodes in his life for *The Spectator* (later collected in *Come Here till I Tell You*, 1960) led to his being offered a column in the *Sunday Times*. There he perfected the style which allowed him to 'toss up a trifle of experience and keep it in the air with great dexterity for minutes before letting it spin away into fantasy' (*The Times*). When E. G. (Ned) Sherrin suggested he should become one of the resident talkers in BBC television's *Not so Much a Programme, More a Way of Life*, he decided to risk trying out his stammer on a mass audience. In the end Campbell used his stammer to point up jokes—or, often, to make ordinary statements sound as if they were jokes. Later he won more kudos in the *Call my Bluff* series in the protracted battle with Frank Muir's team. Gratifying though it was for him to receive tributes, as he often did, for giving the stammer a new image, he always insisted that he would willingly have got rid of it if he could.

Campbell's public profile increased sales of his books: fifteen were published, chiefly for the Christmas market, in the space of twenty-three years. Most of them were collections of his articles, the exceptions being *My Life and Easy Times* (1967), his autobiography, which was also a moving tribute to his father, and *How to Become a Scratch Golfer* (1963), a light-hearted look back over one of the two recreations he listed in *Who's Who* (the other being, simply, 'pleasure'). As a golfer he had in fact been quite close to international standard, on one occasion surviving four rounds of the Irish open amateur championship, defeating a leading Walker cup contender in the process.

Campbell's second marriage was dissolved in 1966 and in the same year he married Vivienne, previously wife of Charles Orme, and daughter of Charles Knight MC. He had worked with her for years on film and television scripts. After their marriage they went to live in the south of France, where they remained—except when television and other commitments brought him back to England—until he died of viral pneumonia, following a few years of ill health, in University College Hospital, London, on 9 November 1980. He was succeeded in the barony by his brother Michael Mussen (*b.* 1924).

Campbell had succeeded his father as Lord Glenavy in 1963, but he rarely reminded anyone of his title. Thanks to his stammer, his height, and his imposing appearance—he had something of the look of a Roman emperor about him—he became a well-known and much imitated public figure, remembered as a skilled humorist and raconteur.

BRIAN INGLIS, *rev.* CLARE L. TAYLOR

Sources P. Campbell, *My life and easy times* (1967) [repr. 1988] · U. O'Connor, 'Patrick Campbell: a biographical memoir', *The Campbell companion: the best of Patrick Campbell* (1987) [repr. 1994] · Burke, *Peerage* · *The Times* (11 Nov 1980) · b. cert. · d. cert. · m. cert. [Cherry Margaret Lowson Lawson]
Archives TCD, family corresp. and papers

Campbell, Pryse, of Cawdor (1727–1768). *See under* Campbell family of Cawdor (*per.* 1511–1821).

Campbell, Reginald John (1867–1956), Congregational minister and Church of England clergyman, was born on 29 August 1867 at 2 Norfolk Villas, Jamaica Level, Bermondsey, London, the second of four sons and one daughter of John Campbell, a United Methodist Free Church minister, and his wife, Mary Johnstone. His parents were of Ulster Presbyterian stock. He was registered at birth as John Wesley Campbell, which name also appears on his first marriage certificate, but he matriculated as Reginald John Campbell, the names by which he was commonly known.

Educated privately in Ulster (where he spent some of his childhood), at grammar school, and University College in Nottingham, he matriculated as a commoner at Christ Church, Oxford, in 1892 after some years as a schoolteacher. He took a second class in modern history in 1895 and proceeded MA in 1902. He was made an honorary DD

Reginald John Campbell (1867–1956), by Lena Connell

in 1919. He married first, in 1889, Mary Elizabeth (1861–1924), daughter of James Slack of Nottingham; and second, in 1927, Ethel Gertrude Smith (1885–1943).

Already confirmed as an Anglican, and moving in Anglo-Catholic circles, it was assumed that Campbell would take holy orders in the Church of England. However, in a period of crisis, he rejected Anglo-Catholic assumptions and unexpectedly, under the influence of A. M. Fairbairn, principal of Mansfield College, became minister of the Congregationalist Union Street Chapel, Brighton. The congregation rallied strongly under his leadership, though it was as much Anglican as nonconformist in composition. It was during these years that he embarked upon a wide range of reading in theology, philosophy, and spirituality. His nonconformity was eclectic. He had a considerable pulpit presence but was not given to histrionics. His delicate features, crowned by an early shock of snow-white hair, expressed spiritual refinement and insight but also revealed physical vulnerability. He was already no stranger to nervous breakdown. Publication of volumes of sermons brought him a wider audience, and prominent Liberal politicians beat a path to his dinner table. His political Liberalism at this time, however, did not altogether banish his early exposure to strong Ulster sentiment. A visit to Cape Town in 1900, for the sake of his health, resulted in his catching both enteric and imperial fever: God had given to the British certain powers which other races had not.

Campbell's reputation spread, and in May 1903 he took up duties as minister of the City Temple—'the cathedral of nonconformity'—in London. On his opening Sunday the total congregations, morning and evening, came to 7000 people. He was expected to preach twice on Sundays and at a popular Thursday lunchtime service. The sermons, which addressed both issues of the day and doctrinal questions, were instantly published and attracted much attention both in Britain and in the United States. Concerning the contemporary educational controversy, Campbell declared that he was unwilling to pay 'the parson's rate'. Some of his leading nonconformist colleagues, even so, felt that he was too gentle with the Church of England, although a particular assault which Campbell made on sacerdotalism accorded with Lloyd George's view of sound doctrine. The fact was that Campbell found it difficult to reconcile the conflicting strands in his upbringing and environment. He lived perpetually on edge.

The New Theology controversy which erupted in 1907 accentuated these tensions. Originating in a press interview Campbell gave to the *Daily Mail*, the term reflected, in his words, an attitude and a spirit rather than a creed. At great speed, Campbell wrote a book, *The New Theology* (1907), which produced further controversy and public fame. Groups of disciples sprang to his defence, and organized a national movement to spread his ideas throughout the country. Traditional exposition of the fall or of the blood-atonement, Campbell suggested, was not only misleading but unethical. There is ample testimony to the interest the book aroused. Orthodox theologians, however, suggested that it revealed that Campbell had never been trained in theology. According to the *British Weekly*, A. M. Fairbairn described the book as 'a farrago of nonsense' (4 April 1907), and James Denney wrote scornfully in private about 'half-educated sophists who write New Theologies' (Denney, 85). Campbell was apparently even subject to death threats. Undeterred, he took up the 'social gospel', put himself at the disposal of the Independent Labour Party, and produced a volume entitled *Christianity and the Social Order* (1907). Campbell was elected to the executive of the Fabian Society in 1908 and shared platforms with Keir Hardie. He supported votes for women and divorce. The conflicting demands on his time and energy, however, created tensions which Campbell found increasingly difficult to handle. Suffering from ill health, he gradually withdrew from public commitments. There were suspicions that he was meditating a return to the Church of England. On his own account, he was influenced by criticism of the New Theology by the Anglican Charles Gore.

Campbell's support for the war in 1914 was politically important. He paid a short visit to the western front. Lloyd George made his first public statement on the war in the City Temple. Campbell's stance upset Liberals and socialists of pacifist inclination. In 1915 he stopped the publication of his book on the New Theology and shortly afterwards resigned from the City Temple. In the same year, he was ordained in the Church of England and joined the staff of Birmingham Cathedral. In 1916 he published an autobiography which conveyed the message that his decision had been logical since he had never been a thoroughbred English nonconformist. It was a blow to dissent to lose a man many regarded as the most dynamic figure in its ranks. Even so, he claimed to be only exchanging a more perfect for a less perfect churchmanship.

Campbell's Anglican career thereafter was far less exposed to public scrutiny. It transpired that as vicar of Christ Church, Westminster, Campbell could not continue in the kind of ministry he had exercised as a nonconformist. Years from 1924 until 1930 back in Brighton at Trinity Chapel were more successful. He was appointed to a residential canonry at Chichester in 1930, a post he held until 1936. For the next decade he remained at Chichester as chancellor, where he reviewed books regularly in the religious press and wrote devotional and biographical studies, an activity continued in retirement after 1946. In 1947, in a private letter, Campbell wrote that no man could have done more to have avoided publicity than he had done for a generation. Before 1914, on the other hand, he had received it, perhaps courted it, in ample measure. He died at his home, Heatherdene, at Fairwarp, near Uckfield, Sussex, on 1 March 1956. KEITH ROBBINS

Sources R. J. Campbell, *A spiritual pilgrimage* (1916) • K. Robbins, 'The spiritual pilgrimage of the Rev. R. J. Campbell', *Journal of Ecclesiastical History*, 30 (1979), 261–76 • K. Robbins, *History, religion and identity in modern Britain* (1993) • C. T. Bateman, *R. J. Campbell, M. A., pastor of the City Temple* (1903) • A. H. Wilkinson, *Rev. R. J. Campbell: the man and his message* (1907) • *The Times* (1 March 1956) • b. cert. • d. cert. • m. certs. • J. Foster, *Oxford men, 1880–1892: with a record of their schools, honours, and degrees* (1893) • *British Weekly* (4 April 1907) • J. Denney, *Letters of Principal James Denney to W. Robertson Nicoll, 1893–1917* (1920) • *CGPLA Eng. & Wales* (1956)

Likenesses L. Connell, photograph, NPG [*see illus.*] • Spy [L. Ward], pen-and-ink drawing, NPG; repro. in *VF* (24 Nov 1904)

Wealth at death £12,997 10s. 2d.: probate, 14 May 1956, *CGPLA Eng. & Wales*

Campbell, Robert (*d.* 1722), Presbyterian minister, probably born in Scotland, was licensed to preach by the presbytery of Dunoon. He went to Ireland and settled at Ray, co. Donegal, where he was ordained in 1671 by a presbytery then known as the Laggan meeting. Its members got into trouble by proclaiming a 'publike fast' for 17 February 1681. Campbell and three others were examined at Raphoe and Dublin, and, having been tried at Lifford assizes, were fined £20 each and required to give a written engagement not to offend again. They refused to do either, and so were detained in custody at Lifford, but after eight months' confinement were released (20 April 1682) on paying a reduced fine. While thus detained they were allowed to preach every Sunday in turn, and were occasionally let out surreptitiously by their keepers to hold services in the country. During the troubles of 1689 Campbell went back to Scotland, where he was called to Rosneath, Dunbartonshire, on 17 August. He accepted on 3 December, and officiated until Whitsunday 1691, after which he went back to Ray, where he is recorded as being on 21 May. He was called to Donaghmore on 21 December 1692, but the Laggan meeting on 8 February 1693 decided that he should remain at Ray. He was moderator of the general synod in 1694 at Antrim. On 2 July 1695 the Laggan presbytery placed his name first among three, one of whom was to act as a commissioner to William III in Flanders, to ask for 'legal liberty' and redress of grievances. It is not certain that this commission was ever carried out, but if it was, Campbell was not involved, as he is recorded as present at presbytery meetings on 30 July and 22 August 1695.

Campbell published a funeral sermon for Mary II in 1695, and a further volumes of sermons in 1696. He was married to Margaret Kelso, though details of the union are unknown; the marriage produced one son, Hugh, and two daughters, Agnes and Sarah. Patrick Vance was ordained at Ray on 23 December 1719 as Campbell's assistant and successor. Campbell died at Ray on 5 October 1722.

ALEXANDER GORDON, *rev.* ALEXANDER DU TOIT

Sources *Fasti Scot.*, new edn, 3.363, 7.527 • A. G. Lecky, *In the days of the Laggan presbytery* (1908) • J. S. Reid and W. D. Killen, *History of the Presbyterian church in Ireland*, new edn, 3 vols. (1867) • *A history of congregations in the Presbyterian Church in Ireland, 1610–1982*, Presbyterian Church in Ireland (1982) • T. Witherow, *Historical and literary memorials of presbyterianism in Ireland, 1623–1731* (1879) • J. Irving, *The book of Dunbartonshire*, 3 vols. (1879) • C. Innes, ed., *Munimenta alme Universitatis Glasguensis / Records of the University of Glasgow from its foundation till 1727*, 3, Maitland Club, 72 (1854)

Campbell, Robert. *See* MacGregor, Robert (*bap.* 1671, *d.* 1734).

Campbell, Robert (1769–1846), colonial merchant, was born on 28 April 1769 at Cathcart Square, Greenock, Renfrewshire, fourth surviving child of ten born to John Campbell (1727–1797), laird of Ashfield, writer, and town clerk, and his wife, Agnes, *née* Paterson (1729–1792). The three Campbell sons were 'bred merchant', and largely financed by their father. Robert was educated well, probably at the local borough school or with private tuition, before apparently joining his brother William in trading. In 1797 Robert followed his eldest brother, John, to Calcutta, where he was admitted to partnership in Campbell, Clarke & Co., later Campbell & Co. In April 1798 he was despatched to New South Wales with a speculative cargo, to investigate the fate of a previous venture wrecked on the Australian coast.

Recognizing the opportunity to open a regular trade with Botany Bay, Campbell acquired land at Sydney Cove for a warehouse and wharf, and returned with another cargo in February 1800. On 17 September 1801 he married Sophia (Sophy) Palmer (1777–1833), the artistically talented sister of the commissary, John Palmer. As Sydney's first resident merchant, Campbell negotiated government contracts for supplies from India, including cargoes of desperately needed cattle. By 1804 goods worth £50,000 lay in his store, and his restrained prices and generous credit caused grateful settlers to acknowledge this means of escape from the former 'mercenary unsparing Hand of Avarice and Extortion' (Steven, 60). To create a trade staple, Campbell financed local sealing and whaling, and to free this successful industry from mercantilist regulations he took a cargo of colonial produce to London in 1805. As the shipment contravened East India Company monopoly rights his ship was formally seized, but, with the intervention of Sir Joseph Banks and William Wilberforce, commercial loss was avoided and permission secured for the entry of a second cargo. Concurrently the Grenville ministry prepared a bill intended to free the trade of New South Wales but this significant policy did not survive its loss of office in 1807.

Campbell returned to Sydney in August 1806, some days after Governor Bligh, who welcomed him as 'just and humane and a gentleman like merchant' (Steven, 153). Already aware of dormant opposition, Bligh drew Campbell into his administration, appointing him magistrate and naval officer, then virtually colonial treasurer. As naval officer Campbell had the responsibility for confiscating the spirit stills from John Macarthur's ship, precipitating open resistance to the governor. Active and courageous during the insurrection, Campbell was arrested and dismissed from his posts by the rebels, and later tried by a rebel court—whose authority he persisted in rejecting—for refusing appointment as coroner. He remained a pillar of support for Bligh's persecuted allies, but his trading was destructively supervised in reprisal. Campbell was one of the first to be officially reinstated by Governor Macquarie but was compelled to sail for London as a witness for Bligh before he could order his affairs. He gave evidence at Lieutenant-Colonel Johnston's court martial in 1811 and the following April appeared before the select committee on transportation. In 1811 his London agent failed spectacularly, reputedly £30,000 in Campbell's debt. Though contriving to postpone collapse, he returned to Sydney in 1815 in all but utter ruin.

Campbell & Co. was liquidated. With house, premises, and lands mortgaged, the family lived frugally on rents until outstanding debts were honoured. By 1820, free of all connection with India, Campbell had opened a modest agency, and in 1827 admitted his sons John and Robert [*see below*] to partnership. Survival was aided by landholding. Campbell had purchased a large estate, Ashfield, in 1803 to accommodate rejected contract cattle. In 1806 one of his ships was wrecked in government service. In 1825 he was finally compensated by a grant of 5000 acres (Duntroon) to which he added many thousand acres by purchase. By the 1840s he owned the choicest selections on the Limestone plains—later the site of Canberra—while his stock also grazed on vast squatting runs.

Raised a Presbyterian, Campbell latterly gravitated towards the Church of England. He was a consistent benefactor, endowing churches and schools, was the agent for the London Missionary Society, and managed a savings bank for 'the industrious poor', popularly known as Campbell's bank. At the founding of the first Sydney chamber of commerce (1826) his name, as 'father of the mercantile community' (*Sydney Gazette*, 8 July 1826), was placed ahead of all other members. Survived by six of his seven children, Campbell died on 15 April 1846 at Duntroon, and was buried on 27 April in the family vault of St John's Anglican Church cemetery, Parramatta.

Robert Campbell (1804–1859), Campbell's second son, was born at Wharf House, Campbell's Wharf, Sydney, and educated in England (1810–19). On his return he joined his father's agency. He became a leader of the campaign to end convict transportation, first in the 1830s and again in 1846 when the threat of revival involved him in a celebrated public meeting and petition of dissent. In mid-1849 he chaired two further meetings, and was subsequently a delegate to the 'anti-felon' Australasian League. He was a liberal and democratic member of the legislative council (1851–6) and legislative assembly (1856–9), and was colonial treasurer in 1856, and again from 1858. He died at Duntroon, and was buried in the family vault at Parramatta.

The elder Robert Campbell's nephew, **Robert Campbell junior** (1789–1851), merchant, was born at Greenock, Renfrewshire, the son of William Campbell, town clerk, and his wife, Jean Morrison. He accompanied his uncle to Sydney in 1806 to become a clerk in Campbell & Co., but raised personal capital by discreet dealing. In 1813 he went into business independently and, acquiring a partner in 1835, traded also as Campbell & Co. During the economic collapse of the 1840s his company was administered by trustees, but the partnership recovered strongly, handling wool and gold. Dashing, convivial, and romantic, as well as shrewd, he was prominent in Sydney life. A director (1830–51) and president (1843–51) of the Bank of New South Wales, he was a pioneer of the Sydney turf, at one time owning a Persian stallion, Hector, the foundation sire of Australian bloodstock. Campbell died at Sydney, and was buried in Waverley cemetery.

MARGARET STEVEN

Sources M. Steven, *Merchant Campbell, 1769–1846* (1965), bibliography • C. E. T. Newman, *The spirit of Wharf House* (1961) • J. Kerr and H. Falkus, *From Sydney Cove to Duntroon* (1982) • J. M. Ward, *Earl Grey and the Australian colonies, 1846–1857: a study of self-government and self-interest* (1958) • R. H. Goddard, *The life and times of James Milson* (1955) • F. M. Bladen, ed., *Historical records of New South Wales*, 7 vols. (1892–1901), vols. 3–7 • [F. Watson], ed., *Historical records of Australia*, 1st ser., 6–12 (1916–19); 17–20 (1923–4) • *Sydney Morning Herald* (23 Oct 1846) • *Sydney Morning Herald* (12 June 1849) • *Sydney Morning Herald* (19 June 1849) • *Sydney Morning Herald* (9 April 1859) • *Australian* (3 Nov 1825) • *Australian* (10 Nov 1825) • *Australian* (30 Oct 1837) • *Australian* (28 April 1859) [Robert Campbell (1804–1859)] • *Sydney Gazette* (28 Nov 1812) • *Sydney Gazette* (24 July 1813) • *Sydney Gazette* (31 July 1813) • *Sydney Gazette* (6 Nov 1813) • *Sydney Gazette* (8 July 1826) • *Sydney Gazette* (1814–21) • Mitchell L., NSW, Robert Campbell MSS • *AusDB* • parish register, Middle Greenock, 28 April 1769 [births] • parish register, St Philip's, Sydney, Australia, 17 Sept 1801; 16 Sept 1835 [Robert Campbell (1804–1859); marriage] • d. cert. [Robert Campbell (1804–1859)]

Archives Mitchell L., NSW, MSS | BL OIOC, corresp. relating to East India Company, MS Eur. D 556 • Mitchell L., NSW, daybook and Charles Hook letter-book [microfilm] • State Archives of New South Wales, Sydney, supreme court MSS

Likenesses C. Rodius, charcoal sketch, 1834 (with C. E. T. Newman; after photograph), Mitchell L., NSW • oils, Royal Military College, Duntroon House, Canberra, Australia • photograph, Mitchell L., NSW

Wealth at death leading mercantile house; extensive lands and stock, and considerable personal establishment: will

Campbell, Robert, junior (1789–1851). *See under* Campbell, Robert (1769–1846).

Campbell, Robert (1804–1859). *See under* Campbell, Robert (1769–1846).

Campbell, Robert Calder (1798–1857), army officer in the East India Company and writer, was born in Scotland, son of the Revd Pryce Campbell, minister of Arderseir, Nair. In 1817 he obtained a cadetship in the East India Company's service, and became a lieutenant on the Madras establishment on 2 October 1818 and captain on 3 October 1826. He served with the 43rd Madras native infantry in the First Anglo-Burmese War of 1826–7. He was invalided in 1831, and promoted major in 1836. Campbell, who was described by *The Athenaeum* as 'a graceful writer of the minor prose and poetry of his time, and a kind-hearted scholar and gentleman', was a frequent contributor to magazines. His publications (under the name Calder Campbell) included *Lays from the East* (1831) and *Episodes in the War-Life of a Soldier, with Sketches in Prose and Verse* (1857). He died at his residence in University Street, London, on 13 May 1857. H. M. Chichester, *rev.* James Lunt

Sources C. Campbell [R. C. Campbell], *Episodes in the war-life of a soldier … in prose and verse* (1857) • Dodwell [E. Dodwell] and Miles [J. S. Miles], eds., *Alphabetical list of the officers of the Indian army: with the dates of their respective promotion, retirement, resignation, or death … from the year 1760 to the year … 1837* (1838) • Dodwell [E. Dodwell] and Miles [J. S. Miles], eds., *Alphabetical list of the Honourable East India Company's Bengal civil servants, from the year 1780 to the year 1838* (1839) • *The Athenaeum* (23 May 1857), 664 • *GM*, 3rd ser., 2 (1857), 742 • Boase, *Mod. Eng. biog.*

Campbell, Sir Ronald Hugh (1883–1953), diplomatist, was born in London on 27 September 1883, the eldest son of Sir Francis Alexander Campbell (1852–1911), assistant under-secretary of state for foreign affairs from 1902 to 1911, and his wife, Dora Edith, daughter of Hugh Hammersley, army agent and banker. He was educated at Haileybury College and in June 1907 passed a competitive examination and was appointed a clerk in the Foreign Office. On 30 April 1908 he married Helen (*d.* 1949), daughter of Richard Graham. They had a son and a daughter. In October 1910 Campbell was appointed an acting third secretary in the diplomatic service, and in November of that year he accompanied Sir Arthur Paget on a special embassy to the courts of Munich, Stuttgart, and Sofia to announce the accession of George V. In the following year he was in attendance on the representative of Venezuela at the coronation. From October 1913 to July 1919 he was private secretary to the permanent under-secretary and in January 1919 he was promoted second secretary while in attendance at the Paris peace conference. From July 1919 to December 1920 he was private secretary to Lord Curzon, acting secretary of state. He was appointed CMG in 1917 and promoted first secretary in September 1919.

Having in April 1928 been promoted counsellor at the Foreign Office, Campbell was in November 1929 appointed envoy-extraordinary and minister-plenipotentiary in Paris, where he often acted as chargé d'affaires. With his perfect command of French, he made many friends in official circles and proved himself a shrewd observer and an able negotiator. He was appointed minister to Belgrade in August 1935 and KCMG in January 1936. His lucid and well-balanced dispatches revealed an exceptional insight into the shifting pattern of Yugoslavia's foreign policy, subjected as it then was to mounting Nazi–fascist pressures.

In July 1939 Campbell was promoted to succeed Sir Eric Phipps as ambassador at Paris. He was sworn of the privy council, and took up his new appointment early in November. Calm, unruffled, as impeccable in unravelling knotty problems as in his personal appearance, he was endowed with the sturdiest common sense, an infinite capacity for taking pains, and a dry sense of humour; it was said that he wrote with such meticulous care that he never needed to correct a draft telegram. When the Germans invaded France in May 1940 this unassuming and gently persuasive Scot soon found his qualities as a diplomatist put to the severest test. Major-General Sir Edward Spears, who liaised on Churchill's behalf with French premier Paul Reynaud, perceived 'a real toughness under the smoothness of his exterior, an unflinching purpose at the back of his non-committal manner' (Spears, 178). Campbell took part on 11 June 1940 in the exodus of the French government from Paris: first to Tours, and three days later to Bordeaux. In intensely trying conditions he attempted to prevail on the French leaders to transfer overseas at least the nucleus of a government and to place their fleet beyond the range of axis interference. After the signature of the Franco-German armistice had made it useless for him to remain at Bordeaux, he embarked for England on 22 June. On his return home he rejoined the Foreign Office and was promoted GCMG.

In November 1940 Campbell was appointed ambassador to Lisbon with a specific brief to maintain Portugal's benevolent neutrality and help prevent Spain from entering the war on the side of the axis powers. In mid-December 1941 Anglo-Portuguese relations came near to breaking-point as a result of the unannounced entry of Australian and Dutch troops into Portuguese Timor to protect the colony from invasion by the Japanese. Campbell's dogged resourcefulness prevented the crisis from becoming an open quarrel. His masterly telegrams stressed the vital importance of the Anglo-Portuguese alliance for British Atlantic strategy and the need to avoid further alienating the Portuguese government and its leader, the dictator Dr Antonio Salazar. They were also reinforced by a visit to London. As a result an agreement was brought about that the troops would be withdrawn as soon as Portuguese forces arrived to replace them. The Japanese seized the island before this arrangement could be completed—which was fortunate, as Churchill intended that the Dutch and Australians should stay. In the summer of 1943 Campbell received the emissaries of Marshal Badoglio, who had been appointed Italian premier following the fall of Mussolini, when they arrived in Lisbon to sue for an armistice. In the same year he presided over the delicate negotiations which led to the grant of Portuguese facilities in the Azores to the allied forces. The Azores played an increasingly significant role in the build-up of American forces before and after the D-day landings in 1944. The negotiations over the Azores had been preceded by a great deal of preparation by Campbell and his staff, not least being his contribution to a series of secret conversations between Portuguese and British military staffs from the winter of 1941. Campbell's unremitting efforts also secured for Britain the lion's share of Portugal's vital supplies of wolfram ore (tungsten).

> Campbell … was just our man, courteous to everybody, rich in experience, dispassionate in his judgement … assuring us, with a touch of the best Foreign Office cynicism, that nothing was ever as serious as we thought it was. One day … when things had gone very wrong and we expected an explosion, he broke off the meeting and rang for the chef to tell him there was just time to make a better apple charlotte for lunch, 'You know, the brown stuff on top must crunch and taste burnt'. We all loved him. (Eccles, 99)

In July 1945 his superbly handled mission in Portugal came to an end and he retired.

It was appropriate that a man of Campbell's exemplary patience should have been an expert angler and that, with his keen eye for precise detail, he also excelled as a skilled cabinet-maker. The last years of his life were clouded by the death in 1949 of his charming and vivacious wife, Helen, and by the death of his daughter. He died at Lymington Hospital, Lymington, Hampshire, on 16 November 1953, of an intestinal obstruction. His son, Robin, who survived him, had been severely wounded in the attempt to kidnap Rommel during the North African campaign.

In 2002, many years after Campbell's death, it emerged that he had saved the lives of some 1000 Jews from Nazi-occupied central Europe, while ambassador in Lisbon, by arranging visas for them to flee to Mauritius, and by persuading the Portuguese authorities to issue transit or entrance visas. His actions led *The Times* to describe him as 'a British Oskar Schindler' (*The Times*, 5 April 2002), after the Sudeten German who had saved a similar number of Jews in German-occupied Poland.

John Balfour, *rev.* Anthony Adamthwaite

Sources *The Times* (17 Nov 1953) · E. M. Gates, *End of the affair: the collapse of the Anglo-French alliance, 1939–40* (1981) · *The diaries of Sir Alexander Cadogan, 1938–1945*, ed. D. Dilks (1971) · D. Eccles, *By safe hand* (1983) · G. Stone, *The oldest ally: Britain and the Portuguese connection, 1936–1941* (1994) · E. Spears, *Assignment to catastrophe* (1954) · C. Gladwyn, *The Paris embassy* (1976) · *WWW, 1951–60* · Burke, *Peerage* · *FO List* (1945) · personal knowledge (1971) [John Balfour] · private information (2004) [Professor Glyn Stone] · d. cert. · *The Times* (5 April 2002)
Archives PRO, private office MSS, FO 800/523-3/1 | Bodl. Oxf., corresp. with Rumbold · Cumbria AS, Carlisle, letters to Lord Howard of Penrith · Lpool RO, corresp. with seventeenth earl of Derby | FILM IWM FVA, news footage
Likenesses W. Stoneman, photograph, 1938, NPG · photograph, repro. in *The Times* (5 April 2002)
Wealth at death £28,847 19*s*. 9*d*.: probate, 3 Feb 1954, *CGPLA Eng. & Wales*

Campbell, (Ignatius) Royston Dunnachie [Roy] (**1901–1957**), poet and writer, was born in Durban, Natal, on 2 October 1901, the fourth child of a leading Durban physician, Samuel George Campbell (*d.* 1926), the son of a Scottish settler, and his wife, Margaret, daughter of James Dunnachie of Glenboig, Lanarkshire. Campbell had a free-ranging childhood, provided at an early age by his extended family of soldiers, farmers, hunters, athletes, and administrators with horses, guns, buck to shoot, fish to catch, and great areas of country in which to wander. Though he was much less active than he later liked to pretend he had been, he attributed to this fortunate childhood his adult enthusiasm for physical pursuits, his love of energy, violence, and colour (in writing as in life), and his dislike of mechanization and urban living. He completed his schooling at Durban Boys' High School in 1917, and after a year at Natal University College in Pietermaritzburg sailed for England at the end of the First World War, intending to read English at Merton College, Oxford. He failed to gain entry to the university, and instead spent a year living in Oxford in a back street, reading widely, notably the Elizabethan and Jacobean poets.

It was at Oxford that Campbell threw off the teetotalism of his family and took to drink; he was to be dependent on alcohol for the rest of his life. It was there, too, that he discovered his bisexual nature; he had a number of transitory affairs with men and women at Oxford. From the musician William Walton he learned the importance of dedicating himself entirely to art, and through Walton obtained introductions to the composer Philip Heseltine, the Sitwells, Wyndham Lewis, and T. S. Eliot.

One of his lovers of this period, the critic T. W. Earp, took Campbell to London, Berlin, and Paris, and steered him in the direction of the French symbolists. When Campbell left Oxford and went down to London, he shared a flat with Earp and (for a time) Aldous Huxley. Here, supported by Earp and an allowance from his father, he moved on the fringes of the London art world, and lived a leisurely, drifting life, travelling cheaply in France during the summer and taking any odd jobs that came to hand. He was tall and powerfully built, with the insolent good looks captured in the portrait Augustus John painted of him around this time.

In 1921 Campbell met and fell in love with a painter, Mary Garman (*d.* 1979), one of several beautiful daughters of a Birmingham doctor. Mary Garman had run away to London with her sister Kathleen, and was mixing with artists much as Campbell had been doing. After a period during which Campbell lived with both Mary and her sister, causing scandal even in bohemia, he and Mary married on 11 February 1922, and settled in a converted cowshed in the Welsh village of Aberdaron. Here their first daughter, Teresa, was born, and here Campbell finished the long poem that was to be published by Jonathan Cape in 1924, *The Flaming Terrapin*. This work was an immediate success and brought Campbell to prominence almost overnight, for in its energy, its cascading prodigality of imagery, and its strangeness of setting, it seemed a breath of fresh air to

(Ignatius) Royston Dunnachie Campbell (1901–1957), by Augustus John, *c.*1924

critics and readers grown accustomed to the genteel tones of the Georgian verse fashionable at the time.

Buoyed by this success, Campbell moved his family to South Africa, where his second daughter, Anna, was born in 1926. He founded a monthly magazine, *Voorslag* ('Whiplash'), which he ran with the help of William Plomer and Laurens van der Post. However their attacks on the colour bar alarmed *Voorslag's* financial backer. Campbell, refusing to be called to heel, resigned after two issues and returned to Europe, taking his revenge on Durban's commercial crassness in a long satirical poem, *The Wayzgoose* (1928). He followed up this energetic lampoon with another entitled *The Georgiad* (1931), this time with a British target, a sense of persecution having been awakened in him by the passionate love affair which his wife, Mary, had during 1927 with Vita Sackville-West, whose guests the Campbells had been for some months in Kent. Campbell associated Vita Sackville-West and her diplomatist husband, Harold Nicolson, with the ruling class of Britain, and came to see in them everything he most disliked.

During 1928–33 Campbell lived in southern France and from 1933 to 1936 in Spain; his love of southern Europe is evident everywhere in his poetry of this period, notably in the finest of his collections of verse, *Adamastor* (1930). His continued friendship with Wyndham Lewis brought him into contact with many of the central movements of modernism, and some of his work of the early 1930s shows the influence of futurism—paradoxically, for Campbell disliked machines and 'progress' as much as the Italian futurist Marinetti exulted in them. *Choosing a Mast* (1931), *Pomegranates* (1932), and *Flowering Reeds* (1933) exemplify his preoccupations at this time.

Campbell's emotional involvement in the Spanish Civil War is evident in many of the poems written after 1936; several reflect his direct experience of the fighting in Toledo, where he was living when the war broke out. His sympathies were for the nationalists (a result chiefly of his conversion to Catholicism), although he never fought for them as he claimed to have done. The most striking of his Spanish Civil War poems were the fine lyrics of *Mithraic Emblems* and the long and partisan poem *Flowering Rifle*, which glorified Franco and did Campbell's reputation great harm.

Campbell joined the British army in 1942, although he was by now over forty and in poor health. He served in east Africa, first in training with Wingate's commando force and then, after being permanently disabled in an accident, as a coast-watcher for German submarines. His wartime experiences gave rise to the poems he published in *Talking Bronco* (1946), in which he continued to depict himself as struggling single-handedly against a hostile social and literary establishment in Britain.

After the war Campbell worked as a clerk on the War Damage Commission in London before joining the BBC as a talks producer. For a short period he edited an unsuccessful magazine, *The Catacomb*, which espoused a right-wing position in British politics. His most important post-war publications were translations: *The Poems of St John of the Cross* (1951), Baudelaire's *Poems: a Translation of 'Les fleurs du mal'* (1952), two novels by Eça de Queirós, six Spanish plays, and the poems of Paco d'Arcos. His translations, particularly of St John of the Cross, are masterful works of art in their own right. He also showed himself to be a sensitive critic in a book on Garcia Lorca, interspersed with his fine translations of Lorca's poems, *Lorca* (1952), and in a critical volume on Wyndham Lewis, published posthumously. During the last years of his life, from 1952, he lived in Sintra in Portugal. He was killed in a car crash near Sintra on 23 April 1957. He was buried four days later at the cemetery of São Pedro, Sintra. PETER F. ALEXANDER

Sources L. Abrahams, 'Roy Campbell: conquistador-refugee', *Theoria*, 8 (1954), 46–65 • P. F. Alexander, *Roy Campbell: a critical biography* (1982) • P. F. Alexander, 'Campbell, Plomer, Van der Post and *Voorslag*', *English in Africa*, 7/2 (1980), 50–59 • P. F. Alexander, 'Roy Campbell, William Plomer and the Bloomsbury group', *Journal of Commonwealth Literature*, 18/1 (1983), 120–27 • [L. Whistler], 'The poetry of statement', *TLS* (24 March 1950), 184 • BBC WAC • B. Bergonzi, 'Roy Campbell: outsider on the right', *Journal of Contemporary History*, 2 (1967), 133–47 • B. Bergonzi, *The turn of a century* (1973) • E. Campbell, *Sam Campbell: a story of Natal* (privately printed, Durban, 1949) • J. Ciardi, 'Muscles and manners', *The Nation* (Dec 1955), 515 • R. N. Currey, *Poets of the 1939–1945 war* (1960) • U. Durham L., archives and special collections, William Plomer MSS • W. H. Gardner, 'Voltage of delight!', *The Month*, new ser., 19 (1958), 5–17, 133–47 • C. J. D. Harvey, 'The poetry of Roy Campbell', *Standpunte* (Oct 1950), 53–9 • Ransom HRC, Campbell MSS • H. Kenner, 'Narcissist of action', *Poetry*, 82 (June 1953), 169–75 • A. Kershaw, ed., *Salute to Roy Campbell* (1984) • Killie Campbell Africana Library, Durban,

South Africa • U. Krige, 'The poetry of Roy Campbell: a few aspects', in *Poems of Roy Campbell*, ed. U. Krige (1960) • U. Krige, 'Roy Campbell as lyrical poet', *English Studies in Africa*, 1/2 (Sept 1958), 81–94 • A. C. Lyle, *Poetic justice: a memoir of my father, Roy Campbell* (1986) • A. Paton, 'Roy Campbell: poet and man', *Theoria*, 9 (1957), 19–31 • W. Plomer, 'Voorslag-days', *London Magazine, a Monthly Review of Literature*, 6/9 (1959), 46–52 • D. S. J. Parsons, *Roy Campbell: a descriptive and annotated bibliography* (1981) • R. Campbell, *Light on a dark horse* (1951) • J. Povey, *Roy Campbell* (1977) • E. Sitwell, 'Roy Campbell', *Poetry*, 92 (April 1958), 42–8 • R. Smith, 'Roy Campbell and his French sources', *Comparative Literature*, 22/1 (1970), 1–18 • R. Smith, *Lyric and polemic* (1973) • South African National Library, Cape Town, South Africa • F. J. Temple, ed., *Hommage à Roy Campbell* (1958) • D. Wright, *Roy Campbell* (1961) • private information (2004) [Mrs Mary Campbell]

Archives BBC WAC, corresp. with BBC staff members • BL, corresp. in Society of Authors archive, Add. MS 63217 • Harvard U., Houghton L., letters and MSS • Killie Campbell Africana Library, Durban, corresp., family papers • Ransom HRC, literary papers • U. Reading, corresp. • University of Indiana, Bloomington, Lilly Library, literary papers • University of Saskatchewan, Saskatoon, Canada, corresp. and literary papers • York University, Toronto, archives, corresp. and literary papers | Bodl. Oxf., letters to Martyn Skinner • Durban City Library, corresp. • Johannesburg City Library, corresp. • National English Literary Museum, Grahamstown, corresp. • Rhodes University, Corey Library, corresp. • U. Durham, archives and special collections, letters to William Plomer • University of Cape Town Library, corresp. with C. J. Sibbett, incl. poems • Witwatersrand University, corresp. | SOUND BBC Archives, Reading

Likenesses A. John, portrait, *c.*1924, Pittsburgh Art Gallery, Pennsylvania [*see illus.*]

Wealth at death £496 10*s.* 5*d.*: administration, 1 Jan 1958, *CGPLA Eng. & Wales*

Campbell, (Renton) Stuart (**1908–1966**), journalist, was born in Kensal Rise, London, on 4 June 1908, the third child of John Campbell, a printer's manager from Scotland, and his wife, Florence Harmsworth. He was educated at Lavender Hill School and at Wandsworth Technical Institute Secondary School. Encouraged by his father he quickly embarked on a career in newspapers, starting as a junior reporter on the *Hendon and Finchley Times*, from which he went on to the *Woking Gazette* and the *Nottingham Guardian*. He was still a reporter when in 1933 he moved to the Manchester office of the *News Chronicle* and then, in 1935, to the *Daily Mirror* in London. In that year he also married Joan Mary Algernon (*d.* 1977), of Nottingham, with whom he had one daughter. In 1937 he was appointed assistant editor of the *Sunday Pictorial* under Hugh Cudlipp. From then on he was a Sunday newspaperman of the watchdog breed.

When Cudlipp joined the forces early in the Second World War, Campbell became editor of the *Sunday Pictorial*. The paper was already making a name as a campaigner for populist causes, and Campbell developed that reputation. The *Pictorial* took up many issues on behalf of soldiers and their families and investigated numerous complaints of profiteering. Campbell trained his reporters in the art of detecting, trapping, and exposing ration dodgers, oppressive landlords, petrol thieves, and other villains of the home front. It was a role he relished as an ardent, although undogmatic, socialist and as a passionate believer in the journalist as crusader. Libel actions were an inevitable hazard and in the course of fighting them Campbell acquired considerable legal agility.

Cudlipp's return to the *Pictorial* in 1946 meant that Campbell was an editor without a newspaper. But he was quickly promised the editorship of the *People*, a Sunday newspaper owned by Odhams Press. The paper was then edited by Harry Ainsworth, who was soon due to retire. In the meantime Campbell became managing editor, running the paper without interference save for timid occasional grumbles from Ainsworth. The grumbles arose because Campbell systematically removed or transformed editorial features which he regarded as almost criminally soporific and out of date, replacing them with his own brand of sharp, topical, combative reporting and comment. Within two years, having also completely redesigned the *People*'s layout and typography, Campbell had a newspaper which, in his view, would appeal to a new post-war generation far more demanding than their parents of entertainment, sensation, and information. He retained one highly successful feature of the old *People*, its confession series written by, or ghosted for, the famous and the notorious. But Campbell's confessionals were often those of obscure people, whose experiences somehow reflected the unacknowledged hopes or fears of his readers. He was a master of the telling headline that sold these articles, for example: 'I took a lorry ride to shame', 'I was a G.I.'s slave bride', and 'Because my skin is black'.

It was, however, in the investigation and exposure of criminal and social wrongdoing that Campbell put his distinctive stamp on popular journalism. Disclosure has always been the business of newspapers. Campbell went a stage further for he not only printed the results of his reporters' enquiries but he also produced the evidence on which those conclusions were based. Thus when in 1950 the *People* disclosed that the Messina brothers were running an empire of prostitution in London his reporter, Duncan Webb, set out the whole course of his investigation, showing how he had traced the women to their various addresses and had established their links with the gang exploiting them. It was a pattern that Campbell followed with equal success in exposures of bribery among footballers, slum landlordism, fake religions, and numerous other social scandals. His techniques were adopted by other newspapers, especially the 'quality Sundays'. All of them, like the *People* itself, gained in circulation as a result.

The *People*'s success was also due to its highly personal flavour. It spoke with one voice—Campbell's. He wrote or rewrote a great part of the paper himself. Reporters' and even columnists' copy was often no more to him than raw material for moulding by the master. His immediate assistants caught Campbell's tone, and articles which he did not have time to edit himself came out with his accent. The note was often strident, especially when evil was being denounced. Articles usually carried black and white moral judgements; as a journalist Campbell knew no greys and, as a stern Caledonian by upbringing, he tended to hark back to hellfire. Campbell did not even leave sport to the experts. He often edited sporting features and constantly briefed sports columnists. His own regular contribution to the paper was the 'Man o' the people' column, for a time written by Gilbert Harding. In it he and Harding produced miniature exposés of the type carried on other pages, often campaigning on behalf of victims of officialdom. Campbell encouraged Harding to start an annual Christmas appeal for charities, which was remarkably successful and remained a feature of the paper that Campbell always cherished.

In 1957 Campbell succeeded Ainsworth as editor. The change meant little. He had been in effective command of the paper for years and remained so until his death. But his elevation did, for the first time in his professional life, give him an uneasy place in the journalists' establishment. From 1961 to 1964 he was a member of the Press Council, whose occasional strictures on his editorial methods he had often scorned. He believed in getting 'the story', even if in the getting he sometimes violated the Press Council canon. But he did come to realize, under his colleagues' influence, the need to improve standards of taste and responsibility in popular newspapers.

Accused more than once as an editor of invasion of privacy, away from his newspaper Campbell was himself a very private man. When he went home to Stella Cottage, near Farnham, where the Stella of Jonathan Swift once lived, he practised family seclusion. Always approachable in office hours by staff and visitors alike, he discouraged callers to his home. Once, when acquaintances were walking around the house in the hope of finding him in, he lay prone on the kitchen floor for half an hour to avoid detection, reading a book. He read, gardened, and fished enthusiastically. But his passion was newspapers. He died at Stella Cottage on 1 February 1966 and was cremated at Aldershot on 7 February. NAT ROTHMAN, *rev.*

Sources *The Times* (3 Feb 1966) • H. Cudlipp, *Walking on the water* (1976) • H. P. Levy, *The Press Council: history, procedure and cases* (1967) • *WWW* • *CGPLA Eng. & Wales* (1966)
Likenesses photograph, repro. in *The Times*
Wealth at death £27,779: probate, 4 April 1966, *CGPLA Eng. & Wales*

Campbell, Sybil (1889–1977), barrister and first woman stipendiary magistrate, was born on 9 October 1889 in Ceylon, the eldest of the three daughters and a son of Neill Graeme Campbell (1859–1940) of Auchendarroch, tea company agent, and his wife, Maude Georgiana (*d.* 1950), daughter of Sir William Bovill, chief justice of common pleas. She was educated at home by her mother on postal instructions from the Parents' National Educational Union until 1903, then at a private school at Dunardarigh, Berwickshire, followed by a finishing school at Paris during the winter of 1906–7. She entered Girton College, Cambridge, in 1908, where she took the natural sciences tripos part one in 1911 and the economics tripos part two in 1912. In 1913 she was appointed an investigating officer for the trade board charged to monitor minimum wages in the sweated industries, most of whose workers were women. Her work involved visiting the roughest parts of many cities to inspect working conditions and her parents

Sybil Campbell (1889–1977), by unknown photographer, *c.*1940

insisted she carry a gun—which she did, hidden and unloaded. In 1918 she became an enforcement officer in the Ministry of Food.

In January 1920 Sybil Campbell entered as a student at the Middle Temple, and became, in 1922, one of the first women to be called to the bar. From 1923 to 1936 she had chambers in the Temple and also practised on the midland circuit. She was a metropolitan chairman of the court of referees, and was also the first secretary of the Cambridge University Women's Appointments Board, from 1930 to 1939. She was a supporter of Crosby Hall, the former home of Sir Thomas More, now dismantled and moved from the City for re-erection in Chelsea, and acquired as the headquarters of the British Federation of University Women (BFUW). Her indefatigable energy and vision as appeal chairman largely ensured the building of Crosby Hall's international hall of residence for women graduates in 1927. She represented the BFUW at council meetings of the International Federation of University Women at Madrid (1928) and Budapest (1934). In 1938 a refugee from Nazi persecution who was supported by the BFUW came to her attention; she ensured that Dr Erna Hollitscher's nephew, a former political prisoner in Germany, also found asylum in Britain, being 'guaranteed' by her own mother, and that Dr Hollitscher herself became refugee secretary at Crosby Hall. After the Second World War, Sybil Campbell resumed her appeal work for the building and scholarships funds for Crosby Hall, remaining a director until 1968 and vice-president of the BFUW until her death. The papers of the BFUW are now located at the Women's Library, London, and the former Sybil Campbell Library at Crosby Hall is now housed at 28 Great James Street, London, after Crosby Hall was lost to public ownership when the London residuary body sold all its remaining assets following the abolition of the Greater London council in 1986.

Sybil Campbell's public profile after 1945 was not that of champion of young women scholars, however, but that of judicial scourge of poor first offenders. Soon after her appointment by the home secretary, Herbert Morrison, on 3 April 1945, as the first British woman judge, becoming stipendiary magistrate at Tower Bridge police court, she was attacked in the *South London Press*. Her sentencing policy in her first months had almost doubled the national level of recourse to imprisonment instead of fines for first offenders. One man was gaoled for stealing four small Christmas puddings; another given six weeks for stealing three bars of soap. Five thousand factory workers demonstrated in protest at the latter sentence and various south London trades councils, the local branch of the Women's Co-operative Guild, and one ward of the local Labour Party called for her dismissal. It was suggested that her wartime experience as assistant divisional food officer (enforcement) when she had trapped food profiteers and black marketeers, for which she was appointed OBE in 1942, accounted for the draconian severity of her sentencing policy in the post-war Britain of austerity rationing. Eventually the outcry against her died down. Some of it had been fuelled not just by genuine social outrage but also by misogyny—and by the self-interest of dockers who had long held pilfering to be their perk. Several appeals against her sentences were upheld; in other cases it was discovered that the supposed 'first offenders' were in fact petty criminals. Sybil Campbell herself had increasing recourse to probation. When she retired at seventy-two in 1961, she had won a reputation for toughness but fairness, patient sympathy with the inarticulate and nervous in her court, and even a humane concern with conditions in prisons, borstals, and probation hostels, all of which she visited—a then almost unprecedented step for a judge. She had also been briefly the honorary secretary of the David Isaacs Fund for the Poor of London as a signal to magistrates that they had a duty to help mitigate the poverty that could breed crime.

Sybil Campbell retired to her family home at Lochgilphead, Argyll, with its 8 acres of wild garden, azaleas, and rhododendrons, until crippling arthritis and heart trouble forced her to go into the Bon Secours Nursing Home, 40 Mansion House Road, Langside, Glasgow, where she died on 29 August 1977. She was buried at Lochgilphead. SYBIL OLDFIELD

Sources K. B. Beauman, *Sybil Campbell, OBE, MA, F.R.Hist.Soc.* (The Sybil Campbell Library Committee, British Federation of University Women, 1987) • P. Polden, 'The lady of Tower Bridge: Sybil Campbell, England's first woman judge', *Women's History Review*, 8 (1999), 505–26 • M. Gledstone, 'Sybil Campbell', *The University Women's Review*, 40 (July 1950) • *The Times* (1 Sept 1977) • 'Cassandra, or, The lady of Tower Bridge', *Sunday Pictorial* (5 Jan 1947) • 'A Portia come to judgement', *Glasgow Herald* (16 April 1948) • C. Dyhouse, 'The British Federation of University Women and the status of women in universities, 1907–1939', *Women's History Review*, 4 (1995), 465–85 • K. T. Butler and H. I. McMorran, eds., *Girton College register, 1869–1946* (1948)

Archives Girton Cam. • Women's Library, London, British Federation of University Women archives

Likenesses photograph, *c*.1940, Girton Cam. [*see illus.*] • J. Pannett, chalk, 1966, Girton Cam. • photograph, repro. in *Glasgow Herald* • photograph, repro. in *Strand Magazine* (July 1949) • photograph, repro. in Gledstone, 'Sybil Campbell' • photograph, repro. in *The Times*

Wealth at death £25,693.97: confirmation, 5 Jan 1978, *CCI* • £622.57—held in trust in England: additional estate, 5 Jan 1978, *CCI*

Campbell, Thomas (1733–1795), Church of Ireland clergyman and traveller, was born on 4 May 1733 at Glack, co. Tyrone, the eldest son of Moses Campbell, curate to the archdeacon of Armagh and afterwards rector of the parish of Killeshill, and Elizabeth Johnston of Tully, co. Monaghan. His mother was the sister of George Johnston, MP for Portarlington (1727–30), and Baptist Johnston, MP for Monaghan borough (1747–53) and high sheriff of that county in 1728. It seems Campbell was married, possibly to Jane Holmes.

Following an education at home, Campbell entered Trinity College, Dublin, and graduated BA in 1756 and MA in 1761. After taking orders in 1761, he became curate of Clogher until 1772, when he was collated to the prebend of Tyholland, and in 1773 he was made chancellor of St Macartin's, Clogher. Described by Mrs Thrale as 'A fine showy talking man' (Clifford, 1), Campbell was, according to Boswell, 'so good humoured a man … and so thankful for any civilities … that he was quite like a pet sheep' (ibid., 2). But in later years numerous requests to preach special charity sermons show he was recognized as one of the best pulpit orators in Ireland.

However, it is for Boswell's portrait and for his 1775 diary, written during his visit to London, that Campbell is best remembered. The diary was not published until 1854 after its discovery in an office of the supreme court in Sydney, Australia, where it had been taken by the writer's nephew at the turn of the nineteenth century. Containing notes of seven visits to England over the period 1775–92 it gives an Irishman's day-to-day impressions of England and the English. Although the second visit in 1776–7 appears to have been the longest, the 1775 trip is the only one for which there is a detailed account. The most valuable aspect is his portrayal of his days with Dr Johnson and his circle including the Thrales, Boswell, and Joshua Reynolds. Campbell was a shrewd, somewhat contemptuous observer. On reading the volume in 1859 Macaulay observed that Johnson 'could swear and swear even before a parson when in a passion' (Clifford, x).

While in London Campbell was dismayed by the lack of knowledge shown concerning his homeland. To remedy this, and the resultant bad policies made on Ireland's behalf, he published a *Philosophical Survey of the South of Ireland in a Series of Letters to John Watkinson, MD* in 1778. Alongside sketches of the social life, local traditions, and historical background of Ireland, Campbell called for free trade for the island, the relaxation of the penal codes, and a union between Great Britain and Ireland. The volume also contained, for the first time in print, Johnson's epitaph on Goldsmith. Boswell styled the *Survey* 'a very entertaining book, which has, however, one fault—that it assumes the fictitious character of an Englishman' (Boswell, 609).

In 1783 Campbell co-operated on the new edition of William Camden's *Britannia*, on the advice and with the assistance of Edmund Burke, who lent him his valuable collection of Irish manuscripts. He then began work on *Strictures on Ecclesiastical and Literary History of Ireland from the Most Ancient of Times till the Introduction of the Roman Ritual and the Establishment of Papal Supremacy by Henry II*. To this was added a *Sketch of the Constitution and Government of Ireland Down to 1783*, a book which went some way to display Campbell's patriot politics. In response the *Gentleman's Magazine* concluded that the historians Charles Vallancy and Charles O'Connor had been 'driven from their strong holds of fanciful and far fetched etymology' (*GM*, 336). Besides these books, Campbell wrote a portion of the memoir of Goldsmith which appeared posthumously in Bishop Percy's 1801 edition of the poet's works. Yet despite his achievements, Campbell's death in London, on 20 June 1795 at the age of sixty-two, went largely unnoticed in English literary circles.

NORMAN MACCOLL, *rev.* ROSEMARY RICHEY

Sources J. L. Clifford, *Dr Campbell's diary of a visit to England in 1775* (1947) • J. Boswell, *Life of Johnson*, ed. R. W. Chapman, rev. J. D. Fleeman, new edn (1970); repr. with introduction by P. Rogers (1980) • Nichols, *Illustrations*, 7.759–809 • *EdinR*, 110 (1859), 322–42 • *GM*, 1st ser., 60 (1790), 318–19, 333–7
Archives BL, Egerton MSS

Campbell, Thomas (1777–1844), poet, was born in High Street, Glasgow, on 27 July 1777, the youngest child of Alexander Campbell (1710–1801) and Margaret, *née* Campbell (1736–1812).

Early life and education, 1777–1798 Thomas Campbell's father had built up a tobacco importing business which was disastrously affected by the American War of Independence, but the family did not forfeit its social standing, and Thomas himself was baptized by Thomas Reid, at that time professor of moral philosophy in Glasgow University. There was little money to spare, and much consequent pressure on the children to work hard and make their own way in the world. Four of Campbell's brothers spent part of their working lives in British Guiana, and a fifth had an unprosperous career in textiles in Germany and France. Two sisters became governesses, and a third worked in a boarding-school.

Campbell proved to be an exemplary pupil at Glasgow grammar school, and achieved even greater success at Glasgow University, which he entered in 1791 with a view to entering the ministry of the Church of Scotland. He showed unusual facility in writing verse, submitting essays in rhyme when prose was expected. One of these exercises, on the origin of evil, is a fair adaptation of the method of Pope's *Essay on Man*. He won prizes, and acquired a reputation as a debater and translator. In his

Thomas Campbell (1777–1844), by Sir Thomas Lawrence, *c.*1820

fourth year at university his father's income was still further reduced by the loss of a chancery suit, and Thomas was obliged to spend the summer vacation working as a tutor in a family on the island of Mull. He returned to the university for one further session, and attended John Millar's lectures on Roman law. Thirty years later, when Campbell was promoting his plan for a university in London, he recalled Millar's 'electrifying' lectures with an enthusiasm which suggests a lifelong influence. They probably reinforced the radical convictions already generated by his indignation at the savage sentences passed for alleged sedition on those moderate reformers Thomas Muir and Joseph Gerrald; Campbell had attended their trial before the notorious Lord Braxfield in Edinburgh.

On leaving Glasgow University in 1795 Campbell again spent a summer as a tutor in the highlands, this time at Dounie, near Crinan, in Argyll. In the autumn he spent two months in Edinburgh in an attempt to take up law, but got no further than working as a copying clerk. He was introduced to Dr Robert Anderson, editor of the monumental *Complete Edition of the Poets of Great Britain*, and through him to the publisher Robert Mundell, for whom he is said to have prepared an abridgement of Bryan Edwards's *West Indies*.

Although Campbell returned to Glasgow, and had plans for a literary periodical there, he was unable to earn a sufficient income, and considered crossing the Atlantic to make for himself a career in trade, as his brothers had done. But poor health at this time discouraged him from emigrating, and in 1798 he settled in Edinburgh, working as a tutor and picking up such literary work as he could. In time he met many talented literary figures, notably Dugald Stewart, Archibald Alison (author of a celebrated essay on taste), and the young Francis Jeffrey.

***The Pleasures of Hope* (1799) and European travels, 1799–1802** On 27 April 1799 Mundell published Campbell's *The Pleasures of Hope*. It was an immediate success, and created eager expectations of future greatness. As the engineer Thomas Telford told Alison, Campbell would surpass 'your Pindars, your Drydens, and your Grays': he looked more like a Scottish Milton or Shakespeare, or even something better (Beattie, 1.395). The poem's popularity is an indication of the prevailing taste, still far more at ease with eighteenth-century didactic poetry than with the innovations of Wordsworth and Coleridge's *Lyrical Ballads*. But the poem was also fortunate in its timing. It was peculiarly welcome to those in sympathy with political reform who were at their most despondent over the bloodshed of the French Revolution. Campbell's poem found ways of asserting radical sentiments that avoided the deadly charge of association with 'French principles'. He denounced the destroyers of Polish liberty, and breathed vengeance on the oppressors of India and supporters of the slave trade. A second part was equally welcome in its rejection of a scepticism that reduced humanity to a 'frail and feverish being of an hour' (*The Pleasures of Hope*, line 338). But Campbell never had confidence that he could sustain the reputation thus early established. He was unable to develop his next poetical project, a celebration of Edinburgh to be called 'The Queen of the North', beyond a few fragments.

In 1800, though, Campbell sought to qualify himself further as a man of letters by travelling to Germany, as Coleridge and Wordsworth had done, to learn the language and acquaint himself with a literature that had for some years been recognized as exceptionally vital and innovative. He went to Hamburg and stayed there for some weeks, meeting the aged poet Friedrich Gottlieb Klopstock and other established writers. Later in the summer he went to Regensburg in Bavaria. While he was there a French army attacked and took the city, and Campbell witnessed some of the fighting at close quarters. The occupation itself seems to have caused him little inconvenience, and he went on to Munich, where he was on good terms with French officers, and given protection to pass through the whole army of Moreau, the commanding general.

Campbell returned to Hamburg for the winter, and stayed in the neighbouring city of Altona, at that time under Danish rule, as was the entire north bank of the River Elbe. So when war threatened between Britain and Denmark in March 1801 he quickly extricated himself, travelling home in a ship that was harried by a Danish privateer. In Altona he was infected with a venereal disease, probably syphilis, which further impaired his never robust health. But his enforced leisure produced some of the short poems that considerably enhanced his popularity, notably 'The Exile of Erin', inspired by his friendship with Anthony MacCann, a survivor of the Irish rising of 1798 who was living in Hamburg.

This friendship, together with Campbell's association with French officers in Bavaria, prompted an inquiry into his loyalty by the sheriff of Edinburgh. But by now his reputation was established in influential circles around Lord Holland in London as well as among the literati of Edinburgh. He was further secured by the patronage of Gilbert Elliot, Lord Minto, who had recently returned from Vienna where he had been British envoy: he was anxious to learn about conditions in French-occupied Bavaria, and was impressed by this talented young observer. Minto had been a close associate of Edmund Burke, but tolerated Campbell's outspoken radicalism, perhaps thinking that he would grow out of it.

Marriage, and later works, 1802–1819 With the restoration of peace in 1802 Campbell considered returning to the continent to collect material for a travel narrative, possibly extending to Turkey and Persia. The publisher Archibald Constable supported the project, but the renewal of war in 1803 made it impracticable, and the success of a new edition of *The Pleasures of Hope*, which included such poems as 'Hohenlinden', convinced Campbell that he could live by his pen in London. He was, indeed, tempted by the possibility in 1804 of a professorial chair at the University of Vilna, then under Russian rule. But he prudently decided that his interest in the regeneration of Poland would make such a post unacceptably perilous. Besides, on 10 October 1803 he had married Matilda Sinclair (*c*.1780–1828), the daughter of a cousin of his mother's, and they soon had a family to consider. There were two sons, both named after friends: Thomas Telford, born in 1804, and Alison, born in 1805. Both were unfortunate, as Alison died of scarlet fever in 1810, and Thomas became incapacitated by some kind of mental illness in adolescence, from which he never recovered. The early years of the marriage were overshadowed by anxieties about Campbell's own health and his finances. He supported himself with hackwork such as *The Annals of Great Britain* (1807), although, as he complained to Walter Scott, the publishers knew of his dependence on them and took advantage of it. But in 1805, with the support of lords Minto and Holland, he was awarded a pension of £200 a year. His father had died in 1801, and he gave generous support to his widowed mother and his sisters, so that the pension did not do a great deal to ease his own situation. But it was something, and successive editions of his poems and the publication in 1809 of *Gertrude of Wyoming* supplemented a still rather modest income.

Gertrude of Wyoming was well received, although not as extravagantly as *The Pleasures of Hope*. Its vision of pastoral innocence evoked only to be destroyed by the savagery of war (embodied in this case by Mohawk allies of the British) was in tune with an increasing taste for pathos. Jeffrey, indeed, regretted the 'fastidious timidity' which led Campbell to refine away much of the original grandeur of his design (*Edinburgh Review*, 14, 1809, 19; Beattie, 2.172). But the poem retained its popularity for many years, particularly in the United States. Still, like *The Pleasures of Hope*, it has proved less enduring than short and apparently unsophisticated poems such as 'Hohenlinden' and 'Lord Ullin's Daughter'.

In 1812 Campbell found a new source of income as a result of the expanding demand for public lectures, and gave a successful series at the Royal Institution on poetry. Later he was received enthusiastically in Liverpool and Birmingham, and Scott suggested he should allow himself to be offered a chair at Edinburgh University. This he declined, but his success as a lecturer contributed to the good reception of his *Specimens of the British Poets* (1819). The project had been in hand since 1805, originally as a collaboration with Walter Scott, but it was completed by Campbell at irregular intervals, the poet complaining that he had to wade through oceans of bad poetry 'where not a fish is to be caught' (Beattie, 2.47). The range and unfamiliarity of what was eventually chosen confirm the editor's diligence, but the book achieved its main notoriety because of a brief defence of Pope against what Campbell saw as a depreciation by his most recent editor, William Lisle Bowles. There followed a controversy on what Bowles called 'the invariable principles of poetry', in which Byron came to play the leading role.

Magazine editing, and involvement with London and Glasgow universities, 1820–1830 Campbell now entered on what was to prove the most successful venture of his life, the editing of the *New Monthly Magazine*. The periodical had been founded in 1814 in opposition to the radical *Monthly Magazine*, but had not prospered, and the publisher, Henry Colburn, sought to change its character by enlisting a distinguished editor. Although Campbell's background was reformist his friendships crossed party lines, and his cosmopolitan interests and sympathies made him an ideal choice. Immediately before taking up his editorial duties he travelled for half a year in Germany, looking for contributors, reporting back to Colburn on writers he had met, and promising not to involve him in unprofitable expense.

In the routine business of an editor Campbell was notoriously incompetent, unsystematic, and dilatory. He was fortunate in his assistant editor, Cyrus Redding, whose recollections of their partnership are an engaging mixture of affection and exasperation. Mrs Campbell herself was a great resource, supplying much of the order and system of which her husband was incapable, and her death on 9 May 1828 left him bereft in more ways than one. But Campbell's role was indispensable. It was he who insisted on high standards from his contributors, while exercising considerable tact in his rejections. He kept his rather unscrupulous publisher firmly in his place. Without Campbell, too, the magazine would have had a less cosmopolitan flavour.

It was while Campbell was editor of the *New Monthly* that he published his last substantial poem, *Theodric* (1824), but by common consent it was a failure. On the other hand, as a public man he had the distinction of successfully promoting the idea of establishing a university in London. He was discussing the project with Francis Place and others in 1824, and on 9 February 1825 published a formal proposal in *The Times*. It is evident that Campbell was inspired by memories of Glasgow and by what he had seen of German universities, insisting that much expense could be saved by students' living at home, thus enabling greater numbers to enter higher education. The scheme was strongly supported by radicals and utilitarian reformers, and aroused fierce hostility among conservatives, for whom the absence of religious education seemed even more sinister than giving the workers ideas above their station. Once the project was under way Campbell ceased to take much part in it, and Henry Brougham took the lead and rather more of the credit than Campbell felt was his due. But the very existence of the University College always gave him pleasure.

In 1826 Campbell was elected rector of Glasgow University, and took the duties of his office with unprecedented seriousness, examining the management of the university and protecting the interests of the students. Such was his popularity that he was re-elected for two further years, to the considerable annoyance of the authorities, who considered his third re-election to be illegal.

Support for Polish independence, and final years, 1830–1844 Campbell's most conspicuous intervention in public life, however, was his championship of the Polish people. As early as 1799 in *The Pleasures of Hope* his lament for Tadeusz Kosciuszko had associated him with that subjected nation's aspirations. When in 1830 the Poles were animated by the July revolution in France to establish their own independence, Campbell rejoiced. But in 1831 the Russians crushed the insurrection, driving thousands of Poles into exile. Campbell took the lead in mobilizing public opinion against the British government's indifference, and initiated an Association of the Friends of Poland to look after the welfare of the exiles. One friend spoke of Campbell's 'real heart-felt sorrow' for this beloved country: 'he identified all his feelings, nay his very being with it' (Beattie, 3.119). He had given up the *New Monthly Magazine* in 1830 and involved himself with another journal, *The Metropolitan*, but this did not prevent his assisting *Polonia*, a magazine aimed at maintaining interest in the Polish cause.

In his later years, in spite of persistent ill health, Campbell continued his career as an author, although with competence rather than distinction. His biography of Sarah Siddons (1834) is a pleasant portrait of the great actress, whom Campbell had known since his arrival in London thirty years earlier. His *Life of Petrarch* (1841), though not a scholarly work, is a reconsideration of the poet which is unpretentious and perceptive. In another genre, *Letters from the South* (1837) records an adventurous visit to Algeria in 1834. He provides a judicious assessment of the virtues and shortcomings of the new French regime, but is also impressed by the eloquent lamentation of a 'native poet' on the fall of Algiers. These books kept his name before the public, as did many successive editions of his poetry, some of them handsomely illustrated by J. M. W. Turner. It was a particular pleasure to him that he was greatly admired in his native Scotland, where he was given the freedom of the city of Edinburgh, and Glasgow students established a Campbell Club in his honour.

In 1843, in search of a healthier climate, Campbell moved with his niece Mary from London to Boulogne, but the change did not help him, and a diseased liver led to his death there, at 5 rue St Jean, on 15 June 1844. He was buried in Westminster Abbey on 3 July with considerable pomp; and, if one observer can be believed, a clap of thunder, nicely timed, added a touch of sublimity to the ceremony (Hall, 358). A group of Polish exiles attended to express their gratitude to the poet who had served their unfortunate country so powerfully. A Colonel Szyrma scattered over the coffin a handful of earth from the grave of the man commemorated in *The Pleasures of Hope* as 'Warsaw's last champion', Tadeusz Kosciuszko.

GEOFFREY CARNALL

Sources *Life and letters of Thomas Campbell*, ed. W. Beattie, 3 vols. (1849) • M. R. Miller, *Thomas Campbell* (1978) • C. Redding, *Literary reminiscences and memoirs of Thomas Campbell*, 2 vols. (1860) • T. Campbell, *Complete poetical works*, ed. J. L. Robertson (1907) • J. G. Lockhart, *Memoirs of the life of Sir Walter Scott*, 7 vols. (1837–8) • T. Constable, *Archibald Constable and his literary correspondents*, 3 vols. (1873) • *New Monthly Magazine* (1821–30) • L. Hunt, *The autobiography of Leigh Hunt, with reminiscences of friends and contemporaries*, 3 vols. (1850) • H. H. Bellot, *University College, London, 1826–1926* (1929) • S. C. Hall, *A book of memories of great men and women of the age* (1871) • *Polonia* (1832) • W. L. Bowles, *The invariable principles of poetry* (1819) • 'Life', *Poetical works of Thomas Campbell and Oliver Goldsmith* (1858)

Archives Harvard U., Houghton L., literary MSS and papers • Hunt. L., letters and literary MSS • LUL, article, draft poem, and letters • Mitchell L., Glas., corresp. and literary MSS; letters and literary fragments • NL Scot., letters and papers; corresp. • NL Scot. • UCL, letters and poems • University of Dundee, archives, corresp., literary MSS, and notebook • V&A NAL, letters incl. to Colburn, publisher | BL, letters to Lady Holland, Add. MSS 51846–51849 • BL, Place MSS • BL, letters as sponsor of Royal Literary Fund, loan no. 96 • Bodl. Oxf., corresp. with Noel and Byron families • Bodl. Oxf., letters to J. Richardson • Derbys. RO, letters to F. C. Arkwright • Lpool RO, letters to members of the Roscoe family • NL Scot., letters to Robert Anderson; letters and poems to Richard Bentley; corresp. with Archibald Constable; letters to Sir Walter Scott • U. Leeds, Brotherton L., letters to John Richardson • UCL, letters to Lord Brougham • V&A, letters to Colburn • Yale U., Beinecke L., letters to Margaret Coates

Likenesses T. Lawrence, chalk, pencil, and watercolour, 1808, Scot. NPG • J. Henning, pencil drawing, 1813, NPG • T. Lawrence, oils, *c.*1820, NPG [*see illus.*] • S. W. Reynolds, mezzotint, pubd 1822 (after T. Phillips), NPG • E. H. Baily, marble bust, 1826, Art Gallery and Museum, Glasgow • S. W. Reynolds, mezzotint, 1826 (after J. Lonsdale), BM, NPG • D. Maclise, watercolour drawing, 1830, V&A • Count D'Orsay, pencil and chalk drawing, 1832, NPG • D. Maclise, watercolour drawing, 1833, V&A • E. Finden, stipple, 1841 (after T. Phillips), BM • H. Room, oils, 1841, Scot. NPG • W. Brockedon, black and red chalk drawing, 1842, NPG • W. Brockedon, chalk drawing, 1847, NPG • W. C. Marshall, marble statue, exh. RA 1849, Westminster Abbey • A. Craig, oils, Art Gallery and Museum, Glasgow • mezzotint, NPG

Campbell, Thomas (1791–1858), sculptor, was born in Tolbooth parish, Edinburgh, on 1 May 1791, and baptized there on 21 November, the son of Douglas Campbell, 'gentleman servant', and his wife, Helen Thorburn. Thomas's younger brother James (1810–1833) became his pupil and studio assistant in Rome and, latterly, in London. Apprenticed at an early age to John Marshall, marble cutter of Leith Walk, Edinburgh, Campbell received his first recorded independent commission as a figure sculptor about 1813, when he executed two freestone heads for the portico of St Mary's Chapel (now St Mary's Metropolitan Cathedral). By 1816, after modelling a bust of Professor Robert Blair in 1815 (University of Edinburgh; probably carved in marble subsequently in Rome), he had attracted the patronage of Gilbert Innes of Stow (*d.* 1832), depute governor of the Royal Bank of Scotland. Innes's financial support, comprising a loan repayment scheme sustained over at least a decade, facilitated Campbell's admission to the Royal Academy Schools on 8 January 1818, and from 1819 his extended residence in Rome. While in London he received informal tuition from Joseph Nollekens, served as a journeyman to Edward Hodges Baily, and obtained an introduction to Sir Thomas Lawrence from Henry Raeburn.

In the winter of 1818 Campbell studied in Paris, where the dowager duchess of Devonshire supplied him with a letter of introduction to Antonio Canova in Rome. In the following year he secured access to Canova and Thorvaldsen, with both of whom he was to maintain an amicable association. This dual association enabled him to secure for the Trustees' Academy in Edinburgh, as the accredited agent of the board of trustees for manufactures in Scotland, first casts after selected works by both sculptors, complemented by numerous casts after the antique. In 1820 he opened at piazza Mignanelli 12 the studio that he was to occupy until 1829. Among the first portrait busts of Edinburgh sitters to be rendered in marble were those of Innes, modelled in 1816–17 and carved by 1821 (plaster cast in the Scottish National Portrait Gallery; marble replica by an unknown sculptor, 1843, in the Royal Highland and Agricultural Society of Scotland), and of Raeburn, modelled in 1818 and carved in 1822 (Scottish National Portrait Gallery). By 1826, when he executed for George IV marble busts of Pope Pius VII and Cardinal Consalvi (Royal Collection, after originals by Bertel Thorvaldsen), Campbell was the doyen of Scottish expatriate sculptors in Rome. He numbered among his patrons for bust portraiture the sixth duke of Devonshire (bronze, 1823; marble of Princess Pauline Borghese, 1824, Chatsworth, Derbyshire); the tenth duke of Hamilton; the eighth Baron Kinnaird; the eighth earl of Lauderdale; and Lord Balgonie, later earl of Leven and Melville.

The immediate proximity of Canova and Thorvaldsen stimulated Campbell's periodic experimentation with ideal sculpture in marble, including several bas-reliefs on classical themes. His group *Cupid and Psyche*, originally submitted to the duke of Bedford, was completed for Christopher Nisbet Hamilton (formerly at Biel, Scotland) and exhibited at the Royal Academy in 1830. *Ganymede*, in progress by 1825, was Campbell's contribution to the Universal Exhibition in Paris in 1855 (now known only from the plaster cast in the Victoria and Albert Museum). For

Lord Kinnaird, and at Byron's instigation, Campbell executed in 1822 an exquisite group of Arthur Fitzgerald Kinnaird, *The Young Ascanius* (Kinnaird loan to the National Gallery of Scotland, Edinburgh), and, for the duke of Leeds, a similar group of Lord Conyers Osborne, *The Young Hannibal* (priv. coll.).

Campbell's chequered career as a monumental sculptor began in 1824 with two highly prestigious commissions. Executed from sittings granted that year, his marble seated figure of Princess Pauline Borghese was eventually delivered to the duke of Devonshire in 1840 as a pendant to Canova's *Madame Mère* (both at Chatsworth). The contemporaneous commission for a bronze dismounted equestrian monument to the fourth earl of Hopetoun (St Andrew Square, Edinburgh), secured in public competition against Samuel Joseph, was not fulfilled until 1834. Through his tardiness Campbell forfeited both a potential nomination for the Scott Monument in 1834 and the wider opportunity to become Scotland's leading monumental sculptor. His marginalization obtained despite a twenty-year private association with the fifth duke of Buccleuch; this was initiated in 1828 with a heroic marble statue of the first duke of Wellington, followed by the marble allegorical monument to the dowager duchess of Buccleuch for St Edmund's Church, Warkton, Northamptonshire (*c*.1830), and the recumbent marble monument to Lady Courtown for Kiltennel church, co. Wexford.

During the winter of 1829–30 Campbell returned permanently to London with commissions estimated in total at £30,000. He established a studio at 28 Leicester Square and then, by 1834, at 16 Great Marlborough Street, exhibiting almost annually at the Royal Academy until 1857. While he was principally in demand for his bust portraiture, both in marble and in bronze, Campbell's later monumental projects undertaken in London included Captain Sir William Hoste in marble for St Paul's Cathedral (1834); the bronze of the duke of York for the esplanade of Edinburgh Castle (1830–39, a successor to the marble monument erected in the United Service Club in Pall Mall in 1829); the granite monument to the fifth duke of Gordon for Aberdeen (1839–44), his last Scottish commission; the Sarah Siddons marble monument for Westminster Abbey (1845); and the bronze statue of Lord George Bentinck (1851) in Cavendish Square, London.

These commissions notwithstanding, Campbell's reputed mismanagement of his financial affairs had reduced his personal estate to less than £600 by the time that he died, a lifelong bachelor, on 4 February 1858 at 1 Great Castle Street, London. He was buried on 12 February in Kensal Green cemetery. His remaining stock-in-trade, including an alto-relievo of Sarah Siddons (*c*.1843) in the National Portrait Gallery, London, was said to have been dispersed at an unrecorded posthumous studio sale. An oil portrait of Campbell (now unlocated) was painted in London in 1838 by Christian Albrecht Jensen for the Danish archaeologist Peter Oluf Brøndsted, an associate of Thorvaldsen, and exhibited at the Copenhagen Salon in 1839.

HELEN E. SMAILES

Sources T. L. Donaldson, *Art Journal* (1858), 107–8 • R. L. Woodward, 'Nineteenth century Scottish sculpture', PhD diss., U. Edin., 1979, vol. 1, pp. 56–9; vol. 3, pp. 41–5 • H. E. Smailes, 'Thomas Campbell and Laurence Macdonald: the Roman solution to the Scottish sculptor's dilemma', *Virtue and vision: sculpture and Scotland, 1540–1990*, ed. F. Pearson (1991) • Thomas Campbell, correspondence to Gilbert Innes of Stow, 1817–25, NA Scot., Innes of Stow muniments, GD 113 • W. M. Parker, 'A note on the Hopetoun monument', *Book of the Old Edinburgh Club*, 22 (1938), 28–37 • H. Smailes, 'Thomas Campbell and the "camera lucida": the Buccleuch statue of the 1st duke of Wellington', *Burlington Magazine*, 129/1016 (Nov 1987), 709–14 • H. Smailes, 'A history of the statue gallery at the Trustees' Academy in Edinburgh and the acquisition of the Albacini casts in 1838', *Journal of the History of Collections*, 3 (1991), 125–43 • T. Campbell, letter-book, NL Scot., MS 146 • Graves, *RA exhibitors*, 1 (1905), 386–7 • C. B. de Laperriere, ed., *The Royal Scottish Academy exhibitors, 1826–1990*, 4 vols. (1991), vol. 1, pp. 274–5 • d. cert. • *CGPLA Eng. & Wales* (1858) • bap. reg. Scot.

Archives NA Scot., bundle of letters • NL Scot., corresp. • NL Scot., letter-book | Chatsworth House, Derbyshire, bound volume of receipts and letters concerning sixth duke of Devonshire's sculptural commissions • Museo Biblioteca Archivio, Bassano del Grappa, Italy, Epistolare comune, III/217/2494 and 1493 • Museo Biblioteca Archivio, Bassano del Grappa, Italy, Epistolario scelto, II/193/1790 • NA Scot., corresp. with Gilbert Innes of Stow, GD 113 • NA Scot., letter-book of the board of trustees for manufactures in Scotland, NG 1/3/22 • NA Scot., minute book of the board of trustees for manufactures in Scotland, NG 1/1/34 • NA Scot., Royal Institution papers, NG 1/41/4 • Thorvaldsens Museum, Copenhagen, Denmark, Campbell/Thorvaldsen letters • U. Edin. L., Laing manuscripts, La.II.426 (96–98)

Likenesses C. A. Jensen, oils, 1838; formerly Brøndsted collection

Wealth at death under £600: administration, 7 July 1858, *CGPLA Eng. & Wales*

Campbell, Lady Victoria (1854–1910), philanthropist, was born on 22 May 1854 at Carlton House, London, the third daughter and eighth of twelve children born to George Douglas *Campbell, eighth duke of Argyll (1823–1900), and his first wife, Lady Elizabeth Georgiana Sutherland-Leveson-Gower (1824–1878). At the request of the monarch, Lady Victoria was named for Queen Victoria, whose mistress of the robes, the duchess of Sutherland, was Lady Victoria's maternal grandmother.

In 1859, at the age of five, Lady Victoria contracted poliomyelitis and all efforts to reverse the effects of the disease, including surgery, were unsuccessful. She was left without the use of her legs and was eventually fitted with braces which she wore throughout her life. For much of each year during 1859–68 she resided near the London and Brighton clinics of her chief orthopaedist, Matthias Roth. Her doctors strengthened her legs by a series of exercises and taught her to manage crutches. She spent the rest of her time in one of the three family homes: Inveraray Castle in Argyllshire, Rosneath Castle in Dunbartonshire, and Argyll House in London. Lady Victoria was tutored by a governess, Georgina Johnstone, and by Elizabeth Knowles, who was her lifelong companion when she was away from her family.

In 1868 Lady Victoria developed a life-threatening lung abscess. Her decision to devote her life to God's service after her recovery in 1870 was the result of this illness. The

Lady Victoria Campbell (1854–1910), by William Crooke, 1895

form such service should take was, however, not immediately clear to her. Meanwhile, she helped to nurse her mother, who had been left partially incapacitated by a stroke in 1868. But the strain of nursing her mother until the duchess's death in 1878 caused Lady Victoria to have a nervous breakdown during 1878–9.

Following these traumatic events, Lady Victoria resolved to devote her life and energies to working on behalf of the Church of Scotland. Since her father's remarriage in 1881 relieved her of the necessity of presiding over the duke's households, Lady Victoria determined to establish her residence on one of the three Scottish Western Isles (Iona, Mull, and Tiree) that were part of the Argyll estate. In 1886 she chose to make her home on Tiree, where crofter disaffection was causing difficulties for the duke.

Most of the work undertaken by Lady Victoria took the form of organizing mothers' clubs, sewing clubs, Women's Guilds, and YWCA branches for the women and girls in the western islands. In response to various community needs, she also established milk and soup kitchens and a school of woodcarving for the young men of Tiree, and secured nurses for each district in the islands. As Gaelic was still predominant on the islands, Lady Victoria learned the language, in which she occasionally taught Bible classes. Writing under the pseudonym Hebridean, she was also one of the island's best-known publicists, writing frequent letters on the islanders' problems to the British press.

Lady Victoria demonstrated great courage in landing on the islands during storms and bad weather, which evoked considerable admiration and respect among the inhabitants. Since she could not walk easily, she had to be assisted off the vessels in ports which often did not have a pier. She finally secured the construction of a pier for Tiree, but did not live to use it.

In addition to her work on the western islands, Lady Victoria, who held no official church position, also founded Women's Guilds at St Columba's and Crown Court churches in London. She served as the first president of the Women's Guild of Crown Court Church from its inception in 1890 until her death, which took place in Edinburgh on 6 July 1910. She was buried in Liberton parish churchyard in Edinburgh. JOAN B. HUFFMAN

Sources Lady F. Balfour, *Lady Victoria Campbell* (1911) · F. Balfour, *Ne obliviscaris: dinna forget*, 2 vols. [1930] · Inveraray Castle, Inveraray, Campbell MSS · B. E. C. Dugdale, *Family homespun* (1940) · D. E. Meek, 'Campbell, Lady Victoria', *DSCHT*, 130–31 · private information (2004) · d. cert.

Archives Inveraray Castle, Inveraray | NA Scot., Balfour MSS

Likenesses W. Crooke, photograph, 1895, repro. in Balfour, *Lady Victoria Campbell* [*see illus.*] · stained-glass window, 1990, Crown Court Church, London

Wealth at death £14,320 4*s*. 2*d*.: confirmation, 26 Oct 1910, *CCI*

Campbell, Victor Lindsey Arbuthnot (1875–1956), naval officer and Antarctic explorer, was born on 20 August 1875 at 16 Adelaide Crescent, Hove, Sussex, son of Captain Hugh Campbell RN, commander of the royal yacht *Victoria and Albert*, and his wife, Lucy Eleanor Archer. Educated at Eton College, Victor Campbell is said to have run away three times before his father agreed to let him join the Merchant Navy (Huxley, 274). He was subsequently admitted to the Royal Navy on 31 October 1895.

Commissioned acting sub-lieutenant, Campbell served in HMS *President* and HMS *Victory*, joining HMS *Cordelia* in March 1896, which brought him to Newfoundland, a place which left a lasting impression on him. In 1901 he resigned his commission and the following year married Lillian Mary Settle (*d*. 1953), daughter of Major-General Sir Henry Hamilton Settle RE KCB DSO. Their son Nigel was born in 1903. Subsequently the family spent their summer months in Sand, Norway, where Campbell was introduced to the art of ski running, a skill which in due course was to serve him well in the Antarctic with Captain Scott. Then in 1909 tragedy struck when Campbell's sister-in-law was drowned in a boating accident in Sandefjord, an event which so affected his wife that the marriage began to founder. It seems likely that this event played some part in deciding Campbell to sign on with Scott's British Antarctic expedition in 1910 as first officer of SY *Terra Nova*.

An archetypal naval officer of his time, Campbell was dubbed 'the Wicked Mate' by the ship's party, a nickname that implied the mixture of respect, awe, and affection with which he was regarded. Following his supervision of the landing of the stores at the expedition's base at Cape Evans, Ross Island, in January 1911, Campbell was selected by Scott to command a six-man eastern party to explore King Edward VII Land. They were to be landed there by *Terra Nova*, but in the event heavy ice frustrated this plan. On the return voyage Campbell and his men unexpectedly encountered the Norwegian explorer, Roald Amundsen, at the Bay of Whales planning the raid on the south pole which was subsequently to defeat Scott. Following a brief exchange of news Campbell continued towards his second objective, Cape Adare, with what had now become the northern party, pausing only to leave news for Scott of Amundsen's intentions.

The story of the northern party is well recorded by one of its members, the geologist Raymond Priestley, in his book *Antarctic Adventure* (1914). More recently Campbell's own diaries were published as *The Wicked Mate* (1988). The other members included Surgeon-Commander G. Murray Levick, petty officers G. F. Browning and G. P. Abbott, and seaman A. B. H. Dickason. The party's objective was to carry out a scientific survey of the Cape Adare region, a frustrating mission since the topography of the area prohibited all access to the interior. Thanks to Campbell's capable leadership morale was maintained and some useful science accomplished. In January 1912 the northern party was picked up by *Terra Nova* and landed on ice-clad Inaccessible Island to geologize for six weeks. When the ship subsequently failed to relieve them Campbell and his men were compelled to overwinter in a hastily improvised snow cave 12 feet by 9 in area and 5½ feet high. In it they managed to survive for seven months during one of the worst winters then on record, subsisting mainly on seal and penguin meat. That they survived was largely due to Campbell's leadership. His word was law. To maintain discipline he drew an imaginary line bisecting the cave, one half of which was the 'messdeck', the other the 'quarterdeck'. Thus nothing could be officially heard in one half that had been spoken in the other. At last on 30 September 1912 the northern party set off for Cape Evans; they traversed a distance of 230 miles over hazardous crevassed terrain and reached base camp on 6 November 1912. Here they learned of the deaths of the pole party. Campbell then took over the command pending their final relief by *Terra Nova* in January 1913.

Back in London the death of Scott and his companions overshadowed the sufferings and remarkable survival of the northern party. Campbell, ever reticent, was content to receive a gold watch from the Royal Geographical Society and the praise of its president, Lord Curzon, for whom 'no more brilliant thing has ever been accomplished in the history of Arctic and Antarctic exploration' (*Wicked Mate*, 12). In 1913 he was raised to the rank of commander for his part in the expedition. During the summer of 1914 he was employed by the Northern Exploration Company to lead a mineral prospecting expedition to Spitsbergen, but this was abruptly terminated by the outbreak of war. His wartime career was exemplary. He saw action in the Dardanelles and was awarded the DSO to which a bar was subsequently added for service in the Dover patrol. In 1918, aboard HMS *Warwick*, he took part in the Zeebrugge raid and in 1919 was appointed OBE for service in north Russia. Following further commands in the Atlantic Fleet he was promoted captain in 1922, before retiring to his beloved Newfoundland.

In 1926 Campbell's wife, Lillian, divorced him, and two years later he married Marit Fabritious, daughter of a Norwegian artist and a former lady-in-waiting to Queen Maud of Norway. During the Second World War he served for a time as senior naval officer, Trinidad, returning to Newfoundland in 1941 to live in the settlement of Black Duck on the west coast. He finally retired to neighbouring Corner Brook where he died on 19 November 1956 and where he was buried with full military honours. A neighbour once described Campbell as 'the finest of a fine breed, so modest and yet with some quality about him so that you would follow him anywhere' (*Wicked Mate*, 14). His contribution to Scott's last expedition has undoubtedly been much underestimated. H. G. R. KING

Sources *The wicked mate: the Antarctic diary of Victor Campbell*, ed. H. G. R. King (1988) • R. E. Priestley, *Antarctic adventure: Scott's northern party* (1914); repr. (1974) • R. E. Priestley, 'Captain V. L. A. Campbell, DSO, RN', *GJ*, 123 (1957), 131–2 • E. Huxley, *Scott of the Antarctic* (1977) • F. Debenham, *Polar Record*, 8 (1956–7), 466 • b. cert. • *The Eton register*, 8 vols. (privately printed, Eton, 1903–32)

Archives Newfoundland Memorial University, St John's, papers, library, and artefacts • Scott Polar RI | FILM BFI NFTVA, *Ninety degrees south*, 1933

Likenesses photographs, Scott Polar RI

Campbell, William (*d.* 1805), minister of the Presbyterian General Synod of Ulster, was born in High Street, Newry, co. Down, the son of Robert Campbell, a merchant of Newry. He received a good education locally before matriculating from Glasgow University in November 1744. He was licensed by Armagh presbytery in 1750 and became tutor in the Bagwell family, of Clonmel, with whom he spent seven years in France from 1751. He was briefly imprisoned in Paris for refusing to kneel while the host was being carried in the streets. On his return to Ireland in 1758 he married his cousin Jane, daughter of Robert Carlile of Newry; they had eleven children. In the following year he was ordained minister of the non-subscribing Presbyterian congregation at Antrim.

In 1764 Campbell became minister of the First Armagh congregation, which was in connection with the general synod, and in 1773 acted as moderator at the synod at Lurgan. A strong opponent of subscription to the Westminster confession, in 1782 he moved to repeal the rule of 1705 that required subscription before ordination, and nearly won over synod. In the same year he proposed a scheme for a university in the north of Ireland, in an unpublished pamphlet addressed to Walter Hussey Burgh, but the scheme foundered, largely because of Henry Grattan's opposition. In 1783 Campbell directed his energies towards procuring an increase in the *regium donum*, the crown grant to Irish Presbyterian ministers, which then yielded only £9 to each minister. He led the synod's discussions with the Dublin Castle administration, seeking to secure an increase of £5500 a year to the grant, which would have provided each minister with an income of £40. But the interference of Lord Hillsborough, who suspected Ulster Presbyterians' connection with the volunteers and the movement for parliamentary reform, ensured that only £1000 was offered and furthermore deprived the synod of half of the increased grant, which was instead given to the rival Secession church. Though 'bitterly disappointed' (McBride, 151) Campbell was rewarded for his efforts by a presentation of plate by the synod in 1784 and awarded the degree of DD by Glasgow University.

In 1787 Campbell joined in the controversy stirred up by Richard Woodward, bishop of Cloyne, over his claim that none but episcopalians could be loyal to the monarchy and state. In two pamphlets, *A Vindication of the Principles and Character of the Presbyterians in Ireland* (1787) and *An Examination of the Bishop of Cloyne's Defence of his Principles*

(1788), Campbell surveyed the history of his co-religionists to demonstrate that they had always upheld the constitution. In 1788 he applied for the post of the synod's agent for the *regium donum* but was defeated by a large majority in favour of Robert Black. Dismayed at this snub and by now nearly blind, Campbell decided to leave Ulster. On 14 September 1789 he resigned Armagh and took charge of the small congregation at Clonmel, co. Tipperary. Though his published writings are eloquent and effective he was a dull and long-winded preacher and published only one sermon, his synodical sermon of 1774. He died on 17 November 1805 and was succeeded at Clonmel by James Worrall. Only three of his children survived him. ALEXANDER GORDON, *rev.* S. J. SKEDD

Sources W. I. Addison, ed., *The matriculation albums of the University of Glasgow from 1728 to 1858* (1913), 31 • J. S. Reid and W. D. Killen, *History of the Presbyterian church in Ireland*, new edn, 3 (1867), 353ff., 362ff. • T. Witherow, *Historical and literary memorials of presbyterianism in Ireland, 1731–1800* (1880), 173–86 • I. R. McBride, *Scripture politics: Ulster Presbyterians and Irish radicalism in the late eighteenth century* (1998) • J. McConnell and others, eds., *Fasti of the Irish Presbyterian church, 1613–1840*, rev. S. G. McConnell, 2 vols. in 12 pts (1935–51), 134

Archives Presbyterian Historical Society of Ireland, Belfast, MSS

Campbell [*née* Maxwell], **Willielma, Viscountess Glenorchy (1741–1786)**, evangelical activist and benefactor, was the younger daughter of prosperous parents, William Maxwell (*d.* 1741), medical practitioner of Kirkcudbright, and his wife, Elizabeth Hairstanes (*d. c.*1806) of Craig. Willielma was born on 2 September 1741 after her father's death. The only other child of the marriage was her sister, Mary, countess of Sutherland, who died in 1766. After twelve years of widowhood her mother married a judge, Charles Erskine, Lord Alva (1680–1763), and the introduction of her daughters to Edinburgh society led to their marrying into the peerage. Willielma married John Campbell, Viscount Glenorchy (1738–1771), the son and heir of John Campbell, third earl of Breadalbane, and Arabella Pershall, on 26 September 1761. After their marriage the earl gave Taymouth Castle, Perthshire, to his son, who also inherited Great Sugnall House, Staffordshire, from his mother.

While resident at Great Sugnall, Lady Glenorchy became acquainted with the Hill family who lived nearby at Hawkstone Park, Shropshire. The Revd Rowland Hill and his sister were both Calvinistic Methodists, and Lady Glenorchy added Methodist principles to her native Presbyterianism in 1765. Five years later she reopened St Mary's Chapel in Niddry's Wynd in the old town of Edinburgh, where she invited Presbyterians, Episcopalians, and Wesleyans to preach in turn. The experiment, as might be expected, was unsuccessful and probably short-lived. On 14 November 1771 her husband died and as there were no children Lady Glenorchy was free to embark on a career of encouraging evangelical preaching. She consulted Lady Huntingdon about her intentions, and began by restoring a church at Strathfillan on the Taymouth estates. She provided an endowment and appointed a missionary, subsequently transferring responsibility to the Society in Scotland for Propagating Christian Knowledge.

Willielma Campbell, Viscountess Glenorchy (1741–1786), by Robert Scott, pubd 1804

In 1774 she opened the chapel which she had built midway between the old and new towns of Edinburgh (later part of Princes Street Gardens and Waverley Station). The chapel was intended to provide additional accommodation for the growing population of Edinburgh. Although intended to be part of the Church of Scotland, Lady Glenorchy refused to allow a *quoad sacra* parish to be formed and wished to retain the appointment of the minister in her own hands. Inevitably this led to problems with the presbytery, and by October 1776 she was so frustrated and in such poor health that she proposed to abandon Scotland for England.

Arriving at Exmouth at the end of the year she soon found an opportunity to build a chapel there. For its minister she provided a Scottish graduate, Robert Winton, to conduct services on Scottish Presbyterian principles. For the Edinburgh chapel she found a solution by appointing English Calvinistic Methodist ministers who could defy the presbytery. Having discovered the ease with which chapels could be opened in England she confined most of her future efforts to that country. In 1781 she opened a chapel in Carlisle, in 1783 another at Matlock Bath, and in 1786 two more at Workington and Bristol. The latter was commenced with the aid of a legacy of £2500 from her friend Lady Henrietta Hope, but it was not completed until after Lady Glenorchy's death. She died in Edinburgh on 17 July and was buried on 24 July 1786 in her chapel there.

The completion of Hope Chapel at Bristol and her other affairs was left in the hands of her friend Lady Maxwell, despite her Wesleyan opinions. Unfortunately Lady Glenorchy left her affairs in some disorder with a will and an unsigned codicil. After all her assets in Scotland and England had been valued there was a deficit of £3733 11*s.* ¼*d.* on the legacies and annuities in her will, while the codicil (if valid) and a claim by the Edinburgh chapel trustees would increase it to £8673 11*s.* ¾*d.* Most of the money available went to complete Hope Chapel, leaving the other congregations dependent on their own resources. All her English chapels eventually became Congregational and all except Exmouth were either closed or absorbed by other congregations. Her Edinburgh chapel was taken over by the Church of Scotland in 1844, closed, and demolished. After the Disruption of 1843 most of the congregation opened a Free Church at Greenside Place (Lady Glenorchy's Church North). Twenty years later the Church of Scotland revived the name for a chapel in Old Roxburgh Place (Lady Glenorchy's Church South). As a result of reunion and amalgamations neither church now bears the name of Willielma, Viscountess Glenorchy.

EDWIN WELCH

Sources W. Atherton, *The life of Darcy, Lady Maxwell* (1852) • T. S. Jones, *The life of Willielma Viscountess Glenorchy* (1822) • D. P. Thomson, *Lady Glenorchy and her churches* (1822) • Edinburgh chapel records, NA Scot., CH2 • GEC, *Peerage*
Archives NA Scot., letters to Anna Bruce of Arnot
Likenesses A. Ramsay, oils, 1750, Dunrobin Castle, Sutherland • R. Scott, engraving, pubd 1804, NPG [*see illus.*] • Hopwood, stipple, pubd 1815, NPG • D. Martin, oils, Scot. NPG
Wealth at death negative value: NA Scot., CH2/129

Campden. For this title name *see* Hicks, Baptist, first Viscount Campden (1551?–1629); Noel, Edward, second Viscount Campden (*bap.* 1582, *d.* 1643); Noel, Baptist, third Viscount Campden (*bap.* 1611, *d.* 1682).

Campeggi [Campeggio]**, Lorenzo** (**1471/2–1539**), diplomat and bishop of Salisbury, was born in Milan, the eldest of the five sons of Giovanni Zaccaria Campeggi and Dorotea di Tommaso Tebaldi. He took his doctorate in canon and civil law at Bologna in 1500, the same year in which he married Francesca Guastavillani with whom he had five children. When she died in 1509 Campeggi began an ecclesiastical career under Julius II's patronage. Named *auditore della sacra rota*—a judge in the principal papal court—in 1510, he moved to Rome in 1511. He was quickly appointed to two diplomatic missions, both against the council of Pisa, first to the emperor Maximilian, who gave him the bishopric of Feltre in 1512 (held until 1520), and then in 1512–13 to the duke of Milan. In 1513 he returned to Germany seeking a league against the Turks. Leo X promoted him cardinal on 1 July 1517, and Maximilian made him cardinal-protector of the Holy Roman empire. On 3 March 1518 he received a commission to travel to England as part of Leo's peace policy. This gave Thomas Wolsey the chance to gain a legation for himself by using permission for Campeggi to enter England as leverage, and then to outmanoeuvre the new legate once he arrived, taking over the process of peace-making which led to the treaty of London (1519).

Showered with gifts by both king and cardinal, Campeggi became a stout English partisan, as well as an imperialist. Although formally appointed cardinal-protector of England only on 22 January 1523, he effectively filled that office from his return to Rome, when he also became a member of the Segnatura di Giustizia and a papal secretary. Despite his new official role, however, Campeggi was not involved in much English business, except for the referring of episcopal provisions in consistory. The election of Adrian VI in 1522 cemented Campeggi's position in the curia and as agent of England. For Adrian, Campeggi composed 'De depravato statu ecclesiae' which proposed many radical reforms of papal bureaucracy. On 2 December 1524 he received the bishopric of Salisbury, which he had been promised in 1518. The election of Clement VII in 1523 further exalted Campeggi's status. He was then also a member of Johann Goritz's humanist sodality. Clement made him bishop of Bologna on 2 December 1523 (held until 1525) and then on 9 January 1524 legate to the diet of Nuremberg.

During the sack of Rome in 1527 Campeggi lost everything. Clement, who fled to Orvieto, left him behind as papal legate in the city, just when the time came of his greatest utility to England. Wolsey and Henry VIII expected Campeggi to be malleable when they proposed that a papal co-legate should decide on Henry's divorce from Katherine of Aragon in co-operation with Wolsey. Campeggi had, however, already given a legal opinion to the pope which leaned heavily in the direction of validating the marriage in the event of its being proved invalid. Nevertheless he was named legate on 8 June 1528, after a joint commission to him with Wolsey had been agreed on 13 April. Clement intended to use Campeggi as a cover for his own tergiversations, as the legate came to suspect. Campeggi arrived in London on 8 October 1528 and was subjected to the first of many sessions with Wolsey and Henry, the first English king to sue before a papal judge in person. They also tried to bribe him, probably promising him the bishopric of Durham, although they did not pay his expenses as they had offered to do.

As a strong imperialist, Campeggi found himself in an almost impossible position, since Charles V, Katherine of Aragon's nephew, was determined to prevent the divorce and pressurized Campeggi almost as much as the English did. The deciding point in law for Campeggi was Julius's dispensation for Henry and Katherine's marriage in the full form recently discovered in Spain. In Katherine's possession from early in 1528, she showed it to Campeggi in October, and he took it to invalidate his commission, since the latter failed to cover the Spanish document. He tried to make the case disappear on 23 July 1529 by proroguing it until October, but this act had been forestalled by the pope's advocation of the matter to Rome a week earlier. On his way back to Rome, Campeggi met Charles and Clement in Bologna, where the pope made over to Campeggi the castle of Dozza and the emperor took the family under his protection. Charles later (2 September 1530) gave Campeggi the Spanish bishopric of Huesca and Jaca, which he held until 17 June 1534 when he became bishop of Candia (Crete) (until 1536); in 1532, moreover, when making Campeggi's son Gianbattista bishop of Majorca, the emperor reserved the administration of the see to the young man's father. Campeggi was legate to the diet of Augsburg in 1530, where he pursued intense negotiations with Philip Melanchthon at the same time as he took a hard line with the German protestants.

By 20 May 1531 Henry had dismissed Campeggi as protector. In August 1533 he lost the revenues of Salisbury, and on 21 March 1534 was deprived by act of parliament. By coincidence immediately afterwards he helped to bring the king's case to its conclusion, in consistory's declaration of the validity of Henry's marriage to Katherine, given on 23 March. Campeggi joined the commission which decided Henry's excommunication in 1535, and also that of 1538 which determined to publish it. He remained protector of Germany until his death, at the same time devoting much energy to insuring the future of his family; he left two sons, two brothers, and one nephew as bishops. He was named legate to the general council called first for Mantua and then for Vicenza, only the first session of which, in May 1538, he attended. He died on 25 July 1539, aged sixty-seven, and was buried in Santa Maria in Trastevere; in 1571 at least some of his bones were transferred to the church of Santi Marta e Bernardino that he had built in Bologna. T. F. MAYER

Sources E. V. Cardinal, *Cardinal Lorenzo Campeggio, legate to the courts of Henry VIII and Charles V* (1935) • S. Skalweit, 'Campeggi, Lorenzo', *Dizionario biografico degli Italiani*, ed. A. M. Ghisalberti, 17 (Rome, 1974) • C. Eubel and others, eds., *Hierarchia Catholica medii et recentioris aevi*, 2nd edn, 3, ed. W. van Gulik, C. Eubel, and L. Schmitz-Kallenberg (Münster, 1923) • B. M. Hallman, *Italian cardinals, reform and the church as property, 1492–1563* (1985) • W. E. Wilkie, *The cardinal protectors of England: Rome and the Tudors before the Reformation* (1974)

Archives Archivio di Stato, Bologna, Fondo Malvezzi-Campeggi | Archivio Segreto Vaticano • BL • PRO

Likenesses E. Harding, stipple, pubd 1793, NPG • Dürer?, portrait, Palazzo dell'Università, Bologna • medal, Hult. Arch., Augustin Rischgitz collection

Campion, Edmund [St Edmund Campion] (**1540–1581**), Jesuit and martyr, was probably one of the Sawston branch of the Campion family and was born in London on 25 January 1540, son of a citizen and bookseller.

Education and early career Campion was educated at a grammar school in London, then at Christ's Hospital and St Paul's where, in August 1553, he won a silver pen in an inter-school literary competition. When, in September 1553, Queen Mary rode through London for her coronation, he was chosen to deliver the scholar's oration to her. In 1558 Campion, promoted by the Grocers' Company, entered the new Oxford college of St John's, founded by Sir Thomas White. There 'I studied philosophy for seven years and theology for about six—Aristotle, positive theology and the Fathers' (Reynolds, 38). On 20 November 1561 he was admitted to the BA degree. After graduating MA in 1564 he and his close friend Gregory Martin were elected fellows of St John's. He acquired a wide reputation as a tutor and lecturer, whose speech and manners were imitated by students, and in 1565 he was appointed to the university committee dealing with dispensations from degree requirements. The long-standing belief that his first public oration at Oxford was at the burial of Amy Robsart, Robert Dudley's wife, has recently been questioned.

When Queen Elizabeth I visited Oxford University in late August 1566, Campion welcomed her on its behalf. He was also one of the scholars chosen to debate what determined the movement of the tides and whether the lower bodies of the universe were regulated by the higher. As a result of his performance he gained the patronage of Robert Dudley, now earl of Leicester. In September that year he also received a Grocers' Company exhibition, which carried with it the condition that he preach at Paul's Cross if required. In order that he could satisfy this requirement, Richard Cheyney, bishop of Gloucester, ordained him deacon in March 1569 and gave him the Gloucestershire living of Sherborne. They became well acquainted and in 1572 Campion corresponded with the bishop even after his own recantation of protestantism. Meanwhile, during the 1560s his Oxford career flourished. He became noted for his orations, which included Sir Thomas White's funeral discourse in 1567. The following year he was elected junior proctor, a prestigious university office with wide-ranging administrative and financial responsibilities.

On 23 March 1569 Campion supplicated for the degree of BTh, because he had studied theology for five years. Six months later, on 6 October, St John's College awarded him a five-year travelling scholarship. By then Campion had been in a religious dilemma for some years. A future Church of England archbishop, Tobie Matthew, who in 1564 was present at one of his orations, observed that 'against his conscience' he took the oath against papal supremacy rather than miss the chance to display his skill as a speaker. According to Robert Persons, Campion had always been a Catholic, but he was swayed by the praise heaped upon him and tempted by the prospect of preferment. When, in 1568, he came under prolonged pressure from the Grocers' Company to preach in accordance with the terms of his exhibition, he procrastinated, repeatedly requesting delays for various reasons. Finally he resigned the exhibition. His ordination in 1569 was rapidly followed by 'a remorse of conscience and a detestation of mind' (Reynolds, 41). After completing his year's duties as junior proctor he did not take up the St John's scholarship, nor did he stay to take his BTh degree. In August 1570 he left Oxford and made his way to Dublin.

In Ireland Campion had been invited by James Stanihurst, Dublin's recorder, speaker of the Irish House of Commons, and father of Richard, one of his students. It was there that he wrote a work which has not survived, *De homine academico*, describing the desirable qualities and responsibilities of a student; and one which has, his *History of Ireland*, in which Richard Stanihurst had a hand. The *History of Ireland*, which he wrote in ten weeks in 1571, was dedicated to his patron, the earl of Leicester, in the hope that he might become a patron to Ireland and as an acknowledgement of 'the general heap of your bounties' (*Two Histories of Ireland*, no pagination). When he wrote how often—at Windsor, Rycote, and the court—Leicester had 'not ceased to further with advice and to countenance with authority, the hope and expectation of me a single student', Campion revealed the frequency of his contact with the queen's favourite since her Oxford visit of 1566. His *History of Ireland* may also have been intended as a defence of the policies and practices of Sir Henry Sidney, who was Elizabeth's chief governor of Ireland between 1565 and 1571, the Stanihursts' friend, and Leicester's brother-in-law. As 'naked and simple' as his *History of Ireland* was:

> it could never have grown to any proportion in such post-haste, except I had entered into such familiar society and daily table-talk with the worshipful Esquire James Stanihurst … Who beside all courtesy of Hospitality, and a thousand loving turns … both by word and written monuments, and by the benefit of his own Library, nourished most effectually mine endeavour. (*Two Histories of Ireland*, no pagination)

The work was revised by Richard Stanihurst, incorporated in Raphael Holinshed's *Chronicles* in the 1587 edition, and then edited and published in Dublin by Sir James Ware in his *Two Histories of Ireland* of 1633. A manuscript copy of Campion's *History of Ireland*, dated 1571, was given by Henry Howard, duke of Norfolk, to the library of the College of Arms in London in 1678. Campion's Catholicism must have been public knowledge because, after the pope's excommunication of Queen Elizabeth in 1570, Sir Henry Sidney warned James Stanihurst that he was at risk. He was conveyed out of Dublin by the Stanihursts, in June 1571 he was at Drogheda, and finally, masquerading as a servant of the earl of Kildare's steward, he was smuggled to England.

The Society of Jesus Campion arrived in England in time to witness the trial of John Storey, who had upheld papal authority. His first attempt to go abroad failed when he was seized in mid-channel and returned to England. At his second attempt he was successful and he proceeded to the English College at Douai. There he was reunited with his old Oxford friends, Gregory Martin and Richard Bristow. He recanted, studied divinity, was ordained subdeacon, took his BTh in 1572, and taught as a professor of rhetoric. Early in 1573 he went to Rome on foot, perhaps as a penance, in order to become a Jesuit. He arrived between the death of the society's general and the appointment of his successor, Everard Mercurian. So it was not until August 1573 that he entered the novitiate. Between 1573 and 1580 he served first as a novice in Brünn (Brno), in Moravia, and Prague, in Bohemia, and then as teacher of philosophy and rhetoric and a Latin preacher in Prague. During those years he was visited by Sir Henry Sidney's son Philip (in 1576), he was ordained deacon and priest by the archbishop of Prague (1578), and he also wrote and produced Latin dramas: on Abraham, King Saul, and also on St Ambrose and the emperor Theodosius, which was performed at the imperial court in 1577. Then, on 9 December 1579, William Allen, writing from Rome, sent him a letter of recall.

The English mission: purposes, problems, and preparations The Jesuits' role in the mission dates from a meeting in Rome in 1575, when Allen, Persons, and others agreed that 'conversion' of England was their prime objective. Mercurian, general of the society from 1573 to 1580, had serious misgivings about the project, especially that it would be viewed as a political, not religious, venture. Although Mercurian's doubts were eventually overcome, the Jesuit dilemma was a serious one: that they would be regarded as the pope's political agents, attempting to enforce Gregory XIII's bull which, in 1570, had excommunicated Elizabeth I. This danger was heightened as Campion and Persons began the Jesuit mission in 1580, because Nicholas Sander, another Englishman and a papal nuncio, was in Ireland, supporting Spanish-assisted rebels against English rule.

Campion, like Mercurian, had his doubts. Allen's letter of December 1579 was followed in March 1580 by the official summons to serve in the mission. Campion left Prague on 25 March and proceeded to Rome via Munich, Innsbruck, and Padua, arriving in Rome on 5 April 1580. He resented his removal from Prague. As he later told Allen, 'Do you think that my labours in England will countervail all this travail, as well as my absence from Bohemia where, though I did not much, yet was I not idle nor unemployed, and that also against heretics' (McCoog, *The Reckoned Expense*, 126–7). On 20 June he expressed his worry concerning hostile English preparations for their arrival when he wrote to Mercurian about 'something positively like a clamour that heralds our approach. Only divine Providence can counteract this kind of publicity' (ibid., 127). By then Mercurian had issued the mission's official objectives: to strengthen the Catholics' faith and to bring back those who, through ignorance or temptation, had been lost.

On 14 April 1580 Campion and Persons had an audience with the pope, who answered questions and granted a number of faculties, in particular an *explanatio* which released English Catholics from implementing the 1570 bull until its terms could be enforced. On 18 April Campion, Persons, a Jesuit lay brother Ralph Emerson, and others left Rome. Campion refused the offer of new apparel, declaring that 'to him that went to be hanged in England any apparel was sufficient' (Reynolds, 63). They travelled to Bologna, Milan, and Geneva, where Campion rashly tried to engage Theodore Beza in religious debate, thereby putting the entire party at risk. On 31 May they reached Rheims. There the party broke up and, in order to lessen the chance of detection, travelled separately by different routes into England. The three Jesuits proceeded to St Omer. Persons entered England first and then, on 24 June, Campion (disguised as a travelling jewel salesman from Dublin) and Emerson crossed from Calais to Dover. On arrival they were arrested and taken before the mayor of Dover, who resolved to send them to London but changed his mind and discharged them. They hurried to London, where they were sheltered in a house rented by

George Gilbert, who was a wealthy young convert to Catholicism and Persons's friend.

Campion's mission, 1580–1581 On 29 June 1580 Campion risked discovery when Thomas, Lord Paget, organized a venue for him to preach in Smithfield. A fortnight later, in Southwark, he and Persons met secular clergy to reassure them that their mission was apostolical not political. Nevertheless, some resented their arrival, which had intensified persecution. The Jesuits then withdrew to Hoxton, where Campion composed an address to the privy council which became known to his opponents as his 'Challenge' or 'Brag'. It was a challenge to debate religion with councillors, university scholars, and lawyers, confident that 'no one Protestant nor all the Protestants living … can maintain their doctrine in disputation'. He knew the cost which the mission might entail, but it was worthwhile. 'The expense is reckoned, the enterprise is begun; it is of God; it cannot be withstood' (McCoog, *The Reckoned Expense*, 128 and n. 35). Campion's text was committed to Thomas Pound, a Catholic prisoner on brief parole from the Marshalsea. Pound allowed copies to be made and soon it was widely circulated. It quickly provoked published protestant replies from William Charke, who called Campion a traitor, Meredith Hanmer, and others.

In early August 1580 the two Jesuits separated and Campion moved through Berkshire, Oxfordshire, and Northamptonshire, ministering to Catholics and, in accordance with Mercurian's instruction, dealing with the wealthier families, who could give them security and shelter. They met again in October 1580 in Uxbridge. As a result of that meeting Campion wrote the *Rationes decem*, finishing it by the end of March 1581. First printed at Stonor Park, Oxfordshire, it was published in Latin and the vernacular at various places in France, Germany, Italy, and Poland, especially in the years 1582–4. (Two important subsequent editions were *Decem rationes, et alia opuscula eius selecta* by P. Silvester Petra-Sancta, 1631, and *Campian Englished*, by a 'Priest of the Catholic and Roman Church', 1632.) At the same time Campion continued to travel and minister clandestinely in England. His route between October and Christmas 1580 is not known. A letter written to Mercurian in November, explaining how the 'Brag' had unintentionally been circulated, printed, and published, bears no address.

Between Christmas 1580 and Easter of 1581 Campion's route through Nottinghamshire, Derbyshire, Yorkshire, and Lancashire can be traced from the later confessions of his Catholic hosts. Meanwhile, the hunt for him intensified, especially after the premature release of his 'Brag'. The privy council letter of 1 December 1580 stating that the queen intended to 'make some example of [Jesuits] by punishment, to the terror of others' (*APC*, 12.271), the proclamation of 10 January 1581, ordering the arrest of Jesuits, and the statute 23 Eliz. 1 c.1, which made it treason to convert the queen's subjects to 'the Romish religion': together these amounted to a declaration of war on the Jesuit mission. Campion, however, remained free. He sent the manuscript of *Rationes decem* to Persons some time after Easter 1581. The Latin text was printed on Persons's private press at Stonor, where Campion arrived in mid-May, and by June copies were available. *Rationes decem* concerned the ten points of the Catholic case which he would have used if the protestants had taken up his 'Challenge' or 'Brag'. He concluded with an appeal to the queen that 'the day will surely come that will show thee clearly which of the two have loved thee, the Society of Jesus or the brood of Luther' (Reynolds, 104). On 27 June 1581 printed copies were secretly spread on the benches of the Oxford University church of St Mary's, before the convocation at which student supplicants for degrees were required to defend their theses. After this publicity coup the two Jesuits left Stonor on 11 July. When they parted, Campion and Emerson were due to go north to Lancashire, but they first detoured to stay overnight at Lyford Grange, the Catholic household of Edward Yates, in Berkshire. Although they left next day, Campion was persuaded to return by a messenger from importunate visitors who had just missed him. It was during his return visit that George Eliot, a Catholic informer who had previously served in the household of Lady Petre at Ingatestone in Essex, alerted the authorities to his presence. On 17 July 1581 Campion, two other priests, and seven laymen were arrested.

Imprisonment, interrogation, torture, and disputation The prisoners were taken under escort, by the high sheriff of Berkshire, through Abingdon and Henley to Colnbrook. From there to London their hands were tied and their feet were bound under their horses' bellies, while Campion bore on his hat the inscription 'THE SEDITIOUS JESUIT'. When he arrived at the Tower he was at first placed in the 'Little Ease', where a prisoner could neither stand upright nor lie stretched out. On 25 or 26 July he was taken by river to meet the earl of Leicester, Sir Christopher Hatton, and the lord chancellor, Thomas Bromley, at the house of the last named. The long-standing story that Queen Elizabeth was also present has recently been shown to be 'no more than a figment of the imaginations of Campion's biographers' (Colthorpe, 199). According to Burghley, at the meeting Campion 'stiffly denieth to answer any question of moment'. His obstinacy may explain why, on 30 July 1581, the privy council ordered him to be further examined and, if he refused 'to answer truly and directly to such things as by them shall be demanded … then to deal with him by the Rack' (*APC*, 13.144).

The record of Campion's interrogations, sometimes under torture, extends over three months to the end of October 1581. According to the Venetian and Spanish ambassadors he suffered not only the rack, but also metal spikes driven between the flesh and fingernails and the nails pulled out. It is impossible to determine how many times he was examined and how often he was tortured. Nor is there any evidence that his interrogators, John Hammond, Robert Beale, and Thomas Norton, extracted confessions of a treasonable nature. He named many of those who had sheltered him and they were in due course, during or after his life, examined and often fined or imprisoned. However—as he declared at Tyburn, his place of execution—he does not appear to have revealed where he said mass, and he certainly did not renounce his faith.

Indeed he was allowed to defend it when the government staged a disputation as he had requested in his 'Brag'. It was, however, designed to be a one-sided affair, the purposes of which were to demonstrate the government's fairness and to discredit the Jesuit. During the four sessions held in the Tower, on 31 August, 18, 23, and 27 September, he had to contest with a team of protestant divines chosen by the bishop of London. They had adequate time and assistance to prepare their case and books on hand during the conference. 'Right opposite upon a stool was set Mr Campion Jesuit, having only his Bible' (BL, Harleian MS 422, no. 23). He had been informed of the event and the subjects of discussion only a few hours before. However, some of his fellow prisoners were allowed to attend the first conference and one of them, Ralph Sherwin, assisted him.

During the four sessions Campion had no part in the choice of the topics for debate: justification by faith, the nature of the church, the eucharist, and the canon and authority of the scriptures. His role was purely responsive and confined to answering challenges and criticisms made by the protestant contestants. Some protestants, such as Bishop Aylmer of London, doubted the wisdom of the disputation, to which the public was admitted and about which stories, unflattering to Campion's adversaries, were circulating. After the opening session Norton, who was repeatedly involved in examining Campion, claimed that the Jesuit was exploiting the occasion. In particular, the government disputants' choice of new topics for each session enabled him to claim that 'they come prepared and he unprepared'. Because there were no rules of debate, he was able to deviate, distort, retract, and engage in 'bragging and impertinent and insolent speeches' (Strype, *Aylmer*, 35–6), and, as there was no screening of those attending, his sympathizers turned up. Although Norton drafted a set of advices for the more effective staging of the remaining meetings, dissatisfaction continued to be voiced by Bishop Aylmer and others. The government finally ended the affair, when it cancelled a fifth session, scheduled for 13 October.

Both contemporary and later verdicts on Campion and his performance were predictably diverse. One of the disputants, John Walker, damned him as 'degenerate from an Englishman, an apostate in religion … unloyal to his Prince', seeking 'to plant secretly the blasphemous Mass' (Reynolds, 144). William Camden wrote that 'he never had so much ado to maintain [his ten reasons], neither answered he to that expectation which himself had formerly given' (Camden, 2.415). However, even Anthony Munday, who condemned him as a traitor, acknowledged that he performed well in the disputation. Action was taken by the privy council against Oliver Cawood and others who publicly stated that he had discomfited his adversaries, but it could not prevent the circulation of popular ballads which mocked the established church's performance. The disputation had two other consequences: it resulted in a flurry of protestant and Catholic polemical pamphlets; and the favourable impression which Campion made on Philip Howard, earl of Arundel, who was in the audience, contributed to his conversion to Catholicism.

Indictment, trial, and execution On 12 November 1581, over six weeks after the last day of the disputation and more than a fortnight after the council's order for what appears to have been Campion's final racking, he, together with six other imprisoned priests and a layman, was indicted before the grand jury in Westminster Hall. Originally the government had intended to charge him with treason for pretending to have the power to withdraw Elizabeth's subjects from 'the religion now by her supreme authority established within this realm of England to the Roman religion' and for persuading them to promise obedience to the papacy (BL, Lansdowne MS 33, fols. 156–7). The indictment was then changed in two ways. Campion was charged together with three absentees—William Allen, Nicholas Morton, and Robert Persons—and thirteen incarcerated priests and others. The charge was also altered to treasonable conspiracy, first hatched in Rome and Rheims, to raise rebellion, invite foreign invasion, overthrow and kill the queen, and alter both the government and religion. So the basis of the charge shifted from religion to political conspiracy, from the act of 1581 to the treason statute of 1351. When the prisoners pleaded 'not guilty' to the indictment, they were ordered, as custom required, to hold up their hands. The effects of racking prevented Campion from doing so without assistance.

On 20 November 1581 Campion and seven other priests were brought to trial in Westminster Hall. The prosecution was conducted by Serjeant Edmund Anderson, the attorney-general and solicitor-general. Their principal witnesses were George Eliot, who had procured Campion's arrest, Anthony Munday, Charles Sledd, and H. Caddy, who claimed to have talked with or eavesdropped on the 'conspirators' abroad. Campion bore the brunt both of his own defence and that of his fellow prisoners, as he criticized trial by 'conjectural surmises, without proof of the crime, sufficient evidence and substantial witness' and as he reminded the court that 'probabilities, aggravations, invectives, are not the balance wherein justice must be weighed, but witnesses, oaths, and apparent guiltiness' (Reynolds, 171–2). His performance was such that, when the jury retired after three hours, their acquittal was widely expected. However, they were all found guilty and condemned to be hanged, drawn, and quartered. When Wray, the presiding judge, asked why they should not die, Campion, acting as spokesman for the defendants, reputedly declared that, while they were prepared to die, adherence to their faith was not treason and they remained the queen's loyal subjects. When sentence was passed Campion began a hymn of praise, *Te Deum laudamus*, and the other prisoners joined in, to the evident wonderment of the packed court. Between his trial and execution he was visited by his sister and by George Eliot. Then, on 1 December 1581 he, together with Ralph Sherwin and Alexander Briant, was drawn to Tyburn. His attempts to address the crowd were interrupted by questions, from Sir Francis Knollys and others, about his opinions on the 1570 bull, his loyalty to the pope, and his alleged treason. The Catholic Thomas Alfield, who was 'present and very near', reported that 'Campion was asked for which queen he prayed … [H]e answered, yea for Elizabeth your queen and my queen … And so he meekly and sweetly yielded his soul unto his Saviour, protesting that he died a perfect catholic' (Alfield, no pagination).

Significance This lies partly in the controversy provoked by Campion's career, arrest, torment, the charges against him, and his trial and death. He was condemned and killed for offending Edward III's treason law. Anthony Munday and George Eliot attacked him in print as a treasonable conspirator. The officially sponsored pamphlet *A particular declaration or testimony of the undutiful and traiterous affection born against her majesty* in 1582 justified the condemnation of Campion and the other executed priests. A proclamation of 1 April that year condemned all Jesuits 'coming into these her dominions in such secret manner' as traitors. Reports of the cruelties inflicted on Campion and other Jesuits obliged Lord Burghley and Thomas Norton to publish in 1583–4, in several languages, defences of official actions against men who were not regarded as religious martyrs but as political traitors. The papal *explanatio* which Campion and Persons had received from Gregory XIII, suspending the queen's excommunication for the time being, enabled her government to represent them as disloyal practitioners of political expedience.

By contrast, the early Catholic responses—martyrologies and defences of Campion's virtues and reputation—published for a European audience in 1582–4 claimed that he was a victim of religious persecution. Persons addressed the privy council, Alfield rebutted Munday, and Allen replied to Burghley. Praise of the martyred Jesuit's qualities and disposition came from all quarters. In the 1586 edition of Holinshed's *Chronicles*, his former student Richard Stanihurst described him as 'so rare a clerk, who was so upright in conscience, so deep in judgement, so ripe in eloquence'. Just before the Jesuit mission began, Campion was described in the Douai diary as an excellent dialectician, good theologian, and 'in speech so polished and eloquent as to have few equals' (Morey, 194–5; McCoog, *The Reckoned Expense*, 127 and n.). Antonio Possevino, who had known Campion in Prague, and possibly in Rome, during the 1570s, extolled his zeal and saintliness. Persons, who acquired and for ever after carried on his person a piece of the rope used in his execution, wrote that '[N]ow I take him rather for my patron than for my brother, whose steps I beseech Christ I may be worthy to follow' (Reynolds, 212). To Alfield he was:

> an honour to our country, a glass and mirror, a light and lantern, a pattern and example to youth, to age, to learned, to unlearned, to religious, and to the laity of all sort, state, and condition of modesty, gravity, eloquence, knowledge, virtue and piety. (Alfield, no pagination)

Anthony Wood, writing in the seventeenth century, observed that:

> All writers, whether protestant or popish, say that he was a man of most admirable parts, an elegant orator, a subtle philosopher and disputant, and an exact preacher whether in English or Latin tongue, of a sweet disposition and a well-polished man. (Wood, *Ath. Oxon.*, 1.475)

Campion was canonized in 1970.

Michael A. R. Graves

Sources E. E. Reynolds, *Campion and Parsons: the Jesuit mission of 1580–1* (1980) • T. M. McCoog, *The Society of Jesus in Ireland, Scotland, and England, 1541–1588* (1996) • T. M. McCoog, ed., *The reckoned expense: Edmund Campion and the early English Jesuits* (1996) • *APC*, 1580–82 • *Campian Englished, or, A translation of the ten reasons, in which Edmund Campian, priest, insisted in his challenge to the universities of Oxford and Cambridge* (1632) • T. Alfield, *A true reporte of the death and martyrdome of M. Campion Jesuite and preiste, and M. Sherwin and M. Bryan preistes at Tiborne the first of December 1581* (1581) • G. Camdeno [W. Camden], *Annales rerum Anglicarum et Hibernicarum regnante Elizabetha* (1615) • Wood, *Ath. Oxon.*, new edn, 1.473 • M. Carrafiello, 'English Catholicism and the Jesuit mission of 1580–1581', *HJ*, 37 (1994), 761–74 • H. Foley, ed., *Records of the English province of the Society of Jesus*, 7 vols. in 8 (1875–83) • R. Holinshed and others, eds., *The chronicles of England, Scotland and Ireland*, 2nd edn, ed. J. Hooker, 2 (1586) • T. M. McCoog, '"The Flower of Oxford": the role of Edmund Campion in early recusant polemics', *Sixteenth Century Journal*, 24 (1993), 899–913 • J. Strype, *Annals of the Reformation and establishment of religion … during Queen Elizabeth's happy reign*, new edn, 2–3 (1824) • indictments of Edmund Campion and others, BL, Lansdowne MS 33, nos. 64–5 • J. Strype, *Historical collections of the life and acts of … John Aylmer*, new edn (1821) • M. Colthorpe, 'Edmund Campion's alleged interview with Queen Elizabeth I in 1581', *Recusant History*, 17 (1984–5), 197–200 • 'Relation of a disputation in the Towre', BL, Harleian MS 422, no. 22, fol. 136; no. 23, fol. 148 • A. Morey, *The Catholic subjects of Elizabeth I* (1978) • P. L. Hughes and J. F. Larkin, eds., *Tudor royal proclamations*, 2 (1969), no. 660 • [J. Ware], ed., *Two histories of Ireland* (1633)

Archives Archivum Romanum Societatis Iesu, Rome, Fondo Gesuitico, letters • BL, corresp. and papers, Harley MSS • Coll. Arms, history of Ireland, Arundel MS 115 • Stonyhurst College, Lancashire, Archives of the British Province of the Society of Jesus, letters • Trinity Cam., history of Ireland, MS 754 | BL, Lansdowne MSS • PRO, state papers (domestic)

Likenesses line engraving, pubd 1819, BM, NPG • J. Neefs, line engraving, BM, NPG • portrait, Campion Hall, Oxford

Campion, Frederick Henry (1872–1957), Church of England clergyman, was born on 8 September 1872 at Danny Park, Hurstpierpoint, Sussex, second son of Colonel William Henry Campion and his wife, Gertrude, daughter of Henry Bouverie William Brand, first Viscount Hampden. Educated at Eton College, and New College, Oxford (BA 1895, MA 1908), he arrived in Sydney in November 1895 as private secretary and tutor in the household of Henry Robert Brand, second Viscount Hampden, governor of New South Wales. A first-class shot and a fine horseman, he afterwards declared that while shooting out of Warren in far western New South Wales he was shocked by the spiritual destitution of bush-dwellers. Having discussed plans to overcome this neglect with the Anglican bishop of Bathurst, C. E. Camidge, and his chaplain, E. H. Lea, Campion returned to England, entered Wells Theological College (1896) and was made deacon (25 September 1898) and priested (21 December 1899) by the bishop of Lichfield. While curate of St Mary, Handsworth, diocese of Lichfield, his name appeared on the Church Association's 'black list' of ritualist clergy. With a colleague from theological college, C. H. S. Matthews, Campion returned to New South Wales to test his plans for a bush brotherhood of celibate priests, on minimal stipends, travelling in bush districts with quarterly reunions at their home base. Both Campion and Matthews were initially licensed, on 9 January 1902, as curates to Lea, recently appointed rector of Dubbo, New South Wales. Campion took responsibility for what was known as the 'home district', the outlying portions of the parishes of Warren and Narromine, northwest of Dubbo. In 1903 he began a regular fundraising campaign in Sydney, organized by a committee with viceregal connections; these spring 'raids' were noted for their drawing-room meetings and visits to the leading Anglican church schools and St Paul's College, University of Sydney.

In August 1903 Camidge laid the foundation stone of Brotherhood House, Dubbo, a substantial red-brick building with wide verandahs and a chapel, built on land given by the bishop. After Lea's successful fund-raising trip to England, the Brotherhood of the Good Shepherd was formally established in May 1904, with Campion as both principal and chairman of directors. Until 1923 the brotherhood was registered as a limited liability company under the New South Wales Companies Act. Campion was an able chair of a board meeting: due to his guidance, his foundation became the most stable of all the Australian bush brotherhoods.

Following his marriage on 19 November 1907 to Noël Blaxland, great-granddaughter of the Australian pioneer explorer Gregory Blaxland, Campion returned to England, as vicar of West Grinstead (1908), of Leigh (1916), and of Tillington (1930–48), all in the diocese of Chichester. In 1915–19, he served as a chaplain in France. In 1932–48, he was rural dean of Petworth and in 1938 became a prebendary of Chichester Cathedral. An avowed high-churchman, he always disclaimed being Anglo-Catholic. In 1908 he became foundation treasurer of the 'home committee' of the Brotherhood of the Good Shepherd, affiliated with the SPG, which enjoyed the enthusiastic support of the bishop of London, A. F. Winnington Ingram. He afterwards was made a life member; his extended family were staunch supporters. Long commissary for successive bishops of Bathurst, he returned to Australia once, in 1924, but in 1952 led the challenge to the Brotherhood, at its golden jubilee, to extend its ministry to the Northern Territory of Australia. He died at the Cottage Hospital, Petworth, on 27 January 1957, survived by his son.

Like his elder brother Sir William Campion, governor of Western Australia (1924–31), Frederick was tall, with clear blue eyes, and bald before he was thirty. The brothers represented that generation of Englishmen whose sense of responsibility saw them serve in war and in the more remote corners of empire. RUTH FRAPPELL

Sources *Bush Brother* [Dubbo, NSW] (Sept 1904) · *Bush Brother* [Dubbo, NSW] (Oct 1905) · *Bush Brother* [Dubbo, NSW] (Nov 1906) · *Bush Brother* [Dubbo, NSW] (Jan 1908) · *Bush Brother* [Dubbo, NSW] (March 1957) · *The Times* (6 Feb 1957) · *The Anglican* [Sydney] (17 Feb 1957) · *The Anglican* [Sydney] (22 Feb 1957) · C. H. S. Matthews, *A parson in the Australian bush* (1908) · R. M. Frappell, 'The Australian bush brotherhoods and their English origins', *Journal of Ecclesiastical History*, 47 (1996), 82–97 · b. cert. · *CGPLA Eng. & Wales* (1957)

Wealth at death £6144 19*s*. 3*d*.: probate, 1 April 1957, *CGPLA Eng. & Wales*

Campion, George Bryant (1796–1870), watercolour painter, initially painted landscapes and topographical views but later specialized in military subjects and studies of uniforms. Nothing is known of his family background and training. He exhibited ten works at the Society of British Artists from 1829 and was one of the earliest members of the New Watercolour Society (later the Royal Institute of Painters in Water Colours), where, up to 1869, he showed over 400 watercolours and was vice-president from 1839 to 1841. He worked in chalks and watercolour, usually on grey or light brown paper. He taught drawing to private pupils and, from 1841, was instructor of drawing at the Royal Military Academy, Woolwich.

Campion produced four lithographs of coaching scenes after James Pollard (1837); six lithographic illustrations each for *Principal Evolutions of the Royal Horse Artillery* and *Principal Evolutions of the Royal Artillery*, published by Rudolph Ackermann in 1846; seventeen plates for *The History of the Corps of Royal Sappers and Miners* by T. W. J. Connolly (1855); and four topographical illustrations for George Virtue's *Views of Kent* (1832). In 1854 he painted six views of the camp at Chobham, Surrey, for Queen Victoria. Two watercolours of the Windsor review of 1869, offered to the queen, were purchased by her son, Prince Arthur, whose governor described Campion as 'a very eccentric old man, [who] will have his own way' (Royal Archives, Add. A 15/1452, 15 July 1869). Campion was married and had at least three children. He died on 1 April 1870 at his home, 49 Woolwich Common, Woolwich, London. From 9 December of that year a sale of 700 of his remaining pictures, sketches, and studies was held at Christies. An exhibition of seventy of his works was held at Walker's Galleries, London, in March and April 1935; a critic in *The Times* wrote that 'his pictures of manœuvres and camps are interesting from the military point of view, but his larger pictures suffer from an over-elaboration of detail and monotony of tone' (12 March 1935). The print room at the Mellon Center, Yale University, contains many of his best works. DELIA MILLAR

Sources *Walker's Monthly*, 87 (March 1935), 1–2 · *Walker's Monthly*, 88 (April 1935), 3 · Mallalieu, *Watercolour artists* · Wood, *Vic. painters*, 3rd edn · A. Wilson, *A dictionary of British military painters* (1972) · *DNB* · A. E. H. Miller and N. P. Dawnay, *Military drawings and paintings in the collection of her majesty the queen*, 2 vols. (1966–70), vol. 2 · D. Millar, *The Victorian watercolours and drawings in the collection of her majesty the queen*, 1 (1995) · d. cert. · *CGPLA Eng. & Wales* (1871)

Likenesses photograph, repro. in *Walker's Monthly*, 87, 1

Wealth at death under £1000: probate, 13 March 1871, *CGPLA Eng. & Wales*

Campion, Gilbert Francis Montriou, **Baron Campion** (**1882–1958**), civil servant, was born at Simla on 11 May 1882, the eldest son of John Montriou Campion, later chief engineer, Punjab, in the public works department of India, and his wife, Grace Hannah, daughter of Abraham Collis Anderson, of co. Kilkenny. He was educated at Bedford School and won a classical scholarship to Hertford College, Oxford, where he gained first-class honours in both classical moderations (1903) and *literae humaniores* (1905). Though he took the civil service examination in 1906 he decided to accept the nomination of Sir

Courtenay Ilbert to a clerkship in the House of Commons.

Campion's interest in comparative parliamentary procedure was shown early on when he and his colleague, W. P. Johnston, suggested to Ilbert that they should visit the principal countries in Europe and gather information about their respective systems. The results of their investigations were placed at the disposal of the select committee on procedure, 1914, and appended to their minutes of evidence. On the outbreak of war Campion joined the army and became a captain in the Army Service Corps. He was invalided home from France and in 1917 was appointed secretary to the conference on the reform of the second chamber presided over by Lord Bryce, who warmly commended Campion's wide knowledge of parliamentary institutions at home and abroad. In 1919 Campion was appointed secretary to the conference on devolution presided over by Speaker Lowther. The scheme of regional grand councils proposed by Lowther is believed to have been substantially Campion's work. In January 1920 Campion married Hilda Mary, daughter of William Alfred Spafford; she was principal of the Darlington Training College for women teachers. There were no children.

In 1921 Campion became second clerk assistant, and in 1929, the year before his promotion to clerk assistant, he published *An Introduction to the Procedure of the House of Commons*, which was conceived originally as a manual of first aid for members, but was in fact a complete account of the procedure of the house. In 1937 he succeeded Sir Horace Dawkins as clerk of the house and when war broke out in 1939 he was responsible for organizing the move to Church House and the procedural innovations required by security.

The publication in 1946 of the fourteenth edition of Sir Thomas Erskine May's century old classic *Parliamentary Practice* marked the end of twelve years' labour for Campion and established his reputation as a master of parliamentary procedure. This massive work was rearranged and largely rewritten under his editorship. A historical introduction, which he had hoped to expand into a separate volume, outlined briefly the results of modern research.

In 1945 the Labour government, faced with a heavy legislative programme, invited Campion to submit a comprehensive scheme of reform to a select committee on procedure. Although his more radical proposals for lessening the legislative burden on the house were rejected, his suggestions provided a framework for discussion, and the changes finally agreed upon were incorporated in the fifteenth edition of Erskine May (1950), edited by Campion with the assistance of T. G. B. Cocks.

After the war the movement towards self-government in the colonies stimulated the demand for information and guidance from Westminster, and Campion authorized the first official visits of a clerk to Commonwealth legislatures. In July 1948 he retired, and his outstanding services to the Commons were recognized in tributes from Herbert Morrison, the leader of the house, and Winston Churchill on behalf of the opposition. The following month Campion set out on an official tour of Commonwealth parliaments, in the course of which he visited Ceylon, Australia, New Zealand, South Africa, Rhodesia, Nyasaland, Kenya, and Sudan. In 1949 he made a similar visit to the legislatures of Canada. Owing to ill health he never wrote the book which would have contained the results of these investigations, but he contributed some impressions of the earlier tour at intervals to the *Sunday Times*.

On his return from these travels Campion was appointed the first clerk of the consultative assembly of the Council of Europe, which met at Strasbourg. The difficulties and weaknesses of this novel experiment in European co-operation were discussed by Campion in articles contributed to the *Sunday Times* (30 July 1950) and *The Times* (13 November 1950). His early interest in comparative procedure had come to fruition in 1946 when he was elected president of the autonomous section of secretaries-general of the Inter-Parliamentary Union. On his initiative the material was collected for the handbook of *European Parliamentary Procedure*, which he compiled jointly with D. W. S. Lidderdale and published in 1953.

Campion ranks with the greatest of his predecessors at the table of the house. By temperament a scholar and somewhat shy in his dealings with people, his humanity and sense of humour made him much more than the pre-eminent practitioner of his profession. His power of analysis and lucid expression made him the ideal expositor of the intricacies of procedure; his grasp of principle, combined with his wide knowledge of historical precedent and contemporary parallel, gave to his views on the British parliamentary system a unique authority.

Campion was appointed CB in 1932, KCB in 1938, GCB in 1948, and was raised to the peerage as Baron Campion in 1950. Hertford College made him an honorary fellow in 1946 and the University of Oxford conferred on him an honorary DCL in 1950. He was a keen golfer and in 1948 won the parliamentary golf handicap. He died at his home, Little Bowes, Abinger Hammer, near Dorking, on 6 April 1958. K. R. MACKENZIE, *rev.* MARK POTTLE

Sources *The Times* (11 May 1946) • *The Times* (13 Nov 1950) • *The Times* (7 April 1958) • *The Times* (11 April 1958) • personal knowledge (1971) • private information (1971) • *CGPLA Eng. & Wales* (1958)
Archives HLRO, corresp. and papers
Likenesses Vandyk, photograph, NPG
Wealth at death £10,194 17*s.* 11*d.*: probate, 1958, *CGPLA Eng. & Wales*

Campion, Sir Harry (1905–1996), statistician, was born on 20 May 1905 at 103 Church Road, Kersley, near Farnworth, in the county of Lancashire, the only son of John Henry Campion, journeyman woodcutting machinist, and his wife, Mary Ann Telford. He had one sister, Hannah Elvin Campion, who predeceased him, dying on 25 September 1995. He was brought up in Worsley and educated at Farnworth grammar school, from where he obtained in 1923 a Charles John Adam scholarship (worth £40 per annum) at Manchester University to read for the degree of bachelor of commerce which he obtained in 1926 with distinction in economics. He went on to graduate MA (commerce) in 1928 and was appointed Robert Ottley lecturer (part-time) in statistics at Manchester University in September 1930. He served for three years as statistician to the Cotton Trade Statistical Bureau, producing a regular digest of statistics for the joint committee of cotton trade organizations, experience which was to be of great value in producing official statistical digests later. After a year in the United States as a Rockefeller foundation fellow in 1932, he became in 1933 Robert Ottley lecturer in economics and subsequently in 1936 reader in economic statistics at Manchester University. He became the secretary to the economics research section in the university, separate from the teaching of economics and one of the earliest groups of its kind in Britain, and published a book, *Distribution of the National Capital*, with Professor George Daniels in 1936 (following a paper read to the Manchester Statistical Society), and a second book, *Public and Private Property in Great Britain*, in 1939.

In December 1939 Campion was seconded from Manchester to join the central economic intelligence service, which had been created as part of the War Cabinet Office. His job was to help organize the statistics needed for a continuous survey of financial and economic plans which had been set up under Lord Stamp earlier in 1939 with war on the horizon. At the same time Churchill had appointed Professor Lindemann (later Lord Cherwell) as his personal adviser, and this led to the creation of the prime minister's statistical section. In order to consolidate the work and to prevent the confusion arising from more than one set of figures, the central statistical office (CSO) was set up in January 1941 and Campion became its head shortly after, remaining in this position until his retirement in 1967. Campion later gave the following account of his first day in the Cabinet Office:

> I was asked about figures of employment in the engineering industry. Should they ask the Board of Trade or the Ministry of Labour for them? When I told them the figures they wanted were already there in the Ministry of Labour Gazette, there was no copy of the Gazette available in the Cabinet Office but it would be ordered. So I went out myself at lunchtime and bought a copy at the Stationery Office in Kingsway. The copy the Office ordered arrived a week later. (talk, 29 Oct 1984)

During his absence in Whitehall, the University of Manchester had established a new chair in statistics to which Campion had been appointed, but his involvement in the CSO led him to give this up in October 1944.

At the request of the United Nations Campion was seconded in 1946 for a year to organize the birth of the UN statistical office. Campion's assignment to the UN consequently established the CSO—and Campion at its head—at the forefront of the development of official statistics internationally as well as in the UK. He gave a comprehensive paper to the Royal Statistical Society in 1949 on the development of international statistics and another in 1957 on economic statistics in the UK. On his return, Campion was involved in the many improvements and developments in UK statistics following the publication of the white paper on employment policy in 1944. The *Monthly Digest of Statistics* first appeared in 1946, and the Statistics of Trade Act, which provided the general legal basis in the UK for the collection of official statistics and for obtaining information for the appreciation of economic trends, was passed in 1947.

Further improvements in official statistics, in which Campion as director of the CSO took the lead, followed the famous 'Bradshaw' speech in 1956 by Harold Macmillan ('we were always, as it were, looking up the train in last year's Bradshaw'). However, in 1966 government statistics again came under criticism in a report of the estimates committee, although a Treasury witness (Mr Wynne Godley) was able to say that 'the statistical service we are given has improved absolutely out of all recognition in the last ten years'. The committee conceded, however, that 'their comments, however critical, have been made with a full awareness of the extent of this transformation' (fourth report from the estimates committee). The committee recommended various changes to the organization of government statistics; the director's post was to be upgraded to permanent secretary rank, and the title changed to director of the central statistical office and head of the government statistical service. Soon after the report was published, however, Campion retired (in March 1967) after twenty-six years as director of the CSO, and these changes were implemented in 1968 under his successor, Sir Claus Moser.

Campion was the UK member of the Statistical Commission of the UN from 1947 to 1967 and president of the International Statistical Institute from 1963 to 1967. He was also active in the Conference of European Statisticians which was set up in 1953 as a regional organization of statisticians under the auspices of the UN, and in the conferences of Commonwealth statisticians which were revived in 1955, continuing the pre-war tradition of 'conferences of Government officers engaged in dealing with statistics in the British Empire'. These activities gave him an international reputation. He was also a big man physically, although somewhat taciturn and inarticulate; his reaction to a query was: 'The thing is …', and it was left to his officials to penetrate the obscurity. Nevertheless he succeeded in getting things done. His distinction in the statistical profession was recognized by his presidency of the Royal Statistical Society (1957–9) and the International Statistical Institute (1963–7), by the appointment as CBE (1945), CB (1949), KCB (1957), and by his being made an honorary LLD of Manchester on his retirement. He was also awarded the Royal Statistical Society's Guy medal in silver in 1950 in recognition of his work in the fields of national and international statistics. He never married. He died of bronchopneumonia and ischaemic heart disease on 24 May 1996 at Northwick Park Hospital, Brent, London; and was cremated on 30 May 1996 at the Breakspear crematorium in Ruislip, Middlesex, where his ashes were buried. He left the residue of his estate to be divided equally between the Royal Statistical Society and the Manchester Statistical Society. Wulf Rudoe

Sources R. Ward and T. Doggett, *Keeping score: the first fifty years of the central statistical office* (1991) • *The Guardian* (4 June 1996) • *The Independent* (5 June 1996) • *The Times* (22 June 1996) • *Journal of the Royal Statistical Society: series A*, 160 (1997), 148–54 • 'Sub-committee on economic affairs: fourth report', *Parl. papers* (1966–7), vol. 12, no. 246 • talk by H. Campion on the history of the origins of the CSO, 29 Oct 1984 • *WWW* [forthcoming] • d. cert. • b. cert. • Bradley and Jones, funeral directors, Love Lane, Pinner, Middlesex

Likenesses photograph, Royal Statistical Society, London • photograph, repro. in *The Times* • photograph, repro. in *The Independent*

Wealth at death £417,764: probate, 9 Aug 1996, *CGPLA Eng. & Wales*

Campion, Mary Anne (*c.*1687–1706), singer and dancer, was born of lowly parents, her father having possibly been a servant of William Cavendish, first duke of Devonshire. She displayed a precocious talent on the stage; aged eleven, she was a member of Christopher Rich's company and sang at a performance of *Phaeton* in March 1698. She sang at Drury Lane over the following seasons; in May 1699 she spoke the epilogue to the second part of *The Famous History of the Rise and Fall of Massaniello* and danced an entry, with Weaver and Cottin, in *The Pilgrim* on 6 July 1700. At her benefit at Drury Lane on 22 June 1703 she exhibited her range of talent, performing a duet with bass Richard Leveridge in 'a mad song' by Henry Purcell, and other songs by John Weldon; dancing with De Ruel; and accompanying Visconti on the harpsichord in a performance of *Love's Contrivance*, presented for the entertainment of the king of Denmark's envoy (*Daily Courant*, 22 June 1703). She was fluent in Italian. She occasionally performed at York Buildings, and she commanded good fees; in 1702 she was paid the considerable sum of £3 4*s.* 6*d.* for performing Weldon's prize music composed to accompany Congreve's *The Judgment of Paris* at Lincoln's Inn Fields for the duke of Bedford. In July of that year another benefit for her was advertised at Drury Lane, in 'Oronoko … with several dances by Mrs Campion and others'.

Campion's last public stage performance was probably on 14 March 1704, after which she retired at the behest of William Cavendish, first duke of Devonshire, whose fancy she had attracted. Installed in Bolton Street, Westminster, she and the duke, then in his sixties and already provided with a wife, sundry other mistresses, and their offspring, enjoyed a fecund relationship that brought them a daughter known as Mary Anne Cavendish. In early 1706 Campion contracted a severe fever, and she died on 19 May 1706. Devonshire buried her in his family church at Latimer, Buckinghamshire, where he set up a lavish tomb of freestone, black marble, and alabaster, celebrating at length her beauty and virtue. In her will, drawn up on 23 April, she left her house and all her valuables to create an income for her daughter when she reached twenty-one. The duke died in London on 18 August 1707, 'afflicted with dropsy, gout, the stone and repentence' (Highfill, Burnim & Langhans, *BDA*, 32), but the probable falsity of this repentance occupied the first section of the scurrilous tract by John Dunton *The Hazard of a Death Bed Repentance* (1708):

> Had the Duke aggravated his lewdness with Miss Heneage, Miss Campion, etc., but more especially had he lamented having a bastard child when he had one foot in the grave … [a reference to Campion's unfortunate offspring] he should have detected and lamented his mean adultery of tempting an actress out of the Playhouse (I mean Mrs Anne Campion) and doating on her to that degree, as to erect a tomb to her memory in Latimer's Chancel, he disgraced himself by ordering a Latin epitaph to be set on the tomb of one of his concubines … erected a tomb to perpetuate the memory of a lewd strumpet. (Dunton, 24–5)

ANITA MCCONNELL

Sources J. Dunton, *The hazard of a death bed repentance* (1708) • Highfill, Burnim & Langhans, *BDA* • W. Van Lennep and others, eds., *The London stage, 1660–1800*, pts 1–2 (1960–65) • M. Tilmouth, 'A calendar of references to music in newspapers published in London and the provinces (1660–1719)', *Royal Musical Association Research Chronicle*, 1 (1961)

Campion, Thomas (1567–1620), poet and musician, was born in London on 12 February 1567 and baptized on the following day at St Andrew's, Holborn, the second child of John Campion (*d.* 1576) and Lucy, *née* Searle (*d.* 1580), widow of Roger Trigg. John entered the Middle Temple in 1565, and obtained a post as cursitor to the chancery court the following year; Vivian conjectures that he and his family may have lived in the cursitor's office in Chancery Lane. By 1581, however, the successive marriages of Lucy to Augustine Steward in 1577, and then of Steward to Anne (*née* Argall), the widow of Thomas Sisley, left Thomas Campion under the guardianship of two step-parents. Of his early education nothing is known, but he was sent by Steward in May 1581 to Peterhouse, Cambridge, as a gentleman pensioner, where he remained until 1584, leaving without taking a degree. Steward carefully recorded the £20 p.a. he paid for Campion and for his other stepson, Thomas Sisley, for tuition and maintenance.

The experience of Cambridge left a much less obvious mark upon Campion than did his subsequent education at Gray's Inn, where he was admitted on 27 April 1586. Although, again, he proceeded to no formal qualification, he participated in the revels of 1588, acting in an unidentified comedy played before Lord Burghley, and he contributed songs to *Gesta Grayorum*, presented at court in 1594. By this time his lyric, 'Harke, all you ladies', had appeared in print appended to Thomas Newman's surreptitious edition of Sir Philip Sidney's *Astrophil and Stella* in 1591 (the attribution of other poems from this collection to Campion is dubious), and he had attracted the praise of George Peele in his *Honour of the Garter* (1593). In 1595, about the time when Campion probably left Gray's Inn, his first major work, the Latin *Poemata*, was published. From the evidence of several epigrams in this volume Vivian speculated, with some plausibility, that he had served under Sir Robert Carey in Essex's expedition to aid Henry IV against the Catholic League in 1591–2.

Apart from a commendatory epigram to John Dowland's *First Booke of Songs and Ayres* (1597) and Meres's praise of his Latin poetry in *Palladis tamia* (1598), Campion disappears from view until the publication, in 1601, of the first among the works upon which his reputation now chiefly rests, *A Booke of Ayres*. It was a joint production with his friend Philip Rosseter, Campion providing both words and music for the first half, Rosseter the music for the second (the words of these latter songs are almost certainly not by Campion). Campion's preface 'To the reader' sets out his determination to write airs of an epigrammatic concentration, eschewing musical complexity and elaborate word-painting, tenets to which he remained faithful throughout his career. Rosseter's dedication of the work to Sir Thomas Monson speaks of 'the manie particular favours' that Campion acknowledged he had received, suggesting that this noted patron of music and musicians had supported him for some time. In 1602 appeared Campion's *Observations in the Art of English Poesie*, the last, and subtlest, of the forlorn Elizabethan attempts to regulate English verse by the rules of classical metrics. One of the songs in *A Booke of Ayres*, 'Come let us sound', united the quantitative scansion of the verse to music exactly reproducing the metre, after the fashion of French *musique mesurée*, and it was to France that Campion went in his final pursuit of professional qualification, emerging from the University of Caen in 1605 with the degree of MD.

In 1607 Campion moved on to a larger stage as he received his first commission to provide a masque at court for the marriage of James's Scottish favourite, James Hay. It was perhaps Monson who commended Campion to the earls of Salisbury and Suffolk, the likely sponsors of the event, and he produced a work deft in its consideration of the vexed topic of the union of England and Scotland, and remarkable for its exceptionally detailed account of the deployment of musical resources in its performance. There is then silence until 1613, Campion's most productive year. On 14 February he provided the subtle and elaborate *The Lords' Masque* to celebrate the marriage of Princess Elizabeth to Frederick, elector palatine. This was followed, on 27–8 April, by *The Caversham Entertainment*, gracefully designed to welcome Queen Anne to the house of Sir William Knollys, the son-in-law of Thomas Howard, earl of Suffolk. On 26 December Campion's *The Somerset Masque* was performed to celebrate the marriage of Suffolk's daughter, Frances Howard, recently and controversially divorced from her first husband, the earl of Essex, to the king's favourite, Robert Carr, a work which struggles bravely to counter the gossip and rumour that surrounded the event. In the same year appeared the *Songs of Mourning*, lamenting in exquisite verse (with music by John Coprario) the death of Prince Henry in 1612, and (probably) the undated *Two Bookes of Ayres*, one of secular, the other of sacred songs. Perhaps to the same period belongs the treatise on composition, *A New Way of Making Fowre Parts*, sufficiently well-regarded to be incorporated in John Playford's *Introduction to the Skill of Music* (1660). In 1615, however, Carr and Frances Howard were accused of having poisoned Sir Thomas Overbury two years earlier. Monson and Campion were caught up in this scandal, for their part in the appointment of Gervase Elwes as lieutenant of the Tower. Campion was questioned on his receipt of money on Monson's behalf from Elwes as payment for securing his post, and though he was immediately cleared, Monson remained in prison until adjudged innocent in 1617. In January 1616 Campion was permitted to attend his patron as his doctor, and his next publication, *The Third and Fourth Booke of Ayres* (1617?) was offered as a tribute to Monson's patience and fortitude.

Campion's final publication was a much revised and expanded second edition of his Latin poetry, *Tho. Campiani epigrammatum libri II* (1619), but at some point after 1612 he had written his longest and most ambitious Latin poem, 'De pulverea coniuratione' ('On the Gunpowder Plot'), which survives in one manuscript, dedicated to King James (Cambridge, Sidney Sussex College, MS 59). The vehemently anti-Jesuit polemic of this poem suggests that Campion was not, as his patron was suspected of being, a Catholic.

Campion declared in the preface to *Two Bookes* that his aim was 'to couple my Wordes and Notes lovingly together', and it is for his graceful dexterity in this art that he is now chiefly remembered. In his own time his Latin verse was highly regarded, but only in recent years have the merits of his court masques, his most ambitious productions, begun to be acknowledged fully.

Campion died on 1 March 1620 and was buried the same day at St Dunstan-in-the-West, Fleet Street. In his nuncupative will he left the £22 of which he was possessed to Philip Rosseter 'and he wished that his estate had bin farre more'. DAVID LINDLEY

Sources P. Vivian, *Campion's works* (1909) · C. R. Wilson, 'Campion, Thomas', *New Grove* · R. W. Innes Smith, *English-speaking students of medicine at the University of Leyden* (1932) · BL, Egerton MS 2599 · C. R. Wilson, *Words and notes coupled lovingly together: Thomas Campion, a critical study* (1989) · D. Lindley, *Thomas Campion* (1986) · E. Lowbury, T. Salter, and A. Young, *Thomas Campion: poet, composer, physician* (1970) · R. Sowerby, *De pulverea coniuratione*, ed. D. Lindley (1987) · L. Bradner, 'References to Chaucer in Campion's *Poemata*', *Review of English Studies*, 12 (1936), 322–3 · J. W. Binns, *The Latin poetry of English poets* (1974), 1–25 · R. W. Berringer, 'Thomas Campion's share in *A booke of ayres*', *Publications of the Modern Language Association of America*, 58 (1943), 938 · D. Lindley, 'Campion and Rosseter: the ascription of *A booke of ayres*', *N&Q*, 228 (1983), 416
Wealth at death £22: Vivian, *Campion's works*, xlvii

Campion, William. *See* Wigmore, William (*c*.1599–1665).

Campoli, Alfredo (1906–1991), violinist, was born on 20 October 1906 in Rome, the son of Romeo Campoli, an orchestral leader and violin professor at the Accademia di Santa Cecilia, and his wife, Elvira, *née* Celi, an opera singer. From the age of four he was taught the violin by his father, who had him listen to recordings of the Italian baritone singer Mattia Battistini in order to acquire a bel canto style of playing. The family moved to London in 1911, and at the age of ten the young prodigy made his début as a soloist. He then gave recitals, and won several first prizes and two gold medals, one of which was at the London music festival in 1919 for his performance of Mendelssohn's violin concerto. In the same year he gave a brilliant first recital at the Wigmore Hall, and in 1921 a series of six impressive recitals there resulted in his engagement to play for the International Celebrity Concerts. So, at the age of fifteen, he toured the British Isles with the singers Dame Nellie Melba and Dame Clara Butt. He became a very successful

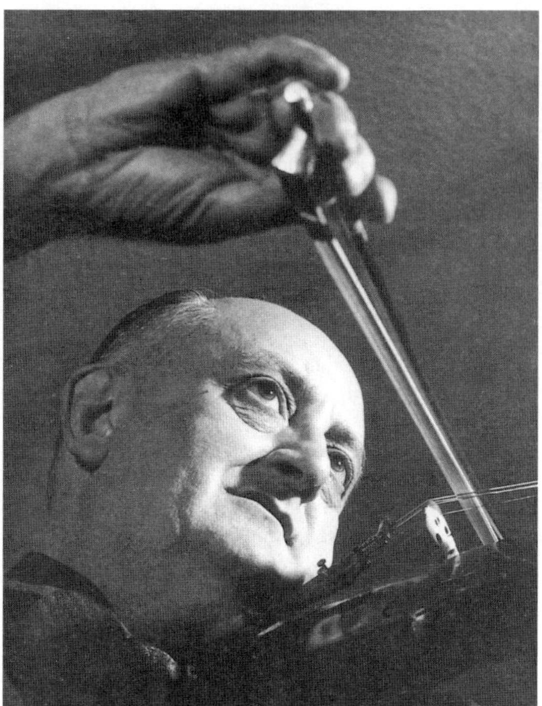

Alfredo Campoli (1906–1991), by Ronald M. Franks

concert artist over the next few years. He also spent time in light music, and in 1926 was asked to form a small group to record light classics, of which a serenade by Heykins became a great favourite. Campoli's Salon Orchestra played at the Trocadero Grill Room in 1927 and at the Dorchester Hotel in 1931. This experience proved useful because during the depression of the 1930s, when life was difficult for most classical musicians, Campoli managed to earn a living with his Salon Orchestra, which gained immense popularity through its hundreds of broadcasts of light music, public concerts, and many recordings. The serious side of his career was maintained by giving recitals and performances of concertos throughout the country, and he first appeared at the Henry Wood Promenade Concerts in 1938, when he performed Paganini's concerto no. 1.

Regarded as an enemy alien when the Second World War broke out in 1939, Campoli was barred from performing in public, but he obtained British naturalization in the same year, disbanded his orchestra, and spent the war years playing in concerts for the troops at home and overseas. At the same time he worked at expanding his classical repertory. In 1942 he married Joy Burbridge, who had been Sir Adrian Boult's secretary. Campoli performed the Brahms violin concerto at a Prom concert in 1944 and the Tchaikovsky concerto the following year.

After the war Campoli resumed his classical concert career and, despite some initial snobbery by those who regarded him simply as a 'salon' player, he soon gained a reputation for his artistry and fine interpretations and appeared under such conductors as Sir Thomas Beecham, Sir Adrian Boult, Sir Malcolm Sargent, and Sir John Barbirolli. He also played abroad, and in 1950 he toured Australia and New Zealand. He made his American début in 1953 with the New York Philharmonic at Carnegie Hall, playing Lalo's *Symphonie espagnole*, then toured America and Canada. In Russia in 1956 he performed the Walton concerto, and he became very popular there. At one concert in Leningrad an enthusiastic audience had him play eleven encores. In 1955 he gave the première in Moscow of the Bliss concerto, which was dedicated to him. He gave many recitals with the pianist Gerald Moore, and during the 1960s formed a duo with the pianist Valerie Tryon. In 1978 he gave a recital at the Wigmore Hall.

When he retired at the age of seventy-five his wife said that Campoli put his Dragonetti Stradivarius of 1700 'away and never took it out of the case again' (*Daily Telegraph*, 30 March 1991). Unusually, this Stradivarius still had its original peg-holes and neck. Campoli continued to teach at his Highgate home, was an excellent croquet and bridge player, read books on music, bridge, and tennis, and owned more than 2000 records. When younger, he played tennis and table tennis and was south London junior snooker champion. His sense of humour was revealed by Monica Parkhurst: his reason for being known professionally as Campoli was that 'when it was announced "Alfredo Campoli is now going to play …", he believed people tended to hear "I'm afraid old Campoli is now going to play …"' (*The Independent*, 5 April 1991).

Campoli was a greatly loved and respected performer whose Italian singing style of playing was coupled with a dazzling technique and a warm, sweet, beautiful tone. He kept all four fingers on the bow (except, of course, for *sautillé*), would not use a shoulder-rest, disliked gymnastics, and practised every day. From his many recordings a number of gems, such as the Bruch, Mendelssohn, and Elgar concertos, have been reissued on CD. He died on 27 March 1991 at Princes Risborough, survived by his wife.

JEAN M. HAIG-WHITELEY

Sources *Daily Telegraph* (30 March 1991) · *The Times* (30 March 1991) · *The Independent* (30 March 1991) · *The Independent* (5 April 1991) · 'Alfredo Campoli, Italian/British violinist', *Annual Obituary* (1991), 126–7 · Grove, *Dict. mus.* (1954) · M. Campbell, *The great violinists* (1980) · *New Grove* · W. Henley, *Antonio Stradivari* (1961) · *WWW* [forthcoming]

Archives SOUND BL NSA, *Talking about music*, 85, 1LP0152067 S1 BD3 · BL NSA, *Talking about music*, 209, 1LP0202188 S1 BD1 · BL NSA, performance recording

Likenesses R. M. Franks, photograph, NPG [*see illus.*] · photograph, repro. in *Daily Telegraph* · photograph, repro. in *The Times* · photograph, repro. in Campbell, *Great violinists*, 179 · three photographs, Hult. Arch.

Wealth at death £132,967: probate, 12 July 1991, *CGPLA Eng. & Wales*

Camps, Francis Edward (1905–1972), forensic scientist, was born on 28 June 1905 at Teddington, Middlesex, the eldest of the three sons of Percy William Leopold Camps (1878–1956), a general practitioner and surgeon, and his wife, Alice, daughter of Joseph Redfern, of Matlock. He was educated at Marlborough College, Guy's Hospital, the School of Tropical Medicine at Liverpool, and Neuchâtel

University, Switzerland. He qualified MRCS LRCP (1928), MB BS (London 1930), MD (1933), DTMH (Liverpool 1931), FRCPath. (1964), and FRCP (1968).

After qualifying in medicine in 1928 Camps practised first as a house physician at Guy's Hospital and then as a junior partner in general practice in rural Essex. In 1935 he abandoned clinical medicine and became a pathologist at the Chelmsford and Essex Hospital, specializing in bacteriology and epidemiology. There the Essex coroners sought his help in improving the standard of post-mortem reports, and he became increasingly involved with criminal cases. It was not, however, until after the Second World War that Camps turned to forensic medicine as a full-time career. He started lecturing at the London Hospital Medical College in 1945, being appointed lecturer in 1953, reader in 1954, and professor in 1963. On his retirement in 1970 he became emeritus professor, having established the department as a leader in its field. Apart from lecturing to undergraduates and postgraduates at the London Hospital, Camps lectured in forensic medicine at the medical schools of the Royal Free Hospital, the Middlesex Hospital, and University College Hospital. He examined in the medical faculties of five British universities, and played a large part in persuading the Society of Apothecaries to set up the diploma in medical jurisprudence. He was consultant pathologist to the Emergency Medical Service during the war, holder of a travelling fellowship of the Kellogg Foundation, and honorary consultant in forensic medicine to the army (1964–70), an appointment he particularly valued.

Camps was tireless in his enthusiasm and advocacy for his subject and served on many committees, including the British Medical Association special committee on the recognition of intoxication in the relation of alcohol to road accidents (1951), the coroners' rules committee of the Home Office (1953), the mortuaries' committee of the Ministry of Housing and Local Government (1955), and the Home Office Scientific Advisory Council (1965). He was a founder of the British Association in Forensic Medicine in 1950, and was its president in 1958–60. He was the moving force behind the formation of the British Academy of Forensic Sciences in 1959, and served as its president (1963) and secretary-general (1960–71). He edited its journal, *Medicine, Science and the Law*, from 1960 until his death, at which time he was president of the Society for the Study of Addiction and vice-president of the Foundation for the Study of Infant Deaths.

Camps married three times. His first wife, Dulcie Williams, was a nurse whom he met when working at Guy's Hospital. They had a son and two daughters, but later divorced. In 1942 he married Mary Ross Mackenzie MD, a pathologist and daughter of James Ross Mackenzie, lecturer in anaesthesia at Aberdeen. They had a son and a daughter. She died in 1970, and two years later Camps married Ann Elizabeth Robinson PhD FRIC, a toxicologist at the London Hospital. Camps held strong views, sometimes in opposition to his colleagues, and had exceptional stamina. He worked hard in the mortuary, laboratory, and court, and also as a lecturer, writer, and broadcaster; he rarely refused a case or an invitation to speak. He published several books, many of which are landmarks in forensic medicine; as editor of the second edition of *Gradwohl's Legal Medicine* (1968), he won the Swiney prize in 1969. He travelled widely, being particularly concerned to advance his subject in other countries, and was well known in the United States.

Of the large number of important cases in which Camps was involved, perhaps the best-known were those of Hume, Christie, and Emmett Dunne. He was deeply interested in Jack the Ripper. As a person, Camps was impressive but modest, enthusiastic and charming. He was popular with students, and they with him. Outside his work, his interests included fishing and gardening. He was a delightful host or guest, having a rich sense of humour, and also a loyal, devoted friend, and a stimulating colleague and teacher.

A heavy smoker, Camps was convinced that he had inoperable cancer, when he died of a ruptured gastric ulcer at the Chelmsford and Essex Hospital on 8 July 1972. His wife survived him. A memorial service was held in the parish church of St Augustine with St Philip, Stepney Way, London. J. M. CAMERON, *rev.* K. D. WATSON

Sources R. Jackson, *Francis Camps: famous case histories of the celebrated pathologist* (1975) • H. B. M., *The Lancet* (15 July 1972), 139–40 • J. M. C., 'F. E. Camps', *BMJ* (22 July 1972), 239 • *The Times* (10 July 1972) • *The Times* (11 July 1972) • *The Times* (14 July 1972) • *The Times* (21 July 1972) • *The Times* (1 Sept 1972) • Munk, *Roll* • J. M. Cameron, 'Professor Francis Edward Camps', *London Hospital Gazette*, 75 (1972), 3–5 • *Medical Directory* • Marlborough College register • *Medicine, Science and the Law*, 12 (1972), 229–30 • *Plarr's surgeons of England*, ed. D. Power, 2 vols. (1930) • papers on forensic medicine, Royal London Hospital, archives • *Gradwohl's legal medicine*, 3rd edn (1976) • private information (1986) • personal knowledge (1986) • *CGPLA Eng. & Wales* (1972) • *WWW*

Archives Royal London Hospital, archives

Likenesses photograph, *c.*1962, Royal London Hospital, archives • photograph, repro. in *Gradwohl's legal medicine*

Wealth at death £41,906: administration, 22 Aug 1972, *CGPLA Eng. & Wales*

Campsall, Richard (*c.*1280–*c.*1330), theologian, was born at Campsall, in the West Riding of Yorkshire, probably between 1280 and 1285. He first appears as a bachelor in arts at Balliol College, Oxford; by 1306 he was regent master in arts at Merton College; a papal letter of 1317 addresses him as bachelor in theology, and by 1322 he was a master in theology. Between 1306 and 1322 he is named repeatedly in Merton rolls. On 10 January 1326, as bursar and procurator, Campsall was locum tenens for the chancellor of the university in a dispute with the mayor of Oxford, who had moved the town pillory: Campsall negotiated a new location for it and absolved the mayor from the chancellor's excommunication. On his death *c.*1330 five volumes owned by Campsall went to Merton: a glossed psalter, two works by Augustine, one by Hugh of St Victor, and 'some works' by Anselm, all of them missing when the catalogue of 1350–60 was drawn up. Campsall was buried in the college chapel at Merton; his tombstone has been securely identified, despite having been moved, and despite the disappearance of both a brass cross 'on steps' and of the inscription, still visible in the seventeenth century: 'Orate pro anima Magistri Ricardi de Camsale sacre pagine Professor … hic jacet tumulatum' (Wood, 1.23–4). Campsall should not be confused with a namesake who was rector of St Martin's, Canterbury.

The catalogue of St Augustine's Abbey, Canterbury, ascribes two works to Campsall—*Questiones super tres libros phisicorum* and *Notabilitates eiusdem super omnes libros phisicorum*—but neither is known to be extant. Campsall's certain writings are a series of twenty disputed questions of c.1306 on the *Prior Analytics*; a disputed question, *Whether Matter Can Be Without Form*; aphorisms *On Contingency and Foreknowledge*, extant in one manuscript, but also in a Bologna printing of 1496 from a slightly variant manuscript base; and a short essay on the universal. All have been published by Synan. There survives also a brief treatment of 'Whether one can act against one's conscience' (Etzkorn, 322). But a truncated *Logica Campsale Anglici, valde utilis et realis contra Ocham*, long ascribed to Campsall, cannot be his. Modern scholars suggest that Campsall's works may be supplemented through citations by contemporaries of his opinions which probably stem from a lost writing on the *Sentences*. He is credited with a solution of paralogisms on the Trinity ('The Father is God; the Son is God; therefore, the Father is the Son'), first by invoking the 'rule of Anselm', that in divinity all is one unless blocked by a relation, and second by pronouncing such syllogisms invalid owing to the 'fallacy of accident'. In the summary division of fourteenth-century thinkers into Scotists and Ockhamists, Campsall may count as mildly Ockhamist (Synan, 2.3, 4), or alternatively Ockham as Campsallist (Tachau, 'The influence of Richard Campsall', 123). EDWARD A. SYNAN

Sources E. A. Synan, *The works of Richard of Campsall*, ed. {}, 2 vols. (1968–82) • G. J. Etzkorn, 'The codex Paris Nat. Lat. 15805', *Archivum Franciscanum Historicum*, 80 (1987), 321–33, esp. 332 • H. G. Gelber, 'Logic and the Trinity: a clash of values in scholastic thought, 1300–1335', PhD diss., 2 vols., University of Wisconsin, USA, 1974, 2.206–10 • K. H. Tachau, 'The influence of Richard Campsall on fourteenth century Oxford thought', *From Ockham to Wyclif*, ed. A. Hudson and M. Wilks, SCH, Subsidia, 5 (1987), 109–23 • K. H. Tachau, 'Richard Campsall as a theologian: new evidence', *Historia philosophiae medii aevi: Studien zur Geschichte der Philosophie des Mittelalters*, ed. B. Mojsisch and O. Pluta (Amsterdam, 1991), 979–1002 • A. Bott, *The monuments in Merton College chapel* (1964), 12, 14 • A. Wood, *The history and antiquities of the colleges and halls in the University of Oxford*, ed. J. Gutch (1786); appx (1790), 1.23, 24 • F. M. Powicke, *The medieval books of Merton College* (1931), 54, 57–9, 114, 167 • M. R. James, *The ancient libraries of Canterbury and Dover* (1903), p. 300, no. 973 • M. R. James, *A descriptive catalogue of the manuscripts in the library of Gonville and Caius College*, 2 (1908), 665ff. • W. J. Courtenay, *Adam Wodeham: an introduction to his life and writings* (1978), 60–61

Campsie, Henry (*fl.* **1688–1689**). *See under* Campsie, John (*d.* 1689).

Campsie, John (*d.* **1689**), local politician, of whose origins, background, and early life nothing is known, was by the 1680s a Londonderry merchant, and was elected mayor of the corporation of Londonderry six times between the years 1681 and 1688. In 1687 the government of Richard Talbot, earl of Tyrconnell followed a policy of remodelling the corporations so that Roman Catholics would be admitted. Under Campsie's mayoralty, Londonderry held out. A writ of *quo warranto* was issued in the court of exchequer and judgment was entered against the corporation. Although a new charter granted by James II was issued on 3 August 1687, Campsie managed to stay in office until 12 October 1688 when he was replaced by Cormack O'Neil.

In order to ensure the city's obedience, Tyrconnell planned to garrison Londonderry with Catholic troops. Pursuant to his orders, the protestant garrison of William Stewart, Viscount Mountjoy left the city on 23 November 1688, but when the replacement garrison tried to enter the city on 7 December 1688, thirteen apprentice boys, with the tacit approval of Campsie and the old protestant corporation, shut the gates. Fearful of the consequences of this act of rebellion, Campsie wrote to Mountjoy on 9 December 1688 distancing himself from the actions of 'the rabble in their heat' (Hempton, 255) and resolving 'always to bear true faith and allegiance' (ibid.) to James II. Since the shutting of the gates, he wrote, a plot to massacre the protestants in Ulster had been discovered and 'we cannot but think it a most wonderful Providence of God, to stir up the mobile for our safety, and preservation of the peace of the kingdom against such bloody attempts as these northern people had formed against us' (ibid.). On the next day he signed a letter, which was delivered by David Cairnes, begging the Irish Society in London for help.

King James's charter of 1687 was in effect swept away when Campsie was unanimously re-elected mayor on 2 January 1689. On 21 March, after civil war had broken out, he took the new oath of allegiance and publicly proclaimed King William and Queen Mary. He died in Londonderry after a short illness on 11 April 1689, a week before James's army arrived outside the city and laid siege to it. He was succeeded as mayor by Gervais Squire. Nothing is known of Campsie's wife but his second son, **Henry Campsie** (*fl.* 1688–1689), apprentice boy and army officer, was the leader of the gang of apprentice boys who seized the keys and locked the city gates against Lord Antrim's regiment on 7 December 1688. Later that day he was shot and wounded by a sentry as he tried to seize the magazine. He was commissioned lieutenant in 1689 and served throughout the siege of Londonderry, during which he was attainted by the Jacobite parliament in Dublin.

PIERS WAUCHOPE

Sources J. Hempton, ed., *The siege and history of Londonderry* (1861) • C. D. Milligan, *History of the siege of Londonderry, 1689* (1951) • J. G. Simms, *Jacobite Ireland, 1685–91* (1969)

Camrose. For this title name *see* Berry, William Ewert, first Viscount Camrose (1879–1954).

Camulacus (*fl.* **5th cent.?**). *See under* Meath, saints of (*act.* *c.*400–*c.*900).

Camville, Gerard de. *See* Canville, Gerard de (*d.* 1214).

Camville, Thomas de. *See* Canville, Sir Thomas de (*d.* 1234/5).

Canabre, Anthony (*fl.* 1595–1609). *See under* American Indians in England (*act. c.*1500–1609).

Canal, Giovanni Antonio [*known as* Canaletto] (**1697–1768**), painter, was born on 17 October 1697 in the district of San Lio, Venice, and was baptized on 30 October in the church of San Lio, the eldest of four children of Bernardo Canal (1674–1744), painter, and his wife, Artemisia Barbieri (*fl.* 1694–1739). The Canal family, whose lineage is traceable in Venice from the mid-sixteenth century, were 'cittadini originari', a class immediately below the patrician, which permitted them to use a coat of arms.

Canaletto, as the artist came to be known at an early stage in his career, was presumably trained by his father, who seems to have been employed primarily in the production of stage scenery. It is as an assistant to his father in this activity that Canaletto is first recorded, in Venice and also subsequently, in 1719–20, in Rome. The statements of Orlandi and Zanetti that it was on this—his only—visit to Rome that he was first inspired to paint and draw his surroundings are borne out by the earliest works attributable to him. An album, later broken up, of twenty-three drawings of views of Rome (of which one sheet is in the Hessischen Landesmuseum, Darmstadt, and the remainder in the British Museum) and a group of a dozen views of Rome and *capricci* (imaginary assemblages of buildings, often incorporating real elements) reflect Canaletto's training in scenography. Their authenticity has, until recently, often been questioned (but see the catalogue of Christies, London, sale 16 December 1998, lot 76, for a documented example).

Canaletto probably returned to Venice in 1720, when he was inscribed in the Venetian painters' guild, and after a modest start his work shows a remarkably rapid development during the 1720s. His first dated painting, a very large *Capriccio of Classical Ruins and a Pyramid*, signed and dated 1723 (priv. coll., Italy), and its pendant (priv. coll., Switzerland), painted for the Giovanelli family's villa at Noventa Padovana, already surpass in technical skill, inventiveness (and size) anything in this genre produced by contemporaries. They were closely followed by two allegorical paintings to which Canaletto contributed architectural elements: *Capriccio: Tomb of Lord Somers, with Ruins and Landscape* (priv. coll., England) and *Capriccio: Tomb of Archbishop Tillotson* (priv. coll.). These were executed in collaboration with G. B. Cimaroli and G. B. Piazzetta (in the former) and G. B. Cimaroli and G. B. Pittoni (in the latter). By this time, however, he had begun to appreciate, as had his predecessor Luca Carlevarijs (1663–1730), the first of the great Venetian view painters, now nearing the end of a long career, that the demand for views of Venice among foreign visitors to the city offered far greater market potential than did any local interest in *capricci*. The two allegorical tombs had been painted for the Irish impresario and agent Owen McSwiny, and were preceded by six large views of the piazza and piazzetta San Marco (Royal Collection) executed *c.*1723 for the English merchant banker Joseph Smith (for some years British consul there) and by a set of four Venetian views of *c.*1724 presumably painted for Prince Josef Wenzel von Liechtenstein (Museo Thyssen-Bornemisza, Madrid, and Ca' Rezzonico, Venice). His earliest documented Venetian views, a set of four supplied for Stefano Conti of Lucca in 1725–6 (priv. coll.), are the last major commission he was to execute for an Italian. These and the roughly contemporary *Venice: Santa Maria della Carità from the Campo San Vidal* ('The Stonemason's Yard', National Gallery, London) display a mastery of perspective and skill at defining form and texture, combined with an acute sensitivity to atmospheric effects of light, rendered with a vivacity of brushwork completely new to Italian view painting. These qualities, and the small, bustling figures, show why contemporaries were already praising Canaletto's work as truer to nature than Carlevarijs's. All, however, include distortions intended to 'improve' reality for pictorial effect, a feature of the artist's approach at all stages of his career, and one which would seem to refute the often-repeated assertion that he relied heavily on the use of the camera obscura.

Giovanni Antonio Canal [Canaletto] (**1697–1768**), by Antonio Visentini, pubd 1735 (after Gian Battista Piazzetta)

By the end of the 1720s Canaletto had demonstrated his ability to paint with equal success on a small scale, in nine views executed, exceptionally, on copper. There are pairs at Goodwood, Sussex, Chatsworth, Derbyshire, Holkham Hall, Norfolk, and in a Belgian private collection; and a single plate in the Musée de Strasbourg. These show his native city bathed in sunshine, delineated with considerable attention to detail and populated by townsfolk going about their everyday business, all characteristics of his mature style which was crystallizing in these years. In 1729–30 Canaletto added to his repertory the depiction, pioneered by Carlevarijs, of ceremonial events and festivals, in two pairs of large canvases celebrating the visits to Venice of the French comte de Gergy (Hermitage Museum, St Petersburg, and Pushkin Museum, Moscow) and the Spanish conde de Bolagnos (priv. coll., Milan). He had also gained a reputation for being complicated. Owen McSwiny, writing to the duke of Richmond in 1727, noted that:

> The fellow is whimsical and varys his prices every day: and he that has a mind to have any of his work, must not seem to be too fond of it, for he'l be the worse treated for it, both in the price and the painting too. (MS letter, 28 Nov 1727, W. Sussex RO, Chichester)

One of the few people who seems not to have found him difficult to deal with was Joseph Smith, with whom Canaletto's fortunes are inextricably bound up from the late 1720s to the early 1750s. Consul Smith, himself one of the foremost collectors in Venice, acquired over three decades no fewer than fifty paintings by the artist, which he housed in his palace on the Grand Canal and eventually sold *en bloc* to George III in 1762, along with 142 drawings, over a quarter of Canaletto's surviving work in that medium. He was a superb draughtsman, whether making rough sketches on the spot or executing finished compositions intended for the use of engravers or as finished works. It was the more finished type of drawing which appealed to Smith and the sale fortunately ensured the preservation of Smith's collection intact to the present day as the single most important group of Canaletto's works (Royal Collection). Another large collection of his drawings is in the British Museum. An album of engravings by Antonio Visentini of fourteen of Consul Smith's collection of paintings was published in 1735. This served to disseminate Canaletto's compositions widely and to enhance his fame, as well as providing, on the frontispiece, the only reliable record of the artist's appearance. A second edition followed in 1742, augmented by engravings of a further twenty-four paintings which had been handled but not retained by Smith. Smith was already acting as an agent and intermediary in the sale of Canaletto's work to English collectors by 1730, when he supplied pairs of canvases to Hugh Howard and Samuel Hill (Museum of Fine Arts, Houston, and Tatton Park, Cheshire). These were followed by a constant flow of commissions throughout the 1730s, the decade which marks the peak of Canaletto's career, including the two large series of (relatively small) Venetian views now at Woburn Abbey and formerly in the Harvey collection. The masterpiece of these years, *Venice: the Riva degli Schiavoni Looking West* (Sir John Soane's Museum, London), was, however, painted not for Consul Smith but for the other great foreign collector resident in Venice, Marshal von der Schulenburg. With the demand for Canaletto's work came a need to delegate to assistants, who included in the late 1730s and early 1740s his nephew Bernardo Bellotto, the only artist to rival him as the greatest Italian view painter of the eighteenth century. The involvement of assistants contributes to an increasing hardening of the delineation of the architectural elements of his views, while the treatment of the figures is increasingly calligraphic.

The outbreak of the War of the Austrian Succession in 1741 restricted travel to Venice and helped to diminish the number of commissions for paintings of Venetian views. Canaletto had, however, shown an appetite for new challenges from the onset of the decade, making a tour of the Brenta Canal in 1740–41 to gather fresh subject matter and working on a series of thirty-one etchings. He also turned back to ancient Rome and to *capricci* for the subjects of series of paintings executed for Consul Smith in 1742–4, years in which many pictures are, exceptionally, signed and dated. His style shows a new coldness of light, similar to that characteristic of Bellotto's paintings from the outset, above all in the masterpiece of these years, *Venice: the Upper Reaches of the Grand Canal with San Simeone Piccolo* (National Gallery, London).

The greatest challenge was provided by Canaletto's move to London in May 1746. There he was to remain for ten years, resident at 16 Silver Street (now 41 Beak Street), north of Golden Square, except for an eight-month return to Venice in 1750–51. Although his English paintings, for which he adopted a lighter tonality, vary in quality, they amount to a definitive depiction of eighteenth-century London (as in *London: the Thames from Somerset House Terrace towards the City* and *London: the Thames from Somerset House Terrace towards Westminster*, both Royal Collection), and many country seats, and Canaletto soon found himself as busy as he had been in the 1730s. Groups or pairs of pictures executed for the dukes of Richmond, Northumberland, and Beaufort and Prince Lobkowicz are still in the possession of their descendants, while groups painted for Lord Brooke, later earl of Warwick (five views of Warwick Castle), Baron King, and Thomas Hollis (views of London including Westminster Bridge, St Paul's Cathedral, and a *capriccio* of buildings in Whitehall), have been dispersed. Large views of St James's Park (presumably the painting owned by the Sir Andrew Lloyd Webber Art Foundation) and of Chelsea College (its canvas divided at an early date into two parts; one now in the Museo Nacional de Bellas Artes, Havana, Cuba, and the other at Blickling Hall, Norfolk), were apparently executed as speculations in 1749 and 1751 respectively. Canaletto's activity in England had a stimulating effect on local topographical painters, most notably Samuel Scott and William Marlow.

Four large Venetian views executed shortly after his return to Italy for the German businessman Sigmund Streit (Gemäldegalerie, Berlin) show Canaletto's powers undiminished, but many works of his later years are small, dark in tone, and populated by exaggeratedly calligraphic figures. One of the very few recorded personal encounters between the artist and English clients took place in 1761 or 1762, when John Crewe, later first Baron Crewe, and the Revd John Hinchliffe encountered him in the piazza San Marco 'making a sketch of the Campanile', according to Hinchliffe's grandson (Links, *Canaletto*, 195–7). Only in 1763 did he receive official recognition, being elected to the Venetian Academy and appointed prior of the Collegio dei Pittori. Canaletto died in Venice, of fever, on 19 April 1768, possibly in the house in which he had been born. He was unmarried. Despite his modest lifestyle he left his three sisters almost nothing except for a small investment in property made on his return visit to Venice in 1750. Canaletto was buried in the communal tomb of the confraternity of the Santissimo Spirito in the church of San Lio, Venice. CHARLES BEDDINGTON

Sources W. G. Constable, *Canaletto*, rev. J. G. Links, 2nd edn, 2 vols. (1989) • J. G. Links, *Canaletto*, rev. edn (1994) • K. Baetjer and J. G. Links, *Canaletto* (1989) [exhibition catalogue, Metropolitan Museum of Art, New York, 30 Oct 1989 – 31 Jan 1990] • M. Liversidge and J. Farrington, eds., *Canaletto and England* (1993) [exhibition catalogue, Birmingham Gas Hall Exhibition Gallery, Birmingham, 14 Oct 1993 – 9 Jan 1994] • K. T. Parker, *The drawings of Antonio Canaletto in the collection of his majesty the king at Windsor Castle* (1948) • J. G. Links, *Canaletto and his patrons* (1977) • W. L. Barcham, *The imaginary view scenes of Antonio Canaletto* (New York, 1977) • A. Corboz, *Canaletto: una Venezia immaginaria* (Milan, c.1985) • J. G. Links, *A supplement to W. G. Constable's 'Canaletto'* (1998) • K. T. Parker and C. Crawley, *The drawings of Antonio Canaletto in the collection of her majesty the queen at Windsor Castle*, new edn (1990) • C. Miller, *Fifty drawings by Canaletto from the Royal Library, Windsor Castle* (1983) • R. Bromberg, *Canaletto's etchings*, rev. 2nd edn (1993)

Likenesses A. Visentini, engraving (after monochrome portrait by G. B. Piazzetta), repro. in A. Visentini, *Prospectus magni canalis Venetiarum* (Venice, 1735), frontispiece [*see illus.*]

Wealth at death 2588/11 ducats: report, 27 May 1768, Archivio di Stato, Venice, Inquisitorato alle Acque, Busta 167; Calculi intestati, Fascicolo 71

Canaletto. *See* Canal, Giovanni Antonio (1697–1768).

Canaries, James (1653/4–1698), episcopalian minister, was the son of Thomas Canaries (*c*.1615–1677), minister of Kinnaird, Perthshire, and his wife, Margaret Leighton. After attending St Andrews University he began trials before the presbytery of Perth in January 1671. His ministerial training ended when he and two other students were allegedly involved in a drunken escapade, after which he is reported to have gone to serve in Dunbarton's regiment in France. In order to train for the Roman Catholic priesthood he entered Douai College on 27 March 1678, aged twenty-four, but, after a period in Rome, left in March 1681 and returned to Scotland.

During 1681–2 Canaries held a bursary in the presbytery of Dunkeld, and taught in that of St Andrews, which admitted him into communion in January 1682, and licensed him to preach on 24 October 1683. In addition to unpublished attacks on Roman Catholicism, in 1684 the ambitious convert proclaimed his renewed protestantism in *A Discourse Representing the Sufficient Manifestation of the Will of God to his Church*, a lengthy work dedicated to the chancellor, the earl of Perth. It perhaps helped him to obtain the parish of Selkirk, to which he was licensed in February 1685. Another fulsome dedication to Perth accompanied *A Sermon Preacht at Selkirk upon the 29th of May 1685*, in which he celebrated the Restoration and strongly upheld the doctrine of non-resistance. In February 1686 Canaries controversially preached against his erstwhile faith, later claiming that far from stirring up sedition, he espoused loyalty to the crown and the protestant religion, and sought to persuade his hearers to trust King James's assurances to the church. Alexander Cairncross, archbishop of Glasgow, was obliged to suspend him, but was said to have given him £20 towards his journey to London, where the bishop of Ely and others approved his sermon. In 1686 it was printed as *Rome's Additions to Christianity*, and he was made DD at St Andrews. Cairncross was deprived for failing to silence him but Canaries's suspension ended in December 1687.

On 30 January 1689 Canaries's *A Sermon Preached at Edinburgh, in the East Church of St Giles*, on the anniversary of Charles I's martyrdom, attacked rebellion against a lawful king, but remarkably proposed that when a ruler acted arbitrarily his subjects might judge his conduct. Although such contractual arguments generally failed to loosen his brethren's allegiance to James VII during the revolution settlement, Canaries duly acknowledged William and Mary as sovereigns. Surviving accusations before the privy council and attacks on his manse during September 1689, he endured the odium of lobbying for the Williamite episcopalians who struggled to secure themselves in their parishes without being subject to presbyterian church government. He officially remained parish minister at Selkirk until October 1691, when the presbytery declared the charge vacant on the grounds of desertion. Canaries had followed William to The Hague early that year, and was appointed his chaplain and clerk of the closet. Despite having access to the king, who desired an accommodation in church government, his vital role in consolidating episcopalian support failed when the general assembly of 1692 refused to receive the majority of episcopalian applicants. In addition to his personal kindness towards Canaries and his wife, Lady Anne Erskine, daughter of the earl of Buchan, the king rewarded the exhausted agent in March 1692 with the vicarage of St Helen's, Abingdon, Berkshire. There he compiled the main text of *The Epitome of Scotch-Presbytery* (1692) and clashed with a Quaker parishioner, Oliver Sansom, who recorded their disputes. He died in May 1698; administration of his estate was granted to his widow on 27 May. TRISTRAM CLARKE

Sources *Fasti Scot.*, new edn, vols. 2 and 5 • A. Philip, 'Dr. Canaries: a vicar of Bray', *The evangel in Gowrie* (1911), 151–63 • G. Grub, *An ecclesiastical history of Scotland*, 4 vols. (1861), vol. 3 • *Historical notices of Scotish affairs, selected from the manuscripts of Sir John Lauder of Fountainhall*, ed. D. Laing, 2, Bannatyne Club, 87 (1848) • T. Clarke, 'The Williamite episcopalians and the Glorious Revolution in Scotland', *Records of the Scottish Church History Society*, 24 (1990–92), 33–51 • J. Canaries, letters to the Revd Robert Wylie, 1691–2, NL Scot., Wodrow MS 26, fols. 308–31 • registers of the Scottish college at Douai, 1678–81, NA Scot., RH4/18 • *CSP dom.*, 1691–2 • J. Canaries, *A sermon preached at Edinburgh … upon the 30th of January, 1689*, ed. T. Harris (2000) • *The life of Oliver Sansom* (1848) • W. L. Mathieson, *Politics and religion: a study in Scottish history from the Reformation to the revolution*, 2 vols. (1902) • J. Hunter, *The diocese and presbytery of Dunkeld, 1660–1689*, 2 [1917], 124 • Berks. RO, D/A1/184/110

Archives NL Scot., Wodrow MSS

Wealth at death see administration, Berks. RO, D/A1/184/110

Cancellar, James (*fl.* 1542–1565), religious author, is first recorded with certainty in 1542, receiving a stipend of £13 from the new collegiate establishment of Canterbury

Cathedral. By the end of Edward VI's reign, as a former lay clerk of Canterbury, he had been recruited to the Chapel Royal, and it was as a chorister and 'dayly oratour' there that he dedicated to Queen Mary *The Pathe of Obedience*, a work directed against those 'seditious, rebellious and disobedient' views and actions which disfigured the reputation of the English people abroad. On 27 July 1554 Cancellar swore an oath of canonical obedience as proctor for Hugh Barret, priest—admitted that day through the patronage of Archbishop Cranmer to the hospital of Peter Poor and to the rectory of St Margaret, Canterbury—and a mandate was issued for his induction. Meanwhile, he continued to submit propaganda to the press, having issued early in 1554 *A Treatise*, against the 'pernicious opinions of those obstinate people of Kent', lately involved in Wyatt's rebellion. In this book he singled out for particular attention *The Vocacyon* by 'the mad, frantic friar Bale'—that is, John Bale, deprived bishop of Ossory in Ireland. Cancellar's new work, like *The Pathe*, demanded obedience to the lawful authority, both of the Church of Rome and of the queen, for 'there is no power but of God only'. Unhappily for the author, events did not bear out this assertion in the sense in which he made it. Faced with the choice between old church and new queen, he found it expedient in 1559 to have his name entered on the pardon roll of Elizabeth, sealing the decision with his issue of *A godly meditation of the soule … aptlye translated out of the French into English by the right highe and most vertuous Princess Elizabeth*.

Bale, meanwhile, had taken the opportunity furnished by his being a prebendary of Canterbury from 1560 to 1563 to launch a scathing rebuttal of his opponent's earlier attack, mocking his lack of university training and deriding him as a 'typeller', careerist, and cheat. Both Cancellar, who seems to have retained or renewed his links with Canterbury, and John Twyne, headmaster of Canterbury Free School, were denounced by Bale as encouraging the continuation of popish practices, such as the celebrations he witnessed in the town in July 1561. Bale confronted his opponent personally over his earlier slanders, and took the opportunity to extract a promise of a public retraction, though this was never printed. Cancellar, having been quick to make his peace with the authorities, set about finding a new patron. By 1565 he seems to have found one, in the person of 'my singular and very good lord Robert Dudley' to whom he dedicated *The Alphabet of Prayers*, a work which ran to several editions. After this time, however, nothing is known of Cancellar.

STEPHEN WRIGHT

Sources E. J. Baskerville, 'A religious disturbance in Canterbury, June 1561', *Historical Research*, 65 (1992), 340–48 • C. Woodruff and W. W. Danks, *Memorials of the cathedral and priory of Christ in Canterbury* (1912) • J. Cancellar, *The pathe of obedience* (1553) • J. Cancellar, *The alphabet of prayers* (1565) • *VCH Kent*, vol. 2 • D. M. Loades, *The reign of Mary Tudor: politics, government and religion in England, 1553–58* (1979) • A. G. Dickens, *The English Reformation*, 2nd edn (1989) • *Fasti Angl., 1541–1857*, [Canterbury] • R. Bowers, 'The liturgy of the cathedral and its music, c.1075–1642', *A history of Canterbury Cathedral, 598–1982*, ed. P. Collinson and others (1995), 408–50

Candidus [Hwita, Wizo] (*fl.* **793–802**), theologian, born probably before *c.*770 in England, was one of Alcuin's closest pupils and, arguably, a leading philosophical and theological thinker in the years around 800. He went to the continent probably in 793 and returned to Lindisfarne a year later, but from *c.*794–5 he seems to have remained on the continent, spending about a year with Arno, bishop of Salzburg, in 798, and travelling to Rome with Arno in 799, and again to Rome in 800–01. Alcuin, who nicknamed him Candidus—presumably on the basis of his English name Hwita ('white')—refers to him often in his poems and letters; he was willing to entrust confidential material to him, and he used him as a messenger to Charlemagne and as a link with Bishop Arno. In 801–2 Candidus clearly belonged to Charlemagne's court circle. After this time it is unclear what happened to him. Perhaps he died; or he may be the Waso (Wiso, Wizo) who was bishop of Trier from 804 to *c.*809.

Two works are attributed in early manuscripts to a Candidus: *De passione domini* (in Munich, Bayerische Staatsbibliothek, clm 14614, 14645, 14740, 6389; BL, Harley MS 3034; and edited in *Patrologia Latina*, 106.57–104) and a letter to a monk about whether Christ could see God with his corporeal eyes (in Munich, Bayerische Staatsbibliothek, clm 14614, 13581; Dümmler, ed., *Epistolae Karolini Aevi*, 4.557–61). The *De passione* is a commentary on the passion as presented in all four gospels, drawing particularly on Bede and Alcuin, but with some more original touches. The letter, which stresses the incorporeality of God, is based especially on Augustine's letter (letter 147) to Paulina. Earlier scholars wondered whether the Candidus in question was Wizo or another Candidus, Bruun, a monk of Fulda (before *c.*780–845); from the provenance of manuscripts and the sources used, Ineichen-Eder has definitely resolved the question in favour of Wizo. A didactic letter, based mainly on Alcuin (also using Augustine and Isidore), whose anonymous author describes himself as Blancidius may well also be Wizo's (Dümmler, ed., *Epistolae Karolini Aevi*, 484–90).

Candidus's claim to have been a thinker of some importance rests, however, on three other compositions, for which there are good, though conjectural reasons, to think that he was responsible as author or compiler. In Munich, Bayerische Staatsbibliothek, clm 6407 (written *c.*800), there is a set of fifteen theological and philosophical passages (the Munich Passages, edited in Marenbon, *From the Circle*, 152–66), which include, besides extracts and adaptations from Augustine and Claudianus Mamertus, more original, though still derivative, discussions of the Trinity and the existence of God and exercises in logical technique. One of the passages is entitled *Dicta Candidi presbiteri de imagine Dei*. Although the passage from which it develops, called *Dicta Albini de imagine Dei*, is probably not an original composition by Alcuin (despite the title's claim: Albinus was one of Alcuin's pen-names), the *Dicta Candidi* has every appearance of being Candidus's own work, and Candidus is the most plausible candidate for having written or compiled the whole set of passages.

Material in Munich, Bayerische Staatsbibliothek, clm

18961 (of the second half of the ninth century), makes this surmise more likely. This manuscript contains most of the Munich Passages, as part of a longer collection of philosophical and theological extracts from Boethius, Augustine, and Plato, and original pieces. It states explicitly that the author of the *Dicta Candidi* also wrote two of the original pieces. It is also quite probable that Candidus wrote the three sermons and the passage on the number three (Marenbon, *From the Circle*, 168–70) which precede the (anonymous) copy of his *De passione domini* in BL, Harley MS 3034 (early ninth century). The passage on the number three, especially, shows the same combination of borrowing from authorities (in this case, Augustine's *De musica*) and homespun philosophizing as that which characterizes the Munich Passages. JOHN MARENBON

Sources J. Marenbon, *From the circle of Alcuin to the school of Auxerre: logic, theology, and philosophy in the early middle ages*, Cambridge Studies in Medieval Life and Thought (1981) • E. Dümmler, ed., *Epistolae Karolini aevi*, MGH Epistolae [quarto], 4 (Berlin, 1895) • C. E. Ineichen-Eder, 'Theologisches und philosophisches Lehrmaterial aus dem Alcuin-Kreise', *Deutsches Archiv für Erforschung des Mittelalters*, 34 (1978), 192–201 • C. E. Ineichen-Eder, 'Candidus-Brun von Fulda: Maler, Lehrer and Schriftsteller', *Hrabanus Maurus und seine Schule*, ed. W. Böhne (1980), 182–92 • J. Marenbon, 'Alcuin, the council of Frankfort and the beginnings of medieval philosophy', *Das Frankfurter Konzil von 794: kristallisationspunkt karolingischer kultur* [Frankfurt 1994], ed. R. Berndt, 2 (Mainz, 1997), 603–15 • D. A. Bullough, 'Alcuin and the kingdom of heaven: liturgy, theology, and the Carolingian age', *Carolingian essays: Andrew W. Mellon lectures in early Christian studies*, ed. U.-R. Blumenthal (1983); repr. in D. A. Bullough, *Carolingian renewal: sources and heritage* (1991), 161–240 • G. Morin, 'Un saint de Maestricht rendu à l'histoire', *Revue Bénédictine*, 8 (1891), 176–83 • T. Sickel, 'Alcuinstudien 1', *Sitzungsberichten der philosophische-historische Klasse der kaiserliche Akademie der Wissenschaften Wien*, 79 (1875), 461–550, 534–41
Archives Bayerische Staatsbibliothek, Munich, clm 13581, 14614, 14645, 14740, 6389, 6407, 18961 • BL, Harley MS 3034

Candler [*née* More], **Ann** (1740–1814), poet, was born on 18 November 1740 at Yoxford, Suffolk, one of the children of William More, a glove maker in Yoxford, and his wife (1696/1697–1751), a daughter of Thomas Holder of Woodbridge. In 1750, after 'falling into reduced circumstances', her father (then 'between forty and fifty'), encouraged by her mother's desire for 'decent and respectable' living conditions, moved the family to Ipswich. One year later, at fifty-four, Ann's mother died (Candler, 1–2).

Raised by her father, Ann was self-taught and 'early evinced a fondness for reading' and for thinking critically about literature, especially travel books, dramas, and romances, but not poetry (Candler, 2–3). She declined writing lessons that her father offered to finance; instead, Ann observed and imitated his penmanship using chalk and pen. Ironically, she first wrote in verse.

In 1762 Ann married a man named Candler, a cottager of Sproughton, a village approximately 3 miles from Ipswich. From 1763 until 1766 Candler served in the militia, limiting family visits to 'twenty-eight days every summer'. Candler's remote employment and alcohol addiction kept Ann and her children destitute. Temporary relief came after the fourth child's birth through Ann's inheritance from a maiden aunt. In 1777 Candler secretly re-enlisted in the guards at Colchester, exacerbating the family's financial woes. Stricken for eleven weeks, Ann put four of her six children into the Tattingstone house of industry; she kept 'the eldest about fourteen, [and] the youngest a year and half old' with her. Although two friends paid for their rent, and others' donations covered their board, she later regretted splitting up her family and not entering all of them in Tattingstone (Candler, 5–9).

While on leave, Candler returned home and 'incessantly importuned' Ann to resettle in London. Once they arrived in April 1779, Candler abandoned Ann and the youngest daughter, Clara; he used the Gordon riots in 1780 to justify sudden army duty and a prolonged stay with guards in St James's Park after the riots had subsided. Late in 1780 Ann left for Sproughton, her travel costs paid by her husband's uncle. She eventually took refuge in Tattingstone workhouse, and gave birth to twin sons on 20 March 1781. Soon after she had written 'On the Birth of Twin Sons in 1781', both twins died.

In 1783, when Candler came back discharged, Ann joined him for seven weeks; but his sickness and her depleted funds made them both return to the workhouse. Candler recovered and dismissed himself in six months; by then Ann finally had resolved not to live with him; they never saw each other again. Later she wrote, 'All I can urge to extenuate, or palliate my folly is, that he was my husband, and the father of my children, and that my affection for him was unbounded' (Candler, 10). Blaming herself for an 'unhappy marriage for nearly forty years', she accepted Tattingstone as 'a severe penance for my indiscretion in leaving my comfortable cottage in Sproughton' in 1777. Even about her *Memoirs* Ann remarked, 'I have not endeavoured to exculpate myself, or to justify my proceedings: no, I stand self-convicted, self-condemned' (Candler, 15).

From Tattingstone Candler wrote several poems that appeared in the *Ipswich Journal*. They include 'On the Death of a Most Benevolent Gentleman' (about Metcalfe Russell of Sproughton, 1785), 'To the Inhabitants of Yoxford' (1787), and two songs that bear the same dedicatory inscription—'The Invitation to Spring' (1788) and 'To Miss F—N' (1789). The *Ipswich Journal* (17 September 1814) also ascribes the following uncollected, religious poems to her: 'A paraphrase of the 5th chapter of the 2nd book of Kings'; the 'History of Joseph, in an address to a young man'; and the 'Life of Elijah the prophet', which probably appeared in that journal from 1790 onwards.

After 1790, when the poet Elizabeth Cobbold heard about Candler, she became a beneficiary of the 'popularity of poetry and charity' (Maddox, 17). By 1800 Cobbold with other female patrons proposed to publish Candler's work by subscription to end her twenty-year stay at Tattingstone. This 'cross-class collaboration' effected publication of the modestly titled *Poetical Attempts, by Ann Candler, a Suffolk Cottager, with a Short Narrative of her Life*. Private sales of over 500 copies paid for Ann's relocation by 24 May 1802 to furnished lodgings at Copdock, close to 'her favorite village of Sproughton' and near her married daughter Lucy (Candler, 15–17). Officially published in

1803, this 68-page octavo volume (including the subscribers' list) was distributed in Ipswich and London.

Largely autobiographical, Candler's poems dramatize her as a working-class mother; as a 'lone recluse … with the dregs of human kind' (as self-portrayed in 'Reflections on my own situation, written in T—tt—ngst—ne house of industry, February 1802'); as an abused spouse; and as a humble, charming, and appreciative friend. Her verse sometimes belies and askews her 'industrious' social status with its occasional allusions to literary genres (like eastern fairy tales), 'traditionally above her station' (Landry, 274), and with her appropriation of an 'elite literary form' which appealed to her patrons (Maddox, 32). The poetical chasm Ann constructs between herself and other inmates, using derogatory descriptions, exposes a 'class conscious snobbery' that subverts her social protest. Yet, simultaneously, her verse tersely registers a stronger 'indictment of contemporary charitable practices than Crabbe's indictment of the institution of the poorhouse as itself perpetuating vices in *The Borough*' (ibid., 279). She described her *Memoirs* attached to the poems as 'The short and simple annals of the poor' (Candler, 1).

Of Candler's nine children, five sons and four daughters, three boys died in infancy (one infant she memorialized in 'The Mother's Feelings on the Loss of her Child'). Writing to a generous but condescending editor (Cobbold) and patrons in 1801, Ann admitted to pain caused by not having heard from 'my eldest son and daughter for many years'. Two of the daughters married: one 'indifferently … and settled in London'; Lucy lived in Copdock, 'the *contented happy Cottager!*' to a 'sober industrious man'; and Clara worked as a live-in domestic for John Cook of Holton Hall near Stratford (Candler, 4). Candler died on 6 September 1814, at Holton, Suffolk.

Jennett Humphreys, *rev.* Angela M. Leonard

Sources A. Candler, *Poetical attempts, by Ann Candler, a Suffolk cottager, with a short narrative of her life* (1803); repr. in *Rare printed autobiographies covering thirty-three women's lives, 1713–1859* (1999), pt 1 of *Women's autobiographies from Cambridge University Library* · *Ipswich Journal* (17 Sept 1814) · D. Landry, *The muses of resistance: laboring-class women's poetry in Britain, 1739–1796* (1990) · A. N. Maddox, '"The industrial sisterhood": collaboration in writing by English working-class women, 1781–1822', MA diss., Appalachian State University, 1997 · B. P. Kanner, *Women in context: two hundred years of British women autobiographers* (1997) · P. R. Feldman, ed., *British women poets of the Romantic era: an anthology* (1997) · G. Davis and B. A. Joyce, *Poetry by women to 1900: a bibliography of American and British writers* (1991) · C. Buck, ed., *The Bloomsbury guide to women's literature* (1992) · J. Todd, ed., *A dictionary of British and American women writers, 1660–1800* (1984) · R. Ackermann, *The microcosm of London* (1808)

Candler [Gillet]**, Matthias** (1605–1663), topographer and Church of England clergyman, son of William Gillet or Candler (*c.*1580–1612), schoolmaster, of Yoxford, Suffolk, and his wife, Hannah (*c.*1585–1649), daughter of William Fiske and Anna Anstye of South Elmham St James, was born on 24 February 1605 at Yoxford and baptized at St Peter's, Yoxford, on 6 March. He entered Trinity College, Cambridge, as a sizar in 1620, graduated BA in 1624, but was of Peterhouse when he proceeded MA in 1628. On 18 May 1625 he married Anne (*bap.* 1604, *d.* 1662), daughter of Peter Devereux, rector of Rattlesden, and they had three sons and two daughters, of whom the eldest, Philip (1629–1689), was from 1670, like his son and namesake after him, master of Woodbridge School, Suffolk. On 18 December 1625 Candler was ordained at Norwich, and on 16 December 1629 he was instituted to the vicarage of Coddenham, Suffolk, which he held until his death. His churchmanship will have suited his patrons, the Bacons of Shrubland: after a visitation in 1636 he was admonished for nonconformity by Bishop Matthew Wren; ten years later he signed the petition concerning church government to the House of Lords, and was chosen to serve on the local presbyterian classis.

In the mid-1650s Candler made extensive and detailed collections for the history of Suffolk; his circle was wide and he recorded much from his own knowledge, full of colourful personal description. There are at least seven different manuscript versions in the Bodleian Library, Society of Antiquaries, College of Arms, and British Library; in combination they are a rich source of church and parish notes, pedigrees, arms, and details of gentry families. Some copies have additions by the elder Philip Candler and William Blois of Grundisburgh (*d.* 1673).

Anne Candler died in December 1662. Calamy was wrong to list Candler as ejected: he died in office at Coddenham on 6 December 1663, leaving his eldest son a tenement in Yoxford. In 1696 John Fairfax wrote most warmly to Henry Sampson about his old friend: 'he never was forward for conformity … all, far and near, flock'd after his Ministry … He still taught them the good old savoury Truths, by which men best get to Heaven' (*Calamy rev.*, 100–01). Candler, Fairfax observed, 'had really been a fit man to have wrote the Antiquities of his Country [county]' (ibid.). The challenge to publish his valuable work stands.

J. M. Blatchly

Sources will, PRO, PROB 11/312, sig. 144 · J. Browne, *A history of Congregationalism and memorials of the churches in Norfolk and Suffolk* (1877) · *Calamy rev.*, 100–01 · J. M. Blatchly, *Topographers of Suffolk*, 5th edn (1988), 10 · *IGI*

Archives BL, county notes, Add. MS 15520 · BL, Harley MS 6071 · Bodl. Oxf., pedigrees, etc., Tanner MSS 180, 226, 257, 324 · S. Antiquaries, Lond., arms in contemporary colours, MS 667 | Coll. Arms, 'Ryece's Suffolk' given by Edward Thurlow

Candlish, John (1816–1874), glass bottle manufacturer and politician, was born at Tarset, near Bellingham in Northumberland, and baptized on 28 April 1816, the eldest son of John Candlish (*b.* 1793), farmer, and his wife, Mary, *née* Robson. Following the death of his wife about 1820, the elder John Candlish moved to Sunderland, where his brother Robert was the manager of Ayres Quay bottle works. Here he found work as a labourer.

The family was Presbyterian, of Scottish descent. Candlish received an education at dissenting schools, first locally, but then at the well-regarded Dr Dodd's academy in North Shields, before returning to Sunderland at the age of eleven to work in the bottle works. When he was fourteen his uncle's influence secured him an apprenticeship with a draper, Robert Tate, a position that gave him opportunities to continue his education by studying

French and joining a debating society. During this period Candlish joined the Baptists with whom he continued to worship throughout his life. In 1836 he began his commercial career as a partner in a drapery business.

Candlish's early career was varied. He moved from enterprise to enterprise with a restlessness that seems to bear out one contemporary verdict which named his only failing as ambition. Various drapery undertakings were followed in 1836 by the purchase of a newspaper, the *Sunderland Beacon*, which failed within six months; this was followed by other short-lived ventures into coal exporting, and, in 1844, shipbuilding. Candlish's yard at Southwick was said to have produced some fine ships but few profits. In 1845 he married his cousin Elizabeth Candlish, of Ayres Quay, and in July 1851 returned to publishing by founding the *Sunderland News*, a move which reflected his growing political ambitions. Other interests in the early 1850s included the Sunderland Gas Company and a small glassworks.

The turning point of Candlish's commercial career came in 1855 when he acquired the lease of a glass bottle works at Seaham harbour on the co. Durham coast. This coal-fired works manufactured the traditional black bottles used for wine and beer under the name the Londonderry Bottle Works. Under Candlish's ownership production expanded and large contracts were secured with brewers and government departments. In 1858 Candlish purchased a second site, at Diamond Hall in Sunderland, and by 1872 had six glasshouses at Seaham and four at Diamond Hall, making him one of the largest manufacturers of black bottles in Europe. The Londonderry Bottle Works was justly celebrated in its day for its good labour relations.

Candlish entered public life in 1848 when he was elected to Sunderland council, representing the west ward. By upbringing and early inclination he was Conservative but transferred his loyalties to the twin causes of radicalism and free trade during the campaign against the corn laws. He was an energetic advocate of reforms in sanitary and financial administration, became mayor in 1858 and 1861, and filled a number of other public offices in Sunderland, notably chairman of the board of guardians. He was made a JP in 1862 and subsequently a county magistrate and deputy lieutenant of the county. During the early 1860s he extended his business interests to a Middlesbrough iron shipbuilding firm, Candlish, Fox & Co., and the Thornleigh Colliery Company. Both these ventures failed and for the last ten years of his life Candlish's energies were taken up by national politics.

Candlish's first attempt to secure one of Sunderland's two parliamentary seats ended in disappointment when in 1865 he was beaten into third place by two tory candidates. The following year a by-election brought success, which was consolidated in the general election of 1868 when the newly enfranchised electorate of Sunderland threw its weight firmly behind the radicals. In parliament Candlish had a high attendance rate and a record of interventions in most of the discussions on major legislation of the period. The activity which brought him most public attention was his criticism of the cost and management of the Abyssinian expedition, which led to his chairmanship of two select committees on the subject between 1868 and 1870. Candlish's record in national politics attracted some criticism in Sunderland for not being sufficiently radical and in April 1871 a meeting in his home town passed a vote of confidence in him despite, according to *The Times*, 'considerable opposition'. His parliamentary connections led to the marriage in 1869 of his only daughter, Elizabeth Penelope, to William Shepherd Allen, MP for Newcastle under Lyme.

Candlish had visited India in the autumn of 1870 and this event was blamed for the subsequent breakdown of his health. He died on 17 March 1874 in Cannes, France, and was buried in Ryhope cemetery in Sunderland. He was commemorated in his home town by a statue, erected in October 1875. CATHERINE ROSS

Sources W. Brockie, *Sunderland notables: natives, residents, and visitors* (1894), 321–33 • *Newcastle Daily Chronicle* (19 March 1874) • *Political life and speeches of John Candlish, member for Sunderland from 1866–1874* (1886) • G. E. Milburn and S. T. Miller, eds., *Sunderland: river, town and people* (1990) • *The Times* (18 April 1871), 11 • *IGI* • m. cert.

Likenesses cartoon, 1868, Sunderland Museum; repro. in Milburn and Miller, eds., *Sunderland* • C. Bacon, statue, 1875, Mowbray Park, Sunderland

Wealth at death under £40,000: probate, 22 July 1874, *CGPLA Eng. & Wales*

Candlish, Robert Smith (1806–1873), Free Church of Scotland minister and theologian, was born on 23 March 1806 in Nicolson Street, Edinburgh, the youngest child of James Candlish (1760–1806), a medical lecturer, and his wife, Jane Smith (1768–1854). When he was only five weeks old, his father died, probably of a brain haemorrhage; the medical case was considered to be of such interest to the medical profession that it was recorded in Dr Abercrombie's book *Pathological and Practical Researches on Diseases of the Brain and Spinal Cord* (1828). Robert was a peculiar-, but interesting-looking, child, 'somewhat delicate and rather timid' (Wilson, 7). He had a delicate, fair complexion, a large forehead, and very long eyelashes, but a very small body. His early education was undertaken at home by his brother James, his sister, and his mother, who ran the household with the strictest economy: 'out of debt, out of danger' was a favourite maxim (ibid., 6).

Candlish matriculated at Glasgow University on 10 October 1818, and graduated MA in 1823, having won a number of prizes. In 1823–6 he undertook divinity studies at Glasgow Divinity Hall. He loved hill climbing and rambling, and enjoyed the beauty of natural scenery. He also enjoyed rowing, fishing, and sea swimming. He was a favourite with the professors, especially with 'Cockie Young', the Greek professor; soon Candlish became known as 'Little Cockie'. It is not surprising, therefore, that when the professors were requested, in 1826, to select their most able student to be sent as a tutor to Eton, Candlish was chosen. He remained there for two unhappy years, finding it difficult to be accepted and describing it as 'my place of exile' (ibid., 36). He returned to Scotland, and was licensed to preach by Glasgow presbytery on 6

Robert Smith Candlish (1806–1873), by David Octavius Hill and Robert Adamson

August 1828. He became an assistant to Dr Gibb at St Andrew's Church, Glasgow.

When Gibb died in June 1831, Candlish was offered the chance to teach Latin at Glasgow University. Instead, he became assistant to a Mr Gregor at Bonhill near Glasgow. While preaching, he had an awkward way of habitually shrugging up one shoulder, which made it look deformed; he would begin to scream or screech, and would gesticulate wildly. But once these mannerisms, which remained a life-long feature of his preaching, ceased to be regarded, many were convinced that a great preacher had appeared. In January 1834 he became a temporary assistant to a Mr Martin at St George's Church, Edinburgh. That spring he also received an offer from Regent Square Church, London. Candlish declined the English proposal when St George's resolved to have him appointed as assistant and successor to Martin. On 27 May 1834 Martin died suddenly, and Candlish was ordained minister in August. On 6 January 1835 he married Janet Brock, a lady described as possessing 'the ornament of a meek and quiet spirit' (ibid., 59); they had ten children. Candlish possessed a keen sense of fun: this came to the fore when he became a family man, playfully relaxing in the company of his children.

On 19 July 1836 Candlish was tempted by, but declined, the offer to become minister of Greenside church, Edinburgh. At the 1839 assembly he rose from virtual obscurity to become a leader in the non-intrusionist party, ultimately second only to Thomas Chalmers. It was Candlish who had Hugh Miller of Cromarty appointed as editor of what became the influential Edinburgh newspaper *The Witness*. In 1841 he was nominated to the new chair in biblical criticism at Edinburgh University. However, he was criticized quite severely in the House of Lords for disregarding the legal interdicts issued against preaching in Strathbogie, and his appointment was cancelled. He then took a leading part in the discussions concerning the church's relationship with the state. In the same year Princeton University conferred upon him a DD. Candlish's writings were many, but he made a particularly valuable contribution in the field of biblical exegesis. His most notable achievements in this area included the sections he wrote for *The Exposition of the Book of Genesis* (1842), his *Life in a Risen Saviour* (1858), and *The Two Great Commandments* (1860).

Just before the Disruption, Candlish was nearly drowned, when a steamer capsized on the Firth of Forth on 9 January 1843. Despite this crisis, he went on to play a major part in the events of the Disruption, becoming an influential leader in the Free Church of Scotland. He became minister of Free St George's, which was opened on 28 May 1843.

Candlish was passionately in favour of the provision of religious education in schools, a cause for which he spent much time campaigning. In 1846 he was appointed convenor of the education committee of the Free Church. In 1847 the assembly proposed him for the post of divinity professor at New College, Edinburgh. Once again, St George's protested, but this time he intimated to them his willingness 'to spend and be spent' in any office to which the church might call him (ibid., 407). However, his successor soon died and Candlish resigned his new post to resume his ministry at St George's.

In Candlish's preaching the doctrine of the atonement played a prominent part. For him atonement was not merely satisfaction of the law, but the start of a new life. He preached powerfully that God does not only save sinners from hell, but also gives them an eternal life of joy and peace, which begins immediately following conversion. He ably advanced these views in his important work *The Atonement*, published in 1845. In 1861 Candlish was appointed moderator of the general assembly and, in the following year, principal of New College. A movement was established to support him, Thomas Guthrie stating: 'I need not tell you how much the Christian Church in general, and the Free Church in particular, owes to the remarkable talents, warm-hearted piety, genius, unselfish devotedness, and Herculean labours, as I may say, of Dr Candlish' (ibid., 532).

In the spring of 1864 Candlish delivered his first important Cunningham lecture on the subject of the fatherhood of God. His theology was quite conservative, but these lectures created some degree of controversy. He began by denying the idea of a universal fatherhood of God, arguing instead for a filial relationship of God with believers only, and that by adoption. Edinburgh University conferred a DD on him on 24 April 1865. Throughout his life,

Candlish took an active part in a number of other important areas of church life: the movement for church union; educational arrangements for ministerial candidates; the sabbath observance movement; the anti-slavery campaign; and the church's mission to the Jews.

After Candlish had experienced a number of illnesses, including some severe attacks of gout, his health deteriorated quite rapidly. In October 1873 he was so weak that he could not even continue to take nourishment. He died on Sunday 19 October 1873 at 11.35 p.m. He was buried at the old Calton cemetery on Friday 24 October 1873, with large numbers of mourners attending.

Candlish was a man of rare ability. He was a clear, profound, and perceptive thinker, a first-class debater, and an inspiring preacher. He took a leading role in the cause of the Disruption and subsequently held a similar role in the affairs of the Free Church of Scotland. Much of the success of the Free Church in its formative years is directly attributable to Candlish's unstinting efforts on its behalf.

MICHAEL D. MCMULLEN

Sources *DNB* • *Fasti Scot.* • W. Ewing, ed., *Annals of the Free Church of Scotland, 1843–1900*, 1 (1914), 116–17 • W. Wilson, *Memorials of Robert Smith Candlish* (1880) • J. Macleod, *Scottish theology in relation to church history since the Reformation*, [3rd edn] (1974), 271–5 • A. L. Drummond and J. Bulloch, *The church in Victorian Scotland, 1843–1874* (1975), 12–16 • R. A. Riesen, '"Higher criticism" in the Free Church Fathers', *SCHS records*, 20/2 (1979), 119–42 • D. K. McKim, ed., *Encyclopedia of the reformed faith* (1992) • S. J. Brown and M. Fry, *Scotland in the age of the disruption* (1993), 84–94 • *DSCHT*, 134

Archives U. Edin., New College | NRA Scotland, priv. coll., letters to Sir George Sinclair

Likenesses B. W. Crombie, etching, 1839, NPG • W. Brodie, bust; formerly at St George's Free Church, Edinburgh • Elliott & Fry, two photographs, NPG • D. O. Hill & R. Adamson, photograph, Scot. NPG [*see illus.*] • Moffat, carte-de-visite, NPG • photograph, repro. in Wilson, *Memorials*

Wealth at death £3642 12*s*. 11*d*.: inventory, 6 Jan 1874, NA Scot., SC 70/1/166, p. 129

Cane, Andrew (*c*.1589–1656x61), goldsmith and actor, was the son of Robert Cane of Windsor, butcher; he may be the otherwise unnamed 'Keane', son of Robert Kene and Lucresia Andrews, who was baptized at the parish church of St John, Windsor, on 2 March 1589. He was apprenticed to Richard Cane, his elder brother, for ten years beginning in August 1602, and took his oath as a freeman of the Goldsmiths' Company in January 1611. By January 1612 he had evidently established his own shop, and he took on the first of nine apprentices who bound themselves to him over the following forty-two years, at least two of whom worked as actors concurrently with their training as goldsmiths.

Cane may have returned to his native district to marry: on 1 June 1612 an Andrew Keine married Mary Homses(?) at the church of St John, Eton; a son, Richard, was baptized there on 28 February 1613. Seven years later Thomas Cane, son of Andrew and Mary Cane, was baptized at St Leonard, Shoreditch. However, if any of these entries are indeed connected with Andrew Cane the goldsmith this first family would appear to have died out. At his death Cane's widow was called Anne (*née* Spencer), and the only surviving child, called 'my son' by Anne in her will, was Edward, made free as a goldsmith by patrimony in 1649, and hence likely to have been born in the 1620s. By 1656 Edward had established a shop in Bishopsgate, and his own son Andrew in turn took up the trade of his grandfather.

Quite when Cane began his theatrical career is unclear, but since by 1622 he was described as among 'the chief of them at the Phoenix' it was by then well developed. For the next twenty years he was a leading player with a number of companies, performing not only at the Phoenix or Cockpit in Drury Lane, but also at the Fortune, the Salisbury Court playhouse, and the Red Bull. Cane specialized in comic roles, and was renowned as a fool well after the theatres had closed (1642–60); as a fictional figure he appears as Quick in the pamphlet dialogue *The Stage-Players' Complaint* (1641). In the tradition of Tarlton he performed jigs and extempore entertainments as well as formal dramatic parts, and was known for a spirited, rapid style of delivery.

By early 1624 Cane had joined the troupe playing at the Fortune Playhouse, then known as the Palsgrave's Company. In January of that year he was named by his dying colleague Francis Grace to administer the payment of Grace's player's share to his creditors; in the same year Cane put his name, with other players, to a bond of agreement drawn up by the actor and manager Richard Gunnell, a document which thirty years later remained the subject of a dispute with Gunnell's heirs, his daughter Margaret and her husband, the actor William Wintersel. After 1625, when the Palsgrave's Company disbanded, little is known of Cane's theatrical activities for the following six years, although he may have joined the King and Queen of Bohemia's Company, which also played at the Fortune.

Late in 1631 Cane emerged as the leading player of a new troupe in the service of the infant Prince Charles, established by special licence. By that date the company was already performing at the relatively new playhouse in Salisbury Court, featuring the play *Holland's Leaguer* by Shakerley Marmion, in which Cane played Trimalchio, '*a humorous gallant*', and his two apprentices John Wright and Arthur Savill the female roles of Millicent and Quartilla. By 1633 the company had moved to the larger Red Bull Playhouse, and in 1640 they moved once again to the Fortune. Cane's only other known part, though it remains unnamed, was in a satirical play, *The Whore New Vamped*, which in 1639 led to Cane being accused of libelling two London aldermen, associated with the wine monopoly.

Prince Charles's Company received royal patronage throughout the eleven years of its existence, playing relatively frequently at court, and accompanying the king and queen on progress as far as Nottinghamshire and southern Derbyshire in the summer of 1634. The company also toured independently: Cane was granted permission to play in Norwich, for example, in March 1636.

Cane appears to have continued business as a goldsmith even during the years of his eminence on the stage. In September 1633 the company wardens fined him for defective wares: those named indicate that he dealt in domestic and decorative silver goods. His shop was in the parish of St

Giles Cripplegate, near to the theatres at which he followed his parallel career. He was still in London at the end of 1642 when he took part in a riotous demonstration at Guildhall designed to get petitions heard by the mayor and council, but thereafter he left for Oxford, where he enlisted in the army and worked in the royalist mint. Cane had returned to London by the later 1640s, resuming his trade as goldsmith as well as taking part in some surreptitious playing: he was arrested while performing at the Red Bull in January 1650.

Cane's last formal activity as a goldsmith was probably to attend the court at which his apprentice Nathaniel Cooper was granted his freedom, in January 1656. He died within the next few years, in his later sixties or early seventies; his wife, Anne, describes herself as his widow in the will she made in May 1661. She left cash bequests of £200, and the will is framed in a way which suggests that Edward Cane had already received his patrimony. Andrew Cane appears to have died a man of moderate wealth.

JOHN H. ASTINGTON

Sources G. E. Bentley, *The Jacobean and Caroline stage*, 7 vols. (1941–68) · apprentices' book and court minutes, Worshipful Company of Goldsmiths, London · W. Ingram, 'Arthur Savill, stage player', *Theatre Notebook*, 37 (1983), 21–22 · E. A. J. Honigmann and S. Brock, eds., *Playhouse wills, 1558–1642: an edition of wills by Shakespeare and his contemporaries in the London theatre* (1993) · parish books of St John, New Windsor, Society of Genealogists, Berks. RO [transcript] · parish books of St John, Eton, Buckinghamshire, Mormon Family History Centre (MFM) · will, GL, MS 9052/14 [Anne Decane] · will, GL, 9171/41 [Edward de Cayne], fol. 371 · G. E. Bentley, 'The troubles of a Caroline acting troupe: Prince Charles's Company', *Huntington Library Quarterly*, 41 (1977–8), 217–49 · E. Nungezer, *A dictionary of actors* (New Haven, 1929) · L. Horson, *The commonwealth and Restoration stage* (Cambridge, MA, 1928) · W. S. Prideaux, *Memorials of the Goldsmiths' Company*, 2 vols. (1896)

Likenesses woodcut (of Cane?), repro. in *The stage-players' complaint* (1641)

Wealth at death apparently moderately wealthy: will [Anne Decane], GL, MS 9052/14

Cane, Elizabeth Bridget. *See* Armitstead, Elizabeth Bridget (1750–1842).

Cane, Robert (1807–1858), Irish nationalist, was born at Kilkenny. His mother's maiden name was Scott. After serving an apprenticeship as a pharmacist he found the means of attending the College of Surgeons, Dublin, and in 1831 was admitted as a member of the Royal College of Surgeons, London. He returned to Kilkenny in 1832 and entered on a highly successful medical career. He held appointments with various public institutions and acquired a lucrative private practice, with the family of the marquess of Ormond among his many aristocratic clients. He published a series of papers on medicine and public health, and was awarded the MD of the University of Glasgow in 1842. He dispensed his wealth very generously.

Cane married the daughter of an army officer and with her had eight children, five of whom survived him. A fine platform orator, he took a highly prominent part in public and political matters, and was the chief promoter of the repeal movement in Kilkenny. In 1844 and again in 1849 he was elected mayor of Kilkenny. He sympathized generally with the Young Ireland party. He withheld support from the insurrection of 1848, but was arrested on 29 July, and detained for some weeks under the terms of the Habeas Corpus Suspension Act (11 & 12 Vict. c35). In 1853 he originated the Celtic Union, a semi-political and semi-literary society, one of the purposes of which was the publication of works relating to the history of Ireland. In connection with the society he edited a magazine, *The Celt*, the first number of which appeared on 1 August 1857. Its inspiration was clearly drawn from Thomas Davis and *The Nation* newspaper of the 1840s. At his home in William Street, Cane hosted gatherings for the contributors, many of them significant practitioners of nationalist journalism and literature in subsequent decades, including William Kenealy, Robert Dwyer Joyce, and Charles J. Kickham. In the March 1858 issue Cane put forward a detailed proposal for the revival of nationalist political organization. On 16 August 1858, following a few days' illness, he died at his home, 8 William Street, Kilkenny. A splendid public funeral preceded his burial in St John's Roman Catholic cemetery, Maudlin Street, Kilkenny, on the 20th. Cane's *History of the Williamite and Jacobite wars of Ireland from their origin to the capture of Athlone* was published in 1859.

R. V. COMERFORD

Sources *Irish Quarterly Review*, 8/31 (1859), 1004–96 · *Medical Directory for Ireland* (1853) · *Medical Directory for Ireland* (1859) · *Croly's Medical Directory* (1846) · *Freeman's Journal* [Dublin] (16 Aug 1858) · *Tipperary Free Press* (20 Aug 1858)

Wealth at death under £2010: probate, 17 Aug 1858, *CGPLA Ire.*

Cane, Stephen Percival [Percy] (1881–1976), garden designer and writer, was born on 20 September 1881 at High Street, Braintree, Essex, the eldest of the five children of William Stephen Cane, a corn dealer, and his wife, Ellen Wagstaff. He spent his childhood at Bocking Mill on the River Blackwater, near Braintree, and was educated privately from 1891 at a school run by Lygon Graham Pakenham. From February 1903 to January 1908 he worked for Crittalls, the firm of window manufacturers owned by family friends. A visit to the garden at Easton Lodge, designed in 1902 by Harold Peto (1854–1933) for the countess of Warwick, inspired him to become a garden designer.

Cane left Crittalls and enrolled at Chelmsford College of Science and Art to study art and architecture. The principal, C. H. Baskett, offered him an introduction to the secretary of the Architectural Association, F. R. Yerbury. Cane arranged to study part-time, as a pupil of one of the senior students, Stephen Rowland Pierce (1896–1966), who was later vice-president of the Royal Institute of British Architects (RIBA) from 1951 to 1955. He began a career in journalism in 1915 by writing for *My Garden, Illustrated*, a monthly magazine which he owned and edited from May 1918 to June 1920. He finished his training by studying at the Chelmsford County School of Horticulture in 1918, and by 1919 was established in London as a garden architect.

Within a decade Cane had become one of the most sought-after designers of his day, and had received commissions for Llannerch Park, north Wales (1927–9); Ivy House, Hampstead, for Anna Pavlova (1926); Bodens Ride, Ascot (1929); and Hascombe Court, Godalming (1928–9). He designed gardens in Britain, France, Austria, and Greece, for the British pavilion at the New York World Fair (1939), for the King's House, Burhill, for the Royal Warrant Holders' Association (1935), and for Hungerdown House, Seagry, Wiltshire (1945–6). After the Second World War he received a number of large commissions, which gave him the scope to design on a grand scale: Falkland Palace, Fife (1947); the imperial palace, Addis Ababa, for Emperor Haile Selassie (1955); and his most important undertaking, Dartington Hall, Devon, for Leonard and Dorothy Elmhirst (from 1945 onwards), where his work survives in excellent condition. Westfields, at Oakley in Bedfordshire (1953–64), has all the characteristic Cane features at their best: a glade of flowering trees and shrubs, a rock and water garden of Westmorland stone, a formal lily pool, and a paved rose garden. The artist Harold White illustrated Cane's design proposals from the 1920s to the 1950s. The landscape architect and pioneer of the modern movement in gardens Christopher Tunnard (1910–1979) and Frank Clark (1902–1971), landscape designer, author, and teacher, were both articled to Cane from 1932 to late 1934.

Cane worked mainly in the larger private gardens, and remained one of the most prominent designers from the 1930s to the 1950s. His commissions provided the material for his books on garden design: *Modern Gardens, British and Foreign* (1926–7), *Garden Design of Today* (1934), *The Earth is my Canvas* (1956), and *The Creative Art of Garden Design* (1967). He contributed articles on gardens to *The Studio* magazine during the 1920s and from 1930 to 1938 served as founder editor of the quarterly journal *Garden Design*. From 1921 until 1953 he exhibited regularly at the Chelsea flower show, where he was awarded eight gold (1936, 1937, 1938, 1947, 1948, 1949, 1951, 1952) and three silver-gilt medals (1934, 1935, 1950). Although very much a lone worker, he was appreciative of contemporary designers; at one stage he joined the Institute of Landscape Architects but later resigned. A small, reserved, dapper man, he was a perfectionist in his work. Modest and courteous in character, he allowed his social life to revolve round his career, and he never married.

In 1926 Cane described successful garden design as

> the inclusion of formal terraces and gardens suitable to the character of the house, and the relation and contrast of these with beautifully balanced glades and planting … It is the harmonious relation of the garden to the house, and of the gardens to the surrounding scenery. (*Modern Gardens, British and Foreign*, 1926–7, 1–2)

He drew inspiration from the Italianate garden designs of Peto and greatly admired the aesthetics and carefully prescribed rules of Japanese gardens. He chose shrubs and trees of Japanese origin—evergreen azaleas, maples, and flowering cherries—and his rock and water gardens were often designed in the Japanese spirit, with a precise placing of rocks and shrubs and an atmosphere of elegant reserve. Cane coined the use of the word glade and gave it a particular significance in the context of his garden designs: with curving borders of ornamental trees and shrubs, glades were a manageable alternative to labour-intensive bedding schemes. Cane was concerned about cost-effective garden schemes: in April 1957 he took part in a symposium promoted by the Royal Horticultural Society entitled 'Garden design in relation to reduction of labour and maintenance costs', with Brenda Colvin and L. Milner White.

In 1963 Cane was awarded the Royal Horticultural Society's Veitch memorial medal for his work as a designer of gardens and a landscape architect. He continued to practise as a garden architect in London until September 1972, when he suffered a severe stroke. He spent his last years in a nursing home, Eastfield House, Whitchurch, Oxfordshire, paid for by the Elmgrant Trust, and died on 23 February 1976 in St Mary's Hospital, Wallingford, Oxfordshire.

CHARLOTTE JOHNSON

Sources R. Webber, *Percy Cane … garden designer* (1975) • P. Cane, *The earth is my canvas* (1956) • R. Desmond, *Bibliography of British gardens* (1984) • 'The gardens at Dartington Hall', *Journal of the Royal Horticultural Society*, 79 (1954), 246–56 • B. Colvin, P. Cane, and L. Milner White, 'Garden design in relation to reduction of labour and maintenance costs', *Journal of the Royal Horticultural Society*, 82 (1957), 294–302 • *Landscape and Garden* (summer 1936), 90–92 • 'King's first visit to the King's House', *ILN* (11 July 1936) • A. Hellyer, 'A Percy Cane period piece', *Country Life*, 170 (1981), 26–8 • F. Gunn, 'Gardens of their time and ours', *Country Life* (28 July 1994), 68–71 • *WWW* • J. Brown, *The English garden in our time* (1987) • b. cert. • d. cert.

Archives High Cross House, Dartington, Devon, Dartington Hall records, gardens • National Trust for Scotland, planting plan for Falkland Palace, Fife (1948) • NRA, priv. coll., drg. nos. 3/403/5442 and 2/403/5409 • Royal Horticultural Society, London, plans

Likenesses photograph, repro. in P. Cane, *The creative art of garden design* (1967), jacket • photographs, repro. in Webber, *Percy Cane*, frontispiece, p. 138

Wealth at death £5781: probate, 9 July 1976, *CGPLA Eng. & Wales*

Canes, Vincent [*alias* Thomas Bodwill; *name in religion* John Baptist] (**1608–1672**), Franciscan friar, was born, he implies in his writings, on the borders of Nottinghamshire and Leicestershire, where his family had gone as a result of religious persecution. The 'Necrology' of the Franciscans describes him as 'Comitatus Lecestriensis' (Trappes-Lomax, 259). Brought up a protestant, he went at eighteen to Cambridge, where he remained for two years. He moved to London and, having travelled in the Netherlands, Germany, France, and Flanders, returned to England 'to participate of the miseries which our civil wars[,] then commenced upon pretens of a purer reformation and further elongation from popery, did bring upon us' (Canes, 269). Having been converted to Catholicism, Canes entered the Franciscan order at Douai, where he became lecturer in theology and professor of divinity, presumably at the monastery of St Bonaventure. He was appointed to defend the Catholic faith against attackers, notably Edward Stillingfleet, and was praised for his execution of his task. His name in religion was John Baptist, and his alias, according to the 'Necrology', was Thomas Bodwill.

Canes describes himself on the title-page of his best-known work, *Fiat lux*, as 'a friend to men of all Religions'. This style captures the central thrust of Canes's work—eirenic, peaceful, accommodating. His first work, *The Reclaimed Papist* (1655), is written entertainingly in the form of a dialogue between a Catholic knight and a protestant lady whom the knight is courting. It shows Canes's characteristically lively imagination and plain style. He writes of the dedicatee, John Compton, as if he, Canes, were in Compton's service. *Fiat lux*, to which there were many respondents, including John Owen, Daniel Whitby, and Stillingfleet, appeared in 1661; an enlarged second edition, dedicated to Elizabeth, countess of Arundel and Sussex, and mother to Cardinal Howard, was published the following year. There was a third enlarged edition in 1665. When Canes replied to his critics he always did so with amiability. There is, he writes in the second edition of *Fiat lux*, 'no rationall motive for disputes and animosities about matters of Religion' (Canes, 13), and describes charity as 'the great rule of our happiness and square of all perfection' (ibid., 396). He responded to John Owen's *Animadversions upon Fiat lux* with his *Epistle*, published in 1661. Canes's *Diaphanta, or, Three Attendants on Fiat lux* (1665) continued his response to Owen and constitutes his reply to Whitby and Jeremy Taylor. Canes here also answered Peter du Moulin, William Denton, and Stillingfleet, and his *Account of Dr. Still[ing]Fleet's Late Book Against the Church of Rome* (1672) was included in his *Tōi katholicōi Stillingfleeton, or, An account given to a Catholick friend of Dr. Stillingfleet's late book against the Roman church, together with a short postil upon his text, in three letters by I. V. C.* (1672). His references, notably in *Diaphanta* (1665), and in *Fiat lux* to the Benedictine monk Serenus Cressy, suggest his connection to other pacific voices and he would have known Christopher Davenport, a fellow Franciscan and contemporary. Hurter's *Nomenclator* recognizes his intellectual context, for Canes is discussed after the entry on Davenport and in conjunction with Cressy and Kenelm Digby.

Canes died on 21 June 1672 in his 63rd year in London 'in or, near, Somerset House in the Strand', and 'was buried in the vault under the chappel belonging to that house' (Wood, *Ath. Oxon.*, 4.107). PATRICIA C. BRÜCKMANN

Sources V. Canes, *Fiat lux* (1662) • R. Trappes-Lomax, ed., *The English Franciscan nuns, 1619–1821, and the Friars Minor of the same province, 1618–1761*, Catholic RS, 24 (1922), 259–314 • G. Oliver, *Collections illustrating the history of the Catholic religion in the counties of Cornwall, Devon, Dorset, Somerset, Wilts, and Gloucester* (1857) • H. Hurter, ed., *Nomenclator literarius theologiae Catholicae: theologos exhibens aetate, natione disciplinis distinctos*, 3rd edn, 5 vols. in 6 (Innsbruck, 1903–13) • T. H. Clancy, *English Catholic books, 1641–1700: a bibliography*, rev. edn (1996) • Wood, *Ath. Oxon.*, new edn, 4.107

Canetti, Elias (1905–1994), author, was born on 25 July 1905 at Ruse in Bulgaria, the eldest son of Jacques Canetti (*d.* 1913) and Mathilde Arditi. His parents were both Sephardic Jews whose first language was Ladino, a mixture of medieval Spanish, Hebrew, Turkish, and other elements. They also spoke German and Canetti grew up hearing a medley of languages in multi-ethnic Ruse.

In 1911 the family moved to Manchester, where Canetti picked up English. On the death of his father from a heart attack in 1913, the family moved again, this time to Vienna, where they remained for another three years, and where Canetti's domineering mother forced him to learn German by rote. In 1916 they moved to Zürich, where Canetti spent some of the happiest years of his life. His education was multinational—schooling in Manchester and various European cities was followed by study at the University of Vienna, from where he graduated with a doctorate in chemistry in 1929.

While writing his first and only novel, the massive epic *Die Blendung* (*Auto da fe*) in 1934, Canetti married Venetia Taubner-Calderón (*d.* 1963), who appears in the three volumes of his memoirs as Veza. The English translation of this novel appeared in 1946, and met with a puzzled response from British critics and the public; its pessimism and fragmented narrative structure presented a strenuous challenge to readers. Further revised editions in German received respectful recognition, so that in 1966 Canetti was awarded the literature prize of the city of Vienna, and in 1972 the Georg Büchner prize.

When Canetti visited Prague for the first time, in May 1937, on a visit to Oskar Kokoschka, he walked the streets of the old city, absorbed not just in the beauty of the architecture, but in the sounds of the unknown language he heard all around him. He cherished the spoken word, in whatever language it manifested itself to his ears, as a priceless personal possession. It lies at the very heart of all his writings.

In 1939, after the *Anschluss*, Canetti took refuge in Britain and settled in Hampstead, where he remained until 1994 and where he wrote his major work, *Masse und Macht* (*Crowds and Power*), in 1960, translated into English in 1962. It was perhaps partly his passion for language that led Canetti to study the psychopathology of power as expressed through the sound and fury of mass movements of society. Canetti was a man who had experienced the violence of crowds as well as the killing quality of certain kinds of dictatorial hectoring language in the social and economic turmoils of Berlin, Zürich, and Vienna. Among the dominating figures of the work are teachers, Shiʿi Muslims, religious extremists, Byzantine emperors, and men of overweening authority like orchestral conductors—'all were raided as examples of the component elements of power' (*The Times*, 19 Aug 1994).

Paradoxically, that agitated, febrile existence in changing communities was to turn Canetti into a semi-recluse. But for someone who was to become a linguist and a writer with a universal vision he started out with the inestimable advantage of being born into a large, talkative, highly dramatic family circle. Later he was able to move with ease in the cultural circles of European cities in which it is natural for educated people to express themselves in several languages, often with inventive fluency.

Canetti's collected plays were issued as *Dramen* in 1964. They were largely unactable, though *Die Befristeten* (*The Numbered*) was given an English production in 1956. An excellent study of Kakfa, *Der andere Prozess* (*Kafka's other Trial*) was issued in 1969.

Veza died in 1963, childless. Canetti married again in

1971 and he and his second wife, Hera Buschor (*d.* 1988), had a daughter, Johanna. He took up a second residence in Zürich, where he composed his other major works, the three absorbing volumes of autobiography: *Der Ohrenzeuge* (*Earwitness*) (1974), *Die gerettete Zunge* (*The Tongue Set Free*) (1977), and *Die Fackel im Ohr* (*The Torch in my Ear*) (1980). In 1981 he was awarded the Nobel prize for literature, and his work was eulogized as being in the great tradition of other Austrian writers of genius, Robert Musil and Hermann Broch. A further volume, *Das Augenspiel Lebensgeschichte*, translated as *The Secret Eye of the Clock*, appeared in 1990. Elias Canetti died on 14 August 1994, at his Zürich home, Klosbachstrasse 88. JAMES KIRKUP

Sources *WW* (1992) · *International who's who* (1994–5) · E. Canetti, *Der Ohrenzeuge* (1974) · E. Canetti, *Die gerettete Zunge* (1977) · E. Canetti, *Die Fackel im Ohr* (1980) · *The Times* (19 Aug 1994) · d. cert.
Likenesses H. Tappe, photograph, *c.*1985, Hult. Arch. · M.-L. von Motesiczky, oils, 1992, NPG
Wealth at death £6423—effects in England: administration with will, 30 July 1997, *CGPLA Eng. & Wales*

Canigiani [Caniziani], **Gherardo** (1424–1484), merchant, was born in Florence, the son of Bernardo di Gherardo Canigiani and his wife, Papera di messer Tommaso Sacchetti. In 1457 he stated that he had a daughter aged twelve named Piera, but nothing is known of his wife. He came to England in 1446 as a factor of the Medici company and probably never returned to Florence. After 1460 he became prominent in the Medici's commercial affairs in England. From 1461 he appears as a lender to the crown and a supplier of textiles to the court. These connections explain why he was used by Edward IV in 1464 as an agent to visit Scotland and distribute bribes to the nobility there. In 1465 the Medici branch in London was reformed by an *accomandita* designating Canigiani and Giovanni de' Bardi as the managers in London. Canigiani contributed £300 to the capital of the branch. From this time he became increasingly independent and prominent in London business.

A series of large loans were made to Edward IV in Canigiani's name. It is impossible to be certain on each occasion whether he was lending Medici money or his own, but the probability is that he was doing business for the Medici. The main loans were £5354 19*s.* 10*d.* in November 1466, £8468 18*s.* 8*d.* in November 1467, £1000 in August 1468, £2610 9*s.* in December 1468, £3225 6*s.* 8*d.* in January 1469, £6600 in July 1471, and £4566 1*s.* 8*d.* in March 1474. Between 1466 and 1471 they totalled over £26,000. These loans were at least partially repaid. In 1468 Canigiani received an elaborate jewel in pawn. He was also at the same time involved in more ordinary trading activities, again presumably doing business on behalf of the Medici. Licences to make substantial exports of wool, cloth, and metal to the Mediterranean at this time were doubtless also intended to repay royal debts. There are documents which show him exporting wool and tin and importing pepper and madder. In 1468 Canigiani advanced money for the payment of the dowry of Margaret of York when she was married to Charles the Bold, duke of Burgundy. It is therefore uncertain whether he was making an overall profit for the Medici, and whether the loans to Edward IV were necessary in order to secure privileges for trade and further business. Lorenzo de' Medici took over control of the Medici position at Florence and its banks elsewhere in Europe in 1469. In 1468 another Medici representative, Angelo Tani, had been sent to London by Piero de' Medici, Lorenzo's father, and had expressed disquiet at the large sums lent to the crown and the slow repayment of them. Lorenzo expressed disquiet himself in 1470, and two years later sent Cristofano Spini to London with instructions to encourage Tommaso Portinari, the Medici manager in Bruges, to keep control of the London business.

Canigiani was probably removed from the Medici branch in 1473. The main cause of the sacking may have been Spini's hostile criticism; it is clear that the two men became bitter enemies. Another consideration may have been the disaster which occurred in April 1473, when a galley loaded with Medici goods on its way from Zeeland to Southampton and Pisa was captured by pirates from Danzig. Canigiani attempted to reduce the damage by sending large numbers of cloths to be exported in the accompanying galley, which managed to reach Southampton. But he was replaced as Medici representative in London by Tommaso Guidetti.

Perhaps in response to Medici disapproval, Canigiani secured denization on 3 November 1473. By January 1474 he was already married to Elizabeth, widow of Sir John Stockton, with whom he had a son in 1476. He evidently retained the approval of the king. In December 1473 he was granted the position of keeper of the exchange at Calais, jointly with William Hatteclyffe (*d.* 1480), the king's secretary, for seven years, and this was renewed for four years in 1480. In July 1474 he was granted the manor of Great Linford, Buckinghamshire, and custody of the lands of Alice Lovel. Lorenzo de' Medici's *Promemoria* of 1478, a statement about the finances of his company, stated that the losses of his London branch amounted to 78,000 ducats (about £14,000 sterling), but still the Medici continued to do business in London. It is not clear how far Canigiani was responsible for the losses. He died in 1484. GEORGE HOLMES

Sources M. Mallett, 'Canigiani, Gherardo', *Dizionario biografico degli Italiani*, ed. A. M. Ghisalberti, 18 (Rome, 1975) · M. E. Mallett, 'Anglo-Florentine commercial relations, 1465–91', *Economic History Review*, 2nd ser., 15 (1962–3) · *Lettere*, ed. N. Rubinstein (Florence, 1977–) · *Chancery records* · R. de Roover, *Il banco Medici dalle origini al declino, 1397–1494* (1970) · L. Lyell and F. D. Watney, eds., *Acts of court of the Mercers' Company, 1453–1527* (1936) · A. H. Thomas and P. E. Jones, eds., *Calendar of plea and memoranda rolls preserved among the archives of the corporation of the City of London at the Guildhall*, 6 vols. (1926–61) · G. Holmes, 'Lorenzo de' Medici's London branch', *Progress and problems in medieval England: essays in honour of Edward Miller*, ed. R. Britnell and J. Hatcher (1996), 273–85 · P. Nightingale, *A medieval mercantile community: the Grocers' Company and the politics and trade of London, 1000–1485* (1995) · Catasti, Archivi di Stato, Florence · Mediceo avanti il Principato, Archivi di Stato, Florence · exchequer records, PRO

Canir (*fl.* **6th cent.**). *See under* Munster, saints of (*act. c.*450–*c.*700).

Cann, Abraham (*bap.* 1794, *d.* 1864), wrestler, the son of Robert Cann, a farmer and a wrestler in Devon, and his wife, Mary, was baptized at Colebrooke, near Crediton, Devon, on 2 December 1794. Having inherited from his father a love of sport, he soon defeated John Jordan, Flower, Wreyford, Simon Webber, and the other best wrestlers in Devon, and carried off the prizes at all the places where he became a competitor. He won early fame wrestling in the Devon fashion—namely, wearing shoes and endeavouring to disable his adversary by violently kicking him on the legs. He was a handsome man of athletic build with black curly hair, and was noted for his rapidity of movement. Wrestling was currently popular in London and there on 21 September 1826, at The Eagle tavern, City Road, wrestling without shoes, Cann won the first prize against James Warren of Redruth (conspicuous for his bravery at the time of the loss of the *Kent*, Indiaman, in 1825). As acknowledged champion of Devon, he now had his most famous contest, against James Polkinghorne, the champion of Cornwall, 6 feet 2 inches tall and weighing 320 lb. This match, which was for £200 a side for the best of three back falls, took place at Tamar Green, Morice Town, near Devonport, on 23 October 1826, before more than 12,000 spectators. After a long struggle the two men had thrown each other in turn. Disputed falls followed on either side and Polkinghorne left the ring claiming victory, but after much wrangling the match was declared to be drawn. After further successes in London and Leeds, Cann was eventually beaten by the young Cornishman Oliver, and he spent many years as the proprietor of an inn. In 1861 Lord Palmerston headed a subscription among west-country gentlemen, by which the sum of £200 was presented to the former champion. Cann died at Colebrooke on 7 April 1864. He had four brothers—James (the most noted of them), Robert, George, and William—all of whom were wrestlers. He married a lady 'connected with a most respectable family'.

Abraham Cann (*bap.* 1794, *d.* 1864), by unknown artist, *c.*1850

G. C. Boase, *rev.* Dennis Brailsford

Sources P. Egan, *Pierce Egan's book of sports* (1832), 53–4, 326–35 · *Sporting Magazine* (1826–7) · *The Times* (23 Sept 1826) · *Illustrated Sporting News* (7 May 1864), 100–01, 111 · d. cert.

Likenesses portrait, *c.*1850, Exeter City Museums and Art Gallery [*see illus.*] · H. B., lithograph, BM · two portraits, repro. in *Illustrated Sporting News*

Cannan, Charles (1858–1919), Aristotelian scholar and publisher, was born at Richmond, Surrey, on 2 August 1858, son of David Alexander Cannan (1820–1877), a building contractor of Kirkcudbrightshire, and his wife, Jane Dorothea Claude (1822–1861), a Sunday school teacher of Huguenot descent. His brother was the economist Edwin *Cannan (1861–1935). He was educated at Clifton College and at Corpus Christi College, Oxford. Cannan was elected fellow of Trinity College, Oxford, in 1884. He became classical tutor and dean in 1884, and junior bursar in 1887.

After an accomplished period as an unorthodox tutor and lecturer Cannan was elected a delegate of Oxford University Press in 1895, and the direction of his career was determined when in 1898 the delegates appointed him their secretary in succession to Philip Lyttelton Gell. He remained in the post until his death, and made Oxford what he deemed 'it ought to be: the first Press in the world' (Sutcliffe, 107). In 1891 he married Mary Wedderburn (1857–1943), daughter of Andrew Wedderburn of Glencair, Kirkcudbrightshire. They had three daughters: Dorothea, who married the printer and assistant secretary to the delegates John Johnson; Joanna Maxwell *Cannan (1896–1961), children's writer; and May. Cannan died at his home, Magdalen Gate House, Oxford, on 15 December 1919, his wife surviving him; he was buried three days later in Holywell cemetery.

During his secretaryship Cannan promoted great expansion in the press's business and in the number of its branches overseas. By nature conservative and cautious, he seldom seemed to initiate far-reaching changes of policy. He conceived of the press as an institution possessing inherited characters and a natural growth. He saw himself as fostering its growth rather than as giving it new directions.

Cannan's greatest reform concerned the press's London office. From here, Henry Frowde had distributed titles and managed the Bible and prayer book business. Cannan saw that the time had come for Oxford men to direct the office. The changes which he made, especially Humphrey Milford's appointment as publisher in 1913, turned the London office into a real university department. Cannan also encouraged fresh projects, including *The Oxford Book of English Verse*, the Oxford Classical Texts, and the revival of the seventeenth-century Fell types, notably in Robert Bridges' *The Yattendon Hymnal* (1899). He was secretary when in 1917 the descendants of George Smith offered the *Dictionary of National Biography* to the press. Cannan was already in dispute with Sidney Lee, hitherto the editor,

Charles Cannan (1858–1919), by Gillman & Co., 1918

about a contract and the acceptance of the *Dictionary of National Biography* was problematic. John Johnson, the assistant secretary, recalled in a letter: 'Cannan hated Sidney Lee, had quarrelled with Sir Charles Firth … disliked A. F. Pollard and altogether regarded the D.N.B. as a white elephant. They were the most melancholy Delegates meetings I ever remember before the gift was finally accepted' (Matthew, 7).

Cannan was a conservative and an imperialist, but not a party man. Local affairs interested him, and he sat on Oxford city council. He was an influential presence on Oxford's committee of appointments, but made few public appearances. He rarely left Oxford except on mountaineering holidays. Rugby football, proofs of *The Oxford English Dictionary*, the daily newspaper, and Aristotle were his other pastimes. His single, anonymous book was the *Selecta ex organo Aristotelio capitula* (1897).

Cannan's manner was formidable. His enthusiasms were unspoken. His tone was dry, even cynical. He had a mean opinion of human intelligence in general, and not a very high one of human probity. His last weapon, which he used ruthlessly, was silence. This is, perhaps, not the description of a great man, or even a lovable one. Yet Cannan was both. Those who knew him saw a man of great intellectual power and subtlety; of rare determination; and of unselfish devotion to the things he loved.

MARTIN MAW

Sources *DNB* • P. Sutcliffe, *The Oxford University Press: an informal history* (1978) • M. W. Cannan, *Grey ghosts and voices* (1976) • *Oxford Magazine* (23 Jan 1920), 167–9 • *Oxford Magazine* (12 March 1920), 276–7 • *The Times* (16 Dec 1919) • *The Periodical*, 7 (1920), 99–102 • *The Clarendonian*, 1 (1919), 97–8 • *WWW* • Foster, *Alum. Oxon.* • H. C. G. Matthew, *Leslie Stephen and the 'New Dictionary of National Biography'* (1997)

Archives Bodl. Oxf., letters to Gilbert Murray • Bodl. Oxf., corresp. with Sir Aurel Stein

Likenesses Gillman & Co., photograph, 1918, NPG [*see illus.*] • E. Walker, photogravure, *c.*1918, NPG • photographs

Wealth at death £18,367 16*s.* 8*d.*: probate, 11 Feb 1920, *CGPLA Eng. & Wales*

Cannan, Edwin (1861–1935), economist, was born on 3 February 1861 at Funchal, Madeira, son of David Alexander Cannan (1820–1877) of Kirkcudbrightshire, formerly a manufacturer's agent, and his wife, Jane Dorothea (1822–1861), formerly Claude. Charles *Cannan was his elder brother; an elder sister was born in the mid-1850s while David and Jane were in Australia, but she died in infancy. A substantial legacy was left to Jane in 1854; it was her poor health during the later 1850s that precipitated first a move from Richmond, Surrey, to Bournemouth, and subsequently to Madeira. She died there thirteen days after giving birth to Edwin, who was named after his godfather, Edwin Chadwick, a close friend of David Cannan (Kadish, *Oxford Economists*, 6–7). David Cannan and his two sons soon returned to Bournemouth to live with his older sister, Agnes, and then, following her death in 1864, with another sister, Margaret. In 1868 David married Eliza Weekes and the family moved to her school, Aschan House; Eliza, however, died in the following year.

Edwin Cannan, who was colour-blind, tone-deaf, and of a delicate constitution, attended Aschan House School, and then in 1876 followed his brother, Charles, to Clifton College, the family having moved to Bristol so that Edwin might attend as a day boy. The following year David Cannan died while touring Ireland, bequeathing to each of his sons, neither yet twenty, a comfortable private income. Edwin entered Balliol College, Oxford, in January 1881 as a commoner, and moved with his aunt Margaret into rooms at 24 St Giles', where they were to share a simple daily routine for many years. Poor health during the spring of 1882 prompted Edwin to abandon his plans to sit for an honours degree; instead in 1884 he took a pass degree, and then embarked on a trip around the world with his aunt (Kadish, *Oxford Economists*, 10). Having returned to Oxford, Edwin began to work up an essay on Saint-Simon (1675–1755) for the Lothian prize, which he was awarded in 1885.

Cannan's fragile health ruled out the peripatetic rigours of lecturing for the Oxford extension, and in any event his private income meant that he was not, like many of his contemporaries, impelled into teaching political economy to earn a living. Another essay was entered, unsuccessfully, for the Cobden prize in 1886; a revised section was published as *Elementary Political Economy* (1888), and his 1889 paper to the Fabian Society (E. Cannan, 'Economics and socialism', in *The Economic Outlook*, 1912, 53–86) also built on the Cobden essay. Through this latter paper he came to know Sidney Webb, who later persuaded Cannan to join the part-time staff of the London School of Economics (LSE) when it opened in 1895. This proved to be a turning point in Cannan's life, for the vigour that he brought to the school belied the fragile health of his youth. He was appointed professor of political economy in 1907, the year of his marriage, on 12 June, at Cheltenham, in a Presbyterian ceremony, to his second cousin, Margaret Mary (Rita) Cullen (*b.* 1870/71), daughter of David Cullen (deceased), who had been deputy surgeon-general; they had one son, David Ricardo, who died in 1918. Cannan retired from his LSE chair in 1926 after joining with Graham Wallas and A. L. Bowley as a founder editor of the school's journal *Economica*.

Oxford was at the centre of academic economics in Britain during the 1880s. Interest in political economy was linked to a wider concern for social reform and Irish home rule, both of which found expression in a number of university and college societies in which Cannan actively participated. Among his student contemporaries were W. J. Ashley, E. C. K. Gonner, Langford Price, and H. L. Smith, while Alfred Marshall succeeded Arnold Toynbee for a brief spell as tutor at Balliol in 1883 before leaving at the end of 1884 for Cambridge. At this time in Oxford political economy was taught in the context of modern history, and a broadly historical approach marked Oxford economics well into the twentieth century. Early influenced by the historian A. L. Smith, Cannan's Lothian essay is an unremarkable historical biography of the life and times not of the social thinker Saint-Simon, but of an aristocratic predecessor. *Elementary Political Economy* is, however, a broadly unhistorical text, expounding classical principles with aggressive common sense, notable mainly for a wilful avoidance of the term 'capital' and a consequent resort to obscure circumlocution. As his *Times* obituarist later observed, 'In controversy he may not always have hit the right nail, but he hit it on the head, and hit it very hard' (*The Times*, 9 April 1935).

The History of the Theories of Production and Distribution (1893) is by contrast a work of some scholarship, but even a cursory glance reveals that Cannan's approach was at once more analytical and critical than historical. He eschewed formal and mathematical reasoning, judging his subject matter in terms of current 'good sense', a quality he rarely encountered in his reading of the classical economists. Alfred Marshall, he thought, was too soft on these writers; W. S. Jevons provided the underlying theoretical principles by which all economics, past and present, should be measured. By this standard the classical economists were woefully inadequate, argued Cannan (Maloney, 70), but as practical responses to contemporary problems their abstractions made more sense. Cannan criticized past economic theory from the standpoint of modern economics, and then used history to account for its shortcomings—the reverse of what one might have expected of a historically inclined economist. This was because he saw himself primarily as an economic theorist building upon, and renovating where necessary, the established body of classical doctrine—for he remained until his death a classical rather than a neo-classical theorist, despite his admiration for the work of Jevons.

Cannan's most lasting contribution was as an editor of Adam Smith, where his acuity and scholarship are displayed at their best. In 1895 a chance encounter with an Edinburgh lawyer brought into his hands a set of student notes from Smith's Glasgow lectures of 1763. Since Smith's executors had (on Smith's instructions) destroyed most of his papers when he died, the discovery of this notebook contributed significantly to understanding of the work. Cannan published the notes as *Lectures on Justice, Police, Revenue and Arms* (1896), and this edition was not superseded until an augmented edition appeared in 1978. Similarly, in 1904 he published an edition of Smith's *Wealth of Nations* that remained the standard critical text until 1976.

In the early 1890s Cannan became a regular contributor on legislative and administrative matters to the new Oxford-based *Economic Review*, and developed an especial interest in the evolution of local government taxation. This formed the subject of his first course of lectures at the LSE in 1895, published the following year (1896) as an account of the early modern statutory foundation of local systems of taxation. His teaching for the school developed rapidly, combining in his core lectures the history of economics with an appraisal of recent economic theory based upon a critical evaluation of Marshallian economics. The first-year lectures on economic principles that he gave were written up as the introductory textbook *Wealth* (1914), a copy of which was placed in a time capsule under a foundation-stone for an extension laid at the school by the king in May 1920 (*Economic Journal*, 30, 1920, 278–9). The second- and third-year theory lectures delivered from the early 1900s until his retirement were likewise written up and published (1929).

Cannan's commitment to teaching at the LSE contrasts with his earlier Oxford years, but he continued to live in Oxford, commuting daily on the train. Lionel Robbins, a student after the First World War, reported that he was a poor, though informative, lecturer, lacking familiarity with modern economic developments (Robbins, *Autobiography*, 83–6)—by which Robbins probably means American and European developments, for Cannan had attended Marshall's lectures in the winter of 1891–2 and demonstrates in *A Review of Economic Theory* an easy familiarity with Marshallian principles. Cannan belonged to an earlier age, when historical and practical interests went naturally together. This was also true of his interest in local government, for he was elected by the university to Oxford city council in 1896 and served his city for many years. At the national level his chief engagement was as a critic of economic administration. Anticipating the question 'What did you do in the Great War?' in the preface to a collection of occasional pieces and letters dating from the period 1914–26, he responds: 'I protested' (E. Cannan, *An Economist's Protest*, 1927, v). War finance and its inflationary domestic impact prompted an interest in earlier debates on paper money, which led to an edition of the 1810 bullion report coupled with a lengthy essay on its historical context entirely within the same combative spirit (1919).

Cannan was a keen gardener and a cyclist who never walked if he could cycle, 'at any time prepared to ride a hundred miles, and the story is told that when he failed to find a book at the Bodleian, he merely said "—then I must go on to the British Museum"' (Bowley, 392). He died on 8 April 1935 of pneumonia and cardiac failure at Bournemouth Hydropathic, Durley Gardens, Bournemouth; his funeral was held on 11 April at Wolvercote, Oxford. He was survived by his wife. KEITH TRIBE

Sources BLPES, Cannan MSS · *The Times* (9 April 1935) · A. L. Bowley, 'Edwin Cannan', *Economic Journal*, 45 (1935), 385–92 · L. Robbins, 'A student's recollections of Edwin Cannan', *Economic Journal*, 45 (1935), 393–8 · T. E. Gregory, 'Edwin Cannan: a personal impression', *Economica*, new ser., 2 (1935), 365–79 · T. E. Gregory and H. Dalton, *London essays in economics: in honour of Edwin Cannan* (1927) · F. A. Hayek, 'Edwin Cannan', *Zeitschrift für Nationalökonomie*, 6 (1935), 246–50; repr. in *The collected works of F. A. Hayek*, ed. B. Caldwell, 9: *Contra Keynes and Cambridge, essays, correspondence* (1995), 64–9 · L. Robbins, *Autobiography of an economist* (1971) · A. Kadish, *The Oxford economists in the late nineteenth century* (1982) · J. Maloney, *Marshall, orthodoxy and the professionalisation of economics* (1985) · A. Kadish, 'Oxford economists in the later nineteenth century', *The market for political economy: the advent of economics in British university culture, 1850–1905*, ed. A. Kadish and K. Tribe (1993), 42–76 · D. P. O'Brien, 'Edwin Cannan: economic theory and the history of economic thought', *Reseach in the History of Economic Thought and Methodology*, 17 (1999), 1–21 · m. cert. · d. cert. · *DNB*

Archives Balliol Oxf., notebooks · BLPES, corresp. and papers | BLPES, corresp. relating to Royal Economic Society · King's AC Cam., letters to J. M. Keynes

Likenesses portrait, repro. in Gregory and Dalton, eds., *London essays in economics*, frontispiece

Wealth at death £57,304 9s. 0d.: probate, 16 July 1935, *CGPLA Eng. & Wales*

Cannan, Gilbert Eric (1884–1955), translator and writer, was born on 25 June 1884 at 24 Great Cheetham Street West, in Broughton, Manchester. One of nine children, he was the second son of Henry Angus Cannan, an ill-paid Scottish shipping clerk, and (Grace Charlotte) Violet, the daughter of the Revd Francis Arbuthnot Wright, an Anglican clergyman whose enthusiasms and hospitality did not match his income. Cannan's parents were loving, but feckless, and as a child Cannan wondered sometimes whether he was a changeling. Overshadowed by Angus, his tough-minded and clever elder brother, he was given to long bouts of crying, which were probably the first symptoms of the insanity which was eventually to cast a cloud over his life. Cannan attended Ducie Avenue board school from where, to his parents' surprise, he won a foundation scholarship to Manchester grammar school in 1898. Here he quickly made his mark in modern languages, winning prizes every year until he left in 1902, with an open modern languages exhibition to King's College, Cambridge, partly on the strength of a brilliant essay on Schiller. At Cambridge he was noted for an aloofness, which may have masked a sense of insecurity. He read voraciously in German, French, and English, made no close friends, and left with a formidable knowledge of European culture, but only a pass degree, which suggests either a breakdown in health, or a failure to adhere to the prescribed texts.

After university Cannan read for the bar, but later abandoned the law in order to write. He was tall and fair with an emperor's nose, and also quickly gained a foothold in literary and theatrical circles. Following a passionate but unconsummated love affair with Kathleen Bruce, who married Robert Scott, the explorer, Cannan became involved with Mary, *née* Ansell (1868/9–1950), James Barrie's wife, while working as secretary of the Society for the Abolition of Censorship. In 1909 he was cited as the co-respondent in the divorce which ensued and, against the advice of H. G. Wells and others, married her out of a sense of chivalry on 28 April 1910.

Cannan started his translation of Romain Rolland's four-volume masterpiece, *Jean Christophe*, in 1907. His own first novel, *Peter Homunculus* (1909), was published in the year he became a theatre critic and, from that time on, novels, reviews, sociological and philosophical books, short plays, poems, and translations poured from Cannan's pen. In 1913 he reached a wider public with *Round the Corner*, a novel based on the life of his maternal grandfather and family, whose perverse and flamboyant lifestyle gave Cannan ample scope for a dense and deeply felt story. Other novels draw on the lives of his paternal forebears and relatives: *Little Brother* (1912) cruelly depicts Edwin *Cannan (1861–1935), the economist, who supported Cannan financially until his marriage, and in *The Stucco House* (1917) is a vivid portrait of Cannan's grandfather, James Cannan, a provincial journalist, bank clerk, and theatre critic for the *Manchester News*. At twenty-five, Cannan declared, he had a very clear conception of the industrial revolution seen through the spiritual history of his family.

In 1913 the Cannans moved to a converted windmill in Cholesbury, Buckinghamshire, where they entertained writers and artists, including D. H. Lawrence, Katherine Mansfield, David Garnett, and Compton Mackenzie. They were also taken up by Ottoline Morrell. Mark Gertler used the mill's garage as a studio; Vladimir Polunin decorated Cannan's study with a frieze; and S. S. Koteliansky worked with him on translations from the Russian. In 1916 Cannan's novel *Mendel*, based on the life of Mark Gertler, caused outrage. His marriage broke up; he fled to London, and, living alone in shabby rooms, became increasingly unstable, but continued to write and translate.

On 11 April 1918 Mary Cannan was granted a judicial separation after Cannan fell in love with a radiant nineteen-year-old South African, Gwen Wilson, an affair which probably postponed his final breakdown. The couple rented a studio in St John's Wood, London, and took as a lodger Henry Mond, later Lord Melchett. This arrangement subsequently resulted in a *ménage à trois* which became a talking point in literary London. In 1920, while Cannan was lecturing in North America and raising money for D. H. Lawrence, Mond married Gwen Wilson, a blow from which Cannan never recovered. Desolate, he travelled across Africa, mostly by horse, sending back dispatches to the *New York Freeman*, which were published in a book, *Letters from a Distance* (1923). On his return, homeless and alone but still writing, he descended into violent madness. Certified insane in April 1924, Cannan became a patient in The Priory, Roehampton, London, where he wrote paranoic letters destined for the dustbin. His translation of *A. O. Barnabooth: his Diary* came out to good reviews that autumn.

In fifteen hectic years Cannan wrote twenty-seven books, countless articles, scores of poems, and at least fourteen one- and two-act plays, of which the best-known were *Everybody's Husband* (1917) and *Miles Dixon*, which the *Manchester Guardian* critic likened to the work of Synge. In 1913 Henry James had described Cannan as one of four up-and-coming authors, with D. H. Lawrence 'in the dusty rear' (Farr, 116). St John Hankin remarked that 'Shaw, Barker and Galsworthy all believe Cannan is going to wipe them out' (ibid., 88). Such praise caused resentment. Lawrence in a furious moment called Cannan a 'soap pill' (J. Boulton, ed., *The Letters of D. H. Lawrence*, 7 vols., 1979–93) and Lytton Strachey described him as 'an empty bucket' (Farr, 65). Yet few knew his fate, for only Gwen Melchett and, later, Edwin Cannan's widow, Rita, were allowed to visit him at The Priory.

In 1952 Cannan was moved to a freer regime at Holloway Sanatorium, Virginia Water, Surrey, where he died of cancer on 30 June 1955, leaving one possession, a barrister's moth-eaten wig. He was cremated in Woking.

DIANA FARR

Sources private information (2004) [family] · D. Farr, *Gilbert Cannan: a Georgian prodigy* (1978) · M. Ansell, *Dogs and men* (1924) · M. Ansell, *Happy houses* (1912) · M. Ansell, *The happy garden* (1912) · J. M. Barrie, *Letters*, ed. V. Meynell (1942) · D. Garnett, *The golden echo* (1953) · *The collected letters of D. H. Lawrence*, ed. H. T. Moore, 2 vols. (1962) · *Ottoline: the early memoirs of Lady Ottoline Morrell*, ed. R. Gathorne-Hardy (1963) · *Ottoline at Garsington: memoirs of Lady Ottoline Morrell, 1915–1918*, ed. R. Gathorne-Hardy (1974) · F. Swinnerton, *The Georgian literary scene, 1910–1935*, rev. edn (1969) · b. cert. · m. cert. · d. cert.

Archives CUL, corresp. and papers, incl. letters with biographer · Yale U., Beinecke L. | BL, letters to S. S. Koteliansky, Add. MS 48974, fols. 1, 5–12, 72–3 · CUL, letters to Lady Kennet · JRL, letters to Allan Monkhouse · Merton Oxf., Max Beerbohm collection, letters · NYPL, Berg collection, letters · Ransom HRC, letters to Ottoline Morrell and Compton Mackenzie · University of Illinois, Chicago, Rare Book Library, H. G. Wells collection, letters

Likenesses M. Gertler, portrait, 1915–16, AM Oxf.

Wealth at death £413 16*s*. 6*d*.: administration, 10 May 1956, *CGPLA Eng. & Wales*

Cannan [*married name* Pullein-Thompson], **Joanna Maxwell (1896–1961)**, novelist and children's writer, was born on 27 May 1896 at Magdalen Gate House, Oxford, the third and youngest daughter of Charles *Cannan (1858–1919), dean of Trinity College, Oxford, and secretary to the delegates of Oxford University Press, and his wife, Mary (1857–1943), daughter of Andrew Wedderburn, a Scot in the Indian Civil Service. Charles Cannan was intellectual, immersed in Aristotelian scholarship, and Mary Cannan preferred adult company. Apart from three mornings a week at Wychwood School, their daughters lived in solitude at home, playing out romantic dramas based on favourite books, or the heroic tales of their Scottish ancestors. Holidays spent riding and boating in the highlands, or climbing in the Lake District and Switzerland, reinforced their ideals of courage and determination. Cannan grew up with a lifelong philosophy of persevering against the odds, and meeting success or failure with light-hearted gallantry.

Cannan was educated at Wychwood School in Oxford from 1902 to 1913, and then went to finishing school in Paris. She planned to study at the Slade School of Fine Art, but the 1914–18 war prevented this. On 11 June 1918 she married Captain Harold James Pullein-Thompson (1885–1957), son of James Pullein-Thompson, a Church of England clergyman ministering in London, and his wife, Emily, *née* Darbyshire. He had an impressive war record, and Cannan admired his commanding ways with waiters and taxi drivers, but his inability to make a peacetime living shook her. Marooned in suburban Wimbledon, she determined to earn money herself by writing. Her first novel, *The Misty Valley* (1922), was well received, and followed quickly by others, until in 1931 Cannan felt wealthy enough to buy The Grove, Peppard Common, a white Oxfordshire dower house.

Here, with her husband, four children, and innumerable animals, Cannan created a congenially bohemian lifestyle. After her restricted childhood she wanted freedom for her family and herself. There might be domestic and financial crises, bantams in the kitchen and hiccups with the boiler, but, ensconced in her small parlour, she worked away steadily at her novels. These were witty, satirical, even cynical, and usually well reviewed. She presented clashes between idealists and materialists, with no easy solutions. Often she drew on her own experiences. *The Misty Valley* dissects a difficult marriage; *High Table* (1930) depicts Oxford dons; *Ithuriel's Hour* (1931) portrays the stresses of mountaineering. Later in her career she tried some traditional English detective stories. From *Death at The Dog* (1940) to *Murder Included* (1950), they featured a socially inept detective, Pryce, who became a further butt for Cannan's sarcastic wit.

A Pony for Jean (1936) was Cannan's first children's story. Previously pony books were animal biographies, like *Black Beauty*. Cannan, watching her children and their ponies, switched the focus of interest to the rider, establishing a major new trend, later followed by her daughters, Josephine, Diana, and Christine Pullein-Thompson. After Cannan most 'pony books' were 'rider books', stories of children schooling much-loved, if recalcitrant, ponies; yet hers, with their passion for animals and country life, and their stylish writing, remain pre-eminent. Jean, the brave determined girl who is also the heroine of two sequels, *Another Pony for Jean* (1938) and *More Ponies for Jean* (1943), is a self-portrait; while the Pullein-Thompson girls provided inspiration for the lively, horsy children of *They Bought her a Pony* (1944), who bicker, and fall off, and make gymkhana stars of their unpromising mounts.

Small, slight, and fair, with myopic grey-green eyes, Cannan lived enthusiastically, but hard work and wartime privations undermined her health. In 1952 tuberculosis was diagnosed. Weakened further by surgery, she died of heart failure following influenza at Blandford Cottage Hospital, Dorset, on 22 April 1961, reciting Landor's 'I strove with none, for none was worth my strife' to maintain her courage to the end. She was buried at Fairmile cemetery, Henley-on-Thames. ANGELA BULL

Sources J. Pullein-Thompson, D. Pullein-Thompson, and C. Pullein-Thompson, *Fair girls on grey horses* (1996) • M. W. Cannan, *Grey ghosts and voices* (1976) • J. Pullein-Thompson, 'Masterpiece on a tight rein', *Oxford Mail* (18 Dec 1987) • A. Bull, 'Joanna Cannan', *Souvenir*, 2 (summer 1986) • private information (2004) [D. Farr]

Canne, John (*d.* 1667?), Independent minister and printer, may have been born in Bristol; details of his parents and early life are unknown. He possibly matriculated at Christ's College, Cambridge, in 1602. In the 1620s he was the 'teacher' of Deadman's Place Independent Church, London, after the congregation's return from exile in Ireland. By 1632 he was in Amsterdam where he worked for a printer and where, having first reconciled some members of Henry Ainsworth's congregation, he became leader of the English Brownists. Here he published his most important book, *A Necessitie of Separation from the Church of England, Proved by the Nonconformists' Principles* (1634), which called for total separation from the Church of England since its ministry, worship, constitution, and government were fatally corrupt.

Canne's press seems to have been the successor to that of the exiled English church in Amsterdam, bearing the 'Richt Right' impress. The report of one of Archbishop Laud's agents in the Low Countries that a number of the books held there were subversive was accurate: the press printed material advocating the overthrow of bishops, rejecting the parish church because it had no way of excluding the unregenerate, and censuring those who listened to its clergy. In 1637 Canne was fined £300 by an Amsterdam tribunal for printing literature prejudicial to Charles I. The press apparently embodied Canne's own major convictions, and its products can plausibly be seen to have 'helped to create the Millenarian agitation which issued in the Fifth Monarchism of the 1650s' (Wilson). The impress ceased after 1641, when unlicensed printing became possible in England, and the press probably returned to the printing of small bibles.

In 1639 Canne had replied to John Robinson's criticism of *A Necessitie of Separation* with *A Stay Against Straying*, which asserted 'the unlawfulness of hearing the ministers of all false churches'. By 1640, when he visited England, he held millenarian views. A claim that in 1642 Canne, as an Anabaptist, founded the first Baptist church in Bristol on the basis of principles outlined in *A Necessitie of Separation* is without foundation. He remained in Amsterdam until at least 1645, although he kept in touch with events in England.

By 1647 Canne was in London where he became chaplain to Colonel Robert Lilburne. Having previously been associated with Levellers such as Robert Overton he turned against them in the crisis of that year and wrote attacking them as atheists. He was also involved in the publication in 1647 of an annotated reference Bible, the best work of its kind to that date, which was to form the basis of many later editions. Over the next few years he also wrote tracts supporting the trial of Charles I, denouncing the national covenant, and exhorting the government to make best use of its victories in Ireland and Scotland. From 1650 he was chaplain to Colonel Robert Overton in Hull, where he was so popular with the army that he was given permission to wall up the arches between the chancel and the main part of the parish church for his meetings. In the remainder of the church the preacher John Shaw boasted that he had 'constantly above 3000 hearers' (*DNB*): Shaw and Canne clashed on a number of occasions and in various places on the fundamental issue of separation, and inaugurated a major pamphlet debate.

Canne had supported the execution of the king as 'God's work', and he worked tirelessly for the Commonwealth, apparently succeeding Marchamount Nedham as its newswriter. The Rump's failure to extirpate the established church rankled, however. In 1653 Canne's *A Voyce from the Temple* supported Cromwell as the one who would guide England in the last days, and he was reported to exercise considerable influence with the council of state. On 9 June that year he was given by the government an exclusive licence for seven years to print another edition of the annotated Bible, but eventually the failure of Cromwell's regime too to introduce thoroughgoing reformation of church and state produced disillusionment. In *Truth with Time* (1656) Canne warned that 'none of the last seven plagues … are yet poured out'. As the Fifth Monarchists' 'most significant spokesman' (G. F. Nuttall, *Visible Saints*, 1957, 147) Canne, with other leaders, broke with Cromwell in September 1656. This period was a difficult one for Canne, who attributed to his constant harassment by the authorities the deaths of his daughter Deliverance, buried at Holy Trinity, Hull, on 18 December 1656, and of his wife, Agnees, buried there on 20 January 1657. His expulsion from the town about this time drew from his antagonist Shaw a stinging epigram:

> Is John departed? Is Canne dead and gone?
> Farewell to both, to Canne and eke to John;
> Yet being dead take this advice from me,
> Let not them both in one grave buried be;
> But lay John here, and lay Canne thereabout,
> For if they both should meet, they would fall out.

In *The End of Time* (1657), which had prefaces by bellicose Fifth Monarchist leaders Christopher Freake and John Rogers, Canne predicted Cromwell's demise within three and a half years, suggesting that he was in fact the 'little horn' in the book of Daniel, while Freake compared the protector to Barabbas. Canne never advocated violent insurrection, being confident that God would begin his reign of a thousand years at his own appointed time. However, in April 1658, just two months after the crushing of Venner's ill-fated rising, Canne was arrested while preaching at a Fifth Monarchist service in Swan Alley, Coleman Street, London, after a meeting with others in a house in Bartholomew Lane—an incident described in *A Narrative wherein is Faithfully Set Forth the Sufferings of John Canne* (1658). Canne and others were brought before magistrates; some were fined and imprisoned, but no charges were brought. Within three days of the ending of the protectorate,

Canne, in *A Seasonable Word to the Parliament Men* (1659), welcomed the restoration of civil liberties to the people, but feared nothing would be done for 'the vindication of God's glory'. He initially supported the government, becoming its official newswriter and editing the papers *Mercurius Politicus* and the *Public Intellegencer*, but he was removed in August.

After the Restoration, Canne continued active propagation of his Fifth Monarchist views. By 1664 he was back in Amsterdam, from where he issued a revised version of his annotated Bible, a useful, painstaking work which was reprinted many times over the next century and later translated into Welsh. Canne died in Amsterdam, probably in 1667. ROGER HAYDEN

Sources *A necessitie of separation from the Church of England, proved by the nonconformists' principles, by John Canne*, ed. C. Stovel, Hanserd Knollys Society (1849) · C. Burrage, 'Was John Canne a Baptist? A study of contemporary evidence', *Transactions of the Baptist Historical Society*, 3 (1912–13), 212–46 · J. Wilson, 'Another look at John Canne', *Church History*, 33 (1964), 34–48 · A. E. Trout, 'Nonconformity in Hull', *Transactions of the Congregational Historical Society*, 9 (1924–6), 29–43, 78–85 · *DNB* · R. Hayden, ed., *The records of a church in Christ in Bristol, 1640–1687*, Bristol RS, 27 (1974), 11–16 · B. Evans, *Early English Baptists* (1864), 2.108 · B. C. Weber, 'Canne, John', Greaves & Zaller, *BDBR* · C. P. Rogers, *The Fifth Monarchy men* (1966) · B. S. Capp, *The Fifth Monarchy Men: a study in seventeenth-century English millenarianism* (1972) · A. Lawrence, *Parliamentary army chaplains, 1642–1651*, Royal Historical Society Studies in History, 59 (1990), 108–9

Cannicus. *See* Cainnech moccu Dálann (521/527–599/600) *under* Munster, saints of (*act. c.*450–*c.*700).

Canning, Charles John, **Earl Canning** (1812–1862), governor-general and first viceroy of India, was born on 14 December 1812 at Gloucester Lodge, an Italianate villa between Kensington and Brompton to the west of London, the third of the four children of George *Canning (1770–1827), foreign secretary and prime minister, and his wife, Joan (1776/7–1837), daughter of General John Scott of Balcomie, Scotland. The Canning family was of Anglo-Irish extraction, while Canning's mother's family, of Scottish descent, was connected to those of Henry Dundas and Lord George Bentinck.

Early years and government service Charles Canning's education was begun at a private school at Putney, and continued at Eton College, which he attended from September 1824 to December 1828. After spending some months studying at a private school operated by a Bedfordshire clergyman, the Revd Thomas Shore, where he met and made friends with the future Lord Harris, a fellow pupil and afterwards governor of Madras, Canning entered Christ Church, Oxford, in December 1829. Among his contemporaries at Christ Church were W. E. Gladstone and the future lords Dalhousie and Elgin, who preceded and followed him as governor-general of India. In 1833 Canning took his degree with first-class honours in classics and a second in mathematics. Two years later, on 5 September 1835, he married Charlotte Stuart (1817–1861) [*see* Canning, Charlotte], elder daughter of Lord Stuart de Rothesay. In August 1836 Canning secured election to parliament as tory member for Warwick. His two elder

Charles John Canning, Earl Canning (1812–1862), by Richard Beard, 1840s?

brothers having both previously died, the second by drowning at Madeira, Canning succeeded on the death of his mother in March 1837 to the peerage which had been created in her favour after her husband's death ten years before. On 24 April 1837 he took his seat in the House of Lords as Viscount Canning of Kilbrahan, county Kilkenny (Ireland).

On the formation of Sir Robert Peel's government in 1841, Lord Canning was appointed under-secretary of state for foreign affairs. He retained that post until the end of 1845, when he became chief commissioner for woods and forests for the final few months prior to the collapse of Peel's government in mid-1846. Canning continued to be a follower of Peel during the remainder of that statesman's life, and, adhering after Peel's death in 1850 to the Peelite party, he declined Lord Derby's offer of the foreign secretaryship when the tory leader attempted unsuccessfully to form an administration on the resignation of Lord John Russell in February 1851. In January 1853 he joined Lord Aberdeen's whig–Peelite coalition government as postmaster-general, but without a place in the cabinet. He continued in this position until Lord Palmerston, who had become prime minister in 1855, nominated him to succeed Lord Dalhousie as governor-general of India. During his years in charge of the postal service Canning reorganized the department in order to ensure the success of the penny post scheme, and secured a place in it for the originator of the scheme, Rowland Hill, who was appointed sole secretary in 1854. Canning also began the practice of submitting to parliament annual reports on the working of the department. In his work as postmaster-general Canning established the reputation for administrative ability, judicious reflection, and careful inquiry that were subsequently to mark his Indian career. As Hill wrote of his superior,

> he is not a man likely to act upon advice in great matters without first being convinced of its soundness; but at the same time … his great ability, diligence, and candour, were likely to bring the means of substantial conviction within his reach. (Maclagan, 18)

Canning assumed the government of India from Lord Dalhousie on 29 February 1856 after a three-month voyage to Calcutta with stops at Bombay and Madras, at the latter place staying with his old schoolfriend Lord Harris, governor of that presidency. Convinced that Britain had a duty to remake India in its own progressive image, Dalhousie had set on foot energetic efforts to introduce the structures of the modern administrative state into the subcontinent and to extend the reach of British authority. To him India owed its railways and telegraphs, its legislative council, and a renewed commitment to a western educational system. Most notably, Dalhousie had overseen the conquest of the Punjab; he had refused to allow the rulers of Nagpur, Satara, and Jhansi to adopt heirs in order to continue their princely rule; in his last month in office he had, over the anguished protests of its ruler, forcibly annexed the rich mid-Gangetic state of Oudh; and in all these territories he had placed in charge officials instructed to displace old aristocratic and landed classes in favour of the settled village and peasant communities. The confidence that India could somehow be reshaped into a modern liberal society was never wholly to disappear, but the tumultuous events of Canning's governor-generalship, above all the uprising of 1857–8, forced Britain dramatically to reconsider its vision of empire and its strategies of imperial governance. Indeed, even before taking office, Canning had been aware of the uncertainties which attended imperial authority. As he told the East India Company directors at a banquet prior to his departure, with an ominous prescience,

> We must not forget that in the sky of India, serene as it is, a cloud may arise, at first no bigger than a man's hand, but which growing larger and larger, may at last threaten to burst, and overwhelm us with ruin. (Kaye, 1.378)

Confronting mutiny and revolt, 1857 During his first year in office Canning had to confront a crisis in Persia, where, along with its neighbour Afghanistan, the British in India endeavoured always, as part of the Great Game in central Asia, to insure in power regimes favourable to themselves rather than their Russian rival. Fearful of the extension of Russian influence in Persia, and through it into western Afghanistan, especially the key city of Herat, which Persian forces had recently occupied, Canning declared war on Persia and sent an expeditionary force into the Persian Gulf. In the end Persia evacuated Herat, and the amir of Afghanistan was given a subsidy to enable him to defend his own territory. During this year as well the first indications arose of impending difficulties in the management of the company's Bengal army. Although the sepoy soldiers of that army had from the outset been enlisted only for duty within India itself, Canning, anxious to provide an adequate garrison for the newly conquered territory of Lower Burma, altered the conditions of employment to require sepoys to serve wherever the army might be sent. This apparent breach of faith, with its corollary, abhorrent to many Hindus on religious grounds, that they might be forced to cross the sea, began the process that, in an army already gorged with conquest and short of officers, was to lead to mutiny. Prompted by the distribution of cartridges for the new Lee Enfield rifles greased with beef and pork fat, which triggered widespread fear of loss of caste among the Bengal sepoys, incidents of indiscipline mounted throughout the first months of 1857 until, on 10 May, the garrison at Meerut murdered its officers, marched on Delhi, massacred the city's European residents, and installed the pensioned Mughal king as ruler. In the course of a few weeks troops throughout northern India, comprising the bulk of the Bengal army, joined the mutiny; at the same time disaffected princes, landholders, and even peasant communities across the extensive region from Delhi to Bihar took advantage of the anarchy that followed the killing or flight of British officials to right grievances, settle old scores, or simply make claims for power and authority on their own behalf. The revolt was especially widespread in the recently annexed province of Oudh, where many of the mutinous sepoys had their homes, and where the dispossessed royal family and landholders provided popular leadership.

Although Canning had not anticipated the scale of the outbreak—indeed no one had—he moved promptly to secure those areas that remained under British control, above all the Punjab under John Lawrence, and he sought reinforcements for the limited British force in India, most immediately by diverting to India troops on their way to China. Inevitably, as the person in charge of the government at the time, he was subjected to intense criticism, especially by the panic-stricken British residents of Calcutta. In part this was due to his refusal to accord this small but influential community any special favour. The white populace resented Canning's reluctance to allow them to form a regiment of volunteers, which, when ultimately enrolled, did very little; they were infuriated by his insistence upon placing the English as well as the Indian language press under censorship; and, hot with passion, they recoiled from his determination, reinforced by his aloof and taciturn personality, to conduct business as usual whenever possible. At the heart of Canning's differences with his countrymen was the nature of the punishment to be meted out to the Indian people. Driven by a fear and anxiety common to colonial settlers in a land they could not wholly master, the British in India sought during 1857 to assuage their desperate sense of vulnerability by a policy of wholesale vengeance in which all Indians were assumed to be untrustworthy and hence complicit in the uprising. This vindictive spirit infused civil and military officers as well as non-official residents, and found its most unbridled expression during the course of General James Neill's march up-country, during which Indians were killed indiscriminately without regard for their behaviour during the revolt. This spirit gained renewed strength from the Cawnpore massacre, in which English women, seen as symbols of English moral purity, were killed (though, contrary to widespread reports, not raped) by mutineers. From the beginning Canning set his face against this cry for bloody revenge. Most notably, in the so-called Clemency Resolution of 31 July 1857, he endeavoured to restrain the activities of the sanguinary special commissions set up to try suspected rebels by withdrawing from them the power of punishing mutineers other than those charged with specific acts, such as the murder of their officers. Continued severity, he cautioned, would only embitter the people and make more difficult the restoration of order. Savagely attacked in the press, this resolution earned the governor-general the derisory title of 'Clemency' Canning; later, when passions had cooled, this title honourably vindicated his commitment to justice and moderation. Nevertheless, a year of racial animosity, by raising walls of mistrust and suspicion, left an enduring mark on the relations between Briton and Indian. No longer could the British so easily adopt towards their Indian subjects what G. O. Trevelyan called 'the lively interest, the credulous partiality of yore' (Metcalf, 296–7).

Policy initiatives, 1858–1859 As the tide of battle shifted in British favour, Canning had to decide how to treat not just the mutinous soldiers but those numerous landholders and peasant communities who had joined the revolt. In Oudh, where participation in the uprising was nearly universal, he determined upon a policy of confiscation. By the so-called Oudh proclamation of March 1858, issued on the occasion of the fall of Lucknow, all proprietary right in the soil in the province with the exception of the lands of five named individuals was forfeit to the government. For the remainder their lives and honour alone were guaranteed, with further indulgence dependent upon evidence of good behaviour and support for the British in the restoration of order. The apparent harshness of this proclamation provoked immediate and widespread protest, above all by the Oudh chief commissioner James Outram, who claimed that the act would drive the province's landholders to a prolonged and desperate resistance. At home the president of the Board of Control, Lord Ellenborough, denounced the proclamation as an act pronouncing 'the disinherison of a people' fighting to secure their legitimate rights and property, while in parliament the issue nearly brought down the recently installed Derby government. Canning, defiant, refused to resign, and throughout justified confiscation as the only act that could avoid an appearance of rewarding rebellion. He insisted further that only 'the distinct orders of superior authority', not mere threats or other rational argument, could move such people as the Indian landholders (Metcalf, 144–5). In the end neither he nor the local authorities, anxious to secure a prompt end to the revolt, could avoid coming to terms with the powerful Oudh chieftains whose opposition fuelled it. As the British armies slowly advanced across the countryside, the *talukdari* chieftains, with only a few exceptions largely along the border with Nepal, submitted, and were rewarded with the return of their estates. Indeed, for the most part, the larger chieftains were treated with such leniency that they obtained not only the lands they had held at the outbreak of the mutiny but those that had been taken from them during the initial settlement of 1856 as well.

The 1858 settlement in Oudh announced a fundamental shift in the British attitude towards India's peoples, and how they should be governed. Angered by the support the Oudh peasantry, the presumed beneficiaries of the province's annexation, had offered to their old chieftains during the revolt, the British turned upon them a cold hostility. As, Canning wrote, 'our endeavour to better, as we thought, the village occupants in Oudh has not been appreciated by them', they deserved 'little consideration from us'. He went on further to argue, on behalf of the new policy of supporting Oudh's rural chieftains, that 'the talookdaree system is the ancient, indigenous, and cherished system of the country' (Metcalf, 133, 148). In doing so Canning effectively undercut the assumptions that had sustained the liberal imperialism of the era of Bentinck and Dalhousie. If the Oudh villagers did not pursue what men like Canning saw as their own best interest, but instead clung irrationally to their traditional ways, then the larger enterprise of reform was pointless if not fraught with danger. That loyalty to their deposed king and sepoy brethren, as well as the need to possess powerful patrons in a time of anarchy, might adequately explain why the villagers' behaviour made no difference to the British, obsessed with meting out punishment for ingratitude. Hence the British unhesitatingly overturned the 1856 settlement, and consigned the bulk of the Oudh peasantry to the status of tenants-at-will on the estates of landlords awarded full proprietary rights.

In the years following the mutiny, although support for Western education was never halted—indeed, in 1857, at the height of the uprising, Canning inaugurated India's first three universities, at Calcutta, Bombay, and Madras—still the predominant objective of British policy, as the secretary of state Charles Wood wrote to Canning in 1860, was 'to enlist on our side, and to employ in our service, those natives who have, from their birth or their position, a natural influence in the country' (Metcalf, 172). Moved by these new, more conservative principles, in the years after the mutiny Canning sought ways to enhance the position not only of the landed élite in the British Indian provinces, but the rulers of India's many princely states as well. For the most part, although the princes dispossessed by Dalhousie's annexations had taken a prominent part in the uprising, those who had retained their thrones stayed loyal. Indeed, they were, as Canning wrote, 'breakwaters to the storm which would otherwise have swept over us in one great wave'. The lesson he drew was obvious—that Britain must abandon the policy of annexation, and instead secure India's remaining princes on their thrones. Following a durbar in Lucknow in 1859, in which he awarded the Oudh *talukdars* patents of ownership over their restored estates, Canning undertook an extended tour of upper India, in which he met and rewarded princes from throughout the region. Some, especially Maharaja Jang Bahadur of Nepal and the Sikh chieftains of the Punjab, were given monetary or territorial awards in recognition of their military support in the critical early months of the uprising. The most sought-after boon, however, was the right of adoption; for it protected a state from being taken over by the British government, as had occurred under Dalhousie, when a prince died without issue. As paramount power Britain still retained the right to intervene in the governance of the princely states, but their independent existence was now secure. Convinced that the princes possessed a 'sympathy with and a hold over the feelings and hearts of the common herd which they cannot bequeath to us', Canning in 1860 awarded patents of adoption to all sovereign ruling chiefs (Metcalf, 224). This act inaugurated an alliance between Britain and India's princely rulers that was to endure until 1947.

Reconstruction of civil government, 1858–1861 The mutiny forced Britain to consider afresh the way it represented itself as an imperial power. Although the East India Company was not charged with responsibility for the uprising, nevertheless the British government took advantage of the occasion to bring to an end this ancient corporation, with the cumbrous administrative structure it had spawned. As the first step towards creating a new Indian empire, the country was placed instead under the direct governance of the crown. Canning inaugurated the new government on 1 November 1858, and so became the first viceroy of India. In 1859 he was raised to an earldom. Two years later, in 1861, seeking further to cement the ties between the monarch and her Indian subjects, he oversaw the creation of a new order of knighthood, the Star of India. The coveted distinction of membership of this order was restricted to senior British officials and the highest-ranked Indian princes. Canning took advantage of the transfer of India to the crown to reorganize the structure of its government. He secured the enactment, after years of delay, of Macaulay's penal code, and codes of civil and criminal procedure prepared under his predecessor. He also undertook reform of the governor-general's executive and legislative councils. Empowered by the Indian Councils Act of 1861, he organized the executive council on a departmental basis, with each member responsible for a defined portfolio. No legally separate legislative council was created under this act, but the executive council was enlarged for the purposes of legislation by the addition of up to twelve nominated members, of whom half were to be non-official. Canning took advantage of this enlarged membership to appoint the first Indian members to the council. Increasingly, over time its Indian members made of this local legislature a forum for criticism of the government and its measures. Nevertheless, despite these appointments, Canning had no intention of encouraging the development of representative institutions in India. For him the admission of Indians to the legislature served much the same purpose as did the simultaneous award of magisterial powers to selected chieftains and landlords. In each case, in order to forestall the ignorance and lack of understanding of India among the British, which had opened the way to the 1857 uprising, it was essential to bring Indians, especially the 'native aristocracy', into the government, where they could be 'turned to useful purposes', and their voices heard; but power had always to be kept firmly in British hands. In similar fashion, the uprising set on foot a renewed determination on the part of the British to know India better so as to be able more effectively to control it. Canning authorized the first archaeological survey of the country's ancient monuments, under General Sir Alexander Cunningham, and he began the use of the recently invented process of photography for the purposes of ethnography. Underlying this enterprise was a conviction that different caste groups represented distinct racial types, so that a photograph of one 'typical' member of an ethnic group provided a means of identifying the characteristics of physiognomy, dress, and manners that defined the whole. The eight-volume compilation of photographs initially collected by Canning for his own personal use was eventually published by the government as *The People of India* (1868). From this beginning followed the subsequent voluminous surveys of India's castes and tribes.

Questions of finance consumed much of Canning's energy during the final years of his viceroyalty. Suppression of the mutiny had drained India's resources, and driven the government deeply into debt. By 1859 the total Indian debt had grown to nearly £1 hundred million, as contrasted with £60 million two years before, and the annual interest charges now consumed some £4.5 million. James Wilson, who was appointed finance member in 1859, put forward a number of measures to restore the country's financial equilibrium. Among these was an income tax, the first in India's history, seen as a way to reach the commercial classes who were not liable for the ordinary taxes on land and its produce. The tax elicited fierce opposition in the legislative council, among the judiciary, and in the provincial governments. Sir Charles Trevelyan, as governor of Madras, fearing the tax might re-ignite hostility towards Britain, launched an attack on the entire financial scheme of such intensity as to bring about his recall to England in 1860. Nevertheless, Canning persevered with his reforms, securing, together with the income tax, a licence tax on traders, the introduction of a paper currency, and more rigorous audit procedures.

Together, by the end of Canning's viceroyalty, though the new taxes were scaled back as time went on, these reforms had reduced the government deficit to an insignificant amount. At the same time this financial reorganization opened the way to the extensive railway and public works construction of the later nineteenth century that tied India, as an exporter of raw materials, ever more tightly into the world economy centred on Great Britain. Indeed, Canning's final years, with the outbreak of the American Civil War, witnessed the beginning of the great Indian cotton boom.

Last days and historical significance Unlike later viceroys of the age of railways, Canning was unable to make a regular pilgrimage to the Simla hills for the summer months. The crisis of the mutiny, with the subsequent administrative reorganization, kept him in the plains for all but a few months of his extended six-year stay in India. He even abandoned one intended hill retreat to return to Calcutta from Simla at the height of the hot weather in 1860 to deal with the crisis precipitated by Trevelyan's opposition to the income tax. In November 1861 Lady Canning died of malaria and was buried at Barrackpore, outside Calcutta. By the time Canning handed over charge of India to his successor, James Bruce, eighth earl of Elgin, on 12 March

1862, an observer described him as 'pale, wan, toilworn, and grief-stricken' (Temple, 230). No sooner had Canning returned to London than he fell ill with an abscess of the liver. He died at his home, 10 Grosvenor Square, London, on 17 June 1862; four days later he was buried in Westminster Abbey near his father's grave. Canning left no heir, so his title and honours became extinct on his death. He bequeathed his extensive property to his sister's younger son, Hubert de Burgh, later Lord Clanricarde. In 1916, on Clanricarde's death, Canning's property, with his papers, came into the possession of the earls of Harewood.

Of Canning's character the fullest account is that prepared by Lord Granville, his friend from their shared schooldays onward. As Granville recollected in 1890, and as his viceregal labours in India made manifest, Canning 'had extraordinary powers of continuous work for months and years', together with an insistence upon absolute truthfulness such that 'inaccuracy of any kind was what he was most severe upon in others'. Although Granville spoke of him as 'one of my greatest friends', still he had to admit that Canning possessed 'some natural reserve', such that he himself would not willingly have confided in him (Maclagan, 24–6). Richard Temple, who knew him in India, spoke of Canning as 'calm, grave, reflective … but more than ordinarily deliberate in forming a definite conclusion, and cautious in taking action on such a decision when formed' (Temple, 164).

From the very beginning, as British writers looked back at Canning's career, his handling of the mutiny crisis always took pride of place. Richard Temple praised him as 'Canning the Just', while his first biographer, H. S. Cunningham, spoke of him as standing 'unmoved and immovable', ruling 'with firmness, confidence, magnanimity, with calm inflexible justice', while the storm raged about him. For the British at the time, and for decades after, Canning stood forth always as the saviour of the raj, 'high on the list of those great officers of state, whose services to their country entitle them to the esteem and gratitude of every loyal Englishman' (Cunningham, 13, 15; Temple, 185). Oddly, perhaps because his reputation became so closely identified with the Indian uprising, Canning's place as an individual in the historiography of the modern British empire remains curiously ill-defined. Apart from Cunningham's brief 1891 biography in the Rulers of India series, Canning's life has received only one full-length treatment, based on a study of his rich private papers, that of Michael Maclagan in his *'Clemency' Canning* (1962). Nor has Canning been much caught up in the enduring historiographical controversies about the nature and character of the mutiny. Those who sought in British policy, to use Disraeli's words, 'adequate causes' for the outbreak, have always turned to Canning's predecessor Lord Dalhousie, and made of his reforms the breeding-ground for Indian disaffection. Indian nationalist historians, on their side, casting all the British together as colonialists, have sought to emphasize the character of the uprising as, if not 'the first war of independence', then as the revolt of an oppressed people. In similar fashion, modern historians have been less interested in the doings of individuals than in assessing the patterns of support for the revolt, the larger racial antagonisms it released, and the varied ways in which its suppression committed the British to a new strategy of governance for India. Nevertheless, among the rulers of British India during the long years of the Victorian era, Lord Canning has fared better than most. Never the subject of such enduring contention as Dalhousie or Curzon, he has yet escaped the fate of most of his successors, who, apart from Lord Ripon, have for the most part been consigned to a deserved obscurity. Canning remains a figure central to any understanding of the climactic event of the British raj in India, the uprising of 1857, and the reconstruction that followed.

THOMAS R. METCALF

Sources M. Maclagan, *'Clemency' Canning* (1962) • H. S. Cunningham, *Earl Canning* (1891) • T. R. Metcalf, *The aftermath of revolt: India, 1857–1870* (1964) • R. Temple, *Men and events of my time in India* (1882) • J. W. Kaye, *A history of the Sepoy War in India, 1857–1858*, 3 vols. (1864–76)

Archives W. Yorks. AS, Leeds, corresp. and papers | BL, corresp. with Lord Aberdeen, Add. MSS 43249–43255 • BL, letters to C. A. Ellis, Add. MS 45176 • BL, family corresp., Add. MS 47469 • BL, corresp. with W. E. Gladstone, Add. MS 44117 • BL, corresp. with Sir Robert Peel, Add. MSS 40490–40603 • BL, corresp. with Lord Strathnairn, Add. MS 42806 • BL OIOC, corresp. with Sir George Clerk, Eur. MS D 538 • BL OIOC, corresp. with Cuthbert Davidson, Eur. MS D 728 • BL OIOC, corresp. with Sir J. P. Grant, Eur. MS F 127 • BL OIOC, corresp. with first Baron Lyveden, Eur. MS F 231 • BL OIOC, letters to Robert Vernon Smith, Eur. MS B 324 • BL OIOC, corresp. with Sir George Yule, Eur. MS E 357 • Borth. Inst., letters to Sir Charles Wood • Ches. & Chester ALSS, letters to Lord and Lady De Tabley • Lpool RO, letters to fourteenth earl of Derby • Lpool RO, corresp. with fifteenth earl of Derby • NA Scot., corresp. with Lord Dalhousie • NAM, department of film and sound, letters to Sir James Outram • Norfolk RO, corresp. with Sir Henry Bulwer • priv. coll., letters to Lord and Lady Sydney • PRO, corresp. with William Petrie, FO 352 • U. Nott. L., department of manuscripts and special collections • U. Nott. L., department of manuscripts and special collections, letters to duke of Portland • W. Yorks. AS, Leeds, corresp. with Lord Clanricarde

Likenesses W. Barclay, miniature, exh. RA 1836, Harewood House, West Yorkshire • R. Beard, daguerreotype, 1840–1849?, NPG [*see illus.*] • G. Richmond, chalk drawing, 1851, NPG • Mayall, two cartes-de-visite, *c*.1860, NPG • engraving, 1861 (after G. Richmond), repro. in *ILN* • G. Hayter, portrait, exh. 1868, Harewood House, West Yorkshire • J. H. Foley, statue, 1874, Calcutta, India • J. H. Foley, statue, Westminster Abbey, London • C. A. Momewick, portrait, Government House, Calcutta, India • M. Noble, bust, priv. coll. • J. Partridge, group portrait (*The fine arts commissioners, 1846*), NPG • G. Richmond, portrait (*Lord Canning in India*), NPG • W. Roffe, stipple (after photograph by Mayall), BM, NPG • W. Simpson, group portrait, watercolour (*Canning's return visit to the maharajah of Kashmir, 1860*), BL OIOC • photographs, BL OIOC

Wealth at death under £250,000: probate, 5 Aug 1862, *CGPLA Eng. & Wales*

Canning [*née* Stuart], **Charlotte Elizabeth**, Countess **Canning (1817–1861)**, courtier and vicereine of India, was born at the British embassy in Paris on 31 March 1817, the elder of the two daughters of Sir Charles *Stuart, later Baron Stuart de Rothesay (1779–1845), diplomatist, and his wife, Lady Elizabeth Yorke (1789–1867), daughter of the third earl of Hardwicke. Like her sister Louisa [*see* Beresford, Louisa, marchioness of Waterford], Charlotte Stuart

Charlotte Elizabeth Canning, Countess Canning (1817–1861), by unknown photographer

was celebrated for her beauty, piety, and artistic talent. Her appearance was enthusiastically described in 1853: 'She is very dark, with splendid eyes and rich black hair and the most classic outline of head and face' (*Letters of the Hon. Mrs Edward Twisleton*, 139). At eighteen she married, on 5 September 1835, Charles John *Canning (1812–1862), only surviving son of the prime minister, George *Canning, and heir to his mother's viscountcy.

The early years of the marriage, which was childless, were spent in establishing Canning's political career, and in travel on the continent. Then in May 1842 Charlotte Canning was invited to become a lady of the bedchamber to Queen Victoria. This appointment, which entailed spending a fortnight in waiting on the queen three times a year, shaped her life for the next thirteen years. Although at this period the queen was too wrapped up in her husband to have much interest in the friendship of her courtiers, Lady Canning was a particular favourite, not least because she won the approval of Prince Albert. The prince was notorious for being unwilling even to talk to the ladies of the household, but Charlotte Canning's character was so impeccable that he unbent sufficiently to deem her 'such a distinguished person' (*Letters of Queen Victoria*, 1st ser., 3.609). Her quiet charm, tolerance, and capacity for enjoyment endeared Lady Canning to the queen, and her artistic talents made her indispensable. Photography was in its infancy, and the queen herself seldom had time to make a complete visual record of the places she visited, so Charlotte Canning was often her choice of attendant for expeditions where her pencils and watercolours could be put to good use. Thus she accompanied the royal party on a yachting trip to the west country and to France in August 1843, and in the following month to Belgium. In 1844 she went with them on their second excursion to Scotland, staying at Blair Castle, and in 1845 on the visit to Albert's homeland of Coburg and Gotha. Lady Canning's facility with a pencil was matched by her ability to draw vivid word-pictures, and her many letters are a valuable mine of social detail.

Charlotte Canning was a devout high-churchwoman, and active in many charitable causes. As chairwoman of the committee of the Institution for the Care of Sick Gentlewomen in Distressed Circumstances, she had been responsible for the appointment of Florence Nightingale as superintendent of their hospital in Henley Street in 1853; she was criticized for not seeking the permission of Miss Nightingale's parents. Then with the outbreak of the Crimean War, Lady Canning was heavily involved in the interviewing and selection of nurses to accompany Florence Nightingale to Scutari.

In June 1855 Lord Canning accepted the post of governor-general of India. '[I] will not take any part in the decision but only be ready to follow like a dog' (Surtees, 193), his wife wrote, rather dispiritedly. They left London in November, travelling to Calcutta via Paris, Malta, and Egypt, pausing in Bombay, Ceylon, and Madras before reaching their destination on 29 February 1856. The queen thanked her for her first letter, from Cairo, envying her former lady-in-waiting the opportunity to see the wonders of the East, though not its inconveniences: 'If it was not for the heat & the *insects* how much I should like to see India', she wrote (ibid., 197). Lady Canning now experienced court life from the other side, presiding over the society of the British in India, as well as being the hostess at the governor-general's court. With no formal duties, no family, a husband inevitably preoccupied with affairs of state, no British ladies of sufficiently high social status to make friends, and only very limited contact with Indian ladies, it was a lonely and challenging life. She was fortunate in the selection of her husband's aides-de-camp, who provided her regular companionship, even if, like Johnny Stanley, they had a tendency to fall in love with her.

The year of the Indian mutiny, 1857, put a tremendous emotional and physical strain on the Cannings. Charlotte was kept well away from the dangerous areas, but she gathered information assiduously, keeping the queen informed in detail of the events as they unfolded, and was able to dispel some of the worst atrocity stories: 'there is not a particle of evidence of the poor women having been "ill-used" anywhere', she wrote (Surtees, 245). (Death, murder, starvation, and the mutilation of corpses did not compare to the horror felt at the idea of interracial rape.) To Lady Canning, the queen was able regularly to express her complete confidence in the beleaguered Canning, who was under continual pressure from the British at home and in India to exact a bloody retribution. Canning was able to rely on his wife to communicate with his colleagues in Britain when the pressures of the situation overwhelmed his correspondence. Lord Granville read a letter of hers to the cabinet in October 1857, drawing from the prime minister, Lord Palmerston, 'a compliment at the expense of her sex. "Ah, ah, a capital letter, unlike a lady's letter; it is all to the point, ah, ah"' (Fitzmaurice, 1.261).

The revolt over, Canning was elevated to an earldom,

the government of India was removed from the hands of the East India Company, and the governor-generalship was transformed into a viceroyalty. The new vicereine travelled widely throughout India, from Madras in the south, to the borders of Tibet in the north. She sketched and painted as she went, and wrote detailed accounts of her travels to her family and to the queen. Despite the difficulties, she had come to enjoy India, but was looking forward to her frequently postponed return to England, which was set for January 1862. In October 1861 she journeyed through Darjeeling, to the borders of Sikkim, and saw Mount Everest, but her mind was on home and planning for the future there. She returned to Calcutta on 8 November, clearly suffering from 'jungle fever', or malaria. Four days later she was confined to bed, and shortly afterwards her mind started wandering, and she died at 2.30 in the morning of 18 November. She was buried the following day in the viceroy's garden at Barrackpore, 'looking upon that reach of the grand river which she was so fond of drawing,—shaded from the glare of the sun by high trees,—and amongst the bright shrubs and flowers in which she had so much pleasure' (*Letters of Queen Victoria*, 1st ser., 3.608). The queen received news of Charlotte's death as her own husband lay dying; when Canning followed his wife to the grave seven months later, she thought him blessed: 'How enviable to follow so soon the partner of your life! How I pray it may be God's will to let me follow mine soon!' (*Letters of Queen Victoria*, 2nd ser., 1.36). K. D. Reynolds

Sources V. Surtees, *Charlotte Canning* (1975) • A. J. C. Hare, *The story of two noble lives*, 3 vols. (1893) • *The letters of Queen Victoria*, ed. A. C. Benson, Lord Esher [R. B. Brett], and G. E. Buckle, 9 vols. (1907–32), 1st–2nd ser. • E. G. Petty-Fitzmaurice, *The life of Granville George Leveson Gower, second Earl Granville*, 2nd edn, 2 vols. (1905) • *Letters of the Hon. Mrs Edward Twisleton* (1928) • Burke, *Peerage* (1907) • K. D. Reynolds, *Aristocratic women and political society in Victorian Britain* (1998)

Archives W. Yorks. AS, Leeds, corresp. and MSS | BL, letters to W. Gladstone, Add. MSS 44362–44392 • BL OIOC, letters to Queen Victoria and family, Photo Eur. 321

Likenesses F. X. Winterhalter, oils, 1849, priv. coll. • J. Barrett, group portrait, oils, 1856, NPG • photograph; Christies, 6 Nov 1953, lot 19 [*see illus.*]

Wealth at death under £6000: administration, 1 Sept 1862, *CGPLA Eng. & Wales*

Canning [*married name* Treat], **Elizabeth** (1734–1773), convicted perjurer, was born on 17 September 1734 in the City of London, the eldest of five surviving children of William Canning (*d.* 1751) and his wife, Elizabeth, who continued her husband's business of sawyer after his death. The family occupied two rooms in Aldermanbury Postern, London. Canning's schooling was limited to no more than a few months at a writing school. From the age of fifteen or sixteen she lived outside the family as a maidservant, first in the household of a neighbouring publican and then, from October 1752, in the house of Edward Lyon, a carpenter in Aldermanbury. She was considered by employers and neighbours to be hard-working and of good character.

Despite being 'an obscure damsel, of low degree' (Smollett, 1.154), Canning became the centre of the most famous English criminal mystery of her century. The events and trials that followed her disappearance on 1 January 1753 excited Londoners for over a year and a half, bringing violent mobs on to the streets. Her own story when, emaciated and half-clad, she reappeared after an absence of twenty-eight days was that she had been abducted in Moorfields by two ruffians who robbed her, partly stripped her, stunned her with a blow to the temple, and then dragged her to a house on the Hertfordshire road. There, she alleged, an old woman had asked her to 'go their way' (become a prostitute), but she refused. The woman cut off her stays and forced her into an upstairs room, where she remained confined for almost a month, with only a jug of water and some pieces of bread to live on, supplemented by a small mince pie she had in her pocket. On 29 January she escaped through a window and walked all the way back to her mother's house. When she told her story to friends and neighbours, one of them was convinced that she had been taken to a house of ill fame belonging to Susannah (Mother) Wells at Enfield Wash, some 10 miles out of London. Two days later the story was repeated before an alderman at the Guildhall and a warrant was issued for the apprehension of Mother Wells. On 1 February Canning, her mother, and a number of friends travelled to Enfield Wash, accompanied by an officer of the lord mayor. Canning was taken from room to room and, with some discrepancies, identified the loft as the place in which she had been held captive. Among the house's inhabitants on the day, she selected a Gypsy, Mary Squires, as the woman who had cut off her stays and thrust her into the loft. A local magistrate committed Squires for trial for stealing the stays, with Susannah Wells as accessory.

Six days later Canning was examined by Henry Fielding, the novelist, in his capacity as justice of the peace for Middlesex and Westminster. Fielding was quickly convinced of her truthfulness and issued a warrant against all in Mother Wells's household. Subsequent proceedings were conducted with some laxity. Virtue Hall, from the Wells house, was bullied into telling a story closely resembling Canning's and, with the aid of Canning's solicitor, incorporated this in a written statement. Squires and Wells faced trial on 21 February 1753 in a packed Old Bailey. Much of the case depended on the conflicting evidence of Canning and Squires. The latter's defence was that she and her family were travelling around Dorset at the time of the alleged abduction. Canning retold her tale, corroborated by Hall, while three defence witnesses supported Squires's alibi. (A number of others had been prevented by the mob from entering the sessions house.) The jury found Squires and Wells guilty, and five days later Wells was sentenced to branding on the thumb and six months in gaol, while Squires was sentenced to death by hanging. In her statement before receiving sentence, Squires pleaded an alibi in which the details differed from the defence evidence at the trial.

Sir Crisp Gascoyne, lord mayor of London, had presided

ex officio at the Old Bailey and was far from content with the turn of events. Disturbed by inconsistencies in the testimony on the Canning side, he made inquiries leading to new material which seemed abundantly to support Squires. Moreover, Virtue Hall recanted her corroboration of the Canning version of events. After examining further Enfield witnesses Gascoyne presented a memorial to the king, who granted Squires a stay of execution, followed by a free pardon in May 1753. Wells, on the other hand, was left to serve out her sentence and was released from Newgate only on 21 August. Canning, meanwhile, was indicted for perjury on 9 June.

These actions gave rise to an avalanche of newspaper articles, pamphlets, engravings, and caricatures between March and July 1753. Two factions did battle: on the one side were ranged the 'Canningites' and on the other the 'Egyptians', who supported Mary Squires. The paper war did more to strengthen certainties on each side than to change minds. The printed word was no doubt more influential in the chocolate houses than among the mob on the streets, wholly devoted to the Canning cause. Yet the press played some part in heightening their passions too, by reinforcing firmly lodged stereotypes of wicked Gypsies and a poor innocent girl refusing to yield her honour. Fielding was among the first to enter the lists, with *A Clear State of the Case of Elizabeth Canning*. Several refutations followed quickly, the most notable of which were *The Story of Elizabeth Canning Considered*, by John Hill, who was keen to pay off old scores with Fielding, and Allan Ramsay's *A Letter to the Right Honourable the Earl of — Concerning the Affair of Elizabeth Canning*, an elegant piece on which, years later, Voltaire based his own inaccurate *Histoire d'Elisabeth Canning, et de Jean Calas* (1762), where he presented the case as a glorious vindication of English justice and assumed, as Ramsay had done, that Canning was covering up a confinement.

After nearly eight months of legal manoeuvres, Canning was summoned again to the Old Bailey on 29 April 1754 to be tried for wilful and corrupt perjury. The trial occupied seven days, during which two great masses of completely contradictory testimony were dissected. Thirty-seven witnesses swore that, at the relevant time, Squires was in Dorset or travelling from it, but twenty-two others testified that they had seen her at or near Mother Wells's house. Four witnesses claimed to have seen Canning at Enfield Wash or being dragged there, while thirteen bore testimony against her being there. No one produced any evidence to show where Canning might have been if she was not at Wells's house. The bewildered jury brought in a qualified verdict: 'guilty of perjury, but not wilful or corrupt'. This the recorder declined to accept, and the jury retired again to return a verdict of 'guilty of wilful and corrupt perjury; recommended to mercy'. Subsequently two of the jurymen made affidavits that the verdict was not according to their consciences. On 30 May 1754, when judgment was to be delivered, the members of the court proved almost evenly divided. The final vote in favour of a month's imprisonment followed by seven years' transportation was passed by a bare majority of nine to eight; the minority would have preferred six months' imprisonment only. Transportation was effected in August and Canning sailed for New England.

The guilty verdict renewed the spate of printed polemic. Canning's main pursuer entered the field with *An Address to the Liverymen of the City of London, from Sir Crisp Gascoyne*. For his advocacy of the 'Egyptian' cause Gascoyne met with violence and threats to his life, along with a good deal of mud-slinging, both literal and figurative. The Canningites reacted with a battery of four repudiations. Not until August of that year did the tide of print begin to ebb again.

Canning's place of exile was Wethersfield in Connecticut, where her supporters in England had arranged for her to live in the household of the Revd Elisha Williams, who died shortly after her arrival. She had a following even in New England, where many thought her unjustly treated. She was courted by John Treat, great-nephew of the former governor, Robert Treat, and married him on 24 November 1756. While her husband was serving in a campaign against the French she bore a son, Joseph Canning Treat, in June 1758. A daughter, Elizabeth, was born in November 1761, after Treat had settled down again with his small family. Canning lived out her life at Wethersfield, giving birth to two more sons, and there she died suddenly in June 1773. The *Connecticut Courant* (444, 22–9 June 1773) recorded the recent death of 'Mrs Elizabeth Treat, wife of Mr Treat, formerly the famous Elizabeth Canning'.

During the nineteen years Canning spent in New England, no further light was shed on what had happened during her four-week disappearance in January 1753. There has been no lack of theories. In the twentieth century alone, no fewer than six book-length analyses sought, with varying degrees of partisanship, to explain the discrepancies and fill in some of the gaps. Neither the 'Canningite' nor the 'Egyptian' cause has died from lack of adherents. ANGUS FRASER

Sources F. Hargrave, ed., *A complete collection of state-trials*, 4th edn, 11 vols. (1776–81) • J. Treherne, *The Canning enigma* (1989) • J. Moore, *The appearance of truth: the story of Elizabeth Canning and eighteenth-century narrative* (1994) • L. B. McCue, 'Elizabeth Canning in print', *Elizabethan studies and other essays in honor of George F. Reynolds* (1945), 223–32 • T. Smollett, *Continuation of the 'Complete history of England'*, 5 vols. (1760–65) • parish register (baptism), 13/10/1734, St Andrew by the Wardrobe, London • *Connecticut Courant*, 444 (22–9 June 1773)

Likenesses L. P. Boitard, line engraving, pubd 1754, BM, NPG • T. Worlidge, etching, 1754, BM • portrait, 1754 (*Elizabeth Canning from a sketch taken in the sessions house during her trial*), BM • J. Macardell, mezzotint (after W. Smith), BM • T. Worlidge, pencil drawing, BM • prints, BM, NPG

Canning, George (1770–1827), prime minister and parodist, was born in Marylebone, Middlesex, on 11 April 1770, the son of George Canning (1736–1771) and his wife, Mary Ann Costello (1747?–1827). His parents were both Irish; he described himself as 'an Irishman born in London' (Temperley, *Life*, 16) and identified himself with the Irish demand for Catholic emancipation, but he visited Ireland only once, in 1824. His father was the eldest son of Stratford Canning (1703–1775), a cantankerous protestant

George Canning (1770–1827), by Sir Thomas Lawrence, 1825

gentleman with a modest estate at Garvagh in co. Londonderry and a house in Dublin. George senior took his BA at Trinity College, Dublin, in 1754, but was sent by his father to London in 1757 to prevent him making an unacceptable marriage. There, on an allowance of £150 p.a., he read for the bar and was called at the Middle Temple in 1764. But 'it would appear that [he] was a lover of literature and pleasure, and excessively averse to the dull study of the profession to which his life was doomed to be devoted' (Rede, 8 n.). His circle included journalists, actors, and politicians, and he was a friend and supporter of Wilkes. He published at least one political pamphlet and some verses, including a translation (1766) of five books of Polignac's *Anti-Lucretius*, which he dedicated to Queen Charlotte as 'a poem, calculated to promote the cause of religion, and virtue, by overturning the pillars of immorality, and atheism'. He ran up large debts, which his father paid off in return for his renouncing his right to inherit the family estates. His wife, whom he married in Marylebone parish church on 21 May 1768, was beautiful, spirited, and on her mother's side from a good family—her guardian and maternal grandfather was Colonel Guydickens of Wigmore Street, formerly known as Guy Dickens, who had been British envoy in Berlin (1740–41), Stockholm (1742–8), and St Petersburg (1749–55), and whose son Gustavus was a gentleman usher in the queen's household—but she had no money of her own.

Childhood and education George was the second of their three children and the only one to reach adulthood. On the boy's first birthday George senior died. Stratford's allowance to his son lapsed, and he would allow Mary Ann only £40 p.a., which was given for the children and on condition that she stayed in England. Her resources were so inadequate that she decided to try to make a living as an actress. Garrick, perhaps at the request of the queen, gave her a chance at Drury Lane in November 1773, but she did not succeed there. She then turned to provincial theatres, where she had better luck. By becoming an actress she excluded herself from respectable society, and she soon made matters worse by becoming the mistress of the dissolute actor Samuel Reddish. The couple had five children and she called herself Mrs Reddish. Canning's early years were spent touring provincial theatres with his mother and Reddish, and he later reminisced about a humble school at which he had within a month 'got through … by far the greater part of a gingerbread alphabet' (*The Microcosm*, 1, 1786, 434).

In 1778, however, the Canning family came dramatically to the boy's rescue. They provided money to pay for his maintenance and education, and his uncle Stratford, well established as a merchant banker in the City, became his guardian and took him into his home in Clement's Lane. He was sent to his first respectable school, Hyde Abbey, Winchester, in 1778 and to Eton College in 1782. On the death of his paternal grandmother in 1786 he 'came into possession of the fortune left me by my grandfather, about 400*l*. per annum' (Raven, 51). His uncle, the younger Stratford, died in May 1787, and Canning's legal guardian now became William Borrowes, Stratford's business partner. He continued to spend much time with Stratford's widow, Hetty (Mehitabel), and her family, who moved to Wanstead; but, especially as he lost sympathy with her whig views, he felt his closest family ties with his aunt Elizabeth and her husband, the Revd William Leigh, who lived first in Norwich and then at Ashbourne Hall in Derbyshire.

It was part of the arrangement of 1778 that Canning was not allowed to see his mother, of whom he was clearly very fond. However, they wrote to each other regularly. In 1783 she married Richard Hunn, a draper of Plymouth, who then himself took up acting and with whom she had at least three more children. Only in 1786 was Canning permitted to see her again. When he received his inheritance, he persuaded his guardian to make his mother an allowance of £50 out of it. For the rest of her life, which lasted until March 1827, he supported her and her children financially and in other ways, and wrote to her frequently and informatively, but she remained a source of embarrassment to him and he saw her only rarely and circumspectly.

Canning's Eton career was a triumph almost without parallel. He proved a brilliant classic, came top of the school, and excelled at public orations. He gathered round him a circle of friends who remained close to him throughout his life, especially John Hookham Frere and Charles Ellis. He and Frere, with John (Easley) Smith and Robert (Bobus) Smith, wrote and published a magazine called *The Microcosm* (1786–7), made up of elegant and witty articles that scoffed at literary criticism, sentimental novels, aristocratic pretension, and the like. This publication achieved remarkable fame and was four times reprinted. Canning's part in it, though he had written under the pseudonym Gregory Griffin, was known and widely admired, not least by George III and Queen Charlotte.

From Eton Canning went up in 1787 to Christ Church, Oxford, where his successes continued. He won college and university prizes for Latin verse and was made a student (fellow) of his college. He acquired many new friends, mostly of high social standing: pre-eminently Robert Banks Jenkinson, later to be his political colleague, on and off, for nearly forty years; Lord Boringdon, owner of Saltram House in Devon; Lord Morpeth, heir to the earldom of Carlisle and to Castle Howard; Lord Holland; Charles Moore, son of the wealthy archbishop of Canterbury; William Sturges Bourne; and Lord Granville Leveson-Gower, son of the marquess of Stafford. Some of them, with Lord Henry Spencer, whom Canning had known at Eton, formed with less well-connected undergraduates a select college debating society, the members of which sported a uniform that paid homage to Demosthenes, Cicero, Pitt, and Fox. Cyril Jackson, the dean of Christ Church, who was to give guidance to Canning for many years, suggested to him that he should resign from the club because his being a member implied that he wanted to go into politics rather than to succeed at his intended profession, the law. Canning complied, to the annoyance of his friends, writing:

> I am already, God knows, too much inclined, both by my own sanguine wishes and the connections with which I am most intimate, and whom I above all others revere, to aim at the House of Commons, as the only path to the only desirable thing in this world, the gratification of ambition; while at the same time every tie of common sense, of fortune, of duty, draws me to the study of a profession. (Newton, 24–5)

The incident encapsulates Canning's predicament: how could a man, however talented, whose origins were dubious and income small, aspire to a political career when MPs were not paid and parliamentary candidates almost always had to shell out large sums to be elected, and when it was axiomatic that nearly every minister would be a peer or the son of a peer?

Canning as disciple of Pitt, 1792–1801 Canning had entered Lincoln's Inn in 1787 and in 1790–92 read seriously for the bar. But he could not be content with making a legal career, and in the summer of 1792 he decided after all to seek a seat in the Commons. His goal, he said, was to become a privy councillor 'at thirty'—an ambition he was to achieve. His views while at Eton and Oxford had been whiggish, strengthened by the example of his father and by his guardian Stratford Canning's friendship with the opposition leaders—Fox had willingly given advice about the young man's career, and Sheridan regarded him as his *élève*. Canning wrote verses scoffing at Jenkinson's Pittite stance in the Regency crisis, and his attitude during the first three years of the French Revolution was that a nation was entitled to establish a republican government if it saw fit, and that the experiment was one from which Britain would be able to draw useful lessons. He enjoyed taking part in the debates of popular societies in London. George III was reported as saying late in 1792 that 'Mr. Canning's republican principles had done great harm at Christ Church' (Marshall, 26). But by then Canning had aligned himself with Pitt. On 26 July 1792, having received encouragement through intermediaries, he wrote to the prime minister in the strictest confidence saying

> that however I was in habits of friendship and familiarity with some of the most eminent men in Opposition, yet I was in no way bound to them by any personal or political obligation, but felt myself perfectly at liberty to choose my own party.

He had not the means to 'do anything towards bringing myself into Parliament, nor should I like to be brought in by an individual … it was with himself personally that I was ambitious of being connected'. Pitt replied warmly, expressing himself happy to 'facilitate' Canning's entry into the Commons when an 'opening' presented itself. The two men met on 15 August, and the understanding was confirmed, the prime minister accepting that Canning might take a different stance from his own on the Test Act and on 'speculative subjects especially' so long as he showed 'a general good disposition towards Government' (ibid., 33–7).

When this agreement became generally known, Canning was accused of betraying both his friends and his principles, and the charge was repeated throughout his career. He explained his motives at length, but even so they are not entirely clear. In some respects his opinions were changing: the course of the revolution had persuaded him that to embark on constitutional reform was too risky, and he particularly criticized Sheridan and his friends for founding the Association of the Friends of the People in April 1792. From this time he consistently defended the unreformed electoral system. His move towards Pitt must have been encouraged by his friendship with Jenkinson and other supporters of government, perhaps especially the Leighs. He must have realized that there was more room for an able young commoner in Pitt's entourage than in Fox's, and that Pitt alone was in a position to procure him a political career on his own terms, terms which no other impecunious aspirant of the time dreamed of proposing. He wanted to be not merely an MP but a minister, a professional politician in an age that expected this ambition, in the rare cases where it existed, to be concealed. This unique approach paid off. In March 1793, in accordance with his principles as stated to Pitt, he refused the offer of a seat from the duke of Portland, despite the duke's political importance, growing sympathy with the government, and readiness to bear the costs of election. However, he took care to retain good relations with the duke, writing verses for his installation as chancellor of the University of Oxford in July 1793. In the same month he became, through Pitt's good offices, MP for Newtown in the Isle of Wight.

Frere said Canning

> had much more in common with Pitt than anyone else about him, and his love for Pitt was quite filial, and Pitt's feeling for him was more that of a father than of a mere political leader. I am sure that from the first Pitt marked Canning out as his political heir. (Thorne, 3.380)

Although Canning was to disagree with Pitt's political strategy during the Addington ministry, the compact made between them in 1792 was broken only by Pitt's death in 1806, if then. Canning declared in 1812, 'my political allegiance lies buried in his grave' (Therry, 6.326), and claimed always to pursue the line that his mentor would have taken.

The friendship was obvious to all once Canning entered the Commons. After some moderately successful early speeches he was asked to second the address on 30 December 1794. On that and later occasions he distinguished himself in defence of the government's war policy. On 16 June 1795 he confessed to Pitt his hopes of office on grounds both of ambition and poverty, but it took the prime minister some time—from Canning's point of view too long—to find him an appropriate place. It was not until January 1796 that Canning took up one of the two under-secretaryships at the Foreign Office under Lord Grenville. Pitt and Grenville had gone to great trouble to make this opening for him: Aust, the previous under-secretary, had been found another post and promised a pension for his wife.

This was one of the most onerous of all government offices, though it brought with it a salary of only £1500 a year. Canning was so swamped by dispatches that he had to work far into the night and give up much of the hectic social round of soirées, dinners, and theatregoing that he had described in his letter-journal written for the Leighs from November 1793 to August 1795. At the general election of 1796 Pitt procured for him, at no cost and without conditions, a seat at Wendover. The war was now going so badly that negotiations with France were initiated: from October to December 1796 his friend the earl of Malmesbury, accompanied by George Ellis, cousin of Charles, was in Paris, and from July to September 1797 in Lille, attempting unsuccessfully to treat with the Directory. The king and Grenville disapproved of the second mission and Canning found himself the channel both for the foreign secretary's discouraging instructions to Malmesbury and for Pitt's 'most private' and more constructive letters to him. Perhaps as a reward for his discretion and dexterity, Pitt appointed him in September 1797 to the clerkship of the alienations, a sinecure worth £700 p.a.

Canning now became the principal mover in a unique project to commend the policies of the government and condemn the revolutionary cause by the publication of a journal, *The Anti-Jacobin*. It had Pitt's blessing, and he contributed to it in a small way; its editor was William Gifford, and Canning's main collaborators were Frere and George Ellis. It appeared every Monday from 20 November 1797 to 9 July 1798. It owed much of its fame to verses written by Canning in whole or part, some of them parodies of poets who supported the opposition, such as 'The Friend of Humanity and the Knife-Grinder', mocking Southey and the idealization of the poor. Another parody of Southey ended:

> Reason philosophy fiddledum diddledum,
> Peace and Fraternity higgledy piggledy.

In 'New Morality', which appeared in the last issue, Canning and Frere ridiculed a whig's foreign policy:

> A steady patriot of the world alone,
> The friend of every country—but his own.

Apart from verses, the paper contained extensive sections of news and attacks on other journals' misrepresentations. It sold the considerable number of 2500 copies, attracted a lot of notice both admiring and hostile, and was evidently justified in its claim to have helped to swing public opinion in favour of the ministry and the war. Although it was all anonymous, it was generally known that Canning was its inspiration. During the same period he further assisted government propaganda by approaching the cartoonist Gillray. He had been impatient to see himself caricatured, which occurred for the first time late in 1796. In the following year he took to suggesting subjects to Gillray, and helped procure him a pension.

More conventionally, Canning as under-secretary made notable speeches in support of the government's foreign policy, among which that of 11 December 1798 was the first he published. It led Lord Minto to call him 'a very rising as well as aspiring person in England' (Thorne, 381). He spoke on several occasions in support of the abolition of the slave trade and succeeded on 3 April 1798 in carrying a resolution (with no legal force) to prevent the cultivation of new land in the West Indies by slave labour. In the following year he defended the proposed union with Ireland as a necessary measure and one that would make possible Catholic emancipation.

In March 1799 Canning's wish to be released from 'three years of slavery' (Thorne, 381) and 'the *disagreeableness*' of serving Grenville (Hinde, 57) was satisfied by his appointment as a commissioner of the Board of Control for India; but he remained discontented and hoped to be made a secretary of state. In May 1800 he received instead the additional office of joint paymaster, which carried with it an 'admirable' house and membership of the privy council. By this time he was seen as the head of a small party of MPs whose votes he expected to control and for whom he sought office: he had, for example, procured for Frere the succession to his under-secretaryship, for which he proved totally unfitted. It was a unique group in being led by a person who held only minor office and had neither fortune nor social standing. Most of his political friends were also his personal friends, attracted to him at school or university by his brilliance, the 'vivacity of his conversation' (Newton, 17), his flights of fancy, and his effervescent sense of fun. They were amused, as others were not, by his habit of bestowing unflattering nicknames on all and sundry, his elaborate practical jokes, and the wit and sarcasm that he directed against those he thought foolish or mistaken. At first too histrionic, he was developing into a great speaker: his height, good looks, jet-black hair, penetrating eye, and sonorous voice gave him a commanding presence; using very few notes, he knew how to marshal an elaborate argument in long sentences of involved syntax, passing easily through light humour and withering invective to an eloquent peroration.

Pitt declared that all Canning now needed to enable him to lead a party with success was to make a good marriage. It is not known that he had any sexually significant relationships with women until in June 1799 he met and was attracted by the princess of Wales, now separated from the prince. She apparently made a pass at him, and the brief liaison, innocent though it seems to have been, was to cause him difficulties when the prince came to the throne in 1820. Fortunately, in August 1799 he went to stay at Walmer Castle, Pitt's house, as warden of the Cinque Ports, where he met Joan Scott (*d.* 1837), a girl of about twenty-two with a fortune generally put at £100,000. He fell in love with her. Joan had expected to be alarmed by Canning, 'to be wearied and oppressed by constant endeavours at shining in conversation, by unmerciful raillery and I know not what' (Hinde, 74), but instead found him captivating. Her parents were dead and she regarded her eldest sister's husband, the marquess of Titchfield, heir to the duke of Portland, as her guardian. He made the predictable objections, but Joan eventually overrode them, and the marriage took place at Brook Street Chapel on 8 July 1800, solemnized by uncle Leigh, with Frere as best man and Pitt as a witness. Canning bought a country house, South Hill, near Bracknell, which he had refurbished by Soane, and his wife became pregnant. Their son (Charles) George was born on 25 April 1801.

Political difficulties, 1801–1807 Since 1778 Canning's career had advanced spectacularly and with scarcely a set-back. In February 1801 it went into reverse, when Pitt resigned after the king refused to allow him to propose Catholic emancipation, which he considered himself honour-bound to do. He was succeeded by Addington, whom Canning regarded with contempt and delighted to ridicule. Pitt asked his followers to join the new ministry, but Canning decided that he could not do so, though he was induced by Pitt to send a letter of support. However, he soon began attacking the new prime minister and his government, calling it 'a conspiracy against all the talents of all sides, and sorts' (Thorne, 383). His successor as paymaster, Lord Glenbervie, described on 1 April 1801 the hostility he had aroused:

> I find the town is full of abuse on Canning. His hot-bed promotions, his saucy manners, and his satirical songs and indiscreet epigrams and buffoonery have already indisposed almost all Pitt's friends. … His conduct has opened many mouths of friends and foes, which had been kept sealed by the knowledge of Pitt's favour or the dread of his own wit. He now may perhaps long repent, though he will probably never subdue the indiscretion of that prurient and boyish vanity which postpones every consideration of decorum, respect for yourself as well as others, and good nature, to the momentary fame and applause of a good thing or an attempt at one. (ibid., 382)

Canning disapproved of the government's policy of making peace with France but was persuaded to absent himself from the debate on the preliminaries in November. At the general election of 1802 he had to buy a seat at Tralee.

Canning continued to regard Pitt as his leader and hero, promoting a birthday dinner for him on 28 May, attended by 975 persons, for which he wrote the song 'The Pilot that Weathered the Storm'. On 8 December he made a passionate defence of Pitt in the Commons against an attack by Sheridan: 'Away with the cant of "measures, not men", the idle supposition that it is the harness and not the horses that draw the chariot along' (Hinde, 113). But he could not persuade Pitt to take the role that he and his followers cast for him, of heading an opposition to displace Addington, even when war broke out again in May 1803. Canning, so conscious of being restrained and frustrated by his loyalty to Pitt, could not, it seems, understand that Pitt felt himself similarly caught in a false position by his obligations to the king. Canning continued to show animus against Addington and all those who had joined his ministry, especially two Pittites of his own age who had thereby beaten him into the cabinet: Viscount Castlereagh, who in 1802 had become president of the Board of Control, and his old Christ Church friend Jenkinson, who was foreign secretary throughout the ministry and became Lord Hawkesbury in 1803. When Pitt finally returned to office in May 1804, retaining many supporters of Addington, Canning received only the minor but well-paid post of treasurer of the navy. He took pride in the part he had taken in giving Nelson the instructions that made possible the victory at Trafalgar, but he was understandably disaffected at being excluded from the cabinet. Though Pitt promised to find a way of bringing him into it, he had not done so by the time he died in January 1806.

Canning was prepared to remain in office under the new ministry of Grenville, which included both Fox and Addington (now Lord Sidmouth), but he was virtually dismissed and went into opposition. He was very soon concocting—with Castlereagh, Hawkesbury, and Spencer Perceval—a scheme to get the Pittites back into office. In the summer of 1806 they appealed directly to the king behind the ministry's back and received a favourable though temporizing answer. Grenville and other ministers would have liked to capture Canning at least, recognizing that he would greatly strengthen them in the Commons, but in August he refused to join unless guaranteed five places for Pittites in the cabinet. Just after Canning's refusal Fox died, and the government called a general election at which Canning was elected for his old seat at Newtown, this time at considerable expense to himself. He now sold South Hill and took his family to reside at Hinckley, Leicestershire. This apparently bizarre decision was provoked by the serious lameness of his son George, which a Mr Chesher of Hinckley was believed to be the best person to treat.

Foreign secretary, 1807–1809 In the new year the situation was entirely changed by the rupture between George III and Grenville over a bill to allow Roman Catholics to hold commissions in the army. The king, confident of Pittite support, dismissed the ministry. It was replaced by a government under the nominal headship of the ailing duke of Portland, in which, after much manoeuvring, Canning was appointed foreign secretary on 25 March 1807. Another general election followed at which Canning was provided with a Treasury seat at Hastings. He at once emerged as the government's chief spokesman in the Commons: his speech of 30 June was described by Perceval, the leader of the house, as 'one of the most brilliant speeches which he or any other man ever delivered' (Thorne, 388–9). He also appeared to dominate the cabinet. Britain, though perhaps secure in the control of the sea, 'never stood more alone'. In the previous year Napoleon had promulgated his Continental System, intended to cut off all British trade with the entire continent. His annihilation of Prussia at Jena in October 1806 was followed in June 1807 by his destruction of the Russian army at Friedland; and his meeting at Tilsit with Tsar Alexander on 9 July was rightly taken to presage an alliance between them against Britain. The government considered it of paramount importance to preserve the remaining uncommitted countries, Denmark and Portugal, and especially their navies, from Napoleon's control, and it was Canning who effectively directed the measures it took to achieve these ends. A large fleet and an expeditionary force were sent to back up the demand of an envoy, Francis Jackson, that the prince regent of Denmark should accept an alliance with Britain and hand over his navy to Britain for the duration of the war. When he refused Jackson's demand, which was presented with much less diplomacy than Canning had intended, Copenhagen was bombarded and Zealand invaded, and the Danish fleet was duly seized.

Canning defended his high-handed policy triumphantly in a series of Commons speeches in February and March 1807: 'he leaped about,' said Sydney Smith, 'touched facts with his wand, turned yes into no, and no into yes' ('Peter Plymley's letters', *Works*, 3 vols., 1848, 3.113n.). Canning's admirers, then and since, have seen this as one of his greatest achievements. Temperley claimed that it

> at least kept the seas of England inviolate and the shores of Ireland uninvaded. It averted the threatened closure of the Sound and enabled English troops to be sent to reinforce Sweden. … The presence of the British fleet in the Baltic at least induced the Tsar to suspend his adoption of the Continental system, and his declaration of war until the extreme close of the year 1807. (Temperley, *Life*, 78–9)

Schroeder, Canning's most recent and most powerful critic, focusing on Canning's ulterior aims, namely to give Russia pause and to strengthen the resolve of Sweden, declares that the expedition was 'if a crime, even more a blunder'. Zealand had to be abandoned almost as soon as occupied; Russia's declaration of war was 'speeded up' by the attack on Copenhagen, and a follow-up expedition to Sweden in 1808 had to be withdrawn. But Schroeder has to admit that the seizure of the Danish fleet was a success of some importance, which contrasted with the contemporary failure of three expeditions promoted by the Grenville ministry to Buenos Aires, the Dardanelles, and Egypt.

To secure Portugal and her fleet Canning signed a treaty with her ambassador on 22 October, under which the regent would leave Europe and establish himself in Brazil. When the regent hesitated to ratify the treaty, Canning ordered a blockade which forced him to comply. The Portuguese navy was seized just as a French army entered Lisbon. As in the Danish case, what followed was less successful. A Spanish rebellion against French influence greatly excited British public opinion, and a force initially under Sir Arthur Wellesley was dispatched to Portugal to assist it. After he had won a battle at Vimeiro, he agreed to an armistice which was followed by the convention of Cintra, the terms of which were negotiated by a commander placed over him and were considered in Britain to have turned victory into humiliation. Canning acquiesced in most of them but with obvious chagrin, blaming Castlereagh as secretary for war for not having disavowed the convention from the start. Another attempt to assist the Spaniards ended early in 1809 with the retreat of Sir John Moore to Corunna. In this case Canning had not only to defend a general in whom he had never felt confidence but also to criticize his friend Frere, whom he had sent as British representative to the rebel government.

Canning was now thoroughly frustrated with the divided conduct of the war. In March 1809 he told Portland that he would resign if the government were not strengthened—by which he meant, first and foremost, removing Castlereagh from the War Office. By May the prime minister, the king, Lord Eldon, and Castlereagh's uncle, Lord Camden, were all working on the assumption that Castlereagh would be moved and were busy devising schemes to achieve this by reshuffling the cabinet. George III authorized Camden to break the news to Castlereagh, but he kept on finding he could not bring himself to do it. Late in July Portland screwed himself up to tell Castlereagh but, before he could do so, had an epileptic fit and the issue became subsumed into the wider question of who should replace Portland as prime minister. Negotiations continued for two more months. Canning said that the choice lay between him and Perceval, and that he would not serve under Perceval. By early September Canning had offered to resign four more times since March. He shocked George III on 12 September by baldly telling him, unasked, that he was ready to form a government. But Castlereagh had at last discovered what had been going on and put the blame on Canning for what seemed like a long course of duplicity. He sent Canning a challenge to a duel. Canning, though he had asked for Castlereagh's removal, had certainly not been responsible for the shilly-shallying of Camden and Portland. But he felt he had to accept the challenge, despite having never fired a pistol in his life. He made his will and wrote a touching farewell letter to his wife. The duel was fought on Putney Heath on 21 September: Canning was wounded but survived. Those in the know criticized Castlereagh for unreasonable overreaction, but the fault was very generally believed to lie with Canning. An immediate result was the appointment of Perceval as prime minister, with neither Canning nor Castlereagh in the cabinet. Even apart from the tragicomedy of the Castlereagh business, Canning had overplayed his hand. He obviously believed, as others like Portland and Perceval often said, that the ministry could not manage the Commons without him. He arrogantly supposed that he alone could give the war coherent and effective direction, and he certainly had exceptional energy, a grand strategic vision, and the ability to appeal to the house and the country. 'Canning's failure to produce any other convincing reason for his resignation suggests that a bid for power was the real reason', and he made it far too blatantly. Lord Eldon angrily described him as 'vanity in human form' (Hinde, 230–31).

Canning had met Sir Walter Scott in 1806, and two years later, with George Ellis, they founded, as a rival to the *Edinburgh Review*, the *Quarterly Review*, the editor of which was William Gifford of *The Anti-Jacobin*. It became for over a century the semi-official organ of central toryism. Canning seems to have written little for it but he took a continuing and constructive interest in it, and no other minister could have made this important contribution to the development of the party. In the early months of 1809 he purchased Gloucester Lodge, Old Brompton, with the idea of re-establishing his family in the London area.

Out of office, 1809–1816, and MP for Liverpool For the next three years Canning was in the wilderness, but giving the government general and valued support in the Commons. George III's insanity recurred late in 1810, and early in the following year the prince of Wales became regent. Though he did not, as expected, put the whigs in power, he kept on trying to find ways of 'strengthening' his ministry. A by-product of these negotiations was that Wellesley, who had become foreign secretary in December 1809, resigned in February 1812. To Canning's mortification, it was Castlereagh whom Perceval appointed to succeed him. The assassination of the prime minister on 11 May 1812 gave Canning, who had been toying with opposition, another chance of major office. Jenkinson, who had succeeded his father as Lord Liverpool, was eventually confirmed as prime minister, and in July set about capturing Canning. He promoted a reconciliation between him and Castlereagh, who offered to surrender the Foreign Office but insisted on retaining the leadership of the House of Commons. Canning, egged on by his friends, rejected the offer as humiliating. He had overreached himself again.

A general election was called at the end of 1812 in which Canning stood and was elected for Liverpool, free of expense. This was a landmark in his career and in the history of his party. Liverpool, one of the burgeoning cities of the industrial revolution, built on the Atlantic trade, had one of the largest electorates in the country, over 4000. Although the Anglican corporation exercised much influence in elections, this was one of the very few constituencies in the country where new commercial and industrial wealth could assert itself. The town's economy was seriously affected by the war and the orders in council, measures taken while Canning was in office to counter Napoleon's Continental System. The whigs had procured the nomination of Brougham, who had been waging an effective campaign against them outside as well as inside parliament. The tories, led by John Gladstone, father of the prime minister, wanted a plausible alternative candidate. They found one in Canning, whose eloquence and political standing would ensure that the interests of the borough were adequately represented in the Commons without committing it to whiggism. He repeatedly told them that he would not support parliamentary reform and that he favoured Catholic emancipation, which was an unpopular cause in Liverpool; and he defended the orders in council as necessary to the prosecution of the war.

Canning had always believed that the tories need not surrender the media to the whigs. He had shown in *The Anti-Jacobin* and the *Quarterly Review* that the press could be used on the side of toryism. He now accepted the challenge of campaigning and appealing by his speeches to opinion in a popular constituency and beyond, something that almost no established politician except Fox—and particularly no tory—had ever attempted. By whatever combination of corruption and conviction, Canning came top of the poll. He then had to attend numerous celebratory dinners in Liverpool, and also in Manchester, where he forcefully defended the system that denied the place representation. In Liverpool a Canning Club was founded in 1812. He told his mother:

> it certainly has been gratifying, and glorious beyond my most sanguine dreams of *popular* ambition. I may have looked to be a Minister—but I hardly ever thought that it would have fallen in my way to come in so close contact with so large a portion of the people, and to be so received. (Hinde, 262)

Liverpool was an extremely demanding seat. His constituents supplied an office and a secretary but expected him to consult them, act for them, and report to them. He pleased them by voting for the end of the East India Company's trade monopoly in 1813. He retained the seat at a by-election in 1816 and the two general elections of 1818 and 1820, but gave it up in 1822, to be succeeded as MP by William Huskisson, by then his principal lieutenant.

Despite his election victory of 1812, at Westminster Canning's situation was dismal. He felt so dispirited that he officially dissolved his little parliamentary party, as its members, he thought, were suffering by their devotion to him. His attendance at Westminster became less regular. He wrote to Leveson-Gower on 22 October 1813:

> At *present* …—while the station in Europe and in history, which I have thrown away, is full before my eyes; while I am alive to the sense of conscious ridicule (to say nothing of the sense of public duty) as having refused the management of the mightiest scheme of politics which this country ever engaged in … from a miserable point of etiquette—one absolutely unintelligible … at a distance of more than six miles from Palace Yard—I really think I am much better at home. (Hinde, 267)

In the summer of 1814 Lord Liverpool made him an offer which both pandered to these feelings and made it easier for him to take his invalid son to a better climate. The

Canningites would become avowed supporters of the government; Liverpool would give ministerial posts to Huskisson and Sturges Bourne, a viscountcy to Leveson-Gower, and an earldom to Boringdon; and Canning himself would be sent to Lisbon, in 'a great, splendid anomalous situation wholly out of the line of ordinary missions' (ibid., 269), at a salary of £14,000 p.a., to receive the regent of Portugal back from Brazil. Canning accepted, and sailed from Portsmouth in November, to the accompaniment of accusations of jobbery from the whigs. The embassy proved a serious task, since the regent did not return and Canning had difficult dealings with his council, especially when they felt threatened by Napoleon's Hundred Days. After Waterloo the mission was terminated, but Canning and his family remained abroad. He thus took no part at all in the peacemaking of 1814–15 or in the cabinet and public discussions about it.

India and the queen's affair, 1816–1822 While still in Portugal, in March 1816, Canning was offered by Liverpool, and accepted, the comparatively humble post of president of the Board of Control within the cabinet. In this post his main contribution was to give distinctly limited support and reluctant approval to the remarkably successful campaigns of the governor-general, Moira, against the Pindaris and the Marathas, which greatly extended the area of central India under British control. In parliament and outside he powerfully defended the government's measures of 1817 and 1819 (Six Acts) to curb domestic unrest. In speeches in Lancashire, as well as in the Commons, he strongly supported the magistrates' actions at Peterloo, playing on the fears of sober citizens for their property and security. However, his position in the cabinet did not give him much influence on general issues, except perhaps on foreign policy. He opposed, with little immediate result, Castlereagh's 'very questionable policy' of agreeing to regular meetings with 'despotic allies' (Thorne, 401; Temperley, *Foreign Policy*, 43–4). But ministers' attitudes were shifting, as was clearly shown in the classic state paper of 1820, in which Castlereagh declared emphatically that Britain's policy was non-intervention in the affairs of other states. This document certainly owed something to Canning's advocacy and drafting.

The accession of George IV in 1820 made the position of his queen the great issue of politics, putting Canning in special difficulty because he had been her friend—even if not, as the king believed, her lover. When she arrived in England in June Canning offered to resign, but was persuaded to stay on. Though he supported the government's policy, he infuriated George by expressing sympathy for her in the Commons. He rode out numerous royal tantrums but decided on 12 December 1820 that he must resign, ostensibly because he did not approve of her being treated as a guilty party. Since it seemed he could never hope to achieve his ambition of succeeding Castlereagh as foreign secretary and leader of the house, he had asked Liverpool early in 1820 for the succession to Moira as governor-general of Bengal. A spell in that post would restore his precarious financial position: much of his wife's fortune had been either spent or invested in a Lincolnshire estate that produced only a low return; without a ministerial salary his annual income was only £2200. In 1821–2 Liverpool tried strenuously to persuade the king to allow him back into the cabinet, but George obstinately refused to have him, and the prime minister concluded that the only way in which the ministry could avoid 'the greatest inconvenience' from his presence in the Commons would be to dispatch him to India. In March 1822 he accepted the governor-generalship. In May, believing that this would be his last opportunity, he obtained a majority in the Commons for a symbolic measure of Catholic emancipation, allowing Catholic peers to take their seats, but the Lords rejected the bill.

Foreign secretary, 1822–1827 On 12 August Canning's career was transformed by another stroke of fate: Castlereagh committed suicide. It was universally expected that Canning would succeed him, but the prime minister met intransigent opposition to this proposal from the king. Meanwhile Canning continued his preparations to go to India and went off to a round of farewell dinners and speeches at Liverpool. George IV gave way only after all members of the cabinet, including Peel and Wellington and the other opponents of Catholic emancipation, declared that Canning's appointment was necessary to the government's position in the Commons. At last, on 9 September, Liverpool was able to offer Canning the foreign secretaryship and the lead in the Commons, and on the 13th he accepted. He was elected for the government borough of Harwich early in 1823.

Canning's accession was the most conspicuous of a series of ministerial changes during the years 1821–3 which made Liverpool's government seem 'new', 'liberal', and 'popular'. Foreign affairs were the main business of governments in the days before parliamentary reform, and the issues with which he had to deal greatly excited the public. The force of his oratory and the vigour and mastery of his dispatches, which he made a point of publishing much more freely than any of his predecessors, ensured that he cut an exceptional figure as foreign secretary both at home and abroad; and it was he and his foreign policy that were generally taken to embody the new attitude of the government.

The Congress of Verona met in October 1822 and found itself unexpectedly concerned with possible intervention by the allied great powers to quell a revolt in Spain. Canning instructed Wellington, the British representative, to oppose such intervention, and in this succeeded. At the opening of parliament on 4 February 1823 the speech from the throne, opposing all intervention, was so well received that the opposition moved no amendment to the address. However France, with Chateaubriand as chief minister, was anxious to intervene on her own account, and this Canning could not prevent. After the French invasion in April, Canning made a powerful speech hostile to France and sympathetic to Spain, announcing that Britain would be neutral and publishing a large selection of diplomatic correspondence to justify his policy. When he came to answer his critics, he called himself 'an enthusiast for national independence', but stressed the blessings that Britain derived from remaining at peace. He won the vote by 372 to 20. In October he defended his policy in a great speech at Plymouth, where he was receiving the freedom of the borough.

Through most of Canning's period as foreign secretary, it was a major question whether to recognize the Latin American republics that had rebelled against Spain. Although Castlereagh had accepted that recognition was only a matter of time, the king and Wellington were violently opposed to it. They were infuriated by Canning's appeals to public opinion and his avowed sympathy with nationalist feeling, and they intrigued with foreign diplomats and tory dissidents against him. It was only with the strong support of Liverpool, and by threatening to resign and inform the public about the king's machinations, that Canning obtained the recognition of Buenos Aires in August 1824, and Colombia and Mexico early in 1825. 'Behold,' he wrote, 'the New World established, and if we do not throw it away, ours' (Hinde 372). Once he had carried these points, the king abandoned his long-standing vendetta against him, became almost his ally, and took to showing him the diplomatic correspondence he received as king of Hanover.

Canning's old involvement with Portugal was revived. The regent had actually returned to Lisbon in 1821 and accepted a constitutional regime, but it was overthrown two years later. In order to restore something like it and to maintain British influence in Portugal, Canning ordered intervention by the British navy, which he claimed was different in principle from intervention by an army. A pro-British regime was established early in 1825, and soon afterwards a British representative negotiated the recognition by Portugal (and Britain) of Brazilian independence. At the end of 1826, however, an invasion of Portugal from Spain led to Canning's proposing, and the Commons' enthusiastically supporting, the dispatch of a military expedition to preserve her liberties—intervention which he claimed was justified because it was designed to defeat the intervention of other powers and thereby to preserve the principle of non-intervention.

Canning's other main preoccupation in foreign policy was the Eastern question, especially as it was affected by the Greek revolt against Turkey in 1821, with which Russia sympathized. He recognized the rebels as belligerents in 1823 on purely pragmatic grounds, insisting that Britain remain completely neutral. He evaded attending an international congress on the issue desired by Tsar Alexander, but he sent Wellington to St Petersburg to try to get an agreement with the new Tsar Nicholas. On 4 April 1826 Wellington signed there a protocol declaring that, subject to Turkish agreement which Canning believed could be obtained, the Greeks would receive a measure of autonomy. In July 1827 England, Russia, and France signed the treaty of London intended to implement this protocol. At Canning's death the question was unresolved, but when the allied fleet, exceeding its instructions, destroyed the Turkish navy at the battle of Navarino on 20 October, Greek independence was secured. Canning received much of the credit for it from liberals, and corresponding blame from the tory ultras.

It is Canning's foreign policy from 1822 to 1827 on which his reputation mainly depends. The business of the Foreign Office vastly increased in these years, and his capacity for work—in particular his ability to reel off with amazing rapidity beautifully phrased and argued dispatches—was the admiration of his staff. It is symbolic that he, alone of foreign secretaries, actually took up residence at the Foreign Office in 1825, having sold Gloucester Lodge. Temperley, his greatest admirer, characterized his policy as:

> non-intervention; no European police system; every nation for itself, and God for us all; balance of power; respect for facts, not for abstract theories; respect for treaty rights, but caution in extending them … a republic is as good a member of the comity of nations as a monarch. 'England not Europe.' 'Our foreign policy cannot be conducted against the will of the nation.' 'Europe's domain extends to the shores of the Atlantic, England's begins there.' (Temperley, *Foreign Policy*, 470–71)

Canning's conduct of foreign policy was often taken as a touchstone by Victorian politicians, and Palmerston declared himself his disciple.

The major criticisms levelled at Canning's policy are of two kinds. First, it has been maintained that it differed from Castlereagh's in style rather than in substance. That their styles were widely different cannot be questioned: Castlereagh's prose was notoriously awkward, whereas Canning's speeches and dispatches were eloquent and ruthlessly clear, though not always tactful; and his appeal to public opinion in speeches both inside and outside the Commons, and by the publication of dispatches, was unprecedented. He claimed to rest his policy on Castlereagh's state paper of 1820; and, if the thinking behind that document was genuinely Castlereagh's, then he anticipated much of Canning's policy. But contemporary ultras, liberals, and radicals were united in their conviction that it was novel. 'A malevolent meteor', Metternich described him, 'a revolution in himself alone' (Hinde, 462). The second main line of criticism rules out the first. This view, expressed most ably by Schroeder, is that Canning's policy was utterly and deplorably different from Castlereagh's, in that it abandoned the beneficent new system established at Vienna to maintain the peace of Europe, and substituted an ultimately irresponsible dedication to British interests narrowly conceived. It is further suggested that Canning tuned his foreign policy to procure himself applause and serve his domestic political ambitions. He certainly wrote flippant dispatches—one of them, famously, in rhyme—to the rather too numerous friends for whom he had found diplomatic posts. But it is very questionable that his foreign policy, bitterly contested as it was by the king, ministers, and many of his own party, was calculated to advance his domestic career. And the essential difficulty about Schroeder's view is that it is impossible to imagine the European rulers of the nineteenth century, particularly those of Austria, adapting themselves in a series of congresses to the economic, social, political, and intellectual developments of the age.

Prime minister, April–August 1827 Like his predecessor, Canning was terribly overworked through being leader of the Commons as well as foreign secretary. As leader he had, of course, to master many subjects. None moved him or troubled him more than Catholic emancipation, which he wished to promote but which continued to be the subject of bitter division within his own party. 'Consider a little', he wrote in 1825, when he was trying to carry a limited measure of emancipation,

> what it is to go into the House, as I did on Monday at five in the afternoon, remain there till two in the morning; then to have for sleep, refreshment, and such business as will not stand still, only twelve hours; then a Cabinet from two to four, then to be in the House again from five to nine, to get up to speak for two hours at eleven, and to get to bed not before five. (Hinde, 398)

On economic and fiscal policy Canning was less well informed and less dogmatic than Liverpool, Peel, and Huskisson, but he backed the reformers, helped to argue their economic measures through the house, and became identified with them. On the mitigation of the corn laws he was more personally engaged, and a speech he made on the subject in 1825 infuriated the tory ultras. He argued for taking account of 'the progress of political knowledge', adding: 'those who resist indiscriminately all improvement as innovation, may find themselves compelled at last to submit to innovations, although they are not improvements' (Hinde, 403). His stance on these matters, as on foreign policy, was more agreeable to the opposition than to many tories.

At the general election of 1826, in which Canning was returned for Newport, Isle of Wight, the divisions within the government on the Catholic question and the corn laws were only too obvious, and the results suggested that English opinion was hostile to emancipation. Liverpool was growing increasingly despondent about keeping the cabinet together when he had an incapacitating stroke on 17 February 1827. Most people assumed that Canning would succeed him and, after a lengthy delay during which other possibilities were canvassed, the king appointed him prime minister on 12 April. But Wellington and his friends had become so jaundiced about Canning's foreign policy, his 'Catholic' and 'liberal' sympathies, his ambition, his intellectual arrogance, and what they saw as his untrustworthiness that they refused to serve under an avowedly 'Catholic' premier. The king was furious with them and took up Canning's challenge: 'Sir, your father broke the domination of the Whigs. I hope Your Majesty will not endure that of the Tories' (Hinde, 443). Canning managed to persuade a few minor 'protestants' to stay on, but made up his cabinet largely from liberal tories and, after protracted negotiations, a contingent of moderate whigs led by the marquess of Lansdowne. All had to agree not to propose either parliamentary reform or the repeal of the Test Act. Among tories Robinson became Viscount Goderich and secretary for war and the colonies, and Huskisson president of the Board of Trade; Lord Dudley became foreign secretary, and initially Sturges Bourne was made home secretary, and Canning's brother-in-law, the duke of Portland, lord privy seal. All these were undoubted Canningites and the last three quite untried in office. Lord Palmerston, who had languished in minor office since 1809, entered the cabinet, and Canning himself took the chancellorship of the exchequer. William Lamb was made Irish secretary. When Lansdowne joined the cabinet in May he took no portfolio, but two months later he became home secretary and Carlisle, another crony of Canning's, lord privy seal, while Sturges Bourne and Portland were relegated to lesser roles. Brougham and many whigs sat on the government side of the house, and Althorp soon joined them in support of 'a government actuated by liberal and enlightened principles' (ibid., 453). Canning had to give up his parliamentary seat when made first lord of the Treasury, and was returned at a by-election for Seaford.

The ministry found its position in the Commons difficult, and in the strongly tory Lords almost impossible. It failed to get through a modification of the corn laws. Canning was subjected to personal attacks of unusual violence. A month after his mother's death and a week after Canning had taken office as prime minister Grey, who had always disliked him, declared in the Lords that he was disqualified for the post because his mother had been an actress; and the tory ultras denounced him for having allegedly betrayed his tory principles and friends. But the government's greatest weakness was Canning's health. For some years he had been suffering ever more frequently from prostrating attacks of what was called gout. It was clear to everyone that he was under enormous strain. He had caught a chill, like several other ministers, while waiting two hours in St George's Chapel, Windsor, for the funeral of the duke of York on 5 January, and never fully recovered. He got worse in July, when the duke of Devonshire lent him Chiswick House to give him some respite. On 30 July he told the king that he did not know what was wrong with him but he was ill all over. Doctors said he was suffering from an inflammation of the liver and the lungs. He died at Chiswick, in the room in which Fox had died, on 8 August.

The coalition ministry was continued under Goderich as prime minister but lasted only until January 1828. Its significance was not in its achievement but in its formation and composition. Although the more rigorous whigs, especially Grey, had refused to serve, the cabinet anticipated the reforming ministry that he was to create in 1830: it was the bridge over which Robinson, Palmerston, and other liberal tories passed to become parliamentary reformers. The refusal of office by Wellington and Peel marked the decisive split between them and the liberal tories, despite a brief reunion in the early stages of Wellington's administration of 1828. In his youth Canning had been part of the movement of the whigs into coalition with Pitt against the threat of the French Revolution. Now he was part creator and part victim of the movement of public opinion in the country and in parliament away from the paranoiac fear of change at home and abroad which the French Revolution and Napoleon had induced: victim both because in emphasizing the liberal elements of Pitt's heritage he lost his natural support across the tory party, and because he was so virulently attacked for it. The scenario was never forgotten by those who had observed it. When on 8 June 1846 Lord George Bentinck, Canning's nephew and private secretary, denounced Peel's proposal to repeal the corn laws, his backers flung against Peel the taunt: 'Who killed Mr Canning?' In 1886 Gladstone said of Canning, who remained always one of his heroes, that he had 'emancipated this country from its servitude to the Holy Alliance; and for so doing he was more detested by the upper classes of this country than any man has been during the present century' (H. C. G. Matthew, *Gladstone, 1875–1898*, 1995, 97).

Canning's death produced an outpouring of sympathy from press and public. It was emphasized that he was one of the people, untitled, without inherited wealth and connections, who had made his way to the top by his own ability and exertions. His early childhood had been passed in by far the poorest, and socially the most dubious, circumstances of any man who achieved major political office before the appointment of the first Labour cabinet in 1924; and he remained the only man without a title to have become foreign secretary until Ramsay MacDonald took the office. He received a public funeral and was buried in Westminster Abbey on 16 August, close to Pitt. His wife, Joan, lived until 1837, jealously defending his political record. She was created a viscountess in 1828, when parliament granted an annual pension of £3000 to the Canning family. Canning was survived by two sons, William Pitt (1802–1828), who was a naval officer and drowned at an early age, and Charles John *Canning (1812–1862), who became governor-general of India. His daughter, Harriet (1801–1876), married Ulick John de Burgh, the first marquess of Clanricarde (1802–1874).

Estimate Canning was one of the handful of men who have brought transcendent talents to the practice of politics in Britain. His contemporaries all recognized him as a man of outstanding ability and personality, about whom it was impossible to be neutral. His gifts were limited in scope: though he was a steadfast supporter of the Church of England, he was uninterested in theology; he confessed to being wholly unmusical; and he took no part in sport of any kind. His recreations were conversation, literature, playgoing, and, when it became possible after the war, continental travel. His knowledge of the classics was recognized as exceptional. He was a fluent and witty versifier, and his wicked parodies of Southey, which led to the withdrawal of the originals, hold their place in modern collections. His and George Ellis's take-off of contemporary German drama, *The Rovers*, was performed at the Haymarket in 1811.

As a minister Canning was formidably hard-working. But his greatest skill and weapon was his style, as expressed in his dispatches but most notably in his speeches. Time and again his oratory saved the day for himself and his colleagues in the Commons, and after 1812 it won him a unique reputation in the country. Among the elaborate images for which he was notorious the following, from a speech at Liverpool on 30 August 1822, a fortnight before he became foreign secretary for the second time, was perhaps the most striking and characteristic:

> What should we think of that philosopher, who, in writing, at the present day, a treatise upon naval architecture and the theory of navigation, should omit wholly from his calculations that new and mighty power ... which walks the water, like a giant rejoicing in his course;—stemming alike the tempest and the tide;—accelerating intercourse, shortening distances;—creating, as it were, unexpected neighbourhoods, and new combinations of social and commercial relation;—and giving to the fickleness of winds and faithlessness of waves the certainty and steadiness of a highway upon the land? ... the power of STEAM. ... So, in political science, he who, speculating on the British Constitution, should content himself with marking the distribution of acknowledged technical powers between the House of Lords, the House of Commons, and the Crown, and assigning to each their separate provinces, ... and should think that he had thus described the British Constitution as it acts and as it is influenced in its action; but should omit from his enumeration that mighty power of Public Opinion, embodied in a Free Press, which pervades, and checks, and perhaps, in the last resort, nearly governs the whole;—such a man would, surely, give but an imperfect view of the government of England as it now is. (Therry, *Speeches*, 6.404–05)

Only Canning, among the politicians of his time, offered the proof that in the unreformed system a man of the people could reach the summit of politics, and that public opinion could be effectively mobilized in support, first, of reaction against the French Revolution, and then of a liberal tory government opposed to parliamentary reform.

DEREK BEALES

Sources J. Bagot, ed., *George Canning and his friends*, 2 vols. (1909) • *The speeches of the Right Honourable George Canning with a memoir of his life*, ed. R. Therry, 6 vols. (1828) • *Speeches of the Right Hon. George Canning delivered on public occasions in Liverpool* (1825) • *The letter-journal of George Canning, 1793–1795*, ed. P. Jupp, CS, 4th ser., 41 (1991) • J. J. Raven, 'Some letters of George Canning (mostly unpublished)', *Anglo-Saxon Review*, 3 (1899), 45–51 • A. Aspinall, ed., *The formation of Canning's ministry, February to August 1827*, CS, 3rd ser., 59 (1937) • *Some official correspondence of George Canning*, ed. E. J. Stapleton, 2 vols. (1887) • [J. Styles], *Memoirs of the life of the Right Honourable George Canning*, 2 vols. (1828) • L. T. Rede, *Memoir of the Right Honourable George Canning* (1827) • A. G. Stapleton, *The political life of the Rt. Hon. George Canning*, 3 vols. (1831) • J. F. Newton, *The early days of George Canning* (1828) • R. Bell, *The life of the Rt. Hon. George Canning* (1846) • W. Hinde, *George Canning* (1973) • R. G. Thorne, 'Canning, George I', HoP, *Commons* • D. Marshall, *The rise of George Canning* (1938) • H. W. V. Temperley, *Life of Canning* (1905) • P. J. V. Rolo, *George Canning* (1965) • P. Dixon, *Canning* (1976) • G. Festing, *John Hookham Frere and his friends* (1899) • H. Temperley, *The foreign policy of Canning, 1822–1827* (1925) • A. Aspinall, 'The Canningite party', *TRHS*, 4th ser., 17 (1934), 177–226 • W. R. Brock, *Lord Liverpool and liberal toryism, 1820 to 1827* (1941) • D. Gray, *Spencer Perceval: the evangelical prime minister, 1762–1812* (1963) • S. Lane-Poole, *The life of ... Stratford Canning*, 2 vols. (1888) • A. Mitchell, *The whigs in opposition, 1815–1830* (1967) • F. O'Gorman, *The whig party and the French Revolution* (1967) • S. Watson, *The reign of George III* (1960) • E. L. Woodward, *The age of reform, 1815–1870* (1938) • C. Collyer, unpublished article on George Canning, priv. coll. • P. Schroeder, *The transformation of European politics, 1763–1848* (1994) • N. Gash, *Lord Liverpool* (1984) • E. Halévy, *The liberal awakening, 1815–1830* (1926) • J. Ehrman, *The* *younger Pitt*, 2–3 (1983–96) • B. Whittingham-Jones, 'Liverpool's political clubs, 1812–1830', *Transactions of the Historic Society of Lancashire and Cheshire*, 111 (1959), 117–38 • C. R. Middleton, *The administration of British foreign policy, 1782–1846* (1977) • S. Schwartzberg, 'The lion and the phoenix — British policy toward the "Greek question", 1821–32', *Middle Eastern Studies*, 24 (1988), 139–77 • A. Cunningham, 'The philhellenes, Canning and Greek independence', *Middle Eastern Studies*, 14 (1978), 151–81 • D. B. Horn, ed., *British diplomatic representatives, 1689–1789*, CS, 3rd ser., 46 (1932)

Archives BL, journals of tours in Europe written by G. R. Chinnery, Add. MSS 64093–64095 • Duke U., Perkins L., letters • Harewood House, Leeds • Harvard U., Houghton L., papers • Lpool RO, letters • NRA, priv. coll., corresp. and papers • PRO, papers relating to Spain and Greece, FO 800/229–31 • St Deiniol's Library, Hawarden, corresp. and papers as MP for Liverpool • U. Mich., Clements L., political and diplomatic corresp. • W. Yorks. AS, Leeds, political corresp., diaries, and papers; corresp. and papers | All Souls Oxf., letters to Sir Charles Vaughan • BL, corresp. with William A'Court, Add. MSS 41541–41555 • BL, corresp. with Lord Bathurst, loan 57 • BL, letters to E. Bootle-Wilbraham, Add. MS 46841 • BL, corresp. with J. Hookham Frere, Add. MS 38833 • BL, letters to James Willoughby Gordon, Add. MS 49476 • BL, corresp. with Sir Robert Gordon, Add. MSS 42314, 42317 • BL, corresp. with Lord Grenville, Add. MS 58960 • BL, letters to Lord Grenville, Add. MSS 69038, 69076 • BL, letters to Thomas Grenville, Add. MS 41856 • BL, corresp. with Lord Holland, Add. MS 51598 • BL, corresp. with William Huskisson, Add. MSS 38736–38749 • BL, corresp. with earls of Liverpool, Add. MSS 38193–38412, 38738–38748, *passim* • BL, corresp. with Lord Melbourne, Add. MSS 60399–60483 • BL, corresp. with Lord Morley, Add. MSS 48219–48221 • BL, corresp. with Sir Arthur Paget, Add. MS 48391 • BL, corresp. with Sir Robert Peel, Add. MS 40311 • BL, corresp. with George Rose, Add. MS 42773 • BL, letters to Sir George Henry Rose, Add. MS 42790 • BL, letters to Lord Skelmersdale, Add. MS 46841 • BL, corresp. with Lord Wellesley, Add. MSS 37286–37297, *passim* • BL, corresp. with William Windham, Add. MS 37844 • BL OIOC, letters to W. P. Amherst, MSS Eur. F 140 • BL OIOC, corresp. relating to East India Company, MSS Eur. F 142 • Bodl. Oxf., letters to Comte Louis D'Antraigues, MS Don d 92 • Bodl. Oxf., corresp. with Spencer Perceval, Eng. Hist. MS 261 (copies) • Bodl. Oxf., Talbot MSS, corresp. with Third Baron Talbot of Malahide • Bodl. Oxf., letters to William Wilberforce • Chatsworth House, Derbyshire, letters to duke of Devonshire • CKS, letters to William Pitt, etc. • CUL, corresp. with Spencer Perceval • Cumbria AS, Carlisle, corresp. with Lord Lowther • Derbys. RO, letters to Lord St Helens • Derbys. RO, letters to Sir R. J. Wilmot-Horton • Devon RO, corresp. with Lord Sidmouth • Durham RO, letters from Lord Castlereagh • Hants. RO, letters to James Harris • Hants. RO, corresp. with William Wickham • Harrowby Manuscript Trust, Sandon Hall, Stafford, letters to Lord and Lady Harrowby • Manx National Heritage Library, Douglas, letters to Drinkwater family of Kirby, Isle of Man • Morgan L., corresp. with Lord Wellesley • NA Scot., corresp. with Lord Binning • NA Scot., letters to Sir Alexander Hope • NA Scot., corresp. with Lord Melville • NL Scot., corresp. with Sir George Henry Rose, MS 3797 • NL Scot., corresp. with Sir Walter Scott, MSS 3875–3904 • NL Scot., letters to Lord Stuart De Rothesay, MSS 6216–6229 • NRA, priv. coll., corresp. with Sir Charles Bagot • NRA, priv. coll., corresp. with Spencer Perceval • NRA, priv. coll., corresp. with Sir John Sinclair • PRO, corresp. with Stratford Canning, FO 352 • PRO, corresp. with Lord Cowley, FO 519 • PRO, Foreign Office MSS, FO 800/229–231 • PRO, corresp. with first Earl Granville, PRO 30/29 • PRO, corresp. with William Pitt, PRO 30/8 • RA, corresp. with Thomas Lawrence • Royal Arch., letters to George III • Sheff. Arch., letters to Lord Wharncliffe • Shrops. RRC, corresp. with third Baron Berwick • St Deiniol's Library, Hawarden, corresp. with Sir John Gladstone • Staffs. RO, letters to Lord Hatherton • TCD, letters to second earl of Donoughmore • TCD, Hely-Hutchinson MSS • U. Durham L., letters to Viscount Ponsonby • U. Mich., Clements L., J. W. Croker MSS • U. Nott. L., Cavendish-Bentinck MSS • U. Nott. L., corresp. with duke of Portland • University of Sydney Library, letters to H. J. Richman • W. Yorks. AS, Leeds, letters to Lord Clanricarde • W. Yorks. AS, Leeds, De Burgh MSS • W. Yorks. AS, Leeds, letters to his cousin Elizabeth • W. Yorks. AS, Leeds, Stapleton MSS • W. Yorks. AS, Leeds, letters to half-sister Mary Thompson

Likenesses T. Gainsborough, oils, *c.*1787, Harewood House, West Yorkshire • J. Hoppner, oils, 1797, Eton • T. Lawrence, oils, 1809, Christ Church Oxf. • J. Nollekens, marble bust, 1810, Wellington Museum, Apsley House, London • W. Ward, mezzotint, pubd 1813 (after oil painting by T. Stewardson, exh. RA 1813), NG Ire. • F. Chantrey, pencil drawing, *c.*1818, NPG • F. Chantrey, marble bust, 1819, Palace of Westminster, London • F. Chantrey, marble bust, 1821, NPG • T. Lawrence, oils, exh. RA 1825, Harewood House, West Yorkshire • T. Lawrence, oils, 1825, NPG [*see illus.*] • D. D'Angers, bronze bust, 1827, Musée d'Angers, France • C. Turner, mezzotint, pubd 1827 (after T. Lawrence), BM, NPG • F. Chantrey, statue, *c.*1829, Westminster Abbey, London • R. Westmacott, statue, 1832, Parliament Square, London • Cruickshank, caricature, BM • Doyle, caricature, BM • K. A. Hickel, group portrait, oils (*The House of Commons, 1793*), NPG • caricatures, BM

Wealth at death under £39,000: Aspinall, ed., *The formation of Canning's ministry*

Canning, Hubert George de Burgh, second marquess of Clanricarde (1832–1916), landlord in Ireland, was born on 30 November 1832, the younger son of Ulick John de Burgh, first marquess and fourteenth earl of Clanricarde (1802–1874), and his wife, Lady Harriet, the only daughter of George Canning. He was on poor terms with his father and identified with his mother's family. Later there were unfounded rumours that his biological father was a Russian nobleman. Educated at Harrow School, he entered the diplomatic service in 1852, and was for ten years attaché at Turin, retiring in 1863 after inheriting (in 1862) the fortune of his maternal uncle, Earl Canning, whose surname he assumed. His financial position had previously been extremely precarious, which is said to have been the cause of his lifelong miserliness. In 1867 the death of his elder brother made him heir to the marquessate. He succeeded his brother as Liberal MP for co. Galway (1867–71). The home rule victory in the by-election after his resignation marked the decline of landlord influence; he later denounced his tenants' 'disloyalty' to his father in 1871.

After his father's death in 1874, Clanricarde lived in rented rooms in London, never visiting his east Galway estates. He lived frugally, apart from the acquisition of an art collection, and allegedly engaged in money lending. In later life he enjoyed ice-skating. Although his estates were not highly rented he saw them as his absolute property, and denied that the tenants had any moral right to object to the contract by which they held them. With the rise of land agitation after the bad harvests of 1879, this unyielding attitude, coupled with his unsociable personality and his position as the stereotypical absentee landlord whose relationship with his tenants was merely that of rent-receiver, made him a major target; his financial resources enabled him to resist effectively. His obduracy brought him into conflict even with some of his land agents; he is alleged to have told one: 'If my tenants think they can intimidate me by shooting you, they are very much mistaken'.

In 1886 the Clanricarde estates became a major battleground for the Plan of Campaign, whereby tenants demanded rent reductions and, if refused, paid the reduced rent to their representatives. Of 1159 tenants 186 were evicted after organized resistance, and 'emergency men' placed in vacant holdings; boycotting and agrarian violence followed. Several tenant leaders and sympathizers were imprisoned. Even unionists saw Clanricarde as a political liability. One request for troops to assist with evictions was refused, and chief secretary A. J. Balfour privately advocated the compulsory purchase of his estates. (This was rejected by the cabinet as interference with property rights.)

Even after the collapse of the Plan, Clanricarde refused any compromise and opposed the policy of land purchase promoted by successive governments. The east Galway area remained a centre of unrest. His eviction of a Loughrea shopkeeper for political activities led to the passage of the 1907 Town Tenants' Act, and Clanricarde made a rare speech in the House of Lords against the 1907 Evicted Tenants' Act. The 1909 Birrell Land Act allowed the compulsory purchase of his estate and reinstatement of evicted tenants, but as he used every legal expedient to resist, not until July 1915 did the land court finally convey the estate to the congested districts board.

Clanricarde died at his home, 13 Hanover Square, London, on 12 April 1916 and was buried in London; some time previously he was evicted from The Albany due to refusal to pay an increased rent. Although heterosexual he never married. His marquessate became extinct; his cousin the marquess of Sligo inherited the earldom of Clanricarde, while his fortune was bequeathed to his great-nephew Lord Lascelles (later earl of Harewood).

S. L. Gwynn, *rev.* Patrick Maume

Sources *Irish Times* (14 April 1916) • M. Shiel and D. Roche, eds., *A forgotten campaign* (1986) • L. M. Geary, *The plan of campaign, 1886–1891* (1986) • V. Crossman, *Politics, law and order in nineteenth-century Ireland* (1996) • *WWW* • Burke, *Peerage* • W. S. Blunt, *The land war in Ireland: being a personal narrative of events* (1912) • E. Longford [E. H. Pakenham, countess of Longford], *A pilgrimage of passion: the life of Wilfrid Scawen Blunt* (1979)

Likenesses L. Ward, oils, 1919, Harewood House, West Yorkshire • Spy [L. Ward], chromolithograph caricature, NPG; repro. in *VF* (22 Jan 1900) • H. Tonks, drawing, posthumous, Harewood House, West Yorkshire • cartoon, repro. in *Weekly Freeman* (17 Dec 1887) • portrait, repro. in Shiel and Roche, eds., *Forgotten campaign*

Wealth at death £2,500,000: probate, 1916, *CGPLA Eng. & Wales*

Canning, Richard (1708–1775), religious controversialist and topographer, was born in Plymouth on 30 September 1708, the son of Richard Canning (*d.* 1726) and his wife, Margaret (*d.* 1734). His father retired from the navy after twenty years' service as a courageous naval commander and in 1712 took the family to Ipswich, where he 'through resentment of party, founded on mis-reported facts, died a private Captain' (memorial inscription, St Helen's, Ipswich) in 1726, aged fifty-seven. By then Canning had passed through Westminster School, where he was King's scholar in 1723, to St Catharine's College, Cambridge, where he graduated BA in 1729, before proceeding MA at Peterhouse six years later. He became perpetual curate at St Lawrence, Ipswich, in 1734 and soon added other livings near by: Harkstead, Freston, Rushmere St Andrew, and Thornham Magna. From 1738 to 1756 and from 1766 to 1768 he held four livings at once. He married Cordelia Westhorp at St Dunstan-in-the-East, London, on 25 July 1739. They had a son and daughter who were christened Richard and Cordelia. His wife died in December 1751, at the age of thirty-six. Their son, after being educated at Emmanuel College, succeeded Canning at Harkstead in 1769, and their daughter died unmarried, also aged thirty-six, in 1780.

Canning was a pillar of Anglican life in Suffolk, and a leading member of the clerical, literary, and musical circles to which the young Thomas Gainsborough belonged until he left for Bath in 1759. Canning's formal and rather humourless portrait by his friend survives. Intolerant of dissent, he wrote several pamphlets replying robustly to vindications of separatism by the Presbyterian Charles Owen and the deist Henry Dodwell the younger. As a tory, he ran an unofficial opposition to the whigs who were then running the Ipswich corporation. Having learned that he was preparing to publish, under a fairly transparent cloak of anonymity, a criticism of the corporation's handling of borough charities, the bailiffs in 1746 rejected his very practical offer of a thousand armorial book-plates to guard against further losses from the valuable library of the town preachers. This snub, however, did not deter him from exposing past mismanagement the following year, when he published his *Account of the gifts and legacies that have been given and bequeathed to charitable uses in the town of Ipswich* (1747), which was revised for a second edition in 1819. In 1754 he published translations of *The Principal Charters which have been Granted to Ipswich*, which he hoped would keep the corporation, now tory, on the right lines.

In the *Illustrations of the Literary History of the Eighteenth Century*, John Nichols confidently called Canning editor of the second edition of *The Suffolk Traveller*, an early road book published by John Kirby in 1735 and reissued, much enlarged, in 1764 over the original author's name. The printed prospectus, however, named Kirby's second and third sons, Joshua and William, and there were substantial additions made by Thomas Martin and John Tanner. Andrew Baldrey, Joshua Kirby's business partner, provided the county and road maps; others of the separate hundreds and of Ipswich exist only as originals. Canning's part was presumably to prepare the much revised edition for the publisher John Shave.

Of his eight published works, only two sermons disclose Canning's identity, and he published nothing more after 1764. In 1770 the bailiffs, by now whigs again, began litigation over various stipends, including his; four years later he won. A widower for twenty-four years, he died in the parish of St Margaret, Ipswich, on 8 June 1775 and was buried in St Helen's, Ipswich, six days later. His daughter's memorial inscription praised his universal benevolence to town charities. Canning did more than criticize earlier trustees of the Ipswich charities, for he gave generously himself, and his son, who died without progeny in 1789, left £10,000 to the SPCK. J. M. BLATCHLY

Sources Nichols, *Illustrations*, 6.538–45 · G. R. Clarke, *The history and description of the town and borough of Ipswich* (1830), 205, 315 · memorial inscription, St Helen's Church, Ipswich · Ipswich Great Court Book, Suffolk RO, Ipswich, C5/14/9, 1750–77 · J. Welch, *The list of the queen's scholars of St Peter's College, Westminster*, ed. [C. B. Phillimore], new edn (1852) · Venn, *Alum. Cant.* · parish register (marriage), London, St Dunstan-in-the-East, 1739 · parish register (burial), Ipswich, St Helen's, 1775

Likenesses T. Gainsborough, portrait, oils, *c*.1755 (half-length), Christchurch Mansion, Ipswich

Wealth at death over £10,000

Canning, Sir Samuel (1823–1908), civil and electrical engineer, was born at Ogbourne St Andrew, Wiltshire, on 21 July 1823, the son of Robert Canning of Ogbourne St Andrew, and his wife, Frances Hyde. Educated at Salisbury, he gained his first engineering experience (1844–9) with Locke and Errington on the Great Western Railway extensions, and as resident engineer on the Liverpool, Ormskirk, and Preston Railway. From railway work he turned in 1852 to submarine telegraphy, and entering the service of Glass, Elliot & Co., cable manufacturers, he laid in 1855–6 the Canadian cable connecting Cape Breton Island with Newfoundland.

In 1857 Canning assisted Charles Bright with the first Atlantic cable, and he was on board HMS *Agamemnon* during the submergence of the cable in 1857 and 1858. Subsequently, until 1865, while in the service of Glass, Elliot & Co., he laid cables in the deep waters of the Mediterranean and other seas. He married on 27 September 1859 Elizabeth Ann (*d.* 1909), daughter of William Henry Gale of Grately, Hampshire; they had three sons and three daughters.

When the Telegraph Construction and Maintenance Company was formed in 1865, Canning was appointed its chief engineer, and in that capacity had charge of the manufacture and laying of the Atlantic cables of 1865 and 1866, for which the company were the contractors. This work involved the preparation and fitting-out of the *Great Eastern*. On 2 August 1865 the cable broke in 2000 fathoms of water. After a second cable had been successfully laid by the *Great Eastern* (13–27 July 1866), Canning set to work to recover the broken cable, using special grappling machinery, which he devised for the purpose. After several failures, the cable was eventually recovered on 2 September 1866. For these services he was knighted in 1866; the king of Portugal conferred upon him the order of St Jago d'Espada, and the Liverpool chamber of commerce presented him with a gold medal. In 1869 he laid the French Atlantic cable between Brest and Duxbury, Massachusetts.

After his retirement from the service of the Telegraph Construction Company, Canning practised as a consulting engineer in matters connected with telegraphy, and, among other work, superintended the laying of the Marseilles–Algiers and other cables for the India Rubber, Gutta Percha, and Telegraph Works Company, acting later as adviser to the West Indian and Panama and other telegraph companies. When the firm of Callender's decided to adapt their bitumen products to the manufacture of insulated cable, they hired Canning to advise them on the acquisition of machinery for wire work. He was appointed to Callender's board in March 1883, but resigned in December after a dispute over his remuneration. He was a member of both the Institution of Civil Engineers and the Institution of Electrical Engineers. He died at Whatley, Twyford, Hampshire, on 24 September 1908, and was buried on 29 September in Kensal Green cemetery, London.

W. F. SPEAR, *rev.* ANITA MCCONNELL

Sir Samuel Canning (1823–1908), by Beatrice Bright, 1897

Sources *PICE*, 175 (1908–9), 316–17 · *The Times* (26 Sept 1908), 11e · R. M. Morgan, *Callender's, 1882–1945* (1982), chaps. 1–2 · private information (1912) · *The Times* (30 Sept 1908), 11a [funeral] · m. cert. · d. cert.

Likenesses B. Bright, oils, 1897, NPG [*see illus.*] · bust, Inst. CE

Wealth at death £109 1*s*. 8*d*.: probate, 24 Oct 1908, *CGPLA Eng. & Wales*

Canning, Stratford, Viscount Stratford de Redcliffe (1786–1880), diplomatist, born on 4 November 1786 in St Clement's Lane in the City of London, was the fourth son and youngest child of Stratford Canning (*d.* 1787), and his wife, Mehitabel (Hetty) Patrick (*d.* 1831), the daughter of a Dublin merchant. He was the first cousin of George Canning, later prime minister. Although the Canning family originated from the west of England, this branch had been resident in Ireland since the seventeenth century.

Family and education The elder Stratford Canning was disinherited by his father, 'Counsellor' Canning (another Stratford), who also disinherited George Canning's father,

Stratford Canning, Viscount Stratford de Redcliffe (1786–1880), by George Frederic Watts, 1856–7

in both cases because he disapproved of their marriages. The second Stratford Canning went to London and became a merchant and banker. His most famous son was born in what the younger Stratford himself later described as 'a narrow dingy street' near the Mansion House, when it was still usual for even prosperous men to live on their business premises. His father died only six months later and the family moved to Wanstead in Essex, although Stratford's strong-minded mother continued to run the firm until his eldest brother was old enough to take over.

Although the family complained of their reduced circumstances, poverty is relative and Stratford, after a dame-school at Snaresbrook (1790–92) and a preparatory school in Hackney (1792–5), was sent to Eton College (1795–1806) and King's College, Cambridge (1806–8). At Eton, where he was a king's scholar, he was at first more interested in games than in scholarship—curious in a man who later in life prided himself on keeping very fit without ever taking exercise. One tutor, John Sumner, later archbishop of Canterbury, however, caught his interest and persuaded him to study.

The playwright Richard Brinsley Sheridan and the politician Charles James Fox were friends of the family, but the most important continuing influence on Stratford was his older cousin George Canning. Probably at his invitation Stratford visited the House of Commons frequently and was awed by the oratory of the younger Pitt. Eton boys were welcome at Windsor and on a famous occasion Stratford, in reply to a question, told George III that he was in the sixth form. The king replied that he was then 'a much greater man than I can ever make you' (Lane-Poole, 1.16). Unlike George Canning, Stratford did not distinguish himself at Eton although he did, with three friends—Richard Wellesley (the son of the marquess), John Rennell, and Gally Knight—publish a weekly literary journal, *The Miniature*, in imitation of George Canning's *The Microcosm*.

Canning's career at Cambridge, where he occupied the rooms that had once belonged to Robert Walpole, was even less remarkable. After only two terms George Canning, then foreign secretary, offered him a post as précis writer at the Foreign Office. Stratford divided his time between Cambridge and his cousin's house in Downing Street, where he first met foreign diplomats. Later the same year (October 1807) Stratford was sent with Anthony Merry's mission to try to restore relations with Denmark after the British bombardment of Copenhagen. He wrote an account to his sister, much of it later published in Lane-Poole's *Life* (1.31–6).

Early diplomatic missions Stratford Canning returned briefly to Cambridge (where he eventually proceeded MA in 1813) but, in May 1808, was asked to accompany Robert Adair's mission to Constantinople. The background to this, as to the Copenhagen mission, was the Napoleonic wars. In 1805 Britain, Russia, and Turkey had seemed united against France but the third coalition quickly fell apart. French influence in Turkey increased and in November 1806 a Russian army entered the principalities of Moldavia and Wallachia to combat this. In December Turkey declared war on Russia. The British mounted an unsuccessful naval demonstration in support of their Russian ally and, in January 1807, the British ambassador, Charles Arbuthnot, left Constantinople. In July 1807, however, France and Russia became allies by the treaty of Tilsit. Adair's task was to restore relations between Britain and Turkey. A peace treaty, the treaty of the Dardanelles, was concluded between them in January 1809.

This mission marked Stratford Canning's first serious involvement in diplomacy and also his introduction to Constantinople, where he was to gain his later fame. Adair chose to leave in 1810, leaving the 24-year-old Canning as minister-plenipotentiary in charge of a key embassy. A secret clause of the 1809 treaty had provided for the possibility of Britain acting as mediator to restore peace between Russia and Turkey.

By 1812 the Turks wished for peace and Napoleon's threat to invade Russia made the British anxious to see Russian troops freed from the Turkish war to fight the French. The signature of the treaty of Bucharest between Turkey and Russia on 28 May 1812 was Canning's first diplomatic success and, in the eyes of his official biographer, Lane-Poole, remained his greatest. Canning may have exaggerated his own role. Other influences were brought to bear on the sultan, Mahmud, including that of his half-French mother, who opposed Napoleon. But Canning played a clever, if at times risky, game, by showing the Turks papers obtained by British intelligence, designed to prove that Napoleon was plotting with Austria to partition the Ottoman empire. At the same time he communicated with the Russians and urged them to moderation.

Canning also had some success in safeguarding British trade in the Levant but he was glad to return to London in 1812. He had several times asked to come home, where he believed the real action to be. He hoped to establish a political or literary career but made little headway, although he was associated with the foundation of the *Quarterly Review*, a tory reply to the whig *Edinburgh Review*. He declined to accompany Lord Aberdeen's mission to Austria in 1813 as secretary of embassy on the grounds that, since he had already been minister-plenipotentiary, it would be a demotion. He visited Paris at the time of the signature of the first treaty of Paris in the spring of 1814. He saw his later enemy the future Tsar Nicholas, but they seem to have met only formally, if at all. He did meet Lord Castlereagh, from whom he solicited a job.

Switzerland In June 1814 Canning accepted Castlereagh's offer of the post of minister-plenipotentiary in Switzerland. Napoleon had bound the Swiss cantons closely to France. Canning's first task, together with other allied representatives, notably the Russian plenipotentiary, Count Capo d'Istria, was to create a new federal Switzerland, whose neutrality would be guaranteed by the powers, to act as a barrier to French expansion towards either Italy or Germany. It was a difficult task, not only because of boundary disputes with France but also because of the political, linguistic, and religious divisions among the Swiss cantons.

In October 1814 Castlereagh summoned Canning to Vienna. Nominally, Canning's task was to bring the new Swiss constitution for approval by the congress but Castlereagh was short of good juniors and Canning was employed in a number of capacities. Vienna gave him an opportunity to observe all the leading statesmen of Europe: the duke of Wellington, for whom Canning developed a deep admiration; the Austrian Metternich, whom on the whole Canning liked; and the French representative Talleyrand, whose conversion from revolutionary to staunch conservative amused him. Canning was back in Switzerland before the battle of Waterloo and tried, unsuccessfully, to galvanize the Swiss into fighting Napoleon. His pleasure at Waterloo was darkened by the death in action of his brother Charles, to whom he had always been close.

Once the Swiss constitution had been approved at Vienna and Swiss neutrality guaranteed by the second treaty of Paris of November 1815, there was, as Canning admitted in a letter to his mother, virtually nothing to do in Switzerland. He found Bern society dull and Zürich worse. He escaped occasionally for walking tours in the mountains or visits to Italy. His decision to leave may have been compounded by private tragedy. On 3 August 1816, while on leave in England, he had married a family friend, Harriet Raikes, the daughter of Thomas Raikes, a governor of the Bank of England, but she died in childbirth in Switzerland on 16 June the following year. The child did not survive. In 1819 Canning was recalled at his own request.

Washington In September 1819 Canning accepted a three-year posting to Washington. Washington was then not a popular posting. To reach it involved a six to eight weeks' crossing of the Atlantic by sailing ship. Canning was lucky. He left Spithead in August 1820 on HMS *Spartan* and arrived in less than six weeks. Understandably, he was fascinated on his arrival by the new invention, the steamship. Washington was still a very primitive place. Canning recorded that Pennsylvania Avenue was 'the only thing approaching our notion of a street'. He added:

> The trees are cut down to the distance of a mile or more in every direction round the houses, and their former place is occupied partly by a naked undulating common, partly by marshes covered with coppice wood and inhabited by frogs, snipes and woodcocks. (Lane-Poole, 1.299–300)

So little was procurable on the other side of the Atlantic that Canning took with him, as well as a French cook, his carriage, his furniture, and stores including wines. It had taken four days to load all 70 tons of it.

Washington still rated only a minister-plenipotentiary rather than a full ambassador, but Canning hoped that, if he were successful there, he might like his predecessor, Charles Bagot, win immediate promotion to a major embassy, although his real ambition was still for a political career in London. Washington seemed a good place to make an impression. Serious questions were outstanding, some, although not all of them, lingering on from the Anglo-American War of 1812–14. The most acute was the suppression of the slave trade and the connected question of the right of search. Both Britain and the United States had independently declared the trade illegal in 1807. It had been outlawed by the Congress of Vienna in 1815 and Britain had secured agreements with a number of powers to allow the Royal Navy to police the prohibition by searching suspected slave ships. The United States refused to grant such a right, partly because of the claims Britain had made to 'impress' (conscript) British seamen from foreign ships during the Napoleonic wars. Almost as serious was the fact that the exact demarcation of the boundary between the United States and British North America still remained unresolved and a sharp dispute arose about ownership of the Columbia River.

The Americans were not in a conciliatory mood and Canning was not the most yielding of ambassadors. The American secretary of state, John Quincy Adams, while respecting Canning's integrity, complained, 'He is a proud, high-tempered Englishman … of all the foreign ministers with whom I have had occasion to treat, the man who has most tried my temper' (Lane-Poole, 1.308). In 1822 Stratford's cousin George Canning became foreign secretary again. He made a bold bid to persuade the Americans to join Britain in preventing the conservative powers of Europe from helping Spain to regain her colonies in South and Central America. President Monroe considered it but rejected it in favour of the unilateral proclamation of the Monroe doctrine, forbidding further European colonization, which could be regarded as anti-British as well as anti-Spanish. In short, Stratford Canning was not notably successful in Washington. He was, however, employed immediately on his return to Britain, together with William Huskisson, the president of the Board of Trade, and Richard Rush, the American minister in London, to conclude a convention settling the main points at issue between the two countries. These included the slave trade, the boundary disputes, and certain questions relating to West Indies trade and fisheries. The convention was signed in February 1824 but rejected by the American senate.

Canning had been sworn of the privy council when he took up his American post in 1820 but his career was not progressing well. Several attempts by George Canning to secure him a government job in London had failed. Instead he was sent on a special mission to Russia in November 1824. One issue was the boundary of Russian America (Alaska) but a more pressing question was the Greek war of independence from Turkey. George Canning had already recognized the Greeks as belligerents, although more for the protection of British commerce than because he supported them.

Stratford Canning travelled by way of Vienna, where both Metternich and the emperor endeavoured to persuade him that George Canning was wrong to separate Britain from the concert that the tsar, Alexander I, was trying to organize to deal with the situation. The Austrians were prepared to condemn the Greeks as simple rebels, but the tsar's sympathy with his co-religionists made his position more complicated. When he arrived in St Petersburg, Canning found the tsar and the chancellor, Count Nesselrode, prepared to discuss the boundary between Alaska and British North America, on which agreement was reached, but they declined to enter into any bilateral negotiations on Greece outside the intended conference. Canning left St Petersburg in April 1825 with a major part of his mission unfulfilled.

The Greek revolt Immediately on his return Canning was appointed ambassador in Constantinople by his cousin George. Before he left London he married, on 3 September 1825, Eliza Charlotte (*d.* 25 Nov 1882), the daughter of James Alexander, MP for Somerhill, a girl of barely eighteen. She accompanied him to Constantinople. He returned there without enthusiasm, expecting the mission to be a short one. George Canning had secured the promise of Lord Liverpool, then prime minister, that he should be the next vice-president of the Board of Trade, with a seat in parliament. George Canning's death in August 1827 ended his hopes of preferment. He remained in Constantinople until 1829.

The Greek war of independence was still the most important question. Stratford had a rather warmer sympathy for the Greek cause than his cousin, having decided during his first mission to Constantinople that the Ottoman empire was so corrupt that it was unlikely to survive. He witnessed a striking illustration of Ottoman brutality in action the following year in the massacre of the janizaries, the élite corps of the sultan's army, after a failed rebellion. But, whatever the defects of the Turks, no British ambassador could ignore the dangers of an increase of Russian influence in the region.

In 1827 George Canning tried to tie the hands of France and Russia by the treaty of London, which bound all these powers to offer mediation, armed if necessary, between Greece and Turkey. The unforeseen result in October 1827 was the battle of Navarino, in which a combined Anglo-Franco-Russian fleet virtually annihilated a Turco-Egyptian one. George Canning was already dead and his successor, the duke of Wellington, whose principal concern was a collapse of Turkish power (which would benefit the Russians), was horrified. In Wellington's eyes Stratford Canning bore some of the responsibility because of an unguarded phrase he had used to the British admiral Edward Codrington. Codrington, dissatisfied by the vagueness of his orders, had sought clarification from the ambassador. Canning, in a private letter, had told him that, if all other means were exhausted, he would have to enforce his instructions 'by cannon-shot' (Lane-Poole, 1.449).

News of Navarino greatly alarmed the British, French, and Russian ambassadors in Constantinople. Canning received private intelligence from a British naval officer. When he placed the note in the French ambassador's hands, 'the colour forsook his face and presently turning to me, he said "Trois têtes dans un bonnet—n'est-ce pas?" I could have added "et dans un panin, peut-être—qui sait?"' (Lane-Poole, 1.451)—not only three heads wearing a single cap but together in a guillotine basket perhaps. All three ambassadors thought it prudent to slip quietly away from Constantinople, even though they had not been officially recalled by their governments. Stratford Canning, his wife, and staff walked through the city in the dark to board a small merchant vessel they had hired and bluffed their way through the Dardanelles, before being picked up by a British frigate.

Canning returned to London. By now the French were assuming the initiative: a French army had been dispatched to Greece. It was not yet safe for the ambassadors to return to Constantinople but they were instructed to proceed to Corfu, and later to Poros, to try to secure a settlement based on an autonomous, but not yet independent, Greece. Its boundaries were not yet decided; in its most restricted form it would have been limited to the Morea (Peloponnese) plus certain, also undetermined, islands.

In May 1828 the fourth earl of Aberdeen became Wellington's foreign secretary. Aberdeen, a classical scholar, had travelled in Greece as a young man and had less fear of Russia and more sympathy with Greek aspirations than his chief. There was undoubtedly a discrepancy between his private letters, in which he encouraged Canning to get the best deal he could for the Greeks, and the official dispatches, which reflected Wellington's views.

The situation in the Near East was now both complex and dangerous. Russia had gone to war with Turkey but the fiction was maintained that they were only at war in the Black Sea, so that Russia might continue to act with Britain and France as a neutral mediator in the Greek war. In December 1828 the three ambassadors agreed the Poros protocol. Greece should have a frontier from the Gulf of Arta to the Gulf of Volo. The islands of Candia (Crete), Samos, and Euboea should be included in the new state. Greece would remain a tributary state of Turkey but be constituted as a hereditary monarchy, with the allies choosing the monarch. Wellington compelled Aberdeen to rebuke Canning for going beyond his instructions. Aberdeen, unhappily conscious that he had encouraged Canning, tried to soothe him in private letters. Canning would have none of it, angrily resigned, and left for home. Thus began the tension between Canning and Aberdeen which was still unresolved at the time of the Crimean War.

Return to British politics Canning was always discreet in subsequent references to the quarrels of 1828–9, and on his return to Britain he was awarded the GCB. In 1830 Aberdeen insisted, against the wishes of the duke of Wellington, who now had little time for Canning, on employing him to draw up the statement of the British claims on the north-east boundary question between Canada and the United States, which was about to be submitted to the arbitration of the king of the Netherlands. (The arbitration failed because the Americans would not accept the king's award.)

For a time it looked as if Canning would turn back to his original ambition of a career in politics at home. In 1828 he had been elected MP for Old Sarum, one of the most notorious rotten boroughs, then in the gift of his father-in-law, James Alexander. In the 1830 election he stood, unsuccessfully, for Leominster. He withdrew his intended candidature for Southampton on discovering that he had no chance there. In 1831 he was returned for Stockbridge but that was another 'closed' borough—Canning paid £1000 for his nomination—which was scheduled to go under the Reform Bill of 1832. Curiously, Canning who was to dominate the politics of Constantinople for a generation as the 'Great Ambassador', was a failure in the Commons. He rarely spoke, and when he did, he was overcome by nerves. With the death of George Canning, there was no group to which he could unreservedly commit himself.

Almost in spite of himself, Canning was drawn back into diplomacy. Lord Palmerston had succeeded Aberdeen at the Foreign Office in November 1830 and was dissatisfied with Robert Gordon, Aberdeen's brother, who had succeeded Canning in Constantinople. Wellington had still been determined to curb Russian influence and a conference in London in March 1829 modified the Poros protocol to Greece's disadvantage. However, the Russian victory over Turkey and the imposition of the treaty of Adrianople in September 1829, although it increased the duke's anxiety, made the British position untenable. Instead, the British and French joined the Russians in insisting upon a completely independent Greece, although without Crete.

Special missions In the autumn of 1831 Palmerston asked Canning to return to Constantinople on a special mission. He went out by way of Brindisi, Corfu, Corinth, and Nauplia, the temporary seat of the Greek government. Although he was hailed as a hero by the Greeks, he found them in disarray and split into factions. Palmerston later thanked him warmly for his work there: 'The Conference are [*sic*] delighted with what you did in the Morea, and all agree how lucky it was that you should have dropped down there at the moment you did' (letter from Palmerston, 7 March 1832; Lane-Poole, 1.498). Canning took pleasure in the first opportunity he had had to explore Greece itself, including Athens. He arrived in Constantinople on 28 January 1832 to find the Turks more conciliatory to the Christians than in the past but determined to drag the negotiations out. Only in July was the convention signed. Palmerston again expressed himself well satisfied with Canning's work but, to the latter's disgust, did not consult him about subsequent decisions and Canning entirely disapproved of the selection of the young Prince Otho of Bavaria as the new king of Greece.

Canning returned to Britain in September 1832, delighted to find that his wife had given birth to a son. (One child had died earlier in Constantinople and Canning had been reluctant to leave his wife, who was pregnant and unwell, the previous autumn.) There seems to have been no suggestion that the child was other than healthy at birth but a serious illness in infancy left him a permanent invalid and he predeceased his father, who had such high hopes for him.

Immediately on his return from Constantinople, Canning was gazetted as ambassador to Russia, but he never took up his appointment because, in an extraordinary diplomatic incident, Tsar Nicholas I indicated that he would not receive him. No fully satisfactory explanation has ever been given, although Canning himself suspected intrigues by the wife of the Russian ambassador, the arch-intriguer Princess Lieven. Nicholas implied that Canning had personally slighted him but Canning protested that, if he had, it could only have been by inadvertently failing to call on him when he had been on his special mission to Alexander I in 1825. Joseph Planta, the permanent under-secretary, suspected that the tsar simply did not want an ambassador who was so well informed about the eastern question, and such theories gained general acceptance after the Crimean War. At the time the British government professed itself baffled and indignant and did not formally replace Canning (by Lord Durham) until 1835, although Canning's appointment was cancelled in July 1833.

While still nominally ambassador to St Petersburg, Canning was sent on a special mission to Madrid in 1833 to try to compose the differences between the rival claimants to the Portuguese throne, Dom Pedro (who had abdicated in favour of his daughter Maria Gloriosa in order to remain emperor of Brazil) and his brother Dom Miguel. The eastern powers favoured the conservative Miguel; Palmerston preferred Maria, as did the French; but the Portuguese, who disliked Pedro's abdication, probably preferred Miguel. Canning did not expect success. He had written to Palmerston from Paris, 'I little thought a year ago that there was anything in negotiation more impossible than the Greek question but the enigma of the two Doms beats it hollow' (letter to Palmerston, 17 Dec 1832; Lane-Poole, 2.26). He subsequently blamed Palmerston for not giving him the full facts and came home indignant at being sent on 'a fool's errand' (ibid.).

Domestic politics Canning still hankered after a career in domestic politics. His wife and father-in-law disapproved, because accepting a seat in parliament would mean surrendering his diplomatic 'pension' (in effect a retainer) of £1200 per annum and Canning, who now had three daughters as well as an invalid son to support, was not a rich man. Nevertheless, when approached by Lord George Bentinck, Canning agreed to stand for King's Lynn in 1835. He retained the seat in the 1837 and 1841 elections but relinquished it in 1842, when he turned back seriously to diplomacy.

Canning had been disappointed not to be offered any government job, except the governorship of Canada, during the short-lived Peel administration of 1834–5 but, apart from his inability to speak in the house, his political position was unclear. He regarded himself as a moderate and sometimes described himself as a liberal conservative. At this time he associated himself most closely with Lord Stanley. Stanley, together with Sir James Graham, the earl of Ripon, and the duke of Richmond, had parted company with Lord Melbourne's administration over an Irish church question. They were moving towards Sir Robert Peel but did not accept office from him until 1841. In the late 1830s Canning did occasionally speak effectively on foreign policy issues in the Commons, including Spain, the Russian occupation of Cracow and, most notably, the *Vixen* incident, when the Russians seized a British ship which had broken their blockade of the Circassian coast. Nevertheless, Peel still did not offer him any post, except again Canada, in 1841.

Canning now turned to the foreign secretary, his old friend and adversary (their relations were always ambiguous) the earl of Aberdeen, and virtually demanded an embassy. The ranks of potential Conservative ambassadors were thin (senior diplomats still habitually changed with a change of government) and Aberdeen offered him Constantinople. Canning had no wish to return to Turkey but accepted. It was to prove the beginning of one of the most important embassies of the Victorian period.

Ambassador to Constantinople The Near East was comparatively quiet in the 1840s. The major crisis which had seen Mehmet Ali, the pasha of Egypt, challenge the sultan and the great powers of Europe drawn into what could have been a very dangerous confrontation, had been resolved for the time being. Great power intervention had ejected Ibrahim, Mehmet Ali's son, from Syria and the powers had composed their own differences in the Straits convention of 1841. But the underlying problem remained. If the sprawling Ottoman empire collapsed, Europe would almost certainly go to war over the spoils. To Canning, as to others, the only practical alternative now seemed to be the reform of the empire, which would at least buy time.

The chances of reform looked better after the promulgation of the Gulhané (or Rose Chamber) decree in November 1839. This would have provided for the reform of the judicial system, taxation, and the army and improved the civil rights of non-Muslims. Unfortunately, by the time Canning arrived in January 1842, it was clear that the decree had been mainly a play for Western support against Mehmet Ali and that the forces of reaction were again in control. Aberdeen had specifically instructed Canning to strive for the enforcement of the 1839 reforms. Canning did this with a vigour that sometimes left the foreign secretary nervous. He worked partly by exercising direct influence on the new and pliable, but weak, Sultan Abdul Mejid, and partly by co-operating after 1845 with Reshid Pasha, the grand vizier, who, although a somewhat venal character, was a reformer and westernizer.

The ambassador had a clear duty to protect British citizens. Particular problems arose about natives of Malta and the Ionian Islands, who had claims to British citizenship and who, in the words of Canning's official biographer, 'were clever enough to absorb a large amount of the British trade in the Levant, and unprincipled enough to constitute the most conspicuous class of criminals' (Lane-Poole, 2.87). In 1843–4 many of these problems were shifted to the consular jurisdiction. But Canning, who had a genuine burning sense of justice, was prepared to intervene, if no other help was at hand, on behalf of Americans, Armenians, and Nestorians. His intervention in one case had important consequences. A young Armenian had converted to Islam and then turned back to Christianity. According to Islamic law he was condemned, and later publicly executed, for apostasy. Canning remonstrated and eventually secured from the sultan an undertaking that the Porte would take 'effectual measures' to ensure that such executions did not take place in future—a promise the sultan was not always able to fulfil. The story was a *cause célèbre* at the time (told in full in 'Correspondence relating to the executions in Turkey for apostacy from Islamism', *Parl. papers*, 1844, 51). Canning also persuaded the sultan to forbid torture in judicial processes. He worked hard for the implementation of the religious toleration promised in 1839, for Jews as well as Christians, and persuaded the Porte to allow the building of a protestant cathedral (St George's) in Jerusalem.

Canning was also drawn into conflicts in Lebanon, where the war against Ibrahim had re-ignited all the old antagonisms between the Maronites and the Druses. Some degree of devolution and the separation of the warring factions gave Lebanon a decade of comparative peace and prosperity. A serious situation also arose from a border dispute between Turkey and Persia. Although he had no official instructions on the subject, Canning sent one of his attachés and a British officer to mediate a boundary. Austin Henry Layard arrived in Constantinople by chance in the summer of 1842, fresh from exploring the disputed region. Canning made use of his knowledge and thereafter supported Layard in his archaeological enterprises.

He provided £200 for Layard's 1846 excavations at Nimrud, as well as securing firmans. The work was only later supported by the British Museum, which, as a result, obtained a major collection of statues and carvings that first introduced Assyrian art to the British public. Canning also secured important marbles from the ruins of the mausoleum at Halicarnassus for the British Museum and subsequently, in the 1850s, supported Charles Newton's work there.

European crisis, 1848 Canning came home on leave in 1846. The change of government made his future uncertain but Palmerston decided to reappoint him. His return to Constantinople was delayed by the crises that overtook Europe in 1848, preceded by the outbreak of civil war in Switzerland in 1847. The great powers, who had guaranteed the Swiss state at Vienna in 1815, agreed to offer their joint mediation and Canning was dispatched as the British mediator. By the time he reached Bern, the matter had been resolved by the victory of the federal forces over the rebellious Sonderbund. Canning did, however, persuade the federal forces not to enter Neuchâtel, which had declared its neutrality. Neuchâtel had an ambiguous position as a possession of the king of Prussia as well as a member of the Swiss confederation, and a federal invasion might have triggered the great power intervention that Britain was anxious to avoid.

Canning finally left for Constantinople in March 1848. Europe was so disturbed that it seemed doubtful whether the ambassador, let alone his family, should undertake the journey. In the event, his wife and three daughters accompanied him. He was instructed to take a roundabout route through Brussels, Hanover, Berlin, Dresden, Vienna, and Munich and accredited to each of these courts. Nominally, he was to take soundings about the situation in Greece. In practice, he made careful observations of the progress of revolution throughout Europe. Only in Vienna on 2 May did they actually become involved in a disturbance but, a few weeks later, at Trieste, Canning aboard HMS *Antelope* had to negotiate with the Sardinian fleet on behalf of the Austrians, at some personal risk. His attempts to mediate in Athens resulted only in a temporary quarrel with an old ally, General Church, who had played an important role in the liberation of Greece.

Return to the Near East Canning arrived back in Constantinople with mixed feelings. He still professed to dislike the city but he also hoped to see through the reforms he had helped to initiate a few years earlier. His success was more limited than his biographer Lane-Poole believed. In particular, he worked hard to secure equality for non-Muslims. One of the most judicious historians of the period, H. W. V. Temperley, came to the conclusion that, although Christians, including the Greek *rayas*, were granted more privileges and protection, political equality was as distant as ever. Whether or not Turkey could be reformed was one of the questions underlying British attitudes to the Crimean War. In 1849 more immediate crises arose out of the revolutions in Europe. Lajos Kossuth, the Hungarian leader, and General Joseph Bem, the Polish leader, as well as a large number of lesser rebels, fled to Turkey. Russia and Austria demanded their extradition. Canning and the French ambassador, General Aupick, persuaded the Porte to refuse. Palmerston backed Canning and he was authorized to summon the British Mediterranean Fleet under Admiral Parker to Besika Bay, just outside the Dardanelles. The Straits convention of 1841 forbade foreign warships to enter the Dardanelles when Turkey was at peace. In November 1849 Parker caused an international sensation by entering the straits, ostensibly and perhaps genuinely, under stress of bad weather. By then a compromise had been reached by which the Turks did not surrender the fugitives and Canning sent the fleet away, but Russia and Austria remained indignant at the ambassador's conduct.

Despite this, Lord Stanley, when it seemed possible that he would be called upon to form a government in 1851, seriously considered offering Canning the Foreign Office. When he did form a government in 1852, however, the office went to Lord Malmesbury. He also sent Lord Cowley, who had once served under Canning, to Paris, the embassy Canning would have liked for himself. It seems to have been as a peace offering (although Canning always indignantly repudiated that suggestion) that he was offered a peerage and became Viscount Stratford de Redcliffe; he took his title from the church of St Mary Redcliffe in Bristol, with which his family had historically been associated.

Canning returned to Britain in 1852 and this time did not expect ever to go back to Constantinople. He was, after all, sixty-six years of age. In the event the new coalition government, headed by the earl of Aberdeen, sent him back in April 1853. The appointment surprised many. Notoriously, Aberdeen and Canning did not get on, although Aberdeen always seems to have respected Canning and, after the quarrel in 1829, actually fostered his career. In 1853 the general consensus in the cabinet was that only Canning could handle the rapidly developing crisis at Constantinople.

Outbreak of the Crimean War The greatest controversy of Stratford de Redcliffe's career has always centred on how far, if at all, he was responsible for the outbreak of the Crimean War in March 1854 between Russia and the alliance of Britain, France, and Turkey. By this time he was the 'Great Elchi' in Constantinople. 'Elchi' simply means 'ambassador' but no one doubted his exceptional position. He had been in Constantinople intermittently since 1808 and more or less continuously since 1841. He was a man of considerable physical presence and completely master of his subject. He was capable of exceptionally hard work—on at least one occasion he worked thirty hours at a stretch—and drove his assistants near to breakdowns. He was known to have a volcanic temper, especially when under stress, and irrevocably antagonized some; but he was readily forgiven by others, who recognized him as a basically generous man with a strong sense of justice. It seems to have been a real concern for justice and human rights, as well as for British prestige and interests, that led him to intervene so vigorously in favour of reform in Turkey in the 1840s.

Like all ambassadors of his generation, Stratford de Redcliffe was accustomed to making many independent decisions. Communications were still slow. Situations could change fundamentally before instructions could be received from London, even if London realized the urgency. He had been left almost without instructions at the time of the treaty of Bucharest in 1812. At the height of the refugee crisis in 1849, even the utmost exertions of the queen's messengers could not get Palmerston's instructions to him in less than a fortnight. (See the account of Captain Townley's epic ride in Lane-Poole, 2.194–7.) The telegraph was coming into use in the 1850s but the route was neither complete nor secure. There is no evidence that Stratford de Redcliffe wilfully disobeyed instructions and, when he used his discretion to delay their implementation, it was in the cause of peace.

Stratford de Redcliffe returned to Constantinople in 1853 to find the situation already tense. Napoleon III's championing of the rights of the Latin Christians had, almost inevitably, called forth a response from Tsar Nicholas, championing the Greek Orthodox Christians. Canning's mediation settled the apparently trivial, but deeply symbolic, quarrel about rights over the holy places in Jerusalem and Bethlehem, within weeks. Unfortunately, the tsar had noted the success of the Austrian Count Leiningen's bullying tactics in securing concessions in the Balkans. He sent the bombastic Prince Menshikov to demand guarantees from the sultan. Menshikov sailed away empty-handed in May 1853. Stratford de Redcliffe had been conciliatory, but neither he nor London was sure whether Menshikov was simply demanding the fulfilment of existing treaties, which would have been entirely acceptable, or demanding the recognition of a Russian protectorate over all the Greek Orthodox subjects of the sultan, which would have been regarded as highly dangerous. To put pressure on the Turks, in July the Russians occupied the Danubian principalities of Moldavia and Wallachia. This was an act of war but the European powers begged the Turks not to respond until diplomacy had been given a chance. Stratford de Redcliffe did what he could but could not prevent the Turks from declaring war in October 1853.

In the meantime the great powers had met in Vienna and drawn up a compromise proposal, the Vienna note. Russia had been a party to the negotiations. The Turks had not, and Turkey rejected the Vienna note. One of the most serious charges against Stratford de Redcliffe is that he persuaded the Turks to reject it. The evidence suggests that, at most, he urged caution. If he did, he proved justified because the later interpretation of the note by the Russian chancellor, Nesselrode, showed that he interpreted it to mean the acceptance of Menshikov's more extreme demands.

Although Russia and Turkey were technically at war, the tsar assured the other powers that he would do nothing to escalate the crisis unless attacked. The so-called 'massacre' of Sinope, when a Russian squadron sank a Turkish fleet off Turkey's Black Sea coast in November 1853, at first looked like a clear breach of that promise, although later information suggested that, like Navarino, it had been an accidental encounter. Disillusioned with Russian good faith, the British cabinet agreed with France to send fleets into the Black Sea and demand that the Russian fleet return to its home port of Sevastopol.

The course of the war Throughout, Stratford de Redcliffe, far from being warlike, tried to put a brake on proceedings. At the beginning of June the British and French fleets had been ordered to Besika Bay as a precaution. Palmerston wanted the ambassador to be given authority to summon the British fleet to Constantinople if necessary, but only in September did Aberdeen, the prime minister, and Clarendon, the foreign secretary, authorize it. The ambassador had not asked for this authority and, at first, did not exercise it. He acted only when the categorical instructions of 8 October 1853 to call up the fleet reached him on the 15th—and even then he delayed the summons until the 20th.

Unfortunately, Stratford de Redcliffe was disliked and distrusted by some members of the cabinet. He was suspicious of Russian intentions and privately made no secret of the fact. His ability to influence the Turkish government was probably exaggerated. As a result, although virtually all the evidence is now in the public domain and has been minutely analysed by scholars, almost all of whom have acquitted him, he is still occasionally offered up as a scapegoat for the outbreak of a muddled and unsatisfactory war.

Once war had broken out, Stratford de Redcliffe's labours increased. He was now called upon not only to exercise diplomatic functions but, as the 'man on the spot', to concern himself with accommodation and supplies for the army and, eventually, the medical problems that brought Florence Nightingale and her nurses to Scutari. He worked day and night and told his wife that he was 'a red-hot horseshoe between the anvil and half a dozen sledge-hammers' (Lane-Poole, 2.366). The British and French had meant to drive the Russians out of the principalities, but the Russians pre-empted that move by withdrawing and leaving them in the keeping of neutral Austria. The Crimean campaign was decided upon to knock out the main Russian naval base of Sevastopol. Stratford de Redcliffe himself paid two visits to the front in 1855. Sevastopol did not fall until September 1855. Stratford de Redcliffe was bitterly disappointed by the peace treaty of Paris of March 1856, mainly because it applied no pressure for continued reform in Turkey.

Resignation and retirement Stratford de Redcliffe left Constantinople on leave in December 1857. Although he was now over seventy and exhausted by four strenuous years, he intended to return to try to complete his reforming work, but when Palmerston, now prime minister, was defeated in February 1858, he decided to resign. Although Stratford de Redcliffe had always regarded himself as a Conservative, Palmerston was the politician to whom he was temperamentally closest and Palmerston had staunchly supported his ambassador against both the criticisms of his conduct before the Crimean War and the ill-founded charges that his neglect had led to the loss of Kars to the Russians in 1855.

Lord Stratford de Redcliffe returned briefly to Constantinople in the autumn of 1858 to take formal leave of the sultan. He already regretted his resignation. He lived to the age of ninety-three with his mental faculties unimpaired, and he found life without official duties boring. He divided his time between London and his country house, Frant Court, Frant, near Tunbridge Wells. He resumed his scholarly studies in history and the classics. He had always had literary ambitions and throughout his life had written (and translated) poetry of some elegance. Lord Byron had admired his poem on Napoleon. In 1866 he published *Shadows of the Past* and in 1876 *The Exile in Calauria* and *Alfred the Great in Athelney*. He wrote occasional verse on the unification of Germany and on the battle of Isandlwana. Comparative religion interested him and his private papers contain notes on books and sermons on Christianity and Islam. In his retirement he wrote two religious works, *Why am I a Christian?* (1873) and *The Greatest of Miracles* (1876). Perhaps significantly he once told a friend, 'I am a believer of its [Christianity's] grander parts. I accept it *en grand*' (Anderson, xiii). He also wrote memoirs of his long official life, which provided the basis for Lane-Poole's biography. These memoirs cannot now be traced, and have probably been destroyed.

Stratford de Redcliffe attended the House of Lords regularly and spoke as a cross-bencher. His technical prowess as a speaker was no better than when he had been in the Commons but his reputation commanded respect. He normally spoke on foreign policy questions, including Italy in 1859, the French intervention in Syria in 1861, the Ionian Islands in 1864, and the insurrection in Crete in 1867. His stance was generally conservative but still with his old concern for justice and religious tolerance. One of his rare domestic speeches was in favour of equality for Jews. He was disappointed never to be offered office but he was given the Order of the Garter, a rare distinction for a diplomat, in 1869.

Like Palmerston, Stratford de Redcliffe disapproved of the building of the Suez Canal, which he feared Britain would not be able to control, and in 1862 became chairman of the rival project, the Euphrates Valley Railway Company. At the time of the eastern crisis of the late 1870s he wrote frequent and substantial letters to *The Times* and contributed articles to the *Nineteenth Century*. These pieces were subsequently published in a collection by Dean A. P. Stanley in 1881. Stanley had first met Lord Stratford de Redcliffe in Constantinople in 1853 and preached the sermon at his funeral at Frant on 21 August 1880, a week after the viscount's death at Frant Court.

MURIEL E. CHAMBERLAIN

Sources S. Lane-Poole, *The life of … Stratford Canning*, 2 vols. (1888); repr. (1976) • H. W. V. Temperley, *England and the Near East: the Crimea* (1936) • H. W. V. Temperley, 'The last phase of Stratford de Redcliffe', *EngHR*, 47 (1932), 216–59 • H. W. V. Temperley, 'Stratford de Redcliffe and the origins of the Crimean War [pt 1]', *EngHR*, 48 (1933), 601–21 • H. W. V. Temperley, 'The alleged violations of the Straits convention by Stratford de Redcliffe between June and September 1853', *EngHR*, 49 (1934), 657–72 • H. W. V. Temperley, 'Stratford de Redcliffe and the origins of the Crimean War [pt 2]', *EngHR*, 49 (1934), 265–98 • *FO List* (1881) • Burke, *Peerage* • M. E. Chamberlain, *Lord Aberdeen: a political biography* (1983) • M. S. Anderson, *The eastern question, 1774–1923* (1966) • S. F. Bernis, *A diplomatic history of the United States* (1955) • A. W. Kinglake, *The invasion of the Crimea*, [new edn], 9 vols. (1901) • V. J. Puryear, *England, Russia and the Straits question, 1844–56* (1931) • D. M. Goldfrank, *The origins of the Crimean War* (1994) • N. Rich, *Why the Crimean War?* (1985) • A. D. Lambert, *The Crimean War: British grand strategy, 1853–56* (1990) • D. Wetzel, *The Crimean War: a diplomatic history* (1985) • J. B. Conaches, *Britain and the Crimea, 1855–6* (1987) • J. H. Harris [third earl of Malmesbury], *Memoirs of an ex-minister: an autobiography*, new edn (1885) • E. F. Malcolm-Smith, *Life of Stratford de Redcliffe* (1933)

Archives PRO, corresp. and papers, FO 352 • PRO, papers relating to special mission, FO 9/101 • W. Yorks. AS, Leeds, family corresp. • Wellcome L., corresp. | Balliol Oxf., letters to David Morier; corresp. with David Urquhart • BL, corresp. with Lord Aberdeen, Add. MSS 43118–43119, 43138–43139, 43185–43187 • BL, corresp. with James Brant, Add. MS 42565 • BL, corresp. with W. E. Gladstone, Add. MSS 44355–44464, *passim* • BL, corresp. with Sir Robert Gordon, Add. MS 43216 • BL, corresp. with Sir Robert Peel, Add. MSS 40424–40600, *passim* • BL, corresp. with Lord Strathrain, Add. MS 42798 • BL, corresp. with Lord Westmorland, M/527/2 [microfilm] • Bodl. Oxf., letters to Friedrich Max Müller • Bodl. Oxf., corresp. with Sir J. G. Wilkinson [incl. some copies] • Derbys. RO, letters to R. J. Wilmot-Horton • Durham RO, letters to Lord Londonderry • Hants. RO, corresp. with Lord Malmesbury • Herts. ALS, letters to Sir Harford Jones • King's Cam., letters to Aupick • Lpool RO, letters to fourteenth earl of Derby • LUL, Loyd MSS • NAM, corresp. with Lord Raglan • NL Scot., corresp. with Lord Melville • NMM, corresp. with Sir William Parker • Norfolk RO, corresp. with Sir Henry Lytton Bulwer • NRA, priv. coll., corresp. with Robert Curzon • PRO, letters to Lord Cowley, FO 519 • PRO, corresp. with Lord Granville, PRO 30/29 • PRO, corresp. with Lord John Russell, PRO 30/22 • PRO, letters to Odo Russell, FO 918 • U. Hull, Brynmor Jones L., letters to Sir Henry Hotham • U. Nott. L., letters to Sir Andrew Buchanan • U. Nott. L., corresp. with duke of Newcastle • U. Nott. L., Pelham MSS • U. Southampton L., corresp. with Lord Palmerston • W. Yorks. AS, Leeds, letters to Lord Canning

Likenesses A. Robertson, miniature, *c*.1815 (aged twenty-nine) • G. Richmond, chalk drawing, 1853, NPG • G. F. Watts, oils, 1856–7, NPG [*see illus.*] • R. Lehmann, drawing, 1859, BM • J. E. Boehm, marble bust, 1864, Gov. Art Coll.; plaster cast, NPG • H. R. Graves, oils, exh. RA 1865, Eton • H. Herkomer, oils, 1879, King's Cam. • statue, 1884, Westminster Abbey • G. Glanville, photograph, NPG • G. Romney, double portrait (as a child)

Wealth at death under £18,000: probate, 6 Oct 1880, *CGPLA Eng. & Wales*

Cannon, George [*pseud.* Erasmus Perkins] (**1789–1854**), freethinker and publisher, was born in London. His parents and early education remain unknown, but he later hinted at a dissenting background, and he was well versed in French as well as philosophy, theology, and literature. Between 1812 and 1815 he became a solicitor at 1 Staple Inn. In 1815 he also took out a dissenting minister's licence within the corporation of London. However, he never openly practised in either profession, preferring to channel his devious energies and talents into the world of letters. Cannon's obscurity was in large part deliberate: throughout a long literary life he published nothing under his real name, taking care to employ a maze of pseudonyms, aliases, and literary frontmen. His significance lies in showing how an unrespectable Georgian literary underworld intersected with and influenced the transmission of such major cultural and intellectual movements as the European Enlightenment and English Romanticism. He edited and published key texts of Enlightenment free thought, romantic poetry, and libertinist pornography.

Cannon's radical and sceptical proclivities surfaced in 1812 when he became a founding signatory of Major John Cartwright's solidly whig-radical Union for Parliamentary Reform and a correspondent in the controversies of the Freethinking Christians, an ultra-rationalist Christian sect led by prosperous drink merchant and City radical Samuel Thompson. The following year Cannon graduated to a politically more extreme circle which gathered at Peckham Lodge, home of banker Timothy Brown, who entertained radical literati and in 1813 masterminded the publishing of Baron d'Holbach's corrosively sceptical tract, *Ecce homo*. This work espoused atheistic materialism and scoffed at Christ's morality: Cannon's chief role was to publicize it in a series of learned and witty articles which appeared in *Cobbett's Political Register* between 3 December 1814 and 8 April 1815 under the pseudonym of Reverend Erasmus Perkins. Their cleverness momentarily shook William Cobbett's faith, and Erasmus Perkins became Cannon's most persistent literary and political persona: he relished posing as an elderly, learned, and tolerant dissenting minister who suavely undermined Christianity while affecting to support it. During the early Regency years Cannon was to publish, edit, or translate several pungently anti-Christian tracts under this name, including a defence of Holbachian materialism, and a substantial freethinking periodical, the *Theological Inquirer, or, Polemical Magazine*, which ran from March to September 1815. The latter carried an impressive range of literary extracts from European sceptical classics, as well as original articles, stories, and poems by local freethinkers.

A strong commitment to freedom of religious opinion, coupled with a relish for conspiracy and subterfuge, also brought Cannon into contact with more fugitive pressmen–radicals such as the veteran bookseller Daniel Isaac Eaton. Cannon bawled court-room advice into Eaton's deaf ears when the ailing bookseller was prosecuted by the government in 1812 for publishing blasphemous libels in freethinking works by Freret, Helvetius, and Paine. Eaton's circle overlapped with that of another veteran of the 1790s, agrarian revolutionary Thomas Spence, whose small band of mainly artisan disciples included numbers of experienced insurrectionary plotters and millenarian enthusiasts. With the peace of 1815 a period of post-war unrest produced renewed demands for political and economic reform and also lifted Spence's followers to short-lived prominence within the London radical movement. The reports of Home Office spies and informers show that Cannon's role in Spencean underground circles was that of a self-conscious Svengali and *philosophe*: he gave legal advice to ultra-radicals accused of treason; he preached and debated at blasphemous chapels; he ghosted legal defences; and he wrote or edited seditious popular periodicals and tracts, usually under the names of humbler radical pressmen who were prepared to accept legal liability. There is also evidence that on several occasions he deliberately hoaxed or misinformed government spies, none of whom managed to obtain a clear sense of his identity.

Cannon's publishing activities in the Regency years add to mounting evidence that metropolitan radical extremists forged links with some of the younger literary romantics. Ironically, the shadowy philosopher–publisher Cannon played a crucial role in bringing Percy Shelley's early poetry out of obscurity. Mary Shelley's *Journal* (*Journal*, ed. F. L. Jones, 1947, 36–7) shows that Cannon met the Shelleys in January 1815, though he had several years earlier revealed in print his knowledge of Percy's expulsion from Oxford for espousing atheist ideas. The Shelleys recoiled from Cannon's pretensions, but they evidently welcomed his eagerness to publish controversial atheistic writings. Soon after, the *Theological Inquirer* carried Shelley's 'Refutation of deism' followed by the ardently revolutionary poem *Queen Mab*, hitherto privately published but now reproduced in extract form with a commentary from a former shoemaker littérateur, R. C. Fair (vol. 1.34–9, 105–10, 205–9, 358–62, 446–8). Cannon was also seeing William Godwin at this time, though there is no suggestion of their collaboration until possibly 1821 when, in partnership with another radical bookseller, William Benbow, Cannon issued a cheap duodecimo edition of *Queen Mab* under the false imprint of William Baldwin, New York. Cannon's shadowy presence can also be discerned in the frontispiece of the most important of all pirated Shelley publications, a scholarly two-volume edition of *Poems* issued in 1834 under the imprint of a minor former radical publisher turned pornographer, John Ascham.

It is not clear when Cannon moved similarly from a political to a pornographic underground. H. S. Ashbee, who knew him slightly, claims that Cannon began publishing erotica as early as 1815, but the first certain evidence of such interests are several bawdy, though not necessarily illegal, French libertinist works which he translated and published in partnership with Benbow during the early 1820s. By the end of the decade, however, Cannon was being classed by police and magistrates as a fully professional trader in obscene publications, who specialized mainly in expensive flagellation literature designed explicitly for sexual arousal. Early in 1831 he was sentenced to twelve months' imprisonment in Tothill Fields for obscene libel; his listed publications included the first known British edition of *Juliette, ou, Les prospérités du vice* by the marquis de Sade. Cannon's involvement with such dangerous but commercially lucrative works was in part an extension of his earlier activities; there were close philosophical links between Enlightenment freethought, anti-clerical obscenity, and French libertinist literature—

all of which combined hostility to Christianity with a celebration of hedonistic natural sexuality. The collapse of the radical book market during the relatively prosperous 1820s also provided a different kind of incentive for transferring covert skills to a burgeoning branch of the publishing trade, and several other of Cannon's former radical associates similarly became professional pornographers at this time. Over the next two decades Cannon was to publish English editions of more than twenty French libertinist writers, including well-known works of Chorier and Mirabeau. During the 1841 census he was living and working, with his wife, Mary, and two daughters, in the rabbit warren of 2 Great Mays Buildings, St Martin's Lane, London. His legendary repertoire of clandestine tricks failed to avert several bouts of imprisonment. When his premises were raided for the last time in December 1853, police officers seized 2115 obscene prints, 9 copper plates, and 81 expensive obscene books. During this bout of imprisonment he died in the Middlesex House of Correction, Clerkenwell, on 7 June 1854 from fever and general debility. As an avowed believer in feminist and sexually libertarian principles, he might have been pleased that his wife, Mary (*d. c.*1864), continued the pornography business for a further ten years.

IAIN MCCALMAN

Sources I. McCalman, *Radical underworld: prophets, revolutionaries, and pornographers in London, 1795–1840* (1988) • W. St Clair, *The Godwins and the Shelleys: the biography of a family* (1989), appx 3 • I. D. McCalman, 'Unrespectable radicalism: infidels and pornography in early nineteenth-century England', *Past and Present*, 104 (1984), 74–110 • D. Thomas, *A long time burning: the history of censorship in England* (1969) • L. S. Boas, '"Erasmus Perkins" and Shelley', *Modern Language Notes*, 70 (1955), 408–13 • Pisansu Fraxi [H. S. Ashbee], *Index librorum prohibitorum: being notes bio-biblio-icono-graphical, on curious and uncommon books* (1877) • *Theological Inquirer, or, Polemical Magazine*, 1 (MarchxSept 1815) • J. Dinwiddy, 'William Cobbett, George Houston and freethought', *N&Q*, 222 (1977), 325–9 • E. Perkins [G. Cannon], 'Letter to Justice Best', *Deists Magazine* (1820), 201–2 • E. Perkins [G. Cannon], 'On religious persecution', *Cobbett's Weekly Political Register* (3 Dec 1814–8 April 1815) [letters 1–8] • *Mary Shelley's journal*, ed. F. L. Jones (1947), 413–14 • P. J. Kearney, ed., *The Private Case: an annotated bibliography of the Private Case Erotica Collection in the British (Museum) Library* (1981) • d. cert. • census returns, 1841 • chancery solicitors' records, admission registers, G. Cannon, Staple Inn, 1812, PRO, MS 216/4

Archives CLRO, session records • PRO, chancery solicitors' records | BL, Reddie MSS, Add. MSS 38828–38830 • PRO, HO files • king's bench records

Cannon, Herbert Graham (1897–1963), zoologist, was born on 14 April 1897 at Wimbledon, Surrey, the third of the four children of David William Cannon, a compositor in the firm of Eyre and Spottiswoode, and his wife, Alice, the daughter of Charles Graham, who owned and drove one of the first horse-buses to run in south London.

When Cannon was about five years old the family moved to Brixton. He attended the local council school, from where he won a scholarship to Wilson's Grammar School in Camberwell. Following a serious accident at the age of sixteen, when he fell from a window while sleepwalking (and suffered several compound fractures), he found strenuous exercise impossible. In 1916, being unfit for war service, Cannon went up to Cambridge as a choral scholar of Christ's College to read for the natural sciences tripos. In 1918 he passed part one with first-class honours in zoology, chemistry, and physiology. Instead of continuing with part two, he obtained leave of absence to take up a temporary post as naturalist in the board of fisheries laboratory at Conwy, returning to Cambridge in January 1919 to complete the three years of residence necessary for the BA degree.

For a while Cannon thought of taking up research in experimental zoology, for which he was well qualified. However, he was unable to get a post in Cambridge and, encouraged by his experiences at Conwy with a variety of living marine animals, he turned his attention to the problems of interpreting animal structure and the nature of animals' developmental processes in terms of their functional significance and adaptational value.

In 1920 Cannon was appointed a demonstrator in the department of zoology at Imperial College, London, under Professor E. W. MacBride, a powerful and provocative advocate of the Lamarckian view of the evolution of organisms through the inheritance of acquired characters. Through MacBride, Cannon became friendly with W. T. Calman, deputy keeper of zoology in the British Museum (Natural History), and an authority on Crustacea, a subphylum which appealed strongly to Cannon as material for research; and in 1922 he began the long series of skilful investigations of the embryology, feeding mechanisms, and general anatomy of the Crustacea which established his reputation as a zoologist.

In 1926 Cannon was appointed to the chair of zoology at Sheffield University, where in the space of five years he published several important papers, three in collaboration with Sidnie Milana Manton (1902–1979). It had long been known that many crustaceans can feed by filtering small organisms from the surrounding water, and that by complicated limb movements they can themselves generate feeding currents, thus drawing food to their mouths. Together with Manton, Cannon studied the structure and motion of the limbs in relation to feeding currents made visible through the movements of particles and dyes. Limb movements were analysed by stroboscopic viewing and the sites of filtration and particle transfer traced by microscopic examination of sections of animals with their limbs carefully preserved in their natural relationships.

In 1927 Cannon married Annie Helen (Nannie), a zoologist, and graduate of Edinburgh, the daughter of Edwin J. Fyfe of Edinburgh. The couple had four children, and the marriage was happy.

Cannon was regarded as a fine lecturer. He used plain language delivered with an actor's generous use of gestures and emphasis, and he was watchful of the responses of his audience. Forthright and uncompromising in the defence of his beliefs, and quick to react to criticism, he was nevertheless warm-hearted and generous. He took an especial pleasure in beautiful things, whether they were natural or artefacts. His main hobby was the collection and annotation of elegantly worked swords and furnishings, on which he was an authority. In his later years his thoughts turned to evolutionary topics, and he wrote *The Evolution of Living Things* (1958) and *Lamarck and Modern Genetics* (1959).

Cannon was elected a fellow of the Royal Society of Edinburgh in 1927 and a fellow of the Royal Society in 1935. He died in St Bartholomew's Hospital, London, on 6 January 1963, shortly after being flown home from Las Palmas, where he had become seriously ill while on a recuperative voyage. ERIC SMITH, *rev.*

Sources J. E. Smith, *Memoirs FRS*, 9 (1963), 55–68 • *CGPLA Eng. & Wales* (1963)
Likenesses photograph, repro. in *Memoirs FRS*, 54
Wealth at death £2661 13*s*.: probate, 18 April 1963, *CGPLA Eng. & Wales*

Cannon, John (1684–1743), excise official and autobiographer, was born on 28 March 1684, the third but eldest surviving child of John Cannon (*b*. 1648), smallholder and butcher, and his wife, Elizabeth Hooper (*b*. 1644), in the small central Somerset village of West Lidford. His life progressed

> from a schoolboy to a ploughboy, and from a ploughboy to an excise man, and from an excise man to a maltster and from a maltster to an almost nothing except a schoolmaster, so that I might be called the tennis ball of fortune. (Money, 367)

And indeed, the modest achievements of Cannon's essentially provincial but varied life would have little impact on the historical record, except that he produced and preserved a 600-page memoir of that life, which is currently preserved in the holdings of the Somerset Archive and Record Service.

'Memoirs of the birth, education, life and death of Mr John Cannon, sometime officer of the excise & writing master at Mere, Glastenbury & West Lydford in the county of Somerset' is the most comprehensive and detailed autobiography of any non-élite British individual created during the eighteenth century. In it Cannon details his family background, his education and experience as a young farm labourer, his sexual life and intellectual life, and his time and concerns as an excise officer and finally as a teacher, neighbour, father, and husband.

Cannon grew up on his father's smallholding in West Lidford and was educated at a series of private venture schools in the village. By the age of thirteen he had become reasonably fluent in Latin and was eager to pursue his education. But his parents' economic circumstances were such that he was forced to 'become a mere clod hopper for a time' (Cannon, 30), working first for his father and later for his uncle. The sections of the memoir which describe this period in Cannon's life give details of the organization of agriculture and of labour in this part of Somerset and of Cannon's extensive social life. Perhaps the most outstanding details refer to his adolescent sexual behaviour in the context of courtship conducted at local fairs, masturbation, and a more serious relationship with one of his uncle's farm servants, Mary Rose, with whom he contracted an informal marriage by exchanging vows and a broken shilling. He also gives details of the medical treatment of a variety of injuries, and of his own use of magic.

After a quarrel with his uncle about the correct way to plough a field, Cannon was forced to leave West Lidford and received a commission in the excise in 1707, at the age of twenty-three. Over the next thirteen years he worked for the excise at Reading, Watlington, and Shepton Mallet. During this period both his activities as an excise officer and his broader social activities are discussed in detail, as is his sexual behaviour. He married a domestic servant, Susannah (*b*. 1691), daughter of Francis Deane of West Wycombe, in 1714 and they had two daughters and two surviving sons.

Cannon was dismissed from the excise in 1720 and first attempted to set himself up as a maltster, later earning his living as a schoolmaster and as a paid writer, accountant, and surveyor in the towns and countryside around West Lidford. Cannon died in West Lidford in 1743, having created the memoir over the previous two to three years.

The memoir itself is a complex mixture of genres, Cannon describes it as:

> an account of his family, ancestors, marriage with choice dissertations, epigrams, epitaphs, recipes in physick & surgery, occurrences & brief descriptions of famous men & sayings with the topography of some cities, towns and places in which he was conversant—very diverting and useful as also ornamental. (Cannon, title-page)

But it is much more than this; despite having been largely ignored by historians, the memoir represents a detailed insight into the interior world of a member of that ill-studied group, the lower middling sort of eighteenth-century provincial England. TIM HITCHCOCK

Sources J. Cannon, 'Memoirs of the birth, education, life and death of Mr John Cannon, sometime officer of the excise & writing master at Mere, Glastenbury & West Lydford', Som. ARS, DD/SAS C/1193/4 • T. Hitchcock, 'Sociability and misogyny in the life of John Cannon, 1684–1743', *English masculinities, 1660–1800*, ed. T. Hitchcock and M. Cohen (1999), 25–43 • J. Money, 'Teaching on the market-place, or, "Caesar adsum jam forte: Pompey aderat": the retailing of knowledge in provincial England during the eighteenth century', *Consumption and the world of goods*, ed. J. Brewer and R. Porter (1993), 335–77 • T. Hitchcock, *English sexualities, 1700–1800* (1997)
Archives Som. ARS, diary, DD/SAS C/1193/4

Cannon, Sir Leslie (1920–1970), trade unionist, was born on 21 February 1920 in Cudworth Street, Wigan, Lancashire, the fourth of seven children born to James (Jim) Cannon, a miner, and his wife, Ellen (Nellie) Turner. He was brought up in poverty in Wigan between the wars. His father worked only sporadically after being victimized following the general strike of 1926. Family income came from temporary work such as newspaper rounds and selling firewood done by Cannon and his brothers. Les Cannon always acknowledged the influence of his father, who was a bookish man, joining the fledgeling Communist Party in 1920 only to leave it later over a dispute within the party over A. J. Cook, the miners' leader.

Cannon won a scholarship to the Junior Technical School of Wigan and District Mining and Technical, but left aged fifteen to work as a van delivery boy. However, he was accepted a year later as an apprentice electrician by Wigan corporation. During his apprenticeship, he successfully studied at Wigan Technical College to ordinary national certificate level.

Cannon joined the Electrical Trades Union (ETU) on 1 May 1936, and the Communist Party in 1939. Both his trade union and political views were influenced heavily by the triumph of fascism in Europe. However, he took little part in union or political affairs before 1941. He worked in a reserved occupation in the Tyneside shipyards, exempted from military service due to ear infections. He returned to Wigan in 1941 after Russia entered the war, and began a meteoric rise in the union at the same time as its leadership fell under communist influence nationally.

Elected district secretary of the union in 1942, and to the national executive in 1945 aged twenty-five, Cannon was re-elected unopposed for his Lancashire seat at every election until 1954, when he became the ETU's education officer at its shop steward training college at Esher in Surrey. As a young communist 'high-flyer' within a communist-dominated union, he was spokesman on many key issues for the union in the period 1946–54 as the cold war intensified. Other unions resented the ETU for acting as a frequent spokesman for the Communist Party view of international and domestic affairs, often contradicting official Labour policy. Cannon's contribution to this period was especially influential in raising questions about the new discipline of 'work study', the social usefulness of automation, the need for the Communist Party to affiliate to the Labour Party, youth issues, and support for East European 'workers' states'. It was in this context that he met and quickly married his wife, Olga Julinava, in Czechoslovakia on 25 August 1947. Communist Party secretary Harry Pollitt was to be best man, but because of the short notice Willie Gallagher MP officiated instead. Two sons were born, Oleg in 1950 and Martin in 1952.

While teaching at Esher from 1954 to 1957 Cannon's disillusion with the Communist Party developed. First, he returned to his father's view that Britain was too wedded to the Labour Party/trade union tradition to make a Leninist approach to political change in Britain possible. Second, his wife's family in Czechoslovakia were cruelly treated by the communist authorities, despite Cannon's influence within the highest echelons of the British Communist Party. Third, he resented some of the cruder power politics within the ETU. The Communist Party leadership of the ETU had failed to defend him when he was dismissed in 1950 from English Electric in Lancashire after a strike, and the union never paid him what he expected when he gave up his executive council seat to go to Esher.

Cannon was especially moved by Khrushchov's speech to the Twentieth Congress of the Soviet Communist Party in 1956, in which Stalin's crimes were first revealed. Cannon's suggested reform documents were sent to the British Communist Party just as the invasion of Hungary by Soviet troops prompted large numbers of communists to leave the party.

Cannon resigned from the party in November 1956. His communist opponents set about isolating him. He lost his job at Esher College in April 1957 when the ETU leadership shut the college for financial reasons, following the union's expenditure incurred during the 1957 engineering strikes. He was forced back into being an electrician.

Instead of taking up a different job—perhaps in the law, which already interested him—Cannon set about opposing the Communist Party leadership of the ETU. He was greatly assisted in this by the events in Hungary, which brought together similar-minded former communists in the union such as Frank Chapple and Mark Young. There was also growing media interest in the communist domination of the ETU. Cannon had an immediate focus for opposition, as an executive council election was due in south-east England. The seat was held by Communist Party member Jack Frazer, seen by many as the successor to the president of the union, Frank Foulkes. Five years earlier, Cannon would have been that obvious choice.

This 1957 election was rigged in favour of Frazer, as was later demonstrated in court. Cannon, who himself failed to gain election in 1957, toured the union's branches with sympathetic colleagues for three years amassing evidence on the methods used by the communists to corrupt ETU elections that would convince a court. The election to the ETU general secretaryship in 1959 was also rigged, and Cannon and John Byrne, district secretary in Glasgow, issued writs for alleged fraud. When their case was heard by the High Court in 1961, Mr Justice Winn declared the election void. This led to fair elections and the eventual defeat of the disgraced communists. Cannon was reinstated at Esher. In 1963 he was elected president of the union by a huge majority, and re-elected in 1968. Success was assured when he reformed the union in tandem with Frank Chapple, the new ETU general secretary.

Cannon's period in office was short, but his impact enormous. He initiated revolutionary negotiating priorities to raise the standard of living for skilled craftsmen. In electrical contracting and the electricity supply industry he introduced productivity-based negotiations. In 1965 he was elected to the TUC general council, where he supported an incomes policy but only as far as it flexibly rewarded those who had higher skills. He gave evidence to the 1965 royal commission on trade unions and employer organizations, suggesting radical changes in trade union structure and purpose. Within the ETU he abolished the mechanisms through which the Communist Party had controlled the union and led the way to merger with the plumbing trades union in 1968. He sat on the Industrial Reorganization Corporation, which attempted structural reform of British companies, and the National Economic Development Council.

Cannon's manner was readily abrasive, sometimes interpreted as arrogance, and his preferred style was often combative on behalf of the issues he cared about. He led the most bitter struggle to rescue the democratic integrity of a union and prevent, by example, such corruption gaining a widespread hold within the labour movement. He showed how unions could contribute intellectual resources in modernizing out-of-date work practices. Cannon died of cancer at the Mount Vernon Hospital, Northwood, Middlesex, on 9 December 1970. His knighthood was gazetted in the new year honours list in 1971.

JOHN LLOYD

Sources ETU Conference Reports and Executive Minutes, 1940–1971, Amalgamated Engineering and Electrical Union head office, Bromley, Kent · O. Cannon and J. R. L. Anderson, *The road from Wigan pier: a biography of Les Cannon* (1973) · U. Warwick Mod. RC, Sir Leslie Cannon archive, MS 137 · Warwick University, Electrical Trades Union archive, MS 387 · F. Chapple, *Sparks fly: a trade union life* (1984) · K. Mason, *Front seat* (1981) · C. H. Rolph, *All those in favour* (1962) · 'The road from Wigan pier: Les Cannon talks to Nicholas Wooley', *The Listener* (28 Jan 1971) · b. cert. · d. cert.

Archives U. Warwick Mod. RC, corresp. and papers | Electrical Trades Union, London, MS 387 · JRL, letters to the *Manchester Guardian* | SOUND BBC WAC, 'The road from Wigan pier: Les Cannon talks to Nicholas Wooley' [recorded 27 Nov 1970]

Wealth at death £30,769: probate, 15 Oct 1971, *CGPLA Eng. & Wales*

Cannon, Richard (1779–1865), civil servant and military historian, was educated at Christ's Hospital, London. On 1 January 1802 he was appointed to a clerkship at the Horse Guards, one of fifteen clerks administering the adjutant-general's department. In 1805 he was made principal clerk of the adjutant-general's office, which appointment he held for nearly fifty years. Reputedly, William IV proposed that a series of regimental histories should be compiled, whereby the general public could be apprised of the distinguished services rendered by the regiments of the British army. By a Horse Guards order, dated 1 January 1836, from General Lord Hill, commander-in-chief, a historic account of every regiment in the British army was to be published under the superintendence of the adjutant-general, Sir John Macdonald, and the work of compilation was entrusted by royal warrant to Cannon. He started immediately and the first volume to be published was a history of the Life Guards in 1837.

In the next sixteen years 'historical records' of sixty-eight regiments were produced, all twenty-four regiments of cavalry and forty-three regiments of infantry (half of those on the establishment at that time). All were prepared under Cannon's direction, except the history of the Royal Horse Guards or Oxford Blues (issued as part of the series in 1847), which was written by Captain Edmund Packe of that regiment. Cannon's warrant expired on the death of William IV but was renewed on Victoria's accession to the throne. Unfortunately the official funding was not maintained and Cannon endeavoured to finance the project from his own pocket, consequently running into serious pecuniary difficulties.

Cannon was married with two sons and four daughters; his wife and his eldest son, Richard, predeceased him. He lived at Stockwell and, at the end of his life, at Kennington. Some time after 1850 he suffered 'a cerebral infection', probably a stroke, and he retired in January 1854 after fifty-two years' service, on his full salary of £800 a year. When he died on 30 October 1865 at 15 rue de la Constitution, Antwerp, the full extent of his liabilities became apparent. His three unmarried daughters, Sophia, Susan, and Emily, were reduced to petitioning the prime minister for pensions. Cannon was buried at St Mark's, Kennington, Surrey.

The last title in the 'Richard Cannon series' was published in 1853, but several second or revised editions were subsequently published under different managements. Cannon's volumes were authoritative and readable, well produced and often well illustrated. If somewhat lacking in the human interest expected of modern historians, Cannon nevertheless set a standard for succeeding regimental historians to emulate.

JAMES LUNT

Sources R. Cannon, preface, *Historical record of the sixteenth, or the queen's regiment of light dragoons, lancers* (1842) · R. Perkins, *Regiments and corps of the British empire and Commonwealth, 1758–1993: a critical bibliography* (1994), 18–19 · O. Wheeler, *The war office past and present* (1914) · War office lists · private information (2004) · J. M. Brereton, 'Records of the regiment', *Journal of the Society for Army Historical Research*, 74 (1996), 107–20 · *CGPLA Eng. & Wales* (1866)

Likenesses C. Baugniet, lithograph, 1850, BM, NPG

Wealth at death under £200: probate, 9 March 1866, *CGPLA Eng. & Wales*

Cannon, Robert (1663–1722), dean of Lincoln, was born on 13 August 1663 in London, the son of John Cannon and his wife, Marie. He was educated at Eton College and King's College, Cambridge, where he matriculated in 1681, graduated BA in 1685, and proceeded MA in 1689, BD in 1702, and DD in 1707. He became a fellow of King's (1684) and was given the position of taxor (1697). He was ordained deacon in London on 20 September 1685, and became the chaplain to Chelsea College. He was made rector of Bexwell, Norfolk (1707–8), and at the same time received the archdeaconry of Norfolk. On 20 August 1709 Cannon married Elizabeth Moore, daughter of John Moore, bishop of Ely, who made Cannon a prebendary of Ely. The couple had at least three children: Charles (*b.* 1713), Anne (*b.* 1716), and Thomas (*b.* 1720). Later Cannon became rector of Bluntisham, Huntingdonshire (1709–14), and rector of Newton, Isle of Ely (1714–16).

Cannon was associated with the whig statesman Charles Townshend, second Viscount Townshend, and was considered one of 'his devoted creatures' (BL, Add. MS 9200, fol. 22*r*) by one contemporary. Cannon was also a low-churchman, with a reputation for sceptical views on religion. His long-term acquaintance the Arian William Whiston called Cannon 'one of the greatest Scepticks that ever was born' (Whiston, 110). Whiston even claimed that Cannon privately rejected the Thirty-Nine Articles and at one point considered leaving the church, but was persuaded to stay by Lord Townshend (ibid., 112). Cannon is reported to have told the religious radical John Jackson that the primary function of religion was to maintain peace within the state, and that he would always support the state religion, regardless of whether it was protestantism, Catholicism, or even Islam (ibid., 112).

His low-church views led Cannon to participate in several ecclesiastical controversies. In 1711, when the convocation censured William Whiston for heresy, Cannon successfully attempted to reduce the number of charges made against him. This support surprised even Whiston himself. On 22 February 1712 Cannon moved in convocation to censure a high-church sermon of Thomas Brett, which strongly supported priestly absolution. A few months later he published his reasons for his actions in a pamphlet, *An Account of Two Motions* (1712), in which he denied such powers to the clergy and argued in favour of convocation taking action against anyone who attempted to raise the powers of the clergy too high.

Cannon received the prebend of Westminster in 1715 and was later made sub-almoner to the king (1716–22). In 1717 he became involved in the notorious Bangorian controversy, precipitated by Benjamin Hoadly, bishop of Bangor. He was a member of the committee set up in convocation to examine Hoadly's *A Preservative* (1716) and his sermon *The Nature of the Kingdom* (1717). The committee condemned Hoadly's extreme latitudinarian views, and on 14 May 1717 Cannon sent a copy of the committee's report to Hoadly, along with a letter in which he fully endorsed the report's findings. Later that year he published a pamphlet called *A Vindication of the Proceedings*, explaining his reasons for condemning Hoadly. Some contemporaries saw Cannon's involvement as being instigated by his associate Lord Townshend (BL, Add. MS 9200, fol. 22*r*), yet Cannon was probably moved to respond by his own religious beliefs. One anonymous writer saw Cannon's stand against Hoadly as uncharacteristic, in view of Cannon's own notoriously low-church views. In a satirical pamphlet this writer declared that owing to his role in the censure of Hoadly, Cannon ran 'the risque of being counted *Orthodox*' (*A Letter*, 17). However, Cannon's stand against Hoadly was not really due to Hoadly's low-church religious beliefs; rather, Cannon felt Hoadly's views destroyed the inextricable relationship between church and state, and thus jeopardized the stability of the government and nation.

Cannon became vicar of Christ Church Greyfriars, London (1718), and in 1721 he was made prebendary and dean of Lincoln. He died on 28 March 1722, and was buried on 31 March in the south aisle of Westminster Abbey. His death left Cannon's widow and family in such 'necessitous circumstances' (Harwood, 266) that the king granted them a pension of £120 per annum.

Rebecca Louise Warner

Sources Venn, *Alum. Cant.* • W. Whiston, *Memoirs of the life and writings of Mr William Whiston: containing memoirs of several of his friends also* (1749) • T. Harwood, *Alumni Etonenses, or, A catalogue of the provosts and fellows of Eton College and King's College, Cambridge, from the foundation in 1443 to the year 1797* (1797) • E. Duffy, '"Whiston's affair": the trials of a primitive Christian, 1709–1714', *Journal of Ecclesiastical History*, 27 (1976), 129–50 • T. Lathbury, *History of convocation of the Church of England from the earliest period to the year 1742* (1853) • *A letter from the Right Reverend G-lb-rt, late lord bishop of S-m, to the Right Reverend B-nj-m-n, l-d b-p of Bangor* (1717) • J. L. Chester, ed., *The marriage, baptismal, and burial registers of the collegiate church or abbey of St Peter, Westminster*, Harleian Society, 10 (1876) • J. Bentham, *The history and antiquities of the conventual and cathedral church of Ely* (1771) • collections of Revd U. Etough, part II, BL, Add. MS 9200 • *IGI*

Wealth at death presumed poor: Harwood, *Alumni Etonenses*, 267

Cannon, Thomas [Tom] (**1846–1917**), jockey and racehorse trainer, the elder son of Thomas H. Cannon, a Windsor livery stable keeper, and his wife, Harriett Townsend, was born on 23 April 1846 in Eton, where his father later kept the George Hotel. At the age of thirteen he was apprenticed to a Mr Sextie, who ran a small training stable in Wiltshire. His first win came the following year when, weighing only 3 st 12 lb, he piloted Lord Portsmouth's My Uncle to victory in a six-furlong heats race at Plymouth. In 1872 he became champion jockey with eighty-seven winners. He rode only one Derby winner—Shotover in 1882—but his thirty-two years in the saddle brought him twelve other English classics, several major French victories, and a career total of 1544 winners.

Cannon was one of the four outstanding professional jockeys of the second half of the nineteenth century, along with George Fordham, John Osborne, and Fred Archer. Fordham and Cannon were both attached to John Day's Danebury stables and George acted as Tom's mentor, teaching him the advantage which could be gained from steadying a horse before the final effort. To this Cannon added his own gentle touch. He rarely used his whip and was renowned for his ability to coax the best from even a highly strung two-year-old. Indeed many contemporaries regarded him as unequalled in his handling of young horses. His one fault, shared with other jockeys, was his habit of attempting to win by the narrowest possible margin in an attempt to deceive the handicapper, though his judgement was such that it cost him fewer races than most. What he did not share with other jockeys of the time—Archer, Fordham, and Osborne excepted—was a reputation for dishonesty: no trace of scandal tinged his career.

While still a professional jockey Cannon turned to training, taking over the lease of the Danebury stables at Stockbridge, Hampshire, from his father-in-law, John Day, in 1879, though he did not take actual possession until after Day's death three years later. Most of the horses which he trained he also owned, many of them in partnership with Tom Robinson of High Wycombe; the most celebrated were Reminder (third in the 1894 Derby), Curzon (second the following year), and Playfair (winner of the 1888 Grand National). His ownership, breeding, and training of horses meant that at times he had over eighty animals in his care. Nevertheless George Lampton, turf raconteur, maintained that Cannon was better at training riders than horses and certainly three leading jockeys—John Watts, Sam Loates, and W. T. (Jack) Robinson—served their apprenticeships at Danebury. He also passed on his riding knowledge to Arthur Coventry, an outstanding gentleman rider, as well as to his own sons. His colours last appeared on a course in 1913 but he had relinquished training well before that, when part of the Danebury training grounds passed into the hands of a lady who refused to allow racehorses on her land. Stockbridge races, at which Cannon served as clerk of the course from 1892 to 1898, had to be abandoned for the same reason.

Cannon was physically slight, riding as a lightweight for

Thomas [Tom] **Cannon (1846–1917)**, by Bassano, 1895

most of his career, but he was a graceful jockey to whom the epithet 'polished' was often applied by contemporaries. Although he was said rarely to smile when racing, he had a sense of humour: in his later years as a trainer he often allowed early-morning visitors to mount a little hog-maned horse which he later revealed to be Duke of Palma, informing his guests that they could therefore rightfully claim to have ridden the winner of the Cambridgeshire.

Cannon's first marriage was to John Day's daughter Catherine (Kate). Three of their sons made a name on the racetrack: Tom junior lost by a length to his father in the 1888 Eclipse Stakes; Kempton (named after the course), in strict contrast to the upright seat of his father, was an English pioneer of the crouched, 'monkey-on-a-stick' riding style introduced to Britain by American jockeys in the 1890s; Mornington (Morny), like both Kempton and his father, won a Derby, as well as the Hanworth Plate at Kempton Park in 1891, when his father, in his last race, finished third. Another son, Charles, also became a jockey, and a daughter, Margaret, married Ernest Piggott, a steeplechase rider; their son Keith was the father of the jockey Lester Piggott. Kate died in 1891 and Cannon later remarried but his second wife also predeceased him. His younger brother Joe was a renowned racehorse trainer.

Cannon suffered recurrent ill health for the last two decades of his life and after a final, long, wearying illness, in which dropsy supervened on serious heart trouble, he died on 13 July 1917 at his Grosvenor Hotel, Stockbridge, Hampshire, where he had settled after the death of his second wife. He left the bulk of his estate, valued at £5306 gross, to his son Ronald Portland, whom he advised 'to make his will'.

WRAY VAMPLEW

Sources *Bloodstock Breeders Review* (1917) · *The Times* (26 Sept 1917) · Earl of Suffolk and Berkshire, H. Peek, and F. G. Aflalo, eds., *Encyclopaedia of sport* (1900) · H. C. Howard, W. G. Craven, and others, *Racing and steeple-chasing* (1886) · W. Vamplew, *The turf: a social and economic history of horse racing* (1976) · *DNB* · G. Lampton, *Men and horses I have known* (1924)

Likenesses photograph, 1890–99, repro. in L. Rasmussen and M. Napier, *Treasures of the Bloodstock Breeders Review* (1990) · Bassano, photograph, 1895, NPG [*see illus.*]

Wealth at death £5306 12*s.* 7*d.*: probate, 21 Sept 1917, *CGPLA Eng. & Wales*

Canot, Peter Charles (*c.*1710–1777/8), engraver, is said to have been born in France about 1710 and to have been the brother of the painter Philippe Canot. He may have been in England as early as 1735, the probable date of a set of hunting prints after John Wootton; these were engraved with Louis Truchy, for whom Canot may have worked. Later he found employment with Arthur Pond, for whom he engraved two paintings by Claude and Gaspar Poussin (1744). He established a reputation as an engraver of shipping and for different light effects on water with a set of twelve sea pieces after Peter Monamy, which were published by John Bowles in February 1746. This specialization was consolidated with further publications, notably views of dockyards for Thomas Milton (1753–6), of Mount Edgecumbe for George Lambert, and of Westminster and London bridges (1758), for Samuel Scott. In 1758 Canot began a lasting collaboration with the painter Richard Paton, for whom he engraved a series of large prints of naval engagements.

Canot was a remarkably prolific line engraver. In 1755 he took on as an apprentice Christopher Norton, who soon proved himself a gifted assistant. Canot undertook frequent commissions to engrave views of gardens and of London, as well as landscapes, seascapes, and fox-hunting scenes after a variety of contemporary artists. The outbreak of war brought the studio further business, fulfilling the public demand for views of America and of amphibious victories such as those at Quebec (1759) and Havana (1762). Meanwhile Canot had begun to publish for himself, having settled by 1755 at the Golden Head in Chapel Street, near Soho Square. He formed a close alliance with his compatriots Jean Pillement, a designer, and Charles Leviez, who was both dancing-master at Drury Lane theatre and also a notable art dealer. Canot's house was the principal English outlet for Pillement's prints; he also published paintings by David Teniers and other fashionable Dutch and Flemish artists. In 1763 his listing in Thomas Mortimer's directory as a 'Landscape engraver remarkable also for Sea Pieces' recognized his eminence and specialization.

The exhibitions of the Society of Artists increased Canot's renown; he came to the notice of the king with a view of the embarkation of Queen Charlotte from Stade. A view of Boston in New England shown in 1764 was one of nineteen prints that he exhibited at the society between 1760 and 1769. Also exhibited were his print of Richard

Wilson's *Bridge over the River Taafe* (1766) and his first four engravings for John Boydell's *Collection of Prints Engraved after the most Capital Paintings in England*. In 1770, together with his friend Francis Ravenet, he was elected one of the original associate engravers of the Royal Academy; according to Robert Strange, he had always been aligned with the faction of artists which broke away to found the academy. Between 1770 and 1776 he exhibited with the academy, showing further engravings after Paton, and after Nicolaes Berghem and Claude. A sensitive engraver with a delicate touch, Canot was the finest contemporary exponent of scenes with water. In 1768 he had retired with Ravenet to a house opposite the Mother Redcap on Hampstead Road, where he died in late 1777 or early 1778, having just completed a prestigious set of prints of the battle of Chesma Bay, commissioned from Paton by Catherine the Great. On 11 February 1778 the auctioneer John Greenwood advertised in the *Morning Chronicle* that the following week he would sell 'The genuine Collection of Prints of the late ingenious Mr Canot, Engraver'. Canot's prints may be found in the British Museum, the National Maritime Museum at Greenwich, and the Bioliothèque Nationale in Paris. TIMOTHY CLAYTON

Sources Y. Sjöberg and F. Gardey, eds., *Inventaire du fonds français: graveurs du XVIIIe siècle* (1977) · F. E. Joubert, *Manuel de l'amateur d'estampes*, 3 vols. (Paris, 1821) · T. Clayton, *The English print, 1688–1802* (1997) · *Morning Chronicle* (11 Feb 1778) · private information (2004) · Graves, *Soc. Artists* · T. Mortimer, *The universal director* (1763) · Redgrave, *Artists*

Cant, Andrew (1584/1590–1663), Church of Scotland minister, was most likely born in Aberdeenshire, but possibly in Haddingtonshire; nothing definite is known of his family. He was educated at the grammar school and at King's College, Aberdeen, where he graduated MA in 1612 and was appointed humanist in 1614. About 1614 he was apparently invited by some people in Edinburgh to become their minister, but nothing came of it. Before 13 December 1617 he became minister at Alford, Aberdeenshire. He married Margaret Irvine (*d.* 1679); they had three sons, James, Alexander, and Andrew (*d.* 1685), and two daughters, Margaret (*d.* 1660) and Sarah (*d.* 1673), who married, in 1647, Alexander *Jaffray (1614–1673) of Aberdeen.

Some time after 26 October 1629 Cant resigned from Alford in order to become tutor to the son of Alexander, Lord Forbes of Pitsligo, Aberdeenshire. By November 1633 Forbes had presented Cant to the new living of Pitsligo. On 7 September 1636 he was admitted a burgess of Aberdeen. Unlike most of the ministers in the area he was a strong supporter of the covenants, and in October 1637 he encouraged protest to the privy council about the introduction of the prayer book. On 13 June 1638 he preached in Greyfriars Church, Edinburgh, a sermon eventually published (1699), and in July he was appointed a member of the delegation sent under the leadership of Alexander Henderson to argue the presbyterian case in Aberdeen, the scene of the only organized opposition to the national covenant, headed by the 'Aberdeen doctors'.

By November 1638 Cant was in Glasgow, where he took part in the assembly which abolished episcopacy. On the presentation of the earl of Lothian he was instituted on 20 May 1639 as minister of Newbattle, Edinburghshire. In 1640 he became a chaplain to the covenanting army. Although it is claimed that he may have been deprived of this position for circulating Samuel Rutherford's *Lex rex*, it seems more likely, in view of his political sentiments, that he was drawn away by the offer of the charge of St Nicholas, Aberdeen, to which he was instituted in December 1641.

Cant was a member of all the commissions of assembly between 1642 and 1649, and on 10 July 1650 was elected moderator of the general assembly. He was a devoted royalist, and on one occasion during the Cromwellian occupation of Aberdeen uttered from the pulpit such strong sentiments on duty to the king that some officers present drew their swords and threatened him. He apparently defied them with the courage and eloquence for which he was well known.

In 1651 Cant became rector of King's College, Aberdeen, and joined the protesters; the *Letter from the Protestors* (1653) was published under his name. While theses published at Aberdeen in 1654 and 1658 are probably the work of his son Andrew—an Andrew Cant had been admitted to Marischal College there by November 1650—*Euchē basilikē, Votum pro rege* (1661) looks like his celebration of the Restoration. However, on 9 December 1662 Cant was among those summoned before the privy council for seditious carriage.

Cant died on 27 or 30 April 1663 in Aberdeen. He was survived by his wife and several of his children, including Andrew Cant, who was principal of the University of Edinburgh from 1675 until his death in 1685.

W. G. BLAIKIE, *rev.* R. P. WELLS

Sources *Fasti Scot.*, new edn, 1.332, 6.37, 118, 234, 7.440, 8.79 · J. Spalding, *Memorialls of the trubles in Scotland and in England, AD 1624 – AD 1645*, ed. J. Stuart, 2 vols., Spalding Club, [21, 23] (1850–51) · D. Calderwood, *The history of the Kirk of Scotland*, ed. T. Thomson and D. Laing, 8 vols., Wodrow Society, 7 (1842–9), vol. 7, pp. 448, 516, 580, 627 · R. Wodrow, *Analecta, or, Materials for a history of remarkable providences, mostly relating to Scotch ministers and Christians*, ed. [M. Leishman], 4 vols., Maitland Club, 60 (1842–3), vol. 2, pp. 154, 161, 189, 374; vol. 3, pp. 126, 414 · J. Stuart, ed., *Selections from the records of the kirk session, presbytery, and synod of Aberdeen*, Spalding Club, 15 (1846) · J. Stuart, ed., *Extracts from the council register of the burgh of Aberdeen, 1625–1747*, 2 vols., Scottish Burgh RS, 8–9 (1871–2) · *The historical works of Sir James Balfour*, ed. J. Haig, 2–4 (1824–5) · J. Row, *The history of the Kirk of Scotland, from the year 1558 to August 1637*, ed. D. Laing, Wodrow Society, 4 (1842), 494–5 · J. Gordon, *History of Scots affairs from 1637–1641*, ed. J. Robertson and G. Grub, 3 vols., Spalding Club, 1, 3, 5 (1841) · Anderson, *Scot. nat.*, 1.586–7 · Chambers, *Scots.*, rev. T. Thomson (1875), 1.315–17 · G. Grub, *An ecclesiastical history of Scotland*, 4 vols. (1861), vol. 3, pp. 13, 77, 143, 164, 182, 206 · *DSCHT*

Archives U. Aberdeen L., lectures on logic

Likenesses S. Freeman, stipple (after unknown artist), BM, NPG; repro. in Chambers, *Scots.*

Cantebrig, John de. *See* Cambridge, Sir John (*d.* 1335).

Cantelowe, Sir William (*d.* 1464), merchant, is first recorded in 1427, when a complaint was lodged against him and his wife, Margaret. He was then described as a mercer. A Thomas Cantelowe, mercer, mentioned in 1410, may have been his father. In the 1430s William Cantelowe achieved some prominence as an administrator appointed by the crown: in 1431 he was collector of lay subsidy, in 1432 collector of alien subsidy and custom on cloth, both at London; from 1436 to 1440 he was victualler of Calais—a responsible and demanding post, after the French attack of 1436. In 1441 the council decided, apparently after some debate, to allow him to ship wool to Calais independently of staple regulations, presumably in order to recover money due to him as victualler, and in 1442 he had permission to recover £1506, a further sum owed to him as victualler.

Cantelowe is recorded as having many dealings with alien merchants, which were evidently connected with his activity in royal finance. In 1434 he guaranteed that a consignment of wool exported by Milanese to Antwerp would go on to Milan, and in 1440 he guaranteed another consignment going via Middelburg to Milan. Between 1440 and 1443 he is reported as engaged in buying fabrics from Lucchese and Venetians and selling cloth to them. In 1445 he was giving credit at Calais as a stapler for wool purchases by Dutch merchants. In the following year he became alderman for Cripplegate, a position he held until 1461. It was at this time that his substantial financial advances to the crown began. In 1445 he had lent money for the journey of Margaret of Anjou to England, before her marriage to Henry VI. In 1449 he was a contributor to the staple loan of £10,700, and acted as agent for the other contributors in arranging assignments in repayment. Cantelowe was sheriff of London in 1448–9. In the latter year he paid 500 marks owed by the crown to Jean de Luxembourg, the Bastard of St Pol, and in 1450 he advanced £800 for the new college at Eton and was allowed, in return, to ship 300 sacks of wool from Southampton through the Strait of Gibraltar without paying customs or subsidies. This was apparently the background to an unusual shipment of 466 pokes of wool from Southampton to Pisa in 1451. The wool was handled on arrival by branches of the Salviati family and sold by them at Florence, the proceeds then being returned to their branch at London. Cantelowe had been dealing with the Salviati of London, to whom he had a debt of over £4200, built up over several years for payments to woolmen, exchange payments at Bruges, and even drafts of cash. This debt was now cancelled by the proceeds of the sale at Florence, and it is clear that the Salviati had in fact financed the shipment for Cantelowe.

Cantelowe continued to be closely associated with the crown in the early 1450s. In 1450 he was one of those said in a political poem to be responsible for the corruption at court. In the same year he was master of the Mercers' Company, a post he also held in 1456 and 1462. In 1451 he was involved in a loan for the expenses of the king's household, while in 1454 he and others made a loan of £304. In view of his connections with alien merchants and royal finance it is surprising that he was punished as a result of the London riots against the Italians in April 1456. As master of the Mercers he promised the mayor on 3 May that they would keep the peace, and he was himself imprisoned in Dudley Castle from October to December. The reason for the mercers' conduct was no doubt displeasure caused by the commercial policy of the crown, the favour it showed to aliens, and its neglect of staple privileges. Whether this displeasure was really shared by Cantelowe is not known. In any case the position was changed by the accession of Edward IV, which resulted in Cantelowe's being knighted in 1461; in the same year he was exonerated from duties as an alderman on the grounds of age and infirmity. He died in 1464 (his will, dated 21 February, was proved on 11 May), leaving property for life to his second wife, Elizabeth, with remainders to his sons Thomas, William, and Henry, and his daughters Anne, Joan, and Katherine. He was described as being of St Mary Magdalen, Milk Street, in London, and of Faversham. There were lands in Kent, Hertfordshire, and Bedfordshire. GEORGE HOLMES

Sources J. L. Bolton, 'The city of London and the crown, 1456–61', *London Journal*, 12 (1986), 11–24 • G. A. Holmes, 'Anglo-Florentine trade in 1451', *EngHR*, 108 (1993), 371–86 • *Chancery records* • N. H. Nicolas, ed., *Proceedings and ordinances of the privy council of England*, 7 vols., RC, 26 (1834–7) • S. L. Thrupp, *The merchant class of medieval London, 1300–1500* (1948) • A. B. Beaven, ed., *The aldermen of the City of London, temp. Henry III–[1912]*, 2 vols. (1908–13) • E. Power and M. Postan, *Studies in English trade in the fifteenth century* (1933) • *Registrum Thome Wolsey cardinalis ecclesie Wintoniensis administratoris*, ed. H. Chitty, CYS, 32 (1926) • exchequer, queen's remembrancer, customs accounts, PRO, E 122 • exchequer, queen's remembrancer, memoranda rolls, PRO, E 159 • Scuola Normale, Pisa, Archivio Salviati

Archives PRO, exchequer, queen's remembrancer, customs accounts, E 122 • PRO, exchequer, queen's remembrancer, memoranda rolls, E 159 • Scuola Normale, Pisa, Archivio Salviati

Cantelupe, Fulk de. *See* Cantilupe, Fulk de (*d.* 1217/18).

Cantelupe, George de. *See* Cantilupe, Sir George de (1251–1273).

Cantelupe, Nicholas de. *See* Cantilupe, Nicholas, third Lord Cantilupe (*c.*1301–1355).

Cantelupe, Roger de. *See* Cantilupe, Roger de (*d.* 1258/9).

Cantelupe, Walter de. *See* Cantilupe, Walter de (*c.*1195–1266).

Cantelupe, William de. *See* Cantilupe, William (I) de (*d.* 1239); Cantilupe, William (II) de (*d.* 1251); Cantilupe, William (III) de (*d.* 1254).

Canterbury. For this title name *see* Sutton, Charles Manners-, first Viscount Canterbury (1780–1845); Sutton, John Henry Thomas Manners-, third Viscount Canterbury (1814–1877).

Canterbury, Alexander of (*fl.* **1100–1109**), Benedictine monk and religious writer, emerges out of obscurity after the return of Archbishop *Anselm from his first exile in September 1100. The archbishop picked him out from the community of Christ Church, Canterbury, and made him a member of his household along with Baldwin of Tournai, Eadmer, and Eustace. In the autumn of 1101 Anselm sent Alexander and Baldwin to Rome as archiepiscopal envoys with the royal envoys Gerard of York, Herbert de

Losinga, and Robert of Limesey. They were sent to achieve a mitigation of the Lenten decrees of 1099 forbidding lay investiture of clerics. The mission lasted from October 1101 to May 1102 and on their return the two embassies made contradictory statements about their negotiations with the pope. The bishops maintained that the pope had granted a mitigation, while the two monks asserted firmly that no such mitigation had been granted.

Since an ensuing exchange of letters between Henry I and Paschal II, and between Anselm and Paschal, did not clarify matters Anselm agreed to undertake in person a third attempt to solve the conflict between king and pope. He set out for Rome on 26 April 1103, with Baldwin, Eadmer, Alexander, and Eustace. When, in late summer 1103, the party passed through the territory of Countess Matilda of Tuscany, Anselm employed Alexander as his messenger to the powerful and reform-minded lady of Canossa. Since the mitigation of the decrees was not achieved Anselm and his company were told while they were at Lyons, on about 20 December 1103, not to return to England. This was the start of Anselm's second exile, shared by the monks of his household until their return to Canterbury in September 1106. Alexander remained a member of the household until Anselm's death on 21 April 1109, after which he disappears into obscurity again.

As a member of the archiepiscopal household Alexander seems to have enjoyed Anselm's high esteem, and to have taken on some of the duties Eadmer had originally performed: sacristan for the archbishop's liturgical functions, reporter of Anselm's public sermons during mass and in the chapter house, and collector of his discourses, arranged (according to Alexander) not in any special order, but each preserving as well as possible the thread of Anselm's talk. These constitute the *Dicta Anselmi*, revised and copied at the request of Anselm's nephew Anselm. However, this work represents only part of the original record; the remainder was borrowed or even stolen without Alexander's knowledge, and is thus lost. To the twenty chapters of the *Dicta Anselmi* Alexander added thirty-two chapters of *Miracula*. In one of them, chapter 39, Alexander is himself the subject of a miracle; another displays Anselm performing one. Alexander heard about many of the miracles in Anselm's company, both in Rome and during the latter's second exile. He seems to have reproduced Anselm's train of thought accurately in the *Dicta Anselmi* but to be less reliable in the *Miracula*.

After Anselm's death Alexander, as his trusted secretary, appears to have been the curator of his literary remains, preserved in LPL, MS 59 (L). While Southern maintains that the entire manuscript was compiled between 1125 and 1130, close scrutiny seems to indicate that the main part of L (fols. 1–160v) was copied by the Canterbury scribe Thidricus under Anselm's own supervision, while the added quires making up La (fols. 160v–190v) were the work of Alexander, in 1109 or 1110. WALTER FRÖHLICH

Sources 'Epistolae Anselmi', ed. F. S. Schmitt, *S. Anselmi Cantuariensis archiepiscopi opera omnia*, 3–5 (1938–61), *epp.* 217–21, 223, 225, 247, 250–51, 265, 280, 284, 311, 325 · *The letters of Saint Anselm of Canterbury*, ed. and trans. W. Fröhlich, 3 vols. (1990–94), vol. 2, pp. 189–90, 292–3, vol. 3, pp. 3, 11–14, 38–9 · R. W. Southern and F. S. Schmitt, eds., *Memorials of Saint Anselm* (1969), 19–30, 105–270 · *Eadmeri Historia novorum in Anglia*, ed. M. Rule, Rolls Series, 81 (1884), 132 · Eadmer, *The life of St Anselm, archbishop of Canterbury*, ed. and trans. R. W. Southern, 2nd edn, OMT (1972), xiii–xiv, 131–2 · R. W. Southern, *Saint Anselm: a portrait in a landscape* (1990), 244, 368, 389–90

Archives LPL, MS 59 (L)

Canterbury, Eadmer of. *See* Eadmer of Canterbury (*b. c.*1060, *d.* in or after 1126).

Canterbury, Gervase of (*b. c.*1145, *d.* in or after 1210), Benedictine monk, chronicler, and topographer, was a member of the cathedral priory of Christ Church, Canterbury, where he was professed by Archbishop Thomas Becket early in 1163. Becket also ordained him, but not necessarily on the same occasion, and on balance it is likely that Gervase was born *c.*1145. He appears to have spent his whole adult life in the convent, holding office as sacrist from 1193 to 1197, and dying (undoubtedly at Canterbury) in or soon after 1210. The day as well as the year of his death is uncertain, as three Gervases figure in the Canterbury obituaries. He had a brother, Thomas, who was also a monk of Christ Church. If Thomas is to be identified with the monk associated with Becket who was known as Thomas of Maidstone, Gervase too may have been a Kentishman, possibly born at Maidstone. On the other hand the priory received land worth 2 mancuses in Canterbury when Gervase was professed, so his family probably had property and influence in the city. Whatever his origins, the monastery and its history became his principal concern, but his intellectual curiosity and his observations give his work a wider interest, ranging from the king's authority to ecclesiastical geography, the detection of forgeries, and the watercourses of England. His career is one measure of the purposeful vigour of his house in the twelfth century.

Gervase of Canterbury says that he attended Becket's funeral, and he witnessed the destruction of the cathedral choir by fire in 1174, which he subsequently described in vivid detail. He had probably evinced some historical interests by 1186, when the convent became embroiled with Archbishop Baldwin, and Gervase was asked to study the background to the dispute. He may already have begun an investigation on his own account which issued in his *Imaginacio*, or statement, of Baldwin's earlier contention with the monks of St Augustine's, in which he presents formally the arguments on either side. He then used the same device to summarize the even more acrimonious struggle between the archbishop and the chapter, but he ranged widely in search of historical material, and began to apply it in other ways. He shows, as Stubbs remarked, no sign of a training in canon law, and when he devised the *Imaginaciones* he was presumably searching for a style. He eventually found his métier in the course of the chapter's own battle with Baldwin, which continued until 1190, when Baldwin went on crusade with Richard I.

What was at issue was first the archbishop's authority

over the convent, which in practice was slight, and then his need of financial support from the priory's revenues to maintain the onerous business of the primacy, together with his distinct but associated need for the means of patronage. Lacking the power to appoint to prebends in the cathedral, Baldwin sought to found a collegiate church, first at Hackington outside Canterbury, and later at Lambeth, in which he could maintain and reward his chaplains and advisers with canonries. The proposal aroused perfervid opposition from the monks, who wished neither to sustain the archbishop's household themselves, nor yet to see him take his problems elsewhere. Their anger was redoubled when Archbishop Hubert Walter revived the scheme in his turn.

Both prelates were defeated by the convent's pertinacious opposition. Gervase of Canterbury took some part in the negotiations as well as in the ordinary business of the house, and he almost certainly had a hand in the extensive correspondence which the convent maintained in support of its claims. At the same time he found his real purpose as the historian of Christ Church. In that role he was ready to do justice to anyone, even an archbishop, who was not at odds with the convent. About 1188 he began the work that he called his *Chronica*, running from 1100 to his own day, and which he prefaced with the *Imaginaciones*, a selection of letters on the dispute with Baldwin, and his celebrated account of the fire of 1174 and the sumptuous rebuilding of the choir by William de Sens and his successor as master mason, William the Englishman.

Beyond the *Chronica* Gervase compiled a shorter but wider ranging text called the *Gesta regum*, incorporating material from Geoffrey of Monmouth's *History of the Kings of Britain*, and from other works available to him in the cathedral library. Beginning with Brut's Albion, he seems to have carried the narrative down to 1210, after which it was continued by other hands. He also composed a series of lives of the archbishops of Canterbury under the title of *Acta pontificum Cantuariensis ecclesie*, from the arrival of St Augustine to the death of Hubert Walter in 1205, and the monastic topography which he called the *Mappa mundi*.

Gervase of Canterbury says that when Sens was bedridden after falling in the choir he entrusted supervision of the works to a particular monk, who may well have been Gervase himself. Everything that he sees and describes, from the rescue of the relics in 1174 to the final glory of the new choir, redounds to the honour of the saint, but his graphic description of the fire, and his account of the progress and detail of the new work, is also characterized by an informed interest in its architecture and furnishing. Besides a passionate regard for the place, he had an intense feeling for the structure itself, and his description of its design and its spatial effect is the best observed extant account of such a building down to his time, and for some centuries afterwards.

Though Gervase's work is narrowly focused upon the cathedral and its clergy, its accomplishment led him much further afield. His underlying concern is to recapture and preserve the past. He describes the choir which was burned and the choir which replaced it, and he also gathers together all that he can about the earlier structure and condition of the church, so that it may not be forgotten. His critical sense is variable, but that was not for want of reflection. He discusses technical questions of chronology, and of the authentication of historical texts. He distinguishes, in theory though not always in practice, the chronicle, with its sequential narration of events and its frank reliance upon diverse sources, from the literary grace and elevating purpose of history. Like his contemporary Richard of Devizes he is influenced by the traditions of romance when he is consciously writing history, but his powers of observation were good. He preserves some important texts, such as the terms of Henry II's inquest of sheriffs in 1170, and he is an interesting, though manifestly partial, witness of the early years of John's reign.

Comparison of Gervase of Canterbury and Richard of Devizes can extend usefully beyond a mere consideration of technique. Both were Benedictines, and comfortably aware of their membership of the church's élite. Both were literate, and widely read by common standards. Both were regularly in touch with the royal court and in some measure responsive to its culture. They both had a high regard for their houses, but whereas Richard saw that Winchester had no rivals, Gervase was aware that Canterbury was unique.

It has been plausibly suggested that the well-known plan of the water supply at Christ Church which is preserved in the manuscript known as the Eadwine psalter is Gervase's work. He certainly had a topographical sense, and an intense desire to record detail systematically. He had in fact some of the temperament of the later antiquaries. His *Mappa mundi* is a tabular account of the monastic houses, castles, and watercourses in each English county. It has its defects, but there is no parallel to it until the seventeenth century. Yet just as his researches made him aware of methodological problems, so his observation of the royal court made him critical of the influence of courtiers, and interested in the constraints that were beginning to work upon the king. In that his attitude prefigures the critical stance of the St Albans chroniclers in Henry III's reign.

There are three principal manuscripts of the works of Gervase of Canterbury, all later than his own day. The earliest is BL, Cotton MS Vespasian B.xix, of *c.*1250, the next Cambridge, Trinity College, MS 644, and the third Cambridge, Corpus Christi College, MS 438, both of the later thirteenth century. The *Acta pontificum* was printed by Sir Roger Twysden in his *Decem scriptores* (1652), and the whole corpus edited by Stubbs as *The Historical Works of Gervase of Canterbury* for the Rolls Series in 1879–80.

G. H. MARTIN

Sources *The historical works of Gervase of Canterbury*, ed. W. Stubbs, 2 vols., Rolls Series, 73 (1879–80) · A. Gransden, *Historical writing in England*, 1 (1974), 253–60 · M. Gibson, 'Normans and Angevins, 1070–1220', *A history of Canterbury Cathedral, 598–1982*, ed. P. Collinson and others (1995), 38–68 · C. R. Cheney, *Hubert Walter* (1967) ·

The Eadwine Psalter: text, image, monastic culture in twelfth-century Canterbury, ed. M. Gibson, T. A. Heslop, and R. W. Pfaff (1992)

Archives BL, Cotton MS Vesp. B.xix • CCC Cam., MS 438 • Trinity Cam., MS 644

Canterbury, John of [John Bellesmains] (*c*.1120–1204?), archbishop of Lyons, was born in Canterbury. His sobriquet, Bellesmains ('Fair Hands'), a common nickname in the twelfth century, gave rise to the mistaken belief that he was a member of the ecclesiastically important Belmeis family; in fact his family was connected with tenants of the archbishop of Canterbury. Given this lack of social distinction, he was fortunate in the place of his upbringing. Much later he was locally remembered as the most outstanding pupil educated in the city. Since there is no evidence that he studied abroad, his high reputation for eloquence and learning may be a tribute to the quality of the Canterbury schools.

The crucial step in John's early career was his appointment as clerk in the household of Archbishop Theobald; he was already installed there before Becket's advent in 1146. In this stimulating environment he developed two abiding convictions: that papal authority must be respected (Gilbert Foliot remarked on his devotion to the pope in 1146), and that ecclesiastical and secular jurisdictions should be sharply distinguished. More immediately, Theobald's household provided him with a network of influential friends. It was said that John, Thomas Becket, and Roger de Pont l'Évêque formed a cartel to assist one another's promotion; certainly they were all soon successful. Of John's everyday work in this period all that remains is his witnessing of thirteen archiepiscopal charters. But his recorded visit to Italy may have occurred about 1150; a stay at the papal curia would explain subsequent papal interest in him.

In 1152 John failed to acquire the archdeaconry of Middlesex, despite the support of Pope Eugenius III, but he became prebendary of St Pancras. In 1153 he was provided by Pope Anastasius IV to the treasurership of the church of York, shortly before his old friend Roger de Pont l'Évêque was elevated to the archbishopric there. John was now an influential figure within the English church, as the substantial number of charters he witnessed attests. He was asked to assist his old friends and to uphold Canterbury interests in the north. His inclusion among those deputed by Becket in 1162 to fetch his pallium from the pope in Montpellier is proof of the new archbishop's continuing attachment to him. As treasurer of York John served the young Henry II. In 1157 he was among the counsellors supporting the abbot of Battle and Richard de Lucy, the king's justiciar, against the claims of Bishop Hilary, bishop of Chichester. But in 1158 he defined the limits of his loyalty to his temporal lord by emphatically denying Henry any jurisdiction over the criminous dean of Scarborough. Here he unequivocally took a stand on the issue that was to dominate church–state relations in England in the 1160s.

The papal schism of 1159 saw John and Archbishop Roger as Alexander III's devoted champions. By 1162 Henry II had energetically embraced Alexander's cause, especially in his own French territories. Hence his choice of John as bishop of Poitiers. John was consecrated by Alexander III at Déols in September 1162, and took his oath of fidelity to the archbishop of Bordeaux at the Council of Tours in 1163. Henry expected the new bishop to act as a focus of loyalty to him in the troubled duchy of Aquitaine. The surviving evidence, though incomplete, suggests that John fulfilled this duty throughout the twenty years of his pontificate, despite the many difficulties he faced. He apparently supported Patrick, earl of Salisbury, Henry's commander, in the dangerous rebellion of 1168, in which Patrick himself was killed; he remained loyal during the 1173–4 revolt of Henry's sons; and he earned much praise for his efforts in 1176 in defeating the invasion of the count of Angoulême. He frequently attended Henry's courts; at Henry's behest he participated in the ceremony by which the young Prince Richard (the future Richard I) was recognized as duke of Aquitaine in June 1172; and he witnessed Henry's purchase of the *conté* of La Marche in 1177. For the most part, John would have pleased his royal master.

The one fly in the ointment was the Becket conflict, which seriously strained John's loyalty to Henry, both because he was Becket's friend and because on the issue of criminous clerks he was sure that Becket was right. His letters from this period, his only surviving literary works, shed light on his troubles. In 1163 he complained that his efforts to persuade Alexander III to support Becket more vigorously were interpreted by Henry as signs of insubordination. By June 1164, he had withdrawn from negotiations with the pope, handing them over to Guichard, abbot of Pontigny, a respected and independent figure. When Becket took refuge in Pontigny at the end of 1164, John was so depressed that he talked of joining the archbishop in exile. In his anger, Henry had attempted to impose severe limitations on episcopal jurisdiction within the diocese of Poitiers, limitations which the bishop saw as infringements on the liberties of his church. In 1166 John of Salisbury (*d*. 1180) heard a rumour that the bishop had been poisoned; Arnulf, bishop of Lisieux, also expressed concern for his safety.

By January 1169 John was back in royal favour, presumably because he had contributed to the king's defeat of the rebellion of 1168. During the peace conference with the rebels at Montmirail, Henry impulsively urged John to make Becket more flexible. John's efforts in this direction proved abortive because he misrepresented to the archbishop the extent of Henry's proposed concessions, thereby earning for himself a hurt rebuke from Becket and sharp criticism from John of Salisbury. The bishop played no part in the subsequent negotiations, but was present at Fréteval in 1170 when the terms for the archbishop's return to England were finally agreed. John's letters to Becket reveal him to have been a loyal but not uncritical friend. Becket's murder buried all criticism. John became an ardent supporter of the cult of the new martyr saint. He made two much publicized pilgrimages to the shrine at Canterbury, and attested two miracles performed by St Thomas. Alexander III in 1174 made him 'legate of the Apostolic see' in recognition of his zeal in this cause. The kiss of peace he exchanged with the now penitent Henry II at Canterbury on his 1174 pilgrimage marked the end of a tense period for him.

There are signs that, as bishop of Poitiers, John slowly won over opposition in the diocese. His relations with the archbishops of Bordeaux ran smoothly; he was often called on as an arbitrator and conciliator in local feuds. He made urgent efforts to protect churches from the depredations of lay lords, especially Rouillé, beset by Hugh of Lusignan, and Angles, oppressed by the young Duke Richard. He acquired the affection of the clergy of Poitiers; he perhaps contributed something to the design of the Gothic chevet in the new cathedral. His departure from the diocese in 1182 was apparently deeply regretted.

In 1178 Count Raymond V of Toulouse appealed to the pope for help against the heretics who flourished in his *conté*. Henry II nominated John of Canterbury to the commission sent there under Cardinal Peter of St Chrysogonus. Despite its sparse results, John's eloquence in the cause of orthodoxy must have made an impression. This, and his presence at the Third Lateran Council, of 1179, weighed with Lucius III when he provided him in 1182 to the archbishopric of Narbonne. But before his installation the canons of Lyons pressed for John as their archbishop, and Lucius concurred. The canons' chief concern was to avoid an imperial nominee; but their recently deceased archbishop, Guichard, the former abbot of Pontigny, had often praised John.

John was enthroned as archbishop of Lyons in 1183, inheriting and asserting that see's supremacy over the archdioceses of Rouen, Rheims, and Sens. When the French king Philip Augustus claimed regalia in Autun during the vacancy of the bishopric, John moved swiftly to obtain an apology from that normally intransigent monarch. There were no other challenges to Lyons's supremacy during John's pontificate. If an account written more than fifty years later can be credited, the first task that John faced was that of driving out of the city the religious activist Peter Valdes and his followers, who had failed to keep their promise made at the Third Lateran Council not to preach unless invited to do so by the clergy. After their expulsion the so-called Poor Men of Lyons scattered to spread abroad their message and their resentment. John co-operated to such effect with the canons who had chosen him that in 1185 they brought out a new edition of the church's statutes, covering both disciplinary and liturgical matters. He turned the newly founded chapel of Fourvière into a collegiate church with a substantial endowment and nine canons. He may even have contributed to the decoration of the pavement in the apse in the cathedral church of St John.

John's secular role was more problematic. In 1157 Frederick Barbarossa had conceded rule over the city of Lyons to the archbishop and chapter. But at that time the archbishop had been a staunch imperialist. Concerned to maintain the rights of his see, John went in 1184 to Verona to secure from the emperor the confirmation of this privilege. Similarly he acquired from Philip Augustus confirmation of the treaty of 1173, which had established ecclesiastical lordship over lands in Lyons once belonging to the count of Forez. His diplomacy thus set the ecclesiastical principality of Lyons on firm foundations for the foreseeable future. This, however, made John, that convinced believer in the distinction between *regnum* and *sacerdotium*, into a secular ruler. He built castles to defend the area, he attacked the brigands who infested the roads, he demolished the strongholds of robbers. Usually he delegated to his seneschal the task of punishing miscreants. But he grew increasingly unhappy about the position. In 1193 he asked Pope Celestine III for permission to resign on grounds of ill health. In April the pope reluctantly agreed.

On his departure, the church of Lyons granted John an anniversary mass and a generous annual pension. In 1194, after another pilgrimage to Canterbury, he retired to Clairvaux. When Hugh, bishop of Lincoln, called upon him there, he was meditating on the Psalms. His meditations provoked intellectual problems which, characteristically, he referred to the pope for resolution. Innocent III wrote considered replies to several of John's difficulties. John was probably still alive when the pope sent the last of these letters in December 1203. His death followed shortly thereafter; his anniversary is kept at Lyons on 24 April.

JEAN DUNBABIN

Sources J. C. Robertson and J. B. Sheppard, eds., *Materials for the history of Thomas Becket, archbishop of Canterbury*, 7 vols., Rolls Series, 67 (1875–85) · *The letters of John of Salisbury*, ed. and trans. H. E. Butler and W. J. Millor, rev. C. N. L. Brooke, 2 vols., OMT (1979–86) [Lat. orig. with parallel Eng. text] · E. Searle, ed., *The chronicle of Battle Abbey*, OMT (1980) · Adam of Eynsham, *Magna vita sancti Hugonis / The life of Saint Hugh of Lincoln*, ed. D. L. Douie and D. H. Farmer, 2 vols., OMT (1961–2) · *Radulfi de Diceto … opera historica*, ed. W. Stubbs, 2 vols., Rolls Series, 68 (1876) · *Chronica magistri Rogeri de Hovedene*, ed. W. Stubbs, 4 vols., Rolls Series, 51 (1868–71) · *The letters of Arnulf of Lisieux*, ed. F. Barlow, CS, 3rd ser., 61 (1939) · P. Pouzet, *L'anglais Jean dit Bellesmains (1122–1204?): évêque de Poitiers, puis archevêque de Lyons* (Lyon, 1927) · F. Barlow, *Thomas Becket* (1986) · C. Duggan, 'Bishop John and Archdeacon Richard of Poitiers: their roles in the Becket dispute', *Thomas Becket* [Sédières 1973], ed. R. Foreville (1975), 72–83 · C. T. Clay, 'The early treasurers of York', *Yorkshire Archaeological Journal*, 35 (1940–43), 7–34, esp. 11–19 · W. Stubbs, ed., *Chronicles and memorials of the reign of Richard I*, 2: *Epistolae Cantuarienses*, Rolls Series, 38 (1865), 513, 541–3 · B. Galland, *Deux archevêchés entre la France et l'Empire: les archévêques de Vienne du milieu di XIIᵉ au milieu du XIVᵉ siècle* (1994) · W. Map, *De nugis curialium / Courtiers' trifles*, ed. and trans. M. R. James, rev. C. N. L. Brooke and R. A. B. Mynors, OMT (1983)

Canterbury, Michael (*fl.* **1275–1321**), master mason, appears to have been a native of Canterbury, where he is first recorded as master mason to the cathedral priory. In 1275/6 and 1277 the treasurer of the priory paid him wages and travel expenses for his work on the new 'prior's house' (in reality a row of high-quality stone-built houses for rent) in Cheapside, London, to the north of the church of St Mary-le-Bow. In 1290, and in other years which cannot be fixed, he was renting from the priory several properties in the Northgate parish of the city. Most of Michael Canterbury's later documented works were in or near

London, but that he continued to be active in Canterbury is suggested by his purchase of a messuage there in 1293 and by the existence in and around the city of several works of *c.*1292–1308 which are in his style, including the tomb of Archbishop John Peckham (*d.* 1292), the choir enclosure and chapter house (*c.*1304), all at the cathedral, and the chancel of Chartham church (of which the cathedral priory was rector), in progress by 1294.

The London 'prior's house' may well have served to advertise Canterbury's work to Edward I, for by Michaelmas 1291 he was making the penultimate and second most costly of the series of great crosses built to the memory of Queen Eleanor, that which stood in Cheapside barely a stone's throw from St Mary-le-Bow. No doubt the Cheapside cross was in its turn a recommendation to further employment by the king, for in April 1292 work started on Canterbury's most important commission, St Stephen's Chapel in Westminster Palace. Although building advanced very rapidly on what was clearly a high-priority project, it was halted by the financial crisis of 1297 and was not to be resumed until 1320. The 1292–7 campaign encompassed the ground-floor chapel of St Mary and the lower parts of the walls of the main upper chapel, and also generated many hundreds of worked stones which were carefully stored for eventual use. It seems likely, therefore, that the chapel was completed essentially to Canterbury's designs.

Despite its simple format and relatively small size, St Stephen's was the most complex and innovatory design of its time. Much of the formal repertory of the English Decorated style, and indeed of European late Gothic architecture generally, was pioneered here, including lierne vaults, curvilinear tracery patterns, and walls treated as tabernacle-work. The principle underlying the formal complexity—that of treating the two interiors and the exterior of the chapel as a means of generating three highly contrasted 'modes' or styles—was grasped by only a handful of leading early fourteenth-century English architects. One of its earliest and most sophisticated applications is on a work almost certainly by Michael Canterbury himself, the gatehouse of St Augustine's Abbey, Canterbury, whose crenellations received royal licence in 1308. Here the three modes of St Stephen's Chapel have their counterparts on a single façade: the heavy supporting mode of the lower chapel on the storey containing the entrance arch; the tabernacle-clad treatment of the interior of the upper chapel on the niche-encrusted first floor; and the flat linear mode of the lateral exterior elevations on the uppermost parts of the octagonal turrets, which are themselves modelled on the corner turrets of St Stephen's. In its overall form, though not in its rich treatment, the St Augustine's gatehouse is the prototype of the kind of structure built at the entrance to many ambitious domestic and collegiate complexes from the fourteenth to the sixteenth centuries. Canterbury's work as a designer of tomb architecture is likely to have included the two most ambitious English funerary monuments of *c.*1300, those of Edmund Crouchback, earl of Lancaster (*d.* 1296), at Westminster, and Bishop William of Louth (*d.* 1298) in Ely Cathedral.

Documentary evidence for Canterbury's later years is sparse. In 1306 he prepared Wolvesey Palace, Winchester, for the lying-in of Queen Margaret and in 1315 he had charge of building a wall round Eltham Manor in Kent. Although not strictly a royal project, the works at the London Dominicans, where Canterbury is mentioned in 1312 heading a team of twenty-four masons, were almost certainly patronized by Edward II, who occasionally resided there. Possibly a London citizen since the 1270s, Canterbury was serving in 1313 as one of the city's sworn surveyors of masons' work and in March 1316 he was a member of a commission of masons appointed to oversee paving in the city. He is last heard of at Michaelmas 1321, when he received a robe in his capacity as master mason of St Stephen's Chapel.

Thomas Canterbury (*fl.* 1323–1335), master mason, may have been the son of Michael Canterbury, who was married to a woman named Mary. Thomas was master mason at St Stephen's from 1323 until the cessation of work early in 1326, and again from 1332 to 1335. For unspecified works at the chapel of the London Guildhall he was paid £6 17*s.* in 1332. His authorship of one of the two earliest works of Perpendicular architecture—the first phase of the remodelling of the eastern parts of St Peter's Abbey (now the cathedral) at Gloucester, the south transept of *c.*1331–7—is suggested by its formal indebtedness to St Stephen's and by the involvement of the king. The probability that Thomas Canterbury died in or soon after 1335 also favours the attribution, for the next phases of work, the choir and presbytery built *c.*1337–60, were clearly designed by a different architect.

CHRISTOPHER WILSON

Sources J. Harvey and A. Oswald, *English mediaeval architects: a biographical dictionary down to 1550*, 2nd edn (1984), 45 • H. M. Colvin and others, eds., *The history of the king's works*, 6 vols. (1963–82), vol. 1, pp. 207, 483–4, 510–12, 514; vol. 2 • C. Wilson, 'The origins of the Perpendicular style and its development to *c.*1360', PhD diss., U. Lond., 1980, 28–111 • J. H. Harvey, 'The origin of the Perpendicular style', *Studies in building history*, ed. E. M. Jope [1961], 134–65, esp. 141–50, 161–2 • H. M. Chew and W. Kellaway, eds., *London assize of nuisance, 1301–1431: a calendar*, London RS, 10 (1973), 42, no. 205

Canterbury, Nigel of [Nigel Wireker or Whiteacre] (*c.***1135–1198?**), writer and Benedictine monk, was a member of his order at Christ Church, Canterbury. If recent findings are true, his father was Gilbert de Sarneis, from Guernsey, and he had a sister Agatha and a brother Ivo. His name is given variously as Cantuariensis (*Commentarii*), Wireker (Bale), Wetekre (BL, Cotton MS Julius A.vii), de Longo Campo (BL, Cotton MS Vespasian D.xix), usually translated de Longchamp(s), and most recently Whiteacre (Urry; Rigg). There is no Nigel in the family tree of William de Longchamp, the chancellor, and, in his writings to William, Nigel never mentions a family relationship or even a shared name. If Nigel's father was Gilbert de Sarneis, he would not bear the surname de Longchamp(s) as either a patronym or a toponym. Canterbury records include several people toponymically named after the village of

Whiteacre (including Watekere, Watacra, and Whetecre, meaning 'wheat-field'), which could also have been known as the 'long field' (on which Nigel could have Latinized his name, playfully alluding to the future chancellor). When he sent his *Tractatus* to William de Longchamp, he told it to avoid the *lingua materna* and use just the *lingua paterna*. From this it has been inferred that his father spoke French and his mother English, but *paterna* could conceivably refer to Latin and *materna* to the vernacular.

Nigel appears to have studied in Paris (of which he shows some knowledge in the *Speculum stultorum*). By 1170 he had become a monk at Christ Church, Canterbury; he claims (*Tractatus*, ed. Boutemy, 151) to have known Becket personally; although his phraseology is biblical, there is no reason to doubt the fact. A letter of John of Salisbury (*Letters of John of Salisbury*, *ep.* 284), written in 1168, is addressed to a 'magister Nigellus'. In the quarrels of the 1180s between the monks of Christ Church and Baldwin, archbishop of Canterbury, Nigel naturally took the side of the monks; he was devoted to Prior Honorius, who died in 1188 while appealing to the pope against Baldwin. In 1189 Nigel was one of the monks who led a deputation to Richard I to oppose the appointment of Richard Norreys as prior. In 1193 he addressed his *Tractatus* to William de Longchamp. John Leland says he was precentor, but none of the three Nigels in the Canterbury obit lists is named precentor. The date of his death is also uncertain: the final datable entry in his commentary on the *Historia ecclesiastica* was made in 1194, and a monk named N died in 1198; it is not unreasonable to infer that this was Nigel. On his death Nigel bequeathed some personal books to the Christ Church Library.

Of Nigel's writings, the first six listed here are verse. His most popular work was the *Speculum stultorum*, in 3900 lines of elegiac couplets. After a verse prologue to a William (often assumed to be Longchamp, but this is uncertain), this satirical beast-epic tells the adventures of Burnellus, an ass who wanted a longer tail to match his ears; finally he is recaptured and loses his ears. The poem satirizes doctors, university students, and novel religious orders. A prose letter to William explicates some points of the allegory. The date is usually given as 1179–80, since Louis VII of France (*d.* 1180) is still alive, but there is also an allusion to a lawsuit of the Grandmontines of 1187–8. The section on religious orders was later supplemented by verses against the friars. The poem was used by Chaucer ('The Nun's Priest's Tale') and Gower (*Vox clamantis* and *Confessio amantis*).

Another five works are in BL, Cotton MS Vespasian D.xix, headed 'Nigelli de Longo Campo'. *Miracula sancte Dei genitricis Marie* (edited by Ziolkowski) contains eighteen stories, based on William of Malmesbury's collection. The *Passio sancti Laurentii Martiris* (also edited by Ziolkowski) is based on the *Passio polychronii* (an anonymous collection of passions of early martyrs). The *Vita Pauli primi heremite* (edited by Kaiser) is based on the life by Jerome. *Minor Poems* (edited by Ziolkowski) include moral, religious, and topical poems (St Catherine, Becket, and Prior Honorius). *Versus de archiepiscopis Cantuariensis ecclesie* (edited by Boutemy) ends with Richard (*d.* 1184).

The only extant and certain prose work is the *Tractatus contra curiales*, addressed in 1193 to William de Longchamp, bishop of Ely and chancellor of England. This purports to be friendly advice, but is in fact a strongly worded attack, illustrating the incompatibility of secular and ecclesiastical offices and showing that William has broken every single vow that he made on becoming a bishop. It was accompanied by a verse letter *Postquam tristis hiems*. It was edited by Boutemy, with the fullest account of Nigel's life and works.

Nigel also wrote marginal notes (including a few poems), described by Ziolkowski, on a text of Peter Comestor's *Historia ecclesiastica* (now Cambridge, Trinity College, MS B.15.5, one of the books bequeathed to Christ Church by Nigel).

Other attributed works are spurious, lost, or doubtful. The *Adversus barbariem* (*Si mihi credideris*) is in fact the verse *Entheticus* (here meaning 'introduction') to John of Salisbury's *Polycraticus*; the erroneous attribution is due to its interest in Canterbury.

John Leland listed a *Distinctiones super Vetus et Novum Testamentum*; this was a book owned by Nigel, but not written by him; it may have incorporated some of the other biblical commentaries attributed to him. Leland's other attribution, *Excerptiones ex Guarnerio Gregoriano super 'Moralia in Job'*, has not been identified. A verse life of St Eustace has been attributed to him because it is in a manuscript containing other works by Nigel and because of a supposed stylistic resemblance. A. G. Rigg

Sources *Nigellus de Longchamp dit Wireker*, ed. A. Boutemy, 1: *Introduction, Tractatus contra curiales et officiales clericos* (Paris, 1959) • *Nigel of Canterbury: the passion of St Lawrence, epigrams, and marginal poems*, ed. and trans. J. Ziolkowski (1994) • A. G. Rigg, *A history of Anglo-Latin literature, 1066–1422* (1992), esp. 102–5 • *Nigel of Canterbury: miracles of the Virgin Mary, in verse*, ed. J. Ziolkowski (1986) • N. Wireker, *Speculum stultorum*, ed. J. H. Mozley and R. R. Raymo (Berkeley, CA, 1960) • L. M. Kaiser, 'A critical edition of Nigel Wireker's *Vita Sancti Pauli primi eremitae*', *Classical Folia*, 14 (1969), 63–81 • A. G. Rigg, 'Nigel of Canterbury: what was his name?', *Medium Aevum*, 56 (1987), 304–7 • W. Urry, *Canterbury under the Angevin kings* (1967), 153–4 • *The letters of John of Salisbury*, ed. and trans. H. E. Butler and W. J. Millor, rev. C. N. L. Brooke, OMT, 2: *The later letters, 1163–1180* (1979) [Lat. orig. with parallel Eng. text] • W. Stubbs, ed., *Chronicles and memorials of the reign of Richard I*, 2: *Epistolae Cantuarienses*, Rolls Series, 38 (1865) • M. R. James, *The ancient libraries of Canterbury and Dover* (1903), p. 101, nos. 1084–91 • *Commentarii de scriptoribus Britannicis, auctore Joanne Lelando*, ed. A. Hall, 1 (1709), 228 • Bale, *Cat.*, 245–6 • Bale, *Index*, 310–12

Archives BL, Cotton MS Julius A.vii • BL, Cotton MS Vespasian D.xix | Trinity Cam., MS B.15.5

Wealth at death bequeathed books to Christ Church, Canterbury: James, *Ancient libraries*

Canterbury, Odo of (*d.* 1200), theologian and abbot of Battle, was probably a native of Kent. All that is known of his immediate family is that his brother Adam and a close relative (perhaps an uncle) named Ralph were Cistercian monks at Igny; another kinsman, John, was chaplain of Harrietsham in Kent.

Monk of Christ Church The first notices of Odo occur when he was already a Benedictine monk at Christ Church Priory, Canterbury. They are by John of Salisbury, who was in the service of three successive archbishops of Canterbury from soon after 1147 until 1176. In his *Entheticus maior*, probably composed *c*.1155, John writes warmly of certain Canterbury monks, among them Odo, who 'is an avid reader of books, yet most of all loves those which speak of Christ' (trans. van Laarhoven, 1675–6); and in the *Entheticus in Policraticum*, finished before September 1159, he tells his book to go to Canterbury and 'If you are able, convey my best wishes to Odo' (pp. 191–2). Late in 1164 or soon after John, now in exile with his master Thomas Becket, wrote to a Master Odo in England, evidently no mean biblical scholar. By this date the epithet 'master' frequently implied time spent in the schools, and if John's addressee was Odo of Canterbury, it could mean that he had had formal scholastic training, probably at Paris.

By now (and since 1163 at least) Odo was sub-prior of Christ Church. He had made a good start in his vocation as a monk; but for the next seven years his career and reputation were to suffer as he struggled to find a middle way through the dispute between Henry II and Archbishop Thomas Becket. In 1163 the archbishop sent him to Rome to protest on his behalf against the claim of the archbishop of York to the right to carry his cross in the southern province. In 1166, however, the convent was ordered by the royal justices to appeal against Becket; in 1167 Odo wrote to Richard of Ilchester, archdeacon of Poitiers and a royal official, explaining the difficulty of his position and pleading for help. In the meantime he and Prior Wibert were recipients of a letter from John of Salisbury, chiding them for withholding financial support for the legal expenses of the exiled archbishop.

Candidate for Canterbury Odo was himself chosen as prior soon after 16 May 1168, but without the archbishop's assent. Becket wished to depose him, and late in 1169 Odo felt obliged to withdraw for a time from Christ Church. He now incurred the pope's displeasure, first for allegedly disregarding the papal prohibition of the young king's coronation on 24 May 1170, and later for even aiding and abetting Becket's death. The martyred Becket was said to have foretold Odo's impending removal from Canterbury to a Christ Church monk, who in his prayers complained of the prior's lack of firmness. None the less, like John of Salisbury himself, Odo continued to maintain a moderate stance. On 21 December 1171 he succeeded in having Christ Church freed from the ecclesiastical censure passed on it because of the archbishop's murder within its walls. At this stage he must have had the support of at least a majority of his monks, for in the following year they began a long and fruitless campaign to have Odo elected as Becket's successor.

Gervase of Canterbury recounts the wearisome and inconclusive series of meetings in England and Normandy, between the king and the monks led by Odo himself, from September 1172 until April 1173. Odo, in a firm but courteous speech, defended their right of 'free election' and their tradition of having a monk as archbishop, blaming the king's unilateral appointment of a secular clerk—Becket—for the troubles that had followed. The king did not at this stage reveal his will, but it would not be surprising if the speech displeased him. Eventually the monks were ordered to meet with the bishops of the province. At the meeting, held in May 1173, the monks put forward as their preferred candidates Odo and Richard, prior of Dover. Gilbert Foliot, bishop of London, as the bishops' spokesman, praised Odo, but none the less expressed their preference for Richard. This may have represented the king's real wishes, for Richard of Dover was one of two monks sent to the king with a message from the council. Possibly Odo too understood this, for Richard was formally elected on 3 June, and Odo wrote to the pope on the convent's behalf supporting 'their' choice.

Abbot of Battle On 5 September 1174 Christ Church was destroyed by fire. On 1 July 1175 Odo attended a royal council at Woodstock, hoping to obtain, in place of the monastery's burned charters, new ones worded similarly to the exemplary privileges of Battle Abbey (which were in fact forgeries). For this purpose the monks of Battle were summoned to be present. As it happened, their abbey had been without a head for four years, and the monks, impressed by Odo's demeanour, nominated him as their abbot. At first Odo refused the position, but after due persuasion yielded, and was elected on 10 July. Odo arrived at Battle on 4 August, receiving the blessing from Archbishop Richard on Sunday 28 September, at Malling. In the following year Odo was summoned to Westminster by the papal legate, Cardinal Hugo Pierleone, to defend the abbey's right to the patronage of the church of Wye against Geoffrey de Lacy. He appealed in vain for assistance to Gerard Pucelle, afterwards bishop of Lichfield, to Bartholomew, bishop of Exeter, and to John of Salisbury. But at last Waleran, the future bishop of Rochester, pleaded Odo's cause, and, Gerard now supporting him, effected a compromise.

When Archbishop Richard died in 1184 the monks of Canterbury once more nominated Odo for archbishop, and again the king refused to accept him. The new archbishop was Baldwin of Forde, who was soon involved in a serious quarrel with the monks over his intention to found a collegiate church at Hackington near Canterbury. On 13 January 1187 Odo was appointed by Pope Urban III as one of the commissioners to remonstrate with Baldwin, and on 1 March he was directed to ensure that the archbishop obeyed the papal mandate ordering him to restore to the monks revenues that he had appropriated for the use of his new church. Baldwin's response was equivocal, and the commissioners contented themselves with rescinding a sentence of deposition already pronounced by him against the prior. Once again Odo found himself caught in the crossfire between the pope and the king's representatives, with his attempted moderation judged unsatisfactory by others.

On 9 May Urban rebuked Odo for his lukewarmness, and sent a fresh mandate. The justiciar Ranulf de Glanville, however, forbade Odo to act, and in July the monks complained to Urban that Odo and his colleagues were prevaricating out of fear, and needed explicit instructions if they were to act with the firmness expected of them. On 3 October the pope sent another mandate to the archbishop, with instructions to the commissioners to ensure its execution. Odo does not figure in the dispute after this date, although in January 1188 the monks made a final appeal to him for assistance. On 3 September of the following year Odo was at Westminster for the coronation of Richard I. In January 1192, when the see of Canterbury was again vacant, the monks turned to him once more for support in the assertion of their right of free election. Odo died on 20 or 21 January 1200. He was buried in Battle Abbey, where John Leland saw his tomb, a slab of black Lydd marble.

A model abbot This bare chronicle of events gives little hint of the man's character. In public life he was obviously by temperament a moderate, whether through wisdom or weakness. Despite that he was evidently held in high esteem by John of Salisbury, by the monks of Canterbury and Battle, but not by Henry II or Thomas Becket. In the end he was remembered, and has in modern times been characterized, not for his public role, but as a model monastic leader: prudent, eloquent, learned, and devout. The Battle Abbey chronicler says that, although he was strict in life and conversation, he consorted freely with his monks; only he did not sleep in the dormitory, because he suffered from a disorder of the stomach which he had to doctor privately. He praises Odo for his humility and modesty, and for his diligence in expounding the scriptures, saying that he could preach alike in French, Latin, and English.

Odo's conservative Benedictine background, his learning, and interest in preaching and biblical exposition are reflected in his surviving writings which, though not widely disseminated, survive in a handful of manuscripts written in or soon after his lifetime, both in England and on the continent. His commentary on *Kings*, probably written at the end of his life, was never completed and is very likely no more than a draft, given the absence of a prologue and its restricted and repetitive vocabulary. None the less it illustrates his profound knowledge of the scriptures, and suggests that he may even have known some Hebrew. But he could clearly write better than this, and the prologue to his sermon collection is a late example of the elegant monastic style of Latinity which owed much to Anselm and Bec.

Writings These last two works, and an unprinted commentary on the Pentateuch, are certainly Odo's; other attributions are uncertain, owing to confusion with writers of the same name, notably Odo of Cheriton, Eudes de Morimond (*d.* 1161), and Eudes de Châteauroux (*d.* 1273). The following works—excluding some which are certainly not his—are attributed to Odo of Canterbury: 1 Commentary on the Pentateuch, unprinted; copies listed in Sharpe, 402. Genesis–Numbers only are in CUL, MS Dd.7.15 (early 13th century, ascribed to Odo); Cambridge, Corpus Christi College, MS 54 (late 12th century, ascribed to Odo); Bodl. Oxf., MS Bodley 331, fols. 1–168 (St Albans, 1250–1300, ascribed to Eudes de Morimond); and Oxford, All Souls College, MS 12 (12th–13th century, ascribed to Isidore). Cambridge, Queens' College, MS 8 (late 12th century, with a 14th century ascription to Haimo), also contains Deuteronomy, though the attribution is uncertain. Other copies are attested at the monastic houses of Christ Church, Canterbury, Waverley, and Warden. 2 Commentary on Kings, ed. C. de Clercq as *Le commentaire d'Odon de Canterbury sur les livres des Rois*, Centre des Recherches Historiques (Ventimiglia, 1980), from the only surviving manuscript, CUL, Gg.4.17 (Christ Church, Canterbury, 13th century); Leland saw another copy at Battle Abbey. 3 'Odo prior de moribus ecclesiae', not known to survive (copy recorded at Christ Church, Canterbury, early 13th century). 4 Letters: to Richard of Ilchester, in *Patrologia Latina*, 190.1003–5; to his brother Adam, then a novice at Igny, in J. Mabillon, *Vetera Analecta* (1675–85), vol. 1, pp. 349–59; to accompany a copy of Benedict's miracles of St Thomas sent to Adam and Ralph, in Robertson and Sheppard, vol. 2, p. xlix; to Pope Alexander III, in JS, *Letters*, no. 311, pp. 760–67. 5 Sermons: Twenty sermons with a prologue, addressed to Odo's brother Adam (in which the collection is called 'Solacium peregrinorum'), in Bruges, Grand Séminaire, MS 406, fols. 1–123*v*; the prologue ed. A. Pattin, 'Un manuscrit du xiie siècle de l'ancienne abbaye d'Eename retrouvé' (Bruges, Grand Séminaire, MS 406), *Scriptorium*, 44 (1990), 79–91. The same sermons, with seven more, from fourteen other manuscripts, ed. C. de Clercq, *The Latin Sermons of Odo of Canterbury* (Brussels, 1983); Pattin questions the authenticity of the seven sermons edited by de Clercq not in the Bruges manuscript; all twenty-seven are listed in J. B. Schneyer, *Repertorium der lateinischen Sermones des Mittelalters*, 11 vols. (Münster, 1969–90); vol. 4, pp. 392–4. A collection was seen by Leland at Waverley. 6 Odo of Canterbury may be identifiable with the Englishman named Odo who, between 1140 and 1148, probably wrote the anti-Jewish theological *summa* called *Ysagoge in theologiam*, ed. A. Landgraf, 'Écrits théologiques de l'école d'Abélard', *Spicilegium Sacrum Lovaniense*, 14 (1934), 61–298. On its authorship and characteristics see D. E. Luscombe, 'The authorship of the *Ysagoge in theologiam*', *Archives d'Histoire Doctrinale et Littéraire du Moyen Âge*, 35 (1969), 7–16; and D. E. Luscombe, *The School of Peter Abelard* (1969), 236–44. R. M. Thomson

Sources E. Searle, ed., *The chronicle of Battle Abbey*, OMT (1980) • R. Sharpe, *A handlist of the Latin writers of Great Britain and Ireland before 1540* (1997), 402–3 • D. Knowles, *The monastic order in England*, 2nd edn (1963) • C. de Clercq, *Le commentaire d'Odon de Canterbury sur les livres des Rois* (Ventimiglia, 1980) • C. de Clercq, *The Latin sermons of Odo of Canterbury* (Brussels, 1983) • D. Knowles, C. N. L. Brooke, and V. C. M. London, eds., *The heads of religious houses, England and Wales, 1: 940–1216* (1972) • J. Leclercq, 'Profession monastique, baptême, et pénitence d'après Odon de Cantorbéry', *Analecta Monastica*, 2nd ser. (1953), 124–40 • H. Mayr-Harting, 'Henry II and the papacy', *Journal of Ecclesiastical History*, 16 (1965), 39–53 • J. Greatrex, *Biographical register of the English cathedral priories of the province of Canterbury* (1997) • John of Salisbury, *Entheticus maior et minor*, ed. and trans. J. van Laarhoven, 3 vols. (Leiden, 1987) • *The letters of John of Salisbury*, ed. and trans. H. E. Butler and W. J. Millor, rev. C. N. L. Brooke, 2 vols., OMT (1979–86) [Lat. orig. with parallel Eng. text] • W. Stubbs, ed., *Chronicles and memorials of the reign of Richard I*, 2: *Epistolae Cantuarienses*, Rolls Series, 38 (1865) • *Radulfi de Diceto … opera historica*, ed. W. Stubbs, 2 vols., Rolls Series, 68 (1876) • *The historical works of Gervase of Canterbury*, ed. W. Stubbs, 2 vols., Rolls Series, 73 (1879–80) • F. Liverani, ed., *Spicilegium liberianum*, 1 vol. in 3 pts (Florence, 1863) • *Joannis Lelandi antiquarii de rebus Britannicis collectanea*, ed. T. Hearne, [3rd edn], 6 vols. (1774) • *Materials for the history of Thomas Becket, archbishop of Canterbury*, 2, ed. J. C. Robertson, Rolls Series, 67 (1876) • A. Pattin, 'Un manuscrit du xiie siècle de l'ancienne abbaye d'Eename retrouvé (Bruges, Grand Séminaire ms. 406)', *Scriptorium*, 44 (1990), 79–91 • J. Mabillon, *Veterum analectum*, 4 vols. (Paris, 1675–85), vol. 1, p. 349–59 • Odo, 'Epistolae', *Patrologia Latina*, 190 (1854), 1003–5 • J. B. Schneyer, *Repertorium der lateinischen Sermones des Mittelalters: für die Zeit von 1150–1350*, 4 (Münster, 1972), 392–4 • A. Landgraf, 'Écrits théologiques de l'école d'Abélard', *Spicilegium Sacrum Lovaniense*, 14 (1934), 61–298 • D. E. Luscombe, 'The authorship of the *Ysagoge in theologiam*', *Archives d'Histoire Doctrinale et Littéraire du Moyen Âge*, 35 (1968), 7–16 • D. E. Luscombe, *The school of Peter Abelard: the influence of Abelard's thought in the early scholastic period* (1969)

Archives All Souls Oxf., MS 12 • Bodl. Oxf., MS Bodley, 331, fols. 1–168 • CCC Cam., MS 54 • CUL, MS Dd.7.15 • CUL, MS Gg.4.17 • Grand Séminaire, Bruges, MS 406, fols. 1–123v • Queens' College, Cambridge, MS 8

Canterbury, Reginald of (*fl.* *c.*1100–*c.*1109), poet and Benedictine monk, has been the subject of a series of biographical misunderstandings (exemplified in the *Dictionary of National Biography*). These were satisfactorily clarified by F. Liebermann in 1888, although precision is hard to attain. He was born about the middle of the eleventh century at 'Fagia', probably Faye-le-Vineuse in north-eastern Poitou in France; he seems to have had some connection with the abbey of Noyers near Tours. Some time later he went to England and became a monk at St Augustine's, Canterbury, certainly before 1100, possibly much earlier: he was thoroughly Anglicized and refers to *gens Anglica nostra*, but retained an affection for his homeland and a literary distaste for beer. Although he had many correspondents, his activities are hard to date precisely; his epic *Malchus* was completed by 1106, when Anselm was about to return from his second exile, and before the deaths in 1107 of Lanzo, prior of Lewes, and Arnulph, prior of Christ Church. He was still alive in 1109, when Thomas (II), archbishop of York (1109–14), sent a poem to him.

Reginald was one of the most imaginative and versatile Latin poets in the first generation after the Norman conquest. His major work was a verse epic in Latin, in 6 books of over 3000 lines, on the life of the desert saint Malchus, based on the life by Jerome. Malchus was a monk who left his abbey in Syria to visit his aged mother; he was captured by bandits, enslaved, forced into marriage (but maintained his chastity), and finally escaped after several adventures. Reginald's first version, in 1706 lines, is in Oxford, Merton College, MS 241, and changes Jerome's first-person narration into a third-person report. The final version, expanded by Virgilian digressions and many entirely new incidents, was three times the length; each book was intended for recitation in a single performance. In a letter to Baldwin, *primicerius* of Rochester Abbey (not prior, but perhaps precentor), he explains the nature of poetic licence.

Reginald sent the *Malchus* to several people besides Baldwin: to the famous poet Hildebert, whose letter (*Patrologia Latina*, 171.292) compliments Reginald; to Gilbert Crispin, abbot of Westminster, who had encouraged him to write it; to Hugh, sub-prior of St Pancras at Lewes; to Lambert, prior of St Bertin; to Anselm in exile; to Arnulph, prior of Christ Church, Canterbury; to Étienne, abbot of Noyers; to Thomas (II), archbishop of York; and to the hagiographer Goscelin.

Reginald wrote many other poems, including one to his old town of Faye and its lord, Aimeric, a series on Canterbury and its saints, and one (or perhaps two) to Anselm the younger, later abbot of Bury St Edmunds, at this time on a visit to England (before 1109). He was particularly interested in metre and experimented with various types, mainly rhymed hexameters, but he wrote one poem entirely in pentameters, and to an Osbern he wrote one in sapphics, recommending the study of Horace for would-be poets. He has also been credited with a series of verse prayers. The fullest collection of his poems is in Bodl. Oxf., MS Laud misc. 40, a Rochester manuscript, and probably a presentation copy made for Baldwin. A. G. RIGG

Sources *Vita Sancti Malchi*, ed. L. R. Lind, Illinois Studies in Language and Literature (1942) • F. Liebermann, 'Reginald von Canterbury', *Neues Archiv*, 13 (1888), 519–56 • T. Wright, ed., *The Anglo-Latin satirical poets and epigrammatists of the twelfth century*, 2, Rolls Series, 59 (1872), 2.259–67 • A. G. Rigg, *A history of Anglo-Latin literature, 1066–1422* (1992), 24–30 • M. Manitius, *Geschichte der lateinischen Literatur des Mittelalters*, 3 (1931), 840–46 • N. K. Rasmüssen, 'Bénédictions de matines attribuées à Réginald de Cantorbéry', *Classica et Mediaevalia*, 25 (1964), 215–23 • Hildebert, 'Epistola XV', *Patrologia Latina*, 171 (1854), 292

Archives Bodl. Oxf., MS Laud misc. 40 • Merton Oxf., MS 241

Canterbury, Thomas (*fl.* 1323–1335). *See under* Canterbury, Michael (*fl.* 1275–1321).

Cantillon, Richard (*c.*1680–1734), banker and economist, was born in Ballyheigue, co. Kerry, in Ireland, the son of Richard Cantillon and his wife, Bridget. His family, of Norman origin, were dispossessed of their lands by the Williamite confiscations and he was forced to emigrate to continental Europe. From Paris he travelled to Spain where he worked for James Brydges (later to become Lord Carnarvon, and still later the duke of Chandos), the British paymaster-general to the forces abroad, during the latter stages of the War of the Spanish Succession. Brydges made a fortune from profiteering on the army's contracts and it appears that Cantillon worked as a type of accountant for him.

From Spain Cantillon returned to Paris, where he assumed control of the close to bankrupt bank of his second cousin, the Chevalier Richard Cantillon. When Bolingbroke fled to Paris in March 1715 Cantillon arranged the payment of £20,000 from Brydges to Bolingbroke. In 1718 Cantillon made contact with the increasingly successful Scottish banker John Law. Along with Law and Joseph Edward Gage, Cantillon established a company to colonize a tract of land in French Louisiana. His brother Bernard Cantillon headed a team of sixty people which attempted to colonize the concession, an attempt which met with only limited success.

Cantillon was already an investor in the shares of Law's Company of the West, which became popularly known as the Mississippi Company. These shares opened at a price of about 150 livres in 1717. By August 1719 they were worth over 2000 livres. Cantillon, fearing that the market for these shares had overheated, liquidated a sizeable part of his holdings and retired to Italy. He had underestimated Law's ability to captivate the French public. In the last week of August 1719 Law proposed a daring plan for his company to take over not only the tax farms but also the totality of the French national debt. Simply put, Law wanted to convert high interest-paying *rentes* (government debt) into equity of the company. These plans caused the share price to rise to over 10,000 livres in October 1719. Such was Law's success that the British government decided to copy part of it by allowing the South Sea Company to take over the British national debt, a move which led to the South Sea Bubble of 1720.

Cantillon had mistimed the demise of the Mississippi Company. But he returned to France in the spring of 1720 more convinced than ever that the system would collapse. Using his economic theory, he believed that it was impossible for Law to expand the money supply, reduce the rate of interest, and revalue the exchange rate simultaneously. Something had to give. He speculated against the French exchange rate to such an extent that Law threatened him with incarceration in the Bastille and Cantillon was obliged to leave France. During the summer of 1720, when his system was coming under intensive pressure, Law attempted to coax Cantillon back to France to assist him in restructuring the system. Cantillon hesitated at this offer to become Law's assistant but eventually, believing that the system was doomed, declined the offer. The unlikely pairing of a Scot and an Irishman running the French economy was not to be.

Cantillon's speculation in John Law's Mississippi system made him a fortune of over 20 million livres. He also made considerable profits from purchasing put options (the right to sell at a predetermined price) during the height of the South Sea Bubble. When share prices collapsed in London in August 1720 Cantillon's put options became extremely profitable. His successful speculation in shares and other financial instruments reinforced his view that the monetary system had to be based on intrinsically valuable metals such as gold and silver. He was a convinced metallist who disapproved of the type of financial innovation that characterized Law's period of policy making. These metallist views feature in Cantillon's one known economic work.

The *Essai sur la nature du commerce en général* was published in 1755 with the imprint of Fletcher Gyles 'dans Holborn'. In reality the book was published clandestinely but with a *permission tacite*, by Guillyn in Paris. It was soon acknowledged that it had been written by the late Richard Cantillon. The book is incomplete. Cantillon intended to back up his economic theory with empirical evidence from a statistical supplement. Though he refers on a number of occasions to this supplement in the first book of the *Essai* it was never published.

Cantillon's *Essai* is notable for its model building, its analysis of market forces and the role of the entrepreneur, its outline of the circular flow of income, and its monetary theory. Cantillon was the first real model builder in economics. His method was to conceptualize the essentials of the economic world and represent them in a simplified model which became more and more complex through the provision of further interlocking elements. To achieve this, in Cartesian style, he stripped the economy down to its bare essentials to determine the fundamental forces at work. He started with a landlord-dominated, barter, command economy which was closed off from the rest of the world. In this primitive structure three socio-economic classes, the landlord, overseers, and workers, interacted. By degrees he transformed this structure from a command economy to a market economy, from a barter system to a monetary system, and from a closed economy to an open economy.

The transformation from the command economy to a market economy necessitated the replacement of the overseer class, whose only function was to relay the commands of the landlord to the worker, by entrepreneurs. Cantillon concisely defined the function of the entrepreneurs as that of buying at a known price to sell at an unknown price. Cantillon's definition gave the entrepreneur a key role in the formulation of market prices. In his structure there was no mechanism for market transactors to be presented with the market clearing range of prices. The prices of goods bought in one market were transformed into prices in other markets by the entrepreneur. If the entrepreneur's price-setting behaviour was accurate, he made money; if not, he lost and risked having to move out of this particular commercial activity.

Money is introduced into the model because of the way it is perceived to facilitate the smooth functioning of the system, but at the same time its introduction did not produce any overall increase in economic activity. This is not to say that Cantillon felt that money was unimportant. Indeed the importance he attached to it is shown by the three chapters that he devoted to the circulation of money in book 2 of the *Essai*. It was in the first of these chapters that he introduced the circular flow of income into his model in order to determine the overall amount of money needed in an economy. To show this Cantillon produced the doctrine of the three rents (*les trois rentes*).

In Cantillon's stylized model of the three rents the absentee landlords spent all the income they derived from the first rent in the city, with farmers spending more than half of the third rent (that is, one-sixth of agricultural income) on urban commodities. This meant that more than half of the agricultural income was destined for expenditure in the cities. Cantillon further assumed that half of the population lived in cities and that consequently the inhabitants of cities consumed more than half the produce of the land. Thus the farmers exported more than half of the agricultural output to the cities and with the income earned paid the landlord's rent and bought urban commodities equivalent to one-sixth of agricultural output. In this way the expenditure of the landlords and the farmers on commodities produced in the cities generated income for urban dwellers and so enabled them to purchase agricultural output. One person's expenditure forms another person's income, derived through the creation of commodities.

The analysis of the circular flow of income and expenditure, which may have been influenced in part by Law's 'island model' in chapter 7 of *Money and Trade* (1705), was not Cantillon's major objective. It was an analysis that he carried out in order to ascertain the equilibrium quantity of money required in the economy. By examining the flow of income Cantillon believed he could determine how much money was needed to meet this income requirement in the economy. In determining the amount of money needed he was then able to assess the effects of excessive increases in the money supply, resulting from financial innovations, on prices and the balance of payments.

Cantillon's view of the consequences of an expansion in the money supply was that it raised expenditure which 'gradually brings about increased prices'. This did not lead him to advocate a crude quantity theory of money that prices rose proportionately with the increases in the money supply. Instead he analysed the channels through which monetary expansion influences expenditure. He detailed a variety of different sources of monetary expansion, including gold or silver mining, capital inflows, and a balance of trade surplus. He then outlined the different ways in which such expansions of the money supply could influence output, prices, and the balance of payments. In examining the ways in which money influenced economic activity he produced one of the first statements of the self-adjusting specie-flow mechanism of the balance of payments.

Cantillon's analysis of the specie-flow mechanism was more comprehensive than that of David Hume, credited as the originator of this approach, in the *Political Discourses* (1752). Unlike Hume, Cantillon's approach incorporated both a relative price effect and a cash balance effect. He recognized, through his distinction between traded and non-traded goods, that the impact of an increase in the money supply on prices was dependent on the openness of the economy.

Cantillon's model building had a policy message. By analysing the equilibrium amount of money required in a money-using, open, market economy he wanted to show how the economy would reject any financial innovation which caused an excessive increase in the money supply. He had lived through the financial innovations of Law's Mississippi system and the South Sea Bubble. While never mentioning either Law or the Mississippi system by name, the final paragraph of the *Essai* suggests that part of Cantillon's motivation in writing his book was to provide an intellectual refutation to Law's system.

The *Essai* had a significant influence in developing François Quesnay's circular flow of income, encapsulated in the *Tableau économique* (1758), and Adam Smith's theory of resource allocation in *An Inquiry into the Nature and Causes of the Wealth of Nations* (1776). Schumpeter remarked on the former:

> Cantillon was the first to make this circular flow concrete and explicit, to give us a bird's eye view of economic life. In other words, he was the first to draw a *tableau économique*. And, barring differences that hardly affect essentials, this *tableau* is the same as Quesnay's though Cantillon did not actually condense it into a table. (Schumpeter, 222)

In distinguishing between market price and intrinsic value and showing how resources moved into those sectors where the market price was above intrinsic value, and away from those sectors where market price was below intrinsic value, Cantillon influenced Adam Smith's famous analysis in chapter 7, book 1, of the *Wealth of Nations* where the latter made the distinction between market price and natural price.

Despite Cantillon's influence on Quesnay, the physiocrats, and Adam Smith, the *Essai* fell into oblivion during the nineteenth century until reassessed by William Stanley Jevons in 1881; he described it as 'the cradle of political economy'. Henry Higgs provided the first English translation of the *Essai*, alongside the French text (1931). The Institut National d'Études Démographiques encouraged French readership of the *Essai* by republishing it (1952, 1996), and in 1979 Takumi Tsuda published a manuscript copy of the *Essai* located in Rouen. Recent studies by A. E. Murphy (*Richard Cantillon: Entrepreneur and Economist*, 1986), and A. Brewer (*Richard Cantillon: Pioneer of Economic Theory*, 1992) have further increased interest in Cantillon.

Cantillon's success in speculating against Law's system was marred by subsequent lawsuits. The Paris-based clients of his bank, most notably Lady Mary Herbert, her father, the duke of Powis, her brother Lord Montgomery, and her aspiring but never-to-be husband, Joseph Edward Gage, contended that Cantillon had fraudulently profited by selling their shares at high prices. These shares had been lodged as collateral for the loans which Cantillon's bank had lent them. Through their Parisian agent, the lame Dublin apothecary Christopher Balfe, Lady Mary and her family took a variety of civil and criminal suits against Cantillon in both London and Paris during the 1720s and 1730s. Though Cantillon was arrested and temporarily imprisoned in Paris, it must be emphasized that none of these legal actions succeeded.

In February 1722 Cantillon married Mary Anne O'Mahony (1701–1751), the daughter of Count Daniel O'Mahony, a hero on the French side during the battle of Cremona (October 1701), and his wife, Cecilia Weld. Mary Anne was regarded as one of the beauties of her age and her portrait was painted by Largillière. The only child to survive of Cantillon's marriage to Mary Anne was a daughter, Henrietta (*b.* 1728), who later married William Mathias Howard, third earl of Stafford.

Cantillon was apparently murdered by his French cook, who also set fire to his house in London's Albemarle Street on 14 May 1734; the murdered corpse was seemingly burnt to ashes in the fire. Cantillon's neighbour, Lord Bolingbroke, searched through ashes for the body. According to parish records, Cantillon's remains were buried in St Pancras parish church on 10 July 1734. There is also the possibility that Cantillon may have used the fire as a subterfuge to exit from Europe and the many pressing lawsuits which he faced. Six months after his demise in Albemarle Street a mysterious Chevalier de Louvigny arrived in the Dutch colony of Surinam, arousing the suspicion of the Dutch authorities, who sent a search party into the jungle after him. They failed to locate the Chevalier de Louvigny but found a chest of papers belonging to Richard Cantillon. Why had the mysterious Chevalier de Louvigny travelled with a heavy case containing these incriminating documents to South America and then into the jungle of Surinam? Was it a case of the French cook posing as the chevalier or could it have been Cantillon himself?

After his demise, his widow, Mary Anne, married in 1736 François Bulkeley, a personal friend of Montesquieu. She died on 17 February 1751 and Bulkeley died in 1756.

ANTOIN E. MURPHY

Sources A. E. Murphy, *Richard Cantillon: entrepreneur and economist* (1986) • J. A. Schumpeter, *History of economic analysis*, ed. E. B. Schumpeter, new edn (1981) • R. Cantillon, *Essai sur la nature du commerce en général* (1755) • R. Cantillon, *Essai sur la nature du commerce en général*, trans. H. Higgs (1931) • R. Cantillon, *Essai sur la nature du commerce en général*, ed. A. Sauvy and others (Paris, 1952); repr. (1997) • A. Brewer, *Richard Cantillon: pioneer of economic theory* (1992) • W. S. Jevons, 'Richard Cantillon and the nationality of political economy', *Contemporary Review*, 39 (1881), 61–80 • R. Cantillon, *Essai sur la nature du commerce en général*, ed. T. Tsuda (Tokyo, 1979) • *London Journal* (18 May 1734)

Cantilupe [Cantelupe], **Fulk de** (*d.* 1217/18), administrator, is first recorded in 1198 as a member of the household of Count John of Mortain, the future king. From 1200 to 1201 he was sheriff of Berkshire. In the spring and summer of 1203 he organized the collection of ships, mariners, and naval stores along the Seine for the king. In 1207, with Reginald of Cornhill, he was given custody of the see of Canterbury, and according to Wendover expelled the monks. King John warranted all sales made by him from the estates of the chapter. In January 1208, however, the see was turned over to new custodians, possibly owing to Innocent III's order that Fulk and Reginald be excommunicated, given on 27 August 1207. Cantilupe heard forest pleas in Shropshire in 1212, and was named by Wendover as one of the king's 'evil counsellors' (Paris, *Chron.*); his role in the civil war was that of custodian of rebel escheats.

Cantilupe was granted various manors and custodies during his career. As count of Mortain John gave him land in Oxenbourne, Hampshire. By 1204 he held the royal demesne manor of Calne, Wiltshire; after Michaelmas 1214 Calstone Wellington, also in Wiltshire, was added; in addition he held the manors of Burton, Northamptonshire, and Shopland, Essex. Before 1207 he held unspecified land in what is now co. Cork, Ireland. He held the lands of the countess of Perche in custody as early as 1208–9, and made his first return for the honour to the exchequer at Michaelmas 1210. By Michaelmas 1211 he also had custody of the barony of Warin de Munchensi.

Cantilupe died between 4 November 1217, when seisin of Burton was restored to him, and 6 March 1218, when Calne and Calstone Wellington were taken into the hands of the king. He took the habit of a templar before his death. He probably died childless, as no one in 1229 could claim hereditary right; Calne and Calstone were granted in 1218 to his nephew William (I) de *Cantilupe.

B. W. HOLDEN

Sources *Chancery records* (RC) • *Chancery records* • *Pipe rolls* • Paris, *Chron.*, 2.516, 533 • *Ann. mon.*, 2.80, 259 • H. Hall, ed., *The Red Book of the Exchequer*, 3 vols., Rolls Series, 99 (1896) • *The historical works of Gervase of Canterbury*, ed. W. Stubbs, 2: *The minor works comprising the Gesta regum with its continuation, the Actus pontificum and the Mappa mundi*, Rolls Series, 73 (1880), lxxxix–xc • *VCH Hampshire and the Isle of Wight*, 3.64 • A. Hughes, *List of sheriffs for England and Wales: from the earliest times to AD 1831*, PRO (1898); repr. (New York, 1963) • L. Landon, *The itinerary of King Richard I*, PRSoc., new ser., 13 (1935), 131

Cantilupe, Sir George de (1251–1273), baron, sprung from a Norman family native to Cantelu near Caen, was born at his father's castle of Abergavenny on 7 April 1251, the eldest son of William (III) de *Cantilupe (*d.* 1254) and Eva (*d.* 1255), daughter of William (V) de Briouze. Through his mother he was heir to major portions of the Briouze baronies of Abergavenny and Totnes, and through his father to the baronies of Eaton Bray in Bedfordshire and Bulwick in Northamptonshire.

Aged only three at the death of his father, he was brought up as a ward of the Lord Edward [*see* Edward I], eldest son of Henry III, although, according to the chronicler Matthew Paris, in 1257 his lands were briefly transferred to the custody of Queen Eleanor, Edward's mother, who exploited them harshly. In 1254 before the death of his father Cantilupe had been betrothed to Margaret, daughter of Edmund de Lacy, earl of Lincoln (*d.* 1258). Although the marriage seems never to have been formalized, the Lacy family continued to take an interest in the Cantilupe estate, so that in April 1270 Edmund's son Henry de Lacy, together with Roger (III) de Mortimer, a kinsman of Cantilupe's mother, fined 800 marks with the Lord Edward on Cantilupe's behalf, presumably to acquire his wardship. Later that year Cantilupe witnessed a charter together with Henry de Lacy, and on 13 October 1272 it was in company with Lacy and Edmund, son of Richard, earl of Cornwall, that he was knighted at Westminster by Henry III. He achieved his majority in April 1273 at the age of twenty-one, and around 23 April, St George's day, was restored to possession of his estates. On 8 September that same year he confirmed a grant of land to Dunstable Priory made by one of his subtenants, and died only a few days later on 14 September 1273. His lands were partitioned thereafter between his two sisters, Joan, the wife of Henry Hastings (*d.* 1269), who inherited Cantilupe's share of the barony of Abergavenny, and Millicent, widow of John de Montalt, from 1268 married to Eudo de la *Zouche (*d.* 1279) [*see under* Zouche family], who inherited the remainder of his vast estate. Joan was succeeded by John Hastings (*d.* 1313), Millicent by William la Zouche (*d.* 1352). NICHOLAS VINCENT

Sources *Chancery records* • Paris, *Chron.* • *Ann. mon.* • I. J. Sanders, *English baronies: a study of their origin and descent, 1086–1327* (1960) • G. H. Fowler, ed., *A digest of the charters preserved in the cartulary of the priory of Dunstable*, Bedfordshire Historical RS, 10 (1926) • *CIPM*, 2, no. 17 • *Calendar of the fine rolls*, PRO, 1 (1911), 12–13

Cantilupe [Cantelupe]**, Nicholas, third Lord Cantilupe** (*c.*1301–1355), soldier, administrator, and justice, was a son of William de Cantilupe, first Lord Cantilupe (1262–1308), and Eve Boltby (*d.* after 1314), formerly the wife of Alan of Walkingham, and succeeded his elder brother, William, second Lord Cantilupe, about 1321. He married, first, Tiffany, and their son, William, was born about 1325. He was knighted on 19 April 1326. In July Cantilupe and his men were accused of assault at Withcall, Lincolnshire. An effective and devoted royal servant, he gained his first military experience fighting the Scots during the same period, with Edward II in 1319, with Aymer de Valence, earl of Pembroke, in 1322, and with Hugh Audley in 1327. His judicial career began in 1328, was interrupted when he went overseas in August 1329, but resumed during the early 1330s, when he played a key role in crown attempts to restore order in the north-east midlands. A man of notable religious conviction, he went on pilgrimage overseas in September 1333. In April 1335 he was appointed keeper of Berwick, and henceforth travelled back and forth between England and Scotland on military and judicial business. In January 1336 he was summoned to parliament for the first time.

With the outbreak of the Hundred Years' War Cantilupe's journeys extended to the continent. He sailed to Antwerp with the earl of Derby in July 1338, and was there in November with Edward III. Having returned to England he re-embarked for the Low Countries with soldiers and material the following July. He spent most of 1340 in England on judicial and taxational business, but was one of the confidants who accompanied the king on his vengeful return from Ghent in November, and was instrumental in the purge that ensued. During December and January Edward twice sent him to Canterbury to summon Archbishop Stratford to London, and commissioned him to try corruption and other crimes throughout the north-east midlands. At Lincoln he duly presided over a great inquiry at which a case first brought before him eleven months previously was resolved, when a former sheriff confessed to having stolen a beached whale belonging to the countess of Lincoln. He spent most of 1341 vigorously pursuing his commissions, then was summoned to fight the Scots. In January 1342 this summons was countermanded by orders that he proceed to London to complete plans for a proposed expedition to Gascony, which in turn was overtaken by events as war broke out in Brittany. About this time he married his second wife, Joan Littlebury (*d.* 1362), formerly the wife of William, Lord Kyme, and holder of extensive Lincolnshire lands. In May he was appointed to treat regarding the war in France, and in October sailed to Brest with the earl of Derby, returning to England the following spring. During 1344–5 he received a series of judicial commissions. In January 1346 he became suddenly and seriously ill; he was exempted from public duties, and played no part in the great campaigns of 1346–7. By October 1346, however, he had recovered sufficiently to act once more as a justice, and during 1347–8 he received further judicial commissions. In October 1349 he hosted at Hereford the translation of the relics of St Thomas of Hereford (Thomas de *Cantilupe), his kinsman. During 1352 he was commissioned to maintain sea defences and array troops in Lincolnshire. In 1354 he received his final summons to parliament and final judicial commission.

Cantilupe acted predominantly in Nottinghamshire, Derbyshire, and Lincolnshire, the counties in which his principal residences—Greasley, Ilkeston, and Withcall—were situated. He inherited Ravensthorpe, Yorkshire, and other Boltby lands after the death of his maternal stepbrother, William Walkingham. In 1337 Roger Lestrange of Knockin granted him for life the castle of Clifford, Herefordshire, and other lands which Roger had inherited from Abel Lestrange. He received licence to crenellate Greasley in April 1340. Between 1339 and 1354 he received a series of licences to endow the Carthusian priory of Beauvale, which he founded within his park at Greasley in December 1343. He also founded Cantilupe College in Lincoln Cathedral close, whose priests celebrated at the altar of St Nicholas within the cathedral. He died on 31 July 1355, and, having previously excluded his son and heir, William, from his succession, was succeeded by William's son Nicholas, then aged thirteen. Nicholas Cantilupe forged a career on the basis of his ability, his intimacy with Edward III, and the trust placed in him as a regional lieutenant. RICHARD PARTINGTON

Sources *Chancery records* • GEC, *Peerage* • W. Dugdale, *The baronage of England*, 2 vols. (1675–6) • B. W. McLane, ed., *The 1341 royal inquest in Lincolnshire*, Lincoln RS, 78 (1988) • Rymer, *Foedera*, 3rd edn, vol. 2/3–4 • Tout, *Admin. hist.*, vol. 3 • M. McKisack, *The fourteenth century* (1959) • R. Midmer, *English mediaeval monasteries, 1066–1540* (1979) • R. Barber, *Edward, prince of Wales and Aquitaine: a biography of the Black Prince* (1978) • Emden, *Oxf.*

Cantilupe [Cantelupe]**, Nicholas** (*d.* 1441), Carmelite friar and historian, was born in Wales, the son of William Cantilupe and a descendant of the noble Cantilupe family. Having joined the Carmelite order in Bristol in his youth, he studied at Cambridge, where he completed a doctorate in theology *c.*1420. In 1423 he is named in local records as prior of the Carmelite house in Northampton. According to the antiquary John Bale, Cantilupe died there on 27 September 1441. Bale also claims that he was a close friend of Humphrey, duke of Gloucester, and prior of Carmelite houses in Cambridge, Bristol, and Gloucester.

Of the five Latin historical and exegetical works attributed to Cantilupe, three are extant. The first two, *In laudem ordinis Carmelitarum* (BL, Harley MS 1819, fols. 153*v*–156*v*) and *Supplementa historiarum* (Bodl. Oxf., MS Bodley 73, fols. 61*r*–61*v*), deal with the glorious past and present of the Carmelite order; they survive in copies made by Bale, who used them in his own writings on the Carmelite order.

Cantilupe's third and most influential work is a foundation myth of the University of Cambridge, the *Historiola de antiquitate et origine almae et immaculatae universitatis Cantebrigiae*. Probably written before 1423, the *Historiola* attempts to upstage rival myths about the antiquity of the University of Oxford by taking the origins of Cambridge back to the pre-Christian past. After an account of the foundation of Cambridge by the mythical prince Cantaber, Cantilupe narrates the evolution of the university against the 'historical' background of the equally inventive *Historia regum Britanniae* of Geoffrey of Monmouth. The *Historiola* interpolates copies of a number of fabricated papal bulls and royal charters, the earliest (dated 541) granted to the university by King Arthur. These spurious bulls assumed importance in the 'Barnwell process' (1430–31), when Cambridge University adduced them as evidence of its ancient privileges in a successful attempt to claim exemption from the jurisdiction of the bishop of Ely.

Ten manuscripts of the *Historiola* have so far been located; Cantilupe's holograph notes for his history survive on folio 220 of Copenhagen, Kongelige Bibliotek, MS Gl. Kgl. Sam. 1653, a volume of medical treatises which Cantilupe may have owned. The *Historiola* was copied into the official Cambridge University register, the Black Book, and it appears to have been known to John Lydgate, who drew on it for his 'Verses on Cambridge'. Sixteenth- and seventeenth-century protagonists in the debate about the relative antiquity of Cambridge and Oxford, such as John Caius and Brian Twyne, duly refer to Cantilupe's contribution to the subject. The *Historiola* was edited, for the first and the last time, by Thomas Hearne in 1719.

AD PUTTER

Sources N. Cantalupus, 'Historiola de antiquitate et origine universitatis Cantebrigiensis', in *Thomae Sprotti Chronica*, ed. T. Hearnius (1719), 221–80 • N. Cantalupus and R. Parker, *The history and antiquities of the University of Cambridge* (1721) • R. Sharpe, *A hand-list of the Latin writers of Great Britain and Ireland before 1540* (1997) [lists nine MSS of the *Historiola*, to which should be added Gon. and Caius Cam., MS 194 (100), fols. 88–97] • Bale, *Cat.*, 1.585 • *History of Barnwell Abbey* (1786) • J. Lydgate, 'Verses on Cambridge', *The minor poems of John Lydgate*, ed. H. N. MacCracken, 2 vols., EETS, original ser., 192 (1934), vol. 2, pp. 652–4 [1934 for 1933] • J. C. Cox and C. A. Markham, eds., *The records of the borough of Northampton*, 1, ed. C. A. Markham (1898), 359–62 • C. H. Cooper, *Annals of Cambridge*, 1 (1842) • R. Copsey, *Biographical register of medieval Carmelites in England* [forthcoming] • Emden, *Cam.*, 120 • J. Parker, *The early history of Oxford*, OHS, 3 (1885) • C. de S. E. de Villiers, ed., *Bibliotheca Carmelitana*, 2 vols. (Orléans, 1752), vol. 2, pp. 482–3 • W. Dugdale, *The baronage of England*, 2 vols. (1675–6)

Archives BL, Harley MS 1819, fols. 153*v*–156*v* • Bodl. Oxf., MS Bodley 73, fols. 61*r*–61*v* • Gon. & Caius Cam., MS 194, fols. 88–97 • Kongelige Bibliotek, Copenhagen, MS GP. Kgl. Sam. 1653, fol. 220

Cantilupe [Cantelupe], **Roger de** (*d.* **1258/9**), lawyer, was described in 1234 by Bishop Alexander of Stainsby as following in the footsteps of his father, who had been hanged as a traitor. It has therefore been surmised that he was the son of the Roger de Cantilupe whom the Dunstable annalist describes as an Essex knight charged in 1225 with breach of the king's peace, and hanged after defeat in a duel. But the identification cannot be regarded as certain. The sons of the man hanged in 1225 were reported to have been disinherited and outlawed, and no such fate is recorded of the younger Roger. He was university-educated, being styled *magister* by 1220. He probably attended Oxford, since he was several times involved in the affairs of religious houses in and around the town. Active as an arbitrator, and as a papal judge-delegate and -subdelegate, his expertise in canon law brought him to the king's attention, and in 1231–2 he acted as Henry III's representative at the papal curia. He must also have been knowledgeable in the common law, for in 1232 he was a justice itinerant, sitting in Nottinghamshire, Derbyshire, and Cambridgeshire, only to be disgraced late in July for involvement in the disturbances directed against foreigners provided to English benefices. But that involvement was probably unimportant, for he was soon back in the king's service, and at the end of 1233 was given an annual retaining fee of 50 marks (£33 6*s.* 8*d.*), while in 1234 he was close enough to the centre of affairs to be insulted by Bishop Stainsby at Westminster.

Cantilupe continued to act for the king; early in 1244 he was sent back to Rome on royal business, in 1245 he was Henry III's proctor in an apparent dispute with the bishop of Bath and Wells, and in 1246 he represented the king in a controversy over the election of an abbess for Shaftesbury. He was also employed by others, advising Christ Church Priory, Canterbury, in the early 1240s. His rewards from the king included the prebend of Cantlers (possibly named from him) in St Paul's, London, by 1240, gifts of money, robes, game, and timber, and grants of at least three wardships. He came to hold lands in several counties, especially Essex and East Anglia. His sister Alice married Ignatius of Clifton, a Somerset landowner, and their son Roger was in 1257 pardoned with Cantilupe for hunting in the king's forests in Wiltshire, where Cantilupe also had land. He was still alive at the end of May 1258, but had died by 15 June 1259, when his prebend was granted to Walter of Merton.

HENRY SUMMERSON

Sources *Chancery records* • *Ann. mon.*, vol. 3 • Paris, *Chron.*, 3.201, 268 • *Curia regis rolls preserved in the Public Record Office* (1922–), vol. 10, p. 3 • Emden, *Oxf.* • J. E. Sayers, *Papal judges delegate in the province of Canterbury, 1198–1254* (1971) • *Fasti Angl., 1066–1300*, [St Paul's, London] • E. Green, ed., *Pedes finium, commonly called, feet of fines, for the county of Somerset*, Somerset RS, 6: *Richard I to Edward I, 1196–1307* (1892), 154 • N. Adams and C. Donahue, eds., *Select cases from the ecclesiastical courts of the province of Canterbury, c. 1200–1301*, SeldS, 95 (1981) • D. Crook, *Records of the general eyre*, Public Record Office Handbooks, 20 (1982), 88 • *CPR, 1247–66*

Cantilupe, Thomas de [St Thomas of Hereford] (*c.***1220–1282**), bishop of Hereford, was born at his father's manor of Hambleden, Buckinghamshire.

Early life and education Thomas's grandfather William (I) de *Cantilupe and father, William (II) de *Cantilupe (*d.* 1251), had served as stewards of the households of John and Henry III. His mother, Millicent, daughter of the Norman baron Hugh de Gournai, was the widow of Amaury de Montfort, count of Évreux. Thomas, one of five brothers, was third in a family of seven or eight children. His eldest brother, William (III) de *Cantilupe, succeeded their father and married Eva de Briouze of Brecon; the second brother, Hugh, entered the church, eventually to become archdeacon of Gloucester; and the younger brothers, John and Nicholas, seem to have become knights. Thomas himself appears from the start to have been destined for the church. He came under the tutelage of his paternal uncle, the influential Walter de *Cantilupe, who was bishop of Worcester from 1236 until his death in 1266. By about 1237 Thomas may have been at Oxford; he joined Hugh at Paris in the early 1240s where the brothers pursued arts degrees while keeping a stately establishment which even Louis IX visited. The two Cantilupes attended the First Council of Lyons in 1245, where Thomas was appointed papal chaplain by Innocent IV (*r.* 1243–54), and also received a dispensation allowing him to hold benefices in plurality, a privilege that he was to use to advantage in later years. After attaining his MA at Paris he studied civil law at Orléans under Guido de Guinis, whose legal and administrative interests seem to have been practical, rather than theoretical. Thomas returned to Paris to dedicate himself to canon law, by which time the two brothers were keeping separate households. Thomas returned to Oxford and completed his studies in canon law *c.*1255, incepting as a doctor in that faculty. In 1261 he was elected chancellor of the university, possibly (in addition to his own merits) because it was advantageous to the university to have as chancellor a man whom Henry III seemed to favour, and who was also the nephew of the bishop of Worcester. During his term in that office Thomas exhibited the traits that were to remain characteristic of him: highly conscious of his own authority, he was inflexibly determined that students should know their place, though he also seems to have been impartial in his administration.

Montfortian connections Cantilupe opened a new phase in his life when, as a result of his involvement in the political conflicts increasingly affecting the kingdom, he went in December 1263 to Amiens, to represent baronial interests in their disputes with Henry III. He drafted the three documents through which the barons' case was submitted to the arbitrament of Louis IX. It has been suggested that Thomas was drawn to Montfort's cause because of the influence of his uncle, Bishop Walter, a close friend of Montfort. Walter, like Simon de Montfort, had played a part in the governance of the realm but, again like the earl of Leicester, had suffered dismissal from royal office by Henry III. Many ecclesiastics supported the earl because he seemed to be a defender of church liberties. In addition Montfort was supported by Thomas's cousin Peter de Montfort (no relation of Simon's), and had been a friend of Thomas's brother William. The French king's rejection of the baronial proposals, in the mise of Amiens of January 1264, was the catalyst that brought Montfortians into open conflict with Henry and, eventually, with the Lord Edward. After Simon de Montfort's victory at Lewes in May of 1264, the magnate council of nine, and a compliant Henry III, in February 1265 appointed Thomas de Cantilupe chancellor of England. Though his execution of duties as chancellor seems to have been of brief duration, the acts he carried out were performed with his usual fastidious attention to detail and consciousness of responsibility. In charge of the king's seal from 25 February to 7 May 1265, Cantilupe took instructions from Montfort, the council of nine, and the king, who, with his own hands, folded a writ granting Cantilupe and his chancery staff a pay rise designed, presumably, to obviate the need for, or suspicions of, bribery under the new chancellor's regime. That Cantilupe was his own man is illustrated by his objection to a writ of early March issued by the council of nine; and his characteristic sense of responsibility is also suggested in that Cantilupe himself (and not, as by then was the custom, the king) was recorded as the 'giver' of four out of six charters. Practice reverted to earlier methods after his departure from office. Cantilupe also seems to have been much more careful to record the authority whereby royal letters were issued, since about 64 per cent of approximately 170 letters in the close rolls recorded while he held office bear notes regarding such authorization. The reasons for his leaving office as chancellor (though he held the title after 7 May) are not known with certainty. There are indications that he had intended to continue in that position. In any case the confusion of events following Edward's escape in late May 1264, and the decisive battle of Evesham on 4 August 1265, put an end to the Montfortian experiment and to this phase of Cantilupe's career.

Further education After Evesham Cantilupe left England. Though restored to royal favour as early as February 1266, he remained abroad for several years, studying theology at Paris, where the Franciscan scholar John Pecham (*d.* 1292), eventually archbishop of Canterbury and Cantilupe's enemy, was also to be found, both as a student and (by 1270) as a doctor of theology. At the university Cantilupe lectured, presumably without interjecting controversial views, on the Epistles and the Apocalypse. There is no evidence for his reaction to the debates between Dominicans and Franciscans arising from the ideas of Thomas Aquinas, then at Paris, or, indeed, for his attitude to any contemporary contentious issues in theology. By about 1272 he had returned to Oxford where, in June 1273, he became a doctor of theology, his inception being conducted by the Dominican Robert Kilwardby, who had been consecrated archbishop of Canterbury only a few months earlier on 26 February 1273. Pecham had also returned to England, serving as lector to the Oxford Franciscans between 1271 and 1275. Once again appointed chancellor of the university, in January 1274 Cantilupe played an important part in quelling a student riot between the 'northerners' and the 'southerners'. But this was to be his last significant act at Oxford. He was evidently not attracted to the intellectual challenges offered by canon law and theology; his interests were more practical. He soon attained an office in which his administrative skills were to be expertly applied.

Bishop of Hereford In May 1274, with his nephew William de Cantilupe, Thomas attended the Second Council of Lyons where, as at the first Lyons council, he was made a papal chaplain. By that time several church livings had come to him, some in plurality. He accumulated wealth as archdeacon of Stafford, precentor and canon of York, canon of London, and as the holder of several parish livings. When not visiting his parishes he resided in London. In 1274 he attained another office which was prefatory to his highest ecclesiastical attainment (apart from his canonization). He was appointed to the prebend of Preston in Hereford diocese by Bishop John le Breton; and when Breton died the next year on 12 May 1275, the canons, following the wishes of the deceased, on 15 June 1275 elected Cantilupe their bishop. The temporalities were restored on 26 June, and he was consecrated by Archbishop Kilwardby on 8 September 1275. As bishop of Hereford Cantilupe was, as usual, protective of his rights and privileges. His episcopal register, the first to survive for Hereford diocese, shows evidence of good administrative intentions: there were attempts, early on, to establish orderly distinctions in the recorded matter, but soon these divisions were neglected, being replaced by the sometimes disorganized entries that betoken a working document, with all its imperfections (some materials from his register have found their way into that of his successor, Richard Swinfield). In spite of its disarray the register shows Cantilupe to have been a diligent administrator of his diocese, one who preached to his flock through an interpreter, who was intolerant of non-resident, pluralist (his own pluralism was licensed), or untitled (that is, without a church to provide a living) clergy, and who perambulated his diocese carrying out confirmations and visitations of parishes and monasteries alike. One of these visits, to Leominster, suggests in a small incident how sensitive was Cantilupe in matters involving his diocesan authority. Learning that the monks had blocked a door used by the laity to gain access to the church, he ordered the door's removal, which was resisted by the monks. (After his death the Leominster monks would provide accommodation to Archbishop Pecham while the latter attempted to force the Hereford canons to accept an archiepiscopal visitation; Pecham, typically, reversed Cantilupe's orders about the door.) Because of Cantilupe's sensitivity to his diocesan rights, and because at the same time the diocesan boundaries were themselves not everywhere clearly established, conflicts arose between the bishop and those whom he identified as encroachers, be they laymen or ecclesiastics. Thus he quarrelled, at one time or another, with the bishop of St Asaph, the bishop of St David's, Prince Llywelyn (*d.* 1282), and Gilbert de Clare, earl of Gloucester (*d.* 1295), and at the time of his death he was involved in a dispute with his archbishop.

Even with this heavy burden as diocesan Cantilupe found time and energy to assist in the administration of the realm. The single extant account of debate within Edward I's council, recording an outburst by Cantilupe, dates from February 1276 (this suggests that he had become a member of this privileged group of royal advisers before that time). A Jewish convert to Christianity had sought royal licence to prosecute Christian forgers. Cantilupe's emotional appeal to the king to refuse such an application was successful, an example of the bishop of Hereford's stern sense of propriety and conservatism, as well as his dislike of Jews, who were to be expelled from the kingdom in 1290.

Quarrels with Archbishop Pecham That a man such as Thomas de Cantilupe eventually became embroiled with John Pecham, archbishop of Canterbury from 1279 to 1292, is not a matter for surprise. Pecham, like Cantilupe, was not a humble man, whatever may have been anticipated from the archbishop's scholarly, Franciscan background. Though the new archbishop, who liked to style himself legate and metropolitan, may have cowed many of his suffragans, Cantilupe was not among that group. When it became clear that Pecham would claim jurisdiction over such issues as the probate of wills involving property lying in more than one diocese, and that he would accept appeals, in general, made from any diocese to his own provincial court (the court of arches in London) with little or no reference to the jurisdictional claims of individual bishops, a discomfiture was felt in many dioceses. Cantilupe, seeing the direction that matters were taking, removed himself to Normandy from 1280 to 1281, while his official, Master Robert of Gloucester, issued appeals to the pope in his name and bore the brunt of the archbishop's fiery mandates. When Cantilupe returned to his see in late 1281, the issues had not been resolved. Far from it: the disputes over jurisdictional authority worsened until, at Lambeth in February of 1282, Pecham pronounced against the bishop of Hereford what he considered to be an excommunication (which papal commissioners, in 1307, determined had been no excommunication at all, since it was not properly promulgated). Cantilupe disregarded this action, taking his appeals against Pecham to the pope, who was then at Orvieto. In June 1282 Cantilupe met Martin IV (*r.* 1281–5). The canonization record suggests that their discussions were amiable. When the pope moved to Montefiascone, Cantilupe followed; by early July he had lodged in cramped quarters at Castrum Florenti (Ferento, now in ruins) some 10 kilometres from Montefiascone. While his petitions and appeals were being reviewed by Martin's cardinals Cantilupe fell ill, and on 18 August he made his will. Having received confession and absolution from the papal penitentiary, on the night of 25 August 1282 he died, attended by his long-time servant, Robert Deynte. Following a requiem mass and eulogy delivered by the Franciscan cardinal Jerome, later Pope Nicholas IV (*r.* 1288–92), Cantilupe's flesh and viscera were buried at the monastery of San Severo outside Orvieto. His bones were returned to England by John de Clare, a prominent member of the bishop's household.

After receiving news of his adversary's death, by October 1282 Pecham had entered the diocese of Hereford where he began his attempts, which have all the appearances of a quest for revenge, to strengthen his control over that see. One victim of the archbishop's wrath was Cantilupe's dedicated official, Robert of Gloucester, whom Pecham fined and bound to a humiliating penance.

Furthermore, even though on 3 December 1282 the archbishop was presented with a document (dated at Orvieto, 5 September 1282) which confirmed the last confession and absolution of Cantilupe (and thereby implied that the bishop was not an excommunicate at his death), Pecham ignored this; continuing to treat him as an excommunicate, he refused to allow the burial of the bishop's bones in Hereford Cathedral. Only after further negotiations in which the dead man's cause was upheld by Edmund, earl of Cornwall (who had seen to the burial of Cantilupe's heart at Ashridge), did Pecham in January 1283 give permission for his burial.

Canonization and reputation Thus, early in 1283, Cantilupe's remains were placed under a slab in the east end of Hereford Cathedral, where they remained until moved into a table tomb (to which a shrine-like superstructure was added) in the north transept in April 1287, a reburial arranged by his successor Richard Swinfield (*d.* 1317). Swinfield became a tireless promoter of Cantilupe's canonization. Between 1287 and 1312 nearly 500 miracles were recorded as evidence of his sanctity, a figure surpassed in the surviving records of medieval England only by the 700 attributed to Thomas Becket. Swinfield's attempts to secure the canonization of his predecessor had little immediate success, though after an inquisition authorized by Clement V (*r.* 1305–14) found that Cantilupe had died in communion with the church, the pope ordered an investigation of his life and miracles, which took place in London and Hereford. Both inquisitorial processes occurred in 1307, the results surviving in two manuscripts now in the Vatican Library (MSS Vat. lat. 4015 and 4016). Continued support for the bishop's cause, by Edward I and Edward II and by many other secular and ecclesiastical magnates, resulted in his canonization on 17 April 1320.

St Thomas's feast day was fixed, for reasons not fully apparent, on 2 October. A new shrine was constructed in the east end of the cathedral. On 25 October 1349, in the presence of Edward III and many other lay and clerical notables, his bones were translated from the north transept to this new location. There the remains lay undisturbed until 1538, when, along with much else that represented papal authority in England, the shrine, its ornaments, and its contents were removed. Thomas's bones seem to have been preserved until the seventeenth century by local Catholics, but thereafter their dispersal was all but complete; some remains said to be his are still honoured in England at Belmont Abbey in Herefordshire, Stonyhurst, and Downside. The tomb in which his bones remained between 1287 and 1349 stands empty in Hereford Cathedral. Other posthumous memorials, apart from several references in bishops' registers and in miscellaneous cathedral documents, include liturgical remains (along with a fifteenth-century motet), representations in glass and, probably, some of the fabric of the cathedral itself, paid for in part from offerings by pilgrims to the shrine. Thomas de Cantilupe was the penultimate figure of English history to have achieved official, papal, canonization during the middle ages (the last medieval recipient of this honour was Osmund, bishop of Salisbury, canonized in 1456).

Appearance and personality No writings or sermons of Thomas de Cantilupe have been found, of his letters nothing beyond the formulaic statements that his clerks entered into his register. Very little else would be known about him were it not for the canonization process of 1307. The forty-three witnesses to that inquiry who testified to the bishop's saintly life (many more testified about his posthumous miracles), provide few clues about what he was like as a man. Among the physical descriptions of him, the only notes that seem to reflect more than the commonplaces of medieval biography are remarks about his long (or large) nose, his ruddy complexion, full head of hair, and his grey and ginger beard. The façade of the efficient, aloof, supremely controlled individual, one who (as bishop) refused to kiss his own sister lest immodesty be suggested, failed him on only a few recorded occasions. One of these occurred during his quarrel with the archbishop—Cantilupe, so a canonization witness claimed, on learning that Pecham might have excommunicated him, pounded upon the archbishop's door in Lambeth Palace, crying out for a copy of the excommunication document. The incident in Edward I's council concerning the converted Jew is another occasion that moved Cantilupe to outraged threats and tears. He seems to have been acutely sensitive to the obligations and privileges of people of his own elevated class, whether he was exercising the authority that pertained to academic administration, to the government of the realm, or to the office of bishop. In all these roles he showed himself to be conscientious and diligent, efficient, a man to whom any sort of frivolity was abhorrent. Apart from the hagiographical topoi concerning his sobriety, open-handedness, seriousness, and devotion to his God, Thomas de Cantilupe leaves the impression of having been a man capable of immense dedication to such tasks as he believed were worthy of him.

R. C. FINUCANE

Sources Biblioteca Apostolica Vaticana, Vatican City, MSS Vat. lat. 4015–4016 · R. G. Griffiths and W. W. Capes, eds., *Registrum Thome de Cantilupo, episcopi Herefordensis*, CYS, 2 (1907) · *The register of Richard de Swinfield, bishop of Hereford* (AD 1283–1317), ed. W. W. Capes, CYS, 6 (1909) · W. W. Capes, ed., *Charters and records of Hereford Cathedral*, Cantilupe Society (1908) · J. Catto, 'The academic career of Thomas Cantilupe', *St Thomas Cantilupe, bishop of Hereford: essays in his honour*, ed. M. Jancey (1982), 45–55 · D. A. Carpenter, 'St. Thomas Cantilupe: his political career', *St Thomas Cantilupe, bishop of Hereford: essays in his honour*, ed. M. Jancey (1982), 57–72 · D. M. Smith, 'Thomas Cantilupe's register: the administration of the diocese of Hereford, 1272–1282', *St Thomas Cantilupe, bishop of Hereford: essays in his honour*, ed. M. Jancey (1982), 83–101 · R. C. Finucane, 'The Cantilupe–Pecham controversy', *St Thomas Cantilupe, bishop of Hereford: essays in his honour*, ed. M. Jancey (1982), 103–123 · R. C. Finucane, 'Cantilupe as thaumaturge: pilgrims and their "miracles"', *St Thomas Cantilupe, bishop of Hereford: essays in his honour*, ed. M. Jancey (1982), 137–44 · P. E. Morgan, 'The effect of the pilgrim cult of St Thomas Cantilupe on Hereford Cathedral', *St Thomas Cantilupe, bishop of Hereford: essays in his honour*, ed. M. Jancey (1982), 145–52 · P. Barrett, 'A saint in the calendar: the effect of the canonization of

St Thomas Cantilupe on the liturgy', *St Thomas Cantilupe, bishop of Hereford: essays in his honour*, ed. M. Jancey (1982), 153–7 • B. Trowell and A. Wathey, 'John Benet's *Lux fulget ex Anglia–O pater pietatis–Salve Thoma*', *St Thomas Cantilupe, bishop of Hereford: essays in his honour*, ed. M. Jancey (1982), 159–80 • I. Barrett, 'The relics of St Thomas Cantilupe', *St Thomas Cantilupe, bishop of Hereford: essays in his honour*, ed. M. Jancey (1982), 181–5 • P. H. Daly, 'The attitude of the English Franciscans to St Thomas Cantilupe', *Franziskanische Studien*, 66 (1984), 251–64 • R. C. Finucane, 'The changing fortunes of a curative shrine: St Thomas Cantilupe', *Miracles and pilgrims* (1977), 173–88; repr. (1995) • R. C. Finucane, 'Pilgrimage in daily life: aspects of medieval communication reflected in the newly-established cult of Thomas Cantilupe (d. 1282), its dissemination and effects upon outlying Herefordshire villagers', *Wallfahrt und Alltag in Mittelalter und früher Neuzeit* [Krems an der Donau 1990], ed. G. Jaritz and B. Schuh (Vienna, 1992), 165–217 • P. H. Daly, 'The process of canonization in the thirteenth and early fourteenth centuries', *St Thomas Cantilupe, bishop of Hereford: essays in his honour*, ed. M. Jancey (1982), 125–35 • J. Webb, ed., *A roll of the household expenses of Richard de Swinfield, bishop of Hereford, during part of the years 1289 and 1290*, CS, 59, 62 (1853–5) • N. D. S. Martin, 'The life of St Thomas of Hereford', *St Thomas Cantilupe, bishop of Hereford: essays in his honour*, ed. M. Jancey (1982), 15–19 • M. Prestwich, *English politics in the thirteenth century* (1990)

Cantilupe, Walter de (*c.*1195–1266), bishop of Worcester, was the second son of William (I) de *Cantilupe (*d.* 1239), a Norman by birth, who served as steward of the household to King John. Walter's elder brother, William (II) de *Cantilupe, held the same position in the household of Henry III; Walter's nephews included Thomas de Cantilupe, the future bishop of Hereford, and Peter de Montfort, both of whom later associated with their uncle in supporting the cause of Simon de *Montfort. After attending the schools, possibly at Oxford, Walter entered royal service. As a king's clerk, as yet in minor orders, he was presented by the crown to a series of parish livings (Eyton in 1208, Burton and Worfield in 1215, Long Itchington, Rampisham, Preston, Priors Hardwick, and a moiety of Stokes in 1216, Hinxworth in 1219, Penrith in 1222, and Bulwick in 1227) and finally, on 22 July 1231, to a canonry and prebend in Lichfield Cathedral. Whether or not he held all these livings simultaneously, he was evidently a pluralist, and as such was not wholly disinterested when, at the legatine council of 1237, he pleaded the cause of many noble pluralists, 'who have until now lived honourably, giving what hospitality they could and dispensing alms with open doors,' who were threatened with impoverishment by being reduced to a single benefice each (Paris, 3.418).

In 1227 Cantilupe served as the king's proctor at the Roman curia, dealing with litigation involving the interests of the crown. He was one of those who brought the pallium from Rome for Archbishop Richard Grant in the autumn of 1229. In January 1235 he was one of three envoys sent to France to bear truce proposals to Louis IX and to swear on Henry III's behalf to observe the conditions of the truce. It was evidently as a trusted royal servant and nominee of the king that he was elected bishop of Worcester on 30 August 1236. The king's assent was signified on 9 September, and the temporalities of his see were handed over to him on the 27th. As bishop-elect, he

Walter de Cantilupe (*c.*1195–1266), tomb effigy

was dispatched in January 1237 to the papal curia on the king's business, and while he was there, at Viterbo on 3 May, Pope Gregory IX consecrated him bishop, having previously ordained him deacon and priest. Possibly it was the irregularity of his position as a pluralist without the requisite dispensations that had made it necessary to defer his consecration until it could be performed by the pope. His enthronement at Worcester on 13 October 1237 was attended by the king and queen as well as by the archbishop of Canterbury, Edmund of Abingdon, and the papal legate, Cardinal Otto.

Cantilupe proved himself a zealous diocesan bishop, sharing with Bishop Grosseteste of Lincoln a concern for the reform of abuses and the improvement of pastoral standards. The synodal statutes he promulgated for the Worcester diocese in 1240, frequently revised and updated, provided a model for the legislation of several of his episcopal colleagues. A noteworthy feature of his ordinances was the attention they gave to instructing the parish clergy in their duties, especially those who had to hear confessions, for whom he provided a detailed summary of moral theology. In 1240 he obtained papal sanction for a drive to remove married clergy from parishes and to deprive those who had succeeded their fathers in their benefices. His zeal for the religious life was manifested by his repeated and searching visitations of the monastic houses of his diocese, and his deposition of lax superiors. His claim to approve the appointment of monastic obedientiaries and his insistence on the adoption of properly audited accounting methods were to involve him in conflicts with the abbot of Gloucester and with the monks of his own cathedral priory.

Cantilupe displayed the same energy in protecting and extending the temporal and spiritual rights of his see. He successfully claimed the town and churches of Dudley for the Worcester diocese, against the claims of the Coventry and Lichfield diocese. A long-standing dispute between successive bishops of Worcester and Evesham Abbey over jurisdiction in the Vale of Evesham was terminated by papal judges in 1248 in the abbey's favour, but in return for renouncing his claims over the churches of the vale, Cantilupe acquired patronal rights in three other churches. An invasion of the bishop's secular rights in the hundred of Oswaldslow by William Beauchamp, the sheriff of Worcester, who held the view of frankpledge in the episcopal manors, was countered by a sentence of excommunication, a judgment for which, despite the king's displeasure, Cantilupe obtained papal confirmation.

Cantilupe received a number of papal commissions to serve as a judge-delegate or to execute papal mandates. In 1244, on the instructions of Innocent IV, he joined the bishop of Hereford and the archdeacon of Canterbury in warning the king, under threat of interdict, to desist from his refusal to accept the translation of William of Raleigh from Norwich to the see of Winchester. With other English prelates he attended the Council of Lyons in 1245. In 1247 he was commissioned to preach the crusade in England and collect funds for the purpose. In 1250 he followed King Henry's example by taking the cross himself, and was authorized by the pope to use the money collected in his diocese from offerings and the redemption of crusading vows. But, like the king, he never fulfilled his undertaking to go to the East.

A friend of Grosseteste, Simon de Montfort, and the Franciscan Adam Marsh, Cantilupe became an active member of a group of learned and idealistic churchmen who were critical of the policies of Henry III. He was chosen to sit on the committee of bishops and magnates which drafted the abortive constitution of 1244, designed to exercise control over the expenditure of a subsidy that had been reluctantly granted to the king. With Grosseteste, he vociferously opposed a papal mandate allocating the king the proceeds of a tenth levied upon the incomes of the clergy. When Montfort was arraigned before the king in 1252 for his conduct as governor of Gascony, Cantilupe loyally defended the earl in the face of Henry's accusations. From 1255 onwards he was chief spokesman for the clerical opposition to Henry's acceptance of the Sicilian crown for his second son, Edmund, and to underwriting the debts incurred by the king and the pope in prosecuting this ill-conceived plan. In 1257 he was one of those sent to France to negotiate terms of a permanent peace.

As a conspicuous critic of the king's policy, Cantilupe played a leading role in the revolutionary events of the years 1258–65. At the Oxford parliament of June 1258 he was the only cleric chosen by the baronial side to serve on the committee of twenty-four which drafted the provisions of Oxford, and he was subsequently elected a member of the standing council imposed upon the king by the new constitution. He was the leading member of a deputation sent by the council in January 1259 to intercept Richard, earl of Cornwall, newly crowned king of the Romans, at St Omer, in order to refuse him entry to the country until he had sworn to observe the Oxford provisions; and later that year he was appointed one of the councillors to act as regents while the king was absent in France. Following King Henry's recovery of power in 1261, Cantilupe remained a stalwart supporter of Montfort and an unyielding upholder of the provisions. He put his name to the baronial letters submitting the cause of the reformers to the arbitration of Louis IX, and his nephew, Thomas de Cantilupe, was entrusted with expounding the baronial case to Louis at Amiens.

In the drift to civil war that followed Louis's verdict for the king in the mise of Amiens of 23 January 1264, Cantilupe made a number of unsuccessful attempts at conciliation. In March 1264, together with the bishops of Winchester, London, and Chichester, he held talks with the king's representatives at Brackley and Oxford, offering baronial acceptance of Louis's verdict on condition that King Henry expelled unacceptable aliens from court and allowed the council to nominate his ministers. In May, he and Henry of Sandwich, bishop of London, accompanied Montfort's army on the march to Lewes, and on the eve of the battle made a last effort to mediate between Montfort and the king. But after this overture failed, Cantilupe exhorted Montfort's troops to confess their sins, gave them absolution, and blessed them.

The legitimacy of the regime set up by Montfort after his victory was challenged by the papal legate, Cardinal Guy Foulquois, who from Boulogne, where he stayed under the wing of King Louis, summoned Montfort and his accomplices before him and ordered the annulment of the provisions under threat of interdict. Cantilupe was sent to Boulogne with the bishops of London and Winchester to put the baronial case, but the legate was immovable and they returned with orders to execute the papal sentence against Montfort and his allies. According to Thomas Wykes, the men of the Cinque Ports met the party and threw the papal letters into the sea. Cantilupe remained loyal to Montfort to the end. He endeavoured without success to arbitrate in the dispute between the earl and Gilbert de Clare, earl of Gloucester, that fatally weakened the baronial party. Montfort slept at his manor of Kempsey the night before the battle of Evesham, and on the morning of 4 August 1265 Cantilupe celebrated mass for his friend. In the aftermath of the battle, the king initiated proceedings against the bishops who had supported Montfort, and Cantilupe together with four others was suspended by the papal legate, Cardinal Ottobuono, and ordered to Rome to receive the judgment of the pope. But after the battle he had retired broken-hearted to his manor of Blockley, Gloucestershire, and he died there on 12 February 1266, his case still unresolved. He was buried in Worcester Cathedral. A zealous pastor, a scholar, and an idealist, as the spiritual mentor of one of the most radical political movements of the middle ages, he ranks among the greatest ecclesiastical leaders of his generation.

C. H. LAWRENCE

Sources Paris, *Chron.* • *Ann. mon.* • *Roberti Grosseteste episcopi quondam Lincolniensis epistolae*, ed. H. R. Luard, Rolls Series, 25 (1861) • *Chancery records* • F. M. Powicke and C. R. Cheney, eds., *Councils and synods with other documents relating to the English church, 1205–1313*, 1 (1964) • *CEPR letters*, vol. 1 • R. F. Treharne and I. J. Sanders, eds., *Documents of the baronial movement of reform and rebellion, 1258–1267* (1973) • Emden, *Oxf.* • W. E. Lunt, *Financial relations of the papacy with England to 1327* (1939) • F. M. Powicke, *King Henry III and the Lord Edward: the community of the realm in the thirteenth century*, 2 vols. (1947) • M. Jancey, ed., *St Thomas Cantilupe, bishop of Hereford: essays in his honour* (1982) • J. R. Maddicott, *Simon de Montfort* (1994)

Likenesses tomb effigy, Worcester Cathedral [*see illus.*]

Cantilupe [Cantelupe]**, William (I) de** (*d.* **1239**), baron and administrator, was of Norman descent, probably the son of Walter de Cantilupe, in 1166 a minor landholder in Essex and Lincolnshire. His wife, Mazilia, brought William land in Kent. By 1198 Cantilupe was steward of the household of John, count of Mortain, the future king. From 1200 to 1204 he was sheriff of Worcestershire, and in 1204 also under-sheriff of Herefordshire, in charge of an unspecified castle treasury. Cantilupe took part in the ineffectual expedition to Poitou of 1205; in that same year he was granted the manor of Eaton Bray, Bedfordshire, which became the *caput* of the Cantilupe barony. In 1208 he was given the custody of the see of Worcester, and was a justice in Nottinghamshire; in 1209 he was appointed sheriff of Warwickshire and Leicestershire, and Kenilworth Castle became his chief residence. He supervised elections to the vacant sees of York and Carlisle in 1214, with William Brewer, and in 1215–16 was granted a number of manors belonging to rebels, and was commissioned to treat with those who might return into the king's peace. Wendover's description of him as one of John's 'evil counsellors' (Paris, *Chron.*) probably owes much to Cantilupe's role as a gaoler of baronial hostages. Wendover also suggests that Cantilupe may have wavered in his loyalty after the rebel seizure of London in 1215, but this is belied by the stream of royal writs sent to him in 1215–16. In 1215 he also witnessed the royal declaration of free election to sees and abbeys.

Cantilupe continued to participate in government under Henry III. In 1217 he was at Mountsorrel and at the battle of Lincoln. In March 1218 he witnessed the treaty of Worcester with Llywelyn ab Iorwerth, and was an itinerant justice in Bedfordshire. For 1217/18 he was also a baron of the exchequer. In 1219 he was a commissioner investigating encroachments on the royal forests in Oxfordshire, Buckinghamshire, and Herefordshire. He remained sheriff of Warwickshire and Leicestershire until 1223, when he was sent to sit with the barons of the exchequer. He joined Ranulf (III) of Chester's armed demonstration at the Tower against the government of Hubert de Burgh in November 1223; his motive was almost certainly the threatened resumption of his custodies of Kenilworth and the royal manors of Calne and Calstone, Wiltshire. He submitted at Northampton on 30 December, however, and joined the royal siege of Bedford in the summer of 1224. He was consequently able to retain Calne and Calstone. In 1225 he was allowed £1084 at the exchequer for war expenses under John; this cancelled a list of debts that included increments due on county farms, scutages, and the fine for the custody of the lands and heir of Robert Chandos. Cantilupe served in Wales in 1228, Brittany in 1230, and Wales again in 1231.

Cantilupe was able to survive the faction-fighting of Henry III's early reign, siding with Hubert de Burgh or Peter des Roches as necessary. His position as royal steward brought him into close contact with the kings whom he served; for example, his seal was sometimes used to authenticate the letters of the young Henry III. This closeness probably aided his political survival; it also provided the entrée to court for his son William (II) de *Cantilupe. Moreover it gave Cantilupe opportunities for collecting custodies and wardships, and thereby to raise his family's status. He died on 7 April 1239 and was succeeded by his son. His second son, Walter de *Cantilupe, was bishop of Worcester.

B. W. HOLDEN

Sources *Chancery records* (RC) • *Chancery records* • F. Palgrave, ed., *Rotuli curiae regis: rolls and records of the court held before the king's justiciars or justices*, 2 vols., RC, 27 (1835) • Paris, *Chron.*, 2.533, 588, 610; 3.15, 18, 83, 529 • *Ann. mon.*, 3.87 • I. J. Sanders, *English baronies: a study of their origin and descent, 1086–1327* (1960), 39–40 • D. A. Carpenter, *The minority of Henry III* (1990) • H. Hall, ed., *The Red Book of the Exchequer*, 3 vols., Rolls Series, 99 (1896) • A. Hughes, *List of sheriffs for England and Wales: from the earliest times to AD 1831*, PRO (1898); repr. (New York, 1963) • L. Landon, *The itinerary of King Richard I*, PRSoc., new ser., 13 (1935), 131

Cantilupe [Cantelupe]**, William (II) de** (*d.* **1251**), baron and administrator, was the son of William (I) de *Cantilupe (*d.* 1239) and his wife, Mazilia. His brother was Walter de *Cantilupe, bishop of Worcester. Like his father he was named by Roger of Wendover as one of King John's 'evil counsellors' (Paris, *Chron.*). Before 1216 he had married Millicent (or Maud), the daughter of Hugh de Gournai and widow of Amaury de Montfort, earl of Gloucester and count of Évreux (*d.* 1210x13). This marriage brought him six and a half fees in Oxfordshire, but also involved him in legal disputes over dower with Gilbert de Clare, earl of Hertford and Gloucester. In 1217 he was at the siege of Mountsorrel and at the battle of Lincoln.

By the mid-1220s Cantilupe was a follower of Earl Ranulf (III) of Chester, and witnessed many of his charters. He participated in Ranulf's armed demonstration at the Tower of London in November 1223 but then submitted with the earl. He joined Chester on the king's expedition to Brittany in 1230. He was one of the executors of Ranulf's will in 1234, and remained in the service of the new earl, John the Scot. In 1236 he went on pilgrimage to Santiago de Compostela. He moved to the royal household in 1238, being appointed steward, and then sheriff of Nottinghamshire and Derbyshire in 1239. In 1238 he was also given the custody and marriage of Eva, one of the heirs of William (V) de Briouze, along with the honour of Abergavenny and half the honour of Totnes in Devon. He proceeded to marry Eva to his son William by July 1241, at a stroke enlarging the family holdings well beyond what they had been under his father.

In 1241 Cantilupe was one of the English arbitrators with Dafydd of Gwynedd. Along with the archbishop of York and the bishop of Carlisle, he was appointed one of the keepers of the realm during the king's Poitevin expedition of 1242. He was one of the proctors of the English baronage at the Council of Lyons in 1245, delivering a lengthy complaint against Roman exactions. He died on 22 February 1251. His widow was in 1255 appointed a custodian of Henry III's young daughter, Margaret, queen of Scots, and died in 1260. William was succeeded by his son William (III) de *Cantilupe; he had four other sons, of whom Thomas de *Cantilupe, the third-born, became bishop of Hereford and a saint.

Following his father into royal service, Cantilupe demonstrated by his appointments as arbitrator and diplomatic representative, and above all as a custodian of the kingdom in the king's absence, the continuing trust in and reliance upon his household which Henry III showed in the late 1230s and 1240s. His obtaining the custody of Eva de Briouze shows the rewards available to those close to the king, and made the Cantilupes for a time a power on the Welsh march. B. W. HOLDEN

Sources *Chancery records* (RC) • *Chancery records* • Paris, *Chron.*, 2.533; 3.18, 83; 4.365, 420; 5.224 and n. 3, 272 • *Ann. mon.*, 3.159, 167, 181; 4.440, 127 • I. J. Sanders, *English baronies: a study of their origin and descent, 1086–1327* (1960), 39–40 • G. Barraclough, ed., *The charters of the Anglo-Norman earls of Chester, c.1071–1237*, Lancashire and Cheshire RS, 126 (1988), 416 • A. Hughes, *List of sheriffs for England and Wales: from the earliest times to AD 1831*, PRO (1898); repr. (New York, 1963)

Cantilupe, William (III) de (*d.* 1254), baron, was the son of William (II) de *Cantilupe (*d.* 1251), steward to Henry III. In 1238 William (II) acquired the wardship and marriage of Eva, one of the coheirs of William (V) de Briouze (*d.* 1230), and by July 1241 Eva and William (III) were married. The Cantilupe family lands lay at Eaton Bray, Bedfordshire, and at Aston Cantlow, Warwickshire. By his marriage, however, William (III) became lord of Abergavenny and an important marcher baron; after 1245 he and his wife acquired additional lands in the marches and in the south-west through the inheritance of Eva's mother, Eva Marshal, one of the coheirs to the Marshal earldom of Pembroke.

His wife's inheritance brought Cantilupe into fierce conflict with John of Monmouth between 1248 and 1253 over Penrhos Castle, a conflict that may lie behind Matthew Paris's story, otherwise uncorroborated, that the king treated Cantilupe harshly in 1251 on his succession to his father's estates. Otherwise his relations with the king were consistently good. He served on Henry's military expedition of 1242–3 to Gascony, and from January 1243 received an annual fee of £50 at the exchequer. He also received frequent gifts of deer and timber from the royal forests. In 1253–4 he served again with the king in Gascony, emerging as one of the king's most important courtiers. He was still with the king in mid-July 1254, but must have returned to England soon afterwards, perhaps in ill health. He died on 25 September 1254 and was buried at Studley Priory, Warwickshire, where his grandfather, William (I), was also buried. Simon de Montfort, earl of Leicester, a distant relative who had served with him in Gascony, and Humphrey (V) de Bohun, earl of Hereford and the husband of Eva's sister Eleanor, laid his body in the grave. Like others of his family, Cantilupe was devoted to the crusade, and left a substantial sum of money in his will to redeem his own unfulfilled crusading vow. This money eventually went to William de Valence, the king's half-brother, to forward his own crusading intentions.

Eva de Cantilupe died around 20 July 1255. Of their three children, Sir George de *Cantilupe died childless in 1273, soon after he came of age. His inheritance then passed to his two elder sisters: Joanna (*d.* 1271), who married Henry Hastings (*d.* 1269), and whose son John inherited Abergavenny; and Millicent (*d.* 1299), who married first John de Montalt and second Eudo de la Zouche (*d.* 1279), and whose son William Zouche (*d.* 1352) eventually inherited Eaton Bray. ROBERT C. STACEY

Sources *Chancery records* (RC) • Paris, *Chron.* • *Ann. mon.* • I. J. Sanders, *English baronies: a study of their origin and descent, 1086–1327* (1960) • D. A. Carpenter, 'St. Thomas Cantilupe: his political career', *St Thomas Cantilupe, bishop of Hereford: essays in his honour*, ed. M. Jancey (1982), 57–72 • J. R. Maddicott, *Simon de Montfort* (1994) • C. Roberts, ed., *Excerpta è rotulis finium in Turri Londinensi asservatis, Henrico Tertio rege, AD 1216–1272*, 2 vols., RC, 32 (1835–6) • *CIPM*, vol. 1 • F. Michel, C. Bémont, and Y. Renouard, eds., *Rôles Gascons*, 4 vols. (1885–1962), vols., 1–3

Wealth at death wealthy: *CIPM*

Cantlie, Sir James (1851–1926), physician and medical administrator, was born on 17 January 1851 at Keithmore Farm, Dufftown, Banffshire, the eldest son of William and Janet Cantlie. Growing up on his father's farm, he absorbed a strong sense of duty and obligation, and the ethics of the Scottish clan remained with him throughout his life. Often in the course of his long medical career he would offer his services free of charge, and he took a great interest in the welfare of those less fortunate than himself. The forthright manner in which he was later to express many of his views on social issues can also be attributed to the formative influences of his childhood, especially that of his father, who was known as the 'biggest Tory in Banffshire', on account of his massive size and independent, though conservative, views. Cantlie resembled his father in both these respects, and his broad shoulders, strong arms, and deep chest made him a powerful boxer and batsman. His pride in his Scottish ancestry also showed itself in his enduring interest in the music, poetry, and language of his homeland.

The young James Cantlie received his education first at Botriphnie's School in the nearby village of Drummuir and then, from the age of thirteen, at Milne's Institution at Fochabers, Speyside. Two years later Cantlie passed the bursary examination for the University of Aberdeen, where he matriculated in 1866. At Aberdeen Cantlie studied both sciences and arts; he graduated in 1871 MA in natural science. By this time he had taken the decision to enter the medical profession and to this end he began training at Aberdeen. After one year he left to join his friend J. Mitchell Bruce at the Charing Cross Hospital, London, for the summer session; he returned to Aberdeen to graduate MB CM in 1873 with honourable distinction.

Cantlie next returned to London to take up a post as instructor in anatomy at the Charing Cross Hospital, where he later became demonstrator in anatomy, house physician, house surgeon, and surgical registrar successively. During his time there he developed an interest in first aid, as the hospital received many accident victims. This led him to join the newly formed St John Ambulance Association, in which he became an instructor. His interest in first aid also extended to the battlefield, and in 1882 he joined the London Scottish Volunteers as a surgeon; this service convinced Cantlie that medical aid for non-regular forces was too inflexible, owing to the strong attachments that developed between medical officers and their regiments. A more flexible system was needed, whereby a pool of medical labour would be available for work wherever it was most needed. This was the inspiration behind the Volunteer Medical Staff Corps (established in 1883), which was the brainchild of Cantlie and the army medical reformer George Evatt.

Later in 1883 Cantlie, together with eleven other civilian doctors and six army regulars, volunteered for service in Egypt, where their knowledge of first aid was needed in the treatment of victims of a cholera epidemic. This marked the beginning of Cantlie's lifelong interest in tropical diseases and whetted his appetite for medical work overseas. Before leaving for Egypt, Cantlie became engaged to Mabel Barclay Brown (*d.* 1921), whose father was also a volunteer with the London Scottish. The couple were married in 1884 and had four sons, one of whom—Neil—went on to become director-general of the Army Medical Service.

While in London, Cantlie also developed an interest in the physical condition of the urban poor. He was appalled by the sanitary conditions in the area around Charing Cross and became convinced, too, that lack of fresh air and exercise was leaving an indelible mark on the population—a taint transmitted from one generation to the next. These views were expressed in a controversial paper read at the Parkes Museum in 1885, entitled 'Degeneracy among Londoners', which argued that the poor health and physique of many Londoners was in large part attributable to the absence of ozone from the air they breathed, since overcrowding and industrial pollution had diminished the gas in cities. Cantlie's opinions were widely discussed in the press, in which he was portrayed as a somewhat eccentric and ridiculous figure.

It may have been the unfavourable response to his paper that led Cantlie to accept an invitation from Dr Patrick Manson to replace him at his practice in Hong Kong, though by this time Cantlie's interest in medicine in tropical regions was already firmly established. After arriving in Hong Kong with his wife early in 1887 he threw himself into his work with characteristic vigour. He was actively involved in all aspects of medical work in the colony, including public health, and established the Vaccine Institute, which afterwards provided Hong Kong with a regular supply of high-quality vaccine against smallpox. Cantlie was also involved in fighting an epidemic of bubonic plague in 1895, which experience later led to his appointment as an adviser to the India Office after bubonic plague arrived in Bombay in 1896. However, Cantlie's most lasting achievement in Hong Kong was the establishment of a medical college for Chinese students, located at the Alice Memorial Hospital. One of the first to graduate from the college, which opened in October 1887, was Sun Yatsen, who in 1911 became the first president of the Chinese republic.

In 1896, after nine exhausting years in Hong Kong, Cantlie returned to London to take the chair of applied anatomy at the Charing Cross Hospital. Soon afterwards he was informed that Sun Yatsen had been kidnapped and imprisoned at the Chinese legation in London and that he was to be sent to China to face trial (and almost certain execution) for sedition. Cantlie immediately organized a watch on the legation, which ultimately involved the Metropolitan Police. At the same time, news of the kidnap reached the press, which mounted a successful campaign for the release of Sun Yatsen. Sun remained a friend of the Cantlies until his death in 1925.

By virtue of his experiences in Hong Kong, Cantlie had gained a reputation as an expert in tropical diseases and he began to build up a successful private practice in this field. He was famed particularly for his treatment of tropical liver abscess, on which he wrote many articles. His interest in tropical medicine also led to his decision to found, with Dr William Simpson (a former health officer in Calcutta), a new journal devoted to the subject: the *Journal of Tropical Medicine and Hygiene*, which was first published in August 1898. Cantlie remained an editor of the journal for twenty-three years. He also assisted Patrick Manson in his efforts to establish a school of tropical medicine in London. These efforts were successful and Cantlie became the first surgeon and lecturer in tropical surgery at the London School of Tropical Medicine, which opened in 1899.

Cantlie's return to London also reawakened his interest in the physical condition of the British people, and his reflections on this subject were published in 1906 under the title *Physical Efficiency*. In many respects the book was typical of the alarmist writings on physical deterioration which abounded in the period after the Second South African War, but some of the opinions expressed in it were rather idiosyncratic, even by the standards of the time. Among other things Cantlie believed that all prospective wives should be required to pass an examination in cookery before they could obtain a marriage licence.

Cantlie's other great, enduring commitment was to first aid and organizations for emergency medical aid. He continued his association with St John's and the volunteers, and he acted as an adviser to the War Office on the establishment of the medical section of the Territorial Force (later the Territorial Army), formed in 1907. During the

First World War he and his wife also became commandants in the British Red Cross Society, which was charged with co-ordinating voluntary medical aid. As well as their duties with the Red Cross, the Cantlies found time to found a College of Ambulance (which continued in existence until 1923) and a humanitarian corps to aid those in distress because of disease or poverty. For these services Cantlie was made a knight of the British empire in 1918 and, in the following year, his wife was appointed OBE for her wartime work with voluntary aid detachments under the Red Cross. In 1919 Cantlie also received an honorary LLD degree from the University of Aberdeen.

These honours marked the peak of Cantlie's career, after which his life was blighted by sadness and physical decline. Cantlie never fully recovered from his exertions during the war and from the death of his beloved wife on 21 December 1921. In 1925 he retired to live near his sister in Scotland and the following January he experienced a severe haemorrhage, which led to his being admitted to a nursing home in Aberdeen. After moving to a succession of nursing institutions, Cantlie died at Dorset Square, London, on 28 May 1926. He was buried at Cottered cemetery, Buntingford, Hertfordshire. His lifelong friend, Dr J. Mitchell Bruce, remembered Cantlie as 'essentially an inventor … a pioneer in things great and small' (*BMJ*, 5 June 1926, 972), and this is probably the best description of his long and varied career. MARK HARRISON

Sources N. Cantlie and G. Searer, *Sir James Cantlie: a romance in medicine* (1939) • J. C. Stewart, *The quality of mercy: the lives of Sir James Cantlie* (1983) • *BMJ* (5 June 1926), 971–2 • *The Lancet* (5 June 1926), 1121–2 • J. R. Harris, 'Sir James Cantlie (1851–1926)', *Journal of Tropical Medicine*, 76 (1973), 185–6 • *WWW*

Archives Wellcome L., diaries, case books, and lectures • Wellcome L., papers relating to Sir James Cantlie and Lady Mabel Cantlie | Wellcome L., lectures, diaries, casebooks • Wellcome L., Royal Army Medical Corps muniment collection

Likenesses H. H. Salomon, oils (after photograph), Wellcome L. • F. C. Stoate, photograph, Wellcome L. • photograph, repro. in Cantlie and Searer, *Sir James Cantlie* • photograph, repro. in Stewart, *The quality of mercy*

Wealth at death £721 6*s*. 6*d*.: administration with will, 23 Nov 1926, *CGPLA Eng. & Wales*

Canton, John (*bap.* **1718**, *d.* **1772**), experimental philosopher and schoolmaster, was born at Stroud, Gloucestershire, and baptized in the old chapel there on 31 July 1718, the son of John Canton, a broadcloth weaver. He was expected to follow his father's trade, and left school early to start an apprenticeship. He persisted with his studies in the evenings, however, and his father was eventually persuaded to allow him to go to London to follow a career more suited to his talents. He first boarded with Dr Henry Miles, dissenting minister at Tooting and himself a native of Stroud, who had encouraged him in his studies. Then in May 1737 he articled himself to Samuel Watkins, master of the Spital Square Academy, London. Here he remained for the rest of his days. After five years' training he entered into partnership with Watkins and in 1745 succeeded him as proprietor of the school, which was a well-regarded establishment and continued to be so under Canton.

In London, Canton became a contributor of riddles and verses to the *Gentleman's* and *London* magazines, and he supplied calculations of lunar eclipses to the *Ladies' Diary*. An active group of practically inclined mathematicians and instrument makers was emerging in London at this period, and Canton, whose amiable character and manners were remarked upon, found himself in congenial company. On Christmas day 1744 he married Penelope Colebrooke, niece of the London banker James Colebrooke, and together they raised three sons.

John Canton (*bap.* **1718**, *d.* **1772**), by unknown artist, 1740s

Canton was caught up by the enthusiasm for electrical experimentation following the discovery in 1746 of the so-called Leiden experiment, in which a glass jar partly filled with water that was then electrified was found to deliver, in some mysterious way, a much more powerful shock than any previously known. Canton is reported to have been among the first to repeat the experiment successfully. Although he was later to make important contributions in this field, his first published effort, two problems in the *Gentleman's Magazine* in January 1747, received a sneering response from Benjamin Wilson and John Smeaton. Comments on current thermometrical practice, published in the following year, fared better. They displayed a clarity of understanding still rare at the time, not long after the first reliable thermometers had been invented, and revealed that Canton had embarked on a programme of systematic meteorological recording.

Much more original was Canton's invention of a technique for magnetizing iron bars to produce artificial magnets. A way of doing this had been discovered shortly before by Gowin Knight, who kept the method secret while he sought to exploit its commercial possibilities; these were considerable on account of the consequential improvements to the mariner's compass. Knight's success encouraged others to take up the subject. Canton seems to have begun experimenting in 1747 out of frustration at the price Knight wanted to charge him for a pair of magnets. His first successes led him to toy briefly with the idea of going into business himself. He showed his method to visitors including David Fordyce, professor at Aberdeen, who may have been responsible for Canton's being awarded an MA degree by King's College, Aberdeen, in April 1750. John Michell in Cambridge had also been experimenting on producing magnets and in 1750 published his method. This prompted Canton to report his own, very similar, technique to the Royal Society, of which he had that year become a fellow. Michell accused him of plagiarism but no one in London believed the charge since they knew that Canton had been producing magnets for several years. So unconvinced of the allegation were members of the Royal Society, indeed, that the society awarded him its Copley medal for 1751 for his work.

Canton retained his interest in electricity. In 1752 he was the first person in England to repeat the successful French trial of Benjamin Franklin's proposed experiment to demonstrate the electrical character of lightning, by drawing electricity from thunderclouds with a conducting wire pointed skywards from the window of his school. A year later he published his major contribution to the subject, on what became known as electrostatic induction. In his experiments, extremely simple in conception, the behaviour of a pair of suspended cork balls, sometimes electrified and sometimes not, was observed under different circumstances as the balls were approached by variously electrified objects. The experiments bore crucially on one of the leading questions in electrical theory at the time, the nature and properties of the supposed atmospheres of electric fluid that were thought to surround electrified bodies and give rise to the attractions or repulsions between them. Canton interpreted his experiments within the overall theoretical framework laid out shortly before by Franklin, though he envisaged atmospheres not as static accumulations of electric fluid, as Franklin did, but in more dynamic terms. His work forced Franklin and others to elaborate their own ideas more fully, but few at first followed Aepinus, who in 1759 abandoned the notion of atmospheres altogether and relied instead on a fully articulated action-at-a-distance theory of electrical action. Canton did, however, in the same year confirm Aepinus's experiments on the extraordinary electrical properties of the tourmaline crystal, which provided important new evidence in support of Franklin's notion that two opposing modes of electrification were possible in nature. He was also sufficiently persuaded by Aepinus's discussion that he eventually abandoned his dynamic view of an electrical atmosphere, seeing it instead in quasi-field terms as an alteration in the state of the electric fluid in the air surrounding an electrified body.

Canton was by this time widely regarded as one of the leading English experimental philosophers of his day. His standing was further enhanced by his demonstration in 1762 that, contrary to what had long been believed, water was compressible. The experiment was difficult and Canton's interpretation was controversial. It brought him nomination in 1764 for a second Copley medal, but the award was delayed for almost a year, pending an investigation by a Royal Society committee. In some of his other papers presented to the society Canton discussed the diurnal variation of the compass needle; reported observations of the transits of Mercury (1753) and Venus (1761 and 1769) across the face of the sun; announced the discovery of 'Canton's phosphor', a strongly phosphorescent compound produced from sulphur and calcined oyster shells; and argued (correctly) that the luminescence of sea water was due to decaying organic matter.

Canton attended meetings of the Royal Society regularly and was elected three times, in 1751, 1754, and 1763, to serve on the society's council. Fond of good company, he was a leading spirit in the dining club comprising mostly dissenting ministers and schoolmasters, liberal in politics and interested in natural philosophy, that Franklin, a regular attender when in London, called the 'Club of Honest Whigs'. Canton and Franklin became firm friends and, with another honest whig, Richard Price, provided crucial support for Joseph Priestley in the early stages of his literary and scientific career. Devoted to his profession and to the science to which he had contributed so notably, Canton died at a comparatively early age on 22 March 1772, his 'close and sedentary life' being blamed by his friends for the dropsy that carried him off. The Spital Square Academy was carried on by his second son, William.

R. W. Home

Sources A. Kippis and others, eds., *Biographia Britannica, or, The lives of the most eminent persons who have flourished in Great Britain and Ireland*, 2nd edn, 3 (1784) • *DSB*, 3.51–2 • J. L. Heilbron, *Electricity in the 17th and 18th centuries: a study of early modern physics* (1979) • E. N. Harvey, *A history of luminescence* (1957) • V. W. Crane, 'The Club of Honest Whigs: friends of science and liberty', *William and Mary Quarterly*, 23 (1966), 210–33 • R. W. Home, *Electricity and experimental physics in eighteenth-century Europe* (1992) • *A scientific autobiography of Joseph Priestley*, ed. R. E. Schofield (1966) • [A. De Morgan], 'The Canton papers [pt 1]', *The Athenaeum* (6 Jan 1849), 5–7 • [A. De Morgan], 'The Canton papers [pt 2]', *The Athenaeum* (17 Feb 1849), 162–4 • [A. De Morgan], 'The Canton papers [pt 3]', *The Athenaeum* (14 April 1849), 375 • P. Rivoire, ed., *Traités sur les aimants artificiels* (1753) • parish register (baptism), 31 July 1718, Stroud, Gloucester CRO

Archives NA Scot., papers relating to pneumatic experiments • RS, corresp. and papers

Likenesses oils, 1740–49, NPG [*see illus.*] • portrait (photographic copy), RS, Canton MSS

Canton, William (1845–1926), poet and journalist, the eldest son of Thomas Canton of the colonial civil service and his wife, Mary Thomas, was born on 27 October 1845 on the island of Chushan, off the coast of China. His father died in Jamaica when he was nine, and his schooldays were spent in France, where 'the sudden discovery of a cromlech in a cornfield inspired him with a passion for antiquity', which became perhaps the most individual quality of his writing. His parents were Catholics, and for a while he studied for the priesthood at the Benedictine College at Douai in Picardy. But as a young man he left the Roman Catholic church and became a protestant. Early friendships, and the estrangement inevitable from his change of faith, found utterance in the lyric 'The Comrades' (published in a collection of the same name, 1902) and in his beautiful story 'The Lost Brother' (published in *A Child's Book of Saints*, 1898). From 1867 he was a teacher and journalist in London. In 1873 his long poem 'Through the Ages: the Legend of a Stone Axe', published in the *New Quarterly Magazine*, aroused T. H. Huxley's enthusiasm as 'the first attempt to use the raw material of science' for poetry. In 1874 Canton married Emma (*d.* 1880), daughter of Charles Moore. The only child of the marriage, a daughter, died in 1877 and was commemorated in *The Invisible Playmate* (1894), the first prose work which won him recognition.

In 1876 Canton began fifteen years of writing for papers in Glasgow, initially as editor of the *Glasgow Weekly Herald* and then as sub-editor and leader writer of the *Glasgow Herald*, which made many assume him to be a Scot—and as such he was attacked in T. W. H. Crosland's diatribe *The Unspeakable Scot*. In 1882 he married his second wife, Annie Elizabeth, daughter of John Ingham Taylor of Manchester, a civil engineer; a daughter, Winifred Vida, was born in 1890 and a son, Guy Desmond, in 1896. In 1891 Canton went to London as general manager to the publishers Isbister & Co., and shortly after became sub-editor of the *Contemporary Review* and editor of the *Sunday Magazine*. He also wrote a large amount of prose and verse for *Good Words*. However, he made his reputation by his own independent work. *A Lost Epic and other Poems* appeared in 1887 and won the admiration of Max Müller, T. E. Brown, and Walter Pater. The 'W. V.' (Winifred Vida) books—*The Invisible Playmate* (1894), *W. V. her Book* (1896), *A Child's Book of Saints* (1898), *In Memory of W. V.* (1901)—gained him a large public.

Winifred Vida died in 1901, and Canton then undertook the task of writing the official *History of the British and Foreign Bible Society* in the hope that the heavy workload would prove an anodyne. It occupied nine years of conscientious labour, and when he at last emerged into literary daylight he found himself all but forgotten. Thereafter, his work was all definitely commissioned. Much was in small popular books for the Bible Society, the last being finished, with the exception of the final chapter, the night before he died. Imaginative relief came rarely to him, but it did so notably in *The Story of St Elizabeth of Hungary* (1912). He was granted a civil-list pension in 1912, and in 1925 his friends collected a sum to mark his eightieth birthday. In the same year, Ernest Benn Ltd published a short selection of his verse in their Augustan series, compiled mainly by his lifelong friend and admirer Edward J. Thompson, the first author of this memoir. On 2 May 1926 Canton died at Hendon, London, where he had lived since 1912.

Canton's verse lacked lyrical impulse, except in the elegiac poems included in *In Memory of W. V.* An earlier generation considered his poems of childhood his finest achievement, but a later age may well consider them marred by a cult of the trivial, the domestic, or the merely pretty. His longer poems are of two kinds: classical, influenced, but remaining individual, by Tennyson's 'Oenone' and 'Tithonus' and, still more, by Robert Browning's 'Cleon' and 'Artemis Prologises'; and those that must be termed antiquarian. The latter are a good expression of the immense change in imaginative outlook which followed the mid-Victorian discovery of the almost immeasurable antiquity of man and of animal life generally. The 'W. V.' books are the best of his prose works, written in a whimsical, light style, allusive in a poetical and not merely scholarly fashion, and often profoundly moving. His eager, courageous spirit, which expression in literature was so often clogged and jaded, showed itself in his private letters; very few who received his correspondence destroyed any of it, notably the first author of this piece himself. E. J. THOMPSON, *rev.* NILANJANA BANERJI

Sources *The poems of William Canton* (1927) [foreword by G. D. Canton] · A. H. Miles, ed., *The poets and the poetry of the nineteenth century*, 7 (1906) [note by J. A. Noble] · personal knowledge (1937) · private information (1937)

Archives NRA, corresp. and literary papers | Bodl. Oxf., corresp. with E. J. Thompson · U. Leeds, Brotherton L., letters to Edmund Gosse

Likenesses J. Russell & Sons, photograph, NPG · photograph, repro. in *Poems of William Canton* (1927)

Cantrell, Henry (*bap.* 1684, *d.* c.1773), Church of England clergyman and religious controversialist, was baptized on 17 September 1684 at St Oswald's, Ashbourne, Derbyshire, the son of Simon Cantrell (1658–1744). He was educated at Derby School, and then admitted sizar at Emmanuel College, Cambridge, matriculating in 1701. He proceeded to his BA in 1705 and his MA in 1710. He was ordained at Lichfield in 1709. In March 1712 he was presented by the corporation of Derby to the vicarage of St Alkmund, Derby, newly created from a perpetual curacy following its endowment by Samuel Goodwin, gentleman. He held the living until his death. The corporation further endowed the living in 1713 with the small tithes. Cantrell immediately attacked dissenters, preaching that 'Dissenting teachers have no authority to baptize, and consequently that children … sprinkled by 'em, ought to baptiz'd by an Episcopal minister' (St Alkmund's register, 5 Nov 1712). His refusal to bury children baptized by dissenting ministers provoked a major controversy involving Ferdinando Shaw (1674–1745), minister of the Presbyterian meeting in Derby, and more than twenty pamphlets were issued by local authors. It formed part of a wider attack by high-churchmen on Presbyterian ordination. In answer to Shaw's *Validity of Baptism Administred by Dissenting Ministers* (1713), Cantrell published the *Invalidity of the Lay-Baptisms of Dissenting Teachers, Prov'd from Scripture and Antiquity* (1714). Cantrell had the better of the scholarly argument, but his bishop refused to countenance the practice of denying burial to those baptized by dissenting ministers. None the less, the Presbyterians in Derby were forced to establish their own burial-ground in 1714. Shaw's claim that Charles I had not received baptism from an episcopal minister provoked Cantrell's major work, *The royal martyr a true Christian, or, A confutation of a late assertion, viz. that King Charles I had only the lay-baptism of a Presbyterian-teacher*. The original research in the heralds' office in Edinburgh was not Cantrell's work, but information from the high-church friends of Arthur Charlett, master of University College, Oxford.

Cantrell was a quarrelsome man whose high-church opinions gave him an exalted view of the rights of the clergy and of the church. As a result he was in frequent conflict with his parishioners in defending even the smallest clerical right or privilege. Before his induction he clashed with his vestry over the right to choose one of the churchwardens. Subsequently he was involved in disputes over the disposal of the sacrament money, control of the parish register, the misappropriation of the communion wine, and the planting of trees in the churchyard by which he did 'so darken the Church & injure the rights of the parish to bury' (St Alkmund's vestry book, 307). His lawsuit with the corporation over the small tithes, which they originally gave him but later removed because he behaved himself 'very Insolently & Indecently' to the mayor (BL, MS Stowe 119, fol. 76*v*), cost him grievously although the case was eventually decided in his favour in 1729. Cantrell typically saw his defence of his right to small tithes against 'their sacrilegious usurpation' as part of a wider defence of clerical rights (Bodl. Oxf., MS Ballard 25, fol. 40*v*). Indeed, he claimed that the suit was commenced by the corporation about the time of the publication of his *Invalidity* 'to ruine me' (ibid., fol. 42*v*). Forced to sell much of his library, 'as good as any of my Brethren here of my age' (ibid., fol. 42*v*), he appealed to the Oxford colleges for charity. He was offered the vicarage of Brecon (which he declined after some months' trial) through the influence of his 'good friend' Dr Sacheverell, the high-church incendiary. When Dr Michael Hutchinson was in dispute with the Derby corporation over his resignation of All Saints in 1727, Cantrell, acting as his substitute, opposed the corporation's nominee by occupying the pulpit. William Hutton's claim in his *History of Derby* (1791) that in 1745 Cantrell drank the Pretender's health 'on his knees' is probably untrue. There is no evidence that he was a Jacobite.

Cantrell had one moment of national significance. His action as surrogate in granting a marriage licence for the clandestine marriage of Annabella, daughter of Robert Wilmot of Osmaston, Derbyshire, provoked the 1733 Ecclesiastical Courts Bill to reform abuses. Cantrell's commonplace book and publications provide evidence of his scholarship. In 1760 he sent Samuel Pegge, the Derbyshire antiquary, information on the history of Derby and St Alkmund's Church. He married twice, first, Constance (1695/6–1725), who died on 24 May 1725, and second, on 2 August 1732, Jane, daughter of Joseph Cradock, rector of Markfield, Leicestershire. William (1716–1787), his eldest surviving son with his first wife, was rector of St Michael, Stamford, and later of Normanton. Cantrell died probably in or about 1773. DAVID L. WYKES

Sources vestry book, St Alkmund's parish, Derby, 1698–1783, Derbys. RO, D916A/PV 1/1 · register, St Alkmund's parish, Derby, 1538–1751, Derbys. RO, D916A/PI 1/1 · H. Cantrell, commonplace book, Derbys. RO, D916A/PI 69 · H. Cantrell, letters to the Revd Dr Arthur Charlett, Bodl. Oxf., MS Ballard 25, fols. 40*r*–64*r* · J. C. Cox and W. H. S. Hope, *The chronicles of the collegiate church or free chapel of All Saints, Derby* (1881) · J. C. Cox, *Notes on the churches of Derbyshire*, 4: *The hundreds of Morleston and Litchurch* (1879), 4.90–93, 116–17 · copy of lease by mayor and burgesses of Derby to Henry Cantrell, vicar of St Alkmund's, Derby, 27 May 1732, BL, Woolley MS 6671, fols. 229–236 · 'The case between the corporation of Derby and Mr [Henry] Cantrell', 1715, BL, MS Stowe 119, fols. 74*r*–90*r* · Bishop's Visitation, July 1710–Oct 1723, Lichfield RO, B/V/1/94 · Consistory Court Books, Jan 1712–June 1716, Lichfield RO, B/C/2/92–3 · Cause Papers, Lichfield RO, B/C/5/1714, tithe case · Venn, *Alum. Cant.* · Foster, *Alum. Oxon.* · L. Eardley-Smith, *Derby and the forty-five* (1933), 14 · B. Tacchella, ed., *The Derby School register, 1570–1901* (1902), 8 · F. Shaw, *The validity of baptism administred by dissenting ministers* (1713) · parish register, St Oswald's, Ashbourne, Derbyshire, 17 Sept 1684, Derbys. RO [baptism]

Archives Derbys. RO, St Alkmund's parish records, commonplace book, D916A/PI 69 | Bodl. Oxf., MS Ballard 25

Cantwell, Andrew (*d.* 1764), physician, was born in co. Tipperary, Ireland, and studied medicine in France, graduating from Montpellier University in 1729. In 1732 he attempted, but failed, to secure the succession to the chair of medicine at Montpellier, left vacant by the death of Jean Astruc. In 1735 Cantwell moved to Paris and continued his medical studies, becoming doctor of the Paris faculty in 1742. He was appointed professor of surgery in the Latin language at Paris in 1750; in 1760 he became professor of the same subject in French; and in 1762 professor of pharmacy. Cantwell was one of the bitterest and most persistent opponents of inoculation against smallpox, which was widely adopted in western Europe during the second half of the eighteenth century. In spite of the censure of many clergymen and of many members of the medical profession, inoculation became first established in England, and Cantwell accordingly paid an extended visit to England in order to study the practice and its results. Cantwell initially embraced inoculation after reading a pamphlet by James Jurin, an English physician who demonstrated statistically the lower risks of inoculation over natural smallpox. Cantwell witnessed at least five inoculations, all successful, but none the less was not convinced of the benefits of inoculation.

Cantwell attacked the practice in two works, published in Paris: *Dissertation sur l'inoculation* (1755) and *Tableau de la petite vérole* (1758). In his *Dissertation* he presented several case histories where inoculation resulted in either death or disfigurement, and instances of inoculated individuals who later contracted natural smallpox. Cantwell also dismissed statistical arguments put forth by James Jurin and Charles Marie de La Condamine which indicated the lower risks of inoculated over natural smallpox, because these statistics were based on very different population groups. Only the healthy got inoculated, while it was mostly the poor who succumbed to smallpox. Further, Cantwell argued that inoculation caused smallpox epidemics, thus increasing the mortality due to this disease. These arguments resurfaced in England in the 1770s and 1780s when the benefits of general and partial inoculations were debated.

Cantwell also wrote numerous medical treatises in Latin and French and served as an important conduit between the medical communities of France and Britain.

His translations of English works into French included Hans Sloane's *An Account of a Medicine for Soreness, Weakness, and other Distempers of the Eyes* (1745), and Stephen Hales's *An account of some experiments and observations on Mrs. Stephens's medicines for dissolving the stone* (1740).

Cantwell was elected a fellow of the Royal Society in 1738, and contributed several articles to the *Philosophical Transactions*. He died at Paris on 11 July 1764.

ANDREA RUSNOCK

Sources N. F. J. Eloy, *Dictionnaire historique de la médecine ancienne et moderne*, 4 vols. (Mons, 1778), vol. 1 • A. J. L. Jourdan, ed., *Biographie médicale*, 7 vols. (1820–25) • *The record of the Royal Society of London*, 4th edn (1940)

Canute. *See* Cnut (*d.* 1035).

Canvane, Peter (1720–1786), physician, was born on St George's Island, Bermuda. He studied medicine at Rheims, graduating MD in 1742; in 1743 he went to Leiden and in 1744 he became a licentiate of the Royal College of Physicians, London. He practised for many years in St Kitts, in the West Indies, and afterwards settled in Bath. He became a fellow of the Royal Society in 1765, and shares with Thomas Fraser, an army surgeon, the credit of introducing castor oil into Britain, having had large experience of its use in medicine in the West Indies. He published a pamphlet, *A Dissertation on the Oleum palmae Christi, sive, Oleum ricini*, on the subject in 1765. Canvane later retired to the continent; he died in Brussels in 1786.

G. T. BETTANY, *rev.* CAROLINE OVERY

Sources Munk, *Roll* • R. W. Innes Smith, *English-speaking students of medicine at the University of Leyden* (1932) • P. J. Wallis and R. V. Wallis, *Eighteenth century medics*, 2nd edn (1988)

Canville [Camville], **Gerard de** (*d.* 1214), administrator, was a member of a Norman family originating from Canville-les-Deux-Églises (Seine-Inférieure). He was the son of Richard de *Canville [*see under* Canville, Richard de], lord of Middleton Stoney, Oxfordshire, and his first wife, Alice. His father came to prominence during the reign of Stephen, of whom he was a loyal supporter, and continued to serve under Henry II until his death in 1176, when Gerard succeeded him in nearly all his lands. After 1174 Gerard de Canville was a regular witness to royal *acta*; he enjoyed Henry II's favour, and in 1180 was excused £800 of his father's debts in Normandy. Some time before 1185 he married Nicola de la *Haie (*d.* 1230), eldest daughter of Richard de la Haie, hereditary castellan of Lincoln, who had died in 1169, and widow of William Fitzerneis. Through her he acquired both the castellanship and her inheritance in England and Normandy. Following the accession of Richard I these, as well as the shrievalty of Lincoln, were confirmed to Canville for 700 marks.

In 1191 Canville—'a factious and untrustworthy man' according to Richard of Devizes (*Chronicon*, 30), 'a man rich and noble' as William of Newburgh has it (William of Newburgh, *Historia rerum Anglicarum*, ed. R. Howlett, Rolls Series, 1884, 1.337)—did homage to John, count of Mortain, the future king, for Lincoln Castle. Thereupon William de Longchamp (*d.* 1197), the chancellor, removed Canville from the shrievalty, replaced him with William de Stuteville (*d.* 1203), and ordered the surrender of the castle. When this was refused, Canville appealed to John; Longchamp promptly besieged the castle, which was fiercely defended by Nicola. Canville and John then besieged Nottingham and Tickhill, and their capture of these castles brought a compromise at Winchester, which included the restoration of Canville to office until his case could be heard in the royal court. Soon afterwards the chancellor secured Canville's excommunication.

Gerard de Canville was a committed supporter of John, who also appointed him keeper of the honour of Wallingford, and backed the count in his rebellion of 1193. As a consequence, on Richard I's return in 1194 he lost his estates and offices, and was replaced as sheriff by Simon of Kyme (*d.* 1220). He recovered his forfeit land (but not his offices) and the king's goodwill in return for a payment of 2000 marks, while his wife owed the king 300 marks for licence to marry an otherwise unrecorded daughter to anyone save an enemy of the king. Through the chancellor's efforts he was also indicted before the royal court for refusing to give up to royal justice robbers he was allegedly protecting, and for his support of Count John at Nottingham and Tickhill, charges he denied and offered to disprove in battle.

After John's accession Canville was regranted Lincoln Castle. He was also appointed sheriff of Lincolnshire, a post he held until 1205. Thereafter he remained until his death a loyal servant of the crown, though comparatively little is known of his career. He was present at Lincoln, perhaps by virtue of office, when William, king of Scots, did homage to John in 1200, and as sheriff he supported the men of Holland, Lincolnshire, in their long-running marshland dispute with Crowland Abbey. In 1208 he supervised the administration of the revenues of the diocese of Lincoln during the interdict, and in 1208–9 served as itinerant justice in Lincolnshire and Cambridgeshire.

Canville's inherited lands comprised lands given to his father in Northamptonshire at Kings Sutton and Duddington, and a fee in Oxfordshire, which was centred on Middleton Stoney where there was a castle and where he was granted a weekly market in 1201, and included the manors of Godington, Oxfordshire, and Avington, Berkshire. The advowson of Middleton was granted to Barlings Priory, Lincolnshire, a Premonstratensian foundation of his wife's family. He seems also to have retained the nine fees the family held of the honour of Mowbray in 1166, which had probably derived from the Stuteville honour. Additionally he held a number of fees in Lincolnshire through his wife.

Canville had at least one daughter, and in 1200 he married his son, Richard, to Eustachia, daughter and heir of Gilbert Basset, and widow of Thomas de Verdon, after offering £1000 for the wardship. Survived by his wife, Gerard de Canville died shortly before January 1215, when his lands passed to Richard, a supporter of the baronial revolt, who died soon after February 1217.

BRIAN GOLDING

Sources *Chronica magistri Rogeri de Hovedene*, ed. W. Stubbs, 4 vols., Rolls Series, 51 (1868–71) • *Chronicon Richardi Divisensis / The Chronicle* *of Richard of Devizes*, ed. J. T. Appleby (1963) • *Pipe rolls* • J. H. Round, ed., *Ancient charters, royal and private, prior to AD 1200*, PRSoc., 10 (1888), 91–2 • *Chancery records* • F. Hill, *Medieval Lincoln* (1965) • *VCH Oxfordshire*, vol. 6 • L. C. Loyd, *The origins of some Anglo-Norman families*, ed. C. T. Clay and D. C. Douglas, Harleian Society, 103 (1951) • D. M. P. Stenton, *English justice between the Norman conquest and the Great Charter, 1066–1215* (1965) • S. Painter, *The reign of King John* (1966) • R. Howlett, ed., *Chronicles of the reigns of Stephen, Henry II, and Richard I*, 1, Rolls Series, 82 (1884) • *CClR, 1227–31*, 458

Canville, Richard de (*d.* **1176**). *See under* Canville, Richard de (*d.* 1191).

Canville [Camville], **Richard de** (*d.* **1191**), soldier, was the son of **Richard de Canville** (*d.* 1176) and his second wife, Millicent, widow of Robert Marmion (*d.* 1143/4), and came of a family originating at Canville-les-Deux-Églises near Yvetot in upper Normandy. In England their most substantial landholding comprised nine knights' fees in the counties of Leicester, Northampton, and Warwick, in 1166 held from the honour of Mowbray by Walter de Canville, who was believed to be a cousin of Richard the elder. The latter also acquired lands in Essex, Warwickshire, and Somerset, and in addition obtained the manor of Stanton Harcourt in Oxfordshire as part of the marriage portion of his second wife, Millicent, a cousin of Adeliza of Louvain (*d.* 1151), second wife of Henry I. He served as a leading member of the household of King Stephen and later of Henry II, by whom he was rewarded with the custody of valuable estates at Little Stretton in Leicestershire and Sutton in Northamptonshire. He accounted as sheriff of Berkshire in 1156, and in 1176 was sent as an envoy to Sicily over the marriage of Henry II's daughter Joan. He died in Apulia that same year, having earlier made numerous gifts to the religious, including the Cistercian abbey of Combe in Warwickshire, which he founded in 1150. He was succeeded in the bulk of his estate by his eldest son, Gerard de *Canville, his son of his first marriage, to Alice.

Richard de Canville the younger (*d.* 1191), who followed his father into the service of Henry II, appears to have inherited his father's land at Stretton and his mother's interest in the manor of Stanton Harcourt. In 1189 he attended the coronation of Richard I, and was appointed one of the commanders of Richard's crusading fleet. He embarked in the spring of 1190 and negotiated a truce at Lisbon with the king of Portugal, before arriving with his ships at Marseilles, where he was joined by King Richard. At Messina in Sicily he was one of the sureties for a truce between Richard and King Tancred, and in the summer of 1191 was appointed joint governor of Cyprus, with Robert of Thornham (*d.* 1211). However, he fell ill soon afterwards, and having rejoined the king at Acre in the Holy Land, died there in June 1191. By his marriage to Hawise, daughter of Walter Fitzwilliam, he acquired the barony of Whalton in Northumberland, but in 1188, in an exchange agreed with his sister-in-law Constance and her husband, Ralph de Crammaville, resigned his rights at Whalton in exchange for land in Leicestershire. His estates at Little Stretton and Stanton Harcourt passed after his death to his daughter Isabella, married to Robert de Harcourt.

NICHOLAS VINCENT

Sources *Reg. RAN* • *Sir Christopher Hatton's Book of seals*, ed. L. C. Loyd and D. M. Stenton, Northamptonshire RS, 15 (1950) • *Chronica magistri Rogeri de Hovedene*, ed. W. Stubbs, 4 vols., Rolls Series, 51 (1868–71) • L. Landon, *The itinerary of King Richard I*, PRSoc., new ser., 13 (1935) • Kenilworth cartulary, BL, Additional charters, 28324, 28326, Add. MS 47677, fols. 363–367 • Coll. Arms, Glover MS B, fol. 9 • D. E. Greenway, ed., *Charters of the honour of Mowbray, 1107–1191* (1972) • P. M. Barnes and C. F. Slade, eds., *A medieval miscellany for Doris Mary Stenton*, PRSoc., new ser., 36 (1962) • *Calendar of the manuscripts of the dean and chapter of Wells*, 1, HMC, 12 (1907) • J. G. Jenkins, ed., *The cartulary of Missenden Abbey*, 3 (1962) • B. R. Kemp, ed., *Reading Abbey cartularies*, 2 vols., CS, 4th ser., 31, 33 (1986–7)

Canville [Camville], **Sir Thomas de** (*d.* **1234/5**), landowner and justice, was the son of Hugh de Canville (*d. c.*1194) and his wife, Christiana, the daughter of William the Monk. His father's family had lands in several counties in southern England and East Anglia, and especially at Shenfield and Fobbing in Essex, and at Westerham in Kent, and took their name from Canville-les-Deux-Églises in Normandy (Seine-Maritime). By 1194 Thomas was old enough to serve with Richard I in Normandy; he was a knight by Easter 1206, when he was named as a juror of the grand assize in Kent. Although he normally paid scutage instead of performing military service, in 1210 he accompanied John to Ireland. By December 1215, however, he had joined the baronial rebels, and his Oxfordshire manor of Godington was confiscated. But following the ending of the civil war he made his peace with the government of Henry III, and in September and October 1217 his lands were restored to him. An apparent report of his death, which in August 1220 led to the grant of custody of his lands and heir to Philip of Oldcotes, proved to be an exaggeration, but Canville played no part in public life for several years afterwards, though he was sufficiently in favour in 1227 to be granted a weekly market and yearly fair at Fobbing, and a weekly market at Westerham.

In September 1227, however, Thomas de Canville was appointed a justice to serve under Martin of Pattishall in eyres in Kent, Essex, and Hertfordshire, and in 1228 and for at least the first two terms of 1229 he also acted as a justice in the common bench. The reasons for his appointment are not apparent, and he is not known to have served again in either capacity after Easter term 1229. He did not go to Brittany with Henry III in 1230, but in 1232 he was one of the collectors of that year's fortieth in Kent. Canville was still alive in July 1234, but was dead by 22 January 1235. He was survived by his wife, Agnes, whose surname is unknown; by 26 July 1236 she had remarried; her new husband was William de Mareny, an Essex landowner. It is likely that she was the mother of Canville's two sons, Robert and John, both of whom were minors at their father's death. The wardship of Robert, the elder son, together with his lands and marriage, was granted to Hamo le Crevequer for a payment of £400. Thomas de Canville was twice a benefactor of nunneries: in or before 1208 he gave land at Fobbing to Barking Abbey, Essex, while after the death of his mother he gave Godington church to Elstow Priory, Oxfordshire. By 1221 he had repented of this second gift, and was denying that he had made it. But the resulting lawsuit ended in April 1222 with

Canville's confirmation of his grant, while in return the nuns 'received him and his heirs in all good works and orisons which shall be done in the abbey' (Salter, 66).

HENRY SUMMERSON

Sources *Chancery records* [PRO and RC] • *Pipe rolls*, 6 Richard I – 17 John • *Curia regis rolls preserved in the Public Record Office* (1922–), vols. 3, 7, 13–14 • T. D. Hardy, ed., *Rotuli de oblatis et finibus*, RC (1835) • H. C. M. Lyte and others, eds., *Liber feodorum: the book of fees*, 3 vols. (1920–31) • C. A. F. Meekings, *Studies in 13th century justice and administration* (1981) • D. Crook, *Records of the general eyre*, Public Record Office Handbooks, 20 (1982) • H. E. Salter, ed., *Feet of fines for Oxfordshire, 1195–1291*, Oxfordshire RS, 12 (1930), 66 • C. Roberts, ed., *Excerpta è rotulis finium in Turri Londinensi asservatis, Henrico Tertio rege, AD 1216–1272*, 1, RC, 32 (1835), 272

Wealth at death custody of lands and heirs valued at £400: Roberts, ed., *Excerpta è rotulis*, 1.272

Canynges, William (1402–1474), merchant and ecclesiastical benefactor, was one of the younger of seven children of John Canynges, clothier and merchant of Bristol, and his wife, Joan Wotton. He was born into a notably successful Bristol family. William Canynges (*d.* 1396) was a wealthy clothier who was five times mayor of Bristol and three times MP. John Canynges, the elder William's second son, died young in 1405 but served twice as mayor and once as MP. His widow, Joan, married by 1408 as her second husband Thomas Young, a man intent on gain who eventually twice served as mayor. He and Joan had two sons. Siblings on both sides flourished. William's elder brother, Thomas Canynges, became a grocer in London and was elected alderman of Aldgate ward in 1445 and lord mayor of London in 1456–7; the elder stepbrother, John Young, also became a London grocer, alderman, and, in 1466–7, lord mayor; the younger stepbrother, Thomas Young (*d.* 1476), trained as a lawyer in the Middle Temple but returned to Bristol and served as recorder from 1441 and as an MP in every parliament, save one, from 1435 to 1455. Interestingly, each time that Canynges represented Bristol, his half-brother was the other MP. William Canynges was thus a member of a prominent family, influential in Bristol and beyond. By 1429 he had made a good marriage, to Joan Burton, a member of another of Bristol's more eminent families; his stepbrother, Thomas, married Joan's sister, Isabel. Canynges had two sons, William and John, both of whom he attempted to set up as country gentlemen; each was married but predeceased their father and died childless. With Canynges's death the dynasty in Bristol petered out.

A substantial legacy of more than £100 from his father's estate was an early advantage to Canynges's commercial career, as were his family connections, but stamina and talent proved more enduring assets. Canynges advanced rapidly, and his youthful undertakings, as bailiff of Bristol in 1432 and constable of the staple in 1436, bespeak early success. He became a grocer in London in 1441, and his name never appears in the aulnage returns, so he seems not to have followed family tradition as a clothier. Rather he devoted his attention to foreign trade and, eventually, to shipping. His trading ventures were directed both towards south-western Europe, with cloth his main commodity (he invested in Robert Sturmy's disastrous Mediterranean venture of 1457), and towards Iceland, the Baltic, and Scandinavia, exporting cloth and importing fish. The breadth of Canynges's interests may explain his success in what were lean years for Bristol. Later he made an unorthodox career decision. The evidence is patchy, but Canynges apparently withdrew from shipping his own merchandise and committed his capital to carrying the goods of others. William Worcester's *Itinerary* mentions nine ships built by Canynges and a tenth lost off Iceland. Given that, to contemporaries, a 200 ton ship was large, two of Canynges's ships, the *Mary Canynges* and the *Mary Redcliffe* at 400 and 500 tons respectively, were big, and the *Mary and John*, at 900 tons, having cost £2666 13*s.* 4*d.* according to Worcester, was a monster. The combined tonnage of Canynges's ships was just short of 3000 tons, and for eight years (presumably in the late 1450s and early 1460s) Canynges employed over 800 men on them. If Worcester is to be trusted, such statistics only emphasize Canynges's pre-eminence in Bristol's mid-fifteenth-century economy.

In these circumstances, the effort that Canynges devoted to Bristol's government is remarkable. He was co-opted to the town council before he reached the age of thirty and served for almost forty years. Having become a bailiff in 1432, he served as sheriff in 1438, and then, in September 1441, when he was less than forty years of age, he was elected mayor for the first time. As well as the stamina needed to discharge a busy round of duties, his next four elections to the office—in 1449, 1456, 1461, and 1466—affirm his effectiveness. Canynges served as one of Bristol's MPs in 1439, 1450–51, and in 1455. During the second of these terms his half-brother, Thomas, a servant by then of Richard, duke of York (*d.* 1460), moved for the recognition of the duke as heir to the king, for which he was imprisoned. Canynges seems to have shared Young's political allegiance: he prevented, during his third mayoralty, the sale in Bristol of gunpowder to be used to the disadvantage of York's cause, and, on the duke's instructions, occupied Bristol Castle 'against the purposed malice' of the duke of Somerset. Canynges also lent Edward IV 500 marks at the start of his reign, and was mayor when the new king visited Bristol in September 1461. In this context Worcester's unconfirmed report that later in Edward's reign Canynges had to pay the king a fine of £2000 *pro pace sua habenda* ('for having peace') is puzzling. What can be said, though, is that the death of his wife, Joan, in mid- or late September 1467, marked a profound turning point. Canynges took holy orders. Whether this prompted Edward's action or whether it was its result (as some contemporaries hinted, Canynges eschewing the remarriage which Edward commanded) is an imponderable.

On 19 September 1467 Bishop John Carpenter of Worcester (*d.* 1476) admitted Canynges, already rector of St Alban's, Worcester, to the order of acolyte, and on 16 April 1468 ordained him priest, collating him both to a canonry in the collegiate church of Westbury-on-Trym and to the prebend of Goodringhill, which gave him a place and voice in the chapter of Westbury. Canynges sang his first mass that Whitsuntide in St Mary Redcliffe. Joan's death prompted Canynges to give fuller expression to a piety previously suggested by the licence of 1454 permitting him to have divine service celebrated within his dwelling house in Redcliffe. He was immensely generous to the parish church of St Mary, repairing and enriching its fabric, greatly adding to its jewels and equipment, and substantially augmenting its auxiliary clergy—his two perpetual chantries, founded in 1466 and 1467, provided for two priests, and an endowment of £340 re-established the two 'St Mary priests' and three clerks. After his wife's death Canynges moved to Westbury, and Bishop Carpenter, who rebuilt and reformed the college there apparently with financial assistance from Canynges, made him dean in June 1469. This he remained for the last five years of his life, trade and town government being now concerns of the past. William Canynges died in November 1474, possibly on the 17th or 19th, and in death his two spiritual allegiances were combined, with a funeral service at Westbury and burial at St Mary Redcliffe. Canynges was buried with his wife in the south aisle in a specially constructed tomb surmounted with their effigies, the male in mayoral robes. Another effigy in canonical vestments in the south transept, said to be of Canynges, was moved from Westbury at its dissolution. CLIVE BURGESS

Sources E. E. Williams, *The chantries of William Canynges in St Mary Redcliffe, Bristol, with a survey of chantries in general and some events in the lives of the Canynges family* (1950) • J. Sherborne, *William Canynges, 1402–1474* (1985) • E. M. Carus-Wilson, ed., *The overseas trade of Bristol in the later middle ages*, 2nd edn (1967) • E. M. Carus-Wilson, *Medieval merchant venturers* (1954) • *Itineraries [of] William Worcestre*, ed. J. H. Harvey, OMT (1969) • P. Nightingale, *A medieval mercantile community: the Grocers' Company and the politics and trade of London, 1000–1485* (1995) • *The maire of Bristowe is kalendar, by Robert Ricart*, ed. L. Toulmin Smith, CS, new ser., 5 (1872)

Likenesses J. Jehner, mezzotint, 1787, BM, NPG • H. Engle, etching, BM, NPG • tomb effigies, St Mary Redcliffe, Bristol

Caparne [*formerly* Caparn], **William John** (1855–1940), artist and horticulturist, was born in Newark-on-Trent, Nottinghamshire, on 17 November 1855, the eldest child of William Horner Caparn, an organist and music teacher, and his wife, Sophia (*b.* 1839/40), the daughter of William Warwick. His father grew irises, and his grandfather and an uncle made their living as seedsmen; as a boy he accompanied the latter to flower shows. The Caparn family was prominent in the civic life of Newark at that period, and a former mayor of that name was perhaps Caparn's great-grandfather.

Brought up in a family in which artistry was valued, Caparn no doubt received every encouragement in a talent for drawing he is said to have displayed from an early age; whether or where that was developed by formal training, however, is unclear. By the age of sixteen he was teaching at an art school, and five years later he was appointed to the newly created position of drawing-master at Oundle School in Northamptonshire, for which he received only a small retainer. There Caparn impinged on general notice only as painter of the drop curtain and scenery for the annual school play. With a private studio of his own he was consequently left with the time and energy to build a reputation professionally, and he was soon exhibiting at the Royal Academy and other leading British galleries.

Marriage, on 5 August 1879, brought Caparn not only a wife, Louisa Jane Atkins (1859/60–1894), and presently a daughter and then a son as well, but also the first garden of his own, in Oundle. Soon he was specializing in bulbous irises, collecting and growing the different species in an unheated greenhouse and painting them as they flowered. Though he was ever averse to being categorized as a floral artist, the superlative results of this merging of his two passions were to win him many Royal Horticultural Society medals. They also brought commissions to provide wood-block illustrations for a book on those plants by a fellow enthusiast, the Cambridge physiologist Michael Foster, and a series of plates of daffodils for a famed grower of those, Peter Barr. Through selective breeding of irises Caparn went on to secure new and more brilliant colours, larger and more numerous blooms, and taller stems—and numerous Royal Horticultural Society awards for those as well. A particular triumph was the surprise emergence, from crosses between a medley of species, of an entirely new group, the 'intermediate' bearded irises, linking the early dwarf kinds to those flowering in late summer. In all Caparn is estimated to have introduced as many as a hundred new varieties into cultivation. An energetic supporter of the Iris Society, he was later elected to honorary membership of both that and its counterpart in America.

The first half of Caparn's life ended abruptly in 1894. The early death of his wife coincided with the arrival at the school of its great reforming headmaster F. W. Sanderson, bent on introducing a curriculum with a novel emphasis on science and engineering. Caparn was required to make way for someone able to teach mechanical drawing, though he was allowed to stay on until the end of the following year.

Reeling from these blows, Caparn took refuge in his painting and embarked on a new life in the relative isolation of Guernsey, adding an 'e' to his surname as if to symbolize the break with the past and the severing of links with England. He may have chosen the island for health reasons, but its benign climate also made it a centre of horticultural propagation, which may have influenced his decision to move there. Determined not to be distracted or compromised by further efforts at earning a living, Caparne opted thenceforward for a reclusive life of austerity with his daughter, Winifred, as sole companion. Through past sales of his work and commissions, which included paintings of the gardens of the wealthy along the French and Italian rivieras, together with perhaps some modest legacies, he had presumably accumulated just enough capital for the two to survive on. The first twenty years of that existence must have been constricted, but about 1920 Caparne acquired a tiny plot on a windswept cliff-top on the island's south coast, put up a ramshackle bungalow, turned a disused tramcar into a studio, and, in face of scepticism from friends, produced from the parched scrubland, with the aid of two substantial greenhouses, a garden of such profusion and interest as to become one of Guernsey's show-pieces. Here he specialized for a time in orchids, though he later turned to South African bulbs, saxifrages, succulents, and cacti.

Caparne's output as an artist was now prolific, and his watercolours and pastels from this period, possibly his most creative one, demonstrate greater spontaneity. Although he held at least two exhibitions locally, he painted essentially for himself, seldom dating his work and parting with pictures only reluctantly—and then as gifts, rarely if ever for money. Some are of value to historians in that they depict the insides of the packing sheds and greenhouses of the local horticultural industry, since largely lost.

Photographs of Caparne show the neat black beard sported by the young schoolmaster replaced in later years by a white and bushy one, but the tall, good-looking man remained recognizably the same. Spared ill health until almost the end, he was still defying the near-total blindness that developed in his last four years to work on one final picture when he died at his home, Bon Port Studio, in the parish of St Martin, on 31 January 1940. Most of his unsold work passed to his daughter, Winifred, at the time of whose death in 1972 it still remained little known. However, after 1980 much returned to Guernsey (Guernsey Museum and Art Gallery, St Peter Port), where several exhibitions have done much to bring about a major upgrading of Caparne's reputation, artistically no less than commercially. D. E. ALLEN

Sources R. Cole, ed., *Caparne, 1856–1940* (1990) [exhibition catalogue, Guernsey Museum and Art Gallery] · *Gardeners' Chronicle*, 3rd ser., 107 (1940), 121–2 · W. G. Walker, *A history of the Oundle schools* (1956) · *Pigot's Nottinghamshire directory* (1837) · *Pigot's Nottinghamshire directory* (1844) · *Pigot's Nottinghamshire directory* (1845) · W. White, *History, gazetteer, and directory of Nottinghamshire* (1832) · *White's Nottinghamshire directory* (1844) · *White's Nottinghamshire directory* (1845) · census returns for Newark, 1861 · b. cert. · m. cert.

Likenesses group portrait, photograph, repro. in Walker, *History of the Oundle schools*, pl. 32 · photographs, repro. in Cole, ed., *Caparne*

Cape, (Herbert) Jonathan (1879–1960), publisher, was born in London on 15 November 1879, the youngest of the seven children of Jonathan Cape, builder's clerk of Cumbrian origin, and his wife, Caroline Page. He received little formal education, and at the age of sixteen he started his career as an errand-boy for Hatchards bookshop in Piccadilly. Four years later, in 1899, he joined the English house of the American publishers Harper & Brothers, where he worked as a travelling salesman, first in the provinces and later in London. In 1904 he moved to the English publisher Gerald Duckworth as London traveller, and later became manager. On 13 June 1907 he married Edith Louisa (1880/1881–1919), the daughter of Francis Creak, an ironmonger. They had two daughters.

In the First World War, Cape served in the Royal Army Ordnance Corps, where he reached the rank of captain. After the war he returned to Duckworth, but early in 1920 he went as manager to the Medici Society: its chief products were coloured reproductions of paintings, with some

(Herbert) Jonathan Cape (1879–1960), by unknown photographer, *c.*1930

book publishing on the side. There he met George Wren Howard, fourteen years his junior, who after taking a degree at Cambridge had fought in the war and was now learning the business. Cape quickly saw that Howard had a fine sense of design in book production, as well as a good business head; the two became friends and allies. After some months they decided that there was no future for them where they were, and that they had better start a new firm of their own. Howard managed to borrow his share of their exiguous starting capital from his father; Cape with no such resource was compelled to look elsewhere. All the time he had been with Duckworth the firm's most profitable author had been Elinor Glyn, and Cape had always advocated cheap editions of her books, which Duckworth had steadfastly refused to issue. Cape persuaded Duckworth to lease him the 'shilling rights' of Elinor Glyn's books, which he republished under the imprint Page & Co.: the profits of this venture helped to provide Cape with his share of the necessary capital.

One thing more was needful: a literary adviser, and for this Cape and Howard engaged Edward Garnett (husband of Constance Garnett), the ablest and most influential publisher's reader of recent time, whom Cape had known at Duckworths. He stayed with Cape until his death in 1937, and it was largely his literary judgement, coupled with Howard's production, which gained the new firm its outstanding reputation for quality during the next two decades.

The firm of Jonathan Cape opened its doors at 11 Gower Street, Bloomsbury, London, on 1 January 1921, and its first publication was a reissue of *Travels in Arabia Deserta* by C. M. Doughty, originally issued in 1888 with no success. This new edition, in two volumes at the huge price of 9 guineas, seemed so risky that it was initially issued jointly with the Medici Society. But its success was prompt and substantial, and long before its appearance it had won the new firm one of its strongest supporters. Knowing that T. E. Lawrence was interested in the book, they persuaded him to write a long introduction for nothing. This eventually led to the firm's publishing Lawrence's *Revolt in the Desert* (1927), *Seven Pillars of Wisdom* (1935), and *The Mint* (1955).

In 1922 Cape purchased the business of A. C. Fifield, a small publisher of independence and judgement, thus adding the works of Samuel Butler, H. G. Wells, Laurence Housman, Lancelot Hogben, and W. H. Davies to his growing list. Cape also regularly visited the United States in search of books, and he led the London publishing industry in importing work by American authors. He was the English publisher of three future Nobel prize-winners (Sinclair Lewis, Ernest Hemingway, and Eugene O'Neill), as well as H. L. Mencken, Sherwood Anderson, Louis Bromfield, Dorothy Canfield, Robert Frost, Carl Sandburg, Edna St Vincent Millay, Margaret Mead, Lewis Mumford, Herman Wouk, and James M. Cain. In 1929 he went into partnership with Harrison Smith to set up a short-lived American company, which published William Faulkner's *As I Lay Dying* (1930).

In 1925 Cape's firm moved to its lasting home at 30 Bedford Square, from which in due course appeared the first, and most of the subsequent, works of H. E. Bates, Duff Cooper, Eric Linklater, J. E. Neale, and C. V. Wedgwood. The children's books of Hugh Lofting and Arthur Ransome were perennially successful, and when Cape heard that Stanley Baldwin was planning to speak at the Royal Literary Fund dinner about *Precious Bane* (1924) by Mary Webb, which Cape had published, he speedily bought the rights of her earlier books from their original publishers and reissued them in an immensely popular collected edition. Cape's many cheap series, of which the Travellers' Library was the most prominent, set a new standard of quality and appearance, and held the field until the arrival of paperbacks. Ten of the first Penguin books were Cape titles: he soon came to regret selling the rights, since the resulting paperback revolution killed his own hardcover reprints.

Several Cape books won the James Tait Black memorial prize, including Percy Lubbock's *Earlham* (1922), Liam O'Flaherty's *The Informer* (1925), and E. H. Young's *Miss Mole* (1930). He also published Robert Graves's *Goodbye to All That* (1929), James Joyce's *Stephen Hero* (1944), Arthur Koestler's *Darkness at Noon* (1940), and works by Roy Campbell, Christopher Isherwood, Henry Williamson, André Maurois, Malcolm Lowry, and Alan Paton.

On 1 October 1927 Cape married again; his second wife was Olyve Vida (1894/1895–1931) who had been an employee in the firm. She was the daughter of M. G. Blackmon, and had recently divorced her first husband, Thomas James. They went on to have a son and a daughter.

Cape won notoriety by publishing Radclyffe Hall's lesbian novel *The Well of Loneliness* (1928), an affair he handled with questionable judgement. When a reviewer, James Douglas, denounced the book as pornographic, Cape appealed to the home secretary, Sir William Joynson-Hicks, who predictably threatened to ban it. Cape then announced that he would cease publication, but he leased the rights to a Parisian press, which smuggled copies into Britain until they were seized by the police. In the subsequent trial Cape's barrister bungled the defence, and the novel was ruled obscene. Fearful of another clash with the censors, Cape was to pass up the opportunity to publish work by Samuel Beckett, Norman Mailer's *The Deer Park* (1955), and Vladimir Nabokov's *Lolita* (1955). He also expurgated fiction by Hemingway and Irwin Shaw. Although he had a low opinion of *Casino Royale* (1953), Cape took on Ian Fleming's James Bond thrillers, which eventually sold millions and generated nearly all of the firm's profits.

Ten years after the death of his second wife, Cape married again, on 16 October 1941. His third wife was Kathleen Mary Webb (1906/1907–1953), the widowed daughter of Philip Wilson, a former librarian at the British Museum. They had one son.

Cape knew his own limitations and stuck to what he knew: general publishing and high-quality books (never attempting to enter the educational, technical, or specialist markets, of which he was ignorant), and his standard remained unusually high. In this he was helped, first by Edward Garnett, and later by the diverse talents of Hamish Miles, David Garnett, Guy Chapman, J. E. Neale, C. V. Wedgwood, Daniel George, and William Plomer.

Cape was a tall, handsome man of commanding stature. He was an extremely hard worker, always keeping the same hours as the most junior member of his staff. By some he was considered a hard man, and he was certainly a shrewd one, but he had a humorous as well as a sentimental side and could sometimes be prevailed upon. He seldom became close personal friends with his authors, but they respected his integrity and admired his thorough knowledge of publishing. Except for reading, and the governorship of Frensham Heights, the co-educational school, he had no other interests. Publishing was his life, and although he suffered two strokes in 1954, he worked at it until his death at his home, 128 Bedford Court Mansions, London, from heart failure on 10 February 1960.

RUPERT HART-DAVIS, *rev.* JONATHAN ROSE

Sources M. S. Howard, *Jonathan Cape, publisher* (1971) · L. Dickson, *Radclyffe Hall at the well of loneliness* (1975) · G. Jefferson, *Edward Garnett: a life in literature* (1982) · V. M. Thompson, *'Not a suitable hobby for an airman': T. E. Lawrence as publisher* (1986) · J. Rose, 'Jonathan Cape Limited', *British literary publishing houses, 1881–1965*, ed. J. Rose and P. J. Anderson, DLitB, 112 (1991) · U. Reading, Jonathan Cape archives · personal knowledge (1971) · private information (1971) · m. certs. · d. cert.

Archives U. Reading | Ransom HRC, letters to T. E. Lawrence

Likenesses photograph, *c.*1930, Jonathan Cape Ltd, London [*see illus.*] · C. Colahan, oils, Jonathan Cape Ltd, London · photographs, repro. in Howard, *Jonathan Cape* · photographs, Jonathan Cape Ltd, London

Wealth at death £121,395 8*s.*: probate, 23 March 1960, *CGPLA Eng. & Wales*

Cape, William (1773–1847). *See under* Cape, William Timothy (1806–1863).

Cape, William Timothy (1806–1863), educationist, born at Walworth, Surrey, on 25 October 1806, was the eldest son of the seven children of **William Cape** (1773–1847), banker and schoolmaster, who was born in Ireby, Cumberland, and who had married Mary Ann Knight (*d.* after 1822) of Tenterden, Kent, in 1805. William Timothy was educated at Merchant Taylors' School, London, with a view to entering the church, and showed great proficiency in his studies. The elder Cape was resident manager of the bank of Brown, Cobb & Co., Lombard Street, but when it failed in 1816 he turned to the importing of tea and finally decided to emigrate. Having obtained letters from Lord Bathurst to Sir Thomas Brisbane, the governor, William Cape, accompanied by his eldest son, sailed for Van Diemen's Land in November 1821. In 1822 they moved to Sydney, where in 1823 the father took over a private school, the Sydney Academy, where William Timothy helped him. In 1824 William Cape became principal of the Sydney public school, with his son as assistant master. After a brief spell at the Sydney Public Free Grammar School, William Timothy Cape became headmaster in 1829, on the resignation of his father. William Cape had had an accident in 1829 which left him lame. He died in Sydney on 19 November 1847.

In 1829, however, William Timothy Cape reopened a private school in Sydney. On 9 April 1831 he married Jane (1811/12–1858), daughter of William Jaques of the survey department. When the high school called Sydney College was founded in 1835, Cape transferred his private pupils to it, and was elected headmaster. He held this office until 1841 when he resigned and in the next year he founded a new private school, Elfred House, at Paddington, Sydney.

Cape was an exacting but popular schoolmaster who strove to fire his pupils with a desire for education and public service, to extend education to poorer boys by helping to found the Sydney Mechanics' School of Art in 1833 (and teaching in it), and to remove education from the damaging sectarian disputes then current. He retired in 1856 and after his wife died on 16 January 1858 he threw himself into public life, in quick succession becoming member of parliament for Wollombi (1859), commissioner of national education, a magistrate, and fellow of St Paul's College within the University of Sydney.

In 1855–6 Cape made a brief visit to England, and went back in 1860 with his younger children, in order to collect educational information. He died of smallpox at 124 Warwick Street, Pimlico, London, on 14 June 1863. His funeral at Brompton was attended by almost all the Australians then in London. His former pupils erected a tablet (destroyed in 1941) to his memory in St Andrew's Cathedral, Sydney.

JOHN WESTBY-GIBSON, *rev.* ELIZABETH BAIGENT

Sources S. H. Smith, 'William Timothy Cape and other pioneers of secondary education in Australia', *Royal Australian Historical Society Journal and Proceedings*, 5 (1919), 201–25 · *GM*, 3rd ser., 15 (1863), 114 · *AusDB* · *CGPLA Eng. & Wales* (1863)

Archives Mitchell L., NSW
Wealth at death under £300: administration, 26 June 1863, *CGPLA Eng. & Wales*

Capel, Arthur, first Baron Capel of Hadham (1604–1649), soldier and politician, was born on 20 February 1604 at Hadham Hall, Hertfordshire, the only son of Sir Henry Capel (*d.* 1622) of Hadham Parva and Theodosia, daughter of Sir Edward Montagu of Boughton, Northamptonshire. He was baptized in Hadham Parva church on 11 March 1604. He matriculated at Queens' College, Cambridge, in the Lent term of 1619. On 28 November 1627 he married Elizabeth (1609/10–1661), the heir of Sir Charles Morrison of Cassiobury, Hertfordshire, and when he joined her estates to his own inheritance on the death of his grandfather, Arthur, in April 1632 (his father having died on 29 April 1622) he became one of the richest men in England. His lands were scattered across ten counties, and brought him a reputed annual income of £7000.

Capel carried on the life of a country gentleman for the rest of the 1630s, and avoided national affairs, perhaps in part because of a disaffection with the government of Charles I, which was so marked in his Montagu cousins. In 1639 he refused to contribute to the king's war against the Scots, and although he made no mark upon the Short Parliament of 1640, in which he represented Hertfordshire, he produced an instant impression upon the Long Parliament when it met in November. Sitting again for Hertfordshire, he became the first MP to present a petition from his shire against the policies of Charles I's personal rule. He also manifested a marked distrust of Roman Catholics, and voted for the death of Charles's principal servant, the earl of Strafford. During the same period, from November 1640 to May 1641, however, he also displayed marked hostility towards the Scottish covenanters who were the allies of the parliamentary radicals, and in particular towards their determination to convert the English church to a Scottish model. His vote against Strafford vexed his conscience ever after; he later confessed that he had given it 'out of base fear of a prevailing party' (Capel 138–9). His opposition to the personal rule had derived from a natural conservatism, which was now offended more by the king's critics. Sensing a potential ally, Charles raised him to the peerage on 5 August 1641.

Capel repaid his monarch from the Lords by opposing the militia ordinance in the crisis of the following winter, and when in May 1642 Charles began to summon his supporters to York, he was one of the first to answer the call. Parliament ordered his impeachment in July, and he subsequently provided the money to raise a hundred horse for the royal army and served himself in the king's life guard, charging with it at Edgehill. In March 1643 he was given his own military command, as lieutenant-general of north Wales, Cheshire, Shropshire, and Worcestershire. He had made his base at Shrewsbury by 23 March, although his commission was not signed until 4 April; his haste may have been due to a parliamentarian advance in Cheshire, the repulse of which became his first duty.

Capel's qualifications for the post were wealth and loyalty, for he lacked any experience of military responsibility, and the result was disastrous. He certainly had disadvantages, for his region had been drained of manpower and money for the royal army, and parliament reinforced his local opponents twice over. On the other hand, he possessed some able officers and initially faced enemy forces in only one of the nine counties upon the resources of which he could draw. In the event, his operations were expensive, cumbersome, and predictable. His attacks on enemy strongholds were always beaten off and the parliamentarian forces ran rings round him in the field. As a result, while consistently disposing of more men than his opponents, he lost more of Cheshire and half of Shropshire. In October 1643 his army was shattered in an attack on Wem, leaving the way open for the enemy to occupy north-east Wales and encircle Chester. He was detested by the local gentry and made the subject of mocking ballads by commoners. It is not surprising that on 19 December he was replaced in his regional command by a proven soldier, although he received an official welcome upon his return to court in recognition that he had done his best and spent large quantities of his own fortune in the process. On 30 April 1643 parliament had responded to his military appointment by granting his estates to its commander-in-chief, the earl of Essex, and Capel had borrowed heavily against the remnants of his property still in royalist territory.

For the whole of 1644 Capel apparently remained in Oxford awaiting further employment, provided in February 1645 when he was made one of the commissioners sent to Uxbridge for fruitless peace negotiations. On 14 February he was given a longer-term post as one of a council of advisers to the prince of Wales, charged with the administration of the royalist west country. Capel was allotted the additional responsibility of raising and commanding a regiment of foot and one of horse as guards for the prince. Between March 1645 and March 1646 he carried out these duties diligently, until the final surrender of the western royalist army. Then he followed the prince of Wales into exile, first in Scilly and then in Jersey, where on 24 June 1646 he quit the prince's service following the decision that the boy should join the queen in France; again, Capel's suspicion of Catholics had surfaced. He wintered in the island and then returned to England, where on 13 March 1647 he petitioned the House of Lords to be allowed to compound for his estates. After a short period of house arrest, he was set at liberty.

Capel immediately returned to abetting the intrigues of the king, keeping in especially close contact with Charles I when the latter was at Hampton Court in the autumn and colluding in his decision to flee to the Isle of Wight. He was subsequently commissioned by the prince of Wales as commander-in-chief for East Anglia in the royalist risings planned for 1648, and on 9 June he joined a rendezvous of royalist rebels at Chelmsford to play this part. Three days later his forces were penned into Colchester by the main parliamentarian army, Capel himself fighting with a pike to cover the retreat into the town, and there they remained until they were finally starved into surrender on 27 August. Capel was imprisoned, first in Windsor Castle and then in the Tower of London, and in October he was impeached by parliament. His process was delayed by the events leading up to the trial and execution of Charles himself, and he used the easy terms upon which friends could visit him to obtain a rope. With this he escaped from the Tower, wading the moat once he had got over the walls, only to be betrayed by a Thames waterman who was engaged to row him from a hiding place at the Temple to one in Lambeth.

This time there was no escape. On 8 March 1649 parliament voted for Capel's death, together with that of two other royalist nobles, and he was beheaded outside Westminster Hall on the following day. He died with conspicuous courage and declined the services of a parliamentarian minister. Instead, he had received the private ministrations of the royalist George Morley, later bishop of Winchester, and confessed to him that his part in voting

Arthur Capel, first Baron Capel of Hadham (1604–1649), by Cornelius Johnson, *c.*1640 [*The Capel Family*]

for the execution of Strafford had troubled him right up until this moment, when he atoned for it with an identical death. He was buried on 20 March, in the church at Hadham Parva where he had been baptized.

A collection of Capel's meditations was first published in 1654, and reveal him to have been prim, sober, and pious, with a rigid devotion to duty and a profound attachment to the Sacraments in the Anglican form. He seems to have been unusually tall, to judge both by his feat in wading the Tower moat and by a quip of his upon the Edgehill campaign, that a barn in which he had spent the night was the first bed large enough to fit him which he had found since the march began. He and his wife, Elizabeth, had five sons and four daughters, including Mary *Somerset, first duchess of Beaufort; she lived until 26 January 1661 and was buried beside her husband at Hadham. She therefore survived long enough to see the Restoration, but missed (by only three months) the considerable act of reward and revenge which Charles II made to her family for the services of the martyred noble who had once been his councillor. In his coronation honours list, in April, he raised the eldest of Capel's five sons, also Arthur *Capel, to the earldom of Essex, thereby granting him the title of the man to whom the Long Parliament had once awarded his father's confiscated (and now restored) estates.

RONALD HUTTON

Sources A. Capel, *Excellent contemplations, divine and moral* (1683) · *The manuscripts of the duke of Beaufort … the earl of Donoughmore*, HMC, 27 (1891), 16–45 · *Report on the manuscripts of the late Reginald Rawdon Hastings*, 4 vols., HMC, 78 (1928–47), vol. 2, pp. 97–105 · *The manuscripts of his grace the duke of Portland*, 10 vols., HMC, 29 (1891–1931), vol. 1, pp. 141–58, 217, 269 · Bodl. Oxf., MSS Clarendon 24–27 · William Salt Library, Stafford, Salt MS 45 · *JHL*, 5 (1642–3), 115; 9 (1646–7), 78 · J. Rushworth, *Historical collections*, 2nd edn, 2/2 (1680), 1243; 3 (1692) · W. Phillips, ed., 'The Ottley papers relating to the civil war [pt 2]', *Transactions of the Shropshire Archaeological and Natural History Society*, 2nd ser., 7 (1895), 241–360, esp. 278–348 · NL Wales, Llanfair-Brynodol papers, 43–54 · NL Wales, Crosse of Shawe Hill MSS 1097–1123 · T. W. Barlow, *Cheshire: its historical and literary associations, illustrated in a series of biographical sketches*, [new edn] (1855), 164–7 · R. Clutterbuck, ed., *The history and antiquities of the county of Hertford*, 3 vols. (1815–27) · GEC, *Peerage* · R. Hutton, *The royalist war effort, 1642–1646* (1982)

Likenesses C. Johnson, group portrait, *c.*1640 (with his family), NPG [*see illus.*] · miniature, 1647 (after J. Hoskins?), NPG · oils, *c.*1680–1700 (after H. Paert), NPG · miniature, 19th cent. (after J. Hoskins), NPG · R. Dunkarton, mezzotint, pubd 1815, BM, NPG

Wealth at death approx. £7000 p.a.: Clutterbuck, ed., *History and antiquities*, 1.244

Capel, Arthur, first earl of Essex (*bap.* **1632**, *d.* **1683**), politician and conspirator, was born at Little Hadham, Hertfordshire, and baptized there on 28 January 1632, the eldest son of Arthur *Capel, first Baron Capel (1604–1649), and his wife, Elizabeth Morrison (1609/10–1661), daughter and heir of Sir Charles Morrison, baronet, of Cassiobury Park, Hertfordshire, and his wife, Mary. Nothing substantive is known of the younger Arthur's education. While his father defended Colchester in July 1648, Arthur, though unwell, was taken from his home by parliamentary troops and paraded outside the town in an unsuccessful attempt to persuade his father to surrender. Following his father's execution on 9 March 1649, Capel succeeded to the title, though he recovered the family estates only in 1651 after petitioning parliament. At Petworth, Sussex, on 19 May 1653, he married Lady Elizabeth Percy (1636–1718), fifth daughter of Algernon Percy, earl of Northumberland, and his first wife, Anne, daughter of William *Cecil, second earl of Salisbury. Following the death of her brother Joceline in May 1670, Elizabeth became the last heir of the Percy family. Capel was also linked to Henry *Somerset, marquess of Worcester, who married Capel's eldest sister, Mary, after the death of her first husband, Henry, Lord Beauchamp. Capel's sister Theodosia wed Henry *Hyde, second earl of Clarendon. Of all Capel's relatives, his cousin Algernon *Sidney had the most influence on him. Capel and his wife had six sons (Algernon, Charles, Arthur, Henry, Algernon, and Arthur) and two daughters (Elizabeth and Anne), of whom only the younger Algernon and Anne lived to maturity.

Early career, 1660–1672 Capel's political career began with his appointment on 7 July 1660 as lord lieutenant and *custos rotulorum* of Hertfordshire. In August, when the House of Lords permitted him to except one person from the Act of Indemnity in retribution for his father's execution, he named the former sheriff, Sir Edmund Wareing. Charles created Capel Viscount Malden and earl of Essex on 20 April 1661. His early years in the Lords were marked by relatively light committee service, including those concerned with censorship, merchants' insurance, and gambling. He evinced concern in May 1662 for a constitutionally strong House of Lords by joining thirteen other peers in asserting that supply bills could begin in either house. In December 1666 Essex was one of four peers who conferred with a Commons' delegation about Viscount Mordant's impeachment. Essex was named to some thirty committees in 1667, including those dealing with London's rebuilding, plague victims, the suppression of atheism and profanity, trade with Scotland, preventing the sale of offices, and the trial of peers. In January 1667 he formally dissented from the peers' refusal to permit victims of the London fire from appealing adverse judicial decisions to the Lords. After the Commons impeached the first earl of Clarendon, Essex served on the committee to explain the Lords' dissent. During this period he took on additional administrative responsibilities as a commissioner to examine both the public accounts and merchants trading with France (January 1667), and as lord lieutenant of Wiltshire (February 1668).

Essex visited the baths at Bourbon in 1667, and while he was in Paris Henrietta Maria sounded him out about a possible alliance between Irish Catholics and the French. After he returned to England he moved his country home from Hadham Hall to Cassiobury, where he began adding state rooms. In the meantime he was appointed to more committees in the Lords, including those for expanding trade, collecting the hearth tax, and preventing highway robberies. He chaired the grand committees to limit trials in parliament and for land registers. The latter was the result of one of three recommendations he announced to the house in November 1669 from the committee on trade; the others were a reduction in the interest rate to 4 per cent and increased naturalization. The following month he reported the trade committee's recommendation to relax the penal laws as another means to increase commerce.

In August 1669 Charles decided to send Essex as an ambassador-extraordinary to the Danish court, authorizing £1500 for equipage and an additional £840 for other expenses. Frederick III's death in February 1670 delayed Essex's departure, enabling him to oppose the second conventicle bill. In March and early April he was named to more than a dozen other committees in the Lords, including those concerning union with Scotland and rebuilding London churches. He also chaired the grand committee for the sale of fee-farm rents. Anticipating problems regarding the Danes' expected insistence on striking the English flag, Essex obtained instructions from the earl of Arlington before departing. When Essex's ship refused to strike its flag as it sailed through the Sound, the Danes fired a shot into its rigging. Upon landing Essex, citing treaties recognizing the right of English ships to sail in Danish waters without saluting, demanded an apology; the governor of Kronberg was ordered to Copenhagen to render one. After negotiating a commercial treaty in July, Essex returned to England, arriving on 1 September. By December he was again very active in the Lords, serving on numerous committees before leaving for Ireland in July 1672. Among them were committees concerned with the Merchant Adventurers, the excise, impositions, the plantation trade, and the production of flax and hemp. His firm commitment to protestantism was undoubtedly a factor in his appointment to committees to prevent the growth of Catholicism (March 1671) and to encourage sabbath observance (April 1671). After Charles resolved early the following year to replace Lord Berkeley of Stratton, a Catholic sympathizer, with Essex as lord lieutenant of Ireland, he appointed Essex to the privy council on 17 April. At this time Essex was not identified with any faction.

Essex in Ireland, 1672–1677 During his tenure as lord lieutenant Essex's principal challenges involved regulating the corporations; securing adequate finances, especially to pay the army; dealing with Catholics and protestant nonconformists, both of which were potentially destabilizing forces; and preserving Phoenix Park. Dealing with these problems was complicated by unresolved fears about the stability of landholdings and shifting political currents at court. Essex enjoyed a solid working relationship with Arlington, whose support he cultivated, and he benefited by executing the king's command to terminate the earl of Orrery's lord presidency of Munster, and Berkeley's of Connaught, thereby strengthening the lord lieutenant's authority.

After arriving in Dublin on 5 August Essex received the ceremonial sword from Berkeley. In keeping with his instructions he drafted regulations for the corporations, giving him the right to approve all chief magistrates and requiring all officers, aldermen, common councillors, and guild members to take the oaths of allegiance and supremacy unless exempted by the lord lieutenant. Unlike Orrery, Essex thought Catholics should be permitted to live in corporate towns as a means to increase commerce and taxation, but he was chary of allowing them to serve as magistrates for fear that protestants would emigrate. When nine or ten Catholics won seats on the Dublin common council Essex exempted them from the oath of supremacy, prompting strenuous opposition from the earl of Anglesey and Dudley Loftus, master in chancery. Responding to complaints, Charles suspended the regulations before ordering Essex to exclude the Catholics.

Arthur Capel, first earl of Essex (*bap.* 1632, *d.* 1683), by Sir Peter Lely, *c.*1653 [with his wife, Elizabeth, countess of Essex]

Security was another pressing concern. Following the disbandment of some units and the transfer of others to England, only thirty-three of sixty-one foot companies and twenty-three of thirty-three troops remained. Fifteen days after arriving in Dublin Essex protested to Arlington that recently disbanded soldiers, having not been paid, suffered terribly; faced with creditors, Essex feared, they would become robbers. Arms and ammunition were in short supply, and forts such as Athlone Castle were in disrepair. He faced criticism when he announced plans to relocate military units to strategic locations, but he proceeded in the interests of security, in part by requiring each troop to spend two months a year on duty in Dublin. Essex wanted to reorganize the army, relying on fewer nobles and more on officers who were 'bred to the trade' (*CSP dom.*, 1673, 16), and he endeavoured to prevent officers from selling their commands. Essex relied on the army rather than the militia to maintain order, fearing the latter would include numerous former Cromwellian troops and Scottish presbyterians who would prove unreliable if troubles erupted in England. Consequently, in June 1674 he opposed Orrery's request to establish a militia in Munster under his command. The relationship between Orrery and Essex was further strained by the lord lieutenant's refusal to let Orrery keep cannons at Charleville or mounted guns at Castlemartyr.

Essex's problems with Irish finances were primarily due to the tax-farm of Orrery's nephew, Viscount Ranelagh, which dated to Christmas 1670. In 1672 Essex had instructions to see that Ranelagh and his partners collected the annual revenue of £300,000 and to collect their payments assiduously. However, Ranelagh soon resented Essex's oversight and reporting of financial matters to Arlington, and Essex in turn complained that Ranelagh received instructions directly from London rather than through him. He also opposed Ranelagh's practice of letting soldiers' arrears mount before paying a fraction of what the government owed. The failure of Ranelagh's agents to account for receipts frustrated Essex, though he admitted they were collecting funds more expeditiously than he could, and he informed Charles in 1673 that a proposal for the crown to assume direct control of revenue collection could be disruptive. Relations between Essex and Ranelagh worsened two months later when the latter blamed Essex for failing to disburse payments in a timely manner. After Ranelagh became vice-treasurer in June 1674, his agents in Ireland were virtually unsupervised, but Essex's attempt to provide oversight angered Ranelagh.

Essex's policies were generally constructive. For the most part he was reluctant to reward suitors with grants of Irish money or land. In November 1674 he rejected a proposed political alliance arranged by the duke of Hamilton with the duchess of Portsmouth because he would have had to provide money or other considerations; the cost of such friendship, in his view, was not worthwhile. The principal threat was from the royal court. In February 1673 Charles ordered Essex to give the duke of Buckingham a pension of £2400 per annum for twenty years, to be paid from Irish revenue, but Essex successfully resisted Charles's proposed grant of Phoenix Park to the duchess of Cleveland. The terms had been artfully crafted so the gift would not take effect until the conclusion of Essex's lord lieutenancy, but he objected on principle, citing the park's value to future governors. When Arlington, the earl of Shaftesbury, and others supported Essex, Charles yielded on the condition that the duchess receive lands of equal value. Essex's concern for Ireland's well-being was also manifest in his efforts to end oppressive governmental practices, including the charging of excessive fees, even by his own secretaries. He opposed reversions of offices on the grounds that recipients had no incentive to acquire qualities essential for effective service. Convinced that the Irish woollen industry should be encouraged, he opposed any endeavour to prohibit the sale of Irish wool in England on the grounds that Irish competition with England in foreign markets would disadvantage the English. Faced with a shortage of small coins in Ireland, he opposed draining the kingdom's silver to obtain them, suggesting instead that England remit coins to pay for the fortification of Kinsale harbour. He also objected to the plan of Sir William Petty and Sir Henry Ingoldsby to give the king £12,000 to £20,000 per annum for the right to lands with concealed titles, for this, he argued, would threaten the settlement. In March 1674 he called for an end within two years to inquiries about uncertain land titles on the grounds that owners would not undertake improvements in their holdings as long as titles were insecure. Late in his administration Essex took pleasure in settling titles in Connaught, relieving numerous poor families who had been kept off their land for years.

In his dealings with Irish Catholics Essex preferred moderation, though instructions from London called for firm action. In September 1673 the committee on Irish affairs ordered him to expel Catholics from the army, towns, and local offices and to exile Catholic clergy, but he protested to Arlington the following month that Catholics were legally entitled to live in corporate towns subject to restrictions on their ability to purchase or lease property. He was reluctant to lose the economic benefits of substantial traders whatever their religious views. However, he issued a proclamation on 27 October commanding Peter Talbot and all archbishops, bishops, abbots, and others exercising ecclesiastical jurisdiction by papal authority to leave Ireland and suppressing all seminaries, convents, friaries, and Catholic schools; he reiterated the orders on 27 April 1674. Another proclamation, dated 8 November 1673, prohibited Catholics from keeping firearms, though in practice he allowed them to retain weapons for self-defence. Essex tolerated quiescent priests, particularly those who had subscribed the Irish remonstrance, and he deemed Oliver Plunket, archbishop of Armagh, more conformable to the government than any other Catholic prelate in Ireland. Essex was particularly tolerant of friars who followed Peter Walsh, for they provided intelligence about Catholic activity. The most dangerous Catholic cleric in Ireland, Essex thought, was John O'Molony, bishop of Killaloe, who tried to heal the breach between factions that the earl had encouraged. Essex was prepared to incarcerate only clergy who threatened security, and his goal, as he told his brother, Sir Henry Capel, was to render justice to Catholics and protestants impartially.

To deal with the nonconformists Essex proposed that Charles issue a declaration of indulgence, licensing some dissenters while forbidding others from meeting. For security reasons he banned conventicles in garrisons such as Londonderry, but even there he permitted presbyterians to meet outside the city walls. He steered a course between Church of Ireland hardliners on the one hand and militant covenanters on the other. Ties between Ulster Scots and covenanters in Scotland concerned him, especially the prospect that the former might support another covenanter rebellion. When an uprising seemed imminent in Scotland in 1674, Essex dispatched additional troops to Carrickfergus, Belfast, Londonderry, and Charlemont. During the summer of 1676 he punished preachers who urged presbyterians to subscribe the covenant, and his efforts to restrain militant covenanters paid off when Irish presbyterians did not rise in support of the Bothwell rebels in 1679.

Essex faced problems of a different sort with the Irish bandits, or tories, especially in Ulster and the mountains of the south-west. Periodically he resorted to frontier justice, as in August 1673 when he permitted the McGuires to apprehend as many tories as possible, promising pardons should any tories be killed. The following January he expressed a willingness to pardon criminals (other than murderers) who caught tories, insisting that killing suspected tories must be a last remedy. A proclamation issued in summer 1674 permitted the killing of housebreakers.

In personal terms the Irish years entailed both hardship and opportunity. For nearly two months in autumn 1672 Essex was very ill, suffering from headaches, fever, and a temporary inability to use a hand, and the following February the death of his daughter devastated him. He found diversion in hunting, which enabled him to become better acquainted with the country gentry. While he was in Ireland he battled the duke of Monmouth for the right to the late earl of Northumberland's estate. His effort to purchase Essex House in London, valued at £7000, was badly mismanaged by his brother and Sir William Harbord, who allowed a builder to acquire the property; not even a grant of £13,000 from Charles, which the earl of Danby had recommended, enticed the builder to sell. Essex did, however, have enough money to continue his expansion at Cassiobury.

As early as March 1674 rumours of Essex's recall circulated and in May he instructed his brother to alert Arlington that Orrery and Ranelagh were plotting his overthrow. Although Charles expressed confidence in Essex in January 1675, the reports continued, encouraging the earl's opponents in the Dublin common council. With Charles's permission, Essex returned to London in July, leaving Ireland in the care of Sir Arthur Forbes and Archbishop James Margetson. On good terms with Danby and the earl of Lauderdale, Essex frequently conferred with the duke of Ormond regarding Irish affairs, but relations with James, duke of York and Heneage Finch were cool. Essex's attempt to gain control of Irish finances prompted Ranelagh and Viscount Conway to ally against him, and his opposition to Danby and Ranelagh's plan to funnel £20,000 per annum from Ireland into the English Treasury increased tension. He worried about a plan to replace him as lord lieutenant with Monmouth, while Conway, Orrery, and Viscount Granard would govern the country as lords justices, but James, unwilling to see Monmouth's stature enhanced, opposed the scheme. Essex was active in the Lords during his sojourn in England, serving on various committees, including those dealing with the trial of peers, Catholic recusants, and the recall of soldiers in French service. With Shaftesbury, Viscount Halifax, Lord Wharton, and others, he voted in November 1675 for an address asking Charles to dissolve parliament.

Shortly before Essex returned to Ireland in May 1676 he protested to Danby about the woeful state of its troops, fortifications, and stores. To remedy this £50,000 was required, he said, but only £20,000 had been allocated. Indeed, that summer the army's arrears amounted to £139,000, prompting Essex to complain to his brother: 'I am so much concerned at it that … I had rather loose not only my place but even my life than see these poor men … thus oppressed' (Pike, 74). Convinced that Ranelagh could have raised the money for which he contracted, Essex concluded that Charles should dismiss him. By early 1677 Ranelagh was complaining that Essex was oppressing him, and Essex, increasingly bitter, denounced Ranelagh's agents in Ireland as cutpurses and cheats. By April Charles, tired of the feuding, decided to remove Essex. Pleased that his replacement would be Ormond rather than Conway, Essex remained in Dublin until the duke's arrival in August.

From crown servant to conspirator, 1677–1683 After Essex returned from Ireland he lived at his house in St James's Square, London, and at Cassiobury Park. His new state rooms featured mantles of Irish marble, carvings by Grinling Gibbons, and a painting by Antonio Verro, and his sizeable library included parliamentary rolls and journals. Modelled on those at Versailles, his gardens featured black cherry and other fruit trees, a trout stream, and ponds. He also owned other manors in Hertfordshire, Essex, Suffolk, and Norfolk, former church lands in Nottinghamshire, and rental property in London and Derbyshire.

By 3 December 1677 Essex had returned to the Lords. Increasingly a critic of corruption and Catholic influence at court, Essex joined Halifax and the second earl of Clarendon in supporting Shaftesbury's petition for release from prison in February 1678, thus increasing his alienation from Danby. As a member of the privy council and its foreign affairs committee he remained interested in Ireland, particularly its security in the event of an Anglo-French war. When Essex called in March for war against France, Charles appointed him, the earl of Bridgewater, and Viscount Fauconberg to negotiate an alliance with the Spanish and Dutch ministers. In addition to his extensive committee assignments in the Lords, during the spring

Essex helped audit Ranelagh's accounts. Well before the disclosure of the alleged Popish Plot he evinced concern with Catholicism, and he was thus an obvious person to sit on the Lords' investigatory committee, which he periodically chaired, working closely with Shaftesbury, Halifax, the earl of Winchester, and Buckingham. In October he urged Charles to banish Catholics from London, and the following month he endorsed Shaftesbury's call for James's removal from public office. Besides chairing the Lords' committees concerned with the militia, a new test, and the exclusion of Catholics from specified trades, Essex was among the peers who interrogated the Catholic lords in the Tower, particularly Viscount Stafford. By late December Danby regarded Essex, Shaftesbury, Halifax, and Monmouth as his principal enemies, and his list of foes also included the Commons' group allied with Essex, notably his brother, Harbord, and Sir Cyril Wyche. In the first Exclusion Parliament Essex chaired the Lords' grand committee considering a bill to disable and banish Danby, and Essex voted for his attainder. However, he thought Danby's offences did not equal those of the popish plotters.

Essex angered many of his country allies when, on 26 March 1679, he became first lord of the Treasury. On a motion by Sir William Coventry the Commons gave him a vote of confidence, but Shaftesbury and Halifax, according to Sir William Temple, resented Essex's breach of an agreement to accept offices together or not at all. Essex and Halifax quickly mended the rift, allying with Temple and the earl of Sunderland in the spring to check the ascendancy of Monmouth and Shaftesbury, whose strong opposition to James they did not share. During this period, Essex, haunted by the prospect of Catholics burning his children at Smithfield, continued to investigate the Popish Plot. His assignments in the Lords included committees concerned with banishing Catholics from London and securing habeas corpus rights. In April he was a member of the Lords' delegation that urged Charles to instruct Ormond to disarm Catholics, to banish Catholics who exercised Rome's jurisdiction, and to provide Irish forces with additional arms and ammunition. Still committed to reform, Essex introduced a bill to prohibit the lord treasurer, Treasury commissioners, or Ireland's lord lieutenant from acquiring any estate by royal grant or selling any offices, but it died in committee.

Charles reorganized the privy council on 20 April, appointing Shaftesbury its president (at the urging of Essex, Finch, and Sunderland) and retaining Essex as first lord of the Treasury. Essex also served on the council's committees for foreign and Irish affairs. At Sunderland's request Essex joined him and Halifax in the so-called triumvirate. When the Lords debated the bishops' right to vote in capital cases in May, Essex stood with Shaftesbury, Buckingham, and Wharton in opposition, and he worked with Shaftesbury in evaluating Solomon de Fobert's proposal for a royal military academy. However, in late May Essex broke with Monmouth when the triumvirate advised Charles to prorogue parliament to head off further inflammatory addresses concerning the succession. Unlike Monmouth and Shaftesbury, the triumvirate and Temple opposed James's exclusion, preferring to impose limits on him should he become king. Following Monmouth's defeat of the Bothwell Bridge rebels on 22 June the triumvirate, fearing his triumphal return, urged Charles to dissolve parliament, which he did on 10 July. Essex's relations with Shaftesbury were also cool, for the latter was afraid Essex's retrenchment at the Treasury would enable Charles to govern longer before summoning another parliament. Likewise, tension between Essex and Ormond had been growing since at least the spring, when Ormond's son, Ossory, depicted Essex as one of his father's bitterest enemies. Rumours that Essex, Halifax, and the earl of Radnor aspired to the lord lieutenantcy exacerbated matters. In June, when Essex pressed Ormond to pay £13,000 in arrears to the army, the duke countered by complaining about the deplorable condition of the fortifications and stores left by Essex. Although Essex wanted an effective army in Ireland, he protested in July when Charles organized a new company of guards in England, noting popular concern that this unit was the beginning of a standing army and worrying about its cost to the Treasury.

When Charles became ill in August 1679, the triumvirate, fearing Monmouth would seize power if the king died, summoned James from Brussels. The duke distrusted Essex and Halifax because they supported limitations, averring that they did 'not love a monarky as it was in England' (*Dartmouth MSS*, 1.36). By the time James reached London on 2 September, Charles had recovered. The ensuing months were among the most crucial in Essex's career. Increasingly concerned about arbitrary government, Charles's reliance on monetary grants from France, and the perceived Catholic threat, he unsuccessfully urged the king on 9 November to have parliament meet; a week later he resigned from the Treasury. In recent months he had drawn closer to Shaftesbury, who shared his belief in the need to continue investigating alleged Catholic plotting. Although Essex contemplated resigning from the privy council, he decided against this owing to Shaftesbury's advice and his own continuing concerns about Ireland. In the absence of a parliament, Essex also needed his council seat as a base from which to investigate alleged Catholic conspiracies. In March he and Shaftesbury presented evidence of an Irish plot to the council and, at Essex's urging, Shaftesbury dispatched agents to Ireland to investigate Peter Talbot, the Catholic archbishop of Dublin, and Oliver Plunket. By mid-April, however, Essex, much to Shaftesbury's annoyance, was having doubts about the reality of an Irish conspiracy, though he changed his mind again, according to Gilbert Burnet, after hearing further testimony. During the summer Essex, Shaftesbury, and Wharton were in frequent contact with Titus Oates and Israel Tong. With parliament scheduled to convene in October, Essex, Halifax, and others persuaded Charles to send James to Scotland.

In the Lords, Essex's primary concern was preserving the realm from Catholicism, a concern sustained by his participation on the committee to investigate the plotting and the subcommittee concerned with the reputed Irish conspiracy. Breaking with Halifax, he voted on 15 November to exclude James from the succession. When that bill failed Essex drafted the heads of an association bill that would require clergy, nobles, MPs, office-holders, and others to subscribe a bond to defend the king, and provide for them to take up arms when Charles died, defending the realm until parliament could convene. Essex also helped prepare for Stafford's trial. Faced with James's opposition to limitations, Essex, Shaftesbury, and the earl of Salisbury attacked the duke and his supporters in late December, warning Charles that good relations with his subjects were impossible unless James were excluded. For opposing Charles's decision to dissolve parliament, Essex, Sunderland, and Temple were removed from the council on 24 January 1681. The following day Essex, Shaftesbury, and others petitioned Charles to have parliament meet at Westminster rather than Oxford, condemned the impact of the prorogations and dissolutions on the conspiracy investigations, and protested against the presence of Catholics and their adherents in the royal guards. Pressed by Charles to identify Catholic guards, Essex retorted that he meant anyone who supported James. For this, Charles dismissed Essex as lord lieutenant of Hertfordshire on 28 January. During the third Exclusion Parliament Essex and Shaftesbury monitored the case of the Irish Catholic Edward Fitzharris, a government informer who had attempted to implicate whig leaders in treason. Both peers formally protested the Lords' refusal to hear impeachment charges against Fitzharris, and both attended his trial in king's bench. When Fitzharris's wife, Anne, was arrested in June on charges of misprision of treason, she accused Essex of having urged her husband to blame the plot on Charles, James, Catherine of Braganza, and Danby, but the accusations were not taken seriously. When Shaftesbury was arrested in July on charges of treason, Essex and other prominent whigs offered to be sureties, but the judge declined Shaftesbury's petition for habeas corpus. At Shaftesbury's trial in November, Essex was among the whigs in attendance as a show of support. He had also been at Stephen College's trial in July.

In the autumn Essex, Sunderland, and Sidney advised Charles to declare war on France, hoping this would compel him to summon another parliament. Essex, who supported a Dutch alliance, had conferred with William of Orange when the latter visited England in July. By December Essex, Lord Howard of Escrick, Sir Patience Ward, and two former sheriffs of London were taking evidence against fabricators of an alleged 'Presbyterian' plot, and they reportedly worried that Charles might charge them with treason. With an eye to self-defence, Essex, Shaftesbury, and other whig leaders attended dinner parties in March 1682 to discuss the forthcoming London shrieval elections, the outcome of which would be crucial for the selection of jurors should they be tried. When the whig candidates were set aside in June, Essex concluded that the people were free to defend themselves from arbitrary government. He summoned Thomas Walcott, whose dissident activities he had encountered as lord lieutenant, from Ireland; in the ensuing months Walcott became one of Shaftesbury's key aides. In mid-September Shaftesbury, the earl of Salisbury, and John Locke went to Cassiobury, where they presumably discussed their options with Essex. The sense of danger must have heightened when Monmouth was arrested less than two weeks later; Essex and Shaftesbury visited him in prison. When plans for an uprising proved abortive, Shaftesbury fled to the Netherlands, secretly consulting Essex and Salisbury before his departure. According to Burnet, Shaftesbury's flight relieved Essex.

Following Shaftesbury's death in January 1683, Essex, Sidney, Monmouth, Howard, Lord William Russell, and John Hampden began exploring plans for an insurrection. Monmouth and Essex reportedly sought Salisbury's backing. Interested in an alliance with the earl of Argyll and his Scottish supporters, the six invited Lord Melville, Sir John Cochrane, and Sir Hugh Campbell of Cessnock to London. However, the six were divided in their aims, with Essex, Sidney, and Hampden favouring a republic, whereas the others preferred a monarchy. Influenced by Sidney and the Jesuit Juan de Mariana's *De rege et regis institutione*, Essex was now acting on his belief that subjects could restrain or overthrow princes who violated the trust vested in them. Monmouth and Russell kept Ford, Lord Grey generally apprised of their discussions; on 20 December 1682 Grey had named Essex a trustee of his estate. Sidney in turn persuaded Essex, Monmouth, and Russell to take John Wildman into their confidence. On 24 April Locke went to Cassiobury, where he summoned Essex to an urgent meeting of the cabal, but the earl arrived too late. At the next meeting Essex and Sidney offered to draft a revolutionary declaration, but this they apparently never did. Following the initial disclosure of the plotting and the first arrests on 19 June, Essex had time to escape, but he eschewed this course because of the implications for Russell, who was apprehended on the 26th. Arrested at Cassiobury on 9 July, Essex was incarcerated the following day in the same rooms in the Tower where his father had been held before his execution. When examined, Essex professed to know of no plot, admitting only that he might have been at Russell's house when Sidney and Monmouth were there, that he had visited Hampden, and that he and the earl of Bedford had called on Salisbury while Monmouth was present.

The cause of Essex's death on 13 July has been vigorously disputed. According to the government he slashed his throat with a razor; this was the judgment of the coroner's inquest, though there is some evidence the jurors were coerced. The whig attorney Lawrence Braddon, Robert Ferguson, and Henry Danvers attempted to prove Essex was murdered as part of a conspiracy to conceal Catholic activity and ensure Russell's conviction, but they undermined their arguments by incorporating baseless allegations. Advocates of the case for suicide point to Essex's distress upon arriving at the Tower, his agitated and confused state before his death, the belief of his wife and brother that he committed suicide, and his wife's intervention to halt the parliamentary investigation into his death in 1689. A compelling case for homicide rests on two surgeons' description of the fatal wound, which extended from ear to ear, severing the jugular veins, the oesophagus, and the trachea, and cutting deep enough to nick the vertebrae at the back of the neck. The instrument that supposedly did this was a handleless French razor between 4¼ and 4½ inches long, which the user had to grasp in his fingers. This would leave between 2¼ and 2¾ inches of blade exposed, but the cut was between 3 and 4 inches deep. On the eve of his death Essex had instructed his steward to take notes during Russell's trial, which would have been pointless had he intended to commit suicide the next morning. Moreover, concerned about his safety in the Tower, he had ordered his cook to prepare his food in silver vessels. His servant reportedly testified to the coroner's jury that Essex ate a hearty breakfast the morning of his death and showed no signs of emotional distress. Finally, given the fact that his father had died for Charles I, Essex was likely to have received mercy from Charles II. The assassin was almost certainly John Holland, Sunderland's erstwhile servant, aided by a Major Webster. The idea may have been Sunderland's; having supported exclusion, he was now intent on winning James's favour. From the duke's perspective, Essex's apparent suicide, timed to coincide with Russell's trial, would (and did) have a powerful impact, virtually assuring Russell's conviction and demonstrating the conspiracy's reality. If Russell escaped, so too might Essex and their compatriots. Sunderland and James had motive and opportunity to commission Essex's assassination. His body was probably buried in the Tower shortly after his death, and later reburied at Watford.

In his will, dated 28 February 1681, Essex had placed most of his estate in the hands of his brother as trustee for his heirs. Professing no desire to profit by Essex's death, Charles permitted Sir Henry to have the estate in October. The king also allowed Essex's widow to have the clothing, jewellery, plate, paintings, and household goods bequeathed to her.

A rather tall, slender man, Essex had a sober disposition. Although he has been accused of being driven by ambition, especially a desire to resume the lord lieutenancy, he was primarily motivated by an intense dislike of arbitrary government, the squandering of public funds, and an increasing concern about the perils of Catholicism, not because of its theology but owing to its tradition of persecution and Rome's jurisdictional claims. Burnet's assertion that Essex had no fixed religious principles misread his willingness to tolerate Catholics and nonconformists as long as they posed no threat to security. Charles deemed Essex stiff and sullen, yet he appreciated his administrative skills, as did his colleagues in the Lords. Like Buckingham, Essex was vocal in defending the Lords' judicial rights. John Evelyn, his friend for nearly two decades, praised Essex as a 'judicious & pondering person, not illiterate beyond the rate of most noble-men in this age, very well Versed in our English Histories & Affaires' (Evelyn, 4.201). Indeed, Essex seems to have loved his library as much as his gardens. He focused his reading on subjects relevant to affairs of state, and his library included transcriptions of various state trials, including those of Buckingham and Surrey in Henry VIII's reign, Arundel and Norfolk in Elizabeth's reign, and Ralegh and Cobham. Imbued with a strong sense of service to his sovereign, Essex embraced radical courses only when compelled by concern for political liberty and self-preservation. Heavily influenced by Algernon Sidney, his dedication to parliamentary government and protestantism places him in the tradition of the fourth earl of Bedford, John Pym, and the elder John Hampden. RICHARD L. GREAVES

Sources PRO, State papers, Charles II, SP29/331–334 · BL, Stowe MSS 201–217 · *JHL*, 11–14 (1660–91) · *CSP dom.*, *1661–2*; *1667–70*; *1672–83* · W. A. Shaw, ed., *Calendar of treasury books*, 1–8, PRO (1904–23) · O. Airy, ed., *Essex papers*, CS, new ser., 47 (1890) · C. E. Pike, ed., *Selections from the correspondence of Arthur Capel, earl of Essex, 1675–1677*, CS, 3rd ser., 24 (1913) · *The manuscripts of the marquis of Ormonde*, [old ser.], 3 vols., HMC, 36 (1895–1909), vols. 1–2 · *Calendar of the manuscripts of the marquess of Ormonde*, new ser., 8 vols., HMC, 36 (1902–20), vols. 3–7 · R. L. Greaves, *God's other children: protestant nonconformists and the emergence of denominational churches in Ireland* (1997) · R. L. Greaves, *Secrets of the kingdom: British radicals from the Popish Plot to the revolution of 1688–89* (1992) · J. Scott, *Algernon Sidney and the Restoration crisis, 1677–1683* (1991) · *The life and letters of Sir George Savile … first marquis of Halifax*, ed. H. C. Foxcroft, 2 vols. (1898) · K. H. D. Haley, *The first earl of Shaftesbury* (1968) · *Burnet's History of my own time*, ed. O. Airy, new edn, 2 vols. (1897–1900) · GEC, *Peerage*, new edn, 5.145 · M. Knights, *Politics and opinion in crisis, 1678–1681* (1994) · Evelyn, *Diary* · *Seventh report*, HMC, 6 (1879) · *The manuscripts of the House of Lords*, 4 vols., HMC, 17 (1887–94) · *Ninth report*, 2, HMC, 8 (1884) · *The manuscripts of the earl of Dartmouth*, 3 vols., HMC, 20 (1887–96), vol. 1 · *VCH Hertfordshire*, vol. 4 · PRO, PROB 11/375, sig. 40 · *DNB*

Archives BL, estate charters and rolls, Add. Ch 64889–66125; 71032–71074 · BL, family, estate, and state papers, Add. MSS 40625–40632 · BL, Irish lieutenancy corresp., letter-books, and papers, Stowe MSS 200–217 · BL, register of letters, Add. MS 28031 · Bodl. Oxf., letters and dispatches as lord lieutenant of Ireland, Add. C33–37 [copies] · Inner Temple, London, letter-book as lord lieutenant of Ireland | BL, Add. MS 36786 · BL, corresp. with Henry Coventry, Add. MSS 25122–25123 · BL, corresp. with Lord Danby, Egerton MS 3327 · Bodl. Oxf., Western MSS, 11839; 30231–30235 · Longleat House, Wiltshire, letters to Henry Coventry

Likenesses P. Lely, double portrait, *c.*1653 (with his wife), NPG [*see illus.*] · E. Lutterell, mezzotint, pubd after 1661 (after P. Lely), NG Ire.; version, NG Ire. · B. Picart, line engraving, 1724 (after P. Lely), BM, NPG · G. Bower, silver medal, BM · P. Lely, double portrait, oils (with his wife), Yale U. CBA · P. Lely, drawing, Staatliche Graphische Sammlung, Munich · P. Lely, oils (as a young man), Badminton House, Gloucestershire · P. Lely, oils, Syon House, Brentford, Middlesex

Wealth at death see will, PRO, PROB 11/375, sig. 40

Capel, Henry, **Baron Capel of Tewkesbury** (*bap.* **1638**, *d.* **1696**), politician and government official, was baptized on 6 March 1638 at Hadham Parva, Hertfordshire. He was the second son of Arthur *Capel, first Baron Capel of Hadham (1604–1649), politician and royalist leader, and his wife, Elizabeth (1609/10–1661), daughter and heir of Sir Charles Morrison. Capel's father fought for the king in the civil wars and was executed on the orders of parliament in March 1649. About February 1659 Capel married Dorothy (1641/2–1721), daughter and coheir of Richard Bennet, of Kew, Surrey, and his second wife, Mary, daughter of Richard Leman of Ipswich. The couple, who had no children, lived at Kew where Capel spent much time improving his gardens, which later became the nucleus of the Royal Botanic Gardens at Kew. His efforts were praised by John Evelyn, whose diary records several visits to 'my worthy friends Sir Hen. Capel's' (Evelyn, 4.144). Capel was knighted, no doubt in recognition of his father's royalism, at Charles II's coronation on 23 April 1661.

In 1660, having inherited Tewkesbury Barton manor, Capel was elected for Tewkesbury and represented the borough in all succeeding parliaments until 1681. In the 1660s he made little impact on the Commons but in the 1670s both he and his elder brother Arthur *Capel, earl of Essex, moved into opposition, eventually becoming committed whigs. Capel was a member of the Irish privy council from April 1673 to March 1685 and of the English privy council from April 1679 to January 1680, and was first lord of the Admiralty from February 1679 to February 1680. In the parliamentary sessions of 1680–81 he was a strong supporter of the exclusion of the future James II from the succession. He appears to have had no involvement in the Rye House plot of 1683, although his brother Essex was arrested and died in the Tower.

After the revolution of 1688 and the installation of William and Mary, Capel was restored to the English privy council on 14 February 1689 and made a lord of the Treasury, a position which, however, he only held until 1690 thanks to William's increasing estrangement from the whigs over fiscal and other matters. He sat for Cockermouth in 1689 and Tewkesbury from 1690 until being created first Baron Capel of Tewkesbury on 11 April 1692. He was said to have tried to prevent the arrest in 1690 or 1691, on suspicion of treason, of Henry *Hyde, earl of Clarendon who, although at the opposite end of the political spectrum, was Capel's former brother-in-law through his marriage to Capel's sister Theodosia (*d.* 1661). His appointment as one of the lords justices of Ireland in June 1693 gave Capel his first opportunity under the new regime to make a significant political impact, but he initially had to share power with his tory fellow lords justices Sir Cyril Wyche and William Duncombe. The tory lord chancellor, Sir Charles Porter, was also a powerful figure.

Capel was a partisan figure in Ireland, endeavouring from the start to build up links with the political leaders of the 1692 Irish parliament, which had been prematurely prorogued by the previous lord lieutenant, Lord Sydney, primarily because of its efforts to investigate alleged misappropriation of funds and other abuses by his administration. In correspondence to the king and the secretary of state, the earl of Shrewsbury, Capel praised Irish opposition leaders and urged compromise with them. In May 1695 he was appointed lord deputy and allowed to promote some of his supporters within the administration and to summon a new parliament. The most prominent of these supporters were Robert Rochfort and Alan Brodrick, who became attorney- and solicitor-general respectively. Lord Chancellor Porter, however, remained powerful and Capel sought to undermine him by sending over hints to London about the alleged (and unproven) pro-Catholic sentiments of Porter and his associates.

Although from the start it was clear that Porter's supporters were in the majority in the new House of Commons, the 1695 parliamentary session was in fact a very successful one from Capel's point of view. Rochfort was elected speaker and the parliament, thanks to a compromise negotiated with Capel on its powers to initiate money bills, approved a large supply and also passed the first anti-popery laws. These were not 'party' issues. There was, however, an attempt by Capel's supporters to impeach Porter (on the dubious grounds of undue favouritism to Catholics and Jacobites) which failed by 121 votes to 77. Capel's correspondence does little to dispel Porter's accusation that he was directly involved in the effort to remove Porter.

By this time Capel's health was failing and he concentrated in his last few months in office on strengthening his control over the administration and making arrangements for successors. Porter claimed that a 'select cabinet', consisting of Capel and a handful of his supporters, was excluding him from all significant political and military decisions (PRO NIre., De Ros MSS, D638/18/39). Capel appointed two close allies, Lord Blessington and Brigadier William Wolseley, to serve as lords justices during his final illness and (he hoped) to continue as such after his death. His power to appoint lords justices to serve after his death was disputed by most of the judiciary in Ireland and England and also by Shrewsbury, and despite his personnel changes Capel still only had the support of a minority on the Irish privy council, a point emphasized after his death when the council elected Porter as sole lord justice. Capel died at the lord lieutenant's country residence at Chapelizod on 30 May 1696 and was buried at Hadham on 8 September 1696. 'A violent party man' according to Lord Dartmouth, Capel was also disparaged by Bishop Burnet as a 'naturally vain, as well as a weak man' (HoP, *Commons, 1660–90*). His widow died on 7 June 1721 at Kew and was buried there. THOMAS DOYLE

Sources *Report on the manuscripts of his grace the duke of Buccleuch and Queensberry … preserved at Montagu House*, 3 vols. in 4, HMC, 45 (1899–1926), vol. 2 • PRO NIre., De Ros MSS, D 638/18 • *CSP dom.*, *1693* • T. G. Doyle, 'Parliament and politics in Williamite Ireland, 1690–1703', MA diss., University College Dublin, 1992, chaps. 3–5 • T. Doyle, 'Politics, religion and society in protestant Ireland, 1700–1710', PhD diss., National University of Ireland, 1996, 22–35 • *DNB* • GEC, *Peerage*, new edn, 3.6 • TCD, Southwell MS 1179, fols. 38–9 • B. D. Henning, 'Capel, Hon. Henry', HoP, *Commons, 1660–90* • Evelyn, *Diary*

Archives PRO NIre., De Ros MSS, D638/18

Capel, James (1789–1872), stockbroker and philanthropist, was born on 22 January 1789 at Kempsey, Worcestershire, the second child and eldest son of Henry Capel of Kempsey and his wife, Elizabeth Goile, of Fowicke, Worcestershire. James Capel married Marion Mary Cundy, who was probably the cousin of his father (she was the granddaughter of Henry Capel's grandfather, James Capel of Droitwich). They had four sons and five daughters.

James Capel went to London to enter the office of his cousin John Capel, a registered bill broker of 96 Cornhill, London, but in 1806 became a clerk in the office of Antrobus and Wood, stockbrokers. In 1813 he became a member of the London stock exchange, and a partner, at which time the firm changed its name to Antrobus, Brown, and Capel. In 1816 he was sworn a stockbroker as a member of the London Framework Knitters' Company, and in 1822 his firm changed its name again, becoming Marjoribanks, Capel, & Co., and moved to new premises at 5 Throgmorton Street. The partnership was divided into seventeen parts, of which Marjoribanks and Capel each took five, Norbury three, Alexander Trotter two, and Richard White two. In 1837 the firm again changed its name, becoming James Capel, Norbury, Trotter & Co., and James Capel became the senior partner. His son James Bury Capel was a partner in the firm by about 1844. The partnership was reconstituted in 1850, with James Capel controlling eight of the thirty shares, and again in 1864, when the firm became officially known as James Capel & Co., although it had long been informally known in this way.

The early nineteenth century was a period of rapid development in the stock exchange, which had acquired its own premises in 1802. British funds were the principal securities traded, together with East India Company, South Sea Company, and Bank of England stock. From the second decade of the nineteenth century the stock exchange was listing canal shares and by the mid-1830s railway company shares were also listed. By 1824 there were 156 companies quoted, and by 1842 this number had risen to 755, but in spite of this rapid growth, as late as 1853 British funds amounted to three-quarters of the total nominal value of securities quoted on the stock exchange. The stockbroking firm with which James Capel was associated was one of the principal dealers in government funds. After 1815 foreign government securities also began to make their appearance in the London stock exchange. James Capel became a member of the foreign committee. In the 1840s trading in these securities became increasingly difficult and the Spanish government proposed to repudiate its bonds. James Capel became chairman of the Spanish Bondholders' Committee and as such persuaded both the London stock exchange and the Paris bourse to suspend dealings in these bonds. Eventually, in 1852, the Spanish government was persuaded to give up this proposal and James Capel was presented with a piece of plate by grateful Spanish bondholders.

In 1841 fraud and forgery upon a considerable scale in exchequer bills were uncovered, and James Capel gave evidence before the Treasury committee appointed to investigate the matter. The mid-1840s saw rapid growth in dealings in railway shares, a period known as the 'railway mania'. James Capel & Co. played some part in railway company flotation and in 1849 James Capel gave evidence before the House of Lords select committee on railway accounts. By 1847 James Capel & Co., with five partners, was one of the two largest stockbroking firms in the London stock exchange, the other being Lawrence, Cazenove, and Pearson.

James Capel became one of the trustees and managers of the stock exchange in 1843, and chairman in 1853, when he oversaw the rebuilding of the premises of the stock exchange. He also became a member, and for twenty-five years chairman, of the Stock Exchange Fund for Decayed Members. By now he was living at 37 Fitzroy Square, London. He became treasurer of the London Orphan Asylum at Watford and remained in this office for eighteen years.

Marion Mary Capel died in Pisa at some time before 1861. James Capel himself died on 18 November 1872, at his home, 62 Westbourne Terrace, London. At the time of his death Capel was the oldest member of the stock exchange and was described by a contemporary as:

> a man of the strictest honour, untarnished reputation, exemplary in all business transactions, shrewd in his perceptions, keenly alive to the fluctuations of the market, clever at bargains for his clients, yet ever ready to act in a spirit of liberality in his dealings with his brother members of the Stock Exchange. (Guildhall MS 15096)

MICHAEL REED

Sources *The Times* (19 Nov 1872) • M. C. Reed, *A history of James Capel & Co.* (privately printed, London, 1975) • E. V. Morgan and W. A. Thomas, *The stock exchange: its history and functions*, 2nd edn (1969) • 'Exchequer bills forgery: report of the commissioners', *Parl. papers* (1842), 18.139, no. 409 • 'Select committee of the House of Lords on … the railway acts: first report', *Parl. papers* (1849), vol. 10, no. 371 [audit of accounts] • GL, James Capel & Co. MSS, Guildhall MS 15096

Archives GL, James Capel & Co. MSS, Guildhall MS 15096

Likenesses portrait (after photograph formerly in the possession of James Capel & Co.), repro. in Reed, *History of James Capel & Co.*

Wealth at death under £140,000: probate, 1872, *CGPLA Eng. & Wales*

Capel, Richard (1586–1656), Church of England clergyman and physician, was born in Gloucester, a younger son of Christopher Capel, a godly alderman of the city whose family came from Herefordshire, and his wife, Grace, daughter of Richard Hands. He matriculated from St Alban Hall, Oxford, on 19 June 1601, aged fourteen, was elected a demy of Magdalen College in 1604, graduated BA on 4 February 1605, and proceeded MA on 14 December 1607. From 1608 to 1614 he was a fellow of Magdalen, and recognized as one of the puritan tutors prominent in the college at that period; Accepted Frewen, the future archbishop of York, was one of his students. Friendship with Sir Thomas Overbury, son of the recorder of Gloucester, took Capel to court in attendance on the earl of Somerset until Overbury's death in 1613. That year he was instituted to the rectory of Eastington, Gloucestershire. At an unknown date he married Dorothy, daughter of William Plumstead of Plumstead, Norfolk; she died on 14 September 1622, aged twenty-eight. By late 1628 Capel had got married again, possibly to Marie, the wife mentioned in his will. He had at least four sons, Christopher, who matriculated from Magdalen College, Oxford, on 23 October 1635, aged sixteen, Daniel, Nathaniel, and John, and two daughters.

According to the memoir written by his friend Valentine Marshall, Capel 'was a very living Library, a full storehouse of all kinde of good Literature no lesse than a little University' (Marshall, 'To the reader'). In the later 1620s

Capel edited and published a number of treatises composed by his favourite student, William Pemble, who had died at his house at Eastington in 1623, including *An Introduction to the Worthy Receiving of the Sacrament of the Lord's Supper* (1628). On the title-page of Pemble's *Vindiciae gratiae* (1627), Capel emphasized that in the Magdalen Hall lectures reproduced there 'the maine sinews of ARMINIUS doctrine are cut asunder' (Cliffe, 87). Marshall claimed that Capel himself, although 'lively' in his prayers, was convinced of the lawfulness of set forms and 'lived and died a true Orthodox Divine according to the knowne doctrine of the Church of England' (Marshall), but placed him close to the great puritan writers John Dod, Richard Cleaver, and Arthur Hildersam. Anthony Wood ascribes to Capel *God's Valuation of Man's Soul* (1632), and he was certainly the author of *Tentations: their Nature, Danger, Cure* (1633), a 456 page work dedicated to Sir William Guise and commended to 'the Christian Reader' by the eminent preacher Richard Sibbes as written by 'this godly Minister (my Christian friend) … [who] besides faithfulnesse, and fruitfulnesse in his ministry, hath beene a good proficient in the schoole of temptation himself'. When the Book of Sports was reissued that year Capel declined to read it in his church and, voluntarily resigning his rectory, obtained from the bishop of Gloucester a licence to practise medicine. He then settled at Pitchcombe, near Stroud.

On the outbreak of the civil war Capel's elder brother William, an alderman of Gloucester, was briefly suspected of royalist sympathies, but Capel himself seems to have early aligned with parliament and to have resumed the exercise of his ministerial functions. He was nominated to the Westminster assembly in 1643 but did not sit. According to Marshall, he was still preaching twice on Sundays when he suddenly died at Pitchcombe on 21 September 1656; he was buried in the church there. His will, dated 22 May 1655, which left land in Westgate Street, Gloucester, and in the parishes of Pitchcombe, Haresfield, and Frampton-on-Severn, was proved by his widow, Marie, on 16 January 1657. His son Daniel, who had graduated BA from Magdalen College in 1649 and proceeded MA in 1651, received all Capel's books. Successively minister of Morton, Alderley, and (from 26 March 1658) Shipton Moyne, all in Gloucestershire, Daniel Capel was listed by Edmund Calamy as having been ejected for nonconformity, but he subscribed on 22 August 1662. By July 1663 he had left the living and removed to Stroud, where he practised medicine and attended the parish church; he was buried there on 24 September 1679.

THOMPSON COOPER, *rev.* VIVIENNE LARMINIE

Sources V. Marshall, *Capel's remains* (1658) • Foster, *Alum. Oxon.* • Wood, *Ath. Oxon.*, new edn, 3.421 • PRO, PROB 11/261, fols. 132r–133r • *Calamy rev.* • B. Brook, *The lives of the puritans*, 3 (1813), 259–60 • A. R. Warmington, *Civil war, interregnum and Restoration in Gloucestershire, 1640–1672* (1997) • J. T. Cliffe, *The puritan gentry: the great puritan families of early Stuart England* (1984), 36, 85, 84, 148–9

Capel, Sir Thomas Bladen (1776–1853), naval officer, youngest son of William Capel, fourth earl of Essex (1732–1799) and his second wife, Harriet (*d.* 12 March 1821), daughter of Colonel Thomas Bladen, was born on 25 August 1776, and entered in the books of the frigate *Phaeton* as captain's servant on 22 March 1782; it was ten years before he actually joined. After serving on the Newfoundland and home stations and being present as midshipman of the *Sans Pareil* in the action against *L'Orient* in Abu Qir Bay on 23 July 1795, he was, on 5 April 1797, promoted lieutenant and appointed to the frigate *Cambrian*, on the home station. In April 1798 he was appointed to the *Vanguard*, bearing the flag of Nelson, and, during the Mediterranean cruise which culminated in the battle of the Nile, acted as Nelson's signal officer. On 4 August 1798 he was appointed by Nelson to command the brig *Mutine* and sent home with duplicate dispatches, which, because of the capture of the *Leander*, brought the first news of the victory to England, on 2 October. His commander's commission was at once confirmed, and on 27 December he was advanced to post rank. On 5 January 1799 he was appointed to the frigate *Arab*, for the West Indian station. In July 1800 he was transferred to the *Meleager*, which on 9 June 1801 was wrecked in the Gulf of Mexico. In August 1802 he was appointed to the *Phoebe* (36 guns), in which he served in the Mediterranean for the three following years, and was present at Trafalgar, where he assisted in taking prize the French ships *Swiftsure* and *Bahama*.

On his return to England, Capel sat as a member of the court-martial on Sir Robert Calder, and on 27 December was appointed to the *Endymion* (40 guns), in which he again went to the Mediterranean, carrying Mr Arbuthnot, the British ambassador, to Constantinople, where he remained while the negotiations were pending, and on their failure brought Arbuthnot back to Malta. The *Endymion* was afterwards one of the fleet which, under Sir John Duckworth, forced the passage of the Dardanelles, on 19 February and 3 March 1807, in which she was struck by two enormous stone shot, upwards of 2 feet in diameter, and weighing nearly 800 lb, fortunately without sustaining much damage.

In December 1811 Capel was appointed to the *Hogue*, on the North American station, where he remained during the war with the United States, at one point commanding a small squadron blockading the American frigates in New London. In June 1815 he was nominated a CB. On 10 May 1816 he married Harriet Catherine (*d.* 30 July 1866), only daughter of Francis George Smyth of Upper Brook Street, London; they had no children.

In December 1821 Capel was appointed to command the yacht *Royal George*, where he remained until advanced to be rear-admiral on 27 May 1825. On 20 May 1832 he was made a KCB, and from May 1834 to July 1837 was commander-in-chief in the East Indies, with his flag in the *Winchester* (50 guns). He became vice-admiral on 10 January 1837, admiral on 28 April 1847, and GCB on 7 April 1852. He was commanding officer at Portsmouth from 1848 to 1852. He died at 22 Rutland Gate, Hyde Park, London, on 4 March 1853.

J. K. LAUGHTON, *rev.* ROGER MORRISS

Sources J. Marshall, *Royal naval biography*, 2/1 (1824), 195–8 · O'Byrne, *Naval biog. dict.* · *GM*, 2nd ser., 39 (1853), 540 · Boase, *Mod. Eng. biog.* · Burke, *Peerage*

Archives BL, letters to Sir Charles Napier, Add. MSS 40044–40045

Wealth at death under £12,000—personalty: *GM*

Capel, Thomas John (1836–1911), Roman Catholic priest, born at Ardmore, co. Waterford, on 28 October 1836, was the eldest son of John Capel and his wife, Mary Fitzgerald. His father, after service in the navy, joined the coastguard service and was stationed at Hastings, where Thomas received his early education from the parish priest before being placed in the care of the Revd J. M. Glennie, a Tractarian convert to Roman Catholicism resident at Brook Green, Hammersmith. In 1851 Glennie became the founding principal of St Mary's Roman Catholic Teacher Training College at Brook Green, and in 1853 Capel was one of the first students to obtain a teaching certificate there. From 1854 he taught at the normal school attached to the college, while studying for the priesthood. He was ordained priest by Cardinal Wiseman in his private chapel at York Place on 28 August 1859. Unusually, he did not attend a seminary, so it must be presumed that he was ordained on his own patrimony. The source of his private income is unknown.

In 1863 Capel retired for reasons of health to Pau, in the Basses-Pyrénées, where he acted as English Catholic chaplain, earned a reputation as a preacher and controversialist, and made some fashionable converts. While there he became acquainted with Charles Scott Murray, the patron of A. W. Pugin, who on his return to England in 1867 engaged him as his chaplain at Danesfield, near Marlow, Buckinghamshire. Scott Murray introduced him to John Patrick Crichton-Stuart, third marquess of Bute, then an undergraduate at Christ Church, Oxford, who adopted him as his spiritual director. In 1868 he paid several visits to Oxford, where his eloquence and charm produced an outbreak of Roman fever among the undergraduates of Christ Church, to the alarm of Dean Liddell. According to Bute, on the last day of his visit in December, after having 'operated privately on some rationalists' he drew an 'immense congregation' to his sermon at the Catholic chapel in St Clements (Blair, 71–2). Capel's reception of Bute into the Roman Catholic church on 8 December 1868 attracted much publicity. Early in 1869 he and Bute departed from Nice on the latter's yacht for a cruise to the Holy Land, calling *en route* at Rome, where they had a private audience of Pope Pius IX, who appointed Capel a papal chamberlain, with the title of Monsignor.

Attached to the pro-cathedral at Kensington on his return to England in 1869, Capel rapidly made his mark in London society and won over a number of titled converts. In 1870 he appeared, thinly disguised, as the worldly-wise and casuistical Monsignor Catesby in Disraeli's novel *Lothair* (1870). Two years later life converged with art when in April 1872 Disraeli was one of the witnesses at the wedding of Bute (Lothair) in Brompton Oratory, Capel celebrating the nuptial mass and Manning (Cardinal Grandison) performing the ceremony. On 7 September 1872, in its 'Men of the day' series, *Vanity Fair* profiled Capel as an 'apostle to the genteel', 'if not an admirer, at least a great controller of the fair sex', who had 'probably made and unmade more important marriages than any man or mamma in the country'.

In February 1873, with the backing of the duke of Norfolk and Lord Petre, Capel opened a Catholic public school at Kensington which was intended to attract the sons of the Catholic aristocracy away from Eton and Harrow. Impressed by his dynamism, Cardinal Manning appointed him in 1874 to the rectorship of his Catholic university which opened at Kensington in January 1875. The appointment was unanimously approved by the English Catholic hierarchy. The staff included scholars of the calibre of St G. Jackson Mivart, Frederick Apthorp Paley, and Charles Stanton Devas, and in three years the number of undergraduates rose from seventeen to fifty, but the scheme was handicapped by the opposition of the Jesuits and by a lack of co-operation from Newman, who declined an invitation to become a member of the senate. Capel devoted his principal energies to his school, and there were complaints that the university students were inadequately supervised. In 1878 a committee of investigation discovered that Capel had kept no accounts and was heavily in debt. On being requested to resign he threatened to sue the hierarchy for damages, and in order to avoid the scandal of a court case Manning was obliged to come to a private financial settlement. The university was wound up and Capel's school also closed, its patrons having withdrawn their support. A further charge of misconduct, involving young women, led to his suspension by Manning. Capel vigorously denied the charges and carried the case to Rome, where he had influential allies. In September 1882 he secured an acquittal, but Manning threatened to resign his see if he were allowed to return to England, and appealed to a higher authority. By a decree of 6 February 1887, valid worldwide, Capel was finally suspended from the exercise of his priestly faculties.

Meanwhile, in 1883 Capel had migrated to the United States, where he undertook a highly successful lecture tour of the eastern and mid-western states before settling in 1885 at San Francisco, where he lived in some style. In 1886 he took up permanent residence at Arno Ranch, near Galt, in northern California, as the guest of Mrs Alice Valensin, whose son he tutored. He continued to publish pamphlets in defence of ultramontane doctrine, and was befriended by Thomas Grace, the bishop of Sacramento, at whose residence he died on 23 October 1911. The entry he supplied to the *American Catholic Who's Who* of 1911 gives a somewhat misleading account of his meteoric career.

G. Martin Murphy

Sources V. A. McClelland, *English Roman Catholics and higher education, 1830–1903* (1973) · E. S. Purcell, *Life of Cardinal Manning*, 2 (1896), 497–505, 581–4 · D. O. H. Blair, *John Patrick, 3rd marquess of Bute: a memoir* (1921) · *VF* (7 Sept 1872) · T. Cooper and others, *Men of mark: a gallery of contemporary portraits*, 1 (1876), 32 · *The Times* (25 Oct 1911), 11 · *American Catholic who's who* (1911) · *Annual report of the Catholic Poor-School Committee*, 6 (1853), 14, 87 · P. Fletcher, *Recollections of a ransomer* (1924), 16 · Lord Braye [A. T. T. W. Edgell], *Fewness of my days: a life in two centuries* (1927), 70–76 · *Catholic Directory* (1912)

Likenesses Lock & Whitfield, woodburytype, NPG; repro. in T. Cooper, *Men of mark: a gallery of contemporary portraits* (1876) • London Stereoscopic Co., two cartes-de-visite, NPG • C. A. Loye, watercolour, NPG; repro. in *VF* (7 Sept 1872) • lithograph, NPG; repro. in *Whitehall Review* (24 Aug 1878)

Capel, William, third earl of Essex (1697–1743), diplomatist and courtier, was the eldest son of Algernon Capel, second earl of Essex (1670–1710), and Lady Mary (*d.* 1726), the eldest daughter of William Bentinck, first earl of Portland. Nothing is known of his education, but in 1718 he was appointed gentleman of the bedchamber to the prince of Wales, an office he continued to hold after the prince's accession to the throne as George II. On 27 November of that year Capel married Lady Jane Hyde, the eldest surviving daughter of Henry Hyde, second earl of Clarendon, at Petersham, Surrey. Jane died on 3 January 1724, leaving Capel with four daughters. In 1722 he was constituted lord lieutenant of Hertfordshire, and in 1725 he was made a knight of the Order of the Thistle. On 3 February 1726 he married his second wife, Elizabeth Russell (*d.* 1784), the youngest daughter of Wriothesley, second duke of Bedford, with whom he had four daughters and two sons.

In 1727 Capel was appointed keeper of St James's and Hyde parks, a position which he resigned on 4 December 1739 on being appointed captain yeoman of the guard. Between 1731 and 1736 he served as minister-plenipotentiary and then as ambassador-extraordinary to the king of Sardinia at Turin. On 12 February 1735 he was sworn of the privy council, and on 20 February 1738 he was made a knight companion of the Order of the Garter. He died at Watford on 8 January 1743, and was buried there on 17 January. The peerage then passed to his second son, William Anne (1732–1799).

T. F. Henderson, *rev.* Philip Carter

Sources GEC, *Peerage* • D. B. Horn, ed., *British diplomatic representatives, 1689–1789*, CS, 3rd ser., 46 (1932) • *GM*, 1st ser., 13 (1743), 51 • A. Collins, *The peerage of England: containing a genealogical and historical account of all the peers of England*

Archives BL, diplomatic corresp., Add. MSS 27730–27738, 60387 | BL, letters from Benjamin Keene, Add. MSS 43416–43421, *passim* • BL, corresp. with duke of Newcastle, Add. MSS 32689–32793, *passim* • BL, letters to Thomas Robinson, Add. MSS 23785–23797, *passim* • NRA, priv. coll., corresp. with first Earl Waldegrave

Capell, Edward (1713–1781), literary scholar, elder son of the Revd Gamaliel Capell, was born at Troston Hall, near Bury, Suffolk, on 11 June 1713. There were four other children. Capell was educated at Bury grammar school. On 15 May 1730 Capell was admitted a pensioner at St Catharine's College, Cambridge. Six days earlier he had been admitted to the Middle Temple. Pegge says that in his youth 'he was a professed beau, and much inclined to gallantry, as well as gaiety in dress' (Pegge, 474). Capell was called to the bar on 27 January 1738.

Thanks to a long-standing connection with the family of the duke of Grafton, Capell was made deputy inspector of plays following the Licensing Act of 1737. The same patron caused his appointment as groom of the privy chamber in 1745. The combined income of these posts was reckoned at £300 per annum. With the manors of Troston and Stanton, which he inherited from his father who died in 1756, Capell was financially independent. He seems to have been a cautious licenser, objecting in 1773 to Antonio Sacchini's opera *Tamerlano* that it was 'too like the present state of our royal family' (Walpole, *Corr.*, 39.169). As part of his duties Capell was in regular contact with the actor-manager David Garrick, who became his closest friend and supporter, though Capell is supposed to have said that Garrick 'spoke many speeches in Shakespeare without understanding them' (Pegge, 474). In 1756 Garrick asked Capell to draw up an inventory or catalogue of his extensive collection of drama, which Capell had been consulting; this formed the basic catalogue for the eventual transfer of the collection to the British Museum and stimulated further collecting by both men. One further fruit of this alliance was a performing version of Shakespeare's *Antony and Cleopatra*, 'fitted for the stage by abridging only' (1758). The printing was done by Dryden Leach, who observed Capell's idiosyncratic system of punctuation and sigla. In 1759 Capell and Garrick commissioned a portrait of Shakespeare, from the Chandos portrait, now in Trinity College, Cambridge.

Edward Capell (1713–1781), by Francesco Bartolozzi, pubd 1779 (after Louis François Roubiliac, 1759)

In 1745 Capell had been struck by the unsystematic editing of Shakespeare performed by Thomas Hanmer and had begun working on a new edition. By 1750 he had collected all the recent editions of Shakespeare, the folios, and most of the known quartos. A transcript of the complete plays was begun on 25 November 1749 and completed on 1 August 1766; this survives in Trinity College, Cambridge, but the story that Capell transcribed Shakespeare ten times testifies only to contemporaries' sense of his obsessional nature. In 1760 Capell published *Prolusions* as a manifesto: an edition of ballads, poems, and *Edward the Third*, a play ascribed to Shakespeare. The texts were 'compiled with great care from the several originals, and offered to the public as specimens of the integrity that should be found in the editions of worthy authors'. Again, the printing and punctuation (with a system of signs for asides, gestures, changes of address and even for irony) caused a minor stir in literary circles. Thomas Percy learned something from the volume and Percy and Capell hunted and borrowed books for and from each other in the early 1760s.

In 1767 Capell began to publish his long-prepared edition of Shakespeare. The first sheet of the edition went to press in September 1760, and the last in August 1765, just as Johnson's edition was being published (Warburton asked Garrick to persuade Capell not to publish at all, given the authority of Johnson's edition). Capell was paid £300, somewhat less than Johnson and previous editors. The edition (in ten small octavo volumes, 1767–8) was warmly dedicated to the duke of Grafton. The introduction was written in an antiquated style, causing Johnson (with *The Tempest* in mind) to remark: 'If the man would have come to me, I would have endeavoured to "endow his purposes with words;" for, as it is, "he doth gabble monstrously"' (Boswell, *Life*, 4.5). The edition was presented in accordance with the principles established in *Prolusions*, with few on-page notes. It was the first edition to be prepared from a complete transcript rather than a marked-up copy of the previous edition, and it marked a change of editorial policy in which the *textus receptus* was rejected in favour of an unusually meticulous collation of the early quartos and first folio. Pegge records that Lord Dacre wrote to Capell as the 'Restorer of Shakespeare', and that Capell wept on reading the letter. Capell was the first to drop Rowe's anecdotal account of Shakespeare's life; he set the agenda for the documentary research of Edmund Malone into Shakespearian chronology and biography.

About 1760 Capell built himself a house near the sea at Hastings, at a cost of about £5000. Each year he lived here from May to October, 'equally unknowing and unknown' (Pegge, 475). Otherwise Capell lived in London at Essex Court, and latterly in 5 Brick Court, Middle Temple, where he became increasingly reclusive. Pegge describes his personal habits as extremely fastidious. A 'disposition naturally upon the fret' (ibid.) was soured by disappointment. Capell did not name those who had contributed to his edition, and in turn much of his labours were either anticipated or appropriated by other scholars. In *A Letter to George Hardinge* (1777), ostensibly by the Revd John Collins, George Steevens was accused of plagiarism from Capell; it was rumoured that Steevens had bribed the printer to let him have the sheets as they were printed off, and that he sat up at night to copy them. Malone vied with Capell for possession of early printed books; they bargained for access to each other's collections with strained politeness.

On his sixty-sixth birthday Capell donated his collection of 245 volumes (including 55 Shakespeare quartos), to Trinity College, Cambridge, where his brother Robert was a senior fellow. Steevens compiled a catalogue of the collection (1779); a fuller catalogue was published by W. W. Greg in 1903. The collection also contains work on an edition of Milton's *Paradise Lost*, as well as a treatise on phonetics, which Capell had been interested in since the 1740s. In 1774 Capell published the first volume of *Notes and Various Readings to Shakespeare*, promised in the edition of 1767–8. This contained notes and variants to nine plays, and a glossary. When the Dillys were unable to sell it, he recalled the remaining copies. Hardinge later persuaded Capell to publish the *Notes* by subscription at a guinea a volume; in a letter to Horace Walpole Hardinge claims 'There is a knot of Booksellers formed against him, because he is (I will not say the best, but) the only Editor of Shakspeare' (Pegge, 3.203). Walpole did not subscribe, and the list was rather respectable than numerous. Capell himself died before the project was finished, and it was edited in three quarto volumes (1783) by Collins, who in a dedication to Lord Dacre extended his complaints about Steevens's plagiarism. The first volume was a reissue with new preliminaries of the volume issued in 1774. The second volume included the first substantial attempt at a chronology of Shakespeare's plays. The third volume consisted of *The School of Shakespeare*, an anthology of extracts from the literature of Shakespeare's day which might have formed sources for the plays; it also included *Notitia dramatica*, Capell's bibliography of printed drama. The awkwardness of using separate notes and variants alongside the edition in a much smaller format contributed to the neglect of the overall editorial project. Johnson complained that the notes were 'just sufficient to select the black hairs from the white for the use of the periwig makers' (Francklin, 115).

Pegge describes Capell as a 'personable, well-made man, of the middle stature', who 'had much of the carriage, manners, and sentiments of a gentleman' (Pegge, 473). In later life Capell was afflicted with a 'scorbutic humour' which coarsened his features; Pegge implies that visits to brothels during his youth affected his constitution and eventually caused his death. Capell died on 24 February 1781 at Brick Court and was buried without epitaph at Fornham All Saints, Suffolk. In his will (PRO, PROB 11/1075, sig. 123 [1781]), dated 12 February 1780, Capell left a series of annuities to his surviving sisters, his nieces, and his servants; he made further bequests to his godson and executors. The Hastings house was sold and added to his personal estate, to cover the publication costs of *Notes and Various Readings*; the real estate was bequeathed for life to his brother Robert Capell, who survived him only until 1 November 1781, and then to his nephew Capell Loft, the residuary legatee. The copyright of *Notes and Various Readings* was left to John Collins in a rare personal testimony to their friendship.

PAUL BAINES

Sources S. Pegge, 'Brief memoir of Edward Capell', Nichols, *Illustrations*, 1.465–76; 3.203 • A. Walker, 'Edward Capell and his editions of "Shakespeare"', *Studies in Shakespeare*, ed. P. Alexander (1964), 132–40 • *Monthly Review*, 69 (1783), 483–8 • Nichols, *Lit. anecdotes*, 5.597; 8.535, 540, 662; 9.425 • G. W. Stone and G. M. Kahrl, *David Garrick: a critical biography* (1979), 174–7, 182, 190–93 • P. Martin, *Edmond Malone, Shakespearean scholar: a literary biography* (1995) • B. Vickers, ed., *Shakespeare: the critical heritage*, 5: 1765–1774 (1979), 32–5 • S. E. Sen, *Capell and Malone, and modern critical bibliography* (1960) • C. Francklin, *Shakespeare domesticated: the eighteenth-century editions* (1991), 28–9, 112–16 • *The correspondence of Thomas Percy and Thomas Warton*, ed. M. G. Robinson and L. Dennis (1951), vol. 3 of *The Percy letters*, ed. C. Brooks, D. N. Smith, and A. F. Falconer (1944–88) • *The correspondence of Thomas Percy and William Shenstone*, ed. C. Brooks (1977), vol. 7 of *The Percy letters*, ed. C. Brooks, D. N. Smith, and A. F. Falconer (1944–88) • Boswell, *Life*, 4.5 • Venn, *Alum. Cant.* • *GM*, 1st ser., 87/1 (1817), 157

Archives Folger • Trinity Cam., collection | Yale U., Osborn collection
Likenesses F. Bartolozzi, line engraving (after plaster medallion by L. F. Roubiliac, 1759), BM, NPG; repro. in E. Capell, *Notes and various readings to Shakespeare*, 3 vols. (1779–80) [*see illus.*] • A. Smith, print (after L. F. Roubiliac), repro. in J. Bell, ed., *The dramatic writings of Will. Shakespeare*, 20 vols. (1705–88) • oils (of Capell?), St Catharine's College, Cambridge
Wealth at death real estate in Suffolk and Sussex; monetary bequests amounting to several thousands of pounds: will, 1781, PRO, PROB 11/1075, sig. 123; Nichols, *Illustrations*, 1.473n

Capern, Edward (1819–1894), poet, was born at Tiverton, Devon, on 21 January 1819, the son of Edward Capern, a baker, and his wife, Elizabeth. His parents were poor and at the age of eight he began to earn his living in a Derby lace factory at Barnstaple. The detailed work damaged his eyesight and he was forced to abandon it in 1847. On 26 October of that year Capern married Jane Trick (1819/20–1894), a dressmaker and the daughter of William and Elizabeth Trick of Ashford by Barnstaple, Devon. They had two children: a son, Charles (*b.* 1848/9), and a daughter, Milly (1852/3–*c.*1860). In May 1848 he became a rural postman walking between Bideford and Appledore, earning 10*s.* 6*d.* per week. He lost his job in September 1849 when alterations in the post occurred but was reappointed in December 1851. His route took him between Bideford and Buckland Brewer, a 13 mile round trip, which he completed for a number of years on foot and later with a pony and trap.

It was about this time that Capern began to write verse for the 'Poet's corner' of the *North Devon Journal*, and his poems were soon in great demand at country gatherings. William Frederick Rock of Barnstaple, a stationer and philanthropist, enlisted the help of subscribers such as W. S. Landor, Alfred Lord Tennyson, Charles Dickens, and Charles Kingsley to publish *Poems by Edward Capern, Rural Postman of Bideford, Devon* (1856). The little volume received lavish praise. Landor lauded a number of the poems in his *Letters* and dedicated 'Antony and Octavius' to Capern. Froude eulogized him in *Fraser's Magazine*, while *The Athenaeum* spoke no less highly of his work. The 1000 copies of the first edition sold out in three months and the book is said to have earned Capern £150. So impressed was Palmerston with Capern's poem 'The Lion Flag of England', about the Crimean War, that on 23 November 1857 he bestowed on the rural postman a civil-list pension of £40, which was raised in 1865 to £60. The poem, which contains the lines

Hurrah! For dear old England!
Come, Britons, one and all,
Strike on, strike hard, strike sure

was also sent as a broadsheet to the troops.

In 1858 Capern issued his *Ballads and Songs*, dedicated to Lady Burdett-Coutts. William Ormond, in his *Recollections of Edward Capern* (1860), depicted the postman-poet as an unassuming, simple, and self-taught man, at one with nature and beloved by everyone. Capern with his clear and ruddy complexion was, Ormond wrote, 'the very *beau idéal* of a sound, hale, and hearty Englishman' and his voice exuded the 'full, rich, unctuous tones to which at all times it is so pleasing to listen, and so invariably suggestive of a sunny and generous disposition' (Ormond, 7–8).

In 1862 Capern's *Devonshire Melodist*, a selection from his songs with his own musical airs, appeared. In the preface to his collection *Wayside Warbles* (1865) Capern reinforced his image as the unspoilt country versifier. He explained that his poems were composed 'in the open air, while doing duty as a rural postman', 'the rude bar of a Devonshire stile or field-gate' serving as a writing desk (Capern, *Wayside Warbles*, v–vi). His daughter Milly died about 1860 and, having celebrated her in his early poems, Capern now mourned her with, among others, 'The Robin is Weeping', 'Disconsolate', and 'The Voice from the Cloud'.

With his health in decline, Capern retired in 1866 on a pension of £8 9*s.* 5*d.* and in 1868 he left Marine Gardens, Bideford, to settle at Harborne, near Birmingham, to be close to his son Charles. Capern had considerable success as a lecturer in the midlands and often contributed to Tom Hood's weekly penny paper *Fun*. He also saw a good deal of the American blacksmith and reformer Elihu Burritt, then the US consular agent at Birmingham. The two men often went on long walks together, all the while discussing nature, poetry, and philosophy. Capern's final book of poems, *Sungleams and Shadows*, appeared in 1881.

Capern returned to Devon in 1884, on account of his wife Jane's ill health, 'full of honours and rich in friends', with 'a purse containing a hundred sovereigns' (Wright, 72), and settled at Braunton, near Bideford. In later life his beard was snow white and he sported round spectacles. In February 1894 his 'blithe and bonnie Janie', who inspired many of his poems, died and it seems that he never quite recovered from the shock (ibid., 73). Edward Capern died on 4 June 1894 at home, Brookdale House, Braunton, Devon. Lady Burdett-Coutts insisted on paying for the funeral and his coffin was draped in the lion flag of England, topped with a laurel wreath. He was buried on 9 June next to his wife at St Augustine's churchyard at Heanton Puncherdon, overlooking the vale of the Torridge. His request to have his postman's handbell buried with him was not carried out because the bell could not be found in time. It was, however, later fixed in a niche in the headstone, which was also inscribed with lines from Alfred Austin, the poet laureate.

THOMAS SECCOMBE, *rev.* JANE POTTER

Sources P. H. W. Almy, 'The Postman Poet of Bideford: Edward Capern', *Sunday Magazine* (July 1896), 447–52 • W. Ormond, *Recollections of Edward Capern* (1860) • *Biograph and Review*, 1st ser., 2 (1879), 479–83 • W. H. K. Wright, *West-country poets: their lives and works* (1896) • www.john.lerwell.btinternet.co.uk/personal/postpoet.htm (8 July 2002) • Boase, *Mod. Eng. biog.* • *CGPLA Eng. & Wales* (1894) • *IGI*
Likenesses W. Widgery, oils, 1857, Bideford Public Library, Devon • photograph, *c.*1890, repro. in Wright, *West-country poets* • E. Williams, oils, Bideford Public Library, Devon
Wealth at death £98 5*s.*: probate, 3 July 1894, *CGPLA Eng. & Wales*

Capes, William Wolfe (1834–1914), Church of England clergyman and classical scholar, was the third son of Joseph Capes, an employee of the Royal Mint and a bookseller in Paternoster Row, London, and his wife, Anne, daughter of Joseph Wolfe, of Reading. He was born on 1

January 1834 in the parish of St Michael-le-Querne, London, probably in Paternoster Row. He was admitted to St Paul's School, London, on 31 January 1843. A keen pedestrian, he used to walk to school daily from Norwood, where his parents then lived; at sixteen he began to travel abroad (he continued these journeys throughout his life), making an expedition, mainly on foot, from the Netherlands to Rome. In 1852 he went up to Oxford, as Michel exhibitioner at Queen's College. The foundation of the college was then being thrown open, and in 1854 Capes was elected to a taberdarship, previously a closed scholarship. He had in 1853 obtained first classes at moderations in classics and mathematics, and in the final honour schools in 1855 he obtained a first class in classics and a second class in mathematics.

Capes was elected fellow of Queen's on 11 December 1856, and as tutor found himself responsible for all the college teaching in *literae humaniores*. He proceeded MA in 1858, and remained a fellow of Queen's until 1870. He was ordained in 1865, and served briefly as curate at Abbot's Anne, near Andover. He returned to college work, and was junior proctor in 1865–6, and examiner in *literae humaniores* in 1867–9, 1873–5, and 1878–9. In 1869 he was presented by his college to the rectory of Bramshott, Hampshire, which he held for thirty-two years. On 23 August 1870 he married Mary (1836/7–1908), daughter of John Leadbeater, of Blackburn. Bramshott was an extensive agricultural parish and, with as many as fourteen gatherings on Sundays for teaching and worship, the services of his wife, his curate, the schoolmasters, and other laymen were called on. But Capes spent three or four days in the middle of each week of term in Oxford, and was from 1870 to 1887 university reader of ancient history. From 1876 to 1886 he was elected fellow and tutor of Hertford College. At this time Capes published *The Early Roman Empire* (1874) and *The Age of the Antonines* (1877), both in a series of Epochs of Ancient History, *University Life in Ancient Athens* (1877), a course of lectures based on Greek inscriptions, and *Stoicism* (1883). Several of these were reissued in the twentieth century. He also prepared editions of some of the texts newly introduced as set books for university honours courses. An edition of Livy, books xxi and xxii (1880), which was reprinted as late as 1960, was followed by one of Sallust (1884) and the part of Polybius containing the history of the Achaean league (1888). Capes was select preacher to the university (1873–4), rural dean of Petersfield, and honorary canon of Winchester from 1894 to 1903. His *History of the English Church in the Fourteenth and Fifteenth Centuries* (1900) was the third volume of an eight-volume work on *The English Church*. Although reprinted in 1968, it had by then very largely outlived its usefulness.

Capes resigned the rectory of Bramshott in 1901 and settled for a while at Addington, Kent, where he wrote *Rural Life in Hampshire* (1903), an account of the neighbourhood of Bramshott. In 1903 he was collated to a residentiary canonry in Hereford Cathedral, and in 1908 he published *The Charters and Records of Hereford Cathedral* with a long introduction containing a valuable account of the constitution of the cathedral. In the late twentieth century this was still a useful work, not least as others have proved reluctant to improve on it. Capes had earlier founded the Cantilupe Society, which succeeded in a few years in printing all the pre-Reformation registers of the bishops of Hereford. Six of these he himself edited, and he took an active interest in the work of his colleagues. He was one of the first scholars to apply himself to publishing this sort of record and is remembered for his early lead, even if his editions have not themselves stood the test of time. He also began arranging and cataloguing the valuable cathedral library, but this he had not finished at his death, on 30 October 1914 at his home in the cathedral close at Hereford. He and his wife were both buried at Bramshott. They had no children. J. R. MAGRATH, *rev.* ELIZABETH BAIGENT

Sources J. Percival, 'A memoir of Canon Capes', in *The register of Thomas Poltone*, ed. W. W. Capes (1916), i–xxiv · personal knowledge (1927) · private information (1927) · Foster, *Alum. Oxon.* · *WWW* · m. cert. · *CGPLA Eng. & Wales* (1914)

Wealth at death £41,977 9s. 0d.: probate, 3 Dec 1914, *CGPLA Eng. & Wales*

Capetanakis, Demetrios (1912–1944), poet and literary critic, was born in Smyrna (now Izmir in Turkey) on 22 January 1912, the son of Apostolos Capetanakis, a medical doctor from Zagora in Pelion, who settled in Athens in 1922. Demetrios was educated at Athens University, where he studied political science and economics. In Greece he published several philosophical works, including *Apo ton agōna ton psychikōs monou* ('The struggle of the solitary soul', 1934) and *Mythologia tou ōraiou* ('The mythology of beauty', 1937). He studied at Heidelberg University (1934–6) under Karl Jaspers, where he obtained the degree of DPhil, writing a dissertation entitled *Liebe und Zeit* ('Love and time'). In Germany he came under the influence of the writings of the German poet Stefan George. He later rejected George's influence, saying in his essay on George that in his attitudes he 'was one of those who prepared the way for the Nazis' (Lehmann, *Demetrios Capetanakis*, 89).

In 1939, with a British Council scholarship, Capetanakis arrived in England, where he spent the remainder of his brief life. At Cambridge he was a pupil of Dadie Rylands at King's College. It was there that he met John Lehmann, the editor of *New Writing* and of *Penguin New Writing*, who became a close friend. While he said of Lehmann, 'away from you I am just nothing' (Wright, 129) and 'all I have created up to now was the work of both of us' (ibid., 128), it seems unlikely that he and Lehmann were lovers. Much of his writing appeared in Lehmann's periodicals, in the wartime evolution of which he was very active, contributing essays, poems, and translations of Greek poetry.

Capetanakis was fluent in French and German and had written in both languages. On his arrival in England he began to write in English. Capetanakis wrote major essays on Rimbaud, Dostoevsky, and Proust, as well as briefer pieces on Thomas Gray and Horace Walpole, Charlotte Brontë, 'A view of English poetry', and 'Notes on some contemporary writers'. The ideas in these essays may well derive from his time with the existentialist Karl Jaspers: 'Silence is what surrounds our lives' (Lehmann, *Demetrios*

Capetanakis, 136); 'It is only when we dare to face unreality, nothingness, that we become real' (ibid., 131).

It is in his dozen or so poems in English that Capetanakis shows himself to be remarkable—not merely because they are written by someone who had studied English for only a few months before coming to England, but because of their power, directness, and economy. They are reminiscent of Emily Dickinson, whom Capetanakis was precocious in admiring. In his essay on Dostoevsky he spoke of 'two kinds of writers: those whose world is protected by a hedge … and those whose world is not protected by anything against the powers of nothingness' (Lehmann, *Demetrios Capetanakis*, 104). His poems are clearly the work of a writer who does not see his world as 'protected'. His poem 'Abel' expresses starkly the ambiguous relation of victim and perpetrator that we have to evil:

> The ageless ambiguity of things
> Which makes our life mean death, our love be hate.
> My blood that streams across the bedroom sings:
> 'I am my brother opening the gate!'

Edith Sitwell, who championed Capetanakis's poetry, said of this poem that in it 'the central problem of humanity is finding words' (ibid., 38).

Capetanakis had a profound effect on those who knew him. William Plomer wrote:

> Of his physical presence the chief feature was his dark eyes, glowing with intelligence and feeling. He was slight in build and had delicate, nervous hands … the whole face was harmonious … it had a kind of radiance, an effect of luminosity. (Lehmann, *Demetrios Capetanakis*, 183)

John Lehmann said, 'he entered into your mind and heart with an uncanny power of imaginative understanding' (Lehmann, *I am my Brother*, 119).

Capetanakis left Cambridge in 1941 to join the press office of the Greek embassy in London; but before that he showed signs of the leukaemia which eventually killed him, though it was not then correctly diagnosed. Shortly after arriving in London, he found himself in hospital; but he rallied sufficiently to continue his activities, and looked forward to a long period of literary work. By autumn 1942 he was ill again, and was sent to Devon to rest. In 1943 he was invited to the Cadbury's Manor Farm in Birmingham to assist in training members of the Friends' Ambulance Unit who would be working in Greece at its liberation. He returned to London, but his apparent recovery did not continue. He had fits of dizziness and was finally admitted to the Westminster Hospital in London, where he died on 9 March 1944.

Capetanakis's funeral was held at the Greek cathedral in Bayswater and he was interred in the Greek enclosure at Norwood cemetery. His passing was commemorated in a volume edited and published in 1947 by John Lehmann, *Demetrios Capetanakis: a Greek Poet in England*, bringing together his writings in English along with recollections by friends. A. T. Tolley

Sources J. Lehmann, ed., *Demetrios Capetanakis: a Greek poet in England* (1947) • J. Lehmann, *I am my brother* (1960) • A. Wright, *John Lehmann: a pagan adventure* (1998) • A. T. Tolley, *The poetry of the forties* (1985) • *Pangosmio viografiko lexiko* [Universal biographical dictionary], 9 vols. (Athens, 1983–8) • G. T. Zoras, ed., *Megalē enkyklopaideia tēs neoellēnikēs logotechnias* [Encyclopaedia of modern Greek literature], 12 vols. (Athens, 1968) • personal knowledge (2004) • private information (2004) [Greek embassy, Ottawa; T. Fotiou] • d. cert.
Archives Hellenic Literary and Historical Archives, Athens, Greece | U. Texas, John Lehmann archive, MSS
Likenesses H. Wild, photograph, repro. in Lehmann, ed., *Demetrios Capetanakis*, frontispiece • H. Wild, photograph, repro. in Lehmann, *I am my brother*, facing p. 153

Capgrave, John (1393–1464), prior of Bishop's Lynn, theologian, and historian, was born on 21 April 1393. Nothing is known of his family, unless an older John Capgrave, who took the degree of doctor of theology at Oxford in 1390, and was also an Augustinian friar, was his uncle. Some early biographers, notably Bale, confused the two John Capgraves. A native of Bishop's Lynn, Norfolk—'My cuntre is Northfolke, of the town of Lynne' (*Life of St Katharine*, 16)—in 1406 he witnessed the departure from Lynn of Henry IV's daughter, Philippa, to marry Eric IX, king of Denmark. Apart from a period of study he spent most of his life in Bishop's Lynn. Capgrave presumably entered the order of Augustinian friars, at their friary in Lynn, about 1410, some six or seven years before his ordination to the priesthood in 1416–17, and his early training probably took place in the *studium grammaticale* in the Bishop's Lynn friary. He studied theology for five years at the order's *studium generale provinciae* in London until 1421–2, his presence in London in 1421 being confirmed by his notice of the jubilation of the crowd at the birth of Henry VI on 6 December. Indeed, by 1421 Capgrave had already become lector, permitted to teach in any school of the order except a *studium generale ordinis*, as recorded by the consent given by the prior-general on 8 April 1421.

From London Capgrave was licensed by the prior-general (13 April 1422) to further his studies in Cambridge at the order's *studium generale ordinis*. There he had to deliver an examinatory sermon in Latin, which he did in 1422, and later he wrote up an English version of it as his *Tretis* on the twelve orders who followed the rule of St Augustine. On 20 March 1423 Capgrave graduated bachelor of theology, sanctioned by the prior-general, and subsequently became master of theology, probably in 1425. According to Roth his progress from ordination to the magisterium was 'the fastest promotion on record' among English Augustinian friars (Roth, 1.174), justification, no doubt, for Leland's report that Capgrave 'stuck to his books like a limpet to its rocks' (*Commentarii*, 2.453). According to the usual practice he probably remained in Cambridge as master regent until 1427. Capgrave's earliest work was his *Life of St Norbert* in English verse, composed before 1422. In 1440 he added an envoi dedicating the work to John Wygenhale, abbot of the Premonstratensian abbey at West Dereham, Norfolk. From 1427 onwards he presumably continued to be engaged in teaching and literary activity, and about twenty-five works attributed to him by his biographers, but since lost, probably belonged to the period 1427–38. His lost biblical commentaries *In regum* were dedicated to Humphrey, duke of Gloucester (*d.* 1447), and John Lowe, prior provincial of the Augustinian friars from 1427 to 1433, and later bishop of St Asaph. His commentary *In Genesim*, begun on 11 October 1437 and completed on 21 September 1438, Capgrave personally presented to Duke Humphrey at Woodstock on 1 January 1439. Presumably encouraged, between 17 January 1439 and 6 May 1440 he wrote his commentary *In Exodum*, but the preface shows signs of frustration with Duke Humphrey as a literary patron. In 1440 Capgrave was the named beneficiary of a small bequest by John Spycer of Bishop's Lynn.

On Passion Sunday (2 April) 1441 Capgrave was present at the laying of the foundation stone of King's College, Cambridge, by Henry VI. About 1442 he wrote his *Concordia* 'made to reform charity' between the Augustinian friars and the Augustinian canons (Capgrave, *Tretis*, in *Lives of St Augustine and St Gilbert*, 146), a work (now lost) which was dedicated to John Watford, abbot of the Augustinian canons at Northampton. By 1445 he had also written his *Life of St Katharine*, his only other work in English verse besides his *Norbert*. On 1 August 1446 Capgrave, now presumably prior of the Augustinian friary at Bishop's Lynn, was host for Henry VI's visit there, a notice of which Capgrave added to his exemplar copy of his *De illustribus Henricis* (Cambridge, Corpus Christi College, MS 408). Capgrave must have remained prior, as he is recorded in office in 1456. In 1449–50 Capgrave visited Rome for the holy year of jubilee, funded by Sir Thomas Tuddenham (*d.* 1462), lord of the manor of Oxborough and keeper of the great wardrobe in the royal household (1446–50). It was ostensibly for him that Capgrave wrote his *Solace of Pilgrimes*, a guide to Rome. Before 1451 Capgrave also wrote his *Life of St Augustine*, and in 1451 he completed his *Life of St Gilbert*. The *Gilbert* and the *Tretis* were both dedicated to Nicholas Reysby, master-general of the Gilbertine order of Sempringham. About 1452 Capgrave wrote his *Manipulus doctrinae Christianae*, now lost, dedicated to Cardinal John Kemp, archbishop of Canterbury (1452–4). On 22 July 1453 Capgrave was elected prior provincial and on 6 August 1455 he was re-elected for a further two-year term at Lynn. On 21 April 1456 he was present at the Augustinian friary in Oxford for the reception of Edmund Rede of Boarstall. After vacating his position as prior provincial in 1457 Capgrave wrote his biblical commentary *In Actus Apostolorum*. In return for the kindness of visiting him while he was ill in Rome, he dedicated this work to William Grey, king's proctor in Rome in 1450, and now bishop of Ely (1454–78). His treatise on the creeds, *De fidei symbolis* (*c.*1462), was also dedicated to Grey. Another work completed *c.*1462–3 was the *Abbreviacion of Cronicles*. On the accession of Edward IV in 1461 the dedicatory preface was added, in which Edward was compared favourably with the failed Henry VI. Capgrave died on 12 August 1464 at Bishop's Lynn.

Capgrave was the most learned of all English Augustinian friars, and his output of literary works was outstanding. He wrote commentaries (in Latin) on most of the books of the Bible, also other theological works, a chronicle, two works *De viris illustribus*, saints' lives, and a guide to Rome. This collection of forty-one works (seven of which are in English) is very similar in scope to those produced by some early church fathers. Modestly describing himself as 'a man somewhat endowed with learning' (*Lives of St Augustine and St Gilbert*, 1), he played on his name in Latin to call himself, in the preface to *De fidei symbolis*, Johannes de Monumento Pileato (John of the Grave with the Scholar's Cap) (*Liber de illustribus Henricis*, 213). Most of his works were written at the behest of a particular individual or were addressed to a specific dedicatee: biblical commentaries and other theological works were dedicated to bishops (Lowe, Kemp, and Grey) and to Duke Humphrey; the lives of saints who inspired or founded religious orders were dedicated to the heads of (houses of) those orders (Wygenhale, Reysby, Watford); and secular biographical and historical works were dedicated to kings. Only twelve of Capgrave's works, including all seven English ones, have survived, most of them in a group of manuscripts closely associated with the author. Eight survive in manuscripts written by the author (*Norbert*, *Augustine*, *Gilbert*, *Tretis*, *De illustribus Henricis*, *Solace*, *Acts*, *Abbreviacion of Cronicles*) and three in manuscripts written by another scribe but revised by the author (*Genesis*, *Exodus*, *Creeds*). Several presentation copies survive—*Norbert* for Wygenhale, *Genesis* and *Exodus* for Duke Humphrey, *Acts* and *Creeds* for Grey, possibly also *Solace* for Tuddenham, and *Abbreviacion of Cronicles* for Edward IV.

Leland, Bale, and their followers probably overestimated Capgrave's importance as a hagiographer by erroneously associating him with the *Nova legenda Anglie*, an alphabetical rearrangement of John Tynemouth's *Sanctilogium*. His theological works, written at the end of an era, attracted little attention. His saints' lives are interesting for their treatment of their sources. His most important historical work, the *Abbreviacion of Cronicles*, provides a framework for world history within an Augustinian providential scheme, drawing its English material from the St Albans chronicles by Thomas Walsingham and others, the version used by Capgrave being superior to those now surviving. Capgrave is also important for the light his manuscript materials shed on late medieval 'publication'. PETER J. LUCAS

Sources *John Capgrave's 'Abbreviacion of cronicles'*, ed. P. J. Lucas, EETS, 285 (1983) · A. de Meijer, 'John Capgrave, O.E.S.A.', *Augustiniana*, 5 (1955), 400–40 · A. de Meijer, 'John Capgrave, O.E.S.A.', *Augustiniana*, 7 (1957), 118–48, 531–75 · P. J. Lucas, 'John Capgrave, OSA (1393–1464), scribe and publisher', *Transactions of the Cambridge Bibliographical Society*, 5 (1969–71), 1–35 · *Johannis Capgrave Liber de illustribus Henricis*, ed. F. C. Hingeston, Rolls Series, 7 (1858) · *John Capgrave's Lives of St Augustine and St Gilbert of Sempringham*, ed. J. J. Munro, EETS, 140 (1910); repr. (1971) [incl. *Tretis*] · *The life of St Katharine of Alexandria by John Capgrave*, ed. C. Horstmann, EETS, 100 (1893); repr. (1973) · P. J. Lucas, 'A bequest to the Austin friars in the will of John Spycer, 1439–40', *Norfolk Archaeology*, 41 (1990–93), 482–9 · F. X. Roth, *The English Austin friars, 1249–1538*, 2 vols. (1961–6) · H. E. Salter and A. H. Cooke, eds., *The Boarstall cartulary*, OHS, 88 (1930) · *Commentarii de scriptoribus Britannicis, auctore Joanne Lelando*, ed. A. Hall, 2 vols. (1709) · Bale, *Cat.* · P. J. Lucas, 'John Capgrave and the *Nova legenda Anglie*: a survey', *The Library*, 5th ser., 25 (1970), 1–10

Archives All Souls Oxf., MSS · BL, Add. MS 36704 · BL, papers · Bodl. Oxf., MSS · CCC Cam., MSS · CCC Cam., MS 408 · CUL, chronicle of England to 1417 · Hunt. L., MSS · Oriel College, Oxford,

MSS • Santa Monica, Rome, general archives, OESA, MSS • University College, Cambridge, MSS

Likenesses miniature (presenting his book to Duke Humphrey, 1438, Lynn), Oriel College, Oxford, MS 32; repro. in de Meijer, 'John Capgrave, O.E.S.A.', *Augustiniana*, 7 (1957) • miniature (presenting his book to Duke Humphrey, 1440, Lynn), Bodl. Oxf., MS Duke Humphrey b.1; repro. in P. J. Lucas, 'John Capgrave, friar of Lynn', *The Historian*, 44 (1994), 23–4 • miniature (presenting his book to John Wygenhale, 1440, Lynn), Hunt. L., MS HM 55; repro. in J. Capgrave, *The life of St Norbert*, ed. C. L. Smetana (1977)

Caplin, Roxey Ann [*formerly* Emily Roxey Caplin] (**1793–1888**), corset maker, writer, and lecturer on health, was born in Canada, the daughter of English settlers; Canadian Indians taught her canoeing and swimming as a child. Probably trained as a milliner, she married about 1835, and by 1839 was living in London. Her husband, Jean François Isidore Caplin (*c*.1790–*c*.1872), used his knowledge of anatomy, gained as a Paris medical student, to treat spinal deformities. He moved to London about 1830. In 1838 he patented (no. 7640) a front-opening corset with a back adjusted by pulleys and wheels. In 1839 Madame Caplin appeared in the London Post Office directory as a 'wholesale and retail milliner and patentee of the mechanical corset' (her name was given as Emily Roxey, then Roxey Ann from 1849).

From 1841 the couple were listed at 58 Berners Street, London. Jean François Caplin, called an orthopaedic corset maker and later an 'orthorachidiste', registered designs for a mannequin in 1841 and the Hygean or Corporiform Corset in 1849. However, the Athenée des Arts de Paris's commendation stated that it was invented and manufactured by his wife. In 1843 the *Court Magazine* commented:

> Madame Caplin has made the manufacture of Corsets a complete study, embracing at once the several designs of anatomy, geometry, drawing and mechanics ... the artist may be traced in all, and her system of measurement is at once perfect and infallible. (R. A. Caplin, *Health and Beauty*, frontispiece)

The Caplins' knowledge of anatomy, fashion, and commerce created a highly successful product.

In 1849 Jean François Caplin lectured in Manchester on spinal deformities, then in the early 1850s, while retaining their London base, husband and wife had premises in Princes Street, and the Manchester Hygiaenic Gymnasium [*sic*] was run from their Pendleton home. Invalid boarders were cured by exercise, diet, and good corsetry. Its prospectus reassured parents that 'Independently of the maternal care of Madame Caplin, a well educated governess of the highest respectability, residing in the establishment, will devote her whole attention to the requirements and comforts of the young ladies' (J. F. I. Caplin, 'Prospectus').

Madame Caplin's corsets and Monsieur's portable gymnasium were awarded medals at the 1851 Great Exhibition and examples of their corsets survive in the Museum of London. Royal patronage followed, according to James Torrington Spencer Lidstone's *Londoniad* (1856), which described Madame thus:

> You'll an incarnation of the Graces meet
> At No. 58, in Berners-street;
> A deity in human form enshrined;
> Gracious demeanour, and a courtly mien,
> Learning and worth are thine, great Nature's queen.
> (Lidstone, 60)

Jean François Caplin became a doctor of medicine in 1854, perhaps for his electrochemical bath which used the principle of electroplating to expel poisons from the body. In 1855 he opened the Hygeinic Gymnasium and Kinesitherapic Institution for Ladies and Children, at 9 York Place, Portman Square, London, which soon became the Hydro-Galvano Therapeutic Institution. His many books describe the bath, with testimonies to its effectiveness for an astonishing range of illnesses.

Madame Caplin now advertised extensive alterations to Berners Street, to show her 'numerous inventions for the purpose of preserving the health and displaying the natural beauties of the female form' (R. A. Caplin, *The Needle*, 60). She also lectured upstairs in her Ladies Anatomical Gallery where, 'in addition to Canova's Anatomical Venus and the Venus de Medici, hundreds of magnificent models, executed with the utmost fidelity to nature, exhibit every organ of the body and the whole course of embryology' (ibid.). This was 'quite distinct from the rest of the Establishment, and a visit to one does not necessarily involve a sight of the other' (ibid.).

Roxey Caplin wrote her first book in 1856. *Health and beauty, or, Corsets and clothing, constructed in accordance with the physiological laws of the human body* gave a history of stays, culminating in her own Hygeinic Corset, which had been 'pirated or attempted by almost every staymaker in London and Paris' (R. A. Caplin, *Health and Beauty*, 51). *The Needle: its History and Utility* (1860) concentrated on the history of the needle since Homer's day, and the clothing it created. She noted 'so far as ornament is concerned… no genuine and earnest effort has yet been made to adapt the dress to the body, in such a manner as shall preserve the health and display the natural beauties of the human figure'. She decried the appalling conditions in the clothing trades, but hoped the sewing machine would improve 'the condition of those whose woes have been so beautifully and pathetically described by dear Tom Hood'.

Roxey Caplin ran her business at Berners Street until her death. In 1876 she co-wrote *Women in the Reign of Queen Victoria*. This praised the recent increase in physical exercise and work opportunities for women, but called for dress reform. From the 1870s she lived in Mortlake with her bookkeeper and three servants. Although she claimed to be a widow of sixty-four in the 1881 census, when she died of old age and gangrene at Cambridge Lodge, Mortlake, East Sheen, Surrey, on 2 August 1888, her death certificate gave her age as ninety-five. SARAH LEVITT

Sources S. Levitt, *Victorians unbuttoned: registered designs for clothing, their makers and wearers, 1839–1900* (1986), 26–30 • R. A. Caplin, *Health and beauty, or, Corsets and clothing* (1856) • R. A. Caplin, *The needle: its history and utility* (1860) • R. A. Caplin and J. Mill, *Women in the reign of Queen Victoria* [1876] • J. F. I. Caplin, *Selection of documents and autograph letters in testimony of the cures effected by the electro-chemical bath of J. F. I. Caplin* (1865) • J. F. I. Caplin, 'Prospectus of the Manchester Hygiaenic Gymnasium', *Catalogue of the works exhibited in* *the British section of the exhibition … together with exhibitors' prospectuses*, 10 (1856) • J. T. S. Lidstone, *The Londoniad: a grand national poem on the arts* (1856) • registered design, 1841, PRO, BT 42, no. 669 • registered design, 1849, PRO, BT 45, no. 1995 • PO street directories, London, Mortlake, and Manchester • census returns for Mortlake, 1881 • d. cert.

Likenesses C. Silvy, photograph, *c.*1864, repro. in Caplin, *Selection of documents* • photogravure photograph, *c.*1875, repro. in Caplin and Mill, *Women in the reign of Queen Victoria*

Wealth at death £6452 19*s*. 10*d*.: probate, 5 Sept 1888, *CGPLA Eng. & Wales*

Capon [Salcot], **John** (*d.* 1557), bishop of Salisbury, was probably a native of Salcot in Essex. Nothing is known of his parents or upbringing, and he is not to be confused with the John Salkott who received a degree in civil law at Cambridge in 1489. On 16 May 1502 he was ordained deacon as a Benedictine monk in St John's Abbey, Colchester. He attended Cambridge University, taking the degrees of BTh in 1512 and DTh in 1515, and by 18 February 1517 had become prior of St John's. His brother William *Capon was Thomas Wolsey's chaplain, enabling John to procure favours from the cardinal, and he also established a relationship with Thomas Cromwell, then one of Wolsey's agents. It was probably through Wolsey's influence that Capon was elected abbot of St Benet of Hulme, Norfolk, on 18 February 1517. He also preached at court on at least two occasions.

Despite Wolsey's fall, Capon rose through service to the government during the 1530s. In February 1530 he was one of the twenty-nine delegates chosen on behalf of Cambridge University to pronounce upon Henry VIII's marriage to Katherine of Aragon. In the very next month, perhaps as a reward for siding with the king on this issue, he was translated to Hyde Abbey in Winchester, and in August 1533 he was nominated bishop of Bangor, an appointment he may have owed to the support of Anne Boleyn. He was consecrated by Archbishop Cranmer on 19 April 1534, and the temporalities were restored on the 28th. In the meantime, on 23 November 1533, he preached at Paul's Cross when Elizabeth Barton, 'the Holy Maid of Kent', and her followers did public penance there. His sermon, no doubt delivered to an official brief, was later repeated at Canterbury by Nicholas Heath, albeit with modifications by Cranmer, when Barton did penance there a fortnight later. Capon preached again at Paul's Cross in 1536, as part of Cranmer's campaign for evangelical reform.

Capon never seems to have resided at Bangor, and admitted to being hampered by his ignorance of Welsh. He employed his brother William as his vicar-general, and it was through others that he made efforts to preach the royal supremacy and implement reform; these were, however, obstructed by quarrels among leading gentry families. On 30 April 1539 he resigned Hyde Abbey (which he had been permitted to hold *in commendam* with his impoverished diocese) to the king, and on 21 July he was elected bishop of Salisbury. Royal assent was given on the 31st, the temporalities were restored on 1 August, and he was enthroned by proxy on the 19th. For the rest of Henry VIII's reign and during that of Edward VI Capon acquiesced in the various changes in religion. In 1539 he was named to a committee for the revision of doctrine. In 1542 he was assigned Corinthians in the abortive project of revising the Great Bible, and in the following year he and Thomas Goodrich, bishop of Ely, were appointed examiners of church books. He was also involved in the prosecution of several heretics. In 1549 he was present when the Act of Uniformity was passed in the House of Lords; his position is not indicated, but he was not among those who opposed the act, and indeed, in the following year he set about implementing it through a visitation of his diocese.

Following Mary's accession in 1553 Capon reverted to Catholicism, prompting later protestant apologists to denounce him as a time-server. He was allowed to retain his bishopric, but because of his age he was excused attendance at Mary's coronation and at all her parliaments. During her reign there were at least seventy-three deprivations in his diocese (a ratio of one in six for the diocese as a whole); the exact cause can seldom be determined, but in many cases the bishop and his officers were probably enforcing the injunctions of 1554 against clerical marriage. Six people were executed for heresy. According to John Foxe, Capon examined three of them, but he is not said to have been involved in their condemnation. The bishop also examined two individuals who were condemned by his chancellor and imprisoned for heresy, but were not burnt, while outside his diocese he served on the commission that tried Rowland Taylor, John Bradford, and Laurence Saunders, who were all burnt in 1555. Capon died on 6 October 1557, possibly the victim of an influenza epidemic, and was buried in Salisbury Cathedral on the south side of the choir. His will, drawn up on 18 July, divided his possessions among his servants.

ANGELO J. LOUISA

Sources Cooper, *Ath. Cantab.*, 1.171–2, 550 • Venn, *Alum. Cant.*, 1/1.290 • *LP Henry VIII* • *The acts and monuments of John Foxe*, ed. S. R. Cattley, 8 vols. (1837–41), vol. 5, pp. 89, 465, 470–72, 482–4, 486–7, 489, 491–2, 494; vol. 6, p. 690; vol. 7, p. 773; vol. 8, pp. 103, 506–7, 631 • registers of Nicholas Shaxton, John Capon, vacancy period of 1557–1560, and John Jewell, Wilts. & Swindon RO • A. J. Louisa, 'The Marian bishops: a study of the backgrounds and ecclesiastical activities of the Marian episcopate', PhD diss., University of Minnesota, 1985, 66, 68, 131, 144–5 (nn. 10, 11), 165, 228, 234 • *Fasti Angl., 1300–1541*, [Salisbury] • *Fasti Angl., 1300–1541*, [Welsh dioceses] • L. E. Whatmore, ed., 'The sermon against the Holy Maid of Kent and her adherents … 1533', *EngHR*, 58 (1943), 463–75 • L. B. Smith, *Tudor prelates and politics, 1536–1558* (1953), 28, 37, 143–4 (n. 37), 149, 283, 305, 307 • J. Ridley, *Thomas Cranmer* (1962), 29, 98, 178, 227, 239 • will, PRO, PROB 11/39, sig. 41 • *VCH Berkshire*, 2.23–34 • *VCH Wiltshire*, 3.27–32, 184–6 • D. MacCulloch, *Thomas Cranmer: a life* (1996), 100, 105–7, 117, 121 (n. 124), 125, 189, 242, 291 (n. 180), 301 • E. W. Ives, *Anne Boleyn* (1986), 303–4 (n. 6) • G. Williams, *Wales and the Reformation* (1997) • Emden, *Cam.*, 503

Archives Wilts. & Swindon RO, Act Book 1, 1554–1558 • Wilts. & Swindon RO, Detecta Book 2, 1556 • Wilts. & Swindon RO, registers of Nicholas Shaxton, John Capon, vacancy period of 1557–1560, and John Jewell

Wealth at death see will, PRO, PROB 11/39, sig. 41

Capon, William (*c.*1480–1550), college head, younger brother of John *Capon, bishop of Salisbury, was born at Salcot, Essex. He was educated at Cambridge University, where he graduated BA in 1499 (when he was probably about nineteen or twenty), MA in 1502, and DD in 1517. He became a fellow of St Catharine's in 1509, proctor in 1509–10, and on 21 July 1516 master of Jesus College, a position he held until his resignation on 10 November 1546. Capon's sympathy for the new humanistic learning attracted the attention of Cardinal Wolsey, who made him his almoner and, in 1528, dean of his college at Ipswich. Capon nominated Thomas Cranmer, then a fellow of Jesus College, for a canonry at Wolsey's college in Oxford; Cranmer declined the offer, but he and Capon remained on good terms for a time after Cranmer's elevation to Canterbury.

Capon received considerable preferment. In 1516 he became vicar of Great Shelford, near Cambridge, and in 1517–32 he was vicar of St Mary Woolchurch, London. At various times he held the livings of Barkway, Hertfordshire (which he resigned in 1534); Duxford St Peter, Cambridgeshire; Berkeley, Gloucestershire; Simondsbury, Dorset; North Stoneham, Hampshire; and St Mary's, Southampton. At least some of these were held in plurality and non-residence. Capon was also dean of Tettenhall, Staffordshire, in 1533–48; prebendary of Combe, second stall, in Wells Cathedral, in 1535–50; and prebendary of Torleton in Salisbury Cathedral, in 1541–50. While his brother was bishop of Bangor (1534–9), William Capon served as vicar-general of the diocese. His appointment as archdeacon of Anglesey in 1537 was cancelled when it was discovered that the previous incumbent was still alive; Capon received instead the prebend of Llanfair, which he held until his death in 1550.

Capon was a distinguished academic and founded Southampton School. He was sympathetic to Henry VIII's early reforms in the church. A coolness seems to have developed between him and Cranmer as the latter's views became more distinctively protestant. Edward VI's commissioners dismantled altars and broke images at Jesus College in 1549, suggesting that the old ritual had continued there in Capon's time. He left the finances of the college in some disarray. Little seems known of him after he retired from the mastership in 1546. He died in 1550, some time before 7 October. BARRIE WILLIAMS

Sources Venn, *Alum. Cant.* • *Fasti Angl.*, *1541–1857*, [Bath and Wells] • *Fasti Angl.*, *1541–1857*, [Salisbury] • A. Gray and F. Brittain, *A history of Jesus College, Cambridge*, rev. edn (1960) • A. I. Pryce, *The diocese of Bangor in the sixteenth century* (1923) • D. MacCulloch, *Thomas Cranmer: a life* (1996) • H. Ellis, ed., *Original letters illustrative of English history*, 1st ser., 1 (1824), 185

Archives NL Wales, register of Mag. William Capon, S.T.P. Vicar General of John Capon, bishop

Capon, William (1757–1827), scene-painter, architectural draughtsman, and architect, was born in Norwich on 6 October 1757, the son of Christopher Capon, portrait painter, and his wife, Anne, and was baptized at St Stephen's Church, Norwich, on 19 February 1758. At first he studied under his father but, preferring architecture, he moved to London and became a pupil of Michael Novosielski (1750–1795), under whom he learned the art of theatrical scene-painting. He assisted Novosielski in building and decorating the Italian Opera House in the Haymarket, London (1790–91)—at that time the largest theatre in Europe after La Scala, Milan—and in designing some buildings, including the theatre, at Ranelagh Gardens. In 1780 he designed a small theatre off Wells Street, north of Oxford Street, and in 1794 a theatre for Edward Stratford, second earl of Aldborough, at Belan House, co. Kildare. In the same year he was engaged as scene-painter at the newly completed Drury Lane Theatre by the actor–manager John Kemble, whom he greatly assisted in his efforts to represent plays with historical accuracy.

Both at Drury Lane and, after 1802, at Covent Garden Capon's reconstructions of medieval buildings, based on his studies of historic English architecture, were greatly admired. Among these were a view of the Old Palace of Westminster in the fifteenth century; the Tower of London for *Richard III*; an 'Anglo-Norman hall' for *Hamlet*; the council chamber at Crosby House for *Jane Shore*; a state chamber at the time of Edward III; a baronial hall in the reign of Edward IV; and a Tudor hall of the period of Henry VII. He made drawings of the interiors of Drury Lane and Covent Garden, which were exhibited in 1800 and 1802. His Drury Lane sets were destroyed when the theatre burned down in 1809 but many of his surviving drawings are in the local history collection of Westminster City Library, and others are in the British Museum. Some of these were reproduced by the London Topographical Society as *A series of drawings by William Capon (1757–1827) of the central part of the City of Westminster* (1923) and *A Series of Views of Westminster 1801–1805 by William Capon* (1924), and others, by H. M. Colvin, in 'Views of the Old Palace of Westminster', in *Architectural History*, volume 9 (1966). Two typical theatrical scenes, from Capon's drawings at Stratford upon Avon, were illustrated in the *Magazine of Art*, volume 18 (1894–5). From 1805 onwards he also worked for the Royal Circus and for the theatre at Bath. In June 1804 he was appointed architectural draughtsman to Frederick, duke of York (1763–1827).

Capon lived in Westminster for over thirty years. He shared the antiquarian interests of his friend and fellow architectural draughtsman John Carter (1748–1817) and both artists made extensive studies of the antiquities of the palace and abbey. Capon was one of the earliest of such draughtsmen to distinguish the architecture of various periods by representing them using different colours. His colour-coded ground plans of the Old Palace of Westminster and the substructure of the abbey are said to have occupied him for thirty years. The plan of the former was purchased by the Society of Antiquaries in 1826 for 120 guineas, and was engraved by James Basire (1796–1869) and published by the society in 1828.

From 1788 until his death Capon regularly exhibited chiefly architectural drawings and some landscapes at the

Royal Academy, and also sent topographical drawings to the School of Artists, the British Institution, and the Society of British Artists. Though his main interest was Gothic architecture his last work is said to have been a design for a Doric church. His earlier ambition to become surveyor to Westminster Abbey was never realized.

Capon died at his house in North Street, Westminster, on 26 September 1827, aged sixty-nine. A portrait of him, engraved by W. Bond from a miniature by W. Bone, appeared in *The Gentleman's Magazine* (*GM*, 98/1). The background shows Capon's design intended for a national monument, comprising a pyramidal building 205 feet high to be erected on Shooter's Hill, Kent.

RICHARD RIDDELL

Sources *DNB* • Colvin, *Archs.* • R. Brown, H. M. Colvin, and A. J. Taylor, eds., *The history of the king's works*, 1 (1963), frontispiece • [H. M. Colvin], ed., 'Views of the old Palace of Westminster', *Architectural History*, 9 (1966) [whole issue] • W. J. Lawrence, 'Art in the theatre, the pioneers of modern English stage mounting: William Capon', *Magazine of Art*, 18 (1894–5), 289–92 • *GM*, 1st ser., 97/2 (1827), 374–7 • *GM*, 1st ser., 98/1 (1828), 105–7 • *GM*, 1st ser., 99/1 (1829), 227 • *A series of views of Westminster 1801–1805 by William Capon*, London Topographical Society Publications (1924) • *A series of drawings by William Capon (1757–1827) of the central part of the City of Westminster*, London Topographical Society Publications (1923) • sale catalogue of drawings by William Capon, Bodl. Oxf., MS Douce CC.284 • *IGI*

Archives Shakespeare Birthplace Trust RO, Stratford upon Avon, papers

Likenesses W. Bond, engraving (after miniature by W. Bone), BM, NPG; repro. in *GM*, 98/1 (1828), 105

PICTURE CREDITS

Burton, Decimus (1800–1881)—© National Portrait Gallery, London

Burton, Henry (*bap.* 1578, *d.* 1647/8)—© National Portrait Gallery, London

Burton, Hezekiah (*bap.* 1632, *d.* 1681)—The Master and Fellows, Magdalene College, Cambridge

Burton, Isabel, Lady Burton (1831–1896)—© National Portrait Gallery, London

Burton, Sir Montague Maurice (1885–1952)—© reserved; Manchester University Press; photograph National Portrait Gallery, London

Burton, Richard (1925–1984)—© Bob Penn; collection National Portrait Gallery, London

Burton, Sir Richard Francis (1821–1890)—© National Portrait Gallery, London

Burton, Robert (1577–1640)—Principal and Fellows of Brasenose College, Oxford

Burton, William (1575–1645)—© National Portrait Gallery, London

Bury, John Bagnell (1861–1927)—© National Portrait Gallery, London

Bury, Richard (1287–1345)—Chapter of Durham Cathedral

Busby, Sir Matthew (1909–1994)—© Sefton Samuels / National Portrait Gallery, London

Busby, Thomas (1754–1838)—© Copyright The British Museum

Busby Babes (*act.* 1953–1958)—© Popperfoto

Bush, Alan Dudley (1900–1995)—© National Portrait Gallery, London

Bushe, Charles Kendal (1767–1843)—National Gallery of Ireland

Buss, Frances Mary (1827–1894)—© National Portrait Gallery, London

Butler, Agnata Frances (1867–1931)—© National Portrait Gallery, London

Butler, Alban (1709–1773)—© National Portrait Gallery, London

Butler, Arthur John (1844–1910)—© National Portrait Gallery, London

Butler, Charles (1750–1832)—© National Portrait Gallery, London

Butler, Lady (Charlotte) Eleanor (1739–1829)—© National Portrait Gallery, London

Butler, Elizabeth Southerden, Lady Butler (1846–1933)—© National Portrait Gallery, London

Butler, Eliza Marian (1885–1959)—© National Portrait Gallery, London

Butler, Frank Hedges (1855–1928)—© National Portrait Gallery, London

Butler, George (1819–1890)—© National Portrait Gallery, London

Butler, Sir (Spencer) Harcourt (1869–1938)—© National Portrait Gallery, London

Butler, Henry Montagu (1833–1918)—© Estate of Sir William Rothenstein / National Portrait Gallery, London

Butler, James, first duke of Ormond (1610–1688)—Kedleston Hall, The Scarsdale Collection (The National Trust). Photograph: Photographic Survey, Courtauld Institute of Art, London

Butler, James, second duke of Ormond (1665–1745)—by kind permission of the Examination Schools, Oxford

Butler, Sir James Ramsay Montagu (1889–1975)—© National Portrait Gallery, London

Butler, Joseph (1692–1752)—by kind permission of the Lord Bishop of Durham and the Church Commissioners of England. Photograph: Photographic Survey, Courtauld Institute of Art, London

Butler, Josephine Elizabeth (1828–1906)—© National Portrait Gallery, London

Butler, Sir Montagu Sherard Dawes (1873–1952)—© National Portrait Gallery, London

Butler, Richard Austen [Rab], Baron Butler of Saffron Walden (1902–1982)—© National Portrait Gallery, London

Butler, Sir Richard Harte Keatinge (1870–1935)—© National Portrait Gallery, London

Butler, Samuel (*bap.* 1613, *d.* 1680)—© National Portrait Gallery, London

Butler, Samuel (1835–1902)—Alexander Turnbull Library, National Library of New Zealand, Te Puna Matauranga o Aotearoa (G-546)

Butler, Thomas, tenth earl of Ormond and third earl of Ossory (1531–1614)—photograph by courtesy Sotheby's Picture Library, London

Butler, Thomas, sixth earl of Ossory (1634–1680)—© National Portrait Gallery, London

Butler, William (1535–1618)—© National Portrait Gallery, London

Butlin, Sir William Heygate Edmund Colborne [Billy] (1899–1980)—© National Portrait Gallery, London

Butt, Dame Clara Ellen (1872–1936)—© National Portrait Gallery, London

Butt, Isaac (1813–1879)—by courtesy of the National Gallery of Ireland

Butterfield, Sir Herbert (1900–1979)—Master and Fellows of Peterhouse, Cambridge

Butterfield, William (1814–1900)—by permission of the Warden and Fellows of Keble College, Oxford

Butts, Sir William (*c.*1485–1545)—© Isabella Stewart Gardner Museum, Boston

Buxton, Charles (1822–1871)—© National Portrait Gallery, London

Buxton, Sydney Charles, Earl Buxton (1853–1934)—© National Portrait Gallery, London

Buxton, Sir Thomas Fowell, first baronet (1786–1845)—© National Portrait Gallery, London

Byfield, Adoniram (*d.* 1658x60)—© National Portrait Gallery, London

Byfield, Nicholas (1578/9–1622)—by permission of Dr Williams's Library

Byng, George, first Viscount Torrington (1663–1733)—© National Portrait Gallery, London

Byng, Julian Hedworth George, Viscount Byng of Vimy (1862–1935)—© National Portrait Gallery, London

Byrd, William (1674–1744)—The Virginia Historical Society, Richmond, Virginia

Byres, James, of Tonley (1734–1817)—© National Portrait Gallery, London

Byrom, John (1692–1763)—© National Portrait Gallery, London

Byron, (Augusta) Ada (1815–1852)—© Crown copyright in photograph: UK Government Art Collection

Byron, George Gordon Noel, sixth Baron Byron (1788–1824)—© Crown copyright in photograph: UK Government Art Collection

Byron, Henry James (1835–1884)—© National Portrait Gallery, London

Byron, John, first Baron Byron (1598/9–1652)—® reserved

Bythell, John Kenworthy (1840–1916)—© Manchester City Art Galleries

Bywater, Ingram (1840–1914)—© Tate, London, 2004

Caccia, Harold Anthony, Baron Caccia (1905–1990)—© National Portrait Gallery, London

Cadbury, Dame Elizabeth Mary (1858–1951)—© National Portrait Gallery, London

Cadbury, George (1839–1922)—by kind permission of Cadbury Trebor Bassett

Cadbury, Laurence John (1889–1982)—© National Portrait Gallery, London

Cadell, Francis (1822–1879)—La Trobe Picture Collection, State Library of Victoria

Cadell, Thomas, the elder (1742–1802)—© National Portrait Gallery, London

Cadman, John, first Baron Cadman (1877–1941)—© National Portrait Gallery, London

Cadogan, Sir Alexander George Montagu (1884–1968)—© National Portrait Gallery, London

Cadogan, George Henry, fifth Earl Cadogan (1840–1915)—© National Portrait Gallery, London

Cadogan, William, Earl Cadogan (1671/2–1726)—© National Portrait Gallery, London

Cadogan, William (1711–1797)—by permission of the Royal College of Physicians, London

Caesar (100–44 BC)—© Copyright The British Museum

Caesar, Sir Julius (*bap.* 1558, *d.* 1636)—© National Portrait Gallery, London

Cahill, Daniel William (1796–1864)—© National Portrait Gallery, London

Caillard, Sir Vincent Henry Penalver (1856–1930)—© National Portrait Gallery, London

Caine, Sir (Thomas Henry) Hall (1853–1931)—© National Portrait Gallery, London

Caine, William Sproston (1842–1903)—© National Portrait Gallery, London

Caird, Edward (1835–1908)—© National Portrait Gallery, London

Caird, George Bradford (1917–1984)—photograph reproduced by courtesy of The British Academy

Caird, Sir James (1816–1892)—© National Portrait Gallery, London

Caird, John (1820–1898)—© National Portrait Gallery, London

Caird, (Alice) Mona (1854–1932)—© National Portrait Gallery, London

Cairncross, Sir Alexander Kirkland (1911–1998)—© National Portrait Gallery, London

Cairnes, John Elliot (1823–1875)—Picture reproduced courtesy of the James Hardiman Library, National University of Ireland, Galway

Cairns, Hugh McCalmont, first Earl Cairns (1819–1885)—by kind permission of the Board of Trinity College Dublin

Calamy, Benjamin (*bap.* 1646, *d.* 1685/6)—© National Portrait Gallery, London

Calamy, Edmund (1600–1666)—© National Portrait Gallery, London

Calamy, Edmund (1671–1732)—© National Portrait Gallery, London

Caldecott, Sir Andrew (1884–1951)—© National Portrait Gallery, London

Caldecott, Randolph (1846–1886)—Aberdeen Art Gallery and Museums Collections

Calder, Peter Ritchie, Baron Ritchie-Calder (1906–1982)—© National Portrait Gallery, London

Calderwood, Margaret (1715–1774)—in the collection of the Dundas-Bekker Family; photograph courtesy the Scottish National Portrait Gallery

Caldwell, Andrew (1733–1808)—by courtesy of the National Gallery of Ireland

Caldwell, John (1628–1679)—© National Portrait Gallery, London

Callaghan, Sir George Astley (1852–1920)—© National Portrait Gallery, London

Callard, Sir (Eric) John (1913–1998)—© reserved; News International Syndication; photograph National Portrait Gallery, London

Callcott, Sir Augustus Wall (1770–1844)—© National Portrait Gallery, London

Callcott, John Wall (1766–1821)—© National Portrait Gallery, London

Callcott, Maria, Lady Callcott (1785–1842)—© National Portrait Gallery, London

Callow, William (1812–1908)—© National Portrait Gallery, London

Callwell, Sir Charles Edward (1859–1928)—© reserved

Calman, Melville (1931–1994)—© Stephen Hyde; collection National Portrait Gallery, London

Calthorpe, Sir Somerset Arthur Gough (1864–1937)—© National Portrait Gallery, London

Calvert, Cecil, second Baron Baltimore (1605–1675)—© National Portrait Gallery, London

Calvert, Charles Alexander (1828–1879)—V&A Images, The Victoria and Albert Museum

Calvert, Edward (1799–1883)—© reserved

Calvert, George, first Baron Baltimore (1579/80–1632)—© reserved

Calvert, (James) Michael (1913–1998)—© reserved; News International Syndication; photograph National Portrait Gallery, London

Calvert, Thomas Christopher [Kit] (1903–1984)—Wensleydale

Cam, Helen Maud (1885–1968)—The Mistress and Fellows, Girton College, Cambridge

Cambridge, Richard Owen (1717–1802)—© National Portrait Gallery, London

Camden, William (1551–1623)—private collection. Photograph: Photographic Survey, Courtauld Institute of Art, London

Cameron, Sir Charles, first baronet (1841–1924)—© National Portrait Gallery, London

Cameron, Charles Hay (1795–1880)—private collection; photograph National Portrait Gallery, London

Cameron, Sir David Young (1865–1945)—© National Portrait Gallery, London

Cameron, Sir Donald Charles (1872–1948)—© National Portrait Gallery, London

Cameron, Sir Ewen, of Lochiel (1629–1719)—Scottish National Portrait Gallery

Cameron, (Mark) James Walter (1911–1985)—© Paul Joyce / National Portrait Gallery, London

Cameron, John (1771–1815)—Ashmolean Museum, Oxford

Cameron, Sir John, Lord Cameron (1900–1996)—© reserved / courtesy of the University of Edinburgh's Collections

Cameron, Julia Margaret (1815–1879)—© National Portrait Gallery, London

Cameron, Katharine (1874–1965)—© reserved; collection National Library of Scotland, Edinburgh; photograph National Portrait Gallery, London

Cameron, Verney Lovett (1844–1894)—The Royal Geographical Society, London

Camoys, Thomas, Baron Camoys (*c.*1350–1420/21)—reproduced by courtesy of H. M. Stutchfield, F.S.A., Hon. Secretary of the Monumental Brass Society

Campbell, Sir Duncan, of Glenorchy (1551x4–1631)—Scottish National Portrait Gallery

Campbell, Alexander (1788–1866)—by permission of Bethany College, West Virginia

Campbell, Amabel Hume-, *suo jure* Countess De Grey (1751–1833)—© National Portrait Gallery, London

Campbell, Archibald, seventh earl of Argyll (1575/6–1638)—in a private Scottish collection

Campbell, Archibald, marquess of Argyll (1605x7–1661)—Scottish National Portrait Gallery

Campbell, Archibald, ninth earl of Argyll (1629–1685)—© National Portrait Gallery, London

Campbell, Archibald, third duke of Argyll (1682–1761)—© Glasgow Museums

Campbell, Archibald Campbell, first Baron Blythswood (1835–1908)—© National Portrait Gallery, London

Campbell, Beatrice Stella [Mrs Patrick Campbell] (1865–1940)—V&A Images, The Victoria and Albert Museum

Campbell, Colin, Baron Clyde (1792–1863)—© National Portrait Gallery, London

Campbell, Donald Malcolm (1921–1967)—© Peter Keen; collection National Portrait Gallery, London

Campbell, Duncan (*c.*1680–1730)—© National Portrait Gallery, London

Campbell [Gunning], Elizabeth, duchess of Argyll and *suo jure* Baroness Hamilton of Hameldon (*bap.* 1733, *d.* 1790)—Board of Trustees of the National Museums and Galleries on Merseyside (Lady Lever Art Gallery, Port Sunlight)

Campbell, Frederick Archibald Vaughan, third Earl Cawdor (1847–1911)—© National Portrait Gallery, London

Campbell, George (1719–1796)—© National Portrait Gallery, London

Campbell, Sir George (1824–1892)—© National Portrait Gallery, London

Campbell, George Douglas, eighth duke of Argyll in the peerage of Scotland, and first duke of Argyll in the peerage of the United Kingdom (1823–1900)—© National Portrait Gallery, London

Campbell, Gertrude Elizabeth [Lady Colin Campbell] (1857–1911)—© National Portrait Gallery, London

Campbell, Herbert (1844–1904)—© National Portrait Gallery, London

Campbell, Sir Ilay, of Succoth, first baronet (1734–1823)—Ashmolean Museum, Oxford

Campbell, John, first earl of Loudoun (1598–1662)—© Copyright The British Museum

Campbell, John, first earl of Breadalbane and Holland (1634–1717)—Scottish National Portrait Gallery

Campbell, John, second duke of Argyll and duke of Greenwich (1680–1743)—© National Portrait Gallery, London

Campbell, John, third earl of Breadalbane and Holland (*bap.* 1696, *d.* 1782)—Scottish National Portrait Gallery

Campbell, John, fourth earl of Loudoun (1705–1782)—Christie's Images Ltd. (2004)

Campbell, John (1766–1840)—© National Portrait Gallery, London

Campbell, John, first Baron Campbell of St Andrews (1779–1861)—© National Portrait Gallery, London

Campbell, John Charles (1894–1942)—The Imperial War Museum, London

Campbell, John George Edward Henry Douglas Sutherland, marquess of Lorne and ninth duke of Argyll (1845–1914)—© National Portrait Gallery, London

Campbell, John McLeod (1800–1872)—© National Portrait Gallery, London

Campbell, John Middleton, Baron Campbell of Eskan (1912–1994)—© National Portrait Gallery, London

Campbell, John Ross (1894–1969)—Getty Images - Hulton Archive

Campbell, Lewis (1830–1908)—© National Portrait Gallery, London

Campbell, Sir Malcolm (1885–1948)—© National Portrait Gallery, London

Campbell, Reginald John (1867–1956)—© reserved; collection National Portrait Gallery, London

Campbell, (Ignatius) Royston Dunnachie (1901–1957)—© courtesy the Artist's Estate / Bridgeman Art Library; Carnegie Institute, Pittsburgh, USA

Campbell, Sybil (1889–1977)—The Mistress and Fellows, Girton College, Cambridge

Campbell, Thomas (1777–1844)—© National Portrait Gallery, London

Campbell, Lady Victoria (1854–1910)—© National Portrait Gallery, London

Campbell, Willielma, Viscountess Glenorchy (1741–1786)—© National Portrait Gallery, London

Campoli, Alfredo (1906–1991)—© Estate of Ronald Franks; collection National Portrait Gallery, London

Canal, Giovanni Antonio [Canaletto] (1697–1768)—The Royal Collection © 2004 HM Queen Elizabeth II

Candlish, Robert Smith (1806–1873)—Scottish National Portrait Gallery

Cann, Abraham (*bap.* 1794, *d.* 1864)—Exeter City Museums & Art Gallery

Cannan, Charles (1858–1919)—© National Portrait Gallery, London

Canning, Charles John, Earl Canning (1812–1862)—© National Portrait Gallery, London

Canning, Charlotte Elizabeth, Countess Canning (1817–1861)—Christie's Images Ltd. (2004)

Canning, George (1770–1827)—© National Portrait Gallery, London

Canning, Sir Samuel (1823–1908)—© Institution of Civil Engineers; collection National Portrait Gallery, London

Canning, Stratford, Viscount Stratford de Redcliffe (1786–1880)—© National Portrait Gallery, London

Cannon, Thomas [Tom] (1846–1917)—© National Portrait Gallery, London

Cantilupe, Walter de (*c.*1195–1266)—photograph by Mr Christopher Guy, Worcester Cathedral Archaeologist. Reproduced by permission of the Chapter of Worcester Cathedral, UK

Canton, John (*bap.* 1718, *d.* 1772)—© National Portrait Gallery, London

Cape, (Herbert) Jonathan (1879–1960)—© reserved; collection Jonathan Cape Ltd; photograph National Portrait Gallery, London

Capel, Arthur, first Baron Capel of Hadham (1604–1649)—© National Portrait Gallery, London

Capel, Arthur, first earl of Essex (*bap.* 1632, *d.* 1683)—© National Portrait Gallery, London

Capell, Edward (1713–1781)—© National Portrait Gallery, London